SCRABBLE

BRAND Crossword Game

DICTIONARY

Collins

HarperCollins Publishers
Westerhill Road
Bishopbriggs
Glasgow
G64 2QT
Great Britain

Third edition 2011

Reprint 10 9 8 7 6 5 4 3 2 1

© HarperCollins Publishers 2006,
2010, 2011

ISBN 978-0-00-743606-4

www.collinslanguage.com

A catalogue record for this book is
available from the British Library

Typeset by Davidson Publishing
Solutions, Glasgow

Printed in Great Britain by
Clays Ltd, St Ives plc

Acknowledgements
We would like to thank those
authors and publishers who kindly
gave permission for copyright
materials to be used in the Collins
Word Web. We would also like to
thank Times Newspapers Ltd for
providing valuable data.

Contents

Introduction

Collins SCRABBLE™ Dictionary is an invaluable tool for any competitive or club player, as well as for those who play with their friends and family. This is the third edition of the dictionary in paperback, and it contains over 2,000 new words recently added to the official SCRABBLE™ word list, reflecting the ways the English language continues to grow and change, as well as the enduring popularity of the game itself.

This dictionary contains every word of between two and nine letters, with either a definition or a cross-reference to a defined root word.

It allows every SCRABBLE™ player, whether a beginner or veteran, access to the definitions of all the most useful words in SCRABBLE™, enabling them to learn words by meaning rather than simply as combinations of letters. For many players, definitions are the key to remembering words, and to using them in SCRABBLE™, and the ability to check meanings, inflections, and variant spellings will add interest to most social games.

The definitions are succinct and practical. In many cases, only a single definition is given, and in general only those parts of speech necessary for existing inflections are included. Cross-referred words include noun plurals, verb inflections, the comparative and superlative forms of adjectives, and variant spellings. Adjectives formed with obvious suffixes, such as -*like* and -*less*, are also cross-referred to the root word when the meaning is easily deduced.

Some of the exciting new additions from the realm of computing are SCROBBLE, WIKI, and VLOG (as well as the verbs FACEBOOK and MYSPACE from the world of social media); new borrowings from other languages include ALU and GOBI from India, UMRA and MEDRESA from the Middle East, and KOGAL from Japan; while slang and informal English have given us BLINGY, INNIT, and THANG.

However, of greatest strategic importance to the game are the two new words featuring Q without U: FIQH, Islamic jurisprudence; and QIN, a Chinese stringed instrument like a zither.

In any SCRABBLE™ game, most words will be between two and nine letters in length. Therefore, this book contains only those words, and does not include words between 10 and 15 letters in length. This accounts for the omission of some plurals and inflected forms of words that are themselves in the dictionary.

Unlike a conventional dictionary, every word in each section is listed in strict alphabetical order, regardless of the relationship between words. Thus there may be many words between the singular form of a noun and its plural. This strict alphabetization allows rapid checking of words – which is particularly important during SCRABBLE™ tournaments.

Collins would like to give warm thanks to Darryl Francis, Allan Simmons, and David Sutton for their enormous contribution to the wordlist in this dictionary. They worked tirelessly with the editorial team to get this right. Any errors – and all the definitions in this book – are the responsibility of the publisher.

Using the SCRABBLE™ Dictionary

This book includes all playable words of two to nine letters in length, in one straight alphabetical list. These words are either defined or cross-referred. Cross-referred words include noun plurals, verb inflections, the comparative and superlative forms of adjectives, and variant spellings. Adjectives formed with obvious suffixes, such as -*like* and -*less* are also cross-referred to the root word.

In *Collins SCRABBLE™ Dictionary*, only a single definition is given for each part of speech, and in general only those parts of speech necessary for existing inflections are included. Definitions are based on those of the *Collins English Dictionary*, complete and unabridged, but have been shortened to make them more concise. Some definitions have been specifically written for this product.

Word order	*Collins SCRABBLE™ Dictionary* is in strict alphabetical order.
Offensive terms	there may be words in *Collins SCRABBLE™ Dictionary* that most or some players might consider derogatory, offensive, or even taboo. These are labelled *offensive* in the dictionary.
Accents	as English language SCRABBLE™ tiles are not accented, no accents are shown in *Collins SCRABBLE™ Dictionary*.
Main entry words	printed in bold capitals, eg:

AA

All entry words, in one alphabetical sequence, eg:

AA
AAH
AAHED
AAL
AALI

Parts of Speech	shown in italics as an abbreviation, eg:
	AA *n*
	When more than one part of speech is given, the change of part of speech is shown after an arrow, eg:
	ABANDON *vb* desert or leave
	▷ *n* lack of inhibition
Cross-references	noun plurals, verb inflections, comparatives and superlatives, and derivatives are all cross-referred to their root form, eg:
	ABASH *vb* cause to feel ill at ease, embarrassed, or confused
	...
	ABASHES > ABASH
	ABASHING > ABASH
	ABASHLESS > ABASH
	ABASHMENT > ABASH
Variant forms	variant forms and synonyms are cross-referred to the most commonly-used form of a word, eg:
	CAFTAN *same as* **>** KAFTAN
	noun plurals, verb inflections, comparatives, superlatives, and derivatives of the variant form are all cross-referred to the root form of that particular variant, eg:
	CAFTAN *same as* **>** KAFTAN
	...
	CAFTANS > CAFTAN
Phrases	when a word is most comonly used in a phrase, the phrase is given in italics and defined, eg:
	BANGALORE as in *bangalore torpedo* explosive device in a long metal tube, used to blow gaps in barbed-wire barriers

Aa

AA *n* volcanic rock consisting of angular blocks of lava with a very rough surface
AAH *vb* exclaim in pleasure or surprise
AAHED > AAH
AAHING > AAH
AAHS > AAH
AAL *n* Asian shrub or tree
AALII *n* bushy sapindaceous shrub with small greenish flowers and sticky foliage
AALIIS > AALII
AALS > AAL
AARDVARK *n* S African anteater with long ears and snout
AARDVARKS > AARDVARK
AARDWOLF *n* nocturnal mammal of southern Africa which feeds on termites and insect larvae
AARGH *same as* > ARGH
AARRGH *same as* > ARGH
AARRGHH *same as* > ARGH
AARTI *n* Hindu ceremony in which lights with wicks soaked in ghee are lit and offered up to one or more deities
AARTIS > AARTI
AAS > AA
AASVOGEL *n* South African bird of prey
AASVOGELS > AASVOGEL
AB *n* abdominal muscle
ABA *n* type of cloth from Syria, made of goat hair or camel hair
ABAC *n* mathematical diagram
ABACA *n* Philippine plant, related to the banana
ABACAS > ABACA
ABACI > ABACUS
ABACK *adv* towards the back; backwards
ABACS > ABAC
ABACTINAL *adj* (of organisms showing radial symmetry) situated away from or opposite to the mouth
ABACTOR *n* cattle thief
ABACTORS > ABACTOR
ABACUS *n* beads on a wire frame, used for doing calculations
ABACUSES > ABACUS

ABAFT *adv* closer to the rear of (a ship) ▷ *adj* closer to the stern of a ship
ABAKA *n* abaca
ABAKAS > ABAKA
ABALONE *n* edible sea creature with a shell lined with mother of pearl
ABALONES > ABALONE
ABAMP *same as* > ABAMPERE
ABAMPERE *n* cgs unit of current in the electromagnetic system
ABAMPERES > ABAMPERE
ABAMPS > ABAMP
ABAND *vb* abandon
ABANDED > ABAND
ABANDING > ABAND
ABANDON *vb* desert or leave (one's wife, children, etc) ▷ *n* lack of inhibition
ABANDONED *adj* deserted
ABANDONEE *n* person to whom something is formally relinquished, esp an insurer having the right to salvage a wreck
ABANDONER > ABANDON
ABANDONS > ABANDON
ABANDS > ABAND
ABAPICAL *adj* away from or opposite the apex
ABAS > ABA
ABASE *vb* humiliate or degrade (oneself)
ABASED > ABASE
ABASEDLY > ABASE
ABASEMENT > ABASE
ABASER > ABASE
ABASERS > ABASE
ABASES > ABASE
ABASH *vb* cause to feel ill at ease, embarrassed, or confused
ABASHED *adj* embarrassed and ashamed
ABASHEDLY > ABASHED
ABASHES > ABASH
ABASHING > ABASH
ABASHLESS > ABASH
ABASHMENT > ABASH
ABASIA *n* disorder affecting ability to walk
ABASIAS > ABASIA
ABASING > ABASE
ABASK *adv* in pleasant warmth
ABATABLE > ABATE
ABATE *vb* make or become less strong
ABATED > ABATE

ABATEMENT *n* diminution or alleviation
ABATER > ABATE
ABATERS > ABATE
ABATES > ABATE
ABATING > ABATE
ABATIS *n* rampart of felled trees bound together, placed with their branches outwards
ABATISES > ABATIS
ABATOR *n* person who effects an abatement
ABATORS > ABATOR
ABATTIS *same as* > ABATIS
ABATTISES > ABATTIS
ABATTOIR *n* place where animals are killed for food
ABATTOIRS > ABATTOIR
ABATTU *adj* dejected
ABATURE *n* trail left by hunted stag
ABATURES > ABATURE
ABAXIAL *adj* facing away from the axis, as the surface of a leaf
ABAXILE *adj* away from the axis
ABAYA *n* Arab outer garment
ABAYAS > ABAYA
ABB *n* yarn used in weaving
ABBA *n* title for a bishop in the Coptic Church
ABBACIES > ABBACY
ABBACY *n* office or jurisdiction of an abbot or abbess
ABBAS > ABBA
ABBATIAL *adj* of or relating to an abbot, abbess, or abbey
ABBE *n* French abbot
ABBED *adj* displaying well-developed abdominal muscles
ABBES > ABBE
ABBESS *n* nun in charge of a convent
ABBESSES > ABBESS
ABBEY *n* dwelling place of, or a church belonging to, a community of monks or nuns
ABBEYS > ABBEY
ABBOT *n* head of an abbey of monks
ABBOTCIES > ABBOT
ABBOTCY > ABBOT
ABBOTS > ABBOT

ABBOTSHIP > ABBOT
ABBS > ABB
ABCEE *n* alphabet
ABCEES > ABCEE
ABCOULOMB *n* cgs unit of electric charge in the electromagnetic system
ABDABS *n* highly nervous state
ABDICABLE > ABDICATE
ABDICANT > ABDICATE
ABDICATE *vb* give up (the throne or a responsibility)
ABDICATED > ABDICATE
ABDICATES > ABDICATE
ABDICATOR > ABDICATE
ABDOMEN *n* part of the body containing the stomach and intestines
ABDOMENS > ABDOMEN
ABDOMINA > ABDOMEN
ABDOMINAL > ABDOMEN
ABDUCE *vb* abduct
ABDUCED > ABDUCE
ABDUCENS as in *abducens nerve* either of the sixth pair of cranial nerves, which supply the lateral rectus muscle of the eye
ABDUCENT *adj* (of a muscle) abducting
ABDUCES > ABDUCE
ABDUCING > ABDUCE
ABDUCT *vb* carry off, kidnap
ABDUCTED > ABDUCT
ABDUCTEE > ABDUCT
ABDUCTEES > ABDUCT
ABDUCTING > ABDUCT
ABDUCTION *n* act of taking someone away by force or cunning
ABDUCTOR > ABDUCT
ABDUCTORS > ABDUCT
ABDUCTS > ABDUCT
ABEAM *adj* at right angles to the length of a ship or aircraft
ABEAR *vb* bear or behave
ABEARING > ABEAR
ABEARS > ABEAR
ABED *adv* in bed
ABEGGING *adj* in the act of begging for money etc
ABEIGH *adv* aloof
ABELE *n* white poplar tree
ABELES > ABELE
ABELIA *n* garden plant with pink or white flowers
ABELIAN > ABELIA
ABELIAS > ABELIA

a

ABELMOSK n tropical plant with yellow-and-crimson flowers and musk-scented seeds
ABELMOSKS > ABELMOSK
ABERNETHY n crisp unleavened biscuit
ABERRANCE > ABERRANT
ABERRANCY > ABERRANT
ABERRANT adj showing aberration ▷ n person whose behaviour is considered to be aberrant
ABERRANTS > ABERRANT
ABERRATE vb deviate from what is normal or correct
ABERRATED > ABERRATE
ABERRATES > ABERRATE
ABESSIVE n grammatical case indicating absence
ABESSIVES > ABESSIVE
ABET vb help or encourage in wrongdoing
ABETMENT > ABET
ABETMENTS > ABET
ABETS > ABET
ABETTAL > ABET
ABETTALS > ABET
ABETTED > ABET
ABETTER > ABET
ABETTERS > ABET
ABETTING > ABET
ABETTOR > ABET
ABETTORS > ABET
ABEYANCE n state of being suspended or put aside temporarily
ABEYANCES > ABEYANCE
ABEYANCY n abeyance
ABEYANT > ABEYANCE
ABFARAD n cgs unit of capacitance in the electromagnetic system
ABFARADS > ABFARAD
ABHENRIES > ABHENRY
ABHENRY n cgs unit of inductance in the electromagnetic system
ABHENRYS > ABHENRY
ABHOR vb detest utterly
ABHORRED > ABHOR
ABHORRENT adj hateful, loathsome
ABHORRER > ABHOR
ABHORRERS > ABHOR
ABHORRING > ABHOR
ABHORS > ABHOR
ABID > ABIDE
ABIDANCE > ABIDE
ABIDANCES > ABIDE
ABIDDEN > ABIDE
ABIDE vb endure, put up with
ABIDED > ABIDE
ABIDER > ABIDE
ABIDERS > ABIDE
ABIDES > ABIDE
ABIDING adj lasting ▷ n action of one who abides
ABIDINGLY > ABIDING
ABIDINGS > ABIDING
ABIES n fir tree
ABIETIC as in abietic acid a yellowish powder used in

lacquers, varnishes, and soap
ABIGAIL n maid for a lady
ABIGAILS > ABIGAIL
ABILITIES > ABILITY
ABILITY n competence, power
ABIOGENIC adj abiogenetic
ABIOSES > ABIOSIS
ABIOSIS n absence of life
ABIOTIC > ABIOSIS
ABITUR n German final-year school examination
ABITURS > ABITUR
ABJECT adj utterly miserable ▷ vb throw down
ABJECTED > ABJECT
ABJECTING > ABJECT
ABJECTION > ABJECT
ABJECTLY > ABJECT
ABJECTS > ABJECT
ABJOINT vb cut off
ABJOINTED > ABJOINT
ABJOINTS > ABJOINT
ABJURE vb deny or renounce on oath
ABJURED > ABJURE
ABJURER > ABJURE
ABJURERS > ABJURE
ABJURES > ABJURE
ABJURING > ABJURE
ABLATE vb remove by ablation
ABLATED > ABLATE
ABLATES > ABLATE
ABLATING > ABLATE
ABLATION n surgical removal of an organ or part
ABLATIONS > ABLATION
ABLATIVAL > ABLATIVE
ABLATIVE n case of nouns in Latin and other languages, indicating source, agent, or instrument of action ▷ adj (in certain inflected languages such as Latin) denoting a case of nouns, pronouns, and adjectives indicating the agent in passive sentences or the instrument, manner, or place of the action described by the verb
ABLATIVES > ABLATIVE
ABLATOR n heat shield of a space vehicle, which melts or wears away during re-entry into the earth's atmosphere
ABLATORS > ABLATOR
ABLAUT n vowel gradation, esp in Indo-European languages
ABLAUTS > ABLAUT
ABLAZE adj burning fiercely ▷ adv on fire
ABLE adj capable, competent ▷ vb enable
ABLED adj having a range of physical powers as specified

ABLEGATE n papal envoy
ABLEGATES > ABLEGATE
ABLEISM n discrimination against disabled or handicapped people
ABLEISMS > ABLEISM
ABLEIST > ABLEISM
ABLEISTS > ABLEISM
ABLER > ABLE
ABLES > ABLE
ABLEST > ABLE
ABLET n freshwater fish
ABLETS > ABLET
ABLING > ABLE
ABLINGS adv possibly
ABLINS adv Scots word meaning perhaps
ABLOOM adj in flower
ABLOW adj blooming
ABLUENT n substance used for cleansing
ABLUENTS > ABLUENT
ABLUSH adj blushing
ABLUTED adj washed thoroughly
ABLUTION n ritual washing of a priest's hands or of sacred vessels
ABLUTIONS > ABLUTION
ABLY adv competently or skilfully
ABMHO n unit of electrical conductance
ABMHOS > ABMHO
ABNEGATE vb deny to oneself
ABNEGATED > ABNEGATE
ABNEGATES > ABNEGATE
ABNEGATOR > ABNEGATE
ABNORMAL adj not normal or usual ▷ n abnormal person or thing
ABNORMALS > ABNORMAL
ABNORMITY > ABNORMAL
ABNORMOUS > ABNORMAL
ABO > ABORIGINE
ABOARD adv on, in, onto, or into (a ship, plane, or plane) ▷ adj on, in, onto, or into (a ship, plane, or train)
ABODE n home, dwelling ▷ vb forebode
ABODED > ABODE
ABODEMENT > ABODE
ABODES > ABODE
ABODING > ABODE
ABOHM n cgs unit of resistance in the electromagnetic system: equivalent to 10^{-9}ohm
ABOHMS > ABOHM
ABOIDEAU n dyke with a sluicegate that allows flood water to drain but keeps the sea water out
ABOIDEAUS > ABOIDEAU
ABOIDEAUX > ABOIDEAU
ABOIL adj boiling
ABOITEAU same as > ABOIDEAU
ABOITEAUS > ABOITEAU
ABOITEAUX > ABOITEAU
ABOLISH vb do away with
ABOLISHED > ABOLISH

ABOLISHER > ABOLISH
ABOLISHES > ABOLISH
ABOLITION n act of abolishing or the state of being abolished
ABOLLA n Roman cloak
ABOLLAE > ABOLLA
ABOLLAS > ABOLLA
ABOMA n South American snake
ABOMAS > ABOMA
ABOMASA > ABOMASUM
ABOMASAL > ABOMASUM
ABOMASI > ABOMASUS
ABOMASUM n fourth and last compartment of the stomach of ruminants, which receives and digests food from the psalterium and passes it on to the small intestine
ABOMASUS n abomasum
ABOMINATE vb dislike intensely
ABONDANCE same as > ABUNDANCE
ABOON Scots word for > ABOVE
ABORAL adj away from or opposite the mouth
ABORALLY > ABORAL
ABORD vb accost
ABORDED > ABORD
ABORDING > ABORD
ABORDS > ABORD
ABORE > ABEAR
ABORIGEN n aborigine
ABORIGENS > ABORIGEN
ABORIGIN n aborigine
ABORIGINE n original inhabitant of a country or region, esp Australia
ABORIGINS > ABORIGIN
ABORNE adj Shakespearean form of auburn
ABORNING > ABEAR
ABORT vb have an abortion or perform an abortion on ▷ n premature termination or failure of (a space flight, military operation, etc)
ABORTED > ABORT
ABORTEE n woman having an abortion
ABORTEES > ABORTEE
ABORTER > ABORT
ABORTERS > ABORT
ABORTING > ABORT
ABORTION n operation to end a pregnancy
ABORTIONS > ABORTION
ABORTIVE adj unsuccessful
ABORTS > ABORT
ABORTUARY n place where abortions are carried out
ABORTUS n aborted fetus
ABORTUSES > ABORTUS
ABOS > ABO
ABOUGHT > ABY
ABOULIA same as > ABULIA
ABOULIAS > ABOULIA
ABOULIC > ABOULIA

ABOUND *vb* be plentiful
ABOUNDED > ABOUND
ABOUNDING > ABOUND
ABOUNDS > ABOUND
ABOUT *adv* nearly, approximately
ABOUTS *prep* about
ABOVE *adv* over or higher (than) ▷ *n* something that is or appears above
ABOVES > ABOVE
ABRACHIA *n* condition of having no arms
ABRACHIAS > ABRACHIA
ABRADABLE > ABRADE
ABRADANT > ABRADE
ABRADANTS > ABRADE
ABRADE *vb* scrape away or wear down by friction
ABRADED > ABRADE
ABRADER > ABRADE
ABRADERS > ABRADE
ABRADES > ABRADE
ABRADING > ABRADE
ABRAID *vb* awake
ABRAIDED > ABRAID
ABRAIDING > ABRAID
ABRAIDS > ABRAID
ABRAM *adj* auburn
ABRASAX *same as* > ABRAXAS
ABRASAXES > ABRASAX
ABRASION *n* scraped area on the skin
ABRASIONS > ABRASION
ABRASIVE *adj* harsh and unpleasant in manner ▷ *n* substance for cleaning or polishing by rubbing
ABRASIVES > ABRASIVE
ABRAXAS *n* ancient charm composed of Greek letters: originally believed to have magical powers and inscribed on amulets, etc, but from the second century AD personified by Gnostics as a deity, the source of divine emanations
ABRAXASES > ABRAXAS
ABRAY *vb* awake
ABRAYED > ABRAY
ABRAYING > ABRAY
ABRAYS > ABRAY
ABRAZO *n* embrace
ABRAZOS > ABRAZO
ABREACT *vb* alleviate (emotional tension) through abreaction
ABREACTED > ABREACT
ABREACTS > ABREACT
ABREAST *adj* side by side
ABREGE *n* abridgment
ABREGES > ABREGE
ABRI *n* shelter or place of refuge, esp in wartime
ABRICOCK *n* apricot
ABRICOCKS > ABRICOCK
ABRIDGE *vb* shorten by using fewer words
ABRIDGED > ABRIDGE
ABRIDGER > ABRIDGE
ABRIDGERS > ABRIDGE

ABRIDGES > ABRIDGE
ABRIDGING > ABRIDGE
ABRIM *adj* full to the brim
ABRIN *n* poisonous compound
ABRINS > ABRIN
ABRIS > ABRI
ABROACH *adj* (of a cask, barrel, etc) tapped
ABROAD *adv* in a foreign country ▷ *adj* (of news, rumours, etc) in general circulation ▷ *n* foreign place
ABROADS > ABROAD
ABROGABLE *adj* able to be abrogated
ABROGATE *vb* cancel (a law or agreement) formally
ABROGATED > ABROGATE
ABROGATES > ABROGATE
ABROGATOR > ABROGATE
ABROOKE *vb* bear or tolerate
ABROOKED > ABROOKE
ABROOKES > ABROOKE
ABROOKING > ABROOKE
ABROSIA *n* condition involving refusal to eat
ABROSIAS > ABROSIA
ABRUPT *adj* sudden, unexpected ▷ *n* abyss
ABRUPTER > ABRUPT
ABRUPTEST > ABRUPT
ABRUPTION *n* breaking off of a part or parts from a mass
ABRUPTLY > ABRUPT
ABRUPTS > ABRUPT
ABS > AB
ABSCESS *n* inflamed swelling containing pus ▷ *vb* form a swelling containing pus
ABSCESSED > ABSCESS
ABSCESSES > ABSCESS
ABSCIND *vb* cut off
ABSCINDED > ABSCIND
ABSCINDS > ABSCIND
ABSCISE *vb* separate or be separated by abscission
ABSCISED > ABSCISE
ABSCISES > ABSCISE
ABSCISIC *adj* as in *abscisic acid* a type of acid
ABSCISIN *n* plant hormone
ABSCISING > ABSCISE
ABSCISINS > ABSCISIN
ABSCISS *n* cutting off
ABSCISSA *n* cutting off
ABSCISSAE > ABSCISSA
ABSCISSAS > ABSCISSA
ABSCISSE *n* cutting off
ABSCISSES > ABSCISSE
ABSCISSIN *n* plant hormone
ABSCOND *vb* leave secretly
ABSCONDED > ABSCOND
ABSCONDER > ABSCOND
ABSCONDS > ABSCOND
ABSEIL *vb* go down a steep drop by a rope fastened at the top and tied around

one's body ▷ *n* instance of abseiling
ABSEILED > ABSEIL
ABSEILING > ABSEIL
ABSEILS > ABSEIL
ABSENCE *n* being away
ABSENCES > ABSENCE
ABSENT *adj* not present ▷ *vb* stay away
ABSENTED > ABSENT
ABSENTEE *n* person who should be present but is not
ABSENTEES > ABSENTEE
ABSENTER > ABSENT
ABSENTERS > ABSENT
ABSENTING > ABSENT
ABSENTLY *adv* in an absent-minded or preoccupied manner
ABSENTS > ABSENT
ABSEY *n* alphabet
ABSEYS > ABSEY
ABSINTH *same as* > ABSINTHE
ABSINTHE *n* strong green aniseed-flavoured liqueur
ABSINTHES > ABSINTHE
ABSINTHS > ABSINTH
ABSIT *n* overnight leave from college
ABSITS > ABSIT
ABSOLUTE *adj* complete, perfect ▷ *n* something that is absolute
ABSOLUTER > ABSOLUTE
ABSOLUTES > ABSOLUTE
ABSOLVE *vb* declare to be free from blame or sin
ABSOLVED > ABSOLVE
ABSOLVER > ABSOLVE
ABSOLVERS > ABSOLVE
ABSOLVES > ABSOLVE
ABSOLVING > ABSOLVE
ABSONANT *adj* unnatural and unreasonable
ABSORB *vb* soak up (a liquid)
ABSORBANT *n* absorbent substance
ABSORBATE *n* absorbed substance
ABSORBED *adj* engrossed
ABSORBENT *adj* able to absorb liquid ▷ *n* substance that absorbs
ABSORBER *n* person or thing that absorbs
ABSORBERS > ABSORBER
ABSORBING *adj* occupying one's interest or attention
ABSORBS > ABSORB
ABSTAIN *vb* choose not to do something
ABSTAINED > ABSTAIN
ABSTAINER > ABSTAIN
ABSTAINS > ABSTAIN
ABSTERGE *vb* cleanse
ABSTERGED > ABSTERGE
ABSTERGES > ABSTERGE
ABSTINENT *adj* refraining from a certain activity
ABSTRACT *adj* existing as a

quality or idea rather than a material object ▷ *n* summary ▷ *vb* summarize
ABSTRACTS > ABSTRACT
ABSTRICT *vb* release
ABSTRICTS > ABSTRICT
ABSTRUSE *adj* not easy to understand
ABSTRUSER > ABSTRUSE
ABSURD *adj* incongruous or ridiculous ▷ *n* conception of the world, esp in Existentialist thought, as neither designed nor predictable but irrational and meaningless
ABSURDER > ABSURD
ABSURDEST > ABSURD
ABSURDISM *n* belief that life is meaningless
ABSURDIST > ABSURDISM
ABSURDITY > ABSURD
ABSURDLY > ABSURD
ABSURDS > ABSURD
ABTHANE *n* ancient Scottish church territory
ABTHANES > ABTHANE
ABUBBLE *adj* bubbling
ABUILDING *adj* being built
ABULIA *n* pathological inability to take decisions
ABULIAS > ABULIA
ABULIC > ABULIA
ABUNA *n* male head of Ethiopian family
ABUNAS > ABUNA
ABUNDANCE *n* copious supply
ABUNDANCY *n* abundance
ABUNDANT *adj* plentiful
ABUNE *Scots word for* > ABOVE
ABURST *adj* bursting
ABUSABLE > ABUSE
ABUSAGE *n* wrong use
ABUSAGES > ABUSAGE
ABUSE *vb* use wrongly ▷ *n* prolonged ill-treatment
ABUSED > ABUSE
ABUSER > ABUSE
ABUSERS > ABUSE
ABUSES > ABUSE
ABUSING > ABUSE
ABUSION *n* wrong use or deception
ABUSIONS > ABUSION
ABUSIVE *adj* rude or insulting
ABUSIVELY > ABUSIVE
ABUT *vb* be next to or touching
ABUTILON *n* shrub with showy white, yellow, or red flowers
ABUTILONS > ABUTILON
ABUTMENT *n* construction that supports the end of a bridge
ABUTMENTS > ABUTMENT
ABUTS > ABUT
ABUTTAL *same as* > ABUTMENT
ABUTTALS > ABUTTAL

ABUTTED > ABUT
ABUTTER n owner of adjoining property
ABUTTERS > ABUTTER
ABUTTING > ABUT
ABUZZ adj noisy, busy with activity etc
ABVOLT n cgs unit of potential difference in the electromagnetic system
ABVOLTS > ABVOLT
ABWATT n cgs unit of power in the electromagnetic system, equal to the power dissipated when a current of 1 abampere flows across a potential difference of 1 abvolt: equivalent to 10^{-7} watt
ABWATTS > ABWATT
ABY vb pay the penalty for
ABYE same as > ABY
ABYEING > ABYE
ABYES > ABYE
ABYING > ABY
ABYS > ABY
ABYSM archaic word for > ABYSS
ABYSMAL adj extremely bad, awful
ABYSMALLY > ABYSMAL
ABYSMS > ABYSM
ABYSS n very deep hole or chasm
ABYSSAL adj of or belonging to the ocean depths, esp below 2000 metres (6500 feet)
ABYSSES > ABYSS
ACACIA n tree or shrub with yellow or white flowers
ACACIAS > ACACIA
ACADEME n place of learning
ACADEMES > ACADEME
ACADEMIA n academic world
ACADEMIAS > ACADEMIA
ACADEMIC adj of an academy or university ▷ n lecturer or researcher at a university
ACADEMICS > ACADEMIC
ACADEMIES > ACADEMY
ACADEMISM n adherence to rules and traditions in art, literature, etc
ACADEMIST > ACADEMY
ACADEMY n society to advance arts or sciences
ACAI n berry found in Brazilian rainforest
ACAIS > ACAI
ACAJOU n type of mahogany used by cabinet-makers in France
ACAJOUS > ACAJOU
ACALCULIA n inability to make simple mathematical calculations
ACALEPH n invertebrate of the former taxonomic group which included the jellyfishes

ACALEPHAE > ACALEPH
ACALEPHAN > ACALEPH
ACALEPHE n acaleph
ACALEPHES > ACALEPHE
ACALEPHS > ACALEPH
ACANTH n acanthus
ACANTHA n thorn or prickle
ACANTHAE > ACANTHA
ACANTHAS > ACANTHA
ACANTHI > ACANTHUS
ACANTHIN n organic chemical used in medicine
ACANTHINE adj of or resembling an acanthus
ACANTHINS > ACANTHIN
ACANTHOID adj resembling a spine
ACANTHOUS adj of an acanthus
ACANTHS > ACANTH
ACANTHUS n prickly plant
ACAPNIA n lack of carbon dioxide
ACAPNIAS > ACAPNIA
ACARBOSE n diabetes medicine
ACARBOSES > ACARBOSE
ACARI > ACARUS
ACARIAN > ACARUS
ACARIASES > ACARIASIS
ACARIASIS n infestation of the hair follicles and skin with acarids, esp mites
ACARICIDE n any drug or formulation for killing acarids
ACARID n member of the group of small arachnids which includes the ticks and mites ▷ adj of or relating to these arachnids
ACARIDAN same as > ACARID
ACARIDANS > ACARIDAN
ACARIDEAN > ACARID
ACARIDIAN > ACARID
ACARIDS > ACARID
ACARINE n acarid
ACARINES > ACARINE
ACAROID adj resembling a mite or tick
ACAROLOGY n study of mites and ticks
ACARPOUS adj (of plants) producing no fruit
ACARUS n type of mites which is a serious pests of stored flour, grain, etc
ACATER n buyer of provisions
ACATERS > ACATER
ACATES n provisions
ACATHISIA same as > AKATHISIA
ACATOUR n buyer of provisions
ACATOURS > ACATOUR
ACAUDAL adj having no tail
ACAUDATE same as > ACAUDAL
ACAULINE adj having no stem
ACAULOSE same as

> ACAULINE
ACAULOUS adj having a short stem or no stem
ACCA n academic
ACCABLE adj dejected or beaten
ACCAS > ACCA
ACCEDE vb consent or agree (to)
ACCEDED > ACCEDE
ACCEDENCE > ACCEDE
ACCEDER > ACCEDE
ACCEDERS > ACCEDE
ACCEDES > ACCEDE
ACCEDING > ACCEDE
ACCEND vb set alight
ACCENDED > ACCEND
ACCENDING > ACCEND
ACCENDS > ACCEND
ACCENSION > ACCEND
ACCENT n distinctive style of pronunciation of a local, national, or social group ▷ vb place emphasis on
ACCENTED > ACCENT
ACCENTING > ACCENT
ACCENTOR n small sparrow-like songbird of Europe and Asia
ACCENTORS > ACCENTOR
ACCENTS > ACCENT
ACCENTUAL adj of, relating to, or having accents
ACCEPT vb receive willingly
ACCEPTANT adj receiving willingly
ACCEPTED adj generally approved
ACCEPTEE n person who has been accepted
ACCEPTEES > ACCEPTEE
ACCEPTER > ACCEPT
ACCEPTERS > ACCEPT
ACCEPTING > ACCEPT
ACCEPTIVE adj ready to accept
ACCEPTOR n person or organization on which a draft or bill of exchange is drawn after liability has been accepted, usually by signature
ACCEPTORS > ACCEPTOR
ACCEPTS > ACCEPT
ACCESS n means of or right to approach or enter ▷ vb obtain (data) from a computer
ACCESSARY same as > ACCESSORY
ACCESSED > ACCESS
ACCESSES > ACCESS
ACCESSING > ACCESS
ACCESSION n taking up of an office or position ▷ vb make a record of (additions to a collection)
ACCESSORY n supplementary part or object ▷ adj supplementary
ACCIDENCE n inflectional morphology
ACCIDENT n mishap, often causing injury

ACCIDENTS > ACCIDENT
ACCIDIA same as > ACCIDIE
ACCIDIAS > ACCIDIA
ACCIDIE n spiritual sloth
ACCIDIES > ACCIDIE
ACCINGE vb put a belt around
ACCINGED > ACCINGE
ACCINGES > ACCINGE
ACCINGING > ACCINGE
ACCIPITER n hawk with short rounded wings and a long tail
ACCITE vb summon
ACCITED > ACCITE
ACCITES > ACCITE
ACCITING > ACCITE
ACCLAIM vb applaud, praise ▷ n enthusiastic approval
ACCLAIMED > ACCLAIM
ACCLAIMER > ACCLAIM
ACCLAIMS > ACCLAIM
ACCLIMATE vb adapt or become accustomed to a new climate or environment
ACCLIVITY n upward slope, esp of the ground
ACCLIVOUS > ACCLIVITY
ACCLOY vb choke or clog
ACCLOYED > ACCLOY
ACCLOYING > ACCLOY
ACCLOYS > ACCLOY
ACCOAST vb accost
ACCOASTED > ACCOAST
ACCOASTS > ACCOAST
ACCOIED > ACCOY
ACCOIL n welcome ▷ vb gather together
ACCOILS > ACCOIL
ACCOLADE n award or praise ▷ vb give an award or praise
ACCOLADED > ACCOLADE
ACCOLADES > ACCOLADE
ACCOMPANY vb go along with
ACCOMPT vb account
ACCOMPTED > ACCOMPT
ACCOMPTS > ACCOMPT
ACCORAGE vb encourage
ACCORAGED > ACCORAGE
ACCORAGES > ACCORAGE
ACCORD n agreement, harmony ▷ vb fit in with
ACCORDANT adj in conformity or harmony
ACCORDED > ACCORD
ACCORDER > ACCORD
ACCORDERS > ACCORD
ACCORDING adj in proportion
ACCORDION n portable musical instrument played by moving the two sides apart and together, and pressing a keyboard or buttons to produce the notes
ACCORDS > ACCORD
ACCOST vb approach and

speak to, often aggressively ▷ *n* greeting

ACCOSTED > ACCOST

ACCOSTING > ACCOST

ACCOSTS > ACCOST

ACCOUNT *n* report, description ▷ *vb* judge to be

ACCOUNTED > ACCOUNT

ACCOUNTS > ACCOUNT

ACCOURAGE *vb* encourage

ACCOURT *vb* entertain

ACCOURTED > ACCOURT

ACCOURTS > ACCOURT

ACCOUTER *same as* > ACCOUTRE

ACCOUTERS > ACCOUTER

ACCOUTRE *vb* provide with equipment or dress, esp military

ACCOUTRED > ACCOUTRE

ACCOUTRES > ACCOUTRE

ACCOY *vb* soothe

ACCOYED > ACCOY

ACCOYING > ACCOY

ACCOYLD > ACCOIL

ACCOYS > ACCOY

ACCREDIT *vb* give official recognition to

ACCREDITS > ACCREDIT

ACCRETE *vb* grow or cause to grow together

ACCRETED > ACCRETE

ACCRETES > ACCRETE

ACCRETING > ACCRETE

ACCRETION *n* gradual growth

ACCRETIVE > ACCRETION

ACCREW *vb* accrue

ACCREWED > ACCREW

ACCREWING > ACCREW

ACCREWS > ACCREW

ACCROIDES *n* red alcohol-soluble resin

ACCRUABLE > ACCRUE

ACCRUAL *n* act of accruing

ACCRUALS > ACCRUAL

ACCRUE *vb* increase gradually

ACCRUED > ACCRUE

ACCRUES > ACCRUE

ACCRUING > ACCRUE

ACCUMBENT *adj* (of plant parts and plants) lying against some other part or thing

ACCURACY *n* faithful representation of the truth

ACCURATE *adj* exact, correct

ACCURSE *vb* curse

ACCURSED *adj* under a curse

ACCURSES > ACCURSE

ACCURSING > ACCURSE

ACCURST *same as* > ACCURSED

ACCUSABLE > ACCUSE

ACCUSABLY > ACCUSE

ACCUSAL *n* accusation

ACCUSALS > ACCUSAL

ACCUSANT *n* person who accuses

ACCUSANTS > ACCUSANT

ACCUSE *vb* charge with wrongdoing

ACCUSED *n* person or people accused of a crime in a court

ACCUSER > ACCUSE

ACCUSERS > ACCUSE

ACCUSES > ACCUSE

ACCUSING > ACCUSE

ACCUSTOM *vb* make used to

ACCUSTOMS > ACCUSTOM

ACE *n* playing card with one symbol on it ▷ *adj* excellent ▷ *vb* serve an ace in racquet sports

ACED > ACE

ACEDIA *same as* > ACCIDIE

ACEDIAS > ACEDIA

ACELDAMA *n* place with ill feeling

ACELDAMAS > ACELDAMA

ACELLULAR *adj* not made up of or containing cells

ACENTRIC *adj* without a centre ▷ *n* acentric chromosome or fragment

ACENTRICS > ACENTRIC n

ACEPHALIC *adj* having no head or one that is reduced and indistinct, as certain insect larvae

ACEQUIA *n* irrigation ditch

ACEQUIAS > ACEQUIA

ACER *n* type of tree cultivated for its brightly coloured foliage

ACERATE *same as* > ACERATED

ACERATED *adj* having sharp points

ACERB *adj* bitter

ACERBATE *vb* embitter or exasperate

ACERBATED > ACERBATE

ACERBATES > ACERBATE

ACERBER > ACERB

ACERBEST > ACERB

ACERBIC *adj* harsh or bitter

ACERBITY *n* bitter speech or temper

ACEROLA *n* cherry-like fruit

ACEROLAS > ACEROLA

ACEROSE *adj* shaped like a needle, as pine leaves

ACEROUS *same as* > ACEROSE

ACERS > ACER

ACERVATE *adj* growing in heaps or clusters

ACERVULI > ACERVULUS

ACERVULUS *n* spore-producing part of plant

ACES > ACE

ACESCENCE > ACESCENT

ACESCENCY > ACESCENT

ACESCENT *adj* slightly sour or turning sour ▷ *n* something that is turning sour

ACESCENTS > ACESCENT

ACETA > ACETUM

ACETABULA *n* deep cuplike cavities on the side of the hipbones that receive the head of the thighbone

ACETAL *n* 1,1-diethoxyethane, a colourless volatile liquid used as a solvent and in perfumes

ACETALS > ACETAL

ACETAMID *same as* > ACETAMIDE

ACETAMIDE *n* white or colourless soluble deliquescent crystalline compound

ACETAMIDS > ACETAMID

ACETATE *n* salt or ester of acetic acid

ACETATED *adj* combined with acetic acid

ACETATES > ACETATE

ACETIC *adj* of or involving vinegar

ACETIFIED > ACETIFY

ACETIFIER > ACETIFY

ACETIFIES > ACETIFY

ACETIFY *vb* become or cause to become acetic acid or vinegar

ACETIN *n* type of acetate

ACETINS > ACETIN

ACETONE *n* colourless liquid used as a solvent

ACETONES > ACETONE

ACETONIC > ACETONE

ACETOSE *same as* > ACETOUS

ACETOUS *adj* containing, producing, or resembling acetic acid or vinegar

ACETOXYL *n* medicine used to treat acne

ACETOXYLS > ACETOXYL

ACETUM *n* solution that has dilute acetic acid as solvent

ACETYL *n* of, consisting of, or containing the monovalent group CH_3CO-

ACETYLATE *vb* introduce an acetyl group into (a chemical compound)

ACETYLENE *n* colourless flammable gas used in welding metals

ACETYLIC > ACETYL

ACETYLIDE *n* any of a class of carbides in which the carbon is present as a diatomic divalent ion (C_2^{2-}). They are formally derivatives of acetylene

ACETYLS > ACETYL

ACH *interj* Scots expression of surprise

ACHAENIA > ACHAENIUM

ACHAENIUM *n* achene

ACHAGE *n* pain

ACHAGES > ACHAGE

ACHALASIA *n* failure of the cardiac sphincter of the oesophagus to relax, resulting in difficulty in swallowing

ACHAR *n* spicy pickle made from mango

ACHARNE *adj* furiously violent

ACHARS > ACHAR

ACHARYA *n* prominent religious teacher and spiritual guide

ACHARYAS > ACHARYA

ACHATES *same as* > ACATES

ACHE *n* dull continuous pain ▷ *vb* be in or cause continuous dull pain

ACHED > ACHE

ACHENE *n* dry one-seeded indehiscent fruit with the seed distinct from the fruit wall. It may be smooth, as in the buttercup, or feathery, as in clematis

ACHENES > ACHENE

ACHENIA > ACHENIUM

ACHENIAL > ACHENE

ACHENIUM *n* achene

ACHENIUMS > ACHENIUM

ACHES > ACHE

ACHIER > ACHY

ACHIEST > ACHY

ACHIEVE *vb* gain by hard work or ability

ACHIEVED > ACHIEVE

ACHIEVER > ACHIEVE

ACHIEVERS > ACHIEVE

ACHIEVES > ACHIEVE

ACHIEVING > ACHIEVE

ACHILLEA *n* type of plant with white, yellow, or purple flowers, often grown in gardens

ACHILLEAS > ACHILLEA

ACHIMENES *n* tropical plant of the S America with showy red, blue, or white tubular flowers

ACHINESS > ACHY

ACHING > ACHE

ACHINGLY > ACHE

ACHINGS > ACHE

ACHIOTE *n* annatto

ACHIOTES > ACHIOTE

ACHIRAL *adj* of a tuber producing arrowroot

ACHKAN *n* man's coat in India

ACHKANS > ACHKAN

ACHOLIA *n* condition involving lack of bile secretion

ACHOLIAS > ACHOLIA

ACHOO *interj* sound of a sneeze

ACHROMAT *n* lens designed to bring light of two chosen wavelengths to the same focal point, thus reducing chromatic aberration

ACHROMATS > ACHROMAT

ACHROMIC *adj* colourless

ACHROMOUS *same as* > ACHROMIC

ACHY *adj* affected by a continuous dull pain

ACICLOVIR *same as* > ACYCLOVIR

ACICULA n needle-shaped part, such as a spine, prickle, or crystal

ACICULAE > ACICULA

ACICULAR > ACICULA

ACICULAS > ACICULA

ACICULATE adj having aciculae

ACICULUM n needle-like bristle that provides internal support for the appendages (chaetae) of some polychaete worms

ACICULUMS > ACICULUM

ACID n one of a class of compounds, corrosive and sour when dissolved in water, that combine with a base to form a salt ▷ adj containing acid

ACIDEMIA n abnormally high level of acid in blood

ACIDEMIAS > ACIDEMIA

ACIDER > ACID

ACIDEST > ACID

ACIDHEAD n person who uses LSD

ACIDHEADS > ACIDHEAD

ACIDIC adj containing acid

ACIDIER > ACID

ACIDIEST > ACID

ACIDIFIED > ACIDIFY

ACIDIFIER > ACIDIFY

ACIDIFIES > ACIDIFY

ACIDIFY vb convert into acid

ACIDITIES > ACIDITY

ACIDITY n quality of being acid

ACIDLY > ACID

ACIDNESS > ACID

ACIDOPHIL adj (of cells or cell contents) easily stained by acid dyes ▷ n acidophil organism

ACIDOSES > ACIDOSIS

ACIDOSIS n condition characterized by an abnormal increase in the acidity of the blood and extracellular fluids

ACIDOTIC > ACIDOSIS

ACIDS > ACID

ACIDULATE vb make slightly acid or sour

ACIDULENT same as > ACIDULOUS

ACIDULOUS adj rather sour

ACIDURIA n abnormally high level of acid in urine

ACIDURIAS > ACIDURIA

ACIDY > ACID

ACIERAGE n iron-plating of metal

ACIERAGES > ACIERAGE

ACIERATE vb change (iron) into steel

ACIERATED > ACIERATE

ACIERATES > ACIERATE

ACIFORM adj shaped like a needle

ACINAR adj of small sacs

ACING > ACE

ACINI > ACINUS

ACINIC > ACINUS

ACINIFORM adj shaped like a bunch of grapes

ACINOSE > ACINUS

ACINOUS > ACINUS

ACINUS n any of the terminal saclike portions of a compound gland

ACKEE n tropical African tree cultivated in the Caribbean for its edible fruit

ACKEES > ACKEE

ACKER same as > ACCA

ACKERS > ACKER

ACKNEW > ACKNOW

ACKNOW vb recognize

ACKNOWING > ACKNOW

ACKNOWN > ACKNOW

ACKNOWNE adj aware

ACKNOWS > ACKNOW

ACLINIC adj unbending

ACMATIC adj highest or ultimate

ACME n highest point of achievement or excellence

ACMES > ACME

ACMIC same as > ACMATIC

ACMITE n chemical with pyramid-shaped crystals

ACMITES > ACMITE

ACNE n pimply skin disease

ACNED adj marked by acne

ACNES > ACNE

ACNODAL > ACNODE

ACNODE n point whose coordinates satisfy the equation of a curve although it does not lie on the curve

ACNODES > ACNODE

ACOCK adv cocked

ACOELOUS adj not having a stomach

ACOEMETI n order of monks

ACOLD adj feeling cold

ACOLUTHIC adj of an afterimage

ACOLYTE n follower or attendant

ACOLYTES > ACOLYTE

ACOLYTH n acolyte

ACOLYTHS > ACOLYTH

ACONITE n poisonous plant with hoodlike flowers

ACONITES > ACONITE

ACONITIC > ACONITE

ACONITINE n poison made from aconite

ACONITUM same as > ACONITE

ACONITUMS > ACONITUM

ACORN n nut of the oak tree

ACORNED adj covered with acorns

ACORNS > ACORN

ACOSMISM n belief that no world exists outside the mind

ACOSMISMS > ACOSMISM

ACOSMIST > ACOSMISM

ACOSMISTS > ACOSMISM

ACOUCHI n South American rodent with a white-tipped tail

ACOUCHIES > ACOUCHY

ACOUCHIS > ACOUCHI

ACOUCHY same as > ACOUCHI

ACOUSTIC adj of sound and hearing

ACOUSTICS n science of sounds

ACQUAINT vb make familiar, inform

ACQUAINTS > ACQUAINT

ACQUEST n something acquired

ACQUESTS > ACQUEST

ACQUIESCE vb agree to what someone wants

ACQUIGHT vb acquit

ACQUIGHTS > ACQUIGHT

ACQUIRAL > ACQUIRE

ACQUIRALS > ACQUIRE

ACQUIRE vb gain, get

ACQUIRED > ACQUIRE

ACQUIREE n one who acquires

ACQUIREES > ACQUIREE

ACQUIRER > ACQUIRE

ACQUIRERS > ACQUIRE

ACQUIRES > ACQUIRE

ACQUIRING > ACQUIRE

ACQUIS n as in acquis communautaire body of law accumulated by the European Union

ACQUIST n acquisition

ACQUISTS > ACQUIST

ACQUIT vb pronounce (someone) innocent

ACQUITE vb acquit

ACQUITES > ACQUITE

ACQUITING > ACQUITE

ACQUITS > ACQUIT

ACQUITTAL n deliverance and release of a person appearing before a court on a charge of crime, as by a finding of not guilty

ACQUITTED > ACQUIT

ACQUITTER > ACQUIT

ACRASIA n lack of willpower

ACRASIAS > ACRASIA

ACRASIN n chemical produced by slime moulds

ACRASINS > ACRASIN

ACRATIC > ACRASIA

ACRAWL adv crawling

ACRE n measure of land, 4840 square yards (4046.86 square metres)

ACREAGE n land area in acres ▷ adj of or relating to a large allotment of land, esp in a rural area

ACREAGES > ACREAGE

ACRED adj having acres of land

ACRES > ACRE

ACRID adj pungent, bitter

ACRIDER > ACRID

ACRIDEST > ACRID

ACRIDIN n acridine

ACRIDINE n colourless crystalline solid

ACRIDINES > ACRIDINE

ACRIDINS > ACRIDIN

ACRIDITY > ACRID

ACRIDLY > ACRID

ACRIDNESS > ACRID

ACRIMONY n bitterness and resentment felt about something

ACRITARCH n type of fossil

ACRITICAL adj not critical

ACROBAT n person skilled in gymnastic feats requiring agility and balance

ACROBATIC > ACROBAT

ACROBATS > ACROBAT

ACRODONT adj (of the teeth of some reptiles) having no roots and being fused at the base to the margin of the jawbones ▷ n acrodont reptile

ACRODONTS > ACRODONT

ACRODROME adj (of the veins of a leaf) running parallel to the edges of the leaf and fusing at the tip

ACROGEN n any flowerless plant, such as a fern or moss, in which growth occurs from the tip of the main stem

ACROGENIC > ACROGEN

ACROGENS > ACROGEN

ACROLECT n most correct form of language

ACROLECTS > ACROLECT

ACROLEIN n colourless or yellowish flammable poisonous pungent liquid

ACROLEINS > ACROLEIN

ACROLITH n (esp in ancient Greek sculpture) a wooden, often draped figure with only the head, hands, and feet in stone

ACROLITHS > ACROLITH

ACROMIA > ACROMION

ACROMIAL > ACROMION

ACROMION n outermost edge of the spine of the shoulder blade

ACRONIC adj acronical

ACRONICAL adj occurring at sunset

ACRONYCAL same as > ACRONICAL

ACRONYM n word formed from the initial letters of other words, such as NASA

ACRONYMIC > ACRONYM

ACRONYMS > ACRONYM

ACROPETAL adj (of leaves and flowers) produced in order from the base upwards so that the youngest are at the apex

ACROPHOBE n person afraid of heights

ACROPHONY n use of symbols to represent sounds

ACROPOLIS n citadel of an ancient Greek city

ACROSOMAL > ACROSOME

ACROSOME n structure at the tip of a sperm cell

ACROSOMES > ACROSOME

ACROSPIRE n first shoot developing from the plumule of a germinating grain seed

ACROSS adv from side to side (of)

ACROSTIC n lines of writing in which the first or last letters of each line spell a word or saying

ACROSTICS > ACROSTIC

ACROTER n plinth bearing a statue, etc, at either end or at the apex of a pediment

ACROTERIA n acroters

ACROTERS > ACROTER

ACROTIC adj of a surface

ACROTISM n absence of pulse

ACROTISMS > ACROTISM

ACRYLATE n chemical compound in plastics and resins

ACRYLATES > ACRYLATE

ACRYLIC adj (synthetic fibre, paint, etc) made from acrylic acid ▷ n man-made fibre used for clothes and blankets

ACRYLICS > ACRYLIC

ACRYLYL n type of monovalent group

ACRYLYLS > ACRYLYL

ACT n thing done ▷ vb do something

ACTA n minutes of meeting

ACTABLE > ACT

ACTANT n (in valency grammar) a noun phrase functioning as the agent of the main verb of a sentence

ACTANTS > ACTANT

ACTED > ACT

ACTIN n protein that participates in many kinds of cell movement, including muscle contraction, during which it interacts with filaments of a second protein, myosin

ACTINAL adj of or denoting the oral part of a radiate animal, such as a jellyfish, sea anemone, or sponge, from which the rays, tentacles, or arms grow

ACTINALLY > ACTINAL

ACTING n art of an actor ▷ adj temporarily performing the duties of

ACTINGS > ACTING

ACTINIA n type of sea anemone common in rock pools

ACTINIAE > ACTINIA

ACTINIAN n sea-anemone

ACTINIANS > ACTINIAN

ACTINIAS > ACTINIA

ACTINIC adj (of radiation) producing a photochemical effect

ACTINIDE n member of the actinide series

ACTINIDES > ACTINIDE

ACTINISM > ACTINIC

ACTINISMS > ACTINIC

ACTINIUM n radioactive chemical element

ACTINIUMS > ACTINIUM

ACTINOID adj having a radiate form, as a sea anemone or starfish ▷ n member of the actinide series

ACTINOIDS > ACTINOID

ACTINON same as > ACTINIDE

ACTINONS > ACTINON

ACTINOPOD n type of single-celled invertebrate

ACTINS > ACTIN

ACTION n process of doing something ▷ vb put into effect

ACTIONED > ACTION

ACTIONER n film with a fast-moving plot, usually containing scenes of violence

ACTIONERS > ACTIONER

ACTIONING > ACTION

ACTIONIST n activist

ACTIONS > ACTION

ACTIVATE vb make active

ACTIVATED > ACTIVATE

ACTIVATES > ACTIVATE

ACTIVATOR > ACTIVATE

ACTIVE adj moving, working ▷ n active form of a verb

ACTIVELY > ACTIVE

ACTIVES > ACTIVE

ACTIVISE same as > ACTIVIZE

ACTIVISED > ACTIVISE

ACTIVISES > ACTIVISE

ACTIVISM n policy of taking direct and often militant action to achieve an end, esp a political or social one

ACTIVISMS > ACTIVISM

ACTIVIST > ACTIVISM

ACTIVISTS > ACTIVISM

ACTIVITY n state of being active

ACTIVIZE vb make active

ACTIVIZED > ACTIVIZE

ACTIVIZES > ACTIVIZE

ACTON n jacket or jerkin, originally of quilted cotton, worn under a coat of mail

ACTONS > ACTON

ACTOR n person who acts in a play, film, etc

ACTORISH > ACTOR

ACTORLY adj of or relating to an actor

ACTORS > ACTOR

ACTRESS n woman who acts in a play, film, broadcast, etc

ACTRESSES > ACTRESS

ACTRESSY adj exaggerated and affected in manner

ACTS > ACT

ACTUAL adj existing in reality

ACTUALISE same as > ACTUALIZE

ACTUALIST n person dealing in hard fact

ACTUALITE n humorous word for truth

ACTUALITY n reality

ACTUALIZE vb make actual or real

ACTUALLY adv really, indeed

ACTUALS npl commercial commodities that can be bought and used

ACTUARIAL > ACTUARY

ACTUARIES > ACTUARY

ACTUARY n statistician who calculates insurance risks

ACTUATE vb start up (a device)

ACTUATED > ACTUATE

ACTUATES > ACTUATE

ACTUATING > ACTUATE

ACTUATION > ACTUATE

ACTUATOR > ACTUATE

ACTUATORS > ACTUATE

ACTURE n action

ACTURES > ACTURE

ACUATE adj sharply pointed

ACUITIES > ACUITY

ACUITY n keenness of vision or thought

ACULEATE adj cutting ▷ n an insect, such as a bee, with a sting

ACULEATED same as > ACULEATE

ACULEATES > ACULEATE

ACULEI > ACULEUS

ACULEUS n prickle or spine, such as the thorn of a rose

ACUMEN n ability to make good judgments

ACUMENS > ACUMEN

ACUMINATE adj narrowing to a sharp point, as some types of leaf ▷ vb make pointed or sharp

ACUMINOUS > ACUMEN

ACUPOINT n any of the specific points on the body where a needle is inserted in acupuncture or pressure is applied in acupressure

ACUPOINTS > ACUPOINT

ACUSHLA n Irish endearment

ACUSHLAS > ACUSHLA

ACUTANCE n physical rather than subjective measure of the sharpness of a photographic image

ACUTANCES > ACUTANCE

ACUTE adj severe ▷ n accent (') over a letter to indicate the quality or length of its sound, as in café

ACUTELY > ACUTE

ACUTENESS > ACUTE

ACUTER > ACUTE

ACUTES > ACUTE

ACUTEST > ACUTE

ACYCLIC adj not cyclic

ACYCLOVIR n drug used against herpes

ACYL n member of the monovalent group of atoms RCO-

ACYLATE vb introduce an acyl group into a compound

ACYLATED > ACYLATE

ACYLATES > ACYLATE

ACYLATING > ACYLATE

ACYLATION n introduction into a chemical compound of an acyl group

ACYLOIN n organic chemical compound

ACYLOINS > ACYLOIN

ACYLS > ACYL

AD n advertisement

ADAGE n wise saying, proverb

ADAGES > ADAGE

ADAGIAL > ADAGE

ADAGIO adv (piece to be played) slowly and gracefully ▷ n movement or piece to be performed slowly

ADAGIOS > ADAGIO

ADAMANCE n being adamant

ADAMANCES > ADAMANCE

ADAMANCY n being adamant

ADAMANT adj unshakable in determination or purpose ▷ n any extremely hard or apparently unbreakable substance

ADAMANTLY > ADAMANT

ADAMANTS > ADAMANT

ADAMSITE n yellow poisonous crystalline solid that readily sublimes

ADAMSITES > ADAMSITE

ADAPT vb alter for new use or new conditions

ADAPTABLE > ADAPT

ADAPTED > ADAPT

ADAPTER same as > ADAPTOR

ADAPTERS > ADAPTER

ADAPTING > ADAPT

ADAPTION n adaptation

ADAPTIONS > ADAPTION

ADAPTIVE > ADAPT

ADAPTOGEN n any of various natural substances used in herbal medicine to normalize and regulate the systems of the body

ADAPTOR n device for connecting several electrical appliances to a single socket

ADAPTORS > ADAPTOR

ADAPTS > ADAPT

ADAW vb subdue

ADAWED > ADAW

ADAWING > ADAW**

a

ADAWS > ADAW
ADAXIAL adj facing towards the axis, as the surface of a leaf that faces the stem
ADAYS adv daily
ADD vb combine (numbers or quantities)
ADDABLE > ADD
ADDAX n N African light-coloured antelope with ribbed spiralled horns
ADDAXES > ADDAX
ADDEBTED adj indebted
ADDED > ADD
ADDEDLY > ADD
ADDEEM vb adjudge
ADDEEMED > ADDEEM
ADDEEMING > ADDEEM
ADDEEMS > ADDEEM
ADDEND n any of a set of numbers that is to be added
ADDENDA > ADDENDUM
ADDENDS > ADDEND
ADDENDUM n addition
ADDENDUMS > ADDENDUM
ADDER n small poisonous snake
ADDERS > ADDER
ADDERWORT n plant of the dock family
ADDIBLE adj addable
ADDICT n person who is unable to stop taking drugs ▷ vb cause (someone or oneself) to become dependent (on something, esp a narcotic drug)
ADDICTED > ADDICT
ADDICTING > ADDICT
ADDICTION n condition of being abnormally dependent on some habit, esp compulsive dependency on narcotic drugs
ADDICTIVE adj causing addiction
ADDICTS > ADDICT
ADDIES > ADDY
ADDING n act or instance of addition ▷ adj of, for, or relating to addition
ADDINGS > ADDING n
ADDIO interj farewell ▷ n cry of addio
ADDITION n adding
ADDITIONS > ADDITION
ADDITIVE n something added, esp to a foodstuff, to improve it or prevent deterioration ▷ adj characterized or produced by addition
ADDITIVES > ADDITIVE
ADDITORY adj adding to something
ADDLE vb make or become confused or muddled ▷ adj indicating a confused or muddled state
ADDLED > ADDLE
ADDLEMENT > ADDLE
ADDLES > ADDLE
ADDLING > ADDLE

ADDOOM vb adjudge
ADDOOMED > ADDOOM
ADDOOMING > ADDOOM
ADDOOMS > ADDOOM
ADDORSED adj back to back
ADDRESS n place where a person lives ▷ vb mark the destination, as on an envelope
ADDRESSED > ADDRESS
ADDRESSEE n person addressed
ADDRESSER > ADDRESS
ADDRESSES > ADDRESS
ADDRESSOR > ADDRESS
ADDREST > ADDRESS
ADDS > ADD
ADDUCE vb mention something as evidence or proof
ADDUCED > ADDUCE
ADDUCENT > ADDUCE
ADDUCER > ADDUCE
ADDUCERS > ADDUCE
ADDUCES > ADDUCE
ADDUCIBLE > ADDUCE
ADDUCING > ADDUCE
ADDUCT vb (of a muscle) to draw or pull (a leg, arm, etc) towards the median axis of the body ▷ n compound formed by direct combination of two or more different compounds or elements
ADDUCTED > ADDUCT
ADDUCTING > ADDUCT
ADDUCTION > ADDUCT
ADDUCTIVE > ADDUCE
ADDUCTOR n muscle that adducts
ADDUCTORS > ADDUCTOR
ADDUCTS > ADDUCT
ADDY n e-mail address
ADEEM vb cancel
ADEEMED > ADEEM
ADEEMING > ADEEM
ADEEMS > ADEEM
ADEMPTION n failure of a specific legacy, as by a testator disposing of the subject matter in his lifetime
ADENINE n purine base present in tissues of all living organisms as a constituent of the nucleic acids DNA and RNA and of certain coenzymes
ADENINES > ADENINE
ADENITIS n inflammation of a gland or lymph node
ADENOID adj of or resembling a gland
ADENOIDAL adj having a nasal voice caused by swollen adenoids
ADENOIDS npl tissue at the back of the throat
ADENOMA n tumour, usually benign, occurring in glandular tissue
ADENOMAS > ADENOMA
ADENOMATA > ADENOMA

ADENOSES > ADENOSIS
ADENOSINE n nucleoside formed by the condensation of adenine and ribose
ADENOSIS n disease of glands
ADENYL n enzyme
ADENYLIC as in adenylic acid nucleotide consisting of adenine, ribose or deoxyribose, and a phosphate group
ADENYLS > ADENYL
ADEPT n very skilful (person) ▷ adj proficient in something requiring skill
ADEPTER > ADEPT
ADEPTEST > ADEPT
ADEPTLY > ADEPT
ADEPTNESS > ADEPT
ADEPTS > ADEPT
ADEQUACY > ADEQUATE
ADEQUATE adj sufficient, enough
ADERMIN n vitamin
ADERMINS > ADERMIN
ADESPOTA n anonymous writings
ADESSIVE n grammatical case denoting place
ADESSIVES > ADESSIVE
ADHAN n call to prayer
ADHANS > ADHAN
ADHARMA n wickedness
ADHARMAS > ADHARMA
ADHERABLE > ADHERE
ADHERE vb stick (to)
ADHERED > ADHERE
ADHERENCE > ADHERE
ADHEREND n something attached by adhesive
ADHERENDS > ADHEREND
ADHERENT n devotee, follower ▷ adj sticking or attached
ADHERENTS > ADHERENT
ADHERER > ADHERE
ADHERERS > ADHERE
ADHERES > ADHERE
ADHERING > ADHERE
ADHESION n sticking (to)
ADHESIONS > ADHESION
ADHESIVE n substance used to stick things together ▷ adj able to stick to things
ADHESIVES > ADHESIVE
ADHIBIT vb administer or apply
ADHIBITED > ADHIBIT
ADHIBITS > ADHIBIT
ADHOCRACY n management that responds to urgent problems rather than planning to avoid them
ADIABATIC adj (of a thermodynamic process) taking place without loss or gain of heat ▷ n curve or surface on a graph representing the changes in two or more characteristics (such as

pressure and volume) of a system undergoing an adiabatic process
ADIAPHORA n matters of indifference
ADIEU n goodbye
ADIEUS > ADIEU
ADIEUX > ADIEU
ADIOS sentence substitute Spanish for goodbye
ADIPIC as in adipic acid colourless crystalline solid used in the preparation of nylon
ADIPOCERE n waxlike fatty substance formed during the decomposition of corpses
ADIPOCYTE n fat cell that accumulates and stores fats
ADIPOSE adj of or containing fat ▷ n animal fat
ADIPOSES > ADIPOSIS
ADIPOSIS n obesity
ADIPOSITY > ADIPOSE
ADIPOUS adj made of fat
ADIPSIA n complete lack of thirst
ADIPSIAS > ADIPSIA
ADIT n almost horizontal shaft into a mine, for access or drainage
ADITS > ADIT
ADJACENCE > ADJACENT
ADJACENCY > ADJACENT
ADJACENT adj near or next (to) ▷ n side lying between a specified angle and a right angle in a right-angled triangle
ADJACENTS > ADJACENT
ADJECTIVE n word that adds information about a noun or pronoun ▷ adj additional or dependent
ADJIGO n SW Australian yam plant with edible tubers
ADJIGOS > ADJIGO
ADJOIN vb be next to
ADJOINED > ADJOIN
ADJOINING adj being in contact
ADJOINS > ADJOIN
ADJOINT n type of mathematical matrix
ADJOINTS > ADJOINT
ADJOURN vb close (a court) at the end of a session
ADJOURNED > ADJOURN
ADJOURNS > ADJOURN
ADJUDGE vb declare (to be)
ADJUDGED > ADJUDGE
ADJUDGES > ADJUDGE
ADJUDGING > ADJUDGE
ADJUNCT n something incidental added to something else
ADJUNCTLY > ADJUNCT
ADJUNCTS > ADJUNCT
ADJURE vb command (to do)
ADJURED > ADJURE

ADJURER > ADJURE
ADJURERS > ADJURE
ADJURES > ADJURE
ADJURING > ADJURE
ADJUROR > ADJURE
ADJURORS > ADJURE
ADJUST *vb* adapt to new conditions
ADJUSTED > ADJUST
ADJUSTER > ADJUST
ADJUSTERS > ADJUST
ADJUSTING > ADJUST
ADJUSTIVE > ADJUST
ADJUSTOR > ADJUST
ADJUSTORS > ADJUST
ADJUSTS > ADJUST
ADJUTAGE *n* nozzle
ADJUTAGES > ADJUTAGE
ADJUTANCY > ADJUTANT
ADJUTANT *n* army officer in charge of routine administration
ADJUTANTS > ADJUTANT
ADJUVANCY > ADJUVANT
ADJUVANT *adj* aiding or assisting ▷ *n* something that aids or assists
ADJUVANTS > ADJUVANT
ADLAND *n* advertising industry and the people who work in it
ADLANDS > ADLAND
ADMAN *n* man who works in advertising
ADMASS *n* mass advertising
ADMASSES > ADMASS
ADMEASURE *vb* measure out (land, etc) as a share
ADMEN > ADMAN
ADMIN *n* administration
ADMINICLE *n* something contributing to prove a point without itself being complete proof
ADMINS > ADMIN
ADMIRABLE *adj* deserving or inspiring admiration
ADMIRABLY > ADMIRABLE
ADMIRAL *n* highest naval rank
ADMIRALS > ADMIRAL
ADMIRALTY *n* office or jurisdiction of an admiral
ADMIRANCE *n* admiration
ADMIRE *vb* regard with esteem and approval
ADMIRED > ADMIRE
ADMIRER > ADMIRE
ADMIRERS > ADMIRE
ADMIRES > ADMIRE
ADMIRING > ADMIRE
ADMISSION *n* permission to enter
ADMISSIVE > ADMISSION
ADMIT *vb* confess, acknowledge
ADMITS > ADMIT
ADMITTED > ADMIT
ADMITTEE *n* one who admits
ADMITTEES > ADMITTEE
ADMITTER > ADMIT

ADMITTERS > ADMIT
ADMITTING > ADMIT
ADMIX *vb* mix or blend
ADMIXED > ADMIX
ADMIXES > ADMIX
ADMIXING > ADMIX
ADMIXT > ADMIX
ADMIXTURE *n* mixture
ADMONISH *vb* reprove sternly
ADMONITOR > ADMONISH
ADNASCENT *adj* growing with something else
ADNATE *adj* growing closely attached to an adjacent part or organ
ADNATION > ADNATE
ADNATIONS > ADNATE
ADNEXA *npl* organs adjoining the uterus
ADNEXAL > ADNEXA
ADNOMINAL *n* word modifying a noun ▷ *adj* of or relating to an adnoun
ADNOUN *n* adjective used as a noun
ADNOUNS > ADNOUN
ADO *n* fuss, trouble
ADOBE *n* sun-dried brick
ADOBELIKE > ADOBE
ADOBES > ADOBE
ADOBO *n* Philippine dish
ADOBOS > ADOBO
ADONIS *n* beautiful young man
ADONISE *vb* adorn
ADONISED > ADONISE
ADONISES > ADONISE
ADONISING > ADONISE
ADONIZE *vb* adorn
ADONIZED > ADONIZE
ADONIZES > ADONIZE
ADONIZING > ADONIZE
ADOORS *adv* at the door
ADOPT *vb* take (someone else's child) as one's own
ADOPTABLE > ADOPT
ADOPTED *adj* having been adopted
ADOPTEE *n* one who has been adopted
ADOPTEES > ADOPTEE
ADOPTER *n* person who adopts
ADOPTERS > ADOPTER
ADOPTING > ADOPT
ADOPTION > ADOPT
ADOPTIONS > ADOPT
ADOPTIOUS *adj* adopted
ADOPTIVE *adj* related by adoption
ADOPTS > ADOPT
ADORABLE *adj* very attractive
ADORABLY > ADORABLE
ADORATION *n* deep love or esteem
ADORE *vb* love intensely
ADORED > ADORE
ADORER > ADORE
ADORERS > ADORE
ADORES > ADORE
ADORING > ADORE
ADORINGLY > ADORE

ADORN *vb* decorate, embellish
ADORNED > ADORN
ADORNER > ADORN
ADORNERS > ADORN
ADORNING > ADORN
ADORNMENT > ADORN
ADORNS > ADORN
ADOS > ADO
ADOWN *adv* down
ADOZE *adv* asleep
ADPRESS *vb* press together
ADPRESSED > ADPRESS
ADPRESSES > ADPRESS
ADRAD *adj* afraid
ADREAD *vb* dread
ADREADED > ADREAD
ADREADING > ADREAD
ADREADS > ADREAD
ADRED *adj* filled with dread
ADRENAL *adj* near the kidneys ▷ *n* adrenal gland
ADRENALIN *n* hormone secreted by the adrenal glands in response to stress
ADRENALLY > ADRENAL
ADRENALS > ADRENAL
ADRIFT *adv* drifting
ADROIT *adj* quick and skilful
ADROITER > ADROIT
ADROITEST > ADROIT
ADROITLY > ADROIT
ADRY *adj* dry
ADS > AD
ADSCRIPT *n* serf
ADSCRIPTS > ADSCRIPT
ADSORB *vb* (of a gas or vapour) condense and form a thin film on a surface
ADSORBATE *n* substance that has been or is to be adsorbed on a surface
ADSORBED > ADSORB
ADSORBENT *adj* capable of adsorption ▷ *n* material, such as activated charcoal, on which adsorption can occur
ADSORBER > ADSORB
ADSORBERS > ADSORB
ADSORBING > ADSORB
ADSORBS > ADSORB
ADSUKI *same as >* ADZUKI
ADSUKIS > ADSUKI
ADSUM *sentence substitute* I am present
ADUKI *same as >* ADZUKI
ADUKIS > ADUKI
ADULARIA *n* white or colourless glassy variety of orthoclase
ADULARIAS > ADULARIA
ADULATE *vb* flatter or praise obsequiously
ADULATED > ADULATE
ADULATES > ADULATE
ADULATING > ADULATE
ADULATION *n* uncritical admiration
ADULATOR > ADULATE
ADULATORS > ADULATE
ADULATORY *adj* expressing praise, esp obsequiously

ADULT *adj* fully grown, mature ▷ *n* adult person or animal
ADULTERER *n* person who has committed adultery
ADULTERY *n* sexual unfaithfulness of a husband or wife
ADULTHOOD > ADULT
ADULTLIKE > ADULT
ADULTLY > ADULT
ADULTNESS > ADULT
ADULTRESS *n* US word for a female adulterer
ADULTS > ADULT
ADUMBRAL *adj* shadowy
ADUMBRATE *vb* outline
ADUNC *adj* hooked
ADUNCATE *adj* hooked
ADUNCATED *adj* hooked
ADUNCITY *n* quality of being hooked
ADUNCOUS *adj* hooked
ADUST *vb* dry up or darken by heat
ADUSTED > ADUST
ADUSTING > ADUST
ADUSTS > ADUST
ADVANCE *vb* go or bring forward ▷ *n* forward movement ▷ *adj* done or happening before an event
ADVANCED *adj* at a late stage in development
ADVANCER > ADVANCE
ADVANCERS > ADVANCE
ADVANCES > ADVANCE
ADVANCING > ADVANCE
ADVANTAGE *n* more favourable position or state
ADVECT *vb* move horizontally in air
ADVECTED > ADVECT
ADVECTING > ADVECT
ADVECTION *n* transferring of heat in a horizontal stream of gas
ADVECTIVE > ADVECTION
ADVECTS > ADVECT
ADVENE *vb* add as extra
ADVENED > ADVENE
ADVENES > ADVENE
ADVENING > ADVENE
ADVENT *n* arrival
ADVENTIVE *adj* (of a species) introduced to a new area and not yet established there ▷ *n* such a plant or animal
ADVENTS > ADVENT
ADVENTURE *n* exciting and risky undertaking or exploit ▷ *vb* take a risk or put at risk
ADVERB *n* word that adds information about a verb, adjective, or other adverb
ADVERBIAL *n* word or group of words playing the grammatical role of an adverb ▷ *adj* of or relating to an adverb or adverbial
ADVERBS > ADVERB
ADVERSARY *n* opponent or enemy

a

ADVERSE adj unfavourable

ADVERSELY > ADVERSE

ADVERSER > ADVERSE

ADVERSEST > ADVERSE

ADVERSITY n very difficult or hard circumstances

ADVERT ▷ vb draw attention (to)

ADVERTED > ADVERT

ADVERTENT adj heedful

ADVERTING > ADVERT

ADVERTISE vb present or praise (goods or services) to the public in order to encourage sales

ADVERTIZE same as > ADVERTISE

ADVERTS > ADVERT

ADVEW vb look at

ADVEWED > ADVEW

ADVEWING > ADVEW

ADVEWS > ADVEW

ADVICE n recommendation as to what to do

ADVICEFUL > ADVICE

ADVICES > ADVICE

ADVISABLE adj prudent, sensible

ADVISABLY > ADVISABLE

ADVISE vb offer advice to

ADVISED adj considered, thought-out

ADVISEDLY > ADVISED

ADVISEE n person receiving advice

ADVISEES > ADVISEE

ADVISER n person who offers advice, e.g. on careers to students or school pupils

ADVISERS > ADVISER

ADVISES > ADVISE

ADVISING > ADVISE

ADVISINGS > ADVISE

ADVISOR same as > ADVISER

ADVISORS > ADVISOR

ADVISORY adj giving advice ▷ n statement giving advice or a warning

ADVOCAAT n liqueur with a raw egg base

ADVOCAATS > ADVOCAAT

ADVOCACY n active support of a cause or course of action

ADVOCATE vb propose or recommend ▷ n person who publicly supports a cause

ADVOCATED > ADVOCATE

ADVOCATES > ADVOCATE

ADVOCATOR n person who advocates

ADVOUTRER n adulterer

ADVOUTRY n adultery

ADVOWSON n right of presentation to a vacant benefice

ADVOWSONS > ADVOWSON

ADWARD vb award

ADWARDED > ADWARD

ADWARDING > ADWARD

ADWARDS > ADWARD

ADWARE n type of computer software that collects information about a user's browsing patterns in order to display relevant advertisements in his or her Web browser

ADWARES > ADWARE

ADWOMAN n woman working in advertising

ADWOMEN > ADWOMAN

ADYNAMIA n loss of vital power or strength, esp as the result of illness

ADYNAMIAS > ADYNAMIA

ADYNAMIC > ADYNAMIA

ADYTA > ADYTUM

ADYTUM n most sacred place of worship in an ancient temple from which the laity was prohibited

ADZ same as > ADZE

ADZE n tool with an arched blade at right angles to the handle ▷ vb use an adze

ADZED > ADZE

ADZES > ADZE

ADZING > ADZE

ADZUKI n type of leguminous plant with yellow flowers and pods containing edible brown seeds

ADZUKIS > ADZUKI

AE det one

AECIA > AECIUM

AECIAL > AECIUM

AECIDIA > AECIDIUM

AECIDIAL > AECIDIUM

AECIDIUM same as > AECIUM

AECIUM n globular or cup-shaped structure in some rust fungi in which aeciospores are produced

AEDES n type of mosquito which transmits yellow fever and dengue

AEDICULE n opening such as a door or a window, framed by columns on either side, and a pediment above

AEDICULES > AEDICULE

AEDILE n magistrate of ancient Rome in charge of public works, games, buildings, and roads

AEDILES > AEDILE

AEDINE adj of a species of mosquito

AEFALD adj single

AEFAULD adj single

AEGIRINE n green mineral

AEGIRINES > AEGIRINE

AEGIRITE n green mineral

AEGIRITES > AEGIRITE

AEGIS n sponsorship, protection

AEGISES > AEGIS

AEGLOGUE n eclogue

AEGLOGUES > AEGLOGUE

AEGROTAT n (in British and certain other universities, and, sometimes, schools) a certificate allowing a candidate to pass an examination although he has missed all or part of it through illness

AEGROTATS > AEGROTAT

AEMULE vb emulate

AEMULED > AEMULE

AEMULES > AEMULE

AEMULING > AEMULE

AENEOUS adj brass-coloured or greenish-gold

AENEUS n aquarium fish

AEOLIAN adj of or relating to the wind

AEOLIPILE n device illustrating the reactive forces of a gas jet: usually a spherical vessel mounted so as to rotate and equipped with angled exit pipes from which steam within it escapes

AEOLIPYLE same as > AEOLIPILE

AEON n immeasurably long period of time

AEONIAN adj everlasting

AEONIC > AEON

AEONS > AEON

AEPYORNIS n type of large extinct flightless bird whose remains have been found in Madagascar

AEQUORIN n type of protein

AEQUORINS > AEQUORIN

AERATE vb put gas into (a liquid), as when making a fizzy drink

AERATED > AERATE

AERATES > AERATE

AERATING > AERATE

AERATION > AERATE

AERATIONS > AERATE

AERATOR > AERATE

AERATORS > AERATE

AERIAL adj in, from, or operating in the air ▷ n metal pole, wire, etc, for receiving or transmitting radio or TV signals

AERIALIST n trapeze artist or tightrope walker

AERIALITY > AERIAL

AERIALLY > AERIAL

AERIALS > AERIAL

AERIE a variant spelling (esp US) of > EYRIE

AERIED adj in a very high place

AERIER > AERY

AERIES > AERIE

AERIEST > AERY

AERIFIED > AERIFY

AERIFIES > AERIFY

AERIFORM adj having the form of air

AERIFY vb change or cause to change into a gas

AERIFYING > AERIFY

AERILY > AERY

AERO n of or relating to aircraft or aeronautics

AEROBAT n person who does stunt flying

AEROBATIC adj pertaining to stunt flying

AEROBATS > AEROBAT

AEROBE n organism that requires oxygen to survive

AEROBES > AEROBE

AEROBIA > AEROBIUM

AEROBIC adj designed for or relating to aerobics

AEROBICS n exercises designed to increase the amount of oxygen in the blood

AEROBIONT n organism needing oxygen to live

AEROBIUM same as > AEROBE

AEROBOMB n bomb dropped from aircraft

AEROBOMBS > AEROBOMB

AEROBOT n unmanned aircraft used esp in space exploration

AEROBOTS > AEROBOT

AEROBRAKE vb use airbrakes to slow aircraft

AERODART n metal arrow dropped from an aircraft as a weapon

AERODARTS > AERODART

AERODROME n small airport

AERODUCT n air duct

AERODUCTS > AERODUCT

AERODYNE n any heavier-than-air machine, such as an aircraft, that derives the greater part of its lift from aerodynamic forces

AERODYNES > AERODYNE

AEROFOIL n part of an aircraft, such as the wing, designed to give lift

AEROFOILS > AEROFOIL

AEROGEL n colloid that has a continuous solid phase containing dispersed gas

AEROGELS > AEROGEL

AEROGRAM n airmail letter on a single sheet of paper that seals to form an envelope

AEROGRAMS > AEROGRAM

AEROGRAPH n airborne instrument recording meteorological conditions

AEROLITE n stony meteorite consisting of silicate minerals

AEROLITES > AEROLITE

AEROLITH n meteorite

AEROLITHS > AEROLITH

AEROLITIC > AEROLITE

AEROLOGIC > AEROLOGY

AEROLOGY n study of the atmosphere, particularly its upper layers

AEROMANCY n using weather observation to foretell the future

AEROMETER n instrument

for determining the mass or density of a gas, esp air

AEROMETRY n branch of physics concerned with the mechanical properties of gases, esp air

AEROMOTOR n aircraft engine

AERONAUT n person who flies in a lighter-than-air craft, esp the pilot or navigator

AERONAUTS > AERONAUT

AERONOMER n scientist studying atmosphere

AERONOMIC > AERONOMY

AERONOMY n science of the earth's upper atmosphere

AEROPAUSE n region of the upper atmosphere above which aircraft cannot fly

AEROPHAGY n spasmodic swallowing of air

AEROPHOBE n person suffering from aerophobia

AEROPHONE n wind instrument

AEROPHONE n device for playing a wind instrument

AEROPHYTE another name for > EPIPHYTE

AEROPLANE n powered flying vehicle with fixed wings

AEROPULSE n type of jet engine

AEROS > AERO

AEROSAT n communications satellite

AEROSATS > AEROSAT

AEROSCOPE n device for observing the atmosphere

AEROSHELL n parachute used to slow spacecraft

AEROSOL n pressurized can from which a substance can be dispensed as a fine spray

AEROSOLS > AEROSOL

AEROSPACE n earth's atmosphere and space beyond ⊳ adj of rockets or space vehicles

AEROSPIKE n type of rocket engine

AEROSTAT n lighter-than-air craft, such as a balloon

AEROSTATS > AEROSTAT

AEROTAXES > AEROTAXIS

AEROTAXIS n movement away from or towards oxygen

AEROTONE n bath incorporating air jets for massage

AEROTONES > AEROTONE

AEROTRAIN n train driven by a jet engine

AERUGO (esp of old bronze) another name for > VERDIGRIS

AERUGOS > AERUGO

AERY adj lofty,

insubstantial, or visionary

AESC n rune

AESCES > AESC

AESCULIN n chemical in horse-chestnut bark

AESCULINS > AESCULIN

AESIR n chief of the Norse gods

AESTHESES > AESTHESIS

AESTHESIA n normal ability to experience sensation, perception, or sensitivity

AESTHESIS variant of > ESTHESIS

AESTHETE n person who has or affects an extravagant love of art

AESTHETES > AESTHETE

AESTHETIC adj relating to the appreciation of art and beauty ⊳ n principle or set of principles relating to the appreciation of art and beauty

AESTIVAL adj of or occurring in summer

AESTIVATE vb pass the summer

AETHER same as > ETHER

AETHEREAL a variant spelling of > ETHEREAL

AETHERIC > AETHER

AETHERS > AETHER

AETIOLOGY n philosophy or study of causation

AFALD adj single

AFAR adv at, from, or to a great distance ⊳ n great distance

AFARA n African tree

AFARAS > AFARA

AFARS > AFAR

AFAWLD adj single

AFEAR vb frighten

AFEARD an archaic or dialect word for > AFRAID

AFEARED same as > AFEARD

AFEARING > AFEAR

AFEARS > AFEAR

AFEBRILE adj without fever

AFF adv off

AFFABLE adj friendly and easy to talk to

AFFABLY > AFFABLE

AFFAIR n event or happening

AFFAIRE n love affair

AFFAIRES > AFFAIRE

AFFAIRS npl personal or business interests

AFFEAR vb frighten

AFFEARD > AFFEAR

AFFEARE vb frighten

AFFEARED > AFFEAR

AFFEARES > AFFEARE

AFFEARING > AFFEAR

AFFEARS > AFFEAR

AFFECT vb act on, influence ⊳ n emotion associated with an idea or set of ideas

AFFECTED adj displaying affectation

AFFECTER > AFFECT

AFFECTERS > AFFECT

AFFECTING adj arousing feelings of pity

AFFECTION n fondness or love

AFFECTIVE adj relating to affects

AFFECTS > AFFECT

AFFEER vb assess

AFFEERED > AFFEER

AFFEERING > AFFEER

AFFEERS > AFFEER

AFFERENT adj bringing or directing inwards to a part or an organ of the body, esp towards the brain or spinal cord ⊳ n nerve that conveys impulses towards an organ of the body

AFFERENTS > AFFERENT

AFFIANCE vb bind (a person or oneself) in a promise of marriage ⊳ n solemn pledge, esp a marriage contract

AFFIANCED > AFFIANCE

AFFIANCES > AFFIANCE

AFFIANT n person who makes an affidavit

AFFIANTS > AFFIANT

AFFICHE n poster or advertisement, esp one drawn by an artist, as for the opening of an exhibition

AFFICHES > AFFICHE

AFFIDAVIT n written statement made on oath

AFFIED > AFFY

AFFIES > AFFY

AFFILIATE vb (of a group) link up with a larger group ⊳ n person or organization that is affiliated with another

AFFINAL > AFFINE

AFFINE adj of, characterizing, or involving transformations which preserve collinearity, esp in classical geometry, those of translation, rotation and reflection in an axis ⊳ n relation by marriage

AFFINED adj closely related

AFFINELY > AFFINE

AFFINES > AFFINE

AFFINITY n close connection or liking

AFFIRM vb declare to be true

AFFIRMANT > AFFIRM

AFFIRMED > AFFIRM

AFFIRMER > AFFIRM

AFFIRMERS > AFFIRM

AFFIRMING > AFFIRM

AFFIRMS > AFFIRM

AFFIX vb attach or fasten ⊳ n word or syllable added to a word to change its meaning

AFFIXABLE > AFFIRM

AFFIXAL > AFFIX

AFFIXED > AFFIX

AFFIXER > AFFIX

AFFIXERS > AFFIX

AFFIXES > AFFIX

AFFIXIAL > AFFIX

AFFIXING > AFFIX

AFFIXMENT > AFFIX

AFFIXTURE > AFFIX

AFFLATED adj inspired

AFFLATION n inspiration

AFFLATUS n impulse of creative power or inspiration, esp in poetry, considered to be of divine origin

AFFLICT vb give pain or grief to

AFFLICTED > AFFLICT

AFFLICTER n one who afflicts

AFFLICTS > AFFLICT

AFFLUENCE n wealth

AFFLUENCY n affluence

AFFLUENT adj having plenty of money ⊳ n tributary stream

AFFLUENTS > AFFLUENT

AFFLUENZA n guilt or lack of motivation experienced by people who have made or inherited large amounts of money

AFFLUX n flowing towards a point

AFFLUXES > AFFLUX

AFFLUXION n flow towards something

AFFOORD vb consent

AFFOORDED > AFFOORD

AFFOORDS > AFFOORD

AFFORCE vb strengthen

AFFORCED > AFFORCE

AFFORCES > AFFORCE

AFFORCING > AFFORCE

AFFORD vb have enough money to buy

AFFORDED > AFFORD

AFFORDING > AFFORD

AFFORDS > AFFORD

AFFOREST vb plant trees on

AFFORESTS > AFFOREST

AFFRAP vb strike

AFFRAPPED > AFFRAP

AFFRAPS > AFFRAP

AFFRAY n noisy fight, brawl ⊳ vb frighten

AFFRAYED > AFFRAY

AFFRAYER > AFFRAY

AFFRAYERS > AFFRAY

AFFRAYING > AFFRAY

AFFRAYS > AFFRAY

AFFRENDED adj brought back into friendship

AFFRET n furious attack

AFFRETS > AFFRET

AFFRICATE n composite speech sound consisting of a stop and a fricative articulated at the same point

a

AFFRIGHT vb frighten ▷ n sudden terror

AFFRIGHTS > AFFRIGHT

AFFRONT n insult ▷ vb hurt someone's pride or dignity

AFFRONTE adj facing

AFFRONTED > AFFRONT

AFFRONTEE adj facing

AFFRONTS > AFFRONT

AFFUSION n baptizing of a person by pouring water onto his head

AFFUSIONS > AFFUSION

AFFY vb trust

AFFYDE > AFFY

AFFYING > AFFY

AFGHAN n type of biscuit

AFGHANI n standard monetary unit of Afghanistan, divided into 100 puli

AFGHANIS > AFGHANI

AFGHANS > AFGHAN

AFIELD adj away from one's usual surroundings or home

AFIRE adj on fire

AFLAJ > FALAJ

AFLAME adj burning

AFLATOXIN n toxin produced by a fungus growing on peanuts, maize, etc, which causes liver disease (esp cancer) in humans

AFLOAT adj floating ▷ adv floating

AFLUTTER adv in or into a nervous or excited state

AFOOT adj happening, in operation ▷ adv happening

AFORE adv before

AFOREHAND adv beforehand

AFORESAID adj referred to previously

AFORETIME adv formerly

AFOUL adj in or into a state of difficulty, confusion, or conflict (with)

AFRAID adj frightened

AFREET n powerful evil demon or giant monster

AFREETS > AFREET

AFRESH adv again, anew

AFRIT same as > AFREET

AFRITS > AFRIT

AFRO n bush-like frizzy hairstyle

AFRONT adv in front

AFROS > AFRO

AFT adv at or towards the rear of a ship or aircraft ▷ adj at or towards the rear of a ship or aircraft

AFTER adv at a later time

AFTERBODY n any discarded part that continues to trail a satellite, rocket, etc, in orbit

AFTERCARE n support given to a person discharged from a hospital or prison

AFTERCLAP n unexpected consequence

AFTERDAMP n poisonous gas formed after the explosion of firedamp in a coal mine

AFTERDECK n unprotected deck behind the bridge of a ship

AFTEREYE vb gaze at someone or something that has passed

AFTEREYED > AFTEREYE

AFTEREYES > AFTEREYE

AFTERGAME n second game that follows another

AFTERGLOW n glow left after a source of light has gone

AFTERHEAT n heat generated in a nuclear reactor after it has been shut down, produced by residual radioactivity in the fuel elements

AFTERINGS n last of the milk drawn in milking

AFTERLIFE n life after death

AFTERMATH n results of an event considered together

AFTERMOST adj closer or closest to the rear or (in a vessel) the stern

AFTERNOON n time between noon and evening

AFTERPAIN n pain that comes after a while

AFTERPEAK n space behind the aftermost bulkhead, often used for storage

AFTERS n sweet course of a meal

AFTERSHOW n party held after a public performance of a play or film

AFTERSUN n moisturizing lotion applied to the skin to soothe sunburn and avoid peeling

AFTERSUNS > AFTERSUN

AFTERTAX adj after tax has been paid

AFTERTIME n later period

AFTERWARD adv after an earlier event or time

AFTERWORD n epilogue or postscript in a book, etc

AFTMOST adj furthest towards rear

AFTOSA n foot-and-mouth disease

AFTOSAS > AFTOSA

AG n agriculture

AGA n title of respect, often used with the title of a senior position

AGACANT adj irritating

AGACANTE adj irritating

AGACERIE n coquetry

AGACERIES > AGACERIE

AGAIN adv once more

AGAINST prep in opposition or contrast to

AGALACTIA n absence or failure of secretion of milk

AGALLOCH another name for > EAGLEWOOD

AGALLOCHS > AGALLOCH

AGALWOOD n eaglewood

AGALWOODS > AGALWOOD

AGAMA n type of small terrestrial lizard which inhabits warm regions of the Old World

AGAMAS > AGAMA

AGAMETE n reproductive cell, such as the merozoite of some protozoans, that develops into a new form without fertilization

AGAMETES > AGAMETE

AGAMI n South American bird

AGAMIC adj asexual

AGAMID same as > AGAMA

AGAMIDS > AGAMID

AGAMIS > AGAMI

AGAMOGONY n asexual reproduction in protozoans that is characterized by multiple fission

AGAMOID n lizard of the agamid type

AGAMOIDS > AGAMOID

AGAMONT another name for > SCHIZONT

AGAMONTS > AGAMONT

AGAMOUS adj without sex

AGAPAE > AGAPE

AGAPAI > AGAPE

AGAPE adj (of the mouth) wide open ▷ n love feast among the early Christians

AGAPEIC > AGAPE

AGAPES > AGAPE

AGAR n jelly-like substance obtained from seaweed and used as a thickener in food

AGARIC n fungus with gills on the underside of the cap, such as a mushroom

AGARICS > AGARIC

AGAROSE n gel used in chemistry

AGAROSES > AGAROSE

AGARS > AGAR

AGAS > AGA

AGAST adj aghast

AGATE n semiprecious form of quartz with striped colouring ▷ adv on the way

AGATES > AGATE

AGATEWARE n ceramic ware made to resemble agate or marble

AGATISE same as > AGATIZE

AGATISED > AGATISE

AGATISES > AGATISE

AGATISING > AGATISE

AGATIZE vb turn into agate

AGATIZED > AGATIZE

AGATIZES > AGATIZE

AGATIZING > AGATIZE

AGATOID adj like agate

AGAVE n tropical American plant with tall flower stalks and thick leaves

AGAVES > AGAVE

AGAZE adj gazing at something

AGAZED adj amazed

AGE n length of time a person or thing has existed ▷ vb make or grow old

AGED adj old

AGEDLY > AGED

AGEDNESS > AGED

AGEE adj awry, crooked, or ajar ▷ adv awry

AGEING n fact or process of growing old ▷ adj becoming or appearing older

AGEINGS > AGEING

AGEISM n discrimination against people on the grounds of age

AGEISMS > AGEISM

AGEIST > AGEISM

AGEISTS > AGEISM

AGELAST n someone who never laughs

AGELASTIC > AGELAST

AGELASTS > AGELAST

AGELESS adj apparently never growing old

AGELESSLY > AGELESS

AGELONG adj lasting for a very long time

AGEMATE n person the same age as another person

AGEMATES > AGEMATE

AGEN archaic form of > AGAIN

AGENCIES > AGENCY

AGENCY n organization providing a service

AGENDA n list of things to be dealt with, esp at a meeting

AGENDAS same as > AGENDA

AGENDUM same as > AGENDA

AGENDUMS same as > AGENDA

AGENE n chemical used to whiten flour

AGENES > AGENE

AGENESES > AGENESIS

AGENESIA n imperfect development

AGENESIAS > AGENESIA

AGENESIS n (of an animal or plant) imperfect development

AGENETIC > AGENESIS

AGENISE same as > AGENIZE

AGENISED > AGENISE

AGENISES > AGENISE

AGENISING > AGENISE

AGENIZE vb whiten using agene

AGENIZED > AGENIZE

AGENIZES > AGENIZE

AGENIZING > AGENIZE

AGENT n person acting on behalf of another ▷ vb act

as an agent
AGENTED > AGENT
AGENTIAL > AGENT
AGENTING > AGENT
AGENTINGS > AGENT
AGENTIVAL *adj* of the performer of an action
AGENTIVE *adj* (in some inflected languages) denoting a case of nouns, etc, indicating the agent described by the verb ▷ *n* agentive case
AGENTIVES > AGENTIVE
AGENTRIES > AGENTRY
AGENTRY *n* acting as agent
AGENTS > AGENT
AGER *n* something that ages
AGERATUM *n* tropical American plant with thick clusters of purplish-blue flowers
AGERATUMS > AGERATUM
AGERS > AGER
AGES > AGE
AGEUSIA *n* lack of the sense of taste
AGEUSIAS > AGEUSIA
AGGADA *n* explanation in Jewish literature
AGGADAH *same as* **>** AGGADA
AGGADAHS > AGGADAH
AGGADAS > AGGADA
AGGADIC *adj* of aggada
AGGADOT > AGGADA
AGGADOTH > AGGADA
AGGER *n* earthwork or mound forming a rampart, esp in a Roman military camp
AGGERS *adj* aggressive
AGGIE *n* American agricultural student
AGGIES > AGGIE
AGGRACE *vb* add grace to
AGGRACED > AGGRACE
AGGRACES > AGGRACE
AGGRACING > AGGRACE
AGGRADE *vb* build up the level of (any land surface) by the deposition of sediment
AGGRADED > AGGRADE
AGGRADES > AGGRADE
AGGRADING > AGGRADE
AGGRATE *vb* gratify
AGGRATED > AGGRATE
AGGRATES > AGGRATE
AGGRATING > AGGRATE
AGGRAVATE *vb* make worse
AGGREGATE *n* total ▷ *adj* gathered into a mass ▷ *vb* combine into a whole
AGGRESS *vb* attack first or begin a quarrel
AGGRESSED > AGGRESS
AGGRESSES > AGGRESS
AGGRESSOR *n* person or body that engages in aggressive behaviour
AGGRI *adj* of African beads

AGGRIEVE *vb* grieve
AGGRIEVED *adj* upset and angry
AGGRIEVES > AGGRIEVE
AGGRO *n* aggressive behaviour
AGGROS > AGGRO
AGGRY *adj* of African beads
AGHA *same as* **>** AGA
AGHAS > AGHA
AGHAST *adj* overcome with amazement or horror
AGILA *n* eaglewood
AGILAS > AGILA
AGILE *adj* nimble, quick-moving
AGILELY > AGILE
AGILENESS > AGILE
AGILER > AGILE
AGILEST > AGILE
AGILITIES > AGILE
AGILITY > AGILE
AGIN *prep* against, opposed to
AGING *same as* **>** AGEING
AGINGS > AGING
AGINNER *n* someone who is against something
AGINNERS > AGINNER
AGIO *n* difference between the nominal and actual values of a currency
AGIOS > AGIO
AGIOTAGE *n* business of exchanging currencies
AGIOTAGES > AGIOTAGE
AGISM *same as* **>** AGEISM
AGISMS > AGISM
AGIST *vb* care for and feed (cattle or horses) for payment
AGISTED > AGIST
AGISTER *n* person who grazes cattle for money
AGISTERS > AGISTER
AGISTING > AGIST
AGISTMENT > AGEISM
AGISTOR *n* person who grazes cattle for money
AGISTORS > AGISTOR
AGISTS > AGIST
AGITA *n* acid indigestion
AGITABLE > AGITATE
AGITANS as in *paralysis agitans* Parkinson's disease
AGITAS > AGITA
AGITATE *vb* disturb or excite
AGITATED > AGITATE
AGITATES > AGITATE
AGITATING > AGITATE
AGITATION *n* state of excitement, disturbance, or worry
AGITATIVE > AGITATE
AGITATO *adv* (to be performed) in an agitated manner
AGITATOR *n* person who agitates for or against a cause, etc
AGITATORS > AGITATOR
AGITPOP *n* use of pop music to promote political

propaganda
AGITPOPS > AGITPOP
AGITPROP *n* political agitation and propaganda
AGITPROPS > AGITPROP
AGLARE *adj* glaring
AGLEAM *adj* glowing
AGLEE *same as* **>** AGLEY
AGLET *n* metal sheath or tag at the end of a shoelace, ribbon, etc
AGLETS > AGLET
AGLEY *adj* awry
AGLIMMER *adj* glimmering
AGLITTER *adj* sparkling, glittering
AGLOO *same as* **>** AGLU
AGLOOS > AGLOO
AGLOSSAL > AGLOSSIA
AGLOSSATE > AGLOSSIA
AGLOSSIA *n* congenital absence of the tongue
AGLOSSIAS > AGLOSSIA
AGLOW *adj* glowing
AGLU *n* breathing hole made in ice by a seal
AGLUS > AGLU
AGLY *Scots word for* **>** WRONG
AGLYCON *n* chemical compound
AGLYCONE *n* chemical compound
AGLYCONES > AGLYCONE
AGLYCONS > AGLYCON
AGMA *n* symbol used to represent a velar nasal consonant
AGMAS > AGMA
AGMINATE *adj* gathered or clustered together
AGNAIL *another name for* **>** HANGNAIL
AGNAILS > AGNAIL
AGNAME *n* name additional to first name and surname
AGNAMED *adj* having an agname
AGNAMES > AGNAME
AGNATE *adj* related by descent from a common male ancestor ▷ *n* male or female descendant by male links from a common male ancestor
AGNATES > AGNATE
AGNATHAN *n* type of jawless eel-like aquatic vertebrate
AGNATHANS > AGNATHAN
AGNATHOUS *adj* (esp of lampreys and hagfishes) lacking jaws
AGNATIC > AGNATE
AGNATICAL > AGNATE
AGNATION > AGNATE
AGNATIONS > AGNATE
AGNISE *vb* acknowledge
AGNISED > AGNISE
AGNISES > AGNISE
AGNISING > AGNISE
AGNIZE *vb* acknowledge
AGNIZED > AGNIZE
AGNIZES > AGNIZE
AGNIZING > AGNIZE

AGNOMEN *n* fourth name or second cognomen occasionally acquired by an ancient Roman
AGNOMENS > AGNOMEN
AGNOMINA > AGNOMEN
AGNOMINAL > AGNOMEN
AGNOSIA *n* loss or diminution of the power to recognize familiar objects or people, usually as a result of brain damage
AGNOSIAS > AGNOSIA
AGNOSIC > AGNOSIA
AGNOSTIC *n* person who believes that it is impossible to know whether God exists ▷ *adj* of agnostics
AGNOSTICS > AGNOSTIC
AGO *adv* in the past
AGOG *adj* eager or curious
AGOGE *n* ancient Greek tempo
AGOGES > AGOGE
AGOGIC *n* musical accent
AGOGICS > AGOGIC
AGOING *adj* moving
AGON *n* (in ancient Greece) a festival at which competitors contended for prizes. Among the best known were the Olympic, Pythian, Nemean, and Isthmian Games
AGONAL *adj* of agony
AGONE *an archaic word for* **>** AGO
AGONES > AGON
AGONIC *adj* forming no angle
AGONIES > AGONY
AGONISE *same as* **>** AGONIZE
AGONISED > AGONISE
AGONISES > AGONISE
AGONISING > AGONISE
AGONIST *n* any muscle that is opposed in action by another muscle
AGONISTES *n* person suffering inner struggle
AGONISTIC *adj* striving for effect
AGONISTS > AGONIST
AGONIZE *vb* worry greatly
AGONIZED > AGONIZE
AGONIZES > AGONIZE
AGONIZING > AGONIZE
AGONS > AGON
AGONY *n* extreme physical or mental pain
AGOOD *adv* seriously or earnestly
AGORA *n* marketplace in Athens, used for popular meetings, or any similar place of assembly in ancient Greece
AGORAE > AGORA
AGORAS > AGORA
AGOROT > AGORA
AGOROTH *n* agorot
AGOUTA *n* Haitian rodent
AGOUTAS > AGOUTA

a

AGOUTI n rodent of Central and South America and the Caribbean with long legs and hooflike claws, valued for its meat

AGOUTIES >AGOUTI

AGOUTIS >AGOUTI

AGOUTY n agouti

AGRAFE same as >AGRAFFE

AGRAFES >AGRAFE

AGRAFFE n fastening consisting of a loop and hook, formerly used in armour and clothing

AGRAFFES >AGRAFFE

AGRAPHA same as >AGRAPHON

AGRAPHIA n loss of the ability to write, resulting from a brain lesion

AGRAPHIAS >AGRAPHIA

AGRAPHIC >AGRAPHIA

AGRAPHON n saying of Jesus not in Gospels

AGRARIAN adj of land or agriculture ▷ n person who favours the redistribution of landed property

AGRARIANS >AGRARIAN

AGRASTE >AGGRACE

AGRAVIC adj of zero gravity

AGREE vb be of the same opinion

AGREEABLE adj pleasant and enjoyable

AGREEABLY >AGREEABLE

AGREED adj determined by common consent

AGREEING >AGREE

AGREEMENT n agreeing

AGREES >AGREE

AGREGE n winner in examination for university teaching post

AGREGES >AGREGE

AGREMENS n amenities

AGREMENT n diplomatic approval of a country

AGREMENTS n amenities

AGRESTAL adj (of uncultivated plants such as weeds) growing on cultivated land

AGRESTIAL adj agrestal

AGRESTIC adj rural

AGRIA n appearance of pustules

AGRIAS >AGRIA

AGRIMONY n yellow-flowered plant with bitter-tasting fruits

AGRIN adv grinning

AGRIOLOGY n study of primitive peoples

AGRISE vb fill with fear

AGRISED >AGRISE

AGRISES >AGRISE

AGRISING >AGRISE

AGRIZE vb fill with fear

AGRIZED >AGRIZE

AGRIZES >AGRIZE

AGRIZING >AGRIZE

AGRODOLCE n Italian sweet-and-sour sauce

AGROLOGIC >AGROLOGY

AGROLOGY n scientific study of soils and their potential productivity

AGRONOMIC >AGRONOMY

AGRONOMY n science of soil management and crop production

AGROUND adv onto the bottom of shallow water ▷ adj on or onto the ground or bottom, as in shallow water

AGRYPNIA n inability to sleep

AGRYPNIAS >AGRYPNIA

AGRYZE vb fill with fear

AGRYZED >AGRYZE

AGRYZES >AGRYZE

AGRYZING >AGRYZE

AGS >AG

AGTERSKOT n final payment to a farmer for crops

AGUACATE n avocado

AGUACATES >AGUACATE

AGUE n periodic fever with shivering

AGUED adj suffering from fever

AGUELIKE >AGUE

AGUES >AGUE

AGUEWEED n N American plant with clusters of pale blue-violet or white flowers

AGUEWEEDS >AGUEWEED

AGUISE vb dress

AGUISED >AGUISE

AGUISES >AGUISE

AGUISH >AGUE

AGUISHLY >AGUE

AGUISING >AGUISE

AGUIZE vb dress

AGUIZED >AGUIZE

AGUIZES >AGUIZE

AGUIZING >AGUIZE

AGUNA n (in Jewish law) woman whose husband will not grant her a divorce

AGUNAH same as >AGUNA

AGUNOT >AGUNA

AGUTI n agouti

AGUTIS >AGUTI

AH vb say ah

AHA interj exclamation expressing triumph, surprise, etc, according to the intonation of the speaker

AHCHOO interj sound made by someone sneezing

AHEAD adv in front

AHEAP adv in a heap

AHED >AH

AHEIGHT adv at height

AHEM interj clearing of the throat in order to attract attention

AHEMERAL adj not constituting a full 24-hour day

AHENT adv behind

AHI n yellowfin tuna

AHIGH adv at height

AHIMSA n (in Hindu, Buddhist, and Jainist philosophy) the law of reverence for, and nonviolence to, every form of life

AHIMSAS >AHIMSA

AHIND adv behind

AHING >AH

AHINT adv behind

AHIS >AHI

AHISTORIC adj not related to history; not historical

AHOLD n holding

AHOLDS >AHOLD

AHORSE adv on horseback

AHOY interj hail used to call a ship

AHS >AH

AHULL adv with sails furled

AHUNGERED adj very hungry

AHUNGRY adj very hungry

AHURU n type of small pink cod of SW Pacific waters

AHURUHURU same as >AHURU

AHURUS >AHURU

AI n shaggy-coated slow-moving animal of South America

AIA n female servant in East

AIAS >AIA

AIBLINS Scots word for >PERHAPS

AID n (give) assistance or support ▷ vb help financially or in other ways

AIDA n cotton fabric with a natural mesh

AIDANCE n help

AIDANCES >AIDANCE

AIDANT adj helping

AIDAS >AIDA

AIDE n assistant

AIDED >AID

AIDER >AID

AIDERS >AID

AIDES >AIDE

AIDFUL adj helpful

AIDING >AID

AIDLESS adj without help

AIDMAN n military medical assistant

AIDMEN >AIDMAN

AIDOI adj of the genitals

AIDOS Greek word for >SHAME

AIDS >AID

AIERIES >AIERY

AIERY n eyrie

AIGA n Māori word for family

AIGAS >AIGA

AIGHT adv all right

AIGLET same as >AGLET

AIGLETS >AIGLET

AIGRET same as >AIGRETTE

AIGRETS >AIGRET

AIGRETTE n long plume worn on hats or as a headdress, esp one of long egret feathers

AIGRETTES >AIGRETTE

AIGUILLE n rock mass or mountain peak shaped like a needle

AIGUILLES >AIGUILLE

AIKIDO n Japanese system of self-defence employing similar principles to judo, but including blows from the hands and feet

AIKIDOS >AIKIDO

AIKONA interj South African expression meaning no

AIL vb trouble, afflict

AILANTHIC >AILANTHUS

AILANTHUS n type of deciduous tree with small greenish flowers and winged fruits, planted in Europe and N America

AILANTO n Asian tree

AILANTOS >AILANTO

AILED >AIL

AILERON n movable flap on an aircraft wing which controls rolling

AILERONS >AILERON

AILETTE n shoulder armour

AILETTES >AILETTE

AILING adj sickly

AILMENT n illness

AILMENTS >AILMENT

AILS >AIL

AIM vb point (a weapon or missile) or direct (a blow or remark) at a target ▷ n aiming

AIMED >AIM

AIMER >AIM

AIMERS >AIM

AIMFUL adj with purpose or intention

AIMFULLY >AIMFUL

AIMING >AIM

AIMLESS adj having no purpose

AIMLESSLY >AIMLESS

AIMS >AIM

AIN variant of >AYIN

AINE adj French word for elder (male)

AINEE adj French word for elder (female)

AINGA n Māori word for village

AINGAS >AINGA

AINS >AIN

AINSELL n Scots word meaning own self

AINSELLS >AINSELL

AIOLI n garlic mayonnaise

AIOLIS >AIOLI

AIR n mixture of gases forming the earth's atmosphere ▷ vb make known publicly

AIRBAG n safety device in a car, consisting of a bag that inflates automatically in an accident to protect the driver or passenger

AIRBAGS > AIRBAG

AIRBASE n centre from which military aircraft operate

AIRBASES > AIRBASE

AIRBOARD n inflatable body board

AIRBOARDS > AIRBOARD

AIRBOAT n shallow-draught boat powered by an aeroplane engine on a raised structure for use in swamps

AIRBOATS > AIRBOAT

AIRBORNE adj carried by air

AIRBOUND adj heading into the air

AIRBRICK n brick with holes in it, put into the wall of a building for ventilation

AIRBRICKS > AIRBRICK

AIRBRUSH n atomizer that sprays paint by compressed air ▷ vb paint using an airbrush

AIRBURST n explosion of a bomb, shell, etc, in the air ▷ vb (of a bomb, shell, etc) to explode in the air

AIRBURSTS > AIRBURST

AIRBUS n commercial passenger aircraft

AIRBUSES > AIRBUS

AIRBUSSES > AIRBUS

AIRCHECK n recording of a radio broadcast

AIRCHECKS > AIRCHECK

AIRCOACH n bus travelling to and from an airport

AIRCON n air conditioner

AIRCONS > AIRCON

AIRCRAFT n any machine that flies, such as an aeroplane

AIRCREW n crew of an aircraft

AIRCREWS > AIRCREW

AIRDATE n date of a programme broadcast

AIRDATES > AIRDATE

AIRDRAWN adj imaginary

AIRDROME same as > AERODROME

AIRDROMES > AIRDROME

AIRDROP n delivery of supplies, troops, etc, from an aircraft by parachute ▷ vb deliver (supplies, etc) by an airdrop

AIRDROPS > AIRDROP

AIRED > AIR

AIRER n device on which clothes are hung to dry

AIRERS > AIRER

AIREST > AIR

AIRFARE n money for an aircraft ticket

AIRFARES > AIRFARE

AIRFIELD n place where aircraft can land and take off

AIRFIELDS > AIRFIELD

AIRFLOW n flow of air in a wind tunnel or past a moving aircraft, car, train, etc

AIRFLOWS > AIRFLOW

AIRFOIL same as > AEROFOIL

AIRFOILS > AIRFOIL

AIRFRAME n body of an aircraft, excluding its engines

AIRFRAMES > AIRFRAME

AIRGAP n gap between parts in an electrical machine

AIRGAPS > AIRGAP

AIRGLOW n faint light from the upper atmosphere in the night sky, esp in low latitudes

AIRGLOWS > AIRGLOW

AIRGRAPH n photographic reduction of a letter for sending airmail

AIRGRAPHS > AIRGRAPH

AIRGUN n gun fired by compressed air

AIRGUNS > AIRGUN

AIRHEAD n person who is stupid or incapable of serious thought

AIRHEADED > AIRHEAD

AIRHEADS > AIRHEAD

AIRHOLE n hole that allows the passage of air

AIRHOLES > AIRHOLE

AIRIER > AIRY

AIRIEST > AIRY

AIRILY adv in a light-hearted and casual manner

AIRINESS n quality or condition of being fresh, light, or breezy

AIRING n exposure to air for drying or ventilation

AIRINGS > AIRING

AIRLESS adj stuffy

AIRLIFT n transport of troops or cargo by aircraft when other routes are blocked ▷ vb transport by airlift

AIRLIFTED > AIRLIFT

AIRLIFTS > AIRLIFT

AIRLIKE > AIR

AIRLINE n company providing scheduled flights for passengers and cargo

AIRLINER n large passenger aircraft

AIRLINERS > AIRLINER

AIRLINES > AIRLINE

AIRLOCK n air bubble blocking the flow of liquid in a pipe

AIRLOCKS > AIRLOCK

AIRMAIL n system of sending mail by aircraft ▷ adj of, used for, or concerned with airmail ▷ vb send by airmail

AIRMAILED > AIRMAIL

AIRMAILS > AIRMAIL

AIRMAN n member of the air force

AIRMEN > AIRMAN

AIRMOBILE adj using aircraft as transport

AIRN Scots word for > IRON

AIRNED > AIRN

AIRNING > AIRN

AIRNS > AIRN

AIRPARK n car park at airport

AIRPARKS > AIRPARK

AIRPLANE same as > AEROPLANE

AIRPLANES > AIRPLANE

AIRPLAY n broadcast performances of a record on radio

AIRPLAYS > AIRPLAY

AIRPORT n airfield for civilian aircraft, with facilities for aircraft maintenance and passengers

AIRPORTS > AIRPORT

AIRPOST n system of delivering mail by air

AIRPOSTS > AIRPOST

AIRPOWER n strength of a nation's air force

AIRPOWERS > AIRPOWER

AIRPROOF vb make something airtight

AIRPROOFS > AIRPROOF

AIRPROX n near collision involving aircraft

AIRPROXES > AIRPROX

AIRS npl manners put on to impress people

AIRSCAPE n picture or view of sky

AIRSCAPES > AIRSCAPE

AIRSCREW n aircraft propeller

AIRSCREWS > AIRSCREW

AIRSHAFT n shaft for ventilation

AIRSHAFTS > AIRSHAFT

AIRSHED n air over a particular geographical area

AIRSHEDS > AIRSHED

AIRSHIP n lighter-than-air self-propelled aircraft

AIRSHIPS > AIRSHIP

AIRSHOT n (in golf) shot that misses the ball completely, but counts as a stroke

AIRSHOTS > AIRSHOT

AIRSHOW n occasion when an air base is open to the public and a flying display and, usually, static exhibitions are held

AIRSHOWS > AIRSHOW

AIRSICK adj nauseated from travelling in an aircraft

AIRSIDE n part of an airport nearest the aircraft

AIRSIDES > AIRSIDE

AIRSPACE n atmosphere above a country, regarded as its territory

AIRSPACES > AIRSPACE

AIRSPEED n speed of an aircraft relative to the air in which it moves

AIRSPEEDS > AIRSPEED

AIRSTOP n helicopter landing-place

AIRSTOPS > AIRSTOP

AIRSTREAM n wind, esp at a high altitude

AIRSTRIKE n attack by military aircraft

AIRSTRIP n cleared area where aircraft can take off and land

AIRSTRIPS > AIRSTRIP

AIRT n direction or point of the compass, esp the direction of the wind ▷ vb direct

AIRTED > AIRT

AIRTH same as > AIRT

AIRTHED > AIRTH

AIRTHING > AIRTH

AIRTHS > AIRTH

AIRTIGHT adj sealed so that air cannot enter

AIRTIME n time allocated to a particular programme, topic, or type of material on radio or television

AIRTIMES > AIRTIME

AIRTING > AIRT

AIRTS > AIRT

AIRWARD adj into air

AIRWARDS adv into air

AIRWAVE n radio wave used in radio and television broadcasting

AIRWAVES > AIRWAVE

AIRWAY n air route used regularly by aircraft

AIRWAYS > AIRWAY

AIRWISE adv towards the air

AIRWOMAN > AIRMAN

AIRWOMEN > AIRMAN

AIRWORTHY adj (of aircraft) fit to fly

AIRY adj well-ventilated

AIS > AI

AISLE n passageway separating seating areas in a church, theatre, etc, or row of shelves in a supermarket

AISLED > AISLE

AISLELESS > AISLE

AISLES > AISLE

AISLEWAY n aisle

AISLEWAYS > AISLEWAY

AISLING Irish word for > DREAM

AISLINGS > AISLING

AIT n islet, esp in a river

AITCH n letter h or the sound represented by it

AITCHBONE n cut of beef from the rump bone

AITCHES > AITCH

AITS > AIT

AITU n half-human half-divine being

AITUS > AITU

AIVER n a working horse

a

AIVERS > AIVER

AIZLE n Scots word for hot ashes

AIZLES > AIZLE

AJAR adv (of a door) partly open ▷ adj not in harmony

AJEE same as **>** AGEE

AJIVA n Jainist term for non-living thing

AJIVAS > AJIVA

AJOWAN n plant related to caraway

AJOWANS > AJOWAN

AJUGA n garden plant

AJUGAS > AJUGA

AJUTAGE n nozzle

AJUTAGES > AJUTAGE

AJWAN n plant related to caraway

AJWANS > AJWAN

AKA n type of New Zealand vine

AKARYOTE n cell without a nucleus

AKARYOTES > AKARYOTE

AKARYOTIC > AKARYOTE

AKAS > AKA

AKATEA n New Zealand vine with white flowers

AKATEAS > AKATEA

AKATHISIA n inability to sit still because of uncontrollable movement caused by reaction to drugs

AKE vb old spelling of ache

AKEAKE n New Zealand tree

AKEAKES > AKEAKE

AKED > AKE

AKEDAH n binding of Isaac in Bible

AKEDAHS > AKEDAH

AKEE same as **>** ACKEE

AKEES > AKEE

AKELA n adult leader of a pack of Cub Scouts

AKELAS > AKELA

AKENE same as **>** ACHENE

AKENES > AKENE

AKENIAL > ACHENE

AKES > AKE

AKHARA n (in India) gymnasium

AKHARAS > AKHARA

AKIMBO as in with arms akimbo with hands on hips and elbows projecting outwards

AKIN adj related by blood

AKINESES > AKINESIS

AKINESIA n loss of power to move

AKINESIAS > AKINESIA

AKINESIS n loss of power to move

AKINETIC > AKINESIA

AKING > AKE

AKIRAHO n small New Zealand shrub with white flowers

AKIRAHOS > AKIRAHO

AKITA n large powerfully-built dog of a Japanese breed with erect ears, a typically white coat, and a large full tail carried curled over its back

AKITAS > AKITA

AKKAS slang word for **>** MONEY

AKOLUTHOS n leader of Byzantine Varangian Guard

AKRASIA n weakness of will

AKRASIAS > AKRASIA

AKRATIC > AKRASIA

AKVAVIT same as **>** AQUAVIT

AKVAVITS > AKVAVIT

AL same as **>** AAL

ALA n wing or flat winglike process or structure, such as a part of some bones and cartilages

ALAAP n part of raga in Indian music

ALAAPS > ALAAP

ALABAMINE old name for **>** ASTATINE

ALABASTER n soft white translucent stone ▷ adj of or resembling alabaster

ALACHLOR n type of herbicide

ALACHLORS > ALACHLOR

ALACK archaic or poetic word for **>** ALAS

ALACKADAY same as **>** ALACK

ALACRITY n speed, eagerness

ALAE > ALA

ALAIMENT old spelling of **>** ALLAYMENT

ALAIMENTS > ALAIMENT

ALALAGMOI **>** ALALAGMOS

ALALAGMOS n ancient Greek war cry

ALALIA n complete inability to speak

ALALIAS > ALALIA

ALAMEDA n public walk or promenade lined with trees, often poplars

ALAMEDAS > ALAMEDA

ALAMO n poplar tree

ALAMODE n soft light silk used for shawls and dresses, esp in the 19th century

ALAMODES > ALAMODE

ALAMORT adj exhausted and downcast

ALAMOS > ALAMO

ALAN n member of ancient European nomadic people

ALAND vb come onto land

ALANDS > ALAND

ALANE Scots word for **>** ALONE

ALANG n type of grass in Malaysia

ALANGS > ALANG

ALANIN n alanine

ALANINE n nonessential aliphatic amino acid that occurs in many proteins

ALANINES > ALANINE

ALANINS > ALANIN

ALANNAH interj my child: used as a term of address or endearment ▷ n. cry of alannah

ALANNAHS > ALANNAH

ALANS > ALAN

ALANT n flowering plant used in herbal medicine

ALANTS > ALANT

ALANYL n chemical found in proteins

ALANYLS > ALANYL

ALAP n Indian vocal music without words

ALAPA n part of raga in Indian music

ALAPAS > ALAPA

ALAPS > ALAP

ALAR adj relating to, resembling, or having wings or alae

ALARM n sudden fear caused by awareness of danger ▷ vb fill with fear

ALARMABLE > ALARM

ALARMED > ALARM

ALARMEDLY > ALARM

ALARMING > ALARM

ALARMISM > ALARMIST

ALARMISMS **>** ALARMIST

ALARMIST n person who alarms others needlessly ▷ adj causing needless alarm

ALARMISTS > ALARMIST

ALARMS > ALARM

ALARUM n alarm, esp a call to arms ▷ vb raise the alarm

ALARUMED > ALARUM

ALARUMING > ALARUM

ALARUMS > ALARUM

ALARY adj of, relating to, or shaped like wings

ALAS adv unfortunately, regrettably

ALASKA n dessert made of cake and ice cream

ALASKAS > ALASKA

ALASTOR n avenging demon

ALASTORS > ALASTOR

ALASTRIM n form of smallpox

ALASTRIMS > ALASTRIM

ALATE adj having wings or winglike extensions ▷ n winged insect

ALATED adj having wings

ALATES > ALATE

ALATION n state of having wings

ALATIONS > ALATION

ALAY vb allay

ALAYED > ALAY

ALAYING > ALAY

ALAYS > ALAY

ALB n long white robe worn by a Christian priest

ALBA n song of lament

ALBACORE n tuna found in warm seas, eaten for food

ALBACORES > ALBACORE

ALBARELLI **>** ALBARELLO

ALBARELLO n jar for drugs

ALBAS > ALBA

ALBATA n variety of German silver consisting of nickel, copper, and zinc

ALBATAS > ALBATA

ALBATROSS n large sea bird with very long wings

ALBE old word for **>** ALBEIT

ALBEDO n ratio of the intensity of light reflected from an object, such as a planet, to that of the light it receives from the sun

ALBEDOES > ALBEDO

ALBEDOS > ALBEDO

ALBEE archaic form of **>** ALBEIT

ALBEIT conj even though

ALBERGHI > ALBERGO

ALBERGO n Italian word for inn

ALBERT n kind of watch chain usually attached to a waistcoat

ALBERTITE n black solid variety of bitumen that has a conchoidal fracture and occurs in veins in oil-bearing strata

ALBERTS > ALBERT

ALBESCENT adj shading into, growing, or becoming white

ALBESPINE old name for **>** HAWTHORN

ALBESPYNE old name for **>** HAWTHORN

ALBICORE n species of tunny

ALBICORES > ALBICORE

ALBINAL > ALBINO

ALBINESS n female albino

ALBINIC > ALBINO

ALBINISM > ALBINO

ALBINISMS > ALBINO

ALBINO n person or animal with white skin and hair and pink eyes

ALBINOISM > ALBINO

ALBINOS > ALBINO

ALBINOTIC > ALBINO

ALBITE n colourless, milky-white, yellow, pink, green, or black mineral

ALBITES > ALBITE

ALBITIC > ALBITE

ALBITICAL > ALBITE

ALBITISE vb turn into albite

ALBITISED > ALBITISE

ALBITISES > ALBITISE

ALBITIZE vb turn into albite

ALBITIZED > ALBITIZE

ALBITIZES > ALBITIZE

ALBIZIA n mimosa

ALBIZIAS > ALBIZIA

ALBIZZIA n mimosa

ALBIZZIAS > ALBIZZIA

ALBS > ALB

ALBUGO n opacity of the cornea

ALBUGOS > ALBUGO

ALBUM n book with blank pages for keeping photographs or stamps in

ALBUMEN same as > ALBUMIN

ALBUMENS > ALBUMEN

ALBUMIN n protein found in blood plasma, egg white, milk, and muscle

ALBUMINS > ALBUMIN

ALBUMOSE the US name for > PROTEOSE

ALBUMOSES > ALBUMOSE

ALBUMS > ALBUM

ALBURNOUS > ALBURNUM

ALBURNUM former name for > SAPWOOD

ALBURNUMS > ALBURNUM

ALBUTEROL n drug used to treat lung diseases

ALCADE same as > ALCALDE

ALCADES > ALCADE

ALCAHEST same as > ALKAHEST

ALCAHESTS > ALCAHEST

ALCAIC n verse consisting of strophes with four tetrametric lines

ALCAICS > ALCAIC

ALCAIDE n commander of a fortress or castle

ALCAIDES > ALCAIDE

ALCALDE n (in Spain and Spanish America) the mayor or chief magistrate in a town

ALCALDES > ALCALDE

ALCARRAZA n Spanish water container

ALCATRAS n pelican

ALCAYDE n alcaide

ALCAYDES > ALCAYDE

ALCAZAR n any of various palaces or fortresses built in Spain by the Moors

ALCAZARS > ALCAZAR

ALCHEMIC > ALCHEMY

ALCHEMIES > ALCHEMY

ALCHEMISE same as > ALCHEMIZE

ALCHEMIST n person who practises alchemy

ALCHEMIZE vb alter (an element, metal, etc) by alchemy

ALCHEMY n medieval form of chemistry concerned with trying to turn base metals into gold and to find the elixir of life

ALCHERA n (in the mythology of Australian Aboriginal peoples) mythical Golden Age of the past

ALCHERAS > ALCHERA

ALCHYMIES > ALCHYMY

ALCHYMY old spelling of > ALCHEMY

ALCID n bird of the auk family

ALCIDINE adj relating to a family of sea birds including the auks, guillemots, and puffins

ALCIDS > ALCID

ALCO same as > ALKO

ALCOHOL n colourless flammable liquid present in intoxicating drinks

ALCOHOLIC adj of alcohol ▷ n person addicted to alcohol

ALCOHOLS > ALCOHOL

ALCOLOCK n breath-alcohol ignition-interlock device, which is fitted to the ignition in certain motor vehicles. The driver must blow into a tube and, if his or her breath contains too much alcohol, a lock is activated to prevent the vehicle starting

ALCOLOCKS > ALCOLOCK

ALCOOL n form of pure grain spirit distilled in Quebec

ALCOOLS > ALCOOL

ALCOPOP n alcoholic drink that tastes like a soft drink

ALCOPOPS > ALCOPOP

ALCORZA n Spanish sweet

ALCORZAS > ALCORZA

ALCOS > ALCO

ALCOVE n recess in the wall of a room

ALCOVED adj with or in an alcove

ALCOVES > ALCOVE

ALDEA n Spanish village

ALDEAS > ALDEA

ALDEHYDE n one of a group of chemical compounds derived from alcohol by oxidation

ALDEHYDES > ALDEHYDE

ALDEHYDIC > ALDEHYDE

ALDER n tree related to the birch

ALDERFLY n insect with large broad-based hind wings, which produces aquatic larvae

ALDERMAN n formerly, senior member of a local council

ALDERMEN > ALDERMAN

ALDERN adj made of alder wood

ALDERS > ALDER

ALDICARB n crystalline compound used as a pesticide

ALDICARBS > ALDICARB

ALDOL n colourless or yellowish oily liquid

ALDOLASE n enzyme present in the body

ALDOLASES > ALDOLASE

ALDOLS > ALDOL

ALDOSE n sugar that contains the aldehyde group or is a hemiacetal

ALDOSES > ALDOSE

ALDOXIME n oxime formed by reaction between hydroxylamine and an aldehyde

ALDOXIMES > ALDOXIME

ALDRIN n brown to white poisonous crystalline solid

ALDRINS > ALDRIN

ALE n kind of beer

ALEATORIC same as > ALEATORY

ALEATORY adj dependent on chance

ALEBENCH n bench at alehouse

ALEC same as > ALECK

ALECITHAL adj (of an ovum) having little or no yolk

ALECK n irritatingly oversmart person

ALECKS > ALECK

ALECOST another name for > COSTMARY

ALECOSTS > ALECOST

ALECS > ALEC

ALEE adj on or towards the lee

ALEF n first letter of Hebrew alphabet

ALEFS > ALEF

ALEFT adv at or to left

ALEGAR n malt vinegar

ALEGARS > ALEGAR

ALEGGE vb alleviate

ALEGGED > ALEGGE

ALEGGES > ALEGGE

ALEGGING > ALEGGE

ALEHOUSE n public house

ALEHOUSES > ALEHOUSE

ALEMBIC n anything that distils or purifies, esp an obsolete vessel used for distillation

ALEMBICS > ALEMBIC

ALEMBROTH n mercury compound in alchemy

ALENCON n elaborate lace worked on a hexagonal mesh

ALENCONS > ALENCON

ALENGTH adv at length

ALEPH n first letter in the Hebrew alphabet

ALEPHS > ALEPH

ALEPINE n type of cloth

ALEPINES > ALEPINE

ALERCE n wood of the sandarac tree

ALERCES > ALERCE

ALERION n eagle in heraldry

ALERIONS > ALERION

ALERT adj watchful, attentive ▷ n warning of danger ▷ vb warn of danger

ALERTED > ALERT

ALERTER > ALERT

ALERTEST > ALERT

ALERTING > ALERT

ALERTLY > ALERT

ALERTNESS > ALERT

ALERTS > ALERT

ALES > ALE

ALETHIC adj of or relating to such philosophical concepts as truth, necessity, possibility, contingency, etc

ALEURON n outer protein-rich layer of certain seeds, esp of cereal grains

ALEURONE same as > ALEURON

ALEURONES > ALEURONE

ALEURONIC > ALEURON

ALEURONS > ALEURON

ALEVIN n young fish, esp a young salmon or trout

ALEVINS > ALEVIN

ALEW n cry to call hunting hounds

ALEWASHED adj showing effects of beer drinking

ALEWIFE n North American fish

ALEWIVES > ALEWIFE

ALEWS > ALEW

ALEXANDER n cocktail made with creme de cacao

ALEXIA n disorder of the central nervous system characterized by impaired ability to read

ALEXIAS > ALEXIA

ALEXIC > ALEXIA

ALEXIN n complement

ALEXINE same as > ALEXIN

ALEXINES > ALEXINE

ALEXINIC > ALEXIN

ALEXINS > ALEXIN

ALEYE vb allay

ALEYED > ALEYE

ALEYES > ALEYE

ALEYING > ALEYE

ALF n uncultivated Australian

ALFA n type of grass

ALFAKI n expert in Muslim law

ALFAKIS > ALFAKI

ALFALFA n kind of plant used to feed livestock

ALFALFAS > ALFALFA

ALFAQUI n expert in Muslim law

ALFAQUIN n expert in Muslim law

ALFAQUINS > ALFAQUIN

ALFAQUIS > ALFAQUI

ALFAS > ALFA

ALFERECES > ALFEREZ

ALFEREZ n Spanish standard-bearer

ALFILARIA n plant with finely divided leaves and small pink or purplish flowers

ALFILERIA same as > ALFILARIA

ALFORJA n saddlebag made of leather or canvas

ALFORJAS > ALFORJA

ALFREDO adj cooked with a cheese and egg sauce

ALFRESCO adj in the open air ▷ adv in the open air

ALFS > ALF

ALGA n unicellular or multicellular organism formerly classified as a plant

ALGAE > ALGA

ALGAECIDE n substance for killing algae

ALGAL > ALGA

ALGAROBA same as > ALGARROBA

ALGAROBAS > ALGAROBA

ALGARROBA n edible pod of these trees

ALGARROBO n carob

ALGAS > ALGA

ALGATE adv anyway

ALGATES adv anyway

ALGEBRA n branch of mathematics using symbols to represent numbers

ALGEBRAIC adj of or relating to algebra

ALGEBRAS > ALGEBRA

ALGERINE n soft striped woollen cloth

ALGERINES > ALGERINE

ALGESES > ALGESIS

ALGESIA n capacity to feel pain

ALGESIAS > ALGESIA

ALGESIC > ALGESIA

ALGESIS n feeling of pain

ALGETIC > ALGESIA

ALGICIDAL > ALGICIDE

ALGICIDE n any substance that kills algae

ALGICIDES > ALGICIDE

ALGID adj chilly or cold

ALGIDITY > ALGID

ALGIDNESS > ALGID

ALGIN n gelatinous solution obtained as a by-product in the extraction of iodine from seaweed

ALGINATE n salt or ester of alginic acid

ALGINATES > ALGINATE

ALGINIC as in alginic acid powdery substance extracted from kelp

ALGINS > ALGIN

ALGOID adj resembling or relating to algae

ALGOLOGY n branch of biology concerned with the study of algae

ALGOMETER n instrument for measuring sensitivity to pressure or to pain

ALGOMETRY > ALGOMETER

ALGOR n chill

ALGORISM n Arabic or decimal system of counting

ALGORISMS > ALGORISM

ALGORITHM n logical arithmetical or computational procedure for solving a problem

ALGORS > ALGOR

ALGUACIL n Spanish law officer

ALGUACILS > ALGUACIL

ALGUAZIL n Spanish law officer

ALGUAZILS > ALGUAZIL

ALGUM n type of wood mentioned in Bible

ALGUMS > ALGUM

ALIAS adv also known as ▷ n false name

ALIASES > ALIAS

ALIASING n error in a vision or sound signal arising from limitations in the system that generates or processes the signal

ALIASINGS > ALIASING

ALIBI n plea of being somewhere else when a crime was committed ▷ vb provide someone with an alibi

ALIBIED > ALIBI

ALIBIES > ALIBI

ALIBIING > ALIBI

ALIBIS > ALIBI

ALIBLE adj nourishing

ALICANT n wine from Alicante in Spain

ALICANTS > ALICANT

ALICYCLIC adj (of an organic compound) having aliphatic properties, in spite of the presence of a ring of carbon atoms

ALIDAD same as > ALIDADE

ALIDADE n surveying instrument used in plane-tabling for drawing lines of sight on a distant object and taking angular measurements

ALIDADES > ALIDADE

ALIDADS > ALIDAD

ALIEN adj foreign ▷ n foreigner ▷ vb transfer (property, etc) to another

ALIENABLE adj able to be transferred to another owner

ALIENAGE > ALIEN

ALIENAGES > ALIEN

ALIENATE vb cause to become hostile

ALIENATED > ALIENATE

ALIENATES > ALIENATE

ALIENATOR > ALIENATE

ALIENED > ALIEN

ALIENEE n person to whom a transfer of property is made

ALIENEES > ALIENEE

ALIENER > ALIEN

ALIENERS > ALIEN

ALIENING > ALIEN

ALIENISM n study and treatment of mental illness

ALIENISMS > ALIENISM

ALIENIST n psychiatrist who specializes in the legal aspects of mental illness

ALIENISTS > ALIENIST

ALIENLY > ALIEN

ALIENNESS > ALIEN

ALIENOR n person who transfers property to another

ALIENORS > ALIENOR

ALIENS > ALIEN

ALIF n first letter of Arabic alphabet

ALIFORM adj wing-shaped

ALIFS > ALIF

ALIGARTA n alligator

ALIGARTAS > ALIGARTA

ALIGHT vb step out of (a vehicle) ▷ adj on fire ▷ adv on fire

ALIGHTED > ALIGHT

ALIGHTING > ALIGHT

ALIGHTS > ALIGHT

ALIGN vb bring (a person or group) into agreement with the policy of another

ALIGNED > ALIGN

ALIGNER > ALIGN

ALIGNERS > ALIGN

ALIGNING > ALIGN

ALIGNMENT n arrangement in a straight line

ALIGNS > ALIGN

ALIKE adj like, similar ▷ adv in the same way

ALIKENESS > ALIKE

ALIMENT n something that nourishes or sustains the body or mind ▷ vb support or sustain

ALIMENTAL > ALIMENT

ALIMENTED > ALIMENT

ALIMENTS > ALIMENT

ALIMONIED adj provided with alimony

ALIMONIES > ALIMONY

ALIMONY n allowance paid under a court order to a separated or divorced spouse

ALINE a rare spelling of > ALIGN

ALINED > ALINE

ALINEMENT > ALINE

ALINER > ALINE

ALINERS > ALINE

ALINES > ALINE

ALINING > ALINE

ALIPED n animal, like the bat, whose toes are joined by a membrane that serves as a wing ▷ adj (of bats and similar animals) having the digits connected by a wing like membrane

ALIPEDS > ALIPED

ALIPHATIC adj (of an organic compound) having an open chain structure

ALIQUANT adj denoting or belonging to a number that is not an exact divisor of a given number

ALIQUOT adj of or denoting an exact divisor of a number ▷ n exact divisor

ALIQUOTS > ALIQUOT

ALISMA n marsh plant

ALISMAS > ALISMA

ALISON same as > ALYSSUM

ALISONS > ALISON

ALIST adj leaning over

ALIT rare past tense and past participle of > ALIGHT

ALITERACY > ALITERATE

ALITERATE n person who is able to read but disinclined to do so ▷ adj of or relating to aliterates

ALIUNDE adj from a source extrinsic to the matter, document, or instrument under consideration

ALIVE adj living, in existence

ALIVENESS > ALIVE

ALIYA n immigration to Holy Land

ALIYAH n immigration to the Holy Land

ALIYAHS > ALIYAH

ALIYAS > ALIYA

ALIYOS n remission of sin in Jewish faith

ALIYOT > ALIYAH

ALIYOTH > ALIYAH

ALIZARI n madder from Middle East

ALIZARIN n brownish-yellow powder or orange-red crystalline solid

ALIZARINE n alizarin

ALIZARINS > ALIZARIN

ALIZARIS > ALIZARI

ALKAHEST n hypothetical universal solvent sought by alchemists

ALKAHESTS > ALKAHEST

ALKALI n substance which combines with acid and neutralizes it to form a salt

ALKALIC adj (of igneous rocks) containing large amounts of alkalis, esp sodium and potassium

ALKALIES > ALKALI

ALKALIFY vb make or become alkaline

ALKALIN adj leaning over

ALKALINE adj having the properties of or containing an alkali

ALKALIS > ALKALI

ALKALISE same as > ALKALIZE

ALKALISED > ALKALISE

ALKALISER > ALKALISE

ALKALISES > ALKALISE

ALKALIZE vb make alkaline

ALKALIZED > ALKALIZE

ALKALIZER > ALKALIZE

ALKALIZES > ALKALIZE

ALKALOID n any of a group of organic compounds containing nitrogen

ALKALOIDS > ALKALOID

ALKALOSES > ALKALOSIS

ALKALOSIS n abnormal increase in the alkalinity of the blood and extracellular fluids

ALKALOTIC > ALKALOSIS

ALKANE n any saturated hydrocarbon with the general formula C_nH_{2n+2}

ALKANES > ALKANE

ALKANET n European plant whose roots yield a red dye

ALKANETS > ALKANET

ALKANNIN same as > ALKANET

ALKANNINS > ALKANNIN

ALKENE n type of unsaturated hydrocarbon

ALKENES > ALKENE

ALKIE same as > ALKY

ALKINE n alkyne

ALKINES > ALKINE

ALKO n heavy drinker or alcoholic

ALKOS > ALKO

ALKOXIDE n chemical compound containing oxygen

ALKOXIDES > ALKOXIDE

ALKOXY adj of type of chemical compound containing oxygen

ALKY n heavy drinker or alcoholic

ALKYD n synthetic resin

ALKYDS > ALKYD

ALKYL n of or containing the monovalent group C_nH_{2n+1}

ALKYLATE vb add alkyl group to a compound

ALKYLATED > ALKYLATE

ALKYLATES > ALKYLATE

ALKYLIC > ALKYL

ALKYLS > ALKYL

ALKYNE n an unsaturated aliphatic hydrocarbon

ALKYNES > ALKYNE

ALL adj whole quantity or number (of) ▷ adv wholly, entirely ▷ n entire being, effort, or property

ALLANITE n rare black or brown mineral

ALLANITES > ALLANITE

ALLANTOIC > ALLANTOIS

ALLANTOID adj relating to or resembling the allantois

ALLANTOIN n chemical used in cosmetics

ALLANTOIS n membranous sac growing out of the ventral surface of the hind gut of embryonic reptiles, birds, and mammals. It combines with the chorion to form the mammalian placenta

ALLATIVE n word in grammatical case denoting movement towards

ALLATIVES > ALLATIVE

ALLAY vb reduce (fear or anger)

ALLAYED > ALLAY

ALLAYER > ALLAY

ALLAYERS > ALLAY

ALLAYING > ALLAY

ALLAYINGS > ALLAY

ALLAYMENT n mitigation

ALLAYS > ALLAY

ALLCOMERS n everyone who comes

ALLEDGE vb allege

ALLEDGED > ALLEDGE

ALLEDGES > ALLEDGE

ALLEDGING > ALLEDGE

ALLEE n avenue

ALLEES > ALLEE

ALLEGE vb state without proof

ALLEGED adj stated but not proved

ALLEGEDLY adv reportedly

ALLEGER > ALLEGE

ALLEGERS > ALLEGE

ALLEGES > ALLEGE

ALLEGGE vb alleviate

ALLEGGED > ALLEGGE

ALLEGGES > ALLEGGE

ALLEGGING > ALLEGGE

ALLEGIANT n loyalty

ALLEGING > ALLEGE

ALLEGORIC adj used in, containing, or characteristic of allegory

ALLEGORY n story with an underlying meaning as well as the literal one

ALLEGRO adv (piece to be played) in a brisk lively manner ▷ n piece or passage to be performed in a brisk lively manner

ALLEGROS > ALLEGRO

ALLEL n form of gene

ALLELE n any of two or more genes that are responsible for alternative characteristics, such as smooth or wrinkled seeds in peas

ALLELES > ALLELE

ALLELIC > ALLELE

ALLELISM > ALLELE

ALLELISMS > ALLELE

ALLELS > ALLEL

ALLELUIA n song of praise to God

ALLELUIAH interj alleluia

ALLELUIAS > ALLELUIA

ALLEMANDE n first movement of the classical suite, composed in a moderate tempo in a time signature of four-four

ALLENARLY adv solely

ALLERGEN n substance capable of causing an allergic reaction

ALLERGENS > ALLERGEN

ALLERGIC adj having or caused by an allergy ▷ n person suffering from an allergy

ALLERGICS > ALLERGIC

ALLERGIES > ALLERGY

ALLERGIN n allergen

ALLERGINS > ALLERGIN

ALLERGIST n physician skilled in the diagnosis and treatment of diseases or conditions caused by allergy

ALLERGY n extreme sensitivity to a substance, which causes the body to react to it

ALLERION n eagle in heraldry

ALLERIONS > ALLERION

ALLETHRIN n clear viscous amber-coloured liquid

ALLEVIANT n medical treatment that reduces pain but does not cure the underlying problem

ALLEVIATE vb lessen (pain or suffering)

ALLEY n narrow street or path

ALLEYCAT n homeless cat that roams in back streets

ALLEYCATS > ALLEYCAT

ALLEYED adj having alleys

ALLEYS > ALLEY

ALLEYWAY n narrow passage with buildings or walls on both sides

ALLEYWAYS > ALLEYWAY

ALLHEAL n any of several plants reputed to have healing powers, such as selfheal and valerian

ALLHEALS > ALLHEAL

ALLIABLE adj able to form an alliance

ALLIANCE n state of being allied

ALLIANCES > ALLIANCE

ALLICE n species of fish

ALLICES > ALLICE

ALLICHOLY n melancholy

ALLICIN n chemical found in garlic

ALLICINS > ALLICIN

ALLIED adj joined, as by treaty, agreement, or marriage

ALLIES > ALLY

ALLIGARTA n alligator

ALLIGATE vb join together

ALLIGATED > ALLIGATE

ALLIGATES > ALLIGATE

ALLIGATOR n reptile of the crocodile family, found in the southern US and China

ALLIS n species of fish

ALLISES > ALLIS

ALLIUM n type of plant of the family including the onion, garlic, shallot, leek, and chive

ALLIUMS > ALLIUM

ALLNESS n being all

ALLNESSES > ALLNESS

ALLNIGHT adj lasting all night

ALLOBAR n form of element

ALLOBARS > ALLOBAR

ALLOCABLE > ALLOCATE

ALLOCARPY n production of fruit through cross-fertilization

ALLOCATE vb assign to

someone or for a particular purpose

ALLOCATED > ALLOCATE

ALLOCATES > ALLOCATE

ALLOCATOR > ALLOCATE

ALLOD same as > ALLODIUM

ALLODIA > ALLODIUM

ALLODIAL adj (of land) held as an allodium

ALLODIUM n lands held in absolute ownership, free from such obligations as rent or services due to an overlord

ALLODIUMS > ALLODIUM

ALLODS > ALLOD

ALLODYNIA n pain caused by a normally painless stimulus

ALLOGAMY n cross-fertilization in flowering plants

ALLOGENIC adj having different genes

ALLOGRAFT n tissue graft from a donor genetically unrelated to the recipient

ALLOGRAPH n document written by a person who is not a party to it

ALLOMERIC adj of similar crystalline structure

ALLOMETRY n study of the growth of part of an organism in relation to the growth of the entire organism

ALLOMONE n chemical substance secreted externally by certain animals, such as insects, affecting the behaviour or physiology of another species detrimentally

ALLOMONES > ALLOMONE

ALLOMORPH n any of the phonological representations of a single morpheme

ALLONGE n paper extension to bill of exchange

ALLONGES > ALLONGE

ALLONS interj French word meaning let's go

ALLONYM n name, often one of historical significance or that of another person, assumed by a person, esp an author

ALLONYMS > ALLONYM

ALLOPATH n person who practises or is skilled in allopathy

ALLOPATHS > ALLOPATH

ALLOPATHY n orthodox method of treating disease, by using drugs that produce an effect opposite to the effect of the disease being treated, as contrasted with homeopathy

ALLOPATRY n condition of taking place or existing in areas that are geographically separated from one another

ALLOPHANE n variously coloured amorphous mineral consisting of hydrated aluminium silicate and occurring in cracks in some sedimentary rocks

ALLOPHONE n any of several speech sounds that are regarded as contextual or environmental variants of the same phoneme

ALLOPLASM n part of the cytoplasm that is specialized to form cilia, flagella, and similar structures

ALLOSAUR n any large carnivorous bipedal dinosaur common in North America in late Jurassic times

ALLOSAURS > ALLOSAUR

ALLOSTERY n condition of an enzyme in which the structure and activity of the enzyme are modified by the binding of a metabolic molecule

ALLOT vb assign as a share or for a particular purpose

ALLOTMENT n distribution

ALLOTROPE n any of two or more physical forms in which an element can exist

ALLOTROPY n existence of an element in two or more physical forms

ALLOTS > ALLOT

ALLOTTED > ALLOT

ALLOTTEE n person to whom something is allotted

ALLOTTEES > ALLOTTEE

ALLOTTER n person who allots

ALLOTTERS > ALLOTTER

ALLOTTERY n something allotted

ALLOTTING > ALLOT

ALLOTYPE n additional type specimen selected because of differences from the original type specimen, such as opposite sex or morphological details

ALLOTYPES > ALLOTYPE

ALLOTYPIC > ALLOTYPE

ALLOTYPY n existence of allotypes

ALLOVER n fabric completely covered with a pattern

ALLOVERS > ALLOVER

ALLOW vb permit

ALLOWABLE adj permissible

ALLOWABLY > ALLOWABLE

ALLOWANCE n amount of money given at regular intervals

ALLOWED > ALLOW

ALLOWEDLY adv by general

admission or agreement

ALLOWING > ALLOW

ALLOWS > ALLOW

ALLOXAN n chemical found in uric acid

ALLOXANS > ALLOXAN

ALLOY n mixture of two or more metals ▷ vb mix (metals)

ALLOYED > ALLOY

ALLOYING > ALLOY

ALLOYS > ALLOY

ALLOZYME n any one of a number of different structural forms of the same enzyme encoded by a different allele

ALLOZYMES > ALLOZYME

ALLS > ALL

ALLSEED n any of several plants that produce many seeds, such as knotgrass

ALLSEEDS > ALLSEED

ALLSORTS n assorted sweets

ALLSPICE n spice made from the berries of a tropical American tree

ALLSPICES > ALLSPICE

ALLUDE vb refer indirectly to

ALLUDED > ALLUDE

ALLUDES > ALLUDE

ALLUDING > ALLUDE

ALLURE n attractiveness ▷ vb entice or attract

ALLURED > ALLURE

ALLURER > ALLURE

ALLURERS > ALLURE

ALLURES > ALLURE

ALLURING adj extremely attractive

ALLUSION n indirect reference

ALLUSIONS > ALLUSION

ALLUSIVE adj containing or full of allusions

ALLUVIA > ALLUVIUM

ALLUVIAL adj of or relating to alluvium ▷ n soil consisting of alluvium

ALLUVIALS > ALLUVIAL

ALLUVION n wash of the sea or of a river

ALLUVIONS > ALLUVION

ALLUVIUM n fertile soil deposited by flowing water

ALLUVIUMS > ALLUVIUM

ALLY vb unite or be united, esp formally, as by treaty, confederation, or marriage ▷ n country, person, or group allied with another

ALLYING > ALLY

ALLYL n of, consisting of, or containing the monovalent group CH_2:$CHCH_2$

ALLYLIC > ALLYL

ALLYLS > ALLYL

ALLYOU pron all of you

ALMA n Egyptian dancing girl

ALMAGEST n medieval treatise concerning

alchemy or astrology

ALMAGESTS > ALMAGEST

ALMAH n Egyptian dancing girl

ALMAHS > ALMAH

ALMAIN n German dance

ALMAINS > ALMAIN

ALMANAC n yearly calendar with detailed information on anniversaries, phases of the moon, etc

ALMANACK same as > ALMANAC

ALMANACKS > ALMANACK

ALMANACS > ALMANAC

ALMANDINE n deep violet-red garnet

ALMANDITE n form of garnet

ALMAS > ALMA

ALME n Egyptian dancing girl

ALMEH n Egyptian dancing girl

ALMEHS > ALMEH

ALMEMAR n (in Ashkenazic usage) the raised platform in a synagogue on which the reading desk stands

ALMEMARS > ALMEMAR

ALMERIES > ALMERY

ALMERY n cupboard for church vessels

ALMES > ALME

ALMIGHTY adj all-powerful ▷ adv extremely

ALMIRAH n cupboard

ALMIRAHS > ALMIRAH

ALMNER n almoner

ALMNERS > ALMNER

ALMOND n edible oval-shaped nut which grows on a small tree

ALMONDS > ALMOND

ALMONDY > ALMOND

ALMONER n formerly, a hospital social worker

ALMONERS > ALMONER

ALMONRIES > ALMONRY

ALMONRY n house of an almoner, usually the place where alms were given

ALMOST adv very nearly

ALMOUS Scots word for > ALMS

ALMS npl gifts to the poor

ALMSGIVER n one who gives alms

ALMSHOUSE n (formerly) a house, financed by charity, which offered accommodation to the poor

ALMSMAN n person who gives or receives alms

ALMSMEN > ALMSMAN

ALMSWOMAN n woman who gives or receives alms

**ALMSWOMEN > ** ALMSWOMAN

ALMUCE n fur-lined hood or cape formerly worn by members of certain religious orders, more recently by canons of

France

ALMUCES > ALMUCE

ALMUD n Spanish unit of measure

ALMUDE n Spanish unit of measure

ALMUDES > ALMUDE

ALMUDS > ALMUD

ALMUG n type of wood mentioned in Bible

ALMUGS > ALMUG

ALNAGE n measurement in ells

ALNAGER n inspector of cloth

ALNAGERS > ALNAGER

ALNAGES > ALNAGE

ALNICO n alloy of various metals including iron, nickel, and cobalt

ALNICOS > ALNICO

ALOCASIA n type of tropical plant

ALOCASIAS > ALOCASIA

ALOD n feudal estate with no superior

ALODIA > ALODIUM

ALODIAL > ALODIUM

ALODIUM same as > ALLODIUM

ALODIUMS > ALODIUM

ALODS > ALOD

ALOE n plant with fleshy spiny leaves

ALOED adj containing aloes

ALOES another name for > EAGLEWOOD

ALOETIC > ALOE

ALOETICS > ALOE

ALOFT adv in the air ▷ adj in or into a high or higher place

ALOGIA n inability to speak

ALOGIAS > ALOGIA

ALOGICAL adj without logic

ALOHA a Hawaiian word for > HELLO

ALOHAS > ALOHA

ALOIN n bitter crystalline compound derived from various species of aloe: used as a laxative and flavouring agent

ALOINS > ALOIN

ALONE adv without anyone or anything else

ALONELY > ALONE

ALONENESS > ALONE

ALONG adv forward

ALONGSIDE adv beside (something)

ALONGST adv along

ALOO n (in Indian cookery) potato

ALOOF adj distant or haughty in manner

ALOOFLY > ALOOF

ALOOFNESS > ALOOF

ALOOS > ALOO

ALOPECIA n loss of hair

ALOPECIAS > ALOPECIA

ALOPECIC > ALOPECIA

ALOPECOID > ALOPECIA

a

ALOUD adv in an audible voice ▷ adj in a normal voice

ALOW adj in or into the lower rigging of a vessel, near the deck

ALOWE Scots word for > ABLAZE

ALP n high mountain

ALPACA n Peruvian llama

ALPACAS > ALPACA

ALPACCA same as > ALPACA

ALPACCAS > ALPACCA

ALPARGATA n Spanish sandal

ALPEEN n Irish cudgel

ALPEENS > ALPEEN

ALPENGLOW n reddish light on the summits of snow-covered mountain peaks at sunset or sunrise

ALPENHORN same as > ALPHORN

ALPHA n first letter in the Greek alphabet

ALPHABET n set of letters used in writing a language

ALPHABETS > ALPHABET

ALPHAS > ALPHA

ALPHASORT vb arrange in alphabetical order

ALPHATEST vb subject (an experimental product such as computer software) to an initial test

ALPHORN n wind instrument used in the Swiss Alps, consisting of a very long tube of wood or bark with a cornet-like mouthpiece

ALPHORNS > ALPHORN

ALPHOSIS n absence of skin pigmentation, as in albinism

ALPHYL n univalent radical

ALPHYLS > ALPHYL

ALPINE adj of high mountains ▷ n mountain plant

ALPINELY > ALPINE

ALPINES > ALPINE

ALPINISM > ALPINIST

ALPINISMS > ALPINIST

ALPINIST n mountain climber

ALPINISTS > ALPINIST

ALPS > ALP

ALREADY adv before the present time

ALRIGHT adj all right

ALS > AL

ALSIKE n clover native to Europe and Asia

ALSIKES > ALSIKE

ALSO adv in addition, too

ALSOON same as > ALSOONE

ALSOONE adv as soon

ALT n octave directly above the treble staff

ALTAR n table used for Communion in Christian churches

ALTARAGE n donations placed on altar for priest

ALTARAGES > ALTARAGE

ALTARS > ALTAR

ALTARWISE adv in the position of an altar

ALTER vb make or become different

ALTERABLE > ALTER

ALTERABLY > ALTER

ALTERANT n alternative

ALTERANTS > ALTERANT

ALTERCATE vb argue, esp heatedly

ALTERED > ALTER

ALTERER > ALTER

ALTERERS > ALTER

ALTERING > ALTER

ALTERITY n quality of being different

ALTERN adj alternate

ALTERNANT adj alternating

ALTERNAT n practice of deciding precedence by lot

ALTERNATE vb (cause to) occur by turns ▷ adj occurring by turns ▷ n person who substitutes for another in his absence

ALTERNATS > ALTERNAT

ALTERNE n neighbouring but different plant group

ALTERNES > ALTERNE

ALTERS > ALTER

ALTESSE n French word for highness

ALTESSES > ALTESSE

ALTEZA n Spanish word for highness

ALTEZAS > ALTEZA

ALTEZZA n Italian word for highness

ALTEZZAS > ALTEZZA

ALTHAEA n plant such as the hollyhock, having tall spikes of showy white, yellow, or red flowers

ALTHAEAS > ALTHAEA

ALTHEA same as > ALTHAEA

ALTHEAS > ALTHEA

ALTHO conj short form of although

ALTHORN n valved brass musical instrument belonging to the saxhorn or flügelhorn families

ALTHORNS > ALTHORN

ALTHOUGH conj despite the fact that; even though

ALTIGRAPH n instrument that measures altitude

ALTIMETER n instrument that measures altitude

ALTIMETRY n science of measuring altitudes, as with an altimeter

ALTIPLANO n high plateau

ALTISSIMO adj (of music) very high in pitch ▷ n as in in altissimo the octave commencing an octave above the treble clef

ALTITUDE n height above sea level

ALTITUDES > ALTITUDE

ALTO n (singer with) the highest adult male voice ▷ adj denoting such an instrument, singer, or voice

ALTOIST n person who plays the alto saxophone

ALTOISTS > ALTOIST

ALTOS > ALTO

ALTRICES npl altricial birds

ALTRICIAL adj (of the young of some species of birds after hatching) naked, blind, and dependent on the parents for food ▷ n altricial bird, such as a pigeon

ALTRUISM n unselfish concern for the welfare of others

ALTRUISMS > ALTRUISM

ALTRUIST > ALTRUISM

ALTRUISTS > ALTRUISM

ALTS > ALT

ALU same as > ALOO

ALUDEL n pear-shaped vessel, open at both ends, formerly used with similar vessels for collecting condensates, esp for subliming mercury

ALUDELS > ALUDEL

ALULA n tuft of feathers attached to the first digit of a bird

ALULAE > ALULA

ALULAR > ALULA

ALULAS > ALULA

ALUM n double sulphate of aluminium and potassium

ALUMIN n aluminium oxide

ALUMINA n aluminium oxide

ALUMINAS > ALUMINA

ALUMINATE n salt of the ortho or meta acid forms of aluminium hydroxide

ALUMINE n French word for alumina

ALUMINES > ALUMINE

ALUMINIC adj of aluminium

ALUMINISE same as > ALUMINIZE

ALUMINIUM n light silvery-white metal that does not rust

ALUMINIZE vb cover with aluminium

ALUMINOUS adj resembling aluminium

ALUMINS > ALUMIN

ALUMINUM same as > ALUMINIUM

ALUMINUMS > ALUMINUM

ALUMISH adj like alum

ALUMIUM old name for > ALUMINIUM

ALUMIUMS > ALUMIUM

ALUMNA n female graduate of a school, college, etc

ALUMNAE > ALUMNA

ALUMNI > ALUMNUS

ALUMNUS n graduate of a college

ALUMROOT n North American plants having small white, reddish, or green bell-shaped flowers and astringent roots

ALUMROOTS > ALUMROOT

ALUMS > ALUM

ALUMSTONE same as > ALUNITE

ALUNITE n white, grey, or reddish mineral

ALUNITES > ALUNITE

ALURE n area behind battlements

ALURES > ALURE

ALUS > ALU

ALVEARIES > ALVEARY

ALVEARY n beehive

ALVEATED adj with vaults like beehive

ALVEOLAR adj of, relating to, or resembling an alveolus ▷ n alveolar consonant, such as the speech sounds written t, d, and s in English

ALVEOLARS > ALVEOLAR

ALVEOLATE adj having many alveoli

ALVEOLE n alveolus

ALVEOLES > ALVEOLE

ALVEOLI > ALVEOLUS

ALVEOLUS n any small pit, cavity, or saclike dilation, such as a honeycomb cell, a tooth socket, or the tiny air sacs in the lungs

ALVINE adj of or relating to the intestines or belly

ALWAY same as > ALWAYS

ALWAYS adv at all times

ALYSSUM n garden plant with small yellow or white flowers

ALYSSUMS > ALYSSUM

AM see > BE

AMA n vessel for water

AMABILE adj sweet

AMADAVAT same as > AVADAVAT

AMADAVATS > AMADAVAT

AMADODA npl grown men

AMADOU n spongy substance made from certain fungi, used as tinder to light fires and in medicine to stop bleeding

AMADOUS > AMADOU

AMAH n (in the East, formerly) a nurse or maidservant

AMAHS > AMAH

AMAIN adv with great strength, speed, or haste

AMAKOSI > INKHOSI

AMALGAM n blend or combination

AMALGAMS > AMALGAM

AMANDINE n protein found in almonds

AMANDINES > AMANDINE

AMANDLA n political slogan

calling for power to the Black population

AMANDLAS > AMANDLA

AMANITA n type of fungus

AMANITAS > AMANITA

AMANITIN n poison from amanita

AMANITINS > AMANITIN

AMARACUS n marjoram

AMARANT n amaranth

AMARANTH n imaginary flower that never fades

AMARANTHS > AMARANTH

AMARANTIN n protein

AMARANTS > AMARANT

AMARELLE n variety of sour cherry that has pale red fruit and colourless juice

AMARELLES > AMARELLE

AMARETTI > AMARETTO

AMARETTO n Italian liqueur with a flavour of almonds

AMARETTOS > AMARETTO

AMARNA adj pertaining to the reign of the Pharaoh Akhenaton

AMARONE n strong dry red Italian wine

AMARONES > AMARONE

AMARYLLID n plant of the amaryllis family

AMARYLLIS n lily-like plant with large red, pink, or white flowers

AMAS > AMA

AMASS vb collect or accumulate

AMASSABLE > AMASS

AMASSED > AMASS

AMASSER > AMASS

AMASSERS > AMASS

AMASSES > AMASS

AMASSING > AMASS

AMASSMENT > AMASS

AMATE vb match

AMATED > AMATE

AMATES > AMATE

AMATEUR n person who engages in a sport or activity as a pastime rather than as a profession ▷ adj not professional

AMATEURS > AMATEUR

AMATING > AMATE

AMATION n lovemaking

AMATIONS > AMATION

AMATIVE a rare word for **>** AMOROUS

AMATIVELY > AMATIVE

AMATOL n explosive mixture of ammonium nitrate and TNT, used in shells and bombs

AMATOLS > AMATOL

AMATORIAL same as **>** AMATORY

AMATORIAN > AMATORY

AMATORY adj relating to romantic or sexual love

AMAUROSES > AMAUROSIS

AMAUROSIS n blindness, esp when occurring

without observable damage to the eye

AMAUROTIC > AMAUROSIS

AMAUT n hood on an Inuit woman's parka for carrying a child

AMAUTS > AMAUT

AMAZE vb surprise greatly, astound

AMAZED > AMAZE

AMAZEDLY > AMAZE

AMAZEMENT n incredulity or great astonishment

AMAZES > AMAZE

AMAZING adj causing wonder or astonishment

AMAZINGLY > AMAZING

AMAZON n any tall, strong, or aggressive woman

AMAZONIAN > AMAZON

AMAZONITE n green variety of microcline used as a gemstone

AMAZONS > AMAZON

AMBACH same as **>** AMBATCH

AMBACHES > AMBACH

AMBAGE n ambiguity

AMBAGES > AMBAGE

AMBAGIOUS > AMBAGE

AMBAN n Chinese official

AMBANS > AMBAN

AMBARI same as **>** AMBARY

AMBARIES > AMBARY

AMBARIS > AMBARI

AMBARY n tropical Asian plant that yields a fibre similar to jute

AMBASSAGE n embassy

AMBASSIES > AMBASSY

AMBASSY n embassy

AMBATCH n tree or shrub of the Nile Valley, valued for its light-coloured wood

AMBATCHES > AMBATCH

AMBEER n saliva coloured by tobacco juice

AMBEERS > AMBEER

AMBER n clear yellowish fossil resin ▷ adj brownish-yellow

AMBERED adj fixed in amber

AMBERGRIS n waxy substance secreted by the sperm whale, used in making perfumes

AMBERIES > AMBERY

AMBERINA n type of glassware

AMBERINAS > AMBERINA

AMBERITE n powder like amber

AMBERITES > AMBERITE

AMBERJACK n type of large fish with golden markings when young, found in Atlantic waters

AMBEROID n synthetic amber made by compressing pieces of amber and other resins together at a high temperature

AMBEROIDS > AMBEROID

AMBEROUS adj like amber

AMBERS > AMBER

AMBERY adj like amber

AMBIANCE same as **>** AMBIENCE

AMBIANCES > AMBIANCE

AMBIENCE n atmosphere of a place

AMBIENCES > AMBIENCE

AMBIENT adj surrounding ▷ n ambient music

AMBIENTS > AMBIENT

AMBIGUITY n possibility of interpreting an expression in more than one way

AMBIGUOUS adj having more than one possible meaning

AMBIPOLAR adj (of plasmas and semiconductors) involving both positive and negative charge carriers

AMBIT n limits or boundary

AMBITION n desire for success

AMBITIONS > AMBITION

AMBITIOUS adj having a strong desire for success

AMBITS > AMBIT

AMBITTY adj crystalline and brittle

AMBIVERT n person who is intermediate between an extrovert and an introvert

AMBIVERTS > AMBIVERT

AMBLE vb walk at a leisurely pace ▷ n leisurely walk or pace

AMBLED > AMBLE

AMBLER > AMBLE

AMBLERS > AMBLE

AMBLES > AMBLE

AMBLING n walking at a leisurely pace

AMBLINGS > AMBLING

AMBLYOPIA n impaired vision with no discernible damage to the eye or optic nerve

AMBLYOPIC > AMBLYOPIA

AMBO n either of two raised pulpits from which the gospels and epistles were read in early Christian churches

AMBOINA same as **>** AMBOYNA

AMBOINAS > AMBOINA

AMBONES > AMBO

AMBOS > AMBO

AMBOYNA n mottled curly-grained wood of an Indonesian tree, used in making furniture

AMBOYNAS > AMBOYNA

AMBRIES > AMBRY

AMBROID same as **>** AMBEROID

AMBROIDS > AMBROID

AMBROSIA n anything delightful to taste or smell

AMBROSIAL > AMBROSIA

AMBROSIAN > AMBROSIA

AMBROSIAS > AMBROSIA

AMBROTYPE n early type of glass negative that could be made to appear as a positive by backing it with black varnish or paper

AMBRY n recessed cupboard in the wall of a church near the altar, used to store sacred vessels, etc

AMBSACE n double ace, the lowest throw at dice

AMBSACES > AMBSACE

AMBULACRA n radial bands on the ventral surface of echinoderms, such as the starfish and sea urchin, on which the tube feet are situated

AMBULANCE n motor vehicle designed to carry sick or injured people

AMBULANT adj moving about from place to place

AMBULANTS > AMBULANT

AMBULATE vb wander about or move from one place to another

AMBULATED > AMBULATE

AMBULATES > AMBULATE

AMBULATOR n person who walks

AMBULETTE n motor vehicle designed for transporting ill or handicapped people

AMBUSCADE n ambush ▷ vb ambush or lie in ambush

AMBUSCADO n ambuscade

AMBUSH n act of waiting in a concealed position to make a surprise attack ▷ vb attack from a concealed position

AMBUSHED > AMBUSH

AMBUSHER > AMBUSH

AMBUSHERS > AMBUSH

AMBUSHES > AMBUSH

AMBUSHING > AMBUSH

AME n soul

AMEARST old form of **>** AMERCE

AMEBA same as **>** AMOEBA

AMEBAE > AMEBA

AMEBAN > AMEBA

AMEBAS > AMEBA

AMEBEAN same as **>** AMOEBEAN

AMEBIASES > AMEBIASIS

AMEBIASIS n disease caused by amoeba

AMEBIC > AMEBA

AMEBOCYTE n any cell having properties similar to an amoeba, such as shape, mobility, and ability to engulf particles

AMEBOID same as **>** AMOEBOID

AMEER n (formerly) the ruler of Afghanistan

AMEERATE n country ruled by an ameer

AMEERATES > AMEERATE

AMEERS > AMEER

AMEIOSES > AMEIOSIS

AMEIOSIS n absence of pairing of chromosomes during meiosis

AMELCORN n variety of wheat

AMELCORNS > AMELCORN

AMELIA n congenital absence of arms or legs

AMELIAS > AMELIA

AMEN n term used at the end of a prayer or religious statement ▷ vb say amen

AMENABLE adj likely or willing to cooperate

AMENABLY > AMENABLE

AMENAGE vb tame

AMENAGED > AMENAGE

AMENAGES > AMENAGE

AMENAGING > AMENAGE

AMENAUNCE n person's bearing

AMEND vb make small changes to correct or improve (something)

AMENDABLE > AMEND

AMENDE n public apology and reparation made to satisfy the honour of the person wronged

AMENDED > AMEND

AMENDER > AMEND

AMENDERS > AMEND

AMENDES > AMENDE

AMENDING > AMEND

AMENDMENT n improvement or correction

AMENDS n recompense or compensation given or gained for some injury, insult, etc

AMENE adj pleasant

AMENED > AMEN

AMENING > AMEN

AMENITIES > AMENITY

AMENITY n useful or enjoyable feature

AMENS > AMEN

AMENT n mentally deficient person

AMENTA > AMENTUM

AMENTAL > AMENTUM

AMENTIA n severe mental deficiency, usually congenital

AMENTIAS > AMENTIA

AMENTS > AMENT

AMENTUM same as > AMENT

AMERCE vb punish by a fine

AMERCED > AMERCE

AMERCER > AMERCE

AMERCERS > AMERCE

AMERCES > AMERCE

AMERCING > AMERCE

AMERICIUM n white metallic element artificially produced from plutonium

AMES > AME

AMESACE same as > AMBSACE

AMESACES > AMESACE

AMETHYST n bluish-violet variety of quartz used as a gemstone ▷ adj purple or violet

AMETHYSTS > AMETHYST

AMETROPIA n loss of ability to focus images on the retina, caused by an imperfection in the refractive function of the eye

AMETROPIC > AMETROPIA

AMI n male friend

AMIA n species of fish

AMIABLE adj friendly, pleasant-natured

AMIABLY > AMIABLE

AMIANTHUS n any of the fine silky varieties of asbestos

AMIANTUS n amianthus

AMIAS > AMIA

AMICABLE adj friendly

AMICABLY > AMICABLE

AMICE n rectangular piece of white linen worn by priests around the neck and shoulders under the alb or, formerly, on the head

AMICES > AMICE

AMICI > AMICUS

AMICUS n Latin for friend

AMID prep in the middle of, among ▷ n amide

AMIDASE n enzyme

AMIDASES > AMIDASE

AMIDE n any organic compound containing the group ·CONH$_2$

AMIDES > AMIDE

AMIDIC > AMIDE

AMIDIN n form of starch

AMIDINE n crystalline compound

AMIDINES > AMIDINE

AMIDINS > AMIDIN

AMIDMOST adv in the middle

AMIDO adj containing amide

AMIDOGEN n chemical compound derived from ammonia

AMIDOGENS > AMIDOGEN

AMIDOL n chemical used in developing photographs

AMIDOLS > AMIDOL

AMIDONE n pain-killing drug

AMIDONES > AMIDONE

AMIDS same as > AMID

AMIDSHIP adj in the middle of a ship

AMIDSHIPS adv at or towards the middle of a ship ▷ adj at, near, or towards the centre of a vessel

AMIDST same as > AMID

AMIE n female friend

AMIES > AMIE

AMIGA n Spanish female friend

AMIGAS > AMIGA

AMIGO n friend

AMIGOS > AMIGO

AMILDAR n manager in India

AMILDARS > AMILDAR

AMIN same as > AMINE

AMINE n organic base formed by replacing one or more of the hydrogen atoms of ammonia by organic groups

AMINES > AMINE

AMINIC > AMINE

AMINITIES > AMINITY

AMINITY n amenity

AMINO n of, consisting of, or containing the group of atoms -NH$_2$

AMINS > AMIN

AMIR n (formerly) the ruler of Afghanistan

AMIRATE > AMIR

AMIRATES > AMIR

AMIRS > AMIR

AMIS > AMI

AMISES > AMI

AMISS adv wrongly, badly ▷ adj wrong, faulty ▷ n evil deed

AMISSES > AMISS

AMISSIBLE adj likely to be lost

AMISSING adj missing

AMITIES > AMITY

AMITOSES > AMITOSIS

AMITOSIS n unusual form of cell division in which the nucleus and cytoplasm divide by constriction without the formation of chromosomes

AMITOTIC > AMITOSIS

AMITROLE n pesticide

AMITROLES > AMITROLE

AMITY n friendship

AMLA n species of Indian tree

AMLAS > AMLA

AMMAN same as > AMTMAN

AMMANS > AMMAN

AMMETER n instrument for measuring electric current

AMMETERS > AMMETER

AMMINE n compound that has molecules containing one or more ammonia molecules bound to another molecule, group, or atom by coordinate bonds

AMMINES > AMMINE

AMMINO adj containing ammonia molecules

AMMIRAL old word for > ADMIRAL

AMMIRALS > AMMIRAL

AMMO n ammunition

AMMOCETE n ammocoete

AMMOCETES > AMMOCETE

AMMOCOETE n larva of primitive jawless vertebrates, such as the lamprey, that lives buried in mud and feeds on microorganisms

AMMON n Asian wild sheep

AMMONAL n explosive made by mixing TNT, ammonium nitrate, and aluminium powder

AMMONALS > AMMONAL

AMMONATE same as > AMMINE

AMMONATES > AMMONATE

AMMONIA n strong-smelling alkaline gas containing hydrogen and nitrogen

AMMONIAC n strong-smelling gum resin obtained from the stems of a N Asian plant

AMMONIACS > AMMONIAC

AMMONIAS > AMMONIA

AMMONIATE vb unite or treat with ammonia

AMMONIC adj of or concerned with ammonia or ammonium compounds

AMMONICAL > AMMONIC

AMMONIFY vb treat or impregnate with ammonia or a compound of ammonia

AMMONITE n fossilized spiral shell of an extinct sea creature

AMMONITES > AMMONITE

AMMONITIC > AMMONITE

AMMONIUM n type of monovalent chemical group

AMMONIUMS > AMMONIUM

AMMONO adj using ammonia

AMMONOID n type of fossil

AMMONOIDS > AMMONOID

AMMONS > AMMON

AMMOS > AMMO

AMNESIA n loss of memory

AMNESIAC > AMNESIA

AMNESIACS > AMNESIA

AMNESIAS > AMNESIA

AMNESIC > AMNESIA

AMNESICS > AMNESIA

AMNESTIC adj relating to amnesia

AMNESTIED > AMNESTY

AMNESTIES > AMNESTY

AMNESTY n general pardon for offences against a government ▷ vb overlook or forget (an offence)

AMNIA > AMNION

AMNIC adj relating to amnion

AMNIO n amniocentesis

AMNION n innermost of two membranes enclosing an embryo

AMNIONIC > AMNION

AMNIONS > AMNION

AMNIOS > AMNIO

AMNIOTE n any vertebrate animal, such as a reptile, bird, or mammal, that possesses an amnion, chorion, and allantois during embryonic development

AMNIOTES > AMNIOTE
AMNIOTIC *adj* of or relating to the amnion
AMNIOTOMY *n* breaking of the membrane surrounding a fetus to induce labour
AMOEBA *n* microscopic single-celled animal able to change its shape
AMOEBAE > AMOEBA
AMOEBAEAN *adj* of or relating to lines of verse dialogue that answer each other alternately
AMOEBAN > AMOEBA
AMOEBAS > AMOEBA
AMOEBEAN *same as* > AMOEBAEAN
AMOEBIC > AMOEBA
AMOEBOID *adj* of, related to, or resembling amoebae
AMOK *n* state of murderous frenzy, originally observed among Malays
AMOKS > AMOK
AMOKURA *n* type of white tropical sea bird with a red beak and long red tail feathers
AMOKURAS > AMOKURA
AMOLE *n* American plant
AMOLES > AMOLE
AMOMUM *n* plant of ginger family
AMOMUMS > AMOMUM
AMONG *prep* in the midst of
AMONGST *same as* > AMONG
AMOOVE *vb* stir someone's emotions
AMOOVED > AMOOVE
AMOOVES > AMOOVE
AMOOVING > AMOOVE
AMORAL *adj* without moral standards
AMORALISM > AMORAL
AMORALIST > AMORAL
AMORALITY > AMORAL
AMORALLY > AMORAL
AMORANCE *n* condition of being in love
AMORANCES > AMORANCE
AMORANT > AMORANCE
AMORCE *n* small percussion cap
AMORCES > AMORCE
AMORET *n* sweetheart
AMORETS > AMORET
AMORETTI > AMORETTO
AMORETTO *n* (esp in painting) a small chubby naked boy representing a cupid
AMORETTOS > AMORETTO
AMORINI > AMORINO
AMORINO *same as* > AMORETTO
AMORISM > AMORIST
AMORISMS > AMORIST
AMORIST *n* lover or a writer about love
AMORISTIC > AMORIST
AMORISTS > AMORIST
AMORNINGS *adv* each

morning
AMOROSA *n* lover
AMOROSAS > AMOROSA
AMOROSITY *n* quality of being amorous
AMOROSO *adv* (to be played) lovingly ▷ *n* rich sweetened sherry of a dark colour
AMOROSOS > AMOROSO
AMOROUS *adj* feeling, showing, or relating to sexual love
AMOROUSLY > AMOROUS
AMORPHISM > AMORPHOUS
AMORPHOUS *adj* without distinct shape
AMORT *adj* in low spirits
AMORTISE *same as* > AMORTIZE
AMORTISED > AMORTISE
AMORTISES > AMORTISE
AMORTIZE *vb* pay off (a debt) gradually by periodic transfers to a sinking fund
AMORTIZED > AMORTIZE
AMORTIZES > AMORTIZE
AMOSITE *n* form of asbestos
AMOSITES > AMOSITE
AMOTION *n* act of removing
AMOTIONS > AMOTION
AMOUNT *n* extent or quantity ▷ *vb* be equal or add up to
AMOUNTED > AMOUNT
AMOUNTING > AMOUNT
AMOUNTS > AMOUNT
AMOUR *n* (secret) love affair
AMOURETTE *n* minor love affair
AMOURS > AMOUR
AMOVE *vb* stir someone's emotions
AMOVED > AMOVE
AMOVES > AMOVE
AMOVING > AMOVE
AMOWT *same as* > AMAUT
AMOWTS > AMOWT
AMP *n* ampere ▷ *vb* excite or become excited
AMPASSIES > AMPASSY
AMPASSY *n* ampersand
AMPED > AMP
AMPERAGE *n* strength of an electric current measured in amperes
AMPERAGES > AMPERAGE
AMPERE *n* basic unit of electric current
AMPERES > AMPERE
AMPERSAND *n* character (&), meaning and
AMPERZAND *n* ampersand
AMPHIBIA *n* class of amphibians
AMPHIBIAN *n* type of animal that lives on land but breeds in water
AMPHIBOLE *n* any of a large group of minerals consisting of the silicates of calcium, iron, magnesium, sodium, and aluminium

AMPHIBOLY *n* ambiguity of expression, esp where due to a grammatical construction
AMPHIGORY *n* piece of nonsensical writing in verse or, less commonly, prose
AMPHIOXI > AMPHIOXUS
AMPHIOXUS *another name for the* > LANCELET
AMPHIPATH *adj* of or relating to a molecule that possesses both hydrophobic and hydrophilic elements
AMPHIPOD *n* type of marine or freshwater crustacean with a flat body
AMPHIPODS > AMPHIPOD
AMPHOLYTE *n* electrolyte that can be acid or base
AMPHORA *n* two-handled ancient Greek or Roman jar
AMPHORAE > AMPHORA
AMPHORAL > AMPHORA
AMPHORAS > AMPHORA
AMPHORIC *adj* resembling the sound produced by blowing into a bottle. Amphoric breath sounds are heard through a stethoscope placed over a cavity in the lung
AMPING > AMP
AMPLE *adj* more than sufficient
AMPLENESS > AMPLE
AMPLER > AMPLE
AMPLEST > AMPLE
AMPLEXUS *n* mating in amphibians
AMPLIDYNE *n* magnetic amplifier
AMPLIFIED > AMPLIFY
AMPLIFIER *n* device used to amplify a current or sound signal
AMPLIFIES > AMPLIFY
AMPLIFY *vb* increase the strength of (a current or sound signal)
AMPLITUDE *n* greatness of extent
AMPLOSOME *n* stocky body type
AMPLY *adv* fully or generously
AMPOULE *n* small sealed glass vessel containing liquid for injection
AMPOULES > AMPOULE
AMPS > AMP
AMPUL *n* ampoule
AMPULE *same as* > AMPOULE
AMPULES > AMPULE
AMPULLA *n* dilated end part of certain tubes in the body
AMPULLAE > AMPULLA
AMPULLAR > AMPULLA
AMPULLARY > AMPULLA
AMPULS > AMPUL
AMPUTATE *vb* cut off (a

limb or part of a limb) for medical reasons
AMPUTATED > AMPUTATE
AMPUTATES > AMPUTATE
AMPUTATOR > AMPUTATE
AMPUTEE *n* person who has had a limb amputated
AMPUTEES > AMPUTEE
AMREETA *same as* > AMRITA
AMREETAS > AMREETA
AMRIT *n* sanctified solution of sugar and water used in the Amrit Ceremony
AMRITA *n* ambrosia of the gods that bestows immortality
AMRITAS > AMRITA
AMRITS > AMRIT
AMSINCKIA *n* Californian herb
AMTMAN *n* magistrate in parts of Europe
AMTMANS > AMTMAN
AMTRAC *n* amphibious tracked vehicle
AMTRACK *n* amphibious tracked vehicle
AMTRACKS > AMTRACK
AMTRACS > AMTRAC
AMU *n* unit of mass
AMUCK *same as* > AMOK
AMUCKS > AMUCK
AMULET *n* something carried or worn as a protection against evil
AMULETIC > AMULET
AMULETS > AMULET
AMUS > AMU
AMUSABLE *adj* capable of being amused
AMUSE *vb* cause to laugh or smile
AMUSEABLE *same as* > AMUSABLE
AMUSED > AMUSE
AMUSEDLY > AMUSE
AMUSEMENT *n* state of being amused
AMUSER > AMUSE
AMUSERS > AMUSE
AMUSES > AMUSE
AMUSETTE *n* type of light cannon
AMUSETTES > AMUSETTE
AMUSIA *n* inability to recognize musical tones
AMUSIAS > AMUSIA
AMUSIC > AMUSIA
AMUSING *adj* mildly entertaining
AMUSINGLY > AMUSING
AMUSIVE *adj* deceptive
AMYGDAL *n* almond
AMYGDALA *n* almond-shaped part, such as a tonsil or a lobe of the cerebellum
AMYGDALAE > AMYGDALA
AMYGDALE *n* vesicle in a volcanic rock, formed from a bubble of escaping gas, that has become filled with light-coloured minerals,

such as quartz and calcite

MYGDALES > AMYGDALE

MYGDALIN n white soluble bitter-tasting crystalline glycoside extracted from bitter almonds

MYGDALS > AMYGDAL

MYGDULE same as > AMYGDALE

MYGDULES > AMYGDULE

MYL n of, consisting of, or containing any of eight isomeric forms of the monovalent group C_5H_{11}–

MYLASE n enzyme, present in saliva, that helps to change starch into sugar

MYLASES > AMYLASE

MYLENE another name (no longer in technical usage) for > PENTENE

MYLENES > AMYLENE

MYLIC adj of or derived from amyl

MYLOGEN n soluble part of starch

MYLOGENS > AMYLOGEN

MYLOID n complex protein resembling starch, deposited in tissues in some degenerative diseases ▷ adj starchlike

MYLOIDAL > AMYLOID

MYLOIDS > AMYLOID

MYLOPSIN n enzyme of the pancreatic juice that converts starch into sugar

MYLOSE n minor component (about 20 per cent) of starch, consisting of long unbranched chains of glucose units. It is soluble in water and gives an intense blue colour with iodine

MYLOSES > AMYLOSE

MYLS > AMYL

MYLUM another name for > STARCH

MYLUMS > AMYLUM

MYOTONIA another name for > MYOTONIA

N adj form of **a** used before vowels, and sometimes before 'h'

NA adv (of ingredients in a prescription) in equal quantities ▷ n collection of reminiscences, sketches, etc, of or about a person or place

NABAENA n type of freshwater alga sometimes found in drinking water, giving it a fishy taste and smell

NABAENAS > ANABAENA

NABANTID n type of spiny-finned fish of the family which includes the fighting fish, climbing perch, and gourami

NABAS n type of fish

NABASES > ANABASIS

ANABASIS n march of Cyrus the Younger and his Greek mercenaries from Sardis to Cunaxa in Babylonia in 401 BC

ANABATIC adj (of air currents) rising upwards, esp up slopes

ANABIOSES > ANABIOSIS

ANABIOSIS n ability to return to life after apparent death

ANABIOTIC > ANABIOSIS

ANABLEPS n type of tropical freshwater fish with eyes adapted for seeing both in air and water

ANABOLIC adj of or relating to anabolism

ANABOLISM n metabolic process in which body tissues are synthesized from food

ANABOLITE n product of anabolism

ANABRANCH n stream that leaves a river and enters it again further downstream

ANACHARIS n water plant

ANACLINAL adj (of valleys and similar formations) progressing in a direction opposite to the dip of the surrounding rock strata

ANACLISES > ANACLITIC

ANACLISIS > ANACLITIC

ANACLITIC adj of or relating to relationships that are characterized by the strong dependence of one person on others or another

ANACONDA n large S American snake which kills by constriction

ANACONDAS > ANACONDA

ANACRUSES > ANACRUSIS

ANACRUSIS n one or more unstressed syllables at the beginning of a line of verse

ANADEM n garland for the head

ANADEMS > ANADEM

ANAEMIA n deficiency in the number of red blood cells

ANAEMIAS > ANAEMIA

ANAEMIC adj having anaemia

ANAEROBE n organism that does not require oxygen

ANAEROBES > ANAEROBE

ANAEROBIA same as > ANAEROBES

ANAEROBIC adj not requiring oxygen

ANAGLYPH n stereoscopic picture consisting of two images of the same object, taken from slightly

different angles

ANAGLYPHS > ANAGLYPH

ANAGLYPHY > ANAGLYPH

ANAGOGE n allegorical or spiritual interpretation, esp of sacred works such as the Bible

ANAGOGES > ANAGOGE

ANAGOGIC > ANAGOGE

ANAGOGIES > ANAGOGY

ANAGOGY same as > ANAGOGE

ANAGRAM n word or phrase made by rearranging the letters of another word or phrase

ANAGRAMS > ANAGRAM

ANAL adj of the anus

ANALCIME same as > ANALCITE

ANALCIMES > ANALCIME

ANALCIMIC > ANALCIME

ANALCITE n white, grey, or colourless zeolite mineral

ANALCITES > ANALCITE

ANALECTA same as > ANALECTS

ANALECTIC > ANALECTS

ANALECTS npl selected literary passages from one or more works

ANALEMMA n graduated scale shaped like a figure of eight that indicates the daily declination of the sun

ANALEMMAS > ANALEMMA

ANALEPTIC adj (of a drug, etc) stimulating the central nervous system ▷ n any drug, such as doxapram, that stimulates the central nervous system

ANALGESIA n absence of pain

ANALGESIC adj (drug) relieving pain ▷ n drug that relieves pain

ANALGETIC n painkilling drug

ANALGIA same as > ANALGESIA

ANALGIAS > ANALGIA

ANALITIES > ANALITY

ANALITY n quality of being psychologically anal

ANALLY > ANAL

ANALOG same as > ANALOGUE

ANALOGA > ANALOGON

ANALOGIC > ANALOGY

ANALOGIES > ANALOGY

ANALOGISE same as > ANALOGIZE

ANALOGISM > ANALOGIZE

ANALOGIST > ANALOGY

ANALOGIZE vb use analogy

ANALOGON n analogue

ANALOGONS > ANALOGON

ANALOGOUS adj similar in some respects

ANALOGS > ANALOG

ANALOGUE n something

that is similar in some respects to something else ▷ adj displaying information by means of a dial

ANALOGUES > ANALOGUE

ANALOGY n similarity in some respects

ANALYSAND n any person who is undergoing psychoanalysis

ANALYSE vb make an analysis of (something)

ANALYSED > ANALYSE

ANALYSER > ANALYSE

ANALYSERS > ANALYSE

ANALYSES > ANALYSIS

ANALYSING > ANALYSE

ANALYSIS n separation of a whole into its parts for study and interpretation

ANALYST n person skilled in analysis

ANALYSTS > ANALYST

ANALYTE n substance that is being analyzed

ANALYTES > ANALYTE

ANALYTIC adj relating to analysis ▷ n analytical logic

ANALYTICS > ANALYTIC

ANALYZE same as > ANALYSE

ANALYZED > ANALYZE

ANALYZER > ANALYZE

ANALYZERS > ANALYZE

ANALYZES > ANALYZE

ANALYZING > ANALYZE

ANAMNESES > ANAMNESIS

ANAMNESIS n ability to recall past events

ANAMNIOTE n any vertebrate animal, such as a fish or amphibian, that lacks an amnion, chorion, and allantois during embryonic development

ANAN interj expression of failure to understand

ANANA n pineapple

ANANAS n plant related to the pineapple

ANANASES > ANANAS

ANANDROUS adj (of flowers) having no stamens

ANANKE n unalterable necessity

ANANKES > ANANKE

ANANTHOUS adj (of higher plants) having no flowers

ANAPAEST n metrical foot of three syllables, the first two short, the last long

ANAPAESTS > ANAPAEST

ANAPEST same as > ANAPAEST

ANAPESTIC > ANAPEST

ANAPESTS > ANAPEST

ANAPHASE n third stage of mitosis, during which the chromatids separate and migrate towards opposite ends of the spindle

ANAPHASES > ANAPHASE

ANAPHASIC > ANAPHASE

ANAPHOR n word referring back to a previous word

ANAPHORA n use of a word such as a pronoun that has the same reference as a word previously used in the same discourse

ANAPHORAL > ANAPHORA

ANAPHORAS > ANAPHORA

ANAPHORIC adj of or relating to anaphorism

ANAPHORS > ANAPHOR

ANAPLASIA n reversion of plant or animal cells to a simpler less differentiated form

ANAPLASTY n plastic surgery

ANAPTYXES > ANAPTYXIS

ANAPTYXIS n insertion of a short vowel between consonants in order to make a word more easily pronounceable

ANARCH n instigator or personification of anarchy

ANARCHAL > ANARCHY

ANARCHIAL > ANARCHY

ANARCHIC > ANARCHY

ANARCHIES > ANARCHY

ANARCHISE vb make anarchic

ANARCHISM n doctrine advocating the abolition of government

ANARCHIST n person who advocates the abolition of government

ANARCHIZE vb make anarchic

ANARCHS > ANARCH

ANARCHY n lawlessness and disorder

ANARTHRIA n loss of the ability to speak coherently

ANARTHRIC > ANARTHRIA

ANAS > ANA

ANASARCA n generalized accumulation of serous fluid within the subcutaneous connective tissue, resulting in oedema

ANASARCAS > ANASARCA

ANASTASES > ANASTASIS

ANASTASIS n Christ's harrowing of hell

ANASTATIC > ANASTASIS

ANATA n (in Theravada Buddhism) the belief that since all things are constantly changing, there can be no such thing as a permanent, unchanging self

ANATAS > ANATA

ANATASE n rare blue or black mineral

ANATASES > ANATASE

ANATEXES > ANATEXIS

ANATEXIS n partial melting of rocks

ANATHEMA n detested person or thing

ANATHEMAS > ANATHEMA

ANATMAN same as > ANATA

ANATMANS > ANATMAN

ANATOMIC > ANATOMY

ANATOMIES > ANATOMY

ANATOMISE same as > ANATOMIZE

ANATOMIST n expert in anatomy

ANATOMIZE vb dissect (an animal or plant)

ANATOMY n science of the structure of the body

ANATOXIN n bacterial toxin used in inoculation

ANATOXINS > ANATOXIN

ANATROPY n (of a plant ovule) condition of being inverted during development by a bending of the stalk (funicle) attaching it to the carpule

ANATTA n annatto

ANATTAS > ANATTA

ANATTO same as > ANNATTO

ANATTOS > ANATTO

ANAXIAL adj asymmetrical

ANBURIES > ANBURY

ANBURY n soft spongy tumour occurring in horses and oxen

ANCE dialect form of > ONCE

ANCESTOR n person from whom one is descended

ANCESTORS > ANCESTOR

ANCESTRAL adj of or inherited from ancestors ▷ n relation that holds between x and y if there is a chain of instances of a given relation leading from x to y

ANCESTRY n lineage or descent

ANCHO n chili pepper

ANCHOR n heavy hooked device attached to a boat by a cable and dropped overboard to fasten the ship to the sea bottom ▷ vb fasten with or as if with an anchor

ANCHORAGE n place where boats can be anchored

ANCHORED > ANCHOR

ANCHORESS > ANCHORITE

ANCHORET n achorite

ANCHORETS > ANCHORET

ANCHORING > ANCHOR

ANCHORITE n religious recluse

ANCHORMAN n broadcaster in a central studio who links up and presents items from outside camera units and other studios

ANCHORMEN > ANCHORMAN

ANCHORS npl brakes of a motor vehicle

ANCHOS > ANCHOS

ANCHOVETA n type of small anchovy of the American Pacific, used as bait by tuna fishermen

ANCHOVIES > ANCHOVY

ANCHOVY n small strong-tasting fish

ANCHUSA n Eurasian plant with rough hairy stems and leaves and blue flowers

ANCHUSAS > ANCHUSA

ANCHUSIN same as > ALKANET

ANCHUSINS > ANCHUSIN

ANCHYLOSE same as > ANKYLOSE

ANCIENT adj dating from very long ago ▷ n member of a civilized nation in the ancient world, esp a Greek, Roman, or Hebrew

ANCIENTER > ANCIENT

ANCIENTLY adv in ancient times

ANCIENTRY n quality of being ancient

ANCIENTS > ANCIENT

ANCILE n mythical Roman shield

ANCILIA > ANCILE

ANCILLA n Latin word for servant

ANCILLAE > ANCILLA

ANCILLARY adj supporting the main work of an organization ▷ n subsidiary or auxiliary thing or person

ANCILLAS > ANCILLA

ANCIPITAL adj flattened and having two edges

ANCLE old spelling of > ANKLE

ANCLES > ANCLE

ANCOME n inflammation

ANCOMES > ANCOME

ANCON n projecting bracket or console supporting a cornice

ANCONAL > ANCON

ANCONE same as > ANCON

ANCONEAL > ANCON

ANCONES > ANCONE

ANCONOID > ANCON

ANCORA adv Italian for encore

ANCRESS n female anchorite

ANCRESSES > ANCRESS

AND n additional matter or problem

ANDANTE adv (piece to be played) moderately slowly ▷ n passage or piece to be performed moderately slowly

ANDANTES > ANDANTE

ANDANTINI > ANDANTINO

ANDANTINO adv slightly faster or slower than andante ▷ n passage or piece to be performed in this way

ANDESINE n feldspar mineral of the plagioclase series

ANDESINES > ANDESINE

ANDESITE n fine-grained tan or grey volcanic rock

ANDESITES > ANDESITE

ANDESITIC > ANDESITE

ANDESYTE n andesite

ANDESYTES > ANDESYTE

ANDIRON n iron stand for supporting logs in a fireplace

ANDIRONS > ANDIRON

ANDOUILLE n spicy smoked pork sausage with a blackish skin

ANDRADITE n yellow, green, or brownish-black garnet

ANDRO n type of sex hormone

ANDROECIA n stamens of flowering plants collectively

ANDROGEN n any of several steroids, produced as hormones by the testes or made synthetically, that promote development of male sexual organs and male secondary sexual characteristics

ANDROGENS > ANDROGEN

ANDROGYNE n person having both male and female sexual characteristics and genital tissues

ANDROGYNY n condition of having male and female characteristics

ANDROID n robot resembling a human ▷ adj resembling a human being

ANDROIDS > ANDROID

ANDROLOGY n branch of medicine concerned with diseases and conditions specific to men

ANDROMEDA n type of shrub

ANDROS > ANDRO

ANDS > AND

ANDVILE old form of > ANVIL

ANDVILES > ANDVILE

ANE Scots word for > ONE

ANEAR adv nearly ▷ vb approach

ANEARED > ANEAR

ANEARING > ANEAR

ANEARS > ANEAR

ANEATH Scots word for > BENEATH

ANECDOTA n unpublished writings

ANECDOTAL adj containing or consisting exclusively of anecdotes rather than connected discourse or research conducted under controlled conditions

ANECDOTE n short

amusing account of an incident

ANECDOTES > ANECDOTE

ANECDOTIC > ANECDOTE

ANECDYSES > ANECDYSIS

ANECDYSIS n period between moults in arthropods

ANECHOIC adj having a low degree of reverberation of sound

ANELACE same as > ANLACE

ANELACES > ANELACE

ANELASTIC adj not elastic

ANELE vb anoint, esp to give extreme unction to

ANELED > ANELE

ANELES > ANELE

ANELING > ANELE

ANELLI npl pasta shaped like small rings

ANEMIA n anaemia

ANEMIAS > ANEMIA

ANEMIC same as > ANAEMIC

ANEMOGRAM n record produced by anemograph

ANEMOLOGY n study of winds

ANEMONE n plant with white, purple, or red flowers

ANEMONES > ANEMONE

ANEMOSES > ANEMOSIS

ANEMOSIS n cracking in timber caused by wind affecting growing tree

ANENST dialect word for > AGAINST

ANENT prep lying against

ANERGIA n anergy

ANERGIAS > ANERGIA

ANERGIC > ANERGY

ANERGIES > ANERGY

ANERGY n lack of energy

ANERLY Scots word for > ONLY

ANEROID adj not containing a liquid ▷ n barometer that does not contain liquid

ANEROIDS > ANEROID

ANES > ANE

ANESTRA > ANESTRUS

ANESTRI > ANESTRUS

ANESTROUS > ANESTRUS

ANESTRUM n anestrus

ANESTRUS same as > ANOESTRUS

ANETHOL n substance derived from oil of anise

ANETHOLE n white water-soluble crystalline substance with a liquorice-like odour

ANETHOLES > ANETHOLE

ANETHOLS > ANETHOL

ANETIC adj medically soothing

ANEUPLOID adj (of polyploid cells or organisms) having a chromosome number that

is not an exact multiple of the haploid number ▷ n cell or individual of this type

ANEURIN a less common name for > THIAMINE

ANEURINS > ANEURIN

ANEURISM same as > ANEURYSM

ANEURISMS > ANEURISM

ANEURYSM n permanent swelling of a blood vessel

ANEURYSMS > ANEURYSM

ANEW adv once more

ANGA n a part in Indian music

ANGAKOK n Inuit shaman

ANGAKOKS > ANGAKOK

ANGARIA n species of shellfish

ANGARIAS > ANGARIA

ANGARIES > ANGARY

ANGARY n right of a belligerent state to use the property of a neutral state or to destroy it if necessary, subject to payment of full compensation to the owners

ANGAS > ANGA

ANGASHORE n miserable person given to complaining

ANGEKKOK n Inuit shaman

ANGEKKOKS > ANGEKKOK

ANGEKOK n Inuit shaman

ANGEKOKS > ANGEKOK

ANGEL n spiritual being believed to be an attendant or messenger of God ▷ vb provide financial support for

ANGELED > ANGEL

ANGELFISH n South American aquarium fish with large fins

ANGELHOOD n state of being an angel

ANGELIC adj very kind, pure, or beautiful

ANGELICA n aromatic plant

ANGELICAL same as > ANGELIC

ANGELICAS > ANGELICA

ANGELING > ANGEL

ANGELS > ANGEL

ANGELUS n series of prayers recited in the morning, at midday, and in the evening, commemorating the Annunciation and Incarnation

ANGELUSES > ANGELUS

ANGER n fierce displeasure or extreme annoyance ▷ vb make (someone) angry

ANGERED > ANGER

ANGERING > ANGER

ANGERLESS > ANGER

ANGERLY adv old form of angrily

ANGERS > ANGER

ANGICO n South American tree

ANGICOS > ANGICO

ANGINA n heart disorder causing sudden severe chest pains

ANGINAL > ANGINA

ANGINAS > ANGINA

ANGINOSE > ANGINA

ANGINOUS > ANGINA

ANGIOGRAM n X-ray picture obtained by angiography

ANGIOLOGY n branch of medical science concerned with the blood vessels and the lymphatic system

ANGIOMA n tumour consisting of a mass of blood vessels or lymphatic vessels

ANGIOMAS > ANGIOMA

ANGIOMATA > ANGIOMA

ANGKLUNG n Asian musical instrument

ANGKLUNGS > ANGKLUNG

ANGLE n space between or shape formed by two lines or surfaces that meet ▷ vb bend or place (something) at an angle

ANGLED > ANGLE

ANGLEDUG n earthworm

ANGLEDUGS > ANGLEDUG

ANGLEPOD n American wild flower

ANGLEPODS > ANGLEPOD

ANGLER n person who fishes with a hook and line

ANGLERS > ANGLER

ANGLES > ANGLE

ANGLESITE n white or grey secondary mineral

ANGLEWISE > ANGLE

ANGLEWORM n earthworm used as bait by anglers

ANGLICE adv in English

ANGLICISE same as > ANGLICIZE

ANGLICISM n word, phrase, or idiom peculiar to the English language, esp as spoken in England

ANGLICIST n expert in or student of English literature or language

ANGLICIZE vb make or become English in outlook, form, etc

ANGLIFIED > ANGLIFY

ANGLIFIES > ANGLIFY

ANGLIFY same as > ANGLICIZE

ANGLING n art or sport of fishing with a hook and line

ANGLINGS > ANGLING

ANGLIST same as > ANGLICIST

ANGLISTS > ANGLIST

ANGLO n White inhabitant of the US not of Latin extraction

ANGLOPHIL n person having admiration for England or the English

ANGLOS > ANGLO

ANGOLA same as > ANGORA

ANGOPHORA n Australian tree related to the eucalyptus

ANGORA n variety of goat, cat, or rabbit with long silky hair

ANGORAS > ANGORA

ANGOSTURA n bitter aromatic bark

ANGRIER > ANGRY

ANGRIES > ANGRY

ANGRIEST > ANGRY

ANGRILY > ANGRY

ANGRINESS > ANGRY

ANGRY adj full of anger ▷ n angry person

ANGST n feeling of anxiety

ANGSTIER > ANGSTY

ANGSTIEST > ANGSTY

ANGSTROM n unit of length used to measure wavelengths

ANGSTROMS > ANGSTROM

ANGSTS > ANGST

ANGSTY adj displaying or feeling angst, esp in a self-conscious manner

ANGUIFORM adj shaped like a snake

ANGUINE adj of, relating to, or similar to a snake

ANGUIPED adj having snakes for legs

ANGUIPEDE adj having snakes for legs

ANGUISH n great mental pain ▷ vb afflict or be afflicted with anguish

ANGUISHED adj feeling or showing great mental pain

ANGUISHES > ANGUISH

ANGULAR adj (of a person) lean and bony

ANGULARLY > ANGULAR

ANGULATE adj having angles or an angular shape ▷ vb make or become angular

ANGULATED > ANGULATE

ANGULATES > ANGULATE

ANGULOSE adj having angles

ANGULOUS adj having angles

ANHEDONIA n inability to feel pleasure

ANHEDONIC > ANHEDONIA

ANHEDRAL n downward inclination of an aircraft wing in relation to the lateral axis

ANHINGA n type of bird

ANHINGAS > ANHINGA

ANHUNGRED adj very hungry

ANHYDRASE n enzyme that catalyzes the removal of water

ANHYDRIDE n substance that combines with water to form an acid

ANHYDRITE n colourless or greyish-white mineral found in sedimentary rocks

a .

a

ANHYDROUS adj containing no water

ANI n tropical American bird with black plumage, a long square-tipped tail, and a hooked bill

ANICCA n (in Theravada Buddhism) the belief that all things, including the self, are impermanent and constantly changing: the first of the three basic characteristics of existence

ANICCAS > ANICCA

ANICONIC adj (of images of deities, symbols, etc) not portrayed in a human or animal form

ANICONISM > ANICONIC

ANICONIST > ANICONIC

ANICUT n dam in India

ANICUTS > ANICUT

ANIDROSES > ANIDROSIS

ANIDROSIS n absence of sweating

ANIGH adv near

ANIGHT adv at night

ANIL n West Indian shrub, from which indigo is obtained

ANILE adj of or like a feeble old woman

ANILIN n aniline

ANILINE n colourless oily liquid obtained from coal tar and used for making dyes, plastics, and explosives

ANILINES > ANILINE

ANILINGUS n sexual stimulation involving oral contact with the anus

ANILINS > ANILIN

ANILITIES > ANILE

ANILITY > ANILE

ANILS > ANIL

ANIMA n feminine principle as present in the male unconscious

ANIMACIES > ANIMACY

ANIMACY n state of being animate

ANIMAL n living creature with specialized sense organs and capable of voluntary motion, esp one other than a human being ▷ adj of animals

ANIMALIAN > ANIMAL

ANIMALIC > ANIMAL

ANIMALIER n painter or sculptor of animal subjects, esp a member of a group of early 19th-century French sculptors who specialized in realistic figures of animals, usually in bronze

ANIMALISE same as > ANIMALIZE

ANIMALISM n preoccupation with physical matters

ANIMALIST > ANIMALISM

ANIMALITY n animal instincts of human beings

ANIMALIZE vb make (a person) brutal or sensual

ANIMALLY adv physically

ANIMALS > ANIMAL

ANIMAS > ANIMA

ANIMATE vb give life to ▷ adj having life

ANIMATED adj interesting and lively

ANIMATELY > ANIMATE

ANIMATER same as > ANIMATOR

ANIMATERS > ANIMATER

ANIMATES > ANIMATE

ANIMATIC n animated film sequence

ANIMATICS > ANIMATIC

ANIMATING > ANIMATE

ANIMATION n technique of making cartoon films

ANIMATISM n belief that inanimate objects have consciousness

ANIMATIST > ANIMATISM

ANIMATO adv (to be performed) in a lively manner

ANIMATOR n person who makes animated cartoons

ANIMATORS > ANIMATOR

ANIME n type of Japanese animated film with themes and styles similar to manga comics

ANIMES > ANIME

ANIMI > ANIMUS

ANIMIS > ANIMI

ANIMISM n belief that natural objects possess souls

ANIMISMS > ANIMISM

ANIMIST > ANIMISM

ANIMISTIC > ANIMISM

ANIMISTS > ANIMISM

ANIMOSITY n hostility, hatred

ANIMUS n hatred, animosity

ANIMUSES > ANIMUS

ANION n ion with negative charge

ANIONIC > ANION

ANIONS > ANION

ANIRIDIA n absence of the iris, due to a congenital condition or an injury

ANIRIDIAS > ANIRIDIA

ANIRIDIC > ANIRIDIA

ANIS > ANI

ANISE n plant with liquorice-flavoured seeds

ANISEED n liquorice-flavoured seeds of the anise plant

ANISEEDS > ANISEED

ANISES > ANISE

ANISETTE n liquorice-flavoured liqueur made from aniseed

ANISETTES > ANISETTE

ANISIC > ANISE

ANISOGAMY n type of sexual reproduction in which the gametes are dissimilar, either in size alone or in size and form

ANISOLE n colourless pleasant-smelling liquid used as a solvent

ANISOLES > ANISOLE

ANKER n old liquid measure for wine

ANKERITE n greyish to brown mineral that resembles dolomite

ANKERITES > ANKERITE

ANKERS > ANKER

ANKH n T-shaped cross with a loop on the top, which symbolized eternal life in ancient Egypt

ANKHS > ANKH

ANKLE n joint between the foot and leg ▷ vb move

ANKLEBONE the nontechnical name for > TALUS

ANKLED > ANKLE

ANKLES > ANKLE

ANKLET n ornamental chain worn round the ankle

ANKLETS > ANKLET

ANKLING > ANKLE

ANKLONG n Asian musical instrument

ANKLONGS > ANKLONG

ANKLUNG n Asian musical instrument

ANKLUNGS > ANKLUNG

ANKUS n stick used, esp in India, for goading elephants

ANKUSES > ANKUS

ANKUSH n Indian weapon

ANKUSHES > ANKUSH

ANKYLOSE vb (of bones in a joint, etc) to fuse or stiffen by ankylosis

ANKYLOSED > ANKYLOSE

ANKYLOSES > ANKYLOSE

ANKYLOSIS n abnormal immobility of a joint, caused by a fibrous growth

ANKYLOTIC > ANKYLOSIS

ANLACE n medieval short dagger with a broad tapering blade

ANLACES > ANLACE

ANLAGE n organ or part in the earliest stage of development

ANLAGEN > ANLAGE

ANLAGES > ANLAGE

ANLAS same as > ANLACE

ANLASES > ANLAS

ANN n old Scots word for a widow's pension

ANNA n former Indian coin worth one sixteenth of a rupee

ANNAL n recorded events of one year

ANNALISE vb record in annals

ANNALISED > ANNALISE

ANNALISES > ANNALISE

ANNALIST > ANNAL

ANNALISTS > ANNAL

ANNALIZE vb record in annals

ANNALIZED > ANNALIZE

ANNALIZES > ANNALIZE

ANNALS > ANNAL

ANNAS > ANNA

ANNAT n singular of annates

ANNATES npl first year's revenue of a see, an abbacy or a minor benefice, paid to the pope

ANNATS > ANNAT

ANNATTA n annatto

ANNATTAS > ANNATTA

ANNATTO n small tropical American tree with red or pinkish flowers and seeds that yield a dye

ANNATTOS > ANNATTO

ANNEAL vb toughen (metal or glass) by heating and slow cooling ▷ n act of annealing

ANNEALED > ANNEAL

ANNEALER > ANNEAL

ANNEALERS > ANNEAL

ANNEALING > ANNEAL

ANNEALS > ANNEAL

ANNECTENT adj connecting

ANNELID n type of worm with a segmented body, such as an earthworm

ANNELIDAN > ANNELID

ANNELIDS > ANNELID

ANNEX vb seize (territory)

ANNEXABLE > ANNEX

ANNEXE n extension to a building

ANNEXED > ANNEX

ANNEXES > ANNEXE

ANNEXING > ANNEX

ANNEXION n old form of annexation

ANNEXIONS > ANNEXION

ANNEXMENT > ANNEX

ANNEXURE n something that is added

ANNEXURES > ANNEXURE

ANNICUT n dam in India

ANNICUTS > ANNICUT

ANNO adv Latin for in the year

ANNONA n American tree or shrub

ANNONAS > ANNONA

ANNOTATE vb add notes to (a written work)

ANNOTATED > ANNOTATE

ANNOTATES > ANNOTATE

ANNOTATOR > ANNOTATE

ANNOUNCE vb make known publicly

ANNOUNCED > ANNOUNCE

ANNOUNCER n person who introduces radio or television programmes

ANNOUNCES > ANNOUNCE

ANNOY vb irritate or displease

ANNOYANCE *n* feeling of being annoyed
ANNOYED > ANNOY
ANNOYER > ANNOY
ANNOYERS > ANNOY
ANNOYING *adj* causing irritation or displeasure
ANNOYS > ANNOY
ANNS > ANN
ANNUAL *adj* happening once a year ▷ *n* plant that completes its life cycle in a year
ANNUALISE same as > ANNUALIZE
ANNUALIZE *vb* calculate (a rate) for or as if for a year
ANNUALLY > ANNUAL
ANNUALS > ANNUAL
ANNUITANT *n* person in receipt of or entitled to an annuity
ANNUITIES > ANNUITY
ANNUITY *n* fixed sum paid every year
ANNUL *vb* declare (something, esp a marriage) invalid
ANNULAR *adj* ring-shaped ▷ *n* ring finger
ANNULARLY > ANNULAR
ANNULARS > ANNULAR
ANNULATE *adj* having, composed of, or marked with rings ▷ *n* annelid
ANNULATED > ANNULATE
ANNULATES > ANNULATE
ANNULET *n* moulding in the form of a ring, as at the top of a column adjoining the capital
ANNULETS > ANNULET
ANNULLI > ANNULUS
ANNULLED > ANNUL
ANNULLING > ANNUL
ANNULMENT *n* formal declaration that a contract or marriage is invalid
ANNULOSE *adj* (of earthworms, crustaceans, and similar animals) having a body formed of a series of rings
ANNULS > ANNUL
ANNULUS *n* area between two concentric circles
ANNULUSES > ANNULUS
ANOA *n* type of small cattle
ANOAS > ANOA
ANOBIID *n* any type of beetle
ANOBIIDS > ANOBIID
ANODAL > ANODE
ANODALLY > ANODE
ANODE *n* positive electrode in a battery, valve, etc
ANODES > ANODE
ANODIC > ANODE
ANODISE same as > ANODIZE
ANODISED > ANODISE
ANODISES > ANODISE
ANODISING > ANODISE
ANODIZE *vb* coat (metal) with a protective oxide film

by electrolysis
ANODIZED > ANODIZE
ANODIZES > ANODIZE
ANODIZING > ANODIZE
ANODONTIA *n* congenital absence of teeth
ANODYNE *n* something that relieves pain or distress ▷ *adj* relieving pain or distress
ANODYNES > ANODYNE
ANODYNIC > ANODYNE
ANOESES > ANOESIS
ANOESIS *n* feeling without understanding
ANOESTRA > ANOESTRUS
ANOESTRI > ANOESTRUS
ANOESTRUM same as > ANOESTRUS
ANOESTRUS *n* period of sexual inactivity between two periods of oestrus in many mammals
ANOETIC > ANOESIS
ANOINT *vb* smear with oil as a sign of consecration
ANOINTED > ANOINT
ANOINTER > ANOINT
ANOINTERS > ANOINT
ANOINTING > ANOINT
ANOINTS > ANOINT
ANOLE *n* type of lizard
ANOLES > ANOLE
ANOLYTE *n* part of electrolyte around anode
ANOLYTES > ANOLYTE
ANOMALIES > ANOMALY
ANOMALOUS *adj* different from the normal or usual order or type
ANOMALY *n* something that deviates from the normal, irregularity
ANOMIC > ANOMIE
ANOMIE *n* lack of social or moral standards
ANOMIES > ANOMIE
ANOMY same as > ANOMIE
ANON *adv* in a short time, soon
ANONYM *n* anonymous person or publication
ANONYMA *n* promiscuous woman
ANONYMAS > ANONYMA
ANONYMISE same as > ANONYMIZE
ANONYMITY > ANONYMOUS
ANONYMIZE *vb* organize in a way that preserves anonymity
ANONYMOUS *adj* by someone whose name is unknown or withheld
ANONYMS > ANONYM
ANOOPSIA *n* squint in which the eye turns upwards
ANOOPSIAS > ANOOPSIA
ANOPHELES *n* type of mosquito which transmits the malaria parasite to man
ANOPIA *n* inability to see
ANOPIAS > ANOPIA

ANOPSIA *n* squint in which the eye turns upwards
ANOPSIAS > ANOPSIA
ANORAK *n* light waterproof hooded jacket
ANORAKS > ANORAK
ANORECTAL *adj* of the anus and rectum
ANORECTIC > ANOREXIA
ANORETIC *n* anorectic
ANORETICS > ANORETIC
ANOREXIA *n* psychological disorder characterized by fear of becoming fat and refusal to eat
ANOREXIAS > ANOREXIA
ANOREXIC > ANOREXIA
ANOREXICS > ANOREXIA
ANOREXIES > ANOREXY
ANOREXY old name for > ANOREXIA
ANORTHIC another word for > TRICLINIC
ANORTHITE *n* white to greyish-white or reddish-white mineral
ANOSMATIC > ANOSMIA
ANOSMIA *n* loss of the sense of smell, usually as the result of a lesion of the olfactory nerve, disease in another organ or part, or obstruction of the nasal passages
ANOSMIAS > ANOSMIA
ANOSMIC > ANOSMIA
ANOTHER *adj* one more
ANOUGH *adj* enough
ANOUROUS *adj* having no tail
ANOVULANT *n* drug preventing ovulation
ANOVULAR *adj* without ovulation
ANOW *adj* old form of enough
ANOXAEMIA *n* deficiency in the amount of oxygen in the arterial blood
ANOXAEMIC > ANOXAEMIA
ANOXEMIA same as > ANOXAEMIA
ANOXEMIAS > ANOXEMIA
ANOXEMIC > ANOXEMIA
ANOXIA *n* lack or absence of oxygen
ANOXIAS > ANOXIA
ANOXIC > ANOXIA
ANS as in *ifs and ans* things that might have happened, but which did not.
ANSA *n* either end of Saturn's rings
ANSAE > ANSA
ANSATE *adj* having a handle or handle-like part
ANSATED *adj* ansate
ANSERINE *adj* of or resembling a goose ▷ *n* chemical compound
ANSERINES > ANSERINE
ANSEROUS same as > ANSERINE
ANSWER *n* reply to a question, request, letter,

etc ▷ *vb* give an answer (to)
ANSWERED > ANSWER
ANSWERER > ANSWER
ANSWERERS > ANSWER
ANSWERING > ANSWER
ANSWERS > ANSWER
ANT *n* small insect living in highly-organized colonies
ANTA *n* pilaster attached to the end of a side wall or sometimes to the side of a doorway
ANTACID *n* substance that counteracts acidity, esp in the stomach ▷ *adj* having the properties of this substance
ANTACIDS > ANTACID
ANTAE > ANTA
ANTALGIC *n* pain-relieving drug
ANTALGICS > ANTALGIC
ANTALKALI *n* substance that neutralizes alkalis
ANTAR old word for > CAVE
ANTARA *n* South American panpipes
ANTARAS > ANTARA
ANTARCTIC *adj* relating to Antarctica
ANTARS > ANTAR
ANTAS > ANTA
ANTBEAR *n* aardvark
ANTBEARS > ANTBEAR
ANTBIRD *n* any of various dull-coloured South American passerine birds that typically feed on ants
ANTBIRDS > ANTBIRD
ANTE *n* player's stake in poker ▷ *vb* place (one's stake) in poker
ANTEATER *n* mammal which feeds on ants by means of a long snout
ANTEATERS > ANTEATER
ANTECEDE *vb* go before, as in time, order, etc
ANTECEDED > ANTECEDE
ANTECEDES > ANTECEDE
ANTECHOIR *n* part of a church in front of the choir, usually enclosed by screens, tombs, etc
ANTED > ANTE
ANTEDATE *vb* precede in time ▷ *n* earlier date
ANTEDATED > ANTEDATE
ANTEDATES > ANTEDATE
ANTEED > ANTE
ANTEFIX *n* carved ornament at the eaves of a roof to hide the joint between the tiles
ANTEFIXA > ANTEFIX
ANTEFIXAE > ANTEFIX
ANTEFIXAL > ANTEFIX
ANTEFIXES > ANTEFIX
ANTEING > ANTE
ANTELOPE *n* deerlike mammal with long legs and horns
ANTELOPES > ANTELOPE
ANTELUCAN *adj* before daylight

a

ANTENATAL adj during pregnancy, before birth ▷ n examination during pregnancy

ANTENATI n people born before certain date

ANTENNA n insect's feeler

ANTENNAE > ANTENNA

ANTENNAL > ANTENNA

ANTENNARY > ANTENNA

ANTENNAS > ANTENNA

ANTENNULE n one of a pair of small mobile appendages on the heads of crustaceans in front of the antennae, usually having a sensory function

ANTEPAST n appetizer

ANTEPASTS > ANTEPAST

ANTERIOR adj the front

ANTEROOM n small room leading into a larger one, often used as a waiting room

ANTEROOMS > ANTEROOM

ANTES > ANTE

ANTETYPE n earlier form

ANTETYPES > ANTETYPE

ANTEVERT vb displace (an organ or part) by tilting it forward

ANTEVERTS > ANTEVERT

ANTHELIA > ANTHELION

ANTHELION n faint halo sometimes seen in polar or high altitude regions around the shadow of an object cast onto a thick cloud bank or fog

ANTHELIX n prominent curved fold of cartilage just inside the outer rim of the external ear

ANTHEM n song of loyalty, esp to a country ▷ vb provide with an anthem

ANTHEMED > ANTHEM

ANTHEMIA > ANTHEMION

ANTHEMIC > ANTHEM

ANTHEMING > ANTHEM

ANTHEMION n floral design, used esp in ancient Greek and Roman architecture and decoration, usually consisting of honeysuckle, lotus, or palmette leaf motifs

ANTHEMS > ANTHEM

ANTHER n part of a flower's stamen containing pollen

ANTHERAL > ANTHER

ANTHERID n antheridium

ANTHERIDS > ANTHERID

ANTHERS > ANTHER

ANTHESES > ANTHESIS

ANTHESIS n time when a flower becomes sexually functional

ANTHILL n mound of soil, leaves, etc, near the entrance of an ants' nest, carried and deposited there by the ants while constructing the nest

ANTHILLS > ANTHILL

ANTHOCARP n fruit developing from many flowers

ANTHOCYAN n any of a class of water-soluble glycosidic pigments

ANTHODIA > ANTHODIUM

ANTHODIUM another name for > CAPITULUM

ANTHOID adj resembling a flower

ANTHOLOGY n collection of poems or other literary pieces by various authors

ANTHOTAXY n arrangement of flowers on a stem or parts on a flower

ANTHOZOAN n type of marine invertebrate with a body in the form of a polyp, such as corals, sea anemones, and sea pens

ANTHOZOIC > ANTHOZOAN

ANTHRACES > ANTHRAX

ANTHRACIC adj of anthrax

ANTHRAX n dangerous disease of cattle and sheep, communicable to humans

ANTHRAXES > ANTHRAX

ANTHROPIC adj of or relating to human beings

ANTHURIUM n tropical American plant cultivated as a house plant for its showy foliage and flowers

ANTI adj opposed (to) ▷ n opponent of a party, policy, or attitude

ANTIABUSE adj designed to prevent abuse

ANTIACNE adj inhibiting the development of acne

ANTIAGING adj resisting the effects of ageing

ANTIAIR adj countering attack by aircraft or missile

ANTIALIEN adj designed to prevent foreign animal or plant species from becoming established

ANTIAR another name for > UPAS

ANTIARIN n poison derived from antiar

ANTIARINS > ANTIARIN

ANTIARMOR adj designed or equipped to combat armoured vehicles

ANTIARS > ANTIAR

ANTIATOM n atom composed of antiparticles, in which the nucleus contains antiprotons with orbiting positrons

ANTIATOMS > ANTIATOM

ANTIAUXIN n substance acting against auxin

ANTIBIAS adj countering bias

ANTIBLACK adj hostile to black people

ANTIBODY n protein produced in the blood, which destroys bacteria

ANTIBOSS adj acting against bosses

ANTIBUG adj acting against computer bugs

ANTIBUSER n person who opposes the policy of transporting students to faraway schools to achieve racial balance

ANTIC n actor in a ludicrous or grotesque part ▷ adj fantastic

ANTICAL adj (of the position of plant parts) in front of or above another part

ANTICALLY > ANTICAL

ANTICAR n opposed to cars

ANTICHLOR n substance used to remove chlorine from a material after bleaching or to neutralize the chlorine present

ANTICISE same as > ANTICIZE

ANTICISED > ANTICISE

ANTICISES > ANTICISE

ANTICITY adj opposed to cities

ANTICIVIC adj opposed to citizenship

ANTICIZE vb play absurdly

ANTICIZED > ANTICIZE

ANTICIZES > ANTICIZE

ANTICK vb perform antics

ANTICKE adj old form of antique

ANTICKED > ANTICK

ANTICKING > ANTICK

ANTICKS > ANTICK

ANTICLINE n fold of rock raised up into a broad arch so that the strata slope down on both sides

ANTICLING adj acting against clinging

ANTICLY adv grotesquely

ANTICODON n element of RNA

ANTICOLD adj preventing or fighting the common cold

ANTICOUS adj on the part of a flower furthest from the stem

ANTICRACK adj protecting a computer against unauthorized access

ANTICRIME adj preventing or fighting crime

ANTICS npl absurd acts or postures

ANTICULT n organisation that is opposed to religious cults

ANTICULTS > ANTICULT

ANTIDORA n bread used in Russian Orthodox Communion

ANTIDOTAL > ANTIDOTE

ANTIDOTE n substance that counteracts a poison ▷ vb counteract with an antidote

ANTIDOTED > ANTIDOTE

ANTIDOTES > ANTIDOTE

ANTIDRAFT adj opposed to conscription

ANTIDRUG adj intended to discourage illegal drug use

ANTIDUNE n sand hill or inclined bedding plane that forms a steep slope against the direction of a fast-flowing current

ANTIDUNES > ANTIDUNE

ANTIELITE adj opposed to elitism

ANTIENT old spelling of > ANCIENT

ANTIENTS > ANTIENT

ANTIFAT adj acting to remove or prevent fat

ANTIFLU adj acting against influenza

ANTIFOAM adj allowing gas to escape rather than form foam

ANTIFOG adj preventing the buildup of moisture on a surface

ANTIFRAUD adj acting against fraud

ANTIFUR adj opposed to the wearing of fur garments

ANTIGANG adj designed to restrict the activities of criminal gangs

ANTIGAY adj hostile to homosexuals

ANTIGEN n substance causing the blood to produce antibodies

ANTIGENE n antigen

ANTIGENES > ANTIGENE

ANTIGENIC > ANTIGEN

ANTIGENS > ANTIGEN

ANTIGLARE adj cutting down glare

ANTIGRAFT adj designed to reduce corruption

ANTIGUN adj opposed to the possession of guns

ANTIHELIX same as > ANTHELIX

ANTIHERO n central character in a book, film, etc, who lacks the traditional heroic virtues

ANTIHUMAN adj inhuman

ANTIJAM adj preventing jamming

ANTIKING n rival to an established king

ANTIKINGS > ANTIKING

ANTIKNOCK n substance added to motor fuel to reduce knocking in the engine caused by too rapid combustion

ANTILABOR adj opposed to labor interests

ANTILEAK adj preventing leaks

ANTILEFT adj opposed to

the left wing in politics

ANTILIFE adj in favour of abortion

ANTILIFER n person in favour of abortion

ANTILOCK adj designed to prevent overbraking

ANTILOG n number whose logarithm to a given base is a given number

ANTILOGS > ANTILOG

ANTILOGY n contradiction in terms

ANTIMACHO adj opposed to macho attitudes

ANTIMALE adj opposed to men

ANTIMAN adj opposed to men

ANTIMASK n interlude in a masque

ANTIMASKS > ANTIMASK

ANTIMERE n part or organ of a bilaterally or radially symmetrical organism that corresponds to a similar structure on the other side of the axis, such as the right or left limb of a four-legged animal

ANTIMERES > ANTIMERE

ANTIMERIC > ANTIMERE

ANTIMINE adj designed to counteract landmines

ANTIMONIC adj of or containing antimony in the pentavalent state

ANTIMONY n brittle silvery-white metallic element

ANTIMONYL n of, consisting of, or containing the monovalent group SbO-

ANTIMUON n antiparticle of a muon

ANTIMUONS > ANTIMUON

ANTIMUSIC n music intended to overthrow traditional conventions and expectations

ANTIMYCIN n antibiotic drug

ANTING n placing or rubbing of ants by birds on their feathers. The body fluids of the ants are thought to repel parasites

ANTINGS > ANTING

ANTINODAL > ANTINODE

ANTINODE n point at which the amplitude of one of the two kinds of displacement in a standing wave has maximum value. Generally the other kind of displacement has its minimum value at this point

ANTINODES > ANTINODE

ANTINOISE n sound generated so that it is out of phase with a noise, such as that made by an engine, in order to reduce the noise level by interference

ANTINOME n opposite

ANTINOMES > ANTINOME

ANTINOMIC > ANTINOMY

ANTINOMY n contradiction between two laws or principles that are reasonable in themselves

ANTINOVEL n type of prose fiction in which conventional elements of the novel are rejected

ANTINUKE same as > ANTINUKER

ANTINUKER n person who is opposed to nuclear weapons or energy

ANTINUKES > ANTINUKE

ANTIPAPAL adj opposed to the pope

ANTIPARTY adj opposed to a political party

ANTIPASTI > ANTIPASTO

ANTIPASTO n appetizer in an Italian meal

ANTIPATHY n dislike, hostility

ANTIPHON n hymn sung in alternate parts by two groups of singers

ANTIPHONS > ANTIPHON

ANTIPHONY n antiphonal singing of a musical composition by two choirs

ANTIPILL adj opposed to the use of the contraceptive pill

ANTIPODAL adj of or relating to diametrically opposite points on the earth's surface

ANTIPODE n exact or direct opposite

ANTIPODES npl any two places diametrically opposite one another on the earth's surface

ANTIPOLAR > ANTIPOLE

ANTIPOLE n opposite pole

ANTIPOLES > ANTIPOLE

ANTIPOPE n pope set up in opposition to the one chosen by church laws

ANTIPOPES > ANTIPOPE

ANTIPORN adj opposed to pornography

ANTIPOT adj opposed to illegal use of marijuana

ANTIPRESS adj hostile to the news media

ANTIPYIC n drug acting against suppuration

ANTIPYICS > ANTIPYIC

ANTIQUARK n antiparticle of a quark

ANTIQUARY n student or collector of antiques or ancient works of art

ANTIQUATE vb make obsolete or old-fashioned

ANTIQUE n object of an earlier period, valued for its beauty, workmanship, or age ▷ adj made in an earlier period ▷ vb give an antique appearance to

ANTIQUED > ANTIQUE

ANTIQUELY > ANTIQUE

ANTIQUER n collector of antiques

ANTIQUERS > ANTIQUE

ANTIQUES > ANTIQUE

ANTIQUEY adj having the appearance of an antique

ANTIQUING > ANTIQUE

ANTIQUITY n great age

ANTIRADAR adj preventing detection by radar

ANTIRAPE adj protecting against rape

ANTIRED adj of a particular colour of antiquark

ANTIRIOT adj (of police officers, equipment, measures, etc) designed for or engaged in the control of crowds

ANTIROCK adj designed to prevent a vehicle from rocking

ANTIROLL adj designed to prevent a vehicle from tilting

ANTIROYAL adj opposed to the monarchy

ANTIRUST adj (of a product or procedure) effective against rust ▷ n substance or device that prevents rust

ANTIRUSTS > ANTIRUST

ANTIS > ANTI

ANTISAG adj preventing sagging

ANTISCIAN n person living on other side of equator

ANTISENSE adj acting in opposite way to RNA

ANTISERA > ANTISERUM

ANTISERUM n blood serum containing antibodies used to treat or provide immunity to a disease

ANTISEX adj opposed to sexual activity

ANTISHAKE adj (in photography) intended to reduce blurring caused by movement ▷ n antishake technology

ANTISHARK adj protecting against sharks

ANTISHIP adj designed for attacking ships

ANTISHOCK n one of a pair of walking poles designed to reduce stress on the knees

ANTISKID adj intended to prevent skidding

ANTISLEEP adj acting to prevent sleep

ANTISLIP adj acting to prevent slipping

ANTISMOG adj reducing smog

ANTISMOKE adj preventing smoke

ANTISMUT adj opposed to obscene material

ANTISNOB n person opposed to snobbery

ANTISNOBS > ANTISNOB

ANTISOLAR adj opposite to the sun

ANTISPAM adj intended to prevent spam

ANTISPAST n group of four syllables in poetic metre

ANTISTAT n substance preventing static electricity

ANTISTATE adj opposed to state authority

ANTISTATS > ANTISTAT

ANTISTICK adj preventing things from sticking to a surface

ANTISTORY n story without a plot

ANTISTYLE n style that rejects traditional aesthetics

ANTITANK adj (of weapons) designed to destroy military tanks

ANTITAX adj opposed to taxation

ANTITHEFT adj (of a device, campaign, system, etc) designed to prevent theft

ANTITHET n example of antithesis

ANTITHETS > ANTITHET

ANTITOXIC > ANTITOXIN

ANTITOXIN n (serum containing) an antibody that acts against a toxin

ANTITRADE n wind blowing in the opposite direction to a trade wind

ANTITRAGI n cartilaginous projections of the external ear opposite the tragus

ANTITRUST adj (of laws) opposing business monopolies ▷ n regulating or opposing trusts, monopolies, cartels, or similar organizations, esp in order to prevent unfair competition

ANTITUMOR adj acting against tumours

ANTITYPAL > ANTITYPE

ANTITYPE n person or thing that is foreshadowed or represented by a type or symbol, esp a character or event in the New Testament prefigured in the Old Testament

ANTITYPES > ANTITYPE

ANTITYPIC > ANTITYPE

ANTIULCER adj used to treat ulcers

ANTIUNION adj opposed to union

ANTIURBAN adj opposed to city life

ANTIVENIN n antitoxin that counteracts a specific venom, esp snake venom

ANTIVENOM n venom antidote

ANTIVIRAL adj inhibiting the growth of viruses ▷ n any antiviral drug: used to treat diseases caused by viruses, such as herpes infections and AIDS

ANTIVIRUS adj relating to software designed to protect computer files from viruses ▷ n such a piece of software

ANTIWAR adj opposed to war

ANTIWEAR adj preventing wear

ANTIWEED adj killing or preventing weeds

ANTIWHITE adj hostile to white people

ANTIWOMAN adj hostile to women

ANTIWORLD n hypothetical or supposed world or universe composed of antimatter

ANTLER n branched horn of a male deer

ANTLERED adj having antlers

ANTLERS > ANTLER

ANTLIA n butterfly proboscis

ANTLIAE > ANTLIA

ANTLIATE adj relating to antlia

ANTLIKE adj of or like an ant or ants

ANTLION n type of insect resembling a dragonfly, mostly found in tropical regions

ANTLIONS > ANTLION

ANTONYM n word that means the opposite of another

ANTONYMIC > ANTONYM

ANTONYMS > ANTONYM

ANTONYMY n use of antonyms

ANTPITTA n S American bird whose diet consists mainly of ants

ANTPITTAS > ANTPITTA

ANTRA > ANTRUM

ANTRAL > ANTRUM

ANTRE n cavern or cave

ANTRES > ANTRE

ANTRORSE adj directed or pointing upwards or forwards

ANTRUM n natural cavity, esp in a bone

ANTRUMS > ANTRUM

ANTS > ANT

ANTSIER > ANTSY

ANTSIEST > ANTSY

ANTSINESS > ANTSY

ANTSY adj restless, nervous, and impatient

ANTWACKIE adj old-fashioned

ANUCLEATE adj without a nucleus

ANURAL adj without a tail

ANURAN n type of tailless amphibian with very long hind legs specialized for hopping, such as frogs and toads

ANURANS > ANURAN

ANURESES > ANURESIS

ANURESIS n inability to urinate even though urine is formed by the kidneys and retained in the urinary bladder

ANURETIC > ANURESIS

ANURIA n complete suppression of urine formation, often as the result of a kidney disorder

ANURIAS > ANURIA

ANURIC > ANURIA

ANUROUS adj lacking a tail

ANUS n opening at the end of the alimentary canal, through which faeces are discharged

ANUSES > ANUS

ANVIL n heavy iron block on which metals are hammered into particular shapes ▷ vb forge on an anvil

ANVILED > ANVIL

ANVILING > ANVIL

ANVILLED > ANVIL

ANVILLING > ANVIL

ANVILS > ANVIL

ANVILTOP n type of stormcloud formation

ANVILTOPS > ANVILTOP

ANXIETIES > ANXIETY

ANXIETY n state of being anxious

ANXIOUS adj worried and tense

ANXIOUSLY > ANXIOUS

ANY adj one or some, no matter which ▷ adv at all

ANYBODIES > ANYBODY

ANYBODY n any person at random

ANYHOW adv anyway

ANYMORE adv at present

ANYON n (in mathematics) projective representation of a Lie group

ANYONE pron any person ▷ n any person at random

ANYONES > ANYONE

ANYONS > ANYON

ANYPLACE adv in, at, or to any unspecified place

ANYROAD a northern English dialect word for > ANYWAY

ANYTHING pron any object, event, or action whatever ▷ n any thing at random

ANYTHINGS > ANYTHING

ANYTIME adv at any time

ANYWAY adv at any rate, nevertheless

ANYWAYS nonstandard word for > ANYWAY

ANYWHEN adv at any time

ANYWHERE adv in, at, or to any place

ANYWHERES nonstandard word for > ANYWHERE

ANYWISE adv in any way or manner

ANZIANI n Italian word for councillors

AORIST n tense of the verb in classical Greek and in certain other inflected languages, indicating past action without reference to whether the action involved was momentary or continuous

AORISTIC > AORIST

AORISTS > AORIST

AORTA n main artery of the body, carrying oxygen-rich blood from the heart

AORTAE > AORTA

AORTAL > AORTA

AORTAS > AORTA

AORTIC > AORTA

AORTITIS n inflammation of the aorta

AOUDAD n N African wild mountain sheep with curved horns and long hair covering the neck and forelegs

AOUDADS > AOUDAD

APACE adv swiftly

APACHE n Parisian gangster or ruffian

APACHES > APACHE

APADANA n ancient Persian palace hall

APADANAS > APADANA

APAGE interj Greek word meaning go away

APAGOGE n reduction to absurdity

APAGOGES > APAGOGE

APAGOGIC > APAGOGE

APAID > APAY

APANAGE same as > APPANAGE

APANAGED adj having apanage

APANAGES > APANAGE

APAREJO n kind of packsaddle made of stuffed leather cushions

APAREJOS > APAREJO

APART adv to pieces or in pieces

APARTHEID n former official government policy of racial segregation in S Africa

APARTMENT n room in a building

APARTNESS > APART

APATETIC adj of or relating to coloration that disguises and protects an animal

APATHATON old word for > EPITHET

APATHETIC adj having or showing little or no emotion

APATHIES > APATHY

APATHY n lack of interest or enthusiasm

APATITE n pale green to purple mineral, found in igneous rocks

APATITES > APATITE

APATOSAUR n long-necked dinosaur

APAY vb old word meaning satisfy

APAYD > APAY

APAYING > APAY

APAYS > APAY

APE n tailless monkey such as the chimpanzee or gorilla ▷ vb imitate

APEAK adj in a vertical or almost vertical position

APED > APE

APEDOM n state of being an ape

APEDOMS > APEDOM

APEEK adv nautical word meaning vertically

APEHOOD n state of being ape

APEHOODS > APEHOOD

APELIKE > APE

APEMAN n extinct primate thought to have been the forerunner of true humans

APEMEN > APEMAN

APEPSIA n digestive disorder

APEPSIAS > APEPSIA

APEPSIES > APEPSY

APEPSY n apepsia

APER n person who apes

APERCU n outline

APERCUS > APERCU

APERIENT adj having a mild laxative effect ▷ n mild laxative

APERIENTS > APERIENT

APERIES > APERY

APERIODIC adj not periodic

APERITIF n alcoholic drink taken before a meal

APERITIFS > APERITIF

APERITIVE n laxative

APERS > APER

APERT adj open

APERTNESS > APERT

APERTURAL > APERTURE

APERTURE n opening or hole

APERTURED adj having an aperture

APERTURES > APERTURE

APERY n imitative behaviour

APES > APE

APESHIT adj crazy or furious

APETALIES > APETALOUS

APETALOUS adj (of flowering plants) having no petals

APETALY > APETALOUS

APEX n highest point

APEXES > APEX

PGAR as in *apgar score* system for determining the condition of an infant at birth

PHAGIA *n* refusal or inability to swallow

PHAGIAS > APHAGIA

PHAKIA *n* absence of the lens of an eye, congenital or otherwise

PHAKIAS > APHAKIA

PHANITE *n* any fine-grained rock, such as a basalt, containing minerals that cannot be distinguished with the naked eye

PHANITES > APHANITE

PHANITIC > APHANITE

PHASIA *n* disorder of the central nervous system that affects the ability to speak and understand words

PHASIAC > APHASIA

PHASIACS > APHASIA

PHASIAS > APHASIA

PHASIC > APHASIA

PHASICS > APHASIA

PHELIA > APHELION

PHELIAN > APHELION

PHELION *n* point of a planet's orbit that is farthest from the sun

PHELIONS > APHELION

PHERESES > APHERESIS

PHERESIS *n* omission of a letter or syllable at the beginning of a word

PHERETIC > APHERESIS

PHESES > APHESIS

PHESIS *n* gradual disappearance of an unstressed vowel at the beginning of a word

PHETIC > APHESIS

PHETISE *vb* lose a vowel at the beginning of a word

PHETISED > APHETISE

PHETISES > APHETISE

PHETIZE *vb* lose a vowel at the beginning of a word

PHETIZED > APHETIZE

PHETIZES > APHETIZE

PHICIDE *n* substance for killing aphids

PHICIDES > APHICIDE

PHID *n* small insect which sucks the sap from plants

PHIDES > APHIS

PHIDIAN > APHID

PHIDIANS > APHID

PHIDIOUS > APHID

PHIDS > APHID

PHIS *n* type of aphid such as the blackfly

PHOLATE *n* type of pesticide

PHOLATES > APHOLATE

PHONIA *n* loss of the voice caused by damage to the vocal tract

PHONIAS > APHONIA

APHONIC *adj* affected with aphonia ▷ *n* person affected with aphonia

APHONICS > APHONIC

APHONIES > APHONY

APHONOUS > APHONIA

APHONY *same as* > APHONIA

APHORISE *same as* > APHORIZE

APHORISED > APHORISE

APHORISER > APHORISE

APHORISES > APHORISE

APHORISM *n* short clever saying expressing a general truth

APHORISMS > APHORISM

APHORIST > APHORISM

APHORISTS > APHORISM

APHORIZE *vb* write or speak in aphorisms

APHORIZED > APHORIZE

APHORIZER > APHORIZE

APHORIZES > APHORIZE

APHOTIC *adj* characterized by or growing in the absence of light

APHRODITE *n* North American butterfly

APHTHA *n* small ulceration on a mucous membrane, as in thrush, caused by a fungal infection

APHTHAE > APHTHA

APHTHOUS > APHTHA

APHYLLIES > APHYLLOUS

APHYLLOUS *adj* (of plants) having no leaves

APHYLLY > APHYLLOUS

APIACEOUS *adj* parsley-like

APIAN *adj* of, relating to, or resembling bees

APIARIAN *adj* of or relating to the breeding and care of bees ▷ *n* apiarist

APIARIANS > APIARIAN

APIARIES > APIARY

APIARIST *n* beekeeper

APIARISTS > APIARIST

APIARY *n* place where bees are kept

APICAL *adj* of, at, or being an apex ▷ *n* sound made with the tip of the tongue

APICALLY > APICAL

APICALS > APICAL

APICES *plural of* > APEX

APICIAN *adj* of fine or dainty food

APICULATE *adj* (of leaves) ending in a short sharp point

APICULI > APICULUS

APICULUS *n* short sharp point

APIECE *adv* each

APIEZON as in *apiezon oil* oil left by distillation

APIMANIA *n* extreme enthusiasm for bees

APIMANIAS > APIMANIA

APING > APE

APIOL *n* substance formerly used to assist menstruation

APIOLOGY *n* study of bees

APIOLS > APIOL

APISH *adj* stupid or foolish

APISHLY > APISH

APISHNESS > APISH

APISM *n* behaviour like an ape

APISMS > APISM

APIVOROUS *adj* eating bees

APLANAT *n* aplanatic lens

APLANATIC *adj* (of a lens or mirror) free from spherical aberration

APLANATS > APLANAT

APLANETIC *adj* (esp of some algal and fungal spores) nonmotile or lacking a motile stage

APLASIA *n* congenital absence or abnormal development of an organ or part

APLASIAS > APLASIA

APLASTIC *adj* relating to or characterized by aplasia

APLENTY *adv* in plenty

APLITE *n* light-coloured fine-grained acid igneous rock with a sugary texture, consisting of quartz and feldspars

APLITES > APLITE

APLITIC > APLITE

APLOMB *n* calm self-possession

APLOMBS > APLOMB

APLUSTRE *n* stern ornament on an ancient Greek ship

APLUSTRES > APLUSTRE

APNEA *same as* > APNOEA

APNEAL > APNEA

APNEAS > APNEA

APNEIC > APNEA

APNEUSES > APNEUSIS

APNEUSIS *n* protracted gasping inhalation followed by short inefficient exhalation, which can cause asphyxia

APNEUSTIC *adj* of or relating to apneusis

APNOEA *n* temporary inability to breathe

APNOEAL > APNOEA

APNOEAS > APNOEA

APNOEIC > APNOEA

APO *n* type of protein

APOAPSES > APOAPSIS

APOAPSIS *n* point in an orbit furthest from the object orbited

APOCARP *n* apocarpous gynoecium or fruit

APOCARPS > APOCARP

APOCARPY *n* presence of many carpels

APOCOPATE *vb* omit the final sound or sounds of (a word)

APOCOPE *n* omission of the final sound or sounds of a word

APOCOPES > APOCOPE

APOCOPIC > APOCOPE

APOCRINE *adj* denoting a type of glandular secretion in which part of the secreting cell is lost with the secretion, as in mammary glands

APOCRYPHA *n* writings or statements of uncertain authority

APOD *n* animal without feet

APODAL *adj* (of snakes, eels, etc) without feet

APODE *n* animal without feet

APODES > APODE

APODICTIC *adj* unquestionably true by virtue of demonstration

APODOSES > APODOSIS

APODOSIS *n* consequent of a conditional statement

APODOUS *same as* > APODAL

APODS > APOD

APOENZYME *n* protein component that together with a coenzyme forms an enzyme

APOGAEIC > APOGEE

APOGAMIC > APOGAMY

APOGAMIES > APOGAMY

APOGAMOUS > APOGAMY

APOGAMY *n* type of reproduction, occurring in some ferns, in which the sporophyte develops from the gametophyte without fusion of gametes

APOGEAL > APOGEE

APOGEAN > APOGEE

APOGEE *n* point of the moon's or a satellite's orbit that is farthest from the earth

APOGEES > APOGEE

APOGEIC > APOGEE

APOGRAPH *n* exact copy

APOGRAPHS > APOGRAPH

APOLLO *n* strikingly handsome youth

APOLLOS > APOLLO

APOLOG *same as* > APOLOGUE

APOLOGAL > APOLOGUE

APOLOGIA *n* formal written defence of a cause

APOLOGIAE > APOLOGIA

APOLOGIAS > APOLOGIA

APOLOGIES > APOLOGY

APOLOGISE *same as* > APOLOGIZE

APOLOGIST *n* person who formally defends a cause

APOLOGIZE *vb* make an apology

APOLOGS > APOLOG

APOLOGUE *n* allegory or moral fable

APOLOGUES > APOLOGUE

APOLOGY *n* expression of regret for wrongdoing

APOLUNE n point in a lunar orbit when a spacecraft is at its greatest distance from the moon

APOLUNES > APOLUNE

APOMICT n organism, esp a plant, produced by apomixis

APOMICTIC > APOMIXIS

APOMICTS > APOMICT

APOMIXES > APOMIXIS

APOMIXIS n (esp in plants) any of several types of asexual reproduction, such as parthenogenesis and apogamy, in which fertilization does not take place

APOOP adv on the poop deck

APOPHASES > APOPHASIS

APOPHASIS n device of mentioning a subject by stating that it will not be mentioned

APOPHATIC adj of theology that says God is indescribable

APOPHONY n change in the quality of vowels

APOPHYGE n outward curve at each end of the shaft of a column, adjoining the base or capital

APOPHYGES > APOPHYGE

APOPHYSES > APOPHYSIS

APOPHYSIS n process, outgrowth, or swelling from part of an animal or plant

APOPLAST n nonprotoplasmic component of a plant, including the cell walls and intercellular material

APOPLASTS > APOPLAST

APOPLEX vb afflict with apoplexy

APOPLEXED > APOPLEX

APOPLEXES > APOPLEX

APOPLEXY n stroke

APOPTOSES > APOPTOSIS

APOPTOSIS n programmed death of some of an organism's cells as part of its natural growth and development

APOPTOTIC > APOPTOSIS

APORETIC > APORIA

APORIA n doubt, real or professed, about what to do or say

APORIAS > APORIA

APORT adj on or towards the port side

APOS > APO

APOSITIA n unwillingness to eat

APOSITIAS > APOSITIA

APOSITIC > APOSITIA

APOSPORIC > APOSPORY

APOSPORY n development of the gametophyte from the sporophyte without the formation of spores

APOSTACY same as > APOSTASY

APOSTASY n abandonment of one's religious faith or other belief

APOSTATE n person who has abandoned his or her religion, political party, or cause ▷ adj guilty of apostasy

APOSTATES > APOSTATE

APOSTATIC > APOSTATE

APOSTIL n marginal note

APOSTILLE n apostil

APOSTILS > APOSTIL

APOSTLE n one of the twelve disciples chosen by Christ to preach his gospel

APOSTLES > APOSTLE

APOSTOLIC adj of or relating to the Apostles or their teachings

APOTHECE n obsolete word for shop

APOTHECES > APOTHECE

APOTHECIA n cup-shaped structures that contain the asci, esp in lichens

APOTHEGM n short cryptic remark containing some general or generally accepted truth; maxim

APOTHEGMS > APOTHEGM

APOTHEM n perpendicular line or distance from the centre of a regular polygon to any of its sides

APOTHEMS > APOTHEM

APOZEM n medicine dissolved in water

APOZEMS > APOZEM

APP n application program

APPAID > APPAY

APPAIR vb old form of impair

APPAIRED > APPAIR

APPAIRING > APPAIR

APPAIRS > APPAIR

APPAL vb dismay, terrify

APPALL same as > APPAL

APPALLED > APPALL

APPALLING adj dreadful, terrible

APPALLS > APPALL

APPALOOSA n North American horse breed

APPALS > APPAL

APPALTI > APPALTO

APPALTO n Italian word for contact

APPANAGE n land or other provision granted by a king for the support of a member of the royal family, esp a younger son

APPANAGED adj having appanage

APPANAGES > APPANAGE

APPARAT n Communist Party organization in the former Soviet Union and other states

APPARATS > APPARAT

APPARATUS n equipment for a particular purpose

APPAREL n clothing ▷ vb clothe, adorn, etc

APPARELED > APPAREL

APPARELS > APPAREL

APPARENCY old word for > APPARENT

APPARENT adj readily seen, obvious ▷ n heir apparent

APPARENTS > APPARENT

APPARITOR n officer who summons witnesses and executes the orders of an ecclesiastical and (formerly) a civil court

APPAY old word for > SATISFY

APPAYD > APPAY

APPAYING > APPAY

APPAYS > APPAY

APPEACH old word for > ACCUSE

APPEACHED > APPEACH

APPEACHES > APPEACH

APPEAL vb make an earnest request ▷ n earnest request

APPEALED > APPEAL

APPEALER > APPEAL

APPEALERS > APPEAL

APPEALING adj attractive or pleasing

APPEALS > APPEAL

APPEAR vb become visible or present

APPEARED > APPEAR

APPEARER > APPEAR

APPEARERS > APPEAR

APPEARING > APPEAR

APPEARS > APPEAR

APPEASE vb pacify (a person) by yielding to his or her demands

APPEASED > APPEASE

APPEASER > APPEASE

APPEASERS > APPEASE

APPEASES > APPEASE

APPEASING > APPEASE

APPEL n stamp of the foot, used to warn of one's intent to attack

APPELLANT n person who makes an appeal to a higher court

APPELLATE adj of appeals

APPELLEE n person who is accused or appealed against

APPELLEES > APPELLEE

APPELLOR n person initiating a law case

APPELLORS > APPELLOR

APPELS > APPEL

APPEND vb join on, add

APPENDAGE n thing joined on or added

APPENDANT adj attached, affixed, or added ▷ n person or thing attached or added

APPENDED > APPEND

APPENDENT same as > APPENDANT

APPENDING > APPEND

APPENDIX n separate additional material at the end of a book

APPENDS > APPEND

APPERIL old word for > PERIL

APPERILL old word for > PERIL

APPERILLS > APPERILL

APPERILS > APPERIL

APPERTAIN vb belong to

APPESTAT n neural control centre within the hypothalamus of the brain that regulates the sense of hunger and satiety

APPESTATS > APPESTAT

APPETENCE n craving or desire

APPETENCY same as > APPETENCE

APPETENT adj eager

APPETIBLE adj old word meaning desirable

APPETISE vb stimulate the appetite

APPETISED > APPETISE

APPETISER same as > APPETIZER

APPETISES > APPETISE

APPETITE n desire for food or drink

APPETITES > APPETITE

APPETIZE vb stimulate the appetite

APPETIZED > APPETIZE

APPETIZER n thing eaten or drunk to stimulate the appetite

APPETIZES > APPETIZE

APPLAUD vb show approval of by clapping one's hands

APPLAUDED > APPLAUD

APPLAUDER > APPLAUD

APPLAUDS > APPLAUD

APPLAUSE n approval shown by clapping one's hands

APPLAUSES > APPLAUSE

APPLE n round firm fleshy fruit that grows on trees

APPLECART n cart used to carry apples

APPLEJACK n brandy made from apples

APPLES > APPLE

APPLET n computing program that runs within a page on the World Wide Web

APPLETS > APPLET

APPLEY adj resembling or tasting like an apple

APPLIABLE adj applicable

APPLIANCE n device with a specific function

APPLICANT n person who applies for something

APPLICATE adj applied

practicably

APPLIED adj (of a skill, science, etc) put to practical use

APPLIER > APPLY

APPLIERS > APPLY

APPLIES > APPLY

APPLIQUE n decoration or trimming of one material sewn or otherwise fixed onto another ▷ vb sew or fix (a decoration) on as an appliqué

APPLIQUED > APPLIQUE

APPLIQUES > APPLIQUE

APPLY vb make a formal request

APPLYING > APPLY

APPOINT vb assign to a job or position

APPOINTED > APPOINT

APPOINTEE n person who is appointed

APPOINTER > APPOINT

APPOINTOR n person to whom a power to nominate persons to take property is given by deed or will

APPOINTS > APPOINT

APPORT n production of objects by apparently supernatural means at a spiritualists' seance

APPORTION vb divide out in shares

APPORTS > APPORT

APPOSABLE adj capable of being apposed or brought into apposition

APPOSE vb place side by side or near to each other

APPOSED > APPOSE

APPOSER > APPOSE

APPOSERS > APPOSE

APPOSES > APPOSE

APPOSING > APPOSE

APPOSITE adj suitable, apt

APPRAISAL n assessment of the worth or quality of a person or thing

APPRAISE vb estimate the value or quality of

APPRAISED > APPRAISE

APPRAISEE n person being appraised

APPRAISER > APPRAISE

APPRAISES > APPRAISE

APPREHEND vb arrest and take into custody

APPRESS vb press together

APPRESSED > APPRESS

APPRESSES > APPRESS

APPRISE vb make aware (of)

APPRISED > APPRISE

APPRISER > APPRISE

APPRISERS > APPRISE

APPRISES > APPRISE

APPRISING > APPRISE

APPRIZE same as > APPRISE

APPRIZED > APPRIZE

APPRIZER > APPRIZE

APPRIZERS > APPRIZE

APPRIZES > APPRIZE

APPRIZING > APPRIZE

APPRO n approval

APPROACH vb come near or nearer (to) ▷ n approaching or means of approaching

APPROBATE vb accept as valid

APPROOF old word for > TRIAL

APPROOFS > APPROOF

APPROS > APPRO

APPROVAL n consent

APPROVALS > APPROVAL

APPROVE vb consider good or right

APPROVED > APPROVE

APPROVER > APPROVE

APPROVERS > APPROVE

APPROVES > APPROVE

APPROVING > APPROVE

APPS > APP

APPUI n support

APPUIED > APPUY

APPUIS > APPUI

APPULSE n very close approach of two celestial bodies so that they are in conjunction but no eclipse or occultation occurs

APPULSES > APPULSE

APPULSIVE > APPULSE

APPUY vb support

APPUYED > APPUY

APPUYING > APPUY

APPUYS > APPUY

APRACTIC > APRAXIA

APRAXIA n disorder of the central nervous system caused by brain damage and characterized by impaired ability to carry out purposeful muscular movements

APRAXIAS > APRAXIA

APRAXIC > APRAXIA

APRES prep French word for after

APRICATE vb bask in sun

APRICATED > APRICATE

APRICATES > APRICATE

APRICOCK old word for > APRICOT

APRICOCKS > APRICOT

APRICOT n yellowish-orange juicy fruit like a small peach ▷ adj yellowish-orange

APRICOTS > APRICOT

APRIORISM n philosophical doctrine that there may be genuine knowledge independent of experience

APRIORIST > APRIORISM

APRIORITY n condition of being innate in the mind

APRON n garment worn over the front of the body to protect the clothes ▷ vb equip with an apron

APRONED > APRON

APRONFUL n amount held in an apron

APRONFULS > APRONFUL

APRONING > APRON

APRONLIKE > APRON

APRONS > APRON

APROPOS adv appropriate(ly)

APROTIC adj (of solvents) neither accepting nor donating hydrogen ions

APSARAS n Hindu water sprite

APSARASES > APSARAS

APSE n arched or domed recess, esp in a church

APSES > APSE

APSIDAL > APSIS

APSIDES > APSIS

APSIDIOLE n small arch

APSIS n either of two points lying at the extremities of the elliptical orbit of a planet or satellite

APSO n Tibetan terrier

APSOS > APSO

APT adj having a specified tendency ▷ vb be fitting

APTAMER n artificially-created DNA or RNA molecule with therapeutic properties

APTAMERS > APTAMER

APTED > APT

APTER > APT

APTERAL adj (esp of a classical temple) not having columns at the sides

APTERIA > APTERIUM

APTERISM > APTEROUS

APTERISMS > APTEROUS

APTERIUM n bare patch on the skin of a bird

APTEROUS adj (of insects) without wings, as silverfish and springtails

APTERYX n kiwi (the bird)

APTERYXES > APTERYX

APTEST > APT

APTING > APT

APTITUDE n natural ability

APTITUDES > APTITUDE

APTLY > APT

APTNESS > APT

APTNESSES > APT

APTOTE n noun without inflections

APTOTES > APTOTE

APTOTIC > APTOTE

APTS > APT

APYRASE n enzyme

APYRASES > APYRASE

APYRETIC > APYREXIA

APYREXIA n absence of fever

APYREXIAS > APYREXIA

AQUA n water

AQUABATIC adj of gymnastic feats in water

AQUABOARD n board used to ride on water

AQUACADE same as > AQUASHOW

AQUACADES > AQUACADE

AQUADROME n venue for water sports

AQUAE > AQUA

AQUAFARM vb cultivate fish or shellfish

AQUAFARMS > AQUAFARM

AQUAFER n aquifer

AQUAFERS > AQUAFER

AQUAFIT n type of aerobic exercise done in water

AQUAFITS > AQUAFIT

AQUALUNG n mouthpiece attached to air cylinders, worn for underwater swimming

AQUALUNGS > AQUALUNG

AQUANAUT n person who lives and works underwater

AQUANAUTS > AQUANAUT

AQUAPHOBE n person afraid of water

AQUAPLANE n board on which a person stands to be towed by a motorboat ▷ vb ride on an aquaplane

AQUAPORIN n any one of a group of proteins in cell membranes that allow the passage of water across the membrane

AQUARELLE n method of watercolour painting in transparent washes

AQUARIA > AQUARIUM

AQUARIAL adj > AQUARIUM

AQUARIAN n person who keeps an aquarium

AQUARIANS > AQUARIAN

AQUARIIST n old form of > AQUARIST

AQUARIST n curator of an aquarium

AQUARISTS > AQUARIST

AQUARIUM n tank in which fish and other underwater creatures are kept

AQUARIUMS > AQUARIUM

AQUAROBIC adj pertaining to exercises performed standing up in a swimming pool

AQUAS > AQUA

AQUASHOW n exhibition of swimming and diving, often accompanied by music

AQUASHOWS > AQUASHOW

AQUATIC adj living in or near water ▷ n marine or freshwater animal or plant

AQUATICS npl water sports

AQUATINT n print like a watercolour, produced by etching copper ▷ vb etch (a block, etc) in aquatint

AQUATINTA n aquatint

AQUATINTS > AQUATINT

AQUATONE n fitness exercise in water

AQUATONES > AQUATONE

AQUAVIT n grain- or potato-based spirit from the Scandinavian countries, flavoured with aromatic seeds and spices, esp caraway

AQUAVITS > AQUAVIT

AQUEDUCT n structure carrying water across a valley or river

AQUEDUCTS > AQUEDUCT

AQUEOUS adj of, like, or containing water

AQUEOUSLY > AQUEOUS

AQUIFER n deposit of rock, such as sandstone, containing water that can be used to supply wells

AQUIFERS > AQUIFER

AQUILEGIA another name for > COLUMBINE

AQUILINE adj (of a nose) curved like an eagle's beak

AQUILON n name for the north wind

AQUILONS > AQUILON

AQUIVER adv quivering

AR n letter R

ARAARA another name for > TREVALLY

ARAARAS > ARAARA

ARABA n Asian carriage

ARABESK > ARABA

ARABESK same as > ARABESQUE

ARABESKS > ARABESK

ARABESQUE n ballet position in which one leg is raised behind and the arms are extended ▷ adj designating, of, or decorated in this style

ARABIC as in gum arabic gum exuded by certain acacia trees

ARABICA n high-quality coffee bean

ARABICAS > ARABICA

ARABICISE same as > ARABICIZE

ARABICIZE vb make or become Arabic

ARABILITY n suitability of land for growing crops

ARABIN n essence of gum arabic

ARABINOSE n pentose sugar in plant gums

ARABINS > ARABIN

ARABIS n type of plant which forms low-growing mats with downy grey foliage and white flowers

ARABISE vb make or become Arab

ARABISED > ARABISE

ARABISES > ARABISE

ARABISING > ARABISE

ARABIZE vb make or become Arab

ARABIZED > ARABIZE

ARABIZES > ARABIZE

ARABIZING > ARABIZE

ARABLE adj suitable for growing crops on ▷ n arable land or farming

ARABLES > ARABLE

ARACEOUS same as > AROID

ARACHIS n Brazilian plant

ARACHISES > ARACHIS

ARACHNID n eight-legged invertebrate, such as a spider, scorpion, tick, or mite

ARACHNIDS > ARACHNID

ARACHNOID n middle of the three membranes that cover the brain and spinal cord ▷ adj of or relating to the middle of the three meninges

ARAGONITE n generally white or grey mineral, found in sedimentary rocks

ARAISE vb old form of raise

ARAISED > ARAISE

ARAISES > ARAISE

ARAISING > ARAISE

ARAK same as > ARRACK

ARAKS > ARAK

ARALIA n type of plant grown in greenhouses or as a house plant for its decorative evergreen foliage

ARALIAS > ARALIA

ARAME n Japanese edible seaweed

ARAMES > ARAME

ARAMID n synthetic fibre

ARAMIDS > ARAMID

ARANEID n type of arachnid of the order which comprises the spiders

ARANEIDAN > ARANEID

ARANEIDS > ARANEID

ARANEOUS adj like a spider's web

ARAPAIMA n very large primitive freshwater teleost fish that occurs in tropical S America

ARAPAIMAS > ARAPAIMA

ARAPONGA n South American bird with a bell-like call

ARAPONGAS > ARAPONGA

ARAPUNGA n South American bird with a bell-like call

ARAPUNGAS > ARAPUNGA

ARAR n African tree

ARAROBA n Brazilian leguminous tree

ARAROBAS > ARAROBA

ARARS > ARAR

ARAUCARIA n type of coniferous tree of S America, Australia, and Polynesia, such as the monkey puzzle and bunya-bunya

ARAYSE vb old form of raise

ARAYSED > ARAYSE

ARAYSES > ARAYSE

ARAYSING > ARAYSE

ARB short for > ARBITRAGE

ARBA n Asian carriage

ARBALEST n large medieval crossbow, usually cocked by mechanical means

ARBALESTS > ARBALEST

ARBALIST same as > ARBALEST

ARBALISTS > ARBALIST

ARBAS > ARBA

ARBELEST n arbalest

ARBELESTS > ARBELEST

ARBITER n person empowered to judge in a dispute

ARBITERS > ARBITER

ARBITRAGE n purchase of currencies, securities, or commodities in one market for immediate resale in others in order to profit from unequal prices

ARBITRAL adj of or relating to arbitration

ARBITRARY adj based on personal choice or chance, rather than reason

ARBITRATE vb settle (a dispute) by arbitration

ARBITRESS n female arbitrator

ARBITRIUM n power to decide

ARBLAST n arbalest

ARBLASTER > ARBLAST

ARBLASTS > ARBLAST

ARBOR n revolving shaft or axle in a machine

ARBOREAL adj of or living in trees

ARBORED adj having arbors

ARBOREOUS adj thickly wooded

ARBORES > ARBOR

ARBORET n old name for an area planted with shrubs

ARBORETA > ARBORETUM

ARBORETS > ARBORET

ARBORETUM n place where rare trees or shrubs are cultivated

ARBORIO n as in arborio rice variety of round-grain rice used for making risotto

ARBORIOS > ARBORIO

ARBORISE same as > ARBORIZE

ARBORISED > ARBORISE

ARBORISES > ARBORISE

ARBORIST n specialist in the cultivation of trees

ARBORISTS > ARBORIST

ARBORIZE vb give or take on a treelike branched appearance

ARBORIZED > ARBORIZE

ARBORIZES > ARBORIZE

ARBOROUS adj of trees

ARBORS > ARBOR

ARBOUR n glade sheltered by trees

ARBOURED adj having arbours

ARBOURS > ARBOUR

ARBOVIRAL > ARBOVIRUS

ARBOVIRUS n any one of a group of viruses that cause such diseases as encephalitis and dengue and are transmitted to

humans by arthropods, esp insects and ticks

ARBS > ARB

ARBUSCLE n small tree

ARBUSCLES > ARBUSCLE

ARBUTE old name for > ARBUTUS

ARBUTEAN > ARBUTUS

ARBUTES > ARBUTE

ARBUTUS n evergreen shrub with strawberry-like berries

ARBUTUSES > ARBUTUS

ARC n part of a circle or other curve ▷ vb form an arc

ARCADE n covered passageway lined with shops ▷ vb provide with an arcade

ARCADED > ARCADE

ARCADES > ARCADE

ARCADIA n traditional idealized rural setting

ARCADIAN n person who leads a rural life

ARCADIANS > ARCADIAN

ARCADIAS > ARCADIA

ARCADINGS > ARCADE

ARCADINGS > ARCADE

ARCANA n either of the two divisions of a pack of tarot cards

ARCANAS > ARCANA

ARCANE adj mysterious and secret

ARCANELY > ARCANE

ARCANIST n person with secret knowledge

ARCANISTS > ARCANIST

ARCANUM n profound secret or mystery known only to initiates

ARCANUMS > ARCANUM

ARCATURE n small-scale arcade

ARCATURES > ARCATURE

ARCCOSINE n trigonometric function

ARCED > ARC

ARCH n curved structure supporting a bridge or roof ▷ vb (cause to) form an arch ▷ adj superior, knowing

ARCHAEA n order of prokaryotic microorganisms

ARCHAEAL same as > ARCHAEAN

ARCHAEAN n type of microorganism

ARCHAEANS > ARCHAEAN

ARCHAEI > ARCHAEUS

ARCHAEON same as > ARCHAEAN

ARCHAEUS n spirit believed to inhabit a living thing

ARCHAIC adj ancient

ARCHAICAL same as > ARCHAIC

ARCHAISE same as > ARCHAIZE

ARCHAISED > ARCHAISE

ARCHAISER > ARCHAISE

ARCHAISES > ARCHAISE

ARCHAISM n archaic word or phrase

ARCHAISMS > ARCHAISM

ARCHAIST > ARCHAISM

ARCHAISTS > ARCHAISM

ARCHAIZE vb give an archaic appearance or character to, as by the use of archaisms

ARCHAIZED > ARCHAIZE

ARCHAIZER > ARCHAIZE

ARCHAIZES > ARCHAIZE

ARCHANGEL n chief angel

ARCHDRUID n chief or principal druid

ARCHDUCAL adj of or relating to an archduke, archduchess, or archduchy

ARCHDUCHY n territory of an archduke or archduchess

ARCHDUKE n duke of specially high rank

ARCHDUKES > ARCHDUKE

ARCHEAN > ARCHAEAN

ARCHED adj provided with or spanned by an arch or arches

ARCHEI > ARCHEUS

ARCHENEMY n chief enemy

ARCHER n person who shoots with a bow and arrow

ARCHERESS n female archer

ARCHERIES > ARCHERY

ARCHERS > ARCHER

ARCHERY n art or sport of shooting with a bow and arrow

ARCHES > ARCH

ARCHEST > ARCH

ARCHETYPE n perfect specimen

ARCHEUS n spirit believed to inhabit a living thing

ARCHFIEND n the chief of fiends or devils

ARCHFOE n chief enemy

ARCHFOES > ARCHFOE

ARCHICARP n female reproductive structure in ascomycetous fungi that consists of a cell or hypha and develops into the ascogonium

ARCHIL a variant spelling of > ORCHIL

ARCHILOWE n treat given in return

ARCHILS > ARCHIL

ARCHIMAGE n great magician or wizard

ARCHINE n Russian unit of length equal to about 71 cm

ARCHINES > ARCHINE

ARCHING > ARCH

ARCHINGS > ARCH

ARCHITECT n person qualified to design and supervise the construction of buildings

ARCHITYPE n primitive original from which others derive

ARCHIVAL > ARCHIVE

ARCHIVE n collection of records or documents ▷ vb store (documents, data, etc) in an archive or other repository

ARCHIVED > ARCHIVE

ARCHIVES > ARCHIVE

ARCHIVING > ARCHIVE

ARCHIVIST n person in charge of archives

ARCHIVOLT n moulding around an arch, sometimes decorated

ARCHLET n small arch

ARCHLETS > ARCHLET

ARCHLUTE n old bass lute

ARCHLUTES > ARCHLUTE

ARCHLY > ARCH

ARCHNESS > ARCH

ARCOLOGY n study of the origins of things

ARCHON n (in ancient Athens) one of the nine chief magistrates

ARCHONS > ARCHON

ARCHONTIC > ARCHON

ARCHOSAUR n early type of dinosaur

ARCHRIVAL n chief rival

ARCHSTONE n wedge-shaped stone forming the curved part of an arch

ARCHWAY n passageway under an arch

ARCHWAYS > ARCHWAY

ARCHWISE adv like an arch

ARCIFORM adj shaped like an arch

ARCING > ARC

ARCINGS > ARC

ARCKED > ARC

ARCKING > ARC

ARCKINGS > ARC

ARCMIN n 1/60 of a degree of an angle

ARCMINS > ARCMIN

ARCMINUTE n unit of angular measurement, 1/60 of a degree

ARCO adv musical direction meaning with bow ▷ n bow of a stringed instrument

ARCOGRAPH n instrument used for drawing arcs without using a central point

ARCOLOGY n architecture blending buildings with the natural environment

ARCOS > ARCO

ARCS > ARC

ARCSEC n 1/3600 of a degree of an angle

ARCSECOND n unit used in astronomy

ARCSECS > ARCSEC

ARCSINE n trigonometrical function

ARCSINES > ARCSINE

ARCTIC adj very cold ▷ n high waterproof overshoe with buckles

ARCTICS > ARCTIC

ARCTIID n type of moth of the family which includes the ermine and tiger moths

ARCTIIDS > ARCTIID

ARCTOID adj like a bear

ARCTOPHIL n arctophile

ARCUATE adj shaped or bent like an arc or bow

ARCUATED same as > ARCUATE

ARCUATELY > ARCUATE

ARCUATION n use of arches or vaults in buildings

ARCUS n circle around the cornea of the eye

ARCUSES > ARCUS

ARD n primitive plough

ARDEB n unit of dry measure used in Egypt and other Middle Eastern countries. In Egypt it is approximately equal to 0.195 cubic metres

ARDEBS > ARDEB

ARDENCIES > ARDENT

ARDENCY > ARDENT

ARDENT adj passionate

ARDENTLY > ARDENT

ARDOR same as > ARDOUR

ARDORS > ARDOR

ARDOUR n passion

ARDOURS > ARDOUR

ARDRI n Irish high king

ARDRIGH n Irish high king

ARDRIGHS > ARDRIGH

ARDRIS > ARDRI

ARDS > ARD

ARDUOUS adj hard to accomplish, strenuous

ARDUOUSLY > ARDUOUS

ARE n unit of measure, 100 square metres ▷ vb used as the singular form with you

AREA n part or region

AREACH vb old form of reach

AREACHED > AREACH

AREACHES > AREACH

AREACHING > AREACH

AREAD vb old word meaning declare

AREADING > AREAD

AREADS > AREAD

AREAE > AREA

AREAL > AREA

AREALLY > AREA

AREAR n old form of arrear

AREAS > AREA

AREAWAY n passageway between parts of a building or between different buildings

AREAWAYS > AREAWAY

ARECA n tall SE Asian palm tree with white flowers and orange or red egg-shaped nuts

ARECAS > ARECA

ARECOLINE n drug derived from betel nut

ARED > AREAD

AREDD > AREAD

AREDE vb old word

meaning declare

AREDES > AREDE

AREDING > AREDE

AREFIED > AREFY

AREFIES > AREFY

AREFY vb dry up

AREFYING > AREFY

AREG a plural of > ERG

AREIC adj relating to area

ARENA n seated enclosure for sports events

ARENAS > ARENA

ARENATION n use of hot sand as a medical poultice

ARENE n aromatic hydrocarbon

ARENES > ARENE

ARENITE n any arenaceous rock

ARENITES > ARENITE

ARENITIC > ARENITE

ARENOSE adj sandy

ARENOUS adj sandy

AREOLA n small circular area, such as the coloured ring around the human nipple

AREOLAE > AREOLA

AREOLAR > AREOLA

AREOLAS > AREOLA

AREOLATE > AREOLA

AREOLATED adj areolate

AREOLE n space outlined on a surface, such as an area between veins on a leaf or on an insect's wing

AREOLES > AREOLE

AREOLOGY n study of the planet Mars

AREOMETER n instrument for measuring the density of liquids

AREOSTYLE n building with widely-spaced columns

AREPA n Colombian cornmeal cake

AREPAS > AREPA

ARERE adv old word meaning backwards

ARES > ARE

ARET vb old word meaning entrust

ARETE n sharp ridge separating two cirques or glacial valleys in mountainous regions

ARETES > ARETE

ARETHUSA n N American orchid with one long narrow leaf and one rose-purple flower fringed with yellow

ARETHUSAS > ARETHUSA

ARETS > ARET

ARETT vb old word meaning entrust

ARETTED > ARETT

ARETTING > ARETT

ARETTS > ARETT

AREW adv old word meaning in a row

ARF n barking sound

ARFS > ARF

ARGAL same as > ARGALI
ARGALA n Indian stork
ARGALAS > ARGALA
ARGALI n large wild sheep of central Asia, the male of which has massive curving horns
ARGALIS > ARGALI
ARGALS > ARGAL
ARGAN n Moroccan tree
ARGAND n lamp with a hollow circular wick
ARGANDS > ARGAND
ARGANS > ARGAN
ARGEMONE n prickly poppy
ARGEMONES > ARGEMONE
ARGENT n silver
ARGENTAL adj of or containing silver
ARGENTIC adj of or containing silver in the divalent or trivalent state
ARGENTINE adj of, relating to, or resembling silver ▷ n type of small silver fish
ARGENTITE n dark grey mineral that consists of silver sulphide, usually in cubic crystalline forms, and occurs in veins, often with native silver. It is found esp in Mexico, Nevada, and Saxony and is an important source of silver. Formula: Ag_2S
ARGENTOUS adj of or containing silver in the monovalent state
ARGENTS > ARGENT
ARGENTUM an obsolete name for > SILVER
ARGENTUMS > ARGENTUM
ARGH interj cry of pain
ARGHAN n agave plant
ARGHANS > ARGHAN
ARGIL n clay, esp potters' clay
ARGILLITE n any argillaceous rock, esp a hardened mudstone
ARGILS > ARGIL
ARGINASE n type of enzyme
ARGINASES > ARGINASE
ARGININE n essential amino acid of plant and animal proteins, necessary for nutrition and for the production of excretory urea
ARGININES > ARGININE
ARGLE vb quarrel
ARGLED > ARGLE
ARGLES > ARGLE
ARGLING > ARGLE
ARGOL n crude potassium hydrogentartrate, deposited as a crust on the sides of wine vats
ARGOLS > ARGOL
ARGON n inert gas found in the air
ARGONAUT n paper nautilus

ARGONAUTS > ARGONAUT
ARGONON n inert gas
ARGONONS > ARGONON
ARGONS > ARGON
ARGOSIES > ARGOSY
ARGOSY n large merchant ship
ARGOT n slang or jargon
ARGOTIC > ARGOT
ARGOTS > ARGOT
ARGUABLE adj capable of being disputed
ARGUABLY adv it can be argued that
ARGUE vb try to prove by giving reasons
ARGUED > ARGUE
ARGUER > ARGUE
ARGUERS > ARGUE
ARGUES > ARGUE
ARGUFIED > ARGUFY
ARGUFIER > ARGUFY
ARGUFIERS > ARGUFY
ARGUFIES > ARGUFY
ARGUFY vb argue or quarrel, esp over something trivial
ARGUFYING > ARGUFY
ARGUING > ARGUE
ARGULI > ARGULUS
ARGULUS n parasite on fish
ARGUMENT n quarrel
ARGUMENTA n appeals to reason
ARGUMENTS > ARGUMENT
ARGUS n any of various brown butterflies
ARGUSES > ARGUS
ARGUTE adj shrill or keen
ARGUTELY > ARGUTE
ARGYLE adj made of knitted or woven material with a diamond-shaped pattern of two or more colours ▷ n sock made of this
ARGYLES > ARGYLE
ARGYLL n sock with diamond pattern
ARGYLLS > ARGYLL
ARGYRIA n staining of skin by exposure to silver
ARGYRIAS > ARGYRIA
ARGYRITE n mineral containing silver sulphide
ARGYRITES > ARGYRITE
ARHAT n Buddhist, esp a monk who has achieved enlightenment and at death passes to nirvana
ARHATS > ARHAT
ARHATSHIP > ARHAT
ARHYTHMIA n irregular heartbeat
ARHYTHMIC > ARHYTHMIA
ARIA n elaborate song for solo voice, esp one from an opera
ARIARY n currency of Madagascar
ARIAS > ARIA
ARID adj parched, dry
ARIDER > ARID

ARIDEST > ARID
ARIDITIES > ARID
ARIDITY > ARID
ARIDLY > ARID
ARIDNESS > ARID
ARIEL n type of Arabian gazelle
ARIELS > ARIEL
ARIETTA n short relatively uncomplicated aria
ARIETTAS > ARIETTA
ARIETTE same as > ARIETTA
ARIETTES > ARIETTE
ARIGHT adv rightly
ARIKI n first-born male or female in a notable family
ARIKIS > ARIKI
ARIL n appendage on certain seeds, such as those of the yew and nutmeg, developed from or near the funicle of the ovule and often brightly coloured and fleshy
ARILED adj having an aril
ARILLARY adj having an aril
ARILLATE > ARILLATED
ARILLATED adj having an aril
ARILLI > ARILLUS
ARILLODE n structure in certain seeds that resembles an aril but is developed from or near the micropyle of the ovule
ARILLODES > ARILLODE
ARILLOID adj of or like an aril
ARILLUS n aril
ARILS > ARIL
ARIOSE adj songlike
ARIOSI > ARIOSO
ARIOSO n recitative with the lyrical quality of an aria
ARIOSOS > ARIOSO
ARIOT adv riotously
ARIPPLE adv in ripples
ARIS n Cockney slang for buttocks
ARISE vb come about
ARISEN > ARISE
ARISES > ARISE
ARISH n field that has been mown
ARISHES > ARISH
ARISING > ARISE
ARISTA n stiff bristle such as the awn of some grasses and cereals
ARISTAE > ARISTA
ARISTAS > ARISTA
ARISTATE > ARISTA
ARISTO n aristocrat
ARISTOS > ARISTO
ARISTOTLE n bottle
ARK n boat built by Noah, which survived the Flood ▷ vb place in an ark
ARKED > ARK
ARKING > ARK
ARKITE n passenger in ark
ARKITES > ARKITE

ARKOSE n sandstone consisting of grains of feldspar and quartz cemented by a mixture of quartz and clay minerals
ARKOSES > ARKOSE
ARKOSIC > ARKOSE
ARKS > ARK
ARLE vb make downpayment
ARLED > ARLE
ARLES > ARLE
ARLING > ARLE
ARM n either of the upper limbs from the shoulder to the wrist ▷ vb supply with weapons
ARMADA n large number of warships
ARMADAS > ARMADA
ARMADILLO n small S American mammal covered in strong bony plates
ARMAGNAC n dry brown brandy
ARMAGNACS > ARMAGNAC
ARMAMENT n military weapons
ARMAMENTS > ARMAMENT
ARMATURE n revolving structure in an electric motor or generator, wound with coils carrying the current
ARMATURED > ARMATURE
ARMATURES > ARMATURE
ARMBAND n band of material worn round the arm, such as one bearing an identifying mark, etc, or a black one indicating mourning
ARMBANDS > ARMBAND
ARMCHAIR n upholstered chair with side supports for the arms ▷ adj taking no active part
ARMCHAIRS > ARMCHAIR
ARMED adj equipped with or supported by arms, armour, etc
ARMER > ARM
ARMERS > ARM
ARMET n close-fitting medieval visored helmet with a neck guard
ARMETS > ARMET
ARMFUL n as much as can be held in the arms
ARMFULS > ARMFUL
ARMGAUNT adj word in Shakespeare of uncertain meaning
ARMHOLE n opening in a garment through which the arm passes
ARMHOLES > ARMHOLE
ARMIES > ARMY
ARMIGER n person entitled to bear heraldic arms, such as a sovereign or nobleman
ARMIGERAL > ARMIGER
ARMIGERO n armiger
ARMIGEROS > ARMIGERO
ARMIGERS > ARMIGER

ARMIL n bracelet

ARMILLA n bracelet

ARMILLAE > ARMILLA

ARMILLARY adj of or relating to bracelets

ARMILLAS > ARMILLA

ARMILS > ARMIL

ARMING n act of taking arms or providing with arms

ARMINGS > ARMING

ARMISTICE n agreed suspension of fighting

ARMLESS > ARM

ARMLET n band worn round the arm

ARMLETS > ARMLET

ARMLIKE > ARM

ARMLOAD n amount carried in the arms

ARMLOADS > ARMLOAD

ARMLOCK vb grip someone's arms

ARMLOCKED > ARMLOCK

ARMLOCKS > ARMLOCK

ARMOIRE n large cabinet, originally used for storing weapons

ARMOIRES > ARMOIRE

ARMONICA n glass harmonica

ARMONICAS > ARMONICA

ARMOR same as > ARMOUR

ARMORED same as > ARMOURED

ARMORER same as > ARMOURER

ARMORERS > ARMORER

ARMORIAL adj of or relating to heraldry or heraldic arms ▷ n book of coats of arms

ARMORIALS > ARMORIAL

ARMORIES > ARMORY

ARMORING > ARMOR

ARMORIST n heraldry expert

ARMORISTS > ARMORIST

ARMORLESS > ARMOR

ARMORS > ARMOR

ARMORY same as > ARMOURY

ARMOUR n metal clothing formerly worn to protect the body in battle ▷ vb equip or cover with armour

ARMOURED adj having a protective covering

ARMOURER n maker, repairer, or keeper of arms or armour

ARMOURERS > ARMOURER

ARMOURIES > ARMOURY

ARMOURING > ARMOUR

ARMOURS > ARMOUR

ARMOURY n place where weapons are stored

ARMOZEEN n material used for clerical gowns

ARMOZEENS > ARMOZEEN

ARMOZINE n material used for clerical gowns

ARMOZINES > ARMOZINE

ARMPIT n hollow under the arm at the shoulder

ARMPITS > ARMPIT

ARMREST n part of a chair or sofa that supports the arm

ARMRESTS > ARMREST

ARMS > ARM

ARMSFUL > ARMFUL

ARMURE n silk or wool fabric with a small cobbled pattern

ARMURES > ARMURE

ARMY n military land forces of a nation

ARMYWORM n caterpillar of a widely distributed noctuid moth

ARMYWORMS > ARMYWORM

ARNA n Indian water buffalo

ARNAS > ARNA

ARNATTO n annatto

ARNATTOS > ARNATTO

ARNICA n N temperate or arctic plant typically having yellow flowers

ARNICAS > ARNICA

ARNOTTO n annatto

ARNOTTOS > ARNOTTO

ARNUT n plant with edible tubers

ARNUTS > ARNUT

AROBA n Asian carriage

AROBAS > AROBA

AROHA n love, compassion, or affection

AROHAS > AROHA

AROID n type of plant of the family which includes the arum, calla, and anthurium

AROIDS > AROID

AROINT vb drive away

AROINTED > AROINT

AROINTING > AROINT

AROINTS > AROINT

AROLLA n European pine tree

AROLLAS > AROLLA

AROMA n pleasant smell

AROMAS > AROMA

AROMATASE n enzyme involved in the production of oestrogen

AROMATIC adj having a distinctive pleasant smell ▷ n something, such as a plant or drug, that gives off a fragrant smell

AROMATICS > AROMATIC

AROMATISE same as > AROMATIZE

AROMATIZE vb make aromatic

AROSE past tense of > ARISE

AROUND adv on all sides (of)

AROUSABLE > AROUSE

AROUSAL > AROUSE

AROUSALS > AROUSE

AROUSE vb stimulate, make active

AROUSED > AROUSE

AROUSER > AROUSE

AROUSERS > AROUSE

AROUSES > AROUSE

AROUSING > AROUSE

AROW adv in a row

AROYNT vb old word meaning to drive away

AROYNTED > AROYNT

AROYNTING > AROYNT

AROYNTS > AROYNT

ARPA n website concerned with structure of the internet

ARPAS > ARPA

ARPEGGIO n notes of a chord played or sung in quick succession

ARPEGGIOS > ARPEGGIO

ARPEN n old French measure of land

ARPENS > ARPEN

ARPENT n former French unit of length equal to 190 feet (approximately 58 metres)

ARPENTS > ARPENT

ARPILLERA n Peruvian wall-hanging

ARQUEBUS n portable long-barrelled gun dating from the 15th century

ARRACACHA n S American plant

ARRACK n alcoholic drink distilled from grain or rice

ARRACKS > ARRACK

ARRAH interj Irish exclamation

ARRAIGN vb bring (a prisoner) before a court to answer a charge

ARRAIGNED > ARRAIGN

ARRAIGNER > ARRAIGN

ARRAIGNS > ARRAIGN

ARRANGE vb plan

ARRANGED > ARRANGE

ARRANGER > ARRANGE

ARRANGERS > ARRANGE

ARRANGES > ARRANGE

ARRANGING > ARRANGE

ARRANT adj utter, downright

ARRANTLY > ARRANT

ARRAS n tapestry wall-hanging

ARRASED adj having an arras

ARRASENE n material used in embroidery

ARRASENES > ARRASENE

ARRASES > ARRAS

ARRAUGHT > AREACH

ARRAY n impressive display or collection ▷ vb arrange in order

ARRAYAL > ARRAY

ARRAYALS > ARRAY

ARRAYED > ARRAY

ARRAYER > ARRAY

ARRAYERS > ARRAY

ARRAYING > ARRAY

ARRAYMENT n act of arraying

ARRAYS > ARRAY

ARREAR n singular of arrears

ARREARAGE same as > ARREARS

ARREARS npl money owed

ARRECT adj pricked up

ARREEDE vb old word meaning declare

ARREEDES > ARREEDE

ARREEDING > ARREEDE

ARREST vb take (a person) into custody ▷ n act of taking a person into custody

ARRESTANT n substance that stops a chemical reaction

ARRESTED > ARREST

ARRESTEE n arrested person

ARRESTEES > ARRESTEE

ARRESTER n person who arrests

ARRESTERS > ARRESTER

ARRESTING adj attracting attention, striking

ARRESTIVE adj making something stop

ARRESTOR n person or thing that arrests

ARRESTORS > ARRESTOR

ARRESTS > ARREST

ARRET n judicial decision

ARRETS > ARRET

ARRHIZAL adj without roots

ARRIAGE n Scottish feudal service

ARRIAGES > ARRIAGE

ARRIBA interj exclamation of pleasure or approval

ARRIDE vb old word meaning gratify

ARRIDED > ARRIDE

ARRIDES > ARRIDE

ARRIDING > ARRIDE

ARRIERE adj French word meaning old-fashioned

ARRIERO n Spanish word for mule driver

ARRIEROS > ARRIERO

ARRIS n sharp edge at the meeting of two surfaces at an angle with one another, as at two adjacent sides of a stone block

ARRISES > ARRIS

ARRISH n corn stubble

ARRISHES > ARRISH

ARRIVAL n arriving

ARRIVALS > ARRIVAL

ARRIVANCE n old word meaning people who have arrived

ARRIVANCY n arrivance

ARRIVE vb reach a place or destination

ARRIVED > ARRIVE

ARRIVER > ARRIVE

ARRIVERS > ARRIVE

ARRIVES > ARRIVE

ARRIVING > ARRIVE

ARRIVISME n unscrupulous ambition

ARRIVISTE n person who is unscrupulously ambitious

ARROBA n unit of weight

used in some Spanish-speaking countries

ARROBAS > ARROBA

ARROGANCE > ARROGANT

ARROGANCY > ARROGANT

ARROGANT *adj* proud and overbearing

ARROGATE *vb* claim or seize without justification

ARROGATED > ARROGATE

ARROGATES > ARROGATE

ARROGATOR > ARROGATE

ARROW *n* pointed shaft shot from a bow

ARROWED *adj* having an arrow pattern

ARROWHEAD *n* pointed tip of an arrow

ARROWING > ARROW

ARROWLESS > ARROW

ARROWLIKE > ARROW

ARROWROOT *n* nutritious starch obtained from the root of a W Indian plant

ARROWS > ARROW

ARROWWOOD *n* any of various trees or shrubs, esp certain viburnums, having long straight tough stems formerly used by North American Indians to make arrows

ARROWWORM *n* type of small marine invertebrate with an elongated transparent body

ARROWY *adj* like an arrow

ARROYO *n* steep-sided stream bed that is usually dry except after heavy rain

ARROYOS > ARROYO

ARS > AR

ARSE *n* buttocks or anus ▷ *vb* play the fool

ARSED > ARSE

ARSEHOLE *n* anus

ARSEHOLED *adj* very drunk

ARSEHOLES > ARSEHOLE

ARSENAL *n* place where arms and ammunition are made or stored

ARSENALS > ARSENAL

ARSENATE *n* salt or ester of arsenic acid

ARSENATES > ARSENATE

ARSENIATE *n* arsenate

ARSENIC *n* toxic grey element ▷ *adj* of or containing arsenic

ARSENICAL *adj* of or containing arsenic ▷ *n* drug or insecticide containing arsenic

ARSENICS > ARSENIC

ARSENIDE *n* compound in which arsenic is the most electronegative element

ARSENIDES > ARSENIDE

ARSENIOUS *adj* of or containing arsenic in the trivalent state

ARSENITE *n* salt or ester of arsenous acid, esp a salt containing the ion $A_sO_3^{3-}$

ARSENITES > ARSENITE

ARSENO *adj* containing arsenic

ARSENOUS *same as* **>** ARSENIOUS

ARSES > ARSIS

ARSEY *adj* aggressive, irritable, or argumentative

ARSHEEN *n* old measure of length in Russia

ARSHEENS > ARSHEEN

ARSHIN *n* old measure of length in Russia

ARSHINE *n* old measure of length in Russia

ARSHINES > ARSHINE

ARSHINS > ARSHIN

ARSIER > ARSY

ARSIEST > ARSY

ARSINE *n* colourless poisonous gas used in the manufacture of organic compounds, to dope transistors, and as a military poisonous gas

ARSINES > ARSINE

ARSING > ARSE

ARSINO *adj* containing arsine

ARSIS *n* (in classical prosody) the long syllable or part on which the ictus falls in a metrical foot

ARSON *n* crime of intentionally setting property on fire

ARSONIST > ARSON

ARSONISTS > ARSON

ARSONITE *n* person committing arson

ARSONITES > ARSONITE

ARSONOUS *adj* of arson

ARSONS > ARSON

ARSY *same as* **>** ARSEY

ART *n* creation of works of beauty, esp paintings or sculpture

ARTAL *a plural of* **>** ROTL

ARTEFACT *n* something made by human beings

ARTEFACTS > ARTEFACT

ARTEL *n* (in the former Soviet Union) a cooperative union or organization, esp of producers, such as peasants

ARTELS > ARTEL

ARTEMISIA *n* type of herbaceous plant of the N hemisphere, such as mugwort, sagebrush, and wormwood

ARTERIAL *adj* of an artery ▷ *n* major road

ARTERIALS > ARTERIAL

ARTERIES > ARTERY

ARTERIOLE *n* any of the small subdivisions of an artery that form thin-walled vessels ending in capillaries

ARTERITIS *n* inflammation of an artery

ARTERY *n* one of the tubes carrying blood from the heart

ARTESIAN as in *artesian well* well sunk through impermeable strata receiving water from an area at a higher altitude than that of the well

ARTFUL *adj* cunning, wily

ARTFULLY > ARTFUL

ARTHOUSE *n* cinema which shows artistic films

ARTHOUSES > ARTHOUSE

ARTHRITIC > ARTHRITIS

ARTHRITIS *n* painful inflammation of a joint or joints

ARTHRODIA *n* joint

ARTHROPOD *n* animal, such as a spider or insect, with jointed limbs and a segmented body

ARTHROSES > ARTHROSIS

ARTHROSIS *n* disease of joint

ARTI *n* ritual performed in homes and temples in which incense and light is offered to a deity

ARTIC *n* articulated vehicle

ARTICHOKE *n* flower head of a thistle-like plant, cooked as a vegetable

ARTICLE *n* written piece in a magazine or newspaper ▷ *vb* bind by a written contract

ARTICLED > ARTICLE

ARTICLES > ARTICLE

ARTICLING > ARTICLE

ARTICS > ARTIC

ARTICULAR *adj* of or relating to joints

ARTIER > ARTY

ARTIES > ARTY

ARTIEST > ARTY

ARTIFACT *same as* **>** ARTEFACT

ARTIFACTS > ARTIFACT

ARTIFICE *n* clever trick

ARTIFICER *n* craftsman

ARTIFICES > ARTIFICE

ARTILLERY *n* large-calibre guns

ARTILY > ARTY

ARTINESS > ARTY

ARTIS > ARTI

ARTISAN *n* skilled worker, craftsman

ARTISANAL > ARTISAN

ARTISANS > ARTISAN

ARTIST *n* person who produces works of art, esp paintings or sculpture

ARTISTE *n* professional entertainer such as a singer or dancer

ARTISTES > ARTISTE

ARTISTIC *adj* of or characteristic of art or artists

ARTISTRY *n* artistic skill

ARTISTS > ARTIST

ARTLESS *adj* free from deceit or cunning

ARTLESSLY > ARTLESS

ARTS > ART

ARTSIER > ARTSY

ARTSIES > ARTSY

ARTSIEST > ARTSY

ARTSINESS > ARTSY

ARTSMAN *old word for* **>** CRAFTSMAN

ARTSMEN > ARTSMAN

ARTSY *adj* interested in the arts ▷ *n* person interested in the arts

ARTWORK *n* all the photographs and illustrations in a publication

ARTWORKS > ARTWORK

ARTY *adj* having an affected interest in art ▷ *n* person interested in art

ARUGOLA *n* salad plant

ARUGOLAS > ARUGOLA

ARUGULA *another name for* **>** ROCKET

ARUGULAS > ARUGULA

ARUHE *n* edible root of a fern

ARUHES > ARUHE

ARUM *n* type of plant with arrow-shaped leaves and a typically white spathe

ARUMS > ARUM

ARUSPEX *variant spelling of* **>** HARUSPEX

ARUSPICES > ARUSPEX

ARVAL *adj* of ploughed land

ARVICOLE *n* water rat

ARVICOLES > ARVICOLE

ARVO *n* afternoon

ARVOS > ARVO

ARY *dialect form of* **>** ANY

ARYBALLOS *n* ancient Greek flask

ARYL *n* of, consisting of, or containing an aromatic group

ARYLS > ARYL

ARYTENOID *adj* denoting either of two small cartilages of the larynx that are attached to the vocal cords ▷ *n* arytenoid cartilage or muscle

ARYTHMIA *n* any variation

ARYTHMIAS > ARYTHMIA

ARYTHMIC > ARYTHMIA

AS *adv* used to indicate amount or extent in comparisons ▷ *n* ancient Roman unit of weight

ASAFETIDA *n* bitter resin with an unpleasant onion-like smell

ASANA *n* any of various postures in yoga

ASANAS > ASANA

ASAR > AS

ASARUM *n* dried strong-scented root of the wild ginger plant: a flavouring agent and source of an aromatic oil used in perfumery, formerly used in medicine

ASARUMS > ASARUM

ASBESTIC > ASBESTOS

ASBESTINE > ASBESTOS

ASBESTOS n fibrous mineral which does not burn

ASBESTOUS > ASBESTOS

ASBESTUS n asbestos

ASCARED adj afraid

ASCARID n type of parasitic nematode worm, such as the common roundworm

ASCARIDES > ASCARID

ASCARIDS > ASCARID

ASCARIS n ascarid

ASCAUNT adv old word meaning slantwise

ASCEND vb go or move up

ASCENDANT adj dominant or influential

ASCENDED > ASCEND

ASCENDENT same as > ASCENDANT

ASCENDER n part of certain lower-case letters, such as b or h, that extends above the body of the letter

ASCENDERS > ASCENDER

ASCENDEUR n metal grip that is threaded on a rope and can be alternately tightened and slackened as an aid to climbing the rope: used attached to slings for the feet and waist

ASCENDING adj moving upwards

ASCENDS > ASCEND

ASCENSION n act of ascending

ASCENSIVE adj moving upwards

ASCENT n ascending

ASCENTS > ASCENT

ASCERTAIN vb find out definitely

ASCESES > ASCESIS

ASCESIS n exercise of self-discipline

ASCETIC adj (person) abstaining from worldly pleasures and comforts ▷ n person who abstains from worldly comforts and pleasures

ASCETICAL ascetic

ASCETICS > ASCETIC

ASCI > ASCUS

ASCIAN n person living in the tropics

ASCIANS > ASCIAN

ASCIDIA > ASCIDIUM

ASCIDIAN n type of minute marine invertebrate, such as the sea squirt

ASCIDIANS > ASCIDIAN

ASCIDIATE > ASCIDIUM

ASCIDIUM n part of a plant that is shaped like a pitcher, such as the modified leaf of the pitcher plant

ASCITES n accumulation of serous fluid in the peritoneal cavity

ASCITIC > ASCITES

ASCITICAL > ASCITES

ASCLEPIAD n Greek verse form

ASCLEPIAS n type of plant often grown as a garden or greenhouse plant for its showy orange-scarlet or purple flowers

ASCOCARP n (in some ascomycetous fungi) a globular structure containing the asci

ASCOCARPS > ASCOCARP

ASCOGONIA n female reproductive bodies in some fungi

ASCONCE adv old form of askance

ASCORBATE n salt of ascorbic acid

ASCORBIC as in ascorbic acid white crystalline vitamin present in plants, esp citrus fruits, tomatoes, and green vegetables

ASCOSPORE n one of the spores (usually eight in number) that are produced in an ascus

ASCOT n cravat with wide square ends, usually secured with an ornamental stud

ASCOTS > ASCOT

ASCRIBE vb attribute, as to a particular origin

ASCRIBED > ASCRIBE

ASCRIBES > ASCRIBE

ASCRIBING > ASCRIBE

ASCUS n saclike structure that produces (usually) eight ascospores during sexual reproduction in ascomycetous fungi such as yeasts and mildews

ASDIC an early form of > SONAR

ASDICS > ASDIC

ASEA adv towards the sea

ASEISMIC adj denoting a region free of earthquakes

ASEITIES > ASEITY

ASEITY n existence derived from itself, having no other source

ASEPALOUS adj (of a plant or flower) having no sepals

ASEPSES > ASEPSIS

ASEPSIS n aseptic condition

ASEPTATE adj not divided into cells or sections by septa

ASEPTIC adj free from harmful bacteria ▷ n aseptic substance

ASEPTICS > ASEPTIC

ASEXUAL adj without sex

ASEXUALLY > ASEXUAL

ASH n powdery substance left when something is burnt ▷ vb reduce to ashes

ASHAKE adv shaking

ASHAME vb make ashamed

ASHAMED adj feeling shame

ASHAMEDLY > ASHAMED

ASHAMES > ASHAME

ASHAMING > ASHAME

ASHCAKE n cornmeal bread

ASHCAKES > ASHCAKE

ASHCAN n large metal dustbin

ASHCANS > ASHCAN

ASHED > ASH

ASHEN adj pale with shock

ASHERIES > ASHERY

ASHERY n place where ashes are made

ASHES > ASH

ASHET n shallow oval dish or large plate

ASHETS > ASHET

ASHFALL n dropping of ash from a volcano

ASHFALLS > ASHFALL

ASHIER > ASHY

ASHIEST > ASHY

ASHINE adv old word meaning shining

ASHINESS > ASHY

ASHING > ASH

ASHIVER adv shivering

ASHKEY n winged fruit of the ash

ASHKEYS > ASHKEY

ASHLAR n square block of hewn stone used in building ▷ vb build with ashlars

ASHLARED > ASHLAR

ASHLARING > ASHLAR

ASHLARS > ASHLAR

ASHLER same as > ASHLAR

ASHLERED > ASHLER

ASHLERING > ASHLER

ASHLERS > ASHLER

ASHLESS > ASH

ASHMAN n man who shovels ashes

ASHMEN > ASHMAN

ASHORE adv towards or on land ▷ adj on land, having come from the water

ASHPLANT n walking stick made from an ash sapling

ASHPLANTS > ASHPLANT

ASHRAF > SHERIF

ASHRAM n religious retreat where a Hindu holy man lives

ASHRAMA n stage in Hindu spiritual life

ASHRAMAS > ASHRAMA

ASHRAMITE n person living in an ashram

ASHRAMS > ASHRAM

ASHTANGA n type of yoga

ASHTANGAS > ASHTANGA

ASHTRAY n receptacle for tobacco ash and cigarette butts

ASHTRAYS > ASHTRAY

ASHY adj pale greyish

ASIAGO n either of two varieties (ripened or fresh) of a cow's-milk cheese produced in NE Italy

ASIAGOS > ASIAGO

ASIDE adv one side ▷ n remark not meant to be heard by everyone present

ASIDES > ASIDE

ASINICO n old Spanish word for fool

ASINICOS > ASINICO

ASININE adj stupid, idiotic

ASININELY > ASININE

ASININITY > ASININE

ASK vb say or write (something) in a form that requires an answer

ASKANCE adv with an oblique glance ▷ vb turn aside

ASKANCED > ASKANCE

ASKANCES > ASKANCE

ASKANCING > ASKANCE

ASKANT same as > ASKANCE

ASKANTED > ASKANT

ASKANTING > ASKANT

ASKANTS > ASKANT

ASKARI n (in East Africa) a soldier or policeman

ASKARIS > ASKARI

ASKED > ASK

ASKER > ASK

ASKERS > ASK

ASKESES > ASKESIS

ASKESIS n practice of self-discipline

ASKEW adj one side, crooked

ASKEWNESS > ASKEW

ASKING > ASK

ASKINGS > ASK

ASKLENT Scots word for > ASLANT

ASKOI > ASKOS

ASKOS n ancient Greek vase

ASKS > ASK

ASLAKE vb slake

ASLAKED > ASLAKE

ASLAKES > ASLAKE

ASLAKING > ASLAKE

ASLANT adv at a slant (to), slanting (across)

ASLEEP adj sleeping

ASLOPE adj sloping

ASLOSH adj awash

ASMEAR adj smeared

ASMOULDER adv old word meaning smouldering

ASOCIAL n person who avoids social contact

ASOCIALS > ASOCIAL

ASP n small poisonous snake

ASPARAGUS n plant whose shoots are cooked as a vegetable

ASPARKLE adv sparkling

ASPARTAME n artificial sweetener

ASPARTATE n enzyme found in blood

ASPARTIC as in aspartic acid nonessential amino acid that is a component of proteins and acts as a neurotransmitter

ASPECT *n* feature or element ▷ *vb* look at
ASPECTED > ASPECT
ASPECTING > ASPECT
ASPECTS > ASPECT
ASPECTUAL *adj* of or relating to grammatical aspect
ASPEN *n* kind of poplar tree ▷ *adj* trembling
ASPENS > ASPEN
ASPER *n* former Turkish monetary unit, a silver coin, worth 1/120 of a piastre
ASPERATE *adj* (of plant parts) having a rough surface due to a covering of short stiff hairs ▷ *vb* make rough
ASPERATED > ASPERATE
ASPERATES > ASPERATE
ASPERGE *vb* sprinkle
ASPERGED > ASPERGE
ASPERGER > ASPERGE
ASPERGERS > ASPERGE
ASPERGES > ASPERGE
ASPERGILL *n* perforated instrument used to sprinkle holy water
ASPERGING > ASPERGE
ASPERITY *n* roughness of temper
ASPERMIA *n* failure to form or emit semen
ASPERMIAS > ASPERMIA
ASPEROUS same as > ASPERATE
ASPERS > ASPER
ASPERSE *vb* spread false rumours about
ASPERSED > ASPERSE
ASPERSER > ASPERSE
ASPERSERS > ASPERSE
ASPERSES > ASPERSE
ASPERSING > ASPERSE
ASPERSION *n* disparaging or malicious remark
ASPERSIVE > ASPERSE
ASPERSOIR *n* sprinkler for holy water
ASPERSOR > ASPERSE
ASPERSORS > ASPERSE
ASPERSORY *n* sprinkler for holy water
ASPHALT *n* black hard tarlike substance used for road surfaces etc ▷ *vb* cover with asphalt
ASPHALTED > ASPHALT
ASPHALTER *n* person who lays asphalt
ASPHALTIC > ASPHALT
ASPHALTS > ASPHALT
ASPHALTUM *n* asphalt
ASPHERIC *adj* not spherical
ASPHODEL *n* plant with clusters of yellow or white flowers
ASPHODELS > ASPHODEL
ASPHYXIA *n* suffocation
ASPHYXIAL > ASPHYXIA
ASPHYXIAS > ASPHYXIA

ASPHYXIES > ASPHYXY
ASPHYXY *n* same as > ASPHYXIA
ASPIC *n* savoury jelly used to coat meat, eggs, fish, etc
ASPICK old word for > ASP
ASPICKS > ASPICK
ASPICS > ASPIC
ASPIDIA > ASPIDIUM
ASPIDIOID > ASPIDIUM
ASPIDIUM *n* variety of fern
ASPINE old word for > ASPEN
ASPINES > ASPINE
ASPIRANT *n* person who aspires ▷ *adj* aspiring or striving
ASPIRANTS > ASPIRANT
ASPIRATA *n* rough stop
ASPIRATAE > ASPIRATA
ASPIRATE *vb* pronounce with an *h* sound ▷ *n* *h* sound ▷ *adj* (of a stop) pronounced with a forceful and audible expulsion of breath
ASPIRATED > ASPIRATE
ASPIRATES > ASPIRATE
ASPIRATOR *n* device for removing fluids from a body cavity by suction
ASPIRE *vb* yearn (for), hope (to do or be)
ASPIRED > ASPIRE
ASPIRER > ASPIRE
ASPIRERS > ASPIRE
ASPIRES > ASPIRE
ASPIRIN *n* drug used to relieve pain and fever
ASPIRING > ASPIRE
ASPIRINS > ASPIRIN
ASPIS *n* horned viper
ASPISES > ASPIS
ASPISH *adj* like an asp
ASPLENIUM *n* type of fern
ASPORT *vb* old word meaning take away
ASPORTED > ASPORT
ASPORTING > ASPORT
ASPORTS > ASPORT
ASPOUT *adv* spouting
ASPRAWL *adv* sprawling
ASPREAD *adv* spreading
ASPRO *n* associate professor at an academic institution
ASPROS > ASPRO
ASPROUT *adv* sprouting
ASPS > ASP
ASQUAT *adv* squatting
ASQUINT *adj* with a glance from the corner of the eye, esp a furtive one
ASRAMA *n* stage in Hindu spiritual life
ASRAMAS > ASRAMA
ASS *n* donkey
ASSAGAI same as > ASSEGAI
ASSAGAIED > ASSAGAI
ASSAGAIS > ASSAGAI
ASSAI *adv* (usually preceded by a musical direction) very ▷ *n* Brazilian

palm tree with small dark purple fleshy edible fruit
ASSAIL *vb* attack violently
ASSAILANT *n* person who attacks another, either physically or verbally
ASSAILED > ASSAIL
ASSAILER > ASSAIL
ASSAILERS > ASSAIL
ASSAILING > ASSAIL
ASSAILS > ASSAIL
ASSAIS > ASSAI
ASSAM *n* (in Malaysia) tamarind as used in cooking
ASSAMS > ASSAM
ASSART *vb* clear ground for cultivation
ASSARTED > ASSART
ASSARTING > ASSART
ASSARTS > ASSART
ASSASSIN *n* person who murders a prominent person
ASSASSINS > ASSASSIN
ASSAULT *n* violent attack ▷ *vb* attack violently
ASSAULTED > ASSAULT
ASSAULTER > ASSAULT
ASSAULTS > ASSAULT
ASSAY *n* analysis of a substance, esp a metal, to ascertain its purity ▷ *vb* make such an analysis
ASSAYABLE > ASSAY
ASSAYED > ASSAY
ASSAYER > ASSAY
ASSAYERS > ASSAY
ASSAYING > ASSAY
ASSAYINGS > ASSAY
ASSAYS > ASSAY
ASSEGAAI same as > ASSEGAI
ASSEGAAIS > ASSEGAI
ASSEGAI *n* slender spear used in S Africa ▷ *vb* spear with an assegai
ASSEGAIED > ASSEGAI
ASSEGAIS > ASSEGAI
ASSEMBLE *vb* collect or congregate
ASSEMBLED > ASSEMBLE
ASSEMBLER *n* person or thing that assembles
ASSEMBLES > ASSEMBLE
ASSEMBLY *n* assembled group
ASSENT *n* agreement or consent ▷ *vb* agree or consent
ASSENTED > ASSENT
ASSENTER *n* person supporting another's nomination
ASSENTERS > ASSENTER
ASSENTING > ASSENT
ASSENTIVE > ASSENT
ASSENTOR *n* any of the eight voters legally required to endorse the nomination of a candidate in a parliamentary or local election in addition to the nominator and seconder

ASSENTORS > ASSENTOR
ASSENTS > ASSENT
ASSERT *vb* declare forcefully
ASSERTED > ASSERT
ASSERTER > ASSERT
ASSERTERS > ASSERT
ASSERTING > ASSERT
ASSERTION *n* positive statement, usu. made without evidence
ASSERTIVE *adj* confident and direct in dealing with others
ASSERTOR > ASSERT
ASSERTORS > ASSERT
ASSERTORY *adj* making affirmation
ASSERTS > ASSERT
ASSES > ASS
ASSESS *vb* judge the worth or importance of
ASSESSED > ASSESS
ASSESSES > ASSESS
ASSESSING > ASSESS
ASSESSOR *n* person who values property for taxation or insurance purposes
ASSESSORS > ASSESSOR
ASSET *n* valuable or useful person or thing
ASSETLESS > ASSET
ASSETS > ASSET
ASSEVER *vb* old form of asseverate
ASSEVERED > ASSEVER
ASSEVERS > ASSEVER
ASSEZ *adv* (as part of a musical direction) fairly
ASSHOLE same as > ARSEHOLE
ASSHOLES > ASSHOLE
ASSIDUITY *n* constant and close application
ASSIDUOUS *adj* hard-working
ASSIEGE *vb* old form of besiege
ASSIEGED > ASSIEGE
ASSIEGES > ASSIEGE
ASSIEGING > ASSIEGE
ASSIENTO *n* slave trade treaty between Britain and Spain
ASSIENTOS > ASSIENTO
ASSIGN *vb* appoint (someone) to a job or task ▷ *n* person to whom property is assigned
ASSIGNAT *n* paper money issued by the Constituent Assembly in 1789, backed by the confiscated land of the Church and the émigrés
ASSIGNATS > ASSIGNAT
ASSIGNED > ASSIGN
ASSIGNEE *n* person to whom some right, interest, or property is transferred
ASSIGNEES > ASSIGNEE
ASSIGNER > ASSIGN
ASSIGNERS > ASSIGN
ASSIGNING > ASSIGN

ASSIGNOR n person who transfers or assigns property

ASSIGNORS > ASSIGNOR

ASSIGNS > ASSIGN

ASSIST vb give help or support ▷ n pass by a player which enables another player to score a goal

ASSISTANT n helper ▷ adj junior or deputy

ASSISTED > ASSIST

ASSISTER > ASSIST

ASSISTERS > ASSIST

ASSISTING > ASSIST

ASSISTIVE adj providing a means of reducing a physical impairment

ASSISTOR > ASSIST

ASSISTORS > ASSIST

ASSISTS > ASSIST

ASSIZE n sitting of a legislative assembly or administrative body

ASSIZED > ASSIZE

ASSIZER n weights and measures official

ASSIZERS > ASSIZER

ASSIZES > ASSIZE

ASSIZING > ASSIZE

ASSLIKE > ASS

ASSOCIATE vb connect in the mind ▷ n partner in business ▷ adj having partial rights or subordinate status

ASSOIL vb absolve

ASSOILED > ASSOIL

ASSOILING > ASSOIL

ASSOILS > ASSOIL

ASSOILZIE vb old Scots word meaning absolve

ASSONANCE n rhyming of vowel sounds but not consonants

ASSONANT > ASSONANCE

ASSONANTS > ASSONANCE

ASSONATE vb show assonance

ASSONATED > ASSONATE

ASSONATES > ASSONATE

ASSORT vb arrange or distribute into groups of the same type

ASSORTED adj consisting of various types mixed together

ASSORTER > ASSORT

ASSORTERS > ASSORT

ASSORTING > ASSORT

ASSORTIVE > ASSORT

ASSORTS > ASSORT

ASSOT vb old word meaning make infatuated

ASSOTS > ASSOT

ASSOTT vb besot

ASSOTTED > ASSOT

ASSOTTING > ASSOT

ASSUAGE vb relieve (pain, grief, thirst, etc)

ASSUAGED > ASSUAGE

ASSUAGER > ASSUAGE

ASSUAGERS > ASSUAGE

ASSUAGES > ASSUAGE

ASSUAGING > ASSUAGE

ASSUASIVE > ASSUAGE

ASSUETUDE n state of being accustomed

ASSUMABLE > ASSUME

ASSUMABLY > ASSUME

ASSUME vb take to be true without proof

ASSUMED adj false

ASSUMEDLY > ASSUME

ASSUMER > ASSUME

ASSUMERS > ASSUME

ASSUMES > ASSUME

ASSUMING adj expecting too much ▷ n action of one who assumes

ASSUMINGS > ASSUMING

ASSUMPSIT n (before 1875) an action to recover damages for breach of an express or implied contract or agreement that was not under seal

ASSURABLE > ASSURE

ASSURANCE n assuring or being assured

ASSURE vb promise or guarantee

ASSURED adj confident ▷ n beneficiary under a life assurance policy

ASSUREDLY > ASSURED

ASSUREDS > ASSURED

ASSURER > ASSURE

ASSURERS > ASSURE

ASSURES > ASSURE

ASSURGENT adj (of leaves, stems, etc) curving or growing upwards

ASSURING > ASSURE

ASSUROR > ASSURE

ASSURORS > ASSURE

ASSWAGE old spelling of > ASSUAGE

ASSWAGED > ASSWAGE

ASSWAGES > ASSWAGE

ASSWAGING > ASSWAGE

ASTABLE adj not stable

ASTARE adv staring

ASTART old word for > START

ASTARTED > ASTART

ASTARTING > ASTART

ASTARTS > ASTART

ASTASIA n inability to stand

ASTASIAS > ASTASIA

ASTATIC adj not static

ASTATIDE n binary compound of astatine with a more electropositive element

ASTATIDES > ASTATIDE

ASTATINE n radioactive nonmetallic element

ASTATINES > ASTATINE

ASTATKI n fuel derived from petroleum

ASTATKIS > ASTATKI

ASTEISM n use of irony

ASTEISMS > ASTEISM

ASTELIC > ASTELY

ASTELIES > ASTELY

ASTELY n lack of central cylinder in plants

ASTER n plant with daisy-like flowers

ASTERIA n gemstone with starlike light effect

ASTERIAS > ASTERIA

ASTERID n variety of flowering plant

ASTERIDS > ASTERID

ASTERISK n star-shaped symbol (*) used in printing or writing to indicate a footnote, etc ▷ vb mark with an asterisk

ASTERISKS > ASTERISK

ASTERISM n three asterisks arranged in a triangle to draw attention to the text that follows

ASTERISMS > ASTERISM

ASTERN adv at or towards the stern of a ship ▷ adj at or towards the stern of a ship

ASTERNAL adj not connected or joined to the sternum

ASTEROID n any of the small planets that orbit the sun between Mars and Jupiter ▷ adj of, relating to, or belonging to the class Asteroidea

ASTEROIDS > ASTEROID

ASTERS > ASTER

ASTERT vb start

ASTERTED > ASTERT

ASTERTING > ASTERT

ASTERTS > ASTERT

ASTHENIA n abnormal loss of strength

ASTHENIAS > ASTHENIA

ASTHENIC adj of, relating to, or having asthenia ▷ n person having long limbs and a small trunk

ASTHENICS > ASTHENIC

ASTHENIES > ASTHENY

ASTHENY same as > ASTHENIA

ASTHMA n illness causing difficulty in breathing

ASTHMAS > ASTHMA

ASTHMATIC adj of, relating to, or having asthma ▷ n person who has asthma

ASTHORE n Irish endearment

ASTHORES > ASTHORE

ASTICHOUS adj not arranged in rows

ASTIGMIA n defect of a lens resulting in the formation of distorted images

ASTIGMIAS > ASTIGMIA

ASTILBE n E Asian and N American plant cultivated for its ornamental spikes of pink or white flowers

ASTILBES > ASTILBE

ASTIR adj out of bed

ASTOMATAL adj having no stomata

ASTOMOUS adj having no mouth

ASTONE vb old form of > ASTONISH

ASTONED > ASTONE

ASTONES > ASTONE

ASTONIED adj stunned

ASTONIES > ASTONY

ASTONING > ASTONE

ASTONISH vb surprise greatly

ASTONY vb old form of > ASTONISH

ASTONYING > ASTONY

ASTOOP adv stooping

ASTOUND vb overwhelm with amazement

ASTOUNDED > ASTOUND

ASTOUNDS > ASTOUND

ASTRACHAN same as > ASTRAKHAN

ASTRADDLE adj with a leg on either side of something

ASTRAGAL n small convex moulding, usually with a semicircular cross section

ASTRAGALI n bones of the ankles that articulate with the leg bones to form ankle joints

ASTRAGALS > ASTRAGAL

ASTRAKHAN n dark curly fleece of lambs from Astrakhan in Russia

ASTRAL adj of stars ▷ n oil lamp

ASTRALLY > ASTRAL

ASTRALS > ASTRAL

ASTRAND adv on shore

ASTRANTIA n flowering plant

ASTRAY adv off the right path

ASTRICT vb bind, confine, or constrict

ASTRICTED > ASTRICT

ASTRICTS > ASTRICT

ASTRIDE adv with a leg on either side (of) ▷ adj with a leg on either side

ASTRINGE vb cause contraction

ASTRINGED > ASTRINGE

ASTRINGER n person who keeps goshawks

ASTRINGES > ASTRINGE

ASTROCYTE n any of the star-shaped cells in the tissue supporting the brain and spinal cord (neuroglia)

ASTRODOME n transparent dome on the top of an aircraft, through which observations can be made, esp of the stars

ASTROFELL n plant in Spenser's poetry

ASTROID n hypocycloid having four cusps

ASTROIDS > ASTROID

ASTROLABE n instrument formerly used to measure

the altitude of stars and planets

ASTROLOGY n study of the alleged influence of the stars, planets, and moon on human affairs

ASTRONAUT n person trained for travelling in space

ASTRONOMY n scientific study of heavenly bodies

ASTROPHEL n plant in Spenser's poetry

ASTRUT adv old word meaning in a protruding way

ASTUCIOUS adj old form of astute

ASTUCITY n quality of being astute

ASTUN vb old form of astonish

ASTUNNED > ASTUN

ASTUNNING > ASTUN

ASTUNS > ASTUN

ASTUTE adj perceptive or shrewd

ASTUTELY > ASTUTE

ASTUTER > ASTUTE

ASTUTEST > ASTUTE

ASTYLAR adj without columns or pilasters

ASUDDEN adv old form of suddenly

ASUNDER adv into parts or pieces ▷ adj into parts or pieces

ASWARM adj filled, esp with moving things

ASWAY adv swaying

ASWIM adv floating

ASWING adv swinging

ASWIRL adv swirling

ASWOON adv swooning

ASYLA > ASYLUM

ASYLEE n person who is granted asylum

ASYLEES > ASYLEE

ASYLLABIC adj not functioning in the manner of a syllable

ASYLUM n refuge or sanctuary

ASYLUMS > ASYLUM

ASYMMETRY n lack of symmetry

ASYMPTOTE n straight line closely approached but never met by a curve

ASYNAPSES > ASYNAPSIS

ASYNAPSIS n failure of pairing of chromosomes at meiosis

ASYNDETA > ASYNDETON

ASYNDETIC adj (of a catalogue or index) without cross references

ASYNDETON n omission of a conjunction between the parts of a sentence

ASYNERGIA n lack of coordination between muscles or parts, as occurs in cerebellar disease

ASYNERGY same as **>** ASYNERGIA

ASYSTOLE n absence of heartbeat

ASYSTOLES > ASYSTOLE

ASYSTOLIC > ASYSTOLE

AT n Laotian monetary unit worth one hundredth of a kip

ATAATA n grazing marine gastropod

ATAATAS > ATAATA

ATABAL n N African drum

ATABALS > ATABAL

ATABEG n Turkish ruler

ATABEGS > ATABEG

ATABEK n Turkish ruler

ATABEKS > ATABEK

ATABRIN n drug formerly used for treating malaria

ATABRINE same as **>** ATABRIN

ATABRINES > ATABRINE

ATABRINS > ATABRINE

ATACAMITE n mineral containing copper

ATACTIC adj (of a polymer) having a random sequence of the stereochemical arrangement of groups or carbon atoms in the chain

ATAGHAN a variant of **>** YATAGHAN

ATAGHANS > ATAGHAN

ATALAYA n watchtower in Spain

ATALAYAS > ATALAYA

ATAMAN n elected leader of the Cossacks

ATAMANS > ATAMAN

ATAMASCO n N American lily

ATAMASCOS > ATAMASCO

ATAP n palm tree of S Asia

ATAPS > ATAP

ATARACTIC adj able to calm or tranquillize ▷ n ataractic drug

ATARAXIA n calmness or peace of mind

ATARAXIAS > ATARAXIA

ATARAXIC same as **>** ATARACTIC

ATARAXICS > ATARAXIC

ATARAXIES > ATARAXY

ATARAXY same as **>** ATARAXIA

ATAVIC > ATAVISM

ATAVISM n recurrence of a trait present in distant ancestors

ATAVISMS > ATAVISM

ATAVIST > ATAVISM

ATAVISTIC adj of or relating to reversion to a former or more primitive type

ATAVISTS > ATAVISM

ATAXIA n lack of muscular coordination

ATAXIAS > ATAXIA

ATAXIC > ATAXIA

ATAXICS > ATAXIA

ATAXIES > ATAXY

ATAXY same as **>** ATAXIA

ATCHIEVE vb old form of **>** ACHIEVE

ATCHIEVED > ATCHIEVE

ATCHIEVES > ATCHIEVE

ATE past tense of **>** EAT

ATEBRIN n drug formerly used to treat malaria

ATEBRINS > ATEBRIN

ATECHNIC adj without technical ability

ATELIC adj of action without end

ATELIER n workshop, artist's studio

ATELIERS > ATELIER

ATEMOYA n tropical fruit tree

ATEMOYAS > ATEMOYA

ATEMPORAL adj not governed by time

ATENOLOL n type of beta-blocker

ATENOLOLS > ATENOLOL

ATES n shop selling confectionery

ATHAME n (in Wicca) witch's ceremonial knife, usually with a black handle, used in rituals rather than for cutting or carving

ATHAMES > ATHAME

ATHANASY n absence of death

ATHANOR n alchemist's furnace

ATHANORS > ATHANOR

ATHEISE vb speak atheistically

ATHEISED > ATHEISE

ATHEISES > ATHEISE

ATHEISING > ATHEISE

ATHEISM n belief that there is no God

ATHEISMS > ATHEISM

ATHEIST > ATHEISM

ATHEISTIC > ATHEISM

ATHEISTS > ATHEISM

ATHEIZE vb speak atheistically

ATHEIZED > ATHEIZE

ATHEIZES > ATHEIZE

ATHEIZING > ATHEIZE

ATHELING n (in Anglo-Saxon England) a prince of any of the royal dynasties

ATHELINGS > ATHELING

ATHEMATIC adj not based on themes

ATHENAEUM n institution for the promotion of learning

ATHENEUM same as **>** ATHENAEUM

ATHENEUMS > ATHENEUM

ATHEOLOGY n opposition to theology

ATHEOUS adj without a belief in god

ATHERINE n small fish

ATHERINES > ATHERINE

ATHEROMA n fatty deposit on or within the inner lining of an artery, often causing

an obstruction to the blood flow

ATHEROMAS > ATHEROMA

ATHETESES > ATHETESIS

ATHETESIS n dismissal of a text as not genuine

ATHETISE vb reject as not genuine

ATHETISED > ATHETISE

ATHETISES > ATHETISE

ATHETIZE vb reject as not genuine

ATHETIZED > ATHETIZE

ATHETIZES > ATHETIZE

ATHETOID > ATHETOSIS

ATHETOSES > ATHETOSIS

ATHETOSIC > ATHETOSIS

ATHETOSIS n condition characterized by uncontrolled rhythmic writhing movement, esp of fingers, hands, head, and tongue, caused by cerebral lesion

ATHETOTIC > ATHETOSIS

ATHIRST adj having an eager desire

ATHLETA n old form of **>** ATHLETE

ATHLETAS > ATHLETA

ATHLETE n person trained in or good at athletics

ATHLETES > ATHLETE

ATHLETIC adj physically fit or strong

ATHLETICS n track and field events

ATHODYD another name for **>** RAMJET

ATHODYDS > ATHODYD

ATHRILL adv feeling thrills

ATHROB adv throbbing

ATHROCYTE n cell able to store matter

ATHWART adv transversely

ATIGI n type of parka worn by the Inuit in Canada

ATIGIS > ATIGI

ATILT adj in a tilted or inclined position

ATIMIES > ATIMY

ATIMY n loss of honour

ATINGLE adv tingling

ATISHOO n sound of a sneeze

ATISHOOS > ATISHOO

ATLANTES > ATLAS

ATLAS n book of maps

ATLASES > ATLAS

ATLATL n Native American throwing stick

ATLATLS > ATLATL

ATMA same as **>** ATMAN

ATMAN n personal soul or self

ATMANS > ATMAN

ATMAS > ATMA

ATMOLOGY n study of aqueous vapour

ATMOLYSE vb separate gases by filtering

ATMOLYSED > ATMOLYSE
ATMOLYSES > ATMOLYSIS
ATMOLYSIS *n* method of separating gases that depends on their differential rates of diffusion through a porous substance
ATMOLYZE *vb* separate gases by filtering
ATMOLYZED > ATMOLYZE
ATMOLYZES > ATMOLYZE
ATMOMETER *n* instrument for measuring the rate of evaporation of water into the atmosphere
ATMOMETRY > ATMOMETER
ATOC *n* skunk
ATOCIA *n* inability to have children
ATOCIAS > ATOCIA
ATOCS > ATOC
ATOK *n* skunk
ATOKAL *adj* having no children
ATOKE *n* part of a worm
ATOKES > ATOKE
ATOKOUS *adj* having no children
ATOKS > ATOK
ATOLL *n* ring-shaped coral reef enclosing a lagoon
ATOLLS > ATOLL
ATOM *n* smallest unit of matter which can take part in a chemical reaction
ATOMIC *adj* of or using atomic bombs or atomic energy
ATOMICAL > ATOMIC
ATOMICITY *n* state of being made up of atoms
ATOMICS *n* science of atoms
ATOMIES > ATOMY
ATOMISE *same as*
> ATOMIZE
ATOMISED > ATOMISE
ATOMISER *same as*
> ATOMIZER
ATOMISERS > ATOMISER
ATOMISES > ATOMISE
ATOMISING > ATOMISE
ATOMISM *n* ancient philosophical theory that the ultimate constituents of the universe are atoms
ATOMISMS > ATOMISM
ATOMIST > ATOMISM
ATOMISTIC > ATOMISM
ATOMISTS > ATOMISM
ATOMIZE *vb* reduce to atoms or small particles
ATOMIZED > ATOMIZE
ATOMIZER *n* device for discharging a liquid in a fine spray
ATOMIZERS > ATOMIZER
ATOMIZES > ATOMIZE
ATOMIZING > ATOMIZE
ATOMS > ATOM
ATOMY *n* atom or minute particle

ATONABLE > ATONE
ATONAL *adj* (of music) not written in an established key
ATONALISM > ATONAL
ATONALIST > ATONAL
ATONALITY *n* absence of or disregard for an established musical key in a composition
ATONALLY > ATONAL
ATONE *vb* make amends (for sin or wrongdoing)
ATONEABLE > ATONE
ATONED > ATONE
ATONEMENT *n* something done to make amends for wrongdoing
ATONER > ATONE
ATONERS > ATONE
ATONES > ATONE
ATONIA *n* lack of normal muscle tone
ATONIAS > ATONIA
ATONIC *adj* (of a syllable, word, etc) carrying no stress ▷ *n* unaccented or unstressed syllable, word
ATONICITY > ATONIC
ATONICS > ATONIC
ATONIES > ATONY
ATONING > ATONE
ATONINGLY > ATONE
ATONY *n* lack of normal tone or tension, as in muscles
ATOP *adv* on top
ATOPIC *adj* of or relating to hereditary hypersensitivity to certain allergens
ATOPIES > ATOPY
ATOPY *n* hereditary tendency to be hypersensitive to certain allergens
ATRAMENT *n* old word meaning black liquid
ATRAMENTS > ATRAMENT
ATRAZINE *n* white crystalline compound
ATRAZINES > ATRAZINE
ATREMBLE *adv* trembling
ATRESIA *n* absence of or unnatural narrowing of a body channel
ATRESIAS > ATRESIA
ATRESIC > ATRESIA
ATRETIC > ATRESIA
ATRIA > ATRIUM
ATRIAL > ATRIUM
ATRIP *adj* (of an anchor) no longer caught on the bottom
ATRIUM *n* upper chamber of either half of the heart
ATRIUMS > ATRIUM
ATROCIOUS *adj* extremely cruel or wicked
ATROCITY *n* wickedness
ATROPHIA *n* wasting disease
ATROPHIAS > ATROPHIA
ATROPHIC > ATROPHY
ATROPHIED > ATROPHY

ATROPHIES > ATROPHY
ATROPHY *n* wasting away of an organ or part ▷ *vb* (cause to) waste away
ATROPIA *n* atropine
ATROPIAS > ATROPIA
ATROPIN *same as*
> ATROPINE
ATROPINE *n* poisonous alkaloid obtained from deadly nightshade
ATROPINES > ATROPINE
ATROPINS > ATROPIN
ATROPISM *n* condition caused by using belladonna
ATROPISMS > ATROPISM
ATROPOUS *adj* growing straight
ATS > AT
ATT *n* old Siamese coin
ATTABOY *sentence substitute* expression of approval or exhortation
ATTACH *vb* join, fasten, or connect
ATTACHE *n* a specialist attached to a diplomatic mission
ATTACHED *adj* fond of
ATTACHER > ATTACH
ATTACHERS > ATTACH
ATTACHES > ATTACH
ATTACHING > ATTACH
ATTACK *vb* launch a physical assault (against) ▷ *n* act of attacking
ATTACKED > ATTACK
ATTACKER > ATTACK
ATTACKERS > ATTACK
ATTACKING > ATTACK
ATTACKMAN *n* attacking player in sport
ATTACKMEN
> ATTACKMAN
ATTACKS > ATTACK
ATTAGIRL *humorous feminine version of*
> ATTABOY
ATTAIN *vb* achieve or accomplish (a task or aim)
ATTAINDER *n* (formerly) the extinction of a person's civil rights resulting from a sentence of death or outlawry on conviction for treason or felony
ATTAINED > ATTAIN
ATTAINER > ATTAIN
ATTAINERS > ATTAIN
ATTAINING > ATTAIN
ATTAINS > ATTAIN
ATTAINT *vb* pass judgment of death or outlawry upon (a person) ▷ *n* dishonour
ATTAINTED > ATTAINT
ATTAINTS > ATTAINT
ATTAP *n* palm tree of South Asia
ATTAPS > ATTAP
ATTAR *n* fragrant oil made from roses
ATTARS > ATTAR
ATTASK *old word for*
> CRITICIZE

ATTASKED > ATTASK
ATTASKING > ATTASK
ATTASKS > ATTASK
ATTASKT > ATTASK
ATTEMPER *vb* modify by blending
ATTEMPERS > ATTEMPER
ATTEMPT *vb* try, make an effort ▷ *n* effort or endeavour
ATTEMPTED > ATTEMPT
ATTEMPTER > ATTEMPT
ATTEMPTS > ATTEMPT
ATTEND *vb* be present at
ATTENDANT *n* person who assists, guides, or provides a service ▷ *adj* accompanying
ATTENDED > ATTEND
ATTENDEE *n* person who is present at a specified event
ATTENDEES > ATTENDEE
ATTENDER > ATTEND
ATTENDERS > ATTEND
ATTENDING > ATTEND
ATTENDS > ATTEND
ATTENT *old word for*
> ATTENTION
ATTENTAT *n* attempt
ATTENTATS > ATTENTAT
ATTENTION *n* concentrated direction of the mind
ATTENTIVE *adj* giving attention
ATTENTS > ATTENT
ATTENUANT *adj* causing dilution or thinness, esp of the blood ▷ *n* attenuant drug or agent
ATTENUATE *vb* weaken or become weak ▷ *adj* diluted, weakened, slender, or reduced
ATTERCOP *n* spider
ATTERCOPS > ATTERCOP
ATTEST *vb* affirm the truth of, be proof of
ATTESTANT > ATTEST
ATTESTED *adj* (of cattle) certified to be free from a disease, such as tuberculosis
ATTESTER > ATTEST
ATTESTERS > ATTEST
ATTESTING > ATTEST
ATTESTOR > ATTEST
ATTESTORS > ATTEST
ATTESTS > ATTEST
ATTIC *n* space or room within the roof of a house
ATTICISE *same as*
> ATTICIZE
ATTICISED > ATTICISE
ATTICISES > ATTICISE
ATTICISM *n* elegant, simple, and clear expression
ATTICISMS > ATTICISM
ATTICIST > ATTICISM
ATTICISTS > ATTICISM
ATTICIZE *vb* conform or adapt to the norms of Attica

ATTICIZED > ATTICIZE
ATTICIZES > ATTICIZE
ATTICS > ATTIC
ATTIRE *n* fine or formal clothes ▷ *vb* dress, esp in fine elegant clothes
ATTIRED > ATTIRE
ATTIRES > ATTIRE
ATTIRING > ATTIRE
ATTIRINGS > ATTIRE
ATTITUDE *n* way of thinking and behaving
ATTITUDES > ATTITUDE
ATTOLASER *n* high-power laser capable of producing pulses with a duration measured in attoseconds
ATTOLLENS *adj* (of muscle) used to lift
ATTOLLENT *adj* muscle used in lifting
ATTONCE *adv* old word for at once
ATTONE *vb* old word meaning appease
ATTONED > ATTONE
ATTONES > ATTONE
ATTONING > ATTONE
ATTORN *vb* acknowledge a new owner of land as one's landlord
ATTORNED > ATTORN
ATTORNEY *n* person legally appointed to act for another
ATTORNEYS > ATTORNEY
ATTORNING > ATTORN
ATTORNS > ATTORN
ATTRACT *vb* arouse the interest or admiration of
ATTRACTED > ATTRACT
ATTRACTER > ATTRACT
ATTRACTOR > ATTRACT
ATTRACTS > ATTRACT
ATTRAHENS *adj* (of muscle) drawing towards
ATTRAHENT *adj* something that attracts
ATTRAP *vb* adorn
ATTRAPPED > ATTRAP
ATTRAPS > ATTRAP
ATTRIBUTE *vb* regard as belonging to or produced by ▷ *n* quality or feature representative of a person or thing
ATTRIST *vb* old word meaning to sadden
ATTRISTED > ATTRIST
ATTRISTS > ATTRIST
ATTRIT *vb* wear down or dispose of gradually
ATTRITE *vb* wear down
ATTRITED > ATTRITE
ATTRITES > ATTRITE
ATTRITING > ATTRITE
ATTRITION *n* constant wearing down to weaken or destroy
ATTRITIVE > ATTRITION
ATTRITS > ATTRIT
ATTRITTED > ATTRIT
ATTUENT *adj* carrying out attuition

ATTUITE *vb* perceive by attuition
ATTUITED > ATTUITE
ATTUITES > ATTUITE
ATTUITING > ATTUITE
ATTUITION *n* way of mentally perceiving something
ATTUITIVE > ATTUITION
ATTUNE *vb* adjust or accustom (a person or thing)
ATTUNED > ATTUNE
ATTUNES > ATTUNE
ATTUNING > ATTUNE
ATUA *n* spirit or demon
ATUAS > ATUA
ATWAIN *adv* old word meaning into two parts
ATWEEL *Scots word for* > WELL
ATWEEN *an archaic or Scots word for* > BETWEEN
ATWITTER *adv* twittering
ATWIXT *old word for* > BETWEEN
ATYPIC *adj* not typical
ATYPICAL *adj* not typical
AUA *n* yellow-eye mullet
AUAS > AUA
AUBADE *n* song or poem appropriate to or greeting the dawn
AUBADES > AUBADE
AUBERGE *n* inn or tavern
AUBERGES > AUBERGE
AUBERGINE *n* dark purple tropical fruit, cooked and eaten as a vegetable
AUBRETIA *same as* > AUBRIETIA
AUBRETIAS > AUBRETIA
AUBRIETA *same as* > AUBRIETIA
AUBRIETAS > AUBRIETA
AUBRIETIA *n* trailing plant with purple flowers
AUBURN *adj* (of hair) reddish-brown ▷ *n* moderate reddish-brown colour
AUBURNS > AUBURN
AUCEPS *n* old word meaning person who catches hawks
AUCEPSES > AUCEPS
AUCTION *n* public sale in which articles are sold to the highest bidder ▷ *vb* sell by auction
AUCTIONED > AUCTION
AUCTIONS > AUCTION
AUCTORIAL *adj* of or relating to an author
AUCUBA *n* Japanese laurel
AUCUBAS > AUCUBA
AUDACIOUS *adj* recklessly bold or daring
AUDACITY > AUDACIOUS
AUDAD *n* wild African sheep
AUDADS > AUDAD
AUDIAL *adj* of sound

AUDIBLE *adj* loud enough to be heard ▷ *n* change of playing tactics called by the quarterback when the offence is lined up at the line of scrimmage ▷ *vb* call an audible
AUDIBLED > AUDIBLE
AUDIBLES > AUDIBLE
AUDIBLING > AUDIBLE
AUDIBLY > AUDIBLE
AUDIENCE *n* group of spectators or listeners
AUDIENCES > AUDIENCE
AUDIENCIA *n* court in South America
AUDIENT *n* person who hears
AUDIENTS > AUDIENT
AUDILE *n* person who possesses a faculty for auditory imagery that is more distinct than his visual or other imagery ▷ *adj* of or relating to such a person
AUDILES > AUDILE
AUDING *n* practice of listening to try to understand
AUDINGS > AUDING
AUDIO *adj* of sound or hearing ▷ *n* of or relating to sound or hearing
AUDIOBOOK *n* recorded reading of a book
AUDIOGRAM *n* graphic record of the acuity of hearing of a person obtained by means of an audiometer
AUDIOLOGY *n* scientific study of hearing, often including the treatment of persons with hearing defects
AUDIOPHIL *n* audiophile
AUDIOS > AUDIO
AUDIOTAPE *n* tape for recording sound
AUDIPHONE *n* type of hearing aid consisting of a diaphragm that, when placed against the upper teeth, conveys sound vibrations to the inner ear
AUDIT *n* official examination of business accounts ▷ *vb* examine (business accounts) officially
AUDITABLE > AUDIT
AUDITED > AUDIT
AUDITEE *n* one who is audited
AUDITEES > AUDITEE
AUDITING > AUDIT
AUDITION *n* test of a performer's ability for a particular role or job ▷ *vb* test or be tested in an audition
AUDITIONS > AUDITION
AUDITIVE *n* person who learns primarily by listening

AUDITIVES > AUDITIVE
AUDITOR *n* person qualified to audit accounts
AUDITORIA *n* areas of concert halls, theatres, schools, etc, in which audiences sit
AUDITORS > AUDITOR
AUDITORY *adj* of or relating to hearing
AUDITRESS *n* female auditor
AUDITS > AUDIT
AUE *interj* Māori exclamation
AUF *old word for* > OAF
AUFGABE *n* word used in psychology to mean task
AUFGABES > AUFGABE
AUFS > AUF
AUGEND *n* number to which another number, the addend, is added
AUGENDS > AUGEND
AUGER *n* tool for boring holes
AUGERS > AUGER
AUGHT *adv* in any least part ▷ *n* less common word for 'nought' (zero)
AUGHTS > AUGHT
AUGITE *n* black or greenish-black mineral
AUGITES > AUGITE
AUGITIC > AUGITE
AUGMENT *vb* increase or enlarge ▷ *n* (in Greek and Sanskrit grammar) a vowel or diphthong prefixed to a verb to form a past tense
AUGMENTED > AUGMENT
AUGMENTER > AUGMENT
AUGMENTOR > AUGMENT
AUGMENTS > AUGMENT
AUGUR *vb* be a sign of (future events) ▷ *n* (in ancient Rome) a religious official who observed and interpreted omens and signs to help guide the making of public decisions
AUGURAL > AUGUR
AUGURED > AUGUR
AUGURER *old word for* > AUGUR
AUGURERS > AUGURER
AUGURIES > AUGURY
AUGURING > AUGUR
AUGURS > AUGUR
AUGURSHIP > AUGUR
AUGURY *n* foretelling of the future
AUGUST *adj* dignified and imposing ▷ *n* auguste
AUGUSTE *n* type of circus clown who usually wears battered ordinary clothes and is habitually maladroit or unlucky
AUGUSTER > AUGUST
AUGUSTES > AUGUSTE
AUGUSTEST > AUGUST
AUGUSTLY > AUGUST
AUGUSTS > AUGUST
AUK *n* northern sea bird

with short wings and black-and-white plumage

AUKLET n type of small auk

AUKLETS > AUKLET

AUKS > AUK

AULA n hall

AULARIAN n Oxford University student belonging to hall

AULARIANS > AULARIAN

AULAS > AULA

AULD a Scots word for > OLD

AULDER > AULD

AULDEST > AULD

AULIC adj relating to a royal court

AULNAGE n measurement in ells

AULNAGER n inspector of cloth

AULNAGERS > AULNAGER

AULNAGES > AULNAGE

AULOI > AULOS

AULOS n ancient Greek pipes

AUMAIL old word for > ENAMEL

AUMAILED > AUMAIL

AUMAILING > AUMAIL

AUMAILS > AUMAIL

AUMBRIES > AUMBRY

AUMBRY same as > AMBRY

AUMIL n manager in India

AUMILS > AUMIL

AUNE n old French measure of length

AUNES > AUNE

AUNT n father's or mother's sister

AUNTER old word for > ADVENTURE

AUNTERS > AUNTER

AUNTHOOD > AUNT

AUNTHOODS > AUNT

AUNTIE n aunt

AUNTIES > AUNTY

AUNTLIER > AUNTLY

AUNTLIEST > AUNTLY

AUNTLIKE > AUNT

AUNTLY adj of or like an aunt

AUNTS > AUNT

AUNTY same as > AUNTIE

AURA n distinctive air or quality of a person or thing

AURAE > AURA

AURAL adj of or using the ears or hearing

AURALITY > AURAL

AURALLY > AURAL

AURAR plural of > EYRIR

AURAS > AURA

AURATE n salt of auric acid

AURATED adj combined with auric acid

AURATES > AURATE

AUREATE adj covered with gold, gilded

AUREATELY > AUREATE

AUREI > AUREUS

AUREITIES > AUREITY

AUREITY n attributes of gold

AURELIA n large jellyfish

AURELIAN n person who studies butterflies and moths

AURELIANS > AURELIAN

AURELIAS > AURELIA

AUREOLA same as > AUREOLE

AUREOLAE > AUREOLA

AUREOLAS > AUREOLA

AUREOLE n halo

AUREOLED > AUREOLE

AUREOLES > AUREOLE

AUREOLING > AUREOLE

AURES > AURIS

AUREUS n gold coin of the Roman Empire

AURIC adj of or containing gold in the trivalent state

AURICLE n upper chamber of the heart

AURICLED > AURICLE

AURICLES > AURICLE

AURICULA n alpine primrose with leaves shaped like a bear's ear

AURICULAE > AURICULA

AURICULAR adj of, relating to, or received by the sense or organs of hearing ▷ n auricular feather

AURICULAS > AURICULA

AURIFIED > AURIFY

AURIFIES > AURIFY

AURIFORM adj shaped like an ear

AURIFY vb turn into gold

AURIFYING > AURIFY

AURIS n medical word for ear

AURISCOPE n medical instrument for examinig the external ear

AURIST a former name for > AUDIOLOGY

AURISTS > AURIST

AUROCHS n recently extinct European wild ox

AUROCHSES > AUROCHS

AURORA n bands of light sometimes seen in the sky in polar regions

AURORAE > AURORA

AURORAL > AURORA

AURORALLY > AURORA

AURORAS > AURORA

AUROREAN adj of dawn

AUROUS adj of or containing gold, esp in the monovalent state

AURUM n gold

AURUMS > AURUM

AUSFORM vb temper steel

AUSFORMED > AUSFORM

AUSFORMS > AUSFORM

AUSLANDER n German word meaning foreigner

AUSPEX same as > AUGUR

AUSPICATE vb inaugurate with a ceremony intended to bring good fortune

AUSPICE n patronage or guidance

AUSPICES > AUSPICE

AUSTENITE n solid solution of carbon in face-centred-cubic gamma iron, usually existing above 723°C

AUSTERE adj stern or severe

AUSTERELY > AUSTERE

AUSTERER > AUSTERE

AUSTEREST > AUSTERE

AUSTERITY n state of being austere

AUSTRAL adj southern ▷ n former monetary unit of Argentina equal to 100 centavos, replaced by the peso

AUSTRALES > AUSTRAL

AUSTRALIS adj Australian

AUSTRALS > AUSTRAL

AUSUBO n tropical tree

AUSUBOS > AUSUBO

AUTACOID n any natural internal secretion, esp one that exerts an effect similar to a drug

AUTACOIDS > AUTACOID

AUTARCH n absolute ruler

AUTARCHIC > AUTARCHY

AUTARCHS > AUTARCH

AUTARCHY n absolute power or autocracy

AUTARKIC > AUTARKY

AUTARKIES > AUTARKY

AUTARKIST > AUTARKY

AUTARKY n policy of economic self-sufficiency

AUTECIOUS adj (of parasites, esp the rust fungi) completing the entire life cycle on a single species of host

AUTECISM > AUTECIOUS

AUTECISMS > AUTECIOUS

AUTEUR n director whose creative influence on a film is so great as to be considered its author

AUTEURISM > AUTEUR

AUTEURIST > AUTEUR

AUTEURS > AUTEUR

AUTHENTIC adj known to be real, genuine

AUTHOR n writer of a book etc ▷ vb write or originate

AUTHORED > AUTHOR

AUTHORESS n female author

AUTHORIAL > AUTHOR

AUTHORING n creation of documents, esp multimedia documents

AUTHORISE same as > AUTHORIZE

AUTHORISH > AUTHOR

AUTHORISM n condition of being author

AUTHORITY n power to command or control others

AUTHORIZE vb give authority to

AUTHORS > AUTHOR

AUTISM n disorder characterized by lack of

response to people and limited ability to communicate

AUTISMS > AUTISM

AUTIST n autistic person

AUTISTIC > AUTISM

AUTISTICS > AUTISM

AUTISTS > AUTIST

AUTO n automobile ▷ vb travel in an automobile

AUTOBAHN n German motorway

AUTOBAHNS > AUTOBAHN

AUTOBUS n motor bus

AUTOBUSES > AUTOBUS

AUTOCADE another name for > MOTORCADE

AUTOCADES > AUTOCADE

AUTOCAR n motor car

AUTOCARP n fruit produced through self-fertilization

AUTOCARPS > AUTOCARP

AUTOCARS > AUTOCAR

AUTOCIDAL adj (of insect pest control) effected by the introduction of sterile or genetically altered individuals into the wild population

AUTOCLAVE n apparatus for sterilizing objects by steam under pressure ▷ vb put in or subject to the action of an autoclave

AUTOCOID n hormone

AUTOCOIDS > AUTOCOID

AUTOCRACY n government by an autocrat

AUTOCRAT n ruler with absolute authority

AUTOCRATS > AUTOCRAT

AUTOCRIME n crime of stealing a car

AUTOCRINE adj relating to self-stimulation through production of a factor and its receptor

AUTOCROSS n motor-racing over a rough course

AUTOCUE n electronic television prompting device

AUTOCUES > AUTOCUE

AUTOCUTIE n young and attractive but inexperienced female television presenter

AUTOCYCLE n bicycle powered or assisted by a small engine

AUTODYNE adj denoting or relating to an electrical circuit in which the same elements and valves are used as oscillator and detector ▷ n autodyne circuit

AUTODYNES > AUTODYNE

AUTOECISM n (of a parasite) completion of an entire lifecycle on a single species of host

AUTOED > AUTO

AUTOFLARE *n* automatic landing system in aircraft

AUTOFOCUS *n* camera system in which the lens is focused automatically

AUTOGAMIC > AUTOGAMY

AUTOGAMY *n* self-fertilization in flowering plants

AUTOGENIC *adj* produced from within

AUTOGENY *n* hypothetical process by which living organisms first arose on earth from nonliving matter

AUTOGIRO *n* self-propelled aircraft resembling a helicopter but with an unpowered rotor

AUTOGIROS > AUTOGIRO

AUTOGRAFT *n* tissue graft obtained from one part of a patient's body for use on another part

AUTOGRAPH *n* handwritten signature of a (famous) person ▷ *vb* write one's signature on or in

AUTOGUIDE *n* traffic information transmission system

AUTOGYRO *same as* > AUTOGIRO

AUTOGYROS > AUTOGYRO

AUTOHARP *n* zither-like musical instrument

AUTOHARPS > AUTOHARP

AUTOICOUS *adj* (of plants, esp mosses) having male and female reproductive organs on the same plant

AUTOING > AUTO

AUTOLATRY *n* self-worship

AUTOLOGY *n* study of oneself

AUTOLYSE *vb* undergo or cause to undergo autolysis

AUTOLYSED > AUTOLYSE

AUTOLYSES > AUTOLYSE

AUTOLYSIN *n* any agent that produces autolysis

AUTOLYSIS *n* destruction of cells and tissues of an organism by enzymes produced by the cells themselves

AUTOLYTIC > AUTOLYSIS

AUTOLYZE *same as* > AUTOLYSE

AUTOLYZED > AUTOLYZE

AUTOLYZES > AUTOLYZE

AUTOMAGIC *adj* done with such ease and speed that it seems like magic

AUTOMAKER *n* car manufacturer

AUTOMAN *n* car manufacturer

AUTOMAT *n* vending machine

AUTOMATA > AUTOMATON

AUTOMATE *vb* make (a manufacturing process) automatic

AUTOMATED > AUTOMATE

AUTOMATES > AUTOMATE

AUTOMATIC *adj* (of a device) operating mechanically by itself ▷ *n* self-loading firearm

AUTOMATON *n* robot

AUTOMATS > AUTOMAT

AUTOMEN > AUTOMAN

AUTOMETER *n* small device inserted in a photocopier to enable the process of copying to begin and to record the number of copies made

AUTONOMIC *adj* occurring involuntarily or spontaneously

AUTONOMY *n* self-government

AUTONYM *n* writing published under the real name of an author

AUTONYMS > AUTONYM

AUTOPEN *n* mechanical device used to produce imitation signatures

AUTOPENS > AUTOPEN

AUTOPHAGY *n* consumption of one's own tissue

AUTOPHOBY *n* reluctance to refer to oneself

AUTOPHONY *n* medical diagnosis by listening to vibration of one's own voice in patient

AUTOPHYTE *n* autotrophic plant, such as any green plant

AUTOPILOT *n* automatic pilot

AUTOPISTA *n* Spanish motorway

AUTOPOINT *n* point-to-point race in cars

AUTOPSIA *n* autopsy

AUTOPSIAS > AUTOPSIA

AUTOPSIC > AUTOPSY

AUTOPSIED > AUTOPSY

AUTOPSIES > AUTOPSY

AUTOPSIST > AUTOPSY

AUTOPSY *n* examination of a corpse to determine the cause of death

AUTOPTIC > AUTOPSY

AUTOPUT *n* motorway in the former Yugoslavia

AUTOPUTS > AUTOPUT

AUTOREPLY *n* email facility for sending automatic replies

AUTOROUTE *n* French motorway

AUTOS > AUTO

AUTOSAVE *n* computer facility for automatically saving data ▷ *vb* save (computer data) automatically

AUTOSAVED > AUTOSAVE

AUTOSAVES > AUTOSAVE

AUTOSCOPY *n* hallucination in which one sees oneself

AUTOSOMAL > AUTOSOME

AUTOSOME *n* any chromosome that is not a sex chromosome

AUTOSOMES > AUTOSOME

AUTOSPORE *n* nonmotile algal spore that develops adult characteristics before being released

AUTOTELIC *adj* justifying itself

AUTOTEST *n* motor race in which standard cars are driven round a circuit

AUTOTESTS > AUTOTEST

AUTOTIMER *n* device for turning a system on and off automatically at times predetermined by advance setting

AUTOTOMIC > AUTOTOMY

AUTOTOMY *n* casting off by an animal of a part of its body, to facilitate escape when attacked

AUTOTOXIC > AUTOTOXIN

AUTOTOXIN *n* any poison or toxin formed in the organism upon which it acts

AUTOTROPH *n* organism capable of manufacturing complex organic nutritive compounds from simple inorganic sources

AUTOTUNE *n* software package that automatically manipulates a recording of a vocal track until it is in tune regardless of whether or not the original performance was in tune

AUTOTUNES > AUTOTUNE

AUTOTYPE *n* photographic process for producing prints in black and white, using a carbon pigment ▷ *vb* process using autotype

AUTOTYPED > AUTOTYPE

AUTOTYPES > AUTOTYPE

AUTOTYPIC > AUTOTYPE

AUTOTYPY > AUTOTYPE

AUTOVAC *n* vacuum pump in a car petrol tank

AUTOVACS > AUTOVAC

AUTUMN *n* season between summer and winter

AUTUMNAL *adj* of, occurring in, or characteristic of autumn

AUTUMNS > AUTUMN

AUTUMNY *adj* like autumn

AUTUNITE *n* yellowish fluorescent radioactive mineral

AUTUNITES > AUTUNITE

AUXESES > AUXESIS

AUXESIS *n* growth in animal or plant tissues resulting from an increase in cell size without cell division

AUXETIC *n* something that promotes growth

AUXETICS > AUXETIC

AUXILIAR *old word for* > AUXILIARY

AUXILIARS > AUXILIAR

AUXILIARY *adj* secondary or supplementary ▷ *n* person or thing that supplements or supports

AUXIN *n* any of various plant hormones, such as indoleacetic acid, that promote growth and control fruit and flower development. Synthetic auxins are widely used in agriculture and horticulture

AUXINIC > AUXIN

AUXINS > AUXIN

AUXOCYTE *n* any cell undergoing meiosis, esp an oocyte or spermatocyte

AUXOCYTES > AUXOCYTE

AUXOMETER *n* instrument for measuring magnification

AUXOSPORE *n* diatom cell before its silicaceous cell wall is formed

AUXOTONIC *adj* (of muscle contraction) occurring against increasing force

AUXOTROPH *n* mutant strain of microorganism having nutritional requirements additional to those of the normal organism

AVA *adv* at all ▷ *n* Polynesian shrub

AVADAVAT *n* Asian weaverbird with usu red plumage, often kept as a cagebird

AVADAVATS > AVADAVAT

AVAIL *vb* be of use or advantage (to) ▷ *n* use or advantage

AVAILABLE *adj* obtainable or accessible

AVAILABLY > AVAILABLE

AVAILE *old word for* > LOWER

AVAILED > AVAIL

AVAILES > AVAILE

AVAILFUL *old word for* > USEFUL

AVAILING > AVAIL

AVAILS > AVAIL

AVAL *adj* of a grandparent

AVALANCHE *n* mass of snow or ice falling down a mountain ▷ *vb* come down overwhelmingly (upon)

AVALE *old word for* > LOWER

AVALED > AVALE

AVALES > AVALE

AVALING > AVALE

AVANT *prep* before

AVANTI *interj* forward!

AVANTIST *n* proponent of the avant-garde

AVANTISTS > AVANTIST
AVARICE n greed for wealth
AVARICES > AVARICE
AVAS > AVA
AVASCULAR adj (of certain tissues, such as cartilage) lacking blood vessels
AVAST sentence substitute stop! cease!
AVATAR n appearance of a god in animal or human form
AVATARS > AVATAR
AVAUNT sentence substitute go away! depart! ▷ vb go away; depart
AVAUNTED > AVAUNT
AVAUNTING > AVAUNT
AVAUNTS > AVAUNT
AVE n expression of welcome or farewell
AVEL a variant of **>** OVEL
AVELLAN adj of hazelnuts
AVELLANE adj of hazelnuts
AVELS > AVEL
AVENGE vb take revenge in retaliation for (harm done) or on behalf of (a person harmed)
AVENGED > AVENGE
AVENGEFUL > AVENGE
AVENGER > AVENGE
AVENGERS > AVENGE
AVENGES > AVENGE
AVENGING > AVENGE
AVENIR n future
AVENIRS > AVENIR
AVENS n any of several temperate or arctic rosaceous plants
AVENSES > AVENS
AVENTAIL n front flap of a helmet
AVENTAILE n aventail
AVENTAILS > AVENTAIL
AVENTRE old word for **>** THRUST
AVENTRED > AVENTRE
AVENTRES > AVENTRE
AVENTRING > AVENTRE
AVENTURE old form of **>** ADVENTURE
AVENTURES > AVENTURE
AVENTURIN n dark-coloured glass, usually green or brown, spangled with fine particles of gold, copper, or some other metal
AVENUE n wide street
AVENUES > AVENUE
AVER vb state to be true
AVERAGE n typical or normal amount or quality ▷ adj usual or typical ▷ vb calculate the average of
AVERAGED > AVERAGE
AVERAGELY > AVERAGE
AVERAGES > AVERAGE
AVERAGING > AVERAGE
AVERMENT > AVER
AVERMENTS > AVER
AVERRABLE > AVER

AVERRED > AVER
AVERRING > AVER
AVERS > AVER
AVERSE adj disinclined or unwilling
AVERSELY > AVERSE
AVERSION n strong dislike
AVERSIONS > AVERSION
AVERSIVE n tool or technique intended to repel animals etc
AVERSIVES > AVERSIVE
AVERT vb turn away
AVERTABLE > AVERT
AVERTED > AVERT
AVERTEDLY > AVERT
AVERTER > AVERT
AVERTERS > AVERT
AVERTIBLE > AVERT
AVERTING > AVERT
AVERTS > AVERT
AVES > AVE
AVGAS n aviation fuel
AVGASES > AVGAS
AVGASSES > AVGAS
AVIAN adj of or like a bird ▷ n bird
AVIANISE same as **>** AVIANIZE
AVIANISED > AVIANISE
AVIANISES > AVIANISE
AVIANIZE vb modify microorganisms in a chicken embryo
AVIANIZED > AVIANIZE
AVIANIZES > AVIANIZE
AVIANS > AVIAN
AVIARIES > AVIARY
AVIARIST n person who keeps an aviary
AVIARISTS > AVIARIST
AVIARY n large cage or enclosure for birds
AVIATE vb pilot or fly in an aircraft
AVIATED > AVIATE
AVIATES > AVIATE
AVIATIC adj pertaining to aviation
AVIATING > AVIATE
AVIATION n art of flying aircraft
AVIATIONS > AVIATION
AVIATOR n pilot of an aircraft
AVIATORS > AVIATOR
AVIATRESS > AVIATOR
AVIATRICE > AVIATOR
AVIATRIX > AVIATOR
AVICULAR adj of small birds
AVID adj keen or enthusiastic
AVIDER > AVID
AVIDEST > AVID
AVIDIN n protein, found in egg-white, that combines with biotin to form a stable compound that cannot be absorbed, leading to a biotin deficiency in the consumer
AVIDINS > AVIDIN
AVIDITIES > AVIDITY

AVIDITY n quality or state of being avid
AVIDLY > AVID
AVIDNESS > AVID
AVIETTE n aeroplane driven by human strength
AVIETTES > AVIETTE
AVIFAUNA n all the birds in a particular region
AVIFAUNAE > AVIFAUNA
AVIFAUNAL > AVIFAUNA
AVIFAUNAS > AVIFAUNA
AVIFORM adj like a bird
AVIGATOR another word for **>** AVIATOR
AVIGATORS > AVIGATOR
AVINE adj of birds
AVION n aeroplane
AVIONIC > AVIONICS
AVIONICS n science and technology of electronics applied to aeronautics and astronautics
AVIONS > AVION
AVIRULENT adj (esp of bacteria) not virulent
AVISANDUM n consideration of a law case by a judge
AVISE old word for **>** ADVISE
AVISED > AVISE
AVISEMENT > AVISE
AVISES > AVISE
AVISING > AVISE
AVISO n boat carrying messages
AVISOS > AVISO
AVITAL adj of a grandfather
AVIZANDUM n judge's or court's decision to consider a case privately before giving judgment
AVIZE old word for **>** ADVISE
AVIZED > AVIZE
AVIZEFULL > AVIZE
AVIZES > AVIZE
AVIZING > AVIZE
AVO n Macao currency unit
AVOCADO n pear-shaped tropical fruit with a leathery green skin and yellowish-green flesh
AVOCADOES > AVOCADO
AVOCADOS > AVOCADO
AVOCATION n occupation
AVOCET n long-legged wading bird with a long slender upward-curving bill
AVOCETS > AVOCET
AVODIRE n African tree
AVODIRES > AVODIRE
AVOID vb prevent from happening
AVOIDABLE > AVOID
AVOIDABLY > AVOID
AVOIDANCE n act of keeping away from or preventing from happening
AVOIDANT adj (of behaviour) demonstrating a tendency to avoid

intimacy or interaction with others
AVOIDED > AVOID
AVOIDER > AVOID
AVOIDERS > AVOID
AVOIDING > AVOID
AVOIDS > AVOID
AVOISION n nonpayment of tax
AVOISIONS > AVOISION
AVOPARCIN n type of antibiotic
AVOS > AVO
AVOSET n avocet
AVOSETS > AVOSET
AVOUCH vb vouch for
AVOUCHED > AVOUCH
AVOUCHER > AVOUCH
AVOUCHERS > AVOUCH
AVOUCHES > AVOUCH
AVOUCHING > AVOUCH
AVOURE old word for **>** AVOWAL
AVOURES > AVOURE
AVOUTERER old word for **>** ADULTERER
AVOUTRER old word for **>** ADULTERER
AVOUTRERS > AVOUTRER
AVOUTRIES > AVOUTRY
AVOUTRY old word for **>** ADULTERY
AVOW vb state or affirm
AVOWABLE > AVOW
AVOWABLY > AVOW
AVOWAL > AVOW
AVOWALS > AVOW
AVOWED > AVOW
AVOWEDLY > AVOW
AVOWER > AVOW
AVOWERS > AVOW
AVOWING > AVOW
AVOWRIES > AVOWRY
AVOWRY old word for **>** AVOWAL
AVOWS > AVOW
AVOYER n former Swiss magistrate
AVOYERS > AVOYER
AVRUGA n herring roe with a smoky flavour, sometimes used as a less expensive alternative to caviar
AVRUGAS > AVRUGA
AVULSE vb take away by force
AVULSED > AVULSE
AVULSES > AVULSE
AVULSING > AVULSE
AVULSION n forcible tearing away or separation of a bodily structure or part, either as the result of injury or as an intentional surgical procedure
AVULSIONS > AVULSION
AVUNCULAR adj (of a man) friendly, helpful, and caring towards someone younger
AVYZE old word for **>** ADVISE
AVYZED > AVYZE
AVYZES > AVYZE

AVYZING > AVYZE
AW variant of **>** ALL
AWA adv away
AWAIT vb wait for
AWAITED > AWAIT
AWAITER > AWAIT
AWAITERS > AWAIT
AWAITING > AWAIT
AWAITS > AWAIT
AWAKE vb emerge or rouse from sleep ▷ adj not sleeping
AWAKED > AWAKE
AWAKEN vb awake
AWAKENED > AWAKEN
AWAKENER > AWAKEN
AWAKENERS > AWAKEN
AWAKENING n start of a feeling or awareness in someone
AWAKENS > AWAKEN
AWAKES > AWAKE
AWAKING > AWAKE
AWAKINGS > AWAKE
AWANTING adj missing
AWARD vb give (something, such as a prize) formally ▷ n something awarded, such as a prize
AWARDABLE > AWARD
AWARDED > AWARD
AWARDEE > AWARD
AWARDEES > AWARD
AWARDER > AWARD
AWARDERS > AWARD
AWARDING > AWARD
AWARDS > AWARD
AWARE adj having knowledge, informed
AWARENESS > AWARE
AWARER > AWARE
AWAREST > AWARE
AWARN vb old form of warn
AWARNED > AWARN
AWARNING > AWARN
AWARNS > AWARN
AWASH adv washed over by water ▷ adj washed over by water
AWATCH adv watching
AWATO n New Zealand caterpillar
AWATOS > AWATO
AWAVE adv in waves
AWAY adv from a place ▷ adj not present ▷ n game played or won at an opponent's ground
AWAYDAY n day trip taken for pleasure
AWAYDAYS > AWAYDAY
AWAYES old word for **>** AWAY
AWAYNESS > AWAY
AWAYS > AWAY
AWDL n traditional Welsh poem
AWDLS > AWDL
AWE n wonder and respect mixed with dread ▷ vb fill with awe
AWEARIED old word for **>** WEARY
AWEARY old form of **>** WEARY
AWEATHER adj towards the weather
AWED > AWE
AWEE adv for a short time
AWEEL interj Scots word meaning well
AWEIGH adj (of an anchor) no longer hooked onto the bottom
AWEING > AWE
AWELESS > AWE
AWES > AWE
AWESOME adj inspiring awe
AWESOMELY > AWESOME
AWESTRUCK adj filled with awe
AWETO n New Zealand caterpillar
AWETOS > AWETO
AWFUL adj very bad or unpleasant ▷ adv very
AWFULLER > AWFUL
AWFULLEST > AWFUL
AWFULLY adv in an unpleasant way
AWFULNESS > AWFUL
AWFY adv (Scots) awfully, extremely
AWHAPE old word for **>** AMAZE
AWHAPED > AWHAPE
AWHAPES > AWHAPE
AWHAPING > AWHAPE
AWHATO n New Zealand caterpillar
AWHATOS > AWHATO
AWHEEL adv on wheels
AWHEELS same as **>** AWHEEL
AWHETO n New Zealand caterpillar
AWHETOS > AWHETO
AWHILE adv for a brief time
AWHIRL adv whirling
AWING > AWE
AWK n type of computer programming language
AWKS > AWK
AWKWARD adj clumsy or ungainly
AWKWARDER > AWKWARD
AWKWARDLY > AWKWARD
AWL n pointed tool for piercing wood, leather, etc
AWLBIRD n woodpecker
AWLBIRDS > AWLBIRD
AWLESS > AWE
AWLS > AWL
AWLWORT n type of small stemless aquatic plant of the N hemisphere, with slender sharp-pointed leaves and minute white flowers
AWLWORTS > AWLWORT
AWMOUS Scots word for **>** ALMS
AWMRIE n cupboard for church vessels
AWMRIES > AWMRIE
AWMRY n cupboard for church vessels
AWN n any of the bristles growing from the flowering parts of certain grasses and cereals
AWNED > AWN
AWNER n machine for removing awns
AWNERS > AWNER
AWNIER > AWNY
AWNIEST > AWNY
AWNING n canvas roof supported by a frame to give protection against the weather
AWNINGED adj sheltered with awning
AWNINGS > AWNING
AWNLESS > AWN
AWNS > AWN
AWNY adj having awns
AWOKE past tense of **>** AWAKE
AWOKEN > AWAKE
AWOL n person who is absent without leave
AWOLS > AWOL
AWORK adv old word meaning at work
AWRACK adv in wrecked condition
AWRONG adv old word meaning wrongly
AWRY adj with a twist to one side, askew
AWSOME adj old form of awesome
AX same as **>** AXE
AXAL adj of an axis
AXE n tool with a sharp blade for felling trees or chopping wood ▷ vb dismiss (employees), restrict (expenditure), or terminate (a project)
AXEBIRD n nightjar of northern Queensland and New Guinea with a cry that sounds like a chopping axe
AXEBIRDS > AXEBIRD
AXED > AXE
AXEL n jump in which the skater takes off from the forward outside edge of one skate, makes one and a half, two and a half, or three and a half turns in the air, and lands on the backward outside edge of the other skate
AXELS > AXEL
AXEMAN n man who wields an axe, esp to cut down trees
AXEMEN > AXEMAN
AXENIC adj (of a biological culture or culture medium) free from other microorganisms
AXES > AXIS
AXIAL adj forming or of an axis
AXIALITY > AXIAL
AXIALLY > AXIAL
AXIL n angle where the stalk of a leaf joins a stem
AXILE adj of, relating to, or attached to the axis
AXILEMMA same as **>** AXOLEMMA
AXILEMMAS > AXILEMMA
AXILLA n area on the undersurface of a bird's wing corresponding to the armpit
AXILLAE > AXILLA
AXILLAR same as **>** AXILLARY
AXILLARS > AXILLAR
AXILLARY adj of, relating to, or near the armpit ▷ n one of the feathers growing from the axilla of a bird's wing
AXILLAS > AXILLA
AXILS > AXIL
AXING > AXE
AXINITE n crystalline substance
AXINITES > AXINITE
AXIOLOGY n theory of values, moral or aesthetic
AXIOM n generally accepted principle
AXIOMATIC adj containing axioms
AXIOMS > AXIOM
AXION n type of hypothetical elementary particle
AXIONS > AXION
AXIS n (imaginary) line round which a body can rotate or about which an object or geometrical figure is symmetrical
AXISED adj having an axis
AXISES > AXIS
AXITE n type of gunpowder
AXITES > AXITE
AXLE n shaft on which a wheel or pair of wheels turns
AXLED adj having axle
AXLES > AXLE
AXLETREE n bar fixed across the underpart of a wagon or carriage that has rounded ends on which the wheels revolve
AXLETREES > AXLETREE
AXLIKE > AX
AXMAN same as **>** AXEMAN
AXMEN > AXMAN
AXOID n type of curve
AXOIDS > AXOID
AXOLEMMA n membrane that encloses the axon of a nerve cell
AXOLEMMAS > AXOLEMMA
AXOLOTL n aquatic salamander of central America
AXOLOTLS > AXOLOTL
AXON n long threadlike extension of a nerve cell that conducts nerve impulses from the cell body
AXONAL > AXON
AXONE same as **>** AXON
AXONEMAL > AXONEME
AXONEME n part of cell consisting of proteins
AXONEMES > AXONEME

AXONES > AXONE
AXONIC > AXON
AXONS > AXON
AXOPLASM *n* part of cell
AXOPLASMS > AXOPLASM
AXSEED *n* crown vetch
AXSEEDS > AXSEED
AY *adv* ever ▷ *n* expression of agreement
AYAH *n* (in parts of the former British Empire) a native maidservant or nursemaid
AYAHS > AYAH
AYAHUASCA *n* type of Brazilian plant
AYAHUASCO *n* South American vine
AYATOLLAH *n* Islamic religious leader in Iran
AYE *n* affirmative vote or voter ▷ *adv* always
AYELP *adv* yelping
AYENBITE *old word for* **>** REMORSE
AYENBITES > AYENBITE
AYES > AYE
AYGRE *old word for* **>** EAGER
AYIN *n* 16th letter in the Hebrew alphabet
AYINS > AYIN
AYONT *adv* beyond
AYRE *old word for* **>** AIR
AYRES > AYRE
AYRIE *old word for* **>** EYRIE
AYRIES > AYRIE
AYS > AY
AYU *n* small Japanese fish
AYURVEDA *n* ancient medical treatise on the art of healing and prolonging life
AYURVEDAS > AYURVEDA
AYURVEDIC > AYURVEDA
AYUS > AYU
AYWORD *n* old word

meaning byword
AYWORDS > AYWORD
AZALEA *n* garden shrub grown for its showy flowers
AZALEAS > AZALEA
AZAN *n* call to prayer five times a day, usually by a muezzin from a minaret
AZANS > AZAN
AZEDARACH *n* astringent bark of the chinaberry tree, formerly used as an emetic and cathartic
AZEOTROPE *n* mixture of liquids that boils at a constant temperature, at a given pressure, without a change in composition
AZEOTROPY > AZEOTROPE
AZERTY *n* common European version of typewriter keyboard layout with the characters a, z, e, r, t, and y positioned on the top row of alphabetic characters at the left side of the keyboard
AZIDE *n* type of chemical compound
AZIDES > AZIDE
AZIDO *adj* containing an azide
AZIMUTH *n* arc of the sky between the zenith and the horizon
AZIMUTHAL > AZIMUTH
AZIMUTHS > AZIMUTH
AZINE *n* any organic compound having a six-membered ring containing at least one nitrogen atom
AZINES > AZINE
AZIONE *n* musical drama
AZIONES > AZIONE
AZLON *n* fibre made from

protein
AZLONS > AZLON
AZO *adj* of, consisting of, or containing the divalent group -N:N-
AZOIC *adj* without life
AZOLE *n* organic five-membered ring compound containing one or more atoms in the ring, the number usually being specified by a prefix
AZOLES > AZOLE
AZOLLA *n* tropical water fern
AZOLLAS > AZOLLA
AZON *n* type of drawing paper
AZONAL *adj* not divided into zones
AZONIC *adj* not confined to a zone
AZONS > AZON
AZOTAEMIA *a less common name for* **>** URAEMIA
AZOTAEMIC > AZOTAEMIA
AZOTE *an obsolete name for* **>** NITROGEN
AZOTED > AZOTE
AZOTEMIA *same as* **>** AZOTAEMIA
AZOTEMIAS > AZOTEMIA
AZOTEMIC > AZOTAEMIC
AZOTES > AZOTE
AZOTH *n* panacea postulated by Paracelsus
AZOTHS > AZOTH
AZOTIC *adj* of, containing, or concerned with nitrogen
AZOTISE *same as* **>** AZOTIZE
AZOTISED > AZOTISE
AZOTISES > AZOTISE
AZOTISING > AZOTISE
AZOTIZE *vb* combine or treat with nitrogen or a

nitrogen compound
AZOTIZED > AZOTIZE
AZOTIZES > AZOTIZE
AZOTIZING > AZOTIZE
AZOTOUS *adj* containing nitrogen
AZOTURIA *n* presence of excess nitrogen in urine
AZOTURIAS > AZOTURIA
AZUKI *same as* **>** ADZUKI
AZUKIS > AZUKI
AZULEJO *n* Spanish porcelain tile
AZULEJOS > AZULEJO
AZURE *n* (of) the colour of a clear blue sky ▷ *adj* deep blue
AZUREAN *adj* azure
AZURES > AZURE
AZURINE *n* blue dye
AZURINES > AZURINE
AZURITE *n* azure-blue mineral associated with copper deposits
AZURITES > AZURITE
AZURN *old word for* **>** AZURE
AZURY *adj* bluish
AZYGIES > AZYGY
AZYGOS *n* biological structure not in a pair
AZYGOSES > AZYGOS
AZYGOUS *adj* developing or occurring singly
AZYGOUSLY > AZYGOUS
AZYGY *n* state of not being joined in pair
AZYM *n* unleavened bread
AZYME *n* unleavened bread
AZYMES > AZYME
AZYMITE *n* member of a church using unleavened bread in the Eucharist
AZYMITES > AZYMITE
AZYMOUS *adj* unleavened
AZYMS > AZYM

Bb

BA n symbol for the soul in Ancient Egyptian religion

BAA vb make the characteristic bleating sound of a sheep ⊳ n cry made by a sheep

BAAED > BAA

BAAING > BAA

BAAINGS > BAA

BAAL n any false god or idol

BAALEBOS n master of the house

BAALIM > BAAL

BAALISM > BAAL

BAALISMS > BAAL

BAALS > BAAL

BAAS South African word for > BOSS

BAASES > BAAS

BAASKAAP same as > BAASKAP

BAASKAAPS > BAASKAAP

BAASKAP n (in South Africa) control by Whites of non-Whites

BAASKAPS > BAASKAP

BAASSKAP same as > BAASKAP

BAASSKAPS > BAASSKAP

BABA n small cake of leavened dough, sometimes mixed with currants and usually soaked in rum

BABACO n greenish-yellow egg-shaped fruit

BABACOOTE n large lemur

BABACOS > BABACO

BABALAS adj drunk

BABAS > BABA

BABASSU n Brazilian palm tree with hard edible nuts that yield an oil used to make soap, margarine, etc

BABASSUS > BABASSU

BABBELAS same as > BABALAS

BABBITRY > BABBITTRY

BABBITT vb line (a bearing) or face (a surface) with Babbitt metal or a similar soft alloy

BABBITTED > BABBITT

BABBITTRY n narrow-minded materialism

BABBITTS > BABBITT

BABBLE vb talk excitedly or foolishly ⊳ n muddled or foolish speech

BABBLED > BABBLE

BABBLER n person who babbles

BABBLERS > BABBLER

BABBLES > BABBLE

BABBLIER > BABBLE

BABBLIEST > BABBLE

BABBLING > BABBLE

BABBLINGS > BABBLE

BABBLY > BABBLE

BABE n baby

BABEL n confused mixture of noises or voices

BABELDOM > BABEL

BABELDOMS > BABEL

BABELISH > BABEL

BABELISM > BABEL

BABELISMS > BABEL

BABELS > BABEL

BABES > BABE

BABESIA n parasite causing infection in cattle

BABESIAS > BABESIA

BABICHE n thongs or lacings of rawhide

BABICHES > BABICHE

BABIED > BABY

BABIER > BABY

BABIES > BABY

BABIEST > BABY

BABIRUSA n Indonesian wild pig with an almost hairless skin and huge curved canine teeth

BABIRUSAS > BABIRUSA

BABIRUSSA same as > BABIRUSA

BABKA n cake

BABKAS > BABKA

BABLAH n type of acacia

BABLAHS > BABLAH

BABOO same as > BABU

BABOOL n type of acacia

BABOOLS > BABOOL

BABOON n large monkey with a pointed face and a long tail

BABOONERY n uncouth behaviour

BABOONISH adj uncouth

BABOONS > BABOON

BABOOS > BABOO

BABOOSH same as > BABOUCHE

BABOOSHES > BABOOSH

BABOUCHE n Middle-Eastern slipper

BABOUCHES > BABOUCHE

BABU n title or form of address used in India

BABUCHE same as > BABOUCHE

BABUCHES > BABUCHE

BABUDOM > BABU

BABUDOMS > BABU

BABUISM > BABU

BABUISMS > BABU

BABUL n N African and Indian tree with small yellow flowers, which is a source of gum arabic, tannin, and hardwood

BABULS > BABUL

BABUS > BABU

BABUSHKA n headscarf tied under the chin, worn by Russian peasant women

BABUSHKAS > BABUSHKA

BABY n very young child or animal ⊳ adj comparatively small of its type ⊳ vb treat as a baby

BABYDOLL n woman's short nightdress

BABYDOLLS > BABYDOLL

BABYFOOD n puréed food for babies

BABYFOODS > BABYFOOD

BABYHOOD > BABY

BABYHOODS > BABY

BABYING > BABY

BABYISH > BABY

BABYISHLY > BABY

BABYPROOF adj safe for babies to handle ⊳ vb make babyproof

BABYSAT > BABYSIT

BABYSIT vb look after a child in its parents' absence

BABYSITS > BABYSIT

BAC n baccalaureate

BACALAO n dried salt cod

BACALAOS > BACALAO

BACCA n berry

BACCAE > BACCA

BACCARA same as > BACCARAT

BACCARAS > BACCARA

BACCARAT n card game involving gambling

BACCARATS > BACCARAT

BACCARE same as > BACKARE

BACCAS > BACCA

BACCATE adj like a berry in form, texture, etc

BACCATED > BACCATE

BACCHANAL n follower of Bacchus ⊳ adj of or relating to Bacchus

BACCHANT n priest or votary of Bacchus

BACCHANTE n priestess or female votary of Bacchus

BACCHANTS > BACCHANT

BACCHIAC > BACCHIUS

BACCHIAN same as > BACCHIC

BACCHIC adj riotously drunk

BACCHII > BACCHIUS

BACCHIUS n metrical foot of one short syllable followed by two long ones

BACCIES > BACCY

BACCIFORM adj shaped like a berry

BACCO n tobacco

BACCOES > BACCO

BACCOS > BACCO

BACCY n tobacco

BACH same as > BATCH

BACHA n Indian English word for young child

BACHARACH n German wine

BACHAS > BACHA

BACHCHA n Indian English word for young child

BACHCHAS > BACHCHA

BACHED > BACH

BACHELOR n unmarried man

BACHELORS > BACHELOR

BACHES > BACH

BACHING > BACH

BACHS > BACH

BACILLAR same as > BACILLARY

BACILLARY adj of or caused by bacilli

BACILLI > BACILLUS

BACILLUS n rod-shaped bacterium

BACK n rear part of the human body, from the neck to the pelvis ⊳ vb (cause to) move backwards ⊳ adj situated behind ⊳ adv at, to, or towards the rear

BACKACHE n ache or pain in one's back

BACKACHES > BACKACHE

BACKARE interj instruction to keep one's distance; back off

BACKBAND n back support

BACKBANDS > BACKBAND

BACKBEAT n second and fourth beats in music written in even time or, in more complex time signatures, the last beat of the bar

BACKBEATS > BACKBEAT

BACKBENCH n lower-ranking seats in Parliament

BACKBEND n gymnastic exercise in which the trunk is bent backwards until the hands touch the floor

BACKBENDS > BACKBEND

BACKBIT > BACKBITE

BACKBITE vb talk spitefully about an absent person

BACKBITER > BACKBITE

BACKBITES > BACKBITE

BACKBLOCK n singular of backblock: bush or remote farming area

BACKBOARD n board that is placed behind something to form or support its back

BACKBOND n legal document

BACKBONDS > BACKBOND

BACKBONE n spinal column

BACKBONED > BACKBONE

BACKBONES > BACKBONE

BACKBURN vb clear (an area of bush) by creating a fire that burns in the opposite direction from the wind ▷ n act or result of backburning

BACKBURNS > BACKBURN

BACKCAST n backward casting of fishing rod ▷ vb cast a fishing rod backwards

BACKCASTS > BACKCAST

BACKCHAT n impudent replies

BACKCHATS > BACKCHAT

BACKCHECK vb (in ice hockey) return from attack to defence

BACKCLOTH n painted curtain at the back of a stage set

BACKCOMB vb comb (the hair) towards the roots to give more bulk to a hairstyle

BACKCOMBS > BACKCOMB

BACKCOURT n part of the court between the service line and the baseline

BACKCROSS vb mate (a hybrid of the first generation) with one of its parents ▷ n offspring so produced

BACKDATE vb make (a document) effective from a date earlier than its completion

BACKDATED > BACKDATE

BACKDATES > BACKDATE

BACKDOOR adj secret, underhand, or obtained through influence

BACKDOWN n abandonment of an earlier claim

BACKDOWNS > BACKDOWN

BACKDRAFT n reverse movement of air

BACKDROP vb provide a backdrop to (something)

BACKDROPS > BACKDROP

BACKDROPT > BACKDROP

BACKED adj having a back or backing

BACKER n person who gives financial support

BACKERS > BACKER

BACKET n shallow box

BACKETS > BACKET

BACKFALL n fall onto the back

BACKFALLS > BACKFALL

BACKFIELD n quarterback and running backs in a team

BACKFILE n archives of a newspaper or magazine

BACKFILES > BACKFILE

BACKFILL vb refill an excavated trench, esp (in archaeology) at the end of an investigation ▷ n soil used to do this

BACKFILLS > BACKFILL

BACKFIRE vb (of a plan) fail to have the desired effect ▷ n (in an engine) explosion of unburnt gases in the exhaust system

BACKFIRED > BACKFIRE

BACKFIRES > BACKFIRE

BACKFISCH n young girl

BACKFIT vb overhaul nuclear power plant

BACKFITS > BACKFIT

BACKFLIP n backwards somersault

BACKFLIPS > BACKFLIP

BACKFLOW n reverse flow

BACKFLOWS > BACKFLOW

BACKHAND n stroke played with the back of the hand facing the direction of the stroke ▷ adv with a backhand stroke ▷ vb play (a shot) backhand

BACKHANDS > BACKHAND

BACKHAUL vb transmit data

BACKHAULS > BACKHAUL

BACKHOE n digger ▷ vb dig with a backhoe

BACKHOED > BACKHOE

BACKHOES > BACKHOE

BACKHOUSE n toilet

BACKIE n ride on the back of someone's bicycle

BACKIES > BACKIE

BACKING n support

BACKINGS > BACKING

BACKLAND n undeveloped land behind a property

BACKLANDS > BACKLAND

BACKLASH n sudden and adverse reaction ▷ vb create a sudden and adverse reaction

BACKLESS adj (of a dress) low-cut at the back

BACKLIFT n backward movement of bat

BACKLIFTS > BACKLIFT

BACKLIGHT vb illuminate (something) from behind

BACKLIST n publisher's previously published books that are still available ▷ vb put on a backlist

BACKLISTS > BACKLIST

BACKLIT adj illuminated from behind

BACKLOAD n load for lorry on return journey ▷ vb load a lorry for a return journey

BACKLOADS > BACKLOAD

BACKLOG n accumulation of things to be dealt with

BACKLOGS > BACKLOG

BACKLOT n area outside a film or television studio used for outdoor filming

BACKLOTS > BACKLOT

BACKMOST adj furthest back

BACKOUT n instance of withdrawing (from an agreement, etc)

BACKOUTS > BACKOUT

BACKPACK n large pack carried on the back ▷ vb go hiking with a backpack

BACKPACKS > BACKPACK

BACKPEDAL vb retract or modify a previous opinion, principle, etc

BACKPIECE n tattoo on the back

BACKPLATE n plate of armour which guards the back

BACKRA n white person

BACKRAS > BACKRA

BACKREST n support for the back of something

BACKRESTS > BACKREST

BACKROOM n place where research or planning is done, esp secret research in wartime

BACKROOMS > BACKROOM

BACKRUSH n seaward return of wave

BACKS > BACK

BACKSAW n small handsaw stiffened along its upper edge by a metal section

BACKSAWS > BACKSAW

BACKSEAT n seat at the back, esp of a vehicle

BACKSEATS > BACKSEAT

BACKSET n reversal

BACKSETS > BACKSET

BACKSEY n sirloin

BACKSEYS > BACKSEY

BACKSHISH same as > BAKSHEESH

BACKSHORE n area of beach above high tide mark

BACKSIDE n buttocks

BACKSIDES > BACKSIDE

BACKSIGHT n sight of a rifle nearer the stock

BACKSLAP vb demonstrate effusive joviality

BACKSLAPS > BACKSLAP

BACKSLASH n slash which slopes to the left)

BACKSLID > BACKSLIDE

BACKSLIDE vb relapse into former bad habits

BACKSPACE vb move a typewriter carriage or computer cursor backwards ▷ n typewriter key that effects such a movements

BACKSPEER same as > BACKSPEIR

BACKSPEIR vb interrogate

BACKSPIN n backward spin given to a ball to reduce its speed at impact

BACKSPINS > BACKSPIN

BACKSTAB vb attack deceitfully

BACKSTABS > BACKSTAB

BACKSTAGE adj behind the stage in a theatre ▷ adv behind the stage in a theatre ▷ n area behind the stage in a theatre

BACKSTAIR adj underhand

BACKSTALL n backward flight of a kite

BACKSTAMP n mark stamped on the back of an envelope ▷ vb mark with a backstamp

BACKSTAY n stay leading aft from the upper part of a mast to the deck or stern

BACKSTAYS > BACKSTAY

BACKSTOP n screen or fence to prevent balls leaving the playing area ▷ vb provide with backing or support

BACKSTOPS > BACKSTOP

BACKSTORY n events assumed before a story begins

BACKSWEPT adj slanting backwards

BACKSWING n backward movement of a bat, etc

BACKSWORD a broad-bladed sword

BACKTRACK vb return by the same route by which one has come

BACKUP n support or reinforcement

BACKUPS > BACKUP

BACKVELD n (in South Africa) remote sparsely populated area

BACKVELDS > BACKVELD

BACKWARD same as > BACKWARDS

BACKWARDS adv towards the rear

BACKWASH n water washed backwards by the motion of a boat ▷ vb remove oil from (combed wool)

BACKWATER n isolated or backward place or condition ▷ vb reverse the direction of a boat, esp to

b

push the oars of a rowing boat

BACKWOOD > BACKWOODS

BACKWOODS npl remote sparsely populated area

BACKWORD n act or an instance of failing to keep a promise or commitment

BACKWORDS > BACKWORD

BACKWORK n work carried out under the ground

BACKWORKS > BACKWORK

BACKWRAP n back support

BACKWRAPS > BACKWRAP

BACKYARD n yard at the back of a house, etc

BACKYARDS > BACKYARD

BACLAVA same as **>** BAKLAVA

BACLAVAS > BACLAVA

BACLOFEN n drug used to treat stroke victims

BACLOFENS > BACLOFEN

BACON n salted or smoked pig meat

BACONER n pig that weighs between 83 and 101 kg, from which bacon is cut

BACONERS > BACONER

BACONS > BACON

BACS > BAC

BACTERIA npl large group of microorganisms

BACTERIAL > BACTERIA

BACTERIAN > BACTERIA

BACTERIAS > BACTERIA

BACTERIC > BACTERIA

BACTERIN n vaccine prepared from bacteria

BACTERINS > BACTERIN

BACTERISE same as **>** BACTERIZE

BACTERIUM n single bacteria

BACTERIZE vb subject to bacterial action

BACTEROID n type of rodlike bacterium occurring in the gut of man and animals

BACULA > BACULUM

BACULINE adj relating to flogging

BACULITE n fossil

BACULITES > BACULITE

BACULUM n bony support in the penis of certain mammals, esp the carnivores

BACULUMS > BACULUM

BAD adj not good **▷** n unfortunate or unpleasant events collectively **▷** adv badly

BADASS n tough or aggressive person **▷** adj tough or aggressive

BADASSED > BADASS

BADASSES > BADASS

BADDER > BAD

BADDEST > BAD

BADDIE n bad character in a story, film, etc, esp an opponent of the hero

BADDIES > BADDIE

BADDISH > BAD

BADDY same as **>** BADDIE

BADE > BID

BADGE n emblem worn to show membership, rank, etc **▷** vb put a badge on

BADGED > BADGE

BADGELESS > BADGE

BADGER n nocturnal burrowing mammal of Europe, Asia, and N America with a black and white head **▷** vb pester or harass

BADGERED > BADGER

BADGERING > BADGER

BADGERLY > BADGER

BADGERS > BADGER

BADGES > BADGE

BADGING > BADGE

BADINAGE n playful and witty conversation **▷** vb engage in badinage

BADINAGED > BADINAGE

BADINAGES > BADINAGE

BADINERIE n name given in the 18th century to a type of quick, light movement in a suite

BADIOUS adj chestnut; brownish-red

BADLAND > BADLANDS

BADLANDS npl any deeply eroded barren area

BADLY adv poorly

BADMAN n hired gunman, outlaw, or criminal

BADMASH n evil-doer **▷** adj naughty or bad **▷** n hooligan

BADMASHES > BADMASH

BADMEN > BADMAN

BADMINTON n game played with rackets and a shuttlecock, which is hit back and forth over a high net

BADMOUTH vb speak unfavourably about (someone or something)

BADMOUTHS > BADMOUTH

BADNESS > BAD

BADNESSES > BAD

BADS > BAD

BADWARE n software designed to harm a computer system

BADWARES > BADWARE

BAEL n type of spiny Indian tree

BAELS > BAEL

BAETYL n magical meteoric stone

BAETYLS > BAETYL

BAFF vb strike ground with golf club

BAFFED > BAFF

BAFFIES npl slippers

BAFFING > BAFF

BAFFLE vb perplex or puzzle **▷** n device to limit or regulate the flow of fluid, light, or sound

BAFFLED > BAFFLE

BAFFLEGAB n insincere speech

BAFFLER > BAFFLE

BAFFLERS > BAFFLE

BAFFLES > BAFFLE

BAFFLING adj impossible to understand

BAFFS > BAFF

BAFFY n golf club

BAFT n coarse fabric

BAFTS > BAFT

BAG n flexible container with an opening at one end **▷** vb put into a bag

BAGARRE n brawl

BAGARRES > BAGARRE

BAGASS same as **>** BAGASSE

BAGASSE n pulp remaining after the extraction of juice from sugar cane or similar plants: used as fuel and for making paper, etc

BAGASSES > BAGASSE

BAGATELLE n something of little value

BAGEL n hard ring-shaped bread roll

BAGELS > BAGEL

BAGFUL n amount (of something) that can be held in a bag

BAGFULS > BAGFUL

BAGGAGE n suitcases packed for a journey

BAGGAGES > BAGGAGE

BAGGED > BAG

BAGGER n person who packs groceries

BAGGERS > BAGGER

BAGGIE n plastic bag

BAGGIER > BAGGY

BAGGIES > BAGGY

BAGGIEST > BAGGY

BAGGILY > BAGGY

BAGGINESS > BAGGY

BAGGING > BAG

BAGGINGS > BAG

BAGGIT n unspawned salmon

BAGGITS > BAGGIT

BAGGY same as **>** BAGIE

BAGH n (in India and Pakistan) a garden

BAGHOUSE n dust-filtering chamber

BAGHOUSES > BAGHOUSE

BAGHS > BAGH

BAGIE n turnip

BAGIES > BAGIE

BAGLESS adj (esp of a vacuum cleaner) not containing a bag

BAGLIKE > BAG

BAGMAN n travelling salesman

BAGMEN > BAGMAN

BAGNETTE variant of **>** BAGUETTE

BAGNETTES > BAGNETTE

BAGNIO n brothel

BAGNIOS > BAGNIO

BAGPIPE vb play the bagpipes

BAGPIPED > BAGPIPE

BAGPIPER > BAGPIPES

BAGPIPERS > BAGPIPES

BAGPIPES npl musical wind instrument with reed pipes and an inflatable bag

BAGPIPING > BAGPIPE

BAGS > BAG

BAGSFUL > BAGFUL

BAGUET same as **>** BAGUETTE

BAGUETS > BAGUET

BAGUETTE n narrow French stick loaf

BAGUETTES > BAGUETTE

BAGUIO n hurricane

BAGUIOS > BAGUIO

BAGWASH n laundry that washes clothes without drying or pressing them

BAGWASHES > BAGWASH

BAGWIG n 18th-century wig with hair pushed back into a bag

BAGWIGS > BAGWIG

BAGWORM n type of moth

BAGWORMS > BAGWORM

BAH interj expression of contempt or disgust

BAHADA same as **>** BAJADA

BAHADAS > BAHADA

BAHADUR n title formerly conferred by the British on distinguished Indians

BAHADURS > BAHADUR

BAHT n standard monetary unit of Thailand, divided into 100 satang

BAHTS > BAHT

BAHU n (in India) daughter-in-law

BAHUS > BAHU

BAHUT n decorative cabinet

BAHUTS > BAHUT

BAHUVRIHI n class of compound words consisting of two elements the first of which is the specific feature of the second

BAIDARKA n narrow hunting boat

BAIDARKAS > BAIDARKA

BAIGNOIRE n low-level theatre box

BAIL n money deposited with a court as security for a person's reappearance in court **▷** vb pay bail for (a person)

BAILABLE adj eligible for release on bail

BAILBOND n document in which a prisoner and one or more sureties guarantee that the prisoner will attend the court hearing of the charges against him if he is released on bail

BAILBONDS > BAILBOND

BAILED > BAIL

BAILEE n person to whom the possession of goods is transferred under a bailment

BAILEES > BAILEE

BAILER > BAIL

BAILERS > BAIL

BAILEY n outermost wall or court of a castle

BAILEYS > BAILEY

BAILIE n (in Scotland) a municipal magistrate

BAILIES > BAILIE

BAILIFF n sheriff's officer who serves writs and summonses

BAILIFFS > BAILIFF

BAILING > BAIL

BAILIWICK n area a person is interested in or operates in

BAILLI n magistrate

BAILLIAGE n magistrate's area of authority

BAILLIE variant of > BAILIE

BAILLIES > BAILLIE

BAILLIS > BAILLI

BAILMENT n contractual delivery of goods in trust to a person for a specific purpose

BAILMENTS > BAILMENT

BAILOR n person who retains ownership of goods but entrusts possession of them to another under a bailment

BAILORS > BAILOR

BAILOUT n instance of helping (a person, organization, etc) out of a predicament

BAILOUTS > BAILOUT

BAILS > BAIL

BAILSMAN n one standing bail for another

BAILSMEN > BAILSMAN

BAININ n Irish collarless jacket made of white wool

BAININS > BAININ

BAINITE n mixture of iron and iron carbide found in incompletely hardened steels, produced when austenite is transformed at temperatures between the pearlite and martensite ranges

BAINITES > BAINITE

BAIRN n child

BAIRNISH > BAIRN

BAIRNLIER > BAIRN

BAIRNLIKE > BAIRN

BAIRNLY > BAIRN

BAIRNS > BAIRN

BAISEMAIN n kissing of the hand

BAIT n piece of food on a hook or in a trap to attract fish or animals ▷ vb put a piece of food on or in (a hook or trap)

BAITED > BAIT

BAITER > BAIT

BAITERS > BAIT

BAITFISH n small fish used as bait

BAITH adj both

BAITING > BAIT

BAITINGS > BAIT

BAITS > BAIT

BAIZA n Omani unit of currency

BAIZAS > BAIZA

BAIZE n woollen fabric used to cover billiard and card tables ▷ vb line or cover with such fabric

BAIZED > BAIZE

BAIZES > BAIZE

BAIZING > BAIZE

BAJADA n sloping surface formed from rock deposits

BAJADAS > BAJADA

BAJAN n freshman at Aberdeen University

BAJANS > BAJAN

BAJRA n Indian millet

BAJRAS > BAJRA

BAJREE variant of > BAJRA

BAJREES > BAJREE

BAJRI variant of > BAJRA

BAJRIS > BAJRI

BAJU n Malay jacket

BAJUS > BAJU

BAKE vb cook by dry heat as in an oven ▷ n party at which the main dish is baked

BAKEAPPLE n cloudberry

BAKEBOARD n board for bread-making

BAKED > BAKE

BAKEHOUSE same as > BAKERY

BAKELITE n tradename for any one of a class of thermosetting resins used as electric insulators and for making plastic ware, telephone receivers, etc

BAKELITES > BAKELITE

BAKEMEAT n pie

BAKEMEATS > BAKEMEAT

BAKEN > BAKE

BAKEOFF n baking competition

BAKEOFFS > BAKEOFF

BAKER n person whose business is to make or sell bread, cakes, etc

BAKERIES > BAKERY

BAKERS > BAKER

BAKERY n place where bread, cakes, etc are baked or sold

BAKES > BAKE

BAKESHOP n bakery

BAKESHOPS > BAKESHOP

BAKESTONE n flat stone in an oven

BAKEWARE n dishes for baking

BAKEWARES > BAKEWARE

BAKGAT adj fine, excellent, marvellous

BAKHSHISH same as > BAKSHEESH

BAKING n process of cooking bread, cakes, etc ▷ adj (esp of weather) very hot and dry

BAKINGS > BAKING

BAKKIE n small truck

BAKKIES > BAKKIE

BAKLAVA n rich cake of Middle Eastern origin consisting of thin layers of pastry filled with nuts and honey

BAKLAVAS > BAKLAVA

BAKLAWA same as > BAKLAVA

BAKLAWAS > BAKLAWA

BAKRA n White person, esp one from Britain ▷ adj (of people) White, esp British

BAKRAS > BAKRA

BAKSHEESH n (in some Eastern countries) money given as a tip ▷ vb give such money to (a person)

BAKSHISH same as > BAKSHEESH

BAL n balmoral

BALACLAVA n close-fitting woollen hood that covers the ears and neck, as originally worn by soldiers in the Crimean War

BALADIN n dancer

BALADINE n female dancer

BALADINES > BALADINE

BALADINS > BALADIN

BALALAIKA n guitar-like musical instrument with a triangular body

BALANCE n stability of mind or body ▷ vb weigh in a balance

BALANCED adj having weight equally distributed

BALANCER n person or thing that balances

BALANCERS > BALANCER

BALANCES > BALANCE

BALANCING > BALANCE

BALANITIS n inflammation of the glans penis, usually due to infection

BALAS n red variety of spinel, used as a gemstone

BALASES > BALAS

BALATA n tropical American tree yielding a latex-like sap

BALATAS > BALATA

BALBOA n standard currency unit of Panama, divided into 100 centesimos

BALBOAS > BALBOA

BALCONET n small balcony

BALCONETS > BALCONET

BALCONIED > BALCONY

BALCONIES > BALCONY

BALCONY n platform on the outside of a building with a rail along the outer edge

BALD adj having little or no hair on the scalp ▷ vb make bald

BALDACHIN n richly ornamented silk and gold brocade

BALDAQUIN same as > BALDACHIN

BALDED > BALD

BALDER > BALD

BALDEST > BALD

BALDFACED same as > BALD

BALDHEAD n person with a bald head

BALDHEADS > BALDHEAD

BALDICOOT another name for > COOT

BALDIE same as > BALDY

BALDIER > BALDY

BALDIES > BALDY

BALDIEST > BALDY

BALDING adj becoming bald

BALDISH > BALD

BALDLY > BALD

BALDMONEY another name for > SPIGNEL

BALDNESS > BALD

BALDPATE n person with a bald head

BALDPATED > BALDPATE

BALDPATES > BALDPATE

BALDRIC n wide silk sash or leather belt worn over the right shoulder to the left hip for carrying a sword, etc

BALDRICK same as > BALDRIC

BALDRICKS > BALDRICK

BALDRICS > BALDRIC

BALDS > BALD

BALDY adj bald ▷ n bald person

BALE same as > BAIL

BALECTION same as > BOLECTION

BALED > BALE

BALEEN n whalebone

BALEENS > BALEEN

BALEFIRE n bonfire

BALEFIRES > BALEFIRE

BALEFUL adj vindictive or menacing

BALEFULLY > BALEFUL

BALER > BAIL

BALERS > BALE

BALES > BALE

BALING > BALE

BALISAUR n badger-like animal

BALISAURS > BALISAUR

BALISE n electronic beacon used on a railway

BALISES > BALISE

BALISTA same as > BALLISTA

BALISTAE > BALISTA

BALISTAS > BALISTA

BALK vb stop short, esp suddenly or unexpectedly ▷ n roughly squared heavy timber beam

BALKANISE variant of > BALKANIZE

BALKANIZE vb divide (a territory) into small warring states

BALKED > BALK

BALKER > BALK
BALKERS > BALK
BALKIER > BALKY
BALKIEST > BALKY
BALKILY > BALKY
BALKINESS > BALKY
BALKING > BALK
BALKINGLY > BALK
BALKINGS > BALK
BALKLINE n line delimiting the balk area on a snooker table
BALKLINES > BALKLINE
BALKS > BALK
BALKY adj inclined to stop abruptly and unexpectedly
BALL n round or nearly round object, esp one used in games ▷ vb form into a ball
BALLABILE n part of ballet where all dancers perform
BALLABILI > BALLABILE
BALLAD n narrative poem or song ▷ vb sing or write a ballad
BALLADE n verse form consisting of three stanzas and an envoy, all ending with the same line
BALLADED > BALLAD
BALLADEER n singer of ballads ▷ vb perform as a balladeer
BALLADES > BALLADE
BALLADIC > BALLAD
BALLADIN same as > BALADIN
BALLADINE same as > BALADINE
BALLADING > BALLAD
BALLADINS > BALLADIN
BALLADIST > BALLAD
BALLADRY n ballad poetry or songs
BALLADS > BALLAD
BALLAN n species of fish
BALLANS > BALLAN
BALLANT vb write a ballad
BALLANTED > BALLANT
BALLANTS > BALLANT
BALLAST n substance, such as sand, used to stabilize a ship when it is not carrying cargo ▷ vb give stability or weight to
BALLASTED > BALLAST
BALLASTER > BALLAST
BALLASTS > BALLAST
BALLAT vb write a ballad
BALLATED > BALLAT
BALLATING > BALLAT
BALLATS > BALLAT
BALLCLAY n clay suitable for ceramics
BALLCLAYS > BALLCLAY
BALLCOCK n device for regulating the flow of a liquid into a tank, cistern, etc, consisting of a floating ball mounted at one end of an arm and a valve at the other end that opens and closes as the ball falls and rises
BALLCOCKS > BALLCOCK
BALLED > BALL
BALLER n ball-game player
BALLERINA n female ballet dancer
BALLERINE > BALLERINA
BALLERS > BALLER
BALLET n classical style of expressive dancing based on conventional steps
BALLETED > BALLAD
BALLETIC > BALLET
BALLETING > BALLET
BALLETS > BALLET
BALLGAME n any game played with a ball
BALLGAMES > BALLGAME
BALLHAWK n skilled baseball player
BALLHAWKS > BALLHAWK
BALLIES > BALLY
BALLING > BALL
BALLINGS > BALL
BALLISTA n ancient catapult for hurling stones, etc
BALLISTAE > BALLISTA
BALLISTAS > BALLISTA
BALLISTIC adj of or relating to ballistics
BALLIUM same as > BAILEY
BALLIUMS > BALLIUM
BALLOCKS same as > BOLLOCKS
BALLON n light, graceful quality
BALLONET n air or gas compartment in a balloon or nonrigid airship, used to control buoyancy and shape
BALLONETS > BALLONET
BALLONNE n bouncing step
BALLONNES > BALLONNE
BALLONS > BALLON
BALLOON n inflatable rubber bag used as a plaything or decoration ▷ vb fly in a balloon
BALLOONED > BALLOON
BALLOONS > BALLOON
BALLOT n method of voting ▷ vb vote or ask for a vote from
BALLOTED > BALLOT
BALLOTEE > BALLOT
BALLOTEES > BALLOT
BALLOTER > BALLOT
BALLOTERS > BALLOT
BALLOTING > BALLOT
BALLOTINI n small glass beads
BALLOTS > BALLOT
BALLOW n heavy club
BALLOWS > BALLOW
BALLPARK n stadium used for baseball games
BALLPARKS > BALLPARK
BALLPEEN as in ballpeen

hammer type of hammer
BALLPOINT n pen with a tiny ball bearing as a writing point
BALLROOM n large hall for dancing
BALLROOMS > BALLROOM
BALLS npl testicles
BALLSIER > BALLSY
BALLSIEST > BALLSY
BALLSY adj courageous and spirited
BALLUP n something botched or muddled
BALLUPS > BALLUP
BALLUTE n inflatable balloon parachute
BALLUTES > BALLUTE
BALLY another word for > BALLYHOO
BALLYARD n baseball ground
BALLYARDS > BALLYARD
BALLYHOO n exaggerated fuss ▷ vb advertise or publicize by sensational or blatant methods
BALLYHOOS > BALLYHOO
BALLYRAG same as > BULLYRAG
BALLYRAGS > BALLYRAG
BALM n aromatic substance used for healing and soothing ▷ vb apply balm to
BALMACAAN n man's knee-length loose flaring overcoat with raglan sleeves
BALMED > BALM
BALMIER > BALMY
BALMIEST > BALMY
BALMILY > BALMY
BALMINESS > BALMY
BALMING > BALM
BALMLIKE > BALM
BALMORAL n laced walking shoe
BALMORALS > BALMORAL
BALMS > BALM
BALMY adj (of weather) mild and pleasant
BALNEAL adj of or relating to baths or bathing
BALNEARY same as > BALNEAL
BALONEY n foolish talk; nonsense
BALONEYS > BALONEY
BALOO n bear
BALOOS > BALOO
BALS > BAL
BALSA n very light wood from a tropical American tree
BALSAM n type of fragrant balm ▷ vb embalm
BALSAMED > BALSAM
BALSAMIC > BALSAM
BALSAMING > BALSAM
BALSAMS > BALSAM
BALSAMY > BALSAM
BALSAS > BALSA
BALSAWOOD same as

> BALSA
BALTHASAR same as > BALTHAZAR
BALTHAZAR n wine bottle holding the equivalent of sixteen normal bottles (approximately 12 litres)
BALTI n spicy Indian dish served in a metal dish
BALTIC adj very cold
BALTIS > BALTI
BALU same as > BALOO
BALUN n device for coupling two electrical circuit elements, such as an aerial and its feeder cable, where one is balanced and the other is unbalanced
BALUNS > BALUN
BALUS > BALU
BALUSTER n set of posts supporting a rail ▷ adj (of a shape) swelling at the base and rising in a concave curve to a narrow stem or neck
BALUSTERS > BALUSTER
BALZARINE n light fabric
BAM vb cheat
BAMBI n born-again middle-aged biker: an affluent middle-aged man who rides a powerful motorbike
BAMBINI > BAMBINO
BAMBINO n young child, esp an Italian one
BAMBINOS > BAMBINO
BAMBIS > BAMBI
BAMBOO n tall treelike tropical grass with hollow stems
BAMBOOS > BAMBOO
BAMBOOZLE vb cheat or mislead
BAMMED > BAM
BAMMER > BAM
BAMMERS > BAM
BAMMING > BAM
BAMPOT n fool
BAMPOTS > BAMPOT
BAMS > BAM
BAN vb prohibit or forbid officially ▷ n official prohibition
BANAK n type of Central American tree
BANAKS > BANAK
BANAL adj ordinary and unoriginal
BANALER > BANAL
BANALEST > BANAL
BANALISE > BANAL
BANALISED > BANAL
BANALISES > BANAL
BANALITY > BANAL
BANALIZE > BANAL
BANALIZED > BANAL
BANALIZES > BANAL
BANALLY > BANAL
BANANA n yellow crescent-shaped fruit
BANANAS adj crazy
BANAUSIAN > BANAUSIC

BANAUSIC *adj* merely mechanical

BANC as in *in banc* sitting as a full court

BANCO *n* call made in gambling games

BANCOS > BANCO

BANCS > BANC

BAND *n* group of musicians playing together ▷ *vb* unite

BANDA *n* African thatched hut

BANDAGE *n* piece of material used to cover a wound or wrap an injured limb ▷ *vb* cover with a bandage

BANDAGED > BANDAGE

BANDAGER > BANDAGE

BANDAGERS > BANDAGE

BANDAGES > BANDAGE

BANDAGING > BANDAGE

BANDAID *adj* (of a solution or remedy) temporary

BANDALORE *n* old-fashioned type of yo-yo

BANDANA *same as* > BANDANNA

BANDANAS > BANDANA

BANDANNA *n* large brightly coloured handkerchief or neckerchief

BANDANNAS > BANDANNA

BANDAR *n* species of monkey

BANDARI *n* Indian English word for female monkey

BANDARIS > BANDARI

BANDARS > BANDAR

BANDAS > BANDA

BANDBOX *n* lightweight usually cylindrical box for hats

BANDBOXES > BANDBOX

BANDBRAKE *n* type of brake

BANDEAU *n* narrow ribbon worn round the head

BANDEAUS > BANDEAU

BANDEAUX > BANDEAU

BANDED > BAND

BANDEIRA *n* 17th-century Portuguese slave-hunting expedition in Brazil

BANDEIRAS > BANDEIRA

BANDELET *n* moulding round top of column

BANDELETS > BANDELET

BANDELIER *same as* > BANDOLEER

BANDER > BAND

BANDEROL *same as* > BANDEROLE

BANDEROLE *n* narrow flag usually with forked ends

BANDEROLS > BANDEROL

BANDERS > BAND

BANDFISH *n* Mediterranean fish with an elongated body

BANDH *n* (in India) a general strike

BANDHS > BANDH

BANDICOOT *n* ratlike Australian marsupial

BANDIED > BANDY

BANDIER > BANDY

BANDIES > BANDY

BANDIEST > BANDY

BANDINESS > BANDY

BANDING *n* practice of grouping schoolchildren according to ability to ensure a balanced intake at different levels of ability to secondary school

BANDINGS > BANDING

BANDIT *n* robber, esp a member of an armed gang

BANDITO *n* Mexican bandit

BANDITOS > BANDITO

BANDITRY > BANDIT

BANDITS > BANDIT

BANDITTI > BANDIT

BANDITTIS > BANDIT

BANDMATE *n* fellow member of band

BANDMATES > BANDMATE

BANDOBAST *same as* > BANDOBUST

BANDOBUST *n* (in India and Pakistan) an arrangement

BANDOG *n* ferocious dog

BANDOGS > BANDOG

BANDOLEER *same as* > BANDOLIER

BANDOLEON *same as* > BANDONEON

BANDOLERO *n* highwayman

BANDOLIER *n* shoulder belt for holding cartridges

BANDOLINE *n* glutinous hair dressing, used (esp formerly) to keep the hair in place

BANDONEON *n* type of square concertina, esp used in Argentina

BANDONION *same as* > BANDONEON

BANDOOK *same as* > BUNDOOK

BANDOOKS > BANDOOK

BANDORA *same as* > BANDORE

BANDORAS > BANDORA

BANDORE *n* 16th-century plucked musical instrument resembling a lute but larger and fitted with seven pairs of metal strings

BANDORES > BANDORE

BANDROL *same as* > BANDEROLE

BANDROLS > BANDROL

BANDS > BAND

BANDSAW *n* power saw with continuous blade

BANDSAWS > BANDSAW

BANDSHELL *n* bandstand concave at back

BANDSMAN *n* player in a musical band

BANDSMEN > BANDSMAN

BANDSTAND *n* roofed outdoor platform for a band

BANDSTER *n* binder of wheat sheaves

BANDSTERS > BANDSTER

BANDURA *n* type of lute

BANDURAS > BANDURA

BANDWAGON *n* type of wagon

BANDWIDTH *n* range of frequencies within a given waveband used for a particular transmission

BANDY *adj* having legs curved outwards at the knees ▷ *vb* exchange (words) in a heated manner

BANDYING > BANDY

BANDYINGS > BANDY

BANDYMAN *n* carriage or cart

BANDYMEN > BANDYMAN

BANE *n* person or thing that causes misery or distress ▷ *vb* cause harm or distress to (someone)

BANEBERRY *n* type of plant with small white flowers and red or white poisonous berries

BANED > BANE

BANEFUL *adj* destructive, poisonous, or fatal

BANEFULLY > BANEFUL

BANES > BANE

BANG *vb* make a short explosive noise

BANGALAY *n* Australian tree valued for its hard red wood

BANGALAYS > BANGALAY

BANGALORE as in *bangalore torpedo* explosive device in a long metal tube, used to blow gaps in barbed-wire barriers

BANGALOW *n* Australian palm tree native to New South Wales and Queensland

BANGALOWS > BANGALOW

BANGED > BANG

BANGER *n* old decrepit car

BANGERS > BANGER

BANGING > BANG

BANGKOK *n* type of straw hat

BANGKOKS > BANGKOK

BANGLE *n* bracelet worn round the arm or the ankle

BANGLED > BANGLE

BANGLES > BANGLE

BANGS > BANG

BANGSRING *same as* > BANXRING

BANGSTER *n* ruffian

BANGSTERS > BANGSTER

BANGTAIL *n* horse's tail cut straight across but not through the bone

BANGTAILS > BANGTAIL

BANI > BAN

BANIA *same as* > BANYAN

BANIAN *same as* > BANYAN

BANIANS > BANIAN

BANIAS > BANIA

BANING > BANE

BANISH *vb* send (someone) into exile

BANISHED > BANISH

BANISHER > BANISH

BANISHERS > BANISH

BANISHES > BANISH

BANISHING > BANISH

BANISTER *same as* > BANNISTER

BANISTERS *npl* railing supported by posts on a staircase

BANJAX *vb* ruin; destroy

BANJAXED > BANJAX

BANJAXES > BANJAX

BANJAXING > BANJAX

BANJO *n* guitar-like musical instrument with a circular body

BANJOES > BANJO

BANJOIST > BANJO

BANJOISTS > BANJO

BANJOS > BANJO

BANJULELE *n* small banjo

BANK *n* institution offering services such as the safekeeping and lending of money ▷ *vb* deposit (cash or cheques) in a bank

BANKABLE *adj* likely to ensure financial success

BANKBOOK *n* book held by depositors at certain banks, in which the bank enters a record of deposits, withdrawals, and earned interest

BANKBOOKS > BANKBOOK

BANKCARD *n* card guaranteeing payment of cheque

BANKCARDS > BANKCARD

BANKED > BANK

BANKER *n* manager or owner of a bank

BANKERLY > BANKER

BANKERS > BANKER

BANKET *n* gold-bearing conglomerate found in South Africa

BANKETS > BANKET

BANKING *same as* > BANK

BANKINGS > BANK

BANKIT *same as* > BANQUETTE

BANKITS > BANKIT

BANKNOTE *n* piece of paper money

BANKNOTES > BANKNOTE

BANKROLL *n* roll of currency notes ▷ *vb* provide the capital for

BANKROLLS > BANKROLL

BANKRUPT *n* person declared by a court to be unable to pay his or her debts ▷ *adj* financially ruined ▷ *vb* make bankrupt

BANKRUPTS > BANKRUPT

BANKS > BANK

BANKSIA *n* Australian evergreen tree or shrub

BANKSIAS > BANKSIA

BANKSIDE *n* riverside

BANKSIDES > BANKSIDE

BANKSMAN *n* crane driver's

helper, who signals instructions to the driver for the movement of the crane and its jib

BANKSMEN > BANKSMAN

BANLIEUE n suburb of a city

BANLIEUES > BANLIEUE

BANNABLE > BAN

BANNED > BAN

BANNER n long strip of cloth displaying a slogan, advertisement, etc ▷ vb (of a newspaper headline) to display (a story) prominently ▷ adj outstandingly successful

BANNERAL same as > BANDEROLE

BANNERED > BANNER

BANNERET n small banner

BANNERETS > BANNERET

BANNERING > BANNER

BANNEROL same as > BANDEROLE

BANNEROLS > BANNEROL

BANNERS > BANNER

BANNET n bonnet

BANNETS > BANNET

BANNING > BAN

BANNISTER same as > BANISTERS

BANNOCK n round flat cake made from oatmeal or barley

BANNOCKS > BANNOCK

BANNS npl public declaration, esp in a church, of an intended marriage

BANOFFEE n filling for a pie, consisting of toffee and banana

BANOFFEES > BANOFFEE

BANOFFI same as > BANOFFEE

BANOFFIS > BANOFFI

BANQUET n elaborate formal dinner ▷ vb hold or take part in a banquet

BANQUETED > BANQUET

BANQUETER > BANQUET

BANQUETS > BANQUET

BANQUETTE n upholstered bench

BANS same as > BANNS

BANSELA same as > BONSELA

BANSELAS > BANSELA

BANSHEE n (in Irish folklore) female spirit whose wailing warns of a coming death

BANSHEES > BANSHEE

BANSHIE same as > BANSHEE

BANSHIES > BANSHIE

BANT n string ▷ vb tie with string

BANTAM n small breed of chicken

BANTAMS > BANTAM

BANTED > BANT

BANTENG n wild ox

BANTENGS > BANTENG

BANTER vb tease jokingly ▷ n teasing or joking conversation

BANTERED > BANTER

BANTERER > BANTER

BANTERERS > BANTER

BANTERING > BANTER

BANTERS > BANTER

BANTIES > BANTY

BANTING > BANT

BANTINGS > BANT

BANTLING n young child

BANTLINGS > BANTLING

BANTS > BANT

BANTU n offensive name for a person who speaks a Bantu language

BANTUS > BANTU

BANTY n bantam

BANXRING n tree-shrew

BANXRINGS > BANXRING

BANYA n traditional Russian steam bath

BANYAN n Indian tree whose branches grow down into the soil forming additional trunks

BANYANS > BANYAN

BANYAS > BANYA

BANZAI interj patriotic cheer, battle cry, or salutation

BANZAIS > BANZAI

BAOBAB n African tree with a thick trunk and angular branches

BAOBABS > BAOBAB

BAP n large soft bread roll

BAPS > BAP

BAPTISE same as > BAPTIZE

BAPTISED > BAPTISE

BAPTISER > BAPTISE

BAPTISERS > BAPTISE

BAPTISES > BAPTISE

BAPTISIA n species of wild flower

BAPTISIAS > BAPTISIA

BAPTISING > BAPTISE

BAPTISM n Christian religious ceremony in which a person is immersed in or sprinkled with water as a sign of being cleansed from sin and accepted into the Church

BAPTISMAL > BAPTISM

BAPTISMS > BAPTISM

BAPTIST n one who baptizes

BAPTISTRY n part of a Christian church in which baptisms are carried out

BAPTISTS > BAPTIST

BAPTIZE vb perform baptism on

BAPTIZED > BAPTIZE

BAPTIZER > BAPTIZE

BAPTIZERS > BAPTIZE

BAPTIZES > BAPTIZE

BAPTIZING > BAPTIZE

BAPU n spiritual father

BAPUS > BAPU

BAR n rigid usually straight length of metal, wood, etc, that is longer than it is wide or thick, used esp as a barrier or as a structural or mechanical part ▷ vb fasten or secure with a bar

BARACAN same as > BARRACAN

BARACANS > BARACAN

BARACHOIS n (in the Atlantic Provinces of Canada) a shallow lagoon formed by a sand bar

BARAGOUIN n incomprehensible language

BARASINGA n type of deer

BARATHEA n fabric made of silk and wool or cotton and rayon, used esp for coats

BARATHEAS > BARATHEA

BARATHRUM n abyss

BARAZA n place where public meetings are held

BARAZAS > BARAZA

BARB n cutting remark ▷ vb provide with a barb or barbs

BARBAL adj of a beard

BARBARIAN n member of a primitive or uncivilized people ▷ adj uncivilized or brutal

BARBARIC adj cruel or brutal

BARBARISE same as > BARBARIZE

BARBARISM n condition of being backward or ignorant

BARBARITY n state of being barbaric or barbarous

BARBARIZE vb make or become barbarous

BARBAROUS adj uncivilized

BARBASCO n S American plant

BARBASCOS > BARBASCO

BARBASTEL n insectivorous forest bat

BARBATE adj having tufts of long hairs

BARBATED > BARBATE

BARBE n Waldensian missionary

BARBECUE n grill on which food is cooked over hot charcoal, usu. outdoors ▷ vb cook (food) on a barbecue

BARBECUED > BARBECUE

BARBECUER > BARBECUE

BARBECUES > BARBECUE

BARBED > BARB

BARBEL n long thin growth that hangs from the jaws of certain fishes, such as the carp

BARBELL n long metal rod to which heavy discs are attached at each end for weightlifting

BARBELLS > BARBELL

BARBELS > BARBEL

BARBEQUE same as > BARBECUE

BARBEQUED > BARBEQUE

BARBEQUES > BARBEQUE

BARBER n person who cuts men's hair and shaves beards ▷ vb cut the hair of

BARBERED > BARBER

BARBERING > BARBER

BARBERRY n shrub with orange or red berries

BARBERS > BARBER

BARBES > BARBE

BARBET n type of small tropical brightly coloured bird with short weak wings and a sharp stout bill

BARBETS > BARBET

BARBETTE n (formerly) an earthen platform inside a parapet, from which heavy guns could fire over the top

BARBETTES > BARBETTE

BARBICAN n walled defence to protect a gate or drawbridge of a fortification

BARBICANS > BARBICAN

BARBICEL n any of the minute hooks on the barbules of feathers that interlock with those of adjacent barbules

BARBICELS > BARBICEL

BARBIE short for > BARBECUE

BARBIES > BARBIE

BARBING > BARB

BARBITAL same as > BARBITONE

BARBITALS > BARBITAL

BARBITONE n long-acting barbiturate used medicinally, usually in the form of the sodium salt, as a sedative or hypnotic

BARBLESS > BARB

BARBOLA n small models of flowers, etc made from plastic paste

BARBOLAS > BARBOLA

BARBOTINE n clay used in making decorated pottery

BARBS > BARB

BARBULE n very small barb

BARBULES > BARBULE

BARBUT n open-faced helmet

BARBUTS > BARBUT

BARBWIRE n barbed wire

BARBWIRES > BARBWIRE

BARBY same as > BARBECUE

BARCA n boat

BARCAROLE n Venetian boat song

BARCAS > BARCA

BARCHAN n crescent-shaped shifting sand dune, convex on the windward side and steeper and concave on the leeward

BARCHANE same as > BARCHAN

BARCHANES > BARCHANE

BARCHANS > BARCHAN

BARCODE n machine-readable code printed on goods

BARCODED *adj* having a barcode

BARCODES > BARCODE

BARD *n* poet ▷ *vb* place a piece of pork fat on

BARDASH *n* kept boy in a homosexual relationship

BARDASHES > BARDASH

BARDE *same as* > BARD

BARDED > BARDE

BARDES > BARDE

BARDIC > BARD

BARDIE *n* type of Australian grub

BARDIER > BARD

BARDIES > BARDIE

BARDIEST > BARD

BARDING > BARD

BARDISM > BARD

BARDISMS > BARD

BARDLING *n* inferior poet

BARDLINGS > BARDLING

BARDO *n* (in Tibetan Buddhism) the state of the soul between its death and its rebirth

BARDOS > BARDO

BARDS > BARD

BARDSHIP > BARD

BARDSHIPS > BARD

BARDY > BARD

BARE *adj* unclothed, naked ▷ *vb* uncover

BAREBACK *adv* (of horse-riding) without a saddle ▷ *vb* ride bareback

BAREBACKS > BAREBACK

BAREBOAT *n* boat chartered without crew, provisions, etc

BAREBOATS > BAREBOAT

BAREBONE *n* computer casing containing bare essentials

BAREBONED *adj* short of resources

BAREBONES > BAREBONE

BARED > BARE

BAREFACED *adj* shameless or obvious

BAREFIT *same as* > BAREFOOT

BAREFOOT *adv* with the feet uncovered

BAREGE *n* light silky gauze fabric made of wool ▷ *adj* made of such a fabric

BAREGES > BAREGE

BAREGINE *n* curative ingredient in thermal waters

BAREGINES > BAREGINE

BAREHAND *vb* handle with bare hands

BAREHANDS > BAREHAND

BAREHEAD *adv* with head unvovered

BARELAND as in *bareland croft* refers to a croft with no croft house

BARELY *adv* only just

BARENESS > BARE

BARER > BARE

BARES > BARE

BARESARK *another word for* > BERSERK

BARESARKS > BARESARK

BAREST > BARE

BARF *vb* vomit ▷ *n* act of vomiting

BARFED > BARF

BARFING > BARF

BARFLIES > BARFLY

BARFLY *n* person who frequents bars

BARFS > BARF

BARFUL *adj* presenting difficulties

BARGAIN *n* agreement establishing what each party will give, receive, or perform in a transaction ▷ *vb* negotiate the terms of an agreement

BARGAINED > BARGAIN

BARGAINER > BARGAIN

BARGAINS > BARGAIN

BARGANDER *same as* > BERGANDER

BARGE *n* flat-bottomed boat used to transport freight ▷ *vb* push violently

BARGED > BARGE

BARGEE *n* person in charge of a barge

BARGEES > BARGEE

BARGEESE > BARGOOSE

BARGELLO *n* zigzag tapestry stitch

BARGELLOS > BARGELLO

BARGEMAN *same as* > BARGEE

BARGEMEN > BARGEMAN

BARGEPOLE *n* long pole used to propel a barge

BARGES > BARGE

BARGEST *same as* > BARGHEST

BARGESTS > BARGEST

BARGHEST *n* mythical goblin in the shape of a dog

BARGHESTS > BARGHEST

BARGING > BARGE

BARGOON *Canadian word for* > BARGAIN

BARGOONS > BARGOON

BARGOOSE *n* type of goose; sheldrake

BARGUEST *same as* > BARGHEST

BARGUESTS > BARGUEST

BARHOP *vb* visit several bars in succession

BARHOPPED > BARHOP

BARHOPS > BARHOP

BARIATRIC *adj* of the treatment of obesity

BARIC *adj* of or containing barium

BARILLA *n* impure mixture of sodium carbonate and sodium sulphate obtained from the ashes of certain plants, such as the saltworts

BARILLAS > BARILLA

BARING > BARE

BARISH *adj* quite thinly covered

BARISTA *n* person who makes and sells coffee in a coffee bar

BARISTAS > BARISTA

BARITE *n* colourless or white mineral consisting of barium sulphate in orthorhombic crystalline form, occurring in sedimentary rocks and with sulphide ores: a source of barium.

BARITES > BARITE

BARITONAL > BARITONE

BARITONE *n* (singer with) the second lowest adult male voice ▷ *adj* relating to or denoting a baritone

BARITONES > BARITONE

BARIUM *n* soft white metallic element

BARIUMS > BARIUM

BARK *vb* (of a dog) make its typical loud abrupt cry

BARKAN *same as* > BARCHAN

BARKANS > BARKAN

BARKED > BARK

BARKEEP *n* barkeeper

BARKEEPER *another name (esp US) for* > BARTENDER

BARKEEPS > BARKEEP

BARKEN *vb* become dry with a bark-like outer layer

BARKENED > BARKEN

BARKENING > BARKEN

BARKENS > BARKEN

BARKER *n* person at a fairground who calls loudly to passers-by in order to attract customers

BARKERS > BARKER

BARKHAN *same as* > BARCHAN

BARKHANS > BARKHAN

BARKIER > BARKY

BARKIEST > BARKY

BARKING *adj* mad ▷ *adv* extremely

BARKLESS > BARK

BARKS > BARK

BARKY *adj* having the texture or appearance of bark

BARLEDUC *n* French preserve made of currants

BARLEDUCS > BARLEDUC

BARLESS > BAR

BARLEY *n* tall grasslike plant cultivated for grain ▷ *sentence substitute* cry for truce or respite from the rules of a game

BARLEYS > BARLEY

BARLOW *n* type of strong knife

BARLOWS > BARLOW

BARM *n* yeasty froth on fermenting malt liquors

BARMAID *n* woman who serves in a pub

BARMAIDS > BARMAID

BARMAN *same as* > BARTENDER

BARMBRACK *n* loaf of bread with currants in it

BARMEN > BARMAN

BARMIE *same as* > BARMY

BARMIER > BARMY

BARMIEST > BARMY

BARMINESS > BARMY

BARMKIN *n* protective wall around castle

BARMKINS > BARMKIN

BARMPOT *n* foolish or deranged person

BARMPOTS > BARMPOT

BARMS > BARM

BARMY *adj* insane

BARN *n* large building on a farm used for storing grain ▷ *vb* keep in a barn

BARNACLE *n* shellfish that lives attached to rocks, ship bottoms, etc

BARNACLED > BARNACLE

BARNACLES > BARNACLE

BARNBRACK *same as* > BARMBRACK

BARNED > BARN

BARNET *n* hair

BARNETS > BARNET

BARNEY *n* noisy fight or argument ▷ *vb* argue or quarrel

BARNEYED > BARNEY

BARNEYING > BARNEY

BARNEYS > BARNEY

BARNIER > BARNY

BARNIEST > BARNY

BARNING > BARN

BARNLIKE > BARN

BARNS > BARN

BARNSTORM *vb* tour rural districts putting on shows or making speeches in a political campaign

BARNY *adj* reminiscent of a barn

BARNYARD *n* yard adjoining a barn

BARNYARDS > BARNYARD

BAROCCO *same as* > BAROQUE

BAROCCOS > BAROCCO

BAROCK *same as* > BAROQUE

BAROCKS > BAROCK

BAROGRAM *n* record of atmospheric pressure traced by a barograph or similar instrument

BAROGRAMS > BAROGRAM

BAROGRAPH *n* barometer that automatically keeps a record of changes in atmospheric pressure

BAROLO *n* red Italian wine

BAROLOS > BAROLO

BAROMETER *n* instrument for measuring atmospheric pressure

BAROMETRY > BAROMETER

BAROMETZ *n* fern whose woolly rhizoma resemble a lamb

b

BARON n member of the lowest rank of nobility

BARONAGE n barons collectively

BARONAGES > BARONAGE

BARONESS n woman holding the rank of baron

BARONET n commoner who holds the lowest hereditary British title

BARONETCY n rank, position, or patent of a baronet

BARONETS > BARONET

BARONG n broad-bladed cleaver-like knife used in the Philippines

BARONGS > BARONG

BARONIAL adj of, relating to, or befitting a baron or barons

BARONIES > BARONY

BARONNE n baroness

BARONNES > BARONNE

BARONS > BARON

BARONY n domain or rank of a baron

BAROPHILE n a living organism that grows best in conditions of high atmospheric pressure

BAROQUE n highly ornate style of art, architecture, or music from the late 16th to the early 18th century ▷ adj ornate in style

BAROQUELY > BAROQUE

BAROQUES > BAROQUE

BAROSAUR n large dinosaur

BAROSAURS > BAROSAUR

BAROSCOPE n any instrument for measuring atmospheric pressure, esp a manometer with one side open to the atmosphere

BAROSTAT n device for maintaining constant pressure, such as one used in an aircraft cabin

BAROSTATS > BAROSTAT

BAROTITIS n inflammation of the ear caused by a change in air pressure

BAROUCHE n four-wheeled horse-drawn carriage, popular in the 19th century, having a retractable hood over the rear half, seats inside for two couples facing each other, and a driver's seat outside at the front

BAROUCHES > BAROUCHE

BARP n hillock or bank of stones

BARPERSON n person who serves in a pub: used esp in advertisements

BARPS > BARP

BARQUE n sailing ship, esp one with three masts

BARQUES > BARQUE

BARQUETTE n boat-shaped pastry shell

BARRA n barramundi

BARRABLE > BAR

BARRACAN n thick, strong fabric

BARRACANS > BARRACAN

BARRACE n record of teams entering a sports contest

BARRACES > BARRACE

BARRACK vb criticize loudly or shout against (a team or speaker)

BARRACKED > BARRACK

BARRACKER > BARRACK

BARRACKS npl building used to accommodate military personnel

BARRACOON n (formerly) a temporary place of confinement for slaves or convicts, awaiting transportation

BARRACUDA n tropical sea fish

BARRAGE n continuous delivery of questions, complaints, etc ▷ vb attack or confront with a barrage

BARRAGED > BARRAGE

BARRAGES > BARRAGE

BARRAGING > BARRAGE

BARRANCA n ravine or precipice

BARRANCAS > BARRANCA

BARRANCO same as > BARRANCA

BARRANCOS > BARRANCO

BARRAS > BARRA

BARRAT n fraudulent dealings

BARRATER same as > BARRATOR

BARRATERS > BARRATER

BARRATOR n person guilty of barratry

BARRATORS > BARRATOR

BARRATRY n (formerly) the vexatious stirring up of quarrels or bringing of lawsuits

BARRATS > BARRAT

BARRE n rail at hip height used for ballet practice ▷ vb execute guitar chords by laying the index finger over some or all of the strings so that the pitch of each stopped string is simultaneously raised ▷ adv by using the barré

BARRED > BAR

BARREED > BARRE

BARREFULL same as > BARFUL

BARREING > BARRE

BARREL n cylindrical container with rounded sides and flat ends ▷ vb put in a barrel

BARRELAGE > BARREL

BARRELED > BARREL

BARRELFUL same as > BARREL

BARRELING > BARREL

BARRELLED > BARREL

BARRELS > BARREL

BARREN adj (of a woman or female animal) incapable of producing offspring

BARRENER > BARREN

BARRENEST > BARREN

BARRENLY > BARREN

BARRENS npl (in North America) a stretch of usually level land that is sparsely vegetated or barren

BARRES > BARRE

BARRET n small flat cap resembling a biretta

BARRETOR n quarrelsome person

BARRETORS > BARRETOR

BARRETRY same as > BARRATRY

BARRETS > BARRET

BARRETTE n clasp or pin for holding women's hair in place

BARRETTER same as > BARRETOR

BARRETTES > BARRETTE

BARRICADE n barrier, esp one erected hastily for defence ▷ vb erect a barricade across (an entrance)

BARRICADO same as > BARRICADE

BARRICO n small container for liquids

BARRICOES > BARRICO

BARRICOS > BARRICO

BARRIE adj very good

BARRIER n anything that prevents access, progress, or union ▷ vb create or form a barrier

BARRIERED > BARRIER

BARRIERS > BARRIER

BARRIES > BARRY

BARRIEST > BARRIE

BARRING > BAR

BARRINGS > BAR

BARRIO n Spanish-speaking quarter in a town or city, esp in the US

BARRIOS > BARRIO

BARRISTER n lawyer qualified to plead in a higher court

BARRO adj embarrassing

BARROOM n room or building where alcoholic drinks are served over a counter

BARROOMS > BARROOM

BARROW n wheelbarrow

BARROWFUL same as > BARROW

BARROWS > BARROW

BARRULET n narrow band across heraldic shield

BARRULETS > BARRULET

BARRY n mistake or blunder

BARS > BAR

BARSTOOL n high stool in bar

BARSTOOLS > BARSTOOL

BARTEND vb serve drinks from a bar

BARTENDED > BARTEND

BARTENDER n man who serves in a bar

BARTENDS > BARTEND

BARTER vb trade (goods) in exchange for other goods ▷ n trade by the exchange of goods

BARTERED > BARTER

BARTERER > BARTER

BARTERERS > BARTER

BARTERING > BARTER

BARTERS > BARTER

BARTISAN same as > BARTIZAN

BARTISANS > BARTISAN

BARTIZAN n small turret projecting from a wall, parapet, or tower

BARTIZANS > BARTIZAN

BARTON n farmyard

BARTONS > BARTON

BARTSIA n type of semiparasitic plant

BARTSIAS > BARTSIA

BARWARE n glasses, etc used in a bar

BARWARES > BARWARE

BARWOOD n red wood from small African tree

BARWOODS > BARWOOD

BARYE n unit of pressure in the cgs system equal to one dyne per square centimetre. 1 barye is equivalent to 1 microbar

BARYES > BARYE

BARYON n elementary particle that has a mass greater than or equal to that of the proton

BARYONIC adj of or relating to a baryon

BARYONS > BARYON

BARYTA same as > BARITE

BARYTAS > BARYTA

BARYTE same as > BARYTA

BARYTES > BARYTE

BARYTIC > BARYTA

BARYTON n bass viol with sympathetic strings as well as its six main strings

BARYTONE adj having the last syllable unaccented ▷ n word in which the last syllable is unaccented

BARYTONES > BARYTONE

BARYTONS > BARYTON

BAS > BA

BASAL adj of, at, or constituting a base

BASALLY > BASAL

BASALT n dark volcanic rock

BASALTES n unglazed black stoneware

BASALTIC > BASALT

BASALTINE adj resembling basalt

BASALTS > BASALT

BASAN n sheepskin tanned in bark

BASANITE n black basaltic rock containing

plagioclase, augite, olivine, and nepheline, leucite, or analcite, formerly used as a touchstone

BASANITES > BASANITE

BASANS > BASAN

BASANT *n* Pakistani spring festival

BASANTS > BASANT

BASCINET *same as* > BASINET

BASCINETS > BASCINET

BASCULE *n* drawbridge that operates by a counterbalanced weight

BASCULES > BASCULE

BASE *n* bottom or supporting part of anything ▷ *vb* use as a basis (for) ▷ *adj* dishonourable or immoral

BASEBALL *n* team game in which runs are scored by hitting a ball with a bat then running round four bases

BASEBALLS > BASEBALL

BASEBAND *n* transmission technique using a narrow range of frequencies that allows only one message to be telecommunicated at a time

BASEBANDS > BASEBAND

BASEBOARD *n* board functioning as the base of anything

BASEBORN *adj* born of humble parents

BASED > BASE

BASEEJ *npl* Iranian volunteer militia

BASELARD *n* short sword

BASELARDS > BASELARD

BASELESS *adj* not based on fact

BASELINE *n* value or starting point on an imaginary scale with which other things are compared

BASELINER *n* tennis player who plays most of his or her shots from the back of the court

BASELINES > BASELINE

BASELY > BASE

BASEMAN *n* fielder positioned near a base

BASEMEN > BASEMAN

BASEMENT *n* partly or wholly underground storey of a building

BASEMENTS > BASEMENT

BASEN *Spencerian spelling of* > BASIN

BASENESS > BASE

BASENJI *n* small smooth-haired breed of dog of African origin having a tightly curled tail and an inability to bark

BASENJIS > BASENJI

BASEPLATE *n* flat supporting plate or frame

BASER > BASE

BASES > BASIS

BASEST > BASE

BASH *vb* hit violently or forcefully ▷ *n* heavy blow

BASHAW *n* important or pompous person

BASHAWISM > BASHAW

BASHAWS > BASHAW

BASHED > BASH

BASHER > BASH

BASHERS > BASH

BASHES > BASH

BASHFUL *adj* shy or modest

BASHFULLY > BASHFUL

BASHING > BASH

BASHINGS > BASH

BASHLESS *adj* not ashamed

BASHLIK *n* Caucasian hood

BASHLIKS > BASHLIK

BASHLYK *same as* > BASHLIK

BASHLYKS > BASHLYK

BASHMENT *same as* > DANCEHALL

BASHMENTS > BASHMENT

BASHO *n* grand tournament in sumo wrestling

BASIC *adj* of or forming a base or basis ▷ *n* fundamental principle, fact, etc

BASICALLY *adv* in a fundamental or elementary manner

BASICITY *n* state of being a base

BASICS > BASIC

BASIDIA > BASIDIUM

BASIDIAL > BASIDIUM

BASIDIUM *n* structure, produced by basidiomycetous fungi after sexual reproduction, in which spores are formed at the tips of projecting slender stalks

BASIFIED > BASIFY

BASIFIER > BASIFY

BASIFIERS > BASIFY

BASIFIES > BASIFY

BASIFIXED *adj* (of an anther) attached to the filament by its base

BASIFUGAL *a less common word for* > ACROPETAL

BASIFY *vb* make basic

BASIFYING > BASIFY

BASIJ *same as* > BASEEJ

BASIL *n* aromatic herb used in cooking

BASILAR *adj* of or situated at a base

BASILARY *same as* > BASILAR

BASILECT *n* debased dialect

BASILECTS > BASILECT

BASILIC > BASILICA

BASILICA *n* rectangular church with a rounded end and two aisles

BASILICAE > BASILICA

BASILICAL > BASILICA

BASILICAN > BASILICA

BASILICAS > BASILICA

BASILICON *n* healing ointment

BASILISK *n* legendary serpent said to kill by its breath or glance

BASILISKS > BASILISK

BASILS > BASIL

BASIN *n* round open container

BASINAL > BASIN

BASINED > BASIN

BASINET *n* close-fitting medieval helmet of light steel usually with a visor

BASINETS > BASINET

BASINFUL *n* amount a basin will hold

BASINFULS > BASINFUL

BASING > BASE

BASINLIKE > BASIN

BASINS > BASIN

BASION *n* (in anatomy) midpoint on the forward border of the foramen magnum

BASIONS > BASION

BASIPETAL *adj* (of leaves and flowers) produced in order from the apex downwards so that the youngest are at the base

BASIS *n* fundamental principles etc from which something is started or developed

BASK *vb* lie in or be exposed to something, esp pleasant warmth

BASKED > BASK

BASKET *n* container made of interwoven strips of wood or cane

BASKETFUL *n* as much as a basket will hold

BASKETRY *n* art or practice of making baskets

BASKETS > BASKET

BASKING > BASK

BASKS > BASK

BASMATI *n* variety of long-grain rice with slender aromatic grains, used for savoury dishes

BASMATIS > BASMATI

BASNET *same as* > BASINET

BASNETS > BASNET

BASOCHE *n* society of medieval French lawyers who performed comic plays

BASOCHES > BASOCHE

BASON *same as* > BASIN

BASONS > BASON

BASOPHIL *adj* (of cells or cell contents) easily stained by basic dyes ▷ *n* basophil cell, esp a leucocyte

BASOPHILE *same as* > BASOPHIL

BASOPHILS > BASOPHIL

BASQUE *n* tight-fitting bodice for women

BASQUED > BASQUE

BASQUES > BASQUE

BASQUINE *n* tight-fitting bodice

BASQUINES > BASQUINE

BASS *vb* speak or sing in a low pitch

BASSE *same as* > BASS

BASSED > BASS

BASSER > BASS

BASSES > BASS

BASSEST > BASS

BASSET *n* long low smooth-haired breed of hound with short strong legs and long ears ▷ *vb* outcrop

BASSETED > BASSET

BASSETING > BASSET

BASSETS > BASSET

BASSETT *same as* > BASSET

BASSETTED > BASSET

BASSETTS > BASSET

BASSI > BASSO

BASSIER > BASSY

BASSIEST > BASSY

BASSINET *n* wickerwork or wooden cradle or pram, usually hooded

BASSINETS > BASSINET

BASSING > BASS

BASSIST *n* player of a double bass, esp in a jazz band

BASSISTS > BASSIST

BASSLINE *n* (in jazz, rock, and pop music) part played by the bass guitar

BASSLINES > BASSLINE

BASSLY > BASS

BASSNESS > BASS

BASSO *n* singer with a bass voice

BASSOON *n* low-pitched woodwind instrument

BASSOONS > BASSOON

BASSOS > BASSO

BASSWOOD *n* N American linden tree

BASSWOODS > BASSWOOD

BASSY *adj* manifesting strong bass tones

BAST *n* fibrous material obtained from the phloem of jute, hemp, flax, lime, etc, used for making rope, matting, etc

BASTA *interj* enough; stop

BASTARD *n* offensive term for an obnoxious or despicable person ▷ *adj* offensive term meaning illegitimate by birth

BASTARDLY > BASTARD

BASTARDRY *n* malicious or cruel behaviour

BASTARDS > BASTARD

BASTARDY *n* condition of being a bastard

BASTE *vb* moisten (meat) during cooking with hot fat

BASTED > BASTE

BASTER > BASTE

b

BASTERS > BASTE

BASTES > BASTE

BASTI n (in India) a slum inhabited by poor people

BASTIDE n small isolated house in France

BASTIDES > BASTIDE

BASTILE same as **>** BASTILLE

BASTILES > BASTILE

BASTILLE n prison

BASTILLES > BASTILLE

BASTINADE same as **>** BASTINADO

BASTINADO n punishment or torture by beating on the soles of the feet with a stick ▷ vb beat (a person) in this way

BASTING n loose temporary stitches

BASTINGS > BASTING

BASTION n projecting part of a fortification

BASTIONED > BASTION

BASTIONS > BASTION

BASTIS > BASTI

BASTLE n fortified house

BASTLES > BASTLE

BASTO n ace of clubs in certain card games

BASTOS > BASTO

BASTS > BAST

BASUCO n cocaine-based drug

BASUCOS > BASUCO

BAT n any of various types of club used to hit the ball in certain sports ▷ vb strike with or as if with a bat

BATABLE > BAT

BATATA n sweet potato

BATATAS > BATATA

BATAVIA n variety of lettuce with smooth pale green leaves

BATAVIAS > BATAVIA

BATBOY n boy who works at baseball game

BATBOYS > BATBOY

BATCH n group of people or things dealt with at the same time ▷ vb group (items) for efficient processing

BATCHED > BATCH

BATCHER > BATCH

BATCHERS > BATCH

BATCHES > BATCH

BATCHING > BATCH

BATCHINGS > BATCH

BATE vb (of hawks) to jump violently from a perch or the falconer's fist, often hanging from the leash while struggling to escape

BATEAU n light flat-bottomed boat used on rivers in Canada and the northern US

BATEAUX > BATEAU

BATED > BATE

BATELESS > BATE

BATELEUR n African bird of prey with a short tail and long wings

BATELEURS > BATELEUR

BATEMENT n reduction

BATEMENTS > BATEMENT

BATES > BATE

BATFISH n type of angler fish with a flattened scaleless body

BATFISHES > BATFISH

BATFOWL vb catch birds by temporarily blinding them with light

BATFOWLED > BATFOWL

BATFOWLER > BATFOWL

BATFOWLS > BATFOWL

BATGIRL n girl who works at baseball games

BATGIRLS > BATGIRL

BATH n large container in which to wash the body ▷ vb wash in a bath

BATHCUBE n cube of soluble scented material for use in a bath

BATHCUBES > BATHCUBE

BATHE vb swim in open water for pleasure

BATHED > BATHE

BATHER > BATHE

BATHERS npl swimming costume

BATHES > BATHE

BATHETIC adj containing or displaying bathos

BATHHOUSE n building containing baths, esp for public use

BATHING > BATHE

BATHLESS > BATH

BATHMAT n mat to stand on after a bath

BATHMATS > BATHMAT

BATHMIC > BATHMISM

BATHMISM n growth-force

BATHMISMS > BATHMISM

BATHOLITE same as **>** BATHOLITH

BATHOLITH n very large irregular-shaped mass of igneous rock, esp granite, formed from an intrusion of magma at great depth, esp one exposed after erosion of less resistant overlying rocks

BATHORSE n officer's packhorse

BATHORSES > BATHORSE

BATHOS n sudden ludicrous change in speech or writing from a serious subject to a trivial one

BATHOSES > BATHOS

BATHROBE n loose-fitting garment for wear before or after a bath or swimming

BATHROBES > BATHROBE

BATHROOM n room with a bath, sink, and usu. a toilet

BATHROOMS > BATHROOM

BATHS > BATH

BATHTUB n bath, esp one not permanently fixed

BATHTUBS > BATHTUB

BATHWATER n used or unused water in a bathtub

BATHYAL adj denoting or relating to an ocean depth of between 200 and 2000 metres (about 100 and 1000 fathoms), corresponding to the continental slope

BATHYBIUS n gelatinous substance on seabed

BATHYLITE same as **>** BATHOLITH

BATHYLITH same as **>** BATHOLITH

BATIK n process of printing fabric using wax to cover areas not to be dyed ▷ vb treat material with this process

BATIKED > BATIK

BATIKING > BATIK

BATIKS > BATIK

BATING > BATE

BATISTE n fine plain-weave cotton fabric: used esp for shirts and dresses

BATISTES > BATISTE

BATLER n flat piece of wood for beating clothes, etc before washing

BATLERS > BATLER

BATLET same as **>** BATLER

BATLETS > BATLET

BATLIKE > BAT

BATMAN n officer's servant in the armed forces

BATMEN > BATMAN

BATOLOGY n study of brambles

BATON n thin stick used by the conductor of an orchestra ▷ vb carry or wave a baton

BATONED > BATON

BATONING > BATON

BATONS > BATON

BATOON same as **>** BATON

BATOONED > BATOON

BATOONING > BATOON

BATOONS > BATOON

BATRACHIA n group of amphibians including frogs and toads

BATS > BAT

BATSMAN n person who bats or specializes in batting

BATSMEN > BATSMAN

BATSWING adj in the form of the wing of a bat

BATSWOMAN > BATSMAN

BATSWOMEN > BATSMAN

BATT same as **>** BAT

BATTA n soldier's allowance

BATTALIA n arrangement of army prepared for battle

BATTALIAS > BATTALIA

BATTALION n army unit consisting of three or more companies

BATTAS > BATTA

BATTEAU same as **>** BATEAU

BATTEAUX > BATTEAU

BATTED > BAT

BATTEL vb make fertile

BATTELED > BATTEL

BATTELER > BATTEL

BATTELERS > BATTEL

BATTELING > BATTEL

BATTELLED > BATTEL

BATTELS > BATTEL

BATTEMENT n extension of one leg forwards, sideways, or backwards, either once or repeatedly

BATTEN n strip of wood fixed to something, esp to hold it in place ▷ vb strengthen or fasten with battens

BATTENED > BATTEN

BATTENER > BATTEN

BATTENERS > BATTEN

BATTENING > BATTEN

BATTENS > BATTEN

BATTER vb hit repeatedly ▷ n mixture of flour, eggs, and milk, used in cooking

BATTERED adj subjected to persistent physical violence, esp by a close relative living in the same house

BATTERER n person who batters someone

BATTERERS > BATTERER

BATTERIE n movement in ballet involving the legs beating together

BATTERIES > BATTERY

BATTERING n act or practice of battering someone

BATTERO n heavy club

BATTEROS > BATTERO

BATTERS > BATTER

BATTERY n device that produces electricity in a torch, radio, etc ▷ adj kept in series of cages for intensive rearing

BATTIER > BATTY

BATTIES > BATTY

BATTIEST > BATTY

BATTIK same as **>** BATIK

BATTIKS > BATTIK

BATTILL old spelling of **>** BATTLE

BATTILLED > BATTILL

BATTILLS > BATTILL

BATTINESS > BATTY

BATTING > BAT

BATTINGS > BAT

BATTLE n fight between large armed forces ▷ vb struggle

BATTLEAX same as **>** BATTLEAXE

BATTLEAXE n kind of axe formerly used in battle

BATTLEBUS n coach that transports politicians and their advisers round the country during an election campaign

BATTLED > BATTLE

BATTLER > BATTLE

BATTLERS > BATTLE
BATTLES > BATTLE
BATTLING > BATTLE
BATTOLOGY n unnecessary repetition of words
BATTS > BATT
BATTU adj (in ballet) involving a beating movement
BATTUE n beating of woodland or cover to force game to flee in the direction of hunters
BATTUES > BATTUE
BATTUTA n (in music) a beat
BATTUTAS > BATTUTA
BATTUTO n (in Italian cookery) selection of chopped herbs
BATTUTOS > BATTUTO
BATTY adj eccentric or crazy ▷ n bottom; bum
BATWING adj shaped like the wings of a bat, as a black tie, collar, etc
BATWOMAN n female servant in any of the armed forces
BATWOMEN > BATWOMAN
BAUBEE same as > BAWBEE
BAUBEES > BAUBEE
BAUBLE n trinket of little value
BAUBLES > BAUBLE
BAUBLING > BAUBLE
BAUCHLE vb shuffle along
BAUCHLED > BAUCHLE
BAUCHLES > BAUCHLE
BAUCHLING > BAUCHLE
BAUD n unit used to measure the speed of transmission of electronic data
BAUDEKIN old variant of > BALDACHIN
BAUDEKINS > BAUDEKIN
BAUDRIC same as > BALDRIC
BAUDRICK same as > BALDRIC
BAUDRICKE same as > BALDRIC
BAUDRICKS > BAUDRICK
BAUDRICS > BAUDRIC
BAUDRONS n name for a cat
BAUDS > BAUD
BAUERA n small evergreen Australian shrub
BAUERAS > BAUERA
BAUHINIA n type of climbing or shrubby plant of tropical and warm regions, widely cultivated for ornament
BAUHINIAS > BAUHINIA
BAUK same as > BALK
BAUKED > BAUK
BAUKING > BAUK
BAUKS > BAUK
BAULK same as > BALK
BAULKED > BALK
BAULKER > BALK

BAULKERS > BALK
BAULKIER > BAULKY
BAULKIEST > BAULKY
BAULKILY > BALKY
BAULKING > BALK
BAULKS > BALK
BAULKY same as > BALKY
BAUR n humorous anecdote; joke
BAURS > BAUR
BAUSOND adj (of animal) dappled with white spots
BAUXITE n claylike substance that is the chief source of aluminium
BAUXITES > BAUXITE
BAUXITIC > BAUXITE
BAVARDAGE n chattering
BAVAROIS n cold dessert consisting of a rich custard set with gelatine and flavoured in various ways
BAVIN n impure limestone
BAVINS > BAVIN
BAWBEE n former Scottish silver coin
BAWBEES > BAWBEE
BAWBLE same as > BAUBLE
BAWBLES > BAWBLE
BAWCOCK n fine fellow
BAWCOCKS > BAWCOCK
BAWD n person who runs a brothel, esp a woman
BAWDIER > BAWDY
BAWDIES > BAWDY
BAWDIEST > BAWDY
BAWDILY > BAWDY
BAWDINESS > BAWDY
BAWDKIN same as > BALDACHIN
BAWDKINS > BAWDKIN
BAWDRIC n heavy belt to support sword
BAWDRICS > BAWDRIC
BAWDRIES > BAWDRY
BAWDRY n obscene talk or language
BAWDS > BAWD
BAWDY adj (of writing etc) containing humorous references to sex ▷ n obscenity or eroticism, esp in writing or drama
BAWL vb shout or weep noisily ▷ n loud shout or cry
BAWLED > BAWL
BAWLER > BAWL
BAWLERS > BAWL
BAWLEY n small fishing boat
BAWLEYS > BAWLEY
BAWLING > BAWL
BAWLINGS > BAWL
BAWLS > BAWL
BAWN n fortified enclosure
BAWNEEN same as > BAININ
BAWNEENS > BAWNEEN
BAWNS > BAWN
BAWR same as > BAUR
BAWRS > BAWR
BAWSUNT adj black and white in colour
BAWTIE n name for a dog

BAWTIES > BAWTIE
BAWTY same as > BAWTIE
BAXTER old variant of > BAKER
BAXTERS > BAXTER
BAY n wide semicircular indentation of a shoreline ▷ vb howl in deep tones
BAYADEER same as > BAYADERE
BAYADEERS > BAYADEER
BAYADERE n dancing girl, esp one serving in a Hindu temple ▷ adj (of fabric, etc) having horizontal stripes
BAYADERES > BAYADERE
BAYAMO n Cuban strong wind
BAYAMOS > BAYAMO
BAYARD n bay horse
BAYARDS > BAYARD
BAYBERRY n tropical American tree that yields an oil used in making bay rum
BAYE vb bathe
BAYED > BAY
BAYES > BAYE
BAYING > BAY
BAYLE n barrier
BAYLES > BAYLE
BAYMAN n fisherman
BAYMEN > BAYMAN
BAYONET n sharp blade that can be fixed to the end of a rifle ▷ vb stab with a bayonet
BAYONETED > BAYONET
BAYONETS > BAYONET
BAYOU n (in the southern US) a sluggish marshy tributary of a lake or river
BAYOUS > BAYOU
BAYS > BAY
BAYT same as > BATE
BAYTED > BAYT
BAYTING > BAYT
BAYTS > BAYT
BAYWOOD n light soft wood of a tropical American mahogany tree
BAYWOODS > BAYWOOD
BAYYAN n Islamic declaration
BAYYANS > BAYYAN
BAZAAR n sale in aid of charity
BAZAARS > BAZAAR
BAZAR same as > BAZAAR
BAZARS > BAZAR
BAZAZZ same as > PIZZAZZ
BAZAZZES > BAZAZZ
BAZILLION same as > GAZILLION
BAZOO a US slang word for > MOUTH
BAZOOKA n portable rocket launcher that fires an armour-piercing projectile
BAZOOKAS > BAZOOKA
BAZOOMS npl woman's breasts
BAZOOS > BAZOO

BAZOUKI same as > BOUZOUKI
BAZOUKIS > BAZOUKI
BAZZAZZ same as > PIZZAZZ
BAZZAZZES > BAZZAZZ
BDELLIUM n African or W Asian tree that yields a gum resin
BDELLIUMS > BDELLIUM
BE vb exist or live
BEACH n area of sand or pebbles on a shore ▷ vb run or haul (a boat) onto a beach
BEACHBALL n light ball for playing on beach
BEACHBOY n male lifeguard on beach
BEACHBOYS > BEACHBOY
BEACHCOMB vb collect objects, seashells, etc on seashore
BEACHED > BEACH
BEACHES > BEACH
BEACHGOER n person who goes to the beach
BEACHHEAD n beach captured by an attacking army on which troops can be landed
BEACHIER > BEACHY
BEACHIEST > BEACHY
BEACHING > BEACH
BEACHSIDE adj situated near a beach
BEACHWEAR n clothes suitable for the beach
BEACHY adj with gentle sandy slopes
BEACON n fire or light on a hill or tower, used as a warning ▷ vb guide or warn
BEACONED > BEACON
BEACONING > BEACON
BEACONS > BEACON
BEAD n small piece of plastic, wood, etc, pierced for threading on a string to form a necklace etc ▷ vb decorate with beads
BEADBLAST n jet of small glass beads blown from a nozzle under air or steam pressure ▷ vb clean or treat (a surface) with a beadblast
BEADED > BEAD
BEADER n person making things with beads
BEADERS > BEADER
BEADHOUSE n chapel
BEADIER > BEADY
BEADIEST > BEADY
BEADILY > BEADY
BEADINESS > BEADY
BEADING n strip of moulding used for edging furniture
BEADINGS > BEADING
BEADLE n (formerly) a minor parish official who acted as an usher
BEADLEDOM n petty officialdom

b

BEADLES > BEADLE
BEADLIKE > BEAD
BEADMAN same as
> BEADSMAN
BEADMEN > BEADMAN
BEADROLL n list of persons for whom prayers are to be offered
BEADROLLS > BEADROLL
BEADS > BEAD
BEADSMAN n person who prays for another's soul, esp one paid or fed for doing so
BEADSMEN > BEADSMAN
BEADWORK same as
> BEADING
BEADWORKS > BEADWORK
BEADY adj small, round, and glittering
BEAGLE n small hound with short legs and drooping ears ▷ vb hunt with beagles, normally on foot
BEAGLED > BEAGLE
BEAGLER n person who hunts with beagles
BEAGLERS > BEAGLER
BEAGLES > BEAGLE
BEAGLING > BEAGLE
BEAGLINGS > BEAGLE
BEAK n projecting horny jaws of a bird ▷ vb strike with the beak
BEAKED > BEAK
BEAKER n large drinking cup
BEAKERFUL n amount of liquid in a full beaker
BEAKERS > BEAKER
BEAKIER > BEAK
BEAKIEST > BEAK
BEAKLESS > BEAK
BEAKLIKE > BEAK
BEAKS > BEAK
BEAKY > BEAK
BEAM n broad smile ▷ vb smile broadly
BEAMED > BEAM
BEAMER n full-pitched ball bowled at the batsman's head
BEAMERS > BEAMER
BEAMIER > BEAM
BEAMIEST > BEAM
BEAMILY > BEAM
BEAMINESS > BEAM
BEAMING > BEAM
BEAMINGLY > BEAM
BEAMINGS > BEAM
BEAMISH adj smiling
BEAMISHLY > BEAMISH
BEAMLESS > BEAM
BEAMLET n small beam
BEAMLETS > BEAMLET
BEAMLIKE > BEAM
BEAMS > BEAM
BEAMY > BEAM
BEAN n seed or pod of various plants, eaten as a vegetable or used to make coffee etc ▷ vb strike on the head
BEANBAG n small cloth bag

filled with dried beans and thrown in games
BEANBAGS > BEANBAG
BEANBALL n baseball intended to hit batter's head
BEANBALLS > BEANBALL
BEANED > BEAN
BEANERIES > BEANERY
BEANERY n cheap restaurant
BEANFEAST n any festive or merry occasion
BEANIE n close-fitting woollen hat
BEANIES > BEANY
BEANING > BEAN
BEANLIKE > BEAN
BEANO n celebration or party
BEANOS > BEANO
BEANPOLE n tall thin person
BEANPOLES > BEANPOLE
BEANS > BEAN
BEANSTALK n stem of a bean plant
BEANY same as > BEANIE
BEAR vb support or hold up (something) ▷ n type of omnivorous mammal with a large head, long shaggy coat, and strong claws
BEARABLE adj endurable
BEARABLY > BEARABLE
BEARBERRY n type of shrub
BEARBINE n type of bindweed
BEARBINES > BEARBINE
BEARCAT n lesser panda
BEARCATS > BEARCAT
BEARD n hair growing on the lower parts of a man's face ▷ vb oppose boldly
BEARDED > BEARD
BEARDIE n another name for bearded loach
BEARDIER > BEARDY
BEARDIES > BEARDIE
BEARDIEST > BEARDY
BEARDING > BEARD
BEARDLESS adj without a beard
BEARDS > BEARD
BEARDY adj having a beard
BEARE same as > BEAR
BEARED > BEAR
BEARER n person who carries, presents, or upholds something
BEARERS > BEARER
BEARES > BEARE
BEARGRASS n North American plant
BEARHUG n wrestling hold in which the arms are locked tightly round an opponent's chest and arms
BEARHUGS > BEARHUG
BEARING > BEAR
BEARINGS > BEAR
BEARISH adj like a bear
BEARISHLY > BEARISH

BEARLIKE > BEAR
BEARNAISE n rich sauce made from egg yolks, lemon juice or wine vinegar, butter, shallots, herbs, and seasoning
BEARS > BEAR
BEARSKIN n tall fur helmet worn by some British soldiers
BEARSKINS > BEARSKIN
BEARWARD n bear keeper
BEARWARDS > BEARWARD
BEARWOOD another name for > CASCARA
BEARWOODS > BEARWOOD
BEAST n large wild animal ▷ vb torture someone using excessive physical exercise
BEASTED > BEAST
BEASTHOOD > BEAST
BEASTIE n small animal
BEASTIES > BEASTIE
BEASTILY > BESTIAL
BEASTING > BEAST
BEASTINGS same as > BEESTINGS
BEASTLIER > BEASTLY
BEASTLIKE > BEAST
BEASTLY adj unpleasant or disagreeable ▷ adv extremely
BEASTS > BEAST
BEAT vb strike with or as if with a series of violent blows; dash or pound repeatedly (against) ▷ n stroke or blow ▷ adj totally exhausted
BEATABLE > BEAT
BEATBOX n drum machine simulated by a human voice
BEATBOXER n person who practices beatboxing
BEATBOXES > BEATBOX
BEATEN > BEAT
BEATER n device used for beating
BEATERS > BEATER
BEATH vb dry; heat
BEATHED > BEATH
BEATHING > BEATH
BEATHS > BEATH
BEATIER > BEATY
BEATIEST > BEATY
BEATIFIC adj displaying great happiness
BEATIFIED > BEATIFY
BEATIFIES > BEATIFY
BEATIFY vb declare (a dead person) to be among the blessed in heaven: the first step towards canonization
BEATING > BEAT
BEATINGS > BEAT
BEATITUDE n any of the blessings on the poor, meek, etc, in the Sermon on the Mount
BEATLESS > BEAT
BEATNIK n young person in the late 1950s who rebelled against

conventional attitudes etc
BEATNIKS > BEATNIK
BEATS > BEAT
BEATY adj (of music) having a strong rhythm
BEAU n boyfriend or admirer
BEAUCOUP n large amount
BEAUCOUPS > BEAUCOUP
BEAUFET same as > BUFFET
BEAUFETS > BEAUFET
BEAUFFET same as > BUFFET
BEAUFFETS > BEAUFFET
BEAUFIN same as > BIFFIN
BEAUFINS > BEAUFIN
BEAUISH adj vain and showy
BEAUS > BEAU
BEAUT n person or thing that is outstanding or distinctive ▷ adj good or excellent ▷ interj exclamation of joy or pleasure
BEAUTEOUS adj beautiful
BEAUTIED > BEAUTY
BEAUTIES > BEAUTY
BEAUTIFUL adj very attractive to look at
BEAUTIFY vb make beautiful
BEAUTS > BEAUT
BEAUTY n combination of all the qualities of a person or thing that delight the senses and mind ▷ interj expression of approval or agreement ▷ vb make beautiful
BEAUTYING > BEAUTY
BEAUX > BEAU
BEAUXITE same as > BAUXITE
BEAUXITES > BEAUXITE
BEAVER n amphibious rodent with a big flat tail ▷ vb work steadily or assiduously
BEAVERED > BEAVER
BEAVERIES > BEAVERY
BEAVERING > BEAVER
BEAVERS > BEAVER
BEAVERY n place for keeping beavers
BEBEERINE n alkaloid, resembling quinine, obtained from the bark of the greenheart and other plants
BEBEERU n tropical American tree
BEBEERUS > BEBEERU
BEBLOOD vb stain with blood
BEBLOODED > BEBLOOD
BEBLOODS > BEBLOOD
BEBOP same as > BOP
BEBOPPED > BEBOP
BEBOPPER > BEBOP
BEBOPPERS > BEBOP
BEBOPPING > BEBOP
BEBOPS > BEBOP

BEBUNG *n* vibrato effect on clavichord

BEBUNGS > BEBUNG

BECALL *vb* use insulting words about someone

BECALLED > BECALL

BECALLING > BECALL

BECALLS > BECALL

BECALM *vb* make calm

BECALMED *adj* (of a sailing ship) motionless through lack of wind

BECALMING > BECALM

BECALMS > BECALM

BECAME > BECOME

BECAP *vb* put cap on

BECAPPED > BECAP

BECAPPING > BECAP

BECAPS > BECAP

BECARPET *vb* lay carpet on

BECARPETS > BECARPET

BECASSE *n* woodcock

BECASSES > BECASSE

BECAUSE *conj* on account of the fact that; on account of being; since

BECCACCIA *n* woodcock

BECCAFICO *n* European songbird, eaten as a delicacy in Italy and other countries

BECHALK *vb* mark with chalk

BECHALKED > BECHALK

BECHALKS > BECHALK

BECHAMEL *n* thick white sauce flavoured with onion and seasoning

BECHAMELS > BECHAMEL

BECHANCE *vb* happen (to)

BECHANCED > BECHANCE

BECHANCES > BECHANCE

BECHARM *vb* delight

BECHARMED > BECHARM

BECHARMS > BECHARM

BECK *n* stream ▷ *vb* attract someone's attention by nodding or gesturing

BECKE *same as* > BEAK

BECKED > BECK

BECKES > BECKE

BECKET *n* clevis forming part of one end of a sheave, used for securing standing lines by means of a thimble

BECKETS > BECKET

BECKING > BECK

BECKON *vb* summon with a gesture ▷ *n* summoning gesture

BECKONED > BECKON

BECKONER > BECKON

BECKONERS > BECKON

BECKONING > BECKON

BECKONS > BECKON

BECKS > BECK

BECLAMOR *vb* clamour excessively

BECLAMORS > BECLAMOR

BECLASP *vb* embrace

BECLASPED > BECLASP

BECLASPS > BECLASP

BECLOAK *vb* dress in cloak

BECLOAKED > BECLOAK

BECLOAKS > BECLOAK

BECLOG *vb* put clogs on

BECLOGGED > BECLOG

BECLOGS > BECLOG

BECLOTHE *vb* put clothes on

BECLOTHED > BECLOTHE

BECLOTHES > BECLOTHE

BECLOUD *vb* cover or obscure with a cloud

BECLOUDED > BECLOUD

BECLOUDS > BECLOUD

BECLOWN *vb* clown around

BECLOWNED > BECLOWN

BECLOWNS > BECLOWN

BECOME *vb* come to be

BECOMES > BECOME

BECOMING *adj* attractive or pleasing ▷ *n* any process of change

BECOMINGS > BECOMING

BECOWARD *vb* make cowardly

BECOWARDS > BECOWARD

BECQUEREL *n* SI unit of activity of a radioactive source

BECRAWL *vb* crawl all over

BECRAWLED > BECRAWL

BECRAWLS > BECRAWL

BECRIME *vb* make someone guilty of a crime

BECRIMED > BECRIME

BECRIMES > BECRIME

BECRIMING > BECRIME

BECROWD *vb* crowd with something

BECROWDED > BECROWD

BECROWDS > BECROWD

BECRUST *vb* cover with crust

BECRUSTED > BECRUST

BECRUSTS > BECRUST

BECUDGEL *vb* arm with cudgel

BECUDGELS > BECUDGEL

BECURL *vb* curl

BECURLED > BECURL

BECURLING > BECURL

BECURLS > BECURL

BECURSE *vb* curse

BECURSED > BECURSE

BECURSES > BECURSE

BECURSING > BECURSE

BECURST > BECURSE

BED *n* piece of furniture on which to sleep ▷ *vb* plant in a bed

BEDABBLE *vb* dabble; moisten

BEDABBLED > BEDABBLE

BEDABBLES > BEDABBLE

BEDAD *interj* by God (oath)

BEDAGGLE *vb* soil by trailing through dirt

BEDAGGLED > BEDAGGLE

BEDAGGLES > BEDAGGLE

BEDAMN *vb* damn

BEDAMNED > BEDAMN

BEDAMNING > BEDAMN

BEDAMNS > BEDAMN

BEDARKEN *vb* make dark

BEDARKENS > BEDARKEN

BEDASH *vb* sprinkle with liquid

BEDASHED > BEDASH

BEDASHES > BEDASH

BEDASHING > BEDASH

BEDAUB *vb* smear with something sticky or dirty

BEDAUBED > BEDAUB

BEDAUBING > BEDAUB

BEDAUBS > BEDAUB

BEDAWIN *same as* > BEDOUIN

BEDAWINS > BEDAWIN

BEDAZE *vb* daze

BEDAZED > BEDAZE

BEDAZES > BEDAZE

BEDAZING > BEDAZE

BEDAZZLE *vb* dazzle or confuse, as with brilliance

BEDAZZLED > BEDAZZLE

BEDAZZLES > BEDAZZLE

BEDBATH *n* washing of a sick person in bed

BEDBATHS > BEDBATH

BEDBOARD *n* base of bed

BEDBOARDS > BEDBOARD

BEDBUG *n* small blood-sucking wingless insect that infests dirty houses

BEDBUGS > BEDBUG

BEDCHAIR *n* adjustable chair to support invalid in bed

BEDCHAIRS > BEDCHAIR

BEDCOVER *n* cover for bed

BEDCOVERS > BEDCOVER

BEDDABLE *adj* sexually attractive

BEDDED > BED

BEDDER *n* (at some universities) a college servant employed to keep students' rooms in order

BEDDERS > BEDDER

BEDDING > BED

BEDDINGS > BED

BEDE *n* prayer

BEDEAFEN *vb* deafen

BEDEAFENS > BEDEAFEN

BEDECK *vb* cover with decorations

BEDECKED > BEDECK

BEDECKING > BEDECK

BEDECKS > BEDECK

BEDEGUAR *n* growth found on rosebushes

BEDEGUARS > BEDEGUAR

BEDEHOUSE *same as* > BEADHOUSE

BEDEL *archaic spellings of* > BEADLE

BEDELL *same as* > BEADLE

BEDELLS > BEDELL

BEDELS > BEDEL

BEDELSHIP > BEDEL

BEDEMAN *same as* > BEADSMAN

BEDEMEN > BEDEMAN

BEDERAL *same as* > BEDRAL

BEDERALS > BEDERAL

BEDES > BEDE

BEDESMAN *same as* > BEADSMAN

BEDESMEN > BEDESMAN

BEDEVIL *vb* harass, confuse, or torment

BEDEVILED > BEDEVIL

BEDEVILS > BEDEVIL

BEDEW *vb* wet or cover with or as if with drops of dew

BEDEWED > BEDEW

BEDEWING > BEDEW

BEDEWS > BEDEW

BEDFAST *an archaic word for* > BEDRIDDEN

BEDFELLOW *n* temporary associate

BEDFRAME *n* framework of bed

BEDFRAMES > BEDFRAME

BEDGOWN *n* night dress

BEDGOWNS > BEDGOWN

BEDHEAD *n* untidy state of hair, esp caused by sleeping

BEDHEADS > BEDHEAD

BEDIAPER *vb* put a nappy on

BEDIAPERS > BEDIAPER

BEDIDE > BEDYE

BEDIGHT *vb* array or adorn ▷ *adj* adorned or bedecked

BEDIGHTED > BEDIGHT

BEDIGHTS > BEDIGHT

BEDIM *vb* make dim or obscure

BEDIMMED > BEDIM

BEDIMMING > BEDIM

BEDIMPLE *vb* form dimples in

BEDIMPLED > BEDIMPLE

BEDIMPLES > BEDIMPLE

BEDIMS > BEDIM

BEDIRTIED > BEDIRTY

BEDIRTIES > BEDIRTY

BEDIRTY *vb* make dirty

BEDIZEN *vb* dress or decorate gaudily or tastelessly

BEDIZENED > BEDIZEN

BEDIZENS > BEDIZEN

BEDLAM *n* noisy confused situation

BEDLAMISM > BEDLAM

BEDLAMITE *n* lunatic

BEDLAMP *n* bedside light

BEDLAMPS > BEDLAMP

BEDLAMS > BEDLAM

BEDLESS > BED

BEDLIKE *adj* like a bed

BEDMAKER *n* person who makes beds

BEDMAKERS > BEDMAKER

BEDMATE *n* person who shares a bed

BEDMATES > BEDMATE

BEDOTTED *adj* scattered; strewn

BEDOUIN *n* member of any of the nomadic tribes of Arabs inhabiting the deserts of Arabia, Jordan, and Syria, as well as parts of the Sahara

BEDOUINS > BEDOUIN

BEDPAN *n* shallow bowl used as a toilet by bedridden people

BEDPANS > BEDPAN
BEDPLATE n heavy metal platform or frame to which an engine or machine is attached
BEDPLATES > BEDPLATE
BEDPOST n vertical support on a bedstead
BEDPOSTS > BEDPOST
BEDQUILT n padded bed cover
BEDQUILTS > BEDQUILT
BEDRAGGLE vb make (hair, clothing, etc) limp, untidy, or dirty, as with rain or mud
BEDRAIL n rail or board along the side of a bed that connects the headboard with the footboard
BEDRAILS > BEDRAIL
BEDRAL n minor church official
BEDRALS > BEDRAL
BEDRAPE vb adorn
BEDRAPED > BEDRAPE
BEDRAPES > BEDRAPE
BEDRAPING > BEDRAPE
BEDRENCH vb drench
BEDRID same as
> BEDRIDDEN
BEDRIDDEN adj confined to bed because of illness or old age
BEDRIGHT n rights expected in the marital bed
BEDRIGHTS > BEDRIGHT
BEDRITE same as
> BEDRIGHT
BEDRITES > BEDRITE
BEDRIVEL vb drivel around
BEDRIVELS > BEDRIVEL
BEDROCK n solid rock beneath the surface soil
BEDROCKS > BEDROCK
BEDROLL n portable roll of bedding, such as a sleeping bag, used esp for sleeping in the open
BEDROLLS > BEDROLL
BEDROOM n room used for sleeping ▷ adj containing references to sex
BEDROOMED adj containing specified number of bedrooms
BEDROOMS > BEDROOM
BEDROP vb drop on
BEDROPPED > BEDROP
BEDROPS > BEDROP
BEDROPT > BEDROP
BEDRUG vb drug excessively
BEDRUGGED > BEDRUG
BEDRUGS > BEDRUG
BEDS > BED
BEDSHEET n sheet for bed
BEDSHEETS > BEDSHEET
BEDSIDE n area beside a bed ▷ adj placed at or near the side of the bed
BEDSIDES > BEDSIDE
BEDSIT n furnished sitting room with a bed
BEDSITS > BEDSIT

BEDSITTER same as
> BEDSIT
BEDSOCKS n socks worn in bed
BEDSONIA n bacterium causing diseases such as trachoma
BEDSONIAS > BEDSONIA
BEDSORE n ulcer on the skin, caused by a lengthy period of lying in bed due to illness
BEDSORES > BEDSORE
BEDSPREAD n top cover on a bed
BEDSPRING vb spring supporting mattress on bed
BEDSTAND n bedside table
BEDSTANDS > BEDSTAND
BEDSTEAD n framework of a bed
BEDSTEADS > BEDSTEAD
BEDSTRAW n plant with small white or yellow flowers
BEDSTRAWS > BEDSTRAW
BEDTICK n case containing stuffing in mattress
BEDTICKS > BEDTICK
BEDTIME n time when one usually goes to bed
BEDTIMES > BEDTIME
BEDU adj relating to beduins
BEDUCK vb duck under water
BEDUCKED > BEDUCK
BEDUCKING > BEDUCK
BEDUCKS > BEDUCK
BEDUIN variant of
> BEDOUIN
BEDUINS > BEDUIN
BEDUMB vb make dumb
BEDUMBED > BEDUMB
BEDUMBING > BEDUMB
BEDUMBS > BEDUMB
BEDUNCE vb cause to look or feel foolish
BEDUNCED > BEDUNCE
BEDUNCES > BEDUNCE
BEDUNCING > BEDUNCE
BEDUNG vb spread with dung
BEDUNGED > BEDUNG
BEDUNGING > BEDUNG
BEDUNGS > BEDUNG
BEDUST vb cover with dust
BEDUSTED > BEDUST
BEDUSTING > BEDUST
BEDUSTS > BEDUST
BEDWARD adj towards bed
BEDWARDS adv towards bed
BEDWARF vb hamper growth of
BEDWARFED > BEDWARF
BEDWARFS > BEDWARF
BEDWARMER n metal pan containing hot coals, formerly used to warm a bed
BEDWETTER n person who

urinates in bed
BEDYDE > BEDYE
BEDYE vb dye
BEDYED > BEDYE
BEDYEING > BEDYE
BEDYES > BEDYE
BEE n insect that makes wax and honey
BEEBEE n air rifle
BEEBEES > BEEBEE
BEEBREAD n mixture of pollen and nectar prepared by worker bees and fed to the larvae
BEEBREADS > BEEBREAD
BEECH n tree with a smooth greyish bark
BEECHEN > BEECH
BEECHES > BEECH
BEECHIER > BEECH
BEECHIEST > BEECH
BEECHMAST n nuts of beech tree
BEECHNUT n small brown triangular edible nut of the beech tree
BEECHNUTS > BEECHNUT
BEECHWOOD n wood of beech tree
BEECHY > BEECH
BEEDI n Indian cigarette
BEEDIE same as **>** BEEDI
BEEDIES > BEEDI
BEEF n flesh of a cow, bull, or ox ▷ vb complain
BEEFALO n cross between cow and buffalo
BEEFALOES > BEEFALO
BEEFALOS > BEEFALO
BEEFCAKE n musclemen as displayed in photographs
BEEFCAKES > BEEFCAKE
BEEFEATER n yeoman warder at the Tower of London
BEEFED > BEEF
BEEFIER > BEEFY
BEEFIEST > BEEFY
BEEFILY > BEEFY
BEEFINESS > BEEFY
BEEFING > BEEF
BEEFLESS > BEEF
BEEFS > BEEF
BEEFSTEAK n piece of beef that can be grilled, fried, etc, cut from any lean part of the animal
BEEFWOOD n any of various trees that produce very hard wood
BEEFWOODS > BEEFWOOD
BEEFY adj like beef
BEEGAH same as **>** BIGHA
BEEGAHS > BEEGAH
BEEHIVE n structure in which bees live
BEEHIVES > BEEHIVE
BEEKEEPER n person who keeps bees for their honey
BEELIKE > BEE
BEELINE n most direct route between two places ▷ adj make a beeline for

(something)
BEELINED > BEELINE
BEELINES > BEELINE
BEELINING > BEELINE
BEEN > BE
BEENAH n understanding; insight
BEENAHS > BEENAH
BEENTO n person who has resided in Britain, esp during part of his education ▷ adj of, relating to, or characteristic of such a person
BEENTOS > BEENTO
BEEP n high-pitched sound, like that of a car horn ▷ vb (cause to) make this noise
BEEPED > BEEP
BEEPER > BEEP
BEEPERS > BEEP
BEEPING > BEEP
BEEPS > BEEP
BEER n alcoholic drink brewed from malt and hops
BEERAGE n brewing industry
BEERAGES > BEERAGE
BEERHALL n large public room where beer is consumed
BEERHALLS > BEERHALL
BEERIER > BEERY
BEERIEST > BEERY
BEERILY > BEERY
BEERINESS > BEERY
BEERS > BEER
BEERY adj smelling or tasting of beer
BEES > BEE
BEESOME same as
> BISSON
BEESTING adj as in beesting lips of lips, pouting
BEESTINGS n first milk secreted by the mammary glands of a cow or similar animal immediately after giving birth
BEESTUNG adj as in beestung lips of lips, pouting
BEESWAX n wax secreted by bees, used in polishes etc ▷ vb polish with such wax
BEESWAXED > BEESWAX
BEESWAXES > BEESWAX
BEESWING n light filmy crust of tartar that forms in port and some other wines after long keeping in the bottle
BEESWINGS > BEESWING
BEET n plant with an edible root and leaves ▷ vb improve or make better
BEETED > BEET
BEETFLIES > BEETFLY
BEETFLY n type of fly which is a common pest of beets and mangel-wurzels
BEETING > BEET
BEETLE n insect with a hard wing cover on its back ▷ adj overhang or jut ▷ vb scuttle or scurry

BEETLED > BEETLE
BEETLER *n* one who operates a beetling machine
BEETLERS > BEETLER
BEETLES > BEETLE
BEETLING > BEETLE
BEETROOT *n* type of beet plant with a dark red root
BEETROOTS > BEETROOT
BEETS > BEET
BEEVES > BEEF
BEEYARD *n* place where bees are kept
BEEYARDS > BEEYARD
BEEZER *n* person or chap ▷ *adj* excellent
BEEZERS > BEEZER
BEFALL *vb* happen to (someone)
BEFALLEN > BEFALL
BEFALLING > BEFALL
BEFALLS > BEFALL
BEFANA *n* Italian gift-bearing good fairy
BEFANAS > BEFANA
BEFELD > BEFALL
BEFELL > BEFALL
BEFFANA *same as* > BEFANA
BEFFANAS > BEFFANA
BEFINGER *vb* mark by handling
BEFINGERS > BEFINGER
BEFINNED *adj* with fins
BEFIT *vb* be appropriate or suitable for
BEFITS > BEFIT
BEFITTED > BEFIT
BEFITTING > BEFIT
BEFLAG *vb* decorate with flags
BEFLAGGED > BEFLAG
BEFLAGS > BEFLAG
BEFLEA *vb* infect with fleas
BEFLEAED > BEFLEA
BEFLEAING > BEFLEA
BEFLEAS > BEFLEA
BEFLECK *vb* fleck
BEFLECKED > BEFLECK
BEFLECKS > BEFLECK
BEFLOWER *vb* decorate with flowers
BEFLOWERS > BEFLOWER
BEFLUM *vb* fool; deceive
BEFLUMMED > BEFLUM
BEFLUMS > BEFLUM
BEFOAM *vb* cover with foam
BEFOAMED > BEFOAM
BEFOAMING > BEFOAM
BEFOAMS > BEFOAM
BEFOG *vb* surround with fog
BEFOGGED > BEFOG
BEFOGGING > BEFOG
BEFOGS > BEFOG
BEFOOL *vb* make a fool of
BEFOOLED > BEFOOL
BEFOOLING > BEFOOL
BEFOOLS > BEFOOL
BEFORE *adv* indicating something earlier in time, in front of, or preferred to ▷ *prep* preceding in space or

time
BEFORTUNE *vb* happen to
BEFOUL *vb* make dirty or foul
BEFOULED > BEFOUL
BEFOULER > BEFOUL
BEFOULERS > BEFOUL
BEFOULING > BEFOUL
BEFOULS > BEFOUL
BEFRET *vb* fret about something
BEFRETS > BEFRET
BEFRETTED > BEFRET
BEFRIEND *vb* become friends with
BEFRIENDS > BEFRIEND
BEFRINGE *vb* decorate with fringe
BEFRINGED > BEFRINGE
BEFRINGES > BEFRINGE
BEFUDDLE *vb* confuse, muddle, or perplex
BEFUDDLED > BEFUDDLE
BEFUDDLES > BEFUDDLE
BEG *vb* solicit (money, food, etc), esp in the street
BEGAD *interj* emphatic exclamation
BEGALL *vb* make sore by rubbing
BEGALLED > BEGALL
BEGALLING > BEGALL
BEGALLS > BEGALL
BEGAN > BEGIN
BEGAR *n* compulsory labour
BEGARS > BEGAR
BEGAT > BEGET
BEGAZE *vb* gaze about or around
BEGAZED > BEGAZE
BEGAZES > BEGAZE
BEGAZING > BEGAZE
BEGEM *vb* decorate with gems
BEGEMMED > BEGEM
BEGEMMING > BEGEM
BEGEMS > BEGEM
BEGET *vb* cause or create
BEGETS > BEGET
BEGETTER > BEGET
BEGETTERS > BEGET
BEGETTING > BEGET
BEGGAR *n* person who begs, esp one who lives by begging ▷ *vb* be beyond the resources of
BEGGARDOM > BEGGAR
BEGGARED > BEGGAR
BEGGARIES > BEGGARY
BEGGARING > BEGGAR
BEGGARLY *adj* meanly inadequate
BEGGARS > BEGGAR
BEGGARY *n* extreme poverty or need
BEGGED > BEG
BEGGING > BEG
BEGGINGLY > BEG
BEGGINGS > BEG
BEGHARD *n* member of a Christian brotherhood that was founded in Flanders in the 13th century and

followed a life based on that of the Beguines
BEGHARDS > BEGHARD
BEGIFT *vb* give gift or gifts to
BEGIFTED > BEGIFT
BEGIFTING > BEGIFT
BEGIFTS > BEGIFT
BEGILD *vb* gild
BEGILDED > BEGILD
BEGILDING > BEGILD
BEGILDS > BEGILD
BEGILT > BEGILD
BEGIN *vb* start
BEGINNE *same as* > BEGINNING
BEGINNER *n* person who has just started learning to do something
BEGINNERS > BEGINNER
BEGINNES > BEGINNE
BEGINNING *n* start
BEGINS > BEGIN
BEGIRD *vb* surround
BEGIRDED > BEGIRD
BEGIRDING > BEGIRD
BEGIRDLE *vb* surround with girdle
BEGIRDLED > BEGIRDLE
BEGIRDLES > BEGIRDLE
BEGIRDS > BEGIRD
BEGIRT > BEGIRD
BEGLAD *vb* make glad
BEGLADDED > BEGLAD
BEGLADS > BEGLAD
BEGLAMOR *same as* > BEGLAMOUR
BEGLAMORS > BEGLAMOR
BEGLAMOUR *vb* glamorize
BEGLERBEG *n* governor in the Ottoman empire
BEGLOOM *vb* make gloomy
BEGLOOMED > BEGLOOM
BEGLOOMS > BEGLOOM
BEGNAW *vb* gnaw at
BEGNAWED > BEGNAW
BEGNAWING > BEGNAW
BEGNAWS > BEGNAW
BEGO *vb* harrass; beset
BEGOES > BEGO
BEGOGGLED *adj* wearing goggles
BEGOING > BEGO
BEGONE > BEGO
BEGONIA *n* tropical plant with waxy flowers
BEGONIAS > BEGONIA
BEGORAH *same as* > BEGORRA
BEGORED *adj* smear with gore
BEGORRA *interj* emphatic exclamation, regarded as a characteristic utterance of Irishmen
BEGORRAH *same as* > BEGORRA
BEGOT *past participle of* > BEGET
BEGOTTEN *past participle of* > BEGET
BEGRIM *same as* > BEGRIME
BEGRIME *vb* make dirty

BEGRIMED > BEGRIME
BEGRIMES > BEGRIME
BEGRIMING > BEGRIME
BEGRIMMED > BEGRIM
BEGRIMS > BEGRIM
BEGROAN *vb* groan at
BEGROANED > BEGROAN
BEGROANS > BEGROAN
BEGRUDGE *vb* envy (someone) the possession of something
BEGRUDGED > BEGRUDGE
BEGRUDGER > BEGRUDGE
BEGRUDGES > BEGRUDGE
BEGS > BEG
BEGUILE *vb* cheat or mislead
BEGUILED > BEGUILE
BEGUILER > BEGUILE
BEGUILERS > BEGUILE
BEGUILES > BEGUILE
BEGUILING *adj* charming, often in a deceptive way
BEGUIN *another name for* > BEGHARD
BEGUINAGE *n* convent for members of beguine sisterhood
BEGUINE *n* S American dance
BEGUINES > BEGUINE
BEGUINS > BEGUIN
BEGULF *vb* overwhelm
BEGULFED > BEGULF
BEGULFING > BEGULF
BEGULFS > BEGULF
BEGUM *n* Muslim woman of high rank
BEGUMS > BEGUM
BEGUN *past participle of* > BEGIN
BEGUNK *vb* delude; trick
BEGUNKED > BEGUNK
BEGUNKING > BEGUNK
BEGUNKS > BEGUNK
BEHALF *n* interest, part, benefit, or respect
BEHALVES > BEHALF
BEHAPPEN *vb* befall
BEHAPPENS > BEHAPPEN
BEHATTED *adj* wearing a hat
BEHAVE *vb* act or function in a particular way
BEHAVED > BEHAVE
BEHAVER > BEHAVE
BEHAVERS > BEHAVE
BEHAVES > BEHAVE
BEHAVING > BEHAVE
BEHAVIOR *same as* > BEHAVIOUR
BEHAVIORS > BEHAVIOR
BEHAVIOUR *n* manner of behaving
BEHEAD *vb* remove the head from
BEHEADAL > BEHEAD
BEHEADALS > BEHEAD
BEHEADED > BEHEAD
BEHEADER > BEHEAD
BEHEADERS > BEHEAD
BEHEADING > BEHEAD
BEHEADS > BEHEAD
BEHELD > BEHOLD

b

b

BEHEMOTH n huge person or thing
BEHEMOTHS > BEHEMOTH
BEHEST n order or earnest request
BEHESTS > BEHEST
BEHIGHT vb entrust
BEHIGHTS > BEHIGHT
BEHIND adv indicating position to the rear, lateness, responsibility, etc ⊳ n buttocks ⊳ prep in or to a position further back than ⊳ adj in a position further back
BEHINDS > BEHIND
BEHOLD vb look (at)
BEHOLDEN adj indebted or obliged
BEHOLDER > BEHOLD
BEHOLDERS > BEHOLD
BEHOLDING > BEHOLD
BEHOLDS > BEHOLD
BEHOOF n advantage or profit
BEHOOFS > BEHOOF
BEHOOVE same as
> BEHOVE
BEHOOVED > BEHOOVE
BEHOOVES > BEHOOVE
BEHOOVING > BEHOOVE
BEHOTE same as
> BEHIGHT
BEHOTES > BEHOTE
BEHOTING > BEHOTE
BEHOVE vb be necessary or fitting for
BEHOVED > BEHOVE
BEHOVEFUL adj useful; of benefit
BEHOVELY adj useful
BEHOVES > BEHOVE
BEHOVING > BEHOVE
BEHOWL vb howl at
BEHOWLED > BEHOWL
BEHOWLING > BEHOWL
BEHOWLS > BEHOWL
BEIGE n pale brown ⊳ n very light brown, sometimes with a yellowish tinge, similar to the colour of undyed wool
BEIGEL same as **>** BAGEL
BEIGELS > BEIGEL
BEIGES > BEIGE
BEIGIER > BEIGE
BEIGIEST > BEIGE
BEIGNE variant of
> BEIGNET
BEIGNES > BEIGNE
BEIGNET n square deep-fried pastry served hot and sprinkled with icing sugar
BEIGNETS > BEIGNET
BEIGY > BEIGE
BEIN adj financially comfortable
BEING > BE
BEINGLESS > BE
BEINGNESS > BE
BEINGS > BE
BEINKED adj daubed with ink

BEINNESS > BEIN
BEJABBERS same as
> BEJABERS
BEJABERS interj by Jesus!
BEJADE vb jade; tire
BEJADED > BEJADE
BEJADES > BEJADE
BEJADING > BEJADE
BEJANT same as **>** BAJAN
BEJANTS > BEJANT
BEJEEBERS same as
> BEJABERS
BEJEEZUS same as
> BEJESUS
BEJESUIT vb convert to Jesuitism
BEJESUITS > BEJESUIT
BEJESUS interj exclamation of surprise ⊳ n as in the bejesus mild expletive
BEJESUSES > BEJESUS
BEJEWEL vb decorate with or as if with jewels
BEJEWELED same as
> BEJEWEL
BEJEWELS > BEJEWEL
BEJUMBLE vb jumble up
BEJUMBLED > BEJUMBLE
BEJUMBLES > BEJUMBLE
BEKAH n half shekel
BEKAHS > BEKAH
BEKISS vb smother with kisses
BEKISSED > BEKISS
BEKISSES > BEKISS
BEKISSING > BEKISS
BEKNAVE vb treat as knave
BEKNAVED > BEKNAVE
BEKNAVES > BEKNAVE
BEKNAVING > BEKNAVE
BEKNIGHT vb esteem
BEKNIGHTS > BEKNIGHT
BEKNOT vb tie knot or knots in
BEKNOTS > BEKNOT
BEKNOTTED > BEKNOT
BEKNOWN adj known about
BEL n unit for comparing two power levels or measuring the intensity of a sound, equal to 10 decibels
BELABOR same as
> BELABOUR
BELABORED > BELABOR
BELABORS > BELABOR
BELABOUR vb attack verbally or physically
BELABOURS > BELABOUR
BELACE vb decorate with lace
BELACED > BELACE
BELACES > BELACE
BELACING > BELACE
BELADIED > BELADY
BELADIES > BELADY
BELADY vb call a lady
BELADYING > BELADY
BELAH n Australian tree which yields a useful timber
BELAHS > BELAH
BELAMIES > BELAMY
BELAMOURE n loved one

BELAMY n close friend
BELAR same as **>** BELAH
BELARS > BELAR
BELATE vb cause to be late
BELATED adj late or too late
BELATEDLY > BELATED
BELATES > BELATE
BELATING > BELATE
BELAUD vb praise highly
BELAUDED > BELAUD
BELAUDING > BELAUD
BELAUDS > BELAUD
BELAY vb secure a line to a pin or cleat ⊳ n attachment (of a climber) to a mountain by tying the rope off round a rock spike, piton, nut, etc, to safeguard the party in the event of a fall
BELAYED > BELAY
BELAYER > BELAY
BELAYERS > BELAY
BELAYING > BELAY
BELAYS > BELAY
BELCH vb expel wind from the stomach noisily through the mouth ⊳ n act of belching
BELCHED > BELCH
BELCHER > BELCH
BELCHERS > BELCH
BELCHES > BELCH
BELCHING > BELCH
BELDAM n old woman, esp an ugly or malicious one
BELDAME same as
> BELDAM
BELDAMES > BELDAME
BELDAMS > BELDAM
BELEAGUER vb trouble persistently
BELEAP vb leap over
BELEAPED > BELEAP
BELEAPING > BELEAP
BELEAPS > BELEAP
BELEAPT > BELEAP
BELEE vb put on sheltered side
BELEED > BELEE
BELEEING > BELEE
BELEES > BELEE
BELEMNITE n type of extinct marine mollusc related to the cuttlefish
BELEMNOID adj shaped like a dart
BELFRIED adj with a belfry
BELFRIES > BELFRY
BELFRY n part of a tower where bells are hung
BELGA n former Belgian monetary unit worth five francs
BELGARD n kind gaze
BELGARDS > BELGARD
BELGAS > BELGA
BELIE vb show to be untrue
BELIED > BELIE
BELIEF n faith or confidence
BELIEFS > BELIEF
BELIER > BELIE

BELIERS > BELIE
BELIES > BELIE
BELIEVE vb accept as true or real
BELIEVED > BELIEVE
BELIEVER > BELIEVE
BELIEVERS > BELIEVE
BELIEVES > BELIEVE
BELIEVING > BELIEVE
BELIKE adv perhaps
BELIQUOR vb cause to be drunk
BELIQUORS > BELIQUOR
BELITTLE vb treat as having little value or importance
BELITTLED > BELITTLE
BELITTLER > BELITTLE
BELITTLES > BELITTLE
BELIVE adv speedily
BELL n hollow, usu. metal, cup-shaped instrument that emits a ringing sound when struck ⊳ vb utter (such a cry)
BELLBIND n bindweed-type climber
BELLBINDS > BELLBIND
BELLBIRD n Australasian bird with bell-like call
BELLBIRDS > BELLBIRD
BELLBOY n man or boy employed in a hotel, club, etc, to carry luggage and answer calls for service
BELLBOYS > BELLBOY
BELLCOTE n small roofed structure for bell
BELLCOTES > BELLCOTE
BELLE n beautiful woman, esp the most attractive woman at a function
BELLED > BELL
BELLEEK n kind of thin fragile porcelain with a lustrous glaze
BELLEEKS > BELLEEK
BELLES > BELLE
BELLETER n person who makes bells
BELLETERS > BELLETER
BELLHOP same as
> BELLBOY
BELLHOPS > BELLHOP
BELLIBONE n beautiful and good woman
BELLICOSE adj warlike and aggressive
BELLIED > BELLY
BELLIES > BELLY
BELLING > BELL
BELLINGS > BELL
BELLMAN n man who rings a bell, esp (formerly) a town crier
BELLMEN > BELLMAN
BELLOCK vb shout
BELLOCKED > BELLOCK
BELLOCKS > BELLOCK
BELLOW vb make a low deep cry like that of a bull ⊳ n loud deep roar
BELLOWED > BELLOW
BELLOWER > BELLOW

BELLOWERS > BELLOW
BELLOWING > BELLOW
BELLOWS npl instrument for pumping a stream of air into something
BELLPULL n handle, rope, or cord pulled to operate a doorbell or servant's bell
BELLPULLS > BELLPULL
BELLS > BELL
BELLWORT n N American plant with slender bell-shaped yellow flowers
BELLWORTS > BELLWORT
BELLY n part of the body of a vertebrate which contains the intestines ▷ vb (cause to) swell out
BELLYACHE n pain in the abdomen ▷ vb complain repeatedly
BELLYBAND n strap around the belly of a draught animal, holding the shafts of a vehicle
BELLYFUL n more than one can tolerate
BELLYFULS > BELLYFUL
BELLYING > BELLY
BELLYINGS > BELLY
BELLYLIKE > BELLY
BELOMANCY n art of divination using arrows
BELON n type of oyster
BELONG vb be the property of
BELONGED > BELONG
BELONGER n native-born Caribbean
BELONGERS > BELONGER
BELONGING n secure relationship
BELONGS > BELONG
BELONS > BELON
BELOVE vb love
BELOVED adj dearly loved ▷ n person dearly loved
BELOVEDS > BELOVED
BELOVES > BELOVE
BELOVING > BELOVE
BELOW adv at or to a position lower than, under ▷ prep at or to a position lower than
BELOWS same as > BELLOWS
BELS > BEL
BELT n band of cloth, leather, etc, worn usu. around the waist ▷ vb fasten with a belt
BELTED > BELT
BELTER n outstanding person or event
BELTERS > BELTER
BELTING n material used to make a belt or belts ▷ adj excellent
BELTINGS > BELTING
BELTLESS > BELT
BELTLINE n line separating car's windows from main body
BELTLINES > BELTLINE
BELTMAN n (formerly) the

member of a beach life-saving team who swam out with a line attached to his belt
BELTMEN > BELTMAN
BELTS > BELT
BELTWAY n people and institutions located in the area bounded by the Washington Beltway, taken to be politically and socially out of touch with the rest of America and much given to political intrigue
BELTWAYS > BELTWAY
BELUGA n large white sturgeon of the Black and Caspian Seas, from which caviar and isinglass are obtained
BELUGAS > BELUGA
BELVEDERE n building designed and situated to look out on pleasant scenery
BELYING > BELIE
BEMA n speaker's platform in the assembly in ancient Athens
BEMAD vb cause to become mad
BEMADAM vb call a person madam
BEMADAMED > BEMADAM
BEMADAMS > BEMADAM
BEMADDED > BEMAD
BEMADDEN vb cause to become mad
BEMADDENS > BEMADDEN
BEMADDING > BEMAD
BEMADS > BEMAD
BEMAS > BEMA
BEMATA > BEMA
BEMAUL vb maul
BEMAULED > BEMAUL
BEMAULING > BEMAUL
BEMAULS > BEMAUL
BEMAZED adj amazed
BEMBEX n type of wasp
BEMBEXES > BEMBEX
BEMBIX same as > BEMBEX
BEMBIXES > BEMBIX
BEMEAN a less common word for > DEMEAN
BEMEANED > BEMEAN
BEMEANING > BEMEAN
BEMEANS > BEMEAN
BEMEANT > BEMEAN
BEMEDAL vb decorate with medals
BEMEDALED > BEMEDAL
BEMEDALS > BEMEDAL
BEMETE vb measure
BEMETED > BEMETE
BEMETES > BEMETE
BEMETING > BEMETE
BEMINGLE vb mingle
BEMINGLED > BEMINGLE
BEMINGLES > BEMINGLE
BEMIRE vb soil with or as if with mire
BEMIRED > BEMIRE
BEMIRES > BEMIRE

BEMIRING > BEMIRE
BEMIST vb cloud with mist
BEMISTED > BEMIST
BEMISTING > BEMIST
BEMISTS > BEMIST
BEMIX vb mix thoroughly
BEMIXED > BEMIX
BEMIXES > BEMIX
BEMIXING > BEMIX
BEMIXT > BEMIX
BEMOAN vb express sorrow or dissatisfaction about
BEMOANED > BEMOAN
BEMOANER > BEMOAN
BEMOANERS > BEMOAN
BEMOANING > BEMOAN
BEMOANS > BEMOAN
BEMOCK vb mock
BEMOCKED > BEMOCK
BEMOCKING > BEMOCK
BEMOCKS > BEMOCK
BEMOIL vb soil with mud
BEMOILED > BEMOIL
BEMOILING > BEMOIL
BEMOILS > BEMOIL
BEMONSTER vb treat as monster
BEMOUTH vb endow with mouth
BEMOUTHED > BEMOUTH
BEMOUTHS > BEMOUTH
BEMUD vb cover with mud
BEMUDDED > BEMUD
BEMUDDING > BEMUD
BEMUDDLE vb confound
BEMUDDLED > BEMUDDLE
BEMUDDLES > BEMUDDLE
BEMUDS > BEMUD
BEMUFFLE vb muffle up
BEMUFFLED > BEMUFFLE
BEMUFFLES > BEMUFFLE
BEMURMUR vb murmur at
BEMURMURS > BEMURMUR
BEMUSE vb confuse
BEMUSED adj puzzled or confused
BEMUSEDLY > BEMUSED
BEMUSES > BEMUSE
BEMUSING > BEMUSE
BEMUZZLE vb put muzzle on
BEMUZZLED > BEMUZZLE
BEMUZZLES > BEMUZZLE
BEN n mountain peak ▷ adv in ▷ adj inner
BENADRYL n tradename of an antihistamine drug used in sleeping tablets
BENADRYLS > BENADRYL
BENAME an archaic word for > NAME
BENAMED > BENAME
BENAMES > BENAME
BENAMING > BENAME
BENCH n long seat ▷ vb put a person on a bench
BENCHED > BENCH
BENCHER n member of the governing body of one of the Inns of Court, usually a judge or a Queen's Counsel
BENCHERS > BENCHER
BENCHES > BENCH
BENCHIER > BENCHY

BENCHIEST > BENCHY
BENCHING > BENCH
BENCHLAND n level ground at foot of mountains
BENCHLESS > BENCH
BENCHMARK n criterion by which to measure something ▷ vb measure or test against a benchmark
BENCHTOP adj for use at bench
BENCHY adj (of a hillside) hollowed out in benches
BEND vb (cause to) form a curve ▷ n curved part
BENDABLE > BEND
BENDAY vb (printing) reproduce using Benday technique
BENDAYED > BENDAY
BENDAYING > BENDAY
BENDAYS > BENDAY
BENDED > BEND
BENDEE same as > BENDY
BENDEES > BENDEE
BENDER n drinking bout
BENDERS > BENDER
BENDIER > BENDY
BENDIEST > BENDY
BENDING > BEND
BENDINGLY > BEND
BENDINGS > BEND
BENDLET n narrow diagonal stripe on heraldic shield
BENDLETS > BENDLET
BENDS > BEND
BENDWAYS same as > BENDWISE
BENDWISE adv diagonally
BENDY adj flexible or pliable ▷ n okra
BENDYS > BENDY
BENE n blessing
BENEATH prep below ▷ adv below
BENEDICK n recently-married man
BENEDICKS > BENEDICK
BENEDICT n newly married man
BENEDICTS > BENEDICT
BENEDIGHT adj blessed
BENEFACT vb be benefactor to
BENEFACTS > BENEFACT
BENEFIC adj a rare word for beneficent
BENEFICE n church office providing its holder with an income ▷ vb provide with a benefice
BENEFICED > BENEFICE
BENEFICES > BENEFICE
BENEFIT n something that improves or promotes ▷ vb do or receive good
BENEFITED > BENEFIT
BENEFITER > BENEFIT
BENEFITS > BENEFIT
BENEMPT a past participle of > NAME
BENEMPTED > BENEMPT
BENES > BENE

b

b

BENET vb trap (something) in a net
BENETS > BENET
BENETTED > BENET
BENETTING > BENET
BENGA n type of Kenyan popular music featuring guitars
BENGALINE n heavy corded fabric, esp silk with woollen or cotton cord
BENGAS > BENGA
BENI n sesame plant
BENIGHT vb shroud in darkness
BENIGHTED adj ignorant or uncultured
BENIGHTEN same as **>** BENIGHT
BENIGHTER > BENIGHT
BENIGHTS > BENIGHT
BENIGN adj showing kindliness
BENIGNANT adj kind or gracious
BENIGNER > BENIGN
BENIGNEST > BENIGN
BENIGNITY n kindliness
BENIGNLY > BENIGN
BENIS > BENI
BENISEED n sesame
BENISEEDS > BENISEED
BENISON n blessing, esp a spoken one
BENISONS > BENISON
BENITIER n basin for holy water
BENITIERS > BENITIER
BENJ another word for **>** BHANG
BENJAMIN same as **>** BENZOIN
BENJAMINS > BENJAMIN
BENJES > BENJ
BENNE another name for **>** SESAME
BENNES > BENNE
BENNET n Eurasian and N African plant with yellow flowers
BENNETS > BENNET
BENNI n sesame
BENNIES > BENNY
BENNIS > BENNI
BENNY n amphetamine tablet, esp benzedrine: a stimulant
BENOMYL n fungicide, derived from imidazole, used on cereal and fruit crops: suspected of being carcinogenic
BENOMYLS > BENOMYL
BENS > BEN
BENT adj not straight ▷ n personal inclination, propensity, or aptitude
BENTGRASS n variety of grass
BENTHAL > BENTHOS
BENTHIC > BENTHOS
BENTHOAL > BENTHON
BENTHON same as **>** BENTHOS

BENTHONIC > BENTHOS
BENTHONS > BENTHON
BENTHOS n animals and plants living at the bottom of a sea or lake
BENTHOSES > BENTHOS
BENTIER > BENTY
BENTIEST > BENTY
BENTO n thin lightweight box divided into compartments, which contain small separate dishes comprising a Japanese meal
BENTONITE n valuable clay, formed by the decomposition of volcanic ash, that swells as it absorbs water: used as a filler in the building, paper, and pharmaceutical industries
BENTOS > BENTO
BENTS > BENT
BENTWOOD n wood bent in moulds, used mainly for furniture ▷ adj made from such wood
BENTWOODS > BENTWOOD
BENTY adj covered with bentgrass
BENUMB vb make numb or powerless
BENUMBED > BENUMB
BENUMBING > BENUMB
BENUMBS > BENUMB
BENZAL n transparent crystalline substance
BENZALS > BENZAL
BENZENE n flammable poisonous liquid used as a solvent, insecticide, etc
BENZENES > BENZENE
BENZENOID adj similar to benzene
BENZIDIN same as **>** BENZIDINE
BENZIDINE n grey or reddish poisonous crystalline powder
BENZIDINS > BENZIDINE
BENZIL n yellow compound radical
BENZILS > BENZIL
BENZIN same as **>** BENZINE
BENZINE n volatile liquid used as a solvent
BENZINES > BENZINE
BENZINS > BENZIN
BENZOATE n any salt or ester of benzoic acid, containing the group C_6H_5COO- or the ion $C_6H_5COO^-$
BENZOATES > BENZOATE
BENZOIC adj of, containing, or derived from benzoic acid or benzoin
BENZOIN n gum resin obtained from various Javanese and Sumatran trees, used in ointments, perfume, etc
BENZOINS > BENZOIN

BENZOL n crude form of benzene, containing toluene, xylene, and other hydrocarbons, obtained from coal tar or coal gas and used as a fuel
BENZOLE same as **>** BENZOL
BENZOLES > BENZOLE
BENZOLINE n unpurified benzene
BENZOLS > BENZOL
BENZOYL n of, consisting of, or containing the monovalent group C_6H_5CO-
BENZOYLS > BENZOYL
BENZYL n of, consisting of, or containing the monovalent group $C_6H_5CH_2$
BENZYLIC > BENZYL
BENZYLS > BENZYL
BEPAINT vb dye; paint
BEPAINTED > BEPAINT
BEPAINTS > BEPAINT
BEPAT vb pat
BEPATCHED adj mended with or covered in patches
BEPATS > BEPAT
BEPATTED > BEPAT
BEPATTING > BEPAT
BEPEARL vb decorate with pearls
BEPEARLED > BEPEARL
BEPEARLS > BEPEARL
BEPELT vb pelt energetically
BEPELTED > BEPELT
BEPELTING > BEPELT
BEPELTS > BEPELT
BEPEPPER vb shower with small missiles
BEPEPPERS > BEPEPPER
BEPESTER vb pester persistently
BEPESTERS > BEPESTER
BEPIMPLE vb form pimples on
BEPIMPLED > BEPIMPLE
BEPIMPLES > BEPIMPLE
BEPITIED > BEPITY
BEPITIES > BEPITY
BEPITY vb feel great pity for
BEPITYING > BEPITY
BEPLASTER vb cover in thick plaster
BEPLUMED adj decorated with feathers
BEPOMMEL vb beat vigorously
BEPOMMELS > BEPOMMEL
BEPOWDER vb cover with powder
BEPOWDERS > BEPOWDER
BEPRAISE vb praise highly
BEPRAISED > BEPRAISE
BEPRAISES > BEPRAISE
BEPROSE vb (of poetry) reduce to prose
BEPROSED > BEPROSE
BEPROSES > BEPROSE
BEPROSING > BEPROSE

BEPUFF vb puff up
BEPUFFED > BEPUFF
BEPUFFING > BEPUFF
BEPUFFS > BEPUFF
BEQUEATH vb dispose of (property) as in a will
BEQUEATHS > BEQUEATH
BEQUEST n legal gift of money or property by someone who has died
BEQUESTS > BEQUEST
BERAKE vb rake thoroughly
BERAKED > BERAKE
BERAKES > BERAKE
BERAKING > BERAKE
BERASCAL vb accuse of being rascal
BERASCALS > BERASCAL
BERATE vb scold harshly
BERATED > BERATE
BERATES > BERATE
BERATING > BERATE
BERAY vb soil; defile
BERAYED > BERAY
BERAYING > BERAY
BERAYS > BERAY
BERBERE n hot-tasting Ethiopian paste made from garlic, cayenne pepper, coriander, and other spices often used in stews
BERBERES > BERBERE
BERBERIN same as **>** BERBERINE
BERBERINE n yellow bitter-tasting alkaloid obtained from barberry
BERBERINS > BERBERIN
BERBERIS n shrub with red berries
BERBICE as in berbice chair large armchair with long arms that can be folded inwards to act as leg rests
BERCEAU n arched trellis for climbing plants
BERCEAUX > BERCEAU
BERCEUSE n lullaby
BERCEUSES > BERCEUSE
BERDACHE n Native American transvestite
BERDACHES > BERDACHE
BERDASH same as **>** BERDACHE
BERDASHES > BERDASH
BERE n barley
BEREAVE vb deprive (of) something or someone valued, esp through death
BEREAVED adj having recently lost a close friend or relative through death
BEREAVEN > BEREAVE
BEREAVER > BEREAVE
BEREAVERS > BEREAVE
BEREAVES > BEREAVE
BEREAVING > BEREAVE
BEREFT adj deprived
BERES > BERE
BERET n round flat close-fitting brimless cap
BERETS > BERET
BERETTA n type of pistol
BERETTAS > BERETTA

BERG n iceberg

BERGAMA n type of Turkish rug

BERGAMAS > BERGAMA

BERGAMASK n person from Bergamo

BERGAMOT n small Asian tree, the fruit of which yields an oil used in perfumery

BERGAMOTS > BERGAMOT

BERGANDER n species of duck

BERGEN n large rucksack with a capacity of over 50 litres

BERGENIA n evergreen ground-covering plant

BERGENIAS > BERGENIA

BERGENS > BERGEN

BERGERE n type of French armchair

BERGERES > BERGERE

BERGFALL n avalanche

BERGFALLS > BERGFALL

BERGHAAN same as **>** BERGMEHL

BERGHAANS > BERGHAAN

BERGMEHL n light powdery variety of calcite

BERGMEHLS > BERGMEHL

BERGOMASK same as **>** BERGAMASK

BERGS > BERG

BERGYLT n large northern marine food fish

BERGYLTS > BERGYLT

BERHYME vb mention in poetry

BERHYMED > BERHYME

BERHYMES > BERHYME

BERHYMING > BERHYME

BERIBERI n disease, endemic in E and S Asia, caused by dietary deficiency of thiamine (vitamin B_1). It affects the nerves to the limbs, producing pain, paralysis, and swelling

BERIBERIS > BERIBERI

BERIMBAU n Brazilian single-stringed bowed instrument, used to accompany capoeira

BERIMBAUS > BERIMBAU

BERIME same as **>** BERHYME

BERIMED > BERIME

BERIMES > BERIME

BERIMING > BERIME

BERINGED adj wearing a ring or rings

BERK n stupid person

BERKELIUM n radioactive element

BERKO adj berserk

BERKS > BERK

BERLEY n bait scattered on water to attract fish ▷ vb scatter (bait) on water

BERLEYED > BERLEY

BERLEYING > BERLEY

BERLEYS > BERLEY

BERLIN n fine wool yarn

used for tapestry work, etc

BERLINE same as **>** BERLIN

BERLINES > BERLINE

BERLINS > BERLIN

BERM n narrow grass strip between the road and the footpath in a residential area ▷ vb create a berm

BERME same as **>** BERM

BERMED > BERM

BERMES > BERME

BERMING > BERM

BERMS > BERM

BERMUDAS npl close-fitting shorts that come down to the knees

BERNICLE n barnacle goose: a N European goose that has a black-and-white head and body and grey wings

BERNICLES > BERNICLE

BEROB vb rob

BEROBBED > BEROB

BEROBBING > BEROB

BEROBED adj wearing a robe

BEROBS > BEROB

BEROUGED adj wearing rouge

BERRET same as **>** BERET

BERRETS > BERRET

BERRETTA same as **>** BIRETTA

BERRETTAS > BERRETTA

BERRIED > BERRY

BERRIES > BERRY

BERRIGAN n Australian tree with hanging branches

BERRIGANS > BERRIGAN

BERRY n small soft stoneless fruit ▷ vb bear or produce berries

BERRYING > BERRY

BERRYINGS > BERRY

BERRYLESS > BERRY

BERRYLIKE > BERRY

BERSEEM n Mediterranean clover grown as a forage crop and to improve the soil

BERSEEMS > BERSEEM

BERSERK adj frenziedly violent or destructive ▷ n member of a class of ancient Norse warriors who worked themselves into a frenzy before battle and fought with insane fury and courage

BERSERKER same as **>** BERSERK

BERSERKLY > BERSERK

BERSERKS > BERSERK

BERTH n bunk in a ship or train ▷ vb dock (a ship)

BERTHA n wide deep capelike collar, often of lace, usually to cover up a low neckline

BERTHAGE n place for mooring boats

BERTHAGES > BERTHAGE

BERTHAS > BERTHA

BERTHE n type of lace collar

BERTHED > BERTH

BERTHES > BERTHE

BERTHING > BERTH

BERTHS > BERTH

BERYL n hard transparent mineral

BERYLINE > BERYL

BERYLLIA n beryllium oxide

BERYLLIAS > BERYLLIA

BERYLLIUM n toxic silvery-white metallic element

BERYLS > BERYL

BES variant of **>** BETH

BESAINT vb give saint status to

BESAINTED > BESAINT

BESAINTS > BESAINT

BESANG > BESING

BESAT > BESIT

BESAW > BESEE

BESCATTER vb strew

BESCORCH vb scorch badly

BESCOUR vb scour thoroughly

BESCOURED > BESCOUR

BESCOURS > BESCOUR

BESCRAWL vb cover with scrawls

BESCRAWLS > BESCRAWL

BESCREEN vb conceal with screen

BESCREENS > BESCREEN

BESEE vb provide for; mind

BESEECH vb ask earnestly

BESEECHED > BESEECH

BESEECHER > BESEECH

BESEECHES > BESEECH

BESEEING > BESEE

BESEEKE same as **>** BESEECH

BESEEKES > BESEEKE

BESEEKING > BESEEKE

BESEEM vb be suitable for

BESEEMED > BESEEM

BESEEMING > BESEEM

BESEEMLY > BESEEM

BESEEMS > BESEEM

BESEEN > BESEE

BESEES > BESEE

BESES > BES

BESET vb trouble or harass constantly

BESETMENT > BESET

BESETS > BESET

BESETTER > BESET

BESETTERS > BESET

BESETTING adj tempting, harassing, or assailing

BESHADOW vb darken with shadow

BESHADOWS > BESHADOW

BESHAME vb cause to feel shame

BESHAMED > BESHAME

BESHAMES > BESHAME

BESHAMING > BESHAME

BESHINE vb illuminate

BESHINES > BESHINE

BESHINING > BESHINE

BESHIVER vb shatter

BESHIVERS > BESHIVER

BESHONE > BESHINE

BESHOUT vb shout about

BESHOUTED > BESHOUT

BESHOUTS > BESHOUT

BESHREW vb wish evil on

BESHREWED > BESHREW

BESHREWS > BESHREW

BESHROUD vb cover with a shroud

BESHROUDS > BESHROUD

BESIDE prep at, by, or to the side of

BESIDES prep in addition ▷ adv in addition

BESIEGE vb surround with military forces

BESIEGED > BESIEGE

BESIEGER > BESIEGE

BESIEGERS > BESIEGE

BESIEGES > BESIEGE

BESIEGING > BESIEGE

BESIGH vb sigh for

BESIGHED > BESIGH

BESIGHING > BESIGH

BESIGHS > BESIGH

BESING vb sing about joyfully

BESINGING > BESING

BESINGS > BESING

BESIT vb suit; fit

BESITS > BESIT

BESITTING > BESIT

BESLAVE vb treat as slave

BESLAVED > BESLAVE

BESLAVER vb fawn over

BESLAVERS > BESLAVER

BESLAVES > BESLAVE

BESLAVING > BESLAVE

BESLIME vb cover with slime

BESLIMED > BESLIME

BESLIMES > BESLIME

BESLIMING > BESLIME

BESLOBBER vb slobber over

BESLUBBER same as **>** BESLOBBER

BESMEAR vb smear over

BESMEARED > BESMEAR

BESMEARER > BESMEAR

BESMEARS > BESMEAR

BESMILE vb smile on

BESMILED > BESMILE

BESMILES > BESMILE

BESMILING > BESMILE

BESMIRCH vb tarnish (someone's name or reputation)

BESMOKE vb blacken with smoke

BESMOKED > BESMOKE

BESMOKES > BESMOKE

BESMOKING > BESMOKE

BESMOOTH vb smooth

BESMOOTHS > BESMOOTH

BESMUDGE vb blacken

BESMUDGED > BESMUDGE

BESMUDGES > BESMUDGE

BESMUT vb blacken with smut

BESMUTCH same as **>** BESMIRCH

BESMUTS > BESMUT

BESMUTTED > BESMUT

BESNOW vb cover with snow

b

BESNOWED > BESNOW
BESNOWING > BESNOW
BESNOWS > BESNOW
BESOGNIO n worthless person
BESOIN n need
BESOINS > BESOIN
BESOM n broom made of twigs ▷ vb sweep with a besom
BESOMED > BESOM
BESOMING > BESOM
BESOMS > BESOM
BESONIAN same as
> BEZONIAN
BESONIANS > BESONIAN
BESOOTHE vb soothe
BESOOTHED > BESOOTHE
BESOOTHES > BESOOTHE
BESORT vb fit
BESORTED > BESORT
BESORTING > BESORT
BESORTS > BESORT
BESOT vb make stupid or muddled
BESOTS > BESOT
BESOTTED adj infatuated
BESOTTING > BESOT
BESOUGHT a past participle of **>** BESEECH
BESOULED adj having a soul
BESPAKE > BESPOKE
BESPANGLE vb cover or adorn with or as if with spangles
BESPAT > BESPIT
BESPATE > BESPIT
BESPATTER vb splash, e.g. with dirty water
BESPEAK vb indicate or suggest
BESPEAKS > BESPEAK
BESPECKLE vb mark with speckles
BESPED > BESPEED
BESPEED vb get on with (doing something)
BESPEEDS > BESPEED
BESPICE vb flavour with spices
BESPICED > BESPICE
BESPICES > BESPICE
BESPICING > BESPICE
BESPIT vb cover with spittle
BESPITS > BESPIT
BESPOKE adj (esp of a suit) made to the customer's specifications
BESPOKEN > BESPEAK
BESPORT vb amuse oneself
BESPORTED > BESPORT
BESPORTS > BESPORT
BESPOT vb mark with spots
BESPOTS > BESPOT
BESPOTTED > BESPOT
BESPOUSE vb marry
BESPOUSED > BESPOUSE
BESPOUSES > BESPOUSE
BESPOUT vb speak pretentiously
BESPOUTED > BESPOUT

BESPOUTS > BESPOUT
BESPREAD vb cover (a surface) with something
BESPREADS > BESPREAD
BESPRENT adj sprinkled over
BEST adj most excellent of a particular group etc ▷ adv in a manner surpassing all others ▷ n utmost effort ▷ vb defeat
BESTAD same as
> BESTEAD
BESTADDE same as
> BESTEAD
BESTAIN vb stain
BESTAINED > BESTAIN
BESTAINS > BESTAIN
BESTAR vb decorate with stars
BESTARRED > BESTAR
BESTARS > BESTAR
BESTEAD vb serve; assist
BESTEADED > BESTEAD
BESTEADS > BESTEAD
BESTED > BEST
BESTI Indian English word for **>** SHAME
BESTIAL adj brutal or savage
BESTIALLY > BESTIAL
BESTIALS > BESTIAL
BESTIARY n medieval collection of descriptions of animals
BESTICK vb cover with sharp points
BESTICKS > BESTICK
BESTILL vb cause to be still
BESTILLED > BESTILL
BESTILLS > BESTILL
BESTING > BEST
BESTIR vb cause (oneself) to become active
BESTIRRED > BESTIR
BESTIRS > BESTIR
BESTIS > BESTI
BESTORM vb assault
BESTORMED > BESTORM
BESTORMS > BESTORM
BESTOW vb present (a gift) or confer (an honour)
BESTOWAL > BESTOW
BESTOWALS > BESTOW
BESTOWED > BESTOW
BESTOWER > BESTOW
BESTOWERS > BESTOW
BESTOWING > BESTOW
BESTOWS > BESTOW
BESTREAK vb streak
BESTREAKS > BESTREAK
BESTREW vb scatter or lie scattered over (a surface)
BESTREWED > BESTREW
BESTREWN > BESTREW
BESTREWS > BESTREW
BESTRID > BESTRIDE
BESTRIDE vb have or put a leg on either side of
BESTRIDES > BESTRIDE
BESTRODE > BESTRIDE
BESTROW same as
> BESTREW

BESTROWED > BESTROW
BESTROWN > BESTROW
BESTROWS > BESTROW
BESTS > BEST
BESTUCK > BESTICK
BESTUD vb set with, or as with studs
BESTUDDED > BESTUD
BESTUDS > BESTUD
BESUITED adj wearing a suit
BESUNG > BESING
BESWARM vb swarm over
BESWARMED > BESWARM
BESWARMS > BESWARM
BET n agreement between two parties that a sum of money or other stake will be paid by the loser to the party who correctly predicts the outcome of an event ▷ vb make or place a bet with (a person or persons)
BETA n second letter in the Greek alphabet, a consonant, transliterated as b
BETACISM vb type of speech impediment
BETACISMS > BETACISM
BETAINE n sweet-tasting alkaloid that occurs in the sugar beet
BETAINES > BETAINE
BETAKE as in betake oneself go
BETAKEN > BETAKE
BETAKES > BETAKE
BETAKING > BETAKE
BETAS > BETA
BETATOPIC adj (of atoms) differing in proton number by one, theoretically as a result of emission of a beta particle
BETATRON n type of particle accelerator for producing high-energy beams of electrons
BETATRONS > BETATRON
BETATTER vb make ragged
BETATTERS > BETATTER
BETAXED adj burdened with taxes
BETCHA interj bet you
BETE same as **>** BEET
BETED > BETE
BETEEM vb accord
BETEEME same as
> BETEEM
BETEEMED > BETEEM
BETEEMES > BETEEME
BETEEMING > BETEEM
BETEEMS > BETEEM
BETEL n Asian climbing plant, the leaves and nuts of which can be chewed
BETELNUT n seed of the betel palm, chewed with betel leaves and nuts by people in S and SE Asia as a digestive stimulant and narcotic

BETELNUTS > BETELNUT
BETELS > BETEL
BETES > BETE
BETH n second letter of the Hebrew alphabet transliterated as b
BETHANK vb thank
BETHANKED > BETHANK
BETHANKIT n grace spoken before meal
BETHANKS > BETHANK
BETHEL n seaman's chapel
BETHELS > BETHEL
BETHESDA n church building of certain Christian denominations
BETHESDAS > BETHESDA
BETHINK vb cause (oneself) to consider or meditate
BETHINKS > BETHINK
BETHORN vb cover with thorns
BETHORNED > BETHORN
BETHORNS > BETHORN
BETHOUGHT > BETHINK
BETHRALL vb make slave of
BETHRALLS > BETHRALL
BETHS > BETH
BETHUMB vb (of books) wear by handling
BETHUMBED > BETHUMB
BETHUMBS > BETHUMB
BETHUMP vb thump hard
BETHUMPED > BETHUMP
BETHUMPS > BETHUMP
BETHWACK vb strike hard with flat object
BETHWACKS > BETHWACK
BETID > BETIDE
BETIDE vb happen (to)
BETIDED > BETIDE
BETIDES > BETIDE
BETIDING > BETIDE
BETIGHT > BETIDE
BETIME vb befall
BETIMED > BETIME
BETIMES > BETIME
BETIMING > BETIME
BETING > BETE
BETISE n folly or lack of perception
BETISES > BETISE
BETITLE vb give title to
BETITLED > BETITLE
BETITLES > BETITLE
BETITLING > BETITLE
BETOIL vb tire through hard work
BETOILED > BETOIL
BETOILING > BETOIL
BETOILS > BETOIL
BETOKEN vb indicate or signify
BETOKENED > BETOKEN
BETOKENS > BETOKEN
BETON n concrete
BETONIES > BETONY
BETONS > BETON
BETONY n North American plant
BETOOK the past tense of
> BETAKE

ETOSS vb toss about
ETOSSED > BETOSS
ETOSSES > BETOSS
ETOSSING > BETOSS
ETRAY vb hand over or expose (one's nation, friend, etc) treacherously to an enemy
ETRAYAL > BETRAY
ETRAYALS > BETRAY
ETRAYED > BETRAY
ETRAYER > BETRAY
ETRAYERS > BETRAY
ETRAYING > BETRAY
ETRAYS > BETRAY
ETREAD vb tread over
ETREADS > BETREAD
ETRIM vb decorate
ETRIMMED > BETRIM
ETRIMS > BETRIM
ETROD > BETREAD
ETRODDEN > BETREAD
ETROTH vb promise to marry or to give in marriage
ETROTHAL n engagement to be married
ETROTHED adj engaged to be married ⊳ n person to whom one is engaged
ETROTHS > BETROTH
ETS > BET
ETTA n fighting fish
ETTAS > BETTA
ETTED > BET
ETTER adj more excellent than others ⊳ adv in a more excellent manner ⊳ npl one's superiors ⊳ vb improve upon
ETTERED > BETTER
ETTERING > BETTER
ETTERS > BETTER
ETTIES > BETTY
ETTING > BET
ETTINGS > BET
ETTONG n short-nosed rat kangaroo
ETTONGS > BETTONG
ETTOR n person who bets
ETTORS > BETTOR
ETTY n type of short crowbar
ETUMBLED adj thrown into disorder
ETWEEN adv indicating position in the middle, alternatives, etc ⊳ prep at a point intermediate to two other points in space, time, etc
ETWEENS > BETWEEN
ETWIXT adv between
EUNCLED adj having many uncles
EURRE n butter
EURRES > BEURRE
EVATRON n proton synchrotron at the University of California
EVATRONS > BEVATRON
EVEL n slanting edge ⊳ vb slope
EVELED > BEVEL
EVELER > BEVEL

BEVELERS > BEVEL
BEVELING > BEVEL
BEVELLED > BEVEL
BEVELLER > BEVEL
BEVELLERS > BEVEL
BEVELLING > BEVEL
BEVELMENT > BEVEL
BEVELS > BEVEL
BEVER n snack
BEVERAGE n drink
BEVERAGES > BEVERAGE
BEVERS > BEVER
BEVIES > BEVY
BEVOMIT vb vomit over
BEVOMITED > BEVOMIT
BEVOMITS > BEVOMIT
BEVOR n armour protecting lower part of face
BEVORS > BEVOR
BEVUE n careless error
BEVUES > BEVUE
BEVVIED > BEVVY
BEVVIES > BEVVY
BEVVY n alcoholic drink ⊳ vb drink alcohol
BEVVYING > BEVVY
BEVY n flock or group
BEWAIL vb express great sorrow over
BEWAILED > BEWAIL
BEWAILER > BEWAIL
BEWAILERS > BEWAIL
BEWAILING > BEWAIL
BEWAILS > BEWAIL
BEWARE vb be on one's guard (against)
BEWARED > BEWARE
BEWARES > BEWARE
BEWARING > BEWARE
BEWEARIED > BEWEARY
BEWEARIES > BEWEARY
BEWEARY vb cause to be weary
BEWEEP vb express grief through weeping
BEWEEPING > BEWEEP
BEWEEPS > BEWEEP
BEWENT > BEGO
BEWEPT > BEWEEP
BEWET vb make wet
BEWETS > BEWET
BEWETTED > BEWET
BEWETTING > BEWET
BEWHORE vb treat as whore
BEWHORED > BEWHORE
BEWHORES > BEWHORE
BEWHORING > BEWHORE
BEWIG vb adorn with wig
BEWIGGED > BEWIG
BEWIGGING > BEWIG
BEWIGS > BEWIG
BEWILDER vb confuse utterly
BEWILDERS > BEWILDER
BEWINGED adj having wings
BEWITCH vb attract and fascinate
BEWITCHED > BEWITCH
BEWITCHER > BEWITCH
BEWITCHES > BEWITCH
BEWORM vb fill with worms
BEWORMED > BEWORM

BEWORMING > BEWORM
BEWORMS > BEWORM
BEWORRIED > BEWORRY
BEWORRIES > BEWORRY
BEWORRY vb beset with worry
BEWRAP vb wrap up
BEWRAPPED > BEWRAP
BEWRAPS > BEWRAP
BEWRAPT > BEWRAP
BEWRAY an obsolete word for > BETRAY
BEWRAYED > BEWRAY
BEWRAYER > BEWRAY
BEWRAYERS > BEWRAY
BEWRAYING > BEWRAY
BEWRAYS > BEWRAY
BEY n (in the Ottoman empire) a title given to senior officers, provincial governors, and certain other officials
BEYLIC n province ruled over by bey
BEYLICS > BEYLIC
BEYLIK same as > BEYLIC
BEYLIKS > BEYLIK
BEYOND prep at or to a point on the other side of ⊳ adv at or to the far side of something ⊳ n unknown, esp life after death
BEYONDS > BEYOND
BEYS > BEY
BEZ n part of deer's horn
BEZANT n medieval Byzantine gold coin
BEZANTS > BEZANT
BEZAZZ another word for > PIZZAZZ
BEZAZZES > BEZAZZ
BEZEL n sloping edge of a cutting tool
BEZELS > BEZEL
BEZES > BEZ
BEZIL archaic word for > ALCOHOLIC
BEZILS > BEZIL
BEZIQUE n card game for two or more players
BEZIQUES > BEZIQUE
BEZOAR n hard mass, such as a stone or hairball, in the stomach and intestines of animals, esp ruminants, and man: formerly thought to be an antidote to poisons
BEZOARDIC adj relating to bezoar
BEZOARS > BEZOAR
BEZONIAN n knave or rascal
BEZONIANS > BEZONIAN
BEZZANT same as > BEZANT
BEZZANTS > BEZZANT
BEZZAZZ > BEZAZZ
BEZZAZZES > BEZAZZ
BEZZLE vb drink to excess
BEZZLED > BEZZLE
BEZZLES > BEZZLE
BEZZLING > BEZZLE
BHAGEE same as > BHAJI

BHAGEES > BHAGEE
BHAI n Indian form of address for a man
BHAIS > BHAI
BHAJAN n singing of devotional songs and hymns
BHAJANS > BHAJAN
BHAJEE same as > BHAJI
BHAJEES > BHAGEE
BHAJI n Indian deep-fried savoury of chopped vegetables in spiced batter
BHAJIA > BHAJI
BHAJIS > BHAJI
BHAKTA n Hindu term for devotee of God
BHAKTAS > BHAKTA
BHAKTI n loving devotion to God leading to nirvana
BHAKTIS > BHAKTI
BHANG n preparation of Indian hemp used as a narcotic and intoxicant
BHANGRA n type of traditional Punjabi folk music combined with elements of Western pop music
BHANGRAS > BHANGRA
BHANGS > BHANG
BHARAL n wild Himalayan sheep with a bluish-grey coat and round backward-curving horns
BHARALS > BHARAL
BHAT n currency of Thailand
BHAVAN n (in India) a large house or building
BHAVANS > BHAVAN
BHAWAN same as > BHAVAN
BHAWANS > BHAWAN
BHEESTIE same as > BHEESTY
BHEESTIES > BHEESTY
BHEESTY same as > BHISHTI
BHEL same as > BAEL
BHELPURI n Indian dish of puffed rice and vegetables
BHELPURIS > BHELPURI
BHELS > BHEL
BHIKHU n fully ordained Buddhist monk
BHIKHUS > BHIKHU
BHIKKHUNI n fully ordained Buddhist nun
BHINDI same as > BINDHI
BHINDIS > BHINDI
BHISHTI n (formerly in India) a water-carrier
BHISHTIS > BHISHTI
BHISTEE same as > BHISHTI
BHISTEES > BHISTEE
BHISTI same as > BHISHTI
BHISTIE same as > BHISHTI
BHISTIES > BHISTIE
BHISTIS > BHISHTI
BHOONA same as > BHUNA
BHOONAS > BHOONA
BHOOT same as > BHUT

b

BHOOTS > BHOOT
BHUNA *n* Indian sauce
BHUNAS > BHUNA
BHUT *n* Hindu term for type of ghost
BHUTS > BHUT
BI *short for* > BISEXUAL
BIACETYL *adj* liquid with strong odour
BIACETYLS > BIACETYL
BIACH *n* slang term for a subordinate or inferior person
BIACHES > BIACH
BIALI *same as* > BIALY
BIALIES > BIALY
BIALIS > BIALI
BIALY *n* type of bagel
BIALYS > BIALY
BIANNUAL *adj* occurring twice a year ▷ *n* something that happens biannually
BIANNUALS > BIANNUAL
BIAS *n* mental tendency, esp prejudice ▷ *vb* cause to have a bias ▷ *adj* slanting obliquely ▷ *adv* obliquely
BIASED > BIAS
BIASEDLY > BIAS
BIASES > BIAS
BIASING > BIAS
BIASINGS > BIAS
BIASNESS > BIAS
BIASSED > BIAS
BIASSEDLY > BIAS
BIASSES > BIAS
BIASSING > BIAS
BIATCH *same as* > BIACH
BIATCHES > BIATCH
BIATHLETE *n* athlete taking part in biathlon
BIATHLON *n* contest in which skiers with rifles shoot at four targets along a 20-kilometre (12.5-mile) cross-country course
BIATHLONS > BIATHLON
BIAXAL *same as* > BIAXIAL
BIAXIAL *adj* (esp of a crystal) having two axes
BIAXIALLY > BIAXIAL
BIB *same as* > BIBCOCK
BIBACIOUS *adj* tending to drink to excess
BIBASIC *adj* with two bases
BIBATION *n* drinking to excess
BIBATIONS > BIBATION
BIBB *n* wooden support on a mast for the trestletrees
BIBBED > BIB
BIBBER *n* drinker
BIBBERIES > BIBBERY
BIBBERS > BIBBER
BIBBERY *n* drinking to excess
BIBBING > BIB
BIBBLE *n* pebble
BIBBLES > BIBBLE
BIBBS > BIBB
BIBCOCK *n* tap with a nozzle bent downwards

BIBCOCKS > BIBCOCK
BIBELOT *n* attractive or curious trinket
BIBELOTS > BIBELOT
BIBFUL *as in* spill a bibful to divulge secrets
BIBFULS > BIBFUL
BIBLE *n* any book containing the sacred writings of a religion
BIBLES > BIBLE
BIBLESS > BIB
BIBLICAL *adj* of, occurring in, or referring to the Bible
BIBLICISM *n* bible-learning
BIBLICIST > BIBLICISM
BIBLIKE > BIB
BIBLIOTIC *n* study of books
BIBLIST *same as* > BIBLICIST
BIBLISTS > BIBLIST
BIBS > BIB
BIBULOUS *adj* addicted to alcohol
BICAMERAL *adj* (of a legislature) consisting of two chambers
BICARB *n* bicarbonate of soda
BICARBS > BICARB
BICAUDAL *adj* having two tails
BICCIES > BICCY
BICCY *n* biscuit
BICE *n* medium blue colour
BICENTRIC *adj* having two centres
BICEP *same as* > BICEPS
BICEPS *n* muscle with two origins, esp the muscle that flexes the forearm
BICEPSES > BICEPS
BICES > BICE
BICHIR *n* African freshwater fish with an elongated body
BICHIRS > BICHIR
BICHORD *adj* having two strings for each note
BICHROME *adj* having two colours
BICIPITAL *adj* having two heads
BICKER *vb* argue over petty matters ▷ *n* petty squabble
BICKERED > BICKER
BICKERER > BICKER
BICKERERS > BICKER
BICKERING > BICKER
BICKERS > BICKER
BICKIE *short for* > BISCUIT
BICKIES > BICKIE
BICOASTAL *adj* relating to both the east and west coasts of the US
BICOLOR *same as* > BICOLOUR
BICOLORED *same as* > BICOLOUR

BICOLORS > BICOLOR
BICOLOUR *adj* two-coloured
BICOLOURS > BICOLOUR
BICONCAVE *adj* (of a lens) having concave faces on both sides
BICONVEX *adj* (of a lens) having convex faces on both sides
BICORN *adj* having two horns or hornlike parts
BICORNATE *same as* > BICORN
BICORNE *same as* > BICORN
BICORNES > BICORNE
BICORNS > BICORN
BICRON *n* billionth part of a metre
BICRONS > BICRON
BICUSPID *adj* having two points ▷ *n* bicuspid tooth
BICUSPIDS > BICUSPID
BICYCLE *n* vehicle with two wheels, one behind the other, pedalled by the rider ▷ *vb* ride a bicycle
BICYCLED > BICYCLE
BICYCLER > BICYCLE
BICYCLERS > BICYCLE
BICYCLES > BICYCLE
BICYCLIC *adj* of, forming, or formed by two circles, cycles, etc
BICYCLING > BICYCLE
BICYCLIST > BICYCLE
BID *vb* offer (an amount) in attempting to buy something, esp in competition with others as at an auction ▷ *n* offer of a specified amount, as at an auction
BIDARKA *n* canoe covered in animal skins, esp sealskin, used by the Inuit of Alaska
BIDARKAS > BIDARKA
BIDARKEE *same as* > BIDARKA
BIDARKEES > BIDARKEE
BIDDABLE *adj* obedient
BIDDABLY > BIDDABLE
BIDDEN > BID
BIDDER > BID
BIDDERS > BID
BIDDIES > BIDDY
BIDDING > BID
BIDDINGS > BID
BIDDY *n* woman, esp an old gossipy one
BIDE *vb* stay or continue
BIDED > BIDE
BIDENT *n* instrument with two prongs
BIDENTAL *n* sacred place where lightning has struck
BIDENTALS > BIDENTAL
BIDENTATE > BIDENT
BIDENTS > BIDENT
BIDER > BIDE
BIDERS > BIDE
BIDES > BIDE

BIDET *n* low basin for washing the genital area
BIDETS > BIDET
BIDI *same as* > BEEDI
BIDING > BIDE
BIDINGS > BIDE
BIDIS > BIDI
BIDON *n* oil drum
BIDONS > BIDON
BIDS > BID
BIELD *n* shelter ▷ *vb* shelter or take shelter
BIELDED > BIELD
BIELDIER > BIELDY
BIELDIEST > BIELDY
BIELDING > BIELD
BIELDS > BIELD
BIELDY *adj* sheltered
BIEN *adv* well
BIENNALE *n* event occurring every two years
BIENNALES > BIENNALE
BIENNIA > BIENNIUM
BIENNIAL *adj* occurring every two years ▷ *n* plant that completes its life cycle in two years
BIENNIALS > BIENNIAL
BIENNIUM *n* period of two years
BIENNIUMS > BIENNIUM
BIER *n* stand on which a corpse or coffin rests before burial
BIERS > BIER
BIESTINGS *same as* > BEESTINGS
BIFACE *n* prehistoric stone tool
BIFACES > BIFACE
BIFACIAL *adj* having two faces or surfaces
BIFARIOUS *adj* having parts arranged in two rows on either side of a central axis
BIFF *n* blow with the fist ▷ *vb* give (someone) such a blow
BIFFED > BIFF
BIFFER *n* someone, such as a sportsperson, who has a reputation for hitting hard
BIFFERS > BIFFER
BIFFIES > BIFFY
BIFFIN *n* variety of red cooking apple
BIFFING > BIFF
BIFFINS > BIFFIN
BIFFO *n* fighting or aggressive behaviour ▷ *adj* aggressive
BIFFOS > BIFFO
BIFFS > BIFF
BIFFY *n* outdoor toilet
BIFID *adj* divided into two by a cleft in the middle
BIFIDITY > BIFID
BIFIDLY > BIFID
BIFILAR *adj* having two parallel threads, as in the suspension of certain measuring instruments

BIFILARLY > BIFILAR

BIFLEX *adj* bent or flexed in two places

BIFOCAL *adj* having two different focuses

BIFOCALED *adj* wearing bifocals

BIFOCALS *npl* spectacles with lenses permitting near and distant vision

BIFOLD *adj* that can be folded in two places

BIFOLIATE *adj* having only two leaves

BIFORATE *adj* having two openings, pores, or perforations

BIFORKED *adj* two-pronged

BIFORM *adj* having or combining the characteristics of two forms, as a centaur

BIFORMED *same as* **>** BIFORM

BIFTAH *same as* **>** BIFTER

BIFTAHS > BIFTAH

BIFTER *n* cannabis cigarette

BIFTERS > BIFTER

BIFURCATE *vb* fork into two branches **▷** *adj* forked into two branches

BIG *adj* of considerable size, height, number, or capacity **▷** *adv* on a grand scale **▷** *vb* build

BIGA *n* chariot drawn by two horses

BIGAE > BIGA

BIGAMIES > BIGAMY

BIGAMIST > BIGAMY

BIGAMISTS > BIGAMY

BIGAMOUS > BIGAMY

BIGAMY *n* crime of marrying a person while still legally married to someone else

BIGARADE *n* Seville orange

BIGARADES > BIGARADE

BIGAROON *same as* **>** BIGARREAU

BIGAROONS > BIGAROON

BIGARREAU *n* any of several heart-shaped varieties of sweet cherry that have firm flesh

BIGEMINAL *adj* double; twinned

BIGEMINY *n* heart complaint

BIGENER *n* hybrid between individuals of different genera

BIGENERIC *adj* (of a hybrid plant) derived from parents of two different genera

BIGENERS > BIGENER

BIGEYE *n* type of tropical or subtropical red marine fish with very large eyes and rough scales

BIGEYES > BIGEYE

BIGFEET > BIGFOOT

BIGFOOT *n* yeti **▷** *vb* throw one's weight around

BIGFOOTED > BIGFOOT

BIGFOOTS > BIGFOOT

BIGG *n* type of barley

BIGGED > BIG

BIGGER > BIG

BIGGEST > BIG

BIGGETY *same as* **>** BIGGITY

BIGGIE *n* something big or important

BIGGIES > BIGGIE

BIGGIN *n* plain close-fitting cap, often tying under the chin, worn in the Middle Ages and by children in the 17th century

BIGGING > BIG

BIGGINGS > BIG

BIGGINS > BIGGIN

BIGGISH > BIG

BIGGITY *adj* conceited

BIGGON *same as* **>** BIGGIN

BIGGONS > BIGGON

BIGGS > BIGG

BIGGY *same as* **>** BIGGIE

BIGHA *n* in India, unit for measuring land

BIGHAS > BIGHA

BIGHEAD *n* conceited person

BIGHEADED > BIGHEAD

BIGHEADS > BIGHEAD

BIGHORN *n* large wild mountain sheep of N America and NE Asia, the male of which has massive curved horns

BIGHORNS > BIGHORN

BIGHT *n* long curved shoreline **▷** *vb* fasten or bind with a bight

BIGHTED > BIGHT

BIGHTING > BIGHT

BIGHTS > BIGHT

BIGLY > BIG

BIGMOUTH *n* noisy, indiscreet, or boastful person

BIGMOUTHS > BIGMOUTH

BIGNESS > BIG

BIGNESSES > BIG

BIGNONIA *n* tropical American climbing shrub, cultivated for its trumpet-shaped yellow or reddish flowers

BIGNONIAS > BIGNONIA

BIGOS *n* Polish stew

BIGOSES > BIGOS

BIGOT *n* person who is intolerant, esp regarding religion or race

BIGOTED > BIGOT

BIGOTEDLY > BIGOT

BIGOTRIES > BIGOTRY

BIGOTRY *n* attitudes, behaviour, or way of thinking of a bigot

BIGOTS > BIGOT

BIGS > BIG

BIGSTICK *adj* of or relating to irresistible military strength

BIGTIME *adj* important

BIGUANIDE *n* any of a class of compounds some of which are used in the treatment of certain forms of diabetes

BIGWIG *n* important person

BIGWIGS > BIGWIG

BIHOURLY *adj* occurring every two hours

BIJECTION *n* mathematical function or mapping that is both an injection and a surjection and therefore has an inverse

BIJECTIVE *adj* (of a function, relation, etc) associating two sets in such a way that every member of each set is uniquely paired with a member of the other

BIJOU *adj* (of a house) small but elegant **▷** *n* something small and delicately worked

BIJOUS > BIJOU

BIJOUX > BIJOU

BIJUGATE *adj* (of compound leaves) having two pairs of leaflets

BIJUGOUS *same as* **>** BIJUGATE

BIJWONER *same as* **>** BYWONER

BIJWONERS > BIJWONER

BIKE *same as* **>** BICYCLE

BIKED > BIKE

BIKER *n* person who rides a motorcycle

BIKERS > BIKER

BIKES > BIKE

BIKEWAY *n* cycle lane

BIKEWAYS > BIKEWAY

BIKIE *n* member of a motorcycle gang

BIKIES > BIKIE

BIKING > BIKE

BIKINGS > BIKE

BIKINI *n* woman's brief two-piece swimming costume

BIKINIED > BIKINI

BIKINIS > BIKINI

BIKKIE *slang word for* **>** BISCUIT

BIKKIES > BIKKIE

BILABIAL *adj* of, relating to, or denoting a speech sound articulated using both lips **▷** *n* bilabial speech sound

BILABIALS > BILABIAL

BILABIATE *adj* divided into two lips

BILANDER *n* small two-masted cargo ship

BILANDERS > BILANDER

BILATERAL *adj* affecting or undertaken by two parties

BILAYER *n* part of cell membrane

BILAYERS > BILAYER

BILBERRY *n* bluish-black edible berry

BILBIES > BILBY

BILBO *n* (formerly) a sword with a marked temper and elasticity

BILBOA *same as* **>** BILBO

BILBOAS > BILBOA

BILBOES > BILBO

BILBOS > BILBO

BILBY *n* Australian marsupial with long pointed ears and grey fur

BILE *n* bitter yellow fluid secreted by the liver **▷** *vb* boil

BILECTION *same as* **>** BOLECTION

BILED > BILE

BILES > BILE

BILESTONE *another name for* **>** GALLSTONE

BILEVEL *n* hairstyle with two different lengths

BILEVELS > BILEVEL

BILGE *n* nonsense **▷** *vb* (of a vessel) to take in water at the bilge

BILGED > BILGE

BILGES > BILGE

BILGIER > BILGE

BILGIEST > BILGE

BILGING > BILGE

BILGY > BILGE

BILHARZIA *n* disease caused by infestation of the body with blood flukes

BILIAN *n* type of tree used for its wood

BILIANS > BILIAN

BILIARIES > BILIARY

BILIARY *adj* of bile, the ducts that convey bile, or the gall bladder **▷** *n* disease found in dogs

BILIMBI *n* type of fruit-bearing tree

BILIMBING *same as* **>** BILIMBI

BILIMBIS > BILIMBI

BILINEAR *adj* of or referring to two lines

BILING > BILE

BILINGUAL *adj* involving or using two languages **▷** *n* bilingual person

BILIOUS *adj* sick, nauseous

BILIOUSLY > BILIOUS

BILIRUBIN *n* orange-yellow pigment in the bile

BILITERAL *adj* relating to two letters

BILK *vb* cheat, esp by not paying **▷** *n* swindle or cheat

BILKED > BILK

BILKER > BILK

BILKERS > BILK

BILKING > BILK

BILKS > BILK

BILL *n* money owed for goods or services supplied

▷ *vb* to send or present an account for payment to (a person)

BILLABLE *adj* that can be charged to a client

BILLABONG *n* stagnant pool in an intermittent stream

BILLBOARD *n* large outdoor board for displaying advertisements

BILLBOOK *n* business record of bills received, paid, etc

BILLBOOKS > BILLBOOK

BILLBUG *n* type of weevil

BILLBUGS > BILLBUG

BILLED > BILL

BILLER *n* stem of a plant

BILLERS > BILLER

BILLET *vb* assign a lodging to (a soldier) ▷ *n* accommodation for a soldier in civil lodgings

BILLETED > BILLET

BILLETEE > BILLET

BILLETEES > BILLET

BILLETER > BILLET

BILLETERS > BILLET

BILLETING > BILLET

BILLETS > BILLET

BILLFISH *n* type of fish with elongated jaws, such as the spearfish and marlin

BILLFOLD *n* small folding case, usually of leather, for holding paper money, documents, etc

BILLFOLDS > BILLFOLD

BILLHEAD *n* printed form for making out bills

BILLHEADS > BILLHEAD

BILLHOOK *n* tool with a hooked blade, used for chopping etc

BILLHOOKS > BILLHOOK

BILLIARD *n* (modifier) of or relating to billiards

BILLIARDS *n* game played on a table with balls and a cue

BILLIE *same as >* BILLY

BILLIES > BILLY

BILLING *n* relative importance of a performer or act as reflected in the prominence given in programmes, advertisements, etc

BILLINGS > BILLING

BILLION *n* one thousand million ▷ *det* amounting to a billion

BILLIONS > BILLION

BILLIONTH > BILLION

BILLMAN *n* person who uses a billhook

BILLMEN > BILLMAN

BILLON *n* alloy consisting of gold or silver and a base metal, usually copper, used esp for coinage

BILLONS > BILLON

BILLOW *n* large sea wave ▷ *vb* rise up or swell out

BILLOWED > BILLOW

BILLOWIER > BILLOWY

BILLOWING > BILLOW

BILLOWS > BILLOW

BILLOWY *adj* full of or forming billows

BILLS > BILL

BILLY *n* metal can or pot for cooking on a camp fire

BILLYBOY *n* type of river barge

BILLYBOYS > BILLYBOY

BILLYCAN *same as >* BILLY

BILLYCANS > BILLYCAN

BILLYCOCK *n* any of several round-crowned brimmed hats of felt, such as the bowler

BILLYO as in *like billyo* phrase used to emphasize or intensify something

BILLYOH *same as >* BILLYO

BILLYOHS > BILLYOH

BILLYOS > BILLYO

BILOBAR *same as >* BILOBATE

BILOBATE *adj* divided into or having two lobes

BILOBATED *same as >* BILOBATE

BILOBED *same as >* BILOBATE

BILOBULAR *adj* having two lobules

BILOCULAR *adj* divided into two chambers or cavities

BILSTED *n* American gum tree

BILSTEDS > BILSTED

BILTONG *n* strips of dried meat

BILTONGS > BILTONG

BIMA *same as >* BEMA

BIMAH *same as >* BEMA

BIMAHS > BIMAH

BIMANAL *same as >* BIMANOUS

BIMANOUS *adj* (of man and the higher primates) having two hands distinct in form and function from the feet

BIMANUAL *adj* using or requiring both hands

BIMAS > BIMA

BIMBASHI *n* Turkish military official

BIMBASHIS > BIMBASHI

BIMBETTE *n* particularly unintelligent bimbo

BIMBETTES > BIMBETTE

BIMBLE as in *bimble box* type of dense Australian tree

BIMBO *n* attractive but empty-headed young person, esp a woman

BIMBOES > BIMBO

BIMBOS > BIMBO

BIMENSAL *adj* occurring every two months

BIMESTER *n* period of two months

BIMESTERS > BIMESTER

BIMETAL *n* material made from two sheets of metal

BIMETALS > BIMETAL

BIMETHYL *another word for >* ETHANE

BIMETHYLS > BIMETHYL

BIMODAL *adj* having two modes

BIMONTHLY *adj* every two months ▷ *adv* every two months ▷ *n* periodical published every two months

BIMORPH *n* assembly of two piezoelectric crystals cemented together so that an applied voltage causes one to expand and the other to contract, converting electrical signals into mechanical energy. Conversely, bending can generate a voltage: used in loudspeakers, gramophone pick-ups, etc

BIMORPHS > BIMORPH

BIN *n* container for rubbish or for storing grain, coal, etc ▷ *vb* put in a rubbish bin

BINAL *adj* twofold

BINARIES > BINARY

BINARISM *n* state of being binary

BINARISMS > BINARISM

BINARY *adj* composed of, relating to, or involving two ▷ *n* something composed of two parts or things

BINATE *adj* occurring in two parts or in pairs

BINATELY > BINATE

BINAURAL *adj* relating to, having, or hearing with both ears

BIND *vb* make secure with or as if with a rope ▷ *n* annoying situation

BINDABLE > BIND

BINDER *n* firm cover for holding loose sheets of paper together

BINDERIES > BINDERY

BINDERS > BINDER

BINDERY *n* bookbindery

BINDHI *same as >* BINDI

BINDHIS > BINDHI

BINDI *n* decorative dot worn in the middle of the forehead, esp by Hindu women

BINDING > BIND

BINDINGLY > BIND

BINDINGS > BIND

BINDIS > BINDI

BINDLE *n* small packet

BINDLES > BINDLE

BINDS > BIND

BINDWEED *n* plant that twines around a support

BINDWEEDS > BINDWEED

BINE *n* climbing or twining stem of any of various plants, such as the woodbine or bindweed

BINER *n* clip used by climbers

BINERS > BINER

BINERVATE *adj* having two nerves

BINES > BINE

BING *n* heap or pile, esp of spoil from a mine

BINGE *n* bout of excessive indulgence, esp in drink ▷ *vb* indulge in a binge (esp of eating or drinking)

BINGED > BINGE

BINGEING > BINGE

BINGER *n* person who is addicted to crack cocaine

BINGERS > BINGER

BINGES > BINGE

BINGHI *n* Australian derogatory slang for an Aboriginal person

BINGHIS > BINGHI

BINGIES > BINGY

BINGING > BINGE

BINGLE *n* minor crash or upset, as in a car or on a surfboard ▷ *vb* layer (hair)

BINGLED > BINGLE

BINGLES > BINGLE

BINGLING > BINGLE

BINGO *n* gambling game in which numbers are called out and covered by the players on their individual cards ▷ *sentence substitute* cry by the winner of a game of bingo

BINGOES > BINGO

BINGOS > BINGO

BINGS > BING

BINGY *Australian slang for >* STOMACH

BINIOU *n* small high-pitched Breton bagpipe

BINIOUS > BINIOU

BINIT *n* (computing) early form of bit

BINITS > BINIT

BINK *n* ledge

BINKS > BINK

BINMAN *another name for >* DUSTMAN

BINMEN > BINMAN

BINNACLE *n* box holding a ship's compass

BINNACLES > BINNACLE

BINNED > BIN

BINNING > BIN

BINOCLE *n* binocular-style telescope

BINOCLES > BINOCLE

BINOCS > BINOCULAR

BINOCULAR *adj* involving both eyes

BINOMIAL *adj* consisting of two terms ▷ *n* mathematical expression consisting of two terms, such as $3x + 2y$

BINOMIALS > BINOMIAL

BINOMINAL *adj* of or denoting the binomial

omenclature ▷ n wo-part taxonomic name

NOVULAR adj relating to derived from two different ova

NS > BIN

NT n derogatory term for girl

NTS > BINT

NTURONG n arboreal SE sian mammal with long haggy black hair

NUCLEAR adj having wo nuclei

O short for > BIOGRAPHY

OACTIVE adj able to teract with living system

OASSAY n method of etermining the oncentration, activity, or ffect of a change to ubstance by testing its ffect on a living organism nd comparing this with he activity of an agreed tandard ▷ vb subject to a ioassay

OASSAYS > BIOASSAY

OBANK n large store of uman samples for medical esearch

OBANKS > BIOBANK

OBLAST same as BIOPLAST

OBLASTS > BIOBLAST

OCENOSE adj living ogether in mutual ependence

OCHEMIC adj of or elating to chemical ompounds, reactions, etc, ccurring in living rganisms

OCHIP n small glass or licon plate containing an rray of biochemical nolecules or structures, sed as a biosensor or in ene sequencing

OCHIPS > BIOCHIP

OCIDAL > BIOCIDE

OCIDE n substance used o destroy living things

OCIDES > BIOCIDE

OCLEAN adj free from armful bacteria

OCYCLE n cycling of hemicals through the iosphere

OCYCLES > BIOCYCLE

ODATA n information egarding an individual's ducation and work istory, esp in the context f a selection process

ODIESEL n biofuel ntended for use in diesel ngines

ODOT n temperature-ensitive device stuck to he skin in order to monitor tress

ODOTS > BIODOT

OENERGY n energy erived from organic natter

BIOETHIC > BIOETHICS

BIOETHICS n study of ethical problems arising from biological research and its applications in such fields as organ transplantation, genetic engineering, or artificial insemination

BIOFACT n item of biological information

BIOFACTS > BIOFACT

BIOFILM n thin layer of living organisms

BIOFILMS > BIOFILM

BIOFOULER n animal that obstructs or pollutes the environment

BIOFUEL n gaseous, liquid, or solid substance of biological origin that is used as a fuel ▷ vb fuel (a vehicle, etc) using biofuel

BIOFUELED adj running on biofuel

BIOFUELS > BIOFUEL

BIOG short form of > BIOGRAPHY

BIOGAS n gaseous fuel produced by the fermentation of organic waste

BIOGASES > BIOGAS

BIOGASSES > BIOGAS

BIOGEN n hypothetical protein assumed to be the basis of the formation and functioning of body cells and tissues

BIOGENIC adj originating from a living organism

BIOGENIES > BIOGENY

BIOGENOUS > BIOGENY

BIOGENS > BIOGEN

BIOGENY n principle that a living organism must originate from a parent form similar to itself

BIOGRAPH vb write biography of

BIOGRAPHS > BIOGRAPH

BIOGRAPHY n account of a person's life by another person

BIOGS > BIOG

BIOHAZARD n material of biological origin that is hazardous to humans

BIOHERM n mound of material laid down by sedentary marine organisms, esp a coral reef

BIOHERMS > BIOHERM

BIOLOGIC adj of or relating to biology ▷ n drug, such as a vaccine, that is derived from a living organism

BIOLOGICS > BIOLOGIC

BIOLOGIES > BIOLOGY

BIOLOGISM n explaining human behaviour through biology

BIOLOGIST > BIOLOGY

BIOLOGY n study of living

organisms

BIOLYSES > BIOLYSIS

BIOLYSIS n death and dissolution of a living organism

BIOLYTIC > BIOLYSIS

BIOMARKER n substance, physiological characteristic, gene, etc that indicates, or may indicate, the presence of disease, a physiological abnormality, or a psychological condition

BIOMASS n total number of living organisms in a given area

BIOMASSES > BIOMASS

BIOME n major ecological community, extending over a large area and usually characterized by a dominant vegetation

BIOMES > BIOME

BIOMETER n device for measuring natural radiation

BIOMETERS > BIOMETER

BIOMETRIC adj of any automated system using physiological or behavioural traits as a means of identification.

BIOMETRY n analysis of biological data using mathematical and statistical methods, especially for purposes of identification

BIOMINING n using plants, etc to collect precious metals for extraction

BIOMORPH n form or pattern resembling living thing

BIOMORPHS > BIOMORPH

BIONIC adj having a part of the body that is operated electronically

BIONICS n study of biological functions in order to develop electronic equipment that operates similarly

BIONOMIC > BIONOMICS

BIONOMICS a less common name for > ECOLOGY

BIONOMIES > BIONOMY

BIONOMIST > BIONOMICS

BIONOMY n laws of life

BIONT n living thing

BIONTIC > BIONT

BIONTS > BIONT

BIOPARENT n biological parent

BIOPHILIA n innate love for the natural world, supposed to be felt universally by humankind

BIOPHOR n hypothetical material particle

BIOPHORE same as > BIOPHOR

BIOPHORES > BIOPHORE

BIOPHORS > BIOPHOR

BIOPIC n film based on the life of a famous person

BIOPICS > BIOPIC

BIOPIRACY n use of wild plants by international companies to develop medicines, without recompensing the countries from which they are taken

BIOPIRATE > BIOPIRACY

BIOPLASM n living matter

BIOPLASMS > BIOPLASM

BIOPLAST n very small unit of bioplasm

BIOPLASTS > BIOPLAST

BIOPSIC > BIOPSY

BIOPSIED > BIOPSY

BIOPSIES > BIOPSY

BIOPSY n examination of tissue from a living body ▷ vb perform a biopsy on

BIOPSYING > BIOPSY

BIOPTIC > BIOPSY

BIOREGION n area in which climate and environment are consistent

BIORHYTHM n complex recurring pattern of physiological states, believed to affect physical, emotional, and mental states

BIOS > BIO

BIOSAFETY n precautions taken to control the cultivation and distribution of genetically modified crops and products

BIOSCOPE n kind of early film projector

BIOSCOPES > BIOSCOPE

BIOSCOPY n examination of a body to determine whether it is alive

BIOSENSOR n device used to monitor living systems

BIOSOCIAL adj relating to the interaction of biological and social elements

BIOSOLID n residue from treated sewage

BIOSOLIDS > BIOSOLID

BIOSPHERE n part of the earth's surface and atmosphere inhabited by living things

BIOSTABLE adj resistant to the effects of microorganisms

BIOSTATIC adj of or relating to the branch of biology that deals with the structure of organisms in relation to their function

BIOSTROME n rock layer consisting of a deposit of organic material, such as fossils

BIOTA n plant and animal life of a particular region or period

BIOTAS > BIOTA

BIOTECH n biotechnology
BIOTECHS > BIOTECH
BIOTERROR n use of biological weapons by terrorists
BIOTIC adj of or relating to living organisms ▷ n living organism
BIOTICAL same as > BIOTIC
BIOTICS > BIOTIC
BIOTIN n vitamin of the B complex, abundant in egg yolk and liver
BIOTINS > BIOTIN
BIOTITE n black or dark green mineral of the mica group
BIOTITES > BIOTITE
BIOTTTIC > BIOTITE
BIOTOPE n small area, such as the bark of a tree, that supports its own distinctive community
BIOTOPES > BIOTOPE
BIOTOXIN n toxic substance produced by a living organism
BIOTOXINS > BIOTOXIN
BIOTRON n climate-control chamber
BIOTRONS > BIOTRON
BIOTROPH n parasitic organism, esp a fungus
BIOTROPHS > BIOTROPH
BIOTURBED adj stirred by organisms
BIOTYPE n group of genetically identical plants within a species, produced by apomixis
BIOTYPES > BIOTYPE
BIOTYPIC > BIOTYPE
BIOVULAR adj (of twins) from two separate eggs
BIOWEAPON n living organism or a toxic product manufactured from it, used to kill or incapacitate
BIPACK n obsolete filming process
BIPACKS > BIPACK
BIPAROUS adj producing offspring in pairs
BIPARTED adj divided into two parts
BIPARTITE adj consisting of two parts
BIPARTY adj involving two parties
BIPED n animal with two feet ▷ adj having two feet
BIPEDAL adj having two feet
BIPEDALLY > BIPEDAL
BIPEDS > BIPED
BIPHASIC adj having two phases
BIPHENYL n white or colourless crystalline solid used as a heat-transfer agent
BIPHENYLS > BIPHENYL
BIPINNATE adj (of pinnate leaves) having the

leaflets themselves divided into smaller leaflets
BIPLANE n aeroplane with two sets of wings, one above the other
BIPLANES > BIPLANE
BIPOD n two-legged support or stand
BIPODS > BIPOD
BIPOLAR adj having two poles
BIPRISM n prism having a highly obtuse angle to facilitate beam splitting
BIPRISMS > BIPRISM
BIPYRAMID n geometrical form consisting of two pyramids with a common polygonal base
BIRACIAL adj for, representing, or including members of two races, esp White and Black
BIRADIAL adj showing both bilateral and radial symmetry, as certain sea anemones
BIRADICAL n molecule with two centres
BIRAMOSE same as > BIRAMOUS
BIRAMOUS adj divided into two parts, as the appendages of crustaceans
BIRCH n tree with thin peeling bark ▷ vb flog with a birch
BIRCHBARK as in birchbark biting Native Canadian craft in which designs are bitten onto bark from birch trees
BIRCHED > BIRCH
BIRCHEN > BIRCH
BIRCHES > BIRCH
BIRCHING > BIRCH
BIRCHIR same as > BICHIR
BIRCHIRS > BIRCHIR
BIRD n creature with feathers and wings, most types of which can fly ▷ vb hunt for birds
BIRDBATH n small basin or trough for birds to bathe in, usually in a garden
BIRDBATHS > BIRDBATH
BIRDBRAIN n stupid person
BIRDCAGE n wire or wicker cage in which captive birds are kept
BIRDCAGES > BIRDCAGE
BIRDCALL n characteristic call or song of a bird
BIRDCALLS > BIRDCALL
BIRDDOG n dog used or trained to retrieve game birds
BIRDDOGS > BIRDDOG
BIRDED > BIRD
BIRDER n birdwatcher
BIRDERS > BIRDER
BIRDFARM n place where birds are kept
BIRDFARMS > BIRDFARM

BIRDFEED n food for birds
BIRDFEEDS > BIRDFEED
BIRDHOUSE n small shelter or box for birds to nest in
BIRDIE n score of one stroke under par for a hole ▷ vb play (a hole) in one stroke under par
BIRDIED > BIRDIE
BIRDIEING > BIRDIE
BIRDIES > BIRDIE
BIRDING > BIRD
BIRDINGS > BIRD
BIRDLIFE n birds collectively
BIRDLIKE > BIRD
BIRDLIME n sticky substance smeared on twigs to catch small birds ▷ vb smear (twigs) with birdlime to catch (small birds)
BIRDLIMED > BIRDLIME
BIRDLIMES > BIRDLIME
BIRDMAN n man concerned with birds, such as a fowler or ornithologist
BIRDMEN > BIRDMAN
BIRDS > BIRD
BIRDSEED n mixture of various kinds of seeds for feeding cage birds
BIRDSEEDS > BIRDSEED
BIRDSEYE n type of primrose
BIRDSEYES > BIRDSEYE
BIRDSFOOT n type of plant with pods shaped like a bird's foot
BIRDSHOT n small pellets designed for shooting birds
BIRDSHOTS > BIRDSHOT
BIRDSONG n musical call of a bird or birds
BIRDSONGS > BIRDSONG
BIRDWATCH vb watch birds
BIRDWING n type of butterfly
BIRDWINGS > BIRDWING
BIREME n ancient galley having two banks of oars
BIREMES > BIREME
BIRETTA n stiff square cap worn by the Catholic clergy
BIRETTAS > BIRETTA
BIRIANI same as > BIRYANI
BIRIANIS > BIRIANI
BIRIYANI same as > BIRIANI
BIRIYANIS > BIRIYANI
BIRK n birch tree ▷ adj consisting or made of birch
BIRKEN adj relating to the birch tree
BIRKIE n spirited or lively person ▷ adj lively
BIRKIER > BIRKIE
BIRKIES > BIRKIE
BIRKIEST > BIRKIE
BIRKS > BIRK
BIRL same as > BURL
BIRLE same as > BURL

BIRLED > BIRL
BIRLER > BIRL
BIRLERS > BIRL
BIRLES > BIRLE
BIRLIEMAN n judge dealing with local law
BIRLIEMEN > BIRLIEMAN
BIRLING > BIRL
BIRLINGS > BIRL
BIRLINN n small Scottish book
BIRLINNS > BIRLINN
BIRLS > BIRL
BIRO n tradename of a kind of ballpoint pen
BIROS > BIRO
BIRR vb make or cause to make a whirring sound ▷ whirring sound
BIRRED > BIRR
BIRRETTA same as > BIRETTA
BIRRETTAS > BIRRETTA
BIRRING > BIRR
BIRROTCH n Ethiopian monetary unit
BIRRS > BIRR
BIRSE n bristle
BIRSES > BIRSE
BIRSIER > BIRSY
BIRSIEST > BIRSY
BIRSLE vb roast
BIRSLED > BIRSLE
BIRSLES > BIRSLE
BIRSLING > BIRSLE
BIRSY adj bristly
BIRTH n process of bearing young ▷ vb give birth to
BIRTHDAY n anniversary of the day of one's birth
BIRTHDAYS > BIRTHDAY
BIRTHDOM n birthright
BIRTHDOMS > BIRTHDOM
BIRTHED > BIRTH
BIRTHING > BIRTH
BIRTHINGS > BIRTH
BIRTHMARK n blemish on the skin formed before birth
BIRTHNAME n name person was born with
BIRTHRATE n ratio of live births in a specified area group, etc, to the population of that area, etc, usually expressed per 1000 population per year
BIRTHROOT n N American plant whose roots were formerly used by the American Indians as an aid in childbirth
BIRTHS > BIRTH
BIRTHWORT n type of climbing plant once believed to ease childbirth
BIRYANI n any of a variety of Indian dishes made with rice, highly flavoured and coloured with saffron or turmeric, mixed with meat or fish
BIRYANIS > BIRYANI
BIS adv twice ▷ sentence substitute encore! again!

ISCACHA *same as* > VISCACHA

ISCACHAS > BISCACHA

ISCOTTI > BISCOTTO

ISCOTTO *n* small Italian biscuit

ISCUIT *n* small flat dry sweet or plain cake ▷ *adj* pale brown

ISCUITS > BISCUIT

ISCUITY *adj* reminiscent of biscuit

ISE *n* cold dry northerly wind in Switzerland and the neighbouring parts of France and Italy, usually in the spring

ISECT *vb* divide into two equal parts

ISECTED > BISECT

ISECTING > BISECT

ISECTION > BISECT

ISECTOR *n* straight line or plane that bisects an angle

ISECTORS > BISECTOR

ISECTRIX *n* bisector of the angle between the optic axes of a crystal

ISECTS > BISECT

ISERIAL *adj* in two rows

ISERIATE *adj* (of plant parts, such as petals) arranged in two whorls, cycles, rows, or series

ISERRATE *adj* (of leaf margins, etc) having serrations that are themselves serrate

ISES > BISE

ISEXUAL *adj* sexually attracted to both men and women ▷ *n* bisexual person

ISEXUALS > BISEXUAL

ISH *n* mistake

ISHES > BISH

ISHOP *n* clergyman who governs a diocese ▷ *vb* make a bishop

ISHOPDOM *n* jurisdiction of bishop

ISHOPED > BISHOP

ISHOPESS > BISHOP

ISHOPING > BISHOP

ISHOPRIC *n* diocese or office of a bishop

ISHOPS > BISHOP

ISK *a less common spelling of* > BISQUE

ISKS > BISK

ISMAR *n* type of weighing scale

ISMARS > BISMAR

ISMILLAH *interj* in the name of Allah, a preface to all except one of the surahs of the Koran, used by Muslims as a blessing before eating or some other action

ISMUTH *n* pinkish-white metallic element

ISMUTHAL > BISMUTH

ISMUTHIC *adj* of or

containing bismuth in the pentavalent state

BISMUTHS > BISMUTH

BISNAGA *n* type of cactus

BISNAGAS > BISNAGA

BISOM *same as* > BESOM

BISOMS > BISOM

BISON *same as* > BUFFALO

BISONS > BISON

BISONTINE *adj* relating to bison

BISPHENOL *n* synthetic organic compound used to make plastics and resins

BISQUE *n* thick rich soup made from shellfish

BISQUES > BISQUE

BISSON *adj* blind

BIST *a form of the second person singular of* > BE

BISTABLE *adj* (of an electronic system) having two stable states ▷ *n* bistable system

BISTABLES > BISTABLE

BISTATE *adj* involving two states

BISTER *same as* > BESTIR

BISTERED > BISTER

BISTERS > BISTER

BISTORT *n* Eurasian plant with a spike of small pink flowers

BISTORTS > BISTORT

BISTOURY *n* long surgical knife with a narrow blade

BISTRE *n* transparent water-soluble brownish-yellow pigment made by boiling the soot of wood, used for pen and wash drawings

BISTRED > BISTRE

BISTRES > BISTRE

BISTRO *n* small restaurant

BISTROIC > BISTRO

BISTROS > BISTRO

BISULCATE *adj* marked by two grooves

BISULFATE *n* bisulphate

BISULFIDE *n* bisulphide

BISULFITE *n* bisulphite

BIT *n* small piece, portion, or quantity

BITABLE > BITE

BITCH *n* female dog, fox, or wolf ▷ *vb* complain or grumble

BITCHED > BITCH

BITCHEN *same as* > BITCHING

BITCHERY *n* spiteful talk

BITCHES > BITCH

BITCHFEST *n* malicious and spiteful discussion of people, events, etc

BITCHIER > BITCHY

BITCHIEST > BITCHY

BITCHILY > BITCHY

BITCHING *adj* wonderful or excellent

BITCHY *adj* spiteful or malicious

BITE *vb* grip, tear, or

puncture the skin, as with the teeth or jaws ▷ *n* act of biting

BITEABLE > BITE

BITEPLATE *n* device used by dentists

BITER > BITE

BITERS > BITE

BITES > BITE

BITESIZE *adj* small enough to put in the mouth whole

BITEWING *n* dental x-ray film

BITEWINGS > BITEWING

BITING > BITE

BITINGLY > BITE

BITINGS > BITE

BITLESS *adj* without a bit

BITMAP *n* picture created by colour or shading on a visual display unit ▷ *vb* create a bitmap of

BITMAPPED > BITMAP

BITMAPS > BITMAP

BITO *n* African and Asian tree

BITONAL *adj* consisting of black and white tones

BITOS > BITO

BITOU *as in bitou bush* type of sprawling woody shrub

BITS > BIT

BITSER *n* mongrel dog

BITSERS > BITSER

BITSIER > BITSY

BITSIEST > BITSY

BITSTOCK *n* handle or stock of a tool into which a drilling bit is fixed

BITSTOCKS > BITSTOCK

BITSTREAM *n* sequence of digital data

BITSY *adj* very small

BITT *n* one of a pair of strong posts on the deck of a ship for securing mooring and other lines ▷ *vb* secure (a line) by means of a bitt

BITTACLE *same as* > BINNACLE

BITTACLES > BITTACLE

BITTE *interj* you're welcome

BITTED > BITT

BITTEN > BITE

BITTER *adj* having a sharp unpleasant taste ▷ *n* beer with a slightly bitter taste ▷ *adv* very ▷ *vb* make or become bitter

BITTERED > BITTER

BITTERER > BITTER

BITTEREST > BITTER

BITTERING > BITTER

BITTERISH > BITTER

BITTERLY > BITTER

BITTERN *n* wading marsh bird with a booming call

BITTERNS > BITTERN

BITTERNUT *n* E North American hickory tree with thin-shelled nuts and bitter kernels

BITTERS *npl* bitter-tasting

spirits flavoured with plant extracts

BITTIE *n* small piece

BITTIER > BITTY

BITTIES > BITTIE

BITTIEST > BITTY

BITTINESS > BITTY

BITTING > BITT

BITTINGS > BITT

BITTOCK *n* small amount

BITTOCKS > BITTOCK

BITTOR *n* bittern

BITTORS > BITTOR

BITTOUR *same as* > BITTOR

BITTOURS > BITTOUR

BITTS > BITT

BITTUR *same as* > BITTOR

BITTURS > BITTUR

BITTY *adj* lacking unity, disjointed

BITUMED *adj* covered with bitumen

BITUMEN *n* black sticky substance obtained from tar or petrol

BITUMENS > BITUMEN

BIUNIQUE *adj* one-to-one correspondence

BIVALENCE *n* semantic principle that there are exactly two truth values, so that every meaningful statement is either true or false

BIVALENCY > BIVALENT

BIVALENT *adj* (of homologous chromosomes) associated together in pairs ▷ *n* structure formed during meiosis consisting of two homologous chromosomes associated together

BIVALENTS > BIVALENT

BIVALVATE *same as* > BIVALVE

BIVALVE *adj* (marine mollusc) with two hinged segments to its shell ▷ *n* sea creature, such as an oyster or mussel, that has a shell consisting of two hinged valves and breathes through gills

BIVALVED > BIVALVE

BIVALVES > BIVALVE

BIVARIANT *same as* > BIVARIATE

BIVARIATE *adj* (of a distribution) involving two random variables, not necessarily independent of one another

BIVIA > BIVIUM

BIVINYL *another word for* > BUTADIENE

BIVINYLS > BIVINYL

BIVIOUS *adj* offering a choice of two different ways

BIVIUM *n* parting of ways

BIVOUAC *n* temporary camp in the open air ▷ *vb* camp in a bivouac

b

b

BIVOUACKS > BIVOUAC
BIVOUACS > BIVOUAC
BIVVIED > BIVVY
BIVVIES > BIVVY
BIVVY n small tent or shelter ▷ vb camp in a bivouac
BIVVYING > BIVVY
BIWEEKLY adv every two weeks ▷ n periodical published every two weeks
BIYEARLY adv every two years
BIZ n business
BIZARRE adj odd or unusual ▷ n bizarre thing
BIZARRELY > BIZARRE
BIZARRES > BIZARRE
BIZARRO n bizarre person
BIZARROS > BIZARRO
BIZAZZ same as > PIZAZZ
BIZAZZES > BIZAZZ
BIZCACHA same as > VISCACHA
BIZCACHAS > BIZCACHA
BIZE n dry, cold wind in France
BIZES > BIZE
BIZNAGA same as > BISNAGA
BIZNAGAS > BIZNAGA
BIZONAL > BIZONE
BIZONE n place comprising two zones
BIZONES > BIZONE
BIZZES > BIZ
BIZZIES > BIZZY
BIZZO n empty and irrelevant talk or ideas
BIZZOS > BIZZO
BIZZY n policeman
BLAB vb reveal (secrets) indiscreetly
BLABBED > BLAB
BLABBER vb talk without thinking ▷ n person who blabs
BLABBERED > BLABBER
BLABBERS > BLABBER
BLABBING > BLAB
BLABBINGS > BLAB
BLABBY adj talking too much; indiscreet
BLABS > BLAB
BLACK adj of the darkest colour, like coal ▷ n darkest colour ▷ vb make black
BLACKBALL vb exclude from a group ▷ n hard boiled sweet with black-and-white stripes
BLACKBAND n type of iron ore
BLACKBIRD n common European thrush ▷ vb (formerly) to kidnap and sell into slavery
BLACKBODY n hypothetical body that would be capable of absorbing all the electromagnetic radiation falling on it
BLACKBOY n grass tree
BLACKBOYS > BLACKBOY

BLACKBUCK n Indian antelope, the male of which has spiral horns, a dark back, and a white belly
BLACKBUTT n Australian eucalyptus tree with hard wood used as timber
BLACKCAP n brownish-grey warbler, the male of which has a black crown
BLACKCAPS > BLACKCAP
BLACKCOCK n male of the black grouse
BLACKDAMP n air that is low in oxygen content and high in carbon dioxide as a result of an explosion in a mine
BLACKED > BLACK
BLACKEN vb make or become black
BLACKENED > BLACKEN
BLACKENER > BLACKEN
BLACKENS > BLACKEN
BLACKER > BLACK
BLACKEST > BLACK
BLACKFACE n performer made up to imitate a Black person
BLACKFIN n type of tuna
BLACKFINS > BLACKFIN
BLACKFISH n small dark Australian estuary fish
BLACKFLY n type of black aphid that infests beans, sugar beet, and other plants
BLACKGAME n large N European grouse
BLACKGUM n US tree
BLACKGUMS > BLACKGUM
BLACKHEAD n black-tipped plug of fatty matter clogging a skin pore
BLACKING n preparation for giving a black finish to shoes, metals, etc
BLACKINGS > BLACKING
BLACKISH > BLACK
BLACKJACK n pontoon or a similar card game ▷ vb hit with or as if with a kind of truncheon
BLACKLAND n dark soil
BLACKLEAD another name for > GRAPHITE
BLACKLEG n person who continues to work during a strike ▷ vb refuse to join a strike
BLACKLEGS > BLACKLEG
BLACKLIST n list of people or organizations considered untrustworthy etc ▷ vb put on a blacklist
BLACKLY > BLACK
BLACKMAIL n act of attempting to extort money by threats ▷ vb (attempt to) obtain money by blackmail
BLACKNESS > BLACK
BLACKOUT n extinguishing of all light as a precaution against an air attack

BLACKOUTS > BLACKOUT
BLACKPOLL n N American warbler, the male of which has a black-and-white head
BLACKS > BLACK
BLACKTAIL n variety of mule deer having a black tail
BLACKTOP n bituminous mixture used for paving
BLACKTOPS > BLACKTOP
BLACKWASH n wash for colouring a surface black
BLACKWOOD n tall Australian acacia tree which yields highly valued black timber
BLAD same as > BLAUD
BLADDED > BLAD
BLADDER n sac in the body where urine is held
BLADDERED adj intoxicated
BLADDERS > BLADDER
BLADDERY > BLADDER
BLADDING > BLAD
BLADE n cutting edge of a weapon or tool
BLADED > BLADE
BLADELESS > BLADE
BLADELIKE > BLADE
BLADER n person skating with in-line skates
BLADERS > BLADER
BLADES > BLADE
BLADEWORK n rowing technique
BLADIER > BLADY
BLADIEST > BLADY
BLADING n act or instance of skating with in-line skates
BLADINGS > BLADING
BLADS > BLAD
BLADY as in blady grass coarse leafy Australasian grass
BLAE adj bluish-grey
BLAEBERRY another name for > BILBERRY
BLAER > BLAE
BLAES n hardened clay or shale, esp when crushed and used to form the top layer of a sports pitch: bluish-grey or reddish in colour
BLAEST > BLAE
BLAFF n West Indian stew
BLAFFS > BLAFF
BLAG vb obtain by wheedling or cadging ▷ n robbery, esp with violence
BLAGGED > BLAG
BLAGGER > BLAG
BLAGGERS > BLAG
BLAGGING > BLAG
BLAGGINGS > BLAG
BLAGS > BLAG
BLAGUE n pretentious but empty talk
BLAGUER > BLAGUE
BLAGUERS > BLAGUE
BLAGUES > BLAGUE

BLAGUEUR n bluffer
BLAGUEURS > BLAGUEUR
BLAH n worthless or silly talk ▷ adj uninteresting ▷ vb talk nonsense or boringly
BLAHED > BLAH
BLAHING > BLAH
BLAHS > BLAH
BLAIN n blister, blotch, or sore on the skin
BLAINS > BLAIN
BLAISE same as > BLAES
BLAIZE same as > BLAES
BLAM n representation of the sound of a bullet being fired
BLAMABLE > BLAME
BLAMABLY > BLAME
BLAME vb consider (someone) responsible ▷ n responsibility for something that is wrong
BLAMEABLE > BLAME
BLAMEABLY > BLAME
BLAMED euphemistic word for > DAMNED
BLAMEFUL adj deserving blame
BLAMELESS adj free from blame
BLAMER > BLAME
BLAMERS > BLAME
BLAMES > BLAME
BLAMING > BLAME
BLAMS > BLAM
BLANCH vb become white or pale
BLANCHED > BLANCH
BLANCHER > BLANCH
BLANCHERS > BLANCH
BLANCHES > BLANCH
BLANCHING > BLANCH
BLANCO n whitening substance ▷ vb whiten (something) with blanco
BLANCOED > BLANCO
BLANCOING > BLANCO
BLANCOS > BLANCO
BLAND adj dull and uninteresting ▷ n bland thing ▷ vb as in bland out to become bland
BLANDED > BLAND
BLANDER > BLAND
BLANDEST > BLAND
BLANDING > BLAND
BLANDISH vb persuade by mild flattery
BLANDLY > BLAND
BLANDNESS > BLAND
BLANDS > BLAND
BLANK adj not written on ▷ n empty space ▷ vb cross out, blot, or obscure
BLANKED > BLANK
BLANKER > BLANK
BLANKEST > BLANK
BLANKET n large thick cloth used as covering for a bed ▷ adj applying to a wide group of people, situations, conditions, etc ▷ vb cover as with a blanket

BLANKETED > BLANKET
BLANKETS > BLANKET
BLANKETY adv euphemism for any taboo word
BLANKING > BLANK
BLANKINGS > BLANK
BLANKLY > BLANK
BLANKNESS > BLANK
BLANKS > BLANK
BLANQUET n variety of pear
BLANQUETS > BLANQUET
BLARE vb sound loudly and harshly ▷ n loud harsh noise
BLARED > BLARE
BLARES > BLARE
BLARING > BLARE
BLARNEY n flattering talk ▷ vb cajole with flattery
BLARNEYED > BLARNEY
BLARNEYS > BLARNEY
BLART vb sound loudly and harshly
BLARTED > BLART
BLARTING > BLART
BLARTS > BLART
BLASE adj indifferent or bored through familiarity
BLASH n splash
BLASHES > BLASH
BLASHIER > BLASHY
BLASHIEST > BLASHY
BLASHY adj windy and rainy
BLASPHEME vb speak disrespectfully of (God or sacred things)
BLASPHEMY n behaviour or language that shows disrespect for God or sacred things
BLAST n explosion ▷ vb blow up (a rock etc) with explosives ▷ interj expression of annoyance
BLASTED adv extreme or extremely ▷ adj blighted or withered
BLASTEMA n mass of undifferentiated animal cells that will develop into an organ or tissue: present at the site of regeneration of a lost part
BLASTEMAL > BLASTEMA
BLASTEMAS > BLASTEMA
BLASTEMIC > BLASTEMA
BLASTER > BLAST
BLASTERS > BLAST
BLASTIE n ugly creature
BLASTIER > BLASTY
BLASTIES > BLASTIE
BLASTIEST > BLASTY
BLASTING n distortion of sound caused by overloading certain components of a radio system
BLASTINGS > BLASTING
BLASTMENT n something that frustrates one's plans
BLASTOFF n launching of a rocket
BLASTOFFS > BLASTOFF

BLASTOID n extinct echinoderm found in fossil form
BLASTOIDS > BLASTOID
BLASTOMA n tumour composed of embryonic tissue that has not yet developed a specialized function
BLASTOMAS > BLASTOMA
BLASTOPOR n opening of the archenteron in the gastrula that develops into the anus of some animals
BLASTS > BLAST
BLASTULA n early form of an animal embryo that develops from a morula, consisting of a sphere of cells with a central cavity
BLASTULAE > BLASTULA
BLASTULAR > BLASTULA
BLASTULAS > BLASTULA
BLASTY adj gusty
BLAT vb cry out or bleat like a sheep
BLATANCY > BLATANT
BLATANT adj glaringly obvious
BLATANTLY > BLATANT
BLATE adj shy; ill at ease
BLATER > BLATE
BLATEST > BLATE
BLATHER vb speak foolishly ▷ n foolish talk
BLATHERED > BLATHER
BLATHERER > BLATHER
BLATHERS > BLATHER
BLATS > BLAT
BLATT n newspaper
BLATTANT same as > BLATANT
BLATTED > BLAT
BLATTER n, vb prattle
BLATTERED > BLATTER
BLATTERS > BLATTER
BLATTING > BLAT
BLATTS > BLATT
BLAUBOK n South African antelope
BLAUBOKS > BLAUBOK
BLAUD vb slap
BLAUDED > BLAUD
BLAUDING > BLAUD
BLAUDS > BLAUD
BLAW vb blow
BLAWED > BLAW
BLAWING > BLAW
BLAWN > BLAW
BLAWORT n harebell
BLAWORTS > BLAWORT
BLAWS > BLAW
BLAY n small river fish
BLAYS > BLAY
BLAZAR n type of active galaxy
BLAZARS > BLAZAR
BLAZE n strong fire or flame ▷ vb burn or shine brightly
BLAZED > BLAZE
BLAZER n lightweight jacket, often in the colours of a school etc

BLAZERED > BLAZER
BLAZERS > BLAZER
BLAZES npl hell
BLAZING > BLAZE
BLAZINGLY > BLAZING
BLAZON vb proclaim publicly ▷ n coat of arms
BLAZONED > BLAZON
BLAZONER > BLAZON
BLAZONERS > BLAZON
BLAZONING > BLAZON
BLAZONRY n art or process of describing heraldic arms in proper form
BLAZONS > BLAZON
BLEACH vb make or become white or colourless ▷ n bleaching agent
BLEACHED > BLEACH
BLEACHER > BLEACH
BLEACHERS npl tier of seats in a sports stadium, etc, that are unroofed and inexpensive
BLEACHERY n place where bleaching is carried out
BLEACHES > BLEACH
BLEACHING > BLEACH
BLEAK adj exposed and barren ▷ n type of slender silvery freshwater fish found in slow-flowing rivers
BLEAKER > BLEAK
BLEAKEST > BLEAK
BLEAKISH > BLEAK
BLEAKLY > BLEAK
BLEAKNESS > BLEAK
BLEAKS > BLEAK
BLEAKY same as > BLEAK
BLEAR vb make (eyes or sight) dim with or as if with tears ▷ adj bleary
BLEARED > BLEAR
BLEARER > BLEAR
BLEAREST > BLEAR
BLEAREYED adj with eyes blurred, as with old age or after waking
BLEARIER > BLEARY
BLEARIEST > BLEARY
BLEARILY > BLEARY
BLEARING > BLEAR
BLEARS > BLEAR
BLEARY adj with eyes dimmed, as by tears or tiredness
BLEAT vb (of a sheep, goat, or calf) utter its plaintive cry ▷ n cry of sheep, goats, and calves
BLEATED > BLEAT
BLEATER > BLEAT
BLEATERS > BLEAT
BLEATING > BLEAT
BLEATINGS > BLEAT
BLEATS > BLEAT
BLEB n fluid-filled blister on the skin
BLEBBIER > BLEB
BLEBBIEST > BLEB
BLEBBING n formation of bleb
BLEBBINGS > BLEB
BLEBBY > BLEB

BLEBS > BLEB
BLED > BLEED
BLEE n complexion; hue
BLEED vb lose or emit blood
BLEEDER n despicable person
BLEEDERS > BLEEDER
BLEEDING > BLEED
BLEEDINGS > BLEED
BLEEDS > BLEED
BLEEP n high-pitched signal or beep ▷ vb make such a noise
BLEEPED > BLEEP
BLEEPER n small portable radio receiver that makes a bleeping signal
BLEEPERS > BLEEPER
BLEEPING > BLEEP
BLEEPS > BLEEP
BLEES > BLEE
BLELLUM n babbler; blusterer
BLELLUMS > BLELLUM
BLEMISH n defect or stain ▷ vb spoil or tarnish
BLEMISHED > BLEMISH
BLEMISHER > BLEMISH
BLEMISHES > BLEMISH
BLENCH vb shy away, as in fear
BLENCHED > BLENCH
BLENCHER > BLENCH
BLENCHERS > BLENCH
BLENCHES > BLENCH
BLENCHING > BLENCH
BLEND vb mix or mingle (components or ingredients) ▷ n mixture
BLENDE n mineral consisting mainly of zinc sulphide
BLENDED > BLEND
BLENDER n electrical appliance for puréeing vegetables etc
BLENDERS > BLENDER
BLENDES > BLENDE
BLENDING > BLEND
BLENDINGS > BLEND
BLENDS > BLEND
BLENNIES > BLENNY
BLENNIOID n type of small, mainly marine spiny-finned fish with an elongated body, such as the blennies, butterfly, and gunnel
BLENNY n small fish with a tapering scaleless body
BLENT a past participle of > BLEND
BLEOMYCIN n drug used to treat cancer
BLERT n foolish person
BLERTS > BLERT
BLESBOK n S African antelope with a deep reddish-brown coat and a white blaze between the eyes
BLESBOKS > BLESBOK
BLESBUCK same as > BLESBOK

BLESBUCKS > BLESBUCK

BLESS vb make holy by means of a religious rite

BLESSED > BLESS

BLESSEDER > BLESS

BLESSEDLY > BLESS

BLESSER > BLESS

BLESSERS > BLESS

BLESSES > BLESS

BLESSING > BLESS

BLESSINGS > BLESS

BLEST > BLESS

BLET n state of softness or decay in certain fruits, such as the medlar, brought about by overripening ▷ vb go soft

BLETHER same as > BLATHER

BLETHERED > BLETHER

BLETHERER > BLETHER

BLETHERS > BLETHER

BLETS > BLET

BLETTED > BLET

BLETTING > BLET

BLEUATRE adj blueish

BLEW > BLOW

BLEWART same as > BLAWORT

BLEWARTS > BLEWART

BLEWITS n type of edible fungus with a pale brown cap and a bluish stalk

BLEWITSES > BLEWITS

BLEY same as > BLAY

BLEYS > BLEY

BLIGHT n person or thing that spoils or prevents growth ▷ vb cause to suffer a blight

BLIGHTED > BLIGHT

BLIGHTER n irritating person

BLIGHTERS > BLIGHTER

BLIGHTIES > BLIGHTY

BLIGHTING > BLIGHT

BLIGHTS > BLIGHT

BLIGHTY n home country; home leave

BLIKSEM interj South African expression of surprise

BLIMBING same as > BILIMBI

BLIMBINGS > BLIMBING

BLIMEY interj exclamation of surprise or annoyance

BLIMP n small airship

BLIMPISH adj complacent and reactionary

BLIMPS > BLIMP

BLIMY same as > BLIMEY

BLIN Scots word for > BLIND

BLIND adj unable to see ▷ vb deprive of sight ▷ n covering for a window

BLINDAGE n (esp formerly) a protective screen or structure, as over a trench

BLINDAGES > BLINDAGE

BLINDED > BLIND

BLINDER same as > BLIND

BLINDERS same as > BLIND

BLINDEST > BLIND

BLINDFISH n any of various small fishes, esp the cavefish, that have rudimentary or functionless eyes and occur in subterranean streams

BLINDFOLD vb prevent (a person) from seeing by covering the eyes ▷ n piece of cloth used to cover the eyes ▷ adv with the eyes covered by a cloth

BLINDGUT same as > CAECUM

BLINDGUTS > BLINDGUT

BLINDING n sand or grit spread over a road surface to fill up cracks ▷ adj making one blind or as if blind

BLINDINGS > BLINDING

BLINDLESS > BLIND

BLINDLY > BLIND

BLINDNESS > BLIND

BLINDS > BLIND

BLINDSIDE vb take (someone) by surprise

BLINDWORM same as > SLOWWORM

BLING adj flashy ▷ n ostentatious jewellery

BLINGER > BLING

BLINGEST > BLING

BLINGIER > BLINGY

BLINGIEST > BLINGY

BLINGING adj flashy and expensive

BLINGLISH n spoken English mixed with Black slang

BLINGS > BLING

BLINGY same as > BLING adj

BLINI npl Russian pancakes made of buckwheat flour and yeast

BLINIS same as > BLINI

BLINK vb close and immediately reopen (the eyes) ▷ n act of blinking

BLINKARD n something that twinkles

BLINKARDS > BLINKARD

BLINKED > BLINK

BLINKER vb provide (a horse) with blinkers ▷ n flashing light for sending messages, as a warning device, etc, such as a direction indicator on a road vehicle

BLINKERED adj considering only a narrow point of view

BLINKERS same as > BLIND

BLINKING adv extreme or extremely

BLINKS > BLINK

BLINNED > BLIN

BLINNING > BLIN

BLINS > BLIN

BLINTZ n thin pancake folded over a filling usually of apple, cream cheese, or meat

BLINTZE same as > BLINTZ

BLINTZES > BLINTZE

BLINY same as > BLINI

BLIP n spot of light on a radar screen indicating the position of an object ▷ vb produce such a noise

BLIPPED > BLIP

BLIPPING > BLIP

BLIPS > BLIP

BLIPVERT n very short television advertisement

BLIPVERTS > BLIPVERT

BLISS n perfect happiness ▷ vb make or become perfectly happy

BLISSED > BLISS

BLISSES > BLISS

BLISSFUL adj serenely joyful or glad

BLISSING > BLISS

BLISSLESS > BLISS

BLIST archaic form of > BLESSED

BLISTER n small bubble on the skin ▷ vb (cause to) have blisters

BLISTERED > BLISTER

BLISTERS > BLISTER

BLISTERY > BLISTER

BLIT vb move or copy (a block of data) from one location to another in a computer's memory

BLITE n type of herb

BLITES > BLITE

BLITHE adj casual and indifferent

BLITHEFUL same as > BLITHE

BLITHELY > BLITHE

BLITHER same as > BLETHER

BLITHERED > BLITHER

BLITHERS > BLITHER

BLITHEST > BLITHE

BLITS > BLIT

BLITTED > BLIT

BLITTER n circuit that transfers large amounts of data within a computer's memory

BLITTERS > BLITTER

BLITTING > BLIT

BLITZ n violent and sustained attack by aircraft ▷ vb attack suddenly and intensively

BLITZED > BLITZ

BLITZER > BLITZ

BLITZERS > BLITZ

BLITZES > BLITZ

BLITZING > BLITZ

BLIVE same as > BELIVE

BLIZZARD n blinding storm of wind and snow

BLIZZARDS > BLIZZARD

BLIZZARDY > BLIZZARD

BLOAT vb cause to swell, as with liquid or air ▷ n abnormal distention of the abdomen in cattle, sheep, etc, caused by accumulation of gas in the stomach

BLOATED adj swollen, as with a liquid, air, or wind

BLOATER n salted smoked herring

BLOATERS > BLOATER

BLOATING > BLOAT

BLOATINGS > BLOAT

BLOATS > BLOAT

BLOATWARE n software with more features than necessary

BLOB n soft mass or drop ▷ vb put blobs, as of ink or paint, on

BLOBBED > BLOB

BLOBBIER > BLOB

BLOBBIEST > BLOB

BLOBBING > BLOB

BLOBBY > BLOB

BLOBS > BLOB

BLOC n people or countries combined by a common interest

BLOCK n large solid piece of wood, stone, etc ▷ vb obstruct or impede by introducing an obstacle

BLOCKABLE > BLOCK

BLOCKADE n sealing of a place to prevent the passage of goods ▷ vb impose a blockade on

BLOCKADED > BLOCKADE

BLOCKADER > BLOCKADE

BLOCKADES > BLOCKADE

BLOCKAGE n act of blocking or state of being blocked

BLOCKAGES > BLOCKAGE

BLOCKBUST vb (try to) bring about the sale of property at a bargain price by stirring up fears of racial change in an area

BLOCKED adj functionally impeded by amphetamine

BLOCKER n person or thing that blocks

BLOCKERS > BLOCKER

BLOCKHEAD n stupid person

BLOCKHOLE n lines marked near stumps on cricket pitch

BLOCKIE n owner of a small property, esp a farm

BLOCKIER > BLOCKY

BLOCKIES > BLOCKIE

BLOCKIEST > BLOCKY

BLOCKING n interruption of anode current in a valve because of the application of a high negative voltage to the grid

BLOCKINGS > BLOCKING

BLOCKISH adj lacking vivacity or imagination

BLOCKS > BLOCK

BLOCKSHIP n ship used to block a river or channel and prevent its being used

b

BLOCKWORK n
wall-building style

BLOCKY adj like a block, esp
in shape and solidity

BLOCS > BLOC

BLOG n journal written
on-line and accessible to
users of the internet ▷ vb
write a blog

BLOGGED > BLOG vb

BLOGGER > BLOG

BLOGGERS > BLOG

BLOGGING > BLOG

BLOGGINGS > BLOG

BLOGRING n group of
blogs joined in a ring

BLOGRINGS > BLOGRING

BLOGROLL n list of blogs

BLOGROLLS > BLOGROLL

BLOGS > BLOG

BLOKART n single-seat
three-wheeled vehicle
propelled by the wind

BLOKARTS > BLOKART

BLOKE n man

BLOKEDOM n state of being
a bloke

BLOKEDOMS > BLOKEDOM

BLOKEISH adj denoting or
exhibiting the
characteristics believed
typical of an ordinary man

BLOKES > BLOKE

BLOKEY same as
> BLOKEISH

BLOKIER > BLOKEY

BLOKIEST > BLOKEY

BLOKISH same as
> BLOKEISH

BLONCKET adj blue-grey

BLOND adj (of men's hair) of
a light colour ▷ n person,
esp a man, having
light-coloured hair and skin

BLONDE n fair-haired
(person) ▷ adj (of hair) fair

BLONDER > BLONDE

BLONDES > BLONDE

BLONDEST > BLONDE

BLONDINE vb dye hair
blonde

BLONDINED > BLONDINE

BLONDINES > BLONDINE

BLONDING n act or an
instance of dyeing hair
blonde

BLONDINGS > BLONDING

BLONDISH > BLOND

BLONDNESS > BLOND

BLONDS > BLOND

BLOOD n red fluid that flows
around the body ▷ vb
initiate (a person) to war or
hunting

BLOODBATH n massacre

BLOODED adj (of horses,
cattle, etc) of good
breeding

BLOODFIN n silvery
red-finned S American
freshwater fish, popular in
aquariums

BLOODFINS > BLOODFIN

BLOODIED > BLOODY

BLOODIER > BLOODY

BLOODIES > BLOODY

BLOODIEST > BLOODY

BLOODILY > BLOODY

BLOODING > BLOOD

BLOODINGS > BLOOD

BLOODLESS adj without
blood or bloodshed

BLOODLIKE > BLOOD

BLOODLINE n all the
members of a family group
over generations, esp
regarding characteristics
common to that group

BLOODLUST n desire to see
bloodshed

BLOODRED adj having a
deep red colour

BLOODROOT n N American
plant with a single whitish
flower and a fleshy red root
that yields a red dye

BLOODS > BLOOD

BLOODSHED n slaughter or
killing

BLOODSHOT adj (of an eye)
inflamed

BLOODWOOD n any of
several species of
Australian eucalyptus that
exude a red sap

BLOODWORM n red
wormlike aquatic larva of
the midge

BLOODWORT n plant with
red dye in roots

BLOODY adj covered with
blood ▷ adv extreme or
extremely ▷ vb stain with
blood

BLOODYING > BLOODY

BLOOEY adj out of order;
faulty

BLOOIE same as > BLOOEY

BLOOK n book published on
a blog

BLOOKS > BLOOK

BLOOM n blossom on a
flowering plant ▷ vb (of
flowers) open

BLOOMED adj (of a lens)
coated with a thin film of
magnesium fluoride or
some other substance to
reduce the amount of light
lost by reflection

BLOOMER n stupid mistake

BLOOMERS npl woman's
baggy knickers

BLOOMERY n place in
which malleable iron is
produced directly from iron
ore

BLOOMIER > BLOOMY

BLOOMIEST > BLOOMY

BLOOMING adj extreme or
extremely

BLOOMLESS > BLOOM

BLOOMS > BLOOM

BLOOMY adj having a fine
whitish coating on the
surface, such as on the rind
of a cheese

BLOOP vb (baseball) hit a
ball into air beyond infield

BLOOPED > BLOOP

BLOOPER n stupid mistake

BLOOPERS > BLOOPER

BLOOPING > BLOOP

BLOOPS > BLOOP

BLOOSME same as
> BLOSSOM

BLOOSMED > BLOOSME

BLOOSMES > BLOOSME

BLOOSMING > BLOOSME

BLOOTERED adj drunk

BLOQUISTE n supporter
of autonomy for Quebec

BLORE n strong blast of
wind

BLORES > BLORE

BLOSSOM n flowers of a
plant ▷ vb (of plants)
flower

BLOSSOMED > BLOSSOM

BLOSSOMS > BLOSSOM

BLOSSOMY > BLOSSOM

BLOT n spot or stain ▷ vb
cause a blemish in or on

BLOTCH n discoloured area
or stain ▷ vb become or
cause to become marked
by such discoloration

BLOTCHED > BLOTCH

BLOTCHES > BLOTCH

BLOTCHIER > BLOTCHY

BLOTCHILY > BLOTCHY

BLOTCHING > BLOTCH

BLOTCHY adj covered in or
marked by blotches

BLOTLESS > BLOT

BLOTS > BLOT

BLOTTED > BLOT

BLOTTER n sheet of
blotting paper

BLOTTERS > BLOTTER

BLOTTIER > BLOTTY

BLOTTIEST > BLOTTY

BLOTTING n blot analysis

BLOTTINGS > BLOTTING

BLOTTO adj extremely
drunk

BLOTTY adj covered in
blots

BLOUBOK same as
> BLAUBOK

BLOUBOKS > BLOUBOK

BLOUSE n woman's
shirtlike garment ▷ vb
hang or cause to hang in
full loose folds

BLOUSED > BLOUSE

BLOUSES > BLOUSE

BLOUSIER > BLOUSY

BLOUSIEST > BLOUSY

BLOUSILY > BLOUSY

BLOUSING > BLOUSE

BLOUSON n short loose
jacket with a tight waist

BLOUSONS > BLOUSON

BLOUSY adj loose;
blouse-like

BLOVIATE vb discourse at
length

BLOVIATED > BLOVIATE

BLOVIATES > BLOVIATE

BLOW vb (of air, the wind,
etc) move ▷ n hard hit

BLOWBACK n escape to the
rear of gases formed during

the firing of a weapon or in
a boiler, internal-
combustion engine, etc

BLOWBACKS > BLOWBACK

BLOWBALL n dandelion
seed head

BLOWBALLS > BLOWBALL

BLOWBY n leakage of gas
past the piston of an engine
at maximum pressure

BLOWBYS > BLOWBY

BLOWDOWN n accident in a
nuclear reactor in which a
cooling pipe bursts causing
the loss of essential coolant

BLOWDOWNS > BLOWDOWN

BLOWED > BLOW

BLOWER n mechanical
device, such as a fan, that
blows

BLOWERS > BLOWER

BLOWFISH a popular name
for > PUFFER

BLOWFLIES > BLOWFLY

BLOWFLY n fly that lays its
eggs in meat

BLOWGUN same as
> BLOWPIPE

BLOWGUNS > BLOWGUN

BLOWHARD n boastful
person ▷ adj blustering or
boastful

BLOWHARDS > BLOWHARD

BLOWHOLE n nostril of a
whale

BLOWHOLES > BLOWHOLE

BLOWIE n bluebottle

BLOWIER > BLOWY

BLOWIES > BLOWIE

BLOWIEST > BLOWY

BLOWINESS > BLOWY

BLOWING n moving of air

BLOWINGS > BLOWING

BLOWJOB slang term for
> FELLATIO

BLOWJOBS > BLOWJOB

BLOWLAMP another name for
> BLOWTORCH

BLOWLAMPS > BLOWLAMP

BLOWN > BLOW

BLOWOFF n discharge of a
surplus fluid

BLOWOFFS > BLOWOFF

BLOWOUT n sudden loss of
air in a tyre

BLOWOUTS > BLOWOUT

BLOWPIPE n long tube
from which darts etc are
shot by blowing

BLOWPIPES > BLOWPIPE

BLOWS > BLOW

BLOWSE n large, red-faced
woman

BLOWSED same as
> BLOWSY

BLOWSES > BLOWSE

BLOWSIER > BLOWSY

BLOWSIEST > BLOWSY

BLOWSILY > BLOWSY

BLOWSY adj fat, untidy, and
red-faced

BLOWTORCH n small
burner producing a very hot
flame

BLOWTUBE n tube for blowing air or oxygen into a flame to intensify its heat

BLOWTUBES > BLOWTUBE

BLOWUP n fit of temper

BLOWUPS > BLOWUP

BLOWY adj windy

BLOWZE variant of > BLOWSE

BLOWZED same as > BLOWSY

BLOWZES > BLOWZE

BLOWZIER > BLOWZY

BLOWZIEST > BLOWZY

BLOWZILY > BLOWZY

BLOWZY same as > BLOWSY

BLUB a slang word for > BLUBBER

BLUBBED > BLUB

BLUBBER n, vb sob without restraint ▷ adj swollen or fleshy ▷ n fat of whales, seals, etc

BLUBBERED > BLUBBER

BLUBBERER > BLUBBER

BLUBBERS > BLUBBER

BLUBBERY adj containing, or like blubber

BLUBBING > BLUB

BLUBS > BLUB

BLUCHER n high shoe with laces over the tongue

BLUCHERS > BLUCHER

BLUDE Scots form of > BLOOD

BLUDES > BLUDE

BLUDGE vb evade work ▷ n easy task

BLUDGED > BLUDGE

BLUDGEON n short thick club ▷ vb hit with a bludgeon

BLUDGEONS > BLUDGEON

BLUDGER n person who scrounges

BLUDGERS > BLUDGER

BLUDGES > BLUDGE

BLUDGING > BLUDGE

BLUDIE Scots form of > BLOODY

BLUDIER > BLUDIE

BLUDIEST > BLUDIE

BLUDY same as > BLUDIE

BLUE n colour of a clear unclouded sky ▷ adj of the colour blue ▷ vb make or become blue

BLUEBACK n type of salmon

BLUEBACKS > BLUEBACK

BLUEBALL n type of European herb

BLUEBALLS > BLUEBALL

BLUEBEARD n any man who murders his wife or wives

BLUEBEAT n type of West Indian pop music of the 1960s

BLUEBEATS > BLUEBEAT

BLUEBELL n flower with blue bell-shaped flowers

BLUEBELLS > BLUEBELL

BLUEBERRY n very small

blackish edible fruit that grows on a North American shrub

BLUEBILL another name for > SCAUP

BLUEBILLS > BLUEBILL

BLUEBIRD n North American songbird with a blue plumage

BLUEBIRDS > BLUEBIRD

BLUEBLOOD n royal or aristocratic person

BLUEBOOK n (in Britain) a government publication, usually the report of a commission

BLUEBOOKS > BLUEBOOK

BLUEBUCK same as > BLAUBOK

BLUEBUCKS > BLUEBUCK

BLUEBUSH n blue-grey herbaceous Australian shrub

BLUECAP another name for > BLUETIT

BLUECAPS > BLUECAP

BLUECOAT n person who wears blue uniform

BLUECOATS > BLUECOAT

BLUECURLS n North American plant

BLUED > BLUE

BLUEFIN another name for > TUNNY

BLUEFINS > BLUEFIN

BLUEFISH n type of bluish marine food and game fish

BLUEGILL n common N American sunfish, an important freshwater food and game fish

BLUEGILLS > BLUEGILL

BLUEGOWN n in past, pauper, recipient of blue gown on King's birthday

BLUEGOWNS > BLUEGOWN

BLUEGRASS n any of several North American bluish-green grasses

BLUEGUM n tall fast-growing widely cultivated Australian tree with aromatic leaves, bark that peels off in shreds, and hard timber

BLUEGUMS > BLUEGUM

BLUEHEAD n type of fish

BLUEHEADS > BLUEHEAD

BLUEING > BLUE

BLUEINGS > BLUE

BLUEISH same as > BLUISH

BLUEJACK n type of oak tree

BLUEJACKS > BLUEJACK

BLUEJAY n common N American jay with bright blue plumage and greyish-white underparts

BLUEJAYS > BLUEJAY

BLUEJEANS n blue denim jeans

BLUELINE n blue-toned photographic proof

BLUELINER n machine for

making blueprints

BLUELINES > BLUELINE

BLUELY > BLUE

BLUENESS > BLUE

BLUENOSE n puritanical or prudish person

BLUENOSED > BLUENOSE

BLUENOSES > BLUENOSE

BLUEPOINT n type of small oyster

BLUEPRINT n photographic print of a plan ▷ vb make a blueprint of (a plan)

BLUER > BLUE

BLUES npl type of music

BLUESHIFT n shift in the spectral lines of a stellar spectrum

BLUESIER > BLUES

BLUESIEST > BLUES

BLUESMAN n blues musician

BLUESMEN > BLUESMAN

BLUEST > BLUE

BLUESTEM n type of tall grass

BLUESTEMS > BLUESTEM

BLUESTONE n blue-grey sandstone containing much clay, used for building and paving

BLUESY > BLUES

BLUET n N American plant with small four-petalled blue flowers

BLUETICK n fast-running dog

BLUETICKS > BLUETICK

BLUETIT n small European bird with a blue crown, wings, and tail and yellow underparts

BLUETITS > BLUETIT

BLUETS > BLUET

BLUETTE n short, brilliant piece of music

BLUETTES > BLUETTE

BLUEWEED n Eurasian weed with blue flowers and pink buds

BLUEWEEDS > BLUEWEED

BLUEWING n type of duck

BLUEWINGS > BLUEWING

BLUEWOOD n type of Mexican shrub

BLUEWOODS > BLUEWOOD

BLUEY adj bluish ▷ n informal Australian word meaning blanket

BLUEYS > BLUEY

BLUFF vb pretend to be confident in order to influence (someone) ▷ n act of bluffing ▷ adj good-naturedly frank and hearty

BLUFFABLE > BLUFF

BLUFFED > BLUFF

BLUFFER > BLUFF

BLUFFERS > BLUFF

BLUFFEST > BLUFF

BLUFFING > BLUFF

BLUFFLY > BLUFF

BLUFFNESS > BLUFF

BLUFFS > BLUFF

BLUGGIER > BLUGGY

BLUGGIEST > BLUGGY

BLUGGY same as > BLOODY

BLUID Scots word for > BLOOD

BLUIDIER > BLUID

BLUIDIEST > BLUID

BLUIDS > BLUID

BLUIDY > BLUID

BLUIER > BLUEY

BLUIEST > BLUEY

BLUING same as > BLUE

BLUINGS > BLUE

BLUISH adj slightly blue

BLUME Scots word for > BLOOM

BLUMED > BLUME

BLUMES > BLUME

BLUMING > BLUME

BLUNDER n clumsy mistake ▷ vb make a blunder

BLUNDERED > BLUNDER

BLUNDERER > BLUNDER

BLUNDERS > BLUNDER

BLUNGE vb mix (clay or a similar substance) with water in order to form a suspension for use in ceramics

BLUNGED > BLUNGE

BLUNGER n large vat in which the contents, esp clay and water, are mixed by rotating arms

BLUNGERS > BLUNGER

BLUNGES > BLUNGE

BLUNGING > BLUNGE

BLUNK vb ruin; botch

BLUNKED > BLUNK

BLUNKER > BLUNK

BLUNKERS > BLUNK

BLUNKING > BLUNK

BLUNKS > BLUNK

BLUNT adj not having a sharp edge or point ▷ vb make less sharp ▷ n cannabis cigarette

BLUNTED > BLUNT

BLUNTER > BLUNT

BLUNTEST > BLUNT

BLUNTHEAD n frequent user of marijuana

BLUNTING > BLUNT

BLUNTISH > BLUNT

BLUNTLY > BLUNT

BLUNTNESS > BLUNT

BLUNTS > BLUNT

BLUR vb make or become vague or less distinct ▷ n something vague, hazy, or indistinct

BLURB n promotional description, as on the jacket of a book ▷ vb describe or recommend in a blurb

BLURBED > BLURB

BLURBING > BLURB

BLURBIST n writer of blurbs

BLURBISTS > BLURBIST

BLURBS > BLURB

BLURRED > BLUR

BLURREDLY >BLUR
BLURRIER >BLUR
BLURRIEST >BLUR
BLURRILY >BLUR
BLURRING >BLUR
BLURRY >BLUR
BLURS >BLUR
BLURT vb utter suddenly and involuntarily
BLURTED >BLURT
BLURTER >BLURT
BLURTERS >BLURT
BLURTING >BLURT
BLURTINGS >BLURT
BLURTS >BLURT
BLUSH vb become red in the face, esp from embarrassment or shame ▷ n reddening of the face
BLUSHED >BLUSH
BLUSHER n cosmetic for giving the cheeks a rosy colour
BLUSHERS >BLUSHER
BLUSHES >BLUSH
BLUSHET n modest young woman
BLUSHETS >BLUSHET
BLUSHFUL >BLUSH
BLUSHING >BLUSH
BLUSHINGS >BLUSH
BLUSHLESS >BLUSH
BLUSTER vb speak loudly or in a bullying way ▷ n empty threats or protests
BLUSTERED >BLUSTER
BLUSTERER >BLUSTER
BLUSTERS >BLUSTER
BLUSTERY >BLUSTER
BLUSTROUS adj inclined to bluster
BLUTWURST n blood sausage
BLYPE n piece of skin peeled off after sunburn
BLYPES >BLYPE
BO interj, n exclamation uttered to startle or surprise someone, esp a child in a game
BOA n large nonvenomous snake
BOAB short for >BAOBAB
BOABS >BOAB
BOAK same as >BOKE
BOAKED >BOAK
BOAKING >BOAK
BOAKS >BOAK
BOAR n uncastrated male pig
BOARD n long flat piece of sawn timber ▷ vb go aboard (a train, aeroplane, etc)
BOARDABLE >BOARD
BOARDED >BOARD
BOARDER n person who pays rent in return for accommodation in someone else's home
BOARDERS >BOARDER
BOARDING n act of embarking on an aircraft, train, ship, etc
BOARDINGS >BOARDING

BOARDLIKE >BOARD
BOARDMAN n man who carries a sandwich board
BOARDMEN >BOARDMAN
BOARDROOM n room where the board of a company meets
BOARDS >BOARD
BOARDWALK n promenade, esp along a beach, usually made of planks
BOARFISH n type of spiny-finned marine fish with a compressed body, a long snout, and large eyes
BOARHOUND n dog used to hunt boar
BOARISH adj coarse, cruel, or sensual
BOARISHLY >BOARISH
BOARS >BOAR
BOART same as >BORT
BOARTS >BOART
BOAS >BOA
BOAST vb speak too proudly about one's talents etc ▷ n bragging statement
BOASTED >BOAST
BOASTER >BOAST
BOASTERS >BOAST
BOASTFUL adj tending to boast
BOASTING >BOAST
BOASTINGS >BOAST
BOASTLESS >BOAST
BOASTS >BOAST
BOAT n small vehicle for travelling across water ▷ vb travel in a boat
BOATABLE adj able to be carried by boat
BOATBILL n nocturnal tropical American wading bird with a broad flattened bill
BOATBILLS >BOATBILL
BOATED >BOAT
BOATEL n waterside hotel catering for boating people
BOATELS >BOATEL
BOATER n flat straw hat
BOATERS >BOATER
BOATFUL >BOAT
BOATFULS >BOAT
BOATHOOK n pole with a hook at one end, used aboard a vessel for fending off other vessels or obstacles or for catching a line or mooring buoy
BOATHOOKS >BOATHOOK
BOATHOUSE n shelter by the edge of a river, lake, etc, for housing boats
BOATIE n boating enthusiast
BOATIES >BOATIE
BOATING n rowing, sailing, or cruising in boats as a form of recreation
BOATINGS >BOATING
BOATLIFT n evacuation by boat
BOATLIFTS >BOATLIFT
BOATLIKE >BOAT

BOATLOAD n amount of cargo or number of people held by a boat or ship
BOATLOADS >BOATLOAD
BOATMAN n man who works on, hires out, or repairs boats
BOATMEN >BOATMAN
BOATNECK n wide open neck on garment
BOATNECKS >BOATNECK
BOATS >BOAT
BOATSMAN same as >BOATMAN
BOATSMEN >BOATSMAN
BOATSWAIN n petty officer on a merchant ship or a warrant officer on a warship who is responsible for the maintenance of the ship and its equipment
BOATTAIL n type of blackbird
BOATTAILS >BOATTAIL
BOATYARD n place where boats are kept, repaired, etc
BOATYARDS >BOATYARD
BOB vb move or cause to move up and down repeatedly, as while floating in water ▷ n short abrupt movement, as of the head
BOBA n type of Chinese tea
BOBAC same as >BOBAK
BOBACS >BOBAC
BOBAK n type of marmot
BOBAKS >BOBAK
BOBAS >BOBA
BOBBED >BOB
BOBBEJAAN n baboon
BOBBER n type of float for fishing
BOBBERIES >BOBBERY
BOBBERS >BOBBER
BOBBERY n mixed pack of hunting dogs, often not belonging to any of the hound breeds ▷ adj noisy or excitable
BOBBIES >BOBBY
BOBBIN n reel on which thread is wound
BOBBINET n netted fabric of hexagonal mesh, made on a lace machine
BOBBINETS >BOBBINET
BOBBING >BOB
BOBBINS >BOBBIN
BOBBISH >CHEERY
BOBBITT vb sever the penis of
BOBBITTED >BOBBITT
BOBBITTS >BOBBITT
BOBBLE n small ball of material, usu for decoration ▷ vb (of a ball) to bounce erratically because of an uneven playing surface
BOBBLED >BOBBLE
BOBBLES >BOBBLE
BOBBLIER >BOBBLY
BOBBLIEST >BOBBLY
BOBBLING >BOBBLE

BOBBLY adj (of fabric) covered in small balls; worn
BOBBY n policeman
BOBBYSOCK n ankle-length sock worn esp by teenage girls
BOBBYSOX npl bobbysocks
BOBCAT n N American feline mammal with reddish-brown fur with dark spots or stripes, tufted ears, and a short tail
BOBCATS >BOBCAT
BOBECHE n candle drip-catcher
BOBECHES >BOBECHE
BOBFLOAT n small buoyant float, usually consisting of a quill stuck through a piece of cork
BOBFLOATS >BOBFLOAT
BOBLET n two-man bobsleigh
BOBLETS >BOBLET
BOBOL n fraud carried out by one or more persons with access to public funds in collusion with someone in a position of authority ▷ vb commit a bobol
BOBOLINK n American songbird, the male of which has a white back and black underparts in the breeding season
BOBOLINKS >BOBOLINK
BOBOLLED >BOBOL
BOBOLLING >BOBOL
BOBOLS >BOBOL
BOBOTIE n dish of curried mince
BOBOTIES >BOBOTIE
BOBOWLER n large moth
BOBOWLERS >BOBOWLER
BOBS >BOB
BOBSLED same as >BOBSLEIGH
BOBSLEDS >BOBSLED
BOBSLEIGH n sledge for racing down an icy track ▷ vb ride on a bobsleigh
BOBSTAY n strong stay between a bowsprit and the stem of a vessel for holding down the bowsprit
BOBSTAYS >BOBSTAY
BOBTAIL n docked tail ▷ adj having the tail cut short ▷ vb dock the tail of
BOBTAILED >BOBTAIL
BOBTAILS >BOBTAIL
BOBWEIGHT n balance weight
BOBWHEEL n poetic device
BOBWHEELS >BOBWHEEL
BOBWHITE n brown N American quail, a popular game bird, the male of which has white markings on the head
BOBWHITES >BOBWHITE
BOBWIG n type of short wig
BOBWIGS >BOBWIG
BOCACCIO n edible American fish

BOCACCIOS > BOCACCIO
BOCAGE n wooded countryside characteristic of northern France, with small irregular-shaped fields and many hedges and copses
BOCAGES > BOCAGE
BOCCA n mouth
BOCCAS > BOCCA
BOCCE same as > BOCCIE
BOCCES > BOCCE
BOCCI same as > BOCCIE
BOCCIA same as > BOCCIE
BOCCIAS > BOCCIA
BOCCIE n Italian version of bowls played on a lawn smaller than a bowling green
BOCCIES > BOCCIE
BOCCIS > BOCCI
BOCHE n derogatory slang for a German soldier
BOCHES > BOCHE
BOCK a variant spelling of > BOKE
BOCKED > BOCK
BOCKEDY adj (of a structure, piece of furniture, etc) unsteady
BOCKING > BOCK
BOCKS > BOCK
BOCONCINI npl small pieces of mozzarella
BOD n person
BODACH n old man
BODACHS > BODACH
BODACIOUS adj impressive or remarkable
BODDLE same as > BODLE
BODDLES > BODDLE
BODE vb portend or presage
BODED > BODE
BODEFUL adj portentous
BODEGA n shop in a Spanish-speaking country that sells wine
BODEGAS > BODEGA
BODEGUERO n wine seller or grocer
BODEMENT > BODE
BODEMENTS > BODE
BODES > BODE
BODGE vb make a mess of
BODGED > BODGE
BODGER adj worthless or second-rate
BODGERS > BODGER
BODGES > BODGE
BODGIE n unruly or uncouth young man, esp in the 1950s ▷ adj inferior
BODGIER > BODGIE
BODGIES > BODGIE
BODGIEST > BODGIE
BODGING > BODGE
BODHI as in bodhi tree holy tree of Buddhists
BODHRAN n shallow one-sided drum popular in Irish and Scottish folk music
BODHRANS > BODHRAN
BODICE n upper part of a dress

BODICES > BODICE
BODIED > BODY
BODIES > BODY
BODIKIN n little body
BODIKINS > BODIKIN
BODILESS adj having no body or substance
BODILY adj relating to the body ▷ adv by taking hold of the body
BODING > BODE
BODINGLY > BODE
BODINGS > BODE
BODKIN n blunt large-eyed needle
BODKINS > BODKIN
BODLE n small obsolete Scottish coin
BODLES > BODLE
BODRAG n enemy attack
BODRAGS > BODRAG
BODS > BOD
BODY n entire physical structure of an animal or human
BODYBOARD n surfboard that is shorter and blunter than the standard board and on which the surfer lies rather than stands
BODYCHECK n obstruction of another player ▷ vb deliver a bodycheck to (an opponent)
BODYGUARD n person or group of people employed to protect someone
BODYING > BODY
BODYLINE n (in cricket) fast bowling aimed at the batsman's body
BODYLINES > BODYLINE
BODYSHELL n external shell of a motor vehicle
BODYSUIT n one-piece undergarment for a baby
BODYSUITS > BODYSUIT
BODYSURF vb ride a wave by lying on it without a surfboard
BODYSURFS > BODYSURF
BODYWORK n outer shell of a motor vehicle
BODYWORKS > BODYWORK
BOEHMITE n grey, red, or brown mineral that consists of alumina in rhombic crystalline form and occurs in bauxite
BOEHMITES > BOEHMITE
BOEP n South African word for a big belly
BOEPS > BOEP
BOERBUL n crossbred mastiff used esp as a watchdog
BOERBULL same as > BOERBUL
BOERBULLS > BOERBULL
BOERBULS > BOERBUL
BOEREWORS n spiced sausage
BOERTJIE South African word for > FRIEND

BOERTJIES > BOERTJIE
BOET n brother
BOETS > BOET
BOEUF as in boeuf bourguignon casserole of beef, vegetables, herbs, etc, cooked in red wine
BOFF n boffin ▷ vb hit
BOFFED > BOFF
BOFFIN n scientist or expert
BOFFING > BOFF
BOFFINS > BOFFIN
BOFFO adj very good
BOFFOLA n great success
BOFFOLAS > BOFFOLA
BOFFOS > BOFFO
BOFFS > BOFF
BOG n wet spongy ground ▷ vb mire or delay
BOGAN n youth who dresses and behaves rebelliously
BOGANS > BOGAN
BOGART vb monopolize or keep (something, esp a marijuana cigarette) to oneself selfishly
BOGARTED > BOGART
BOGARTING > BOGART
BOGARTS > BOGART
BOGBEAN same as > BUCKBEAN
BOGBEANS > BOGBEAN
BOGEY n evil or mischievous spirit ▷ vb play (a hole) in one stroke over par
BOGEYED > BOGEY
BOGEYING > BOGEY
BOGEYISM n demonization
BOGEYISMS > BOGEYISM
BOGEYMAN n frightening person, real or imaginary, used as a threat, esp to children
BOGEYMEN > BOGEYMAN
BOGEYS > BOGEY
BOGGARD same as > BOGGART
BOGGARDS > BOGGARD
BOGGART n ghost or poltergeist
BOGGARTS > BOGGART
BOGGED > BOG
BOGGER n lavatory
BOGGERS > BOGGER
BOGGIER > BOG
BOGGIEST > BOG
BOGGINESS > BOG
BOGGING > BOG
BOGGISH > BOG
BOGGLE vb be surprised, confused, or alarmed
BOGGLED > BOGGLE
BOGGLER > BOGGLE
BOGGLERS > BOGGLE
BOGGLES > BOGGLE
BOGGLING > BOGGLE
BOGGY > BOG
BOGIE same as > BOGEY
BOGIED > BOGIE
BOGIEING > BOGIE
BOGIES > BOGY
BOGLAND n area of wetland

BOGLANDS > BOGLAND
BOGLE n rhythmic dance performed to ragga music ▷ vb to perform such a dance
BOGLED > BOGLE
BOGLES > BOGLE
BOGLING > BOGLE
BOGMAN n body of a person found preserved in a peat bog
BOGMEN > BOGMAN
BOGOAK n oak or other wood found preserved in peat bogs; bogwood
BOGOAKS > BOGOAK
BOGONG n large nocturnal Australian moth
BOGONGS > BOGONG
BOGS > BOG
BOGUS adj not genuine
BOGUSLY > BOGUS
BOGUSNESS > BOGUS
BOGWOOD same as > BOGOAK
BOGWOODS > BOGWOOD
BOGY same as > BOGEY
BOGYISM same as > BOGEYISM
BOGYISMS > BOGYISM
BOGYMAN same as > BOGEYMAN
BOGYMEN > BOGYMAN
BOH same as > BO
BOHEA n black Chinese tea, once regarded as the choicest, but now as an inferior grade
BOHEAS > BOHEA
BOHEMIA n area frequented by unconventional (esp creative) people
BOHEMIAN adj unconventional in lifestyle or appearance ▷ n person, esp an artist or writer, who lives an unconventional life
BOHEMIANS > BOHEMIAN
BOHEMIAS > BOHEMIA
BOHO short for > BOHEMIAN
BOHOS > BOHO
BOHRIUM n element artificially produced in minute quantities
BOHRIUMS > BOHRIUM
BOHS > BOH
BOHUNK n derogatory name for a labourer from east or central Europe
BOHUNKS > BOHUNK
BOI n lesbian who dresses like a boy
BOIL vb (cause to) change from a liquid to a vapour so quickly that bubbles are formed ▷ n state or action of boiling
BOILABLE > BOIL
BOILED > BOIL
BOILER n piece of equipment which provides hot water
BOILERIES > BOILERY
BOILERS > BOILER

BOILERY n place where water is boiled to extract salt

BOILING adj very hot ▷ n sweet

BOILINGLY > BOILING

BOILINGS > BOILING

BOILOFF n quantity of liquified gases lost in evaporation

BOILOFFS > BOILOFF

BOILOVER n surprising result in a sporting event, esp in a horse race

BOILOVERS > BOILOVER

BOILS > BOIL

BOING vb rebound making a noise

BOINGED > BOING

BOINGING > BOING

BOINGS > BOING

BOINK same as > BOING

BOINKED > BOINK

BOINKING > BOINK

BOINKS > BOINK

BOIS > BOI

BOISERIE n finely crafted wood-carving

BOISERIES > BOISERIE

BOITE n artist's portfolio

BOITES > BOITE

BOK n S African antelope

BOKE vb retch or vomit ▷ n retch

BOKED > BOKE

BOKES > BOKE

BOKING > BOKE

BOKO slang word for > NOSE

BOKOS > BOKO

BOKS > BOK

BOLA n missile used by gauchos and Indians of South America, consisting of two or more heavy balls on a cord. It is hurled at a running quarry, such as an ox or rhea, so as to entangle its legs

BOLAR adj relating to clay

BOLAS same as > BOLA

BOLASES > BOLAS

BOLD adj confident and fearless ▷ n boldface

BOLDEN vb make bold

BOLDENED > BOLDEN

BOLDENING > BOLDEN

BOLDENS > BOLDEN

BOLDER > BOLD

BOLDEST > BOLD

BOLDFACE n weight of type characterized by thick heavy lines ▷ vb print in boldface

BOLDFACED > BOLDFACE

BOLDFACES > BOLDFACE

BOLDLY > BOLD

BOLDNESS > BOLD

BOLDS > BOLD

BOLE n tree trunk

BOLECTION n stepped moulding covering and projecting beyond the joint between two members having surfaces at different levels

BOLERO n (music for) traditional Spanish dance

BOLEROS > BOLERO

BOLES > BOLE

BOLETE n type of fungus

BOLETES > BOLETE

BOLETI > BOLETUS

BOLETUS n type of fungus, often edible, with a brownish umbrella-shaped cap

BOLETUSES > BOLETUS

BOLIDE n large exceptionally bright meteor that often explodes

BOLIDES > BOLIDE

BOLINE n (in Wicca) a knife, usually sickle-shaped and with a white handle, used for gathering herbs and carving symbols

BOLINES > BOLINE

BOLIVAR n standard monetary unit of Venezuela, equal to 100 céntimos

BOLIVARES > BOLIVAR

BOLIVARS > BOLIVAR

BOLIVIA n type of woollen fabric

BOLIVIANO n (until 1963 and from 1987) the standard monetary unit of Bolivia, equal to 100 centavos

BOLIVIAS > BOLIVIA

BOLIX same as > BOLLOCKS

BOLIXED > BOLIX

BOLIXES > BOLIX

BOLIXING > BOLIX

BOLL n rounded seed capsule of cotton, flax, etc ▷ vb form into a boll

BOLLARD n short thick post used to prevent the passage of motor vehicles

BOLLARDS > BOLLARD

BOLLED > BOLL

BOLLEN > BOLL

BOLLETRIE n type of W Indian tree

BOLLING > BOLL

BOLLIX same as > BOLLOCKS

BOLLIXED > BOLLIX

BOLLIXES > BOLLIX

BOLLIXING > BOLLIX

BOLLOCK vb rebuke severely

BOLLOCKED > BOLLOCK

BOLLOCKS npl testicles ▷ interj exclamation of annoyance, disbelief, etc ▷ vb rebuke severely

BOLLOX same as > BOLLOCKS

BOLLOXED > BOLLOX

BOLLOXES > BOLLOX

BOLLOXING > BOLLOX

BOLLS > BOLL

BOLLWORM n any of various moth caterpillars that feed on and destroy cotton bolls

BOLLWORMS > BOLLWORM

BOLO n large single-edged knife, originating in the Philippines

BOLOGNA n type of sausage

BOLOGNAS > BOLOGNA

BOLOGNESE n Italian meat and tomato sauce

BOLOGRAPH n record made by a bolometer

BOLOMETER n sensitive instrument for measuring radiant energy by the increase in the resistance of an electrical conductor

BOLOMETRY > BOLOMETER

BOLONEY a variant spelling of > BALONEY

BOLONEYS > BOLONEY

BOLOS > BOLO

BOLSHEVIK n any political radical

BOLSHIE adj difficult or rebellious ▷ n any political radical

BOLSHIER > BOLSHIE

BOLSHIES > BOLSHY

BOLSHIEST > BOLSHIE

BOLSHY same as > BOLSHIE

BOLSON n desert valley surrounded by mountains, with a shallow lake at the centre

BOLSONS > BOLSON

BOLSTER vb support or strengthen ▷ n long narrow pillow

BOLSTERED > BOLSTER

BOLSTERER > BOLSTER

BOLSTERS > BOLSTER

BOLT n sliding metal bar for fastening a door etc ▷ vb run away suddenly

BOLTED > BOLT

BOLTER > BOLT

BOLTERS > BOLT

BOLTHEAD n glass receptacle used in chemistry

BOLTHEADS > BOLTHEAD

BOLTHOLE n place of escape from danger

BOLTHOLES > BOLTHOLE

BOLTING > BOLT

BOLTINGS > BOLT

BOLTLESS > BOLT

BOLTLIKE > BOLT

BOLTONIA n N American plant with daisy-like flowers with white, violet, or pinkish rays

BOLTONIAS > BOLTONIA

BOLTROPE n rope sewn to the foot or luff of a sail to strengthen it

BOLTROPES > BOLTROPE

BOLTS > BOLT

BOLUS same as > BOLE

BOLUSES > BOLUS

BOMA n enclosure, esp a palisade or fence of thorn bush, set up to protect a camp, herd of animals, etc

BOMAS > BOMA

BOMB n container fitted with explosive material ▷ vb attack with bombs

BOMBABLE > BOMB

BOMBARD vb attack with heavy gunfire or bombs ▷ n ancient type of cannon that threw stone balls

BOMBARDE n alto wind instrument similar to the oboe or medieval shawm, used mainly in Breton traditional music

BOMBARDED > BOMBARD

BOMBARDER > BOMBARD

BOMBARDES > BOMBARDE

BOMBARDON n brass instrument of the tuba type, similar to a sousaphone

BOMBARDS > BOMBARD

BOMBASINE same as > BOMBAZINE

BOMBAST n pompous language ▷ vb speak pompous language

BOMBASTED > BOMBAST

BOMBASTER > BOMBAST

BOMBASTIC > BOMBAST

BOMBASTS > BOMBAST

BOMBAX n type of S American tree

BOMBAXES > BOMBAX

BOMBAZINE n twill fabric, usually of silk and worsted, formerly worn dyed black for mourning

BOMBE n dessert of ice cream lined or filled with custard, cake crumbs, etc ▷ adj (of furniture) having a projecting swollen shape

BOMBED > BOMB

BOMBER n aircraft that drops bombs

BOMBERS > BOMBER

BOMBES > BOMBE

BOMBESIN n hormone found in brain

BOMBESINS > BOMBESIN

BOMBILATE same as > BOMBINATE

BOMBINATE vb make a buzzing noise

BOMBING > BOMB

BOMBINGS > BOMB

BOMBLET n small bomb

BOMBLETS > BOMBLET

BOMBLOAD n quantity of bombs carried at one time

BOMBLOADS > BOMBLOAD

BOMBO n inferior wine

BOMBORA n submerged reef

BOMBORAS > BOMBORA

BOMBOS > BOMBO

BOMBPROOF adj able to withstand the impact of a bomb

BOMBS > BOMB

BOMBSHELL n shocking or unwelcome surprise

BOMBSIGHT n mechanical or electronic device in an aircraft for aiming bombs

BOMBSITE n area where

b

the buildings have been destroyed by bombs

BOMBSITES > BOMBSITE

BOMBYCID n type of moth of the family which includes the silkworm moth, found mostly in Africa and SE Asia

BOMBYCIDS > BOMBYCID

BOMBYCOID adj of or like bombycids

BOMBYX n type of moth

BOMBYXES > BOMBYX

BOMMIE n outcrop of coral reef

BOMMIES > BOMMIE

BON adj good

BONA n goods

BONACI n type of fish

BONACIS > BONACI

BONAMANI > BONAMANO

BONAMANO n gratuity

BONAMIA n parasite

BONAMIAS > BONAMIA

BONANZA n sudden good luck or wealth

BONANZAS > BONANZA

BONASSUS same as > BONASUS

BONASUS n European bison

BONASUSES > BONASUS

BONBON n sweet

BONBONS > BONBON

BONCE n head

BONCES > BONCE

BOND n something that binds, fastens or holds together ▷ vb bind

BONDABLE > BOND

BONDAGE n slavery

BONDAGER > BONDAGE

BONDAGERS > BONDAGE

BONDAGES > BONDAGE

BONDED adj consisting of, secured by, or operating under a bond or bonds

BONDER same as > BONDSTONE

BONDERS > BONDER

BONDING n process by which individuals become emotionally attached to one another

BONDINGS > BONDING

BONDLESS > BOND

BONDMAID n unmarried female serf or slave

BONDMAIDS > BONDMAID

BONDMAN same as > BONDSMAN

BONDMEN > BONDMAN

BONDS > BOND

BONDSMAN n person bound by bond to act as surety for another

BONDSMEN > BONDSMAN

BONDSTONE n long stone or brick laid in a wall as a header

BONDUC n type of North American tree

BONDUCS > BONDUC

BONDWOMAN n female slave

BONDWOMEN > BONDWOMAN

BONE n any of the hard parts in the body that form the skeleton ▷ vb remove the bones from (meat for cooking etc)

BONEBLACK n black residue from the destructive distillation of bones, containing about 10 per cent carbon and 80 per cent calcium phosphate, used as a decolorizing agent and pigment

BONED > BONE

BONEFISH n type of silvery marine game fish occurring in warm shallow waters

BONEHEAD n stupid or obstinate person

BONEHEADS > BONEHEAD

BONELESS > BONE

BONEMEAL n product of dried and ground animal bones, used as a fertilizer or in stock feeds

BONEMEALS > BONEMEAL

BONER n blunder

BONERS > BONER

BONES > BONE

BONESET n N American plant with flat clusters of small white flowers

BONESETS > BONESET

BONETIRED adj completely exhausted

BONEY same as > BONY

BONEYARD an informal name for a > CEMETERY

BONEYARDS > BONEYARD

BONEYER > BONEY

BONEYEST > BONEY

BONFIRE n large outdoor fire

BONFIRES > BONFIRE

BONG n deep reverberating sound, as of a large bell ▷ vb make a deep reverberating sound

BONGED > BONG

BONGING > BONG

BONGO n small drum played with the fingers

BONGOES > BONGO

BONGOIST n bongo player

BONGOISTS > BONGOIST

BONGOS > BONGO

BONGRACE n shade for face

BONGRACES > BONGRACE

BONGS > BONG

BONHAM n piglet

BONHAMS > BONHAM

BONHOMIE n cheerful friendliness

BONHOMIES > BONHOMIE

BONHOMMIE same as > BONHOMIE

BONHOMOUS adj exhibiting bonhomie

BONIATO n sweet potato

BONIATOS > BONIATO

BONIBELL same as > BONNIBELL

BONIBELLS > BONIBELL

BONIE same as > BONNY

BONIER > BONY

BONIEST > BONY

BONIFACE n pub landlord

BONIFACES > BONIFACE

BONILASSE n an attractive young woman

BONINESS > BONY

BONING > BONE

BONINGS > BONE

BONISM n doctrine that the world is good, although not the best of all possible worlds

BONISMS > BONISM

BONIST > BONISM

BONISTS > BONISM

BONITA slang term for > HEROIN

BONITAS > BONITA

BONITO n small tunny-like marine food fish

BONITOES > BONITO

BONITOS > BONITO

BONJOUR interj hello

BONK vb have sex with

BONKED > BONK

BONKERS adj crazy

BONKING > BONK

BONKINGS > BONK

BONKS > BONK

BONNE n housemaid or female servant

BONNES > BONNE

BONNET n metal cover over a vehicle's engine ▷ vb place a bonnet on

BONNETED > BONNET

BONNETING > BONNET

BONNETS > BONNET

BONNIBELL n beautiful girl

BONNIE same as > BONNY

BONNIER > BONNY

BONNIES > BONNY

BONNIEST > BONNY

BONNILY > BONNY

BONNINESS > BONNY

BONNOCK n thick oatmeal cake

BONNOCKS > BONNOCK

BONNY adj beautiful ▷ adv agreeably or well

BONOBO n type of anthropoid ape of central W Africa

BONOBOS > BONOBO

BONSAI n ornamental miniature tree or shrub

BONSELA n small gift of money

BONSELAS > BONSELA

BONSELLA same as > BONSELA

BONSELLAS > BONSELLA

BONSOIR interj good evening

BONSPELL same as > BONSPIEL

BONSPELLS > BONSPIEL

BONSPIEL n curling match

BONSPIELS > BONSPIEL

BONTEBOK n S African antelope with a deep reddish-brown coat with a white blaze, tail, and rump patch

BONTEBOKS > BONTEBOK

BONUS n something given, paid, or received above what is due or expected

BONUSES > BONUS

BONXIE n great skua

BONXIES > BONXIE

BONY adj having many bones

BONZA same as > BONZER

BONZE n Chinese or Japanese Buddhist priest or monk

BONZER adj excellent

BONZES > BONZE

BOO interj shout of disapproval ▷ vb shout 'boo' to show disapproval

BOOAI same as > BOOHAI

BOOAIS > BOOAI

BOOAY same as > BOOHAI

BOOAYS > BOOAY

BOOB n foolish mistake ▷ vb make a foolish mistake ▷ adj of poor quality, similar to that provided in prison

BOOBED > BOOB

BOOBHEAD n repeat offender in a prison

BOOBHEADS > BOOBHEAD

BOOBIALLA n type of tree or shrub

BOOBIE same as > BOOBY

BOOBIES > BOOBY

BOOBING > BOOB

BOOBIRD n person who boos

BOOBIRDS > BOOBIRD

BOOBISH > BOOB

BOOBOISIE n group of people considered as (stupid

BOOBOO n blunder

BOOBOOK n small spotted Australian brown owl

BOOBOOKS > BOOBOOK

BOOBOOS > BOOBOO

BOOBS > BOOB

BOOBY n foolish person

BOOBYISH > BOOBY

BOOBYISM > BOOBY

BOOBYISMS > BOOBY

BOOCOO same as > BEAUCOUP

BOOCOOS > BOOCOO

BOODIE n type of kangaroo

BOODIED > BOODY

BOODIES > BOODY

BOODLE n money or valuables, esp when stolen, counterfeit, or used as a bribe ▷ vb give or receive money corruptly or illegally

BOODLED > BOODLE

BOODLER > BOODLE

BOODLERS > BOODLE

BOODLES > BOODLE

BOODLING > BOODLE

BOODY vb sulk

BOODYING > BOODY

BOOED > BOO

b

BOOFHEAD n stupid person
BOOFHEADS > BOOFHEAD
BOOFIER > BOOFY
BOOFIEST > BOOFY
BOOFY adj muscular and strong but stupid
BOOGALOO n type of dance performed to rock and roll music ▷ vb dance a boogaloo
BOOGALOOS > BOOGALOO
BOOGER n dried mucous from the nose
BOOGERMAN American form of > BOGEYMAN
BOOGERMEN > BOOGERMAN
BOOGERS > BOOGER
BOOGEY same as > BOOGIE
BOOGEYED > BOOGEY
BOOGEYING > BOOGEY
BOOGEYMAN same as > BOGEYMAN
BOOGEYMEN > BOGEYMAN
BOOGEYS > BOOGEY
BOOGIE vb dance to fast pop music ▷ n session of dancing to pop music
BOOGIED > BOOGIE
BOOGIEING > BOOGIE
BOOGIEMAN same as > BOGEYMAN
BOOGIEMEN > BOOGIEMAN
BOOGIES > BOOGIE
BOOGY same as > BOOGIE
BOOGYING > BOOGY
BOOGYMAN same as > BOGEYMAN
BOOGYMEN > BOOGYMAN
BOOH same as > BOO
BOOHAI as in up the boohai thoroughly lost
BOOHAIS > BOOHAI
BOOHED > BOOH
BOOHING > BOOH
BOOHOO vb sob or pretend to sob noisily ▷ n distressed or pretended sobbing
BOOHOOED > BOOHOO
BOOHOOING > BOOHOO
BOOHOOS > BOOHOO
BOOHS > BOOH
BOOING > BOO
BOOJUM n American tree
BOOJUMS > BOOJUM
BOOK n number of pages bound together between covers ▷ vb reserve (a place, passage, etc) in advance
BOOKABLE > BOOK
BOOKCASE n piece of furniture containing shelves for books
BOOKCASES > BOOKCASE
BOOKED > BOOK
BOOKEND n one of a pair of usually ornamental supports for holding a row of books upright
BOOKENDS > BOOKEND
BOOKER > BOOK

BOOKERS > BOOK
BOOKFUL > BOOK
BOOKFULS > BOOK
BOOKIE short for > BOOKMAKER
BOOKIER > BOOKY
BOOKIES > BOOKIE
BOOKIEST > BOOKY
BOOKING n reservation, as of a table or seat
BOOKINGS > BOOKING
BOOKISH adj fond of reading
BOOKISHLY > BOOKISH
BOOKLAND n common land given to private owner
BOOKLANDS > BOOKLAND
BOOKLESS > BOOK
BOOKLET n thin book with paper covers
BOOKLETS > BOOKLET
BOOKLICE > BOOKLOUSE
BOOKLIGHT n small light that can be clipped onto a book for reading by
BOOKLORE n knowledge or beliefs gleaned from books
BOOKLORES > BOOKLORE
BOOKLOUSE n wingless insect that feeds on bookbinding paste, etc
BOOKMAKER n person whose occupation is taking bets
BOOKMAN n learned person
BOOKMARK n person whose occupation is taking bets ▷ vb identify and store (a website) so that one can return to it quickly and easily
BOOKMARKS > BOOKMARK
BOOKMEN > BOOKMAN
BOOKOO same as > BOOCOO
BOOKOOS > BOOKOO
BOOKPLATE n label bearing the owner's name and an individual design or coat of arms, pasted into a book
BOOKRACK n rack for holding books
BOOKRACKS > BOOKRACK
BOOKREST n stand for supporting open book
BOOKRESTS > BOOKREST
BOOKS > BOOK
BOOKSHELF n shelf for books
BOOKSHOP n shop where books are sold
BOOKSHOPS > BOOKSHOP
BOOKSIE same as > BOOKSY
BOOKSIER > BOOKSY
BOOKSIEST > BOOKSY
BOOKSTALL n stall or stand where periodicals, newspapers, or books are sold
BOOKSTAND n support for open book
BOOKSTORE same as > BOOKSHOP
BOOKSY adj inclined to be

bookish or literary
BOOKWORK n academic study
BOOKWORKS > BOOKWORK
BOOKWORM n person devoted to reading
BOOKWORMS > BOOKWORM
BOOKY adj bookish
BOOL n bowling bowl ▷ vb play bowls
BOOLED > BOOL
BOOLING > BOOL
BOOLS > BOOL
BOOM vb make a loud deep echoing sound ▷ n loud deep echoing sound
BOOMBOX n portable stereo system
BOOMBOXES > BOOMBOX
BOOMED > BOOM
BOOMER n large male kangaroo
BOOMERANG n curved wooden missile which can be made to return to the thrower ▷ vb (of a plan) recoil unexpectedly
BOOMERS > BOOMER
BOOMIER > BOOMY
BOOMIEST > BOOMY
BOOMING > BOOM
BOOMINGLY > BOOM
BOOMINGS > BOOM
BOOMKIN n short boom projecting from the deck of a ship, used to secure the main-brace blocks or to extend the lower edge of the foresail
BOOMKINS > BOOMKIN
BOOMLET n small boom in business, birth rate, etc
BOOMLETS > BOOMLET
BOOMS > BOOM
BOOMSLANG n large greenish venomous tree-living snake of southern Africa
BOOMTOWN n town that is enjoying sudden prosperity or has grown rapidly
BOOMTOWNS > BOOMTOWN
BOOMY adj characterized by heavy bass sound
BOON n something extremely useful, helpful, or beneficial
BOONDOCK > BOONDOCKS
BOONDOCKS n remote rural area
BOONER n young working-class person from Canberra
BOONERS > BOONER
BOONG n offensive term for a Black person
BOONGA n offensive term for a Pacific Islander
BOONGARY n tree kangaroo of NE Queensland, Australia
BOONGAS > BOONGA
BOONGS > BOONG
BOONIES short form of > BOONDOCKS

BOONLESS > BOON
BOONS > BOON
BOOR n rude or insensitive person
BOORD obsolete spelling of > BOARD
BOORDE obsolete spelling of > BOARD
BOORDES > BOORDE
BOORDS > BOORD
BOORISH adj ill-mannered, clumsy, or insensitive
BOORISHLY > BOORISH
BOORKA same as > BURKA
BOORKAS > BOORKA
BOORS > BOOR
BOORTREE same as > BOURTREE
BOORTREES > BOORTREE
BOOS > BOO
BOOSE same as > BOOZE
BOOSED > BOOSE
BOOSES > BOOSE
BOOSHIT adj very good
BOOSING > BOOSE
BOOST n encouragement or help ▷ vb improve
BOOSTED > BOOST
BOOSTER n small additional injection of a vaccine
BOOSTERS > BOOSTER
BOOSTING > BOOST
BOOSTS > BOOST
BOOT n outer covering for the foot that extends above the ankle ▷ vb kick
BOOTABLE > BOOT
BOOTBLACK another word for > SHOEBLACK
BOOTCUT adj (of trousers) slightly flared at the bottom of the legs to fit over boots
BOOTED adj wearing boots
BOOTEE n baby's soft shoe
BOOTEES > BOOTEE
BOOTERIES > BOOTERY
BOOTERY n shop where boots and shoes are sold
BOOTH n small partly enclosed cubicle
BOOTHOSE n stocking worn with boots
BOOTHS > BOOTH
BOOTIE n Royal Marine
BOOTIES > BOOTY
BOOTIKIN n small boot
BOOTIKINS > BOOTIKIN
BOOTING > BOOT
BOOTJACK n device that grips the heel of a boot to enable the foot to be withdrawn easily
BOOTJACKS > BOOTJACK
BOOTLACE n strong lace for fastening a boot
BOOTLACES > BOOTLACE
BOOTLAST n foot shape placed in boots or shoes to keep their shape
BOOTLASTS > BOOTLAST
BOOTLEG adj produced, distributed, or sold illicitly

b

▷*vb* make, carry, or sell (illicit goods) ▷ *n* something made or sold illicitly, such as alcohol during Prohibition in the US
BOOTLEGS > BOOTLEG
BOOTLESS *adj* of little or no use
BOOTLICK *vb* seek favour by servile or ingratiating behaviour towards (someone, esp someone in authority)
BOOTLICKS > BOOTLICK
BOOTMAKER *n* person who makes boots and shoes
BOOTS > BOOT
BOOTSTRAP *n* leather or fabric loop on the back or side of a boot
BOOTY *n* valuable articles obtained as plunder
BOOZE *n* (consume) alcoholic drink ▷ *vb* drink alcohol, esp in excess
BOOZED > BOOZE
BOOZER *n* person who is fond of drinking
BOOZERS > BOOZER
BOOZES > BOOZE
BOOZEY *same as* > BOOZY
BOOZIER > BOOZY
BOOZIEST > BOOZY
BOOZILY > BOOZY
BOOZINESS > BOOZY
BOOZING > BOOZE
BOOZINGS > BOOZE
BOOZY *adj* inclined to or involving excessive drinking of alcohol
BOP *vb* dance to pop music ▷ *n* form of jazz with complex rhythms and harmonies
BOPEEP *n* quick look; peek
BOPEEPS > BOPEEP
BOPPED > BOP
BOPPER > BOP
BOPPERS > BOP
BOPPING > BOP
BOPS > BOP
BOR *n* neighbour
BORA *n* Aboriginal ceremony
BORACES > BORAX
BORACHIO *n* pig's skin wine carrier
BORACHIOS > BORACHIO
BORACIC *same as* > BORIC
BORACITE *n* white mineral that forms salt deposits of magnesium borate
BORACITES > BORACITE
BORAGE *n* Mediterranean plant with star-shaped blue flowers
BORAGES > BORAGE
BORAK *n* rubbish
BORAKS > BORAK
BORAL *n* type of fine powder
BORALS > BORAL
BORANE *n* any compound of boron and hydrogen, used in the synthesis of

other boron compounds and as high-energy fuels
BORANES > BORANE
BORAS > BORA
BORATE *n* salt or ester of boric acid. Salts of boric acid consist of BO$_3$ and BO$_4$ units linked together ▷ *vb* treat with borax, boric acid, or borate
BORATED > BORATE
BORATES > BORATE
BORATING > BORATE
BORAX *n* soluble white mineral occurring in alkaline soils and salt deposits
BORAXES > BORAX
BORAZON *n* extremely hard form of boron nitride
BORAZONS > BORAZON
BORD *obsolete spelling of* > BOARD
BORDAR *n* smallholder who held cottage in return for menial work
BORDARS > BORDAR
BORDE *obsolete spelling of* > BOARD
BORDEAUX *adj* any of several wines produced around Bordeaux
BORDEL *same as* > BORDELLO
BORDELLO *n* brothel
BORDELLOS > BORDELLO
BORDELS > BORDEL
BORDER *n* dividing line between political or geographical regions ▷ *vb* provide with a border
BORDEREAU *n* memorandum or invoice prepared for a company by an underwriter, containing a list of reinsured risks
BORDERED > BORDER
BORDERER *n* person who lives in a border area, esp the border between England and Scotland
BORDERERS > BORDERER
BORDERING > BORDER
BORDERS > BORDER
BORDES > BORDE
BORDS > BORD
BORDURE *n* outer edge of a shield, esp when decorated distinctively
BORDURES > BORDURE
BORE *vb* make (someone) weary by being dull
BOREAL *adj* of or relating to the north or the north wind
BOREALIS *as in aurora borealis* lights seen around the North Pole
BOREAS *n* name for the north wind
BOREASES > BOREAS
BORECOLE *another name for* > KALE
BORECOLES > BORECOLE
BORED > BORE
BOREDOM *n* state of being bored

BOREDOMS > BOREDOM
BOREE *same as* > MYALL
BOREEN *n* country lane or narrow road
BOREENS > BOREEN
BOREES > BOREE
BOREHOLE *n* hole driven into the ground to obtain geological information, release water, etc
BOREHOLES > BOREHOLE
BOREL *adj* unlearned
BORER *n* machine or hand tool for boring holes
BORERS > BORER
BORES > BEAR
BORESCOPE *n* long narrow device for inspection of, e.g. bore
BORESOME *adj* boring
BORGHETTO *n* settlement outside city walls
BORGO *n* small attractive medieval village
BORGOS > BORGO
BORIC *adj* of or containing boron
BORIDE *n* compound in which boron is the most electronegative element, esp a compound of boron and a metal
BORIDES > BORIDE
BORING *n* act or process of making or enlarging a hole ▷ *adj* dull
BORINGLY > BORING
BORINGS > BORING
BORK *vb* dismiss from job unfairly
BORKED > BORK
BORKING > BORK
BORKS > BORK
BORLOTTI *as in borlotti bean* variety of kidney bean
BORM *vb* smear with paint, oil, etc
BORMED > BORM
BORMING > BORM
BORMS > BORM
BORN *adj* possessing certain qualities from birth
BORNA *as in borna disease* viral disease found in mammals, esp horses
BORNE > BEAR
BORNEOL *n* white solid terpene alcohol
BORNEOLS > BORNEOL
BORNITE *n* mineral consisting of a sulphide of copper and iron that tarnishes to purple
BORNITES > BORNITE
BORNITIC > BORNITE
BORNYL *as in bornyl alcohol* white solid alcohol from a Malaysian tree
BORNYLS > BORNYL
BORON *n* element used in hardening steel
BORONIA *n* Australian aromatic flowering shrub
BORONIAS > BORONIA
BORONIC > BORON

BORONS > BORON
BOROUGH *n* town or district with its own council
BOROUGHS > BOROUGH
BORREL *adj* ignorant
BORRELIA *n* type of bacterium
BORRELIAS > BORRELIA
BORRELL *same as* > BORREL
BORROW *vb* obtain (something) temporarily
BORROWED > BORROW
BORROWER > BORROW
BORROWERS > BORROW
BORROWING > BORROW
BORROWS > BORROW
BORS > BORS
BORSCH *same as* > BORSCHT
BORSCHES > BORSCH
BORSCHT *n* Russian soup based on beetroot
BORSCHTS > BORSCHT
BORSHCH *same as* > BORSCHT
BORSHCHES > BORSHCH
BORSHT *same as* > BORSCHT
BORSHTS > BORSHT
BORSIC *n* strong light composite material of boron fibre and silicon carbide used in aviation
BORSICS > BORSIC
BORSTAL *n* (formerly in Britain) prison for young criminals
BORSTALL *same as* > BORSTAL
BORSTALLS > BORSTALL
BORSTALS > BORSTAL
BORT *n* inferior grade of diamond used for cutting and drilling or, in powdered form, as an industrial abrasive
BORTIER > BORT
BORTIEST > BORT
BORTS > BORT
BORTSCH *same as* > BORSCHT
BORTSCHES > BORTSCH
BORTY > BORT
BORTZ *same as* > BORT
BORTZES > BORTZ
BORZOI *n* tall dog with a long silky coat
BORZOIS > BORZOI
BOS > BO
BOSBERAAD *n* meeting in an isolated venue to break a political deadlock
BOSBOK *same as* > BUSHBUCK
BOSBOKS > BOSBOK
BOSCAGE *n* mass of trees and shrubs
BOSCAGES > BOSCAGE
BOSCHBOK *same as* > BUSHBUCK
BOSCHBOKS > BOSCHBOK
BOSCHE *same as* > BOCHE
BOSCHES > BOSCHE

BOSCHVARK same as > BUSHPIG

BOSCHVELD same as > BUSHVELD

BOSH n empty talk, nonsense

BOSHBOK same as > BUSHBUCK

BOSHBOKS > BOSHBOK

BOSHES > BOSH

BOSHTA same as > BOSHTER

BOSHTER adj excellent

BOSHVARK same as > BOSCHVARK

BOSHVARKS > BOSHVARK

BOSIE n (in cricket) another term for googly

BOSIES > BOSIE

BOSK n small wood of bushes and small trees

BOSKAGE same as > BOSCAGE

BOSKAGES > BOSKAGE

BOSKER adj excellent

BOSKET n clump of small trees or bushes

BOSKETS > BOSKET

BOSKIER > BOSKY

BOSKIEST > BOSKY

BOSKINESS > BOSKY

BOSKS > BOSK

BOSKY adj containing or consisting of bushes or thickets

BOSOM n chest of a person, esp the female breasts ▷ adj very dear ▷ vb embrace

BOSOMED > BOSOM

BOSOMIER > BOSOMY

BOSOMIEST > BOSOMY

BOSOMING > BOSOM

BOSOMS > BOSOM

BOSOMY adj (of a woman) having large breasts

BOSON n any of a group of elementary particles, such as a photon or pion, that has zero or integral spin and obeys the rules of Bose-Einstein statistics

BOSONIC > BOSON

BOSONS > BOSON

BOSQUE same as > BOSK

BOSQUES > BOSQUE

BOSQUET same as > BOSKET

BOSQUETS > BOSQUET

BOSS n raised knob or stud ▷ vb employ, supervise, or be in charge of ▷ adj excellent

BOSSBOY n Black African foreman of a gang of workers

BOSSBOYS > BOSSBOY

BOSSDOM n bosses collectively

BOSSDOMS > BOSSDOM

BOSSED > BOSS

BOSSER > BOSS

BOSSES > BOSS

BOSSEST > BOSS

BOSSET n either of the rudimentary antlers found in young deer

BOSSETS > BOSSET

BOSSIER > BOSSY

BOSSIES > BOSSY

BOSSIEST > BOSSY

BOSSILY > BOSSY

BOSSINESS > BOSSY

BOSSING n act of shaping malleable metal, such as lead cladding, with mallets to fit a surface

BOSSINGS > BOSSING

BOSSISM n domination or the system of domination of political organizations by bosses

BOSSISMS > BOSSISM

BOSSY same as > BOSS

BOSTANGI n imperial Turkish guard

BOSTANGIS > BOSTANGI

BOSTHOON n boor

BOSTHOONS > BOSTHOON

BOSTON n card game for four, played with two packs

BOSTONS > BOSTON

BOSTRYX n phenomenon in which flowers develop on one side only

BOSTRYXES > BOSTRYX

BOSUN same as > BOATSWAIN

BOSUNS > BOSUN

BOT n larva of a botfly, which typically develops inside the body of a horse, sheep, or man

BOTA n leather container

BOTANIC same as > BOTANICAL

BOTANICA n botany

BOTANICAL adj of or relating to botany or plants ▷ n any drug or pesticide that is made from parts of a plant

BOTANICAS > BOTANICA

BOTANICS > BOTANIC

BOTANIES > BOTANY

BOTANISE same as > BOTANIZE

BOTANISED > BOTANISE

BOTANISER > BOTANIZE

BOTANISES > BOTANISE

BOTANIST > BOTANY

BOTANISTS > BOTANY

BOTANIZE vb collect or study plants

BOTANIZED > BOTANIZE

BOTANIZER > BOTANIZE

BOTANIZES > BOTANIZE

BOTANY n study of plants

BOTARGO n relish consisting of the roe of mullet or tunny, salted and pressed into rolls

BOTARGOES > BOTARGO

BOTARGOS > BOTARGO

BOTAS > BOTA

BOTCH vb spoil through clumsiness ▷ n badly done piece of work or repair

BOTCHED > BOTCH

BOTCHEDLY > BOTCH

BOTCHER > BOTCH

BOTCHERS > BOTCH

BOTCHERY n instance of botching

BOTCHES > BOTCH

BOTCHIER > BOTCHY

BOTCHIEST > BOTCHY

BOTCHILY > BOTCHY

BOTCHING > BOTCH

BOTCHINGS > BOTCH

BOTCHY adj clumsily done or made

BOTE n compensation given for injury or damage to property

BOTEL same as > BOATEL

BOTELS > BOTEL

BOTES > BOTE

BOTFLIES > BOTFLY

BOTFLY n type of stout-bodied hairy fly, the larvae of which are parasites of man, sheep, and horses

BOTH pron two considered together ▷ adj two considered together ▷ det two

BOTHAN n unlicensed drinking house

BOTHANS > BOTHAN

BOTHER vb take the time or trouble ▷ n trouble, fuss, or difficulty ▷ interj exclamation of slight annoyance

BOTHERED > BOTHER

BOTHERING > BOTHER

BOTHERS > BOTHER

BOTHIE same as > BOTHY

BOTHIES > BOTHY

BOTHOLE n hole made by the larva of the botfly

BOTHOLES > BOTHOLE

BOTHRIA > BOTHRIUM

BOTHRIUM n groove-shaped sucker on tapeworm

BOTHRIUMS > BOTHRIUM

BOTHY n hut used for temporary shelter

BOTHYMAN n man who lives in bothy

BOTHYMEN > BOTHYMAN

BOTNET n network of infected computers

BOTNETS > BOTNET

BOTONE adj having lobes at the ends

BOTONEE same as > BOTONE

BOTONNEE same as > BOTONE

BOTRYOID adj shaped like a bunch of grapes

BOTRYOSE same as > BOTRYOID

BOTRYTIS n type of fungus which causes plant diseases

BOTS n digestive disease of horses and some other animals caused by the presence of botfly larvae in the stomach

BOTT same as > BOT

BOTTARGA same as > BOTARGO

BOTTARGAS > BOTTARGA

BOTTE n thrust or hit

BOTTED > BOT

BOTTEGA n workshop; studio

BOTTEGAS > BOTTEGA

BOTTES > BOTTE

BOTTIES > BOTTY

BOTTINE n light boot for women or children

BOTTINES > BOTTINE

BOTTING > BOT

BOTTLE n container for holding liquids ▷ vb put in a bottle

BOTTLED > BOTTLE

BOTTLEFUL same as > BOTTLE

BOTTLER n exceptional person or thing

BOTTLERS > BOTTLER

BOTTLES > BOTTLE

BOTTLING > BOTTLE

BOTTLINGS > BOTTLE

BOTTOM n lowest, deepest, or farthest removed part of a thing ▷ adj lowest or last ▷ vb provide with a bottom

BOTTOMED > BOTTOM

BOTTOMER n pit worker

BOTTOMERS > BOTTOMER

BOTTOMING n lowest level of foundation material for a road or other structure

BOTTOMRY n contract whereby the owner of a ship borrows money to enable the vessel to complete the voyage and pledges the ship as security for the loan

BOTTOMS > BOTTOM

BOTTOMSET as in bottomset bed fine sediment deposited at the front of a growing delta

BOTTONY same as > BOTONE

BOTTS > BOTT

BOTTY n diminutive for bottom

BOTULIN n potent toxin produced by a bacterium in imperfectly preserved food, etc, which causes botulism

BOTULINAL > BOTULIN

BOTULINS > BOTULIN

BOTULINUM n botulin-secreting bacterium

BOTULINUS n type of bacterium whose toxins (botulins) cause botulism

BOTULISM n severe food poisoning

BOTULISMS > BOTULISM

BOUBOU n long flowing garment worn by men and women in Mali, Nigeria, Senegal, and some other parts of Africa

b

b

BOUBOUS > BOUBOU

BOUCHE n notch cut in top corner of shield

BOUCHEE n small pastry case filled with a savoury mixture, served hot with cocktails or as an hors d'oeuvre

BOUCHEES > BOUCHEE

BOUCLE n looped yarn giving a knobbly effect ▷ adj of or designating such a yarn or fabric

BOUCLEE n support for a cue in billiards formed by doubling the first finger so that its tip is aligned with the thumb at its second joint, to form a loop through which the cue may slide

BOUCLEES > BOUCLEE

BOUCLES > BOUCLE

BOUDERIE n sulkiness

BOUDERIES > BOUDERIE

BOUDIN n French version of a black pudding

BOUDINS > BOUDIN

BOUDOIR n woman's bedroom or private sitting room

BOUDOIRS > BOUDOIR

BOUFFANT adj (of a hairstyle) having extra height through backcombing ▷ n bouffant hair style

BOUFFANTS > BOUFFANT

BOUFFE n type of light or satirical opera common in France during the 19th century

BOUFFES > BOUFFE

BOUGE vb move

BOUGED > BOUGE

BOUGES > BOUGE

BOUGET n budget

BOUGETS > BOUGET

BOUGH n large branch of a tree

BOUGHED > BOUGH

BOUGHLESS > BOUGH

BOUGHPOT n container for displaying boughs

BOUGHPOTS > BOUGHPOT

BOUGHS > BOUGH

BOUGHT > BUY

BOUGHTEN a dialect word for > BUY

BOUGHTS > BUY

BOUGIE n long slender semiflexible cylindrical instrument for inserting into body passages, such as the rectum or urethra, to dilate structures, introduce medication, etc

BOUGIES > BOUGIE

BOUGING > BOUGE

BOUILLI n stew

BOUILLIS > BOUILLI

BOUILLON n thin clear broth or stock

BOUILLONS > BOUILLON

BOUK n bulk; volume

BOUKS > BOUK

BOULDER n large rounded rock ▷ vb convert into boulders

BOULDERED > BOULDER

BOULDERER > BOULDER

BOULDERS > BOULDER

BOULDERY > BOULDER

BOULE same as > BOULLE

BOULES n game, popular in France, in which metal bowls are thrown to land as close as possible to a target ball

BOULEVARD n wide, usu. tree-lined, street

BOULLE adj denoting or relating to a type of marquetry of patterned inlays of brass and tortoiseshell, occasionally with other metals such as pewter, much used on French furniture from the 17th century ▷ n something ornamented with such marquetry

BOULLES > BOULLE

BOULT same as > BOLT

BOULTED > BOULT

BOULTER > BOLT

BOULTERS > BOLT

BOULTING > BOULT

BOULTINGS > BOULT

BOULTS > BOULT

BOUN vb prepare to go out

BOUNCE vb (of a ball etc) rebound from an impact ▷ n act of rebounding

BOUNCED > BOUNCE

BOUNCER n person employed at a disco etc to remove unwanted people

BOUNCERS > BOUNCER

BOUNCES > BOUNCE

BOUNCIER > BOUNCY

BOUNCIEST > BOUNCY

BOUNCILY > BOUNCY

BOUNCING adj vigorous and robust

BOUNCY adj lively, exuberant, or self-confident

BOUND > BIND

BOUNDABLE > BIND

BOUNDARY n dividing line that indicates the farthest limit

BOUNDED adj (of a set) having a bound, esp where a measure is defined in terms of which all the elements of the set, or the differences between all pairs of members, are less than some value, or else all its members lie within some other well-defined set

BOUNDEN adj morally obligatory

BOUNDER n morally reprehensible person

BOUNDERS > BOUNDER

BOUNDING > BIND

BOUNDLESS adj unlimited

BOUNDNESS > BIND

BOUNDS npl limit

BOUNED > BOUN

BOUNING > BOUN

BOUNS > BOUN

BOUNTEOUS adj giving freely

BOUNTIED > BOUNTY

BOUNTIES > BOUNTY

BOUNTIFUL adj plentiful

BOUNTREE another name for > BOUNTREE

BOUNTREES > BOUNTREE

BOUNTY n generosity

BOUNTYHED n generosity

BOUQUET n bunch of flowers

BOUQUETS > BOUQUET

BOURASQUE n violent storm

BOURBON n whiskey made from maize

BOURBONS > BOURBON

BOURD n prank

BOURDER n prankster

BOURDERS > BOURDER

BOURDON n 16-foot organ stop of the stopped diapason type

BOURDONS > BOURDON

BOURDS > BOURD

BOURG n French market town, esp one beside a castle

BOURGEOIS n middle-class (person) ▷ adj characteristic of or comprising the middle class

BOURGEON same as > BURGEON

BOURGEONS > BOURGEON

BOURGS > BOURG

BOURKHA same as > BURKA

BOURKHAS > BOURKHA

BOURLAW same as > BYRLAW

BOURLAWS > BOURLAW

BOURN n (in S Britain) stream

BOURNE same as > BOURN

BOURNES > BOURNE

BOURNS > BOURN

BOURREE n traditional French dance in fast duple time

BOURREES > BOURREE

BOURRIDE n Mediterranean fish soup

BOURRIDES > BOURRIDE

BOURSE n stock exchange of continental Europe, esp Paris

BOURSES > BOURSE

BOURSIER n stock-exchange worker

BOURSIERS > BOURSIER

BOURSIN n tradename of a smooth white creamy cheese, often flavoured with garlic

BOURSINS > BOURSIN

BOURTREE n elder tree

BOURTREES > BOURTREE

BOUSE vb raise or haul with a tackle

BOUSED > BOUSE

BOUSES > BOUSE

BOUSIER > BOUSY

BOUSIEST > BOUSY

BOUSING > BOUSE

BOUSOUKI same as > BOUZOUKI

BOUSOUKIA > BOUSOUKI

BOUSOUKIS > BOUSOUKI

BOUSY adj drunken; boozy

BOUT n period of activity or illness

BOUTADE n outburst

BOUTADES > BOUTADE

BOUTIQUE n small clothes shop

BOUTIQUES > BOUTIQUE

BOUTIQUEY adj typical of boutiques

BOUTON n knob-shaped contact between nerve fibres

BOUTONNE adj reserved or inhibited

BOUTONNEE same as > BOUTONNE

BOUTONS > BOUTON

BOUTS > BOUT

BOUVARDIA n flowering plant

BOUVIER n large powerful dog of a Belgian breed, having a rough shaggy coat: used esp for cattle herding and guarding

BOUVIERS > BOUVIER

BOUZOUKI n Greek stringed musical instrument

BOUZOUKIA > BOUZOUKI

BOUZOUKIS > BOUZOUKI

BOVATE n obsolete measure of land

BOVATES > BOVATE

BOVID n type of ruminant, hollow-horned mammal such as sheep, goats, cattle, antelopes, and buffalo

BOVIDS > BOVID

BOVINE n domesticated bovine mammal

BOVINELY > BOVINE

BOVINES > BOVINE

BOVINITY > BOVINE

BOVVER n rowdiness, esp caused by gangs of teenage youths

BOVVERS > BOVVER

BOW vb lower (one's head) or bend (one's knee or body) as a sign of respect or shame ▷ n movement made when bowing

BOWAT n lamp

BOWATS > BOWAT

BOWBENT adj bent; bow-like

BOWED adj lowered, bent forward, or curved

BOWEL n intestine, esp the

large intestine ▷ *vb* remove the bowels

BOWELED > BOWEL

BOWELING > BOWEL

BOWELLED > BOWEL

BOWELLESS > BOWEL

BOWELLING > BOWEL

BOWELS > BOWEL

BOWER *n* shady leafy shelter ▷ *vb* surround as with a bower

BOWERBIRD *n* songbird of Australia and New Guinea, the males of which build bower-like display grounds to attract females

BOWERED > BOWER

BOWERIES > BOWER

BOWERING > BOWER

BOWERS > BOWER

BOWERY > BOWER

BOWES > BOUGH

BOWET *same as* > BOWAT

BOWETS > BOWET

BOWFIN *n* primitive N American freshwater bony fish with an elongated body and a very long dorsal fin

BOWFINS > BOWFIN

BOWFRONT *adj* having a front that curves outwards

BOWGET *obsolete variant of* > BUDGET

BOWGETS > BOWGET

BOWHEAD *n* type of large-mouthed arctic whale

BOWHEADS > BOWHEAD

BOWHUNTER *n* person hunting with bow and arrows

BOWIE as in *bowie knife* type of hunting knife

BOWING *n* technique of using the bow in playing a violin, viola, cello, or related instrument

BOWINGLY > BOWING

BOWINGS > BOWING

BOWKNOT *n* decorative knot usually having two loops and two loose ends

BOWKNOTS > BOWKNOT

BOWL *n* round container with an open top ▷ *vb* roll smoothly along the ground

BOWLDER *same as* > BOULDER

BOWLDERS > BOWLDER

BOWLED > BOWL

BOWLEG *n* a leg curving outwards like a bow between the ankle and the thigh

BOWLEGGED *adj* having legs that curve outwards like a bow

BOWLEGS > BOWLEG

BOWLER *n* player who sends (a ball) towards the batsman

BOWLERS > BOWLER

BOWLESS > BOW

BOWLFUL *same as* > BOWL

BOWLFULS > BOWLFUL

BOWLIKE > BOW

BOWLINE *n* line used to keep the sail taut against the wind

BOWLINES > BOWLINE

BOWLING *n* game in which bowls are rolled at a group of pins

BOWLINGS > BLOW

BOWLLIKE > BOWL

BOWLS *n* game played on a very smooth area of grass in which opponents roll biased wooden bowls as near a small bowl (the jack) as possible

BOWMAN *n* archer

BOWMEN > BOWMAN

BOWNE *same as* > BOUN

BOWNED > BOWNE

BOWNES > BOWNE

BOWNING > BOWNE

BOWPOT *same as* > BOUGHPOT

BOWPOTS > BOWPOT

BOWR *n* muscle

BOWRS > BOWR

BOWS > BOW

BOWSAW *n* saw with a thin blade in a bow-shaped frame

BOWSAWS > BOWSAW

BOWSE *same as* > BOUSE

BOWSED > BOWSE

BOWSER *n* tanker containing fuel for aircraft, military vehicles, etc

BOWSERS > BOWSER

BOWSES > BOWSE

BOWSEY *same as* > BOWSIE

BOWSEYS > BOWSEY

BOWSHOT *n* distance an arrow travels from the bow

BOWSHOTS > BOWSHOT

BOWSIE *n* low-class, mean or obstreperous person

BOWSIES > BOWSIE

BOWSING > BOWSE

BOWSPRIT *n* spar projecting from the bow of a sailing ship

BOWSPRITS > BOWSPRIT

BOWSTRING *n* string of an archer's bow

BOWSTRUNG > BOWSTRING

BOWWOW *n* imitation of the bark of a dog ▷ *vb* make a noise like a dog

BOWWOWED > BOWWOW

BOWWOWING > BOWWOW

BOWWOWS > BOWWOW

BOWYANG *n* band worn round trouser leg below knee

BOWYANGS > BOWYANG

BOWYER *n* person who makes or sells archery bows

BOWYERS > BOWYER

BOX *n* container with a firm flat base and sides ▷ *vb* put into a box

BOXBALL *n* street ball game

BOXBALLS > BOXBALL

BOXBERRY *n* fruit of the partridgeberry or wintergreen

BOXBOARD *n* tough paperboard made from wood and wastepaper pulp: used for making boxes, etc

BOXBOARDS > BOXBOARD

BOXCAR *n* closed railway freight van

BOXCARS > BOXCAR

BOXED > BOX

BOXEN > BOX

BOXER *n* person who participates in the sport of boxing

BOXERCISE *n* system of sustained exercises combining boxing movements with aerobic activities

BOXERS > BOXER

BOXES > BOX

BOXFISH *another name for* > TRUNKFISH

BOXFISHES > BOXFISH

BOXFUL *same as* > BOX

BOXFULS > BOX

BOXHAUL *vb* bring (a square-rigger) onto a new tack by backwinding the foresails and steering hard round

BOXHAULED > BOXHAUL

BOXHAULS > BOXHAUL

BOXIER > BOXY

BOXIEST > BOXY

BOXILY > BOXY

BOXINESS > BOXY

BOXING *n* sport of fighting with the fists

BOXINGS > BOXING

BOXKEEPER *n* person responsible for theatre boxes

BOXLIKE > BOX

BOXPLOT *n* (in statistics) type of graph

BOXPLOTS > BOXPLOT

BOXROOM *n* small room in which boxes, cases, etc may be stored

BOXROOMS > BOXROOM

BOXTHORN *n* matrimony vine

BOXTHORNS > BOXTHORN

BOXTIES *n* Irish potato cake

BOXTY *n* type of Irish potato pancake

BOXWALLAH *n* salesman

BOXWOOD *n* hard yellow wood of the box tree, used to make tool handles, etc

BOXWOODS > BOXWOOD

BOXY *adj* squarish or chunky

BOY *n* male child ▷ *vb* act the part of a boy in a play

BOYAR *n* member of an old order of Russian nobility, ranking immediately below the princes: abolished by Peter the Great

BOYARD *same as* > BOYAR

BOYARDS > BOYARD

BOYARISM > BOYAR

BOYARISMS > BOYAR

BOYARS > BOYAR

BOYAU *n* connecting trench

BOYAUX > BOYAU

BOYCHICK *same as* > BOYCHIK

BOYCHICKS > BOYCHICK

BOYCHIK *n* young boy

BOYCHIKS > BOYCHIK

BOYCOTT *vb* refuse to deal with (an organization or country) ▷ *n* instance of boycotting

BOYCOTTED > BOYCOTT

BOYCOTTER > BOYCOTT

BOYCOTTS > BOYCOTT

BOYED > BOY

BOYF *n* boyfriend

BOYFRIEND *n* male friend with whom a person is romantically or sexually involved

BOYFS > BOYF

BOYG *n* troll-like mythical creature

BOYGS > BOYG

BOYHOOD *n* state or time of being a boy

BOYHOODS > BOYHOOD

BOYING > BOY

BOYISH *adj* of or like a boy in looks, behaviour, or character, esp when regarded as attractive or endearing

BOYISHLY > BOYISH

BOYKIE *n* chap or fellow

BOYKIES > BOYKIE

BOYLA *n* Australian Aboriginal word for magician

BOYLAS > BOYLA

BOYO *n* boy or young man: often used in direct address

BOYOS > BOYO

BOYS > BOY

BOYSHORTS *npl* women's underpants resembling close-fitting shorts

BOYSIER > BOYSY

BOYSIEST > BOYSY

BOYSY *adj* suited to or typical of boys or young men

BOZO *n* man, esp a stupid one

BOZOS > BOZO

BOZZETTI > BOZZETTO

BOZZETTO *n* small sketch of planned work

BRA *same as* > BRASSIERE

BRAAI *vb* grill or roast (meat) over open coals

BRAAIED > BRAAI

BRAAIING > BRAAI

BRAAIS > BRAAI

BRAATA *n* small portion added to a purchase of food by a market vendor, to encourage the customer to return

b

b

BRAATAS *same as* > BRAATA

BRAATASES > BRAATAS

BRABBLE *rare word for* > SQUABBLE

BRABBLED > BRABBLE

BRABBLER > BRABBLE

BRABBLERS > BRABBLE

BRABBLES > BRABBLE

BRABBLING > BRABBLE

BRACCATE *adj* (of birds) having feathered legs

BRACCIA > BRACCIO

BRACCIO *n* former unit of measurement; length of man's arm

BRACE *n* object fastened to something to straighten or support it ▷ *vb* steady or prepare (oneself) for something unpleasant

BRACED > BRACE

BRACELET *n* ornamental chain or band for the wrist

BRACELETS *npl* handcuffs

BRACER *n* person or thing that braces

BRACERO *n* Mexican World War II labourer

BRACEROS > BRACERO

BRACERS > BRACER

BRACES *npl* pair of straps worn over the shoulders for holding up the trousers

BRACH *n* bitch hound

BRACHAH *n* blessing

BRACHAHS > BRACHAH

BRACHES > BRACH

BRACHET *same as* > BRACH

BRACHETS > BRACHET

BRACHIA > BRACHIUM

BRACHIAL *adj* of or relating to the arm or to an armlike part or structure ▷ *n* brachial part or structure

BRACHIALS > BRACHIAL

BRACHIATE *adj* having widely divergent paired branches ▷ *vb* (of some arboreal apes and monkeys) swing by the arms from one hold to the next

BRACHIUM *n* arm, esp the upper part

BRACHOT > BRACHAH

BRACHS > BRACH

BRACING *adj* refreshing and invigorating ▷ *n* system of braces used to strengthen or support

BRACINGLY > BRACING

BRACINGS > BRACING

BRACIOLA *n* Italian meat roulade

BRACIOLAS > BRACIOLA

BRACIOLE > BRACIOLA

BRACIOLES > BRACIOLA

BRACK *same as* > BARMBRACK

BRACKEN *n* large fern

BRACKENS > BRACKEN

BRACKET *n* pair of characters used to enclose a section of writing ▷ *vb* put in brackets

BRACKETED > BRACKET

BRACKETS > BRACKET

BRACKISH *adj* (of water) slightly salty

BRACKS > BRACK

BRACONID *n* type of fly with parasitic larva

BRACONIDS > BRACONID

BRACT *n* leaf at the base of a flower

BRACTEAL > BRACT

BRACTEATE *adj* (of a plant) having bracts ▷ *n* fine decorated dish or plate of precious metal

BRACTED > BRACT

BRACTEOLE *n* secondary bract subtending a flower within an inflorescence

BRACTLESS > BRACT

BRACTLET *variant of* > BRACTEOLE

BRACTLETS > BRACTLET

BRACTS > BRACT

BRAD *n* small tapered nail with a small head

BRADAWL *n* small boring tool

BRADAWLS > BRADAWL

BRADDED > BRAD

BRADDING > BRAD

BRADOON *same as* > BRIDOON

BRADOONS > BRADOON

BRADS > BRAD

BRAE *n* hill or slope

BRAEHEID *n* summit of a hill or slope

BRAEHEIDS > BRAEHEID

BRAES > BRAE

BRAG *vb* speak arrogantly and boastfully ▷ *n* boastful talk or behaviour

BRAGGART *n* person who boasts loudly ▷ *adj* boastful

BRAGGARTS > BRAGGART

BRAGGED > BRAG

BRAGGER > BRAG

BRAGGERS > BRAG

BRAGGEST > BRAG

BRAGGIER > BRAGGY

BRAGGIEST > BRAGGY

BRAGGING > BRAG

BRAGGINGS > BRAG

BRAGGY *adj* boastful

BRAGLY > BRAG

BRAGS > BRAG

BRAHMA *n* heavy breed of domestic fowl with profusely feathered legs and feet

BRAHMAN *n* member of highest Hindu caste

BRAHMANI *n* woman of the highest Hindu caste

BRAHMANIS > BRAHMANI

BRAHMANS > BRAHMAN

BRAHMAS > BRAHMA

BRAHMIN *same as* > BRAHMAN

BRAHMINS > BRAHMIN

BRAID *vb* interweave (hair, thread, etc) ▷ *n* length of hair etc that has been braided ▷ *adj* broad ▷ *adv* broadly

BRAIDE *adj* given to deceit

BRAIDED *adj* (of a river or stream) flowing in several shallow interconnected channels separated by banks of deposited material

BRAIDER > BRAID

BRAIDERS > BRAID

BRAIDEST > BRAID

BRAIDING *n* braids collectively

BRAIDINGS > BRAIDING

BRAIDS > BRAID

BRAIL *n* one of several lines fastened to the leech of a fore-and-aft sail to aid in furling it ▷ *vb* furl (a fore-and-aft sail) using brails

BRAILED > BRAIL

BRAILING > BRAIL

BRAILLE *n* system of writing for the blind consisting of raised dots that can be interpreted by touch ▷ *vb* print or write using this method

BRAILLED > BRAILLE

BRAILLER *n* device for producing text in braille

BRAILLERS > BRAILLER

BRAILLES > BRAILLE

BRAILLING > BRAILLE

BRAILLIST *n* braille transcriber

BRAILS > BRAIL

BRAIN *n* soft mass of nervous tissue in the head ▷ *vb* hit (someone) hard on the head

BRAINBOX *n* skull

BRAINCASE *n* part of cranium that covers brain

BRAINDEAD *adj* having suffered irreversible stoppage of breathing due to brain damage

BRAINED > BRAIN

BRAINFART *n* idea expressed without much previous thought

BRAINFOOD *n* food containing nutrients that promote brain function

BRAINIAC *n* highly intelligent person

BRAINIACS > BRAINIAC

BRAINIER > BRAINY

BRAINIEST > BRAINY

BRAINILY > BRAINY

BRAINING > BRAIN

BRAINISH *adj* impulsive

BRAINLESS *adj* stupid

BRAINPAN *n* skull

BRAINPANS > BRAINPAN

BRAINS > BRAIN

BRAINSICK *adj* relating to or caused by insanity

BRAINSTEM *n* stalklike part of the brain consisting of the medulla oblongata, the midbrain, and the pons Varolii

BRAINWASH *vb* cause (a person) to alter his or her beliefs, esp by methods based on isolation, sleeplessness, etc

BRAINWAVE *n* sudden idea

BRAINY *adj* clever

BRAIRD *vb* appear as shoots

BRAIRDED > BRAIRD

BRAIRDING > BRAIRD

BRAIRDS > BRAIRD

BRAISE *vb* cook slowly in a covered pan with a little liquid

BRAISED > BRAISE

BRAISES > BRAISE

BRAISING > BRAISE

BRAIZE *same as* > BRAISE

BRAIZES > BRAIZE

BRAK *n* crossbred dog ▷ *adj* (of water) slightly salty

BRAKE *same as* > BRACKEN

BRAKEAGE > BRAKE

BRAKEAGES > BRAKE

BRAKED > BRAKE

BRAKELESS > BRAKE

BRAKEMAN *n* crew member of a goods or passenger train. His duties include controlling auxiliary braking power and inspecting the train

BRAKEMEN > BRAKEMAN

BRAKES > BRAKE

BRAKESMAN *n* pithead winch operator

BRAKESMEN > BRAKESMAN

BRAKIER > BRAKY

BRAKIEST > BRAKY

BRAKING > BRAKE

BRAKS > BRAK

BRAKY *adj* brambly

BRALESS > BRA

BRAMBLE *n* Scots word for blackberry

BRAMBLED > BRAMBLE

BRAMBLES > BRAMBLE

BRAMBLIER > BRAMBLE

BRAMBLING *n* Eurasian finch with a speckled head and back and, in the male, a reddish brown breast and darker wings and tail

BRAMBLY > BRAMBLE

BRAME *n* powerful feeling of emotion

BRAMES > BRAME

BRAN *n* husks of cereal grain

BRANCARD *n* couch on shafts, carried between two horses

BRANCARDS > BRANCARD

BRANCH *n* secondary stem of a tree ▷ *vb* (of stems, roots, etc) divide, then develop in different directions

BRANCHED > BRANCH

BRANCHER *n* young bird learning to fly

BRANCHERS > BRANCHER
BRANCHERY n branches
BRANCHES > BRANCH
BRANCHIA n gill in aquatic animals
BRANCHIAE > BRANCHIA
BRANCHIAL adj of or relating to the gills of an aquatic animal, esp a fish
BRANCHIER > BRANCH
BRANCHING > BRANCH
BRANCHLET n small branch
BRANCHY > BRANCH
BRAND n particular product ▷ vb mark with a brand
BRANDADE n French puréed fish dish
BRANDADES > BRANDADE
BRANDED adj identifiable as being the product of a particular manufacturer or marketing company
BRANDER > BRAND
BRANDERED > BRAND
BRANDERS > BRAND
BRANDIED > BRANDY
BRANDIES > BRANDY
BRANDING > BRAND
BRANDINGS > BRAND
BRANDISE n three-legged metal stand for cooking pots
BRANDISES > BRANDISE
BRANDISH vb wave (a weapon etc) in a threatening way ▷ n threatening or defiant flourish
BRANDLESS > BRAND
BRANDLING n type of small red earthworm found in manure and used as bait by anglers
BRANDRETH n framework of bars used for cooking meat over fire
BRANDS > BRAND
BRANDY n alcoholic spirit distilled from wine ▷ vb give brandy to
BRANDYING > BRANDY
BRANE n hypothetical component of string theory
BRANES > BRANE
BRANGLE vb quarrel noisily
BRANGLED > BRANGLE
BRANGLES > BRANGLE
BRANGLING > BRANGLE
BRANK vb walk with swaggering gait
BRANKED > BRANK
BRANKIER > BRANKY
BRANKIEST > BRANKY
BRANKING > BRANK
BRANKS npl (formerly) iron bridle used to restrain scolding women
BRANKY adj ostentatious
BRANLE n old French country dance performed in a linked circle
BRANLES > BRANLE
BRANNED > BRAN

BRANNER n person or machine that treats metal with bran
BRANNERS > BRANNER
BRANNIER > BRANNY
BRANNIEST > BRANNY
BRANNIGAN n noisy quarrel
BRANNING > BRAN
BRANNY adj having the appearance or texture of bran
BRANS > BRAN
BRANSLE another word for > BRANTLE
BRANSLES > BRANSLE
BRANT n type of small goose of northern coastal regions, with dark grey plumage and a short neck
BRANTAIL n singing bird with red tail
BRANTAILS > BRANTAIL
BRANTLE n French country dance
BRANTLES > BRANTLE
BRANTS > BRANT
BRAS > BRA
BRASCO n lavatory
BRASCOS > BRASCO
BRASERO n metal grid for burning coals
BRASEROS > BRASERO
BRASES > BRA
BRASH adj offensively loud, showy, or self-confident ▷ n loose rubbish, such as broken rock, hedge clippings, etc ▷ vb assault
BRASHED > BRASH
BRASHER > BRASH
BRASHES > BRASH
BRASHEST > BRASH
BRASHIER > BRASHY
BRASHIEST > BRASHY
BRASHING > BRASH
BRASHLY > BRASH
BRASHNESS > BRASH
BRASHY adj loosely fragmented
BRASIER same as > BRAZIER
BRASIERS > BRASIER
BRASIL same as > BRAZIL
BRASILEIN same as > BRAZILEIN
BRASILIN same as > BRAZILIN
BRASILINS > BRASILIN
BRASILS > BRASIL
BRASS n alloy of copper and zinc ▷ vb make irritated or annoyed
BRASSAGE n amount charged by government for making coins
BRASSAGES > BRASSAGE
BRASSARD n identifying armband or badge
BRASSARDS > BRASSARD
BRASSART same as > BRASSARD
BRASSARTS > BRASSART
BRASSED > BRASS

BRASSERIE n restaurant serving drinks and cheap meals
BRASSES > BRASS
BRASSET same as > BRASSART
BRASSETS > BRASSET
BRASSICA n any plant of the cabbage and turnip family
BRASSICAS > BRASSICA
BRASSIE n former name for a club, a No. 2 wood, originally having a brass-plated sole and with a shallower face than a driver to give more loft
BRASSIER > BRASSY
BRASSIERE n bra
BRASSIES > BRASSIE
BRASSIEST > BRASSY
BRASSILY > BRASSY
BRASSING > BRASS
BRASSISH > BRASS
BRASSWARE n items made of brass
BRASSY same as > BRASSIE
BRAST same as > BURST
BRASTING > BRAST
BRASTS > BRAST
BRAT n unruly child
BRATCHET n hunting dog
BRATCHETS > BRATCHET
BRATLING n small badly-behaved child
BRATLINGS > BRATLING
BRATPACK n group of precocious and successful young actors, writers, etc
BRATPACKS > BRATPACK
BRATS > BRAT
BRATTICE n partition of wood or treated cloth used to control ventilation in a mine ▷ vb fit with a brattice
BRATTICED > BRATTICE
BRATTICES > BRATTICE
BRATTIER > BRAT
BRATTIEST > BRAT
BRATTISH same as > BRATTICE
BRATTLE vb make a rattling sound
BRATTLED > BRATTLE
BRATTLES > BRATTLE
BRATTLING > BRATTLE
BRATTY > BRAT
BRATWURST n type of small pork sausage
BRAUNCH old variant of > BRANCH
BRAUNCHED > BRAUNCH
BRAUNCHES > BRAUNCH
BRAUNITE n brown or black mineral
BRAUNITES > BRAUNITE
BRAVA n professional assassin
BRAVADO n showy display of self-confidence ▷ vb behave with bravado
BRAVADOED > BRAVADO
BRAVADOES > BRAVADO

BRAVADOS > BRAVADO
BRAVAS > BRAVA
BRAVE adj having or showing courage, resolution, and daring ▷ n Native American warrior ▷ vb confront with resolution or courage
BRAVED > BRAVE
BRAVELY > BRAVE
BRAVENESS > BRAVE
BRAVER > BRAVE
BRAVERIES > BRAVE
BRAVERS > BRAVE
BRAVERY > BRAVE
BRAVES > BRAVE
BRAVEST > BRAVE
BRAVI > BRAVO
BRAVING > BRAVE
BRAVO interj well done! ▷ n cry of 'bravo' ▷ vb cry or shout 'bravo'
BRAVOED > BRAVO
BRAVOES > BRAVO
BRAVOING > BRAVO
BRAVOS > BRAVO
BRAVURA n display of boldness or daring
BRAVURAS > BRAVURA
BRAVURE > BRAVURA
BRAW adj fine or excellent, esp in appearance or dress ▷ npl best clothes
BRAWER > BRAW
BRAWEST > BRAW
BRAWL n noisy fight ▷ vb fight noisily
BRAWLED > BRAWL
BRAWLER > BRAWL
BRAWLERS > BRAWL
BRAWLIE adj in good health
BRAWLIER > BRAWLIE
BRAWLIEST > BRAWLIE
BRAWLING > BRAWL
BRAWLINGS > BRAWL
BRAWLS > BRAWL
BRAWLY > BRAW
BRAWN n physical strength
BRAWNED > BRAWN
BRAWNIER > BRAWNY
BRAWNIEST > BRAWNY
BRAWNILY > BRAWNY
BRAWNS > BRAWN
BRAWNY adj muscular and strong
BRAWS n fine apparel
BRAXIES > BRAXY
BRAXY n acute and usually fatal bacterial disease of sheep
BRAY vb (of a donkey) utter its loud harsh sound ▷ n donkey's loud harsh sound
BRAYED > BRAY
BRAYER > BRAY
BRAYERS > BRAY
BRAYING > BRAY
BRAYS > BRAY
BRAZA n Spanish unit of measurement
BRAZAS > BRAZA
BRAZE vb join (two metal surfaces) with brass ▷ n

high-melting solder or alloy used in brazing

BRAZED > BRAZE

BRAZELESS > BRAZE

BRAZEN *adj* shameless and bold ▷ *vb* face and overcome boldly or shamelessly

BRAZENED > BRAZEN

BRAZENING > BRAZEN

BRAZENLY > BRAZEN

BRAZENRY *adj* audacity

BRAZENS > BRAZEN

BRAZER > BRAZE

BRAZERS > BRAZE

BRAZES > BRAZE

BRAZIER *n* portable container for burning charcoal or coal

BRAZIERS > BRAZIER

BRAZIERY > BRAZIER

BRAZIL *n* red wood obtained from various tropical leguminous trees, used for cabinetwork

BRAZILEIN *n* red crystalline solid

BRAZILIN *n* pale yellow soluble crystalline solid

BRAZILINS > BRAZILIN

BRAZILS > BRAZIL

BRAZING > BRAZE

BREACH *n* breaking of a promise, obligation, etc ▷ *vb* break (a promise, law, etc)

BREACHED > BREACH

BREACHER > BREACH

BREACHERS > BREACH

BREACHES > BREACH

BREACHING > BREACH

BREAD *n* food made by baking a mixture of flour and water or milk ▷ *vb* cover (food) with breadcrumbs before cooking

BREADBOX *n* airtight container for bread, cakes, etc

BREADED > BREAD

BREADHEAD *n* person solely concerned with money

BREADIER > BREADY

BREADIEST > BREADY

BREADING > BREAD

BREADLESS > BREAD

BREADLINE *n* queue of people waiting for free food given as charity

BREADNUT *n* type of Central American and Carbbean tree

BREADNUTS > BREADNUT

BREADROOM *n* place where bread is kept on ship

BREADROOT *n* central N American leguminous plant with an edible starchy root

BREADS > BREAD

BREADTH *n* extent of something from side to side

BREADTHS > BREADTH

BREADY *adj* having the appearance or texture of bread

BREAK > BRACKEN

BREAKABLE *adj* capable of being broken ▷ *n* fragile easily broken article

BREAKAGE *n* act or result of breaking

BREAKAGES > BREAKAGE

BREAKAWAY *n* (consisting of) a dissenting group who have left a larger unit ▷ *adj* dissenting ▷ *vb* leave hastily or escape

BREAKBACK *adj* backbreaking; arduous

BREAKBEAT *n* type of electronic dance music

BREAKBONE as in *breakbone fever* dengue

BREAKDOWN *n* act or instance of breaking down

BREAKER *n* large wave

BREAKERS > BREAKER

BREAKEVEN *n* the level of commercial activity at which the total cost and total revenue of a business enterprise are equal

BREAKFAST *n* first meal of the day ▷ *vb* eat breakfast

BREAKING > BRACKEN

BREAKINGS > BRACKEN

BREAKNECK *adj* fast and dangerous

BREAKOFF *n* act or an instance of breaking off or stopping

BREAKOFFS > BREAKOFF

BREAKOUT *n* escape, esp from prison or confinement

BREAKOUTS > BREAKOUT

BREAKS > BRACKEN

BREAKTIME *n* period of rest or recreation, esp at school

BREAKUP *n* separation or disintegration

BREAKUPS > BREAKUP

BREAKWALL *n* breakwater

BREAM *n* Eurasian freshwater fish with a compressed body covered with silvery scales ▷ *vb* clean debris (from the bottom of a vessel)

BREAMED > BREAM

BREAMING > BREAM

BREAMS > BREAM

BREARE *same as* > BRIER

BREARES > BREARE

BREASKIT *same as* > BRISKET

BREASKITS > BREASKIT

BREAST *n* either of the (two soft fleshy milk-secreting glands on a woman's chest ▷ *vb* reach the summit of

BREASTED > BREAST

BREASTFD *adj* fed at mother's breast

BREASTING > BREAST

BREASTPIN *n* brooch

worn on the breast, esp to close a garment

BREASTS > BREAST

BREATH *n* taking in and letting out of air during breathing

BREATHE *vb* take in oxygen and give out carbon dioxide

BREATHED *adj* relating to or denoting a speech sound for whose articulation the vocal cords are not made to vibrate

BREATHER *n* short rest

BREATHERS > BREATHER

BREATHES > BREATHE

BREATHFUL > BREATH

BREATHIER > BREATHY

BREATHILY > BREATHY

BREATHING *n* passage of air into and out of the lungs to supply the body with oxygen

BREATHS > BREATH

BREATHY *adj* (of the speaking voice) accompanied by an audible emission of breath

BRECCIA *n* rock consisting of angular fragments embedded in a finer matrix, formed by erosion, impact, volcanic activity, etc

BRECCIAL > BRECCIA

BRECCIAS > BRECCIA

BRECCIATE > BRECCIA

BRECHAM *n* straw horse-collar

BRECHAMS > BRECHAM

BRECHAN *same as* > BRECHAM

BRECHANS > BRECHAN

BRED *n* person who lives in a small remote place

BREDE *archaic spelling of* > BRAID

BREDED > BREDE

BREDES > BREDE

BREDIE *n* meat and vegetable stew

BREDIES > BREDIE

BREDING > BREDE

BREDREN > BRETHREN

BREDRENS > BREDREN

BREDRIN *same as* > BRETHREN

BREDRINS > BREDRIN

BREDS > BRED

BREE *n* broth, stock, or juice

BREECH *n* buttocks ▷ *vb* fit (a gun) with a breech

BREECHED > BREECH

BREECHES *npl* trousers extending to just below the knee

BREECHING *n* strap of a harness that passes behind a horse's haunches

BREED *vb* produce new or improved strains of (domestic animals or plants) ▷ *n* group of animals etc within a (species that have certain clearly defined

characteristics

BREEDER *n* person who breeds plants or animals

BREEDERS > BREEDER

BREEDING > BREED

BREEDINGS > BREED

BREEDS > BREED

BREEKS *npl* trousers

BREEM *same as* > BREME

BREENGE *vb* lunge forward ▷ *n* violent movement

BREENGED > BREENGE

BREENGES > BREENGE

BREENGING > BREENGE

BREER *another word for* > BRAIRD

BREERED > BREER

BREERING > BREER

BREERS > BREER

BREES > BREE

BREESE *same as* > BREEZE

BREESES > BREESE

BREEST *same as* > BREAST

BREESTS > BREAST

BREEZE *n* gentle wind ▷ *vb* move quickly or casually

BREEZED > BREEZE

BREEZES > BREEZE

BREEZEWAY *n* roofed passageway connecting two buildings, sometimes with the sides enclosed

BREEZIER > BREEZY

BREEZIEST > BREEZY

BREEZILY > BREEZY

BREEZING > BREEZE

BREEZY *adj* windy

BREGMA *n* point on the top (of the skull where the coronal and sagittal sutures meet: in infants this corresponds to the anterior fontanelle

BREGMATA > BREGMA

BREGMATE > BREGMA

BREGMATIC > BREGMA

BREHON *n* (formerly) judge in Ireland

BREHONS > BREHON

BREI *vb* speak with a uvular r, esp in Afrikaans

BREID *n* bread

BREIDS > BREID

BREIING > BREI

BREINGE *same as* > BREENGE

BREINGED > BREINGE

BREINGES > BREINGE

BREINGING > BREINGE

BREIS > BREI

BREIST *Scot word for* > BREAST

BREISTS > BREIST

BREKKIES > BREKKY

BREKKY *slang word for* > BREAKFAST

BRELOQUE *n* charm attached to watch chain

BRELOQUES > BRELOQUE

BREME *adj* well-known

BREN *n* type of machine gun

BRENNE *vb* burn

BRENNES > BRENNE

BRENNING > BREN

BRENS > BREN

BRENT n type of goose ⊳ adj steep

BRENTER > BRENT

BRENTEST > BRENT

BRENTS > BRENT

BRER n brother: usually prefixed to a name

BRERE same as > BRIER

BRERES > BRERE

BRERS > BRER

BRESAOLA n (in Italian cookery) air-dried, salted beef

BRESAOLAS > BRESAOLA

BRETASCHE another word for > BRATTICE

BRETESSE another word for > BRATTICE

BRETESSES > BRETESSE

BRETHREN > BROTHER

BRETON n hat with an upturned brim and a rounded crown

BRETONS > BRETON

BRETTICE same as > BRATTICE

BRETTICED > BRETTICE

BRETTICES > BRETTICE

BREVE n accent (brevhere), placed over a vowel to indicate that it is short or is pronounced in a specified way

BREVES > BREVE

BREVET n document entitling a commissioned officer to hold temporarily a higher military rank without the appropriate pay and allowances ⊳ vb promote by brevet

BREVETCY > BREVET

BREVETE adj patented

BREVETED > BREVET

BREVETING > BREVET

BREVETS > BREVET

BREVETTED > BREVET

BREVIARY n book of prayers to be recited daily by a Roman Catholic priest

BREVIATE n summary

BREVIATES > BREVIATE

BREVIER n (formerly) size of printer's type approximately equal to 8 point

BREVIERS > BREVIER

BREVIS same as > BREWIS

BREVISES > BREVIS

BREVITIES > BREVITY

BREVITY n shortness

BREW vb make (beer etc) by steeping, boiling, and fermentation ⊳ n beverage produced by brewing

BREWAGE n product of brewing

BREWAGES > BREWAGE

BREWED > BREW

BREWER > BREW

BREWERIES > BREWERY

BREWERS > BREW

BREWERY n place where beer etc is brewed

BREWING n quantity of a beverage brewed at one time

BREWINGS > BREWING

BREWIS n bread soaked in broth, gravy, etc

BREWISES > BREWIS

BREWPUB n pub that incorporates a brewery on its premises

BREWPUBS > BREWPUB

BREWS > BREW

BREWSKI n beer

BREWSKIES > BREWSKI

BREWSKIS > BREWSKI

BREWSTER n person, particularly a woman, who brews

BREWSTERS > BREWSTER

BREY same as > BREI

BREYED > BREY

BREYING > BREY

BREYS > BREY

BRIAR n S European shrub with a hard woody root (briarroot)

BRIARD n medium-sized dog of an ancient French sheep-herding breed having a long rough coat of a single colour

BRIARDS > BRIARD

BRIARED > BRIAR

BRIARROOT n hard woody root of the briar, used for making tobacco pipes

BRIARS > BRIAR

BRIARWOOD same as > BRIARROOT

BRIARY > BRIAR

BRIBABLE > BRIBE

BRIBE vb offer or give something to someone to gain favour, influence, etc ⊳ n something given or offered as a bribe

BRIBEABLE > BRIBE

BRIBED > BRIBE

BRIBEE n one who is bribed

BRIBEES > BRIBEE

BRIBER > BRIBE

BRIBERIES > BRIBERY

BRIBERS > BRIBE

BRIBERY n process of giving or taking bribes

BRIBES > BRIBE

BRIBING > BRIBE

BRICABRAC n miscellaneous small objects, esp furniture and curios, kept because they are ornamental or rare

BRICHT Scot word for > BRIGHT

BRICHTER > BRICHT

BRICHTEST > BRICHT

BRICK n (rectangular block of) baked clay used in building ⊳ vb build, enclose, or fill with bricks

BRICKBAT n blunt criticism

BRICKBATS > BRICKBAT

BRICKCLAY n clay for making bricks

BRICKED > BRICK

BRICKEN adj made of brick

BRICKIE n bricklayer

BRICKIER > BRICKY

BRICKIES > BRICKIE

BRICKIEST > BRICKY

BRICKING > BRICK

BRICKINGS > BRICK

BRICKKILN n kiln for making bricks

BRICKLE variant of > BRITTLE

BRICKLES > BRICKLE

BRICKLIKE > BRICK

BRICKS > BRICK

BRICKWALL same as > BRICOLE

BRICKWORK n structure, such as a wall, built of bricks

BRICKY same as > BRICKIE

BRICKYARD n place in which bricks are made, stored, or sold

BRICOLAGE n jumbled effect produced by the close proximity of buildings from different periods and in different architectural styles

BRICOLE n shot in which the cue ball touches a cushion after striking the object ball and before touching another ball

BRICOLES > BRICOLE

BRIDAL adj of a bride or a wedding ⊳ n wedding or wedding feast

BRIDALLY > BRIDAL

BRIDALS > BRIDAL

BRIDE n woman who has just been or is about to be married

BRIDECAKE n wedding cake

BRIDED > BRIDE

BRIDEMAID n old form of bridesmaid

BRIDEMAN n bridegroom's attendant

BRIDEMEN > BRIDEMAN

BRIDES > BRIDE

BRIDESMAN same as > BRIDEMAN

BRIDESMEN > BRIDESMAN

BRIDEWELL n house of correction

BRIDGABLE > BRIDGE

BRIDGE n structure for crossing a river etc ⊳ vb build a bridge over (something)

BRIDGED > BRIDGE

BRIDGES > BRIDGE

BRIDGING n one or more timber struts fixed between floor or roof joists to stiffen the construction and distribute the loads

BRIDGINGS > BRIDGING

BRIDIE n semicircular pie containing meat and onions

BRIDIES > BRIDIE

BRIDING > BRIDE

BRIDLE n headgear for controlling a horse ⊳ vb show anger or indignation

BRIDLED > BRIDLE

BRIDLER > BRIDLE

BRIDLERS > BRIDLE

BRIDLES > BRIDLE

BRIDLEWAY n path for riding horses

BRIDLING > BRIDLE

BRIDOON n horse's bit: small snaffle used in double bridles

BRIDOONS > BRIDOON

BRIE same as > BREE

BRIEF adj short in duration ⊳ n condensed statement or written synopsis ⊳ vb give information and instructions to (a person)

BRIEFCASE n small flat case for carrying papers, books, etc

BRIEFED > BRIEF

BRIEFER > BRIEF

BRIEFERS > BRIEF

BRIEFEST > BRIEF

BRIEFING n meeting at which detailed information or instructions are given, as for military operations, etc

BRIEFINGS > BRIEFING

BRIEFLESS adj (said of a barrister) without clients

BRIEFLY > BRIEF

BRIEFNESS > BRIEF

BRIEFS npl men's or women's underpants without legs

BRIER same as > BRIAR

BRIERED > BRIER

BRIERIER > BRIER

BRIERIEST > BRIER

BRIERROOT same as > BRIARROOT

BRIERS > BRIER

BRIERWOOD same as > BRIARROOT

BRIERY > BRIER

BRIES > BRIE

BRIG n two-masted square-rigged ship

BRIGADE n army unit smaller than a division ⊳ vb organize into a brigade

BRIGADED > BRIGADE

BRIGADES > BRIGADE

BRIGADIER n high-ranking army officer

BRIGADING > BRIGADE

BRIGALOW n type of acacia tree

BRIGALOWS > BRIGALOW

BRIGAND n bandit

BRIGANDRY > BRIGAND

BRIGANDS > BRIGAND

BRIGHT adj emitting or reflecting much light ⊳ adv brightly

BRIGHTEN vb make or become bright or brighter

BRIGHTENS > BRIGHTEN
BRIGHTER > BRIGHT
BRIGHTEST > BRIGHT
BRIGHTISH > BRIGHT
BRIGHTLY > BRIGHT
BRIGHTS npl high beam of the headlights of a motor vehicle
BRIGS > BRIG
BRIGUE vb solicit
BRIGUED > BRIGUE
BRIGUES > BRIGUE
BRIGUING > BRIGUE
BRIGUINGS > BRIGUE
BRIK n Tunisian deep-fried spicy pastry filled with fish or meat and sometimes an egg
BRIKI same as > CEZVE
BRIKIS > BRIKI
BRIKS > BRIKI
BRILL n type of European flatfish popular as a food fish
BRILLER > BRILL
BRILLEST > BRILL
BRILLIANT adj shining with light ▷ n popular circular cut for diamonds and other gemstones in the form of two many-faceted pyramids (the top one truncated) joined at their bases
BRILLO n tradename for a type of scouring pad impregnated with a detergent
BRILLOS > BRILLO
BRILLS > BRILL
BRIM n upper rim of a vessel ▷ vb fill or be full to the brim
BRIMFUL adj completely filled with
BRIMFULL same as > BRIMFUL
BRIMFULLY > BRIMFUL
BRIMING n phosphorescence of sea
BRIMINGS > BRIMING
BRIMLESS > BRIM
BRIMMED > BRIM
BRIMMER n vessel, such as a glass or bowl, filled to the brim
BRIMMERS > BRIMMER
BRIMMING > BRIM
BRIMS > BRIM
BRIMSTONE n sulphur
BRIMSTONY > BRIMSTONE
BRIN n thread of silk from silkworm
BRINDED adj streaky or patchy
BRINDISI n song sung in celebration
BRINDISIS > BRINDISI
BRINDLE n brindled animal
BRINDLED adj brown or grey streaked with a darker colour
BRINDLES > BRINDLE
BRINE n salt water ▷ vb

soak in or treat with brine
BRINED > BRINE
BRINELESS > BRINE
BRINER > BRINE
BRINERS > BRINE
BRINES > BRINE
BRING vb carry, convey, or take to a designated place or person
BRINGDOWN n cause to be elated and then suddenly depressed, as from using drugs
BRINGER > BRING
BRINGERS > BRING
BRINGING > BRING
BRINGINGS > BRING
BRINGS > BRING
BRINIER > BRINY
BRINIES > BRINY
BRINIEST > BRINY
BRININESS > BRINY
BRINING > BRINE
BRINISH > BRINE
BRINJAL n dark purple tropical fruit, cooked and eaten as a vegetable
BRINJALS > BRINJAL
BRINJARRY n grain trader
BRINK n edge of a steep place
BRINKMAN n one who goes in for brinkmanship
BRINKMEN > BRINKMAN
BRINKS > BRINK
BRINNIES > BRINNY
BRINNY n stone, esp when thrown
BRINS > BRIN
BRINY adj very salty
BRIO n liveliness
BRIOCHE n soft roll or loaf made from a very light yeast dough, sometimes mixed with currants
BRIOCHES > BRIOCHE
BRIOLETTE n pear-shaped gem cut with long triangular facets
BRIONIES > BRIONY
BRIONY same as > BRYONY
BRIOS > BRIO
BRIQUET same as > BRIQUETTE
BRIQUETS > BRIQUET
BRIQUETTE n block of compressed coal dust ▷ vb make into the form of a brick or bricks
BRIS n ritual circumcision of male babies, usually at eight days old, regarded as the formal entry of the child to the Jewish community
BRISANCE n shattering effect or power of an explosion or explosive
BRISANCES > BRISANCE
BRISANT > BRISANCE
BRISE n type of jump
BRISES > BRIS
BRISK adj lively and quick ▷ vb enliven
BRISKED > BRISK

BRISKEN vb make or become more lively or brisk
BRISKENED > BRISKEN
BRISKENS > BRISKEN
BRISKER > BRISK
BRISKEST > BRISK
BRISKET n beef from the breast of a cow
BRISKETS > BRISKET
BRISKIER same as > BRISKY
BRISKIEST > BRISKY
BRISKING > BRISK
BRISKISH > BRISK
BRISKLY > BRISK
BRISKNESS > BRISK
BRISKS > BRISK
BRISKY another word for > BRISK
BRISLING same as > SPRAT
BRISLINGS > BRISLING
BRISS same as > BRIS
BRISSES > BRIS
BRISTLE n short stiff hair ▷ vb (cause to) stand up like bristles
BRISTLED > BRISTLE
BRISTLES > BRISTLE
BRISTLIER > BRISTLE
BRISTLING > BRISTLE
BRISTLY > BRISTLE
BRISTOL as in bristol board type of heavy cardboard
BRISTOLS npl woman's breasts
BRISURE n mark of cadency in heraldry
BRISURES > BRISURE
BRIT n young of a herring, sprat, or similar fish
BRITANNIA n coin bearing figure of Britannia
BRITCHES same as > BREECHES
BRITH same as > BRIS
BRITHS > BRITH
BRITS > BRIT
BRITSCHKA n light open carriage
BRITSKA same as > BRITZKA
BRITSKAS > BRITSKA
BRITT n young herring or sprat
BRITTANIA variant spelling of > BRITANNIA
BRITTLE adj hard but easily broken ▷ n crunchy sweet made with treacle and nuts
BRITTLED > BRITTLE
BRITTLELY > BRITTLE
BRITTLER > BRITTLE
BRITTLES > BRITTLE
BRITTLEST > BRITTLE
BRITTLING > BRITTLE
BRITTLY > BRITTLE
BRITTS > BRITT
BRITZKA n long horse-drawn carriage with a folding top over the rear seat and a rear-facing front seat

BRITZKAS > BRITZKA
BRITZSKA same as > BRITZKA
BRITZSKAS > BRITZSKAS
BRIZE same as > BREEZE
BRIZES > BRIZE
BRO n family member
BROACH vb introduce (a topic) for discussion ▷ n spit for roasting meat
BROACHED > BROACH
BROACHER > BROACH
BROACHERS > BROACH
BROACHES > BROACH
BROACHING > BROACH
BROAD adj having great breadth or width ▷ n woman
BROADAX same as > BROADAXE
BROADAXE n broad-bladed axe
BROADAXES > BROADAXE
BROADBAND n telecommunication transmission technique using a wide range of frequencies
BROADBEAN n variety of bean
BROADBILL n tropical African and Asian bird with bright plumage and a short wide bill
BROADBRIM n broad-brimmed hat, esp one worn by the Quakers in the 17th century
BROADCAST n programme or announcement on radio or television ▷ vb transmit (a programme or announcement) on radio or television ▷ adj dispersed over a wide area ▷ adv far and wide
BROADEN vb make or become broad or broader
BROADENED > BROADEN
BROADENER > BROADEN
BROADENS > BROADEN
BROADER > BROAD
BROADEST > BROAD
BROADISH > BROAD
BROADLEAF n any tobacco plant having broad leaves, used esp in making cigars
BROADLINE n company dealing in large volumes of cheap products
BROADLOOM adj of or designating carpets woven on a wide loom ▷ n of or designating carpets or carpeting woven on a wide loom to obviate the need for seams
BROADLY > BROAD
BROADNESS > BROAD
BROADS > BROAD
BROADSIDE n strong verbal or written attack ▷ adv with a broader side facing an object

BROADTAIL n highly valued black wavy fur obtained from the skins of newly born karakul lambs

BROADWAY n wide road

BROADWAYS > BROADWAY

BROADWISE adv rare form of breadthwise

BROCADE n rich fabric woven with a raised design ▷ vb weave with such a design

BROCADED > BROCADE

BROCADES > BROCADE

BROCADING > BROCADE

BROCAGE another word for > BROKERAGE

BROCAGES > BROCAGE

BROCARD n basic principle of civil law

BROCARDS > BROCARD

BROCATEL n heavy upholstery brocade

BROCATELS > BROCATEL

BROCCOLI n type of cabbage with greenish flower heads

BROCCOLIS > BROCCOLI

BROCH n (in Scotland) a circular dry-stone tower large enough to serve as a fortified home

BROCHAN n type of thin porridge

BROCHANS > BROCHAN

BROCHE adj woven with a raised design, as brocade

BROCHED > BROCHE

BROCHES > BROCHE

BROCHETTE n skewer used for holding pieces of meat or vegetables while grilling

BROCHING > BROCHE

BROCHO same as > BRACHAH

BROCHOS > BROCHO

BROCHS > BROCH

BROCHURE n booklet that contains information about a product or service

BROCHURES > BROCHURE

BROCK n badger

BROCKAGE same as > BROKERAGE

BROCKAGES > BROCKAGE

BROCKED adj having different colours

BROCKET n small tropical American deer with small unbranched antlers

BROCKETS > BROCKET

BROCKIT same as > BROCKED

BROCKRAM another word for > BRECCIA

BROCKRAMS > BROCKRAM

BROCKS > BROCK

BROCOLI same as > BROCCOLI

BROCOLIS > BROCOLI

BROD vb prod

BRODDED > BROD

BRODDING > BROD

BRODDLE vb poke or pierce (something)

BRODDLED > BRODDLE

BRODDLES > BRODDLE

BRODDLING > BRODDLE

BRODEKIN another word for > BUSKIN

BRODEKINS > BRODEKIN

BRODKIN same as > BRODEKIN

BRODKINS > BRODKIN

BRODS > BROD

BROEKIES npl underpants

BROG n bradawl

BROGAN n heavy laced, usually ankle-high, work boot

BROGANS > BROGAN

BROGGED > BROG

BROGGING > BROG

BROGH same as > BROCH

BROGHS > BROGH

BROGS > BROG

BROGUE n sturdy walking shoe

BROGUEISH > BROGUE

BROGUERY > BROGUE

BROGUES > BROGUE

BROGUISH > BROGUE

BROIDER archaic word for > EMBROIDER

BROIDERED > BROIDER

BROIDERER > BROIDER

BROIDERS > BROIDER

BROIDERY n old form of embroidery

BROIL vb cook by direct heat under a grill ▷ n process of broiling

BROILED > BROIL

BROILER n young tender chicken for roasting

BROILERS > BROILER

BROILING > BROIL

BROILS > BROIL

BROKAGE another word for > BROKERAGE

BROKAGES > BROKAGE

BROKE vb negotiate or deal

BROKED > BROKE

BROKEN > BRACKEN

BROKENLY > BRACKEN

BROKER n agent who buys or sells goods, securities, etc ▷ vb act as a broker (in)

BROKERAGE n commission charged by a broker

BROKERED > BROKER

BROKERIES > BROKERY

BROKERING > BROKER

BROKERS > BROKER

BROKERY n work done by broker

BROKES > BROKE

BROKING > BROKE

BROKINGS > BROKE

BROLGA n large grey Australian crane with a trumpeting call

BROLGAS > BROLGA

BROLLIES > BROLLY

BROLLY n umbrella

BROMAL n yellowish oily synthetic liquid formerly used medicinally as a sedative and hypnotic

BROMALS > BROMAL

BROMATE same as > BROMINATE

BROMATED > BROMATE

BROMATES > BROMATE

BROMATING > BROMATE

BROME n type of grass

BROMELAIN n enzyme in pineapples

BROMELIA n type of plant

BROMELIAD n tropical American plant with a rosette of fleshy leaves

BROMELIAS > BROMELIA

BROMELIN n protein-digesting enzyme found in pineapple and extracted for use in treating joint pain and inflammation, hay fever, and various other conditions

BROMELINS > BROMELIN

BROMEOSIN another name for > EOSIN

BROMES > BROME

BROMIC adj of or containing bromine in the trivalent or pentavalent state

BROMID same as > BROMIDE

BROMIDE n chemical compound used in medicine and photography

BROMIDES > BROMIDE

BROMIDIC adj ordinary

BROMIDS > BROMID

BROMIN same as > BROMINE

BROMINATE vb treat or react with bromine

BROMINE n dark red liquid element that gives off a pungent vapour

BROMINES > BROMINE

BROMINISM same as > BROMISM

BROMINS > BROMIN

BROMISE same as > BROMIZE

BROMISED > BROMIZE

BROMISES > BROMIZE

BROMISING > BROMIZE

BROMISM n poisoning caused by the excessive intake of bromine or compounds containing bromine

BROMISMS > BROMISM

BROMIZE vb treat with bromine

BROMIZED > BROMIZE

BROMIZES > BROMIZE

BROMIZING > BROMIZE

BROMMER n S African word for bluebottle

BROMMERS > BROMMER

BROMO n something that contains bromide

BROMOFORM n heavy colourless liquid substance with a sweetish taste

BROMOS > BROMO

BRONC same as > BRONCO

BRONCHI > BRONCHUS

BRONCHIA npl bronchial tubes

BRONCHIAL adj of the bronchi

BRONCHIUM n medium-sized bronchial tube

BRONCHO same as > BRONCO

BRONCHOS > BRONCHO

BRONCHUS n either of the two branches of the windpipe

BRONCO n (in the US) wild or partially tamed pony

BRONCOS > BRONCO

BRONCS > BRONC

BROND n old form of brand

BRONDS > BROND

BRONDYRON n sword

BRONZE n alloy of copper and tin ▷ adj made of, or coloured like, bronze ▷ vb (esp of the skin) make or become brown

BRONZED > BRONZE

BRONZEN adj made of or the colour of bronze

BRONZER n cosmetic applied to the skin to simulate a sun tan

BRONZERS > BRONZER

BRONZES > BRONZE

BRONZIER > BRONZE

BRONZIEST > BRONZE

BRONZIFY vb cause to become colour of bronze

BRONZING n blue pigment producing a metallic lustre when ground into paint media at fairly high concentrations

BRONZINGS > BRONZING

BRONZITE n type of orthopyroxene often having a metallic or pearly sheen

BRONZITES > BRONZITE

BRONZY > BRONZE

BROO n brow of hill

BROOCH n ornament with a pin, worn fastened to clothes ▷ vb decorate with a brooch

BROOCHED > BROOCH

BROOCHES > BROOCH

BROOCHING > BROOCH

BROOD n number of birds produced at one hatching ▷ vb (of a bird) sit on or hatch eggs

BROODED > BROOD

BROODER n enclosure or other structure, usually heated, used for rearing young chickens or other fowl

BROODERS > BROODER

BROODIER > BROODY

BROODIEST > BROODY

BROODILY > BROODY

BROODING > BROOD

BROODINGS > BROOD

BROODLESS > BROOD

BROODMARE n mare for breeding

BROODS > BROOD

BROODY adj moody and sullen

BROOK n small stream ▷ vb bear or tolerate

BROOKABLE > BROOK

BROOKED > BROOK

BROOKIE n brook trout

BROOKIES > BROOKIE

BROOKING > BROOK

BROOKITE n reddish-brown to black mineral

BROOKITES > BROOKITE

BROOKLET n small brook

BROOKLETS > BROOKLET

BROOKLIKE > BROOK

BROOKLIME n type of blue-flowered trailing plant of N America, Europe or Asia, which grows in moist places

BROOKS > BROOK

BROOKWEED n type of white-flowered plant of Europe or North America, growing in moist places

BROOL n low roar

BROOLS > BROOL

BROOM n long-handled sweeping brush ▷ vb sweep with a broom

BROOMBALL n type of ice hockey played with broom

BROOMCORN n variety of sorghum, the long stiff flower stalks of which can be used to make brooms

BROOMED > BROOM

BROOMIER > BROOMY

BROOMIEST > BROOMY

BROOMING > BROOM

BROOMRAPE n type of plant which grows as brownish small-flowered leafless parasites on the roots of other plants

BROOMS > BROOM

BROOMY adj covered with growth of broom

BROOS > BROO

BROOSE n race at country wedding

BROOSES > BROOSE

BROS > BRO

BROSE n oatmeal or pease porridge, sometimes with butter or fat added

BROSES > BROSE

BROSIER > BROSY

BROSIEST > BROSY

BROSY adj smeared with porridge

BROTH n soup, usu. containing vegetables

BROTHEL n house where men pay to have sex with prostitutes

BROTHELS > BROTHEL

BROTHER n boy or man with the same parents as another person ▷ interj exclamation of amazement, disgust,

surprise, disappointment, etc ▷ vb treat someone like a brother

BROTHERED > BROTHER

BROTHERLY adj of or like a brother, esp in showing loyalty and affection ▷ adv in a brotherly way

BROTHERS > BROTHER

BROTHIER > BROTHY

BROTHIEST > BROTHY

BROTHS > BROTH

BROTHY adj having appearance or texture of broth

BROUGH same as > BROCH

BROUGHAM n horse-drawn closed carriage with a raised open driver's seat in front

BROUGHAMS > BROUGHAM

BROUGHS > BROUGH

BROUGHT > BRING

BROUGHTA same as > BRAATA

BROUGHTAS same as > BRAATA

BROUHAHA n loud confused noise

BROUHAHAS > BROUHAHA

BROUZE same as > BROOSE

BROUZES > BROUZE

BROW n part of the face (from the eyes to the hairline)

BROWALLIA n flowering plant

BROWBAND n strap of a horse's bridle that goes across the forehead

BROWBANDS > BROWBAND

BROWBEAT vb frighten (someone) with threats

BROWBEATS > BROWBEAT

BROWED adj having a brow

BROWLESS > BROW

BROWN n colour of earth or wood ▷ adj (of bread) made from wheatmeal or wholemeal flour ▷ vb make or become brown

BROWNED > BROWN

BROWNER > BROWN

BROWNEST > BROWN

BROWNIE n small square nutty chocolate cake

BROWNIER > BROWN

BROWNIES > BROWNIE

BROWNIEST > BROWN

BROWNING n substance used to darken gravies

BROWNINGS > BROWNING

BROWNISH > BROWN

BROWNNESS > BROWN

BROWNNOSE vb be abjectly subservient

BROWNOUT n dimming or reduction in the use of electric lights in a city, esp to conserve electric power or as a defensive precaution in wartime

BROWNOUTS > BROWNOUT

BROWNS > BROWN

BROWNTAIL as in browntail

moth kind of moth

BROWNY > BROWN

BROWRIDGE n ridge of bone over eyes

BROWS > BROW

BROWSABLE > BROWSE

BROWSE vb look through (a book or articles for sale) in a casual manner ▷ n instance of browsing

BROWSED > BROWSE

BROWSER n software package that enables a user to read hypertext, esp on the Internet

BROWSERS > BROWSER

BROWSES > BROWSE

BROWSIER > BROWSE

BROWSIEST > BROWSE

BROWSING > BROWSE

BROWSINGS > BROWSE

BROWST n brewing (of ale, tea)

BROWSTS > BROWST

BROWSY > BROWSE

BRR same as > BRRR

BRRR interj used to suggest shivering

BRU South African word for > FRIEND

BRUCELLA n type of bacterium

BRUCELLAE > BRUCELLA

BRUCELLAS > BRUCELLA

BRUCHID n type of beetle

BRUCHIDS > BRUCHID

BRUCIN same as > BRUCINE

BRUCINE n bitter poisonous alkaloid resembling strychnine

BRUCINES > BRUCINE

BRUCINS > BRUCIN

BRUCITE n white translucent mineral

BRUCITES > BRUCITE

BRUCKLE adj brittle

BRUGH n large house

BRUGHS > BRUGH

BRUHAHA same as > BROUHAHA

BRUHAHAS > BRUHAHA

BRUILZIE same as > BRULZIE

BRUILZIES > BRUILZIE

BRUIN n name for a bear, used in children's tales, fables, etc

BRUINS > BRUIN

BRUISE n discoloured area on the skin caused by an injury ▷ vb cause a bruise on

BRUISED > BRUISE

BRUISER n strong tough person

BRUISERS > BRUISER

BRUISES > BRUISE

BRUISING adj causing bruises, as by a blow ▷ n bruise or bruises

BRUISINGS > BRUISING

BRUIT vb report ▷ n abnormal sound heard

within the body during auscultation, esp a heart murmur

BRUITED > BRUIT

BRUITER > BRUIT

BRUITERS > BRUIT

BRUITING > BRUIT

BRUITS > BRUIT

BRULE n shortened form of the archaic word for a mixed-race person of Canadian Indian and White (usually French-Canadian) ancestry

BRULES > BRULE

BRULOT n coffee-based alcoholic drink, served flaming

BRULOTS > BRULOT

BRULYIE same as > BRULYIE

BRULYIES > BRULYIE

BRULZIE n noisy dispute

BRULZIES > BRULZIE

BRUMAL adj of, characteristic of, or relating to winter

BRUMBIES > BRUMBY

BRUMBY n wild horse

BRUME n heavy mist or fog

BRUMES > BRUME

BRUMMAGEM n something that is cheap and flashy, esp imitation jewellery

BRUMMER same as > BROMMER

BRUMMERS > BRUMMER

BRUMOUS > BRUME

BRUNCH n breakfast and lunch combined ▷ vb eat brunch

BRUNCHED > BRUNCH

BRUNCHER > BRUNCH

BRUNCHERS > BRUNCH

BRUNCHES > BRUNCH

BRUNCHING > BRUNCH

BRUNET adj dark brown

BRUNETS > BRUNET

BRUNETTE n girl or woman with dark brown hair ▷ adj dark brown

BRUNETTES > BRUNETTE

BRUNG > BRING

BRUNIZEM n prairie soil

BRUNIZEMS > BRUNIZEM

BRUNT n main force or shock of a blow, attack, etc ▷ vb suffer the main force or shock of a blow, attack, etc

BRUNTED > BRUNT

BRUNTING > BRUNT

BRUNTS > BRUNT

BRUS > BRU

BRUSH n device made of bristles, wires, etc used for cleaning, painting, etc ▷ vb clean, scrub, or paint with a brush

BRUSHBACK n (baseball) ball intended to hit the batter

BRUSHED adj treated with a brushing process to raise the nap and give a softer and warmer finish

BRUSHER > BRUSH

BRUSHERS > BRUSH

BRUSHES > BRUSH

BRUSHFIRE n fire in bushes and scrub

BRUSHIER > BRUSHY

BRUSHIEST > BRUSHY

BRUSHING > BRUSH

BRUSHINGS > BRUSH

BRUSHLAND n land characterized by patchy shrubs

BRUSHLESS > BRUSH

BRUSHLIKE > BRUSH

BRUSHMARK n indented lines sometimes left by the bristles of a brush on a painted surface

BRUSHOFF n an abrupt dismissal or rejection

BRUSHOFFS > BRUSHOFF

BRUSHUP n the act or an instance of tidying one's appearance

BRUSHUPS > BRUSHUP

BRUSHWOOD n cut or broken-off tree branches and twigs

BRUSHWORK n characteristic manner of applying paint with a brush

BRUSHY adj like a brush

BRUSK same as > BRUSQUE

BRUSKER > BRUSK

BRUSKEST > BRUSK

BRUSQUE adj blunt or curt in manner or speech

BRUSQUELY > BRUSQUE

BRUSQUER > BRUSQUE

BRUSQUEST > BRUSQUE

BRUSSELS adj as in brussels sprout small cabbage-like vegetable

BRUSSEN adj bold

BRUST same as > BURST

BRUSTING > BRUST

BRUSTS > BRUST

BRUT adj (of champagne or sparkling wine) very dry ▷ n very dry champagne

BRUTAL adj cruel and vicious

BRUTALISE same as > BRUTALIZE

BRUTALISM n austere architectural style of the 1950s on, characterized by the use of exposed concrete and angular shapes

BRUTALIST > BRUTALISM

BRUTALITY > BRUTAL

BRUTALIZE vb make or become brutal

BRUTALLY > BRUTAL

BRUTE n brutal person ▷ adj wholly instinctive or physical, like an animal

BRUTED > BRUTE

BRUTELIKE > BRUTE

BRUTELY > BRUTE

BRUTENESS > BRUTE

BRUTER n diamond cutter

BRUTERS > BRUTER

BRUTES > BRUTE

BRUTIFIED > BRUTIFY

BRUTIFIES > BRUTIFY

BRUTIFY less common word for > BRUTALIZE

BRUTING n diamond cutting

BRUTINGS > BRUTING

BRUTISH adj of or like an animal

BRUTISHLY > BRUTISH

BRUTISM n stupidity; vulgarity

BRUTISMS > BRUTISM

BRUTS > BRUT

BRUX vb grind one's teeth

BRUXED > BRUX

BRUXES > BRUX

BRUXING > BRUX

BRUXISM n habit of grinding the teeth, esp unconsciously

BRUXISMS > BRUXISM

BRYOLOGY n branch of botany concerned with the study of bryophytes

BRYONIES > BRYONY

BRYONY n wild climbing hedge plant

BRYOPHYTE n type of plant such as mosses, liverworts, or hornworts, which has stems and leaves but lacks roots and reproduces by spores

BRYOZOAN n type of aquatic invertebrate which forms colonies of polyps

BRYOZOANS > BRYOZOAN

BUAT same as > BOWAT

BUATS > BUAT

BUAZE n fibrous African plant

BUAZES > BUAZE

BUB n youngster

BUBA another name for > YAWS

BUBAL n any of various antelopes, esp an extinct N African variety of hartebeest

BUBALE n large antelope

BUBALES > BUBALE

BUBALINE adj (of antelopes) related to or resembling the bubal

BUBALIS same as > BUBAL

BUBALISES > BUBALIS

BUBALS > BUBAL

BUBAS > BUBA

BUBBA n ordinary American person

BUBBAS > BUBBA

BUBBIES > BUBBY

BUBBLE n ball of air in a liquid or solid ▷ vb form bubbles

BUBBLED > BUBBLE

BUBBLEGUM n type of chewing gum that can be blown into large bubbles

BUBBLER n drinking fountain in which the water is forced in a stream from a small vertical nozzle

BUBBLERS > BUBBLER

BUBBLES > BUBBLE

BUBBLIER > BUBBLY

BUBBLIES > BUBBLY

BUBBLIEST > BUBBLY

BUBBLING > BUBBLE

BUBBLY adj excited and lively ▷ n champagne

BUBBY n old word for woman's breast

BUBINGA n reddish-brown wood from African tree

BUBINGAS > BUBINGA

BUBKES n very small amount

BUBKIS n nothing

BUBO n inflammation and swelling of a lymph node, esp in the armpit or groin

BUBOED > BUBO

BUBOES > BUBO

BUBONIC > BUBO

BUBS > BUB

BUBU same as > BOUBOU

BUBUKLE n red spot on skin

BUBUKLES > BUBUKLE

BUBUS > BUBU

BUCARDO n type of Spanish mountain goat, recently extinct

BUCARDOS > BUCARDO

BUCATINI npl pasta in the shape of long tubes

BUCCAL adj of or relating to the cheek

BUCCALLY > BUCCAL

BUCCANEER n pirate ▷ vb be or act like a buccaneer

BUCCANIER same as > BUCCANEER

BUCCINA n curved Roman horn

BUCCINAS > BUCCINA

BUCELLAS n type of Portuguese white wine

BUCENTAUR n state barge of Venice from which the doge and other officials dropped a ring into the sea on Ascension Day to symbolize the ceremonial marriage of the state with the Adriatic

BUCHU n S African shrub whose leaves are used as an antiseptic and diuretic

BUCHUS > BUCHU

BUCK n male of the goat, hare, kangaroo, rabbit, and reindeer ▷ vb (of a horse etc) jump with legs stiff and back arched

BUCKAROO n cowboy

BUCKAROOS > BUCKAROO

BUCKAYRO same as > BUCKAROO

BUCKAYROS > BUCKAYRO

BUCKBEAN n type of marsh plant with white or pink flowers

BUCKBEANS > BUCKBEAN

BUCKBOARD n open four-wheeled horse-drawn carriage with the seat attached to a flexible board between the front and rear axles

BUCKBRUSH n American shrub

BUCKED > BUCK

BUCKEEN n (in Ireland) poor young man who aspires to the habits and dress of the wealthy

BUCKEENS > BUCKEEN

BUCKER > BUCK

BUCKEROO same as > BUCKAROO

BUCKEROOS > BUCKEROO

BUCKERS > BUCK

BUCKET vb open-topped roughly cylindrical container ▷ vb rain heavily

BUCKETED > BUCKET

BUCKETFUL same as > BUCKET

BUCKETING > BUCKET

BUCKETS > BUCKET

BUCKEYE n N American tree with erect clusters of white or red flowers and prickly fruits

BUCKEYES > BUCKEYE

BUCKHORN n horn from a buck, used for knife handles, etc

BUCKHORNS > BUCKHORN

BUCKHOUND n hound, smaller than a staghound, used for hunting the smaller breeds of deer, esp fallow deer

BUCKIE n whelk or its shell

BUCKIES > BUCKIE

BUCKING > BUCK

BUCKINGS > BUCK

BUCKISH > BUCK

BUCKISHLY > BUCK

BUCKLE n clasp for fastening a belt or strap ▷ vb fasten or be fastened with a buckle

BUCKLED > BUCKLE

BUCKLER n small round shield worn on the forearm ▷ vb defend

BUCKLERED > BUCKLER

BUCKLERS > BUCKLER

BUCKLES > BUCKLE

BUCKLING another name for > BLOATER

BUCKLINGS > BUCKLING

BUCKO n lively young fellow: often a term of address

BUCKOES > BUCKO

BUCKOS > BUCKO

BUCKRA n (used contemptuously by Black people, esp in the US) White man

BUCKRAKE n large rake attached to tractor

BUCKRAKES > BUCKRAKE

BUCKRAM n cotton or linen cloth stiffened with size, etc, used in lining or stiffening clothes, bookbinding, etc ▷ *vb* stiffen with buckram

BUCKRAMED > BUCKRAM

BUCKRAMS > BUCKRAM

BUCKRAS > BUCKRA

BUCKS > BUCK

BUCKSAW *n* woodcutting saw having its blade set in a frame and tensioned by a turnbuckle across the back of the frame

BUCKSAWS > BUCKSAW

BUCKSHEE *adj* free

BUCKSHEES > BUCKSHEE

BUCKSHISH *n* tip, present or gift

BUCKSHOT *n* large lead pellets used for shooting game

BUCKSHOTS > BUCKSHOT

BUCKSKIN *n* skin of a male deer ▷ *adj* greyish-yellow

BUCKSKINS *npl* (in the US and Canada) breeches, shoes, or a suit of buckskin

BUCKSOM *same as* **> BUXOM**

BUCKTAIL *n* in fishing, fly with appearance of minnow

BUCKTAILS > BUCKTAIL

BUCKTEETH > BUCKTOOTH

BUCKTHORN *n* thorny shrub whose berries were formerly used as a purgative

BUCKTOOTH *n* projecting upper front tooth

BUCKU *same as* **> BUCHU**

BUCKUS > BUCKU

BUCKWHEAT *n* small black grain used for making flour

BUCKYBALL *n* ball-like polyhedral carbon molecule of the type found in buckminsterfullerene and other fullerenes

BUCKYTUBE *n* tube of carbon atoms structurally similar to buckminsterfullerene

BUCOLIC *adj* of the countryside or country life ▷ *n* pastoral poem

BUCOLICAL > BUCOLIC

BUCOLICS > BUCOLIC

BUD *n* swelling on a plant that develops into a leaf or flower ▷ *vb* produce buds

BUDA *n* derogatory Indian English word for an old man

BUDAS > BUDA

BUDDED > BUD

BUDDER > BUD

BUDDERS > BUD

BUDDHA *n* person who has achieved a state of perfect enlightenment

BUDDHAS > BUDDHA

BUDDIED > BUDDY

BUDDIER > BUDDY

BUDDIES > BUDDY

BUDDIEST > BUDDY

BUDDING > BUDDY

BUDDINGS > BUDDY

BUDDLE *n* sloping trough in which ore is washed ▷ *vb* wash (ore) in a buddle

BUDDLED > BUDDLE

BUDDLEIA *n* shrub with long spikes of purple flowers

BUDDLEIAS > BUDDLEIA

BUDDLES > BUDDLE

BUDDLING > BUDDLE

BUDDY *n* friend ▷ *vb* act as a friend to ▷ *adj* friendly

BUDDYING > BUDDY

BUDGE *vb* move slightly ▷ *n* lambskin dressed for the fur to be worn on the outer side

BUDGED > BUDGE

BUDGER > BUDGE

BUDGEREE *adj* good

BUDGERO *same as* **> BUDGEROW**

BUDGEROS > BUDGERO

BUDGEROW *n* barge use on Ganges

BUDGEROWS > BUDGEROW

BUDGERS > BUDGE

BUDGES > BUDGE

BUDGET *n* financial plan for a period of time ▷ *vb* plan the expenditure of (money or time) ▷ *adj* cheap

BUDGETARY > BUDGET

BUDGETED > BUDGET

BUDGETEER > BUDGET

BUDGETER > BUDGET

BUDGETERS > BUDGET

BUDGETING > BUDGET

BUDGETS > BUDGET

BUDGIE *n* short form of budgerigar

BUDGIES > BUDGIE

BUDGING > BUDGE

BUDI *n* derogatory Indian English word an for old woman

BUDIS > BUDI

BUDLESS > BUD

BUDLIKE > BUD

BUDMASH > BADMASH

BUDMASHES > BUDMASH

BUDO *n* combat and spirit in martial arts

BUDOS > BUDO

BUDS > BUD

BUDWORM *n* pest that eats tree leaves and buds

BUDWORMS > BUDWORM

BUFF *n* soft flexible undyed leather ▷ *adj* dull yellowish-brown ▷ *vb* clean or polish with soft material

BUFFA > BUFFO

BUFFABLE > BUFF

BUFFALO *n* member of the cattle tribe with upward-curving horns, mostly found in game reserves in S and E Africa ▷ *vb* confuse

BUFFALOED > BUFFALO

BUFFALOES > BUFFALO

BUFFALOS > BUFFALO

BUFFE > BUFFO

BUFFED > BUFF

BUFFEL as in *buffel grass* grass used for pasture in Africa, India, and Australia

BUFFER *same as* **> BUFF**

BUFFERED > BUFFER

BUFFERING > BUFFER

BUFFERS > BUFFER

BUFFEST > BUFF

BUFFET *n* counter where drinks and snacks are served ▷ *vb* knock against or about

BUFFETED > BUFFET

BUFFETER > BUFFET

BUFFETERS > BUFFET

BUFFETING *n* response of an aircraft structure to buffet, esp an irregular oscillation of the tail

BUFFETS > BUFFET

BUFFI > BUFFO

BUFFIER > BUFFY

BUFFIEST > BUFFY

BUFFING > BUFF

BUFFINGS > BUFFING

BUFFO *n* (in Italian opera of the 18th century) comic part, esp one for a bass

BUFFOON *n* clown or fool

BUFFOONS > BUFFOON

BUFFOS > BUFFO

BUFFS > BUFF

BUFFY *adj* having appearance or texture of buff

BUFO *n* type of toad

BUFOS > BUFO

BUFOTALIN *n* principal poisonous substance in the skin and saliva of the common European toad

BUFTIE *n* homosexual man

BUFTIES > BUFTIE

BUFTY *same as* **> BUFTIE**

BUG *n* insect ▷ *vb* irritate

BUGABOO *n* imaginary source of fear

BUGABOOS > BUGABOO

BUGBANE *n* European plant whose flowers are reputed to repel insects

BUGBANES > BUGBANE

BUGBEAR *n* thing that causes obsessive anxiety

BUGBEARS > BUGBEAR

BUGEYE *n* oyster-dredging boat

BUGEYES > BUGEYE

BUGGAN *n* evil spirit

BUGGANE *same as* **> BUGGAN**

BUGGANES > BUGGANE

BUGGANS > BUGGAN

BUGGED > BUG

BUGGER *n* unpleasant or difficult person or thing ▷ *vb* tire ▷ *interj* exclamation of annoyance or disappointment

BUGGERED > BUGGER

BUGGERIES > BUGGERY

BUGGERING > BUGGER

BUGGERS > BUGGER

BUGGERY *n* anal intercourse

BUGGIER > BUGGY

BUGGIES > BUGGY

BUGGIEST > BUGGY

BUGGIN *same as* **> BUGGAN**

BUGGINESS > BUGGY

BUGGING > BUG

BUGGINGS > BUG

BUGGINS > BUGGIN

BUGGY *n* light horse-drawn carriage having two or four wheels ▷ *adj* infested with bugs

BUGHOUSE *n* offensive name for a mental hospital or asylum ▷ *adj* offensive word for insane

BUGHOUSES > BUGHOUSE

BUGLE *n* instrument like a small trumpet ▷ *vb* play or sound (on) a bugle

BUGLED > BUGLE

BUGLER > BUGLE

BUGLERS > BUGLE

BUGLES > BUGLE

BUGLET *n* small bugle

BUGLETS > BUGLET

BUGLEWEED *same as* **> BUGLE**

BUGLING > BUGLE

BUGLOSS *n* hairy Eurasian plant with clusters of blue flowers

BUGLOSSES > BUGLOSS

BUGONG *same as* **> BOGONG**

BUGONGS > BUGONG

BUGOUT *n* act of running away

BUGOUTS > BUGOUT

BUGS > BUG

BUGSEED *n* form of tumbleweed

BUGSEEDS > BUGSEED

BUGSHA *same as* **> BUQSHA**

BUGSHAS > BUGSHA

BUGWORT *another name for* **> BUGBANE**

BUGWORTS > BUGWORT

BUHL *same as* **> BOULLE**

BUHLS > BUHL

BUHLWORK *n* woodwork with decorative inlay

BUHLWORKS > BUHLWORK

BUHR *same as* **> BURR**

BUHRS > BURR

BUHRSTONE *n* hard tough rock containing silica, fossils, and cavities, formerly used as a grindstone

BUHUND *n* type of Norwegian dog

BUHUNDS > BUHUND

BUIBUI *n* piece of black cloth worn as a shawl by Muslim women, esp on the E African coast

BUIBUIS > BUIBUI

BUIK *same as* **> BOOK**

BUIKS > BUIK

BUILD *vb* make, construct,

or form by joining parts or materials ▷ *n* shape of the body

BUILDABLE *adj* suitable for building on

BUILDDOWN *n* planned reduction

BUILDED ▷ BUILD

BUILDER *n* person who constructs houses and other buildings

BUILDERS ▷ BUILDER

BUILDING ▷ BUILD

BUILDINGS ▷ BUILD

BUILDS ▷ BUILD

BUILDUP *n* gradual approach to a climax or critical point

BUILDUPS ▷ BUILDUP

BUILT ▷ BUILD

BUIRDLIER ▷ BUIRDLY

BUIRDLY *adj* well-built

BUIST *vb* brand sheep with identification mark

BUISTED ▷ BUIST

BUISTING ▷ BUIST

BUISTS ▷ BUIST

BUKE *same as* ▷ BOOK

BUKES ▷ BUKE

BUKKAKE *n* type of sexual practice

BUKKAKES ▷ BUKKAKE

BUKSHEE *n* person in charge of paying wages

BUKSHEES ▷ BUKSHEE

BUKSHI *same as* ▷ BUKSHEE

BUKSHIS ▷ BUKSHI

BULB *n* onion-shaped root which grows into a flower or plant ▷ *vb* form into the shape of a bulb

BULBAR *adj* of or relating to a bulb, esp the medulla oblongata

BULBED ▷ BULB

BULBEL *same as* ▷ BULBIL

BULBELS ▷ BULBEL

BULBIL *n* small bulblike organ of vegetative reproduction growing in leaf axils or on flower stalks of plants such as the onion and tiger lily

BULBILS ▷ BULBIL

BULBING ▷ BULB

BULBLET *n* small bulb at base of main bulb

BULBLETS ▷ BULBLET

BULBOSITY ▷ BULBOUS

BULBOUS *adj* round and fat

BULBOUSLY ▷ BULBOUS

BULBS ▷ BULB

BULBUL *n* songbird of tropical Africa and Asia, with brown plumage and often a distinct crest

BULBULS ▷ BULBUL

BULGE *n* swelling on a normally flat surface ▷ *vb* swell outwards

BULGED ▷ BULGE

BULGER ▷ BULGE

BULGERS ▷ BULGE

BULGES ▷ BULGE

BULGHUR *same as* ▷ BULGUR

BULGHURS ▷ BULGHUR

BULGIER ▷ BULGE

BULGIEST ▷ BULGE

BULGINE *same as* ▷ BULLGINE

BULGINES ▷ BULGINE

BULGINESS ▷ BULGE

BULGING ▷ BULGE

BULGINGLY ▷ BULGE

BULGUR *n* kind of dried cracked wheat

BULGURS ▷ BULGUR

BULGY ▷ BULGE

BULIMIA *n* disorder characterized by compulsive overeating followed by vomiting

BULIMIAC ▷ BULIMIA

BULIMIAS ▷ BULIMIA

BULIMIC ▷ BULIMIA

BULIMICS ▷ BULIMIA

BULIMIES ▷ BULIMIA

BULIMUS ▷ BULIMIA

BULIMUSES ▷ BULIMIA

BULIMY ▷ BULIMIA

BULK *n* volume, size, or magnitude of something ▷ *vb* cohere or cause to cohere in a mass

BULKAGE ▷ BULK

BULKAGES ▷ BULK

BULKED ▷ BULK

BULKER *n* ship that carries unpackaged cargo, usually consisting of a single dry commodity, such as coal or grain

BULKERS ▷ BULKER

BULKHEAD *n* partition in a ship or aeroplane

BULKHEADS ▷ BULKHEAD

BULKIER ▷ BULKY

BULKIEST ▷ BULKY

BULKILY ▷ BULKY

BULKINESS ▷ BULKY

BULKING *n* expansion of excavated material to a volume greater than that of the excavation from which it came

BULKINGS ▷ BULKING

BULKS ▷ BULK

BULKY *adj* very large and massive, esp so as to be unwieldy

BULL *adj* any male bovine animal, esp one that is sexually mature

BULLA *n* leaden seal affixed to a papal bull, having a representation of Saints Peter and Paul on one side and the name of the reigning pope on the other

BULLACE *n* small Eurasian tree of which the damson is the cultivated form

BULLACES ▷ BULLACE

BULLAE ▷ BULLA

BULLARIES ▷ BULLARY

BULLARY *n* boilery for preparing salt

BULLATE *adj* puckered or blistered in appearance

BULLBARS *n* large protective metal grille on the front of some vehicles, esp four-wheel-drive vehicles

BULLBAT *another name for* ▷ NIGHTHAWK

BULLBATS ▷ BULLBAT

BULLBRIER *n* prickly American vine

BULLDOG *n* thickset dog with a broad head and a muscular body

BULLDOGS ▷ BULLDOG

BULLDOZE *vb* demolish or flatten with a bulldozer

BULLDOZED ▷ BULLDOZE

BULLDOZER *n* powerful tractor for moving earth

BULLDOZES ▷ BULLDOZE

BULLDUST *n* fine dust

BULLDUSTS ▷ BULLDUST

BULLDYKE *n* mannish lesbian

BULLDYKES ▷ BULLDYKE

BULLED ▷ BULL

BULLER *vb* make bubbling sound

BULLERED ▷ BULLER

BULLERING ▷ BULLER

BULLERS ▷ BULLER

BULLET *n* small piece of metal fired from a gun ▷ *vb* move extremely quickly

BULLETED ▷ BULLET

BULLETIN *n* short official report or announcement ▷ *vb* make known by bulletin

BULLETING ▷ BULLET

BULLETINS ▷ BULLETIN

BULLETRIE *n* W Indian fruit tree

BULLETS ▷ BULLET

BULLFIGHT *n* public show in which a matador kills a bull

BULLFINCH *n* common European songbird

BULLFROG *n* large American frog with a deep croak

BULLFROGS ▷ BULLFROG

BULLGINE *n* steam locomotive

BULLGINES ▷ BULLGINE

BULLHEAD *n* type of small northern mainly marine fish with a large head covered with bony plates and spines

BULLHEADS ▷ BULLHEAD

BULLHORN *n* portable loudspeaker having a built-in amplifier and microphone

BULLHORNS ▷ BULLHORN

BULLIED ▷ BULLY

BULLIER ▷ BULLY

BULLIES ▷ BULLY

BULLIEST ▷ BULLY

BULLING ▷ BULL

BULLINGS ▷ BULL

BULLION *n* gold or silver in the form of bars

BULLIONS ▷ BULLION

BULLISH *adj* like a bull

BULLISHLY ▷ BULLISH

BULLNECK *n* enlarged neck

BULLNECKS ▷ BULLNECK

BULLNOSE *n* rounded exterior angle, as where two walls meet

BULLNOSES ▷ BULLNOSE

BULLOCK *n* castrated bull ▷ *vb* work hard and long

BULLOCKED ▷ BULLOCK

BULLOCKS ▷ BULLOCK

BULLOCKY *n* driver of a team of bullocks

BULLOSA *as in epidermolysis bullosa* type of genetic skin disorder

BULLOUS *adj* blistered

BULLPEN *n* large cell where prisoners are confined together temporarily

BULLPENS ▷ BULLPEN

BULLPOUT *n* type of fish

BULLPOUTS ▷ BULLPOUT

BULLRING *n* arena for staging bullfights

BULLRINGS ▷ BULLRING

BULLRUSH *same as* ▷ BULRUSH

BULLS ▷ BULL

BULLSHAT ▷ BULLSHIT

BULLSHIT *n* exaggerated or foolish talk ▷ *vb* talk bullshit to

BULLSHITS ▷ BULLSHIT

BULLSHOT *n* cocktail of vodka and beef stock

BULLSHOTS ▷ BULLSHOT

BULLSNAKE *n* American burrowing snake

BULLWADDY *n* N Australian tree which grows in dense thickets

BULLWEED *n* knapweed

BULLWEEDS ▷ BULLWEED

BULLWHACK *vb* flog with short whip

BULLWHIP *n* long tapering heavy whip, esp one of plaited rawhide ▷ *vb* whip with a bullwhip

BULLWHIPS ▷ BULLWHIP

BULLY *n* person who hurts, persecutes, or intimidates weaker people ▷ *vb* hurt, intimidate, or persecute (a weaker or smaller person), esp to make him do something ▷ *adj* dashing

BULLYBOY *n* ruffian or tough, esp a hired one

BULLYBOYS ▷ BULLYBOY

BULLYCIDE *n* suicide as a result of bullying

BULLYING ▷ BULLY

BULLYISM ▷ BULLY

BULLYISMS ▷ BULLY

BULLYRAG *vb* bully, esp by means of cruel practical jokes

BULLYRAGS ▷ BULLYRAG

BULNBULN another name for >LYREBIRD

BULNBULNS >BULNBULN

BULRUSH n tall stiff reed

BULRUSHES >BULRUSH

BULRUSHY >BULRUSH

BULSE n purse or bag for diamonds

BULSES >BULSE

BULWADDEE same as >BULLWADDY

BULWADDY same as >BULLWADDY

BULWARK n wall used as a fortification ▷vb defend or fortify with or as if with a bulwark

BULWARKED >BULWARK

BULWARKS >BULWARK

BUM n buttocks or anus ▷vb get by begging ▷adj of poor quality

BUMALO same as >BUMMALO

BUMALOTI same as >BUMMALOTI

BUMALOTIS >BUMALOTI

BUMBAG n small bag attached to a belt and worn round the waist

BUMBAGS >BUMBAG

BUMBAZE vb confuse; bewilder

BUMBAZED >BUMBAZE

BUMBAZES >BUMBAZE

BUMBAZING >BUMBAZE

BUMBLE vb speak, do, or move in a clumsy way ▷n blunder or botch

BUMBLEBEE n large hairy bee

BUMBLED >BUMBLE

BUMBLEDOM n self-importance in a minor office

BUMBLER >BUMBLE

BUMBLERS >BUMBLE

BUMBLES >BUMBLE

BUMBLING >BUMBLE

BUMBLINGS >BUMBLE

BUMBO n drink with gin or rum, nutmeg, lemon juice, etc

BUMBOAT n any small boat used for ferrying supplies or goods for sale to a ship at anchor or at a mooring

BUMBOATS >BUMBOAT

BUMBOS >BUMBO

BUMELIA n thorny shrub

BUMELIAS >BUMELIA

BUMF n official documents or forms

BUMFLUFF n soft and fluffy growth of hair on the chin of an adolescent

BUMFLUFFS >BUMFLUFF

BUMFS >BUMF

BUMFUCK n remote or insignificant place

BUMFUCKS >BUMFUCK

BUMFUZZLE vb confuse

BUMKIN same as >BUMPKIN

BUMKINS >BUMKIN

BUMMALO n Bombay duck

BUMMALOS >BUMMALO

BUMMALOTI another word for >BUMMALO

BUMMAREE n dealer at Billingsgate fish market

BUMMAREES >BUMMAREE

BUMMED >BUM

BUMMEL n stroll

BUMMELS >STROLL

BUMMER n unpleasant or disappointing experience

BUMMERS >BUMMER

BUMMEST >BUM

BUMMING >BUM

BUMMLE Scots variant of >BUMBLE

BUMMLED >BUMMLE

BUMMLES >BUMMLE

BUMMLING >BUMMLE

BUMMOCK n submerged mass of ice projecting downwards

BUMMOCKS >BUMMOCK

BUMP vb knock or strike with a jolt ▷n dull thud from an impact or collision

BUMPED >BUMP

BUMPER n bar on the front and back of a vehicle to protect against damage ▷adj unusually large or abundant ▷vb toast with a bumper

BUMPERED >BUMPER

BUMPERING >BUMPER

BUMPERS >BUMPER

BUMPH same as >BUMF

BUMPHS >BUMPH

BUMPIER >BUMPY

BUMPIEST >BUMPY

BUMPILY >BUMPY

BUMPINESS >BUMPY

BUMPING >BUMP

BUMPINGS >BUMP

BUMPKIN n awkward simple country person

BUMPKINLY >BUMPKIN

BUMPKINS >BUMPKIN

BUMPOLOGY n humorous word for phrenology

BUMPS >BUMP

BUMPTIOUS adj offensively self-assertive

BUMPY adj having an uneven surface

BUMS >BUM

BUMSTER adj (of trousers) cut low so as to reveal the top part of the buttocks

BUMSTERS npl trousers cut so that the top lies just above the cleft of the buttocks

BUMSUCKER n toady

BUN n small sweet bread roll or cake

BUNA n synthetic rubber formed by polymerizing butadiene or by copolymerizing it with such compounds as acrylonitrile or styrene

BUNAS >BUNA

BUNCE n windfall; boom ▷vb charge someone too much money

BUNCED >BUNCE

BUNCES >BUNCE

BUNCH n number of things growing, fastened, or grouped together ▷vb group or be grouped together in a bunch

BUNCHED >BUNCH

BUNCHES npl hairstyle in which hair is tied into two sections on either side of the head at the back

BUNCHIER >BUNCHY

BUNCHIEST >BUNCHY

BUNCHILY >BUNCHY

BUNCHING >BUNCH

BUNCHINGS >BUNCH

BUNCHY adj composed of or resembling bunches

BUNCING >BUNCE

BUNCO n swindle, esp one by confidence tricksters ▷vb swindle

BUNCOED >BUNCO

BUNCOING >BUNCO

BUNCOMBE same as >BUNKUM

BUNCOMBES >BUNCOMBE

BUNCOS >BUNCO

BUND n embankment or German federation ▷vb form into an embankment

BUNDE >BUND

BUNDED >BUND

BUNDH same as >BANDH

BUNDHS >BUNDH

BUNDIED >BUNDY

BUNDIES >BUNDY

BUNDING >BUND

BUNDIST >BUND

BUNDISTS >BUND

BUNDLE n number of things gathered loosely together ▷vb cause to go roughly or unceremoniously

BUNDLED >BUNDLE

BUNDLER >BUNDLE

BUNDLERS >BUNDLE

BUNDLES >BUNDLE

BUNDLING >BUNDLE

BUNDLINGS >BUNDLE

BUNDOBUST same as >BANDOBAST

BUNDOOK n rifle

BUNDOOKS >BUNDOOK

BUNDS >BUND

BUNDT n type of sweet cake

BUNDTS >BUNDT

BUNDU n largely uninhabited wild region far from towns

BUNDUS >BUNDU

BUNDWALL n concrete or earth wall surrounding a storage tank containing crude oil or its refined product, designed to hold the contents of the tank in the event of a rupture or leak

BUNDWALLS >BUNDWALL

BUNDY n time clock at work ▷vb register arrival or departure from work on a time clock

BUNDYING >BUNDY

BUNFIGHT n tea party

BUNFIGHTS >BUNFIGHT

BUNG n stopper for a cask etc ▷vb close with a bung

BUNGALOID n bungalow-type house

BUNGALOW n one-storey house

BUNGALOWS >BUNGALOW

BUNGED >BUNG

BUNGEE n strong elastic cable

BUNGEES >BUNGEE

BUNGER n firework

BUNGERS >BUNGER

BUNGEY same as >BUNGEE

BUNGEYS >BUNGEY

BUNGHOLE n hole in a cask or barrel through which liquid can be drained

BUNGHOLES >BUNGHOLE

BUNGIE same as >BUNGEE

BUNGIES >BUNGY

BUNGING >BUNG

BUNGLE vb spoil through incompetence ▷n blunder or muddle

BUNGLED >BUNGLE

BUNGLER >BUNGLE

BUNGLERS >BUNGLE

BUNGLES >BUNGLE

BUNGLING >BUNGLE

BUNGLINGS >BUNGLE

BUNGS >BUNG

BUNGWALL n Australian fern with an edible rhizome

BUNGWALLS >BUNGWALL

BUNGY >BUNGEE

BUNIA same as >BUNNIA

BUNIAS >BUNIA

BUNION n inflamed swelling on the big toe

BUNIONS >BUNION

BUNJE same as >BUNGEE

BUNJEE same as >BUNGEE

BUNJEES >BUNJEE

BUNJES >BUNJE

BUNJIE same as >BUNGEE

BUNJIES >BUNJIE

BUNJY same as >BUNGEE

BUNK n narrow shelflike bed ▷vb prepare to sleep

BUNKED >BUNK

BUNKER n sand-filled hollow forming an obstacle on a golf course ▷vb drive (the ball) into a bunker

BUNKERED >BUNKER

BUNKERING >BUNKER

BUNKERS >BUNKER

BUNKHOUSE n (in the US and Canada) building containing the sleeping quarters of workers on a ranch

BUNKING >BUNK

BUNKMATE n person who sleeps in the same quarters as another

BUNKMATES > BUNKMATE

BUNKO same as > BUNCO

BUNKOED > BUNKO

BUNKOING > BUNKO

BUNKOS > BUNKO

BUNKUM n nonsense

BUNKUMS > BUNKUM

BUNN same as > BUN

BUNNET same as > BONNET

BUNNETS > BUNNET

BUNNIA n Hindu shopkeeper

BUNNIAS > BUNNIA

BUNNIES > BUNNY

BUNNS > BUNN

BUNNY n child's word for a rabbit

BUNODONT adj (of the teeth of certain mammals) having cusps that are separate and rounded

BUNRAKU n Japanese form of puppet theatre in which the puppets are usually about four feet high, with moving features as well as limbs and each puppet is manipulated by up to three puppeteers who remain onstage

BUNRAKUS > BUNRAKU

BUNS npl buttocks

BUNSEN as in bunsen burner gas burner used in scientific labs

BUNSENS > BUNSEN

BUNT vb butt (of an animal) (something) with the head or horns ▷ n act or an instance of bunting

BUNTAL n straw obtained from leaves of the talipot palm

BUNTALS > BUNTAL

BUNTED > BUNT

BUNTER n batter who deliberately taps ball lightly

BUNTERS > BUNTER

BUNTIER > BUNT

BUNTIEST > BUNT

BUNTING n decorative flags

BUNTINGS > BUNTING

BUNTLINE n one of several lines fastened to the foot of a square sail for hauling it up to the yard when furling

BUNTLINES > BUNTLINE

BUNTS > BUNT

BUNTY > BUNT

BUNYA n tall dome-shaped Australian coniferous tree

BUNYAS > BUNYA

BUNYIP n legendary monster said to live in swamps and lakes

BUNYIPS > BUNYIP

BUOY n floating marker anchored in the sea ▷ vb prevent from sinking

BUOYAGE n system of buoys

BUOYAGES > BUOYAGE

BUOYANCE same as > BUOYANCY

BUOYANCES > BUOYANCE

BUOYANCY n ability to float in a liquid or to rise in a fluid

BUOYANT adj able to float

BUOYANTLY > BUOYANT

BUOYED > BUOY

BUOYING > BUOY

BUOYS > BUOY

BUPKES same as > BUBKES

BUPKIS same as > BUBKIS

BUPKUS same as > BUBKES

BUPLEVER n type of plant

BUPLEVERS > BUPLEVER

BUPPIE n affluent young Black person

BUPPIES > BUPPY

BUPPY variant of > BUPPY

BUPRESTID n type of mainly tropical beetle, the adults of which are brilliantly coloured

BUPROPION n antidepressant drug used to help people stop smoking

BUQSHA n former Yemeni coin

BUQSHAS > BUQSHA

BUR same as > BURR

BURA same as > BURAN

BURAN n blizzard, with the wind blowing from the north and reaching gale force

BURANS > BURAN

BURAS > BURA

BURB n suburb

BURBLE vb make a bubbling sound ▷ n bubbling or gurgling sound

BURBLED > BURBLE

BURBLER > BURBLE

BURBLERS > BURBLE

BURBLES > BURBLE

BURBLIER > BURBLY

BURBLIEST > BURBLY

BURBLING > BURBLE

BURBLINGS > BURBLE

BURBLY adj burbling

BURBOT n freshwater fish of the cod family that has barbels around its mouth

BURBOTS > BURBOT

BURBS > BURB

BURD Scots form of > BIRD

BURDASH n fringed sash worn over coat

BURDASHES > BURDASH

BURDEN n heavy load ▷ vb put a burden on

BURDENED > BURDEN

BURDENER > BURDEN

BURDENERS > BURDEN

BURDENING > BURDEN

BURDENOUS > BURDEN

BURDENS > BURDEN

BURDIE Scots form of > BIRDIE

BURDIES > BURDIE

BURDIZZO n surgical instrument used to castrate animals

BURDIZZOS > BURDIZZO

BURDOCK n weed with prickly burrs

BURDOCKS > BURDOCK

BURDS > BURD

BUREAU n office that provides a service

BUREAUS > BUREAU

BUREAUX > BUREAU

BURET same as > BURETTE

BURETS > BURET

BURETTE n glass tube for dispensing known volumes of fluids

BURETTES > BURETTE

BURG n fortified town

BURGAGE n (in England) tenure of land or tenement in a town or city, which originally involved a fixed money rent

BURGAGES > BURGAGE

BURGANET same as > BURGONET

BURGANETS > BURGANET

BURGEE n triangular or swallow-tailed flag flown from the mast of a merchant ship for identification and from the mast of a yacht to indicate its owner's membership of a particular yacht club

BURGEES > BURGEE

BURGEON vb develop or grow rapidly ▷ n bud of a plant

BURGEONED > BURGEON

BURGEONS > BURGEON

BURGER n hamburger

BURGERS > BURGER

BURGESS n (in England) citizen or freeman of a borough

BURGESSES > BURGESS

BURGH n Scottish borough

BURGHAL > BURGH

BURGHER n citizen

BURGHERS > BURGHER

BURGHS > BURGH

BURGHUL same as > BULGUR

BURGHULS > BURGHUL

BURGLAR n person who enters a building to commit a crime, esp theft ▷ vb burgle

BURGLARED > BURGLAR

BURGLARS > BURGLAR

BURGLARY n crime of entering a building as a trespasser to commit theft or another offence

BURGLE vb break into (a house, shop, etc)

BURGLED > BURGLE

BURGLES > BURGLE

BURGLING > BURGLE

BURGONET n light 16th-century helmet, usually made of steel, with hinged cheekpieces

BURGONETS > BURGONET

BURGOO n porridge

BURGOOS > BURGOO

BURGOUT same as > BURGOO

BURGOUTS > BURGOUT

BURGRAVE n military governor of a German town or castle, esp in the 12th and 13th centuries

BURGRAVES > BURGRAVE

BURGS > BURG

BURGUNDY adj dark-purplish red

BURHEL same as > BHARAL

BURHELS > BURHEL

BURIAL n burying of a dead body

BURIALS > BURIAL

BURIED > BURY

BURIER n person or thing that buries

BURIERS > BURIER

BURIES > BURY

BURIN n steel chisel used for engraving metal, wood, or marble

BURINIST > BURIN

BURINISTS > BURIN

BURINS > BURIN

BURITI n type of palm tree

BURITIS > BURITI

BURK same as > BERK

BURKA same as > BURQA

BURKAS > BURKA

BURKE vb murder in such a way as to leave no marks on the body, usually by suffocation

BURKED > BURKE

BURKER > BURKE

BURKERS > BURKE

BURKES > BURKE

BURKHA n all-enveloping garment worn by Muslim women

BURKHAS > BURKHA

BURKING > BURKE

BURKITE > BURKE

BURKITES > BURKE

BURKS > BURK

BURL n small knot or lump in wool ▷ vb remove the burls from (cloth)

BURLADERO n safe area for bull-fighter in bull ring

BURLAP n coarse fabric woven from jute, hemp, or the like

BURLAPS > BURLAP

BURLED > BURL

BURLER > BURL

BURLERS > BURL

BURLESK same as > BURLESQUE

BURLESKS > BURLESK

BURLESQUE n artistic work which satirizes a subject by caricature ▷ adj of or characteristic of a burlesque ▷ vb represent or imitate (a person or thing) in a ludicrous way

BURLETTA n type of comic opera

BURLETTAS > BURLETTA

BURLEY same as > BERLEY

BURLEYCUE same as > BURLESQUE

b

BURLEYED > BURLEY
BURLEYING > BURLEY
BURLEYS > BURLEY
BURLIER > BURLY
BURLIEST > BURLY
BURLILY > BURLY
BURLINESS > BURLY
BURLING > BURL
BURLS > BURL
BURLY adj (of a person) broad and strong
BURN vb be or set on fire ▷ n injury or mark caused by fire or exposure to heat
BURNABLE > BURN
BURNABLES > BURN
BURNED > BURN
BURNER n part of a stove or lamp that produces the flame
BURNERS > BURNER
BURNET n type of rose
BURNETS > BURNET
BURNIE n sideburn
BURNIES > BURNIE
BURNING > BURN
BURNINGLY > BURN
BURNINGS > BURN
BURNISH vb make smooth and shiny by rubbing ▷ n shiny finish
BURNISHED > BURNISH
BURNISHER > BURNISH
BURNISHES > BURNISH
BURNOOSE same as > BURNOUS
BURNOOSED > BURNOUS
BURNOOSES > BURNOOSE
BURNOUS n long circular cloak with a hood, worn esp by Arabs
BURNOUSE same as > BURNOUS
BURNOUSED > BURNOUS
BURNOUSES > BURNOUSE
BURNOUT n failure of a mechanical device from excessive heating
BURNOUTS > BURNOUT
BURNS > BURN
BURNSIDE n land along side of burn
BURNSIDES > BURNSIDE
BURNT > BURN
BUROO n government office from which unemployment benefit is distributed
BUROOS > BUROO
BURP n belch ▷ vb belch
BURPED > BURP
BURPEE n type of physical exercise movement
BURPEES > BURPEE
BURPING > BURP
BURPS > BURP
BURQA n long enveloping garment worn by Muslim women in public, covering all but the wearer's eyes
BURQAS > BURQA
BURR n small power-driven hand-operated rotary file, esp for removing burrs or for machining recesses ▷ vb

form a rough edge on (a workpiece)
BURRAMYS n very rare Australian mountain pigmy possum
BURRAWANG n Australian plant with fernlike leaves and an edible nut
BURRED > BURR
BURREL same as > BHARAL
BURRELL variant of > BHARAL
BURRELLS > BURRELL
BURRELS > BURREL
BURRER n person who removes burrs
BURRERS > BURRER
BURRHEL same as > BURREL
BURRHELS > BURRHEL
BURRIER > BURRY
BURRIEST > BURRY
BURRING > BURR
BURRITO n tortilla folded over a filling of minced beef, chicken, cheese, or beans
BURRITOS > BURRITO
BURRO n donkey, esp one used as a pack animal
BURROS > BURRO
BURROW n hole dug in the ground by a rabbit etc ▷ vb dig holes in the ground
BURROWED > BURROW
BURROWER > BURROW
BURROWERS > BURROW
BURROWING > BURROW
BURROWS > BURROW
BURRS > BURR
BURRSTONE same as > BUHRSTONE
BURRY adj full of or covered in burs
BURS > BUR
BURSA n small fluid-filled sac that reduces friction between movable parts of the body, esp at joints
BURSAE > BURSA
BURSAL > BURSA
BURSAR n treasurer of a school, college, or university
BURSARIAL adj of, relating to, or paid by a bursar or bursary
BURSARIES > BURSARY
BURSARS > BURSAR
BURSARY n scholarship
BURSAS > BURSA
BURSATE > BURSA
BURSE n flat case used at Mass as a container for the corporal
BURSEED n type of plant
BURSEEDS > BURSEED
BURSERA adj of a type of gum tree
BURSES > BURSE
BURSICON n hormone, produced by the insect brain, that regulates processes associated with ecdysis, such as darkening of the cuticle

BURSICONS > BURSICON
BURSIFORM adj shaped like a pouch or sac
BURSITIS n inflammation of a bursa, esp one in the shoulder joint
BURST vb break or cause to break open or apart suddenly and noisily, esp from internal pressure ▷ n sudden breaking open or apart ▷ adj broken apart
BURSTED > BURST
BURSTEN > BURST
BURSTER > BURST
BURSTERS > BURST
BURSTING > BURST
BURSTONE same as > BUHRSTONE
BURSTONES > BURSTONE
BURSTS > BURST
BURTHEN archaic word for > BURDEN
BURTHENED > BURTHEN
BURTHENS > BURTHEN
BURTON n type of hoisting tackle
BURTONS > BURTON
BURWEED n any of various plants that bear burs, such as the burdock
BURWEEDS > BURWEED
BURY vb place in a grave
BURYING > BURY
BUS n large motor vehicle for carrying passengers between stops ▷ vb travel by bus
BUSBAR n electrical conductor, maintained at a specific voltage and capable of carrying a high current, usually used to make a common connection between several circuits in a system
BUSBARS > BUSBAR
BUSBIES > BUSBY
BUSBOY n waiter's assistant
BUSBOYS > BUSBOY
BUSBY n tall fur hat worn by some soldiers
BUSED > BUS
BUSERA n Ugandan alcoholic drink made from millet: sometimes mixed with honey
BUSERAS > BUSERA
BUSES > BUS
BUSGIRL n waiter's assistant
BUSGIRLS > BUSGIRL
BUSH n dense woody plant, smaller than a tree ▷ vb fit a bush to (a casing or bearing)
BUSHBABY n small African tree-living mammal with large eyes
BUSHBUCK n small nocturnal spiral-horned antelope of Africa, with a reddish-brown coat with a few white markings

BUSHBUCKS > BUSHBUCK
BUSHCRAFT n ability and experience in matters concerned with living in the bush
BUSHED adj extremely tired
BUSHEL n obsolete unit of measure equal to 8 gallons (36.4 litres) ▷ vb alter or mend (a garment)
BUSHELED > BUSHEL
BUSHELER > BUSHEL
BUSHELERS > BUSHEL
BUSHELING > BUSHEL
BUSHELLED > BUSHEL
BUSHELLER > BUSHEL
BUSHELMAN > BUSHEL
BUSHELMEN > BUSHEL
BUSHELS > BUSHEL
BUSHER > BUSH
BUSHERS > BUSH
BUSHES > BUSH
BUSHFIRE n uncontrolled fire in the bush
BUSHFIRES > BUSHFIRE
BUSHFLIES > BUSHFLY
BUSHFLY n small black Australian fly that breeds in faeces and dung
BUSHGOAT n S African antelope
BUSHGOATS > BUSHGOAT
BUSHIDO n feudal code of the Japanese samurai, stressing self-discipline, courage and loyalty
BUSHIDOS > BUSHIDO
BUSHIE same as > BUSHY
BUSHIER > BUSHY
BUSHIES > BUSHY
BUSHIEST > BUSHY
BUSHILY > BUSHY
BUSHINESS > BUSHY
BUSHING same as > BUSH
BUSHINGS > BUSHING
BUSHLAND n land characterized by natural vegetation
BUSHLANDS > BUSHLAND
BUSHLESS > BUSH
BUSHLIKE > BUSH
BUSHMAN n person who lives or travels in the bush
BUSHMEAT n meat taken from any animal native to African forests, including species that may be endangered or not usually eaten outside Africa
BUSHMEATS > BUSHMEAT
BUSHMEN > BUSHMAN
BUSHPIG n wild brown or black forest pig of tropical Africa and Madagascar
BUSHPIGS > BUSHPIG
BUSHTIT n small grey active North American songbird
BUSHTITS > BUSHTIT
BUSHVELD n bushy countryside
BUSHVELDS > BUSHVELD
BUSHWA n nonsense

BUSHWAH same as
> BUSHWA
BUSHWAHS > BUSHWAH
BUSHWALK vb hike through
bushland
BUSHWALKS > BUSHWALK
BUSHWAS > BUSHWA
BUSHWHACK vb ambush
BUSHWOMAN > BUSHMAN
BUSHWOMEN > BUSHMAN
BUSHY adj (of hair) thick
and shaggy ▷ n person
who lives in the bush
BUSIED > BUSY
BUSIER > BUSY
BUSIES > BUSY
BUSIEST > BUSY
BUSILY adv in a busy
manner
BUSINESS n purchase and
sale of goods and services
BUSINESSY adj of,
relating to, typical of, or
suitable for the world of
commercial or industrial
business
BUSING > BUS
BUSINGS > BUS
BUSK vb act as a busker ▷ n
strip of whalebone, wood,
steel, etc, inserted into the
front of a corset to stiffen it
BUSKED > BUSK
BUSKER > BUSK
BUSKERS > BUSK
BUSKET n bouquet
BUSKETS > BUSKET
BUSKIN n (formerly)
sandal-like covering for the
foot and leg, reaching the
calf and usually laced
BUSKINED adj relating to
tragedy
BUSKING > BUSK
BUSKINGS > BUSK
BUSKINS > BUSKIN
BUSKS > BUSK
BUSKY same as > BOSKY
BUSLOAD n number of
people bus carries
BUSLOADS > BUSLOAD
BUSMAN n person who
drives a bus
BUSMEN > BUSMAN
BUSS archaic or dialect word
for > KISS
BUSSED > BUS
BUSSES > BUS
BUSSING > BUS
BUSSINGS > BUS
BUSSU n type of palm tree
BUSSUS > BUSSU
BUST n chest of a human
being, esp a woman's
bosom ▷ adj broken ▷ vb
burst or break
BUSTARD n bird with long
strong legs, a heavy body, a
long neck, and speckled
plumage
BUSTARDS > BUSTARD
BUSTED > BUST
BUSTEE same as > BASTI
BUSTEES > BUSTEE

BUSTER n person or thing
destroying something as
specified
BUSTERS > BUSTER
BUSTI same as > BASTI
BUSTIC n type of small
American tree
BUSTICATE vb break
BUSTICS > BUSTIC
BUSTIER n close-fitting
strapless women's top
BUSTIERS > BUSTIER
BUSTIEST > BUSTY
BUSTINESS > BUSTY
BUSTING > BUST
BUSTINGS > BUST
BUSTIS > BUSTI
BUSTLE vb hurry with a
show of activity or energy
▷ n energetic and noisy
activity
BUSTLED > BUSTLE
BUSTLER > BUSTLE
BUSTLERS > BUSTLE
BUSTLES > BUSTLE
BUSTLINE n shape or size
of woman's bust
BUSTLINES > BUSTLINE
BUSTLING > BUSTLE
BUSTS > BUST
BUSTY adj (of a woman)
having a prominent bust
BUSULFAN n drug used to
treat cancer
BUSULFANS > BUSULFAN
BUSUUTI n long garment
with short sleeves and a
square neckline, worn by
Ugandan women, esp in S
Uganda
BUSUUTIS > BUSUUTI
BUSY adj actively employed
▷ vb keep (someone, esp
oneself) busy
BUSYBODY n meddlesome
or nosy person
BUSYING > BUSY
BUSYNESS > BUSY
BUSYWORK n unproductive
work
BUSYWORKS > BUSYWORK
BUT prep except ▷ adv only
▷ n outer room of a
two-roomed cottage:
usually the kitchen
BUTADIENE n colourless
easily liquefiable
flammable gas
BUTANE n gas used for fuel
BUTANES > BUTANE
BUTANOIC as in butanoic
acid kind of acid
BUTANOL n colourless
substance
BUTANOLS > BUTANOL
BUTANONE n colourless
soluble flammable liquid
used mainly as a solvent for
resins
BUTANONES > BUTANONE
BUTCH adj markedly or
aggressively masculine ▷ n
lesbian who is noticeably
masculine
BUTCHER n person who

slaughters animals or sells
their meat ▷ vb kill and
prepare (animals) for meat
BUTCHERED > BUTCHER
BUTCHERER > BUTCHER
BUTCHERLY > BUTCHER
BUTCHERS > BUTCHER
BUTCHERY n senseless
slaughter
BUTCHES > BUTCH
BUTCHEST > BUTCH
BUTCHING > BUTCH
BUTCHINGS > BUTCH
BUTCHNESS > BUTCH
BUTE n drug used illegally
to dope horses
BUTENE n pungent
colourless gas
BUTENES > BUTENE
BUTEO n type of American
hawk
BUTEONINE adj of hawks
BUTEOS > BUTEO
BUTES > BUTE
BUTLE vb act as butler
BUTLED > BUTLE
BUTLER n chief male
servant ▷ vb act as a butler
BUTLERAGE > BUTLER
BUTLERED > BUTLER
BUTLERIES > BUTLERY
BUTLERING > BUTLER
BUTLERS > BUTLER
BUTLERY n butler's room
BUTLES > BUTLE
BUTLING > BUTLE
BUTMENT same as
> ABUTMENT
BUTMENTS > BUTMENT
BUTS > BUT
BUTSUDAN n (in Buddhism)
small household altar
BUTSUDANS > BUTSUDAN
BUTT n thicker or blunt end
of something, such as the
end of the stock of a rifle
▷ vb strike or push with the
head or horns
BUTTALS n abuttal
BUTTE n isolated steep
flat-topped hill
BUTTED > BUTT
BUTTER n edible fatty
yellow solid made form
cream ▷ vb put butter on
BUTTERBUR n Eurasian
plant with fragrant whitish
or purple flowers and
woolly stems
BUTTERCUP n small yellow
flower
BUTTERED > BUTTER
BUTTERFAT n fatty
substance of milk from
which butter is made,
consisting of a mixture of
glycerides, mainly butyrin,
olein, and palmitin
BUTTERFLY n insect with
brightly coloured wings
BUTTERIER > BUTTERY
BUTTERIES > BUTTERY
BUTTERINE n artificial
butter made partly from

milk
BUTTERING > BUTTER
BUTTERNUT n E North
American walnut tree
BUTTERS > BUTTER
BUTTERY n (in some
universities) room in which
food and drink are sold to
students ▷ adj containing,
like, or coated with butter
BUTTES > BUTTE
BUTTHEAD n stupid person
BUTTHEADS > BUTTHEAD
BUTTIES > BUTTY
BUTTING > BUTT
BUTTINSKI same as
> BUTTINSKY
BUTTINSKY n busybody
BUTTLE vb act as butler
BUTTLED > BUTTLE
BUTTLES > BUTTLE
BUTTLING > BUTTLE
BUTTOCK n either of the
two fleshy masses that
form the human rump ▷ vb
perform a kind of wrestling
manoeuvre on a person
BUTTOCKED > BUTTOCK
BUTTOCKS > BUTTOCK
BUTTON n small disc or
knob sewn to clothing,
which can be passed
through a slit in another
piece of fabric to fasten
them ▷ vb fasten with
buttons
BUTTONED > BUTTON
BUTTONER > BUTTON
BUTTONERS > BUTTON
BUTTONING > BUTTON
BUTTONS n page boy
BUTTONY > BUTTON
BUTTRESS n structure to
support a wall ▷ vb support
with, or as if with, a
buttress
BUTTS > BUTT
BUTTSTOCK n part of gun
BUTTY n sandwich
BUTTYMAN n offensive
term for a homosexual
BUTTYMEN > BUTTYMAN
BUTUT n Gambian
monetary unit worth one
hundredth of a dalasi
BUTUTS > BUTUT
BUTYL adj of or containing
any of four isomeric forms
of the group C_4H_9 ▷ n of,
consisting of, or containing
any of four isomeric forms
of the group C_4H_9.
BUTYLATE vb introduce
butyl into (compound)
BUTYLATED > BUTYLATE
BUTYLATES > BUTYLATE
BUTYLENE same as
> BUTENE
BUTYLENES > BUTYLENE
BUTYLS > BUTYL
BUTYRAL n type of resin
BUTYRALS > BUTYRAL
BUTYRATE n any salt or
ester of butyric acid
BUTYRATES > BUTYRATE

b

b

BUTYRIC as in *butyric acid* type of acid

BUTYRIN *n* colourless liquid ester or oil found in butter. It is formed from butyric acid and glycerine

BUTYRINS > BUTYRIN

BUTYROUS *adj* butyraceous

BUTYRYL *n* radical of butyric acid

BUTYRYLS > BUTYRYL

BUVETTE *n* roadside café

BUVETTES > BUVETTE

BUXOM *adj* (of a woman) healthily plump and full-bosomed

BUXOMER > BUXOM

BUXOMEST > BUXOM

BUXOMLY > BUXOM

BUXOMNESS > BUXOM

BUY *vb* acquire by paying money for ▷ *n* thing acquired through payment

BUYABLE > BUY

BUYABLES > BUY

BUYBACK *n* repurchase by a company of some or all of its shares from an investor, who acquired them by putting venture capital into the company when it was formed

BUYBACKS > BUYBACK

BUYER *n* customer

BUYERS > BUYER

BUYING *n* as in *panic buying* the buying up of large quantities of something feared to be scarce

BUYINGS > BUYING

BUYOFF *n* purchase

BUYOFFS > BUYOFF

BUYOUT *n* purchase of a company, esp by its former management or staff

BUYOUTS > BUYOUT

BUYS > BUY

BUZKASHI *n* game played in Afghanistan, in which opposing teams of horsemen strive for possession of the headless carcass of a goat

BUZKASHIS > BUZKASHI

BUZUKI *same as* > BOUZOUKI

BUZUKIA > BUZUKI

BUZUKIS > BUZUKI

BUZZ *n* rapidly vibrating humming sound ▷ *vb* make a humming sound

BUZZARD *n* bird of prey of the hawk family

BUZZARDS > BUZZARD

BUZZBAIT *n* fishing lure with small blades that stir the water

BUZZBAITS > BUZZBAIT

BUZZCUT *n* very short haircut

BUZZCUTS > BUZZCUT

BUZZED > BUZZ

BUZZER *n* electronic device that produces a buzzing sound as a signal

BUZZERS > BUZZER

BUZZES > BUZZ

BUZZIER > BUZZY

BUZZIEST > BUZZY

BUZZING > BUZZ

BUZZINGLY > BUZZ

BUZZINGS > BUZZ

BUZZKILL *n* someone or something that spoils the enjoyment of others

BUZZKILLS > BUZZKILL

BUZZWIG *n* bushy wig

BUZZWIGS > BUZZWIG

BUZZWORD *n* word, often originating in a particular jargon, that becomes a vogue word in the community as a whole or among a particular group

BUZZWORDS > BUZZWORD

BUZZY *adj* making a buzzing sound

BWANA *n* (in E Africa) master, often used as a respectful form of address

BWANAS > BWANA

BWAZI *same as* > BUAZE

BWAZIS > BWAZI

BY *prep* indicating the doer of an action, nearness, movement past, time before or during which, etc ▷ *adv* near ▷ *n* bye

BYCATCH *n* unwanted fish and other sea animals caught in a fishing net along with the desired kind of fish

BYCATCHES > BYCATCH

BYCOKET *n* former Italian high-crowned hat

BYCOKETS > BYCOKET

BYDE *same as* > BIDE

BYDED > BYDE

BYDES > BYDE

BYDING > BYDE

BYE *n* situation where a player or team wins a round by having no opponent ▷ *interj* goodbye ▷ *sentence substitute* goodbye

BYELAW *n* rule made by a local authority for the regulation of its affairs or management of the area it governs

BYELAWS > BYELAW

BYES > BYE

BYGONE *adj* past

BYGONES > BYGONE

BYKE *same as* > BICYCLE

BYKED > BICYCLE

BYKES > BICYCLE

BYKING > BICYCLE

BYLANDER *same as* > BILANDER

BYLANDERS > BYLANDER

BYLANE *n* side lane or alley off a road

BYLANES > BYLANE

BYLAW *n* rule made by a local authority

BYLAWS > BYLAW

BYLINE *n* line under the title of a newspaper or magazine article giving the author's name ▷ *vb* give a byline to

BYLINED > BYLINE

BYLINER > BYLINE

BYLINERS > BYLINE

BYLINES > BYLINE

BYLINING > BYLINE

BYLIVE *same as* > BELIVE

BYNAME *n* nickname

BYNAMES > BYNAME

BYNEMPT > BENAME

BYPASS *n* main road built to avoid a city ▷ *vb* go round or avoid

BYPASSED > BYPASS

BYPASSES > BYPASS

BYPASSING > BYPASS

BYPAST > BYPASS

BYPATH *n* little-used path or track, esp in the country

BYPATHS > BYPATH

BYPLACE *n* private place

BYPLACES > BYPLACE

BYPLAY *n* secondary action or talking carried on apart while the main action proceeds, esp in a play

BYPLAYS > BYPLAY

BYPRODUCT *n* secondary product

BYRE *n* shelter for cows

BYREMAN *n* man who works in byre

BYREMEN > BYREMAN

BYRES > BYRE

BYREWOMAN *n* woman who works in byre

BYREWOMEN > BYREWOMAN

BYRL *same as* > BIRL

BYRLADY *interj* short for By Our Lady

BYRLAKIN *interj* By Our Ladykin

BYRLAW *same as* > BYLAW

BYRLAWS > BYRLAW

BYRLED > BYRL

BYRLING > BYRL

BYRLS > BYRL

BYRNIE *n* archaic word for coat of mail

BYRNIES > BYRNIE

BYROAD *n* secondary or side road

BYROADS > BYROAD

BYROOM *n* private room

BYROOMS > BYROOM

BYS > BY

BYSSAL *adj* of mollusc's byssus

BYSSI > BYSSUS

BYSSINE *adj* made from flax

BYSSOID *adj* consisting of fine fibres

BYSSUS *n* mass of strong threads secreted by a sea mussel or similar mollusc that attaches the animal to a hard fixed surface

BYSSUSES > BYSSUS

BYSTANDER *n* person present but not involved

BYSTREET *n* obscure or secondary street

BYSTREETS > BYSTREET

BYTALK *n* trivial conversation

BYTALKS > BYTALK

BYTE *n* group of bits processed as one unit of data

BYTES > BYTE

BYTOWNITE *n* rare mineral

BYWAY *n* minor road

BYWAYS > BYWAY

BYWONER *n* poor tenant-farmer

BYWONERS > BYWONER

BYWORD *n* person or thing regarded as a perfect example of something

BYWORDS > BYWORD

BYWORK *n* work done outside usual working hours

BYWORKS > BYWORK

BYZANT *same as* > BEZANT

BYZANTINE *adj* of, characteristic of, or relating to Byzantium or the Byzantine Empire

BYZANTS > BYZANT

Cc

CAA *a Scot word for* > CALL
CAED > CAA
CAAING > CAA
CAAS > CAA
CAATINGA *n* Brazilian semi-arid scrub forest
CAATINGAS > CAATINGA
CAB *n* taxi ▷ *vb* take a taxi
CABA *same as* > CABAS
CABAL *n* small group of political plotters ▷ *vb* form a cabal
CABALA *a variant spelling of* > KABBALAH
CABALAS > CABALA
CABALETTA *n* final section of an aria
CABALETTE > CABALETTA
CABALISM > CABALA
CABALISMS > CABALA
CABALIST > CABALA
CABALISTS > CABALA
CABALLED > CABAL
CABALLER > CABAL
CABALLERO *n* Spanish gentleman
CABALLERS > CABAL
CABALLINE *adj* pertaining to a horse
CABALLING > CABAL
CABALS > CABAL
CABANA *n* tent used as a dressing room by the sea
CABANAS > CABANA
CABARET *n* dancing and singing show in a nightclub
CABARETS > CABARET
CABAS *n* reticule
CABBAGE *n* vegetable with a large head of green leaves ▷ *vb* steal
CABBAGED > CABBAGE
CABBAGES > CABBAGE
CABBAGEY > CABBAGE
CABBAGING > CABBAGE
CABBAGY > CABBAGE
CABBALA *a variant spelling of* > KABBALAH
CABBALAH *same as* > CABBALA
CABBALAHS > CABBALA
CABBALAS > CABBALA
CABBALISM > CABBALA
CABBALIST > CABBALA
CABBED > CAB
CABBIE *n* taxi driver
CABBIES > CABBIE
CABBING > CAB
CABBY *same as* > CABBIE

CABDRIVER *n* taxi-driver
CABER *n* tree trunk tossed in competition at Highland games
CABERNET *n* type of grape, or the red wine made from it
CABERNETS > CABERNET
CABERS > CABER
CABESTRO *n* halter made from horsehair
CABESTROS > CABESTRO
CABEZON *n* large food fish of N American Pacific coastal waters, with greenish flesh
CABEZONE *same as* > CABEZON
CABEZONES > CABEZON
CABEZONS > CABEZON
CABILDO *n* Spanish municipal council
CABILDOS > CABILDO
CABIN *n* compartment in a ship or aircraft ▷ *vb* confine in a small space
CABINED > CABIN
CABINET *n* piece of furniture with drawers or shelves
CABINETRY *n* cabinetmaking
CABINETS > CABINET
CABINING > CABIN
CABINMATE *n* sharer of cabin
CABINS > CABIN
CABLE *n* strong thick rope; a wire or bundle of wires that conduct electricity ▷ *vb* send (someone) a message by cable
CABLECAST *n* broadcast on cable
CABLED > CABLE
CABLEGRAM *n* message sent by cable
CABLER *n* cable broadcasting company
CABLERS > CABLER
CABLES > CABLE
CABLET *n* small cable, esp a cable-laid rope that has a circumference of less than 25 centimetres (ten inches)
CABLETS > CABLET
CABLEWAY *n* system for moving people or bulk materials in which suspended cars, buckets, etc, run on cables that extend between terminal towers

CABLEWAYS > CABLEWAY
CABLING > CABLE
CABLINGS > CABLE
CABMAN *n* driver of a cab
CABMEN > CABMAN
CABOB *vb* roast on a skewer
CABOBBED > CABOB
CABOBBING > CABOB
CABOBS > CABOB
CABOC *n* type of Scottish cheese
CABOCEER *n* in African history, indigenous representative appointed by his leader to deal with European slave traders
CABOCEERS > CABOCEER
CABOCHED *adj* in heraldry, with the face exposed, but neck concealed
CABOCHON *n* smooth domed gem, polished but unfaceted
CABOCHONS > CABOCHON
CABOCS > CABOC
CABOMBA *n* type of aquatic plant
CABOMBAS > CABOMBA
CABOODLE *n* lot, bunch, or group
CABOODLES > CABOODLE
CABOOSE *n* guard's van on a train
CABOOSES > CABOOSE
CABOSHED *same as* > CABOCHED
CABOTAGE *n* coastal navigation or shipping, esp within the borders of one country
CABOTAGES > CABOTAGE
CABOVER *adj* of or denoting a truck or lorry in which the cab is over the engine
CABRE *adj* heraldic term designating an animal rearing
CABRESTA *variant of* > CABESTRO
CABRESTAS > CABRESTA
CABRESTO *variant of* > CABESTRO
CABRESTOS > CABRESTO
CABRETTA *n* soft leather obtained from the skins of certain South American or African sheep
CABRETTAS > CABRETTA

CABRIE *n* pronghorn antelope
CABRIES > CABRIE
CABRILLA *n* type of food fish occurring in warm seas around Florida and the Caribbean
CABRILLAS > CABRILLA
CABRIO *short for* > CABRIOLET
CABRIOLE *n* type of furniture leg, popular in the first half of the 18th century, in which an upper convex curve descends tapering to a concave curve
CABRIOLES > CABRIOLE
CABRIOLET *n* small horse-drawn carriage with a folding hood
CABRIOS > CABRIO
CABRIT *n* pronghorn antelope
CABRITS > CABRIT
CABS > CAB
CABSTAND *n* taxi-rank
CABSTANDS > CABSTAND
CACA *n* heroin
CACAFOGO *same as* > CACAFUEGO
CACAFOGOS > CACAFUEGO
CACAFUEGO *n* spitfire
CACAO *same as* > COCOA
CACAOS > COCOA
CACAS > CACA
CACHACA *n* white Brazilian rum made from sugar cane
CACHACAS > CACHACA
CACHAEMIA *n* poisoned condition of the blood
CACHAEMIC > CACHAEMIA
CACHALOT *n* sperm whale
CACHALOTS > CACHALOT
CACHE *n* hidden store of weapons or treasure ▷ *vb* store in a cache
CACHECTIC > CACHEXIA
CACHED > CACHE
CACHEPOT *n* ornamental container for a flowerpot
CACHEPOTS > CACHEPOT
CACHES > CACHE
CACHET *n* prestige, distinction ▷ *vb* apply a commemorative design to an envelope, as a first-day cover
CACHETED > CACHET
CACHETING > CACHET

CACHETS > CACHET

CACHEXIA *n* generally weakened condition of body or mind resulting from any debilitating chronic disease

CACHEXIAS > CACHEXIA

CACHEXIC > CACHEXIA

CACHEXIES > CACHEXIA

CACHEXY *same as* **>** CACHEXIA

CACHING > CACHE

CACHOLONG *n* a type of opal

CACHOLOT *same as* **>** CACHALOT

CACHOLOTS > CACHALOT

CACHOU *same as* **>** CATECHU

CACHOUS > CATECHU

CACHUCHA *n* graceful Spanish solo dance in triple time

CACHUCHAS > CACHUCHA

CACIQUE *n* American Indian chief in a Spanish-speaking region

CACIQUES > CACIQUE

CACIQUISM *n* (esp in Spanish America) government by local political bosses

CACK *n* excrement

CACKIER > CACKY

CACKIEST > CACKY

CACKLE *vb* laugh shrilly ▷ *n* cackling noise

CACKLED > CACKLE

CACKLER > CACKLE

CACKLERS > CACKLE

CACKLES > CACKLE

CACKLING > CACKLE

CACKS > CACK

CACKY *adj* of or like excrement

CACODEMON *n* evil spirit or devil

CACODOXY *n* heterodoxy

CACODYL *n* oily poisonous liquid with a strong garlic smell

CACODYLIC > CACODYL

CACODYLS > CACODYL

CACOEPIES > CACOEPY

CACOEPY *n* bad or mistaken pronunciation

CACOETHES *n* uncontrollable urge or desire, esp for something harmful

CACOETHIC **>** CACOETHES

CACOGENIC *adj* reducing the quality of a race

CACOLET *n* seat fitted to the back of a mule

CACOLETS > CACOLET

CACOLOGY *n* bad choice of words

CACOMIXL *n* carnivorous mammal

CACOMIXLE *same as* **>** CACOMIXL

CACOMIXLS > CACOMIXL

CACONYM *n* erroneous name

CACONYMS > CACONYM

CACONYMY > CACONYM

CACOON *n* large seed of the sword-bean

CACOONS > CACOON

CACOPHONY *n* harsh discordant sound

CACOTOPIA *n* dystopia, the opposite of utopia

CACTI > CACTUS

CACTIFORM *adj* cactus-like

CACTOID *adj* resembling a cactus

CACTUS *n* fleshy desert plant with spines but no leaves

CACTUSES > CACTUS

CACUMEN *n* apex

CACUMINA > CACUMEN

CACUMINAL *adj* relating to or denoting a consonant articulated with the tip of the tongue turned back towards the hard palate ▷ *n* consonant articulated in this manner

CAD *n* dishonourable man

CADAGA *n* eucalyptus tree of tropical and subtropical Australia with a smooth green trunk

CADAGAS > CADAGA

CADAGI *same as* **>** CADAGA

CADAGIS > CADAGI

CADASTER *n* official register showing details of ownership, boundaries, and value of real property in a district, made for taxation purposes

CADASTERS > CADASTER

CADASTRAL > CADASTER

CADASTRE *same as* **>** CADASTER

CADASTRES > CADASTER

CADAVER *n* corpse

CADAVERIC > CADAVER

CADAVERS > CADAVER

CADDICE *same as* **>** CADDIS

CADDICES > CADDIS

CADDIE *n* person who carries a golfer's clubs ▷ *vb* act as a caddie

CADDIED > CADDIE

CADDIES > CADDIE

CADDIS *n* type of coarse woollen yarn, braid, or fabric

CADDISED *adj* trimmed with a type of ribbon

CADDISES > CADDIS

CADDISFLY *n* small fly

CADDISH > CAD

CADDISHLY > CAD

CADDY *same as* **>** CADDIE

CADDYING > CADDIE

CADDYSS *same as* **>** CADDIS

CADDYSSES > CADDIS

CADE *n* juniper tree ▷ *adj* (of a young animal) left by its mother and reared by

humans, usually as a pet

CADEAU *n* present

CADEAUX > CADEAU

CADEE *old form of* **>** CADET

CADEES > CADEE

CADELLE *n* type of beetle that feeds on flour, grain, and other stored foods

CADELLES > CADELLE

CADENCE *n* rise and fall in the pitch of the voice ▷ *vb* modulate musically

CADENCED > CADENCE

CADENCES > CADENCE

CADENCIES > CADENCY

CADENCING > CADENCE

CADENCY *same as* **>** CADENCE

CADENT *adj* having cadence

CADENTIAL > CADENT

CADENZA *n* complex solo passage in a piece of music

CADENZAS > CADENZA

CADES > CADE

CADET *n* young person training for the armed forces or police

CADETS > CADET

CADETSHIP > CADET

CADGE *vb* get (something) by taking advantage of someone's generosity

CADGED > CADGE

CADGER *n* person who cadges

CADGERS > CADGER

CADGES > CADGE

CADGIER > CADGY

CADGIEST > CADGY

CADGING > CADGE

CADGY *adj* cheerful

CADI *n* judge in a Muslim community

CADIE *n* messenger

CADIES > CADIE

CADIS > CADI

CADMIC > CADMIUM

CADMIUM *n* bluish-white metallic element used in alloys

CADMIUMS > CADMIUM

CADRANS *n* instrument used in gemcutting

CADRANSES > CADRANS

CADRE *n* small group of people selected and trained to form the core of a political organization or military unit

CADRES > CADRE

CADS > CAD

CADUAC *n* windfall

CADUACS > CADUAC

CADUCEAN > CADUCEUS

CADUCEI > CADUCEUS

CADUCEUS *n* staff entwined with two serpents and bearing a pair of wings at the top, carried by Hermes (Mercury) as messenger of the gods

CADUCITY *n* perishableness

CADUCOUS *adj* (of parts of

a plant or animal) shed during the life of the organism

CAECA > CAECUM

CAECAL > CAECUM

CAECALLY > CAECUM

CAECILIAN *n* type of tropical limbless amphibian resembling an earthworm

CAECITIS *n* inflammation of the caecum

CAECUM *n* pouch at the beginning of the large intestine

CAEOMA *n* aecium in some rust fungi that has no surrounding membrane

CAEOMAS > CAEOMA

CAERULE *same as* **>** CERULE

CAERULEAN *same as* **>** CERULEAN

CAESAR *n* any emperor, autocrat, dictator, or other powerful ruler

CAESAREAN *n* surgical incision through the abdominal and uterine walls in order to deliver a baby

CAESARIAN *variant spelling of* **>** CAESAREAN

CAESARISM *n* imperialism

CAESARS > CAESAR

CAESE *interj* Shakespearean interjection

CAESIOUS *adj* having a waxy bluish-grey coating

CAESIUM *n* silvery-white metallic element used in photocells

CAESIUMS > CAESIUM

CAESTUS *same as* **>** CESTUS

CAESTUSES > CAESTUS

CAESURA *n* pause in a line of verse

CAESURAE > CAESURA

CAESURAL > CAESURA

CAESURAS > CAESURA

CAESURIC > CAESURA

CAFARD *n* feeling of severe depression

CAFARDS > CAFARD

CAFE *n* small or inexpensive restaurant serving light refreshments

CAFES > CAFE

CAFETERIA *n* self-service restaurant

CAFETIERE *n* kind of coffeepot in which boiling water is poured onto ground coffee and a plunger fitted with a metal filter is pressed down, forcing the grounds to the bottom

CAFETORIA *variant of* **>** CAFETERIA

CAFF *n* café

CAFFEIN *same as* **>** CAFFEINE

CAFFEINE *n* stimulant found in tea and coffee

CAFFEINES > CAFFEINE
CAFFEINIC *adj* of or containing caffeine
CAFFEINS > CAFFEINE
CAFFEISM *n* addiction to caffeine
CAFFEISMS > CAFFEISM
CAFFILA *n* caravan train
CAFFILAS > CAFFILA
CAFFS > CAFF
CAFILA *same as* > CAFFILA
CAFILAS > CAFILA
CAFTAN *same as* > KAFTAN
CAFTANED *adj* wearing caftan
CAFTANS > CAFTAN
CAG *same as* > CAGOULE
CAGANER *n* figure of a squatting defecating person, a traditional character in Catalan Christmas crèche scenes
CAGANERS > CAGANER
CAGE *n* enclosure of bars or wires, for keeping animals or birds ▷ *vb* confine in a cage
CAGED > CAGE
CAGEFUL *n* amount which fills a cage to capacity
CAGEFULS > CAGEFUL
CAGELIKE > CAGE
CAGELING *n* bird kept in a cage
CAGELINGS > CAGELING
CAGER *n* basketball player
CAGERS > CAGER
CAGES > CAGE
CAGEWORK *n* something constructed as if from the bars of a cage
CAGEWORKS > CAGEWORK
CAGEY *adj* reluctant to go into details
CAGEYNESS > CAGEY
CAGIER > CAGEY
CAGIEST > CAGEY
CAGILY > CAGEY
CAGINESS > CAGY
CAGING > CAGE
CAGMAG *adj* done shoddily ▷ *vb* chat idly
CAGMAGGED > CAGMAG
CAGMAGS > CAGMAG
CAGOT *n* member of a class of French outcasts
CAGOTS > CAGOT
CAGOUL *same as* > CAGOULE
CAGOULE *n* lightweight hooded waterproof jacket
CAGOULES > CAGOULE
CAGOULS > CAGOUL
CAGS > CAG
CAGY *same as* > CAGEY
CAGYNESS > CAGY
CAHIER *n* notebook
CAHIERS > CAHIER
CAHOOT *n* partnership
CAHOOTS > CAHOOT
CAHOW *n* Bermuda petrel
CAHOWS > CAHOW
CAID *n* Moroccan district administrator
CAIDS > CAID
CAILLACH *same as* > CAILLEACH
CAILLACHS > CAILLACH
CAILLE *n* quail
CAILLEACH *n* old woman
CAILLES > CAILLE
CAILLIACH *same as* > CAILLEACH
CAIMAC *same as* > CAIMACAM
CAIMACAM *n* Turkish governor of a sanjak
CAIMACAMS > CAIMACAM
CAIMACS > CAIMAC
CAIMAN *same as* > CAYMAN
CAIMANS > CAIMAN
CAIN *n* (in Scotland and Ireland) payment in kind, usually farm produce paid as rent
CAINS > CAIN
CAIQUE *n* long narrow light rowing skiff used on the Bosporus
CAIQUES > CAIQUE
CAIRD *n* travelling tinker
CAIRDS > CAIRD
CAIRN *n* mound of stones erected as a memorial or marker
CAIRNED *adj* marked by a cairn
CAIRNGORM *n* yellow or brownish quartz gemstone
CAIRNIER > CAIRNY
CAIRNIEST > CAIRNY
CAIRNS > CAIRN
CAIRNY *adj* covered with cairns
CAISSON *same as* > COFFERDAM
CAISSONS > CAISSON
CAITIFF *n* cowardly or base person ▷ *adj* cowardly
CAITIFFS > CAITIFF
CAITIVE *n* captive
CAITIVES > CAITIVE
CAJAPUT *same as* > CAJUPUT
CAJAPUTS > CAJAPUT
CAJEPUT *same as* > CAJUPUT
CAJEPUTS > CAJEPUT
CAJOLE *vb* persuade by flattery
CAJOLED > CAJOLE
CAJOLER > CAJOLE
CAJOLERS > CAJOLE
CAJOLERY > CAJOLE
CAJOLES > CAJOLE
CAJOLING > CAJOLE
CAJON *n* Peruvian wooden box used as a drum
CAJONES > CAJON
CAJUN *n* music of the Cajun people, combining blues and European folk music
CAJUPUT *n* small tree or shrub native to the East Indies and Australia, with whitish flowers and leaves
CAJUPUTS > CAJUPUT

CAKE *n* sweet food baked from a mixture of flour, eggs, etc ▷ *vb* form into a hardened mass or crust
CAKED > CAKE
CAKES > CAKE
CAKEWALK *n* dance based on a march with intricate steps, originally performed by African-Americans with the prize of a cake for the best performers ▷ *vb* perform the cakewalk
CAKEWALKS > CAKEWALK
CAKEY > CAKE
CAKIER > CAKE
CAKIEST > CAKE
CAKINESS > CAKE
CAKING > CAKE
CAKINGS > CAKE
CAKY > CAKE
CALABASH *n* type of large round gourd
CALABAZA *n* variety of squash
CALABAZAS > CALABAZA
CALABOGUS *n* mixed drink containing rum, spruce beer, and molasses
CALABOOSE *n* prison
CALABRESE *n* kind of green sprouting broccoli
CALADIUM *n* type of tropical plant widely cultivated as a potted plant for its colourful variegated foliage
CALADIUMS > CALADIUM
CALALOO *same as* > CALALU
CALALOOS > CALALOO
CALALU *n* edible leaves of various plants, used as greens or in making thick soups
CALALUS > CALALU
CALAMANCO *n* glossy woollen fabric woven with a checked design that shows on one side only
CALAMAR *n* any member of the squid family
CALAMARI *n* squid cooked for eating, esp cut into rings and fried in batter
CALAMARIS > CALAMARI
CALAMARS > CALAMAR
CALAMARY *variant of* > CALAMARI
CALAMATA *same as* > KALAMATA
CALAMATAS > CALAMATA
CALAMI > CALAMUS
CALAMINE *n* pink powder consisting chiefly of zinc oxide, used in skin lotions and ointments ▷ *vb* apply calamine
CALAMINED > CALAMINE
CALAMINES > CALAMINE
CALAMINT *n* aromatic Eurasian plant with clusters of purple or pink flowers
CALAMINTS > CALAMINT

CALAMITE *n* type of extinct treelike plant related to the horsetails
CALAMITES > CALAMITE
CALAMITY *n* disaster
CALAMUS *n* tropical Asian palm, some species of which are a source of rattan and canes
CALANDO *adv* (to be performed) with gradually decreasing tone and speed
CALANDRIA *n* cylindrical vessel through which vertical tubes pass, esp one forming part of an evaporator, heat exchanger, or nuclear reactor
CALANTHE *n* type of orchid
CALANTHES > CALANTHE
CALASH *n* horse-drawn carriage with low wheels and a folding top
CALASHES > CALASH
CALATHEA *n* S American plant often grown as a greenhouse or house plant for its variegated leaves
CALATHEAS > CALATHEA
CALATHI > CALATHUS
CALATHOS *same as* > CALATHUS
CALATHUS *n* vase-shaped basket represented in ancient Greek art, used as a symbol of fruitfulness
CALAVANCE *n* type of pulse
CALCANEA > CALCANEUS
CALCANEAL > CALCANEUS
CALCANEAN > CALCANEUS
CALCANEI > CALCANEUS
CALCANEUM *same as* > CALCANEUS
CALCANEUS *n* largest tarsal bone, forming the heel in man
CALCAR *n* spur or spurlike process, as on the leg of a bird or the corolla of a flower
CALCARATE > CALCAR
CALCARIA > CALCAR
CALCARINE > CALCAR
CALCARS > CALCAR
CALCEATE *vb* to shoe
CALCEATED > CALCEATE
CALCEATES > CALCEATE
CALCED *adj* wearing shoes
CALCEDONY *n* a microcrystalline often greyish form of quartz with crystals arranged in parallel fibres: a gemstone.
CALCES > CALX
CALCIC *adj* of, containing, or concerned with lime or calcium
CALCICOLE *n* any plant that thrives in lime-rich soils
CALCIFIC *adj* forming or

causing to form lime or chalk

CALCIFIED > CALCIFY

CALCIFIES > CALCIFY

CALCIFUGE n any plant that thrives in acid soils but not in lime-rich soils

CALCIFY vb harden by the depositing of calcium salts

CALCIMINE n white or pale tinted wash for walls ▷ vb cover with calcimine

CALCINE vb oxidize (a substance) by heating

CALCINED > CALCINE

CALCINES > CALCINE

CALCINING > CALCINE

CALCITE n colourless or white form of calcium carbonate

CALCITES > CALCITE

CALCITIC > CALCITE

CALCIUM n silvery-white metallic element found in bones, teeth, limestone, and chalk

CALCIUMS > CALCIUM

CALCRETE another name for **>** CALICHE

CALCRETES > CALCRETE

CALCSPAR another name for **>** CALCITE

CALCSPARS > CALCSPAR

CALCTUFA another name for **>** TUFA

CALCTUFAS > CALCTUFA

CALCTUFF another name for **>** TUFA

CALCTUFFS > CALCTUFF

CALCULAR adj relating to calculus

CALCULARY adj relating to stone

CALCULATE vb solve or find out by a mathematical procedure or by reasoning

CALCULI > CALCULUS

CALCULOSE adj relating to calculi

CALCULOUS adj of or suffering from a stonelike accretion of minerals and salts found in ducts or hollow organs of the body

CALCULUS n branch of mathematics dealing with infinitesimal changes to a variable number or quantity

CALDARIA > CALDARIUM

CALDARIUM n (in ancient Rome) a room for taking hot baths

CALDERA n large basin-shaped crater at the top of a volcano, formed by the collapse or explosion of the cone

CALDERAS > CALDERA

CALDRON same as **>** CAULDRON

CALDRONS > CALDRON

CALECHE a variant of **>** CALASH

CALECHES > CALECHE

CALEFIED > CALEFY

CALEFIES > CALEFY

CALEFY vb to make warm

CALEFYING > CALEFY

CALEMBOUR n pun

CALENDAL > CALENDS

CALENDAR n chart showing a year divided up into months, weeks, and days ▷ vb enter in a calendar

CALENDARS > CALENDAR

CALENDER n machine in which paper or cloth is smoothed by passing it between rollers ▷ vb smooth in such a machine

CALENDERS > CALENDER

CALENDRER > CALENDER

CALENDRIC > CALENDAR

CALENDRY n place where calendering is carried out

CALENDS npl first day of each month in the ancient Roman calendar

CALENDULA n marigold

CALENTURE n mild fever of tropical climates, similar in its symptoms to sunstroke

CALESA n horse-drawn buggy

CALESAS > CALESA

CALESCENT adj increasing in heat

CALF n young cow, bull, elephant, whale, or seal

CALFDOZER n small bulldozer

CALFLESS > CALF

CALFLICK another word for **>** COWLICK

CALFLICKS > CALFLICK

CALFLIKE > CALF

CALFS > CALF

CALFSKIN n fine leather made from the skin of a calf

CALFSKINS > CALFSKIN

CALIATOUR n red sandalwood

CALIBER same as **>** CALIBRE

CALIBERED > CALIBER

CALIBERS > CALIBER

CALIBRATE vb mark the scale or check the accuracy of (a measuring instrument)

CALIBRE n person's ability or worth

CALIBRED > CALIBRE

CALIBRES > CALIBRE

CALICES > CALIX

CALICHE n bed of sand or clay in arid regions cemented by calcium carbonate, sodium chloride, and other soluble minerals

CALICHES > CALICHE

CALICLE same as **>** CALYCLE

CALICLES > CALICLE

CALICO n white cotton fabric

CALICOES > CALICO

CALICOS > CALICO

CALICULAR > CALYCLE

CALID adj warm

CALIDITY > CALID

CALIF same as **>** CALIPH

CALIFATE same as **>** CALIPHATE

CALIFATES > CALIFATE

CALIFONT n gas water heater

CALIFONTS > CALIFONT

CALIFS > CALIF

CALIGO n speck on the cornea causing poor vision

CALIGOES > CALIGO

CALIGOS > CALIGO

CALIMA n Saharan dust-storm

CALIMAS > CALIMA

CALIMOCHO n Spanish cocktail consisting of cola and red wine

CALIOLOGY n the study of birds' nests

CALIPASH n greenish glutinous edible part of the turtle found next to the upper shell, considered a delicacy

CALIPEE n yellow glutinous edible part of the turtle found next to the lower shell, considered a delicacy

CALIPEES > CALIPEE

CALIPER same as **>** CALLIPER

CALIPERED > CALLIPER

CALIPERS > CALLIPER

CALIPH n Muslim ruler

CALIPHAL > CALIPH

CALIPHATE n office, jurisdiction, or reign of a caliph

CALIPHS > CALIPH

CALISAYA n bark of a type of tropical tree from which quinine is extracted

CALISAYAS > CALISAYA

CALIVER n type of musket

CALIVERS > CALIVER

CALIX n cup

CALK same as **>** CAULK

CALKED > CALK

CALKER > CALK

CALKERS > CALK

CALKIN same as **>** CALK

CALKING > CALK

CALKINGS > CALK

CALKINS > CALK

CALKS > CALK

CALL vb name ▷ n cry, shout

CALLA n S African plant with a white funnel-shaped spathe enclosing a yellow spadix

CALLABLE adj (of a security) subject to redemption before maturity

CALLAIDES > CALLAIS

CALLAIS n green stone found as beads and ornaments in the late

Neolithic and early Bronze Age of W Europe

CALLALOO n leafy green vegetable

CALLALOOS > CALLALOO

CALLAN same as **>** CALLANT

CALLANS > CALLAN

CALLANT n youth

CALLANTS > CALLANT

CALLAS > CALLA

CALLBACK n telephone call made in response to an earlier call

CALLBACKS > CALLBACK

CALLBOARD n notice board listing opportunities for performers

CALLBOY n person who notifies actors when it is time to go on stage

CALLBOYS > CALLBOY

CALLED > CALL

CALLEE n computer function being used

CALLEES > CALLEE

CALLER n person or thing that calls, esp a person who makes a brief visit ▷ adj (of food, esp fish) fresh

CALLERS > CALLER

CALLET n scold

CALLETS > CALLET

CALLID adj cunning

CALLIDITY > CALLID

CALLIGRAM n poem in which words are positioned so as to create a visual image of the subject on the page

CALLING n vocation, profession

CALLINGS > CALLING

CALLIOPE n steam organ

CALLIOPES > CALLIOPE

CALLIPASH same as **>** CALIPASH

CALLIPEE same as **>** CALIPEE

CALLIPEES > CALLIPEE

CALLIPER n metal splint for supporting the leg ▷ vb measure the dimensions of (an object) with callipers

CALLIPERS > CALLIPER

CALLOP n edible Australian freshwater fish, often golden or pale yellow in colour

CALLOPS > CALLOP

CALLOSE n carbohydrate, a polymer of glucose, found in plants, esp in the sieve tubes

CALLOSES > CALLOSE

CALLOSITY same as **>** CALLUS

CALLOUS adj showing no concern for other people's feelings ▷ vb make or become callous

CALLOUSED > CALLOUS

CALLOUSES > CALLOUS

CALLOUSLY > CALLOUS

CALLOW adj young and

inexperienced ▷ n someone young and inexperienced

CALLOWER > CALLOW

CALLOWEST > CALLOW

CALLOWS > CALLOW

CALLS > CALL

CALLTIME n time available for making calls on a mobile phone

CALLTIMES > CALLTIME

CALLUNA n type of heather

CALLUNAS > CALLUNA

CALLUS n area of thick hardened skin ▷ vb produce or cause to produce a callus

CALLUSED > CALLUS

CALLUSES > CALLUS

CALLUSING > CALLUS

CALM adj not agitated or excited ▷ n peaceful state ▷ vb make or become calm

CALMANT n sedative

CALMANTS > CALMANT

CALMATIVE adj (of a remedy or agent) sedative ▷ n sedative remedy or drug

CALMED > CALM

CALMER > CALM

CALMEST > CALM

CALMIER > CALMY

CALMIEST > CALMY

CALMING > CALM

CALMINGLY > CALM

CALMINGS > CALM

CALMLY > CALM

CALMNESS > CALM

CALMS > CALM

CALMSTANE same as > CAMSTONE

CALMSTONE same as > CAMSTONE

CALMY adj tranquil

CALO n military servant

CALOMEL n colourless tasteless powder

CALOMELS > CALOMEL

CALORIC adj of heat or calories ▷ n hypothetical elastic fluid formerly postulated as the embodiment of heat

CALORICS > CALORIC

CALORIE n unit of measurement for the energy value of food

CALORIES > CALORIE

CALORIFIC adj of calories or heat

CALORISE same as > CALORIZE

CALORISED > CALORISE

CALORISES > CALORISE

CALORIST n believer in caloric theory

CALORISTS > CALORIST

CALORIZE vb coat (a ferrous metal) by spraying with aluminium powder and then heating

CALORIZED > CALORIZE

CALORIZES > CALORIZE

CALORY same as > CALORIE

CALOS > CALO

CALOTTE n skullcap worn by Roman Catholic clergy

CALOTTES > CALOTTE

CALOTYPE n early photographic process invented by W. H. Fox Talbot, in which the image was produced on paper treated with silver iodide and developed by sodium thiosulphite

CALOTYPES > CALOTYPE

CALOYER n monk of the Greek Orthodox Church, esp of the Basilian Order

CALOYERS > CALOYER

CALP n type of limestone

CALPA n Hindu unit of time

CALPAC n large black brimless hat made of sheepskin or felt, worn by men in parts of the Near East

CALPACK same as > CALPAC

CALPACKS > CALPACK

CALPACS > CALPAC

CALPAIN n type of enzyme

CALPAINS > CALPAIN

CALPAS > CALPA

CALPS > CALP

CALQUE n CAULK

CALQUED > CALQUE

CALQUES > CALQUE

CALQUING > CALQUE

CALTHA n marsh marigold

CALTHAS > CALTHA

CALTHROP same as > CALTHROP

CALTHROPS > CALTROP

CALTRAP same as > CALTROP

CALTRAPS > CALTRAP

CALTROP n floating Asian plant

CALTROPS > CALTROP

CALUMBA n Mozambiquan root used for medicinal purposes

CALUMBAS > CALUMBA

CALUMET n peace pipe

CALUMETS > CALUMET

CALUMNIES > CALUMNY

CALUMNY n false or malicious statement

CALUTRON n device used for the separation of isotopes

CALUTRONS > CALUTRON

CALVADOS n type of apple brandy

CALVARIA n top part of the skull of vertebrates

CALVARIAL > CALVARIUM

CALVARIAN > CALVARIUM

CALVARIAS > CALVARIA

CALVARIES > CALVARY

CALVARIUM same as > CALVARIA

CALVARY n representation of Christ's crucifixion, usually sculptured and in the open air

CALVE vb give birth to a calf

CALVED > CALVE

CALVER vb prepare fish for cooking

CALVERED > CALVER

CALVERING > CALVER

CALVERS > CALVER

CALVES > CALF

CALVING > CALVE

CALVITIES n baldness

CALX n powdery metallic oxide formed when an ore or mineral is roasted

CALXES > CALX

CALYCATE > CALYX

CALYCEAL adj resembling a calyx

CALYCES > CALYX

CALYCINAL same as > CALYCINE

CALYCINE adj relating to, belonging to, or resembling a calyx

CALYCLE n cup-shaped structure, as in the coral skeleton

CALYCLED > CALYCLE

CALYCLES > CALYCLE

CALYCOID adj resembling a calyx

CALYCULAR > CALYCLE

CALYCULE n bracts surrounding the base of the calyx

CALYCULES > CALYCULE

CALYCULI > CALYCULUS

CALYCULUS same as > CALYCLE

CALYPSO n West Indian song with improvised topical lyrics

CALYPSOES > CALYPSO

CALYPSOS > CALYPSO

CALYPTER n alula

CALYPTERA same as > CALYPTRA

CALYPTERS > CALYPTER

CALYPTRA n membranous hood covering the spore-bearing capsule of mosses and liverworts

CALYPTRAS > CALYPTRA

CALYX n outer leaves that protect a flower bud

CALYXES > CALYX

CALZONE n folded pizza filled with cheese, tomatoes, etc

CALZONES > CALZONE

CALZONI > CALZONE

CAM n device that converts a circular motion to a to-and-fro motion ▷ vb furnish (a machine) with a cam

CAMA n hybrid offspring of a camel and a llama

CAMAIEU n cameo

CAMAIEUX > CAMAIEU

CAMAIL n neck and shoulders covering of mail worn with and laced to the basinet

CAMAILED > CAMAIL

CAMAILS > CAMAIL

CAMAN n wooden stick used to hit the ball in shinty

CAMANACHD n shinty

CAMANS > CAMAN

CAMARILLA n group of confidential advisers, esp formerly, to the Spanish kings

CAMARON n shrimp

CAMARONS > CAMARON

CAMAS same as > CAMASS

CAMASES > CAMAS

CAMASH same as > CAMASS

CAMASHES > CAMASH

CAMASS n type of North American plant

CAMASSES > CAMASS

CAMBER n slight upward curve to the centre of a surface ▷ vb form or be formed with a surface that curves upwards to its centre

CAMBERED > CAMBER

CAMBERING > CAMBER

CAMBERS > CAMBER

CAMBIA > CAMBIUM

CAMBIAL > CAMBIUM

CAMBIFORM > CAMBIUM

CAMBISM > CAMBIST

CAMBISMS > CAMBIST

CAMBIST n dealer or expert in foreign exchange

CAMBISTRY > CAMBIST

CAMBISTS > CAMBIST

CAMBIUM n meristem that increases the girth of stems and roots by producing additional xylem and phloem

CAMBIUMS > CAMBIUM

CAMBOGE n type of gum resin

CAMBOGES > CAMBOGE

CAMBOGIA another name for > GAMBOGE

CAMBOGIAS > CAMBOGIA

CAMBOOSE n cabin built as living quarters for a gang of lumbermen

CAMBOOSES > CAMBOOSE

CAMBREL a variant of > GAMBREL

CAMBRELS > CAMBREL

CAMBRIC n fine white linen fabric

CAMBRICS > CAMBRIC

CAMCORDER n combined portable video camera and recorder

CAME > COME

CAMEL n humped mammal that can survive long periods without food or water in desert regions

CAMELBACK n type of locomotive

CAMELEER n camel-driver

CAMELEERS > CAMELEER

CAMELEON same as > CHAMELEON

CAMELEONS > CAMELEON
CAMELHAIR n hair of camel
CAMELIA same as > CAMELLIA
CAMELIAS > CAMELIA
CAMELID adj of or relating to camels ▷ n any animal of the camel family
CAMELIDS > CAMELID
CAMELINE n material made from camel hair
CAMELINES > CAMELINE
CAMELISH > CAMEL
CAMELLIA n evergreen ornamental shrub with white, pink, or red flowers
CAMELLIAS > CAMELLIA
CAMELLIKE > CAMEL
CAMELOID n member of the camel family
CAMELOIDS > CAMELOID
CAMELOT n supposedly idyllic period or age
CAMELOTS > CAMELOT
CAMELRIES > CAMELRY
CAMELRY n troops mounted on camels
CAMELS > CAMEL
CAMEO n brooch or ring with a profile head carved in relief ▷ vb to appear in a brief role
CAMEOED > CAMEO
CAMEOING > CAMEO
CAMEOS > CAMEO
CAMERA n apparatus used for taking photographs or pictures for television or cinema
CAMERAE > CAMERA
CAMERAL adj of or relating to a judicial or legislative chamber
CAMERAMAN n man who operates a camera for television or cinema
CAMERAMEN > CAMERAMAN
CAMERAS > CAMERA
CAMERATED adj vaulted
CAMES same as > CANVAS
CAMESE same as > CAMISE
CAMESES > CAMESE
CAMION n lorry, or, esp formerly, a large dray
CAMIONS > CAMION
CAMIS n light robe
CAMISA n smock
CAMISADE same as > CAMISADO
CAMISADES > CAMISADE
CAMISADO n (formerly) an attack made under cover of darkness
CAMISADOS > CAMISADO
CAMISAS > CAMISA
CAMISE n loose light shirt, smock, or tunic originally worn in the Middle Ages
CAMISES > CAMISE
CAMISIA n surplice
CAMISIAS > CAMISIA
CAMISOLE n woman's

bodice-like garment
CAMISOLES > CAMISOLE
CAMLET n tough waterproof cloth
CAMLETS > CAMLET
CAMMED > CAM
CAMMIE n webcam award
CAMMIES > CAMMIE
CAMMING > CAM
CAMO short for camouflage
CAMOGIE n form of hurling played by women
CAMOGIES > CAMOGIE
CAMOMILE n aromatic plant, used to make herbal tea
CAMOMILES > CAMOMILE
CAMOODI a Caribbean name for > ANACONDA
CAMOODIS > CAMOODI
CAMORRA n secret criminal group
CAMORRAS > CAMORRA
CAMORRIST > CAMORRA
CAMOS > CAMO
CAMOTE n type of sweet potato
CAMOTES > CAMOTE
CAMOUFLET n type of bomb used in a seige to collapse an enemy's tunnel
CAMP vb stay in a camp ▷ adj effeminate or homosexual ▷ adj (place for) temporary lodgings consisting of tents, huts, or cabins
CAMPAGNA same as > CHAMPAIGN
CAMPAGNAS > CAMPAGNA
CAMPAGNE > CAMPAGNA
CAMPAIGN n series of coordinated activities designed to achieve a goal ▷ vb take part in a campaign
CAMPAIGNS > CAMPAIGN
CAMPANA n bell or bell shape
CAMPANAS > CAMPANA
CAMPANERO n South American bellbird
CAMPANILE n bell tower, usu. one not attached to another building
CAMPANILI > CAMPANILE
CAMPANIST n expert on bells
CAMPANULA n plant with blue or white bell-shaped flowers
CAMPCRAFT n skills required when camping
CAMPEACHY adj as in campeachy wood kind of wood
CAMPEADOR n champion; term applied especially to El Cid
CAMPED > CAMP
CAMPER n person who lives or temporarily stays in a tent, cabin, etc
CAMPERIES > CAMPERY
CAMPERS > CAMPER

CAMPERY n campness
CAMPESINO n Latin American rural peasant
CAMPEST > CAMP
CAMPFIRE n outdoor fire in a camp, esp one used for cooking or as a focal point for community events
CAMPFIRES > CAMPFIRE
CAMPHANE n one of the terpene hydrocarbons
CAMPHANES > CAMPHANE
CAMPHENE n colourless crystalline insoluble terpene
CAMPHENES > CAMPHENE
CAMPHINE n type of solvent
CAMPHINES > CAMPHINE
CAMPHIRE an archaic name for > HENNA
CAMPHIRES > CAMPHIRE
CAMPHOL another word for > BORNEOL
CAMPHOLS > CAMPHOL
CAMPHONE n combined mobile phone and digital camera
CAMPHONES > CAMPHONE
CAMPHOR n aromatic crystalline substance used medicinally and in mothballs
CAMPHORIC > CAMPHOR
CAMPHORS > CAMPHOR
CAMPI > CAMPO
CAMPIER > CAMPY
CAMPIEST > CAMPY
CAMPILY > CAMPY
CAMPINESS > CAMPY
CAMPING > CAMP
CAMPINGS > CAMP
CAMPION n red, pink, or white wild flower
CAMPIONS > CAMPION
CAMPLE vb to argue
CAMPLED > CAMPLE
CAMPLES > CAMPLE
CAMPLING > CAMPLE
CAMPLY > CAMP
CAMPNESS > CAMP
CAMPO n level or undulating savanna country, esp in the uplands of Brazil
CAMPODEID n member of the Campodea genus of bristle-tails
CAMPONG n in Malaysia, a village
CAMPONGS > CAMPONG
CAMPOREE n local meeting or assembly of Scouts
CAMPOREES > CAMPOREE
CAMPOS > CAMPO
CAMPOUT n camping trip
CAMPOUTS > CAMPOUT
CAMPS > CAMP
CAMPSHIRT n short-sleeved shirt
CAMPSITE n area on which holiday makers may pitch a tent
CAMPSITES > CAMPSITE
CAMPSTOOL n folding

stool
CAMPUS n grounds of a university or college ▷ vb to restrict a student to campus, as a punishment
CAMPUSED > CAMPUS
CAMPUSES > CAMPUS
CAMPUSING > CAMPUS
CAMPY adj effeminate
CAMS > CAM
CAMSHAFT n part of an engine consisting of a rod to which cams are fixed
CAMSHAFTS > CAMSHAFT
CAMSHO adj crooked
CAMSHOCH same as > CAMSHO
CAMSTAIRY adj perverse
CAMSTANE same as > CAMSTONE
CAMSTANES > CAMSTONE
CAMSTEARY same as > CAMSTAIRY
CAMSTONE n a limestone used for whitening stone doorsteps
CAMSTONES > CAMSTONE
CAMUS n type of loose robe
CAMUSES > CAMUS
CAMWOOD n W African leguminous tree whose hard wood was formerly used to make a red dye
CAMWOODS > CAMWOOD
CAN vb be able to ▷ n metal container for food or liquids
CANADA n canada goose
CANADAS > CANADA
CANAIGRE n southern US dock, the root of which yields a substance used in tanning
CANAIGRES > CANAIGRE
CANAILLE n masses or rabble
CANAILLES > CANAILLE
CANAKIN same as > CANNIKIN
CANAKINS > CANAKIN
CANAL n artificial waterway ▷ vb dig a canal through
CANALBOAT n boat made for canals
CANALED > CANAL
CANALING > CANAL
CANALISE same as > CANALIZE
CANALISED > CANALIZE
CANALISES > CANALIZE
CANALIZE vb give direction to
CANALIZED > CANALIZE
CANALIZES > CANALIZE
CANALLED > CANAL
CANALLER n canal boat worker
CANALLERS > CANALLER
CANALLING > CANAL
CANALS > CANAL
CANAPE n small piece of bread or toast with a savoury topping
CANAPES > CANAPE

CANARD n false report

CANARDS > CANARD

CANARIED > CANARY

CANARIES > CANARY

CANARY n small yellow songbird often kept as a pet ▷ vb perform a dance called the canary

CANARYING > CANARY

CANASTA n card game like rummy, played with two packs

CANASTAS > CANASTA

CANASTER n coarsely broken dried tobacco leaves

CANASTERS > CANASTER

CANBANK n container for receiving cans for recycling

CANBANKS > CANBANK

CANCAN n lively high-kicking dance performed by a female group

CANCANS > CANCAN

CANCEL vb stop (something that has been arranged) from taking place ▷ n new leaf or section of a book replacing a defective one, one containing errors, or one that has been omitted

CANCELBOT n computer program that deletes unwanted mailings to Internet usergroups

CANCELED > CANCEL

CANCELEER vb (of a hawk) to turn in flight when a stoop fails, in order to re-attempt it

CANCELER > CANCEL

CANCELERS > CANCEL

CANCELIER a variant of > CANCELEER

CANCELING > CANCEL

CANCELLED > CANCEL

CANCELLER > CANCEL

CANCELLI n any lattice-like structures

CANCELS > CANCEL

CANCER n serious disease resulting from a malignant growth or tumour

CANCERATE vb to become cancerous

CANCERED adj affected by cancer

CANCEROUS > CANCER

CANCERS > CANCER

CANCHA n toasted maize

CANCHAS > CANCHA

CANCRINE adj crab-like

CANCROID adj resembling a cancerous growth ▷ n skin cancer, esp one of only moderate malignancy

CANCROIDS > CANCROID

CANDELA n unit of luminous intensity

CANDELAS > CANDELA

CANDENT adj emitting light as a result of being heated to a high temperature

CANDID adj honest and straightforward ▷ n unposed photograph

CANDIDA n yeastlike parasitic fungus which causes thrush

CANDIDACY > CANDIDATE

CANDIDAL > CANDIDA

CANDIDAS > CANDIDA

CANDIDATE n person seeking a job or position

CANDIDER > CANDID

CANDIDEST > CANDID

CANDIDLY > CANDID

CANDIDS > CANDID

CANDIE n South Indian unit of weight

CANDIED adj coated with sugar

CANDIES > CANDY

CANDIRU n parasitic freshwater catfish of the Amazon region

CANDIRUS > CANDIRU

CANDLE n stick of wax enclosing a wick, which is burned to produce light ▷ vb test by holding up to a candle

CANDLED > CANDLE

CANDLELIT adj lit by the light of candles

CANDLENUT n tropical Asian and Polynesian tree

CANDLEPIN n bowling pin, as used in skittles, tenpin bowling, candlepins, etc

CANDLER > CANDLE

CANDLERS > CANDLE

CANDLES > CANDLE

CANDLING > CANDLE

CANDOCK n type of water lily, or horsetail

CANDOCKS > CANDOCK

CANDOR same as > CANDOUR

CANDORS > CANDOR

CANDOUR n honesty and straightforwardness

CANDOURS > CANDOUR

CANDY n sweet or sweets ▷ vb make sweet

CANDYGRAM n message accompanied by sweets

CANDYING > CANDY

CANDYMAN n drug-dealer, esp one who targets young people

CANDYMEN > CANDYMAN

CANDYTUFT n garden plant with clusters of white, pink, or purple flowers

CANE n stem of the bamboo or similar plant ▷ vb beat with a cane

CANEBRAKE n thicket of canes

CANED > CANE

CANEFRUIT n fruit, like the raspberry, which grows on woody-stemmed plants

CANEGRUB n Australian grub that feeds on sugarcane

CANEGRUBS > CANEGRUB

CANEH n Hebrew unit of length

CANEHS > CANEH

CANELLA n fragrant cinnamon-like inner bark of a W Indian tree, used as a spice and in medicine

CANELLAS > CANELLA

CANELLINI n white kidney bean

CANEPHOR n sculpted figure carrying a basket on its head

CANEPHORA same as > CANEPHORE

CANEPHORE same as > CANEPHOR

CANEPHORS > CANEPHOR

CANER > CANE

CANERS > CANE

CANES > CANE

CANESCENT adj white or greyish due to the presence of numerous short white hairs

CANEWARE n type of unglazed stoneware

CANEWARES > CANEWARE

CANFIELD n gambling game adapted from a type of patience

CANFIELDS > CANFIELD

CANFUL n amount a can will hold

CANFULS > CANFUL

CANG same as > CANGUE

CANGLE vb to wrangle

CANGLED > CANGLE

CANGLES > CANGLE

CANGLING > CANGLE

CANGS > CANG

CANGUE n (formerly in China) a large wooden collar worn by petty criminals as a punishment

CANGUES > CANGUE

CANICULAR adj of or relating to the star Sirius or its rising

CANID n animal of the dog family

CANIDS > CANID

CANIER > CANY

CANIEST > CANY

CANIKIN same as > CANNIKIN

CANIKINS > CANIKIN

CANINE adj of or like a dog ▷ n sharp pointed tooth between the incisors and the molars

CANINES > CANINE

CANING n beating with a cane as a punishment

CANINGS > CANING

CANINITY > CANINE

CANISTEL n Caribbean fruit

CANISTELS > CANISTEL

CANISTER n metal container ▷ vb to put into canisters

CANISTERS > CANISTER

CANITIES n grey hair

CANKER n ulceration, ulcerous disease ▷ vb infect or become infected with or as if with canker

CANKERED > CANKER

CANKERING > CANKER

CANKEROUS adj having cankers

CANKERS > CANKER

CANKERY adj like a canker

CANKLE n thickened calfs on an overweight person

CANKLES > CANKLE

CANN vb direct a ship's steering

CANNA n type of tropical plant with broad leaves, cultivated for its red or yellow showy flowers

CANNABIC > CANNABIS

CANNABIN n greenish-black poisonous resin obtained from the Indian hemp plant

CANNABINS > CANNABIN

CANNABIS n Asian plant with tough fibres

CANNACH n cotton grass

CANNACHS > CANNACH

CANNAE vb can not

CANNAS > CANNA

CANNED > CAN

CANNEL n type of dull coal

CANNELON n type of meat loaf

CANNELONI npl pasta in the shape of tubes, which are usually stuffed

CANNELONS > CANNELON

CANNELS > CANNEL

CANNELURE n groove or fluting, esp one around the cylindrical part of a bullet

CANNER n person or organization whose job is to can foods

CANNERIES > CANNERY

CANNERS > CANNER

CANNERY n factory where food is canned

CANNIBAL n person who eats human flesh

CANNIBALS > CANNIBAL

CANNIE same as > CANNY

CANNIER > CANNY

CANNIEST > CANNY

CANNIKIN n small can, esp one used as a drinking vessel

CANNIKINS > CANNIKIN

CANNILY > CANNY

CANNINESS > CANNY

CANNING > CAN

CANNINGS > CAN

CANNISTER same as > CANISTER

CANNOLI n Sicilian pudding of pasta shells filled with sweetened ricotta

CANNOLIS > CANNOLI

CANNON n gun of large calibre ▷ vb to collide (with)

CANNONADE n continuous heavy gunfire ▷ vb attack (a target) with cannon
CANNONED > CANNON
CANNONEER n (formerly) a soldier who served and fired a cannon
CANNONIER same as > CANNONEER
CANNONING > CANNON
CANNONRY n volley of artillery fire
CANNONS > CANNON
CANNOT vb can not
CANNS > CANN
CANNULA n narrow tube for insertion into a bodily cavity, as for draining off fluid, introducing medication, etc
CANNULAE > CANNULA
CANNULAR adj shaped like a cannula
CANNULAS > CANNULA
CANNULATE vb insert a cannula into ▷ adj shaped like a cannula
CANNY adj shrewd, cautious ▷ adv quite
CANOE n light narrow open boat propelled by a paddle or paddles ▷ vb use a canoe
CANOEABLE > CANOE
CANOED > CANOE
CANOEINGS > CANOE
CANOEIST > CANOE
CANOEISTS > CANOE
CANOER > CANOE
CANOERS > CANOE
CANOES > CANOE
CANOEWOOD n type of tree
CANOLA n cooking oil extracted from a variety of rapeseed developed in Canada
CANOLAS > CANOLA
CANON n priest serving in a cathedral
CANONESS n woman belonging to any one of several religious orders and living under a rule but not under a vow
CANONIC same as > CANONICAL
CANONICAL adj conforming with canon law
CANONISE same as > CANONIZE
CANONISED > CANONISE
CANONISER > CANONISE
CANONISES > CANONISE
CANONIST n specialist in canon law
CANONIZE vb declare (a person) officially to be a saint
CANONIZED > CANONIZE
CANONIZER > CANONIZE
CANONIZES > CANONIZE
CANONRIES > CANONRY
CANONRY n office, benefice, or status of a

canon
CANONS > CANON
CANOODLE vb kiss and cuddle
CANOODLED > CANOODLE
CANOODLER > CANOODLE
CANOODLES > CANOODLE
CANOPIC adj of ancient Egyptian vase
CANOPIED > CANOPY
CANOPIES > CANOPY
CANOPY n covering above a bed, door, etc ▷ vb cover with or as if with a canopy
CANOPYING > CANOPY
CANOROUS adj tuneful
CANS > CAN
CANSFUL > CANFUL
CANSO n love song
CANSOS > CANSO
CANST vb form of 'can' used with the pronoun thou or its relative form
CANSTICK n candlestick
CANSTICKS > CANSTICK
CANT n insincere talk ▷ vb use cant ▷ adj oblique
CANTABANK n itinerant singer
CANTABILE adv flowing and melodious ▷ n piece or passage performed in this way
CANTAL n French cheese
CANTALA n tropical American plant, the agave
CANTALAS > CANTALA
CANTALOUP n type of melon
CANTALS > CANTAL
CANTAR variant form of > KANTAR
CANTARS > CANTAR
CANTATA n musical work consisting of arias, duets, and choruses
CANTATAS > CANTATA
CANTATE n 98th psalm sung as a nonmetrical hymn
CANTATES > CANTATE
CANTDOG same as > CANTHOOK
CANTDOGS > CANTDOG
CANTED > CANT
CANTEEN n restaurant attached to a workplace or school
CANTEENS > CANTEEN
CANTER vb move at gait between trot and gallop
CANTERED > CANTER
CANTERING > CANTER
CANTERS > CANTER
CANTEST > CANT
CANTHAL > CANTHUS
CANTHARI > CANTHARUS
CANTHARID n type of beetle with a soft elongated body
CANTHARIS n type of soldier beetle
CANTHARUS n large two-handled pottery cup

CANTHI > CANTHUS
CANTHITIS n inflammation of canthus
CANTHOOK n wooden pole with a hook used for handling logs
CANTHOOKS > CANTHOOK
CANTHUS n inner or outer corner or angle of the eye, formed by the natural junction of the eyelids
CANTIC > CANT
CANTICLE n short hymn with words from the Bible
CANTICLES > CANTICLE
CANTICO vb to dance as part of an act of worship
CANTICOED > CANTICO
CANTICOS > CANTICO
CANTICOY same as > CANTICO
CANTICOYS > CANTICOY
CANTICUM n canticle
CANTICUMS > CANTICUM
CANTIER > CANTY
CANTIEST > CANTY
CANTILENA n smooth flowing style in the writing of vocal music
CANTILY > CANTY
CANTINA n bar or wine shop, esp in a Spanish-speaking country
CANTINAS > CANTINA
CANTINESS > CANTY
CANTING > CANT
CANTINGLY > CANT
CANTINGS > CANT
CANTION n song
CANTIONS > CANTION
CANTLE n back part of a saddle that slopes upwards ▷ vb to set up, or stand, on high
CANTLED > CANTLE
CANTLES > CANTLE
CANTLET n piece
CANTLETS > CANTLET
CANTLING > CANTLE
CANTO same as > CANTUS
CANTON n political division of a country, esp Switzerland ▷ vb divide into cantons
CANTONAL > CANTON
CANTONED > CANTON
CANTONING > CANTON
CANTONISE vb to divide into cantons
CANTONIZE same as > CANTONISE
CANTONS > CANTON
CANTOR n man employed to lead services in a synagogue
CANTORIAL adj of or relating to a precentor
CANTORIS adj (in antiphonal music) to be sung by the cantorial side of a choir
CANTORS > CANTOR
CANTOS > CANTO
CANTRAIP n witch's spell

or charm
CANTRAIPS > CANTRAIP
CANTRAP same as > CANTRAIP
CANTRAPS > CANTRAP
CANTRED n district comprising a hundred villages
CANTREDS > CANTRED
CANTREF same as > CANTRED
CANTREFS > CANTREF
CANTRIP n magic spell ▷ adj (of an effect) produced by black magic
CANTRIPS > CANTRIP
CANTS > CANT
CANTUS n medieval form of church singing
CANTY adj lively
CANULA same as > CANNULA
CANULAE > CANULA
CANULAR adj shaped like a cannula
CANULAS > CANULA
CANULATE same as > CANNULATE
CANULATED > CANULATE
CANULATES > CANULATE
CANVAS n heavy coarse cloth used for sails and tents, and for oil painting ▷ vb to cover with, or be applied to, canvas
CANVASED > CANVAS
CANVASER > CANVAS
CANVASERS > CANVAS
CANVASES > CANVAS
CANVASING > CANVAS
CANVASS vb try to get votes or support (from) ▷ n canvassing
CANVASSED > CANVASS
CANVASSER > CANVASS
CANVASSES > CANVASS
CANY adj cane-like
CANYON n deep narrow valley
CANYONEER n canyon explorer
CANYONING n sport of going down a canyon river by any of various means
CANYONS > CANYON
CANZONA n type of 16th- or 17th-century contrapuntal music, usually for keyboard, lute, or instrumental ensemble
CANZONAS > CANZONA
CANZONE n Provençal or Italian lyric, often in praise of love or beauty
CANZONES > CANZONE
CANZONET n short, cheery, or lively Italian song
CANZONETS > CANZONET
CANZONI > CANZONA
CAP n soft close-fitting covering for the head ▷ vb cover or top with something
CAPA n type of Spanish cloak

CAPABLE adj having the ability (for)

CAPABLER > CAPABLE

CAPABLEST > CAPABLE

CAPABLY > CAPABLE

CAPACIOUS adj roomy

CAPACITOR n device for storing electrical charge

CAPACITY n ability to contain, absorb, or hold ▷ adj of the maximum amount or number possible

CAPARISON n decorated covering for a horse or other animal, esp (formerly) for a warhorse ▷ vb put a caparison on

CAPAS > CAPA

CAPE n short cloak ▷ vb to cut and remove the hide of an animal

CAPED > CAPE

CAPELAN another word for > CAPELIN

CAPELANS > CAPELAN

CAPELET n small cape

CAPELETS > CAPELET

CAPELIN n type of small marine food fish occurring in northern and Arctic seas

CAPELINE n cap-shaped bandage to cover the head or an amputation stump

CAPELINES > CAPELINE

CAPELINS > CAPELIN

CAPELLET n wen-like swelling on a horse

CAPELLETS > CAPELLET

CAPELLINE same as > CAPELINE

CAPELLINI n type of pasta

CAPER n high-spirited prank ▷ vb skip about

CAPERED > CAPER

CAPERER > CAPER

CAPERERS > CAPER

CAPERING > CAPER

CAPERS npl pickled flower buds of a Mediterranean shrub used in sauces

CAPES > CAPE

CAPESKIN n soft leather obtained from the skins of a type of lamb or sheep having hairlike wool ▷ adj made of this leather

CAPESKINS > CAPESKIN

CAPEWORK n use of the cape by the matador in bullfighting

CAPEWORKS > CAPEWORK

CAPEX n capital expenditure

CAPEXES > CAPEX

CAPFUL n quantity held by a (usually bottle) cap

CAPFULS > CAPFUL

CAPH n letter of the Hebrew alphabet

CAPHS > CAPH

CAPI > CAPO

CAPIAS n (formerly) a writ directing a sheriff or other officer to arrest a named person

CAPIASES > CAPIAS

CAPILLARY n very fine blood vessel ▷ adj (of a tube) having a fine bore

CAPING > CAPE

CAPITA > CAPUT

CAPITAL n chief city of a country ▷ adj involving or punishable by death

CAPITALLY adv in an excellent manner

CAPITALS > CAPITAL

CAPITAN another name for > HOGFISH

CAPITANI > CAPITANO

CAPITANO n chief; captain

CAPITANOS > CAPITANO

CAPITANS > CAPITAN

CAPITATE adj shaped like a head, as certain flowers or inflorescences

CAPITATED adj having fixed upper limit

CAPITAYN n captain

CAPITAYNS > CAPITAYN

CAPITELLA n plural form of singular: capitellum, an enlarged knoblike structure at the end of a bone that forms an articulation with another bone

CAPITOL n (in America) building housing the state legislature

CAPITOLS > CAPITOL

CAPITULA > CAPITULUM

CAPITULAR adj of or associated with a cathedral chapter ▷ n member of a cathedral chapter

CAPITULUM n racemose inflorescence in the form of a disc of sessile flowers, the youngest at the centre. It occurs in the daisy and related plants

CAPIZ n bivalve shell of a mollusc found esp in the Philippines, used in jewellery, ornaments, lampshades, etc

CAPIZES > CAPIZ

CAPLE n horse

CAPLES > CAPLE

CAPLESS > CAP

CAPLET n medicinal tablet, usually oval in shape, coated in a soluble substance

CAPLETS > CAPLET

CAPLIN same as > CAPELIN

CAPLINS > CAPLIN

CAPMAKER > CAP

CAPMAKERS > CAP

CAPO n device fitted across the strings of a guitar or similar instrument so as to raise the pitch

CAPOCCHIA n fool

CAPOEIRA n combination of martial art and dance, which originated among African slaves in 19th-century Brazil

CAPOEIRAS > CAPOEIRA

CAPON n castrated cock fowl fattened for eating

CAPONATA n Sicilian antipasto relish

CAPONATAS > CAPONATA

CAPONIER n covered passageway built across a ditch as a military defence

CAPONIERE same as > CAPONIER

CAPONIERS > CAPONIER

CAPONISE same as > CAPONIZE

CAPONISED > CAPONISE

CAPONISES > CAPONISE

CAPONIZE vb make (a cock) into a capon

CAPONIZED > CAPONIZE

CAPONIZES > CAPONIZE

CAPONS > CAPON

CAPORAL n strong coarse dark tobacco

CAPORALS > CAPORAL

CAPOS > CAPO

CAPOT n winning of all the tricks by one player ▷ vb score a capot (against)

CAPOTASTO same as > CAPO

CAPOTE n long cloak or soldier's coat, usually with a hood

CAPOTES > CAPOTE

CAPOTS > CAPOT

CAPOTTED > CAPOT

CAPOTTING > CAPOT

CAPOUCH same as > CAPUCHE

CAPOUCHES > CAPOUCH

CAPPED > CAP

CAPPER > CAP

CAPPERS > CAP

CAPPING > CAP

CAPPINGS > CAP

CAPRATE n any salt of capric acid

CAPRATES > CAPRATE

CAPRIC adj (of a type of acid) smelling of goats

CAPRICCI > CAPRICCIO

CAPRICCIO n lively piece composed freely and without adhering to the rules for any specific musical form

CAPRICE same as > CAPRICCIO

CAPRICES > CAPRICE

CAPRID n any member of the goat family

CAPRIDS > CAPRID

CAPRIFIED > CAPRIFY

CAPRIFIES > CAPRIFY

CAPRIFIG n wild variety of fig of S Europe and SW Asia

CAPRIFIGS > CAPRIFIG

CAPRIFOIL variant of > CAPRIFOLE

CAPRIFOLE n honeysuckle

CAPRIFORM adj goatlike

CAPRIFY vb induce figs to ripen

CAPRINE adj of or resembling a goat

CAPRIOLE n upward but not forward leap made by a horse ▷ vb perform a capriole

CAPRIOLED > CAPRIOLE

CAPRIOLES > CAPRIOLE

CAPRIS npl women's tight-fitting trousers

CAPROATE n any salt of caproic acid

CAPROATES > CAPROATE

CAPROCK n layer of rock that overlies a salt dome

CAPROCKS > CAPROCK

CAPROIC as in caproic acid oily acid found in milk

CAPRYLATE n any salt of caprylic acid

CAPRYLIC variant of > CAPRIC

CAPS > CAP

CAPSAICIN n colourless crystalline bitter alkaloid

CAPSICIN n liquid or resin extracted from capsicum

CAPSICINS > CAPSICIN

CAPSICUM n kind of pepper used as a vegetable or as a spice

CAPSICUMS > CAPSICUM

CAPSID n outer protein coat of a mature virus

CAPSIDAL > CAPSID

CAPSIDS > CAPSID

CAPSIZAL > CAPSIZE

CAPSIZALS > CAPSIZE

CAPSIZE vb (of a boat) overturn accidentally

CAPSIZED > CAPSIZE

CAPSIZES > CAPSIZE

CAPSIZING > CAPSIZE

CAPSOMER n one of the units making up a viral capsid

CAPSOMERE n any of the protein units that together form the capsid of a virus

CAPSOMERS > CAPSOMER

CAPSTAN n rotating cylinder round which a ship's rope is wound

CAPSTANS > CAPSTAN

CAPSTONE n one of a set of slabs on the top of a wall, building, etc

CAPSTONES > CAPSTONE

CAPSULAR adj relating to a capsule

CAPSULARY same as > CAPSULAR

CAPSULATE adj within or formed into a capsule

CAPSULE n soluble gelatine case containing a dose of medicine ▷ adj very concise ▷ vb to contain within a capsule

CAPSULED > CAPSULE

CAPSULES > CAPSULE

CAPSULING > CAPSULE

CAPSULISE same as > CAPSULIZE

C

CAPSULIZE vb state (information) in a highly condensed form

CAPTAIN n commander of a ship or civil aircraft ▷ vb be captain of

CAPTAINCY > CAPTAIN

CAPTAINED > CAPTAIN

CAPTAINRY n condition or skill of being a captain

CAPTAINS > CAPTAIN

CAPTAN n type of fungicide

CAPTANS > CAPTAN

CAPTION n title or explanation accompanying an illustration ▷ vb provide with a caption

CAPTIONED > CAPTION

CAPTIONS > CAPTION

CAPTIOUS adj tending to make trivial criticisms

CAPTIVATE vb attract and hold the attention of

CAPTIVE n person kept in confinement ▷ adj kept in confinement ▷ vb to take prisoner

CAPTIVED > CAPTIVE

CAPTIVES > CAPTIVE

CAPTIVING > CAPTIVE

CAPTIVITY n state of being kept in confinement

CAPTOPRIL n drug used to treat high blood pressure and congestive heart failure

CAPTOR n person who captures a person or animal

CAPTORS > CAPTOR

CAPTURE vb take by force ▷ n capturing

CAPTURED > CAPTURE

CAPTURER > CAPTURE

CAPTURERS > CAPTURE

CAPTURES > CAPTURE

CAPTURING > CAPTURE

CAPUCCIO n hood

CAPUCCIOS > CAPUCCIO

CAPUCHE n large hood or cowl, esp that worn by Capuchin friars

CAPUCHED adj hooded

CAPUCHES > CAPUCHE

CAPUCHIN n S American monkey with thick hair on the top of its head

CAPUCHINS > CAPUCHIN

CAPUERA variant of > CAPOEIRA

CAPUERAS > CAPUERA

CAPUL same as > CAPLE

CAPULS > CAPUL

CAPUT n main or most prominent part of an organ or structure

CAPYBARA n very large S American rodent

CAPYBARAS > CAPYBARA

CAR n motor vehicle designed to carry a small number of people

CARABAO n water buffalo

CARABAOS > CARABAO

CARABID n type of usu dark-coloured beetle such as the bombardier and other ground beetles

CARABIDS > CARABID

CARABIN same as > CARBINE

CARABINE same as > CARBINE

CARABINER a variant spelling of > KARABINER

CARABINES > CARABINE

CARABINS > CARABIN

CARACAL n lynx with reddish fur, which inhabits deserts of N Africa and S Asia

CARACALS > CARACAL

CARACARA n type of large carrion-eating bird of prey of S North, Central, and S America, with long legs and a naked face

CARACARAS > CARACARA

CARACK same as > CARRACK

CARACKS > CARACK

CARACOL same as > CARACOLE

CARACOLE n half turn to the right or left ▷ vb execute a half turn to the right or left

CARACOLED > CARACOLE

CARACOLER > CARACOLE

CARACOLES > CARACOLE

CARACOLS > CARACOL

CARACT n sign or symbol

CARACTS > CARACT

CARACUL n black loosely curled fur obtained from the skins of newly born lambs of the karakul sheep

CARACULS > CARACUL

CARAFE n glass bottle for serving water or wine

CARAFES > CARAFE

CARAGANA n pea tree

CARAGANAS > CARAGANA

CARAGEEN same as > CARRAGEEN

CARAGEENS > CARAGEEN

CARAMBA n Spanish interjection similar to 'wow!'

CARAMBOLA n yellow edible star-shaped fruit that grows on a Brazilian tree

CARAMBOLE vb make a carom or carambola (shot in billiards)

CARAMEL n chewy sweet made from sugar and milk ▷ vb to turn into caramel

CARAMELS > CARAMEL

CARANGID n type of marine fish with a compressed body and deeply forked tail, such as the horse mackerel, pompano, and pilot fish

CARANGIDS > CARANGID

CARANGOID same as > CARANGID

CARANNA n gumlike substance

CARANNAS > CARANNA

CARAP n crabwood

CARAPACE n hard upper shell of tortoises and crustaceans

CARAPACED adj having carapace

CARAPACES > CARAPACE

CARAPAX n carapace

CARAPAXES > CARAPAX

CARAPS > CARAP

CARASSOW same as > CURASSOW

CARASSOWS > CARASSOW

CARAT n unit of weight of precious stones

CARATE n tropical disease

CARATES > CARATE

CARATS > CARAT

CARAUNA same as > CARANNA

CARAUNAS > CARAUNA

CARAVAN n large enclosed vehicle for living in, designed to be towed by a car or horse ▷ vb travel or have a holiday in a caravan

CARAVANCE same as > CALAVANCE

CARAVANED > CARAVAN

CARAVANER n person who holidays in a caravan

CARAVANS > CARAVAN

CARAVEL n two- or three-masted sailing ship, esp one with a broad beam, high poop deck, and lateen rig that was used by the Spanish and Portuguese in the 15th and 16th centuries

CARAVELLE variant of > CARAVEL

CARAVELS > CARAVEL

CARAWAY n plant whose seeds are used as a spice

CARAWAYS > CARAWAY

CARB n carbohydrate

CARBACHOL n carbamylcholine, a cholinergic agent

CARBAMATE n salt or ester of carbamic acid

CARBAMIC as in carbamic acid hypothetical compound known only in carbamate salts

CARBAMIDE another name for > UREA

CARBAMINO adj relating to the compound produced when carbon dioxide reacts with an amino group

CARBAMOYL same as > CARBAMYL

CARBAMYL n radical from carbamic acid

CARBAMYLS > CARBAMYL

CARBANION n negatively charged organic ion in which most of the negative charge is localized on a carbon atom

CARBARN n streetcar depot

CARBARNS > CARBARN

CARBARYL n organic compound of the carbamate group

CARBARYLS > CARBARYL

CARBAZOLE n colourless insoluble solid obtained from coal tar

CARBEEN n Australian eucalyptus tree with drooping branches and grey bark

CARBEENS > CARBEEN

CARBENE n neutral divalent free radical, such as methylene: CH_2

CARBENES > CARBENE

CARBIDE n compound of carbon with a metal

CARBIDES > CARBIDE

CARBIES > CARBY

CARBINE n light automatic rifle

CARBINEER n (formerly) a soldier equipped with a carbine

CARBINES > CARBINE

CARBINIER same as > CARBINEER

CARBINOL same as > METHANOL

CARBINOLS > CARBINOL

CARBO n carbohydrate

CARBOLIC as in carbolic acid phenol, when it is used as a disinfectant

CARBOLICS > CARBOLIC

CARBOLISE same as > CARBOLIZE

CARBOLIZE another word for > PHENOLATE

CARBON n nonmetallic element occurring in charcoal, graphite, and diamond, found in all organic matter

CARBONADE n stew of beef and onions cooked in beer

CARBONADO n piece of meat, fish, etc, scored and grilled ▷ vb score and grill (meat, fish, etc)

CARBONARA n pasta sauce containing cream, bacon and cheese

CARBONATE n salt or ester of carbonic acid ▷ vb form or turn into a carbonate

CARBONIC adj containing carbon

CARBONISE same as > CARBONIZE

CARBONIUM as in carbonium ion type of positively charged organic ion

CARBONIZE vb turn into carbon as a result of heating

CARBONOUS > CARBON

CARBONS > CARBON

CARBONYL n of, consisting of, or containing the divalent group =CO

CARBONYLS > CARBONYL

CARBORA n former name for the koala

CARBORAS > CARBORA
CARBOS > CARBO
CARBOXYL as in *carboxyl group* functional group in organic acids
CARBOXYLS > CARBOXYL
CARBOY *n* large bottle with a protective casing
CARBOYED > CARBOY
CARBOYS > CARBOY
CARBS > CARB
CARBUNCLE *n* inflamed boil
CARBURATE *same as* > CARBURET
CARBURET *vb* combine or mix (a gas) with carbon or carbon compounds ▷ *vb* to combine with carbon
CARBURETS > CARBURET
CARBURISE *same as* > CARBONIZE
CARBURIZE *same as* > CARBONIZE
CARBY *n* short for carburettor
CARCAJOU *a North American name for* > WOLVERINE
CARCAJOUS > CARCAJOU
CARCAKE *n* (formerly, in Scotland) a cake traditionally made for Shrove Tuesday
CARCAKES > CARCAKE
CARCANET *n* jewelled collar or necklace
CARCANETS > CARCANET
CARCASE *same as* > CARCASS
CARCASED > CARCASE
CARCASES > CARCASE
CARCASING > CARCASE
CARCASS *n* dead body of an animal ▷ *vb* to make a carcass of
CARCASSED > CARCASS
CARCASSES > CARCASS
CARCEL *n* French unit of light
CARCELS > CARCEL
CARCERAL *adj* relating to prison
CARCINOID *n* small serotonin-secreting tumour
CARCINOMA *n* malignant tumour
CARD *n* piece of thick stiff paper or cardboard used for identification, reference, or sending greetings or messages ▷ *vb* comb out fibres of wool or cotton before spinning
CARDAMINE *n* bittercress
CARDAMOM *n* spice obtained from the seeds of a tropical plant
CARDAMOMS > CARDAMOM
CARDAMON *same as* > CARDAMOM
CARDAMONS > CARDAMON
CARDAMUM *same as* > CARDAMOM

CARDAMUMS > CARDAMUM
CARDAN as in *cardan joint* type of universal joint
CARDBOARD *n* thin stiff board made from paper pulp ▷ *adj* without substance
CARDCASE *n* small case for holding business cards
CARDCASES > CARDCASE
CARDECU *n* old French coin (a quarter of a crown)
CARDECUE *same as* > CARDECU
CARDECUES > CARDECUE
CARDECUS > CARDECU
CARDED > CARD
CARDER > CARD
CARDERS > CARD
CARDI *n* cardigan
CARDIA *n* lower oesophageal sphincter
CARDIAC *adj* of the heart ▷ *n* person with a heart disorder
CARDIACAL > CARDIAC
CARDIACS > CARDIAC
CARDIAE > CARDIA
CARDIALGY *n* pain in or near the heart
CARDIAS > CARDIA
CARDIE *short for* > CARDIGAN
CARDIES > CARDIE
CARDIGAN *n* knitted jacket
CARDIGANS > CARDIGAN
CARDINAL *n* any of the high-ranking clergymen of the RC Church who elect the Pope and act as his counsellors ▷ *adj* fundamentally important
CARDINALS > CARDINAL
CARDING > CARD
CARDINGS > CARD
CARDIO *adj* exercising heart
CARDIOID *n* heart-shaped curve generated by a fixed point on a circle as it rolls around another fixed circle of equal radius
CARDIOIDS > CARDIOID
CARDIOS > CARDIO
CARDIS > CARDI
CARDITIC > CARDITIS
CARDITIS *n* inflammation of the heart
CARDON *n* variety of cactus
CARDONS > CARDON
CARDOON *n* thistle-like S European plant with spiny leaves, purple flowers, and an edible leafstalk
CARDOONS > CARDOON
CARDPHONE *n* public telephone operated by the insertion of a phonecard instead of coins
CARDPUNCH *n* device for putting data from a CPU onto punched cards
CARDS > CARD
CARDSHARP *n* professional card player who cheats
CARDUUS *n* thistle

CARDUUSES > CARDUUS
CARDY *same as* > CARDIE
CARE *vb* be concerned ▷ *n* careful attention, caution
CARED > CARE
CAREEN *vb* tilt over to one side
CAREENAGE > CAREEN
CAREENED > CAREEN
CAREENER > CAREEN
CAREENERS > CAREEN
CAREENING > CAREEN
CAREENS > CAREEN
CAREER *n* series of jobs in a profession or occupation that a person has through their life ▷ *vb* rush in an uncontrolled way ▷ *adj* having chosen to dedicate his or her life to a particular occupation
CAREERED > CAREER
CAREERER > CAREER
CAREERERS > CAREER
CAREERING > CAREER
CAREERISM > CAREERIST
CAREERIST *n* person who seeks advancement by any possible means
CAREERS > CAREER
CAREFREE *adj* without worry or responsibility
CAREFUL *adj* cautious in attitude or action
CAREFULLY > CAREFUL
CAREGIVER *same as* > CARER
CARELESS *adj* done or acting with insufficient attention
CARELINE *n* telephone service set up by a company or other organization to provide its customers or clients with information about its products or services
CARELINES > CARELINE
CAREME *n* period of Lent
CAREMES > CAREME
CARER *n* person who looks after someone who is ill or old, often a relative
CARERS > CARER
CARES > CARE
CARESS *n* gentle affectionate touch or embrace ▷ *vb* touch gently and affectionately
CARESSED > CARESS
CARESSER > CARESS
CARESSERS > CARESS
CARESSES > CARESS
CARESSING > CARESS
CARESSIVE *adj* caressing
CARET *n* symbol indicating a place in written or printed matter where something is to be inserted
CARETAKE *vb* to work as a caretaker
CARETAKEN > CARETAKE
CARETAKER *n* person employed to look after a

place ▷ *adj* performing the duties of an office temporarily
CARETAKES > CARETAKE
CARETOOK > CARETAKE
CARETS > CARET
CAREWARE *n* computer software licensed in exchange for a donation to charity
CAREWARES > CAREWARE
CAREWORN *adj* showing signs of worry
CAREX *n* any member of the sedge family
CARFARE *n* fare that a passenger is charged for a ride on a bus, etc
CARFARES > CARFARE
CARFAX *n* place where principal roads or streets intersect, esp a place in a town where four roads meet
CARFAXES > CARFAX
CARFOX *same as* > CARFAX
CARFOXES > CARFOX
CARFUFFLE *a variant spelling of* > KERFUFFLE
CARFUL *n* maximum number of people a car will hold
CARFULS > CARFUL
CARGEESE > CARGOOSE
CARGO *n* goods carried by a ship, aircraft, etc ▷ *vb* to load
CARGOED > CARGO
CARGOES > CARGO
CARGOING > CARGO
CARGOOSE *n* crested grebe
CARGOS > CARGO
CARHOP *n* waiter or waitress at a drive-in restaurant ▷ *vb* work as a carhop
CARHOPPED > CARHOP
CARHOPS > CARHOP
CARIACOU *n* type of deer
CARIACOUS > CARIACOU
CARIAMA *another word for* > SERIEMA
CARIAMAS > CARIAMA
CARIBE *n* piranha
CARIBES > CARIBE
CARIBOU *n* large N American reindeer
CARIBOUS > CARIBOU
CARICES > CAREX
CARIED *adj* (of teeth) decayed
CARIERE *obsolete word for* > CAREER
CARIERES > CARIERE
CARIES *n* tooth decay
CARILLON *n* set of bells played by keyboard or mechanically ▷ *vb* play a carillon
CARILLONS > CARILLON
CARINA *n* keel-like part or ridge, as in the breastbone of birds or the fused lower petals of a leguminous flower

CARINAE > CARINA

CARINAL adj keel-like

CARINAS > CARINA

CARINATE adj having a keel or ridge

CARINATED same as > CARINATE

CARING adj feeling or showing care and compassion for other people ▷ n practice or profession of providing social or medical care

CARINGLY > CARING

CARINGS > CARING

CARIOCA n Brazilian dance similar to the samba

CARIOCAS > CARIOCA

CARIOLE n small open two-wheeled horse-drawn vehicle

CARIOLES > CARIOLE

CARIOSE same as > CARIOUS

CARIOSITY > CARIOUS

CARIOUS adj (of teeth or bone) affected with caries

CARITAS n divine love; charity

CARITASES > CARITAS

CARITATES > CARITAS

CARJACK vb attack (a car driver) to rob them or to steal the car ▷ vb to steal a car, by force, from a person who is present

CARJACKED > CARJACK

CARJACKER > CARJACK

CARJACKS > CARJACK

CARJACOU variation of > CARIACOU

CARJACOUS > CARJACOU

CARK vb break down

CARKED > CARK

CARKING > CARK

CARKS > CARK

CARL another word for > CHURL

CARLE same as > CARL

CARLES > CARLE

CARLESS > CAR

CARLIN same as > CARLING

CARLINE same as > CARLING

CARLINES > CARLINE

CARLING n fore-and-aft beam in a vessel, used for supporting the deck, esp around a hatchway or other opening

CARLINGS > CARLING

CARLINS > CARLING

CARLISH adj churlish

CARLOAD n amount that can be carried by a car

CARLOADS > CARLOAD

CARLOCK n type of Russian isinglass

CARLOCKS > CARLOCK

CARLOT n boor

CARLOTS > CARLOT

CARLS > CARL

CARMAKER n car manufacturing company

CARMAKERS > CARMAKER

CARMAN n man who drives a car or cart

CARMELITE n member of an order of mendicant friars

CARMEN > CARMAN

CARMINE adj vivid red ▷ n vivid red colour, sometimes with a purplish tinge

CARMINES > CARMINE

CARN n cairn

CARNAGE n extensive slaughter of people

CARNAGES > CARNAGE

CARNAHUBA same as > CARNAUBA

CARNAL adj of a sexual or sensual nature ▷ vb act in a carnal manner

CARNALISE vb to sensualise

CARNALISM > CARNALISE

CARNALIST > CARNALISE

CARNALITY > CARNAL

CARNALIZE same as > CARNALISE

CARNALLED > CARNAL

CARNALLY > CARNAL

CARNALS > CARNAL

CARNAROLI n variety of short-grain rice used for risotto

CARNATION n cultivated plant with fragrant white, pink, or red flowers

CARNAUBA n Brazilian fan palm tree

CARNAUBAS > CARNAUBA

CARNELIAN n reddish-yellow gemstone

CARNEOUS adj fleshy

CARNET n customs licence permitting motorists to take their cars across certain frontiers

CARNETS > CARNET

CARNEY same as > CARNY

CARNEYED > CARNEY

CARNEYING > CARNEY

CARNEYS > CARNEY

CARNIE same as > CARNY

CARNIED > CARNY

CARNIER > CARNY

CARNIES > CARNY

CARNIEST > CARNY

CARNIFEX n executioner

CARNIFIED > CARNIFY

CARNIFIES > CARNIFY

CARNIFY vb (esp of lung tissue, as the result of pneumonia) to be altered so as to resemble skeletal muscle

CARNITINE n type of white betaine

CARNIVAL n festive period with processions, music, and dancing in the street

CARNIVALS > CARNIVAL

CARNIVORA n members of a group of carnivorous mammals

CARNIVORE n meat-eating animal

CARNIVORY n state of being carnivore

CARNOSAUR n meat-eating dinosaur

CARNOSE adj fleshy

CARNOSITY n fleshy protrusion

CARNOTITE n radioactive yellow mineral

CARNS > CARN

CARNY vb coax or cajole or act in a wheedling manner ▷ n person who works in a carnival ▷ adj sly

CARNYING > CARNY

CARNYX n bronze Celtic war trumpet

CARNYXES > CARNYX

CAROACH same as > CAROCHE

CAROACHES > CAROACH

CAROB n pod of a Mediterranean tree, used as a chocolate substitute

CAROBS > CAROB

CAROCH same as > CAROCHE

CAROCHE n stately ceremonial carriage used in the 16th and 17th centuries

CAROCHES > CAROCHE

CAROL n joyful Christmas hymn ▷ vb sing carols

CAROLED > CAROL

CAROLER > CAROL

CAROLERS > CAROL

CAROLI > CAROLUS

CAROLING > CAROL

CAROLINGS > CAROL

CAROLLED > CAROL

CAROLLER > CAROL

CAROLLERS > CAROL

CAROLLING > CAROL

CAROLS > CAROL

CAROLUS n any of several coins struck in the reign of a king called Charles, esp an English gold coin from the reign of Charles I

CAROLUSES > CAROLUS

CAROM n shot in which the cue ball is caused to contact one object ball after another ▷ vb to carambole

CAROMED > CAROM

CAROMEL vb to turn into caramel

CAROMELS > CAROMEL

CAROMING > CAROM

CAROMS > CAROM

CARON n inverted circumflex

CARONS > CARON

CAROTENE n any of four orange-red hydrocarbons, found in many plants, converted to vitamin A in the liver

CAROTENES > CAROTENE

CAROTID n either of the two arteries supplying blood to the head ▷ adj of either of these arteries

CAROTIDAL > CAROTID

CAROTIDS > CAROTID

CAROTIN same as > CAROTENE

CAROTINS > CAROTIN

CAROUSAL n merry drinking party

CAROUSALS > CAROUSAL

CAROUSE vb have a merry drinking party

CAROUSED > CAROUSE

CAROUSEL n revolving conveyor belt for luggage or photographic slides

CAROUSELS > CAROUSEL

CAROUSER > CAROUSE

CAROUSERS > CAROUSE

CAROUSES > CAROUSE

CAROUSING same as > CAROUSAL

CARP n large freshwater fish ▷ vb complain, find fault

CARPACCIO n Italian dish of thin slices of raw meat or fish

CARPAL n wrist bone

CARPALE same as > CARPAL

CARPALES > CARPAL

CARPALIA > CARPAL

CARPALS > CARPAL

CARPED > CARP

CARPEL n female reproductive organ of a flowering plant

CARPELS > CARPEL

CARPENTER n person who makes or repairs wooden structures ▷ vb do the work of a carpenter

CARPENTRY n skill or work of a carpenter

CARPER > CARP

CARPERS > CARP

CARPET n heavy fabric for covering floors ▷ vb cover with a carpet

CARPETBAG n travelling bag made of carpeting

CARPETED > CARPET

CARPETING n carpet material or carpets in general

CARPETS > CARPET

CARPHONE n phone designed for use in a car

CARPHONES > CARPHONE

CARPI > CARPUS

CARPING adj tending to make petty complaints ▷ n petty complaint

CARPINGLY > CARPING

CARPINGS > CARPING

CARPOLOGY n branch of botany concerned with the study of fruits and seeds

CARPOOL vb (of a group of people) to share the use of a single car to travel to work or school

CARPOOLED > CARPOOL

CARPOOLER > CARPOOL

CARPOOLS > CARPOOL

CARPORT n shelter for a car, consisting of a roof supported by posts

CARPORTS > CARPORT

CARPS > CARP

CARPUS n set of eight bones of the wrist

CARR n area of bog or fen in which scrub, esp willow, has become established

CARRACK n galleon sailed in the Mediterranean as a merchantman in the 15th and 16th centuries

CARRACKS > CARRACK

CARRACT same as > CARRACK

CARRACTS > CARRACT

CARRAGEEN n edible red seaweed of North America and N Europe

CARRAT same as > CARAT

CARRATS > CARRAT

CARRAWAY same as > CARAWAY

CARRAWAYS > CARRAWAY

CARRECT same as > CARRACK

CARRECTS > CARRECT

CARREFOUR n public square, esp one at the intersection of several roads

CARREL n small individual study room or private desk, often in a library, where a student or researcher can work undisturbed

CARRELL same as > CARREL

CARRELLS > CARRELL

CARRELS > CARREL

CARRIAGE n one of the sections of a train for passengers

CARRIAGES > CARRIAGE

CARRICK as in carrick bend type of knot

CARRIED > CARRY

CARRIER n person or thing that carries something

CARRIERS > CARRIER

CARRIES > CARRY

CARRIOLE same as > CARIOLE

CARRIOLES > CARRIOLE

CARRION n dead and rotting flesh

CARRIONS > CARRION

CARRITCH n catechism

CARROCH variant of > CAROCHE

CARROCHES > CAROM

CARROM same as > CAROM

CARROMED > CARROM

CARROMING > CARROM

CARROMS > CARROM

CARRON as in carron oil ointment of limewater and linseed oil

CARRONADE n obsolete naval gun of short barrel and large bore

CARROT n long tapering orange root vegetable

CARROTIER > CARROTY

CARROTIN n carotene

CARROTINS > CARROTIN

CARROTS > CARROT

CARROTTOP n facetious term for a person with red hair

CARROTY adj (of hair) reddish-orange

CARROUSEL a variant spelling of > CAROUSEL

CARRS > CARR

CARRY vb take from one place to another

CARRYALL n light four-wheeled horse-drawn carriage usually designed to carry four passengers

CARRYALLS > CARRYALL

CARRYBACK n amount carried back in accounting

CARRYCOT n light portable bed for a baby, with handles and a hood

CARRYCOTS > CARRYCOT

CARRYING > CARRY

CARRYON n fuss or commotion

CARRYONS > CARRYON

CARRYOUT n hot cooked food bought in a shop for consumption elsewhere

CARRYOUTS > CARRYOUT

CARRYOVER n sum or balance carried forward in accounting

CARRYTALE n gossip

CARS > CAR

CARSE n riverside area of flat fertile alluvium

CARSES > CARSE

CARSEY slang word for > TOILET

CARSEYS > CARSEY

CARSHARE same as > CARPOOL

CARSHARED > CARSHARE

CARSHARES > CARSHARE

CARSICK adj nauseated from riding in a car

CART n open two-wheeled horse-drawn vehicle for carrying goods or passengers ▷ vb carry, usu. with some effort

CARTA n charter

CARTABLE > CART

CARTAGE n process or cost of carting

CARTAGES > CARTAGE

CARTAS > CARTA

CARTE n fencing position

CARTED > CART

CARTEL n association of competing firms formed to fix prices

CARTELISE same as > CARTELIZE

CARTELISM > CARTEL

CARTELIST > CARTEL

CARTELIZE vb form or be formed into a cartel

CARTELS > CARTEL

CARTER > CART

CARTERS > CART

CARTES > CARTE

CARTFUL n amount a cart can hold

CARTFULS > CARTFUL

CARTHORSE n large heavily built horse

CARTILAGE n strong flexible tissue forming part of the skeleton

CARTING > CART

CARTLOAD n amount a cart can hold

CARTLOADS > CARTLOAD

CARTOGRAM n map showing statistical information in diagrammatic form

CARTOLOGY n theory of mapmaking

CARTON n container made of cardboard or waxed paper ▷ vb enclose (goods) in a carton

CARTONAGE n material from which mummy masks and coffins were made

CARTONED > CARTON

CARTONING > CARTON

CARTONS > CARTON

CARTOON n humorous or satirical drawing ▷ vb to depict in a cartoon

CARTOONED > CARTOON

CARTOONS > CARTOON

CARTOONY > CARTOON

CARTOP adj designed to be transported on top of a vehicle

CARTOPPER n anything designed to be transported on top of a vehicle

CARTOUCH same as > CARTOUCHE

CARTOUCHE n ornamental tablet or panel in the form of a scroll

CARTRIDGE n casing containing an explosive charge and bullet for a gun

CARTROAD n road for carts to drive on

CARTROADS > CARTROAD

CARTS > CART

CARTULARY n collection of charters or records, esp relating to the title to an estate or monastery

CARTWAY n way by which carts travel

CARTWAYS > CARTWAY

CARTWHEEL n sideways somersault supported by the hands with legs outstretched ▷ vb to perform a cartwheel movement

CARUCAGE n tax due on a carucate

CARUCAGES > CARUCAGE

CARUCATE n area of land an oxen team could plough in a year

CARUCATES > CARUCATE

CARUNCLE n fleshy outgrowth on the heads of certain birds, such as a cock's comb

CARUNCLES > CARUNCLE

CARVACROL n aromatic phenol found in oregano

CARVE vb cut to form an object

CARVED > CARVE

CARVEL same as > CARAVEL

CARVELS > CARVEL

CARVEN an archaic or literary past participle of > CARVE

CARVER n carving knife

CARVERIES > CARVERY

CARVERS > CARVER

CARVERY n restaurant where customers pay a set price for unrestricted helpings of carved meat and other food

CARVES > CARVE

CARVIES > CARVY

CARVING n figure or design produced by carving stone or wood

CARVINGS > CARVING

CARVY n caraway seed

CARWASH n drive-through structure containing automated equipment for washing cars

CARWASHES > CARWASH

CARYATIC > CARYATID

CARYATID n supporting column in the shape of a female figure

CARYATIDS > CARYATID

CARYOPSES > CARYOPSIS

CARYOPSIS n dry seedlike fruit having the pericarp fused to the seed coat of the single seed: produced by the grasses

CARYOTIN variant of > KARYOTIN

CARYOTINS > CARYOTIN

CASA n house

CASABA n kind of winter muskmelon having a yellow rind and sweet juicy flesh

CASABAS > CASABA

CASAS > CASA

CASAVA same as > CASSAVA

CASAVAS > CASAVA

CASBAH n citadel of a N African city

CASBAHS > CASBAH

CASCABEL n knoblike protrusion on the rear part of the breech of an obsolete muzzle-loading cannon

CASCABELS > CASCABEL

CASCABLE same as > CASCABEL

CASCABLES > CASCABLE

CASCADE n waterfall ▷ vb flow or fall in a cascade

CASCADED > CASCADE

CASCADES > CASCADE

CASCADING > CASCADE

CASCADURA n Trinidadian fish

CASCARA n bark of a N American shrub, used as a laxative

CASCARAS > CASCARA

CASCHROM n wooden hand-plough

CASCHROMS > CASCHROM

CASCO n Argentinian homestead

CASCOS > CASCO

CASE n instance, example ▷ vb inspect (a building) with the intention of burgling it

CASEASE n proteolytic enzyme formed by certain bacteria that activates the solution of albumin and casein in milk and cheese

CASEASES > CASEASE

CASEATE vb undergo caseation

CASEATED > CASEATE

CASEATES > CASEATE

CASEATING > CASEATE

CASEATION n formation of cheese from casein during the coagulation of milk

CASEBOOK n book in which records of legal or medical cases are kept

CASEBOOKS > CASEBOOK

CASEBOUND another word for > HARDBACK

CASED > CASE

CASEFIED > CASEFY

CASEFIES > CASEFY

CASEFY vb make or become similar to cheese

CASEFYING > CASEFY

CASEIC adj relating to cheese

CASEIN n a phosphoprotein, precipitated from milk by the action of rennin, forming the basis of cheese: used in the manufacture of plastics and adhesives

CASEINATE n protein found in milk

CASEINS > CASEIN

CASELOAD n number of cases that someone like a doctor or social worker deals with at any one time

CASELOADS > CASELOAD

CASEMAKER n in bookbinding, machine that makes stiff covers for hardbacks

CASEMAN n in printing, a person who sets and corrects type

CASEMATE n armoured compartment in a ship or fortification in which guns are mounted

CASEMATED > CASEMATE

CASEMATES > CASEMATE

CASEMEN > CASEMAN

CASEMENT n window that is hinged on one side

CASEMENTS > CASEMENT

CASEMIX n mix or type of patients treated by a hospital or medical unit

CASEMIXES > CASEMIX

CASEOSE n peptide produced by the peptic digestion of the casein

CASEOSES > CASEOSE

CASEOUS adj of or like cheese

CASERN n (formerly) a billet or accommodation for soldiers in a town

CASERNE same as > CASERN

CASERNES > CASERNE

CASERNS > CASERN

CASES > CASE

CASETTE variant of > CASSETTE

CASETTES > CASETTE

CASEVAC vb evacuate (a casualty) from a combat zone, usu by air

CASEVACED > CASEVAC

CASEVACS > CASEVAC

CASEWORK n social work based on close study of the personal histories and circumstances of individuals and families

CASEWORKS > CASEWORK

CASEWORM n caddis worm

CASEWORMS > CASEWORM

CASH n banknotes and coins ▷ adj of, for, or paid in cash ▷ vb obtain cash for

CASHABLE > CASH

CASHAW n winter squash

CASHAWS > CASHAW

CASHBACK n discount offered in return for immediate payment

CASHBACKS > CASHBACK

CASHBOOK n journal in which cash receipts and payments are recorded

CASHBOOKS > CASHBOOK

CASHBOX n box for holding cash

CASHBOXES > CASHBOX

CASHED > CASH

CASHES > CASH

CASHEW n edible kidney-shaped nut

CASHEWS > CASHEW

CASHIER n person responsible for handling cash in a bank, shop, etc ▷ vb dismiss with dishonour from the armed forces

CASHIERED > CASHIER

CASHIERER > CASHIER

CASHIERS > CASHIER

CASHING > CASH

CASHLESS adj functioning, operated, or performed without using coins or banknotes for money transactions but instead using credit cards or electronic transfer of funds

CASHMERE n fine soft wool obtained from goats

CASHMERES > CASHMERE

CASHOO n catechu

CASHOOS > CASHOO

CASHPOINT n cash dispenser

CASIMERE same as > CASSIMERE

CASIMERES > CASIMERE

CASIMIRE variant of > CASSIMERE

CASIMIRES > CASIMIRE

CASING n protective case, covering

CASINGS > CASING

CASINI > CASINO

CASINO n public building or room where gambling games are played

CASINOS > CASINO

CASITA n small house

CASITAS > CASITA

CASK n barrel used to hold alcoholic drink ▷ vb put into a cask

CASKED > CASK

CASKET n small box for valuables ▷ vb put into a casket

CASKETED > CASKET

CASKETING > CASKET

CASKETS > CASKET

CASKIER > CASKY

CASKIEST > CASKY

CASKING > CASK

CASKS > CASK

CASKSTAND n frame on which a cask rests

CASKY adj (of wine) having a musty smell due to resting too long in the cask

CASPASE n type of enzyme

CASPASES > CASPASE

CASQUE n helmet or a helmet-like process or structure, as on the bill of most hornbills

CASQUED > CASQUE

CASQUES > CASQUE

CASSABA same as > CASABA

CASSABAS > CASSABA

CASSAREEP n juice of the bitter cassava root, boiled down to a syrup and used as a flavouring, esp in West Indian cookery

CASSATA n ice cream, originating in Italy, usually containing nuts and candied fruit

CASSATAS > CASSATA

CASSATION n (esp in France) annulment, as of a judicial decision by a higher court

CASSAVA n starch obtained from the roots of a tropical American plant, used to make tapioca

CASSAVAS > CASSAVA

CASSENA same as > CASSINA

CASSENAS > CASSENA

CASSENE same as > CASSINA

CASSENES > CASSENE

CASSEROLE n covered dish in which food is cooked slowly, usu. in an oven ▷ vb cook in a casserole

CASSETTE n plastic container for magnetic tape

CASSETTES > CASSETTE

CASSIA n tropical plant whose pods yield a mild laxative

CASSIAS > CASSIA

CASSIMERE n woollen suiting cloth of plain or twill weave

CASSINA n American tree

CASSINAS > CASSINA

CASSINE same as > CASSINA

CASSINES > CASSINE

CASSINGLE n cassette single

CASSINO n card game for two to four players in which players pair cards from their hands with others exposed on the table

CASSINOS > CASSINO

CASSIS n blackcurrant cordial

CASSISES > CASSIS

CASSOCK n long tunic, usu black, worn by priests

CASSOCKED > CASSOCK

CASSOCKS > CASSOCK

CASSONADE n raw sugar

CASSONE n highly-decorated Italian dowry chest

CASSONES > CASSONE

CASSOULET n stew originating from France, made from haricot beans and goose, duck, pork, etc

CASSOWARY n large flightless bird of Australia and New Guinea

CASSPIR n armoured military vehicle

CASSPIRS > CASSPIR

CAST n actors in a play or film collectively ▷ vb select (an actor) to play a part in a play or film

CASTABLE adj able to be cast

CASTANET > CASTANETS

CASTANETS npl musical instrument, used by Spanish dancers, consisting of curved pieces of hollow wood clicked together in the hand

CASTAWAY n shipwrecked person ▷ adj shipwrecked or put adrift ▷ vb cause (a ship, person, etc) to be shipwrecked or abandoned

CASTAWAYS > CASTAWAY

CASTE n any of the hereditary classes into which Hindu society is divided

ASTED *adj* having a caste

ASTEISM *n* belief in, and adherence to, the caste system

ASTEISMS > CASTEISM

ASTELESS *adj* having no caste

ASTELLA > CASTELLUM

ASTELLAN *n* keeper or governor of a castle

ASTELLUM *n* fort

ASTER *n* person or thing that casts

ASTERS > CASTER

ASTES > CASTE

ASTIGATE *vb* reprimand severely

ASTING > CAST

ASTINGS > CAST

ASTLE *n* large fortified building, often built as a ruler's residence ▷ *vb* (in chess) move (the king) two squares laterally on the first rank and place the nearest rook on the square passed over by the king

ASTLED *adj* like a castle in construction

ASTLES > CASTLE

ASTLING > CASTLE

ASTOCK *n* kale stalk

ASTOCKS > CASTOCK

ASTOFF *n* person or thing that has been discarded or abandoned

ASTOFFS > CASTOFF

ASTOR *same as* > CASTER

ASTOREUM *n* oil secreted from the beaver, used as bait by trappers

ASTORIES > CASTORY

ASTORS > CASTOR

ASTORY *n* dye derived from beaver pelts

ASTRAL *adj* relating to camps

ASTRATE *vb* remove the testicles of

ASTRATED > CASTRATE

ASTRATER > CASTRATE

ASTRATES > CASTRATE

ASTRATI > CASTRATO

ASTRATO *n* (in 17th- and 18th-century opera) a male singer whose testicles are removed before puberty, allowing the retention of a soprano or alto voice

ASTRATOR > CASTRATE

ASTRATOS > CASTRATO

ASTS > CAST

ASUAL *adj* careless, nonchalant ▷ *n* occasional worker

ASUALISE *vb* to make (a regular employee) into a casual worker

ASUALISM > CASUALISE

ASUALIZE *same as* > CASUALISE

ASUALLY > CASUAL

ASUALS > CASUAL

ASUALTY *n* person killed

or injured in an accident or war

CASUARINA *n* Australian tree with jointed green branches

CASUIST *n* person, esp a theologian, who attempts to resolve moral dilemmas by the application of general rules and the careful distinction of special cases

CASUISTIC > CASUIST

CASUISTRY *n* reasoning that is misleading or oversubtle

CASUISTS > CASUIST

CASUS *n* event

CAT *n* small domesticated furry mammal ▷ *vb* flog with a cat-'o-nine-tails

CATABASES > CATABASIS

CATABASIS *n* descent or downward movement

CATABATIC > CATABASIS

CATABOLIC *adj* of a metabolic process in which complex molecules are broken down into simple ones with the release of energy

CATACLASM *n* breaking down

CATACLYSM *n* violent upheaval

CATACOMB *n* underground burial place, esp the galleries at Rome, consisting of tunnels with vaults or niches leading off them for tombs

CATACOMBS > CATACOMB

CATAFALCO *n* temporary raised platform on which a body lies in state before or during a funeral

CATALASE *n* enzyme that catalyses the decomposition of hydrogen peroxide

CATALASES > CATALASE

CATALATIC *adj* relating to catalase

CATALEPSY *n* trancelike state in which the body is rigid

CATALEXES > CATALEXIS

CATALEXIS *n* the state of lacking a syllable in the last foot of a line of poetry

CATALO *same as* > CATTALO

CATALOES > CATALO

CATALOG *same as* > CATALOGUE

CATALOGED > CATALOGUE

CATALOGER > CATALOGUE

CATALOGIC > CATALOG

CATALOGS > CATALOG

CATALOGUE *n* book containing details of items

for sale ▷ *vb* enter (an item) in a catalogue

CATALOS > CATALO

CATALPA *n* tree of N America and Asia with bell-shaped whitish flowers

CATALPAS > CATALPA

CATALYSE *vb* speed up (a chemical reaction) by a catalyst

CATALYSED > CATALYSE

CATALYSER > CATALYSE

CATALYSES > CATALYSIS

CATALYSIS *n* acceleration of a chemical reaction by the action of a catalyst

CATALYST *n* substance that speeds up a chemical reaction without itself changing

CATALYSTS > CATALYST

CATALYTIC *adj* of or relating to catalysis

CATALYZE *same as* > CATALYSE

CATALYZED > CATALYZE

CATALYZER > CATALYZE

CATALYZES > CATALYZE

CATAMARAN *n* boat with twin parallel hulls

CATAMENIA *another word for* > MENSES

CATAMITE *n* boy kept as a homosexual partner

CATAMITES > CATAMITE

CATAMOUNT *n* any of various medium-sized felines, such as the puma or lynx

CATAPAN *n* governor in the Byzantine Empire

CATAPANS > CATAPAN

CATAPHOR *n* word that refers to or stands for another word used later

CATAPHORA *n* use of a word such as a pronoun that has the same reference as a word used subsequently in the same discourse

CATAPHORS > CATAPHOR

CATAPHYLL *n* simplified form of plant leaf, such as a scale leaf or cotyledon

CATAPLASM *another name for* > POULTICE

CATAPLEXY *n* sudden temporary paralysis, brought on by severe shock

CATAPULT *n* Y-shaped device with a loop of elastic, used by children for firing stones ▷ *vb* shoot forwards or upwards violently

CATAPULTS > CATAPULT

CATARACT *n* eye disease in which the lens becomes opaque

CATARACTS > CATARACT

CATARHINE *adj* having a thin or narrow nose

CATARRH *n* excessive

mucus in the nose and throat, during or following a cold

CATARRHAL > CATARRH

CATARRHS > CATARRH

CATASTA *n* platform on which slaves were presented for sale

CATASTAS > CATASTA

CATATONIA *n* form of schizophrenia characterized by stupor, with outbreaks of excitement

CATATONIC > CATATONIA

CATATONY *another word for* > CATATONIA

CATAWBA *n* type of red North American grape

CATAWBAS > CATAWBA

CATBIRD *n* North American songbird whose call resembles the mewing of a cat

CATBIRDS > CATBIRD

CATBOAT *n* sailing vessel with a single mast, set well forward and often unstayed, and a large sail, usually rigged with a gaff

CATBOATS > CATBOAT

CATBRIER *n* greenbrier

CATBRIERS > CATBRIER

CATCALL *n* derisive whistle or cry ▷ *vb* utter such a call (at)

CATCALLED > CATCALL

CATCALLER > CATCALL

CATCALLS > CATCALL

CATCH *vb* seize, capture ▷ *n* device for fastening a door, window, etc

CATCHABLE > CATCH

CATCHALL *n* something designed to cover a variety of situations

CATCHALLS > CATCHALL

CATCHCRY *n* well-known much-used phrase, perhaps associated with a particular group

CATCHED *rarely used past tense of* > CATCH

CATCHEN *same as* > CATCH

CATCHER *n* person or thing that catches, esp in a game or sport

CATCHERS > CATCHER

CATCHES > CATCH

CATCHFLY *n* type of plant with sticky calyxes and stems on which insects are trapped

CATCHIER > CATCHY

CATCHIEST > CATCHY

CATCHING > CATCH

CATCHINGS > CATCH

CATCHMENT *n* structure in which water is collected

CATCHPOLE *n* (in medieval England) a sheriff's officer who arrested debtors

CATCHPOLL *same as* > CATCHPOLE

CATCHT same as > CATCHED

CATCHUP a variant spelling (esp US) of > KETCHUP

CATCHUPS > CATCHUP

CATCHWEED n goosegrass

CATCHWORD n well-known and frequently used phrase

CATCHY adj (of a tune) pleasant and easily remembered

CATCLAW n type of shrub; black bead

CATCLAWS > CATCLAW

CATCON n catalytic converter

CATCONS > CATCON

CATE n delicacy

CATECHIN n soluble yellow solid substance found in mahogany wood

CATECHINS > CATECHIN

CATECHISE same as > CATECHIZE

CATECHISM n instruction on the doctrine of a Christian Church in a series of questions and answers

CATECHIST > CATECHIZE

CATECHIZE vb instruct by using a catechism

CATECHOL n colourless crystalline phenol found in resins and lignins

CATECHOLS > CATECHOL

CATECHU n astringent resinous substance obtained from certain tropical plants, used in medicine, tanning, and dyeing

CATECHUS > CATECHU

CATEGORIC adj unqualified

CATEGORY n class, group

CATELOG obsolete word for > CATALOGUE

CATELOGS > CATELOG

CATENA n connected series, esp of patristic comments on the Bible

CATENAE > CATENA

CATENANE n type of chemical compound in which the molecules have two or more rings that are interlocked like the links of a chain

CATENANES > CATENANE

CATENARY n curve assumed by a heavy uniform flexible cord hanging freely from two points ▷ adj of, resembling, relating to, or constructed using a catenary or suspended chain

CATENAS > CATENA

CATENATE vb arrange or be arranged in a series of chains or rings

CATENATED > CATENATE

CATENATES > CATENATE

CATENOID n geometrical surface generated by rotating a catenary about its axis

CATENOIDS > CATENOID

CATER vb provide what is needed or wanted, esp food or services

CATERAN n (formerly) a member of a band of brigands and marauders in the Scottish highlands

CATERANS > CATERAN

CATERED > CATER

CATERER n person whose job is to provide food for social events such as parties and weddings

CATERERS > CATERER

CATERESS n female caterer

CATERING n supplying of food for a social event

CATERINGS > CATERING

CATERS > CATER

CATERWAUL n wail, yowl ▷ vb make a yowling noise like a cat

CATES npl choice dainty food

CATFACE n deformity of the surface of a tree trunk, caused by fire or disease

CATFACES > CATFACE

CATFACING n disorder that affects tomatoes, causing scarring of the fruit

CATFALL n line used as a tackle for hoisting an anchor to the cathead

CATFALLS > CATFALL

CATFIGHT n fight between two women

CATFIGHTS > CATFIGHT

CATFISH n fish with whisker-like barbels round the mouth

CATFISHES > CATFISH

CATFLAP n small flap in a door to let a cat go through

CATFLAPS > CATFLAP

CATGUT n strong cord used to string musical instruments and sports rackets

CATGUTS > CATGUT

CATHARISE vb to purify

CATHARIZE same as > CATHARISE

CATHARSES > CATHARSIS

CATHARSIS n relief of strong suppressed emotions

CATHARTIC adj causing catharsis ▷ n drug that causes catharsis

CATHEAD n fitting at the bow of a vessel for securing the anchor when raised

CATHEADS > CATHEAD

CATHECT vb to invest mental or emotional energy in

CATHECTED > CATHECT

CATHECTIC adj of or relating to cathexis

CATHECTS > CATHECT

CATHEDRA n bishop's throne

CATHEDRAE > CATHEDRA

CATHEDRAL n principal church of a diocese

CATHEDRAS > CATHEDRA

CATHEPSIN n proteolytic enzyme responsible for the autolysis of cells after death

CATHEPTIC > CATHEPSIN

CATHETER n tube inserted into a body cavity to drain fluid

CATHETERS > CATHETER

CATHETUS n straight line or radius perpendicular to another line or radius

CATHEXES > CATHEXIS

CATHEXIS n concentration of psychic energy on a single goal

CATHISMA n short hymn used as a response

CATHISMAS > CATHISMA

CATHODAL > CATHODE

CATHODE > negative electrode, by which electrons leave a circuit

CATHODES > CATHODE

CATHODIC > CATHODE

CATHOLE n hole in a ship through which ropes are passed

CATHOLES > CATHOLE

CATHOLIC adj (of tastes or interests) covering a wide range ▷ n member of the Roman Catholic Church

CATHOLICS > CATHOLIC

CATHOLYTE same as > CATOLYTE

CATHOOD n state of being a cat

CATHOODS > CATHOOD

CATHOUSE a slang word for > BROTHEL

CATHOUSES > CATHOUSE

CATION n positively charged ion

CATIONIC > CATION

CATIONS > CATION

CATJANG n tropical shrub

CATJANGS > CATJANG

CATKIN n drooping flower spike of certain trees

CATKINATE adj like catkin

CATKINS > CATKIN

CATLIKE > CAT

CATLIN same as > CATLING

CATLING n long double-edged surgical knife for amputations

CATLINGS > CATLING

CATLINS > CATLIN

CATMINT n Eurasian plant with scented leaves that attract cats

CATMINTS > CATMINT

CATNAP vb doze ▷ n short sleep or doze

CATNAPER > CATNAP

CATNAPERS > CATNAP

CATNAPPED > CATNAP

CATNAPPER > CATNAP

CATNAPS > CATNAP

CATNEP same as > CATMINT

CATNEPS > CATNEP

CATNIP same as > CATMINT

CATNIPS > CATMINT

CATOLYTE n part of the electrolyte that surrounds the cathode in an electrolytic cell

CATOLYTES > CATOLYTE

CATOPTRIC adj relating to reflection

CATRIGGED adj rigged like a catboat

CATS > CAT

CATSKIN n skin and/or fur of a cat

CATSKINS > CATSKIN

CATSPAW n person used by another as a tool

CATSPAWS > CATSPAW

CATSUIT n one-piece usually close-fitting trouser suit

CATSUITS > CATSUIT

CATSUP a variant (esp US) of > KETCHUP

CATSUPS > CATSUP

CATTABU n cross between common cattle and zebu

CATTABUS > CATTABU

CATTAIL n reed mace

CATTAILS > CATTAIL

CATTALO n hardy breed of cattle developed by crossing the American bison with domestic cattle

CATTALOES > CATTALO

CATTALOS > CATTALO

CATTED > CAT

CATTERIES > CATTERY

CATTERY n place where cats are bred or looked after

CATTIE same as > CATTY

CATTIER > CATTY

CATTIES > CATTY

CATTIEST > CATTY

CATTILY > CATTY

CATTINESS > CATTY

CATTING > CAT

CATTISH > CAT

CATTISHLY > CAT

CATTLE npl domesticated cows and bulls

CATTLEMAN n person who breeds, rears, or tends cattle

CATTLEMEN > CATTLEMAN

CATTLEYA n tropical American orchid cultivated for its purplish-pink or white showy flowers

CATTLEYAS > CATTLEYA

CATTY adj spiteful ▷ n unit of weight, used esp in China, equal to about one and a half pounds or about

0.67 kilogram

ATWALK *n* narrow pathway or platform

ATWALKS > CATWALK

ATWORKS *n* machinery on a drilling platform

ATWORM *n* type of carnivorous worm about 10cm (4in) long, often dug for bait

ATWORMS > CATWORM

AUCHEMAR *n* nightmare

AUCUS *n* local committee or faction of a political party ▷ *vb* hold a caucus

AUCUSED > CAUCUS

AUCUSES > CAUCUS

AUCUSING > CAUCUS

AUCUSSED > CAUCUS

AUCUSSES > CAUCUS

AUDA *n* area behind the anus of an animal

AUDAD *adv* towards the tail or posterior part

AUDAE > CAUDA

AUDAL *adj* at or near an animal's tail

AUDALLY > CAUDAL

AUDATE *adj* having a tail or a tail-like appendage ▷ *n* lizard-like amphibian

AUDATED *same as* > CAUDATE

AUDATES > CAUDATE

AUDATION > CAUDATE

AUDEX *n* thickened persistent stem base of some herbaceous perennial plants

AUDEXES > CAUDEX

AUDICLE *n* stalk to which an orchid's pollen masses are attached

AUDICLES > CAUDICLE

AUDILLO *n* (in Spanish-speaking countries) a military or political leader

AUDILLOS > CAUDILLO

AUDLE *n* hot spiced wine drink made with gruel, formerly used medicinally ▷ *vb* make such a drink

AUDLED > CAUDLE

AUDLES > CAUDLE

AUDLING > CAUDLE

AUDRON *Spenserian spelling of* > CAULDRON

AUDRONS > CAUDRON

AUF *n* cage for holding live fish in the water

AUGHT > CATCH

AUK *n* type of barite

AUKER *n* one who caulks

AUKERS > CAUKER

AUKS > CAUK

AUL *n* membrane sometimes covering a child's head at birth

AULD *a Scot word for* > COLD

AULDER > CAULD

AULDEST > CAULD

AULDRIFE *adj*

susceptible to cold

CAULDRON *n* large pot used for boiling

CAULDRONS > CAULDRON

CAULDS > CAULD

CAULES > CAULIS

CAULICLE *n* small stalk or stem

CAULICLES > CAULICLE

CAULICULI *n* plural form of singular cauliculus: another word for caulicle

CAULIFORM *adj* resembling a caulis

CAULINARY *another word for* > CAULINE

CAULINE *adj* relating to or growing from a plant stem

CAULIS *n* main stem of a plant

CAULK *vb* fill in (cracks) with paste etc

CAULKED > CAULK

CAULKER > CAULK

CAULKERS > CAULK

CAULKING > CAULK

CAULKINGS > CAULK

CAULKS > CAULK

CAULOME *n* plant's stem structure, considered as a whole

CAULOMES > CAULOME

CAULS > CAUL

CAUM *same as* > CAM

CAUMED > CAUM

CAUMING > CAUM

CAUMS > CAUM

CAUMSTANE *same as* > CAMSTONE

CAUMSTONE *same as* > CAMSTONE

CAUP *n* type of quaich

CAUPS > CAUP

CAUSA *n* reason or cause

CAUSABLE > CAUSE

CAUSAE > CAUSA

CAUSAL *adj* of or being a cause ▷ *n* something that suggests a cause

CAUSALGIA *n* burning sensation along the course of a peripheral nerve together with local changes in the appearance of the skin

CAUSALGIC > CAUSALGIA

CAUSALITY *n* relationship of cause and effect

CAUSALLY > CAUSAL

CAUSALS > CAUSAL

CAUSATION *n* relationship of cause and effect

CAUSATIVE *adj* producing an effect ▷ *n* causative form or class of verbs

CAUSE *n* something that produces a particular effect ▷ *vb* be the cause of

CAUSED > CAUSE

CAUSELESS > CAUSE

CAUSEN *old infinitive of* > CAUSE

CAUSER > CAUSE

CAUSERIE *n* informal talk or conversational piece of writing

CAUSERIES > CAUSERIE

CAUSERS > CAUSE

CAUSES > CAUSE

CAUSEWAY *n* raised path or road across water or marshland

CAUSEWAYS > CAUSEWAY

CAUSEY *n* cobbled street ▷ *vb* cobble

CAUSEYED > CAUSEY

CAUSEYS > CAUSEY

CAUSING > CAUSE

CAUSTIC *adj* capable of burning by chemical action ▷ *n* caustic substance

CAUSTICAL > CAUSTIC

CAUSTICS > CAUSTIC

CAUTEL *n* craftiness

CAUTELOUS > CAUTEL

CAUTELS > CAUTEL

CAUTER *n* cauterising instrument

CAUTERANT *same as* > CAUTERY

CAUTERIES > CAUTERY

CAUTERISE *same as* > CAUTERIZE

CAUTERISM > CAUTERIZE

CAUTERIZE *vb* burn (a wound) with heat or a caustic agent to prevent infection

CAUTERS > CAUTER

CAUTERY *n* coagulation of blood or destruction of body tissue by cauterizing

CAUTION *n* care, esp in the face of danger ▷ *vb* warn, advise

CAUTIONED > CAUTION

CAUTIONER > CAUTION

CAUTIONRY *n* in Scots law, standing surety

CAUTIONS > CAUTION

CAUTIOUS *adj* showing caution

CAUVES > CAUF

CAVA *n* Spanish sparkling wine produced by a method similar to that used for champagne

CAVALCADE *n* procession of people on horseback or in cars

CAVALERO *n* cavalier

CAVALEROS > CAVALERO

CAVALETTI *n* bars supported on low stands used in dressage and horse jumping

CAVALIER *adj* showing haughty disregard ▷ *n* gallant gentleman

CAVALIERS > CAVALIER

CAVALLA *n* type of tropical fish

CAVALLAS > CAVALLA

CAVALLIES > CAVALLY

CAVALLY *same as* > CAVALLA

CAVALRIES > CAVALRY

CAVALRY *n* part of the army orig. on horseback, but now often using fast armoured vehicles

CAVAS > CAVA

CAVASS *n* Turkish armed police officer

CAVASSES > CAVASS

CAVATINA *n* solo song resembling a simple aria

CAVATINAS > CAVATINA

CAVATINE > CAVATINA

CAVE *n* hollow in the side of a hill or cliff ▷ *vb* hollow out

CAVEAT *n* warning ▷ *vb* to introduce a caveat

CAVEATED > CAVEAT

CAVEATING > CAVEAT

CAVEATOR *n* person who enters a caveat

CAVEATORS > CAVEATOR

CAVEATS > CAVEAT

CAVED > CAVE

CAVEFISH *n* type of small freshwater fish living in subterranean and other waters in S North America

CAVEL *n* drawing of lots among miners for an easy and profitable place at the coalface

CAVELIKE *adj* resembling a cave

CAVELS > CAVEL

CAVEMAN *n* prehistoric cave dweller

CAVEMEN > CAVEMAN

CAVENDISH *n* tobacco that has been sweetened and pressed into moulds to form bars

CAVER > CAVING

CAVERN *n* large cave ▷ *vb* shut in or as if in a cavern

CAVERNED > CAVERN

CAVERNING > CAVERN

CAVERNOUS *adj* like a cavern in vastness, depth, or hollowness

CAVERNS > CAVERN

CAVERS > CAVING

CAVES > CAVE

CAVESSON *n* kind of hard noseband, used (esp formerly) in breaking a horse in

CAVESSONS > CAVESSON

CAVETTI > CAVETTO

CAVETTO *n* concave moulding, shaped to a quarter circle in cross section

CAVETTOS > CAVETTO

CAVIAR *n* salted sturgeon roe, regarded as a delicacy

CAVIARE *same as* > CAVIAR

CAVIARES > CAVIARE

CAVIARIE *same as* > CAVIAR

CAVIARIES > CAVIARIE

CAVIARS > CAVIAR

CAVICORN *adj* (of sheep, goats, etc) having hollow horns as distinct from the solid antlers of deer ▷ *n* sheep, goats, etc with hollow horns as distinct from the solid antlers of deer

CAVICORNS > CAVICORN

CAVIE *n* hen coop

CAVIER *same as* **> CAVIAR**

CAVIERS > CAVIER

CAVIES > CAVY

CAVIL *vb* make petty objections ▷ *n* petty objection

CAVILED > CAVIL

CAVILER > CAVIL

CAVILERS > CAVIL

CAVILLED > CAVIL

CAVILLER > CAVIL

CAVILLERS > CAVIL

CAVILLING > CAVIL

CAVILS > CAVIL

CAVING *n* sport of exploring caves

CAVINGS > CAVING

CAVITARY *adj* containing cavities

CAVITATE *vb* to form cavities or bubbles

CAVITATED > CAVITATE

CAVITATES > CAVITATE

CAVITIED > CAVITY

CAVITIES > CAVITY

CAVITY *n* hollow space

CAVORT *vb* skip about

CAVORTED > CAVORT

CAVORTER > CAVORT

CAVORTERS > CAVORT

CAVORTING > CAVORT

CAVORTS > CAVORT

CAVY *n* type of small S American rodent with a thickset body and a very small tail

CAW *n* cry of a crow, rook, or raven ▷ *vb* make this cry

CAWED > CAW

CAWING > CAW

CAWINGS > CAW

CAWK *same as* **> CAUK**

CAWKER *n* metal projection on a horse's shoe to prevent slipping

CAWKERS > CAWKER

CAWKS > CAWK

CAWS > CAW

CAXON *n* type of wig

CAXONS > CAXON

CAY *n* low island or bank composed of sand and coral fragments

CAYENNE *n* very hot condiment, bright red in colour, made from dried capsicums

CAYENNED *adj* seasoned with cayenne

CAYENNES > CAYENNE

CAYMAN *n* S American reptile similar to an alligator

CAYMANS > CAYMAN

CAYS > CAY

CAYUSE *n* small American Indian pony used by cowboys

CAYUSES > CAYUSE

CAZ *short for* **> CASUAL**

CAZIQUE *same as* **> CACIQUE**

CAZIQUES > CAZIQUE

CEANOTHUS *n* N American shrub grown for its ornamental, often blue, flower clusters

CEAS *same as* **> CAESE**

CEASE *vb* bring or come to an end

CEASED > CEASE

CEASEFIRE *n* temporary truce

CEASELESS *adj* without stopping

CEASES > CEASE

CEASING > CEASE

CEASINGS > CEASE

CEAZE *obsolete spelling of* **> SEIZE**

CEAZED > CEAZE

CEAZES > CEAZE

CEAZING > CEAZE

CEBADILLA *same as* **> SABADILLA**

CEBID *n* any member of the Cebidae family of New World monkeys

CEBIDS > CEBID

CEBOID *same as* **> CEBID**

CEBOIDS > CEBOID

CECA > CECUM

CECAL > CECUM

CECALLY > CECUM

CECILS *n* fried meatballs

CECITIES > CECITY

CECITIS *n* inflammation of the c(a)ecum

CECITISES > CECITIS

CECITY *n* rare word for blindness

CECROPIA *n* large North American moth

CECROPIAS > CECROPIA

CECROPIN *n* antimicrobial peptide originally derived from the cecropia moth

CECROPINS > CECROPIN

CECUM *same as* **> CAECUM**

CEDAR *n* evergreen coniferous tree ▷ *adj* made of the wood of a cedar tree

CEDARBIRD *n* type of waxwing

CEDARED *adj* covered with cedars

CEDARN *adj* relating to cedar

CEDARS > CEDAR

CEDARWOOD *n* wood of any of the cedar trees

CEDARY *adj* like cedar

CEDE *vb* surrender (territory or legal rights)

CEDED > CEDE

CEDER > CEDE

CEDERS > CEDE

CEDES > CEDE

CEDI *n* standard monetary unit of Ghana, divided into 100 pesewas

CEDILLA *n* character placed under a c in some languages, to show that it is pronounced s, not k

CEDILLAS > CEDILLA

CEDING > CEDE

CEDIS > CEDI

CEDRATE *n* citron

CEDRATES > CEDRATE

CEDRINE *adj* relating to cedar

CEDULA *n* form of identification in Spanish-speaking countries

CEDULAS > CEDULA

CEE *n* third letter of the alphabet

CEES > CEE

CEIBA *n* type of tropical tree

CEIBAS > CEIBA

CEIL *vb* line (a ceiling) with plaster, boarding, etc

CEILED > CEIL

CEILER > CEIL

CEILERS > CEIL

CEILI *variant spelling of* **> CEILIDH**

CEILIDH *n* informal social gathering for singing and dancing, esp in Scotland

CEILIDHS > CEILIDH

CEILING *n* inner upper surface of a room ▷ *vb* make a ceiling

CEILINGED > CEILING

CEILINGS > CEILING

CEILIS > CEILI

CEILS > CEIL

CEINTURE *n* belt

CEINTURES > CEINTURE

CEL *short for* **> CELLULOID**

CELADON *n* type of porcelain having a greyish-green glaze: mainly Chinese

CELADONS > CELADON

CELANDINE *n* wild plant with yellow flowers

CELEB *n* celebrity

CELEBRANT *n* person who performs a religious ceremony

CELEBRATE *vb* hold festivities to mark (a happy event, anniversary, etc)

CELEBRITY *n* famous person

CELEBS > CELEB

CELECOXIB *n* type of anti-inflammatory drug

CELERIAC *n* variety of celery with a large turnip-like root

CELERIACS > CELERIAC

CELERIES > CELERY

CELERITY *n* swiftness

CELERY *n* vegetable with long green crisp edible stalks

CELESTA *n* instrument like a small piano in which key-operated hammers strike metal plates

CELESTAS > CELESTA

CELESTE *same as* **> CELESTA**

CELESTES > CELESTE

CELESTIAL *adj* heavenly, divine

CELESTINE *same as* **> CELESTITE**

CELESTITE *n* white, red or blue mineral

CELIAC *same as* **> COELIAC**

CELIACS > CELIAC

CELIBACY > CELIBATE

CELIBATE *adj* unmarried or abstaining from sex, esp because of a religious vow of chastity ▷ *n* celibate person

CELIBATES > CELIBATE

CELIBATIC *adj* celibate

CELL *n* smallest unit of an organism that is able to function independently

CELLA *n* inner room of a classical temple, esp the room housing the statue of a deity

CELLAE > CELLA

CELLAR *n* underground room for storage ▷ *vb* store in a cellar

CELLARAGE *n* area of a cellar

CELLARED > CELLAR

CELLARER *n* monastic official responsible for food, drink, etc

CELLARERS > CELLARER

CELLARET *n* case, cabinet or sideboard with compartments for holding wine bottles

CELLARETS > CELLARET

CELLARING > CELLAR

CELLARIST *same as* **> CELLARER**

CELLARMAN *n* person in charge of a cellar

CELLARMEN > CELLARMAN

CELLAROUS *adj* relating a cellar

CELLARS > CELLAR

CELLARWAY *n* way into cellar

CELLBLOCK *n* group of prison cells

CELLED *adj* cellular

CELLI > CELLO

CELLING *n* formation of cells

CELLIST > CELLO

CELLISTS > CELLO

CELLMATE *n* person with whom a prisoner shares a prison cell

CELLMATES > CELLMATE

CELLO *n* large low-pitched instrument of the violin family

CELLOIDIN *n* nitrocellulose compound derived from pyroxylin, used in a solution of alcohol and ether for embedding specimens before cutting sections for microscopy

CELLOS > CELLO

CELLOSE n a disaccharide obtained by the hydrolysis of cellulose by cellulase.

CELLOSES > CELLOSE

CELLPHONE n portable telephone operated by cellular radio

CELLS > CELL

CELLULAR adj of or consisting of cells ▷ n cellular phone

CELLULARS > CELLULAR

CELLULASE n any enzyme that converts cellulose to the disaccharide cellobiose

CELLULE n very small cell

CELLULES > CELLULE

CELLULITE n fat deposits under the skin alleged to resist dieting

CELLULOID n kind of plastic used to make toys and, formerly, photographic film

CELLULOSE n main constituent of plant cell walls, used in making paper, plastics, etc

CELLULOUS > CELLULOSE

CELOM same as > COELOM

CELOMATA > CELOM

CELOMIC > CELOM

CELOMS > CELOM

CELOSIA same as > COCKSCOMB

CELOSIAS > CELOSIA

CELOTEX n tradename for a type of insulation board

CELOTEXES > CELOTEX

CELS > CEL

CELSITUDE n loftiness

CELT n stone or metal axelike instrument with a bevelled edge

CELTS > CELT

CEMBALI > CEMBALO

CEMBALIST > CEMBALO

CEMBALO n harpsichord

CEMBALOS > CEMBALO

CEMBRA n Swiss pine

CEMBRAS > CEMBRA

CEMENT n fine grey powder mixed with water and sand to make mortar or concrete ▷ vb join, bind, or cover with cement

CEMENTA > CEMENTUM

CEMENTED > CEMENT

CEMENTER > CEMENT

CEMENTERS > CEMENT

CEMENTING > CEMENT

CEMENTITE n hard brittle compound of iron and carbon

CEMENTS > CEMENT

CEMENTUM n thin bonelike tissue that covers the dentine in the root of a tooth

CEMENTUMS > CEMENTUM

CEMETERY n place where dead people are buried

CEMITARE obsolete spelling of > SCIMITAR

CEMITARES > CEMITARE

CENACLE n supper room, esp one on an upper floor

CENACLES > CENACLE

CENDRE adj ash-blond

CENOBITE same as > COENOBITE

CENOBITES > CENOBITE

CENOBITIC > CENOBITE

CENOTAPH n monument honouring soldiers who died in a war

CENOTAPHS > CENOTAPH

CENOTE n (esp in the Yucatán peninsula) a natural well formed by the collapse of an overlying limestone crust: often used as a sacrificial site by the Mayas

CENOTES > CENOTE

CENOZOIC adj of or relating to the most recent geological era, characterized by the development and increase of the mammals

CENS n type of annual property rent

CENSE vb burn incense near or before (an altar, shrine, etc)

CENSED > CENSE

CENSER n container for burning incense

CENSERS > CENSER

CENSES > CENSE

CENSING > CENSE

CENSOR n person authorized to examine films, books, etc, to ban or cut anything considered obscene or objectionable ▷ vb ban or cut parts of (a film, book, etc)

CENSORED > CENSOR

CENSORIAL > CENSOR

CENSORIAN > CENSOR

CENSORING > CENSOR

CENSORS > CENSOR

CENSUAL > CENSUS

CENSURE n severe disapproval ▷ vb criticize severely

CENSURED > CENSURE

CENSURER > CENSURE

CENSURERS > CENSURE

CENSURES > CENSURE

CENSURING > CENSURE

CENSUS n official count of a population ▷ vb to conduct a census

CENSUSED > CENSUS

CENSUSES > CENSUS

CENSUSING > CENSUS

CENT n hundredth part of a monetary unit such as the dollar or euro

CENTAGE n rate per hundred

CENTAGES > CENTAGE

CENTAI > CENTAS

CENTAL n unit of weight equal to 100 pounds (45.3 kilograms)

CENTALS > CENTAL

CENTARE same as > CENTIARE

CENTARES > CENTARE

CENTAS n monetary unit of Lithuania, worth one hundredth of a litas

CENTAUR n mythical creature with the head, arms, and torso of a man, and the lower body and legs of a horse

CENTAUREA n type of plant of the genus which includes the cornflower and knapweed

CENTAURIC adj integrating mind and body

CENTAURS > CENTAUR

CENTAURY n Eurasian plant with purplish-pink flowers, formerly believed to have medicinal properties

CENTAVO n monetary unit worth one hundredth of the main unit of currency in Portugal and many Latin American countries

CENTAVOS > CENTAVO

CENTENARY n 100th anniversary or its celebration ▷ adj of or relating to a period of 100 years

CENTENIER n in Jersey, a local police officer

CENTER same as > CENTRE

CENTERED > CENTER

CENTERING same as > CENTRING

CENTERS > CENTER

CENTESES > CENTESIS

CENTESIMI > CENTESIMO

CENTESIMO n former monetary unit of Italy, San Marino, and the Vatican City worth one hundredth of a lira

CENTESIS n surgical puncturing part of the body with a hollow needle, to extract fluid

CENTIARE n unit of area equal to one square metre

CENTIARES > CENTIARE

CENTIGRAM n one hundredth of a gram

CENTILE n one of 99 actual or notional values of a variable dividing its distribution into 100 groups with equal frequencies

CENTILES > CENTILE

CENTIME n monetary unit worth one hundredth of a franc

CENTIMES > CENTIME

CENTIMO n monetary unit of Costa Rica, Paraguay, Peru, and Venezuela. It is worth one hundredth of their respective standard currency units

CENTIMOS > CENTIMO

CENTINEL obsolete variant of > SENTINEL

CENTINELL obsolete variant of > SENTINEL

CENTINELS > CENTINEL

CENTIPEDE n small wormlike creature with many legs

CENTNER n unit of weight equivalent to 100 pounds (45.3 kilograms)

CENTNERS > CENTNER

CENTO n piece of writing, esp a poem, composed of quotations from other authors

CENTOIST n one who composes centos

CENTOISTS > CENTOIST

CENTONATE adj having many patches

CENTONEL obsolete variant of > SENTINEL

CENTONELL obsolete variant of > SENTINEL

CENTONELS > CENTONEL

CENTONES > CENTO

CENTONIST same as > CENTOIST

CENTOS > CENTO

CENTRA > CENTRUM

CENTRAL adj of, at, or forming the centre ▷ n workplace serving as a telecommunications facility

CENTRALER > CENTRAL

CENTRALLY > CENTRAL

CENTRALS > CENTRAL

CENTRE n middle point or part ▷ vb put in the centre of something

CENTRED adj mentally and emotionally confident, focused, and well-balanced

CENTREING same as > CENTRING

CENTRES > CENTRE

CENTRIC adj being central or having a centre

CENTRICAL same as > CENTRIC

CENTRIES > CENTRY

CENTRING n temporary structure, esp one made of timber, used to support an arch during construction

CENTRINGS > CENTRING

CENTRIOLE n either of two rodlike bodies in most animal cells that form the poles of the spindle during mitosis

CENTRISM > CENTRIST

CENTRISMS > CENTRIST

CENTRIST n person favouring political moderation

CENTRISTS > CENTRIST
CENTRODE n locus produced by plotting course of the instantaneous centre of two bodies in relative motion
CENTRODES > CENTRODE
CENTROID n centre of mass of an object of uniform density, esp of a geometric figure
CENTROIDS > CENTROID
CENTRUM n main part or body of a vertebra
CENTRUMS > CENTRUM
CENTRY obsolete variant of > SENTRY
CENTS > CENT
CENTU n Lithuanian money unit
CENTUM adj denoting or belonging to the Indo-European languages in which original velar stops (k) were not palatalized ⊳ n hundred
CENTUMS > CENTUM
CENTUMVIR n one of the Roman judges who sat in civil cases
CENTUPLE n one hundredfold
CENTUPLED > CENTUPLE
CENTUPLES > CENTUPLE
CENTURIAL adj of or relating to a Roman century
CENTURIES > CENTURY
CENTURION n (in ancient Rome) officer commanding 100 men
CENTURY n period of 100 years
CEORL n freeman of the lowest class in Anglo-Saxon England
CEORLISH > CEORL
CEORLS > CEORL
CEP n another name for > PORCINO
CEPACEOUS adj having an onion-like smell or taste
CEPAGE n grape variety or type of wine
CEPAGES > CEPAGE
CEPE another spelling of > CEP
CEPES > CEPE
CEPHALAD adv towards the head or anterior part
CEPHALATE adj possessing a head
CEPHALIC adj of or relating to the head ⊳ n remedy for pains in the head
CEPHALICS > CEPHALIC
CEPHALIN n phospholipid, similar to lecithin, that occurs in the nerve tissue and brain
CEPHALINS > CEPHALIN
CEPHALOUS adj with a head

CEPHEID n type of variable star with a regular cycle of variations in luminosity
CEPHEIDS > CEPHEID
CEPS > CEP
CERACEOUS adj waxlike or waxy
CERAMAL same as > CERMET
CERAMALS > CERAMAL
CERAMIC n hard brittle material made by heating clay to a very high temperature ⊳ adj made of ceramic
CERAMICS n art of producing ceramic objects
CERAMIDE n any of a class of biologically important compounds used as moisturizers in skin-care preparations
CERAMIDES > CERAMIDE
CERAMIST > CERAMICS
CERAMISTS > CERAMICS
CERASIN n meta-arabinic acid
CERASINS > CERASIN
CERASTES n type of venomous snake, esp the horned viper
CERASTIUM n mouse-eared chickweed
CERATE n hard ointment or medicated paste consisting of lard or oil mixed with wax or resin
CERATED adj (of certain birds, such as the falcon) having a cere
CERATES > CERATE
CERATIN same as > KERATIN
CERATINS > CERATIN
CERATITIS same as > KERATITIS
CERATODUS n type of extinct lungfish common in Cretaceous and Triassic times
CERATOID adj having the shape or texture of animal horn
CERBEREAN adj of or resembling Cerberus, the three-headed dog that guarded the entrance to Hades in Greek mythology
CERBERIAN same as > CERBEREAN
CERCAL adj of or relating to a tail
CERCARIA n one of the larval forms of trematode worms. It has a short forked tail and resembles an immature adult
CERCARIAE > CERCARIA
CERCARIAL > CERCARIA
CERCARIAN > CERCARIA
CERCI > CERCUS
CERCIS n type of tree or shrub of the genus which includes the redbud and

Judas tree
CERCISES > CERCIS
CERCOPID n froghopper or spittlebug
CERCOPIDS > CERCOPID
CERCUS n one of a pair of sensory appendages at the tip of the abdomen of some insects and other arthropods
CERE n soft waxy swelling, containing the nostrils, at the base of the upper beak of a parrot ⊳ vb wrap (a corpse) in a cerecloth
CEREAL n grass plant with edible grain, such as oat or wheat
CEREALIST n expert in cereals
CEREALS > CEREAL
CEREBELLA n plural of singular cerebellum: one of the major divisions of the vertebrate brain
CEREBRA > CEREBRUM
CEREBRAL same as > CACUMINAL
CEREBRALS > CEREBRAL
CEREBRATE vb use the mind
CEREBRIC > CEREBRUM
CEREBROID > CEREBRUM
CEREBRUM n main part of the brain
CEREBRUMS > CEREBRUM
CERECLOTH n waxed waterproof cloth of a kind formerly used as a shroud
CERED > CERE
CEREMENT n any burial clothes
CEREMENTS > CEREMENT
CEREMONY n formal act or ritual
CEREOUS adj waxlike
CERES > CERE
CERESIN n white wax extracted from ozocerite
CERESINE same as > CERESIN
CERESINES > CERESINE
CERESINS > CERESIN
CEREUS n type of tropical American cactus
CEREUSES > CEREUS
CERGE n large altar candle
CERGES > CERGE
CERIA n ceric oxide
CERIAS > CERIA
CERIC adj of or containing cerium in the tetravalent state
CERING > CERE
CERIPH same as > SERIF
CERIPHS > CERIPH
CERISE adj cherry-red ⊳ n moderate to dark red colour
CERISES > CERISE
CERITE n hydrous silicate of cerium
CERITES > CERITE
CERIUM n steel-grey metallic element

CERIUMS > CERIUM
CERMET n any of several materials consisting of a metal matrix with ceramic particles disseminated through it. They are hard and resistant to high temperatures
CERMETS > CERMET
CERNE obsolete variant of > ENCIRCLE
CERNED > CERNE
CERNES > CERNE
CERNING > CERNE
CERNUOUS adj (of some flowers or buds) drooping
CERO n type of large spiny-finned food fish of warm American coastal regions of the Atlantic
CEROGRAPH n writing on wax
CEROMANCY n divination by interpreting significance of shapes formed when melted wax is dropped into water
CEROON n hide-covered bale
CEROONS > CEROON
CEROS > CERO
CEROTIC as in cerotic acid white insoluble odourless wax
CEROTYPE n process for preparing a printing plate by engraving a wax-coated copper plate and then using this as a mould for an electrotype
CEROTYPES > CEROTYPE
CEROUS adj of or containing cerium in the trivalent state
CERRADO n vast area of tropical savanna in Brazil
CERRADOS > CERRADO
CERRIAL adj relating to the cerris
CERRIS n Turkey oak
CERRISES > CERRIS
CERT n certainty
CERTAIN adj positive and confident
CERTAINER > CERTAIN
CERTAINLY adv without doubt ⊳ sentence substitute by all means
CERTAINTY n state of being sure
CERTES adv with certainty
CERTIE n as in by my certie assuredly
CERTIFIED > CERTIFY
CERTIFIER > CERTIFY
CERTIFIES > CERTIFY
CERTIFY vb confirm, attest to
CERTITUDE n confidence, certainty
CERTS > CERT
CERTY n as in by my certy assuredly
CERULE adj sky-blue
CERULEAN n deep blue

colour ▷ *n* light shade of blue

CERULEANS > CERULEAN

CERULEIN *n* type of dyestuff

CERULEINS > CERULEIN

CERULEOUS *adj* sky-blue

CERUMEN *n* soft brownish-yellow wax secreted by glands in the auditory canal of the external ear

CERUMENS > CERUMEN

CERUSE *n* white lead

CERUSES > CERUSE

CERUSITE *same as* > CERUSSITE

CERUSITES > CERUSITE

CERUSSITE *n* usually white mineral, found in veins

CERVELAS *n* French garlicky pork sausage

CERVELAT *n* smoked sausage made from pork and beef

CERVELATS > CERVELAT

CERVEZA *n* Spanish word for beer

CERVEZAS > CERVEZA

CERVICAL *adj* of or relating to the neck or cervix

CERVICES > CERVIX

CERVICUM *n* flexible region between the prothorax and head in insects

CERVICUMS > CERVICUM

CERVID *n* type of ruminant mammal such as the deer, characterized by the presence of antlers

CERVIDS > CERVID

CERVINE *adj* resembling or relating to a deer

CERVIX *n* narrow entrance of the womb

CERVIXES > CERVIX

CESAREAN *variant of* > CAESAREAN

CESAREANS > CESAREAN

CESAREVNA *n* wife of a Russian tsar's eldest son

CESARIAN US *variant of* > CAESAREAN

CESARIANS > CESARIAN

CESIOUS *same as* > CAESIOUS

CESIUM *same as* > CAESIUM

CESIUMS > CESIUM

CESPITOSE *adj* growing in dense tufts

CESS *n* any of several special taxes, such as a land tax in Scotland ▷ *vb* tax or assess for taxation

CESSATION *n* ceasing

CESSE *obsolete variant of* > CEASE

CESSED > CESS

CESSER *n* coming to an end of a term interest or annuity

CESSERS > CESSER

CESSES > CESS

CESSING > CESS

CESSION *n* ceding

CESSIONS > CESSION

CESSPIT *same as* > CESSPOOL

CESSPITS > CESSPIT

CESSPOOL *n* covered tank or pit for collecting and storing sewage or waste water

CESSPOOLS > CESSPOOL

CESTA *n* in jai alai, the basket used to throw and catch the pelota

CESTAS > CESTA

CESTI > CESTUS

CESTODE *n* type of parasitic flatworm such as the tapeworms

CESTODES > CESTODE

CESTOI > CESTOS

CESTOID *adj* (esp of tapeworms and similar animals) ribbon-like in form ▷ *n* ribbon-like worm

CESTOIDS > CESTOID

CESTOS *same as* > CESTUS

CESTOSES > CESTOS

CESTUI *n* "the one (who)"; legal term, used in certain phrases, to designate a person

CESTUIS > CESTUI

CESTUS *n* girdle of Aphrodite (Venus) decorated to cause amorousness

CESTUSES > CESTUS

CESURA *a variant spelling of* > CAESURA

CESURAE > CESURA

CESURAL > CESURA

CESURAS > CESURA

CESURE *same as* > CAESURA

CESURES > CESURE

CETACEAN *n* fish-shaped sea mammal such as a whale or dolphin ▷ *adj* relating to these mammals

CETACEANS > CETACEAN

CETACEOUS *same as* > CETACEAN

CETANE *n* colourless liquid hydrocarbon, used as a solvent

CETANES > CETANE

CETE *n* group of badgers

CETERACH *n* scale-fern

CETERACHS > CETERACH

CETES > CETE

CETOLOGY *n* branch of zoology concerned with the study of whales (cetaceans)

CETRIMIDE *n* quaternary ammonium compound used as a detergent

CETUXIMAB *n* monoclonal antibody used to treat cancer

CETYL *n* univalent alcohol radical

CETYLS > CETYL

CESSES > CESS

CESSING > CESS

CESSION *n* ceding

CETYWALL *n* valerian

CETYWALLS > CETYWALL

CEVADILLA *same as* > SABADILLA

CEVAPCICI *n* sausages made with beef and paprika

CEVICHE *n* Peruvian seafood dish

CEVICHES > CEVICHE

CEVITAMIC as in *cevitamic acid* ascorbic (acid)

CEYLANITE *same as* > CEYLONITE

CEYLONITE *n* pleonaste

CEZVE *n* small metal pot for brewing coffee

CEZVES > CEZVE

CH *pron* obsolete from of I

CHA *n* tea

CHABAZITE *n* pink, white, or colourless zeolite mineral

CHABLIS *n* dry white French wine

CHABOUK *n* type of whip

CHABOUKS > CHABOUK

CHABUK *same as* > CHABOUK

CHABUKS > CHABUK

CHACE *obsolete variant of* > CHASE

CHACED > CHACE

CHACES > CHACE

CHACHKA *n* cheap trinket

CHACHKAS > CHACHKA

CHACING > CHACE

CHACK *vb* to bite

CHACKED > CHACK

CHACKING > CHACK

CHACKS > CHACK

CHACMA *n* type of baboon with coarse greyish hair, occurring in S and E Africa

CHACMAS > CHACMA

CHACO *same as* > SHAKO

CHACOES > CHACO

CHACONINE *n* toxic substance found in potatoes

CHACONNE *n* musical form consisting of a set of variations on a repeated melodic bass line

CHACONNES > CHACONNE

CHACOS > CHACO

CHAD *n* small pieces removed during the punching of holes in punch cards, printer paper, etc

CHADAR *same as* > CHUDDAR

CHADARIM > CHEDER

CHADARS > CHADAR

CHADDAR *same as* > CHUDDAR

CHADDARS > CHADDAR

CHADDOR *same as* > CHUDDAR

CHADDORS > CHADDOR

CHADLESS *adj* (of a keypunch) not producing chads

CHADO *n* Japanese tea ceremony

CHADOR *same as* > CHUDDAR

CHADORS > CHADOR

CHADOS > CHADO

CHADRI *n* shroud which covers the body from head to foot, usually worn by females in Islamic countries

CHADS > CHAD

CHAEBOL *n* large, usually family-owned, business group in South Korea

CHAEBOLS > CHAEBOL

CHAETA *n* any of the chitinous bristles on the body of such annelids as the earthworm and the lugworm: used in locomotion

CHAETAE > CHAETA

CHAETAL > CHAETA

CHAETODON *n* butterfly fish

CHAETOPOD *n* type of annelid worm

CHAFE *vb* make sore or worn by rubbing

CHAFED > CHAFE

CHAFER *n* large beetle

CHAFERS > CHAFER

CHAFES > CHAFE

CHAFF *n* grain husks ▷ *vb* tease good-naturedly

CHAFFED > CHAFF

CHAFFER *vb* haggle

CHAFFERED > CHAFFER

CHAFFERER > CHAFFER

CHAFFERS > CHAFFER

CHAFFERY *n* bargaining

CHAFFIER > CHAFF

CHAFFIEST > CHAFF

CHAFFINCH *n* small European songbird

CHAFFING > CHAFF

CHAFFINGS > CHAFF

CHAFFRON *same as* > CHAMFRON

CHAFFRONS > CHAFFRON

CHAFFS > CHAFF

CHAFFY > CHAFF

CHAFING > CHAFE

CHAFT *n* jaw

CHAFTS > CHAFT

CHAGAN *n* Mongolian royal or imperial title

CHAGANS > CHAGAN

CHAGRIN *n* annoyance and disappointment ▷ *vb* embarrass and annoy

CHAGRINED > CHAGRIN

CHAGRINS > CHAGRIN

CHAI *n* tea, esp as made in India with added spices

CHAIN *n* flexible length of connected metal links ▷ *vb* restrict or fasten with or as if with a chain

CHAINE *adj* (of a dance turn) producing a full rotation for every two steps taken ▷ *vb* produce a full rotation for every two steps taken

CHAINED > CHAIN

CHAINES > CHAINE
CHAINFALL n type of hoist
CHAINING > CHAIN
CHAINLESS adj having no chain
CHAINLET n small chain
CHAINLETS > CHAINLET
CHAINMAN n person who does the chaining in a survey
CHAINMEN > CHAINMAN
CHAINS > CHAIN
CHAINSAW n motor-driven saw with teeth linked in a continuous chain ▷ vb operate a chainsaw
CHAINSAWS > CHAINSAW
CHAINSHOT n cannon shot of two balls joined by a chain
CHAINWORK n work linked or looped in the manner of a chain
CHAIR n seat with a back, for one person ▷ vb preside over (a meeting)
CHAIRDAYS n old age
CHAIRED > CHAIR
CHAIRING > CHAIR
CHAIRLIFT n series of chairs suspended from a moving cable for carrying people up a slope
CHAIRMAN n person in charge of a company's board of directors or a meeting ▷ vb to act as chairman of
CHAIRMANS > CHAIRMAN
CHAIRMEN > CHAIRMAN
CHAIRS > CHAIR
CHAIS > CHAI
CHAISE n light horse-drawn carriage
CHAISES > CHAISE
CHAKALAKA n relish made from tomatoes, onions, and spices
CHAKRA n (in yoga) any of the seven major energy centres in the body
CHAKRAS > CHAKRA
CHAL n in Romany, person or fellow
CHALAH same as
> CHALLAH
CHALAHS > CHALAH
CHALAN vb (in India) to cause an accused person to appear before a magistrate
CHALANS > CHALAN
CHALAZA n one of a pair of spiral threads of albumen holding the yolk of a bird's egg in position
CHALAZAE > CHALAZA
CHALAZAL > CHALAZA
CHALAZAS > CHALAZA
CHALAZIA > CHALAZION
CHALAZION n small cyst on the eyelid resulting from chronic inflammation of a meibomian gland
CHALCID n type of tiny hymenopterous insect

whose larvae are parasites of other insects
CHALCIDS > CHALCID
CHALCOGEN n any of the elements oxygen, sulphur, selenium, tellurium, or polonium, of group 6A of the periodic table
CHALDER n former Scottish dry measure
CHALDERS > CHALDER
CHALDRON n unit of capacity equal to 36 bushels. Formerly used in the US for the measurement of solids, being equivalent to 1.268 cubic metres. Used in Britain for both solids and liquids, it is equivalent to 1.309 cubic metres
CHALDRONS > CHALDRON
CHALEH same as
> CHALLAH
CHALEHS > CHALEH
CHALET n kind of Swiss wooden house with a steeply sloping roof
CHALETS > CHALET
CHALICE n large goblet
CHALICED adj (of plants) having cup-shaped flowers
CHALICES > CHALICE
CHALK n soft white rock consisting of calcium carbonate ▷ vb draw or mark with chalk
CHALKED > CHALK
CHALKFACE n work or art of teaching in a school
CHALKIER > CHALK
CHALKIEST > CHALK
CHALKING > CHALK
CHALKLIKE > CHALK
CHALKPIT n quarry for chalk
CHALKPITS > CHALKPIT
CHALKS > CHALK
CHALKY > CHALK
CHALLA same as
> CHALLAH
CHALLAH n bread, usually in the form of a plaited loaf, traditionally eaten by Jews to celebrate the Sabbath
CHALLAHS > CHALLAH
CHALLAN same as
> CHALAN
CHALLANS > CHALLAN
CHALLAS > CHALLA
CHALLENGE n demanding or stimulating situation ▷ vb issue a challenge to
CHALLIE same as
> CHALLIS
CHALLIES > CHALLIE
CHALLIS n lightweight plain-weave fabric of wool, cotton, etc, usually with a printed design
CHALLISES > CHALLIS
CHALLOT > CHALLAH
CHALLOTH > CHALLAH
CHALLY same as
> CHALLIS

CHALONE n any internal secretion that inhibits a physiological process or function
CHALONES > CHALONE
CHALONIC > CHALONE
CHALOT > CHALAH
CHALOTH > CHALAH
CHALS > CHAL
CHALUMEAU n early type of reed instrument, precursor of the clarinet
CHALUPA n Mexican dish
CHALUPAS > CHALUPA
CHALUTZ n member of an organization of immigrants to Israeli agricultural settlements
CHALUTZES > CHALUTZ
CHALUTZIM > CHALUTZ
CHALYBEAN adj (of steel) of superior quality
CHALYBITE another name for **>** SIDERITE
CHAM an archaic word for
> KHAN
CHAMADE n (formerly) a signal by drum or trumpet inviting an enemy to a parley
CHAMADES > CHAMADE
CHAMBER n hall used for formal meetings ▷ vb act lasciviously
CHAMBERED > CHAMBER
CHAMBERER n lascivious person
CHAMBERS npl judge's room for hearing private cases not taken in open court
CHAMBRAY n smooth light fabric of cotton, linen, etc, with white weft and a coloured warp
CHAMBRAYS > CHAMBRAY
CHAMBRE adj (of wine) at room temperature
CHAMELEON n small lizard that changes colour to blend in with its surroundings
CHAMELOT same as
> CAMLET
CHAMELOTS > CHAMELOT
CHAMETZ n leavened food which may not be eaten during Passover
CHAMETZES > CHAMETZ
CHAMFER same as **>** CHASE
CHAMFERED > CHAMFER
CHAMFERER > CHAMFER
CHAMFERS > CHAMFER
CHAMFRAIN same as
> CHAMFRON
CHAMFRON n piece of armour for a horse's head
CHAMFRONS > CHAMFRON
CHAMISA n American shrub
CHAMISAL n place overgrown with chamiso
CHAMISALS > CHAMISAL
CHAMISAS > CHAMISA
CHAMISE same as

> CHAMISO
CHAMISES > CHAMISE
CHAMISO n fourwing saltbush
CHAMISOS > CHAMISO
CHAMLET same as
> CAMLET
CHAMLETS > CHAMLET
CHAMMIED > CHAMMY
CHAMMIES > CHAMMY
CHAMMY same as
> CHAMOIS
CHAMMYING > CHAMMY
CHAMOIS n small mountain antelope or a pice of leather from its skin, used for polishing ▷ vb polish with a chamois
CHAMOISED > CHAMOIS
CHAMOISES > CHAMOIS
CHAMOIX same as
> CHAMOIS
CHAMOMILE same as
> CAMOMILE
CHAMP vb chew noisily
CHAMPAC n type of tree of India and the E Indies, whose yellow flowers yield an oil used in perfumes
CHAMPACA same as
> CHAMPAC
CHAMPACAS > CHAMPACA
CHAMPACS > CHAMPAC
CHAMPAGNE n sparkling white French wine ▷ adj denoting a luxurious lifestyle
CHAMPAIGN n expanse of open level or gently undulating country
CHAMPAK same as
> CHAMPAC
CHAMPAKS > CHAMPAK
CHAMPART n granting of land to a person, on condition that a portion of the crops will be given to the seller
CHAMPARTS > CHAMPART
CHAMPED > CHAMP
CHAMPER > CHAMP
CHAMPERS n champagne
CHAMPERTY n (formerly) an illegal bargain between a party to litigation and an outsider whereby the latter agrees to pay for the action and thereby share in any proceeds recovered
CHAMPIER > CHAMPY
CHAMPIEST > CHAMPY
CHAMPING > CHAMP
CHAMPION n overall winner of a competition ▷ vb support ▷ adj excellent ▷ adv very well
CHAMPIONS > CHAMPION
CHAMPLEVE adj of or relating to a process of enamelling by which grooves are cut into a metal base and filled with enamel colours ▷ n object enamelled by this process
CHAMPS > CHAMP

CHAMPY adj (of earth) churned up (by cattle, for example)

CHAMS > CHAM

CHANA n (in Indian cookery) chickpeas

CHANAS > CHANA

CHANCE n likelihood, probability ▷ vb risk, hazard

CHANCED > CHANCE

CHANCEFUL > CHANCE

CHANCEL n part of a church containing the altar and choir

CHANCELS > CHANCEL

CHANCER n unscrupulous or dishonest opportunist who is prepared to try any dubious scheme for making money or furthering his own ends

CHANCERS > CHANCER

CHANCERY n Lord Chancellor's court, now a division of the High Court of Justice

CHANCES > CHANCE

CHANCEY same as > CHANCY

CHANCIER > CHANCY

CHANCIEST > CHANCY

CHANCILY > CHANCY

CHANCING > CHANCE

CHANCRE n small hard growth which is the first sign of syphilis

CHANCRES > CHANCRE

CHANCROID n soft venereal ulcer, esp of the male genitals, caused by a bacterial infection ▷ adj relating to or resembling a chancroid or chancre

CHANCROUS > CHANCRE

CHANCY adj uncertain, risky

CHANDELLE n abrupt climbing turn almost to the point of stalling, in which an aircraft's momentum is used to increase its rate of climb ▷ vb carry out a chandelle

CHANDLER n dealer, esp in ships' supplies

CHANDLERS > CHANDLER

CHANDLERY n business, warehouse, or merchandise of a chandler

CHANFRON same as > CHAMFRON

CHANFRONS > CHANFRON

CHANG n loud discordant noise

CHANGA interj in Indian English, an expression of approval or agreement

CHANGE n becoming different ▷ vb make or become different

CHANGED > CHANGE

CHANGEFUL adj often changing

CHANGER > CHANGE

CHANGERS > CHANGE

CHANGES > CHANGE

CHANGEUP n type of baseball pitch

CHANGEUPS > CHANGEUP

CHANGING > CHANGE

CHANGS > CHANG

CHANK n shell of several types of sea conch, used to make bracelets

CHANKS > CHANK

CHANNEL n band of broadcasting frequencies ▷ vb direct or convey through a channel

CHANNELED > CHANNEL

CHANNELER > CHANNEL

CHANNELS > CHANNEL

CHANNER n gravel

CHANNERS > CHANNER

CHANOYO a variant of > CHADO

CHANOYOS > CHANOYO

CHANOYU same as > CHADO

CHANOYUS > CHADO

CHANSON n song

CHANSONS > CHANSON

CHANT vb utter or sing (a slogan or psalm) ▷ n rhythmic or repetitious slogan

CHANTABLE > CHANT

CHANTAGE n blackmail

CHANTAGES > CHANTAGE

CHANTED > CHANT

CHANTER n (on bagpipes) pipe on which the melody is played

CHANTERS > CHANTER

CHANTEUSE n female singer, esp in a nightclub or cabaret

CHANTEY the usual US spelling of > SHANTY

CHANTEYS > CHANTEY

CHANTIE n chamber pot

CHANTIES > CHANTY

CHANTILLY as in chantilly lace delicate ornamental lace

CHANTING > CHANT

CHANTINGS > CHANTING

CHANTOR same as > CHANTER

CHANTORS > CHANTOR

CHANTRESS n female chanter

CHANTRIES > CHANTRY

CHANTRY n endowment for the singing of Masses for the soul of the founder or others designated by him

CHANTS > CHANT

CHANTY same as > SHANTY

CHANUKIAH a variant spelling of > HANUKIAH

CHAO n Vietnamese rice porridge

CHAOLOGY n study of chaos theory

CHAORDIC adj combining elements of chaos and order

CHAOS n complete disorder or confusion

CHAOSES > CHAOS

CHAOTIC > CHAOS

CHAP n man or boy ▷ vb (of the skin) to make or become raw and cracked, esp by exposure to cold

CHAPARRAL n (in the southwestern US) a dense growth of shrubs and trees, esp evergreen oaks

CHAPATI n (in Indian cookery) flat thin unleavened bread

CHAPATIES > CHAPATI

CHAPATIS > CHAPATI

CHAPATTI same as > CHAPATI

CHAPATTIS > CHAPATTI

CHAPBOOK n book of popular ballads, stories, etc, formerly sold by chapmen or pedlars

CHAPBOOKS > CHAPBOOK

CHAPE n metal tip or trimming for a scabbard

CHAPEAU n hat

CHAPEAUS > CHAPEAU

CHAPEAUX > CHAPEAU

CHAPEL n place of worship with its own altar, within a church

CHAPELESS > CHAPE

CHAPELRY n district legally assigned to and served by an Anglican chapel

CHAPELS > CHAPEL

CHAPERON n (esp formerly) an older or married woman who accompanies or supervises a young unmarried woman on social occasions ▷ vb act as a chaperon to

CHAPERONE same as > CHAPERON

CHAPERONS > CHAPERON

CHAPES > CHAPE

CHAPESS n woman

CHAPESSES > CHAPESS

CHAPITER same as > CAPITAL

CHAPITERS > CHAPITER

CHAPKA same as > CZAPKA

CHAPKAS > CHAPKA

CHAPLAIN n clergyman attached to a chapel, military body, or institution

CHAPLAINS > CHAPLAIN

CHAPLESS adj lacking a lower jaw

CHAPLET n garland for the head ▷ vb create a garland

CHAPLETED > CHAPLET

CHAPLETS > CHAPLET

CHAPMAN n travelling pedlar

CHAPMEN > CHAPMAN

CHAPPAL n one of a pair of sandals, usually of leather, worn in India

CHAPPALS > CHAPPAL

CHAPPATI same as > CHAPATI

CHAPPATIS > CHAPPATI

CHAPPED > CHAP

CHAPPESS same as > CHAPESS

CHAPPIE n man or boy

CHAPPIER > CHAPPY

CHAPPIES > CHAPPIE

CHAPPIEST > CHAPPY

CHAPPING > CHAP

CHAPPY adj (of skin) chapped

CHAPRASSI n in India, during the British Empire, an office messenger

CHAPS > CHAP

CHAPSTICK n cylinder of a substance for preventing or soothing chapped lips

CHAPT adj chapped

CHAPTER n division of a book ▷ vb divide into chapters

CHAPTERAL > CHAPTER

CHAPTERED > CHAPTER

CHAPTERS > CHAPTER

CHAPTREL n capital of a pillar supporting an arch

CHAPTRELS > CHAPTREL

CHAQUETA n South American cowboy jacket

CHAQUETAS > CHAQUETA

CHAR vb blacken by partial burning ▷ n charwoman

CHARA n type of green freshwater algae

CHARABANC n coach for sightseeing

CHARACID same as > CHARACIN

CHARACIDS > CHARACIN

CHARACIN n type of small carnivorous freshwater fish of Central and S America and Africa

CHARACINS > CHARACIN

CHARACT n distinctive mark

CHARACTER n combination of qualities distinguishing a person, group, or place

CHARACTS > CHARACT

CHARADE n absurd pretence

CHARADES n game in which one team acts out each syllable of a word or phrase, which the other team has to guess

CHARANGA n type of orchestra used in performing traditional Cuban music

CHARANGAS > CHARANGA

CHARANGO n Andean ten-stringed mandolin

CHARANGOS > CHARANGO

CHARAS another name for > HASHISH

CHARASES > CHARAS

CHARBROIL vb to grill over charcoal

CHARCOAL n black substance formed by partially burning wood

▷ adj very dark grey ▷ vb write, draw, or blacken with charcoal

CHARCOALS > CHARCOAL

CHARCOALY > CHARCOAL

CHARD n variety of beet with large succulent leaves and thick stalks, used as a vegetable

CHARDS > CHARD

CHARE same as > CHAR

CHARED > CHAR

CHARES > CHAR

CHARET obsolete variant of > CHARIOT

CHARETS > CHARET

CHARGE vb ask as a price ▷ n price charged

CHARGED > CHARGE

CHARGEFUL adj expensive

CHARGER n device for charging an accumulator

CHARGERS > CHARGER

CHARGES > CHARGE

CHARGING > CHARGE

CHARGRILL vb to grill over charcoal

CHARIDEE n jocular spelling of charity, as pronounced in a mid-Atlantic accent

CHARIDEES > CHARIDEE

CHARIER > CHARY

CHARIEST > CHARY

CHARILY adv cautiously

CHARINESS n state of being chary

CHARING > CHAR

CHARIOT n two-wheeled horse-drawn vehicle used in ancient times in wars and races ▷ vb to ride in a chariot

CHARIOTED > CHARIOT

CHARIOTS > CHARIOT

CHARISM same as > CHARISMA

CHARISMA n person's power to attract or influence people

CHARISMAS > CHARISMA

CHARISMS > CHARISM

CHARITIES > CHARITY

CHARITY n organization that gives help, such as money or food, to those in need

CHARIVARI n discordant mock serenade to newlyweds, made with pans, kettles, etc ▷ vb make such a serenade

CHARK vb to char

CHARKA same as > CHARKHA

CHARKAS > CHARKA

CHARKED > CHARK

CHARKHA n (in India) a spinning wheel, esp for cotton

CHARKHAS > CHARKHA

CHARKING > CHARK

CHARKS > CHARK

CHARLADY same as > CHARWOMAN

CHARLATAN n person who claims expertise that he or she does not have

CHARLEY as in charley horse muscle stiffness after strenuous exercise

CHARLEYS > CHARLEY

CHARLIE n fool

CHARLIER as in charlier shoe special light horseshoe

CHARLIES > CHARLIE

CHARLOCK n weed with hairy leaves and yellow flowers

CHARLOCKS > CHARLOCK

CHARLOTTE n dessert made with fruit and bread or cake crumbs

CHARM n attractive quality ▷ vb attract, delight

CHARMED adj delighted or fascinated

CHARMER n attractive person

CHARMERS > CHARMER

CHARMEUSE n trademark for a lightweight fabric with a satin-like finish

CHARMFUL adj highly charming or enchanting

CHARMING adj attractive

CHARMLESS adj devoid of charm

CHARMONIA npl elementary particles containing an antiquark and a charm quark

CHARMS > CHARM

CHARNECO n type of sweet wine

CHARNECOS > CHARNECO

CHARNEL adj ghastly ▷ n ghastly thing

CHARNELS > CHARNEL

CHAROSET n dish of chopped fruit, nuts and wine, eaten at Passover

CHAROSETH same as > CHAROSET

CHAROSETS > CHAROSET

CHARPAI same as > CHARPOY

CHARPAIS > CHARPAI

CHARPIE n lint pieces used to make surgical dressings

CHARPIES > CHARPIE

CHARPOY n bedstead of woven webbing or hemp stretched on a wooden frame on four legs, common in India

CHARPOYS > CHARPOY

CHARQUI n meat, esp beef, cut into strips and dried

CHARQUID > CHARQUI

CHARQUIS > CHARQUI

CHARR same as > CHAR

CHARRED > CHAR

CHARRIER > CHARRY

CHARRIEST > CHARRY

CHARRING > CHAR

CHARRO n Mexican cowboy

CHARROS > CHARRO

CHARRS > CHARR

CHARRY adj of or relating to charcoal

CHARS > CHAR

CHART n graph, table, or diagram showing information ▷ vb plot the course of

CHARTA n charter

CHARTABLE > CHART

CHARTAS > CHARTA

CHARTED > CHART

CHARTER n document granting or demanding certain rights ▷ vb hire by charter

CHARTERED adj officially qualified to practise a profession

CHARTERER > CHARTER

CHARTERS > CHARTER

CHARTING > CHART

CHARTISM n historical reform movement in Britain

CHARTISMS > CHARTISM

CHARTIST n supporter of chartism

CHARTISTS > CHARTIST

CHARTLESS adj not mapped

CHARTS > CHART

CHARVER n derogatory term for a young woman

CHARVERS > CHARVER

CHARWOMAN n woman whose job is to clean other people's homes

CHARWOMEN > CHARWOMAN

CHARY adj wary, careful

CHAS > CHA

CHASE vb run after quickly in order to catch or drive away ▷ n chasing, pursuit

CHASEABLE > CHASE

CHASED > CHASE

CHASEPORT n porthole through which a chase gun is fired

CHASER n milder drink drunk after another stronger one

CHASERS > CHASER

CHASES > CHASE

CHASING > CHASE

CHASINGS > CHASE

CHASM n deep crack in the earth ▷ vb create a chasm

CHASMAL > CHASM

CHASMED > CHASM

CHASMIC > CHASM

CHASMIER > CHASMY

CHASMIEST > CHASMY

CHASMS > CHASM

CHASMY adj full of chasms

CHASSE n one of a series of gliding steps in ballet in which the same foot always leads ▷ vb perform either of these steps

CHASSED > CHASSE

CHASSEED > CHASSE

CHASSEING > CHASSE

CHASSEPOT n breech-loading bolt-action rifle formerly used by the French Army

CHASSES > CHASSE

CHASSEUR n member of a unit specially trained and equipped for swift deployment ▷ adj designating or cooked in a sauce consisting of white wine and mushrooms

CHASSEURS > CHASSEUR

CHASSIS n frame, wheels and mechanical parts of a vehicle

CHASTE adj abstaining from sex outside marriage or altogether

CHASTELY > CHASTE

CHASTEN vb subdue by criticism

CHASTENED > CHASTEN

CHASTENER > CHASTEN

CHASTENS > CHASTEN

CHASTER > CHASTE

CHASTEST > CHASTE

CHASTISE vb scold severely

CHASTISED > CHASTISE

CHASTISER > CHASTISE

CHASTISES > CHASTISE

CHASTITY n state of being chaste

CHASUBLE n long sleeveless robe worn by a priest when celebrating Mass

CHASUBLES > CHASUBLE

CHAT n informal conversation ▷ vb have an informal conversation

CHATBOT n computer program in the form of a virtual e-mail correspondent that can reply to messages from computer users

CHATBOTS > CHATBOT

CHATCHKA variant of > TCHOTCHKE

CHATCHKAS > CHATCHKA

CHATCHKE same as > TCHOTCHKE

CHATCHKES > CHATCHKE

CHATEAU n French castle

CHATEAUS > CHATEAU

CHATEAUX > CHATEAU

CHATELAIN same as > CASTELLAN

CHATLINE n telephone service enabling callers to join in general conversatio with each other

CHATLINES > CHATLINE

CHATON n in jewellery, a stone with a reflective metal foil backing

CHATONS > CHATON

CHATOYANT adj having changeable lustre ▷ n gemstone with a changeable lustre

CHATROOM n site on the Internet where users have group discussions by e-ma

CHATROOMS > CHATROOM

CHATS > CHAT

CHATTA *n* umbrella
CHATTAS > CHATTA
CHATTED > CHAT
CHATTEL *n* item of movable personal property
CHATTELS > CHATTEL
CHATTER *vb* speak quickly and continuously about unimportant things ▷ *n* idle talk
CHATTERED > CHATTER
CHATTERER *same as* > COTINGA
CHATTERS > CHATTER
CHATTERY > CHATTER
CHATTI *n* (in India) an earthenware pot
CHATTIER > CHATTY
CHATTIES > CHATTI
CHATTIEST > CHATTY
CHATTILY > CHATTY
CHATTING > CHAT
CHATTIS > CHATTI
CHATTY *adj* (of a person) fond of friendly, informal conversation
CHAUFE *obsolete variant of* > CHAFE
CHAUFED > CHAUFE
CHAUFER *same as* > CHAUFFER
CHAUFERS > CHAUFER
CHAUFES > CHAUFE
CHAUFF *obsolete variant of* > CHAFE
CHAUFFED > CHAUFF
CHAUFFER *n* small portable heater or stove
CHAUFFERS > CHAUFFER
CHAUFFEUR *n* person employed to drive a car for someone ▷ *vb* act as driver for (someone)
CHAUFFING > CHAUFF
CHAUFFS > CHAUFF
CHAUFING > CHAUFE
CHAUMER *n* chamber
CHAUMERS > CHAUMER
CHAUNCE *archaic variant of* > CHANCE
CHAUNCED > CHAUNCE
CHAUNCES > CHAUNCE
CHAUNCING > CHAUNCE
CHAUNGE *archaic variant of* > CHANGE
CHAUNGED > CHAUNGE
CHAUNGES > CHAUNGE
CHAUNGING > CHAUNGE
CHAUNT *a less common variant of* > CHANT
CHAUNTED > CHAUNT
CHAUNTER > CHAUNT
CHAUNTERS > CHAUNT
CHAUNTING > CHAUNT
CHAUNTRY *same as* > CHANTRY
CHAUNTS > CHAUNT
CHAUSSES *n* tight-fitting medieval garment covering the feet and legs, usually made of chain mail
CHAUSSURE *n* any type of footwear
CHAUVIN *n* chauvinist

CHAUVINS > CHAUVIN
CHAV *n* informal derogatory word for a young working-class person who wears casual sports clothes
CHAVE *vb* old dialect term for "I have"
CHAVENDER *n* chub
CHAVETTE *n* informal derogatory word for a young working-class female who wears casual sports clothes
CHAVETTES > CHAVETTE
CHAVISH > CHAV
CHAVS > CHAV
CHAVVIER > CHAVVY
CHAVVIEST > CHAVVY
CHAVVY *adj* relating to or like a chav
CHAW *vb* chew (tobacco), esp without swallowing it ▷ *n* something chewed, esp a plug of tobacco
CHAWBACON *n* bumpkin
CHAWDRON *n* entrails
CHAWDRONS > CHAWDRON
CHAWED > CHAW
CHAWER > CHAW
CHAWERS > CHAW
CHAWING > CHAW
CHAWK *n* jackdaw
CHAWKS > CHAWK
CHAWS > CHAW
CHAY *n* plant of the madder family
CHAYA *same as* > CHAY
CHAYAS > CHAYA
CHAYOTE *n* tropical American climbing plant with edible pear-shaped fruit enclosing a single huge seed
CHAYOTES > CHAYOTE
CHAYROOT *n* root of the chay plant
CHAYROOTS > CHAYROOT
CHAYS > CHAY
CHAZAN *same as* > CANTOR
CHAZANIM > CHAZAN
CHAZANS > CHAZAN
CHAZZAN *variant of* > CHAZAN
CHAZZANIM > CHAZZAN
CHAZZANS > CHAZZAN
CHAZZEN *same as* > CHAZZAN
CHAZZENIM > CHAZZEN
CHAZZENS > CHAZZEN
CHE *pron* dialectal form meaning "I"
CHEAP *adj* costing relatively little ▷ *adv* at very little cost ▷ *n* bargain ▷ *vb* take the cheapest thing
CHEAPED > CHEAP
CHEAPEN *vb* lower the reputation of
CHEAPENED > CHEAPEN
CHEAPENER > CHEAPEN
CHEAPENS > CHEAPEN
CHEAPER > CHEAP
CHEAPEST > CHEAP
CHEAPIE *n* something

inexpensive
CHEAPIES > CHEAPIE
CHEAPING > CHEAP
CHEAPISH > CHEAP
CHEAPJACK *n* person who sells cheap and shoddy goods ▷ *adj* shoddy or inferior
CHEAPLY > CHEAP
CHEAPNESS > CHEAP
CHEAPO *n* very cheap and possibly shoddy thing
CHEAPOS > CHEAPO
CHEAPS > CHEAP
CHEAPY *same as* > CHEAPIE
CHEAT *vb* act dishonestly to gain profit or advantage ▷ *n* person who cheats
CHEATABLE > CHEAT
CHEATED > CHEAT
CHEATER > CHEAT
CHEATERS > CHEAT
CHEATERY *n* cheating
CHEATING > CHEAT
CHEATINGS > CHEAT
CHEATS > CHEAT
CHEBEC *n* type of boat
CHEBECS > CHEBEC
CHECHAKO *same as* > CHEECHAKO
CHECHAKOS > CHECHAKO
CHECHAQUO *same as* > CHEECHAKO
CHECHIA *n* Berber skullcap
CHECHIAS > CHECHIA
CHECK *vb* examine or investigate ▷ *n* control designed to ensure accuracy
CHECKABLE > CHECK
CHECKBOOK *n* American word for chequebook
CHECKED > CHECK
CHECKER *same as* > CHEQUER
CHECKERED *same as* > CHEQUERED
CHECKERS *n* game for two players using a checkerboard and 12 checkers each. The object is to jump over and capture the opponent's pieces
CHECKIER > CHECKY
CHECKIEST > CHECKY
CHECKING > CHECK
CHECKLESS *adj* without check or restraint
CHECKLIST *vb* check items, facts, etc, against those in a list used for verification
CHECKMARK *vb* make a mark of approval or verification
CHECKMATE *n* winning position in which an opponent's king is under attack and unable to escape ▷ *vb* place the king of (one's opponent) in checkmate ▷ *interj* call made when placing an opponent's king in

checkmate
CHECKOFF *n* procedure where an employer pays the employee's union dues straight from his or her salary
CHECKOFFS > CHECKOFF
CHECKOUT *n* counter in a supermarket, where customers pay
CHECKOUTS > CHECKOUT
CHECKRAIL *another word for* > GUARDRAIL
CHECKREIN *n* bearing rein
CHECKROOM *n* place at a railway station, airport, etc, where luggage may be left for a small charge with an attendant for safekeeping
CHECKROW *n* row of plants, esp corn, in which the spaces between adjacent plants are equal to those between adjacent rows to facilitate cultivation ▷ *vb* plant in checkrows
CHECKROWS > CHECKROW
CHECKS > CHECK
CHECKSUM *n* digit representing the number of bits of information transmitted, attached to the end of a message, to verify the integrity of data
CHECKSUMS > CHECKSUM
CHECKUP *n* thorough medical examination ▷ *vb* investigate or make an inquiry into (a person's character, evidence, etc), esp when suspicions have been aroused
CHECKUPS > CHECKUP
CHECKY *adj* having squares of alternating tinctures or furs
CHEDDAR *n* type of smooth hard yellow or whitish cheese
CHEDDARS > CHEDDAR
CHEDDARY > CHEDDAR
CHEDDITE *n* explosive made by mixing a powdered chlorate or perchlorate with a fatty substance, such as castor oil
CHEDDITES > CHEDDITE
CHEDER *n* (in Western countries) elementary religious education classes, usually outside normal school hours
CHEDERS > CHEDER
CHEDITE *same as* > CHEDDITE
CHEDITES > CHEDITE
CHEECHAKO *n* local name for a newcomer to Alaska
CHEEK *n* either side of the face below the eye ▷ *vb* speak impudently to
CHEEKBONE *n* bone at the top of the cheek, just below the eye

CHEEKED > CHEEK
CHEEKFUL *n* quantity that can be held in a cheek
CHEEKFULS > CHEEKFUL
CHEEKIER > CHEEKY
CHEEKIEST > CHEEKY
CHEEKILY > CHEEKY
CHEEKING > CHEEK
CHEEKLESS > CHEEK
CHEEKS > CHEEK
CHEEKY *adj* impudent, disrespectful
CHEEP *n* young bird's high-pitched cry ▷ *vb* utter a cheep
CHEEPED > CHEEP
CHEEPER > CHEEP
CHEEPERS > CHEEP
CHEEPING > CHEEP
CHEEPS > CHEEP
CHEER *vb* applaud or encourage with shouts ▷ *n* shout of applause or encouragement
CHEERED > CHEER
CHEERER > CHEER
CHEERERS > CHEER
CHEERFUL *adj* having a happy disposition
CHEERIER > CHEERY
CHEERIEST > CHEERY
CHEERILY > CHEERY
CHEERING > CHEER
CHEERIO *interj* goodbye ▷ *n* small red cocktail sausage ▷ *sentence substitute* farewell greeting
CHEERIOS > CHEERIO
CHEERLEAD *vb* to lead a crowd in formal cheers at sports events
CHEERLED > CHEERLEAD
CHEERLESS *adj* dreary, gloomy
CHEERLY *adv* cheerful or cheerfully
CHEERO *same as* > CHEERIO
CHEEROS > CHEERO
CHEERS *interj* drinking toast ▷ *sentence substitute* drinking toast
CHEERY *adj* cheerful
CHEESE *n* food made from coagulated milk curd ▷ *vb* stop
CHEESED > CHEESE
CHEESES > CHEESE
CHEESEVAT *n* in cheesemaking, vat in which curds are formed and cut
CHEESIER > CHEESY
CHEESIEST > CHEESY
CHEESILY > CHEESY
CHEESING > CHEESE
CHEESY *adj* like cheese
CHEETAH *n* large fast-running spotted African wild cat
CHEETAHS > CHEETAH
CHEEWINK *same as* > CHEWINK
CHEEWINKS > CHEEWINK

CHEF *n* cook in a restaurant ▷ *vb* to work as a chef
CHEFDOM *n* state or condition of being a chef
CHEFDOMS > CHEFDOM
CHEFED > CHEF
CHEFFED > CHEF
CHEFFING > CHEF
CHEFING > CHEF
CHEFS > CHEF
CHEGOE *same as* > CHIGGER
CHEGOES > CHIGGER
CHEILITIS *n* inflammation of the lip(s)
CHEKA *n* secret police set up in Russia in 1917
CHEKAS > CHEKA
CHEKIST *n* member of the cheka
CHEKISTS > CHEKIST
CHELA *n* disciple of a religious teacher
CHELAE > CHELA
CHELAS > CHELA
CHELASHIP > CHELA
CHELATE *n* coordination compound in which a metal atom or ion is bound to a ligand at two or more points on the ligand, so as to form a heterocyclic ring containing a metal atom ▷ *adj* of or possessing chelae ▷ *vb* form a chelate
CHELATED > CHELATE
CHELATES > CHELATE
CHELATING > CHELATE
CHELATION *n* process by which a chelate is formed
CHELATOR > CHELATE
CHELATORS > CHELATE
CHELICERA *n* one of a pair of appendages on the head of spiders and other arachnids: often modified as food-catching claws
CHELIFORM *adj* shaped like a chela
CHELIPED *n* (on a arthropod) either of two legs which each carry a claw
CHELIPEDS > CHELIPED
CHELLUP *n* noise
CHELLUPS > CHELLUP
CHELOID *a variant spelling of* > KELOID
CHELOIDAL > CHELOID
CHELOIDS > CHELOID
CHELONE *n* hardy N American plant grown for its white, rose, or purple flower spikes
CHELONES > CHELONE
CHELONIAN *n* type of reptile such as the tortoises and turtles, in which most of the body is enclosed in a protective bony capsule
CHELP *vb* (esp of women or children) to chatter or speak out of turn
CHELPED > CHELP
CHELPING > CHELP

CHELPS > CHELP
CHEMIC *vb* to bleach ▷ *n* chemist
CHEMICAL *n* substance used in or resulting from a reaction involving changes to atoms or molecules ▷ *adj* of chemistry or chemicals
CHEMICALS > CHEMICAL
CHEMICKED > CHEMIC
CHEMICS > CHEMIC
CHEMISE *n* woman's loose-fitting slip
CHEMISES > CHEMISE
CHEMISM *n* chemical action
CHEMISMS > CHEMISM
CHEMISORB *vb* take up (a substance) by chemisorption
CHEMIST *n* shop selling medicines and cosmetics
CHEMISTRY *n* science of the composition, properties, and reactions of substances
CHEMISTS > CHEMIST
CHEMITYPE *n* process by which a relief impression is obtained from an engraving
CHEMITYPY > CHEMITYPE
CHEMMIES > CHEMMY
CHEMMY *n* gambling card game
CHEMO *n* short form of chemotherapy
CHEMOKINE *n* type of protein
CHEMOS > CHEMO
CHEMOSORB *same as* > CHEMISORB
CHEMOSTAT *n* apparatus for growing bacterial cultures at a constant rate by controlling the supply of nutrient medium
CHEMPADUK *n* Malaysian evergreen tree
CHEMURGIC > CHEMURGY
CHEMURGY *n* branch of chemistry concerned with the industrial use of organic raw materials, esp materials of agricultural origin
CHENAR *n* oriental plane tree
CHENARS > CHENAR
CHENET *another word for* > GENIP
CHENETS > CHENET
CHENILLE *n* (fabric of) thick tufty yarn
CHENILLES > CHENILLE
CHENIX *n* ancient measure, slightly more than a quart
CHENIXES > CHENIX
CHENOPOD *n* type of plant of the family which includes the beet, mangel-wurzel, spinach, and goosefoot

CHENOPODS > CHENOPOD
CHEONGSAM *n* straight dress, usually of silk or cotton, with a stand-up collar and a slit in one side of the skirt, worn by Chinese women
CHEQUE *n* written order to one's bank to pay money from one's account
CHEQUER *n* piece used in Chinese chequers ▷ *vb* make irregular in colour or character
CHEQUERED *adj* marked by varied fortunes
CHEQUERS *n* game of draughts
CHEQUES > CHEQUE
CHEQUIER > CHEQUY
CHEQUIEST > CHEQUY
CHEQUING as in *chequing account* (in Canada) account against which cheques can be drawn
CHEQUY *same as* > CHECKY
CHER *adj* dear or expensive
CHERALITE *n* rare phosphate-silicate of Thorium and Calcium
CHERE *feminine variant of* > CHER
CHERIMOYA *n* large tropical fruit with custardlike flesh
CHERISH *vb* cling to (an idea or feeling)
CHERISHED > CHERISH
CHERISHER > CHERISH
CHERISHES > CHERISH
CHERMOULA *n* type of marinade used in N African cookery
CHERNOZEM *n* black soil, rich in humus and carbonates, in cool or temperate semiarid regions, as the grasslands of Russia
CHEROOT *n* cigar with both ends cut flat
CHEROOTS > CHEROOT
CHERRIED > CHERRY
CHERRIER > CHERRY
CHERRIES > CHERRY
CHERRIEST > CHERRY
CHERRY *n* small red or black fruit with a stone ▷ *adj* deep red ▷ *vb* to cheer
CHERRYING > CHERRY
CHERT *n* microcrystalline form of silica usually occurring as bands or layers of pebbles in sedimentary rock. Formula: SiO_2. Varieties include flint, lyddite (Lydian stone)
CHERTIER > CHERT
CHERTIEST > CHERT
CHERTS > CHERT
CHERTY > CHERT
CHERUB *n* angel, often represented as a winged child
CHERUBIC > CHERUB

CHERUBIM > CHERUB

CHERUBIMS > CHERUB

CHERUBIN n cherub ▷ adj cherubic

CHERUBINS > CHERUBIN

CHERUBS > CHERUB

CHERUP same as > CHIRRUP

CHERUPED > CHERUP

CHERUPING > CHERUP

CHERUPS > CHERUP

CHERVIL n aniseed-flavoured herb

CHERVILS > CHERVIL

CHESHIRE n breed of American pig

CHESHIRES > CHESHIRE

CHESIL n gravel or shingle

CHESILS > CHESIL

CHESNUT rare variant of > CHESTNUT

CHESNUTS > CHESNUT

CHESS n game for two players with 16 pieces each, played on a chequered board of 64 squares

CHESSEL n mould used in cheese-making

CHESSELS > CHESSEL

CHESSES > CHESS

CHESSMAN n piece used in chess

CHESSMEN > CHESSMAN

CHEST n front of the body, from neck to waist ▷ vb to hit with the chest, as with a ball in football

CHESTED > CHEST

CHESTFUL n amount a chest will hold

CHESTFULS > CHESTFUL

CHESTIER > CHESTY

CHESTIEST > CHESTY

CHESTILY > CHESTY

CHESTING > CHEST

CHESTNUT n reddish-brown edible nut ▷ adj (of hair or a horse) reddish-brown

CHESTNUTS > CHESTNUT

CHESTS > CHEST

CHESTY adj symptomatic of chest disease

CHETAH same as > CHEETAH

CHETAHS > CHETAH

CHETH same as > HETH

CHETHS > CHETH

CHETNIK n member of a Serbian nationalist paramilitary group

CHETNIKS > CHETNIK

CHETRUM n monetary unit in Bhutan

CHETRUMS > CHETRUM

CHEVAL as in cheval glass full-length mirror that can swivel

CHEVALET n bridge of a stringed musical instrument

CHEVALETS > CHEVALET

CHEVALIER n member of the French Legion of Honour

CHEVELURE n nebulous part of the tail of a comet

CHEVEN n chub

CHEVENS > CHEVEN

CHEVEREL n kid or goatskin leather

CHEVERELS > CHEVEREL

CHEVERIL same as > CHEVEREL

CHEVERILS > CHEVERIL

CHEVERON same as > CHEVRON

CHEVERONS > CHEVERON

CHEVERYE same as > CHIEFERY

CHEVERYES > CHEVERYE

CHEVET n semicircular or polygonal east end of a church, esp a French Gothic church, often with a number of attached apses

CHEVETS > CHEVET

CHEVIED > CHEVY

CHEVIES > CHEVY

CHEVILLE n peg of a stringed musical instrument

CHEVILLES > CHEVILLE

CHEVIN same as > CHEVEN

CHEVINS > CHEVIN

CHEVIOT n type of British sheep reared for its wool

CHEVIOTS > CHEVIOT

CHEVRE n any cheese made from goats' milk

CHEVRES > CHEVRE

CHEVRET n type of goats' cheese

CHEVRETS > CHEVRET

CHEVRETTE n skin of a young goat

CHEVRON n V-shaped pattern, esp on the sleeve of a military uniform to indicate rank ▷ vb make a chevron

CHEVRONED > CHEVRON

CHEVRONS > CHEVRON

CHEVRONY adj in heraldry, bearing chevrons

CHEVY same as > CHIVY

CHEVYING > CHEVY

CHEW vb grind (food) between the teeth ▷ n act of chewing

CHEWABLE > CHEW

CHEWED > CHEW

CHEWER > CHEW

CHEWERS > CHEW

CHEWET n type of meat pie

CHEWETS > CHEWET

CHEWIE n chewing gum

CHEWIER > CHEWY

CHEWIES > CHEWY

CHEWIEST > CHEWY

CHEWINESS > CHEWY

CHEWING > CHEW

CHEWINK n towhee

CHEWINKS > CHEWINK

CHEWS > CHEW

CHEWY adj requiring a lot of chewing ▷ n dog's rubber toy

CHEZ prep at the home of

CHI n 22nd letter of the Greek alphabet, a consonant, transliterated as ch or rarely kh

CHIA n plant of the mint family

CHIACK vb tease or banter ▷ n good-humoured banter

CHIACKED > CHIACK

CHIACKING > CHIACK

CHIACKS > CHIACK

CHIANTI n dry red Italian wine

CHIANTIS > CHIANTI

CHIAO n Chinese coin equal to one tenth of one yuan

CHIAREZZA n (in music) clarity

CHIAREZZE > CHIAREZZA

CHIAS > CHIA

CHIASM same as > CHIASMA

CHIASMA n cross-shaped connection produced by the crossing over of pairing chromosomes during meiosis

CHIASMAL > CHIASMA

CHIASMAS > CHIASMA

CHIASMATA > CHIASMA

CHIASMI > CHIASMUS

CHIASMIC > CHIASMA

CHIASMS > CHIASMA

CHIASMUS n reversal of the order of words in the second of two parallel phrases

CHIASTIC > CHIASMUS

CHIAUS same as > CHOUSE

CHIAUSED > CHIAUS

CHIAUSES > CHIAUS

CHIAUSING > CHIAUS

CHIB vb in Scots English, stab or slash with a sharp weapon ▷ n sharp weapon

CHIBBED > CHIB

CHIBBING > CHIB

CHIBOL n spring onion

CHIBOLS > CHIBOL

CHIBOUK n Turkish tobacco pipe with an extremely long stem

CHIBOUKS > CHIBOUK

CHIBOUQUE same as > CHIBOUK

CHIBS > CHIB

CHIC adj stylish, elegant ▷ n stylishness, elegance

CHICA n Spanish young girl

CHICALOTE n type of poppy of the southwestern US and Mexico with prickly leaves and white or yellow flowers

CHICANA n female chicano

CHICANAS > CHICANA

CHICANE n obstacle in a motor-racing circuit ▷ vb deceive or trick by chicanery

CHICANED > CHICANE

CHICANER > CHICANE

CHICANERS > CHICANE

CHICANERY n trickery, deception

CHICANES > CHICANE

CHICANING > CHICANE

CHICANO n American citizen of Mexican origin

CHICANOS > CHICANO

CHICAS > CHICA

CHICCORY a variant spelling of > CHICORY

CHICER > CHIC

CHICEST > CHIC

CHICH another word for > CHICKPEA

CHICHA n Andean drink made from fermented maize

CHICHAS > CHICHA

CHICHES > CHICKPEA

CHICHI adj affectedly pretty or stylish ▷ n quality of being affectedly pretty or stylish

CHICHIER > CHICHI

CHICHIEST > CHICHI

CHICHIS > CHICHI

CHICK n baby bird

CHICKADEE n small North American songbird

CHICKAREE n American red squirrel

CHICKEE n opensided, thatched building on stilts

CHICKEES > CHICKEE

CHICKEN n domestic fowl ▷ adj cowardly ▷ vb to lose one's nerve

CHICKENED > CHICKEN

CHICKENS > CHICKEN

CHICKLING n small chick

CHICKORY same as > CHICORY

CHICKPEA n edible yellow pealike seed

CHICKPEAS > CHICKPEA

CHICKS > CHICK

CHICKWEED n weed with small white flowers

CHICLE n gumlike substance obtained from the sapodilla

CHICLES > CHICLE

CHICLY > CHIC

CHICNESS > CHIC

CHICO n spiny chenopodiaceous shrub

CHICON same as > CHICORY

CHICONS > CHICON

CHICORIES > CHICORY

CHICORY n plant whose leaves are used in salads

CHICOS > CHICO

CHICS > CHIC

CHID > CHIDE

CHIDDEN > CHIDE

CHIDE vb rebuke, scold

CHIDED > CHIDE

CHIDER > CHIDE

CHIDERS > CHIDE

CHIDES > CHIDE

CHIDING > CHIDE

CHIDINGLY > CHIDE

CHIDINGS > CHIDE

CHIDLINGS n intestines of a pig prepared as a dish

CHIEF n head of a group of people ▷ adj most important

CHIEFDOM n any tribal social group led by a chief

CHIEFDOMS > CHIEFDOM

CHIEFER > CHIEF

CHIEFERY n lands belonging to a chief

CHIEFESS n female chief

CHIEFEST > CHIEF

CHIEFLESS adj lacking a chief

CHIEFLING n petty chief

CHIEFLY adv especially ▷ adj of or relating to a chief or chieftain

CHIEFRIES > CHIEFRY

CHIEFRY same as > CHIEFERY

CHIEFS > CHIEF

CHIEFSHIP n state of being a chief

CHIEFTAIN n leader of a tribe

CHIEL n young man

CHIELD same as > CHIEL

CHIELDS > CHIEL

CHIELS > CHIEL

CHIFFON n fine see-through fabric ▷ adj made of chiffon

CHIFFONS > CHIFFON

CHIFFONY > CHIFFON

CHIGETAI n variety of the Asiatic wild ass of Mongolia

CHIGETAIS > CHIGETAI

CHIGGA n informal Australian derogatory word for a young working-class person from Hobart, Tasmania

CHIGGAS > CHIGGA

CHIGGER n parasitic larva of any of various mites, which causes intense itching of human skin

CHIGGERS > CHIGGER

CHIGNON n knot of hair pinned up at the back of the head ▷ vb make a chignon

CHIGNONED > CHIGNON

CHIGNONS > CHIGNON

CHIGOE same as > CHIGGER

CHIGOES > CHIGOE

CHIGRE same as > CHIGGER

CHIGRES > CHIGRE

CHIHUAHUA n tiny short-haired dog

CHIK n slatted blind

CHIKARA n Indian seven-stringed musical instrument

CHIKARAS > CHIKARA

CHIKHOR same as > CHUKAR

CHIKHORS > CHIKHOR

CHIKOR same as > CHUKAR

CHIKORS > CHIKOR

CHIKS > CHIK

CHILBLAIN n

inflammation of the fingers or toes, caused by exposure to cold

CHILD n young human being, boy or girl ▷ vb to give birth

CHILDBED n condition of giving birth to a child

CHILDBEDS > CHILDBED

CHILDCARE n care provided for children without homes (or with a seriously disturbed home life) by a local authority

CHILDE n young man of noble birth

CHILDED > CHILD

CHILDER dialect variant of > CHILDREN

CHILDES > CHILDE

CHILDHOOD n time or condition of being a child

CHILDING > CHILD

CHILDISH adj immature, silly

CHILDLESS > CHILD

CHILDLIER > CHILD

CHILDLIKE adj innocent, trustful

CHILDLY > CHILD

CHILDNESS n nature of a child

CHILDREN > CHILD

CHILDS > CHILD

CHILE a variant spelling of > CHILLI

CHILES > CHILE

CHILI same as > CHILLI

CHILIAD n group of one thousand

CHILIADAL > CHILIAD

CHILIADIC > CHILIAD

CHILIADS > CHILIAD

CHILIAGON n thousand-sided polygon

CHILIARCH n commander of a thousand men

CHILIASM n belief in the Second Coming of Christ

CHILIASMS > CHILIASM

CHILIAST > CHILIASM

CHILIASTS > CHILIASM

CHILIDOG n hot dog served with chilli sauce

CHILIDOGS > CHILIDOG

CHILIES > CHILI

CHILIS > CHILI

CHILL n feverish cold ▷ vb make (something) cool or cold ▷ adj unpleasantly cold

CHILLADA n spicy Mexican dish made of fried vegetables and pulses

CHILLADAS > CHILLADA

CHILLED > CHILL

CHILLER n cooling or refrigerating device

CHILLERS > CHILLER

CHILLEST > CHILL

CHILLI n small red or green hot-tasting capsicum pod, used in cooking

CHILLIER > CHILLY

CHILLIES > CHILLI

CHILLIEST > CHILLY

CHILLILY > CHILLY

CHILLING > CHILL

CHILLINGS > CHILL

CHILLIS > CHILLI

CHILLNESS > CHILL

CHILLS > CHILL

CHILLUM n short pipe, usually of clay, used esp for smoking cannabis

CHILLUMS > CHILLUM

CHILLY adj moderately cold

CHILOPOD n type of arthropod of the class which includes the centipedes

CHILOPODS > CHILOPOD

CHILTEPIN n variety of chilli pepper

CHIMAERA same as > CHIMERA

CHIMAERAS > CHIMAERA

CHIMAERIC > CHIMAERA

CHIMAR same as > CHIMERE

CHIMARS > CHIMAR

CHIMB same as > CHIME

CHIMBLEY same as > CHIMNEY

CHIMBLEYS > CHIMBLEY

CHIMBLIES > CHIMBLY

CHIMBLY same as > CHIMNEY

CHIMBS > CHIME

CHIME n musical ringing sound of a bell or clock ▷ vb make a musical ringing sound

CHIMED > CHIME

CHIMER > CHIME

CHIMERA n unrealistic hope or idea

CHIMERAS > CHIMERA

CHIMERE n sleeveless red or black gown, part of a bishop's formal dress though not a vestment

CHIMERES > CHIMERE

CHIMERIC same as > CHIMERA

CHIMERID n fish of the genus Chimaera

CHIMERIDS > CHIMERID

CHIMERISM n medical condition in which a person possesses two genetically distinct sets of cells

CHIMERS > CHIME

CHIMES > CHIME

CHIMINEA n free-standing outdoor fireplace with a rounded body

CHIMINEAS > CHIMINEA

CHIMING > CHIME

CHIMLA same as > CHIMNEY

CHIMLAS > CHIMLA

CHIMLEY same as > CHIMNEY

CHIMLEYS > CHIMLEY

CHIMNEY n hollow vertical structure for carrying away smoke from a fire ▷ vb to

climb two vertical, parallel, chimney-like rock faces

CHIMNEYED > CHIMNEY

CHIMNEYS > CHIMNEY

CHIMO interj Inuit greeting and toast

CHIMP n chimpanzee

CHIMPS > CHIMP

CHIN n part of the face below the mouth ▷ vb hit someone in the chin

CHINA n fine earthenware or porcelain

CHINAMAN n in cricket, a ball bowled by a left-handed bowler to a right-handed batsman that spins from off to leg

CHINAMEN > CHINAMAN

CHINAMPA n in Mesoamerican agriculture, an artificially created island used for growing crops

CHINAMPAS > CHINAMPA

CHINAR same as > CHINAR

CHINAROOT n bristly greenbrier

CHINARS > CHENAR

CHINAS > CHINA

CHINAWARE n articles made of china, esp those made for domestic use

CHINBONE n front part of the mandible which forms the chin

CHINBONES > CHINBONE

CHINCAPIN n dwarf chestnut tree

CHINCH another name for a > BEDBUG

CHINCHES > CHINCH

CHINCHIER > CHINCHY

CHINCHY adj tightfisted

CHINCOUGH n whooping cough

CHINDIT n Allied soldier fighting behind the Japanese lines in Burma during World War II

CHINDITS > CHINDIT

CHINE same as > CHIME

CHINED > CHINE

CHINES > CHINE

CHINESE adj of or relating to China

CHINING > CHINE

CHINK n small narrow opening ▷ vb make a light ringing sound

CHINKAPIN same as > CHINCAPIN

CHINKARA n Indian gazelle

CHINKARAS > CHINKARA

CHINKED > CHINK

CHINKIE n offensive term for a (takeaway) meal of Chinese food

CHINKIER > CHINK

CHINKIES > CHINKIE

CHINKIEST > CHINK

CHINKING > CHINK

CHINKS > CHINK

CHINKY > CHINK

CHINLESS adj having a receding chin

CHINNED > CHIN

CHINNING > CHIN

CHINO *n* durable cotton twill cloth

CHINONE *n* benzoquinone

CHINONES > CHINONE

CHINOOK *n* warm dry southwesterly wind blowing down the eastern slopes of the Rocky Mountains

CHINOOKS > CHINOOK

CHINOS *npl* trousers made of a kind of hard-wearing cotton

CHINOVNIK *n* Russian official or bureaucrat

CHINS > CHIN

CHINSTRAP *n* strap on a helmet which fastens under the chin

CHINTS *obsolete variant of* > CHINTZ

CHINTSES > CHINTS

CHINTZ *n* printed cotton fabric with a glazed finish

CHINTZES > CHINTZ

CHINTZIER > CHINTZY

CHINTZY *adj* of or covered with chintz

CHINWAG *n* chat

CHINWAGS > CHINWAG

CHIP *n* strip of potato, fried in deep fat ▷ *vb* break small pieces from

CHIPBOARD *n* thin board made of compressed wood particles

CHIPMUCK *another word for* > CHIPMUCK

CHIPMUCKS > CHIPMUCK

CHIPMUNK *n* small squirrel-like N American rodent with a striped back

CHIPMUNKS > CHIPMUNK

CHIPOCHIA *same as* > CAPOCCHIA

CHIPOLATA *n* small sausage

CHIPOTLE *n* dried chilli pepper

CHIPOTLES > CHIPOTLE

CHIPPABLE > CHIP

CHIPPED > CHIP

CHIPPER *vb* chirp or chatter

CHIPPERED > CHIPPER

CHIPPERS > CHIPPER

CHIPPIE *same as* > CHIPPY

CHIPPIER > CHIPPY

CHIPPIES > CHIPPY

CHIPPIEST > CHIPPY

CHIPPING > CHIP

CHIPPINGS > CHIP

CHIPPY *n* fish-and-chip shop ▷ *adj* resentful or oversensitive about being perceived as inferior

CHIPS > CHIP

CHIPSET *n* highly integrated circuit on the motherboard of a computer that controls many of its data transfer functions

CHIPSETS > CHIPSET

CHIRAGRA *n* gout occurring in the hands

CHIRAGRAS > CHIRAGRA

CHIRAGRIC > CHIRAGRA

CHIRAL > CHIRALITY

CHIRALITY *n* configuration or handedness (left or right) of an asymmetric, optically active chemical compound

CHIRIMOYA *same as* > CHERIMOYA

CHIRK *vb* to creak, like a door ▷ *adj* spritely; high-spirited

CHIRKED > CHIRK

CHIRKER > CHIRK

CHIRKEST > CHIRK

CHIRKING > CHIRK

CHIRKS > CHIRK

CHIRL *vb* to warble

CHIRLED > CHIRL

CHIRLING > CHIRL

CHIRLS > CHIRL

CHIRM *n* chirping of birds ▷ *vb* (esp of a bird) to chirp

CHIRMED > CHIRM

CHIRMING > CHIRM

CHIRMS > CHIRM

CHIRO *n* an informal name for chiropractor

CHIROLOGY *n* palmistry

CHIRONOMY *n* art of hand movement in oratory or theatrical performance

CHIROPODY *n* treatment of the feet, esp the treatment of corns, verrucas, etc

CHIROPTER *n* type of bat

CHIROS > CHIRO

CHIRP *vb* (of a bird or insect) make a short high-pitched sound ▷ *n* chirping sound

CHIRPED > CHIRP

CHIRPER > CHIRP

CHIRPERS > CHIRP

CHIRPIER > CHIRPY

CHIRPIEST > CHIRPY

CHIRPILY > CHIRPY

CHIRPING > CHIRP

CHIRPS > CHIRP

CHIRPY *adj* lively and cheerful

CHIRR *vb* (esp of certain insects, such as crickets) to make a shrill trilled sound ▷ *n* sound of chirring

CHIRRE *same as* > CHIRR

CHIRRED > CHIRR

CHIRREN *n* dialect form of children

CHIRRES > CHIRRE

CHIRRING > CHIRR

CHIRRS > CHIRR

CHIRRUP *vb* (of some birds) to chirp repeatedly ▷ *n* chirruping sound

CHIRRUPED > CHIRRUP

CHIRRUPER > CHIRRUP

CHIRRUPS > CHIRRUP

CHIRRUPY > CHIRRUP

CHIRT *vb* to squirt

CHIRTED > CHIRT

CHIRTING > CHIRT

CHIRTS > CHIRT

CHIRU *n* Tibetan antelope with a dense woolly pinkish-brown fleece, prized as the source of shahtoosh wool

CHIRUS > CHIRU

CHIS > CHI

CHISEL *n* metal tool with a sharp end for shaping wood or stone ▷ *vb* carve or form with a chisel

CHISELED *same as* > CHISELLED

CHISELER > CHISEL

CHISELERS > CHISEL

CHISELING > CHISEL

CHISELLED *adj* finely or sharply formed

CHISELLER *n* person who uses a chisel

CHISELS > CHISEL

CHIT *n* short official note, such as a receipt ▷ *vb* to sprout

CHITAL *n* type of deer

CHITALS > CHITAL

CHITCHAT *n* chat, gossip ▷ *vb* gossip

CHITCHATS > CHITCHAT

CHITIN *n* tough substance forming the outer layer of the bodies of arthropods

CHITINOID > CHITIN

CHITINOUS > CHITIN

CHITINS > CHITIN

CHITLIN *n* pig intestine cooked and served as a dish

CHITLING > CHITLINGS

CHITLINGS *same as* > CHIDLINGS

CHITLINS > CHITLIN

CHITON *n* (in ancient Greece and Rome) a loose woollen tunic worn knee length by men and full length by women

CHITONS > CHITON

CHITOSAN *n* polysaccharide derived from chitin

CHITOSANS > CHITOSAN

CHITS > CHIT

CHITTED > CHIT

CHITTER *vb* twitter or chirp

CHITTERED > CHITTER

CHITTERS > CHITTER

CHITTIER > CHIT

CHITTIES > CHITTY

CHITTIEST > CHIT

CHITTING > CHIT

CHITTY *adj* childish ▷ *vb* sprout

CHIV *n* knife ▷ *vb* stab (someone)

CHIVALRIC > CHIVALRY

CHIVALRY *n* courteous behaviour, esp by men towards women

CHIVAREE *n* charivari ▷ *vb* to perform a chivaree

CHIVAREED > CHIVAREE

CHIVAREES > CHIVAREE

CHIVARI *same as* > CHARIVARI

CHIVARIED > CHIVARI

CHIVARIES > CHIVARI

CHIVE *n* small Eurasian purple-flowered plant whose long slender hollow leaves are used in cooking ▷ *vb* file or cut off

CHIVED > CHIVE

CHIVES *same as* > CHIVE

CHIVIED > CHIVY

CHIVIES > CHIVY

CHIVING > CHIVE

CHIVS > CHIV

CHIVVED > CHIV

CHIVVIED > CHIVVY

CHIVVIES > CHIVVY

CHIVVING > CHIV

CHIVVY *same as* > CHIVY

CHIVVYING > CHIVVY

CHIVY *vb* harass or nag ▷ *n* hunt

CHIVYING > CHIVY

CHIYOGAMI *n* type of highly decorated Japanese craft paper

CHIZ *n* cheat ▷ *vb* cheat

CHIZZ *same as* > CHIZ

CHIZZED > CHIZ

CHIZZES > CHIZ

CHIZZING > CHIZ

CHLAMYDES > CHLAMYS

CHLAMYDIA *n* type of bacteria responsible for some sexually transmitted diseases

CHLAMYS *n* woollen cloak worn by ancient Greek soldiers

CHLAMYSES > CHLAMYS

CHLOASMA *n* appearance on a person's skin, esp of the face, of patches of darker skin colour: associated with hormonal changes caused by liver disease or the use of oral contraceptives

CHLOASMAS > CHLOASMA

CHLORACNE *n* disfiguring skin disease that results from contact with or ingestion or inhalation of certain chlorinated aromatic hydrocarbons

CHLORAL *n* colourless oily liquid with a pungent odour, made from chlorine and acetaldehyde and used in preparing chloral hydrate and DDT

CHLORALS > CHLORAL

CHLORATE *n* type of chemical salt

CHLORATES > CHLORATE

CHLORDAN *same as* > CHLORDANE

CHLORDANE *n* white insoluble toxic solid

CHLORDANS > CHLORDAN

CHLORELLA *n* type of microscopic unicellular green alga, some species of which are used in the preparation of human food

CHLORIC *adj* of or containing chlorine in the pentavalent state

CHLORID *n* type of chlorine compound

CHLORIDE *n* compound of chlorine and another substance

CHLORIDES > CHLORIDE

CHLORIDIC > CHLORIDE

CHLORIDS > CHLORID

CHLORIN *same as* > CHLORINE

CHLORINE *n* strong-smelling greenish-yellow gaseous element, used to disinfect water

CHLORINES > CHLORINE

CHLORINS > CHLORIN

CHLORITE *n* any of a group of green soft secondary minerals consisting of the hydrated silicates of aluminium, iron, and magnesium in monoclinic crystalline form: common in metamorphic rocks

CHLORITES > CHLORITE

CHLORITIC > CHLORITE

CHLOROSES > CHLOROSIS

CHLOROSIS *n* disorder, formerly common in adolescent women, characterized by pale greenish-yellow skin, weakness, and palpitation and caused by insufficient iron in the body

CHLOROTIC > CHLOROSIS

CHLOROUS *adj* of or containing chlorine in the trivalent state

CHOANA *n* posterior nasal aperture

CHOANAE > CHOANA

CHOBDAR *n* in India and Nepal, king's macebearer or attendant

CHOBDARS > CHOBDAR

CHOC *short form of* > CHOCOLATE

CHOCCIER > CHOCCY

CHOCCIES > CHOCCY

CHOCCIEST > CHOCCY

CHOCCY *n* chocolate ▷ *adj* made of, tasting of, smelling of, or resembling chocolate

CHOCHO *same as* > CHAYOTE

CHOCHOS > CHOCHO

CHOCK *n* block or wedge used to prevent a heavy object from moving ▷ *vb* secure by a chock ▷ *adv* as closely or tightly as possible

CHOCKED > CHOCK

CHOCKER *adj* full up

CHOCKFUL *adj* filled to capacity

CHOCKFULL *variant of* > CHOCKFUL

CHOCKING > CHOCK

CHOCKO *same as* > CHOCO

CHOCKOS > CHOCKO

CHOCKS > CHOCK

CHOCO *n* member of the Australian army

CHOCOLATE *n* sweet food made from cacao seeds ▷ *adj* dark brown

CHOCOLATY > CHOCOLATE

CHOCOS > CHOCO

CHOCS > CHOC

CHOCTAW *n* turn from the inside edge of one skate to the outside edge of the other or vice versa

CHOCTAWS > CHOCTAW

CHODE > CHIDE

CHOENIX *same as* > CHENIX

CHOENIXES > CHOENIX

CHOG *n* core of a piece of fruit

CHOGS > CHOG

CHOICE *n* choosing ▷ *adj* of high quality

CHOICEFUL *adj* fickle

CHOICELY > CHOICE

CHOICER > CHOICE

CHOICES > CHOICE

CHOICEST > CHOICE

CHOIR *n* organized group of singers, esp in church ▷ *vb* to sing in chorus

CHOIRBOY *n* boy who sings in a church choir

CHOIRBOYS > CHOIRBOY

CHOIRED > CHOIR

CHOIRGIRL *n* girl who sings in a choir

CHOIRING > CHOIR

CHOIRLIKE > CHOIR

CHOIRMAN *n* man who sings in a choir

CHOIRMEN > CHOIRMAN

CHOIRS > CHOIR

CHOKE *vb* hinder or stop the breathing of (a person) by strangling or smothering ▷ *n* device controlling the amount of air that is mixed with the fuel in a petrol engine

CHOKEABLE > CHOKE

CHOKEBORE *n* shotgun bore that becomes narrower towards the muzzle so that the shot is not scattered

CHOKECOIL *n* type of electronic inductor

CHOKED *adj* disappointed or angry

CHOKEDAMP *another word for* > BLACKDAMP

CHOKEHOLD *n* act of holding a person's neck across the windpipe, esp from behind

CHOKER *n* tight-fitting necklace

CHOKERS > CHOKER

CHOKES > CHOKE

CHOKEY *n* a slang word for prison ▷ *adj* involving, caused by, or causing choking

CHOKEYS > CHOKEY

CHOKIDAR *n* in India, a gatekeeper

CHOKIDARS > CHOKIDAR

CHOKIER > CHOKEY

CHOKIES > CHOKEY

CHOKIEST > CHOKEY

CHOKING > CHOKE

CHOKINGLY > CHOKE

CHOKO *n* pear-shaped fruit of a tropical American vine, eaten as a vegetable

CHOKOS > CHOKO

CHOKRA *n* in India, a boy or young man

CHOKRAS > CHOKRA

CHOKRI *n* in India, a girl or young woman

CHOKRIS > CHOKRI

CHOKY *same as* > CHOKEY

CHOLA *n* Hispanic girl

CHOLAEMIA *n* toxic medical condition indicated by the presence of bile in the blood

CHOLAEMIC > CHOLAEMIA

CHOLAS > CHOLA

CHOLATE *n* salt of cholic acid

CHOLATES > CHOLATE

CHOLECYST *n* gall bladder

CHOLELITH *n* gallstone

CHOLEMIA *same as* > CHOLAEMIA

CHOLEMIAS > CHOLEMIA

CHOLENT *n* meal usually consisting of a stew of meat, potatoes, and pulses prepared before the Sabbath on Friday and left to cook until eaten for Sabbath lunch

CHOLENTS > CHOLENT

CHOLER *n* bad temper

CHOLERA *n* serious infectious disease causing severe vomiting and diarrhoea

CHOLERAIC > CHOLERA

CHOLERAS > CHOLERA

CHOLERIC *adj* bad-tempered

CHOLEROID > CHOLERA

CHOLERS > CHOLER

CHOLI *n* short-sleeved bodice, as worn by Indian women

CHOLIAMB *n* imperfect iambic trimeter, with a spondee as the last foot

CHOLIAMBS > CHOLIAMB

CHOLIC *as in cholic acid* crystalline acid found in bile

CHOLINE *n* colourless viscous soluble alkaline substance present in animal tissues, esp as a constituent of lecithin: used as a supplement to the diet of poultry and in medicine for preventing the accumulation of fat in the liver

CHOLINES > CHOLINE

CHOLIS > CHOLI

CHOLLA *n* type of spiny cactus of the southwestern US and Mexico, with cylindrical stem segments

CHOLLAS > CHOLLA

CHOLLERS *npl* jowls or cheeks

CHOLO *n* chicano gangster

CHOLOS > CHOLO

CHOLTRIES > CHOLTRY

CHOLTRY *n* caravanserai

CHOMETZ *same as* > CHAMETZ

CHOMETZES > CHOMETZ

CHOMMIE *n* (in informal South African English) friend

CHOMMIES > CHOMMIE

CHOMP *vb* chew noisily ▷ *n* act or sound of chewing in this manner

CHOMPED > CHOMP

CHOMPER > CHOMP

CHOMPERS > CHOMP

CHOMPING > CHOMP

CHOMPS > CHOMP

CHON *n* North and South Korean monetary unit worth one hundredth of a won

CHONDRAL *adj* of or relating to cartilage

CHONDRE *another word for* > CHONDRULE

CHONDRES > CHONDRE

CHONDRI > CHONDRUS

CHONDRIFY *vb* become or convert into cartilage

CHONDRIN *n* resilient translucent bluish-white substance that forms the matrix of cartilage

CHONDRINS > CHONDRIN

CHONDRITE *n* stony meteorite consisting mainly of silicate minerals in the form of chondrules

CHONDROID *adj* resembling cartilage

CHONDROMA *n* benign cartilaginous growth or neoplasm

CHONDRULE *n* one of the small spherical masses of mainly silicate minerals present in chondrites

CHONDRUS *n* cartilage

CHOOF *vb* go away

CHOOFED > CHOOF

CHOOFING > CHOOF

CHOOFS > CHOOF

CHOOK *n* hen or chicken ▷ *vb* make the sound of a hen of chicken

CHOOKED > CHOOK

CHOOKIE *same as* > CHOOK

CHOOKIES > CHOOK

CHOOKING > CHOOK

CHOOKS > CHOOK

CHOOM n Englishman

CHOOMS > CHOOM

CHOON n slang term for music that one likes

CHOONS > CHOON

CHOOSE vb select from a number of alternatives

CHOOSER > CHOOSE

CHOOSERS > CHOOSE

CHOOSES > CHOOSE

CHOOSEY same as > CHOOSY

CHOOSIER > CHOOSY

CHOOSIEST > CHOOSY

CHOOSING > CHOOSE

CHOOSY adj fussy, hard to please

CHOP vb cut with a blow from an axe or knife ▷ n cutting or sharp blow

CHOPHOUSE n restaurant specializing in steaks, grills, chops, etc

CHOPIN same as > CHOPINE

CHOPINE n sandal-like shoe on tall wooden or cork bases popular in the 18th century

CHOPINES > CHOPINE

CHOPINS > CHOPIN

CHOPLOGIC n person who uses excessively subtle or involved logic

CHOPPED > CHOP

CHOPPER n helicopter ▷ vb travel by helicopter

CHOPPERED > CHOPPER

CHOPPERS > CHOPPER

CHOPPIER > CHOPPY

CHOPPIEST > CHOPPY

CHOPPILY > CHOPPY

CHOPPING > CHOP

CHOPPINGS > CHOP

CHOPPY adj (of the sea) fairly rough

CHOPS > CHOP

CHOPSOCKY n genre of martial arts film

CHOPSTICK n one of a pair of thin sticks used as eating utensils

CHORAGI > CHORAGUS

CHORAGIC > CHORAGUS

CHORAGUS n leader of a chorus

CHORAL adj of a choir

CHORALE n slow stately hymn tune

CHORALES > CHORALE

CHORALIST n singer or composer of chorals

CHORALLY > CHORAL

CHORALS > CHORAL

CHORD n straight line joining two points on a curve ▷ vb provide (a melodic line) with chords

CHORDA n in anatomy, a cord

CHORDAE > CHORDA

CHORDAL > CHORD

CHORDATE n type of animal with a long fibrous rod just above the gut to support the body, such as the vertebrates

CHORDATES > CHORDATE

CHORDED > CHORD

CHORDEE n painful penile erection, a symptom of gonorrhoea

CHORDEES > CHORDEE

CHORDING n distribution of chords throughout a piece of harmony

CHORDINGS > CHORDING

CHORDS > CHORD

CHORDWISE adv in the direction of an aerofoil chord ▷ adj moving in this direction

CHORE n routine task ▷ vb to carry out chores

CHOREA n disorder of the nervous system characterized by uncontrollable brief jerky movements

CHOREAL > CHOREA

CHOREAS > CHOREA

CHOREATIC > CHOREA

CHORED > CHORE

CHOREE n trochee

CHOREES > CHOREE

CHOREGI > CHOREGUS

CHOREGIC > CHOREGUS

CHOREGUS n in ancient Greece, the producer/ financier of a dramatist's works

CHOREIC > CHOREA

CHOREMAN n handyman

CHOREMEN > CHOREMAN

CHOREOID adj resembling chorea

CHORES > CHORE

CHOREUS same as > CHOREE

CHOREUSES > CHOREUS

CHORIA > CHORION

CHORIAL > CHORION

CHORIAMB n metrical foot used in classical verse consisting of four syllables, two short ones between two long ones

CHORIAMBI > CHORIAMB

CHORIAMBS > CHORIAMB

CHORIC adj of, like, for, or in the manner of a chorus, esp of singing, dancing, or the speaking of verse

CHORINE n chorus girl

CHORINES > CHORINE

CHORING > CHORE

CHORIOID same as > CHOROID

CHORIOIDS > CHORIOID

CHORION n outer of two membranes that form a sac around the embryonic reptile, bird, or mammal

CHORIONIC > CHORION

CHORIONS > CHORION

CHORISES > CHORISIS

CHORISIS n

multiplication of leaves etc by branching or splitting

CHORISM > CHORISIS

CHORISMS > CHORISIS

CHORIST > CHORIST

CHORISTER n singer in a choir

CHORISTS > CHORIST

CHORIZO n kind of highly seasoned pork sausage of Spain or Mexico

CHORIZONT n person who challenges the authorship of a work

CHORIZOS > CHORIZO

CHOROID adj resembling the chorion, esp in being vascular ▷ n brownish vascular membrane of the eyeball between the sclera and the retina

CHOROIDAL > CHOROID

CHOROIDS > CHOROID

CHOROLOGY n study of the causal relations between geographical phenomena occurring within a particular region

CHORRIE n dilapidated old car

CHORRIES > CHORRIE

CHORTEN n Buddhist shrine

CHORTENS > CHORTEN

CHORTLE vb chuckle in amusement ▷ n amused chuckle

CHORTLED > CHORTLE

CHORTLER > CHORTLE

CHORTLERS > CHORTLE

CHORTLES > CHORTLE

CHORTLING > CHORTLE

CHORUS n large choir ▷ vb sing or say together

CHORUSED > CHORUS

CHORUSES > CHORUS

CHORUSING > CHORUS

CHORUSSED > CHORUS

CHORUSSES > CHORUS

CHOSE > CHOOSE

CHOSEN > CHOOSE

CHOSES > CHOOSE

CHOTA adj (in British Empire Indian usage) small

CHOTT a variant spelling of > SHOTT

CHOTTS > CHOTT

CHOU n type of cabbage

CHOUGH n large black Eurasian and N African bird of the crow family

CHOUGHS > CHOUGH

CHOULTRY same as > CHOLTRY

CHOUNTER same as > CHUNTER

CHOUNTERS > CHOUNTER

CHOUSE vb to cheat

CHOUSED > CHOUSE

CHOUSER > CHOUSE

CHOUSERS > CHOUSE

CHOUSES > CHOUSE

CHOUSH n Turkish messenger

CHOUSHES > CHOUSH

CHOUSING > CHOUSE

CHOUT n blackmail

CHOUTS > CHOUT

CHOUX > CHOU

CHOW n thick-coated dog with a curled tail, orig. from China ▷ vb eat

CHOWCHOW same as > CHOW

CHOWCHOWS > CHOWCHOW

CHOWDER n thick soup containing clams or fish ▷ vb to make a chowder of

CHOWDERED > CHOWDER

CHOWDERS > CHOWDER

CHOWED > CHOW

CHOWHOUND n person who loves eating

CHOWING > CHOW

CHOWK n marketplace or market area

CHOWKIDAR same as > CHOKIDAR

CHOWKS > CHOWK

CHOWRI n fly-whisk

CHOWRIES > CHOWRI

CHOWRIS > CHOWRI

CHOWRY same as > CHOWRI

CHOWS > CHOW

CHOWSE same as > CHOWSE

CHOWSED > CHOWSE

CHOWSES > CHOWSE

CHOWSING > CHOWSE

CHOWTIME n mealtime

CHOWTIMES > CHOWTIME

CHRESARD n amount of water present in the soil that is available to plants

CHRESARDS > CHRESARD

CHRISM n consecrated oil used for anointing in some churches

CHRISMA > CHRISMON

CHRISMAL n chrism container

CHRISMALS > CHRISMAL

CHRISMON n monogram and symbol of Christ's name

CHRISMONS > CHRISMON

CHRISMS > CHRISM

CHRISOM same as > CHRISM

CHRISOMS > CHRISOM

CHRISTEN vb baptize

CHRISTENS > CHRISTEN

CHRISTIAN adj exhibiting kindness or goodness

CHRISTIE same as > CHRISTY

CHRISTIES > CHRISTIE

CHRISTOM same as > CHRISOM

CHRISTOMS > CHRISTOM

CHRISTY n skiing turn for stopping or changing direction quickly

CHROMA n attribute of a colour that enables an observer to judge how much chromatic colour it contains irrespective of achromatic colour present

CHROMAKEY n (in colour television) a special effect in which a coloured background can be eliminated and a different background substituted
CHROMAS > CHROMA
CHROMATE n any salt or ester of chromic acid
CHROMATES > CHROMATE
CHROMATIC adj of colour or colours
CHROMATID n either of the two strands into which a chromosome divides during mitosis. They separate to form daughter chromosomes at anaphase
CHROMATIN n part of the nucleus of a cell that forms the chromosomes and can easily be dyed
CHROME n anything plated with chromium ▷ vb plate with chromium ▷ vb to chromium-plate ▷ adj of or having the appearance of chrome
CHROMED > CHROME
CHROMEL n nickel-based alloy containing about 10 per cent chromium, used in heating elements
CHROMELS > CHROMEL
CHROMENE n chemical compound
CHROMENES > CHROMENE
CHROMES > CHROME
CHROMIC adj of or containing chromium in the trivalent state
CHROMIDE n any member of the cichlid family of fish
CHROMIDES > CHROMIDE
CHROMIDIA n chromatins in cell cytoplasm
CHROMIER > CHROME
CHROMIEST > CHROMY
CHROMING > CHROME
CHROMINGS > CHROME
CHROMISE same as
> CHROMIZE
CHROMISED > CHROMISE
CHROMISES > CHROMISE
CHROMITE n brownish-black mineral which is the only commercial source of chromium
CHROMITES > CHROMITE
CHROMIUM n grey metallic element used in steel alloys and for electroplating
CHROMIUMS > CHROMIUM
CHROMIZE vb chrome-plate
CHROMIZED > CHROMIZE
CHROMIZES > CHROMIZE
CHROMO n picture produced by the process of making coloured prints by lithography
CHROMOGEN n compound that forms coloured compounds on oxidation
CHROMOS > CHROMO

CHROMOUS adj of or containing chromium in the divalent state
CHROMY > CHROME
CHROMYL n of, consisting of, or containing the divalent radical CrO_2
CHROMYLS > CHROMYL
CHRONAXIE n minimum time required for excitation of a nerve or muscle when the stimulus is double the minimum (threshold) necessary to elicit a basic response
CHRONAXY same as
> CHRONAXIE
CHRONIC adj (of an illness) lasting a long time ▷ n chronically-ill patient
CHRONICAL > CHRONIC
CHRONICLE n record of events in order of occurrence ▷ vb record in or as if in a chronicle
CHRONICS > CHRONIC
CHRONON n unit of time equal to the time that a photon would take to traverse the diameter of an electron: about 10^{-24}seconds
CHRONONS > CHRONON
CHRYSALID adj of or relating to a chrysalis
CHRYSALIS n insect in the stage between larva and adult, when it is in a cocoon
CHRYSANTH n chrysanthemum
CHTHONIAN adj of or relating to the underworld
CHTHONIC same as
> CHTHONIAN
CHUB n European freshwater fish of the carp family
CHUBASCO n in Mexico, a hurricane
CHUBASCOS > CHUBASCO
CHUBBIER > CHUBBY
CHUBBIEST > CHUBBY
CHUBBILY > CHUBBY
CHUBBY adj plump and round
CHUBS > CHUB
CHUCK vb throw ▷ n cut of beef from the neck to the shoulder
CHUCKED > CHUCK
CHUCKER n person who throws something
CHUCKERS > CHUCKER
CHUCKHOLE n pothole
CHUCKIE n small stone
CHUCKIES > CHUCKIE
CHUCKING > CHUCK
CHUCKLE vb laugh softly ▷ n soft laugh
CHUCKLED > CHUCKLE
CHUCKLER > CHUCKLE
CHUCKLERS > CHUCKLE
CHUCKLES > CHUCKLE
CHUCKLING > CHUCKLE
CHUCKS > CHUCK

CHUCKY same as
> CHUCKIE
CHUDDAH same as
> CHUDDAR
CHUDDAHS > CHUDDAH
CHUDDAR n large shawl or veil worn by Muslim or Hindu women that covers them from head to foot
CHUDDARS > CHUDDAR
CHUDDER same as
> CHUDDAR
CHUDDERS > CHUDDER
CHUDDIES npl underpants
CHUDDY n chewing gum
CHUFA n type of sedge of warm regions of the Old World, with nutlike edible tubers
CHUFAS > CHUFA
CHUFF vb (of a steam engine) move while making a puffing sound ▷ n. puffing sound of or as if a steam engine ▷ adj boorish
CHUFFED adj very pleased
CHUFFER > CHUFF
CHUFFEST > CHUFF
CHUFFIER > CHUFFY
CHUFFIEST > CHUFFY
CHUFFING > CHUFF
CHUFFS > CHUFF
CHUFFY adj boorish and surly
CHUG n short dull sound like the noise of an engine ▷ vb operate or move with this sound
CHUGALUG vb to gulp down a drink in one go
CHUGALUGS > CHUGALUG
CHUGGED > CHUG
CHUGGER > CHUG
CHUGGERS > CHUG
CHUGGING > CHUG
CHUGS > CHUG
CHUKAR n common Indian partridge with red legs and bill and a black-barred sandy plumage
CHUKARS > CHUKAR
CHUKKA n period of play in polo
CHUKKAR same as
> CHUKKA
CHUKKARS > CHUKKAR
CHUKKAS > CHUKKA
CHUKKER same as
> CHUKKA
CHUKKERS > CHUKKER
CHUKOR same as > CHUKAR
CHUKORS > CHUKOR
CHUM n close friend ▷ vb be or become an intimate friend (of)
CHUMASH n printed book containing one of the Five Books of Moses
CHUMASHES > CHUMASH
CHUMASHIM > CHUMASH
CHUMLEY same as
> CHIMNEY
CHUMLEYS > CHUMLEY
CHUMMAGE n formerly, fee paid by a prisoner for sole

occupancy of a cell
CHUMMAGES > CHUMMAGE
CHUMMED > CHUM
CHUMMIER > CHUMMY
CHUMMIES > CHUMMY
CHUMMIEST > CHUMMY
CHUMMILY > CHUMMY
CHUMMING > CHUM
CHUMMY adj friendly ▷ n chum
CHUMP n stupid person ▷ vb chew noisily
CHUMPED > CHUMP
CHUMPING n collecting wood for bonfires on Guy Fawkes Day
CHUMPINGS > CHUMPING
CHUMPS > CHUMP
CHUMS > CHUM
CHUMSHIP n friendship
CHUMSHIPS > CHUMSHIP
CHUNDER vb vomit ▷ n vomit
CHUNDERED > CHUNDER
CHUNDERS > CHUNDER
CHUNK n thick solid piece ▷ vb to break up into chunks
CHUNKED > CHUNK
CHUNKIER > CHUNKY
CHUNKIEST > CHUNKY
CHUNKILY > CHUNKY
CHUNKING n grouping together of a number of items by the mind, after which they can be remembered as a single item, such as a word or a musical phrase
CHUNKINGS
> CHUNKING
CHUNKS > CHUNK
CHUNKY adj (of a person) broad and heavy
CHUNNEL n rail tunnel beneath the English Channel, linking England and France
CHUNNELS > CHUNNEL
CHUNNER same as
> CHUNTER
CHUNNERED > CHUNNER
CHUNNERS > CHUNNER
CHUNTER vb mutter or grumble incessantly in a meaningless fashion
CHUNTERED > CHUNTER
CHUNTERS > CHUNTER
CHUPATI same as
> CHUPATTI
CHUPATIS > CHUPATI
CHUPATTI variant spellings of > CHAPATI
CHUPATTIS > CHUPATTI
CHUPATTY same as
> CHUPATTI
CHUPPA variant of
> CHUPPAH
CHUPPAH n canopy under which a marriage is performed
CHUPPAHS > CHUPPAH
CHUPPAS > CHUPPA
CHUPPOT > CHUPPAH

CHUPPOTH *same as*
> CHUPPOT

CHUPRASSY *same as*
> CHAPRASSI

CHUR *interj* expression of
agreement

CHURCH *n* building for
public Christian worship
▷ *vb* bring (someone, esp a
woman after childbirth) to
church for special
ceremonies

CHURCHED > CHURCH

CHURCHES > CHURCH

CHURCHIER > CHURCHY

CHURCHING > CHURCH

CHURCHISM *n* adherence
to the principles of an
established church

CHURCHLY *adj* appropriate
to, associated with, or
suggestive of church life
and customs

CHURCHMAN *n* clergyman

CHURCHMEN
> CHURCHMAN

CHURCHWAY *n* way or road
that leads to a church

CHURCHY *adj* like a church,
church service, etc

CHURIDAR as in *churidar
pyjamas* long tight-fitting
trousers, worn by Indian
men and women

CHURIDARS > CHURIDAR

CHURINGA *n* sacred
amulet of the native
Australians

CHURINGAS > CHURINGA

CHURL *n* surly ill-bred
person

CHURLISH *adj* surly and
rude

CHURLS > CHURL

CHURN *n* machine in which
cream is shaken to make
butter ▷ *vb* stir (cream)
vigorously to make butter

CHURNED > CHURN

CHURNER > CHURN

CHURNERS > CHURN

CHURNING *n* quantity of
butter churned at any one
time

CHURNINGS > CHURNING

CHURNMILK *n* buttermilk

CHURNS > CHURN

CHURR *same as* > CHIRR

CHURRED > CHURR

CHURRING > CHURR

CHURRO *n* Spanish dough
stick snack

CHURROS > CHURRO

CHURRS > CHURR

CHURRUS *n* hemp resin

CHURRUSES > CHURRUS

CHUSE *obsolete variant of*
> CHOOSE

CHUSES > CHUSE

CHUSING > CHUSE

CHUT *interj* expression of
surprise or annoyance ▷ *vb*
make such an expression

CHUTE *n* steep slope down
which things may be slid

▷ *vb* to descend by a chute

CHUTED > CHUTE

CHUTES > CHUTE

CHUTING > CHUTE

CHUTIST > CHUTE

CHUTISTS > CHUTE

CHUTNEE *same as*
> CHUTNEY

CHUTNEES > CHUTNEE

CHUTNEY *n* pickle made
from fruit, vinegar, spices,
and sugar

CHUTNEYS > CHUTNEY

CHUTZPA *same as*
> CHUTZPAH

CHUTZPAH *n* unashamed
self-confidence

CHUTZPAHS > CHUTZPAH

CHUTZPAS > CHUTZPA

CHYACK *same as* > CHIACK

CHYACKED > CHYACK

CHYACKING > CHYACK

CHYACKS > CHYACK

CHYLDE *archaic word for*
> CHILD

CHYLE *n* milky fluid formed
in the small intestine
during digestion

CHYLES > CHYLE

CHYLIFIED > CHYLIFY

CHYLIFIES > CHYLIFY

CHYLIFY *vb* to be turned
into chyle

CHYLOUS > CHYLE

CHYLURIA *n* presence of
chyle in urine

CHYLURIAS > CHYLURIA

CHYME *n* thick fluid mass of
partially digested food that
leaves the stomach

CHYMES > CHYME

CHYMIC *same as* > CHEMIC

CHYMICS > CHYMIC

CHYMIFIED > CHYMIFY

CHYMIFIES > CHYMIFY

CHYMIFY *vb* to form into
chyme

CHYMIST *same as*
> CHEMIST

CHYMISTRY *same as*
> CHEMISTRY

CHYMISTS > CHYMIST

CHYMOSIN *another name for*
> RENNIN

CHYMOSINS > CHYMOSIN

CHYMOUS > CHYME

CHYND *adj* chined

CHYPRE *n* perfume made
from sandalwood

CHYPRES > CHYPRE

CHYTRID *n* variety of
fungus

CHYTRIDS > CHYTRID

CIABATTA *n* type of bread
made with olive oil

CIABATTAS > CIABATTA

CIABATTE > CIABATTA

CIAO *an informal word for*
> HELLO

CIBATION *n* feeding

CIBATIONS > CIBATION

CIBOL *same as* > CHIBOL

CIBOLS > CIBOL

CIBORIA > CIBORIUM

CIBORIUM *n* goblet-
shaped lidded vessel used
to hold consecrated wafers
in Holy Communion

CIBOULE *same as*
> CHIBOL

CIBOULES > CIBOULE

CICADA *n* large insect that
makes a high-pitched
drone

CICADAE > CICADA

CICADAS > CICADA

CICALA *same as* > CICADA

CICALAS > CICALA

CICALE > CICALA

CICATRICE *n* scar

CICATRISE *same as*
> CICATRIZE

CICATRIX *n* scar

CICATRIZE *vb* (of a
wound or defect in tissue)
to close or be closed by scar
formation

CICELIES > CICELY

CICELY *n* type of plant

CICERO *n* measure for type
that is somewhat larger
than the pica

CICERONE *n* person who
guides and informs
sightseers ▷ *vb* to act as a
cicerone

CICERONED > CICERONE

CICERONES > CICERONE

CICERONI > CICERONE

CICEROS > CICERO

CICHLID *n* type of tropical
freshwater fish popular in
aquariums

CICHLIDAE *n* cichlids

CICHLIDS > CICHLID

CICHLOID > CICHLID

CICINNUS *n* scorpioid
cyme

CICISBEI > CICISBEO

CICISBEO *n* escort or
lover of a married woman,
esp in 18th-century Italy

CICISBEOS > CICISBEO

CICLATON *n* rich material
of silk and gold

CICLATONS > CICLATON

CICLATOUN *same as*
> CICLATON

CICOREE *same as*
> CHICORY

CICOREES > CICOREE

CICUTA *n* spotted hemlock

CICUTAS > CICUTA

CICUTINE *same as*
> CONIINE

CICUTINES > CICUTINE

CID *n* leader

CIDARIS *n* sea urchin

CIDARISES > CIDARIS

CIDE *Shakespearean variant
of* > DECIDE

CIDED > CIDE

CIDER *n* alcoholic drink
made from fermented
apple juice

CIDERKIN *n* weak type of
cider

CIDERKINS > CIDERKIN

CIDERS > CIDER

CIDERY > CIDER

CIDES > CIDE

CIDING > CIDE

CIDS > CID

CIEL *same as* > CEIL

CIELED > CIEL

CIELING > CIEL

CIELINGS > CIEL

CIELS > CIEL

CIERGE *same as* > CERGE

CIERGES > CIERGE

CIG *same as* > CIGARETTE

CIGAR *n* roll of cured
tobacco leaves for smoking

CIGARET *same as*
> CIGARETTE

CIGARETS > CIGARET

CIGARETTE *n* thin roll of
shredded tobacco in thin
paper, for smoking

CIGARILLO *n* small cigar
often only slightly larger
than a cigarette

CIGARLIKE > CIGAR

CIGARS > CIGAR

CIGGIE *same as*
> CIGARETTE

CIGGIES > CIGGIE

CIGGY *same as*
> CIGARETTE

CIGS > CIG

CIGUATERA *n* food
poisoning caused by a toxin
in seafood

CILANTRO *same as*
> CORIANDER

CILANTROS > CILANTRO

CILIA > CILIUM

CILIARY *adj* of or relating
to cilia

CILIATE *n* type of
protozoan

CILIATED > CILIATE

CILIATELY > CILIATE

CILIATES > CILIATE

CILIATION > CILIATE

CILICE *n* haircloth fabric
or garment

CILICES > CILICE

CILICIOUS *adj* made of
hair

CILIOLATE *adj* covered
with minute hairs, as some
plants

CILIUM *n* short thread
projecting from a cell,
whose rhythmic beating
causes movement

CILL *a variant spelling (used
in the building industry) for*
> SILL

CILLS > CILL

CIMAR *same as* > CYMAR

CIMARS > CIMAR

CIMBALOM *n* type of
dulcimer, esp of Hungary

CIMBALOMS > CIMBALOM

CIMELIA *n* (especially,
ecclesiastical) treasures

CIMEX *n* type of
heteropterous insect, esp
the bedbug

CIMICES > CIMEX

CIMIER n crest of a helmet

CIMIERS > CIMIER

CIMINITE n type of igneous rock

CIMINITES > CIMINITE

CIMMERIAN adj very dark or gloomy

CIMOLITE n clayey, whitish mineral

CIMOLITES > CIMOLITE

CINCH n easy task ▷ vb fasten a girth around (a horse)

CINCHED > CINCH

CINCHES > CINCH

CINCHING > CINCH

CINCHINGS > CINCH

CINCHONA same as > CALISAYA

CINCHONAS > CINCHONA

CINCHONIC > CINCHONA

CINCINNUS same as > CICINNUS

CINCT adj encircled

CINCTURE n something, such as a belt or girdle, that goes around another thing ▷ vb to encircle

CINCTURED > CINCTURE

CINCTURES > CINCTURE

CINDER n piece of material that will not burn, left after burning coal ▷ vb burn to cinders

CINDERED > CINDER

CINDERING > CINDER

CINDEROUS > CINDER

CINDERS > CINDER

CINDERY > CINDER

CINE as in cine camera camera able to film moving pictures

CINEAST same as > CINEASTE

CINEASTE n enthusiast for films

CINEASTES > CINEASTE

CINEASTS > CINEAST

CINEMA n place for showing films

CINEMAS > CINEMA

CINEMATIC > CINEMA

CINEOL n colourless oily liquid with a camphor-like odour and a spicy taste

CINEOLE same as > CINEOL

CINEOLES > CINEOLE

CINEOLS > CINEOL

CINEPHILE n film enthusiast

CINEPLEX n (tradename for) a large cinema complex

CINERAMIC adj relating to a cinematic process producing widescreen images

CINERARIA n garden plant with daisy-like flowers

CINERARY adj of (someone's) ashes

CINERATOR same as > CREMATOR

CINEREA n grey matter of

the brain and nervous system

CINEREAL adj ashy

CINEREAS > CINEREA

CINEREOUS adj of a greyish colour

CINERIN n either of two organic compounds used as insecticides

CINERINS > CINERIN

CINES > CINE

CINGULA > CINGULUM

CINGULAR adj ring-shaped

CINGULATE > CINGULUM

CINGULUM n girdle-like part, such as the ridge round the base of a tooth or the band of fibres connecting parts of the cerebrum

CINNABAR n heavy red mineral containing mercury

CINNABARS > CINNABAR

CINNAMIC > CINNAMON

CINNAMON n spice obtained from the bark of an Asian tree

CINNAMONS > CINNAMON

CINNAMONY > CINNAMON

CINNAMYL n univalent radical of cinnamic compounds

CINNAMYLS > CINNAMYL

CINQUAIN n stanza of five lines

CINQUAINS > CINQUAIN

CINQUE n number five in cards, dice, etc

CINQUES > CINQUE

CION same as > SCION

CIONS > CION

CIOPPINO n Italian rich fish stew

CIOPPINOS > CIOPPINO

CIPHER n system of secret writing ▷ vb put (a message) into secret writing

CIPHERED > CIPHER

CIPHERER > CIPHER

CIPHERERS > CIPHER

CIPHERING > CIPHER

CIPHERS > CIPHER

CIPHONIES > CIPHONY

CIPHONY n ciphered telephony; process of enciphering audio information, producing encrypted speech

CIPOLIN n Italian marble with alternating white and green streaks

CIPOLINS > CIPOLIN

CIPOLLINO same as > CIPOLIN

CIPPI > CIPPUS

CIPPUS n pillar bearing an inscription

CIRCA prep approximately, about

CIRCADIAN adj of biological processes that occur regularly at 24-hour intervals

CIRCAR n in India, part of a province

CIRCARS > CIRCAR

CIRCINATE adj (of part of a plant, such as a young fern) coiled so that the tip is at the centre

CIRCITER prep around, about

CIRCLE n perfectly round geometric figure, line, or shape ▷ vb move in a circle (round)

CIRCLED > CIRCLE

CIRCLER > CIRCLE

CIRCLERS > CIRCLE

CIRCLES > CIRCLE

CIRCLET n circular ornament worn on the head

CIRCLETS > CIRCLET

CIRCLING > CIRCLE

CIRCLINGS > CIRCLE

CIRCLIP n flat spring ring split at one point so that it can be sprung open, passed over a shaft or spindle, and allowed to close into a closely fitting annular recess to form a collar on the shaft. A similar design can be closed to pass into a bore and allowed to spring out into an annular recess to form a shoulder in the bore

CIRCLIPS > CIRCLIP

CIRCS npl circumstances

CIRCUIT n complete route or course, esp a circular one ▷ vb make or travel in a circuit around (something)

CIRCUITAL > CIRCUIT

CIRCUITED > CIRCUIT

CIRCUITRY n electrical circuit(s)

CIRCUITS > CIRCUIT

CIRCUITY n (of speech, reasoning, etc) a roundabout or devious quality

CIRCULAR adj in the shape of a circle ▷ n letter for general distribution

CIRCULARS > CIRCULAR

CIRCULATE vb send, go, or pass from place to place or person to person

CIRCUS n (performance given by) a travelling company of acrobats, clowns, performing animals, etc

CIRCUSES > CIRCUS

CIRCUSSY > CIRCUS

CIRCUSY > CIRCUS

CIRE adj (of fabric) treated with a heat or wax process to make it smooth ▷ n such a surface on a fabric

CIRES > CIRE

CIRL n bird belonging to the bunting family

CIRLS > CIRL

CIRQUE n steep-sided

semicircular hollow found in mountainous areas

CIRQUES > CIRQUE

CIRRATE adj bearing or resembling cirri

CIRRHOSED > CIRRHOSIS

CIRRHOSES > CIRRHOSIS

CIRRHOSIS n serious liver disease, often caused by drinking too much alcohol

CIRRHOTIC > CIRRHOSIS

CIRRI > CIRRUS

CIRRIFORM adj cirrus-like

CIRRIPED same as > CIRRIPEDE

CIRRIPEDE n type of marine crustacean of the subclass including the barnacles

CIRRIPEDS > CIRRIPED

CIRROSE same as > CIRRATE

CIRROUS same as > CIRRATE

CIRRUS n high wispy cloud

CIRSOID adj resembling a varix

CIS adj having two groups of atoms on the same side of a double bond

CISALPINE adj on this (the southern) side of the Alps, as viewed from Rome

CISCO n whitefish, esp the lake herring of cold deep lakes of North America

CISCOES > CISCO

CISCOS > CISCO

CISELEUR n person who is expert in ciselure

CISELEURS > CISELEUR

CISELURE n art or process of chasing metal

CISELURES > CISELURE

CISLUNAR adj of or relating to the space between the earth and the moon

CISPADANE adj on this (the southern) side of the River Po, as viewed from Rome

CISPLATIN n cytotoxic drug that acts by preventing DNA replication and hence cell division, used in the treatment of tumours, esp of the ovary and testis

CISSIER > CISSY

CISSIES > CISSY

CISSIEST > CISSY

CISSIFIED another word for > SISSY

CISSING n appearance of pinholes, craters, etc, in paintwork due to poor adhesion of the paint to the surface

CISSINGS > CISSING

CISSOID n geometric curve whose two branches

meet in a cusp at the origin and are asymptotic to a line parallel to the y-axis

CISSOIDS > CISSOID

CISSUS n type of climbing plant sometimes grown as a greenhouse or house plant for its shiny green or mottled leaves

CISSUSES > CISSUS

CISSY same as > SISSY

CIST n wooden box for holding ritual objects used in ancient Rome and Greece ▷ vb make a cist

CISTED > CIST

CISTERN n water tank, esp one that holds water for flushing a toilet

CISTERNA n sac or partially closed space containing body fluid, esp lymph or cerebrospinal fluid

CISTERNAE > CISTERNA

CISTERNAL > CISTERN

CISTERNS > CISTERN

CISTIC adj cist-like

CISTRON n section of a chromosome that encodes a single polypeptide chain

CISTRONIC > CISTRON

CISTRONS > CISTRON

CISTS > CIST

CISTUS n type of plant

CISTUSES > CISTUS

CISTVAEN n pre-Christian stone coffin or burial chamber

CISTVAENS > CISTVAEN

CIT n pejorative term for a town dweller

CITABLE > CITE

CITADEL n fortress in a city

CITADELS > CITADEL

CITAL n court summons

CITALS > CITAL

CITATION n commendation for bravery

CITATIONS > CITATION

CITATOR n legal publication listing cases and statutes, their history and current status

CITATORS > CITATOR

CITATORY > CITATION

CITE vb quote, refer to

CITEABLE > CITE

CITED > CITE

CITER > CITE

CITERS > CITE

CITES > CITE

CITESS n female cit

CITESSES > CITESS

CITHARA n stringed musical instrument of ancient Greece and elsewhere, similar to the lyre and played with a plectrum

CITHARAS > CITHARA

CITHARIST n player of the cithara

CITHER same as

> CITTERN

CITHERN same as

> CITTERN

CITHERNS > CITHERN

CITHERS > CITHER

CITHREN same as

> CITHARA

CITHRENS > CITHREN

CITIED adj having cities

CITIES > CITY

CITIFIED > CITIFY

CITIFIES > CITIFY

CITIFY vb cause to conform to or adopt the customs, habits, or dress of city people

CITIFYING > CITIFY

CITIGRADE adj relating to (fast-moving) wolf spiders

CITING > CITE

CITIZEN n native or naturalized member of a state or nation

CITIZENLY > CITIZEN

CITIZENRY n citizens collectively

CITIZENS > CITIZEN

CITO adv swiftly

CITOLA n type of medieval stringed instrument

CITOLAS > CITOLA

CITOLE a rare word for

> CITTERN

CITOLES > CITOLE

CITRAL n yellow volatile liquid with a lemon-like odour, found in oils of lemon grass, orange, and lemon and used in perfumery

CITRALS > CITRAL

CITRANGE n type of acidic and aromatic orange

CITRANGES > CITRANGE

CITRATE n any salt or ester of citric acid

CITRATED adj treated with a citrate

CITRATES > CITRATE

CITREOUS adj of a greenish-yellow colour

CITRIC adj of or derived from citrus fruits or citric acid

CITRIN n vitamin P

CITRINE n brownish-yellow variety of quartz: a gemstone

CITRINES > CITRINE

CITRININ n a mycotoxin

CITRININS > CITRININ

CITRINS > CITRIN

CITRON n lemon-like fruit of a small Asian tree

CITRONS > CITRON

CITROUS same as

> CITRUS

CITRUS n type of tropical or subtropical tree or shrub of the genus which includes the orange, lemon, lime, and grapefruit

CITRUSES > CITRUS

CITRUSSY adj having or resembling the taste or colour of a citrus fruit

CITRUSY same as

> CITRUSSY

CITS > CIT

CITTERN n medieval stringed instrument resembling a lute but having wire strings and a flat back

CITTERNS > CITTERN

CITY n large or important town

CITYFIED > CITYFY

CITYFIES > CITYFY

CITYFY same as > CITIFY

CITYFYING > CITYFY

CITYSCAPE n urban landscape

CITYWARD adv towards a city

CITYWIDE adj occurring throughout a city

CIVE same as > CHIVE

CIVES > CIVE

CIVET n spotted catlike African mammal

CIVETLIKE > CIVET

CIVETS > CIVET

CIVIC adj of a city or citizens

CIVICALLY > CIVIC

CIVICISM n principle of civil government

CIVICISMS > CIVICISM

CIVICS n study of the rights and responsibilities of citizenship

CIVIE same as > CIVVY

CIVIES > CIVIE

CIVIL adj relating to the citizens of a state as opposed to the armed forces or the Church

CIVILIAN adj not belonging to the armed forces ▷ n person who is not a member of the armed forces or police

CIVILIANS > CIVILIAN

CIVILISE same as

> CIVILIZE

CIVILISED same as

> CIVILIZED

CIVILISER > CIVILISE

CIVILISES > CIVILISE

CIVILIST n civilian

CIVILISTS > CIVILIST

CIVILITY n polite or courteous behaviour

CIVILIZE vb refine or educate (a person)

CIVILIZED adj having a high state of culture and social development

CIVILIZER > CIVILIZE

CIVILIZES > CIVILIZE

CIVILLY > CIVIL

CIVILNESS > CIVIL

CIVILS > CIVIL

CIVISM n good citizenship

CIVISMS > CIVISM

CIVVIES > CIVVY

CIVVY n civilian

CIZERS archaic spelling of

> SCISSORS

CLABBER vb to cover with mud

CLABBERED > CLABBER

CLABBERS > CLABBER

CLACH n stone

CLACHAN n small village

CLACHANS > CLACHAN

CLACHS > CLACH

CLACK n sound made by two hard objects striking each other ▷ vb make this sound

CLACKBOX n casing enclosing a clack

CLACKDISH n formerly, a dish carried by a beggar

CLACKED > CLACK

CLACKER n object that makes a clacking sound

CLACKERS > CLACKER

CLACKING > CLACK

CLACKS > CLACK

CLAD vb bond a metal to (another metal), esp to form a protective coat

CLADDAGH n Irish ring

CLADDAGHS > CLADDAGH

CLADDED adj covered with cladding

CLADDER > CLAD

CLADDERS > CLAD

CLADDIE another name for

> KORARI

CLADDIES > CLADDIE

CLADDING > CLOTHE

CLADDINGS > CLOTHE

CLADE n group of organisms considered as having evolved from a common ancestor

CLADES > CLADE

CLADISM > CLADIST

CLADISMS > CLADIST

CLADIST n proponent of cladistics: a method of grouping animals that makes use of lines of descent rather than structural similarities

CLADISTIC > CLADIST

CLADISTS > CLADIST

CLADODE n flattened stem resembling and functioning as a leaf, as in butcher's-broom

CLADODES > CLADODE

CLADODIAL > CLADODE

CLADOGRAM n treelike diagram illustrating the development of a clade

CLADS > CLAD

CLAES Scots word for

> CLOTHES

CLAFOUTI same as

> CLAFOUTIS

CLAFOUTIS n French baked pudding

CLAG n sticky mud ▷ vb stick, as mud

CLAGGED > CLAG

CLAGGIER > CLAGGY

CLAGGIEST > CLAGGY

CLAGGING > CLAG

CLAGGY adj stickily clinging, as mud

CLAGS > CLAG

CLAIM vb assert as a fact ▷ n assertion that something is true

CLAIMABLE > CLAIM

CLAIMANT n person who makes a claim

CLAIMANTS > CLAIMANT

CLAIMED > CLAIM

CLAIMER > CLAIM

CLAIMERS > CLAIM

CLAIMING > CLAIM

CLAIMS > CLAIM

CLAM n edible shellfish with a hinged shell ▷ vb gather clams

CLAMANCY n urgency

CLAMANT adj noisy

CLAMANTLY > CLAMANT

CLAMBAKE n picnic, often by the sea, at which clams, etc, are baked

CLAMBAKES > CLAMBAKE

CLAMBE old variant of > CLIMB

CLAMBER vb climb awkwardly ▷ n climb performed in this manner

CLAMBERED > CLAMBER

CLAMBERER > CLAMBER

CLAMBERS > CLAMBER

CLAME archaic variant of > CLAIM

CLAMES > CLAIM

CLAMLIKE > CLAM

CLAMMED > CLAM

CLAMMER n person who gathers clams

CLAMMERS > CLAMMER

CLAMMIER > CLAMMY

CLAMMIEST > CLAMMY

CLAMMILY > CLAMMY

CLAMMING > CLAM

CLAMMY adj unpleasantly moist and sticky

CLAMOR same as > CLAMOUR

CLAMORED > CLAMOR

CLAMORER > CLAMOR

CLAMORERS > CLAMOR

CLAMORING > CLAMOR

CLAMOROUS > CLAMOR

CLAMORS > CLAMOR

CLAMOUR n loud protest ▷ vb make a loud noise or outcry

CLAMOURED > CLAMOUR

CLAMOURER > CLAMOUR

CLAMOURS > CLAMOUR

CLAMP n tool with movable jaws for holding things together tightly ▷ vb fasten with a clamp

CLAMPDOWN n sudden restrictive measure

CLAMPED > CLAMP

CLAMPER n spiked metal frame fastened to the sole of a shoe to prevent slipping on ice ▷ vb to tread heavily

CLAMPERED > CLAMPER

CLAMPERS > CLAMPER

CLAMPING > CLAMP

CLAMPS > CLAMP

CLAMS > CLAM

CLAMSHELL n dredging bucket that is hinged like the shell of a clam

CLAMWORM the US name for the > RAGWORM

CLAMWORMS > CLAMWORM

CLAN n group of families with a common ancestor, esp among Scottish Highlanders

CLANG vb make a loud ringing metallic sound ▷ n ringing metallic sound

CLANGBOX n device fitted to a jet-engine to change the direction of thrust

CLANGED > CLANG

CLANGER n obvious mistake

CLANGERS > CLANGER

CLANGING > CLANG

CLANGINGS > CLANG

CLANGOR same as > CLANGOUR

CLANGORED > CLANGOR

CLANGORS > CLANGOR

CLANGOUR n loud continuous clanging sound ▷ vb make or produce a loud resonant noise

CLANGOURS > CLANGOUR

CLANGS > CLANG

CLANK n harsh metallic sound ▷ vb make such a sound

CLANKED > CLANK

CLANKIER > CLANKY

CLANKIEST > CLANKY

CLANKING > CLANK

CLANKINGS > CLANK

CLANKS > CLANK

CLANKY adj making clanking sounds

CLANNISH adj (of a group) tending to exclude outsiders

CLANS > CLAN

CLANSHIP n association of families under the leadership of a chieftain

CLANSHIPS > CLANSHIP

CLANSMAN n man belonging to a clan

CLANSMEN > CLANSMAN

CLAP vb applaud by hitting the palms of one's hands sharply together ▷ n act or sound of clapping

CLAPBOARD n long thin timber board with one edge thicker than the other, used esp in the US and Canada in wood-frame construction by lapping each board over the one below ▷ vb cover with such boards

CLAPBREAD n type of cake made from oatmeal

CLAPDISH same as > CLACKDISH

CLAPNET n net that can be closed instantly by pulling a string

CLAPNETS > CLAPNET

CLAPPED > CLAP

CLAPPER n piece of metal inside a bell, which causes it to sound when struck against the side ▷ vb make a sound like a clapper

CLAPPERED > CLAPPER

CLAPPERS > CLAPPER

CLAPPING > CLAP

CLAPPINGS > CLAP

CLAPS > CLAP

CLAPT > CLAP

CLAPTRAP n foolish or pretentious talk

CLAPTRAPS > CLAPTRAP

CLAQUE n group of people hired to applaud

CLAQUER same as > CLAQUEUR

CLAQUERS > CLAQUER

CLAQUES > CLAQUE

CLAQUEUR n member of a claque

CLAQUEURS > CLAQUEUR

CLARAIN n one of the four major lithotypes of banded coal

CLARAINS > CLARAIN

CLARENCE n closed four-wheeled horse-drawn carriage, having a glass front

CLARENCES > CLARENCE

CLARENDON n style of boldface roman type

CLARET n dry red wine from Bordeaux ▷ adj purplish-red ▷ vb to drink claret

CLARETED > CLARET

CLARETING > CLARET

CLARETS > CLARET

CLARIES > CLARY

CLARIFIED > CLARIFY

CLARIFIER > CLARIFY

CLARIFIES > CLARIFY

CLARIFY vb make (a matter) clear and unambiguous

CLARINET n keyed woodwind instrument with a single reed

CLARINETS > CLARINET

CLARINI > CLARINO

CLARINO adj of or relating to a high passage for the trumpet in 18th-century music ▷ n high register of the trumpet

CLARINOS > CLARINO

CLARION n obsolete high-pitched trumpet ▷ adj clear and ringing ▷ vb proclaim loudly

CLARIONED > CLARION

CLARIONET same as > CLARINET

CLARIONS > CLARION

CLARITIES > CLARITY

CLARITY n clearness

CLARKIA n N American plant cultivated for its red, purple, or pink flowers

CLARKIAS > CLARKIA

CLARO n mild light-coloured cigar

CLAROES > CLARO

CLAROS > CLARO

CLARSACH n Celtic harp of Scotland and Ireland

CLARSACHS > CLARSACH

CLART vb to dirty

CLARTED > CLART

CLARTHEAD n slow-witted or stupid person

CLARTIER > CLARTY

CLARTIEST > CLARTY

CLARTING > CLART

CLARTS npl lumps of mud, esp on shoes

CLARTY adj dirty, esp covered in mud

CLARY n European plant with aromatic leaves and blue flowers

CLASH vb come into conflict ▷ n fight, argument

CLASHED > CLASH

CLASHER > CLASH

CLASHERS > CLASH

CLASHES > CLASH

CLASHING > CLASH

CLASHINGS > CLASH

CLASP n device for fastening things ▷ vb grasp or embrace firmly

CLASPED > CLASP

CLASPER > CLASP

CLASPERS npl paired organ of male insects, used to clasp the female during copulation

CLASPING > CLASP

CLASPINGS > CLASP

CLASPS > CLASP

CLASPT old inflection of > CLASP

CLASS n group of people sharing a similar social position ▷ vb place in a class

CLASSABLE > CLASS

CLASSED > CLASS

CLASSER > CLASS

CLASSERS > CLASS

CLASSES > CLASSIS

CLASSIBLE adj able to be classed

CLASSIC adj being a typical example of something ▷ n author, artist, or work of art of recognized excellence

CLASSICAL adj of or in a restrained conservative style

CLASSICO adj (of Italian wines) coming from the centre of a specific wine-growing region

CLASSICS npl the. a body of literature regarded as great or lasting, esp that of ancient Greece or Rome

CLASSIER > CLASSY

CLASSIEST > CLASSY

CLASSIFIC adj relating to classification

CLASSIFY vb divide into groups with similar characteristics

CLASSILY > CLASSY

CLASSING > CLASS

CLASSINGS > CLASS

CLASSIS n governing body of elders or pastors

CLASSISM n belief that people from certain social or economic classes are superior to others

CLASSISMS > CLASSISM

CLASSIST > CLASSISM

CLASSISTS > CLASSISM

CLASSLESS adj not belonging to a class

CLASSMAN n graduate of Oxford University with a classed honours degree

CLASSMATE n friend or contemporary in the same class of a school

CLASSMEN > CLASSMAN

CLASSON n elementary atomic particle

CLASSONS > CLASSON

CLASSROOM n room in a school where lessons take place

CLASSWORK n school work done in class

CLASSY adj stylish and elegant

CLAST n fragment of a clastic rock

CLASTIC adj (of sedimentary rock, etc) composed of fragments of pre-existing rock that have been transported some distance from their points of origin ▷ n clast

CLASTICS > CLASTIC

CLASTS > CLAST

CLAT n irksome or troublesome task ▷ vb to scrape

CLATCH vb to move making a squelching sound

CLATCHED > CLATCH

CLATCHES > CLATCH

CLATCHING > CLATCH

CLATHRATE adj resembling a net or lattice ▷ n solid compound in which molecules of one substance are physically trapped in the crystal lattice of another

CLATS > CLAT

CLATTED > CLAT

CLATTER n (make) a rattling noise ▷ vb make a rattling noise, as when hard objects hit each other

CLATTERED > CLATTER

CLATTERER > CLATTER

CLATTERS > CLATTER

CLATTERY > CLATTER

CLATTING > CLAT

CLAUCHT vb to seize by force

CLAUCHTED > CLAUCHT

CLAUCHTS > CLAUCHT

CLAUGHT same as > CLAUCHT

CLAUGHTED > CLAUGHT

CLAUGHTS > CLAUGHT

CLAUSAL > CLAUSE

CLAUSE n section of a legal document

CLAUSES > CLAUSE

CLAUSTRA > CLAUSTRUM

CLAUSTRAL same as > CLOISTRAL

CLAUSTRUM n thin layer of gret matter in the brain

CLAUSULA n type of cadence in polyphony

CLAUSULAE > CLAUSULA

CLAUSULAR > CLAUSE

CLAUT same as > CLAT

CLAUTED > CLAUT

CLAUTING > CLAUT

CLAUTS > CLAUT

CLAVATE adj shaped like a club with the thicker end uppermost

CLAVATED same as > CLAVATE

CLAVATELY > CLAVATE

CLAVATION > CLAVATE

CLAVE n one of a pair of hardwood sticks struck together to make a hollow sound, esp to mark the beat of Latin-American dance music

CLAVECIN n harpsichord

CLAVECINS > CLAVECIN

CLAVER vb talk idly ▷ n idle talk

CLAVERED > CLAVER

CLAVERING > CLAVER

CLAVERS > CLAVER

CLAVES > CLAVE

CLAVI > CLAVUS

CLAVICLE n either of the two bones connecting the shoulder blades with the upper part of the breastbone

CLAVICLES > CLAVICLE

CLAVICORN n type of beetle such as the ladybirds, characterized by club-shaped antennae

CLAVICULA n clavicle

CLAVIE n tar-barrel traditionally set alight in Moray in Scotland on Hogmanay

CLAVIER n any keyboard instrument

CLAVIERS > CLAVIER

CLAVIES > CLAVIE

CLAVIFORM same as > CLAVATE

CLAVIGER n key- or club-bearer

CLAVIGERS > CLAVIGER

CLAVIS n key

CLAVULATE adj club-shaped

CLAVUS n corn on the toe

CLAW n sharp hooked nail of a bird or beast ▷ vb tear with claws or nails

CLAWBACK n recovery of a sum of money

CLAWBACKS > CLAWBACK

CLAWED > CLAW

CLAWER > CLAW

CLAWERS > CLAW

CLAWING > CLAW

CLAWLESS > CLAW

CLAWLIKE adj resembling a claw or claws

CLAWS > CLAW

CLAXON same as > KLAXON

CLAXONS > CLAXON

CLAY n fine-grained earth, soft when moist and hardening when baked, used to make bricks and pottery ▷ vb cover or mix with clay

CLAYBANK n dull brownish-orange colour

CLAYBANKS > CLAYBANK

CLAYED > CLAY

CLAYEY > CLAY

CLAYIER > CLAY

CLAYIEST > CLAY

CLAYING > CLAY

CLAYISH > CLAY

CLAYLIKE > CLAY

CLAYMORE n large two-edged sword formerly used by Scottish Highlanders

CLAYMORES > CLAYMORE

CLAYPAN n layer of stiff impervious clay situated just below the surface of the ground, which holds water after heavy rain

CLAYPANS > CLAYPAN

CLAYS > CLAY

CLAYSTONE n compact very fine-grained rock consisting of consolidated clay particles

CLAYTONIA n low-growing N American succulent plant

CLAYWARE n pottery

CLAYWARES > CLAYWARE

CLEAN adj free from dirt or impurities ▷ vb make (something) free from dirt ▷ adv completely

CLEANABLE > CLEAN

CLEANED > CLEAN

CLEANER n person or thing that removes dirt

CLEANERS > CLEANER

CLEANEST > CLEAN

CLEANING n act of cleaning something

CLEANINGS > CLEANING

CLEANLIER > CLEANLY

CLEANLILY > CLEANLY

CLEANLY adv easily or smoothly ▷ adj habitually clean or neat

CLEANNESS > CLEAN

CLEANS > CLEAN

CLEANSE vb make clean

CLEANSED > CLEANSE

CLEANSER n cleansing agent, such as a detergent

CLEANSERS > CLEANSER

CLEANSES > CLEANSE

CLEANSING > CLEANSE

CLEANSKIN n unbranded animal

CLEANUP n process of cleaning up or eliminating something

CLEANUPS > CLEANUP

CLEAR adj free from doubt or confusion ▷ adv in a clear or distinct manner ▷ vb make or become clear

CLEARABLE > CLEAR

CLEARAGE n clearance

CLEARAGES > CLEARAGE

CLEARANCE n clearing

CLEARCOLE n type of size containing whiting ▷ vb paint (a wall) with this size

CLEARCUT n act of felling all trees in area

CLEARCUTS > CLEARCUT

CLEARED > CLEAR

CLEARER > CLEAR

CLEARERS > CLEAR

CLEAREST > CLEAR

CLEAREYED adj having good judgment

CLEARING n treeless area in a wood

CLEARINGS > CLEARING

CLEARLY adv in a clear, distinct, or obvious manner

CLEARNESS > CLEAR

CLEARS > CLEAR

CLEARSKIN same as > CLEANSKIN

CLEARWAY n stretch of road on which motorists may stop in an emergency

CLEARWAYS > CLEARWAY

CLEARWEED n plant like nettle

CLEARWING n type of moth

CLEAT n wedge ▷ vb supply or support with a cleat or cleats

CLEATED > CLEAT

CLEATING > CLEAT

CLEATS > CLEAT

CLEAVABLE > CLEAVE

CLEAVAGE n space between a woman's breasts, as revealed by a low-cut dress

CLEAVAGES > CLEAVAGE

CLEAVE vb split apart ▷ n split

CLEAVED > CLEAVE

CLEAVER n butcher's heavy knife with a square blade

CLEAVERS n plant with small white flowers and sticky fruits

CLEAVES > CLEAVE

CLEAVING > CLEAVE

CLEAVINGS > CLEAVE

CLECHE adj (in heraldry) voided so that only a narrow border is visible

CLECK vb (of birds) to hatch ▷ n piece of gossip

CLECKED > CLECK
CLECKIER > CLECK
CLECKIEST > CLECK
CLECKING > CLECK
CLECKINGS > CLECK
CLECKS > CLECK
CLECKY > CLECK
CLEEK n large hook, such as one used to land fish ▷ vb to seize
CLEEKED > CLEEK
CLEEKING > CLEEK
CLEEKIT > CLEEK
CLEEKS > CLEEK
CLEEP same as > CLEPE
CLEEPED > CLEEP
CLEEPING > CLEEP
CLEEPS > CLEEP
CLEEVE n cliff
CLEEVES > CLEEVE
CLEF n symbol at the beginning of a stave to show the pitch
CLEFS > CLEF
CLEFT > CLEAVE
CLEFTED > CLEAVE
CLEFTING > CLEAVE
CLEFTS > CLEAVE
CLEG another name for a > HORSEFLY
CLEGS > CLEG
CLEIDOIC as in cleidoic egg egg of birds and insects
CLEIK same as > CLEEK
CLEIKS > CLEEK
CLEITHRAL adj covered with a roof
CLEM vb be hungry or cause to be hungry
CLEMATIS n climbing plant with large colourful flowers
CLEMENCY n kind or lenient treatment
CLEMENT adj (of weather) mild
CLEMENTLY > CLEMENT
CLEMMED > CLEM
CLEMMING > CLEM
CLEMS > CLEM
CLENCH vb close or squeeze (one's teeth or fist) tightly ▷ n firm grasp or grip
CLENCHED > CLENCH
CLENCHER > CLENCH
CLENCHERS > CLENCH
CLENCHES > CLENCH
CLENCHING > CLENCH
CLEOME n type of herbaceous or shrubby plant cultivated for its clusters of white or purplish flowers
CLEOMES > CLEOME
CLEOPATRA n type of yellow butterfly, the male of which has its wings flushed with orange
CLEPE vb call by the name of
CLEPED > CLEPE
CLEPES > CLEPE
CLEPING > CLEPE
CLEPSYDRA n ancient

device for measuring time by the flow of water or mercury through a small aperture
CLEPT > CLEPE
CLERGIES > CLERGY
CLERGY n priests and ministers as a group
CLERGYMAN n member of the clergy
CLERGYMEN > CLERGYMAN
CLERIC n member of the clergy
CLERICAL adj of clerks or office work
CLERICALS npl distinctive dress of a clergyman
CLERICATE n clerical post
CLERICITY n condition of being a clergyman
CLERICS > CLERIC
CLERID n beetle that preys on other insects
CLERIDS > CLERID
CLERIHEW n form of comic or satiric verse, consisting of two couplets and containing the name of a well-known person
CLERIHEWS > CLERIHEW
CLERISIES > CLERISY
CLERISY n learned or educated people
CLERK n employee in an office, bank, or court who keeps records, files, and accounts ▷ vb work as a clerk
CLERKDOM > CLERK
CLERKDOMS > CLERK
CLERKED > CLERK
CLERKESS n female office clerk
CLERKING > CLERK
CLERKISH > CLERK
CLERKLIER > CLERKLY
CLERKLIKE adj acting in a scholarly manner
CLERKLING n young or inexperienced clerk
CLERKLY adj of or like a clerk ▷ adv in the manner of a clerk
CLERKS > CLERK
CLERKSHIP > CLERK
CLERUCH n settler in a cleruchy
CLERUCHIA same as > CLERUCHY
CLERUCHS > CLERUCH
CLERUCHY n (in the ancient world) a special type of Athenian colony, in which settlers retained their Athenian citizenship and the community remained a political dependency of Athens
CLEUCH same as > CLOUGH
CLEUCHS > CLEUCH
CLEUGH same as > CLOUGH
CLEUGHS > CLEUGH
CLEVE same as > CLEEVE
CLEVEITE n crystalline

variety of the mineral uraninite
CLEVEITES > CLEVEITE
CLEVER adj intelligent, quick at learning
CLEVERER > CLEVER
CLEVEREST > CLEVER
CLEVERISH > CLEVER
CLEVERLY > CLEVER
CLEVES > CLEEVE
CLEVIS n U-shaped component of a shackle for attaching a drawbar to a plough or similar implement
CLEVISES > CLEVIS
CLEW n ball of thread, yarn, or twine ▷ vb coil or roll into a ball
CLEWED > CLEW
CLEWING > CLEW
CLEWS > CLEW
CLIANTHUS n Australian or NZ plant with slender scarlet flowers
CLICHE n expression or idea that is no longer effective because of overuse ▷ vb use a cliché (in speech or writing)
CLICHED > CLICHE
CLICHEED > CLICHE
CLICHES > CLICHE
CLICK n short sharp sound ▷ vb make this sound
CLICKABLE adj (of a website) having links that can be accessed by clicking a computer mouse
CLICKED > CLICK
CLICKER > CLICK
CLICKERS > CLICK
CLICKET vb make a click
CLICKETED > CLICKET
CLICKETS > CLICKET
CLICKING > CLICK
CLICKINGS > CLICK
CLICKLESS > CLICK
CLICKS > CLICK
CLICKWRAP adj (of agreement) consented to by user clicking computer button
CLIED > CLY
CLIENT n person who uses the services of a professional person or company
CLIENTAGE same as > CLIENTELE
CLIENTAL > CLIENT
CLIENTELE n clients collectively
CLIENTS > CLIENT
CLIES > CLY
CLIFF n steep rock face, esp along the sea shore ▷ vb scale a cliff
CLIFFED > CLIFF
CLIFFHANG vb (of a serial or film) to end on a note of suspense
CLIFFHUNG > CLIFFHANG
CLIFFIER > CLIFF

CLIFFIEST > CLIFF
CLIFFLIKE > CLIFF
CLIFFS > CLIFF
CLIFFY > CLIFF
CLIFT same as > CLIFF
CLIFTED > CLIFF
CLIFTIER > CLIFF
CLIFTIEST > CLIFF
CLIFTS > CLIFF
CLIFTY > CLIFF
CLIMACTIC adj consisting of, involving, or causing a climax
CLIMATAL > CLIMATE
CLIMATE n typical weather conditions of an area ▷ vb acclimatize
CLIMATED > CLIMATE
CLIMATES > CLIMATE
CLIMATIC > CLIMATE
CLIMATING > CLIMATE
CLIMATISE vb in Australia, adapt or become accustomed to a new climate or environment
CLIMATIZE same as > CLIMATISE
CLIMATURE n clime
CLIMAX n most intense point of an experience, series of events, or story ▷ vb reach a climax
CLIMAXED > CLIMAX
CLIMAXES > CLIMAX
CLIMAXING > CLIMAX
CLIMB vb go up, ascend ▷ n climbing
CLIMBABLE > CLIMB
CLIMBDOWN n act of backing down from opinion
CLIMBED > CLIMB
CLIMBER n person or thing that climbs
CLIMBERS > CLIMBER
CLIMBING > CLIMB
CLIMBINGS > CLIMB
CLIMBS > CLIMB
CLIME n place or its climate
CLIMES > CLIME
CLINAL > CLINE
CLINALLY > CLINE
CLINAMEN n bias
CLINAMENS > CLINAMEN
CLINCH vb settle (an argument or agreement) decisively ▷ n movement in which one competitor holds on to the other to avoid punches
CLINCHED > CLINCH
CLINCHER n something decisive
CLINCHERS > CLINCHER
CLINCHES > CLINCH
CLINCHING > CLINCH
CLINE n continuous variation in form between members of a species having a wide variable geographical or ecological range
CLINES > CLINE
CLING vb hold tightly or stick closely ▷ n tendency

of cotton fibres in a sample to stick to each other

CLINGED > CLING

CLINGER > CLING

CLINGERS > CLING

CLINGFILM n thin polythene material for wrapping food

CLINGFISH n type of small marine fish with a flattened elongated body and a sucking disc beneath the head for clinging to rocks, etc

CLINGIER > CLING

CLINGIEST > CLING

CLINGING > CLING

CLINGS > CLING

CLINGY > CLING

CLINIC n building where outpatients receive medical treatment or advice

CLINICAL adj of a clinic

CLINICIAN n physician, psychiatrist, etc, who specializes in clinical work as opposed to one engaged in laboratory or experimental studies

CLINICS > CLINIC

CLINIQUE same as > CLINIC

CLINIQUES > CLINIC

CLINK n (make) a light sharp metallic sound ▷ vb make a light sharp metallic sound

CLINKED > CLINK

CLINKER n fused coal left over in a fire or furnace ▷ vb form clinker during burning

CLINKERED > CLINKER

CLINKERS > CLINKER

CLINKING > CLINK

CLINKS > CLINK

CLINOAXES > CLINOAXIS

CLINOAXIS n in a monoclinic crystal, the lateral axis which forms an oblique angle with the vertical axis

CLINOSTAT n apparatus for studying tropisms in plants, usually a rotating disc to which the plant is attached so that it receives an equal stimulus on all sides

CLINQUANT adj glittering, esp with tinsel ▷ n tinsel or imitation gold leaf

CLINT n section of a limestone pavement separated from adjacent sections by solution fissures

CLINTONIA n type of temperate plant with white, greenish-yellow, or purplish leaves, broad ribbed leaves, and blue berries

CLINTS > CLINT

CLIP vb cut with shears or scissors ▷ n short extract of a film

CLIPART n large collection of simple drawings stored in a computer

CLIPARTS > CLIPART

CLIPBOARD n portable writing board with a clip at the top for holding paper

CLIPE same as > CLYPE

CLIPED > CLIPE

CLIPES > CLIPE

CLIPING > CLIPE

CLIPPABLE > CLIP

CLIPPED > CLIP

CLIPPER n fast commercial sailing ship

CLIPPERS npl tool for clipping

CLIPPIE n bus conductress

CLIPPIES > CLIPPIE

CLIPPING same as > CLIP

CLIPPINGS > CLIP

CLIPS > CLIP

CLIPSHEAR n earwig

CLIPSHEET n sheet of paper with text printed on one side only

CLIPT old inflection of > CLIP

CLIQUE n small exclusive group ▷ vb to form a clique

CLIQUED > CLIQUE

CLIQUES > CLIQUE

CLIQUEY adj exclusive, confined to a small group

CLIQUIER > CLIQUEY

CLIQUIEST > CLIQUEY

CLIQUING > CLIQUE

CLIQUISH > CLIQUE

CLIQUISM > CLIQUE

CLIQUISMS > CLIQUE

CLIQUY same as > CLIQUEY

CLIT same as > CLITORIS

CLITELLA > CLITELLUM

CLITELLAR > CLITELLUM

CLITELLUM n thickened saddle-like region of epidermis in earthworms and leeches whose secretions bind copulating worms together and later form a cocoon around the eggs

CLITHRAL same as > CLEITHRAL

CLITIC adj (of a word) incapable of being stressed, usually pronounced as if part of the word that follows or precedes it ▷ n clitic word

CLITICISE same as > CLITICIZE

CLITICIZE vb pronounce as part of following or preceding word

CLITICS > CLITIC

CLITORAL > CLITORIS

CLITORIC > CLITORIS

CLITORIS n small sexually

sensitive organ at the front of the vulva

CLITS > CLIT

CLITTER vb to stridulate

CLITTERED > CLITTER

CLITTERS > CLITTER

CLIVERS same as > CLEAVERS

CLIVIA n plant belonging to the Amaryllid family

CLIVIAS > CLIVIA

CLOACA n cavity in most animals, except higher mammals, into which the alimentary canal and the genital and urinary ducts open

CLOACAE > CLOACA

CLOACAL > CLOACA

CLOACAS > CLOACA

CLOACINAL > CLOACA

CLOACITIS n inflammation of the cloaca in birds, including domestic fowl, and other animals with a common opening of the urinary and gastrointestinal tracts

CLOAK n loose sleeveless outer garment ▷ vb cover or conceal

CLOAKED > CLOAK

CLOAKING > CLOAK

CLOAKROOM n room where coats may be left temporarily

CLOAKS > CLOAK

CLOAM adj made of clay or earthenware ▷ n clay or earthenware pots, dishes, etc, collectively

CLOAMS > CLOAM

CLOBBER vb hit ▷ n belongings, esp clothes

CLOBBERED > CLOBBER

CLOBBERS > CLOBBER

CLOCHARD n tramp

CLOCHARDS > CLOCHARD

CLOCHE n cover to protect young plants

CLOCHES > CLOCHE

CLOCK n instrument for showing the time ▷ vb record (time) with a stopwatch

CLOCKED > CLOCK

CLOCKER > CLOCK

CLOCKERS > CLOCK

CLOCKING > CLOCK

CLOCKINGS > CLOCK

CLOCKLIKE > CLOCK

CLOCKS > CLOCK

CLOCKWISE adj in the direction in which the hands of a clock rotate

CLOCKWORK n mechanism similar to the kind in a clock, used in wind-up toys

CLOD n lump of earth ▷ vb pelt with clods

CLODDED > CLOD

CLODDIER > CLOD

CLODDIEST > CLOD

CLODDING > CLOD

CLODDISH > CLOD

CLODDY > CLOD

CLODLY > CLOD

CLODPATE n dull or stupid person

CLODPATED adj stupid

CLODPATES > CLODPATE

CLODPOLE same as > CLODPOLL

CLODPOLES > CLODPOLE

CLODPOLL same as > CLODPATE

CLODPOLLS > CLODPOLL

CLODS > CLOD

CLOFF n cleft of a tree

CLOFFS > CLOFF

CLOG vb obstruct ▷ n wooden or wooden-soled shoe

CLOGDANCE n dance performed in clogs

CLOGGED > CLOG

CLOGGER n clogmaker

CLOGGERS > CLOGGER

CLOGGIER > CLOG

CLOGGIEST > CLOG

CLOGGILY > CLOG

CLOGGING > CLOG

CLOGGINGS > CLOG

CLOGGY > CLOG

CLOGS > CLOG

CLOISON n partition

CLOISONNE n design made by filling in a wire outline with coloured enamel ▷ adj of, relating to, or made by cloisonné

CLOISONS > CLOISON

CLOISTER n covered pillared arcade, usu. in a monastery ▷ vb confine or seclude in or as if in a monastery

CLOISTERS > CLOISTER

CLOISTRAL adj of, like, or characteristic of a cloister

CLOKE same as > CLOAK

CLOKED > CLOKE

CLOKES > CLOKE

CLOKING > CLOKE

CLOMB a past tense and past participle of > CLIMB

CLOMP same as > CLUMP

CLOMPED > CLOMP

CLOMPING > CLOMP

CLOMPS > CLOMP

CLON same as > CLONE

CLONAL > CLONE

CLONALLY > CLONE

CLONE n animal or plant produced artificially from the cells of another animal or plant, and identical to the original ▷ vb produce as a clone

CLONED > CLONE

CLONER > CLONE

CLONERS > CLONE

CLONES > CLONE

CLONIC > CLONUS

CLONICITY > CLONUS

CLONIDINE n antihypertensive drug

CLONING > CLONE

CLONINGS > CLONE

CLONISM *n* series of clonic spasms

CLONISMS > CLONISM

CLONK *vb* make a loud dull thud ▷ *n* loud thud

CLONKED > CLONK

CLONKING > CLONK

CLONKS > CLONK

CLONS > CLON

CLONUS *n* type of convulsion characterized by rapid contraction and relaxation of a muscle

CLONUSES > CLONUS

CLOOP *n* sound made when a cork is drawn from a bottle

CLOOPS > CLOOP

CLOOT *n* hoof

CLOOTIE as in *clootie dumpling* kind of dumpling

CLOOTS > CLOOT

CLOP *vb* make or move along with a sound as of a horse's hooves striking the ground ▷ *n* sound of this nature

CLOPPED > CLOP

CLOPPING > CLOP

CLOPS > CLOP

CLOQUE *n* fabric with an embossed surface

CLOQUES > CLOQUE

CLOSABLE > CLOSE

CLOSE *vb* shut ▷ *n* end, conclusion ▷ *adj* near ▷ *adv* closely, tightly ▷ *n* passageway leading to a tenement building

CLOSEABLE > CLOSE

CLOSED > CLOSE

CLOSEDOWN *n* closure or stoppage of operations

CLOSEHEAD *n* entrance to a close

CLOSELY > CLOSE

CLOSENESS > CLOSE

CLOSEOUT *n* termination of an account on which the margin is exhausted

CLOSEOUTS > CLOSEOUT

CLOSER > CLOSE

CLOSERS > CLOSE

CLOSES > CLOSE

CLOSEST > CLOSE

CLOSET *n* cupboard ▷ *adj* private, secret ▷ *vb* shut (oneself) away in private

CLOSETED > CLOSET

CLOSETFUL *n* quantity that may be contained in a closet

CLOSETING > CLOSET

CLOSETS > CLOSET

CLOSEUP *n* photo taken close to subject

CLOSEUPS > CLOSEUP

CLOSING > CLOSE

CLOSINGS > CLOSE

CLOSURE *n* closing ▷ *vb* (in a deliberative body) to end (debate) by closure

CLOSURED > CLOSURE

CLOSURES > CLOSURE

CLOSURING > CLOSURE

CLOT *n* soft thick lump formed from liquid ▷ *vb* form soft thick lumps

CLOTBUR *n* burdock

CLOTBURS > CLOTBUR

CLOTE *n* burdock

CLOTES > CLOTE

CLOTH *n* (piece of) woven fabric

CLOTHE *vb* put clothes on

CLOTHED > CLOTHE

CLOTHES *n* garments

CLOTHIER *n* maker or seller of clothes or cloth

CLOTHIERS > CLOTHIER

CLOTHING > CLOTHE

CLOTHINGS > CLOTHE

CLOTHLIKE > CLOTH

CLOTHS > CLOTH

CLOTPOLL *same as* > CLODPOLL

CLOTPOLLS > CLOTPOLL

CLOTS > CLOT

CLOTTED > CLOT

CLOTTER *vb* to clot

CLOTTERED > CLOTTER

CLOTTERS > CLOTTER

CLOTTIER > CLOTTY

CLOTTIEST > CLOTTY

CLOTTING > CLOT

CLOTTINGS > CLOT

CLOTTISH > CLOT

CLOTTY *adj* full of clots

CLOTURE *n* closure in the US Senate ▷ *vb* end (debate) in the US Senate by cloture

CLOTURED > CLOTURE

CLOTURES > CLOTURE

CLOTURING > CLOTURE

CLOU *n* crux; focus

CLOUD *n* mass of condensed water vapour floating in the sky ▷ *vb* become cloudy

CLOUDAGE *n* mass of clouds

CLOUDAGES > CLOUDAGE

CLOUDED > CLOUD

CLOUDIER > CLOUDY

CLOUDIEST > CLOUDY

CLOUDILY > CLOUDY

CLOUDING > CLOUD

CLOUDINGS > CLOUD

CLOUDLAND *n* realm or fantasy or impractical notions

CLOUDLESS > CLOUD

CLOUDLET *n* small cloud

CLOUDLETS > CLOUDLET

CLOUDLIKE > CLOUD

CLOUDS > CLOUD

CLOUDTOWN *n* cloudland

CLOUDY *adj* having a lot of clouds

CLOUGH *n* gorge or narrow ravine

CLOUGHS > CLOUGH

CLOUR *vb* to thump or dent

CLOURED > CLOUR

CLOURING > CLOUR

CLOURS > CLOUR

CLOUS > CLOU

CLOUT *n* hard blow ▷ *vb* hit hard

CLOUTED > CLOUT

CLOUTER > CLOUT

CLOUTERLY *adj* clumsy

CLOUTERS > CLOUT

CLOUTING > CLOUT

CLOUTS > CLOUT

CLOVE *n* tropical evergreen myrtaceous tree

CLOVEN > CLEAVE

CLOVER *n* plant with three-lobed leaves

CLOVERED *adj* covered with clover

CLOVERS > CLOVER

CLOVERY > CLOVER

CLOVES > CLOVE

CLOVIS as in *clovis point* flint projectile dating from the 10th millennium bc

CLOW *n* clove

CLOWDER *n* collective terms for a group of cats

CLOWDERS > CLOWDER

CLOWN *n* comic entertainer in a circus ▷ *vb* behave foolishly

CLOWNED > CLOWN

CLOWNERY > CLOWN

CLOWNFISH *n* small, brightly-coloured tropical fish

CLOWNING > CLOWN

CLOWNINGS > CLOWN

CLOWNISH > CLOWN

CLOWNS > CLOWN

CLOWS > CLOW

CLOY *vb* make weary or cause weariness through an excess of something initially pleasurable or sweet

CLOYED > CLOY

CLOYES > CLOYE

CLOYING *adj* sickeningly sweet

CLOYINGLY > CLOYING

CLOYLESS *adj* not cloying

CLOYMENT *n* satiety

CLOYMENTS > CLOYMENT

CLOYS > CLOY

CLOYSOME *adj* cloying

CLOZAPINE *n* drug used to treat mental illness

CLOZE as in *cloze test* test of the ability to understand text

CLOZES > CLOZE

CLUB *n* association of people with common interests ▷ *vb* hit with a club

CLUBABLE *same as* > CLUBBABLE

CLUBBABLE *adj* suitable to be a member of a club

CLUBBED > CLUB

CLUBBER *n* person who regularly frequents nightclubs and similar establishments

CLUBBERS > CLUBBER

CLUBBIER > CLUBBY

CLUBBIEST > CLUBBY

CLUBBILY > CLUBBY

CLUBBING > CLUB

CLUBBINGS > CLUB

CLUBBISH *adj* clubby

CLUBBISM *n* advantage gained through membership of a club or clubs

CLUBBISMS > CLUBBISM

CLUBBIST > CLUBBISM

CLUBBISTS > CLUBBISM

CLUBBY *adj* sociable, esp effusively so

CLUBFACE *n* face of golf club

CLUBFACES > CLUBFACE

CLUBFEET > CLUBFOOT

CLUBFOOT *n* congenital deformity of the foot

CLUBHAND *n* congenital deformity of the hand

CLUBHANDS > CLUBHAND

CLUBHAUL *vb* force (a sailing vessel) onto a new tack, esp in an emergency

CLUBHAULS > CLUBHAUL

CLUBHEAD *n* head of golf club

CLUBHEADS > CLUBHEAD

CLUBHOUSE *n* premises of a sports or other club, esp a golf club

CLUBLAND *n* (in Britain) the area of London around St. James's, which contains most of the famous London clubs

CLUBLANDS > CLUBLAND

CLUBMAN *n* man who is an enthusiastic member of a club or clubs

CLUBMEN > CLUBMAN

CLUBROOM *n* room in which a club meets

CLUBROOMS > CLUBROOM

CLUBROOT *n* disease of cabbages

CLUBROOTS > CLUBROOT

CLUBRUSH *n* any rush of the genus Scirpus

CLUBS > CLUB

CLUBWOMAN *n* woman who is an enthusiastic member of a club or clubs

CLUBWOMEN > CLUBWOMAN

CLUCK *n* low clicking noise made by a hen ▷ *vb* make this noise

CLUCKED > CLUCK

CLUCKIER > CLUCKY

CLUCKIEST > CLUCKY

CLUCKING > CLUCK

CLUCKS > CLUCK

CLUCKY *adj* wishing to have a baby

CLUDGIE *n* toilet

CLUDGIES > CLUDGIE

CLUE *n* something that helps to solve a mystery or puzzle ▷ *vb* help solve a mystery or puzzle

CLUED > CLUE

CLUEING > CLUE
CLUELESS adj stupid
CLUES > CLUE
CLUING > CLUE
CLUMBER n type of thickset spaniel
CLUMBERS > CLUMBER
CLUMP n small group of things or people ▷ vb walk heavily
CLUMPED > CLUMP
CLUMPER > CLUMP
CLUMPERS > CLUMP
CLUMPIER > CLUMP
CLUMPIEST > CLUMP
CLUMPING > CLUMP
CLUMPISH > CLUMP
CLUMPLIKE > CLUMP
CLUMPS > CLUMP
CLUMPY > CLUMP
CLUMSIER > CLUMSY
CLUMSIEST > CLUMSY
CLUMSILY > CLUMSY
CLUMSY adj lacking skill or physical coordination
CLUNCH n hardened clay
CLUNCHES > CLUNCH
CLUNG > CLING
CLUNK n dull metallic sound ▷ vb make such a sound
CLUNKED > CLUNK
CLUNKER n dilapidated old car or other machine
CLUNKERS > CLUNKER
CLUNKIER > CLUNKY
CLUNKIEST > CLUNKY
CLUNKING > CLUNK
CLUNKS > CLUNK
CLUNKY adj making a clunking noise
CLUPEID n type of widely distributed soft-finned fish, typically with oily flesh, such as the herrings, sardines, and shad
CLUPEIDS > CLUPEID
CLUPEOID n type of soft-finned fish belonging to the order which includes the herrings, salmon, and tarpon
CLUPEOIDS > CLUPEOID
CLUSIA n tree of the tropical American genus Clusia
CLUSIAS > CLUSIA
CLUSTER n small close group ▷ vb gather in clusters
CLUSTERED > CLUSTER
CLUSTERS > CLUSTER
CLUSTERY > CLUSTER
CLUTCH vb grasp tightly ▷ n device enabling two revolving shafts to be connected and disconnected, esp in a motor vehicle
CLUTCHED > CLUTCH
CLUTCHES > CLUTCH
CLUTCHING > CLUTCH
CLUTCHY adj (of a person) tending to cling

CLUTTER vb scatter objects about (a place) untidily ▷ n untidy mess
CLUTTERED > CLUTTER
CLUTTERS > CLUTTER
CLUTTERY adj full of clutter
CLY vb to steal or seize
CLYING > CLY
CLYPE vb tell tales ▷ n person who tells tales
CLYPEAL > CLYPEUS
CLYPEATE a CLYPEUS
CLYPED > CLYPE
CLYPEI > CLYPEUS
CLYPES > CLYPE
CLYPEUS n cuticular plate on the head of some insects between the labrum and the frons
CLYPING > CLYPE
CLYSTER a former name for an > ENEMA
CLYSTERS > CLYSTER
CNEMIAL > CNEMIS
CNEMIDES > CNEMIS
CNEMIS n shin or tibia
CNIDA n nematocyst
CNIDAE > CNIDA
CNIDARIAN n type of invertebrate of the phylum which comprises the coelenterates
COACH n long-distance bus ▷ vb train, teach
COACHABLE adj capable of being coached
COACHDOG n Dalmatian dog
COACHDOGS > COACHDOG
COACHED > COACH
COACHEE n person who receives training from a coach, esp in business or office practice
COACHEES > COACHEE
COACHER > COACH
COACHERS > COACH
COACHES > COACH
COACHIER > COACHY
COACHIES > COACHY
COACHIEST > COACHY
COACHING > COACH
COACHINGS > COACH
COACHLINE n decorative line on the bodywork of a vehicle
COACHLOAD n quantity that a coach can carry
COACHMAN n driver of a horse-drawn coach or carriage
COACHMEN > COACHMAN
COACHWHIP n whipsnake
COACHWOOD n Australian tree yielding light aromatic wood used for furniture etc
COACHWORK n body of a car
COACHY n coachman ▷ adj resembling or pertaining to a coach
COACT vb to act together
COACTED > COACT
COACTING > COACT

COACTION n any relationship between organisms within a community
COACTIONS > COACTION
COACTIVE > COACTION
COACTOR > COACT
COACTORS > COACT
COACTS > COACT
COADAPTED adj adapted to one another
COADJUTOR n bishop appointed as assistant to a diocesan bishop
COADMIRE vb to admire together
COADMIRED > COADMIRE
COADMIRES > COADMIRE
COADMIT vb to admit together
COADMITS > COADMIT
COADUNATE same as > CONNATE
COAEVAL n contemporary
COAEVALS > COAEVAL
COAGENCY n joint agency
COAGENT > COAGENCY
COAGENTS > COAGENCY
COAGULA > COAGULUM
COAGULANT n substance causing coagulation
COAGULASE n any enzyme that causes coagulation of blood
COAGULATE vb change from a liquid to a semisolid mass ▷ n solid or semisolid substance produced by coagulation
COAGULUM n any coagulated mass
COAGULUMS > COAGULUM
COAITA n spider monkey
COAITAS > COAITA
COAL n black rock consisting mainly of carbon, used as fuel ▷ vb take in, or turn into coal
COALA same as > KOALA
COALAS > COALA
COALBALL n in coal, nodule containing petrified plant or animal remains
COALBALLS > COALBALL
COALBIN n bin for holding coal
COALBINS > COALBIN
COALBOX n box for holding coal
COALBOXES > COALBOX
COALED > COAL
COALER n ship, train, etc, used to carry or supply coal
COALERS > COALER
COALESCE vb come together, merge
COALESCED > COALESCE
COALESCES > COALESCE
COALFACE n exposed seam of coal in a mine
COALFACES > COALFACE
COALFIELD n area with coal under the ground
COALFISH n type of dark-coloured food fish

occurring in northern seas
COALHOLE n small coal cellar
COALHOLES > COALHOLE
COALHOUSE n shed or building for storing coal
COALIER > COAL
COALIEST > COAL
COALIFIED > COALIFY
COALIFIES > COALIFY
COALIFY vb to turn into coal
COALING > COAL
COALISE vb to form a coalition
COALISED > COALISE
COALISES > COALISE
COALISING > COALISE
COALITION n temporary alliance, esp between political parties
COALIZE same as > COALISE
COALIZED > COALIZE
COALIZES > COALIZE
COALIZING > COALIZE
COALLESS adj without coal
COALMAN n man who delivers coal
COALMEN > COALMAN
COALMINE n mine from which coal is extracted
COALMINER > COALMINE
COALMINES > COALMINE
COALPIT n pit from which coal is extracted
COALPITS > COALPIT
COALS > COAL
COALSACK n dark nebula near the constellation Cygnus
COALSACKS > COALSACK
COALSHED n shed in which coal is stored
COALSHEDS > COALSHED
COALY > COAL
COALYARD n yard in which coal is stored
COALYARDS > COALYARD
COAMING n raised frame round a ship's hatchway for keeping out water
COAMINGS > COAMING
COANCHOR vb to co-present a TV programme
COANCHORS > COANCHOR
COANNEX vb to annex with something else
COANNEXED > COANNEX
COANNEXES > COANNEX
COAPPEAR vb to appear jointly
COAPPEARS > COAPPEAR
COAPT vb to secure
COAPTED > COAPT
COAPTING > COAPT
COAPTS > COAPT
COARB n spiritual successor
COARBS > COARB
COARCTATE adj (of a pupa) enclosed in a hard barrel-shaped case (puparium), as in the

housefly ▷ vb (esp of the aorta) to become narrower

COARSE adj rough in texture

COARSELY > COARSE

COARSEN vb make or become coarse

COARSENED > COARSEN

COARSENS > COARSEN

COARSER > COARSE

COARSEST > COARSE

COARSISH > COARSE

COASSIST vb to assist jointly

COASSISTS > COASSIST

COASSUME vb to assume jointly

COASSUMED > COASSUME

COASSUMES > COASSUME

COAST n place where the land meets the sea ▷ vb move by momentum, without the use of power

COASTAL > COAST

COASTALLY > COAST

COASTED > COAST

COASTER n small mat placed under a glass

COASTERS > COASTER

COASTING > COAST

COASTINGS > COAST

COASTLAND n land fringing a coast

COASTLINE n outline of a coast

COASTS > COAST

COASTWARD adv towards the coast

COASTWISE adv along the coast

COAT n outer garment with long sleeves ▷ vb cover with a layer

COATDRESS n garment that can be worn as a coat or a dress

COATE same as > QUOTE

COATED adj covered with an outer layer, film, etc

COATEE n short coat, esp for a baby

COATEES > COATEE

COATER n machine that applies a coating to something

COATERS > COATER

COATES > COATE

COATI n type of omnivorous mammal of Central and S America, with a long flexible snout and a brindled coat

COATING n covering layer

COATINGS > COATING

COATIS > COATI

COATLESS adj without a coat

COATRACK n rack for hanging coats on

COATRACKS > COATRACK

COATROOM n cloakroom

COATROOMS > COATROOM

COATS > COAT

COATSTAND n stand for hanging coats on

COATTAIL n long tapering tail at the back of a man's tailored coat

COATTAILS > COATTAIL

COATTEND vb to attend jointly

COATTENDS > COATTEND

COATTEST vb to attest jointly

COATTESTS > COATTEST

COAUTHOR n person who shares the writing of a book, article, etc, with another ▷ vb be the joint author of (a book, article, etc)

COAUTHORS > COAUTHOR

COAX vb persuade gently

COAXAL same as > COAXIAL

COAXED > COAX

COAXER > COAX

COAXERS > COAX

COAXES > COAX

COAXIAL adj (of a cable) transmitting by means of two concentric conductors separated by an insulator

COAXIALLY > COAXIAL

COAXING > COAX

COAXINGLY > COAX

COB n stalk of an ear of maize ▷ vb beat, esp on the buttocks

COBAEA n tropical American climbing shrub grown for its large trumpet-shaped purple or white flowers

COBAEAS > COBAEA

COBALAMIN n vitamin B12

COBALT n brittle silvery-white metallic element

COBALTIC adj of or containing cobalt, esp in the trivalent state

COBALTINE same as > COBALTITE

COBALTITE n rare silvery-white mineral

COBALTOUS adj of or containing cobalt in the divalent state

COBALTS > COBALT

COBB same as > COB

COBBED > COB

COBBER n friend

COBBERS > COBBER

COBBIER > COBBY

COBBIEST > COBBY

COBBING > COB

COBBLE n cobblestone ▷ vb pave (a road) with cobblestones

COBBLED > COBBLE

COBBLER n shoe mender

COBBLERS npl nonsense ▷ interj exclamation of strong disagreement

COBBLERY n shoemaking or shoemending

COBBLES npl coal in small rounded lumps

COBBLING > COBBLE

COBBLINGS > COBBLE

COBBS > COBB

COBBY adj short and stocky

COBIA n large dark-striped game fish of tropical and subtropical seas

COBIAS > COBIA

COBLE n small single-masted flat-bottomed fishing boat

COBLES > COBLE

COBLOAF n round loaf of bread

COBLOAVES > COBLOAF

COBNUT another name for > HAZELNUT

COBNUTS > COBNUT

COBRA n venomous hooded snake of Asia and Africa

COBRAS > COBRA

COBRIC > COBRA

COBRIFORM adj cobra-like

COBS > COB

COBURG n rounded loaf with a cross cut on the top

COBURGS > COBURG

COBWEB n spider's web

COBWEBBED > COBWEB

COBWEBBY > COBWEB

COBWEBS > COBWEB

COBZA n Romanian lute

COBZAS > COBZA

COCA n dried leaves of a S American shrub which contain cocaine

COCAIN same as > COCAINE

COCAINE n addictive drug used as a narcotic and as an anaesthetic

COCAINES > COCAINE

COCAINISE same as > COCAINIZE

COCAINISM n use of cocaine

COCAINIST n cocaine addict

COCAINIZE vb anaesthetize with cocaine

COCAINS > COCAIN

COCAPTAIN vb to captain jointly

COCAS > COCA

COCCAL > COCCUS

COCCI > COCCUS

COCCIC > COCCUS

COCCID n type of homopterous insect of the family which includes the scale insects

COCCIDIA > COCCIDIUM

COCCIDIUM n any parasitic protozoan of the order Coccidia

COCCIDS > COCCID

COCCO n taro

COCCOID > COCCUS

COCCOIDAL > COCCUS

COCCOIDS > COCCUS

COCCOLITE n variety of pyroxene

COCCOLITH n any of the round calcareous plates in

chalk formations: formed the outer layer of unicellular plankton

COCCOS > COCCO

COCCOUS > COCCUS

COCCUS n any spherical or nearly spherical bacterium, such as a staphylococcus

COCCYGEAL > COCCYX

COCCYGES > COCCYX

COCCYGIAN > COCCYX

COCCYX n bone at the base of the spinal column

COCCYXES > COCCYX

COCH obsolete variant of > COACH

COCHAIR vb to chair jointly

COCHAIRED > COCHAIR

COCHAIRS > COCHAIR

COCHES > COCH

COCHIN n large breed of domestic fowl

COCHINEAL n red dye obtained from a Mexican insect, used for food colouring

COCHINS > COCHIN

COCHLEA n spiral tube in the internal ear, which converts sound vibrations into nerve impulses

COCHLEAE > COCHLEA

COCHLEAR adj of or relating to the cochlea ▷ n spoonful

COCHLEARE variant of > COCHLEAR

COCHLEARS > COCHLEAR

COCHLEAS > COCHLEA

COCHLEATE adj shaped like a snail's shell

COCINERA n in Mexico, a female cook

COCINERAS > COCINERA

COCK n male bird, esp of domestic fowl ▷ vb draw back (the hammer of a gun) to firing position

COCKADE n feather or rosette worn on a hat as a badge

COCKADED > COCKADE

COCKADES > COCKADE

COCKAMAMY adj ridiculous or nonsensical

COCKAPOO n cross between a cocker spaniel and a poodle

COCKAPOOS > COCKAPOO

COCKATEEL same as > COCKATIEL

COCKATIEL n crested Australian parrot with a greyish-brown and yellow plumage

COCKATOO n crested parrot of Australia or the East Indies

COCKATOOS > COCKATOO

COCKBILL vb to tilt up one end of

COCKBILLS > COCKBILL

COCKBIRD n male bird

COCKBIRDS > COCKBIRD

COCKBOAT n any small boat

COCKBOATS > COCKBOAT

COCKCROW n daybreak

COCKCROWS > COCKCROW

COCKED > COCK

COCKER n devotee of cockfighting ▷ vb pamper or spoil by indulgence

COCKERED > COCKER

COCKEREL n young domestic cock

COCKERELS > COCKEREL

COCKERING > COCKER

COCKERS > COCKER

COCKET n document issued by a customs officer

COCKETS > COCKET

COCKEYE n eye affected with strabismus or one that squints

COCKEYED adj crooked, askew

COCKEYES > COCKEYE

COCKFIGHT n fight between two gamecocks fitted with sharp metal spurs

COCKHORSE n rocking horse

COCKIER > COCKY

COCKIES > COCKY

COCKIEST > COCKY

COCKILY > COCKY

COCKINESS n conceited self-assurance

COCKING > COCK

COCKISH adj wanton

COCKLE n edible shellfish ▷ vb fish for cockles

COCKLEBUR n type of coarse weed with spiny burs

COCKLED > COCKLE

COCKLEERT a Southwest English dialect variant of > COCKCROW

COCKLEMAN n man who collects cockles

COCKLEMEN > COCKLEMAN

COCKLER n person employed to gather cockles

COCKLERS > COCKLER

COCKLES > COCKLE

COCKLIKE adj resembling a cock

COCKLING > COCKLE

COCKLINGS > COCKLING

COCKLOFT n small loft, garret, or attic

COCKLOFTS > COCKLOFT

COCKMATCH n cockfight

COCKNEY n native of London, esp if its East End ▷ adj characteristic of cockneys or their dialect

COCKNEYFY vb cause (one's speech, manners, etc) to fit the stereotyped idea of a cockney

COCKNEYS > COCKNEY

COCKNIFY same as > COCKNEYFY

COCKPIT n pilot's compartment in an aircraft

COCKPITS > COCKPIT

COCKROACH n beetle-like insect which is a household pest

COCKS > COCK

COCKSCOMB n comb of a domestic cock

COCKSFOOT n type of Eurasian grass, cultivated as a pasture grass in N America and S Africa

COCKSHIES > COCKSHY

COCKSHOT another name for > COCKSHY

COCKSHOTS > COCKSHOT

COCKSHUT n dusk

COCKSHUTS > COCKSHUT

COCKSHY n target aimed at in throwing games

COCKSIER > COCKSY

COCKSIEST > COCKSY

COCKSPUR n spur on the leg of a cock

COCKSPURS > COCKSPUR

COCKSURE adj overconfident, arrogant

COCKSWAIN same as > COXSWAIN

COCKSY adj cocky

COCKTAIL n mixed alcoholic drink

COCKTAILS > COCKTAIL

COCKUP n something done badly ▷ vb ruin or spoil

COCKUPS > COCKUP

COCKY adj conceited and overconfident ▷ n farmer whose farm is regarded as small or of little account

COCO n coconut palm

COCOA n powder made from the seed of the cacao tree

COCOANUT same as > COCONUT

COCOANUTS > COCONUT

COCOAS > COCOA

COCOBOLA n type of rosewood

COCOBOLAS > COCOBOLA

COCOBOLO same as > COCOBOLA

COCOBOLOS > COCOBOLO

COCOMAT n mat made from coconut fibre

COCOMATS > COCOMAT

COCONUT n large hard fruit of a type of palm tree

COCONUTS > COCONUT

COCOON n silky protective covering of a silkworm ▷ vb wrap up tightly for protection

COCOONED > COCOON

COCOONERY n place where silkworms feed and make cocoons

COCOONING > COCOON

COCOONS > COCOON

COCOPAN n (in South Africa) a small wagon running on narrow-gauge railway lines used in mines

COCOPANS > COCOPAN

COCOPLUM n tropical shrub, also known as icaco, or its fruit

COCOPLUMS > COCOPLUM

COCOS > COCO

COCOTTE n small fireproof dish in which individual portions of food are cooked

COCOTTES > COCOTTE

COCOUNSEL vb to counsel jointly

COCOYAM n either of two food plants of West Africa, the taro or the yantia, both of which have edible underground stems

COCOYAMS > COCOYAM

COCOZELLE n variety of squash

COCREATE vb to create jointly

COCREATED > COCREATE

COCREATES > COCREATE

COCREATOR > COCREATE

COCTILE adj made by exposing to heat

COCTION n boiling

COCTIONS > COCTION

COCULTURE vb to culture together

COCURATOR n joint curator

COCUSWOOD n wood from a tropical American leguminous tree, used for inlaying, musical instruments, etc

COD n large food fish of the North Atlantic ▷ adj having the character of an imitation or parody ▷ vb make fun of

CODA n final part of a musical composition

CODABLE adj capable of being coded

CODAS > CODA

CODDED > COD

CODDER n cod fisherman or his boat

CODDERS > CODDER

CODDING > COD

CODDLE vb pamper, overprotect ▷ n stew made from ham and bacon scraps

CODDLED > CODDLE

CODDLER > CODDLE

CODDLERS > CODDLE

CODDLES > CODDLE

CODDLING > CODDLE

CODE n system of letters, symbols, or prearranged signals by which messages can be communicated secretly or briefly ▷ vb put into code

CODEBOOK n book containing the means to decipher a code

CODEBOOKS > CODEBOOK

CODEBTOR n fellow debtor

CODEBTORS > CODEBTOR

CODEC n set of equipment that encodes an analogue speech or video signal into digital form for

transmission purposes and at the receiving end decodes the digital signal into a form close to its original

CODECS > CODEC

CODED > CODE

CODEIA n codeine

CODEIAS > CODEIA

CODEIN same as > CODEINE

CODEINA obsolete variant of > CODEINE

CODEINAS > CODEINA

CODEINE n drug used as a painkiller

CODEINES > CODEINE

CODEINS > CODEIN

CODELESS adj lacking a code

CODEN n unique six-character code assigned to a publication for identification purposes

CODENAME same as > CODEWORD

CODENAMES > CODEWORD

CODENS > CODEN

CODER n person or thing that codes

CODERIVE vb to derive jointly

CODERIVED > CODERIVE

CODERIVES > CODERIVE

CODERS > CODER

CODES > CODE

CODESIGN vb to design jointly

CODESIGNS > CODESIGN

CODETTA n short coda

CODETTAS > CODETTA

CODEVELOP vb to develop jointly

CODEWORD n (esp in military use) a word used to identify a classified plan, operation, etc

CODEWORDS > CODEWORD

CODEX n volume of manuscripts of an ancient text

CODFISH n cod

CODFISHES > CODFISH

CODGER n old man

CODGERS > CODGER

CODICES > CODEX

CODICIL n addition to a will

CODICILS > CODICIL

CODIFIED > CODIFY

CODIFIER > CODIFY

CODIFIERS > CODIFY

CODIFIES > CODIFY

CODIFY vb organize (rules or procedures) systematically

CODIFYING > CODIFY

CODILLA n coarse tow of hemp and flax

CODILLAS > CODILLA

CODILLE n in the cardgame ombre, term indicating that the game is won

CODILLES > CODILLE
CODING > CODE
CODINGS > CODE
CODIRECT vb to direct jointly
CODIRECTS > CODIRECT
CODIST n codifier
CODISTS > CODIST
CODLIN same as **> CODLING**
CODLING n young cod
CODLINGS > CODLING
CODLINS > CODLIN
CODOLOGY n art or practice of bluffing or deception
CODOMAIN n set of values that a function is allowed to take
CODOMAINS > CODOMAIN
CODON n unit that consists of three adjacent bases on a DNA molecule that determines the position of a specific amino acid in a protein molecule during protein synthesis
CODONS > CODON
CODPIECE n bag covering the male genitals, attached to the breeches
CODPIECES > CODPIECE
CODRIVE vb take alternate turns driving a car with another person
CODRIVEN > CODRIVE
CODRIVER n one of two drivers who take turns to drive a car
CODRIVERS > CODRIVER
CODRIVES > CODRIVE
CODRIVING > CODRIVE
CODROVE > CODRIVE
CODS > COD
COED adj educating both sexes together ▷ n school or college that educates both sexes together
COEDIT vb edit (a book, newspaper, etc) jointly
COEDITED > COEDIT
COEDITING > COEDIT
COEDITOR > COEDIT
COEDITORS > COEDIT
COEDITS > COEDIT
COEDS > COED
COEFFECT n secondary effect
COEFFECTS > COEFFECT
COEHORN n type of small artillery mortar
COEHORNS > COEHORN
COELIAC adj of or relating to the abdomen ▷ n person who has coeliac disease
COELIACS > COELIAC
COELOM n body cavity of many multicellular animals, situated in the mesoderm and containing the digestive tract and other visceral organs
COELOMATA n animals possessing a coelom
COELOMATE adj possessing a coelom

COELOME same as **> COELOM**
COELOMES > COELOME
COELOMIC > COELOM
COELOMS > COELOM
COELOSTAT n astronomical instrument consisting of a plane mirror mounted parallel to the earth's axis and rotated about this axis once every two days so that light from a celestial body, esp the sun, is reflected onto a second mirror, which reflects the beam into a telescope
COEMBODY vb to embody jointly
COEMPLOY vb to employ together
COEMPLOYS > COEMPLOY
COEMPT vb buy up something in its entirety
COEMPTED > COEMPT
COEMPTING > COEMPT
COEMPTION n buying up of the complete supply of a commodity
COEMPTS > COEMPT
COENACLE same as **> CENACLE**
COENACLES > COENACLE
COENACT vb to enact jointly
COENACTED > COENACT
COENACTS > COENACT
COENAMOR vb enamour jointly
COENAMORS > COENAMOR
COENDURE vb to endure together
COENDURED > COENDURE
COENDURES > COENDURE
COENOBIA > COENOBIUM
COENOBITE n member of a religious order in a monastic community
COENOBIUM n monastery or convent
COENOCYTE n mass of protoplasm containing many nuclei and enclosed by a cell wall: occurs in many fungi and some algae
COENOSARC n system of protoplasmic branches connecting the polyps of colonial organisms such as corals
COENURE variant form of **> COENURUS**
COENURES > COENURE
COENURI > COENURUS
COENURUS n encysted larval form of a type of tapeworm with many encapsulated heads
COENZYME n nonprotein organic molecule that forms a complex with certain enzymes and is essential for their activity
COENZYMES > COENZYME
COEQUAL n equal ▷ adj of

the same size, rank, etc
COEQUALLY > COEQUAL
COEQUALS > COEQUAL
COEQUATE vb to equate together
COEQUATED > COEQUATE
COEQUATES > COEQUATE
COERCE vb compel, force
COERCED > COERCE
COERCER > COERCE
COERCERS > COERCE
COERCES > COERCE
COERCIBLE > COERCE
COERCIBLY > COERCE
COERCING > COERCE
COERCION n act or power of coercing
COERCIONS > COERCION
COERCIVE > COERCE
COERECT vb to erect together
COERECTED > COERECT
COERECTS > COERECT
COESITE n polymorph of silicon dioxide
COESITES > COESITE
COETERNAL adj existing together eternally
COEVAL n contemporary ▷ adj contemporary
COEVALITY > COEVAL
COEVALLY > COEVAL
COEVALS > COEVAL
COEVOLVE vb to evolve together
COEVOLVED > COEVOLVE
COEVOLVES > COEVOLVE
COEXERT vb to exert together
COEXERTED > COEXERT
COEXERTS > COEXERT
COEXIST vb exist together, esp peacefully despite differences
COEXISTED > COEXIST
COEXISTS > COEXIST
COEXTEND vb extend or cause to extend equally in space or time
COEXTENDS > COEXTEND
COFACTOR n number associated with an element in a square matrix, equal to the determinant of the matrix formed by removing the row and column in which the element appears from the given determinant
COFACTORS > COFACTOR
COFEATURE vb to feature together
COFF vb buy
COFFED > COFF
COFFEE n drink made from the roasted and ground seeds of a tropical shrub ▷ adj medium-brown
COFFEEPOT n pot in which coffee is brewed or served
COFFEES > COFFEE
COFFER n chest, esp for storing valuables ▷ vb store
COFFERDAM n watertight

enclosure pumped dry to enable construction work to be done
COFFERED > COFFERDAM
COFFERING > COFFERDAM
COFFERS > COFFERDAM
COFFIN n box in which a corpse is buried or cremated ▷ vb place in or as in a coffin
COFFINED > COFFIN
COFFING > COFF
COFFINING > COFFIN
COFFINITE n uranium-bearing silicate mineral
COFFINS > COFFIN
COFFLE n (esp formerly) a line of slaves, beasts, etc, fastened together ▷ vb to fasten together in a coffle
COFFLED > COFFLE
COFFLES > COFFLE
COFFLING > COFFLE
COFFRET n small coffer
COFFRETS > COFFRET
COFFS > COFF
COFINANCE vb to finance jointly
COFIRING n combustion of two different types of fuel at the same time
COFIRINGS > COFIRING
COFOUND vb to found jointly
COFOUNDED > COFOUND
COFOUNDER > COFOUND
COFOUNDS > COFOUND
COFT > COFF
COG n one of the teeth on the rim of a gearwheel ▷ vb roll (cast-steel ingots) to convert them into blooms
COGENCE > COGENT
COGENCES > COGENT
COGENCIES > COGENT
COGENCY > COGENT
COGENER n congener
COGENERS > COGENER
COGENT adj forcefully convincing
COGENTLY > COGENT
COGGED > COG
COGGER n deceiver
COGGERS > COGGER
COGGIE n quaich or drinking cup
COGGIES > COGGIE
COGGING > COG
COGGINGS > COG
COGGLE vb wobble or rock
COGGLED > COGGLE
COGGLES > COGGLE
COGGLIER > COGGLE
COGGLIEST > COGGLE
COGGLING > COGGLE
COGGLY > COGGLE
COGIE same as **> COGGIE**
COGIES > COGIE
COGITABLE adj conceivable
COGITATE vb think deeply about

COGITATED > COGITATE
COGITATES > COGITATE
COGITATOR > COGITATE
COGITO n philosophical theory that one must exist because one is capable of thought
COGITOS > COGITO
COGNAC n French brandy
COGNACS > COGNAC
COGNATE adj derived from a common original form ⊳ n cognate word or language
COGNATELY > COGNATE
COGNATES > COGNATE
COGNATION > COGNATE
COGNISANT same as > COGNIZANT
COGNISE same as > COGNIZE
COGNISED > COGNISE
COGNISER > COGNISE
COGNISERS > COGNISE
COGNISES > COGNISE
COGNISING > COGNISE
COGNITION n act or experience of knowing or acquiring knowledge
COGNITIVE adj of or relating to cognition
COGNIZANT adj aware
COGNIZE vb perceive, become aware of, or know
COGNIZED > COGNIZE
COGNIZER > COGNIZE
COGNIZERS > COGNIZE
COGNIZES > COGNIZE
COGNIZING > COGNIZE
COGNOMEN n nickname
COGNOMINA > COGNOMEN
COGNOSCE vb in Scots law, to give judgment upon
COGNOSCED > COGNOSCE
COGNOSCES > COGNOSCE
COGNOVIT n in law, a defendant's confession that the case against him is just
COGNOVITS > COGNOVIT
COGON n type of coarse tropical grass used for thatching
COGONS > COGON
COGS > COG
COGUE n wooden pail or drinking vessel
COGUES > COGUE
COGWAY n rack railway
COGWAYS > COGWAY
COGWHEEL same as > GEARWHEEL
COGWHEELS > COGWHEEL
COHAB n cohabitor
COHABIT vb live together as husband and wife without being married
COHABITED > COHABIT
COHABITEE > COHABIT
COHABITER > COHABIT
COHABITS > COHABIT
COHABS > COHAB
COHEAD vb to head jointly

COHEADED > COHEAD
COHEADING > COHEAD
COHEADS > COHEAD
COHEIR n person who inherits jointly with others
COHEIRESS > COHEIR
COHEIRS > COHEIR
COHEN same as > KOHEN
COHENS > COHEN
COHERE vb hold or stick together
COHERED > COHERE
COHERENCE n logical or natural connection or consistency
COHERENCY same as > COHERENCE
COHERENT adj logical and consistent
COHERER n electrical component formerly used to detect radio waves, consisting of a tube containing loosely packed metal particles. The waves caused the particles to cohere, thereby changing the current through the circuit
COHERERS > COHERER
COHERES > COHERE
COHERING > COHERE
COHERITOR n coheir
COHESIBLE adj capable of cohesion
COHESION n sticking together
COHESIONS > COHESION
COHESIVE adj sticking together to form a whole
COHIBIT vb to restrain
COHIBITED > COHIBIT
COHIBITS > COHIBIT
COHO n type of Pacific salmon
COHOBATE vb redistil (a distillate), esp by allowing it to mingle with the remaining matter
COHOBATED > COHOBATE
COHOBATES > COHOBATE
COHOE same as > COHO
COHOES > COHO
COHOG n quahog, an edible clam
COHOGS > COHOG
COHOLDER n joint holder
COHOLDERS > COHOLDER
COHORN same as > COEHORN
COHORNS > COEHORN
COHORT n band of associates
COHORTS > COHORT
COHOS > COHO
COHOSH n type of North American plant
COHOSHES > COHOSH
COHOST vb to host jointly
COHOSTED > COHOST
COHOSTESS vb (of a woman) to host jointly
COHOSTING > COHOST
COHOSTS > COHOST

COHOUSING n type of housing with some shared facilities
COHUNE n tropical American feather palm whose large nuts yield an oil similar to coconut oil
COHUNES > COHUNE
COHYPONYM n word which is one of multiple hyponyms of another word
COIF vb arrange the hair of ⊳ n close-fitting cap worn in the Middle Ages
COIFED adj wearing a coif
COIFFE vb to coiffure
COIFFED > COIF
COIFFES > COIFFE
COIFFEUR n hairdresser
COIFFEURS > COIFFEUR
COIFFEUSE > COIFFEUR
COIFFING > COIF
COIFFURE n hairstyle ⊳ vb dress or arrange (the hair)
COIFFURED > COIFFURE
COIFFURES > COIFFURE
COIFING > COIF
COIFS > COIF
COIGN vb wedge ⊳ n quoin
COIGNE same as > COIGN
COIGNED > COIGN
COIGNES > COIGNE
COIGNING > COIGN
COIGNS > COIGN
COIL vb wind in loops ⊳ n something coiled
COILED > COIL
COILER > COIL
COILERS > COIL
COILING > COIL
COILS > COIL
COIN n piece of metal money ⊳ vb invent (a word or phrase)
COINABLE > COIN
COINAGE n coins collectively
COINAGES > COINAGE
COINCIDE vb happen at the same time
COINCIDED > COINCIDE
COINCIDES > COINCIDE
COINED > COIN
COINER > COIN
COINERS > COIN
COINFECT vb infect at same time as other infection
COINFECTS > COINFECT
COINFER vb infer jointly
COINFERS > COINFER
COINHERE vb to inhere together
COINHERED > COINHERE
COINHERES > COINHERE
COINING > COIN
COININGS > COIN
COINMATE n fellow inmate
COINMATES > COINMATE
COINOP adj (of a machine) operated by putting a coin in a slot
COINS > COIN
COINSURE vb insure jointly

COINSURED > COINSURE
COINSURER > COINSURE
COINSURES > COINSURE
COINTER vb to inter together
COINTERS > COINTER
COINTREAU n tradename for a French orange liqueur
COINVENT vb to invent jointly
COINVENTS > COINVENT
COIR n coconut fibre, used for matting
COIRS > COIR
COISTREL n knave
COISTRELS > COISTREL
COISTRIL same as > COISTREL
COISTRILS > COISTRIL
COIT n buttocks
COITAL > COITUS
COITALLY > COITUS
COITION same as > COITUS
COITIONAL > COITION
COITIONS > COITION
COITS > COIT
COITUS n sexual intercourse
COITUSES > COITUS
COJOIN vb to conjoin
COJOINED > COJOIN
COJOINING > COJOIN
COJOINS > COJOIN
COJONES npl testicles
COKE n solid fuel left after gas has been distilled from coal ⊳ vb become or convert into coke
COKED > COKE
COKEHEAD n cocaine addict
COKEHEADS > COKEHEAD
COKELIKE > COKE
COKERNUT same as > COCONUT
COKERNUTS > COKERNUT
COKES n fool
COKESES > COKES
COKIER > COKY
COKIEST > COKY
COKING > COKE
COKULORIS n palette with irregular holes, placed between lighting and camera to prevent glare
COKY adj like coke
COL n high mountain pass
COLA n dark brown fizzy soft drink
COLANDER n perforated bowl for straining or rinsing foods
COLANDERS > COLANDER
COLAS > COLA
COLBIES > COLBY
COLBY n type of mild-tasting hard cheese
COLBYS > COLBY
COLCANNON n dish, originating in Ireland, of potatoes and cabbage or other greens boiled and mashed together

COLCHICA > COLCHICUM
COLCHICUM n type of Eurasian liliaceous plant, such as the autumn crocus
COLCOTHAR n finely powdered form of ferric oxide produced by heating ferric sulphate and used as a pigment and as jewellers' rouge
COLD adj lacking heat ▷ n lack of heat
COLDBLOOD n any heavy draught-horse
COLDCOCK vb to knock to the ground
COLDCOCKS > COLDCOCK
COLDER > COLD
COLDEST > COLD
COLDHOUSE n unheated greenhouse
COLDIE n cold can or bottle of beer
COLDIES > COLDIE
COLDISH > COLD
COLDLY > COLD
COLDNESS > COLD
COLDS > COLD
COLE same as > CABBAGE
COLEAD vb to lead together
COLEADER > COLEAD
COLEADERS > COLEAD
COLEADING > COLEAD
COLEADS > COLEAD
COLECTOMY n surgical removal of part or all of the colon
COLED > COLEAD
COLEOPTER n aircraft that has an annular wing with the fuselage and engine on the centre line
COLES > COLE
COLESEED n common rape or cole
COLESEEDS > COLESEED
COLESLAW n salad dish of shredded raw cabbage in a dressing
COLESLAWS > COLESLAW
COLESSEE n joint lessee
COLESSEES > COLESSEE
COLESSOR n joint lessor
COLESSORS > COLESSOR
COLETIT n coal tit
COLETITS > COLETIT
COLEUS n Old World plant cultivated for its variegated leaves, typically marked with red, yellow, or white
COLEUSES > COLEUS
COLEWORT same as > CABBAGE
COLEWORTS > CABBAGE
COLEY same as > COALFISH
COLEYS > COLEY
COLIBRI n hummingbird
COLIBRIS > COLIBRI
COLIC n severe pains in the stomach and bowels
COLICIN n bacteriocidal protein
COLICINE n antibacterial protein

COLICINES > COLICINE
COLICINS > COLICIN
COLICKIER > COLICKY
COLICKY adj relating to or suffering from colic
COLICROOT n N American plant with tubular white or yellow flowers and a bitter root formerly used to relieve colic
COLICS > COLIC
COLICWEED n type of plant such as the squirrel corn and Dutchman's-breeches
COLIES > COLY
COLIFORM n type of bacteria of the intestinal tract
COLIFORMS > COLIFORM
COLIN n quail
COLINEAR same as > COLLINEAR
COLINS > COLIN
COLIPHAGE n bacteriophage
COLISEUM n large building, such as a stadium or theatre, used for entertainments, sports, etc
COLISEUMS > COLISEUM
COLISTIN n polymyxin antibiotic
COLISTINS > COLISTIN
COLITIC > COLITIS
COLITIS n inflammation of the colon
COLITISES > COLITIS
COLL vb to embrace
COLLAGE n art form in which various materials or objects are glued onto a surface ▷ vb to make a collage
COLLAGED > COLLAGE
COLLAGEN n protein found in cartilage and bone that yields gelatine when boiled
COLLAGENS > COLLAGEN
COLLAGES > COLLAGE
COLLAGING > COLLAGE
COLLAGIST > COLLAGE
COLLAPSAR n collapsed star, either a white dwarf, neutron star, or black hole
COLLAPSE vb fall down suddenly ▷ n collapsing
COLLAPSED > COLLAPSE
COLLAPSES > COLLAPSE
COLLAR n part of a garment round the neck ▷ vb seize, arrest
COLLARD n variety of the cabbage with a crown of edible leaves
COLLARDS > COLLARD
COLLARED > COLLAR
COLLARET n small collar
COLLARETS > COLLARET
COLLARING > COLLAR
COLLARS > COLLAR
COLLATE vb gather together, examine, and put in order

COLLATED > COLLATE
COLLATES > COLLATE
COLLATING > COLLATE
COLLATION n collating
COLLATIVE adj involving collation
COLLATOR n person or machine that collates texts or manuscripts
COLLATORS > COLLATOR
COLLEAGUE n fellow worker, esp in a profession
COLLECT vb gather together ▷ n short prayer
COLLECTED adj calm and controlled
COLLECTOR n person who collects objects as a hobby
COLLECTS > COLLECT
COLLED > COLL
COLLEEN n girl
COLLEENS > COLLEEN
COLLEGE n place of higher education
COLLEGER n member of a college
COLLEGERS > COLLEGER
COLLEGES > COLLEGE
COLLEGIA > COLLEGIUM
COLLEGIAL adj of or relating to a college
COLLEGIAN n member of a college
COLLEGIUM n (in the former Soviet Union) a board in charge of a department
COLLET n (in a jewellery setting) a band or coronet-shaped claw that holds an individual stone ▷ vb mount in a collet
COLLETED > COLLET
COLLETING > COLLET
COLLETS > COLLET
COLLICULI n plural form of singular colliculus: small elevation, as on the surface of the optic lobe of the brain
COLLIDE vb crash together violently
COLLIDED > COLLIDE
COLLIDER n particle accelerator in which beams of particles are made to collide
COLLIDERS > COLLIDER
COLLIDES > COLLIDE
COLLIDING > COLLIDE
COLLIE n silky-haired sheepdog
COLLIED > COLLY
COLLIER n coal miner
COLLIERS > COLLIER
COLLIERY n coal mine
COLLIES > COLLY
COLLIGATE vb connect or link together
COLLIMATE vb adjust the line of sight of (an optical instrument)
COLLINEAR adj lying on the same straight line
COLLING n embrace

COLLINGS > COLLING
COLLINS n tall fizzy iced drink made with gin, vodka, rum, etc, mixed with fruit juice, soda water, and sugar
COLLINSES > COLLINS
COLLINSIA n N American plant with blue, white, or purple flowers
COLLISION n violent crash between moving objects
COLLOCATE vb (of words) occur together regularly
COLLODION n colourless or yellow syrupy liquid that consists of a solution of pyroxylin in ether and alcohol: used in medicine and in the manufacture of photographic plates, lacquers, etc
COLLODIUM same as > COLLODION
COLLOGUE vb confer confidentially
COLLOGUED > COLLOGUE
COLLOGUES > COLLOGUE
COLLOID n suspension of particles in a solution ▷ adj of or relating to the gluelike translucent material found in certain degenerating tissues
COLLOIDAL adj of, denoting, or having the character of a colloid
COLLOIDS > COLLOID
COLLOP n small slice of meat
COLLOPS > COLLOP
COLLOQUE vb to converse
COLLOQUED > COLLOQUE
COLLOQUES > COLLOQUE
COLLOQUIA n plural form of singular colloquium: informal gathering
COLLOQUY n conversation or conference
COLLOTYPE n method of lithographic printing from a flat surface of hardened gelatine: used mainly for fine-detail reproduction in monochrome or colour
COLLOTYPY > COLLOTYPE
COLLS > COLL
COLLUDE vb act in collusion
COLLUDED > COLLUDE
COLLUDER > COLLUDE
COLLUDERS > COLLUDE
COLLUDES > COLLUDE
COLLUDING > COLLUDE
COLLUSION n secret or illegal cooperation
COLLUSIVE > COLLUSION
COLLUVIA > COLLUVIUM
COLLUVIAL > COLLUVIUM
COLLUVIES n offscourings

COLLUVIUM n mixture of rock fragments from the bases of cliffs

COLLY n soot or grime, such as coal dust ▷ vb begrime

COLLYING > COLLY

COLLYRIA > COLLYRIUM

COLLYRIUM a technical name for an > EYEWASH

COLOBI > COLOBUS

COLOBID > COLOBUS

COLOBOMA n structural defect of the eye, esp in the choroid, retina, or iris

COLOBOMAS > COLOBOMA

COLOBUS n type of leaf-eating arboreal Old World monkey of W and central Africa, with a slender body, long silky fur, and a long tail

COLOBUSES > COLOBUS

COLOCATE vb to locate together

COLOCATED > COLOCATE

COLOCATES > COLOCATE

COLOCYNTH n type of Mediterranean and Asian climbing plant with bitter-tasting fruit

COLOG n logarithm of the reciprocal of a number

COLOGNE n mild perfume

COLOGNED > COLOGNE

COLOGNES > COLOGNE

COLOGS > COLOG

COLOMBARD n grape used to make wine

COLON n punctuation mark (:)

COLONE variant of > COLON

COLONEL n senior commissioned army or air-force officer

COLONELCY > COLONEL

COLONELS > COLONEL

COLONES > COLONE

COLONI > COLONUS

COLONIAL n inhabitant of a colony ▷ adj of or inhabiting a colony or colonies

COLONIALS > COLONIAL

COLONIC adj of or relating to the colon ▷ n irrigation of the colon by injecting large amounts of fluid high into the colon

COLONICS > COLONIC

COLONIES > COLONY

COLONISE same as > COLONIZE

COLONISED > COLONISE

COLONISER > COLONISE

COLONISES > COLONISE

COLONIST n settler in a colony

COLONISTS > COLONIST

COLONITIS same as > COLITIS

COLONIZE vb make into a colony

COLONIZED > COLONIZE

COLONIZER > COLONIZE

COLONIZES > COLONIZE

COLONNADE n row of columns

COLONS > COLON

COLONUS n ancient Roman farmer

COLONY n group of people who settle in a new country but remain under the rule of their homeland

COLOPHON n publisher's symbol on a book

COLOPHONS > COLOPHON

COLOPHONY another name for > ROSIN

COLOR same as > COLOUR

COLORABLE > COLOR

COLORABLY > COLOR

COLORADO adj (of a cigar) of middling colour and strength

COLORANT n any substance that imparts colour, such as a pigment, dye, or ink

COLORANTS > COLORANT

COLORBRED adj (of animals) bred for their colour

COLORCAST vb broadcast in colour

COLORED US spelling of > COLOURED

COLOREDS > COLORED

COLORER > COLOR

COLORERS > COLOR

COLORFAST adj variant of colourfast: (of a fabric) having a colour that does not run when washed

COLORFUL > COLOR

COLORIFIC adj producing, imparting, or relating to colour

COLORING > COLOUR

COLORINGS > COLOUR

COLORISE same as > COLOURIZE

COLORISED > COLORISE

COLORISER > COLORISE

COLORISES > COLORISE

COLORISM > COLOR

COLORISMS > COLOR

COLORIST > COLOR

COLORISTS > COLOR

COLORIZE same as > COLOURIZE

COLORIZED > COLOURIZE

COLORIZER > COLORIZE

COLORIZES > COLORIZE

COLORLESS > COLOR

COLORMAN same as > COLOURMAN

COLORMEN > COLORMAN

COLORS > COLOR

COLORWAY variant of > COLOURWAY

COLORWAYS > COLORWAY

COLORY same as > COLOURY

COLOSSAL adj very large

COLOSSEUM same as > COLISEUM

COLOSSI > COLOSSUS

COLOSSUS n huge statue

COLOSTOMY n operation to form an opening from the colon onto the surface of the body, for emptying the bowel

COLOSTRAL > COLOSTRUM

COLOSTRIC > COLOSTRUM

COLOSTRUM n thin milky secretion from the nipples that precedes and follows true lactation. It consists largely of serum and white blood cells

COLOTOMY n colonic incision

COLOUR n appearance of things as a result of reflecting light ▷ vb apply colour to

COLOURANT same as > COLORANT

COLOURED adj having colour ▷ n person who is not white

COLOUREDS > COLOURED

COLOURER > COLOUR

COLOURERS > COLOUR

COLOURFUL adj with bright or varied colours

COLOURING n application of colour

COLOURISE same as > COLOURIZE

COLOURIST n person who uses colour, esp an artist

COLOURIZE vb add colour electronically to (an old black-and-white film)

COLOURMAN n person who deals in paints

COLOURMEN > COLOURMAN

COLOURS > COLOUR

COLOURWAY n one of several different combinations of colours in which a given pattern is printed on fabrics, wallpapers, etc

COLOURY adj possessing colour

COLPITIS another name for > VAGINITIS

COLPOTOMY n surgical incision into the wall of the vagina

COLS > COL

COLT n young male horse ▷ vb to fool

COLTAN n metallic ore found esp in the E Congo, consisting of columbite and tantalite and used as a source of tantalum

COLTANS > COLTAN

COLTED > COLT

COLTER same as > COULTER

COLTERS > COULTER

COLTING > COLT

COLTISH adj

inexperienced

COLTISHLY > COLTISH

COLTS > COLT

COLTSFOOT n weed with yellow flowers and heart-shaped leaves

COLTWOOD n plant mentioned in Spenser's Faerie Queene

COLTWOODS > COLTWOOD

COLUBRIAD n epic poem about a snake

COLUBRID n type of snake such as the grass snake and whip snakes

COLUBRIDS > COLUBRID

COLUBRINE adj of or resembling a snake

COLUGO n flying lemur

COLUGOS > COLUGO

COLUMBARY n dovecote

COLUMBATE n niobate

COLUMBIC another word for > NIOBIC

COLUMBINE n garden flower with five petals ▷ adj of, relating to, or resembling a dove

COLUMBITE n black mineral occurring in coarse granite

COLUMBIUM the former name of > NIOBIUM

COLUMBOUS another word for > NIOBOUS

COLUMEL n in botany, the central column in a capsule

COLUMELLA n central part of the spore-producing body of some fungi and mosses

COLUMELS > COLUMEL

COLUMN n pillar ▷ vb create a column

COLUMNAL > COLUMN

COLUMNAR > COLUMN

COLUMNEA n flowering plant

COLUMNEAS > COLUMNEA

COLUMNED > COLUMN

COLUMNIST n journalist who writes a regular feature in a newspaper

COLUMNS > COLUMN

COLURE n either of two great circles on the celestial sphere, one of which passes through the celestial poles and the equinoxes and the other through the poles and the solstices

COLURES > COLURE

COLY n S African arboreal bird with a soft hairlike plumage, crested head, and very long tail

COLZA n oilseed rape, a Eurasian plant with bright yellow flowers

COLZAS > COLZA

COMA n state of deep unconsciousness

COMADE > COMAKE

COMAE > COMA

COMAKE vb to make together

COMAKER > COMAKE

COMAKERS > COMAKE

COMAKES > COMAKE

COMAKING > COMAKE

COMAL > COMA

COMANAGE vb to manage jointly

COMANAGED > COMANAGE

COMANAGER > COMANAGE

COMANAGES > COMANAGE

COMARB same as > COARB

COMARBS > COMARB

COMART n covenant

COMARTS > COMART

COMAS > COMA

COMATE adj having tufts of hair ▷ n companion

COMATES > COMATE

COMATIC > COMA

COMATIK variant of > KOMATIK

COMATIKS > COMATIK

COMATOSE adj in a coma

COMATULA same as > COMATULID

COMATULAE > COMATULID

COMATULID n any of a group of crinoid echinoderms, including the feather stars, in which the adults are free-swimming

COMB n toothed implement for arranging the hair ▷ vb use a comb on

COMBAT vb fight, struggle ▷ n fight or struggle

COMBATANT n fighter ▷ adj fighting

COMBATED > COMBAT

COMBATER > COMBAT

COMBATERS > COMBAT

COMBATING > COMBAT

COMBATIVE adj eager or ready to fight, argue, etc

COMBATS > COMBAT

COMBATTED > COMBAT

COMBE same as > COMB

COMBED > COMB

COMBER n long curling wave

COMBERS > COMBER

COMBES > COMBE

COMBI n combination boiler

COMBIER > COMBY

COMBIES > COMBY

COMBIEST > COMBY

COMBINATE adj betrothed

COMBINE vb join together ▷ n association of people or firms for a common purpose

COMBINED n competitive event consisting of two skiing competitions

COMBINEDS > COMBINE

COMBINER > COMBINE

COMBINERS > COMBINE

COMBINES > COMBINE

COMBING > COMB

COMBINGS npl loose hair or fibres removed by combing, esp from animals

COMBINING > COMBINE

COMBIS > COMBI

COMBLE n apex; zenith

COMBLES > COMBLE

COMBLESS adj without a comb

COMBLIKE adj resembling a comb

COMBO n small group of jazz musicians

COMBOS > COMBO

COMBOVER n hairstyle in which thinning hair is combed over the scalp

COMBOVERS > COMBOVER

COMBRETUM n any tree or shrub belonging to the genus Combretum

COMBS > COMB

COMBUST adj (of a star or planet) invisible for a period between 24 and 30 days each year due to its proximity to the sun ▷ vb burn

COMBUSTED > COMBUST

COMBUSTOR n combustion system of a jet engine or ramjet, comprising the combustion chamber, the fuel injection apparatus, and the igniter

COMBUSTS > COMBUST

COMBWISE adv in the manner of a comb

COMBY adj comb-like ▷ n combination boiler

COME vb move towards a place, arrive

COMEBACK n return to a former position ▷ vb return, esp to the memory

COMEBACKS > COMEBACK

COMEDDLE vb mix

COMEDDLED > COMEDDLE

COMEDDLES > COMEDDLE

COMEDIAN n entertainer who tells jokes

COMEDIANS > COMEDIAN

COMEDIC adj of or relating to comedy

COMEDIES > COMEDY

COMEDO the technical name for > BLACKHEAD

COMEDONES > COMEDO

COMEDOS > COMEDO

COMEDOWN n decline in status ▷ vb come to a place regarded as lower

COMEDOWNS > COMEDOWN

COMEDY n humorous play, film, or programme

COMELIER > COMELY

COMELIEST > COMELY

COMELILY > COMELY

COMELY adj nice-looking

COMEMBER n fellow member

COMEMBERS > COMEMBER

COMEOVER n person who has come from Britain to the Isle of Man to settle

COMEOVERS > COMEOVER

COMER n person who comes

COMERS > COMER

COMES > COME

COMET n heavenly body with a long luminous tail

COMETARY > COMET

COMETH > COME

COMETHER n coaxing; allure

COMETHERS > COMETHER

COMETIC > COMET

COMETS > COMET

COMFIER > COMFY

COMFIEST > COMFY

COMFINESS > COMFY

COMFIT n sugar-coated sweet

COMFITS > COMFIT

COMFITURE n confiture

COMFORT n physical ease or wellbeing ▷ vb soothe, console

COMFORTED > COMFORT

COMFORTER n person or thing that comforts

COMFORTS > COMFORT

COMFREY n tall plant with bell-shaped flowers

COMFREYS > COMFREY

COMFY adj comfortable

COMIC adj humorous, funny ▷ n comedian

COMICAL adj amusing

COMICALLY > COMICAL

COMICE n kind of pear

COMICES > COMICE

COMICS > COMIC

COMING > COME

COMINGLE same as > COMMINGLE

COMINGLED > COMMINGLE

COMINGLES > COMINGLE

COMINGS > COME

COMIQUE n comic actor

COMIQUES > COMIQUE

COMITADJI n Balkan guerrilla fighter

COMITAL adj relating to a count or earl

COMITATUS n leader's retinue

COMITIA n ancient Roman assembly that elected officials and exercised judicial and legislative authority

COMITIAL > COMITIA

COMITIAS > COMITIA

COMITIES > COMITY

COMITY n friendly politeness, esp between different countries

COMIX n comic books in general

COMM as in comm badge small wearable badge-shaped radio transmitter and receiver

COMMA n punctuation mark (,)

COMMAND vb order ▷ n authoritative instruction that something must be done

COMMANDED > COMMAND

COMMANDER n military officer in command of a group or operation

COMMANDO n (member of) a military unit trained for swift raids in enemy territory

COMMANDOS > COMMANDO

COMMANDS > COMMAND

COMMAS > COMMA

COMMATA > COMMA

COMMENCE vb begin

COMMENCED > COMMENCE

COMMENCER > COMMENCE

COMMENCES > COMMENCE

COMMEND vb praise

COMMENDAM n temporary holding of an ecclesiastical benefice

COMMENDED > COMMEND

COMMENDER > COMMEND

COMMENDS > COMMEND

COMMENSAL adj (of two different species of plant or animal) living in close association, such that one species benefits without harming the other ▷ n commensal plant or animal

COMMENT n remark ▷ vb make a comment

COMMENTED > COMMENT

COMMENTER > COMMENT

COMMENTOR > COMMENT

COMMENTS > COMMENT

COMMER same as > COMER

COMMERCE n buying and selling, trade ▷ vb to trade

COMMERCED > COMMERCE

COMMERCES > COMMERCE

COMMERE n female compere

COMMERES > COMMERE

COMMERGE vb to merge together

COMMERGED > COMMERGE

COMMERGES > COMMERGE

COMMERS > COMMER

COMMIE adj communist

COMMIES > COMMIE

COMMINATE vb to anathematise

COMMINGLE vb mix or be mixed

COMMINUTE vb break (a bone) into several small fragments

COMMIS n apprentice waiter or chef ▷ adj (of a waiter or chef) apprentice

COMMISSAR n (formerly) official responsible for political education in Communist countries

COMMIT vb perform (a crime or error)

COMMITS > COMMIT

COMMITTAL n act of committing or pledging

COMMITTED > COMMIT

COMMITTEE n group of people appointed to perform a specified service or function

COMMITTER > COMMIT

COMMIX *a rare word for* >MIX

COMMIXED > COMMIX

COMMIXES > COMMIX

COMMIXING > COMMIX

COMMIXT > COMMIX

COMMO *short for* > COMMUNIST

COMMODE *n* seat with a hinged flap concealing a chamber pot

COMMODES > COMMODE

COMMODIFY *vb* to make into a commodity

COMMODITY *n* something that can be bought or sold

COMMODO *same as* > COMODO

COMMODORE *n* senior commissioned officer in the navy

COMMON *adj* occurring often ▷ *n* area of grassy land belonging to a community ▷ *vb* sit at table with strangers

COMMONAGE *n* use of something, esp a pasture, in common with others

COMMONED > COMMON

COMMONER *n* person who does not belong to the nobility

COMMONERS > COMMONER

COMMONEST > COMMON

COMMONEY *n* playing marble of a common sort

COMMONEYS > COMMONEY

COMMONING > COMMON

COMMONLY *adv* usually

COMMONS *n* people not of noble birth viewed as forming a political order

COMMORANT *n* resident

COMMOS > COMMO

COMMOT *n* in medieval Wales, a division of land

COMMOTE *same as* > COMMOT

COMMOTES > COMMOTE

COMMOTION *n* noisy disturbance

COMMOTS > COMMOT

COMMOVE *vb* disturb

COMMOVED > COMMOVE

COMMOVES > COMMOVE

COMMOVING > COMMOVE

COMMS *npl* communications

COMMUNAL *adj* shared

COMMUNARD *n* member of a commune

COMMUNE *n* group of people who live together and share everything ▷ *vb* feel very close (to)

COMMUNED > COMMUNE

COMMUNER > COMMUNE

COMMUNERS > COMMUNE

COMMUNES > COMMUNE

COMMUNING > COMMUNE

COMMUNION *n* sharing of thoughts or feelings

COMMUNISE *same as* > COMMUNIZE

COMMUNISM *n* belief that all property and means of production should be shared by the community

COMMUNIST *n* supporter of any form of communism ▷ *adj* of, characterized by, favouring, or relating to communism

COMMUNITY *n* all the people living in one district

COMMUNIZE *vb* make (property) public

COMMUTATE *vb* reverse the direction of (an electric current)

COMMUTE *vb* travel daily to and from work ▷ *n* journey made by commuting

COMMUTED > COMMUTE

COMMUTER *n* person who commutes to and from work

COMMUTERS > COMMUTER

COMMUTES > COMMUTE

COMMUTING > COMMUTE

COMMUTUAL *adj* mutual

COMMY *same as* > COMMIE

COMODO *adv* (to be performed) at a convenient relaxed speed

COMONOMER *n* monomer that, with another, constitutes a copolymer

COMORBID *adj* (of illness) happening at same time as other illness

COMOSE *another word for* > COMATE

COMOUS *adj* hairy

COMP *n* person who sets and corrects type ▷ *vb* set or correct type

COMPACT *adj* closely packed ▷ *n* small flat case containing a mirror and face powder ▷ *vb* pack closely together

COMPACTED > COMPACT

COMPACTER > COMPACT

COMPACTLY > COMPACT

COMPACTOR *n* machine which compresses waste material for easier disposal

COMPACTS > COMPACT

COMPADRE *n* masculine friend

COMPADRES > COMPADRE

COMPAGE *obsolete form of* > COMPAGES

COMPAGES *n* structure or framework

COMPAND *vb* (of a transmitter signal) to compress before, and expand after, transmission

COMPANDED > COMPAND

COMPANDER *n* system for improving the signal-to-noise ratio of a signal at a transmitter or recorder by first compressing the volume

range of the signal and then restoring it to its original amplitude level at the receiving or reproducing apparatus

COMPANDOR *same as* > COMPANDER

COMPANDS > COMPAND

COMPANIED > COMPANY

COMPANIES > COMPANY

COMPANING > COMPANY

COMPANION *n* person who associates with or accompanies someone ▷ *vb* accompany or be a companion to

COMPANY *n* business organization ▷ *vb* associate or keep company with someone

COMPARE *vb* examine (things) and point out the resemblances or differences

COMPARED > COMPARE

COMPARER > COMPARE

COMPARERS > COMPARE

COMPARES > COMPARE

COMPARING > COMPARE

COMPART *vb* to divide into parts

COMPARTED > COMPART

COMPARTS > COMPART

COMPAS *n* rhythm in flamenco

COMPASS *n* instrument for showing direction, with a needle that points north ▷ *vb* encircle or surround

COMPASSED > COMPASS

COMPASSES > COMPASS

COMPAST *adj* rounded

COMPEAR *vb* in Scots law, to appear in court

COMPEARED > COMPEAR

COMPEARS > COMPEAR

COMPED > COMP

COMPEER *n* person of equal rank, status, or ability ▷ *vb* to equal

COMPEERED > COMPEER

COMPEERS > COMPEER

COMPEL *vb* force (to be or do)

COMPELLED > COMPEL

COMPELLER > COMPEL

COMPELS > COMPEL

COMPEND *n* compendium

COMPENDIA *n* plural form of singular compendium: book containing a collection of useful hints

COMPENDS > COMPEND

COMPER *n* person who regularly enters competitions in newspapers, magazines, etc, esp competitions offering consumer goods as prizes

COMPERE *n* person who presents a stage, radio, or television show ▷ *vb* be the compere of

COMPERED > COMPERE

COMPERES > COMPERE

COMPERING > COMPERE

COMPERS > COMPER

COMPESCE *vb* to curb

COMPESCED > COMPESCE

COMPESCES > COMPESCE

COMPETE *vb* try to win or achieve (a prize, profit, etc)

COMPETED > COMPETE

COMPETENT *adj* having the skill or knowledge to do something well

COMPETES > COMPETE

COMPETING > COMPETE

COMPILE *vb* collect and arrange (information), esp to make a book

COMPILED > COMPILE

COMPILER *n* person who compiles information

COMPILERS > COMPILER

COMPILES > COMPILE

COMPILING > COMPILE

COMPING > COMP

COMPITAL *adj* pertaining to crossroads

COMPLAIN *vb* express resentment or displeasure

COMPLAINS > COMPLAIN

COMPLAINT *n* complaining

COMPLEAT *an archaic spelling of* > COMPLETE

COMPLECT *vb* interweave or entwine

COMPLECTS > COMPLECT

COMPLETE *adj* thorough, absolute ▷ *vb* finish

COMPLETED > COMPLETE

COMPLETER > COMPLETE

COMPLETES > COMPLETE

COMPLEX *adj* made up of parts ▷ *n* whole made up of parts ▷ *vb* to form a complex

COMPLEXED > COMPLEX

COMPLEXER > COMPLEX

COMPLEXES > COMPLEX

COMPLEXLY > COMPLEX

COMPLEXUS *n* complex

COMPLIANT *adj* complying, obliging, or yielding

COMPLICE *n* associate or accomplice

COMPLICES > COMPLICE

COMPLICIT *adj* involved in a crime or questionable act

COMPLIED > COMPLY

COMPLIER > COMPLY

COMPLIERS > COMPLY

COMPLIES > COMPLY

COMPLIN *same as* > COMPLINE

COMPLINE *n* last service of the day in the Roman Catholic Church

COMPLINES > COMPLINE

COMPLINS > COMPLIN

COMPLISH *vb* accomplish

COMPLOT *n* plot or conspiracy ▷ *vb* plot together

COMPLOTS > COMPLOT

COMPLUVIA n plural form of singular compluvium: an unroofed space over the atrium in a Roman house, though which rain fell and was collected

COMPLY vb act in accordance (with)

COMPLYING > COMPLY

COMPO n mixture of materials, such as mortar, plaster, etc ▷ adj intended to last for several days

COMPONE same as > COMPONY

COMPONENT adj (being) part of a whole ▷ n constituent part or feature of a whole

COMPONY adj made up of alternating metal and colour, colour and fur, or fur and metal

COMPORT vb behave (oneself) in a specified way

COMPORTED > COMPORT

COMPORTS > COMPORT

COMPOS > COMPO

COMPOSE vb put together

COMPOSED adj calm

COMPOSER n person who writes music

COMPOSERS > COMPOSER

COMPOSES > COMPOSE

COMPOSING > COMPOSE

COMPOSITE adj made up of separate parts ▷ n something composed of separate parts ▷ vb merge related motions from local branches of (a political party, trade union, etc) so as to produce a manageable number of proposals for discussion at national level

COMPOST n decayed plants used as a fertilizer ▷ vb make (vegetable matter) into compost

COMPOSTED > COMPOST

COMPOSTER n bin or other container used to turn garden waste into compost

COMPOSTS > COMPOST

COMPOSURE n calmness

COMPOT same as > COMPOTE

COMPOTE n fruit stewed with sugar

COMPOTES > COMPOTE

COMPOTIER n dish for holding compote

COMPOTS > COMPOT

COMPOUND adj (thing, esp chemical) made up of two or more combined parts or elements ▷ vb combine or make by combining ▷ n fenced enclosure containing buildings

COMPOUNDS > COMPOUND

COMPRADOR n (formerly in China and some other Asian countries) a native agent of a foreign enterprise

COMPRESS vb squeeze together ▷ n pad applied to stop bleeding or cool inflammation

COMPRINT vb to print jointly

COMPRINTS > COMPRINT

COMPRISAL > COMPRISE

COMPRISE vb be made up of or make up

COMPRISED > COMPRISE

COMPRISES > COMPRISE

COMPRIZE same as > COMPRISE

COMPRIZED > COMPRIZE

COMPRIZES > COMPRIZE

COMPS > COMP

COMPT obsolete variant of > COUNT

COMPTABLE n countable

COMPTED > COMPT

COMPTER n formerly, a prison

COMPTERS > COMPT

COMPTIBLE same as > COMPTABLE

COMPTING > COUNT

COMPTROLL obsolete variant of > CONTROL

COMPTS > COUNT

COMPULSE vb to compel

COMPULSED > COMPULSE

COMPULSES > COMPULSE

COMPUTANT n calculator

COMPUTE vb calculate, esp using a computer ▷ n calculation

COMPUTED > COMPUTE

COMPUTER n electronic machine that stores and processes data

COMPUTERS > COMPUTER

COMPUTES > COMPUTE

COMPUTING n activity of using computers and writing programs for them ▷ adj of or relating to computers

COMPUTIST n one who computes

COMRADE n fellow member of a union or socialist political party

COMRADELY > COMRADE

COMRADERY n comradeship

COMRADES > COMRADE

COMS npl one-piece woollen undergarment with longs sleeves and legs

COMSYMP n Communist Party sympathizer

COMSYMPS > COMSYMP

COMTE n European nobleman

COMTES > COMTE

COMUS n wild party

COMUSES > COMUS

CON vb deceive, swindle ▷ n convict ▷ prep with

CONACRE n farming land let for a season or eleven months ▷ vb to let conacre

CONACRED > CONACRE

CONACRES > CONACRE

CONACRING > CONACRE

CONARIA > CONARIUM

CONARIAL > CONARIUM

CONARIUM n pineal gland

CONATION n element in psychological processes that tends towards activity or change and appears as desire, volition, and striving

CONATIONS > CONATION

CONATIVE adj denoting an aspect of verbs in some languages used to indicate the effort of the agent in performing the activity described by the verb

CONATUS n effort or striving of natural impulse

CONCAUSE n shared cause

CONCAUSES > CONCAUSE

CONCAVE adj curving inwards ▷ vb make concave

CONCAVED > CONCAVE

CONCAVELY > CONCAVE

CONCAVES > CONCAVE

CONCAVING > CONCAVE

CONCAVITY n state or quality of being concave

CONCEAL vb cover and hide

CONCEALED > CONCEAL

CONCEALER > CONCEAL

CONCEALS > CONCEAL

CONCEDE vb admit to be true

CONCEDED > CONCEDE

CONCEDER > CONCEDE

CONCEDERS > CONCEDE

CONCEDES > CONCEDE

CONCEDING > CONCEDE

CONCEDO interj I allow; I concede (a point)

CONCEIT n too high an opinion of oneself ▷ vb like or be able to bear (something, such as food or drink)

CONCEITED adj having an excessively high opinion of oneself

CONCEITS > CONCEIT

CONCEITY adj full of conceit

CONCEIVE vb imagine, think

CONCEIVED > CONCEIVE

CONCEIVER > CONCEIVE

CONCEIVES > CONCEIVE

CONCENT n concord, as of sounds, voices, etc

CONCENTER same as > CONCENTRE

CONCENTRE vb converge or cause to converge on a common centre

CONCENTS > CONCENT

CONCENTUS n vocal harmony

CONCEPT n abstract or general idea

CONCEPTI > CONCEPTUS

CONCEPTS > CONCEPT

CONCEPTUS n any product of conception, including the embryo, foetus and surrounding tissue

CONCERN n anxiety, worry ▷ vb worry (someone)

CONCERNED adj interested, involved

CONCERNS > CONCERN

CONCERT n musical entertainment

CONCERTED adj done together

CONCERTI > CONCERTO

CONCERTO n large-scale composition for a solo instrument and orchestra

CONCERTOS > CONCERTO

CONCERTS > CONCERT

CONCETTI > CONCETTO

CONCETTO n conceit, ingenious thought

CONCH same as > CONCHA

CONCHA n any bodily organ or part resembling a shell in shape, such as the external ear

CONCHAE > CONCHA

CONCHAL > CONCHA

CONCHAS > CONCHA

CONCHATE adj shell-shaped

CONCHE vb (in chocolate-making) to use a conche (machine which mixes and smooths the chocolate mass)

CONCHED > CONCHE

CONCHES > CONCHE

CONCHIE n conscientious objector

CONCHIES > CONCHIE

CONCHING > CONCHE

CONCHITIS n inflammation of the outer ear

CONCHO n American metal ornament

CONCHOID n type of plane curve

CONCHOIDS > CONCHOID

CONCHOS > CONCHO

CONCHS > CONCH

CONCHY same as > CONCHIE

CONCIERGE n (in France) caretaker in a block of flats

CONCILIAR adj of, from, or by means of a council, esp an ecclesiastical one

CONCISE adj brief and to the point ▷ vb mutilate

CONCISED > CONCISE

CONCISELY > CONCISE

CONCISER > CONCISE

CONCISES > CONCISE

CONCISEST > CONCISE

CONCISING > CONCISE

CONCISION n quality of being concise

CONCLAVE n secret meeting

CONCLAVES > CONCLAVE

CONCLUDE vb decide by reasoning

CONCLUDED > CONCLUDE

CONCLUDER > CONCLUDE

CONCLUDES > CONCLUDE
CONCOCT *vb* make up (a story or plan)
CONCOCTED > CONCOCT
CONCOCTER > CONCOCT
CONCOCTOR > CONCOCT
CONCOCTS > CONCOCT
CONCOLOR *adj* of a single colour
CONCORD *n* state of peaceful agreement, harmony ▷ *vb* to agree
CONCORDAL > CONCORD
CONCORDAT *n* pact or treaty
CONCORDED > CONCORD
CONCORDS > CONCORD
CONCOURS *n* contest
CONCOURSE *n* large open public place where people can gather
CONCREATE *vb* to create at the same time
CONCRETE *n* mixture of cement, sand, stone, and water, used in building ▷ *vb* cover with concrete ▷ *adj* made of concrete
CONCRETED > CONCRETE
CONCRETES > CONCRETE
CONCREW *vb* to grow together
CONCREWED > CONCREW
CONCREWS > CONCREW
CONCUBINE *n* woman living in a man's house but not married to him and kept for his sexual pleasure
CONCUPIES > CONCUPY
CONCUPY *n* concupiscence
CONCUR *vb* agree
CONCURRED > CONCUR
CONCURS > CONCUR
CONCUSS *vb* injure (the brain) by a fall or blow
CONCUSSED > CONCUSS
CONCUSSES > CONCUSS
CONCYCLIC *adj* (of a set of geometric points) lying on a common circle
COND *old inflection of >* CON
CONDEMN *vb* express disapproval of
CONDEMNED > CONDEMN
CONDEMNER > CONDEMN
CONDEMNOR > CONDEMN
CONDEMNS > CONDEMN
CONDENSE *vb* make shorter
CONDENSED *adj* (of printers' type) narrower than usual for a particular height
CONDENSER *same as* **> CAPACITOR**
CONDENSES > CONDENSE
CONDER *n* person who directs the steering of a vessel
CONDERS > CONDER
CONDIDDLE *vb* to steal
CONDIE *n* culvert; tunnel
CONDIES > CONDIE
CONDIGN *adj* (esp of a

punishment) fitting
CONDIGNLY > CONDIGN
CONDIMENT *n* seasoning for food, such as salt or pepper
CONDITION *n* particular state of being ▷ *vb* train or influence to behave in a particular way
CONDO *n* condominium
CONDOES > CONDO
CONDOLE *vb* express sympathy with someone in grief, pain, etc
CONDOLED > CONDOLE
CONDOLENT *adj* expressing sympathy with someone in grief
CONDOLER > CONDOLE
CONDOLERS > CONDOLE
CONDOLES > CONDOLE
CONDOLING > CONDOLE
CONDOM *n* rubber sheath worn on the penis or in the vagina during sexual intercourse to prevent conception or infection
CONDOMS > CONDOM
CONDONE *vb* overlook or forgive (wrongdoing)
CONDONED > CONDONE
CONDONER > CONDONE
CONDONERS > CONDONE
CONDONES > CONDONE
CONDONING > CONDONE
CONDOR *n* large vulture of S America
CONDORES > CONDOR
CONDORS > CONDOR
CONDOS > CONDO
CONDUCE *vb* lead or contribute (to a result)
CONDUCED > CONDUCE
CONDUCER > CONDUCE
CONDUCERS > CONDUCE
CONDUCES > CONDUCE
CONDUCING > CONDUCE
CONDUCIVE *adj* likely to lead (to)
CONDUCT *n* management of an activity ▷ *vb* carry out (a task)
CONDUCTED > CONDUCT
CONDUCTI > CONDUCTUS
CONDUCTOR *n* person who conducts musicians
CONDUCTS > CONDUCT
CONDUCTUS *n* medieval liturgical composition
CONDUIT *n* channel or tube for fluid or cables
CONDUITS > CONDUIT
CONDYLAR > CONDYLE
CONDYLE *n* rounded projection on the articulating end of a bone, such as the ball portion of a ball-and-socket joint
CONDYLES > CONDYLE
CONDYLOID *adj* of or resembling a condyle
CONDYLOMA *n* skin tumour near the anus or genital organs, esp as a result of syphilis

CONE *n* object with a circular base, tapering to a point ▷ *vb* shape like a cone or part of a cone
CONED > CONE
CONELRAD *n* US defence and information system for use in the event of air attack
CONELRADS > CONELRAD
CONENOSE *n* bloodsucking bug of the genus Triatoma
CONENOSES > CONENOSE
CONEPATE *same as* **> CONEPATL**
CONEPATES > CONEPATE
CONEPATL *n* skunk
CONEPATLS > CONEPATL
CONES > CONE
CONEY *same as* **>** CONY
CONEYS > CONEY
CONF *n* online forum
CONFAB *n* conversation ▷ *vb* converse
CONFABBED > CONFAB
CONFABS > CONFAB
CONFECT *vb* prepare by combining ingredients
CONFECTED > CONFECT
CONFECTS > CONFECT
CONFER *vb* discuss together
CONFEREE *n* person who takes part in a conference
CONFEREES > CONFEREE
CONFERRAL > CONFER
CONFERRED > CONFER
CONFERREE *same as* **> CONFEREE**
CONFERRER > CONFER
CONFERS > CONFER
CONFERVA *n* type of threadlike green alga typically occurring in fresh water
CONFERVAE > CONFERVA
CONFERVAL > CONFERVA
CONFERVAS > CONFERVA
CONFESS *vb* admit (a fault or crime)
CONFESSED > CONFESS
CONFESSES > CONFESS
CONFESSOR *n* priest who hears confessions
CONFEST *adj* admitted
CONFESTLY *adv* confessedly
CONFETTI *n* small pieces of coloured paper thrown at weddings
CONFETTO *n* sweetmeat
CONFIDANT *n* person confided in
CONFIDE *vb* tell someone (a secret)
CONFIDED > CONFIDE
CONFIDENT *adj* sure, esp of oneself
CONFIDER > CONFIDE
CONFIDERS > CONFIDE
CONFIDES > CONFIDE
CONFIDING *adj* trusting
CONFIGURE *vb* to design or set up

CONFINE *vb* keep within bounds ▷ *n* limit
CONFINED *adj* enclosed or restricted
CONFINER > CONFINE
CONFINERS > CONFINE
CONFINES > CONFINE
CONFINING > CONFINE
CONFIRM *vb* prove to be true
CONFIRMED *adj* firmly established in a habit or condition
CONFIRMEE *n* person to whom a confirmation is made
CONFIRMER > CONFIRM
CONFIRMOR *n* person who makes a confirmation
CONFIRMS > CONFIRM
CONFISEUR *n* confectioner
CONFIT *n* preserve
CONFITEOR *n* Catholic prayer asking for forgiveness
CONFITS > CONFIT
CONFITURE *n* confection, preserve of fruit, etc
CONFIX *vb* to fasten
CONFIXED > CONFIX
CONFIXES > CONFIX
CONFIXING > CONFIX
CONFLATE *vb* combine or blend into a whole
CONFLATED > CONFLATE
CONFLATES > CONFLATE
CONFLICT *n* disagreement ▷ *vb* be incompatible
CONFLICTS > CONFLICT
CONFLUENT *adj* flowing together or merging ▷ *n* stream that flows into another, usually of approximately equal size
CONFLUX *n* merging or following togther, especially of rivers
CONFLUXES > CONFLUX
CONFOCAL *adj* having a common focus or common foci
CONFORM *vb* comply with accepted standards or customs
CONFORMAL *adj* (of a transformation) preserving the angles of the depicted surface
CONFORMED > CONFORM
CONFORMER > CONFORM
CONFORMS > CONFORM
CONFOUND *vb* astound, bewilder
CONFOUNDS > CONFOUND
CONFRERE *n* colleague
CONFRERES > CONFRERE
CONFRERIE *n* brotherhood
CONFRONT *vb* come face to face with
CONFRONTE *adj* in heraldry, (of two animals) face to face
CONFRONTS > CONFRONT

C

CONFS > CONF

CONFUSE vb mix up

CONFUSED adj lacking a clear understanding of something

CONFUSES > CONFUSE

CONFUSING adj causing bewilderment

CONFUSION n mistaking one person or thing for another

CONFUTE vb prove wrong

CONFUTED > CONFUTE

CONFUTER > CONFUTE

CONFUTERS > CONFUTE

CONFUTES > CONFUTE

CONFUTING > CONFUTE

CONGA n dance performed by a number of people in single file ▷ vb dance the conga

CONGAED > CONGA

CONGAING > CONGA

CONGAS > CONGA

CONGE n permission to depart or dismissal, esp when formal ▷ vb to take one's leave

CONGEAL vb (of a liquid) become thick and sticky

CONGEALED > CONGEAL

CONGEALER > CONGEAL

CONGEALS > CONGEAL

CONGED > CONGE

CONGEE same as > CONGE

CONGEED > CONGEE

CONGEEING > CONGEE

CONGEES > CONGEE

CONGEING > CONGE

CONGENER n member of a class, group, or other category, esp any animal of a specified genus

CONGENERS > CONGENER

CONGENIAL adj pleasant, agreeable

CONGENIC adj (of inbred animal cells) genetically identical except for a single gene locus

CONGER n large sea eel

CONGERIES n collection of objects or ideas

CONGERS > CONGER

CONGES > CONGE

CONGEST vb crowd or become crowded to excess

CONGESTED adj crowded to excess

CONGESTS > CONGEST

CONGIARY n Roman emperor's gift to the people or soldiers

CONGII > CONGIUS

CONGIUS n unit of liquid measure equal to 1 Imperial gallon

CONGLOBE vb to gather into a globe or ball

CONGLOBED > CONGLOBE

CONGLOBES > CONGLOBE

CONGO same as > CONGOU

CONGOES > CONGOU

CONGOS > CONGO

CONGOU n kind of black tea from China

CONGOUS > CONGOU

CONGRATS sentence substitute congratulations

CONGREE vb to agree

CONGREED > CONGREE

CONGREES > CONGREE

CONGREET vb (of two or more people) to greet one another

CONGREETS > CONGREET

CONGRESS n formal meeting for discussion

CONGRUE vb to agree

CONGRUED > CONGRUE

CONGRUENT adj similar, corresponding

CONGRUES > CONGRUE

CONGRUING > CONGRUE

CONGRUITY > CONGRUOUS

CONGRUOUS adj appropriate or in keeping

CONI > CONUS

CONIA same as > CONIINE

CONIAS > CONIINE

CONIC adj having the shape of a cone

CONICAL adj cone-shaped

CONICALLY > CONIC

CONICINE same as > CONIINE

CONICINES > CONICINE

CONICITY > CONICAL

CONICS n branch of geometry concerned with the parabola, ellipse, and hyperbola

CONIDIA > CONIDIUM

CONIDIAL > CONIDIUM

CONIDIAN > CONIDIUM

CONIDIUM n asexual spore formed at the tip of a specialized filament in certain types of fungi

CONIES > CONY

CONIFER n cone-bearing tree, such as the fir or pine

CONIFERS > CONIFER

CONIFORM adj cone-shaped

CONIINE n colourless poisonous soluble liquid alkaloid found in hemlock

CONIINES > CONIINE

CONIMA n gum resin from the conium hemlock tree

CONIMAS > CONIMA

CONIN same as > CONIINE

CONINE same as > CONIINE

CONINES > CONINE

CONING > CONE

CONINS > CONIN

CONIOLOGY a variant spelling of > KONIOLOGY

CONIOSES > CONIOSIS

CONIOSIS n any disease or condition caused by dust inhalation

CONIUM n N temperate umbelliferous plant, esp hemlock

CONIUMS > CONIUM

CONJECT vb to conjecture

CONJECTED > CONJECT

CONJECTS > CONJECT

CONJEE vb prepare as, or in, a conjee (a gruel of boiled rice and water)

CONJEED > CONJEE

CONJEEING > CONJEE

CONJEES > CONJEE

CONJOIN vb join or become joined

CONJOINED > CONJOIN

CONJOINER > CONJOIN

CONJOINS > CONJOIN

CONJOINT adj united, joint, or associated

CONJUGAL adj of marriage

CONJUGANT n either of a pair of organisms or gametes undergoing conjugation

CONJUGATE vb inflect (a verb) systematically

CONJUNCT adj joined ▷ n one of the propositions or formulas in a conjunction

CONJUNCTS > CONJUNCT

CONJUNTO n style of Mexican music

CONJUNTOS > CONJUNTO

CONJURE vb perform tricks that appear to be magic

CONJURED > CONJURE

CONJURER same as > CONJUROR

CONJURERS > CONJUROR

CONJURES > CONJURE

CONJURIES > CONJURY

CONJURING n performance of tricks that appear to defy natural laws ▷ adj denoting or relating to such tricks or entertainment

CONJUROR n person who performs magic tricks for people's entertainment

CONJURORS > CONJUROR

CONJURY n magic

CONK n nose ▷ vb strike (someone) on the head or nose

CONKED > CONK

CONKER n nut of the horse chestnut

CONKERS n game played with conkers tied on strings

CONKIER > CONKY

CONKIEST > CONKY

CONKING > CONK

CONKS > CONK

CONKY adj affected by the timber disease, conk

CONN same as > CON

CONNATE adj existing in a person or thing from birth

CONNATELY > CONNATE

CONNATION n joining of similar parts or organs

CONNATURE n sharing a common nature or character

CONNE same as > CON

CONNECT vb join together

CONNECTED adj joined or linked together

CONNECTER > CONNECT

CONNECTOR > CONNECT

CONNECTS > CONNECT

CONNED > CON

CONNER same as > CONDER

CONNERS > CONNER

CONNES > CONNE

CONNEXION n act or state of connecting

CONNEXIVE adj connective

CONNIE n tram or bus conductor

CONNIES > CONNIE

CONNING > CON

CONNINGS > CON

CONNIVE vb allow (wrongdoing) by ignoring it

CONNIVED > CONNIVE

CONNIVENT adj (of parts of plants and animals) touching without being fused, as some petals, insect wings, etc

CONNIVER > CONNIVE

CONNIVERS > CONNIVE

CONNIVERY n act of conniving

CONNIVES > CONNIVE

CONNIVING > CONNIVE

CONNOTATE vb to connote

CONNOTE vb (of a word, phrase, etc) to imply or suggest (associations or ideas) other than the literal meaning

CONNOTED > CONNOTE

CONNOTES > CONNOTE

CONNOTING > CONNOTE

CONNOTIVE adj act or state of connecting

CONNS > CONN

CONNUBIAL adj of marriage

CONODONT n any of various small Palaeozoic toothlike fossils derived from an extinct eel-like marine animal

CONODONTS > CONODONT

CONOID n geometric surface formed by rotating a parabola, ellipse, or hyperbola about one axis ▷ adj conical, cone-shaped

CONOIDAL same as > CONOID

CONOIDIC > CONOID

CONOIDS > CONOID

CONOMINEE n joint nominee

CONQUER vb defeat

CONQUERED > CONQUER

CONQUERER variant of > CONQUEROR

CONQUEROR > CONQUER

CONQUERS > CONQUER

CONQUEST n conquering

CONQUESTS > CONQUEST

CONQUIAN same as > COONCAN

CONQUIANS > COONCAN

CONS > CON

CONSCIENT adj conscious

CONSCIOUS adj alert and awake ▷ n conscious part of the mind

CONSCRIBE vb to enrol compulsorily

CONSCRIPT n person enrolled for compulsory military service ▷ vb enrol (someone) for compulsory military service

CONSEIL n advice

CONSEILS > CONSEIL

CONSENSUS n general agreement

CONSENT n agreement, permission ▷ vb permit, agree to

CONSENTED > CONSENT

CONSENTER > CONSENT

CONSENTS > CONSENT

CONSERVE vb protect from harm, decay, or loss ▷ n jam containing large pieces of fruit

CONSERVED > CONSERVE

CONSERVER > CONSERVE

CONSERVES > CONSERVE

CONSIDER vb regard as

CONSIDERS > CONSIDER

CONSIGN vb put somewhere

CONSIGNED > CONSIGN

CONSIGNEE n person, agent, organization, etc, to which merchandise is consigned

CONSIGNER same as > CONSIGNOR

CONSIGNOR n person, enterprise, etc, that consigns goods

CONSIGNS > CONSIGN

CONSIST vb be composed (of)

CONSISTED > CONSIST

CONSISTS > CONSIST

CONSOCIES n natural community with a single dominant species

CONSOL n consolidated annuity, a British government bond

CONSOLATE vb to console

CONSOLE vb comfort in distress ▷ n panel of controls for electronic equipment

CONSOLED > CONSOLE

CONSOLER > CONSOLE

CONSOLERS > CONSOLE

CONSOLES > CONSOLE

CONSOLING > CONSOLE

CONSOLS npl irredeemable British government securities carrying annual interest rates of two and a half or four per cent

CONSOLUTE adj (of two or more liquids) mutually soluble in all proportions

CONSOMME n thin clear meat soup

CONSOMMES > CONSOMME

CONSONANT n speech sound made by partially or completely blocking the breath stream ▷ adj agreeing (with)

CONSONOUS adj harmonious

CONSORT vb keep company (with) ▷ n husband or wife of a monarch

CONSORTED > CONSORT

CONSORTER > CONSORT

CONSORTIA n plural form of singular consortium: association of financiers, companies etc

CONSORTS > CONSORT

CONSPIRE vb plan a crime together in secret

CONSPIRED > CONSPIRE

CONSPIRER > CONSPIRE

CONSPIRES > CONSPIRE

CONSPUE vb spit on with contempt

CONSPUED > CONSPUE

CONSPUES > CONSPUE

CONSPUING > CONSPUE

CONSTABLE n police officer of the lowest rank

CONSTANCY n quality of having a resolute mind, purpose, or affection

CONSTANT adj continuous ▷ n unvarying quantity

CONSTANTS > CONSTANT

CONSTATE vb to affirm

CONSTATED > CONSTATE

CONSTATES > CONSTATE

CONSTER obsolete variant of > CONSTRUE

CONSTERED > CONSTRUE

CONSTERS > CONSTRUE

CONSTRAIN vb compel, force

CONSTRICT vb make narrower by squeezing

CONSTRUAL n act of construing

CONSTRUCT vb build or put together ▷ n complex idea resulting from the combination of simpler ideas

CONSTRUE vb interpret ▷ n something that is construed, such as a piece of translation

CONSTRUED > CONSTRUE

CONSTRUER > CONSTRUE

CONSTRUES > CONSTRUE

CONSUL n official representing a state in a foreign country

CONSULAGE n duty paid by merchants for a consul's protection of their goods while abroad

CONSULAR n anyone of consular rank

CONSULARS > CONSULAR

CONSULATE n workplace or position of a consul

CONSULS > CONSUL

CONSULT vb go to for advice or information

CONSULTA n official planning meeting

CONSULTAS > CONSULTA

CONSULTED > CONSULT

CONSULTEE n person who is consulted

CONSULTER > CONSULT

CONSULTOR > CONSULT

CONSULTS > CONSULT

CONSUME vb eat or drink

CONSUMED > CONSUME

CONSUMER n person who buys goods or uses services

CONSUMERS > CONSUMER

CONSUMES > CONSUME

CONSUMING > CONSUME

CONSUMPT n quantity used up; consumption

CONSUMPTS > CONSUMPT

CONTACT n communicating ▷ vb get in touch with ▷ interj (formerly) a call made by the pilot to indicate that an aircraft's ignition is switched on and that the engine is ready for starting by swinging the propeller

CONTACTED > CONTACT

CONTACTEE n person contacted by aliens

CONTACTOR n type of switch for repeatedly opening and closing an electric circuit. Its operation can be mechanical, electromagnetic, or pneumatic

CONTACTS > CONTACT

CONTADINA n female Italian farmer

CONTADINE > CONTADINA

CONTADINI > CONTADINO

CONTADINO n Italian farmer

CONTAGIA > CONTAGIUM

CONTAGION n passing on of disease by contact

CONTAGIUM n specific virus or other direct cause of any infectious disease

CONTAIN vb hold or be capable of holding

CONTAINED > CONTAIN

CONTAINER n object used to hold or store things in

CONTAINS > CONTAIN

CONTANGO n (formerly, on the London Stock Exchange) postponement of payment for and delivery of stock from one account day to the next ▷ vb arrange such a postponement of payment (for)

CONTANGOS > CONTANGO

CONTE n tale or short story, esp of adventure

CONTECK n contention

CONTECKS > CONTECK

CONTEMN vb regard with contempt

CONTEMNED > CONTEMN

CONTEMNER > CONTEMN

CONTEMNOR > CONTEMN

CONTEMNS > CONTEMN

CONTEMPER vb to modify

CONTEMPO adj contemporary

CONTEMPT n dislike and disregard

CONTEMPTS > CONTEMPT

CONTEND vb deal with

CONTENDED > CONTEND

CONTENDER > CONTEND

CONTENDS > CONTEND

CONTENT n meaning or substance of a piece of writing ▷ adj satisfied with things as they are ▷ vb make (someone) content

CONTENTED adj satisfied with one's situation or life

CONTENTLY > CONTENT

CONTENTS > CONTENT

CONTES > CONTE

CONTESSA n Italian countess

CONTESSAS > CONTESSA

CONTEST n competition or struggle ▷ vb dispute, object to

CONTESTED > CONTEST

CONTESTER > CONTEST

CONTESTS > CONTEST

CONTEXT n circumstances of an event or fact

CONTEXTS > CONTEXT

CONTICENT adj silent

CONTINENT n one of the earth's large masses of land ▷ adj able to control one's bladder and bowels

CONTINUA > CONTINUUM

CONTINUAL adj constant

CONTINUE vb (cause to) remain in a condition or place

CONTINUED > CONTINUE

CONTINUER > CONTINUE

CONTINUES > CONTINUE

CONTINUO n continuous bass part, usu. played on a keyboard instrument

CONTINUOS > CONTINUO

CONTINUUM n continuous series

CONTLINE n space between the bilges of stowed casks

CONTLINES > CONTLINE

CONTO n former Portuguese monetary unit worth 1000 escudos

CONTORNO n in Italy, side dish of salad or vegetables

CONTORNOS > CONTORNO

CONTORT vb twist out of shape

CONTORTED adj twisted out of shape

CONTORTS > CONTORT

CONTOS > CONTO

CONTOUR n outline ▷ vb shape so as to form or

follow the contour of something

CONTOURED > CONTOUR

CONTOURS > CONTOUR

CONTRA n counterargument

CONTRACT n (document setting out) a formal agreement ▷ vb make a formal agreement (to do something)

CONTRACTS > CONTRACT

CONTRAIL n aeroplane's vapour trail

CONTRAILS > CONTRAIL

CONTRAIR adj contrary

CONTRALTI > CONTRALTO

CONTRALTO n (singer with) the lowest female voice ▷ adj of or denoting a contralto

CONTRARY n complete opposite ▷ adj opposed, completely different ▷ adv in opposition

CONTRAS > CONTRA

CONTRAST n obvious difference ▷ vb compare in order to show differences

CONTRASTS > CONTRAST

CONTRASTY adj (of a photograph or subject) having sharp gradations in tone, esp between light and dark areas

CONTRAT old form of > CONTRACT

CONTRATE adj (of gears) having teeth set at a right angle to the axis

CONTRATS > CONTRAT

CONTRIST vb to make sad

CONTRISTS > CONTRIST

CONTRITE adj sorry and apologetic

CONTRIVE vb make happen

CONTRIVED adj planned or artificial

CONTRIVER > CONTRIVE

CONTRIVES > CONTRIVE

CONTROL n power to direct something ▷ vb have power over

CONTROLE adj officially registered

CONTROLS > CONTROL

CONTROUL obsolete variant of > CONTROL

CONTROULS > CONTROUL

CONTUMACY n obstinate disobedience

CONTUMELY n scornful or insulting treatment

CONTUND vb to pummel

CONTUNDED > CONTUND

CONTUNDS > CONTUND

CONTUSE vb injure (the body) without breaking the skin

CONTUSED > CONTUSE

CONTUSES > CONTUSE

CONTUSING > CONTUSE

CONTUSION n bruise

CONTUSIVE > CONTUSE

CONUNDRUM n riddle

CONURBAN adj relating to an urban region

CONURBIA n conurbations considered collectively

CONURBIAS > CONURBIA

CONURE n small American parrot

CONURES > CONURE

CONUS n any of several cone-shaped structures, such as the conus medullaris, the lower end of the spinal cord

CONVECT vb to circulate hot air by convection

CONVECTED > CONVECT

CONVECTOR n heater that gives out hot air

CONVECTS > CONVECT

CONVENE vb gather or summon for a formal meeting

CONVENED > CONVENE

CONVENER n person who calls a meeting

CONVENERS > CONVENER

CONVENES > CONVENE

CONVENING > CONVENE

CONVENOR same as > CONVENER

CONVENORS > CONVENOR

CONVENT n building where nuns live ▷ vb to summon

CONVENTED > CONVENT

CONVENTS > CONVENT

CONVERGE vb meet or join

CONVERGED > CONVERGE

CONVERGES > CONVERGE

CONVERSE vb have a conversation ▷ n opposite or contrary ▷ adj reversed or opposite

CONVERSED > CONVERSE

CONVERSER > CONVERSE

CONVERSES > CONVERSE

CONVERSO n medieval Spanish Jew converting to Catholicism

CONVERSOS > CONVERSO

CONVERT vb change in form, character, or function ▷ n person who has converted to a different belief or religion

CONVERTED > CONVERT

CONVERTER n person or thing that converts

CONVERTOR same as > CONVERTER

CONVERTS > CONVERT

CONVEX adj curving outwards ▷ vb make convex

CONVEXED > CONVEX

CONVEXES > CONVEX

CONVEXING > CONVEX

CONVEXITY n state or quality of being convex

CONVEXLY > CONVEX

CONVEY vb communicate (information)

CONVEYAL n act or means of conveying

CONVEYALS > CONVEYAL

CONVEYED > CONVEY

CONVEYER same as > CONVEYOR

CONVEYERS > CONVEYER

CONVEYING > CONVEY

CONVEYOR n person or thing that conveys

CONVEYORS > CONVEYOR

CONVEYS > CONVEY

CONVICT vb declare guilty ▷ n person serving a prison sentence ▷ adj convicted

CONVICTED > CONVICT

CONVICTS > CONVICT

CONVINCE vb persuade by argument or evidence

CONVINCED > CONVINCE

CONVINCER > CONVINCE

CONVINCES > CONVINCE

CONVIVE vb to feast together

CONVIVED > CONVIVE

CONVIVES > CONVIVE

CONVIVIAL adj sociable, lively

CONVIVING > CONVIVE

CONVO n conversation

CONVOCATE vb to call together

CONVOKE vb call together

CONVOKED > CONVOKE

CONVOKER > CONVOKE

CONVOKERS > CONVOKE

CONVOKES > CONVOKE

CONVOKING > CONVOKE

CONVOLUTE vb form into a twisted, coiled, or rolled shape ▷ adj rolled longitudinally upon itself

CONVOLVE vb wind or roll together

CONVOLVED > CONVOLVE

CONVOLVES > CONVOLVE

CONVOS > CONVO

CONVOY n group of vehicles or ships travelling together ▷ vb escort while in transit

CONVOYED > CONVOY

CONVOYING > CONVOY

CONVOYS > CONVOY

CONVULSE vb (of part of the body) undergo violent spasms

CONVULSED > CONVULSE

CONVULSES > CONVULSE

CONY n rabbit

COO vb (of a dove or pigeon) make a soft murmuring sound ▷ n sound of cooing ▷ interj exclamation of surprise, awe, etc

COOCH n slang term for vagina

COOCHES > COOCH

COOCOO old spelling of > CUCKOO

COOED > COO

COOEE interj call to attract attention ▷ vb utter this call ▷ n calling distance

COOEED > COOEE

COOEEING > COOEE

COOEES > COOEE

COOER > COO

COOERS > COO

COOEY same as > COOEE

COOEYED > COOEY

COOEYING > COOEY

COOEYS > COOEY

COOF n simpleton

COOFS > COOF

COOING > COO

COOINGLY > COO

COOINGS > COO

COOK vb prepare (food) by heating ▷ n person who cooks food

COOKABLE > COOK

COOKBOOK n book containing recipes and instructions for cooking

COOKBOOKS > COOKBOOK

COOKED > COOK

COOKER n apparatus for cooking heated by gas or electricity

COOKERIES > COOKERY

COOKERS > COOKER

COOKERY n art of cooking

COOKEY same as > COOKIE

COOKEYS > COOKEY

COOKHOUSE n place for cooking, esp a camp kitchen

COOKIE n biscuit

COOKIES > COOKIE

COOKING > COOK

COOKINGS > COOK

COOKLESS adj devoid of a cook

COOKMAID n maid who assists a cook

COOKMAIDS > COOKMAID

COOKOFF n cookery competition

COOKOFFS > COOKOFF

COOKOUT n party where a meal is cooked and eaten out of doors

COOKOUTS > COOKOUT

COOKROOM n room in which food is cooked

COOKROOMS > COOKROOM

COOKS > COOK

COOKSHACK n makeshift building in which food is cooked

COOKSHOP n shop that sells cookery equipment

COOKSHOPS > COOKSHOP

COOKSTOVE n stove for cooking

COOKTOP n flat unit for cooking in saucepans or the top part of a stove

COOKTOPS > COOKTOP

COOKWARE n cooking utensils

COOKWARES > COOKWARE

COOKY same as > COOKIE

COOL adj moderately cold ▷ vb make or become cool ▷ n coolness

COOLABAH n Australian tree that grows along rivers, with smooth bark and long narrow leaves

COOLABAHS > COOLABAH

COOLAMON *n* shallow dish of wood or bark, used for carrying water

COOLAMONS > COOLAMON

COOLANT *n* fluid used to cool machinery while it is working

COOLANTS > COOLANT

COOLDOWN *n* gentle stretching exercises after strenuous activity, to allow the heart rate gradually to return to normal

COOLDOWNS > COOLDOWN

COOLED > COOL

COOLER *n* container for making or keeping things cool

COOLERS > COOLER

COOLEST > COOL

COOLHOUSE *n* greenhouse in which a cool temperature is maintained

COOLIBAH *same as* **>** COOLABAH

COOLIBAHS > COOLIBAH

COOLIBAR *same as* **>** COOLABAH

COOLIBARS > COOLIBAR

COOLIE *n* unskilled Oriental labourer

COOLIES > COOLIE

COOLING *n* as in *regenerative cooling* a method of cooling rocket combustion chambers

COOLINGLY > COOL

COOLINGS > COOLING

COOLISH > COOL

COOLLY > COOL

COOLNESS > COOL

COOLS > COOL

COOLTH *n* coolness

COOLTHS > COOLTH

COOLY *same as* **>** COOLIE

COOM *n* waste material, such as dust from coal, grease from axles, etc ▷ *vb* to blacken

COOMB *same as* **>** COMB

COOMBE *same as* **>** COMB

COOMBES > COOMBE

COOMBS > COOMB

COOMED > COOM

COOMIER > COOMY

COOMIEST > COOMY

COOMING > COOM

COOMS > COOM

COOMY *adj* grimy

COON *n* raccoon

COONCAN *n* card game for two players, similar to rummy

COONCANS > COONCAN

COONDOG *n* dog trained to hunt raccoons

COONDOGS > COONDOG

COONHOUND *n* dog for hunting raccoons

COONS > COON

COONSKIN *n* pelt of a raccoon

COONSKINS > COONSKIN

COONTIE *n* evergreen plant of S Florida, with large dark green leathery leaves

COONTIES > COONTIE

COONTY *same as* **>** COONTIE

COOP *n* cage or pen for poultry ▷ *vb* confine in a restricted area

COOPED > COOP

COOPER *n* person who makes or repairs barrels ▷ *vb* make or mend (barrels, casks, etc)

COOPERAGE *n* craft, place of work, or products of a cooper

COOPERATE *vb* work or act together

COOPERED > COOPER

COOPERIES > COOPERY

COOPERING > COOPER

COOPERS > COOPER

COOPERY *same as* **>** COOPERAGE

COOPING > COOP

COOPS > COOP

COOPT *vb* add (someone) to a group by the agreement of the existing members

COOPTED > COOPT

COOPTING > COOPT

COOPTION > COOPT

COOPTIONS > COOPT

COOPTS > COOPT

COORDINAL *adj* (of animals or plants) belonging to the same order

COORIE *same as* **>** COURIE

COORIED > COORIE

COORIEING > COORIE

COORIES > COORIE

COOS > COO

COOSEN *same as* **>** COZEN

COOSENED > COOSEN

COOSENING > COOSEN

COOSENS > COOSEN

COOSER *n* stallion

COOSERS > COOSER

COOSIN *same as* **>** COZEN

COOSINED > COOSIN

COOSINING > COOSIN

COOSINS > COOSIN

COOST *Scots form of* **>** CAST

COOT *n* small black water bird

COOTCH *n* hiding place ▷ *vb* hide

COOTCHED > COOTCH

COOTCHES > COOTCH

COOTCHING > COOTCH

COOTER *n* type of freshwater turtle

COOTERS > COOTER

COOTIE > LOUSE

COOTIES > COOTIE

COOTIKIN *n* gaiter

COOTIKINS > COOTIKIN

COOTS > COOT

COOZE *n* US and Canadian taboo slang word for the female genitals

COOZES > COOZE

COP *same as* **>** COPPER

COPACETIC *adj* very good

COPAIBA *n* resin obtained from certain tropical S American trees, used in varnishes and ointments

COPAIBAS > COPAIBA

COPAIVA *same as* **>** COPAIBA

COPAIVAS > COPAIVA

COPAL *n* resin used in varnishes

COPALM *n* aromatic brown resin obtained from the sweet gum tree

COPALMS > COPALM

COPALS > COPAL

COPARCENY *n* form of joint ownership of property

COPARENT *n* fellow parent

COPARENTS > COPARENT

COPARTNER *n* partner or associate

COPASETIC *same as* **>** COPACETIC

COPASTOR *n* fellow pastor

COPASTORS > COPASTOR

COPATAINE *adj* (of a hat) high-crowned

COPATRIOT *n* fellow patriot

COPATRON *n* fellow patron

COPATRONS > COPATRON

COPAY *n* amount payable for treatment by person with medical insurance

COPAYMENT *n* fee paid for medical insurance

COPAYS > COPAY

COPE *vb* deal successfully (with) ▷ *n* large ceremonial cloak worn by some Christian priests

COPECK *same as* **>** KOPECK

COPECKS > COPECK

COPED > COPE

COPEMATE *n* partner

COPEMATES > COPEMATE

COPEN *n* shade of blue

COPENS > COPEN

COPEPOD *n* type of minute crustacean of marine and fresh waters, which is an important constituent of plankton

COPEPODS > COPEPOD

COPER *n* horse-dealer ▷ *vb* smuggle liquor to deep-sea fishermen

COPERED > COPER

COPERING > COPER

COPERS > COPER

COPES > COPE

COPESETIC *same as* **>** COPACETIC

COPESTONE *same as* **>** CAPSTONE

COPIED > COPY

COPIER *n* machine that copies

COPIERS > COPIER

COPIES > COPY

COPIHUE *n* Chilean bellflower

COPIHUES > COPIHUE

COPILOT *n* second pilot of an aircraft

COPILOTS > COPILOT

COPING *n* sloping top row of a wall

COPINGS > COPING

COPIOUS *adj* abundant, plentiful

COPIOUSLY > COPIOUS

COPITA *n* tulip-shaped sherry glass

COPITAS > COPITA

COPLANAR *adj* lying in the same plane

COPLOT *vb* plot together

COPLOTS > COPLOT

COPLOTTED > COPLOT

COPOLYMER *n* chemical compound of high molecular weight formed by uniting the molecules of two or more different compounds (monomers)

COPOUT *n* act of avoiding responsibility

COPOUTS > COPOUT

COPPED > COPPER

COPPER *n* soft reddish-brown metal ▷ *adj* reddish-brown ▷ *vb* coat or cover with copper

COPPERAH *same as* **>** COPRA

COPPERAHS > COPPERAH

COPPERAS *n* ferrous sulphate

COPPERED > COPPER

COPPERING > COPPER

COPPERISH *adj* copper-like

COPPERS > COPPER

COPPERY > COPPER

COPPICE *n* small group of trees growing close together ▷ *vb* trim back (trees or bushes) to form a coppice

COPPICED > COPPICE

COPPICES > COPPICE

COPPICING > COPPICE

COPPIES > COPPY

COPPIN *n* ball of thread

COPPING > COPPER

COPPINS > COPPIN

COPPLE *n* hill rising to a point

COPPLES > COPPLE

COPPRA *same as* **>** COPRA

COPPRAS > COPPRA

COPPY *n* small wooden stool

COPRA *n* dried oil-yielding kernel of the coconut

COPRAH *same as* **>** COPRA

COPRAHS > COPRAH

COPRAS > COPRA

COPREMIA *n* poisoning due to chronic constipation

COPREMIAS > COPREMIA

COPREMIC > COPREMIA

COPRESENT *vb* to present jointly

COPRINCE n fellow prince

COPRINCES > COPRINCE

COPRODUCE vb to produce jointly

COPRODUCT n joint product

COPROLITE n any of various rounded stony nodules thought to be the fossilized faeces of Palaeozic-Cenozoic vertebrates

COPROLITH n hard stony mass of dried faeces

COPROLOGY n preoccupation with excrement

COPROSMA n Australasian shrub sometimes planted for ornament

COPROSMAS > COPROSMA

COPROZOIC adj (of animals) living in dung

COPS > COPPER

COPSE same as > COPPICE

COPSED > COPSE

COPSES > COPSE

COPSEWOOD n brushwood

COPSHOP n police station

COPSHOPS > COPSHOP

COPSIER > COPSY

COPSIEST > COPSY

COPSING > COPSE

COPSY adj having copses

COPTER n helicopter

COPTERS > COPTER

COPUBLISH vb to publish jointly

COPULA n verb used to link the subject and complement of a sentence

COPULAE > COPULA

COPULAR > COPULA

COPULAS > COPULA

COPULATE vb have sexual intercourse

COPULATED > COPULATE

COPULATES > COPULATE

COPURIFY vb to purify together

COPY n thing made to look exactly like another ▷ vb make a copy of

COPYABLE > COPY

COPYBOOK n book of specimens for imitation

COPYBOOKS > COPYBOOK

COPYBOY n formerly, in journalism, boy who carried copy and ran errands

COPYBOYS > COPYBOY

COPYCAT n person who imitates or copies someone ▷ vb to imitate with great attention to detail

COPYCATS > COPYCAT

COPYDESK n desk where newspaper copy is edited

COPYDESKS > COPYDESK

COPYEDIT vb prepare text for printing by styling, correcting, etc

COPYEDITS > COPYEDIT

COPYFIGHT n legal battle

over the use of a copyright

COPYGIRL n female copyboy

COPYGIRLS > COPYGIRL

COPYGRAPH n process for copying type

COPYHOLD n tenure less than freehold of land in England evidenced by a copy of the Court roll

COPYHOLDS > COPYHOLD

COPYING > COPY

COPYISM n slavish copying

COPYISMS > COPYISM

COPYIST n person who makes written copies

COPYISTS > COPYIST

COPYLEFT n permission to use something free of charge ▷ vb use copyright law to make (work, esp software) free to use

COPYLEFTS > COPYLEFT

COPYREAD vb subedit

COPYREADS > COPYREAD

COPYRIGHT n exclusive legal right to reproduce and control a book, work of art, etc ▷ vb take out a copyright on ▷ adj protected by copyright

COPYTAKER n (esp in a newspaper office) a person employed to type reports as journalists dictate them over the telephone

COQUET vb behave flirtatiously

COQUETRY n flirtation

COQUETS > COQUET

COQUETTE n woman who flirts

COQUETTED > COQUET

COQUETTES > COQUETTE

COQUILLA n type of South American nut

COQUILLAS > COQUILLA

COQUILLE n any dish, esp seafood, served in a scallop shell

COQUILLES > COQUILLE

COQUINA n soft limestone consisting of shells, corals, etc, that occurs in parts of the US

COQUINAS > COQUINA

COQUITO n Chilean palm tree yielding edible nuts and a syrup

COQUITOS > COQUITO

COR interj exclamation of surprise, amazement, or admiration

CORACLE n small round boat of wicker covered with skins

CORACLES > CORACLE

CORACOID n paired ventral bone of the pectoral girdle in vertebrates

CORACOIDS > CORACOID

CORAGGIO interj exhortation to hold one's nerve

CORAL n hard substance

formed from the skeletons of very small sea animals ▷ adj orange-pink

CORALLA > CORALLUM

CORALLINE n type of red alga impregnated with calcium carbonate

CORALLITE n skeleton of a coral polyp

CORALLOID same as > CORALLINE

CORALLUM n skeleton of any zoophyte

CORALROOT n N temperate leafless orchid with small yellow-green or purple flowers and branched roots resembling coral

CORALS > CORAL

CORALWORT n coralroot or toothwort

CORAM prep before, in the presence of

CORANACH same as > CORONACH

CORANACHS > CORANACH

CORANTO same as > COURANTE

CORANTOES > CORANTO

CORANTOS > CORANTO

CORBAN n gift to God

CORBANS > CORBAN

CORBE obsolete variant of > CORBEL

CORBEAU n blackish green colour

CORBEAUS > CORBEAU

CORBEIL n carved ornament in the form of a basket of fruit, flowers, etc

CORBEILLE same as > CORBEIL

CORBEILS > CORBEIL

CORBEL n stone or timber support sticking out of a wall ▷ vb lay (a stone or brick) so that it forms a corbel

CORBELED > CORBEL

CORBELING n set of corbels stepped outwards, one above another

CORBELLED > CORBEL

CORBELS > CORBEL

CORBES > CORBE

CORBICULA n pollen basket

CORBIE n raven or crow

CORBIES > CORBIE

CORBINA n type of North American whiting

CORBINAS > CORBINA

CORBY same as > CORBIE

CORCASS n in Ireland, marshland

CORCASSES > CORCASS

CORD n thin rope or thick string ▷ adj (of fabric) ribbed ▷ vb bind or furnish with a cord or cords

CORDAGE n lines and rigging of a vessel

CORDAGES > CORDAGE

CORDATE adj heart-shaped

CORDATELY > CORDATE

CORDED adj tied or fastened with cord

CORDELLE vb to tow

CORDELLED > CORDELLE

CORDELLES > CORDELLE

CORDER > CORD

CORDERS > CORD

CORDGRASS n type of coarse grass

CORDIAL adj warm and friendly ▷ n drink with a fruit base

CORDIALLY > CORDIAL

CORDIALS > CORDIAL

CORDIFORM adj heart-shaped

CORDINER n shoemaker

CORDINERS > CORDINER

CORDING > CORD

CORDINGS > CORD

CORDITE n explosive used in guns and bombs

CORDITES > CORDITE

CORDLESS adj (of an electrical appliance) powered by an internal battery, so that there is no cable connecting the appliance itself to the electrical mains

CORDLIKE > CORD

CORDOBA n standard monetary unit of Nicaragua, divided into 100 centavos

CORDOBAS > CORDOBA

CORDON n chain of police, soldiers, etc, guarding an area ▷ vb put or form a cordon (around)

CORDONED > CORDON

CORDONING > CORDON

CORDONNET n type of thread

CORDONS > CORDON

CORDOTOMY n method of pain relief in which nerves are cut

CORDOVAN n fine leather now made principally from horsehide, isolated from the skin layers above and below it and tanned

CORDOVANS > CORDOVAN

CORDS npl trousers made of corduroy

CORDUROY n cotton fabric with a velvety ribbed surface

CORDUROYS npl trousers made of corduroy

CORDWAIN an archaic name for > CORDOVAN

CORDWAINS > CORDWAIN

CORDWOOD n wood that has been cut into lengths of four feet so that it can be stacked in cords

CORDWOODS > CORDWOOD

CORDYLINE n any tree of the genus Cordyline

CORE n central part of certain fruits, containing the seeds ▷ vb remove the core from

CORED > CORE
COREDEEM vb to redeem together
COREDEEMS > COREDEEM
COREGENT n joint regent
COREGENTS > COREGENT
COREIGN vb to reign jointly
COREIGNS > COREIGN
CORELATE same as **>** CORRELATE
CORELATED > CORELATE
CORELATES > CORELATE
CORELESS > CORE
CORELLA n white Australian cockatoo
CORELLAS > CORELLA
COREMIA > COREMIUM
COREMIUM n spore-producing organ of certain fungi
COREOPSIS n American and tropical African plant cultivated for its yellow, brown, or yellow-and-red daisy-like flowers
CORER > CORE
CORERS > CORE
CORES > CORE
COREY n slang word for the penis
COREYS > COREY
CORF n wagon or basket used formerly in mines
CORFHOUSE n shed used for curing salmon and storing nets
CORGI n short-legged sturdy dog
CORGIS > CORGI
CORIA > CORIUM
CORIANDER n plant grown for its aromatic seeds and leaves
CORIES > CORY
CORING > CORE
CORIOUS adj leathery
CORIUM n deep inner layer of the skin, beneath the epidermis, containing connective tissue, blood vessels, and fat
CORIUMS > CORIUM
CORIVAL same as **>** CORRIVAL
CORIVALRY > CORIVAL
CORIVALS > CORIVAL
CORIXID n type of water bug
CORIXIDS > CORIXID
CORK n thick light bark of a Mediterranean oak **>** vb seal with a cork **>** adj made of cork
CORKAGE n restaurant's charge for serving wine bought elsewhere
CORKAGES > CORKAGE
CORKBOARD n thin slab made of granules of cork, used as a floor or wall finish and as an insulator
CORKBORER n tool for cutting a hole in a stopper to insert a glass tube
CORKED adj (of wine)

spoiled through having a decayed cork
CORKER n splendid or outstanding person or thing
CORKERS > CORKER
CORKIER > CORKY
CORKIEST > CORKY
CORKINESS > CORKY
CORKING adj excellent
CORKIR n lichen from which red or purple dye is made
CORKIRS > CORKIR
CORKLIKE > CORK
CORKS > CORK
CORKSCREW n spiral metal tool for pulling corks from bottles **>** adj like a corkscrew in shape **>** vb move in a spiral or zigzag course
CORKTREE n type of evergreen oak tree
CORKTREES > CORKTREE
CORKWING n type of greenish or bluish European fish
CORKWINGS > CORKWING
CORKWOOD n type of small tree of the southeastern US, with very lightweight porous wood
CORKWOODS > CORKWOOD
CORKY same as **>** CORKED
CORM n bulblike underground stem of certain plants
CORMEL n new small corm arising from the base of a fully developed one
CORMELS > CORMEL
CORMIDIA > CORMIDIUM
CORMIDIUM n iteration of the repeating zooid pattern in a siphosome
CORMLIKE adj resembling a corm
CORMOID adj like a corm
CORMORANT n large dark-coloured long-necked sea bird
CORMOUS > CORM
CORMS > CORM
CORMUS n corm
CORMUSES > CORMUS
CORN n cereal plant such as wheat or oats **>** vb feed (animals) with corn, esp oats
CORNACRE same as **>** CONACRE
CORNACRES > CORNACRE
CORNAGE n rent fixed according to the number of horned cattle pastured
CORNAGES > CORNAGE
CORNBALL n person given to mawkish or unsophisticated behaviour
CORNBALLS > CORNBALL
CORNBORER n larva of the pyralid moth
CORNBRAID vb braid hair in cornrows

CORNBRASH n type of limestone which produces good soil for growing corn
CORNBREAD n bread made from maize meal
CORNCAKE n kind of cornmeal flatbread
CORNCAKES > CORNCAKE
CORNCOB n core of an ear of maize, to which the kernels are attached
CORNCOBS > CORNCOB
CORNCRAKE n brown Eurasian bird with a harsh cry
CORNCRIB n ventilated building for the storage of unhusked maize
CORNCRIBS > CORNCRIB
CORNEA n transparent membrane covering the eyeball
CORNEAE > CORNEA
CORNEAL > CORNEA
CORNEAS > CORNEA
CORNED adj (esp of beef) cooked and then preserved or pickled in salt or brine, now often canned
CORNEITIS n inflammation of cornea
CORNEL n type of plant such as the dogwood and dwarf cornel
CORNELIAN same as **>** CARNELIAN
CORNELS > CORNEL
CORNEMUSE n French bagpipe
CORNEOUS adj horny
CORNER n area or angle where two converging lines or surfaces meet **>** vb force into a difficult or inescapable position
CORNERED > CORNER
CORNERING > CORNER
CORNERMAN n in baseball, first baseman
CORNERMEN > CORNERMAN
CORNERS > CORNER
CORNET same as **>** CORNETT
CORNETCY n commission or rank of a cornet
CORNETIST n person who plays the cornet
CORNETS > CORNET
CORNETT n musical instrument consisting of a straight or curved tube of wood or ivory having finger holes like a recorder and a cup-shaped mouthpiece like a trumpet
CORNETTI > CORNETTO
CORNETTO same as **>** CORNETT
CORNETTS > CORNETT
CORNFED adj fed on corn
CORNFIELD n field planted with cereal crops
CORNFLAG n gladiolus
CORNFLAGS > CORNFLAG

CORNFLAKE n singular form of plural cornflakes: toasted flakes made from cornmeal, sold as a breakfast cereal
CORNFLIES > CORNFLY
CORNFLOUR n fine maize flour
CORNFLY n small fly whose larvae cause swollen, gouty stems in cereal crops
CORNHUSK n outer protective covering of an ear of maize
CORNHUSKS > CORNHUSK
CORNI > CORNO
CORNICE n decorative moulding around the top of a wall **>** vb furnish or decorate with or as if with a cornice
CORNICED > CORNICE
CORNICES > CORNICE
CORNICHE n coastal road, esp one built into the face of a cliff
CORNICHES > CORNICHE
CORNICHON n type of small gherkin
CORNICING > CORNICE
CORNICLE n wax-secreting organ on an aphid's abdomen
CORNICLES > CORNICLE
CORNICULA n plural form of singular corniculum: small horn
CORNIER > CORNY
CORNIEST > CORNY
CORNIFIC adj producing horns
CORNIFIED > CORNIFY
CORNIFIES > CORNIFY
CORNIFORM adj horn-shaped
CORNIFY vb turn soft tissue hard
CORNILY > CORNY
CORNINESS > CORNY
CORNING > CORN
CORNIST n horn-player
CORNISTS > CORNIST
CORNLAND n land suitable for growing corn or grain
CORNLANDS > CORNLAND
CORNLOFT n loft for storing corn
CORNLOFTS > CORNLOFT
CORNMEAL n meal made from maize
CORNMEALS > CORNMEAL
CORNMILL n flour mill
CORNMILLS > CORNMILL
CORNMOTH n moth whose larvae feed on grain
CORNMOTHS > CORNMOTH
CORNO n French horn
CORNOPEAN n cornet (the brass musical instrument)
CORNPIPE n musical instrument made from a stalk of corn etc
CORNPIPES > CORNPIPE
CORNPONE n American corn bread

CORNPONES > CORNPONE

CORNROW n hairstyle in which the hair is plaited in close parallel rows ▷ vb style the hair in a cornrow

CORNROWED > CORNROW

CORNROWS > CORNROW

CORNS > CORN

CORNSTALK n stalk or stem of corn

CORNSTONE n mottled green and red limestone

CORNU n part or structure resembling a horn or having a hornlike pattern, such as a cross section of the grey matter of the spinal cord

CORNUA > CORNU

CORNUAL > CORNU

CORNUS n any member of the genus Cornus, such as dogwood

CORNUSES > CORNUS

CORNUTE adj having or resembling cornua ▷ vb to make a cuckold of

CORNUTED same as > CORNUTE

CORNUTES > CORNUTE

CORNUTING > CORNUTE

CORNUTO n cuckold

CORNUTOS > CORNUTO

CORNWORM n cornmoth larva

CORNWORMS > CORNWORM

CORNY adj unoriginal or oversentimental

COROCORE same as > COROCORO

COROCORES > COROCORE

COROCORO n South Asian vessel fitted with outriggers

COROCOROS > COROCORO

CORODIES > CORODY

CORODY n (originally) the right of a lord to receive free quarters from his vassal

COROLLA n petals of a flower collectively

COROLLARY n idea, fact, or proposition which is the natural result of something else ▷ adj consequent or resultant

COROLLAS > COROLLA

COROLLATE adj having a corolla

COROLLINE adj relating to a corolla

CORONA n ring of light round the moon or sun

CORONACH n dirge or lamentation for the dead

CORONACHS > CORONACH

CORONAE > CORONA

CORONAL n circlet for the head ▷ adj of or relating to a corona or coronal

CORONALLY > CORONAL

CORONALS > CORONAL

CORONARY adj of the arteries surrounding the heart ▷ n coronary

thrombosis

CORONAS > CORONA

CORONATE vb to crown

CORONATED > CORONATE

CORONATES > CORONATE

CORONEL n iron head of a tilting spear

CORONELS > CORONEL

CORONER n official responsible for the investigation of violent, sudden, or suspicious deaths

CORONERS > CORONER

CORONET n small crown

CORONETED adj wearing a coronet

CORONETS > CORONET

CORONIS n in Greek grammar, symbol placed over a contracted syllable

CORONISES > CORONIS

CORONIUM n highly-ionized iron and nickel seen as a green line in the solar coronal spectrum

CORONIUMS > CORONIUM

CORONOID adj crown-shaped

COROTATE vb to rotate together

COROTATED > COROTATE

COROTATES > COROTATE

COROZO n tropical American palm whose seeds yield a useful oil

COROZOS > COROZO

CORPORA > CORPUS

CORPORAL n noncommissioned officer in an army ▷ adj of the body

CORPORALE same as > CORPORAL

CORPORALS > CORPORAL

CORPORAS n communion cloth

CORPORATE adj of business corporations

CORPOREAL adj physical or tangible

CORPORIFY vb to embody

CORPOSANT n Saint Elmo's fire

CORPS n military unit with a specific function

CORPSE n dead body ▷ vb laugh or cause to laugh involuntarily or inopportunely while on stage

CORPSED > CORPSE

CORPSES > CORPSE

CORPSING > CORPSE

CORPSMAN n medical orderly or stretcher-bearer

CORPSMEN > CORPSMAN

CORPULENT adj fat or plump

CORPUS n collection of writings, esp by a single author

CORPUSCLE n red or white blood cell

CORPUSES > CORPUS

CORRADE vb (of rivers,

streams, etc) to erode (land) by the abrasive action of rock particles

CORRADED > CORRADE

CORRADES > CORRADE

CORRADING > CORRADE

CORRAL n enclosure for cattle or horses ▷ vb put in a corral

CORRALLED > CORRAL

CORRALS > CORRAL

CORRASION n erosion of rocks caused by fragments transported over them by water, wind, or ice

CORRASIVE > CORRASION

CORREA n Australian evergreen shrub with large showy tubular flowers

CORREAS > CORREA

CORRECT adj free from error, true ▷ vb put right

CORRECTED > CORRECT

CORRECTER > CORRECT

CORRECTLY > CORRECT

CORRECTOR > CORRECT

CORRECTS > CORRECT

CORRELATE vb place or be placed in a mutual relationship ▷ n either of two things mutually related ▷ adj having a mutual, complementary, or reciprocal relationship

CORRIDA the Spanish word for > BULLFIGHT

CORRIDAS > CORRIDA

CORRIDOR n passage in a building or train

CORRIDORS > CORRIDOR

CORRIE same as > CIRQUE

CORRIES > CORRIE

CORRIGENT n corrective

CORRIVAL a rare word for > RIVAL

CORRIVALS > CORRIVAL

CORRODANT > CORRODE

CORRODE vb eat or be eaten away by chemical action or rust

CORRODED > CORRODE

CORRODENT > CORRODE

CORRODER > CORRODE

CORRODERS > CORRODE

CORRODES > CORRODE

CORRODIES > CORRODY

CORRODING > CORRODE

CORRODY same as > CORODY

CORROSION n process by which something, esp a metal, is corroded

CORROSIVE adj (esp of acids or alkalis) capable of destroying solid materials ▷ n corrosive substance, such as a strong acid or alkali

CORRUGATE vb fold into alternate grooves and ridges ▷ adj folded into furrows and ridges

CORRUPT adj open to or involving bribery ▷ vb

make corrupt

CORRUPTED > CORRUPT

CORRUPTER > CORRUPT

CORRUPTLY > CORRUPT

CORRUPTOR > CORRUPT

CORRUPTS > CORRUPT

CORS > COR

CORSAC n type of fox of central Asia

CORSACS > CORSAC

CORSAGE n small bouquet worn on the bodice of a dress

CORSAGES > CORSAGE

CORSAIR n pirate

CORSAIRS > CORSAIR

CORSE n corpse

CORSELET n one-piece undergarment combining a corset and bra

CORSELETS > CORSELET

CORSES > CORSE

CORSET n women's close-fitting undergarment worn to shape the torso ▷ vb dress or enclose in, or as in, a corset

CORSETED > CORSET

CORSETIER n man who makes and fits corsets

CORSETING > CORSET

CORSETRY n making of or dealing in corsets

CORSETS > CORSET

CORSEY n pavement or pathway

CORSEYS > CORSEY

CORSIVE n corrodent

CORSIVES > CORSIVE

CORSLET same as > CORSELET

CORSLETED > CORSLET

CORSLETS > CORSLET

CORSNED n ordeal whereby an accused person had to eat a morsel of bread; swallowing it freely indicated innocence; choking, guilt

CORSNEDS > CORSNED

CORSO n promenade

CORSOS > CORSO

CORTEGE n funeral procession

CORTEGES > CORTEGE

CORTEX n outer layer of the brain or other internal organ

CORTEXES > CORTEX

CORTICAL > CORTEX

CORTICATE adj (of plants, seeds, etc) having a bark, husk, or rind

CORTICES > CORTEX

CORTICOID n steroid hormone

CORTICOSE adj consisting of or like bark

CORTILE n open, internal courtyard

CORTILI > CORTILE

CORTIN n adrenal cortex extract containing cortisone and other hormones

CORTINA n weblike part of certain mushrooms

CORTINAS > CORTINA

CORTINS > CORTIN

CORTISOL n principal glucocorticoid secreted by the adrenal cortex

CORTISOLS > CORTISOL

CORTISONE n steroid hormone used to treat various diseases

CORULER n joint ruler

CORULERS > CORULER

CORUNDUM n hard mineral used as an abrasive

CORUNDUMS > CORUNDUM

CORUSCANT adj giving off flashes of light

CORUSCATE vb sparkle

CORVEE n day's unpaid labour owed by a feudal vassal to his lord

CORVEES > CORVEE

CORVES > CORF

CORVET same as > CURVET

CORVETED > CORVET

CORVETING > CORVET

CORVETS > CORVET

CORVETTE n lightly armed escort warship ▷ vb to participate in social activities with fellow Corvette car enthusiasts

CORVETTED > CORVETTE

CORVETTES > CORVETTE

CORVID n any member of the crow family

CORVIDS > CORVID

CORVINA same as > CORBINA

CORVINAS > CORVINA

CORVINE adj of, relating to, or resembling a crow

CORVUS n type of ancient hook

CORVUSES > CORVUS

CORY n catfish belonging to the South American Corydoras genus

CORYBANT n wild attendant of the goddess Cybele

CORYBANTS > CORYBANT

CORYDALIS n N temperate plant with finely-lobed leaves and spurred yellow or pinkish flowers

CORYLUS n hazel genus

CORYLUSES > CORYLUS

CORYMB n flat-topped flower cluster with the stems growing progressively shorter towards the centre ▷ vb be corymb-like

CORYMBED > CORYMB

CORYMBOSE > CORYMB

CORYMBOUS > CORYMB

CORYMBS > CORYMB

CORYPHAEI n plural form of singular coryphaeus: leader of the chorus

CORYPHE n coryphaeus

CORYPHEE n leading

dancer of a corps de ballet

CORYPHEES > CORYPHEE

CORYPHENE n any fish of the genus Coryphaena

CORYPHES > CORYPHE

CORYZA n acute inflammation of the mucous membrane of the nose, with discharge of mucus

CORYZAL > CORYZA

CORYZAS > CORYZA

COS same as > COSINE

COSCRIPT vb to script jointly

COSCRIPTS > COSCRIPT

COSE vb get cosy

COSEC same as > COSECANT

COSECANT n (in trigonometry) the ratio of the length of the hypotenuse to that of the opposite side in a right-angled triangle

COSECANTS > COSECANT

COSECH n hyperbolic cosecant

COSECHS > COSECH

COSECS > COSEC

COSED > COSE

COSEISMAL adj of or designating points at which earthquake waves are felt at the same time ▷ n such a line on a map

COSEISMIC same as > COSEISMAL

COSES > COSE

COSET n mathematical set

COSETS > COSET

COSEY n tea cosy

COSEYS > COSEY

COSH n heavy blunt weapon ▷ vb hit with a cosh

COSHED > COSH

COSHER vb pamper or coddle

COSHERED > COSHER

COSHERER > COSHER

COSHERERS > COSHER

COSHERIES > COSHERY

COSHERING > COSHER

COSHERS > COSHER

COSHERY n Irish chief's right to lodge at his tenants' houses

COSHES > COSH

COSHING > COSH

COSIE same as > COSY

COSIED > COSY

COSIER n cobbler

COSIERS > COSIER

COSIES > COSY

COSIEST > COSY

COSIGN vb to sign jointly

COSIGNED > COSIGN

COSIGNER > COSIGN

COSIGNERS > COSIGN

COSIGNING > COSIGN

COSIGNS > COSIGN

COSILY > COSY

COSINE n (in trigonometry) ratio of the length of the adjacent side

to that of the hypotenuse in a right-angled triangle

COSINES > COSINE

COSINESS > COSY

COSING > COSE

COSMEA n plant of the genus Cosmos

COSMEAS > COSMEA

COSMESES > COSMESIS

COSMESIS n aesthetic covering on a prosthesis to make it look more natural

COSMETIC n preparation used to improve the appearance of a person's skin ▷ adj improving the appearance only

COSMETICS > COSMETIC

COSMIC adj of the whole universe

COSMICAL > COSMIC

COSMID n segment of DNA

COSMIDS > COSMID

COSMIN same as > COSMINE

COSMINE n substance resembling dentine, forming the outer layer of cosmoid scales

COSMINES > COSMINE

COSMINS > COSMIN

COSMISM n Russian cultural and philosophical movement

COSMISMS > COSMISM

COSMIST > COSMISM

COSMISTS > COSMISM

COSMOCRAT n ruler of the world

COSMOGENY same as > COSMOGONY

COSMOGONY n study of the origin of the universe

COSMOID adj (of the scales of coelacanths and lungfish) consisting of two inner bony layers and an outer layer of cosmine

COSMOLINE n type of petroleum jelly ▷ vb to apply cosmoline to

COSMOLOGY n study of the origin and nature of the universe

COSMONAUT n Russian name for an astronaut

COSMORAMA n lifelike display, using mirrors and lenses, which shows reflections of various views of parts of the world

COSMOS n universe

COSMOSES > COSMOS

COSMOTRON n large type of particle accelerator

COSPHERED adj sharing the same sphere

COSPONSOR vb to sponsor jointly

COSS another name for > KOS

COSSACK n Slavonic warrior-peasant who served in the Russian cavalry under the tsars

COSSACKS > COSSACK

COSSES > COSS

COSSET vb pamper ▷ n any pet animal, esp a lamb

COSSETED > COSSET

COSSETING > COSSET

COSSETS > COSSET

COSSIE n informal name for a swimming costume

COSSIES > COSSIE

COST n amount of money, time, labour, etc, required for something ▷ vb have as its cost

COSTA n riblike part, such as the midrib of a plant leaf

COSTAE > COSTA

COSTAL n strengthening rib of an insect's wing

COSTALGIA n pain in the ribs

COSTALLY > COSTAL

COSTALS > COSTAL

COSTAR n actor who shares the billing with another ▷ vb share the billing with another actor

COSTARD n English variety of apple tree

COSTARDS > COSTARD

COSTARRED > COSTAR

COSTARS > COSTAR

COSTATE adj having ribs

COSTATED same as > COSTATE

COSTE vb to draw near

COSTEAN vb to mine for lodes

COSTEANED > COSTEAN

COSTEANS > COSTEAN

COSTED > COST

COSTER n person who sells fruit, vegetables etc from a barrow

COSTERS > COSTER

COSTES > COSTE

COSTING n as in marginal costing a method of cost accounting

COSTINGS > COSTING

COSTIVE adj having or causing constipation

COSTIVELY > COSTIVE

COSTLESS > COST

COSTLIER > COSTLY

COSTLIEST > COSTLY

COSTLY adj expensive

COSTMARY n herbaceous Asian plant whose fragrant leaves were used as a seasoning and to flavour ale

COSTOTOMY n surgical incision into a rib

COSTREL n flask, usually of earthenware or leather

COSTRELS > COSTREL

COSTS > COST

COSTUME n style of dress of a particular place or time, or for a particular activity ▷ vb provide with a costume

COSTUMED > COSTUME

COSTUMER same as > COSTUMIER

COSTUMERS
> COSTUMIER
COSTUMERY n collective term for costumes
COSTUMES > COSTUME
COSTUMEY adj (stage) costume-like; unrealistic
COSTUMIER n maker or seller of costumes
COSTUMING > COSTUME
COSTUS n Himalayan herb with an aromatic root
COSTUSES > COSTUS
COSY adj warm and snug ▷ n cover for keeping things warm ▷ vb to make oneself snug and warm
COSYING > COSY
COT n baby's bed with high sides ▷ vb entangle or become entangled
COTAN same as
> COTANGENT
COTANGENT n (in trigonometry) the ratio of the length of the adjacent side to that of the opposite side in a right-angled triangle
COTANS > COTANGENT
COTE same as > COT
COTEAU n hillside
COTEAUX > COTEAU
COTED > COT
COTELETTE n cutlet
COTELINE n kind of muslin
COTELINES > COTELINE
COTENANCY > COTENANT
COTENANT n person who holds property jointly or in common with others
COTENANTS > COTENANT
COTERIE n exclusive group, clique
COTERIES > COTERIE
COTES > COTE
COTH n hyperbolic cotangent
COTHS > COTH
COTHURN same as
> COTHURNUS
COTHURNAL
> COTHURNUS
COTHURNI > COTHURNUS
COTHURNS > COTHURNUS
COTHURNUS n buskin worn in ancient Greek tragedy
COTICULAR adj relating to whetstones
COTIDAL adj (of a line on a tidal chart) joining points at which high tide occurs simultaneously
COTILLION n French formation dance of the 18th century
COTILLON same as
> COTILLION
COTILLONS > COTILLION
COTING > COT
COTINGA n tropical American bird such as the umbrella bird and the cock-of-the-rock, with a broad slightly hooked bill

COTINGAS > COTINGA
COTININE n substance used to indicate presence of nicotine
COTININES > COTININE
COTISE same as
> COTTISE
COTISED > COTISE
COTISES > COTISE
COTISING > COTISE
COTLAND n grounds that belong to a cotter
COTLANDS > COTLAND
COTQUEAN n coarse woman
COTQUEANS > COTQUEAN
COTRUSTEE n fellow trustee
COTS > COT
COTT same as > COT
COTTA n short form of surplice
COTTABUS n ancient Greek game involving throwing wine into a vessel
COTTAE > COTTA
COTTAGE n small house in the country ▷ vb engage in homosexual activity in a public lavatory
COTTAGED > COTTAGE
COTTAGER n person who lives in a cottage
COTTAGERS > COTTAGER
COTTAGES > COTTAGE
COTTAGEY adj resembling a cottage
COTTAGING n homosexual activity between men in a public lavatory
COTTAR same as > COTTER
COTTARS > COTTAR
COTTAS > COTTA
COTTED > COT
COTTER n pin or wedge used to secure machine parts ▷ vb secure (two parts) with a cotter
COTTERED > COTTER
COTTERING > COTTER
COTTERS > COTTIER
COTTID n type of fish typically with a large head, tapering body, and spiny fins
COTTIDS > COTTID
COTTIER same as
> COTTER
COTTIERS > COTTIER
COTTING > COT
COTTISE n type of heraldic decoration ▷ vb (in heraldry) decorate with a cottise
COTTISED > COTTISE
COTTISES > COTTISE
COTTISING > COTTISE
COTTOID adj resembling a fish of the genus Cottus
COTTON n white downy fibre covering the seeds of a tropical plant ▷ vb take a liking
COTTONADE n coarse fabric of cotton or mixed

fibres, used for work clothes, etc
COTTONED > COTTON
COTTONING > COTTON
COTTONS > COTTON
COTTONY > COTTON
COTTOWN Scots variant of
> COTTON
COTTOWNS > COTTON
COTTS > COTT
COTTUS n type of fish with four yellowish knobs on its head
COTTUSES > COTTUS
COTURNIX n variety of quail
COTWAL n Indian police officer
COTWALS > COTWAL
COTYLAE > COTYLE
COTYLE n cuplike cavity
COTYLEDON n first leaf of a plant embryo
COTYLES > COTYLE
COTYLOID adj shaped like a cup ▷ n small bone forming part of the acetabular cavity in some mammals
COTYLOIDS > COTYLOID
COTYPE n additional type specimen from the same brood as the original type specimen
COTYPES > COTYPE
COUCAL n type of ground-living bird of Africa, S Asia, and Australia, with long strong legs
COUCALS > COUCAL
COUCH n piece of upholstered furniture for seating more than one person ▷ vb express in a particular way
COUCHANT adj in a lying position
COUCHE adj in heraldry (of a shield), tilted
COUCHED > COUCH
COUCHEE n reception held late at night
COUCHEES > COUCHEE
COUCHER > COUCH
COUCHERS > COUCH
COUCHES > COUCH
COUCHETTE n bed converted from seats on a train or ship
COUCHING n method of embroidery in which the thread is caught down at intervals by another thread passed through the material from beneath
COUCHINGS > COUCHING
COUDE adj (of a reflecting telescope) having plane mirrors positioned to reflect light from the primary mirror along the axis onto a detector
COUGAN n drunk and rowdy person
COUGANS > COUGAN

COUGAR n puma
COUGARS > COUGAR
COUGH vb expel air from the lungs abruptly and noisily ▷ n act or sound of coughing
COUGHED > COUGH
COUGHER > COUGH
COUGHERS > COUGH
COUGHING > COUGH
COUGHINGS > COUGH
COUGHS > COUGH
COUGUAR same as
> COUGAR
COUGUARS > COUGUAR
COULD > CAN
COULDEST same as
> COULDST
COULDST vb form of 'could' used with the pronoun thou or its relative form
COULEE n flow of molten lava
COULEES > COULEE
COULIBIAC n Russian fish pie
COULIS n thin purée of vegetables or fruit, usually served as a sauce surrounding a dish
COULISSE n timber member grooved to take a sliding panel, such as a sluicegate, portcullis, or stage flat
COULISSES > COULISSE
COULOIR n deep gully on a mountain side, esp in the French Alps
COULOIRS > COULOIR
COULOMB n SI unit of electric charge
COULOMBIC > COULOMB
COULOMBS > COULOMB
COULTER n blade at the front of a ploughshare
COULTERS > COULTER
COUMARIC > COUMARIN
COUMARIN n white vanilla-scented crystalline ester, used in perfumes and flavourings and as an anticoagulant
COUMARINS > COUMARIN
COUMARONE n a colourless insoluble aromatic liquid obtained from coal tar and used in the manufacture of synthetic resins
COUMAROU n tonka bean tree, or its seed
COUMAROUS > COUMAROU
COUNCIL n group meeting for discussion or consultation ▷ adj of or by a council
COUNCILOR n member of a council
COUNCILS > COUNCIL
COUNSEL n advice or guidance ▷ vb give guidance to
COUNSELED > COUNSEL
COUNSELEE n one who is counselled

COUNSELOR n person who gives counsel

COUNSELS > COUNSEL

COUNT vb say numbers in order ▷ n counting

COUNTABLE adj capable of being counted

COUNTABLY > COUNTABLE

COUNTBACK n system of deciding the winner of a tied competition by comparing earlier points or scores

COUNTDOWN n counting backwards to zero of the seconds before an event ▷ vb count numbers backwards towards zero, esp in timing such a critical operation

COUNTED > COUNT

COUNTER n long flat surface in a bank or shop, on which business is transacted ▷ vb oppose, retaliate against ▷ adv in the opposite direction

COUNTERED > COUNTER

COUNTERS > COUNTER

COUNTESS n woman holding the rank of count or earl

COUNTIAN n dweller in a given county

COUNTIANS > COUNTIAN

COUNTIES > COUNTY

COUNTING > COUNT

COUNTLESS adj too many to count

COUNTLINE n (in confectionery marketing) a chocolate-based bar

COUNTRIES > COUNTRY

COUNTROL obsolete variant of > CONTROL

COUNTROLS > COUNTROL

COUNTRY n nation

COUNTS > COUNT

COUNTSHIP > COUNT

COUNTY n (in some countries) division of a country ▷ adj upper-class

COUP n successful action ▷ vb turn or fall over

COUPE n sports car with two doors and a sloping fixed roof

COUPED > COUP

COUPEE n (in dance) a forward movement on one leg, with the other slightly bent and raised

COUPEES > COUPEE

COUPER n dealer

COUPERS > COUPER

COUPES > COUPE

COUPING > COUP

COUPLE n two people who are married or romantically involved ▷ vb connect, associate

COUPLED > COUPLE

COUPLEDOM n state of living as a couple, esp when

regarded as being interested in each other to the exclusion of the outside world

COUPLER n link or rod transmitting power between two rotating mechanisms or a rotating part and a reciprocating part

COUPLERS > COUPLER

COUPLES > COUPLE

COUPLET n two consecutive lines of verse, usu. rhyming and of the same metre

COUPLETS > COUPLET

COUPLING n device for connecting things, such as railway carriages

COUPLINGS > COUPLING

COUPON n piece of paper entitling the holder to a discount or gift

COUPONING n in marketing, distribution or redemption of promotional coupons

COUPONS > COUPON

COUPS > COUP

COUPURE n entrenchment made by beseiged forces behind a breach in their defences

COUPURES > COUPURE

COUR obsolete variant of > COVER

COURAGE n ability to face danger or pain without fear

COURAGES > COURAGE

COURANT n courante ▷ adj (of an animal) running

COURANTE n old dance in quick triple time

COURANTES > COURANTE

COURANTO same as > COURANTE

COURANTOS > COURANTO

COURANTS > COURANT

COURB vb to bend

COURBARIL n tropical American tree whose wood is a useful timber and whose gum is a source of copal

COURBED > COURB

COURBETTE same as > CURVET

COURBING > COURB

COURBS > COURB

COURD obsolete variant of > COVERED

COURE obsolete variant of > COVER

COURED > COURE

COURES > COURE

COURGETTE n type of small vegetable marrow

COURIE vb nestle or snuggle

COURIED > COURIE

COURIEING > COURIE

COURIER n person employed to look after holiday-makers ▷ vb send

(a parcel, letter, etc) by courier

COURIERED > COURIER

COURIERS > COURIER

COURIES > COURIE

COURING > COUR

COURLAN another name for > LIMPKIN

COURLANS > COURLAN

COURS > COUR

COURSE n series of lessons or medical treatment ▷ vb (of liquid) run swiftly

COURSED > COURSE

COURSER n swift horse

COURSERS > COURSER

COURSES another word for > MENSES

COURSING n hunting with hounds trained to hunt game by sight

COURSINGS > COURSING

COURT n body which decides legal cases ▷ vb try to gain the love of

COURTED > COURT

COURTEOUS adj polite

COURTER n suitor

COURTERS > COURTER

COURTESAN n mistress or high-class prostitute

COURTESY n politeness, good manners

COURTEZAN same as > COURTESAN

COURTIER n attendant at a royal court

COURTIERS > COURTIER

COURTING > COURT

COURTINGS > COURT

COURTLET n small court

COURTLETS > COURTLET

COURTLIER > COURTLY

COURTLIKE adj courtly

COURTLING n fawning courtier

COURTLY adj ceremoniously polite

COURTROOM n room in which the sittings of a law court are held

COURTS > COURT

COURTSHIP n courting of an intended spouse or mate

COURTSIDE n in sport, area closest to the court

COURTYARD n paved space enclosed by buildings or walls

COUSCOUS n type of semolina used in North African cookery

COUSIN n child of one's uncle or aunt

COUSINAGE n kinship

COUSINLY > COUSIN

COUSINRY n collective term for cousins

COUSINS > COUSIN

COUTA n traditional Australian sailing boat

COUTAS > COUTA

COUTEAU n large

two-edged knife used formerly as a weapon

COUTEAUX > COUTEAU

COUTER n armour designed to protect the elbow

COUTERS > COUTER

COUTH adj refined ▷ n refinement

COUTHER > COUTH

COUTHEST > COUTH

COUTHIE adj sociable

COUTHIER > COUTHIE

COUTHIEST > COUTHIE

COUTHS > COUTH

COUTHY same as > COUTHIE

COUTIL n type of tightly-woven twill cloth

COUTILLE same as > COUTIL

COUTILLES > COUTILLE

COUTILS > COUTIL

COUTURE n high-fashion designing and dressmaking ▷ adj relating to high fashion design and dress-making

COUTURES > COUTURE

COUTURIER n person who designs women's fashion clothes

COUVADE n custom in certain cultures of treating the husband of a woman giving birth as if he were bearing the child

COUVADES > COUVADE

COUVERT another word for > COVER

COUVERTS > COUVERT

COUZIN n South African word for a friend

COUZINS > COUZIN

COVALENCE same as > COVALENCY

COVALENCY n ability to form a bond in which two atoms share a pair of electrons

COVALENT > COVALENCY

COVARIANT n variant that varies leaving certain mathematical relationships it has with another variant (its covariant) unchanged

COVARIATE n statistical variable

COVARIED > COVARY

COVARIES > COVARY

COVARY vb vary together maintaining a certain mathematical relationship

COVARYING > COVARY

COVE n small bay or inlet ▷ vb form an architectural cove in

COVED > COVE

COVELET n small cove

COVELETS > COVELET

COVELLINE same as > COVELLITE

COVELLITE n indigo copper (blue sulphide of copper)

COVEN n meeting of witches

COVENANT n contract ▷ vb agree by a covenant

COVENANTS > COVENANT

COVENS > COVEN

COVENT same as > CONVENT

COVENTS > COVENT

COVER vb place something over, to protect or conceal ▷ n anything that covers

COVERABLE > COVER

COVERAGE n amount or extent covered

COVERAGES > COVERAGE

COVERALL n thing that covers something entirely

COVERALLS > COVERALL

COVERED > COVER

COVERER > COVER

COVERERS > COVER

COVERING another word for > COVER

COVERINGS > COVERING

COVERLESS > COVER

COVERLET n bed cover

COVERLETS > COVERLET

COVERLID same as > COVERLET

COVERLIDS > COVERLID

COVERS > COVER

COVERSED as in coversed sine obsolete function in trigonometry

COVERSINE n function in trigonometry

COVERSLIP n very thin piece of glass placed over a specimen on a glass slide

COVERT adj concealed, secret ▷ n thicket giving shelter to game birds or animals

COVERTLY > COVERT

COVERTS > COVERT

COVERTURE n condition or status of a married woman considered as being under the protection and influence of her husband

COVERUP n concealment of a mistake, crime, etc

COVERUPS > COVERUP

COVES > COVE

COVET vb long to possess (what belongs to someone else)

COVETABLE > COVET

COVETED > COVET

COVETER > COVET

COVETERS > COVET

COVETING > COVET

COVETISE n covetousness

COVETISES > COVETISE

COVETOUS adj jealously longing to possess something

COVETS > COVET

COVEY n small flock of grouse or partridge

COVEYS > COVEY

COVIN n conspiracy between two or more persons to act to the detriment or injury of another

COVING same as > COVE

COVINGS > COVING

COVINOUS adj deceitful

COVINS > COVIN

COVYNE same as > COVIN

COVYNES > COVYNE

COW n mature female of cattle and of certain other mammals, such as the elephant or seal ▷ vb intimidate, subdue

COWAGE n tropical climbing plant whose bristly pods cause severe itching and stinging

COWAGES > COWAGE

COWAL n shallow lake or swampy depression supporting vegetation

COWALS > COWAL

COWAN n drystone waller

COWANS > COWAN

COWARD n person who lacks courage ▷ vb show (someone) up to be a coward

COWARDED > COWARD

COWARDICE n lack of courage

COWARDING > COWARD

COWARDLY adj of or characteristic of a coward

COWARDRY n cowardice

COWARDS > COWARD

COWBANE n N temperate poisonous marsh plant with clusters of small white flowers

COWBANES > COWBANE

COWBELL n bell hung around a cow's neck

COWBELLS > COWBELL

COWBERRY n creeping evergreen shrub of N temperate and arctic regions, with pink or red flowers and edible berries

COWBIND n any of various bryony plants, esp the white bryony

COWBINDS > COWBIND

COWBIRD n American oriole with a dark plumage and short bill

COWBIRDS > COWBIRD

COWBOY n (in the US) ranch worker who herds and tends cattle, usu. on horseback ▷ vb work or behave as a cowboy

COWBOYED > COWBOY

COWBOYING > COWBOY

COWBOYS > COWBOY

COWED > COW

COWEDLY > COW

COWER vb cringe in fear

COWERED > COWER

COWERING > COWER

COWERS > COWER

COWFEEDER n dairyman

COWFISH n type of trunkfish with hornlike spines over the eyes

COWFISHES > COWFISH

COWFLAP n cow dung

COWFLAPS > COWFLAP

COWFLOP n foxglove

COWFLOPS > COWFLOP

COWGIRL n female cowboy

COWGIRLS > COWGIRL

COWGRASS n red clover

COWHAGE same as > COWAGE

COWHAGES > COWHAGE

COWHAND same as > COWBOY

COWHANDS > COWBOY

COWHEARD same as > COWHERD

COWHEARDS > COWHEARD

COWHEEL n heel of a cow, used as cooking ingredient

COWHEELS > COWHEEL

COWHERB n European plant with clusters of pink flowers

COWHERBS > COWHERB

COWHERD n person employed to tend cattle

COWHERDS > COWHERD

COWHIDE n hide of a cow ▷ vb to lash with a cowhide whip

COWHIDED > COWHIDE

COWHIDES > COWHIDE

COWHIDING > COWHIDE

COWHOUSE n byre

COWHOUSES > COWHOUSE

COWIER > COWY

COWIEST > COWY

COWING > COW

COWINNER n joint winner

COWINNERS > COWINNER

COWISH adj cowardly

COWITCH another name for > COWAGE

COWITCHES > COWITCH

COWK vb retch or feel nauseated

COWKED > COWK

COWKING > COWK

COWKS > COWK

COWL same as > COWLING

COWLED adj wearing a cowl

COWLICK n tuft of hair over the forehead

COWLICKS > COWLICK

COWLING n cover on an engine

COWLINGS > COWLING

COWLS > COWL

COWLSTAFF n pole, used by two people, for carrying a vessel

COWMAN n man who owns cattle

COWMEN > COWMAN

COWORKER n fellow worker

COWORKERS > COWORKER

COWP same as > COUP

COWPAT n pool of cow dung

COWPATS > COWPAT

COWPEA n type of tropical climbing plant producing long pods with edible pealike seeds

COWPEAS > COWPEA

COWPED > COWP

COWPIE n cowpat

COWPIES > COWPIE

COWPING > COWP

COWPLOP n cow dung

COWPLOPS > COWPLOP

COWPOKE n cowboy

COWPOKES > COWPOKE

COWPOX n disease of cows, the virus of which is used in the smallpox vaccine

COWPOXES > COWPOX

COWPS > COWP

COWRIE n brightly-marked sea shell

COWRIES > COWRIE

COWRITE vb to write jointly

COWRITER > COWRITE

COWRITERS > COWRITE

COWRITES > COWRITE

COWRITING > COWRITE

COWRITTEN > COWRITE

COWROTE > COWRITE

COWRY same as > COWRIE

COWS > COW

COWSHED n byre

COWSHEDS > COWSHED

COWSKIN same as > COWHIDE

COWSKINS > COWSKIN

COWSLIP n small yellow wild European flower

COWSLIPS > COWSLIP

COWTREE n South American tree that produces latex

COWTREES > COWTREE

COWY adj cowlike

COX n coxswain ▷ vb act as cox of (a boat)

COXA n technical name for the hipbone or hip joint

COXAE > COXA

COXAL > COXA

COXALGIA n pain in the hip joint

COXALGIAS > COXALGIA

COXALGIC > COXALGIA

COXALGIES > COXALGIA

COXALGY same as > COXALGIA

COXCOMB same as > COCKSCOMB

COXCOMBIC > COXCOMB

COXCOMBRY n conceited arrogance or foppishness

COXCOMBS > COXCOMB

COXED > COX

COXES > COX

COXIB n anti-inflammatory drug used to treat osteoarthritis

COXIBS > COXIB

COXIER > COXY

COXIEST > COXY

COXINESS > COXY

COXING > COX

COXITIDES > COXITIS

COXITIS n inflammation of the hip joint

COXLESS > COX

COXSWAIN n person who steers a rowing boat

COXSWAINS > COXSWAIN

COXY adj cocky

COY adj affectedly shy or modest ▷ vb to caress

COYDOG n cross between a coyote and a dog

COYDOGS > COYDOG

COYED > COY

COYER > COY

COYEST > COY

COYING > COY

COYISH > COY

COYISHLY > COY

COYLY > COY

COYNESS > COY

COYNESSES > COY

COYOTE n prairie wolf of N America

COYOTES > COYOTE

COYOTILLO n thorny poisonous shrub of Mexico and the southwestern US

COYPOU same as **>** COYPU

COYPOUS > COYPOU

COYPU n beaver-like aquatic rodent native to S America, bred for its fur

COYPUS > COYPU

COYS > COY

COYSTREL same as **>** COISTREL

COYSTRELS > COYSTREL

COYSTRIL same as **>** COISTREL

COYSTRILS > COYSTRIL

COZ archaic word for **>** COUSIN

COZE vb to chat

COZED > COZE

COZEN vb cheat, trick

COZENAGE > COZEN

COZENAGES > COZEN

COZENED > COZEN

COZENER > COZEN

COZENERS > COZEN

COZENING > COZEN

COZENS > COZEN

COZES > COZE

COZEY n tea cosy

COZEYS > COZEY

COZIE same as **>** COZEY

COZIED > COSY

COZIER n cobbler

COZIERS > COZIER

COZIES > COZEY

COZIEST > COZY

COZILY > COZY

COZINESS > COZY

COZING > COZE

COZY same as **>** COSY

COZYING > COZY

COZZES > COZ

CRAAL vb to enclose in a craal (or kraal)

CRAALED > CRAAL

CRAALING > CRAAL

CRAALS > CRAAL

CRAB n edible shellfish with ten legs, the first pair modified into pincers

CRABAPPLE n tree bearing small sour apple-like fruit

CRABBED > CRAB

CRABBEDLY > CRAB

CRABBER n crab fisherman

CRABBERS > CRABBER

CRABBIER > CRABBY

CRABBIEST > CRABBY

CRABBILY > CRABBY

CRABBING > CRAB

CRABBIT adj bad-tempered

CRABBY adj bad-tempered

CRABEATER n species of seal

CRABGRASS n type of coarse weedy grass

CRABLIKE adj resembling a crab

CRABMEAT n edible flesh of a crab

CRABMEATS > CRABMEAT

CRABS > CRAB

CRABSTICK n stick, cane, or cudgel made of crabapple wood

CRABWISE adv (of motion) sideways

CRABWOOD n tropical American tree

CRABWOODS > CRABWOOD

CRACHACH npl (in Wales) elitists

CRACK vb break or split partially ▷ n sudden sharp noise ▷ adj first-rate, excellent

CRACKA n US derogatory word for a poor White person

CRACKAS > CRACKA

CRACKBACK n in American football, illegal blocking of an opponent

CRACKDOWN n severe disciplinary measures

CRACKED adj damaged by cracking ▷ n sharp noise

CRACKER n thin dry biscuit

CRACKERS adj insane

CRACKET n low stool, often one with three legs

CRACKETS > CRACKET

CRACKHEAD n person addicted to the drug crack

CRACKING adj very fast

CRACKINGS > CRACKING

CRACKJAW adj difficult to pronounce ▷ n word or phrase that is difficult to pronounce

CRACKJAWS > CRACKJAW

CRACKLE vb make small sharp popping noises ▷ n crackling sound

CRACKLED > CRACKLE

CRACKLES > CRACKLE

CRACKLIER > CRACKLY

CRACKLING n crackle

CRACKLY adj making a cracking sound

CRACKNEL n type of hard plain biscuit

CRACKNELS > CRACKNEL

CRACKPOT adj eccentric ▷ n eccentric person

CRACKPOTS > CRACKPOT

CRACKS > CRACK

CRACKSMAN n burglar, esp a safe-breaker

CRACKSMEN > CRACKSMAN

CRACKUP n physical or mental breakdown

CRACKUPS > CRACKUP

CRACKY adj full of cracks

CRACOWE n medieval shoe with a sharply pointed toe

CRACOWES > CRACOWE

CRADLE n baby's bed on rockers ▷ vb hold gently as if in a cradle

CRADLED > CRADLE

CRADLER > CRADLE

CRADLERS > CRADLE

CRADLES > CRADLE

CRADLING n framework of iron or wood, esp as used in the construction of a ceiling

CRADLINGS > CRADLING

CRAFT n occupation requiring skill with the hands ▷ vb make skilfully

CRAFTED > CRAFT

CRAFTER n person doing craftwork

CRAFTERS > CRAFTER

CRAFTIER > CRAFTY

CRAFTIEST > CRAFTY

CRAFTILY > CRAFTY

CRAFTING > CRAFT

CRAFTLESS adj guileless

CRAFTS > CRAFT

CRAFTSMAN n skilled worker

CRAFTSMEN > CRAFTSMAN

CRAFTWORK n handicraft

CRAFTY adj skilled in deception

CRAG n steep rugged rock

CRAGFAST adj stranded on a crag

CRAGGED same as **>** CRAGGY

CRAGGIER > CRAGGY

CRAGGIEST > CRAGGY

CRAGGILY > CRAGGY

CRAGGY adj having many crags

CRAGS > CRAG

CRAGSMAN n rock climber

CRAGSMEN > CRAGSMAN

CRAIC n Irish word meaning fun

CRAICS > CRAIC

CRAIG a Scot word for **>** CRAG

CRAIGS > CRAIG

CRAKE n bird of the rail family, such as the corncrake ▷ vb to boast

CRAKED > CRAKE

CRAKES > CRAKE

CRAKING > CRAKE

CRAM vb force into too small a space ▷ n act or condition of cramming

CRAMBE n any plant of the genus Crambe

CRAMBES > CRAMBE

CRAMBO n word game in which one team says a rhyme or rhyming line for a word or line given by the other team

CRAMBOES > CRAMBO

CRAMBOS > CRAMBO

CRAME n merchant's booth or stall

CRAMES > CRAME

CRAMESIES > CRAMESY

CRAMESY same as **>** CRAMOISY

CRAMFULL adj very full

CRAMMABLE adj able to be crammed or filled

CRAMMED > CRAM

CRAMMER n person or school that prepares pupils for an examination

CRAMMERS > CRAMMER

CRAMMING > CRAM

CRAMOISIE same as **>** CRAMOISY

CRAMOISY adj of a crimson colour ▷ n crimson cloth

CRAMP n painful muscular contraction ▷ vb affect with a cramp

CRAMPBARK n guelder rose

CRAMPED adj closed in

CRAMPER n spiked metal plate used as a brace for the feet in throwing the stone

CRAMPERS > CRAMPER

CRAMPET n cramp iron

CRAMPETS > CRAMPET

CRAMPFISH n electric ray

CRAMPIER > CRAMPY

CRAMPIEST > CRAMPY

CRAMPING > CRAMP

CRAMPIT same as **>** CRAMPET

CRAMPITS > CRAMPIT

CRAMPON n spiked plate strapped to a boot for climbing on ice ▷ vb climb using crampons

CRAMPONED > CRAMPON

CRAMPONS > CRAMPON

CRAMPOON same as **>** CRAMPON

CRAMPOONS > CRAMPOON

CRAMPS > CRAMP

CRAMPY adj affected with cramp

CRAMS > CRAM

CRAN n unit of capacity used for measuring fresh herring, equal to 37.5 gallons

CRANACHAN n Scottish dessert made with oatmeal, cream and whisky

CRANAGE n use of a crane

CRANAGES > CRANAGE

CRANBERRY n sour edible red berry

CRANCH vb to crunch

CRANCHED > CRANCH

CRANCHES > CRANCH

CRANCHING > CRANCH

CRANE n machine for lifting and moving heavy weights ▷ vb stretch (one's neck) to see something

CRANED > CRANE
CRANEFLY n fly with long legs, slender wings, and a narrow body
CRANES > CRANE
CRANIA > CRANIUM
CRANIAL adj of or relating to the skull
CRANIALLY > CRANIAL
CRANIATE adj having a skull or cranium ▷ n vertebrate
CRANIATES > CRANIATE
CRANING > CRANE
CRANIUM n skull
CRANIUMS > CRANIUM
CRANK n arm projecting at right angles from a shaft, for transmitting or converting motion ▷ vb turn with a crank ▷ adj (of a sailing vessel) easily keeled over by the wind
CRANKCASE n metal case that encloses the crankshaft in an internal-combustion engine
CRANKED > CRANK
CRANKER > CRANK
CRANKEST > CRANK
CRANKIER > CRANK
CRANKIEST > CRANK
CRANKILY > CRANK
CRANKING > CRANK
CRANKISH adj somewhat eccentric or bad-tempered
CRANKLE vb to bend or wind
CRANKLED > CRANKLE
CRANKLES > CRANKLE
CRANKLING > CRANKLE
CRANKLY adj vigorously
CRANKNESS n (of a vessel) liability to capsize
CRANKOUS adj fretful
CRANKPIN n short cylindrical pin in a crankshaft, to which the connecting rod is attached
CRANKPINS > CRANKPIN
CRANKS > CRANK
CRANKY same as > CRANK
CRANNIED > CRANNY
CRANNIES > CRANNY
CRANNOG n ancient Celtic lake or bog dwelling dating from the late Bronze Age to the 16th century AD, often fortified and used as a refuge
CRANNOGE same as > CRANNOG
CRANNOGES > CRANNOGE
CRANNOGS > CRANNOG
CRANNY n narrow opening ▷ vb to become full of crannies
CRANNYING > CRANNY
CRANREUCH n hoarfrost
CRANS > CRAN
CRANTS n garland carried in front of a maiden's bier
CRANTSES > CRANTS
CRAP n rubbish, nonsense

▷ vb defecate
CRAPAUD n frog or toad
CRAPAUDS > CRAPAUD
CRAPE same as > CREPE
CRAPED > CRAPE
CRAPELIKE > CRAPE
CRAPES > CRAPE
CRAPIER > CRAPE
CRAPIEST > CRAPE
CRAPING > CRAPE
CRAPLE same as > GRAPPLE
CRAPLES > CRAPLE
CRAPOLA n rubbish
CRAPOLAS > CRAPOLA
CRAPPED > CRAP
CRAPPER n toilet
CRAPPERS > CRAPPER
CRAPPIE n N American freshwater fish
CRAPPIER > CRAPPY
CRAPPIES > CRAPPIE
CRAPPIEST > CRAPPY
CRAPPING > CRAP
CRAPPY adj worthless, lousy
CRAPS > CRAP
CRAPSHOOT n dice game
CRAPULENT adj given to or resulting from excessive eating or drinking
CRAPULOUS same as > CRAPULENT
CRAPY > CRAPE
CRARE n type of trading vessel
CRARES > CRARE
CRASES > CRASIS
CRASH n collision involving a vehicle or vehicles ▷ vb (cause to) collide violently with a vehicle, a stationary object, or the ground ▷ adj requiring or using great effort in order to achieve results quickly
CRASHED > CRASH
CRASHER > CRASH
CRASHERS > CRASH
CRASHES > CRASH
CRASHING adj extreme
CRASHPAD n place to sleep or live temporarily
CRASHPADS > CRASHPAD
CRASIS n fusion or contraction of two adjacent vowels into one
CRASS adj stupid and insensitive
CRASSER > CRASS
CRASSEST > CRASS
CRASSLY > CRASS
CRASSNESS > CRASS
CRATCH n rack for holding fodder for cattle, etc
CRATCHES > CRATCH
CRATE n large wooden container for packing goods ▷ vb put in a crate
CRATED > CRATE
CRATEFUL > CRATE
CRATEFULS > CRATE
CRATER n bowl-shaped opening at the top of a

volcano ▷ vb make or form craters
CRATERED > CRATER
CRATERING > CRATER
CRATERLET n small crater
CRATEROUS > CRATER
CRATERS > CRATER
CRATES > CRATE
CRATHUR same as > CRATUR
CRATHURS > CRATHUR
CRATING > CRATE
CRATON n stable part of the earth's continental crust or lithosphere that has not been deformed significantly for many millions, even hundreds of millions, of years
CRATONIC > CRATON
CRATONS > CRATON
CRATUR n whisky or whiskey
CRATURS > CRATUR
CRAUNCH same as > CRUNCH
CRAUNCHED > CRAUNCH
CRAUNCHES > CRAUNCH
CRAUNCHY > CRAUNCH
CRAVAT n man's scarf worn like a tie ▷ vb wear a cravat
CRAVATS > CRAVAT
CRAVATTED > CRAVAT
CRAVE vb desire intensely
CRAVED > CRAVE
CRAVEN adj cowardly ▷ n coward ▷ vb to make cowardly
CRAVENED > CRAVEN
CRAVENING > CRAVEN
CRAVENLY > CRAVEN
CRAVENS > CRAVEN
CRAVER > CRAVE
CRAVERS > CRAVE
CRAVES > CRAVE
CRAVING n intense desire or longing
CRAVINGS > CRAVING
CRAW n pouchlike part of a bird's oesophagus
CRAWDAD n crayfish
CRAWDADDY n crayfish
CRAWDADS > CRAWDAD
CRAWFISH same as > CRAYFISH
CRAWL vb move on one's hands and knees ▷ n crawling motion or pace
CRAWLED > CRAWL
CRAWLER n servile flatterer
CRAWLERS > CRAWLER
CRAWLIER > CRAWLY
CRAWLIEST > CRAWLY
CRAWLING n defect in freshly applied paint or varnish characterized by bare patches and ridging
CRAWLINGS > CRAWLING
CRAWLS > CRAWL
CRAWLWAY n in a mine, low passageway that can only be negotiated by crawling
CRAWLWAYS > CRAWLWAY
CRAWLY adj feeling or

causing a sensation like creatures crawling on one's skin
CRAWS > CRAW
CRAY n crayfish
CRAYER same as > CRARE
CRAYERS > CRAYER
CRAYFISH n edible shellfish like a lobster
CRAYON n a stick or pencil of coloured wax or clay ▷ vb draw or colour with a crayon
CRAYONED > CRAYON
CRAYONER > CRAYON
CRAYONERS > CRAYON
CRAYONING > CRAYON
CRAYONIST > CRAYON
CRAYONS > CRAYON
CRAYS > CRAY
CRAYTHUR variant of > CRATUR
CRAYTHURS > CRAYTHUR
CRAZE n short-lived fashion or enthusiasm ▷ vb make mad
CRAZED adj wild and uncontrolled
CRAZES > CRAZE
CRAZIER > CRAZY
CRAZIES > CRAZY
CRAZIEST > CRAZY
CRAZILY > CRAZY
CRAZINESS > CRAZY
CRAZING > CRAZE
CRAZY adj ridiculous ▷ n crazy person ▷ n crazy person
CRAZYWEED n locoweed
CREACH same as > CREAGH
CREACHS > CREACH
CREAGH n foray
CREAGHS > CREAGH
CREAK n (make) a harsh squeaking sound ▷ vb make or move with a harsh squeaking sound
CREAKED > CREAK
CREAKIER > CREAK
CREAKIEST > CREAK
CREAKILY > CREAK
CREAKING > CREAK
CREAKS > CREAK
CREAKY > CREAK
CREAM n fatty part of milk ▷ adj yellowish-white ▷ vb beat to a creamy consistency
CREAMCUPS n Californian plant with small cream-coloured or yellow flowers on long stalks
CREAMED > CREAM
CREAMER n powdered milk substitute for use in coffee
CREAMERS > CREAMER
CREAMERY n place where dairy products are made or sold
CREAMIER > CREAMY
CREAMIEST > CREAMY
CREAMILY > CREAMY
CREAMING > CREAM
CREAMLAID adj (of laid

paper) cream-coloured and of a ribbed appearance

CREAMLIKE > CREAM

CREAMPUFF *n* puff pastry filled with cream

CREAMS > CREAM

CREAMWARE *n* type of earthenware with a deep cream body developed about 1720 and widely produced

CREAMWOVE *adj* (of wove paper) cream-coloured and even-surfaced

CREAMY *adj* resembling cream in colour, taste, or consistency

CREANCE *n* long light cord used in falconry

CREANCES > CREANCE

CREANT *adj* formative

CREASE *n* line made by folding or pressing ▷ *vb* crush or line

CREASED > CREASE

CREASER > CREASE

CREASERS > CREASE

CREASES > CREASE

CREASIER > CREASE

CREASIEST > CREASE

CREASING > CREASE

CREASOTE *same as* > CREOSOTE

CREASOTED > CREASOTE

CREASOTES > CREASOTE

CREASY > CREASE

CREATABLE > CREATE

CREATE *vb* make, cause to exist

CREATED > CREATE

CREATES > CREATE

CREATIC *adj* relating to flesh or meat

CREATIN *same as* > CREATINE

CREATINE *n* important metabolite involved in many biochemical reactions and present in many types of living cells

CREATINES > CREATINE

CREATING > CREATE

CREATINS > CREATIN

CREATION *n* creating or being created

CREATIONS > CREATION

CREATIVE *adj* imaginative or inventive ▷ *n* person who is creative professionally

CREATIVES > CREATIVE

CREATOR *n* person who creates

CREATORS > CREATOR

CREATRESS > CREATOR

CREATRIX > CREATOR

CREATURAL > CREATURE

CREATURE *n* animal, person, or other being

CREATURES > CREATURE

CRECHE *n* place where small children are looked after while their parents are working, shopping, etc

CRECHES > CRECHE

CRED *n* short for credibility

CREDAL > CREED

CREDENCE *n* belief in the truth or accuracy of a statement

CREDENCES > CREDENCE

CREDENDA > CREDENDUM

CREDENDUM *n* article of faith

CREDENT *adj* believing or believable

CREDENZA *n* type of small sideboard

CREDENZAS > CREDENZA

CREDIBLE *adj* believable

CREDIBLY > CREDIBLE

CREDIT *n* system of allowing customers to receive goods and pay later ▷ *vb* enter as a credit in an account

CREDITED > CREDIT

CREDITING > CREDIT

CREDITOR *n* person to whom money is owed

CREDITORS > CREDITOR

CREDITS *npl* list of people responsible for the production of a film, programme, or record

CREDO *n* creed

CREDOS > CREDO

CREDS > CRED

CREDULITY *n* willingness to believe something on little evidence

CREDULOUS *adj* too willing to believe

CREE *vb* to soften grain by boiling or soaking

CREED *n* statement or system of (Christian) beliefs or principles

CREEDAL > CREED

CREEDS > CREED

CREEING > CREE

CREEK *n* narrow inlet or bay

CREEKIER > CREEKY

CREEKIEST > CREEKY

CREEKS > CREEK

CREEKY *adj* abounding in creeks

CREEL *n* wicker basket used by anglers ▷ *vb* to fish using creels

CREELED > CREEL

CREELING > CREEL

CREELS > CREEL

CREEP *vb* move quietly and cautiously ▷ *n* creeping movement

CREEPAGE *n* imperceptible movement

CREEPAGES > CREEPAGE

CREEPED > CREEP

CREEPER *n* creeping plant ▷ *vb* train a plant to creep

CREEPERED > CREEPER

CREEPERS > CREEPER

CREEPIE *n* low stool

CREEPIER > CREEPY

CREEPIES > CREEPIE

CREEPIEST > CREEPY

CREEPILY > CREEPY

CREEPING > CREEP

CREEPS > CREEP

CREEPY *adj* causing a feeling of fear or disgust

CREES > CREE

CREESE *same as* > KRIS

CREESED > CREESE

CREESES > CREESE

CREESH *vb* to lubricate

CREESHED > CREESH

CREESHES > CREESH

CREESHIER > CREESHY

CREESHING > CREESH

CREESHY *adj* greasy

CREESING > CREESE

CREM *n* crematorium

CREMAINS *n* cremated remains of a body

CREMANT *adj* (of wine) moderately sparkling

CREMASTER *n* muscle which raises and lowers the scrotum

CREMATE *vb* burn (a corpse) to ash

CREMATED > CREMATE

CREMATES > CREMATE

CREMATING > CREMATE

CREMATION > CREMATE

CREMATOR *n* furnace for cremating corpses

CREMATORS > CREMATOR

CREMATORY *adj* of or relating to cremation or crematoriums

CREME *n* cream ▷ *adj* (of a liqueur) rich and sweet

CREMES > CREME

CREMINI *n* variety of mushroom

CREMINIS > CREMINI

CREMOCARP *n* any fruit, such as anise or fennel, consisting of two united carpels

CREMONA *same as* > CROMORNA

CREMONAS > CREMONA

CREMOR *n* cream

CREMORNE *n* penis

CREMORNES > CREMORNE

CREMORS > CREMOR

CREMOSIN *adj* crimson

CREMS > CREM

CREMSIN *same as* > CREMOSIN

CRENA *n* cleft or notch

CRENAS > CRENA

CRENATE *adj* having a scalloped margin, as certain leaves

CRENATED *same as* > CRENATE

CRENATELY > CRENATE

CRENATION *n* any of the rounded teeth or the notches between them on a crenate structure

CRENATURE *same as* > CRENATION

CRENEL *n* any of a set of openings formed in the top of a wall or parapet and having slanting sides, as in

a battlement ▷ *vb* to crenelate

CRENELATE *vb* supply with battlements

CRENELED > CRENEL

CRENELING > CRENEL

CRENELLE *same as* > CRENEL

CRENELLED > CRENEL

CRENELLES > CRENELLE

CRENELS > CRENEL

CRENSHAW *n* variety of melon

CRENSHAWS > CRENSHAW

CRENULATE *adj* having a margin very finely notched with rounded projections, as certain leaves

CREODONT *n* type of extinct Tertiary mammal, the ancestor of modern carnivores

CREODONTS > CREODONT

CREOLE *n* language developed from a mixture of languages ▷ *adj* of or relating to a creole

CREOLES > CREOLE

CREOLIAN *n* Creole

CREOLIANS > CREOLIAN

CREOLISE *vb* (of a pidgin language) to become the native language of a speech community

CREOLISED *same as* > CREOLIZED

CREOLISES > CREOLISE

CREOLIST *n* student of creole languages

CREOLISTS > CREOLIST

CREOLIZE *same as* > CREOLISE

CREOLIZED *adj* (of a language) incorporating a considerable range of features from one or more unrelated languages, as the result of contact between language communities

CREOLIZES > CREOLIZE

CREOPHAGY *n* act of eating meat

CREOSOL *n* colourless or pale yellow insoluble oily liquid with a smoky odour and a burning taste

CREOSOLS > CREOSOL

CREOSOTE *n* dark oily liquid made from coal tar and used for preserving wood ▷ *vb* treat with creosote

CREOSOTED > CREOSOTE

CREOSOTES > CREOSOTE

CREOSOTIC > CREOSOTE

CREPANCE *n* injury to a horse's hind leg caused by being struck by the shoe of the other hind foot

CREPANCES > CREPANCE

CREPE *n* fabric or rubber with a crinkled texture ▷ *vb* cover or drape with crepe ▷ *vb* to crimp or frizz

CREPED > CREPE

CREPERIE n eating establishment that specializes in pancakes

CREPERIES > CREPERIE

CREPES > CREPE

CREPEY same as > CREPY

CREPIER > CREPY

CREPIEST > CREPY

CREPINESS > CREPY

CREPING > CREPE

CREPITANT > CREPITATE

CREPITATE vb make a rattling or crackling sound

CREPITUS n crackling chest sound heard in pneumonia and other lung diseases

CREPOLINE n light silk material used in dressmaking

CREPON n thin material made of fine wool and/or silk

CREPONS > CREPON

CREPS npl slang term for training shoes

CREPT > CREEP

CREPUSCLE n twilight

CREPY adj (esp of the skin) having a dry wrinkled appearance like crepe

CRESCENDI > CRESCENDO

CRESCENDO n gradual increase in loudness, esp in music ▷ adv gradually getting louder ▷ vb increase in loudness or force

CRESCENT n (curved shape of) the moon as seen in its first or last quarter ▷ adj crescent-shaped

CRESCENTS > CRESCENT

CRESCIVE adj increasing

CRESOL n aromatic compound derived from phenol, existing in three isomeric forms: found in coal tar and creosote and used in making synthetic resins and as an antiseptic and disinfectant

CRESOLS > CRESOL

CRESS n plant with strong-tasting leaves, used in salads

CRESSES > CRESS

CRESSET n metal basket mounted on a pole in which oil or pitch was burned for illumination

CRESSETS > CRESSET

CRESSIER > CRESSY

CRESSIEST > CRESSY

CRESSY > CRESS

CREST n top of a mountain, hill, or wave ▷ vb come to or be at the top of

CRESTA n in cresta run high-speed toboganning down a steep narrow passage of compacted snow and ice

CRESTAL > CREST

CRESTED > CREST

CRESTING same as > CREST

CRESTINGS > CREST

CRESTLESS > CREST

CRESTON n hogback

CRESTONS > CRESTON

CRESTS > CREST

CRESYL n tolyl

CRESYLIC adj of, concerned with, or containing creosote or cresol

CRESYLS > CRESYL

CRETIC n metrical foot consisting of three syllables, the first long, the second short, and the third long

CRETICS > CRETIC

CRETIN n stupid person

CRETINISE vb make (someone) a cretin

CRETINISM n condition arising from a deficiency of thyroid hormone, present from birth, characterized by dwarfism and mental retardation

CRETINIZE same as > CRETINISE

CRETINOID > CRETIN

CRETINOUS > CRETIN

CRETINS > CRETIN

CRETISM n lying

CRETISMS > CRETISM

CRETONNE n heavy printed cotton fabric used in furnishings

CRETONNES > CRETONNE

CRETONS npl spread made from pork fat and onions

CREUTZER n former copper and silver coin of Germany or Austria

CREUTZERS > CREUTZER

CREVALLE n any fish of the family Carangidae

CREVALLES > CREVALLE

CREVASSE n deep open crack in a glacier ▷ vb make a break or fissure in (a dyke, wall, etc)

CREVASSED > CREVASSE

CREVASSES > CREVASSE

CREVETTE n shrimp

CREVETTES > CREVETTE

CREVICE n narrow crack or gap in rock

CREVICED > CREVICE

CREVICES > CREVICE

CREW n people who work on a ship or aircraft ▷ vb serve as a crew member (on)

CREWCUT n very short haircut

CREWCUTS > CREWCUT

CREWE n type of pot

CREWED > CREW

CREWEL n fine worsted yarn used in embroidery ▷ vb to embroider in crewel

CREWELIST > CREWEL

CREWELLED > CREWEL

CREWELS > CREWEL

CREWES > CREWE

CREWING > CREW

CREWLESS adj lacking a crew

CREWMAN n member of a ship's crew

CREWMATE n colleague on the crew of a boat or ship

CREWMATES > CREWMATE

CREWMEN > CREWMAN

CREWNECK n plain round neckline in sweaters

CREWNECKS > CREWNECK

CREWS > CREW

CRIA n baby llama, alpaca, or vicu

CRIANT adj garish

CRIAS > CRIA

CRIB n piece of writing stolen from elsewhere ▷ vb copy (someone's work) dishonestly

CRIBBAGE n card game for two to four players

CRIBBAGES > CRIBBAGE

CRIBBED > CRIB

CRIBBER > CRIB

CRIBBERS > CRIB

CRIBBING > CRIB

CRIBBINGS > CRIB

CRIBBLE vb to sift

CRIBBLED > CRIBBLE

CRIBBLES > CRIBBLE

CRIBBLING > CRIBBLE

CRIBELLA > CRIBELLUM

CRIBELLAR > CRIBELLUM

CRIBELLUM n sievelike spinning organ in certain spiders that occurs between the spinnerets

CRIBLE adj dotted

CRIBRATE adj sievelike

CRIBROSE adj pierced with holes

CRIBROUS > CRIBROSE

CRIBS > CRIB

CRIBWORK same as > CRIB

CRIBWORKS > CRIBWORK

CRICETID n any member of the family Cricetidae, such as the hamster and vole

CRICETIDS > CRICETID

CRICK n muscle spasm or cramp in the back or neck ▷ vb cause a crick in

CRICKED > CRICK

CRICKET n outdoor game played with bats, a ball, and wickets by two teams of eleven ▷ vb play cricket

CRICKETED > CRICKET

CRICKETER > CRICKET

CRICKETS > CRICKET

CRICKEY same as > CRIKEY

CRICKING > CRICK

CRICKS > CRICK

CRICKY same as > CRIKEY

CRICOID adj of or relating to the ring-shaped lowermost cartilage of the larynx ▷ n this cartilage

CRICOIDS > CRICOID

CRIED > CRY

CRIER n (formerly) official who made public announcements

CRIERS > CRIER

CRIES > CRY

CRIKEY interj expression of surprise

CRIM short for > CRIMINAL

CRIME n unlawful act ▷ vb charge with a crime

CRIMED > CRIME

CRIMEFUL adj criminal

CRIMELESS adj innocent

CRIMEN n crime

CRIMES > CRIME

CRIMEWAVE n period of increased criminal activity

CRIMINA > CRIMEN

CRIMINAL n person guilty of a crime ▷ adj of crime

CRIMINALS > CRIMINAL

CRIMINATE vb charge with a crime

CRIMINE interj expression of surprise

CRIMING > CRIME

CRIMINI > CRIMINE

CRIMINIS n accomplice in crime

CRIMINOUS adj criminal

CRIMINY interj cry of surprise

CRIMMER a variant spelling of > KRIMMER

CRIMMERS > CRIMMER

CRIMP vb fold or press into ridges ▷ n act or result of crimping

CRIMPED > CRIMP

CRIMPER > CRIMP

CRIMPERS > CRIMP

CRIMPIER > CRIMP

CRIMPIEST > CRIMP

CRIMPING > CRIMP

CRIMPLE vb crumple, wrinkle, or curl

CRIMPLED > CRIMPLE

CRIMPLES > CRIMPLE

CRIMPLING > CRIMPLE

CRIMPS > CRIMP

CRIMPY > CRIMP

CRIMS > CRIM

CRIMSON adj deep purplish-red ▷ n deep or vivid red colour ▷ vb make or become crimson

CRIMSONED > CRIMSON

CRIMSONS > CRIMSON

CRINAL adj relating to the hair

CRINATE adj having hair

CRINATED same as > CRINATE

CRINE vb to shrivel

CRINED > CRINE

CRINES > CRINE

CRINGE vb flinch in fear ▷ n act of cringing

CRINGED > CRINGE

CRINGER > CRINGE**

CRINGERS > CRINGE
CRINGES > CRINGE
CRINGING > CRINGE
CRINGINGS > CRINGE
CRINGLE n eye at the edge of a sail, usually formed from a thimble or grommet
CRINGLES > CRINGLE
CRINING > CRINE
CRINITE adj covered with soft hairs or tufts ▷ n sedimentary rock
CRINITES > CRINITE
CRINKLE n wrinkle, crease, or fold ▷ vb become slightly creased or folded
CRINKLED > CRINKLE
CRINKLES > CRINKLE
CRINKLIER > CRINKLY
CRINKLIES > CRINKLY
CRINKLING > CRINKLE
CRINKLY adj wrinkled ▷ n old person
CRINOID n type of primitive echinoderm with delicate feathery arms radiating from a central disc, such as feather stars and sea lilies
CRINOIDAL > CRINOID
CRINOIDS > CRINOID
CRINOLINE n hooped petticoat
CRINOSE adj hairy
CRINUM n type of mostly tropical plant with straplike leaves and clusters of lily-like flowers
CRINUMS > CRINUM
CRIOLLO n native or inhabitant of Latin America of European descent, esp of Spanish descent ▷ adj of, relating to, or characteristic of a criollo or criollos
CRIOLLOS > CRIOLLO
CRIOS n multicoloured woven woollen belt traditionally worn by men in the Aran Islands
CRIOSES > CRIOS
CRIPE variant of > CRIPES
CRIPES interj expression of surprise
CRIPPLE n offensive word for a person who is lame or disabled ▷ vb make lame or disabled
CRIPPLED > CRIPPLE
CRIPPLER > CRIPPLE
CRIPPLERS > CRIPPLE
CRIPPLES > CRIPPLE
CRIPPLING adj damaging or injurious
CRIS variant of > KRIS
CRISE n crisis
CRISES > CRISIS
CRISIC adj relating to a crisis
CRISIS n crucial stage, turning point
CRISP adj fresh and firm ▷ n very thin slice of potato fried till crunchy ▷ vb make

or become crisp
CRISPATE adj having a curled or waved appearance
CRISPATED same as > CRISPATE
CRISPED same as > CRISPATE
CRISPEN vb to make crisp
CRISPENED > CRISPEN
CRISPENS > CRISPEN
CRISPER n compartment in a refrigerator for storing salads, vegetables, etc, in order to keep them fresh
CRISPERS > CRISPER
CRISPEST > CRISP
CRISPHEAD n variety of lettuce
CRISPIER > CRISPY
CRISPIES npl as in rice crispies puffed grains of rice, eaten esp as breakfast cereal
CRISPIEST > CRISPY
CRISPILY > CRISPY
CRISPIN n cobbler
CRISPING > CRISP
CRISPINS > CRISPIN
CRISPLY > CRISP
CRISPNESS > CRISP
CRISPS > CRISP
CRISPY adj hard and crunchy
CRISSA > CRISSUM
CRISSAL > CRISSUM
CRISSUM n area or feathers surrounding the cloaca of a bird
CRISTA n structure resembling a ridge or crest, such as that formed by folding of the inner membrane of a mitochondrion
CRISTAE > CRISTA
CRISTATE adj having a crest
CRISTATED same as > CRISTATE
CRIT abbreviation of > CRITICISM
CRITERIA > CRITERION
CRITERIAL > CRITERION
CRITERION n standard of judgment
CRITERIUM n type of bicycle race, involving many laps of a short course
CRITH n unit of weight for gases
CRITHS > CRITH
CRITIC n professional judge of any of the arts
CRITICAL adj very important or dangerous
CRITICISE same as > CRITICIZE
CRITICISM n fault-finding
CRITICIZE vb find fault with
CRITICS > CRITIC
CRITIQUE n critical essay

▷ vb to review critically
CRITIQUED > CRITIQUE
CRITIQUES > CRITIQUE
CRITS > CRIT
CRITTER a dialect word for > CREATURE
CRITTERS > CRITTER
CRITTUR same as > CRITTER
CRITTURS > CRITTUR
CRIVENS interj expression of surprise
CRIVVENS same as > CRIVENS
CROAK vb (of a frog or crow) give a low hoarse cry ▷ n low hoarse sound
CROAKED > CROAK
CROAKER n animal, bird, etc, that croaks
CROAKERS > CROAKER
CROAKIER > CROAK
CROAKIEST > CROAK
CROAKILY > CROAK
CROAKING > CROAK
CROAKINGS > CROAK
CROAKS > CROAK
CROAKY > CROAK
CROC short for > CROCODILE
CROCEATE adj saffron-coloured
CROCEIN n any one of a group of red or orange acid azo dyes
CROCEINE same as > CROCEIN
CROCEINES > CROCEIN
CROCEINS > CROCEIN
CROCEOUS adj saffron-coloured
CROCHE n knob at the top of a deer's horn
CROCHES > CROCHE
CROCHET vb make by looping and intertwining yarn with a hooked needle ▷ n work made in this way
CROCHETED > CROCHET
CROCHETER > CROCHET
CROCHETS > CROCHET
CROCI > CROCUS
CROCINE adj relating to the crocus
CROCK n earthenware pot or jar ▷ vb become or cause to become weak or disabled
CROCKED adj injured
CROCKERY n dishes
CROCKET n carved ornament in the form of a curled leaf or cusp, used in Gothic architecture
CROCKETED > CROCKET
CROCKETS > CROCKET
CROCKING > CROCK
CROCKPOT n tradename for a brand of slow cooker
CROCKPOTS > CROCKPOT
CROCKS > CROCK
CROCODILE n large amphibious tropical reptile
CROCOITE n rare orange

secondary mineral
CROCOITES > CROCOITE
CROCOSMIA n type of S African plant
CROCS > CROC
CROCUS n flowering plant
CROCUSES > CROCUS
CROFT n small farm worked by one family in Scotland ▷ vb farm land as a croft
CROFTED > CROFT
CROFTER n owner or tenant of a small farm, esp in Scotland or northern England
CROFTERS > CROFTER
CROFTING n system or occupation of working land in crofts
CROFTINGS > CROFTING
CROFTS > CROFT
CROG vb ride on a bicycle as a passenger
CROGGED > CROG
CROGGIES > CROGGY
CROGGING > CROG
CROGGY n ride on a bicycle as a passenger
CROGS > CROG
CROISSANT n rich flaky crescent-shaped roll
CROJIK n triangular sail
CROJIKS > CROJIK
CROKINOLE n board game popular in Canada in which players flick wooden discs
CROMACK same as > CRUMMOCK
CROMACKS > CROMACK
CROMB same as > CROME
CROMBEC n African Old World warbler with colourful plumage
CROMBECS > CROMBEC
CROMBED > CROMB
CROMBING > CROMB
CROMBS > CROMB
CROME n hook ▷ vb use a crome
CROMED > CROME
CROMES > CROME
CROMING > CROME
CROMLECH n circle of prehistoric standing stones
CROMLECHS > CROMLECH
CROMORNA n one of the reed stops in an organ
CROMORNAS > CROMORNA
CROMORNE variant of > CROMORNA
CROMORNES > CROMORNE
CRONE n witchlike old woman
CRONES > CRONE
CRONET n hair which grows over the top of a horse's hoof
CRONETS > CRONET
CRONIES > CRONY
CRONISH > CRONE
CRONK adj unfit
CRONKER > CRONK
CRONKEST > CRONK
CRONY n close friend

CRONYISM n practice of appointing friends to high-level, esp political, posts regardless of their suitability

CRONYISMS > CRONYISM

CROODLE vb to nestle close

CROODLED > CROODLE

CROODLES > CROODLE

CROODLING > CROODLE

CROOK n dishonest person ▷ vb bend or curve

CROOKBACK a rare word for > HUNCHBACK

CROOKED adj bent or twisted

CROOKEDER > CROOKED

CROOKEDLY > CROOKED

CROOKER > CROOK

CROOKERY n illegal or dishonest activity

CROOKEST > CROOK

CROOKING > CROOK

CROOKNECK n any type of summer squash

CROOKS > CROOK

CROOL vb spoil

CROOLED > CROOL

CROOLING > CROOL

CROOLS > CROOL

CROON vb sing, hum, or speak in a soft low tone ▷ n soft low singing or humming

CROONED > CROON

CROONER > CROON

CROONERS > CROON

CROONING > CROON

CROONINGS > CROON

CROONS > CROON

CROOVE n animal enclosure

CROOVES > CROOVE

CROP n cultivated plant ▷ vb cut very short

CROPBOUND n poultry disease causing a pendulous crop

CROPFUL n quantity that can be held in the craw

CROPFULL adj satiated

CROPFULS > CROPFUL

CROPLAND n land on which crops are grown

CROPLANDS > CROPLAND

CROPLESS adj without crops

CROPPED > CROP

CROPPER n person who cultivates or harvests a crop

CROPPERS > CROPPER

CROPPIE same as > CROPPY

CROPPIES > CROPPY

CROPPING > CROP

CROPPINGS > CROP

CROPPY n rebel in the Irish rising of 1798

CROPS > CROP

CROPSICK adj sick from excessive food or drink

CROQUANTE n crisp nut-filled chocolate or cake

CROQUET n game played on a lawn in which balls are hit through hoops ▷ vb drive away (another player's ball) by hitting one's own ball when the two are in contact

CROQUETED > CROQUET

CROQUETS > CROQUET

CROQUETTE n fried cake of potato, meat, or fish

CROQUIS n rough sketch

CRORE n (in Indian English) ten million

CROREPATI n (in India) person whose assets are at least 10 million rupees

CRORES > CRORE

CROSIER n staff surmounted by a crook or cross, carried by bishops as a symbol of pastoral office ▷ vb bear or carry such a cross

CROSIERED > CROSIER

CROSIERS > CROSIER

CROSS vb move or go across (something) ▷ n structure, symbol, or mark of two intersecting lines ▷ adj angry, annoyed

CROSSABLE adj capable of being crossed

CROSSARM n in mining, horizontal bar on which a drill is mounted

CROSSARMS > CROSSARM

CROSSBAND vb to set the grain of layers of wood at right angles to one another

CROSSBAR n horizontal bar across goalposts or on a bicycle ▷ vb provide with crossbars

CROSSBARS > CROSSBAR

CROSSBEAM n beam that spans from one support to another

CROSSBILL n finch that has a bill with crossed tips

CROSSBIT > CROSSBITE

CROSSBITE vb to trick

CROSSBOW n weapon consisting of a bow fixed across a wooden stock

CROSSBOWS > CROSSBOW

CROSSBRED adj bred from two different types of animal or plant ▷ n crossbred plant or animal, esp an animal resulting from a cross between two pure breeds

CROSSBUCK n US roadsign used at railroad crossings

CROSSCUT vb cut across ▷ adj cut across ▷ n transverse cut or course

CROSSCUTS > CROSSCUT

CROSSE n light staff with a triangular frame to which a network is attached, used in playing lacrosse

CROSSED > CROSS

CROSSER > CROSS

CROSSERS > CROSS

CROSSES > CROSS

CROSSEST > CROSS

CROSSETTE n in architecture, return in a corner of the architrave of a window or door

CROSSFALL n camber of a road

CROSSFIRE n gunfire crossing another line of fire

CROSSFISH n starfish

CROSSHAIR n one of two fine wires that cross in the focal plane of a gunsight or other optical instrument, used to define the line of sight

CROSSHEAD n subsection or paragraph heading printed within the body of the text

CROSSING n place where a street may be crossed safely

CROSSINGS > CROSSING

CROSSISH > CROSS

CROSSJACK n square sail on a ship's mizzenmast

CROSSLET n cross having a smaller cross near the end of each arm

CROSSLETS > CROSSLET

CROSSLY > CROSS

CROSSNESS > CROSS

CROSSOVER n place at which a crossing is made ▷ adj (of music, fashion, art, etc) combining two distinct styles

CROSSROAD n road that crosses another road

CROSSRUFF n alternate trumping of each other's leads by two partners, or by declarer and dummy ▷ vb trump alternately in two hands of a partnership

CROSSTALK n rapid or witty talk

CROSSTIE n railway sleeper

CROSSTIED adj tied with ropes going across

CROSSTIES > CROSSTIE

CROSSTOWN adj going across town

CROSSTREE n either of a pair of wooden or metal braces on the head of a mast to support the topmast, etc

CROSSWALK n place marked where pedestrians may cross a road

CROSSWAY same as > CROSSROAD

CROSSWAYS same as > CROSSWISE

CROSSWIND n wind that blows at right angles to the direction of travel

CROSSWISE adv across ▷ adj across

CROSSWORD n puzzle in which the solver deduces words suggested by clues and writes them into a grid

CROSSWORT n herbaceous Eurasian plant with pale yellow flowers and whorls of hairy leaves

CROST > CROSS

CROSTINI > CROSTINO

CROSTINIS > CROSTINO

CROSTINO n piece of toasted bread served with a savoury topping

CROTAL n any of various lichens used in dyeing wool, esp for the manufacture of tweeds

CROTALA > CROTALUM

CROTALINE adj relating to rattlesnakes

CROTALISM n posoining due to ingestion of plants of the genus Crotalaria

CROTALS > CROTAL

CROTALUM n ancient castanet-like percussion instrument

CROTCH n part of the body between the tops of the legs ▷ vb have crotch (usu of a piece of clothing) removed

CROTCHED > CROTCH

CROTCHES > CROTCH

CROTCHET n musical note half the length of a minim

CROTCHETS > CROTCHET

CROTCHETY adj bad-tempered

CROTON n type of shrub or tree, the seeds of which yield croton oil

CROTONBUG n species of cockroach

CROTONIC as in crotonic acid type of colourless acid

CROTONS > CROTON

CROTTLE same as > CROTAL

CROTTLES > CROTTLE

CROUCH vb bend low with the legs and body close ▷ n this position

CROUCHED > CROUCH

CROUCHES > CROUCH

CROUCHING > CROUCH

CROUP n throat disease of children, with a cough ▷ vb have croup

CROUPADE n leap by a horse, pulling the hind legs towards the belly

CROUPADES > CROUPADE

CROUPE same as > CROUP

CROUPED > CROUP

CROUPER obsolete variant of > CRUPPER

CROUPERS > CROUPER

CROUPES > CROUPE

CROUPIER n person who collects bets and pays out winnings at a gambling table in a casino

CROUPIERS > CROUPIER

CROUPIEST > CROUP

CROUPILY > CROUP

CROUPING > CROUP

CROUPON n type of

highly-polished flexible leather

CROUPONS > CROUPON

CROUPOUS > CROUP

CROUPS > CROUP

CROUPY > CROUP

CROUSE adj lively, confident, or saucy

CROUSELY > CROUSE

CROUSTADE n pastry case in which food is served

CROUT n sauerkraut

CROUTE n small round of toasted bread on which a savoury mixture is served

CROUTES > CROUTE

CROUTON n small piece of fried or toasted bread served in soup

CROUTONS > CROUTON

CROUTS > CROUT

CROW n large black bird with a harsh call ▷ vb (of a cock) make a shrill squawking sound

CROWBAR n iron bar used as a lever ▷ vb use a crowbar to lever (something)

CROWBARS > CROWBAR

CROWBERRY n low-growing N temperate evergreen shrub with small purplish flowers and black berry-like fruit

CROWBOOT n type of Inuit boot made of fur and leather

CROWBOOTS > CROWBOOT

CROWD n large group of people or things ▷ vb gather together in large numbers

CROWDED > CROWD

CROWDEDLY > CROWD

CROWDER > CROWD

CROWDERS > CROWD

CROWDIE n porridge of meal and water

CROWDIES > CROWDIE

CROWDING > CROWD

CROWDS > CROWD

CROWDY same as > CROWDIE

CROWEA n Australian shrub with pink flowers

CROWEAS > CROWEA

CROWED > CROW

CROWER > CROW

CROWERS > CROW

CROWFEET > CROWFOOT

CROWFOOT n type of plant

CROWFOOTS > CROWFOOT

CROWING > CROW

CROWINGLY > CROW

CROWN n monarch's headdress of gold and jewels ▷ vb put a crown on the head of (someone) to proclaim him or her monarch

CROWNED > CROWN

CROWNER n promotional label consisting of a shaped printed piece of card or paper attached to a product on display

CROWNERS > CROWNER

CROWNET n coronet

CROWNETS > CROWNET

CROWNING n stage of labour when the infant's head is passing through the vaginal opening

CROWNINGS > CROWNING

CROWNLAND n large administrative division of the former empire of Austria-Hungary

CROWNLESS > CROWN

CROWNLET n small crown

CROWNLETS > CROWNLET

CROWNS > CROWN

CROWNWORK n manufacture of artificial crowns for teeth

CROWS > CROW

CROWSFEET > CROWSFOOT

CROWSFOOT n wrinkle at side of eye

CROWSTEP n set of steps to the top of a gable on a building

CROWSTEPS > CROWSTEP

CROZE n recess cut at the end of a barrel or cask to receive the head

CROZER n machine which cuts grooves in cask staves

CROZERS > CROZER

CROZES > CROZE

CROZIER same as > CROSIER

CROZIERS > CROZIER

CROZZLED adj blackened or burnt at the edges

CRU n (in France) a vineyard, group of vineyards, or wine-producing region

CRUBEEN n pig's trotter

CRUBEENS > CRUBEEN

CRUCES > CRUX

CRUCIAL adj very important

CRUCIALLY > CRUCIAL

CRUCIAN n European fish with a dark-green back, a golden-yellow undersurface, and reddish dorsal and tail fins, popular in aquariums

CRUCIANS > CRUCIAN

CRUCIATE adj shaped or arranged like a cross

CRUCIATES > CRUCIATE

CRUCIBLE n pot in which metals are melted

CRUCIBLES > CRUCIBLE

CRUCIFER n type of plant with a corolla of four petals arranged like a cross, such as the brassicas, mustard, cress, and wallflower

CRUCIFERS > CRUCIFER

CRUCIFIED > CRUCIFY

CRUCIFIER > CRUCIFY

CRUCIFIX n model of Christ on the Cross

CRUCIFORM adj

cross-shaped ▷ n geometric curve, shaped like a cross, that has four similar branches asymptotic to two mutually perpendicular pairs of lines

CRUCIFY vb put to death by fastening to a cross

CRUCK n one of a pair of curved wooden timbers supporting the end of the roof in certain types of building

CRUCKS > CRUCK

CRUD n sticky or encrusted substance ▷ interj expression of disgust, disappointment, etc ▷ vb cover with a sticky or encrusted substance

CRUDDED > CRUD

CRUDDIER > CRUDDY

CRUDDIEST > CRUDDY

CRUDDING > CRUD

CRUDDLE vb to curdle

CRUDDLED > CRUDDLE

CRUDDLES > CRUDDLE

CRUDDLING > CRUDDLE

CRUDDY adj dirty or unpleasant

CRUDE adj rough and simple ▷ n crude oil

CRUDELY > CRUDE

CRUDENESS > CRUDE

CRUDER > CRUDE

CRUDES > CRUDE

CRUDEST > CRUDE

CRUDITES npl selection of raw vegetables often served with a variety of dips before a meal

CRUDITIES > CRUDE

CRUDITY > CRUDE

CRUDS > CRUD

CRUDY adj raw

CRUE obsolete variant of > CREW

CRUEL adj delighting in others' pain

CRUELER > CRUEL

CRUELEST > CRUEL

CRUELLER > CRUEL

CRUELLEST > CRUEL

CRUELLS same as > CRUELS

CRUELLY > CRUEL

CRUELNESS > CRUEL

CRUELS n disease of cattle and sheep

CRUELTIES > CRUELTY

CRUELTY n deliberate infliction of pain or suffering

CRUES > CREW

CRUET n small container for salt, pepper, etc, at table

CRUETS > CRUET

CRUISE n sail for pleasure ▷ vb sail from place to place for pleasure

CRUISED > CRUISE

CRUISER n fast warship

CRUISERS > CRUISER

CRUISES > CRUISE

CRUISEWAY n canal used for recreational purposes

CRUISIE same as > CRUIZIE

CRUISIES > CRUISIE

CRUISING > CRUISE

CRUISINGS > CRUISE

CRUIVE n animal enclosure

CRUIVES > CRUIVE

CRUIZIE n oil lamp

CRUIZIES > CRUIZIE

CRULLER n light sweet ring-shaped cake, fried in deep fat

CRULLERS > CRULLER

CRUMB n small fragment of bread or other dry food ▷ vb prepare or cover (food) with breadcrumbs ▷ adj (esp of pie crusts) made with a mixture of biscuit crumbs, sugar, etc

CRUMBED > CRUMB

CRUMBER > CRUMB

CRUMBERS > CRUMB

CRUMBIER > CRUMBY

CRUMBIEST > CRUMBY

CRUMBING > CRUMB

CRUMBLE vb break into fragments ▷ n pudding of stewed fruit with a crumbly topping

CRUMBLED > CRUMBLE

CRUMBLES > CRUMBLE

CRUMBLIER > CRUMBLY

CRUMBLIES n elderly people

CRUMBLING > CRUMBLE

CRUMBLY adj easily crumbled or crumbling

CRUMBS interj expression of dismay or surprise

CRUMBUM n rogue

CRUMBUMS > CRUMBUM

CRUMBY adj full of crumbs

CRUMEN n deer's larmier or tear-pit

CRUMENAL n purse

CRUMENALS > CRUMENAL

CRUMENS > CRUMEN

CRUMHORN n medieval woodwind instrument of bass pitch, consisting of an almost cylindrical tube curving upwards and blown through a double reed covered by a pierced cap

CRUMHORNS > CRUMHORN

CRUMMACK same as > CRUMMOCK

CRUMMACKS > CRUMMACK

CRUMMIE n cow with a crumpled horn

CRUMMIER > CRUMMY

CRUMMIES > CRUMMY

CRUMMIEST > CRUMMY

CRUMMOCK n stick with a crooked head

CRUMMOCKS > CRUMMOCK

CRUMMY adj of poor quality ▷ n lorry that carries loggers to work from their camp

CRUMP vb thud or explode with a loud dull sound ▷ n crunching, thudding, or exploding noise ▷ adj crooked

CRUMPED > CRUMP

CRUMPER > CRUMP

CRUMPEST > CRUMP

CRUMPET n round soft yeast cake, eaten buttered

CRUMPETS > CRUMPET

CRUMPIER > CRUMPY

CRUMPIEST > CRUMPY

CRUMPING > CRUMP

CRUMPLE vb crush, crease ▷ n untidy crease or wrinkle

CRUMPLED > CRUMPLE

CRUMPLES > CRUMPLE

CRUMPLIER > CRUMPLE

CRUMPLING > CRUMPLE

CRUMPLY > CRUMPLE

CRUMPS > CRUMP

CRUMPY adj crisp

CRUNCH vb bite or chew with a noisy crushing sound ▷ n crunching sound

CRUNCHED > CRUNCH

CRUNCHER > CRUNCH

CRUNCHERS > CRUNCH

CRUNCHES > CRUNCH

CRUNCHIE n derogatory word for an Afrikaner

CRUNCHIER > CRUNCH

CRUNCHIES > CRUNCHIE

CRUNCHILY > CRUNCH

CRUNCHING > CRUNCH

CRUNCHY > CRUNCH

CRUNK n form of hip-hop music originating in the Southern US

CRUNKED adj excited or intoxicated

CRUNKLE Scots variant of > CRINKLE

CRUNKLED > CRUNKLE

CRUNKLES > CRUNKLE

CRUNKLING > CRUNKLE

CRUNKS > CRUNK

CRUNODAL > CRUNODE

CRUNODE n point at which two branches of a curve intersect, each branch having a distinct tangent

CRUNODES > CRUNODE

CRUOR n blood clot

CRUORES > CRUOR

CRUORS > CRUOR

CRUPPER n strap that passes from the back of a saddle under a horse's tail

CRUPPERS > CRUPPER

CRURA > CRUS

CRURAL adj of or relating to the leg or thigh

CRUS n leg, esp from the knee to the foot

CRUSADE n medieval Christian war to recover the Holy Land from the Muslims ▷ vb take part in a crusade

CRUSADED > CRUSADE

CRUSADER > CRUSADE

CRUSADERS > CRUSADE

CRUSADES > CRUSADE

CRUSADING > CRUSADE

CRUSADO n former gold or silver coin of Portugal bearing on its reverse the figure of a cross

CRUSADOES > CRUSADO

CRUSADOS > CRUSADO

CRUSE n small earthenware jug or pot

CRUSES > CRUSE

CRUSET n goldsmith's crucible

CRUSETS > CRUSET

CRUSH vb compress so as to injure, break, or crumple ▷ n dense crowd

CRUSHABLE > CRUSH

CRUSHED > CRUSH

CRUSHER > CRUSH

CRUSHERS > CRUSH

CRUSHES > CRUSH

CRUSHING > CRUSH

CRUSIAN variant of > CRUCIAN

CRUSIANS > CRUSIAN

CRUSIE same as > CRUIZIE

CRUSIES > CRUSIE

CRUSILY adj (in heraldry) strewn with crosses

CRUST n hard outer part of something, esp bread ▷ vb cover with or form a crust

CRUSTA n hard outer layer

CRUSTACEA n members of the Crustacea class of arthropods including the lobster

CRUSTAE > CRUSTA

CRUSTAL adj of or relating to the earth's crust

CRUSTATE adj covered with a crust

CRUSTATED same as > CRUSTATE

CRUSTED > CRUST

CRUSTIER > CRUSTY

CRUSTIES > CRUSTY

CRUSTIEST > CRUSTY

CRUSTILY > CRUSTY

CRUSTING > CRUST

CRUSTLESS adj lacking a crust

CRUSTOSE adj having a crustlike appearance

CRUSTS > CRUST

CRUSTY adj having a crust ▷ n dirty type of punk or hippy whose lifestyle involves travelling and squatting

CRUSY same as > CRUIZIE

CRUTCH n long sticklike support with a rest for the armpit, used by a lame person ▷ vb support or sustain (a person or thing) as with a crutch

CRUTCHED > CRUTCH

CRUTCHES > CRUTCH

CRUTCHING > CRUTCH

CRUVE same as > CRUIVE

CRUVES > CRUVE

CRUX n crucial or decisive point

CRUXES > CRUX

CRUZADO same as > CRUSADO

CRUZADOES > CRUZADO

CRUZADOS > CRUZADO

CRUZEIRO n former monetary unit of Brazil, replaced by the cruzeiro real

CRUZEIROS > CRUZEIRO

CRUZIE same as > CRUIZIE

CRUZIES > CRUZIE

CRWTH n ancient stringed instrument of Celtic origin similar to the cithara but bowed in later types

CRWTHS > CRWTH

CRY vb shed tears ▷ n fit of weeping

CRYBABIES > CRYBABY

CRYBABY n person, esp a child, who cries too readily

CRYING > CRY

CRYINGLY > CRY

CRYINGS > CRY

CRYOBANK n place for storing genetic material at low temperature

CRYOBANKS > CRYOBANK

CRYOCABLE n highly conducting electrical cable cooled with a refrigerant such as liquid nitrogen

CRYOGEN n substance used to produce low temperatures

CRYOGENIC adj of the branch of physics concerned with the production of very low temperatures

CRYOGENS > CRYOGEN

CRYOGENY n cryogenic science

CRYOLITE n white or colourless mineral

CRYOLITES > CRYOLITE

CRYOMETER n thermometer for measuring low temperatures

CRYOMETRY > CRYOMETER

CRYONIC > CRYONICS

CRYONICS n practice of freezing a human corpse in the hope of restoring it to life in the future

CRYOPHYTE n organism, esp an alga or moss, that grows on snow or ice

CRYOPROBE n supercooled instrument used in surgery

CRYOSCOPE n any instrument used to determine the freezing point of a substance

CRYOSCOPY n determination of freezing points, esp for the determination of molecular weights by measuring the lowering of the freezing point of a solvent when a known quantity of solute is added

CRYOSTAT n apparatus for maintaining a constant low temperature or a vessel in which a substance is stored at a low temperature

CRYOSTATS > CRYOSTAT

CRYOTRON n miniature switch working at the temperature of liquid helium and depending for its action on the production and destruction of superconducting properties in the conductor

CRYOTRONS > CRYOTRON

CRYPT n vault under a church, esp one used as a burial place

CRYPTADIA n things to be kept hidden

CRYPTAL > CRYPT

CRYPTIC adj obscure in meaning, secret

CRYPTICAL same as > CRYPTIC

CRYPTO n person who is a secret member of an organization or sect

CRYPTOGAM n plant that reproduces by spores not seeds

CRYPTON n krypton

CRYPTONS > CRYPTON

CRYPTONYM n code name

CRYPTOS > CRYPTO

CRYPTS > CRYPT

CRYSTAL n (single grain of) a symmetrically shaped solid formed naturally by some substances ▷ adj bright and clear

CRYSTALS > CRYSTAL

CSARDAS n type of Hungarian folk dance

CSARDASES > CSARDAS

CTENE n locomotor organ found in ctenophores (or comb jellies)

CTENES > CTENE

CTENIDIA > CTENIDIUM

CTENIDIUM n one of the comblike respiratory gills of molluscs

CTENIFORM adj comblike

CTENOID adj toothed like a comb, as the scales of perches

CUADRILLA n matador's assistants in a bullfight

CUATRO n four-stringed guitar

CUATROS > CUATRO

CUB n young wild animal such as a bear or fox ▷ adj young or inexperienced ▷ vb give birth to cubs

CUBAGE same as > CUBATURE

CUBAGES > CUBATURE

CUBANE n rare octahedral hydrocarbon

CUBANELLE n variety of pepper

CUBANES > CUBANE
CUBATURE n
determination of the cubic contents of something
CUBATURES > CUBATURE
CUBBED > CUB
CUBBIER > CUBBY
CUBBIES > CUBBY
CUBBIEST > CUBBY
CUBBING > CUB
CUBBINGS > CUB
CUBBISH > CUB
CUBBISHLY > CUB
CUBBY n a cubbyhole ▷ adj short and plump
CUBBYHOLE n small enclosed space or room
CUBE n object with six equal square sides ▷ vb cut into cubes
CUBEB n SE Asian woody climbing plant with brownish berries
CUBEBS > CUBEB
CUBED > CUBE
CUBER > CUBE
CUBERS > CUBE
CUBES > CUBE
CUBHOOD n state of being a cub
CUBHOODS > CUBHOOD
CUBIC adj having three dimensions ▷ n cubic equation
CUBICA n fine shalloon-like fabric
CUBICAL adj of or related to volume
CUBICALLY > CUBICAL
CUBICAS > CUBICA
CUBICITY n property of being cubelike
CUBICLE n enclosed part of a large room, screened for privacy
CUBICLES > CUBICLE
CUBICLY > CUBIC
CUBICS > CUBIC
CUBICULA > CUBICULUM
CUBICULUM n underground burial chamber in Imperial Rome, such as those found in the catacombs
CUBIFORM adj having the shape of a cube
CUBING > CUBE
CUBISM n style of art in which objects are represented by geometrical shapes
CUBISMS > CUBISM
CUBIST > CUBISM
CUBISTIC > CUBISM
CUBISTS > CUBISM
CUBIT n old measure of length based on the length of the forearm
CUBITAL adj of or relating to the forearm
CUBITI > CUBITUS
CUBITS > CUBIT
CUBITUS n elbow
CUBITUSES > CUBITUS

CUBLESS adj having no cubs
CUBOID adj shaped like a cube ▷ n geometric solid whose six faces are rectangles
CUBOIDAL same as **>** CUBOID
CUBOIDS > CUBOID
CUBS > CUB
CUCKING as in cucking stool stool to which suspected witches, etc, were tied and pelted or ducked into water as punishment
CUCKOLD n man whose wife has been unfaithful ▷ vb be unfaithful to (one's husband)
CUCKOLDED > CUCKOLD
CUCKOLDLY adj possessing the qualities of a cuckold
CUCKOLDOM n state of being a cuckold
CUCKOLDRY > CUCKOLD
CUCKOLDS > CUCKOLD
CUCKOO n migratory bird with a characteristic two-note call, which lays its eggs in the nests of other birds ▷ adj insane or foolish ▷ interj imitation or representation of the call of a cuckoo ▷ vb repeat over and over
CUCKOOED > CUCKOO
CUCKOOING > CUCKOO
CUCKOOS > CUCKOO
CUCULLATE adj shaped like a hood or having a hoodlike part
CUCUMBER n long green-skinned fleshy fruit used in salads
CUCUMBERS > CUCUMBER
CUCURBIT n type of tropical or subtropical creeping plant such as the pumpkin, cucumber, squashes, and gourds
CUCURBITS > CUCURBIT
CUD n partially digested food which a ruminant brings back into its mouth to chew again
CUDBEAR another name for **>** ORCHIL
CUDBEARS > CUDBEAR
CUDDEN n young coalfish
CUDDENS > CUDDEN
CUDDIE same as **>** CUDDY
CUDDIES > CUDDY
CUDDIN same as **>** CUDDEN
CUDDINS > CUDDIN
CUDDLE n hug ▷ vb hold (another person or thing) close or (of two people, etc) to hold each other close, as for affection, comfort, or warmth
CUDDLED > CUDDLE
CUDDLER > CUDDLE
CUDDLERS > CUDDLE
CUDDLES > CUDDLE

CUDDLIER > CUDDLE
CUDDLIEST > CUDDLE
CUDDLING > CUDDLE
CUDDLY > CUDDLE
CUDDY n small cabin in a boat
CUDGEL n short thick stick used as a weapon ▷ vb use a cudgel
CUDGELED > CUDGEL
CUDGELERS > CUDGEL
CUDGELING > CUDGEL
CUDGELLED > CUDGEL
CUDGELLER > CUDGEL
CUDGELS > CUDGEL
CUDGERIE n type of large tropical tree with light-coloured wood
CUDGERIES > CUDGERIE
CUDS > CUD
CUDWEED n type of temperate woolly plant with clusters of whitish or yellow flowers
CUDWEEDS > CUDWEED
CUE n signal to an actor or musician to begin speaking or playing ▷ vb give a cue to
CUED > CUE
CUEING same as **>** FOLDBACK
CUEINGS > CUEING
CUEIST n snooker or billiards player
CUEISTS > CUEIST
CUES > CUE
CUESTA n long low ridge with a steep scarp slope and a gentle back slope, formed by the differential erosion of strata of differing hardness
CUESTAS > CUESTA
CUFF n end of a sleeve ▷ vb hit with an open hand
CUFFED > CUFF
CUFFIN n man
CUFFING > CUFF
CUFFINS > CUFFIN
CUFFLE vb scuffle
CUFFLED > CUFFLE
CUFFLES > CUFFLE
CUFFLESS adj having no cuff(s)
CUFFLING > CUFFLE
CUFFLINK n detachable fastener for shirt cuff
CUFFLINKS > CUFFLINK
CUFFO adv free of charge
CUFFS > CUFF
CUFFUFFLE same as **>** KERFUFFLE
CUIF same as **>** COOF
CUIFS > CUIF
CUING > CUE
CUIRASS n piece of armour, of leather or metal covering the chest and back ▷ vb equip with a cuirass
CUIRASSED > CUIRASS
CUIRASSES > CUIRASS

CUISH same as **>** CUISSE
CUISHES > CUISH
CUISINART n tradename for a type of food processor
CUISINE n style of cooking
CUISINES > CUISINE
CUISINIER n cook
CUISSE n piece of armour for the thigh
CUISSER same as **>** COOSER
CUISSERS > CUISSER
CUISSES > CUISSE
CUIT n ankle
CUITER vb to pamper
CUITERED > CUITER
CUITERING > CUITER
CUITERS > CUITER
CUITIKIN n gaiter
CUITIKINS > CUITIKIN
CUITS > CUIT
CUITTLE vb to wheedle
CUITTLED > CUITTLE
CUITTLES > CUITTLE
CUITTLING > CUITTLE
CUKE n cucumber
CUKES > CUKE
CULCH n mass of broken stones, shells, and gravel that forms the basis of an oyster bed
CULCHES > CULCH
CULCHIE n rough or unsophisticated country-dweller from outside Dublin
CULCHIES > CULCHIE
CULET n flat face at the bottom of a gem
CULETS > CULET
CULEX n type of mosquito
CULEXES > CULEX
CULICES > CULEX
CULICID n type of dipterous insect of the family which comprises the mosquitoes
CULICIDS > CULICID
CULICINE n any member of the genus Culex containing mosquitoes
CULICINES > CULICINE
CULINARY adj of kitchens or cookery
CULL vb choose, gather ▷ n culling
CULLAY n soapbark tree
CULLAYS > CULLAY
CULLED > CULL
CULLENDER same as **>** COLANDER
CULLER n person employed to cull animals
CULLERS > CULLER
CULLET n waste glass for melting down to be reused
CULLETS > CULLET
CULLIED > CULLY
CULLIES > CULLY
CULLING > CULL
CULLINGS > CULL
CULLION n rascal
CULLIONLY > CULLION
CULLIONS > CULLION

CULLIS same as
> COULISSE
CULLISES > CULLIS
CULLS > CULL
CULLY n pal ▷ vb to trick
CULLYING > CULLY
CULLYISM n state of being
a dupe
CULLYISMS > CULLYISM
CULM n coal-mine waste
▷ vb to form a culm or grass
stem
CULMED > CULM
CULMEN n summit
CULMINA > CULMEN
CULMINANT adj highest or
culminating
CULMINATE vb reach the
highest point or climax
CULMING > CULM
CULMS > CULM
CULOTTE > CULOTTES
CULOTTES npl women's
knee-length trousers cut to
look like a skirt
CULPA n act of neglect
CULPABLE adj deserving
blame
CULPABLY > CULPABLE
CULPAE > CULPA
CULPATORY adj expressing
blame
CULPRIT n person guilty of
an offence or misdeed
CULPRITS > CULPRIT
CULT n specific system of
worship ▷ adj very popular
among a limited group of
people
CULTCH same as **>** CULTCH
CULTCHES > CULTCH
CULTER same as
> COULTER
CULTERS > CULTER
CULTI > CULTUS
CULTIC adj of or relating to
a religious cult
CULTIER > CULTY
CULTIEST > CULTY
CULTIGEN n species of
plant that is known only as
a cultivated form and did
not originate from a wild
type
CULTIGENS > CULTIGEN
CULTISH adj intended to
appeal to a small group of
fashionable people
CULTISHLY > CULTISH
CULTISM > CULT
CULTISMS > CULT
CULTIST > CULT
CULTISTS > CULT
CULTIVAR n variety of a
plant that was produced
from a natural species and
is maintained by cultivation
CULTIVARS > CULTIVAR
CULTIVATE vb prepare
(land) to grow crops
CULTLIKE adj resembling
a cult
CULTRATE adj shaped like
a knife blade

CULTRATED same as
> CULTRATE
CULTS > CULT
CULTURAL adj of or
relating to artistic or social
pursuits or events
considered to be valuable
or enlightened
CULTURATI n people
interested in cultural
activities
CULTURE n ideas, customs,
and art of a particular
society ▷ vb grow
(bacteria) for study
CULTURED adj showing
good taste or manners
CULTURES > CULTURE
CULTURING > CULTURE
CULTURIST > CULTURE
CULTUS another word for
> CULT
CULTUSES > CULTUS
CULTY same as **>** CULTISH
CULVER an archaic or poetic
name for **>** PIGEON
CULVERIN n long-range
medium to heavy cannon
used during the 15th, 16th,
and 17th centuries
CULVERINS > CULVERIN
CULVERS > CULVER
CULVERT n drain under a
road or railway
CULVERTS > CULVERT
CUM prep with
CUMACEAN n type of small
marine crustacean, mostly
dwelling on the sea bed but
sometimes found among
the plankton
CUMACEANS > CUMACEAN
CUMARIC > CUMARIN
CUMARIN same as
> COUMARIN
CUMARINS > CUMARIN
CUMARONE variant spelling
of **>** COUMARONE
CUMARONES > CUMARONE
CUMBENT adj lying down
CUMBER vb obstruct or
hinder ▷ n hindrance or
burden
CUMBERED > CUMBER
CUMBERER > CUMBER
CUMBERERS > CUMBER
CUMBERING > CUMBER
CUMBERS > CUMBER
CUMBIA n Colombian style
of music
CUMBIAS > CUMBIA
CUMBRANCE n burden,
obstacle, or hindrance
CUMBROUS adj awkward
because of size, weight, or
height
CUMBUNGI n type of tall
Australian marsh plant
CUMBUNGIS > CUMBUNGI
CUMEC n unit of volumetric
rate of flow
CUMECS > CUMEC
CUMIN n sweet-smelling
seeds of a Mediterranean
plant, used in cooking

CUMINS > CUMIN
CUMMER n gossip
CUMMERS > CUMMER
CUMMIN same as **>** CUMIN
CUMMINS > CUMMIN
CUMQUAT same as
> KUMQUAT
CUMQUATS > CUMQUAT
CUMS > CUM
CUMSHAW n (used, esp
formerly, by beggars in
Chinese ports) a present or
tip
CUMSHAWS > CUMSHAW
CUMULATE vb accumulate
▷ adj heaped up
CUMULATED > CUMULATE
CUMULATES > CUMULATE
CUMULET n variety of
domestic fancy pigeon,
pure white or white with
light red markings
CUMULETS > CUMULET
CUMULI > CUMULUS
CUMULOSE adj full of heaps
CUMULOUS adj resembling
or consisting of cumulus
clouds
CUMULUS n thick white or
dark grey cloud
CUNABULA n cradle
CUNCTATOR n person in
habit of being late
CUNDIES > CUNDY
CUNDUM n early form of
condom
CUNDUMS > CUNDUM
CUNDY n sewer
CUNEAL same as
> CUNEIFORM
CUNEATE adj wedge-
shaped: cuneate leaves are
attached at the narrow end
CUNEATED same as
> CUNEATE
CUNEATELY > CUNEATE
CUNEATIC adj cuneiform
CUNEI > CUNEUS
CUNEIFORM adj (written
in) an ancient system of
writing using wedge-
shaped characters ▷ n
ancient system of writing
using wedge-shaped
characters
CUNETTE n small trench
dug in the main ditch of a
fortification
CUNETTES > CUNETTE
CUNEUS n small
wedge-shaped area of the
cerebral cortex
CUNIFORM same as
> CUNIFORM
CUNIFORMS > CUNIFORM
CUNJEVOI n plant of
tropical Asia and Australia
with small flowers,
cultivated for its edible
rhizome
CUNJEVOIS > CUNJEVOI
CUNNER n fish of the
wrasse family
CUNNERS > CUNNER
CUNNING adj clever at

deceiving ▷ n cleverness at
deceiving
CUNNINGER > CUNNING
CUNNINGLY > CUNNING
CUNNINGS > CUNNING
CUNT n taboo word for
female genitals
CUNTS > CUNT
CUP n small bowl-shaped
drinking container with a
handle ▷ vb form (one's
hands) into the shape of a
cup
CUPBEARER n attendant
who fills and serves wine
cups, as in a royal
household
CUPBOARD n piece of
furniture or alcove with a
door, for storage ▷ vb to
store in a cupboard
CUPBOARDS > CUPBOARD
CUPCAKE n small cake
baked in a cup-shaped foil
or paper case
CUPCAKES > CUPCAKE
CUPEL n refractory pot in
which gold or silver is
refined ▷ vb refine (gold or
silver) by means of
cupellation
CUPELED > CUPEL
CUPELER > CUPEL
CUPELERS > CUPEL
CUPELING > CUPEL
CUPELLED > CUPEL
CUPELLER > CUPEL
CUPELLERS > CUPEL
CUPELLING > CUPEL
CUPELS > CUPEL
CUPFERRON n compound
used in chemical analysis
CUPFUL n amount a cup
will hold
CUPFULS > CUPFUL
CUPGALL n gall found on
oakleaves
CUPGALLS > CUPGALL
CUPHEAD n type of bolt or
rivet with a cup-shaped
head
CUPHEADS > CUPHEAD
CUPID n figure
representing the Roman
god of love
CUPIDITY n greed for
money or possessions
CUPIDS > CUPID
CUPLIKE > CUP
CUPMAN n drinking
companion
CUPMEN > CUPMAN
CUPOLA n domed roof or
ceiling ▷ vb to provide with
a cupola
CUPOLAED > CUPOLA
CUPOLAING > CUPOLA
CUPOLAR > CUPOLA
CUPOLAS > CUPOLA
CUPOLATED > CUPOLA
CUPPA n cup of tea
CUPPAS > CUPPA
CUPPED > CUP
CUPPER same as **>** CUPPA
CUPPERS > CUPPER

CUPPIER > CUPPY
CUPPIEST > CUPPY
CUPPING > CUP
CUPPINGS > CUP
CUPPY adj cup-shaped
CUPREOUS adj of copper
CUPRESSUS n type of tree
CUPRIC adj of or
containing copper in the
divalent state
CUPRITE n red secondary
mineral
CUPRITES > CUPRITE
CUPROUS adj of or
containing copper in the
monovalent state
CUPRUM an obsolete name for
> COPPER
CUPRUMS > CUPRUM
CUPS > CUP
CUPSFUL > CUPFUL
CUPULA n dome-shaped
structure, esp the sensory
structure within the
semicircular canals of the
ear
CUPULAE > CUPULA
CUPULAR same as
> CUPULATE
CUPULATE adj shaped like
a small cup
CUPULE n cup-shaped part
or structure, such as the
cup around the base of an
acorn
CUPULES > CUPULE
CUR n mongrel dog
CURABLE adj capable of
being cured
CURABLY > CURABLE
CURACAO n orange-
flavoured liqueur
CURACAOS > CURACAO
CURACIES > CURACY
CURACOA same as
> CURACAO
CURACOAS > CURACOA
CURACY n work or position
of a curate
CURAGH same as
> CURRACH
CURAGHS > CURAGH
CURANDERA n female faith
healer
CURANDERO n male faith
healer
CURARA same as > CURARE
CURARAS > CURARA
CURARE n poisonous resin
of a S American tree, used
as a muscle relaxant in
medicine
CURARES > CURARE
CURARI same as > CURARE
CURARINE n alkaloid
extracted from curare, used
as a muscle relaxant in
surgery
CURARINES > CURARINE
CURARIS > CURARI
CURARISE same as
> CURARIZE
CURARISED > CURARISE
CURARISES > CURARISE
CURARIZE vb paralyse or

treat with curare
CURARIZED > CURARIZE
CURARIZES > CURARIZE
CURASSOW n gallinaceous
ground-nesting bird with
long legs and tails and,
typically, a distinctive crest
of curled feathers
CURASSOWS > CURASSOW
CURAT n cuirass
CURATE n clergyman who
assists a parish priest ▷ vb
be in charge of (an art
exhibition or museum) ▷ vb
to act as a curator
CURATED > CURATE
CURATES > CURATE
CURATING > CURATE
CURATIVE n something
able to cure ▷ adj able to
cure
CURATIVES > CURATIVE
CURATOR n person in
charge of a museum or art
gallery
CURATORS > CURATOR
CURATORY > CURATOR
CURATRIX n female
curator
CURATS > CURAT
CURB n something that
restrains ▷ vb control,
restrain
CURBABLE adj capable of
being restrained
CURBED > CURB
CURBER > CURB
CURBERS > CURB
CURBING the US spelling of
> KERBING
CURBINGS > CURBING
CURBLESS adj having no
restraint
CURBS > CURB
CURBSIDE n pavement
CURBSIDES > CURBSIDE
CURBSTONE the US spelling
of > KERBSTONE
CURCH n woman's plain cap
or kerchief
CURCHEF same as > CURCH
CURCHEFS > CURCHEF
CURCHES > CURCH
CURCULIO n type of
American weevil
CURCULIOS > CURCULIO
CURCUMA n type of tropical
Asian tuberous plant
CURCUMAS > CURCUMA
CURCUMIN n yellow dye
derived from turmeric
CURCUMINE same as
> CURCUMIN
CURCUMINS > CURCUMIN
CURD n coagulated milk,
used to make cheese ▷ vb
turn into or become curd
CURDED > CURD
CURDIER > CURD
CURDIEST > CURD
CURDINESS > CURD
CURDING > CURD
CURDLE vb turn into curd,
coagulate

CURDLED > CURDLE
CURDLER > CURDLE
CURDLERS > CURDLE
CURDLES > CURDLE
CURDLING > CURDLE
CURDS > CURD
CURDY > CURD
CURE vb get rid of (an illness
or problem) ▷ n (treatment
causing) curing of an illness
or person
CURED > CURE
CURELESS > CURE
CURER > CURE
CURERS > CURE
CURES > CURE
CURET same as > CURETTE
CURETS > CURET
CURETTAGE n process of
using a curette
CURETTE n surgical
instrument for scraping
tissue from body cavities
▷ vb scrape with a curette
CURETTED > CURETTE
CURETTES > CURETTE
CURETTING > CURETTE
CURF n type of limestone
CURFEW n law ordering
people to stay inside their
homes after a specific time
at night
CURFEWS > CURFEW
CURFS > CURF
CURFUFFLE vb make a
kerfuffle
CURIA n papal court and
government of the Roman
Catholic Church
CURIAE > CURIA
CURIAL > CURIA
CURIALISM n
ultramontanism
CURIALIST
> CURIALISM
CURIAS > CURIA
CURIE n standard unit of
radioactivity
CURIES > CURIE
CURIET n cuirass
CURIETS > CURIET
CURING > CURE
CURIO n rare or unusual
object valued as a
collector's item
CURIOS > CURIO
CURIOSA n curiosities
CURIOSITY n eagerness
to know or find out
CURIOUS adj eager to learn
or know
CURIOUSER > CURIOUS
CURIOUSLY > CURIOUS
CURITE n oxide of uranium
and lead
CURITES > CURITE
CURIUM n radioactive
element produced artificially
from plutonium
CURIUMS > CURIUM
CURL n curved piece of hair
▷ vb make (hair) into curls
or (of hair) grow in curls
CURLED > CURL

CURLER n pin or small tube
for curling hair
CURLERS > CURLER
CURLEW n long-billed
wading bird
CURLEWS > CURLEW
CURLI npl curled hairlike
processes on the surface of
the E. coli bacterium, by
means of which it adheres
to and infects wounds
CURLICUE n ornamental
curl or twist ▷ vb to curl or
twist elaborately, as in
curlicues
CURLICUED > CURLICUE
CURLICUES > CURLICUE
CURLIER > CURLY
CURLIES as in have by the
short and curlies have
completely in one's power
CURLIEST > CURLY
CURLILY > CURLY
CURLINESS > CURLY
CURLING n game like
bowls, played with heavy
stones on ice
CURLINGS > CURLING
CURLPAPER n strip of
paper used to roll up and
set a section of hair, usually
wetted, into a curl
CURLS > CURL
CURLY adj tending to curl
CURLYCUE same as
> CURLICUE
CURLYCUES > CURLYCUE
CURN n grain (of corn etc)
CURNEY same as > CURNY
CURNIER > CURNY
CURNIEST > CURNY
CURNS > CURN
CURNY adj granular
CURPEL same as
> CRUPPER
CURPELS > CURPEL
CURR vb to purr
CURRACH a Scot or Irish name
for > CORACLE
CURRACHS > CURRACH
CURRAGH same as
> CURRACH
CURRAGHS > CURRAGH
CURRAJONG same as
> KURRAJONG
CURRAN n black bun
CURRANS > CURRAN
CURRANT n small dried
grape
CURRANTS > CURRANT
CURRANTY > CURRANT
CURRAWONG n Australian
songbird
CURRED > CURR
CURREJONG same as
> KURRAJONG
CURRENCY n money in use
in a particular country
CURRENT adj of the
immediate present ▷ n
flow of water or air in one
direction
CURRENTLY > CURRENT
CURRENTS > CURRENT

CURRICLE n two-wheeled open carriage drawn by two horses side by side
CURRICLES > CURRICLE
CURRICULA n plural form of singular curriculum: course of study in one subject at school or college
CURRIE same as **>** CURRY
CURRIED > CURRY
CURRIER n person who curries leather
CURRIERS > CURRIER
CURRIERY n trade, work, or place of occupation of a currier
CURRIES > CURRY
CURRIJONG same as **>** KURRAJONG
CURRING > CURR
CURRISH adj of or like a cur
CURRISHLY > CURRISH
CURRS > CURR
CURRY n Indian dish of meat or vegetables in a hot spicy sauce **>** vb prepare (food) with curry powder
CURRYCOMB n ridged comb used for grooming horses
CURRYING > CURRY
CURRYINGS > CURRY
CURS > CUR
CURSAL > CURSUS
CURSE vb swear (at) **>** n swearword
CURSED > CURSE
CURSEDER > CURSE
CURSEDEST > CURSE
CURSEDLY > CURSE
CURSENARY same as **>** CURSORARY
CURSER > CURSE
CURSERS > CURSE
CURSES > CURSE
CURSI > CURSUS
CURSING > CURSE
CURSINGS > CURSE
CURSITOR n clerk in the Court of Chancery
CURSITORS > CURSITOR
CURSITORY > CURSITOR
CURSIVE n (handwriting) done with joined letters **>** adj of handwriting or print in which letters are joined in a flowing style
CURSIVELY > CURSIVE
CURSIVES > CURSIVE
CURSOR n movable point of light that shows a specific position on a visual display unit
CURSORARY adj cursory
CURSORES > CURSOR
CURSORIAL adj adapted for running
CURSORILY > CURSORY
CURSORS > CURSOR
CURSORY adj quick and superficial
CURST same as **>** CURSE
CURSTNESS n peevishness
CURSUS n Neolithic parallel earthworks

CURT adj brief and rather rude
CURTAIL vb cut short
CURTAILED > CURTAIL
CURTAILER > CURTAIL
CURTAILS > CURTAIL
CURTAIN n piece of cloth hung at a window or opening as a screen **>** vb provide with curtains
CURTAINED > CURTAIN
CURTAINS npl death or ruin
CURTAL adj cut short **>** n animal whose tail has been docked
CURTALAX same as **>** CURTALAXE
CURTALAXE n cutlass
CURTALS > CURTAL
CURTANA n unpointed sword carried before an English sovereign at a coronation as an emblem of mercy
CURTANAS > CURTANA
CURTATE adj shortened
CURTATION > CURTATE
CURTAXE same as **>** CURTALAXE
CURTAXES > CURTAXE
CURTER > CURT
CURTESIES > CURTESY
CURTEST > CURT
CURTESY n widower's life interest in his wife's estate
CURTILAGE n enclosed area of land adjacent to a dwelling house
CURTLY > CURT
CURTNESS > CURT
CURTSEY same as **>** CURTSY
CURTSEYED > CURTSEY
CURTSEYS > CURTSEY
CURTSIED > CURTSY
CURTSIES > CURTSY
CURTSY n woman's gesture of respect made by bending the knees and bowing the head **>** vb make a curtsy
CURTSYING > CURTSY
CURULE adj (in ancient Rome) of the highest rank, esp one entitled to use a curule chair
CURVATE adj curved
CURVATED same as **>** CURVATE
CURVATION > CURVATE
CURVATIVE adj having curved edges
CURVATURE n curved shape
CURVE n continuously bending line with no straight parts **>** vb form or move in a curve
CURVEBALL n in baseball, a ball pitched in a curving path **>** vb pitch a curveball
CURVED > CURVE
CURVEDLY > CURVE
CURVES > CURVE

CURVESOME adj curvaceous
CURVET n horse's low leap with all four feet off the ground **>** vb make such a leap
CURVETED > CURVET
CURVETING > CURVET
CURVETS > CURVET
CURVETTED > CURVET
CURVEY same as **>** CURVY
CURVIER > CURVE
CURVIEST > CURVE
CURVIFORM adj having a curved form
CURVINESS > CURVY
CURVING > CURVE
CURVITAL adj relating to curvature
CURVITIES > CURVITY
CURVITY n curvedness
CURVY > CURVE
CUSCUS n large Australian nocturnal possum
CUSCUSES > CUSCUS
CUSEC n unit of flow equal to 1 cubic foot per second
CUSECS > CUSEC
CUSH n cushion
CUSHAT n wood pigeon
CUSHATS > CUSHAT
CUSHAW same as **>** CASHAW
CUSHAWS > CUSHAW
CUSHES > CUSH
CUSHIE same as **>** CUSHAT
CUSHIER > CUSHY
CUSHIES > CUSHIE
CUSHIEST > CUSHY
CUSHILY > CUSHY
CUSHINESS > CUSHY
CUSHION n bag filled with soft material, to make a seat more comfortable **>** vb lessen the effects of
CUSHIONED > CUSHION
CUSHIONET n small cushion
CUSHIONS > CUSHION
CUSHIONY > CUSHION
CUSHTY interj exclamation of pleasure, agreement, approval, etc
CUSHY adj easy
CUSK n type of food fish of northern coastal waters, with a single long dorsal fin
CUSKS > CUSK
CUSP n pointed end, esp on a tooth
CUSPAL > CUSP
CUSPATE adj having a cusp or cusps
CUSPATED same as **>** CUSPATE
CUSPED same as **>** CUSPATE
CUSPID n tooth having one point
CUSPIDAL same as **>** CUSPIDATE
CUSPIDATE adj having a cusp or cusps
CUSPIDES > CUSPIS
CUSPIDOR another word

(esp US) for **>** SPITTOON
CUSPIDORE same as **>** CUSPIDOR
CUSPIDORS > CUSPIDOR
CUSPIDS > CUSPID
CUSPIER > CUSPY
CUSPIEST > CUSPY
CUSPIS n in anatomy, tapering structure
CUSPS > CUSP
CUSPY adj (of a computer program) well-designed and user-friendly
CUSS n curse, oath **>** vb swear (at)
CUSSED adj obstinate
CUSSEDLY > CUSSED
CUSSER same as **>** COOSER
CUSSERS > CUSSER
CUSSES > CUSS
CUSSING > CUSS
CUSSO n tree of the rose family
CUSSOS > CUSSO
CUSSWORD n swearword
CUSSWORDS > CUSSWORD
CUSTARD n sweet yellow sauce made from milk and eggs
CUSTARDS > CUSTARD
CUSTARDY > CUSTARD
CUSTOCK same as **>** CASTOCK
CUSTOCKS > CUSTOCK
CUSTODE n custodian
CUSTODES > CUSTODE
CUSTODIAL > CUSTODY
CUSTODIAN n person in charge of a public building
CUSTODIER n custodian
CUSTODIES > CUSTODY
CUSTODY n protective care
CUSTOM n long-established activity or action **>** adj made to the specifications of an individual customer
CUSTOMARY adj usual **>** n statement in writing of customary laws and practices
CUSTOMED adj accustomed
CUSTOMER n person who buys goods or services
CUSTOMERS > CUSTOMER
CUSTOMISE same as **>** CUSTOMIZE
CUSTOMIZE vb make (something) according to a customer's individual requirements
CUSTOMS n duty charged on imports or exports
CUSTOS n superior in the Franciscan religious order
CUSTREL n knave
CUSTRELS > CUSTREL
CUSTUMAL another word for **>** CUSTOMARY
CUSTUMALS > CUSTUMAL
CUSTUMARY n customary
CUSUM n analysis technique used in statistics
CUSUMS > CUSUM
CUT vb open up, penetrate,

wound, or divide with a sharp instrument ▷ *n* act of cutting

CUTANEOUS *adj* of the skin

CUTAWAY *adj* (of a drawing or model) having part of the outside omitted to reveal the inside ▷ *n* man's coat cut diagonally from the front waist to the back of the knees

CUTAWAYS > CUTAWAY

CUTBACK *n* decrease or reduction ▷ *vb* shorten by cutting

CUTBACKS > CUTBACK

CUTBANK *n* steep banking at a bend in a river

CUTBANKS > CUTBANK

CUTCH *same as* > CATECHU

CUTCHA *adj* crude

CUTCHERRY *n* (formerly, in India) government offices and law courts collectively

CUTCHERY *same as* > CUTCHERRY

CUTCHES > CUTCH

CUTDOWN *n* decrease

CUTDOWNS > CUTDOWN

CUTE *adj* appealing or attractive

CUTELY > CUTE

CUTENESS > CUTE

CUTER > CUTE

CUTES > CUTIS

CUTESIE *same as* > CUTESY

CUTESIER > CUTESY

CUTESIEST > CUTESY

CUTEST > CUTE

CUTESY *adj* affectedly cute or coy

CUTEY *same as* > CUTIE

CUTEYS > CUTEY

CUTGLASS *adj* (of an accent) upper-class

CUTGRASS *n* any grass of the genus Leersia

CUTICLE *n* skin at the base of a fingernail or toenail

CUTICLES > CUTICLE

CUTICULA *n* cuticle

CUTICULAE > CUTICULA

CUTICULAR > CUTICLE

CUTIE *n* person regarded as appealing or attractive, esp a girl or woman

CUTIES > CUTIE

CUTIKIN *same as* > CUTIKIN

CUTIKINS > CUTIKIN

CUTIN *n* waxy waterproof substance, consisting of derivatives of fatty acids, that is the main constituent of the plant cuticle

CUTINISE *same as* > CUTINIZE

CUTINISED > CUTINISE

CUTINISES > CUTINISE

CUTINIZE *vb* become or cause to become covered or impregnated with cutin

CUTINIZED > CUTINIZE

CUTINIZES > CUTINIZE

CUTINS > CUTIN

CUTIS *a technical name for the* > SKIN

CUTISES > CUTIS

CUTLAS *same as* > CUTLASS

CUTLASES > CUTLAS

CUTLASS *n* curved one-edged sword formerly used by sailors

CUTLASSES > CUTLASS

CUTLER *n* maker of cutlery

CUTLERIES > CUTLERY

CUTLERS > CUTLER

CUTLERY *n* knives, forks, and spoons

CUTLET *n* small piece of meat like a chop

CUTLETS > CUTLET

CUTLINE *n* caption

CUTLINES > CUTLINE

CUTOFF *n* limit or termination

CUTOFFS > CUTOFF

CUTOUT *n* something that has been cut out from something else

CUTOUTS > CUTOUT

CUTOVER *n* transitional period in IT system changeover, during which old and new systems are working concurrently

CUTOVERS > CUTOVER

CUTPURSE *n* pickpocket

CUTPURSES > CUTPURSE

CUTS > CUT

CUTTABLE *adj* capable of being cut

CUTTAGE *n* propagation by using parts taken from growing plants

CUTTAGES > CUTTAGE

CUTTER *n* person or tool that cuts

CUTTERS > CUTTER

CUTTHROAT *n* person who cuts throats

CUTTIER > CUTTY

CUTTIES > CUTTY

CUTTIEST > CUTTY

CUTTING > CUT

CUTTINGLY > CUT

CUTTINGS > CUT

CUTTLE *vb* to whisper

CUTTLED > CUTTLE

CUTTLES > CUTTLE

CUTTLING > CUTTLE

CUTTO *n* large knife

CUTTOE *same as* > CUTTO

CUTTOES > CUTTO

CUTTY *adj* short or cut short ▷ *n* something cut short, such as a spoon or short-stemmed tobacco pipe

CUTUP *n* joker or prankster

CUTUPS > CUTUP

CUTWATER *n* forward part of the stem of a vessel, which cuts through the water

CUTWATERS > CUTWATER

CUTWORK *n* openwork embroidery in which the pattern is cut away from the background

CUTWORKS > CUTWORK

CUTWORM *n* caterpillar of various types of moth, a pest of young crop plants in N America

CUTWORMS > CUTWORM

CUVEE *n* individual batch or blend of wine

CUVEES > CUVEE

CUVETTE *n* shallow dish or vessel for holding liquid

CUVETTES > CUVETTE

CUZ *n* cousin

CUZZES > CUZ

CUZZIE *n* close friend or family member

CUZZIES > CUZZIE

CWM *same as* > CIRQUE

CWMS > CWM

CWTCH *vb* be snuggled up

CWTCHED > CWTCH

CWTCHES > CWTCH

CWTCHING > CWTCH

CYAN *n* highly saturated green-blue that is the complementary colour of red and forms, with magenta and yellow, a set of primary colours ▷ *adj* of this colour

CYANAMID *same as* > CYANAMIDE

CYANAMIDE *n* white or colourless crystalline soluble weak dibasic acid, which can be hydrolysed to urea

CYANAMIDS > CYANAMID

CYANATE *n* any salt or ester of cyanic acid

CYANATES > CYANATE

CYANIC as in *cyanic acid* colourless poisonous volatile liquid acid

CYANID *same as* > CYANIDE

CYANIDE *n* extremely poisonous chemical compound ▷ *vb* treat with cyanide

CYANIDED > CYANIDE

CYANIDES > CYANIDE

CYANIDING > CYANIDE

CYANIDS > CYANID

CYANIN *same as* > CYANINE

CYANINE *n* blue dye used to extend the sensitivity of photographic emulsions to colours other than blue and ultraviolet

CYANINES > CYANINE

CYANINS > CYANIN

CYANISE *vb* to turn into cyanide

CYANISED > CYANISE

CYANISES > CYANISE

CYANISING > CYANISE

CYANITE *a variant spelling of* > KYANITE

CYANITES > CYANITE

CYANITIC > CYANITE

CYANIZE *same as* > CYANISE

CYANIZED > CYANIZE

CYANIZES > CYANIZE

CYANIZING > CYANIZE

CYANO *adj* containing cyanogen

CYANOGEN *n* poisonous colourless flammable gas

CYANOGENS > CYANOGEN

CYANOSED *adj* affected by cyanosis

CYANOSES > CYANOSIS

CYANOSIS *n* blueness of the skin, caused by a deficiency of oxygen in the blood

CYANOTIC > CYANOSIS

CYANOTYPE *another name for* > BLUEPRINT

CYANS > CYAN

CYANURATE *n* chemical derived from cyanide

CYANURET *n* cyanide

CYANURETS > CYANURET

CYATHI > CYATHUS

CYATHIA > CYATHIUM

CYATHIUM *n* inflorescence of the type found on the poinsettia

CYATHUS *n* ancient measure of wine

CYBER *adj* involving computers

CYBERCAFE *n* café equipped with computer terminals which customers can use to access the internet

CYBERCAST *same as* > WEBCAST

CYBERNATE *vb* control (a manufacturing process) with a servomechanism or (of a process) to be controlled by a servomechanism

CYBERNAUT *n* person using internet

CYBERPET *n* electronic toy that simulates the activities of a pet, requiring the owner to feed, discipline, and entertain it

CYBERPETS > CYBERPET

CYBERPORN *n* pornography on Internet

CYBERPUNK *n* genre of science fiction that features rebellious computer hackers and is set in a dystopian society integrated by computer networks

CYBERSEX *n* exchanging of sexual messages or information via the internet

CYBERWAR *n* information warfare

CYBERWARS > CYBERWAR

CYBORG *n* (in science fiction) a living being whose powers are enhanced by computer implants

CYBORGS > CYBORG

CYBRARIAN n person in charge of computer archives

CYBRID n cytoplasmic hybrid (hybrid resulting from the fusion of a cytoplast and a whole cell)

CYBRIDS > CYBRID

CYCAD n type of tropical or subtropical plant with an unbranched stem and fernlike leaves crowded at the top

CYCADEOID n (now extinct) plant with a woody stem and tough leaves

CYCADS > CYCAD

CYCAS n palm tree of the genus Cycas

CYCASES > CYCAS

CYCASIN n glucoside, toxic to mammals, occurring in cycads

CYCASINS > CYCASIN

CYCLAMATE n salt or ester of cyclamic acid. Certain of the salts have a very sweet taste and were formerly used as food additives and sugar substitutes

CYCLAMEN n plant with red, pink, or white flowers ⊳ adj of a dark reddish-purple colour

CYCLAMENS > CYCLAMEN

CYCLASE n enzyme which acts as a catalyst in the formation of a cyclic compound

CYCLASES > CYCLASE

CYCLE vb ride a bicycle ⊳ n bicycle

CYCLECAR n any light car with an engine capacity of 1100cc or less

CYCLECARS > CYCLECAR

CYCLED > CYCLE

CYCLEPATH n special path for bicycles

CYCLER same as > CYCLIST

CYCLERIES > CYCLERY

CYCLERS > CYCLIST

CYCLERY n business dealing in bicycles and bicycle accessories

CYCLES > CYCLE

CYCLEWAY n path or way designed, and reserved for, cyclists

CYCLEWAYS > CYCLEWAY

CYCLIC adj recurring or revolving in cycles

CYCLICAL n short-term trend, of which reversal is expected ⊳ adj cyclic

CYCLICALS > CYCLIC

CYCLICISM > CYCLIC

CYCLICITY > CYCLIC

CYCLICLY > CYCLIC

CYCLIN n type of protein

CYCLING > CYCLE

CYCLINGS > CYCLE

CYCLINS > CYCLIN

CYCLISE same as > CYCLIZE

CYCLISED > CYCLISE

CYCLISES > CYCLISE

CYCLISING > CYCLISE

CYCLIST n person who rides a bicycle

CYCLISTS > CYCLIST

CYCLITOL n alicyclic compound

CYCLITOLS > CYCLITOL

CYCLIZE vb be cyclical

CYCLIZED > CYCLIZE

CYCLIZES > CYCLIZE

CYCLIZINE n drug used to relieve the symptoms of motion sickness

CYCLIZING > CYCLIZE

CYCLO n type of rickshaw

CYCLOGIRO n aircraft lifted and propelled by pivoted blades rotating parallel to roughly horizontal transverse axes

CYCLOID adj resembling a circle ⊳ n curve described by a point on the circumference of a circle as the circle rolls along a straight line

CYCLOIDAL > CYCLOID

CYCLOIDS > CYCLOID

CYCLOLITH n stone circle

CYCLONAL > CYCLONE

CYCLONE n violent wind moving round a central area

CYCLONES > CYCLONE

CYCLONIC > CYCLONE

CYCLONITE n white crystalline insoluble explosive prepared by the action of nitric acid on hexamethylenetetramine

CYCLOPEAN adj of or relating to the Cyclops

CYCLOPES > CYCLOPS

CYCLOPIAN > CYCLOPS

CYCLOPIC > CYCLOPS

CYCLOPS n type of copepod characterized by having one eye

CYCLORAMA n large picture, such as a battle scene, on the interior wall of a cylindrical room, designed to appear in natural perspective to a spectator in the centre

CYCLOS > CYCLO

CYCLOSES > CYCLOSIS

CYCLOSIS n circulation of cytoplasm or cell organelles, such as food vacuoles in some protozoans

CYCLOTRON n apparatus that accelerates charged particles by means of a strong vertical magnetic field

CYCLUS n cycle

CYCLUSES > CYCLUS

CYDER same as > CIDER

CYDERS > CYDER

CYESES > CYESIS

CYESIS the technical name for > PREGNANCY

CYGNET n young swan

CYGNETS > CYGNET

CYLICES > CYLIX

CYLINDER n solid or hollow body with straight sides and circular ends

CYLINDERS > CYLINDER

CYLINDRIC adj shaped like, or characteristic of a cylinder

CYLIX a variant of > KYLIX

CYMA n moulding with a double curve, part concave and part convex

CYMAE > CYMA

CYMAGRAPH same as > CYMOGRAPH

CYMAR n woman's short fur-trimmed jacket, popular in the 17th and 18th centuries

CYMARS > CYMAR

CYMAS > CYMA

CYMATIA > CYMATIUM

CYMATICS n theory and practice of a therapy whereby sound waves are directed at the body, with the aim of promoting health

CYMATIUM n top moulding of a classical cornice or entablature

CYMBAL n percussion instrument consisting of a brass plate which is struck against another or hit with a stick

CYMBALEER > CYMBAL

CYMBALER > CYMBAL

CYMBALERS > CYMBAL

CYMBALIST > CYMBAL

CYMBALO another name for > DULCIMER

CYMBALOES > CYMBALO

CYMBALOM same as > CIMBALOM

CYMBALOMS > CYMBALOM

CYMBALOS > CYMBALO

CYMBALS > CYMBAL

CYMBIDIA > CYMBIDIUM

CYMBIDIUM n any orchid of the genus Cymbidium

CYMBIFORM adj shaped like a boat

CYMBLING same as > CYMLING

CYMBLINGS > CYMLING

CYME n flower cluster which has a single flower on the end of each stem and of which the central flower blooms first

CYMENE n colourless insoluble liquid with an aromatic odour that exists in three isomeric forms

CYMENES > CYMENE

CYMES > CYME

CYMLIN same as > CYMLING

CYMLING n pattypan squash

CYMLINGS > CYMLING

CYMLINS > CYMLIN

CYMOGENE n mixture of volatile flammable hydrocarbons, mainly butane, obtained in the distillation of petroleum

CYMOGENES > CYMOGENE

CYMOGRAPH n instrument for tracing the outline of an architectural moulding

CYMOID adj resembling a cyme or cyma

CYMOL same as > CYMENE

CYMOLS > CYMOL

CYMOPHANE n yellow or green opalescent variety of chrysoberyl

CYMOSE adj having the characteristics of a cyme

CYMOSELY > CYMOSE

CYMOUS adj relating to a cyme

CYNANCHE n any disease characterised by inflammation and swelling of the throat

CYNANCHES > CYNANCHE

CYNEGETIC adj relating to hunting

CYNIC n person who believes that people always act selfishly ⊳ adj of or relating to Sirius, the Dog Star

CYNICAL adj believing that people always act selfishly

CYNICALLY > CYNICAL

CYNICISM n attitude or beliefs of a cynic

CYNICISMS > CYNICISM

CYNICS > CYNIC

CYNODONT n carnivorous mammal-like reptile of the late Permian and Triassic periods, whose specialized teeth were well developed

CYNODONTS > CYNODONT

CYNOMOLGI n plural form of singular cynomolgus: type of monkey

CYNOSURAL > CYNOSURE

CYNOSURE n centre of attention

CYNOSURES > CYNOSURE

CYPHER same as > CIPHER

CYPHERED > CYPHER

CYPHERING > CYPHER

CYPHERS > CYPHER

CYPRES n legal doctrine stating that a testator's intentions should be carried out as closely as possible

CYPRESES > CYPRES

CYPRESS n evergreen tree with dark green leaves

CYPRESSES > CYPRESS

CYPRIAN n prostitute or dancer

CYPRIANS > CYPRIAN

CYPRID n cypris

CYPRIDES > CYPRIS

CYPRIDS > CYPRID

CYPRINE *adj* relating to carp

CYPRINID *n* type of mainly freshwater fish, usu with toothless jaws and cycloid scales, such as the carp, tench, roach, rudd, and dace

CYPRINIDS > CYPRINID

CYPRINOID *n* type of fish belonging to the suborder which includes cyprinids, electric eels, and loaches

CYPRIS *n* member of the genus Cypris (small bivalve freshwater crustaceans)

CYPRUS *same as* > CYPRESS

CYPRUSES > CYPRUS

CYPSELA *n* dry one-seeded fruit of the daisy and related plants, which resembles an achene but is surrounded by a calyx sheath

CYPSELAE > CYPSELA

CYST *n* (abnormal) sac in the body containing fluid or soft matter

CYSTEIN *same as* > CYSTEINE

CYSTEINE *n* sulphur-containing amino acid

CYSTEINES > CYSTEINE

CYSTEINIC > CYSTEINE

CYSTEINS > CYSTEIN

CYSTIC *adj* of, relating to, or resembling a cyst

CYSTID *n* cystidean

CYSTIDEAN *n* any echinoderm of the class Cystoidea, an extinct order of sea lilies

CYSTIDS > CYSTID

CYSTIFORM *adj* having the form of a cyst

CYSTINE *n* sulphur-containing amino acid

CYSTINES > CYSTINE

CYSTITIS *n* inflammation

of the bladder

CYSTOCARP *n* reproductive body in red algae, developed after fertilization and consisting of filaments bearing carpospores

CYSTOCELE *n* hernia of the urinary bladder, esp one protruding into the vagina

CYSTOID *adj* resembling a cyst or bladder ▷ *n* tissue mass, such as a tumour, that resembles a cyst but lacks an outer membrane

CYSTOIDS > CYSTOID

CYSTOLITH *n* knoblike deposit of calcium carbonate in the epidermal cells of such plants as the stinging nettle

CYSTOTOMY *n* surgical incision into the gall bladder or urinary bladder

CYSTS > CYST

CYTASE *n* cellulose-dissolving enzyme

CYTASES > CYTASE

CYTASTER *another word for* > ASTER

CYTASTERS > CYTASTER

CYTE *n* biological cell

CYTES > CYTE

CYTIDINE *n* nucleoside formed by the condensation of cytosine and ribose

CYTIDINES > CYTIDINE

CYTIDYLIC *as in* cytidylic *acid* nucleotide that is found in DNA

CYTISI > CYTISUS

CYTISINE *n* poisonous alkaloid found in laburnum seeds

CYTISINES > CYTISINE

CYTISUS *n* any plant of the broom genus, Cytisus

CYTODE *n* mass of protoplasm without a nucleus

CYTODES > CYTODE

CYTOGENY *n* origin and development of plant cells

CYTOID *adj* resembling a cell

CYTOKINE *n* any of various proteins, secreted by cells, that carry signals to neighbouring cells. Cytokines include interferon

CYTOKINES > CYTOKINE

CYTOKININ *n* any of a group of plant hormones that promote cell division and retard ageing in plants

CYTOLOGIC > CYTOLOGY

CYTOLOGY *n* study of plant and animal cells

CYTOLYSES > CYTOLYSIS

CYTOLYSIN *n* substance that can partially or completely destroy animal cells

CYTOLYSIS *n* dissolution of cells, esp by the destruction of their membranes

CYTOLYTIC > CYTOLYSIS

CYTOMETER *n* glass slide used to count and measure blood cells

CYTOMETRY *n* counting of blood cells using a cytometer

CYTON *n* main part of a neuron

CYTONS > CYTON

CYTOPENIA *n* blood disorder where there is a deficiency in the blood cells

CYTOPLASM *n* protoplasm of a cell excluding the nucleus

CYTOPLAST *n* intact cytoplasm of a single cell

CYTOSINE *n* white crystalline pyrimidine occurring in nucleic acids

CYTOSINES > CYTOSINE

CYTOSOL *n* solution of proteins and metabolites

inside a biological cell, in which the organelles are suspended

CYTOSOLIC > CYTOSOL

CYTOSOLS > CYTOSOL

CYTOSOME *n* body of a cell excluding its nucleus

CYTOSOMES > CYTOSOME

CYTOTAXES > CYTOTAXIS

CYTOTAXIS *n* movement of cells due to external stimulation

CYTOTOXIC *adj* poisonous to living cells: denoting certain drugs used in the treatment of leukaemia and other cancers

CYTOTOXIN *n* any substance that is poisonous to living cells

CZAPKA *n* leather and felt peaked military helmet of Polish origin

CZAPKAS > CZAPKA

CZAR *same as* > TSAR

CZARDAS *n* Hungarian national dance of alternating slow and fast sections

CZARDASES > CZARDAS

CZARDOM > CZAR

CZARDOMS > CZAR

CZAREVICH *n* son of a czar

CZAREVNA *a variant spelling* (*esp US*) *of* > TSAREVNA

CZAREVNAS > CZAREVNA

CZARINA *variant spellings* (*esp US*) *of* > TSARINA

CZARINAS > CZARINA

CZARISM *a variant spelling* (*esp US*) *of* > TSARISM

CZARISMS > CZARISM

CZARIST > CZARISM

CZARISTS > CZARISM

CZARITSA *n* Russian empress

CZARITSAS > CZARITSA

CZARITZA *same as* > CZARINA

CZARITZAS > CZARINA

CZARS > CZAR

Dd

DA n Burmese knife
DAAL n (in Indian cookery) split pulses
DAALS > DAAL
DAB vb pat lightly ▷ n small amount of something soft or moist
DABBA n in Indian cookery, round metal box used to transport hot food
DABBAS > DABBA
DABBED > DAB
DABBER n pad used by printers for applying ink by hand
DABBERS > DABBER
DABBING > DAB
DABBITIES > DABBITY
DABBITY n temporary tattoo
DABBLE vb be involved in something superficially
DABBLED > DABBLE
DABBLER > DABBLE
DABBLERS > DABBLE
DABBLES > DABBLE
DABBLING > DABBLE
DABBLINGS > DABBLE
DABCHICK n type of small grebe
DABCHICKS > DABCHICK
DABS > DAB
DABSTER n incompetent or amateurish worker
DABSTERS > DABSTER
DACE n small European freshwater fish
DACES > DACE
DACHA n country cottage in Russia
DACHAS > DACHA
DACHSHUND n dog with a long body and short legs
DACITE n volcanic rock
DACITES > DACITE
DACK vb remove the trousers from (someone) by force
DACKED > DACK
DACKER vb walk slowly
DACKERED > DACKER
DACKERING > DACKER
DACKERS > DACKER
DACKING > DACK
DACKS > DACK
DACOIT n (in India and Myanmar) a member of a gang of armed robbers
DACOITAGE n robbery by armed gang
DACOITIES > DACOITY

DACOITS > DACOIT
DACOITY n (in India and Myanmar) robbery by an armed gang
DACQUOISE n cake with meringue layers
DACRON n US tradename for a synthetic polyester fibre or fabric characterized by lightness and crease resistance
DACRONS > DACRON
DACTYL n metrical foot of three syllables, one long followed by two short
DACTYLAR adj poetry term
DACTYLI > DACTYLUS
DACTYLIC same as > DACTYL
DACTYLICS > DACTYLIC
DACTYLIST n poet
DACTYLS > DACTYL
DACTYLUS n tip of a squid's tentacular club
DAD n father ▷ vb act or treat as a father
DADA n nihilistic artistic movement of the early 20th century
DADAH n illegal drugs
DADAHS > DADAH
DADAISM same as > DADA
DADAISMS > DADAISM
DADAIST > DADA
DADAISTIC > DADA
DADAISTS > DADA
DADAS > DADA
DADDED > DAD
DADDIES > DADDY
DADDING > DAD
DADDLE vb walk unsteadily
DADDLED > DADDLE
DADDLES > DADDLE
DADDLING > DADDLE
DADDOCK n core of a dead tree
DADDOCKS > DADDOCK
DADDY n father
DADGUM mild form of > DAMNED
DADO n lower part of an interior wall, below a rail, decorated differently from the upper part ▷ vb provide with a dado
DADOED > DADO
DADOES > DADO
DADOING > DADO
DADOS > DADO
DADS > DAD
DAE a Scot word for > DO

DAEDAL adj skilful or intricate
DAEDALEAN same as > DAEDALIAN
DAEDALIAN adj of, relating to, or resembling the work of Daedalus, the Athenian architect and inventor of Greek mythology
DAEDALIC same as > DAEDALIAN
DAEING > DAE
DAEMON same as > DEMON
DAEMONES > DAEMON
DAEMONIC > DAEMON
DAEMONS > DAEMON
DAES > DAE
DAFF vb frolic
DAFFED > DAFF
DAFFIER > DAFFY
DAFFIES > DAFFY
DAFFIEST > DAFFY
DAFFILY > DAFFY
DAFFINESS > DAFFY
DAFFING > DAFF
DAFFINGS > DAFF
DAFFODIL n yellow trumpet-shaped flower that blooms in spring ▷ adj brilliant yellow
DAFFODILS > DAFFODIL
DAFFS > DAFF
DAFFY another word for > DAFT
DAFT adj foolish or crazy
DAFTAR Indian word for > OFFICE
DAFTARS > DAFTAR
DAFTER > DAFT
DAFTEST > DAFT
DAFTIE n foolish person
DAFTIES > DAFTIE
DAFTLY > DAFT
DAFTNESS > DAFT
DAG n character ▷ vb cut daglocks from sheep
DAGABA n shrine for Buddhist relics
DAGABAS > DAGABA
DAGGA n cannabis
DAGGAS > DAGGA
DAGGED > DAG
DAGGER > DAG
DAGGERED > DAG
DAGGERING > DAG
DAGGERS > DAG
DAGGIER > DAGGY
DAGGIEST > DAGGY
DAGGING > DAG

DAGGINGS > DAG
DAGGLE vb trail through water
DAGGLED > DAGGLE
DAGGLES > DAGGLE
DAGGLING > DAGGLE
DAGGY adj amusing
DAGLOCK n dung-caked lock of wool around the hindquarters of a sheep
DAGLOCKS > DAGLOCK
DAGO n offensive term for a member of a Latin race, esp a Spaniard or Portuguese
DAGOBA n dome-shaped shrine containing relics of the Buddha or a Buddhist saint
DAGOBAS > DAGOBA
DAGOES > DAGO
DAGOS > DAGO
DAGS > DAG
DAGWOOD n European shrub
DAGWOODS > DAGWOOD
DAH n long sound used in combination with the short sound in the spoken representation of Morse and other telegraphic codes
DAHABEAH n houseboat used on the Nile
DAHABEAHS > DAHABEAH
DAHABEEAH n Egyptian houseboat
DAHABIAH same as > DAHABEAH
DAHABIAHS > DAHABIAH
DAHABIEH n Egyptian houseboat
DAHABIEHS > DAHABIEH
DAHABIYA n Egyptian houseboat
DAHABIYAH n Egyptian houseboat
DAHABIYAS > DAHABIYA
DAHABIYEH n Egyptian houseboat
DAHL same as > DHAL
DAHLIA n brightly coloured garden flower
DAHLIAS > DAHLIA
DAHLS > DAHL
DAHOON n evergreen shrub
DAHOONS > DAHOON
DAHS > DAH
DAIDLE vb waddle about
DAIDLED > DAIDLE
DAIDLES > DAIDLE
DAIDLING > DAIDLE

DAIDZEIN n type of protein

DAIDZEINS > DAIDZEIN

DAIKER vb walk slowly

DAIKERED > DAIKER

DAIKERING > DAIKER

DAIKERS > DAIKER

DAIKO n Japanese drum

DAIKON another name for > MOOLI

DAIKONS > DAIKON

DAIKOS > DAIKO

DAILIES > DAILY

DAILINESS > DAILY

DAILY adj occurring every day or every weekday ▷ adv every day ▷ n daily newspaper

DAILYNESS > DAILY

DAIMEN adj occasional

DAIMIO same as > DAIMYO

DAIMIOS > DAIMIO

DAIMOKU n Nichiren Buddhist chant

DAIMOKUS > DAIMOKU

DAIMON same as > DEMON

DAIMONES npl disembodied souls

DAIMONIC > DAIMON

DAIMONS > DAIMON

DAIMYO n (in Japan) one of the territorial magnates who dominated much of the country from about the 11th to the 19th century

DAIMYOS > DAIMYO

DAINE vb condescend

DAINED > DAINE

DAINES > DAINE

DAINING > DAINE

DAINT adj dainty

DAINTIER > DAINTY

DAINTIES > DAINTY

DAINTIEST > DAINTY

DAINTILY > DAINTY

DAINTY adj delicate or elegant ▷ n small cake or sweet

DAIQUIRI n iced drink containing rum, lime juice, and sugar

DAIQUIRIS > DAIQUIRI

DAIRIES > DAIRY

DAIRY n place for the processing or sale of milk and its products ▷ adj of milk or its products

DAIRYING n business of producing, processing, and selling dairy products

DAIRYINGS > DAIRYING

DAIRYMAID n (formerly) woman employed to milk cows

DAIRYMAN n man employed to look after cows

DAIRYMEN > DAIRYMAN

DAIS n raised platform in a hall, used by a speaker

DAISES > DAIS

DAISHIKI n upper garment

DAISHIKIS > DAISHIKI

DAISIED > DAISY

DAISIES > DAISY

DAISY n small wild flower with a yellow centre and white petals

DAK n system of mail delivery or passenger transport by relays of bearers or horses stationed at intervals along a route

DAKER vb walk slowly

DAKERED > DAKER

DAKERHEN n European bird

DAKERHENS > DAKERHEN

DAKERING > DAKER

DAKERS > DAKER

DAKOIT same as > DACOIT

DAKOITI same as > DAKOIT

DAKOITIES > DAKOIT

DAKOITIS > DAKOIT

DAKOITS > DAKOIT

DAKOITY n armed robbery

DAKS an informal name for > TROUSERS

DAL same as > DECALITRE

DALAPON n herbicide

DALAPONS > DALAPON

DALASI n standard monetary unit of The Gambia, divided into 100 bututs

DALASIS > DALASI

DALE n (esp in N England) valley

DALED same as > DALETH

DALEDH n letter of Hebrew alphabet

DALEDHS > DALEDH

DALEDS > DALED

DALES > DALE

DALESMAN n person living in a dale, esp in the dales of N England

DALESMEN > DALESMAN

DALETH n fourth letter of the Hebrew alphabet, transliterated as d or, when final, dh

DALETHS > DALETH

DALGYTE another name for > BILBY

DALGYTES > DALGYTE

DALI n type of tree

DALIS > DALI

DALLE > DALLES

DALLES npl stretch of a river between high rock walls, with rapids and dangerous currents

DALLIANCE n flirtation

DALLIED > DALLY

DALLIER > DALLY

DALLIERS > DALLY

DALLIES > DALLY

DALLOP n semisolid lump

DALLOPS > DALLOP

DALLY vb waste time

DALLYING > DALLY

DALMAHOY n bushy wig

DALMAHOYS > DALMAHOY

DALMATIAN n breed of dog characterized by its striking spotted markings

DALMATIC n wide-sleeved tunic-like vestment open at the sides, worn by deacons and bishops

DALMATICS > DALMATIC

DALS > DAL

DALT n foster child

DALTON n atomic mass unit

DALTONIAN > DALTON

DALTONIC > DALTONISM

DALTONISM n colour blindness, esp the confusion of red and green

DALTONS > DALTON

DALTS > DALT

DAM n barrier built across a river to create a lake ▷ vb build a dam across (a river)

DAMAGE vb harm, spoil ▷ n harm to a person or thing

DAMAGED > DAMAGE

DAMAGER > DAMAGE

DAMAGERS > DAMAGE

DAMAGES npl money awarded as compensation for injury or loss

DAMAGING > DAMAGE

DAMAN n esp the Syrian rock hyrax

DAMANS > DAMAN

DAMAR same as > DAMMAR

DAMARS > DAMMAR

DAMASCENE vb ornament (metal, esp steel) by etching or by inlaying, usually with gold or silver ▷ n design or article produced by this process ▷ adj of or relating to this process

DAMASK n fabric with a pattern woven into it, used for tablecloths etc ▷ vb ornament (metal) by etching or inlaying, usually with gold or silver

DAMASKED > DAMASK

DAMASKEEN vb decorate metal

DAMASKIN vb decorate metal

DAMASKING > DAMASK

DAMASKINS > DAMASKIN

DAMASKS > DAMASK

DAMASQUIN vb decorate metal

DAMASSIN n patterned damask

DAMASSINS > DAMASSIN

DAMBOARD n draughtboard

DAMBOARDS > DAMBOARD

DAMBROD n draughtboard

DAMBRODS > DAMBROD

DAME n woman

DAMES > DAME

DAMEWORT n sweet-scented perennial plant with mauve or white flowers

DAMEWORTS > DAMEWORT

DAMFOOL adj foolish

DAMIANA n herbal medicine

DAMIANAS > DAMIANA

DAMMAR n any of various resins obtained from SE Asian trees used for varnishes, lacquers, bases for oil paints, etc

DAMMARS > DAMMAR

DAMME interj exclamation of surprise

DAMMED > DAM

DAMMER same as > DAMMAR

DAMMERS > DAMMER

DAMMING > DAM

DAMMIT interj exclamation of surprise

DAMN interj exclamation of annoyance ▷ adj extreme(ly) ▷ vb condemn as bad or worthless

DAMNABLE adj annoying

DAMNABLY adv in a detestable manner

DAMNATION interj exclamation of anger ▷ n eternal punishment

DAMNATORY adj threatening or occasioning condemnation

DAMNDEST n utmost

DAMNDESTS > DAMNDEST

DAMNED adj condemned to hell ▷ adv extreme or extremely

DAMNEDER > DAMNED

DAMNEDEST n utmost

DAMNER n person who damns

DAMNERS > DAMNER

DAMNIFIED > DAMNIFY

DAMNIFIES > DAMNIFY

DAMNIFY vb cause loss or damage to (a person)

DAMNING > DAMN

DAMNINGLY > DAMN

DAMNS > DAMN

DAMOISEL same as > DAMSEL

DAMOISELS > DAMOISEL

DAMOSEL same as > DAMSEL

DAMOSELS > DAMOSEL

DAMOZEL same as > DAMSEL

DAMOZELS > DAMOZEL

DAMP adj slightly wet ▷ n slight wetness, moisture ▷ vb make damp

DAMPED > DAMP

DAMPEN vb reduce the intensity of

DAMPENED > DAMPEN

DAMPENER > DAMPEN

DAMPENERS > DAMPEN

DAMPENING > DAMPEN

DAMPENS > DAMPEN

DAMPER n movable plate to regulate the draught in a fire

DAMPERS > DAMPER

DAMPEST > DAMP

DAMPIER > DAMPY

DAMPIEST > DAMPY

DAMPING n moistening or wetting

DAMPINGS > DAMPING

d

DAMPISH > DAMP
DAMPLY > DAMP
DAMPNESS > DAMP
DAMPS > DAMP
DAMPY adj damp
DAMS > DAM
DAMSEL n young woman
DAMSELFLY n type of insect similar to but smaller than a dragonfly
DAMSELS > DAMSEL
DAMSON n small blue-black plumlike fruit
DAMSONS > DAMSON
DAN n in judo, any of the 10 black-belt grades of proficiency
DANAZOL n type of drug
DANAZOLS > DANAZOL
DANCE vb move the feet and body rhythmically in time to music ▷ n series of steps and movements in time to music
DANCEABLE > DANCE
DANCED > DANCE
DANCEHALL n style of dance-oriented reggae
DANCER > DANCE
DANCERS > DANCE
DANCES > DANCE
DANCETTE another name for > CHEVRON
DANCETTEE adj having a zigzag pattern
DANCETTES > DANCETTE
DANCETTY adj having a zigzag pattern
DANCEY adj of, relating to, or resembling dance music
DANCICAL n type of dance show set to pop music
DANCICALS > DANCICAL
DANCIER > DANCEY
DANCIEST > DANCEY
DANCING > DANCE
DANCINGS > DANCE
DANCY adj (of music) appropriate for dancing
DANDELION n yellow-flowered wild plant
DANDER n stroll ▷ vb stroll
DANDERED > DANDER
DANDERING > DANDER
DANDERS > DANDER
DANDIACAL adj like a dandy
DANDIER > DANDY
DANDIES > DANDY
DANDIEST > DANDY
DANDIFIED > DANDIFY
DANDIFIES > DANDIFY
DANDIFY vb dress like or cause to resemble a dandy
DANDILY > DANDY
DANDIPRAT n small English coin minted in the 16th century
DANDLE vb move (a child) up and down on one's knee
DANDLED > DANDLE
DANDLER > DANDLE
DANDLERS > DANDLE
DANDLES > DANDLE

DANDLING > DANDLE
DANDRIFF same as > DANDRUFF
DANDRIFFS > DANDRIFF
DANDRUFF n loose scales of dry dead skin shed from the scalp
DANDRUFFS > DANDRUFF
DANDRUFFY > DANDRUFF
DANDY n man who is overconcerned with the elegance of his appearance ▷ adj very good
DANDYFUNK n ship's biscuit
DANDYISH > DANDY
DANDYISM > DANDY
DANDYISMS > DANDY
DANDYPRAT n English coin
DANEGELD n tax levied in Anglo-Saxon England to provide protection money for, or to finance forces to oppose, Viking invaders
DANEGELDS > DANEGELD
DANEGELT same as > DANEGELD
DANEGELTS > DANEGELT
DANELAGH same as > DANELAW
DANELAGHS > DANELAGH
DANELAW n Danish law and customs of northern, central, and eastern parts of Anglo-Saxon England
DANELAWS > DANELAW
DANEWEED n dwarf elder
DANEWEEDS > DANEWEED
DANEWORT n dwarf elder
DANEWORTS > DANEWORT
DANG a euphemistic word for > DAMN
DANGED > DANG
DANGER n possibility of being injured or killed ▷ vb in archaic usage, endanger
DANGERED > DANGER
DANGERING > DANGER
DANGEROUS adj likely or able to cause injury or harm
DANGERS > DANGER
DANGING > DANG
DANGLE vb hang loosely ▷ n act of dangling or something that dangles
DANGLED > DANGLE
DANGLER > DANGLE
DANGLERS > DANGLE
DANGLES > DANGLE
DANGLIER > DANGLE
DANGLIEST > DANGLE
DANGLING > DANGLE
DANGLINGS > DANGLE
DANGLY > DANGLE
DANGS > DANG
DANIO n type of brightly coloured tropical freshwater fish popular in aquariums
DANIOS > DANIO
DANISH n sweet pastry
DANISHES > DANISH
DANK adj unpleasantly damp and chilly ▷ n

unpleasant damp and chilliness
DANKER > DANK
DANKEST > DANK
DANKISH > DANK
DANKLY > DANK
DANKNESS > DANK
DANKS > DANK
DANNEBROG n Danish flag
DANNIES > DANNY
DANNY n hand (used esp when addressing children)
DANS > DAN
DANSEUR n male ballet dancer
DANSEURS > DANSEUR
DANSEUSE n female ballet dancer
DANSEUSES > DANSEUSE
DANT vb intimidate
DANTED > DANT
DANTHONIA n type of grass of N temperate regions and S America
DANTING > DANT
DANTON same as > DAUNTON
DANTONED > DANTON
DANTONING > DANTON
DANTONS > DANTON
DANTS > DANT
DAP vb fish with a natural or artificial fly on a floss silk line so that the wind makes the fly bob on and off the surface of the water
DAPHNE n ornamental Eurasian shrub with shiny evergreen leaves and clusters of small bell-shaped flowers
DAPHNES > DAPHNE
DAPHNIA n type of water flea with a rounded body in a transparent shell
DAPHNIAS > DAPHNIA
DAPHNID n water flea
DAPHNIDS > DAPHNID
DAPPED > DAP
DAPPER adj (of a man) neat in appearance ▷ n fisherman or -woman who uses a bobbing bait
DAPPERER > DAPPER
DAPPEREST > DAPPER
DAPPERLY > DAPPER
DAPPERS > DAPPER
DAPPING > DAP
DAPPLE vb mark or become marked with spots or patches of a different colour ▷ n mottled or spotted markings ▷ adj marked with dapples or spots
DAPPLED > DAPPLE
DAPPLES > DAPPLE
DAPPLING > DAPPLE
DAPS > DAP
DAPSONE n antimicrobial drug used to treat leprosy and certain types of dermatitis
DAPSONES > DAPSONE
DAQUIRI n rum cocktail

DAQUIRIS > DAQUIRI
DARAF n unit of elastance equal to a reciprocal farad
DARAFS > DARAF
DARB n something excellent
DARBAR n hall in Sikh temple
DARBARS > DARBAR
DARBIES > HANDCUFFS
DARBS > DARB
DARCIES > DARCY
DARCY n unit expressing the permeability coefficient of rock
DARCYS > DARCY
DARE vb be courageous enough to try (to do something) ▷ n challenge to do something risky
DARED > DARE
DAREDEVIL n recklessly bold person ▷ adj recklessly bold or daring
DAREFUL adj daring
DARER > DARE
DARERS > DARE
DARES > DARE
DARESAY vb venture to say
DARG n day's work
DARGA n Muslim shrine
DARGAH n tomb of a Muslim saint
DARGAHS > DARGAH
DARGAS > DARGA
DARGLE n wooded hollow
DARGLES > DARGLE
DARGS > DARG
DARI n variety of sorghum
DARIC n gold coin of ancient Persia
DARICS > DARIC
DARING adj willing to take risks ▷ n courage to do dangerous things
DARINGLY > DARING
DARINGS > DARING
DARIOLE n small cup-shaped mould used for making individual sweet or savoury dishes
DARIOLES > DARIOLE
DARIS > DARI
DARK adj having little or no light ▷ n absence of light ▷ vb in archaic usage, darken
DARKED > DARK
DARKEN vb make or become dark or darker
DARKENED > DARKEN
DARKENER > DARKEN
DARKENERS > DARKEN
DARKENING > DARKEN
DARKENS > DARKEN
DARKER > DARK
DARKEST > DARK
DARKEY same as > DARKY
DARKEYS > DARKEY
DARKFIELD as in darkfield microscope kind of microscope
DARKIE same as > DARKY
DARKIES > DARKY
DARKING > DARK

DARKISH > DARK
DARKLE vb grow dark
DARKLED > DARKLE
DARKLES > DARKLE
DARKLIER > DARK
DARKLIEST > DARK
DARKLING adj in the dark or night
DARKLINGS adv in darkness
DARKLY > DARK
DARKMANS n slang term for night-time
DARKNESS > DARK
DARKNET n covert communication network on the Internet
DARKNETS > DARKNET
DARKROOM n darkened room for processing photographic film
DARKROOMS > DARKROOM
DARKS > DARK
DARKSOME adj dark or darkish
DARKY n offensive word for a Black person
DARLING n much-loved person ▷ adj much-loved
DARLINGLY > DARLING
DARLINGS > DARLING
DARN vb mend (a garment) with a series of interwoven stitches ▷ n patch of darned work
DARNATION mild form of > DAMNATION
DARNDEST n utmost
DARNDESTS > DARNDEST
DARNED adj damned
DARNEDER > DARNED
DARNEDEST a euphemistic word for > DAMNEDEST
DARNEL n weed that grows in grain fields
DARNELS > DARNEL
DARNER > DARN
DARNERS > DARN
DARNING > DARN
DARNINGS > DARN
DARNS > DARN
DAROGHA n in India, manager
DAROGHAS > DAROGHA
DARRAIGN same as > DERAIGN
DARRAIGNE vb clear from guilt
DARRAIGNS > DARRAIGN
DARRAIN vb clear of guilt
DARRAINE vb clear of guilt
DARRAINED > DARRAINE
DARRAINES > DARRAINE
DARRAINS > DARRAIN
DARRAYN vb clear of guilt
DARRAYNED > DARRAYN
DARRAYNS > DARRAYN
DARRE vb dare
DARRED > DARRE
DARRES > DARRE
DARRING > DARRE
DARSHAN n Hindu blessing
DARSHANS > DARSHAN
DART n small narrow

pointed missile that is thrown or shot, esp in the game of darts ▷ vb move or direct quickly and suddenly
DARTBOARD n circular board used as the target in the game of darts
DARTED > DART
DARTER n type of aquatic bird of tropical and subtropical inland waters, with a long slender neck and bill
DARTERS > DARTER
DARTING > DART
DARTINGLY > DART
DARTITIS n nervous twitching while playing darts
DARTLE vb move swiftly
DARTLED > DARTLE
DARTLES > DARTLE
DARTLING > DARTLE
DARTRE n skin disease
DARTRES > DARTRE
DARTROUS adj having a skin disease
DARTS n game in which darts are thrown at a dartboard
DARZI n tailor in India
DARZIS > DARZI
DAS > DA
DASH vb move quickly ▷ n sudden quick movement
DASHBOARD n instrument panel in a vehicle
DASHED > DASH
DASHEEN another name for > TARO
DASHEENS > DASHEEN
DASHEKI n upper garment
DASHEKIS > DASHEKI
DASHER n one of the boards surrounding an ice-hockey rink
DASHERS > DASHER
DASHES > DASH
DASHI n clear stock made from dried fish and kelp
DASHIER > DASHY
DASHIEST > DASHY
DASHIKI n large loose-fitting buttonless upper garment worn esp by Blacks in the US, Africa, and the Caribbean
DASHIKIS > DASHIKI
DASHING adj stylish and attractive
DASHINGLY > DASHING
DASHIS > DASHI
DASHPOT n device for damping vibrations
DASHPOTS > DASHPOT
DASHY adj showy
DASSIE n type of hoofed rodent-like animal
DASSIES > DASSIE
DASTARD n contemptible sneaking coward
DASTARDLY adj wicked and cowardly
DASTARDS > DASTARD
DASTARDY n cowardice

DASYMETER n device for measuring density of gases
DASYPOD n armadillo
DASYPODS > DASYPOD
DASYURE n small marsupial of Australia, New Guinea, and adjacent islands
DASYURES > DASYURE
DATA n information consisting of observations, measurements, or facts
DATABANK n store of a large amount of information, esp in a form that can be handled by a computer
DATABANKS > DATABANK
DATABASE n store of information in a form that can be easily handled by a computer ▷ vb put data into a database
DATABASED > DATABASE
DATABASES > DATABASE
DATABLE > DATE
DATABUS n computing term
DATABUSES > DATABUS
DATACARD n smart card
DATACARDS > DATACARD
DATACOMMS n computing term
DATAFLOW as in dataflow architecture means of arranging computer data processing in which operations are governed by the data present and the processing it requires rather than by a prewritten program that awaits data to be processed
DATAGLOVE n computing term
DATAGRAM n (in computing) self-contained unit of data transmitted in a packet-switched network
DATAGRAMS > DATAGRAM
DATAL adj slow-witted ▷ n day labour
DATALLER n worker paid by the day
DATALLERS > DATALLER
DATALS > DATAL
DATARIA n Roman Catholic office
DATARIAS > DATARIA
DATARIES > DATARY
DATARY n head of the dataria, the papal office that assesses candidates for benefices reserved to the Holy See
DATCHA same as > DACHA
DATCHAS > DATCHA
DATE n specified day of the month ▷ vb mark with the date
DATEABLE > DATE
DATEBOOK n list of forthcoming events
DATEBOOKS > DATEBOOK
DATED adj old-fashioned

DATEDLY > DATED
DATEDNESS > DATED
DATELESS > DATE
DATELINE n information about the place and time a story was written, placed at the top of the article
DATELINED > DATELINE
DATELINES > DATELINE
DATER n person who dates
DATERS > DATER
DATES > DATE
DATING n any of several techniques, such as radioactive dating, dendrochronology, or varve dating, for establishing the age of rocks, palaeontological or archaeological specimens, etc
DATINGS > DATING
DATIVAL > DATIVE
DATIVE adj denoting a case of nouns, pronouns, and adjectives used to express the indirect object ▷ n this grammatical case
DATIVELY > DATIVE
DATIVES > DATIVE
DATO n chief of any of certain Muslim tribes in the Philippine Islands
DATOLITE n colourless mineral
DATOLITES > DATOLITE
DATOS > DATO
DATTO n Datsun car
DATTOS > DATTO
DATUM n single piece of information in the form of a fact or statistic
DATUMS > DATUM
DATURA n type of chiefly Indian plant with large trumpet-shaped flowers, prickly pods, and narcotic properties
DATURAS > DATURA
DATURIC > DATURA
DATURINE n poisonous alkaloid
DATURINES > DATURINE
DAUB vb smear or spread quickly or clumsily ▷ n crude or badly done painting
DAUBE n braised meat stew
DAUBED > DAUB
DAUBER > DAUB
DAUBERIES > DAUBERY
DAUBERS > DAUB
DAUBERY n act or an instance of daubing
DAUBES > DAUBE
DAUBIER > DAUB
DAUBIEST > DAUB
DAUBING > DAUB
DAUBINGLY > DAUB
DAUBINGS > DAUB
DAUBRIES > DAUBRY
DAUBRY n unskilful painting
DAUBS > DAUB
DAUBY > DAUB

DAUD n lump or chunk of something ▷ vb (in dialect) whack
DAUDED >DAUD
DAUDING >DAUD
DAUDS >DAUD
DAUGHTER n female child ▷ adj denoting a cell, chromosome, etc produced by the division of one of its own kind
DAUGHTERS >DAUGHTER
DAULT n foster child
DAULTS >DAULT
DAUNDER vb stroll
DAUNDERED >DAUNDER
DAUNDERS >DAUNDER
DAUNER vb stroll
DAUNERED >DAUNER
DAUNERING >DAUNER
DAUNERS >DAUNER
DAUNT vb intimidate
DAUNTED >DAUNT
DAUNTER >DAUNT
DAUNTERS >DAUNT
DAUNTING adj intimidating or worrying
DAUNTLESS adj fearless
DAUNTON vb dishearten
DAUNTONED >DAUNTON
DAUNTONS >DAUNTON
DAUNTS >DAUNT
DAUPHIN n (formerly) eldest son of the king of France
DAUPHINE n wife of a dauphin
DAUPHINES >DAUPHINE
DAUPHINS >DAUPHIN
DAUR a Scot word for >DARE
DAURED >DAUR
DAURING >DAUR
DAURS >DAUR
DAUT vb fondle
DAUTED >DAUT
DAUTIE n darling
DAUTIES >DAUTIE
DAUTING >DAUT
DAUTS >DAUT
DAVEN vb pray
DAVENED >DAVEN
DAVENING >DAVEN
DAVENPORT n small writing table with drawers
DAVENS >DAVEN
DAVIDIA n Chinese shrub
DAVIDIAS >DAVIDIA
DAVIES >DAVY
DAVIT n crane, usu. one of a pair, at a ship's side, for lowering and hoisting a lifeboat
DAVITS >DAVIT
DAVY n miner's safety lamp
DAW n an archaic, dialect, or poetic name for a jackdaw ▷ vb old word for dawn
DAWAH n practice of educating non-Muslims about the message of Islam
DAWAHS >DAWAH
DAWBAKE n foolish or slow-witted person
DAWBAKES >DAWBAKE

DAWBRIES >DAWBRY
DAWBRY n unskilful painting
DAWCOCK n male jackdaw
DAWCOCKS >DAWCOCK
DAWD vb thump
DAWDED >DAWD
DAWDING >DAWD
DAWDLE vb walk slowly, lag behind
DAWDLED >DAWDLE
DAWDLER >DAWDLE
DAWDLERS >DAWDLE
DAWDLES >DAWDLE
DAWDLING >DAWDLE
DAWDS >DAWD
DAWED >DAW
DAWEN >DAW
DAWING >DAW
DAWISH >DAW
DAWK same as >DAK
DAWKS >DAWK
DAWN n daybreak ▷ vb begin to grow light
DAWNED >DAWN
DAWNER vb stroll
DAWNERED >DAWNER
DAWNERING >DAWNER
DAWNERS >DAWNER
DAWNEY adj (of a person) dull or slow
DAWNING >DAWN
DAWNINGS >DAWN
DAWNLIKE >DAWN
DAWNS >DAWN
DAWS >DAW
DAWSONITE n mineral
DAWT vb fondle
DAWTED >DAWT
DAWTIE n darling
DAWTIES >DAWTIE
DAWTING >DAWT
DAWTS >DAWT
DAY n period of 24 hours
DAYAN n senior rabbi, esp one who sits in a religious court
DAYANIM >DAYAN
DAYANS >DAYAN
DAYBED n narrow bed with a head piece and sometimes a foot piece and back, for day use
DAYBEDS >DAYBED
DAYBOAT n small sailing boat with no sleeping accommodation
DAYBOATS >DAYBOAT
DAYBOOK n book in which the transactions of each day are recorded as they occur
DAYBOOKS >DAYBOOK
DAYBOY n boy who attends a boarding school daily, but returns home each evening
DAYBOYS >DAYBOY
DAYBREAK n time in the morning when light first appears
DAYBREAKS >DAYBREAK
DAYCARE n occupation, treatment, or supervision during the working day for

people who might be at risk if left on their own, or whose usual carers need daytime relief
DAYCARES >DAYCARE
DAYCENTRE n building used for daycare or other welfare services
DAYCH vb thatch
DAYCHED >DAYCH
DAYCHES >DAYCH
DAYCHING >DAYCH
DAYDREAM n pleasant fantasy indulged in while awake ▷ vb indulge in idle fantasy
DAYDREAMS >DAYDREAM
DAYDREAMT >DAYDREAM
DAYDREAMY >DAYDREAM
DAYFLIES >DAYFLY
DAYFLOWER n type of tropical and subtropical plant with narrow pointed leaves and blue or purplish flowers which wilt quickly
DAYFLY another name for >MAYFLY
DAYGIRL n a girl who attends boarding school during the day but returns home in the evening
DAYGIRLS >DAYGIRL
DAYGLO n fluorescent colours
DAYGLOW n fluorescent colours
DAYGLOWS >DAYGLOW
DAYLIGHT n light from the sun
DAYLIGHTS npl consciousness or wits
DAYLILIES >DAYLILY
DAYLILY n any of various plants having lily-like flowers that typically last only one day before being succeeded by others
DAYLIT >DAYLIGHT
DAYLONG adv lasting the entire day
DAYMARE n bad dream during the day
DAYMARES >DAYMARE
DAYMARK n navigation aid
DAYMARKS >DAYMARK
DAYNT adj dainty
DAYPACK n small rucksack
DAYPACKS >DAYPACK
DAYROOM n communal living room in a residential institution
DAYROOMS >DAYROOM
DAYS adv during the day, esp regularly
DAYSACK n rucksack
DAYSACKS >DAYSACK
DAYSAILER same as >DAYSAILOR
DAYSAILOR n small sailing boat with no sleeping accommodation
DAYSHELL n thistle
DAYSHELLS >DAYSHELL
DAYSIDE n side of a planet nearest the sun

DAYSIDES >DAYSIDE
DAYSMAN n umpire
DAYSMEN >DAYSMAN
DAYSPRING a poetic word for >DAWN
DAYSTAR a poetic word for >SUN
DAYSTARS >DAYSTAR
DAYTALE n day labour
DAYTALER n worker paid by the day
DAYTALERS >DAYTALER
DAYTALES >DAYTALE
DAYTIME n time from sunrise to sunset
DAYTIMES >DAYTIME
DAYWEAR n clothes for everyday or informal wear
DAYWEARS >DAYWEAR
DAYWORK n daytime work
DAYWORKER >DAYWORK
DAYWORKS >DAYWORK
DAZE vb stun, by a blow or shock ▷ n state of confusion or shock
DAZED >DAZE
DAZEDLY >DAZE
DAZEDNESS >DAZE
DAZER >DAZE
DAZERS >DAZE
DAZES >DAZE
DAZING >DAZE
DAZZLE vb impress greatly ▷ n bright light that dazzles
DAZZLED >DAZZLE
DAZZLER >DAZZLE
DAZZLERS >DAZZLE
DAZZLES >DAZZLE
DAZZLING >DAZZLE
DAZZLINGS >DAZZLING
DE prep of or from
DEACIDIFY vb removal acid from
DEACON n ordained minister ranking immediately below a priest ▷ vb make a deacon of
DEACONED >DEACON
DEACONESS n (in the early church and in some modern Churches) a female member of the laity with duties similar to those of a deacon
DEACONING >DEACON
DEACONRY n office or status of a deacon
DEACONS >DEACON
DEAD adj no longer alive ▷ n period during which coldness or darkness is most intense ▷ adv extremely ▷ vb in archaic usage, die or kill
DEADBEAT n lazy useless person
DEADBEATS >DEADBEAT
DEADBOLT n bolt operated without a spring
DEADBOLTS >DEADBOLT
DEADBOY >DEADMAN
DEADBOYS >DEADBOY
DEADED >DEAD

DEADEN *vb* make less intense

DEADENED > DEADEN

DEADENER > DEADEN

DEADENERS > DEADEN

DEADENING > DEADEN

DEADENS > DEADEN

DEADER > DEAD

DEADERS > DEAD

DEADEST > DEAD

DEADEYE *n* either of a pair of disclike wooden blocks, supported by straps in grooves around them, between which a line is rove so as to draw them together to tighten a shroud

DEADEYES > DEADEYE

DEADFALL *n* type of trap, used esp for catching large animals, in which a heavy weight falls to crush the prey

DEADFALLS > DEADFALL

DEADHEAD *n* person who does not pay on a bus, at a game, etc ▷ *vb* cut off withered flowers from (a plant)

DEADHEADS > DEADHEAD

DEADHOUSE *n* mortuary

DEADING > DEAD

DEADLIER > DEADLY

DEADLIEST > DEADLY

DEADLIFT *vb* weightlifting term

DEADLIFTS > DEADLIFT

DEADLIGHT *n* bull's-eye let into the deck or hull of a vessel to admit light to a cabin

DEADLINE *n* time limit ▷ *vb* put a time limit on an action, decision, etc

DEADLINED > DEADLINE

DEADLINES > DEADLINE

DEADLOCK *n* point in a dispute at which no agreement can be reached ▷ *vb* bring or come to a deadlock

DEADLOCKS > DEADLOCK

DEADLY *adj* likely to cause death ▷ *adv* extremely

DEADMAN *n* heavy plate, wall, or block buried in the ground that acts as an anchor for a retaining wall, sheet pile, etc, by a tie connecting the two

DEADMEN > DEADMAN

DEADNESS > DEAD

DEADPAN *adv* showing no emotion or expression ▷ *adj* deliberately emotionless ▷ *n* deadpan expression or manner

DEADPANS > DEADPAN

DEADS > DEAD

DEADSTOCK *n* farm equipment

DEADWOOD *n* dead trees or branches

DEADWOODS > DEADWOOD

DEAERATE *vb* remove air from

DEAERATED > DEAERATE

DEAERATES > DEAERATE

DEAERATOR > DEAERATE

DEAF *adj* unable to hear

DEAFBLIND *adj* unable to hear or see

DEAFEN *vb* make deaf, esp temporarily

DEAFENED > DEAFEN

DEAFENING *n* excessively loud

DEAFENS > DEAFEN

DEAFER > DEAF

DEAFEST > DEAF

DEAFISH > DEAF

DEAFLY > DEAF

DEAFNESS > DEAF

DEAIR *vb* reove air from

DEAIRED > DEAIR

DEAIRING > DEAIR

DEAIRS > DEAIR

DEAL *n* agreement or transaction ▷ *vb* inflict (a blow) on ▷ *adj* of fir or pine

DEALATE *adj* (of ants and other insects) having lost their wings, esp by biting or rubbing them off after mating ▷ *n* insect that has shed its wings

DEALATED *same as* > DEALATE

DEALATES > DEALATE

DEALATION > DEALATE

DEALBATE *adj* bleached

DEALER *n* person whose business involves buying and selling

DEALERS > DEALER

DEALFISH *n* long thin fish

DEALING > DEAL

DEALINGS *npl* transactions or business relations

DEALS > DEAL

DEALT > DEAL

DEAMINASE *n* enzyme that breaks down amino compounds

DEAMINATE *vb* remove one or more amino groups from (a molecule)

DEAMINISE *same as* > DEAMINATE

DEAMINIZE *same as* > DEAMINATE

DEAN *n* chief administrative official of a college or university faculty ▷ *vb* punish (a student) by sending them to the dean

DEANED > DEAN

DEANER *n* shilling

DEANERIES > DEANERY

DEANERS > DEANER

DEANERY *n* office or residence of a dean

DEANING > DEAN

DEANS > DEAN

DEANSHIP > DEAN

DEANSHIPS > DEAN

DEAR *n* someone regarded with affection ▷ *adj* much-loved

DEARE *vb* harm

DEARED > DEARE

DEARER > DEAR

DEARES > DEARE

DEAREST > DEAR

DEARESTS > DEAREST

DEARIE *same as* > DEARY

DEARIES > DEARY

DEARING > DEARE

DEARLING *n* darling

DEARLINGS > DEARLING

DEARLY *adv* very much

DEARN *vb* hide

DEARNESS > DEAR

DEARNFUL *adj* secret

DEARNLY > DEARN

DEARNS > DEARN

DEARS > DEAR

DEARTH *n* inadequate amount, scarcity

DEARTHS > DEARTH

DEARY *n* term of affection: now often sarcastic or facetious

DEASH *vb* remove ash from

DEASHED > DEASH

DEASHES > DEASH

DEASHING > DEASH

DEASIL *adv* in the direction of the apparent course of the sun ▷ *n* motion in this direction

DEASILS > DEASIL

DEASIUL *n* motion towards the sun

DEASIULS > DEASIUL

DEASOIL *n* motion towards the sun

DEASOILS > DEASOIL

DEATH *n* permanent end of life in a person or animal

DEATHBED *n* bed where a person is about to die or has just died

DEATHBEDS > DEATHBED

DEATHBLOW *n* thing or event that destroys hope

DEATHCUP *n* poisonous fungus

DEATHCUPS > DEATHCUP

DEATHFUL *adj* murderous

DEATHIER > DEATH

DEATHIEST > DEATH

DEATHLESS *adj* everlasting, because of fine qualities

DEATHLIER > DEATHLY

DEATHLIKE > DEATH

DEATHLY *adv* like death ▷ *adj* resembling death

DEATHS > DEATH

DEATHSMAN *n* executioner

DEATHSMEN > DEATHSMAN

DEATHTRAP *n* building, vehicle, etc, that is considered very unsafe

DEATHWARD *adv* heading towards death

DEATHY > DEATH

DEAVE *vb* deafen

DEAVED > DEAVE

DEAVES > DEAVE

DEAVING > DEAVE

DEAW *n* dew

DEAWIE > DEAW

DEAWS > DEAW

DEAWY > DEAW

DEB *n* debutante

DEBACLE *n* disastrous failure

DEBACLES > DEBACLE

DEBAG *vb* remove the trousers from (someone) by force

DEBAGGED > DEBAG

DEBAGGING > DEBAG

DEBAGS > DEBAG

DEBAR *vb* prevent, bar

DEBARK *vb* remove the bark from (a tree)

DEBARKED > DEBARK

DEBARKER > DEBARK

DEBARKERS > DEBARK

DEBARKING > DEBARK

DEBARKS > DEBARK

DEBARMENT > DEBAR

DEBARRASS *vb* relieve

DEBARRED > DEBAR

DEBARRING > DEBAR

DEBARS > DEBAR

DEBASE *vb* lower in value, quality, or character

DEBASED > DEBASE

DEBASER > DEBASE

DEBASERS > DEBASE

DEBASES > DEBASE

DEBASING > DEBASE

DEBATABLE *adj* not absolutely certain

DEBATABLY > DEBATABLE

DEBATE *n* discussion ▷ *vb* discuss formally

DEBATED > DEBATE

DEBATEFUL *adj* quarrelsome

DEBATER > DEBATE

DEBATERS > DEBATE

DEBATES > DEBATE

DEBATING > DEBATE

DEBAUCH *vb* make (someone) bad or corrupt, esp sexually ▷ *n* instance or period of extreme dissipation

DEBAUCHED > DEBAUCH

DEBAUCHEE *n* man who leads a life of reckless drinking, promiscuity, and self-indulgence

DEBAUCHER > DEBAUCH

DEBAUCHES > DEBAUCH

DEBBIER > DEBBY

DEBBIES > DEBBY

DEBBIEST > DEBBY

DEBBY *n* debutante ▷ *adj* of, or resembling a debutante

DEBE *n* tin

DEBEAK *vb* remove part of the beak of poultry to reduce the risk of such habits as feather-picking or cannibalism

DEBEAKED > DEBEAK

DEBEAKING > DEBEAK
DEBEAKS > DEBEAK
DEBEARD vb remove beard from mussel
DEBEARDED > DEBEARD
DEBEARDS > DEBEARD
DEBEL vb beat in war
DEBELLED > DEBEL
DEBELLING > DEBEL
DEBELS > DEBEL
DEBENTURE n long-term bond bearing fixed interest, issued by a company or a government agency
DEBES > DEBE
DEBILE adj lacking strength
DEBILITY n weakness, infirmity
DEBIT n acknowledgment of a sum owing by entry on the left side of an account ▷ vb charge (an account) with a debt
DEBITED > DEBIT
DEBITING > DEBIT
DEBITOR n person in debt
DEBITORS > DEBITOR
DEBITS > DEBIT
DEBONAIR adj (of a man) charming and refined
DEBONAIRE adj sauve and refined
DEBONE vb remove bones from
DEBONED > DEBONE
DEBONER > DEBONE
DEBONERS > DEBONE
DEBONES > DEBONE
DEBONING > DEBONE
DEBOSH vb debauch
DEBOSHED > DEBOSH
DEBOSHES > DEBOSH
DEBOSHING > DEBOSH
DEBOSS vb carve a design into
DEBOSSED > DEBOSS
DEBOSSES > DEBOSS
DEBOSSING > DEBOSS
DEBOUCH vb move out from a narrow place to a wider one ▷ n outlet or passage, as for the exit of troops
DEBOUCHE same as > DEBOUCH
DEBOUCHED > DEBOUCH
DEBOUCHES > DEBOUCH
DEBRIDE vb remove dead tissue from
DEBRIDED > DEBRIDE
DEBRIDES > DEBRIDE
DEBRIDING > DEBRIDE
DEBRIEF vb receive a report from (a soldier, diplomat, etc) after an event
DEBRIEFED > DEBRIEF
DEBRIEFER > DEBRIEF
DEBRIEFS > DEBRIEF
DEBRIS n fragments of something destroyed
DEBRUISE vb (in heraldry) overlay or partly cover

DEBRUISED > DEBRUISE
DEBRUISES > DEBRUISE
DEBS > DEB
DEBT n something owed, esp money
DEBTED adj in debt
DEBTEE n person owed a debt
DEBTEES > DEBTEE
DEBTLESS > DEBT
DEBTOR n person who owes money
DEBTORS > DEBTOR
DEBTS > DEBT
DEBUD same as > DISBUD
DEBUDDED > DEBUD
DEBUDDING > DEBUD
DEBUDS > DEBUD
DEBUG vb find and remove defects in (a computer program) ▷ n something, esp a computer program, that locates and removes defects in a device, system, etc
DEBUGGED > DEBUG
DEBUGGER > DEBUG
DEBUGGERS > DEBUG
DEBUGGING > DEBUG
DEBUGS > DEBUG
DEBUNK vb expose the falseness of
DEBUNKED > DEBUNK
DEBUNKER > DEBUNK
DEBUNKERS > DEBUNK
DEBUNKING > DEBUNK
DEBUNKS > DEBUNK
DEBUR vb remove burs from (a piece of machined metal)
DEBURR vb remove burrs from (a workpiece)
DEBURRED > DEBURR
DEBURRING > DEBURR
DEBURRS > DEBURR
DEBURS > DEBUR
DEBUS vb unload (goods) or (esp of troops) to alight from a motor vehicle
DEBUSED > DEBUS
DEBUSES > DEBUS
DEBUSING > DEBUS
DEBUSSED > DEBUS
DEBUSSES > DEBUS
DEBUSSING > DEBUS
DEBUT n first public appearance of a performer ▷ vb make a debut
DEBUTANT n person who is making a first appearance in a particular capacity, such as a sportsperson playing in a first game for a team
DEBUTANTE n young upper-class woman being formally presented to society
DEBUTANTS > DEBUTANT
DEBUTED > DEBUT
DEBUTING > DEBUT
DEBUTS > DEBUT
DEBYE n unit of electric dipole moment
DEBYES > DEBYE

DECACHORD n instrument with ten strings
DECAD n ten years
DECADAL > DECADE
DECADE n period of ten years
DECADENCE n deterioration in morality or culture
DECADENCY same as > DECADENCE
DECADENT adj characterized by decay or decline, as in being self-indulgent or morally corrupt ▷ n decadent person
DECADENTS > DECADENT
DECADES > DECADE
DECADS > DECAD
DECAF n decaffeinated coffee ▷ adj decaffeinated
DECAFF n decaffeinated coffee
DECAFFS > DECAFF
DECAFS > DECAF
DECAGON n geometric figure with ten faces
DECAGONAL > DECAGON
DECAGONS > DECAGON
DECAGRAM n ten grams
DECAGRAMS > DECAGRAM
DECAHEDRA n plural form of singular decahedron: solid figure with ten plane faces
DECAL vb transfer (a design) by decalcomania
DECALCIFY vb remove calcium or lime from (bones, teeth, etc)
DECALED > DECAL
DECALING > DECAL
DECALITER same as > DECALITRE
DECALITRE n measure of volume equivalent to 10 litres
DECALLED > DECAL
DECALLING > DECAL
DECALOG same as > DECALOGUE
DECALOGS > DECALOG
DECALOGUE n Ten Commandments
DECALS > DECAL
DECAMETER same as > DECAMETRE
DECAMETRE n unit of length equal to ten metres
DECAMP vb depart secretly or suddenly
DECAMPED > DECAMP
DECAMPING > DECAMP
DECAMPS > DECAMP
DECANAL adj of or relating to a dean or deanery
DECANALLY > DECANAL
DECANE n liquid alkane hydrocarbon
DECANES > DECANE
DECANI adv be sung by the decanal side of a choir
DECANOIC as in decanoic acid white crystalline

insoluble carboxylic acid with an unpleasant odour, used in perfumes and for making fruit flavours
DECANT vb pour (a liquid) from one container to another
DECANTATE vb decant
DECANTED > DECANT
DECANTER n stoppered bottle for wine or spirits
DECANTERS > DECANTER
DECANTING > DECANT
DECANTS > DECANT
DECAPOD n creature, such as a crab, with five pairs of walking limbs ▷ adj of, relating to, or belonging to these creatures
DECAPODAL > DECAPOD
DECAPODAN > DECAPOD
DECAPODS > DECAPOD
DECARB vb decoke
DECARBED > DECARB
DECARBING > DECARB
DECARBS > DECARB
DECARE n ten ares or 1000 square metres
DECARES > DECARE
DECASTERE n ten steres
DECASTICH n poem with ten lines
DECASTYLE n portico consisting of ten columns
DECATHLON n athletic contest with ten events
DECAUDATE vb remove the tail from
DECAY vb become weaker or more corrupt ▷ n process of decaying
DECAYABLE > DECAY
DECAYED > DECAY
DECAYER > DECAY
DECAYERS > DECAY
DECAYING > DECAY
DECAYLESS adj immortal
DECAYS > DECAY
DECCIE n decoration
DECCIES > DECCIE
DECEASE n death
DECEASED adj dead ▷ n dead person
DECEASES > DECEASE
DECEASING > DECEASE
DECEDENT n deceased person
DECEDENTS > DECEDENT
DECEIT n behaviour intended to deceive
DECEITFUL adj full of deceit
DECEITS > DECEIT
DECEIVE vb mislead by lying
DECEIVED > DECEIVE
DECEIVER > DECEIVE
DECEIVERS > DECEIVE
DECEIVES > DECEIVE
DECEIVING > DECEIVE
DECELERON n type of aileron
DECEMVIR n (in ancient Rome) a member of a board

of ten magistrates, esp either of the two commissions established in 451 and 450 BC to revise the laws

DECEMVIRI > DECEMVIR

DECEMVIRS > DECEMVIR

DECENARY *adj* of or relating to a tithing

DECENCIES *npl* generally accepted standards of good behaviour

DECENCY *n* conformity to the prevailing standards of what is right

DECENNARY *same as* > DECENARY

DECENNIA > DECENNIUM

DECENNIAL *adj* lasting for ten years ▷ *n* tenth anniversary or its celebration

DECENNIUM *a less common word for* > DECADE

DECENT *adj* (of a person) polite and morally acceptable

DECENTER *vb* put out of centre

DECENTERS > DECENTER

DECENTEST > DECENT

DECENTLY > DECENT

DECENTRE *vb* put out of centre

DECENTRED > DECENTRE

DECENTRES > DECENTRE

DECEPTION *n* deceiving

DECEPTIVE *adj* likely or designed to deceive

DECEPTORY *adj* deceiving

DECERN *vb* decree or adjudge

DECERNED > DECERN

DECERNING > DECERN

DECERNS > DECERN

DECERTIFY *vb* withdraw or remove a certificate or certification from (a person, organization, or country)

DECESSION *n* departure

DECHEANCE *n* forfeiting

DECIARE *n* one tenth of an are or 10 square metres

DECIARES > DECIARE

DECIBEL *n* unit for measuring the intensity of sound

DECIBELS > DECIBEL

DECIDABLE *adj* able to be decided

DECIDE *vb* (cause to) reach a decision

DECIDED *adj* unmistakable

DECIDEDLY > DECIDED

DECIDER *n* point, goal, game, etc, that determines who wins a match or championship

DECIDERS > DECIDER

DECIDES > DECIDE

DECIDING > DECIDE

DECIDUA *n* specialized mucous membrane that lines the uterus of some

mammals during pregnancy: is shed, with the placenta, at parturition

DECIDUAE > DECIDUA

DECIDUAL > DECIDUA

DECIDUAS > DECIDUA

DECIDUATE > DECIDUA

DECIDUOUS *adj* (of a tree) shedding its leaves annually

DECIGRAM *n* tenth of a gram

DECIGRAMS > DECIGRAM

DECILE *n* one of nine actual or notional values of a variable dividing its distribution into ten groups with equal frequencies: the ninth decile is the value below which 90% of the population lie

DECILES > DECILE

DECILITER *same as* > DECILITRE

DECILITRE *n* measure of volume equivalent to one tenth of a litre

DECILLION *n* (in Britain, France, and Germany) the number represented as one followed by 60 zeros (10^{60})

DECIMAL *n* fraction written in the form of a dot followed by one or more numbers ▷ *adj* relating to or using powers of ten

DECIMALLY > DECIMAL

DECIMALS > DECIMAL

DECIMATE *vb* destroy or kill a large proportion of

DECIMATED > DECIMATE

DECIMATES > DECIMATE

DECIMATOR > DECIMATE

DECIME *n* a former French coin

DECIMES > DECIME

DECIMETER *same as* > DECIMETRE

DECIMETRE *n* unit of length equal to one tenth of a metre

DECIPHER *vb* work out the meaning of (something illegible or in code)

DECIPHERS > DECIPHER

DECISION *n* judgment, conclusion, or resolution

DECISIONS > DECISION

DECISIVE *adj* having a definite influence

DECISORY *adj* deciding

DECISTERE *n* tenth of a stere

DECK *n* area of a ship that forms a floor dress or decorate)

DECKCHAIR *n* folding wooden and canvas chair designed for use outside

DECKED *adj* having a wooden deck or platform

DECKEL *same as* > DECKLE

DECKELS > DECKEL

DECKER > DECK

DECKERS > DECK

DECKHAND *n* seaman assigned various duties, such as mooring and cargo handling, on the deck of a ship

DECKHANDS > DECKHAND

DECKHOUSE *n* houselike cabin on the deck of a ship

DECKING *n* wooden platform in a garden

DECKINGS > DECKING

DECKLE *n* frame used to contain pulp on the mould in the making of handmade paper

DECKLED > DECKLE

DECKLES > DECKLE

DECKO *n* look ▷ *vb* have a look

DECKOED > DECKO

DECKOING > DECKO

DECKOS > DECKO

DECKS > DECK

DECLAIM *vb* speak loudly and dramatically

DECLAIMED > DECLAIM

DECLAIMER > DECLAIM

DECLAIMS > DECLAIM

DECLARANT *n* person who makes a declaration

DECLARE *vb* state firmly and forcefully

DECLARED > DECLARE

DECLARER *n* person who declares

DECLARERS > DECLARER

DECLARES > DECLARE

DECLARING > DECLARE

DECLASS *vb* lower in social status or position

DECLASSE *adj* having lost social standing or status

DECLASSED > DECLASS

DECLASSEE *adj* (of a woman) having lost social standing or status

DECLASSES > DECLASS

DECLAW *vb* remove claws from

DECLAWED > DECLAW

DECLAWING > DECLAW

DECLAWS > DECLAW

DECLINAL *adj* bending down

DECLINANT *adj* heraldry term

DECLINATE *adj* (esp of plant parts) descending from the horizontal in a curve

DECLINE *vb* become smaller, weaker, or less important ▷ *n* gradual weakening or loss

DECLINED > DECLINE

DECLINER > DECLINE

DECLINERS > DECLINE

DECLINES > DECLINE

DECLINING > DECLINE

DECLINIST *n* person believing something is in decline

DECLIVITY *n* downward slope

DECLIVOUS *adj* steep

DECLUTCH *vb* disengage the clutch of a motor vehicle

DECLUTTER *vb* simplify or get rid of mess, disorder, complications, etc

DECO as in *art deco* style of art, jewellery, design, etc

DECOCT *vb* extract the essence from (a substance) by boiling

DECOCTED > DECOCT

DECOCTING > DECOCT

DECOCTION *n* extraction by boiling

DECOCTIVE > DECOCT

DECOCTS > DECOCT

DECOCTURE *n* substance obtained by decoction

DECODE *vb* convert from code into ordinary language

DECODED > DECODE

DECODER > DECODE

DECODERS > DECODE

DECODES > DECODE

DECODING > DECODE

DECOHERER *n* electrical device

DECOKE *n* decarbonize

DECOKED > DECOKE

DECOKES > DECOKE

DECOKING > DECOKE

DECOLLATE *vb* separate (continuous stationery, etc) into individual forms

DECOLLETE *adj* (of a woman's garment) low-cut ▷ *n* low-cut neckline

DECOLOR *vb* bleach

DECOLORED > DECOLOR

DECOLORS > DECOLOR

DECOLOUR *vb* deprive of colour, as by bleaching

DECOLOURS > DECOLOUR

DECOMMIT *vb* withdraw from a commitment or agreed course of action

DECOMMITS > DECOMMIT

DECOMPLEX *adj* repeatedly compound

DECOMPOSE *vb* be broken down through chemical or bacterial action

DECONGEST *vb* relieve congestion in

DECONTROL *vb* free of restraints or controls, esp government controls

DECOR *n* style in which a room or house is decorated

DECORATE *vb* make more attractive by adding something ornamental

DECORATED > DECORATE

DECORATES > DECORATE

DECORATOR *n* person whose profession is the painting and wallpapering of buildings

DECOROUS *adj* polite, calm, and sensible in behaviour

DECORS > DECOR

DECORUM *n* polite and

socially correct behaviour
DECORUMS >DECORUM
DECOS >DECO
DECOUPAGE n art or process of decorating a surface with shapes or illustrations cut from paper, card, etc
DECOUPLE vb separate (joined or coupled subsystems) thereby enabling them to exist and operate separately
DECOUPLED >DECOUPLE
DECOUPLER >DECOUPLE
DECOUPLES >DECOUPLE
DECOY n person or thing used to lure someone into danger ▷ vb lure away by means of a trick
DECOYED >DECOY
DECOYER >DECOY
DECOYERS >DECOY
DECOYING >DECOY
DECOYS >DECOY
DECREASE vb make or become less ▷ n lessening, reduction
DECREASED >DECREASE
DECREASES >DECREASE
DECREE n law made by someone in authority ▷ vb order by decree
DECREED >DECREE
DECREEING >DECREE
DECREER >DECREE
DECREERS >DECREE
DECREES >DECREE
DECREET n final judgment or sentence of a court
DECREETS >DECREET
DECREMENT n act of decreasing
DECREPIT adj weakened or worn out by age or long use
DECRETAL n papal decree ▷ adj of or relating to a decretal or a decree
DECRETALS >DECRETAL
DECRETIST n law student
DECRETIVE adj of a decree
DECRETORY adj of a decree
DECREW vb decrease
DECREWED >DECREW
DECREWING >DECREW
DECREWS >DECREW
DECRIAL >DECRY
DECRIALS >DECRY
DECRIED >DECRY
DECRIER >DECRY
DECRIERS >DECRY
DECRIES >DECRY
DECROWN vb depose
DECROWNED >DECROWN
DECROWNS >DECROWN
DECRY vb express disapproval of
DECRYING >DECRY
DECRYPT vb decode (a message) with or without previous knowledge of its key
DECRYPTED >DECRYPT

DECRYPTS >DECRYPT
DECTET n ten musicians
DECTETS >DECTET
DECUBITAL >DECUBITUS
DECUBITI >DECUBITUS
DECUBITUS n posture adopted when lying down
DECUMAN n large wave
DECUMANS >DECUMAN
DECUMBENT adj lying down or lying flat
DECUPLE vb increase by ten times ▷ n amount ten times as large as a given reference ▷ adj increasing tenfold
DECUPLED >DECUPLE
DECUPLES >DECUPLE
DECUPLING >DECUPLE
DECURIA n group of ten
DECURIAS >DECURIA
DECURIES >DECURY
DECURION n local councillor
DECURIONS >DECURION
DECURRENT adj extending down the stem, esp (of a leaf) having the base of the blade extending down the stem as two wings
DECURSION n state of being decurrent
DECURSIVE adj extending downwards
DECURVE vb curve downwards
DECURVED adj bent or curved downwards
DECURVES >DECURVE
DECURVING >DECURVE
DECURY n (in ancient Rome) a body of ten men
DECUSSATE vb cross or cause to cross in the form of the letter X ▷ adj in the form of the letter X
DEDAL same as >DAEDAL
DEDALIAN adj of Daedalus
DEDANS n open gallery at the server's end of the court
DEDICANT n person who dedicates
DEDICANTS >DEDICANT
DEDICATE vb commit (oneself or one's time) wholly to a special purpose or cause
DEDICATED adj devoted to a particular purpose or cause
DEDICATEE >DEDICATE
DEDICATES >DEDICATE
DEDICATOR >DEDICATE
DEDIMUS n legal term
DEDIMUSES >DEDIMUS
DEDUCE vb reach (a conclusion) by reasoning from evidence
DEDUCED >DEDUCE
DEDUCES >DEDUCE
DEDUCIBLE >DEDUCE
DEDUCIBLY >DEDUCE
DEDUCING >DEDUCE
DEDUCT vb subtract

DEDUCTED >DEDUCT
DEDUCTING >DEDUCT
DEDUCTION n deducting
DEDUCTIVE adj of or relating to deduction
DEDUCTS >DEDUCT
DEE a Scot word for >DIE
DEED n something that is done ▷ vb convey or transfer (property) by deed ▷ adj Scots form of dead
DEEDED >DEED
DEEDER >DEED
DEEDEST >DEED
DEEDFUL adj full of exploits
DEEDIER >DEEDY
DEEDIEST >DEEDY
DEEDILY >DEEDY
DEEDING >DEED
DEEDLESS adj without exploits
DEEDS >DEED
DEEDY adj hard-working
DEEING >DEE
DEEJAY n disc jockey ▷ vb work or act as a disc jockey
DEEJAYED >DEEJAY
DEEJAYING >DEEJAY
DEEJAYS >DEEJAY
DEEK vb look at
DEELY as in deely boppers hairband with two bobbing antennae-like attachments
DEEM vb consider, judge
DEEMED >DEEM
DEEMING >DEEM
DEEMS >DEEM
DEEMSTER n title of one of the two justices in the Isle of Man
DEEMSTERS >DEEMSTER
DEEN n din
DEENS >DEEN
DEEP adj extending or situated far down, inwards, backwards, or sideways ▷ n any deep place on land or under water
DEEPEN vb make or become deeper or more intense
DEEPENED >DEEPEN
DEEPENER >DEEPEN
DEEPENERS >DEEPEN
DEEPENING >DEEPEN
DEEPENS >DEEPEN
DEEPER >DEEP
DEEPEST >DEEP
DEEPFELT adj sincere
DEEPFROZE vb froze in a freezer
DEEPIE n 3D film
DEEPIES >DEEPIE
DEEPLY >DEEP
DEEPMOST adj deepest
DEEPNESS >DEEP
DEEPS >DEEP
DEEPWATER adj seagoing
DEER n large wild animal, the male of which has antlers
DEERBERRY n huckleberry
DEERE adj serious
DEERFLIES >DEERFLY

DEERFLY n insect related to the horsefly
DEERGRASS n type of plant that grows in dense tufts in peat bogs of temperate regions
DEERHOUND n very large rough-coated breed of dog of the greyhound type
DEERLET n ruminant mammal
DEERLETS >DEERLET
DEERLIKE adj like a deer
DEERS >DEER
DEERSKIN n hide of a deer
DEERSKINS >DEERSKIN
DEERWEED n forage plant
DEERWEEDS >DEERWEED
DEERYARD n gathering place for deer
DEERYARDS >DEERYARD
DEES >DEE
DEET n insect-repellent
DEETS >DEET
DEEV n mythical monster
DEEVE vb deafen
DEEVED >DEEVE
DEEVES >DEEVE
DEEVING >DEEVE
DEEVS >DEEV
DEEWAN n chief of a village in India
DEEWANS >DEEWAN
DEF adj very good
DEFACE vb deliberately spoil the appearance of
DEFACED >DEFACE
DEFACER >DEFACE
DEFACERS >DEFACE
DEFACES >DEFACE
DEFACING >DEFACE
DEFAECATE same as >DEFECATE
DEFALCATE vb make wrong use of funds entrusted to one
DEFAME vb attack the good reputation of
DEFAMED >DEFAME
DEFAMER >DEFAME
DEFAMERS >DEFAME
DEFAMES >DEFAME
DEFAMING >DEFAME
DEFAMINGS >DEFAME
DEFANG vb remove the fangs of
DEFANGED >DEFANG
DEFANGING >DEFANG
DEFANGS >DEFANG
DEFAST adj defaced
DEFASTE adj defaced
DEFAT vb remove fat from
DEFATS >DEFAT
DEFATTED >DEFAT
DEFATTING >DEFAT
DEFAULT n failure to do something ▷ vb fail to fulfil an obligation
DEFAULTED >DEFAULT
DEFAULTER n person who defaults
DEFAULTS >DEFAULT
DEFEAT vb win a victory over ▷ n defeating

DEFEATED > DEFEAT
DEFEATER > DEFEAT
DEFEATERS > DEFEAT
DEFEATING > DEFEAT
DEFEATISM n ready acceptance or expectation of defeat
DEFEATIST > DEFEATISM
DEFEATS > DEFEAT
DEFEATURE vb deform
DEFECATE vb discharge waste from the body through the anus
DEFECATED > DEFECATE
DEFECATES > DEFECATE
DEFECATOR > DEFECATE
DEFECT n imperfection, blemish ▷ vb desert one's cause or country to join the opposing forces
DEFECTED > DEFECT
DEFECTING > DEFECT
DEFECTION n act or an instance of defecting
DEFECTIVE adj imperfect, faulty
DEFECTOR > DEFECT
DEFECTORS > DEFECT
DEFECTS > DEFECT
DEFENCE n resistance against attack
DEFENCED > DEFENCE
DEFENCES > DEFENCE
DEFENCING > DEFENCE
DEFEND vb protect from harm or danger
DEFENDANT n person accused of a crime ▷ adj making a defence
DEFENDED > DEFEND
DEFENDER > DEFEND
DEFENDERS > DEFEND
DEFENDING > DEFEND
DEFENDS > DEFEND
DEFENSE same as > DEFENCE
DEFENSED > DEFENSE
DEFENSES > DEFENSE
DEFENSING > DEFENSE
DEFENSIVE adj intended for defence
DEFER vb delay (something) until a future time
DEFERABLE > DEFER
DEFERENCE n polite and respectful behaviour
DEFERENT adj (esp of a bodily nerve, vessel, or duct) conveying an impulse, fluid, etc, outwards, down, or away ▷ n (in the Ptolemaic system) a circle centred on the earth around which the centre of the epicycle was thought to move
DEFERENTS > DEFERENT
DEFERMENT n act of deferring or putting off until another time
DEFERRAL same as > DEFERMENT
DEFERRALS > DEFERRAL

DEFERRED adj withheld over a certain period
DEFERRER > DEFER
DEFERRERS > DEFER
DEFERRING > DEFER
DEFERS > DEFER
DEFFER > DEF
DEFFEST > DEF
DEFFLY archaic word meaning the same as > DEFTLY
DEFFO interj definitely: an expression of agreement or consent
DEFI n challenge
DEFIANCE n open resistance or disobedience
DEFIANCES > DEFIANCE
DEFIANT adj marked by resistance or bold opposition, as to authority
DEFIANTLY > DEFIANT
DEFICIENT adj lacking some essential thing or quality
DEFICIT n amount by which a sum of money is too small
DEFICITS > DEFICIT
DEFIED > DEFY
DEFIER > DEFY
DEFIERS > DEFY
DEFIES > DEFY
DEFILADE n protection provided by obstacles against enemy crossfire from the rear, or observation ▷ vb provide protection for by defilade
DEFILADED > DEFILADE
DEFILADES > DEFILADE
DEFILE vb treat (something sacred or important) without respect ▷ n narrow valley or pass
DEFILED > DEFILE
DEFILER > DEFILE
DEFILERS > DEFILE
DEFILES > DEFILE
DEFILING > DEFILE
DEFINABLE > DEFINE
DEFINABLY > DEFINE
DEFINE vb state precisely the meaning of
DEFINED > DEFINE
DEFINER > DEFINE
DEFINERS > DEFINE
DEFINES > DEFINE
DEFINIENS n word or words used to define or give an account of the meaning of another word, as in a dictionary entry
DEFINING > DEFINE
DEFINITE adj firm, clear, and precise
DEFIS > DEFI
DEFLATE vb (cause to) collapse through the release of air
DEFLATED > DEFLATE
DEFLATER > DEFLATE
DEFLATERS > DEFLATE
DEFLATES > DEFLATE

DEFLATING > DEFLATE
DEFLATION n reduction in economic activity resulting in lower output and investment
DEFLATOR > DEFLATE
DEFLATORS > DEFLATE
DEFLEA vb remove fleas from
DEFLEAED > DEFLEA
DEFLEAING > DEFLEA
DEFLEAS > DEFLEA
DEFLECT vb (cause to) turn aside from a course
DEFLECTED > DEFLECT
DEFLECTOR > DEFLECT
DEFLECTS > DEFLECT
DEFLEX vb turn downwards
DEFLEXED > DEFLEX
DEFLEXES > DEFLEX
DEFLEXING > DEFLEX
DEFLEXION n deflection
DEFLEXURE n act of deflecting
DEFLORATE vb deflower
DEFLOWER vb deprive (a woman) of her virginity
DEFLOWERS > DEFLOWER
DEFLUENT adj running downwards
DEFLUXION n discharge
DEFO interj (slang) definitely
DEFOAM vb remove foam from
DEFOAMED > DEFOAM
DEFOAMER > DEFOAM
DEFOAMERS > DEFOAM
DEFOAMING > DEFOAM
DEFOAMS > DEFOAM
DEFOCUS vb put out of focus
DEFOCUSED > DEFOCUS
DEFOCUSES > DEFOCUS
DEFOG vb clear of vapour
DEFOGGED > DEFOG
DEFOGGER > DEFOG
DEFOGGERS > DEFOG
DEFOGGING > DEFOG
DEFOGS > DEFOG
DEFOLIANT n chemical sprayed or dusted onto trees to cause their leaves to fall, esp to remove cover from an enemy in warfare
DEFOLIATE vb deprive (a plant) of its leaves ▷ adj (of a plant) having shed its leaves
DEFORCE vb withhold (property, esp land) wrongfully or by force from the rightful owner
DEFORCED > DEFORCE
DEFORCER > DEFORCE
DEFORCERS > DEFORCE
DEFORCES > DEFORCE
DEFORCING > DEFORCE
DEFOREST vb clear of trees
DEFORESTS > DEFOREST
DEFORM vb put out of shape or spoil the appearance of

DEFORMED adj disfigured or misshapen
DEFORMER > DEFORM
DEFORMERS > DEFORM
DEFORMING > DEFORM
DEFORMITY n distortion of a body part
DEFORMS > DEFORM
DEFOUL vb defile
DEFOULED > DEFOUL
DEFOULING > DEFOUL
DEFOULS > DEFOUL
DEFRAG vb defragment
DEFRAGGED > DEFRAG
DEFRAGGER > DEFRAG
DEFRAGS > DEFRAG
DEFRAUD vb cheat out of money, property, etc
DEFRAUDED > DEFRAUD
DEFRAUDER > DEFRAUD
DEFRAUDS > DEFRAUD
DEFRAY vb provide money for (costs or expenses)
DEFRAYAL > DEFRAY
DEFRAYALS > DEFRAY
DEFRAYED > DEFRAY
DEFRAYER > DEFRAY
DEFRAYERS > DEFRAY
DEFRAYING > DEFRAY
DEFRAYS > DEFRAY
DEFREEZE vb defrost
DEFREEZES > DEFREEZE
DEFROCK vb deprive (a priest) of priestly status
DEFROCKED > DEFROCK
DEFROCKS > DEFROCK
DEFROST vb make or become free of ice
DEFROSTED > DEFROST
DEFROSTER n device by which the de-icing process of a refrigerator is accelerated, usually by circulating the refrigerant without the expansion process
DEFROSTS > DEFROST
DEFROZE > DEFREEZE
DEFROZEN > DEFREEZE
DEFT adj quick and skilful in movement
DEFTER > DEFT
DEFTEST > DEFT
DEFTLY > DEFT
DEFTNESS > DEFT
DEFUEL vb remove fuel from
DEFUELED > DEFUEL
DEFUELING > DEFUEL
DEFUELLED > DEFUEL
DEFUELS > DEFUEL
DEFUNCT adj no longer existing or operative ▷ n deceased person
DEFUNCTS > DEFUNCT
DEFUND vb stop funds to
DEFUNDED > DEFUND
DEFUNDING > DEFUND
DEFUNDS > DEFUND
DEFUSE vb remove the fuse of (an explosive device)
DEFUSED > DEFUSE
DEFUSER > DEFUSE
DEFUSERS > DEFUEL

DEFUSES > DEFUSE
DEFUSING > DEFUSE
DEFUZE *same as* > DEFUSE
DEFUZED > DEFUZE
DEFUZES > DEFUZE
DEFUZING > DEFUZE
DEFY *vb* resist openly and boldly
DEFYING > DEFY
DEG *vb* water (a plant, etc)
DEGAGE *adj* unconstrained in manner
DEGAME *n* tree of South and Central America
DEGAMES > DEGAME
DEGAMI *same as* > DEGAME
DEGAMIS > DEGAMI
DEGARNISH *vb* remove ornament from
DEGAS *vb* remove gas from (a container, vacuum tube, liquid, adsorbent, etc)
DEGASES > DEGAS
DEGASSED > DEGAS
DEGASSER > DEGAS
DEGASSERS > DEGAS
DEGASSES > DEGAS
DEGASSING > DEGAS
DEGAUSS *n* demagnetize
DEGAUSSED > DEGAUSS
DEGAUSSER > DEGAUSS
DEGAUSSERS > DEGAUSS
DEGAUSSES > DEGAUSS
DEGEARING *n* process in which a company replaces some or all of its fixed-interest loan stock with ordinary shares
DEGENDER *vb* remove reference to gender from
DEGENDERS > DEGENDER
DEGERM *vb* remove germs from
DEGERMED > DEGERM
DEGERMING > DEGERM
DEGERMS > DEGERM
DEGGED > DEG
DEGGING > DEG
DEGLAZE *vb* dilute meat sediments in (a pan) in order to make a sauce or gravy
DEGLAZED > DEGLAZE
DEGLAZES > DEGLAZE
DEGLAZING > DEGLAZE
DEGOUT *n* disgust
DEGOUTS > DEGOUT
DEGRADE *vb* reduce to dishonour or disgrace
DEGRADED > DEGRADE
DEGRADER > DEGRADE
DEGRADERS > DEGRADE
DEGRADES > DEGRADE
DEGRADING *adj* causing humiliation
DEGRAS *n* emulsion used for dressing hides
DEGREASE *vb* remove grease from
DEGREASED > DEGREASE
DEGREASER > DEGREASE
DEGREASES > DEGREASE
DEGREE *n* stage in a scale of relative amount or intensity

DEGREED *adj* having a degree
DEGREES > DEGREE
DEGS > DEG
DEGU *n* small S American rodent
DEGUM *vb* remove gum from
DEGUMMED > DEGUM
DEGUMMING > DEGUM
DEGUMS > DEGUM
DEGUS > DEGU
DEGUST *vb* taste, esp with care or relish
DEGUSTATE *same as* > DEGUST
DEGUSTED > DEGUST
DEGUSTING > DEGUST
DEGUSTS > DEGUST
DEHISCE *vb* (of the seed capsules of some plants) to burst open spontaneously
DEHISCED > DEHISCE
DEHISCENT *adj* (of fruits, anthers, etc) opening spontaneously to release seeds or pollen
DEHISCES > DEHISCE
DEHISCING > DEHISCE
DEHORN *vb* remove or prevent the growth of the horns of (cattle, sheep, or goats)
DEHORNED > DEHORN
DEHORNER > DEHORN
DEHORNERS > DEHORN
DEHORNING > DEHORN
DEHORNS > DEHORN
DEHORT *vb* dissuade
DEHORTED > DEHORT
DEHORTER > DEHORT
DEHORTERS > DEHORT
DEHORTING > DEHORT
DEHORTS > DEHORT
DEHYDRATE *vb* remove water from (food) to preserve it
DEI > DEUS
DEICE *vb* to free or be freed of ice
DEICED > DEICE
DEICER > DEICE
DEICERS > DEICE
DEICES > DEICE
DEICIDAL > DEICIDE
DEICIDE *n* act of killing a god
DEICIDES > DEICIDE
DEICING > DEICE
DEICTIC *adj* proving by direct argument
DEICTICS > DEICTIC
DEID *a Scot word for* > DEAD
DEIDER > DEID
DEIDEST > DEID
DEIDS > DEID
DEIF *a Scot word for* > DEAF
DEIFER > DEIF
DEIFEST > DEIF
DEIFIC *adj* making divine or exalting to the position of a god
DEIFICAL *adj* divine
DEIFIED > DEIFY

DEIFIER > DEIFY
DEIFIERS > DEIFY
DEIFIES > DEIFY
DEIFORM *adj* having the form or appearance of a god
DEIFY *vb* treat or worship as a god
DEIFYING > DEIFY
DEIGN *vb* agree (to do something), but as if doing someone a favour
DEIGNED > DEIGN
DEIGNING > DEIGN
DEIGNS > DEIGN
DEIL *a Scot word for* > DEVIL
DEILS > DEIL
DEINDEX *vb* cause to become no longer index-linked
DEINDEXED > DEINDEX
DEINDEXES > DEINDEX
DEINOSAUR *n* dinosaur
DEIONISE *same as* > DEIONIZE
DEIONISED > DEIONISE
DEIONISER > DEIONISE
DEIONISES > DEIONISE
DEIONIZE *vb* to remove ions from (water, etc), esp by ion exchange
DEIONIZED > DEIONIZE
DEIONIZER > DEIONIZE
DEIONIZES > DEIONIZE
DEIPAROUS *adj* giving birth to a god
DEISEAL *n* clockwise motion
DEISEALS > DEISEAL
DEISHEAL *n* clockwise motion
DEISHEALS > DEISHEAL
DEISM *n* belief in God but not in divine revelation
DEISMS > DEISM
DEIST > DEISM
DEISTIC > DEISM
DEISTICAL > DEISM
DEISTS > DEISM
DEITIES > DEITY
DEITY *n* god or goddess
DEIXES > DEIXIS
DEIXIS *n* use or reference of a deictic word
DEIXISES > DEIXIS
DEJECT *vb* have a depressing effect on ▷ *adj* downcast
DEJECTA *npl* waste products excreted through the anus
DEJECTED *adj* unhappy
DEJECTING > DEJECT
DEJECTION *n* lowness of spirits
DEJECTORY *adj* causing dejection
DEJECTS > DEJECT
DEJEUNE *n* lunch
DEJEUNER *n* lunch
DEJEUNERS > DEJEUNER
DEJEUNES > DEJEUNE
DEKAGRAM *n* ten grams

DEKAGRAMS > DEKAGRAM
DEKALITER *n* ten litres
DEKALITRE *n* ten litres
DEKALOGY *n* series of ten related works
DEKAMETER *n* ten meters
DEKAMETRE *n* ten metres
DEKARE *n* unit of measurement equal to ten ares
DEKARES > DEKARE
DEKE *vb* (in ice hockey or box lacrosse) to draw (a defending player) out of position by faking a shot or movement ▷ *n* such a shot or movement
DEKED > DEKE
DEKEING > DEKE
DEKES > DEKE
DEKING > DEKE
DEKKO *n* look ▷ *vb* have a look
DEKKOED > DEKKO
DEKKOING > DEKKO
DEKKOS > DEKKO
DEL *n* differential operator
DELAINE *n* sheer wool or wool and cotton fabric
DELAINES > DELAINE
DELAPSE *vb* be inherited
DELAPSED > DELAPSE
DELAPSES > DELAPSE
DELAPSING > DELAPSE
DELAPSION *n* falling down
DELATE *vb* (formerly) to bring a charge against
DELATED > DELATE
DELATES > DELATE
DELATING > DELATE
DELATION > DELATE
DELATIONS > DELATE
DELATOR > DELATE
DELATORS > DELATE
DELAY *vb* put off to a later time ▷ *n* act of delaying
DELAYABLE > DELAY
DELAYED > DELAY
DELAYER > DELAY
DELAYERS > DELAY
DELAYING > DELAY
DELAYS > DELAY
DELE *n* sign indicating that typeset matter is to be deleted ▷ *vb* mark (matter to be deleted) with a dele
DELEAD *vb* remove lead from
DELEADED > DELEAD
DELEADING > DELEAD
DELEADS > DELEAD
DELEAVE *vb* separate copies
DELEAVED > DELEAVE
DELEAVES > DELEAVE
DELEAVING > DELEAVE
DELEBLE *adj* able to be deleted
DELECTATE *vb* delight
DELED > DELE
DELEGABLE > DELEGATE
DELEGACY *n* elected standing committee at

some British universities

DELEGATE *n* person chosen to represent others, esp at a meeting ▷ *vb* entrust (duties or powers) to someone

DELEGATED > DELEGATE

DELEGATEE > DELEGATE

DELEGATES > DELEGATE

DELEGATOR > DELEGATE

DELEING > DELE

DELENDA *npl* items for deleting

DELES > DELE

DELETABLE > DELETE

DELETE *vb* remove (something written or printed)

DELETED > DELETE

DELETES > DELETE

DELETING > DELETE

DELETION *n* act of deleting or fact of being deleted

DELETIONS > DELETION

DELETIVE > DELETE

DELETORY > DELETE

DELF *n* kind of earthenware

DELFS > DELF

DELFT *n* tin-glazed earthenware, typically having blue designs on white

DELFTS > DELFT

DELFTWARE *same as* > DELFT

DELI *n* delicatessen

DELIBATE *vb* taste

DELIBATED > DELIBATE

DELIBATES > DELIBATE

DELIBLE *adj* able to be deleted

DELICACY *n* being delicate

DELICATE *adj* fine or subtle in quality or workmanship ▷ *n* delicacy

DELICATES > DELICATE

DELICE *n* delicacy

DELICES > DELICE

DELICIOUS *adj* very appealing to taste or smell

DELICT *n* wrongful act for which the person injured has the right to a civil remedy

DELICTS > DELICT

DELIGHT *n* (source of) great pleasure ▷ *vb* please greatly

DELIGHTED *adj* greatly pleased ▷ *sentence substitute* I should be delighted to!

DELIGHTER > DELIGHT

DELIGHTS > DELIGHT

DELIME *vb* remove lime from

DELIMED > DELIME

DELIMES > DELIME

DELIMING > DELIME

DELIMIT *vb* mark or lay down the limits of

DELIMITED > DELIMIT

DELIMITER > DELIMIT

DELIMITS > DELIMIT

DELINEATE *vb* show by drawing

DELIQUIUM *n* loss of consciousness

DELIRIA > DELIRIUM

DELIRIANT > DELIRIUM

DELIRIOUS *adj* suffering from delirium

DELIRIUM *n* state of excitement and mental confusion, often with hallucinations

DELIRIUMS > DELIRIUM

DELIS > DELI

DELISH *adj* delicious

DELIST *vb* remove from a list

DELISTED > DELIST

DELISTING > DELIST

DELISTS > DELIST

DELIVER *vb* carry (goods etc) to a destination

DELIVERED > DELIVER

DELIVERER > DELIVER

DELIVERLY *adv* quickly

DELIVERS > DELIVER

DELIVERY *n* delivering

DELL *n* small wooded hollow

DELLIES > DELLY

DELLS > DELL

DELLY *n* delicatessen

DELO *an informal word for* > DELEGATE

DELOPE *vb* shoot into the air

DELOPED > DELOPE

DELOPES > DELOPE

DELOPING > DELOPE

DELOS > DELO

DELOUSE *vb* rid (a person or animal) of lice

DELOUSED > DELOUSE

DELOUSER > DELOUSE

DELOUSERS > DELOUSE

DELOUSES > DELOUSE

DELOUSING > DELOUSE

DELPH *n* kind of earthenware

DELPHIC *adj* obscure or ambiguous

DELPHIN *n* fatty substance from dolphin oil

DELPHINIA *n* plural form of singular delphinium: garden plant with blue, white or pink flowers

DELPHS > DELPH

DELS > DEL

DELT *n* deltoid muscle

DELTA *n* fourth letter in the Greek alphabet

DELTAIC > DELTA

DELTAS > DELTA

DELTIC > DELTA

DELTOID *n* thick muscle forming the rounded contour of the outer edge of the shoulder and acting to raise the arm ▷ *adj* shaped like a Greek capital delta

DELTOIDEI *n* deltoid

DELTOIDS > DELTOID

DELTS > DELT

DELUBRUM *n* shrine

DELUBRUMS > DELUBRUM

DELUDABLE > DELUDE

DELUDE *vb* deceive

DELUDED > DELUDE

DELUDER > DELUDE

DELUDERS > DELUDE

DELUDES > DELUDE

DELUDING > DELUDE

DELUGE *n* great flood ▷ *vb* flood

DELUGED > DELUGE

DELUGES > DELUGE

DELUGING > DELUGE

DELUNDUNG *n* spotted mammal

DELUSION *n* mistaken idea or belief

DELUSIONS > DELUSION

DELUSIVE > DELUSION

DELUSORY > DELUSION

DELUSTER *vb* remove the lustre from

DELUSTERS > DELUSTER

DELUXE *adj* rich, elegant, superior, or sumptuous

DELVE *vb* research deeply (for information)

DELVED > DELVE

DELVER > DELVE

DELVERS > DELVE

DELVES > DELVE

DELVING > DELVE

DEMAGOG *same as* > DEMAGOGUE

DEMAGOGED > DEMAGOG

DEMAGOGIC *adj* of, characteristic of, relating to, or resembling a demagogue

DEMAGOGS > DEMAGOG

DEMAGOGUE *n* political agitator who appeals to the prejudice and passions of the mob

DEMAGOGY *n* demagoguery

DEMAIN *n* demesne

DEMAINE *n* demesne

DEMAINES > DEMAINE

DEMAINS > DEMAIN

DEMAN *vb* reduce the workforce of (a plant, industry, etc)

DEMAND *vb* request forcefully ▷ *n* forceful request

DEMANDANT *n* (formerly) the plaintiff in an action relating to real property

DEMANDED > DEMAND

DEMANDER > DEMAND

DEMANDERS > DEMAND

DEMANDING *adj* requiring a lot of time or effort

DEMANDS > DEMAND

DEMANNED > DEMAN

DEMANNING > DEMAN

DEMANS > DEMAN

DEMANTOID *n* bright green variety of andradite garnet

DEMARCATE *vb* mark, fix, or draw the boundaries, limits, etc, of

DEMARCHE *n* move, step, or manoeuvre, esp in diplomatic affairs

DEMARCHES > DEMARCHE

DEMARK *vb* demarcate

DEMARKED > DEMARK

DEMARKET *vb* discourage consumers from buying (a particular product), either because it is faulty or because it could jeopardize the seller's reputation

DEMARKETS > DEMARKET

DEMARKING > DEMARK

DEMARKS > DEMARK

DEMAST *vb* remove the mast from

DEMASTED > DEMAST

DEMASTING > DEMAST

DEMASTS > DEMAST

DEMAYNE *n* demesne

DEMAYNES > DEMAYNE

DEME *n* (in preclassical Greece) the territory inhabited by a tribe

DEMEAN *vb* lower (oneself) in dignity, status, or character

DEMEANE *n* demesne

DEMEANED > DEMEAN

DEMEANES *n* demesne

DEMEANING > DEMEAN

DEMEANOR *same as* > DEMEANOUR

DEMEANORS > DEMEANOR

DEMEANOUR *n* way a person behaves

DEMEANS > DEMEAN

DEMENT *vb* deteriorate mentally, esp because of old age

DEMENTATE *vb* deteriorate mentally

DEMENTED *adj* mad

DEMENTI *n* denial

DEMENTIA *n* state of serious mental deterioration

DEMENTIAL > DEMENTIA

DEMENTIAS > DEMENTIA

DEMENTING > DEMENT

DEMENTIS > DEMENTI

DEMENTS > DEMENT

DEMERARA *n* brown crystallized cane sugar from the Caribbean and nearby countries

DEMERARAN *adj* from Demerara

DEMERARAS > DEMERARA

DEMERGE *vb* separate a company from another with which it was previously merged

DEMERGED > DEMERGE

DEMERGER *n* separation of two or more companies which have previously been merged

DEMERGERS > DEMERGER

DEMERGES > DEMERGE

DEMERGING > DEMERGE

DEMERIT n fault, disadvantage ▷ vb deserve
DEMERITED > DEMERIT
DEMERITS > DEMERIT
DEMERSAL adj living or occurring on the bottom of a sea or a lake
DEMERSE vb immerse
DEMERSED > DEMERSE
DEMERSES > DEMERSE
DEMERSING > DEMERSE
DEMERSION > DEMERSE
DEMES > DEME
DEMESNE n land surrounding a house
DEMESNES > DEMESNE
DEMETON n insecticide
DEMETONS > DEMETON
DEMIC adj of population
DEMIES > DEMY
DEMIGOD n being who is part mortal, part god
DEMIGODS > DEMIGOD
DEMIJOHN n large bottle with a short neck, often encased in wicker
DEMIJOHNS > DEMIJOHN
DEMILUNE n outwork in front of a fort, shaped like a crescent moon
DEMILUNES > DEMILUNE
DEMIMONDE n (esp in the 19th century) class of women considered to be outside respectable society because of promiscuity
DEMIPIQUE n low pique on a saddle
DEMIREP n woman of bad repute, esp a prostitute
DEMIREPS > DEMIREP
DEMISABLE > DEMISE
DEMISE n eventual failure (of something successful) ▷ vb transfer for a limited period
DEMISED > DEMISE
DEMISES > DEMISE
DEMISING > DEMISE
DEMISS adj humble
DEMISSION n relinquishment of or abdication from an office, responsibility, etc
DEMISSIVE adj humble
DEMISSLY > DEMISS
DEMIST vb remove condensation from (a windscreen)
DEMISTED > DEMIST
DEMISTER n device incorporating a heater and/or blower used in a motor vehicle to free the windscreen of condensation
DEMISTERS > DEMISTER
DEMISTING > DEMIST
DEMISTS > DEMIST
DEMIT vb resign (an office, position, etc)
DEMITASSE n small cup used to serve coffee, esp after a meal
DEMITS > DEMIT

DEMITTED > DEMIT
DEMITTING > DEMIT
DEMIURGE n (in the philosophy of Plato) the creator of the universe
DEMIURGES > DEMIURGE
DEMIURGIC > DEMIURGE
DEMIURGUS n demiurge
DEMIVEG n person who eats poultry and fish, but no red meat ▷ adj denoting a person who eats poultry and fish, but no red meat
DEMIVEGES > DEMIVEG
DEMIVOLT n half turn on the hind legs
DEMIVOLTE same as
> DEMIVOLT
DEMIVOLTS > DEMIVOLT
DEMIWORLD n demimonde
DEMO n demonstration, organized expression of public opinion ▷ vb demonstrate
DEMOB vb demobilize
DEMOBBED > DEMOB
DEMOBBING > DEMOB
DEMOBS > DEMOB
DEMOCRACY n government by the people or their elected representatives
DEMOCRAT n advocate of democracy
DEMOCRATS > DEMOCRAT
DEMOCRATY n democracy
DEMODE adj out of fashion
DEMODED adj out of fashion
DEMOED > DEMO
DEMOING > DEMO
DEMOLISH vb knock down or destroy (a building)
DEMOLOGY n demography
DEMON n evil spirit
DEMONESS n female demon
DEMONIAC adj appearing to be possessed by a devil ▷ n person possessed by an evil spirit or demon
DEMONIACS > DEMONIAC
DEMONIAN adj of a demon
DEMONIC adj evil
DEMONICAL adj demonic
DEMONISE same as
> DEMONIZE
DEMONISED > DEMONISE
DEMONISES > DEMONISE
DEMONISM n study of demons
DEMONISMS > DEMONISM
DEMONIST > DEMONISM
DEMONISTS > DEMONISM
DEMONIZE vb make into a demon
DEMONIZED > DEMONIZE
DEMONIZES > DEMONIZE
DEMONRIES > DEMONRY
DEMONRY > DEMON
DEMONS > DEMON
DEMOS n people of a nation regarded as a political unit
DEMOSCENE n computer art subculture
DEMOSES > DEMOS

DEMOTE vb reduce in status or rank
DEMOTED > DEMOTE
DEMOTES > DEMOTE
DEMOTIC adj of the common people ▷ n demotic script of ancient Egypt
DEMOTICS > DEMOTIC
DEMOTING > DEMOTE
DEMOTION > DEMOTE
DEMOTIONS > DEMOTE
DEMOTIST > DEMOTIC
DEMOTISTS > DEMOTIC
DEMOUNT vb remove (a motor, gun, etc) from its mounting or setting
DEMOUNTED > DEMOUNT
DEMOUNTS > DEMOUNT
DEMPSTER same as
> DEEMSTER
DEMPSTERS > DEMPSTER
DEMPT > DEEM
DEMULCENT adj soothing ▷ n drug or agent that soothes the irritation of inflamed or injured skin surfaces
DEMULSIFY vb undergo or cause to undergo a process in which an emulsion is permanently broken down into its constituents
DEMUR vb raise objections or show reluctance ▷ n act of demurring
DEMURE adj quiet, reserved, and rather shy ▷ vb archaic for look demure ▷ n archaic for demure look
DEMURED > DEMURE
DEMURELY > DEMURE
DEMURER > DEMURE
DEMURES > DEMURE
DEMUREST > DEMURE
DEMURING > DEMURE
DEMURRAGE n delaying of a ship, railway wagon, etc, caused by the charterer's failure to load, unload, etc, before the time of scheduled departure
DEMURRAL n act of demurring
DEMURRALS > DEMURRAL
DEMURRED > DEMUR
DEMURRER n pleading that admits an opponent's point but denies that it is a relevant or valid argument
DEMURRERS > DEMURRER
DEMURRING > DEMUR
DEMURS > DEMUR
DEMY n size of printing paper, 17M by 22M inches (444.5 ◊ 571.5 mm)
DEMYSHIP > DEMY
DEMYSHIPS > DEMY
DEMYSTIFY vb remove the mystery from
DEN n home of a wild animal ▷ vb live in or as if in a den
DENAR n standard monetary unit of Macedonia, divided into

100 deni
DENARI > DENAR
DENARIES > DENARIUS
DENARII > DENARIUS
DENARIUS n ancient Roman silver coin, often called a penny in translation
DENARS > DENAR
DENARY adj calculated by tens
DENATURE vb change the nature of
DENATURED > DENATURE
DENATURES > DENATURE
DENAY vb deny
DENAYED > DENAY
DENAYING > DENAY
DENAYS > DENAY
DENAZIFY vb free or declare (people, institutions, etc) freed from Nazi influence or ideology
DENDRIMER n chemical compound with treelike molecular structure
DENDRITE n any of the short branched threadlike extensions of a nerve cell, which conduct impulses towards the cell body
DENDRITES > DENDRITE
DENDRITIC > DENDRITE
DENDROID adj freely branching
DENDRON same as
> DENDRITE
DENDRONS > DENDRON
DENE n narrow wooded valley
DENERVATE vb deprive (a tissue or organ) of its nerve supply
DENES > DENE
DENET vb remove from the Net Book Agreement
DENETS > DENET
DENETTED > DENET
DENETTING > DENET
DENGUE n viral disease transmitted by mosquitoes, characterized by headache, fever, pains in the joints, and a rash
DENGUES > DENGUE
DENI n monetary unit of the Former Yugoslav Republic of Macedonia, worth one hundredth of a denar
DENIABLE adj able to be denied
DENIABLY > DENIABLE
DENIAL n statement that something is not true
DENIALS > DENIAL
DENIED > DENY
DENIER n unit of weight used to measure the fineness of nylon or silk
DENIERS > DENIER
DENIES > DENY
DENIGRATE vb criticize unfairly
DENIM n hard-wearing

cotton fabric, usu. blue
DENIMED *adj* wearing denim
DENIMS *npl* jeans or overalls made of denim
DENIS > DENI
DENITRATE *vb* undergo or cause to undergo a process in which a compound loses a nitro or nitrate group, nitrogen dioxide, or nitric acid
DENITRIFY *vb* undergo or cause to undergo loss or removal of nitrogen compounds or nitrogen
DENIZEN *n* inhabitant ▷ *vb* make a denizen
DENIZENED > DENIZEN
DENIZENS > DENIZEN
DENNED > DEN
DENNET *n* carriage for one horse
DENNETS > DENNET
DENNING > DEN
DENOMINAL *adj* formed from a noun
DENOTABLE > DENOTE
DENOTATE *vb* denote
DENOTATED > DENOTATE
DENOTATES > DENOTATE
DENOTE *vb* be a sign of
DENOTED > DENOTE
DENOTES > DENOTE
DENOTING > DENOTE
DENOTIVE > DENOTE
DENOUNCE *vb* speak vehemently against
DENOUNCED > DENOUNCE
DENOUNCER > DENOUNCE
DENOUNCES > DENOUNCE
DENS > DEN
DENSE *adj* closely packed
DENSELY > DENSE
DENSENESS > DENSE
DENSER > DENSE
DENSEST > DENSE
DENSIFIED > DENSIFY
DENSIFIER > DENSIFY
DENSIFIES > DENSIFY
DENSIFY *vb* make or become dense
DENSITIES > DENSITY
DENSITY *n* degree to which something is filled or occupied
DENT *n* hollow in the surface of something, made by hitting it ▷ *vb* make a dent in
DENTAL *adj* of teeth or dentistry ▷ *n* dental consonant
DENTALIA > DENTALIUM
DENTALITY *n* use of teeth in pronouncing words
DENTALIUM *n* type of mollusc
DENTALLY > DENTAL
DENTALS > DENTAL
DENTARIA *n* botanical term
DENTARIAS > DENTARIA
DENTARIES > DENTARY

DENTARY *n* lower jawbone with teeth
DENTATE *adj* having teeth or teethlike notches
DENTATED *adj* having teeth
DENTATELY > DENTATE
DENTATION *n* state or condition of being dentate
DENTED > DENT
DENTEL *n* architectural term
DENTELLE *n* bookbinding term
DENTELLES > DENTELLE
DENTELS > DENTEL
DENTEX *n* large predatory fish of Mediterranean and E Atlantic waters, with long sharp teeth and powerful jaws
DENTEXES > DENTEX
DENTICLE *n* small tooth or toothlike part, such as any of the placoid scales of sharks
DENTICLES > DENTICLE
DENTIFORM *adj* shaped like a tooth
DENTIL *n* one of a set of small square or rectangular blocks evenly spaced to form an ornamental row, usually under a classical cornice on a building, piece of furniture, etc
DENTILED > DENTIL
DENTILS > DENTIL
DENTIN *same as* > DENTINE
DENTINAL > DENTINE
DENTINE *n* hard dense tissue forming the bulk of a tooth
DENTINES > DENTINE
DENTING > DENT
DENTINS > DENTIN
DENTIST *n* person qualified to practise dentistry
DENTISTRY *n* branch of medicine concerned with the teeth and gums
DENTISTS > DENTIST
DENTITION *n* typical arrangement of teeth in a species
DENTOID *adj* resembling a tooth
DENTS > DENT
DENTULOUS *adj* having teeth
DENTURAL > DENTURE
DENTURE *n* false tooth
DENTURES > DENTURE
DENTURIST *n* person who makes dentures
DENUDATE *adj* denuded ▷ *vb* denude
DENUDATED > DENUDATE
DENUDATES > DENUDATE
DENUDE *vb* remove the covering or protection from
DENUDED > DENUDE
DENUDER > DENUDE

DENUDERS > DENUDE
DENUDES > DENUDE
DENUDING > DENUDE
DENY *vb* declare to be untrue
DENYING > DENY
DENYINGLY > DENY
DEODAND *n* (formerly) a thing that had caused a person's death and was forfeited to the crown for a charitable purpose: abolished 1862
DEODANDS > DEODAND
DEODAR *n* Himalayan cedar with drooping branches
DEODARA *same as* > DEODAR
DEODARAS > DEODARA
DEODARS > DEODAR
DEODATE *n* offering to God
DEODATES > DEODATE
DEODORANT *n* substance applied to the body to mask the smell of perspiration
DEODORISE *same as* > DEODORIZE
DEODORIZE *vb* remove or disguise the smell of
DEONTIC *adj* of or relating to such ethical concepts as obligation and permissibility
DEONTICS > DEONTIC
DEORBIT *vb* go out of orbit
DEORBITED > DEORBIT
DEORBITS > DEORBIT
DEOXIDATE *vb* remove oxygen atoms from
DEOXIDISE *same as* > DEOXIDIZE
DEOXIDIZE *vb* remove oxygen atoms from (a compound, molecule, etc)
DEOXY *adj* having less oxygen than a specified related compound
DEPAINT *vb* depict
DEPAINTED > DEPAINT
DEPAINTS > DEPAINT
DEPANNEUR *n* (in Quebec) a convenience store
DEPART *vb* leave
DEPARTED *adj* dead
DEPARTEE > DEPART
DEPARTEES > DEPART
DEPARTER > DEPART
DEPARTERS > DEPART
DEPARTING > DEPART
DEPARTS > DEPART
DEPARTURE *n* act of departing
DEPASTURE *vb* graze or denude by grazing (a pasture, esp a meadow specially grown for the purpose)
DEPECHE *n* message
DEPECHES > DEPECHE
DEPEINCT *vb* paint
DEPEINCTS > DEPEINCT
DEPEND *vb* put trust (in)
DEPENDANT *same as* > DEPENDENT

DEPENDED > DEPEND
DEPENDENT *adj* depending on someone or something ▷ *n* element in a phrase or clause that is not the governor
DEPENDING > DEPEND
DEPENDS > DEPEND
DEPEOPLE *vb* reduce population
DEPEOPLED > DEPEOPLE
DEPEOPLES > DEPEOPLE
DEPERM *vb* demagnetize
DEPERMED > DEPERM
DEPERMING > DEPERM
DEPERMS > DEPERM
DEPICT *vb* produce a picture of
DEPICTED > DEPICT
DEPICTER > DEPICT
DEPICTERS > DEPICT
DEPICTING > DEPICT
DEPICTION > DEPICT
DEPICTIVE > DEPICT
DEPICTOR > DEPICT
DEPICTORS > DEPICT
DEPICTS > DEPICT
DEPICTURE *a less common word for* > DEPICT
DEPIGMENT *vb* reduce or remove the normal pigmentation of (the skin)
DEPILATE *vb* remove the hair from
DEPILATED > DEPILATE
DEPILATES > DEPILATE
DEPILATOR > DEPILATE
DEPLANE *vb* disembark from an aeroplane
DEPLANED > DEPLANE
DEPLANES > DEPLANE
DEPLANING > DEPLANE
DEPLETE *vb* use up
DEPLETED > DEPLETE
DEPLETER > DEPLETE
DEPLETERS > DEPLETE
DEPLETES > DEPLETE
DEPLETING > DEPLETE
DEPLETION > DEPLETE
DEPLETIVE > DEPLETE
DEPLETORY > DEPLETE
DEPLORE *vb* condemn strongly
DEPLORED > DEPLORE
DEPLORER > DEPLORE
DEPLORERS > DEPLORE
DEPLORES > DEPLORE
DEPLORING > DEPLORE
DEPLOY *vb* organize (troops or resources) into a position ready for immediate action
DEPLOYED > DEPLOY
DEPLOYER > DEPLOY
DEPLOYERS > DEPLOY
DEPLOYING > DEPLOY
DEPLOYS > DEPLOY
DEPLUME *vb* deprive of feathers
DEPLUMED > DEPLUME
DEPLUMES > DEPLUME
DEPLUMING > DEPLUME
DEPOLISH *vb* remove the polish from

d

DEPONE *vb* declare (something) under oath

DEPONED > DEPONE

DEPONENT *n* person who makes a statement on oath ▷ *adj* (of a verb, esp in Latin) having the inflectional endings of a passive verb but the meaning of an active verb

DEPONENTS > DEPONENT

DEPONES > DEPONE

DEPONING > DEPONE

DEPORT *vb* remove forcibly from a country

DEPORTED > DEPORT

DEPORTEE *n* person deported or awaiting deportation

DEPORTEES > DEPORTEE

DEPORTER > DEPORT

DEPORTERS > DEPORT

DEPORTING > DEPORT

DEPORTS > DEPORT

DEPOSABLE > DEPOSE

DEPOSAL *n* deposition; giving of testimony under oath

DEPOSALS > DEPOSAL

DEPOSE *vb* remove from an office or position of power

DEPOSED > DEPOSE

DEPOSER > DEPOSE

DEPOSERS > DEPOSE

DEPOSES > DEPOSE

DEPOSING > DEPOSE

DEPOSIT *vb* put down ▷ *n* sum of money paid into a bank account

DEPOSITED > DEPOSIT

DEPOSITOR *n* person who places or has money on deposit in a bank or similar organization

DEPOSITS > DEPOSIT

DEPOT *n* building where goods or vehicles are kept when not in use ▷ *adj* (of a drug or drug dose) designed for gradual release from the site of an injection so as to act over a long period

DEPOTS > DEPOT

DEPRAVE *vb* make morally bad

DEPRAVED *adj* morally bad

DEPRAVER > DEPRAVE

DEPRAVERS > DEPRAVE

DEPRAVES > DEPRAVE

DEPRAVING > DEPRAVE

DEPRAVITY *n* moral corruption

DEPRECATE *vb* express disapproval of

DEPREDATE *vb* plunder or destroy

DEPREHEND *vb* apprehend

DEPRENYL *n* drug combating effects of ageing

DEPRENYLS > DEPRENYL

DEPRESS *vb* make sad

DEPRESSED *adj* low in spirits

DEPRESSES > DEPRESS

DEPRESSOR *n* person or thing that depresses

DEPRIVAL > DEPRIVE

DEPRIVALS > DEPRIVE

DEPRIVE *vb* prevent from (having or enjoying)

DEPRIVED *adj* lacking adequate living conditions, education, etc

DEPRIVER > DEPRIVE

DEPRIVERS > DEPRIVE

DEPRIVES > DEPRIVE

DEPRIVING > DEPRIVE

DEPROGRAM *vb* free someone from indoctrination

DEPSIDE *n* any ester formed by the condensation of the carboxyl group of one phenolic carboxylic acid with the hydroxyl group of another, found in plant cells

DEPSIDES > DEPSIDE

DEPTH *n* distance downwards, backwards, or inwards

DEPTHLESS *adj* immeasurably deep

DEPTHS > DEPTH

DEPURANT *adj* purifying

DEPURANTS > DEPURANT

DEPURATE *vb* cleanse or purify or to be cleansed or purified

DEPURATED > DEPURATE

DEPURATES > DEPURATE

DEPURATOR > DEPURATE

DEPUTABLE > DEPUTE

DEPUTE *vb* appoint (someone) to act on one's behalf ▷ *n* deputy

DEPUTED > DEPUTE

DEPUTES > DEPUTE

DEPUTIES > DEPUTY

DEPUTING > DEPUTE

DEPUTISE *same as* > DEPUTIZE

DEPUTISED > DEPUTISE

DEPUTISES > DEPUTISE

DEPUTIZE *vb* act as deputy

DEPUTIZED > DEPUTIZE

DEPUTIZES > DEPUTIZE

DEPUTY *n* person appointed to act on behalf of another

DEQUEUE *vb* remove (an item) from a queue of computing tasks

DEQUEUED > DEQUEUE

DEQUEUES > DEQUEUE

DEQUEUING > DEQUEUE

DERACINE *adj* uprooted

DERAIGN *vb* contest (a claim, suit, etc)

DERAIGNED > DERAIGN

DERAIGNS > DERAIGN

DERAIL *vb* cause (a train) to go off the rails ▷ *n* device designed to make rolling stock or locomotives leave the rails to avoid a collision or accident

DERAILED > DERAIL

DERAILER *same as* > DERAIL

DERAILERS > DERAILER

DERAILING > DERAIL

DERAILS > DERAIL

DERANGE *vb* disturb the order or arrangement of

DERANGED > DERANGE

DERANGER > DERANGE

DERANGERS > DERANGE

DERANGES > DERANGE

DERANGING > DERANGE

DERAT *vb* remove rats from

DERATE *vb* assess the value of (some types of property, such as agricultural land) at a lower rate than others for local taxation

DERATED > DERATE

DERATES > DERATE

DERATING > DERATE

DERATINGS > DERATE

DERATION *vb* end rationing of (food, petrol, etc)

DERATIONS > DERATION

DERATS > DERAT

DERATTED > DERAT

DERATTING > DERAT

DERAY *vb* go mad

DERAYED > DERAY

DERAYING > DERAY

DERAYS > DERAY

DERBIES > DERBY

DERBY *n* bowler hat

DERE *vb* injure

DERED > DERE

DERELICT *adj* unused and falling into ruins ▷ *n* social outcast, vagrant

DERELICTS > DERELICT

DEREPRESS *vb* induce operation of gene

DERES > DERE

DERHAM *same as* > DIRHAM

DERHAMS > DERHAM

DERIDE *vb* treat with contempt or ridicule

DERIDED > DERIDE

DERIDER > DERIDE

DERIDERS > DERIDE

DERIDES > DERIDE

DERIDING > DERIDE

DERIG *vb* remove equipment, e.g. from stage set

DERIGGED > DERIG

DERIGGING > DERIG

DERIGS > DERIG

DERING > DERE

DERINGER *same as* > DERRINGER

DERINGERS > DERINGER

DERISIBLE *adj* subject to or deserving of derision

DERISION *n* act of deriding

DERISIONS > DERISION

DERISIVE *adj* mocking, scornful

DERISORY *adj* too small or inadequate to be considered seriously

DERIVABLE > DERIVE

DERIVABLY > DERIVE

DERIVATE *n* derivative

DERIVATES > DERIVATE

DERIVE *vb* take or develop (from)

DERIVED > DERIVE

DERIVER > DERIVE

DERIVERS > DERIVE

DERIVES > DERIVE

DERIVING > DERIVE

DERM *same as* > DERMA

DERMA *n* beef or fowl intestine used as a casing for certain dishes, esp kishke

DERMAL *adj* of or relating to the skin

DERMAS > DERMA

DERMATIC *adj* of skin

DERMATOID *adj* resembling skin

DERMATOME *n* surgical instrument for cutting thin slices of skin, esp for grafting

DERMESTID *n* type of beetle whose larva and adult is destructive to many stored organic materials, such as wool and meat

DERMIC > DERMIS

DERMIS *another name for* > CORIUM

DERMISES > DERMIS

DERMOID *adj* of or resembling skin ▷ *n* congenital cystic tumour whose walls are lined with epithelium

DERMOIDS > DERMOID

DERMS > DERM

DERN *n* concealment

DERNFUL *adj* sorrowful

DERNIER *adj* last

DERNLY *adv* sorrowfully

DERNS > DERN

DERO *n* tramp or derelict

DEROGATE *vb* detract from ▷ *adj* debased or degraded

DEROGATED > DEROGATE

DEROGATES > DEROGATE

DEROS > DERO

DERRICK *n* simple crane ▷ *vb* raise or lower the jib of (a crane)

DERRICKED > DERRICK

DERRICKS > DERRICK

DERRIERE > BUTTOCK

DERRIERES > DERRIERE

DERRIES > DERRY

DERRINGER *n* small large-bored pistol

DERRIS *n* E Indian woody climbing plant

DERRISES > DERRIS

DERRO *n* vagrant

DERROS > DERRO

DERRY *n* derelict house, esp one used by tramps, drug addicts, etc

DERTH *same as* > DEARTH

DERTHS > DERTH

DERV n diesel oil, when used for road transport

DERVISH n member of a Muslim religious order noted for a frenzied whirling dance

DERVISHES > DERVISH

DERVS > DERV

DESALT vb desalinate

DESALTED > DESALT

DESALTER > DESALT

DESALTERS > DESALT

DESALTING > DESALT

DESALTS > DESALT

DESAND vb remove sand from

DESANDED > DESAND

DESANDING > DESAND

DESANDS > DESAND

DESCALE vb remove a hard coating from inside (a kettle or pipe)

DESCALED > DESCALE

DESCALES > DESCALE

DESCALING > DESCALE

DESCANT n tune played or sung above a basic melody ▷ adj denoting the highest member in a family of musical instruments ▷ vb compose or perform a descant (for a piece of music)

DESCANTED > DESCANT

DESCANTER > DESCANT

DESCANTS > DESCANT

DESCEND vb move down (a slope etc)

DESCENDED > DESCEND

DESCENDER same as > DESCEND

DESCENDS > DESCEND

DESCENT n descending

DESCENTS > DESCENT

DESCHOOL vb separate education from the institution of school and operate through the pupil's life experience as opposed to a set curriculum

DESCHOOLS > DESCHOOL

DESCRIBE vb give an account of (something or someone) in words

DESCRIBED > DESCRIBE

DESCRIBER > DESCRIBE

DESCRIBES > DESCRIBE

DESCRIED > DESCRY

DESCRIER > DESCRY

DESCRIERS > DESCRY

DESCRIES > DESCRY

DESCRIVE vb describe

DESCRIVED > DESCRIVE

DESCRIVES > DESCRIVE

DESCRY vb catch sight of

DESCRYING > DESCRY

DESECRATE vb damage or insult (something sacred)

DESEED vb to remove the seeds from (eg a fruit)

DESEEDED > DESEED

DESEEDING > DESEED

DESEEDS > DESEED

DESELECT vb refuse to select (an MP) for re-election

DESELECTS > DESELECT

DESERT n region with little or no vegetation because of low rainfall ▷ vb abandon (a person or place) without intending to return

DESERTED > DESERT

DESERTER > DESERT

DESERTERS > DESERT

DESERTIC adj (of soil) developing in hot climates

DESERTIFY vb turn into desert

DESERTING > DESERT

DESERTION n act of deserting or abandoning or the state of being deserted or abandoned

DESERTS > DESERT

DESERVE vb be entitled to or worthy of

DESERVED > DESERVE

DESERVER > DESERVE

DESERVERS > DESERVE

DESERVES > DESERVE

DESERVING adj worthy of help, praise, or reward ▷ n merit or demerit

DESEX n desexualize

DESEXED > DESEX

DESEXES > DESEX

DESEXING > DESEX

DESHI same as > DESI

DESI adj in Indian English, indigenous or local

DESICCANT adj desiccating or drying ▷ n substance, such as calcium oxide, that absorbs water and is used to remove moisture

DESICCATE vb remove most of the water from

DESIGN vb work out the structure or form of (something), by making a sketch or plans ▷ n preliminary drawing

DESIGNATE vb give a name to ▷ adj appointed but not yet in office

DESIGNED > DESIGN

DESIGNEE n person designated to do something

DESIGNEES > DESIGNEE

DESIGNER n person who draws up original sketches or plans from which things are made ▷ adj designed by a well-known designer

DESIGNERS > DESIGNER

DESIGNFUL adj scheming

DESIGNING adj cunning and scheming

DESIGNS > DESIGN

DESILVER vb remove silver from

DESILVERS > DESILVER

DESINE same as > DESIGN

DESINED > DESINE

DESINENCE n ending or termination, esp an

inflectional ending of a word

DESINENT > DESINENCE

DESINES > DESINE

DESINING > DESINE

DESIPIENT adj foolish

DESIRABLE adj worth having ▷ n person or thing that is the object of desire

DESIRABLY > DESIRABLE

DESIRE vb want very much ▷ n wish, longing

DESIRED > DESIRE

DESIRER > DESIRE

DESIRERS > DESIRE

DESIRES > DESIRE

DESIRING > DESIRE

DESIROUS adj having a desire for

DESIST vb stop (doing something)

DESISTED > DESIST

DESISTING > DESIST

DESISTS > DESIST

DESK n piece of furniture with a writing surface and drawers

DESKBOUND adj engaged in or involving sedentary work, as at an office desk

DESKFAST n breakfast eaten at one's desk at work

DESKFASTS > DESKFAST

DESKILL vb mechanize or computerize (a job) thereby reducing the skill required to do it

DESKILLED > DESKILL

DESKILLS > DESKILL

DESKING n desks and related furnishings in a given space, eg an office

DESKINGS > DESKING

DESKMAN n police officer in charge in police station

DESKMEN > DESKMAN

DESKNOTE n small computer

DESKNOTES > DESKNOTE

DESKS > DESK

DESKTOP adj (of a computer) small enough to use at a desk ▷ n denoting a computer system, esp for word processing, that is small enough to use at a desk

DESKTOPS > DESKTOP

DESMAN n either of two molelike amphibious mammals

DESMANS > DESMAN

DESMID n type of mainly unicellular freshwater green alga

DESMIDIAN > DESMID

DESMIDS > DESMID

DESMINE n type of mineral

DESMINES > DESMINE

DESMODIUM n type of plant

DESMOID adj resembling a tendon or ligament ▷ n very firm tumour of

connective tissue

DESMOIDS > DESMOID

DESMOSOME n structure in the cell membranes of adjacent cells that binds them together

DESNOOD vb remove the snood of a turkey poult to reduce the risk of cannibalism

DESNOODED > DESNOOD

DESNOODS > DESNOOD

DESOEUVRE adj with nothing to do

DESOLATE adj uninhabited and bleak ▷ vb deprive of inhabitants

DESOLATED > DESOLATE

DESOLATER > DESOLATE

DESOLATES > DESOLATE

DESOLATOR > DESOLATE

DESORB vb change from an adsorbed state on a surface to a gaseous or liquid state

DESORBED > DESORB

DESORBING > DESORB

DESORBS > DESORB

DESOXY same as > DEOXY

DESPAIR n total loss of hope ▷ vb lose hope

DESPAIRED > DESPAIR

DESPAIRER n one who despairs

DESPAIRS > DESPAIR

DESPATCH same as > DISPATCH

DESPERADO n reckless person ready to commit any violent illegal act

DESPERATE adj in despair and reckless

DESPIGHT obsolete form of > DESPITE

DESPIGHTS > DESPIGHT

DESPISAL > DESPISE

DESPISALS > DESPISE

DESPISE vb regard with contempt

DESPISED > DESPISE

DESPISER > DESPISE

DESPISERS > DESPISE

DESPISES > DESPISE

DESPISING > DESPISE

DESPITE prep in spite of ▷ n contempt ▷ vb show contempt for

DESPITED > DESPITE

DESPITES > DESPITE

DESPITING > DESPITE

DESPOIL vb plunder

DESPOILED > DESPOIL

DESPOILER > DESPOIL

DESPOILS > DESPOIL

DESPOND vb lose heart or hope

DESPONDED > DESPOND

DESPONDS > DESPOND

DESPOT n person in power who acts unfairly or cruelly

DESPOTAT n despot's domain

DESPOTATE same as > DESPOTAT

DESPOTATS > DESPOTAT

DESPOTIC > DESPOT

DESPOTISM n unfair or cruel government or behaviour

DESPOTS > DESPOT

DESPUMATE vb clarify or purify (a liquid) by skimming a scum from its surface

DESSE n desk

DESSERT n sweet course served at the end of a meal

DESSERTS > DESSERT

DESSES > DESSE

DESTAIN vb remove stain from

DESTAINED > DESTAIN

DESTAINS > DESTAIN

DESTEMPER same as > DISTEMPER

DESTINATE same as > DESTINE

DESTINE vb set apart or appoint (for a certain purpose or person, or to do something)

DESTINED adj certain to be or to do something

DESTINES > DESTINE

DESTINIES > DESTINY

DESTINING > DESTINE

DESTINY n future marked out for a person or thing

DESTITUTE adj having no money or possessions

DESTOCK vb (of a retailer) to reduce the amount of stock held or cease to stock certain products

DESTOCKED > DESTOCK

DESTOCKS > DESTOCK

DESTRIER an archaic word for > WARHORSE

DESTRIERS > DESTRIER

DESTROY vb ruin, demolish

DESTROYED > DESTROY

DESTROYER n small heavily armed warship

DESTROYS > DESTROY

DESTRUCT vb destroy (one's own missile or rocket) for safety ▷ n act of destructing ▷ adj designed to be capable of destroying itself or the object, system, or installation containing it

DESTRUCTO n person who causes havoc or destruction

DESTRUCTS > DESTRUCT

DESUETUDE n condition of not being in use

DESUGAR vb remove sugar from

DESUGARED > DESUGAR

DESUGARS > DESUGAR

DESULFUR same as > DESULPHUR

DESULFURS > DESULFUR

DESULPHUR vb remove sulphur from

DESULTORY adj jumping from one thing to another, disconnected

DESYATIN n Russian unit of area

DESYATINS > DESYATIN

DESYNE same as > DESIGN

DESYNED > DESYNE

DESYNES > DESYNE

DESYNING > DESYNE

DETACH vb disengage and separate

DETACHED adj (of a house) not joined to another house

DETACHER > DETACH

DETACHERS > DETACH

DETACHES > DETACH

DETACHING > DETACH

DETAIL n individual piece of information ▷ vb list fully

DETAILED adj having many details

DETAILER > DETAIL

DETAILERS > DETAIL

DETAILING > DETAIL

DETAILS > DETAIL

DETAIN vb delay (someone)

DETAINED > DETAIN

DETAINEE > DETAIN

DETAINEES > DETAIN

DETAINER n wrongful withholding of the property of another person

DETAINERS > DETAINER

DETAINING > DETAIN

DETAINS > DETAIN

DETANGLE vb remove tangles from (esp hair)

DETANGLED > DETANGLE

DETANGLER n cosmetic product used to detangle hair

DETANGLES > DETANGLE

DETASSEL vb remove top part of corn plant

DETASSELS > DETASSEL

DETECT vb notice

DETECTED > DETECT

DETECTER > DETECT

DETECTERS > DETECT

DETECTING > DETECT

DETECTION n act of noticing, discovering, or sensing something

DETECTIVE n police officer or private agent who investigates crime ▷ adj used in or serving for detection

DETECTOR n instrument used to find something

DETECTORS > DETECTOR

DETECTS > DETECT

DETENT n locking piece of a mechanism, often spring-loaded to check the movement of a wheel in one direction only

DETENTE n easing of tension between nations

DETENTES > DETENTE

DETENTION n imprisonment

DETENTIST n supporter of detente

DETENTS > DETENT

DETENU n prisoner

DETENUE n female prisoner

DETENUES > DETENUE

DETENUS > DETENU

DETER vb discourage (someone) from doing something by instilling fear or doubt

DETERGE vb wash or wipe away

DETERGED > DETERGE

DETERGENT n chemical substance for washing clothes or dishes ▷ adj having cleansing power

DETERGER n detergent

DETERGERS > DETERGER

DETERGES > DETERGE

DETERGING > DETERGE

DETERMENT > DETER

DETERMINE vb settle (an argument or a question) conclusively

DETERRED > DETER

DETERRENT n something that deters ▷ adj tending to deter

DETERRER > DETER

DETERRERS > DETERRER

DETERRING > DETER

DETERS > DETER

DETERSION n act of cleansing

DETERSIVE same as > DETERGENT

DETEST vb dislike intensely

DETESTED > DETEST

DETESTER > DETEST

DETESTERS > DETEST

DETESTING > DETEST

DETESTS > DETEST

DETHATCH vb remove dead grass from lawn

DETHRONE vb remove from a throne or position of power

DETHRONED > DETHRONE

DETHRONER > DETHRONE

DETHRONES > DETHRONE

DETICK vb remove ticks from

DETICKED > DETICK

DETICKER > DETICK

DETICKERS > DETICK

DETICKING > DETICK

DETICKS > DETICK

DETINUE n action brought by a plaintiff to recover goods wrongfully detained

DETINUES > DETINUE

DETONABLE adj that can be detonated

DETONATE vb explode

DETONATED > DETONATE

DETONATES > DETONATE

DETONATOR n small amount of explosive, or a device, used to set off an explosion

DETORSION > DETORT

DETORT vb pervert

DETORTED > DETORT

DETORTING > DETORT

DETORTION > DETORT

DETORTS > DETORT

DETOUR n route that is not the most direct one ▷ vb deviate or cause to deviate from a direct route or course of action

DETOURED > DETOUR

DETOURING > DETOUR

DETOURS > DETOUR

DETOX n treatment to rid the body of poisonous substances ▷ vb undergo treatment to rid the body of poisonous substances, esp alcohol and drugs

DETOXED > DETOX

DETOXES > DETOX

DETOXIFY vb remove poison from

DETOXING > DETOX

DETRACT vb make (something) seem less good

DETRACTED > DETRACT

DETRACTOR > DETRACT

DETRACTS > DETRACT

DETRAIN vb leave or cause to leave a railway train, as passengers, etc

DETRAINED > DETRAIN

DETRAINS > DETRAIN

DETRAQUE n insane person

DETRAQUEE n female insane person

DETRAQUES > DETRAQUE

DETRIMENT n disadvantage or damage

DETRITAL > DETRITUS

DETRITION n act of rubbing or wearing away by friction

DETRITUS n loose mass of stones and silt worn away from rocks

DETRUDE vb force down or thrust away or out

DETRUDED > DETRUDE

DETRUDES > DETRUDE

DETRUDING > DETRUDE

DETRUSION > DETRUDE

DETRUSOR n muscle in the wall of the bladder

DETRUSORS > DETRUSOR

DETUNE vb change pitch of (stringed instrument)

DETUNED > DETUNE

DETUNES > DETUNE

DETUNING > DETUNE

DEUCE vb score deuce in tennis ▷ n score of forty all

DEUCED adj damned

DEUCEDLY > DEUCED

DEUCES > DEUCE

DEUCING > DEUCE

DEUDDARN n two-tiered Welsh dresser

DEUDDARNS > DEUDDARN

DEUS n god

DEUTERATE vb treat or combine with deuterium

DEUTERIC adj (of mineral) formed by metasomatic changes

DEUTERIDE n compound of deuterium with some other element. It is analogous to a hydride

DEUTERIUM n isotope of hydrogen twice as heavy as the normal atom

DEUTERON n nucleus of a deuterium atom, consisting of one proton and one neutron

DEUTERONS > DEUTERON

DEUTON old form of > DEUTERON

DEUTONS > DEUTON

DEUTZIA n shrub with clusters of pink or white flowers

DEUTZIAS > DEUTZIA

DEV same as > DEVA

DEVA n (in Hinduism and Buddhism) divine being or god

DEVALL vb stop

DEVALLED > DEVALL

DEVALLING > DEVALL

DEVALLS > DEVALL

DEVALUATE same as > DEVALUE

DEVALUE vb reduce the exchange value of (a currency)

DEVALUED > DEVALUE

DEVALUES > DEVALUE

DEVALUING > DEVALUE

DEVAS > DEVA

DEVASTATE vb destroy

DEVEIN vb remove vein from

DEVEINED > DEVEIN

DEVEINING > DEVEIN

DEVEINS > DEVEIN

DEVEL same as > DEVVEL

DEVELED > DEVEL

DEVELING > DEVEL

DEVELLED > DEVEL

DEVELLING > DEVEL

DEVELOP vb grow or bring to a later, more elaborate, or more advanced stage

DEVELOPE old form of > DEVELOP

DEVELOPED > DEVELOP

DEVELOPER n person who develops property

DEVELOPES > DEVELOPE

DEVELOPPE n ballet position

DEVELOPS > DEVELOP

DEVELS > DEVEL

DEVERBAL n word deriving from verb

DEVERBALS > DEVERBAL

DEVEST variant spelling of > DIVEST

DEVESTED > DEVEST

DEVESTING > DEVEST

DEVESTS > DEVEST

DEVIANCE n act or state of being deviant

DEVIANCES > DEVIANCE

DEVIANCY same as > DEVIANCE

DEVIANT adj (person)

deviating from what is considered acceptable behaviour ▷ n person whose behaviour deviates from what is considered to be acceptable

DEVIANTS > DEVIANT

DEVIATE vb differ from others in belief or thought

DEVIATED > DEVIATE

DEVIATES > DEVIATE

DEVIATING > DEVIATE

DEVIATION n act or result of deviating

DEVIATIVE adj tending to deviate

DEVIATOR > DEVIATE

DEVIATORS > DEVIATE

DEVIATORY > DEVIATE

DEVICE n machine or tool used for a specific task

DEVICEFUL adj full of devices

DEVICES > DEVICE

DEVIL n evil spirit ▷ vb prepare (food) with a highly flavoured spiced mixture

DEVILDOM n domain of evil spirits

DEVILDOMS > DEVILDOM

DEVILED > DEVIL

DEVILESS n female devil

DEVILET n young devil

DEVILETS > DEVILET

DEVILFISH n manta fish

DEVILING > DEVIL

DEVILINGS > DEVIL

DEVILISH adj cruel or unpleasant ▷ adv extremely

DEVILISM n doctrine of devil

DEVILISMS > DEVILISM

DEVILKIN n small devil

DEVILKINS > DEVILKIN

DEVILLED > DEVIL

DEVILLING > DEVIL

DEVILMENT n mischievous conduct

DEVILRIES > DEVILRY

DEVILRY n mischievousness

DEVILS > DEVIL

DEVILSHIP n character of devil

DEVILTRY same as > DEVILRY

DEVILWOOD n small US tree

DEVIOUS adj insincere and dishonest

DEVIOUSLY > DEVIOUS

DEVISABLE adj (of property, esp realty) capable of being transferred by will

DEVISAL n act of inventing, contriving, or devising

DEVISALS > DEVISAL

DEVISE vb work out (something) in one's mind ▷ n disposition of property by will

DEVISED > DEVISE

DEVISEE n person to whom property, esp realty, is devised by will

DEVISEES > DEVISEE

DEVISER > DEVISE

DEVISERS > DEVISE

DEVISES > DEVISE

DEVISING > DEVISE

DEVISOR n person who devises property, esp realty, by will

DEVISORS > DEVISOR

DEVITRIFY vb change from a vitreous state to a crystalline state

DEVLING n young devil

DEVLINGS > DEVLING

DEVOICE vb make (a voiced speech sound) voiceless

DEVOICED > DEVOICE

DEVOICES > DEVOICE

DEVOICING > DEVOICE

DEVOID adj completely lacking (in)

DEVOIR n duty

DEVOIRS > DEVOIR

DEVOLVE vb pass (power or duties) or (of power or duties) be passed to a successor or substitute

DEVOLVED > DEVOLVE

DEVOLVES > DEVOLVE

DEVOLVING > DEVOLVE

DEVON n bland processed meat in sausage form, eaten cold in slices

DEVONIAN adj of, denoting, or formed in the fourth period of the Palaeozoic era, between the Silurian and Carboniferous periods

DEVONPORT same as > DAVENPORT

DEVONS > DEVON

DEVORE n velvet fabric with a raised pattern created by disintegrating some of the pile with chemicals

DEVORES > DEVORE

DEVOT n devotee

DEVOTE vb apply or dedicate to a particular purpose

DEVOTED adj showing loyalty or devotion

DEVOTEDLY > DEVOTED

DEVOTEE n person who is very enthusiastic about something

DEVOTEES > DEVOTEE

DEVOTES > DEVOTE

DEVOTING > DEVOTE

DEVOTION n strong affection for or loyalty to someone or something

DEVOTIONS > DEVOTION

DEVOTS > DEVOT

DEVOUR vb eat greedily

DEVOURED > DEVOUR

DEVOURER > DEVOUR

DEVOURERS > DEVOUR

DEVOURING > DEVOUR

DEVOURS > DEVOUR

DEVOUT adj deeply religious

DEVOUTER > DEVOUT

DEVOUTEST > DEVOUT

DEVOUTLY > DEVOUT

DEVS > DEV

DEVVEL vb strike with blow

DEVVELLED > DEVVEL

DEVVELS > DEVVEL

DEW n drops of water that form on the ground at night from vapour in the air ▷ vb moisten with or as with dew

DEWAN n (formerly in India) the chief minister or finance minister of a state ruled by an Indian prince

DEWANI n post of dewan

DEWANIS > DEWANI

DEWANNIES > DEWANNY

DEWANNY same as > DEWANI

DEWANS > DEWAN

DEWAR as in dewar flask type of vacuum flask

DEWARS > DEWAR

DEWATER vb remove water from

DEWATERED > DEWATER

DEWATERER > DEWATER

DEWATERS > DEWATER

DEWAX vb remove wax from

DEWAXED > DEWAX

DEWAXES > DEWAX

DEWAXING > DEWAX

DEWBERRY n type of bramble with blue-black fruits

DEWCLAW n nonfunctional claw on a dog's leg

DEWCLAWED > DEWCLAW

DEWCLAWS > DEWCLAW

DEWDROP n drop of dew

DEWDROPS > DEWDROP

DEWED > DEW

DEWFALL n formation of dew

DEWFALLS > DEWFALL

DEWFULL obsolete form of > DUE

DEWIER > DEWY

DEWIEST > DEWY

DEWILY > DEWY

DEWINESS > DEWY

DEWING > DEW

DEWITT vb kill, esp hang unlawfully

DEWITTED > DEWITT

DEWITTING > DEWITT

DEWITTS > DEWITT

DEWLAP n loose fold of skin hanging under the throat in dogs, cattle, etc

DEWLAPPED > DEWLAP

DEWLAPS > DEWLAP

DEWLAPT > DEWLAP

DEWLESS > DEW

DEWOOL vb remove wool from

DEWOOLED > DEWOOL

DEWOOLING > DEWOOL

DEWOOLS > DEWOOL

DEWORM vb rid of worms

d

DEWORMED > DEWORM
DEWORMER > DEWORM
DEWORMERS > DEWORM
DEWORMING > DEWORM
DEWORMS > DEWORM
DEWPOINT n temperature at which water vapour in the air becomes saturated and water droplets begin to form
DEWPOINTS > DEWPOINT
DEWS > DEW
DEWY adj moist with or as with dew
DEX n dextroamphetamine
DEXES > DEX
DEXIE n pill containing dextroamphetamine
DEXIES > DEXIE
DEXTER adj of or on the right side of a shield, etc, from the bearer's point of view ▷ n small breed of red or black beef cattle, originally from Ireland
DEXTERITY n skill in using one's hands
DEXTEROUS adj possessing or done with dexterity
DEXTERS > DEXTER
DEXTRAL adj of, relating to, or located on the right side, esp of the body
DEXTRALLY > DEXTRAL
DEXTRAN n polysaccharide produced by the action of bacteria on sucrose: used as a substitute for plasma in blood transfusions
DEXTRANS > DEXTRAN
DEXTRIN n sticky substance obtained from starch, used as a thickening agent in food
DEXTRINE same as > DEXTRIN
DEXTRINES > DEXTRINE
DEXTRINS > DEXTRIN
DEXTRO adj dextrorotatory or rotating to the right
DEXTRORSE adj (of some climbing plants) growing upwards in a helix from left to right or anticlockwise
DEXTROSE n glucose occurring in fruit, honey, and the blood of animals
DEXTROSES > DEXTROSE
DEXTROUS same as > DEXTEROUS
DEXY same as > DEXIE
DEY n title given to commanders or (from 1710) governors of the Janissaries of Algiers (1671-1830)
DEYS > DEY
DEZINC vb remove zinc from
DEZINCED > DEZINC
DEZINCING > DEZINC
DEZINCKED > DEZINC
DEZINCS > DEZINC
DHAK n tropical Asian tree with bright red flowers,

which yields a red resin used as an astringent
DHAKS > DHAK
DHAL n curry made from lentils or beans
DHALS > DHAL
DHAMMA variant of > DHARMA
DHAMMAS > DHAMMA
DHANSAK n any of a variety of Indian dishes consisting of meat or vegetables braised with water or stock and lentils
DHANSAKS > DHANSAK
DHARMA n moral law or behaviour
DHARMAS > DHARMA
DHARMIC > DHARMA
DHARMSALA n Indian hostel
DHARNA n (in India) a method of obtaining justice, as the payment of a debt, by sitting, fasting, at the door of the person from whom reparation is sought
DHARNAS > DHARNA
DHIMMI n non-Muslim living in a state governed by sharia law
DHIMMIS > DHIMMI
DHOBI n (in India, Malaya, East Africa, etc, esp formerly) a washerman
DHOBIS > DHOBI
DHOL n type of Indian drum
DHOLE n fierce canine mammal of the forests of central and SE Asia, with a reddish-brown coat and rounded ears
DHOLES > DHOLE
DHOLL same as > DHAL
DHOLLS > DHOLL
DHOLS > DHOL
DHOOLIES > DHOOLY
DHOOLY same as > DOOLIE
DHOORA same as > DURRA
DHOORAS > DHOORA
DHOOTI same as > DHOTI
DHOOTIE same as > DHOTI
DHOOTIES > DHOOTIE
DHOOTIS > DHOOTI
DHOTI n long loincloth worn by men in India
DHOTIS > DHOTI
DHOURRA same as > DURRA
DHOURRAS > DHOURRA
DHOW n Arab sailing ship
DHOWS > DHOW
DHURNA same as > DHARNA
DHURNAS > DHURNA
DHURRA same as > DURRA
DHURRAS > DHURRA
DHURRIE same as > DURRIE
DHURRIES > DHURRIE
DHUTI same as > DHOTI
DHUTIS > DHUTI
DI > DEUS
DIABASE n altered dolerite
DIABASES > DIABASE
DIABASIC > DIABASE

DIABETES n disorder in which an abnormal amount of urine containing an excess of sugar is excreted
DIABETIC n person who has diabetes ▷ adj of or having diabetes
DIABETICS > DIABETIC
DIABLE n type of sauce
DIABLERIE n magic or witchcraft connected with devils
DIABLERY same as > DIABLERIE
DIABLES > DIABLE
DIABOLIC adj of the Devil
DIABOLISE same as > DIABOLIZE
DIABOLISM n witchcraft, devil worship
DIABOLIST > DIABOLISM
DIABOLIZE vb make (someone or something) diabolical
DIABOLO n game in which one throws and catches a spinning top on a cord fastened to two sticks held in the hands
DIABOLOGY n study of devils
DIABOLOS > DIABOLO
DIACETYL n aromatic compound
DIACETYLS > DIACETYL
DIACHRONY n change over time
DIACHYLON n acid or salt that contains two acidic hydrogen atoms
DIACHYLUM n plaster containing glycerin with lead salts
DIACID n lead plaster
DIACIDIC adj (of a base, such as calcium hydroxide $Ca(OH)_2$) capable of neutralizing two protons with one of its molecules
DIACIDS > DIACID
DIACODION n herbal remedy aiding sleep
DIACODIUM n syrup of poppies
DIACONAL adj of or associated with a deacon or the diaconate
DIACONATE n position or period of office of a deacon
DIACRITIC n sign above or below a character to indicate phonetic value or stress
DIACT n two-rayed
DIACTINAL adj having two pointed ends
DIACTINE adj two-rayed
DIACTINIC adj able to transmit photochemically active radiation
DIADEM n crown ▷ vb adorn or crown with or as with a diadem

DIADEMED > DIADEM
DIADEMING > DIADEM
DIADEMS > DIADEM
DIADOCHI npl the six Macedonian generals who, after the death of Alexander the Great, fought for control of his empire
DIADOCHY n replacement of one element in a crystal by another
DIADROM n complete course of pendulum
DIADROMS > DIADROM
DIAERESES > DIAERESIS
DIAERESIS n mark placed over a vowel to show that it is pronounced separately from the preceding one, for example in Noël
DIAERETIC > DIAERESIS
DIAGLYPH n figure cut into stone
DIAGLYPHS > DIAGLYPH
DIAGNOSE vb determine by diagnosis
DIAGNOSED > DIAGNOSE
DIAGNOSES > DIAGNOSIS
DIAGNOSIS n discovery and identification of diseases from the examination of symptoms
DIAGONAL adj from corner to corner ▷ n diagonal line
DIAGONALS > DIAGONAL
DIAGRAM n sketch showing the form or workings of something ▷ vb show in or as if in a diagram
DIAGRAMED > DIAGRAM
DIAGRAMS > DIAGRAM
DIAGRAPH n device for enlarging or reducing maps, plans, etc
DIAGRAPHS > DIAGRAPH
DIAGRID n diagonal structure network
DIAGRIDS > DIAGRID
DIAL n face of a clock or watch ▷ vb operate the dial or buttons on a telephone in order to contact (a number)
DIALECT n form of a language spoken in a particular area
DIALECTAL > DIALECT
DIALECTIC n logical debate by question and answer to resolve differences between two views ▷ adj of or relating to logical disputation
DIALECTS > DIALECT
DIALED > DIAL
DIALER > DIAL
DIALERS > DIAL
DIALING > DIAL
DIALINGS > DIAL
DIALIST n dial-maker

DIALISTS > DIALIST

DIALLAGE n green or brownish-black variety of the mineral augite in the form of layers of platelike crystals

DIALLAGES > DIALLAGE

DIALLAGIC > DIALLAGE

DIALLED > DIAL

DIALLEL n interbreeding among a group of parents

DIALLER > DIAL

DIALLERS > DIAL

DIALLING > DIAL

DIALLINGS > DIAL

DIALLIST same as > DIALIST

DIALLISTS > DIALLIST

DIALOG same as > DIALOGUE

DIALOGED > DIALOG

DIALOGER > DIALOG

DIALOGERS > DIALOG

DIALOGIC > DIALOGUE

DIALOGING > DIALOG

DIALOGISE same as > DIALOGIZE

DIALOGISM n deduction with one premise and a disjunctive conclusion

DIALOGIST n person who writes or takes part in a dialogue

DIALOGITE n carbonate mineral

DIALOGIZE vb carry on a dialogue

DIALOGS > DIALOG

DIALOGUE n conversation between two people, esp in a book, film, or play ▷ vb put into the form of a dialogue

DIALOGUED > DIALOGUE

DIALOGUER > DIALOGUE

DIALOGUES > DIALOGUE

DIALS > DIAL

DIALYSATE n liquid used in dialysis

DIALYSE vb separate by dialysis

DIALYSED > DIALYSE

DIALYSER n machine that performs dialysis, esp one that removes impurities from the blood of patients with malfunctioning kidneys

DIALYSERS > DIALYSER

DIALYSES > DIALYSIS

DIALYSING > DIALYSE

DIALYSIS n filtering of blood through a membrane to remove waste products

DIALYTIC > DIALYSIS

DIALYZATE same as > DIALYSATE

DIALYZE same as > DIALYSE

DIALYZED > DIALYZE

DIALYZER same as > DIALYSER

DIALYZERS > DIALYZER

DIALYZES > DIALYZE

DIALYZING > DIALYZE

DIAMAGNET n substance exhibiting diamagnetism

DIAMANTE adj decorated with artificial jewels or sequins ▷ n fabric so covered

DIAMANTES > DIAMANTE

DIAMETER n (length of) a straight line through the centre of a circle or sphere

DIAMETERS > DIAMETER

DIAMETRAL same as > DIAMETRIC

DIAMETRIC adj of a diameter

DIAMIDE n compound containing two amido groups

DIAMIDES > DIAMIDE

DIAMIN same as > DIAMIN

DIAMINE n any chemical compound containing two amino groups in its molecules

DIAMINES > DIAMINE

DIAMINS > DIAMIN

DIAMOND n exceptionally hard, usu. colourless, precious stone ▷ adj (of an anniversary) the sixtieth ▷ vb stud or decorate with diamonds

DIAMONDED > DIAMOND

DIAMONDS > DIAMOND

DIAMYL adj with two amyl groups

DIANDRIES > DIANDRY

DIANDROUS adj (of some flowers or flowering plants) having two stamens

DIANDRY n practice of having two husbands

DIANE as in steak diane kind of steak

DIANODAL adj going through a node

DIANOETIC adj of or relating to thought, esp to discursive reasoning rather than intuition

DIANOIA n perception and experience regarded as lower modes of knowledge

DIANOIAS > DIANOIA

DIANTHUS n type of widely cultivated Eurasian plant, such as the carnation, pink, and sweet william

DIAPASE same as > DIAPASON

DIAPASES > DIAPASE

DIAPASON n either of two stops found throughout the range of a pipe organ

DIAPASONS > DIAPASON

DIAPAUSE vb undergo diapause ▷ n period of suspended development and growth accompanied by decreased metabolism in insects and some other animals. It is correlated with seasonal changes

DIAPAUSED > DIAPAUSE

DIAPAUSES > DIAPAUSE

DIAPENTE n (in classical Greece) the interval of a perfect fifth

DIAPENTES > DIAPENTE

DIAPER n nappy ▷ vb decorate with a geometric pattern

DIAPERED > DIAPER

DIAPERING > DIAPER

DIAPERS > DIAPER

DIAPHONE n set of all realizations of a given phoneme in a language

DIAPHONES > DIAPHONE

DIAPHONIC > DIAPHONY

DIAPHONY n style of two-part polyphonic singing

DIAPHRAGM n muscular partition that separates the abdominal cavity and chest cavity

DIAPHYSES > DIAPHYSIS

DIAPHYSIS n shaft of a long bone

DIAPIR n anticlinal fold in which the brittle overlying rock has been pierced by material, such as salt, from beneath

DIAPIRIC > DIAPIR

DIAPIRISM > DIAPIR

DIAPIRS > DIAPIR

DIAPSID n reptile with two holes in rear of skull

DIAPSIDS > DIAPSID

DIAPYESES > DIAPYESIS

DIAPYESIS n discharge of pus

DIAPYETIC > DIAPYESIS

DIARCH adj (of a vascular bundle) having two strands of xylem

DIARCHAL > DIARCHY

DIARCHIC > DIARCHY

DIARCHIES > DIARCHY

DIARCHY n government by two states, individuals, etc

DIARIAL > DIARY

DIARIAN > DIARY

DIARIES > DIARY

DIARISE same as > DIARIZE

DIARISED > DIARISE

DIARISES > DIARISE

DIARISING > DIARISE

DIARIST n person who writes a diary

DIARISTIC > DIARIST

DIARISTS > DIARIST

DIARIZE vb record in diary

DIARIZED > DIARIZE

DIARIZES > DIARIZE

DIARIZING > DIARIZE

DIARRHEA same as > DIARRHOEA

DIARRHEAL > DIARRHEA

DIARRHEAS > DIARRHEA

DIARRHEIC > DIARRHEA

DIARRHOEA n frequent discharge of abnormally liquid faeces

DIARY n (book for) a record of daily events, appointments, or observations

DIASCIA n S African plant, usu with pink flowers

DIASCIAS > DIASCIA

DIASCOPE n optical projector used to display transparencies

DIASCOPES > DIASCOPE

DIASPORA n dispersion or spreading, as of people originally belonging to one nation or having a common culture

DIASPORAS > DIASPORA

DIASPORE n white, yellowish, or grey mineral

DIASPORES > DIASPORE

DIASPORIC > DIASPORA

DIASTASE n enzyme that converts starch into sugar

DIASTASES > DIASTASIS

DIASTASIC > DIASTASE

DIASTASIS n separation of an epiphysis from the long bone to which it is normally attached without fracture of the bone

DIASTATIC > DIASTASIS

DIASTEM same as > DIASTEMA

DIASTEMA n abnormal space, fissure, or cleft in a bodily organ or part

DIASTEMAS > DIASTEMA

DIASTEMS > DIASTEM

DIASTER n stage in cell division at which the chromosomes are in two groups at the poles of the spindle before forming daughter nuclei

DIASTERS > DIASTER

DIASTOLE n dilation of the chambers of the heart

DIASTOLES > DIASTOLE

DIASTOLIC > DIASTOLE

DIASTRAL > DIASTER

DIASTYLE adj having columns about three diameters apart ▷ n diastyle building

DIASTYLES > DIASTYLE

DIATHERMY n local heating of the body tissues with an electric current for medical or surgical purposes

DIATHESES > DIATHESIS

DIATHESIS n hereditary or acquired susceptibility of the body to one or more diseases

DIATHETIC > DIATHESIS

DIATOM n microscopic unicellular alga

DIATOMIC adj containing two atoms

DIATOMIST n specialist in diatoms

DIATOMITE n soft very fine-grained whitish rock consisting of the siliceous remains of diatoms deposited in the ocean or in ponds or lakes. It is used as an absorbent, filtering medium, insulator, filler, etc

DIATOMS > DIATOM

DIATONIC adj of a regular major or minor scale

DIATRETA > DIATRETUM

DIATRETUM n Roman glass bowl

DIATRIBE n bitter critical attack

DIATRIBES > DIATRIBE

DIATRON n circuit that uses diodes

DIATRONS > DIATRON

DIATROPIC adj relating to a type of response in plants to an external stimulus

DIAXON n bipolar cell

DIAXONS > DIAXON

DIAZEPAM n chemical compound used as a minor tranquillizer and muscle relaxant and to treat acute epilepsy

DIAZEPAMS > DIAZEPAM

DIAZEUXES > DIAZEUXIS

DIAZEUXIS n separation of two tetrachords by interval of a tone

DIAZIN same as > DIAZINE

DIAZINE n organic compound

DIAZINES > DIAZINE

DIAZINON n type of insecticide

DIAZINONS > DIAZINON

DIAZINS > DIAZIN

DIAZO adj of, or relating to the reproduction of documents using the bleaching action of ultraviolet radiation on diazonium salts ▷ n document produced by this method

DIAZOES > DIAZO

DIAZOLE n type of organic compound

DIAZOLES > DIAZOLE

DIAZONIUM n type of chemical group

DIAZOS > DIAZO

DIAZOTISE same as > DIAZOTIZE

DIAZOTIZE vb cause (an aryl amine) to react with nitrous acid to produce a diazonium salt

DIB vb fish by allowing the bait to bob and dip on the surface

DIBASIC adj (of an acid, such as sulphuric acid, H_2SO_4) containing two

acidic hydrogen atoms

DIBBED > DIB

DIBBER same as > DIBBLE

DIBBERS > DIBBER

DIBBING > DIB

DIBBLE n small hand tool used to make holes in the ground for seeds or plants ▷ vb make a hole in (the ground) with a dibble

DIBBLED > DIBBLE

DIBBLER > DIBBLE

DIBBLERS > DIBBLE

DIBBLES > DIBBLE

DIBBLING > DIBBLE

DIBBS n money

DIBBUK variant spelling of > DYBBUK

DIBBUKIM > DIBBUK

DIBBUKKIM > DIBBUK

DIBBUKS > DIBBUK

DIBROMIDE n chemical compound that contains two bromine atoms per molecule

DIBS > DIB

DIBUTYL adj with two butyl groups

DICACIOUS adj teasing

DICACITY n playful teasing

DICACODYL n oily slightly water-soluble poisonous liquid with garlic-like odour

DICAMBA n type of weedkiller

DICAMBAS > DICAMBA

DICAST n (in ancient Athens) a juror in the popular courts chosen by lot from a list of citizens

DICASTERY n congregation

DICASTIC > DICAST

DICASTS > DICAST

DICE n small cube each of whose sides has a different number of spots (1 to 6), used in games of chance ▷ vb cut (food) into small cubes

DICED > DICE

DICENTRA n Asian or N American plant with finely divided leaves and ornamental clusters of drooping flowers

DICENTRAS > DICENTRA

DICENTRIC n abnormal chromosome with two centromeres

DICER > DICE

DICERS > DICE

DICES > DICE

DICEY adj dangerous or risky

DICH interj archaic expression meaning "may it do"

DICHASIA > DICHASIUM

DICHASIAL > DICHASIUM

DICHASIUM n cymose inflorescence in which each branch bearing a flower

gives rise to two other flowering branches, as in the stitchwort

DICHOGAMY n maturation of male and female parts of a flower at different times, preventing automatic self-pollination

DICHONDRA n creeping perennial herb

DICHOPTIC adj having the eyes distinctly separate

DICHORD n two-stringed musical instrument

DICHORDS > DICHORD

DICHOTIC adj relating to or involving the stimulation of each ear simultaneously by different sounds

DICHOTOMY n division into two opposed groups or parts

DICHROIC adj having or consisting of only two colours

DICHROISM n property of a uniaxial crystal, such as tourmaline, of showing a perceptible difference in colour when viewed along two different axes in transmitted white light

DICHROITE n grey or violet-blue dichroic material

DICHROMAT n person able to distinguish only two colours

DICHROMIC adj of or involving only two colours

DICHT vb wipe

DICHTED > DICHT

DICHTING > DICHT

DICHTS > DICHT

DICIER > DICEY

DICIEST > DICEY

DICING > DICE

DICINGS > DICE

DICK n penis ▷ vb penetrate with a penis

DICKED > DICK

DICKENS n euphemism for devil

DICKENSES > DICKENS

DICKER vb trade (goods) by bargaining ▷ n petty bargain or barter

DICKERED > DICKER

DICKERING > DICKER

DICKERS > DICKER

DICKEY same as > DICKY

DICKEYS > DICKEY

DICKHEAD n stupid or despicable man or boy

DICKHEADS > DICKHEAD

DICKIE same as > DICKY

DICKIER > DICKY

DICKIES > DICKY

DICKIEST > DICKY

DICKING > DICK

DICKINGS > DICKING

DICKS > DICK

DICKTIER > DICKTY

DICKTIEST > DICKTY

DICKTY same as > DICTY

DICKY n false shirt front ▷ adj shaky or weak

DICKYBIRD See > DICKY

DICLINIES > DICLINOUS

DICLINISM > DICLINOUS

DICLINOUS adj (of flowering plants) bearing unisexual flowers

DICLINY > DICLINOUS

DICOT n type of flowering plant

DICOTS > DICOT

DICOTYL n a type of flowering plant; dicotyledon

DICOTYLS > DICOTYL

DICROTAL same as > DICROTIC

DICROTIC adj having or relating to a double pulse for each heartbeat

DICROTISM > DICROTIC

DICROTOUS same as > DICROTIC

DICT vb dictate

DICTA > DICTUM

DICTATE vb say aloud for someone else to write down ▷ n authoritative command

DICTATED > DICTATE

DICTATES > DICTATE

DICTATING > DICTATE

DICTATION n act of dictating words to be taken down in writing

DICTATOR n ruler who has complete power

DICTATORS > DICTATOR

DICTATORY adj tending to dictate

DICTATRIX > DICTATOR

DICTATURE n dictatorship

DICTED > DICT

DICTIER > DICTY

DICTIEST > DICTY

DICTING > DICT

DICTION n manner of pronouncing words and sounds

DICTIONAL > DICTION

DICTIONS > DICTION

DICTS > DICT

DICTUM n formal statement

DICTUMS > DICTUM

DICTY adj conceited; snobbish

DICTYOGEN n plant with net-veined leaves

DICUMAROL n anticoagulant drug

DICYCLIC adj having the perianth arranged in two whorls

DICYCLIES > DICYCLIC

DICYCLY > DICYCLIC

DID > DO

DIDACT n instructive person

DIDACTIC adj intended to instruct

DIDACTICS n art or

science of teaching

DIDACTS > DIDACT

DIDACTYL adj having only two toes on each foot ▷ n animal with only two toes on each foot

DIDACTYLS > DIDACTYL

DIDAKAI same as > DIDICOY

DIDAKAIS > DIDAKAI

DIDAKEI same as > DIDICOY

DIDAKEIS > DIDAKEI

DIDAPPER n small grebe

DIDAPPERS > DIDAPPER

DIDDER vb shake with fear

DIDDERED > DIDDER

DIDDERING > DIDDER

DIDDERS > DIDDER

DIDDICOY same as > DIDICOY

DIDDICOYS > DIDDICOY

DIDDIER > DIDDY

DIDDIES > DIDDY

DIDDIEST > DIDDY

DIDDLE vb swindle

DIDDLED > DIDDLE

DIDDLER > DIDDLE

DIDDLERS > DIDDLE

DIDDLES > DIDDLE

DIDDLEY n worthless amount

DIDDLEYS > DIDDLEY

DIDDLIES > DIDDLY

DIDDLING > DIDDLE

DIDDLY n worthless amount

DIDDY n female breast or nipple ▷ adj of or relating to a diddy

DIDELPHIC adj with two genital tubes or ovaries

DIDELPHID n marsupial

DIDICOI same as > DIDICOY

DIDICOIS > DIDICOI

DIDICOY n (in Britain) one of a group of caravan-dwelling roadside people who live like Gypsies but are not true Romanies

DIDICOYS > DIDICOY

DIDIE same as > DIDY

DIDIES > DIDY

DIDJERIDU n Australian Aboriginal wind instrument

DIDO n antic

DIDOES > DIDO

DIDOS > DIDO

DIDRACHM n two-drachma piece

DIDRACHMA same as > DIDRACHM

DIDRACHMS > DIDRACHM

DIDST form of the past tense of > DO

DIDY n woman's breast

DIDYMIUM n mixture of the metallic rare earths neodymium and praseodymium, once thought to be an element

DIDYMIUMS > DIDYMIUM

DIDYMOUS adj in pairs or in two parts

DIDYNAMY n (of stamens) being in two unequal pairs

DIE vb (of a person, animal, or plant) cease all biological activity permanently ▷ n shaped block used to cut or form metal

DIEB n N African jackal

DIEBACK n disease of trees and shrubs characterized by death of the young shoots, which spreads to the larger branches: caused by injury to the roots or attack by bacteria or fungi ▷ vb (of plants) to suffer from dieback

DIEBACKS > DIEBACK

DIEBS > DIEB

DIECIOUS same as > DIOECIOUS

DIED > DIE

DIEDRAL same as > DIHEDRAL

DIEDRALS > DIEDRAL

DIEDRE n large shallow groove or corner in a rock face

DIEDRES > DIEDRE

DIEGESES > DIEGESIS

DIEGESIS n utterance of fact

DIEGETIC adj relating to a factual narrative

DIEHARD n person who resists change or who holds on to an outdated attitude

DIEHARDS > DIEHARD

DIEING > DIE

DIEL n 24-hour period

DIELDRIN n highly toxic insecticide

DIELDRINS > DIELDRIN

DIELYTRA n genus of herbaceous plants

DIELYTRAS > DIELYTRA

DIEMAKER n one who makes dies

DIEMAKERS > DIEMAKER

DIENE n hydrocarbon that contains two carbon-to-carbon double bonds in its molecules

DIENES > DIENE

DIEOFF n process of dying in large numbers

DIEOFFS > DIEOFF

DIERESES > DIERESIS

DIERESIS same as > DIAERESIS

DIERETIC > DIERESIS

DIES > DIE

DIESEL vb drive diesel-fueled vehicle ▷ n diesel engine

DIESELED > DIESEL

DIESELING > DIESEL

DIESELISE same as > DIESELIZE

DIESELIZE vb be equipped with diesel engine

DIESELS > DIESEL

DIESES > DIESIS

DIESINKER n person who engraves dies

DIESIS n (in ancient Greek theory) any interval smaller than a whole tone, esp a semitone in the Pythagorean scale

DIESTER n synthetic lubricant

DIESTERS > DIESTER

DIESTOCK n device holding the dies used to cut an external screw thread

DIESTOCKS > DIESTOCK

DIESTROUS same as > DIOESTRUS

DIESTRUM another word for > DIESTROUS

DIESTRUMS > DIESTRUM

DIESTRUS same as > DIOESTRUS

DIET n food that a person or animal regularly eats ▷ vb follow a special diet so as to lose weight ▷ adj (of food) suitable for a weight-reduction diet

DIETARIAN n dieter

DIETARIES > DIETARY

DIETARILY > DIETARY

DIETARY adj of or relating to a diet ▷ n regulated diet

DIETED > DIET

DIETER > DIET

DIETERS > DIET

DIETETIC adj prepared for special dietary requirements

DIETETICS n study of diet and nutrition

DIETHER n chemical compound

DIETHERS > DIETHER

DIETHYL as in diethyl ether same as > ETHER

DIETHYLS > DIETHYL

DIETICIAN n person who specializes in dietetics

DIETINE n low-ranking diet

DIETINES > DIETINE

DIETING > DIET

DIETINGS > DIET

DIETIST another word for > DIETITIAN

DIETISTS > DIETIST

DIETITIAN same as > DIETICIAN

DIETS > DIET

DIF same as > DIFF

DIFF n (slang) difference

DIFFER vb be unlike

DIFFERED > DIFFER

DIFFERENT adj unlike

DIFFERING > DIFFER

DIFFERS > DIFFER

DIFFICILE adj difficult

DIFFICULT adj requiring effort or skill to do or understand

DIFFIDENT adj lacking self-confidence

DIFFLUENT adj flowing; not fixed

DIFFORM adj irregular in form

DIFFRACT vb cause to undergo diffraction

DIFFRACTS > DIFFRACT

DIFFS > DIFF

DIFFUSE vb spread over a wide area ▷ adj widely spread

DIFFUSED > DIFFUSE

DIFFUSELY > DIFFUSE

DIFFUSER n person or thing that diffuses

DIFFUSERS > DIFFUSER

DIFFUSES > DIFFUSE

DIFFUSING > DIFFUSE

DIFFUSION n act of diffusing or the fact of being diffused

DIFFUSIVE adj characterized by diffusion

DIFFUSOR same as > DIFFUSER

DIFFUSORS > DIFFUSOR

DIFS > DIF

DIG vb cut into, break up, and turn over or remove (earth), esp with a spade ▷ n digging

DIGAMIES > DIGAMY

DIGAMIST > DIGAMY

DIGAMISTS > DIGAMY

DIGAMMA n letter of the Greek alphabet that became obsolete before the classical period of the language.

DIGAMMAS > DIGAMMA

DIGAMOUS > DIGAMY

DIGAMY n second marriage contracted after the termination of the first by death or divorce

DIGASTRIC adj (of certain muscles) having two fleshy portions joined by a tendon ▷ n muscle of the mandible that assists in lowering the lower jaw

DIGENESES > DIGENESIS

DIGENESIS n ability to alternate sexual and asexual means of reproduction

DIGENETIC adj of or relating to digenesis

DIGERATI npl people who earn large amounts of money through internet-related business

DIGEST vb subject to a process of digestion ▷ n shortened version of a book, report, or article

DIGESTANT same as > DIGESTIVE

DIGESTED > DIGEST

DIGESTER n apparatus or vessel, such as an autoclave, in which digestion is carried out

DIGESTERS > DIGESTER

DIGESTIF n something, esp a drink, taken as an aid

to digestion, either before or after a meal

DIGESTIFS > DIGESTIF

DIGESTING > DIGEST

DIGESTION n (body's system for) breaking down food into easily absorbed substances

DIGESTIVE adj relating to digestion

DIGESTOR same as > DIGESTER

DIGESTORS > DIGESTOR

DIGESTS > DIGEST

DIGGABLE adj that can be dug

DIGGED a past tense of > DIG

DIGGER n machine used for digging

DIGGERS > DIGGER

DIGGING > DIG

DIGGINGS npl material that has been dug out

DIGHT vb adorn or equip, as for battle

DIGHTED > DIGHT

DIGHTING > DIGHT

DIGHTS > DIGHT

DIGICAM n digital camera

DIGICAMS > DIGICAM

DIGIPACK n type of packaging for a CD or DVD

DIGIPACKS > DIGIPACK

DIGIT n finger or toe

DIGITAL adj displaying information as numbers rather than with hands and a dial ⊳ n one of the keys on the manuals of an organ or on a piano, harpsichord, etc

DIGITALIN n poisonous amorphous crystalline mixture of glycosides extracted from digitalis leaves and formerly used in treating heart disease.

DIGITALIS n drug made from foxglove leaves, used as a heart stimulant

DIGITALLY > DIGITAL

DIGITALS > DIGITAL

DIGITATE adj (of leaves) having leaflets in the form of a spread hand

DIGITATED same as > DIGITATE

DIGITISE same as > DIGITIZE

DIGITISED > DIGITISE

DIGITISER > DIGITISE

DIGITISES > DIGITISE

DIGITIZE vb transcribe (data) into a digital form for processing by a computer

DIGITIZED adj recorded or stored in digital form

DIGITIZER > DIGITIZE

DIGITIZES > DIGITIZE

DIGITONIN n type of glycoside

DIGITOXIN same as > DIGOXIN

DIGITRON n type of tube, for displaying information,

having a common anode and several cathodes shaped in the form of characters, which can be lit by a glow discharge

DIGITRONS > DIGITRON

DIGITS > DIGIT

DIGITULE n any small finger-like process

DIGITULES > DIGITULE

DIGLOSSIA n existence in a language of a high, or socially prestigious, and a low, or everyday, form, as German and Swiss German in Switzerland

DIGLOSSIC > DIGLOSSIA

DIGLOT n bilingual book

DIGLOTS > DIGLOT

DIGLOTTIC > DIGLOT

DIGLYPH n ornament in Doric frieze with two grooves

DIGLYPHS > DIGLYPH

DIGNIFIED adj calm, impressive, and worthy of respect

DIGNIFIES > DIGNIFY

DIGNIFY vb add distinction to

DIGNITARY n person of high official position

DIGNITIES > DIGNITY

DIGNITY n serious, calm, and controlled behaviour or manner

DIGONAL adj of or relating to a symmetry operation in which the original figure is reconstructed after a 180° turn about an axis

DIGOXIN n glycoside extracted from the leaves of the woolly foxglove

DIGOXINS > DIGOXIN

DIGRAPH n two letters used to represent a single sound, such as gh in tough

DIGRAPHIC > DIGRAPH

DIGRAPHS > DIGRAPH

DIGRESS vb depart from the main subject in speech or writing

DIGRESSED > DIGRESS

DIGRESSER > DIGRESS

DIGRESSES > DIGRESS

DIGS > DIG

DIGYNIAN adj relating to plant class Digynia

DIGYNOUS another word for > DIGYNIAN

DIHEDRA > DIHEDRON

DIHEDRAL adj having or formed by two intersecting planes ⊳ n figure formed by two intersecting planes

DIHEDRALS > DIHEDRAL

DIHEDRON same as > DIHEDRAL

DIHEDRONS > DIHEDRON

DIHYBRID n offspring of two individuals that differ with respect to two pairs of genes

DIHYBRIDS > DIHYBRID

DIHYDRIC adj (of an alcohol) containing two hydroxyl groups per molecule

DIKA n wild mango

DIKAS > DIKA

DIKAST same as > DICAST

DIKASTS > DIKAST

DIKDIK n small African antelope

DIKDIKS > DIKDIK

DIKE same as > DYKE

DIKED > DIKE

DIKER n builder of dikes

DIKERS > DIKER

DIKES > DIKE

DIKETONE as in diphenylene diketone a compound used in dye manufacture, aka anthraquinone

DIKEY adj (of a lesbian) masculine

DIKIER > DIKEY

DIKIEST > DIKEY

DIKING > DIKE

DIKKOP n type of brownish shore bird with a large head and eyes

DIKKOPS > DIKKOP

DIKTAT n dictatorial decree

DIKTATS > DIKTAT

DILATABLE > DILATE

DILATABLY > DILATE

DILATANCY n phenomenon caused by the nature of the stacking or fitting together of particles or granules in a heterogeneous system, such as the solidification of certain sols under pressure, and the thixotropy of certain gels

DILATANT adj tending to dilate ⊳ n something, such as a catheter, that causes dilation

DILATANTS > DILATANT

DILATATE same as > DILATE

DILATATOR same as > DILATOR

DILATE vb make or become wider or larger

DILATED > DILATE

DILATER same as > DILATOR

DILATERS > DILATER

DILATES > DILATE

DILATING > DILATE

DILATION > DILATE

DILATIONS > DILATE

DILATIVE > DILATE

DILATOR n something that dilates an object, esp a surgical instrument for dilating a bodily cavity

DILATORS > DILATOR

DILATORY adj tending or intended to waste time

DILDO n object used as a substitute for an erect penis

DILDOE same as > DILDO

DILDOES > DILDOE

DILDOS > DILDO

DILEMMA n situation offering a choice between two equally undesirable alternatives

DILEMMAS > DILEMMA

DILEMMIC > DILEMMA

DILIGENCE n steady and careful application

DILIGENT adj careful and persevering in carrying out duties

DILL vb flavour with dill ⊳ n sweet-smelling herb

DILLED > DILL

DILLI n dilly bag; small bag, esp one made of plaited grass and used for carrying food

DILLIER > DILLY

DILLIES > DILLY

DILLIEST > DILLY

DILLING > DILL

DILLINGS > DILL

DILLIS > DILLI

DILLS > DILL

DILLY adj foolish ⊳ n person or thing that is remarkable

DILTIAZEM n drug used to treat angina

DILUENT adj causing dilution or serving to dilute ⊳ n substance used for or causing dilution

DILUENTS > DILUENT

DILUTABLE > DILUTE

DILUTE vb make (a liquid) less concentrated, esp by adding water ⊳ adj (of a liquid) thin and watery

DILUTED > DILUTE

DILUTEE > DILUTE

DILUTEES > DILUTE

DILUTER > DILUTE

DILUTES > DILUTE

DILUTING > DILUTE

DILUTION n act of diluting or state of being diluted

DILUTIONS > DILUTION

DILUTIVE adj having effect of decreasing earnings per share

DILUTOR n thing intended to have a diluting effect

DILUTORS > DILUTOR

DILUVIA > DILUVIUM

DILUVIAL adj of a flood, esp the great Flood described in the Old Testament

DILUVIAN same as > DILUVIAL

DILUVION same as > DILUVIUM

DILUVIONS > DILUVION

DILUVIUM n glacial drift

DILUVIUMS > DILUVIUM

DIM adj badly lit ⊳ vb make or become dim

DIMBLE n wooded hollow; dingle

DIMBLES > DIMBLE
DIME n coin of the US and Canada, worth ten cents
DIMENSION n measurement of the size of something in a particular direction ▷ vb shape or cut to specified dimensions
DIMER n molecule made up of two identical molecules bonded together
DIMERIC adj of a dimer
DIMERISE same as > DIMERIZE
DIMERISED > DIMERISE
DIMERISES > DIMERISE
DIMERISM > DIMEROUS
DIMERISMS > DIMEROUS
DIMERIZE vb react or cause to react to form a dimer
DIMERIZED > DIMERIZE
DIMERIZES > DIMERIZE
DIMEROUS adj consisting of or divided into two segments, as the tarsi of some insects
DIMERS > DIMER
DIMES > DIME
DIMETER n line of verse consisting of two metrical feet or a verse written in this metre
DIMETERS > DIMETER
DIMETHYL n ethane
DIMETHYLS > DIMETHYL
DIMETRIC adj of, relating to, or shaped like a quadrilateral
DIMIDIATE adj divided in halves ▷ vb halve (two bearings) so that they can be represented on the same shield
DIMINISH vb make or become smaller, fewer, or less
DIMISSORY adj granting permission to be ordained
DIMITIES > DIMITY
DIMITY n light strong cotton fabric with woven stripes or squares
DIMLY > DIM
DIMMABLE adj that can be dimmed
DIMMED > DIM
DIMMER > DIM
DIMMERS > DIM
DIMMEST > DIM
DIMMING n as in global dimming decrease in the amount of sunlight reaching the earth
DIMMINGS > DIMMING
DIMMISH > DIM
DIMNESS > DIM
DIMNESSES > DIM
DIMORPH n either of two forms of a substance that exhibits dimorphism
DIMORPHIC adj having two distinct forms
DIMORPHS > DIMORPH
DIMOUT n reduction of lighting
DIMOUTS > DIMOUT
DIMP n in Northern English dialect, a cigarette butt
DIMPLE n small natural dent, esp in the cheeks or chin ▷ vb produce dimples by smiling
DIMPLED > DIMPLE
DIMPLES > DIMPLE
DIMPLIER > DIMPLE
DIMPLIEST > DIMPLE
DIMPLING > DIMPLE
DIMPLY > DIMPLE
DIMPS > DIMP
DIMPSIES > DIMPSY
DIMPSY n twilight
DIMS > DIM
DIMWIT n stupid person
DIMWITS > DIMWIT
DIMWITTED > DIMWIT
DIMYARIAN adj with two adductor muscles
DIN n loud unpleasant confused noise ▷ vb instil (something) into someone by constant repetition
DINAR n monetary unit of various Balkan, Middle Eastern, and North African countries
DINARCHY same as > DIARCHY
DINARS > DINAR
DINDLE another word for > DINNLE
DINDLED > DINDLE
DINDLES > DINDLE
DINDLING > DINDLE
DINE vb eat dinner
DINED > DINE
DINER n person eating a meal
DINERIC adj of or concerned with the interface between immiscible liquids
DINERO n money
DINEROS > DINERO
DINERS > DINER
DINES > DINE
DINETTE n alcove or small area for use as a dining room
DINETTES > DINETTE
DINFUL adj noisy
DING n small dent in a vehicle ▷ vb ring or cause to ring, esp with tedious repetition
DINGBAT n any unnamed object, esp one used as a missile
DINGBATS > DINGBAT
DINGDONG n sound of a bell or bells ▷ vb make such a sound
DINGDONGS > DINGDONG
DINGE n dent ▷ vb make a dent in (something)
DINGED > DINGE
DINGER n (in baseball) home run
DINGERS > DINGER
DINGES n jocular word for something whose name is unknown or forgotten
DINGESES > DINGES
DINGEY same as > DINGHY
DINGEYS > DINGEY
DINGHIES > DINGHY
DINGHY n small boat, powered by sails, oars, or a motor ▷ vb ignore or avoid a person or event
DINGIED > DINGEY
DINGIER > DINGY
DINGIES > DINGY
DINGIEST > DINGY
DINGILY > DINGY
DINGINESS > DINGY
DINGING > DINGE
DINGLE n small wooded hollow or valley
DINGLES > DINGLE
DINGO n Australian wild dog ▷ vb act in a cowardly manner
DINGOED > DINGO
DINGOES > DINGO
DINGOING > DINGO
DINGS > DING
DINGUS same as > DINGES
DINGUSES > DINGUS
DINGY adj lacking light ▷ vb ignore or avoid a person or event
DINGYING > DINGY
DINIC n remedy for vertigo
DINICS > DINIC
DINING > DINE
DINITRO adj containing two nitro groups
DINK adj neat or neatly dressed ▷ vb carry (a second person) on a horse, bicycle, etc ▷ n ball struck delicately
DINKED > DINK
DINKER > DINK
DINKEST > DINK
DINKEY n small locomotive
DINKEYS > DINKEY
DINKIE n affluent married childless person ▷ adj designed for or appealing to dinkies
DINKIER > DINKY
DINKIES > DINKIE
DINKIEST > DINKY
DINKING > DINK
DINKLY adj neat
DINKS > DINK
DINKUM n truth or genuineness
DINKUMS > DINKUM
DINKY adj small and neat
DINMONT n neutered sheep
DINMONTS > DINMONT
DINNA vb a Scots word for do not
DINNAE vb (Scots) do not
DINNED > DIN
DINNER vb dine ▷ n main meal of the day, eaten either in the evening or at midday
DINNERED > DINNER
DINNERING > DINNER
DINNERS > DINNER
DINNING > DIN
DINNLE vb shake
DINNLED > DINNLE
DINNLES > DINNLE
DINNLING > DINNLE
DINO n dinosaur
DINOCERAS another name for a > UINTATHERE
DINOMANIA n strong interest in dinosaurs
DINOS > DINO
DINOSAUR n type of extinct prehistoric reptile, many of which were of gigantic size
DINOSAURS > DINOSAUR
DINOTHERE n type of extinct elephant-like mammal with tusks curving downwards and backwards
DINS > DIN
DINT variant of > DENT
DINTED > DINT
DINTING > DINT
DINTLESS > DINT
DINTS > DINT
DIOBOL n ancient Greek coin
DIOBOLON same as > DIOBOL
DIOBOLONS > DIOBOLON
DIOBOLS > DIOBOL
DIOCESAN adj of or relating to a diocese ▷ n bishop of a diocese
DIOCESANS > DIOCESAN
DIOCESE n district over which a bishop has control
DIOCESES > DIOCESE
DIODE n semiconductor device for converting alternating current to direct current
DIODES > DIODE
DIOECIES > DIOECY
DIOECIOUS adj (of plants) having the male and female reproductive organs on separate plants
DIOECISM > DIOECIOUS
DIOECISMS > DIOECIOUS
DIOECY n state of being dioecious
DIOESTRUS n period in mammal's oestral cycle
DIOICOUS same as > DIOECIOUS
DIOL n any of a class of alcohols that have two hydroxyl groups in each molecule
DIOLEFIN n type of polymer
DIOLEFINS > DIOLEFIN
DIOLS > DIOL
DIONYSIAC same as > DIONYSIAN
DIONYSIAN adj wild or orgiastic
DIOPSIDE n colourless or pale-green pyroxene mineral

d

DIOPSIDES >DIOPSIDE
DIOPSIDIC >DIOPSIDE
DIOPTASE n green glassy mineral
DIOPTASES >DIOPTASE
DIOPTER same as >DIOPTRE
DIOPTERS >DIOPTER
DIOPTRAL >DIOPTRE
DIOPTRATE adj (of compound eye) divided by transverse line
DIOPTRE n unit for measuring the refractive power of a lens
DIOPTRES >DIOPTRE
DIOPTRIC adj of or concerned with dioptrics
DIOPTRICS n branch of geometrical optics concerned with the formation of images by lenses
DIORAMA n miniature three-dimensional scene, in which models of figures are seen against a three-dimensional background
DIORAMAS >DIORAMA
DIORAMIC >DIORAMA
DIORISM n definition; clarity
DIORISMS >DIORISM
DIORISTIC >DIORISM
DIORITE n dark coarse-grained igneous plutonic rock consisting of plagioclase feldspar and ferromagnesian minerals such as hornblende
DIORITES >DIORITE
DIORITIC >DIORITE
DIOSGENIN n yam-based substance used in hormone therapy
DIOTA n type of ancient vase
DIOTAS >DIOTA
DIOXAN n colourless insoluble toxic liquid made by heating ethanediol with sulphuric acid
DIOXANE same as >DIOXAN
DIOXANES >DIOXANE
DIOXANS >DIOXAN
DIOXID same as >DIOXIDE
DIOXIDE n oxide containing two oxygen atoms per molecule
DIOXIDES >DIOXIDE
DIOXIDS >DIOXID
DIOXIN n any of a number of mostly poisonous chemical by-products of certain weedkillers
DIOXINS >DIOXIN
DIP vb plunge quickly or briefly into a liquid ▷ n dipping
DIPCHICK same as >DABCHICK
DIPCHICKS >DIPCHICK

DIPEPTIDE n compound consisting of two linked amino acids
DIPHASE adj of, having, or concerned with two phases
DIPHASIC same as >DIPHASE
DIPHENYL another name for >BIPHENYL
DIPHENYLS >DIPHENYL
DIPHONE n combination of two speech sounds
DIPHONES >DIPHONE
DIPHTHONG n union of two vowel sounds in a single compound sound
DIPHYSITE n belief in Christ having both divine and human natures
DIPLEGIA n paralysis of corresponding parts on both sides of the body
DIPLEGIAS >DIPLEGIA
DIPLEGIC >DIPLEGIA
DIPLEX adj (in telecommunications) permitting the transmission of simultaneous signals in both directions
DIPLEXER n device that enables the simultaneous transmission of more than one signal
DIPLEXERS >DIPLEXER
DIPLOE n spongy bone separating the two layers of compact bone of the skull
DIPLOES >DIPLOE
DIPLOGEN n heavy hydrogen
DIPLOGENS >DIPLOGEN
DIPLOIC adj relating to diploe
DIPLOID adj denoting a cell or organism with pairs of homologous chromosomes ▷ n diploid cell or organism
DIPLOIDIC >DIPLOID
DIPLOIDS >DIPLOID
DIPLOIDY >DIPLOID
DIPLOMA vb bestow diploma on ▷ n qualification awarded by a college on successful completion of a course
DIPLOMACY n conduct of the relations between nations by peaceful means
DIPLOMAED >DIPLOMA
DIPLOMAS >DIPLOMA
DIPLOMAT n official engaged in diplomacy
DIPLOMATA n DIPLOMA
DIPLOMATE n any person who has been granted a diploma, esp a physician certified as a specialist
DIPLOMATS >DIPLOMAT
DIPLON another name for >DEUTERON
DIPLONEMA a less common name for >DIPLOTENE

DIPLONS >DIPLON
DIPLONT n animal or plant that has the diploid number of chromosomes in its somatic cells
DIPLONTIC >DIPLONT
DIPLONTS >DIPLONT
DIPLOPIA n visual defect in which a single object is seen in duplicate
DIPLOPIAS >DIPLOPIA
DIPLOPIC >DIPLOPIA
DIPLOPOD n type of arthropod such as the millipede
DIPLOPODS >DIPLOPOD
DIPLOSES >DIPLOSIS
DIPLOSIS n doubling of the haploid number of chromosomes that occurs during fusion of gametes to form a diploid zygote
DIPLOTENE n fourth stage of the prophase of meiosis, during which the paired homologous chromosomes separate except at the places where genetic exchange has occurred
DIPLOZOA n type of parasitic worm
DIPLOZOIC adj (of certain animals) bilaterally symmetrical
DIPLOZOON n type of parasitic worm
DIPNET vb fish using fishing net on pole
DIPNETS >DIPNET
DIPNETTED >DIPNET
DIPNOAN n lungfish
DIPNOANS >DIPNOAN
DIPNOOUS adj having lungs and gills
DIPODIC >DIPODY
DIPODIES >DIPODY
DIPODY n metrical unit consisting of two feet
DIPOLAR >DIPOLE
DIPOLE n two equal but opposite electric charges or magnetic poles separated by a small distance
DIPOLES >DIPOLE
DIPPABLE >DIP
DIPPED >DIP
DIPPER n ladle used for dipping
DIPPERFUL n amount held by scoop
DIPPERS >DIPPER
DIPPIER >DIPPY
DIPPIEST >DIPPY
DIPPINESS >DIPPY
DIPPING >DIP
DIPPINGS >DIP
DIPPY adj odd, eccentric, or crazy
DIPROTIC adj having two hydrogen atoms
DIPS >DIP
DIPSADES >DIPSAS
DIPSAS n type of snake
DIPSHIT n stupid person
DIPSHITS >DIPSHIT

DIPSO n (slang) dipsomaniac or alcoholic
DIPSOS >DIPSO
DIPSTICK n notched rod dipped into a container to measure the level of a liquid
DIPSTICKS >DIPSTICK
DIPSWITCH n switch for dipping a vehicle's headlights
DIPT >DIP
DIPTERA n order of insects with two wings
DIPTERAL adj having a double row of columns
DIPTERAN n dipterous insect ▷ adj having two wings or winglike parts
DIPTERANS >DIPTERAN
DIPTERAS >DIPTERA
DIPTERIST n fly expert
DIPTEROI >DIPTEROS
DIPTERON same as >DIPTERAN
DIPTERONS >DIPTERON
DIPTEROS n Greek building with double columns
DIPTEROUS adj having two wings or winglike parts
DIPTYCA same as >DIPTYCH
DIPTYCAS >DIPTYCA
DIPTYCH n painting on two hinged panels
DIPTYCHS >DIPTYCH
DIQUARK n low-energy configuration of two quarks attracted to one another by virtue of having antisymmetric colours and spins
DIQUARKS >DIQUARK
DIQUAT n type of herbicide
DIQUATS >DIQUAT
DIRAM n money unit of Tajikistan
DIRAMS >DIRAM
DIRDAM same as >DIRDUM
DIRDAMS >DIRDAM
DIRDUM n tumult
DIRDUMS >DIRDUM
DIRE adj disastrous, urgent, or terrible
DIRECT adj (of a route) shortest, straight ▷ adv in a direct manner ▷ vb lead and organize
DIRECTED adj (of a number, line, or angle) having either a positive or negative sign to distinguish measurement in one direction or orientation from that in the opposite direction or orientation
DIRECTER >DIRECT
DIRECTEST >DIRECT
DIRECTING >DIRECT
DIRECTION n course or line along which a person or thing moves, points, or lies
DIRECTIVE n instruction,

order ▷ adj tending to direct

DIRECTLY adv in a direct manner

DIRECTOR n person or thing that directs or controls

DIRECTORS > DIRECTOR

DIRECTORY n book listing names, addresses, and telephone numbers ▷ adj directing

DIRECTRIX n fixed reference line, situated on the convex side of a conic section, that is used when defining or calculating its eccentricity

DIRECTS > DIRECT

DIREFUL same as > DIRE

DIREFULLY > DIREFUL

DIRELY > DIRE

DIREMPT vb separate with force

DIREMPTED > DIREMPT

DIREMPTS > DIREMPT

DIRENESS > DIRE

DIRER > DIRE

DIREST > DIRE

DIRGE n slow sad song of mourning

DIRGEFUL > DIRGE

DIRGELIKE > DIRGE

DIRGES > DIRGE

DIRHAM n standard monetary unit of Morocco, divided into 100 centimes

DIRHAMS > DIRHAM

DIRHEM same as > DIRHAM

DIRHEMS > DIRHEM

DIRIGE n dirge

DIRIGENT adj directing

DIRIGES > DIRIGE

DIRIGIBLE adj able to be steered ▷ n airship

DIRIGISM same as > DIRIGISME

DIRIGISME n control by the state of economic and social matters

DIRIGISMS > DIRIGISM

DIRIGISTE > DIRIGISME

DIRIMENT adj (of an impediment to marriage in canon law) totally invalidating

DIRK n dagger, formerly worn by Scottish Highlanders ▷ vb stab with a dirk

DIRKE variant of > DIRK

DIRKED > DIRK

DIRKES > DIRKE

DIRKING > DIRK

DIRKS > DIRK

DIRL vb tingle; vibrate

DIRLED > DIRL

DIRLING > DIRL

DIRLS > DIRL

DIRNDL n full gathered skirt originating from Tyrolean peasant wear

DIRNDLS > DIRNDL

DIRT vb soil ▷ n unclean substance, filth

DIRTBAG n filthy person

DIRTBAGS > DIRTBAG

DIRTED > DIRT

DIRTIED > DIRTY

DIRTIER > DIRTY

DIRTIES > DIRTY

DIRTIEST > DIRTY

DIRTILY > DIRTY

DIRTINESS > DIRTY

DIRTING > DIRT

DIRTS > DIRT

DIRTY adj covered or marked with dirt ▷ vb make dirty

DIRTYING > DIRTY

DIS same as > DISS

DISA n type of orchid

DISABLE vb make ineffective, unfit, or incapable

DISABLED adj lacking a physical power, such as the ability to walk

DISABLER > DISABLE

DISABLERS > DISABLE

DISABLES > DISABLE

DISABLING > DISABLE

DISABLISM n discrimination against disabled people

DISABLIST > DISABLISM

DISABUSAL > DISABUSE

DISABUSE vb rid (someone) of a mistaken idea

DISABUSED > DISABUSE

DISABUSES > DISABUSE

DISACCORD n lack of agreement or harmony ▷ vb be out of agreement

DISADORN vb deprive of ornamentation

DISADORNS > DISADORN

DISAFFECT vb cause to lose loyalty or affection

DISAFFIRM vb deny or contradict (a statement)

DISAGREE vb argue or have different opinions

DISAGREED > DISAGREE

DISAGREES > DISAGREE

DISALLIED > DISALLY

DISALLIES > DISALLY

DISALLOW vb reject as untrue or invalid

DISALLOWS > DISALLOW

DISALLY vb separate

DISANCHOR vb raise anchor of

DISANNEX vb disunite

DISANNUL vb cancel

DISANNULS > DISANNUL

DISANOINT vb invalidate anointment of

DISAPPEAR vb cease to be visible

DISAPPLY vb make (law) invalid

DISARM vb deprive of weapons

DISARMED > DISARM

DISARMER > DISARM

DISARMERS > DISARM

DISARMING adj removing hostility or suspicion

DISARMS > DISARM

DISARRAY n confusion and lack of discipline ▷ vb throw into confusion

DISARRAYS > DISARRAY

DISAS > DISA

DISASTER n occurrence that causes great distress or destruction

DISASTERS > DISASTER

DISATTIRE vb remove clothes from

DISATTUNE vb render out of tune

DISAVOUCH archaic form of > DISAVOW

DISAVOW vb deny connection with or responsibility for

DISAVOWAL > DISAVOW

DISAVOWED > DISAVOW

DISAVOWER > DISAVOW

DISAVOWS > DISAVOW

DISBAND vb (cause to) cease to function as a group

DISBANDED > DISBAND

DISBANDS > DISBAND

DISBAR vb deprive (a barrister) of the right to practise

DISBARK same as > DISEMBARK

DISBARKED > DISBARK

DISBARKS > DISBARK

DISBARRED > DISBAR

DISBARS > DISBAR

DISBELIEF n refusal or reluctance to believe

DISBENCH vb remove from bench

DISBODIED adj disembodied

DISBOSOM vb disclose

DISBOSOMS > DISBOSOM

DISBOUND adj unbound

DISBOWEL vb disembowel

DISBOWELS > DISBOWEL

DISBRANCH vb remove or cut a branch or branches from (a tree)

DISBUD vb remove superfluous buds, flowers, or shoots from (a plant, esp a fruit tree)

DISBUDDED > DISBUD

DISBUDS > DISBUD

DISBURDEN vb remove a load from (a person or animal)

DISBURSAL > DISBURSE

DISBURSE vb pay out

DISBURSED > DISBURSE

DISBURSER > DISBURSE

DISBURSES > DISBURSE

DISC n flat circular object ▷ vb work (land) with a disc harrow

DISCAGE vb release from cage

DISCAGED > DISCAGE

DISCAGES > DISCAGE

DISCAGING > DISCAGE

DISCAL adj relating to or resembling a disc

DISCALCED adj barefooted: used to denote friars and nuns who wear sandals

DISCANDIE same as > DISCANDY

DISCANDY vb melt; dissolve

DISCANT same as > DESCANT

DISCANTED > DISCANT

DISCANTER > DISCANT

DISCANTS > DISCANT

DISCARD vb get rid of (something or someone) as useless or undesirable ▷ n person or thing that has been cast aside

DISCARDED > DISCARD

DISCARDER > DISCARD

DISCARDS > DISCARD

DISCASE vb remove case from

DISCASED > DISCASE

DISCASES > DISCASE

DISCASING > DISCASE

DISCED > DISC

DISCEPT vb discuss

DISCEPTED > DISCEPT

DISCEPTS > DISCEPT

DISCERN vb see or be aware of (something) clearly

DISCERNED > DISCERN

DISCERNER > DISCERN

DISCERNS > DISCERN

DISCERP vb divide

DISCERPED > DISCERP

DISCERPS > DISCERP

DISCHARGE vb release, allow to go ▷ n substance that comes out from a place

DISCHURCH vb deprive of church membership

DISCI > DISCUS

DISCIDE vb split

DISCIDED > DISCIDE

DISCIDES > DISCIDE

DISCIDING > DISCIDE

DISCIFORM adj disc-shaped

DISCINCT adj loosely dressed, without belt

DISCING > DISC

DISCIPLE vb teach ▷ n follower of the doctrines of a teacher, esp Jesus Christ

DISCIPLED > DISCIPLE

DISCIPLES > DISCIPLE

DISCLAIM vb deny (responsibility for or knowledge of something)

DISCLAIMS > DISCLAIM

DISCLIKE > DISC

DISCLIMAX n climax community resulting from the activities of man or domestic animals in climatic and other conditions that would

d

otherwise support a different type of community

DISCLOSE vb make known

DISCLOSED > DISCLOSE

DISCLOSER > DISCLOSE

DISCLOSES > DISCLOSE

DISCLOST > DISCLOSE

DISCO vb go to a disco ▷ n nightclub where people dance to amplified pop records

DISCOBOLI npl discus throwers

DISCOED > DISCO

DISCOER > DISCO

DISCOERS > DISCO

DISCOID adj like a disc ▷ n disclike object

DISCOIDAL adj like a disc

DISCOIDS > DISCOID

DISCOING > DISCO

DISCOLOGY n study of gramophone records

DISCOLOR same as > DISCOLOUR

DISCOLORS > DISCOLOR

DISCOLOUR vb change in colour, fade

DISCOMFIT vb make uneasy or confused

DISCOMMON vb deprive (land) of the character and status of common, as by enclosure

DISCORD n lack of agreement or harmony between people ▷ vb disagree

DISCORDED > DISCORD

DISCORDS > DISCORD

DISCOS > DISCO

DISCOUNT vb take no account of (something) because it is considered to be unreliable, prejudiced, or irrelevant ▷ n deduction from the full price of something

DISCOUNTS > DISCOUNT

DISCOURE vb discover

DISCOURED > DISCOURE

DISCOURES > DISCOURE

DISCOURSE n conversation ▷ vb speak or write (about) at length

DISCOVER vb be the first to find or to find out about

DISCOVERS > DISCOVER

DISCOVERT adj (of a woman) not under the protection of a husband

DISCOVERY n discovering

DISCREDIT vb damage the reputation of ▷ n damage to someone's reputation

DISCREET adj careful to avoid embarrassment, esp by keeping confidences secret

DISCRETE adj separate, distinct

DISCRETER > DISCRETE

DISCROWN vb deprive of a

crown

DISCROWNS > DISCROWN

DISCS > DISC

DISCUMBER vb disencumber

DISCURE old form of > DISCOVER

DISCURED > DISCURE

DISCURES > DISCURE

DISCURING > DISCURE

DISCURSUS n discursive reasoning

DISCUS n heavy disc-shaped object thrown in sports competitions

DISCUSES > DISCUS

DISCUSS vb consider (something) by talking it over

DISCUSSED > DISCUSS

DISCUSSER > DISCUSS

DISCUSSES > DISCUSS

DISDAIN n feeling of superiority and dislike ▷ vb refuse with disdain

DISDAINED > DISDAIN

DISDAINS > DISDAIN

DISEASE vb make uneasy ▷ n illness, sickness

DISEASED adj having or affected with disease

DISEASES > DISEASE

DISEASING > DISEASE

DISEDGE vb render blunt

DISEDGED > DISEDGE

DISEDGES > DISEDGE

DISEDGING > DISEDGE

DISEMBARK vb get off a ship, aircraft, or bus

DISEMBODY vb free from the body or from physical form

DISEMPLOY vb dismiss from employment

DISENABLE vb cause to become incapable

DISENDOW vb take away an endowment from

DISENDOWS > DISENDOW

DISENGAGE vb release from a connection

DISENROL vb remove from register

DISENROLS > DISENROL

DISENTAIL vb free (an estate) from entail ▷ n act of disentailing

DISENTOMB vb disinter

DISESTEEM vb think little of ▷ n lack of esteem

DISEUR same as > DISEUSE

DISEURS > DISEUR

DISEUSE n (esp formerly) an actress who presents dramatic recitals, usually sung accompanied by music

DISEUSES > DISEUSE

DISFAME n discredit

DISFAMES > DISFAME

DISFAVOR same as > DISFAVOUR

DISFAVORS > DISFAVOR

DISFAVOUR n disapproval or dislike ▷ vb regard or treat with disapproval or dislike

DISFIGURE vb spoil the appearance of

DISFLESH vb reduce flesh of

DISFLUENT adj lacking fluency in speech

DISFOREST same as > DEFOREST

DISFORM vb change form of

DISFORMED > DISFORM

DISFORMS > DISFORM

DISFROCK another word for > UNFROCK

DISFROCKS > DISFROCK

DISGAVEL vb deprive of quality of gavelkind

DISGAVELS > DISGAVEL

DISGEST vb digest

DISGESTED > DISGEST

DISGESTS > DISGEST

DISGODDED adj deprived of religion

DISGORGE vb empty out, discharge

DISGORGED > DISGORGE

DISGORGER n thin notched metal implement for removing hooks from a fish

DISGORGES > DISGORGE

DISGOWN vb remove gown from

DISGOWNED > DISGOWN

DISGOWNS > DISGOWN

DISGRACE n condition of shame, loss of reputation, or dishonour ▷ vb bring shame upon (oneself or others)

DISGRACED > DISGRACE

DISGRACER > DISGRACE

DISGRACES > DISGRACE

DISGRADE vb degrade

DISGRADED > DISGRADE

DISGRADES > DISGRADE

DISGUISE vb change the appearance or manner in order to conceal the identity of (someone or something) ▷ n mask, costume, or manner that disguises

DISGUISED > DISGUISE

DISGUISER > DISGUISE

DISGUISES > DISGUISE

DISGUST n great loathing or distaste ▷ vb sicken, fill with loathing

DISGUSTED > DISGUST

DISGUSTS > DISGUST

DISH n shallow container used for holding or serving food ▷ vb put into a dish

DISHABIT vb dislodge

DISHABITS > DISHABIT

DISHABLE obsolete form of > DISABLE

DISHABLED > DISHABLE

DISHABLES > DISHABLE

DISHALLOW vb make

unholy

DISHCLOTH n cloth for washing dishes

DISHCLOUT same as > DISHCLOTH

DISHDASH same as > DISHDASHA

DISHDASHA n long-sleeved collarless white garment worn by some Muslim men

DISHED adj shaped like a dish

DISHELM vb remove helmet from

DISHELMED > DISHELM

DISHELMS > DISHELM

DISHERIT vb disinherit

DISHERITS > DISHERIT

DISHES > DISH

DISHEVEL vb disarrange (the hair or clothes) of (someone)

DISHEVELS > DISHEVEL

DISHFUL n the amount that a dish is able to hold

DISHFULS > DISHFUL

DISHIER > DISHY

DISHIEST > DISHY

DISHING > DISH

DISHINGS > DISH

DISHLIKE > DISH

DISHOME vb deprive of home

DISHOMED > DISHOME

DISHOMES > DISHOME

DISHOMING > DISHOME

DISHONEST adj not honest or fair

DISHONOR same as > DISHONOUR

DISHONORS > DISHONOR

DISHONOUR vb treat with disrespect ▷ n lack of respect

DISHORN vb remove horns from

DISHORNED > DISHORN

DISHORNS > DISHORN

DISHORSE vb dismount

DISHORSED > DISHORSE

DISHORSES > DISHORSE

DISHOUSE vb deprive of home

DISHOUSED > DISHOUSE

DISHOUSES > DISHOUSE

DISHPAN n large pan for washing dishes, pots, etc

DISHPANS > DISHPAN

DISHRAG n dishcloth

DISHRAGS > DISHRAG

DISHTOWEL n towel for drying dishes and kitchen utensils

DISHUMOUR vb upset; offend

DISHWARE n tableware

DISHWARES > DISHWARE

DISHWATER n water in which dishes and kitchen utensils are or have been washed

DISHY adj good-looking

DISILLUDE vb remove

illusions from

DISIMMURE vb release

DISINFECT vb rid of harmful germs, chemically

DISINFEST vb rid of vermin

DISINFORM vb give wrong information

DISINHUME vb dig up

DISINTER vb dig up

DISINTERS > DISINTER

DISINURE vb render unaccustomed

DISINURED > DISINURE

DISINURES > DISINURE

DISINVENT vb undo the invention or existence of

DISINVEST vb remove investment (from)

DISINVITE vb retract invitation to

DISJASKIT adj fatigued

DISJECT vb break apart

DISJECTED > DISJECT

DISJECTS > DISJECT

DISJOIN vb disconnect or become disconnected

DISJOINED > DISJOIN

DISJOINS > DISJOIN

DISJOINT vb take apart or come apart at the joints ▷ adj (of two sets) having no members in common

DISJOINTS > DISJOINT

DISJUNCT adj not united or joined ▷ n one of the propositions or formulas in a disjunction

DISJUNCTS > DISJUNCT

DISJUNE n breakfast

DISJUNES > DISJUNE

DISK same as > DISC

DISKED > DISK

DISKETTE n floppy disk

DISKETTES > DISKETTE

DISKING > DISK

DISKLESS > DISK

DISKLIKE > DISK

DISKS > DISK

DISLEAF vb remove leaf or leaves from

DISLEAFED > DISLEAF

DISLEAFS > DISLEAF

DISLEAL archaic form of > DISLOYAL

DISLEAVE variant of > DISLEAF

DISLEAVED > DISLEAVE

DISLEAVES > DISLEAVE

DISLIKE vb consider unpleasant or disagreeable ▷ n feeling of not liking something or someone

DISLIKED > DISLIKE

DISLIKEN vb render dissimilar to

DISLIKENS > DISLIKEN

DISLIKER > DISLIKE

DISLIKERS > DISLIKE

DISLIKES > DISLIKE

DISLIKING > DISLIKE

DISLIMB vb remove limbs from

DISLIMBED > DISLIMB

DISLIMBS > DISLIMB

DISLIMN vb efface

DISLIMNED > DISLIMN

DISLIMNS > DISLIMN

DISLINK vb disunite

DISLINKED > DISLINK

DISLINKS > DISLINK

DISLOAD vb unload

DISLOADED > DISLOAD

DISLOADS > DISLOAD

DISLOCATE vb displace (a bone or joint) from its normal position

DISLODGE vb remove (something) from a previously fixed position

DISLODGED > DISLODGE

DISLODGES > DISLODGE

DISLOIGN vb put at a distance

DISLOIGNS > DISLOIGN

DISLOYAL adj not loyal, deserting one's allegiance

DISLUSTRE vb remove lustre from

DISMAL adj gloomy and depressing

DISMALER > DISMAL

DISMALEST > DISMAL

DISMALITY > DISMAL

DISMALLER > DISMAL

DISMALLY > DISMAL

DISMALS npl gloomy state of mind

DISMAN vb remove men from

DISMANNED > DISMAN

DISMANS > DISMAN

DISMANTLE vb take apart piece by piece

DISMASK vb remove mask from

DISMASKED > DISMASK

DISMASKS > DISMASK

DISMAST vb break off the mast or masts of (a sailing vessel)

DISMASTED > DISMAST

DISMASTS > DISMAST

DISMAY vb fill with alarm or depression ▷ n alarm mixed with sadness

DISMAYD > DISMAY

DISMAYED > DISMAY

DISMAYFUL > DISMAY

DISMAYING > DISMAY

DISMAYL vb remove a coat of mail from

DISMAYLED > DISMAYL

DISMAYLS > DISMAYL

DISMAYS > DISMAY

DISME old form of > DIME

DISMEMBER vb remove the limbs of

DISMES > DISME

DISMISS vb remove (an employee) from a job ▷ sentence substitute order to end an activity or give permission to disperse

DISMISSAL n official notice of discharge from employment or service

DISMISSED > DISMISS

DISMISSES > DISMISS

DISMODED adj no longer fashionable

DISMOUNT vb get off a horse or bicycle ▷ n act of dismounting

DISMOUNTS > DISMOUNT

DISNEST vb remove from nest

DISNESTED > DISNEST

DISNESTS > DISNEST

DISOBEY vb neglect or refuse to obey

DISOBEYED > DISOBEY

DISOBEYER > DISOBEY

DISOBEYS > DISOBEY

DISOBLIGE vb disregard the desires of

DISODIUM n compound containing two sodium atoms

DISOMIC adj having an extra chromosome in the haploid state that is homologous to an existing chromosome in this set

DISOMIES > DISOMIC

DISOMY > DISOMIC

DISORBED adj thrown out of orbit

DISORDER n state of untidiness and disorganization ▷ vb upset the order of

DISORDERS > DISORDER

DISORIENT vb cause (someone) to lose their bearings

DISOWN vb deny any connection with (someone)

DISOWNED > DISOWN

DISOWNER > DISOWN

DISOWNERS > DISOWN

DISOWNING > DISOWN

DISOWNS > DISOWN

DISPACE vb move or travel about

DISPACED > DISPACE

DISPACES > DISPACE

DISPACING > DISPACE

DISPARAGE vb speak contemptuously of

DISPARATE adj completely different ▷ n unlike things or people

DISPARITY n inequality or difference

DISPARK vb release

DISPARKED > DISPARK

DISPARKS > DISPARK

DISPART vb separate

DISPARTED > DISPART

DISPARTS > DISPART

DISPATCH vb send off to a destination or to perform a task ▷ n official communication or report, sent in haste

DISPATHY obsolete spelling of > DYSPATHY

DISPAUPER vb state that someone is no longer a pauper

DISPEACE n absence of

peace

DISPEACES > DISPEACE

DISPEL vb destroy or remove

DISPELLED > DISPEL

DISPELLER > DISPEL

DISPELS > DISPEL

DISPENCE same as > DISPENSE

DISPENCED > DISPENCE

DISPENCES > DISPENCE

DISPEND vb spend

DISPENDED > DISPEND

DISPENDS > DISPEND

DISPENSE vb distribute in portions

DISPENSED > DISPENSE

DISPENSER n device, such as a vending machine, that automatically dispenses a single item or a measured quantity

DISPENSES > DISPENSE

DISPEOPLE vb remove inhabitants from

DISPERSAL n act of dispersing or the condition of being dispersed

DISPERSE vb scatter over a wide area ▷ adj or of consisting of the particles in a colloid or suspension

DISPERSED > DISPERSE

DISPERSER > DISPERSE

DISPERSES > DISPERSE

DISPIRIT vb make downhearted

DISPIRITS > DISPIRIT

DISPLACE vb move from the usual location

DISPLACED > DISPLACE

DISPLACER > DISPLACE

DISPLACES > DISPLACE

DISPLANT vb displace

DISPLANTS > DISPLANT

DISPLAY vb make visible or noticeable ▷ n displaying

DISPLAYED > DISPLAY

DISPLAYER > DISPLAY

DISPLAYS > DISPLAY

DISPLE vb punish

DISPLEASE vb annoy or upset

DISPLED > DISPLE

DISPLES > DISPLE

DISPLING > DISPLE

DISPLODE obsolete word for > EXPLODE

DISPLODED > DISPLODE

DISPLODES > DISPLODE

DISPLUME vb remove feathers from

DISPLUMED > DISPLUME

DISPLUMES > DISPLUME

DISPONDEE n (poetry) double foot of two long syllables

DISPONE vb transfer ownership

DISPONED > DISPONE

DISPONEE vb person whom something is disponed to

DISPONEES > DISPONEE
DISPONER > DISPONE
DISPONERS > DISPONE
DISPONES > DISPONE
DISPONGE *same as* > DISPUNGE
DISPONGED > DISPONGE
DISPONGES > DISPONGE
DISPONING > DISPONE
DISPORT *vb* indulge (oneself) in pleasure ▷ *n* amusement
DISPORTED > DISPORT
DISPORTS > DISPORT
DISPOSAL *n* getting rid of something
DISPOSALS > DISPOSAL
DISPOSE *vb* place in a certain order
DISPOSED *adj* willing or eager
DISPOSER > DISPOSE
DISPOSERS > DISPOSE
DISPOSES > DISPOSE
DISPOSING > DISPOSE
DISPOST *vb* remove from post
DISPOSTED > DISPOST
DISPOSTS > DISPOST
DISPOSURE *a rare word for* > DISPOSAL
DISPRAD *old form of* > DISPREAD
DISPRAISE *vb* express disapproval or condemnation of ▷ *n* disapproval, etc, expressed
DISPREAD *vb* spread out
DISPREADS > DISPREAD
DISPRED *old spelling of* > DISPREAD
DISPREDS > DISPRED
DISPRISON *vb* release from captivity
DISPRIZE *vb* scorn
DISPRIZED > DISPRIZE
DISPRIZES > DISPRIZE
DISPROFIT *n* loss
DISPROOF *n* facts that disprove something
DISPROOFS > DISPROOF
DISPROOVE *vb* disapprove of
DISPROVED > DISPROVE
DISPROVEN > DISPROVE
DISPROVER > DISPROVE
DISPROVES > DISPROVE
DISPUNGE *vb* expunge
DISPUNGED > DISPUNGE
DISPUNGES > DISPUNGE
DISPURSE *another word for* > DISBURSE
DISPURSED > DISPURSE
DISPURSES > DISPURSE
DISPURVEY *vb* strip of equipment, provisions, etc
DISPUTANT *n* person who argues ▷ *adj* engaged in argument
DISPUTE *n* disagreement,

argument ▷ *vb* argue about (something)
DISPUTED > DISPUTE
DISPUTER > DISPUTE
DISPUTERS > DISPUTE
DISPUTES > DISPUTE
DISPUTING > DISPUTE
DISQUIET *n* feeling of anxiety ▷ *vb* make (someone) anxious ▷ *adj* uneasy or anxious
DISQUIETS > DISQUIET
DISRANK *vb* demote
DISRANKED > DISRANK
DISRANKS > DISRANK
DISRATE *vb* punish (an officer) by lowering in rank
DISRATED > DISRATE
DISRATES > DISRATE
DISRATING > DISRATE
DISREGARD *vb* give little or no attention to ▷ *n* lack of attention or respect
DISRELISH *vb* have a feeling of aversion for ▷ *n* such a feeling
DISREPAIR *n* condition of being worn out or in poor working order
DISREPUTE *n* loss or lack of good reputation
DISROBE *vb* undress
DISROBED > DISROBE
DISROBER > DISROBE
DISROBERS > DISROBE
DISROBES > DISROBE
DISROBING > DISROBE
DISROOT *vb* uproot
DISROOTED > DISROOT
DISROOTS > DISROOT
DISRUPT *vb* interrupt the progress of
DISRUPTED > DISRUPT
DISRUPTER > DISRUPT
DISRUPTOR > DISRUPT
DISRUPTS > DISRUPT
DISS *vb* treat (a person) with contempt
DISSAVE *vb* spend savings
DISSAVED > DISSAVE
DISSAVES > DISSAVE
DISSAVING > DISSAVE
DISSEAT *vb* unseat
DISSEATED > DISSEAT
DISSEATS > DISSEAT
DISSECT *vb* cut open (a corpse) to examine it
DISSECTED *adj* in the form of narrow lobes or segments
DISSECTOR > DISSECT
DISSECTS > DISSECT
DISSED > DISS
DISSEISE *vb* deprive of seisin
DISSEISED > DISSEISE
DISSEISEE *n* person who is disseised
DISSEISES > DISSEISE
DISSEISIN *n* act of disseising or state of being disseised
DISSEISOR > DISSEISE
DISSEIZE *same as*

> DISSEISE
DISSEIZED > DISSEIZE
DISSEIZEE *n* person who is disseized
DISSEIZES > DISSEIZE
DISSEIZIN *same as* > DISSEISIN
DISSEIZOR > DISSEIZE
DISSEMBLE *vb* conceal one's real motives or emotions by pretence
DISSEMBLY *n* dismantling
DISSENSUS *n* disagreement within group
DISSENT *vb* disagree ▷ *n* disagreement
DISSENTED > DISSENT
DISSENTER > DISSENT
DISSENTS > DISSENT
DISSERT *n* give or make a dissertation; dissertate
DISSERTED > DISSERT
DISSERTS > DISSERT
DISSERVE *vb* do a disservice to
DISSERVED > DISSERVE
DISSERVES > DISSERVE
DISSES > DISS
DISSEVER *vb* break off or become broken off
DISSEVERS > DISSEVER
DISSHIVER *vb* break in pieces
DISSIDENT *n* person who disagrees with and criticizes the government ▷ *adj* disagreeing with the government
DISSIGHT *n* eyesore
DISSIGHTS > DISSIGHT
DISSIMILE *n* comparison using contrast
DISSING > DISS
DISSIPATE *vb* waste or squander
DISSOCIAL *adj* incongruous or irreconcilable
DISSOLUTE *adj* leading an immoral life
DISSOLVE *vb* (cause to) become liquid ▷ *n* scene filmed or televised by dissolving
DISSOLVED > DISSOLVE
DISSOLVER > DISSOLVE
DISSOLVES > DISSOLVE
DISSONANT *adj* discordant
DISSUADE *vb* deter (someone) by persuasion from doing something
DISSUADED > DISSUADE
DISSUADER > DISSUADE
DISSUADES > DISSUADE
DISSUNDER *vb* separate
DISTAFF *n* rod on which wool etc is wound for spinning
DISTAFFS > DISTAFF
DISTAIN *vb* stain; tarnish
DISTAINED > DISTAIN
DISTAINS > DISTAIN
DISTAL *adj* (of a muscle, bone, limb, etc) situated

farthest from the centre, median line, or point of attachment or origin
DISTALLY > DISTAL
DISTANCE *n* space between two points
DISTANCED > DISTANCE
DISTANCES > DISTANCE
DISTANT *adj* far apart
DISTANTLY > DISTANT
DISTASTE *n* dislike, disgust
DISTASTED > DISTASTE
DISTASTES > DISTASTE
DISTAVES > DISTAFF
DISTEMPER *n* highly contagious viral disease of dogs ▷ *vb* paint with distemper
DISTEND *vb* (of part of the body) swell
DISTENDED > DISTEND
DISTENDER > DISTEND
DISTENDS > DISTEND
DISTENT *adj* bloated; swollen
DISTHENE *n* bluish-green mineral
DISTHENES > DISTHENE
DISTHRONE *vb* remove from throne
DISTICH *n* unit of two verse lines
DISTICHAL > DISTICH
DISTICHS > DISTICH
DISTIL *vb* subject to or obtain by distillation
DISTILL *same as* > DISTIL
DISTILLED > DISTIL
DISTILLER *n* person or company that makes strong alcoholic drink, esp whisky
DISTILLS > DISTILL
DISTILS > DISTIL
DISTINCT *adj* not the same
DISTINGUE *adj* distinguished or noble
DISTOME *n* parasitic flatworm
DISTOMES > DISTOME
DISTORT *vb* misrepresent (the truth or facts)
DISTORTED > DISTORT
DISTORTER > DISTORT
DISTORTS > DISTORT
DISTRACT *vb* draw the attention of (a person) away from something
DISTRACTS > DISTRACT
DISTRAIL *n* trail made by aircraft flying through cloud
DISTRAILS > DISTRAIL
DISTRAIN *vb* seize (personal property) to enforce payment of a debt
DISTRAINS > DISTRAIN
DISTRAINT *n* act or process of distraining
DISTRAIT *adj* absent-minded or preoccupied

DISTRAITE *feminine form of* > DISTRAIT

DISTRESS *n* extreme unhappiness ▷ *vb* upset badly

DISTRICT *n* area of land regarded as an administrative or geographical unit ▷ *vb* divide into districts

DISTRICTS > DISTRICT

DISTRIX *n* splitting of the ends of hairs

DISTRIXES > DISTRIX

DISTRUST *vb* regard as untrustworthy ▷ *n* feeling of suspicion or doubt

DISTRUSTS > DISTRUST

DISTUNE *vb* cause to be out of tune

DISTUNED > DISTUNE

DISTUNES > DISTUNE

DISTUNING > DISTUNE

DISTURB *vb* intrude on

DISTURBED *adj* emotionally upset or maladjusted

DISTURBER > DISTURB

DISTURBS > DISTURB

DISTYLE *n* temple with two columns

DISTYLES > DISTYLE

DISULFATE *n* chemical compound containing two sulfate ions

DISULFID *same as* > DISULFIDE

DISULFIDE *n* compound of a base with two atoms of sulfur

DISULFIDS > DISULFID

DISUNION > DISUNITE

DISUNIONS > DISUNITE

DISUNITE *vb* cause disagreement among

DISUNITED > DISUNITE

DISUNITER > DISUNITE

DISUNITES > DISUNITE

DISUNITY *n* dissension or disagreement

DISUSAGE *n* disuse

DISUSAGES > DISUSAGE

DISUSE *vb* stop using ▷ *n* state of being no longer used

DISUSED *adj* no longer used

DISUSES > DISUSE

DISUSING > DISUSE

DISVALUE *vb* belittle

DISVALUED > DISVALUE

DISVALUES > DISVALUE

DISVOUCH *vb* dissociate oneself from

DISYOKE *vb* unyoke

DISYOKED > DISYOKE

DISYOKES > DISYOKE

DISYOKING > DISYOKE

DIT *vb* stop something happening ▷ *n* short sound used, in combination with the long sound in the spoken representation of Morse and other telegraphic codes

DITA *n* tropical African and Asian shrub with large shiny whorled leaves and medicinal bark

DITAL *n* key for raising pitch of lute string

DITALS > DITAL

DITAS > DITA

DITCH *n* narrow channel dug in the earth for drainage or irrigation ▷ *vb* abandon

DITCHED > DITCH

DITCHER > DITCH

DITCHERS > DITCH

DITCHES > DITCH

DITCHING > DITCH

DITCHLESS > DITCH

DITE *vb* set down in writing

DITED > DITE

DITES > DITE

DITHECAL *adj* having two thecae

DITHECOUS *another word for* > DITHECAL

DITHEISM *n* belief in two equal gods

DITHEISMS > DITHEISM

DITHEIST > DITHEISM

DITHEISTS > DITHEISM

DITHELETE *n* one believing that Christ had two wills

DITHELISM *n* belief that Christ had two wills

DITHER *vb* be uncertain or indecisive ▷ *n* state of indecision or agitation

DITHERED > DITHER

DITHERER > DITHER

DITHERERS > DITHER

DITHERIER > DITHER

DITHERING > DITHER

DITHERS > DITHER

DITHERY > DITHER

DITHIOL *n* chemical compound

DITHIONIC as in *dithionic acid* type of acid

DITHYRAMB *n* (in ancient Greece) a passionate choral hymn in honour of Dionysus

DITING > DITE

DITOKOUS *adj* producing two eggs

DITONE *n* interval of two tones

DITONES > DITONE

DITROCHEE *n* double metrical foot

DITS > DIT

DITSIER > DITSY

DITSIEST > DITSY

DITSINESS > DITSY

DITSY *same as* > DITZY

DITT *same as* > DIT

DITTANDER *n* type of plant of coastal Europe, N Africa, and SW Asia, with clusters of small white flowers

DITTANIES > DITTANY

DITTANY *n* aromatic Cretan plant with pink drooping flowers, formerly credited with great medicinal properties

DITTAY *n* accusation; charge

DITTAYS > DITTAY

DITTED > DIT

DITTIED > DITTY

DITTIES > DITTY

DITTING > DIT

DITTIT > DIT

DITTO *n* same ▷ *adv* in the same way ▷ *sentence substitute* used to avoid repeating or to confirm agreement or to confirm an immediately preceding sentence ▷ *vb* copy

DITTOED > DITTO

DITTOING > DITTO

DITTOLOGY *n* interpretation in two ways

DITTOS > DITTO

DITTS > DITT

DITTY *vb* set to music ▷ *n* short simple poem or song

DITTYING > DITTY

DITZ *n* silly scatterbrained person

DITZES > DITZ

DITZIER > DITZY

DITZIEST > DITZY

DITZINESS > DITZY

DITZY *adj* silly and scatterbrained

DIURESES > DIURESIS

DIURESIS *n* excretion of an unusually large quantity of urine

DIURETIC *n* drug that increases the flow of urine ▷ *adj* acting to increase the flow of urine

DIURETICS > DIURETIC

DIURNAL *adj* happening during the day or daily ▷ *n* service book containing all the canonical hours except matins

DIURNALLY > DIURNAL

DIURNALS > DIURNAL

DIURON *n* type of herbicide

DIURONS > DIURON

DIUTURNAL *adj* long-lasting

DIV *n* stupid or foolish person

DIVA *n* distinguished female singer

DIVAGATE *vb* digress or wander

DIVAGATED > DIVAGATE

DIVAGATES > DIVAGATE

DIVALENCE > DIVALENT

DIVALENCY > DIVALENT

DIVALENT *n* element that can unite with two atoms ▷ *adj* having two valencies or a valency of two

DIVALENTS > DIVALENT

DIVAN *n* low backless bed

DIVANS > DIVAN

DIVAS > DIVA

DIVE *vb* plunge headfirst into water ▷ *n* diving

DIVEBOMB *vb* bomb while making steep dives

DIVEBOMBS > DIVEBOMB

DIVED > DIVE

DIVELLENT *adj* separating

DIVER *n* person who works or explores underwater

DIVERGE *vb* separate and go in different directions

DIVERGED > DIVERGE

DIVERGENT *adj* diverging or causing divergence

DIVERGES > DIVERGE

DIVERGING > DIVERGE

DIVERS *adj* various ▷ *det* various

DIVERSE *vb* turn away ▷ *adj* having variety, assorted

DIVERSED > DIVERSE

DIVERSELY > DIVERSE

DIVERSES > DIVERSE

DIVERSIFY *vb* create different forms of

DIVERSING > DIVERSE

DIVERSION *n* official detour used by traffic when a main route is closed

DIVERSITY *n* quality of being different or varied

DIVERSLY > DIVERS

DIVERT *vb* change the direction of

DIVERTED > DIVERT

DIVERTER > DIVERT

DIVERTERS > DIVERT

DIVERTING > DIVERT

DIVERTIVE > DIVERT

DIVERTS > DIVERT

DIVES > DIVE

DIVEST *vb* strip (of clothes)

DIVESTED > DIVEST

DIVESTING > DIVEST

DIVESTS > DIVEST

DIVESTURE > DIVEST

DIVI *alternative spelling of* > DIVVY

DIVIDABLE > DIVIDE

DIVIDANT *adj* distinct

DIVIDE *vb* separate into parts ▷ *n* division, split

DIVIDED *adj* split

DIVIDEDLY > DIVIDED

DIVIDEND *n* sum of money representing part of the profit made, paid by a company to its shareholders

DIVIDENDS > DIVIDEND

DIVIDER *n* screen used to divide a room into separate areas

DIVIDERS *npl* compasses with two pointed arms, used for measuring or dividing lines

DIVIDES > DIVIDE

DIVIDING > DIVIDE

DIVIDINGS > DIVIDE

DIVIDIVI *n* tropical tree

DIVIDIVIS > DIVIDIVI

DIVIDUAL *adj* divisible

DIVIDUOUS adj divided
DIVIED same as
>DIVVIED
DIVINABLE >DIVINE
DIVINATOR n diviner
DIVINE adj of God or a god
▷ vb discover (something)
by intuition or guessing ▷ n
priest who is learned in
theology
DIVINED >DIVINE
DIVINELY >DIVINE
DIVINER >DIVINE
DIVINERS >DIVINE
DIVINES >DIVINE
DIVINEST >DIVINE
DIVING >DIVE
DIVINGS >DIVE
DIVINIFY vb give divine
status to
DIVINING >DIVINE
DIVINISE same as
>DIVINIZE
DIVINISED >DIVINISE
DIVINISES >DIVINISE
DIVINITY n study of
religion
DIVINIZE vb make divine
DIVINIZED >DIVINIZE
DIVINIZES >DIVINIZE
DIVIS >DIVI
DIVISIBLE adj capable of
being divided
DIVISIBLY
>DIVISIBLE
DIVISIM adv separately
DIVISION n dividing,
sharing out
DIVISIONS >DIVISION
DIVISIVE adj tending to
cause disagreement
DIVISOR n number to be
divided into another
number
DIVISORS >DIVISOR
DIVNA vb do not
DIVO n male diva
DIVORCE n legal ending of
a marriage ▷ vb legally end
one's marriage (to)
DIVORCED >DIVORCE
DIVORCEE n person who is
divorced
DIVORCEES >DIVORCEE
DIVORCER >DIVORCE
DIVORCERS >DIVORCE
DIVORCES >DIVORCE
DIVORCING >DIVORCE
DIVORCIVE >DIVORCE
DIVOS >DIVO
DIVOT n small piece of turf
DIVOTS >DIVOT
DIVS >DIV
DIVULGATE vb make
publicly known
DIVULGE vb make known,
disclose
DIVULGED >DIVULGE
DIVULGER >DIVULGE
DIVULGERS >DIVULGE
DIVULGES >DIVULGE
DIVULGING >DIVULGE
DIVULSE vb tear apart
DIVULSED >DIVULSE

DIVULSES >DIVULSE
DIVULSING >DIVULSE
DIVULSION n tearing or
pulling apart
DIVULSIVE
>DIVULSION
DIVVIED >DIVVY
DIVVIER >DIVVY
DIVVIES >DIVVY
DIVVIEST >DIVVY
DIVVY vb divide and share
▷ adj stupid ▷ n stupid
person
DIVVYING >DIVVY
DIVYING same as
>DIVVYING
DIWAN same as >DEWAN
DIWANS >DIWAN
DIXI interj I have spoken
DIXIE n large metal pot for
cooking, brewing tea, etc
DIXIES >DIXIE
DIXIT n statement
DIXITS >DIXIT
DIXY same as >DIXIE
DIYA n small oil lamp, usu
made from clay
DIYAS >DIYA
DIZAIN n ten-line poem
DIZAINS >DIZAIN
DIZEN archaic word for
>BEDIZEN
DIZENED >DIZEN
DIZENING >DIZEN
DIZENMENT >DIZEN
DIZENS >DIZEN
DIZYGOTIC adj developed
from two separately
fertilized eggs
DIZYGOUS another word for
>DIZYGOTIC
DIZZARD n dunce
DIZZARDS >DIZZARD
DIZZIED >DIZZY
DIZZIER >DIZZY
DIZZIES >DIZZY
DIZZIEST >DIZZY
DIZZILY >DIZZY
DIZZINESS >DIZZY
DIZZY adj having or
causing a whirling
sensation ▷ vb make dizzy
DIZZYING >DIZZY
DJEBEL a variant spelling of
>JEBEL
DJEBELS >DJEBEL
DJELLABA n kind of loose
cloak with a hood, worn by
men esp in North Africa and
the Middle East
DJELLABAH same as
>DJELLABA
DJELLABAS >DJELLABA
DJEMBE n W African drum
played by beating with the
hand
DJEMBES >DJEMBE
DJIBBAH same as
>JUBBAH
DJIBBAHS >DJIBBAH
DJIN same as >JINN
DJINN >DJINNI
DJINNI same as >JINNI
DJINNS >DJIN

DJINNY same as >JINNI
DJINS >DJIN
DO vb perform or complete
(a deed or action) ▷ n party,
celebration
DOAB n alluvial land
between two converging
rivers, esp the area
between the Ganges and
Jumna in N India
DOABLE adj capable of
being done
DOABS >DOAB
DOAT same as >DOTE
DOATED >DOAT
DOATER >DOAT
DOATERS >DOAT
DOATING >DOAT
DOATINGS >DOAT
DOATS >DOAT
DOB as in dob in inform
against or report
DOBBED >DOB
DOBBER n informant or
traitor
DOBBERS >DOBBER
DOBBIE same as >DOBBY
DOBBIES >DOBBY
DOBBIN n name for a
horse, esp a workhorse,
often used in children's
tales, etc
DOBBING >DOB
DOBBINS >DOBBIN
DOBBY n attachment to a
loom, used in weaving
small figures
DOBCHICK same as
>DABCHICK
DOBCHICKS >DOBCHICK
DOBHASH n interpreter
DOBHASHES >DOBHASH
DOBIE n cannabis
DOBIES >DOBIE
DOBLA n medieval Spanish
gold coin, probably worth
20 maravedis
DOBLAS >DOBLA
DOBLON a variant spelling of
>DOUBLOON
DOBLONES >DOBLON
DOBLONS >DOBLON
DOBRA n standard
monetary unit of São Tomé
e Principe, divided into 100
cêntimos
DOBRAS >DOBRA
DOBRO n tradename for a
type of acoustic guitar
having a metal resonator
built into the body
DOBROS >DOBRO
DOBS >DOB
DOBSON n larva of
dobsonfly
DOBSONFLY n large North
American insect
DOBSONS >DOBSON
DOBY same as >DOBIE
DOC same as >DOCTOR
DOCENT n voluntary
worker who acts as a guide
in a museum, art gallery,
etc
DOCENTS >DOCENT

DJINNY same as >JINNI
DJINS >DJIN
DOCETIC adj believer in
docetism: a heresy that the
humanity of Christ was
apparent rather than real
DOCHMIAC >DOCHMIUS
DOCHMII >DOCHMIUS
DOCHMIUS n five-syllable
foot
DOCHT >DOW
DOCIBLE adj easily tamed
DOCILE adj (of a person or
animal) easily controlled
DOCILELY >DOCILE
DOCILER >DOCILE
DOCILEST >DOCILE
DOCILITY >DOCILE
DOCIMASY n close
examination
DOCK n enclosed area of
water where ships are
loaded, unloaded, or
repaired ▷ vb bring or be
brought into dock
DOCKAGE n charge levied
upon a vessel for using a
dock
DOCKAGES >DOCKAGE
DOCKED >DOCK
DOCKEN n something of no
value or importance
DOCKENS >DOCKEN
DOCKER n person employed
to load and unload ships
DOCKERS >DOCKER
DOCKET n label on a
package or other delivery,
stating contents, delivery
instructions, etc ▷ vb fix a
docket to (a package or
other delivery)
DOCKETED >DOCKET
DOCKETING >DOCKET
DOCKETS >DOCKET
DOCKHAND n dock labourer
DOCKHANDS >DOCKHAND
DOCKING >DOCK
DOCKINGS >DOCK
DOCKISE same as
>DOCKIZE
DOCKISED >DOCKISE
DOCKISES >DOCKISE
DOCKISING >DOCKISE
DOCKIZE vb convert into
docks
DOCKIZED >DOCKIZE
DOCKIZES >DOCKIZE
DOCKIZING >DOCKIZE
DOCKLAND n area around
the docks
DOCKLANDS >DOCKLAND
DOCKS >DOCK
DOCKSIDE n area next to
dock
DOCKSIDES >DOCKSIDE
DOCKYARD n place where
ships are built or repaired
DOCKYARDS >DOCKYARD
DOCO n (slang)
documentary
DOCOS >DOCO
DOCQUET same as
>DOCKET
DOCQUETED >DOCQUET
DOCQUETS >DOCQUET

DOCS > DOC
DOCTOR n person licensed to practise medicine ▷ vb alter in order to deceive
DOCTORAL > DOCTOR
DOCTORAND n student working towards doctorate
DOCTORATE n highest academic degree in any field of knowledge
DOCTORED > DOCTOR
DOCTORESS n female doctor
DOCTORIAL > DOCTOR
DOCTORING > DOCTOR
DOCTORLY > DOCTOR
DOCTORS > DOCTOR
DOCTRESS same as > DOCTORESS
DOCTRINAL > DOCTRINE
DOCTRINE n body of teachings of a religious, political, or philosophical group
DOCTRINES > DOCTRINE
DOCUDRAMA n film or television programme based on true events, presented in a dramatized form
DOCUMENT n piece of paper providing an official record of something ▷ vb record or report (something) in detail
DOCUMENTS > DOCUMENT
DOCUSOAP n reality television programme in the style of a documentary
DOCUSOAPS > DOCUSOAP
DOD vb clip
DODDARD adj archaic word for missing branches; rotten
DODDED > DOD
DODDER vb move unsteadily ▷ n type of rootless parasitic plant whose twining stems have suckers for drawing nourishment from the host plant
DODDERED > DODDER
DODDERER > DODDER
DODDERERS > DODDER
DODDERIER > DODDER
DODDERING adj shaky, feeble, or infirm, esp from old age
DODDERS > DODDER
DODDERY > DODDER
DODDIER > DODDY
DODDIES > DODDY
DODDIEST > DODDY
DODDING > DOD
DODDIPOLL same as > DODDYPOLL
DODDLE n something easily accomplished
DODDLES > DODDLE
DODDY n bad mood ▷ adj sulky
DODDYPOLL n dunce
DODECAGON n geometric figure with twelve sides

DODGE vb avoid (a blow, being seen, etc) by moving suddenly ▷ n cunning or deceitful trick
DODGEBALL n game in which the players form a circle and try to hit opponents in the circle with a large ball
DODGED > DODGE
DODGEM n bumper car
DODGEMS > DODGEM
DODGER n person who evades a responsibility or duty
DODGERIES > DODGERY
DODGERS > DODGER
DODGERY n deception
DODGES > DODGE
DODGIER > DODGY
DODGIEST > DODGY
DODGINESS > DODGY
DODGING > DODGE
DODGINGS > DODGE
DODGY adj dangerous, risky
DODKIN n coin of little value
DODKINS > DODKIN
DODMAN n snail
DODMANS > DODMAN
DODO n large flightless extinct bird
DODOES > DODO
DODOISM > DODO
DODOISMS > DODO
DODOS > DODO
DODS > DOD
DOE n female deer, hare, or rabbit
DOEK n square of cloth worn on the head by women
DOEKS > DOEK
DOEN > DO
DOER n active or energetic person
DOERS > DOER
DOES > DO
DOESKIN n skin of a deer, lamb, or sheep
DOESKINS > DOESKIN
DOEST > DO
DOETH > DO
DOF informal South African word for > STUPID
DOFF vb take off or lift (one's hat) in polite greeting
DOFFED > DOFF
DOFFER > DOFF
DOFFERS > DOFF
DOFFING > DOFF
DOFFS > DOFF
DOG n domesticated four-legged mammal of many different breeds ▷ vb follow (someone) closely
DOGARESSA n wife of doge
DOGATE n office of doge
DOGATES > DOGATE
DOGBANE n N American plant with bell-shaped white or pink flowers, thought to be poisonous to dogs

DOGBANES > DOGBANE
DOGBERRY n any of certain plants that have berry-like fruits, such as the European dogwood or the bearberry
DOGBOLT n bolt on cannon
DOGBOLTS > DOGBOLT
DOGCART n light horse-drawn two-wheeled cart
DOGCARTS > DOGCART
DOGDOM n world of dogs
DOGDOMS > DOGDOM
DOGE n (formerly) chief magistrate of Venice or Genoa
DOGEAR vb fold down the corner of (a page) ▷ n folded-down corner of a page
DOGEARED > DOGEAR
DOGEARING > DOGEAR
DOGEARS > DOGEAR
DOGEATE n office of doge
DOGEATES > DOGEATE
DOGEDOM n domain of doge
DOGEDOMS > DOGEDOM
DOGES > DOGE
DOGESHIP > DOGE
DOGESHIPS > DOGE
DOGEY same as > DOGIE
DOGEYS > DOGEY
DOGFACE n WW2 US soldier
DOGFACES > DOGFACE
DOGFIGHT vb fight in confused way ▷ n close-quarters combat between fighter aircraft
DOGFIGHTS > DOGFIGHT
DOGFISH n small shark
DOGFISHES > DOGFISH
DOGFOUGHT > DOGFIGHT
DOGFOX n male fox
DOGFOXES > DOGFOX
DOGGED > DOG
DOGGEDER > DOG
DOGGEDEST > DOG
DOGGEDLY > DOG
DOGGER n Dutch fishing vessel with two masts
DOGGEREL n poorly written poetry, usu. comic
DOGGERELS > DOGGEREL
DOGGERIES > DOGGERY
DOGGERMAN n sailor on dogger
DOGGERMEN > DOGGERMAN
DOGGERS > DOGGER
DOGGERY n surly behaviour
DOGGESS n female dog
DOGGESSES > DOGGESS
DOGGIE same as > DOGGY
DOGGIER > DOGGY
DOGGIES > DOGGY
DOGGIEST > DOGGY
DOGGINESS > DOGGY
DOGGING > DOG
DOGGINGS > DOG
DOGGISH adj of or like a dog
DOGGISHLY > DOGGISH
DOGGO adv in hiding and

keeping quiet
DOGGONE interj exclamation of annoyance, disappointment, etc ▷ vb damn ▷ adj damnedest
DOGGONED > DOGGONE
DOGGONER > DOGGONE
DOGGONES > DOGGONE
DOGGONEST > DOGGONE
DOGGONING > DOGGONE
DOGGREL same as > DOGGEREL
DOGGRELS > DOGGREL
DOGGY n child's word for a dog ▷ adj of or like a dog
DOGHANGED same as > HANGDOG
DOGHOLE n squalid dwelling place
DOGHOLES > DOGHOLE
DOGHOUSE n kennel
DOGHOUSES > DOGHOUSE
DOGIE n motherless calf
DOGIES > DOGY
DOGLEG n sharp bend ▷ vb go off at an angle ▷ adj of or with the shape of a dogleg
DOGLEGGED > DOGLEG
DOGLEGS > DOGLEG
DOGLIKE > DOG
DOGMA n doctrine or system of beliefs proclaimed by authority as true
DOGMAN n person who directs the operation of a crane whilst riding on an object being lifted by it
DOGMAS > DOGMA
DOGMATA > DOGMA
DOGMATIC adj habitually stating one's opinions forcefully or arrogantly
DOGMATICS n study of religious dogmas and doctrines
DOGMATISE same as > DOGMATIZE
DOGMATISM > DOGMATIZE
DOGMATIST n dogmatic person
DOGMATIZE vb say or state (something) in a dogmatic manner
DOGMATORY > DOGMA
DOGMEN > DOGMAN
DOGNAP vb carry off and hold (a dog), usually for ransom
DOGNAPED > DOGNAP
DOGNAPER > DOGNAP
DOGNAPERS > DOGNAP
DOGNAPING > DOGNAP
DOGNAPPED > DOGNAP
DOGNAPPER > DOGNAP
DOGNAPS > DOGNAP
DOGROBBER n army cook
DOGS > DOG
DOGSBODY n person who carries out boring tasks for others ▷ vb act as a dogsbody
DOGSHIP n condition of being a dog
DOGSHIPS > DOGSHIP

d

d

DOGSHORES n pieces of wood to prop up boat
DOGSKIN n leather from dog's skin
DOGSKINS > DOGSKIN
DOGSLED n sleigh drawn by dogs
DOGSLEDS > DOGSLED
DOGSLEEP n feigned sleep
DOGSLEEPS > DOGSLEEP
DOGTEETH > DOGTOOTH
DOGTOOTH n carved ornament in the form of four leaflike projections radiating from a raised centre, used in England in the 13th century
DOGTOWN n community of prairie dogs
DOGTOWNS > DOGTOWN
DOGTROT n gently paced trot
DOGTROTS > DOGTROT
DOGVANE n light windvane consisting of a feather or a piece of cloth or yarn mounted on the side of a vessel
DOGVANES > DOGVANE
DOGWATCH n either of two watches aboard ship, from four to six pm or from six to eight pm
DOGWOOD n type of tree or shrub, esp a European species with clusters of small white flowers and black berries
DOGWOODS > DOGWOOD
DOGY same as > DOGIE
DOH n in tonic sol-fa, first degree of any major scale ▷ interj exclamation of annoyance when something goes wrong
DOHS > DOH
DOHYO n sumo wrestling ring
DOHYOS > DOHYO
DOILED same as > DOILT
DOILIES > DOILY
DOILT adj foolish
DOILTER > DOILT
DOILTEST > DOILT
DOILY n decorative lacy paper mat, laid on a plate
DOING > DO
DOINGS npl deeds or actions
DOIT n former small copper coin of the Netherlands
DOITED adj foolish or childish, as from senility
DOITIT same as > DOITED
DOITKIN same as > DOIT
DOITKINS > DOITKIN
DOITS > DOIT
DOJO n room or hall for the practice of martial arts
DOJOS > DOJO
DOL n unit of pain intensity, as measured by dolorimetry
DOLABRATE adj shaped like a hatchet or axe head

DOLCE n dessert ▷ adv (to be performed) gently and sweetly
DOLCES > DOLCE
DOLCETTO n variety of grape for making wine
DOLCETTOS > DOLCETTO
DOLCI > DOLCE
DOLDRUMS npl depressed state of mind
DOLE n money received from the state while unemployed ▷ vb distribute in small quantities
DOLED > DOLE
DOLEFUL adj dreary, unhappy
DOLEFULLY > DOLEFUL
DOLENT adj sad
DOLENTE adv (to be performed) in a sorrowful manner
DOLERITE n dark basic intrusive igneous rock consisting of plagioclase feldspar and a pyroxene, such as augite
DOLERITES > DOLERITE
DOLERITIC > DOLERITE
DOLES > DOLE
DOLESOME same as > DOLEFUL
DOLIA > DOLIUM
DOLICHOS n tropical vines
DOLICHURI n poetic term
DOLINA same as > DOLINE
DOLINAS > DOLINA
DOLINE n shallow usually funnel-shaped depression of the ground surface formed by solution in limestone regions
DOLINES > DOLINE
DOLING > DOLE
DOLIUM n genus of molluscs
DOLL n small model of a human being, used as a toy ▷ vb as in doll up dress up
DOLLAR n standard monetary unit of many countries
DOLLARED adj flagged with a dollar sign
DOLLARISE same as > DOLLARIZE
DOLLARIZE vb replace a country's currency with US dollar
DOLLARS > DOLLAR
DOLLDOM > DOLL
DOLLDOMS > DOLL
DOLLED > DOLL
DOLLHOOD > DOLL
DOLLHOODS > DOLL
DOLLHOUSE n toy house in which dolls and miniature furniture can be put
DOLLIED > DOLLY
DOLLIER n person who operates a dolly
DOLLIERS > DOLLIER
DOLLIES > DOLLY
DOLLINESS > DOLLY

DOLLING > DOLL
DOLLISH > DOLL
DOLLISHLY > DOLL
DOLLOP n lump (of food) ▷ vb serve out (food)
DOLLOPED > DOLLOP
DOLLOPING > DOLLOP
DOLLOPS > DOLLOP
DOLLS > DOLL
DOLLY adj attractive and unintelligent ▷ n wheeled support on which a camera may be mounted; shaped block of lead used to hammer dents out of sheet metal ▷ vb wheel (a camera) backwards or forwards on a dolly
DOLLYBIRD n pretty and fashionable young woman
DOLLYING > DOLLY
DOLMA n vine leaf stuffed with a filling of meat and rice
DOLMADES > DOLMA
DOLMAN n long Turkish outer robe
DOLMANS > DOLMAN
DOLMAS > DOLMA
DOLMEN n prehistoric monument consisting of a horizontal stone supported by vertical stones
DOLMENIC > DOLMEN
DOLMENS > DOLMEN
DOLOMITE n mineral consisting of calcium magnesium carbonate
DOLOMITES > DOLOMITE
DOLOMITIC > DOLOMITE
DOLOR same as > DOLOUR
DOLORIFIC adj causing pain or sadness
DOLOROSO adv (to be performed) in a sorrowful manner
DOLOROUS adj sad, mournful
DOLORS > DOLOR
DOLOS n knucklebone of a sheep, buck, etc, used esp by diviners
DOLOSSE > DOLOS
DOLOSTONE n rock composed of the mineral dolomite
DOLOUR n grief or sorrow
DOLOURS > DOLOUR
DOLPHIN n sea mammal of the whale family, with a beaklike snout
DOLPHINET n female dolphin
DOLPHINS > DOLPHIN
DOLS > DOL
DOLT n stupid person
DOLTISH > DOLT
DOLTISHLY > DOLT
DOLTS > DOLT
DOM n title given to Benedictine, Carthusian, and Cistercian monks and to certain of the canons regular
DOMAIN n field of

knowledge or activity
DOMAINAL > DOMAIN
DOMAINE n French estate where wine is made
DOMAINES > DOMAINE
DOMAINS > DOMAIN
DOMAL adj of a house
DOMANIAL > DOMAIN
DOMATIA > DOMATIUM
DOMATIUM n plant cavity inhabited by commensal insects or mites or, occasionally, microorganisms
DOME n rounded roof built on a circular base ▷ vb cover with or as if with a dome
DOMED > DOME
DOMELIKE > DOME
DOMES > DOME
DOMESDAY same as > DOOMSDAY
DOMESDAYS > DOMESDAY
DOMESTIC adj of one's own country or a specific country ▷ n person whose job is to do housework in someone else's house
DOMESTICS > DOMESTIC
DOMETT n wool and cotton cloth
DOMETTS > DOMETT
DOMIC adj dome-shaped
DOMICAL > DOME
DOMICALLY > DOME
DOMICIL same as > DOMICILE
DOMICILE n place where one lives ▷ vb establish or be established in a dwelling place
DOMICILED > DOMICILE
DOMICILES > DOMICILE
DOMICILS > DOMICIL
DOMIER > DOMY
DOMIEST > DOMY
DOMINANCE n control
DOMINANCY > DOMINANCE
DOMINANT adj having authority or influence ▷ n dominant allele or character
DOMINANTS > DOMINANT
DOMINATE vb control or govern
DOMINATED > DOMINATE
DOMINATES > DOMINATE
DOMINATOR > DOMINATE
DOMINE n clergyman
DOMINEE n minister of the Dutch Reformed Church
DOMINEER vb act with arrogance or tyranny
DOMINEERS > DOMINEER
DOMINEES > DOMINEE
DOMINES > DOMINE
DOMING > DOME
DOMINICAL adj of, relating to, or emanating from Jesus Christ as Lord
DOMINICK n breed of chicken

DOMINICKS > DOMINICK
DOMINIE n minister or clergyman: also used as a term of address
DOMINIES > DOMINIE
DOMINION same as > DOMINIUM
DOMINIONS same as > DOMINION
DOMINIQUE n type of chicken
DOMINIUM n ownership or right to possession of property, esp realty
DOMINIUMS > DOMINIUM
DOMINO n small rectangular block marked with dots, used in dominoes
DOMINOES n game in which dominoes with matching halves are laid together
DOMINOS > DOMINO
DOMOIC as in domoic acid kind of amino acid
DOMS > DOM
DOMY adj having a dome or domes
DON vb put on (clothing) ▷ n member of the teaching staff at a university or college
DONA n Spanish lady
DONAH n woman
DONAHS > DONAH
DONARIES > DONARY
DONARY n thing given for holy use
DONAS > DONA
DONATARY n recipient
DONATE vb give, esp to a charity or organization
DONATED > DONATE
DONATES > DONATE
DONATING > DONATE
DONATION n donating
DONATIONS > DONATION
DONATISM n doctrine and beliefs relating to a schismatic heretical Christian sect originating in N Africa in 311 AD
DONATISMS > DONATISM
DONATIVE n gift or donation ▷ adj of or like a donation
DONATIVES > DONATIVE
DONATOR > DONATE
DONATORS > DONATE
DONATORY n recipient
DONDER vb beat (someone) up ▷ n wretch
DONDERED > DONDER
DONDERING > DONDER
DONDERS > DONDER
DONE > DO
DONEE n person who receives a gift
DONEES > DONEE
DONENESS n extent to which something is cooked
DONEPEZIL n drug used to treat dementia
DONER as in doner kebab

grilled meat and salad served in pitta bread with chilli sauce
DONG n deep reverberating sound of a large bell ▷ vb (of a bell) to make a deep reverberating sound
DONGA n steep-sided gully created by soil erosion
DONGAS > DONGA
DONGED > DONG
DONGING > DONG
DONGLE n electronic device that accompanies a software item to prevent the unauthorized copying of programs
DONGLES > DONGLE
DONGOLA n leather tanned using a particular method
DONGOLAS > DONGOLA
DONGS > DONG
DONING n act of giving blood
DONINGS > DONING
DONJON n heavily fortified central tower of a castle
DONJONS > DONJON
DONKEY n long-eared member of the horse family
DONKEYS > DONKEY
DONKO n tearoom or cafeteria in a factory, wharf area, etc
DONKOS > DONKO
DONNA n Italian lady
DONNARD same as > DONNERT
DONNART same as > DONNERT
DONNAS > DONNA
DONNAT n lazy person
DONNATS > DONNAT
DONNE same as > DONNEE
DONNED > DON
DONNEE n subject or theme
DONNEES > DONNEE
DONNERD adj stupid
DONNERED same as > DONNERT
DONNERT adj stunned
DONNES > DONNE
DONNICKER n toilet
DONNIES > DONNY
DONNIKER same as > DONNICKER
DONNIKERS > DONNIKER
DONNING > DON
DONNISH adj serious and academic
DONNISHLY > DONNISH
DONNISM n loftiness
DONNISMS > DONNISM
DONNOT n lazy person
DONNOTS > DONNOT
DONNY same as > DANNY
DONOR n person who gives blood or organs for use in the treatment of another person
DONORS > DONOR
DONORSHIP > DONOR
DONS > DON
DONSHIP n state or

condition of being a don
DONSHIPS > DONSHIP
DONSIE adj rather unwell
DONSIER > DONSIE
DONSIEST > DONSIE
DONSY same as > DONSIE
DONUT same as > DOUGHNUT
DONUTS > DONUT
DONUTTED > DONUT
DONUTTING > DONUT
DONZEL n man of high birth
DONZELS > DONZEL
DOO a Scot word for > DOVE
DOOB n cannabis cigarette
DOOBIE same as > DOOB
DOOBIES > DOOBIE
DOOBREY n thingumabob
DOOBREYS > DOOBREY
DOOBRIE same as > DOOBREY
DOOBRIES > DOOBRIE
DOOBS > DOOB
DOOCE vb dismiss (an employee) because of comments they have posted on the Internet
DOOCED as in get dooced be dismissed on account of indiscretions written in a blog or on a website
DOOCES > DOOCE
DOOCING > DOOCE
DOOCOT n dovecote
DOOCOTS > DOOCOT
DOODAD same as > DOODAH
DOODADS > DOODAD
DOODAH n unnamed thing, esp an object the name of which is unknown or uncertain
DOODAHS > DOODAH
DOODIES > DOODY
DOODLE vb scribble or draw aimlessly ▷ n shape or picture drawn aimlessly
DOODLEBUG n diviner's rod
DOODLED > DOODLE
DOODLER > DOODLE
DOODLERS > DOODLE
DOODLES > DOODLE
DOODLING > DOODLE
DOODOO n excrement
DOODOOS > DOODOO
DOODY same as > DOODOO
DOOFER n thingamajig
DOOFERS > DOOFER
DOOFUS n slow-witted or stupid person
DOOFUSES > DOOFUS
DOOHICKEY another name for > DOODAH
DOOK n wooden plug driven into a wall to hold a nail, screw, etc ▷ vb dip or plunge
DOOKED > DOOK
DOOKET n dovecote
DOOKETS > DOOKET
DOOKING > DOOK
DOOKS > DOOK
DOOL n boundary marker
DOOLALLY adj out of one's mind

DOOLAN n Roman Catholic
DOOLANS > DOOLAN
DOOLE same as > DOOL
DOOLEE same as > DOOLIE
DOOLEES > DOOLEE
DOOLES > DOOLE
DOOLIE n enclosed couch on poles for carrying passengers
DOOLIES > DOOLIE
DOOLS > DOOL
DOOLY same as > DOOLIE
DOOM n death or a terrible fate ▷ vb destine or condemn to death or a terrible fate
DOOMED > DOOM
DOOMFUL > DOOM
DOOMFULLY > DOOM
DOOMIER > DOOMY
DOOMIEST > DOOMY
DOOMILY > DOOMY
DOOMING > DOOM
DOOMS > DOOM
DOOMSAYER n pessimist
DOOMSDAY n day on which the Last Judgment will occur
DOOMSDAYS > DOOMSDAY
DOOMSMAN n pessimist
DOOMSMEN > DOOMSMAN
DOOMSTER n person habitually given to predictions of impending disaster or doom
DOOMSTERS > DOOMSTER
DOOMWATCH n surveillance of the environment to warn of and prevent harm to it from human factors such as pollution or overpopulation
DOOMY adj despondent or pessimistic
DOON same as > DOWN
DOONA n large quilt used as a bed cover in place of the top sheet and blankets
DOONAS > DOONA
DOOR n hinged or sliding panel for closing the entrance to a building, room, etc
DOORBELL n device for visitors to announce presence at a door
DOORBELLS > DOORBELL
DOORCASE same as > DOORFRAME
DOORCASES > DOORCASE
DOORFRAME n frame that supports a door
DOORJAMB n vertical post forming one side of a door frame
DOORJAMBS > DOORJAMB
DOORKNOB n knob for opening and closing a door
DOORKNOBS > DOORKNOB
DOORKNOCK n fund-raising campaign for charity conducted by seeking donations from door to door
DOORLESS > DOOR

DOORMAN n man employed to be on duty at the entrance to a large public building

DOORMAT n mat for wiping dirt from shoes before going indoors

DOORMATS > DOORMAT

DOORMEN > DOORMAN

DOORN n thorn

DOORNAIL as in *dead as a doornail* dead beyond any doubt

DOORNAILS > DOORNAIL

DOORNBOOM n S African tree with yellow or white flowers

DOORNS > DOORN

DOORPLATE n name-plate on door

DOORPOST same as > DOORJAMB

DOORPOSTS > DOORPOST

DOORS > DOOR

DOORSILL n horizontal member of wood, stone, etc, forming the bottom of a doorframe

DOORSILLS > DOORSILL

DOORSMAN n doorkeeper

DOORSMEN > DOORSMAN

DOORSTEP n step in front of a door

DOORSTEPS > DOORSTEP

DOORSTONE n stone of threshold

DOORSTOP n heavy object or one fixed to the floor, which prevents a door from closing or from striking a wall

DOORSTOPS > DOORSTOP

DOORWAY n opening into a building or room

DOORWAYS > DOORWAY

DOORWOMAN n female doorman

DOORWOMEN > DOORWOMAN

DOORYARD n yard in front of the front or back door of a house

DOORYARDS > DOORYARD

DOOS > DOO

DOOSRA n in cricket, a delivery, bowled by an off-spinner, that turns the opposite way from an off-break

DOOSRAS > DOOSRA

DOOWOP n style of singing in harmony

DOOWOPS > DOOWOP

DOOZER same as > DOOZY

DOOZERS > DOOZER

DOOZIE same as > DOOZY

DOOZIES > DOOZIE

DOOZY n something excellent

DOP vb curtsy ▷ n tot or small drink, usually alcoholic ▷ vb fail to reach the required standard in (an examination, course, etc)

DOPA n precursor to dopamine

DOPAMINE n chemical found in the brain that acts as a neurotransmitter

DOPAMINES > DOPAMINE

DOPANT n element or compound used to dope a semiconductor

DOPANTS > DOPANT

DOPAS > DOPA

DOPATTA n headscarf

DOPATTAS > DOPATTA

DOPE n illegal drug, usu. cannabis ▷ vb give a drug to, esp in order to improve performance in a race ▷ adj excellent

DOPED > DOPE

DOPEHEAD n habitual drug user

DOPEHEADS > DOPEHEAD

DOPER n person who administers dope

DOPERS > DOPER

DOPES > DOPE

DOPESHEET n document giving information on horse races

DOPESTER n person who makes predictions, esp in sport or politics

DOPESTERS > DOPESTER

DOPEY adj half-asleep, drowsy

DOPEYNESS > DOPEY

DOPIAZA n Indian meat or fish dish cooked in onion sauce

DOPIAZAS > DOPIAZA

DOPIER > DOPY

DOPIEST > DOPY

DOPILY > DOPEY

DOPINESS > DOPEY

DOPING > DOPE

DOPINGS > DOPE

DOPPED > DOP

DOPPER n member of an Afrikaner church that practises a stict Calvinism

DOPPERS > DOPPER

DOPPIE n cartridge case

DOPPIES > DOPPIE

DOPPING > DOP

DOPPINGS > DOP

DOPPIO n double measure, esp of espresso coffee

DOPPIOS > DOPPIO

DOPS > DOP

DOPY same as > DOPEY

DOR n European dung beetle that makes a droning sound when it flies

DORAD n South American river fish

DORADO n large marine percoid fish

DORADOS > DORADO

DORADS > DORAD

DORB same as > DORBA

DORBA n stupid, inept, or clumsy person

DORBAS > DORBA

DORBEETLE same as > DOR

DORBS > DORB

DORBUG n type of beetle

DORBUGS > DORBUG

DORE n walleye fish

DOREE n type of fish

DOREES > DOREE

DORES > DORE

DORHAWK n nightjar

DORHAWKS > DORHAWK

DORIC adj rustic

DORIDOID n shell-less mollusc

DORIDOIDS > DORIDOID

DORIES > DORY

DORIS n woman

DORISE same as > DORIZE

DORISED > DORISE

DORISES > DORISE

DORISING > DORISE

DORIZE vb become Doric

DORIZED > DORIZE

DORIZES > DORIZE

DORIZING > DORIZE

DORK n stupid person

DORKIER > DORK

DORKIEST > DORK

DORKINESS > DORK

DORKISH adj stupid or contemptible

DORKS > DORK

DORKY > DORK

DORLACH n quiver of arrows

DORLACHS > DORLACH

DORM same as > DORMITORY

DORMANCY > DORMANT

DORMANT n supporting beam ▷ adj temporarily quiet, inactive, or not being used

DORMANTS > DORMANT

DORMER n window that sticks out from a sloping roof

DORMERED adj having dormer windows

DORMERS > DORMER

DORMICE > DORMOUSE

DORMIE adj (of a player or side) as many holes ahead of an opponent as there are still to play

DORMIENT adj dormant

DORMIN n hormone found in plants

DORMINS > DORMIN

DORMITION n Mary's assumption to heaven

DORMITIVE adj sleep-inducing

DORMITORY n large room, esp at a school, containing several beds ▷ adj (of a town or suburb) having many inhabitants who travel to work in a nearby city

DORMOUSE n small mouselike rodent with a furry tail

DORMS > DORM

DORMY same as > DORMIE

DORNECK same as > DORNICK

DORNECKS > DORNECK

DORNICK n heavy damask cloth, formerly used for vestments, curtains, etc

DORNICKS > DORNICK

DORNOCK n type of coarse fabric

DORNOCKS > DORNOCK

DORONICUM n Eurasian and N African plant with yellow daisy-like flowers

DORP n small town

DORPER n breed of sheep

DORPERS > DORPER

DORPS > DORP

DORR same as > DOR

DORRED > DOR

DORRING > DOR

DORRS > DORR

DORS > DOR

DORSA > DORSUM

DORSAD adj towards the back or dorsal aspect

DORSAL adj of or on the back ▷ n dorsal fin

DORSALLY > DORSAL

DORSALS > DORSAL

DORSE n type of small fish

DORSEL another word for > DOSSAL

DORSELS > DORSEL

DORSER n hanging tapestry

DORSERS > DORSER

DORSES > DORSE

DORSIFLEX adj bending towards the back

DORSUM n the back

DORT vb sulk

DORTED > DORT

DORTER n dormitory

DORTERS > DORTER

DORTIER > DORTY

DORTIEST > DORTY

DORTINESS > DORTY

DORTING > DORT

DORTOUR same as > DORTER

DORTOURS > DORTOUR

DORTS > DORT

DORTY adj haughty, or sullen

DORY n spiny-finned edible sea fish

DOS > DO

DOSAGE same as > DOSE

DOSAGES > DOSAGE

DOSE n specific quantity of a medicine taken at one time ▷ vb give a dose to

DOSED > DOSE

DOSEH n former Egyptian religious ceremony

DOSEHS > DOSEH

DOSEMETER same as > DOSIMETER

DOSER > DOSE

DOSERS > DOSE

DOSES > DOSE

DOSH n money

DOSHES > DOSH

DOSIMETER n instrument for measuring the dose of X-rays or other radiation absorbed by matter or the intensity of a source of radiation

DOSIMETRY
> DOSIMETER

DOSING > DOSE

DOSIOLOGY n study of doses

DOSOLOGY same as > DOSIOLOGY

DOSS vb sleep, esp in a dosshouse ⊳ n bed, esp in a dosshouse

DOSSAL n ornamental hanging, placed at the back of an altar or at the sides of a chancel

DOSSALS > DOSSAL

DOSSED > DOSS

DOSSEL same as > DOSSAL

DOSSELS > DOSSEL

DOSSER n bag or basket for carrying objects on the back

DOSSERET n stone above column supporting an arch

DOSSERETS > DOSSERET

DOSSERS > DOSSER

DOSSES > DOSS

DOSSHOUSE n cheap lodging house for homeless people

DOSSIER n collection of documents about a subject or person

DOSSIERS > DOSSIER

DOSSIL n lint for dressing wound

DOSSILS > DOSSIL

DOSSING > DOSS

DOST a singular form of the present tense (indicative mood) of > DO

DOT n small round mark ⊳ vb mark with a dot

DOTAGE n weakness as a result of old age

DOTAGES > DOTAGE

DOTAL > DOT

DOTANT another word for > DOTARD

DOTANTS > DOTANT

DOTARD n person who is feeble-minded through old age

DOTARDLY > DOTARD

DOTARDS > DOTARD

DOTATION n act of giving a dowry

DOTATIONS > DOTATION

DOTCOM n company that does most of its business on the Internet

DOTCOMMER n person who carries out business on the internet

DOTCOMS > DOTCOM

DOTE vb love to an excessive or foolish degree

DOTED > DOTE

DOTER > DOTE

DOTERS > DOTE

DOTES > DOTE

DOTH a singular form of the present tense of > DO

DOTIER > DOTY

DOTIEST > DOTY

DOTING > DOTE

DOTINGLY > DOTE

DOTINGS > DOTE

DOTISH adj foolish

DOTS > DOT

DOTTED > DOT

DOTTEL same as > DOTTLE

DOTTELS > DOTTEL

DOTTER > DOT

DOTTEREL n rare kind of plover

DOTTERELS > DOTTEREL

DOTTERS > DOT

DOTTIER > DOTTY

DOTTIEST > DOTTY

DOTTILY > DOTTY

DOTTINESS > DOTTY

DOTTING > DOT

DOTTLE n tobacco left in a pipe after smoking ⊳ adj relating to dottle

DOTTLED adj foolish

DOTTLER > DOTTLE

DOTTLES > DOTTLE

DOTTLEST > DOTTLE

DOTTREL same as > DOTTEREL

DOTTRELS > DOTTREL

DOTTY adj rather eccentric

DOTY adj (of wood) rotten

DOUANE n customs house

DOUANES > DOUANE

DOUANIER n customs officer

DOUANIERS > DOUANIER

DOUAR same as > DUAR

DOUARS > DOUAR

DOUBLE adj as much again in number, amount, size, etc ⊳ adv twice over ⊳ n twice the number, amount, size, etc ⊳ vb make or become twice as much or as many

DOUBLED > DOUBLE

DOUBLER > DOUBLE

DOUBLERS > DOUBLE

DOUBLES n game between two pairs of players

DOUBLET n man's close-fitting jacket, with or without sleeves

DOUBLETON n original holding of two cards only in a suit

DOUBLETS > DOUBLET

DOUBLING > DOUBLE

DOUBLINGS > DOUBLE

DOUBLOON n former Spanish gold coin

DOUBLOONS > DOUBLOON

DOUBLURE n decorative lining of vellum or leather, etc, on the inside of a book cover

DOUBLURES > DOUBLURE

DOUBLY adv in a greater degree, quantity, or measure

DOUBT n uncertainty about the truth, facts, or existence of something ⊳ vb question the truth of

DOUBTABLE > DOUBT

DOUBTABLY > DOUBT

DOUBTED > DOUBT

DOUBTER > DOUBT

DOUBTERS > DOUBT

DOUBTFUL adj unlikely ⊳ n person who is undecided or uncertain about an issue

DOUBTFULS > DOUBTFUL

DOUBTING > DOUBT

DOUBTINGS > DOUBT

DOUBTLESS adv probably or certainly ⊳ adj certain

DOUBTS > DOUBT

DOUC n Old World monkey of SE Asia with a bright yellow face surrounded by reddish-brown fur, a white tail, and white hindquarters

DOUCE adj quiet

DOUCELY > DOUCE

DOUCENESS > DOUCE

DOUCEPERE same as > DOUZEPER

DOUCER > DOUCE

DOUCEST > DOUCE

DOUCET n former flute-like instrument

DOUCETS > DOUCET

DOUCEUR n gratuity, tip, or bribe

DOUCEURS > DOUCEUR

DOUCHE n (instrument for applying) a stream of water directed onto or into the body for cleansing or medical purposes ⊳ vb cleanse or treat by means of a douche

DOUCHEBAG n despicable person

DOUCHED > DOUCHE

DOUCHES > DOUCHE

DOUCHING > DOUCHE

DOUCINE n type of moulding for cornice

DOUCINES > DOUCINE

DOUCS > DOUC

DOUGH n thick mixture of flour and water or milk, used for making bread etc

DOUGHBALL n ball of bread used as bait in carp fishing

DOUGHBOY n infantryman, esp in World War I

DOUGHBOYS > DOUGHBOY

DOUGHFACE n Northern Democrat who sided with the South in the American Civil War

DOUGHIER > DOUGHY

DOUGHIEST > DOUGHY

DOUGHLIKE > DOUGH

DOUGHNUT n small cake of sweetened dough fried in deep fat ⊳ vb (of Members of Parliament) to surround (a speaker) during the televising of Parliament to give the impression that the chamber is crowded or the speaker is well supported

DOUGHNUTS > DOUGHNUT

DOUGHS > DOUGH

DOUGHT > DOW

DOUGHTIER > DOUGHTY

DOUGHTILY > DOUGHTY

DOUGHTY adj brave and determined

DOUGHY adj resembling dough in consistency, colour, etc

DOUK same as > DOOK

DOUKED > DOUK

DOUKING > DOUK

DOUKS > DOUK

DOULA n woman who is trained to provide support to women and their families during pregnancy, childbirth, and the period of time following the birth

DOULAS > DOULA

DOULEIA same as > DULIA

DOULEIAS > DOULEIA

DOUM as in doum palm variety of palm tree

DOUMA same as > DUMA

DOUMAS > DOUMA

DOUMS > DOUM

DOUN same as > DOWN

DOUP n bottom

DOUPIONI n type of fabric

DOUPIONIS > DOUPIONI

DOUPPIONI n type of silk yarn

DOUPS > DOUP

DOUR adj sullen and unfriendly

DOURA same as > DURRA

DOURAH same as > DURRA

DOURAHS > DOURAH

DOURAS > DOURA

DOURER > DOUR

DOUREST > DOUR

DOURINE n infectious venereal disease of horses

DOURINES > DOURINE

DOURLY > DOUR

DOURNESS > DOUR

DOUSE vb drench with water or other liquid ⊳ n immersion

DOUSED > DOUSE

DOUSER > DOUSE

DOUSERS > DOUSE

DOUSES > DOUSE

DOUSING > DOUSE

DOUT vb extinguish

DOUTED > DOUT

DOUTER > DOUT

DOUTERS > DOUT

DOUTING > DOUT

DOUTS > DOUT

DOUX adj sweet

DOUZEPER n distinguished person

DOUZEPERS > DOUZEPER

DOVE vb be semi-conscious ⊳ n bird with a heavy body, small head, and short legs

DOVECOT same as > DOVECOTE

DOVECOTE n structure for housing pigeons

DOVECOTES > DOVECOTE

DOVECOTS > DOVECOT

DOVED > DOVE
DOVEISH *adj* dovelike
DOVEKEY *same as* **> DOVEKIE**
DOVEKEYS > DOVEKEY
DOVEKIE *n* small short-billed auk
DOVEKIES > DOVEKIE
DOVELET *n* small dove
DOVELETS > DOVELET
DOVELIKE > DOVE
DOVEN *vb* pray
DOVENED > DOVEN
DOVENING > DOVEN
DOVENS > DOVEN
DOVER *vb* doze ⊳ *n* doze
DOVERED > DOVER
DOVERING > DOVER
DOVERS > DOVER
DOVES > DOVE
DOVETAIL *n* joint containing wedge-shaped tenons ⊳ *vb* fit together neatly
DOVETAILS > DOVETAIL
DOVIE *Scots word for* **> STUPID**
DOVIER > DOVIE
DOVIEST > DOVIE
DOVING > DOVE
DOVISH > DOVE
DOW *vb* archaic word meaning be of worth
DOWABLE *adj* capable of being endowed
DOWAGER *n* widow possessing property or a title obtained from her husband
DOWAGERS > DOWAGER
DOWAR *same as* **> DUAR**
DOWARS > DOWAR
DOWD *n* woman who wears unfashionable clothes
DOWDIER > DOWDY
DOWDIES > DOWDY
DOWDIEST > DOWDY
DOWDILY > DOWDY
DOWDINESS > DOWDY
DOWDS > DOWD
DOWDY *adj* dull and old-fashioned ⊳ *n* dowdy woman
DOWDYISH > DOWDY
DOWDYISM > DOWD
DOWDYISMS > DOWD
DOWED > DOW
DOWEL *n* wooden or metal peg that fits into two corresponding holes to join two adjacent parts ⊳ *vb* join pieces of wood using dowels
DOWELED > DOWEL
DOWELING *n* joining of two pieces of wood using dowels
DOWELINGS > DOWELING
DOWELLED > DOWEL
DOWELLING *same as* **> DOWELING**
DOWELS > DOWEL
DOWER *n* life interest in a part of her husband's

estate allotted to a widow by law ⊳ *vb* endow
DOWERED > DOWER
DOWERIES > DOWERY
DOWERING > DOWER
DOWERLESS > DOWER
DOWERS > DOWER
DOWERY *same as* **> DOWRY**
DOWF *adj* dull; listless
DOWFNESS > DOWF
DOWIE *adj* dull and dreary
DOWIER > DOWIE
DOWIEST > DOWIE
DOWING > DOW
DOWITCHER *n* type of snipelike shore bird of arctic and subarctic N America
DOWL *n* fluff
DOWLAS *n* coarse fabric
DOWLASES > DOWLAS
DOWLE *same as* **> DOWL**
DOWLES > DOWLE
DOWLIER > DOWLY
DOWLIEST > DOWLY
DOWLNE *obsolete form of* **> DOWN**
DOWLNES > DOWLNE
DOWLNEY > DOWLNE
DOWLS > DOWL
DOWLY *adj* dull
DOWN *adv* indicating movement to or position in a lower place ⊳ *adj* depressed, unhappy ⊳ *vb* drink quickly ⊳ *n* soft fine feathers
DOWNA *obsolete Scots form of* **> CANNOT**
DOWNBEAT *adj* gloomy ⊳ *n* first beat of a bar
DOWNBEATS > DOWNBEAT
DOWNBOW *n* (in music) a downward stroke of the bow across the strings
DOWNBOWS > DOWNBOW
DOWNBURST *n* very high-speed downward movement of turbulent air in a limited area for a short time. Near the ground it spreads out from its centre with high horizontal velocities
DOWNCAST *adj* sad, dejected ⊳ *n* ventilation shaft
DOWNCASTS > DOWNCAST
DOWNCOME *same as* **> DOWNCOMER**
DOWNCOMER *n* pipe that connects a cistern to a WC, wash basin, etc
DOWNCOMES > DOWNCOME
DOWNCOURT *adj* in far end a of court
DOWNDRAFT *n* downward air current
DOWNED > DOWN
DOWNER *n* barbiturate, tranquillizer, or narcotic
DOWNERS > DOWNER
DOWNFALL *same as* **> DEADFALL**
DOWNFALLS > DOWNFALL
DOWNFIELD *adj* at far end

of field
DOWNFLOW *n* something that flows down
DOWNFLOWS > DOWNFLOW
DOWNFORCE *n* force produced by air resistance plus gravity that increases the stability of an aircraft or motor vehicle by pressing it downwards
DOWNGRADE *vb* reduce in importance or value
DOWNHAUL, *n* line for hauling down a sail or for increasing the tension at its luff
DOWNHAULS > DOWNHAUL
DOWNHILL *adj* going or sloping down ⊳ *adv* towards the bottom of a hill ⊳ *n* downward slope
DOWNHILLS > DOWNHILL
DOWNHOLE *adj* (in the oil industry) denoting any piece of equipment that is used in the well itself
DOWNIER > DOWNY
DOWNIEST > DOWNY
DOWNINESS > DOWNY
DOWNING > DOWN
DOWNLAND *same as* **> DOWNS**
DOWNLANDS > DOWNLAND
DOWNLESS > DOWN
DOWNLIGHT *n* lamp shining downwards
DOWNLIKE > DOWN
DOWNLINK *n* satellite transmission channel
DOWNLINKS > DOWNLINK
DOWNLOAD *vb* transfer (data) from the memory of one computer to that of another, especially over the Internet ⊳ *n* file transferred in such a way
DOWNLOADS > DOWNLOAD
DOWNMOST *adj* lowest
DOWNPIPE *n* pipe for carrying rainwater from a roof gutter to the ground or to a drain
DOWNPIPES > DOWNPIPE
DOWNPLAY *vb* play down
DOWNPLAYS > DOWNPLAY
DOWNPOUR *n* heavy fall of rain
DOWNPOURS > DOWNPOUR
DOWNRANGE *adv* in the direction of the intended flight path of a rocket or missile
DOWNRIGHT *adv* extreme(ly) ⊳ *adj* absolute
DOWNRIVER *adv* in direction of current
DOWNRUSH *n* instance of rushing down
DOWNS *npl* low grassy hills, esp in S England
DOWNSCALE *vb* reduce in scale
DOWNSHIFT *vb* reduce work hours
DOWNSIDE *n*

disadvantageous aspect of a situation
DOWNSIDES > DOWNSIDE
DOWNSIZE *vb* reduce the number of people employed by (a company)
DOWNSIZED > DOWNSIZE
DOWNSIZER > DOWNSIZE
DOWNSIZES > DOWNSIZE
DOWNSLIDE *n* downward trend
DOWNSLOPE *adv* towards the bottom of a slope
DOWNSPIN *n* sudden downturn
DOWNSPINS > DOWNSPIN
DOWNSPOUT *same as* **> DOWNPIPE**
DOWNSTAGE *adj* or at the front part of the stage ⊳ *adv* at or towards the front of the stage ⊳ *n* front half of the stage
DOWNSTAIR *adj* situated on lower floor
DOWNSTATE *adj* in, or relating to the part of the state away from large cities, esp the southern part ⊳ *adv* towards the southern part of a state ⊳ *n* southern part of a state
DOWNSWING *n* statistical downward trend in business activity, the death rate, etc
DOWNTHROW *n* state of throwing down or being thrown down
DOWNTICK *n* small decrease
DOWNTICKS > DOWNTICK
DOWNTIME *n* time during which a computer or other machine is not working
DOWNTIMES > DOWNTIME
DOWNTOWN *n* central or lower part of a city, esp the main commercial area ⊳ *adv* towards, to, or into this area ⊳ *adj* of, relating to, or situated in the downtown area
DOWNTOWNS > DOWNTOWN
DOWNTREND *n* downward trend
DOWNTROD *adj* downtrodden
DOWNTURN *n* drop in the success of an economy or a business
DOWNTURNS > DOWNTURN
DOWNWARD *same as* **> DOWNWARDS**
DOWNWARDS *adv* from a higher to a lower level, condition, or position
DOWNWASH *n* downward deflection of an airflow, esp one caused by an aircraft wing
DOWNWIND *adj* in the same direction towards which the wind is blowing
DOWNY *adj* covered with soft fine hair or feathers

DOWNZONE vb reduce density of housing in area
DOWNZONED > DOWNZONE
DOWNZONES > DOWNZONE
DOWP same as > DOUP
DOWPS > DOWP
DOWRIES > DOWRY
DOWRY n property brought by a woman to her husband at marriage
DOWS > DOW
DOWSABEL n sweetheart
DOWSABELS > DOWSABEL
DOWSE same as > DOUSE
DOWSED > DOWSE
DOWSER > DOWSE
DOWSERS > DOWSE
DOWSES > DOWSE
DOWSET same as > DOUCET
DOWSETS > DOWSET
DOWSING > DOWSE
DOWT n cigarette butt
DOWTS > DOWT
DOXAPRAM n drug used to stimulate the respiration
DOXAPRAMS > DOXAPRAM
DOXASTIC adj of or relating to belief
DOXASTICS > DOXASTIC
DOXIE same as > DOXY
DOXIES > DOXY
DOXOLOGY n short hymn of praise to God
DOXY n opinion or doctrine, esp concerning religious matters
DOY n beloved person: used esp as an endearment
DOYEN n senior member of a group, profession, or society
DOYENNE > DOYEN
DOYENNES > DOYEN
DOYENS > DOYEN
DOYLEY same as > DOILY
DOYLEYS > DOYLEY
DOYLIES > DOYLY
DOYLY same as > DOILY
DOYS > DOY
DOZE vb sleep lightly or briefly ▷ n short sleep
DOZED adj (of timber or rubber) rotten or decayed
DOZEN vb stun
DOZENED > DOZEN
DOZENING > DOZEN
DOZENS > DOZEN
DOZENTH > DOZEN
DOZENTHS > DOZEN
DOZER > DOZE
DOZERS > DOZE
DOZES > DOZE
DOZIER > DOZY
DOZIEST > DOZY
DOZILY > DOZY
DOZINESS > DOZY
DOZING > DOZE
DOZINGS > DOZE
DOZY adj feeling sleepy
DRAB adj dull and dreary ▷ n light olive-brown colour ▷ vb consort with prostitutes
DRABBED > DRAB

DRABBER n one who frequents low women
DRABBERS > DRABBER
DRABBEST > DRAB
DRABBET n yellowish-brown fabric of coarse linen
DRABBETS > DRABBET
DRABBIER > DRABBY
DRABBIEST > DRABBY
DRABBING > DRAB
DRABBISH adj promiscuous
DRABBLE vb make or become wet or dirty
DRABBLED > DRABBLE
DRABBLER n part fixed to bottom of sail
DRABBLERS > DRABBLER
DRABBLES > DRABBLE
DRABBLING > DRABBLE
DRABBY adj promiscuous
DRABETTE n type of rough linen fabric
DRABETTES > DRABETTE
DRABLER same as > DRABBLE
DRABLERS > DRABLER
DRABLY > DRAB
DRABNESS > DRAB
DRABS > DRAB
DRAC same as > DRACK
DRACAENA n type of tropical plant often cultivated as a house plant for its decorative foliage
DRACAENAS > DRACAENA
DRACENA same as > DRACAENA
DRACENAS > DRACENA
DRACHM same as > DRAM
DRACHMA n former monetary unit of Greece
DRACHMAE > DRACHMA
DRACHMAI > DRACHMA
DRACHMAS > DRACHMA
DRACHMS > DRACHM
DRACK adj (esp of a woman) unattractive
DRACO as in draco lizard flying lizard
DRACONE n large flexible cylindrical container towed by a ship, used for transporting liquids
DRACONES > DRACONE
DRACONIAN adj severe, harsh
DRACONIC same as > DRACONIAN
DRACONISM > DRACONIAN
DRACONTIC same as > DRACONIC
DRAD > DREAD
DRAFF n residue of husks after fermentation of the grain used in brewing, used as a food for cattle
DRAFFIER > DRAFF
DRAFFIEST > DRAFF
DRAFFISH adj worthless
DRAFFS > DRAFF
DRAFFY > DRAFF
DRAFT same as > DRAUGHT

DRAFTABLE > DRAFT
DRAFTED > DRAFT
DRAFTEE n conscript
DRAFTEES > DRAFTEE
DRAFTER > DRAFT
DRAFTERS > DRAFT
DRAFTIER > DRAFTY
DRAFTIEST > DRAFTY
DRAFTILY > DRAFTY
DRAFTING > DRAFT
DRAFTINGS > DRAFT
DRAFTS > DRAFT
DRAFTSMAN adj person skilled in drawing
DRAFTSMEN > DRAFTSMAN
DRAFTY same as > DRAUGHTY
DRAG vb pull with force, esp along the ground ▷ n person or thing that slows up progress
DRAGEE n sweet made of a nut, fruit, etc, coated with a hard sugar icing
DRAGEES > DRAGEE
DRAGGED > DRAG
DRAGGER > DRAG
DRAGGERS > DRAG
DRAGGIER > DRAGGY
DRAGGIEST > DRAGGY
DRAGGING > DRAG
DRAGGINGS > DRAGGING
DRAGGLE vb make or become wet or dirty by trailing on the ground
DRAGGLED > DRAGGLE
DRAGGLES > DRAGGLE
DRAGGLING > DRAGGLE
DRAGGY adj slow or boring
DRAGHOUND n hound used to follow an artificial trail of scent in a drag hunt
DRAGLINE same as > DRAGROPE
DRAGLINES > DRAGLINE
DRAGNET n net used to scour the bottom of a pond or river to search for something
DRAGNETS > DRAGNET
DRAGOMAN n (in some Middle Eastern countries) professional interpreter or guide
DRAGOMANS > DRAGOMAN
DRAGOMEN > DRAGOMAN
DRAGON n mythical fire-breathing monster like a huge lizard
DRAGONESS > DRAGON
DRAGONET n type of small spiny-finned fish with a flat head and a slender brightly coloured body
DRAGONETS > DRAGONET
DRAGONFLY n brightly coloured insect with a long slender body and two pairs of wings
DRAGONISE same as > DRAGONIZE
DRAGONISH > DRAGON
DRAGONISM n vigilance

DRAGONIZE vb turn into dragon
DRAGONNE adj dragonlike
DRAGONS > DRAGON
DRAGOON n heavily armed cavalryman ▷ vb coerce, force
DRAGOONED > DRAGOON
DRAGOONS > DRAGOON
DRAGROPE n rope used to drag military equipment, esp artillery
DRAGROPES > DRAGROPE
DRAGS > DRAG
DRAGSMAN n carriage driver
DRAGSMEN > DRAGSMAN
DRAGSTER n car specially built or modified for drag racing
DRAGSTERS > DRAGSTER
DRAGSTRIP n track for drag racing
DRAIL n weighted hook used in trolling ▷ vb fish with a drail
DRAILED > DRAIL
DRAILING > DRAIL
DRAILS > DRAIL
DRAIN n pipe or channel that carries off water or sewage ▷ vb draw off or remove liquid from
DRAINABLE > DRAIN
DRAINAGE n system of drains
DRAINAGES > DRAINAGE
DRAINED > DRAIN
DRAINER n person or thing that drains
DRAINERS > DRAINER
DRAINING > DRAIN
DRAINPIPE same as > DOWNPIPE
DRAINS > DRAIN
DRAISENE same as > DRAISINE
DRAISENES > DRAISENE
DRAISINE n light rail vehicle
DRAISINES > DRAISINE
DRAKE n male duck
DRAKES > DRAKE
DRAM n small amount of a strong alcoholic drink, esp whisky ▷ vb drink a dram
DRAMA n serious play for theatre, television, or radio
DRAMADIES > DRAMEDY
DRAMADY same as > DRAMEDY
DRAMAS > DRAMA
DRAMATIC adj of or like drama
DRAMATICS n art of acting or producing plays
DRAMATISE same as > DRAMATIZE
DRAMATIST n person who writes plays
DRAMATIZE vb rewrite (a book) in the form of a play
DRAMATURG n literary adviser at a theatre
DRAMEDIES > DRAMEDY

DRAMEDY n television or film drama in which there are important elements of comedy

DRAMMACH n oatmeal mixed with cold water

DRAMMACHS > DRAMMACH

DRAMMED > DRAM

DRAMMING > DRAM

DRAMMOCK same as > DRAMMACH

DRAMMOCKS > DRAMMOCK

DRAMS > DRAM

DRAMSHOP n bar

DRAMSHOPS > DRAMSHOP

DRANGWAY n narrow lane

DRANGWAYS > DRANGWAY

DRANK > DRINK

DRANT vb drone

DRANTED > DRANT

DRANTING > DRANT

DRANTS > DRANT

DRAP a Scot word for > DROP

DRAPABLE > DRAPE

DRAPE vb cover with material, usu. in folds ▷ n piece of cloth hung at a window or opening as a screen

DRAPEABLE > DRAPE

DRAPED > DRAPE

DRAPER n person who sells fabrics and sewing materials

DRAPERIED > DRAPERY

DRAPERIES > DRAPERY

DRAPERS > DRAPER

DRAPERY n fabric or clothing arranged and draped

DRAPES npl material hung at an opening or window to shut out light or to provide privacy

DRAPET n cloth

DRAPETS > DRAPET

DRAPEY adj hanging in loose folds

DRAPIER n draper

DRAPIERS > DRAPIER

DRAPIEST > DRAPEY

DRAPING > DRAPE

DRAPPED > DRAP

DRAPPIE n little drop, esp a small amount of spirits

DRAPPIES > DRAPPIE

DRAPPING > DRAP

DRAPPY n drop (of liquid)

DRAPS > DRAP

DRASTIC n strong purgative ▷ adj strong and severe

DRASTICS > DRASTIC

DRAT interj exclamation of annoyance ▷ vb curse

DRATCHELL n low woman

DRATS > DRAT

DRATTED adj wretched

DRATTING > DRAT

DRAUGHT vb make preliminary plan ▷ n current of cold air, esp in an enclosed space ▷ adj (of an animal) used for pulling heavy loads

DRAUGHTED > DRAUGHT

DRAUGHTER > DRAUGHT

DRAUGHTS n game for two players using a draughtboard and 12 draughtsmen each

DRAUGHTY adj exposed to draughts of air

DRAUNT same as > DRANT

DRAUNTED > DRAUNT

DRAUNTING > DRAUNT

DRAUNTS > DRAUNT

DRAVE archaic past of > DRIVE

DRAW vb sketch (a figure, picture, etc) with a pencil or pen ▷ n raffle or lottery

DRAWABLE > DRAW

DRAWBACK n disadvantage ▷ vb move backwards

DRAWBACKS > DRAWBACK

DRAWBAR n strong metal bar on a tractor, locomotive, etc, bearing a hook or link and pin to attach a trailer, wagon, etc

DRAWBARS > DRAWBAR

DRAWBORE n hole bored through tenon

DRAWBORES > DRAWBORE

DRAWDOWN n decrease

DRAWDOWNS > DRAWDOWN

DRAWEE n person or organization on which a cheque or other order for payment is drawn

DRAWEES > DRAWEE

DRAWER n sliding box-shaped part of a piece of furniture, used for storage

DRAWERFUL n amount contained in drawer

DRAWERS npl undergarment worn on the lower part of the body

DRAWING > DRAW

DRAWINGS > DRAW

DRAWKNIFE n woodcutting tool with two handles at right angles to the blade, used to shave wood

DRAWL vb speak slowly, with long vowel sounds ▷ n drawling manner of speech

DRAWLED > DRAWL

DRAWLER > DRAWL

DRAWLERS > DRAWL

DRAWLIER > DRAWL

DRAWLIEST > DRAWL

DRAWLING > DRAWL

DRAWLS > DRAWL

DRAWLY > DRAWL

DRAWN > DRAW

DRAWNWORK n type of ornamental needlework

DRAWPLATE n plate used to reduce the diameter of wire by drawing it through conical holes

DRAWS > DRAW

DRAWSHAVE same as > DRAWKNIFE

DRAWTUBE n tube, such as one of the component tubes of a telescope, fitting coaxially within another tube through which it can slide

DRAWTUBES > DRAWTUBE

DRAY vb pull using cart ▷ n low cart used for carrying heavy loads

DRAYAGE n act of transporting something a short distance by lorry or other vehicle

DRAYAGES > DRAYAGE

DRAYED > DRAY

DRAYHORSE n large powerful horse used for drawing a dray

DRAYING > DRAY

DRAYMAN n driver of a dray

DRAYMEN > DRAYMAN

DRAYS > DRAY

DRAZEL n low woman

DRAZELS > DRAZEL

DREAD vb anticipate with apprehension or fear ▷ n great fear ▷ adj awesome

DREADED > DREAD

DREADER > DREAD

DREADERS > DREAD

DREADFUL n cheap, often lurid or sensational book or magazine ▷ adj very disagreeable or shocking

DREADFULS > DREADFUL

DREADING > DREAD

DREADLESS > DREAD

DREADLOCK n Rastafarian hair braid

DREADLY > DREAD

DREADS > DREAD

DREAM n imagined series of events experienced in the mind while asleep ▷ vb see imaginary pictures in the mind while asleep ▷ adj ideal

DREAMBOAT n exceptionally attractive person or thing, esp a person of the opposite sex

DREAMED > DREAM

DREAMER n person who dreams habitually

DREAMERS > DREAMER

DREAMERY n dream world

DREAMFUL > DREAM

DREAMHOLE n light-admitting hole in a tower

DREAMIER > DREAMY

DREAMIEST > DREAMY

DREAMILY > DREAMY

DREAMING > DREAM

DREAMINGS > DREAM

DREAMLAND n ideal land existing in dreams or in the imagination

DREAMLESS > DREAM

DREAMLIKE > DREAM

DREAMS > DREAM

DREAMT > DREAM

DREAMTIME n time when the world was new and fresh

DREAMY adj vague or impractical

DREAR same as > DREARY

DREARE obsolete form of > DREAR

DREARER > DREAR

DREARES > DREARE

DREAREST > DREAR

DREARIER > DREARY

DREARIES > DREARY

DREARIEST > DREARY

DREARILY > DREARY

DREARING n sorrow

DREARINGS > DREARING

DREARS > DREAR

DREARY adj dull, boring ▷ n a dreary thing or person

DRECK n rubbish

DRECKIER > DRECK

DRECKIEST > DRECK

DRECKS > DRECK

DRECKSILL n doorstep

DRECKY > DRECK

DREDGE vb clear or search (a river bed or harbour) by removing silt or mud ▷ n machine used to scoop or suck up silt or mud from a river bed or harbour

DREDGED > DREDGE

DREDGER same as > DREDGE

DREDGERS > DREDGER

DREDGES > DREDGE

DREDGING > DREDGE

DREDGINGS > DREDGE

DREE vb endure

DREED > DREE

DREEING > DREE

DREES > DREE

DREG n small quantity

DREGGIER > DREGGY

DREGGIEST > DREGGY

DREGGISH adj foul

DREGGY adj like or full of dregs

DREGS npl solid particles that settle at the bottom of some liquids

DREICH adj dreary

DREICHER > DREICH

DREICHEST > DREICH

DREIDEL n spinning top

DREIDELS > DREIDEL

DREIDL same as > DREIDEL

DREIDLS > DREIDL

DREIGH same as > DREICH

DREIGHER > DREIGH

DREIGHEST > DREIGH

DREK same as > DRECK

DREKS > DREK

DRENCH vb make completely wet ▷ n act or an instance of drenching

DRENCHED > DRENCH

DRENCHER > DRENCH

DRENCHERS > DRENCH

DRENCHES > DRENCH

DRENCHING > DRENCH

DRENT > DRENCH

DREPANID n type of moth of the superfamily which

comprises the hook-tip moths

DREPANIDS > DREPANID

DREPANIUM n type of flower cluster

DRERE obsolete form of > DREAR

DRERES > DRERE

DRERIHEAD n obsolete word for dreary

DRESS n one-piece garment for a woman or girl, consisting of a skirt and bodice and sometimes sleeves ▷ vb put clothes on ▷ adj suitable for a formal occasion

DRESSAGE n training of a horse to perform manoeuvres in response to the rider's body signals

DRESSAGES > DRESSAGE

DRESSED > DRESS

DRESSER n piece of furniture with shelves and with cupboards, for storing or displaying dishes

DRESSERS > DRESSER

DRESSES > DRESS

DRESSIER > DRESSY

DRESSIEST > DRESSY

DRESSILY > DRESSY

DRESSING n sauce for salad

DRESSINGS npl dressed stonework, mouldings, and carved ornaments used to form quoins, keystones, sills, and similar features

DRESSMAKE > DRESSMAKE

DRESSMAKE vb make clothes

DRESSY adj (of clothes) elegant

DREST > DRESS

DREVILL n offensive person

DREVILLS > DREVILL

DREW > DRAW

DREY n squirrel's nest

DREYS > DREY

DRIB vb flow in drops

DRIBBED > DRIB

DRIBBER > DRIB

DRIBBERS > DRIB

DRIBBING > DRIB

DRIBBLE vb (allow to) flow in drops ▷ n small quantity of liquid falling in drops

DRIBBLED > DRIBBLE

DRIBBLER > DRIBBLE

DRIBBLERS > DRIBBLE

DRIBBLES > DRIBBLE

DRIBBLET same as > DRIBLET

DRIBBLETS > DRIBBLET

DRIBBLIER > DRIBBLE

DRIBBLING > DRIBBLE

DRIBBLY > DRIBBLE

DRIBLET n small amount

DRIBLETS > DRIBLET

DRIBS > DRIB

DRICE n pellets of frozen carbon dioxide

DRICES > DRICE

DRICKSIE same as > DRUXY

DRICKSIER > DRICKSIE

DRIED > DRY

DRIEGH adj tedious

DRIER > DRY

DRIERS > DRY

DRIES > DRY

DRIEST > DRY

DRIFT vb be carried along by currents of air or water ▷ n something piled up by the wind or current, such as a snowdrift

DRIFTAGE n act of drifting

DRIFTAGES > DRIFTAGE

DRIFTED > DRIFT

DRIFTER n person who moves aimlessly from place to place or job to job

DRIFTERS > DRIFTER

DRIFTIER > DRIFT

DRIFTIEST > DRIFT

DRIFTING > DRIFT

DRIFTLESS > DRIFT

DRIFTPIN same as > DRIFT

DRIFTPINS > DRIFTPIN

DRIFTS > DRIFT

DRIFTWOOD n wood floating on or washed ashore by the sea

DRIFTY > DRIFT

DRILL n tool or machine for boring holes ▷ vb bore a hole in (something) with or as if with a drill

DRILLABLE > DRILL

DRILLED > DRILL

DRILLER > DRILL

DRILLERS > DRILL

DRILLHOLE n hole drilled in the ground, usu for exploratory purposes

DRILLING same as > DRILL

DRILLINGS > DRILL

DRILLS > DRILL

DRILLSHIP n floating drilling platform

DRILY adv in a dry manner

DRINK vb swallow (a liquid) ▷ n (portion of) a liquid suitable for drinking

DRINKABLE > DRINK

DRINKABLY > DRINK

DRINKER n person who drinks, esp a person who drinks alcohol habitually

DRINKERS > DRINKER

DRINKING > DRINK

DRINKINGS > DRINK

DRINKS > DRINK

DRIP vb (let) fall in drops ▷ n falling of drops of liquid

DRIPLESS > DRIP

DRIPPED > DRIP

DRIPPER > DRIP

DRIPPERS > DRIP

DRIPPIER > DRIPPY

DRIPPIEST > DRIPPY

DRIPPILY > DRIPPY

DRIPPING > DRIP

DRIPPINGS > DRIP

DRIPPY adj mawkish, insipid, or inane

DRIPS > DRIP

DRIPSTONE n form of calcium carbonate existing in stalactites or stalagmites

DRIPT > DRIP

DRISHEEN n pudding made of sheep's intestines filled with meal and sheep's blood

DRISHEENS > DRISHEEN

DRIVABLE > DRIVE

DRIVE vb guide the movement of (a vehicle) ▷ n journey by car, van, etc

DRIVEABLE > DRIVE

DRIVEL n foolish talk ▷ vb speak foolishly

DRIVELED > DRIVEL

DRIVELER > DRIVEL

DRIVELERS > DRIVEL

DRIVELINE n transmission line from engine to wheels of vehicle

DRIVELING > DRIVEL

DRIVELLED > DRIVEL

DRIVELLER > DRIVEL

DRIVELS > DRIVEL

DRIVEN > DRIVE

DRIVER n person who drives a vehicle

DRIVERS > DRIVER

DRIVES > DRIVE

DRIVEWAY n path for vehicles connecting a building to a public road

DRIVEWAYS > DRIVEWAY

DRIVING > DRIVE

DRIVINGLY > DRIVE

DRIVINGS > DRIVE

DRIZZLE n very light rain ▷ vb rain lightly

DRIZZLED > DRIZZLE

DRIZZLES > DRIZZLE

DRIZZLIER > DRIZZLE

DRIZZLING > DRIZZLE

DRIZZLY > DRIZZLE

DROGER n W Indian boat

DROGERS > DROGER

DROGHER same as > DROGER

DROGHERS > DROGHER

DROGUE n any funnel-like device, esp one of canvas, used as a sea anchor

DROGUES > DROGUE

DROGUET n woollen fabric

DROGUETS > DROGUET

DROICH n dwarf

DROICHIER > DROICHY

DROICHS > DROICH

DROICHY adj dwarfish

DROID same as > ANDROID

DROIDS > DROID

DROIL vb carry out boring menial work

DROILED > DROIL

DROILING > DROIL

DROILS > DROIL

DROIT n legal or moral right or claim

DROITS > DROIT

DROLE adj amusing ▷ n scoundrel

DROLER > DROLE

DROLES > DROLE

DROLEST > DROLE

DROLL vb speak wittily ▷ adj quaintly amusing

DROLLED > DROLL

DROLLER > DROLL

DROLLERY n humour

DROLLEST > DROLL

DROLLING > DROLL

DROLLINGS > DROLL

DROLLISH adj somewhat droll

DROLLNESS > DROLL

DROLLS > DROLL

DROLLY > DROLL

DROME same as > AERODROME

DROMEDARE obsolete form of > DROMEDARY

DROMEDARY n camel with a single hump

DROMES > DROME

DROMIC adj relating to running track

DROMICAL same as > DROMIC

DROMOI > DROMOS

DROMON same as > DROMOND

DROMOND n large swift sailing vessel of the 12th to 15th centuries

DROMONDS > DROMOND

DROMONS > DROMON

DROMOS n Greek passageway

DRONE n male bee ▷ vb make a monotonous low dull sound

DRONED > DRONE

DRONER > DRONE

DRONERS > DRONE

DRONES > DRONE

DRONGO n tropical songbird with a glossy black plumage, a forked tail, and a stout bill

DRONGOES > DRONGO

DRONGOS > DRONGO

DRONIER > DRONY

DRONIEST > DRONY

DRONING > DRONE

DRONINGLY > DRONE

DRONISH > DRONE

DRONISHLY > DRONE

DRONKLAP n South African word for a drunkard

DRONKLAPS > DRONKLAP

DRONY adj monotonous

DROOB n pathetic person

DROOBS > DROOB

DROOG n ruffian

DROOGISH > DROOG

DROOGS > DROOG

DROOK same as > DROUK

DROOKED > DROOK

DROOKING > DROOK

DROOKINGS > DROOK

DROOKIT same as > DROUKIT

DROOKS > DROOK

DROOL vb show excessive enthusiasm (for)
DROOLED > DROOL
DROOLIER > DROOLY
DROOLIEST > DROOLY
DROOLING > DROOL
DROOLS > DROOL
DROOLY adj tending to drool
DROOME obsolete form of > DRUM
DROOMES > DRUM
DROOP vb hang downwards loosely ▷ n act or state of drooping
DROOPED > DROOP
DROOPIER > DROOPY
DROOPIEST > DROOPY
DROOPILY > DROOPY
DROOPING > DROOP
DROOPS > DROOP
DROOPY adj hanging or sagging downwards
DROP vb (allow to) fall vertically ▷ n small quantity of liquid forming a round shape
DROPCLOTH n cloth spread on floor to catch drips while painting
DROPFLIES > DROPFLY
DROPFLY n (angling) artificial fly
DROPFORGE vb forge metal between two dies
DROPHEAD as in drophead coupe two-door car with a folding roof and sloping back
DROPHEADS > DROPHEAD
DROPKICK n (in certain ball games) a kick in which the ball is first dropped then kicked as it bounces from the ground
DROPKICKS > DROPKICK
DROPLET n very small drop of liquid
DROPLETS > DROPLET
DROPLIGHT n electric light that may be raised or lowered by means of a pulley or other mechanism
DROPLOCK as in droplock loan type of bank loan
DROPOUT n person who rejects conventional society ▷ vb abandon or withdraw (from an institution or group)
DROPOUTS > DROPOUT
DROPPABLE > DROP
DROPPED > DROP
DROPPER n small tube with a rubber part at one end for drawing up and dispensing drops of liquid
DROPPERS > DROPPER
DROPPING > DROP
DROPPINGS npl faeces of certain animals, such as rabbits or birds
DROPPLE n trickle
DROPPLES > DROPPLE
DROPS > DROP

DROPSHOT n (in tennis) shot in which a softly returned ball just clears the net before falling abruptly
DROPSHOTS > DROPSHOT
DROPSICAL > DROPSY
DROPSIED > DROPSY
DROPSIES > DROPSY
DROPSONDE n radiosonde dropped by parachute
DROPSTONE n calcium carbonate in stalactites
DROPSY n illness in which watery fluid collects in the body
DROPT > DROP
DROPWISE adv in form of a drop
DROPWORT n Eurasian plant with cream-coloured flowers, related to the rose
DROPWORTS > DROPWORT
DROSERA n insectivorous plant
DROSERAS > DROSERA
DROSHKIES > DROSHKY
DROSHKY n open four-wheeled horse-drawn passenger carriage, formerly used in Russia
DROSKIES > DROSKY
DROSKY same as > DROSHKY
DROSS n scum formed on the surfaces of molten metals
DROSSES > DROSS
DROSSIER > DROSS
DROSSIEST > DROSS
DROSSY > DROSS
DROSTDIES > DROSTDY
DROSTDY n office of landdrost
DROSTDYS > DROSTDY
DROUGHT n prolonged shortage of rainfall
DROUGHTS > DROUGHT
DROUGHTY > DROUGHT
DROUK vb drench
DROUKED > DROUK
DROUKING > DROUK
DROUKINGS > DROUK
DROUKIT adj drenched
DROUKS > DROUK
DROUTH same as > DROUGHT
DROUTHIER > DROUTHY
DROUTHS > DROUTH
DROUTHY adj thirsty or dry
DROVE > DRIVE
DROVED > DRIVE
DROVER n person who drives sheep or cattle
DROVERS > DROVER
DROVES > DRIVE
DROVING > DRIVE
DROVINGS > DRIVE
DROW n sea fog
DROWN vb die or kill by immersion in liquid
DROWND dialect form of > DROWN
DROWNDED > DROWND
DROWNDING > DROWND

DROWNDS > DROWND
DROWNED > DROWN
DROWNER > DROWN
DROWNERS > DROWN
DROWNING > DROWN
DROWNINGS > DROWN
DROWNS > DROWN
DROWS > DROW
DROWSE vb be sleepy, dull, or sluggish ▷ n state of being drowsy
DROWSED > DROWSE
DROWSES > DROWSE
DROWSIER > DROWSY
DROWSIEST > DROWSY
DROWSIHED adj old form of drowsy
DROWSILY > DROWSY
DROWSING > DROWSE
DROWSY adj feeling sleepy
DRUB vb beat as with a stick ▷ n blow, as from a stick
DRUBBED > DRUB
DRUBBER > DRUB
DRUBBERS > DRUB
DRUBBING > DRUB
DRUBBINGS > DRUB
DRUBS > DRUB
DRUCKEN adj drunken
DRUDGE n person who works hard at uninteresting tasks ▷ vb work at such tasks
DRUDGED > DRUDGE
DRUDGER > DRUDGE
DRUDGERS > DRUDGE
DRUDGERY n uninteresting work that must be done
DRUDGES > DRUDGE
DRUDGING > DRUDGE
DRUDGISM > DRUDGE
DRUDGISMS > DRUDGE
DRUG n substance used in the treatment or prevention of disease ▷ vb give a drug to (a person or animal) to cause sleepiness or unconsciousness
DRUGGED > DRUG
DRUGGER n druggist
DRUGGERS > DRUGGER
DRUGGET n coarse fabric used as a protective floor-covering, etc
DRUGGETS > DRUGGET
DRUGGIE n drug addict
DRUGGIER > DRUG
DRUGGIES > DRUGGIE
DRUGGIEST > DRUG
DRUGGING > DRUG
DRUGGIST n pharmacist
DRUGGISTS > DRUGGIST
DRUGGY > DRUG
DRUGLORD n criminal who controls the distribution and sale of large quantities of illegal drugs
DRUGLORDS > DRUGLORD
DRUGMAKER n manufacturer of drugs
DRUGS > DRUG
DRUGSTORE n pharmacy where a wide range of goods are available

DRUID n member of an ancient order of priests in Gaul, Britain, and Ireland in the pre-Christian era
DRUIDESS > DRUID
DRUIDIC > DRUID
DRUIDICAL > DRUID
DRUIDISM > DRUID
DRUIDISMS > DRUID
DRUIDRIES > DRUID
DRUIDRY > DRUID
DRUIDS > DRUID
DRUM n percussion instrument sounded by striking a membrane stretched across the opening of a hollow cylinder ▷ vb play (music) on a drum
DRUMBEAT n sound made by beating a drum
DRUMBEATS > DRUMBEAT
DRUMBLE vb be inactive
DRUMBLED > DRUMBLE
DRUMBLES > DRUMBLE
DRUMBLING > DRUMBLE
DRUMFIRE n heavy, rapid, and continuous gunfire, the sound of which resembles rapid drumbeats
DRUMFIRES > DRUMFIRE
DRUMFISH n one of several types of fish that make a drumming sound
DRUMHEAD n part of a drum that is struck
DRUMHEADS > DRUMHEAD
DRUMLIER > DRUMLY
DRUMLIEST > DRUMLY
DRUMLIKE > DRUM
DRUMLIN n streamlined mound of glacial drift, rounded or elongated in the direction of the original flow of ice
DRUMLINS > DRUMLIN
DRUMLY adj dismal; dreary
DRUMMED > DRUM
DRUMMER n person who plays a drum or drums
DRUMMERS > DRUMMER
DRUMMIES > DRUMMY
DRUMMING > DRUM
DRUMMOCK same as > DRAMMOCK
DRUMMOCKS > DRUMMOCK
DRUMMY n (in South Africa) drum majorette
DRUMROLL n continued repeated sound of drum
DRUMROLLS > DRUMROLL
DRUMS > DRUM
DRUMSTICK n stick used for playing a drum
DRUNK > DRINK
DRUNKARD n person who frequently gets drunk
DRUNKARDS > DRUNKARD
DRUNKEN adj drunk or frequently drunk
DRUNKENLY > DRUNKEN
DRUNKER > DRINK
DRUNKEST > DRINK
DRUNKS > DRINK

DRUPE *n* fleshy fruit with a stone, such as the peach or cherry

DRUPEL *same as* **> DRUPELET**

DRUPELET *n* small drupe, usually one of a number forming a compound fruit

DRUPELETS > DRUPELET

DRUPELS > DRUPEL

DRUPES > DRUPE

DRUSE *n* aggregate of small crystals within a cavity, esp those lining a rock or mineral

DRUSEN *npl* small deposits of material on the retina

DRUSES > DRUSE

DRUSIER > DRUSY

DRUSIEST > DRUSY

DRUSY *adj* made of tiny crystals

DRUTHERS *n* preference

DRUXIER > DRUXY

DRUXIEST > DRUXY

DRUXY *adj* (of wood) having decayed white spots

DRY *adj* lacking moisture ▷ *vb* make or become dry

DRYABLE > DRY

DRYAD *n* wood nymph

DRYADES > DRYAD

DRYADIC > DRYAD

DRYADS > DRYAD

DRYASDUST *adj* boringly bookish

DRYBEAT *vb* beat severely

DRYBEATEN > DRYBEAT

DRYBEATS > DRYBEAT

DRYER > DRY

DRYERS > DRY

DRYEST > DRY

DRYING > DRY

DRYINGS > DRY

DRYISH *adj* fairly dry

DRYLAND *adj* of an arid area

DRYLOT *n* livestock enclosure

DRYLOTS > DRYLOT

DRYLY *same as* **> DRILY**

DRYMOUTH *n* condition of insufficient saliva

DRYMOUTHS > DRYMOUTH

DRYNESS > DRY

DRYNESSES > DRY

DRYPOINT *n* copper engraving technique using a hard steel needle

DRYPOINTS > DRYPOINT

DRYS > DRY

DRYSALTER *n* dealer in certain chemical products, such as dyestuffs and gums, and in dried, tinned, or salted foods and edible oils

DRYSTONE *adj* (of a wall) made without mortar

DRYSUIT *n* waterproof rubber suit for wearing in esp cold water

DRYSUITS > DRYSUIT

DRYWALL *n* wall built

without mortar ▷ *vb* build a wall without mortar

DRYWALLED > DRYWALL

DRYWALLS > DRYWALL

DRYWELL *n* type of sewage disposal system

DRYWELLS > DRYWELL

DSO *same as* **> ZHO**

DSOBO *same as* **> ZOBO**

DSOBOS > DSOBO

DSOMO *same as* **> ZHOMO**

DSOMOS > DSOMO

DSOS > DSO

DUAD *a rare word for* **> PAIR**

DUADS > DUAD

DUAL *adj* having two parts, functions, or aspects ▷ *n* dual number ▷ *vb* make (a road) into a dual carriageway

DUALIN *n* explosive substance

DUALINS > DUALIN

DUALISE *same as* **> DUALIZE**

DUALISED > DUALISE

DUALISES > DUALISE

DUALISING > DUALISE

DUALISM *n* state of having or being believed to have two distinct parts or aspects

DUALISMS > DUALISM

DUALIST > DUALISM

DUALISTIC > DUALISM

DUALISTS > DUALISM

DUALITIES > DUALITY

DUALITY *n* state or quality of being two or in two parts

DUALIZE *vb* cause to have two parts

DUALIZED > DUALIZE

DUALIZES > DUALIZE

DUALIZING > DUALIZE

DUALLED > DUAL

DUALLING > DUAL

DUALLY > DUAL

DUALS > DUAL

DUAN *n* poem

DUANS > DUAN

DUAR *n* Arab camp

DUARCHIES > DUARCHY

DUARCHY *same as* **> DIARCHY**

DUARS > DUAR

DUATHLON *n* athletic contest in which each athlete competes in running and cycling events

DUATHLONS > DUATHLON

DUB *vb* give (a person or place) a name or nickname ▷ *n* style of reggae record production involving exaggeration of instrumental parts, echo, etc

DUBBED > DUB

DUBBER > DUB

DUBBERS > DUB

DUBBIN *n* thick grease applied to leather to soften and waterproof it

DUBBING > DUB

DUBBINGS > DUB

DUBBINS > DUBBIN

DUBBO *adj* stupid ▷ *n* stupid person

DUBBOS > DUBBO

DUBIETIES > DUBIETY

DUBIETY *n* state of being doubtful

DUBIOSITY *same as* **> DUBIETY**

DUBIOUS *adj* feeling or causing doubt

DUBIOUSLY > DUBIOUS

DUBITABLE *adj* open to doubt

DUBITABLY > DUBITABLE

DUBITANCY > DUBITATE

DUBITATE *vb* doubt

DUBITATED > DUBITATE

DUBITATES > DUBITATE

DUBNIUM *n* element produced in minute quantities by bombarding plutonium with high-energy neon ions

DUBNIUMS > DUBNIUM

DUBONNET *n* dark purplish-red colour

DUBONNETS > DUBONNET

DUBS > DUB

DUBSTEP *n* genre of electronic music

DUBSTEPS > DUBSTEP

DUCAL *adj* of a duke

DUCALLY > DUCAL

DUCAT *n* former European gold or silver coin

DUCATOON *n* former silver coin

DUCATOONS > DUCATOON

DUCATS > DUCAT

DUCDAME *interj* Shakespearean nonsense word

DUCE *n* leader

DUCES > DUCE

DUCHESS *n* woman who holds the rank of duke ▷ *vb* overwhelm with flattering attention

DUCHESSE *n* type of satin

DUCHESSED > DUCHESS

DUCHESSES > DUCHESS

DUCHIES > DUCHY

DUCHY *n* territory of a duke or duchess

DUCI > DUCE

DUCK *n* water bird with short legs, webbed feet, and a broad blunt bill ▷ *vb* move (the head or body) quickly downwards, to avoid being seen or to dodge a blow

DUCKBILL *n* duckbilled platypus

DUCKBILLS > DUCKBILL

DUCKBOARD *n* board or boards laid so as to form a floor or path over wet or muddy ground

DUCKED > DUCK

DUCKER > DUCK

DUCKERS > DUCK

DUCKFOOT as in *duckfoot quote* chevron-shaped quotation mark

DUCKIE *same as* **> DUCKY**

DUCKIER > DUCKY

DUCKIES > DUCKY

DUCKIEST > DUCKY

DUCKING > DUCK

DUCKINGS > DUCK

DUCKLING *n* baby duck

DUCKLINGS > DUCKLING

DUCKMOLE *another word for* **> DUCKBILL**

DUCKMOLES > DUCKMOLE

DUCKPIN *n* short bowling pin

DUCKPINS > DUCKPIN

DUCKS > DUCK

DUCKSHOVE *vb* evade responsibility

DUCKTAIL *n* Teddy boy's hairstyle

DUCKTAILS > DUCKTAIL

DUCKWALK *vb* walk in a squatting posture

DUCKWALKS > DUCKWALK

DUCKWEED *n* type of small stemless aquatic plant with rounded leaves, which floats on still water in temperate regions

DUCKWEEDS > DUCKWEED

DUCKY *n* darling or dear: used as a term of endearment among women, but now often used in imitation of the supposed usage of homosexual men ▷ *adj* delightful

DUCT *vb* convey via a duct ▷ *n* tube, pipe, or channel through which liquid or gas is conveyed

DUCTAL > DUCT

DUCTED > DUCT

DUCTILE *adj* (of a metal) able to be shaped into sheets or wires

DUCTILELY > DUCTILE

DUCTILITY > DUCTILE

DUCTING > DUCT

DUCTINGS > DUCT

DUCTLESS > DUCT

DUCTS > DUCT

DUCTULE *n* small duct

DUCTULES > DUCTULE

DUCTWORK *n* system of ducts

DUCTWORKS > DUCTWORK

DUD *n* ineffectual person or thing ▷ *adj* bad or useless

DUDDER *n* door-to-door salesman

DUDDERIES > DUDDERY

DUDDERS > DUDDER

DUDDERY *n* place where old clothes are sold

DUDDIE *adj* ragged

DUDDIER > DUDDIE

DUDDIEST > DUDDIE

DUDDY *same as* **> DUDDIE**

DUDE *vb* dress fashionably ▷ *n* man

DUDED > DUDE
DUDEEN n clay pipe with a short stem
DUDEENS > DUDEEN
DUDES > DUDE
DUDGEON n anger or resentment
DUDGEONS > DUDGEON
DUDHEEN n type of pipe
DUDHEENS > DUDHEEN
DUDING > DUDE
DUDISH > DUDE
DUDISHLY > DUDE
DUDISM n being a dude
DUDISMS > DUDISM
DUDS > DUD
DUE vb supply with ▷ adj expected or scheduled to be present or arrive ▷ n something that is owed or required ▷ adv directly or exactly
DUECENTO n thirteenth century (in Italian art)
DUECENTOS > DUECENTO
DUED > DUE
DUEFUL adj proper
DUEL n formal fight with deadly weapons between two people, to settle a quarrel ▷ vb fight in a duel
DUELED > DUEL
DUELER > DUEL
DUELERS > DUEL
DUELING > DUEL
DUELIST > DUEL
DUELISTS > DUEL
DUELLED > DUEL
DUELLER > DUEL
DUELLERS > DUEL
DUELLI > DUELLO
DUELLING > DUEL
DUELLINGS > DUEL
DUELLIST > DUEL
DUELLISTS > DUEL
DUELLO n art of duelling
DUELLOS > DUELLO
DUELS > DUEL
DUELSOME adj given to duelling
DUENDE n Spanish goblin
DUENDES > DUENDE
DUENESS > DUE
DUENESSES > DUE
DUENNA n (esp in Spain) elderly woman acting as chaperone to a young woman
DUENNAS > DUENNA
DUES npl membership fees paid to a club or organization
DUET n piece of music for two performers ▷ vb perform a duet
DUETED > DUET
DUETING > DUET
DUETS > DUET
DUETT same as **>** DUET
DUETTED > DUET
DUETTI > DUETTO
DUETTING > DUET
DUETTINO n simple duet
DUETTINOS > DUETTINO

DUETTIST > DUET
DUETTISTS > DUET
DUETTO same as **>** DUET
DUETTOS > DUETTO
DUETTS > DUETT
DUFF adj broken or useless ▷ vb change the appearance of or give a false appearance to (old or stolen goods) ▷ n rump or buttocks
DUFFED > DUFF
DUFFEL n heavy woollen cloth with a thick nap
DUFFELS > DUFFEL
DUFFER n dull or incompetent person
DUFFERDOM n condition of being a duffer
DUFFERISM same as **>** DUFFERDOM
DUFFERS > DUFFER
DUFFEST > DUFF
DUFFING > DUFF
DUFFINGS > DUFF
DUFFLE same as **>** DUFFEL
DUFFLES > DUFFLE
DUFFS > DUFF
DUFUS same as **>** DOOFUS
DUFUSES > DUFUS
DUG > DIG
DUGITE n medium-sized Australian venomous snake
DUGITES > DUGITE
DUGONG n whalelike mammal of tropical waters
DUGONGS > DUGONG
DUGOUT n (at a sports ground) covered bench where managers and substitutes sit
DUGOUTS > DUGOUT
DUGS > DIG
DUH interj ironic response to a question or statement, implying that the speaker is stupid or that the reply is obvious
DUHKHA same as **>** DUKKHA
DUHKHAS > DUHKHA
DUI > DUO
DUIKER n small African antelope
DUIKERBOK same as **>** DUIKER
DUIKERS > DUIKER
DUING > DUE
DUIT n former Dutch coin
DUITS > DUIT
DUKA n shop
DUKAS > DUKA
DUKE vb fight with fists ▷ n nobleman of the highest rank
DUKED > DUKE
DUKEDOM n title, rank, or position of a duke
DUKEDOMS > DUKEDOM
DUKELING n low-ranking duke
DUKELINGS > DUKELING
DUKERIES > DUKERY
DUKERY n duke's domain

DUKES npl fists
DUKESHIP > DUKE
DUKESHIPS > DUKE
DUKING > DUKE
DUKKA n mix of ground roast nuts and spices, originating in Egypt, and used for sprinkling on meat or as a dip
DUKKAH same as **>** DUKKA
DUKKAHS > DUKKAH
DUKKAS > DUKKA
DUKKHA n (in Theravada Buddhism) the belief that all things are suffering, due to the desire to seek permanence or recognise the self when neither exist: one of the three basic characteristics of existence
DUKKHAS > DUKKHA
DULCAMARA n orange-fruited vine
DULCET adj (of a sound) soothing or pleasant ▷ n soft organ stop
DULCETLY > DULCET
DULCETS > DULCET
DULCIAN n precursor to the bassoon
DULCIANA n sweet-toned organ stop, controlling metal pipes of narrow scale
DULCIANAS > DULCIANA
DULCIANS > DULCIAN
DULCIFIED > DULCIFY
DULCIFIES > DULCIFY
DULCIFY vb make pleasant or agreeable
DULCIMER n tuned percussion instrument consisting of a set of strings stretched over a sounding board and struck with hammers
DULCIMERS > DULCIMER
DULCIMORE former name for **>** DULCIMER
DULCINEA n man's sweetheart
DULCINEAS > DULCINEA
DULCITE n sweet substance
DULCITES > DULCITE
DULCITOL another word for **>** DULCITE
DULCITOLS > DULCITOL
DULCITUDE n sweetness
DULCOSE another word for **>** DULCITE
DULCOSES > DULCOSE
DULE n suffering; misery
DULES > DULE
DULIA n veneration accorded to saints in the Roman Catholic and Eastern Churches, as contrasted with hyperdulia and latria
DULIAS > DULIA
DULL adj not interesting ▷ vb make or become dull
DULLARD n dull or stupid person
DULLARDS > DULLARD

DULLED > DULL
DULLER > DULL
DULLEST > DULL
DULLIER > DULL
DULLIEST > DULL
DULLING > DULL
DULLISH > DULL
DULLISHLY > DULL
DULLNESS > DULL
DULLS > DULL
DULLY > DULL
DULNESS > DULL
DULNESSES > DULL
DULOCRACY n rule by slaves
DULOSES > DULOSIS
DULOSIS n practice of some ants, in which one species forces members of a different species to do the work of the colony
DULOTIC > DULOSIS
DULSE n seaweed with large red edible fronds
DULSES > DULSE
DULY adv in a proper manner
DUMA n elective legislative assembly established by Tsar Nicholas II in 1905: overthrown by the Bolsheviks in 1917
DUMAIST n member of duma
DUMAISTS > DUMAIST
DUMAS > DUMA
DUMB vb silence ▷ adj lacking the power to speak
DUMBBELL n short bar with a heavy ball or disc at each end, used for physical exercise
DUMBBELLS > DUMBBELL
DUMBCANE n West Indian aroid plant
DUMBCANES > DUMBCANE
DUMBED > DUMB
DUMBER > DUMB
DUMBEST > DUMB
DUMBFOUND vb strike dumb with astonishment
DUMBHEAD n dunce
DUMBHEADS > DUMBHEAD
DUMBING > DUMB
DUMBLY > DUMB
DUMBNESS > DUMB
DUMBO n slow-witted unintelligent person
DUMBOS > DUMBO
DUMBS > DUMB
DUMBSHIT n taboo slang word for a stupid person
DUMBSHITS > DUMBSHIT
DUMBSHOW n actions performed without words in a play
DUMBSHOWS > DUMBSHOW
DUMDUM n soft-nosed bullet that expands on impact and causes serious wounds
DUMDUMS > DUMDUM
DUMELA sentence substitute hello

DUMFOUND same as
> DUMBFOUND
DUMFOUNDS > DUMFOUND
DUMKA n Slavonic lyrical
song
DUMKY > DUMKA
DUMMERER n person who
pretends to be dumb
DUMMERERS > DUMMERER
DUMMIED > DUMMY
DUMMIER > DUMMY
DUMMIES > DUMMY
DUMMIEST > DUMMY
DUMMINESS > DUMMY
DUMMKOPF n stupid person
DUMMKOPFS > DUMMKOPF
DUMMY adj sham ▷ n figure
representing the human
form, used for displaying
clothes etc ▷ adj imitation,
substitute ▷ vb prepare a
dummy of (a proposed
book, page, etc)
DUMMYING > DUMMY
DUMOSE adj bushlike
DUMOSITY > DUMOSE
DUMOUS same as > DUMOSE
DUMP vb drop or let fall in a
careless manner ▷ n place
where waste materials are
left
DUMPBIN n free-standing
unit in a bookshop in which
a particular publisher's
books are displayed
DUMPBINS > DUMPBIN
DUMPCART n cart for
dumping without handling
DUMPCARTS > DUMPCART
DUMPED > DUMP
DUMPEE n person dumped
from a relationship
DUMPEES > DUMPEE
DUMPER > DUMP
DUMPERS > DUMP
DUMPIER > DUMPY
DUMPIES > DUMPY
DUMPIEST > DUMPY
DUMPILY > DUMPY
DUMPINESS > DUMPY
DUMPING > DUMP
DUMPINGS > DUMP
DUMPISH same as > DUMPY
DUMPISHLY > DUMPISH
DUMPLE vb form into
dumpling shape
DUMPLED > DUMPLE
DUMPLES > DUMPLE
DUMPLING n small ball of
dough cooked and served
with stew
DUMPLINGS > DUMPLING
DUMPS npl state of
melancholy or depression
DUMPSITE n location of
dump
DUMPSITES > DUMPSITE
DUMPSTER n refuse skip
DUMPSTERS > DUMPSTER
DUMPTRUCK n lorry with a
tipping container
DUMPY n dumpy person
▷ adj short and plump
DUN adj brownish-grey ▷ vb

demand payment from
(a debtor) ▷ n demand for
payment
DUNAM n unit of area
measurement
DUNAMS > DUNAM
DUNCE n person who is
stupid or slow to learn
DUNCEDOM > DUNCE
DUNCEDOMS > DUNCE
DUNCELIKE > DUNCE
DUNCERIES > DUNCERY
DUNCERY n duncelike
behaviour
DUNCES > DUNCE
DUNCH vb push against
gently
DUNCHED > DUNCH
DUNCHES > DUNCH
DUNCHING > DUNCH
DUNCICAL adj duncelike
DUNCISH adj duncelike
DUNCISHLY > DUNCE
DUNDER n cane juice lees
DUNDERS > DUNDER
DUNE n mound or ridge of
drifted sand
DUNELAND n land
characterized by dunes
DUNELANDS > DUNELAND
DUNELIKE > DUNE
DUNES > DUNE
DUNG n faeces from animals
such as cattle ▷ vb cover
(ground) with manure
DUNGAREE n coarse cotton
fabric used chiefly for work
clothes, etc
DUNGAREED adj wearing
dungarees
DUNGAREES > DUNGAREE
DUNGED > DUNG
DUNGEON vb hold captive in
dungeon ▷ n underground
prison cell
DUNGEONED > DUNGEON
DUNGEONER n jailer
DUNGEONS > DUNGEON
DUNGER n old decrepit car
DUNGERS > DUNGER
DUNGHEAP n pile of dung
DUNGHEAPS > DUNGHEAP
DUNGHILL n heap of dung
DUNGHILLS > DUNGHILL
DUNGIER > DUNG
DUNGIEST > DUNG
DUNGING > DUNG
DUNGMERE n cesspool
DUNGMERES > DUNGMERE
DUNGS > DUNG
DUNGY > DUNG
DUNITE n ultrabasic
igneous rock consisting
mainly of olivine
DUNITES > DUNITE
DUNITIC > DUNITE
DUNK vb dip (a biscuit or
bread) in a drink or soup
before eating it
DUNKED > DUNK
DUNKER > DUNK
DUNKERS > DUNK
DUNKING > DUNK
DUNKS > DUNK

DUNLIN n small sandpiper
with a brown back found in
northern regions
DUNLINS > DUNLIN
DUNNAGE n loose material
used for packing cargo
DUNNAGES > DUNNAGE
DUNNAKIN n lavatory
DUNNAKINS > DUNNAKIN
DUNNART n type of
mouselike insectivorous
marsupial of Australia and
New Guinea
DUNNARTS > DUNNART
DUNNED > DUN
DUNNER > DUN
DUNNESS > DUN
DUNNESSES > DUN
DUNNEST > DUN
DUNNIER > DUNNY
DUNNIES > DUNNY
DUNNIEST > DUNNY
DUNNING > DUN
DUNNINGS > DUN
DUNNISH > DUN
DUNNITE n explosive
containing ammonium
picrate
DUNNITES > DUNNITE
DUNNO vb slang for don't
know
DUNNOCK n hedge sparrow
DUNNOCKS > DUNNOCK
DUNNY n in Australia, toilet
▷ adj relating to dunny
DUNS > DUN
DUNSH same as > DUNCH
DUNSHED > DUNSH
DUNSHES > DUNSH
DUNSHING > DUNSH
DUNT n blow ▷ vb strike or
hit
DUNTED > DUNT
DUNTING > DUNT
DUNTS > DUNT
DUO same as > DUET
DUOBINARY adj denoting
a communications system
for coding digital data in
which three data bands are
used, 0, +1, -1
DUODECIMO n book size
resulting from folding a
sheet of paper into twelve
leaves
DUODENA > DUODENUM
DUODENAL > DUODENUM
DUODENARY adj of or
relating to the number 12
DUODENUM n first part of
the small intestine, just
below the stomach
DUODENUMS > DUODENUM
DUOLOG same as
> DUOLOGUE
DUOLOGS > DUOLOG
DUOLOGUE n (in drama)
conversation between only
two speakers
DUOLOGUES > DUOLOGUE
DUOMI > DUOMO
DUOMO n cathedral in Italy
DUOMOS > DUOMO
DUOPOLIES > DUOPOLY

DUOPOLY n situation in
which control of a
commodity or service in a
particular market is vested
in just two producers or
suppliers
DUOPSONY n two rival
buyers controlling sellers
DUOS > DUO
DUOTONE n process for
producing halftone
illustrations using two
shades of a single colour or
black and a colour
DUOTONES > DUOTONE
DUP vb open
DUPABLE > DUPE
DUPATTA n scarf worn in
India
DUPATTAS > DUPATTA
DUPE vb deceive or cheat
▷ n person who is easily
deceived
DUPED > DUPE
DUPER > DUPE
DUPERIES > DUPE
DUPERS > DUPE
DUPERY > DUPE
DUPES > DUPE
DUPING > DUPE
DUPION n silk fabric made
from the threads of double
cocoons
DUPIONS > DUPION
DUPLE adj having two
beats in a bar
DUPLET n pair of electrons
shared between two atoms
in a covalent bond
DUPLETS > DUPLET
DUPLEX vb duplicate ▷ n
apartment on two floors
▷ adj having two parts
DUPLEXED > DUPLEX
DUPLEXER n
telecommunications
system
DUPLEXERS > DUPLEXER
DUPLEXES > DUPLEX
DUPLEXING > DUPLEX
DUPLEXITY > DUPLEX
DUPLICAND n feu duty
doubled
DUPLICATE adj copied
exactly from an original ▷ n
exact copy ▷ vb make an
exact copy of
DUPLICITY n deceitful
behaviour
DUPLIED > DUPLY
DUPLIES > DUPLY
DUPLY vb give a second
reply
DUPLYING > DUPLY
DUPONDII > DUPONDIUS
DUPONDIUS n brass coin of
ancient Rome worth half a
sesterce
DUPPED > DUP
DUPPIES > DUPPY
DUPPING > DUP
DUPPY n spirit or ghost
DUPS > DUP
DURA same as > DURRA
DURABLE adj long-lasting

d

d

DURABLES npl goods that require infrequent replacement

DURABLY > DURABLE

DURAL n alloy of aluminium and copper

DURALS > DURAL

DURALUMIN n light and strong aluminium alloy containing copper, silicon, magnesium, and manganese

DURAMEN another name for > HEARTWOOD

DURAMENS > DURAMEN

DURANCE n imprisonment

DURANCES > DURANCE

DURANT n tough, leathery cloth

DURANTS > DURANT

DURAS > DURA

DURATION n length of time that something lasts

DURATIONS > DURATION

DURATIVE adj denoting an aspect of verbs that includes the imperfective and the progressive ⊳ n durative aspect of a verb

DURATIVES > DURATIVE

DURBAR n (formerly) the court of a native ruler or a governor in India

DURBARS > DURBAR

DURDUM same as > DIRDUM

DURDUMS > DURDUM

DURE vb endure

DURED > DURE

DUREFUL adj lasting

DURES > DURE

DURESS n compulsion by use of force or threats

DURESSE same as > DURESS

DURESSES > DURESS

DURGAH same as > DARGAH

DURGAHS > DURGAH

DURGAN n dwarf

DURGANS > DURGAN

DURGIER > DURGY

DURGIEST > DURGY

DURGY adj dwarflike

DURIAN n SE Asian tree whose very large oval fruits have a hard spiny rind and an evil smell

DURIANS > DURIAN

DURICRUST another name for > CALICHE

DURING prep throughout or within the limit of (a period of time)

DURION same as > DURIAN

DURIONS > DURION

DURMAST n large Eurasian oak tree with lobed leaves

DURMASTS > DURMAST

DURN same as > DARN

DURNDEST same as > DARNEDEST

DURNED > DURN

DURNEDER > DURN

DURNEDEST > DURN

DURNING > DURN

DURNS > DURN

DURO n silver peso of Spain or Spanish America

DUROC n breed of pig

DUROCS > DUROC

DUROMETER n instrument for measuring hardness

DUROS > DURO

DUROY n coarse woollen fabric

DUROYS > DUROY

DURR same as > DURRA

DURRA n Old World variety of sorghum with hairy flower spikes and round seeds, cultivated for grain and fodder

DURRAS > DURRA

DURRIE n cotton carpet made in India, often in rectangular pieces fringed at the ends: sometimes used as a sofa cover, wall hanging, etc

DURRIES > DURRY

DURRS > DURR

DURRY n cigarette

DURST a past tense of > DARE

DURUKULI n S American monkey

DURUKULIS > DURUKULI

DURUM n variety of wheat cultivated mainly in the Mediterranean region, used chiefly to make pastas

DURUMS > DURUM

DURZI n Indian tailor

DURZIS > DURZI

DUSH vb strike hard

DUSHED > DUSH

DUSHES > DUSH

DUSHING > DUSH

DUSK n time just before nightfall, when it is almost dark ⊳ adj shady ⊳ vb make or become dark

DUSKED > DUSK

DUSKEN vb grow dark

DUSKENED > DUSKEN

DUSKENING > DUSKEN

DUSKENS > DUSKEN

DUSKER > DUSK

DUSKEST > DUSK

DUSKIER > DUSKY

DUSKIEST > DUSKY

DUSKILY > DUSKY

DUSKINESS > DUSKY

DUSKING > DUSK

DUSKISH > DUSK

DUSKISHLY > DUSK

DUSKLY > DUSK

DUSKNESS > DUSK

DUSKS > DUSK

DUSKY adj dark in colour

DUST n small dry particles of earth, sand, or dirt ⊳ vb remove dust from (furniture) by wiping

DUSTBIN n large container for household rubbish

DUSTBINS > DUSTBIN

DUSTCART n truck for collecting household rubbish

DUSTCARTS > DUSTCART

DUSTCOAT n light, loose-fitting long coat

DUSTCOATS > DUSTCOAT

DUSTCOVER same as > DUSTSHEET

DUSTED > DUST

DUSTER n cloth used for dusting

DUSTERS > DUSTER

DUSTHEAP n accumulation of refuse

DUSTHEAPS > DUSTHEAP

DUSTIER > DUSTY

DUSTIEST > DUSTY

DUSTILY > DUSTY

DUSTINESS > DUSTY

DUSTING > DUST

DUSTINGS > DUST

DUSTLESS > DUST

DUSTLIKE > DUST

DUSTMAN n man whose job is to collect household rubbish

DUSTMEN > DUSTMAN

DUSTOFF n casualty evacuation helicopter

DUSTOFFS > DUSTOFF

DUSTPAN n short-handled shovel into which dust is swept from floors

DUSTPANS > DUSTPAN

DUSTPROOF adj repelling dust

DUSTRAG n cloth for dusting

DUSTRAGS > DUSTRAG

DUSTS > DUST

DUSTSHEET n large cloth cover to protect furniture from dust

DUSTSTORM n storm with whirling column of dust

DUSTUP n quarrel, fight, or argument

DUSTUPS > DUSTUP

DUSTY adj covered with dust

DUTCH n wife

DUTCHES > DUTCH

DUTCHMAN n piece of wood, metal, etc, used to repair or patch faulty workmanship

DUTCHMEN > DUTCHMAN

DUTEOUS adj dutiful or obedient

DUTEOUSLY > DUTEOUS

DUTIABLE adj (of goods) requiring payment of duty

DUTIED adj liable for duty

DUTIES > DUTY

DUTIFUL adj doing what is expected

DUTIFULLY > DUTIFUL

DUTY n work or a task performed as part of one's job

DUUMVIR n one of two coequal magistrates or officers

DUUMVIRAL > DUUMVIR

DUUMVIRI > DUUMVIR

DUUMVIRS > DUUMVIR

DUVET same as > DOONA

DUVETINE same as > DUVETYN

DUVETINES > DUVETINE

DUVETS > DUVET

DUVETYN n soft napped velvety fabric of cotton, silk, wool, or rayon

DUVETYNE same as > DUVETYN

DUVETYNES > DUVETYNE

DUVETYNS > DUVETYN

DUX n (in Scottish and certain other schools) the top pupil in a class or school

DUXELLES n paste of mushrooms and onions

DUXES > DUX

DUYKER same as > DUIKER

DUYKERS > DUYKER

DVANDVA n class of compound words consisting of two elements having a coordinate relationship as if connected by and

DVANDVAS > DVANDVA

DVORNIK n Russian doorkeeper

DVORNIKS > DVORNIK

DWAAL n state of absent-mindedness

DWAALS > DWAAL

DWALE n deadly nightshade

DWALES > DWALE

DWALM vb faint

DWALMED > DWALM

DWALMING > DWALM

DWALMS > DWALM

DWAM n stupor or daydream ⊳ vb faint or fall ill

DWAMMED > DWAM

DWAMMING > DWAM

DWAMS > DWAM

DWANG n short piece of wood inserted in a timber-framed wall

DWANGS > DWANG

DWARF adj undersized ⊳ n person who is smaller than average ⊳ adj (of an animal or plant) much smaller than the usual size for the species ⊳ vb cause (someone or something) to seem small by being much larger

DWARFED > DWARF

DWARFER > DWARF

DWARFEST > DWARF

DWARFING > DWARF

DWARFISH > DWARF

DWARFISM n condition of being a dwarf

DWARFISMS > DWARFISM

DWARFLIKE > DWARF

DWARFNESS > DWARF

DWARFS > DWARF

DWARVES > DWARF

DWAUM same as > DWAM

DWAUMED > DWAUM

DWAUMING > DWAUM

DWAUMS > DWAUM

DWEEB n stupid or

uninteresting person
DWEEBIER > DWEEBY
DWEEBIEST > DWEEBY
DWEEBISH > DWEEB
DWEEBS > DWEEB
DWEEBY adj like or typical of a dweeb
DWELL vb live, reside ▷ n regular pause in the operation of a machine
DWELLED > DWELL
DWELLER > DWELL
DWELLERS > DWELL
DWELLING > DWELL
DWELLINGS > DWELL
DWELLS > DWELL
DWELT > DWELL
DWILE n floor cloth
DWILES > DWILE
DWINDLE vb grow less in size, strength, or number
DWINDLED > DWINDLE
DWINDLES > DWINDLE
DWINDLING > DWINDLE
DWINE vb languish
DWINED > DWINE
DWINES > DWINE
DWINING > DWINE
DYABLE > DYE
DYAD n operator that is the unspecified product of two vectors. It can operate on a vector to produce either a scalar or vector product
DYADIC adj of or relating to a dyad ▷ n sum of a particular number of dyads
DYADICS > DYADIC
DYADS > DYAD
DYARCHAL > DIARCHY
DYARCHIC > DYARCHY
DYARCHIES > DYARCHY
DYARCHY same as > DIARCHY
DYBBUK n (in the folklore of the cabala) the soul of a dead sinner that has transmigrated into the body of a living person
DYBBUKIM > DYBBUK
DYBBUKKIM > DYBBUK
DYBBUKS > DYBBUK
DYE n colouring substance ▷ vb colour (hair or fabric) by applying a dye
DYEABLE > DYE
DYED > DYE
DYEING > DYE
DYEINGS > DYE
DYELINE same as > DIAZO
DYELINES > DYELINE
DYER > DYE
DYERS > DYE
DYES > DYE
DYESTER n dyer
DYESTERS > DYESTER
DYESTUFF n substance that can be used as a dye or from which a dye can be obtained
DYESTUFFS > DYESTUFF
DYEWEED n plant that produces dye
DYEWEEDS > DYEWEED

DYEWOOD n any wood, such as brazil, from which dyes and pigments can be obtained
DYEWOODS > DYEWOOD
DYING > DIE
DYINGLY > DIE
DYINGNESS > DIE
DYINGS > DIE
DYKE n wall built to prevent flooding ▷ vb embankment or wall built to confine a river to a particular course
DYKED > DYKE
DYKES > DYKE
DYKEY same as > DIKEY
DYKIER > DYKEY
DYKIEST > DYKEY
DYKING > DYKE
DYKON n celebrity admired by lesbians
DYKONS > DYKON
DYNAMETER n instrument for determining the magnifying power of telescopes
DYNAMIC adj full of energy, ambition, and new ideas ▷ n energetic or driving force
DYNAMICAL same as > DYNAMIC
DYNAMICS n branch of mechanics concerned with the forces that change or produce the motions of bodies
DYNAMISE same as > DYNAMIZE
DYNAMISED > DYNAMISE
DYNAMISES > DYNAMISE
DYNAMISM n great energy and enthusiasm
DYNAMISMS > DYNAMISM
DYNAMIST > DYNAMISM
DYNAMISTS > DYNAMISM
DYNAMITE n explosive made of nitroglycerine ▷ vb blow (something) up with dynamite
DYNAMITED > DYNAMITE
DYNAMITER > DYNAMITE
DYNAMITES > DYNAMITE
DYNAMITIC > DYNAMITE
DYNAMIZE vb cause to be dynamic
DYNAMIZED > DYNAMIZE
DYNAMIZES > DYNAMIZE
DYNAMO n device for converting mechanical energy into electrical energy
DYNAMOS > DYNAMO
DYNAMOTOR n electrical machine having a single magnetic field and two independent armature windings of which one acts as a motor and the other a generator: used to convert direct current from a battery into alternating current
DYNAST n hereditary ruler
DYNASTIC > DYNASTY

DYNASTIES > DYNASTY
DYNASTS > DYNAST
DYNASTY n sequence of hereditary rulers
DYNATRON as in dynatron oscillator type of oscillator
DYNATRONS > DYNATRON
DYNE n cgs unit of force
DYNEIN n class of proteins
DYNEINS > DYNEIN
DYNEL n trade name for synthetic fibre
DYNELS > DYNEL
DYNES > DYNE
DYNODE n electrode onto which a beam of electrons can fall, causing the emission of a greater number of electrons by secondary emission. They are used in photomultipliers to amplify the signal
DYNODES > DYNODE
DYNORPHIN n drug used to treat cocaine addiction
DYSBINDIN n gene associated with schizophrenia
DYSCHROA n discolouration of skin
DYSCHROAS > DYSCHROA
DYSCHROIA same as > DYSCHROA
DYSCRASIA n any abnormal physiological condition, esp of the blood
DYSCRASIC > DYSCRASIA
DYSCRATIC > DYSCRASIA
DYSENTERY n infection of the intestine causing severe diarrhoea
DYSGENIC adj of, relating to, or contributing to a degeneration or deterioration in the fitness and quality of a race or strain
DYSGENICS n study of factors capable of reducing the quality of a race or strain, esp the human race
DYSLALIA n defective speech characteristic of those affected by aphasia
DYSLALIAS > DYSLALIA
DYSLECTIC > DYSLEXIA
DYSLEXIA n disorder causing impaired ability to read
DYSLEXIAS > DYSLEXIA
DYSLEXIC > DYSLEXIA
DYSLEXICS > DYSLEXIA
DYSLOGIES > DYSLOGY
DYSLOGY n uncomplimentary remarks
DYSMELIA n condition of missing or stunted limbs
DYSMELIAS > DYSMELIA
DYSMELIC > DYSMELIA
DYSODIL n yellow or green mineral
DYSODILE same as

> DYSODIL
DYSODILES > DYSODILE
DYSODILS > DYSODIL
DYSODYLE same as > DYSODIL
DYSODYLES > DYSODIL
DYSPATHY n dislike
DYSPEPSIA n indigestion
DYSPEPSY same as > DYSPEPSIA
DYSPEPTIC adj relating to or suffering from dyspepsia ▷ n person suffering from dyspepsia
DYSPHAGIA n difficulty in swallowing, caused by obstruction or spasm of the oesophagus
DYSPHAGIC > DYSPHAGIA
DYSPHAGY same as > DYSPHAGIA
DYSPHASIA n disorder of language caused by a brain lesion
DYSPHASIC > DYSPHASIA
DYSPHONIA n any impairment in the ability to speak normally, as from spasm or strain of the vocal cords
DYSPHONIC > DYSPHONIA
DYSPHORIA n feeling of being ill at ease
DYSPHORIC > DYSPHORIA
DYSPLASIA n abnormal development of an organ or part of the body, including congenital absence
DYSPNEA same as > DYSPNOEA
DYSPNEAL > DYSPNEA
DYSPNEAS > DYSPNEA
DYSPNEIC > DYSPNEA
DYSPNOEA n difficulty in breathing or in catching the breath
DYSPNOEAL > DYSPNOEA
DYSPNOEAS > DYSPNOEA
DYSPNOEIC > DYSPNOEA
DYSPNOIC > DYSPNEA
DYSPRAXIA n impairment in the control of the motor system
DYSPRAXIC adj suffering from dyspraxia
DYSTAXIA n lack of muscular coordination resulting in shaky limb movements and unsteady gait
DYSTAXIAS > DYSTAXIA
DYSTECTIC adj difficult to fuse together
DYSTHESIA n unpleasant skin sensation
DYSTHETIC > DYSTHESIA
DYSTHYMIA n characteristics of the neurotic and introverted, including anxiety,

d

depression, and compulsive behaviour

DYSTHYMIC
> DYSTHYMIA

DYSTOCIA *n* abnormal, slow, or difficult childbirth, usually because of disordered or ineffective contractions of the uterus

DYSTOCIAL > DYSTOCIA

DYSTOCIAS > DYSTOCIA

DYSTONIA *n* neurological disorder, caused by disease of the basal ganglia, in which the muscles of the trunk, shoulders, and neck go into spasm, so that the head and limbs are held in unnatural positions

DYSTONIAS > DYSTONIA

DYSTONIC > DYSTONIA

DYSTOPIA *n* imaginary place where everything is as bad as it can be

DYSTOPIAN > DYSTOPIA

DYSTOPIAS > DYSTOPIA

DYSTROPHY *n* any of various bodily disorders, characterized by wasting of tissues

DYSURIA *n* difficult or painful urination

DYSURIAS > DYSURIA

DYSURIC > DYSURIA

DYSURIES > DYSURY

DYSURY *same as*
> DYSURIA

DYTISCID *n* type of carnivorous aquatic beetle with large flattened back legs used for swimming

DYTISCIDS > DYTISCID

DYVOUR *n* debtor

DYVOURIES > DYVOURY

DYVOURS > DYVOUR

DYVOURY *n* bankruptcy

DZEREN *n* Chinese yellow antelope

DZERENS > DZEREN

DZHO *same as* > ZHO

DZHOS > DZHO

DZIGGETAI *a variant of*
> CHIGETAI

DZO *a variant spelling of* > ZO

DZOS > ZO

Ee

EA n river
EACH pron every (one) taken separately ▷ det every (one) of two or more considered individually ▷ adv for, to, or from each one
EACHWHERE adv everywhere
EADISH n aftermath
EADISHES > EADISH
EAGER adj showing or feeling great desire, keen ▷ n eagre
EAGERER > EAGER
EAGEREST > EAGER
EAGERLY > EAGER
EAGERNESS > EAGER
EAGERS > EAGER
EAGLE n bird of prey ▷ vb in golf, score two strokes under par for a hole
EAGLED > EAGLE
EAGLEHAWK n large Australian eagle
EAGLES > EAGLE
EAGLET n young eagle
EAGLETS > EAGLET
EAGLEWOOD n Asian thymelaeaceous tree with fragrant wood that yields a resin used as a perfume
EAGLING > EAGLE
EAGRE n tidal bore, esp of the Humber or Severn estuaries
EAGRES > EAGRE
EALDORMAN n official of Anglo-Saxon England, appointed by the king, who was responsible for law, order, and justice in his shire and for leading his local fyrd in battle
EALDORMEN > EALDORMAN
EALE n beast in Roman legend
EALES > EALE
EAN vb give birth
EANED > EAN
EANING > EAN
EANLING n newborn lamb
EANLINGS > EANLING
EANS > EAN
EAR n organ of hearing, esp the external part of it ▷ vb (of cereal plants) to develop such parts
EARACHE n pain in the ear
EARACHES > EARACHE

EARBALL n (in acupressure) a small ball kept in position in the ear and pressed when needed to relieve stress
EARBALLS > EARBALL
EARBASH vb talk incessantly
EARBASHED > EARBASH
EARBASHER > EARBASH
EARBASHES > EARBASH
EARBOB n earring
EARBOBS > EARBOB
EARBUD n small earphone
EARBUDS > EARBUD
EARCON n sound representing object or event
EARCONS > EARCON
EARD vb bury
EARDED > EARD
EARDING > EARD
EARDROP n pendant earring
EARDROPS npl liquid medication for inserting into the external ear
EARDRUM n thin piece of skin inside the ear which enables one to hear sounds
EARDRUMS > EARDRUM
EARDS > EARD
EARED adj having an ear or ears
EARFLAP n either of two pieces of fabric or fur attached to a cap, which can be let down to keep the ears warm
EARFLAPS > EARFLAP
EARFUL n scolding or telling-off
EARFULS > EARFUL
EARING n line fastened to a corner of a sail for reefing
EARINGS > EARING
EARL n British nobleman ranking next below a marquess
EARLAP same as > EARFLAP
EARLAPS > EARLAP
EARLDOM n rank, title, or dignity of an earl or countess
EARLDOMS > EARLDOM
EARLESS > EAR
EARLIER > EARLY
EARLIES > EARLY
EARLIEST > EARLY
EARLIKE > EAR

EARLINESS > EARLY
EARLOBE n fleshy lower part of the outer ear
EARLOBES > EARLOBE
EARLOCK n curl of hair close to ear
EARLOCKS > EARLOCK
EARLS > EARL
EARLSHIP n title or position of earl
EARLSHIPS > EARLSHIP
EARLY adv before the expected or usual time ▷ adj occurring or arriving before the correct or expected time ▷ n something which is early
EARLYWOOD n light wood made by tree in spring
EARMARK vb set (something) aside for a specific purpose ▷ n distinguishing mark
EARMARKED > EARMARK
EARMARKS > EARMARK
EARMUFF n one of a pair of pads of fur or cloth, joined by a headband, for keeping the ears warm
EARMUFFS > EARMUFF
EARN vb obtain by work or merit
EARNED > EARN
EARNER > EARN
EARNERS > EARN
EARNEST adj serious and sincere ▷ n part payment given in advance, esp to confirm a contract
EARNESTLY > EARNEST
EARNESTS > EARNEST
EARNING > EARN
EARNINGS npl money earned
EARNS > EARN
EARPHONE n receiver for a radio etc, held to or put in the ear
EARPHONES > EARPHONE
EARPICK n instrument for removing ear wax
EARPICKS > EARPICK
EARPIECE n earphone in a telephone receiver
EARPIECES > EARPIECE
EARPLUG n piece of soft material placed in the ear to keep out water or noise
EARPLUGS > EARPLUG
EARRING n ornament for the lobe of the ear

EARRINGED adj wearing earrings
EARRINGS > EARRING
EARS > EAR
EARSHOT n hearing range
EARSHOTS > EARSHOT
EARST adv first; previously
EARSTONE n calcium carbonate crystal in the ear
EARSTONES > EARSTONE
EARTH n planet that we live on ▷ vb connect (a circuit) to earth
EARTHBORN adj of earthly origin
EARTHED > EARTH
EARTHEN adj made of baked clay or earth
EARTHFALL n landslide
EARTHFAST adj method of building
EARTHFLAX n type of asbestos
EARTHIER > EARTHY
EARTHIEST > EARTHY
EARTHILY > EARTHY
EARTHING > EARTH
EARTHLIER > EARTHLY
EARTHLIES > EARTHLY
EARTHLIKE > EARTH
EARTHLING n (esp in poetry or science fiction) an inhabitant of the earth
EARTHLY adj conceivable or possible ▷ n a chance
EARTHMAN n (esp in science fiction) an inhabitant or native of the earth
EARTHMEN > EARTHMAN
EARTHNUT n perennial umbelliferous plant of Europe and Asia, with edible dark brown tubers
EARTHNUTS > EARTHNUT
EARTHPEA n peanut; groundnut
EARTHPEAS > EARTHPEA
EARTHRISE n rising of the earth above the lunar horizon, as seen from a spacecraft emerging from the lunar farside
EARTHS > EARTH
EARTHSET n setting of the earth below the lunar horizon, as seen from a spacecraft emerging from the lunar farside
EARTHSETS > EARTHSET

EARTHSTAR n type of woodland fungus
EARTHWARD adv towards the earth
EARTHWAX n ozocerite
EARTHWOLF n aardvark
EARTHWORK n fortification made of earth
EARTHWORM n worm which burrows in the soil
EARTHY adj coarse or crude
EARWAX nontechnical name for > CERUMEN
EARWAXES > EARWAX
EARWIG n small insect with a pincer-like tail ▷ vb eavesdrop
EARWIGGED > EARWIG
EARWIGGY > EARWIG
EARWIGS > EARWIG
EARWORM n irritatingly catchy tune
EARWORMS > EARWORM
EAS > EA
EASE n freedom from difficulty, discomfort, or worry ▷ vb give bodily or mental ease to
EASED > EASE
EASEFUL adj characterized by or bringing ease
EASEFULLY > EASEFUL
EASEL n frame to support an artist's canvas or a blackboard
EASELED adj mounted on easel
EASELESS > EASE
EASELS > EASEL
EASEMENT n right enjoyed by a landowner of making limited use of his neighbour's land, as by crossing it to reach his own property
EASEMENTS > EASEMENT
EASER > EASE
EASERS > EASE
EASES > EASE
EASIED > EASY
EASIER > EASY
EASIES > EASY
EASIEST > EASY
EASILY adv without difficulty
EASINESS n quality or condition of being easy to accomplish, do, obtain, etc
EASING n as in *quantitative easing* increasing the supply of money to stimulate the economy
EASINGS > EASING
EASLE n hot ash
EASLES > EASLE
EASSEL adv easterly
EASSIL adv easterly
EAST n (direction towards) the part of the horizon where the sun rises ▷ adj in the east ▷ adv in, to, or towards the east ▷ vb move or turn east
EASTABOUT adv in, to, or towards the east

EASTBOUND adj going towards the east
EASTED > EAST
EASTER n most important festival of the Christian Church, commemorating the Resurrection of Christ
EASTERLY adj of or in the east ▷ adv towards the east ▷ n wind from the east
EASTERN adj situated in or towards the east
EASTERNER n person from the east of a country or area
EASTERS > EASTER
EASTING n net distance eastwards made by a vessel moving towards the east
EASTINGS > EASTING
EASTLAND adj relating to land in east
EASTLANDS > EASTLAND
EASTLIN adj easterly
EASTLING adj easterly
EASTLINGS adv eastward
EASTLINS adv eastward
EASTMOST adj furthest east
EASTS > EAST
EASTWARD same as > EASTWARDS
EASTWARDS adv towards the east
EASY adj not needing much work or effort ▷ vb stop rowing
EASYGOING adj relaxed in manner
EASYING > EASY
EAT vb take (food) into the mouth and swallow it
EATABLE adj fit or suitable for eating
EATABLES npl food
EATAGE n grazing rights
EATAGES > EATAGE
EATCHE n adze
EATCHES > EATCHE
EATEN > EAT
EATER > EAT
EATERIE same as > EATERY
EATERIES > EATERY
EATERS > EAT
EATERY n restaurant or eating house
EATH adj easy
EATHE same as > EATH
EATHLY > EATH
EATING > EAT
EATINGS > EAT
EATS > EAT
EAU same as > EA
EAUS > EAU
EAUX > EAU
EAVE n overhanging edge of a roof
EAVED adj having eaves
EAVES > EAVE
EAVESDRIP n water dropping from eaves
EAVESDROP vb listen secretly to a private conversation

EBAUCHE n rough sketch
EBAUCHES > EBAUCHE
EBAYER n any person who buys or sells using the internet auction site, eBay
EBAYERS > EBAYER
EBAYING n buying or selling using the internet auction site eBay
EBAYINGS > EBAYING
EBB vb (of tide water) flow back ▷ n flowing back of the tide
EBBED > EBB
EBBET n type of newt
EBBETS > EBBET
EBBING > EBB
EBBLESS > EBB
EBBS > EBB
EBENEZER n chapel
EBENEZERS > EBENEZER
EBENISTE n cabinetmaker
EBENISTES > EBENISTE
EBIONISE same as > EBIONIZE
EBIONISED > EBIONISE
EBIONISES > EBIONISE
EBIONISM n doctrine that the poor shall be saved
EBIONISMS > EBIONISM
EBIONITIC > EBIONISM
EBIONIZE vb preach ebionism
EBIONIZED > EBIONIZE
EBIONIZES > EBIONIZE
EBON poetic word for > EBONY
EBONICS n dialect used by African-Americans
EBONIES > EBONY
EBONISE same as > EBONIZE
EBONISED > EBONISE
EBONISES > EBONISE
EBONISING > EBONISE
EBONIST n carver of ebony
EBONISTS > EBONIST
EBONITE another name for > VULCANITE
EBONITES > EBONITE
EBONIZE vb stain or otherwise finish in imitation of ebony
EBONIZED > EBONIZE
EBONIZES > EBONIZE
EBONIZING > EBONIZE
EBONS > EBON
EBONY n hard black wood ▷ adj deep black
EBOOK n book in electronic form
EBOOKS > EBOOK
EBRIATE adj drunk
EBRIATED > EBRIATE
EBRIETIES > EBRIETY
EBRIETY n drunkenness
EBRILLADE n jerk on rein, when horse refuses to turn
EBRIOSE adj drunk
EBRIOSITY > EBRIOSE
EBULLIENT adj full of enthusiasm or excitement
EBURNEAN adj made of ivory

EBURNEOUS adj like ivory
ECAD n organism whose form has been affected by its environment
ECADS > ECAD
ECARINATE adj having no carina or keel
ECARTE n card-game for two, played with 32 cards and king high
ECARTES > ECARTE
ECAUDATE adj tailless
ECBOLE n digression
ECBOLES > ECBOLE
ECBOLIC adj hastening labour or abortion ▷ n drug or agent that hastens labour or abortion
ECBOLICS > ECBOLIC
ECCE interj behold
ECCENTRIC adj odd or unconventional ▷ n eccentric person
ECCLESIA n (in informal Church usage) a congregation
ECCLESIAE > ECCLESIA
ECCLESIAL adj ecclesiastical
ECCO interj look there
ECCRINE adj of or denoting glands that secrete externally, esp the numerous sweat glands on the human body
ECCRISES > ECCRISIS
ECCRISIS n excrement
ECCRITIC n purgative
ECCRITICS > ECCRITIC
ECDEMIC adj not indigenous or endemic
ECDYSES > ECDYSIS
ECDYSIAL > ECDYSIS
ECDYSIAST facetious word for > STRIPPER
ECDYSIS n periodic shedding of the cuticle in insects and other arthropods or the outer epidermal layer in reptiles
ECDYSON > ECDYSONE
ECDYSONE n hormone secreted by the prothoracic gland of insects that controls ecdysis and stimulates metamorphosis
ECDYSONES > ECDYSONE
ECDYSONS > ECDYSON
ECESIC > ECESIS
ECESIS n establishment of a plant in a new environment
ECESISES > ECESIS
ECH same as > ECHE
ECHAPPE n leap in ballet
ECHAPPES > ECHAPPE
ECHARD n water that is present in the soil but cannot be absorbed or otherwise utilized by plants
ECHARDS > ECHARD
ECHE vb eke out
ECHED > ECHE
ECHELLE n ladder; scale
ECHELLES > ECHELLE**

ECHELON n level of power or responsibility ▷ vb assemble in echelon

ECHELONED > ECHELON

ECHELONS > ECHELON

ECHES > ECHE

ECHEVERIA n tropical American plant cultivated for its colourful foliage

ECHIDNA n Australian spiny egg-laying mammal

ECHIDNAE > ECHIDNA

ECHIDNAS > ECHIDNA

ECHIDNINE n snake poison

ECHINACEA n N American plant with purple and black flowers

ECHINATE adj covered with spines, bristles, or bristle-like outgrowths

ECHINATED same as > ECHINATE

ECHING > ECHE

ECHINI > ECHINUS

ECHINOID n type of echinoderm of the class which includes the sea urchins and sand dollars

ECHINOIDS > ECHINOID

ECHINUS n ovolo moulding between the shaft and the abacus of a Doric column

ECHINUSES > ECHINUS

ECHIUM n type of Eurasian and African plant

ECHIUMS > ECHIUM

ECHIURAN n spoonworm

ECHIURANS > ECHIURAN

ECHIUROID n marine worm

ECHO n repetition of sounds by reflection of sound waves off a surface ▷ vb repeat or be repeated as an echo

ECHOED > ECHO

ECHOER > ECHO

ECHOERS > ECHO

ECHOES > ECHO

ECHOEY adj producing echoes

ECHOGRAM n record made by echography

ECHOGRAMS > ECHOGRAM

ECHOGRAPH n device that uses sonic waves to measure the depth of water

ECHOIC adj characteristic of or resembling an echo

ECHOIER > ECHOEY

ECHOIEST > ECHOEY

ECHOING > ECHO

ECHOISE same as > ECHOIZE

ECHOISED > ECHOISE

ECHOISES > ECHOISE

ECHOISING > ECHOISE

ECHOISM n onomatopoeia as a source of word formation

ECHOISMS > ECHOISM

ECHOIST > ECHOISM

ECHOISTS > ECHOISM

ECHOIZE vb repeat like echo

ECHOIZED > ECHOIZE

ECHOIZES > ECHOIZE

ECHOIZING > ECHOIZE

ECHOLALIA n tendency to repeat mechanically words just spoken by another person: can occur in cases of brain damage, mental retardation, and schizophrenia

ECHOLALIC > ECHOLALIA

ECHOLESS > ECHO

ECHOS > ECHO

ECHOVIRUS n any of a group of viruses that can cause symptoms of mild meningitis, the common cold, or infections of the intestinal and respiratory tracts

ECHT adj real

ECLAIR n finger-shaped pastry filled with cream and covered with chocolate

ECLAIRS > ECLAIR

ECLAMPSIA n serious condition that can develop towards the end of a pregnancy, causing high blood pressure, swelling, and convulsions

ECLAMPSY same as > ECLAMPSIA

ECLAMPTIC > ECLAMPSIA

ECLAT n brilliant success

ECLATS > ECLAT

ECLECTIC adj selecting from various styles, ideas, or sources ▷ n person who takes an eclectic approach

ECLECTICS > ECLECTIC

ECLIPSE n temporary obscuring of one star or planet by another ▷ vb surpass or outclass

ECLIPSED > ECLIPSE

ECLIPSER > ECLIPSE

ECLIPSERS > ECLIPSE

ECLIPSES > ECLIPSIS

ECLIPSING > ECLIPSE

ECLIPSIS same as > ELLIPSIS

ECLIPTIC n apparent path of the sun ▷ adj of or relating to an eclipse

ECLIPTICS > ECLIPTIC

ECLOGITE n rare coarse-grained basic rock consisting principally of garnet and pyroxene. Quartz, feldspar, etc, may also be present. It is thought to originate by metamorphism or igneous crystallization at extremely high pressure

ECLOGITES > ECLOGITE

ECLOGUE n pastoral or idyllic poem, usually in the form of a conversation or soliloquy

ECLOGUES > ECLOGUE

ECLOSE vb emerge

ECLOSED > ECLOSE

ECLOSES > ECLOSE

ECLOSING > ECLOSE

ECLOSION n emergence of an insect larva from the egg or an adult from the pupal case

ECLOSIONS > ECLOSION

ECO n ecology activist

ECOCIDAL > ECOCIDE

ECOCIDE n total destruction of an area of the natural environment, esp by human agency

ECOCIDES > ECOCIDE

ECOD same as > EGAD

ECOFREAK n environmentalist

ECOFREAKS > ECOFREAK

ECOLODGE n eco-friendly tourist accommodation

ECOLODGES > ECOLODGE

ECOLOGIC > ECOLOGY

ECOLOGIES > ECOLOGY

ECOLOGIST > ECOLOGY

ECOLOGY n study of the relationships between living things and their environment

ECOMAP n diagram showing the relationships between an individual and their community

ECOMAPS > ECOMAP

ECOMMERCE n business transactions conducted on the internet

ECONOBOX n fuel efficient utility vehicle

ECONOMIC adj of economics

ECONOMICS n social science concerned with the production and consumption of goods and services

ECONOMIES > ECONOMY

ECONOMISE same as > ECONOMIZE

ECONOMISM n political theory that regards economics as the main factor in society, ignoring or reducing to simplistic economic terms other factors such as culture, nationality, etc

ECONOMIST n specialist in economics

ECONOMIZE vb reduce expense or waste

ECONOMY n system of interrelationship of money, industry, and employment in a country ▷ adj denoting a class of air travel that is cheaper than first-class

ECONUT n environmentalist

ECONUTS > ECONUT

ECOPHOBIA n fear of home

ECORCHE n anatomical figure without the skin, so that the muscular structure is visible

ECORCHES > ECORCHE

ECOREGION n area defined by its environmental conditions, esp climate, landforms, and soil characteristics

ECOS > ECO

ECOSPHERE n planetary ecosystem, consisting of all living organisms and their environment

ECOSSAISE n lively dance in two-four time

ECOSTATE adj with no ribs or nerves

ECOSYSTEM n system involving interactions between a community and its environment

ECOTAGE n sabotage for ecological motives

ECOTAGES > ECOTAGE

ECOTARIAN n person who eats only eco-friendly food

ECOTONAL > ECOTONE

ECOTONE n zone between two major ecological communities

ECOTONES > ECOTONE

ECOTOUR n holiday taking care not to damage environment

ECOTOURS > ECOTOUR

ECOTOXIC adj harmful to animals, plants or the environment

ECOTYPE n group of organisms within a species that is adapted to particular environmental conditions and therefore exhibits behavioural, structural, or physiological differences from other members of the species

ECOTYPES > ECOTYPE

ECOTYPIC > ECOTYPE

ECPHRASES > ECPHRASIS

ECPHRASIS same as > EKPHRASIS

ECRASEUR n surgical device consisting of a heavy wire loop placed around a part to be removed and tightened until it cuts through

ECRASEURS > ECRASEUR

ECRITOIRE n writing desk with compartments and drawers

ECRU adj pale creamy-brown ▷ n greyish-yellow to a light greyish colour

ECRUS > ECRU

ECSTASES > ECSTASIS

ECSTASIED > ECSTASY

ECSTASIES > ECSTASY

ECSTASIS same as > ECSTASY

e

ECSTASISE *same as* > ECSTASIZE

ECSTASIZE *vb* make or become ecstatic

ECSTASY *n* state of intense delight

ECSTATIC *adj* in a trancelike state of great rapture or delight ▷ *n* person who has periods of intense trancelike joy

ECSTATICS *npl* fits of delight or rapture

ECTASES > ECTASIS

ECTASIA *n* distension or dilation of a duct, vessel, or hollow viscus

ECTASIAS > ECTASIA

ECTASIS *same as* > ECTASIA

ECTATIC > ECTASIA

ECTHYMA *n* local inflammation of the skin characterized by flat ulcerating pustules

ECTHYMAS > ECTHYMA

ECTHYMATA > ECTHYMA

ECTOBLAST *same as* > EPIBLAST

ECTOCRINE *n* substance that is released by an organism into the external environment and influences the development, behaviour, etc, of members of the same or different species

ECTODERM *n* outer germ layer of an animal embryo, which gives rise to epidermis and nervous tissue

ECTODERMS > ECTODERM

ECTOGENIC *adj* capable of developing outside the host

ECTOGENY *n* (of bacteria, etc) development outside the host

ECTOMERE *n* any of the blastomeres that later develop into ectoderm

ECTOMERES > ECTOMERE

ECTOMERIC > ECTOMERE

ECTOMORPH *n* person with a thin body build: said to be correlated with cerebrotonia

ECTOPHYTE *n* parasitic plant that lives on the surface of its host

ECTOPIA *n* congenital displacement or abnormal positioning of an organ or part

ECTOPIAS > ECTOPIA

ECTOPIC > ECTOPIA

ECTOPIES > ECTOPY

ECTOPLASM *n* substance that supposedly is emitted from the body of a medium during a trance

ECTOPROCT *another word for* > BRYOZOAN

ECTOPY *same as* > ECTOPIA

ECTOSARC *n* ectoplasm of an amoeba or any other protozoan

ECTOSARCS > ECTOSARC

ECTOTHERM *n* animal whose body temperature is determined by ambient temperature

ECTOZOA > ECTOZOON

ECTOZOAN *same as* > ECTOZOON

ECTOZOANS > ECTOZOAN

ECTOZOIC > ECTOZOON

ECTOZOON *n* parasitic organism that lives on the outside of its host

ECTROPIC > ECTROPION

ECTROPION *n* condition in which the eyelid turns over exposing some of the inner lid

ECTROPIUM *same as* > ECTROPION

ECTYPAL > ECTYPE

ECTYPE *n* copy as distinguished from a prototype

ECTYPES > ECTYPE

ECU *n* any of various former French gold or silver coins

ECUELLE *n* covered soup bowl with handles

ECUELLES > ECUELLE

ECUMENIC *adj* tending to promote unity among Churches

ECUMENICS > ECUMENIC

ECUMENISM *n* aim of unity among Christian churches throughout the world

ECUMENIST > ECUMENISM

ECURIE *n* team of motor-racing cars

ECURIES > ECURIE

ECUS > ECU

ECZEMA *n* skin disease causing intense itching

ECZEMAS > ECZEMA

ED *n* editor

EDACIOUS *adj* devoted to eating

EDACITIES > EDACIOUS

EDACITY > EDACIOUS

EDAMAME *n* immature soybeans boiled in the pod

EDAMAMES > EDAMAME

EDAPHIC *adj* of or relating to the physical and chemical conditions of the soil, esp in relation to the plant and animal life it supports

EDDIED > EDDY

EDDIES > EDDY

EDDISH *n* pasture grass

EDDISHES > EDDISH

EDDO *same as* > TARO

EDDOES > EDDO

EDDY *n* circular movement of air, water, etc ▷ *vb* move with a circular motion

EDDYING > EDDY

EDELWEISS *n* alpine plant with white flowers

EDEMA *same as* > OEDEMA

EDEMAS > EDEMA

EDEMATA > EDEMA

EDEMATOSE > EDEMA

EDEMATOUS > EDEMA

EDENIC *adj* delightful, like the Garden of Eden

EDENTAL *adj* having few or no teeth

EDENTATE *n* mammal with few or no teeth, such as an armadillo or a sloth ▷ *adj* denoting such a mammal

EDENTATES > EDENTATE

EDGE *n* border or line where something ends or begins ▷ *vb* provide an edge or border for

EDGEBONE *n* aitchbone

EDGEBONES > EDGEBONE

EDGED > EDGE

EDGELESS > EDGE

EDGER > EDGE

EDGERS > EDGE

EDGES > EDGE

EDGEWAYS *adv* with the edge forwards or uppermost

EDGEWISE *same as* > EDGEWAYS

EDGIER > EDGY

EDGIEST > EDGY

EDGILY > EDGY

EDGINESS > EDGY

EDGING *n* anything placed along an edge to finish it ▷ *adj* relating to or used for making an edge

EDGINGS > EDGING

EDGY *adj* nervous or irritable

EDH *n* character of the runic alphabet used to represent the voiced dental fricative

EDHS > EDH

EDIBILITY > EDIBLE

EDIBLE *adj* fit to be eaten

EDIBLES *npl* articles fit to eat

EDICT *n* order issued by an authority

EDICTAL > EDICT

EDICTALLY > EDICT

EDICTS > EDICT

EDIFICE *n* large building

EDIFICES > EDIFICE

EDIFICIAL > EDIFICE

EDIFIED > EDIFY

EDIFIER > EDIFY

EDIFIERS > EDIFY

EDIFIES > EDIFY

EDIFY *vb* improve morally by instruction

EDIFYING > EDIFY

EDILE *variant spelling of* > AEDILE

EDILES > EDILE

EDIT *vb* prepare (a book, film, etc) for publication or broadcast ▷ *n* act of editing

EDITABLE > EDIT

EDITED > EDIT

EDITING > EDIT

EDITINGS > EDIT

EDITION *n* number of copies of a new publication printed at one time ▷ *vb* produce multiple copies of (an original work of art)

EDITIONED > EDITION

EDITIONS > EDITION

EDITOR *n* person who edits

EDITORIAL *n* newspaper article stating the opinion of the editor ▷ *adj* of editing or editors

EDITORS > EDITOR

EDITRESS *n* female editor

EDITRICES > EDITRIX

EDITRIX *n* female editor

EDITRIXES > EDITRIX

EDITS > EDIT

EDS > ED

EDUCABLE *adj* capable of being trained or educated ▷ *n* mentally retarded person who is capable of being educated

EDUCABLES > EDUCABLE

EDUCATE *vb* teach

EDUCATED *adj* having an education, esp a good one

EDUCATES > EDUCATE

EDUCATING > EDUCATE

EDUCATION *n* process of acquiring knowledge and understanding

EDUCATIVE *adj* educating

EDUCATOR *n* person who educates

EDUCATORS > EDUCATOR

EDUCATORY *adj* educative or educational

EDUCE *vb* evolve or develop, esp from a latent or potential state

EDUCED > EDUCE

EDUCEMENT > EDUCE

EDUCES > EDUCE

EDUCIBLE > EDUCE

EDUCING > EDUCE

EDUCT *n* substance separated from another substance without chemical change

EDUCTION *n* something educed

EDUCTIONS > EDUCTION

EDUCTIVE > EDUCE

EDUCTOR > EDUCE

EDUCTORS > EDUCE

EDUCTS > EDUCT

EE *Scots word for* > EYE

EECH *same as* > ECHE

EECHED > EECH

EECHES > EECH

EECHING > EECH

EEJIT *Scots and Irish word for* > IDIOT

EEJITS > EEJIT

EEK *interj* indicating shock or fright

EEL *n* snakelike fish

EELFARE *n* young eel

EELFARES > EELFARE

EELGRASS *n* type of submerged marine plant

with grasslike leaves
EELIER > EEL
EELIEST > EEL
EELLIKE adj resembling an eel
EELPOUT n marine eel-like blennioid fish
EELPOUTS > EELPOUT
EELS > EEL
EELWORM n any of various nematode worms, esp the wheatworm and the vinegar eel
EELWORMS > EELWORM
EELWRACK n grasslike plant growing in seawater
EELWRACKS > EELWRACK
EELY > EEL
EEN > EE
EERIE adj uncannily frightening or disturbing
EERIER > EERIE
EERIEST > EERIE
EERILY > EERIE
EERINESS > EERIE
EERY same as > EERIE
EEVEN n evening
EEVENS > EEVEN
EEVN n evening
EEVNING n evening
EEVNINGS > EEVNING
EEVNS > EEVN
EF n sixth letter of Roman alphabet
EFF vb say the word 'fuck'
EFFABLE adj capable of being expressed in words
EFFACE vb remove by rubbing
EFFACED > EFFACE
EFFACER > EFFACE
EFFACERS > EFFACE
EFFACES > EFFACE
EFFACING > EFFACE
EFFECT n change or result caused by someone or something ▷ vb cause to happen, accomplish
EFFECTED > EFFECT
EFFECTER > EFFECT
EFFECTERS > EFFECT
EFFECTING > EFFECT
EFFECTIVE adj producing a desired result ▷ n serviceman who is equipped and prepared for action
EFFECTOR n nerve ending that terminates in a muscle or gland and provides neural stimulation causing contraction or secretion
EFFECTORS > EFFECTOR
EFFECTS npl personal belongings
EFFECTUAL adj producing the intended result
EFFED > EFF
EFFEIR vb suit
EFFEIRED > EFFEIR
EFFEIRING > EFFEIR
EFFEIRS > EFFEIR
EFFENDI n (in the Ottoman Empire) a title of

respect used to address men of learning or social standing
EFFENDIS > EFFENDI
EFFERE same as > EFFEIR
EFFERED > EFFERE
EFFERENCE > EFFERENT
EFFERENT adj carrying or conducting outwards from a part or an organ of the body, esp from the brain or spinal cord ▷ n nerve that carries impulses outwards from the brain or spinal cord
EFFERENTS > EFFERENT
EFFERES > EFFERE
EFFERING > EFFERE
EFFETE adj powerless, feeble
EFFETELY > EFFETE
EFFICACY n quality of being successful in producing an intended result
EFFICIENT adj functioning effectively with little waste of effort
EFFIERCE vb archaic word meaning make fierce
EFFIERCED > EFFIERCE
EFFIERCES > EFFIERCE
EFFIGIAL > EFFIGY
EFFIGIES > EFFIGY
EFFIGY n image or likeness of a person
EFFING > EFF
EFFINGS > EFF
EFFLUENCE n act or process of flowing out
EFFLUENT n liquid discharged as waste ▷ adj flowing out or forth
EFFLUENTS > EFFLUENT
EFFLUVIA > EFFLUVIUM
EFFLUVIAL > EFFLUVIUM
EFFLUVIUM n unpleasant smell, as of decaying matter or gaseous waste
EFFLUX same as > EFFLUENCE
EFFLUXES > EFFLUX
EFFLUXION same as > EFFLUX
EFFORCE vb force
EFFORCED > EFFORCE
EFFORCES > EFFORCE
EFFORCING > EFFORCE
EFFORT n physical or mental exertion
EFFORTFUL > EFFORT
EFFORTS > EFFORT
EFFRAIDE same as > AFRAID
EFFRAY same as > AFFRAY
EFFRAYS > EFFRAY
EFFS > EFF
EFFULGE vb radiate
EFFULGED > EFFULGE
EFFULGENT adj radiant
EFFULGES > EFFULGE
EFFULGING > EFFULGE
EFFUSE vb pour or flow out

▷ adj (esp of an inflorescence) spreading out loosely
EFFUSED > EFFUSE
EFFUSES > EFFUSE
EFFUSING > EFFUSE
EFFUSION n unrestrained outburst
EFFUSIONS > EFFUSION
EFFUSIVE adj openly emotional, demonstrative
EFS > EF
EFT n dialect or archaic name for a newt ▷ adv again
EFTEST adj nearest at hand
EFTS > EFT
EFTSOON > EFTSOONS
EFTSOONS adv soon afterwards
EGAD n mild oath or expression of surprise
EGADS > EGAD
EGAL adj equal
EGALITE n equality
EGALITES > EGALITY
EGALITIES > EGALITY
EGALITY n equality
EGALLY > EGAL
EGAREMENT n confusion
EGENCE n need
EGENCES > EGENCE
EGENCIES > EGENCY
EGENCY same as > EGENCE
EGER same as > EAGRE
EGERS > EGER
EGEST vb excrete (waste material)
EGESTA npl anything egested, as waste material from the body
EGESTED > EGEST
EGESTING > EGEST
EGESTION > EGEST
EGESTIONS > EGEST
EGESTIVE > EGEST
EGESTS > EGEST
EGG n oval or round object laid by the females of birds and other creatures, containing a developing embryo ▷ vb urge or incite, esp to daring or foolish acts
EGGAR same as > EGGER
EGGARS > EGGAR
EGGBEATER n kitchen utensil for beating eggs, whipping cream, etc
EGGCUP n cup for holding a boiled egg
EGGCUPS > EGGCUP
EGGED > EGG
EGGER n any of various widely distributed moths having brown bodies and wings
EGGERIES > EGGERY
EGGERS > EGGER
EGGERY n place where eggs are laid
EGGFRUIT n fruit of eggplant
EGGFRUITS > EGGFRUIT

EGGHEAD n intellectual person
EGGHEADED > EGGHEAD
EGGHEADS > EGGHEAD
EGGIER > EGGY
EGGIEST > EGGY
EGGING > EGG
EGGLER n egg dealer: sometimes itinerant
EGGLERS > EGGLER
EGGLESS > EGG
EGGMASS n intelligentsia
EGGMASSES > EGGMASS
EGGNOG n drink made of raw eggs, milk, sugar, spice, and brandy or rum
EGGNOGS > EGGNOG
EGGPLANT n dark purple tropical fruit, cooked and eaten as a vegetable
EGGPLANTS > EGGPLANT
EGGS > EGG
EGGSHELL n hard covering round the egg of a bird or animal ▷ adj (of paint) having a very slight sheen
EGGSHELLS > EGGSHELL
EGGWASH n beaten egg for brushing on pastry
EGGWASHES > EGGWASH
EGGWHISK same as > EGGBEATER
EGGWHISKS > EGGWHISK
EGGY adj soaked in or tasting of egg
EGIS rare spelling of > AEGIS
EGISES > EGIS
EGLANTINE n Eurasian rose
EGLATERE archaic name for > EGLANTINE
EGLATERES > EGLATERE
EGLOMISE n gilding
EGMA mispronunciation of > ENIGMA
EGMAS > EGMA
EGO n conscious mind of an individual
EGOISM n excessive concern for one's own interests
EGOISMS > EGOISM
EGOIST n person who is preoccupied with his own interests
EGOISTIC > EGOIST
EGOISTS > EGOIST
EGOITIES > EGOITY
EGOITY n essence of the ego
EGOLESS adj without an ego
EGOMANIA n obsessive concern with fulfilling one's own needs and desires, regardless of the effect on other people
EGOMANIAC > EGOMANIA
EGOMANIAS > EGOMANIA
EGOS > EGO
EGOTHEISM n making god of oneself
EGOTISE same as > EGOTIZE

EGOTISED > EGOTISE

EGOTISES > EGOTISE

EGOTISING > EGOTISE

EGOTISM n concern only for one's own interests and feelings

EGOTISMS > EGOTISM

EGOTIST n conceited boastful person

EGOTISTIC > EGOTIST

EGOTISTS > EGOTIST

EGOTIZE vb talk or write in self-important way

EGOTIZED > EGOTIZE

EGOTIZES > EGOTIZE

EGOTIZING > EGOTIZE

EGREGIOUS adj outstandingly bad

EGRESS same as > EMERSION

EGRESSED > EGRESS

EGRESSES > EGRESS

EGRESSING > EGRESS

EGRESSION same as > EGRESS

EGRESSIVE n speech sound produced with an exhalation of breath

EGRET n lesser white heron

EGRETS > EGRET

EGYPTIAN n type of typeface

EGYPTIANS > EGYPTIAN

EH interj exclamation of surprise or inquiry, or to seek confirmation of a statement or question ▷ vb say 'eh'

EHED > EH

EHING > EH

EHS > EH

EIDE > EIDOS

EIDENT adj diligent

EIDER n Arctic duck

EIDERDOWN n quilt (orig. stuffed with eider feathers)

EIDERS > EIDER

EIDETIC adj (of visual, or sometimes auditory, images) exceptionally vivid and allowing detailed recall of something previously perceived ▷ n person with eidetic ability

EIDETICS > EIDETIC

EIDOGRAPH n device for copying drawings

EIDOLA > EIDOLON

EIDOLIC > EIDOLON

EIDOLON n unsubstantial image

EIDOLONS > EIDOLON

EIDOS n intellectual character of a culture or a social group

EIGENMODE n characteristic vibration pattern

EIGENTONE n characteristic acoustic resonance frequency of a system

EIGHT n one more than seven ▷ adj amounting to eight

EIGHTBALL n black ball in pool

EIGHTEEN n eight and ten ▷ adj amounting to eighteen ▷ det amounting to eighteen

EIGHTEENS > EIGHTEEN

EIGHTFOIL n eight leaved flower shape in heraldry

EIGHTFOLD adj having eight times as many or as much ▷ adv by eight times as many or as much

EIGHTH n (of) number eight in a series ▷ adj coming after the seventh and before the ninth in numbering or counting order, position, time, etc ▷ adv after the seventh person, position, event, etc

EIGHTHLY same as > EIGHTH

EIGHTHS > EIGHTH

EIGHTIES > EIGHTY

EIGHTIETH n one of 80 approximately equal parts of something

EIGHTS > EIGHT

EIGHTSMAN n member of an eight-man team

EIGHTSMEN > EIGHTSMAN

EIGHTSOME n group of eight people

EIGHTVO another word for > OCTAVO

EIGHTVOS > EIGHTVO

EIGHTY n eight times ten ▷ adj amounting to eighty ▷ det amounting to eighty

EIGNE adj firstborn

EIK variant form of > EKE

EIKED > EIK

EIKING > EIK

EIKON variant spelling of > ICON

EIKONES > EIKON

EIKONS > EIKON

EIKS > EIK

EILD n old age

EILDING n fuel

EILDINGS > EILDING

EILDS > EILD

EINA interj exclamation of pain

EINE npl eyes

EINKORN n variety of wheat of Greece and SW Asia

EINKORNS > EINKORN

EINSTEIN n scientific genius

EINSTEINS > EINSTEIN

EIRACK n young hen

EIRACKS > EIRACK

EIRENIC variant spelling of > IRENIC

EIRENICAL same as > IRENIC

EIRENICON n proposition that attempts to harmonize conflicting viewpoints

EISEGESES > EISEGESIS

EISEGESIS n interpretation of a text, esp a biblical text, using one's own ideas

EISEL n vinegar

EISELL same as > EISEL

EISELLS > EISELL

EISELS > EISEL

EISH interj South African exclamation expressive of surprise, agreement, disapproval, etc

EISWEIN n wine made from grapes frozen on the vine

EISWEINS > EISWEIN

EITHER pron one or the other (of two) ▷ adv likewise ▷ det one or the other (of two)

EJACULATE vb eject (semen)

EJECT vb force out, expel

EJECTA npl matter thrown out of a crater by an erupting volcano or during a meteorite impact

EJECTABLE > EJECT

EJECTED > EJECT

EJECTING > EJECT

EJECTION > EJECT

EJECTIONS > EJECT

EJECTIVE adj relating to or causing ejection ▷ n ejective consonant

EJECTIVES > EJECTIVE

EJECTMENT n (formerly) an action brought by a wrongfully dispossessed owner seeking to recover possession of his land

EJECTOR n person or thing that ejects

EJECTORS > EJECTOR

EJECTS > EJECT

EKE vb increase, enlarge, or lengthen

EKED > EKE

EKES > EKE

EKING > EKE

EKISTIC > EKISTICS

EKISTICAL > EKISTICS

EKISTICS n science or study of human settlements

EKKA n type of one-horse carriage

EKKAS > EKKA

EKLOGITE same as > ECLOGITE

EKLOGITES > EKLOGITE

EKPHRASES > EKPHRASIS

EKPHRASIS n description of a visual work of art

EKPWELE n former monetary unit of Equatorial Guinea

EKPWELES > EKPWELE

EKTEXINE n in pollen and spores, the outer of the two layers that make up the exine

EKTEXINES > EKTEXINE

EKUELE same as > EKPWELE

EL n American elevated railway

ELABORATE adj with a lot of fine detail ▷ vb expand upon

ELAEOLITE n nepheline

ELAIN same as > TRIOLEIN

ELAINS > ELAIN

ELAIOSOME n oil-rich body on seeds or fruits that attracts ants, which act as dispersal agents

ELAN n style and vigour

ELANCE vb throw a lance

ELANCED > ELANCE

ELANCES > ELANCE

ELANCING > ELANCE

ELAND n large antelope of southern Africa

ELANDS > ELAND

ELANET n bird of prey

ELANETS > ELANET

ELANS > ELAN

ELAPHINE adj of or like a red deer

ELAPID n mostly tropical type of venomous snake

ELAPIDS > ELAPID

ELAPINE adj of or like an elapid

ELAPSE vb (of time) pass by

ELAPSED > ELAPSE

ELAPSES > ELAPSE

ELAPSING > ELAPSE

ELASTANCE n reciprocal of capacitance

ELASTANE n synthetic fibre that is able to return to its original shape after being stretched

ELASTANES > ELASTANE

ELASTASE n enzyme that digests elastin

ELASTASES > ELASTASE

ELASTIC adj resuming normal shape after distortion ▷ n tape or fabric containing interwoven strands of flexible rubber

ELASTICS > ELASTIC

ELASTIN n fibrous scleroprotein constituting the major part of elastic tissue, such as the walls of arteries

ELASTINS > ELASTIN

ELASTOMER n any material, such as natural or synthetic rubber, that is able to resume its original shape when a deforming force is removed

ELATE vb fill with high spirits, exhilaration, pride or optimism

ELATED adj extremely happy and excited

ELATEDLY > ELATED

ELATER n elaterid beetle

ELATERID n type of beetle of the family which

constitutes the click beetles

ELATERIDS > ELATERID

ELATERIN *n* white crystalline substance found in elaterium, used as a purgative

ELATERINS > ELATERIN

ELATERITE *n* dark brown naturally occurring bitumen resembling rubber

ELATERIUM *n* greenish sediment prepared from the juice of the squirting cucumber, used as a purgative

ELATERS > ELATER

ELATES > ELATE

ELATING > ELATE

ELATION *n* feeling of great happiness and excitement

ELATIONS > ELATION

ELATIVE *adj* (in the grammar of Finnish and other languages) denoting a case of nouns expressing a relation of motion or direction ▷ *n* elative case

ELATIVES > ELATIVE

ELBOW *n* joint between the upper arm and the forearm ▷ *vb* shove or strike with the elbow

ELBOWED > ELBOW

ELBOWING > ELBOW

ELBOWROOM *n* sufficient scope to move or function

ELBOWS > ELBOW

ELCHEE *n* ambassador

ELCHEES > ELCHEE

ELCHI *same as* > ELCHEE

ELCHIS > ELCHI

ELD *n* old age

ELDER *adj* older ▷ *n* older person

ELDERCARE *n* care of elderly

ELDERLIES > ELDERLY

ELDERLY *adj* (fairly) old

ELDERS > ELDER

ELDERSHIP > ELDER

ELDEST *adj* oldest

ELDIN *n* fuel

ELDING *same as* > ELDIN

ELDINGS > ELDING

ELDINS > ELDIN

ELDORADO *n* place of great riches or fabulous opportunity

ELDORADOS > ELDORADO

ELDRESS *n* woman elder

ELDRESSES > ELDRESS

ELDRICH *same as* > ELDRITCH

ELDRITCH *adj* weird, uncanny

ELDS > ELD

ELECT *vb* choose by voting ▷ *adj* appointed but not yet in office

ELECTABLE > ELECT

ELECTED > ELECT

ELECTEE *n* someone who is elected

ELECTEES > ELECTEE

ELECTING > ELECT

ELECTION *n* choosing of representatives by voting

ELECTIONS > ELECTION

ELECTIVE *adj* chosen by election ▷ *n* optional course or hospital placement undertaken by a medical student

ELECTIVES > ELECTIVE

ELECTOR *n* someone who has the right to vote in an election

ELECTORAL *adj* of or relating to elections

ELECTORS > ELECTOR

ELECTRESS *n* female elector

ELECTRET *n* permanently polarized dielectric material

ELECTRETS > ELECTRET

ELECTRIC *adj* produced by, transmitting, or powered by electricity ▷ *n* electric train, car, etc

ELECTRICS > ELECTRIC

ELECTRIFY *vb* adapt for operation by electric power

ELECTRISE *same as* > ELECTRIZE

ELECTRIZE *vb* electrify

ELECTRO *vb* (in printing) make a metallic copy of a page

ELECTRODE *n* conductor through which an electric current enters or leaves a battery, vacuum tube, etc

ELECTROED > ELECTRO

ELECTRON *n* elementary particle in all atoms that has a negative electrical charge

ELECTRONS > ELECTRON

ELECTROS > ELECTRO

ELECTRUM *n* alloy of gold (55·88 per cent) and silver used for jewellery and ornaments

ELECTRUMS > ELECTRUM

ELECTS > ELECT

ELECTUARY *n* paste taken orally, containing a drug mixed with syrup or honey

ELEDOISIN *n* substance extracted from the salivary glands of a small octopus for medical applications

ELEGANCE *n* dignified grace in appearance, movement, or behaviour

ELEGANCES > ELEGANCE

ELEGANCY *same as* > ELEGANCE

ELEGANT *adj* pleasing or graceful in dress, style, or design

ELEGANTLY > ELEGANT

ELEGIAC *adj* mournful or plaintive ▷ *n* elegiac couplet or stanza

ELEGIACAL > ELEGIAC

ELEGIACS > ELEGIAC

ELEGIAST *n* writer of elegies

ELEGIASTS > ELEGIAST

ELEGIES > ELEGY

ELEGISE *same as* > ELEGIZE

ELEGISED > ELEGISE

ELEGISES > ELEGISE

ELEGISING > ELEGISE

ELEGIST > ELEGIZE

ELEGISTS > ELEGIZE

ELEGIT *n* writ delivering debtor's property to plaintiff

ELEGITS > ELEGIT

ELEGIZE *vb* compose an elegy or elegies (in memory of)

ELEGIZED > ELEGIZE

ELEGIZES > ELEGIZE

ELEGIZING > ELEGIZE

ELEGY *n* mournful poem, esp a lament for the dead

ELEMENT *n* component part

ELEMENTAL *adj* of primitive natural forces or passions ▷ *n* spirit or force that is said to appear in physical form

ELEMENTS > ELEMENT

ELEMI *n* fragrant resin obtained from various tropical trees, used to make varnishes, ointments, inks, etc

ELEMIS > ELEMI

ELENCH *n* refutation in logic

ELENCHI > ELENCHUS

ELENCHIC > ELENCHUS

ELENCHS > ELENCH

ELENCHTIC *same as* > ELENCTIC

ELENCHUS *n* refutation of an argument by proving the contrary of its conclusion, esp syllogistically

ELENCTIC *adj* refuting an argument by proving the falsehood of its conclusion

ELEOPTENE *n* liquid part of a volatile oil

ELEPHANT *n* huge four-footed thick-skinned animal with ivory tusks and a long trunk

ELEPHANTS *adj* in Australia, a slang word for drunk

ELEUTHERI *npl* secret society

ELEVATE *vb* raise in rank or status

ELEVATED *adj* higher than normal ▷ *n* railway that runs on an elevated structure

ELEVATEDS > ELEVATED

ELEVATES > ELEVATE

ELEVATING > ELEVATE

ELEVATION *n* raising

ELEVATOR *n* lift for carrying people

ELEVATORS > ELEVATOR

ELEVATORY > ELEVATE

ELEVEN *n* one more than ten ▷ *adj* amounting to eleven ▷ *det* amounting to eleven

ELEVENS > ELEVEN

ELEVENSES *n* mid-morning snack

ELEVENTH *n* (of) number eleven in a series ▷ *adj* coming after the tenth in numbering or counting order, position, time, etc

ELEVENTHS > ELEVENTH

ELEVON *n* aircraft control surface that combines the functions of an elevator and aileron, usually fitted to tailless or delta-wing aircraft

ELEVONS > ELEVON

ELF *n* (in folklore) small mischievous fairy ▷ *vb* entangle (esp hair)

ELFED > ELF

ELFHOOD > ELF

ELFHOODS > ELF

ELFIN *adj* small and delicate ▷ *n* young elf

ELFING > ELF

ELFINS > ELFIN

ELFISH *adj* of, relating to, or like an elf or elves ▷ *n* supposed language of elves

ELFISHLY > ELFISH

ELFLAND *another name for* > FAIRYLAND

ELFLANDS > ELFLAND

ELFLIKE > ELF

ELFLOCK *n* lock of hair, fancifully regarded as having been tangled by the elves

ELFLOCKS > ELFLOCK

ELFS > ELF

ELHI *adj* informal word for or relating to elementary high school

ELIAD *n* glance

ELIADS > ELIAD

ELICHE *n* pasta in the form of spirals

ELICHES > ELICHE

ELICIT *vb* bring about (a response or reaction)

ELICITED > ELICIT

ELICITING > ELICIT

ELICITOR > ELICIT

ELICITORS > ELICIT

ELICITS > ELICIT

ELIDE *vb* omit (a vowel or syllable) from a spoken word

ELIDED > ELIDE

ELIDES > ELIDE

ELIDIBLE > ELIDE

ELIDING > ELIDE

ELIGIBLE *adj* meeting the requirements or qualifications needed ▷ *n* eligible person or thing

ELIGIBLES > ELIGIBLE

ELIGIBLY > ELIGIBLE

ELIMINANT > ELIMINATE

ELIMINATE *vb* get rid of

ELINT *n* electronic intelligence

ELINTS > ELINT

ELISION *n* omission of a syllable or vowel from a spoken word

ELISIONS > ELISION

ELITE *n* most powerful, rich, or gifted members of a group ▷ *adj* of, relating to, or suitable for an elite

ELITES > ELITE

ELITISM *n* belief that society should be governed by a small group of superior people

ELITISMS > ELITISM

ELITIST > ELITISM

ELITISTS > ELITISM

ELIXIR *n* imaginary liquid that can prolong life or turn base metals into gold

ELIXIRS > ELIXIR

ELK *n* large deer of N Europe and Asia

ELKHORN as in *elkhorn fern* fern with a large leaf like an elk's horn

ELKHOUND *n* powerful breed of dog of the spitz type with a thick grey coat and tightly curled tail

ELKHOUNDS > ELKHOUND

ELKS > ELK

ELL *n* obsolete unit of length equal to approximately 45 inches

ELLAGIC *adj* of an acid derived from gallnuts

ELLIPSE *n* oval shape

ELLIPSES > ELLIPSIS

ELLIPSIS *n* omission of letters or words in a sentence

ELLIPSOID *n* surface whose plane sections are ellipses or circles

ELLIPTIC *adj* relating to or having the shape of an ellipse

ELLOPS *same as* > ELOPS

ELLOPSES > ELLOPS

ELLS > ELL

ELLWAND *n* stick for measuring lengths

ELLWANDS > ELLWAND

ELM *n* tree with serrated leaves

ELMEN *adj* of or relating to elm trees

ELMIER > ELMY

ELMIEST > ELMY

ELMS > ELM

ELMWOOD *n* wood from an elm tree

ELMWOODS > ELMWOOD

ELMY *adj* of or relating to elm trees

ELOCUTE *vb* speak as if practising elocution

ELOCUTED > ELOCUTE

ELOCUTES > ELOCUTE

ELOCUTING > ELOCUTE

ELOCUTION *n* art of speaking clearly in public

ELOCUTORY > ELOCUTION

ELODEA *n* type of American plant

ELODEAS > ELODEA

ELOGE *same as* > EULOGY

ELOGES > ELOGE

ELOGIES > ELOGY

ELOGIST > ELOGY

ELOGISTS > ELOGY

ELOGIUM *same as* > EULOGY

ELOGIUMS > ELOGIUM

ELOGY *same as* > EULOGY

ELOIGN *vb* remove (oneself, one's property, etc) to a distant place

ELOIGNED > ELOIGN

ELOIGNER > ELOIGN

ELOIGNERS > ELOIGN

ELOIGNING > ELOIGN

ELOIGNS > ELOIGN

ELOIN *same as* > ELOIGN

ELOINED > ELOIN

ELOINER > ELOIGN

ELOINERS > ELOIGN

ELOINING > ELOIN

ELOINMENT > ELOIGN

ELOINS > ELOIN

ELONGATE *vb* make or become longer ▷ *adj* long and narrow

ELONGATED > ELONGATE

ELONGATES > ELONGATE

ELOPE *vb* (of two people) run away secretly to get married

ELOPED > ELOPE

ELOPEMENT > ELOPE

ELOPER > ELOPE

ELOPERS > ELOPE

ELOPES > ELOPE

ELOPING > ELOPE

ELOPS *n* type of fish

ELOPSES > ELOPS

ELOQUENCE *n* fluent powerful use of language

ELOQUENT *adj* (of speech or writing) fluent and persuasive

ELPEE *n* LP, long-playing record

ELPEES > ELPEE

ELS > EL

ELSE *adv* in addition or more

ELSEWHERE *adv* in or to another place

ELSEWISE *adv* otherwise

ELSHIN *n* cobbler's awl

ELSHINS > ELSHIN

ELSIN *variant of* > ELSHIN

ELSINS > ELSIN

ELT *n* young female pig

ELTCHI *variant of* > ELCHEE

ELTCHIS > ELTCHI

ELTS > ELT

ELUANT *same as* > ELUENT

ELUANTS > ELUANT

ELUATE *n* solution of adsorbed material in the eluent obtained during the process of elution

ELUATES > ELUATE

ELUCIDATE *vb* make (something difficult) clear

ELUDE *vb* escape from by cleverness or quickness

ELUDED > ELUDE

ELUDER > ELUDE

ELUDERS > ELUDE

ELUDES > ELUDE

ELUDIBLE *adj* able to be eluded

ELUDING > ELUDE

ELUENT *n* solvent used for eluting

ELUENTS > ELUENT

ELUSION > ELUDE

ELUSIONS > ELUDE

ELUSIVE *adj* difficult to catch or remember

ELUSIVELY > ELUSIVE

ELUSORY *adj* avoiding the issue

ELUTE *vb* wash out (a substance) by the action of a solvent, as in chromatography

ELUTED > ELUTE

ELUTES > ELUTE

ELUTING > ELUTE

ELUTION > ELUTE

ELUTIONS > ELUTE

ELUTOR > ELUTE

ELUTORS > ELUTE

ELUTRIATE *vb* purify or separate (a substance or mixture) by washing and straining or decanting

ELUVIA > ELUVIUM

ELUVIAL > ELUVIUM

ELUVIATE *vb* remove material suspended in water in a layer of soil by the action of rainfall

ELUVIATED > ELUVIATE

ELUVIATES > ELUVIATE

ELUVIUM *n* mass of sand, silt, etc: a product of the erosion of rocks that has remained in its place of origin

ELUVIUMS > ELUVIUM

ELVAN *n* type of rock

ELVANITE *variant of* > ELVAN

ELVANITES > ELVANITE

ELVANS > ELVAN

ELVER *n* young eel

ELVERS > ELVER

ELVES > ELF

ELVISH *same as* > ELFISH

ELVISHLY > ELVISH

ELYSIAN *adj* delightful, blissful

ELYTRA > ELYTRUM

ELYTRAL > ELYTRON

ELYTROID > ELYTRON

ELYTRON *n* either of the horny front wings of beetles and some other insects, which cover and protect the hind wings

ELYTROUS > ELYTRON

ELYTRUM *same as* > ELYTRON

EM *n* square of a body of any size of type, used as a unit of measurement

EMACIATE *vb* become or cause to become abnormally thin

EMACIATED *adj* abnormally thin

EMACIATES > EMACIATE

EMACS *n* powerful computer program used for creating and editing text

EMACSEN > EMACS

EMAIL *n* electronic mail ▷ *vb* send a message by electronic mail

EMAILED > EMAIL

EMAILER > EMAIL

EMAILERS > EMAILER

EMAILING > EMAIL

EMAILINGS > EMAILING

EMAILS > EMAIL

EMANANT > EMANATE

EMANATE *vb* issue, proceed from a source

EMANATED > EMANATE

EMANATES > EMANATE

EMANATING > EMANATE

EMANATION *n* act or instance of emanating

EMANATIST > EMANATE

EMANATIVE > EMANATE

EMANATOR > EMANATE

EMANATORS > EMANATE

EMANATORY > EMANATE

EMBACE *variant of* > EMBASE

EMBACES > EMBACE

EMBACING > EMBACE

EMBAIL *vb* enclose in a circle

EMBAILED > EMBAIL

EMBAILING > EMBAIL

EMBAILS > EMBAIL

EMBALE *vb* bind

EMBALED > EMBALE

EMBALES > EMBALE

EMBALING > EMBALE

EMBALL *vb* enclose in a circle

EMBALLED > EMBALL

EMBALLING > EMBALL

EMBALLS > EMBALL

EMBALM *vb* preserve (a corpse) from decay by the use of chemicals etc

EMBALMED > EMBALM

EMBALMER > EMBALM

EMBALMERS > EMBALM

EMBALMING > EMBALM

EMBALMS > EMBALM

EMBANK *vb* protect, enclose, or confine (a waterway, road, etc) with an embankment

EMBANKED > EMBANK

EMBANKER > EMBANK

EMBANKERS > EMBANK

EMBANKING > EMBANK

EMBANKS > EMBANK

EMBAR *vb* close in with bars

EMBARGO *n* order by a

government prohibiting trade with a country ▷ *vb* put an embargo on

EMBARGOED > EMBARGO

EMBARGOES > EMBARGO

EMBARK *vb* board a ship or aircraft

EMBARKED > EMBARK

EMBARKING > EMBARK

EMBARKS > EMBARK

EMBARRASS *vb* cause to feel self-conscious or ashamed

EMBARRED > EMBAR

EMBARRING > EMBAR

EMBARS > EMBAR

EMBASE *vb* degrade or debase

EMBASED > EMBASE

EMBASES > EMBASE

EMBASING > EMBASE

EMBASSADE *n* embassy

EMBASSAGE *n* work of an embassy

EMBASSIES > EMBASSY

EMBASSY *n* offices or official residence of an ambassador

EMBASTE > EMBASE

EMBATHE *vb* bathe with water

EMBATHED > EMBATHE

EMBATHES > EMBATHE

EMBATHING > EMBATHE

EMBATTLE *vb* deploy (troops) for battle

EMBATTLED *adj* having a lot of difficulties

EMBATTLES > EMBATTLE

EMBAY *vb* form into a bay

EMBAYED > EMBAY

EMBAYING > EMBAY

EMBAYLD > EMBAIL

EMBAYMENT *n* shape resembling a bay

EMBAYS > EMBAY

EMBED *vb* fix firmly in something solid ▷ *n* journalist accompanying an active military unit

EMBEDDED > EMBED

EMBEDDING *n* practice of assigning or being assigned a journalist to accompany an active military unit

EMBEDMENT > EMBED

EMBEDS > EMBED

EMBELLISH *vb* decorate

EMBER *n* glowing piece of wood or coal in a dying fire

EMBERS > EMBER

EMBEZZLE *vb* steal money that has been entrusted to one

EMBEZZLED > EMBEZZLE

EMBEZZLER > EMBEZZLE

EMBEZZLES > EMBEZZLE

EMBITTER *vb* make (a person) resentful or bitter

EMBITTERS > EMBITTER

EMBLAZE *vb* cause to light up

EMBLAZED > EMBLAZE

EMBLAZER > EMBLAZE

EMBLAZERS > EMBLAZE

EMBLAZES > EMBLAZE

EMBLAZING > EMBLAZE

EMBLAZON *vb* decorate with bright colours

EMBLAZONS > EMBLAZON

EMBLEM *n* object or design that symbolizes a quality, type, or group ▷ *vb* represent or signify

EMBLEMA *n* mosaic decoration

EMBLEMATA > EMBLEMA

EMBLEMED > EMBLEM

EMBLEMING > EMBLEM

EMBLEMISE *same as* > EMBLEMIZE

EMBLEMIZE *vb* function as an emblem of

EMBLEMS > EMBLEM

EMBLIC *n* type of Indian tree

EMBLICS > EMBLIC

EMBLOOM *vb* adorn with blooms

EMBLOOMED > EMBLOOM

EMBLOOMS > EMBLOOM

EMBLOSSOM *vb* adorn with blossom

EMBODIED > EMBODY

EMBODIER > EMBODY

EMBODIERS > EMBODY

EMBODIES > EMBODY

EMBODY *vb* be an example or expression of

EMBODYING > EMBODY

EMBOG *vb* sink down into a bog

EMBOGGED > EMBOG

EMBOGGING > EMBOG

EMBOGS > EMBOG

EMBOGUE *vb* go out through a narrow channel or passage

EMBOGUED > EMBOGUE

EMBOGUES > EMBOGUE

EMBOGUING > EMBOGUE

EMBOIL *vb* enrage or be enraged

EMBOILED > EMBOIL

EMBOILING > EMBOIL

EMBOILS > EMBOIL

EMBOLDEN *vb* encourage (someone)

EMBOLDENS > EMBOLDEN

EMBOLI > EMBOLUS

EMBOLIC *adj* of or relating to an embolus or embolism

EMBOLIES > EMBOLY

EMBOLISE *same as* > EMBOLIZE

EMBOLISED > EMBOLISE

EMBOLISES > EMBOLISE

EMBOLISM *n* blocking of a blood vessel by a blood clot or air bubble

EMBOLISMS > EMBOLISM

EMBOLIZE *vb* cause embolism in (a blood vessel)

EMBOLIZED > EMBOLIZE

EMBOLIZES > EMBOLIZE

EMBOLUS *n* material, such as a blood clot, that blocks

a blood vessel

EMBOLUSES > EMBOLUS

EMBOLY *n* infolding of the outer layer of cells of an organism or part of an organism so as to form a pocket on the surface

EMBORDER *vb* edge or border

EMBORDERS > EMBORDER

EMBOSCATA *n* sudden attack or raid

EMBOSK *vb* hide or cover

EMBOSKED > EMBOSK

EMBOSKING > EMBOSK

EMBOSKS > EMBOSK

EMBOSOM *vb* enclose or envelop, esp protectively

EMBOSOMED > EMBOSOM

EMBOSOMS > EMBOSOM

EMBOSS *vb* mould or carve a decoration on (a surface) so that it stands out from the surface

EMBOSSED *adj* (of a design or pattern) standing out from a surface

EMBOSSER > EMBOSS

EMBOSSERS > EMBOSS

EMBOSSES > EMBOSS

EMBOSSING > EMBOSS

EMBOST > EMBOSS

EMBOUND *vb* surround or encircle

EMBOUNDED > EMBOUND

EMBOUNDS > EMBOUND

EMBOW *vb* design or create (a structure) in the form of an arch or vault

EMBOWED > EMBOW

EMBOWEL *vb* bury or embed deeply

EMBOWELED > EMBOWEL

EMBOWELS > EMBOWEL

EMBOWER *vb* enclose in or, as in a bower

EMBOWERED > EMBOWER

EMBOWERS > EMBOWER

EMBOWING > EMBOW

EMBOWMENT > EMBOW

EMBOWS > EMBOW

EMBOX *vb* put in a box

EMBOXED > EMBOX

EMBOXES > EMBOX

EMBOXING > EMBOX

EMBRACE *vb* clasp in the arms, hug ▷ *n* act of embracing

EMBRACED > EMBRACE

EMBRACEOR *n* person guilty of embracery

EMBRACER > EMBRACE

EMBRACERS > EMBRACE

EMBRACERY *n* offence of attempting by corrupt means to influence a jury or juror, as by bribery or threats

EMBRACES > EMBRACE

EMBRACING > EMBRACE

EMBRACIVE > EMBRACE

EMBRAID *vb* braid or interweave

EMBRAIDED > EMBRAID

EMBRAIDS > EMBRAID

EMBRANGLE *vb* confuse or entangle

EMBRASOR *n* one who embraces

EMBRASORS > EMBRASOR

EMBRASURE *n* door or window having splayed sides so that the opening is larger on the inside

EMBRAVE *vb* adorn or decorate

EMBRAVED > EMBRAVE

EMBRAVES > EMBRAVE

EMBRAVING > EMBRAVE

EMBRAZURE *variant of* > EMBRASURE

EMBREAD *vb* braid

EMBREADED > EMBREAD

EMBREADS > EMBREAD

EMBREATHE *vb* breathe in air

EMBRITTLE *vb* become brittle

EMBROCATE *vb* apply a liniment or lotion to (a part of the body)

EMBROGLIO *same as* > IMBROGLIO

EMBROIDER *vb* decorate with needlework

EMBROIL *vb* involve (a person) in problems

EMBROILED > EMBROIL

EMBROILER > EMBROIL

EMBROILS > EMBROIL

EMBROWN *vb* make or become brown

EMBROWNED > EMBROWN

EMBROWNS > EMBROWN

EMBRUE *variant spelling of* > IMBRUE

EMBRUED > EMBRUE

EMBRUES > EMBRUE

EMBRUING > EMBRUE

EMBRUTE *variant of* > IMBRUTE

EMBRUTED > EMBRUTE

EMBRUTES > EMBRUTE

EMBRUTING > EMBRUTE

EMBRYO *n* unborn creature in the early stages of development

EMBRYOID > EMBRYO

EMBRYOIDS > EMBRYO

EMBRYON *variant of* > EMBRYO

EMBRYONAL *same as* > EMBRYONIC

EMBRYONIC *adj* at an early stage

EMBRYONS > EMBRYON

EMBRYOS > EMBRYO

EMBRYOTIC *variant of* > EMBRYONIC

EMBUS *vb* cause (troops) to board or (of troops) to board a transport vehicle

EMBUSED > EMBUS

EMBUSES > EMBUS

EMBUSIED > EMBUSY

EMBUSIES > EMBUSY

EMBUSING > EMBUS

EMBUSQUE n man who avoids military conscription by obtaining a government job

EMBUSQUES > EMBUSQUE

EMBUSSED > EMBUS

EMBUSSES > EMBUS

EMBUSSING > EMBUS

EMBUSY vb keep occupied

EMBUSYING > EMBUSY

EMCEE n master of ceremonies ▷ vb act as master of ceremonies (for or at)

EMCEED > EMCEE

EMCEEING > EMCEE

EMCEES > EMCEE

EMDASH n long dash in punctuation

EMDASHES > EMDASH

EME n uncle

EMEER variant of > EMIR

EMEERATE variant of > EMIRATE

EMEERATES > EMEERATE

EMEERS > EMEER

EMEND vb remove errors from

EMENDABLE > EMEND

EMENDALS npl funds put aside for repairs

EMENDATE vb make corrections

EMENDATED > EMENDATE

EMENDATES > EMENDATE

EMENDATOR n one who emends a text

EMENDED > EMEND

EMENDER > EMEND

EMENDERS > EMEND

EMENDING > EMEND

EMENDS > EMEND

EMERALD n bright green precious stone ▷ adj bright green

EMERALDS > EMERALD

EMERAUDE archaic variant of > EMERALD

EMERAUDES > EMERAUDE

EMERGE vb come into view

EMERGED > EMERGE

EMERGENCE n act or process of emerging

EMERGENCY n sudden unforeseen occurrence needing immediate action

EMERGENT adj coming into being or notice ▷ n aquatic plant with stem and leaves above the water

EMERGENTS > EMERGENT

EMERGES > EMERGE

EMERGING > EMERGE

EMERIED > EMERY

EMERIES > EMERY

EMERITA adj retired, but retaining an honorary title ▷ n woman who is retired, but retains an honorary title

EMERITAE > EMERITA

EMERITAS > EMERITA

EMERITI > EMERITUS

EMERITUS adj retired, but

retaining an honorary title ▷ n man who is retired, but retains an honorary title

EMEROD n haemorrhoid

EMERODS > EMEROD

EMEROID variant of > EMEROD

EMEROIDS > EMEROID

EMERSE same as > EMERSED

EMERSED adj (of the leaves or stems of aquatic plants) protruding above the surface of the water

EMERSION n act or an instance of emerging

EMERSIONS > EMERSION

EMERY n hard mineral used for smoothing and polishing ▷ vb apply emery to

EMERYING > EMERY

EMES > EME

EMESES > EMESIS

EMESIS technical name for > VOMITING

EMETIC n substance that causes vomiting ▷ adj causing vomiting

EMETICAL same as > EMETIC

EMETICS > EMETIC

EMETIN same as > EMETINE

EMETINE n white bitter poisonous alkaloid

EMETINES > EMETINE

EMETINS > EMETIN

EMEU variant of > EMU

EMEUS > EMEU

EMEUTE n uprising or rebellion

EMEUTES > EMEUTE

EMIC adj of or relating to a significant linguistic unit

EMICANT > EMICATE

EMICATE vb twinkle

EMICATED > EMICATE

EMICATES > EMICATE

EMICATING > EMICATE

EMICATION > EMICATE

EMICTION n passing of urine

EMICTIONS > EMICTION

EMICTORY > EMICTION

EMIGRANT n person who leaves one place or country, esp a native country, to settle in another

EMIGRANTS > EMIGRANT

EMIGRATE vb go and settle in another country

EMIGRATED > EMIGRATE

EMIGRATES > EMIGRATE

EMIGRE n someone who has left his native country for political reasons

EMIGRES > EMIGRE

EMINENCE n position of superiority or fame

EMINENCES > EMINENCE

EMINENCY same as > EMINENCE

EMINENT adj distinguished, well-known

EMINENTLY > EMINENT

EMIR n Muslim ruler

EMIRATE n emir's country

EMIRATES > EMIRATE

EMIRS > EMIR

EMISSARY n agent sent on a mission by a government ▷ adj (of veins) draining blood from sinuses in the dura mater to veins outside the skull

EMISSILE adj able to be emitted

EMISSION n act of giving out heat, light, a smell, etc

EMISSIONS > EMISSION

EMISSIVE > EMISSION

EMIT vb give out

EMITS > EMIT

EMITTANCE > EMIT

EMITTED > EMIT

EMITTER n person or thing that emits

EMITTERS > EMITTER

EMITTING > EMIT

EMLETS as in blood-drop emlets Chilean plant with red-spotted yellow flowers

EMMA n former communications code for the letter A

EMMARBLE vb decorate with marble

EMMARBLED > EMMARBLE

EMMARBLES > EMMARBLE

EMMAS > EMMA

EMMER n variety of wheat grown in mountainous parts of Europe

EMMERS > EMMER

EMMESH variant of > ENMESH

EMMESHED > EMMESH

EMMESHES > EMMESH

EMMESHING > EMMESH

EMMET n tourist or holiday-maker

EMMETROPE n person whose vision is normal

EMMETS > EMMET

EMMEW vb restrict

EMMEWED > EMMEW

EMMEWING > EMMEW

EMMEWS > EMMEW

EMMOVE vb cause emotion in

EMMOVED > EMMOVE

EMMOVES > EMMOVE

EMMOVING > EMMOVE

EMMY n (in the US) one of the gold-plated statuettes awarded annually for outstanding television performances and productions

EMMYS > EMMY

EMO n type of music combining hard rock with emotional lyrics

EMODIN n type of chemical compound

EMODINS > EMODIN

EMOLLIATE vb make soft or smooth

EMOLLIENT adj softening,

soothing ▷ n substance which softens or soothes the skin

EMOLUMENT n fees or wages from employment

EMONG variant of > AMONG

EMONGES variant of > AMONG

EMONGEST variant of > AMONGST

EMONGST variant of > AMONGST

EMOS > EMO

EMOTE vb display exaggerated emotion, as if acting

EMOTED > EMOTE

EMOTER > EMOTE

EMOTERS > EMOTE

EMOTES > EMOTE

EMOTICON n any of several combinations of symbols used in electronic mail and text messaging to indicate the state of mind of the writer, such as :-) to express happiness

EMOTICONS > EMOTICON

EMOTING > EMOTE

EMOTION n strong feeling

EMOTIONAL adj readily affected by or appealing to the emotions

EMOTIONS > EMOTION

EMOTIVE adj tending to arouse emotion

EMOTIVELY > EMOTIVE

EMOTIVISM n theory that moral utterances do not have a truth value but express the feelings of the speaker, so that murder is wrong is equivalent to down with murder

EMOTIVITY > EMOTIVE

EMOVE vb cause to feel emotion

EMOVED > EMOVE

EMOVES > EMOVE

EMOVING > EMOVE

EMPACKET vb wrap up

EMPACKETS > EMPACKET

EMPAESTIC adj embossed

EMPAIRE variant of > IMPAIR

EMPAIRED > EMPAIRE

EMPAIRES > EMPAIRE

EMPAIRING > EMPAIRE

EMPALE less common spelling of > IMPALE

EMPALED > EMPALE

EMPALER > EMPALE

EMPALERS > EMPALE

EMPALES > EMPALE

EMPALING > EMPALE

EMPANADA n Spanish meat-filled pastry

EMPANADAS > EMPANADA

EMPANEL vb enter on a list (names of persons to be summoned for jury service)

EMPANELED > EMPANEL

EMPANELS > EMPANEL

EMPANOPLY vb put armour on

EMPARE variant of
> IMPAIR
EMPARED > EMPARE
EMPARES > EMPARE
EMPARING > EMPARE
EMPARL variant of
> IMPARL
EMPARLED > EMPARL
EMPARLING > EMPARL
EMPARLS > EMPARL
EMPART variant of
> IMPART
EMPARTED > EMPART
EMPARTING > EMPART
EMPARTS > EMPART
EMPATHIC adj of or
relating to empathy
EMPATHIES > EMPATHY
EMPATHISE same as
> EMPATHIZE
EMPATHIST > EMPATHY
EMPATHIZE vb sense and
understand someone else's
feelings as if they were
one's own
EMPATHY n ability to
understand someone else's
feelings as if they were
one's own
EMPATRON vb treat in the
manner of a patron
EMPATRONS > EMPATRON
EMPAYRE variant of
> IMPAIR
EMPAYRED > EMPAYRE
EMPAYRES > EMPAYRE
EMPAYRING > EMPAYRE
EMPEACH variant of
> IMPEACH
EMPEACHED > EMPEACH
EMPEACHES > EMPEACH
EMPENNAGE n rear part of
an aircraft, comprising the
fin, rudder, and tailplane
EMPEOPLE vb bring people
into
EMPEOPLED > EMPEOPLE
EMPEOPLES > EMPEOPLE
EMPERCE variant of
> EMPIERCE
EMPERCED > EMPERCE
EMPERCES > EMPERCE
EMPERCING > EMPERCE
EMPERIES > EMPERY
EMPERISE variant of
> EMPERIZE
EMPERISED > EMPERISE
EMPERISES > EMPERISE
EMPERISH vb damage or
harm
EMPERIZE vb act like an
emperor
EMPERIZED > EMPERIZE
EMPERIZES > EMPERIZE
EMPEROR n ruler of an
empire
EMPERORS > EMPEROR
EMPERY n dominion or
power
EMPHASES > EMPHASIS
EMPHASIS n special
importance or
significance
EMPHASISE same as

> EMPHASIZE
EMPHASIZE vb give
emphasis or prominence to
EMPHATIC adj showing
emphasis ▷ n emphatic
consonant, as used in
Arabic
EMPHATICS > EMPHATIC
EMPHLYSES
> EMPHLYSIS
EMPHLYSIS n outbreak of
blisters on the body
EMPHYSEMA n condition in
which the air sacs of the
lungs are grossly enlarged,
causing breathlessness
EMPIERCE vb pierce or cut
EMPIERCED > EMPIERCE
EMPIERCES > EMPIERCE
EMPIGHT adj attached or
positioned
EMPIRE n group of
territories under the rule of
one state or person
EMPIRES > EMPIRE
EMPIRIC n person who
relies on empirical methods
EMPIRICAL adj relying on
experiment or experience,
not on theory ▷ n posterior
probability of an event
derived on the basis of its
observed frequency in a
sample
EMPIRICS > EMPIRIC
EMPLACE vb put in place or
position
EMPLACED > EMPLACE
EMPLACES > EMPLACE
EMPLACING > EMPLACE
EMPLANE vb board or put
on board an aeroplane
EMPLANED > EMPLANE
EMPLANES > EMPLANE
EMPLANING > EMPLANE
EMPLASTER vb cover with
plaster
EMPLASTIC adj sticky
EMPLEACH variant of
> IMPLEACH
EMPLECTON n type of
masonry filled with rubbish
EMPLECTUM variant of
> EMPLECTON
EMPLONGE variant of
> IMPLUNGE
EMPLONGED > EMPLONGE
EMPLONGES > EMPLONGE
EMPLOY vb engage or make
use of the services of (a
person) in return for money
▷ n state of being employed
EMPLOYE same as
> EMPLOYEE
EMPLOYED > EMPLOY
EMPLOYEE n person who is
hired to work for someone
in return for payment
EMPLOYEES > EMPLOYEE
EMPLOYER n person or
organization that employs
someone
EMPLOYERS > EMPLOYER
EMPLOYES > EMPLOYE
EMPLOYING > EMPLOY

EMPLOYS > EMPLOY
EMPLUME vb put a plume
on
EMPLUMED > EMPLUME
EMPLUMES > EMPLUME
EMPLUMING > EMPLUME
EMPOISON vb embitter or
corrupt
EMPOISONS > EMPOISON
EMPOLDER variant spelling
of > IMPOLDER
EMPOLDERS > EMPOLDER
EMPORIA > EMPORIUM
EMPORIUM n large general
shop
EMPORIUMS > EMPORIUM
EMPOWER vb enable,
authorize
EMPOWERED > EMPOWER
EMPOWERS > EMPOWER
EMPRESS n woman who
rules an empire
EMPRESSE adj keen;
zealous
EMPRESSES > EMPRESS
EMPRISE n chivalrous or
daring enterprise
EMPRISES > EMPRISE
EMPRIZE variant of
> EMPRISE
EMPRIZES > EMPRIZE
EMPT vb empty
EMPTED > EMPT
EMPTIABLE > EMPTY
EMPTIED > EMPTY
EMPTIER > EMPTY
EMPTIERS > EMPTY
EMPTIES > EMPTY
EMPTIEST > EMPTY
EMPTILY > EMPTY
EMPTINESS > EMPTY
EMPTING > EMPT
EMPTINGS variant of
> EMPTINS
EMPTINS npl liquid
leavening agent made from
potatoes
EMPTION n process of
buying something
EMPTIONAL > EMPTION
EMPTIONS > EMPTION
EMPTS > EMPT
EMPTY adj containing
nothing ▷ vb make or
become empty ▷ n empty
container, esp a bottle
EMPTYING > EMPTY
EMPTYINGS > EMPTY
EMPTYSES > EMPTYSIS
EMPTYSIS n act of spitting
up blood
EMPURPLE vb make or
become purple
EMPURPLED > EMPURPLE
EMPURPLES > EMPURPLE
EMPUSA n goblin in Greek
mythology
EMPUSAS > EMPUSA
EMPUSE variant of
> EMPUSA
EMPUSES > EMPUSE
EMPYEMA n collection of
pus in a body cavity, esp in
the chest

EMPYEMAS > EMPYEMA
EMPYEMATA > EMPYEMA
EMPYEMIC > EMPYEMA
EMPYESES > EMPYESIS
EMPYESIS n pus-filled boil
on the skin
EMPYREAL variant of
> EMPYREAN
EMPYREAN n heavens or
sky ▷ adj of or relating to
the sky or the heavens
EMPYREANS > EMPYREAN
EMPYREUMA n smell and
taste associated with
burning vegetable and
animal matter
EMS > EM
EMU n large Australian
flightless bird with long
legs
EMULATE vb attempt to
equal or surpass by
imitating
EMULATED > EMULATE
EMULATES > EMULATE
EMULATING > EMULATE
EMULATION n act of
emulating or imitating
EMULATIVE > EMULATE
EMULATOR > EMULATE
EMULATORS > EMULATE
EMULE variant of
> EMULATE
EMULED > EMULE
EMULES > EMULE
EMULGE vb remove liquid
from
EMULGED > EMULGE
EMULGENCE > EMULGE
EMULGENT > EMULGE
EMULGES > EMULGE
EMULGING > EMULGE
EMULING > EMULE
EMULOUS adj desiring or
aiming to equal or surpass
another
EMULOUSLY > EMULOUS
EMULSIBLE > EMULSIFY
EMULSIFY vb (of two
liquids) join together
EMULSIN n enzyme that is
found in almonds
EMULSINS > EMULSIN
EMULSION n light-
sensitive coating on
photographic film ▷ vb
paint with emulsion paint
EMULSIONS > EMULSION
EMULSIVE > EMULSION
EMULSOID n sol with a
liquid disperse phase
EMULSOIDS > EMULSOID
EMULSOR n device that
emulsifies
EMULSORS > EMULSOR
EMUNCTION
> EMUNCTORY
EMUNCTORY adj of or
relating to a bodily organ or
duct having an excretory
function ▷ n excretory
organ or duct, such as a
skin pore
EMUNGE vb clean or clear
out

EMUNGED > EMUNGE
EMUNGES > EMUNGE
EMUNGING > EMUNGE
EMURE variant of **>** IMMURE
EMURED > EMURE
EMURES > EMURE
EMURING > EMURE
EMUS > EMU
EMYD n freshwater tortoise or terrapin
EMYDE same as **>** EMYD
EMYDES > EMYDE
EMYDS > EMYD
EMYS n freshwater tortoise or terrapin
EN n unit of measurement, half the width of an em
ENABLE vb provide (a person) with the means, opportunity, or authority (to do something)
ENABLED > ENABLE
ENABLER > ENABLE
ENABLERS > ENABLE
ENABLES > ENABLE
ENABLING > ENABLE
ENACT vb establish by law
ENACTABLE > ENACT
ENACTED > ENACT
ENACTING > ENACT
ENACTION > ENACT
ENACTIONS > ENACT
ENACTIVE > ENACT
ENACTMENT > ENACT
ENACTOR > ENACT
ENACTORS > ENACT
ENACTORY > ENACT
ENACTS > ENACT
ENACTURE > ENACT
ENACTURES > ENACT
ENALAPRIL n ACE inhibitor used to treat high blood pressure and congestive heart failure
ENALLAGE n act of using one grammatical form in the place of another
ENALLAGES > ENALLAGE
ENAMEL n glasslike coating applied to metal etc to preserve the surface ▷ vb cover with enamel
ENAMELED > ENAMEL
ENAMELER > ENAMEL
ENAMELERS > ENAMEL
ENAMELING > ENAMEL
ENAMELIST > ENAMEL
ENAMELLED > ENAMEL
ENAMELLER > ENAMEL
ENAMELS > ENAMEL
ENAMINE n type of unsaturated compound
ENAMINES > ENAMINE
ENAMOR same as **>** ENAMOUR
ENAMORADO n beloved one, lover
ENAMORED same as **>** ENAMOURED
ENAMORING > ENAMOR
ENAMORS > ENAMOR
ENAMOUR vb inspire with love
ENAMOURED adj inspired

with love
ENAMOURS > ENAMOUR
ENANTHEMA n ulcer on a mucous membrane
ENARCH variant of **>** INARCH
ENARCHED > ENARCH
ENARCHES > ENARCH
ENARCHING > ENARCH
ENARGITE n sulphide of copper and arsenic
ENARGITES > ENARGITE
ENARM vb provide with arms
ENARMED > ENARM
ENARMING > ENARM
ENARMS > ENARM
ENATE adj growing out or outwards ▷ n relative on the mother's side
ENATES > ENATE
ENATIC adj related on one's mother's side
ENATION > ENATE
ENATIONS > ENATE
ENAUNTER conj in case that
ENCAENIA n festival of dedication or commemoration
ENCAENIAS > ENCAENIA
ENCAGE vb confine in or as in a cage
ENCAGED > ENCAGE
ENCAGES > ENCAGE
ENCAGING > ENCAGE
ENCALM vb becalm, settle
ENCALMED > ENCALM
ENCALMING > ENCALM
ENCALMS > ENCALM
ENCAMP vb set up in a camp
ENCAMPED > ENCAMP
ENCAMPING > ENCAMP
ENCAMPS > ENCAMP
ENCANTHIS n tumour in the eye
ENCAPSULE vb enclose or be enclosed in or as if in a capsule
ENCARPUS n decoration of fruit or flowers on a frieze
ENCASE vb enclose or cover completely
ENCASED > ENCASE
ENCASES > ENCASE
ENCASH vb exchange (a cheque) for cash
ENCASHED > ENCASH
ENCASHES > ENCASH
ENCASHING > ENCASH
ENCASING > ENCASE
ENCASTRE adj (of a beam) fixed at the ends
ENCAUSTIC adj decorated by any process involving burning in colours, esp by inlaying coloured clays and baking or by fusing wax colours to the surface ▷ n process of burning in colours
ENCAVE variant of **>** INCAVE
ENCAVED > ENCAVE

ENCAVES > ENCAVE
ENCAVING > ENCAVE
ENCEINTE n boundary wall enclosing a defended area
ENCEINTES > ENCEINTE
ENCEPHALA n brains
ENCHAFE vb heat up
ENCHAFED > ENCHAFE
ENCHAFES > ENCHAFE
ENCHAFING > ENCHAFE
ENCHAIN vb bind with chains
ENCHAINED > ENCHAIN
ENCHAINS > ENCHAIN
ENCHANT vb delight and fascinate
ENCHANTED > ENCHANT
ENCHANTER > ENCHANT
ENCHANTS > ENCHANT
ENCHARGE vb give into the custody of
ENCHARGED > ENCHARGE
ENCHARGES > ENCHARGE
ENCHARM vb enchant
ENCHARMED > ENCHARM
ENCHARMS > ENCHARM
ENCHASE less common word for **>** CHASE
ENCHASED > ENCHASE
ENCHASER > ENCHASE
ENCHASERS > ENCHASE
ENCHASES > ENCHASE
ENCHASING > ENCHASE
ENCHEASON n reason
ENCHEER vb cheer up
ENCHEERED > ENCHEER
ENCHEERS > ENCHEER
ENCHILADA n Mexican dish of a tortilla filled with meat, served with chilli sauce
ENCHORIAL adj of or used in a particular country: used esp of the popular (demotic) writing of the ancient Egyptians
ENCHORIC same as **>** ENCHORIAL
ENCIERRO n Spanish bull run
ENCIERROS > ENCIERRO
ENCINA n type of oak
ENCINAL > ENCINA
ENCINAS > ENCINA
ENCIPHER vb convert (a message, document, etc) from plain text into code or cipher
ENCIPHERS > ENCIPHER
ENCIRCLE vb form a circle around
ENCIRCLED > ENCIRCLE
ENCIRCLES > ENCIRCLE
ENCLASP vb clasp
ENCLASPED > ENCLASP
ENCLASPS > ENCLASP
ENCLAVE n part of a country entirely surrounded by foreign territory ▷ vb hold in an enclave
ENCLAVED > ENCLAVE
ENCLAVES > ENCLAVE

ENCLAVING > ENCLAVE
ENCLISES > ENCLISIS
ENCLISIS n state of being enclitic
ENCLITIC adj denoting or relating to a monosyllabic word or form that is treated as a suffix of the preceding word ▷ n enclitic word or linguistic form
ENCLITICS > ENCLITIC
ENCLOSE vb surround completely
ENCLOSED > ENCLOSE
ENCLOSER > ENCLOSE
ENCLOSERS > ENCLOSE
ENCLOSES > ENCLOSE
ENCLOSING > ENCLOSE
ENCLOSURE n area of land enclosed by a fence, wall, or hedge
ENCLOTHE vb clothe
ENCLOTHED > ENCLOTHE
ENCLOTHES > ENCLOTHE
ENCLOUD vb hide with clouds
ENCLOUDED > ENCLOUD
ENCLOUDS > ENCLOUD
ENCODABLE > ENCODE
ENCODE vb convert (a message) into code
ENCODED > ENCODE
ENCODER > ENCODE
ENCODERS > ENCODE
ENCODES > ENCODE
ENCODING > ENCODE
ENCOLOUR vb give a colour to
ENCOLOURS > ENCOLOUR
ENCOLPION n religious symbol worn on the breast
ENCOLPIUM variant of **>** ENCOLPION
ENCOLURE n mane of a horse
ENCOLURES > ENCOLURE
ENCOMIA > ENCOMIUM
ENCOMIAST n person who speaks or writes an encomium
ENCOMION variant of **>** ENCOMIUM
ENCOMIUM n formal expression of praise
ENCOMIUMS > ENCOMIUM
ENCOMPASS vb surround
ENCORE interj again, once more ▷ n extra performance due to enthusiastic demand ▷ vb demand an extra or repeated performance of (a work, piece of music, etc) by (a performer)
ENCORED > ENCORE
ENCORES > ENCORE
ENCORING > ENCORE
ENCOUNTER vb meet unexpectedly ▷ n unexpected meeting
ENCOURAGE vb inspire with confidence
ENCRADLE vb put in a cradle
ENCRADLED > ENCRADLE

ENCRADLES > ENCRADLE
ENCRATIES > ENCRATY
ENCRATY n control of one's desires, actions, etc
ENCREASE variant form of > INCREASE
ENCREASED > ENCREASE
ENCREASES > ENCREASE
ENCRIMSON vb make crimson
ENCRINAL > ENCRINITE
ENCRINIC > ENCRINITE
ENCRINITE n sedimentary rock formed almost exclusively from the skeletal plates of crinoids
ENCROACH vb intrude gradually on a person's rights or land
ENCRUST vb cover with a layer of something
ENCRUSTED > ENCRUST
ENCRUSTS > ENCRUST
ENCRYPT vb put (a message) into code
ENCRYPTED > ENCRYPT
ENCRYPTS > ENCRYPT
ENCUMBER vb hinder or impede
ENCUMBERS > ENCUMBER
ENCURTAIN vb cover or surround with curtains
ENCYCLIC n letter sent by the Pope to all bishops
ENCYCLICS > ENCYCLIC
ENCYST vb enclose or become enclosed by a cyst, thick membrane, or shell
ENCYSTED > ENCYST
ENCYSTING > ENCYST
ENCYSTS > ENCYST
END n furthest point or part ▷ vb bring or come to a finish
ENDAMAGE vb cause injury to
ENDAMAGED > ENDAMAGE
ENDAMAGES > ENDAMAGE
ENDAMEBA same as > ENDAMOEBA
ENDAMEBAE > ENDAMEBA
ENDAMEBAS > ENDAMEBA
ENDAMEBIC > ENDAMEBA
ENDAMOEBA same as > ENTAMOEBA
ENDANGER vb put in danger
ENDANGERS > ENDANGER
ENDARCH adj (of a xylem strand) having the first-formed xylem internal to that formed later
ENDARCHY n state of being endarch
ENDART variant of > INDART
ENDARTED > ENDART
ENDARTING > ENDART
ENDARTS > ENDART
ENDASH n short dash in punctuation
ENDASHES > ENDASH
ENDBRAIN n part of the brain

ENDBRAINS > ENDBRAIN
ENDEAR vb cause to be liked
ENDEARED > ENDEAR
ENDEARING adj giving rise to love or esteem
ENDEARS > ENDEAR
ENDEAVOR same as > ENDEAVOUR
ENDEAVORS > ENDEAVOR
ENDEAVOUR vb try ▷ n effort
ENDECAGON n figure with eleven sides
ENDED > END
ENDEICTIC > ENDEIXIS
ENDEIXES > ENDEIXIS
ENDEIXIS n sign or mark
ENDEMIAL same as > ENDEMIC
ENDEMIC adj present within a localized area or peculiar to a particular group of people ▷ n endemic disease or plant
ENDEMICAL adj endemic
ENDEMICS > ENDEMIC
ENDEMISM > ENDEMIC
ENDEMISMS > ENDEMIC
ENDENIZEN vb make a denizen
ENDER > END
ENDERMIC adj (of a medicine) acting by absorption through the skin
ENDERON variant of > ANDIRON
ENDERONS > ENDERON
ENDERS > END
ENDEW variant of > ENDUE
ENDEWED > ENDEW
ENDEWING > ENDEW
ENDEWS > ENDEW
ENDEXINE n inner layer of an exine
ENDEXINES > ENDEXINE
ENDGAME n closing stage of a game of chess, in which only a few pieces are left on the board
ENDGAMES > ENDGAME
ENDGATE n tailboard of a vehicle
ENDGATES > ENDGATE
ENDING n last part or conclusion of something
ENDINGS > ENDING
ENDIRON variant of > ANDIRON
ENDIRONS > ENDIRON
ENDITE variant of > INDICT
ENDITED > ENDITE
ENDITES > ENDITE
ENDITING > ENDITE
ENDIVE n curly-leaved plant used in salads
ENDIVES > ENDIVE
ENDLANG variant of > ENDLONG
ENDLEAF n endpaper in a book
ENDLEAFS > ENDLEAF

ENDLEAVES > ENDLEAF
ENDLESS adj having no end
ENDLESSLY > ENDLESS
ENDLONG adv lengthways or on end
ENDMOST adj nearest the end
ENDNOTE n note at the end of a section of writing
ENDNOTES > ENDNOTE
ENDOBLAST less common name for > ENDODERM
ENDOCARP n inner, usually woody, layer of the pericarp of a fruit, such as the stone of a peach or cherry
ENDOCARPS > ENDOCARP
ENDOCAST n cast made of the inside of a cranial cavity to show the size and shape of a brain
ENDOCASTS > ENDOCAST
ENDOCRINE adj relating to the glands which secrete hormones directly into the bloodstream ▷ n endocrine gland
ENDOCYTIC adj involving absorption of cells
ENDODERM n inner germ layer of an animal embryo, which gives rise to the lining of the digestive and respiratory tracts
ENDODERMS > ENDODERM
ENDODYNE same as > AUTODYNE
ENDOERGIC adj (of a nuclear reaction) occurring with absorption of energy
ENDOGAMIC > ENDOGAMY
ENDOGAMY n marriage within one's own tribe or similar unit
ENDOGEN n plant that increases in size by internal growth
ENDOGENIC > ENDOGEN
ENDOGENS > ENDOGEN
ENDOGENY n development by internal growth
ENDOLYMPH n fluid that fills the membranous labyrinth of the internal ear
ENDOMIXES > ENDOMIXIS
ENDOMIXIS n reorganization of certain nuclei with some protozoa
ENDOMORPH n person with a fat and heavy body build: said to be correlated with viscerotonia
ENDOPHAGY n cannibalism within the same group or tribe
ENDOPHYTE n fungus, or occasionally an alga or other organism, that lives within a plant
ENDOPLASM n inner cytoplasm in some cells, esp protozoa, which is more granular and fluid than the outer cytoplasm

ENDOPOD n inner branch of a two-branched crustacean
ENDOPODS > ENDOPOD
ENDOPROCT n small animal living in water
ENDORPHIN n chemical occurring in the brain, which has a similar effect to morphine
ENDORSE vb give approval to
ENDORSED > ENDORSE
ENDORSEE n person in whose favour a negotiable instrument is endorsed
ENDORSEES > ENDORSEE
ENDORSER > ENDORSE
ENDORSERS > ENDORSE
ENDORSES > ENDORSE
ENDORSING > ENDORSE
ENDORSIVE > ENDORSE
ENDORSOR > ENDORSE
ENDORSORS > ENDORSE
ENDOSARC same as > ENDOPLASM
ENDOSARCS > ENDOSARC
ENDOSCOPE n long slender medical instrument used for examining the interior of hollow organs including the lung, stomach, bladder and bowel
ENDOSCOPY > ENDOSCOPE
ENDOSMOS same as > ENDOSMOSE
ENDOSMOSE n osmosis in which water enters a cell or organism from the surrounding solution
ENDOSOME n sac within a biological cell
ENDOSOMES > ENDOSOME
ENDOSPERM n tissue within the seed of a flowering plant that surrounds and nourishes the developing embryo
ENDOSPORE n small asexual spore produced by some bacteria and algae
ENDOSS vb endorse
ENDOSSED > ENDOSS
ENDOSSES > ENDOSS
ENDOSSING > ENDOSS
ENDOSTEA > ENDOSTEUM
ENDOSTEAL > ENDOSTEUM
ENDOSTEUM n highly vascular membrane lining the marrow cavity of long bones, such as the femur and humerus
ENDOSTYLE n groove or fold in the pharynx of various chordates
ENDOTHERM n animal with warm blood
ENDOTOXIC > ENDOTOXIN
ENDOTOXIN n toxin contained within the protoplasm of an organism, esp a bacterium, and liberated only at death

e

ENDOW vb provide permanent income for
ENDOWED > ENDOW
ENDOWER > ENDOW
ENDOWERS > ENDOW
ENDOWING > ENDOW
ENDOWMENT n money given to an institution, such as a hospital
ENDOWS > ENDOW
ENDOZOA > ENDOZOON
ENDOZOIC adj (of a plant) living within an animal
ENDOZOON variant of > ENTOZOON
ENDPAPER n either of two leaves at the front and back of a book pasted to the inside of the cover
ENDPAPERS > ENDPAPER
ENDPLATE n any usually flat platelike structure at the end of something
ENDPLATES > ENDPLATE
ENDPLAY n way of playing the last few tricks in a hand so that an opponent is forced to make a particular lead ▷ vb force (an opponent) to make a particular lead near the end of a hand
ENDPLAYED > ENDPLAY
ENDPLAYS > ENDPLAY
ENDPOINT n point at which anything is complete
ENDPOINTS > ENDPOINT
ENDRIN n type of insecticide
ENDRINS > ENDRIN
ENDS > END
ENDSHIP n small village
ENDSHIPS > ENDSHIP
ENDUE vb invest or provide, as with some quality or trait
ENDUED > ENDUE
ENDUES > ENDUE
ENDUING > ENDUE
ENDUNGEON vb put in a dungeon
ENDURABLE > ENDURE
ENDURABLY > ENDURE
ENDURANCE n act or power of enduring
ENDURE vb bear (hardship) patiently
ENDURED > ENDURE
ENDURER > ENDURE
ENDURERS > ENDURE
ENDURES > ENDURE
ENDURING adj long-lasting
ENDURO n long-distance race for vehicles, intended to test endurance
ENDUROS > ENDURO
ENDWAYS adv having the end forwards or upwards ▷ adj vertical or upright
ENDWISE same as > ENDWAYS
ENDYSES > ENDYSIS
ENDYSIS n formation of new layers of integument after ecdysis

ENDZONE n (in American football) area at either end of the playing field
ENDZONES > ENDZONE
ENE variant of > EVEN
ENEMA n medicine injected into the rectum to empty the bowels
ENEMAS > ENEMA
ENEMATA > ENEMA
ENEMIES > ENEMY
ENEMY n hostile person or nation, opponent ▷ adj of or belonging to an enemy
ENERGETIC adj having or showing energy and enthusiasm
ENERGIC > ENERGY
ENERGID n nucleus and the cytoplasm associated with it in a syncytium
ENERGIDS > ENERGID
ENERGIES > ENERGY
ENERGISE same as > ENERGIZE
ENERGISED > ENERGISE
ENERGISER > ENERGISE
ENERGISES > ENERGISE
ENERGIZE vb give vigour to
ENERGIZED > ENERGIZE
ENERGIZER > ENERGIZE
ENERGIZES > ENERGIZE
ENERGUMEN n person thought to be possessed by an evil spirit
ENERGY n capacity for intense activity
ENERVATE vb deprive of strength or vitality ▷ adj deprived of strength or vitality
ENERVATED > ENERVATE
ENERVATES > ENERVATE
ENERVATOR > ENERVATE
ENERVE vb enervate
ENERVED > ENERVE
ENERVES > ENERVE
ENERVING > ENERVE
ENES > ENE
ENEW vb force a bird into water
ENEWED > ENEW
ENEWING > ENEW
ENEWS > ENEW
ENFACE vb write, print, or stamp (something) on the face of (a document)
ENFACED > ENFACE
ENFACES > ENFACE
ENFACING > ENFACE
ENFANT n French child
ENFANTS > ENFANT
ENFEEBLE vb weaken
ENFEEBLED > ENFEEBLE
ENFEEBLER > ENFEEBLE
ENFEEBLES > ENFEEBLE
ENFELON vb infuriate
ENFELONED > ENFELON
ENFELONS > ENFELON
ENFEOFF vb invest (a person) with possession of a freehold estate in land
ENFEOFFED > ENFEOFF

ENFEOFFS > ENFEOFF
ENFESTED adj made bitter
ENFETTER vb fetter
ENFETTERS > ENFETTER
ENFEVER vb make feverish
ENFEVERED > ENFEVER
ENFEVERS > ENFEVER
ENFIERCE vb make ferocious
ENFIERCED > ENFIERCE
ENFIERCES > ENFIERCE
ENFILADE n burst of gunfire sweeping from end to end along a line of troops ▷ vb attack with an enfilade
ENFILADED > ENFILADE
ENFILADES > ENFILADE
ENFILED adj passed through
ENFIRE vb set alight
ENFIRED > ENFIRE
ENFIRES > ENFIRE
ENFIRING > ENFIRE
ENFIX variant of > INFIX
ENFIXED > ENFIX
ENFIXES > ENFIX
ENFIXING > ENFIX
ENFLAME variant of > INFLAME
ENFLAMED > ENFLAME
ENFLAMES > ENFLAME
ENFLAMING > ENFLAME
ENFLESH vb make flesh
ENFLESHED > ENFLESH
ENFLESHES > ENFLESH
ENFLOWER vb put flowers on
ENFLOWERS > ENFLOWER
ENFOLD vb cover by wrapping something around
ENFOLDED > ENFOLD
ENFOLDER > ENFOLD
ENFOLDERS > ENFOLD
ENFOLDING > ENFOLD
ENFOLDS > ENFOLD
ENFORCE vb impose obedience (to a law etc)
ENFORCED > ENFORCE
ENFORCER > ENFORCE
ENFORCERS > ENFORCE
ENFORCES > ENFORCE
ENFORCING > ENFORCE
ENFOREST vb make into a forest
ENFORESTS > ENFOREST
ENFORM variant of > INFORM
ENFORMED > ENFORM
ENFORMING > ENFORM
ENFORMS > ENFORM
ENFRAME vb put inside a frame
ENFRAMED > ENFRAME
ENFRAMES > ENFRAME
ENFRAMING > ENFRAME
ENFREE vb release, make free
ENFREED > ENFREE
ENFREEDOM variant of > ENFREE
ENFREEING > ENFREE
ENFREES > ENFREE
ENFREEZE vb freeze

ENFREEZES > ENFREEZE
ENFROSEN > ENFREEZE
ENFROZE > ENFREEZE
ENFROZEN > ENFREEZE
ENG another name for > AGMA
ENGAGE vb take part, participate ▷ adj (of a writer or artist, esp a man) morally or politically committed to some ideology
ENGAGED adj pledged to be married
ENGAGEDLY > ENGAGED
ENGAGEE adj (of a female writer or artist) morally or politically committed to some ideology
ENGAGER > ENGAGE
ENGAGERS > ENGAGE
ENGAGES > ENGAGE
ENGAGING adj charming
ENGAOL vb put into gaol
ENGAOLED > ENGAOL
ENGAOLING > ENGAOL
ENGAOLS > ENGAOL
ENGARLAND vb cover with garlands
ENGENDER vb produce, cause to occur
ENGENDERS > ENGENDER
ENGENDURE > ENGENDER
ENGILD vb cover with or as if with gold
ENGILDED > ENGILD
ENGILDING > ENGILD
ENGILDS > ENGILD
ENGILT > ENGILD
ENGINE n any machine which converts energy into mechanical work ▷ vb put an engine in
ENGINED > ENGINE
ENGINEER n person trained in any branch of engineering ▷ vb plan in a clever manner
ENGINEERS > ENGINEER
ENGINER > ENGINE
ENGINERS > ENGINE
ENGINERY n collection or assembly of engines
ENGINES > ENGINE
ENGINING > ENGINE
ENGINOUS adj ingenious or clever
ENGIRD vb surround
ENGIRDED > ENGIRD
ENGIRDING > ENGIRD
ENGIRDLE variant of > ENGIRD
ENGIRDLED > ENGIRDLE
ENGIRDLES > ENGIRDLE
ENGIRDS > ENGIRD
ENGIRT > ENGIRD
ENGLACIAL adj embedded in, carried by, or running through a glacier
ENGLISH vb put a spinning movement on a billiard ball
ENGLISHED > ENGLISH
ENGLISHES > ENGLISH
ENGLOBE vb surround as if in a globe

ENGLOBED > ENGLOBE
ENGLOBES > ENGLOBE
ENGLOBING > ENGLOBE
ENGLOOM vb make dull or dismal
ENGLOOMED > ENGLOOM
ENGLOOMS > ENGLOOM
ENGLUT vb devour ravenously
ENGLUTS > ENGLUT
ENGLUTTED > ENGLUT
ENGOBE n liquid put on pottery before glazing
ENGOBES > ENGOBE
ENGORE vb pierce or wound
ENGORED > ENGORE
ENGORES > ENGORE
ENGORGE vb clog with blood
ENGORGED > ENGORGE
ENGORGES > ENGORGE
ENGORGING > ENGORGE
ENGORING > ENGORE
ENGOULED adj (in heraldry) with ends coming from the mouths of animals
ENGOUMENT n obsessive liking
ENGRACE vb give grace to
ENGRACED > ENGRACE
ENGRACES > ENGRACE
ENGRACING > ENGRACE
ENGRAFF variant of > ENGRAFT
ENGRAFFED > ENGRAFF
ENGRAFFS > ENGRAFF
ENGRAFT vb graft (a shoot, bud, etc) onto a stock
ENGRAFTED > ENGRAFT
ENGRAFTS > ENGRAFT
ENGRAIL vb decorate or mark (the edge of) (a coin) with small carved notches
ENGRAILED > ENGRAIL
ENGRAILS > ENGRAIL
ENGRAIN variant spelling of > INGRAIN
ENGRAINED > ENGRAIN
ENGRAINER > ENGRAIN
ENGRAINS > ENGRAIN
ENGRAM n physical basis of an individual memory in the brain
ENGRAMMA variant of > ENGRAM
ENGRAMMAS > ENGRAMMA
ENGRAMME variant of > ENGRAM
ENGRAMMES > ENGRAMME
ENGRAMMIC > ENGRAM
ENGRAMS > ENGRAM
ENGRASP vb grasp or seize
ENGRASPED > ENGRASP
ENGRASPS > ENGRASP
ENGRAVE vb carve (a design) onto a hard surface
ENGRAVED > ENGRAVE
ENGRAVEN > ENGRAVE
ENGRAVER > ENGRAVE
ENGRAVERS > ENGRAVE
ENGRAVERY > ENGRAVE
ENGRAVES > ENGRAVE
ENGRAVING n print made from an engraved plate

ENGRENAGE n act of putting into gear
ENGRIEVE vb grieve
ENGRIEVED > ENGRIEVE
ENGRIEVES > ENGRIEVE
ENGROOVE vb put a groove in
ENGROOVED > ENGROOVE
ENGROOVES > ENGROOVE
ENGROSS vb occupy the attention of (a person) completely
ENGROSSED > ENGROSS
ENGROSSER > ENGROSS
ENGROSSES > ENGROSS
ENGS > ENG
ENGUARD vb protect or defend
ENGUARDED > ENGUARD
ENGUARDS > ENGUARD
ENGULF vb cover or surround completely
ENGULFED > ENGULF
ENGULFING > ENGULF
ENGULFS > ENGULF
ENGULPH variant of > ENGULF
ENGULPHED > ENGULPH
ENGULPHS > ENGULPH
ENGYSCOPE n microscope
ENHALO vb surround with or as if with a halo
ENHALOED > ENHALO
ENHALOES > ENHALO
ENHALOING > ENHALO
ENHALOS > ENHALO
ENHANCE vb increase in quality, value, or attractiveness
ENHANCED > ENHANCE
ENHANCER > ENHANCE
ENHANCERS > ENHANCE
ENHANCES > ENHANCE
ENHANCING > ENHANCE
ENHANCIVE > ENHANCE
ENHEARSE variant of > INHEARSE
ENHEARSED > ENHEARSE
ENHEARSES > ENHEARSE
ENHEARTEN vb give heart to, encourage
ENHUNGER vb cause to be hungry
ENHUNGERS > ENHUNGER
ENHYDRITE n type of mineral
ENHYDROS n piece of chalcedony that contains water
ENHYDROUS > ENHYDROS
ENIAC n early type of computer built in the 1940s
ENIACS > ENIAC
ENIGMA n puzzling thing or person
ENIGMAS > ENIGMA
ENIGMATA > ENIGMA
ENIGMATIC > ENIGMA
ENISLE vb put on or make into an island
ENISLED > ENISLE
ENISLES > ENISLE
ENISLING > ENISLE
ENJAMB vb (of a line of

verse) run over into the next line
ENJAMBED > ENJAMB
ENJAMBING > ENJAMB
ENJAMBS > ENJAMB
ENJOIN vb order (someone) to do something
ENJOINDER n order
ENJOINED > ENJOIN
ENJOINER > ENJOIN
ENJOINERS > ENJOIN
ENJOINING > ENJOIN
ENJOINS > ENJOIN
ENJOY vb take joy in
ENJOYABLE > ENJOY
ENJOYABLY > ENJOY
ENJOYED > ENJOY
ENJOYER > ENJOY
ENJOYERS > ENJOY
ENJOYING > ENJOY
ENJOYMENT n act or condition of receiving pleasure from something
ENJOYS > ENJOY
ENKERNEL vb put inside a kernel
ENKERNELS > ENKERNEL
ENKINDLE vb set on fire
ENKINDLED > ENKINDLE
ENKINDLER > ENKINDLE
ENKINDLES > ENKINDLE
ENLACE vb bind or encircle with or as with laces
ENLACED > ENLACE
ENLACES > ENLACE
ENLACING > ENLACE
ENLARD vb put lard on
ENLARDED > ENLARD
ENLARDING > ENLARD
ENLARDS > ENLARD
ENLARGE vb make or grow larger
ENLARGED > ENLARGE
ENLARGEN variant of > ENLARGE
ENLARGENS > ENLARGEN
ENLARGER n optical instrument for making enlarged photographic prints in which a negative is brightly illuminated and its enlarged image is focused onto a sheet of sensitized paper
ENLARGERS > ENLARGER
ENLARGES > ENLARGE
ENLARGING > ENLARGE
ENLEVE adj having been abducted
ENLIGHT vb light up
ENLIGHTED > ENLIGHT
ENLIGHTEN vb give information to
ENLIGHTS > ENLIGHT
ENLINK vb link together
ENLINKED > ENLINK
ENLINKING > ENLINK
ENLINKS > ENLINK
ENLIST vb enter the armed forces
ENLISTED > ENLIST
ENLISTEE > ENLIST
ENLISTEES > ENLIST
ENLISTER > ENLIST

ENLISTERS > ENLIST
ENLISTING > ENLIST
ENLISTS > ENLIST
ENLIT > ENLIGHT
ENLIVEN vb make lively or cheerful
ENLIVENED > ENLIVEN
ENLIVENER > ENLIVEN
ENLIVENS > ENLIVEN
ENLOCK vb lock or secure
ENLOCKED > ENLOCK
ENLOCKING > ENLOCK
ENLOCKS > ENLOCK
ENLUMINE vb illuminate
ENLUMINED > ENLUMINE
ENLUMINES > ENLUMINE
ENMESH vb catch or involve in or as if in a net or snare
ENMESHED > ENMESH
ENMESHES > ENMESH
ENMESHING > ENMESH
ENMEW variant of > EMMEW
ENMEWED > ENMEW
ENMEWING > ENMEW
ENMEWS > ENMEW
ENMITIES > ENMITY
ENMITY n ill will, hatred
ENMOSSED adj having a covering of moss
ENMOVE variant of > EMMOVE
ENMOVED > ENMOVE
ENMOVES > ENMOVE
ENMOVING > ENMOVE
ENNAGE n total number of ens in a piece of matter to be set in type
ENNAGES > ENNAGE
ENNEAD n group or series of nine
ENNEADIC > ENNEAD
ENNEADS > ENNEAD
ENNEAGON another name for > NONAGON
ENNEAGONS > ENNEAGON
ENNEAGRAM n personality system involving nine distinct but interconnected personality types
ENNOBLE vb make noble, elevate
ENNOBLED > ENNOBLE
ENNOBLER > ENNOBLE
ENNOBLERS > ENNOBLE
ENNOBLES > ENNOBLE
ENNOBLING > ENNOBLE
ENNOG n back alley
ENNOGS > ENNOG
ENNUI n boredom, dissatisfaction ▷ vb bore
ENNUIED > ENNUI
ENNUIS > ENNUI
ENNUYE adj bored
ENNUYED > ENNUI
ENNUYEE same as > ENNUYE
ENNUYING > ENNUI
ENODAL adj having no nodes
ENOKI variant of > ENOKITAKE
ENOKIDAKE variant of > ENOKITAKE
ENOKIS > ENOKI

e

ENOKITAKE n Japanese mushroom

ENOL n any organic compound containing the group -CH:CO-, often existing in chemical equilibrium with the corresponding keto form

ENOLASE n type of enzyme

ENOLASES > ENOLASE

ENOLIC > ENOL

ENOLOGIES > ENOLOGY

ENOLOGIST n wine expert

ENOLOGY usual US spelling of > OENOLOGY

ENOLS > ENOL

ENOMOTIES > ENOMOTY

ENOMOTY n division of the Spartan army in ancient Greece

ENOPHILE n lover of wine

ENOPHILES > ENOPHILE

ENORM variant of > ENORMOUS

ENORMITY n great wickedness

ENORMOUS adj very big, vast

ENOSES > ENOSIS

ENOSIS n union of Greece and Cyprus

ENOSISES > ENOSIS

ENOUGH adj as much or as many as necessary ▷ n sufficient quantity ▷ adv sufficiently

ENOUGHS > ENOUGH

ENOUNCE vb enunciate

ENOUNCED > ENOUNCE

ENOUNCES > ENOUNCE

ENOUNCING > ENOUNCE

ENOW archaic word for > ENOUGH

ENOWS > ENOW

ENPLANE vb board an aircraft

ENPLANED > ENPLANE

ENPLANES > ENPLANE

ENPLANING > ENPLANE

ENPRINT n standard photographic print produced from a negative

ENPRINTS > ENPRINT

ENQUEUE vb add (an item) to a queue of computing tasks

ENQUEUED > ENQUEUE

ENQUEUES > ENQUEUE

ENQUEUING > ENQUEUE

ENQUIRE same as > INQUIRE

ENQUIRED > ENQUIRE

ENQUIRER > ENQUIRE

ENQUIRERS > ENQUIRE

ENQUIRES > ENQUIRE

ENQUIRIES > ENQUIRE

ENQUIRING > ENQUIRE

ENQUIRY > ENQUIRE

ENRACE vb bring in a race of people

ENRACED > ENRACE

ENRACES > ENRACE

ENRACING > ENRACE

ENRAGE vb make extremely angry

ENRAGED > ENRAGE

ENRAGEDLY > ENRAGE

ENRAGES > ENRAGE

ENRAGING > ENRAGE

ENRANCKLE vb upset, make irate

ENRANGE vb arrange, organize

ENRANGED > ENRANGE

ENRANGES > ENRANGE

ENRANGING > ENRANGE

ENRANK vb put in a row

ENRANKED > ENRANK

ENRANKING > ENRANK

ENRANKS > ENRANK

ENRAPT > ENRAPTURE

ENRAPTURE vb fill with delight

ENRAUNGE variant of > ENRANGE

ENRAUNGED > ENRAUNGE

ENRAUNGES > ENRAUNGE

ENRAVISH vb enchant

ENRHEUM vb pass a cold on to

ENRHEUMED > ENRHEUM

ENRHEUMS > ENRHEUM

ENRICH vb improve in quality

ENRICHED > ENRICH

ENRICHER > ENRICH

ENRICHERS > ENRICH

ENRICHES > ENRICH

ENRICHING > ENRICH

ENRIDGED adj ridged

ENRING vb put a ring round

ENRINGED > ENRING

ENRINGING > ENRING

ENRINGS > ENRING

ENRIVEN adj ripped

ENROBE vb dress in or as if in a robe

ENROBED > ENROBE

ENROBER > ENROBE

ENROBERS > ENROBE

ENROBES > ENROBE

ENROBING > ENROBE

ENROL vb (cause to) become a member

ENROLL same as > ENROL

ENROLLED > ENROL

ENROLLEE > ENROL

ENROLLEES > ENROL

ENROLLER > ENROL

ENROLLERS > ENROL

ENROLLING > ENROLL

ENROLLS > ENROLL

ENROLMENT n act of enrolling or state of being enrolled

ENROLS > ENROL

ENROOT vb establish (plants) by fixing their roots in the earth

ENROOTED > ENROOT

ENROOTING > ENROOT

ENROOTS > ENROOT

ENROUGH vb roughen

ENROUGHED > ENROUGH

ENROUGHS > ENROUGH

ENROUND vb encircle

ENROUNDED > ENROUND

ENROUNDS > ENROUND

ENS n being or existence in the most general abstract sense

ENSAMPLE n example ▷ vb make an example

ENSAMPLED > ENSAMPLE

ENSAMPLES > ENSAMPLE

ENSATE adj shaped like a sword

ENSCONCE vb settle firmly or comfortably

ENSCONCED > ENSCONCE

ENSCONCES > ENSCONCE

ENSCROLL variant of > INSCROLL

ENSCROLLS > ENSCROLL

ENSEAL vb seal up

ENSEALED > ENSEAL

ENSEALING > ENSEAL

ENSEALS > ENSEAL

ENSEAM vb put a seam on

ENSEAMED > ENSEAM

ENSEAMING > ENSEAM

ENSEAMS > ENSEAM

ENSEAR vb dry

ENSEARED > ENSEAR

ENSEARING > ENSEAR

ENSEARS > ENSEAR

ENSEMBLE n all the parts of something taken together ▷ adv all together or at once ▷ adj (of a film or play) involving several separate but often interrelated story lines

ENSEMBLES > ENSEMBLE

ENSERF vb enslave

ENSERFED > ENSERF

ENSERFING > ENSERF

ENSERFS > ENSERF

ENSEW variant of > ENSUE

ENSEWED > ENSEW

ENSEWING > ENSEW

ENSEWS > ENSEW

ENSHEATH variant of > INSHEATHE

ENSHEATHE variant of > INSHEATHE

ENSHEATHS > ENSHEATH

ENSHELL variant of > INSHELL

ENSHELLED > ENSHELL

ENSHELLS > ENSHELL

ENSHELTER vb shelter

ENSHIELD vb protect

ENSHIELDS > ENSHIELD

ENSHRINE vb cherish or treasure

ENSHRINED > ENSHRINE

ENSHRINEE > ENSHRINE

ENSHRINES > ENSHRINE

ENSHROUD vb cover or hide as with a shroud

ENSHROUDS > ENSHROUD

ENSIFORM adj shaped like a sword blade

ENSIGN n naval flag ▷ vb mark with a sign

ENSIGNCY > ENSIGN

ENSIGNED > ENSIGN

ENSIGNING > ENSIGN

ENSIGNS > ENSIGN

ENSILAGE n process of ensiling green fodder ▷ vb make into silage

ENSILAGED > ENSILAGE

ENSILAGES > ENSILAGE

ENSILE vb store and preserve (green fodder) in an enclosed pit or silo

ENSILED > ENSILE

ENSILES > ENSILE

ENSILING > ENSILE

ENSKIED > ENSKY

ENSKIES > ENSKY

ENSKY vb put in the sky

ENSKYED > ENSKY

ENSKYING > ENSKY

ENSLAVE vb make a slave of (someone)

ENSLAVED > ENSLAVE

ENSLAVER > ENSLAVE

ENSLAVERS > ENSLAVE

ENSLAVES > ENSLAVE

ENSLAVING > ENSLAVE

ENSNARE vb catch in or as if in a snare

ENSNARED > ENSNARE

ENSNARER > ENSNARE

ENSNARERS > ENSNARE

ENSNARES > ENSNARE

ENSNARING > ENSNARE

ENSNARL vb become tangled in

ENSNARLED > ENSNARL

ENSNARLS > ENSNARL

ENSORCEL vb enchant

ENSORCELL variant of > ENSORCEL

ENSORCELS > ENSORCEL

ENSOUL vb endow with a soul

ENSOULED > ENSOUL

ENSOULING > ENSOUL

ENSOULS > ENSOUL

ENSPHERE vb enclose in or as if in a sphere

ENSPHERED > ENSPHERE

ENSPHERES > ENSPHERE

ENSTAMP vb imprint with a stamp

ENSTAMPED > ENSTAMP

ENSTAMPS > ENSTAMP

ENSTATITE n grey, green, yellow, or brown pyroxene mineral consisting of magnesium silicate in orthorhombic crystalline form

ENSTEEP vb soak in water

ENSTEEPED > ENSTEEP

ENSTEEPS > ENSTEEP

ENSTYLE vb give a name to

ENSTYLED > ENSTYLE

ENSTYLES > ENSTYLE

ENSTYLING > ENSTYLE

ENSUE vb come next, result

ENSUED > ENSUE

ENSUES > ENSUE

ENSUING adj following subsequently or in order

ENSURE vb make certain or sure

ENSURED > ENSURE

ENSURER > ENSURE

ENSURERS > ENSURE

ENSURES > ENSURE

ENSURING > ENSURE
ENSWATHE vb bind or wrap
ENSWATHED > ENSWATHE
ENSWATHES > ENSWATHE
ENSWEEP vb sweep across
ENSWEEPS > ENSWEEP
ENSWEPT > ENSWEEP
ENTAIL vb bring about or impose inevitably ▷ n restriction imposed by entailing an estate
ENTAILED > ENTAIL
ENTAILER > ENTAIL
ENTAILERS > ENTAIL
ENTAILING > ENTAIL
ENTAILS > ENTAIL
ENTAME vb make tame
ENTAMEBA same as > ENTAMOEBA
ENTAMEBAE > ENTAMEBA
ENTAMEBAS > ENTAMEBA
ENTAMED > ENTAME
ENTAMES > ENTAME
ENTAMING > ENTAME
ENTAMOEBA n parasitic amoeba that lives in the intestines of man and causes amoebic dysentery
ENTANGLE vb catch or involve in or as if in a tangle
ENTANGLED > ENTANGLE
ENTANGLER > ENTANGLE
ENTANGLES > ENTANGLE
ENTASES > ENTASIS
ENTASIA same as > ENTASIS
ENTASIAS > ENTASIA
ENTASIS n slightly convex curve given to the shaft of a column, pier, or similar structure, to correct the illusion of concavity produced by a straight shaft
ENTASTIC adj (of a disease) characterized by spasms
ENTAYLE variant of > ENTAIL
ENTAYLED > ENTAYLE
ENTAYLES > ENTAYLE
ENTAYLING > ENTAYLE
ENTELECHY n (in the philosophy of Aristotle) actuality as opposed to potentiality
ENTELLUS n langur of S Asia
ENTENDER vb make more tender
ENTENDERS > ENTENDER
ENTENTE n friendly understanding between nations
ENTENTES > ENTENTE
ENTER vb come or go in
ENTERA > ENTERON
ENTERABLE > ENTER
ENTERAL same as > ENTERIC
ENTERALLY > ENTERIC
ENTERATE adj with an intestine separate from the outer wall of the body

ENTERED > ENTER
ENTERER > ENTER
ENTERERS > ENTER
ENTERIC adj intestinal ▷ n infectious disease of the intestines
ENTERICS > ENTERIC
ENTERING > ENTER
ENTERINGS > ENTER
ENTERITIS n inflammation of the intestine, causing diarrhoea
ENTERON n alimentary canal, esp of an embryo or a coelenterate
ENTERONS > ENTERON
ENTERS > ENTER
ENTERTAIN vb amuse
ENTERTAKE vb entertain
ENTERTOOK > ENTERTAKE
ENTETE adj obsessed
ENTETEE variant of > ENTETE
ENTHALPY n thermodynamic property of a system equal to the sum of its internal energy and the product of its pressure and volume
ENTHETIC adj (esp of infectious diseases) introduced into the body from without
ENTHRAL vb hold the attention of
ENTHRALL same as > ENTHRAL
ENTHRALLS > ENTHRALL
ENTHRALS > ENTHRAL
ENTHRONE vb place (someone) on a throne
ENTHRONED > ENTHRONE
ENTHRONES > ENTHRONE
ENTHUSE vb (cause to) show enthusiasm
ENTHUSED > ENTHUSE
ENTHUSES > ENTHUSE
ENTHUSING > ENTHUSE
ENTHYMEME n incomplete syllogism, in which one or more premises are unexpressed as their truth is considered to be self-evident
ENTIA > ENS
ENTICE vb attract by exciting hope or desire, tempt
ENTICED > ENTICE
ENTICER > ENTICE
ENTICERS > ENTICE
ENTICES > ENTICE
ENTICING > ENTICE
ENTICINGS > ENTICE
ENTIRE adj including every detail, part, or aspect of something ▷ n state of being entire
ENTIRELY adv without reservation or exception
ENTIRES > ENTIRE
ENTIRETY n state of being entire or whole

ENTITIES > ENTITY
ENTITLE vb give a right to
ENTITLED > ENTITLE
ENTITLES > ENTITLE
ENTITLING > ENTITLE
ENTITY n separate distinct thing
ENTOBLAST less common name for > ENDODERM
ENTODERM same as > ENDODERM
ENTODERMS > ENTODERM
ENTOIL archaic word for > ENSNARE
ENTOILED > ENTOIL
ENTOILING > ENTOIL
ENTOILS > ENTOIL
ENTOMB vb place (a corpse) in a tomb
ENTOMBED > ENTOMB
ENTOMBING > ENTOMB
ENTOMBS > ENTOMB
ENTOMIC adj denoting or relating to insects
ENTOPHYTE variant of > ENDOPHYTE
ENTOPIC adj situated in its normal place or position
ENTOPROCT n type of marine animal
ENTOPTIC adj (of visual sensation) resulting from structures within the eye itself
ENTOPTICS n study of entoptic visions
ENTOTIC adj of or relating to the inner ear
ENTOURAGE n group of people who assist an important person
ENTOZOA > ENTOZOON
ENTOZOAL > ENTOZOON
ENTOZOAN same as > ENTOZOON
ENTOZOANS > ENTOZOON
ENTOZOIC adj of or relating to an entozoon
ENTOZOON n internal parasite
ENTRAIL vb twist or entangle
ENTRAILED > ENTRAIL
ENTRAILS npl intestines
ENTRAIN vb board or put aboard a train
ENTRAINED > ENTRAIN
ENTRAINER > ENTRAIN
ENTRAINS > ENTRAIN
ENTRALL variant of > ENTRAILS
ENTRALLES variant of > ENTRAILS
ENTRAMMEL vb hamper or obstruct by entangling
ENTRANCE n way into a place ▷ vb delight ▷ adj necessary in order to enter something
ENTRANCED > ENTRANCE
ENTRANCES > ENTRANCE
ENTRANT n person who enters a university, contest, etc
ENTRANTS > ENTRANT

ENTRAP vb trick into difficulty etc
ENTRAPPED > ENTRAP
ENTRAPPER > ENTRAP
ENTRAPS > ENTRAP
ENTREAT vb ask earnestly
ENTREATED > ENTREAT
ENTREATS > ENTREAT
ENTREATY n earnest request
ENTRECHAT n leap in ballet during which the dancer repeatedly crosses his feet or beats them together
ENTRECOTE n beefsteak cut from between the ribs
ENTREE n dish served before a main course
ENTREES > ENTREE
ENTREMES variant of > ENTREMETS
ENTREMETS n dessert
ENTRENCH vb establish firmly
ENTREPOT n warehouse for commercial goods
ENTREPOTS > ENTREPOT
ENTRESOL another name for > MEZZANINE
ENTRESOLS > ENTRESOL
ENTREZ interj enter
ENTRIES > ENTRY
ENTRISM variant of > ENTRYISM
ENTRISMS > ENTRISM
ENTRIST > ENTRYISM
ENTRISTS > ENTRYISM
ENTROLD adj surrounded
ENTROPIC > ENTROPY
ENTROPIES > ENTROPY
ENTROPION n turning inwards of the edge of the eyelid
ENTROPIUM variant of > ENTROPION
ENTROPY n lack of organization
ENTRUST vb put into the care or protection of
ENTRUSTED > ENTRUST
ENTRUSTS > ENTRUST
ENTRY n entrance ▷ adj necessary in order to enter something
ENTRYISM n policy or practice of members of a particular political group joining an existing political party with the intention of changing its principles and policies, instead of forming a new party
ENTRYISMS > ENTRYISM
ENTRYIST > ENTRYISM
ENTRYISTS > ENTRYISM
ENTRYWAY n entrance passage
ENTRYWAYS > ENTRYWAY
ENTWINE vb twist together or around
ENTWINED > ENTWINE
ENTWINES > ENTWINE
ENTWINING > ENTWINE

ENTWIST vb twist together or around

ENTWISTED > ENTWIST

ENTWISTS > ENTWIST

ENUCLEATE vb remove the nucleus from (a cell) ▷ adj (of cells) deprived of their nuclei

ENUF common intentional literary misspelling of > ENOUGH

ENUMERATE vb name one by one

ENUNCIATE vb pronounce clearly

ENURE variant spelling of > INURE

ENURED > ENURE

ENUREMENT > ENURE

ENURES > ENURE

ENURESES > ENURESIS

ENURESIS n involuntary discharge of urine, esp during sleep

ENURETIC > ENURESIS

ENURETICS > ENURESIS

ENURING > ENURE

ENURN same as > INURN

ENURNED same as > INURNED

ENURNING same as > INURNING

ENURNS same as > INURNS

ENVASSAL vb make a vassal of

ENVASSALS > ENVASSAL

ENVAULT vb enclose in a vault; entomb

ENVAULTED > ENVAULT

ENVAULTS > ENVAULT

ENVEIGLE same as > INVEIGLE

ENVEIGLED > ENVEIGLE

ENVEIGLES > ENVEIGLE

ENVELOP vb wrap up, enclose

ENVELOPE n folded gummed paper cover for a letter

ENVELOPED > ENVELOP

ENVELOPER > ENVELOP

ENVELOPES > ENVELOPE

ENVELOPS > ENVELOP

ENVENOM vb fill or impregnate with venom

ENVENOMED > ENVENOM

ENVENOMS > ENVENOM

ENVERMEIL vb dye vermilion

ENVIABLE adj arousing envy, fortunate

ENVIABLY > ENVIABLE

ENVIED > ENVY

ENVIER > ENVY

ENVIERS > ENVY

ENVIES > ENVY

ENVIOUS adj full of envy

ENVIOUSLY > ENVIOUS

ENVIRO n environmentalist

ENVIRON vb encircle or surround

ENVIRONED > ENVIRON

ENVIRONS npl surrounding area, esp of a town

ENVIROS > ENVIRO

ENVISAGE vb conceive of as a possibility

ENVISAGED > ENVISAGE

ENVISAGES > ENVISAGE

ENVISION vb conceive of as a possibility, esp in the future

ENVISIONS > ENVISION

ENVOI same as > ENVOY

ENVOIS > ENVOI

ENVOY n messenger

ENVOYS > ENVOY

ENVOYSHIP > ENVOY

ENVY n feeling of discontent aroused by another's good fortune ▷ vb grudge (another's good fortune, success, or qualities)

ENVYING > ENVY

ENVYINGLY > ENVY

ENVYINGS > ENVY

ENWALL vb wall in

ENWALLED > ENWALL

ENWALLING > ENWALL

ENWALLOW vb sink or plunge

ENWALLOWS > ENWALLOW

ENWALLS > ENWALL

ENWHEEL archaic word for > ENCIRCLE

ENWHEELED > ENWHEEL

ENWHEELS > ENWHEEL

ENWIND vb wind or coil around

ENWINDING > ENWIND

ENWINDS > ENWIND

ENWOMB vb enclose in or as if in a womb

ENWOMBED > ENWOMB

ENWOMBING > ENWOMB

ENWOMBS > ENWOMB

ENWOUND > ENWIND

ENWRAP vb wrap or cover up

ENWRAPPED > ENWRAP

ENWRAPS > ENWRAP

ENWREATH vb surround or encircle with or as with a wreath or wreaths

ENWREATHE same as > ENWREATH

ENWREATHS > ENWREATH

ENZIAN n gentian violet

ENZIANS > ENZIAN

ENZONE vb enclose in a zone

ENZONED > ENZONE

ENZONES > ENZONE

ENZONING > ENZONE

ENZOOTIC adj (of diseases) affecting animals within a limited region ▷ n enzootic disease

ENZOOTICS > ENZOOTIC

ENZYM same as > ENZYME

ENZYMATIC > ENZYME

ENZYME n any of a group of complex proteins that act as catalysts in specific biochemical reactions

ENZYMES > ENZYME

ENZYMIC > ENZYME

ENZYMS > ENZYM

EOAN adj of or relating to the dawn

EOBIONT n hypothetical chemical precursor of a living cell

EOBIONTS > EOBIONT

EOCENE adj of, denoting, or formed in the second epoch of the Tertiary period

EOHIPPUS n earliest horse: an extinct Eocene dog-sized animal of the genus with four-toed forelegs, three-toed hindlegs, and teeth specialized for browsing

EOLIAN adj of or relating to the wind

EOLIENNE n type of fine cloth

EOLIENNES > EOLIENNE

EOLIPILE variant of > AEOLIPILE

EOLIPILES > EOLIPILE

EOLITH n stone, usually crudely broken, used as a primitive tool in Eolithic times

EOLITHIC > EOLITH

EOLITHS > EOLITH

EOLOPILE variant of > AEOLIPILE

EOLOPILES > EOLOPILE

EON n longest division of geological time, comprising two or more eras

EONIAN adj of or relating to an eon

EONISM n adoption of female dress and behaviour by a male

EONISMS > EONISM

EONS > EON

EORL n Anglo-Saxon nobleman

EORLS > EORL

EOSIN n red crystalline water-insoluble derivative of fluorescein

EOSINE same as > EOSIN

EOSINES > EOSINE

EOSINIC > EOSIN

EOSINS > EOSIN

EOTHEN adv from the East

EPACRID n type of heath-like plant

EPACRIDS > EPACRID

EPACRIS n genus of the epacrids

EPACRISES > EPACRIS

EPACT n difference in time, about 11 days, between the solar year and the lunar year

EPACTS > EPACT

EPAENETIC adj eulogistic

EPAGOGE n inductive reasoning

EPAGOGES > EPAGOGE

EPAGOGIC > EPAGOGE

EPANODOS n return to main theme after a digression

EPARCH n bishop or metropolitan in charge of an eparchy

EPARCHATE same as > EPARCHY

EPARCHIAL > EPARCHY

EPARCHIES > EPARCHY

EPARCHS > EPARCH

EPARCHY n diocese of the Eastern Christian Church

EPATANT adj startling or shocking, esp through being unconventional

EPAULE n shoulder of a fortification

EPAULES > EPAULE

EPAULET same as > EPAULETTE

EPAULETS > EPAULET

EPAULETTE n shoulder ornament on a uniform

EPAXIAL adj above the axis

EPAZOTE n type of herb

EPAZOTES > EPAZOTE

EPEDAPHIC adj of or relating to atmospheric conditions

EPEE n straight-bladed sword used in fencing

EPEEIST n one who uses or specializes in using an epee

EPEEISTS > EPEEIST

EPEES > EPEE

EPEIRA same as > EPEIRID

EPEIRAS > EPEIRA

EPEIRIC adj in, of, or relating to a continent

EPEIRID n type of spider

EPEIRIDS > EPEIRID

EPENDYMA n membrane lining the ventricles of the brain and the central canal of the spinal cord

EPENDYMAL > EPENDYMA

EPENDYMAS > EPENDYMA

EPEOLATRY n worship of words

EPERDU adj distracted

EPERDUE adj distracted

EPERGNE n ornamental centrepiece for a table: a stand with holders for sweetmeats, fruit, flowers, etc

EPERGNES > EPERGNE

EPHA same as > EPHAH

EPHAH n Hebrew unit of dry measure equal to approximately one bushel or about 33 litres

EPHAHS > EPHAH

EPHAS > EPHA

EPHEBE n (in ancient Greece) youth about to enter full citizenship, esp one undergoing military training

EPHEBES > EPHEBE

EPHEBI > EPHEBE

EPHEBIC > EPHEBE

EPHEBOI > EPHEBOS

EPHEBOS same as > EPHEBE

EPHEBUS same as > EPHEBE

EPHEDRA n gymnosperm shrub of warm regions of America and Eurasia

EPHEDRAS > EPHEDRA

EPHEDRIN same as > EPHEDRINE

EPHEDRINE n alkaloid used for treatment of asthma and hay fever

EPHEDRINS > EPHEDRIN

EPHELIDES > EPHELIS

EPHELIS n freckle

EPHEMERA n something transitory or short-lived

EPHEMERAE > EPHEMERA

EPHEMERAL adj short-lived ▷ n short-lived organism, such as the mayfly

EPHEMERAS > EPHEMERA

EPHEMERID n mayfly

EPHEMERIS n table giving the future positions of a planet, comet, or satellite

EPHEMERON > EPHEMERA

EPHIALTES n incubus

EPHOD n embroidered vestment believed to resemble an apron with shoulder straps, worn by priests in ancient Israel

EPHODS > EPHOD

EPHOR n (in ancient Greece) one of a board of senior magistrates in any of several Dorian states, esp the five Spartan ephors, who were elected by the vote of all full citizens and who wielded effective power

EPHORAL > EPHOR

EPHORALTY > EPHOR

EPHORATE > EPHOR

EPHORATES > EPHOR

EPHORI > EPHOR

EPHORS > EPHOR

EPIBIOSES > EPIBIOSIS

EPIBIOSIS n any relationship between two organisms in which one grows on the other but is not parasitic on it

EPIBIOTIC > EPIBIOSIS

EPIBLAST n outermost layer of an embryo, which becomes the ectoderm at gastrulation

EPIBLASTS > EPIBLAST

EPIBLEM n outermost cell layer of a root

EPIBLEMS > EPIBLEM

EPIBOLIC > EPIBOLY

EPIBOLIES > EPIBOLY

EPIBOLY n process that occurs during gastrulation in vertebrates, in which cells on one side of the blastula grow over and surround the remaining cells and yolk and eventually form the ectoderm

EPIC n long poem, book, or film about heroic events or actions ▷ adj very impressive or ambitious

EPICAL > EPIC

EPICALLY > EPIC

EPICALYX n series of small sepal-like bracts forming an outer calyx beneath the true calyx in some flowers

EPICANTHI n folds of skin extending vertically over the inner angles of the eyes

EPICARDIA n layers of pericardia in direct contact with the heart

EPICARP n outermost layer of the pericarp of fruits: forms the skin of a peach or grape

EPICARPS > EPICARP

EPICEDE same as > EPICEDIUM

EPICEDES > EPICEDE

EPICEDIA > EPICEDIUM

EPICEDIAL > EPICEDIUM

EPICEDIAN > EPICEDIUM

EPICEDIUM n funeral ode

EPICENE adj having the characteristics of both sexes; hermaphroditic ▷ n epicene person or creature

EPICENES > EPICENE

EPICENISM > EPICENE

EPICENTER same as > EPICENTRE

EPICENTRA n epicentres

EPICENTRE n point on the earth's surface immediately above the origin of an earthquake

EPICIER n grocer

EPICIERS > EPICIER

EPICISM n style or trope characteristic of epics

EPICISMS > EPIC

EPICIST n writer of epics

EPICISTS > EPIC

EPICLESES > EPICLESIS

EPICLESIS n invocation of the Holy Spirit to consecrate the bread and wine of the Eucharist

EPICLIKE adj resembling or reminiscent of an epic

EPICORMIC adj (of a tree shoot or branch) growing from a dormant bud below the bark

EPICOTYL n part of an embryo plant stem above the cotyledons but beneath the terminal bud

EPICOTYLS > EPICOTYL

EPICRANIA n tissue covering the cranium

EPICRISES

> EPICRISIS

EPICRISIS n secondary crisis occurring in the course of a disease

EPICRITIC adj (of certain nerve fibres of the skin) serving to perceive and distinguish fine variations of temperature or touch

EPICS > EPIC

EPICURE n person who enjoys good food and drink

EPICUREAN adj devoted to sensual pleasures, esp food and drink ▷ n epicure

EPICURES > EPICURE

EPICURISE same as > EPICURIZE

EPICURISM > EPICURE

EPICURIZE vb act as an epicure

EPICYCLE n (in the Ptolemaic system) a small circle, around which a planet was thought to revolve

EPICYCLES > EPICYCLE

EPICYCLIC > EPICYCLE

EPIDEMIC n widespread occurrence of a disease ▷ adj (esp of a disease) affecting many people in an area

EPIDEMICS > EPIDEMIC

EPIDERM same as > EPIDERMIS

EPIDERMAL > EPIDERMIS

EPIDERMIC > EPIDERMIS

EPIDERMIS n outer layer of the skin

EPIDERMS > EPIDERM

EPIDICTIC adj designed to display something, esp the skill of the speaker in rhetoric

EPIDOSITE n rock formed of quartz and epidote

EPIDOTE n green mineral consisting of hydrated calcium iron aluminium silicate in monoclinic crystalline form: common in metamorphic rocks

EPIDOTES > EPIDOTE

EPIDOTIC > EPIDOTE

EPIDURAL n spinal anaesthetic injected to relieve pain during childbirth ▷ adj on or over the outermost membrane covering the brain and spinal cord

EPIDURALS > EPIDURAL

EPIFAUNA n animals that live on the surface of the seabed

EPIFAUNAE > EPIFAUNA

EPIFAUNAL > EPIFAUNA

EPIFAUNAS > EPIFAUNA

EPIFOCAL adj situated or occurring at an epicentre

EPIGAEAL same as > EPIGEAL

EPIGAEAN same as > EPIGEAL

EPIGAEOUS same as > EPIGEAL

EPIGAMIC adj attractive to the opposite sex

EPIGEAL adj of or relating to seed germination in which the cotyledons appear above the ground because of the growth of the hypocotyl

EPIGEAN same as > EPIGEAL

EPIGEIC same as > EPIGEAL

EPIGENE adj formed or taking place at or near the surface of the earth

EPIGENIC adj pertaining to the theory of the gradual development of the embryo

EPIGENIST n one who studies or espouses the theory of the gradual development of the embryo

EPIGENOUS adj growing on the surface, esp the upper surface, of an organism or part

EPIGEOUS same as > EPIGEAL

EPIGON same as > EPIGONE

EPIGONE n inferior follower or imitator

EPIGONES > EPIGONE

EPIGONI > EPIGONE

EPIGONIC > EPIGONE

EPIGONISM > EPIGONE

EPIGONOUS > EPIGONE

EPIGONS > EPIGON

EPIGONUS same as > EPIGONE

EPIGRAM n short witty remark or poem

EPIGRAMS > EPIGRAM

EPIGRAPH n quotation at the start of a book

EPIGRAPHS > EPIGRAPH

EPIGRAPHY n study of ancient inscriptions

EPIGYNIES > EPIGYNOUS

EPIGYNOUS adj (of flowers) having the receptacle enclosing and fused with the gynoecium so that the other floral parts arise above it

EPIGYNY > EPIGYNOUS

EPILATE vb remove hair from

EPILATED > EPILATE

EPILATES > EPILATE

EPILATING > EPILATE

EPILATION > EPILATE

EPILATOR n electrical appliance consisting of a metal spiral head that rotates at high speed, plucking unwanted hair

EPILATORS > EPILATOR

e

EPILEPSY n disorder of the nervous system causing loss of consciousness and sometimes convulsions

EPILEPTIC adj of or having epilepsy ▷ n person who has epilepsy

EPILIMNIA n upper layers of water in lakes

EPILITHIC adj (of plants) growing on the surface of rock

EPILOBIUM n willow-herb

EPILOG same as
> EPILOGUE

EPILOGIC > EPILOGUE

EPILOGISE same as
> EPILOGIZE

EPILOGIST > EPILOGUE

EPILOGIZE vb write or deliver epilogues

EPILOGS > EPILOG

EPILOGUE n short speech or poem at the end of a literary work, esp a play

EPILOGUED adj followed by an epilogue

EPILOGUES > EPILOGUE

EPIMER n isomer

EPIMERASE n enzyme that interconverts epimers

EPIMERE n dorsal part of the mesoderm of a vertebrate embryo, consisting of a series of segments

EPIMERES > EPIMERE

EPIMERIC > EPIMERISM

EPIMERISE same as
> EPIMERIZE

EPIMERISM n optical isomerism in which isomers can form about asymmetric atoms within the molecule

EPIMERIZE vb change (a chemical compound) into an epimer

EPIMERS > EPIMER

EPIMYSIA > EPIMYSIUM

EPIMYSIUM n sheath of connective tissue that encloses a skeletal muscle

EPINAOI > EPINAOS

EPINAOS n rear vestibule

EPINASTIC > EPINASTY

EPINASTY n increased growth of the upper surface of a plant part, such as a leaf, resulting in a downward bending of the part

EPINEURAL adj outside a nerve trunk

EPINEURIA n sheaths of connective tissue around bundles of nerve fibres

EPINICIAN
> EPINICION

EPINICION n victory song

EPINIKIAN
> EPINICION

EPINIKION same as
> EPINICION

EPINOSIC adj unhealthy

EPIPHANIC > EPIPHANY

EPIPHANY n moment of great or sudden revelation

EPIPHRAGM n disc of calcium phosphate and mucilage secreted by snails over the aperture of their shells before hibernation

EPIPHYSES
> EPIPHYSIS

EPIPHYSIS n end of a long bone, initially separated from the shaft (diaphysis) by a section of cartilage that eventually ossifies so that the two portions fuse together

EPIPHYTAL > EPIPHYTE

EPIPHYTE n plant that grows on another plant but is not parasitic on it

EPIPHYTES > EPIPHYTE

EPIPHYTIC > EPIPHYTE

EPIPLOIC > EPIPLOON

EPIPLOON n greater omentum

EPIPLOONS > EPIPLOON

EPIPOLIC > EPIPOLISM

EPIPOLISM n fluorescence

EPIROGENY n formation and submergence of continents by broad, relatively slow, displacements of the earth's crust

EPIRRHEMA n address in Greek comedy

EPISCIA n creeping plant

EPISCIAS > EPISCIA

EPISCOPAL adj of or governed by bishops

EPISCOPE n optical device that projects an enlarged image of an opaque object, such as a printed page or photographic print, onto a screen by means of reflected light

EPISCOPES > EPISCOPE

EPISCOPY n area overseen

EPISEMON n emblem

EPISEMONS > EPISEMON

EPISODAL same as
> EPISODIC

EPISODE n incident in a series of incidents

EPISODES > EPISODE

EPISODIAL same as
> EPISODIC

EPISODIC adj occurring at irregular intervals

EPISOMAL > EPISOME

EPISOME n unit of genetic material (DNA) in bacteria, such as a plasmid, that can either replicate independently or can be integrated into the host chromosome

EPISOMES > EPISOME

EPISPERM n protective outer layer of certain seeds

EPISPERMS > EPISPERM

EPISPORE n outer layer of certain spores

EPISPORES > EPISPORE

EPISTASES
> EPISTASIS

EPISTASIS n scum on the surface of a liquid, esp on an old specimen of urine

EPISTASY same as
> EPISTASIS

EPISTATIC
> EPISTASIS

EPISTAXES
> EPISTAXIS

EPISTAXIS technical name for > NOSEBLEED

EPISTEMIC adj of or relating to knowledge or epistemology

EPISTERNA n parts of the sternums of mammals

EPISTLE n letter, esp of an apostle ▷ vb preface

EPISTLED > EPISTLE

EPISTLER n writer of an epistle or epistles

EPISTLERS > EPISTLER

EPISTLES > EPISTLE

EPISTLING > EPISTLE

EPISTOLER same as
> EPISTLER

EPISTOLET n short letter

EPISTOLIC > EPISTLE

EPISTOME n area between the mouth and antennae of crustaceans

EPISTOMES > EPISTOME

EPISTYLE n lowest part of an entablature that bears on the columns

EPISTYLES > EPISTYLE

EPITAPH n commemorative inscription on a tomb ▷ vb compose an epitaph

EPITAPHED > EPITAPH

EPITAPHER > EPITAPH

EPITAPHIC > EPITAPH

EPITAPHS > EPITAPH

EPITASES > EPITASIS

EPITASIS n (in classical drama) part of a play in which the main action develops

EPITAXES > EPITAXIS

EPITAXIAL > EPITAXY

EPITAXIC > EPITAXY

EPITAXIES > EPITAXY

EPITAXIS same as
> EPITAXY

EPITAXY n growth of a thin layer on the surface of a crystal so that the layer has the same structure as the underlying crystal

EPITHECA n outer and older layer of the cell wall of a diatom

EPITHECAE > EPITHECA

EPITHELIA n animal tissues consisting of one or more layers of closely packed cells covering the external and internal surfaces of the body

EPITHEM n external topical application

EPITHEMA > EPITHEM

EPITHEMS > EPITHEM

EPITHESES
> EPITHESIS

EPITHESIS n addition of a letter to the end of a word, so that its sense does not change

EPITHET n descriptive word or name ▷ vb name

EPITHETED > EPITHET

EPITHETIC > EPITHET

EPITHETON same as
> EPITHET

EPITHETS > EPITHET

EPITOME n typical example

EPITOMES > EPITOME

EPITOMIC > EPITOME

EPITOMISE same as
> EPITOMIZE

EPITOMIST
> EPITOMIZE

EPITOMIZE vb be the epitome of

EPITONIC adj undergoing too great a strain

EPITOPE n site on an antigen at which a specific antibody becomes attached

EPITOPES > EPITOPE

EPITRITE n metrical foot with three long syllables and one short one

EPITRITES > EPITRITE

EPIZEUXES
> EPIZEUXIS

EPIZEUXIS n deliberate repetition of a word

EPIZOA > EPIZOON

EPIZOAN same as
> EPIZOON

EPIZOANS > EPIZOAN

EPIZOIC adj (of an animal or plant) growing or living on the exterior of a living animal

EPIZOISM > EPIZOIC

EPIZOISMS > EPIZOIC

EPIZOITE n organism that lives on an animal but is not parasitic on it

EPIZOITES > EPIZOITE

EPIZOON n animal, such as a parasite, that lives on the body of another animal

EPIZOOTIC adj (of a disease) suddenly and temporarily affecting a large number of animals over a large area ▷ n epizootic disease

EPIZOOTY n animal disease

EPOCH n period of notable events

EPOCHA same as > EPOCH

EPOCHAL > EPOCH

EPOCHALLY > EPOCH

EPOCHAS > EPOCHA

EPOCHS > EPOCH

EPODE n part of a lyric ode

that follows the strophe and the antistrophe

EPODES > EPODE

EPODIC > EPODE

EPONYM n name, esp a place name, derived from the name of a real or mythical person

EPONYMIC > EPONYM

EPONYMIES > EPONYM

EPONYMOUS adj after whom a book, play, etc is named

EPONYMS > EPONYM

EPONYMY n derivation of names of places, etc, from those of persons

EPOPEE n epic poem

EPOPEES > EPOPEE

EPOPOEIA same as > EPOPEE

EPOPOEIAS > EPOPOEIA

EPOPT n one initiated into mysteries

EPOPTS > EPOPT

EPOS n body of poetry in which the tradition of a people is conveyed, esp a group of poems concerned with a common epic theme

EPOSES > EPOS

EPOXIDE n compound containing an oxygen atom joined to two different groups that are themselves joined to other groups

EPOXIDES > EPOXIDE

EPOXIDISE same as > EPOXIDIZE

EPOXIDIZE vb form an epoxide

EPOXIED > EPOXY

EPOXIES > EPOXY

EPOXY adj of or containing an oxygen atom joined to two different groups that are themselves joined to other groups ▷ n epoxy resin ▷ vb glue with epoxy resin

EPOXYED > EPOXY

EPOXYING > EPOXY

EPRIS adj enamoured

EPRISE feminine form of > EPRIS

EPSILON n fifth letter of the Greek alphabet, a short vowel, transliterated as e

EPSILONIC adj of or relating to an arbitrary small quantity

EPSILONS > EPSILON

EPSOMITE n sulphate of magnesium

EPSOMITES > EPSOMITE

EPUISE adj exhausted

EPUISEE feminine form of > EPUISE

EPULARY adj of or relating to feasting

EPULATION n feasting

EPULIDES > EPULIS

EPULIS n swelling of the gum, usually as a result of fibrous hyperplasia

EPULISES > EPULIS

EPULOTIC n scarring

EPULOTICS > EPULOTIC

EPURATE vb purify

EPURATED > EPURATE

EPURATES > EPURATE

EPURATING > EPURATE

EPURATION > EPURATE

EPYLLIA > EPYLLION

EPYLLION n miniature epic

EPYLLIONS > EPYLLION

EQUABLE adj even-tempered

EQUABLY > EQUABLE

EQUAL adj identical in size, quantity, degree, etc ▷ n person or thing equal to another ▷ vb be equal to

EQUALED > EQUAL

EQUALI npl pieces for a group of instruments of the same kind

EQUALING > EQUAL

EQUALISE same as > EQUALIZE

EQUALISED > EQUALISE

EQUALISER same as > EQUALIZER

EQUALISES > EQUALISE

EQUALITY n state of being equal

EQUALIZE vb make or become equal

EQUALIZED > EQUALIZE

EQUALIZER n person or thing that equalizes, esp a device to counterbalance opposing forces

EQUALIZES > EQUALIZE

EQUALLED > EQUAL

EQUALLING > EQUAL

EQUALLY > EQUAL

EQUALNESS n equality

EQUALS > EQUAL

EQUANT n circle in which a planet was formerly believed to move

EQUANTS > EQUANT

EQUATABLE > EQUATE

EQUATE vb make or regard as equivalent

EQUATED > EQUATE

EQUATES > EQUATE

EQUATING > EQUATE

EQUATION n mathematical statement that two expressions are equal

EQUATIONS > EQUATION

EQUATIVE adj (in grammar) denoting the equivalence or identity of two terms

EQUATOR n imaginary circle round the earth, equidistant from the poles

EQUATORS > EQUATOR

EQUERRIES > EQUERRY

EQUERRY n officer who acts as an attendant to a member of a royal family

EQUID n any animal of the horse family

EQUIDS > EQUID

EQUIFINAL adj having the same end or result

EQUIMOLAL adj having an equal number of moles

EQUIMOLAR same as > EQUIMOLAL

EQUINAL same as > EQUINE

EQUINE adj of or like a horse ▷ n any animal of the horse family

EQUINELY > EQUINE

EQUINES > EQUINE

EQUINIA n glanders

EQUINIAS > EQUINIA

EQUINITY n horse-like nature

EQUINOX n time of year when day and night are of equal length

EQUINOXES > EQUINOX

EQUIP vb provide with supplies, components, etc

EQUIPAGE n horse-drawn carriage, esp one elegantly equipped and attended by liveried footmen ▷ vb equip

EQUIPAGED > EQUIPAGE

EQUIPAGES > EQUIPAGE

EQUIPE n (esp in motor racing) team

EQUIPES > EQUIPE

EQUIPMENT n set of tools or devices used for a particular purpose

EQUIPOISE n perfect balance ▷ vb offset or balance in weight or force

EQUIPPED > EQUIP

EQUIPPER > EQUIP

EQUIPPERS > EQUIP

EQUIPPING > EQUIP

EQUIPS > EQUIP

EQUISETA > EQUISETUM

EQUISETIC > EQUISETUM

EQUISETUM n type of plant such as the horsetail

EQUITABLE adj fair and reasonable

EQUITABLY > EQUITABLE

EQUITANT adj (of a leaf) having the base folded around the stem so that it overlaps the leaf above and opposite

EQUITES npl cavalry

EQUITIES > EQUITY

EQUITY n fairness

EQUIVALVE adj equipped with identical valves

EQUIVOCAL adj ambiguous

EQUIVOKE same as > EQUIVOQUE

EQUIVOKES > EQUIVOKE

EQUIVOQUE n play on words

ER interj sound made when hesitating in speech

ERA n period of time considered as distinctive

ERADIATE less common word for > RADIATE

ERADIATED > ERADIATE

ERADIATES > ERADIATE

ERADICANT > ERADICATE

ERADICATE vb destroy completely

ERAS > ERA

ERASABLE > ERASE

ERASE vb destroy all traces of

ERASED > ERASE

ERASEMENT > ERASE

ERASER n object for erasing something written

ERASERS > ERASER

ERASES > ERASE

ERASING > ERASE

ERASION n act of erasing

ERASIONS > ERASION

ERASURE n erasing

ERASURES > ERASURE

ERATHEM n stratum of rocks representing a specific geological era

ERATHEMS > ERATHEM

ERBIA n oxide of erbium

ERBIAS > ERBIA

ERBIUM n metallic element of the lanthanide series

ERBIUMS > ERBIUM

ERE prep before ▷ vb plough

ERECT vb build ▷ adj upright

ERECTABLE > ERECT

ERECTED > ERECT

ERECTER same as > ERECTOR

ERECTERS > ERECTER

ERECTILE adj capable of becoming erect from sexual excitement

ERECTING > ERECT

ERECTION n act of erecting or the state of being erected

ERECTIONS > ERECTION

ERECTIVE adj producing erections

ERECTLY > ERECT

ERECTNESS > ERECT

ERECTOR n any muscle that raises a part or makes it erect

ERECTORS > ERECTOR

ERECTS > ERECT

ERED > ERE

ERELONG adv before long

EREMIC adj of or relating to deserts

EREMITAL > EREMITE

EREMITE n Christian hermit

EREMITES > EREMITE

EREMITIC > EREMITE

EREMITISH > EREMITE

EREMITISM > EREMITE

EREMURI > EREMURUS

EREMURUS n type of herb

ERENOW adv long before the present

EREPSIN n mixture of proteolytic enzymes

e

secreted by the small intestine

EREPSINS > EREPSIN

ERES > ERE

ERETHIC > ERETHISM

ERETHISM n abnormally high degree of irritability or sensitivity in any part of the body

ERETHISMS > ERETHISM

ERETHITIC > ERETHISM

EREV n day before

EREVS > EREV

EREWHILE adv short time ago

EREWHILES same as > EREWHILE

ERF n plot of land, usually urban, marked off for building purposes

ERG same as > ERGOMETER

ERGASTIC adj consisting of the non-living by-products of protoplasmic activity

ERGATANER n wingless male ant

ERGATE n worker ant

ERGATES > ERGATE

ERGATIVE adj denoting a type of verb that takes the same noun as either direct object or as subject, with equivalent meaning. Thus, "fuse" is an ergative verb: "He fused the lights" and "The lights fused" have equivalent meaning ▷ n ergative verb

ERGATIVES > ERGATIVE

ERGATOID > ERGATE

ERGO same as > ERGOMETER

ERGODIC adj of or relating to the probability that any state will recur

ERGOGENIC adj giving energy

ERGOGRAM n tracing produced by an ergograph

ERGOGRAMS > ERGOGRAM

ERGOGRAPH n instrument that measures and records the amount of work a muscle does during contraction, its rate of fatigue, etc

ERGOMANIA n excessive desire to work

ERGOMETER n dynamometer

ERGOMETRY n measurement of work done

ERGON n work

ERGONOMIC adj designed to minimize effort

ERGONS > ERGON

ERGOS > ERGO

ERGOT n fungal disease of cereal

ERGOTIC > ERGOT

ERGOTISE same as > ERGOTIZE

ERGOTISED > ERGOTISE

ERGOTISES > ERGOTISE

ERGOTISM n ergot poisoning, producing either burning pains and eventually gangrene in the limbs or itching skin and convulsions

ERGOTISMS > ERGOTISM

ERGOTIZE vb inflict ergotism upon

ERGOTIZED > ERGOTIZE

ERGOTIZES > ERGOTIZE

ERGOTS > ERGOT

ERGS > ERG

ERHU n Chinese two-stringed violin

ERHUS > ERHU

ERIACH same as > ERIC

ERIACHS > ERIACH

ERIC n (in old Irish law) fine paid by a murderer to the family of his victim

ERICA n genus of plants including heathers

ERICAS > ERICA

ERICK same as > ERIC

ERICKS > ERICK

ERICOID adj (of leaves) small and tough, resembling those of heather

ERICS > ERIC

ERIGERON n type of plant

ERIGERONS > ERIGERON

ERING > ERE

ERINGO same as > ERYNGO

ERINGOES > ERINGO

ERINGOS > ERINGO

ERINITE n arsenate of copper

ERINITES > ERINITE

ERINUS n type of plant

ERINUSES > ERINUS

ERIOMETER n device for measuring the diameters of minute particles or fibres

ERIONITE n common form of zeolite

ERIONITES > ERIONITE

ERIOPHYID n type of mite

ERISTIC adj of, relating, or given to controversy or logical disputation, esp for its own sake ▷ n person who engages in logical disputes

ERISTICAL same as > ERISTIC

ERISTICS > ERISTIC

ERK n aircraftman or naval rating

ERKS > ERK

ERLANG n unit of traffic intensity in a telephone system equal to the intensity for a specific period when the average number of simultaneous calls is unity

ERLANGS > ERLANG

ERLKING n malevolent spirit who carries off children

ERLKINGS > ERLKING

ERM interj expression of hesitation

ERMELIN n ermine

ERMELINS > ERMELIN

ERMINE n stoat in northern regions, where it has a white winter coat with a black-tipped tail

ERMINED adj clad in the fur of the ermine

ERMINES > ERMINE

ERN archaic variant of > EARN

ERNE n fish-eating (European) sea eagle

ERNED > ERN

ERNES > ERNE

ERNING > ERN

ERNS > ERN

ERODABLE > ERODE

ERODE vb wear away

ERODED > ERODE

ERODENT > ERODE

ERODENTS > ERODE

ERODES > ERODE

ERODIBLE > ERODE

ERODING > ERODE

ERODIUM n type of geranium

ERODIUMS > ERODIUM

EROGENIC same as > EROGENOUS

EROGENOUS adj sensitive to sexual stimulation

EROS n lust

EROSE adj jagged or uneven, as though gnawed or bitten

EROSELY > EROSE

EROSES > EROS

EROSIBLE adj able to be eroded

EROSION n wearing away of rocks or soil by the action of water, ice, or wind

EROSIONAL > EROSION

EROSIONS > EROSION

EROSIVE > EROSION

EROSIVITY > EROSION

EROSTRATE adj without a beak

EROTEMA n rhetorical question

EROTEMAS > EROTEMA

EROTEME same as > EROTEMA

EROTEMES > EROTEME

EROTESES > EROTESIS

EROTESIS same as > EROTEMA

EROTETIC adj pertaining to a rhetorical question

EROTIC adj relating to sexual pleasure or desire ▷ n person who has strong sexual desires or is especially responsive to sexual stimulation

EROTICA n sexual literature or art

EROTICAL adj erotic

EROTICISE same as > EROTICIZE

EROTICISM n erotic quality or nature

EROTICIST > EROTICISM

EROTICIZE vb regard or present in a sexual way

EROTICS > EROTIC

EROTISE same as > EROTIZE

EROTISED > EROTISE

EROTISES > EROTISE

EROTISING > EROTISE

EROTISM same as > EROTICISM

EROTISMS > EROTISM

EROTIZE vb make erotic

EROTIZED > EROTIZE

EROTIZES > EROTIZE

EROTIZING > EROTIZE

EROTOLOGY n study of erotic stimuli and sexual behaviour

ERR vb make a mistake

ERRABLE adj capable of making a mistake

ERRANCIES > ERRANCY

ERRANCY n state or an instance of erring or a tendency to err

ERRAND n short trip to do something for someone

ERRANDS > ERRAND

ERRANT adj behaving in a manner considered to be unacceptable ▷ n knight-errant

ERRANTLY > ERRANT

ERRANTRY n way of life of a knight errant

ERRANTS > ERRANT

ERRATA > ERRATUM

ERRATAS informal variant of > ERRATA

ERRATIC adj irregular or unpredictable ▷ n rock that has been transported by glacial action

ERRATICAL adj erratic

ERRATICS > ERRATIC

ERRATUM n error in writing or printing

ERRED > ERR

ERRHINE adj causing nasal secretion ▷ n errhine drug or agent

ERRHINES > ERRHINE

ERRING > ERR

ERRINGLY > ERR

ERRINGS > ERR

ERRONEOUS adj incorrect, mistaken

ERROR n mistake, inaccuracy, or misjudgment

ERRORIST n one who makes errors

ERRORISTS > ERRORIST

ERRORLESS > ERROR

ERRORS > ERROR

ERRS > ERR

ERS same as > ERVIL

ERSATZ adj made in imitation ▷ n ersatz substance or article

ERSATZES > ERSATZ

ERSES > ERS

ERST adv long ago

ERSTWHILE adj former

▷ *adv* formerly

ERUCIC as in *erucic acid* crystalline fatty acid derived from rapeseed, mustard seed and wallflower seed

ERUCIFORM *adj* resembling a caterpillar

ERUCT *vb* belch

ERUCTATE *same as* > ERUCT

ERUCTATED > ERUCTATE

ERUCTATES > ERUCTATE

ERUCTED > ERUCT

ERUCTING > ERUCT

ERUCTS > ERUCT

ERUDITE *adj* having great academic knowledge ▷ *n* erudite person

ERUDITELY > ERUDITE

ERUDITES > ERUDITE

ERUDITION > ERUDITE

ERUGO *n* verdigris

ERUGOS > ERUGO

ERUMPENT *adj* bursting out or (esp of plant parts) developing as though bursting through an overlying structure

ERUPT *vb* eject (steam, water, or volcanic material) violently

ERUPTED > ERUPT

ERUPTIBLE > ERUPT

ERUPTING > ERUPT

ERUPTION > ERUPT

ERUPTIONS > ERUPT

ERUPTIVE *adj* erupting or tending to erupt ▷ *n* type of volcanic rock

ERUPTIVES > ERUPTIVE

ERUPTS > ERUPT

ERUV *n* area, circumscribed by a symbolic line, within which certain activities forbidden to Orthodox Jews on the Sabbath are permitted

ERUVIM > ERUV

ERUVIN > ERUV

ERUVS > ERUV

ERVALENTA *n* health food made from lentil and barley flour

ERVEN > ERF

ERVIL *n* type of vetch

ERVILS > ERVIL

ERYNGIUM *n* type of temperate and subtropical plant

ERYNGIUMS > ERYNGIUM

ERYNGO *n* type of plant with toothed or lobed leaves, such as the sea holly

ERYNGOES > ERYNGO

ERYNGOS > ERYNGO

ERYTHEMA *n* patchy inflammation of the skin

ERYTHEMAL > ERYTHEMA

ERYTHEMAS > ERYTHEMA

ERYTHEMIC > ERYTHEMA

ERYTHRINA *n* tropical tree with red flowers

ERYTHRISM *n* abnormal red coloration, as in

plumage or hair

ERYTHRITE *n* sweet crystalline compound extacted from certain algae and lichens

ERYTHROID *adj* red or reddish

ERYTHRON *n* red blood cells and their related tissues

ERYTHRONS > ERYTHRON

ES *n* letter S

ESCABECHE *n* (in Mexican cookery) pickled vegetables and peppers, served as a condiment for fish

ESCALADE *n* assault by the use of ladders, esp on a fortification ▷ *vb* gain access to (a place) by the use of ladders

ESCALADED > ESCALADE

ESCALADER > ESCALADE

ESCALADES > ESCALADE

ESCALADO *n* escalade

ESCALATE *vb* increase in extent or intensity

ESCALATED > ESCALATE

ESCALATES > ESCALATE

ESCALATOR *n* moving staircase

ESCALIER *n* staircase

ESCALIERS > ESCALIER

ESCALLOP *another word for* > SCALLOP

ESCALLOPS > ESCALLOP

ESCALOP *another word for* > SCALLOP

ESCALOPE *n* thin slice of meat, esp veal

ESCALOPED > ESCALOP

ESCALOPES > ESCALOPE

ESCALOPS > ESCALOP

ESCAPABLE > ESCAPE

ESCAPADE *n* mischievous adventure

ESCAPADES > ESCAPADE

ESCAPADO *n* escaped criminal

ESCAPE *vb* get free (of) ▷ *n* act of escaping

ESCAPED > ESCAPE

ESCAPEE *n* person who has escaped

ESCAPEES > ESCAPEE

ESCAPER > ESCAPE

ESCAPERS > ESCAPE

ESCAPES > ESCAPE

ESCAPING > ESCAPE

ESCAPISM *n* taking refuge in fantasy to avoid unpleasant reality

ESCAPISMS > ESCAPISM

ESCAPIST > ESCAPISM

ESCAPISTS > ESCAPISM

ESCAR *same as* > ESKER

ESCARGOT *n* variety of edible snail, usually eaten with a sauce made of melted butter and garlic

ESCARGOTS > ESCARGOT

ESCAROLE *n* variety of endive with broad leaves, used in salads

ESCAROLES > ESCAROLE

ESCARP *n* inner side of the ditch separating besiegers and besieged ▷ *vb* make into a slope

ESCARPED > ESCARP

ESCARPING > ESCARP

ESCARPS > ESCARP

ESCARS > ESCAR

ESCHALOT *another name for* *a* > SHALLOT

ESCHALOTS > ESCHALOT

ESCHAR *n* dry scab or slough, esp one following a burn or cauterization of the skin

ESCHARS > ESCHAR

ESCHEAT *n* private possessions that become state property in the absence of an heir ▷ *vb* attain such property

ESCHEATED > ESCHEAT

ESCHEATOR > ESCHEAT

ESCHEATS > ESCHEAT

ESCHEW *vb* abstain from, avoid

ESCHEWAL > ESCHEW

ESCHEWALS > ESCHEW

ESCHEWED > ESCHEW

ESCHEWER > ESCHEW

ESCHEWERS > ESCHEW

ESCHEWING > ESCHEW

ESCHEWS > ESCHEW

ESCLANDRE *n* scandal or notoriety

ESCOLAR *n* slender spiny-finned fish

ESCOLARS > ESCOLAR

ESCOPETTE *n* carbine

ESCORT *n* people or vehicles accompanying another person for protection or as an honour ▷ *vb* act as an escort to

ESCORTAGE > ESCORT

ESCORTED > ESCORT

ESCORTING > ESCORT

ESCORTS > ESCORT

ESCOT *vb* maintain

ESCOTED > ESCOT

ESCOTING > ESCOT

ESCOTS > ESCOT

ESCOTTED > ESCOT

ESCOTTING > ESCOT

ESCRIBANO *n* clerk

ESCRIBE *vb* draw (a circle) so that it is tangential to one side of a triangle and to the other two sides produced

ESCRIBED > ESCRIBE

ESCRIBES > ESCRIBE

ESCRIBING > ESCRIBE

ESCROC *n* conman

ESCROCS > ESCROC

ESCROL *same as* > ESCROLL

ESCROLL *n* scroll

ESCROLLS > ESCROLL

ESCROLS > ESCROL

ESCROW *n* money, goods, or a written document, such as a contract bond, delivered to a third party

and held by him pending fulfilment of some condition ▷ *vb* place (money, a document, etc) in escrow

ESCROWED > ESCROW

ESCROWING > ESCROW

ESCROWS > ESCROW

ESCUAGE (in medieval Europe) another word for > SCUTAGE

ESCUAGES > ESCUAGE

ESCUDO *n* former monetary unit of Portugal

ESCUDOS > ESCUDO

ESCULENT *adj* edible ▷ *n* any edible substance

ESCULENTS > ESCULENT

ESEMPLASY *n* unification

ESERINE *n* crystalline alkaloid

ESERINES > ESERINE

ESES > ES

ESILE *n* vinegar

ESILES > ESILE

ESKAR *same as* > ESKER

ESKARS > ESKAR

ESKER *n* long winding ridge of gravel, sand, etc, originally deposited by a meltwater stream running under a glacier

ESKERS > ESKER

ESKIES > ESKY

ESKY *n* portable insulated container for keeping food and drink cool

ESLOIN *same as* > ELOIGN

ESLOINED > ESLOIN

ESLOINING > ESLOIN

ESLOINS > ESLOIN

ESLOYNE *same as* > ELOIGN

ESLOYNED > ESLOYNE

ESLOYNES > ESLOYNE

ESLOYNING > ESLOYNE

ESNE *n* household slave

ESNECIES > ESNECY

ESNECY *n* right of the eldest daughter to make the first choice when dividing inheritance

ESNES > ESNE

ESOPHAGI > ESOPHAGUS

ESOPHAGUS *n* part of the alimentary canal between the pharynx and the stomach

ESOTERIC *adj* understood by only a small number of people with special knowledge

ESOTERICA *npl* esoteric things

ESOTERIES > ESOTERIC

ESOTERISM > ESOTERIC

ESOTERY > ESOTERIC

ESOTROPIA *n* condition in which eye turns inwards

ESOTROPIC > ESOTROPIA

ESPADA *n* sword

ESPADAS > ESPADA

ESPAGNOLE *n* tomato and sherry sauce

ESPALIER n shrub or fruit tree trained to grow flat ▷ vb train (a plant) on an espalier

ESPALIERS > ESPALIER

ESPANOL n Spanish person

ESPANOLES > ESPANOL

ESPARTO n grass of S Europe and N Africa used for making rope etc

ESPARTOS > ESPARTO

ESPECIAL adj special

ESPERANCE n hope or expectation

ESPIAL n act or fact of being seen or discovered

ESPIALS > ESPIAL

ESPIED > ESPY

ESPIEGLE adj playful

ESPIER > ESPY

ESPIERS > ESPY

ESPIES > ESPY

ESPIONAGE n spying

ESPLANADE n wide open road used as a public promenade

ESPOUSAL n adoption or support

ESPOUSALS > ESPOUSAL

ESPOUSE vb adopt or give support to (a cause etc)

ESPOUSED > ESPOUSE

ESPOUSER > ESPOUSE

ESPOUSERS > ESPOUSE

ESPOUSES > ESPOUSE

ESPOUSING > ESPOUSE

ESPRESSO n strong coffee made by forcing steam or boiling water through ground coffee beans

ESPRESSOS > ESPRESSO

ESPRIT n spirit, liveliness, or wit

ESPRITS > ESPRIT

ESPUMOSO n sparkling wine

ESPUMOSOS > ESPUMOSO

ESPY vb catch sight of

ESPYING > ESPY

ESQUIRE n courtesy title placed after a man's name ▷ vb escort

ESQUIRED > ESQUIRE

ESQUIRES > ESQUIRE

ESQUIRESS feminine form of > ESQUIRE

ESQUIRING > ESQUIRE

ESQUISSE n sketch

ESQUISSES > ESQUISSE

ESS n letter S

ESSAY n short literary composition ▷ vb attempt

ESSAYED > ESSAY

ESSAYER > ESSAY

ESSAYERS > ESSAY

ESSAYETTE n short essay

ESSAYING > ESSAY

ESSAYISH > ESSAY

ESSAYIST n person who writes essays

ESSAYISTS > ESSAYIST

ESSAYS > ESSAY

ESSE n existence

ESSENCE n most

important feature of a thing which determines its identity

ESSENCES > ESSENCE

ESSENTIAL adj vitally important ▷ n something fundamental or indispensable

ESSES > ESS

ESSIVE n grammatical case

ESSIVES > ESSIVE

ESSOIN n excuse

ESSOINER > ESSOIN

ESSOINERS > ESSOIN

ESSOINS > ESSOIN

ESSONITE variant spelling of > HESSONITE

ESSONITES > ESSONITE

ESSOYNE same as > ESSOIN

ESSOYNES > ESSOYNE

EST n treatment intended to help people towards psychological growth, in which they spend many hours in large groups, deprived of food and water and hectored by stewards

ESTABLISH vb set up on a permanent basis

ESTACADE n defensive arrangement of stakes

ESTACADES > ESTACADE

ESTAFETTE n mounted courier

ESTAMINET n small café, bar, or bistro, esp a shabby one

ESTANCIA n (in Spanish America) a large estate or cattle ranch

ESTANCIAS > ESTANCIA

ESTATE n landed property ▷ vb provide with an estate

ESTATED > ESTATE

ESTATES > ESTATE

ESTATING > ESTATE

ESTEEM n high regard ▷ vb think highly of

ESTEEMED > ESTEEM

ESTEEMING > ESTEEM

ESTEEMS > ESTEEM

ESTER n compound produced by the reaction between an acid and an alcohol

ESTERASE n any of a group of enzymes that hydrolyse esters into alcohols and acids

ESTERASES > ESTERASE

ESTERIFY vb change or cause to change into an ester

ESTERS > ESTER

ESTHESES > ESTHESIS

ESTHESIA US spelling of > AESTHESIA

ESTHESIAS > ESTHESIA

ESTHESIS n esthesia

ESTHETE US spelling of > AESTHETE

ESTHETES > ESTHETE

ESTHETIC > ESTHETE

ESTHETICS > ESTHETE

ESTIMABLE adj worthy of respect

ESTIMABLY > ESTIMABLE

ESTIMATE vb calculate roughly ▷ n approximate calculation

ESTIMATED > ESTIMATE

ESTIMATES > ESTIMATE

ESTIMATOR n person or thing that estimates

ESTIVAL usual US spelling of > AESTIVAL

ESTIVATE usual US spelling of > AESTIVATE

ESTIVATED > ESTIVATE

ESTIVATES > ESTIVATE

ESTIVATOR > ESTIVATE

ESTOC n short stabbing sword

ESTOCS > ESTOC

ESTOILE n heraldic star with wavy points

ESTOILES > ESTOILE

ESTOP vb preclude by estoppel

ESTOPPAGE > ESTOP

ESTOPPED > ESTOP

ESTOPPEL n rule of evidence whereby a person is precluded from denying the truth of a statement of facts he has previously asserted

ESTOPPELS > ESTOPPEL

ESTOPPING > ESTOP

ESTOPS > ESTOP

ESTOVER same as > ESTOVERS

ESTOVERS npl right allowed by law to tenants of land to cut timber, esp for fuel and repairs

ESTRADE n dais or raised platform

ESTRADES > ESTRADE

ESTRADIOL n most potent estrogenic hormone secreted by the mammalian ovary

ESTRAGON another name for > TARRAGON

ESTRAGONS > ESTRAGON

ESTRAL US spelling of > OESTRAL

ESTRANGE vb separate and live apart from (one's spouse)

ESTRANGED adj no longer living with one's spouse

ESTRANGER > ESTRANGE

ESTRANGES > ESTRANGE

ESTRAPADE n attempt by a horse to throw its rider

ESTRAY n stray domestic animal of unknown ownership ▷ vb stray

ESTRAYED > ESTRAY

ESTRAYING > ESTRAY

ESTRAYS > ESTRAY

ESTREAT n true copy of or extract from a court record ▷ vb enforce (a recognizance that has been

forfeited) by sending an extract of the court record to the proper authority

ESTREATED > ESTREAT

ESTREATS > ESTREAT

ESTREPE vb lay waste

ESTREPED > ESTREPE

ESTREPES > ESTREPE

ESTREPING > ESTREPE

ESTRICH n ostrich

ESTRICHES > ESTRICH

ESTRIDGE n ostrich

ESTRIDGES > ESTRIDGE

ESTRILDID n weaver finch

ESTRIN US spelling of > OESTRIN

ESTRINS > ESTRIN

ESTRIOL usual US spelling of > OESTRIOL

ESTRIOLS > ESTRIOL

ESTRO n poetic inspiration

ESTROGEN usual US spelling of > OESTROGEN

ESTROGENS > OESTROGEN

ESTRONE usual US spelling of > OESTRONE

ESTRONES > ESTRONE

ESTROS > ESTRO

ESTROUS > ESTRUS

ESTRUAL > ESTRUS

ESTRUM usual US spelling of > OESTRUM

ESTRUMS > ESTRUM

ESTRUS usual US spelling of > OESTRUS

ESTRUSES > ESTRUS

ESTS > EST

ESTUARIAL > ESTUARY

ESTUARIAN > ESTUARY

ESTUARIES > ESTUARY

ESTUARINE adj formed or deposited in an estuary

ESTUARY n mouth of a river

ESURIENCE > ESURIENT

ESURIENCY > ESURIENT

ESURIENT adj greedy

ET dialect past tense of > EAT

ETA n seventh letter in the Greek alphabet, a long vowel sound

ETACISM n pronunciation of eta as a long vowel sound

ETACISMS > ETACISM

ETAERIO n aggregate fruit, as one consisting of drupes (raspberry) or achenes (traveller's joy)

ETAERIOS > ETAERIO

ETAGE n floor in a multi-storey building

ETAGERE n stand with open shelves for displaying ornaments, etc

ETAGERES > ETAGERE

ETAGES > ETAGE

ETALAGE n display

ETALAGES > ETALAGE

ETALON n device used in spectroscopy to measure wavelengths by interference effects produced by multiple reflections between parallel half-silvered glass or quartz plates

ETALONS > ETALON

ETAMIN same as > ETAMINE

ETAMINE n cotton or worsted fabric of loose weave, used for clothing, curtains, etc

ETAMINES > ETAMINE

ETAMINS > ETAMIN

ETAPE n public storehouse

ETAPES > ETAPE

ETAS > ETA

ETAT n state

ETATISM same as > ETATISME

ETATISME n authoritarian control by the state

ETATISMES > ETATISME

ETATISMS > ETATISM

ETATIST > ETATISME

ETATISTE > ETATISME

ETATISTES > ETATISME

ETATS > ETAT

ETCETERA n number of other items

ETCETERAS npl miscellaneous extra things or people

ETCH vb wear away or cut the surface of (metal, glass, etc) with acid

ETCHANT n any acid or corrosive used for etching

ETCHANTS > ETCHANT

ETCHED > ETCH

ETCHER > ETCH

ETCHERS > ETCH

ETCHES > ETCH

ETCHING n picture printed from an etched metal plate

ETCHINGS > ETCHING

ETEN n giant

ETENS > ETEN

ETERNAL adj without beginning or end ▷ n eternal thing

ETERNALLY > ETERNAL

ETERNALS > ETERNAL

ETERNE archaic or poetic word for > ETERNAL

ETERNISE same as > ETERNIZE

ETERNISED > ETERNISE

ETERNISES > ETERNISE

ETERNITY n infinite time

ETERNIZE vb make eternal

ETERNIZED > ETERNIZE

ETERNIZES > ETERNIZE

ETESIAN adj (of NW winds) recurring annually in the summer in the E Mediterranean ▷ n etesian wind

ETESIANS > ETESIAN

ETH same as > EDH

ETHAL n cetyl alcohol

ETHALS > ETHAL

ETHANAL n colourless volatile pungent liquid

ETHANALS > ETHANAL

ETHANE n odourless flammable gas obtained from natural gas and petroleum

ETHANES > ETHANE

ETHANOATE same as > ACETATE

ETHANOIC as in ethanoic acid acetic acid

ETHANOL same as > ALCOHOL

ETHANOLS > ETHANOL

ETHANOYL n substance consisting of or containing the monovalent group CH_3CO-

ETHANOYLS > ETHANOYL

ETHE adj easy

ETHENE same as > ETHYLENE

ETHENES > ETHENE

ETHEPHON n synthetic plant-growth regulator

ETHEPHONS > ETHEPHON

ETHER n colourless sweet-smelling liquid used as an anaesthetic

ETHERCAP n spider

ETHERCAPS > ETHERCAP

ETHEREAL adj extremely delicate

ETHEREOUS same as > ETHEREAL

ETHERIAL same as > ETHEREAL

ETHERIC > ETHER

ETHERICAL > ETHER

ETHERIFY vb change (a compound, such as an alcohol) into an ether

ETHERION n gas formerly believed to exist in air

ETHERIONS > ETHERION

ETHERISE same as > ETHERIZE

ETHERISED > ETHERISE

ETHERISER > ETHERISE

ETHERISES > ETHERISE

ETHERISH > ETHER

ETHERISM n addiction to ether

ETHERISMS > ETHERISM

ETHERIST > ETHERISM

ETHERISTS > ETHERISM

ETHERIZE vb subject (a person) to the anaesthetic influence of ether fumes

ETHERIZED > ETHERIZE

ETHERIZER > ETHERIZE

ETHERIZES > ETHERIZE

ETHERS > ETHER

ETHIC n moral principle

ETHICAL adj of or based on a system of moral beliefs about right and wrong ▷ n drug available only by prescription

ETHICALLY > ETHICAL

ETHICALS > ETHICAL

ETHICIAN > ETHICS

ETHICIANS > ETHICS

ETHICISE same as > ETHICIZE

ETHICISED > ETHICISE

ETHICISES > ETHICISE

ETHICISM > ETHICS

ETHICIST > ETHICS

ETHICISTS > ETHICS

ETHICIZE vb make or consider as ethical

ETHICIZED > ETHICIZE

ETHICIZES > ETHICIZE

ETHICS n code of behaviour

ETHINYL same as > ETHYNYL

ETHINYLS > ETHINYL

ETHION n type of pesticide

ETHIONINE n type of amino acid

ETHIONS > ETHION

ETHIOPS n dark-coloured chemical compound

ETHIOPSES > ETHIOPS

ETHMOID adj denoting or relating to a bone of the skull that forms part of the eye socket and the nasal cavity ▷ n ethmoid bone

ETHMOIDAL same as > ETHMOID

ETHMOIDS > ETHMOID

ETHNARCH n ruler of a people or province, as in parts of the Roman and Byzantine Empires

ETHNARCHS > ETHNARCH

ETHNARCHY > ETHNARCH

ETHNIC adj relating to a people or group that shares a culture, religion, or language ▷ n member of an ethnic group, esp a minority group

ETHNICAL same as > ETHNIC

ETHNICISM n paganism

ETHNICITY > ETHNIC

ETHNICS > ETHNIC

ETHNOCIDE n extermination of a race

ETHNOGENY n branch of ethnology that deals with the origin of races or peoples

ETHNOLOGY n study of human races

ETHNONYM n name of ethnic group

ETHNONYMS > ETHNONYM

ETHNOS n ethnic group

ETHNOSES > ETHNOS

ETHOGRAM n description of animal's behaviour

ETHOGRAMS > ETHOGRAM

ETHOLOGIC > ETHOLOGY

ETHOLOGY n study of the behaviour of animals in their normal environment

ETHONONE another name for > KETENE

ETHONONES > ETHONONE

ETHOS n distinctive spirit and attitudes of a people, culture, etc

ETHOSES > ETHOS

ETHOXIDE n any of a class of saltlike compounds

ETHOXIDES > ETHOXIDE

ETHOXIES > ETHOXY

ETHOXY > ETHOXYL

ETHOXYL n univalent radical

ETHOXYLS > ETHOXYL

ETHS > ETH

ETHYL adj type of chemical hydrocarbon group

ETHYLATE same as > ETHOXIDE

ETHYLATED > ETHYLATE

ETHYLATES > ETHYLATE

ETHYLENE n poisonous gas used as an anaesthetic and as fuel

ETHYLENES > ETHYLENE

ETHYLENIC > ETHYLENE

ETHYLIC > ETHYL

ETHYLS > ETHYL

ETHYNE another name for > ACETYLENE

ETHYNES > ETHYNE

ETHYNYL n univalent radical

ETHYNYLS > ETHYNYL

ETIC adj (in linguistics) of or relating to items analyzed without consideration of their structural function

ETIOLATE vb become pale and weak

ETIOLATED > ETIOLATE

ETIOLATES > ETIOLATE

ETIOLIN n yellow pigment

ETIOLINS > ETIOLIN

ETIOLOGIC > ETIOLOGY

ETIOLOGY n study of the causes of diseases

ETIQUETTE n conventional code of conduct

ETNA n container used to heat liquids

ETNAS > ETNA

ETOILE n star

ETOILES > ETOILE

ETOUFFEE n spicy Cajun stew

ETOUFFEES > ETOUFFEE

ETOURDI adj foolish

ETOURDIE feminine form of > ETOURDI

ETRANGER n foreigner

ETRANGERE feminine form of > ETRANGER

ETRANGERS > ETRANGER

ETRENNE n New Year's gift

ETRENNES > ETRENNE

ETRIER n short portable ladder or set of webbing loops that can be attached to a karabiner or fifi hook

ETRIERS > ETRIER

ETTERCAP n spider

ETTERCAPS > ETTERCAP

ETTIN n giant

ETTINS > ETTIN

ETTLE vb intend

ETTLED > ETTLE

ETTLES > ETTLE

ETTLING > ETTLE

e

ETUDE *n* short musical composition for a solo instrument, esp intended as a technical exercise

ETUDES > ETUDE

ETUI *n* small usually ornamented case for holding needles, cosmetics, or other small articles

ETUIS > ETUI

ETWEE *same as* > ETUI

ETWEES > ETUI

ETYMA > ETYMON

ETYMIC > ETYMON

ETYMOLOGY *n* study of the sources and development of words

ETYMON *n* earliest form of a word or morpheme, or a reconstructed form, from which another word or morpheme is derived

ETYMONS > ETYMON

ETYPIC *n* unable to conform to type

ETYPICAL *same as* > ETYPIC

EUCAIN *same as* > EUCAINE

EUCAINE *n* crystalline optically active substance formerly used as a local anaesthetic

EUCAINES > EUCAINE

EUCAINS > EUCAIN

EUCALYPT *n* myrtaceous tree

EUCALYPTI *n* eucalypts

EUCALYPTS > EUCALYPT

EUCARYON *same as* > EUKARYOTE

EUCARYONS > EUCARYON

EUCARYOT *same as* > EUKARYOTE

EUCARYOTE *same as* > EUKARYOTE

EUCARYOTS > EUCARYOT

EUCHARIS *n* S American plant cultivated for its large white fragrant flowers

EUCHLORIC > EUCHLORIN

EUCHLORIN *n* explosive gaseous mixture of chlorine and chlorine dioxide

EUCHOLOGY *n* prayer formulary

EUCHRE *n* US and Canadian card game similar to écarté for two to four players, using a poker pack with joker ▷ *vb* prevent (a player) from making his contracted tricks

EUCHRED > EUCHRE

EUCHRES > EUCHRE

EUCHRING > EUCHRE

EUCLASE *n* brittle green gem

EUCLASES > EUCLASE

EUCLIDEAN *adj* of or relating to Euclid (Greek mathematician of Alexandria, 3rd century BC), esp his system of geometry

EUCLIDIAN *same as* > EUCLIDEAN

EUCRITE *n* type of stony meteorite

EUCRITES > EUCRITE

EUCRITIC > EUCRITE

EUCRYPHIA *n* Australian and S American tree or shrub, mostly evergreen, with dark lustrous green leaves and white flowers

EUCYCLIC *adj* (of plants) having the same number of leaves in each whorl

EUDAEMON *same as* > EUDEMON

EUDAEMONS > EUDAEMON

EUDAEMONY *same as* > EUDEMONIA

EUDAIMON *same as* > EUDAEMON

EUDAIMONS > EUDAIMON

EUDEMON *n* benevolent spirit or demon

EUDEMONIA *n* happiness, esp (in the philosophy of Aristotle) that resulting from a rational active life

EUDEMONIC > EUDEMONIA

EUDEMONS > EUDEMON

EUDIALYTE *n* brownish-red mineral

EUGARIE *another name for* > PIPI

EUGARIES > EUGARIE

EUGE *interj* well done!

EUGENIA *n* plant of the clove family

EUGENIAS > EUGENIA

EUGENIC > EUGENICS

EUGENICAL > EUGENICS

EUGENICS *n* study of methods of improving the human race

EUGENISM > EUGENICS

EUGENISMS > EUGENICS

EUGENIST > EUGENICS

EUGENISTS > EUGENICS

EUGENOL *n* colourless or pale yellow oily liquid substance with a spicy taste and an odour of cloves, used in perfumery

EUGENOLS > EUGENOL

EUGH *archaic form of* > YEW

EUGHEN *archaic form of* > YEW

EUGHS > EUGH

EUGLENA *n* type of freshwater unicellular organism

EUGLENAS > EUGLENA

EUGLENID *same as* > EUGLENA

EUGLENIDS > EUGLENID

EUGLENOID > EUGLENA

EUK *vb* itch

EUKARYON *same as* > EUKARYOTE

EUKARYONS > EUKARYON

EUKARYOT *same as* > EUKARYOTE

EUKARYOTE *n* type of organism whose cells each have a distinct nucleus within which the genetic material is contained

EUKARYOTS > EUKARYOT

EUKED > EUK

EUKING > EUK

EUKS > EUK

EULACHAN *same as* > EULACHON

EULACHANS > EULACHAN

EULACHON *n* salmonoid food fish

EULACHONS > EULACHON

EULOGIA *n* blessed bread distributed to members of the congregation after the liturgy, esp to those who have not communed

EULOGIAE > EULOGIA

EULOGIAS > EULOGIA

EULOGIES > EULOGY

EULOGISE *same as* > EULOGIZE

EULOGISED > EULOGISE

EULOGISER > EULOGISE

EULOGISES > EULOGISE

EULOGIST > EULOGIZE

EULOGISTS > EULOGIZE

EULOGIUM *same as* > EULOGY

EULOGIUMS > EULOGIUM

EULOGIZE *vb* praise (a person or thing) highly in speech or writing

EULOGIZED > EULOGIZE

EULOGIZER > EULOGIZE

EULOGIZES > EULOGIZE

EULOGY *n* speech or writing in praise of a person

EUMELANIN *n* dark melanin

EUMERISM *n* collection of similar parts

EUMERISMS > EUMERISM

EUMONG *same as* > EUMUNG

EUMONGS > EUMONG

EUMUNG *n* any of various Australian acacias

EUMUNGS > EUMUNG

EUNUCH *n* castrated man, esp (formerly) a guard in a harem

EUNUCHISE *same as* > EUNUCHIZE

EUNUCHISM > EUNUCH

EUNUCHIZE *vb* castrate

EUNUCHOID *n* one suffering from deficient sexual development

EUNUCHS > EUNUCH

EUOI *n* cry of Bacchic frenzy

EUONYMIN *n* extract derived from the bark of the euonymus

EUONYMINS > EUONYMIN

EUONYMUS *n* type of N temperate tree or shrub

EUOUAE *n* a mnemonic used to recall the sequence of tones in a particular passage of the Gloria

EUOUAES > EUOUAE

EUPAD *n* antiseptic powder

EUPADS > EUPAD

EUPATRID *n* (in ancient Greece) hereditary noble or landowner

EUPATRIDS > EUPATRID

EUPEPSIA *n* good digestion

EUPEPSIAS > EUPEPSIA

EUPEPSIES > EUPEPSY

EUPEPSY *same as* > EUPEPSIA

EUPEPTIC > EUPEPSIA

EUPHAUSID *n* small pelagic shrimplike crustacean

EUPHEMISE *same as* > EUPHEMIZE

EUPHEMISM *n* inoffensive word or phrase substituted for one considered offensive or upsetting

EUPHEMIST > EUPHEMISM

EUPHEMIZE *vb* speak in euphemisms or refer to by means of a euphemism

EUPHENIC *n* of or pertaining to biological improvement

EUPHENICS *n* science of biological improvement

EUPHOBIA *n* fear of good news

EUPHOBIAS > EUPHOBIA

EUPHON *n* glass harmonica

EUPHONIA *same as* > EUPHONY

EUPHONIAS > EUPHONIA

EUPHONIC *adj* denoting or relating to euphony

EUPHONIES > EUPHONY

EUPHONISE *same as* > EUPHONIZE

EUPHONISM *n* use of pleasant-sounding words

EUPHONIUM *n* brass musical instrument, tenor tuba

EUPHONIZE *vb* make pleasant to hear

EUPHONS > EUPHON

EUPHONY *n* pleasing sound

EUPHORBIA *n* type of plant such as the spurge or poinsettia

EUPHORIA *n* sense of elation

EUPHORIAS > EUPHORIA

EUPHORIC > EUPHORIA

EUPHORIES > EUPHORY

EUPHORY *same as* > EUPHORIA

EUPHOTIC *adj* denoting or relating to the uppermost part of a sea or lake down to about 100 metres depth, which receives enough light to enable photosynthesis to take place

EUPHRASIA *n* eyebright

EUPHRASY *same as* > EYEBRIGHT

EUPHROE *n* wooden block with holes through which

the lines of a crowfoot are rove

EUPHROES > EUPHROE
EUPHUISE *same as* > EUPHUIZE
EUPHUISED > EUPHUISE
EUPHUISES > EUPHUISE
EUPHUISM n artificial prose style of the Elizabethan period, marked by extreme use of antithesis, alliteration, and extended similes and allusions
EUPHUISMS > EUPHUISM
EUPHUIST > EUPHUISM
EUPHUISTS > EUPHUISM
EUPHUIZE vb write in euphuism
EUPHUIZED > EUPHUIZE
EUPHUIZES > EUPHUIZE
EUPLASTIC adj healing quickly and well
EUPLOID adj having chromosomes present in an exact multiple of the haploid number ▷ n euploid cell or individual
EUPLOIDS > EUPLOID
EUPLOIDY > EUPLOID
EUPNEA *same as* > EUPNOEA
EUPNEAS > EUPNEA
EUPNEIC > EUPNOEA
EUPNOEA n normal relaxed breathing
EUPNOEAS > EUPNOEA
EUPNOEIC > EUPNOEA
EUREKA n exclamation of triumph at finding something
EUREKAS > EUREKA
EURHYTHMY n rhythmic movement
EURIPI > EURIPUS
EURIPUS n strait or channel with a strong current or tide
EURIPUSES > EURIPUS
EURO n unit of the single currency of the European Union
EUROBOND n bond issued in a eurocurrency
EUROBONDS > EUROBOND
EUROCRAT n member, esp a senior member, of the administration of the European Union
EUROCRATS > EUROCRAT
EUROCREEP n gradual introduction of the euro into use in Britain
EUROKIES > EUROKY
EUROKOUS > EUROKY
EUROKY n ability of an organism to live under different conditions
EURONOTE n form of euro-commercial paper consisting of short-term negotiable bearer notes
EURONOTES > EURONOTE
EUROPHILE n person who admires Europe,

Europeans, or the European Union
EUROPIUM n silvery-white element of the lanthanide series
EUROPIUMS > EUROPIUM
EUROPOP n type of pop music by European artists
EUROPOPS > EUROPOP
EUROS > EURO
EURYBATH n organism that can live at different depths underwater
EURYBATHS > EURYBATH
EURYOKIES > EURYOKY
EURYOKOUS > EURYOKY
EURYOKY *same as* > EUROKY
EURYTHERM n organism that can tolerate widely differing temperatures
EURYTHMIC adj having a pleasing and harmonious rhythm, order, or structure
EURYTHMY n dancing style in which the rhythm of music is expressed through body movements
EURYTOPIC adj (of a species) able to tolerate a wide range of environments
EUSOCIAL adj using division of labour
EUSOL n solution of eupad in water
EUSOLS > EUSOL
EUSTACIES > EUSTATIC
EUSTACY > EUSTATIC
EUSTASIES > EUSTATIC
EUSTASY > EUSTATIC
EUSTATIC adj denoting or relating to worldwide changes in sea level, caused by the melting of ice sheets, movements of the ocean floor, sedimentation, etc
EUSTELE n central cylinder of a seed plant
EUSTELES > EUSTELE
EUSTYLE n building with columns optimally spaced
EUSTYLES > EUSTYLE
EUTAXIA n condition of being easily melted
EUTAXIAS > EUTAXIA
EUTAXIES > EUTAXY
EUTAXITE n banded volcanic rock
EUTAXITES > EUTAXITE
EUTAXITIC > EUTAXITE
EUTAXY n good order
EUTECTIC adj (of a mixture of substances, esp an alloy) having the lowest freezing point of all possible mixtures of the substances ▷ n eutectic mixture
EUTECTICS > EUTECTIC
EUTECTOID n mixture of substances similar to a eutectic, but forming two or three constituents from a solid instead of from a melt ▷ adj concerned with

or suitable for eutectoid mixtures
EUTEXIA *same as* > EUTAXIA
EUTEXIAS > EUTEXIA
EUTHANASE *same as* > EUTHANIZE
EUTHANASY n the act of killing someone painlessly
EUTHANAZE *same as* > EUTHANIZE
EUTHANISE *same as* > EUTHANIZE
EUTHANIZE vb put (someone, esp one suffering from a terminal illness) to death painlessly
EUTHENICS n study of the control of the environment, esp with a view to improving the health and living standards of the human race
EUTHENIST > EUTHENICS
EUTHERIAN n type of mammal with a placenta, whose young reach an advanced state of development before birth
EUTHYMIA n pleasant state of mind
EUTHYMIAS > EUTHYMIA
EUTHYROID n condition of having thyroid glands that function normally
EUTRAPELY n conversational skill
EUTROPHIC adj (of lakes and similar habitats) rich in organic and mineral nutrients and supporting an abundant plant life, which in the process of decaying depletes the oxygen supply for animal life
EUTROPHY > EUTROPHIC
EUTROPIC > EUTROPY
EUTROPIES > EUTROPY
EUTROPOUS > EUTROPY
EUTROPY n regular variation of the crystalline structure of a series of compounds according to atomic number
EUXENITE n rare brownish-black mineral containing erbium, cerium, uranium, columbium, and yttrium
EUXENITES > EUXENITE
EVACUANT adj serving to promote excretion, esp of the bowels ▷ n evacuant agent
EVACUANTS > EVACUANT
EVACUATE vb send (someone) away from a place of danger
EVACUATED > EVACUATE
EVACUATES > EVACUATE
EVACUATOR > EVACUATE
EVACUEE n person evacuated from a place of danger, esp in wartime

EVACUEES > EVACUEE
EVADABLE > EVADE
EVADE vb get away from or avoid
EVADED > EVADE
EVADER > EVADE
EVADERS > EVADE
EVADES > EVADE
EVADIBLE > EVADE
EVADING > EVADE
EVADINGLY > EVADE
EVAGATION n digression
EVAGINATE vb turn (an organ or part) inside out
EVALUABLE > EVALUATE
EVALUATE vb find or judge the value of
EVALUATED > EVALUATE
EVALUATES > EVALUATE
EVALUATOR > EVALUATE
EVANESCE vb fade gradually from sight
EVANESCED > EVANESCE
EVANESCES > EVANESCE
EVANGEL n gospel of Christianity
EVANGELIC adj of, based upon, or following from the gospels
EVANGELS > EVANGEL
EVANGELY n gospel
EVANISH poetic word for > VANISH
EVANISHED > EVANISH
EVANISHES > EVANISH
EVANITION > EVANISH
EVAPORATE vb change from a liquid or solid to a vapour
EVAPORITE n any sedimentary rock, such as rock salt, gypsum, or anhydrite, formed by evaporation of former seas or salt-water lakes
EVASIBLE > EVASION
EVASION n act of evading something, esp a duty or responsibility, by cunning or illegal means
EVASIONAL > EVASION
EVASIONS > EVASION
EVASIVE adj not straightforward
EVASIVELY > EVASIVE
EVE n evening or day before some special event
EVECTION n irregularity in the moon's motion caused by perturbations of the sun and planets
EVECTIONS > EVECTION
EVEJAR n nightjar
EVEJARS > EVEJAR
EVEN adj flat or smooth ▷ adv equally ▷ vb make even ▷ n eve
EVENED > EVEN
EVENEMENT n event
EVENER > EVEN
EVENERS > EVEN
EVENEST > EVEN
EVENFALL n early evening
EVENFALLS > EVENFALL

EVENING n end of the day or early part of the night ▷ adj of or in the evening

EVENINGS adv in the evening, esp regularly

EVENLY > EVEN

EVENNESS > EVEN

EVENS adv (of a bet) winning the same as the amount staked if successful

EVENSONG n evening prayer

EVENSONGS > EVENSONG

EVENT n anything that takes place ▷ vb take part or ride (a horse) in eventing

EVENTED > EVENT

EVENTER > EVENTING

EVENTERS > EVENTING

EVENTFUL adj full of exciting incidents

EVENTIDE n evening

EVENTIDES > EVENTIDE

EVENTING n riding competitions, usu. involving cross-country, jumping, and dressage

EVENTINGS > EVENTING

EVENTLESS > EVENT

EVENTRATE vb open the belly of

EVENTS > EVENT

EVENTUAL adj ultimate

EVENTUATE vb result ultimately (in)

EVER adv at any time

EVERGLADE n large area of submerged marshland

EVERGREEN adj (tree or shrub) having leaves throughout the year ▷ n evergreen tree or shrub

EVERMORE adv for all time to come

EVERNET n hypothetical form of internet that is continuously accessible using a wide variety of devices

EVERNETS > EVERNET

EVERSIBLE > EVERT

EVERSION > EVERT

EVERSIONS > EVERT

EVERT vb turn (an eyelid, the intestines, or some other bodily part) outwards or inside out

EVERTED > EVERT

EVERTING > EVERT

EVERTOR n any muscle that turns a part outwards

EVERTORS > EVERTOR

EVERTS > EVERT

EVERWHERE adv to or in all parts or places

EVERWHICH dialect version of > WHICHEVER

EVERY adj each without exception

EVERYBODY pron every person

EVERYDAY adj usual or ordinary ▷ n ordinary day

EVERYDAYS > EVERYDAY

EVERYMAN n ordinary person; common man

EVERYMEN > EVERYMAN

EVERYONE pron every person

EVERYWAY adv in every way

EVERYWHEN adv to or in all parts or places

EVES > EVE

EVET n eft

EVETS > EVET

EVHOE interj cry of Bacchic frenzy

EVICT vb legally expel (someone) from his or her home

EVICTED > EVICT

EVICTEE > EVICT

EVICTEES > EVICT

EVICTING > EVICT

EVICTION > EVICT

EVICTIONS > EVICT

EVICTOR > EVICT

EVICTORS > EVICT

EVICTS > EVICT

EVIDENCE n ground for belief ▷ vb demonstrate, prove

EVIDENCED > EVIDENCE

EVIDENCES > EVIDENCE

EVIDENT adj easily seen or understood ▷ n item of evidence

EVIDENTLY adv without question

EVIDENTS > EVIDENT

EVIL n wickedness ▷ adj harmful ▷ adv in an evil manner

EVILDOER n wicked person

EVILDOERS > EVILDOER

EVILDOING > EVILDOER

EVILER > EVIL

EVILEST > EVIL

EVILLER > EVIL

EVILLEST > EVIL

EVILLY > EVIL

EVILNESS > EVIL

EVILS > EVIL

EVINCE vb make evident

EVINCED > EVINCE

EVINCES > EVINCE

EVINCIBLE > EVINCE

EVINCIBLY > EVINCE

EVINCING > EVINCE

EVINCIVE > EVINCE

EVIRATE vb castrate

EVIRATED > EVIRATE

EVIRATES > EVIRATE

EVIRATING > EVIRATE

EVITABLE adj able to be avoided

EVITATE archaic word for > AVOID

EVITATED > EVITATE

EVITATES > EVITATE

EVITATING > EVITATE

EVITATION > EVITATE

EVITE archaic word for > AVOID

EVITED > EVITE

EVITERNAL adj eternal

EVITES > EVITE

EVITING > EVITE

EVO informal word for > EVENING

EVOCABLE > EVOKE

EVOCATE vb evoke

EVOCATED > EVOCATE

EVOCATES > EVOCATE

EVOCATING > EVOCATE

EVOCATION n act of evoking

EVOCATIVE adj tending or serving to evoke

EVOCATOR n person or thing that evokes

EVOCATORS > EVOCATOR

EVOCATORY adj evocative

EVOE interj cry of Bacchic frenzy

EVOHE interj cry of Bacchic frenzy

EVOKE vb call or summon up (a memory, feeling, etc)

EVOKED > EVOKE

EVOKER > EVOKE

EVOKERS > EVOKE

EVOKES > EVOKE

EVOKING > EVOKE

EVOLUE n (in the African former colonies of Belgium and France) African person educated according to European principles

EVOLUES > EVOLUE

EVOLUTE n geometric curve that describes the locus of the centres of curvature of another curve ▷ adj having the margins rolled outwards ▷ vb evolve

EVOLUTED > EVOLUTE

EVOLUTES > EVOLUTE

EVOLUTING > EVOLUTE

EVOLUTION n gradual change in the characteristics of living things over successive generations, esp to a more complex form

EVOLUTIVE adj relating to, tending to, or promoting evolution

EVOLVABLE > EVOLVE

EVOLVE vb develop gradually

EVOLVED > EVOLVE

EVOLVENT adj evolving

EVOLVER > EVOLVE

EVOLVERS > EVOLVE

EVOLVES > EVOLVE

EVOLVING > EVOLVE

EVONYMUS same as > EUONYMUS

EVOS > EVO

EVOVAE n a mnemonic used to recall the sequence of tones in a particular passage of the Gloria Patri

EVOVAES > EVOVAE

EVULGATE vb make public

EVULGATED > EVULGATE

EVULGATES > EVULGATE

EVULSE vb extract by force

EVULSED > EVULSE

EVULSES > EVULSE

EVULSING > EVULSE

EVULSION n act of extracting by force

EVULSIONS > EVULSION

EVZONE n soldier in an elite Greek infantry regiment

EVZONES > EVZONE

EWE n female sheep

EWER n large jug with a wide mouth

EWERS > EWER

EWES > EWE

EWEST Scots word for > NEAR

EWFTES Spenserian plural of > EFT

EWGHEN archaic form of > YEW

EWHOW interj expression of pity or regret

EWK vb itch

EWKED > EWK

EWKING > EWK

EWKS > EWK

EWT archaic form of > NEWT

EWTS > EWT

EX prep not including ▷ vb cross out or delete

EXABYTE n very large unit of computer memory

EXABYTES > EXABYTE

EXACT adj correct and complete in every detail ▷ vb demand (payment or obedience)

EXACTA n horse-racing bet in which the first and second horses must be named in the correct order

EXACTABLE > EXACT

EXACTAS > EXACTA

EXACTED > EXACT

EXACTER > EXACT

EXACTERS > EXACT

EXACTEST > EXACT

EXACTING adj making rigorous or excessive demands

EXACTION n act of obtaining or demanding money as a right

EXACTIONS > EXACTION

EXACTLY adv precisely, in every respect ▷ interj just so! precisely!

EXACTMENT n condition of being exact

EXACTNESS > EXACT

EXACTOR > EXACT

EXACTORS > EXACT

EXACTRESS > EXACT

EXACTS > EXACT

EXACUM n type of tropical plant often grown as a greenhouse plant for its bluish-purple platter-shaped flowers

EXACUMS > EXACUM

EXAHERTZ n very large unit of frequency

EXALT vb praise highly

EXALTED adj high or elevated in rank, position, dignity, etc

EXALTEDLY > EXALTED

EXALTER > EXALT
EXALTERS > EXALT
EXALTING > EXALT
EXALTS > EXALT
EXAM n examination
EXAMEN n examination of conscience, usually made daily by Jesuits and others
EXAMENS > EXAMEN
EXAMINANT n examiner
EXAMINATE n examinee
EXAMINE vb look at closely
EXAMINED > EXAMINE
EXAMINEE n person who sits an exam
EXAMINEES > EXAMINEE
EXAMINER > EXAMINE
EXAMINERS > EXAMINE
EXAMINES > EXAMINE
EXAMINING > EXAMINE
EXAMPLAR archaic form of > EXEMPLAR
EXAMPLARS > EXAMPLAR
EXAMPLE n specimen typical of its group
EXAMPLED > EXAMPLE
EXAMPLES > EXAMPLE
EXAMPLING > EXAMPLE
EXAMS > EXAM
EXANIMATE adj lacking life
EXANTHEM same as > EXANTHEMA
EXANTHEMA n skin eruption or rash occurring as a symptom in a disease such as measles or scarlet fever
EXANTHEMS > EXANTHEM
EXAPTED adj biologically adapted
EXAPTIVE adj involving biological adaptation
EXARATE adj (of the pupa of such insects as ants and bees) having legs, wings, antennae, etc, free and movable
EXARATION n writing
EXARCH n head of certain autonomous Orthodox Christian Churches, such as that of Bulgaria and Cyprus ▷ adj (of a xylem strand) having the first-formed xylem external to that formed later
EXARCHAL > EXARCH
EXARCHATE n office, rank, or jurisdiction of an exarch
EXARCHIES > EXARCHY
EXARCHIST n supporter of an exarch
EXARCHS > EXARCH
EXARCHY same as > EXARCHATE
EXCAMB vb exchange
EXCAMBED > EXCAMB
EXCAMBING > EXCAMB
EXCAMBION n exchange, esp of land
EXCAMBIUM same as > EXCAMBION
EXCAMBS > EXCAMB
EXCARNATE vb remove flesh from

EXCAUDATE adj having no tail or tail-like process
EXCAVATE vb unearth buried objects from (a piece of land) methodically to learn about the past
EXCAVATED > EXCAVATE
EXCAVATES > EXCAVATE
EXCAVATOR n large machine used for digging
EXCEED vb be greater than
EXCEEDED > EXCEED
EXCEEDER > EXCEED
EXCEEDERS > EXCEED
EXCEEDING adj very great
EXCEEDS > EXCEED
EXCEL vb be superior to
EXCELLED > EXCEL
EXCELLENT adj exceptionally good
EXCELLING > EXCEL
EXCELS > EXCEL
EXCELSIOR n excellent: used as a motto and as a trademark for various products, esp in the US for fine wood shavings used for packing breakable objects
EXCENTRIC same as > ECCENTRIC
EXCEPT prep other than, not including ▷ vb leave out; omit; exclude
EXCEPTANT n person taking exception
EXCEPTED > EXCEPT
EXCEPTING prep except
EXCEPTION n excepting
EXCEPTIVE adj relating to or forming an exception
EXCEPTOR > EXCEPT
EXCEPTORS > EXCEPT
EXCEPTS > EXCEPT
EXCERPT n passage taken from a book, speech, etc ▷ vb take a passage from a book, speech, etc
EXCERPTA > EXCERPTUM
EXCERPTED > EXCERPT
EXCERPTER > EXCERPT
EXCERPTOR > EXCERPT
EXCERPTS > EXCERPT
EXCERPTUM n excerpt
EXCESS n state or act of exceeding the permitted limits ▷ vb make (a position) redundant
EXCESSED > EXCESS
EXCESSES > EXCESS
EXCESSING > EXCESS
EXCESSIVE adj exceeding the normal or permitted extents or limits
EXCHANGE vb give or receive (something) in return for something else ▷ n act of exchanging
EXCHANGED > EXCHANGE
EXCHANGER n person or thing that exchanges
EXCHANGES > EXCHANGE
EXCHEAT same as > ESCHEAT
EXCHEATS > EXCHEAT
EXCHEQUER n (in Britain

and certain other countries) accounting department of the Treasury, responsible for receiving and issuing funds
EXCIDE vb cut out
EXCIDED > EXCIDE
EXCIDES > EXCIDE
EXCIDING > EXCIDE
EXCIMER n excited dimer formed by the association of excited and unexcited molecules, which would remain dissociated in the ground state
EXCIMERS > EXCIMER
EXCIPIENT n substance, such as sugar or gum, used to prepare a drug or drugs in a form suitable for administration
EXCIPLE n part of a lichen
EXCIPLES > EXCIPLE
EXCISABLE > EXCISE
EXCISE n tax on goods produced for the home market ▷ vb cut out or away
EXCISED > EXCISE
EXCISEMAN n (formerly) a government agent who collected excise and prevented smuggling
EXCISEMEN > EXCISEMAN
EXCISES > EXCISE
EXCISING > EXCISE
EXCISION > EXCISE
EXCISIONS > EXCISE
EXCITABLE adj easily excited
EXCITABLY > EXCITABLE
EXCITANCY n ability to excite
EXCITANT adj able to excite or stimulate ▷ n something, such as a drug or other agent, able to excite
EXCITANTS > EXCITANT
EXCITE vb arouse to strong emotion
EXCITED adj emotionally aroused, esp to pleasure or agitation
EXCITEDLY > EXCITED
EXCITER n person or thing that excites
EXCITERS > EXCITER
EXCITES > EXCITE
EXCITING adj causing excitement
EXCITON n mobile neutral entity in a crystalline solid consisting of an excited electron bound to the hole produced by its excitation
EXCITONIC > EXCITON
EXCITONS > EXCITON
EXCITOR n nerve that, when stimulated, causes increased activity in the organ or part it supplies
EXCITORS > EXCITOR

EXCLAIM vb speak suddenly, cry out
EXCLAIMED > EXCLAIM
EXCLAIMER > EXCLAIM
EXCLAIMS > EXCLAIM
EXCLAVE n part of a country entirely surrounded by foreign territory: viewed from the position of the home country
EXCLAVES > EXCLAVE
EXCLOSURE n area of land, esp in a forest, fenced round to keep out unwanted animals
EXCLUDE vb keep out, leave out
EXCLUDED > EXCLUDE
EXCLUDEE > EXCLUDE
EXCLUDEES > EXCLUDE
EXCLUDER > EXCLUDE
EXCLUDERS > EXCLUDE
EXCLUDES > EXCLUDE
EXCLUDING prep excepting
EXCLUSION n act or an instance of excluding or the state of being excluded
EXCLUSIVE adj excluding everything else ▷ n story reported in only one newspaper
EXCLUSORY > EXCLUSIVE
EXCORIATE vb censure severely
EXCREMENT n waste matter discharged from the body
EXCRETA n excrement
EXCRETAL > EXCRETA
EXCRETE vb discharge (waste matter) from the body
EXCRETED > EXCRETE
EXCRETER > EXCRETE
EXCRETERS > EXCRETE
EXCRETES > EXCRETE
EXCRETING > EXCRETE
EXCRETION > EXCRETE
EXCRETIVE > EXCRETE
EXCRETORY > EXCRETE
EXCUBANT adj keeping guard
EXCUDIT sentence substitute (named person) made this
EXCULPATE vb free from blame or guilt
EXCURRENT adj having an outward flow, as certain pores in sponges, ducts, etc
EXCURSE vb wander
EXCURSED > EXCURSE
EXCURSES > EXCURSE
EXCURSING > EXCURSE
EXCURSION n short journey, esp for pleasure
EXCURSIVE adj tending to digress
EXCURSUS n incidental digression from the main topic under discussion or from the main story in a narrative

EXCUSABLE > EXCUSE
EXCUSABLY > EXCUSE
EXCUSAL > EXCUSE
EXCUSALS > EXCUSE
EXCUSE n explanation offered to justify (a fault etc) ▷ vb put forward a reason or justification for (a fault etc)
EXCUSED > EXCUSE
EXCUSER > EXCUSE
EXCUSERS > EXCUSE
EXCUSES > EXCUSE
EXCUSING > EXCUSE
EXCUSIVE adj excusing
EXEAT n leave of absence from school or some other institution
EXEATS > EXEAT
EXEC n executive
EXECRABLE adj of very poor quality
EXECRABLY > EXECRABLE
EXECRATE vb feel and express loathing and hatred of (someone or something)
EXECRATED > EXECRATE
EXECRATES > EXECRATE
EXECRATOR > EXECRATE
EXECS > EXEC
EXECUTANT n performer, esp of musical works
EXECUTARY n person whose job comprises tasks appropriate to a middle-management executive as well as those traditionally carried out by a secretary
EXECUTE vb put (a condemned person) to death
EXECUTED > EXECUTE
EXECUTER > EXECUTE
EXECUTERS > EXECUTE
EXECUTES > EXECUTE
EXECUTING > EXECUTE
EXECUTION n act of executing
EXECUTIVE n person or group in an administrative position ▷ adj having the function of carrying out plans, orders, laws, etc
EXECUTOR n person appointed to perform the instructions of a will
EXECUTORS > EXECUTOR
EXECUTORY adj (of a law, agreement, etc) coming into operation at a future date
EXECUTRIX n female executor
EXECUTRY n condition of being an executor
EXED > EX
EXEDRA n building, room, portico, or apse containing a continuous bench, used in ancient Greece and Rome for holding discussions

EXEDRAE > EXEDRA
EXEEM same as > EXEME
EXEEMED > EXEEM
EXEEMING > EXEEM
EXEEMS > EXEEM
EXEGESES > EXEGESIS
EXEGESIS n explanation of a text, esp of the Bible
EXEGETE n person who practises exegesis
EXEGETES > EXEGETE
EXEGETIC adj of or relating to exegesis
EXEGETICS n scientific study of exegesis and exegetical methods
EXEGETIST same as > EXEGETE
EXEME vb set free
EXEMED > EXEME
EXEMES > EXEME
EXEMING > EXEME
EXEMPLA > EXEMPLUM
EXEMPLAR n person or thing to be copied, model
EXEMPLARS > EXEMPLAR
EXEMPLARY adj being a good example
EXEMPLE same as > EXAMPLE
EXEMPLES > EXEMPLE
EXEMPLIFY vb show an example of
EXEMPLUM n anecdote that supports a moral point or sustains an argument, used esp in medieval sermons
EXEMPT adj not subject to an obligation etc ▷ vb release from an obligation etc ▷ n person who is exempt from an obligation, tax, etc
EXEMPTED > EXEMPT
EXEMPTING > EXEMPT
EXEMPTION > EXEMPT
EXEMPTIVE > EXEMPT
EXEMPTS > EXEMPT
EXEQUATUR n official authorization issued by a host country to a consular agent, permitting him to perform his official duties
EXEQUIAL > EXEQUY
EXEQUIES > EXEQUY
EXEQUY n funeral rite
EXERCISE n activity to train the body or mind ▷ vb make use of
EXERCISED > EXERCISE
EXERCISER n device with springs or elasticated cords for muscular exercise
EXERCISES > EXERCISE
EXERCYCLE n exercise bicycle
EXERGIES > EXERGY
EXERGONIC adj (of a biochemical reaction) producing energy and therefore occurring spontaneously
EXERGUAL > EXERGUE
EXERGUE n space on the

reverse of a coin or medal below the central design, often containing the date, place of minting, etc
EXERGUES > EXERGUE
EXERGY n maximum amount of useful work obtainable from a system
EXERT vb use (influence, authority, etc) forcefully or effectively
EXERTED > EXERT
EXERTING > EXERT
EXERTION > EXERT
EXERTIONS > EXERT
EXERTIVE > EXERT
EXERTS > EXERT
EXES > EX
EXEUNT vb (they) go out
EXFOLIANT n cosmetic removing dead skin
EXFOLIATE vb peel in scales or layers
EXHALABLE > EXHALE
EXHALANT adj emitting a vapour or liquid ▷ n organ or vessel that emits a vapour or liquid
EXHALANTS > EXHALANT
EXHALE vb breathe out
EXHALED > EXHALE
EXHALENT same as > EXHALANT
EXHALENTS > EXHALENT
EXHALES > EXHALE
EXHALING > EXHALE
EXHAUST vb tire out ▷ n gases ejected from an engine as waste products
EXHAUSTED > EXHAUST
EXHAUSTER > EXHAUST
EXHAUSTS > EXHAUST
EXHEDRA same as > EXEDRA
EXHEDRAE > EXHEDRA
EXHIBIT vb display to the public ▷ n object exhibited to the public
EXHIBITED > EXHIBIT
EXHIBITER > EXHIBIT
EXHIBITOR n person or thing that exhibits
EXHIBITS > EXHIBIT
EXHORT vb urge earnestly
EXHORTED > EXHORT
EXHORTER > EXHORT
EXHORTERS > EXHORT
EXHORTING > EXHORT
EXHORTS > EXHORT
EXHUMATE same as > EXHUME
EXHUMATED > EXHUMATE
EXHUMATES > EXHUMATE
EXHUME vb dig up (something buried, esp a corpse)
EXHUMED > EXHUME
EXHUMER > EXHUME
EXHUMERS > EXHUME
EXHUMES > EXHUME
EXHUMING > EXHUME
EXIES n hysterics
EXIGEANT adj exacting
EXIGEANTE same as

> EXIGEANT
EXIGENCE same as > EXIGENCY
EXIGENCES > EXIGENCE
EXIGENCY n urgent demand or need
EXIGENT adj urgent ▷ n emergency
EXIGENTLY > EXIGENT
EXIGENTS > EXIGENT
EXIGIBLE adj liable to be exacted or required
EXIGUITY > EXIGUOUS
EXIGUOUS adj scanty or meagre
EXILABLE > EXILE
EXILE n prolonged, usu. enforced, absence from one's country ▷ vb expel from one's country
EXILED > EXILE
EXILEMENT same as > EXILE
EXILER > EXILE
EXILERS > EXILE
EXILES > EXILE
EXILIAN > EXILE
EXILIC > EXILE
EXILING > EXILE
EXILITIES > EXILITY
EXILITY n poverty or meagreness
EXIMIOUS adj select and distinguished
EXINE n outermost coat of a pollen grain or a spore
EXINES > EXINE
EXING > EX
EXIST vb have being or reality
EXISTED > EXIST
EXISTENCE n fact or state of being real, live, or actual
EXISTENT adj in existence ▷ n person or a thing that exists
EXISTENTS > EXISTENT
EXISTING > EXIST
EXISTS > EXIST
EXIT n way out ▷ vb go out
EXITANCE n measure of the ability of a surface to emit radiation
EXITANCES > EXITANCE
EXITED > EXIT
EXITING > EXIT
EXITLESS > EXIT
EXITS > EXIT
EXO informal word for > EXCELLENT
EXOCARP same as > EPICARP
EXOCARPS > EXOCARP
EXOCRINE adj relating to a gland, such as the sweat gland, that secretes externally through a duct ▷ n exocrine gland
EXOCRINES > EXOCRINE
EXOCYCLIC adj (of a sea urchin) having the anus situated outside the apical disc
EXOCYTIC adj outside

biological cell

EXOCYTOSE vb secrete substance from within cell

EXODE n exodus

EXODERM same as > ECTODERM

EXODERMAL > EXODERM

EXODERMIS same as > ECTODERM

EXODERMS > EXODERM

EXODES > EXODE

EXODIC > EXODE

EXODISTS > EXODUS

EXODOI > EXODOS

EXODONTIA n branch of dental surgery concerned with the extraction of teeth

EXODOS n processional song performed at the end of a play

EXODUS n departure of a large number of people

EXODUSES > EXODUS

EXOENZYME n extracellular enzyme

EXOERGIC adj (of a nuclear reaction) occurring with evolution of energy

EXOGAMIC > EXOGAMY

EXOGAMIES > EXOGAMY

EXOGAMOUS > EXOGAMY

EXOGAMY n custom or an act of marrying a person belonging to another tribe, clan, or similar social unit

EXOGEN n plant with a stem that develops through the growth of new layers on its outside

EXOGENISM > EXOGENOUS

EXOGENOUS adj having an external origin

EXOGENS > EXOGEN

EXOMION same as > EXOMIS

EXOMIONS > EXOMION

EXOMIS n sleeveless jacket

EXOMISES > EXOMIS

EXON n one of the four officers who command the Yeomen of the Guard

EXONERATE vb free from blame or a criminal charge

EXONIC > EXON

EXONS > EXON

EXONUMIA n objects of interest to numismatists that are not coins, such as medals and tokens

EXONUMIST n collector of medals and tokens

EXONYM n name given to a place by foreigners

EXONYMS > EXONYM

EXOPHAGY n (among cannibals) custom of eating only members of other tribes

EXOPHORIC adj denoting or relating to a pronoun such as "I" or "you", the meaning of which is determined by reference

outside the discourse rather than by a preceding or following expression

EXOPLANET n planet that orbits a star in a solar system other than that of Earth

EXOPLASM another name for > ECTOPLASM

EXOPLASMS > EXOPLASM

EXOPOD same as > EXOPODITE

EXOPODITE n outer projection on the hind legs of some crustaceans

EXOPODS > EXOPOD

EXORABLE adj able to be persuaded or moved by pleading

EXORATION n plea

EXORCISE same as > EXORCIZE

EXORCISED > EXORCISE

EXORCISER > EXORCISE

EXORCISES > EXORCISE

EXORCISM > EXORCIZE

EXORCISMS > EXORCIZE

EXORCIST > EXORCIZE

EXORCISTS > EXORCIZE

EXORCIZE vb expel (evil spirits) by prayers and religious rites

EXORCIZED > EXORCIZE

EXORCIZER > EXORCIZE

EXORCIZES > EXORCIZE

EXORDIA > EXORDIUM

EXORDIAL > EXORDIUM

EXORDIUM n introductory part or beginning, esp of an oration or discourse

EXORDIUMS > EXORDIUM

EXOSMIC > EXOSMOSIS

EXOSMOSE same as > EXOSMOSIS

EXOSMOSES > EXOSMOSIS

EXOSMOSIS n osmosis in which water flows from a cell or organism into the surrounding solution

EXOSMOTIC > EXOSMOSIS

EXOSPHERE n outermost layer of the earth's atmosphere

EXOSPORAL > EXOSPORE

EXOSPORE n outer layer of the spores of some algae and fungi

EXOSPORES > EXOSPORE

EXOSPORIA n exospores

EXOSTOSES > EXOSTOSIS

EXOSTOSIS n abnormal bony outgrowth from the surface of a bone

EXOTERIC adj intelligible to or intended for more than a select or initiated minority

EXOTIC adj having a strange allure or beauty ▷ n non-native plant

EXOTICA npl (collection of) exotic objects

EXOTICISM > EXOTIC

EXOTICIST > EXOTIC

EXOTICS > EXOTIC

EXOTISM > EXOTIC

EXOTISMS > EXOTIC

EXOTOXIC > EXOTOXIN

EXOTOXIN n toxin produced by a microorganism and secreted into the surrounding medium

EXOTOXINS > EXOTOXIN

EXOTROPIA n condition in which eye turns outwards

EXOTROPIC > EXOTROPIA

EXPAND vb make or become larger

EXPANDED adj (of printer's type) wider than usual for a particular height

EXPANDER n device for exercising and developing the muscles of the body

EXPANDERS > EXPANDER

EXPANDING > EXPAND

EXPANDOR same as > EXPANDER

EXPANDORS > EXPANDOR

EXPANDS > EXPAND

EXPANSE n uninterrupted wide area

EXPANSES > EXPANSE

EXPANSILE adj able to expand or cause expansion

EXPANSION n act of expanding

EXPANSIVE adj wide or extensive

EXPAT n short for

EXPATIATE vb speak or write at great length (on)

EXPATS > EXPAT

EXPECT vb regard as probable

EXPECTANT adj expecting or hopeful ▷ n person who expects something

EXPECTED > EXPECT

EXPECTER n person who expects

EXPECTERS > EXPECTER

EXPECTING adj pregnant

EXPECTS > EXPECT

EXPEDIENT n something that achieves a particular purpose ▷ adj suitable to the circumstances, appropriate

EXPEDITE vb hasten the progress of ▷ adj unimpeded or prompt

EXPEDITED > EXPEDITE

EXPEDITER n person who expedites something, esp a person employed in an industry to ensure that work on each job progresses efficiently

EXPEDITES > EXPEDITE

EXPEDITOR same as > EXPEDITER

EXPEL vb drive out with force

EXPELLANT adj forcing

out or having the capacity to force out ▷ n medicine used to expel undesirable substances or organisms from the body, esp worms from the digestive tract

EXPELLED > EXPEL

EXPELLEE > EXPEL

EXPELLEES > EXPEL

EXPELLENT same as > EXPELLANT

EXPELLER > EXPEL

EXPELLERS npl residue remaining after an oilseed has been crushed to expel the oil, used for animal fodder

EXPELLING > EXPEL

EXPELS > EXPEL

EXPEND vb spend, use up

EXPENDED > EXPEND

EXPENDER > EXPEND

EXPENDERS > EXPEND

EXPENDING > EXPEND

EXPENDS > EXPEND

EXPENSE n cost

EXPENSED > EXPENSE

EXPENSES > EXPENSE

EXPENSING > EXPENSE

EXPENSIVE adj high-priced

EXPERT n person with extensive skill or knowledge in a particular field ▷ adj skilful or knowledgeable ▷ vb experience

EXPERTED > EXPERT

EXPERTING > EXPERT

EXPERTISE same as > EXPERTIZE

EXPERTISM > EXPERTIZE

EXPERTIZE vb act as an expert or give an expert opinion (on)

EXPERTLY > EXPERT

EXPERTS > EXPERT

EXPIABLE adj capable of being expiated or atoned for

EXPIATE vb make amends for

EXPIATED > EXPIATE

EXPIATES > EXPIATE

EXPIATING > EXPIATE

EXPIATION n act, process, or a means of expiating

EXPIATOR > EXPIATE

EXPIATORS > EXPIATE

EXPIATORY adj capable of making expiation

EXPIRABLE > EXPIRE

EXPIRANT n one who expires

EXPIRANTS > EXPIRANT

EXPIRE vb finish or run out

EXPIRED > EXPIRE

EXPIRER > EXPIRE

EXPIRERS > EXPIRE

EXPIRES > EXPIRE

EXPIRIES > EXPIRY

EXPIRING > EXPIRE

EXPIRY n end, esp of a contract period

EXPISCATE vb find; fish out

EXPLAIN vb make clear and intelligible

EXPLAINED > EXPLAIN

EXPLAINER > EXPLAIN

EXPLAINS > EXPLAIN

EXPLANT vb transfer (living tissue) from its natural site to a new site or to a culture medium ▷ n piece of tissue treated in this way

EXPLANTED > EXPLANT

EXPLANTS > EXPLANT

EXPLETIVE n swearword ▷ adj expressing no particular meaning, esp when filling out a line of verse

EXPLETORY adj expletive

EXPLICATE vb explain

EXPLICIT adj precisely and clearly expressed ▷ n word used to indicate the end of a book

EXPLICITS > EXPLICIT

EXPLODE vb burst with great violence, blow up

EXPLODED > EXPLODE

EXPLODER > EXPLODE

EXPLODERS > EXPLODE

EXPLODES > EXPLODE

EXPLODING > EXPLODE

EXPLOIT vb take advantage of for one's own purposes ▷ n notable feat or deed

EXPLOITED > EXPLOIT

EXPLOITER > EXPLOIT

EXPLOITS > EXPLOIT

EXPLORE vb investigate

EXPLORED > EXPLORE

EXPLORER > EXPLORE

EXPLORERS > EXPLORE

EXPLORES > EXPLORE

EXPLORING > EXPLORE

EXPLOSION n exploding

EXPLOSIVE adj tending to explode ▷ n substance that causes explosions

EXPO n exposition, large public exhibition

EXPONENT n person who advocates an idea, cause, etc ▷ adj offering a declaration, explanation, or interpretation

EXPONENTS > EXPONENT

EXPONIBLE adj able to be explained

EXPORT n selling or shipping of goods to a foreign country ▷ vb sell or ship (goods) to a foreign country

EXPORTED > EXPORT

EXPORTER > EXPORT

EXPORTERS > EXPORT

EXPORTING > EXPORT

EXPORTS > EXPORT

EXPOS > EXPO

EXPOSABLE > EXPOSE

EXPOSAL > EXPOSE

EXPOSALS > EXPOSE

EXPOSE vb uncover or reveal ▷ n bringing of a crime, scandal, etc to public notice

EXPOSED adj not concealed

EXPOSER > EXPOSE

EXPOSERS > EXPOSE

EXPOSES > EXPOSE

EXPOSING > EXPOSE

EXPOSIT vb state

EXPOSITED > EXPOSIT

EXPOSITOR n person who expounds

EXPOSITS > EXPOSIT

EXPOSTURE n exposure

EXPOSURE n exposing

EXPOSURES > EXPOSURE

EXPOUND vb explain in detail

EXPOUNDED > EXPOUND

EXPOUNDER > EXPOUND

EXPOUNDS > EXPOUND

EXPRESS vb put into words ▷ adj explicitly stated ▷ n fast train or bus stopping at only a few stations ▷ adv by express delivery

EXPRESSED > EXPRESS

EXPRESSER > EXPRESS

EXPRESSES > EXPRESS

EXPRESSLY adv definitely

EXPRESSO variant of > ESPRESSO

EXPRESSOS > ESPRESSO

EXPUGN vb storm

EXPUGNED > EXPUGN

EXPUGNING > EXPUGN

EXPUGNS > EXPUGN

EXPULSE vb expel

EXPULSED > EXPULSE

EXPULSES > EXPULSE

EXPULSING > EXPULSE

EXPULSION n act of expelling or the fact of being expelled

EXPULSIVE adj tending or serving to expel

EXPUNCT vb expunge

EXPUNCTED > EXPUNCT

EXPUNCTS > EXPUNCT

EXPUNGE vb delete, erase, blot out

EXPUNGED > EXPUNGE

EXPUNGER > EXPUNGE

EXPUNGERS > EXPUNGE

EXPUNGES > EXPUNGE

EXPUNGING > EXPUNGE

EXPURGATE vb remove objectionable parts from (a book etc)

EXPURGE vb purge

EXPURGED > EXPURGE

EXPURGES > EXPURGE

EXPURGING > EXPURGE

EXQUISITE adj of extreme beauty or delicacy ▷ n dandy

EXSCIND vb cut off or out

EXSCINDED > EXSCIND

EXSCINDS > EXSCIND

EXSECANT n trigonometric function

EXSECANTS > EXSECANT

EXSECT vb cut out

EXSECTED > EXSECT

EXSECTING > EXSECT

EXSECTION > EXSECT

EXSECTS > EXSECT

EXSERT vb thrust out ▷ adj protruded, stretched out, or (esp of stamens) projecting beyond the corolla of a flower

EXSERTED > EXSERT

EXSERTILE > EXSERT

EXSERTING > EXSERT

EXSERTION > EXSERT

EXSERTS > EXSERT

EXSICCANT > EXSICCATE

EXSICCATE vb dry up

EXSTROPHY n congenital eversion of a hollow organ, esp the urinary bladder

EXSUCCOUS adj without sap or juice

EXTANT adj still existing

EXTASIES > EXTASY

EXTASY same as > ECSTASY

EXTATIC same as > ECSTATIC

EXTEMPORE adj without planning or preparation ▷ adv without planning or preparation

EXTEND vb draw out or be drawn out, stretch

EXTENDANT adj (in heraldry) with wings spread

EXTENDED > EXTEND

EXTENDER n person or thing that extends

EXTENDERS > EXTENDER

EXTENDING > EXTEND

EXTENDS > EXTEND

EXTENSE adj extensive

EXTENSILE adj capable of being extended

EXTENSION n room or rooms added to an existing building ▷ adj denoting something that can be extended or that extends another object

EXTENSITY n that part of sensory perception relating to the spatial aspect of objects

EXTENSIVE adj having a large extent, widespread

EXTENSOR n muscle that extends a part of the body

EXTENSORS > EXTENSOR

EXTENT n range over which something extends, area

EXTENTS > EXTENT

EXTENUATE vb make (an offence or fault) less blameworthy

EXTERIOR n part or surface on the outside ▷ adj of, on, or coming from the outside

EXTERIORS > EXTERIOR

EXTERMINE vb exterminate

EXTERN n person, such as a physician at a hospital, who has an official connection with an institution but does not reside in it

EXTERNAL adj of, situated on, or coming from the outside ▷ n external circumstance or aspect, esp one that is superficial or inessential

EXTERNALS > EXTERNAL

EXTERNAT n day school

EXTERNATS > EXTERNAT

EXTERNE same as > EXTERN

EXTERNES > EXTERNE

EXTERNS > EXTERN

EXTINCT adj having died out ▷ vb extinguish

EXTINCTED > EXTINCT

EXTINCTS > EXTINCT

EXTINE same as > EXINE

EXTINES > EXTINE

EXTIRP vb extirpate

EXTIRPATE vb destroy utterly

EXTIRPED > EXTIRP

EXTIRPING > EXTIRP

EXTIRPS > EXTIRP

EXTOL vb praise highly

EXTOLD archaic past participle of > EXTOL

EXTOLL same as > EXTOL

EXTOLLED > EXTOLL

EXTOLLER > EXTOL

EXTOLLERS > EXTOL

EXTOLLING > EXTOLL

EXTOLLS > EXTOLL

EXTOLMENT > EXTOL

EXTOLS > EXTOL

EXTORSIVE adj intended or tending to extort

EXTORT vb get (something) by force or threats

EXTORTED > EXTORT

EXTORTER > EXTORT

EXTORTERS > EXTORT

EXTORTING > EXTORT

EXTORTION n act of securing money, favours, etc by intimidation or violence

EXTORTIVE > EXTORT

EXTORTS > EXTORT

EXTRA adj more than is usual, expected or needed ▷ n additional person or thing ▷ adv unusually or exceptionally

EXTRABOLD n very bold typeface

EXTRACT vb pull out by force ▷ n something extracted, such as a passage from a book etc

EXTRACTED > EXTRACT

EXTRACTOR n person or thing that extracts

EXTRACTS > EXTRACT

EXTRADITE vb send (an accused person) back to his or her own country for trial

EXTRADOS n outer curve or surface of an arch or vault
EXTRAIT n extracts
EXTRAITS > EXTRAIT
EXTRALITY n diplomatic immunity
EXTRANET n intranet that is modified to allow outsiders access to it, esp one belonging to a business that allows access to customers
EXTRANETS > EXTRANET
EXTRAPOSE vb move (a word or words) to the end of a clause or sentence
EXTRAS > EXTRA
EXTRAUGHT old past participle of > EXTRACT
EXTRAVERT same as > EXTROVERT
EXTREAT n extraction
EXTREATS > EXTREAT
EXTREMA > EXTREMUM
EXTREMAL n clause in a recursive definition that specifies that no items other than those generated by the stated rules fall within the definition
EXTREMALS > EXTREMAL
EXTREME adj of a high or the highest degree or intensity ▷ n either of the two limits of a scale or range
EXTREMELY > EXTREME
EXTREMER > EXTREME
EXTREMES > EXTREME
EXTREMEST > EXTREME
EXTREMISM > EXTREMIST
EXTREMIST n person who favours immoderate methods ▷ adj holding extreme opinions
EXTREMITY n farthest point
EXTREMUM n extreme point
EXTRICATE vb free from complication or difficulty
EXTRINSIC adj not contained or included within
EXTRORSAL same as > EXTRORSE
EXTRORSE adj turned or opening outwards or away from the axis
EXTROVERT adj lively and outgoing ▷ n extrovert person
EXTRUDE vb squeeze or force out
EXTRUDED > EXTRUDE
EXTRUDER > EXTRUDE
EXTRUDERS > EXTRUDE
EXTRUDES > EXTRUDE
EXTRUDING > EXTRUDE
EXTRUSILE adj being thrust or forced out
EXTRUSION n act or process of extruding
EXTRUSIVE adj tending to

extrude
EXTRUSORY > EXTRUDE
EXTUBATE vb remove tube from hollow organ
EXTUBATED > EXTUBATE
EXTUBATES > EXTUBATE
EXUBERANT adj high-spirited
EXUBERATE vb be exuberant
EXUDATE same as > EXUDATION
EXUDATES > EXUDATE
EXUDATION n act of exuding or oozing out
EXUDATIVE > EXUDATION
EXUDE vb (of a liquid or smell) seep or flow out slowly and steadily
EXUDED > EXUDE
EXUDES > EXUDE
EXUDING > EXUDE
EXUL n exile
EXULS > EXUL
EXULT vb be joyful or jubilant
EXULTANCE > EXULTANT
EXULTANCY > EXULTANT
EXULTANT adj elated or jubilant, esp because of triumph or success
EXULTED > EXULT
EXULTING > EXULT
EXULTS > EXULT
EXURB n residential area beyond suburbs
EXURBAN > EXURBIA
EXURBIA n region outside the suburbs of a city, consisting of residential areas that are occupied predominantly by rich commuters
EXURBIAS > EXURBIA
EXURBS > EXURB
EXUVIA n cast-off exoskeleton of animal
EXUVIAE > EXUVIA
EXUVIAL > EXUVIA
EXUVIATE vb shed (a skin or similar outer covering)
EXUVIATED > EXUVIATE
EXUVIATES > EXUVIATE
EXUVIUM n cast-off exoskeleton of animal
EYALET n province of Ottoman Empire
EYALETS > EYALET
EYAS n nestling hawk or falcon, esp one reared for training in falconry
EYASES > EYAS
EYASS same as > EYAS
EYASSES > EYASS
EYE n organ of sight ▷ vb look at carefully or warily
EYEABLE adj pleasant to look at
EYEBALL n ball-shaped part of the eye ▷ vb eye
EYEBALLED > EYEBALL
EYEBALLS > EYEBALL
EYEBANK n place in which

corneas are stored for use in corneal grafts
EYEBANKS > EYEBANK
EYEBAR n bar with flattened ends with holes for connecting pins
EYEBARS > EYEBAR
EYEBATH same as > EYECUP
EYEBATHS > EYEBATH
EYEBEAM n glance
EYEBEAMS > EYEBEAM
EYEBLACK another name for > MASCARA
EYEBLACKS > EYEBLACK
EYEBLINK n very small amount of time
EYEBLINKS > EYEBLINK
EYEBOLT n threaded bolt, the head of which is formed into a ring or eye for lifting, pulling, or securing
EYEBOLTS > EYEBOLT
EYEBRIGHT n type of plant with small white-and-purple flowers, formerly used to treat eye disorders
EYEBROW n line of hair on the bony ridge above the eye ▷ vb equip with artificial eyebrows
EYEBROWED > EYEBROW
EYEBROWS > EYEBROW
EYECUP same as > EYEBATH
EYECUPS > EYECUP
EYED > EYE
EYEDNESS > EYE
EYEDROPS n medicine applied to the eyes in drops
EYEFOLD n fold of skin above eye
EYEFOLDS > EYEFOLD
EYEFUL n view
EYEFULS > EYEFUL
EYEGLASS n lens for aiding defective vision
EYEHOLE n hole through which something, such as a rope, hook, or bar, is passed
EYEHOLES > EYEHOLE
EYEHOOK n hook attached to a ring at the extremity of a rope or chain
EYEHOOKS > EYEHOOK
EYEING > EYE
EYELASH n short hair that grows out from the eyelid
EYELASHES > EYELASH
EYELESS > EYE
EYELET n small hole for a lace or cord to be passed through ▷ vb supply with an eyelet or eyelets
EYELETED > EYELET
EYELETEER n small bodkin or other pointed tool for making eyelet holes
EYELETING > EYELET
EYELETS > EYELET
EYELETTED > EYELET
EYELEVEL adj level with a person's eyes
EYELIAD same as

> OEILLADE
EYELIADS > EYELIAD
EYELID n fold of skin that covers the eye when it is closed
EYELIDS > EYELID
EYELIFT n cosmetic surgery for eyes
EYELIFTS > EYELIFT
EYELIKE > EYE
EYELINER n cosmetic used to outline the eyes
EYELINERS > EYELINER
EYEN npl eyes
EYEOPENER n something surprising
EYEPIECE n lens in a microscope, telescope, etc, into which the person using it looks
EYEPIECES > EYEPIECE
EYEPOINT n position of a lens at which the sharpest image is obtained
EYEPOINTS > EYEPOINT
EYEPOPPER n something that excites the eye
EYER n someone who eyes
EYERS > EYER
EYES > EYE
EYESHADE n opaque or tinted translucent visor, worn on the head like a cap to protect the eyes from glare
EYESHADES > EYESHADE
EYESHADOW n coloured cosmetic put around the eyes so as to enhance their colour or shape
EYESHINE n reflection of light from animal eye at night
EYESHINES > EYESHINE
EYESHOT n range of vision
EYESHOTS > EYESHOT
EYESIGHT n ability to see
EYESIGHTS > EYESIGHT
EYESOME adj attractive
EYESORE n ugly object
EYESORES > EYESORE
EYESPOT n small area of light-sensitive pigment in some protozoans, algae, and other simple organisms
EYESPOTS > EYESPOT
EYESTALK n movable stalk bearing a compound eye at its tip: occurs in crustaceans and some molluscs
EYESTALKS > EYESTALK
EYESTONE n device for removing foreign body from eye
EYESTONES > EYESTONE
EYESTRAIN n fatigue or irritation of the eyes, caused by tiredness or a failure to wear glasses
EYETEETH > EYETOOTH
EYETOOTH n either of the two canine teeth in the upper jaw

EYEWASH *n* nonsense

EYEWASHES > EYEWASH

EYEWATER *n* lotion for the eyes

EYEWATERS > EYEWATER

EYEWEAR *n* spectacles; glasses

EYEWEARS > EYEWEAR

EYEWINK *n* wink of the eye; instant

EYEWINKS > EYEWINK

EYING > EYE

EYLIAD *same as* **>** OEILLADE

EYLIADS > EYLIAD

EYNE *poetic plural of* **>** EYE

EYOT *n* island

EYOTS > EYOT

EYRA *n* reddish-brown variety of the jaguarondi

EYRAS > EYRA

EYRE *n* any of the circuit courts held in each shire from 1176 until the late 13th century

EYRES > EYRE

EYRIE *n* nest of an eagle

EYRIES > EYRIE

EYRIR *n* Icelandic monetary unit worth one hundredth of a krona

EYRY *same as* **>** EYRIE

Ff

FA *same as* > FAH
FAA *Scot word for* > FALL
FAAING > FAA
FAAN > FAA
FAAS > FAA
FAB *adj* excellent ▷ *n* fabrication
FABACEOUS *adj* belonging to the legume family of flowering plants which includes peas and beans
FABBER > FAB
FABBEST > FAB
FABBIER > FABBY
FABBIEST > FABBY
FABBY *same as* > FAB
FABLE *n* story with a moral ▷ *vb* relate or tell (fables)
FABLED *adj* made famous in legend
FABLER > FABLE
FABLERS > FABLE
FABLES > FABLE
FABLIAU *n* comic usually ribald verse tale, of a kind popular in France in the 12th and 13th centuries
FABLIAUX > FABLIAU
FABLING > FABLE
FABLINGS > FABLE
FABRIC *n* knitted or woven cloth
FABRICANT *n* manufacturer
FABRICATE *vb* make up (a story or lie)
FABRICKED *adj* built
FABRICS > FABRIC
FABS > FAB
FABULAR *adj* relating to fables
FABULATE *vb* make up fables
FABULATED > FABULATE
FABULATES > FABULATE
FABULATOR > FABULATE
FABULISE *vb* make up fables
FABULISED > FABULISE
FABULISES > FABULISE
FABULIST *n* person who invents or recounts fables
FABULISTS > FABULIST
FABULIZE *vb* make up fables
FABULIZED > FABULIZE
FABULIZES > FABULIZE
FABULOUS *adj* excellent
FABURDEN *n* early form of counterpoint
FABURDENS > FABURDEN

FACADE *n* front of a building
FACADES > FACADE
FACE *n* front of the head ▷ *vb* look or turn towards
FACEABLE > FACE
FACEBAR *n* wrestling hold in which a wrestler stretches the skin on his opponent's face backwards
FACEBARS > FACEBAR
FACEBOOK *vb* search for (someone) on the Facebook website
FACEBOOKS > FACEBOOK
FACECLOTH *n* small piece of cloth used to wash the face and hands
FACED > FACE
FACEDOWN *vb* confront and force (someone or something) to back down
FACEDOWNS > FACEDOWN
FACELESS *adj* impersonal, anonymous
FACELIFT *n* cosmetic surgery for the face
FACELIFTS > FACELIFT
FACEMAIL *n* computer program which uses an electronically generated face to deliver messages on screen
FACEMAILS > FACEMAIL
FACEMAN *n* miner who works at the coalface
FACEMASK *n* protective mask for the face
FACEMASKS > FACEMASK
FACEMEN > FACEMAN
FACEPLATE *n* perforated circular metal plate that can be attached to the headstock of a lathe in order to hold flat or irregularly shaped workpieces
FACEPRINT *n* digitally recorded representation of a person's face that can be used for security purposes because it is as individual as a fingerprint
FACER *n* difficulty or problem
FACERS > FACER
FACES > FACE
FACET *n* aspect ▷ *vb* cut facets in (a gemstone)
FACETE *adj* witty and humorous

FACETED > FACET
FACETELY > FACETE
FACETIAE *npl* humorous or witty sayings
FACETING > FACET
FACETIOUS *adj* funny or trying to be funny, esp at inappropriate times
FACETS > FACET
FACETTED > FACET
FACETTING > FACET
FACEUP *adj* with the face or surface exposed
FACIA *same as* > FASCIA
FACIAE > FACIA
FACIAL *adj* of or relating to the face ▷ *n* beauty treatment for the face
FACIALIST *n* beautician who specializes in treatments for the face
FACIALLY > FACIAL
FACIALS > FACIAL
FACIAS > FACIA
FACIEND *n* multiplicand
FACIENDS > FACIEND
FACIES *n* general form and appearance of an individual or a group of plants or animals
FACILE *adj* (of a remark, argument, etc) superficial and showing lack of real thought
FACILELY > FACILE
FACILITY *n* skill
FACING *n* lining or covering for decoration or reinforcement
FACINGS > FACING
FACONNE *adj* denoting a fabric with the design woven in ▷ *n* such a fabric
FACONNES > FACONNE
FACSIMILE *n* exact copy ▷ *vb* make an exact copy of
FACT *n* event or thing known to have happened or existed
FACTFUL > FACT
FACTICE *n* soft rubbery material made by reacting sulphur or sulphur chloride with vegetable oil
FACTICES > FACTICE
FACTICITY *n* philosophical process
FACTION *n* (dissenting) minority group within a larger body
FACTIONAL > FACTION

FACTIONS > FACTION
FACTIOUS *adj* of or producing factions
FACTIS *variant of* > FACTICE
FACTISES > FACTIS
FACTITIVE *adj* denoting a verb taking a direct object as well as a noun in apposition, as for example *elect* in *They elected John president*, where *John* is the direct object and *president* is the complement
FACTIVE *adj* (of a linguistic context) giving rise to the presupposition that a sentence occurring in that context is true, as *John regrets that Mary did not attend*
FACTOID *n* piece of unreliable information believed to be true because of the way it is presented or repeated in print
FACTOIDAL > FACTOID
FACTOIDS > FACTOID
FACTOR *n* element contributing to a result ▷ *vb* engage in the business of a factor
FACTORAGE *n* commission payable to a factor
FACTORED > FACTOR
FACTORIAL *n* product of all the integers from one to a given number ▷ *adj* of factorials or factors
FACTORIES > FACTORY
FACTORING *n* business of a factor
FACTORISE *same as* > FACTORIZE
FACTORIZE *vb* calculate the factors of (a number)
FACTORS > FACTOR
FACTORY *n* building where goods are manufactured
FACTOTUM *n* person employed to do all sorts of work
FACTOTUMS > FACTOTUM
FACTS > FACT
FACTSHEET *n* printed sheet containing information relating to items covered in a television or radio programme
FACTUAL *adj* concerning facts rather than opinions or theories

FACTUALLY > FACTUAL

FACTUM n something done, deed

FACTUMS > FACTUM

FACTURE n construction

FACTURES > FACTURE

FACULA n any of the bright areas on the sun's surface, usually appearing just before a sunspot and subject to the same 11-year cycle

FACULAE > FACULA

FACULAR > FACULA

FACULTIES > FACULTY

FACULTY n physical or mental ability

FACUNDITY n eloquence, fluency of speech

FAD n short-lived fashion

FADABLE > FADE

FADAISE n silly remark

FADAISES > FADAISE

FADDIER > FADDY

FADDIEST > FADDY

FADDINESS n excessive fussiness

FADDISH > FAD

FADDISHLY > FAD

FADDISM > FAD

FADDISMS > FAD

FADDIST > FAD

FADDISTS > FAD

FADDLE vb mess around, toy with

FADDLED > FADDLE

FADDLES > FADDLE

FADDLING > FADDLE

FADDY adj unreasonably fussy, particularly about food

FADE vb (cause to) lose brightness, colour, or strength ▷ n act or an instance of fading

FADEAWAY n fading to the point of disappearance

FADEAWAYS > FADEAWAY

FADED > FADE

FADEDLY > FADE

FADEDNESS > FADE

FADEIN n gradual appearance of image on film

FADEINS > FADEIN

FADELESS adj not subject to fading

FADEOUT n gradual disappearance of image on film

FADEOUTS > FADEOUT

FADER > FADE

FADERS > FADE

FADES > FADE

FADEUR n blandness, insipidness

FADEURS > FADEUR

FADGE vb agree ▷ n package of wool in a wool-bale that weighs less than 100 kilograms

FADGED > FADGE

FADGES > FADGE

FADGING > FADGE

FADIER > FADY

FADIEST > FADY

FADING n variation in the strength of received radio signals due to variations in the conditions of the transmission medium

FADINGS > FADING

FADLIKE > FAD

FADO n type of melancholy Portuguese folk song

FADOMETER n instrument used to determine the resistance to fading of a pigment or dye

FADOS > FADO

FADS > FAD

FADY adj faded

FAE Scot word for > FROM

FAECAL adj of, relating to, or consisting of faeces

FAECES npl waste matter discharged from the anus

FAENA n matador's final series of passes with sword and cape before the kill

FAENAS > FAENA

FAERIE n land of fairies

FAERIES > FAERY

FAERY same as > FAERIE

FAFF vb dither or fuss

FAFFED > FAFF

FAFFING > FAFF

FAFFS > FAFF

FAG same as > FAGGOT

FAGACEOUS adj relating to a family of trees, including beech, oak, and chestnut, whose fruit is enclosed in a husk

FAGGED > FAG

FAGGERIES > FAGGERY

FAGGERY n offensive term for homosexuality

FAGGIER > FAG

FAGGIEST > FAG

FAGGING > FAG

FAGGINGS > FAG

FAGGOT n ball of chopped liver, herbs, and bread ▷ vb collect into a bundle or bundles

FAGGOTED > FAGGOT

FAGGOTING n decorative needlework done by tying vertical threads together in bundles

FAGGOTRY n offensive term for homosexuality

FAGGOTS > FAGGOT

FAGGOTY > FAGGOT

FAGGY > FAG

FAGIN n criminal

FAGINS > FAGIN

FAGOT same as > FAGGOT

FAGOTED > FAGOT

FAGOTER > FAGOT

FAGOTERS > FAGOT

FAGOTING same as > FAGGOTING

FAGOTINGS > FAGOTING

FAGOTS > FAGOT

FAGOTTI > FAGOTTO

FAGOTTIST n bassoon player

FAGOTTO n bassoon

FAGS > FAG

FAH n (in tonic sol-fa) fourth degree of any major scale

FAHLBAND n thin bed of schistose rock impregnated with metallic sulphides

FAHLBANDS > FAHLBAND

FAHLERZ n copper ore

FAHLERZES > FAHLERZ

FAHLORE n copper ore

FAHLORES > FAHLORE

FAHS > FAH

FAIBLE variant of > FOIBLE

FAIBLES > FAIBLE

FAIENCE n tin-glazed earthenware

FAIENCES > FAIENCE

FAIK vb grasp

FAIKED > FAIK

FAIKES > FAIK

FAIKING > FAIK

FAIKS > FAIK

FAIL vb be unsuccessful ▷ n instance of not passing an exam or test

FAILED > FAIL

FAILING n weak point ▷ prep in the absence of

FAILINGLY > FAILING

FAILINGS > FAILING

FAILLE n soft light ribbed fabric of silk, rayon, or taffeta

FAILLES > FAILLE

FAILS > FAIL

FAILURE n act or instance of failing

FAILURES > FAILURE

FAIN adv gladly ▷ adj willing or eager

FAINE variant of > FAIN

FAINEANCE > FAINEANT

FAINEANCY > FAINEANT

FAINEANT n lazy person ▷ adj indolent

FAINEANTS > FAINEANT

FAINED > FAIN

FAINER > FAIN

FAINES > FAINE

FAINEST > FAIN

FAINING > FAIN

FAINITES interj cry for truce or respite from the rules of a game

FAINLY > FAIN

FAINNE n small ring-shaped metal badge worn by advocates of the Irish language

FAINNES > FAINNE

FAINNESS > FAIN

FAINS same as > FAINITES

FAINT adj lacking clarity, brightness, or volume ▷ vb lose consciousness temporarily ▷ n temporary loss of consciousness

FAINTED > FAINT

FAINTER > FAINT

FAINTERS > FAINT

FAINTEST > FAINT

FAINTIER > FAINTY

FAINTIEST > FAINTY

FAINTING > FAINT

FAINTINGS > FAINT

FAINTISH > FAINT

FAINTLY > FAINT

FAINTNESS > FAINT

FAINTS > FAINT

FAINTY > FAINT

FAIR adj unbiased and reasonable ▷ adv fairly ▷ n travelling entertainment with sideshows, rides, and amusements ▷ vb join together so as to form a smooth or regular shape or surface

FAIRED > FAIR

FAIRER > FAIR

FAIREST > FAIR

FAIRFACED adj (of brickwork) having a neat smooth unplastered surface

FAIRGOER n person attending fair

FAIRGOERS > FAIRGOER

FAIRIES > FAIRY

FAIRILY > FAIRY

FAIRING n curved metal structure fitted round part of a car, aircraft, etc to reduce drag

FAIRINGS > FAIRING

FAIRISH adj moderately good, well, etc

FAIRISHLY > FAIRISH

FAIRLEAD n block or ring through which a line is rove to keep it clear of obstructions, prevent chafing, or maintain it at an angle

FAIRLEADS > FAIRLEAD

FAIRLY adv moderately

FAIRNESS > FAIR

FAIRS > FAIR

FAIRWAY n smooth area between the tee and the green

FAIRWAYS > FAIRWAY

FAIRY n imaginary small creature with magic powers

FAIRYDOM > FAIRY

FAIRYDOMS > FAIRY

FAIRYHOOD > FAIRY

FAIRYISM > FAIRY

FAIRYISMS > FAIRY

FAIRYLAND n imaginary place where fairies live

FAIRYLIKE > FAIRY

FAIRYTALE n story about fairies or other mythical or magical beings, esp one of traditional origin told to children

FAITH n strong belief, esp without proof

FAITHED adj having faith or a faith

FAITHER Scot word for > FATHER

FAITHERS > FAITHER

FAITHFUL adj loyal

FAITHFULS > FAITHFUL
FAITHING n practising a faith
FAITHLESS adj disloyal or dishonest
FAITHS > FAITH
FAITOR n traitor, impostor
FAITORS > FAITOR
FAITOUR n impostor
FAITOURS > FAITOUR
FAIX interj have faith
FAJITA > FAJITAS
FAJITAS npl Mexican dish of soft tortillas wrapped around fried strips of meat or vegetables
FAKE vb cause something not genuine to appear real or more valuable by fraud ▷ n person, thing, or act that is not genuine ▷ adj not genuine
FAKED > FAKE
FAKEER same as > FAKIR
FAKEERS > FAKEER
FAKEMENT n something false, counterfeit
FAKEMENTS > FAKEMENT
FAKER > FAKE
FAKERIES > FAKE
FAKERY > FAKE
FAKES > FAKE
FAKEY adv (of a skateboarding or snowboarding manoeuvre) performed with the board facing backwards
FAKIE same as > FAKEY
FAKIER > FAKEY
FAKIES > FAKIE
FAKIEST > FAKEY
FAKING > FAKE
FAKIR n Muslim who spurns worldly possessions
FAKIRISM > FAKIR
FAKIRISMS > FAKIR
FAKIRS > FAKIR
FALAFEL n ball or cake of ground spiced chickpeas, deep-fried and often served with pitta bread
FALAFELS > FALAFEL
FALAJ n kind of irrigation channel in ancient Oman
FALANGISM > FALANGIST
FALANGIST n member of the Fascist movement founded in Spain in 1933
FALBALA n gathered flounce, frill, or ruffle
FALBALAS > FALBALA
FALCADE n movement of a horse
FALCADES > FALCADE
FALCATE adj shaped like a sickle
FALCATED > FALCATE
FALCATION > FALCATE
FALCES > FALX
FALCHION n short and slightly curved medieval sword broader towards the point

FALCHIONS > FALCHION
FALCIFORM same as > FALCATE
FALCON n small bird of prey
FALCONER n person who breeds or trains hawks or who follows the sport of falconry
FALCONERS > FALCONER
FALCONET n type of small falcons
FALCONETS > FALCONET
FALCONINE adj of, relating to, or resembling a falcon
FALCONOID n chemical thought to resist cancer
FALCONRY n art of training falcons
FALCONS > FALCON
FALCULA n sharp curved claw, esp of a bird
FALCULAE > FALCULA
FALCULAS > FALCULA
FALCULATE > FALCULA
FALDAGE n feudal right
FALDAGES > FALDAGE
FALDEROL n showy but worthless trifle ▷ vb sing nonsense words
FALDERALS > FALDERAL
FALDEROL same as > FALDERAL
FALDEROLS > FALDEROL
FALDETTA n Maltese woman's garment with a stiffened hood
FALDETTAS > FALDETTA
FALDSTOOL n backless seat, sometimes capable of being folded, used by bishops and certain other prelates
FALL vb drop from a higher to a lower place through the force of gravity ▷ n falling
FALLACIES > FALLACY
FALLACY n false belief
FALLAL n showy ornament, trinket, or article of dress
FALLALERY > FALLAL
FALLALISH adj foppish
FALLALS > FALLAL
FALLAWAY n friendship that has been withdrawn
FALLAWAYS > FALLAWAY
FALLBACK n something that recedes or retreats
FALLBACKS > FALLBACK
FALLBOARD n cover for piano keyboard
FALLEN > FALL
FALLER n any device that falls or operates machinery by falling, as in a spinning machine
FALLERS > FALLER
FALLFISH n large N American freshwater fish resembling the chub
FALLIBLE adj (of a person) liable to make mistakes
FALLIBLY > FALLIBLE

FALLING > FALL
FALLINGS > FALL
FALLOFF n decline or drop
FALLOFFS > FALLOFF
FALLOUT n radioactive particles spread as a result of a nuclear explosion ▷ vb disagree and quarrel ▷ sentence substitute order to leave a parade or disciplinary formation
FALLOUTS > FALLOUT
FALLOW adj (of land) ploughed but left unseeded to regain fertility ▷ n land treated in this way ▷ vb leave (land) unseeded after ploughing and harrowing it
FALLOWED > FALLOW
FALLOWER > FALLOW
FALLOWEST > FALLOW
FALLOWING > FALLOW
FALLOWS > FALLOW
FALLS > FALL
FALSE adj not true or correct ▷ adv in a false or dishonest manner ▷ vb falsify
FALSED > FALSE
FALSEFACE n mask
FALSEHOOD n quality of being untrue
FALSELY > FALSE
FALSENESS > FALSE
FALSER > FALSE
FALSERS n colloquial term for false teeth
FALSES > FALSE
FALSEST > FALSE
FALSETTO n voice pitched higher than one's natural range
FALSETTOS > FALSETTO
FALSEWORK n framework supporting something under construction
FALSIE n pad used to enlarge breast shape
FALSIES > FALSIE
FALSIFIED > FALSIFY
FALSIFIER > FALSIFY
FALSIFIES > FALSIFY
FALSIFY vb alter fraudulently
FALSING > FALSE
FALSISH > FALSE
FALSISM > FALSE
FALSISMS > FALSE
FALSITIES > FALSITY
FALSITY n state of being false
FALTBOAT n collapsible boat made of waterproof material stretched over a light framework
FALTBOATS > FALTBOAT
FALTER vb be hesitant, weak, or unsure ▷ n uncertainty or hesitancy in speech or action
FALTERED > FALTER
FALTERER > FALTER
FALTERERS > FALTER
FALTERING > FALTER
FALTERS > FALTER

FALX n sickle-shaped anatomical structure
FAME n state of being widely known or recognized ▷ vb make known or famous
FAMED > FAME
FAMELESS > FAME
FAMES > FAME
FAMILIAL adj of or relating to the family
FAMILIAR adj well-known ▷ n demon supposed to attend a witch
FAMILIARS n attendant demons
FAMILIES > FAMILY
FAMILISM n practice of a mystical Christian religious sect of the 16th and 17th centuries based upon love
FAMILISMS > FAMILISM
FAMILLE n type of Chinese porcelain
FAMILLES > FAMILLE
FAMILY n group of parents and their children ▷ adj suitable for parents and children together
FAMINE n severe shortage of food
FAMINES > FAMINE
FAMING > FAME
FAMISH vb be or make very hungry or weak
FAMISHED adj very hungry
FAMISHES > FAMISH
FAMISHING > FAMISH
FAMOUS adj very well-known ▷ vb make famous
FAMOUSED > FAMOUS
FAMOUSES > FAMOUS
FAMOUSING > FAMOUS
FAMOUSLY adv excellently
FAMULI > FAMULUS
FAMULUS n (formerly) the attendant of a sorcerer or scholar
FAN n hand-held or mechanical object used to create a current of air for ventilation or cooling ▷ vb blow or cool with a fan
FANAL n lighthouse
FANALS > FANAL
FANATIC n person who is excessively enthusiastic about something ▷ adj excessively enthusiastic
FANATICAL adj surpassing what is normal or accepted in enthusiasm for or belief in something
FANATICS > FANATIC
FANBASE n body of admirers of a particular pop singer, sports team, etc
FANBASES > FANBASE
FANBOY n obsessive fan of a subject or hobby
FANBOYS > FANBOY
FANCIABLE adj sexually attractive
FANCIED adj imaginary

FANCIER n person who is interested in and often breeds plants or animals
FANCIERS > FANCIER
FANCIES > FANCY
FANCIEST > FANCY
FANCIFIED > FANCIFY
FANCIFIES > FANCIFY
FANCIFUL adj not based on fact
FANCIFY vb make more beautiful
FANCILESS > FANCY
FANCILY > FANCY
FANCINESS > FANCY
FANCY adj elaborate, not plain ▷ n sudden irrational liking or desire ▷ vb be sexually attracted to
FANCYING > FANCY
FANCYWORK n ornamental needlework
FAND vb try
FANDANGLE n elaborate ornament
FANDANGO n lively Spanish dance
FANDANGOS > FANDANGO
FANDED > FAND
FANDING > FAND
FANDOM n collectively, the fans of a sport, pastime or person
FANDOMS > FANDOM
FANDS > FAND
FANE n temple or shrine
FANEGA n Spanish unit of measurement
FANEGADA n Spanish unit of land area
FANEGADAS > FANEGADA
FANEGAS > FANEGA
FANES > FANE
FANFARADE n fanfare
FANFARE n short loud tune played on brass instruments ▷ vb perform a fanfare
FANFARED > FANFARE
FANFARES > FANFARE
FANFARING > FANFARE
FANFARON n braggart
FANFARONA n gold chain
FANFARONS > FANFARON
FANFIC n fiction written around previously established characters invented by other authors
FANFICS > FANFIC
FANFOLD vb fold (paper) like a fan
FANFOLDED > FANFOLD
FANFOLDS > FANFOLD
FANG n snake's tooth which injects poison ▷ vb seize
FANGA same as > FANEGA
FANGAS > FANGA
FANGED > FANG
FANGING > FANG
FANGLE vb fashion
FANGLED > FANGLE
FANGLES > FANGLE
FANGLESS > FANG
FANGLIKE > FANG

FANGLING > FANGLE
FANGO n mud from thermal springs in Italy, used in the treatment of rheumatic disease
FANGOS > FANGO
FANGS > FANG
FANION n small flag used by surveyors to mark stations
FANIONS > FANION
FANJET same as > TURBOFAN
FANJETS > FANJET
FANK n sheep pen
FANKLE vb entangle ▷ n tangle
FANKLED > FANKLE
FANKLES > FANKLE
FANKLING > FANKLE
FANKS > FANK
FANLIGHT n semicircular window over a door or window
FANLIGHTS > FANLIGHT
FANLIKE > FAN
FANNED > FAN
FANNEL n ecclesiastical vestment
FANNELL variant of > FANNEL
FANNELLS > FANNELL
FANNELS > FANNEL
FANNER > FAN
FANNERS > FAN
FANNIED > FANNY
FANNIES > FANNY
FANNING > FAN
FANNINGS > FAN
FANNY n taboo word for female genitals ▷ vb waste time; misbehave
FANNYING > FANNY
FANO same as > FANON
FANON n collar-shaped vestment worn by the pope when celebrating mass
FANONS > FANON
FANOS > FANO
FANS > FAN
FANSITE n website aimed at fans of a celebrity, film, etc
FANSITES > FANSITE
FANSUB n fan-produced subtitling of films
FANSUBS > FANSUB
FANTAD n nervous, agitated state
FANTADS > FANTAD
FANTAIL n small New Zealand bird with a tail like a fan
FANTAILED adj having a tail like a fan
FANTAILS > FANTAIL
FANTASIA n musical composition of an improvised nature
FANTASIAS > FANTASIA
FANTASIE same as > FANTASY
FANTASIED > FANTASY
FANTASIES > FANTASY

FANTASISE same as > FANTASIZE
FANTASIST n person who indulges in fantasies
FANTASIZE vb indulge in daydreams
FANTASM archaic spelling of > PHANTASM
FANTASMAL > FANTASM
FANTASMIC > FANTASM
FANTASMS > FANTASM
FANTASQUE n fantasy
FANTAST n dreamer or visionary
FANTASTIC adj very good ▷ n person who dresses or behaves eccentrically
FANTASTRY n condition of being fantastic
FANTASTS > FANTAST
FANTASY n far-fetched notion ▷ adj of a competition in which a participant selects players for an imaginary, ideal team and points are awarded according to the actual performances of the chosen players ▷ vb fantasize
FANTEEG n nervous, agitated state
FANTEEGS > FANTEEG
FANTIGUE variant of > FANTEEG
FANTIGUES > FANTIGUE
FANTOD n crotchety or faddish behaviour
FANTODS > FANTOD
FANTOM archaic spelling of > PHANTOM
FANTOMS > FANTOM
FANTOOSH adj pretentious
FANUM n temple
FANUMS > FANUM
FANWISE adj like a fan
FANWORT n aquatic plant
FANWORTS > FANWORT
FANZINE n magazine produced by fans of a specific interest, soccer club, etc, for fellow fans
FANZINES > FANZINE
FAP adj drunk
FAQIR same as > FAKIR
FAQIRS > FAQIR
FAQUIR variant of > FAQIR
FAQUIRS > FAQIR
FAR adv at, to, or from a great distance ▷ adj remote in space or time ▷ vb go far
FARAD n unit of electrical capacitance
FARADAIC same as > FARADIC
FARADAY n quantity of electricity, used in electrochemical calculations
FARADAYS > FARADAY
FARADIC adj of or concerned with an intermittent asymmetric alternating current such as

that induced in the secondary winding of an induction coil
FARADISE same as > FARADIZE
FARADISED > FARADISE
FARADISER > FARADISE
FARADISES > FARADISE
FARADISM n therapeutic use of faradic currents
FARADISMS > FARADISM
FARADIZE vb treat (an organ or part) with faradic currents
FARADIZED > FARADIZE
FARADIZER > FARADIZE
FARADIZES > FARADIZE
FARADS > FARAD
FARAND adj pleasant or attractive in manner or appearance
FARANDINE n silk and wool cloth
FARANDOLE n lively dance in six-eight or four-four time from Provence
FARAWAY adj very distant
FARAWAYS same as > FARAWAY
FARCE n boisterous comedy ▷ vb enliven (a speech, etc) with jokes
FARCED > FARCE
FARCEMEAT same as > FORCEMEAT
FARCER same as > FARCEUR
FARCERS > FARCER
FARCES > FARCE
FARCEUR n writer of or performer in farces
FARCEURS > FARCEUR
FARCEUSE n female farceur
FARCEUSES > FARCEUSE
FARCI adj (of food) stuffed
FARCICAL adj ludicrous
FARCIE same as > FARCI
FARCIED adj afflicted with farcy
FARCIES > FARCY
FARCIFIED > FARCIFY
FARCIFIES > FARCIFY
FARCIFY vb turn into a farce
FARCIN n equine disease
FARCING > FARCE
FARCINGS > FARCE
FARCINS > FARCIN
FARCY n form of glanders, a bacterial disease of horses
FARD n paint for the face, esp white paint ▷ vb paint (the face) with fard
FARDAGE n material laid beneath or between cargo
FARDAGES > FARDAGE
FARDED > FARD
FARDEL n bundle or burden
FARDELS > FARDEL
FARDEN n farthing
FARDENS > FARDEN
FARDING > FARD
FARDINGS > FARD

FARDS > FARD
FARE n charge for a passenger's journey ▷ vb get on (as specified)
FAREBOX n box where money for bus fares is placed
FAREBOXES > FAREBOX
FARED > FARE
FARER > FARE
FARERS > FARE
FARES > FARE
FAREWELL interj goodbye ▷ n act of saying goodbye and leaving ▷ vb say goodbye ▷ adj parting or closing ▷ sentence substitute goodbye
FAREWELLS > FAREWELL
FARFAL same as **>** FELAFEL
FARFALLE n pasta in bow shapes
FARFALLES > FARFALLE
FARFALS > FARFAL
FARFEL same as **>** FELAFEL
FARFELS same as **>** FARFEL
FARFET adj far-fetched
FARINA n flour or meal made from any kind of cereal grain
FARINAS > FARINA
FARING > FARE
FARINHA n cassava meal
FARINHAS > FARINHA
FARINOSE adj similar to or yielding farina
FARL n thin cake of oatmeal, often triangular in shape
FARLE same as **>** FARL
FARLES > FARLE
FARLS > FARL
FARM n area of land for growing crops or rearing livestock ▷ vb cultivate (land)
FARMABLE > FARM
FARMED adj (of fish or game) reared on a farm rather than caught in the wild
FARMER n person who owns or runs a farm
FARMERESS n female farmer
FARMERIES > FARMERY
FARMERS > FARMER
FARMERY n farm buildings
FARMHAND n person who is hired to work on a farm
FARMHANDS > FARMHAND
FARMHOUSE n house attached to a farm
FARMING n business or skill of agriculture
FARMINGS > FARMING
FARMLAND n land that is used for or suitable for farming
FARMLANDS > FARMLAND
FARMOST > FAR
FARMS > FARM

FARMSTEAD n farm and its buildings
FARMWIFE n woman who works on a farm
FARMWIVES > FARMWIFE
FARMWORK n tasks carried out on a farm
FARMWORKS > FARMWORK
FARMYARD n small area of land enclosed by or around the farm buildings
FARMYARDS > FARMYARD
FARNARKEL vb spend time or act in a careless or inconsequential manner
FARNESOL n colourless aromatic sesquiterpene alcohol found in many essential oils and used in the form of its derivatives in perfumery
FARNESOLS > FARNESOL
FARNESS > FAR
FARNESSES > FAR
FARO n gambling game in which players bet against the dealer on what cards he will turn up
FAROLITO n votive candle
FAROLITOS > FAROLITO
FAROS > FARO
FAROUCHE adj sullen or shy
FARRAGO n jumbled mixture of things
FARRAGOES > FARRAGO
FARRAGOS > FARRAGO
FARRAND variant of **>** FARAND
FARRANT variant of **>** FARAND
FARRED > FAR
FARREN n allotted ground
FARRENS > FARREN
FARRIER n person who shoes horses
FARRIERS > FARRIER
FARRIERY n art, work, or establishment of a farrier
FARRING > FAR
FARROW n litter of piglets ▷ vb (of a sow) give birth ▷ adj (of a cow) not calving in a given year
FARROWED > FARROW
FARROWING > FARROW
FARROWS > FARROW
FARRUCA n flamenco dance performed by men
FARRUCAS > FARRUCA
FARS > FAR
FARSE vb insert into
FARSED > FARSE
FARSEEING adj having shrewd judgment
FARSES > FARSE
FARSIDE n part of the Moon facing away from the Earth
FARSIDES > FARSIDE
FARSING > FARSE
FART n emission of gas from the anus ▷ vb emit gas from the anus
FARTED > FART
FARTHEL same as **>** FARL

FARTHELS > FARTHEL
FARTHER > FAR
FARTHEST > FAR
FARTHING n former British coin equivalent to a quarter of a penny
FARTHINGS > FARTHING
FARTING > FART
FARTLEK n in sport, another name for interval training
FARTLEKS > FARTLEK
FARTS > FART
FAS > FA
FASCES npl (in ancient Rome) a bundle of rods containing an axe with its blade pointing out
FASCI > FASCIO
FASCIA n outer surface of a dashboard
FASCIAE > FASCIA
FASCIAL > FASCIA
FASCIAS > FASCIA
FASCIATE adj (of stems and branches) abnormally flattened due to coalescence
FASCIATED same as **>** FASCIATE
FASCICLE same as **>** FASCICULE
FASCICLED adj in instalments
FASCICLES > FASCICLE
FASCICULE n one part of a printed work that is published in instalments
FASCICULI > FASCICULE
FASCIITIS n inflammation of the fascia of a muscle
FASCINATE vb attract and interest strongly
FASCINE n bundle of long sticks used for filling in ditches and in the construction of embankments, roads, fortifications, etc
FASCINES > FASCINE
FASCIO n political group
FASCIOLA n band
FASCIOLAS > FASCIOLA
FASCIOLE n band
FASCIOLES > FASCIOLE
FASCIS > FASCES
FASCISM n right-wing totalitarian political system characterized by state control and extreme nationalism
FASCISMI > FASCISMO
FASCISMO Italian word for **>** FASCISM
FASCISMS > FASCISM
FASCIST n adherent or practitioner of fascism ▷ adj characteristic of or relating to fascism
FASCISTA Italian word for **>** FASCIST
FASCISTI > FASCISTA
FASCISTIC > FASCIST

FASCISTS > FASCIST
FASCITIS same as **>** FASCIITIS
FASH n worry ▷ vb trouble
FASHED > FASH
FASHERIES > FASHERY
FASHERY n difficulty, trouble
FASHES > FASH
FASHING > FASH
FASHION n style in clothes, hairstyle, etc, popular at a particular time ▷ vb form or make into a particular shape
FASHIONED > FASHION
FASHIONER > FASHION
FASHIONS > FASHION
FASHIONY adj of or relating to fashion
FASHIOUS adj troublesome
FAST adj (capable of) acting or moving quickly ▷ adv quickly ▷ vb go without food, esp for religious reasons ▷ n period of fasting
FASTBACK n car having a back that forms one continuous slope from roof to rear
FASTBACKS > FASTBACK
FASTBALL n ball pitched at the pitcher's top speed
FASTBALLS > FASTBALL
FASTED > FAST
FASTEN vb make or become firmly fixed or joined
FASTENED > FASTEN
FASTENER > FASTEN
FASTENERS > FASTEN
FASTENING n something that fastens something, such as a clasp or lock
FASTENS > FASTEN
FASTER > FAST
FASTERS > FAST
FASTEST > FAST
FASTI n in ancient Rome, days when business could legally be carried out
FASTIE n deceitful act
FASTIES > FASTIE
FASTIGIUM n highest point
FASTING > FAST
FASTINGS > FAST
FASTISH > FAST
FASTLY > FAST
FASTNESS n fortress, safe place
FASTS > FAST
FASTUOUS adj arrogant
FAT adj having excess flesh on the body ▷ n extra flesh on the body
FATAL adj causing death or ruin
FATALISM n belief that all events are predetermined and people are powerless to change their destinies
FATALISMS > FATALISM

FATALIST > FATALISM
FATALISTS > FATALISM
FATALITY n death caused by an accident or disaster
FATALLY adv resulting in death or disaster
FATALNESS > FATAL
FATBACK n fat, usually salted, from the upper part of a side of pork
FATBACKS > FATBACK
FATBIRD n nocturnal bird
FATBIRDS > FATBIRD
FATE n power supposed to predetermine events ▷ vb predetermine
FATED adj destined
FATEFUL adj having important, usu disastrous, consequences
FATEFULLY > FATEFUL
FATES > FATE
FATHEAD n stupid person
FATHEADED adj stupid
FATHEADS > FATHEAD
FATHER n male parent ▷ vb be the father of (offspring)
FATHERED > FATHER
FATHERING > FATHER
FATHERLY adj kind or protective, like a father
FATHERS > FATHER
FATHOM n unit of length, used in navigation, equal to six feet (1.83 metres) ▷ vb understand
FATHOMED > FATHOM
FATHOMER > FATHOM
FATHOMERS > FATHOM
FATHOMING > FATHOM
FATHOMS > FATHOM
FATIDIC adj prophetic
FATIDICAL same as
> FATIDIC
FATIGABLE > FATIGUE
FATIGATE vb fatigue
FATIGATED > FATIGATE
FATIGATES > FATIGATE
FATIGUE n extreme physical or mental tiredness ▷ vb tire out
FATIGUED > FATIGUE
FATIGUES > FATIGUE
FATIGUING > FATIGUE
FATING > FATE
FATISCENT adj having the appearance of being cracked
FATLESS > FAT
FATLIKE > FAT
FATLING n young farm animal fattened for killing
FATLINGS > FATLING
FATLY > FAT
FATNESS > FAT
FATNESSES > FAT
FATS > FAT
FATSIA n type of shrub with large deeply palmate leaves and umbels of white flowers
FATSIAS > FATSIA
FATSO n fat person: used as an insulting or disparaging

term of address
FATSOES > FATSO
FATSOS > FATSO
FATSTOCK n livestock fattened and ready for market
FATSTOCKS > FATSTOCK
FATTED > FAT
FATTEN vb (cause to) become fat
FATTENED > FATTEN
FATTENER > FATTEN
FATTENERS > FATTEN
FATTENING > FATTEN
FATTENS > FATTEN
FATTER > FAT
FATTEST > FAT
FATTIER > FATTY
FATTIES > FATTY
FATTIEST > FATTY
FATTILY > FATTY
FATTINESS > FATTY
FATTING > FAT
FATTISH > FAT
FATTISM n discrimination on the basis of weight, esp prejudice against those considered to be overweight
FATTISMS > FATTISM
FATTIST > FATTISM
FATTISTS > FATTISM
FATTRELS n ends of ribbon
FATTY adj containing fat ▷ n fat person
FATUITIES > FATUITY
FATUITOUS > FATUITY
FATUITY n foolish thoughtlessness
FATUOUS adj foolish
FATUOUSLY > FATUOUS
FATWA n religious decree issued by a Muslim leader ▷ vb issue a fatwa
FATWAH same as **>** FATWA
FATWAHED > FATWAH
FATWAHING > FATWAH
FATWAHS > FATWAH
FATWAING > FATWA
FATWAS > FATWA
FATWOOD n wood used for kindling
FATWOODS > FATWOOD
FAUBOURG n suburb or quarter, esp of a French city
FAUBOURGS > FAUBOURG
FAUCAL adj of or relating to the fauces
FAUCALS > FAUCAL
FAUCES n area between the cavity of the mouth and the pharynx, including the surrounding tissues
FAUCET n tap
FAUCETS > FAUCET
FAUCHION n short sword
FAUCHIONS > FAUCHION
FAUCHON variant of **>** FAUCHION
FAUCHONS > FAUCHON
FAUCIAL same as **>** FAUCAL
FAUGH interj exclamation of

disgust, scorn, etc
FAULCHION variant of **>** FAUCHION
FAULD n piece of armour
FAULDS > FAULD
FAULT n responsibility for something wrong ▷ vb criticize or blame
FAULTED > FAULT
FAULTFUL > FAULT
FAULTIER > FAULTY
FAULTIEST > FAULTY
FAULTILY > FAULTY
FAULTING > FAULT
FAULTLESS adj without fault
FAULTLINE n surface of a fault fracture
FAULTS > FAULT
FAULTY adj badly designed or not working properly
FAUN n (in Roman legend) creature with a human face and torso and a goat's horns and legs
FAUNA n animals of a given place or time
FAUNAE > FAUNA
FAUNAL > FAUNA
FAUNALLY > FAUNA
FAUNAS > FAUNA
FAUNIST > FAUNA
FAUNISTIC > FAUNA
FAUNISTS > FAUNA
FAUNLIKE > FAUN
FAUNS > FAUN
FAUNULA n fauna of a small single environment
FAUNULAE > FAUNULA
FAUNULE same as **>** FAUNULA
FAUNULES > FAUNULE
FAUR Scot word for **>** FAR
FAURD adj favoured
FAURER > FAUR
FAUREST > FAUR
FAUSTIAN adj of or relating to Faust, esp reminiscent of his bargain with the devil
FAUT Scot word for **>** FAULT
FAUTED > FAUT
FAUTEUIL n armchair, the sides of which are not upholstered
FAUTEUILS > FAUTEUIL
FAUTING > FAUT
FAUTOR n patron
FAUTORS > FAUTOR
FAUTS > FAUT
FAUVE adj of the style of the Fauve art movement ▷ n member of the Fauve art movement
FAUVES > FAUVE
FAUVETTE n singing bird, warbler
FAUVETTES > FAUVETTE
FAUVISM > FAUVE
FAUVISMS > FAUVISM
FAUVIST n artist following the Fauve style of painting
FAUVISTS > FAUVIST
FAUX adj false

FAVA n type of bean
FAVAS > FAVA
FAVE short for **>** FAVOURITE
FAVEL adj (of a horse) dun-coloured
FAVELA n (in Brazil) a shanty or shantytown
FAVELAS > FAVELA
FAVELL variant of **>** FAVEL
FAVELLA n group of spores
FAVELLAS > FAVELLA
FAVEOLATE adj pitted with cell-like cavities
FAVER > FAVE
FAVES > FAVE
FAVEST > FAVE
FAVICON n icon displayed before a website's URL
FAVICONS > FAVICON
FAVISM n type of anaemia
FAVISMS > FAVISM
FAVONIAN adj of or relating to the west wind
FAVOR same as **>** FAVOUR
FAVORABLE adj favourable
FAVORABLY adv favourably
FAVORED > FAVOR
FAVORER > FAVOUR
FAVORERS > FAVOUR
FAVORING > FAVOR
FAVORITE same as **>** FAVOURITE
FAVORITES > FAVORITE
FAVORLESS > FAVOR
FAVORS same as **>** FAVOURS
FAVOSE same as **>** FAVEOLATE
FAVOUR n approving attitude ▷ vb prefer
FAVOURED > FAVOUR
FAVOURER > FAVOUR
FAVOURERS > FAVOUR
FAVOURING > FAVOUR
FAVOURITE adj most liked ▷ n preferred person or thing
FAVOURS npl sexual intimacy, as when consented to by a woman
FAVOUS adj resembling honeycomb
FAVRILE n type of iridescent glass
FAVRILES > FAVRILE
FAVUS n infectious fungal skin disease of man and some domestic animals, characterized by formation of a honeycomb-like mass of roundish dry cup-shaped crusts
FAVUSES > FAVUS
FAW n gypsy
FAWN n young deer ▷ adj light yellowish-brown ▷ vb seek attention from (someone) by insincere flattery
FAWNED > FAWN
FAWNER > FAWN
FAWNERS > FAWN

FAWNIER > FAWNY
FAWNIEST > FAWNY
FAWNING > FAWN
FAWNINGLY > FAWN
FAWNINGS > FAWN
FAWNLIKE > FAWN
FAWNS > FAWN
FAWNY adj of a fawn colour
FAWS > FAW
FAX n electronic system for sending facsimiles of documents by telephone ▷ vb send (a document) by this system
FAXED > FAX
FAXES > FAX
FAXING > FAX
FAY n fairy or sprite ▷ adj of or resembling a fay ▷ vb fit or be fitted closely or tightly
FAYALITE n rare brown or black mineral
FAYALITES > FAYALITE
FAYED > FAY
FAYENCE variant of > FAIENCE
FAYENCES > FAYENCE
FAYER > FAY
FAYEST > FAY
FAYING > FAY
FAYNE vb pretend
FAYNED > FAYNE
FAYNES > FAYNE
FAYNING > FAYNE
FAYRE pseudo-archaic spelling of > FAIR
FAYRES > FAYRE
FAYS > FAY
FAZE vb disconcert or fluster
FAZED adj worried or disconcerted
FAZENDA n large estate or ranch
FAZENDAS > FAZENDA
FAZES > FAZE
FAZING > FAZE
FE n variant of Hebrew letter pe, transliterated as f
FEAGUE vb whip or beat
FEAGUED > FEAGUE
FEAGUES > FEAGUE
FEAGUING > FEAGUE
FEAL vb conceal
FEALED > FEAL
FEALING > FEAL
FEALS > FEAL
FEALTIES > FEALTY
FEALTY n (in feudal society) subordinate's loyalty to his ruler or lord
FEAR n distress or alarm caused by impending danger or pain ▷ vb be afraid of (something or someone)
FEARE n companion, spouse
FEARED > FEAR
FEARER > FEAR
FEARERS > FEAR
FEARES > FEARE
FEARFUL adj feeling fear
FEARFULLY adv in a

fearful manner
FEARING > FEAR
FEARLESS > FEAR
FEARS > FEAR
FEARSOME adj terrifying
FEART adj (Scots) afraid
FEASANCE n performance of an act
FEASANCES > FEASANCE
FEASE vb perform an act
FEASED > FEASE
FEASES > FEASE
FEASIBLE adj able to be done, possible
FEASIBLY > FEASIBLE
FEASING > FEASE
FEAST n lavish meal ▷ vb eat a feast
FEASTED > FEAST
FEASTER > FEAST
FEASTERS > FEAST
FEASTFUL adj festive
FEASTING > FEAST
FEASTINGS > FEAST
FEASTLESS > FEAST
FEASTS > FEAST
FEAT n remarkable, skilful, or daring action
FEATED > FEAT
FEATEOUS adj neat
FEATER > FEAT
FEATEST > FEAT
FEATHER n one of the barbed shafts forming the plumage of birds ▷ vb fit or cover with feathers
FEATHERED > FEATHER
FEATHERS > FEATHER
FEATHERY > FEATHER
FEATING > FEAT
FEATLIER > FEAT
FEATLIEST > FEAT
FEATLY > FEAT
FEATOUS variant of > FEATEOUS
FEATS > FEAT
FEATUOUS variant of > FEATEOUS
FEATURE n part of the face, such as the eyes ▷ vb have as a feature or be a feature in
FEATURED adj having features as specified
FEATURELY adj handsome
FEATURES > FEATURE
FEATURING > FEATURE
FEAZE same as > FEEZE
FEAZED > FEAZE
FEAZES > FEAZE
FEAZING > FEAZE
FEBLESSE n feebleness
FEBLESSES > FEBLESSE
FEBRICITY n condition of having a fever
FEBRICULA n slight transient fever
FEBRICULE variant of > FEBRICULA
FEBRIFIC adj causing or having a fever
FEBRIFUGE n any drug or agent for reducing fever ▷ adj serving to reduce

fever
FEBRILE adj very active and nervous
FEBRILITY > FEBRILE
FECAL same as > FAECAL
FECES same as > FAECES
FECHT Scot word for > FIGHT
FECHTER > FECHT
FECHTERS > FECHT
FECHTING > FECHT
FECHTS > FECHT
FECIAL adj heraldic
FECIALS > FECIAL
FECIT (he or she) made it: used formerly on works of art next to the artist's name
FECK vb euphemism for 'fuck'
FECKED > FECK
FECKIN same as > FECKING
FECKING > FECK
FECKLESS adj ineffectual or irresponsible
FECKLY > FECK
FECKS > FECK
FECULA n starch obtained by washing the crushed parts of plants, such as the potato
FECULAE > FECULA
FECULAS > FECULA
FECULENCE > FECULENT
FECULENCY > FECULENT
FECULENT adj filthy, scummy, muddy, or foul
FECUND adj fertile
FECUNDATE vb make fruitful
FECUNDITY n fertility
FED n FBI agent
FEDARIE n accomplice
FEDARIES > FEDARIE
FEDAYEE n (in Arab states) a commando, esp one fighting against Israel
FEDAYEEN > FEDAYEE
FEDELINI n type of pasta
FEDELINIS > FEDELINI
FEDERACY n alliance
FEDERAL adj of a system in which power is divided between one central government and several regional governments ▷ n supporter of federal union or federation
FEDERALLY > FEDERAL
FEDERALS > FEDERAL
FEDERARIE variant of > FEDARIE
FEDERARY variant of > FEDARIE
FEDERATE vb unite in a federation ▷ adj federal
FEDERATED > FEDERATE
FEDERATES > FEDERATE
FEDERATOR > FEDERATE
FEDEX vb send by FedEx
FEDEXED > FEDEX
FEDEXES > FEDEX
FEDEXING > FEDEX
FEDORA n man's soft hat

with a brim
FEDORAS > FEDORA
FEDS > FED
FEE n charge paid to be allowed to do something ▷ vb pay a fee to
FEEB n contemptible person
FEEBLE adj lacking physical or mental power ▷ vb make feeble
FEEBLED > FEEBLE
FEEBLER > FEEBLE
FEEBLES > FEEBLE
FEEBLEST > FEEBLE
FEEBLING > FEEBLE
FEEBLISH > FEEBLE
FEEBLY > FEEBLE
FEEBS > FEEB
FEED vb give food to ▷ n act of feeding
FEEDABLE > FEE
FEEDBACK n information received in response to something done ▷ adv return (part of the output of a system) to its input
FEEDBACKS > FEEDBACK
FEEDBAG n any bag in which feed for livestock is sacked
FEEDBAGS > FEEDBAG
FEEDBOX n trough, manger
FEEDBOXES > FEEDBOX
FEEDER n baby's bib
FEEDERS > FEEDER
FEEDGRAIN n cereal grown to feed livestock
FEEDHOLE n small hole through which cable etc is inserted
FEEDHOLES > FEEDHOLE
FEEDING > FEED
FEEDINGS > FEED
FEEDLOT n area or building where livestock are fattened rapidly for market
FEEDLOTS > FEEDLOT
FEEDS > FEED
FEEDSTOCK n main raw material used in the manufacture of a product
FEEDSTUFF n any material used as a food, esp for animals
FEEDWATER n water, previously purified to prevent scale deposit or corrosion, that is fed to boilers for steam generation
FEEDYARD n place where cattle are kept and fed
FEEDYARDS > FEEDYARD
FEEING > FEE
FEEL vb have a physical or emotional sensation of ▷ n act of feeling
FEELBAD n something inducing depression
FEELER n organ of touch in some animals
FEELERS > FEELER
FEELESS > FEE

FEELGOOD adj causing or characterized by a feeling of self-satisfaction
FEELING > FEEL
FEELINGLY > FEEL
FEELINGS > FEEL
FEELS > FEEL
FEEN n in Irish dialect, an informal word for 'man'
FEENS > FEEN
FEER vb make a furrow
FEERED > FEER
FEERIE n fairyland
FEERIES > FEERIE
FEERIN n furrow
FEERING > FEER
FEERINGS > FEER
FEERINS > FEERIN
FEERS > FEER
FEES > FEE
FEESE vb perturb
FEESED > FEESE
FEESES > FEESE
FEESING > FEESE
FEET > FOOT
FEETFIRST adv with the feet coming first
FEETLESS > FOOT
FEEZE vb beat ▷ n rush
FEEZED > FEEZE
FEEZES > FEEZE
FEEZING > FEEZE
FEG same as > FIG
FEGARIES > FEGARY
FEGARY variant of > VAGARY
FEGS > FEG
FEH > FE
FEHM n medieval German court
FEHME > FEHM
FEHMIC > FEHM
FEHS > FEH
FEIGN vb pretend
FEIGNED > FEIGN
FEIGNEDLY > FEIGN
FEIGNER > FEIGN
FEIGNERS > FEIGN
FEIGNING > FEIGN
FEIGNINGS > FEIGN
FEIGNS > FEIGN
FEIJOA n evergreen myrtaceous shrub of S America
FEIJOADA n Brazilian stew of black beans, meat and vegetables
FEIJOADAS > FEIJOADA
FEIJOAS > FEIJOA
FEINT n sham attack or blow meant to distract an opponent ▷ vb make a feint ▷ adj printing term meaning ruled with faint lines
FEINTED > FEINT
FEINTER > FEINT
FEINTEST > FEINT
FEINTING > FEINT
FEINTS npl leavings of the second distillation of Scotch malt whisky
FEIRIE adj nimble
FEIRIER > FEIRIE

FEIRIEST > FEIRIE
FEIS n Irish music and dance festival
FEISEANNA > FEIS
FEIST n small aggressive dog
FEISTIER > FEISTY
FEISTIEST > FEISTY
FEISTILY > FEISTY
FEISTS > FEIST
FEISTY adj showing courage or spirit
FELAFEL same as > FALAFEL
FELAFELS > FELAFEL
FELCH vb suck semen from the vagina or anus of (a sexual partner)
FELCHED > FELCH
FELCHES > FELCH
FELCHING > FELCH
FELDGRAU n ordinary German soldier (from uniform colour)
FELDGRAUS > FELDGRAU
FELDSCHAR same as > FELDSHER
FELDSCHER same as > FELDSHER
FELDSHER n (in Russia) a medical doctor's assistant
FELDSHERS > FELDSHER
FELDSPAR n hard mineral that is the main constituent of igneous rocks
FELDSPARS > FELDSPAR
FELDSPATH variant of > FELDSPAR
FELICIA n type of African herb
FELICIAS > FELICIA
FELICIFIC adj making or tending to make happy
FELICITER > FELICITY
FELICITY n happiness
FELID n any animal belonging to the cat family
FELIDS > FELID
FELINE adj of cats ▷ n member of the cat family
FELINELY > FELINE
FELINES > FELINE
FELINITY > FELINE
FELL vb cut or knock down ▷ adj cruel or deadly
FELLA nonstandard variant of > FELLOW
FELLABLE > FALL
FELLAH n peasant in Arab countries
FELLAHEEN > FELLAH
FELLAHIN > FELLAH
FELLAHS > FELLAH
FELLAS > FELLA
FELLATE vb perform fellatio on (a person)
FELLATED > FELLATE
FELLATES > FELLATE
FELLATING > FELLATE
FELLATIO n sexual activity in which the penis is stimulated by the partner's mouth

FELLATION same as > FELLATIO
FELLATIOS > FELLATIO
FELLATOR > FELLATIO
FELLATORS > FELLATIO
FELLATRIX > FELLATIO
FELLED > FELL
FELLER n person or thing that fells
FELLERS > FELLER
FELLEST > FELL
FELLIES > FELLY
FELLING > FELL
FELLINGS > FELLING
FELLNESS > FELL
FELLOE n (segment of) the rim of a wheel
FELLOES > FELLOE
FELLOW n man or boy ▷ adj in the same group or condition
FELLOWED > FELLOW
FELLOWING > FELLOW
FELLOWLY adj friendly, companionable
FELLOWMAN n companion
FELLOWMEN > FELLOWMAN
FELLOWS > FELLOW
FELLS > FELL
FELLY same as > FELLOE
FELON n (formerly) person guilty of a felony ▷ adj evil
FELONIES > FELONY
FELONIOUS adj of, involving, or constituting a felony
FELONOUS adj wicked
FELONRIES > FELONRY
FELONRY n felons collectively
FELONS > FELON
FELONY n serious crime
FELSIC adj relating to igneous rock
FELSITE n any fine-grained igneous rock consisting essentially of quartz and feldspar
FELSITES > FELSITE
FELSITIC > FELSITE
FELSPAR same as > FELDSPAR
FELSPARS > FELSPAR
FELSTONE same as > FELSITE
FELSTONES > FELSTONE
FELT n matted fabric ▷ vb become matted
FELTED > FELT
FELTER vb mat together
FELTERED > FELTER
FELTERING > FELTER
FELTERS > FELTER
FELTIER > FELT
FELTIEST > FELT
FELTING n felted material
FELTINGS > FELTING
FELTLIKE > FEEL
FELTS > FELT
FELTY > FELT
FELUCCA n narrow lateen-rigged vessel of the Mediterranean

FELUCCAS > FELUCCA
FELWORT n type of plant of Europe and SW China with purple flowers and rosettes of leaves
FELWORTS > FELWORT
FEM n passive homosexual
FEMAL adj effeminate ▷ n effeminate person
FEMALE adj of the sex which bears offspring ▷ n female person or animal
FEMALES > FEMALE
FEMALITY > FEMALE
FEMALS > FEMAL
FEME n woman or wife
FEMERALL n ventilator or smoke outlet on a roof
FEMERALLS > FEMERALL
FEMES > FEME
FEMETARY variant of > FUMITORY
FEMICIDAL > FEMICIDE
FEMICIDE n killing of females because of their gender
FEMICIDES > FEMICIDE
FEMINACY n feminine character
FEMINAL adj feminine, female
FEMINAZI n militant feminist
FEMINAZIS > FEMINAZI
FEMINEITY n quality of being feminine
FEMINIE n women collectively
FEMININE adj having qualities traditionally regarded as suitable for, or typical of, women ▷ n short for feminine noun
FEMININES > FEMININE
FEMINISE same as > FEMINIZE
FEMINISED > FEMINISE
FEMINISES > FEMINISE
FEMINISM n advocacy of equal rights for women
FEMINISMS > FEMINISM
FEMINIST n person who advocates equal rights for women ▷ adj of, relating to, or advocating feminism
FEMINISTS > FEMINIST
FEMINITY > FEMINAL
FEMINIZE vb make or become feminine
FEMINIZED > FEMINIZE
FEMINIZES > FEMINIZE
FEMITER variant of > FUMITORY
FEMITERS > FEMITER
FEMME n woman or wife
FEMMES > FEMME
FEMMIER > FEMMY
FEMMIEST > FEMMY
FEMMY adj markedly or exaggeratedly feminine in appearance, manner, etc
FEMORA > FEMUR
FEMORAL adj of the thigh
FEMS > FEM

FEMUR n thighbone

FEMURS > FEMUR

FEN n low-lying flat marshy land

FENAGLE variant of > FINAGLE

FENAGLED > FENAGLE

FENAGLES > FENAGLE

FENAGLING > FENAGLE

FENCE n barrier of posts linked by wire or wood, enclosing an area ▷ vb enclose with or as if with a fence

FENCED > FENCE

FENCELESS > FENCE

FENCELIKE > FENCE

FENCER n person who fights with a sword, esp one who practises the art of fencing

FENCEROW n uncultivated land flanking a fence

FENCEROWS > FENCEROW

FENCERS > FENCER

FENCES > FENCE

FENCIBLE n (formerly) a person who undertook military service in immediate defence of his homeland only

FENCIBLES > FENCIBLE

FENCING n sport of fighting with swords

FENCINGS > FENCING

FEND vb give support (to someone, esp oneself) ▷ n shift or effort

FENDED > FEND

FENDER n low metal frame in front of a fireplace

FENDERED adj having a fender

FENDERS > FENDER

FENDIER > FENDY

FENDIEST > FENDY

FENDING > FEND

FENDS > FEND

FENDY adj thrifty

FENESTRA n small opening in or between bones, esp one of the openings between the middle and inner ears

FENESTRAE > FENESTRA

FENESTRAL > FENESTRA

FENESTRAS > FENESTRA

FENI n Goan alcoholic drink

FENIS > FENI

FENITAR variant of > FUMITORY

FENITARS > FENITAR

FENKS n whale blubber

FENLAND > FEN

FENLANDS > FEN

FENMAN > FEN

FENMEN > FEN

FENNEC n type of very small nocturnal desert fox of N Africa and Arabia, with pale fur and enormous ears

FENNECS > FENNEC

FENNEL n fragrant plant whose seeds, leaves, and root are used in cookery

FENNELS > FENNEL

FENNIER > FENNY

FENNIES > FENNY

FENNIEST > FENNY

FENNISH > FEN

FENNY adj boggy or marshy ▷ n feni

FENS > FEN

FENT n piece of waste fabric

FENTANYL n narcotic drug used in medicine to relieve pain

FENTANYLS > FENTANYL

FENTHION n type of pesticide

FENTHIONS > FENTHION

FENTS > FENT

FENUGREEK n Mediterranean plant grown for its heavily scented seeds

FENURON n type of herbicide

FENURONS > FENURON

FEOD same as > FEUD

FEODAL > FEOD

FEODARIES > FEOD

FEODARY > FEOD

FEODS > FEOD

FEOFF same as > FIEF

FEOFFED > FEOFF

FEOFFEE n (in feudal society) a vassal granted a fief by his lord

FEOFFEES > FEOFFEE

FEOFFER > FEOFF

FEOFFERS > FEOFF

FEOFFING > FEOFF

FEOFFMENT n (in medieval Europe) a lord's act of granting a fief to his man

FEOFFOR > FEOFF

FEOFFORS > FEOFF

FEOFFS > FEOFF

FER same as > FAR

FERACIOUS adj fruitful

FERACITY > FERACIOUS

FERAL adj wild ▷ n person who displays such tendencies and appearance

FERALISED same as > FERALIZED

FERALIZED adj once domesticated, but now wild

FERALS > FERAL

FERBAM n black slightly water-soluble fluffy powder used as a fungicide

FERBAMS > FERBAM

FERE n companion ▷ adj fierce

FERER > FERE

FERES > FERE

FEREST > FERE

FERETORY n shrine, usually portable, for a saint's relics

FERIA n weekday, other than Saturday, on which no feast occurs

FERIAE > FERIA

FERIAL adj of or relating to a feria

FERIAS > FERIA

FERINE same as > FERAL

FERITIES > FERAL

FERITY > FERAL

FERLIE same as > FERLY

FERLIED > FERLY

FERLIER > FERLY

FERLIES > FERLY

FERLIEST > FERLY

FERLY adj wonderful ▷ n wonder ▷ vb wonder

FERLYING > FERLY

FERM variant of > FARM

FERMATA another word for > PAUSE

FERMATAS > FERMATA

FERMATE > FERMATA

FERMENT n any agent that causes fermentation ▷ vb (cause to) undergo fermentation

FERMENTED > FERMENT

FERMENTER > FERMENT

FERMENTOR > FERMENT

FERMENTS > FERMENT

FERMI n unit of length used in nuclear physics equal to 10^{-15} metre

FERMION n any of a group of elementary particles, such as a nucleon, that has half-integral spin and obeys Fermi-Dirac statistics

FERMIONIC > FERMION

FERMIONS > FERMION

FERMIS > FERMI

FERMIUM n element artificially produced by neutron bombardment of plutonium

FERMIUMS > FERMIUM

FERMS > FERM

FERN n flowerless plant with fine fronds

FERNALLY n seedless plant that is not a true fern

FERNBIRD n small brown and white New Zealand swamp bird with a fernlike tail

FERNBIRDS > FERNBIRD

FERNERIES > FERNERY

FERNERY n place where ferns are grown

FERNIER > FERN

FERNIEST > FERN

FERNING n production of a fern-like pattern

FERNINGS > FERNING

FERNINST same as > FORNENST

FERNLESS > FERN

FERNLIKE > FERN

FERNS > FERN

FERNSHAW n fern thicket

FERNSHAWS > FERNSHAW

FERNTICLE n freckle

FERNY > FERN

FEROCIOUS adj savagely fierce or cruel

FEROCITY > FEROCIOUS

FERRATE n type of salt

FERRATES > FERRATE

FERREL variant of > FERRULE

FERRELED > FERREL

FERRELING > FERREL

FERRELLED > FERREL

FERRELS > FERREL

FERREOUS adj containing or resembling iron

FERRET n tamed polecat used to catch rabbits or rats ▷ vb hunt with ferrets

FERRETED > FERRET

FERRETER > FERRET

FERRETERS > FERRET

FERRETING > FERRET

FERRETS > FERRET

FERRETY > FERRET

FERRIAGE n transportation by ferry

FERRIAGES > FERRIAGE

FERRIC adj of or containing iron

FERRIED > FERRY

FERRIES > FERRY

FERRITE n any of a group of ferromagnetic highly resistive ceramic compounds

FERRITES > FERRITE

FERRITIC > FERRITE

FERRITIN n protein that contains iron and plays a part in the storage of iron in the body. It occurs in the liver and spleen

FERRITINS > FERRITIN

FERROCENE n reddish-orange insoluble crystalline compound

FERROTYPE n photographic print produced directly in a camera by exposing a sheet of iron or tin coated with a sensitized enamel

FERROUS adj of or containing iron in the divalent state

FERRUGO n disease affecting plants

FERRUGOS > FERRUGO

FERRULE n metal cap to strengthen the end of a stick ▷ vb equip (a stick, etc) with a ferrule

FERRULED > FERRULE

FERRULES > FERRULE

FERRULING > FERRULE

FERRUM Latin word for > IRON

FERRUMS > FERRUM

FERRY n boat for transporting people and vehicles ▷ vb carry by ferry

FERRYBOAT same as > FERRY

FERRYING > FERRY

FERRYMAN n someone who provides a ferry service

FERRYMEN > FERRYMAN

FERTIGATE vb fertilize and irrigate at the same time

FERTILE adj capable of producing young, crops, or vegetation

> FERRULE

FERRELED > FERREL

FERTILELY > FERTILE

FERTILER > FERTILE

FERTILEST > FERTILE

FERTILISE same as > FERTILIZE

FERTILITY n ability to produce offspring, esp abundantly

FERTILIZE vb provide (an animal or plant) with sperm or pollen to bring about fertilization

FERULA n large Mediterranean plant with thick stems and dissected leaves, cultivated for its strongly-scented gum resin

FERULAE > FERULA

FERULAS > FERULA

FERULE same as > FERRULE

FERULED > FERULE

FERULES > FERULE

FERULING > FERULE

FERVENCY another word for > FERVOUR

FERVENT adj intensely passionate and sincere

FERVENTER > FERVENT

FERVENTLY > FERVENT

FERVID same as > FERVENT

FERVIDER > FERVID

FERVIDEST > FERVID

FERVIDITY > FERVID

FERVIDLY > FERVID

FERVOR same as > FERVOUR

FERVOROUS > FERVOUR

FERVORS > FERVOR

FERVOUR n intensity of feeling

FERVOURS > FERVOUR

FES > FE

FESCUE n pasture and lawn grass with stiff narrow leaves

FESCUES > FESCUE

FESS same as > FESSE

FESSE n ordinary consisting of a horizontal band across a shield, conventionally occupying a third of its length and being wider than a bar

FESSED > FESS

FESSES > FESSE

FESSING > FESS

FESSWISE adv in heraldry, with a horizontal band across the shield

FEST n event at which the emphasis is on a particular activity

FESTA n festival

FESTAL adj festive ▷ n festivity

FESTALLY > FESTAL

FESTALS > FESTAL

FESTAS > FESTA

FESTER vb grow worse and increasingly hostile ▷ n small ulcer or sore containing pus

FESTERED > FESTER

FESTERING > FESTER

FESTERS > FESTER

FESTIER > FESTY

FESTIEST > FESTY

FESTILOGY n treatise about church festivals

FESTINATE vb hurry

FESTIVAL n organized series of special events or performances

FESTIVALS > FESTIVAL

FESTIVE adj of or like a celebration

FESTIVELY > FESTIVE

FESTIVITY n happy celebration

FESTIVOUS > FESTIVE

FESTOLOGY variant of > FESTILOGY

FESTOON vb hang decorations in loops ▷ n decorative chain of flowers or ribbons suspended in loops

FESTOONED > FESTOON

FESTOONS > FESTOON

FESTS > FEST

FESTY adj dirty

FET vb fetch

FETA n white salty Greek cheese

FETAL adj of, relating to, or resembling a fetus

FETAS > FETA

FETATION n state of pregnancy

FETATIONS > FETATION

FETCH vb go after and bring back ▷ n ghost or apparition of a living person

FETCHED > FETCH

FETCHER n person or animal that fetches

FETCHERS > FETCHER

FETCHES > FETCH

FETCHING adj attractive

FETE n gala, bazaar, etc, usu held outdoors ▷ vb honour or entertain regally

FETED > FETE

FETERITA n type of sorghum

FETERITAS > FETERITA

FETES > FETE

FETIAL n (in ancient Rome) any of the 20 priestly heralds involved in declarations of war and in peace negotiations ▷ adj of or relating to the fetiales

FETIALES > FETIAL

FETIALIS n priest in ancient Rome

FETIALS > FETIAL

FETICH same as > FETISH

FETICHE variant of > FETICH

FETICHES > FETICH

FETICHISE variant of > FETICHIZE

FETICHISM same as > FETISHISM

FETICHIST > FETISHISM

FETICHIZE vb be excessively or irrationally devoted to an object, activity, etc

FETICIDAL > FETICIDE

FETICIDE n destruction of a fetus in the uterus

FETICIDES > FETICIDE

FETID adj stinking

FETIDER > FETID

FETIDEST > FETID

FETIDITY > FETID

FETIDLY > FETID

FETIDNESS > FETID

FETING > FETE

FETISH n form of behaviour in which sexual pleasure is derived from looking at or handling an inanimate object

FETISHES > FETISH

FETISHISE same as > FETISHIZE

FETISHISM n condition in which the handling of an inanimate object or a specific part of the body other than the sexual organs is a source of sexual satisfaction

FETISHIST > FETISHISM

FETISHIZE vb be excessively or irrationally devoted to (an object, activity, etc)

FETLOCK n projection behind and above a horse's hoof

FETLOCKED adj having fetlocks

FETLOCKS > FETLOCK

FETOLOGY n branch of medicine concerned with the fetus in the uterus

FETOR n offensive stale or putrid odour

FETORS > FETOR

FETOSCOPE n fibreoptic instrument that can be passed through the abdomen of a pregnant woman to enable examination of the fetus and withdrawal of blood for sampling in prenatal diagnosis

FETOSCOPY > FETOSCOPE

FETS > FET

FETT variant of > FET

FETTA variant of > FETA

FETTAS > FETTA

FETTED > FET

FETTER n chain or shackle for the foot ▷ vb restrict

FETTERED > FETTER

FETTERER > FETTER

FETTERERS > FETTER

FETTERING > FETTER

FETTERS > FETTER

FETTING > FET

FETTLE same as > FETTLING

FETTLED > FETTLE

FETTLER n person employed to maintain railway tracks

FETTLERS > FETTLER

FETTLES > FETTLE

FETTLING n refractory material used to line the hearth of puddling furnaces

FETTLINGS > FETTLING

FETTS > FETT

FETTUCINE n type of pasta in the form of narrow ribbons

FETTUCINI same as > FETTUCINE

FETUS n embryo of a mammal in the later stages of development

FETUSES > FETUS

FETWA variant of > FATWA

FETWAS > FETWA

FEU n (in Scotland) right of use of land in return for a fixed annual payment

FEUAR n tenant of a feu

FEUARS > FEUAR

FEUD n long bitter hostility between two people or groups ▷ vb carry on a feud

FEUDAL adj of or like feudalism

FEUDALISE same as > FEUDALIZE

FEUDALISM n medieval system in which people held land from a lord, and in return worked and fought for him

FEUDALIST > FEUDALISM

FEUDALITY n state or quality of being feudal

FEUDALIZE vb make feudal

FEUDALLY > FEUDAL

FEUDARIES > FEUDARY

FEUDARY n holder of land through feudal right

FEUDATORY n person holding a fief ▷ adj relating to or characteristic of the relationship between lord and vassal

FEUDED > FEUD

FEUDING > FEUD

FEUDINGS > FEUD

FEUDIST n person who takes part in a feud or quarrel

FEUDISTS > FEUDIST

FEUDS > FEUD

FEUED > FEU

FEUILLETE n puff pastry

FEUING > FEU

FEUS > FEU

FEUTRE vb place in a resting position

FEUTRED > FEUTRE

FEUTRES > FEUTRE

FEUTRING > FEUTRE

FEVER n (illness causing) high body temperature ▷ vb affect with or as if with fever

FEVERED > FEVER
FEVERFEW n bushy European plant with white flower heads, formerly used medicinally
FEVERFEWS > FEVERFEW
FEVERING > FEVER
FEVERISH adj suffering from fever
FEVERLESS > FEVER
FEVEROUS same as > FEVERISH
FEVERROOT n American wild plant
FEVERS > FEVER
FEVERWEED n plant thought to be medicinal
FEVERWORT n any of several plants considered to have medicinal properties, such as horse gentian and boneset
FEW adj not many
FEWER > FEW
FEWEST > FEW
FEWMET variant of > FUMET
FEWMETS > FEWMET
FEWNESS > FEW
FEWNESSES > FEW
FEWS > FEW
FEWTER variant of > FEUTRE
FEWTERED > FEUTRE
FEWTERING > FEUTRE
FEWTERS > FEUTRE
FEWTRILS n trifles, trivia
FEY adj whimsically strange ▷ vb clean out
FEYED > FEY
FEYER > FEY
FEYEST > FEY
FEYING > FEY
FEYLY > FEY
FEYNESS > FEY
FEYNESSES > FEY
FEYS > FEY
FEZ n brimless tasselled cap, orig. from Turkey
FEZES > FEZ
FEZZED adj wearing a fez
FEZZES > FEZ
FEZZY > FEZ
FIACRE n small four-wheeled horse-drawn carriage, usually with a folding roof
FIACRES > FIACRE
FIANCE n man engaged to be married
FIANCEE n woman who is engaged to be married
FIANCEES > FIANCEE
FIANCES > FIANCE
FIAR n property owner
FIARS n legally fixed price of corn
FIASCHI > FIASCO
FIASCO n ridiculous or humiliating failure
FIASCOES > FIASCO
FIASCOS > FIASCO
FIAT n arbitrary order ▷ vb issue a fiat
FIATED > FIAT

FIATING > FIAT
FIATS > FIAT
FIAUNT n fiat
FIAUNTS > FIAUNT
FIB n trivial lie ▷ vb tell a lie
FIBBED > FIB
FIBBER > FIB
FIBBERIES > FIB
FIBBERY > FIB
FIBBING > FIB
FIBER same as > FIBRE
FIBERED > FIBRE
FIBERFILL same as > FIBREFILL
FIBERISE same as > FIBERIZE
FIBERISED > FIBERISE
FIBERISES > FIBERISE
FIBERIZE vb break into fibres
FIBERIZED > FIBERIZE
FIBERIZES > FIBERIZE
FIBERLESS > FIBRE
FIBERLIKE > FIBER
FIBERS > FIBER
FIBRANNE n synthetic fabric
FIBRANNES > FIBRANNE
FIBRATE n drug used to lower fat levels in the body
FIBRATES > FIBRATE
FIBRE n thread that can be spun into yarn
FIBRED > FIBRE
FIBREFILL n synthetic fibre used as a filling for pillows, quilted materials, etc
FIBRELESS > FIBRE
FIBRES > FIBRE
FIBRIFORM adj having the form of a fibre or fibres
FIBRIL n small fibre
FIBRILAR > FIBRIL
FIBRILLA same as > FIBRIL
FIBRILLAE > FIBRILLA
FIBRILLAR > FIBRIL
FIBRILLIN n kind of protein
FIBRILS > FIBRIL
FIBRIN n white insoluble elastic protein formed when blood clots
FIBRINOID > FIBRIN
FIBRINOUS adj of, containing, or resembling fibrin
FIBRINS > FIBRIN
FIBRO n mixture of cement and asbestos fibre, used in sheets for building
FIBROCYTE n type of fibroblast
FIBROID adj (of structures or tissues) containing or resembling fibres ▷ n benign tumour composed of fibrous connective tissue
FIBROIDS > FIBROID
FIBROIN n tough elastic protein that is the principal component of spiders'

webs and raw silk
FIBROINS > FIBROIN
FIBROLINE n type of yarn
FIBROLITE n trademark name for a type of building board containing asbestos and cement
FIBROMA n benign tumour derived from fibrous connective tissue
FIBROMAS > FIBROMA
FIBROMATA > FIBROMA
FIBROS > FIBRO
FIBROSE vb become fibrous
FIBROSED > FIBROSE
FIBROSES > FIBROSE
FIBROSING > FIBROSE
FIBROSIS n formation of an abnormal amount of fibrous tissue
FIBROTIC > FIBROSIS
FIBROUS adj consisting of, containing, or resembling fibres
FIBROUSLY > FIBROUS
FIBS > FIB
FIBSTER n fibber
FIBSTERS > FIBSTER
FIBULA n slender outer bone of the lower leg
FIBULAE > FIBULA
FIBULAR > FIBULA
FIBULAS > FIBULA
FICE n small aggressive dog
FICES > FICE
FICHE n sheet of film for storing publications in miniaturized form
FICHES > FICHE
FICHU n woman's shawl or scarf of some light material, worn esp in the 18th century
FICHUS > FICHU
FICIN n enzyme
FICINS > FICIN
FICKLE adj changeable, inconstant ▷ vb puzzle
FICKLED > FICKLE
FICKLER > FICKLE
FICKLES > FICKLE
FICKLEST > FICKLE
FICKLING > FICKLE
FICKLY > FICKLE
FICO n worthless trifle
FICOES > FICO
FICOS > FICO
FICTILE adj moulded or capable of being moulded from clay
FICTION n literary works of the imagination, such as novels
FICTIONAL > FICTION
FICTIONS > FICTION
FICTIVE adj of, relating to, or able to create fiction
FICTIVELY > FICTIVE
FICTOR n sculptor
FICTORS > FICTOR
FICUS n type of plant such as the edible fig, often

grown as a greenhouse or house plant
FICUSES > FICUS
FID n spike for separating strands of rope in splicing
FIDDIOUS vb treat someone as Coriolanus, in the eponymous play, dealt with Aufidius
FIDDLE n violin ▷ vb play the violin
FIDDLED > FIDDLE
FIDDLER n person who plays the fiddle
FIDDLERS > FIDDLER
FIDDLES > FIDDLE
FIDDLEY n vertical space above a vessel's engine room extending into its stack
FIDDLEYS > FIDDLEY
FIDDLIER > FIDDLY
FIDDLIEST > FIDDLY
FIDDLING adj trivial
FIDDLY adj awkward to do or use
FIDEISM n theological doctrine that religious truth is a matter of faith and cannot be established by reason
FIDEISMS > FIDEISM
FIDEIST > FIDEISM
FIDEISTIC > FIDEISM
FIDEISTS > FIDEISM
FIDELISMO n belief in, adherence to, or advocacy of the principles of Fidel Castro, the Cuban Communist statesman (born 1927)
FIDELISTA n advocate of fidelismo
FIDELITY n faithfulness
FIDES n faith or trust
FIDGE obsolete word for > FIDGET
FIDGED > FIDGE
FIDGES > FIDGE
FIDGET vb move about restlessly ▷ n person who fidgets
FIDGETED > FIDGET
FIDGETER > FIDGET
FIDGETERS > FIDGET
FIDGETIER > FIDGET
FIDGETING > FIDGET
FIDGETS > FIDGET
FIDGETY > FIDGET
FIDGING > FIDGE
FIDIBUS n spill for lighting a candle or pipe
FIDIBUSES > FIDIBUS
FIDO n generic term for a dog
FIDOS > FIDO
FIDS > FID
FIDUCIAL adj used as a standard of reference or measurement
FIDUCIARY n person bound to act for someone else's benefit, as a trustee ▷ adj of a trust or trustee
FIE adj same as > FEY

FIEF n land granted by a lord in return for war service

FIEFDOM n (in Feudal Europe) the property owned by a lord

FIEFDOMS > FIEFDOM

FIEFS > FIEF

FIELD n piece of land, usu enclosed with a fence or hedge, and used for pasture or growing crops ▷ vb stop, catch, or return (the ball) as a fielder

FIELDED > FIELD

FIELDER n (in certain sports) player whose task is to field the ball

FIELDERS > FIELDER

FIELDFARE n type of large Old World thrush

FIELDING > FIELD

FIELDINGS > FIELD

FIELDMICE npl nocturnal mice

FIELDS > FIELD

FIELDSMAN n fielder

FIELDSMEN > FIELDSMAN

FIELDVOLE n small rodent

FIELDWARD adv towards a field or fields

FIELDWORK n investigation made in the field as opposed to the classroom or the laboratory

FIEND n evil spirit

FIENDISH adj of or like a fiend

FIENDLIKE > FIEND

FIENDS > FIEND

FIENT n fiend

FIENTS > FIENT

FIER same as > FERE

FIERCE adj wild or aggressive

FIERCELY > FIERCE

FIERCER > FIERCE

FIERCEST > FIERCE

FIERE same as > FERE

FIERES > FERE

FIERIER > FIERY

FIERIEST > FIERY

FIERILY > FIERY

FIERINESS > FIERY

FIERS > FIER

FIERY adj consisting of or like fire

FIEST > FIE

FIESTA n religious festival, carnival

FIESTAS > FIESTA

FIFE n small high-pitched flute ▷ vb play (music) on a fife

FIFED > FIFE

FIFER > FIFE

FIFERS > FIFE

FIFES > FIFE

FIFING > FIFE

FIFTEEN n five and ten ▷ adj amounting to fifteen ▷ det amounting to fifteen

FIFTEENER n fifteen-syllable line of poetry

FIFTEENS > FIFTEEN

FIFTEENTH adj coming after the fourteenth in order, position, time, etc. Often written: 15th ▷ n one of 15 equal or nearly equal parts of something

FIFTH n (of) number five in a series ▷ adj of or being number five in a series ▷ adv after the fourth person, position, time, etc

FIFTHLY same as > FIFTH

FIFTHS > FIFTH

FIFTIES > FIFTY

FIFTIETH adj being the ordinal number of fifty in order, position, time, etc. Often written: 50th ▷ n one of 50 equal or approximately equal parts of something

FIFTIETHS > FIFTIETH

FIFTY n five times ten ▷ adj amounting to fifty ▷ det amounting to fifty

FIFTYISH > FIFTY

FIG n soft pear-shaped fruit ▷ vb dress (up) or rig (out)

FIGEATER n large beetle

FIGEATERS > FIGEATER

FIGGED > FIG

FIGGERIES > FIGGERY

FIGGERY n adornment, ornament

FIGGING > FIG

FIGHT vb struggle (against) in battle or physical combat ▷ n aggressive conflict between two (groups of) people

FIGHTABLE > FIGHT

FIGHTBACK n act or campaign of resistance

FIGHTER n boxer

FIGHTERS > FIGHTER

FIGHTING > FIGHT

FIGHTINGS > FIGHT

FIGHTS > FIGHT

FIGJAM n very conceited person

FIGJAMS > FIGJAM

FIGMENT n fantastic notion, invention, or fabrication

FIGMENTS > FIGMENT

FIGO variant of > FICO

FIGOS > FIGO

FIGS > FIG

FIGULINE adj of or resembling clay ▷ n article made of clay

FIGULINES > FIGULINE

FIGURABLE > FIGURE

FIGURAL adj composed of or relating to human or animal figures

FIGURALLY > FIGURAL

FIGURANT n ballet dancer who does group work but no solo roles

FIGURANTE n female figurant

FIGURANTS > FIGURANT

FIGURATE adj exhibiting or produced by figuration

FIGURE n numerical symbol ▷ vb calculate (sums or amounts)

FIGURED adj decorated with a design

FIGUREDLY > FIGURED

FIGURER > FIGURE

FIGURERS > FIGURE

FIGURES > FIGURE

FIGURINE n statuette

FIGURINES > FIGURINE

FIGURING > FIGURE

FIGURIST n user of numbers

FIGURISTS > FIGURIST

FIGWORT n N temperate plant with square stems and small brown or greenish flowers

FIGWORTS > FIGWORT

FIKE vb fidget

FIKED > FIKE

FIKERIES > FIKERY

FIKERY n fuss

FIKES > FIKE

FIKIER > FIKY

FIKIEST > FIKY

FIKING > FIKE

FIKISH adj fussy

FIKY adj fussy

FIL same as > FILS

FILA > FILUM

FILABEG variant of > FILIBEG

FILABEGS > FILABEG

FILACEOUS adj made of threads

FILACER n formerly, English legal officer

FILACERS > FILACER

FILAGGRIN n protein found in skin cells

FILAGREE same as > FILIGREE

FILAGREED > FILAGREE

FILAGREES > FILAGREE

FILAMENT n fine wire in a light bulb that gives out light

FILAMENTS > FILAMENT

FILANDER n species of kangaroo

FILANDERS > FILANDER

FILAR adj of thread

FILAREE n type of storksbill, a weed

FILAREES > FILAREE

FILARIA n type of parasitic nematode worm transmitted to vertebrates by insects, the cause of filariasis

FILARIAE > FILARIA

FILARIAL > FILARIA

FILARIAN > FILARIA

FILARIID adj of or relating to a family of threadlike roundworms

FILARIIDS > FILARIID

FILASSE n vegetable fibre such as jute

FILASSES > FILASSE

FILATORY n machine for making threads

FILATURE n act or process of spinning silk, etc, into threads

FILATURES > FILATURE

FILAZER variant of > FILACER

FILAZERS > FILAZER

FILBERD variant of > FILBERT

FILBERDS > FILBERD

FILBERT n hazelnut

FILBERTS > FILBERT

FILCH vb steal (small amounts)

FILCHED > FILCH

FILCHER > FILCH

FILCHERS > FILCH

FILCHES > FILCH

FILCHING > FILCH

FILCHINGS > FILCH

FILE n box or folder used to keep documents in order ▷ vb place (a document) in a file

FILEABLE > FILE

FILECARD n type of brush with sharp steel bristles, used for cleaning the teeth of a file

FILECARDS > FILECARD

FILED > FILE

FILEFISH n type of tropical triggerfish with a narrow compressed body and a very long dorsal spine

FILEMOT n type of brown colour

FILEMOTS > FILEMOT

FILENAME n arrangement of characters that enables a computer system to permit the user to have access to a particular file

FILENAMES > FILENAME

FILER > FILE

FILERS > FILE

FILES > FILE

FILET variant of > FILLET

FILETED > FILET

FILETING > FILET

FILETS > FILET

FILFOT variant of > FYLFOT

FILFOTS > FILFOT

FILIAL adj of or befitting a son or daughter

FILIALLY > FILIAL

FILIATE vb judicially fix the paternity of (a child, esp one born out of wedlock)

FILIATED > FILIATE

FILIATES > FILIATE

FILIATING > FILIATE

FILIATION n line of descent

FILIBEG n kilt worn by Scottish Highlanders

FILIBEGS > FILIBEG

FILICIDAL > FILICIDE

FILICIDE n act of killing

one's own son or daughter
FILICIDES > FILICIDE
FILIFORM adj having the form of a thread
FILIGRAIN n filigree
FILIGRANE variant of > FILIGRAIN
FILIGREE n delicate ornamental work of gold or silver wire ▷ adj made of filigree ▷ vb decorate with or as if with filigree
FILIGREED > FILIGREE
FILIGREES > FILIGREE
FILII > FILIUS
FILING > FILE
FILINGS npl shavings removed by a file
FILIOQUE n theological term found in the Nicene Creed
FILIOQUES > FILIOQUE
FILISTER same as > FILLISTER
FILISTERS > FILISTER
FILIUS n son
FILL vb make or become full
FILLABLE > FILL
FILLAGREE same as > FILIGREE
FILLE n girl
FILLED > FILL
FILLER n substance that fills a gap or increases bulk
FILLERS > FILLER
FILLES > FILLE
FILLESTER same as > FILLISTER
FILLET n boneless piece of meat ▷ vb remove the bones from
FILLETED > FILLET
FILLETING > FILLET
FILLETS > FILLET
FILLIBEG same as > FILIBEG
FILLIBEGS > FILLIBEG
FILLIES > FILLY
FILLING n substance that fills a gap or cavity, esp in a tooth ▷ adj (of food) substantial and satisfying
FILLINGS > FILLING
FILLIP n something that adds stimulation or enjoyment ▷ vb stimulate or excite
FILLIPED > FILLIP
FILLIPEEN n philopoena
FILLIPING > FILLIP
FILLIPS > FILLIP
FILLISTER n adjustable plane for cutting rabbets, grooves, etc
FILLO variant of > FILO
FILLOS > FILLO
FILLS > FILL
FILLY n young female horse
FILM n sequence of images projected on a screen, creating the illusion of movement ▷ vb photograph with a movie

or video camera ▷ adj connected with films or the cinema
FILMABLE > FILM
FILMCARD n cinema loyalty card
FILMCARDS > FILMCARD
FILMDOM n cinema industry
FILMDOMS > FILMDOM
FILMED > FILM
FILMER n film-maker
FILMERS > FILMER
FILMGOER n person who goes regularly to the cinema
FILMGOERS > FILMGOER
FILMGOING > FILMGOER
FILMI adj in Indian English, of or relating to the Indian film industry or Indian films
FILMIC adj of or suggestive of films or the cinema
FILMIER > FILMY
FILMIEST > FILMY
FILMILY > FILMY
FILMINESS > FILMY
FILMING > FILM
FILMIS > FILMI
FILMISH > FILM
FILMLAND n cinema industry
FILMLANDS > FILMLAND
FILMLESS > FILM
FILMLIKE > FILM
FILMMAKER n person who makes films
FILMS > FILM
FILMSET vb set (type matter) by filmsetting
FILMSETS > FILMSET
FILMSTRIP n strip of film composed of different images projected separately as slides
FILMY adj very thin, delicate
FILO n type of flaky Greek pastry in very thin sheets
FILOPLUME n any of the hairlike feathers that lack vanes and occur between the contour feathers
FILOPODIA n plural form of singular filopodium: ectoplasmic pseudopodium
FILOS > FILO
FILOSE adj resembling or possessing a thread or threadlike process
FILOSELLE n soft silk thread, used esp for embroidery
FILOVIRUS n any member of a family of viruses that includes the agents responsible for Ebola virus disease and Marburg disease
FILS n fractional monetary unit of Bahrain, Iraq, Jordan, and Kuwait, worth one thousandth of a dinar

FILTER n material or device permitting fluid to pass but retaining solid particles ▷ vb remove impurities from (a substance) with a filter
FILTERED > FILTER
FILTERER > FILTER
FILTERERS > FILTER
FILTERING > FILTER
FILTERS > FILTER
FILTH n disgusting dirt
FILTHIER > FILTHY
FILTHIEST > FILTHY
FILTHILY > FILTHY
FILTHS > FILTH
FILTHY adj characterized by or full of filth ▷ adv extremely
FILTRABLE adj capable of being filtered
FILTRATE n filtered gas or liquid ▷ vb remove impurities with a filter
FILTRATED > FILTRATE
FILTRATES > FILTRATE
FILTRE as in cafe filtre a strong black filtered coffee
FILUM n any threadlike structure or part
FIMBLE n male plant of the hemp, which matures before the female plant
FIMBLES > FIMBLE
FIMBRIA n fringe or fringelike margin or border, esp at the opening of the Fallopian tubes
FIMBRIAE > FIMBRIA
FIMBRIAL > FIMBRIA
FIMBRIATE adj having a fringed margin, as some petals, antennae, etc
FIN n any of the firm appendages that are the organs of locomotion and balance in fishes and some other aquatic mammals ▷ vb provide with fins
FINABLE adj liable to a fine
FINAGLE vb get or achieve by craftiness or trickery
FINAGLED > FINAGLE
FINAGLER > FINAGLE
FINAGLERS > FINAGLE
FINAGLES > FINAGLE
FINAGLING > FINAGLE
FINAL adj at the end ▷ n deciding contest between winners of previous rounds in a competition
FINALE n concluding part of a dramatic performance or musical work
FINALES > FINALE
FINALIS n musical finishing note
FINALISE same as > FINALIZE
FINALISED > FINALISE
FINALISER > FINALISE
FINALISES > FINALISE
FINALISM n doctrine that final causes determine the course of all events

FINALISMS > FINALISM
FINALIST n competitor in a final
FINALISTS > FINALIST
FINALITY n condition or quality of being final or settled
FINALIZE vb put into final form
FINALIZED > FINALIZE
FINALIZER > FINALIZE
FINALIZES > FINALIZE
FINALLY adv after a long delay
FINALS npl deciding part of a competition
FINANCE vb provide or obtain funds for ▷ n system of money, credit, and investment
FINANCED > FINANCE
FINANCES > FINANCE
FINANCIAL adj of or relating to finance, finances, or people who manage money
FINANCIER n person involved in large-scale financial business
FINANCING > FINANCE
FINBACK another name for > RORQUAL
FINBACKS > FINBACK
FINCA n Spanish villa
FINCAS > FINCA
FINCH n small songbird with a short strong beak
FINCHED adj with streaks or spots on the back
FINCHES > FINCH
FIND vb discover by chance ▷ n person or thing found, esp when valuable
FINDABLE > FIND
FINDER n small telescope fitted to a larger one
FINDERS > FINDER
FINDING > FIND
FINDINGS > FIND
FINDRAM variant of > FINNAN
FINDRAMS > FINDRAM
FINDS > FIND
FINE adj very good ▷ n payment imposed as a penalty ▷ vb impose a fine on
FINEABLE same as > FINABLE
FINED > FINE
FINEER variant of > VENEER
FINEERED > FINEER
FINEERING > FINEER
FINEERS > FINEER
FINEISH > FINE
FINELESS > FINE
FINELY adv into small pieces
FINENESS n state or quality of being fine
FINER > FINE
FINERIES > FINERY
FINERS > FINE

FINERY n showy clothing

FINES > FINE

FINESPUN adj spun or drawn out to a fine thread

FINESSE n delicate skill ▷ vb bring about with finesse

FINESSED > FINESSE

FINESSER > FINESSE

FINESSERS > FINESSE

FINESSES > FINESSE

FINESSING > FINESSE

FINEST > FINE

FINFISH n fish with fins, as opposed to shellfish

FINFISHES > FINFISH

FINFOOT n type of tropical and subtropical aquatic bird with broadly lobed toes, a long slender head and neck, and pale brown plumage

FINFOOTS > FINFOOT

FINGAN variant of > FINJAN

FINGANS > FINGAN

FINGER n one of the four long jointed parts of the hand ▷ vb touch or handle with the fingers

FINGERED adj marked or dirtied by handling

FINGERER > FINGER

FINGERERS > FINGER

FINGERING n technique of using the fingers in playing a musical instrument

FINGERS > FINGER

FINGERTIP n end joint or tip of a finger

FINI n end; finish

FINIAL n ornament at the apex of a gable or spire

FINIALED adj having a finial or finials

FINIALS > FINIAL

FINICAL another word for > FINICKY

FINICALLY > FINICAL

FINICKETY adj fussy or tricky

FINICKIER > FINICKY

FINICKIN variant of > FINICKY

FINICKING same as > FINICKY

FINICKY adj excessively particular, fussy

FINIKIN variant of > FINICKY

FINIKING variant of > FINICKY

FINING n process of removing undissolved gas bubbles from molten glass

FININGS > FINING

FINIS > FINI

FINISES > FINIS

FINISH vb bring to an end, stop ▷ n end, last part

FINISHED adj perfected

FINISHER n craftsman who carries out the final tasks in a manufacturing process

FINISHERS > FINISHER

FINISHES > FINISH

FINISHING n act or skill of goal scoring

FINITE adj having limits in space, time, or size

FINITELY > FINITE

FINITES > FINITE

FINITISM n view that only those entities may be admitted to mathematics that can be constructed in a finite number of steps, and only those propositions entertained whose truth can be proved in a finite number of steps

FINITISMS > FINITISM

FINITO adj finished

FINITUDE > FINITE

FINITUDES > FINITE

FINJAN n small, handleless coffee cup

FINJANS > FINJAN

FINK n strikebreaker ▷ vb inform (on someone), as to the police

FINKED > FINK

FINKING > FINK

FINKS > FINK

FINLESS > FIN

FINLIKE > FIN

FINMARK n monetary unit of Finland

FINMARKS > FINMARK

FINNAC variant of > FINNOCK

FINNACK variant of > FINNOCK

FINNACKS > FINNACK

FINNACS > FINNAC

FINNAN n smoked haddock

FINNANS > FINNAN

FINNED > FIN

FINNER another name for > RORQUAL

FINNERS > FINNER

FINNESKO n reindeer-skin boot

FINNICKY variant of > FINICKY

FINNIER > FINNY

FINNIEST > FINNY

FINNING > FIN

FINNMARK n Finnish monetary unit

FINNMARKS > FINNMARK

FINNOCHIO variant of > FINOCCHIO

FINNOCK n young sea trout on its first return to fresh water

FINNOCKS > FINNOCK

FINNSKO variant of > FINNESKO

FINNY adj relating to or containing many fishes

FINO n very dry sherry

FINOCCHIO n variety of fennel with celery-like stalks which are eaten as a vegetable

FINOCHIO same as > FINOCCHIO

FINOCHIOS > FINOCHIO

FINOS > FINO

FINS > FIN

FINSKO variant of > FINNESKO

FIORATURA same as > FIORITURA

FIORD same as > FJORD

FIORDS > FIORD

FIORIN n type of temperate perennial grass

FIORINS > FIORIN

FIORITURA n embellishment, esp ornamentation added by the performer

FIORITURE > FIORITURA

FIPPENCE n fivepence

FIPPENCES > FIPPENCE

FIPPLE n wooden plug forming a flue in the end of a pipe, as the mouthpiece of a recorder

FIPPLES > FIPPLE

FIQH n Islamic jurisprudence

FIQHS > FIQH

FIQUE n hemp

FIQUES > FIQUE

FIR n pyramid-shaped tree with needle-like leaves and erect cones

FIRE n state of combustion producing heat, flames, and smoke ▷ vb operate (a weapon) so that a bullet or missile is released

FIREABLE > FIRE

FIREARM n rifle, pistol, or shotgun

FIREARMED adj carrying firearm

FIREARMS > FIREARM

FIREBACK n ornamental iron slab against the back wall of a hearth

FIREBACKS > FIREBACK

FIREBALL n ball of fire at the centre of an explosion

FIREBALLS > FIREBALL

FIREBASE n artillery base from which heavy fire is directed at the enemy

FIREBASES > FIREBASE

FIREBIRD n any of various songbirds having a bright red plumage, esp the Baltimore oriole

FIREBIRDS > FIREBIRD

FIREBOARD n mantelpiece

FIREBOAT n motor vessel with fire-fighting apparatus

FIREBOATS > FIREBOAT

FIREBOMB n bomb that is designed to cause fires ▷ vb detonate such a bomb

FIREBOMBS > FIREBOMB

FIREBOX n furnace chamber of a boiler in a steam locomotive

FIREBOXES > FIREBOX

FIREBRAND n person who causes unrest

FIREBRAT n type of small primitive wingless insect

FIREBRATS > FIREBRAT

FIREBREAK n strip of cleared land to stop the advance of a fire

FIREBRICK n heat-resistant brick used for lining furnaces, fireplaces, etc

FIREBUG n person who deliberately sets fire to property

FIREBUGS > FIREBUG

FIREBUSH as in Chilean firebush South American shrub with scarlet flowers

FIRECLAY n heat-resistant clay used in the making of firebricks, furnace linings, etc

FIRECLAYS > FIRECLAY

FIRECREST n small European warbler with a crown striped with yellow, black, and white

FIRED > FIRE

FIREDAMP n explosive gas, composed mainly of methane, formed in mines

FIREDAMPS > FIREDAMP

FIREDOG n either of a pair of decorative metal stands used to support logs in an open fire

FIREDOGS > FIREDOG

FIREDRAKE n fire-breathing dragon

FIREFANG vb become overheated through decomposition

FIREFANGS > FIREFANG

FIREFIGHT n brief small-scale engagement between opposing military ground forces using short-range light weapons

FIREFLIES > FIREFLY

FIREFLOAT n boat used for firefighting

FIREFLOOD n method of extracting oil from a well by burning some of the oil to increase the rate of flow

FIREFLY n beetle that glows in the dark

FIREGUARD same as > FIREBREAK

FIREHALL n US and Canadian word for fire station

FIREHALLS > FIREHALL

FIREHOUSE n firestation

FIRELESS > FIRE

FIRELIGHT n light from a fire

FIRELIT adj lit by firelight

FIRELOCK n obsolete type of gunlock with a priming mechanism ignited by sparks

FIRELOCKS > FIRELOCK

FIREMAN n man whose job is to put out fires and

rescue people endangered by them

FIREMANIC > FIREMAN

FIREMARK n plaque indicating that a building is insured

FIREMARKS > FIREMARK

FIREMEN > FIREMAN

FIREPAN n metal container for a fire in a room

FIREPANS > FIREPAN

FIREPINK n wildflower belonging to the pink family

FIREPINKS > FIREPINK

FIREPLACE n recess in a room for a fire

FIREPLUG n US and New Zealand name for a fire hydrant

FIREPLUGS > FIREPLUG

FIREPOT n Chinese fondue-like cooking pot

FIREPOTS > FIREPOT

FIREPOWER n amount of fire that may be delivered by a unit or weapon

FIREPROOF adj capable of resisting damage by fire ▷ vb make resistant to fire

FIRER > FIRE

FIREROOM n stokehold

FIREROOMS > FIREROOM

FIRERS > FIRE

FIRES > FIRE

FIRESHIP n vessel loaded with flammable materials, ignited, and directed among enemy warships to set them alight

FIRESHIPS > FIRESHIP

FIRESIDE n hearth

FIRESIDES > FIRESIDE

FIRESTONE n sandstone that withstands intense heat, esp one used for lining kilns, furnaces, etc

FIRESTORM n uncontrollable blaze sustained by violent winds that are drawn into the column of rising hot air over the burning area: often the result of heavy bombing

FIRETHORN n type of evergreen spiny shrub of SE Europe and Asia with bright red or orange fruits, cultivated for ornament

FIRETRAP n building that would burn easily or one without fire escapes

FIRETRAPS > FIRETRAP

FIRETRUCK n fire engine

FIREWALL n appliance that prevents unauthorized access to a computer network from the internet ▷ vb protect (a computer system) or block (unwanted access) with a firewall

FIREWALLS > FIREWALL

FIREWATER n any alcoholic spirit

FIREWEED n any of various plants that appear as first vegetation in burnt-over areas, esp rosebay willowherb

FIREWEEDS > FIREWEED

FIREWOMAN n female firefighter

FIREWOMEN > FIREWOMAN

FIREWOOD n wood for burning

FIREWOODS > FIREWOOD

FIREWORK n device containing chemicals that is ignited to produce spectacular explosions and coloured sparks

FIREWORKS npl show in which fireworks are let off

FIREWORM n cranberry worm

FIREWORMS > FIREWORM

FIRIE n in Australian English, informal word for a firefighter

FIRIES > FIRIE

FIRING n discharge of a firearm

FIRINGS > FIRING

FIRK vb beat

FIRKED > FIRK

FIRKIN n small wooden barrel or similar container

FIRKING > FIRK

FIRKINS > FIRKIN

FIRKS > FIRK

FIRLOT n unit of measurement for grain

FIRLOTS > FIRLOT

FIRM adj not soft or yielding ▷ adv in an unyielding manner ▷ vb make or become firm ▷ n business company

FIRMAMENT n sky or the heavens

FIRMAN n edict of an Oriental sovereign

FIRMANS > FIRMAN

FIRMED > FIRM

FIRMER > FIRM

FIRMERS > FIRM

FIRMEST > FIRM

FIRMING > FIRM

FIRMLESS adj unstable

FIRMLY > FIRM

FIRMNESS > FIRM

FIRMS > FIRM

FIRMWARE n fixed form of software programmed into a read-only memory

FIRMWARES > FIRMWARE

FIRN another name for > NEVE

FIRNS > FIRN

FIRRIER > FIRRY

FIRRIEST > FIRRY

FIRRING n wooden battens used in building construction

FIRRINGS > FIRRING

FIRRY adj of, relating to, or

made from fir trees

FIRS > FIR

FIRST adj earliest in time or order ▷ n person or thing coming before all others ▷ adv before anything else

FIRSTBORN adj eldest of the children in a family ▷ n eldest child in a family

FIRSTHAND adj from the original source

FIRSTLING n first, esp the first offspring

FIRSTLY adv coming before other points, questions, etc

FIRSTNESS > FIRST

FIRSTS npl saleable goods of the highest quality

FIRTH n narrow inlet of the sea, esp in Scotland

FIRTHS > FIRTH

FIRWOOD n wood of the fir tree

FIRWOODS > FIRWOOD

FISC n state or royal treasury

FISCAL adj of government finances, esp taxes ▷ n (in some countries) a public prosecutor

FISCALIST > FISCAL

FISCALLY > FISCAL

FISCALS > FISCAL

FISCS > FISC

FISGIG variant of > FISHGIG

FISGIGS > FISGIG

FISH n cold-blooded vertebrate with gills, that lives in water ▷ vb try to catch fish

FISHABLE > FISH

FISHBALL n fried ball of flaked fish and mashed potato

FISHBALLS > FISHBALL

FISHBOLT n bolt used for fastening a fishplate to a rail

FISHBOLTS > FISHBOLT

FISHBONE n bone of a fish

FISHBONES > FISHBONE

FISHBOWL n goldfish bowl

FISHBOWLS > FISHBOWL

FISHCAKE n mixture of flaked fish and mashed potatoes formed into a flat circular shape

FISHCAKES > FISHCAKE

FISHED > FISH

FISHER n fisherman

FISHERIES > FISHERY

FISHERMAN n person who catches fish for a living or for pleasure

FISHERMEN > FISHERMAN

FISHERS > FISHER

FISHERY n area of the sea used for fishing

FISHES > FISH

FISHEYE n in photography, a lens of small focal length, having a

highly curved protruding front element, that covers an angle of view of almost 180°

FISHEYES > FISHEYE

FISHFUL adj teeming with fish

FISHGIG n pole with barbed prongs for impaling fish

FISHGIGS > FISHGIG

FISHHOOK n sharp hook used in angling, esp one with a barb

FISHHOOKS > FISHHOOK

FISHIER > FISHY

FISHIEST > FISHY

FISHIFIED > FISHIFY

FISHIFIES > FISHIFY

FISHIFY vb change into fish

FISHILY > FISHY

FISHINESS > FISHY

FISHING n job or pastime of catching fish

FISHINGS > FISHING

FISHKILL n mass killing of fish by pollution

FISHKILLS > FISHKILL

FISHLESS > FISH

FISHLIKE > FISH

FISHLINE n line used on a fishing-rod

FISHLINES > FISHLINE

FISHMEAL n ground dried fish used as feed for farm animals or as a fertilizer

FISHMEALS > FISHMEAL

FISHNET n open mesh fabric resembling netting

FISHNETS > FISHNET

FISHPLATE n metal plate holding rails together

FISHPOLE n boom arm for a microphone

FISHPOLES > FISHPOLE

FISHPOND > FISH

FISHPONDS > FISH

FISHSKIN n skin of a fish

FISHSKINS > FISHSKIN

FISHTAIL n nozzle having a long narrow slot at the top, placed over a Bunsen burner to produce a thin fanlike flame ▷ vb slow an aeroplane by moving the tail from side to side

FISHTAILS > FISHTAIL

FISHWAY n fish ladder

FISHWAYS > FISHWAY

FISHWIFE n coarse scolding woman

FISHWIVES > FISHWIFE

FISHWORM n worm used as fishing bait

FISHWORMS > FISHWORM

FISHY adj of or like fish

FISHYBACK n goods supply chain involving container transfer from lorry to ship

FISK vb frisk

FISKED > FISK

FISKING > FISK

FISKS > FISK
FISNOMIE n physiognomy
FISNOMIES > FISNOMIE
FISSATE > FISSILE
FISSILE adj capable of undergoing nuclear fission
FISSILITY > FISSILE
FISSION n splitting
FISSIONAL > FISSION
FISSIONED adj split or broken into parts
FISSIONS > FISSION
FISSIPED adj having toes that are separated from one another, as dogs, cats, bears, and similar carnivores ▷ n fissiped animal
FISSIPEDE > FISSIPED
FISSIPEDS > FISSIPED
FISSIVE > FISSILE
FISSLE vb rustle
FISSLED > FISSLE
FISSLES > FISSLE
FISSLING > FISSLE
FISSURAL > FISSURE
FISSURE n long narrow cleft or crack ▷ vb crack or split apart
FISSURED > FISSURE
FISSURES > FISSURE
FISSURING > FISSURE
FIST n clenched hand ▷ vb hit with the fist
FISTED > FIST
FISTFIGHT n fight using bare fists
FISTFUL n quantity that can be held in a fist or hand
FISTFULS > FISTFUL
FISTIANA n world of boxing
FISTIC adj of or relating to fisticuffs or boxing
FISTICAL > FISTIC
FISTICUFF n cuff or blow
FISTIER > FIST
FISTIEST > FIST
FISTING > FIST
FISTMELE n measure of the width of a hand and the extended thumb, used to calculate the approximate height of the string of a braced bow
FISTMELES > FISTMELE
FISTNOTE n note in printed text preceded by the fist symbol
FISTNOTES > FISTNOTE
FISTS > FIST
FISTULA n long narrow ulcer
FISTULAE > FISTULA
FISTULAR same as > FISTULOUS
FISTULAS > FISTULA
FISTULATE same as > FISTULOUS
FISTULOSE variant of > FISTULOUS
FISTULOUS adj containing, relating to, or resembling a fistula

FISTY > FIST
FIT vb be appropriate or suitable for ▷ adj appropriate ▷ n way in which something fits
FITCH n fur of the polecat or ferret
FITCHE adj pointed
FITCHEE variant of > FITCHE
FITCHES > FITCH
FITCHET same as > FITCH
FITCHETS > FITCHET
FITCHEW archaic name for > POLECAT
FITCHEWS > FITCHEW
FITCHY variant of > FITCHE
FITFUL adj occurring in irregular spells
FITFULLY > FITFUL
FITLIER > FITLY
FITLIEST > FITLY
FITLY adv in a proper manner or place or at a proper time
FITMENT n accessory attached to a machine
FITMENTS > FITMENT
FITNA n state of trouble or chaos
FITNAS > FITNA
FITNESS n state of being fit
FITNESSES > FITNESS
FITS > FIT
FITT n song
FITTABLE > FIT
FITTE variant of > FITT
FITTED > FIT
FITTER > FIT
FITTERS > FIT
FITTES > FITTE
FITTEST > FIT
FITTING > FIT
FITTINGLY > FIT
FITTINGS > FIT
FITTS > FITT
FIVE n one more than four ▷ adj amounting to five ▷ det amounting to five
FIVEFOLD adj having five times as many or as much ▷ adv by five times as many or as much
FIVEPENCE n five-penny coin
FIVEPENNY adj (of a nail) one and three-quarters of an inch in length
FIVEPIN > FIVEPINS
FIVEPINS n bowling game played esp in Canada
FIVER n five-pound note
FIVERS > FIVER
FIVES n ball game resembling squash but played with bats or the hands
FIX vb make or become firm, stable, or secure ▷ n difficult situation
FIXABLE > FIX
FIXATE vb become or

cause to become fixed
FIXATED > FIXATE
FIXATES > FIXATE
FIXATIF variant of > FIXATIVE
FIXATIFS > FIXATIF
FIXATING > FIXATE
FIXATION n obsessive interest in something
FIXATIONS > FIXATION
FIXATIVE n liquid used to preserve or hold things in place ▷ adj serving or tending to fix
FIXATIVES > FIXATIVE
FIXTURE n something that holds an object in place
FIXATURES > FIXATURE
FIXED adj attached or placed so as to be immovable
FIXEDLY > FIXED
FIXEDNESS > FIXED
FIXER n solution used to make a photographic image permanent
FIXERS > FIXER
FIXES > FIX
FIXING n means of attaching one thing to another, as a pipe to a wall, slate to a roof, etc
FIXINGS npl apparatus or equipment
FIXIT n solution to a complex problem
FIXITIES > FIXITY
FIXITY n state or quality of a person's gaze, attitude, or concentration not changing or weakening
FIXIVE > FIX
FIXT adj fixed
FIXTURE n permanently fitted piece of household equipment
FIXTURES > FIXTURE
FIXURE n firmness
FIXURES > FIXURE
FIZ variant of > FIZZ
FIZGIG vb inform on someone to the police
FIZGIGGED > FIZGIG
FIZGIGS > FIZGIG
FIZZ vb make a hissing or bubbling noise ▷ n hissing or bubbling noise
FIZZED > FIZZ
FIZZEN variant of > FOISON
FIZZENS > FIZZEN
FIZZER n anything that fizzes
FIZZERS > FIZZER
FIZZES > FIZZ
FIZZGIG variant of > FISHGIG
FIZZGIGS > FIZZGIG
FIZZIER > FIZZ
FIZZIEST > FIZZ
FIZZINESS > FIZZ
FIZZING > FIZZ
FIZZINGS > FIZZ

FIZZLE vb make a weak hissing or bubbling sound ▷ n hissing or bubbling sound
FIZZLED > FIZZLE
FIZZLES > FIZZLE
FIZZLING > FIZZLE
FIZZY > FIZZ
FJELD n high rocky plateau with little vegetation in Scandinavian countries
FJELDS > FJELD
FJORD n long narrow inlet of the sea between cliffs, esp in Norway
FJORDIC > FJORD
FJORDS > FJORD
FLAB n unsightly body fat
FLABBIER > FLABBY
FLABBIEST > FLABBY
FLABBILY > FLABBY
FLABBY adj having flabby flesh
FLABELLA > FLABELLUM
FLABELLUM n fan-shaped organ or part, such as the tip of the proboscis of a honeybee
FLABS > FLAB
FLACCID adj soft and limp
FLACCIDER > FLACCID
FLACCIDLY > FLACCID
FLACK vb flutter
FLACKED > FLACK
FLACKER vb flutter like a bird
FLACKERED > FLACKER
FLACKERS > FLACKER
FLACKERY > FLACK
FLACKET n flagon
FLACKETS > FLACKET
FLACKING > FLACK
FLACKS > FLACK
FLACON n small stoppered bottle or flask, such as one used for perfume
FLACONS > FLACON
FLAFF vb flap
FLAFFED > FLAFF
FLAFFER vb flutter
FLAFFERED > FLAFFER
FLAFFERS > FLAFFER
FLAFFING > FLAFF
FLAFFS > FLAFF
FLAG n piece of cloth attached to a pole as an emblem or signal ▷ vb mark with a flag or sticker
FLAGELLA > FLAGELLUM
FLAGELLAR > FLAGELLUM
FLAGELLIN n structural protein of bacterial flagella
FLAGELLUM n whiplike outgrowth from a cell that acts as an organ of movement
FLAGEOLET n small instrument like a recorder
FLAGGED > FLAG
FLAGGER > FLAG
FLAGGERS > FLAG
FLAGGIER > FLAGGY
FLAGGIEST > FLAGGY

FLAGGING > FLAG

FLAGGINGS > FLAG

FLAGGY *adj* drooping

FLAGITATE *vb* importune

FLAGLESS > FLAG

FLAGMAN *n* person who has charge of, carries, or signals with a flag, esp a railway employee

FLAGMEN > FLAGMAN

FLAGON *n* wide bottle for wine or cider

FLAGONS > FLAGON

FLAGPOLE *n* pole for a flag

FLAGPOLES > FLAGPOLE

FLAGRANCE > FLAGRANT

FLAGRANCY > FLAGRANT

FLAGRANT *adj* openly outrageous

FLAGS > FLAG

FLAGSHIP *n* admiral's ship

FLAGSHIPS > FLAGSHIP

FLAGSTAFF *same as* **>** FLAGPOLE

FLAGSTICK *n* in golf, pole used to indicate position of hole

FLAGSTONE *n* flat slab of hard stone for paving

FLAIL *vb* wave about wildly ▷ *n* tool formerly used for threshing grain by hand

FLAILED > FLAIL

FLAILING > FLAIL

FLAILS > FLAIL

FLAIR *n* natural ability

FLAIRS > FLAIR

FLAK *n* anti-aircraft fire

FLAKE *n* small thin piece, esp chipped off something ▷ *vb* peel off in flakes

FLAKED > FLAKE

FLAKER > FLAKE

FLAKERS > FLAKE

FLAKES > FLAKE

FLAKEY *same as* **>** FLAKY

FLAKIER > FLAKY

FLAKIES *n* dandruff

FLAKIEST > FLAKY

FLAKILY > FLAKY

FLAKINESS > FLAKY

FLAKING > FLAKE

FLAKS > FLAK

FLAKY *adj* like or made of flakes

FLAM *n* falsehood, deception, or sham ▷ *vb* cheat or deceive

FLAMBE *vb* cook or serve (food) in flaming brandy ▷ *adj* (of food, such as steak or pancakes) served in flaming brandy

FLAMBEAU *n* burning torch, as used in night processions

FLAMBEAUS > FLAMBEAU

FLAMBEAUX > FLAMBEAU

FLAMBEE *same as* **>** FLAMBE

FLAMBEED > FLAMBEE

FLAMBEES > FLAMBEE

FLAMBEING > FLAMBE

FLAMBES > FLAMBE

FLAME *n* luminous burning gas coming from burning material ▷ *vb* burn brightly

FLAMED > FLAME

FLAMELESS > FLAME

FLAMELET > FLAME

FLAMELETS > FLAME

FLAMELIKE > FLAME

FLAMEN *n* (in ancient Rome) any of 15 priests who each served a particular deity

FLAMENCO *n* rhythmical Spanish dance accompanied by a guitar and vocalist

FLAMENCOS > FLAMENCO

FLAMENS > FLAMEN

FLAMEOUT *n* failure of an aircraft jet engine in flight due to extinction of the flame ▷ *vb* (of a jet engine) to fail in flight or to cause (a jet engine) to fail in flight

FLAMEOUTS > FLAMEOUT

FLAMER > FLAME

FLAMERS > FLAME

FLAMES > FLAME

FLAMFEW *n* fantastic trifle

FLAMFEWS > FLAMFEW

FLAMIER > FLAME

FLAMIEST > FLAME

FLAMINES > FLAMEN

FLAMING *adj* burning with flames ▷ *adv* extremely

FLAMINGLY > FLAMING

FLAMINGO *n* large pink wading bird with a long neck and legs

FLAMINGOS > FLAMINGO

FLAMM *variant of* **>** FLAM

FLAMMABLE *adj* easily set on fire

FLAMMED > FLAM

FLAMMING > FLAM

FLAMMS > FLAMM

FLAMMULE *n* small flame

FLAMMULES > FLAMMULE

FLAMS > FLAM

FLAMY > FLAME

FLAN *n* open sweet or savoury tart

FLANCARD *n* armour covering a horse's flank

FLANCARDS > FLANCARD

FLANCH *variant of* **>** FLAUNCH

FLANCHED > FLANCH

FLANCHES > FLANCH

FLANCHING > FLANCH

FLANERIE *n* aimless strolling or lounging

FLANERIES > FLANERIE

FLANES *n* arrows

FLANEUR *n* idler or loafer

FLANEURS > FLANEUR

FLANGE *n* projecting rim or collar ▷ *vb* attach or provide (a component) with a flange

FLANGED > FLANGE

FLANGER > FLANGE

FLANGERS > FLANGE

FLANGES > FLANGE

FLANGING > FLANGE

FLANK *n* part of the side between the hips and ribs ▷ *vb* be at or move along the side of

FLANKED > FLANK

FLANKEN *n* cut of beef

FLANKER *n* one of a detachment of soldiers detailed to guard the flanks, esp of a formation

FLANKERED > FLANKER

FLANKERS > FLANKER

FLANKING > FLANK

FLANKS > FLANK

FLANNEL *n* small piece of cloth for washing the face ▷ *vb* talk evasively

FLANNELED > FLANNEL

FLANNELET *n* cotton imitation of flannel

FLANNELLY > FLANNEL

FLANNELS > FLANNEL

FLANNEN *adj* made of flannel

FLANNENS > FLANNEN

FLANNIE *same as* **>** FLANNY

FLANNIES > FLANNIE

FLANNY *n* a shirt made of flannel

FLANS > FLAN

FLAP *vb* move back and forwards or up and down ▷ *n* action or sound of flapping

FLAPERON *n* control flap on aircraft wing

FLAPERONS > FLAPERON

FLAPJACK *n* chewy biscuit made with oats

FLAPJACKS > FLAPJACK

FLAPLESS > FLAP

FLAPPABLE > FLAP

FLAPPED > FLAP

FLAPPER *n* (in the 1920s) a lively young woman who dressed and behaved unconventionally

FLAPPERS > FLAPPER

FLAPPIER > FLAPPY

FLAPPIEST > FLAPPY

FLAPPING > FLAP

FLAPPINGS > FLAP

FLAPPY *adj* loose

FLAPS > FLAP

FLAPTRACK *n* component in an aircraft wing

FLARE *vb* blaze with a sudden unsteady flame ▷ *n* sudden unsteady flame

FLAREBACK *n* flame in the breech of a gun when fired

FLARED > FLARE

FLARES *npl* trousers with legs that widen below the knee

FLAREUP *n* outbreak of something

FLAREUPS > FLAREUP

FLARIER > FLARE

FLARIEST > FLARE

FLARING > FLARE

FLARINGLY > FLARE

FLARY > FLARE

FLASER *n* type of sedimentary structure in rock

FLASERS > FLASER

FLASH *n* sudden burst of light or flame ▷ *adj* vulgarly showy ▷ *vb* (cause to) burst into flame

FLASHBACK *n* scene in a book, play, or film, that shows earlier events ▷ *vb* return in a novel, film, etc, to a past event

FLASHBULB *n* small light bulb that produces a bright flash of light

FLASHCARD *n* card shown briefly as a memory test

FLASHCUBE *n* in photography, a cube with a bulb that is attached to a camera

FLASHED > FLASH

FLASHER *n* man who exposes himself indecently

FLASHERS > FLASHER

FLASHES > FLASH

FLASHEST > FLASH

FLASHGUN *n* type of electronic flash, attachable to or sometimes incorporated in a camera, that emits a very brief flash of light when the shutter is open

FLASHGUNS > FLASHGUN

FLASHIER > FLASHY

FLASHIEST > FLASHY

FLASHILY > FLASHY

FLASHING *n* watertight material used to cover joins in a roof

FLASHINGS > FLASHING

FLASHLAMP *n* electric lamp producing a flash of intense light

FLASHOVER *n* electric discharge over or around the surface of an insulator

FLASHTUBE *n* tube used in a flashlamp

FLASHY *adj* showy in a vulgar way

FLASK *n* flat bottle for carrying alcoholic drink in the pocket

FLASKET *n* long shallow basket

FLASKETS > FLASKET

FLASKS > FLASK

FLAT *adj* level and horizontal ▷ *adv* in or into a flat position ▷ *n* flat surface ▷ *vb* live in a flat

FLATBACK *n* flat-backed ornament, designed for viewing from front

FLATBACKS > FLATBACK

FLATBED *n* printing machine on which the type forme is carried on a flat bed under a revolving paper-bearing cylinder

FLATBEDS > FLATBED
FLATBOAT n flat-bottomed boat for transporting goods on a canal
FLATBOATS > FLATBOAT
FLATBREAD n type of thin unleavened bread
FLATCAP n Elizabethan man's hat with a narrow down-turned brim
FLATCAPS > FLATCAP
FLATCAR n flatbed
FLATCARS > FLATCAR
FLATETTE n very small flat
FLATETTES > FLATETTE
FLATFEET > FLATFOOT
FLATFISH n sea fish, such as the sole, which has a flat body
FLATFOOT n condition in which the entire sole of the foot is able to touch the ground because of flattening of the instep arch
FLATFOOTS > FLATFOOT
FLATHEAD n common Australian flatfish
FLATHEADS > FLATHEAD
FLATIRON n (formerly) an iron for pressing clothes that was heated by being placed on a stove
FLATIRONS > FLATIRON
FLATLAND n land notable for its levelness
FLATLANDS > FLATLAND
FLATLET n small flat
FLATLETS > FLATLET
FLATLINE vb die or be so near death that the display of one's vital signs on medical monitoring equipment shows a flat line rather than peaks and troughs
FLATLINED > FLATLINE
FLATLINER > FLATLINE
FLATLINES > FLATLINE
FLATLING adv in a flat or prostrate position ⊳ adj with the flat side, as of a sword
FLATLINGS same as > FLATLING
FLATLONG adv prostrate
FLATLY > FLAT
FLATMATE n person with whom one shares a flat
FLATMATES > FLATMATE
FLATNESS > FLAT
FLATPACK n (of a piece of furniture, equipment, or other construction) supplied in pieces packed into a flat box for assembly by the buyer
FLATPACKS > FLATPACK
FLATS > FLAT
FLATSHARE n state of living in a flat where each occupant shares the facilities and expenses ⊳ vb live in a flat with other

people who are not relatives
FLATSTICK adv with great speed or effort
FLATTED > FLAT
FLATTEN vb make or become flat or flatter
FLATTENED > FLATTEN
FLATTENER > FLATTEN
FLATTENS > FLATTEN
FLATTER vb praise insincerely
FLATTERED > FLATTER
FLATTERER > FLATTER
FLATTERS > FLATTER
FLATTERY n excessive or insincere praise
FLATTEST > FLAT
FLATTIE n flat tyre
FLATTIES same as > FLATTIE
FLATTING > FLAT
FLATTINGS > FLAT
FLATTISH adj somewhat flat
FLATTOP n informal name for an aircraft carrier
FLATTOPS > FLATTOP
FLATTY n flat shoe
FLATULENT adj suffering from or caused by too much gas in the intestines
FLATUOUS > FLATUS
FLATUS n gas generated in the alimentary canal
FLATUSES > FLATUS
FLATWARE n cutlery
FLATWARES > FLATWARE
FLATWASH n laundry that can be ironed mechanically
FLATWAYS adv with the flat or broad side down or in contact with another surface
FLATWISE same as > FLATWAYS
FLATWORK n laundry that can be ironed mechanically
FLATWORKS > FLATWORK
FLATWORM n worm, such as a tapeworm, with a flattened body
FLATWORMS > FLATWORM
FLAUGHT vb flutter
FLAUGHTED > FLAUGHT
FLAUGHTER vb cut peat
FLAUGHTS > FLAUGHT
FLAUNCH n cement or mortar slope around a chimney top, manhole, etc, to throw off water ⊳ vb cause to slope in this manner
FLAUNCHED > FLAUNCH
FLAUNCHES > FLAUNCH
FLAUNE variant of > FLAM
FLAUNES > FLAUNE
FLAUNT vb display (oneself or one's possessions) arrogantly ⊳ n act of flaunting
FLAUNTED > FLAUNT
FLAUNTER > FLAUNT
FLAUNTERS > FLAUNT

FLAUNTIER > FLAUNTY
FLAUNTILY > FLAUNTY
FLAUNTING > FLAUNT
FLAUNTS > FLAUNT
FLAUNTY adj characterized by or inclined to ostentatious display or flaunting
FLAUTA n tortilla rolled around a filling
FLAUTAS > FLAUTA
FLAUTIST n flute player
FLAUTISTS > FLAUTIST
FLAVA n individual style
FLAVANOL n type of flavonoid
FLAVANOLS > FLAVANOL
FLAVANONE n flavone-derived compound
FLAVAS > FLAVA
FLAVIN n heterocyclic ketone
FLAVINE same as > FLAVIN
FLAVINES > FLAVINE
FLAVINS > FLAVIN
FLAVONE n crystalline compound occurring in plants
FLAVONES > FLAVONE
FLAVONOID n any of a group of organic compounds that occur as pigments in fruit and flowers
FLAVONOL n flavonoid that occurs in red wine and is said to offer protection against heart disease
FLAVONOLS > FLAVONOL
FLAVOR same as > FLAVOUR
FLAVORED > FLAVOR
FLAVORER > FLAVOR
FLAVORERS > FLAVOR
FLAVORFUL adj flavourful
FLAVORING same as > FLAVOURING
FLAVORIST n blender of ingredients, to create or enhance flavours
FLAVOROUS adj having flavour
FLAVORS > FLAVOR
FLAVORY adj flavoursome
FLAVOUR n distinctive taste ⊳ vb give flavour to
FLAVOURED > FLAVOUR
FLAVOURER > FLAVOUR
FLAVOURS > FLAVOUR
FLAVOURY adj flavoursome
FLAW n imperfection or blemish ⊳ vb make or become blemished, defective, or imperfect
FLAWED > FLAW
FLAWIER > FLAW
FLAWIEST > FLAW
FLAWING > FLAW
FLAWLESS > FLAW
FLAWN variant of > FLAM
FLAWNS > FLAWN
FLAWS > FLAW

FLAWY > FLAW
FLAX n plant grown for its stem fibres and seeds
FLAXEN adj (of hair) pale yellow
FLAXES > FLAX
FLAXIER > FLAXY
FLAXIEST > FLAXY
FLAXSEED n seed of the flax plant, which yields linseed oil
FLAXSEEDS > FLAXSEED
FLAXY same as > FLAXEN
FLAY same as > FLEY
FLAYED > FLAY
FLAYER > FLAY
FLAYERS > FLAY
FLAYING > FLAY
FLAYS > FLAY
FLAYSOME adj frightening
FLEA n small wingless jumping bloodsucking insect
FLEABAG n dirty or unkempt person, esp a woman
FLEABAGS > FLEABAG
FLEABANE n as in Canadian fleabane a small plant thought to ward off fleas
FLEABANES > FLEABANE
FLEABITE n bite of a flea
FLEABITES > FLEABITE
FLEADH n festival of Irish music, dancing, and culture
FLEADHS > FLEADH
FLEAM n lancet used for letting blood
FLEAMS > FLEAM
FLEAPIT n shabby cinema or theatre
FLEAPITS > FLEAPIT
FLEAS > FLEA
FLEASOME > FLEA
FLEAWORT n type of plant, esp a European species with yellow daisy-like flowers and rosettes of downy leaves
FLEAWORTS > FLEAWORT
FLECHE n slender spire, esp over the intersection of the nave and transept ridges of a church roof
FLECHES > FLECHE
FLECHETTE n steel dart or missile dropped from an aircraft, as in World War I
FLECK n small mark, streak, or speck ⊳ vb speckle
FLECKED > FLECK
FLECKER same as > FLECK
FLECKERED > FLECKER
FLECKERS > FLECKER
FLECKIER > FLECKY
FLECKIEST > FLECKY
FLECKING > FLECK
FLECKLESS > FLECK
FLECKS > FLECK
FLECKY > FLECK
FLECTION n act of bending or the state of being bent

FLECTIONS > FLECTION
FLED > FLEE
FLEDGE vb feed and care for (a young bird) until it is able to fly
FLEDGED > FLEDGE
FLEDGES > FLEDGE
FLEDGIER > FLEDGY
FLEDGIEST > FLEDGY
FLEDGING > FLEDGE
FLEDGLING n young bird ▷ adj new or inexperienced
FLEDGY adj feathery or feathered
FLEE vb run away (from)
FLEECE n sheep's coat of wool ▷ vb defraud or overcharge
FLEECED > FLEECE
FLEECER > FLEECE
FLEECERS > FLEECE
FLEECES > FLEECE
FLEECH vb flatter
FLEECHED > FLEECH
FLEECHES > FLEECH
FLEECHING > FLEECH
FLEECIE n person who collects fleeces after shearing and prepares them for baling
FLEECIER > FLEECY
FLEECIES > FLEECIE
FLEECIEST > FLEECY
FLEECILY > FLEECY
FLEECING > FLEECE
FLEECY adj made of or like fleece ▷ n person who collects fleeces after shearing and prepares them for baling
FLEEING > FLEE
FLEER vb grin or laugh at ▷ n derisory glance or grin
FLEERED > FLEER
FLEERER > FLEER
FLEERERS > FLEER
FLEERING > FLEER
FLEERINGS > FLEER
FLEERS > FLEER
FLEES > FLEE
FLEET n number of warships organized as a unit ▷ adj swift in movement ▷ vb move rapidly
FLEETED > FLEET
FLEETER > FLEET
FLEETEST > FLEET
FLEETING adj rapid and soon passing
FLEETLY > FLEET
FLEETNESS > FLEET
FLEETS > FLEET
FLEG vb scare
FLEGGED > FLEG
FLEGGING > FLEG
FLEGS > FLEG
FLEHMEN vb (of mammal) grimace
FLEHMENED > FLEHMEN
FLEHMENS > FLEHMEN
FLEISHIG same as **>** FLEISHIK
FLEISHIK adj (of food)

containing or derived from meat or meat products and therefore to be prepared and eaten separately from dairy foods
FLEME vb drive out
FLEMES > FLEME
FLEMING n native or inhabitant of Flanders or a Flemish-speaking Belgian
FLEMISH vb stow (a rope) in a Flemish coil
FLEMISHED > FLEMISH
FLEMISHES > FLEMISH
FLEMIT > FLEME
FLENCH same as **>** FLENSE
FLENCHED > FLENCH
FLENCHER > FLENCH
FLENCHERS > FLENCH
FLENCHES > FLENCH
FLENCHING > FLENCH
FLENSE vb strip (a whale, seal, etc) of (its blubber or skin)
FLENSED > FLENSE
FLENSER > FLENSE
FLENSERS > FLENSE
FLENSES > FLENSE
FLENSING > FLENSE
FLESH n soft part of a human or animal body
FLESHED > FLESH
FLESHER n person or machine that fleshes hides or skins
FLESHERS > FLESHER
FLESHES > FLESH
FLESHHOOD incarnation
FLESHIER > FLESHY
FLESHIEST > FLESHY
FLESHILY > FLESHY
FLESHING > FLESH
FLESHINGS npl flesh-coloured tights
FLESHLESS > FLESH
FLESHLIER > FLESHLY
FLESHLING n voluptuary
FLESHLY adj carnal
FLESHMENT n act of fleshing
FLESHPOT n pot in which meat is cooked
FLESHPOTS npl places, such as brothels and strip clubs, where sexual desires are catered to
FLESHWORM n flesh-eating worm
FLESHY adj plump
FLETCH same as **>** FLEDGE
FLETCHED > FLETCH
FLETCHER n person who makes arrows
FLETCHERS > FLETCHER
FLETCHES > FLETCH
FLETCHING > FLETCH
FLETTON n type of brick
FLETTONS > FLETTON
FLEURET same as **>** FLEURETTE
FLEURETS > FLEURET
FLEURETTE n ornament resembling a flower
FLEURON n decorative

piece of pastry
FLEURONS > FLEURON
FLEURY same as **>** FLORY
FLEW > FLY
FLEWED adj having large flews
FLEWS npl fleshy hanging upper lip of a bloodhound or similar dog
FLEX n flexible insulated electric cable ▷ vb bend
FLEXAGON n hexagon made from a single pliable strip of triangles
FLEXAGONS > FLEXAGON
FLEXED > FLEX
FLEXES > FLEX
FLEXIBLE adj easily bent
FLEXIBLY > FLEXIBLE
FLEXILE same as **>** FLEXIBLE
FLEXING > FLEX
FLEXION n act of bending a joint or limb
FLEXIONAL > FLEXION
FLEXIONS > FLEXION
FLEXITIME n system permitting variation in starting and finishing times of work
FLEXO n, adj, adv flexography
FLEXOR n any muscle whose contraction serves to bend a joint or limb
FLEXORS > FLEXOR
FLEXOS > FLEXO
FLEXTIME same as **>** FLEXITIME
FLEXTIMER > FLEXTIME
FLEXTIMES > FLEXTIME
FLEXUOSE same as **>** FLEXUOUS
FLEXUOUS adj full of bends or curves
FLEXURAL > FLEXURE
FLEXURE n act of flexing or the state of being flexed
FLEXURES > FLEXURE
FLEY vb be afraid or cause to be afraid
FLEYED > FLEY
FLEYING > FLEY
FLEYS > FLEY
FLIBBERT n small piece or bit
FLIBBERTS > FLIBBERT
FLIC n French police officer
FLICHTER vb flutter
FLICHTERS > FLICHTER
FLICK vb touch or move with the finger or hand in a quick movement ▷ n tap or quick stroke
FLICKABLE > FLICK
FLICKED > FLICK
FLICKER vb shine unsteadily or intermittently ▷ n unsteady brief light
FLICKERED > FLICKER
FLICKERS > FLICKER
FLICKERY > FLICKER
FLICKING > FLICK

FLICKS > FLICK
FLICS > FLIC
FLIED > FLY
FLIER same as **>** FLY
FLIERS > FLY
FLIES > FLY
FLIEST > FLY
FLIGHT n journey by air ▷ vb cause (a ball, dart, etc) to float slowly or deceptively towards its target
FLIGHTED > FLIGHT
FLIGHTIER > FLIGHTY
FLIGHTILY > FLIGHTY
FLIGHTING > FLIGHT
FLIGHTS > FLIGHT
FLIGHTY adj frivolous and fickle
FLIM n five-pound note
FLIMFLAM n nonsense ▷ vb deceive
FLIMFLAMS > FLIMFLAM
FLIMP vb steal
FLIMPED > FLIMP
FLIMPING > FLIMP
FLIMPS > FLIMP
FLIMS > FLIM
FLIMSIER > FLIMSY
FLIMSIES > FLIMSY
FLIMSIEST > FLIMSY
FLIMSILY > FLIMSY
FLIMSY adj not strong or substantial ▷ n thin paper used for making carbon copies of a letter, etc
FLINCH same as **>** FLENSE
FLINCHED > FLINCH
FLINCHER > FLINCH
FLINCHERS > FLINCH
FLINCHES > FLINCH
FLINCHING > FLINCH
FLINDER n fragment
FLINDERS > FLINDER
FLING vb throw, send, or move forcefully or hurriedly ▷ n spell of self-indulgent enjoyment
FLINGER > FLING
FLINGERS > FLING
FLINGING > FLING
FLINGS > FLING
FLINKITE n anhydrous phosphate
FLINKITES > FLINKITE
FLINT n hard grey stone ▷ vb fit or provide with a flint
FLINTED > FLINT
FLINTHEAD n American wading bird
FLINTIER > FLINTY
FLINTIEST > FLINTY
FLINTIFY vb turn to flint
FLINTILY > FLINTY
FLINTING > FLINT
FLINTLIKE > FLINT
FLINTLOCK n obsolete gun in which the powder was lit by a spark from a flint
FLINTS > FLINT
FLINTY adj cruel
FLIP vb throw (something

f

small or light) carelessly ▷ n
snap or tap ▷ adj flippant
FLIPBOOK n book of
drawings made to seem
animated by flipping pages
FLIPBOOKS > FLIPBOOK
FLIPFLOP n rubber sandal
FLIPFLOPS > FLIPFLOP
FLIPPANCY > FLIPPANT
FLIPPANT adj treating
serious things lightly
FLIPPED > FLIP
FLIPPER n limb of a sea
animal adapted for
swimming
FLIPPERS > FLIPPER
FLIPPEST > FLIP
FLIPPIER > FLIPPY
FLIPPIEST > FLIPPY
FLIPPING > FLIP
FLIPPY adj (of clothes)
tending to move to and fro
as the wearer walks
FLIPS > FLIP
FLIPSIDE n reverse or
opposite side
FLIPSIDES > FLIPSIDE
FLIR n forward looking
infrared radar
FLIRS > FLIR
FLIRT vb behave as if
sexually attracted to
someone ▷ n person who
flirts
FLIRTED > FLIRT
FLIRTER > FLIRT
FLIRTERS > FLIRT
FLIRTIER > FLIRT
FLIRTIEST > FLIRT
FLIRTING > FLIRT
FLIRTINGS > FLIRT
FLIRTISH > FLIRT
FLIRTS > FLIRT
FLIRTY > FLIRT
FLISK vb skip
FLISKED > FLISK
FLISKIER > FLISK
FLISKIEST > FLISK
FLISKING > FLISK
FLISKS > FLISK
FLISKY > FLISK
FLIT vb move lightly and
rapidly ▷ n act of flitting
FLITCH n side of pork
salted and cured ▷ vb cut (a
tree trunk) into flitches
FLITCHED > FLITCH
FLITCHES > FLITCH
FLITCHING > FLITCH
FLITE vb scold or rail at ▷ n
dispute or scolding
FLITED > FLITE
FLITES > FLITE
FLITING > FLITE
FLITS > FLIT
FLITT adj fleet
FLITTED > FLIT
FLITTER > FLIT
FLITTERED > FLIT
FLITTERN n bark of young
oak tree
FLITTERNS > FLITTERN
FLITTERS > FLIT
FLITTING > FLIT

FLITTINGS > FLIT
FLIVVER n old, cheap, or
battered car
FLIVVERS > FLIVVER
FLIX n fur ▷ vb have fur
FLIXED > FLIX
FLIXES > FLIX
FLIXING > FLIX
FLOAT vb rest on the
surface of a liquid ▷ n light
object used to help
someone or something
float
FLOATABLE > FLOAT
FLOATAGE same as
> FLOTAGE
FLOATAGES > FLOATAGE
FLOATANT n substance
used in fly-fishing, to help
dry flies to float
FLOATANTS > FLOATANT
FLOATCUT as in floatcut file
file with rows of parallel
teeth
FLOATED > FLOAT
FLOATEL same as
> FLOTEL
FLOATELS > FLOATEL
FLOATER n person or thing
that floats
FLOATERS > FLOATER
FLOATIER > FLOATY
FLOATIEST > FLOATY
FLOATING adj moving
about, changing
FLOATINGS > FLOATING
FLOATS npl footlights
FLOATY adj filmy and light
FLOB vb spit
FLOBBED > FLOB
FLOBBING > FLOB
FLOBS > FLOB
FLOC same as > FLOCK
FLOCCED > FLOC
FLOCCI > FLOCCUS
FLOCCING > FLOC
FLOCCOSE adj consisting
of or covered with woolly
tufts or hairs
FLOCCULAR > FLOCCUS
FLOCCULE n small
aggregate of flocculent
material
FLOCCULES > FLOCCULE
FLOCCULI > FLOCCULUS
FLOCCULUS same as
> FLOCCULE
FLOCCUS n downy or
woolly covering, as on the
young of certain birds ▷ adj
(of a cloud) having the
appearance of woolly tufts
at odd intervals in its
structure
FLOCK n number of animals
of one kind together ▷ vb
gather in a crowd ▷ adj (of
wallpaper) with a velvety
raised pattern
FLOCKED > FLOCK
FLOCKIER > FLOCK
FLOCKIEST > FLOCK
FLOCKING > FLOCK
FLOCKINGS > FLOCK

FLOCKLESS > FLOCK
FLOCKS > FLOCK
FLOCKY > FLOCK
FLOCS > FLOC
FLOE n sheet of floating ice
FLOES > FLOE
FLOG vb beat with a whip or
stick
FLOGGABLE > FLOG
FLOGGED > FLOG
FLOGGER > FLOG
FLOGGERS > FLOG
FLOGGING > FLOG
FLOGGINGS > FLOG
FLOGS > FLOG
FLOKATI n Greek
hand-woven shaggy
woollen rug
FLOKATIS > FLOKATI
FLONG n material, usually
pulped paper or cardboard,
used for making moulds in
stereotyping
FLONGS > FLONG
FLOOD n overflow of water
onto a normally dry area
▷ vb cover or become
covered with water
FLOODABLE > FLOOD
FLOODED > FLOOD
FLOODER > FLOOD
FLOODERS > FLOOD
FLOODGATE n gate used to
control the flow of water
FLOODING n submerging
of land under water, esp
due to heavy rain, a lake or
river overflowing, etc
FLOODINGS > FLOODING
FLOODLESS > FLOOD
FLOODLIT adj illuminated
with a floodlight
FLOODMARK n high-water
mark
FLOODS > FLOOD
FLOODTIDE n rising tide
FLOODWALL n wall built as
a defence against floods
FLOODWAY n conduit for
floodwater
FLOODWAYS > FLOODWAY
FLOOEY adj awry
FLOOIE same as > FLOOEY
FLOOR n lower surface of a
room ▷ vb knock down
FLOORAGE n area of floor
FLOORAGES > FLOORAGE
FLOORED > FLOOR
FLOORER n coup de grâce
FLOORERS > FLOORER
FLOORHEAD n upper side
of a floor timber
FLOORING > FLOOR
FLOORINGS > FLOOR
FLOORLESS > FLOOR
FLOORS > FLOOR
FLOORSHOW n
entertainment on floor of
nightclub
FLOOSIE same as
> FLOOSIE
FLOOSIES > FLOOSIE
FLOOSY variant of
> FLOOSIE

FLOOZIE same as
> FLOOZY
FLOOZIES > FLOOZY
FLOOZY n disreputable
woman
FLOP vb bend, fall, or
collapse loosely or
carelessly ▷ n failure
FLOPHOUSE n cheap
lodging house, esp one
used by tramps
FLOPOVER n TV visual
effect of page being turned
FLOPOVERS > FLOPOVER
FLOPPED > FLOP
FLOPPER > FLOP
FLOPPERS > FLOP
FLOPPIER > FLOPPY
FLOPPIES > FLOPPY
FLOPPIEST > FLOPPY
FLOPPILY > FLOPPY
FLOPPING > FLOP
FLOPPY adj hanging
downwards, loose ▷ n
floppy disk
FLOPS > FLOP
FLOPTICAL n type of
floppy disk
FLOR n yeast formed on the
surface of sherry after
fermentation
FLORA n plants of a given
place or time
FLORAE > FLORA
FLORAL adj consisting of or
decorated with flowers ▷ n
class of perfume
FLORALLY > FLORAL
FLORALS > FLORAL
FLORAS > FLORA
FLOREANT > FLOREAT
FLOREAT vb may (a person,
institution, etc) flourish
FLOREATED same as
> FLORIATED
FLORENCE n type of fennel
FLORENCES > FLORENCE
FLORET n small flower
forming part of a
composite flower head
FLORETS > FLORET
FLORIATED adj having
ornamentation based on
flowers and leaves
FLORICANE n fruiting
stem of plant
FLORID adj with a red or
flushed complexion
FLORIDEAN n member of
the red seaweed family
FLORIDER > FLORID
FLORIDEST > FLORID
FLORIDITY > FLORID
FLORIDLY > FLORID
FLORIER > FLORY
FLORIEST > FLORY
FLORIFORM adj
flower-shaped
FLORIGEN n hypothetical
plant hormone that
induces flowering, thought
to be synthesized in the
leaves as a photoperiodic
response and transmitted
to the flower buds

FLORIGENS > FLORIGEN
FLORIN n former British and Australian coin
FLORINS > FLORIN
FLORIST n seller of flowers
FLORISTIC adj of or relating to flowers or a flora
FLORISTRY > FLORIST
FLORISTS > FLORIST
FLORS > FLOR
FLORUIT prep (he or she) flourished: used to indicate the period when a historical figure, whose birth and death dates are unknown, was most active ▷ n such a period in a person's life
FLORUITS > FLORUIT
FLORULA n flora of a small single environment
FLORULAE > FLORULA
FLORULE same as > FLORULA
FLORULES > FLORULE
FLORY adj containing a fleur-de-lys
FLOSCULAR > FLOSCULE
FLOSCULE n floret
FLOSCULES > FLOSCULE
FLOSH n hopper-shaped box
FLOSHES > FLOSH
FLOSS n fine silky fibres ▷ vb clean (between the teeth) with dental floss
FLOSSED > FLOSS
FLOSSER > FLOSS
FLOSSERS > FLOSS
FLOSSES > FLOSS
FLOSSIE variant of > FLOSSY
FLOSSIER > FLOSSY
FLOSSIES > FLOSSY
FLOSSIEST > FLOSSY
FLOSSILY > FLOSSY
FLOSSING > FLOSS
FLOSSINGS > FLOSS
FLOSSY adj consisting of or resembling floss ▷ n floozy
FLOTA n formerly, Spanish commercial fleet
FLOTAGE n act or state of floating
FLOTAGES > FLOTAGE
FLOTANT adj in heraldry, flying in the air
FLOTAS > FLOTA
FLOTATION n launching or financing of a business enterprise
FLOTE n aquatic perennial grass
FLOTEL n (in the oil industry) an oil rig or boat used as accommodation for workers in off-shore oil fields
FLOTELS > FLOTEL
FLOTES > FLOTE
FLOTILLA n small fleet or fleet of small ships
FLOTILLAS > FLOTILLA
FLOTSAM n floating wreckage

FLOTSAMS > FLOTSAM
FLOUNCE vb go with emphatic movements ▷ n flouncing movement
FLOUNCED > FLOUNCE
FLOUNCES > FLOUNCE
FLOUNCIER > FLOUNCE
FLOUNCING n material, such as lace or embroidered fabric, used for making flounces
FLOUNCY > FLOUNCE
FLOUNDER vb move with difficulty, as in mud ▷ n edible flatfish
FLOUNDERS > FLOUNDER
FLOUR n powder made by grinding grain, esp wheat ▷ vb sprinkle with flour
FLOURED > FLOUR
FLOURIER > FLOUR
FLOURIEST > FLOUR
FLOURING > FLOUR
FLOURISH vb be active, successful, or widespread ▷ n dramatic waving motion
FLOURISHY > FLOURISH
FLOURLESS > FLOUR
FLOURS > FLOUR
FLOURY > FLOUR
FLOUSE vb splash
FLOUSED > FLOUSE
FLOUSES > FLOUSE
FLOUSH variant of > FLOUSE
FLOUSHED > FLOUSH
FLOUSHES > FLOUSH
FLOUSHING > FLOUSH
FLOUSING > FLOUSE
FLOUT vb deliberately disobey (a rule, law, etc)
FLOUTED > FLOUT
FLOUTER > FLOUT
FLOUTERS > FLOUT
FLOUTING > FLOUT
FLOUTS > FLOUT
FLOW vb (of liquid) move in a stream ▷ n act, rate, or manner of flowing
FLOWAGE n act of flowing or overflowing or the state of having overflowed
FLOWAGES > FLOWAGE
FLOWCHART n diagrammatic representation of the sequence of operations or equipment in an industrial process, computer program, etc
FLOWED > FLOW
FLOWER n part of a plant that produces seeds ▷ vb produce flowers, bloom
FLOWERAGE n mass of flowers
FLOWERBED n piece of ground for growing flowers
FLOWERED adj decorated with a floral design
FLOWERER n plant that flowers at a specified time or in a specified way
FLOWERERS > FLOWERER

FLOWERET another name for > FLORET
FLOWERETS > FLOWERET
FLOWERFUL adj having plentiful flowers
FLOWERIER > FLOWERY
FLOWERILY > FLOWERY
FLOWERING adj (of certain species of plants) capable of producing conspicuous flowers
FLOWERPOT n pot in which plants are grown
FLOWERS > FLOWER
FLOWERY adj decorated with a floral design
FLOWING > FLOW
FLOWINGLY > FLOW
FLOWMETER n instrument that measures the rate of flow of a liquid or gas within a pipe or tube
FLOWN > FLY
FLOWS > FLOW
FLOWSTONE n type of speleothem
FLOX as in flox silk type of silk
FLU n any of various viral infections, esp a respiratory or intestinal infection
FLUATE n fluoride
FLUATES > FLUATE
FLUB vb bungle
FLUBBED > FLUB
FLUBBER > FLUB
FLUBBERS > FLUB
FLUBBING > FLUB
FLUBDUB n bunkum
FLUBDUBS > FLUBDUB
FLUBS > FLUB
FLUCTUANT adj inclined to vary or fluctuate
FLUCTUATE vb change frequently and erratically
FLUE n passage or pipe for smoke or hot air
FLUED adj having a flue
FLUELLEN n type of plant
FLUELLENS > FLUELLEN
FLUELLIN same as > FLUELLEN
FLUELLINS > FLUELLIN
FLUENCE > FLUENCY
FLUENCES > FLUENCY
FLUENCIES > FLUENCY
FLUENCY n quality of being fluent, esp facility in speech or writing
FLUENT adj able to speak or write with ease ▷ n variable quantity in fluxions
FLUENTLY > FLUENT
FLUENTS > FLUENT
FLUERIC adj of or relating to fluidics
FLUERICS npl fluidics
FLUES > FLUE
FLUEWORK n collectively, organ stops
FLUEWORKS > FLUEWORK
FLUEY adj involved in, caused by, or like influenza
FLUFF n soft fibres ▷ vb

make or become soft and puffy
FLUFFED > FLUFF
FLUFFER n person employed on a pornographic film set to ensure that male actors are kept aroused
FLUFFERS n fluffer
FLUFFIER > FLUFFY
FLUFFIEST > FLUFFY
FLUFFILY > FLUFFY
FLUFFING > FLUFF
FLUFFS > FLUFF
FLUFFY adj of, resembling, or covered with fluff
FLUGEL n grand piano or harpsichord
FLUGELMAN variant of > FUGLEMAN
FLUGELMEN > FLUGELMAN
FLUGELS > FLUGEL
FLUID n substance able to flow and change its shape ▷ adj able to flow or change shape easily
FLUIDAL > FLUID
FLUIDALLY > FLUID
FLUIDIC > FLUIDICS
FLUIDICS n study and use of systems in which the flow of fluids in tubes simulates the flow of electricity in conductors. Such systems are used in place of electronics in certain applications, such as the control of apparatus
FLUIDIFY vb make fluid
FLUIDISE same as > FLUIDIZE
FLUIDISED > FLUIDISE
FLUIDISER > FLUIDISE
FLUIDISES > FLUIDISE
FLUIDITY n state of being fluid
FLUIDIZE vb make fluid, esp to make (solids) fluid by pulverizing them so that they can be transported in a stream of gas as if they were liquids
FLUIDIZED > FLUIDIZE
FLUIDIZER > FLUIDIZE
FLUIDIZES > FLUIDIZE
FLUIDLIKE > FLUID
FLUIDLY > FLUID
FLUIDNESS > FLUID
FLUIDRAM n British imperial measure
FLUIDRAMS > FLUIDRAM
FLUIDS > FLUID
FLUIER > FLUEY
FLUIEST > FLUEY
FLUISH > FLU
FLUKE n accidental stroke of luck ▷ vb gain, make, or hit by a fluke
FLUKED > FLUKE
FLUKES > FLUKE
FLUKEY same as > FLUKY
FLUKIER > FLUKY
FLUKIEST > FLUKY
FLUKILY > FLUKY

FLUKINESS > FLUKY

FLUKING > FLUKE

FLUKY adj done or gained by an accident, esp a lucky one

FLUME n narrow sloping channel for water ▷ vb transport (logs) in a flume

FLUMED > FLUME

FLUMES > FLUME

FLUMING > FLUME

FLUMMERY n silly or trivial talk

FLUMMOX vb puzzle or confuse

FLUMMOXED > FLUMMOX

FLUMMOXES > FLUMMOX

FLUMP vb move or fall heavily

FLUMPED > FLUMP

FLUMPING > FLUMP

FLUMPS > FLUMP

FLUNG > FLING

FLUNK vb fail ▷ n low grade below the pass standard

FLUNKED > FLUNK

FLUNKER > FLUNK

FLUNKERS > FLUNK

FLUNKEY same as > FLUNKY

FLUNKEYS > FLUNKEY

FLUNKIE same as > FLUNKY

FLUNKIES > FLUNKY

FLUNKING > FLUNK

FLUNKS > FLUNK

FLUNKY n servile person

FLUNKYISM > FLUNKY

FLUOR same as > FLUORSPAR

FLUORENE n white insoluble crystalline solid

FLUORENES > FLUORENE

FLUORESCE vb exhibit fluorescence

FLUORIC adj of, concerned with, or produced from fluorine or fluorspar

FLUORID same as > FLUORIDE

FLUORIDE n compound containing fluorine

FLUORIDES > FLUORIDE

FLUORIDS same as > FLUORID

FLUORIN same as > FLUORINE

FLUORINE n toxic yellow gas: most reactive of all the elements

FLUORINES > FLUORINE

FLUORINS > FLUORIN

FLUORITE same as > FLUORSPAR

FLUORITES > FLUORITE

FLUOROSES > FLUOROSIS

FLUOROSIS n fluoride poisoning, due to ingestion of too much fluoride in drinking water over a long period or to ingestion of pesticides containing fluoride salts. Chronic fluorosis results in mottling

of the teeth of children

FLUOROTIC > FLUOROSIS

FLUORS > FLUOR

FLUORSPAR n white or colourless mineral, consisting of calcium fluoride in crystalline form: the chief ore of fluorine

FLURR vb scatter

FLURRED > FLURR

FLURRIED > FLURRY

FLURRIES > FLURRY

FLURRING > FLURR

FLURRS > FLURR

FLURRY n sudden commotion ▷ vb confuse

FLURRYING > FLURRY

FLUS > FLU

FLUSH vb blush or cause to blush ▷ n blush ▷ adj level with the surrounding surface ▷ adv so as to be level

FLUSHABLE > FLUSH

FLUSHED > FLUSH

FLUSHER > FLUSH

FLUSHERS > FLUSH

FLUSHES > FLUSH

FLUSHEST > FLUSH

FLUSHIER > FLUSHY

FLUSHIEST > FLUSHY

FLUSHING n extra feeding given to ewes before mating to increase the lambing percentage

FLUSHINGS > FLUSHING

FLUSHNESS > FLUSH

FLUSHWORK n decorative treatment of the surface of an outside wall with flints split to show their smooth black surface, combined with dressed stone to form patterns such as tracery or initials

FLUSHY adj ruddy

FLUSTER vb make nervous or upset ▷ n nervous or upset state

FLUSTERED > FLUSTER

FLUSTERS > FLUSTER

FLUSTERY > FLUSTER

FLUSTRATE vb fluster

FLUTE n wind instrument consisting of a tube with sound holes and a mouth hole in the side ▷ vb utter in a high-pitched tone

FLUTED adj having decorative grooves

FLUTELIKE > FLUTE

FLUTER n craftsman who makes flutes or fluting

FLUTERS > FLUTER

FLUTES > FLUTE

FLUTEY > FLUTE

FLUTIER > FLUTE

FLUTIEST > FLUTE

FLUTINA n type of accordion

FLUTINAS > FLUTINA

FLUTING n design of decorative grooves

FLUTINGS > FLUTING

FLUTIST same as > FLAUTIST

FLUTISTS > FLUTIST

FLUTTER vb wave rapidly ▷ n flapping movement

FLUTTERED > FLUTTER

FLUTTERER > FLUTTER

FLUTTERS > FLUTTER

FLUTTERY adj flapping rapidly

FLUTY > FLUTE

FLUVIAL adj of rivers

FLUVIATIC > FLUVIAL

FLUX n constant change or instability ▷ vb make or become fluid

FLUXED > FLUX

FLUXES > FLUX

FLUXGATE n type of magnetometer

FLUXGATES > FLUXGATE

FLUXING > FLUX

FLUXION n rate of change of a function, especially the instantaneous velocity of a moving body

FLUXIONAL > FLUXION

FLUXIONS > FLUXION

FLUXIVE > FLUX

FLUXMETER n any instrument for measuring magnetic flux, usually by measuring the charge that flows through a coil when the flux changes

FLUYT n Dutch sailing ship

FLUYTS > FLUYT

FLY vb move through the air on wings or in an aircraft ▷ n fastening at the front of trousers ▷ adj sharp and cunning

FLYABLE > FLY

FLYAWAY adj (of hair) very fine and soft ▷ n person who is frivolous or flighty

FLYAWAYS > FLYAWAY

FLYBACK n fast return of the spot on a cathode-ray tube after completion of each trace

FLYBACKS > FLYBACK

FLYBANE n type of campion

FLYBANES > FLYBANE

FLYBELT n strip of tsetse-infested land

FLYBELTS > FLYBELT

FLYBLEW > FLYBLOW

FLYBLOW vb contaminate, esp with the eggs or larvae of the blowfly ▷ n egg or young larva of a blowfly, deposited on meat, paper, etc

FLYBLOWN adj covered with blowfly eggs

FLYBLOWS > FLYBLOW

FLYBOAT n any small swift boat

FLYBOATS > FLYBOAT

FLYBOOK n small case or wallet used by anglers for storing artificial flies

FLYBOOKS > FLYBOOK

FLYBOY n air force pilot

FLYBOYS > FLYBOY

FLYBRIDGE n highest navigational bridge on a ship

FLYBY n flight past a particular position or target, esp the close approach of a spacecraft to a planet or satellite for investigation of conditions

FLYBYS > FLYBY

FLYER > FLY

FLYERS > FLY

FLYEST > FLY

FLYHAND n device for transferring printed sheets from the press to a flat pile

FLYHANDS > FLYHAND

FLYING > FLY

FLYINGS > FLY

FLYLEAF n blank leaf at the beginning or end of a book

FLYLEAVES > FLYLEAF

FLYLESS > FLY

FLYMAKER n person who makes fishing flies

FLYMAKERS > FLYMAKER

FLYMAN n stagehand who operates the scenery, curtains, etc, in the flies

FLYMEN > FLYMAN

FLYOFF n total volume of water transferred from the earth to the atmosphere

FLYOFFS > FLYOFF

FLYOVER n road passing over another by a bridge

FLYOVERS > FLYOVER

FLYPAPER n paper with a sticky poisonous coating, used to kill flies

FLYPAPERS > FLYPAPER

FLYPAST n ceremonial flight of aircraft over a given area

FLYPASTS > FLYPAST

FLYPE vb fold back

FLYPED > FLYPE

FLYPES > FLYPE

FLYPING > FLYPE

FLYPITCH n area for unlicensed stalls at markets

FLYPOSTER n person who puts up posters illegally

FLYRODDER n angler using artificial fly

FLYSCH n marine sedimentary facies consisting of a sequence of sandstones, conglomerates, marls, shales, and clays that were formed by erosion during a period of mountain building and subsequently deformed as the mountain building continued

FLYSCHES > FLYSCH

FLYSCREEN n wire-mesh screen over a window to prevent flies from entering a room

FLYSHEET *n* part of tent

FLYSHEETS > FLYSHEET

FLYSPECK *n* small speck of the excrement of a fly ▷ *vb* mark with flyspecks

FLYSPECKS > FLYSPECK

FLYSPRAY *n* insecticide sprayed from an aerosol

FLYSPRAYS > FLYSPRAY

FLYSTRIKE *n* infestation of wounded sheep by blowflies or maggots

FLYTE *same as >* FLITE

FLYTED > FLYTE

FLYTES > FLYTE

FLYTIER *n* person who makes his own fishing flies

FLYTIERS > FLYTIER

FLYTING > FLYTE

FLYTINGS > FLYTE

FLYTRAP *n* any of various insectivorous plants, esp Venus's flytrap

FLYTRAPS > FLYTRAP

FLYWAY *n* usual route used by birds when migrating

FLYWAYS > FLYWAY

FLYWEIGHT *n* boxer weighing up to 112lb (professional) or 51kg (amateur)

FLYWHEEL *n* heavy wheel regulating the speed of a machine

FLYWHEELS > FLYWHEEL

FOAL *n* young of a horse or related animal ▷ *vb* give birth to a foal

FOALED > FOAL

FOALFOOT *n* coltsfoot

FOALFOOTS > FOALFOOT

FOALING > FOAL

FOALS > FOAL

FOAM *n* mass of small bubbles on a liquid ▷ *vb* produce foam

FOAMABLE > FOAM

FOAMED > FOAM

FOAMER *n* (possibly obsessive) enthusiast

FOAMERS > FOAMER

FOAMIER > FOAMY

FOAMIEST > FOAMY

FOAMILY > FOAMY

FOAMINESS > FOAMY

FOAMING > FOAM

FOAMINGLY > FOAM

FOAMINGS > FOAM

FOAMLESS > FOAM

FOAMLIKE > FOAM

FOAMS > FOAM

FOAMY *adj* of, resembling, consisting of, or covered with foam

FOB *n* short watch chain ▷ *vb* cheat

FOBBED > FOB

FOBBING > FOB

FOBS > FOB

FOCACCIA *n* flat Italian bread made with olive oil and yeast

FOCACCIAS > FOCACCIA

FOCAL *adj* of or at a focus

FOCALISE *same as >* FOCUS

FOCALISED > FOCUS

FOCALISES > FOCUS

FOCALIZE *less common word for >* FOCUS

FOCALIZED > FOCALIZE

FOCALIZES > FOCALIZE

FOCALLY > FOCAL

FOCI > FOCUS

FOCIMETER *n* photographic focusing device

FOCOMETER *n* instrument for measuring the focal length of a lens

FOCUS *n* point at which light or sound waves converge ▷ *vb* bring or come into focus

FOCUSABLE > FOCUS

FOCUSED > FOCUS

FOCUSER > FOCUS

FOCUSERS > FOCUS

FOCUSES > FOCUS

FOCUSING > FOCUS

FOCUSINGS > FOCUS

FOCUSLESS > FOCUS

FOCUSSED > FOCUS

FOCUSSES > FOCUS

FOCUSSING > FOCUS

FODDER *n* feed for livestock ▷ *vb* supply (livestock) with fodder

FODDERED > FODDER

FODDERER > FODDER

FODDERERS > FODDER

FODDERING > FODDER

FODDERS > FODDER

FODGEL *adj* buxom

FOE *n* enemy, opponent

FOEDARIE *variant of >* FEDARIE

FOEDARIES > FOEDARIE

FOEDERATI *npl* (in ancient Rome) tribes bound by treaty to support the Roman Empire

FOEHN *same as >* FOHN

FOEHNS > FOEHN

FOEMAN *n* enemy in war

FOEMEN > FOEMAN

FOEN *same as >* FOE

FOES > FOE

FOETAL *same as >* FETAL

FOETATION *same as >* FETATION

FOETICIDE *same as >* FETICIDE

FOETID *same as >* FETID

FOETIDER > FOETID

FOETIDEST > FOETID

FOETIDLY > FOETID

FOETOR *same as >* FETOR

FOETORS > FOETOR

FOETUS *same as >* FETUS

FOETUSES > FOETUS

FOG *n* mass of condensed water vapour in the lower air, often greatly reducing visibility ▷ *vb* cover with steam

FOGASH *n* type of Hungarian pike perch

FOGASHES > FOGASH

FOGBOUND *adj* prevented from operating by fog

FOGBOW *n* faint arc of light sometimes seen in a fog bank

FOGBOWS > FOGBOW

FOGDOG *n* whitish spot sometimes seen in fog near the horizon

FOGDOGS > FOGDOG

FOGEY *n* old-fashioned person

FOGEYDOM > FOGEY

FOGEYDOMS > FOGEY

FOGEYISH > FOGEY

FOGEYISM > FOGEY

FOGEYISMS > FOGEY

FOGEYS > FOGEY

FOGFRUIT *n* wildflower of the verbena family

FOGFRUITS > FOGFRUIT

FOGGAGE *n* grass grown for winter grazing

FOGGAGES > FOGGAGE

FOGGED > FOG

FOGGER *n* device that generates a fog

FOGGERS > FOGGER

FOGGIER > FOG

FOGGIEST > FOG

FOGGILY > FOG

FOGGINESS > FOG

FOGGING > FOG

FOGGY *same as >* FOG

FOGHORN *n* large horn sounded to warn ships in fog

FOGHORNS > FOGHORN

FOGIE *variant of >* FOGEY

FOGIES > FOGIE

FOGLE *n* silk handkerchief

FOGLES > FOGLE

FOGLESS > FOG

FOGMAN *n* person in charge of railway fog-signals

FOGMEN > FOGMAN

FOGOU *n* man-made subterranean passage or chamber found in Cornwall

FOGOUS > FOGOU

FOGRAM *n* fogey

FOGRAMITE > FOGRAM

FOGRAMITY > FOGRAM

FOGRAMS > FOGRAM

FOGS > FOG

FOGY *same as >* FOGEY

FOGYDOM > FOGY

FOGYDOMS > FOGY

FOGYISH > FOGY

FOGYISM > FOGY

FOGYISMS > FOGY

FOH *interj* expression of disgust

FOHN *n* warm dry wind blowing down the northern slopes of the Alps

FOHNS > FOHN

FOIBLE *n* minor weakness or slight peculiarity

FOIBLES > FOIBLE

FOID *n* rock-forming mineral similar to feldspar

FOIDS > FOID

FOIL *vb* ruin (someone's plan) ▷ *n* metal in a thin sheet, esp for wrapping food

FOILABLE > FOIL

FOILBORNE *adj* moving by means of hydrofoils

FOILED > FOIL

FOILING > FOIL

FOILINGS > FOIL

FOILS > FOIL

FOILSMAN *n* person who uses or specializes in using a foil

FOILSMEN > FOILSMAN

FOIN *n* thrust or lunge with a weapon ▷ *vb* thrust with a weapon

FOINED > FOIN

FOINING > FOIN

FOININGLY > FOIN

FOINS > FOIN

FOISON *n* plentiful supply or yield

FOISONS > FOISON

FOIST *vb* force or impose on

FOISTED > FOIST

FOISTER > FOIST

FOISTERS > FOIST

FOISTING > FOIST

FOISTS > FOIST

FOLACIN *n* folic acid

FOLACINS > FOLACIN

FOLATE *n* folic acid

FOLATES > FOLIC

FOLD *vb* bend so that one part covers another ▷ *n* folded piece or part

FOLDABLE > FOLD

FOLDAWAY *adj* (of a bed) able to be folded and put away when not in use

FOLDAWAYS > FOLDAWAY

FOLDBACK *n* (in multitrack recording) a process for returning a signal to a performer instantly

FOLDBACKS > FOLDBACK

FOLDBOAT *another name for >* FALTBOAT

FOLDBOATS > FOLDBOAT

FOLDED > FOLD

FOLDER *n* piece of folded cardboard for holding loose papers

FOLDEROL *same as >* FALDERAL

FOLDEROLS > FOLDEROL

FOLDERS > FOLDER

FOLDING > FOLD

FOLDINGS > FOLDING

FOLDOUT *another name for >* GATEFOLD

FOLDOUTS > FOLDOUT

FOLDS > FOLD

FOLDUP *n* something that folds up

FOLDUPS > FOLDUP

FOLEY *n* footsteps editor

FOLEYS > FOLEY

FOLIA > FOLIUM

FOLIAGE *n* leaves

FOLIAGED *adj* having foliage

FOLIAGES > FOLIAGE

FOLIAR *adj* of or relating to a leaf or leaves

FOLIATE *adj* relating to, possessing, or resembling leaves ▷ *vb* ornament with foliage or with leaf forms such as foils

FOLIATED *adj* ornamented with or made up of foliage or foils

FOLIATES > FOLIATE

FOLIATING > FOLIATE

FOLIATION *n* process of producing leaves

FOLIATURE > FOLIATION

FOLIC as in *folic acid* , any of a group of vitamins of the B complex, occurring in pteroylglutamic acid and its derivatives: used in the treatment of megaloblastic anaemia

FOLIE *n* madness

FOLIES > FOLIE

FOLIO *n* sheet of paper folded in half to make two leaves of a book ▷ *adj* of or made in the largest book size, common esp in early centuries of European printing ▷ *vb* number the leaves of (a book) consecutively

FOLIOED > FOLIO

FOLIOING > FOLIO

FOLIOLATE *adj* possessing or relating to leaflets

FOLIOLE *n* part of a compound leaf

FOLIOLES > FOLIOLE

FOLIOLOSE > FOLIOLE

FOLIOS > FOLIO

FOLIOSE *adj* (of a tree) leaf-bearing

FOLIOUS *adj* foliose

FOLIUM *n* plane geometrical curve consisting of a loop whose two ends, intersecting at a node, are asymptotic to the same line

FOLIUMS > FOLIUM

FOLK *n* people in general ▷ *adj* originating from or traditional to the common people of a country

FOLKIE *n* devotee of folk music ▷ *adj* of or relating to folk music

FOLKIER > FOLKIE

FOLKIES > FOLKIE

FOLKIEST > FOLKIE

FOLKISH > FOLK

FOLKLAND *n* former type of land tenure

FOLKLANDS > FOLKLAND

FOLKLIFE *n* traditional customs, arts, crafts, and other forms of cultural expression of a people

FOLKLIKE > FOLK

FOLKLIVES > FOLKLIFE

FOLKLORE *n* traditional beliefs and stories of a people

FOLKLORES > FOLKLORE

FOLKLORIC > FOLKLORE

FOLKMOOT *n* (in early medieval England) an assembly of the people of a district, town, or shire

FOLKMOOTS > FOLKMOOT

FOLKMOT *same as* > FOLKMOOT

FOLKMOTE *same as* > FOLKMOOT

FOLKMOTES > FOLKMOTE

FOLKMOTS > FOLKMOT

FOLKS > FOLK

FOLKSIER > FOLKSY

FOLKSIEST > FOLKSY

FOLKSILY > FOLKSY

FOLKSONG *n* traditional song

FOLKSONGS > FOLKSONG

FOLKSY *adj* simple and unpretentious

FOLKTALE *n* tale or legend originating among a people and typically becoming part of an oral tradition

FOLKTALES > FOLKTALE

FOLKWAY *singular form of* > FOLKWAYS

FOLKWAYS *npl* traditional and customary ways of living

FOLKY *same as* > FOLKIE

FOLLES > FOLLIS

FOLLICLE *n* small cavity in the body, esp one from which a hair grows

FOLLICLES > FOLLICLE

FOLLIED > FOLLY

FOLLIES > FOLLY

FOLLIS *n* Roman coin

FOLLOW *vb* go or come after

FOLLOWED > FOLLOW

FOLLOWER *n* disciple or supporter

FOLLOWERS > FOLLOWER

FOLLOWING *adj* about to be mentioned ▷ *n* group of supporters ▷ *prep* as a result of

FOLLOWS > FOLLOW

FOLLOWUP *n* further action

FOLLOWUPS > FOLLOWUP

FOLLY *n* foolishness ▷ *vb* behave foolishly

FOLLYING > FOLLY

FOMENT *vb* encourage or stir up (trouble)

FOMENTED > FOMENT

FOMENTER > FOMENT

FOMENTERS > FOMENT

FOMENTING > FOMENT

FOMENTS > FOMENT

FOMES *n* any material, such as bedding or clothing, that may harbour pathogens and therefore convey disease

FOMITE > FOMES

FOMITES > FOMES

FON *vb* compel

FOND *adj* tender, loving ▷ *n* background of a design, as in lace ▷ *vb* dote

FONDA *n* Spanish hotel

FONDANT *n* (sweet made from) flavoured paste of sugar and water ▷ *adj* (of a colour) soft

FONDANTS > FONDANT

FONDAS > FONDA

FONDED > FOND

FONDER > FOND

FONDEST > FOND

FONDING > FOND

FONDLE *vb* caress

FONDLED > FONDLE

FONDLER > FONDLE

FONDLERS > FONDLE

FONDLES > FONDLE

FONDLING > FONDLE

FONDLINGS > FONDLE

FONDLY > FOND

FONDNESS > FOND

FONDS > FOND

FONDU *n* ballet movement, lowering the body by bending the leg(s)

FONDUE *n* Swiss dish of a hot melted cheese sauce into which pieces of bread are dipped ▷ *vb* cook and serve (food) as a fondue

FONDUED > FONDUE

FONDUEING > FONDUE

FONDUES > FONDUE

FONDUING > FONDUE

FONDUS > FONDU

FONE *variant of* > FOE

FONLY *adv* foolishly

FONNED > FON

FONNING > FON

FONS > FON

FONT *n* bowl in a church for baptismal water

FONTAL > FONT

FONTANEL *n* soft membraneous gap in an infant's skull

FONTANELS > FONTANEL

FONTANGE *n* type of tall headdress

FONTANGES > FONTANGE

FONTICULI *npl* fontanelles

FONTINA *n* semihard, pale yellow, mild Italian cheese made from cow's milk

FONTINAS > FONTINA

FONTLET > FONT

FONTLETS > FONT

FONTS > FONT

FOOBAR *same as* > FUBAR

FOOD *n* what one eats; solid nourishment

FOODFUL *adj* supplying abundant food

FOODIE *n* gourmet

FOODIES > FOODIE

FOODISM *n* enthusiasm for and interest in the preparation and consumption of good food

FOODISMS > FOODISM

FOODLESS > FOOD

FOODS > FOOD

FOODSTUFF *n* substance used as food

FOODWAYS *npl* customs and traditions relating to food and its preparation

FOODY *same as* > FOODIE

FOOFARAW *n* vulgar ornamentation

FOOFARAWS > FOOFARAW

FOOL *n* person lacking sense or judgment ▷ *vb* deceive (someone)

FOOLED > FOOL

FOOLERIES > FOOLERY

FOOLERY *n* foolish behaviour

FOOLFISH *n* orange filefish or winter flounder

FOOLHARDY *adj* recklessly adventurous

FOOLING > FOOL

FOOLINGS > FOOL

FOOLISH *adj* unwise, silly, or absurd

FOOLISHER > FOOLISH

FOOLISHLY > FOOLISH

FOOLPROOF *adj* unable to fail

FOOLS > FOOL

FOOLSCAP *n* size of paper, 34.3 × 43.2 centimetres

FOOLSCAPS > FOOLSCAP

FOOSBALL *n* US and Canadian name for table football

FOOSBALLS > FOOSBALL

FOOT *n* part of the leg below the ankle ▷ *vb* kick

FOOTAGE *n* amount of film used

FOOTAGES > FOOTAGE

FOOTBAG *n* sport of keeping small round object off the ground by kicking it

FOOTBAGS > FOOTBAG

FOOTBALL *n* game played by two teams of eleven players kicking a ball in an attempt to score goals

FOOTBALLS > FOOTBALL

FOOTBAR *n* any bar designed as a footrest or to be operated by the foot

FOOTBARS > FOOTBAR

FOOTBATH *n* vessel for bathing the feet

FOOTBATHS > FOOTBATH

FOOTBOARD *n* treadle or foot-operated lever on a machine

FOOTBOY *n* boy servant

FOOTBOYS > FOOTBOY

FOOTBRAKE *n* brake operated with the foot

FOOTCLOTH *obsolete word for* > CAPARISON

FOOTED > FOOT

FOOTER *n* person who goes on foot ▷ *vb* potter

FOOTERED > FOOTER

FOOTERING > FOOTER

FOOTERS > FOOTER
FOOTFALL n sound of a footstep
FOOTFALLS > FOOTFALL
FOOTFAULT n fault that occurs when the server fails to keep both feet behind the baseline until he/she has served
FOOTGEAR another name for > FOOTWEAR
FOOTGEARS > FOOTGEAR
FOOTHILL n lower slope of a mountain or a relatively low hill at the foot of a mountain
FOOTHILLS > FOOTHILL
FOOTHOLD n secure position from which progress may be made
FOOTHOLDS > FOOTHOLD
FOOTIE same as > FOOTY
FOOTIER > FOOTY
FOOTIES > FOOTIE
FOOTIEST > FOOTY
FOOTING n basis or foundation
FOOTINGS > FOOTING
FOOTLE vb loiter aimlessly ▷ n foolishness
FOOTLED > FOOTLE
FOOTLER > FOOTLE
FOOTLERS > FOOTLE
FOOTLES > FOOTLE
FOOTLESS > FOOT
FOOTLIGHT n light illuminating the front of a stage
FOOTLIKE > FOOT
FOOTLING adj trivial ▷ n trifle
FOOTLINGS > FOOTLING
FOOTLOOSE adj free from ties
FOOTMAN n male servant in uniform
FOOTMARK n mark or trace of mud, wetness, etc, left by a person's foot on a surface
FOOTMARKS > FOOTMARK
FOOTMEN > FOOTMAN
FOOTMUFF n muff used to keep the feet warm
FOOTMUFFS > FOOTMUFF
FOOTNOTE n note printed at the foot of a page ▷ vb supply (a page, book, etc) with footnotes
FOOTNOTED > FOOTNOTE
FOOTNOTES > FOOTNOTE
FOOTPACE n normal or walking pace
FOOTPACES > FOOTPACE
FOOTPAD n highwayman, on foot rather than horseback
FOOTPADS > FOOTPAD
FOOTPAGE n errand-boy
FOOTPAGES > FOOTPAGE
FOOTPATH n narrow path for walkers only
FOOTPATHS > FOOTPATH
FOOTPLATE n platform in the cab of a locomotive for the driver

FOOTPOST n post delivered on foot
FOOTPOSTS > FOOTPOST
FOOTPRINT n mark left by a foot
FOOTPUMP n pump operated with the foot
FOOTPUMPS > FOOTPUMP
FOOTRA variant of > FOUTRA
FOOTRACE n race run on foot
FOOTRACES > FOOTRACE
FOOTRAS > FOOTRA
FOOTREST n something that provides a support for the feet, such as a low stool, rail, etc
FOOTRESTS > FOOTREST
FOOTROPE n part of a boltrope to which the foot of a sail is stitched
FOOTROPES > FOOTROPE
FOOTRULE n rigid measure, one foot in length
FOOTRULES > FOOTRULE
FOOTS npl sediment that accumulates at the bottom of a vessel containing any of certain liquids, such as vegetable oil or varnish
FOOTSIE n flirtation involving the touching together of feet
FOOTSIES > FOOTSIE
FOOTSLOG vb march
FOOTSLOGS > FOOTSLOG
FOOTSORE adj having sore or tired feet, esp from much walking
FOOTSTALK n small supporting stalk in animals and plants
FOOTSTALL n pedestal, plinth, or base of a column, pier, or statue
FOOTSTEP n step in walking
FOOTSTEPS > FOOTSTEP
FOOTSTOCK another name for > TAILSTOCK
FOOTSTONE n memorial stone at the foot of a grave
FOOTSTOOL n low stool used to rest the feet on while sitting
FOOTSY variant of > FOOTSIE
FOOTWALL n rocks on the lower side of an inclined fault plane or mineral vein
FOOTWALLS > FOOTWALL
FOOTWAY n way or path for pedestrians, such as a raised walk along the edge of a bridge
FOOTWAYS > FOOTWAY
FOOTWEAR n anything worn to cover the feet
FOOTWEARS > FOOTWEAR
FOOTWEARY adj tired from walking
FOOTWELL n part of a car in which the foot pedals are located

FOOTWELLS > FOOTWELL
FOOTWORK n skilful use of the feet, as in sport or dancing
FOOTWORKS > FOOTWORK
FOOTWORN adj footsore
FOOTY n football ▷ adj mean
FOOZLE vb bungle (a shot) ▷ n bungled shot
FOOZLED > FOOZLE
FOOZLER > FOOZLE
FOOZLERS > FOOZLE
FOOZLES > FOOZLE
FOOZLING > FOOZLE
FOOZLINGS > FOOZLE
FOP n man excessively concerned with fashion ▷ vb act like a fop
FOPLING n vain affected dandy
FOPLINGS > FOPLING
FOPPED > FOP
FOPPERIES > FOPPERY
FOPPERY n clothes, affectations, obsessions, etc, of or befitting a fop
FOPPING > FOP
FOPPISH > FOP
FOPPISHLY > FOP
FOPS > FOP
FOR prep indicating a person intended to benefit from or receive something, span of time or distance, person or thing represented by someone, etc
FORA > FORUM
FORAGE vb search about (for) ▷ n food for cattle or horses
FORAGED > FORAGE
FORAGER > FORAGE
FORAGERS > FORAGE
FORAGES > FORAGE
FORAGING > FORAGE
FORAM n a marine protozoan
FORAMEN n natural hole, esp one in a bone through which nerves pass
FORAMENS > FORAMEN
FORAMINA > FORAMEN
FORAMINAL > FORAMEN
FORAMS > FORAM
FORANE as in vicar forane, in the Roman Catholic church, vicar or priest appointed to act in a certain area of the diocese
FORASMUCH conj since
FORAY n brief raid or attack ▷ vb raid or ravage (a town, district, etc)
FORAYED > FORAY
FORAYER > FORAY
FORAYERS > FORAY
FORAYING > FORAY
FORAYS > FORAY
FORB n any herbaceous plant that is not a grass
FORBAD > FORBID
FORBADE > FORBID

FORBARE > FORBEAR
FORBEAR vb cease or refrain (from doing something)
FORBEARER > FORBEAR
FORBEARS > FORBEAR
FORBID vb prohibit, refuse to allow
FORBIDAL > FORBID
FORBIDALS > FORBIDAL
FORBIDDAL n prohibition
FORBIDDEN adj not permitted by order or law
FORBIDDER > FORBID
FORBIDS > FORBID
FORBODE vb obsolete word meaning forbid ▷ n obsolete word meaning forbidding
FORBODED > FORBODE
FORBODES > FORBODE
FORBODING > FORBODE
FORBORE past tense of > FORBEAR
FORBORNE > FORBEAR
FORBS > FORB
FORBY adv besides
FORBYE same as > FORBY
FORCAT n convict or galley slave
FORCATS > FORCAT
FORCE n strength or power ▷ vb compel, make (someone) do something
FORCEABLE > FORCE
FORCED adj compulsory
FORCEDLY > FORCED
FORCEFUL adj emphatic and confident
FORCELESS > FORCE
FORCEMEAT n mixture of chopped ingredients used for stuffing
FORCEPS npl surgical pincers
FORCEPSES > FORCEPS
FORCER > FORCE
FORCERS > FORCE
FORCES > FORCE
FORCIBLE adj involving physical force or violence
FORCIBLY > FORCIBLE
FORCING > FORCE
FORCINGLY > FORCE
FORCIPATE > FORCEPS
FORCIPES > FORCEPS
FORD n shallow place where a river may be crossed ▷ vb cross (a river) at a ford
FORDABLE > FORD
FORDED > FORD
FORDID > FORDO
FORDING > FORD
FORDLESS > FORD
FORDO vb destroy
FORDOES > FORDO
FORDOING > FORDO
FORDONE > FORDO
FORDONNE as in from fordonne fordone
FORDS > FORD
FORE adj in, at, or towards the front ▷ n front part ▷ interj golfer's shouted

warning to a person in the path of a ball

FOREANENT *prep* opposite

FOREARM *n* arm from the wrist to the elbow ▷ *vb* prepare beforehand

FOREARMED > FOREARM

FOREARMS > FOREARM

FOREBAY *n* reservoir or canal

FOREBAYS > FOREBAY

FOREBEAR *n* ancestor

FOREBEARS > FOREBEAR

FOREBITT *n* post at a ship's foremast for securing cables

FOREBITTS > FOREBITT

FOREBODE *vb* warn of or indicate (an event, result, etc) in advance

FOREBODED > FOREBODE

FOREBODER > FOREBODE

FOREBODES > FOREBODE

FOREBODY *n* part of a ship forward of the foremast

FOREBOOM *n* boom of a foremast

FOREBOOMS > FOREBOOM

FOREBRAIN *n* the part of the brain that develops from the anterior portion of the neural tube

FOREBY *variant of* > FORBY

FOREBYE *variant of* > FORBY

FORECABIN *n* forward cabin on a vessel

FORECADDY *n* caddy who goes ahead of the golfer to point out the ball's location

FORECAR *n* three-wheeled passenger vehicle attached to a motorcycle

FORECARS > FORECAR

FORECAST *vb* predict (weather, events, etc) ▷ *n* prediction

FORECASTS > FORECAST

FORECHECK *vb* in ice-hockey, to try to gain control of the puck while at opponents' end of rink

FORECLOSE *vb* take possession of (property bought with borrowed money which has not been repaid)

FORECLOTH *n* cloth hung over the front of something, especially an altar

FORECOURT *n* courtyard or open space in front of a building

FOREDATE *vb* antedate

FOREDATED > FOREDATE

FOREDATES > FOREDATE

FOREDECK *n* deck between the bridge and the forecastle

FOREDECKS > FOREDECK

FOREDID > FOREDO

FOREDO *same as* > FORDO

FOREDOES > FOREDO

FOREDOING > FOREDO

FOREDONE > FOREDO

FOREDOOM *vb* doom or condemn beforehand

FOREDOOMS > FOREDOOM

FOREFACE *n* muzzle of an animal

FOREFACES > FOREFACE

FOREFEEL *vb* have a premonition of

FOREFEELS > FOREFEEL

FOREFEET > FOREFOOT

FOREFELT > FOREFEEL

FOREFEND *same as* > FORFEND

FOREFENDS > FOREFEND

FOREFOOT *n* either of the front feet of an animal

FOREFRONT *n* most active or prominent position

FOREGLEAM *n* early or premonitory inkling or indication

FOREGO *same as* > FORGO

FOREGOER > FOREGO

FOREGOERS > FOREGO

FOREGOES > FOREGO

FOREGOING *adj* going before, preceding

FOREGONE *adj* gone or completed

FOREGUT *n* anterior part of the digestive tract of vertebrates, between the buccal cavity and the bile duct

FOREGUTS > FOREGUT

FOREHAND *n* stroke played with the palm of the hand facing forward ▷ *adj* (of a stroke) made so that the racket is held with the palm facing the direction of play ▷ *adv* with a forehand stroke ▷ *vb* play (a shot) forehand

FOREHANDS > FOREHAND

FOREHEAD *n* part of the face above the eyebrows

FOREHEADS > FOREHEAD

FOREHENT *vb* seize in advance

FOREHENTS > FOREHENT

FOREHOCK *n* foreleg cut of bacon or pork

FOREHOCKS > FOREHOCK

FOREHOOF *n* front hoof

FOREHOOFS > FOREHOOF

FOREIGN *adj* not of, or in, one's own country

FOREIGNER *n* person from a foreign country

FOREIGNLY > FOREIGN

FOREJUDGE *same as* > FORJUDGE

FOREKING *n* previous king

FOREKINGS > FOREKING

FOREKNEW > FOREKNOW

FOREKNOW *vb* know in advance

FOREKNOWN > FOREKNOW

FOREKNOWS > FOREKNOW

FOREL *n* type of parchment

FORELADY *n* forewoman of a jury

FORELAID > FORELAY

FORELAIN > FORELIE

FORELAND *n* headland, cape, or coastal promontory

FORELANDS > FORELAND

FORELAY *archaic word for* > AMBUSH

FORELAYS > FORELAY

FORELEG *n* either of the front legs of an animal

FORELEGS > FORELEG

FORELEND *vb* give up

FORELENDS > FORELEND

FORELENT > FORELEND

FORELIE *vb* lie in front of

FORELIES > FORELIE

FORELIFT *vb* lift up in front

FORELIFTS > FORELIFT

FORELIMB *n* either of the front or anterior limbs of a four-limbed vertebrate: a foreleg, flipper, or wing

FORELIMBS > FORELIMB

FORELOCK *n* lock of hair over the forehead ▷ *vb* secure (a bolt) by means of a forelock

FORELOCKS > FORELOCK

FORELS > FOREL

FORELYING > FORELIE

FOREMAN *n* person in charge of a group of workers

FOREMAST *n* mast nearest the bow of a ship

FOREMASTS > FOREMAST

FOREMEAN *vb* intend in advance

FOREMEANS > FOREMEAN

FOREMEANT > FOREMEAN

FOREMEN > FOREMAN

FOREMILK *n* first milk drawn from a cow's udder prior to milking

FOREMILKS > FOREMILK

FOREMOST *adv* first in time, place, or importance ▷ *adj* first in time, place, or importance

FORENAME *n* first name

FORENAMED *adj* named or mentioned previously

FORENAMES > FORENAME

FORENIGHT *n* evening

FORENOON *n* morning

FORENOONS > FORENOON

FORENSIC *adj* used in or connected with courts of law

FORENSICS *n* art or study of formal debating

FOREPART *n* first or front part in place, order, or time

FOREPARTS > FOREPART

FOREPAST *adj* bygone

FOREPAW *n* either of the front feet of a land mammal that does not have hooves

FOREPAWS > FOREPAW

FOREPEAK *n* interior part of a vessel that is furthest forward

FOREPEAKS > FOREPEAK

FOREPLAN *vb* plan in advance

FOREPLANS > FOREPLAN

FOREPLAY *n* sexual stimulation before intercourse

FOREPLAYS > FOREPLAY

FOREPOINT *vb* predetermine or indicate in advance

FORERAN > FORERUN

FORERANK *n* first rank

FORERANKS > FORERANK

FOREREACH *vb* keep moving under momentum without engine or sails

FOREREAD *vb* foretell

FOREREADS > FOREREAD

FORERUN *vb* serve as a herald for

FORERUNS > FORERUN

FORES > FORE

FORESAID *less common word for* > AFORESAID

FORESAIL *n* main sail on the foremast of a ship

FORESAILS > FORESAIL

FORESAW > FORESEE

FORESAY *vb* foretell

FORESAYS > FORESAY

FORESEE *vb* see or know beforehand

FORESEEN > FORESEE

FORESEER > FORESEE

FORESEERS > FORESEE

FORESEES > FORESEE

FORESHANK *n* top of the front leg of an animal

FORESHEET *n* sheet of a foresail

FORESHEW *variant of* > FORESHOW

FORESHEWN > FORESHEW

FORESHEWS > FORESHEW

FORESHIP *n* fore part of a ship

FORESHIPS > FORESHIP

FORESHOCK *n* relatively small earthquake heralding the arrival of a much larger one. Some large earthquakes are preceded by a series of foreshocks

FORESHORE *n* part of the shore between high- and low-tide marks

FORESHOW *vb* indicate in advance

FORESHOWN > FORESHOW

FORESHOWS > FORESHOW

FORESIDE *n* front or upper side or part

FORESIDES > FORESIDE

FORESIGHT *n* ability to anticipate and provide for future needs

FORESKIN *n* fold of skin covering the tip of the penis

FORESKINS > FORESKIN

FORESKIRT *n* front skirt of a garment (as opposed to the train)

FORESLACK *variant of* > FORSLACK

FORESLOW *variant of* > FORSLOW

FORESLOWS > FORESLOW
FORESPAKE > FORESPEAK
FORESPEAK vb predict
FORESPEND variant of > FORSPEND
FORESPENT > FORSPEND
FORESPOKE > FORESPEAK
FOREST n large area with a thick growth of trees ▷ vb create a forest (in)
FORESTAGE n part of a stage in front of the curtain
FORESTAIR n external stair
FORESTAL > FOREST
FORESTALL vb prevent or guard against in advance
FORESTAY n adjustable stay leading from the truck of the foremast to the deck, stem, or bowsprit, for controlling the motion or bending of the mast
FORESTAYS > FORESTAY
FORESTEAL > FOREST
FORESTED > FOREST
FORESTER n person skilled in forestry
FORESTERS > FORESTER
FORESTIAL > FOREST
FORESTINE > FOREST
FORESTING > FOREST
FORESTRY n science of planting and caring for trees
FORESTS > FOREST
FORESWEAR vb forgo
FORESWORE > FORESWEAR
FORESWORN > FORESWEAR
FORETASTE n early limited experience of something to come ▷ vb have a foretaste of
FORETEACH vb teach beforehand
FORETEETH > FORETOOTH
FORETELL vb tell or indicate beforehand
FORETELLS > FORETELL
FORETHINK vb have prescience
FORETIME n time already gone
FORETIMES > FORETIME
FORETOKEN n sign of a future event ▷ vb foreshadow
FORETOLD > FORETELL
FORETOOTH another word for an > INCISOR
FORETOP n platform at the top of the foremast
FORETOPS > FORETOP
FOREVER adv without end
FOREVERS > FOREVER
FOREWARD n vanguard
FOREWARDS > FOREWARD
FOREWARN vb warn beforehand

FOREWARNS > FOREWARN
FOREWEIGH vb assess in advance
FOREWENT past tense of > FOREGO
FOREWIND n favourable wind
FOREWINDS > FOREWIND
FOREWING n either wing of the anterior pair of an insect's two pairs of wings
FOREWINGS > FOREWING
FOREWOMAN n woman in charge of a group of workers
FOREWOMEN > FOREWOMAN
FOREWORD n introduction to a book
FOREWORDS > FOREWORD
FOREWORN same as > FORWORN
FOREX n foreign exchange
FOREXES > FOREX
FOREYARD n yard for supporting the foresail of a square-rigger
FOREYARDS > FOREYARD
FORFAIR vb perish
FORFAIRED > FORFAIR
FORFAIRN adj worn out
FORFAIRS > FORFAIR
FORFAITER n someone who purchases receivables from exporters
FORFAULT variant of > FORFEIT
FORFAULTS > FORFAULT
FORFEIT n thing lost or given up as a penalty for a fault or mistake ▷ vb lose as a forfeit ▷ adj lost as a forfeit
FORFEITED > FORFEIT
FORFEITER > FORFEIT
FORFEITS > FORFEIT
FORFEND vb protect or secure
FORFENDED > FORFEND
FORFENDS > FORFEND
FORFEX n pair of pincers, esp the paired terminal appendages of an earwig
FORFEXES > FORFEX
FORFICATE adj (esp of the tails of certain birds) deeply forked
FORFOCHEN Scots word for > EXHAUSTED
FORGAT past tense of > FORGET
FORGATHER vb gather together
FORGAVE > FORGIVE
FORGE n place where metal is worked, smithy ▷ vb make a fraudulent imitation of (something)
FORGEABLE > FORGE
FORGED > FORGE
FORGEMAN > FORGE
FORGEMEN > FORGE
FORGER > FORGE
FORGERIES > FORGERY
FORGERS > FORGE

FORGERY n illegal copy of something
FORGES > FORGE
FORGET vb fail to remember
FORGETFUL adj tending to forget
FORGETIVE adj imaginative and inventive
FORGETS > FORGET
FORGETTER > FORGET
FORGING n process of producing a metal component by hammering
FORGINGS > FORGING
FORGIVE vb cease to blame or hold resentment against, pardon
FORGIVEN > FORGIVE
FORGIVER > FORGIVE
FORGIVERS > FORGIVE
FORGIVES > FORGIVE
FORGIVING adj willing to forgive
FORGO vb do without or give up
FORGOER > FORGO
FORGOERS > FORGO
FORGOES > FORGO
FORGOING > FORGO
FORGONE > FORGO
FORGOT past tense of > FORGET
FORGOTTEN past participle of > FORGET
FORHAILE vb distress
FORHAILED > FORHAILE
FORHAILES > FORHAILE
FORHENT variant of > FOREHENT
FORHENTS > FORHENT
FORHOO vb forsake
FORHOOED > FORHOO
FORHOOIE variant of > FORHOO
FORHOOIED > FORHOOIE
FORHOOIES > FORHOOIE
FORHOOING > FORHOO
FORHOOS > FORHOO
FORHOW variant of > FORHOO
FORHOWED > FORHOW
FORHOWING > FORHOW
FORHOWS > FORHOW
FORINSEC adj foreign
FORINT n standard monetary unit of Hungary, divided into 100 fillér
FORINTS > FORINT
FORJASKIT adj exhausted
FORJESKIT variant of > FORJASKIT
FORJUDGE vb deprive of a right by the judgment of a court
FORJUDGED > FORJUDGE
FORJUDGES > FORJUDGE
FORK n tool for eating food, with prongs and a handle ▷ vb pick up, dig, etc with a fork
FORKBALL n method of pitching in baseball
FORKBALLS > FORKBALL

FORKED adj having a fork or forklike parts
FORKEDLY > FORKED
FORKER > FORK
FORKERS > FORK
FORKFUL > FORK
FORKFULS > FORK
FORKHEAD n forked head of a rod
FORKHEADS > FORKHEAD
FORKIER > FORKY
FORKIEST > FORKY
FORKINESS > FORKY
FORKING > FORK
FORKLESS > FORK
FORKLIFT n vehicle having two power-operated horizontal prongs that can be raised and lowered for loading, transporting, and unloading goods, esp goods that are stacked on wooden pallets
FORKLIFTS > FORKLIFT
FORKLIKE > FORK
FORKS > FORK
FORKSFUL > FORK
FORKTAIL n bird belonging to the flycatcher family
FORKTAILS > FORKTAIL
FORKY adj forked
FORLANA n Venetian dance
FORLANAS > FORLANA
FORLEND variant of > FORELEND
FORLENDS > FORLEND
FORLENT > FORLEND
FORLORN adj lonely and unhappy ▷ n forsaken person
FORLORNER > FORLORN
FORLORNLY > FORLORN
FORLORNS > FORLORN
FORM n shape or appearance ▷ vb give a (particular) shape to or take a (particular) shape
FORMABLE > FORM
FORMABLY > FORM
FORMAL adj of or characterized by established conventions of ceremony and behaviour
FORMALIN n solution of formaldehyde in water, used as a disinfectant or a preservative for biological specimens
FORMALINS > FORMALIN
FORMALISE same as > FORMALIZE
FORMALISM n concern with outward appearances and structure at the expense of content
FORMALIST > FORMALISM
FORMALITY n requirement of custom or etiquette
FORMALIZE vb make official or formal
FORMALLY > FORMAL

FORMALS > FORMAL
FORMAMIDE n amide derived from formic acid
FORMANT n any of several frequency ranges within which the partials of a sound, esp a vowel sound, are at their strongest, thus imparting to the sound its own special quality, tone colour, or timbre
FORMANTS > FORMANT
FORMAT n size and shape of a publication ▷ vb arrange in a format
FORMATE n any salt or ester of formic acid containing the ion HCOO or the group HCOO ▷ vb fly aircraft in formation
FORMATED > FORMATE
FORMATES > FORMATE
FORMATING > FORMATE
FORMATION n forming
FORMATIVE adj of or relating to development ▷ n inflectional or derivational affix
FORMATS > FORMAT
FORMATTED > FORMAT
FORMATTER > FORMAT
FORME n type matter, blocks, etc, assembled in a chase and ready for printing
FORMED > FORM
FORMEE n type of heraldic cross
FORMER adj of an earlier time, previous ▷ n person or thing that forms or shapes
FORMERLY adv in the past
FORMERS > FORMER
FORMES > FORME
FORMFUL adj imaginative
FORMIATE variant of > FORMATE
FORMIATES > FORMIATE
FORMIC adj of, relating to, or derived from ants
FORMICA n tradename for any of various laminated plastic sheets, containing melamine, used esp for heat-resistant surfaces that can be easily cleaned
FORMICANT adj low-tension (of pulse)
FORMICARY n ant hill
FORMICAS > FORMICA
FORMICATE vb crawl around like ants
FORMING > FORM
FORMINGS > FORM
FORMLESS adj without a definite shape or form
FORMOL same as > FORMALIN
FORMOLS > FORMOL
FORMS > FORM
FORMULA n group of numbers, letters, or symbols expressing a

scientific or mathematical rule
FORMULAE > FORMULA
FORMULAIC > FORMULA
FORMULAR adj of or relating to formulas
FORMULARY n book of prescribed formulas ▷ adj of, relating to, or of the nature of a formula
FORMULAS > FORMULA
FORMULATE vb plan or describe precisely and clearly
FORMULISE vb express in a formula
FORMULISM n adherence to or belief in formulas
FORMULIST > FORMULISM
FORMULIZE variant of > FORMULISE
FORMWORK n arrangement of wooden boards, bolts, etc, used to shape reinforced concrete while it is setting
FORMWORKS > FORMWORK
FORMYL n of, consisting of, or containing the monovalent group HCO-
FORMYLS > FORMYL
FORNENST prep situated against or facing towards
FORNENT variant of > FORNENST
FORNICAL > FORNIX
FORNICATE vb have sexual intercourse without being married ▷ adj arched or hooklike in form
FORNICES > FORNIX
FORNIX n any archlike structure, esp the arched band of white fibres at the base of the brain
FORPET n quarter of a peck (measure)
FORPETS > FORPET
FORPINE vb waste away
FORPINED > FORPINE
FORPINES > FORPINE
FORPINING > FORPINE
FORPIT variant of > FORPET
FORPITS > FORPIT
FORRAD adv forward
FORRADER > FORRAD
FORRARDER adv further forward
FORRAY archaic variant of > FORAY
FORRAYED > FORRAY
FORRAYING > FORRAY
FORRAYS > FORRAY
FORREN adj foreign
FORRIT adv forward(s)
FORSAID > FORSAY
FORSAKE vb withdraw support or friendship from
FORSAKEN adj completely deserted or helpless
FORSAKER > FORSAKE
FORSAKERS > FORSAKE
FORSAKES > FORSAKE

FORSAKING > FORSAKE
FORSAY vb renounce
FORSAYING > FORSAY
FORSAYS > FORSAY
FORSLACK vb be neglectful
FORSLACKS > FORSLACK
FORSLOE variant of > FORSLOW
FORSLOED > FORSLOE
FORSLOES > FORSLOE
FORSLOW vb hinder
FORSLOWED > FORSLOW
FORSLOWS > FORSLOW
FORSOOK past tense of > FORSAKE
FORSOOTH adv indeed
FORSPEAK vb bewitch
FORSPEAKS > FORSPEAK
FORSPEND vb exhaust
FORSPENDS > FORSPEND
FORSPENT > FORSPEND
FORSPOKE > FORSPEAK
FORSPOKEN > FORSPEAK
FORSWATT adj sweat-covered
FORSWEAR vb renounce or reject
FORSWEARS > FORSWEAR
FORSWINK vb exhaust through toil
FORSWINKS > FORSWINK
FORSWONCK variant of > FORSWUNK
FORSWORE > FORSWEAR
FORSWORN past participle of > FORSWEAR
FORSWUNK adj overworked
FORSYTHIA n shrub with yellow flowers in spring
FORT n fortified building or place ▷ vb fortify
FORTALICE n small fort or outwork of a fortification
FORTE n thing at which a person excels ▷ adv loudly
FORTED > FORT
FORTES > FORTIS
FORTH adv forwards, out, or away ▷ prep out of
FORTHCAME > FORTHCOME
FORTHCOME vb come forth
FORTHINK vb regret
FORTHINKS > FORTHINK
FORTHWITH adv at once
FORTHY adv therefore
FORTIES > FORTY
FORTIETH adj being the ordinal number of forty in numbering or counting order, position, time, etc. Often written: 40th ▷ n one of 40 approximately equal parts of something
FORTIETHS > FORTIETH
FORTIFIED > FORTIFY
FORTIFIER > FORTIFY
FORTIFIES > FORTIFY
FORTIFY vb make (a place) defensible, as by building walls
FORTILAGE n small fort
FORTING > FORT
FORTIS adj (of a

consonant) articulated with considerable muscular tension of the speech organs or with a great deal of breath pressure or plosion ▷ n consonant, such as English p or f, pronounced with considerable muscular force or breath pressure
FORTITUDE n courage in adversity or pain
FORTLET > FORT
FORTLETS > FORT
FORTNIGHT n two weeks
FORTRESS n large fort or fortified town ▷ vb protect with or as if with a fortress
FORTS > FORT
FORTUITY n chance or accidental occurrence
FORTUNATE adj having good luck
FORTUNE n luck, esp when favourable ▷ vb befall
FORTUNED > FORTUNE
FORTUNES > FORTUNE
FORTUNING > FORTUNE
FORTUNIZE vb make happy
FORTY n four times ten ▷ adj amounting to forty ▷ det amounting to forty
FORTYISH > FORTY
FORUM n meeting or medium for open discussion or debate
FORUMS > FORUM
FORWANDER vb wander far
FORWARD same as > FORWARDS
FORWARDED > FORWARD
FORWARDER n person or thing that forwards
FORWARDLY > FORWARD
FORWARDS adv towards or at a place further ahead in space or time
FORWARN archaic word for > FORBID
FORWARNED > FORWARN
FORWARNS > FORWARN
FORWASTE vb lay waste
FORWASTED > FORWASTE
FORWASTES > FORWASTE
FORWEARY vb exhaust
FORWENT past tense of > FORGO
FORWHY adv for what reason
FORWORN adj weary
FORZA n force
FORZANDI > FORZANDO
FORZANDO another word for > SFORZANDO
FORZANDOS > FORZANDO
FORZATI > FORZATO
FORZATO variant of > FORZANDO
FORZATOS > FORZATO
FORZE > FORZA
FOSCARNET n drug used to treat AIDS
FOSS same as > FOSSE
FOSSA n anatomical

depression, trench, or hollow area

FOSSAE > FOSSA

FOSSAS > FOSSA

FOSSATE adj having cavities or depressions

FOSSE n ditch or moat, esp one dug as a fortification

FOSSED adj having a ditch or moat

FOSSES > FOSSE

FOSSETTE n small depression or fossa, as in a bone

FOSSETTES > FOSSETTE

FOSSICK vb search, esp for gold or precious stones

FOSSICKED > FOSSICK

FOSSICKER > FOSSICK

FOSSICKS > FOSSICK

FOSSIL n hardened remains of a prehistoric animal or plant preserved in rock ▷ adj of, like, or being a fossil

FOSSILISE same as > FOSSILIZE

FOSSILIZE vb turn into a fossil

FOSSILS > FOSSIL

FOSSOR n grave digger

FOSSORIAL adj (of the forelimbs and skeleton of burrowing animals) adapted for digging

FOSSORS > FOSSOR

FOSSULA n small fossa

FOSSULAE > FOSSULA

FOSSULATE adj hollowed

FOSTER vb promote the growth or development of ▷ adj of or involved in fostering a child

FOSTERAGE n act of caring for or bringing up a foster child

FOSTERED > FOSTER

FOSTERER > FOSTER

FOSTERERS > FOSTER

FOSTERING > FOSTER

FOSTERS > FOSTER

FOSTRESS n female fosterer

FOTHER vb stop a leak in a ship's hull

FOTHERED > FOTHER

FOTHERING > FOTHER

FOTHERS > FOTHER

FOU adj full ▷ n bushel

FOUAT n succulent pink-flowered plant

FOUATS > FOUAT

FOUD n sheriff in Orkney and Shetland

FOUDRIE n foud's district or office

FOUDRIES > FOUDRIE

FOUDS > FOUD

FOUER > FOU

FOUEST > FOU

FOUET n archaic word for a whip

FOUETS > FOUET

FOUETTE n step in ballet in

which the dancer stands on one foot and makes a whiplike movement with the other

FOUETTES > FOUETTE

FOUGADE n booby-trapped pit or type of mine

FOUGADES > FOUGADE

FOUGASSE n type of bread made with olive oil

FOUGASSES > FOUGASSE

FOUGHT > FIGHT

FOUGHTEN > FIGHT

FOUGHTIER > FOUGHTY

FOUGHTY adj musty

FOUL adj loathsome or offensive ▷ n violation of the rules ▷ vb make dirty or polluted

FOULARD n soft light fabric of plain-weave or twill-weave silk or rayon, usually with a printed design

FOULARDS > FOULARD

FOULBROOD n disease of honeybees

FOULDER vb flash like lightning

FOULDERED > FOULDER

FOULDERS > FOULDER

FOULE n type of woollen cloth

FOULED > FOUL

FOULER > FOUL

FOULES > FOULE

FOULEST > FOUL

FOULIE n bad mood

FOULIES > FOULIE

FOULING > FOUL

FOULINGS > FOUL

FOULLY > FOUL

FOULMART n polecat

FOULMARTS > FOULMART

FOULNESS n state or quality of being foul

FOULS > FOUL

FOUMART former name for the > POLECAT

FOUMARTS > FOUMART

FOUND vb set up or establish (an institution, etc)

FOUNDED > FOUND

FOUNDER vb break down or fail ▷ n person who establishes an institution, company, society, etc

FOUNDERED > FOUNDER

FOUNDERS > FOUNDER

FOUNDING > FOUND

FOUNDINGS > FOUND

FOUNDLING n abandoned baby

FOUNDRESS > FOUNDER

FOUNDRIES > FOUNDRY

FOUNDRY n place where metal is melted and cast

FOUNDS > FOUND

FOUNT same as > FONT

FOUNTAIN n jet of water

FOUNTAINS > FOUNTAIN

FOUNTFUL adj full of springs

FOUNTS > FOUNT

FOUR n one more than three ▷ adj amounting to four ▷ det amounting to four

FOURBALL n in golf, match for two pairs in which each player uses his own ball, the better score of each pair being counted at every hole

FOURBALLS > FOURBALL

FOURCHEE n type of heraldic cross

FOUREYED adj wearing spectacles

FOURFOLD adj having four times as many or as much ▷ adv by four times as many or as much

FOURGON n long covered wagon, used mainly for carrying baggage, supplies, etc

FOURGONS > FOURGON

FOURPENCE n former English silver coin then worth four pennies

FOURPENNY adj blow, esp with the fist

FOURPLAY n supply of television, internet, landline and mobile phone services by one provider

FOURPLAYS > FOURPLAY

FOURPLEX n building that contains four separate dwellings

FOURS > FOUR

FOURSCORE adj eighty

FOURSES n snack eaten at four o'clock

FOURSOME n group of four people

FOURSOMES > FOURSOME

FOURTEEN n four and ten ▷ adj amounting to fourteen ▷ det amounting to fourteen

FOURTEENS > FOURTEEN

FOURTH n (of) number four in a series ▷ adj of or being number four in a series ▷ adv after the third person, position, event, etc

FOURTHLY > FOURTH

FOURTHS > FOURTH

FOUS > FOU

FOUSSA n Madagascan civet-like animal

FOUSSAS > FOUSSA

FOUSTIER > FOUSTY

FOUSTIEST > FOUSTY

FOUSTY archaic variant of > FUSTY

FOUTER same as > FOOTER

FOUTERED > FOUTER

FOUTERING > FOUTER

FOUTERS > FOUTER

FOUTH n abundance

FOUTHS > FOUTH

FOUTRA n fig; expression of contempt

FOUTRAS > FOUTRA

FOUTRE vb footer

FOUTRED > FOUTRE

FOUTRES > FOUTRE

FOUTRING > FOUTRE

FOVEA n any small pit or depression in the surface of a bodily organ or part

FOVEAE > FOVEA

FOVEAL > FOVEA

FOVEAS > FOVEA

FOVEATE > FOVEA

FOVEATED > FOVEA

FOVEIFORM adj shaped like small pit

FOVEOLA n small fovea

FOVEOLAE > FOVEOLA

FOVEOLAR > FOVEOLA

FOVEOLAS > FOVEOLA

FOVEOLATE > FOVEOLA

FOVEOLE same as > FOVEOLA

FOVEOLES > FOVEOLE

FOVEOLET same as > FOVEOLA

FOVEOLETS > FOVEOLET

FOWL n domestic cock or hen ▷ vb hunt or snare wild birds

FOWLED > FOWL

FOWLER > FOWLING

FOWLERS > FOWLING

FOWLING n shooting or trapping of birds for sport or as a livelihood

FOWLINGS > FOWLING

FOWLPOX n viral infection of poultry and other birds

FOWLPOXES > FOWLPOX

FOWLS > FOWL

FOWTH variant of > FOUTH

FOWTHS > FOWTH

FOX n reddish-brown bushy-tailed animal of the dog family ▷ vb perplex or deceive

FOXBERRY n lingonberry

FOXED > FOX

FOXES > FOX

FOXFIRE n luminescent glow emitted by certain fungi on rotting wood

FOXFIRES > FOXFIRE

FOXFISH n type of shark

FOXFISHES > FOXFISH

FOXGLOVE n tall plant with purple or white flowers

FOXGLOVES > FOXGLOVE

FOXHOLE n small pit dug for protection

FOXHOLES > FOXHOLE

FOXHOUND n dog bred for hunting foxes

FOXHOUNDS > FOXHOUND

FOXHUNT n hunting of foxes with hounds ▷ vb hunt foxes with hounds

FOXHUNTED > FOXHUNT

FOXHUNTER > FOXHUNT

FOXHUNTS > FOXHUNT

FOXIE n fox terrier

FOXIER > FOXY

FOXIES > FOXIE

FOXIEST > FOXY

FOXILY > FOXY

FOXINESS > FOXY

FOXING n piece of leather used to reinforce or trim part of the upper of a shoe

FOXINGS > FOXING
FOXLIKE > FOX
FOXSHARK n thresher shark
FOXSHARKS > FOXSHARK
FOXSHIP n cunning
FOXSHIPS > FOXSHIP
FOXSKIN adj made from the skin of a fox ▷ n skin of a fox
FOXSKINS > FOXSKIN
FOXTAIL n European, Asian, and S American grass with soft cylindrical spikes of flowers, cultivated as a pasture grass
FOXTAILS > FOXTAIL
FOXTROT n ballroom dance with slow and quick steps ▷ vb perform this dance
FOXTROTS > FOXTROT
FOXY adj of or like a fox, esp in craftiness
FOY n loyalty
FOYBOAT n small rowing boat
FOYBOATS > FOYBOAT
FOYER n entrance hall in a theatre, cinema, or hotel
FOYERS > FOYER
FOYLE variant of > FOIL
FOYLED > FOYLE
FOYLES > FOYLE
FOYLING > FOYLE
FOYNE variant of > FOIN
FOYNED > FOYNE
FOYNES > FOYNE
FOYNING > FOYNE
FOYS > FOY
FOZIER > FOZY
FOZIEST > FOZY
FOZINESS > FOZY
FOZY adj spongy
FRA n brother: a title given to an Italian monk or friar
FRAB vb nag
FRABBED > FRAB
FRABBING > FRAB
FRABBIT adj peevish
FRABJOUS adj splendid
FRABS > FRAB
FRACAS n noisy quarrel
FRACASES > FRACAS
FRACK adj bold
FRACKING n method of releasing oil or gas from rock
FRACKINGS > FRACKING
FRACT vb break
FRACTAL n figure or surface generated by successive subdivisions of a simpler polygon or polyhedron, according to some iterative process ▷ adj of, relating to, or involving such a process
FRACTALS > FRACTAL
FRACTED > FRACT
FRACTI > FRACTUS
FRACTING > FRACT
FRACTION n numerical quantity that is not a whole number ▷ vb divide

FRACTIONS > FRACTION
FRACTIOUS adj easily upset and angered
FRACTS > FRACT
FRACTUR variant of > FRAKTUR
FRACTURAL > FRACTURE
FRACTURE n breaking, esp of a bone ▷ vb break
FRACTURED > FRACTURE
FRACTURER > FRACTURE
FRACTURES > FRACTURE
FRACTURS > FRACTUR
FRACTUS n ragged-shaped cloud formation
FRAE Scot word for > FROM
FRAENA > FRAENUM
FRAENUM n fold of membrane or skin, such as the fold beneath the tongue, that supports an organ
FRAENUMS > FRAENUM
FRAG vb kill or wound (a fellow soldier or superior officer) deliberately with an explosive device
FRAGGED > FRAG
FRAGGING > FRAG
FRAGGINGS > FRAG
FRAGILE adj easily broken or damaged
FRAGILELY > FRAGILE
FRAGILER > FRAGILE
FRAGILEST > FRAGILE
FRAGILITY > FRAGILE
FRAGMENT n piece broken off ▷ vb break into pieces
FRAGMENTS > FRAGMENT
FRAGOR n sudden sound
FRAGORS > FRAGOR
FRAGRANCE n pleasant smell
FRAGRANCY same as > FRAGRANCE
FRAGRANT adj sweet-smelling
FRAGS > FRAG
FRAICHEUR n freshness
FRAIL adj physically weak ▷ n rush basket for figs or raisins
FRAILER > FRAIL
FRAILEST > FRAIL
FRAILISH > FRAIL
FRAILLY > FRAIL
FRAILNESS > FRAIL
FRAILS > FRAIL
FRAILTEE variant of > FRAILTY
FRAILTEES > FRAILTEE
FRAILTIES > FRAILTY
FRAILTY n physical or moral weakness
FRAIM n stranger
FRAIMS > FRAIM
FRAISE n neck ruff worn during the 16th century ▷ vb provide a rampart with a palisade
FRAISED > FRAISE
FRAISES > FRAISE
FRAISING > FRAISE
FRAKTUR n style of

typeface, formerly used in German typesetting for many printed works
FRAKTURS > FRAKTUR
FRAMABLE > FRAME
FRAMBESIA n an infectious disease
FRAMBOISE n brandy distilled from raspberries in the Alsace-Lorraine region
FRAME n structure giving shape or support ▷ vb put together, construct
FRAMEABLE > FRAME
FRAMED > FRAME
FRAMELESS > FRAME
FRAMER > FRAME
FRAMERS > FRAME
FRAMES > FRAME
FRAMEWORK n supporting structure
FRAMING n frame, framework, or system of frames
FRAMINGS > FRAMING
FRAMPAL same as > FRAMPOLD
FRAMPLER n quarrelsome person
FRAMPLERS > FRAMPLER
FRAMPOLD adj peevish
FRANC n monetary unit of Switzerland, various African countries, and formerly of France and Belgium
FRANCHISE n right to vote ▷ vb grant (a person, firm, etc) a franchise
FRANCISE same as > FRANCIZE
FRANCISED > FRANCISE
FRANCISES > FRANCISE
FRANCIUM n radioactive metallic element
FRANCIUMS > FRANCIUM
FRANCIZE vb make French
FRANCIZED > FRANCIZE
FRANCIZES > FRANCIZE
FRANCO adj post-free
FRANCOLIN n African or Asian partridge
FRANCS > FRANC
FRANGER n condom
FRANGERS > FRANGER
FRANGIBLE adj breakable or fragile
FRANGLAIS n informal French containing a high proportion of words of English origin
FRANION n lover, paramour
FRANIONS > FRANION
FRANK adj honest and straightforward in speech or attitude ▷ n official mark on a letter permitting delivery ▷ vb put such a mark on (a letter)
FRANKABLE > FRANK
FRANKED > FRANK
FRANKER > FRANK
FRANKERS > FRANK
FRANKEST > FRANK

FRANKFORT same as > FRANKFURT
FRANKFURT n light brown smoked sausage
FRANKING > FRANK
FRANKLIN n (in 14th- and 15th-century England) a substantial landholder of free but not noble birth
FRANKLINS > FRANKLIN
FRANKLY adv in truth
FRANKNESS > FRANK
FRANKS > FRANK
FRANSERIA n American shrub
FRANTIC adj distracted with rage, grief, joy, etc
FRANTICLY > FRANTIC
FRANZIER > FRANZY
FRANZIEST > FRANZY
FRANZY adj irritable
FRAP vb lash down or together
FRAPE adj tightly bound
FRAPPANT adj striking, vivid
FRAPPE adj (of drinks) chilled ▷ n drink consisting of a liqueur, etc, poured over crushed ice
FRAPPED > FRAP
FRAPPEE > FRAPPE
FRAPPES > FRAPPE
FRAPPING > FRAP
FRAPS > FRAP
FRAS > FRA
FRASCATI n dry or semisweet white wine from the Lazio region of Italy
FRASCATIS > FRASCATI
FRASS n excrement or other refuse left by insects and insect larvae
FRASSES > FRASS
FRAT n member of a fraternity
FRATCH n quarrel
FRATCHES > FRATCH
FRATCHETY same as > FRATCHY
FRATCHIER > FRATCHY
FRATCHING > FRATCH
FRATCHY adj quarrelsome
FRATE n friar
FRATER n mendicant friar or a lay brother in a monastery or priory
FRATERIES > FRATER
FRATERNAL adj of a brother, brotherly
FRATERS > FRATER
FRATERY > FRATER
FRATI > FRATE
FRATRIES > FRATER
FRATRY > FRATER
FRATS > FRAT
FRAU n married German woman
FRAUD n (criminal) deception, swindle
FRAUDFUL > FRAUD
FRAUDS > FRAUD
FRAUDSMAN n practitioner

of criminal fraud

FRAUDSMEN
> FRAUDSMAN

FRAUDSTER n person who commits a fraud

FRAUGHAN n a small shrub

FRAUGHANS > FRAUGHAN

FRAUGHT adj tense or anxious ▷ vb archaic word for load ▷ n archaic word for freight

FRAUGHTED > FRAUGHT

FRAUGHTER > FRAUGHT

FRAUGHTS > FRAUGHT

FRAULEIN n unmarried German woman

FRAULEINS > FRAULEIN

FRAUS > FRAU

FRAUTAGE n cargo

FRAUTAGES > FRAUTAGE

FRAWZEY n celebration

FRAWZEYS > FRAWZEY

FRAY n noisy quarrel or conflict ▷ vb make or become ragged at the edge

FRAYED > FRAY

FRAYING > FRAY

FRAYINGS > FRAY

FRAYS > FRAY

FRAZIL n small pieces of ice that form in water moving turbulently enough to prevent the formation of a sheet of ice

FRAZILS > FRAZIL

FRAZZLE n exhausted state ▷ vb tire out

FRAZZLED > FRAZZLE

FRAZZLES > FRAZZLE

FRAZZLING > FRAZZLE

FREAK n abnormal person or thing ▷ adj abnormal ▷ vb streak with colour

FREAKED > FREAK

FREAKERY as in control freakery need to be in control of events

FREAKFUL variant of > FREAKISH

FREAKIER > FREAKY

FREAKIEST > FREAKY

FREAKILY > FREAKY

FREAKING > FREAK

FREAKISH adj of, related to, or characteristic of a freak

FREAKOUT n heightened emotional state

FREAKOUTS > FREAKOUT

FREAKS > FREAK

FREAKY adj weird, peculiar

FRECKLE n small brown spot on the skin ▷ vb mark or become marked with freckles

FRECKLED > FRECKLE

FRECKLES > FRECKLE

FRECKLIER > FRECKLE

FRECKLING > FRECKLE

FRECKLY > FRECKLE

FREDAINE n escapade

FREDAINES > FREDAINE

FREE adj able to act at will, not compelled or restrained

▷ vb release, liberate

FREEBASE n cocaine that has been refined by heating it in ether or some other solvent ▷ vb refine (cocaine) in this way

FREEBASED > FREEBASE

FREEBASER > FREEBASE

FREEBASES > FREEBASE

FREEBEE variant of > FREEBIE

FREEBEES > FREEBEE

FREEBIE n something provided without charge ▷ adj without charge

FREEBIES > FREEBIE

FREEBOARD n space or distance between the deck of a vessel and the water line

FREEBOOT vb act as a freebooter

FREEBOOTS > FREEBOOT

FREEBOOTY > FREEBOOT

FREEBORN adj not born in slavery

FREECYCLE vb recycle an unwanted item by donating it

FREED > FREE

FREEDIVER n person who dives without breathing apparatus

FREEDMAN n man freed from slavery

FREEDMEN > FREEDMAN

FREEDOM n being free

FREEDOMS > FREEDOM

FREEFORM n irregular flowing shape, often used in industrial or fabric design ▷ adj freely flowing, spontaneous

FREEGAN n person who avoids buying consumer goods, recycling discarded goods instead

FREEGANS > FREEGAN

FREEHAND adj drawn without guiding instruments

FREEHOLD n tenure of land for life without restrictions ▷ adj of or held by freehold

FREEHOLDS > FREEHOLD

FREEING > FREE

FREELANCE n (of) a self-employed person doing specific pieces of work for various employers ▷ vb work as a freelance ▷ adv to or as a freelance

FREELOAD vb act as a freeloader

FREELOADS > FREELOAD

FREELY > FREE

FREEMAN n person who has been given the freedom of a city

FREEMASON n member of a guild of itinerant skilled stonemasons, who had a system of secret signs and passwords with which they recognized each other

FREEMEN > FREEMAN

FREENESS > FREE

FREEPHONE n system of telephone use in which the cost of calls in response to an advertisement is borne by the advertiser

FREER n liberator

FREERIDE n extreme form of skiing, snowboarding, or mountain biking

FREERIDES > FREERIDE

FREERS > FREER

FREES > FREE

FREESHEET n newspaper that is distributed free, paid for by its advertisers

FREESIA n plant with fragrant tubular flowers

FREESIAS > FREESIA

FREEST > FREE

FREESTONE n any fine-grained stone, esp sandstone or limestone, that can be cut and worked in any direction without breaking

FREESTYLE n competition, such as in swimming, in which each participant may use a style of his or her choice ▷ vb perform (music, a sport, etc) in a freestyle manner

FREET n omen or superstition

FREETIER > FREETY

FREETIEST > FREETY

FREETS > FREET

FREETY adj superstitious

FREEWARE n computer software that may be distributed and used without payment

FREEWARES > FREEWARE

FREEWAY n motorway

FREEWAYS > FREEWAY

FREEWHEEL vb travel downhill on a bicycle without pedalling ▷ n device in the rear hub of a bicycle wheel that permits it to rotate freely while the pedals are stationary

FREEWILL n apparent human ability to make choices that are not externally determined

FREEWOMAN n woman who is free or at liberty

FREEWOMEN
> FREEWOMAN

FREEWRITE vb write freely without stopping or thinking

FREEWROTE
> FREEWRITE

FREEZABLE > FREEZE

FREEZE vb change from a liquid to a solid by the reduction of temperature, as water to ice ▷ n period of very cold weather

FREEZER n insulated cabinet for cold-storage of

perishable foods

FREEZERS > FREEZER

FREEZES > FREEZE

FREEZING > FREEZE

FREEZINGS > FREEZE

FREIGHT n commercial transport of goods ▷ vb send by freight

FREIGHTED > FREIGHT

FREIGHTER n ship or aircraft for transporting goods

FREIGHTS > FREIGHT

FREIT variant of > FREET

FREITIER > FREITY

FREITIEST > FREITY

FREITS > FREIT

FREITY adj superstitious

FREMD adj alien or strange

FREMDS > FREMD

FREMIT same as > FREMD

FREMITS > FREMIT

FREMITUS n vibration felt by the hand when placed on a part of the body, esp the chest, when the patient is speaking or coughing

FRENA > FRENUM

FRENCH vb (of food) cut into thin strips

FRENCHED > FRENCH

FRENCHES > FRENCH

FRENCHIFY vb make or become French in appearance, behaviour, etc

FRENCHING > FRENCH

FRENETIC adj uncontrolled, excited ▷ n madman

FRENETICS > FRENETIC

FRENNE variant of > FREMD

FRENNES > FRENNE

FRENULA > FRENULUM

FRENULAR > FRENULUM

FRENULUM n strong bristle or group of bristles on the hind wing of some moths and other insects, by which the forewing and hind wing are united during flight

FRENULUMS > FRENULUM

FRENUM same as > FRAENUM

FRENUMS > FRENUM

FRENZICAL > FRENZY

FRENZIED adj filled with or as if with frenzy

FRENZIES > FRENZY

FRENZILY > FRENZY

FRENZY n violent mental derangement ▷ vb make frantic

FRENZYING > FRENZY

FREQUENCE same as > FREQUENCY

FREQUENCY n rate of occurrence

FREQUENT adj happening often ▷ vb visit habitually

FREQUENTS > FREQUENT

FRERE n friar

FRERES > FRERE

FRESCADE n shady place or cool walk

FRESCADES > FRESCADE
FRESCO n watercolour painting done on wet plaster on a wall ▷ vb paint a fresco
FRESCOED > FRESCO
FRESCOER > FRESCO
FRESCOERS > FRESCO
FRESCOES > FRESCO
FRESCOING > FRESCO
FRESCOIST > FRESCO
FRESCOS > FRESCO
FRESH adj newly made, acquired, etc ▷ adv recently ▷ vb freshen
FRESHED > FRESH
FRESHEN vb make or become fresh or fresher
FRESHENED > FRESHEN
FRESHENER > FRESHEN
FRESHENS > FRESHEN
FRESHER n first-year student
FRESHERS > FRESHER
FRESHES > FRESH
FRESHEST > FRESH
FRESHET n sudden overflowing of a river
FRESHETS > FRESHET
FRESHIE n in Indian English, new immigrant to the UK from the Asian subcontinent
FRESHIES > FRESHIE
FRESHING > FRESH
FRESHISH > FRESH
FRESHLY > FRESH
FRESHMAN same as
> FRESHER
FRESHMEN > FRESHMAN
FRESHNESS > FRESH
FRESNEL n unit of frequency equivalent to 10¹²hertz
FRESNELS > FRESNEL
FRET vb be worried ▷ n worried state
FRETBOARD n fingerboard with frets on a stringed musical instrument
FRETFUL adj irritable
FRETFULLY > FRETFUL
FRETLESS > FRET
FRETS > FRET
FRETSAW n fine saw with a narrow blade, used for fretwork
FRETSAWS > FRETSAW
FRETSOME adj vexing
FRETTED > FRET
FRETTER > FRET
FRETTERS > FRET
FRETTIER > FRETTY
FRETTIEST > FRETTY
FRETTING > FRET
FRETTINGS > FRET
FRETTY adj decorated with frets
FRETWORK n decorative carving in wood
FRETWORKS > FRETWORK
FRIABLE adj easily crumbled
FRIAND n small almond

cake
FRIANDE variant of
> FRIAND
FRIANDES > FRIANDE
FRIANDS > FRIAND
FRIAR n member of a male Roman Catholic religious order
FRIARBIRD n Australian honeyeater with a naked head
FRIARIES > FRIARY
FRIARLY > FRIAR
FRIARS > FRIAR
FRIARY n house of friars
FRIB n short heavy-conditioned piece of wool removed from a fleece during classing
FRIBBLE vb fritter away ▷ n wasteful or frivolous person or action ▷ adj frivolous
FRIBBLED > FRIBBLE
FRIBBLER > FRIBBLE
FRIBBLERS > FRIBBLE
FRIBBLES > FRIBBLE
FRIBBLING > FRIBBLE
FRIBBLISH adj trifling
FRIBS > FRIB
FRICADEL variant of
> FRIKKADEL
FRICADELS > FRICADEL
FRICANDO n a larded and braised veal fillet
FRICASSEE n stewed meat served in a thick white sauce ▷ vb prepare (meat) as a fricassee
FRICATIVE n consonant produced by friction of the breath through a partially open mouth, such as (f) or (z) ▷ adj relating to or being a fricative
FRICHT vb frighten
FRICHTED > FRICHT
FRICHTING > FRICHT
FRICHTS > FRICHT
FRICKING adj slang word for absolute
FRICTION n resistance met with by a body moving over another
FRICTIONS > FRICTION
FRIDGE n apparatus in which food and drinks are kept cool ▷ vb archaic word for chafe
FRIDGED > FRIDGE
FRIDGES > FRIDGE
FRIDGING > FRIDGE
FRIED > FRY
FRIEDCAKE n type of doughnut
FRIEND n person whom one knows well and likes ▷ vb befriend
FRIENDED > FRIEND
FRIENDING > FRIEND
FRIENDLY adj showing or expressing liking ▷ n match played for its own sake and not as part of a competition
FRIENDS > FRIEND

FRIER same as **>** FRYER
FRIERS > FRIER
FRIES > FRY
FRIEZE n ornamental band on a wall ▷ vb give a nap to (cloth)
FRIEZED > FRIEZE
FRIEZES > FRIEZE
FRIEZING > FRIEZE
FRIG vb taboo word meaning masturbate ▷ n fridge
FRIGATE n medium-sized fast warship
FRIGATES > FRIGATE
FRIGATOON n Venetian sailing ship
FRIGES > FRIG
FRIGGED > FRIG
FRIGGER > FRIG
FRIGGERS > FRIG
FRIGGING > FRIG
FRIGGINGS > FRIG
FRIGHT n sudden fear or alarm
FRIGHTED > FRIGHT
FRIGHTEN vb scare or terrify
FRIGHTENS > FRIGHTEN
FRIGHTFUL adj horrifying
FRIGHTING > FRIGHT
FRIGHTS > FRIGHT
FRIGID adj (of a woman) sexually unresponsive
FRIGIDER > FRIGID
FRIGIDEST > FRIGID
FRIGIDITY > FRIGID
FRIGIDLY > FRIGID
FRIGOT variant of
> FRIGATE
FRIGOTS > FRIGOT
FRIGS > FRIG
FRIJOL n variety of bean, esp the French bean, extensively cultivated for food in Mexico
FRIJOLE variant of
> FRIJOL
FRIJOLES > FRIJOL
FRIKKADEL n South African meatball
FRILL n gathered strip of fabric attached at one edge ▷ vb adorn or fit with a frill or frills
FRILLED > FRILL
FRILLER > FRILL
FRILLERS > FRILL
FRILLIER > FRILLY
FRILLIES npl flimsy women's underwear
FRILLIEST > FRILLY
FRILLING > FRILL
FRILLINGS > FRILL
FRILLS > FRILL
FRILLY adj with a frill or frills
FRINGE n hair cut short and hanging over the forehead ▷ vb decorate with a fringe ▷ adj (of theatre) unofficial or unconventional
FRINGED > FRINGE

FRINGES > FRINGE
FRINGIER > FRINGY
FRINGIEST > FRINGY
FRINGING > FRINGE
FRINGY adj having a fringe
FRIPON n rogue
FRIPONS > FRIPON
FRIPPER n dealer in old clothes
FRIPPERER same as
> FRIPPER
FRIPPERS > FRIPPER
FRIPPERY n useless ornamentation
FRIPPET n frivolous or flamboyant young woman
FRIPPETS > FRIPPET
FRIS same as **>** FRISKA
FRISBEE n tradename of a light plastic disc, thrown with a spinning motion for recreation or in competition
FRISBEES > FRISBEE
FRISE n fabric with a long normally uncut nap used for upholstery and rugs
FRISEE n endive
FRISEES > FRISEE
FRISES > FRIS
FRISETTE n curly or frizzed fringe, often an artificial hairpiece, worn by women on the forehead
FRISETTES > FRISETTE
FRISEUR n hairdresser
FRISEURS > FRISEUR
FRISK vb move or leap playfully ▷ n playful movement
FRISKA n (in Hungarian music) the fast movement of a piece
FRISKAS > FRISKA
FRISKED > FRISK
FRISKER > FRISK
FRISKERS > FRISK
FRISKET n light rectangular frame, attached to the tympan of a hand printing press, that carries a parchment sheet to protect the nonprinting areas
FRISKETS > FRISKET
FRISKFUL > FRISK
FRISKIER > FRISKY
FRISKIEST > FRISKY
FRISKILY > FRISKY
FRISKING > FRISK
FRISKINGS > FRISK
FRISKS > FRISK
FRISKY adj lively or high-spirited
FRISSON n shiver of fear or excitement
FRISSONS > FRISSON
FRIST archaic word for
> POSTPONE
FRISTED > FRIST
FRISTING > FRIST
FRISTS > FRIST
FRISURE n styling the hair into curls

FRISURES > FRISURE

FRIT n basic materials, partially or wholly fused, for making glass, glazes for pottery, enamel, etc ▷ vb fuse (materials) in making frit

FRITES npl chipped potatoes

FRITFLIES > FRITFLY

FRITFLY n type of small black fly whose larvae are destructive to grain crops

FRITH same as > FIRTH

FRITHBORH n type of pledge

FRITHS > FRITH

FRITS > FRIT

FRITT same as > FRIT

FRITTATA n Italian dish made with eggs and chopped vegetables or meat, resembling a flat thick omelette

FRITTATAS > FRITTATA

FRITTED > FRIT

FRITTER n piece of food fried in batter ▷ vb waste or squander

FRITTERED > FRITTER

FRITTERER > FRITTER

FRITTERS > FRITTER

FRITTING > FRIT

FRITTS > FRITT

FRITURE archaic word for > FRITTER

FRITURES > FRITURE

FRITZ n as in on the fritz state of disrepair

FRITZES > FRITZ

FRIVOL vb behave frivolously

FRIVOLED > FRIVOL

FRIVOLER > FRIVOL

FRIVOLERS > FRIVOL

FRIVOLING > FRIVOL

FRIVOLITY > FRIVOLOUS

FRIVOLLED > FRIVOL

FRIVOLLER > FRIVOL

FRIVOLOUS adj not serious or sensible

FRIVOLS > FRIVOL

FRIZ variant of > FRIZZ

FRIZE n coarse woollen fabric ▷ vb freeze

FRIZED > FRIZE

FRIZER n person who gives nap to cloth

FRIZERS > FRIZER

FRIZES > FRIZE

FRIZETTE same as > FRISETTE

FRIZETTES > FRIZETTE

FRIZING > FRIZE

FRIZZ vb form (hair) into stiff wiry curls ▷ n hair that has been frizzed

FRIZZANTE adj (of wine) slightly effervescent

FRIZZED > FRIZZ

FRIZZER > FRIZZ

FRIZZERS > FRIZZ

FRIZZES > FRIZZ

FRIZZIER > FRIZZY

FRIZZIES n condition of having frizzy hair

FRIZZIEST > FRIZZY

FRIZZILY > FRIZZY

FRIZZING > FRIZZ

FRIZZLE vb cook or heat until crisp and shrivelled ▷ n tight curl

FRIZZLED > FRIZZLE

FRIZZLER > FRIZZLE

FRIZZLERS > FRIZZLE

FRIZZLES > FRIZZLE

FRIZZLIER > FRIZZLE

FRIZZLING > FRIZZLE

FRIZZLY > FRIZZLE

FRIZZY adj (of the hair) in tight crisp wiry curls

FRO adv away ▷ n afro

FROCK n dress ▷ vb invest (a person) with the office or status of a cleric

FROCKED > FROCK

FROCKING n coarse material suitable for making frocks or work clothes

FROCKINGS > FROCKING

FROCKLESS > FROCK

FROCKS > FROCK

FROE n cutting tool with handle and blade at right angles, used for stripping young trees, etc

FROES > FROE

FROG n smooth-skinned tailless amphibian with long back legs used for jumping

FROGBIT n floating aquatic Eurasian plant

FROGBITS > FROGBIT

FROGEYE n plant disease

FROGEYED adj affected by frogeye

FROGEYES > FROGEYE

FROGFISH n type of angler fish whose body is covered with fleshy processes, including a fleshy lure on top of the head

FROGGED adj decorated with frogging

FROGGERY n place where frogs are kept

FROGGIER > FROGGY

FROGGIEST > FROGGY

FROGGING n decorative fastening of looped braid on a coat

FROGGINGS > FROGGING

FROGGY adj like a frog

FROGLET n young frog

FROGLETS > FROGLET

FROGLIKE > FROG

FROGLING n young frog

FROGLINGS > FROGLING

FROGMAN n swimmer with a rubber suit and breathing equipment for working underwater

FROGMARCH vb force (a resisting person) to move by holding his arms ▷ n method of carrying a resisting person in which each limb is held and the victim is face downwards

FROGMEN > FROGMAN

FROGMOUTH n type of nocturnal insectivorous bird of SE Asia and Australia

FROGS > FROG

FROGSPAWN n jelly-like substance containing frog's eggs

FROIDEUR n coldness

FROIDEURS > FROIDEUR

FROING as in toing and froing going back and forth

FROINGS > FROING

FROISE n kind of pancake

FROISES > FROISE

FROLIC vb run and play in a lively way ▷ n lively and merry behaviour ▷ adj full of merriment or fun

FROLICKED > FROLIC

FROLICKER > FROLIC

FROLICKY adj frolicsome

FROLICS > FROLIC

FROM prep indicating the point of departure, source, distance, cause, change of state, etc

FROMAGE as in fromage frais low-fat soft cheese

FROMAGES > FROMAGE

FROMENTY same as > FRUMENTY

FROND n long leaf or leaflike part of a fern, palm, or seaweed

FRONDAGE n fronds collectively

FRONDAGES > FRONDAGE

FRONDED adj having fronds

FRONDENT adj leafy

FRONDEUR n 17th-century French rebel

FRONDEURS > FRONDEUR

FRONDLESS > FROND

FRONDOSE adj leafy or like a leaf

FRONDOUS adj leafy or like a leaf

FRONDS > FROND

FRONS n anterior cuticular plate on the head of some insects, in front of the clypeus

FRONT n fore part ▷ adj of or at the front ▷ vb face (onto)

FRONTAGE n facade of a building

FRONTAGER n owner of a building or land on the front of a street

FRONTAGES > FRONTAGE

FRONTAL adj of, at, or in the front ▷ n decorative hanging for the front of an altar

FRONTALLY > FRONTAL

FRONTALS > FRONTAL

FRONTED > FRONT

FRONTENIS n racket used in Basque ball game

FRONTER > FRONT

FRONTES > FRONS

FRONTIER n area of a country bordering on another

FRONTIERS > FRONTIER

FRONTING > FRONT

FRONTLESS > FRONT

FRONTLET n small decorative loop worn on a woman's forehead, projecting from under her headdress, in the 15th century

FRONTLETS > FRONTLET

FRONTLINE adj of, relating to, or suitable for the front line of a military formation

FRONTLIST n list of books about to be published

FRONTMAN n nominal leader of an organization, etc, who lacks real power or authority, esp one who lends respectability to some nefarious activity

FRONTMEN > FRONTMAN

FRONTON n wall against which pelota or jai alai is played

FRONTONS > FRONTON

FRONTOON variant of > FRONTON

FRONTOONS > FRONTOON

FRONTPAGE adj on or suitable for the front page of a newspaper ▷ vb to place something on the front page of a newspaper

FRONTS > FRONT

FRONTWARD adv towards the front

FRONTWAYS adv with the front forward

FRONTWISE variant of > FRONTWAYS

FRORE adj very cold or frosty

FROREN variant of > FRORE

FRORN variant of > FRORE

FRORNE variant of > FRORE

FRORY adj frozen

FROS > FRO

FROSH n freshman

FROSHES > FROSH

FROST n white frozen dew or mist ▷ vb become covered with frost

FROSTBIT > FROSTBITE

FROSTBITE n destruction of tissue, esp of the fingers or ears, by cold ▷ vb affect with frostbite

FROSTED adj (of glass) having a rough surface to make it opaque ▷ n type of ice cream dish

FROSTEDS > FROSTED

FROSTFISH n American fish appearing in frosty weather

FROSTIER > FROSTY

FROSTIEST > FROSTY

FROSTILY > FROSTY

FROSTING n sugar icing

FROSTINGS > FROSTING
FROSTLESS > FROST
FROSTLIKE > FROST
FROSTLINE n depth to which ground freezes in winter
FROSTNIP n milder form of frostbite
FROSTNIPS > FROSTNIP
FROSTS > FROST
FROSTWORK n patterns made by frost on glass, metal, etc
FROSTY adj characterized or covered by frost
FROTH n mass of small bubbles ▷ vb foam
FROTHED > FROTH
FROTHER > FROTH
FROTHERS > FROTH
FROTHERY n anything insubstantial, like froth
FROTHIER > FROTH
FROTHIEST > FROTH
FROTHILY > FROTH
FROTHING > FROTH
FROTHLESS > FROTH
FROTHS > FROTH
FROTHY > FROTH
FROTTAGE n act or process of taking a rubbing from a rough surface, such as wood, for a work of art
FROTTAGES > FROTTAGE
FROTTEUR n person who rubs against another person's body for a sexual thrill
FROTTEURS > FROTTEUR
FROUFROU n swishing sound, as made by a long silk dress
FROUFROUS > FROUFROU
FROUGHIER > FROUGHY
FROUGHY adj rancid
FROUNCE vb wrinkle
FROUNCED > FROUNCE
FROUNCES > FROUNCE
FROUNCING > FROUNCE
FROUZIER > FROUZY
FROUZIEST > FROUZY
FROUZY same as > FROWZY
FROW same as > FROE
FROWARD adj obstinate
FROWARDLY > FROWARD
FROWARDS > FROWARD
FROWIE variant of > FROUGHY
FROWIER > FROWIE
FROWIEST > FROWIE
FROWN vb wrinkle one's brows in worry, anger, or thought ▷ n frowning expression
FROWNED > FROWN
FROWNER > FROWN
FROWNERS > FROWN
FROWNING > FROWN
FROWNS > FROWN
FROWS > FROW
FROWSIER > FROWSY
FROWSIEST > FROWSY
FROWST n hot and stale atmosphere ▷ vb abandon oneself to such an atmosphere
FROWSTED > FROWST
FROWSTER > FROWST
FROWSTERS > FROWST
FROWSTIER > FROWSTY
FROWSTING > FROWST
FROWSTS > FROWST
FROWSTY adj stale or musty
FROWSY same as > FROWZY
FROWY variant of > FROUGHY
FROWZIER > FROWZY
FROWZIEST > FROWZY
FROWZILY > FROWZY
FROWZY adj dirty or unkempt
FROZE > FREEZE
FROZEN > FREEZE
FROZENLY > FREEZE
FRUCTAN n type of polymer of fructose, present in certain fruits
FRUCTANS > FRUCTAN
FRUCTED adj fruit-bearing
FRUCTIFY vb (cause to) bear fruit
FRUCTIVE adj fruitful
FRUCTOSE n crystalline sugar occurring in many fruits
FRUCTOSES > FRUCTOSE
FRUCTUARY n archaic word for a person who enjoys the fruits of something
FRUCTUATE vb bear fruit
FRUCTUOUS adj productive or fruitful
FRUG vb perform the frug, a 1960s dance
FRUGAL adj thrifty, sparing
FRUGALIST > FRUGAL
FRUGALITY > FRUGAL
FRUGALLY > FRUGAL
FRUGGED > FRUG
FRUGGING > FRUG
FRUGIVORE adj fruit-eating
FRUGS > FRUG
FRUICT obsolete variant of > FRUIT
FRUICTS > FRUICT
FRUIT n part of a plant containing seeds, esp if edible ▷ vb bear fruit
FRUITAGE n process, state, or season of producing fruit
FRUITAGES > FRUITAGE
FRUITCAKE n cake containing dried fruit
FRUITED > FRUIT
FRUITER n fruit grower
FRUITERER n person who sells fruit
FRUITERS > FRUITER
FRUITERY n fruitage
FRUITFUL adj useful or productive
FRUITIER > FRUITY
FRUITIEST > FRUITY
FRUITILY > FRUITY

FRUITING > FRUIT
FRUITINGS > FRUIT
FRUITION n fulfilment of something worked for or desired
FRUITIONS > FRUITION
FRUITIVE adj enjoying
FRUITLESS adj useless or unproductive
FRUITLET n small fruit
FRUITLETS > FRUITLET
FRUITLIKE > FRUIT
FRUITS > FRUIT
FRUITWOOD n wood of a fruit tree
FRUITY adj of or like fruit
FRUMENTY n kind of porridge made from hulled wheat boiled with milk, sweetened, and spiced
FRUMP n dowdy woman ▷ vb mock or taunt
FRUMPED > FRUMP
FRUMPIER > FRUMPY
FRUMPIEST > FRUMPY
FRUMPILY > FRUMPY
FRUMPING > FRUMP
FRUMPISH same as > FRUMPY
FRUMPLE vb wrinkle or crumple
FRUMPLED > FRUMPLE
FRUMPLES > FRUMPLE
FRUMPLING > FRUMPLE
FRUMPS > FRUMP
FRUMPY adj (of a woman, clothes, etc) dowdy, drab, or unattractive
FRUSEMIDE n diuretic used to relieve oedema, for example caused by heart or kidney disease
FRUSH vb break into pieces
FRUSHED > FRUSH
FRUSHES > FRUSH
FRUSHING > FRUSH
FRUST n fragment
FRUSTA > FRUSTUM
FRUSTRATE vb upset or anger ▷ adj frustrated or thwarted
FRUSTS > FRUST
FRUSTULE n hard siliceous cell wall of a diatom
FRUSTULES > FRUSTULE
FRUSTUM n part of a cone or pyramid contained between the base and a plane parallel to the base that intersects the solid
FRUSTUMS > FRUSTUM
FRUTEX n shrub
FRUTICES > FRUTEX
FRUTICOSE adj shrubby
FRUTIFIED > FRUTIFY
FRUTIFIES > FRUTIFY
FRUTIFY vb malapropism for notify; used for comic effect by Shakespeare
FRY vb cook or be cooked in fat or oil ▷ n dish of fried food
FRYABLE > FRY
FRYBREAD n Native

American fried bread
FRYBREADS > FRYBREAD
FRYER n person or thing that fries
FRYERS > FRYER
FRYING > FRY
FRYINGS > FRY
FRYPAN n long-handled shallow pan used for frying
FRYPANS > FRYPAN
FUB vb cheat
FUBAR adj irreparably damaged or bungled
FUBBED > FUB
FUBBERIES > FUBBERY
FUBBERY n cheating
FUBBIER > FUBBY
FUBBIEST > FUBBY
FUBBING > FUB
FUBBY adj chubby
FUBS > FUB
FUBSIER > FUBSY
FUBSIEST > FUBSY
FUBSY adj short and stout
FUCHSIA n ornamental shrub with hanging flowers
FUCHSIAS > FUCHSIA
FUCHSIN n greenish crystalline substance
FUCHSINE same as > FUCHSIN
FUCHSINES > FUCHSINE
FUCHSINS > FUCHSIN
FUCHSITE n form of mica
FUCHSITES > FUCHSITE
FUCI > FUCUS
FUCK vb taboo word meaning to have sexual intercourse (with) ▷ n taboo word for an act of sexual intercourse
FUCKED > FUCK
FUCKER n taboo word for a despicable or obnoxious person
FUCKERS > FUCKER
FUCKHEAD n stupid or contemptible person
FUCKHEADS > FUCKHEAD
FUCKING > FUCK
FUCKINGS > FUCK
FUCKOFF n taboo word for an annoying or unpleasant person
FUCKOFFS > FUCKOFF
FUCKS > FUCK
FUCKUP vb taboo word meaning to damage or bungle ▷ n taboo word meaning an act or an instance of bungling
FUCKUPS > FUCKUP
FUCKWIT n taboo word for a fool or idiot
FUCKWITS > FUCKWIT
FUCOID n type of seaweed
FUCOIDAL n type of seaweed
FUCOIDS > FUCOID
FUCOSE n aldose
FUCOSES > FUCOSE
FUCOUS same as > FUCOIDAL
FUCUS n type of seaweed

typically with greenish-brown slimy fronds

FUCUSED adj archaic word meaning made up with cosmetics

FUCUSES > FUCUS

FUD n rabbit's tail

FUDDIES > FUDDY

FUDDLE vb cause to be intoxicated or confused ▷ n confused state

FUDDLED > FUDDLE

FUDDLER > FUDDLE

FUDDLERS > FUDDLE

FUDDLES > FUDDLE

FUDDLING > FUDDLE

FUDDLINGS > FUDDLE

FUDDY n old-fashioned person

FUDGE n soft caramel-like sweet ▷ vb make (an issue) less clear deliberately ▷ interj mild exclamation of annoyance

FUDGED > FUDGE

FUDGES > FUDGE

FUDGING > FUDGE

FUDS > FUD

FUEHRER n leader: applied esp to Adolf Hitler

FUEHRERS > FUEHRER

FUEL n substance burned or treated to produce heat or power ▷ vb provide with fuel

FUELED > FUEL

FUELER > FUEL

FUELERS > FUEL

FUELING > FUEL

FUELLED > FUEL

FUELLER > FUEL

FUELLERS > FUEL

FUELLING > FUEL

FUELS > FUEL

FUELWOOD n any wood used as a fuel

FUELWOODS > FUELWOOD

FUERO n Spanish code of laws

FUEROS > FUERO

FUFF vb puff

FUFFED > FUFF

FUFFIER > FUFFY

FUFFIEST > FUFFY

FUFFING > FUFF

FUFFS > FUFF

FUFFY adj puffy

FUG n hot stale atmosphere ▷ vb sit in a fug

FUGACIOUS adj passing quickly away

FUGACITY n property of a gas that expresses its tendency to escape or expand

FUGAL adj of, relating to, or in the style of a fugue

FUGALLY > FUGAL

FUGATO adj in the manner or style of a fugue ▷ n movement, section, or piece in this style

FUGATOS > FUGATO

FUGGED > FUG

FUGGIER > FUG

FUGGIEST > FUG

FUGGILY > FUG

FUGGINESS n state or condition of being fuggy

FUGGING > FUG

FUGGY > FUG

FUGHETTA n short fugue

FUGHETTAS > FUGHETTA

FUGIE n runaway

FUGIES > FUGIE

FUGIO n former US copper coin worth one dollar, the first authorized by Congress (1787)

FUGIOS > FUGIO

FUGITIVE n person who flees, esp from arrest or pursuit ▷ adj fleeing

FUGITIVES > FUGITIVE

FUGLE vb act as a fugleman

FUGLED > FUGLE

FUGLEMAN n (formerly) a soldier used as an example for those learning drill

FUGLEMEN > FUGLEMAN

FUGLES > FUGLE

FUGLIER > FUGLY

FUGLIEST > FUGLY

FUGLING > FUGLE

FUGLY adj offensive word for very ugly

FUGS > FUG

FUGU n puffer fish

FUGUE n musical composition in which a theme is repeated in different parts ▷ vb be in a dreamlike, altered state of consciousness

FUGUED > FUGUE

FUGUELIKE > FUGUE

FUGUES > FUGUE

FUGUING > FUGUE

FUGUIST n composer of fugues

FUGUISTS > FUGUIST

FUGUS > FUGU

FUHRER same as > FUEHRER

FUHRERS > FUHRER

FUJI n type of African music

FUJIS > FUJI

FULCRA > FULCRUM

FULCRATE > FULCRUM

FULCRUM n pivot about which a lever turns

FULCRUMS > FULCRUM

FULFIL vb bring about the achievement of (a desire or promise)

FULFILL same as > FULFIL

FULFILLED > FULFILL

FULFILLER > FULFIL

FULFILLS > FULFILL

FULFILS > FULFIL

FULGENCY > FULGENT

FULGENT adj shining brilliantly

FULGENTLY > FULGENT

FULGID same as

> FULGENT

FULGOR n brilliance

FULGOROUS > FULGOR

FULGORS > FULGOR

FULGOUR variant of > FULGOR

FULGOURS > FULGOUR

FULGURAL > FULGURATE

FULGURANT > FULGURATE

FULGURATE vb flash like lightning

FULGURITE n tube of glassy mineral matter found in sand and rock, formed by the action of lightning

FULGUROUS adj flashing like or resembling lightning

FULHAM n loaded die

FULHAMS > FULHAM

FULL adj containing as much or as many as possible ▷ adv completely ▷ vb clean, shrink, and press cloth

FULLAGE n price charged for fulling cloth

FULLAGES > FULLAGE

FULLAM variant of > FULHAM

FULLAMS > FULLAM

FULLAN variant of > FULHAM

FULLANS > FULLAN

FULLBACK n defensive player

FULLBACKS > FULLBACK

FULLBLOOD n person of unmixed race

FULLED > FULL

FULLER n person who fulls cloth for his living ▷ vb forge (a groove) or caulk (a riveted joint) with a fuller

FULLERED > FULLER

FULLERENE n any of various carbon molecules with a polyhedral structure similar to that of buckminsterfullerene, such as C_{60}, C_{76}, and C_{84}

FULLERIDE n compound of a fullerene in which atoms are trapped inside the cage of carbon atoms

FULLERIES > FULLERY

FULLERING > FULLER

FULLERITE n crystalline form of a fullerene

FULLERS > FULLER

FULLERY n place where fulling is carried out

FULLEST > FULL

FULLFACE n in printing, a letter that takes up full body size

FULLFACES > FULLFACE

FULLING > FULL

FULLISH > FULL

FULLNESS > FULL

FULLS > FULL

FULLY adv greatest degree or extent

FULMAR n Arctic sea bird

FULMARS > FULMAR

FULMINANT adj sudden and violent

FULMINATE vb criticize or denounce angrily ▷ n any salt or ester of fulminic acid, esp the mercury salt, which is used as a detonator

FULMINE vb fulminate

FULMINED > FULMINE

FULMINES > FULMINE

FULMINIC adj in fulminic acid, unstable volatile acid known only in solution and in the form of its salts and esters

FULMINING > FULMINE

FULMINOUS adj harshly critical

FULNESS > FULL

FULNESSES > FULL

FULSOME adj distastefully excessive or insincere

FULSOMELY > FULSOME

FULSOMER > FULSOME

FULSOMEST > FULSOME

FULVID variant of

> FULVOUS

FULVOUS adj of a dull brownish-yellow colour

FUM n phoenix, in Chinese mythology

FUMADO n salted, smoked fish

FUMADOES > FUMADO

FUMADOS > FUMADO

FUMAGE n hearth money

FUMAGES > FUMAGE

FUMARASE n enzyme

FUMARASES > FUMARASE

FUMARATE n salt of fumaric acid

FUMARATES > FUMARATE

FUMARIC as in fumaric acid, colourless crystalline acid with a fruity taste, found in some plants and manufactured from benzene

FUMAROLE n vent in or near a volcano from which hot gases, esp steam, are emitted

FUMAROLES > FUMAROLE

FUMAROLIC > FUMAROLE

FUMATORIA npl small airtight chambers for fumigating insects or fungi

FUMATORY n a chamber where insects and fungi are destroyed by fumigation

FUMBLE vb handle awkwardly ▷ n act of fumbling

FUMBLED > FUMBLE

FUMBLER > FUMBLE

FUMBLERS > FUMBLE

FUMBLES > FUMBLE

FUMBLING > FUMBLE

FUME vb be very angry ▷ npl pungent smoke or vapour

FUMED adj (of wood, esp oak) having a dark colour and distinctive grain from

f

exposure to ammonia fumes

FUMELESS > FUME

FUMELIKE > FUME

FUMER > FUME

FUMEROLE *variant of* > FUMAROLE

FUMEROLES > FUMEROLE

FUMERS > FUME

FUMES > FUME

FUMET *n* strong-flavoured liquor from cooking fish, meat, or game: used to flavour sauces

FUMETS > FUMET

FUMETTE *variant of* > FUMET

FUMETTES > FUMETTE

FUMETTI > FUMETTO

FUMETTO *n* speech balloon in a comic or cartoon

FUMIER > FUME

FUMIEST > FUME

FUMIGANT *n* substance used for fumigating

FUMIGANTS > FUMIGANT

FUMIGATE *vb* disinfect with fumes

FUMIGATED > FUMIGATE

FUMIGATES > FUMIGATE

FUMIGATOR > FUMIGATE

FUMING > FUME

FUMINGLY > FUME

FUMITORY *n* chiefly European plant with spurred flowers, formerly used medicinally

FUMOSITY > FUME

FUMOUS > FUME

FUMS > FUM

FUMULI > FUMULUS

FUMULUS *n* smokelike cloud

FUMY > FUME

FUN *n* enjoyment or amusement ▷ *vb* trick

FUNBOARD *n* type of surfboard

FUNBOARDS > FUNBOARD

FUNCKIA *n* a type of plant resembling the lily

FUNCKIAS > FUNCKIA

FUNCTION *n* purpose something exists for ▷ *vb* operate or work

FUNCTIONS > FUNCTION

FUNCTOR *n* performer of a function

FUNCTORS > FUNCTOR

FUND *n* stock of money for a special purpose ▷ *vb* provide money to

FUNDABLE > FUND

FUNDAMENT *n* buttocks

FUNDED > FUND

FUNDER > FUND

FUNDERS > FUND

FUNDI *n* expert or boffin

FUNDIC > FUNDUS

FUNDIE *n* fundamentalist Christian

FUNDIES > FUNDIE

FUNDING > FUND

FUNDINGS > FUND

FUNDIS > FUNDI

FUNDLESS > FUND

FUNDRAISE *vb* raise money for a cause

FUNDS *npl* money that is readily available

FUNDUS *n* base of an organ or the part farthest away from its opening

FUNDY *n* fundamentalist

FUNEBRAL *variant of* > FUNEBRIAL

FUNEBRE *adj* funereal or mournful

FUNEBRIAL *same as* > FUNEREAL

FUNERAL *n* ceremony of burying or cremating a dead person

FUNERALS > FUNERAL

FUNERARY *adj* of or for a funeral

FUNEREAL *adj* gloomy or sombre

FUNEST *adj* lamentable

FUNFAIR *n* entertainment with machines to ride on and stalls

FUNFAIRS > FUNFAIR

FUNFEST *n* enjoyable time

FUNFESTS > FUNFEST

FUNG *same as* > FUNK

FUNGAL *adj* of, derived from, or caused by a fungus or fungi ▷ *n* fungus or fungal infection

FUNGALS > FUNGAL

FUNGI > FUNGUS

FUNGIBLE *n* moveable perishable goods of a sort that may be estimated by number or weight, such as grain, wine, etc ▷ *adj* having the nature or quality of fungibles

FUNGIBLES > FUNGIBLE

FUNGIC > FUNGUS

FUNGICIDE *n* substance that destroys fungi

FUNGIFORM *adj* shaped like a mushroom or similar fungus

FUNGISTAT *n* substance that inhibits the growth of fungi

FUNGO *n* in baseball, act of tossing and hitting the ball ▷ *vb* toss and hit a ball

FUNGOES > FUNGO

FUNGOID *adj* resembling a fungus

FUNGOIDAL > FUNGOID

FUNGOIDS > FUNGOID

FUNGOSITY > FUNGOUS

FUNGOUS *adj* appearing suddenly and spreading quickly like a fungus

FUNGS > FUNG

FUNGUS *n* plant without leaves, flowers, or roots, such as a mushroom or mould

FUNGUSES > FUNGUS

FUNHOUSE *n* amusing place at fairground

FUNHOUSES > FUNHOUSE

FUNICLE *n* stalk that attaches an ovule or seed to the wall of the ovary

FUNICLES > FUNICLE

FUNICULAR *n* cable railway on a mountainside or cliff ▷ *adj* relating to or operated by a rope, cable, etc

FUNICULI > FUNICULUS

FUNICULUS *same as* > FUNICLE

FUNK *n* style of dance music with a strong beat ▷ *vb* avoid (doing something) through fear

FUNKED > FUNK

FUNKER > FUNK

FUNKERS > FUNK

FUNKHOLE *n* dugout

FUNKHOLES > FUNKHOLE

FUNKIA *n* hosta

FUNKIAS > FUNKIA

FUNKIER > FUNKY

FUNKIEST > FUNKY

FUNKILY > FUNKY

FUNKINESS > FUNKY

FUNKING > FUNK

FUNKS > FUNK

FUNKSTER *n* performer or fan of funk music

FUNKSTERS > FUNKSTER

FUNKY *adj* (of music) having a strong beat

FUNNED > FUN

FUNNEL *n* cone-shaped tube for pouring liquids into a narrow opening ▷ *vb* (cause to) move through or as if through a funnel

FUNNELED > FUNNEL

FUNNELING > FUNNEL

FUNNELLED > FUNNEL

FUNNELS > FUNNEL

FUNNER > FUN

FUNNEST > FUN

FUNNIER > FUNNY

FUNNIES *npl* comic strips in a newspaper

FUNNIEST > FUNNY

FUNNILY > FUNNY

FUNNINESS > FUNNY

FUNNING > FUN

FUNNY *adj* comical, humorous ▷ *n* joke or witticism

FUNNYMAN *n* comedian

FUNNYMEN > FUNNYMAN

FUNPLEX *n* large amusement centre

FUNPLEXES > FUNPLEX

FUNS > FUN

FUNSTER *n* funnyman

FUNSTERS > FUNSTER

FUR *n* soft hair of a mammal ▷ *vb* cover or become covered with fur

FURACIOUS *adj* thievish

FURACITY > FURACIOUS

FURAL *n* furfural

FURALS > FURAL

FURAN *n* colourless flammable toxic liquid

heterocyclic compound

FURANE *variant of* > FURAN

FURANES > FURANE

FURANOSE *n* simple sugar containing a furan ring

FURANOSES > FURANOSE

FURANS > FURAN

FURBEARER *n* mammal hunted for its pelt or fur

FURBELOW *n* flounce, ruffle, or other ornamental trim ▷ *vb* put a furbelow on (a garment)

FURBELOWS > FURBELOW

FURBISH *vb* smarten up

FURBISHED > FURBISH

FURBISHER > FURBISH

FURBISHES > FURBISH

FURCA *n* any forklike structure, esp in insects

FURCAE > FURCA

FURCAL > FURCA

FURCATE *vb* divide into two parts ▷ *adj* forked, branching

FURCATED > FURCATE

FURCATELY > FURCATE

FURCATES > FURCATE

FURCATING > FURCATE

FURCATION > FURCATE

FURCRAEA *n* plant belonging to the Agave family

FURCRAEAS > FURCRAEA

FURCULA *n* any forklike part or organ, esp the fused clavicles (wishbone) of birds

FURCULAE > FURCULA

FURCULAR > FURCULA

FURCULUM *same as* > FURCULA

FURDER *same as* > FURTHER

FUREUR *n* rage or anger

FUREURS > FUREUR

FURFAIR *variant of* > FURFUR

FURFAIRS > FURFAIR

FURFUR *n* scurf or scaling of the skin

FURFURAL *n* colourless liquid used as a solvent

FURFURALS > FURFURAL

FURFURAN *same as* > FURAN

FURFURANS > FURFURAN

FURFURES > FURFUR

FURFUROL *variant of* > FURFURAL

FURFUROLE *variant of* > FURFURAL

FURFUROLS > FURFUROL

FURFUROUS > FURFUR

FURFURS > FURFUR

FURIBUND *adj* furious

FURIES > FURY

FURIOSITY > FURIOUS

FURIOSO *adv* in a frantically rushing manner ▷ *n* passage or piece to be performed in this way

FURIOSOS > FURIOSO

FURIOUS *adj* very angry

FURIOUSLY > FURIOUS

FURKID n companion animal

FURKIDS > FURKID

FURL vb roll up and fasten (a sail, umbrella, or flag) ▷ n act or an instance of furling

FURLABLE > FURL

FURLANA variant of > FORLANA

FURLANAS > FURLANA

FURLED > FURL

FURLER > FURL

FURLERS > FURL

FURLESS > FUR

FURLING > FURL

FURLONG n unit of length equal to 220 yards (201.168 metres)

FURLONGS > FURLONG

FURLOUGH n leave of absence ▷ vb grant a furlough to

FURLOUGHS > FURLOUGH

FURLS > FURL

FURMENTY same as > FRUMENTY

FURMETIES > FURMETY

FURMETY same as > FRUMENTY

FURMITIES > FURMITY

FURMITY same as > FRUMENTY

FURNACE n enclosed chamber containing a very hot fire ▷ vb burn in a furnace

FURNACED > FURNACE

FURNACES > FURNACE

FURNACING > FURNACE

FURNIMENT n furniture

FURNISH vb provide (a house or room) with furniture

FURNISHED > FURNISH

FURNISHER > FURNISH

FURNISHES > FURNISH

FURNITURE n large movable articles such as chairs and wardrobes

FUROL variant of > FURFURAL

FUROLE variant of > FURFURAL

FUROLES > FUROLE

FUROLS > FUROL

FUROR same as > FURORE

FURORE n very excited or angry reaction

FURORES > FURORE

FURORS > FUROR

FURPHIES > FURPHY

FURPHY n rumour or fictitious story

FURR vb furrow

FURRED same as > FURRY

FURRIER n dealer in furs

FURRIERS > FURRIER

FURRIERY n occupation of a furrier

FURRIES > FURRY

FURRIEST > FURRY

FURRILY > FURRY

FURRINER n dialect rendering of foreigner

FURRINERS > FURRINER

FURRINESS > FURRY

FURRING > FUR

FURRINGS > FUR

FURROW n trench made by a plough ▷ vb make or become wrinkled

FURROWED > FURROW

FURROWER > FURROW

FURROWERS > FURROW

FURROWING > FURROW

FURROWS > FURROW

FURROWY > FURROW

FURRS > FURR

FURTH adv out

FURTHER adv in addition ▷ adj more distant ▷ vb promote

FURTHERED > FURTHER

FURTHERER > FURTHER

FURTHERS > FURTHER

FURTHEST adv to the greatest degree ▷ adj most distant

FURTIVE adj sly and secretive

FURTIVELY > FURTIVE

FURUNCLE technical name for > BOIL

FURUNCLES > FURUNCLE

FURY n wild anger

FURZE n gorse

FURZES > FURZE

FURZIER > FURZE

FURZIEST > FURZE

FURZY > FURZE

FUSAIN n fine charcoal pencil or stick made from the spindle tree

FUSAINS > FUSAIN

FUSARIA > FUSARIUM

FUSARIUM n type of fungus

FUSAROL variant of > FUSAROLE

FUSAROLE n type of architectural moulding

FUSAROLES > FUSAROLE

FUSAROLS > FUSAROL

FUSBALL same as > FOOSBALL

FUSBALLS > FUSBALL

FUSC adj dark or dark-brown

FUSCOUS adj of a brownish-grey colour

FUSE n cord containing an explosive for detonating a bomb ▷ vb (cause to) fail as a result of a blown fuse

FUSED > FUSE

FUSEE n (in early clocks and watches) a spirally grooved spindle, functioning as an equalizing force during the unwinding of the mainspring

FUSEES > FUSEE

FUSEL n mixture of amyl alcohols, propanol, and butanol: a by-product in the distillation of fermented liquors used as a source of amyl alcohols

FUSELAGE n body of an aircraft

FUSELAGES > FUSELAGE

FUSELESS > FUSE

FUSELIKE > FUSE

FUSELS > FUSEL

FUSES > FUSE

FUSHION n spirit

FUSHIONS > FUSHION

FUSIBLE adj capable of being melted

FUSIBLY > FUSIBLE

FUSIDIC as in fusidic acid kind of acid

FUSIFORM adj elongated and tapering at both ends

FUSIL n light flintlock musket

FUSILE adj easily melted

FUSILEER same as > FUSILIER

FUSILEERS > FUSILEER

FUSILIER n soldier of certain regiments

FUSILIERS > FUSILIER

FUSILLADE n continuous discharge of firearms ▷ vb attack with a fusillade

FUSILLI n spiral-shaped pasta

FUSILLIS > FUSILLI

FUSILS > FUSIL

FUSING > FUSE

FUSION n melting ▷ adj of a style of cooking that combines traditional Western techniques and ingredients with those used in Eastern cuisine

FUSIONAL > FUSION

FUSIONISM n favouring of coalitions among political groups

FUSIONIST > FUSIONISM

FUSIONS > FUSION

FUSS n needless activity or worry ▷ vb make a fuss

FUSSBALL same as > FOOSBALL

FUSSBALLS > FUSSBALL

FUSSED > FUSS

FUSSER > FUSS

FUSSERS > FUSS

FUSSES > FUSS

FUSSIER > FUSSY

FUSSIEST > FUSSY

FUSSILY > FUSSY

FUSSINESS > FUSSY

FUSSING > FUSS

FUSSPOT n person who is difficult to please and complains often

FUSSPOTS > FUSSPOT

FUSSY adj inclined to fuss

FUST vb become mouldy

FUSTED > FUST

FUSTET n wood of the Venetian sumach shrub

FUSTETS > FUSTET

FUSTIAN n (formerly) a hard-wearing fabric of cotton mixed with flax or wool ▷ adj cheap

FUSTIANS > FUSTIAN

FUSTIC n large tropical American tree

FUSTICS > FUSTIC

FUSTIER > FUSTY

FUSTIEST > FUSTY

FUSTIGATE vb beat

FUSTILUGS n fat person

FUSTILY > FUSTY

FUSTINESS > FUSTY

FUSTING > FUST

FUSTOC variant of > FUSTIC

FUSTOCS > FUSTOC

FUSTS > FUST

FUSTY adj stale-smelling

FUSULINID n any of various extinct foraminifers

FUSUMA n Japanese sliding door

FUTCHEL n timber support in a carriage

FUTCHELS > FUTCHEL

FUTHARC same as > FUTHARK

FUTHARCS > FUTHARC

FUTHARK n phonetic alphabet consisting of runes

FUTHARKS > FUTHARK

FUTHORC same as > FUTHARK

FUTHORCS > FUTHORC

FUTHORK same as > FUTHARK

FUTHORKS > FUTHORK

FUTILE adj unsuccessful or useless

FUTILELY > FUTILE

FUTILER > FUTILE

FUTILEST > FUTILE

FUTILITY n lack of effectiveness or success

FUTON n Japanese-style bed

FUTONS > FUTON

FUTSAL n form of association football, played indoors with five players on each side

FUTSALS > FUTSAL

FUTTOCK n one of the ribs in the frame of a wooden vessel

FUTTOCKS > FUTTOCK

FUTURAL adj relating to the future

FUTURE n time to come ▷ adj yet to come or be

FUTURES npl commodities bought or sold at an agreed price for delivery at a specified future date

FUTURISM n early 20th-century artistic movement making use of the characteristics of the machine age

FUTURISMS > FUTURISM

FUTURIST > FUTURISM
FUTURISTS > FUTURISM
FUTURITY n future
FUTZ vb fritter time away
FUTZED > FUTZ
FUTZES > FUTZ
FUTZING > FUTZ
FUZE same as > FUSE
FUZED > FUZE
FUZEE same as > FUSEE
FUZEES > FUZEE
FUZES > FUZE
FUZIL variant of > FUSIL
FUZILS > FUZIL
FUZING > FUZE
FUZZ n mass of fine or curly hairs or fibres ▷ vb make or become fuzzy
FUZZBOX n device that distorts the sound of eg an electric guitar
FUZZBOXES > FUZZBOX
FUZZED > FUZZ
FUZZES > FUZZ
FUZZIER > FUZZY
FUZZIEST > FUZZY
FUZZILY > FUZZY
FUZZINESS > FUZZY
FUZZING > FUZZ
FUZZLE vb make drunk
FUZZLED > FUZZLE
FUZZLES > FUZZLE
FUZZLING > FUZZLE
FUZZTONE n device

distorting electric guitar sound
FUZZTONES > FUZZTONE
FUZZY adj of, like, or covered with fuzz
FY variant of > FIE
FYCE variant of > FICE
FYCES > FYCE
FYKE n fish trap consisting of a net suspended over a series of hoops, laid horizontally in the water ▷ vb catch fish in this manner
FYKED > FYKE
FYKES > FYKE
FYKING > FYKE

FYLE variant of > FILE
FYLES > FYLE
FYLFOT rare word for > SWASTIKA
FYLFOTS > FYLFOT
FYNBOS n area of low-growing, evergreen vegetation
FYNBOSES > FYNBOS
FYRD n local militia of an Anglo-Saxon shire, in which all freemen had to serve
FYRDS > FYRD
FYTTE n song
FYTTES > FYTTE

Gg

GAB *vb* talk or chatter ▷ *n* hook or open notch in a rod or lever that drops over the spindle of a valve to form a temporary connection for operating the valve

GABARDINE *n* strong twill cloth used esp for raincoats

GABBA *n* type of electronic dance music

GABBARD *same as* **>GABBART**

GABBARDS >GABBARD

GABBART *n* Scottish sailing barge

GABBARTS >GABBART

GABBAS >GABBA

GABBED >GAB

GABBER >GAB

GABBERS >GAB

GABBIER >GABBY

GABBIEST >GABBY

GABBINESS >GABBY

GABBING >GAB

GABBLE *vb* speak rapidly and indistinctly ▷ *n* rapid indistinct speech

GABBLED >GABBLE

GABBLER >GABBLE

GABBLERS >GABBLE

GABBLES >GABBLE

GABBLING >GABBLE

GABBLINGS >GABBLE

GABBRO *n* dark coarse-grained basic plutonic igneous rock consisting of plagioclase feldspar, pyroxene, and often olivine

GABBROIC >GABBRO

GABBROID *adj* gabbro-like

GABBROS >GABBRO

GABBY *adj* talkative

GABELLE *n* salt tax levied until 1790

GABELLED >GABELLE

GABELLER *n* person who collects the gabelle

GABELLERS >GABELLER

GABELLES >GABELLE

GABERDINE *same as* **>GABARDINE**

GABFEST *n* prolonged gossiping or conversation

GABFESTS >GABFEST

GABIES >GABY

GABION *n* cylindrical metal container filled with stones, used in the construction of underwater foundations

GABIONADE *n* row of gabions submerged in a waterway, stream, river, etc, to control the flow of water

GABIONAGE *n* structure composed of gabions

GABIONED >GABION

GABIONS >GABION

GABLE *n* triangular upper part of a wall between sloping roofs

GABLED >GABLE

GABLELIKE >GABLE

GABLES >GABLE

GABLET *n* small gable

GABLETS >GABLET

GABLING >GABLE

GABNASH *n* chatter

GABNASHES >GABNASH

GABOON *n* dark wood from a western and central African tree, used in plywood, for furniture, and as a veneer

GABOONS >GABOON

GABS >GAB

GABY *n* simpleton

GAD *vb* go about in search of pleasure ▷ *n* carefree adventure

GADABOUT *n* pleasure-seeker

GADABOUTS >GADABOUT

GADARENE *adj* headlong

GADDED >GAD

GADDER >GAD

GADDERS >GAD

GADDI *n* cushion on an Indian prince's throne

GADDING >GAD

GADDIS >GADDI

GADE *same as* **>**GAD

GADES >GADE

GADFLIES >GADFLY

GADFLY *n* fly that bites cattle

GADGE *n* man

GADGES >GADGE

GADGET *n* small mechanical device or appliance

GADGETEER *n* person who delights in gadgetry

GADGETRY *n* gadgets

GADGETS >GADGET

GADGETY >GADGET

GADGIE *n* fellow

GADGIES >GADGIE

GADI *n* Indian throne

GADID *n* type of marine fish of the family which includes the cod, haddock, whiting, and pollack

GADIDS >GADID

GADIS >GADI

GADJE *same as* **>** GADGIE

GADJES >GADJE

GADJO *same as* **>**GORGIO

GADLING *n* vagabond

GADLINGS >GADLING

GADOID *adj* of the cod family of marine fishes ▷ *n* gadoid fish

GADOIDS >GADOID

GADOLINIC *adj* relating to gadolinium, a silvery white metallic element

GADROON *n* moulding composed of a series of convex flutes and curves joined to form a decorative pattern, used esp as an edge to silver articles

GADROONED >GADROON

GADROONS >GADROON

GADS >GAD

GADSMAN *n* person who uses a gad when driving animals

GADSMEN >GADSMAN

GADSO *n* archaic expression of surprise

GADWALL *n* type of duck related to the mallard

GADWALLS >GADWALL

GADZOOKS *interj* mild oath

GAE *Scot word for* **>** GO

GAED >GAE

GAEING >GAE

GAELICISE *vb* adapt to conform to Gaelic spelling and pronunciation

GAELICISM >GAELICISE

GAELICIZE *same as* **>**GAELICISE

GAEN >GAE

GAES >GAE

GAFF *n* stick with an iron hook for landing large fish ▷ *vb* hook or land (a fish) with a gaff

GAFFE *n* social blunder

GAFFED >GAFF

GAFFER *n* foreman or boss

GAFFERS >GAFFER

GAFFES >GAFFE

GAFFING >GAFF

GAFFINGS >GAFF

GAFFS >GAFF

GAFFSAIL *n* quadrilateral fore-and-aft sail on a sailing vessel

GAFFSAILS >GAFFSAIL

GAG *vb* choke or retch ▷ *n* cloth etc put into or tied across the mouth

GAGA *adj* senile

GAGAKU *n* type of traditional Japanese music

GAGAKUS >GAGAKU

GAGE *vb* gauge ▷ *n* (formerly) a glove or other object thrown down to indicate a challenge to fight

GAGEABLE >GAGE

GAGEABLY >GAGE

GAGED >GAGE

GAGER *same as* **>** GAUGER

GAGERS >GAGER

GAGES >GAGE

GAGGED >GAG

GAGGER *n* person or thing that gags

GAGGERIES >GAGGERY

GAGGERS >GAGGER

GAGGERY *n* practice of telling jokes

GAGGING >GAG

GAGGLE *n* disorderly crowd ▷ *vb* (of geese) to cackle

GAGGLED >GAGGLE

GAGGLES >GAGGLE

GAGGLING >GAGGLE

GAGGLINGS >GAGGLE

GAGING >GAGE

GAGMAN *n* person who writes gags for a comedian

GAGMEN >GAGMAN

GAGS >GAG

GAGSTER *n* standup comedian

GAGSTERS >GAGSTER

GAHNITE *n* dark green mineral of the spinel group consisting of zinc aluminium oxide

GAHNITES >GAHNITE

GAID *same as* **>**GAD

GAIDS >GAID

GAIETIES >GAIETY

GAIETY *n* cheerfulness

GAIJIN *n* (in Japan) a foreigner

GAILLARD *same as* **>**GALLIARD

GAILLARDE *same as* **>**GAILLARD

GAILY *adv* merrily

GAIN *vb* acquire or obtain ▷ *n* profit or advantage ▷ *adj* straight or near

GAINABLE > GAIN
GAINED > GAIN
GAINER n person or thing that gains
GAINERS > GAINER
GAINEST > GAIN
GAINFUL adj useful or profitable
GAINFULLY > GAINFUL
GAINING > GAIN
GAININGS npl profits or earnings
GAINLESS > GAIN
GAINLIER > GAINLY
GAINLIEST > GAINLY
GAINLY adj graceful or well-formed ▷ adv conveniently or suitably
GAINS npl profits or winnings
GAINSAID > GAINSAY
GAINSAY vb deny or contradict
GAINSAYER > GAINSAY
GAINSAYS > GAINSAY
GAINST short for > AGAINST
GAIR n strip of green grass on a hillside
GAIRFOWL same as > GAREFOWL
GAIRFOWLS > GAIRFOWL
GAIRS > GAIR
GAIT n manner of walking ▷ vb teach (a horse) a particular gait
GAITA n type of bagpipe played in Spain and Portugal
GAITAS > GAITA
GAITED > GAIT
GAITER n cloth or leather covering for the lower leg
GAITERED adj wearing gaiters
GAITERS > GAITER
GAITING > GAIT
GAITS > GAIT
GAITT Scots word for > GATE
GAITTS > GAITT
GAJO same as > GORGIO
GAJOS > GAJO
GAK n (slang) cocaine
GAKS > GAK
GAL n girl
GALA n festival
GALABEA same as > DJELLABA
GALABEAH same as > DJELLABA
GALABEAHS > GALABEAH
GALABEAS > GALABEA
GALABIA same as > DJELLABA
GALABIAH same as > DJELLABA
GALABIAHS > GALABIAH
GALABIAS > GALABIA
GALABIEH same as > DJELLABA
GALABIEHS > GALABIEH
GALABIYA same as > DJELLABA
GALABIYAH same as

> DJELLABA
GALABIYAS > GALABIYA
GALACTIC adj of the Galaxy or other galaxies
GALACTOSE n white water-soluble monosaccharide found in lactose
GALAGE same as > GALOSH
GALAGES > GALAGE
GALAGO another name for > BUSHBABY
GALAGOS > GALAGO
GALAH n Australian cockatoo with grey wings, back, and crest and a pink body
GALAHS > GALAH
GALANGA same as > GALINGALE
GALANGAL same as > GALINGALE
GALANGALS > GALANGAL
GALANGAS > GALANGAL
GALANT n 18th-century style of music characterized by homophony and elaborate ornamentation
GALANTINE n cold dish of meat or poultry, which is boned, cooked, stuffed, then pressed into a neat shape and glazed
GALANTY as in galanty show pantomime shadow play, esp one in miniature using figures cut from paper
GALAPAGO n tortoise
GALAPAGOS > GALAPAGO
GALAS > GALA
GALATEA n strong twill-weave cotton fabric, striped or plain, for clothing
GALATEAS > GALATEA
GALAVANT same as > GALLIVANT
GALAVANTS > GALAVANT
GALAX n coltsfoot
GALAXES > GALAX
GALAXIES > GALAXY
GALAXY n system of stars
GALBANUM n bitter aromatic gum resin extracted from various Asian plants, used in incense and medicinally
GALBANUMS > GALBANUM
GALDRAGON old Scots word for a > SORCERESS
GALE n strong wind
GALEA n part or organ shaped like a helmet or hood, such as the petals of certain flowers
GALEAE > GALEA
GALEAS > GALEA
GALEATE > GALEA
GALEATED > GALEA
GALEIFORM > GALEA
GALENA n soft bluish-grey mineral consisting of lead sulphide: the chief source of lead
GALENAS > GALENA
GALENGALE same as

> GALINGALE
GALENIC > GALENA
GALENICAL n any drug prepared from plant or animal tissue, esp vegetables, rather than being chemically synthesized ▷ adj denoting or belonging to this group of drugs
GALENITE same as > GALENA
GALENITES > GALENITE
GALENOID adj pertaining to galena
GALERE n group of people having a common interest, esp a coterie of undesirable people
GALERES > GALERE
GALES > GALE
GALETTE n type of savoury pancake
GALETTES > GALETTE
GALILEE n porch or chapel at the entrance to some medieval churches and cathedrals in England
GALILEES > GALILEE
GALINGALE n European plant with rough-edged leaves, reddish spikelets of flowers, and aromatic roots
GALIONGEE n sailor
GALIOT n small swift galley formerly sailed on the Mediterranean
GALIOTS > GALIOT
GALIPOT n resin obtained from several species of pine
GALIPOTS > GALIPOT
GALIVANT same as > GALLIVANT
GALIVANTS > GALIVANT
GALL n impudence ▷ vb annoy
GALLABEA same as > DJELLABA
GALLABEAH same as > DJELLABA
GALLABEAS > GALLABEA
GALLABIA same as > DJELLABA
GALLABIAH same as > DJELLABA
GALLABIAS > GALLABIA
GALLABIEH same as > DJELLABA
GALLABIYA same as > DJELLABA
GALLAMINE n muscle relaxant used in anaesthesia
GALLANT adj brave and noble ▷ n young man who tried to impress women with his fashionable clothes or daring acts ▷ vb court or flirt (with)
GALLANTED > GALLANT
GALLANTER > GALLANT
GALLANTLY > GALLANT
GALLANTRY n showy, attentive treatment of women

GALLANTS > GALLANT
GALLATE n salt of gallic acid
GALLATES > GALLATE
GALLEASS n three-masted lateen-rigged galley used as a warship in the Mediterranean from the 15th to the 18th centuries
GALLED > GALL
GALLEIN n type of dyestuff
GALLEINS > GALLEIN
GALLEON n large three-masted sailing ship of the 15th-17th centuries
GALLEONS > GALLEON
GALLERIA n central court through several storeys of a shopping centre or department store onto which shops or departments open at each level
GALLERIAS > GALLERIA
GALLERIED adj having a gallery or galleries
GALLERIES > GALLERY
GALLERIST n person who owns or runs an art gallery
GALLERY n room or building for displaying works of art ▷ vb tunnel; form an underground gallery
GALLET vb (in roofing) use small pieces of slate mixed with mortar to support an upper slate
GALLETA n low-growing, coarse grass
GALLETAS > GALLETA
GALLETED > GALLET
GALLETING > GALLET
GALLETS > GALLET
GALLEY n kitchen of a ship or aircraft
GALLEYS > GALLEY
GALLFLIES > GALLFLY
GALLFLY n any of several small insects that produce galls in plant tissues, such as the gall wasp and gall midge
GALLIARD n spirited dance in triple time for two persons, popular in the 16th and 17th centuries ▷ adj lively
GALLIARDS > GALLIARD
GALLIASS same as > GALLEASS
GALLIC adj of or containing gallium in the trivalent state
GALLICA n variety of rose
GALLICAN adj of or relating to a movement favouring the restriction of papal control and greater autonomy for the French church
GALLICAS > GORGIO
GALLICISE same as > GALLICIZE
GALLICISM n word or

idiom borrowed from French

GALLICIZE *vb* make or become French in attitude, language, etc

GALLIED > GALLY

GALLIES > GALLY

GALLINAZO *n* black vulture

GALLING *adj* annoying or bitterly humiliating

GALLINGLY > GALLING

GALLINULE *n* moorhen

GALLIOT *same as* > GALIOT

GALLIOTS > GALLIOT

GALLIPOT *same as* > GALIPOT

GALLIPOTS > GALLIPOT

GALLISE *vb* add water and sugar to unfermented grape juice to increase the quantity of wine produced

GALLISED > GALLISE

GALLISES > GALLISE

GALLISING > GALLISE

GALLISISE *vb* gallise

GALLISIZE *same as* > GALLISE

GALLIUM *n* soft grey metallic element used in semiconductors

GALLIUMS > GALLIUM

GALLIVANT *vb* go about in search of pleasure

GALLIVAT *n* Oriental armed vessel

GALLIVATS > GALLIVAT

GALLIWASP *n* type of Central American lizard

GALLIZE *same as* > GALLISE

GALLIZED > GALLIZE

GALLIZES > GALLIZE

GALLIZING > GALLIZE

GALLNUT *n* type of plant gall that resembles a nut

GALLNUTS > GALLNUT

GALLOCK *adj* left-handed

GALLON *n* liquid measure of eight pints, equal to 4.55 litres

GALLONAGE *n* capacity measured in gallons

GALLONS > GALLON

GALLOON *n* narrow band of cord, embroidery, silver or gold braid, etc, used on clothes and furniture

GALLOONED > GALLOON

GALLOONS > GALLOON

GALLOOT *same as* > GALLOOT

GALLOOTS > GALLOOT

GALLOP *n* horse's fastest pace ▷ *vb* go or ride at a gallop

GALLOPADE *n* gallop ▷ *vb* perform a gallopade

GALLOPED > GALLOP

GALLOPER > GALLOP

GALLOPERS > GALLOP

GALLOPING *adj* progressing at or as if at a gallop

GALLOPS > GALLOP

GALLOUS *adj* of or containing gallium in the divalent state

GALLOW *vb* frighten

GALLOWED > GALLOW

GALLOWING > GALLOW

GALLOWS *n* wooden structure used for hanging criminals

GALLOWSES > GALLOWS

GALLS > GALL

GALLSTONE *n* hard mass formed in the gall bladder or its ducts

GALLUMPH *same as* > GALUMPH

GALLUMPHS > GALLUMPH

GALLUS *adj* bold ▷ *n* suspender for trousers

GALLUSED *adj* held up by galluses

GALLUSES > GALLUS

GALLY *vb* frighten

GALLYING > GALLY

GALOCHE *same as* > GALOSH

GALOCHED > GALOCHE

GALOCHES > GALOCHE

GALOCHING > GALOCHE

GALOOT *n* clumsy or uncouth person

GALOOTS > GALOOT

GALOP *n* 19th-century dance in quick duple time ▷ *vb* dance a galop

GALOPADE *same as* > GALOP

GALOPADES > GALOP

GALOPED > GALOP

GALOPIN *n* boy who ran errands for a cook

GALOPING > GALOP

GALOPINS > GALOPIN

GALOPPED > GALOP

GALOPPING > GALOP

GALOPS > GALOP

GALORE *adv* in abundance ▷ *adj* in abundance ▷ *n* abundance

GALORES > GALORE

GALOSH *n* waterproof overshoe ▷ *vb* cover with galoshes

GALOSHE *same as* > GALOSH

GALOSHED > GALOSH

GALOSHES > GALOSH

GALOSHING > GALOSH

GALOWSES *Shakespearean plural for* > GALLOWS

GALRAVAGE *same as* > GILRAVAGE

GALS > GAL

GALTONIA *n* type of bulbous plant with waxy white flowers and a fragrant scent

GALTONIAS > GALTONIA

GALUMPH *vb* leap or move about clumsily

GALUMPHED > GALUMPH

GALUMPHER > GALUMPH

GALUMPHS > GALUMPH

GALUT *same as* > GALUTH

GALUTH *n* exile of Jews from Palestine

GALUTHS > GALUTH

GALUTS > GALUT

GALVANIC *adj* of or producing an electric current generated by chemical means

GALVANISE *same as* > GALVANIZE

GALVANISM *n* electricity, esp when produced by chemical means as in a cell or battery

GALVANIST > GALVANISM

GALVANIZE *vb* stimulate into action ▷ *n* galvanized iron, usually in the form of corrugated sheets as used in roofing

GALVO *n* instrument for measuring electric current

GALVOS > GALVO

GALYAC *same as* > GALYAK

GALYACS > GALYAC

GALYAK *n* smooth glossy fur obtained from the skins of newborn or premature lambs and kids

GALYAKS > GALYAK

GAM *n* school of whales ▷ *vb* (of whales) form a school

GAMA *n* tall perennial grass

GAMAHUCHE *vb* practise cunnilingus or fellatio on ▷ *n* cunnilingus or fellatio

GAMARUCHE *same as* > GAMAHUCHE

GAMAS > GAMA

GAMASH *n* type of gaiter

GAMASHES > GAMASH

GAMAY *n* red grape variety, or the wine made from it

GAMAYS > GAMAY

GAMB *n* in heraldry, the whole foreleg of a beast

GAMBA *n* second-largest member of the viol family

GAMBADE *same as* > GAMBADO

GAMBADES > GAMBADE

GAMBADO *n* leap or gambol; caper ▷ *vb* perform a gambado

GAMBADOED > GAMBADO

GAMBADOES > GAMBADO

GAMBADOS > GAMBADO

GAMBAS > GAMBA

GAMBE *same as* > GAMB

GAMBES > GAMBE

GAMBESON *n* quilted and padded or stuffed leather or cloth garment worn under mail in the Middle Ages and later as a doublet by men and women

GAMBESONS > GAMBESON

GAMBET *n* tattler

GAMBETS > GAMBET

GAMBETTA *n* redshank

GAMBETTAS > GAMBETTA

GAMBIA *same as* > GAMBIER

GAMBIAS > GAMBIA

GAMBIER *n* astringent resinous substance obtained from a tropical Asian climbing plant

GAMBIERS > GAMBIER

GAMBIR *same as* > GAMBIER

GAMBIRS > GAMBIR

GAMBIST *n* person who plays the (viola da) gamba

GAMBISTS > GAMBIST

GAMBIT *n* opening line or move intended to secure an advantage ▷ *vb* sacrifice a chess piece, in opening, to gain a better position

GAMBITED > GAMBIT

GAMBITING > GAMBIT

GAMBITS > GAMBIT

GAMBLE *vb* play games of chance to win money ▷ *n* risky undertaking

GAMBLED > GAMBLE

GAMBLER > GAMBLE

GAMBLERS > GAMBLE

GAMBLES > GAMBLE

GAMBLING > GAMBLE

GAMBLINGS > GAMBLE

GAMBO *n* farm cart

GAMBOES > GAMBO

GAMBOGE *n* gum resin used as a yellow pigment and purgative

GAMBOGES > GAMBOGE

GAMBOGIAN > GAMBOGE

GAMBOGIC > GAMBOGE

GAMBOL *vb* jump about playfully, frolic ▷ *n* frolic

GAMBOLED > GAMBOL

GAMBOLING > GAMBOL

GAMBOLLED > GAMBOL

GAMBOLS > GAMBOL

GAMBREL *n* hock of a horse or similar animal

GAMBRELS > GAMBREL

GAMBROON *n* type of linen cloth

GAMBROONS > GAMBROON

GAMBS > GAMB

GAMBUSIA *n* small fish that feeds on mosquito larvae

GAMBUSIAS > GAMBUSIA

GAME *n* amusement or pastime ▷ *vb* gamble ▷ *adj* brave

GAMECOCK *n* cock bred and trained for fighting

GAMECOCKS > GAMECOCK

GAMED > GAME

GAMELAN *n* type of percussion orchestra common in the East Indies

GAMELANS > GAMELAN

GAMELIKE > GAME

GAMELY *adv* in a brave or sporting manner

GAMENESS *n* courage or bravery

GAMEPLAY *n* plot of a computer or video game or the way that it is played

GAMEPLAYS > GAMEPLAY

g

GAMER n person who plays computer games

GAMERS > GAMER

GAMESIER > GAMESY

GAMESIEST > GAMESY

GAMESMAN n one who practises gamesmanship: the art of winning by cunning practices without actually cheating

GAMESMEN > GAMESMAN

GAMESOME adj full of merriment

GAMEST > GAME

GAMESTER n gambler

GAMESTERS > GAMESTER

GAMESY adj sporty

GAMETAL > GAMETE

GAMETE n reproductive cell

GAMETES > GAMETE

GAMETIC > GAMETE

GAMEY adj having the smell or flavour of game

GAMEYNESS n quality of being gamey

GAMGEE as in gamgee tissue type of wound-dressing

GAMIC adj (esp of reproduction) requiring the fusion of gametes

GAMIER > GAMEY

GAMIEST > GAMEY

GAMILY > GAMEY

GAMIN n street urchin

GAMINE n slim boyish young woman

GAMINERIE n impish behaviour

GAMINES > GAMINE

GAMINESS > GAMEY

GAMING n gambling

GAMINGS > GAMING

GAMINS > GAMIN

GAMMA n third letter of the Greek alphabet

GAMMADIA > GAMMADION

GAMMADION n decorative figure composed of a number of Greek capital gammas, esp radiating from a centre, as in a swastika

GAMMAS > GAMMA

GAMMAT n derogatory term for a Cape Coloured person

GAMMATIA > GAMMATION

GAMMATS > GAMMAT

GAMME n musical scale

GAMMED > GAM

GAMMER n dialect word for an old woman: now chiefly humorous or contemptuous

GAMMERS > GAMMER

GAMMES > GAMME

GAMMIER > GAMMY

GAMMIEST > GAMMY

GAMMING > GAM

GAMMOCK vb clown around

GAMMOCKED > GAMMOCK

GAMMOCKS > GAMMOCK

GAMMON n cured or smoked ham ▷ vb score a double victory in backgammon over

GAMMONED > GAMMON

GAMMONER > GAMMON

GAMMONERS > GAMMON

GAMMONING > GAMMON

GAMMONS > GAMMON

GAMMY adj (of the leg) lame

GAMODEME n isolated breeding population

GAMODEMES > GAMODEME

GAMONE n any chemical substance secreted by a gamete that attracts another gamete during sexual reproduction

GAMONES > GAMONE

GAMP n umbrella

GAMPISH adj bulging

GAMPS > GAMP

GAMS > GAM

GAMUT n whole range or scale (of music, emotions, etc)

GAMUTS > GAMUT

GAMY same as > GAMEY

GAMYNESS > GAMY

GAN vb go

GANACHE n rich icing or filling made of chocolate and cream

GANACHES > GANACHE

GANCH vb impale

GANCHED > GANCH

GANCHES > GANCH

GANCHING > GANCH

GANDER n male goose ▷ vb look

GANDERED > GANDER

GANDERING > GANDER

GANDERISM > GANDER

GANDERS > GANDER

GANDY as in gandy dancer railway track maintenance worker

GANE > GANGUE

GANEF n unscrupulous opportunist who stoops to sharp practice

GANEFS > GANEF

GANEV same as > GANEF

GANEVS > GANEV

GANG n (criminal) group ▷ vb become or act as a gang

GANGBANG n sexual intercourse between one woman and several men one after the other, esp against her will ▷ vb force (a woman) to take part in a gangbang

GANGBANGS > GANGBANG

GANGBOARD n gangway

GANGED > GANG

GANGER n foreman of a gang of labourers

GANGERS > GANGER

GANGING > GANG

GANGINGS > GANG

GANGLAND n criminal underworld

GANGLANDS > GANGLAND

GANGLIA > GANGLION

GANGLIAL > GANGLION

GANGLIAR > GANGLION

GANGLIATE vb form a ganglion

GANGLIER > GANGLY

GANGLIEST > GANGLY

GANGLING adj lanky and awkward

GANGLION n group of nerve cells

GANGLIONS > GANGLION

GANGLY same as > GANGLING

GANGPLANK n portable bridge for boarding or leaving a ship

GANGPLOW n plough designed to produce parallel furrows

GANGPLOWS > GANGPLOW

GANGREL n wandering beggar

GANGRELS > GANGREL

GANGRENE n decay of body tissue as a result of disease or injury ▷ vb become or cause to become affected with gangrene

GANGRENED > GANGRENE

GANGRENES > GANGRENE

GANGS > GANG

GANGSHAG vb participate in group sex with

GANGSHAGS > GANGSHAG

GANGSMAN n foreman

GANGSMEN > GANGSMAN

GANGSTA n member of a street gang

GANGSTAS > GANGSTA

GANGSTER n member of a criminal gang

GANGSTERS > GANGSTER

GANGUE n valueless material in an ore

GANGUES > GANGUE

GANGWAY same as > GANGPLANK

GANGWAYS > GANGWAY

GANISTER n highly refractory siliceous sedimentary rock occurring beneath coal seams: used for lining furnaces

GANISTERS > GANISTER

GANJA n highly potent form of cannabis, usually used for smoking

GANJAH same as > GANJA

GANJAHS > GANJAH

GANJAS > GANJA

GANNED > GAN

GANNET n large sea bird

GANNETRY n gannets' breeding-place

GANNETS > GANNET

GANNING > GAN

GANNISTER same as > GANISTER

GANOF same as > GANEF

GANOFS > GANOF

GANOID adj (of the scales of certain fishes) consisting of an inner bony layer covered with an enamel-like substance ▷ n ganoid fish

GANOIDS > GANOID

GANOIN n substance of which the outer layer of fish scales is composed

GANOINE same as > GANOIN

GANOINES > GANOINE

GANOINS > GANOIN

GANS > GAN

GANSEY n jersey or pullover

GANSEYS > GANSEY

GANT vb yawn

GANTED > GANT

GANTELOPE same as > GAUNTLET

GANTING > GANT

GANTLET n section of a railway where two tracks overlap ▷ vb make railway tracks form a gantlet

GANTLETED > GANTLET

GANTLETS > GANTLET

GANTLINE n line rove through a sheave for hoisting men or gear

GANTLINES > GANTLINE

GANTLOPE same as > GAUNTLET

GANTLOPES > GANTLOPE

GANTRIES > GANTRY

GANTRY n structure supporting something such as a crane or rocket

GANTS > GANT

GANYMEDE n catamite

GANYMEDES > GANYMEDE

GAOL same as > JAIL

GAOLBIRD n person who is or has been confined to gaol, esp repeatedly

GAOLBIRDS > GAOLBIRD

GAOLBREAK n escape from gaol

GAOLED > GAOL

GAOLER > GAOL

GAOLERESS n female gaoler

GAOLERS > GAOL

GAOLING > GAOL

GAOLLESS > GAOL

GAOLS > GAOL

GAP n break or opening

GAPE vb stare in wonder ▷ n act of gaping

GAPED > GAPE

GAPER n person or thing that gapes

GAPERS > GAPER

GAPES n disease of young domestic fowl, characterized by gaping or gasping for breath and caused by gapeworms

GAPESEED n person who stares, mouth agape, at something

GAPESEEDS > GAPESEED

GAPEWORM n type of parasitic worm that lives in the trachea of birds

GAPEWORMS > GAPEWORM

GAPIER >GAPES

GAPIEST >GAPES

GAPING adj wide open ▷ n state of having a gaping mouth

GAPINGLY >GAPING

GAPINGS >GAPING

GAPLESS >GAP

GAPO n forest near a river, regularly flooded in the rainy season

GAPOS >GAPO

GAPOSIS n gap between closed fastenings on a garment

GAPOSISES >GAPOSIS

GAPPED >GAP

GAPPER n in British English, person taking a year out between school and further education

GAPPERS >GAPPER

GAPPIER >GAP

GAPPIEST >GAP

GAPPING n the act of taking a gap year

GAPPINGS >GAPPING

GAPPY >GAP

GAPS >GAP

GAPY >GAPES

GAR same as >GARPIKE

GARAGE n building used to house cars ▷ vb put or keep a car in a garage

GARAGED >GARAGE

GARAGEMAN n car mechanic

GARAGEMEN >GARAGEMAN

GARAGES >GARAGE

GARAGEY adj (of music) in a garage style

GARAGING n accommodation for housing a motor vehicle

GARAGINGS >GARAGING

GARAGIST n person who runs a garage

GARAGISTE n small-scale wine-maker

GARAGISTS >GARAGIST

GARB n clothes ▷ vb clothe

GARBAGE n rubbish

GARBAGES >GARBAGE

GARBAGEY >GARBAGE

GARBAGY >GARBAGE

GARBANZO another name for >CHICKPEA

GARBANZOS >GARBANZO

GARBE n in heraldry, a wheat-sheaf

GARBED >GARBE

GARBES >GARBE

GARBING >GARB

GARBLE vb jumble (a story, quotation, etc), esp unintentionally ▷ n act of garbling

GARBLED adj (of a story etc) jumbled and confused

GARBLER >GARBLE

GARBLERS >GARBLE

GARBLES >GARBLE

GARBLESS >GARB

GARBLING >GARBLE

GARBLINGS >GARBLE

GARBO n dustman

GARBOARD n bottommost plank of a vessel's hull

GARBOARDS >GARBOARD

GARBOIL n confusion or disturbance

GARBOILS >GARBOIL

GARBOLOGY n study of the contents of domestic dustbins to analyse the consumption patterns of households

GARBOS >GARBO

GARBS >GARB

GARBURE n thick soup from Bearn in France

GARBURES >GARBURE

GARCINIA n tropical tree

GARCINIAS >GARCINIA

GARCON n waiter

GARCONS >GARCON

GARDA n member of the police force of the Republic of Ireland

GARDAI >GARDA

GARDANT same as >GUARDANT

GARDANTS >GUARDANT

GARDEN n piece of land for growing flowers, fruit, or vegetables ▷ vb cultivate a garden

GARDENED >GARDEN

GARDENER n person who works in or takes care of a garden as an occupation or pastime

GARDENERS >GARDENER

GARDENFUL n quantity that will fill a garden

GARDENIA n large fragrant white waxy flower

GARDENIAS >GARDENIA

GARDENING n planning and cultivation of a garden

GARDENS >GARDEN

GARDEROBE n wardrobe or the contents of a wardrobe

GARDYLOO n act of throwing slops from a window

GARDYLOOS >GARDYLOO

GARE n filth

GAREFOWL n great auk

GAREFOWLS >GAREFOWL

GARFISH same as >GARPIKE

GARFISHES >GARFISH

GARGANEY n small Eurasian duck, closely related to the mallard

GARGANEYS >GARGANEY

GARGANTUA n monster in Japanese film

GARGARISE vb gargle

GARGARISM n gargle

GARGARIZE same as >GARGARISE

GARGET n inflammation of the mammary gland of domestic animals, esp cattle

GARGETS >GARGET

GARGETY >GARGET

GARGLE vb wash the throat with (a liquid) by breathing out slowly through the liquid ▷ n liquid used for gargling

GARGLED >GARGLE

GARGLER >GARGLE

GARGLERS >GARGLE

GARGLES >GARGLE

GARGLING >GARGLE

GARGOYLE n waterspout carved in the form of a grotesque face, esp on a church ▷ vb provide with gargoyles

GARGOYLED >GARGOYLE

GARGOYLES >GARGOYLE

GARI n thinly sliced pickled ginger, often served with sushi

GARIAL same as >GAVIAL

GARIALS >GARIAL

GARIBALDI n woman's loose blouse with long sleeves popular in the 1860s, copied from the red flannel shirt worn by Garibaldi's soldiers

GARIGUE n open shrubby vegetation of dry Mediterranean regions, consisting of spiny or aromatic dwarf shrubs interspersed with colourful ephemeral species

GARIGUES >GARIGUE

GARIS >GARI

GARISH adj crudely bright or colourful ▷ vb heal

GARISHED >GARISH

GARISHES >GARISH

GARISHING >GARISH

GARISHLY >GARISH

GARJAN same as >GURJUN

GARJANS >GARJAN

GARLAND n wreath of flowers worn or hung as a decoration ▷ vb decorate with garlands

GARLANDED >GARLAND

GARLANDRY n collective term for garlands

GARLANDS >GARLAND

GARLIC n pungent bulb of a plant of the onion family, used in cooking

GARLICKED adj flavoured with garlic

GARLICKY adj containing or resembling the taste or odour of garlic

GARLICS >GARLIC

GARMENT n article of clothing ▷ vb cover or clothe

GARMENTED >GARMENT

GARMENTS >GARMENT

GARNER vb collect or store ▷ n place for storage or safekeeping

GARNERED >GARNER

GARNERING >GARNER

GARNERS >GARNER

GARNET n red semiprecious stone

GARNETS >GARNET

GARNI adj garnished

GARNISH vb decorate (food) ▷ n decoration for food

GARNISHED >GARNISH

GARNISHEE n person upon whom a notice of warning has been served ▷ vb attach (a debt or other property) by a notice of warning

GARNISHER >GARNISH

GARNISHES >GARNISH

GARNISHRY n decoration

GARNITURE n decoration or embellishment

GAROTE same as >GARROTTE

GAROTED >GAROTE

GAROTES >GAROTE

GAROTING >GAROTE

GAROTTE same as >GARROTTE

GAROTTED >GAROTTE

GAROTTER >GAROTTE

GAROTTERS >GAROTTE

GAROTTES >GAROTTE

GAROTTING >GAROTTE

GAROUPA in Chinese and SE Asian cookery, another name for >GROPER

GAROUPAS >GAROUPA

GARPIKE n primitive N and Central American freshwater bony fish with very long toothed jaws and thick scales

GARPIKES >GARPIKE

GARRAN same as >GARRON

GARRANS >GARRAN

GARRE vb compel

GARRED >GAR

GARRES >GARRE

GARRET n attic in a house

GARRETED adj living in a garret

GARRETEER n person who lives in a garret

GARRETS >GARRET

GARRIGUE same as >GARIGUE

GARRIGUES >GARRIGUE

GARRING >GAR

GARRISON n troops stationed in a town or fort ▷ vb station troops in

GARRISONS >GARRISON

GARRON n small sturdy pony bred and used chiefly in Scotland and Ireland

GARRONS >GARRON

GARROT n goldeneye duck

GARROTE same as >GARROTTE

GARROTED >GARROTE

GARROTER >GARROTE

GARROTERS >GARROTE

GARROTES >GARROTE

GARROTING >GARROTE

GARROTS >GARROT

GARROTTE n Spanish method of execution by

strangling ▷ *vb* kill by this method

GARROTTED > GARROTTE

GARROTTER > GARROTTE

GARROTTES > GARROTTE

GARRULITY
> GARRULOUS

GARRULOUS *adj* talkative

GARRYA *n* N American ornamental catkin-bearing evergreen shrub

GARRYAS > GARRYA

GARRYOWEN *n* (in rugby union) high kick forwards followed by a charge to the place where the ball lands

GARS > GAR

GART *vb* compel

GARTER *n* band worn round the leg to hold up a sock or stocking ▷ *vb* secure with a garter

GARTERED > GARTER

GARTERING > GARTER

GARTERS > GARTER

GARTH *n* courtyard surrounded by a cloister

GARTHS > GARTH

GARUDA *n* Hindu god

GARUDAS > GARUDA

GARUM *n* fermented fish sauce

GARUMS > GARUM

GARVEY *n* small flat-bottomed yacht

GARVEYS > GARVEY

GARVIE *n* sprat

GARVIES > GARVIE

GARVOCK *n* sprat

GARVOCKS > GARVOCK

GAS *n* airlike substance that is not liquid or solid ▷ *vb* poison or render unconscious with gas

GASAHOL *n* mixture of petrol and alcohol used as fuel

GASAHOLS > GASAHOL

GASALIER *same as*
> GASOLIER

GASALIERS > GASALIER

GASBAG *n* person who talks too much ▷ *vb* talk in a voluble way, esp about unimportant matters

GASBAGGED > GASBAG

GASBAGS > GASBAG

GASCON *n* boaster

GASCONADE *n* boastful talk, bragging, or bluster ▷ *vb* boast, brag, or bluster

GASCONISM > GASCON

GASCONS > GASCON

GASEITIES > GASEITY

GASEITY *n* state of being gaseous

GASELIER *same as*
> GASOLIER

GASELIERS > GASELIER

GASEOUS *adj* of or like gas

GASES > GAS

GASFIELD *n* area in which natural gas is found underground

GASFIELDS > GASFIELD

GASH *vb* make a long deep cut in ▷ *n* long deep cut ▷ *adj* surplus to requirements ▷ *adj* witty

GASHED > GASH

GASHER > GASH

GASHES > GASH

GASHEST > GASH

GASHFUL *adj* full of gashes

GASHING > GASH

GASHLY *adv* wittily

GASHOLDER *n* large tank for storing gas

GASHOUSE *n* gasworks

GASHOUSES > GASHOUSE

GASIFIED > GASIFY

GASIFIER > GASIFY

GASIFIERS > GASIFY

GASIFIES > GASIFY

GASIFORM *adj* in a gaseous form

GASIFY *vb* change into a gas

GASIFYING > GASIFY

GASKET *n* piece of rubber etc placed between the faces of a metal joint to act as a seal

GASKETS > GASKET

GASKIN *n* lower part of a horse's thigh, between the hock and the stifle

GASKING *same as*
> GASKET

GASKINGS > GASKING

GASKINS > GASKIN

GASLESS > GAS

GASLIGHT *n* lamp in which light is produced by burning gas

GASLIGHTS > GASLIGHT

GASLIT *adj* lit by gas

GASMAN *n* man employed to read household gas meters and install or repair gas fittings, etc

GASMEN > GASMAN

GASOGENE *n* siphon bottle

GASOGENES > GASOGENE

GASOHOL *n* mixture of 80% or 90% petrol with 20% or 10% ethyl alcohol, for use as a fuel in internal-combustion engines

GASOHOLS > GASOHOL

GASOLENE *same as*
> GASOLINE

GASOLENES > GASOLENE

GASOLIER *n* branched hanging fitting for gaslights

GASOLIERS > GASOLIER

GASOLINE *n* petrol

GASOLINES > GASOLINE

GASOLINIC > GASOLINE

GASOMETER *same as*
> GASHOLDER

GASOMETRY *n* measurement of quantities of gases

GASP *vb* draw in breath sharply or with difficulty ▷ *n* convulsive intake of breath

GASPED > GASP

GASPER *n* person who gasps

GASPEREAU *another name for* > ALEWIFE

GASPERS > GASPER

GASPIER > GASP

GASPIEST > GASP

GASPINESS > GASP

GASPING > GASP

GASPINGLY > GASP

GASPINGS > GASP

GASPS > GASP

GASPY > GASP

GASSED > GAS

GASSER *n* drilling or well that yields natural gas

GASSERS > GASSER

GASSES > GAS

GASSIER > GASSY

GASSIEST > GASSY

GASSILY > GASSY

GASSINESS > GASSY

GASSING > GAS

GASSINGS > GAS

GASSY *adj* filled with gas

GAST *vb* frighten

GASTED > GAST

GASTER > GAST

GASTERS > GAST

GASTFULL *adj* dismal

GASTIGHT *adj* not allowing gas to enter or escape

GASTING > GAST

GASTNESS *n* dread

GASTNESSE *same as*
> GASTNESS

GASTRAEA *n* hypothetical primeval form posited by Haeckel

GASTRAEAS > GASTRAEA

GASTRAEUM *n* underside of the body

GASTRAL *adj* relating to the stomach

GASTREA *same as*
> GASTRAEA

GASTREAS > GASTREAS

GASTRIC *adj* of the stomach

GASTRIN *n* polypeptide hormone secreted by the stomach: stimulates secretion of gastric juice

GASTRINS > GASTRIN

GASTRITIC
> GASTRITIS

GASTRITIS *n* inflammation of the stomach lining

GASTROPOD *n* type of mollusc, such as a snail, with a single flattened muscular foot

GASTROPUB *n* pub specializing in high-quality food

GASTRULA *n* saclike animal embryo consisting of three layers of cells (see ectoderm, mesoderm, and endoderm) surrounding a central cavity (archenteron) with a small opening (blastopore) to the exterior

GASTRULAE > GASTRULA

GASTRULAR > GASTRULA

GASTRULAS > GASTRULA

GASTS > GAST

GASWORKS *n* plant where coal gas is made

GAT *n* pistol or revolver

GATE *n* movable barrier, usu hinged, in a wall or fence ▷ *vb* provide with a gate or gates

GATEAU *n* rich elaborate cake

GATEAUS > GATEAU

GATEAUX > GATEAU

GATECRASH *vb* gain entry to (a party, concert, etc) without invitation or payment

GATED > GATE

GATEFOLD *n* oversize page in a book or magazine that is folded in

GATEFOLDS > GATEFOLD

GATEHOUSE *n* building at or above a gateway

GATELEG *adj* (of a table) with one or two drop leaves that are supported when in use by a hinged leg swung out from the frame

GATELESS > GATE

GATELIKE > GATE

GATEMAN *n* gatekeeper

GATEMEN > GATEMAN

GATEPOST *n* post on which a gate is hung

GATEPOSTS > GATEPOST

GATER *variant of* > GATOR

GATERS > GATER

GATES > GATE

GATEWAY *n* entrance with a gate

GATEWAYS > GATEWAY

GATH *n* (in Indian music) second section of a raga

GATHER *vb* assemble ▷ *n* act of gathering

GATHERED > GATHER

GATHERER > GATHER

GATHERERS > GATHER

GATHERING *n* assembly

GATHERS > GATHER

GATHS > GATH

GATING > GATE

GATINGS > GATE

GATLING *as in gatling gun* kind of machinegun

GATOR *shortened form of*
> ALLIGATOR

GATORS > GATOR

GATS > GAT

GATVOL *adj* in South African English, fed up

GAU *n* district set up by the Nazi Party during the Third Reich

GAUCHE *adj* socially awkward

GAUCHELY > GAUCHE

GAUCHER > GAUCHE

GAUCHERIE *n* quality of

being gauche

GAUCHESCO *adj* relating to the folk traditions of the gauchos

GAUCHEST > GAUCHE

GAUCHO *n* S American cowboy

GAUCHOS > GAUCHO

GAUCIE *variant of >* GAUCY

GAUCIER > GAUCY

GAUCIEST > GAUCY

GAUCY *adj* plump or jolly

GAUD *n* article of cheap finery ⊳ *vb* decorate gaudily

GAUDEAMUS *n* first word of a traditional graduation song, hence the song itself

GAUDED > GAUD

GAUDERIES > GAUDERY

GAUDERY *n* cheap finery or display

GAUDGIE *same as* **>** GADGIE

GAUDGIES > GADGIE

GAUDIER > GAUDY

GAUDIES > GAUDY

GAUDIEST > GAUDY

GAUDILY > GAUDY

GAUDINESS > GAUDY

GAUDING > GAUD

GAUDS > GAUD

GAUDY *adj* vulgarly bright or colourful ⊳ *n* celebratory festival or feast held at some schools and colleges

GAUFER *n* wafer

GAUFERS > GAUFER

GAUFFER *same as* **>** GOFFER

GAUFFERED > GAUFFER

GAUFFERS > GAUFFER

GAUFRE *same as* **S** GAUFER

GAUFRES > GAUFRE

GAUGE *vb* estimate or judge ⊳ *n* measuring instrument ⊳ *adj* (of a pressure measurement) measured on a pressure gauge that registers zero at atmospheric pressure

GAUGEABLE > GAUGE

GAUGEABLY > GAUGE

GAUGED > GAUGE

GAUGER *n* person or thing that gauges

GAUGERS > GAUGER

GAUGES > GAUGE

GAUGING > GAUGE

GAUGINGS > GAUGE

GAUJE *same as* **>** GADGIE

GAUJES > GAUJE

GAULEITER *n* person in a position of authority who behaves in an overbearing authoritarian manner

GAULT *n* stiff compact clay or thick heavy clayey soil

GAULTER *n* person who digs gault

GAULTERS > GAULTER

GAULTS > GAULT

GAUM *vb* understand

GAUMED > GAUM

GAUMIER > GAUMY

GAUMIEST > GAUMY

GAUMING > GAUM

GAUMLESS *variant spelling of >* GORMLESS

GAUMS > GAUM

GAUMY *adj* clogged

GAUN > GO

GAUNCH *same as* **>** GANCH

GAUNCHED > GAUNCH

GAUNCHES > GAUNCH

GAUNCHING > GAUNCH

GAUNT *adj* lean and haggard ⊳ *vb* yawn

GAUNTED > GAUNT

GAUNTER > GAUNT

GAUNTEST > GAUNT

GAUNTING > GAUNT

GAUNTLET *n* heavy glove with a long cuff ⊳ *vb* run (or cause to run) the gauntlet

GAUNTLETS > GAUNTLET

GAUNTLY > GAUNT

GAUNTNESS > GAUNT

GAUNTREE *same as* **>** GANTRY

GAUNTREES > GAUNTREE

GAUNTRIES > GAUNTRY

GAUNTRY *same as* **>** GANTRY

GAUNTS > GAUNT

GAUP *same as* **>** GAWP

GAUPED > GAUP

GAUPER > GAUP

GAUPERS > GAUP

GAUPING > GAUP

GAUPS > GAUP

GAUPUS *same as* **>** GAWPUS

GAUPUSES > GAUPUS

GAUR *n* large wild member of the cattle tribe, inhabiting mountainous regions of S Asia

GAURS > GAUR

GAUS > GAU

GAUSS *n* cgs unit of magnetic flux density

GAUSSES > GAUSS

GAUSSIAN *adj* of or relating to the principles established by Karl Friedrich Gauss, the German mathematician

GAUZE *n* transparent loosely-woven fabric, often used for surgical dressings

GAUZELIKE > GAUZE

GAUZES > GAUZE

GAUZIER > GAUZY

GAUZIEST > GAUZY

GAUZILY > GAUZY

GAUZINESS > GAUZY

GAUZY *adj* resembling gauze

GAVAGE *n* forced feeding by means of a tube inserted into the stomach through the mouth

GAVAGES > GAVAGE

GAVE > GIVE

GAVEL *n* small hammer banged on a table by a judge, auctioneer, or chairman to call for

attention ⊳ *vb* use a gavel to restore order

GAVELED > GAVEL

GAVELING > GAVEL

GAVELKIND *n* former system of land tenure peculiar to Kent based on the payment of rent to the lord instead of the performance of services by the tenant

GAVELLED > GAVEL

GAVELLING > GAVEL

GAVELMAN *n* gavelkind tenant

GAVELMEN > GAVELMAN

GAVELOCK *n* iron crowbar

GAVELOCKS > GAVELOCK

GAVELS > GAVEL

GAVIAL as in *false gavial* small crocodile

GAVIALOID *adj* of or like gavials

GAVIALS > GAVIAL

GAVOT *same as* **>** GAVOTTE

GAVOTS > GAVOT

GAVOTTE *n* old formal dance ⊳ *vb* dance a gavotte

GAVOTTED > GAVOTTE

GAVOTTES > GAVOTTE

GAVOTTING > GAVOTTE

GAW *n* as in *weather gaw* partial rainbow

GAWCIER > GAWCY

GAWCIEST > GAWCY

GAWCY *same as* **>** GAUCY

GAWD *same as* **>** GAUD

GAWDS > GAWD

GAWK *vb* stare stupidly ⊳ *n* clumsy awkward person

GAWKED > GAWK

GAWKER > GAWK

GAWKERS > GAWK

GAWKIER > GAWKY

GAWKIES > GAWKY

GAWKIEST > GAWKY

GAWKIHOOD *n* state of being gawky

GAWKILY > GAWKY

GAWKINESS > GAWKY

GAWKING > GAWK

GAWKISH *same as* **>** GAWKY

GAWKISHLY > GAWKY

GAWKS > GAWK

GAWKY *adj* clumsy or awkward ⊳ *n* simpleton

GAWP *vb* stare stupidly

GAWPED > GAWP

GAWPER > GAWP

GAWPERS > GAWP

GAWPING > GAWP

GAWPS > GAWP

GAWPUS *n* silly person

GAWPUSES > GAWPUS

GAWS > GAW

GAWSIE *same as* **>** GAUCY

GAWSIER > GAWSIE

GAWSIEST > GAWSIE

GAWSY *same as* **>** GAUCY

GAY *adj* homosexual ⊳ *n* homosexual

GAYAL *n* type of ox of India and Myanmar, black or brown with white

stockings

GAYALS > GAYAL

GAYDAR *n* supposed ability of a homosexual person to determine whether or not another person is homosexual

GAYDARS > GAYDAR

GAYER > GAY

GAYEST > GAY

GAYETIES > GAYETY

GAYETY *same as* **>** GAIETY

GAYLY > GAY

GAYNESS > GAY

GAYNESSES > GAY

GAYS > GAY

GAYSOME *adj* full of merriment

GAYWINGS *n* flowering wintergreen

GAZABO *n* fellow or companion

GAZABOES > GAZABO

GAZABOS > GAZABO

GAZAL *same as* **>** GHAZAL

GAZALS > GAZAL

GAZANIA *n* S African plant grown for its variegated flowers

GAZANIAS > GAZANIA

GAZAR *n* type of silk cloth

GAZARS > GAZAR

GAZE *vb* look fixedly ⊳ *n* fixed look

GAZEBO *n* summerhouse with a good view

GAZEBOES > GAZEBO

GAZEBOS > GAZEBO

GAZED > GAZE

GAZEFUL *adj* gazing

GAZEHOUND *n* hound such as a greyhound that hunts by sight rather than by scent

GAZELLE *n* small graceful antelope

GAZELLES > GAZELLE

GAZEMENT *n* view

GAZEMENTS > GAZEMENT

GAZER > GAZE

GAZERS > GAZE

GAZES > GAZE

GAZETTE *n* official publication containing announcements ⊳ *vb* announce or report (facts or an event) in a gazette

GAZETTED > GAZETTE

GAZETTEER *n* (part of) a book that lists and describes places ⊳ *vb* list in a gazetteer

GAZETTES > GAZETTE

GAZETTING > GAZETTE

GAZIER > GAZY

GAZIEST > GAZY

GAZILLION *n* in informal English, an extremely large but unspecified number, quantity, or amount

GAZING > GAZE

GAZINGS > GAZE

GAZOGENE *same as* **>** GASOGENE

GAZOGENES > GAZOGENE
GAZON n sod used to cover a parapet in a fortification
GAZONS > GAZON
GAZOO n kazoo
GAZOOKA same as **>** GAZOO
GAZOOKAS > GAZOOKA
GAZOON same as **>** GAZON
GAZOONS > GAZOON
GAZOOS > GAZOO
GAZPACHO n Spanish soup made from tomatoes, peppers, etc, and served cold
GAZPACHOS > GAZPACHO
GAZUMP vb raise the price of a property after verbally agreeing to it with (a prospective buyer) **>** n act or an instance of gazumping
GAZUMPED > GAZUMP
GAZUMPER > GAZUMP
GAZUMPERS > GAZUMP
GAZUMPING > GAZUMP
GAZUMPS > GAZUMP
GAZUNDER vb reduce an offer on a property immediately before exchanging contracts having earlier agreed a higher price with the seller **>** n act or instance of gazundering
GAZUNDERS > GAZUNDER
GAZY adj prone to gazing
GEAL vb congeal
GEALED > GEAL
GEALING > GEAL
GEALOUS Spenserian spelling of **>** JEALOUS
GEALOUSY Spenserian spelling of **>** JEALOUSY
GEALS > GEAL
GEAN n white-flowered tree of Europe, W Asia, and N Africa, the ancestor of cultivated sweet cherries
GEANS > GEAN
GEAR n set of toothed wheels connecting with another or with a rack to change the direction or speed of transmitted motion **>** vb prepare or organize for something
GEARBOX n case enclosing a set of gears in a motor vehicle
GEARBOXES > GEARBOX
GEARCASE n protective casing for gears
GEARCASES > GEARCASE
GEARE Spenserian spelling of **>** JEER
GEARED > GEAR
GEARES > GEARE
GEARHEAD n part in engine gear system
GEARHEADS > GEARHEAD
GEARING n system of gears designed to transmit motion
GEARINGS > GEARING
GEARLESS > GEAR

GEARS > GEAR
GEARSHIFT n lever used to move gearwheels relative to each other, esp in a motor vehicle
GEARWHEEL n one of the toothed wheels in the gears of a motor vehicle
GEASON adj wonderful
GEAT n in casting, the channel through which molten metal runs into a mould
GEATS > GEAT
GEBUR n tenant farmer
GEBURS > GEBUR
GECK vb beguile
GECKED > GECK
GECKING > GECK
GECKO n small tropical lizard
GECKOES > GECKO
GECKOS > GECKO
GECKS > GECK
GED Scots word for **>** PIKE
GEDACT n flutelike stopped metal diapason organ pipe
GEDACTS > GEDACT
GEDDIT interj exclamation meaning do you understand it?
GEDECKT same as **>** GEDACT
GEDECKTS > GEDECKT
GEDS > GED
GEE interj mild exclamation of surprise, admiration, etc **>** vb move (an animal, esp a horse) ahead
GEEBAG n in Irish slang, a disagreeable woman
GEEBAGS > GEEBAG
GEEBUNG n Australian tree or shrub with an edible but tasteless fruit
GEEBUNGS > GEEBUNG
GEECHEE n Black person from the southern states of the US
GEECHEES > GEECHEE
GEED > GEE
GEEGAW same as **>** GEWGAW
GEEGAWS > GEEGAW
GEEING > GEE
GEEK n boring, unattractive person
GEEKDOM > GEEK
GEEKDOMS > GEEK
GEEKED adj highly excited
GEEKIER > GEEK
GEEKIEST > GEEK
GEEKINESS > GEEK
GEEKS > GEEK
GEEKSPEAK n slang word for jargon used by geeks, esp computer enthusiasts
GEEKY > GEEK
GEELBEK n edible marine fish
GEELBEKS > GEELBEK
GEEP n cross between a goat and a sheep
GEEPOUND another name for **>** SLUG

GEEPOUNDS > SLUG
GEEPS > GEEP
GEES > GEE
GEESE > GOOSE
GEEST n area of sandy heathland in N Germany and adjacent areas
GEESTS > GEEST
GEEZ interj expression of surprise
GEEZAH variant spelling of **>** GEEZER
GEEZAHS > GEEZAH
GEEZER n man
GEEZERS > GEEZER
GEFILTE as in gefilte fish dish of fish stuffed with various ingredients
GEFUFFLE same as **>** KERFUFFLE
GEFUFFLED > GEFUFFLE
GEFUFFLES > GEFUFFLE
GEFULLTE as in gefullte fish dish of fish stuffed with various ingredients
GEGGIE Scottish, esp Glaswegian, slang word for the **>** MOUTH
GEGGIES > GEGGIE
GEHLENITE n green mineral consisting of calcium aluminium silicate in tetragonal crystalline form
GEISHA n (in Japan) professional female companion for men
GEISHAS > GEISHA
GEIST n spirit
GEISTS > GEIST
GEIT n border on clothing
GEITS > GEIT
GEL n jelly-like substance, esp one used to secure a hairstyle **>** vb form a gel
GELABLE adj capable of forming a gel
GELADA n NE African baboon with a dark brown mane over the shoulders, a bare red chest, and a ridge muzzle
GELADAS > GELADA
GELANDE as in gelande jump jump made in downhill skiing
GELANT same as **>** GELLANT
GELANTS > GELANT
GELASTIC adj relating to laughter
GELATE vb form a gel
GELATED > GELATE
GELATES > GELATE
GELATI n layered dessert of frozen custard and ice cream
GELATIN same as **>** GELATINE
GELATINE n substance made by boiling animal bones
GELATINES > GELATINE
GELATING > GELATE
GELATINS > GELATIN

GELATION n act or process of freezing a liquid
GELATIONS > GELATION
GELATIS > GELATI
GELATO n Italian frozen dessert, similar to ice cream
GELATOS > GELATO
GELCAP n dose of medicine enclosed in a soluble case of gelatine
GELCAPS > GELCAP
GELD vb castrate **>** n tax on land levied in late Anglo-Saxon and Norman England
GELDED > GELD
GELDER > GELD
GELDERS > GELD
GELDING > GELD
GELDINGS > GELD
GELDS > GELD
GELEE n jelly
GELEES > GELEE
GELID adj very cold, icy, or frosty
GELIDER > GELID
GELIDEST > GELID
GELIDITY > GELID
GELIDLY > GELID
GELIDNESS > GELID
GELIGNITE n type of dynamite used for blasting
GELLANT n compound that forms a solid structure
GELLANTS > GELLANT
GELLED > GEL
GELLIES > GELLY
GELLING > GEL
GELLY same as **>** GELIGNITE
GELOSIES > GELOSY
GELOSY Spenserian spelling of **>** JEALOUSY
GELS > GEL
GELSEMIA > GELSEMIUM
GELSEMINE n alkaloid obtained from gelsemium
GELSEMIUM n type of climbing shrub of SE Asia and North America, esp the yellow jasmine
GELT > GELD
GELTS > GELD
GEM n precious stone or jewel **>** vb set or ornament with gems
GEMATRIA n numerology of the Hebrew language and alphabet
GEMATRIAS > GEMATRIA
GEMCLIP n paperclip
GEMCLIPS > GEMCLIP
GEMEL n in heraldry, parallel bars
GEMELS > GEMEL
GEMFISH n Australian food fish with a delicate flavour
GEMFISHES > GEMFISH
GEMINAL adj occurring in pairs
GEMINALLY > GEMINAL
GEMINATE adj combined in pairs **>** vb arrange or be

arranged in pairs

GEMINATED > GEMINATE

GEMINATES > GEMINATE

GEMINI n expression of surprise

GEMINIES > GEMINY

GEMINOUS adj in pairs

GEMINY n pair

GEMLIKE > GEM

GEMMA n small asexual reproductive structure in liverworts, mosses, etc, that becomes detached from the parent and develops into a new individual

GEMMAE > GEMMA

GEMMAN dialect form of > GENTLEMAN

GEMMATE adj (of some plants and animals) having or reproducing by gemmae ▷ vb produce or reproduce by gemmae

GEMMATED > GEMMATE

GEMMATES > GEMMATE

GEMMATING > GEMMATE

GEMMATION > GEMMATE

GEMMATIVE adj relating to gemmation

GEMMED > GEM

GEMMEN > GEMMAN

GEMMEOUS adj gem-like

GEMMERIES > GEMMERY

GEMMERY n gems collectively

GEMMIER > GEM

GEMMIEST > GEM

GEMMILY > GEM

GEMMINESS > GEM

GEMMING > GEM

GEMMOLOGY same as > GEMOLOGY

GEMMULE n cell or mass of cells produced asexually by sponges and developing into a new individual

GEMMULES > GEMMULE

GEMMY > GEM

GEMOLOGY n branch of mineralogy that is concerned with gems and gemstones

GEMONY same as > JIMINY

GEMOT n (in Anglo-Saxon England) a legal or administrative assembly of a community, such as a shire or hundred

GEMOTE same as > GEMOT

GEMOTES > GEMOTE

GEMOTS > GEMOT

GEMS > GEM

GEMSBOK same as > ORYX

GEMSBOKS > GEMSBOK

GEMSBUCK same as > ORYX

GEMSBUCKS > GEMSBUCK

GEMSHORN n type of medieval flute

GEMSHORNS > GEMSHORN

GEMSTONE n precious or semiprecious stone, esp one which has been cut and polished

GEMSTONES > GEMSTONE

GEMUTLICH adj having a feeling or atmosphere of warmth and friendliness

GEN n information ▷ vb gain information

GENA n cheek

GENAL > GENA

GENAPPE n smooth worsted yarn used for braid, etc

GENAPPES > GENAPPE

GENAS > GENA

GENDARME n member of the French police force

GENDARMES > GENDARME

GENDER n state of being male or female ▷ vb have sex

GENDERED > GENDER

GENDERING > GENDER

GENDERISE same as > GENDERIZE

GENDERIZE vb make distinctions according to gender in or among

GENDERS > GENDER

GENE n part of a cell which determines inherited characteristics

GENEALOGY n (study of) the history and descent of a family or families

GENERA > GENUS

GENERABLE adj able to be generated

GENERAL adj common or widespread ▷ n very senior army officer ▷ vb act as a general

GENERALCY n rank of general

GENERALE singular form of > GENERALIA

GENERALIA n generalities

GENERALLY adv usually

GENERALS > GENERAL

GENERANT n something that generates

GENERANTS > GENERANT

GENERATE vb produce or bring into being

GENERATED > GENERATE

GENERATES > GENERATE

GENERATOR n machine for converting mechanical energy into electrical energy

GENERIC adj of a class, group, or genus ▷ n drug, food product, etc that does not have a trademark

GENERICAL same as > GENERIC

GENERICS > GENERIC

GENEROUS adj free in giving

GENES > GENE

GENESES > GENESIS

GENESIS n beginning or origin

GENET n type of agile catlike mammal of Africa and S Europe, with an elongated head, thick spotted fur, and a very

long tail

GENETIC adj of genes or genetics

GENETICAL same as > GENETIC

GENETICS n study of heredity and variation in organisms

GENETRIX n female progenitor

GENETS > GENET

GENETTE same as > GENET

GENETTES > GENETTE

GENEVA n gin

GENEVAS > GENEVA

GENIAL adj cheerful and friendly

GENIALISE vb make genial

GENIALITY > GENIAL

GENIALIZE same as > GENIALISE

GENIALLY > GENIAL

GENIC adj of or relating to a gene or genes

GENICALLY > GENIC

GENICULAR adj of or relating to the knee

GENIE n (in fairy tales) servant who appears by magic and grants wishes

GENIES > GENIE

GENII > GENIUS

GENIP same as > GENIPAP

GENIPAP n evergreen Caribbean tree with reddish-brown edible orange-like fruits

GENIPAPS > GENIPAP

GENIPS > GENIP

GENISTA n any member of the broom family

GENISTAS > GENISTA

GENISTEIN n substance found in plants, thought to fight cancer

GENITAL adj of the sexual organs or reproduction

GENITALIA same as > GENITALS

GENITALIC > GENITALIA

GENITALLY > GENITAL

GENITALS npl external sexual organs

GENITIVAL > GENITIVE

GENITIVE n grammatical case indicating possession or association ▷ adj denoting a case of nouns, pronouns, and adjectives in inflected languages used to indicate a relation of ownership or association, usually translated by English of

GENITIVES > GENITIVE

GENITOR n biological father as distinguished from the pater or legal father

GENITORS > GENITOR

GENITRIX same as > GENETRIX

GENITURE n birth

GENITURES > GENITURE

GENIUS n (person with) exceptional ability in a particular field

GENIUSES > GENIUS

GENIZAH n repository (usually in a synagogue) for books and other sacred objects which can no longer be used but which may not be destroyed

GENIZAHS > GENIZAH

GENIZOT > GENIZAH

GENIZOTH > GENIZAH

GENLOCK n generator locking device

GENLOCKS > GENLOCK

GENNAKER n type of sail for boats

GENNAKERS > GENNAKER

GENNED > GEN

GENNEL same as > GINNEL

GENNELS > GENNEL

GENNET n female donkey or ass

GENNETS > GENNET

GENNIES > GENNY

GENNING > GEN

GENNY same as > GENOA

GENOA n large triangular jib sail, often with a foot that extends as far aft as the clew of the mainsail

GENOAS > GENOA

GENOCIDAL > GENOCIDE

GENOCIDE n murder of a race of people

GENOCIDES > GENOCIDE

GENOGRAM n expanded family tree

GENOGRAMS > GENOGRAM

GENOISE n rich sponge cake

GENOISES > GENOISE

GENOM same as > GENOME

GENOME n full complement of genetic material within an organism

GENOMES > GENOME

GENOMIC > GENOME

GENOMICS n branch of molecular genetics concerned with the study of genomes

GENOMS > GENOM

GENOTOXIC adj harmful to genetic material

GENOTYPE n genetic constitution of an organism

GENOTYPES > GENOTYPE

GENOTYPIC > GENOTYPE

GENRE n style of literary, musical, or artistic work

GENRES > GENRE

GENRO n group of highly respected elder statesmen in late 19th- and early 20th-century Japan

GENROS > GENRO

GENS n (in ancient Rome) any of a group of aristocratic families, having a common name and claiming descent from

g

a common ancestor in the male line

GENSENG same as > GINSENG

GENSENGS > GENSENG

GENT n gentleman

GENTEEL adj affectedly proper and polite

GENTEELER > GENTEEL

GENTEELLY > GENTEEL

GENTES > GENS

GENTIAN n mountain plant with deep blue flowers

GENTIANS > GENTIAN

GENTIER > GENTY

GENTIEST > GENTY

GENTIL adj gentle

GENTILE n non-Jewish (person) ▷ adj denoting an adjective or proper noun used to designate a place or the inhabitants of a place

GENTILES > GENTILE

GENTILIC adj tribal

GENTILISE vb live like a gentile

GENTILISH adj heathenish

GENTILISM n heathenism

GENTILITY n noble birth or ancestry

GENTILIZE same as > GENTILISE

GENTLE adj mild or kindly ▷ vb tame or subdue (a horse) ▷ n maggot, esp when used as bait in fishing

GENTLED > GENTLE

GENTLEMAN n polite well-bred man

GENTLEMEN > GENTLEMAN

GENTLER > GENTLE

GENTLES > GENTLE

GENTLEST > GENTLE

GENTLING > GENTLE

GENTLY > GENTLE

GENTOO n grey-backed penguin

GENTOOS > GENTOO

GENTRICE n high birth

GENTRICES > GENTRICE

GENTRIES > GENTRY

GENTRIFY vb change the character of a neighbourhood by restoring property or introducing amenities that appeal to the middle classes

GENTRY n informal, often derogatory term for people just below the nobility in social rank

GENTS n men's public toilet

GENTY adj neat

GENU n any knee-like bend in a structure or part

GENUA > GENU

GENUFLECT vb bend the knee as a sign of reverence or deference

GENUINE adj not fake, authentic

GENUINELY > GENUINE

GENUS n group into which a family of animals or plants is divided

GENUSES > GENUS

GEO n (esp in Shetland) a small fjord or gully

GEOBOTANY n study of plants in relation to their geological habitat

GEOCARPIC > GEOCARPY

GEOCARPY n ripening of fruits below ground, as occurs in the peanut

GEOCORONA n outer layer of earth's atmosphere

GEODE n cavity, usually lined with crystals, within a rock mass or nodule

GEODES > GEODE

GEODESIC adj of the geometry of curved surfaces ▷ n shortest line between two points on a curve

GEODESICS > GEODESIC

GEODESIES > GEODESY

GEODESIST > GEODESY

GEODESY n study of the shape and size of the earth

GEODETIC same as > GEODESIC

GEODETICS same as > GEODETIC

GEODIC > GEODE

GEODUCK n king clam

GEODUCKS > GEODUCK

GEOFACT n rock shaped by natural forces, as opposed to a manmade artefact

GEOFACTS > GEOFACT

GEOGENIES > GEOGENY

GEOGENY same as > GEOGONY

GEOGNOSES > GEOGNOSY

GEOGNOSIS same as > GEOGNOSY

GEOGNOST > GEOGNOSY

GEOGNOSTS > GEOGNOSY

GEOGNOSY n study of the origin and distribution of minerals and rocks in the earth's crust: superseded generally by the term 'geology'

GEOGONIC > GEOGONY

GEOGONIES > GEOGONY

GEOGONY n science of the earth's formation

GEOGRAPHY n study of the earth's physical features, climate, population, etc

GEOID n hypothetical surface that corresponds to mean sea level and extends at the same level under the continents

GEOIDAL > GEOID

GEOIDS > GEOID

GEOLATRY n worship of the earth

GEOLOGER > GEOLOGY

GEOLOGERS > GEOLOGY

GEOLOGIAN > GEOLOGY

GEOLOGIC > GEOLOGY

GEOLOGIES > GEOLOGY

GEOLOGISE same as > GEOLOGIZE

GEOLOGIST > GEOLOGY

GEOLOGIZE vb study the geological features of (an area)

GEOLOGY n study of the earth's origin, structure, and composition

GEOMANCER > GEOMANCY

GEOMANCY n prophecy from the pattern made when a handful of earth is cast down or dots are drawn at random and connected with lines

GEOMANT n geomancer

GEOMANTIC > GEOMANCY

GEOMANTS > GEOMANT

GEOMETER n person who is practised in or who studies geometry

GEOMETERS > GEOMETER

GEOMETRIC adj of geometry

GEOMETRID n type of moth, the larvae of which are called measuring worms, inchworms, or loopers

GEOMETRY n branch of mathematics dealing with points, lines, curves, and surfaces

GEOMYOID adj relating to burrowing rodents of the genus Geomys

GEOPHAGIA same as > GEOPHAGY

GEOPHAGY n practice of eating earth, clay, chalk, etc, found in some primitive tribes

GEOPHILIC adj soil-loving

GEOPHONE n device for recording seismic movement

GEOPHONES > GEOPHONE

GEOPHYTE n perennial plant that propagates by means of buds below the soil surface

GEOPHYTES > GEOPHYTE

GEOPHYTIC > GEOPHYTE

GEOPONIC adj of or relating to agriculture, esp as a science

GEOPONICS n science of agriculture

GEOPROBE n probing device used for sampling soil

GEOPROBES > GEOPROBE

GEORGETTE n fine silky fabric

GEORGIC adj agricultural ▷ n poem about rural or agricultural life

GEORGICAL same as > GEORGIC

GEORGICS > GEORGIC

GEOS > GEO

GEOSPHERE n the rigid outer layer of the earth

GEOSTATIC adj denoting or relating to the pressure exerted by a mass of rock or a similar substance

GEOTACTIC > GEOTAXIS

GEOTAXES > GEOTAXIS

GEOTAXIS n movement of an organism in response to the stimulus of gravity

GEOTHERM n line or surface within or on the earth connecting points of equal temperature

GEOTHERMS > GEOTHERM

GEOTROPIC adj of geotropism: the response of a plant to the stimulus of gravity

GER n portable Mongolian dwelling

GERAH n ancient Hebrew unit of weight

GERAHS > GERAH

GERANIAL n cis- isomer of citral

GERANIALS > GERANIAL

GERANIOL n colourless or pale yellow terpine alcohol with an odour of roses, found in many essential oils: used in perfumery

GERANIOLS > GERANIOL

GERANIUM n cultivated plant with red, pink, or white flowers

GERANIUMS > GERANIUM

GERARDIA n any plant of the genus Gerardia

GERARDIAS > GERARDIA

GERBE same as > GARBE

GERBERA n type of plant grown, usually as a greenhouse plant, for its large brightly coloured daisy-like flowers

GERBERAS > GERBERA

GERBES > GARBE

GERBIL n burrowing desert rodent of Asia and Africa

GERBILLE same as > GERBIL

GERBILLES > GERBILLE

GERBILS > GERBIL

GERE Spenserian spelling of > GEAR

GERENT n person who rules or manages

GERENTS > GERENT

GERENUK n slender E African antelope with a long thin neck and backward-curving horns

GERENUKS > GERENUK

GERES > GEAR

GERFALCON same as > GYRFALCON

GERIATRIC n derogatory term for old person ▷ adj of geriatrics or old people

GERLE Spenserian spelling of > GIRL

GERLES > GERLE

GERM n microbe, esp one causing disease ▷ vb sprout

GERMAIN *same as* > GERMEN

GERMAINE *same as* > GERMEN

GERMAINES > GERMAINE

GERMAINS > GERMAIN

GERMAN *n* dance consisting of complicated figures and changes of partners *▷ adj* having the same parents as oneself

GERMANDER *n* type of plant

GERMANE *adj* relevant

GERMANELY > GERMANE

GERMANIC *adj* of or containing germanium in the tetravalent state

GERMANISE *same as* > GERMANIZE

GERMANITE *n* mineral consisting of a complex copper arsenic sulphide containing germanium, gallium, iron, zinc, and lead: an ore of germanium and gallium

GERMANIUM *n* brittle grey element that is a semiconductor

GERMANIZE *vb* adopt or cause to adopt German customs, speech, institutions, etc

GERMANOUS *adj* of or containing germanium in the divalent state

GERMANS > GERMAN

GERMED > GERM

GERMEN *n* mass of undifferentiated cells that gives rise to the germ cells

GERMENS > GERMEN

GERMFREE > GERM

GERMICIDE *n* substance that kills germs

GERMIER > GERMY

GERMIEST > GERMY

GERMIN *same as* > GERMEN

GERMINA > GERMEN

GERMINAL *adj* of or in the earliest stage of development

GERMINANT *adj* in the process of germinating

GERMINATE *vb* (cause to) sprout or begin to grow

GERMINESS > GERMY

GERMING > GERM

GERMINS > GERMIN

GERMLIKE > GERM

GERMPLASM *n* plant genetic material

GERMPROOF *adj* protected against the penetration of germs

GERMS > GERM

GERMY *adj* full of germs

GERNE *vb* grin

GERNED > GERNE

GERNES > GERNE

GERNING > GERNE

GERONIMO *interj* shout given by US paratroopers as they jump into battle

GERONTIC *adj* of or relating to the senescence of an organism

GEROPIGA *n* grape syrup used to sweeten inferior port wines

GEROPIGAS > GEROPIGA

GERS > GER

GERT *adv* in dialect, great or very big

GERTCHA *interj* get out of here!

GERUND *n* noun formed from a verb

GERUNDIAL > GERUND

GERUNDIVE *n* (in Latin grammar) an adjective formed from a verb, expressing the desirability of the activity denoted by the verb *▷ adj* of or relating to the gerund or gerundive

GERUNDS > GERUND

GESNERIA *n* S American plant grown as a greenhouse plant for its large leaves and showy brightly-coloured flowers

GESNERIAD > GESNERIA

GESNERIAS > GESNERIA

GESSAMINE *another word for* > JASMINE

GESSE *Spenserian spelling of* > GUESS

GESSED > GESSE

GESSES > GESSE

GESSING > GESSE

GESSO *n* plaster used for painting or in sculpture *▷ vb* apply gesso to

GESSOED > GESSO

GESSOES > GESSO

GEST *n* notable deed or exploit

GESTALT *n* perceptual pattern or structure possessing qualities as a whole that cannot be described merely as a sum of its parts

GESTALTEN > GESTALT

GESTALTS > GESTALT

GESTANT *adj* laden

GESTAPO *n* any secret state police organization

GESTAPOS > GESTAPO

GESTATE *vb* carry (developing young) in the uterus during pregnancy

GESTATED > GESTATE

GESTATES > GESTATE

GESTATING > GESTATE

GESTATION *n* (period of) carrying of young in the womb between conception and birth

GESTATIVE > GESTATION

GESTATORY > GESTATION

GESTE *same as* > GEST

GESTES > GESTE

GESTIC *adj* consisting of gestures

GESTICAL > GESTIC

GESTS > GEST

GESTURAL > GESTURE

GESTURE *n* movement to convey meaning *▷ vb* gesticulate

GESTURED > GESTURE

GESTURER > GESTURE

GESTURERS > GESTURE

GESTURES > GESTURE

GESTURING > GESTURE

GET *vb* obtain or receive

GETA *n* type of Japanese wooden sandal

GETABLE > GET

GETAS > GETA

GETATABLE *adj* accessible

GETAWAY *n* used in escape

GETAWAYS > GETAWAY

GETS > GET

GETTABLE > GET

GETTER *n* person or thing that gets *▷ vb* remove (a gas) by the action of a getter

GETTERED > GETTER

GETTERING > GETTER

GETTERS > GETTER

GETTING > GET

GETTINGS > GET

GETUP *n* outfit

GETUPS > GETUP

GEUM *n* type of herbaceous plant with compound leaves and red, orange, or white flowers

GEUMS > GEUM

GEWGAW *n* showy but valueless trinket *▷ adj* showy and valueless

GEWGAWED *adj* decorated gaudily

GEWGAWS > GEWGAW

GEY *adv* extremely *▷ adj* gallant

GEYAN *adv* somewhat

GEYER > GEY

GEYEST > GEY

GEYSER *n* spring that discharges steam and hot water

GEYSERITE *n* mineral form of hydrated silica resembling opal, deposited from the waters of geysers and hot springs

GEYSERS > GEYSER

GHARIAL *same as* > GAVIAL

GHARIALS > GHARIAL

GHARRI *same as* > GHARRY

GHARRIES > GHARRY

GHARRIS > GHARRY

GHARRY *n* (in India) horse-drawn vehicle available for hire

GHAST *vb* terrify

GHASTED > GHAST

GHASTFUL *adj* dismal

GHASTING > GHAST

GHASTLIER > GHASTLY

GHASTLY *adj* unpleasant *▷ adv* unhealthily

GHASTNESS *n* dread

GHASTS > GHAST

GHAT *n* (in India) steps leading down to a river

GHATS > GHAT

GHAUT *n* small cleft in a hill through which a rivulet runs down to the sea

GHAUTS > GHAUT

GHAZAL *n* Arabic love poem

GHAZALS > GHAZAL

GHAZEL *same as* > GHAZAL

GHAZELS > GHAZEL

GHAZI *n* Muslim fighter against infidels

GHAZIES > GHAZI

GHAZIS > GHAZI

GHEE *n* (in Indian cookery) clarified butter

GHEES > GHEE

GHERAO *n* form of industrial action in India in which workers imprison their employers on the premises until their demands are met *▷ vb* trap an employer in his office, to indicate the workforce's discontent

GHERAOED > GHERAO

GHERAOES > GHERAO

GHERAOING > GHERAO

GHERAOS > GHERAO

GHERKIN *n* small pickled cucumber

GHERKINS > GHERKIN

GHESSE *Spenserian spelling of* > GUESS

GHESSED > GHESSE

GHESSES > GHESSE

GHESSING > GHESSE

GHEST > GHESSE

GHETTO *n* slum area inhabited by a deprived minority *▷ vb* ghettoize

GHETTOED > GHETTO

GHETTOES > GHETTO

GHETTOING > GHETTO

GHETTOISE *same as* > GHETTOIZE

GHETTOIZE *vb* confine (someone or something) to a particular area or category

GHETTOS > GHETTO

GHI *same as* > GHEE

GHIBLI *n* fiercely hot wind of North Africa

GHIBLIS > GHIBLI

GHILGAI *same as* > GILGAI

GHILGAIS > GHILGAI

GHILLIE *n* type of tongueless shoe with lacing up the instep, originally worn by the Scots *▷ vb* act as a g(h)illie

GHILLIED > GHILLIE

GHILLIES > GHILLIE

GHILLYING > GHILLIE

GHIS > GHI

GHOST *n* disembodied spirit of a dead person *▷ vb* ghostwrite

GHOSTED > GHOST

GHOSTIER > GHOSTY

GHOSTIEST > GHOSTY

g

GHOSTING > GHOST

GHOSTINGS > GHOST

GHOSTLIER > GHOSTLY

GHOSTLIKE > GHOST

GHOSTLY adj frightening in appearance or effect

GHOSTS > GHOST

GHOSTY adj pertaining to ghosts

GHOUL n person with morbid interests

GHOULIE n goblin

GHOULIES > GHOULIE

GHOULISH adj of or relating to ghouls

GHOULS > GHOUL

GHRELIN n hormone that stimulates appetite

GHRELINS > GHRELIN

GHUBAR as in ghubar numeral type of numeral

GHYLL same as > GILL

GHYLLS > GHYLL

GI n loose-fitting white suit worn in judo, karate, and other martial arts

GIAMBEUX n jambeaux; leg armour

GIANT n mythical being of superhuman size ▷ adj huge

GIANTESS same as > GIANT

GIANTHOOD n condition of being a giant

GIANTISM same as > GIGANTISM

GIANTISMS > GIANTISM

GIANTLIER > GIANTLY

GIANTLIKE > GIANT

GIANTLY adj giantlike

GIANTRIES > GIANTRY

GIANTRY n collective term for giants

GIANTS > GIANT

GIANTSHIP n style of address for a giant

GIAOUR n derogatory term for a non-Muslim, esp a Christian, used esp by the Turks

GIAOURS > GIAOUR

GIARDIA n species of parasite

GIARDIAS > GIARDIA

GIB n metal wedge, pad, or thrust bearing, esp a brass plate let into a steam engine crosshead ▷ vb fasten or supply with a gib

GIBBED > GIB

GIBBER vb speak or utter rapidly and unintelligibly ▷ n boulder

GIBBERED > GIBBER

GIBBERING > GIBBER

GIBBERISH n rapid unintelligible talk

GIBBERS > GIBBER

GIBBET n gallows for displaying executed criminals ▷ vb put to death by hanging on a gibbet

GIBBETED > GIBBET

GIBBETING > GIBBET

GIBBETS > GIBBET

GIBBETTED > GIBBET

GIBBING > GIB

GIBBON n agile tree-dwelling ape of S Asia

GIBBONS > GIBBON

GIBBOSE same as > GIBBOUS

GIBBOSITY n state of being gibbous

GIBBOUS adj (of the moon) more than half but less than fully illuminated

GIBBOUSLY > GIBBOUS

GIBBSITE n mineral consisting of hydrated aluminium oxide

GIBBSITES > GIBBSITE

GIBE vb make jeering or scoffing remarks (at) ▷ n derisive or provoking remark

GIBED > GIBE

GIBEL n Prussian carp

GIBELS > GIBEL

GIBER > GIBE

GIBERS > GIBE

GIBES > GIBE

GIBING > GIBE

GIBINGLY > GIBE

GIBLET > GIBLETS

GIBLETS npl gizzard, liver, heart, and neck of a fowl

GIBLI same as > GHIBLI

GIBLIS > GIBLI

GIBS > GIB

GIBSON n martini garnished with onion

GIBSONS > GIBSON

GIBUS n collapsible top hat operated by a spring

GIBUSES > GIBUS

GID n disease of sheep characterized by an unsteady gait and staggering

GIDDAP interj exclamation used to make a horse go faster

GIDDAY interj expression of greeting

GIDDIED > GIDDY

GIDDIER > GIDDY

GIDDIES > GIDDY

GIDDIEST > GIDDY

GIDDILY > GIDDY

GIDDINESS > GIDDY

GIDDUP same as > GIDDYUP

GIDDY adj having or causing a feeling of dizziness ▷ vb make giddy

GIDDYAP same as > GIDDYUP

GIDDYING > GIDDY

GIDDYUP interj exclamation used to make a horse go faster

GIDGEE n small acacia tree, which at times emits an unpleasant smell

GIDGEES > GIDGEE

GIDJEE same as > GIDGEE

GIDJEES > GIDJEE

GIDS > GID

GIE Scot word for > GIVE

GIED > GIVE

GIEING > GIVE

GIEN > GIVE

GIES > GIVE

GIF obsolete word for > IF

GIFT n present ▷ vb make a present of

GIFTABLE adj suitable as gift ▷ n something suitable as gift

GIFTABLES > GIFTABLE

GIFTED adj talented

GIFTEDLY > GIFTED

GIFTEE n person given a gift

GIFTEES > GIFTEE

GIFTING > GIFT

GIFTLESS > GIFT

GIFTS > GIFT

GIFTSHOP n shop selling articles suitable for gifts

GIFTSHOPS > GIFTSHOP

GIFTWARE n anything that may be given as a present

GIFTWARES > GIFTWARE

GIFTWRAP vb wrap (a gift) in decorative wrapping paper

GIFTWRAPS > GIFTWRAP

GIG n single performance by pop or jazz musicians ▷ vb play a gig or gigs

GIGA same as > GIGUE

GIGABIT n unit of information in computing

GIGABITS > GIGABIT

GIGABYTE n one thousand and twenty-four megabytes

GIGABYTES > GIGABYTE

GIGACYCLE same as > GIGAHERTZ

GIGAFLOP n measure of processing speed, consisting of a thousand million floating-point operations a second

GIGAFLOPS > GIGAFLOP

GIGAHERTZ n unit of frequency equal to 10^9 hertz.

GIGANTEAN adj gigantic

GIGANTIC adj enormous

GIGANTISM n excessive growth of the entire body, caused by overproduction of growth hormone by the pituitary gland during childhood or adolescence

GIGAS > GIGA

GIGATON n unit of explosive force

GIGATONS > GIGATON

GIGAWATT n unit of power equal to 1 billion watts

GIGAWATTS > GIGAWATT

GIGGED > GIG

GIGGING > GIG

GIGGIT vb move quickly

GIGGITED > GIGGIT

GIGGITING > GIGGIT

GIGGITS > GIGGIT

GIGGLE vb laugh nervously or foolishly ▷ n such a laugh

GIGGLED > GIGGLE

GIGGLER > GIGGLE

GIGGLERS > GIGGLE

GIGGLES > GIGGLE

GIGGLIER > GIGGLE

GIGGLIEST > GIGGLE

GIGGLING > GIGGLE

GIGGLINGS > GIGGLE

GIGGLY > GIGGLE

GIGHE > GIGA

GIGLET n flighty girl

GIGLETS > GIGLET

GIGLOT same as > GIGLET

GIGLOTS > GIGLOT

GIGMAN n one who places great importance on respectability

GIGMANITY > GIGMAN

GIGMEN > GIGMAN

GIGOLO n man paid by an older woman to be her escort or lover

GIGOLOS > GIGOLO

GIGOT n leg of lamb or mutton

GIGOTS > GIGOT

GIGS > GIG

GIGUE n piece of music, usually in six-eight time and often fugal, incorporated into the classical suite

GIGUES > GIGUE

GILA n large venomous brightly coloured lizard

GILAS > GILA

GILBERT n unit of magnetomotive force

GILBERTS > GILBERT

GILCUP same as > GILTCUP

GILCUPS > GILCUP

GILD vb put a thin layer of gold on

GILDED > GILD

GILDEN adj gilded

GILDER > GILD

GILDERS > GILD

GILDHALL same as > GUILDHALL

GILDHALLS > GILDHALL

GILDING > GILD

GILDINGS > GILD

GILDS > GILD

GILDSMAN > GILD

GILDSMEN > GILD

GILET n waist- or hip-length garment, usually sleeveless, fastening up the front

GILETS > GILET

GILGAI n natural water hole

GILGAIS > GILGAI

GILGIE n type of freshwater crayfish

GILGIES > GILGIE

GILL n radiating structure beneath the cap of a mushroom ▷ vb catch (fish) or (of fish) to be caught in a gill net

GILLAROO n type of brown trout

GILLAROOS > GILLAROO

GILLED > GILL

GILLER > GILL

GILLERS > GILL

GILLET n mare

GILLETS > GILLET

GILLFLIRT n flirtatious woman

GILLIE n (in Scotland) attendant for hunting or fishing ▷ vb act as a gillie

GILLIED > GILLIE

GILLIES > GILLY

GILLING > GILL

GILLION n (no longer in technical use) one thousand million

GILLIONS > GILLION

GILLNET n net designed to catch fish by the gills ▷ vb fish using a gillnet

GILLNETS > GILLNET

GILLS npl breathing organs in fish and other water creatures

GILLY vb act as a gillie

GILLYING > GILLY

GILLYVOR n type of carnation

GILLYVORS > GILLYVOR

GILPEY n mischievous, frolicsome boy or girl

GILPEYS > GILPEY

GILPIES > GILPEY

GILPY same as > GILPEY

GILRAVAGE vb make merry, especially to excess

GILSONITE n very pure form of asphalt found in Utah and Colorado

GILT > GILD

GILTCUP n buttercup

GILTCUPS > GILTCUP

GILTHEAD n type of fish of Mediterranean and European Atlantic waters, with a gold-coloured band between the eyes

GILTHEADS > GILTHEAD

GILTS > GILD

GILTWOOD adj made of wood and gilded

GIMBAL vb support on gimbals

GIMBALED > GIMBAL

GIMBALING > GIMBAL

GIMBALLED > GIMBAL

GIMBALS npl set of pivoted rings which allow nautical instruments to remain horizontal at sea

GIMCRACK adj showy but cheap ▷ n cheap showy trifle or gadget

GIMCRACKS > GIMCRACK

GIMEL n third letter of the Hebrew alphabet

GIMELS > GIMEL

GIMLET n small tool with a screwlike tip for boring holes in wood ▷ adj penetrating or piercing ▷ vb make holes in (wood) using a gimlet

GIMLETED > GIMLET

GIMLETING > GIMLET

GIMLETS > GIMLET

GIMMAL n ring composed of interlocking rings ▷ vb provide with gimmals

GIMMALLED > GIMMAL

GIMMALS > GIMMAL

GIMME interj give me! ▷ n short putt that one is excused by one's opponent from playing because it is considered too easy to miss

GIMMER n year-old ewe

GIMMERS > GIMMER

GIMMES > GIMME

GIMMICK n something designed to attract attention or publicity ▷ vb make gimmicky

GIMMICKED > GIMMICK

GIMMICKRY > GIMMICK

GIMMICKS > GIMMICK

GIMMICKY > GIMMICK

GIMMIE n in golf, an easy putt conceded to one's opponent

GIMMIES > GIMMIE

GIMMOR n mechanical device

GIMMORS > GIMMOR

GIMP n tapelike trimming of silk, wool, or cotton, often stiffened with wire ▷ vb derogatory term for limp

GIMPED > GIMP

GIMPIER > GIMPY

GIMPIEST > GIMPY

GIMPING > GIMP

GIMPS > GIMP

GIMPY same as > GAMMY

GIN n spirit flavoured with juniper berries ▷ vb free (cotton) of seeds with a gin; begin

GING n child's catapult

GINGAL n type of musket mounted on a swivel

GINGALL same as > GINGAL

GINGALLS > GINGALL

GINGALS > GINGAL

GINGE n person with ginger hair

GINGELEY same as > GINGILI

GINGELEYS > GINGELEY

GINGELI same as > GINGILI

GINGELIES > GINGELY

GINGELIS > GINGELI

GINGELLI same as > GINGILI

GINGELLIS > GINGILI

GINGELLY same as > GINGILI

GINGELY same as > GINGILI

GINGER n root of a tropical plant, used as a spice ▷ adj light reddish-brown ▷ vb add the spice ginger to (a dish)

GINGERADE n fizzy drink flavoured with ginger

GINGERED > GINGER

GINGERING > GINGER

GINGERLY adv cautiously ▷ adj cautious

GINGEROUS adj reddish

GINGERS > GINGER

GINGERY adj like or tasting of ginger

GINGES > GINGE

GINGHAM n cotton cloth, usu checked or striped

GINGHAMS > GINGHAM

GINGILI n oil obtained from sesame seeds

GINGILIS > GINGILI

GINGILLI same as > GINGILI

GINGILLIS > GINGILLI

GINGIVA same as > GUM

GINGIVAE > GINGIVA

GINGIVAL > GINGIVA

GINGKO same as > GINKGO

GINGKOES > GINKGO

GINGKOS > GINKGO

GINGLE same as > JINGLE

GINGLES > GINGLE

GINGLYMI > GINGLYMUS

GINGLYMUS n hinge joint

GINGS > GING

GINHOUSE n building where cotton is ginned

GINHOUSES > GINHOUSE

GINK n man or boy, esp one considered to be odd

GINKGO n ornamental Chinese tree

GINKGOES > GINKGO

GINKGOS > GINKGO

GINKS > GINK

GINN same as > JINN

GINNED > GIN

GINNEL n narrow passageway between buildings

GINNELS > GINNEL

GINNER > GIN

GINNERIES > GINHOUSE

GINNERS > GIN

GINNERY another word for > GINHOUSE

GINNIER > GINNY

GINNIEST > GINNY

GINNING > GIN

GINNINGS > GIN

GINNY adj relating to the spirit gin

GINORMOUS adj very large

GINS > GIN

GINSENG n (root of) a plant believed to have tonic and energy-giving properties

GINSENGS > GINSENG

GINSHOP n tavern

GINSHOPS > GINSHOP

GINZO n disparaging term for person of Italian descent

GINZOES > GINZO

GIO same as > GEO

GIOCOSO adv (of music) to be expressed joyfully or playfully

GIOS > GIO

GIP same as > GYP

GIPON another word for > JUPON

GIPONS > GIPON

GIPPED > GIP

GIPPER > GIP

GIPPERS > GIP

GIPPIES > GIPPY

GIPPING > GIP

GIPPO same as > GIPPY

GIPPOES > GIPPO

GIPPOS > GIPPO

GIPPY n starling

GIPS > GIP

GIPSEN obsolete word for > GYPSY

GIPSENS > GIPSEN

GIPSIED > GIPSY

GIPSIES > GIPSY

GIPSY n member of a nomadic people scattered throughout Europe and North America ▷ vb live like a gypsy

GIPSYDOM > GIPSY

GIPSYDOMS > GIPSY

GIPSYHOOD > GIPSY

GIPSYING > GIPSY

GIPSYISH > GIPSY

GIPSYWORT n hairy Eurasian plant with two-lipped white flowers with purple dots on the lower lip

GIRAFFE n African ruminant mammal with a spotted yellow skin and long neck and legs

GIRAFFES > GIRAFFE

GIRAFFID adj giraffe-like

GIRAFFINE adj relating to a giraffe

GIRAFFISH > GIRAFFE

GIRAFFOID adj giraffe-like

GIRANDOLA same as > GIRANDOLE

GIRANDOLE n ornamental branched wall candleholder, usually incorporating a mirror

GIRASOL n type of opal that has a red or pink glow in bright light

GIRASOLE same as > GIRASOL

GIRASOLES > GIRASOLE

GIRASOLS > GIRASOL

GIRD vb put a belt round ▷ n blow or stroke

GIRDED > GIRD

GIRDER n large metal beam

GIRDERS > GIRDER

GIRDING > GIRD

GIRDINGLY > GIRD

GIRDINGS > GIRD

GIRDLE n woman's elastic corset ▷ vb surround or encircle

GIRDLED > GIRDLE

GIRDLER n person or thing that girdles

GIRDLERS > GIRDLER

GIRDLES > GIRDLE

GIRDLING > GIRDLE

GIRDS > GIRD

GIRKIN same as > GHERKIN

GIRKINS > GIRKIN

GIRL n female child

GIRLHOOD n state or time of being a girl

GIRLHOODS > GIRLHOOD

GIRLIE adj (of a magazine, calendar, etc) featuring pictures of naked or scantily clad women ▷ n little girl

GIRLIER > GIRLY

GIRLIES > GIRLIE

GIRLIEST > GIRLY

GIRLISH adj of or like a girl in looks, behaviour, innocence, etc

GIRLISHLY > GIRLISH

GIRLOND obsolete word for > GARLAND

GIRLONDS > GIRLOND

GIRLS > GIRL

GIRLY same as > GIRLIE

GIRN vb snarl

GIRNED > GIRN

GIRNEL n large chest for storing meal

GIRNELS > GIRNEL

GIRNER > GIRN

GIRNERS > GIRN

GIRNIE adj peevish

GIRNIER > GIRNIE

GIRNIEST > GIRNIE

GIRNING > GIRN

GIRNS > GIRN

GIRO n (in some countries) system of transferring money within a post office or bank directly from one account to another

GIROLLE n chanterelle mushroom

GIROLLES > GIROLLE

GIRON n charge consisting of the lower half of a diagonally divided quarter, usually in the top left corner of the shield

GIRONIC > GIRON

GIRONNY adj divided into segments from the fesse point

GIRONS > GIRON

GIROS > GIRO

GIROSOL same as > GIRASOL

GIROSOLS > GIROSOL

GIRR same as > GIRD

GIRRS > GIRR

GIRSH n currency unit of Saudi Arabia

GIRSHES > GIRSH

GIRT vb gird; bind

GIRTED > GIRT

GIRTH n measurement round something ▷ vb fasten a girth on (a horse)

GIRTHED > GIRTH

GIRTHING > GIRTH

GIRTHLINE same as > GIRTLINE

GIRTHS > GIRTH

GIRTING > GIRT

GIRTLINE n gantline

GIRTLINES > GIRTLINE

GIRTS > GIRT

GIS > GI

GISARME n long-shafted battle-axe with a sharp point on the back of the axe head

GISARMES > GISARME

GISM n semen

GISMO same as > GIZMO

GISMOLOGY same as > GIZMOLOGY

GISMOS > GISMO

GISMS > GISM

GIST n substance or main point of a matter

GISTS > GIST

GIT n contemptible person ▷ vb dialect version of get

GITANA n female gypsy

GITANAS > GITANA

GITANO n male gypsy

GITANOS > GITANO

GITE n self-catering holiday cottage for let in France

GITES > GITE

GITS > GIT

GITTARONE n acoustic bass guitar

GITTED > GIT

GITTERN n obsolete medieval stringed instrument resembling the guitar ▷ vb play the gittern

GITTERNED > GITTERN

GITTERNS > GITTERN

GITTIN n Jewish divorce

GITTING > GIT

GIUST same as > JOUST

GIUSTED > GIUST

GIUSTING > GIUST

GIUSTO adv be observed strictly

GIUSTS > GIUST

GIVABLE > GIVE

GIVE vb present (something) to another person ▷ n resilience or elasticity

GIVEABLE > GIVE

GIVEAWAY n something that reveals hidden feelings or intentions ▷ adj very cheap or free

GIVEAWAYS > GIVEAWAY

GIVEBACK n reduction in wages in return for some other benefit, in time of recession

GIVEBACKS > GIVEBACK

GIVED same as > GYVED

GIVEN n assumed fact

GIVENNESS n condition of being given

GIVENS > GIVEN

GIVER > GIVE

GIVERS > GIVE

GIVES > GIVE

GIVING > GIVE

GIVINGS > GIVE

GIZMO n device

GIZMOLOGY n study of gadgets

GIZMOS > GIZMO

GIZZ n wig

GIZZARD n part of a bird's stomach

GIZZARDS > GIZZARD

GIZZEN vb (of wood) to warp

GIZZENED > GIZZEN

GIZZENING > GIZZEN

GIZZENS > GIZZEN

GIZZES > GIZZ

GJETOST n type of Norwegian cheese

GJETOSTS > GJETOST

GJU n type of violin used in Shetland

GJUS > GJU

GLABELLA n smooth elevation of the frontal bone just above the bridge of the nose: a reference point in physical anthropology or craniometry

GLABELLAE > GLABELLA

GLABELLAR > GLABELLA

GLABRATE same as > GLABROUS

GLABROUS adj without hair or a similar growth

GLACE adj preserved in a thick sugary syrup ▷ vb ice or candy (cakes, fruits, etc)

GLACEED > GLACE

GLACEING > GLACE

GLACES > GLACE

GLACIAL adj of ice or glaciers ▷ n ice age

GLACIALLY > GLACIAL

GLACIALS > GLACIAL

GLACIATE vb cover or become covered with glaciers or masses of ice

GLACIATED > GLACIATE

GLACIATES > GLACIATE

GLACIER n slow-moving mass of ice formed by accumulated snow

GLACIERED adj having a glacier or glaciers

GLACIERS > GLACIER

GLACIS n slight incline

GLACISES > GLACIS

GLAD adj pleased and happy ▷ vb become glad ▷ n gladiolus

GLADDED > GLAD

GLADDEN vb make glad

GLADDENED > GLADDEN

GLADDENER > GLADDEN

GLADDENS > GLADDEN

GLADDER > GLAD

GLADDEST > GLAD

GLADDIE same as > GLADDIE

GLADDIES > GLADDIE

GLADDING > GLAD

GLADDON n stinking iris

GLADDONS > GLADDON

GLADE n open space in a forest

GLADELIKE > GLADE

GLADES > GLADE

GLADFUL adj full of gladness

GLADIATE adj shaped like a sword

GLADIATOR n (in ancient Rome) man trained to fight in arenas to provide entertainment

GLADIER > GLADE

GLADIEST > GLADE

GLADIOLA same as > GLADIOLUS

GLADIOLAR > GLADIOLUS

GLADIOLAS > GLADIOLA

GLADIOLE same as > GLADIOLUS

GLADIOLES > GLADIOLE

GLADIOLI > GLADIOLUS

GLADIOLUS n garden plant with sword-shaped leaves

GLADIUS n short sword used by Roman legionaries

GLADIUSES > GLADIUS

GLADLIER > GLAD

GLADLIEST > GLAD

GLADLY > GLAD

GLADNESS > GLAD

GLADS > GLAD

GLADSOME adj joyous or cheerful

GLADSOMER > GLADSOME

GLADSTONE n light four-wheeled horse-drawn vehicle

GLADWRAP n in New Zealand English, thin film for wrapping food ▷ vb cover with gladwrap

GLADWRAPS > GLADWRAP

GLADY > GLADE

GLAIK n prank

GLAIKET same as > GLAIKIT

GLAIKIT adj foolish

GLAIKS > GLAIK

GLAIR n white of egg, esp when used as a size, glaze, or adhesive, usually in bookbinding ▷ vb apply glair to (something)

GLAIRE same as > GLAIR

GLAIRED > GLAIR

GLAIREOUS > GLAIR

GLAIRES > GLAIRE

GLAIRIER > GLAIR

GLAIRIEST > GLAIR

GLAIRIN n viscous deposit found in some mineral waters

GLAIRING > GLAIR

GLAIRINS > GLAIRIN

GLAIRS > GLAIR

GLAIRY > GLAIR

GLAIVE archaic word for > SWORD

GLAIVED adj armed with a sword

GLAIVES > GLAIVE
GLAM n magical illusion ▷ vb make oneself look glamorous
GLAMMED > GLAM
GLAMMIER > GLAMMY
GLAMMIEST > GLAMMY
GLAMMING > GLAM
GLAMMY adj glamorous
GLAMOR same as **>** GLAMOUR
GLAMORED > GLAMOR
GLAMORING > GLAMOR
GLAMORISE same as **>** GLAMORIZE
GLAMORIZE vb cause to be or seem glamorous
GLAMOROUS adj alluring
GLAMORS > GLAMOR
GLAMOUR n alluring charm or fascination ▷ vb bewitch
GLAMOURED adj bewitched
GLAMOURS > GLAMOUR
GLAMPING n camping with luxurious physical comforts
GLAMPINGS > GLAMPING
GLAMS > GLAM
GLANCE vb look rapidly or briefly ▷ n brief look
GLANCED > GLANCE
GLANCER n log or pole used to protect standing trees from damage
GLANCERS > GLANCER
GLANCES > GLANCE
GLANCING > GLANCE
GLANCINGS > GLANCE
GLAND n organ that produces and secretes substances in the body
GLANDERED > GLANDERS
GLANDERS n highly infectious bacterial disease of horses, sometimes transmitted to man
GLANDES > GLANS
GLANDLESS > GLAND
GLANDLIKE > GLAND
GLANDS > GLAND
GLANDULAR adj of or affecting a gland or glands
GLANDULE n small gland
GLANDULES > GLANDULE
GLANS n any small rounded body or glandlike mass, such as the head of the penis
GLARE vb stare angrily ▷ n angry stare ▷ adj smooth and glassy
GLAREAL adj (of a plant) growing in cultivated land
GLARED > GLARE
GLARELESS > GLARE
GLAREOUS adj resembling the white of an egg
GLARES > GLARE
GLARIER > GLARE
GLARIEST > GLARE
GLARINESS > GLARE
GLARING adj conspicuous
GLARINGLY > GLARING
GLARY > GLARE
GLASNOST n policy of

openness and accountability, esp, formerly, in the USSR
GLASNOSTS > GLASNOST
GLASS n hard brittle, usu transparent substance consisting of metal silicates or similar compounds ▷ vb cover with, enclose in, or fit with glass
GLASSED > GLASS
GLASSEN adj glassy
GLASSES npl pair of lenses for correcting faulty vision, in a frame that rests on the nose and hooks behind the ears
GLASSFUL n amount held by a full glass
GLASSFULS > GLASSFUL
GLASSIE same as **>** GLASSY
GLASSIER > GLASSY
GLASSIES > GLASSY
GLASSIEST > GLASSY
GLASSIFY vb turn into glass
GLASSILY > GLASSY
GLASSINE n glazed translucent paper used for book jackets
GLASSINES > GLASSINE
GLASSING > GLASS
GLASSLESS > GLASS
GLASSLIKE > GLASS
GLASSMAN n man whose work is making or selling glassware
GLASSMEN > GLASSMAN
GLASSWARE n articles made of glass
GLASSWORK n production of glassware
GLASSWORM n larva of gnat
GLASSWORT n type of plant of salt marshes, with fleshy stems and scalelike leaves, formerly used in glass-making
GLASSY adj like glass ▷ n glass marble
GLAUCOMA n eye disease
GLAUCOMAS > GLAUCOMA
GLAUCOUS adj covered with a bluish waxy or powdery bloom
GLAUM vb snatch
GLAUMED > GLAUM
GLAUMING > GLAUM
GLAUMS > GLAUM
GLAUR n mud or mire
GLAURIER > GLAUR
GLAURIEST > GLAUR
GLAURS > GLAUR
GLAURY > GLAUR
GLAZE vb fit or cover with glass ▷ n transparent coating
GLAZED > GLAZE
GLAZEN adj glazed
GLAZER > GLAZE
GLAZERS > GLAZE
GLAZES > GLAZE
GLAZIER n person who fits

windows with glass
GLAZIERS > GLAZIER
GLAZIERY > GLAZIER
GLAZIEST > GLAZE
GLAZILY > GLAZE
GLAZINESS > GLAZE
GLAZING n surface of a glazed object
GLAZINGS > GLAZING
GLAZY > GLAZE
GLEAM n small beam or glow of light ▷ vb emit a gleam
GLEAMED > GLEAM
GLEAMER n mirror used to cheat in card games
GLEAMERS > GLEAMER
GLEAMIER > GLEAM
GLEAMIEST > GLEAM
GLEAMING > GLEAM
GLEAMINGS > GLEAM
GLEAMS > GLEAM
GLEAMY > GLEAM
GLEAN vb gather (facts etc) bit by bit
GLEANABLE > GLEAN
GLEANED > GLEAN
GLEANER > GLEAN
GLEANERS > GLEAN
GLEANING > GLEAN
GLEANINGS npl pieces of information that have been gleaned
GLEANS > GLEAN
GLEAVE same as **>** SWORD
GLEAVES > GLEAVE
GLEBA n mass of spores
GLEBAE > GLEBA
GLEBE n land granted to a member of the clergy as part of his or her benefice
GLEBELESS > GLEBE
GLEBES > GLEBE
GLEBIER > GLEBY
GLEBIEST > GLEBY
GLEBOUS adj gleby
GLEBY adj relating to a glebe
GLED n kite
GLEDE same as **>** GLED
GLEDES > GLEDE
GLEDGE vb glance sideways
GLEDGED > GLEDGE
GLEDGES > GLEDGE
GLEDGING > GLEDGE
GLEDS > GLED
GLEE n triumph and delight ▷ vb be full of glee
GLEED n burning ember or hot coal
GLEEDS > GLEED
GLEEFUL adj merry or joyful, esp over someone else's mistake or misfortune
GLEEFULLY > GLEEFUL
GLEEING > GLEE
GLEEK vb jeer
GLEEKED > GLEEK
GLEEKING > GLEEK
GLEEKS > GLEEK
GLEEMAN n minstrel
GLEEMEN > GLEEMAN
GLEENIE n guinea fowl

GLEENIES > GLEENIE
GLEES > GLEE
GLEESOME adj full of glee
GLEET n inflammation of the urethra with a slight discharge of thin pus and mucus: a stage of chronic gonorrhoea ▷ vb discharge gleet
GLEETED > GLEET
GLEETIER > GLEET
GLEETIEST > GLEET
GLEETING > GLEET
GLEETS > GLEET
GLEETY adj gleet
GLEG adj quick
GLEGGER > GLEG
GLEGGEST > GLEG
GLEGLY > GLEG
GLEGNESS > GLEG
GLEI same as **>** GLEY
GLEIS > GLEI
GLEN n deep narrow valley, esp in Scotland
GLENGARRY n brimless Scottish cap with a crease down the crown
GLENLIKE > GLEN
GLENOID adj resembling or having a shallow cavity ▷ n shallow cavity
GLENOIDAL > GLENOID
GLENOIDS > GLENOID
GLENS > GLEN
GLENT same as **>** GLINT
GLENTED > GLENT
GLENTING > GLENT
GLENTS > GLENT
GLEY n bluish-grey compact sticky soil occurring in certain humid regions ▷ vb squint
GLEYED > GLEY
GLEYING > GLEY
GLEYINGS > GLEY
GLEYS > GLEY
GLIA n delicate web of connective tissue that surrounds and supports nerve cells
GLIADIN n protein of cereals, esp wheat, with a high proline content: forms a sticky mass with water that binds flour into dough
GLIADINE same as **>** GLIADIN
GLIADINES > GLIADINE
GLIADINS > GLIADIN
GLIAL > GLIA
GLIAS > GLIA
GLIB adj fluent but insincere or superficial ▷ vb castrate
GLIBBED > GLIB
GLIBBER > GLIB
GLIBBERY adj slippery
GLIBBEST > GLIB
GLIBBING > GLIB
GLIBLY > GLIB
GLIBNESS > GLIB
GLIBS > GLIB
GLID adj moving smoothly and easily

GLIDDER > GLID

GLIDDERY adj slippery

GLIDDEST > GLID

GLIDE vb move easily and smoothly ▷ n smooth easy movement

GLIDED > GLIDE

GLIDEPATH n path followed by aircraft coming in to land

GLIDER n flying phalanger

GLIDERS > GLIDER

GLIDES > GLIDE

GLIDING n sport of flying gliders

GLIDINGLY > GLIDE

GLIDINGS > GLIDING

GLIFF n slap

GLIFFING > GLIFF

GLIFFINGS > GLIFF

GLIFFS > GLIFF

GLIFT n moment

GLIFTS > GLIFT

GLIKE same as > GLEEK

GLIKES > GLIKE

GLIM n light or lamp

GLIME vb glance sideways

GLIMED > GLIME

GLIMES > GLIME

GLIMING > GLIME

GLIMMER vb shine faintly, flicker ▷ n faint gleam

GLIMMERED > GLIMMER

GLIMMERS > GLIMMER

GLIMMERY > GLIMMER

GLIMPSE n brief or incomplete view ▷ vb catch a glimpse of

GLIMPSED > GLIMPSE

GLIMPSER > GLIMPSE

GLIMPSERS > GLIMPSE

GLIMPSES > GLIMPSE

GLIMPSING > GLIMPSE

GLIMS > GLIM

GLINT vb gleam brightly ▷ n bright gleam

GLINTED > GLINT

GLINTIER > GLINT

GLINTIEST > GLINT

GLINTING > GLINT

GLINTS > GLINT

GLINTY > GLINT

GLIOMA n tumour of the brain and spinal cord, composed of neuroglia cells and fibres

GLIOMAS > GLIOMA

GLIOMATA > GLIOMA

GLIOSES > GLIOSIS

GLIOSIS n process leading to scarring in the central nervous system

GLISK n glimpse

GLISKS > GLISK

GLISSADE n gliding step in ballet ▷ vb perform a glissade

GLISSADED > GLISSADE

GLISSADER > GLISSADE

GLISSADES > GLISSADE

GLISSANDI > GLISSANDO

GLISSANDO n slide between two notes in

which all intermediate notes are played

GLISTEN vb gleam by reflecting light ▷ n gleam or gloss

GLISTENED > GLISTEN

GLISTENS > GLISTEN

GLISTER archaic word for > GLITTER

GLISTERED > GLISTER

GLISTERS > GLISTER

GLIT n slimy matter

GLITCH n small problem that stops something from working properly

GLITCHES > GLITCH

GLITCHIER > GLITCH

GLITCHY > GLITCH

GLITS > GLIT

GLITTER vb shine with bright flashes ▷ n sparkle or brilliance

GLITTERED > GLITTER

GLITTERS > GLITTER

GLITTERY > GLITTER

GLITZ n ostentatious showiness ▷ vb make something more attractive

GLITZED > GLITZ

GLITZES > GLITZ

GLITZIER > GLITZY

GLITZIEST > GLITZY

GLITZILY > GLITZY

GLITZING > GLITZ

GLITZY adj showily attractive

GLOAM n dusk

GLOAMING n twilight

GLOAMINGS > GLOAMING

GLOAMS > GLOAM

GLOAT vb regard one's own good fortune or the misfortune of others with smug or malicious pleasure ▷ n act of gloating

GLOATED > GLOAT

GLOATER > GLOAT

GLOATERS > GLOAT

GLOATING > GLOAT

GLOATS > GLOAT

GLOB n rounded mass of thick fluid

GLOBAL adj worldwide

GLOBALISE same as > GLOBALIZE

GLOBALISM n policy which is worldwide in scope

GLOBALIST > GLOBALISM

GLOBALIZE vb put (something) into effect worldwide

GLOBALLY > GLOBAL

GLOBATE adj shaped like a globe

GLOBATED same as > GLOBATE

GLOBBIER > GLOBBY

GLOBBIEST > GLOBBY

GLOBBY adj thick and lumpy

GLOBE n sphere with a map of the earth on it ▷ vb form

or cause to form into a globe

GLOBED > GLOBE

GLOBEFISH another name for > PUFFER

GLOBELIKE > GLOBE

GLOBES > GLOBE

GLOBESITY n informal word for obesity seen as a worldwide social problem

GLOBETROT vb regularly travel internationally

GLOBI > GLOBUS

GLOBIN n protein component of the pigments myoglobin and haemoglobin

GLOBING > GLOBE

GLOBINS > GLOBIN

GLOBOID adj shaped approximately like a globe ▷ n globoid body, such as any of those occurring in certain plant granules

GLOBOIDS > GLOBOID

GLOBOSE adj spherical or approximately spherical ▷ n globose object

GLOBOSELY > GLOBOSE

GLOBOSITY > GLOBOSE

GLOBOUS same as > GLOBOSE

GLOBS > GLOB

GLOBULAR adj shaped like a globe or globule ▷ n globular star cluster

GLOBULARS > GLOBULAR

GLOBULE n small round drop

GLOBULES > GLOBULE

GLOBULET n small globule

GLOBULETS > GLOBULET

GLOBULIN n simple protein found in living tissue

GLOBULINS > GLOBULIN

GLOBULITE n spherical form of crystallite

GLOBULOUS same as > GLOBULAR

GLOBUS n any spherelike structure

GLOBY adj round

GLOCHID n barbed spine on a plant

GLOCHIDIA n plural form of singular glochidium, a barbed hair on some plants

GLOCHIDS > GLOCHID

GLODE > GLIDE

GLOGG n hot alcoholic mixed drink, originally from Sweden, consisting of sweetened brandy, red wine, bitters or other flavourings, and blanched almonds

GLOGGS > GLOGG

GLOIRE n glory

GLOIRES > GLOIRE

GLOM vb attach oneself to or associate oneself with

GLOMERA > GLOMUS

GLOMERATE adj gathered into a compact rounded

mass ▷ vb wind into a ball

GLOMERULE n cymose inflorescence in the form of a ball-like cluster of flowers

GLOMERULI n plural of singular glomerulus: a knot of blood vessels in the kidney

GLOMMED > GLOM

GLOMMING > GLOM

GLOMS > GLOM

GLOMUS n small anastomosis in an artery or vein

GLONOIN n nitroglycerin

GLONOINS > GLONOIN

GLOOM n melancholy or depression ▷ vb look sullen or depressed

GLOOMED > GLOOM

GLOOMFUL > GLOOM

GLOOMIER > GLOOMY

GLOOMIEST > GLOOMY

GLOOMILY > GLOOMY

GLOOMING > GLOOM

GLOOMINGS > GLOOM

GLOOMLESS > GLOOM

GLOOMS > GLOOM

GLOOMY adj despairing or sad

GLOOP vb cover with a viscous substance

GLOOPED > GLOOP

GLOOPIER > GLOOP

GLOOPIEST > GLOOP

GLOOPING > GLOOP

GLOOPS > GLOOP

GLOOPY > GLOOP

GLOP vb cover with a viscous substance

GLOPPED > GLOP

GLOPPIER > GLOP

GLOPPIEST > GLOP

GLOPPING > GLOP

GLOPPY > GLOP

GLOPS > GLOP

GLORIA n silk, wool, cotton, or nylon fabric used esp for umbrellas

GLORIAS > GLORIA

GLORIED > GLORY

GLORIES > GLORY

GLORIFIED > GLORIFY

GLORIFIER > GLORIFY

GLORIFIES > GLORIFY

GLORIFY vb make (something) seem more worthy than it is

GLORIOLE another name for a > HALO

GLORIOLES > GLORIOLE

GLORIOSA n bulbous African tropical plant

GLORIOSAS > GLORIOSA

GLORIOUS adj brilliantly beautiful

GLORY n praise or honour ▷ vb triumph or exalt

GLORYING > GLORY

GLOSS n surface shine or lustre ▷ vb make glossy

GLOSSA n paired tonguelike lobe in the labium of an insect

GLOSSAE >GLOSSA

GLOSSAL >GLOSSA

GLOSSARY n list of special or technical words with definitions

GLOSSAS >GLOSSA

GLOSSATOR n writer of glosses and commentaries, esp (in the Middle Ages) an interpreter of Roman and Canon Law

GLOSSED >GLOSS

GLOSSEME n smallest meaningful unit of a language, such as stress, form, etc

GLOSSEMES >GLOSSEME

GLOSSER >GLOSS

GLOSSERS >GLOSS

GLOSSES >GLOSS

GLOSSIER >GLOSSY

GLOSSIES >GLOSSY

GLOSSIEST >GLOSSY

GLOSSILY >GLOSSY

GLOSSINA n tsetse fly

GLOSSINAS >GLOSSINA

GLOSSING >GLOSS

GLOSSIST same as >GLOSSATOR

GLOSSISTS >GLOSSIST

GLOSSITIC >GLOSSITIS

GLOSSITIS n inflammation of the tongue

GLOSSLESS >GLOSS

GLOSSY adj smooth and shiny ▷ n expensively produced magazine

GLOST n lead glaze used for pottery

GLOSTS >GLOST

GLOTTAL adj of the glottis

GLOTTIC adj of or relating to the tongue or the glottis

GLOTTIDES >GLOTTIS

GLOTTIS n vocal cords and the space between them

GLOTTISES >GLOTTIS

GLOUT vb look sullen

GLOUTED >GLOUT

GLOUTING >GLOUT

GLOUTS >GLOUT

GLOVE n covering for the hand with individual sheaths for each finger and the thumb

GLOVED >GLOVE

GLOVELESS >GLOVE

GLOVER n person who makes or sells gloves

GLOVERS >GLOVER

GLOVES >GLOVE

GLOVING >GLOVE

GLOVINGS >GLOVE

GLOW vb emit light and heat without flames ▷ n glowing light

GLOWED >GLOW

GLOWER n scowl ▷ vb stare angrily

GLOWERED >GLOWER

GLOWERING >GLOWER

GLOWERS >GLOWER

GLOWFLIES >GLOWFLY

GLOWFLY n firefly

GLOWING adj full of praise

GLOWINGLY >GLOWING

GLOWLAMP n small light consisting of two or more electrodes in an inert gas

GLOWLAMPS >GLOWLAMP

GLOWS >GLOW

GLOWSTICK n plastic tube containing a luminescent material, waved or held aloft esp at gigs, raves, etc

GLOWWORM n European beetle, the females and larvae of which bear luminescent organs producing a greenish light

GLOWWORMS >GLOWWORM

GLOXINIA n tropical plant with large bell-shaped flowers

GLOXINIAS >GLOXINIA

GLOZE vb explain away ▷ n flattery or deceit

GLOZED >GLOZE

GLOZES >GLOZE

GLOZING >GLOZE

GLOZINGS >GLOZE

GLUCAGON n polypeptide hormone, produced in the pancreas by the islets of Langerhans, that stimulates the release of glucose into the blood

GLUCAGONS >GLUCAGON

GLUCAN n any polysaccharide consisting of a polymer of glucose, such as cellulose or starch

GLUCANS >GLUCAN

GLUCINA n oxide of glucinum

GLUCINAS >GLUCINA

GLUCINIC >GLUCINIUM

GLUCINIUM former name of >BERYLLIUM

GLUCINUM same as >GLUCINIUM

GLUCINUMS >GLUCINUM

GLUCONATE n compound formed when a mineral is bound to gluconic acid

GLUCOSE n kind of sugar found in fruit

GLUCOSES >GLUCOSE

GLUCOSIC >GLUCOSE

GLUCOSIDE n any of a large group of glycosides that yield glucose on hydrolysis

GLUE n natural or synthetic sticky substance used as an adhesive ▷ vb fasten with glue

GLUEBALL n hypothetical composite subatomic particle

GLUEBALLS >GLUEBALL

GLUED >GLUE

GLUEING >GLUE

GLUELIKE >GLUE

GLUEPOT n container for holding glue

GLUEPOTS >GLUEPOT

GLUER >GLUE

GLUERS >GLUE

GLUES >GLUE

GLUEY >GLUE

GLUEYNESS >GLUE

GLUG n word representing a gurgling sound, as of liquid being poured from a bottle or swallowed ▷ vb drink noisily, taking big gulps

GLUGGABLE adj (of wine) easy and pleasant to drink

GLUGGED >GLUG

GLUGGING >GLUG

GLUGS >GLUG

GLUHWEIN n mulled wine

GLUHWEINS >GLUHWEIN

GLUIER >GLUE

GLUIEST >GLUE

GLUILY >GLUE

GLUINESS >GLUE

GLUING >GLUE

GLUISH >GLUE

GLUM adj sullen or gloomy

GLUME n one of a pair of dry membranous bracts at the base of the spikelet of grasses

GLUMELIKE >GLUME

GLUMELLA n palea

GLUMELLAS >GLUMELLA

GLUMES >GLUME

GLUMLY >GLUM

GLUMMER >GLUM

GLUMMEST >GLUM

GLUMNESS >GLUM

GLUMPIER >GLUMPY

GLUMPIEST >GLUMPY

GLUMPILY >GLUMPY

GLUMPISH >GLUMPY

GLUMPS n state of sulking

GLUMPY adj sullen

GLUMS n gloomy feelings

GLUNCH vb look sullen

GLUNCHED >GLUNCH

GLUNCHES >GLUNCH

GLUNCHING >GLUNCH

GLUON n hypothetical particle believed to be exchanged between quarks in order to bind them together to form particles

GLUONS >GLUON

GLURGE n stories, often sent by email, that are supposed to be true and uplifting, but which are often fabricated and sentimental

GLURGES >GLURGE

GLUT n excessive supply ▷ vb oversupply

GLUTAEAL >GLUTAEUS

GLUTAEI >GLUTAEUS

GLUTAEUS same as >GLUTEUS

GLUTAMATE n any salt of glutamic acid, esp its sodium salt

GLUTAMIC as in glutamic acid nonessential amino acid that plays a part in nitrogen metabolism

GLUTAMINE n

nonessential amino acid occurring in proteins: plays an important role in protein metabolism

GLUTE n same as >GLUTEUS

GLUTEAL >GLUTEUS

GLUTEI >GLUTEUS

GLUTELIN n any of a group of water-insoluble plant proteins found in cereals. They are precipitated by alcohol and are not coagulated by heat

GLUTELINS >GLUTELIN

GLUTEN n protein found in cereal grain

GLUTENIN n type of protein

GLUTENINS >GLUTENIN

GLUTENOUS >GLUTEN

GLUTENS >GLUTEN

GLUTES >GLUTE

GLUTEUS n any of the three muscles of the buttock

GLUTINOUS adj sticky or gluey

GLUTS >GLUT

GLUTTED >GLUT

GLUTTING >GLUT

GLUTTON n greedy person

GLUTTONS >GLUTTON

GLUTTONY n practice of eating too much

GLYCAEMIA n presence of glucose in blood

GLYCAEMIC >GLYCAEMIA

GLYCAN n polysaccharide

GLYCANS >GLYCAN

GLYCATION n the bonding of a sugar molecule to a protein or lipid

GLYCEMIA US spelling of >GLYCAEMIA

GLYCEMIAS >GLYCEMIA

GLYCEMIC >GLYCEMIA

GLYCERIA n manna grass

GLYCERIAS >GLYCERIA

GLYCERIC adj of, containing, or derived from glycerol

GLYCERIDE n any fatty-acid ester of glycerol

GLYCERIN same as >GLYCEROL

GLYCERINE same as >GLYCEROL

GLYCERINS >GLYCERIN

GLYCEROL n colourless odourless syrupy liquid obtained from animal and vegetable fats, used as a solvent, antifreeze, and sweetener, and in explosives

GLYCEROLS >GLYCEROL

GLYCERYL n (something) derived from glycerol by replacing or removing one or more of its hydroxyl groups

GLYCERYLS >GLYCERYL

GLYCIN same as >GLYCINE

g

GLYCINE n nonessential amino acid occurring in most proteins
GLYCINES > GLYCINE
GLYCINS > GLYCIN
GLYCOCOLL n glycine
GLYCOGEN n starchlike carbohydrate stored in the liver and muscles of humans and animals
GLYCOGENS > GLYCOGEN
GLYCOL n another name (not in technical usage) for or a diol
GLYCOLIC > GLYCOL
GLYCOLLIC > GLYCOL
GLYCOLS > GLYCOL
GLYCONIC n verse consisting of a spondee, choriamb and pyrrhic
GLYCONICS > GLYCONIC
GLYCOSE n any of various monosaccharides
GLYCOSES > GLYCOSE
GLYCOSIDE n any of a group of substances, such as digitoxin, derived from monosaccharides by replacing the hydroxyl group by another group
GLYCOSYL n glucose-derived radical
GLYCOSYLS > GLYCOSYL
GLYCYL n radical of glycine
GLYCYLS > GLYCYL
GLYPH n carved channel or groove, esp a vertical one as used on a Doric frieze
GLYPHIC > GLYPH
GLYPHS > GLYPH
GLYPTAL n alkyd resin obtained from polyhydric alcohols and polybasic organic acids or their anhydrides
GLYPTALS > GLYPTAL
GLYPTIC adj of or relating to engraving or carving, esp on precious stones
GLYPTICS n art of engraving precious stones
GMELINITE n zeolitic mineral
GNAMMA variant of > NAMMA
GNAR same as > GNARL
GNARL n any knotty protuberance or swelling on a tree ▷ vb knot or cause to knot
GNARLED adj rough, twisted, and knobbly
GNARLIER > GNARLY
GNARLIEST > GNARLY
GNARLING > GNARL
GNARLS > GNARL
GNARLY adj good
GNARR same as > GNARL
GNARRED > GNARR
GNARRING > GNARR
GNARRS > GNARR
GNARS > GNAR
GNASH vb grind (the teeth) together in anger or pain ▷ n act of gnashing the teeth

GNASHED > GNASH
GNASHER n tooth
GNASHERS npl teeth, esp false ones
GNASHES > GNASH
GNASHING > GNASH
GNASHINGS > GNASHING
GNAT n small biting two-winged fly
GNATHAL same as > GNATHIC
GNATHIC adj of or relating to the jaw
GNATHION n lowest point of the midline of the lower jaw: a reference point in craniometry
GNATHIONS > GNATHION
GNATHITE n appendage of an arthropod that is specialized for grasping or chewing
GNATHITES > GNATHITE
GNATHONIC adj deceitfully flattering
GNATLIKE > GNAT
GNATLING n small gnat
GNATLINGS > GNATLING
GNATS > GNAT
GNATTIER > GNATTY
GNATTIEST > GNATTY
GNATTY adj infested with gnats
GNATWREN n small bird of the gnatcatcher family
GNATWRENS > GNATWREN
GNAW vb bite or chew steadily ▷ n act or an instance of gnawing
GNAWABLE > GNAW
GNAWED > GNAW
GNAWER > GNAW
GNAWERS > GNAW
GNAWING > GNAW
GNAWINGLY > GNAW
GNAWINGS > GNAW
GNAWN > GNAW
GNAWS > GNAW
GNEISS n coarse-grained metamorphic rock
GNEISSES > GNEISS
GNEISSIC > GNEISS
GNEISSOID > GNEISS
GNEISSOSE > GNEISS
GNOCCHI n dumplings made of pieces of semolina pasta, or sometimes potato, used to garnish soup or served alone with sauce
GNOMAE > GNOME
GNOME n imaginary creature like a little old man
GNOMELIKE > GNOME
GNOMES > GNOME
GNOMIC adj of pithy sayings
GNOMICAL same as > GNOMIC
GNOMISH > GNOME
GNOMIST n writer of pithy sayings
GNOMISTS > GNOMIST
GNOMON n stationary arm that projects the shadow

on a sundial
GNOMONIC > GNOMON
GNOMONICS > GNOMON
GNOMONS > GNOMON
GNOSES > GNOSIS
GNOSIS n supposedly revealed knowledge of various spiritual truths, esp that said to have been possessed by ancient Gnostics
GNOSTIC adj of, relating to, or possessing knowledge, esp esoteric spiritual knowledge ▷ n one who knows
GNOSTICAL same as > GNOSTIC
GNOSTICS > GNOSTIC
GNOW n Australian wild bird
GNOWS > GNOW
GNU n ox-like S African antelope
GNUS > GNU
GO vb move to or from a place ▷ n attempt
GOA n Tibetan gazelle with a brownish-grey coat and backward-curving horns
GOAD vb provoke (someone) to take some kind of action, usu in anger ▷ n spur or provocation
GOADED > GOAD
GOADING > GOAD
GOADLIKE > GOAD
GOADS > GOAD
GOADSMAN n person who uses a goad
GOADSMEN > GOADSMAN
GOADSTER n goadsman
GOADSTERS > GOADSTER
GOAF n waste left in old mine workings
GOAFS > GOAF
GOAL n posts through which the ball or puck has to be propelled to score ▷ vb in rugby, to convert a try into a goal
GOALBALL n game played by two teams who compete to score goals by throwing a ball that emits audible sound when in motion. Players, who may be blind or sighted, are blindfolded during play
GOALBALLS > GOALBALL
GOALED > GOAL
GOALIE n goalkeeper
GOALIES > GOALIE
GOALING > GOAL
GOALLESS > GOAL
GOALMOUTH n area in front of the goal
GOALPOST n one of the two posts marking the limit of a goal
GOALPOSTS > GOALPOST
GOALS > GOAL
GOALWARD adv towards a goal
GOALWARDS > GOALWARD
GOANNA n large Australian

lizard
GOANNAS > GOANNA
GOARY variant spelling of > GORY
GOAS > GOA
GOAT n sure-footed ruminant animal with horns
GOATEE n pointed tuft-like beard
GOATEED > GOATEE
GOATEES > GOATEE
GOATFISH n red mullet
GOATHERD n person who looks after a herd of goats
GOATHERDS > GOATHERD
GOATIER > GOAT
GOATIEST > GOAT
GOATISH adj of, like, or relating to a goat
GOATISHLY > GOATISH
GOATLIKE > GOAT
GOATLING n young goat
GOATLINGS > GOATLING
GOATS > GOAT
GOATSKIN n leather made from the skin of a goat
GOATSKINS > GOATSKIN
GOATWEED n plant of the genus Capraria
GOATWEEDS > GOATWEED
GOATY > GOAT
GOB n lump of a soft substance ▷ vb spit
GOBAN n board on which go is played
GOBANG n Japanese board-game
GOBANGS > GOBANG
GOBANS > GOBAN
GOBAR as in gobar numeral kind of numeral
GOBBED > GOB
GOBBELINE same as > GOBLIN
GOBBET n lump, esp of food
GOBBETS > GOBBET
GOBBI > GOBBO
GOBBIER > GOBBY
GOBBIEST > GOBBY
GOBBING > GOB
GOBBLE vb eat hastily and greedily ▷ n rapid gurgling cry of the male turkey ▷ interj imitation of this sound
GOBBLED > GOBBLE
GOBBLER n turkey
GOBBLERS > GOBBLER
GOBBLES > GOBBLE
GOBBLING > GOBBLE
GOBBO n hunchback
GOBBY adj loudmouthed and offensive
GOBI n (in Indian cookery) cauliflower
GOBIES > GOBY
GOBIID n member of the genus Gobius
GOBIIDS > GOBIID
GOBIOID n type of spiny-finned fish of the suborder which includes the goby and mudskipper

GOBIOIDS > GOBIOID

GOBIS > GOBI

GOBLET n drinking cup without handles

GOBLETS > GOBLET

GOBLIN n (in folklore) small malevolent creature

GOBLINS > GOBLIN

GOBO n shield placed around a microphone to exclude unwanted sounds

GOBOES > GOBO

GOBONEE same as > GOBONY

GOBONY adj in heraldry, composed of a row of small, alternately-coloured, squares

GOBOS > GOBO

GOBS > GOB

GOBSHITE n stupid person

GOBSHITES > GOBSHITE

GOBURRA n kookaburra

GOBURRAS > GOBURRA

GOBY n small spiny-finned fish

GOD n spirit or being worshipped as having supernatural power ▷ vb deify

GODCHILD n child for whom a person stands as godparent

GODDAM vb damn

GODDAMMED > GODDAM

GODDAMN interj oath expressing anger, surprise, etc ▷ adj extremely ▷ vb damn

GODDAMNED > GODDAMN

GODDAMNS > GODDAMN

GODDAMS > GODDAM

GODDED > GOD

GODDEN n evening greeting

GODDENS > GODDEN

GODDESS n female divinity

GODDESSES > GODDESS

GODDING > GOD

GODET n triangular piece of material inserted into a garment, such as into a skirt to create a flare

GODETIA n plant with showy flowers

GODETIAS > GODETIA

GODETS > GODET

GODFATHER n male godparent ▷ vb be a godfather to

GODHEAD n essential nature and condition of being a god

GODHEADS > GODHEAD

GODHOOD n state of being divine

GODHOODS > GODHOOD

GODLESS adj wicked or unprincipled

GODLESSLY > GODLESS

GODLIER > GODLY

GODLIEST > GODLY

GODLIKE adj resembling or befitting a god or God

GODLILY > GODLY

GODLINESS > GODLY

GODLING n little god

GODLINGS > GODLING

GODLY adj devout or pious

GODMOTHER n female godparent

GODOWN n (in East Asia and India) warehouse

GODOWNS > GODOWN

GODPARENT n person who promises at a child's baptism to bring the child up as a Christian

GODROON same as > GADROON

GODROONED > GODROON

GODROONS > GODROON

GODS > GOD

GODSEND n something unexpected but welcome

GODSENDS > GODSEND

GODSHIP n divinity

GODSHIPS > GODSHIP

GODSLOT n time in a television or radio schedule traditionally reserved for religious broadcasts

GODSLOTS > GODSLOT

GODSO same as > GADSO

GODSON n male godchild

GODSONS > GODSON

GODSPEED n expression of one's good wishes for a person's success and safety

GODSPEEDS > GODSPEED

GODSQUAD n informal, sometimes derogatory term for any group of evangelical Christians, members of which are regarded as intrusive and exuberantly pious

GODSQUADS > GODSQUAD

GODWARD adv towards God

GODWARDS same as > GODWARD

GODWIT n shore bird with long legs and an upturned bill

GODWITS > GODWIT

GOE same as > GO

GOEL n in Jewish law, blood-avenger

GOELS > GOEL

GOER n person who attends something regularly

GOERS > GOER

GOES > GO

GOEST vb archaic 2nd person sing present of go

GOETH vb archaic 3rd person sing present of go

GOETHITE n black, brown, or yellow mineral consisting of hydrated iron oxide in the form of orthorhombic crystals or fibrous masses

GOETHITES > GOETHITE

GOETIC > GOETY

GOETIES > GOETY

GOETY n witchcraft

GOEY adj go-ahead

GOFER n employee or assistant whose duties include menial tasks such as running errands

GOFERS > GOFER

GOFF obsolete variant of > GOLF

GOFFED > GOFF

GOFFER vb press pleats into (a frill) ▷ n ornamental frill made by pressing pleats

GOFFERED > GOFFER

GOFFERING > GOFFER

GOFFERS > GOFFER

GOFFING > GOFF

GOFFS > GOFF

GOGGA n any small insect

GOGGAS > GOGGA

GOGGLE vb (of the eyes) bulge ▷ n fixed or bulging stare

GOGGLEBOX n television set

GOGGLED > GOGGLE

GOGGLER n big-eyed scad

GOGGLERS > GOGGLER

GOGGLES > GOGGLE

GOGGLIER > GOGGLE

GOGGLIEST > GOGGLE

GOGGLING > GOGGLE

GOGGLINGS > GOGGLE

GOGGLY > GOGGLE

GOGLET n long-necked water-cooling vessel of porous earthenware, used esp in India

GOGLETS > GOGLET

GOGO n disco

GOGOS > GOGO

GOHONZON n (in Nichiren Buddhism) paper scroll to which devotional chanting is directed

GOHONZONS > GOHONZON

GOIER > GOEY

GOIEST > GOEY

GOING > GO

GOINGS > GO

GOITER same as > GOITRE

GOITERED > GOITER

GOITERS > GOITER

GOITRE n swelling of the thyroid gland in the neck

GOITRED > GOITRE

GOITRES > GOITRE

GOITROGEN n substance that induces the formation of a goitre

GOITROUS > GOITRE

GOJI same as > WOLFBERRY

GOJIS > GOJI

GOLCONDA n source of wealth or riches, esp a mine

GOLCONDAS > GOLCONDA

GOLD n yellow precious metal ▷ adj made of gold

GOLDARN euphemistic variant of > GODDAMN

GOLDARNS > GODDAMN

GOLDBRICK vb swindle

GOLDBUG n American beetle with a bright metallic lustre

GOLDBUGS > GOLDBUG

GOLDCREST n small bird with a yellow crown

GOLDEN adj made of gold ▷ vb gild

GOLDENED > GOLDEN

GOLDENER > GOLDEN

GOLDENEST > GOLDEN

GOLDENEYE n type of black-and-white diving duck of northern regions

GOLDENING > GOLDEN

GOLDENLY > GOLDEN

GOLDENROD n tall plant with spikes of small yellow flowers

GOLDENS > GOLDEN

GOLDER > GOLD

GOLDEST > GOLD

GOLDEYE n N American fish with yellowish eyes, silvery sides, and a dark blue back

GOLDEYES > GOLDEYE

GOLDFIELD n area in which there are gold deposits

GOLDFINCH n kind of finch, the male of which has yellow-and-black wings

GOLDFINNY same as > GOLDSINNY

GOLDFISH n orange fish kept in ponds or aquariums

GOLDIER > GOLDY

GOLDIEST > GOLDY

GOLDISH > GOLD

GOLDLESS > GOLD

GOLDMINER n miner who works in a gold mine

GOLDS > GOLD

GOLDSINNY n small European fish

GOLDSIZE n adhesive used to fix gold leaf to a surface

GOLDSIZES > GOLDSIZE

GOLDSMITH n dealer in or maker of gold articles

GOLDSPINK n goldfinch

GOLDSTICK n colonel in the Life Guards who carries out ceremonial duties

GOLDSTONE n dark-coloured glass, usually green or brown, spangled with fine particles of gold, copper, or some other metal

GOLDTAIL as in goldtail moth European moth with white wings and a soft white furry body with a yellow tail tuft

GOLDTONE adj gold-coloured

GOLDURN variant of > GODDAMN

GOLDURNS > GOLDURN

GOLDWORK n gold objects collectively

GOLDWORKS > GOLDWORK

GOLDY adj gold-like

GOLE obsolete spelling of > GOAL

GOLEM n (in Jewish legend) artificially created human being brought to life by supernatural means

g

GOLEMS > GOLEM

GOLES > GOLE

GOLF n outdoor game in which a ball is struck with clubs into a series of holes ▷ vb play golf

GOLFED > GOLF

GOLFER n person who plays golf

GOLFERS > GOLFER

GOLFIANA n golfing collectibles

GOLFIANAS > GOLFIANA

GOLFING > GOLF

GOLFINGS > GOLF

GOLFS > GOLF

GOLGOTHA n place of burial

GOLGOTHAS > GOLGOTHA

GOLIARD n one of a number of wandering scholars in 12th- and 13th-century Europe famed for their riotous behaviour, intemperance, and composition of satirical and ribald Latin verse

GOLIARDIC > GOLIARD

GOLIARDS > GOLIARD

GOLIARDY > GOLIARD

GOLIAS vb behave outrageously

GOLIASED > GOLIAS

GOLIASES > GOLIAS

GOLIASING > GOLIAS

GOLIATH n giant

GOLIATHS > GOLIATH

GOLLAN n yellow flower

GOLLAND same as > GOLLAN

GOLLANDS > GOLLAND

GOLLANS > GOLLAN

GOLLAR same as > GOLLER

GOLLARED > GOLLAR

GOLLARING > GOLLAR

GOLLARS > GOLLAR

GOLLER vb roar

GOLLERED > GOLLER

GOLLERING > GOLLER

GOLLERS > GOLLER

GOLLIED > GOLLY

GOLLIES > GOLLY

GOLLIWOG n soft black-faced doll

GOLLIWOGG same as > GOLLIWOG

GOLLIWOGS > GOLLIWOG

GOLLIWOGS > GOLLIWOG

GOLLOP vb eat or drink (something) quickly or greedily

GOLLOPED > GOLLOP

GOLLOPER > GOLLOP

GOLLOPERS > GOLLOP

GOLLOPING > GOLLOP

GOLLOPS > GOLLOP

GOLLY interj exclamation of mild surprise ▷ n short for golliwog: used chiefly by children ▷ vb spit

GOLLYING > GOLLY

GOLLYWOG same as > GOLLIWOG

GOLLYWOGS > GOLLYWOG

GOLOMYNKA n oily fish found only in Lake Baikal

GOLOSH same as > GALOSH

GOLOSHE same as > GALOSH

GOLOSHED > GOLOSH

GOLOSHES > GOLOSH

GOLOSHING > GOLOSH

GOLOSHOES > GOLOSH

GOLP same as > GOLPE

GOLPE n in heraldry, a purple circle

GOLPES > GOLPE

GOLPS > GOLP

GOMBEEN n usury

GOMBEENS > GOMBEEN

GOMBO same as > GUMBO

GOMBOS > GOMBO

GOMBRO same as > GUMBO

GOMBROON n Persian and Chinese pottery and porcelain wares

GOMBROONS > GOMBROON

GOMBROS > GOMBRO

GOMER n unwanted hospital patient

GOMERAL same as > GOMERIL

GOMERALS > GOMERAL

GOMEREL same as > GOMERIL

GOMERELS > GOMEREL

GOMERIL n slow-witted or stupid person

GOMERILS > GOMERIL

GOMERS > GOMER

GOMOKU another word for > GOBANG

GOMOKUS > GOMOKU

GOMPA n Tibetan monastery

GOMPAS > GOMPA

GOMPHOSES > GOMPHOSIS

GOMPHOSIS n form of immovable articulation in which a peglike part fits into a cavity, as in the setting of a tooth in its socket

GOMUTI n E Indian feather palm whose sweet sap is a source of sugar

GOMUTIS > GOMUTI

GOMUTO same as > GOMUTI

GOMUTOS > GOMUTO

GON n geometrical grade

GONAD n organ producing reproductive cells, such as a testicle or ovary

GONADAL > GONAD

GONADIAL > GONAD

GONADIC > GONAD

GONADS > GONAD

GONDELAY same as > GONDOLA

GONDELAYS > GONDELAY

GONDOLA n long narrow boat used in Venice

GONDOLAS > GONDOLA

GONDOLIER n person who propels a gondola

GONE > GO

GONEF same as > GANEF

GONEFS > GONEF

GONENESS n faintness

from hunger

GONER n person or thing beyond help or recovery

GONERS > GONER

GONFALON n banner hanging from a crossbar, used esp by certain medieval Italian republics or in ecclesiastical processions

GONFALONS > GONFALON

GONFANON same as > GONFALON

GONFANONS > GONFANON

GONG n rimmed metal disc that produces a note when struck ▷ vb sound a gong

GONGED > GONG

GONGING > GONG

GONGLIKE > GONG

GONGS > GONG

GONGSTER n person who strikes a gong

GONGSTERS > GONGSTER

GONGYO n (in Nichiren Buddhism) ceremony, performed twice a day, involving reciting parts of the Lotus Sutra and chanting the Daimoku to the Gohonzon

GONGYOS > GONGYO

GONIA > GONION

GONIATITE n type of extinct cephalopod mollusc similar to an ammonite

GONIDIA > GONIDIUM

GONIDIAL > GONIDIUM

GONIDIC > GONIDIUM

GONIDIUM n green algal cell in the thallus of a lichen

GONIF same as > GANEF

GONIFF same as > GANEF

GONIFFS > GONIFF

GONIFS > GONIF

GONION n point or apex of the angle of the lower jaw

GONIUM n immature reproductive cell

GONK n stuffed toy, often used as a mascot

GONKS > GONK

GONNA vb going to

GONOCOCCI n plural of singular gonococcus: bacterium that causes gonorrhea

GONOCYTE n oocyte or spermatocyte

GONOCYTES > GONOCYTE

GONODUCT n duct leading from a gonad to the exterior, through which gametes pass

GONODUCTS > GONODUCT

GONOF same as > GANEF

GONOFS > GANOF

GONOPH same as > GANEF

GONOPHS > GONOPH

GONOPOD n either member of a pair of appendages that are the external

reproductive organs of insects and some other arthropods

GONOPODS > GONOPOD

GONOPORE n external pore in insects, earthworms, etc, through which the gametes are extruded

GONOPORES > GONOPORE

GONORRHEA n infectious venereal disease

GONOSOME n individuals, collectively, in a colonial animal that are involved with reproduction

GONOSOMES > GONOSOME

GONS > GON

GONYS n lower outline of a bird's bill

GONYSES > GONYS

GONZO adj wild or crazy

GOO n sticky substance

GOOBER another name for > PEANUT

GOOBERS > GOOBER

GOOBIES > GOOBY

GOOBY n spittle

GOOD adj giving pleasure ▷ n benefit

GOODBY same as > GOODBYE

GOODBYE n expression used on parting ▷ interj expression used on parting ▷ sentence substitute farewell: a conventional expression used at leave-taking or parting with people and at the loss or rejection of things or ideas

GOODBYES > GOODBYE

GOODBYS > GOODBY

GOODFACED adj with a handsome face

GOODFELLA n gangster, esp one in the Mafia

GOODIE same as > GOODY

GOODIER > GOODY

GOODIES > GOODY

GOODIEST > GOODY

GOODINESS > GOODY

GOODISH > GOOD

GOODLIER > GOODLY

GOODLIEST > GOODLY

GOODLY adj considerable

GOODMAN n husband

GOODMEN > GOODMAN

GOODNESS n quality of being good ▷ interj exclamation of surprise

GOODNIGHT n conventional expression of farewell used in the evening or at night

GOODS > GOOD

GOODSIRE n grandfather

GOODSIRES > GOODSIRE

GOODTIME adj wildly seeking pleasure

GOODWIFE n mistress of a household

GOODWILL n kindly feeling

GOODWILLS > GOODWILL

GOODWIVES > GOODWIFE

GOODY n hero in a book or film ▷ interj child's exclamation of pleasure ▷ adj smug and sanctimonious
GOODYEAR n euphemistic term for the Devil
GOODYEARS > GOODYEAR
GOOEY adj sticky and soft
GOOEYNESS > GOOEY
GOOF n mistake ▷ vb make a mistake
GOOFBALL n barbiturate sleeping pill
GOOFBALLS > GOOFBALL
GOOFED > GOOF
GOOFIER > GOOFY
GOOFIEST > GOOFY
GOOFILY > GOOFY
GOOFINESS > GOOFY
GOOFING > GOOF
GOOFS > GOOF
GOOFY adj silly or ridiculous
GOOG n egg
GOOGLE vb search for (something) on the internet using a search engine
GOOGLED > GOOGLE
GOOGLES > GOOGLE
GOOGLIES > GOOGLY
GOOGLING > GOOGLE
GOOGLY n ball that spins unexpectedly from off to leg on the bounce
GOOGOL n number represented as one followed by 100 zeros (10¹⁰⁰)
GOOGOLS > GOOGOL
GOOGS > GOOG
GOOIER > GOOEY
GOOIEST > GOOEY
GOOILY > GOOEY
GOOINESS n quality of being gooey
GOOK n derogatory word for a person from a Far Eastern country
GOOKS > GOOK
GOOKY adj sticky and messy
GOOL n corn marigold
GOOLD Scots word for > GOLD
GOOLDS > GOOLD
GOOLEY same as > GOOLIE
GOOLEYS > GOOLEY
GOOLIE n testicle
GOOLIES > GOOLIE
GOOLS > GOOL
GOOLY same as > GOOLIE
GOOMBAH n patron or mentor
GOOMBAHS > GOOMBAH
GOOMBAY n Bahamian soft drink
GOOMBAYS > GOOMBAY
GOON n stupid person
GOONDA n (in India) habitual criminal
GOONDAS > GOONDA
GOONEY n albatross
GOONEYS > GOONEY
GOONIE Scots word for a > GOWN

GOONIER > GOON
GOONIES > GOONIE
GOONIEST > GOON
GOONS > GOON
GOONY > GOON
GOOP n rude or ill-mannered person
GOOPED as in gooped up sticky with goop
GOOPIER > GOOP
GOOPIEST > GOOP
GOOPINESS n quality of being goopy
GOOPS > GOOP
GOOPY > GOOP
GOOR same as > GUR
GOORAL same as > GORAL
GOORALS > GOORAL
GOORIE same as > KURI
GOORIES > GOORIE
GOOROO same as > GURU
GOOROOS > GOOROO
GOORS > GOOR
GOORY same as > KURI
GOOS > GOO
GOOSANDER n type of duck
GOOSE n web-footed bird like a large duck ▷ vb prod (someone) playfully in the bottom
GOOSED > GOOSE
GOOSEFISH another name for > MONKFISH
GOOSEFOOT n type of usu weedy plant with small greenish flowers and leaves shaped like a goose's foot
GOOSEGOB n gooseberry
GOOSEGOBS > GOOSEGOB
GOOSEGOG dialect or informal word for > GOOSEGOG
GOOSEGOGS > GOOSEGOG
GOOSEHERD n person who herds geese
GOOSENECK n pivot between the forward end of a boom and a mast, to allow the boom to swing freely
GOOSERIES > GOOSERY
GOOSERY n place for keeping geese
GOOSES > GOOSE
GOOSEY same as > GOOSY
GOOSEYS > GOOSEY
GOOSIER > GOOSY
GOOSIES > GOOSY
GOOSIEST > GOOSY
GOOSINESS > GOOSY
GOOSING > GOOSE
GOOSY adj of or like a goose
GOPAK n spectacular high-leaping Russian peasant dance for men
GOPAKS > GOPAK
GOPHER n American burrowing rodent ▷ vb burrow
GOPHERED > GOPHER
GOPHERING > GOPHER
GOPHERS > GOPHER
GOPIK n money unit of Azerbaijan

GOPIKS > GOPIK
GOPURA n gateway tower of an Indian temple
GOPURAM same as > GOPURA
GOPURAMS > GOPURAM
GOPURAS > GOPURA
GOR interj God!
GORA n (in informal Indian English) White or fair-skinned male
GORAL n small S Asian goat antelope with a yellowish-grey and black coat and small conical horns
GORALS > GORAL
GORAMIES > GORAMY
GORAMY n GOURAMI
GORAS > GORA
GORBELLY n large belly
GORBLIMEY interj exclamation of surprise or annoyance ▷ n instance of having uttered this exclamation
GORBLIMY same as > GORBLIMEY
GORCOCK n male of the red grouse
GORCOCKS > GORCOCK
GORCROW n carrion crow
GORCROWS > GORCROW
GORDITA n small thick tortilla
GORDITAS > GORDITA
GORE n blood from a wound ▷ vb pierce with horns
GORED > GORE
GOREHOUND n enthusiast of gory horror films
GORES > GORE
GORGE n deep narrow valley ▷ vb eat greedily
GORGEABLE > GORGE
GORGED > GORGE
GORGEDLY > GORGE
GORGEOUS adj strikingly beautiful or attractive
GORGER > GORGE
GORGERIN another name for > NECKING
GORGERINS > GORGERIN
GORGERS > GORGE
GORGES > GORGE
GORGET n collar-like piece of armour worn to protect the throat
GORGETED > GORGET
GORGETS > GORGET
GORGIA n improvised sung passage
GORGIAS > GORGIA
GORGING > GORGE
GORGIO n word used by gypsies for a non-gypsy
GORGIOS > GORGIO
GORGON n terrifying or repulsive woman
GORGONEIA n plural of gorgoneion: representation of a Gorgon's head
GORGONIAN n type of coral with a horny or chalky

branching skeleton, such as the sea fan and red coral
GORGONISE vb turn to stone
GORGONIZE same as > GORGONISE
GORGONS > GORGON
GORHEN n female red grouse
GORHENS > GORHEN
GORI n in informal Indian English, a White or fair-skinned female
GORIER > GORY
GORIEST > GORY
GORILLA n largest of the apes, found in Africa
GORILLAS > GORILLA
GORILLIAN > GORILLA
GORILLINE > GORILLA
GORILLOID > GORILLA
GORILY > GORY
GORINESS > GORY
GORING > GORE
GORINGS > GORE
GORIS > GORI
GORM n foolish person ▷ vb understand
GORMAND same as > GOURMAND
GORMANDS > GOURMAND
GORMED > GORM
GORMIER > GORMY
GORMIEST > GORMY
GORMING > GORM
GORMLESS adj stupid
GORMS > GORM
GORMY adj gormless
GORP same as > GAWP
GORPED > GAWP
GORPING > GAWP
GORPS > GAWP
GORSE n prickly yellow-flowered shrub
GORSEDD n meeting of bards and druids held daily before an eisteddfod
GORSEDDS > GORSEDD
GORSES > GORSE
GORSIER > GORSE
GORSIEST > GORSE
GORSOON n young boy
GORSOONS > GORSOON
GORSY > GORSE
GORY adj horrific or bloodthirsty
GOS > GO
GOSH interj exclamation of mild surprise or wonder
GOSHAWK n large hawk
GOSHAWKS > GOSHAWK
GOSHT n Indian meat dish
GOSHTS > GOSHT
GOSLARITE n hydrated zinc sulphate
GOSLET n pygmy goose
GOSLETS > GOSLET
GOSLING n young goose
GOSLINGS > GOSLING
GOSPEL n any of the first four books of the New Testament ▷ adj denoting a kind of religious music originating in the churches

of the Black people in the Southern US ▷ vb teach the gospel

GOSPELER same as > GOSPELLER

GOSPELERS > GOSPELER

GOSPELISE vb evangelise

GOSPELIZE same as > GOSPELISE

GOSPELLED > GOSPEL

GOSPELLER n person who reads or chants the Gospel in a religious service

GOSPELLY > GOSPEL

GOSPELS > GOSPEL

GOSPODA > GOSPODIN

GOSPODAR n hospodar

GOSPODARS > GOSPODAR

GOSPODIN n Russian title of address, often indicating respect.

GOSPORT n aeroplane communication device

GOSPORTS > GOSPORT

GOSS vb spit

GOSSAMER n very fine fabric

GOSSAMERS > GOSSAMER

GOSSAMERY > GOSSAMER

GOSSAN n oxidised portion of a mineral vein in rock

GOSSANS > GOSSAN

GOSSE variant of > GORSE

GOSSED > GOSS

GOSSES > GOSSE

GOSSIB n gossip

GOSSIBS > GOSSIB

GOSSING > GOSS

GOSSIP n idle talk, esp about other people ▷ vb engage in gossip

GOSSIPED > GOSSIP

GOSSIPER > GOSSIP

GOSSIPERS > GOSSIP

GOSSIPING > GOSSIP

GOSSIPPED > GOSSIP

GOSSIPPER > GOSSIP

GOSSIPRY n idle talk

GOSSIPS > GOSSIP

GOSSIPY > GOSSIP

GOSSOON n boy, esp a servant boy

GOSSOONS > GOSSOON

GOSSYPINE adj cottony

GOSSYPOL n toxic crystalline pigment that is a constituent of cottonseed oil

GOSSYPOLS > GOSSYPOL

GOSTER vb laugh uncontrollably

GOSTERED > GOSTER

GOSTERING > GOSTER

GOSTERS > GOSTER

GOT > GET

GOTCHA as in gotcha lizard Australian name for a crocodile

GOTCHAS > GOTCHA

GOTH n aficionado of Goth music and fashion

GOTHIC adj of or relating to a literary style characterized by gloom,

the grotesque, and the supernatural ▷ n family of heavy script typefaces

GOTHICISE same as > GOTHICIZE

GOTHICISM > GOTHIC

GOTHICIZE vb make gothic in style

GOTHICS > GOTHIC

GOTHITE same as > GOETHITE

GOTHITES > GOTHITE

GOTHS > GOTH

GOTTA vb got to

GOTTEN past participle of > GET

GOUACHE n (painting using) watercolours mixed with glue

GOUACHES > GOUACHE

GOUCH vb become drowsy or lethargic under the influence of narcotics

GOUCHED > GOUCH

GOUCHES > GOUCH

GOUCHING > GOUCH

GOUGE vb scoop or force out ▷ n hole or groove

GOUGED > GOUGE

GOUGER n person or tool that gouges

GOUGERE n choux pastry flavoured with cheese

GOUGERES > GOUGERE

GOUGERS > GOUGER

GOUGES > GOUGE

GOUGING > GOUGE

GOUJEERS same as > GOODYEAR

GOUJON n small strip of fish or chicken, coated in breadcrumbs and deep-fried

GOUJONS > GOUJON

GOUK same as > GOWK

GOUKS > GOUK

GOULASH n rich stew seasoned with paprika

GOULASHES > GOULASH

GOURA n large, crested ground pigeon found in New Guinea

GOURAMI n large SE Asian labyrinth fish used for food and (when young) as an aquarium fish

GOURAMIES > GOURAMI

GOURAMIS > GOURAMI

GOURAS > GOURA

GOURD n fleshy fruit of a climbing plant

GOURDE n standard monetary unit of Haiti, divided into 100 centimes

GOURDES > GOURDE

GOURDIER > GOURDY

GOURDIEST > GOURDY

GOURDLIKE > GOURD

GOURDS > GOURD

GOURDY adj (of horses) swollen-legged

GOURMAND n person who is very keen on food and drink

GOURMANDS > GOURMAND

GOURMET n connoisseur of food and drink

GOURMETS > GOURMET

GOUSTIER > GOUSTY

GOUSTIEST > GOUSTY

GOUSTROUS adj stormy

GOUSTY adj dismal

GOUT n disease causing inflammation of the joints

GOUTFLIES > GOUTFLY

GOUTFLY n fly whose larvae infect crops

GOUTIER > GOUT

GOUTIEST > GOUT

GOUTILY > GOUT

GOUTINESS > GOUT

GOUTS > GOUT

GOUTTE n in heraldry, charge shaped like a drop of liquid

GOUTTES > GOUTTE

GOUTWEED n Eurasian plant with white flowers and creeping underground stems

GOUTWEEDS > GOUTWEED

GOUTWORT n bishop's weed

GOUTWORTS > GOUTWORT

GOUTY > GOUT

GOV n boss

GOVERN vb rule, direct, or control ▷ n ability to be governed

GOVERNALL n government

GOVERNED > GOVERN

GOVERNESS n woman teacher in a private household ▷ vb act as a governess

GOVERNING > GOVERN

GOVERNOR n official governing a province or state

GOVERNORS > GOVERNOR

GOVERNS > GOVERN

GOVS > GOV

GOWAN n any of various yellow or white flowers growing in fields, esp the common daisy

GOWANED > GOWAN

GOWANS > GOWAN

GOWANY > GOWAN

GOWD Scots word for > GOWD

GOWDER > GOWD

GOWDEST > GOWD

GOWDS > GOWD

GOWDSPINK n goldfinch

GOWF vb strike

GOWFED > GOWF

GOWFER > GOWF

GOWFERS > GOWF

GOWFING > GOWF

GOWFS > GOWF

GOWK n stupid person

GOWKS > GOWK

GOWL n substance often found in the corner of the eyes after sleep ▷ vb howl

GOWLAN same as > GOLLAN

GOWLAND same as > GOLLAN

GOWLANDS > GOWLAND

GOWLANS > GOWLAN

GOWLED > GOWL

GOWLING > GOWL

GOWLS > GOWL

GOWN n woman's long formal dress ▷ vb supply with or dress in a gown

GOWNBOY n foundationer schoolboy who wears a gown

GOWNBOYS > GOWNBOY

GOWNED > GOWN

GOWNING > GOWN

GOWNMAN n professional person, such as a lawyer, who wears a gown

GOWNMEN > GOWNMAN

GOWNS > GOWN

GOWNSMAN same as > GOWNMAN

GOWNSMEN > GOWNSMAN

GOWPEN n pair of cupped hands

GOWPENFUL n amount that can be contained in cupped hands

GOWPENS > GOWPEN

GOX n gaseous oxygen

GOXES > GOX

GOY n Jewish word for a non-Jew

GOYIM > GOY

GOYISCH > GOY

GOYISH > GOY

GOYLE n ravine

GOYLES > GOYLE

GOYS > GOY

GOZZAN same as > GOSSAN

GOZZANS > GOZZAN

GRAAL n holy grail

GRAALS > GRAAL

GRAB vb grasp suddenly, snatch ▷ n sudden snatch

GRABBABLE > GRAB

GRABBED > GRAB

GRABBER > GRAB

GRABBERS > GRAB

GRABBIER > GRABBY

GRABBIEST > GRABBY

GRABBING > GRAB

GRABBLE vb scratch or feel about with the hands

GRABBLED > GRABBLE

GRABBLER > GRABBLE

GRABBLERS > GRABBLE

GRABBLES > GRABBLE

GRABBLING > GRABBLE

GRABBY adj greedy or selfish

GRABEN n elongated trough of land produced by subsidence of the earth's crust between two faults

GRABENS > GRABEN

GRABS > GRAB

GRACE n beauty and elegance ▷ vb honour

GRACED > GRACE

GRACEFUL adj having beauty of movement, style, or form

GRACELESS adj lacking elegance

GRACES > GRACE

GRACILE adj gracefully

thin or slender

GRACILES > GRACILIS

GRACILIS n thin muscle on the inner thigh

GRACILITY > GRACILE

GRACING > GRACE

GRACIOSO n clown in Spanish comedy

GRACIOSOS > GRACIOSO

GRACIOUS adj kind and courteous ▷ interj expression of mild surprise or wonder ▷ interj expression of surprise

GRACKLE n American songbird with a dark iridescent plumage

GRACKLES > GRACKLE

GRAD n graduate

GRADABLE adj capable of being graded ▷ n word of this kind

GRADABLES > GRADABLE

GRADATE vb change or cause to change imperceptibly, as from one colour, tone, or degree to another

GRADATED > GRADATE

GRADATES > GRADATE

GRADATIM adv step by step

GRADATING > GRADATE

GRADATION n (stage in) a series of degrees or steps

GRADATORY adj moving step by step

GRADDAN vb dress corn

GRADDANED > GRADDAN

GRADDANS > GRADDAN

GRADE n place on a scale of quality, rank, or size ▷ vb arrange in grades

GRADED > GRADE

GRADELESS > GRADE

GRADELIER > GRADELY

GRADELY adj fine

GRADER n person or thing that grades

GRADERS > GRADER

GRADES > GRADE

GRADIENT n (degree of) slope ▷ adj sloping uniformly

GRADIENTS > GRADIENT

GRADIN n ledge above or behind an altar on which candles, a cross, or other ornaments stand

GRADINE same as > GRADIN

GRADINES > GRADINE

GRADING > GRADE

GRADINGS > GRADING

GRADINI > GRADINO

GRADINO n step above an altar

GRADINS > GRADIN

GRADS > GRAD

GRADUAL adj occurring, developing, or moving in small stages ▷ n antiphon or group of several antiphons, usually from the Psalms, sung or recited immediately after the

epistle at Mass

GRADUALLY > GRADUAL

GRADUALS > GRADUAL

GRADUAND n person who is about to graduate

GRADUANDS > GRADUAND

GRADUATE vb receive a degree or diploma ▷ n holder of a degree

GRADUATED > GRADUATE

GRADUATES > GRADUATE

GRADUATOR > GRADUATE

GRADUS n book of études or other musical exercises arranged in order of increasing difficulty

GRADUSES > GRADUS

GRAECISE same as > GRAECIZE

GRAECISED > GRAECISE

GRAECISES > GRAECISE

GRAECIZE vb make or become like the ancient Greeks

GRAECIZED > GRAECIZE

GRAECIZES > GRAECIZE

GRAFF same as > GRAFT

GRAFFED > GRAFF

GRAFFING > GRAFF

GRAFFITI npl words or drawings scribbled or sprayed on walls etc

GRAFFITIS > GRAFFITI

GRAFFITO n instance of graffiti

GRAFFS > GRAFF

GRAFT n surgical transplant of skin or tissue ▷ vb transplant (living tissue) surgically

GRAFTAGE n in horticulture, the art of grafting

GRAFTAGES > GRAFTAGE

GRAFTED > GRAFT

GRAFTER > GRAFT

GRAFTERS > GRAFT

GRAFTING > GRAFT

GRAFTINGS > GRAFT

GRAFTS > GRAFT

GRAHAM n made of graham flour

GRAHAMS > GRAHAM

GRAIL n any desired ambition or goal

GRAILE same as > GRAIL

GRAILES > GRAILE

GRAILS > GRAIL

GRAIN n seedlike fruit of a cereal plant ▷ vb paint in imitation of the grain of wood or leather

GRAINAGE n duty paid on grain

GRAINAGES > GRAINAGE

GRAINE n eggs of the silkworm

GRAINED > GRAIN

GRAINER > GRAIN

GRAINERS > GRAIN

GRAINES > GRAINE

GRAINIER > GRAINY

GRAINIEST > GRAINY

GRAINING n pattern or

texture of the grain of wood, leather, etc

GRAININGS > GRAINING

GRAINLESS > GRAIN

GRAINS > GRAIN

GRAINY adj resembling, full of, or composed of grain

GRAIP n long-handled gardening fork

GRAIPS > GRAIP

GRAITH vb clothe

GRAITHED > GRAITH

GRAITHING > GRAITH

GRAITHLY > GRAITH

GRAITHS > GRAITH

GRAKLE same as > GRACKLE

GRAKLES > GRAKLE

GRALLOCH n entrails of a deer ▷ vb disembowel (a deer killed in a hunt)

GRALLOCHS > GRALLOCH

GRAM n metric unit of mass equal to one thousandth of a kilogram

GRAMA n type of grass of W North America and S America, often used as a pasture grass

GRAMARIES > GRAMARY

GRAMARY same as > GRAMARYE

GRAMARYE n magic, necromancy, or occult learning

GRAMARYES > GRAMARYE

GRAMAS > GRAMA

GRAMASH n type of gaiter

GRAMASHES > GRAMASH

GRAME n sorrow

GRAMERCY interj many thanks

GRAMES > GRAME

GRAMMA n pasture grass of the South American plains

GRAMMAGE n weight of paper expressed as grams per square metre

GRAMMAGES > GRAMMAGE

GRAMMAR n branch of linguistics dealing with the form, function, and order of words

GRAMMARS > GRAMMAR

GRAMMAS > GRAMMA

GRAMMATIC adj of or relating to grammar

GRAMME same as > GRAME

GRAMMES > GRAM

GRAMOCHE same as > GRAMASH

GRAMOCHES > GRAMOCHE

GRAMP n grandfather

GRAMPA variant of > GRANDPA

GRAMPAS > GRAMPA

GRAMPS > GRAMP

GRAMPUS n dolphin-like mammal

GRAMPUSES > GRAMPUS

GRAMS > GRAM

GRAN n grandmother

GRANA > GRANUM

GRANARIES > GRANARY

GRANARY n storehouse for grain

GRAND adj large or impressive, imposing ▷ n thousand pounds or dollars

GRANDAD n grandfather

GRANDADDY same as > GRANDAD

GRANDADS > GRANDAD

GRANDAM n archaic word for grandmother

GRANDAME same as > GRANDAM

GRANDAMES > GRANDAME

GRANDAMS > GRANDAM

GRANDAUNT n great-aunt

GRANDBABY n very young grandchild

GRANDDAD same as > GRANDDAD

GRANDDADS > GRANDAD

GRANDDAM same as > GRANDAM

GRANDDAMS > GRANDDAM

GRANDE feminine form of > GRAND

GRANDEE n Spanish nobleman of the highest rank

GRANDEES > GRANDEE

GRANDER > GRAND

GRANDEST > GRAND

GRANDEUR n magnificence

GRANDEURS > GRANDEUR

GRANDIOSE adj imposing

GRANDIOSO adv (to be played) in a grand manner

GRANDKID n grandchild

GRANDKIDS > GRANDKID

GRANDLY > GRAND

GRANDMA n grandmother

GRANDMAMA same as > GRANDMA

GRANDMAS > GRANDMA

GRANDNESS > GRAND

GRANDPA n grandfather

GRANDPAPA same as > GRANDPA

GRANDPAS > GRANDPA

GRANDS > GRAND

GRANDSIR same as > GRANDSIRE

GRANDSIRE n grandfather

GRANDSIRS > GRANDSIRE

GRANDSON n male grandchild

GRANDSONS > GRANDSON

GRANFER n grandfather

GRANFERS > GRANFER

GRANGE n country house with farm buildings

GRANGER n keeper or member of a grange

GRANGERS > GRANGER

GRANGES > GRANGE

GRANITA n Italian iced drink

GRANITAS > GRANITA

GRANITE n very hard igneous rock often used in building

GRANITES > GRANITE

GRANITIC > GRANITE

GRANITISE vb form granite

g

GRANITITE n any granite with a high content of biotite

GRANITIZE same as > GRANITISE

GRANITOID > GRANITE

GRANIVORE n animal that feeds on seeds and grain

GRANNAM n old woman

GRANNAMS > GRANNAM

GRANNIE vb defeat (in a game or contest) so that one's opponent does not score a single point

GRANNIED > GRANNY

GRANNIES npl Granny Smith apples

GRANNOM n type of caddis fly esteemed as a bait by anglers

GRANNOMS > GRANNOM

GRANNY n grandmother ▷ vb defeat (in a game or contest) so that one's opponent does not score a single point

GRANNYING > GRANNY

GRANNYISH adj typical of or suitable for an elderly woman

GRANOLA n muesli-like breakfast cereal

GRANOLAS > GRANOLA

GRANOLITH n paving material consisting of a mixture of cement and crushed granite or granite chippings

GRANS > GRAN

GRANT vb consent to fulfil (a request) ▷ n sum of money provided by a government for a specific purpose, such as education

GRANTABLE > GRANT

GRANTED > GRANT

GRANTEE n person to whom a grant is made

GRANTEES > GRANTEE

GRANTER > GRANT

GRANTERS > GRANT

GRANTING > GRANT

GRANTOR n person who makes a grant

GRANTORS > GRANTOR

GRANTS > GRANT

GRANTSMAN n student who specializes in obtaining grants

GRANTSMEN > GRANTSMAN

GRANULAR adj of or like grains

GRANULARY adj granular

GRANULATE vb make into grains

GRANULE n small grain

GRANULES > GRANULE

GRANULITE n granular foliated metamorphic rock in which the minerals form a mosaic of equal-sized granules

GRANULOMA n tumour composed of granulation tissue produced in response to chronic infection, inflammation, a foreign body, or to unknown causes

GRANULOSE less common word for > GRANULAR

GRANULOUS adj consisting of grains or granules

GRANUM n membrane layers in a chloroplast

GRAPE n small juicy green or purple berry, eaten raw or used to produce wine, raisins, currants, or sultanas ▷ vb grope

GRAPED > GRAPE

GRAPELESS > GRAPE

GRAPELICE npl lice that are destructive to grape plants

GRAPELIKE > GRAPE

GRAPERIES > GRAPERY

GRAPERY n building where grapes are grown

GRAPES n abnormal growth, resembling a bunch of grapes, on the fetlock of a horse

GRAPESEED n seed of the grape

GRAPESHOT n bullets which scatter when fired

GRAPETREE n sea grape, a shrubby plant resembling a grapevine

GRAPEVINE n grape-bearing vine

GRAPEY > GRAPE

GRAPH n drawing showing the relation of different numbers or quantities plotted against a set of axes ▷ vb draw or represent in a graph

GRAPHED > GRAPH

GRAPHEME n one of a set of etters or combinations of letters in a given language that serve to distinguish one word from another and usually correspond to or represent phonemes

GRAPHEMES > GRAPHEME

GRAPHEMIC > GRAPHEME

GRAPHENE n layer of graphite one atom thick

GRAPHENES > GRAPHENE

GRAPHIC adj vividly descriptive

GRAPHICAL same as > GRAPHIC

GRAPHICLY > GRAPHIC

GRAPHICS npl diagrams, graphs, etc, esp as used on a television programme or computer screen

GRAPHING > GRAPH

GRAPHITE n soft black form of carbon, used in pencil leads

GRAPHITES > GRAPHITE

GRAPHITIC > GRAPHITE

GRAPHIUM n stylus (for writing)

GRAPHIUMS > GRAPHIUM

GRAPHS > GRAPH

GRAPIER > GRAPE

GRAPIEST > GRAPE

GRAPINESS > GRAPE

GRAPING > GRAPE

GRAPLE same as > GRAPPLE

GRAPLES > GRAPLE

GRAPLIN same as > GRAPNEL

GRAPLINE same as > GRAPNEL

GRAPLINES > GRAPLINE

GRAPLINS > GRAPLIN

GRAPNEL n device with several hooks, used to grasp or secure things

GRAPNELS > GRAPNEL

GRAPPA n spirit distilled from the fermented remains of grapes after pressing

GRAPPAS > GRAPPA

GRAPPLE vb try to cope with (something difficult) ▷ n grapnel

GRAPPLED > GRAPPLE

GRAPPLER > GRAPPLE

GRAPPLERS > GRAPPLE

GRAPPLES > GRAPPLE

GRAPPLING n act of gripping or seizing, as in wrestling

GRAPY same as > GRAPE

GRASP vb grip something firmly ▷ n grip or clasp

GRASPABLE > GRASP

GRASPED > GRASP

GRASPER > GRASP

GRASPERS > GRASP

GRASPING adj greedy or avaricious

GRASPLESS adj relaxed

GRASPS > GRASP

GRASS n common type of plant with jointed stems and long narrow leaves, including cereals and bamboo ▷ vb cover with grass

GRASSBIRD n type of warbler found in long grass and reed beds

GRASSED > GRASS

GRASSER n police informant

GRASSERS > GRASSER

GRASSES > GRASS

GRASSHOOK another name for > SICKLE

GRASSIER > GRASSY

GRASSIEST > GRASSY

GRASSILY > GRASSY

GRASSING > GRASS

GRASSINGS > GRASS

GRASSLAND n land covered with grass

GRASSLESS > GRASS

GRASSLIKE > GRASS

GRASSPLOT n plot of ground overgrown with grass

GRASSQUIT n tropical American finch

GRASSROOT adj relating to the ordinary people, especially as part of the electorate

GRASSUM n in Scots law, lump sum paid when taking up a lease

GRASSUMS > GRASSUM

GRASSY adj covered with, containing, or resembling grass

GRASTE archaic past participle of > GRACE

GRAT > GREET

GRATE vb rub into small bits on a rough surface ▷ n framework of metal bars for holding fuel in a fireplace

GRATED > GRATE

GRATEFUL adj feeling or showing gratitude

GRATELESS > GRATE

GRATER n tool with a sharp surface for grating food

GRATERS > GRATER

GRATES > GRATE

GRATICULE n grid of intersecting lines, esp of latitude and longitude on which a map is drawn

GRATIFIED > GRATIFY

GRATIFIER > GRATIFY

GRATIFIES > GRATIFY

GRATIFY vb satisfy or please ▷ adj giving one satisfaction or pleasure

GRATIN n crust of browned breadcrumbs

GRATINATE vb cook until the juice is absorbed and the surface crisps

GRATINE adj cooked au gratin

GRATINEE vb cook au gratin

GRATINEED > GRATINEE

GRATINEES > GRATINEE

GRATING adj harsh or rasping ▷ n framework of metal bars covering an opening

GRATINGLY > GRATING

GRATINGS > GRATING

GRATINS > GRATIN

GRATIS adj free, for nothing

GRATITUDE n feeling of being thankful for a favour or gift

GRATTOIR n scraper made of flint

GRATTOIRS > GRATTOIR

GRATUITY n money given for services rendered, tip

GRATULANT > GRATULATE

GRATULATE vb greet joyously

GRAUNCH vb crush or destroy

GRAUNCHED > GRAUNCH

GRAUNCHER > GRAUNCH

GRAUNCHES > GRAUNCH

GRAUPEL n soft hail or snow pellets

GRAUPELS > GRAUPEL

GRAV n unit of acceleration equal to the standard acceleration of free fall

GRAVADLAX same as > GRAVLAX

GRAVAMEN n that part of an accusation weighing most heavily against an accused

GRAVAMENS > GRAVAMEN

GRAVAMINA > GRAVAMEN

GRAVE n hole for burying a corpse ▷ adj causing concern ▷ vb cut, carve, sculpt, or engrave ▷ adv to be performed in a solemn manner

GRAVED > GRAVE

GRAVEL n mixture of small stones and coarse sand ▷ vb cover with gravel

GRAVELED > GRAVEL

GRAVELESS > GRAVE

GRAVELIKE > GRAVE

GRAVELING > GRAVEL

GRAVELISH > GRAVEL

GRAVELLED > GRAVEL

GRAVELLY adj covered with gravel

GRAVELS > GRAVEL

GRAVELY > GRAVE

GRAVEN > GRAVE

GRAVENESS > GRAVE

GRAVER n any of various engraving, chasing, or sculpting tools, such as a burin

GRAVERS > GRAVER

GRAVES > GRAVE

GRAVESIDE n area surrounding a grave

GRAVESITE n site of grave

GRAVEST > GRAVE

GRAVEWARD adj moving towards grave

GRAVEYARD n cemetery

GRAVID adj pregnant

GRAVIDA n pregnant woman

GRAVIDAE > GRAVIDA

GRAVIDAS > GRAVIDA

GRAVIDITY > GRAVID

GRAVIDLY > GRAVID

GRAVIES > GRAVY

GRAVING > GRAVE

GRAVINGS > GRAVING

GRAVIS as in myasthenia gravis chronic muscle-weakening disease

GRAVITAS n seriousness or solemnity

GRAVITATE vb be influenced or drawn towards

GRAVITIES > GRAVITY

GRAVITINO n hypothetical subatomic particle

GRAVITON n postulated quantum of gravitational energy

GRAVITONS > GRAVITON

GRAVITY n force of attraction of one object for another, esp of objects to the earth

GRAVLAKS same as > GRAVLAX

GRAVLAX n dry-cured salmon, marinated in salt, sugar, and spices, as served in Scandinavia

GRAVLAXES > GRAVLAX

GRAVS > GRAV

GRAVURE n method of intaglio printing using a plate with many small etched recesses

GRAVURES > GRAVURE

GRAVY n juices from meat in cooking

GRAY same as > GREY

GRAYBACK same as > GREYBACK

GRAYBACKS > GRAYBACK

GRAYBEARD same as > GREYBEARD

GRAYED > GRAY

GRAYER > GRAY

GRAYEST > GRAY

GRAYFISH n dogfish

GRAYFLIES > GRAYFLY

GRAYFLY n trumpet fly

GRAYHOUND US spelling of > GREYHOUND

GRAYING > GRAY

GRAYISH > GRAY

GRAYLAG same as > GREYLAG

GRAYLAGS > GRAYLAG

GRAYLE n holy grail

GRAYLES > GRAYLE

GRAYLING n fish of the salmon family

GRAYLINGS > GRAYLING

GRAYLY > GRAY

GRAYMAIL n tactic to avoid prosecution in espionage case by threatening to expose state secrets during trial

GRAYMAILS > GRAYMAIL

GRAYNESS > GREY

GRAYOUT n in aeronautics, impairment of vision due to lack of oxygen

GRAYOUTS > GRAYOUT

GRAYS > GRAY

GRAYSCALE adj in shades of grey

GRAYWACKE same as > GREYWACKE

GRAYWATER n water that has been used

GRAZABLE > GRAZE

GRAZE vb feed on grass ▷ n slight scratch or scrape

GRAZEABLE > GRAZE

GRAZED > GRAZE

GRAZER > GRAZE

GRAZERS > GRAZE

GRAZES > GRAZE

GRAZIER n person who feeds cattle for market

GRAZIERS > GRAZIER

GRAZING n land on which grass for livestock is grown

GRAZINGLY > GRAZE

GRAZINGS > GRAZING

GRAZIOSO adv (of music) to be played gracefully

GREASE n soft melted animal fat ▷ vb apply grease to

GREASED > GREASE

GREASER n mechanic, esp of motor vehicles

GREASERS > GREASER

GREASES > GREASE

GREASIER > GREASY

GREASIES > GREASY

GREASIEST > GREASY

GREASILY > GREASY

GREASING > GREASE

GREASY adj covered with or containing grease ▷ n shearer

GREAT adj large in size or number ▷ n distinguished person

GREATCOAT n heavy overcoat

GREATEN vb make or become great

GREATENED > GREATEN

GREATENS > GREATEN

GREATER > GREAT

GREATEST n most outstanding individual in a given field

GREATESTS > GREATEST

GREATLY > GREAT

GREATNESS > GREAT

GREATS > GREAT

GREAVE n piece of armour for the shin ▷ vb grieve

GREAVED > GREAVE

GREAVES npl residue left after the rendering of tallow

GREAVING > GREAVE

GREBE n diving water bird

GREBES > GREBE

GREBO same as > GREEBO

GREBOS > GREBO

GRECE n flight of steps

GRECES > GRECE

GRECIAN same as > GRECE

GRECIANS > GRECIAN

GRECISE same as > GRAECIZE

GRECISED > GRECISE

GRECISES > GRECISE

GRECISING > GRECISE

GRECIZE same as > GRAECIZE

GRECIZED > GRECIZE

GRECIZES > GRECIZE

GRECIZING > GRECIZE

GRECQUE n ornament of Greek origin

GRECQUES > GRECQUE

GREE n superiority or victory ▷ vb come or cause to come to agreement or harmony

GREEBO n unkempt or dirty-looking young man

GREEBOES > GREEBO

GREECE same as > GRECE

GREECES > GREECE

GREED n excessive desire for food, wealth, etc

GREEDIER > GREEDY

GREEDIEST > GREEDY

GREEDILY > GREEDY

GREEDLESS > GREED

GREEDS > GREED

GREEDSOME same as > GREEDY

GREEDY adj having an excessive desire for something, such as food or money

GREEGREE same as > GRIGRI

GREEGREES > GREEGREE

GREEING > GREE

GREEK vb represent text as grey lines on a computer screen

GREEKED > GREEK

GREEKING > GREEK

GREEKINGS > GREEK

GREEN adj of a colour between blue and yellow ▷ n colour between blue and yellow ▷ vb make or become green

GREENBACK n inconvertible legal-tender US currency note originally issued during the Civil War in 1862

GREENBELT n zone of farmland, parks, and open country surrounding a town or city

GREENBONE n an eel-like food fish

GREENBUG n common name for Schizaphis graminum

GREENBUGS > GREENBUG

GREENED > GREEN

GREENER n recent immigrant

GREENERS > GREENER

GREENERY n vegetation

GREENEST > GREEN

GREENEYE n small slender fish with pale green eyes

GREENEYES > GREENEYE

GREENFLY n green aphid, a common garden pest

GREENGAGE n sweet green plum

GREENHAND n greenhorn

GREENHEAD n male mallard

GREENHORN n novice

GREENIE n conservationist

GREENIER > GREEN

GREENIES > GREENIE

GREENIEST > GREEN

GREENING n process of making or becoming more aware of environmental considerations

GREENINGS > GREENING

GREENISH > GREEN

GREENLET n type of insectivorous songbird

GREENLETS > GREENLET

GREENLING n type of food fish of the N Pacific Ocean
GREENLIT adj given permission to proceed
GREENLY > GREEN
GREENMAIL n practice of a company buying sufficient shares in another company to threaten takeover and making a quick profit as a result of the threatened company buying back its shares at a higher price ▷ vb carry out the practice of greenmail
GREENNESS > GREEN
GREENROOM n backstage room in a theatre where performers rest or receive visitors
GREENS > GREEN
GREENSAND n olive-green sandstone consisting mainly of quartz and glauconite
GREENSICK adj suffering from greensickness: same as chlorosis
GREENSOME n match for two pairs in which each of the four players tees off and after selecting the better drive the partners of each pair play that ball alternately
GREENTH n greenness
GREENTHS > GREENTH
GREENWASH n superficial or insincere display of concern for the environment that is shown by an organization ▷ vb adopt a 'greenwash' policy
GREENWAY n linear open space, with pedestrian and cycle paths
GREENWAYS > GREENWAY
GREENWEED n woodwaxen
GREENWING n teal
GREENWOOD n forest or wood when the leaves are green
GREENY > GREEN
GREES > GREE
GREESE same as > GRECE
GREESES > GREESE
GREESING > GREESE
GREESINGS > GREESE
GREET vb meet with expressions of welcome ▷ n weeping
GREETE same as > GREET
GREETED > GREET
GREETER n person who greets people at the entrance of a shop, restaurant, casino, etc
GREETERS > GREETER
GREETES > GREETE
GREETING n act or words of welcoming on meeting
GREETINGS > GREETING
GREETS > GREET
GREFFIER n registrar
GREFFIERS > GREFFIER

GREGALE n northeasterly wind occurring in the Mediterranean
GREGALES > GREGALE
GREGARIAN adj gregarious
GREGARINE n type of parasitic protozoan typically occurring in other invertebrates
GREGATIM adv in flocks or crowds
GREGE vb make heavy
GREGO n short, thick jacket
GREGOS > GREGO
GREIGE adj (of a fabric or material) not yet dyed ▷ n unbleached or undyed cloth or yarn
GREIGES > GREIGE
GREIN vb desire fervently
GREINED > GREIN
GREINING > GREIN
GREINS > GREIN
GREISEN n light-coloured metamorphic rock consisting mainly of quartz, white mica, and topaz formed by the pneumatolysis of granite
GREISENS > GREISEN
GREISLY same as > GRISLY
GREMIAL n cloth spread upon the lap of a bishop when seated during Mass
GREMIALS > GREMIAL
GREMLIN n imaginary being blamed for mechanical malfunctions
GREMLINS > GREMLIN
GREMMIE n young surfer
GREMMIES > GREMMIE
GREMMY same as > GREMMIE
GREMOLATA n garnish of finely chopped parsley, garlic and lemon
GREN same as > GRIN
GRENACHE n variety of grape used in wine-making
GRENACHES > GRENACHE
GRENADE n small bomb thrown by hand or fired from a rifle
GRENADES > GRENADE
GRENADIER n soldier of a regiment formerly trained to throw grenades
GRENADINE n syrup made from pomegranates
GRENNED > GREN
GRENNING > GREN
GRENS > GREN
GRESE same as > GRECE
GRESES > GRESE
GRESSING same as > GRECE
GRESSINGS > GRESSING
GREVE same as > GREAVE
GREVES > GREVE
GREVILLEA n any of various Australian evergreen trees and shrubs
GREW vb shudder
GREWED > GROW

GREWHOUND n greyhound
GREWING > GROW
GREWS > GROW
GREWSOME archaic or US spelling of > GRUESOME
GREWSOMER > GREWSOME
GREX n group of plants that has arisen from the same hybrid parent group
GREXES > GREX
GREY adj of a colour between black and white ▷ n grey colour ▷ vb become or make grey
GREYBACK n any of various animals having a grey back, such as the grey whale and the hooded crow
GREYBACKS > GREYBACK
GREYBEARD n old man, esp a sage
GREYED > GREY
GREYER > GREY
GREYEST > GREY
GREYHEN n female of the black grouse
GREYHENS > GREYHEN
GREYHOUND n swift slender dog used in racing
GREYING > GREY
GREYINGS > GREY
GREYISH > GREY
GREYLAG n large grey goose
GREYLAGS > GREYLAG
GREYLIST vb hold (someone) in suspicion, without actually excluding him or her from a particular activity
GREYLISTS > GREYLIST
GREYLY > GREY
GREYNESS > GREY
GREYS > GREY
GREYSCALE n range of grey shades from white to black
GREYSTONE n type of grey rock
GREYWACKE n any dark sandstone or grit having a matrix of clay minerals
GRIBBLE n type of small marine crustacean which bores into and damages submerged wooden structures such as wharves
GRIBBLES > GRIBBLE
GRICE vb (of a railway enthusiast) to collect objects or visit places connected with trains and railways ▷ n object collected or place visited by a railway enthusiast
GRICED > GRICE
GRICER > GRICE
GRICERS > GRICE
GRICES > GRICE
GRICING > GRICE
GRICINGS > GRICE
GRID n network of horizontal and vertical lines, bars, etc
GRIDDED > GRID

GRIDDER n American football player
GRIDDERS > GRIDDER
GRIDDLE n flat iron plate for cooking ▷ vb cook (food) on a griddle
GRIDDLED > GRIDDLE
GRIDDLES > GRIDDLE
GRIDDLING > GRIDDLE
GRIDE vb grate or scrape harshly ▷ n harsh or piercing sound
GRIDED > GRIDE
GRIDELIN n greyish violet colour
GRIDELINS > GRIDELIN
GRIDES > GRIDE
GRIDING > GRIDE
GRIDIRON n frame of metal bars for grilling food ▷ vb cover with parallel lines
GRIDIRONS > GRIDIRON
GRIDLOCK n situation where traffic is not moving ▷ vb (of traffic) to obstruct (an area)
GRIDLOCKS > GRIDLOCK
GRIDS > GRID
GRIECE same as > GRECE
GRIECED > GRIECE
GRIECES > GRIECE
GRIEF n deep sadness
GRIEFER n online game player who intentionally spoils the game for other players
GRIEFERS > GRIEFER
GRIEFFUL adj stricken with grief
GRIEFLESS > GRIEF
GRIEFS > GRIEF
GRIESIE same as > GRISY
GRIESLY same as > GRISY
GRIESY same as > GRISY
GRIEVANCE n real or imaginary cause for complaint
GRIEVANT n any person with a grievance
GRIEVANTS > GRIEVANT
GRIEVE vb (cause to) feel grief ▷ n farm manager or overseer
GRIEVED > GRIEVE
GRIEVER > GRIEVE
GRIEVERS > GRIEVE
GRIEVES > GRIEVE
GRIEVING > GRIEVE
GRIEVINGS > GRIEVE
GRIEVOUS adj very severe or painful
GRIFF n information
GRIFFE n carved ornament at the base of a column, often in the form of a claw
GRIFFES > GRIFFE
GRIFFIN n mythical monster with an eagle's head and wings and a lion's body
GRIFFINS > GRIFFIN
GRIFFON same as > GRIFFIN

GRIFFONS > GRIFFON
GRIFFS > GRIFF
GRIFT vb swindle
GRIFTED > GRIFT
GRIFTER > GRIFT
GRIFTERS > GRIFT
GRIFTING > GRIFT
GRIFTS > GRIFT
GRIG n lively person ▷ vb fish for grigs
GRIGGED > GRIG
GRIGGING > GRIG
GRIGRI n African talisman, amulet, or charm
GRIGRIS > GRIGRI
GRIGS > GRIG
GRIKE n solution fissure, a vertical crack about 0.5 m wide formed by the dissolving of limestone by water, that divides an exposed limestone surface into sections or clints
GRIKES > GRIKE
GRILL n device on a cooker that radiates heat downwards ▷ vb cook under a grill
GRILLADE n grilled food
GRILLADES > GRILLADE
GRILLAGE n arrangement of beams and crossbeams used as a foundation on soft ground
GRILLAGES > GRILLAGE
GRILLE n grating over an opening
GRILLED adj cooked on a grill or gridiron
GRILLER > GRILL
GRILLERS > GRILL
GRILLERY n place where food is grilled
GRILLES > GRILLE
GRILLING > GRILL
GRILLINGS > GRILL
GRILLION n extremely large but unspecified number, quantity, or amount ▷ det amounting to a grillion
GRILLIONS > GRILLION
GRILLROOM n restaurant serving grilled foods
GRILLS > GRILL
GRILLWORK same as > GRILL
GRILSE n salmon on its first return from the sea to fresh water
GRILSES > GRILSE
GRIM adj stern
GRIMACE n ugly or distorted facial expression of pain, disgust, etc ▷ vb make a grimace
GRIMACED > GRIMACE
GRIMACER > GRIMACE
GRIMACERS > GRIMACE
GRIMACES > GRIMACE
GRIMACING > GRIMACE
GRIMALKIN n old cat, esp an old female cat
GRIME n ingrained dirt ▷ vb make very dirty

GRIMED > GRIME
GRIMES > GRIME
GRIMIER > GRIME
GRIMIEST > GRIME
GRIMILY > GRIME
GRIMINESS > GRIME
GRIMING > GRIME
GRIMLY > GRIM
GRIMMER > GRIM
GRIMMEST > GRIM
GRIMNESS > GRIM
GRIMOIRE n textbook of sorcery and magic
GRIMOIRES > GRIMOIRE
GRIMY > GRIME
GRIN vb smile broadly, showing the teeth ▷ n broad smile
GRINCH n person whose lack of enthusiasm or bad temper has a depressing effect on others
GRINCHES > GRINCH
GRIND vb crush or rub to a powder ▷ n hard work
GRINDED obsolete past participle of > GRIND
GRINDELIA n type of coarse American plant with yellow daisy-like flower heads
GRINDER n device for grinding substances
GRINDERS > GRINDER
GRINDERY n place in which tools and cutlery are sharpened
GRINDING > GRIND
GRINDINGS > GRIND
GRINDS > GRIND
GRINGA n female gringo
GRINGAS > GRINGA
GRINGO n person from an English-speaking country: used as a derogatory term by Latin Americans
GRINGOS > GRINGO
GRINNED > GRIN
GRINNER > GRIN
GRINNERS > GRIN
GRINNING > GRIN
GRINNINGS > GRIN
GRINS > GRIN
GRIOT n (in Western Africa) member of a caste responsible for maintaining an oral record of tribal history in the form of music, poetry, and storytelling
GRIOTS > GRIOT
GRIP n firm hold or grasp ▷ vb grasp or hold tightly
GRIPE vb complain persistently ▷ n complaint
GRIPED > GRIPE
GRIPER > GRIPE
GRIPERS > GRIPE
GRIPES > GRIPE
GRIPEY adj causing gripes
GRIPIER > GRIPEY
GRIPIEST > GRIPEY
GRIPING > GRIPE
GRIPINGLY > GRIPE

GRIPLE same as > GRIPPLE
GRIPMAN n cable-car operator
GRIPMEN > GRIPMAN
GRIPPE former name for > INFLUENZA
GRIPPED > GRIP
GRIPPER > GRIP
GRIPPERS > GRIP
GRIPPES > GRIPPE
GRIPPIER > GRIPPY
GRIPPIEST > GRIPPY
GRIPPING > GRIP
GRIPPLE adj greedy ▷ n hook
GRIPPLES > GRIPPLE
GRIPPY adj having grip
GRIPS > GRIP
GRIPSACK n travel bag
GRIPSACKS > GRIPSACK
GRIPT archaic variant of > GRIPPED
GRIPTAPE n rough tape for sticking to a surface to provide a greater grip
GRIPTAPES > GRIPTAPE
GRIPY same as > GRIPEY
GRIS same as > GRECE
GRISAILLE n technique of monochrome painting in shades of grey, as in an oil painting or a wall decoration, imitating the effect of relief
GRISE vb shudder
GRISED > GRISE
GRISELY same as > GRISLY
GRISEOUS adj streaked or mixed with grey
GRISES > GRISE
GRISETTE n (esp formerly) a French working-class girl, esp a pretty or flirtatious one
GRISETTES > GRISETTE
GRISGRIS same as > GRIGRI
GRISING > GRISE
GRISKIN n lean part of a loin of pork
GRISKINS > GRISKIN
GRISLED another word for > GRIZZLED
GRISLIER > GRISLY
GRISLIES > GRISLY
GRISLIEST > GRISLY
GRISLY adj horrifying or ghastly ▷ n large American bear
GRISON n type of mammal of Central and S America with a greyish back and black face and underparts
GRISONS > GRISON
GRISSINI npl thin crisp breadsticks
GRISSINO n Italian breadstick
GRIST n grain for grinding
GRISTER n device for grinding grain
GRISTERS > GRISTER

GRISTLE n tough stringy animal tissue found in meat
GRISTLES > GRISTLE
GRISTLIER > GRISTLE
GRISTLY > GRISTLE
GRISTMILL n mill, esp one equipped with large grinding stones for grinding grain
GRISTS > GRIST
GRISY adj grim
GRIT n rough particles of sand ▷ vb spread grit on (an icy road etc) ▷ adj great
GRITH n security, peace, or protection, guaranteed either in a certain place, such as a church, or for a period of time
GRITHS > GRITH
GRITLESS > GRIT
GRITS > GRIT
GRITSTONE same as > GRIT
GRITTED > GRIT
GRITTER n vehicle that spreads grit on the roads in icy weather
GRITTERS > GRITTER
GRITTEST > GRIT
GRITTIER > GRITTY
GRITTIEST > GRITTY
GRITTILY > GRITTY
GRITTING n spreading grit on road surfaces
GRITTINGS > GRITTING
GRITTY adj courageous and tough
GRIVATION n (in navigation) grid variation
GRIVET n E African monkey with long white tufts of hair on either side of the face
GRIVETS > GRIVET
GRIZE same as > GRECE
GRIZES > GRIZE
GRIZZLE vb whine or complain ▷ n grey colour
GRIZZLED adj grey-haired
GRIZZLER > GRIZZLE
GRIZZLERS > GRIZZLE
GRIZZLES > GRIZZLE
GRIZZLIER > GRIZZLY
GRIZZLIES > GRIZZLY
GRIZZLING > GRIZZLE
GRIZZLY n large American bear ▷ adj somewhat grey
GROAN n deep sound of grief or pain ▷ vb utter a groan
GROANED > GROAN
GROANER n person or thing that groans
GROANERS > GROANER
GROANFUL adj sad
GROANING > GROAN
GROANINGS > GROAN
GROANS > GROAN
GROAT n fourpenny piece
GROATS npl hulled and crushed grain of various cereals

GROCER n shopkeeper selling foodstuffs

GROCERIES npl food and other household supplies

GROCERS > GROCER

GROCERY n business or premises of a grocer

GROCKED same as > GROKKED

GROCKING same as > GROKKING

GROCKLE n tourist, esp one from the Midlands or the North of England

GROCKLES > GROCKLE

GRODIER > GRODY

GRODIEST > GRODY

GRODY adj unpleasant

GROG n spirit, usu rum, and water ▷ vb drink grog

GROGGED > GROG

GROGGERY n grogshop

GROGGIER > GROGGY

GROGGIEST > GROGGY

GROGGILY > GROGGY

GROGGING > GROG

GROGGY adj faint, shaky, or dizzy

GROGRAM n coarse fabric of silk, wool, or silk mixed with wool or mohair, often stiffened with gum, formerly used for clothing

GROGRAMS > GROGRAM

GROGS > GROG

GROGSHOP n drinking place, esp one of disreputable character

GROGSHOPS > GROGSHOP

GROIN n place where the legs join the abdomen ▷ vb provide or construct with groins

GROINED > GROIN

GROINING > GROIN

GROININGS > GROIN

GROINS > GROIN

GROK vb understand completely and intuitively

GROKED same as > GROKKED

GROKING same as > GROKKING

GROKKED > GROK

GROKKING > GROK

GROKS > GROK

GROMA n Roman surveying instrument

GROMAS > GROMA

GROMET same as > GROMMET

GROMETS > GROMET

GROMMET n ring or eyelet

GROMMETED adj having grommets

GROMMETS > GROMMET

GROMWELL n type of hairy plant with small greenish-white, yellow, or blue flowers, and smooth nutlike fruits

GROMWELLS > GROMWELL

GRONE obsolete word for > GROAN

GRONED > GRONE

GRONEFULL same as > GROANFUL

GRONES > GRONE

GRONING > GRONE

GROOF n face, or front of the body

GROOFS > GROOF

GROOLIER > GROOLY

GROOLIEST > GROOLY

GROOLY adj gruesome

GROOM n person who looks after horses ▷ vb make or keep one's clothes and appearance neat and tidy

GROOMED > GROOM

GROOMER > GROOM

GROOMERS > GROOM

GROOMING > GROOM

GROOMINGS > GROOM

GROOMS > GROOM

GROOMSMAN n man who attends the bridegroom at a wedding, usually the best man

GROOMSMEN > GROOMSMAN

GROOVE n long narrow channel in a surface

GROOVED > GROOVE

GROOVER n device that makes grooves

GROOVERS > GROOVER

GROOVES > GROOVE

GROOVIER > GROOVY

GROOVIEST > GROOVY

GROOVILY > GROOVY

GROOVING > GROOVE

GROOVY adj attractive or exciting

GROPE vb feel about or search uncertainly ▷ n instance of groping.

GROPED > GROPE

GROPER n type of large fish of warm and tropical seas

GROPERS > GROPER

GROPES > GROPE

GROPING > GROPE

GROPINGLY > GROPE

GROSBEAK n finch with a large powerful bill

GROSBEAKS > GROSBEAK

GROSCHEN n former Austrian monetary unit worth one hundredth of a schilling

GROSCHENS > GROSCHEN

GROSER n gooseberry

GROSERS > GROSER

GROSERT another word for > GROSER

GROSERTS > GROSERT

GROSET another word for > GROSER

GROSETS > GROSET

GROSGRAIN n heavy ribbed silk or rayon fabric

GROSS adj flagrant ▷ n twelve dozen ▷ vb make as total revenue before deductions ▷ interj exclamation indicating disgust

GROSSART another word for > GROSER

GROSSARTS > GROSSART

GROSSED > GROSS

GROSSER > GROSS

GROSSERS > GROSS

GROSSES > GROSS

GROSSEST > GROSS

GROSSING > GROSS

GROSSLY > GROSS

GROSSNESS > GROSS

GROSSULAR n type of garnet

GROSZ n Polish monetary unit worth one hundredth of a zloty

GROSZE > GROSZ

GROSZY > GROSZ

GROT n rubbish

GROTESQUE adj strangely distorted ▷ n grotesque person or thing

GROTS > GROT

GROTTIER > GROTTY

GROTTIEST > GROTTY

GROTTO n small picturesque cave

GROTTOED adj having grotto

GROTTOES > GROTTO

GROTTOS > GROTTO

GROTTY adj nasty or in bad condition

GROUCH vb grumble or complain ▷ n person who is always complaining

GROUCHED > GROUCH

GROUCHES > GROUCH

GROUCHIER > GROUCHY

GROUCHILY > GROUCHY

GROUCHING > GROUCH

GROUCHY adj bad-tempered

GROUF same as > GROOF

GROUFS > GROUF

GROUGH n natural channel or fissure in a peat moor

GROUGHS > GROUGH

GROUND n surface of the earth ▷ adj on or of the ground ▷ vb base or establish

GROUNDAGE n fee levied on a vessel entering a port or anchored off a shore

GROUNDED adj sensible and down-to-earth

GROUNDEN obsolete variant of > GROUND

GROUNDER n (in baseball) ball that travels along the ground

GROUNDERS > GROUNDER

GROUNDHOG another name for > WOODCHUCK

GROUNDING n basic knowledge of a subject

GROUNDMAN n groundsman

GROUNDMEN > GROUNDMAN

GROUNDNUT n peanut

GROUNDOUT n (in baseball) being put out after hitting a grounder that is fielded and thrown to first base

GROUNDS > GROUND

GROUNDSEL n yellow-flowered weed

GROUP n number of people or things regarded as a unit ▷ vb place or form into a group

GROUPABLE > GROUP

GROUPAGE n gathering people or objects into a group or groups

GROUPAGES > GROUPAGE

GROUPED > GROUP

GROUPER n large edible sea fish

GROUPERS > GROUPER

GROUPIE n ardent fan of a celebrity or of a sport or activity

GROUPIES > GROUPIE

GROUPING n set of people or organizations who act or work together to achieve a shared aim

GROUPINGS > GROUPING

GROUPIST n follower of a group

GROUPISTS > GROUPIST

GROUPLET n small group

GROUPLETS > GROUPLET

GROUPOID n magma

GROUPOIDS > GROUPOID

GROUPS > GROUP

GROUPWARE n software that enables computers within a group or organization to work together, allowing users to exchange electronic-mail messages, access shared files and databases, use video conferencing, etc

GROUPWORK n work done by a group acting together

GROUPY same as > GROUPIE

GROUSE n stocky game bird ▷ vb grumble or complain ▷ adj fine or excellent ▷ adj excellent

GROUSED > GROUSE

GROUSER > GROUSE

GROUSERS > GROUSE

GROUSES > GROUSE

GROUSEST > GROUSE

GROUSING > GROUSE

GROUT n thin mortar ▷ vb fill up with grout

GROUTED > GROUT

GROUTER > GROUT

GROUTERS > GROUT

GROUTIER > GROUTY

GROUTIEST > GROUTY

GROUTING > GROUT

GROUTINGS > GROUT

GROUTS npl sediment or grounds, as from making coffee

GROUTY adj sullen or surly

GROVE n small group of trees

GROVED > GROVE

GROVEL vb behave humbly in order to win a superior's favour

GROVELED > GROVEL
GROVELER > GROVEL
GROVELERS > GROVEL
GROVELESS > GROVE
GROVELING > GROVEL
GROVELLED > GROVEL
GROVELLER > GROVEL
GROVELS > GROVEL
GROVES > GROVE
GROVET *n* wrestling hold in which a wrestler in a kneeling position grips the head of his kneeling opponent with one arm and forces his shoulders down with the other
GROVETS > GROVET
GROW *vb* develop physically
GROWABLE *adj* able to be cultivated
GROWER *n* person who grows plants
GROWERS > GROWER
GROWING > GROW
GROWINGLY > GROW
GROWINGS > GROW
GROWL *vb* make a low rumbling sound ▷ *n* growling sound
GROWLED > GROWL
GROWLER *n* person, animal, or thing that growls
GROWLERS > GROWLER
GROWLERY *n* place to retreat to, alone, when ill-humoured
GROWLIER > GROWL
GROWLIEST > GROWL
GROWLING > GROWL
GROWLINGS > GROWL
GROWLS > GROWL
GROWLY > GROWL
GROWN > GROW
GROWNUP *n* adult
GROWNUPS > GROWNUP
GROWS > GROW
GROWTH *n* growing ▷ *adj* of or relating to growth
GROWTHIER > GROWTHY
GROWTHIST *n* advocate of the importance of economic growth
GROWTHS > GROWTH
GROWTHY *adj* rapid-growing
GROYNE *n* wall built out from the shore to control erosion
GROYNES > GROYNE
GROZING as in *grozing iron* iron for smoothing joints between lead pipes
GRRL as in *riot grrl* young woman who plays or enjoys an aggressively feminist style of punk rock music
GRRLS > GRRL
GRRRL as in *riot grrrl* young woman who plays or enjoys an aggressively feminist style of punk rock music
GRRRLS > GRRRL
GRUB *n* legless insect larva ▷ *vb* search carefully for something by digging or by

moving things about
GRUBBED > GRUB
GRUBBER *n* person who grubs
GRUBBERS > GRUBBER
GRUBBIER > GRUBBY
GRUBBIEST > GRUBBY
GRUBBILY > GRUBBY
GRUBBING > GRUB
GRUBBLE *same as* > GRABBLE
GRUBBLED > GRUBBLE
GRUBBLES > GRUBBLE
GRUBBLING > GRUBBLE
GRUBBY *adj* dirty
GRUBS > GRUB
GRUBSTAKE *n* supplies provided for a prospector on the condition that the donor has a stake in any finds ▷ *vb* furnish with such supplies
GRUBWORM *another word for* > GRUB
GRUBWORMS > GRUBWORM
GRUDGE *vb* be unwilling to give or allow ▷ *n* resentment ▷ *adj* planned or carried out in order to settle a grudge
GRUDGED > GRUDGE
GRUDGEFUL *adj* envious
GRUDGER > GRUDGE
GRUDGERS > GRUDGE
GRUDGES > GRUDGE
GRUDGING > GRUDGE
GRUDGINGS > GRUDGE
GRUE *n* shiver or shudder ▷ *vb* shiver or shudder
GRUED > GRUE
GRUEING > GRUE
GRUEL *n* thin porridge ▷ *vb* subject to exhausting experiences
GRUELED > GRUEL
GRUELER > GRUEL
GRUELERS > GRUEL
GRUELING *same as* > GRUELLING
GRUELINGS > GRUELING
GRUELLED > GRUEL
GRUELLER > GRUEL
GRUELLERS > GRUEL
GRUELLING *adj* exhausting or severe ▷ *n* severe experience, esp severe punishment
GRUELS > GRUEL
GRUES > GRUE
GRUESOME *adj* causing horror and disgust
GRUESOMER > GRUESOME
GRUFE *same as* > GROOF
GRUFES > GRUFE
GRUFF *adj* rough or surly in manner or voice ▷ *vb* talk gruffly
GRUFFED > GRUFF
GRUFFER > GRUFF
GRUFFEST > GRUFF
GRUFFIER > GRUFFY
GRUFFIEST > GRUFFY
GRUFFILY > GRUFFY
GRUFFING > GRUFF

GRUFFISH > GRUFF
GRUFFLY > GRUFF
GRUFFNESS > GRUFF
GRUFFS > GRUFF
GRUFFY *adj* gruff
GRUFTED *adj* dirty
GRUGRU *n* tropical American palm with a spiny trunk and leaves and edible nuts
GRUGRUS > GRUGRU
GRUIFORM *adj* relating to an order of birds, including cranes and bustards
GRUING > GRUE
GRUM *adj* surly
GRUMBLE *vb* complain ▷ *n* complaint
GRUMBLED > GRUMBLE
GRUMBLER > GRUMBLE
GRUMBLERS > GRUMBLE
GRUMBLES > GRUMBLE
GRUMBLIER > GRUMBLE
GRUMBLING > GRUMBLE
GRUMBLY > GRUMBLE
GRUME *n* clot
GRUMES > GRUME
GRUMLY > GRUM
GRUMMER > GRUM
GRUMMEST > GRUM
GRUMMET *same as* > GROMMET
GRUMMETED *adj* having grummets
GRUMMETS > GRUMMET
GRUMNESS > GRUM
GRUMOSE *same as* > GRUMOUS
GRUMOUS *adj* (esp of plant parts) consisting of granular tissue
GRUMP *n* surly or bad-tempered person ▷ *vb* complain or grumble
GRUMPED > GRUMP
GRUMPH *vb* grunt
GRUMPHED > GRUMPH
GRUMPHIE *n* pig
GRUMPHIES > GRUMPHIE
GRUMPHING > GRUMPH
GRUMPHS > GRUMPH
GRUMPHY *same as* > GRUMPHIE
GRUMPIER > GRUMPY
GRUMPIEST > GRUMPY
GRUMPILY > GRUMPY
GRUMPING > GRUMP
GRUMPISH *same as* > GRUMPY
GRUMPS > GRUMP
GRUMPY *adj* bad-tempered
GRUND as in *grund mail* payment for right of burial
GRUNDIES *npl* men's underpants
GRUNDLE *n* perineum
GRUNDLES > GRUNDLE
GRUNGE *n* style of rock music with a fuzzy guitar sound
GRUNGER *n* fan of grunge music
GRUNGERS > GRUNGER
GRUNGES > GRUNGE

GRUNGEY *adj* messy or dirty
GRUNGIER > GRUNGY
GRUNGIEST > GRUNGY
GRUNGY *adj* squalid or seedy
GRUNION *n* Californian marine fish that spawns on beaches
GRUNIONS > GRUNION
GRUNT *vb* make a low short gruff sound, like a pig ▷ *n* pig's sound
GRUNTED > GRUNT
GRUNTER *n* person or animal that grunts, esp a pig
GRUNTERS > GRUNTER
GRUNTING > GRUNT
GRUNTINGS > GRUNT
GRUNTLE *vb* grunt or groan
GRUNTLED > GRUNTLE
GRUNTLES > GRUNTLE
GRUNTLING > GRUNTLE
GRUNTS > GRUNT
GRUPPETTI > GRUPPETTO
GRUPPETTO *n* turn
GRUSHIE *adj* healthy and strong
GRUTCH *vb* grudge
GRUTCHED > GRUTCH
GRUTCHES > GRUTCH
GRUTCHING > GRUTCH
GRUTTEN > GREET
GRUYERE *n* hard flat whole-milk cheese with holes
GRUYERES > GRUYERE
GRYCE *same as* > GRICE
GRYCES > GRYCE
GRYDE *same as* > GRYDE
GRYDED > GRYDE
GRYDES > GRYDE
GRYDING > GRYDE
GRYESY *adj* grey
GRYFON *same as* > GRIFFIN
GRYFONS > GRYFON
GRYKE *same as* > GRIKE
GRYKES > GRYKE
GRYPE *same as* > GRIPE
GRYPES > GRIPE
GRYPHON *same as* > GRIFFIN
GRYPHONS > GRYPHON
GRYPT *archaic form of* > GRIPPED
GRYSBOK *n* small antelope of central and S Africa with small straight horns
GRYSBOKS > GRYSBOK
GRYSELY *same as* > GRISLY
GRYSIE *same as* > GRISY
GU *same as* > GJU
GUACAMOLE *n* spread of mashed avocado, tomato pulp, mayonnaise, and seasoning
GUACHARO *another name for* > OILBIRD
GUACHAROS > GUACHARO

GUACO n any of several tropical American plants whose leaves are used as an antidote to snakebite

GUACOS > GUACO

GUAIAC same as > GUAIACUM

GUAIACOL n yellowish oily creosote-like liquid extracted from guaiacum resin and hardwood tar, used medicinally as an expectorant

GUAIACOLS > GUAIACOL

GUAIACS > GUAIACUM

GUAIACUM n tropical American evergreen tree

GUAIACUMS > GUAIACUM

GUAIOCUM same as > GUAIACUM

GUAIOCUMS > GUAIACUM

GUAN n type of bird of Central and S America

GUANA another word for > IGUANA

GUANABANA n tropical tree or its fruit

GUANACO n S American animal related to the llama

GUANACOS > GUANACO

GUANAS > GUANA

GUANASE n enzyme that converts guanine to xanthine by removal of an amino group

GUANASES > GUANASE

GUANAY n type of cormorant

GUANAYS > GUANAY

GUANAZOLO n form of guanine

GUANGO n rain tree

GUANGOS > GUANGO

GUANIDIN same as > GUANIDINE

GUANIDINE n strongly alkaline crystalline substance, soluble in water and found in plant and animal tissues

GUANIDINS > GUANIDIN

GUANIN same as > GUANINE

GUANINE n white almost insoluble compound: one of the purine bases in nucleic acids

GUANINES > GUANINE

GUANINS > GUANINE

GUANO n dried sea-bird manure, used as fertilizer

GUANOS > GUANO

GUANOSINE n nucleoside consisting of guanine and ribose

GUANS > GUAN

GUANXI n Chinese social concept based on the exchange of favours

GUANXIS > GUANXI

GUANYLIC as in guanylic acid nucleotide consisting of guanine, ribose or deoxyribose, and a phosphate group

GUAR n Indian plant grown as a fodder crop and for the gum obtained from its seeds

GUARANA n type of shrub native to Venezuela

GUARANAS > GUARANA

GUARANI n standard monetary unit of Paraguay, divided into 100 céntimos

GUARANIES > GUARANI

GUARANIS > GUARANI

GUARANTEE n formal assurance, esp in writing, that a product will meet certain standards ▷ vb give a guarantee

GUARANTOR n person who gives or is bound by a guarantee

GUARANTY n pledge of responsibility for fulfilling another person's obligations in case of default

GUARD vb watch over to protect or to prevent escape ▷ n person or group that guards

GUARDABLE > GUARD

GUARDAGE n state of being in the care of a guardian

GUARDAGES > GUARDAGE

GUARDANT adj (of a beast) shown full face ▷ n guardian

GUARDANTS > GUARDANT

GUARDDOG n dog trained to protect premises

GUARDDOGS > GUARDDOG

GUARDED adj cautious or noncommittal

GUARDEDLY > GUARDED

GUARDEE n guardsman, esp considered as representing smartness and dash

GUARDEES > GUARDEE

GUARDER > GUARD

GUARDERS > GUARD

GUARDIAN n keeper or protector ▷ adj protecting or safeguarding

GUARDIANS > GUARDIAN

GUARDING > GUARD

GUARDLESS > GUARD

GUARDLIKE > GUARD

GUARDRAIL n railing at the side of a staircase, road, etc, as a safety barrier

GUARDROOM n room used by guards

GUARDS > GUARD

GUARDSHIP n warship responsible for the safety of other ships in its company

GUARDSMAN n member of the Guards

GUARDSMEN > GUARDSMAN

GUARISH vb heal

GUARISHED > GUARISH

GUARISHES > GUARISH

GUARS > GUAR

GUAVA n yellow-skinned tropical American fruit

GUAVAS > GUAVA

GUAYABERA n type of embroidered men's shirt

GUAYULE n bushy shrub of the southwestern US

GUAYULES > GUAYULE

GUB n white man ▷ vb hit or defeat

GUBBAH same as > GUB

GUBBAHS > GUBBAH

GUBBED > GUB

GUBBING > GUB

GUBBINS n object of little or no value

GUBBINSES > GUBBINS

GUBERNIYA n territorial division of imperial Russia

GUBS > GUB

GUCK n slimy matter

GUCKIER > GUCKY

GUCKIEST > GUCKY

GUCKS > GUCK

GUCKY adj slimy and mucky

GUDDLE vb catch (fish) by groping with the hands under the banks or stones of a stream ▷ n muddle

GUDDLED > GUDDLE

GUDDLES > GUDDLE

GUDDLING > GUDDLE

GUDE Scots word for > GOOD

GUDEMAN n male householder

GUDEMEN > GUDEMAN

GUDES n goods

GUDESIRE n grandfather

GUDESIRES > GUDESIRE

GUDEWIFE n female householder

GUDEWIVES > GUDEWIFE

GUDGEON n small freshwater fish ▷ vb trick or cheat

GUDGEONED > GUDGEON

GUDGEONS > GUDGEON

GUE same as > GJU

GUELDER as in guelder rose kind of shrub

GUENON n slender Old World monkey of Africa with long hind limbs and tail and long hair surrounding the face

GUENONS > GUENON

GUERDON n reward or payment ▷ vb give a guerdon to

GUERDONED > GUERDON

GUERDONER > GUERDON

GUERDONS > GUERDON

GUEREZA n handsome colobus monkey of the mountain forests of Ethiopia

GUEREZAS > GUEREZA

GUERIDON n small ornately-carved table

GUERIDONS > GUERIDON

GUERILLA same as > GUERRILLA

GUERILLAS > GUERILLA

GUERITE n turret used by a sentry

GUERITES > GUERITE

GUERNSEY n seaman's knitted woolen sweater

GUERNSEYS > GUERNSEY

GUERRILLA n member of an unofficial armed force fighting regular forces

GUES > GUE

GUESS vb estimate or draw a conclusion without proper knowledge ▷ n estimate or conclusion reached by guessing

GUESSABLE > GUESS

GUESSED > GUESS

GUESSER > GUESS

GUESSERS > GUESS

GUESSES > GUESS

GUESSING > GUESS

GUESSINGS > GUESS

GUESSWORK n process or results of guessing

GUEST n person entertained at another's house or at another's expense ▷ vb appear as a visiting player or performer

GUESTBOOK n page on a website where users leave comments

GUESTED > GUEST

GUESTEN vb stay as a guest in someone's house

GUESTENED > GUESTEN

GUESTENS > GUESTEN

GUESTING > GUEST

GUESTS > GUEST

GUESTWISE adv as, or in the manner of, a guest

GUFF n nonsense

GUFFAW n crude noisy laugh ▷ vb laugh in this way

GUFFAWED > GUFFAW

GUFFAWING > GUFFAW

GUFFAWS > GUFFAW

GUFFIE Scots word for > PIG

GUFFIES > GUFFIE

GUFFS > GUFF

GUGA n gannet chick

GUGAS > GUGA

GUGGLE vb drink making a gurgling sound

GUGGLED > GUGGLE

GUGGLES > GUGGLE

GUGGLING > GUGGLE

GUGLET same as > GOGLET

GUGLETS > GUGLET

GUICHET n grating, hatch, or small opening in a wall, esp a ticket-office window

GUICHETS > GUICHET

GUID Scot word for > GOOD

GUIDABLE > GUIDE

GUIDAGE n guidance

GUIDAGES > GUIDAGE

GUIDANCE n leadership, instruction, or advice

GUIDANCES > GUIDANCE

GUIDE n person who conducts tour expeditions ▷ vb act as a guide for

GUIDEBOOK n handbook with information for visitors to a place

GUIDED > GUIDE

GUIDELESS > GUIDE

GUIDELINE n set principle for doing something

GUIDEPOST n sign on a post by a road indicating directions

GUIDER > GUIDE

GUIDERS > GUIDE

GUIDES > GUIDE

GUIDESHIP n supervision

GUIDEWAY n track controlling the motion of something

GUIDEWAYS > GUIDEWAY

GUIDEWORD n word at top of dictionary page indicating first entry on page

GUIDING > GUIDE

GUIDINGS > GUIDE

GUIDON n small pennant, used as a marker or standard, esp by cavalry regiments

GUIDONS > GUIDON

GUIDS n possessions

GUILD n organization or club

GUILDER n former monetary unit of the Netherlands

GUILDERS > GUILDER

GUILDHALL n hall where members of a guild meet

GUILDRIES > GUILDRY

GUILDRY n in Scotland, corporation of merchants in a burgh

GUILDS > GUILD

GUILDSHIP n condition of being a member of a guild

GUILDSMAN n man who is a member of a guild

GUILDSMEN > GUILDSMAN

GUILE n cunning or deceit ▷ vb deceive

GUILED > GUILE

GUILEFUL > GUILE

GUILELESS adj free from guile

GUILER n deceiver

GUILERS > GUILER

GUILES > GUILE

GUILING > GUILE

GUILLEMET n (in printing) a duckfoot quote

GUILLEMOT n black-and-white diving sea bird of N hemisphere

GUILLOCHE n ornamental band or border with a repeating pattern of two or more interwoven wavy lines, as in architecture ▷ vb decorate with guilloches

GUILT n fact or state of having done wrong

GUILTIER > GUILTY

GUILTIEST > GUILTY

GUILTILY > GUILTY

GUILTLESS adj innocent

GUILTS > GUILT

GUILTY adj responsible for an offence or misdeed

GUIMBARD n Jew's harp

GUIMBARDS > GUIMBARD

GUIMP same as > GUIMPE

GUIMPE n short blouse with sleeves worn under a pinafore dress ▷ vb make with gimp

GUIMPED > GUIMPE

GUIMPES > GUIMPE

GUIMPING > GUIMPE

GUIMPS > GUIMP

GUINEA n former British monetary unit worth 21 shillings (1.05 pounds)

GUINEAS > GUINEA

GUIPURE n heavy lace that has its pattern connected by threads, rather than supported on a net mesh

GUIPURES > GUIPURE

GUIRO n percussion instrument made from a hollow gourd

GUIROS > GUIRO

GUISARD n guiser

GUISARDS > GUISARD

GUISE n false appearance ▷ vb disguise or be disguised in fancy dress

GUISED > GUISE

GUISER n mummer, esp at Christmas or Halloween revels

GUISERS > GUISER

GUISES > GUISE

GUISING > GUISE

GUISINGS > GUISE

GUITAR n stringed instrument with a flat back and a long neck, played by plucking or strumming

GUITARIST > GUITAR

GUITARS > GUITAR

GUITGUIT n bird belonging to the family Coerebidae

GUITGUITS > GUITGUIT

GUIZER same as > GUISER

GUIZERS > GUIZER

GUL n design used in oriental carpets

GULA n gluttony

GULAG n forced-labour camp

GULAGS > GULAG

GULAR adj of, relating to, or situated in the throat or oesophagus

GULAS > GULA

GULCH n deep narrow valley ▷ vb swallow fast

GULCHED > GULCH

GULCHES > GULCH

GULCHING > GULCH

GULDEN same as > GUILDER

GULDENS > GULDEN

GULE Scots word for > MARIGOLD

GULES n red in heraldry

GULET n wooden Turkish sailing boat

GULETS > GULET

GULF n large deep bay ▷ vb swallow up

GULFED > GULF

GULFIER > GULF

GULFIEST > GULF

GULFING > GULF

GULFLIKE > GULF

GULFS > GULF

GULFWEED n type of brown seaweed

GULFWEEDS > GULFWEED

GULFY > GULF

GULL n long-winged sea bird ▷ vb cheat or deceive

GULLABLE same as > GULLIBLE

GULLABLY > GULLABLE

GULLED > GULL

GULLER n deceiver

GULLERIES > GULLERY

GULLERS > GULLER

GULLERY n breeding-place for gulls

GULLET n muscular tube through which food passes from the mouth to the stomach

GULLETS > GULLET

GULLEY same as > GULLY

GULLEYED > GULLEY

GULLEYING > GULLEY

GULLEYS > GULLEY

GULLIBLE adj easily tricked

GULLIBLY > GULLIBLE

GULLIED > GULLY

GULLIES > GULLY

GULLING > GULL

GULLISH adj stupid

GULLS > GULL

GULLWING adj (of vehicle door) opening upwards

GULLY n channel cut by running water ▷ vb make (channels) in (the ground, sand, etc)

GULLYING > GULLY

GULOSITY n greed or gluttony

GULP vb swallow hastily ▷ n gulping

GULPED > GULP

GULPER > GULP

GULPERS > GULP

GULPH archaic word for > GULF

GULPHS > GULPH

GULPIER > GULP

GULPIEST > GULP

GULPING > GULP

GULPINGLY > GULP

GULPS > GULP

GULPY > GULP

GULS > GUL

GULY adj relating to gules

GUM n firm flesh in which the teeth are set ▷ vb stick with gum

GUMBALL n round piece of chewing gum

GUMBALLS > GUMBALL

GUMBO n mucilaginous pods of okra

GUMBOIL n abscess on the gum

GUMBOILS > GUMBOIL

GUMBOOT n rubber boot

GUMBOOTS npl Wellington boots

GUMBOS > GUMBO

GUMBOTIL n sticky clay formed by the weathering of glacial drift

GUMBOTILS > GUMBOTIL

GUMDROP n hard jelly-like sweet

GUMDROPS > GUMDROP

GUMLANDS npl infertile land from which the original kauri bush has been removed or burnt producing only kauri gum

GUMLESS > GUM

GUMLIKE > GUM

GUMLINE n line where gums meet teeth

GUMLINES > GUMLINE

GUMMA n rubbery tumour characteristic of advanced syphilis, occurring esp on the skin, liver, brain or heart

GUMMAS > GUMMA

GUMMATA > GUMMA

GUMMATOUS > GUMMA

GUMMED > GUM

GUMMER n punch-cutting tool

GUMMERS > GUMMER

GUMMIER > GUMMY

GUMMIES > GUMMY

GUMMIEST > GUMMY

GUMMILY > GUMMY

GUMMINESS > GUMMY

GUMMING > GUM

GUMMINGS > GUM

GUMMITE n orange or yellowish amorphous secondary mineral consisting of hydrated uranium oxides

GUMMITES > GUMMITE

GUMMOSE same as > GUMMOUS

GUMMOSES > GUMMOSE

GUMMOSIS n abnormal production of excessive gum in certain trees, esp fruit trees, as a result of wounding, infection, adverse weather conditions, severe pruning, etc

GUMMOSITY > GUMMOUS

GUMMOUS adj resembling or consisting of gum

GUMMY adj toothless ▷ n type of small crustacean-eating shark whose mouth has bony ridges resembling gums

GUMNUT n hardened seed container of the gumtree

GUMNUTS > GUMNUT

GUMP vb guddle

GUMPED > GUMP

GUMPHION n funeral banner

GUMPHIONS > GUMPHION

GUMPING > GUMP
GUMPS > GUMP
GUMPTION n resourcefulness
GUMPTIONS > GUMPTION
GUMPTIOUS > GUMPTION
GUMS > GUM
GUMSHIELD n plate or strip of soft waxy substance used by boxers to protect the teeth and gums
GUMSHOE n waterproof overshoe ▷ vb act stealthily
GUMSHOED > GUMSHOE
GUMSHOES > GUMSHOE
GUMSUCKER n native-born Australian
GUMTREE n any of various trees that yield gum, such as the eucalyptus, sweet gum, and sour gum
GUMTREES > GUMTREE
GUMWEED n any of several American yellow-flowered plants that have sticky flower heads
GUMWEEDS > GUMWEED
GUMWOOD same as > GUMTREE
GUMWOODS > GUMWOOD
GUN n weapon with a metal tube from which missiles are fired by explosion ▷ vb cause (an engine) to run at high speed
GUNBOAT n small warship
GUNBOATS > GUNBOAT
GUNCOTTON n form of cellulose nitrate used as an explosive
GUNDIES > GUNDY
GUNDOG n dog trained to work with a hunter or gamekeeper
GUNDOGS > GUNDOG
GUNDY n toffee
GUNFIGHT n fight between persons using firearms ▷ vb fight with guns
GUNFIGHTS > GUNFIGHT
GUNFIRE n repeated firing of guns
GUNFIRES > GUNFIRE
GUNFLINT n piece of flint in a flintlock's hammer used to strike the spark that ignites the charge
GUNFLINTS > GUNFLINT
GUNFOUGHT > GUNFIGHT
GUNG as in gung ho extremely or excessively enthusiastic about something
GUNGE n sticky unpleasant substance ▷ vb block or encrust with gunge
GUNGED > GUNGE
GUNGES > GUNGE
GUNGIER > GUNGE
GUNGIEST > GUNGE
GUNGING > GUNGE
GUNGY > GUNGE
GUNHOUSE n on a warship, an armoured rotatable enclosure for guns

GUNHOUSES > GUNHOUSE
GUNITE n cement-sand mortar that is sprayed onto formwork, walls, or rock by a compressed air ejector giving a very dense strong concrete layer: used to repair reinforced concrete, to line tunnel walls or mine airways, etc
GUNITES > GUNITE
GUNK n slimy or filthy substance
GUNKHOLE vb make a series of short boat excursions
GUNKHOLED > GUNKHOLE
GUNKHOLES > GUNKHOLE
GUNKIER > GUNK
GUNKIEST > GUNK
GUNKS > GUNK
GUNKY > GUNK
GUNLAYER n person who aims a ship's gun
GUNLAYERS > GUNLAYER
GUNLESS > GUN
GUNLOCK n mechanism in some firearms that causes the charge to be exploded
GUNLOCKS > GUNLOCK
GUNMAKER n person who makes guns
GUNMAKERS > GUNMAKER
GUNMAN n armed criminal
GUNMEN > GUNMAN
GUNMETAL n alloy of copper, tin, and zinc ▷ adj dark grey
GUNMETALS > GUNMETAL
GUNNAGE n number of guns carried by a warship
GUNNAGES > GUNNAGE
GUNNED > GUN
GUNNEL same as > GUNWALE
GUNNELS > GUNNEL
GUNNEN > GUN
GUNNER n artillery soldier
GUNNERA n type of herbaceous plant found throughout the S hemisphere and cultivated for its large leaves
GUNNERAS > GUNNERA
GUNNERIES > GUNNERY
GUNNERS > GUNNER
GUNNERY n use or science of large guns
GUNNIES > GUNNY
GUNNING > GUN
GUNNINGS > GUN
GUNNY n strong coarse fabric used for sacks
GUNNYBAG same as > GUNNYSACK
GUNNYBAGS > GUNNYBAG
GUNNYSACK n sack made from gunny
GUNPAPER n cellulose nitrate explosive made by treating paper with nitric acid
GUNPAPERS > GUNPAPER
GUNPLAY n use of firearms, as by criminals

GUNPLAYS > GUNPLAY
GUNPOINT n muzzle of a gun
GUNPOINTS > GUNPOINT
GUNPORT n porthole, or other, opening for a gun
GUNPORTS > GUNPORT
GUNPOWDER n explosive mixture of potassium nitrate, sulphur, and charcoal
GUNROOM n (esp in the Royal Navy) the mess allocated to subordinate or junior officers
GUNROOMS > GUNROOM
GUNRUNNER n person who smuggles guns and ammunition
GUNS > GUN
GUNSEL n catamite
GUNSELS > GUNSEL
GUNSHIP n ship or helicopter armed with heavy guns
GUNSHIPS > GUNSHIP
GUNSHOT n shot or range of a gun
GUNSHOTS > GUNSHOT
GUNSIGHT n device on a gun which helps the user to aim
GUNSIGHTS > GUNSIGHT
GUNSMITH n person who manufactures or repairs firearms, esp portable guns
GUNSMITHS > GUNSMITH
GUNSTICK n ramrod
GUNSTICKS > GUNSTICK
GUNSTOCK n wooden handle to which the barrel of a rifle is attached
GUNSTOCKS > GUNSTOCK
GUNSTONE n cannonball
GUNSTONES > GUNSTONE
GUNTER n type of gaffing in which the gaff is hoisted parallel to the mast
GUNTERS > GUNTER
GUNWALE n top of a ship's side
GUNWALES > GUNWALE
GUNYAH n hut or shelter in the bush
GUNYAHS > GUNYAH
GUP n gossip
GUPPIES > GUPPY
GUPPY n small colourful aquarium fish
GUPS > GUP
GUQIN n type of Chinese zither
GUQINS > GUQIN
GUR n unrefined cane sugar
GURAMI same as > GOURAMI
GURAMIS > GURAMI
GURDWARA n Sikh place of worship
GURDWARAS > GURDWARA
GURGE vb swallow up
GURGED > GURGE
GURGES > GURGE
GURGING > GURGE

GURGLE n bubbling noise ▷ vb (of water) to make low bubbling noises when flowing
GURGLED > GURGLE
GURGLES > GURGLE
GURGLET same as > GOGLET
GURGLETS > GURGLET
GURGLING > GURGLE
GURGOYLE same as > GARGOYLE
GURGOYLES > GURGOYLE
GURJUN n S or SE Asian tree that yields a resin
GURJUNS > GURJUN
GURL vb snarl
GURLED > GURL
GURLET n type of pickaxe
GURLETS > GURLET
GURLIER > GURLY
GURLIEST > GURLY
GURLING > GURL
GURLS > GURL
GURLY adj stormy
GURN variant spelling of > GIRN
GURNARD n spiny armour-headed sea fish
GURNARDS > GURNARD
GURNED > GURN
GURNET same as > GURNARD
GURNETS > GURNARD
GURNEY n wheeled stretcher for transporting hospital patients
GURNEYS > GURNEY
GURNING > GURN
GURNS > GURN
GURRAH n type of coarse muslin
GURRAHS > GURRAH
GURRIER n low-class tough ill-mannered person
GURRIERS > GURRIER
GURRIES > GURRY
GURRY n dog-fight
GURS > GUR
GURSH n unit of currency in Saudi Arabia
GURSHES > GURSH
GURU n Hindu or Sikh religious teacher or leader
GURUDOM n state of being a guru
GURUDOMS > GURUDOM
GURUISM > GURU
GURUISMS > GURU
GURUS > GURU
GURUSHIP > GURU
GURUSHIPS > GURU
GUS > GU
GUSH vb flow out suddenly and profusely ▷ n sudden copious flow
GUSHED > GUSH
GUSHER n spurting oil well
GUSHERS > GUSHER
GUSHES > GUSH
GUSHIER > GUSHY
GUSHIEST > GUSHY
GUSHILY > GUSHY
GUSHINESS > GUSHY

GUSHING > GUSH

GUSHINGLY > GUSH

GUSHY adj displaying excessive admiration or sentimentality

GUSLA n Balkan single-stringed musical instrument

GUSLAR n player of the gusla

GUSLARS > GUSLAR

GUSLAS > GUSLA

GUSLE same as > GUSLA

GUSLES > GUSLE

GUSLI n Russian harp-like musical instrument

GUSLIS > GUSLI

GUSSET n piece of material sewn into a garment to strengthen it ▷ vb put a gusset in (a garment)

GUSSETED > GUSSET

GUSSETING > GUSSET

GUSSETS > GUSSET

GUSSIE n young pig

GUSSIED > GUSSY

GUSSIES > GUSSY

GUSSY vb dress elaborately

GUSSYING > GUSSY

GUST n sudden blast of wind ▷ vb blow in gusts

GUSTABLE n anything that can be tasted

GUSTABLES > GUSTABLE

GUSTATION n act of tasting or the faculty of taste

GUSTATIVE > GUSTATION

GUSTATORY > GUSTATION

GUSTED > GUST

GUSTFUL adj tasty

GUSTIE adj tasty

GUSTIER > GUSTY

GUSTIEST > GUSTY

GUSTILY > GUSTY

GUSTINESS > GUSTY

GUSTING > GUST

GUSTLESS adj tasteless

GUSTO n enjoyment or zest

GUSTOES > GUSTO

GUSTOS > GUSTO

GUSTS > GUST

GUSTY adj blowing or occurring in gusts or characterized by blustery weather

GUT n intestine ▷ vb remove the guts from ▷ adj basic or instinctive

GUTBUCKET n highly emotional style of jazz playing

GUTCHER n grandfather

GUTCHERS > GUTCHER

GUTFUL n bellyful

GUTFULS > GUTFUL

GUTLESS adj cowardly

GUTLESSLY > GUTLESS

GUTLIKE > GUT

GUTROT n diarrhoea

GUTROTS > GUTROT

GUTS vb devour greedily

GUTSED > GUTS

GUTSER as in come a gutser fall heavily to the ground

GUTSERS > GUTSER

GUTSES > GUTS

GUTSFUL n bellyful

GUTSFULS > GUTSFUL

GUTSIER > GUTSY

GUTSIEST > GUTSY

GUTSILY > GUTSY

GUTSINESS > GUTSY

GUTSING > GUTS

GUTSY adj courageous

GUTTA n one of a set of small drop-like ornaments, esp as used on the architrave of a Doric entablature ▷ n rubber substance obtained from the coagulated latex of the guttapercha tree

GUTTAE > GUTTA

GUTTAS > GUTTA

GUTTATE adj (esp of plants) covered with small drops or drop-like markings, esp oil glands ▷ vb exude droplets of liquid

GUTTATED same as > GUTTATE

GUTTATES > GUTTATE

GUTTATING > GUTTATE

GUTTATION > GUTTATE

GUTTED > GUT

GUTTER n shallow channel for carrying away water from a roof or roadside ▷ vb (of a candle) burn unsteadily, with wax running down the sides

GUTTERED > GUTTER

GUTTERING n material for gutters

GUTTERS > GUTTER

GUTTERY > GUTTER

GUTTIER > GUTTY

GUTTIES > GUTTY

GUTTIEST > GUTTY

GUTTING > GUT

GUTTLE vb eat greedily

GUTTLED > GUTTLE

GUTTLER > GUTTLE

GUTTLERS > GUTTLE

GUTTLES > GUTTLE

GUTTLING > GUTTLE

GUTTURAL adj (of a sound) produced at the back of the throat ▷ n guttural consonant

GUTTURALS > GUTTURAL

GUTTY n urchin or delinquent ▷ adj courageous

GUTZER n bad fall

GUTZERS > GUTZER

GUV informal name for > GOVERNOR

GUVS > GUV

GUY n man or boy ▷ vb make fun of

GUYED > GUY

GUYING > GUY

GUYLE same as > GUILE

GUYLED > GUYLE

GUYLER > GUYLE

GUYLERS > GUYLE

GUYLES > GUYLE

GUYLINE n guy rope

GUYLINER n eyeliner worn by men

GUYLINERS > GUYLINER

GUYLINES > GUYLINE

GUYLING > GUYLE

GUYOT n flat-topped submarine mountain, common in the Pacific Ocean, usually an extinct volcano whose summit did not reach above the sea surface

GUYOTS > GUYOT

GUYS > GUY

GUYSE same as > GUISE

GUYSES > GUYSE

GUZZLE vb eat or drink greedily

GUZZLED > GUZZLE

GUZZLER n person or thing that guzzles

GUZZLERS > GUZZLER

GUZZLES > GUZZLE

GUZZLING > GUZZLE

GWEDUC same as > GEODUCK

GWEDUCK same as > GEODUCK

GWEDUCKS > GWEDUCK

GWEDUCS > GWEDUCK

GWINE dialect form of > GOING

GWINIAD n powan

GWINIADS > GWINIAD

GWYNIAD n type of freshwater white fish occurring in Lake Bala in Wales

GWYNIADS > GWYNIAD

GYAL same as > GAYAL

GYALS > GYAL

GYBE vb (of a fore-and-aft sail) swing suddenly from one side to the other ▷ n instance of gybing

GYBED > GYBE

GYBES > GYBE

GYBING > GYBE

GYELD n guild

GYELDS > GYELD

GYLDEN adj golden

GYM n gymnasium

GYMBAL same as > GIMBAL

GYMBALS > GYMBAL

GYMKHANA n horse-riding competition

GYMKHANAS > GYMKHANA

GYMMAL same as > GIMMAL

GYMMALS > GYMMAL

GYMNASIA > GYMNASIUM

GYMNASIAL > GYMNASIUM

GYMNASIC > GYMNASIUM

GYMNASIEN > GYMNASIUM

GYMNASIUM n large room with equipment for physical training

GYMNAST n expert in gymnastics

GYMNASTIC adj of, relating to, like, or involving gymnastics

GYMNASTS > GYMNAST

GYMNIC adj gymnastic

GYMNOSOPH n adherent of gymnosophy: belief that food and clothing are detrimental to purity of thought

GYMP same as > GIMP

GYMPED > GYMP

GYMPIE n tall tree with stinging hairs on its leaves

GYMPIES > GYMPIE

GYMPING > GYMP

GYMPS > GYMP

GYMS > GYM

GYMSLIP n tunic or pinafore formerly worn by schoolgirls

GYMSLIPS > GYMSLIP

GYNAE adj gynaecological ▷ n gynaecology

GYNAECEA > GYNAECIUM

GYNAECEUM same as > GYNAECIA

GYNAECIA > GYNAECIUM

GYNAECIUM same as > GYNOECIUM

GYNAECOID adj resembling, relating to, or like a woman

GYNAES > GYNAE

GYNANDRY n hermaphroditism

GYNARCHIC > GYNARCHY

GYNARCHY n government by women

GYNECIA > GYNECIUM

GYNECIC adj relating to the female sex

GYNECIUM same as > GYNOECIUM

GYNECOID same as > GYNAECOID

GYNIATRY n gynaecology: medicine concerned with diseases in women

GYNIE n gynaecology

GYNIES > GYNIE

GYNNEY n guinea hen

GYNNEYS > GYNNEY

GYNNIES > GYNNY

GYNNY same as > GYNNEY

GYNOCRACY n government by women

GYNOECIA > GYNOECIUM

GYNOECIUM n carpels of a flowering plant collectively

GYNOPHOBE n person who hates or fears women

GYNOPHORE n stalk in some plants that bears the gynoecium above the level of the other flower parts

GYNY n gynaecology

GYOZA n Japanese fried dumpling

GYOZAS > GYOZA

GYP vb swindle, cheat, or defraud ▷ n act of cheating

GYPLURE n synthetic version of the gypsy moth

sex pheromone

GYPLURES > GYPLURE

GYPPED > GYP

GYPPER > GYP

GYPPERS > GYP

GYPPIE *same as* > GIPPY

GYPPIES > GYPPY

GYPPING > GYP

GYPPO *n* derogatory term for a gypsy

GYPPOS > GYPPO

GYPPY *same as* > GIPPY

GYPS > GYP

GYPSEIAN *adj* relating to gypsies

GYPSEOUS > GYPSUM

GYPSIED > GYPSY

GYPSIES > GYPSY

GYPSTER *n* swindler

GYPSTERS > GYPSTER

GYPSUM *n* chalklike mineral used to make plaster of Paris

GYPSUMS > GYPSUM

GYPSY *n* member of a nomadic people scattered throughout Europe and North America ▷ *vb* live like a gypsy

GYPSYDOM > GYPSY

GYPSYDOMS > GYPSYDOM

GYPSYHOOD > GYPSY

GYPSYING > GYPSY

GYPSYISH > GYPSY

GYPSYISM *n* state of being a gypsy

GYPSYISMS > GYPSYISM

GYPSYWORT *n* type of Eurasian herb with white flowers

GYRAL *adj* having a circular, spiral, or rotating motion

GYRALLY > GYRAL

GYRANT *adj* gyrating

GYRASE *n* topoisomerase enzyme

GYRASES > GYRASE

GYRATE *vb* rotate or spiral about a point or axis ▷ *adj* curved or coiled into a circle

GYRATED > GYRATE

GYRATES > GYRATE

GYRATING > GYRATE

GYRATION *n* act or process of gyrating

GYRATIONS > GYRATION

GYRATOR *n* electronic circuit that inverts the impedance

GYRATORS > GYRATOR

GYRATORY > GYRATE

GYRE *n* circular or spiral movement or path ▷ *vb* whirl

GYRED > GYRE

GYRENE *n* nickname for a member of the US Marine Corps

GYRENES > GYRENE

GYRES > GYRE

GYRFALCON *n* very large rare falcon of northern regions

GYRI > GYRUS

GYRING > GYRE

GYRO *n* gyrocompass: nonmagnmetic compass that uses a motor-driven gyroscope to indicate true north

GYROCAR *n* two-wheeled car

GYROCARS > GYROCAR

GYRODYNE *n* aircraft that uses a powered rotor to take off and manoeuvre, but uses autorotation when cruising

GYRODYNES > GYRODYNE

GYROIDAL *adj* spiral

GYROLITE *n* silicate

GYROLITES > GYROLITE

GYROMANCY *n* divination by spinning in a circle, then falling on any of various letters that have been written on the ground

GYRON *same as* > GIRON

GYRONIC > GYRON

GYRONNY *same as* > GIRONNY

GYRONS > GYRON

GYROPILOT *n* type of automatic pilot

GYROPLANE *another name for* > AUTOGIRO

GYROS > GYRO

GYROSCOPE *n* disc rotating on an axis that can turn in any direction, so the disc maintains the same position regardless of the movement of the surrounding structure

GYROSE *adj* marked with sinuous lines

GYROSTAT *same as* > GYROSCOPE

GYROSTATS > GYROSTAT

GYROUS *adj* gyrose

GYROVAGUE *n* peripatetic monk

GYRUS *n* convolution

GYRUSES > GYRUS

GYTE *n* spoilt child

GYTES > GYTE

GYTRASH *n* spirit that haunts lonely roads

GYTRASHES > GYTRASH

GYTTJA *n* sediment on lake bottom

GYTTJAS > GYTTJA

GYVE *vb* shackle or fetter ▷ *n* fetters

GYVED > GYVE

GYVES > GYVE

GYVING > GYVE

Hh

HA *interj* exclamation expressing triumph, surprise, or scorn
HAAF *n* deep-sea fishing ground off the Shetland and Orkney Islands
HAAFS > HAAF
HAANEPOOT *n* variety of grape
HAAR *n* cold sea mist or fog off the North Sea
HAARS > HAAR
HABANERA *n* slow Cuban dance in duple time
HABANERAS > HABANERA
HABANERO *n* variety of chilli pepper
HABANEROS > HABANERO
HABDABS *n* highly nervous state
HABDALAH *n* prayer at end of Jewish sabbath
HABDALAHS > HABDALAH
HABERDINE *n* dried cod
HABERGEON *n* light sleeveless coat of mail worn in the 14th century under the plated hauberk
HABILABLE *adj* able to wear clothes
HABILE *adj* skilful
HABIT *n* established way of behaving ▷ *vb* clothe
HABITABLE *adj* fit to be lived in
HABITABLY > HABITABLE
HABITAN *same as* > HABITANT
HABITANS > HABITAN
HABITANT *n* early French settler in Canada or Louisiana or a descendant of one, esp a farmer
HABITANTS > HABITANT
HABITAT *n* natural home of an animal or plant
HABITATS > HABITAT
HABITED *adj* dressed in a habit
HABITING > HABIT
HABITS > HABIT
HABITUAL *adj* done regularly and repeatedly ▷ *n* person with a habit
HABITUALS > HABITUAL
HABITUATE *vb* accustom
HABITUDE *n* habit or tendency
HABITUDES > HABITUDE
HABITUE *n* frequent visitor

to a place
HABITUES > HABITUE
HABITUS *n* general physical state, esp with regard to susceptibility to disease
HABLE *old form of* > ABLE
HABOOB *n* sandstorm
HABOOBS > HABOOB
HABU *n* large venomous snake
HABUS > HABU
HACEK *n* pronunciation symbol in Slavonic language
HACEKS > HACEK
HACENDADO *n* owner of hacienda
HACHIS *n* hash
HACHURE *n* shading of short lines drawn on a map to indicate the degree of steepness of a hill ▷ *vb* mark or show by hachures
HACHURED > HACHURE
HACHURES > HACHURE
HACHURING > HACHURE
HACIENDA *n* ranch or large estate in Latin America
HACIENDAS > HACIENDA
HACK *vb* cut or chop violently ▷ *n* (inferior) writer or journalist ▷ *adj* unoriginal or of a low standard
HACKABLE > HACK
HACKAMORE *n* rope or rawhide halter used for unbroken foals
HACKBERRY *n* American tree or shrub with edible cherry-like fruits
HACKBOLT *n* shearwater
HACKBOLTS > HACKBOLT
HACKBUT *another word for* > ARQUEBUS
HACKBUTS > HACKBUT
HACKED > HACK
HACKEE *n* chipmunk
HACKEES > HACKEE
HACKER *n* computer enthusiast, esp one who breaks into the computer system of a company or government
HACKERIES > HACKERY
HACKERS > HACKER
HACKERY *n* journalism
HACKETTE *n* informal, derogatory term for female journalist

HACKETTES > HACKETTE
HACKIE *n* US word meaning cab driver
HACKIES > HACKIE
HACKING > HACK
HACKINGS > HACK
HACKLE *same as* > HECKLE
HACKLED > HACKLE
HACKLER > HACKLE
HACKLERS > HACKLE
HACKLES *npl* hairs on the back of the neck and the back of a dog, cat, etc, which rise when the animal is angry or afraid
HACKLET *n* kittiwake
HACKLETS > HACKLET
HACKLIER > HACKLY
HACKLIEST > HACKLY
HACKLING > HACKLE
HACKLY *adj* rough or jagged
HACKMAN *n* taxi driver
HACKMEN > HACKMAN
HACKNEY *n* taxi ▷ *vb* make commonplace and banal by too frequent use
HACKNEYED *adj* (of a word or phrase) unoriginal and overused
HACKNEYS > HACKNEY
HACKS > HACK
HACKSAW *n* small saw for cutting metal ▷ *vb* cut with a hacksaw
HACKSAWED > HACKSAW
HACKSAWN > HACKSAW
HACKSAWS > HACKSAW
HACKWORK *n* dull repetitive work
HACKWORKS > HACKWORK
HACQUETON *n* padded jacket worn under chain mail
HAD *vb* Scots form of hold
HADAL *adj* of, relating to, or constituting very deep zones of the oceans
HADARIM > HEDER
HADAWAY *sentence substitute* exclamation urging the hearer to refrain from delay in the execution of a task
HADDEN > HAVE
HADDEST *same as* > HADST
HADDIE *n* finnan haddock
HADDIES > HADDIE
HADDING > HAVE
HADDOCK *n* edible sea fish of N Atlantic

HADDOCKS > HADDOCK
HADE *n* angle made to the vertical by the plane of a fault or vein ▷ *vb* incline from the vertical
HADED > HADE
HADEDAH *n* large grey-green S African ibis
HADEDAHS > HADEDAH
HADES > HADE
HADING > HADE
HADITH *n* body of tradition and legend about Mohammed and his followers, used as a basis of Islamic law
HADITHS > HADITH
HADJ *same as* > HAJJ
HADJEE *same as* > HADJI
HADJEES > HADJEE
HADJES > HADJ
HADJI *same as* > HAJJI
HADJIS > HADJI
HADROME *n* part of xylem
HADROMES > HADROME
HADRON *n* any elementary particle capable of taking part in a strong nuclear interaction and therefore excluding leptons and photons
HADRONIC > HADRON
HADRONS > HADRON
HADROSAUR *n* any one of a large group of duck-billed partly aquatic bipedal dinosaurs
HADS > HAVE
HADST *singular form of the past tense (indicative mood) of* > HAVE
HAE *Scot variant of* > HAVE
HAECCEITY *n* property that uniquely identifies an object
HAED > HAE
HAEING > HAE
HAEM *n* complex red organic pigment containing ferrous iron, present in haemoglobin
HAEMAL *adj* of the blood
HAEMATAL *same as* > HAEMAL
HAEMATEIN *n* dark purple water-insoluble crystalline substance obtained from logwood and used as an indicator and biological stain
HAEMATIC *n* agent that

stimulates the production of red blood cells

HAEMATICS > HAEMATIC

HAEMATIN n dark bluish or brownish pigment containing iron in the ferric state, obtained by the oxidation of haem

HAEMATINS > HAEMATIN

HAEMATITE same as > HEMATITE

HAEMATOID adj resembling blood

HAEMATOMA n tumour of clotted or partially clotted blood

HAEMIC same as > HAEMATIC

HAEMIN n haematin chloride

HAEMINS > HAEMIN

HAEMOCOEL n body cavity of many invertebrates, including arthropods and molluscs, developed from part of the blood system

HAEMOCYTE n any blood cell, esp a red blood cell

HAEMOID same as > HAEMATOID

HAEMONIES > HAEMONY

HAEMONY n plant mentioned in Milton's poetry

HAEMOSTAT n surgical instrument that stops bleeding by compression of a blood vessel

HAEMS > HAEM

HAEN > HAE

HAEREDES > HAERES

HAEREMAI interj Māori expression of welcome

HAEREMAIS > HAEREMAI

HAERES same as > HERES

HAES > HAE

HAET n whit

HAETS > HAET

HAFF n lagoon

HAFFET n side of head

HAFFETS > HAFFET

HAFFIT same as > HAFFET

HAFFITS > HAFFIT

HAFFLIN same as > HALFLING

HAFFLINS > HAFFLIN

HAFFS > HAFF

HAFIZ n title for a person who knows the Koran by heart

HAFIZES > HAFIZ

HAFNIUM n metallic element found in zirconium ores

HAFNIUMS > HAFNIUM

HAFT n handle of an axe, knife, or dagger ▷ vb provide with a haft

HAFTARA same as > HAFTARAH

HAFTARAH n (in Judaism) short reading from the Prophets which follows the reading from the Torah on Sabbaths and festivals

HAFTARAHS > HAFTARAH

HAFTARAS > HAFTARA

HAFTAROT > HAFTARAH

HAFTAROTH > HAFTARAH

HAFTED > HAFT

HAFTER > HAFT

HAFTERS > HAFT

HAFTING > HAFT

HAFTORAH same as > HAFTARAH

HAFTORAHS > HAFTORAH

HAFTOROS > HAFTORAH

HAFTOROT > HAFTORAH

HAFTOROTH > HAFTORAH

HAFTS > HAFT

HAG n ugly old woman ▷ vb hack

HAGADIC same as > HAGGADIC

HAGADIST same as > HAGGADIST

HAGADISTS > HAGADIST

HAGBERRY same as > HACKBERRY

HAGBOLT same as > HACKBOLT

HAGBOLTS > HAGBOLT

HAGBORN adj born of witch

HAGBUSH > ARQUEBUS

HAGBUSHES > HAGBUSH

HAGBUT same as > ARQUEBUS

HAGBUTEER > HAGBUT

HAGBUTS > HAGBUT

HAGBUTTER > HAGBUT

HAGDEN same as > HACKBOLT

HAGDENS > HAGDEN

HAGDON same as > HACKBOLT

HAGDONS > HAGDON

HAGDOWN same as > HACKBOLT

HAGDOWNS > HAGDOWN

HAGFISH n any of various primitive eel-like marine vertebrates

HAGFISHES > HAGFISH

HAGG n boggy place

HAGGADA same as > HAGGADAH

HAGGADAH n book containing the order of service of the traditional Jewish Passover meal

HAGGADAHS > HAGGADAH

HAGGADAS > HAGGADA

HAGGADIC > HAGGADAH

HAGGADIST n writer of Aggadoth

HAGGADOT > HAGGADAH

HAGGADOTH > HAGGADAH

HAGGARD adj looking tired and ill ▷ n hawk that has reached maturity before being caught

HAGGARDLY > HAGGARD

HAGGARDS > HAGGARD

HAGGED > HAG

HAGGING > HAG

HAGGIS n Scottish dish made from sheep's offal, oatmeal, suet, and

seasonings, boiled in a bag made from the sheep's stomach

HAGGISES > HAGGIS

HAGGISH > HAG

HAGGISHLY > HAG

HAGGLE vb bargain or wrangle over a price

HAGGLED > HAGGLE

HAGGLER > HAGGLE

HAGGLERS > HAGGLE

HAGGLES > HAGGLE

HAGGLING > HAGGLE

HAGGS > HAGG

HAGIARCHY n government by saints, holy men, or men in holy orders

HAGIOLOGY n literature about the lives and legends of saints

HAGLET same as > HACKLET

HAGLETS > HAGLET

HAGLIKE > HAG

HAGRIDDEN > HAGRIDE

HAGRIDE vb torment or obsess

HAGRIDER > HAGRIDE

HAGRIDERS > HAGRIDE

HAGRIDES > HAGRIDE

HAGRIDING > HAGRIDE

HAGRODE > HAGRIDE

HAGS > HAG

HAH same as > HA

HAHA n wall or other boundary marker that is set in a ditch so as not to interrupt the landscape

HAHAS > HAHA

HAHNIUM n transuranic element artificially produced from californium

HAHNIUMS > HAHNIUM

HAHS > HAH

HAICK same as > HAIK

HAICKS > HAICK

HAIDUK n rural brigand

HAIDUKS > HAIDUK

HAIK n Arab's outer garment of cotton, wool, or silk, for the head and body

HAIKA > HAIK

HAIKAI same as > HAIKU

HAIKS > HAIK

HAIKU n Japanese verse form in 17 syllables

HAIKUS > HAIKU

HAIL n (shower of) small pellets of ice ▷ vb fall as or like hail ▷ sentence substitute exclamation of greeting

HAILED > HAIL

HAILER > HAIL

HAILERS > HAIL

HAILIER > HAIL

HAILIEST > HAIL

HAILING > HAIL

HAILS > HAIL

HAILSHOT n small scattering shot

HAILSHOTS > HAILSHOT

HAILSTONE n pellet of hail

HAILSTORM n storm during which hail falls

HAILY > HAIL

HAIMISH same as > HEIMISH

HAIN vb Scots word meaning save

HAINCH Scots form of > HAUNCH

HAINCHED > HAINCH

HAINCHES > HAINCH

HAINCHING > HAINCH

HAINED > HAIN

HAINING > HAIN

HAININGS > HAIN

HAINS > HAIN

HAINT same as > HAUNT

HAINTS > HAINT

HAIQUE same as > HAIK

HAIQUES > HAIK

HAIR n threadlike growth on the skin ▷ vb provide with hair

HAIRBALL n compact mass of hair that forms in the stomach of cats, calves, etc, as a result of licking and swallowing the fur, and causes vomiting, coughing, bloat, weight loss, and depression

HAIRBALLS > HAIRBALL

HAIRBAND n band worn around head to control hair

HAIRBANDS > HAIRBAND

HAIRBELL same as > HAREBELL

HAIRBELLS > HAIRBELL

HAIRBRUSH n brush for grooming the hair

HAIRCAP n type of moss

HAIRCAPS > HAIRCAP

HAIRCLOTH n cloth woven from horsehair, used in upholstery

HAIRCUT n act or an instance of cutting the hair

HAIRCUTS > HAIRCUT

HAIRDO n hairstyle

HAIRDOS > HAIRDO

HAIRDRIER same as > HAIRDRYER

HAIRDRYER n hand-held electric device that blows out hot air and is used to dry and, sometimes, assist in styling the hair, as in blow-drying

HAIRED adj with hair

HAIRGRIP n small bent clasp used to fasten the hair

HAIRGRIPS > HAIRGRIP

HAIRIER > HAIRY

HAIRIEST > HAIRY

HAIRIF another name for > CLEAVERS

HAIRIFS > HAIRIF

HAIRINESS > HAIRY

HAIRING > HAIR

HAIRLESS adj having little or no hair ▷ n as in Mexican hairless a small breed of hairless dog

HAIRLIKE > HAIR

HAIRLINE n edge of hair at the top of the forehead ▷ adj very fine or narrow

HAIRLINES > HAIRLINE

HAIRLOCK n lock of hair

HAIRLOCKS > HAIRLOCK

HAIRNET n any of several kinds of light netting worn over the hair to keep it in place

HAIRNETS > HAIRNET

HAIRPIECE n section of false hair added to a person's real hair

HAIRPIN n U-shaped wire used to hold the hair in place

HAIRPINS > HAIRPIN

HAIRS > HAIR

HAIRSPRAY n fixative solution sprayed onto the hair to keep a hairstyle in shape

HAIRST Scots form of > HARVEST

HAIRSTED > HAIRST

HAIRSTING > HAIRST

HAIRSTS > HAIRST

HAIRSTYLE n cut and arrangement of a person's hair

HAIRTAIL n any of various marine spiny-finned fish having a long whiplike scaleless body and long sharp teeth

HAIRTAILS > HAIRTAIL

HAIRWORK n thing made from hair

HAIRWORKS > HAIRWORK

HAIRWORM n any of various hairlike nematode worms

HAIRWORMS > HAIRWORM

HAIRY adj covered with hair

HAIRYBACK n offensive word for an Afrikaner

HAITH interj Scots oath

HAJ same as > HADJ

HAJES > HAJ

HAJI same as > HAJJI

HAJIS > HAJI

HAJJ n pilgrimage a Muslim makes to Mecca

HAJJAH n Muslim woman who has made a pilgrimage to Mecca

HAJJAHS > HAJJAH

HAJJES > HAJJ

HAJJI n Muslim who has made a pilgrimage to Mecca

HAJJIS > HAJJI

HAKA n ceremonial Māori dance with chanting

HAKAM n text written by a rabbi

HAKAMS > HAKAM

HAKARI n Māori ritual feast

HAKARIS > HAKARI

HAKAS > HAKA

HAKE n edible sea fish of N hemisphere

HAKEA n Australian tree or shrub with hard woody fruit

HAKEAS > HAKEA

HAKEEM same as > HAKIM

HAKEEMS > HAKEEM

HAKES > HAKE

HAKIM n Muslim judge, ruler, or administrator

HAKIMS > HAKIM

HAKU in New Zealand English, same as > KINGFISH

HAKUS > HAKU

HALACHA n Jewish religious law

HALACHAS > HALACHA

HALACHIC > HALACHA

HALACHIST > HALACHA

HALACHOT > HALACHA

HALACHOTH > HALACHA

HALAKAH same as > HALACHA

HALAKAHS > HALAKAH

HALAKHA same as > HALACHA

HALAKHAH same as > HALACHA

HALAKHAHS > HALAKHAH

HALAKHAS > HALAKHA

HALAKHIC > HALAKHAH

HALAKHIST > HALAKHAH

HALAKHOT > HALAKHA

HALAKHOTH > HALAKHAH

HALAKIC > HALAKHA

HALAKIST > HALAKHA

HALAKISTS > HALAKHA

HALAKOTH > HALAKHA

HALAL n meat from animals slaughtered according to Muslim law ▷ adj of or relating to such meat ▷ vb kill (animals) in this way

HALALA n money unit in Saudi Arabia

HALALAH same as > HALALA

HALALAHS > HALALAH

HALALAS > HALALA

HALALLED > HALAL

HALALLING > HALAL

HALALS > HALAL

HALATION n fogging usually seen as a bright ring surrounding a source of light: caused by reflection from the back of the film

HALATIONS > HALATION

HALAVAH same as > HALVAH

HALAVAHS > HALAVAH

HALAZONE n type of disinfectant

HALAZONES > HALAZONE

HALBERD n spear with an axe blade

HALBERDS > HALBERD

HALBERT same as > HALBERD

HALBERTS > HALBERT

HALCYON adj peaceful and happy ▷ n (in Greek mythology) fabulous bird associated with the winter solstice

HALCYONIC adj peaceful and happy

HALCYONS > HALCYON

HALE adj healthy, robust ▷ vb pull or drag

HALED > HALE

HALENESS > HALE

HALER same as > HELLER

HALERS > HALER

HALERU > HALER

HALES > HALE

HALEST > HALE

HALF n either of two equal parts ▷ adj denoting one of two equal parts ▷ adv to the extent of half

HALFA n African grass

HALFAS > HALFA

HALFBACK n player positioned immediately behind the forwards

HALFBACKS > HALFBACK

HALFBEAK n type of fish with an elongated body, a short upper jaw, and a long protruding lower jaw

HALFBEAKS > HALFBEAK

HALFEN > HALF

HALFLIFE n time taken for half of the atoms in a radioactive material to undergo decay

HALFLIN same as > HALFLING

HALFLING n person only half-grown

HALFLINGS > HALFLING

HALFLINS > HALFLIN

HALFLIVES > HALFLIFE

HALFNESS > HALF

HALFPACE n landing on staircase

HALFPACES > HALFPACE

HALFPENCE > HALFPENNY

HALFPENNY n former British coin worth half an old penny

HALFPIPE n U-shaped object used in skateboarding stunts

HALFPIPES > HALFPIPE

HALFS > HALF

HALFTIME n rest period between the two halves of a game

HALFTIMES > HALFTIME

HALFTONE n illustration showing lights and shadows by means of very small dots ▷ adj relating to, used in, or made by halftone

HALFTONES > HALFTONE

HALFTRACK n vehicle with caterpillar tracks and wheels

HALFWAY adj at or to half the distance

HALFWIT n foolish or stupid person

HALFWITS > HALFWIT

HALIBUT n large edible flatfish of N Atlantic

HALIBUTS > HALIBUT

HALICORE n dugong

HALICORES > HALICORE

HALID same as > HALIDE

HALIDE n binary compound containing a halogen atom or ion in combination with a more electropositive element

HALIDES > HALIDE

HALIDOM n holy place or thing

HALIDOME same as > HALIDOM

HALIDOMES > HALIDOME

HALIDOMS > HALIDOM

HALIDS > HALID

HALIEUTIC adj of fishing

HALIMOT n court held by lord

HALIMOTE same as > HALIMOT

HALIMOTES > HALIMOTE

HALIMOTS > HALIMOT

HALING > HALE

HALIOTIS n type of shellfish

HALITE n colourless or white mineral sometimes tinted by impurities, found in beds as an evaporite

HALITES > HALITE

HALITOSES > HALITOSIS

HALITOSIS n unpleasant-smelling breath

HALITOTIC > HALITUS

HALITOUS > HALITUS

HALITUS n vapour

HALITUSES > HALITUS

HALL n entrance passage

HALLAH variant spelling of > CHALLAH

HALLAHS > HALLAH

HALLAL same as > HALAL

HALLALI n bugle call

HALLALIS > HALLALI

HALLALLED > HALLAL

HALLALOO same as > HALLOO

HALLALOOS > HALLALOO

HALLALS > HALLAL

HALLAN n partition in cottage

HALLANS > HALLAN

HALLEL n (in Judaism) section of the liturgy consisting of Psalms 113-18, read during the morning service on festivals, Chanukah, and Rosh Chodesh

HALLELS > HALLEL

HALLIAN same as > HALLION

HALLIANS > HALLIAN

HALLIARD same as > HALYARD

HALLIARDS > HALLIARD

HALLING n Norwegian country dance

HALLINGS > HALLING

HALLION n lout

HALLIONS > HALLION

HALLMARK n typical

feature ▷ vb stamp with a hallmark

HALLMARKS >HALLMARK

HALLO same as >HALLOO

HALLOA same as >HALLOO

HALLOAED >HALLOA

HALLOAING >HALLOA

HALLOAS >HALLOA

HALLOED >HALLO

HALLOES >HALLO

HALLOING >HALLO

HALLOO interj shout used to call hounds at a hunt ▷ sentence substitute shout to attract attention, esp to call hounds at a hunt ▷ n shout of "halloo" ▷ vb shout (something) to (someone)

HALLOOED >HALLOO

HALLOOING >HALLOO

HALLOOS >HALLOO

HALLOT >HALLAH

HALLOTH same as >CHALLAH

HALLOUMI n salty white sheep's cheese from Greece or Turkey, usually eaten grilled

HALLOUMIS >HALLOUMI

HALLOW vb consecrate or set apart as being holy

HALLOWED adj regarded as holy

HALLOWER >HALLOW

HALLOWERS >HALLOW

HALLOWING >HALLOW

HALLOWS >HALLOW

HALLS >HALL

HALLSTAND n piece of furniture on which are hung coats, hats, etc

HALLUCAL >HALLUX

HALLUCES >HALLUX

HALLUX n first digit on the hind foot of a mammal, bird, reptile, or amphibian

HALLWAY n entrance area

HALLWAYS >HALLWAY

HALLYON same as >HALLION

HALLYONS >HALLYON

HALM same as >HAULM

HALMA n board game in which players attempt to transfer their pieces from their own to their opponents' bases

HALMAS >HALMA

HALMS >HALM

HALO n ring of light round the head of a sacred figure ▷ vb surround with a halo

HALOBIONT n plant or animal that lives in a salty environment such as the sea

HALOCLINE n gradient in salinity of sea

HALOED >HALO

HALOES >HALO

HALOGEN n any of a group of nonmetallic elements including chlorine and iodine

HALOGENS >HALOGEN

HALOGETON n herbaceous plant

HALOID adj resembling or derived from a halogen ▷ n compound containing halogen atoms in its molecules

HALOIDS >HALOID

HALOING >HALO

HALOLIKE >HALO

HALON n any of a class of chemical compounds derived from hydrocarbons by replacing one or more hydrogen atoms by bromine atoms and other hydrogen atoms by other halogen atoms (chlorine, fluorine, or iodine). Halons are stable compounds that are used in fire extinguishers, although they may contribute to depletion of the ozone layer

HALONS >HALON

HALOPHILE n organism that thrives in an extremely salty environment, such as the Dead Sea

HALOPHILY n ability to live in salty environment

HALOPHOBE n plant unable to live in salty soil

HALOPHYTE n plant that grows in very salty soil, as in a salt marsh

HALOS >HALO

HALOSERE n plant community that originates and develops in conditions of high salinity

HALOSERES >HALOSERE

HALOTHANE n colourless volatile slightly soluble liquid with an odour resembling that of chloroform

HALOUMI same as >HALLOUMI

HALOUMIS >HALOUMI

HALSE vb embrace

HALSED >HALSE

HALSER >HALSE

HALSERS >HALSE

HALSES >HALSE

HALSING >HALSE

HALT vb come or bring to a stop ▷ n temporary stop ▷ adj lame

HALTED >HALT

HALTER n strap round a horse's head with a rope to lead it with ▷ vb put a halter on (a horse)

HALTERE n one of a pair of short projections in dipterous insects that are modified hind wings, used for maintaining equilibrium during flight

HALTERED >HALTER

HALTERES >HALTERE

HALTERING >HALTER

HALTERS >HALTER

HALTING >HALT

HALTINGLY >HALT

HALTINGS >HALT

HALTLESS >HALT

HALTS >HALT

HALUTZ variant spelling of >CHALUTZ

HALUTZIM >HALUTZ

HALVA same as >HALVAH

HALVAH n Eastern Mediterranean, Middle Eastern, or Indian sweetmeat made of honey and containing sesame seeds, nuts, rose water, saffron, etc

HALVAHS >HALVAH

HALVAS >HALVA

HALVE vb divide in half

HALVED >HALVE

HALVER >HALVE

HALVERS >HALVE

HALVES >HALVE

HALVING >HALVE

HALYARD n rope for raising a ship's sail or flag

HALYARDS >HALYARD

HAM n smoked or salted meat from a pig's thigh ▷ vb overact

HAMADA n rocky plateau in desert

HAMADAS >HAMADA

HAMADRYAD n one of a class of nymphs, each of which inhabits a tree and dies with it

HAMADRYAS n type of baboon

HAMAL n (in Middle Eastern countries) a porter, bearer, or servant

HAMALS >HAMAL

HAMAMELIS n any of several trees or shrubs native to E Asia and North America and cultivated as ornamentals

HAMARTIA n flaw in character which leads to the downfall of the protagonist in a tragedy

HAMARTIAS >HAMARTIA

HAMATE adj hook-shaped ▷ n small bone in the wrist

HAMATES >HAMATE

HAMAUL same as >HAMAL

HAMAULS >HAMAUL

HAMBA interj usually offensive term for go away

HAMBLE vb mutilate

HAMBLED >HAMBLE

HAMBLES >HAMBLE

HAMBLING >HAMBLE

HAMBONE vb strike body to provide percussion

HAMBONED >HAMBONE

HAMBONES >HAMBONE

HAMBONING >HAMBONE

HAMBURG same as >HAMBURGER

HAMBURGER n minced beef shaped into a flat disc, cooked and usually served in a bread roll

HAMBURGS >HAMBURG

HAME n a Scots word for home ▷ vb to home

HAMED >HAME

HAMES >HAME

HAMEWITH adv Scots word meaning homewards

HAMFATTER n inferior actor or musician

HAMING >HAME

HAMLET n small village

HAMLETS >HAMLET

HAMMADA same as >HAMADA

HAMMADAS >HAMMADA

HAMMAL same as >HAMAL

HAMMALS >HAMMAL

HAMMAM n bathing establishment, such as a Turkish bath

HAMMAMS >HAMMAM

HAMMED >HAM

HAMMER n tool with a heavy metal head and a wooden handle, used to drive in nails etc ▷ vb hit (as if) with a hammer

HAMMERED >HAMMER

HAMMERER >HAMMER

HAMMERERS >HAMMER

HAMMERING >HAMMER

HAMMERKOP n shark with hammer-shaped head

HAMMERMAN n person working with hammer

HAMMERMEN >HAMMERMAN

HAMMERS >HAMMER

HAMMERTOE n condition in which the toe is permanently bent at the joint

HAMMIER >HAMMY

HAMMIEST >HAMMY

HAMMILY >HAMMY

HAMMINESS >HAMMY

HAMMING >HAM

HAMMOCK same as >HUMMOCK

HAMMOCKS >HAMMOCK

HAMMY adj (of an actor) overacting or tending to overact

HAMOSE adj shaped like a hook

HAMOUS same as >HAMOSE

HAMPER vb make it difficult for (someone or something) to move or progress ▷ n large basket with a lid

HAMPERED >HAMPER

HAMPERER >HAMPER

HAMPERERS >HAMPER

HAMPERING >HAMPER

HAMPERS >HAMPER

HAMPSTER same as >HAMSTER

HAMPSTERS >HAMPSTER

HAMS >HAM

HAMSTER n small rodent

with a short tail and cheek pouches

HAMSTERS > HAMSTER

HAMSTRING *n* tendon at the back of the knee ▷ *vb* make it difficult for (someone) to take any action

HAMSTRUNG > HAMSTRING

HAMULAR > HAMULUS

HAMULATE > HAMULUS

HAMULI > HAMULUS

HAMULOSE > HAMULUS

HAMULOUS > HAMULUS

HAMULUS *n* hook or hooklike process at the end of some bones or between the fore and hind wings of a bee or similar insect

HAMZA *n* sign used in Arabic to represent the glottal stop

HAMZAH *same as >* HAMZA

HAMZAHS > HAMZAH

HAMZAS > HAMZA

HAN *archaic inflected form of >* HAVE

HANAP *n* medieval drinking cup

HANAPER *n* small wickerwork basket, often used to hold official papers

HANAPERS > HANAPER

HANAPS > HANAP

HANCE *same as >* HAUNCH

HANCES > HANCE

HANCH *vb* try to bite

HANCHED > HANCH

HANCHES > HANCH

HANCHING > HANCH

HAND *n* part of the body at the end of the arm, consisting of a palm, four fingers, and a thumb ▷ *vb* pass, give

HANDAX *n* small axe held in one hand

HANDAXES > HANDAX

HANDBAG *n* woman's small bag for carrying personal articles in

HANDBAGS *npl* incident in which people, esp sportsmen, fight or threaten to fight, but without real intent to inflict harm

HANDBALL *n* game in which two teams of seven players try to throw a ball into their opponent's goal ▷ *vb* pass (the ball) with a blow of the fist

HANDBALLS > HANDBALL

HANDBELL *n* bell rung by hand, esp one of a tuned set used in musical performance

HANDBELLS > HANDBELL

HANDBILL *n* small printed notice

HANDBILLS > HANDBILL

HANDBLOWN *adj* (of glass) made by hand

HANDBOOK *n* small reference or instruction book

HANDBOOKS > HANDBOOK

HANDBRAKE *n* brake in a motor vehicle operated by a hand lever

HANDCAR *n* small railway vehicle propelled by hand-pumped mechanism

HANDCARS > HANDCAR

HANDCART *n* simple cart pushed or pulled by hand, used for transporting goods

HANDCARTS > HANDCART

HANDCLAP *n* act of clapping hands

HANDCLAPS > HANDCLAP

HANDCLASP *another word for >* HANDSHAKE

HANDCRAFT *n* handicraft

HANDCUFF *n* one of a linked pair of metal rings designed to be locked round a prisoner's wrists by the police ▷ *vb* put handcuffs on

HANDCUFFS > HANDCUFF

HANDED > HAND

HANDER > HAND

HANDERS > HAND

HANDFAST *n* agreement, esp of marriage, confirmed by a handshake ▷ *vb* betroth or marry (two persons or another person) by joining the hands

HANDFASTS > HANDFAST

HANDFED > HANDFEED

HANDFEED *vb* feed (a person or an animal) by hand

HANDFEEDS > HANDFEED

HANDFUL *n* amount that can be held in the hand

HANDFULS > HANDFUL

HANDGRIP *n* covering, usually of towelling or rubber, that makes the handle of a racket or club easier to hold

HANDGRIPS > HANDGRIP

HANDGUN *n* firearm that can be held, carried, and fired with one hand, such as a pistol

HANDGUNS > HANDGUN

HANDHELD *adj* held in position by the hand ▷ *n* computer that can be held in the hand

HANDHELDS > HANDHELD

HANDHOLD *n* object, crevice, etc, that can be used as a grip or support, as in climbing

HANDHOLDS > HANDHOLD

HANDICAP *n* physical or mental disability ▷ *vb* make it difficult for (someone) to do something

HANDICAPS > HANDICAP

HANDIER > HANDY

HANDIEST > HANDY

HANDILY *adv* in a handy way or manner

HANDINESS > HANDY

HANDING > HAND

HANDISM *n* discrimination against people on the grounds of whether they are left-handed or right-handed

HANDISMS > HANDISM

HANDIWORK *n* result of someone's work or activity

HANDJAR *n* Persian dagger

HANDJARS > HANDJAR

HANDJOB *n* manual stimulation of another person's penis

HANDJOBS > HANDJOB

HANDKNIT *adj* (of a garment) knitted by hand

HANDKNITS > HANDKNIT

HANDLE *n* part of an object that is held so that it can be used ▷ *vb* hold, feel, or move with the hands

HANDLEBAR as in *handlebar moustache:* bushy extended moustache with curled ends that resembles the handlebars of a bicycle

HANDLED > HANDLE

HANDLER *n* person who controls an animal

HANDLERS > HANDLER

HANDLES > HANDLE

HANDLESS > HAND

HANDLIKE > HAND

HANDLING *n* act or an instance of picking up, turning over, or touching something

HANDLINGS > HANDLING

HANDLIST *n* rough list

HANDLISTS > HANDLIST

HANDLOOM *n* weaving device operated by hand

HANDLOOMS > HANDLOOM

HANDMADE *adj* made by hand, not by machine

HANDMAID *n* person or thing that serves as a useful but subordinate purpose

HANDMAIDS > HANDMAID

HANDOFF *n* (in rugby) act of warding off an opposing player with the open hand

HANDOFFS > HANDOFF

HANDOUT *n* clothing, food, or money given to a needy person

HANDOUTS > HANDOUT

HANDOVER *n* transfer or surrender

HANDOVERS > HANDOVER

HANDPASS *vb* (in Australian Rules football) pass the ball by holding it in one hand and striking it with the other

HANDPHONE *n* in SE Asian English, mobile phone

HANDPICK *vb* choose or select with great care, as for a special job or purpose

HANDPICKS > HANDPICK

HANDPLAY *n* fighting with fists

HANDPLAYS > HANDPLAY

HANDPRESS *n* printing press operated by hand

HANDPRINT *n* print of hand

HANDRAIL *n* rail alongside a stairway, to provide support

HANDRAILS > HANDRAIL

HANDROLL *n* large dried-seaweed cone filled with cold rice and other ingredients

HANDROLLS > HANDROLL

HANDS > HAND

HANDSAW *n* any saw for use in one hand only

HANDSAWS > HANDSAW

HANDSEL *n* gift for good luck at the beginning of a new year, new venture, etc ▷ *vb* give a handsel to (a person)

HANDSELED > HANDSEL

HANDSELS > HANDSEL

HANDSET *n* telephone mouthpiece and earpiece in a single unit

HANDSETS > HANDSET

HANDSEWN *adj* sewn by hand

HANDSFUL > HANDFUL

HANDSHAKE *n* act of grasping and shaking a person's hand, such as in greeting or when agreeing on a deal

HANDSOME *adj* (esp of a man) good-looking ▷ *n* term of endearment for a beloved person

HANDSOMER > HANDSOME

HANDSOMES > HANDSOME

HANDSPIKE *n* bar or length of pipe used as a lever

HANDSTAFF *n* staff held in hand

HANDSTAMP *vb* stamp by hand

HANDSTAND *n* act of supporting the body on the hands in an upside-down position

HANDSTURN *n* slightest amount of work

HANDTOWEL *n* towel for drying hands

HANDWHEEL *n* wheel operated by hand

HANDWORK *n* work done by hand rather than by machine

HANDWORKS > HANDWORK

HANDWOVEN *adj* woven by hand

HANDWRIT > HANDWRITE

HANDWRITE *vb* write by hand

HANDWROTE > HANDWRITE

HANDY *adj* convenient, useful

HANDYMAN n man who is good at making or repairing things

HANDYMEN > HANDYMAN

HANDYWORK same as > HANDIWORK

HANEPOOT n variety of muscat grape

HANEPOOTS > HANEPOOT

HANG vb attach or be attached at the top with the lower part free

HANGABLE adj suitable for hanging

HANGAR n large shed for storing aircraft ▷ vb put in a hangar

HANGARED > HANGAR

HANGARING > HANGAR

HANGARS > HANGAR

HANGBIRD n any bird, esp the Baltimore oriole, that builds a hanging nest

HANGBIRDS > HANGBIRD

HANGDOG adj guilty, ashamed ▷ n furtive or sneaky person

HANGDOGS > HANGDOG

HANGED > HANG

HANGER n curved piece of wood, wire, or plastic, with a hook, for hanging up clothes

HANGERS > HANGER

HANGFIRE n failure to fire

HANGFIRES > HANGFIRE

HANGI n Māori oven consisting of a hole in the ground filled with hot stones

HANGING > HANG

HANGINGS > HANG

HANGIS > HANGI

HANGMAN n man who executes people by hanging

HANGMEN > HANGMAN

HANGNAIL n piece of skin partly torn away from the base or side of a fingernail

HANGNAILS > HANGNAIL

HANGNEST same as > HANGBIRD

HANGNESTS > HANGNEST

HANGOUT n place where one lives or that one frequently visits

HANGOUTS > HANGOUT

HANGOVER n headache and nausea as a result of drinking too much alcohol

HANGOVERS > HANGOVER

HANGS > HANG

HANGTAG n attached label

HANGTAGS > HANGTAG

HANGUL n Korean language

HANGUP n emotional or psychological preoccupation or problem

HANGUPS > HANGUP

HANIWA n Japanese funeral offering

HANJAR same as > HANDJAR

HANJARS > HANJAR

HANK n coil, esp of yarn ▷ vb

attach (a sail) to a stay by hanks

HANKED > HANK

HANKER vb desire intensely

HANKERED > HANKER

HANKERER > HANKER

HANKERERS > HANKER

HANKERING > HANKER

HANKERS > HANKER

HANKIE same as > HANKY

HANKIES > HANKY

HANKING > HANK

HANKS > HANK

HANKY n handkerchief

HANSA same as > HANSE

HANSAS > HANSA

HANSE n medieval guild of merchants

HANSEATIC > HANSA

HANSEL same as > HANDSEL

HANSELED > HANSEL

HANSELING > HANSEL

HANSELLED > HANSEL

HANSELS > HANSEL

HANSES > HANSE

HANSOM n formerly, a two-wheeled one-horse carriage with a fixed hood

HANSOMS > HANSOM

HANT same as > HAUNT

HANTED > HANT

HANTING > HANT

HANTLE n good deal

HANTLES > HANTLE

HANTS > HANT

HANUKIAH n candelabrum having nine branches that is lit during the festival of Hanukkah

HANUKIAHS > HANUKIAH

HANUMAN n type of monkey

HANUMANS > HANUMAN

HAO n monetary unit of Vietnam, worth one tenth of a đồng

HAOLE n Hawaiian word for white person

HAOLES > HAOLE

HAOMA n type of ritual drink

HAOMAS > HAOMA

HAOS > HAO

HAP n luck ▷ vb cover up

HAPAX n word that only appears once in a work of literature, or in a body of work by a particular author

HAPAXES > HAPAX

HAPHAZARD adj not organized or planned ▷ n chance

HAPHTARA same as > HAFTARAH

HAPHTARAH same as > HAFTARAH

HAPHTARAS > HAPHTARA

HAPHTAROT > HAPHTARA

HAPKIDO n Korean martial art

HAPKIDOS > HAPKIDO

HAPLESS adj unlucky

HAPLESSLY > HAPLESS

HAPLITE variant of > APLITE

HAPLITES > HAPLITE

HAPLITIC > HAPLITE

HAPLOID adj denoting a cell or organism with unpaired chromosomes ▷ n haploid cell or organism

HAPLOIDIC adj denoting a cell or organism with unpaired chromosomes

HAPLOIDS > HAPLOID

HAPLOIDY > HAPLOID

HAPLOLOGY n omission of a repeated occurrence of a sound or syllable in fluent speech

HAPLONT n organism, esp a plant, that has the haploid number of chromosomes in its somatic cells

HAPLONTIC > HAPLONT

HAPLONTS > HAPLONT

HAPLOPIA n normal single vision

HAPLOPIAS > HAPLOPIA

HAPLOSES > HAPLOSIS

HAPLOSIS n production of a haploid number of chromosomes during meiosis

HAPLOTYPE n collection of genetic markers usually inherited together

HAPLY archaic word for > PERHAPS

HAPPED > HAP

HAPPEN vb take place, occur

HAPPENED > HAPPEN

HAPPENING n event, occurrence ▷ adj fashionable and up-to-the-minute

HAPPENS > HAPPEN

HAPPIED > HAPPY

HAPPIER > HAPPY

HAPPIES > HAPPY

HAPPIEST > HAPPY

HAPPILY > HAPPY

HAPPINESS > HAPPY

HAPPING > HAP

HAPPY adj feeling or causing joy ▷ vb make happy

HAPPYING > HAPPY

HAPS > HAP

HAPTEN n incomplete antigen that can stimulate antibody production only when it is chemically combined with a particular protein

HAPTENE same as > HAPTEN

HAPTENES > HAPTENE

HAPTENIC > HAPTEN

HAPTENS > HAPTEN

HAPTERON n cell or group of cells that occurs in certain plants, esp seaweeds, and attaches the plant to its substratum

HAPTERONS > HAPTERON

HAPTIC adj relating to or based on the sense of touch

HAPTICAL same as > HAPTIC

HAPTICS n science of sense of touch

HAPU n subtribe

HAPUKA another name for > GROPER

HAPUKAS > HAPUKA

HAPUKU same as > HAPUKA

HAPUKUS > HAPUKU

HAPUS > HAPU

HAQUETON same as > HACQUETON

HAQUETONS > HAQUETON

HARAKEKE in New Zealand English, another name for > FLAX

HARAKEKES > HARAKEKE

HARAM n anything that is forbidden by Islamic law

HARAMBEE n work chant used on the E African coast ▷ interj cry of harambee

HARAMBEES > HARAMBEE

HARAMDA same as > HARAMZADA

HARAMDAS > HARAMDA

HARAMDI same as > HARAMZADI

HARAMDIS > HARAMDI

HARAMS > HARAM

HARAMZADA n in Indian English, slang word for an illegitimate male

HARAMZADI n in Indian English, slang word for an illegitimate female

HARANGUE vb address angrily or forcefully ▷ n angry or forceful speech

HARANGUED > HARANGUE

HARANGUER > HARANGUE

HARANGUES > HARANGUE

HARASS vb annoy or trouble constantly

HARASSED > HARASS

HARASSER > HARASS

HARASSERS > HARASS

HARASSES > HARASS

HARASSING > HARASS

HARBINGER n someone or something that announces the approach of something ▷ vb announce the approach or arrival of

HARBOR same as > HARBOUR

HARBORAGE n shelter or refuge, as for a ship

HARBORED > HARBOR

HARBORER > HARBOR

HARBORERS > HARBOR

HARBORFUL n amount a harbour can hold

HARBORING > HARBOR

HARBOROUS adj hospitable

HARBORS > HARBOR

HARBOUR n sheltered port ▷ vb maintain secretly in the mind

HARBOURED > HARBOUR

HARBOURER > HARBOUR

HARBOURS > HARBOUR

HARD adj firm, solid, or rigid

▷ adv with great energy or effort

HARDASS *n* tough person

HARDASSES > HARDASS

HARDBACK *n* book with a stiff cover *▷ adj* of or denoting a hardback

HARDBACKS > HARDBACK

HARDBAKE *n* almond toffee

HARDBAKES > HARDBAKE

HARDBALL as in *play hardball* act in a ruthless or uncompromising way

HARDBALLS > HARDBALL

HARDBEAM same as > HORNBEAM

HARDBEAMS > HARDBEAM

HARDBOARD *n* thin stiff board made of compressed sawdust and wood chips

HARDBOOT *n* type of skiing boot

HARDBOOTS > HARDBOOT

HARDBOUND same as > HARDBACK

HARDCASE *n* tough person

HARDCORE *n* style of rock music with short fast songs and little melody

HARDCORES > HARDCORE

HARDCOURT *adj* (of tennis) played on hard surface

HARDCOVER same as > HARDBACK

HARDEDGE *n* style of painting in which vividly coloured subjects are clearly delineated *▷ adj* of, relating to, or denoting this style of painting

HARDEDGES > HARDEDGE

HARDEN *vb* make or become hard *▷ n* rough fabric made from hards

HARDENED *adj* toughened by experience

HARDENER *n* person or thing that hardens

HARDENERS > HARDENER

HARDENING *n* act or process of becoming or making hard

HARDENS > HARDEN

HARDER > HARD

HARDEST > HARD

HARDFACE *n* uncompromising person

HARDFACES > HARDFACE

HARDGOODS same as > HARDWARE

HARDGRASS *n* coarse grass

HARDHACK *n* woody North American rosaceous plant with downy leaves and clusters of small pink or white flowers

HARDHACKS > HARDHACK

HARDHAT *n* hat made of a hard material for protection, worn esp by construction workers, equestrians, etc *▷ adj* (in US English) characteristic of the presumed

conservative attitudes and prejudices typified by construction workers

HARDHATS > HARDHAT

HARDHEAD same as > HARDHEADS

HARDHEADS *n* thistle-like plant

HARDIER > HARDY

HARDIES > HARDY

HARDIEST > HARDY

HARDIHEAD same as > HARDIHOOD

HARDIHOOD *n* courage or daring

HARDILY *adv* in a hardy manner

HARDIMENT same as > HARDIHOOD

HARDINESS *n* condition or quality of being hardy, robust, or bold

HARDISH > HARD

HARDLINE *adj* uncompromising

HARDLINER > HARDLINE

HARDLY *adv* scarcely or not at all

HARDMAN *n* tough, ruthless, or violent man

HARDMEN > HARDMAN

HARDNESS *n* quality or condition of being hard

HARDNOSE *n* tough person

HARDNOSED *adj* tough, shrewd, and practical

HARDNOSES > HARDNOSE

HARDOKE *n* burdock

HARDOKES > HARDOKE

HARDPACK *n* rigid backpack

HARDPACKS > HARDPACK

HARDPAN *n* hard impervious layer of clay below the soil, resistant to drainage and root growth

HARDPANS > HARDPAN

HARDPARTS *n* skeleton

HARDROCK *adj* (of mining) concerned with extracting minerals other than coal, usually from solid rock *▷ n* tough uncompromising man

HARDROCKS > HARDROCK

HARDS *npl* coarse fibres and other refuse from flax and hemp

HARDSET *adj* in difficulties

HARDSHELL *adj* having a shell or carapace that is thick, heavy, or hard

HARDSHIP *n* suffering

HARDSHIPS > HARDSHIP

HARDSTAND *n* hard surface on which vehicles may be parked

HARDTACK *n* kind of hard saltless biscuit, formerly eaten by sailors

HARDTACKS > HARDTACK

HARDTAIL *n* mountain bike with no rear suspension

HARDTAILS > HARDTAIL

HARDTOP *n* car equipped with a metal or plastic roof that is sometimes detachable

HARDTOPS > HARDTOP

HARDWARE *n* metal tools or implements

HARDWARES > HARDWARE

HARDWIRE *vb* instal permanently in computer

HARDWIRED *adj* (of a circuit or instruction) permanently wired into a computer, replacing separate software

HARDWIRES > HARDWIRE

HARDWOOD *n* wood of a broad-leaved tree such as oak or ash

HARDWOODS > HARDWOOD

HARDY *adj* able to stand difficult conditions *▷ n* any blacksmith's tool made with a square shank so that it can be lodged in a square hole in an anvil

HARE *n* animal like a large rabbit, with longer ears and legs *▷ vb* run (away) quickly

HAREBELL *n* blue bell-shaped flower

HAREBELLS > HAREBELL

HARED > HARE

HAREEM same as > HAREM

HAREEMS > HAREEM

HARELD *n* long-tailed duck

HARELDS > HARELD

HARELIKE > HARE

HARELIP *n* slight split in the upper lip

HARELIPS > HARELIP

HAREM *n* (apartments of) a Muslim man's wives and concubines

HAREMS > HAREM

HARES > HARE

HARESTAIL *n* species of cotton grass

HAREWOOD *n* sycamore wood that has been stained for use in furniture making

HAREWOODS > HAREWOOD

HARIANA *n* Indian breed of cattle

HARIANAS > HARIANA

HARICOT *n* variety of French bean with light-coloured edible seeds, which can be dried and stored

HARICOTS > HARICOT

HARIGALDS *npl* intestines

HARIGALS same as > HARIGALDS

HARIJAN *n* member of an Indian caste once considered untouchable

HARIJANS > HARIJAN

HARIM same as > HAREM

HARIMS > HARIM

HARING > HARE

HARIOLATE *vb* practise divination

HARIRA *n* Moroccan soup made from a variety of

vegetables with lentils, chickpeas, and coriander

HARIRAS > HARIRA

HARISH *adj* like hare

HARISSA *n* hot paste made from chilli peppers, tomatoes, spices, and olive oil

HARISSAS > HARISSA

HARK *vb* listen

HARKED > HARK

HARKEN same as > HEARKEN

HARKENED > HARKEN

HARKENER > HARKEN

HARKENERS > HARKEN

HARKENING > HARKEN

HARKENS > HARKEN

HARKING > HARK

HARKS > HARK

HARL same as > HERL

HARLED > HARL

HARLEQUIN *n* stock comic character with a diamond-patterned costume and mask *▷ adj* in many colours

HARLING > HARL

HARLINGS > HARL

HARLOT *n* prostitute *▷ adj* of or like a harlot

HARLOTRY > HARLOT

HARLOTS > HARLOT

HARLS > HARL

HARM *vb* injure physically, mentally, or morally *▷ n* physical, mental, or moral injury

HARMALA *n* African plant

HARMALAS > HARMALA

HARMALIN *n* chemical derived from harmala

HARMALINE same as > HARMALIN

HARMALINS > HARMALIN

HARMAN *n* constable

HARMANS > HARMAN

HARMATTAN *n* dry dusty wind from the Sahara blowing towards the W African coast, esp from November to March

HARMDOING *n* doing of harm

HARMED > HARM

HARMEL same as > HARMALA

HARMELS > HARMEL

HARMER > HARM

HARMERS > HARM

HARMFUL *adj* causing or tending to cause harm, esp to a person's health

HARMFULLY > HARMFUL

HARMIN same as > HARMALIN

HARMINE same as > HARMALIN

HARMINES > HARMINE

HARMING > HARM

HARMINS > HARMIN

HARMLESS *adj* safe to use, touch, or be near

h

HARMONIC *adj* of harmony ▷ *n* overtone of a musical note produced when that note is played, but not usually heard as a separate note

HARMONICA *n* small wind instrument played by sucking and blowing

HARMONICS *n* science of musical sounds

HARMONIES > HARMONY

HARMONISE *same as* > HARMONIZE

HARMONIST *n* person skilled in the art and techniques of harmony

HARMONIUM *n* keyboard instrument like a small organ

HARMONIZE *vb* sing or play in harmony

HARMONY *n* peaceful agreement and cooperation

HARMOST *n* Spartan governor

HARMOSTS > HARMOST

HARMOSTY *n* office of a harmost

HARMOTOME *n* mineral of the zeolite group

HARMS > HARM

HARN *n* coarse linen

HARNESS *n* arrangement of straps for attaching a horse to a cart or plough ▷ *vb* put a harness on

HARNESSED > HARNESS

HARNESSER > HARNESS

HARNESSES > HARNESS

HARNS > HARN

HARO *interj* cry meaning alas

HAROS > HARO

HAROSET *n* Jewish dish eaten at Passover

HAROSETH *same as* > HAROSET

HAROSETHS > HAROSETH

HAROSETS > HAROSET

HARP *n* large triangular stringed instrument played with the fingers ▷ *vb* play the harp

HARPED > HARP

HARPER > HARP

HARPERS > HARP

HARPIES > HARPY

HARPIN *n* type of protein

HARPING > HARP

HARPINGS *npl* wooden members used for strengthening the bow of a vessel

HARPINS *same as* > HARPINGS

HARPIST > HARP

HARPISTS > HARP

HARPOON *n* barbed spear attached to a rope used for hunting whales ▷ *vb* spear with a harpoon

HARPOONED > HARPOON

HARPOONER > HARPOON

HARPOONS > HARPOON

HARPS > HARP

HARPY *n* nasty or bad-tempered woman

HARPYLIKE > HARPY

HARQUEBUS *variant of* > ARQUEBUS

HARRIDAN *n* nagging or vicious woman

HARRIDANS > HARRIDAN

HARRIED > HARRY

HARRIER *n* cross-country runner

HARRIERS > HARRIER

HARRIES > HARRY

HARROW *n* implement used to break up lumps of soil ▷ *vb* draw a harrow over

HARROWED > HARROW

HARROWER > HARROW

HARROWERS > HARROW

HARROWING > HARROW

HARROWS > HARROW

HARRUMPH *vb* clear or make the noise of clearing the throat

HARRUMPHS > HARRUMPH

HARRY *vb* keep asking (someone) to do something, pester

HARRYING > HARRY

HARSH *adj* severe and difficult to cope with ▷ *vb* ruin or end a state of elation

HARSHED > HARSH

HARSHEN *vb* make harsh

HARSHENED > HARSHEN

HARSHENS > HARSHEN

HARSHER > HARSH

HARSHES > HARSH

HARSHEST > HARSH

HARSHING > HARSH

HARSHLY > HARSH

HARSHNESS > HARSH

HARSLET *same as* > HASLET

HARSLETS > HARSLET

HART *n* adult male deer

HARTAL *n* (in India) the act of closing shops or suspending work, esp in political protest

HARTALS > HARTAL

HARTBEES *same as* > HARTBEEST

HARTBEEST *n* African antelope

HARTELY *archaic spelling of* > HEARTILY

HARTEN *same as* > HEARTEN

HARTENED > HARTEN

HARTENING > HARTEN

HARTENS > HARTEN

HARTLESSE *same as* > HEARTLESS

HARTS > HART

HARTSHORN *n* sal volatile

HARUMPH *same as* > HARRUMPH

HARUMPHED > HARUMPH

HARUMPHS > HARUMPH

HARUSPEX *n* (in ancient Rome) a priest who practised divination, esp by examining the entrails of animals

HARUSPICY > HARUSPEX

HARVEST *n* (season for) the gathering of crops ▷ *vb* gather (a ripened crop)

HARVESTED > HARVEST

HARVESTER *n* harvesting machine, esp a combine harvester

HARVESTS > HARVEST

HAS > HAVE

HASBIAN *n* former lesbian who has become heterosexual or bisexual

HASBIANS > HASBIAN

HASH *n* dish of diced cooked meat and vegetables reheated ▷ *vb* chop into small pieces

HASHED > HASH

HASHEESH *same as* > HASHISH

HASHES > HASH

HASHHEAD *n* regular marijuana user

HASHHEADS > HASHHEAD

HASHIER > HASH

HASHIEST > HASH

HASHING > HASH

HASHINGS > HASHING

HASHISH *n* drug made from the cannabis plant, smoked for its intoxicating effects

HASHISHES > HASHISH

HASHMARK *n* character (#)

HASHMARKS > HASHMARK

HASHY > HASH

HASK *n* archaic name for a basket for transporting fish

HASKS > HASK

HASLET *n* loaf of cooked minced pig's offal, eaten cold

HASLETS > HASLET

HASP *n* clasp that fits over a staple and is secured by a bolt or padlock, used as a fastening ▷ *vb* secure (a door, window, etc) with a hasp

HASPED > HASP

HASPING > HASP

HASPS > HASP

HASS as in *white hass* oatmeal pudding made with sheep's gullet

HASSAR *n* South American catfish

HASSARS > HASSAR

HASSEL *variant of* > HASSLE

HASSELS > HASSEL

HASSES > HASS

HASSIUM *n* element synthetically produced in small quantities by high-energy ion bombardment

HASSIUMS > HASSIUM

HASSLE *n* trouble, bother ▷ *vb* bother or annoy

HASSLED > HASSLE

HASSLES > HASSLE

HASSLING > HASSLE

HASSOCK *n* cushion for kneeling on in church

HASSOCKS > HASSOCK

HASSOCKY > HASSOCK

HAST *singular form of the present tense (indicative mood) of* > HAVE

HASTA *Spanish for* > UNTIL

HASTATE *adj* (of a leaf) having a pointed tip and two outward-pointing lobes at the base

HASTATED *same as* > HASTATE

HASTATELY > HASTATE

HASTE *n* (excessive) quickness ▷ *vb* hasten

HASTED > HASTE

HASTEFUL > HASTE

HASTEN *vb* (cause to) hurry

HASTENED > HASTEN

HASTENER > HASTEN

HASTENERS > HASTEN

HASTENING > HASTEN

HASTENS > HASTEN

HASTES > HASTE

HASTIER > HASTY

HASTIEST > HASTY

HASTILY > HASTY

HASTINESS > HASTY

HASTING > HASTE

HASTINGS > HASTE

HASTY *adj* (too) quick

HAT *n* covering for the head, often with a brim ▷ *vb* supply (a person) with a hat or put a hat on (someone)

HATABLE > HATE

HATBAND *n* band or ribbon around the base of the crown of a hat

HATBANDS > HATBAND

HATBOX *n* box or case for a hat or hats

HATBOXES > HATBOX

HATBRUSH *n* brush for hats

HATCH *vb* (cause to) emerge from an egg ▷ *n* hinged door covering an opening in a floor or wall

HATCHABLE > HATCH

HATCHBACK *n* car with a lifting door at the back

HATCHECK *n* cloakroom

HATCHECKS > HATCHECK

HATCHED > HATCH

HATCHEL *same as* > HECKLE

HATCHELED > HATCHEL

HATCHELS > HATCHEL

HATCHER > HATCH

HATCHERS > HATCH

HATCHERY *n* place where eggs are hatched under artificial conditions

HATCHES > HATCH

HATCHET *n* small axe

HATCHETS > HATCHET

HATCHETY *adj* like a hatchet

HATCHING > HATCH

HATCHINGS > HATCH
HATCHLING *n* young animal that has newly hatched from an egg
HATCHMENT *n* diamond-shaped tablet displaying the coat of arms of a dead person
HATCHWAY *n* opening in the deck of a ship
HATCHWAYS > HATCHWAY
HATE *vb* dislike intensely ▷ *n* intense dislike
HATEABLE > HATE
HATED > HATE
HATEFUL *adj* causing or deserving hate
HATEFULLY > HATEFUL
HATELESS > HATE
HATER > HATE
HATERENT *same as* **>** HATRED
HATERENTS > HATERENT
HATERS > HATE
HATES > HATE
HATFUL *n* amount a hat will hold
HATFULS > HATFUL
HATGUARD *n* string to keep a hat from blowing off
HATGUARDS > HATGUARD
HATH *form of the present tense (indicative mood) of* **>** HAVE
HATHA *as in hatha yoga* form of yoga
HATING > HATE
HATLESS > HAT
HATLIKE > HAT
HATMAKER *n* maker of hats
HATMAKERS > HATMAKER
HATPEG *n* peg to hang hat on
HATPEGS > HATPEG
HATPIN *n* sturdy pin used to secure a woman's hat to her hair, often having a decorative head
HATPINS > HATPIN
HATRACK *n* rack for hanging hats on
HATRACKS > HATRACK
HATRED *n* intense dislike
HATREDS > HATRED
HATS > HAT
HATSFUL > HATFUL
HATSTAND *n* frame or pole equipped with hooks or arms for hanging up hats, coats, etc
HATSTANDS > HATSTAND
HATTED > HAT
HATTER *n* person who makes and sells hats ▷ *vb* annoy
HATTERED > HATTER
HATTERIA *n* species of reptile
HATTERIAS > HATTERIA
HATTERING > HATTER
HATTERS > HATTER
HATTING > HAT
HATTINGS > HAT
HATTOCK *n* small hat
HATTOCKS > HATTOCK

HAUBERK *n* long sleeveless coat of mail
HAUBERKS > HAUBERK
HAUBOIS *same as* **>** HAUTBOY
HAUD *Scot word for* **>** HOLD
HAUDING > HAUD
HAUDS > HAUD
HAUF *Scot word for* **>** HALF
HAUFS > HAUF
HAUGH *n* low-lying often alluvial riverside meadow
HAUGHS > HAUGH
HAUGHT *same as* **>** HAUGHTY
HAUGHTIER > HAUGHTY
HAUGHTILY > HAUGHTY
HAUGHTY *adj* proud, arrogant
HAUL *vb* pull or drag with effort ▷ *n* hauling
HAULAGE *n* (charge for) transporting goods
HAULAGES > HAULAGE
HAULD *Scots word for* **>** HOLD
HAULDS > HAULD
HAULED > HAUL
HAULER *same as* **>** HAULIER
HAULERS > HAULER
HAULIER *n* firm or person that transports goods by road
HAULIERS > HAULIER
HAULING > HAUL
HAULM *n* stalks of beans, peas, or potatoes collectively
HAULMIER > HAULMY
HAULMIEST > HAULMY
HAULMS > HAULM
HAULMY *adj* having haulms
HAULS > HAUL
HAULST *same as* **>** HALSE
HAULT *same as* **>** HAUGHTY
HAULYARD *same as* **>** HALYARD
HAULYARDS > HAULYARD
HAUNCH *n* human hip or fleshy hindquarter of an animal ▷ *vb* in archaic usage, cause (an animal) to come down on its haunches
HAUNCHED > HAUNCH
HAUNCHES > HAUNCH
HAUNCHING > HAUNCH
HAUNT *vb* visit in the form of a ghost ▷ *n* place visited frequently
HAUNTED *adj* frequented by ghosts
HAUNTER > HAUNT
HAUNTERS > HAUNT
HAUNTING *adj* memorably beautiful or sad
HAUNTINGS > HAUNT
HAUNTS > HAUNT
HAURIANT *adj* rising
HAURIENT *same as* **>** HAURIANT
HAUSE *same as* **>** HALSE
HAUSED > HAUSE
HAUSEN *n* variety of

sturgeon
HAUSENS > HAUSEN
HAUSES > HAUSE
HAUSFRAU *n* German housewife
HAUSFRAUS > HAUSFRAU
HAUSING > HAUSE
HAUSTELLA *n* pl of haustellum: tip of the proboscis of an insect
HAUSTORIA *n* pl of haustorium: organ of a parasitic plant that absorbs food and water from host tissues
HAUT *same as* **>** HAUGHTY
HAUTBOIS *same as* **>** HAUTBOY
HAUTBOY *n* type of strawberry
HAUTBOYS > HAUTBOY
HAUTE *adj* French word meaning high
HAUTEUR *n* haughtiness
HAUTEURS > HAUTEUR
HAUYNE *n* blue mineral containing calcium
HAUYNES > HAUYNE
HAVARTI *n* Danish cheese
HAVARTIS > HAVARTI
HAVDALAH *n* ceremony marking the end of the sabbath or of a festival, including the blessings over wine, candles, and spices
HAVDALAHS > HAVDALAH
HAVDOLOH *same as* **>** HAVDALAH
HAVDOLOHS > HAVDOLOH
HAVE *vb* possess, hold
HAVELOCK *n* light-coloured cover for a service cap with a flap extending over the back of the neck to protect the head and neck from the sun
HAVELOCKS > HAVELOCK
HAVEN *n* place of safety ▷ *vb* secure or shelter in or as if in a haven
HAVENED > HAVEN
HAVENING > HAVEN
HAVENLESS > HAVEN
HAVENS > HAVEN
HAVEOUR *same as* **>** HAVIOR
HAVEOURS > HAVEOUR
HAVER *vb* talk nonsense ▷ *n* nonsense
HAVERED > HAVER
HAVEREL *n* fool
HAVERELS > HAVEREL
HAVERING > HAVER
HAVERINGS > HAVER
HAVERS > HAVER
HAVERSACK *n* canvas bag carried on the back or shoulder
HAVERSINE *n* half the value of the versed sine
HAVES > HAVE
HAVILDAR *n* noncommissioned officer in the Indian army, equivalent in rank to

sergeant
HAVILDARS > HAVILDAR
HAVING > HAVE
HAVINGS > HAVE
HAVIOR *same as* **>** HAVIOUR
HAVIORS > HAVIOR
HAVIOUR *n* possession
HAVIOURS > HAVIOUR
HAVOC *n* disorder and confusion ▷ *vb* lay waste
HAVOCKED > HAVOC
HAVOCKER > HAVOC
HAVOCKERS > HAVOC
HAVOCKING > HAVOC
HAVOCS > HAVOC
HAW *n* hawthorn berry ▷ *vb* make an inarticulate utterance
HAWALA *n* Middle Eastern system of money transfer
HAWALAS > HAWALA
HAWBUCK *n* bumpkin
HAWBUCKS > HAWBUCK
HAWED > HAW
HAWFINCH *n* European finch with a stout bill and brown plumage with black-and-white wings
HAWING > HAW
HAWK *n* bird of prey with a short hooked bill and very good eyesight ▷ *vb* offer (goods) for sale in the street or door-to-door
HAWKBELL *n* bell fitted to a hawk's leg
HAWKBELLS > HAWKBELL
HAWKBILL *same as* **>** HAWKSBILL
HAWKBILLS > HAWKBILL
HAWKBIT *n* any of three perennial plants with yellow dandelion-like flowers
HAWKBITS > HAWKBIT
HAWKED > HAWK
HAWKER *n* person who travels from place to place selling goods
HAWKERS > HAWKER
HAWKEY *same as* **>** HOCKEY
HAWKEYED *adj* having extremely keen sight
HAWKEYS > HAWKEY
HAWKIE *n* cow with white stripe on face
HAWKIES > HAWKIE
HAWKING *another name for* **>** FALCONRY
HAWKINGS > HAWKING
HAWKISH *adj* favouring the use or display of force rather than diplomacy to achieve foreign policy goals
HAWKISHLY > HAWKISH
HAWKIT *adj* having a white streak
HAWKLIKE > HAWK
HAWKMOTH *n* powerful narrow-winged moth with the ability to hover over flowers when feeding from the nectar
HAWKMOTHS > HAWKMOTH

h

HAWKNOSE n hooked nose
HAWKNOSES >HAWKNOSE
HAWKS >HAWK
HAWKSBILL n type of turtle
HAWKSHAW n private detective
HAWKSHAWS >HAWKSHAW
HAWKWEED n hairy plant with clusters of dandelion-like flowers
HAWKWEEDS >HAWKWEED
HAWM vb be idle and relaxed
HAWMED >HAWM
HAWMING >HAWM
HAWMS >HAWM
HAWS >HAW
HAWSE vb of boats, pitch violently when at anchor
HAWSED >HAWSE
HAWSEHOLE n one of the holes in the upper part of the bows of a vessel through which the anchor ropes pass
HAWSEPIPE n strong metal pipe through which an anchor rope passes
HAWSER n large rope used on a ship
HAWSERS >HAWSER
HAWSES >HAWSE
HAWSING >HAWSE
HAWTHORN n thorny shrub or tree
HAWTHORNS >HAWTHORN
HAWTHORNY >HAWTHORN
HAY n grass cut and dried as fodder ▷ vb cut, dry, and store (grass, clover, etc) as fodder
HAYBAND n rope made by twisting hay together
HAYBANDS >HAYBAND
HAYBOX n airtight box full of hay or other insulating material used to keep partially cooked food warm and allow cooking by retained heat
HAYBOXES >HAYBOX
HAYCOCK n small cone-shaped pile of hay left in the field until dry enough to carry to the rick or barn
HAYCOCKS >HAYCOCK
HAYED >HAY
HAYER n person who makes hay
HAYERS >HAYER
HAYEY >HAY
HAYFIELD n field of hay
HAYFIELDS >HAYFIELD
HAYFORK n long-handled fork with two long curved prongs, used for moving or turning hay
HAYFORKS >HAYFORK
HAYIER >HAYEY
HAYIEST >HAYEY
HAYING >HAY
HAYINGS >HAY
HAYLAGE n type of hay for animal fodder
HAYLAGES >HAYLAGE

HAYLE n welfare
HAYLES >HAYLE
HAYLOFT n loft for storing hay
HAYLOFTS >HAYLOFT
HAYMAKER n person who helps to cut, turn, toss, spread, or carry hay
HAYMAKERS >HAYMAKER
HAYMAKING >HAYMAKER
HAYMOW n part of a barn where hay is stored
HAYMOWS >HAYMOW
HAYRACK n rack for holding hay for feeding to animals
HAYRACKS >HAYRACK
HAYRAKE n large rake used to collect hay
HAYRAKES >HAYRAKE
HAYRICK same as >HAYSTACK
HAYRICKS >HAYRICK
HAYRIDE n pleasure trip in hay wagon
HAYRIDES >HAYRIDE
HAYS >HAY
HAYSEED n seeds or fragments of grass or straw
HAYSEEDS >HAYSEED
HAYSEL n season for making hay
HAYSELS >HAYSEL
HAYSTACK n large pile of stored hay
HAYSTACKS >HAYSTACK
HAYWARD n parish officer in charge of enclosures and fences
HAYWARDS >HAYWARD
HAYWIRE adj (of things) not functioning properly ▷ n wire for binding hay
HAYWIRES >HAYWIRE
HAZAN same as >CANTOR
HAZANIM >HAZAN
HAZANS >HAZAN
HAZARD n something that could be dangerous ▷ vb put in danger
HAZARDED >HAZARD
HAZARDER >HAZARD
HAZARDERS >HAZARD
HAZARDING >HAZARD
HAZARDIZE same as >HAZARD
HAZARDOUS adj involving great risk
HAZARDRY n taking of risks
HAZARDS >HAZARD
HAZE n mist, often caused by heat ▷ vb make or become hazy
HAZED >HAZE
HAZEL n small tree producing edible nuts ▷ adj (of eyes) greenish-brown
HAZELHEN n type of grouse
HAZELHENS >HAZELHEN
HAZELLY >HAZEL
HAZELNUT n nut of a hazel shrub, which has a smooth shiny hard shell
HAZELNUTS >HAZELNUT

HAZELS >HAZEL
HAZER >HAZE
HAZERS >HAZE
HAZES >HAZE
HAZIER >HAZY
HAZIEST >HAZY
HAZILY >HAZY
HAZINESS >HAZY
HAZING >HAZE
HAZINGS >HAZE
HAZMAT n hazardous material
HAZMATS >HAZMAT
HAZY adj not clear, misty
HAZZAN same as >CANTOR
HAZZANIM >HAZZAN
HAZZANS >HAZZAN
HE pron male person or animal ▷ n male person or animal ▷ interj expression of amusement or derision
HEAD n upper or front part of the body, containing the sense organs and the brain ▷ adj chief, principal ▷ vb be at the top or front of
HEADACHE n continuous pain in the head
HEADACHES >HEADACHE
HEADACHEY same as >HEADACHY
HEADACHY adj suffering from, caused by, or likely to cause a headache
HEADAGE n payment to farmer based on number of animals kept
HEADAGES >HEADAGE
HEADBAND n ribbon or band worn around the head
HEADBANDS >HEADBAND
HEADBANG vb nod one's head violently to the beat of loud rock music
HEADBANGS >HEADBANG
HEADBOARD n vertical board at the top end of a bed
HEADCASE n insane person
HEADCASES >HEADCASE
HEADCHAIR n chair with support for the head
HEADCLOTH n kerchief worn on the head
HEADCOUNT n count of number of people present
HEADDRESS n decorative head covering
HEADED adj having a head or heads
HEADEND n facility from which cable television is transmitted
HEADENDS >HEADEND
HEADER n striking a ball with the head
HEADERS >HEADER
HEADFAST n mooring rope at the bows of a ship
HEADFASTS >HEADFAST
HEADFIRST adv with the head foremost
HEADFISH same as >SUNFISH

HEADFRAME n structure supporting winding machinery at mine
HEADFUCK n taboo slang for experience that is wildly exciting or impressive
HEADFUCKS >HEADFUCK
HEADFUL n amount head will hold
HEADFULS >HEADFUL
HEADGATE n a gate that is used to control the flow of water at the upper end of a lock or conduit
HEADGATES >HEADGATE
HEADGEAR n hats collectively
HEADGEARS >HEADGEAR
HEADGUARD n padded helmet worn to protect the head in contact sports
HEADHUNT vb recruit employee from another company
HEADHUNTS >HEADHUNT
HEADIER >HEADY
HEADIEST >HEADY
HEADILY >HEADY
HEADINESS >HEADY
HEADING same as >HEAD
HEADINGS >HEADING
HEADLAMP same as >HEADLIGHT
HEADLAMPS >HEADLAMP
HEADLAND n area of land jutting out into the sea
HEADLANDS >HEADLAND
HEADLEASE n main lease often subdivided
HEADLESS adj without a head
HEADLIGHT n powerful light on the front of a vehicle
HEADLIKE >HEAD
HEADLINE n title at the top of a newspaper article, esp on the front page
HEADLINED >HEADLINE
HEADLINER n performer given prominent billing
HEADLINES >HEADLINE
HEADLOCK n wrestling hold in which a wrestler locks his opponent's head between the crook of his elbow and the side of his body
HEADLOCKS >HEADLOCK
HEADLONG adj with the head first ▷ adv with the head foremost
HEADMAN n chief or leader
HEADMARK n characteristic
HEADMARKS >HEADMARK
HEADMEN >HEADMAN
HEADMOST less common word for >FOREMOST
HEADNOTE n note at book chapter head
HEADNOTES >HEADNOTE
HEADPEACE archaic form of >HEADPIECE
HEADPHONE n small loudspeaker held against

the ear

HEADPIECE n decorative band at the top of a page, chapter, etc

HEADPIN another word for >KINGPIN

HEADPINS >HEADPIN

HEADRACE n channel that carries water to a water wheel, turbine, etc

HEADRACES >HEADRACE

HEADRAIL n end of the table from which play is started, nearest the baulkline

HEADRAILS >HEADRAIL

HEADREACH n distance made to windward while tacking ▷ vb gain distance over (another boat) when tacking

HEADREST n support for the head, as on a dentist's chair or car seat

HEADRESTS >HEADREST

HEADRIG n edge of ploughed field

HEADRIGS >HEADRIG

HEADRING n African head decoration

HEADRINGS >HEADRING

HEADROOM n space below a roof or bridge which allows an object to pass or stay underneath it without touching it

HEADROOMS >HEADROOM

HEADROPE n rope round an animal's head

HEADROPES >HEADROPE

HEADS adv with the side of a coin which has a portrait of a head on it uppermost

HEADSAIL n any sail set forward of the foremast

HEADSAILS >HEADSAIL

HEADSCARF n scarf for the head, often worn tied under the chin

HEADSET n pair of headphones, esp with a microphone attached

HEADSETS >HEADSET

HEADSHAKE n gesture of shaking head

HEADSHIP n position or state of being a leader, esp the head teacher of a school

HEADSHIPS >HEADSHIP

HEADSHOT n photo of person's head

HEADSHOTS >HEADSHOT

HEADSMAN n (formerly) an executioner who beheaded condemned persons

HEADSMEN >HEADSMAN

HEADSPACE n space between bolt and cartridge in a rifle

HEADSTALL n part of a bridle that fits round a horse's head

HEADSTAND n act or an instance of balancing on the head, usually with the hands as support

HEADSTAY n rope from mast to bow on ship

HEADSTAYS >HEADSTAY

HEADSTICK n piece of wood formerly used in typesetting

HEADSTOCK n part of a machine that supports and transmits the drive to the chuck

HEADSTONE n memorial stone on a grave

HEADWALL n steep slope at the head of a glacial cirque

HEADWALLS >HEADWALL

HEADWARD same as >HEADWARDS

HEADWARDS adv backwards beyond the original source

HEADWATER n highest part of river

HEADWAY same as >HEADROOM

HEADWAYS >HEADWAY

HEADWIND n wind blowing against the course of an aircraft or ship

HEADWINDS >HEADWIND

HEADWORD n key word placed at the beginning of a line, paragraph, etc, as in a dictionary entry

HEADWORDS >HEADWORD

HEADWORK n mental work

HEADWORKS >HEADWORK

HEADY adj intoxicating or exciting

HEAL vb make or become well

HEALABLE >HEAL

HEALD same as >HEDDLE

HEALDED >HEALD

HEALDING >HEALD

HEALDS >HEALD

HEALED >HEAL

HEALEE n person who is being healed

HEALEES >HEALEE

HEALER >HEAL

HEALERS >HEAL

HEALING >HEAL

HEALINGLY >HEAL

HEALINGS >HEAL

HEALS >HEAL

HEALSOME Scots word for >WHOLESOME

HEALTH n normal (good) condition of someone's body ▷ interj exclamation wishing someone good health as part of a toast

HEALTHFUL same as >HEALTHY

HEALTHIER >HEALTHY

HEALTHILY >HEALTHY

HEALTHISM n lifestyle that prioritizes health and fitness over anything else

HEALTHS >HEALTH

HEALTHY adj having good health

HEAME old form of >HOME

HEAP n pile of things one on top of another ▷ vb gather into a pile

HEAPED >HEAP

HEAPER >HEAP

HEAPERS >HEAP

HEAPIER >HEAPY

HEAPIEST >HEAPY

HEAPING adj (of a spoonful) heaped

HEAPS >HEAP

HEAPSTEAD n buildings at mine

HEAPY adj having many heaps

HEAR vb perceive (a sound) by ear

HEARABLE >HEAR

HEARD same as >HERD

HEARDS >HERD

HEARE old form of >HAIR

HEARER >HEAR

HEARERS >HEAR

HEARES >HEARE

HEARIE old form of >HAIRY

HEARING >HEAR

HEARINGS >HEAR

HEARKEN vb listen

HEARKENED >HEARKEN

HEARKENER >HEARKEN

HEARKENS >HEARKEN

HEARS >HEAR

HEARSAY n gossip, rumour

HEARSAYS >HEARSAY

HEARSE n funeral car used to carry a coffin ▷ vb put in hearse

HEARSED >HEARSE

HEARSES >HEARSE

HEARSIER >HEARSY

HEARSIEST >HEARSY

HEARSING >HEARSE

HEARSY adj like a hearse

HEART n organ that pumps blood round the body ▷ vb (of vegetables) form a heart

HEARTACHE n intense anguish

HEARTBEAT n one complete pulsation of the heart

HEARTBURN n burning sensation in the chest caused by indigestion

HEARTED >HEART

HEARTEN vb encourage, make cheerful

HEARTENED >HEARTEN

HEARTENER >HEARTEN

HEARTENS >HEARTEN

HEARTFELT adj felt sincerely or strongly

HEARTFREE adj not in love

HEARTH n floor of a fireplace

HEARTHRUG n rug laid before fireplace

HEARTHS >HEARTH

HEARTIER >HEARTY

HEARTIES >HEARTY

HEARTIEST >HEARTY

HEARTIKIN n little heart

HEARTILY adv thoroughly or vigorously

HEARTING >HEART

HEARTLAND n central region of a country or continent

HEARTLESS adj cruel, unkind

HEARTLET n little heart

HEARTLETS >HEART

HEARTLING n little heart

HEARTLY adv vigorously

HEARTPEA same as >HEARTSEED

HEARTPEAS >HEARTPEA

HEARTS n card game in which players must avoid winning tricks containing hearts or the queen of spades

HEARTSEED n type of vine

HEARTSICK adj deeply dejected or despondent

HEARTSINK n patient who visits a doctor with multiple non-specific symptoms that are impossible to treat

HEARTSOME adj cheering or encouraging

HEARTSORE adj greatly distressed

HEARTWOOD n central core of dark hard wood in tree trunks

HEARTWORM n parasitic nematode worm that lives in the heart and bloodstream of vertebrates

HEARTY adj substantial, nourishing ▷ n comrade, esp a sailor

HEAST same as >HEST

HEASTE same as >HEST

HEASTES >HEASTE

HEASTS >HEAST

HEAT vb make or become hot ▷ n state of being hot

HEATABLE >HEAT

HEATED adj angry and excited

HEATEDLY >HEATED

HEATER n device for supplying heat

HEATERS >HEATER

HEATH n area of open uncultivated land

HEATHBIRD n black grouse

HEATHCOCK same as >BLACKCOCK

HEATHEN n (of) a person who does not believe in an established religion ▷ adj of or relating to heathen peoples

HEATHENRY >HEATHEN

HEATHENS >HEATHEN

HEATHER n low-growing plant with small purple, pinkish, or white flowers, growing on heaths and mountains ▷ adj of a heather colour

HEATHERED >HEATHER

HEATHERS >HEATHER

HEATHERY >HEATHER

HEATHFOWL *Compare*
> MOORFOWL
HEATHIER > HEATH
HEATHIEST > HEATH
HEATHLAND *n* area of
heath
HEATHLESS > HEATH
HEATHLIKE > HEATH
HEATHS > HEATH
HEATHY > HEATH
HEATING *n* device or
system for supplying heat,
esp central heating, to a
building
HEATINGS > HEATING
HEATLESS > HEAT
HEATPROOF > HEAT
HEATS > HEAT
HEATSPOT *n* spot on skin
produced by heat
HEATSPOTS > HEATSPOT
HEATWAVE *n* prolonged
period of unusually hot
weather
HEATWAVES > HEATWAVE
HEAUME *n* (in the 12th and
13th centuries) a large
helmet reaching and
supported by the shoulders
HEAUMES > HEAUME
HEAVE *vb* lift with effort ▷ *n*
heaving
HEAVED > HEAVE
HEAVEN *n* place believed to
be the home of God, where
good people go when they
die
HEAVENLY *adj* of or like
heaven
HEAVENS > HEAVEN
HEAVER > HEAVE
HEAVERS > HEAVE
HEAVES > HEAVE
HEAVIER > HEAVY
HEAVIES > HEAVY
HEAVIEST > HEAVY
HEAVILY > HEAVY
HEAVINESS > HEAVY
HEAVING > HEAVE
HEAVINGS > HEAVE
HEAVY *adj* of great weight
HEAVYSET *adj* stockily
built
HEBDOMAD *n* number
seven or a group of seven
HEBDOMADS > HEBDOMAD
HEBE *n* any of various
flowering shrubs
HEBEN *old form of* > EBONY
HEBENON *n* source of
poison
HEBENONS > HEBENON
HEBENS > HEBEN
HEBES > HEBE
HEBETANT *adj* causing
dullness
HEBETATE *adj* (of plant
parts) having a blunt or soft
point ▷ *vb* make or become
blunted
HEBETATED > HEBETATE
HEBETATES > HEBETATE
HEBETIC *adj* of or relating
to puberty

HEBETUDE *n* mental
dullness or lethargy
HEBETUDES > HEBETUDE
HEBONA *same as*
> HEBENON
HEBONAS > HEBONA
HEBRAISE *same as*
> HEBRAIZE
HEBRAISED > HEBRAISE
HEBRAISES > HEBRAISE
HEBRAIZE *vb* become or
cause to become Hebrew
or Hebraic
HEBRAIZED > HEBRAIZE
HEBRAIZES > HEBRAIZE
HECATOMB *n* (in ancient
Greece or Rome) any great
public sacrifice and feast,
originally one in which 100
oxen were sacrificed
HECATOMBS > HECATOMB
HECH *interj* expression of
surprise
HECHT *same as* > HIGHT
HECHTING > HECHT
HECHTS > HECHT
HECK *interj* mild
exclamation of surprise,
irritation, etc ▷ *n* frame for
obstructing the passage of
fish in a river
HECKLE *vb* interrupt (a
public speaker) with
comments, questions, or
taunts ▷ *n* instrument for
combing flax or hemp
HECKLED > HECKLE
HECKLER > HECKLE
HECKLERS > HECKLE
HECKLES > HECKLE
HECKLING > HECKLE
HECKLINGS > HECKLE
HECKS > HECK
HECOGENIN *n* plant
chemical used in drugs
HECTARE *n* one hundred
ares or 10 000 square
metres (2.471 acres)
HECTARES > HECTARE
HECTIC *adj* rushed or busy
▷ *n* hectic fever or flush
HECTICAL *same as*
> HECTIC
HECTICLY > HECTIC
HECTICS > HECTIC
HECTOGRAM *n* one
hundred grams. 1
hectogram is equivalent to
3.527 ounces.
HECTOR *vb* bully ▷ *n*
blustering bully
HECTORED > HECTOR
HECTORER > HECTOR
HECTORERS > HECTOR
HECTORING > HECTOR
HECTORISM > HECTOR
HECTORLY > HECTOR
HECTORS > HECTOR
HEDDLE *n* one of a set of
frames of vertical wires on
a loom, each wire having an
eye through which a warp
thread can be passed ▷ *vb*
pass thread through heddle
HEDDLED > HEDDLE

HEDDLES > HEDDLE
HEDDLING > HEDDLE
HEDER *variant spelling of*
> CHEDER
HEDERA *See* > IVY
HEDERAL > HEDERA
HEDERAS > HEDERA
HEDERATED *adj* honoured
with crown of ivy
HEDERS > HEDER
HEDGE *n* row of bushes
forming a barrier or
boundary ▷ *vb* be evasive
or noncommittal
HEDGEBILL *n* tool for
pruning a hedge
HEDGED > HEDGE
HEDGEHOG *n* small
mammal with a protective
covering of spines
HEDGEHOGS > HEDGEHOG
HEDGEHOP *vb* (of an
aircraft) to fly close to the
ground, as in crop spraying
HEDGEHOPS > HEDGEHOP
HEDGEPIG *same as*
> HEDGEHOG
HEDGEPIGS > HEDGEPIG
HEDGER > HEDGE
HEDGEROW *n* bushes
forming a hedge
HEDGEROWS > HEDGEROW
HEDGERS > HEDGE
HEDGES > HEDGE
HEDGIER > HEDGE
HEDGIEST > HEDGE
HEDGING > HEDGE
HEDGINGLY > HEDGE
HEDGINGS > HEDGE
HEDGY > HEDGE
HEDONIC > HEDONISM
HEDONICS *n* branch of
psychology concerned with
the study of pleasant and
unpleasant sensations
HEDONISM *n* doctrine that
pleasure is the most
important thing in life
HEDONISMS > HEDONISM
HEDONIST > HEDONISM
HEDONISTS > HEDONISM
HEDYPHANE *n* variety of
lead ore
HEED *n* careful attention
▷ *vb* pay careful attention
to
HEEDED > HEED
HEEDER > HEED
HEEDERS > HEED
HEEDFUL > HEED
HEEDFULLY > HEED
HEEDINESS > HEED
HEEDING > HEED
HEEDLESS *adj* taking no
notice
HEEDS > HEED
HEEDY > HEED
HEEHAW *interj*
representation of the
braying sound of a donkey
▷ *vb* make braying sound
HEEHAWED > HEEHAW
HEEHAWING > HEEHAW
HEEHAWS > HEEHAW

HEEL *n* back part of the foot
▷ *vb* repair the heel of (a
shoe)
HEELBALL *n* mixture of
beeswax and lampblack
used by shoemakers
HEELBALLS > HEELBALL
HEELBAR *n* small shop or
counter where shoes are
repaired
HEELBARS > HEELBAR
HEELED > HEEL
HEELER *n* dog that herds
cattle by biting at their
heels
HEELERS > HEELER
HEELING > HEEL
HEELINGS > HEEL
HEELLESS > HEEL
HEELPIECE *n* piece of a
shoe, stocking, etc,
designed to fit the heel
HEELPLATE *n* reinforcing
piece of metal
HEELPOST *n* post for
carrying the hinges of a
door or gate
HEELPOSTS > HEELPOST
HEELS > HEEL
HEELTAP *n* layer of leather,
etc, in the heel of a shoe
HEELTAPS > HEELTAP
HEEZE *Scots word for*
> HOIST
HEEZED > HEEZE
HEEZES > HEEZE
HEEZIE *n* act of lifting
HEEZIES > HEEZIE
HEEZING > HEEZE
HEFT *vb* assess the weight
of (something) by lifting ▷ *n*
weight
HEFTE *same as* > HEAVE
HEFTED > HEFT
HEFTER > HEFT
HEFTERS > HEFT
HEFTIER > HEFTY
HEFTIEST > HEFTY
HEFTILY > HEFTY
HEFTINESS > HEFTY
HEFTING > HEFT
HEFTS > HEFT
HEFTY *adj* large, heavy, or
strong
HEGARI *n* African sorghum
HEGARIS > HEGARI
HEGEMON *n* person in
authority
HEGEMONIC > HEGEMONY
HEGEMONS > HEGEMON
HEGEMONY *n* political
domination
HEGIRA *n* emigration
escape or flight
HEGIRAS > HEGIRA
HEGUMEN *n* head of a
monastery of the Eastern
Church
HEGUMENE *n* head of Greek
nunnery
HEGUMENES > HEGUMENE
HEGUMENOI
> HEGUMENOS
HEGUMENOS *same as*

> HEGUMEN

HEGUMENS > HEGUMEN

HEGUMENY *n* office of hegumen

HEH *interj* exclamation of surprise or inquiry

HEHS > HEH

HEID *Scot word for* > HEAD

HEIDS > HEID

HEIFER *n* young cow

HEIFERS > HEIFER

HEIGH *same as* > HEY

HEIGHT *n* distance from base to top

HEIGHTEN *vb* make or become higher or more intense

HEIGHTENS > HEIGHTEN

HEIGHTH *obsolete form of* > HEIGHT

HEIGHTHS > HEIGHTH

HEIGHTISM *n* discrimination based on people's heights

HEIGHTS > HEIGHT

HEIL *vb* give a German greeting

HEILED > HEIL

HEILING > HEIL

HEILS > HEIL

HEIMISH *adj* comfortable

HEINIE *n* buttocks

HEINIES > HEINIE

HEINOUS *adj* evil and shocking

HEINOUSLY > HEINOUS

HEIR *n* person entitled to inherit property or rank ▷ *vb* inherit

HEIRDOM *n* succession by right of blood

HEIRDOMS > HEIRDOM

HEIRED > HEIR

HEIRESS *n* woman who inherits or expects to inherit great wealth

HEIRESSES > HEIRESS

HEIRING > HEIR

HEIRLESS > HEIR

HEIRLOOM *n* object that has belonged to a family for generations

HEIRLOOMS > HEIRLOOM

HEIRS > HEIR

HEIRSHIP *n* state or condition of being an heir

HEIRSHIPS > HEIRSHIP

HEISHI *n* Native American shell jewellery

HEIST *n* robbery ▷ *vb* steal or burgle

HEISTED > HEIST

HEISTER > HEIST

HEISTERS > HEIST

HEISTING > HEIST

HEISTS > HEIST

HEITIKI *n* Māori neck ornament of greenstone

HEITIKIS > HEITIKI

HEJAB *same as* > HIJAB

HEJABS > HEJAB

HEJIRA *same as* > HEGIRA

HEJIRAS > HEJIRA

HEJRA *same as* > HEGIRA

HEJRAS > HEJRA

HEKETARA *n* small shrub that has flowers with white petals and yellow centres

HEKETARAS > HEKETARA

HEKTARE *same as* > HECTARE

HEKTARES > HEKTARE

HEKTOGRAM *same as* > HECTOGRAM

HELCOID *adj* having ulcers

HELD > HOLD

HELE as in *hele in* dialect expression meaning insert (cuttings, shoots, etc) into soil before planting to keep them moist

HELED > HELE

HELENIUM *n* plant with daisy-like yellow or variegated flowers

HELENIUMS > HELENIUM

HELES > HELE

HELIAC *same as* > HELIACAL

HELIACAL as in *heliacal rising* rising of a celestial object at approximately the same time as the rising of the sun

HELIAST *n* ancient Greek juror

HELIASTS > HELIAST

HELIBORNE *adj* carried in helicopter

HELIBUS *n* helicopter carrying passengers

HELIBUSES > HELIBUS

HELICAL *adj* spiral

HELICALLY > HELICAL

HELICASE *n* enzyme vital to all living organisms

HELICASES > HELICASE

HELICES > HELIX

HELICITY *n* projection of the spin of an elementary particle on the direction of propagation

HELICLINE *n* spiral-shaped ramp

HELICOID *adj* shaped like a spiral ▷ *n* any surface resembling that of a screw thread

HELICOIDS > HELICOID

HELICON *n* bass tuba made to coil over the shoulder of a band musician

HELICONIA *n* tropical flowering plant

HELICONS > HELICON

HELICOPT *vb* transport using a helicopter

HELICOPTS > HELICOPT

HELICTITE *n* twisted stalactite

HELIDECK *n* landing deck for helicopters on ships, oil platforms, etc

HELIDECKS > HELIDECK

HELIDROME *n* small airport for helicopters

HELILIFT *vb* transport by helicopter

HELILIFTS > HELILIFT

HELIMAN *n* helicopter pilot

HELIMEN > HELIMAN

HELING > HELE

HELIO *n* instrument for sending messages in Morse code by reflecting the sun's rays

HELIODOR *n* clear yellow form of beryl used as a gemstone

HELIODORS > HELIODOR

HELIOGRAM *n* message sent by reflecting the sun's rays in a mirror

HELIOLOGY *n* study of sun

HELIOS > HELIO

HELIOSES > HELIOSIS

HELIOSIS *n* bad effect of overexposure to the sun

HELIOSTAT *n* astronomical instrument used to reflect the light of the sun in a constant direction

HELIOTYPE *n* printing process in which an impression is taken in ink from a gelatine surface that has been exposed under a negative and prepared for printing

HELIOTYPY *same as* > HELIOTYPE

HELIOZOAN *n* type of protozoan, typically having a siliceous shell and stiff radiating cytoplasmic projections

HELIOZOIC > HELIOZOAN

HELIPAD *n* place for helicopters to land and take off

HELIPADS > HELIPAD

HELIPILOT *n* helicopter pilot

HELIPORT *n* airport for helicopters

HELIPORTS > HELIPORT

HELISTOP *n* landing place for helicopter

HELISTOPS > HELISTOP

HELIUM *n* very light colourless odourless gas

HELIUMS > HELIUM

HELIX *n* spiral

HELIXES > HELIX

HELL *n* place believed to be where wicked people go when they die ▷ *vb* act wildly

HELLBENT *adj* intent

HELLBOX *n* (in printing) container for broken type

HELLBOXES > HELLBOX

HELLBROTH *n* evil concoction

HELLCAT *n* spiteful fierce-tempered woman

HELLCATS > HELLCAT

HELLDIVER *n* greyish-brown North American grebe

HELLEBORE *n* plant with white flowers that bloom in winter

HELLED > HELL

HELLENISE *same as* > HELLENIZE

HELLENIZE *vb* make or become like the ancient Greeks

HELLER *n* monetary unit of the Czech Republic and Slovakia

HELLERI *n* Central American fish

HELLERIES > HELLERY

HELLERIS > HELLERI

HELLERS > HELLER

HELLERY *n* wild or mischievous behaviour

HELLFIRE *n* torment of hell, imagined as eternal fire

HELLFIRES > HELLFIRE

HELLHOLE *n* unpleasant or evil place

HELLHOLES > HELLHOLE

HELLHOUND *n* hound of hell

HELLICAT *n* evil creature

HELLICATS > HELLICAT

HELLIER *n* slater

HELLIERS > HELLIER

HELLING > HELL

HELLION *n* rough or rowdy person, esp a child

HELLIONS > HELLION

HELLISH *adj* very unpleasant ▷ *adv* (intensifier)

HELLISHLY > HELLISH

HELLKITE *n* bird of prey from hell

HELLKITES > HELLKITE

HELLO *interj* expression of greeting or surprise ▷ *n* act of saying 'hello' ▷ *sentence substitute* expression of greeting used on meeting a person or at the start of a telephone call ▷ *vb* say hello

HELLOED > HELLO

HELLOES > HELLO

HELLOING > HELLO

HELLOS > HELLO

HELLOVA *same as* > HELLUVA

HELLS > HELL

HELLUVA *adj* (intensifier)

HELLWARD *adj* towards hell

HELLWARDS *adv* towards hell

HELM *n* tiller or wheel for steering a ship ▷ *vb* direct or steer

HELMED > HELM

HELMER *n* film director

HELMERS > HELMER

HELMET *n* hard hat worn for protection

HELMETED > HELMET

HELMETING *n* wearing or provision of a helmet

HELMETS > HELMET

HELMING > HELM

HELMINTH n any parasitic worm, esp a nematode or fluke

HELMINTHS > HELMINTH

HELMLESS > HELM

HELMS > HELM

HELMSMAN n person at the helm who steers the ship

HELMSMEN > HELMSMAN

HELO n helicopter

HELOPHYTE n any perennial marsh plant that bears its overwintering buds in the mud below the surface

HELOS > HELO

HELOT n serf or slave

HELOTAGE same as **>** HELOTISM

HELOTAGES > HELOTAGE

HELOTISM n condition or quality of being a helot

HELOTISMS > HELOTISM

HELOTRIES > HELOTRY

HELOTRY n serfdom or slavery

HELOTS > HELOT

HELP vb make something easier, better, or quicker for (someone) **▷** n assistance or support

HELPABLE > HELP

HELPDESK n place where advice is given by telephone

HELPDESKS > HELPDESK

HELPED > HELP

HELPER > HELP

HELPERS > HELP

HELPFUL adj giving help

HELPFULLY > HELPFUL

HELPING n single portion of food

HELPINGS > HELPING

HELPLESS adj weak or incapable

HELPLINE n telephone line set aside for callers to contact an organization for help with a problem

HELPLINES > HELPLINE

HELPMATE n companion and helper, esp a husband or wife

HELPMATES > HELPMATE

HELPMEET less common word for **>** HELPMATE

HELPMEETS > HELPMEET

HELPS > HELP

HELVE n handle of a hand tool such as an axe or pick **▷** vb fit a helve to (a tool)

HELVED > HELVE

HELVES > HELVE

HELVETIUM same as **>** ASTATINE

HELVING > HELVE

HEM n bottom edge of a garment, folded under and stitched down **▷** vb provide with a hem

HEMAGOG same as **>** HEMAGOGUE

HEMAGOGS > HEMAGOGUE

HEMAGOGUE n haemagogue: drug that promotes the flow of blood

HEMAL same as **>** HAEMAL

HEMATAL same as **>** HEMAL

HEMATEIN same as **>** HAEMATEIN

HEMATEINS > HEMATEIN

HEMATIC same as **>** HAEMATIC

HEMATICS > HEMATIC

HEMATIN same as **>** HAEMATIN

HEMATINE n red dye

HEMATINES > HEMATINE

HEMATINIC same as **>** HAEMATIC

HEMATINS > HEMATIN

HEMATITE n red, grey, or black mineral

HEMATITES > HEMATITE

HEMATITIC > HEMATITE

HEMATOID same as **>** HAEMATOID

HEMATOMA same as **>** HAEMATOMA

HEMATOMAS > HEMATOMA

HEMATOSES > HEMATOSIS

HEMATOSIS n haematosis: oxygenation of venous blood in the lungs

HEMATOZOA n plural of hematozoon: protozoan that is parasitic in the blood

HEMATURIA n the presence of blood or red blood cells in the urine

HEMATURIC > HEMATURIA

HEME same as **>** HAEM

HEMELYTRA n plural of hemelytron: forewing of plant bugs

HEMES > HEME

HEMIALGIA n pain limited to one side of the body

HEMIC same as **>** HAEMATIC

HEMICYCLE n semicircular structure, room, arena, wall, etc

HEMIHEDRY n state of crystal having certain kind of symmetry

HEMIN same as **>** HAEMIN

HEMINA n old liquid measure

HEMINAS > HEMINA

HEMINS > HEMIN

HEMIOLA n rhythmic device involving the superimposition of, for example, two notes in the time of three

HEMIOLAS > HEMIOLA

HEMIOLIA same as **>** HEMIOLA

HEMIOLIAS > HEMIOLIA

HEMIOLIC > HEMIOLA

HEMIONE same as **>** HEMIONUS

HEMIONES > HEMIONE

HEMIONUS n Asian wild ass

HEMIOPIA n defective vision seeing only halves of things

HEMIOPIAS > HEMIOPIA

HEMIOPIC > HEMIOPIA

HEMIOPSIA same as **>** HEMIOPIA

HEMIPOD same as **>** HEMIPODE

HEMIPODE n button quail

HEMIPODES > HEMIPODE

HEMIPODS > HEMIPOD

HEMIPTER n insect with beaklike mouthparts

HEMIPTERS > HEMIPTER

HEMISPACE n area in brain

HEMISTICH n half line of verse

HEMITROPE another name for **>** HEMITROPY

HEMITROPY n state of being a twin

HEMLINE n level to which the hem of a skirt hangs

HEMLINES > HEMLINE

HEMLOCK n poison made from a plant with spotted stems and small white flowers

HEMLOCKS > HEMLOCK

HEMMED > HEM

HEMMER n attachment on a sewing machine for hemming

HEMMERS > HEMMER

HEMMING > HEM

HEMOCOEL same as **>** HAEMOCOEL

HEMOCOELS > HEMOCOEL

HEMOCYTE same as **>** HAEMOCYTE

HEMOCYTES > HEMOCYTE

HEMOID same as **>** HAEMATOID

HEMOLYMPH n blood-like fluid in invertebrates

HEMOLYSE vb break down so that haemoglobin is released

HEMOLYSED > HEMOLYSE

HEMOLYSES > HEMOLYSIS

HEMOLYSIN n haemolysin: substance that breaks down red blood cells

HEMOLYSIS n haemolysis: disintegration of red blood cells

HEMOLYTIC > HEMOLYSIS

HEMOLYZE vb undergo or make undergo hemolysis

HEMOLYZED > HEMOLYZE

HEMOLYZES > HEMOLYZE

HEMOPHILE n haemophile: person with haemophilia

HEMOSTAT same as **>** HAEMOSTAT

HEMOSTATS > HEMOSTAT

HEMOTOXIC > HEMOTOXIN

HEMOTOXIN n substance that destroys red blood cells

HEMP n Asian plant with tough fibres

HEMPEN > HEMP

HEMPIE variant of **>** HEMPY

HEMPIER > HEMPY

HEMPIES > HEMPY

HEMPIEST > HEMPY

HEMPLIKE > HEMP

HEMPS > HEMP

HEMPSEED n seed of hemp

HEMPSEEDS > HEMPSEED

HEMPWEED n climbing weed

HEMPWEEDS > HEMPWEED

HEMPY adj of or like hemp **▷** n rogue

HEMS > HEM

HEMSTITCH n decorative edging stitch, usually for a hem, in which the cross threads are stitched in groups **▷** vb decorate (a hem, etc) with hemstitches

HEN n female domestic fowl **▷** vb lose one's courage

HENBANE n poisonous plant with sticky hairy leaves

HENBANES > HENBANE

HENBIT n European plant with small dark red flowers

HENBITS > HENBIT

HENCE adv from this time **▷** interj begone! away!

HENCHMAN n person employed by someone powerful to carry out orders

HENCHMEN > HENCHMAN

HENCOOP n cage for poultry

HENCOOPS > HENCOOP

HEND vb seize

HENDED > HEND

HENDIADYS n rhetorical device by which two nouns joined by a conjunction are used instead of a noun and modifier

HENDING > HEND

HENDS > HEND

HENEQUEN n agave plant native to Yucatán

HENEQUENS > HENEQUEN

HENEQUIN same as **>** HENEQUEN

HENEQUINS > HENEQUIN

HENGE n circular monument, often containing a circle of stones, dating from the Neolithic and Bronze Ages

HENGES > HENGE

HENHOUSE n coop for hens

HENHOUSES > HENHOUSE

HENIQUEN same as **>** HENEQUEN

HENIQUENS > HENIQUEN

HENIQUIN same as **>** HENIQUEN

HENIQUINS > HENIQUIN

HENLEY n type of sweater

HENLEYS > HENLEY

HENLIKE > HEN

HENNA n reddish dye made from a shrub or tree **▷** vb dye (the hair) with henna

HENNAED > HENNA

HENNAING > HENNA

HENNAS > HENNA
HENNED > HEN
HENNER n challenge
HENNERIES > HENNERY
HENNERS > HENNER
HENNERY n place or farm for keeping poultry
HENNIER > HENNY
HENNIES > HENNY
HENNIEST > HENNY
HENNIN n former women's hat
HENNING > HEN
HENNINS > HENNIN
HENNISH > HEN
HENNISHLY > HEN
HENNY adj like hen ▷ n cock that looks like hen
HENOTIC adj acting to reconcile
HENPECK vb (of a woman) to harass or torment (a man, esp her husband) by persistent nagging
HENPECKED adj (of a man) dominated by his wife
HENPECKS > HENPECK
HENRIES > HENRY
HENRY n unit of electrical inductance
HENRYS > HENRY
HENS > HEN
HENT vb seize ▷ n anything that has been grasped, esp by the mind
HENTED > HENT
HENTING > HENT
HENTS > HENT
HEP same as **>** HIP
HEPAR n compound containing sulphur
HEPARIN n polysaccharide, containing sulphate groups, present in most body tissues: an anticoagulant used in the treatment of thrombosis
HEPARINS > HEPARIN
HEPARS > HEPAR
HEPATIC adj of the liver ▷ n any of various drugs for use in treating diseases of the liver
HEPATICA n woodland plant with white, mauve, or pink flowers
HEPATICAE > HEPATICA
HEPATICAL same as **>** HEPATIC
HEPATICAS > HEPATICA
HEPATICS > HEPATIC
HEPATISE same as **>** HEPATIZE
HEPATISED > HEPATISE
HEPATISES > HEPATISE
HEPATITE n mineral containing sulphur
HEPATITES > HEPATITE
HEPATITIS n inflammation of the liver
HEPATIZE vb turn into liver
HEPATIZED > HEPATIZE
HEPATIZES > HEPATIZE

HEPATOMA n cancer of liver
HEPATOMAS > HEPATOMA
HEPCAT n person who is hep, esp a player or admirer of jazz and swing in the 1940s
HEPCATS > HEPCAT
HEPPER > HEP
HEPPEST > HEP
HEPS > HEP
HEPSTER same as **>** HIPSTER
HEPSTERS > HEPSTER
HEPT archaic spelling of **>** HEAPED
HEPTAD n group or series of seven
HEPTADS > HEPTAD
HEPTAGON n geometric figure with seven sides
HEPTAGONS > HEPTAGON
HEPTANE n alkane found in petroleum and used as an anaesthetic
HEPTANES > HEPTANE
HEPTAPODY n verse with seven beats in rhythm
HEPTARCH > HEPTARCHY
HEPTARCHS **>** HEPTARCHY
HEPTARCHY n government by seven rulers
HEPTOSE n any monosaccharide that has seven carbon atoms per molecule
HEPTOSES > HEPTOSE
HER pron refers to a female person or animal or anything personified as feminine when the object of a sentence or clause ▷ adj belonging to her ▷ det of, belonging to, or associated with her
HERALD n person who announces important news ▷ vb signal the approach of
HERALDED > HERALD
HERALDIC adj of or relating to heraldry
HERALDING > HERALD
HERALDIST > HERALDRY
HERALDRY n study of coats of arms and family trees
HERALDS > HERALD
HERB n plant used for flavouring in cookery, and in medicine
HERBAGE n herbaceous plants collectively, esp those on which animals graze
HERBAGED adj with grass growing on it
HERBAGES > HERBAGE
HERBAL adj of or relating to herbs, usually culinary or medicinal herbs ▷ n book describing and listing the properties of plants
HERBALISM n use of herbal medicine
HERBALIST n person who

grows or specializes in the use of medicinal herbs
HERBALS > HERBAL
HERBAR same as **>** HERBARY
HERBARIA > HERBARIUM
HERBARIAL **>** HERBARIUM
HERBARIAN same as **>** HERBALIST
HERBARIES > HERBARY
HERBARIUM n collection of dried plants that are mounted and classified systematically
HERBARS > HERBAR
HERBARY n herb garden
HERBED adj flavoured with herbs
HERBELET same as **>** HERBLET
HERBELETS > HERBELET
HERBICIDE n chemical used to destroy plants, esp weeds
HERBIER > HERBY
HERBIEST > HERBY
HERBIST same as **>** HERBALIST
HERBISTS > HERBIST
HERBIVORA n animals that eat grass
HERBIVORE n animal that eats only plants
HERBIVORY **>** HERBIVORE
HERBLESS > HERB
HERBLET n little herb
HERBLETS > HERBLET
HERBLIKE > HERB
HERBOLOGY n use or study of herbal medicine
HERBORISE same as **>** HERBORIZE
HERBORIST same as **>** HERBALIST
HERBORIZE vb collect herbs
HERBOSE same as **>** HERBOUS
HERBOUS adj with abundance of herbs
HERBS > HERB
HERBY adj abounding in herbs
HERCOGAMY n prevention of flower pollination
HERCULEAN adj requiring great strength or effort
HERCULES as in hercules beetle very large tropical American beetle
HERCYNITE n mineral containing iron
HERD n group of animals feeding and living together ▷ vb collect into a herd
HERDBOY n boy who looks after herd
HERDBOYS > HERDBOY
HERDED > HERD
HERDEN n type of coarse cloth
HERDENS > HERDEN
HERDER same as

> HERDSMAN
HERDERS > HERDER
HERDESS n female herder
HERDESSES > HERDESS
HERDIC n small horse-drawn carriage with a rear entrance and side seats
HERDICS > HERDIC
HERDING > HERD
HERDLIKE > HERD
HERDMAN same as **>** HERDSMAN
HERDMEN > HERDMAN
HERDS > HERD
HERDSMAN n man who looks after a herd of animals
HERDSMEN > HERDSMAN
HERDWICK n hardy breed of sheep
HERDWICKS > HERDWICK
HERE adv in, at, or to this place or point ▷ n this place
HEREABOUT adv hereabouts
HEREAFTER adv after this point or time ▷ n life after death
HEREAT adv because of this
HEREAWAY same as **>** HEREABOUT
HEREAWAYS dialect form of **>** HERE
HEREBY adv by means of or as a result of this
HEREDES > HERES
HEREDITY n passing on of characteristics from one generation to another
HEREFROM adv from here
HEREIN adv in this place, matter, or document
HEREINTO adv into this place, circumstance, etc
HERENESS n state of being here
HEREOF adv of or concerning this
HEREON archaic word for **>** HEREUPON
HERES npl **>** HERE
HERESIES > HERESY
HERESY n opinion contrary to accepted opinion or belief
HERETIC n person who holds unorthodox opinions
HERETICAL > HERETIC
HERETICS > HERETIC
HERETO adv this place, matter, or document
HERETRIX n in Scots law, female inheritor
HEREUNDER adv (in documents, etc) below this
HEREUNTO archaic word for **>** HERETO
HEREUPON adv following immediately after this
HEREWITH adv with this
HERIED > HERY
HERIES > HERY
HERIOT n (in medieval England) a death duty paid

by villeins and free tenants to their lord, often consisting of the dead man's best beast or chattel

HERIOTS > HERIOT

HERISSE adj with bristles

HERISSON n spiked beam used as fortification

HERISSONS > HERISSON

HERITABLE adj capable of being inherited

HERITABLY > HERITABLE

HERITAGE n something inherited

HERITAGES > HERITAGE

HERITOR n person who inherits

HERITORS > HERITOR

HERITRESS > HERITOR

HERITRIX > HERITOR

HERKOGAMY same as > HERCOGAMY

HERL n barb or barbs of a feather, used to dress fishing flies

HERLING n Scots word for a type of fish

HERLINGS > HERL

HERLS > HERL

HERM n (in ancient Greece) a stone head of Hermes surmounting a square stone pillar

HERMA same as > HERM

HERMAE > HERMA

HERMAEAN adj type of statue

HERMAI > HERMA

HERMANDAD n organization of middle classes in Spain

HERMETIC adj sealed so as to be airtight

HERMETICS n alchemy

HERMETISM n belief in pagan mystical knowledge

HERMETIST > HERMETISM

HERMIT n person living in solitude, esp for religious reasons

HERMITAGE n home of a hermit

HERMITESS n female hermit

HERMITIC > HERMIT

HERMITISM n act of living as hermit

HERMITRY n life as hermit

HERMITS > HERMIT

HERMS > HERM

HERN archaic or dialect word for > HERON

HERNIA n protrusion of an organ or part through the lining of the surrounding body cavity

HERNIAE > HERNIA

HERNIAL > HERNIA

HERNIAS > HERNIA

HERNIATE n form hernia

HERNIATED > HERNIA

HERNIATES > HERNIATE

HERNS > HERN

HERNSHAW same as > HERONSHAW

HERNSHAWS > HERNSHAW

HERO n principal character in a film, book, etc

HEROES > HERO

HEROIC adj courageous

HEROICAL same as > HEROIC

HEROICISE same as > HEROICIZE

HEROICIZE same as > HEROIZE

HEROICLY > HEROIC

HEROICS npl extravagant behaviour

HEROIN n highly addictive drug derived from morphine

HEROINE n principal female character in a novel, play, etc

HEROINES > HEROINE

HEROINISM n addiction to heroin

HEROINS > HEROIN

HEROISE same as > HEROIZE

HEROISED > HEROISE

HEROISES > HEROISE

HEROISING > HEROISE

HEROISM n great courage and bravery

HEROISMS > HEROISM

HEROIZE vb make into hero

HEROIZED > HEROIZE

HEROIZES > HEROIZE

HEROIZING > HEROIZE

HERON n long-legged wading bird

HERONRIES > HERONRY

HERONRY n colony of breeding herons

HERONS > HERON

HERONSEW same as > HERONSHAW

HERONSEWS > HERONSEW

HERONSHAW n young heron

HEROON n temple or monument dedicated to hero

HEROONS > HEROON

HEROS > HERO

HEROSHIP > HERO

HEROSHIPS > HERO

HERPES n any of several inflammatory skin diseases, including shingles and cold sores

HERPESES > HERPES

HERPETIC adj of or relating to any of the herpes diseases ▷ n person suffering from any of the herpes diseases

HERPETICS > HERPETIC

HERPETOID adj like reptile

HERPTILE adj denoting, relating to, or characterizing both reptiles and amphibians

HERRIED > HERRY

HERRIES > HERRY

HERRIMENT n act of plundering

HERRING n important food fish of northern seas

HERRINGER n person or boat catching herring

HERRINGS > HERRING

HERRY vb harry

HERRYING > HERRY

HERRYMENT same as > HERRIMENT

HERS pron something belonging to her

HERSALL n rehearsal

HERSALLS > HERSALL

HERSE n harrow

HERSED adj arranged like a harrow

HERSELF pron feminine singular reflexive form

HERSES > HERSE

HERSHIP n act of plundering

HERSHIPS > HERSHIP

HERSTORY n history from a female point of view or as it relates to women

HERTZ n unit of frequency

HERTZES > HERTZ

HERY vb praise

HERYE same as > HERY

HERYED > HERYE

HERYES > HERYE

HERYING > HERY

HES > HE

HESITANCE > HESITANT

HESITANCY > HESITANT

HESITANT adj undecided or wavering

HESITATE vb be slow or uncertain in doing something

HESITATED > HESITATE

HESITATER > HESITATE

HESITATES > HESITATE

HESITATOR > HESITATE

HESP same as > HASP

HESPED > HESP

HESPERID n species of butterfly

HESPERIDS > HESPERID

HESPING > HESP

HESPS > HESP

HESSIAN n coarse jute fabric

HESSIANS > HESSIAN

HESSITE n black or grey metallic mineral consisting of silver telluride in cubic crystalline form

HESSITES > HESSITE

HESSONITE n orange-brown variety of grossularite garnet

HEST archaic word for > BEHEST

HESTERNAL adj belonging to yesterday

HESTS > HEST

HET n short for heterosexual ▷ adj Scot word for hot

HETAERA n (esp in ancient Greece) a female

prostitute, esp an educated courtesan

HETAERAE > HETAERA

HETAERAS > HETAERA

HETAERIC > HETAERA

HETAERISM n state of being a concubine

HETAERIST > HETAERISM

HETAIRA same as > HETAERA

HETAIRAI > HETAIRA

HETAIRAS > HETAIRA

HETAIRIA n society

HETAIRIAS > HETAIRIA

HETAIRIC > HETAERA

HETAIRISM same as > HETAERISM

HETAIRIST > HETAERISM

HETE same as > HIGHT

HETERO n short for heterosexual

HETERODOX adj differing from accepted doctrines or beliefs

HETERONYM n one of two or more words pronounced differently but spelt alike

HETEROPOD n marine invertebrate with a foot for swimming

HETEROS > HETERO

HETEROSES > HETEROSIS

HETEROSIS n increased size, strength, etc, of a hybrid as compared to either of its parents

HETEROTIC > HETEROSIS

HETES > HETE

HETH n eighth letter of the Hebrew alphabet

HETHER same as > HITHER

HETHS > HETH

HETING > HETE

HETMAN another word for > ATAMAN

HETMANATE > HETMAN

HETMANS > HETMAN

HETS > HET

HETTIE n slang term for a heterosexual

HETTIES > HETTIE

HEUCH Scots word for > CRAG

HEUCHERA n N American plant with heart-shaped leaves and mostly red flowers

HEUCHERAS > HEUCHERA

HEUCHS > HEUCH

HEUGH same as > HEUCH

HEUGHS > HEUGH

HEUREKA same as > EUREKA

HEUREKAS > HEUREKA

HEURETIC same as > HEURISTIC

HEURETICS n use of logic

HEURISM n use of logic

HEURISMS > HEURISM

HEURISTIC adj involving learning by investigation

▷ *n* science of heuristic procedure

HEVEA *n* rubber-producing South American tree

HEVEAS > HEVEA

HEW *vb* cut with an axe

HEWABLE > HEW

HEWED > HEW

HEWER > HEW

HEWERS > HEW

HEWGH *interj* sound made to imitate the flight of an arrow

HEWING > HEW

HEWINGS > HEW

HEWN > HEW

HEWS > HEW

HEX *adj* of or relating to hexadecimal notation ▷ *n* evil spell ▷ *vb* bewitch

HEXACHORD *n* (in medieval musical theory) any of three diatonic scales based upon C, F, and G, each consisting of six notes, from which solmization was developed

HEXACT *n* part of a sponge with six rays

HEXACTS > HEXACT

HEXAD *n* group or series of six

HEXADE *same as* > HEXAD

HEXADES > HEXADE

HEXADIC > HEXAD

HEXADS > HEXAD

HEXAFOIL *n* pattern with six lobes

HEXAFOILS > HEXAFOIL

HEXAGON *n* geometrical figure with six sides

HEXAGONAL *adj* having six sides and six angles

HEXAGONS > HEXAGON

HEXAGRAM *n* star formed by extending the sides of a regular hexagon to meet at six points

HEXAGRAMS > HEXAGRAM

HEXAHEDRA *n* plural of hexahedron: solid figure with six plane faces

HEXAMERAL *adj* arranged in six groups

HEXAMETER *n* verse line consisting of six metrical feet

HEXAMINE *n* type of fuel produced in small solid blocks or tablets for use in miniature camping stoves

HEXAMINES > HEXAMINE

HEXANE *n* liquid alkane existing in five isomeric forms that are found in petroleum and used as solvents

HEXANES > HEXANE

HEXANOIC *as in hexanoic acid* insoluble oily carboxylic acid found in coconut and palm oils and in milk

HEXAPLA *n* edition of the Old Testament compiled by Origen, containing six versions of the text

HEXAPLAR > HEXAPLA

HEXAPLAS > HEXAPLA

HEXAPLOID *adj* with six times the normal number of chromosomes

HEXAPOD *n* six-footed arthropod

HEXAPODAL *adj* relating to the Hexapoda, ie insects

HEXAPODIC > HEXAPODY

HEXAPODS > HEXAPOD

HEXAPODY *n* verse measure consisting of six metrical feet

HEXARCH *adj* (of plant) with six veins

HEXARCHY *n* alliance of six states

HEXASTICH *n* poem, stanza, or strophe that consists of six lines

HEXASTYLE *n* portico or façade with six columns ▷ *adj* having six columns

HEXED > HEX

HEXENE *same as* > HEXYLENE

HEXENES > HEXENE

HEXER > HEX

HEXEREI *n* witchcraft

HEXEREIS > HEXEREI

HEXERS > HEX

HEXES > HEX

HEXING > HEX

HEXINGS > HEX

HEXONE *n* colourless insoluble liquid ketone used as a solvent for organic compounds

HEXONES > HEXONE

HEXOSAN *n* any of a group of polysaccharides that yield hexose on hydrolysis

HEXOSANS > HEXOSAN

HEXOSE *n* monosaccharide, such as glucose, that contains six carbon atoms per molecule

HEXOSES > HEXOSE

HEXYL *adj* of, consisting of, or containing the group of atoms C_6H_{13}, esp the isomeric form of this group, $CH_3(CH_2)_4CH_2$-

HEXYLENE *n* chemical compound similar to ethylene

HEXYLENES > HEXYLENE

HEXYLIC > HEXYL

HEXYLS > HEXYL

HEY *interj* expression of surprise or for catching attention ▷ *vb* perform a country dance

HEYDAY *n* time of greatest success, prime

HEYDAYS > HEYDAY

HEYDEY *variant of* > HEYDAY

HEYDEYS > HEYDEY

HEYDUCK *same as* > HAIDUK

HEYDUCKS > HEYDUCK

HEYED > HEY

HEYING > HEY

HEYS > HEY

HI *interj* hello

HIANT *adj* gaping

HIATAL > HIATUS

HIATUS *n* pause or interruption in continuity

HIATUSES > HIATUS

HIBACHI *n* portable brazier for heating and cooking food

HIBACHIS > HIBACHI

HIBAKUSHA *n* survivor of either of the atomic-bomb attacks on Hiroshima and Nagasaki in 1945

HIBERNAL *adj* of or occurring in winter

HIBERNATE *vb* (of an animal) pass the winter as if in a deep sleep

HIBERNISE > HIBERNIZE

HIBERNIZE *vb* make Irish

HIBISCUS *n* tropical plant with large brightly coloured flowers

HIC *interj* representation of the sound of a hiccup

HICATEE *same as* > HICCATEE

HICATEES > HICATEE

HICCATEE *n* tortoise of West Indies

HICCATEES > HICCATEE

HICCOUGH *same as* > HICCUP

HICCOUGHS > HICCOUGH

HICCUP *n* spasm of the breathing organs with a sharp coughlike sound ▷ *vb* make a hiccup

HICCUPED > HICCUP

HICCUPING > HICCUP

HICCUPPED > HICCUP

HICCUPS > HICCUP

HICCUPY > HICCUP

HICK *n* unsophisticated country person

HICKEY *n* object or gadget: used as a name when the correct name is forgotten, etc

HICKEYS > HICKEY

HICKIE *same as* > HICKEY

HICKIES > HICKIE

HICKISH > HICK

HICKORIES > HICKORY

HICKORY *n* N American nut-bearing tree

HICKS > HICK

HICKWALL *n* green woodpecker

HICKWALLS > HICKWALL

HICKYMAL *n* titmouse

HICKYMALS > HICKYMAL

HID > HIDE

HIDABLE > HIDE

HIDAGE *n* former tax on land

HIDAGES > HIDAGE

HIDALGA *n* Spanish noblewoman

HIDALGAS > HIDALGA

HIDALGO *n* member of the lower nobility in Spain

HIDALGOS > HIDALGO

HIDDEN > HIDE

HIDDENITE *n* green transparent variety of the mineral spodumene, used as a gemstone

HIDDENLY > HIDE

HIDDER *n* young ram

HIDDERS > HIDDER

HIDE *vb* put (oneself or an object) somewhere difficult to see or find ▷ *n* place of concealment, esp for a bird-watcher

HIDEAWAY *n* private place

HIDEAWAYS > HIDEAWAY

HIDEBOUND *adj* unwilling to accept new ideas

HIDED > HIDE

HIDELESS > HIDE

HIDEOSITY > HIDEOUS

HIDEOUS *adj* ugly, revolting

HIDEOUSLY > HIDEOUS

HIDEOUT *n* hiding place, esp a remote place used by outlaws, etc; hideaway

HIDEOUTS > HIDEOUT

HIDER > HIDE

HIDERS > HIDE

HIDES > HIDE

HIDING > HIDE

HIDINGS > HIDE

HIDLING *n* hiding place

HIDLINGS *adv* in secret

HIDLINS *same as* > HIDLINGS

HIDROSES > HIDROSIS

HIDROSIS *n* any skin disease affecting the sweat glands

HIDROTIC > HIDROSIS

HIDROTICS > HIDROSIS

HIE *vb* hurry

HIED > HIE

HIEING > HIE

HIELAMAN *n* Australian Aboriginal shield

HIELAMANS > HIELAMAN

HIELAND *adj* characteristic of Highlanders, esp alluding to their supposed gullibility or foolishness in towns or cities

HIEMAL *less common word for* > HIBERNAL

HIEMS *n* winter

HIERACIUM *n* plant of hawkweed family

HIERARCH *n* person in a position of high-priestly authority

HIERARCHS > HIERARCH

HIERARCHY *n* system of people or things arranged in a graded order

HIERATIC *adj* of or relating to priests ▷ *n* hieratic script of ancient Egypt

HIERATICA *n* type of papyrus

h

HIERATICS > HIERATIC

HIEROCRAT n person who believes in government by religious leaders

HIERODULE n (in ancient Greece) a temple slave, esp a sacral prostitute

HIEROGRAM n sacred symbol

HIEROLOGY n sacred literature

HIERURGY n performance of religious drama or music

HIES > HIE

HIFALUTIN adj pompous or pretentious

HIGGLE less common word for > HAGGLE

HIGGLED > HIGGLE

HIGGLER > HIGGLE

HIGGLERS > HIGGLE

HIGGLES > HIGGLE

HIGGLING > HIGGLE

HIGGLINGS > HIGGLE

HIGH adj being a relatively great distance from top to bottom; tall ▷ adv at or to a height ▷ n a high place or level ▷ vb hie

HIGHBALL n tall drink of whiskey with soda water or ginger ale and ice ▷ vb move at great speed

HIGHBALLS > HIGHBALL

HIGHBORN adj of noble or aristocratic birth

HIGHBOY n tall chest of drawers in two sections, the lower section being a lowboy

HIGHBOYS > HIGHBOY

HIGHBRED adj of noble breeding

HIGHBROW n intellectual and serious person ▷ adj concerned with serious, intellectual subjects

HIGHBROWS > HIGHBROW

HIGHBUSH adj (of bush) growing tall

HIGHCHAIR n long-legged chair with a tray attached, used by a very young child at mealtimes

HIGHED > HIGH

HIGHER n advanced level of the Scottish Certificate of Education ▷ vb raise up

HIGHERED > HIGHER

HIGHERING > HIGHER

HIGHERS > HIGHER

HIGHEST > HIGH

HIGHFLIER same as > HIGHFLYER

HIGHFLYER n person who is extreme in aims, ambition, etc

HIGHING > HIGH

HIGHISH > HIGH

HIGHJACK same as > HIJACK

HIGHJACKS > HIGHJACK

HIGHLAND n relatively high ground

HIGHLANDS > HIGHLAND

HIGHLIFE n style of music combining West African elements with US jazz forms, found esp in the cities of West Africa

HIGHLIFES > HIGHLIFE

HIGHLIGHT n outstanding part or feature ▷ vb give emphasis to

HIGHLY adv extremely

HIGHMAN n dice weighted to make it fall in particular way

HIGHMEN > HIGHMAN

HIGHMOST adj highest

HIGHNESS n condition of being high or lofty

HIGHRISE n tall building

HIGHRISES > HIGHRISE

HIGHROAD n main road

HIGHROADS > HIGHROAD

HIGHS > HIGH

HIGHSPOT n highlight

HIGHSPOTS > HIGHSPOT

HIGHT vb archaic word for name or call

HIGHTAIL vb go or move in a great hurry

HIGHTAILS > HIGHTAIL

HIGHTED > HIGHT

HIGHTH old form of > HEIGHT

HIGHTHS > HIGHTH

HIGHTING n oath

HIGHTOP n top of ship's mast

HIGHTOPS > HIGHTOP

HIGHTS > HIGHT

HIGHVELD n high-altitude grassland region of E South Africa

HIGHVELDS > HIGHVELD

HIGHWAY n main road

HIGHWAYS > HIGHWAY

HIJAB n covering for the head and face, worn by Muslim women

HIJABS > HIJAB

HIJACK vb seize control of (an aircraft or other vehicle) while travelling ▷ n instance of hijacking

HIJACKED > HIJACK

HIJACKER > HIJACK

HIJACKERS > HIJACK

HIJACKING > HIJACK

HIJACKS > HIJACK

HIJINKS n lively enjoyment

HIJRA same as > HIJRAH

HIJRAH same as > HEGIRA

HIJRAHS > HIJRAH

HIJRAS > HIJRA

HIKE n long walk in the country, esp for pleasure ▷ vb go for a long walk

HIKED > HIKE

HIKER > HIKE

HIKERS > HIKE

HIKES > HIKE

HIKING > HIKE

HIKOI n walk or march, esp a Māori protest march ▷ vb take part in such a march

HIKOIED > HIKOI

HIKOIING > HIKOI

HIKOIS > HIKOI

HILA > HILUM

HILAR > HILUS

HILARIOUS adj very funny

HILARITY n mirth and merriment

HILCH vb hobble

HILCHED > HILCH

HILCHES > HILCH

HILCHING > HILCH

HILD same as > HOLD

HILDING n coward

HILDINGS > HILDING

HILI > HILUS

HILL n raised part of the earth's surface, less high than a mountain ▷ vb form into a hill or mound

HILLBILLY n usually disparaging term for an unsophisticated country person

HILLCREST n crest of hill

HILLED > HILL

HILLER > HILL

HILLERS > HILL

HILLFOLK n people living in the hills

HILLFORT n hilltop fortified with ramparts and ditches, dating from the second millennium BC

HILLFORTS > HILLFORT

HILLIER > HILL

HILLIEST > HILL

HILLINESS > HILL

HILLING > HILL

HILLINGS > HILLING

HILLMEN same as > HILLFOLK

HILLO same as > HELLO

HILLOA same as > HALLOA

HILLOAED > HILLOA

HILLOAING > HILLOA

HILLOAS > HILLOA

HILLOCK n small hill

HILLOCKED > HILLOCK

HILLOCKS > HILLOCK

HILLOCKY > HILLOCK

HILLOED > HILLO

HILLOES > HILLO

HILLOING > HILLO

HILLOS > HILLO

HILLS > HILL

HILLSIDE n side of a hill

HILLSIDES > HILLSIDE

HILLSLOPE same as > HILLSIDE

HILLTOP n top of hill

HILLTOPS > HILLTOP

HILLY > HILL

HILT n handle of a sword or knife ▷ vb supply with a hilt

HILTED > HILT

HILTING > HILT

HILTLESS > HILT

HILTS > HILT

HILUM n scar on a seed marking its point of attachment to the seed vessel

HILUS rare word for > HILUM

HIM pron refers to a male person or animal when the object of a sentence or clause ▷ n male person

HIMATIA > HIMATION

HIMATION n (in ancient Greece) a cloak draped around the body

HIMATIONS > HIMATION

HIMBO n slang, usually derogarory term for an attractive but empty-headed man

HIMBOS > HIMBO

HIMS > HIM

HIMSELF pron masculine singular reflexive form

HIN n Hebrew unit of capacity equal to about 12 pints or 3.5 litres

HINAHINA same as > MAHOE

HINAHINAS > HINAHINA

HINAU n New Zealand tree

HINAUS > HINAU

HIND adj situated at the back ▷ n female deer

HINDBERRY n raspberry

HINDBRAIN part of the brain comprising the cerbellum, pons and medulla oblongata

HINDCAST vb test (a mathematical model)

HINDCASTS > HINDCAST

HINDER vb get in the way of ▷ adj situated at the back

HINDERED > HINDER

HINDERER > HINDER

HINDERERS > HINDER

HINDERING > HINDER

HINDERS > HINDER

HINDFEET > HINDFOOT

HINDFOOT n back foot

HINDGUT n part of the vertebrate digestive tract comprising the colon and rectum

HINDGUTS > HINDGUT

HINDHEAD n back of head

HINDHEADS > HINDHEAD

HINDLEG n back leg

HINDLEGS > HINDLEG

HINDMOST > HIND

HINDRANCE n obstruction or snag

HINDS > HIND

HINDSHANK n meat from animal's hind leg

HINDSIGHT n ability to understand, after something has happened, what should have been done

HINDWARD adj at back

HINDWING n back wing

HINDWINGS > HINDWING

HING n asafoetida

HINGE n device for holding together two parts so that one can swing freely ▷ vb depend (on)

HINGED > HINGE

HINGELESS > HINGE

HINGELIKE > HINGE

HINGER *n* tool for making hinges

HINGERS > HINGER

HINGES > HINGE

HINGING > HINGE

HINGS > HING

HINKIER > HINKY

HINKIEST > HINKY

HINKY *adj* strange

HINNIED > HINNY

HINNIES > HINNY

HINNY *n* offspring of a male horse and a female donkey ▷ *vb* whinny

HINNYING > HINNY

HINS > HIN

HINT *n* indirect suggestion ▷ *vb* suggest indirectly

HINTED > HINT

HINTER > HINT

HINTERS > HINT

HINTING > HINT

HINTINGLY > HINT

HINTINGS > HINT

HINTS > HINT

HIOI *n* New Zealand plant of the mint family

HIOIS > HIOI

HIP *n* either side of the body between the pelvis and the thigh ▷ *adj* aware of or following the latest trends ▷ *interj* exclamation used to introduce cheers

HIPBONE *n* either of the two bones that form the sides of the pelvis

HIPBONES > HIPBONE

HIPHUGGER *adj* (of trousers) having a low waist

HIPLESS > HIP

HIPLIKE > HIP

HIPLINE *n* widest part of a person's hips

HIPLINES > HIPLINE

HIPLY > HIP

HIPNESS > HIP

HIPNESSES > HIP

HIPPARCH *n* (in ancient Greece) a cavalry commander

HIPPARCHS > HIPPARCH

HIPPED *adj* having a hip or hips

HIPPEN *n* baby's nappy

HIPPENS > HIPPEN

HIPPER > HIP

HIPPEST > HIP

HIPPIATRY *n* treatment of disease in horses

HIPPIC *adj* of horses

HIPPIE *same as* **>** HIPPY

HIPPIEDOM > HIPPIE

HIPPIEISH > HIPPIE

HIPPIER > HIPPY

HIPPIES > HIPPY

HIPPIEST > HIPPY

HIPPIN *same as* **>** HIPPEN

HIPPINESS > HIPPY

HIPPING *same as* **>** HIPPEN

HIPPINGS > HIPPING

HIPPINS > HIPPIN

HIPPISH *adj* in low spirits

HIPPO *n* hippopotamus

HIPPOCRAS *n* old English drink of wine flavoured with spices

HIPPODAME *n* sea horse

HIPPOLOGY *n* study of horses

HIPPOS > HIPPO

HIPPURIC as in *hippuric acid* crystalline solid excreted in the urine of mammals

HIPPURITE *n* type of fossil

HIPPUS *n* spasm of eye

HIPPUSES > HIPPUS

HIPPY *n* (esp in the 1960s) person whose behaviour and dress imply a rejection of conventional values ▷ *adj* having large hips

HIPPYDOM > HIPPY

HIPPYDOMS > HIPPY

HIPS > HIP

HIPSHOT *adj* having a dislocated hip

HIPSTER *n* enthusiast of modern jazz

HIPSTERS *npl* trousers cut so that the top encircles the hips

HIPT > HIP

HIRABLE > HIRE

HIRAGANA *n* one of the Japanese systems of syllabic writing based on Chinese cursive ideograms. The more widely used of the two current systems, it is employed in newspapers and general literature

HIRAGANAS > HIRAGANA

HIRAGE *n* fee for hiring

HIRAGES > HIRAGE

HIRCINE *adj* of or like a goat, esp in smell

HIRCOSITY *n* quality of being like a goat

HIRE *vb* pay to have temporary use of ▷ *n* hiring

HIREABLE > HIRE

HIREAGE *same as* **>** HIRAGE

HIREAGES > HIREAGE

HIRED > HIRE

HIREE *n* hired person

HIREES > HIRE

HIRELING *n* derogatory term for a person who works only for wages

HIRELINGS > HIRELING

HIRER > HIRE

HIRERS > HIRE

HIRES > HIRE

HIRING > HIRE

HIRINGS > HIRE

HIRLING *n* Scots word for a type of fish

HIRLINGS > HIRLING

HIRPLE *vb* limp ▷ *n* limping gait

HIRPLED > HIRPLE

HIRPLES > HIRPLE

HIRPLING > HIRPLE

HIRRIENT *n* trilled sound

HIRRIENTS > HIRRIENT

HIRSEL *vb* sort into groups

HIRSELED > HIRSEL

HIRSELING > HIRSEL

HIRSELLED > HIRSEL

HIRSELS > HIRSEL

HIRSLE *vb* wriggle or fidget

HIRSLED > HIRSLE

HIRSLES > HIRSLE

HIRSLING > HIRSLE

HIRSTIE *adj* dry

HIRSUTE *adj* hairy

HIRSUTISM > HIRSUTE

HIRUDIN *n* anticoagulant extracted from the mouth glands of leeches

HIRUDINS > HIRUDIN

HIRUNDINE *adj* of or resembling a swallow

HIS *adj* belonging to him

HISH *same as* **>** HISS

HISHED > HISH

HISHES > HISH

HISHING > HISH

HISN *dialect form of* **>** HIS

HISPANISM *n* Spanish turn of phrase

HISPID *adj* covered with stiff hairs or bristles

HISPIDITY > HISPID

HISS *n* sound like that of a long *s* (as an expression of contempt) ▷ *vb* utter a hiss ▷ *interj* exclamation of derision or disapproval

HISSED > HISS

HISSELF *dialect form of* **>** HIMSELF

HISSER > HISS

HISSERS > HISS

HISSES > HISS

HISSIER > HISSY

HISSIES > HISSY

HISSIEST > HISSY

HISSING > HISS

HISSINGLY > HISS

HISSINGS > HISS

HISSY *n* temper tantrum ▷ *adj* sound similar to a hiss

HIST *interj* exclamation used to attract attention or as a warning to be silent ▷ *vb* make hist sound

HISTAMIN *variant of* **>** HISTAMINE

HISTAMINE *n* substance released by the body tissues in allergic reactions

HISTAMINS > HISTAMIN

HISTED > HIST

HISTIDIN *variant of* **>** HISTIDINE

HISTIDINE *n* nonessential amino acid that occurs in most proteins: a precursor of histamine

HISTIDINS > HISTIDIN

HISTIE *same as* **>** HIRSTIE

HISTING > HIST

HISTIOID *same as* **>** HISTOID

HISTOGEN *n* (formerly) any of three layers in an apical meristem that were thought to give rise to the different parts of the plant: the apical meristem is now regarded as comprising two layers

HISTOGENS > HISTOGEN

HISTOGENY > HISTOGEN

HISTOGRAM *n* statistical graph in which the frequency of values is represented by vertical bars of varying heights and widths

HISTOID *adj* (esp of a tumour)

HISTOLOGY *n* study of the tissues of an animal or plant

HISTONE *n* any of a group of basic proteins present in cell nuclei and implicated in the spatial organization of DNA

HISTONES > HISTONE

HISTORIAN *n* writer of history

HISTORIC *adj* famous or significant in history

HISTORIED *adj* recorded in history

HISTORIES > HISTORY

HISTORIFY *vb* make part of history

HISTORISM *n* idea that history influences present

HISTORY *n* (record or account of) past events and developments

HISTRIO *n* actor

HISTRION *same as* **>** HISTRIO

HISTRIONS > HISTRION

HISTRIOS > HISTRIO

HISTS > HIST

HIT *vb* strike, touch forcefully ▷ *n* hitting

HITCH *n* minor problem ▷ *vb* obtain (a lift) by hitchhiking

HITCHED > HITCH

HITCHER > HITCH

HITCHERS > HITCH

HITCHES > HITCH

HITCHHIKE *vb* travel by obtaining free lifts

HITCHIER > HITCH

HITCHIEST > HITCH

HITCHILY > HITCH

HITCHING > HITCH

HITCHY > HITCH

HITHE *n* small harbour

HITHER *adv* or towards this place ▷ *vb* come

HITHERED > HITHER

HITHERING > HITHER

HITHERS > HITHER

HITHERTO *adv* until this time

HITHES > HITHE

HITLESS > HIT

HITMAN *n* professional killer

HITMEN > HITMAN

HITS > HIT

HITTABLE > HIT

HITTER *n* boxer who has a hard punch rather than skill or finesse

HITTERS > HITTER

HITTING > HIT

HIVE *n* structure in which social bees live and rear their young ▷ *vb* cause (bees) to collect or (of bees) to collect inside a hive

HIVED > HIVE

HIVELESS > HIVE

HIVELIKE > HIVE

HIVER *n* person who keeps beehives

HIVERS > HIVER

HIVES *n* allergic reaction in which itchy red or whitish patches appear on the skin

HIVEWARD *adj* towards hive

HIVEWARDS *adv* towards hive

HIVING > HIVE

HIYA *sentence substitute* informal term of greeting

HIZEN *n* type of Japanese porcelain

HIZENS > HIZEN

HIZZ *same as* > HISS

HIZZED > HIZZ

HIZZES > HIZZ

HIZZING > HIZZ

HIZZONER *n* nickname for mayor

HIZZONERS > HIZZONER

HM *interj* sound made to express hesitation or doubt

HMM *same as* > HM

HO *n* derogatory term for a woman ▷ *interj* imitation or representation of the sound of a deep laugh ▷ *vb* halt

HOA *same as* > HO

HOACTZIN *same as* > HOATZIN

HOACTZINS > HOATZIN

HOAED > HOA

HOAGIE *n* sandwich made with long bread roll

HOAGIES > HOAGIE

HOAGY *same as* > HOAGIE

HOAING > HOA

HOAR *adj* covered with hoarfrost ▷ *vb* make hoary

HOARD *n* store hidden away for future use ▷ *vb* save or store

HOARDED > HOARD

HOARDER > HOARD

HOARDERS > HOARD

HOARDING *n* large board for displaying advertisements

HOARDINGS > HOARDING

HOARDS > HOARD

HOARED > HOAR

HOARFROST *n* white ground frost

HOARHEAD *n* person with white hair

HOARHEADS > HOARHEAD

HOARHOUND *same as* > HOREHOUND

HOARIER > HOARY

HOARIEST > HOARY

HOARILY > HOARY

HOARINESS > HOARY

HOARING > HOAR

HOARS > HOAR

HOARSE *adj* (of a voice) rough and unclear

HOARSELY > HOARSE

HOARSEN *vb* make or become hoarse

HOARSENED > HOARSEN

HOARSENS > HOARSEN

HOARSER > HOARSE

HOARSEST > HOARSE

HOARY *adj* grey or white(-haired)

HOAS > HOA

HOAST *n* cough ▷ *vb* cough

HOASTED > HOAST

HOASTING > HOAST

HOASTMAN *n* shipper of coal

HOASTMEN > HOASTMAN

HOASTS > HOAST

HOATCHING *adj* infested

HOATZIN *n* South American bird with a brownish plumage and very small crested head

HOATZINES > HOATZIN

HOATZINS > HOATZIN

HOAX *n* deception or trick ▷ *vb* deceive or play a trick upon

HOAXED > HOAX

HOAXER > HOAX

HOAXERS > HOAX

HOAXES > HOAX

HOAXING > HOAX

HOB *n* flat top part of a cooker, or a separate flat surface, containing gas or electric rings for cooking on ▷ *vb* cut or form with a hob

HOBBED > HOB

HOBBER *n* machine used in making gears

HOBBERS > HOBBER

HOBBIES > HOBBY

HOBBING > HOB

HOBBISH *adj* like a clown

HOBBIT *n* one of an imaginary race of half-size people living in holes

HOBBITRY > HOBBIT

HOBBITS > HOBBIT

HOBBLE *vb* walk lamely ▷ *n* strap, rope, etc, used to hobble a horse

HOBBLED > HOBBLE

HOBBLER > HOBBLE

HOBBLERS > HOBBLE

HOBBLES > HOBBLE

HOBBLING > HOBBLE

HOBBLINGS > HOBBLE

HOBBY *n* activity pursued in one's spare time

HOBBYISM > HOBBY

HOBBYISMS > HOBBY

HOBBYIST > HOBBY

HOBBYISTS > HOBBY

HOBBYLESS > HOBBY

HOBDAY *vb* alleviate (a breathing problem in certain horses) by the surgical operation of removing soft tissue ventricles to pull back the vocal fold

HOBDAYED > HOBDAY

HOBDAYING > HOBDAY

HOBDAYS > HOBDAY

HOBGOBLIN *n* mischievous goblin

HOBJOB *vb* do odd jobs

HOBJOBBED > HOBJOB

HOBJOBBER > HOBJOB

HOBJOBS > HOBJOB

HOBLIKE > HOB

HOBNAIL *n* short nail with a large head for protecting the soles of heavy footwear ▷ *vb* provide with hobnails

HOBNAILED > HOBNAIL

HOBNAILS > HOBNAIL

HOBNOB *vb* be on friendly terms (with)

HOBNOBBED > HOBNOB

HOBNOBBER > HOBNOB

HOBNOBBY > HOBNOB

HOBNOBS > HOBNOB

HOBO *n* tramp or vagrant ▷ *vb* live as hobo

HOBODOM > HOBO

HOBODOMS > HOBO

HOBOED > HOBO

HOBOES > HOBO

HOBOING > HOBO

HOBOISM > HOBO

HOBOISMS > HOBO

HOBOS > HOBO

HOBS > HOB

HOC *adj* Latin for this

HOCK *n* joint in the back leg of an animal such as a horse that corresponds to the human ankle ▷ *vb* pawn

HOCKED > HOCK

HOCKER > HOCK

HOCKERS > HOCK

HOCKEY *n* team game played on a field with a ball and curved sticks

HOCKEYS > HOCKEY

HOCKING > HOCK

HOCKLE *vb* spit

HOCKLED > HOCKLE

HOCKLES > HOCKLE

HOCKLING > HOCKLE

HOCKS > HOCK

HOCKSHOP *n* pawnshop

HOCKSHOPS > HOCKSHOP

HOCUS *vb* take in

HOCUSED > HOCUS

HOCUSES > HOCUS

HOCUSING > HOCUS

HOCUSSED > HOCUS

HOCUSSES > HOCUS

HOCUSSING > HOCUS

HOD *n* open wooden box attached to a pole, for carrying bricks or mortar ▷ *vb* bob up and down

HODAD *n* person who pretends to be a surfer

HODADDIES > HODADDY

HODADDY *same as* > HODAD

HODADS > HODAD

HODDED > HOD

HODDEN *n* coarse homespun cloth produced in Scotland: hodden grey is made by mixing black and white wools

HODDENS > HODDEN

HODDIN *same as* > HODDEN

HODDING > HOD

HODDINS > HODDIN

HODDLE *vb* waddle

HODDLED > HODDLE

HODDLES > HODDLE

HODDLING > HODDLE

HODIERNAL *adj* of the present day

HODJA *n* respectful Turkish form of address

HODJAS > HODJA

HODMAN *n* hod carrier

HODMANDOD *n* snail

HODMEN > HODMAN

HODOGRAPH *n* curve of which the radius vector represents the velocity of a moving particle

HODOMETER *another name for* > ODOMETER

HODOMETRY > HODOMETER

HODOSCOPE *n* any device for tracing the path of a charged particle, esp a particle found in cosmic rays

HODS > HOD

HOE *n* long-handled tool used for loosening soil or weeding ▷ *vb* scrape or weed with a hoe

HOECAKE *n* maize cake

HOECAKES > HOECAKE

HOED > HOE

HOEDOWN *n* boisterous square dance

HOEDOWNS > HOEDOWN

HOEING > HOE

HOELIKE > HOE

HOER > HOE

HOERS > HOE

HOES > HOE

HOG *n* castrated male pig ▷ *vb* take more than one's share of

HOGAN *n* wooden dwelling covered with earth, typical of the Navaho Indians of N America

HOGANS > HOGAN

HOGBACK *n* narrow ridge that consists of steeply inclined rock strata

HOGBACKS > HOGBACK

HOGEN *n* strong alcoholic drink

HOGENS > HOGEN

HOGFISH *n* type of fish

HOGFISHES > HOGFISH

HOGG same as > HOG
HOGGED > HOG
HOGGER > HOG
HOGGEREL n year-old sheep
HOGGERELS > HOGGEREL
HOGGERIES > HOGGERY
HOGGERS > HOG
HOGGERY n hogs collectively
HOGGET n sheep up to the age of one year that has yet to be sheared
HOGGETS > HOGGET
HOGGIN n finely sifted gravel containing enough clay binder for it to be used in its natural form for making paths or roads
HOGGING same as > HOGGIN
HOGGINGS > HOGGING
HOGGINS > HOGGIN
HOGGISH adj selfish, gluttonous, or dirty
HOGGISHLY > HOGGISH
HOGGS > HOGG
HOGH n ridge of land
HOGHOOD n condition of being hog
HOGHOODS > HOGHOOD
HOGHS > HOGH
HOGLIKE > HOG
HOGMANAY n New Year's Eve
HOGMANAYS > HOGMANAY
HOGMANE n short stiff mane
HOGMANES > HOGMANE
HOGMENAY variant of > HOGMANAY
HOGMENAYS > HOGMENAY
HOGNOSE as in hognose snake puff adder
HOGNOSED as in hognosed skunk any of several American skunks having a broad snoutlike nose
HOGNOSES > HOGNOSE
HOGNUT another name for > PIGNUT
HOGNUTS > HOGNUT
HOGS > HOG
HOGSHEAD n large cask
HOGSHEADS > HOGSHEAD
HOGTIE vb tie together the legs or the arms and legs of
HOGTIED > HOGTIE
HOGTIEING > HOGTIE
HOGTIES > HOGTIE
HOGTYING > HOGTIE
HOGWARD n person looking after hogs
HOGWARDS > HOGWARD
HOGWASH n nonsense
HOGWASHES > HOGWASH
HOGWEED n any of several coarse weedy umbelliferous plants, esp cow parsnip
HOGWEEDS > HOGWEED
HOH same as > HO
HOHA adj bored or annoyed
HOHED > HOH

HOHING > HOH
HOHS > HOH
HOI same as > HOY
HOICK vb raise abruptly and sharply
HOICKED > HOICK
HOICKING > HOICK
HOICKS interj cry used to encourage hounds to hunt ▷ vb shout hoicks
HOICKSED > HOICKS
HOICKSES > HOICKS
HOICKSING > HOICKS
HOIDEN same as > HOYDEN
HOIDENED > HOIDEN
HOIDENING > HOIDEN
HOIDENISH > HOIDEN
HOIDENS > HOIDEN
HOIK same as > HOICK
HOIKED > HOIK
HOIKING > HOIK
HOIKS > HOIK
HOING > HO
HOISE same as > HOIST
HOISED > HOISE
HOISES > HOISE
HOISIN n Chinese sweet spicy reddish-brown sauce made from soya beans, sugar, vinegar, and garlic
HOISING > HOISE
HOISINS > HOISIN
HOIST vb raise or lift up ▷ n device for lifting things
HOISTED > HOIST
HOISTER > HOIST
HOISTERS > HOIST
HOISTING > HOIST
HOISTINGS > HOIST
HOISTMAN n person operating a hoist
HOISTMEN > HOISTMAN
HOISTS > HOIST
HOISTWAY n shaft for a hoist
HOISTWAYS > HOISTWAY
HOKA n red cod
HOKAS > HOKA
HOKE vb overplay (a part, etc)
HOKED > HOKE
HOKES > HOKE
HOKEY adj corny
HOKEYNESS > HOKEY
HOKI n fish of New Zealand waters
HOKIER > HOKEY
HOKIEST > HOKEY
HOKILY > HOKEY
HOKINESS > HOKEY
HOKING > HOKE
HOKIS > HOKI
HOKKU same as > HAIKU
HOKONUI n illicit whisky
HOKONUIS > HOKONUI
HOKUM n rubbish, nonsense
HOKUMS > HOKUM
HOKYPOKY n trickery
HOLANDRIC adj relating to Y-chromosomal genes
HOLARCHY n system composed of interacting holons
HOLARD n amount of water

contained in soil
HOLARDS > HOLARD
HOLD vb keep or support in or with the hands or arms ▷ n act or way of holding
HOLDABLE > HOLD
HOLDALL n large strong travelling bag
HOLDALLS > HOLDALL
HOLDBACK n strap of the harness joining the breeching to the shaft, so that the horse can hold back the vehicle
HOLDBACKS > HOLDBACK
HOLDDOWN n control function in a computer
HOLDDOWNS > HOLDDOWN
HOLDEN past participle of > HOLD
HOLDER n person or thing that holds
HOLDERBAT n part of pipe used as fastening
HOLDERS > HOLDER
HOLDFAST n act of gripping strongly
HOLDFASTS > HOLDFAST
HOLDING > HOLD
HOLDINGS > HOLD
HOLDOUT n (in US English) person, country, organization, etc, that continues to resist or refuses to change
HOLDOUTS > HOLDOUT
HOLDOVER n (in US and Canadian English) elected official who continues in office after his term has expired
HOLDOVERS > HOLDOVER
HOLDS > HOLD
HOLDUP n robbery, esp an armed one
HOLDUPS > HOLDUP
HOLE n area hollowed out in a solid ▷ vb make holes in
HOLED > HOLE
HOLELESS > HOLE
HOLES > HOLE
HOLESOM same as > HOLESOME
HOLESOME same as > WHOLESOME
HOLEY adj full of holes
HOLEYER > HOLEY
HOLEYEST > HOLEY
HOLIBUT same as > HALIBUT
HOLIBUTS > HOLIBUT
HOLIDAY n time spent away from home for rest or recreation ▷ vb spend a holiday
HOLIDAYED > HOLIDAY
HOLIDAYER > HOLIDAY
HOLIDAYS > HOLIDAY
HOLIER > HOLY
HOLIES > HOLY
HOLIEST > HOLY
HOLILY adv in a holy, devout, or sacred manner
HOLINESS n state of being holy

HOLING > HOLE
HOLINGS > HOLE
HOLISM n view that a whole is greater than the sum of its parts
HOLISMS > HOLISM
HOLIST > HOLISM
HOLISTIC adj considering the complete person, physically and mentally, in the treatment of an illness
HOLISTS > HOLISM
HOLK vb dig
HOLKED > HOLK
HOLKING > HOLK
HOLKS > HOLK
HOLLA same as > HOLLO
HOLLAED > HOLLA
HOLLAING > HOLLA
HOLLAND n coarse linen cloth, used esp for furnishing
HOLLANDS > HOLLAND
HOLLAS > HOLLA
HOLLER n shout, yell ▷ vb shout or yell
HOLLERED > HOLLER
HOLLERING > HOLLER
HOLLERS > HOLLER
HOLLIDAM same as > HALIDOM
HOLLIDAMS > HOLLIDAM
HOLLIES > HOLLY
HOLLO interj cry for attention, or of encouragement ▷ vb shout
HOLLOA same as > HOLLO
HOLLOAED > HOLLOA
HOLLOAING > HOLLOA
HOLLOAS > HOLLOA
HOLLOED > HOLLO
HOLLOES > HOLLO
HOLLOING > HOLLO
HOLLOO same as > HALLOO
HOLLOOED > HOLLOO
HOLLOOING > HOLLOO
HOLLOOS > HOLLOO
HOLLOS > HOLLO
HOLLOW adj having a hole or space inside ▷ n cavity or space ▷ vb form a hollow in
HOLLOWARE n hollow utensils such as cups
HOLLOWED > HOLLOW
HOLLOWER > HOLLOW
HOLLOWEST > HOLLOW
HOLLOWING > HOLLOW
HOLLOWLY > HOLLOW
HOLLOWS > HOLLOW
HOLLY n evergreen tree with prickly leaves and red berries
HOLLYHOCK n tall garden plant with spikes of colourful flowers
HOLM n island in a river, lake, or estuary
HOLMIA n oxide of holmium
HOLMIAS > HOLMIA
HOLMIC adj of or containing holmium
HOLMIUM n silver-white metallic element, the

compounds of which are highly magnetic

HOLMIUMS > HOLMIUM

HOLMS > HOLM

HOLOCAUST *n* destruction or loss of life on a massive scale

HOLOCENE *adj* of, denoting, or formed in the second and most recent epoch of the Quaternary period, which began 10 000 years ago at the end of the Pleistocene

HOLOCRINE *adj* (of the secretion of glands) characterized by disintegration of the entire glandular cell in releasing its product, as in sebaceous glands

HOLOGAMY *n* condition of having gametes like ordinary cells

HOLOGRAM *n* three-dimensional photographic image

HOLOGRAMS > HOLOGRAM

HOLOGRAPH *n* document handwritten by the author

HOLOGYNIC *adj* passed down through females

HOLOGYNY *n* inheritance of genetic traits through females only

HOLOHEDRA *n* geometrical forms with particular symmetry

HOLON *n* autonomous self-reliant unit, esp in manufacturing

HOLONIC > HOLON

HOLONS > HOLON

HOLOPHOTE *n* device for directing light from lighthouse

HOLOPHYTE *n* plant capable of synthesizing food from inorganic molecules

HOLOPTIC *adj* with eyes meeting at the front

HOLOTYPE *n* original specimen from which a description of a new species is made

HOLOTYPES > HOLOTYPE

HOLOTYPIC > HOLOTYPE

HOLOZOIC *adj* (of animals) obtaining nourishment by feeding on plants or other animals

HOLP *past tense of* > HELP

HOLPEN *past participle of* > HELP

HOLS *npl* holidays

HOLSTEIN *n* breed of cattle

HOLSTEINS > HOLSTEIN

HOLSTER *n* leather case for a pistol, hung from a belt ▷ *vb* return (a pistol) to its holster

HOLSTERED > HOLSTER

HOLSTERS > HOLSTER

HOLT *n* otter's lair

HOLTS > HOLT

HOLY *adj* of God or a god

HOLYDAM *same as* > HALIDOM

HOLYDAME *same as* > HALIDOM

HOLYDAMES > HOLYDAME

HOLYDAMS > HOLYDAM

HOLYDAY *n* day on which a religious festival is observed

HOLYDAYS > HOLYDAY

HOLYSTONE *n* soft sandstone used for scrubbing the decks of a vessel ▷ *vb* scrub (a vessel's decks) with a holystone

HOLYTIDE *n* time for special religious observance

HOLYTIDES > HOLYTIDE

HOM *n* sacred plant of the Parsees and ancient Persians

HOMA *same as* > HOM

HOMAGE *n* show of respect or honour towards someone or something ▷ *vb* render homage to

HOMAGED > HOMAGE

HOMAGER > HOMAGE

HOMAGERS > HOMAGE

HOMAGES > HOMAGE

HOMAGING > HOMAGE

HOMALOID *n* geometrical plane

HOMALOIDS > HOMALOID

HOMAS > HOMA

HOMBRE *slang word for* > MAN

HOMBRES > HOMBRE

HOMBURG *n* man's soft felt hat with a dented crown and a stiff upturned brim

HOMBURGS > HOMBURG

HOME *n* place where one lives ▷ *adj* of one's home, birthplace, or native country ▷ *adv* to or at home ▷ *vb* direct towards (a point or target)

HOMEBIRTH *n* act of giving birth to a child in one's own home

HOMEBODY *n* person whose life and interests are centred on the home

HOMEBOUND *adj* heading for home

HOMEBOY *n* close friend

HOMEBOYS > HOMEBOY

HOMEBRED *adj* raised or bred at home ▷ *n* animal bred at home

HOMEBREDS > HOMEBRED

HOMEBREW *n* home-made beer

HOMEBREWS > HOMEBREW

HOMEBUILT *adj* built at home

HOMEBUYER *n* person buying a home

HOMECOMER *n* person coming home

HOMECRAFT *n* skills used in the home

HOMED > HOME

HOMEFELT *adj* felt personally

HOMEGIRL > HOMEBOY

HOMEGIRLS > HOMEBOY

HOMEGROWN *adj* (esp of fruit and vegetables) produced in one's own country, district, estate, or garden

HOMELAND *n* country from which a person's ancestors came

HOMELANDS > HOMELAND

HOMELESS *adj* having nowhere to live ▷ *npl* people who have nowhere to live

HOMELIER > HOMELY

HOMELIEST > HOMELY

HOMELIKE > HOME

HOMELILY > HOMELY

HOMELY *adj* simple, ordinary, and comfortable

HOMELYN *n* species of ray

HOMELYNS > HOMELYN

HOMEMADE *adj* (esp of cakes, jam, and other foods) made at home or on the premises, esp of high-quality ingredients

HOMEMAKER *n* person, esp a housewife, who manages a home

HOMEOBOX *adj* of genes that regulate cell development

HOMEOMERY *n* condition of being made up of similar parts

HOMEOPATH *n* person who treats disease by the use of small amounts of a drug that produces symptoms like those of the disease being treated

HOMEOSES > HOMEOSIS

HOMEOSIS *n* process of one part coming to resemble another

HOMEOTIC > HOMEOSIS

HOMEOWNER *n* person who owns the home in which he or she lives

HOMEPAGE *n* main page of website

HOMEPAGES > HOMEPAGE

HOMEPLACE *n* person's home

HOMEPORT *n* port where vessel is registered

HOMEPORTS > HOMEPORT

HOMER *n* homing pigeon ▷ *vb* score a home run in baseball

HOMERED > HOMER

HOMERIC *adj* grand or heroic

HOMERING > HOMER

HOMEROOM *n* common room at school

HOMEROOMS > HOMEROOM

HOMERS > HOMER

HOMES > HOME

HOMESICK *adj* sad because missing one's home and family

HOMESITE *n* site for building house

HOMESITES > HOMESITE

HOMESPUN *adj* (of philosophies or opinions) plain and unsophisticated ▷ *n* cloth made at home or made of yarn spun at home

HOMESPUNS > HOMESPUN

HOMESTALL *same as* > HOMESTEAD

HOMESTAND *n* series of games played at a team's home ground

HOMESTAY *n* period spent living as a guest in someone's home

HOMESTAYS > HOMESTAY

HOMESTEAD *n* farmhouse plus the adjoining land

HOMETOWN *n* town where one lives or was born

HOMETOWNS > HOMETOWN

HOMEWARD *adj* going home ▷ *adv* towards home

HOMEWARDS *adv* towards home

HOMEWARE *n* crockery, furniture, and furnishings with which a house, room, etc, is furnished

HOMEWARES > HOMEWARE

HOMEWORK *n* school work done at home

HOMEWORKS > HOMEWORK

HOMEY *same as* > HOMY

HOMEYNESS > HOMEY

HOMEYS > HOMEY

HOMICIDAL *adj* of, involving, or characterized by homicide

HOMICIDE *n* killing of a human being

HOMICIDES > HOMICIDE

HOMIE *short for* > HOMEBOY

HOMIER > HOMY

HOMIES > HOMIE

HOMIEST > HOMY

HOMILETIC *adj* of or relating to a homily or sermon

HOMILIES > HOMILY

HOMILIST > HOMILY

HOMILISTS > HOMILY

HOMILY *n* speech telling people how they should behave

HOMINES > HOMO

HOMINESS > HOMY

HOMING *adj* denoting the ability to return home after travelling great distances ▷ *n* relating to the ability to return home after travelling great distances

HOMINGS > HOMING

HOMINIAN *same as* > HOMINID

HOMINIANS > HOMINIAN

HOMINID *n* man or any extinct forerunner of man

▷ *adj* of or belonging to this family

HOMINIDS > HOMINID

HOMINIES > HOMINY

HOMININ *n* member of zoological family that includes humans and direct ancestors

HOMININE *adj* characteristic of humans

HOMININS > HOMININ

HOMINISE *same as* > HOMINIZE

HOMINISED > HOMINISE

HOMINISES > HOMINISE

HOMINIZE *vb* make suitable for humans

HOMINIZED > HOMINIZE

HOMINIZES > HOMINIZE

HOMINOID *n* manlike animal ▷ *adj* of or like man

HOMINOIDS > HOMINOID

HOMINY *n* coarsely ground maize prepared as a food by boiling in milk or water

HOMME *French word for* > MAN

HOMMES > HOMME

HOMMOCK *same as* > HUMMOCK

HOMMOCKS > HOMMOCK

HOMMOS *same as* > HUMMUS

HOMMOSES > HOMMOS

HOMO *n* homogenized milk

HOMOCERCY *n* condition in fish of having a symmetrical tail

HOMODONT *adj* (of most nonmammalian vertebrates) having teeth that are all of the same type

HOMODYNE *adj* of strengthened radio waves

HOMOEOBOX *same as* > HOMEOBOX

HOMOEOSES > HOMOEOSIS

HOMOEOSIS *n* condition of controlling a system from within

HOMOEOTIC > HOMOEOSIS

HOMOGAMIC > HOMOGAMY

HOMOGAMY *n* condition in which all the flowers of an inflorescence are either of the same sex or hermaphrodite

HOMOGENY *n* similarity in structure of individuals or parts because of common ancestry

HOMOGONY *n* condition in a plant of having stamens and styles of the same length in all the flowers

HOMOGRAFT *n* tissue graft obtained from an organism of the same species as the recipient

HOMOGRAPH *n* word spelt the same as another, but with a different meaning

HOMOLOG *same as* > HOMOLOGUE

HOMOLOGIC *adj* having a related or similar position, structure, etc

HOMOLOGS > HOMOLOG

HOMOLOGUE *n* homologous part or organ

HOMOLOGY *n* condition of being homologous

HOMOLYSES > HOMOLYSIS

HOMOLYSIS *n* dissociation of a molecule into two neutral fragments

HOMOLYTIC > HOMOLYSIS

HOMOMORPH *n* thing same in form as something else

HOMONYM *n* word spelt or pronounced the same as another, but with a different meaning

HOMONYMIC > HOMONYM

HOMONYMS > HOMONYM

HOMONYMY *n* the quality of being pronounced or spelt in the same way

HOMOPHILE *n* rare word for homosexual: person who is sexually attracted to members of the same sex

HOMOPHOBE *n* person who has an intense hatred of homosexuality

HOMOPHONE *n* word pronounced the same as another, but with a different meaning or spelling

HOMOPHONY *n* linguistic phenomenon whereby words of different origins become identical in pronunciation

HOMOPHYLY *n* resemblance due to common ancestry

HOMOPLASY *n* state of being derived from an individual of the same species as the recipient

HOMOPOLAR *adj* of uniform charge

HOMOS > HOMO

HOMOSEX *n* sexual activity between homosexuals

HOMOSEXES > HOMOSEX

HOMOSPORY *n* state of producing spores of one kind only

HOMOSTYLY *n* (in flowers) existence of styles of only one length

HOMOTAXES > HOMOTAXIS

HOMOTAXIC > HOMOTAXIS

HOMOTAXIS *n* similarity of composition and arrangement in rock strata of different ages or in different regions

HOMOTONIC *adj* of same tone

HOMOTONY > HOMOTONIC

HOMOTYPAL *adj* of normal type

HOMOTYPE *n* something

with same structure as something else

HOMOTYPES > HOMOTYPE

HOMOTYPIC *same as* > HOMOTYPAL

HOMOTYPY > HOMOTYPE

HOMOUSIAN *adj* believing God the Son and God the Father to be of the same essence

HOMS > HOM

HOMUNCLE *n* homunculus

HOMUNCLES > HOMUNCLE

HOMUNCULE *n* homunculus

HOMUNCULI *n* plural of homunculus: miniature man

HOMY *adj* like a home

HON *short for* > HONEY

HONAN *n* silk fabric of rough weave

HONANS > HONAN

HONCHO *n* person in charge ▷ *vb* supervise or be in charge of

HONCHOED > HONCHO

HONCHOING > HONCHO

HONCHOS > HONCHO

HOND *old form of* > HAND

HONDA *n* loop through which rope is threaded to make a lasso

HONDAS > HONDA

HONDLE *vb* negotiate on price

HONDLED > HONDLE

HONDLES > HONDLE

HONDLING > HONDLE

HONDS > HOND

HONE *vb* sharpen ▷ *n* fine whetstone used for sharpening edged tools and knives

HONED > HONE

HONER > HONE

HONERS > HONE

HONES > HONE

HONEST *adj* truthful and moral

HONESTER > HONEST

HONESTEST > HONEST

HONESTIES > HONESTY

HONESTLY *adv* in an honest manner ▷ *interj* expression of disgust, surprise, etc

HONESTY *n* quality of being honest

HONEWORT *n* European plant that has clusters of small white flowers

HONEWORTS > HONEWORT

HONEY *n* sweet edible sticky substance made by bees from nectar; term of endearment ▷ *vb* sweeten with or as if with honey

HONEYBEE *n* bee widely domesticated as a source of honey and beeswax

HONEYBEES > HONEYBEE

HONEYBUN *n* term of endearment

HONEYBUNS > HONEYBUN

HONEYCOMB *n* waxy structure of six-sided cells in which honey is stored by bees in a beehive ▷ *vb* pierce or fill with holes, cavities, etc

HONEYDEW *n* sugary substance excreted by aphids and similar insects

HONEYDEWS > HONEYDEW

HONEYED > HONEY

HONEYEDLY > HONEY

HONEYFUL *adj* full of honey

HONEYING > HONEY

HONEYLESS > HONEY

HONEYMOON *n* holiday taken by a newly married couple ▷ *vb* take a honeymoon

HONEYPOT *n* container for honey

HONEYPOTS > HONEYPOT

HONEYS > HONEY

HONEYTRAP *n* scheme in which a victim is lured into a compromising sexual situation that provides the opportunity for blackmail

HONG *n* (in China) a factory, warehouse, etc ▷ *vb* archaic form of hang

HONGI *n* Māori greeting in which people touch noses ▷ *vb* touch noses

HONGIED > HONGI

HONGIES > HONGI

HONGIING > HONGI

HONGING > HONG

HONGIS > HONGI

HONGS > HONG

HONIED *same as* > HONEY

HONIEDLY > HONEY

HONING > HONE

HONK *n* sound made by a car horn ▷ *vb* (cause to) make this sound

HONKED > HONK

HONKER *n* person or thing that honks

HONKERS > HONKER

HONKEY *same as* > HONKY

HONKEYS > HONKEY

HONKIE *same as* > HONKY

HONKIES > HONKY

HONKING > HONK

HONKS > HONK

HONKY *n* derogatory slang for White man or White men collectively

HONOR *same as* > HONOUR

HONORABLE *adj* possessing high principles

HONORABLY *adv* in an honourable way

HONORAND *n* person being honoured

HONORANDS > HONORAND

HONORARIA *n* fee pain for a nominally free service

HONORARY *adj* held or given only as an honour

HONORED > HONOR

HONOREE *same as* > HONORAND

HONOREES > HONOREE

HONORER > HONOUR
HONORERS > HONOUR
HONORIFIC adj showing respect
HONORING > HONOR
HONORLESS > HONOUR
HONORS same as > HONOURS
HONOUR n sense of honesty and fairness ▷ vb give praise and attention to
HONOURED > HONOUR
HONOUREE n person who is honoured
HONOUREES > HONOUREE
HONOURER > HONOUR
HONOURERS > HONOUR
HONOURING > HONOUR
HONOURS > HONOUR
HONS > HON
HOO interj expression of joy, excitement, etc
HOOCH n alcoholic drink, esp illicitly distilled spirits
HOOCHES > HOOCH
HOOCHIE n immoral woman
HOOCHIES > HOOCHIE
HOOD n head covering, often attached to a coat or jacket ▷ vb cover with or as if with a hood
HOODED adj (of a garment) having a hood
HOODIA n any of several southern African succulent plants whose sap has appetite-suppressing properties
HOODIAS > HOODIA
HOODIE n hooded sweatshirt
HOODIER > HOOD
HOODIES > HOODIE
HOODIEST > HOOD
HOODING > HOOD
HOODLESS > HOOD
HOODLIKE > HOOD
HOODLUM n violent criminal, gangster
HOODLUMS > HOODLUM
HOODMAN n blindfolded person in blindman's buff
HOODMEN > HOODMAN
HOODMOLD n moulding over door or window
HOODMOLDS > HOODMOLD
HOODOO n (cause of) bad luck ▷ vb bring bad luck to
HOODOOED > HOODOO
HOODOOING > HOODOO
HOODOOISM > HOODOO
HOODOOS > HOODOO
HOODS > HOOD
HOODWINK vb trick, deceive
HOODWINKS > HOODWINK
HOODY > HOOD
HOOEY n nonsense ▷ interj nonsense
HOOEYS > HOOEY
HOOF n horny covering of the foot of a horse, deer, etc ▷ vb kick or trample with

the hooves
HOOFBEAT n sound made by hoof on the ground
HOOFBEATS > HOOFBEAT
HOOFBOUND adj (of a horse) having dry contracted hooves, with resultant pain and lameness
HOOFED adj having a hoof or hoofs
HOOFER n professional dancer
HOOFERS > HOOFER
HOOFING > HOOF
HOOFLESS > HOOF
HOOFLIKE > HOOF
HOOFPRINT n mark made by hoof on ground
HOOFROT n disease of hoof
HOOFROTS > HOOFROT
HOOFS > HOOF
HOOK n curved piece of metal, plastic, etc, used to hang, hold, or pull something ▷ vb fasten or catch (as if) with a hook
HOOKA same as > HOOKAH
HOOKAH n oriental pipe in which smoke is drawn through water and a long tube
HOOKAHS > HOOKAH
HOOKAS > HOOKA
HOOKCHECK n in ice hockey, act of hooking an opposing player
HOOKED adj bent like a hook
HOOKER n prostitute
HOOKERS > HOOKER
HOOKEY same as > HOOKY
HOOKEYS > HOOKEY
HOOKIER > HOOKY
HOOKIES > HOOKY
HOOKIEST > HOOKY
HOOKING > HOOK
HOOKLESS > HOOK
HOOKLET n little hook
HOOKLETS > HOOKLET
HOOKLIKE > HOOK
HOOKNOSE n nose with a pronounced outward and downward curve
HOOKNOSED > HOOKNOSE
HOOKNOSES > HOOKNOSE
HOOKS > HOOK
HOOKUP n contact of an aircraft in flight with the refuelling hose of a tanker aircraft
HOOKUPS > HOOKUP
HOOKWORM n blood-sucking worm with hooked mouthparts
HOOKWORMS > HOOKWORM
HOOKY n truancy, usually from school (esp in the phrase play hooky) ▷ adj hooklike
HOOLACHAN n Highland reel
HOOLEY n lively party
HOOLEYS > HOOLEY
HOOLICAN same as

> HOOLACHAN
HOOLICANS > HOOLICAN
HOOLIE same as > HOOLEY
HOOLIER > HOOLY
HOOLIES > HOOLIE
HOOLIEST > HOOLY
HOOLIGAN n rowdy young person
HOOLIGANS > HOOLIGAN
HOOLOCK n Indian gibbon
HOOLOCKS > HOOLOCK
HOOLY adj careful or gentle
HOON n loutish youth who drives irresponsibly ▷ vb drive irresponsibly
HOONED > HOON
HOONING > HOON
HOONS > HOON
HOOP n rigid circular band, used esp as a child's toy or for animals to jump through in the circus ▷ vb surround with or as if with a hoop
HOOPED > HOOP
HOOPER rare word for > COOPER
HOOPERS > HOOPER
HOOPING > HOOP
HOOPLA n fairground game in which hoops are thrown over objects in an attempt to win them
HOOPLAS > HOOPLA
HOOPLESS > HOOP
HOOPLIKE > HOOP
HOOPOE n bird with a pinkish-brown plumage and a fanlike crest
HOOPOES > HOOPOE
HOOPOO same as > HOOPOE
HOOPOOS > HOOPOO
HOOPS > HOOP
HOOPSKIRT n skirt stiffened by hoops
HOOPSTER n basketball player
HOOPSTERS > HOOPSTER
HOOR n unpleasant or difficult thing
HOORAH same as > HURRAH
HOORAHED > HOORAH
HOORAHING > HOORAH
HOORAHS > HOORAH
HOORAY same as > HURRAH
HOORAYED > HOORAY
HOORAYING > HOORAY
HOORAYS > HOORAY
HOORD same as > HOARD
HOORDS > HOORD
HOOROO same as > HURRAH
HOORS > HOOR
HOOSEGOW slang word for > JAIL
HOOSEGOWS > HOOSEGOW
HOOSGOW same as > JAIL
HOOSGOWS > JAIL
HOOSH vb shoo away
HOOSHED > HOOSH
HOOSHES > HOOSH
HOOSHING > HOOSH
HOOT n sound of a car horn ▷ vb sound (a car horn) ▷ interj exclamation of

impatience or dissatisfaction: a supposed Scotticism
HOOTCH same as > HOOCH
HOOTCHES > HOOTCH
HOOTED > HOOT
HOOTER n device that hoots
HOOTERS > HOOTER
HOOTIER > HOOT
HOOTIEST > HOOT
HOOTING > HOOT
HOOTNANNY n informal performance by folk singers
HOOTS same as > HOOT
HOOTY > HOOT
HOOVE same as > HEAVE
HOOVED > HOOVE
HOOVEN > HOOVE
HOOVER vb vacuum-clean (a carpet, furniture, etc)
HOOVERED > HOOVER
HOOVERING > HOOVER
HOOVERS > HOOVER
HOOVES > HOOF
HOOVING > HOOVE
HOP vb jump on one foot ▷ n instance of hopping
HOPBIND n stalk of the hop
HOPBINDS > HOPBIND
HOPBINE same as > HOPBIND
HOPBINES > HOPBINE
HOPDOG n species of caterpillar
HOPDOGS > HOPDOG
HOPE vb want (something) to happen or be true ▷ n expectation of something desired
HOPED > HOPE
HOPEFUL adj having, expressing, or inspiring hope ▷ n person considered to be on the brink of success
HOPEFULLY adv in a hopeful manner
HOPEFULS > HOPEFUL
HOPELESS adj having or offering no hope
HOPER > HOPE
HOPERS > HOPE
HOPES > HOPE
HOPHEAD n heroin or opium addict
HOPHEADS > HOPHEAD
HOPING > HOPE
HOPINGLY > HOPE
HOPLITE n (in ancient Greece) a heavily armed infantryman
HOPLITES > HOPLITE
HOPLITIC > HOPLITE
HOPLOLOGY n study of weapons or armour
HOPPED > HOP
HOPPER n container for storing substances such as grain or sand
HOPPERCAR same as > HOPPER
HOPPERS > HOPPER
HOPPIER > HOPPY

HOPPIEST > HOPPY

HOPPING > HOP

HOPPINGS > HOP

HOPPLE *same as* > HOBBLE

HOPPLED > HOPPLE

HOPPLER > HOPPLE

HOPPLERS > HOPPLE

HOPPLES > HOPPLE

HOPPLING > HOPPLE

HOPPUS as in *hoppus foot* unit of volume for round timber

HOPPY *adj* tasting of hops

HOPS > HOP

HOPSACK *n* roughly woven fabric of wool, cotton, etc, used for clothing

HOPSACKS > HOPSACK

HOPSCOTCH *n* children's game of hopping in a pattern drawn on the ground

HOPTOAD *n* toad

HOPTOADS > HOPTOAD

HORA *n* traditional Israeli or Romanian circle dance

HORAH *same as* > HORA

HORAHS > HORAH

HORAL *less common word for* > HOURLY

HORARY *adj* relating to the hours

HORAS > HORA

HORDE *n* large crowd ▷ *vb* form, move in, or live in a horde

HORDED > HORDE

HORDEIN *n* simple protein, rich in proline, that occurs in barley

HORDEINS > HORDEIN

HORDEOLA > HORDEOLUM

HORDEOLUM *n* (in medicine) stye

HORDES > HORDE

HORDING > HORDE

HORDOCK *same as* > HARDOKE

HORDOCKS > HORDOCK

HORE *same as* > HOAR

HOREHOUND *n* plant that produces a bitter juice formerly used as a cough medicine

HORI *n* derogatory term for Māori

HORIATIKI *n* traditional Greek salad consisting of tomatoes, cucumber, onion, olives, and feta cheese

HORIS > HORI

HORIZON *n* apparent line that divides the earth and the sky

HORIZONAL > HORIZON

HORIZONS > HORIZON

HORKEY *same as* > HOCKEY

HORKEYS > HORKEY

HORLICKS as in *make a horlicks* make a mistake or a mess

HORME *n* (in the psychology of C. G. Jung) fundamental vital energy

HORMES > HORME

HORMESES > HORMESIS

HORMESIS *n* beneficial effect of exposure to a very small amount of a toxic substance

HORMETIC *adj* relating to hormesis

HORMIC > HORME

HORMONAL > HORMONE

HORMONE *n* substance secreted by certain glands which stimulates certain organs of the body

HORMONES > HORMONE

HORMONIC > HORMONE

HORN *n* one of a pair of bony growths sticking out of the heads of cattle, sheep, etc ▷ *vb* provide with a horn or horns

HORNBAG *n* in Australian slang, a promiscuous woman

HORNBAGS > HORNBAG

HORNBEAK *n* garfish

HORNBEAKS > HORNBEAK

HORNBEAM *n* tree with smooth grey bark

HORNBEAMS > HORNBEAM

HORNBILL *n* bird with a bony growth on its large beak

HORNBILLS > HORNBILL

HORNBOOK *n* page bearing a religious text or the alphabet, held in a frame with a thin window of flattened cattle horn over it

HORNBOOKS > HORNBOOK

HORNBUG *n* stag beetle

HORNBUGS > HORNBUG

HORNED *adj* having a horn, horns, or hornlike parts

HORNER *n* dealer in horn

HORNERS > HORNER

HORNET *n* large wasp with a severe sting

HORNETS > HORNET

HORNFELS *n* hard compact fine-grained metamorphic rock formed by the action of heat from a magmatic intrusion on neighbouring sedimentary rocks

HORNFUL *n* amount a horn will hold

HORNFULS > HORNFUL

HORNGELD *n* feudal rent based on number of cattle

HORNGELDS > HORNGELD

HORNIER > HORNY

HORNIEST > HORNY

HORNILY > HORNY

HORNINESS > HORNY

HORNING > HORN

HORNINGS > HORN

HORNISH *adj* like horn

HORNIST *n* horn player

HORNISTS > HORNIST

HORNITO *n* small vent in volcano

HORNITOS > HORNITO

HORNLESS > HORN

HORNLET *n* small horn

HORNLETS > HORNLET

HORNLIKE > HORN

HORNPIPE *n* (music for a) solo dance, traditionally performed by sailors

HORNPIPES > HORNPIPE

HORNPOUT *n* catfish

HORNPOUTS > HORNPOUT

HORNS > HORN

HORNSTONE *same as* > HORNFELS

HORNTAIL *n* wasplike insect

HORNTAILS > HORNTAIL

HORNWORK *n* bastion in fortifications

HORNWORKS > HORNWORK

HORNWORM *n* caterpillar of hawk moth

HORNWORMS > HORNWORM

HORNWORT *n* aquatic plant

HORNWORTS > HORNWORT

HORNWRACK *n* yellowish bryozoan or sea mat sometimes found on beaches after a storm

HORNY *adj* of or like horn

HORNYHEAD *n* species of fish

HORNYWINK *n* lapwing

HOROEKA *n* New Zealand tree

HOROEKAS > HOROEKA

HOROKAKA *n* low-growing New Zealand plant with fleshy branches and pink or white flowers

HOROKAKAS > HOROKAKA

HOROLOGE *rare word for* > TIMEPIECE

HOROLOGER *n* an expert maker of timepieces

HOROLOGES > HOROLOGE

HOROLOGIA *n* plural of horologium: clocktower

HOROLOGIC > HOROLOGY

HOROLOGY *n* art of making clocks and watches or of measuring time

HOROMETRY *n* measurement of time

HOROPITO *n* New Zealand plant

HOROPITOS > HOROPITO

HOROPTER *n* locus of all points in space that stimulate points on each eye that yield the same visual direction as each other

HOROPTERS > HOROPTER

HOROSCOPE *n* prediction of a person's future based on the positions of the planets, sun, and moon at his or her birth

HOROSCOPY *n* casting and interpretation of horoscopes

HORRENT *adj* bristling

HORRIBLE *adj* disagreeable, unpleasant ▷ *n* horrible thing

HORRIBLES > HORRIBLE

HORRIBLY *adv* in a horrible manner

HORRID *adj* disagreeable, unpleasant

HORRIDER > HORRID

HORRIDEST > HORRID

HORRIDLY > HORRID

HORRIFIC *adj* causing horror

HORRIFIED *adj* terrified

HORRIFIES > HORRIFY

HORRIFY *vb* cause to feel horror or shock

HORROR *n* (thing or person causing) terror or hatred ▷ *adj* having a frightening subject, usually concerned with the supernatural

HORRORS *npl* fit of depression or anxiety ▷ *interj* expression of dismay, sometimes facetious

HORS as in *hors d'oeuvre* appetizer

HORSE *n* large animal with hooves, a mane, and a tail, used for riding and pulling carts etc ▷ *vb* provide with a horse

HORSEBACK *n* horse's back

HORSEBEAN *n* broad bean

HORSEBOX *n* trailer used for transporting horses

HORSECAR *n* streetcar drawn by horses

HORSECARS > HORSECAR

HORSED > HORSE

HORSEFLY *n* large bloodsucking fly

HORSEHAIR *n* hair from the tail or mane of a horse

HORSEHIDE *n* hide of a horse

HORSELESS > HORSE

HORSELIKE > HORSE

HORSEMAN *n* person skilled in riding

HORSEMEAT *n* flesh of the horse used as food

HORSEMEN > HORSEMAN

HORSEMINT *n* European mint plant

HORSEPLAY *n* rough or rowdy play

HORSEPOND *n* pond where horses drink

HORSEPOX *n* viral infection of horses

HORSERACE *n* race for horses

HORSES > HORSE

HORSESHIT *n* rubbish

HORSESHOD > HORSESHOE

HORSESHOE *n* protective U-shaped piece of iron nailed to a horse's hoof, regarded as a symbol of good luck ▷ *vb* fit with a horseshoe

HORSETAIL *n* plant with small dark toothlike leaves

HORSEWAY *n* road for horses

HORSEWAYS > HORSEWAY

h

HORSEWEED *n* US name for Canadian fleabane

HORSEWHIP *n* whip with a long thong, used for managing horses ▷ *vb* beat (a person or animal) with such a whip

HORSEY *adj* very keen on horses

HORSIER > HORSY

HORSIEST > HORSY

HORSILY > HORSEY

HORSINESS > HORSEY

HORSING > HORSE

HORSINGS > HORSE

HORSON *same as* > WHORESON

HORSONS > HORSON

HORST *n* ridge of land that has been forced upwards between two parallel faults

HORSTE *variant of* > HORST

HORSTES > HORSTE

HORSTS > HORST

HORSY *same as* > HORSEY

HORTATION > HORTATORY

HORTATIVE *same as* > HORTATORY

HORTATORY *adj* encouraging

HOS > HO

HOSANNA *interj* exclamation of praise to God ▷ *n* act of crying "hosanna" ▷ *vb* cry hosanna

HOSANNAED > HOSANNA

HOSANNAH *same as* > HOSANNA

HOSANNAHS > HOSANNAH

HOSANNAS > HOSANNA

HOSE *n* flexible pipe for conveying liquid ▷ *vb* water with a hose

HOSED > HOSE

HOSEL *n* socket in head of golf club

HOSELIKE > HOSE

HOSELS > HOSEL

HOSEMAN *n* fireman in charge of hose

HOSEMEN > HOSEMAN

HOSEN > HOSE

HOSEPIPE *n* hose

HOSEPIPES > HOSEPIPE

HOSER *n* person who swindles or deceives others

HOSERS > HOSER

HOSES > HOSE

HOSEY *vb* claim possession

HOSEYED > HOSEY

HOSEYING > HOSEY

HOSEYS > HOSEY

HOSIER *n* person who sells stockings, etc

HOSIERIES > HOSIERY

HOSIERS > HOSIER

HOSIERY *n* stockings, socks, and tights collectively

HOSING > HOSE

HOSPICE *n* nursing home for the terminally ill

HOSPICES > HOSPICE

HOSPITAGE *n* behaviour of guest

HOSPITAL *n* place where people who are ill are looked after and treated

HOSPITALE *n* lodging

HOSPITALS > HOSPITAL

HOSPITIA > HOSPITIUM

HOSPITIUM *same as* > HOSPICE

HOSPODAR *n* (formerly) the governor or prince of Moldavia or Wallachia under Ottoman rule

HOSPODARS > HOSPODAR

HOSS *n* horse

HOSSES > HOSS

HOST *n* person who entertains guests, esp in his own home ▷ *vb* be the host of

HOSTA *n* ornamental plant

HOSTAGE *n* person who is illegally held prisoner until certain demands are met by other people

HOSTAGES > HOSTAGE

HOSTAS > HOSTA

HOSTED > HOST

HOSTEL *n* building providing accommodation at a low cost for a specific group of people such as students, travellers, homeless people, etc ▷ *vb* stay in hostels

HOSTELED > HOSTEL

HOSTELER *same as* > HOSTELLER

HOSTELERS > HOSTELER

HOSTELING *n* hostelling

HOSTELLED > HOSTEL

HOSTELLER *n* person who stays at youth hostels

HOSTELRY *n* inn, pub

HOSTELS > HOSTEL

HOSTESS *n* woman who receives and entertains guests, esp in her own house ▷ *vb* act as hostess

HOSTESSED > HOSTESS

HOSTESSES > HOSTESS

HOSTIE *n* informal Australian word for an air hostess

HOSTIES > HOSTIE

HOSTILE *adj* unfriendly ▷ *n* hostile person

HOSTILELY > HOSTILE

HOSTILES > HOSTILE

HOSTILITY *n* unfriendly and aggressive feelings or behaviour

HOSTING > HOST

HOSTINGS > HOST

HOSTLER *another name (esp Brit) for* > OSTLER

HOSTLERS > HOSTLER

HOSTLESSE *adj* inhospitable

HOSTLY > HOST

HOSTRIES > HOSTRY

HOSTRY *n* lodging

HOSTS > HOST

HOT *adj* having a high temperature

HOTBED *n* any place encouraging a particular activity

HOTBEDS > HOTBED

HOTBLOOD *n* type of horse

HOTBLOODS > HOTBLOOD

HOTBOX *n* closed room where marijuana is smoked

HOTBOXES > HOTBOX

HOTCAKE *n* pancake

HOTCAKES > HOTCAKE

HOTCH *vb* jog

HOTCHED > HOTCH

HOTCHES > HOTCH

HOTCHING > HOTCH

HOTCHPOT *n* collecting of property so that it may be redistributed in equal shares, esp on the intestacy of a parent who has given property to his children in his lifetime

HOTCHPOTS > HOTCHPOT

HOTDOG *vb* perform a series of manoeuvres in skiing, surfing, etc, esp in a showy manner

HOTDOGGED > HOTDOG

HOTDOGGER > HOTDOG

HOTDOGS > HOTDOG

HOTE > HIGHT

HOTEL *n* commercial establishment providing lodging and meals

HOTELDOM *n* hotel business

HOTELDOMS > HOTELDOM

HOTELIER *n* owner or manager of a hotel

HOTELIERS > HOTELIER

HOTELING *n* office practice in which desk space is booked in advance by an employee as required

HOTELINGS > HOTELING

HOTELLING *same as* > HOTELING

HOTELMAN *n* hotel owner

HOTELMEN > HOTELMAN

HOTELS > HOTEL

HOTEN > HIGHT

HOTFOOT *adv* quickly and eagerly ▷ *vb* move quickly

HOTFOOTED > HOTFOOT

HOTFOOTS > HOTFOOT

HOTHEAD *n* excitable or fiery person

HOTHEADED *adj* impetuous, rash, or hot-tempered

HOTHEADS > HOTHEAD

HOTHOUSE *n* greenhouse

HOTHOUSED *adj* taught intensively

HOTHOUSES > HOTHOUSE

HOTLINE *n* direct telephone link for emergency use

HOTLINES > HOTLINE

HOTLINK *n* area on website connecting to another site

HOTLINKS > HOTLINK

HOTLY > HOT

HOTNESS > HOT

HOTNESSES > HOT

HOTPLATE *n* heated metal surface on an electric cooker

HOTPLATES > HOTPLATE

HOTPOT *n* casserole of meat and vegetables, topped with potatoes

HOTPOTS > HOTPOT

HOTPRESS *vb* subject (paper, cloth, etc) to heat and pressure to give it a smooth surface or extract oil

HOTROD *n* car with an engine that has been radically modified to produce increased power

HOTRODS > HOTROD

HOTS as in *the hots* feeling of lust

HOTSHOT *n* important person or expert, esp when showy

HOTSHOTS > HOTSHOT

HOTSPOT *n* place where wireless broadband services are provided through a wireless local area network

HOTSPOTS > HOTSPOT

HOTSPUR *n* impetuous or fiery person

HOTSPURS > HOTSPUR

HOTTED > HOT

HOTTENTOT as in *hottentot fig* perennial plant with fleshy leaves, showy yellow or purple flowers, and edible fruits

HOTTER *vb* simmer

HOTTERED > HOTTER

HOTTERING > HOTTER

HOTTERS > HOTTER

HOTTEST > HOT

HOTTIE *n* sexually attractive person

HOTTIES > HOTTIE

HOTTING *n* practice of stealing fast cars and putting on a show of skilful but dangerous driving

HOTTINGS > HOTTING

HOTTISH *adj* fairly hot

HOTTY *same as* > HOTTIE

HOUDAH *same as* > HOWDAH

HOUDAHS > HOUDAH

HOUDAN *n* breed of light domestic fowl originally from France, with a distinctive full crest

HOUDANS > HOUDAN

HOUF *same as* > HOWF

HOUFED > HOUF

HOUFF *same as* > HOWF

HOUFFED > HOUFF

HOUFFING > HOUFF

HOUFFS > HOUFF

HOUFING > HOUF

HOUFS > HOUF

HOUGH *n* in Scotland, a cut of meat corresponding to shin ▷ *vb* hamstring

HOUGHED > HOUGH
HOUGHING > HOUGH
HOUGHS > HOUGH
HOUHERE n small evergreen New Zealand tree
HOUHERES > HOUHERE
HOUMMOS same as > HUMMUS
HOUMMOSES > HOUMMOS
HOUMOUS same as > HUMMUS
HOUMOUSES > HOUMOUS
HOUMUS same as > HUMMUS
HOUMUSES > HOUMUS
HOUND n hunting dog ▷ vb pursue relentlessly
HOUNDED > HOUND
HOUNDER > HOUND
HOUNDERS > HOUND
HOUNDFISH n name given to various small sharks or dogfish
HOUNDING > HOUND
HOUNDS > HOUND
HOUNGAN n voodoo priest
HOUNGANS > HOUNGAN
HOUR n twenty-fourth part of a day, sixty minutes
HOURGLASS n device with two glass compartments, containing a quantity of sand that takes an hour to trickle from the top section to the bottom one
HOURI n any of the nymphs of paradise
HOURIS > HOURI
HOURLIES > HOURLY
HOURLONG adj lasting an hour
HOURLY adv (happening) every hour ▷ adj of, occurring, or done once every hour ▷ n something that is done by the hour; someone who is paid by the hour
HOURPLATE n dial of clock
HOURS npl indefinite time
HOUSE n building used as a home ▷ vb give accommodation to ▷ adj (of wine) sold in a restaurant at a lower price than wines on the wine list
HOUSEBOAT n stationary boat used as a home
HOUSEBOY n male domestic servant
HOUSEBOYS > HOUSEBOY
HOUSECARL n (in medieval Europe) a household warrior of Danish kings and noblemen
HOUSECOAT n woman's long loose coat-shaped garment for wearing at home
HOUSED > HOUSE
HOUSEFLY n common fly often found in houses
HOUSEFUL n full amount or number that can be

accommodated in a particular house
HOUSEFULS > HOUSEFUL
HOUSEHOLD n all the people living in a house ▷ adj relating to the running of a household
HOUSEKEEP vb run household
HOUSEKEPT > HOUSEKEEP
HOUSEL vb give the Eucharist to (someone)
HOUSELED > HOUSEL
HOUSELEEK n plant that has a rosette of succulent leaves and pinkish flowers and grows on walls
HOUSELESS > HOUSE
HOUSELINE n tarred marline
HOUSELING > HOUSEL
HOUSELLED > HOUSEL
HOUSELS > HOUSEL
HOUSEMAID n female servant employed to do housework
HOUSEMAN n junior hospital doctor
HOUSEMATE n person who is not part of the same family, but with whom one shares a house
HOUSEMEN > HOUSEMAN
HOUSER > HOUSE
HOUSEROOM n room for storage or lodging
HOUSERS > HOUSE
HOUSES > HOUSE
HOUSESAT > HOUSESIT
HOUSESIT vb live in and look after a house during the absence of its owner or owners
HOUSESITS > HOUSESIT
HOUSETOP n rooftop
HOUSETOPS > HOUSETOP
HOUSEWIFE n woman who runs her own household and does not have a job
HOUSEWORK n work of running a home, such as cleaning, cooking, and shopping
HOUSEY adj of or like house music
HOUSIER > HOUSEY
HOUSIEST > HOUSEY
HOUSING n (providing of) houses
HOUSINGS > HOUSING
HOUSLING adj of sacrament
HOUSTONIA n small North American plant with blue, white or purple flowers
HOUT same as > HOOT
HOUTED > HOUT
HOUTING n type of fish that lives in salt water but spawns in freshwater lakes and is valued for its edible flesh
HOUTINGS > HOUTING

HOUTS > HOUT
HOVE > HEAVE
HOVEA n Australian plant with purple flowers
HOVEAS > HOVEA
HOVED > HEAVE
HOVEL n small dirty house or hut ▷ vb shelter or be sheltered in a hovel
HOVELED > HOVEL
HOVELING > HOVEL
HOVELLED > HOVEL
HOVELLER n man working on boat
HOVELLERS > HOVELLER
HOVELLING > HOVEL
HOVELS > HOVEL
HOVEN > HEAVE
HOVER vb (of a bird etc) remain suspended in one place in the air ▷ n act of hovering
HOVERED > HOVER
HOVERER > HOVER
HOVERERS > HOVER
HOVERFLY n hovering wasp-like fly
HOVERING > HOVER
HOVERPORT n port for hovercraft
HOVERS > HOVER
HOVES > HEAVE
HOVING > HEAVE
HOW adv in what way, by what means ▷ n the way a thing is done ▷ sentence substitute greeting supposed to be or have been used by American Indians and often used humorously
HOWBE same as > HOWBEIT
HOWBEIT adv in archaic usage, however
HOWDAH n canopied seat on an elephant's back
HOWDAHS > HOWDAH
HOWDIE n midwife
HOWDIED > HOWDY
HOWDIES > HOWDY
HOWDY vb greet someone
HOWDYING > HOWDY
HOWE n depression in the earth's surface, such as a basin or valley
HOWES > HOWE
HOWEVER adv nevertheless
HOWF n haunt, esp a public house ▷ vb visit place frequently
HOWFED > HOWF
HOWFF vb visit place frequently
HOWFFED > HOWFF
HOWFFING > HOWFF
HOWFFS > HOWFF
HOWFING > HOWF
HOWFS > HOWF
HOWITZER n large gun firing shells at a steep angle
HOWITZERS > HOWITZER
HOWK vb dig (out or up)
HOWKED > HOWK

HOWKER > HOWK
HOWKERS > HOWK
HOWKING > HOWK
HOWKS > HOWK
HOWL n loud wailing cry ▷ vb utter a howl
HOWLBACK same as > HOWLROUND
HOWLBACKS > HOWLBACK
HOWLED > HOWL
HOWLER n stupid mistake
HOWLERS > HOWLER
HOWLET another word for > OWL
HOWLETS > HOWLET
HOWLING adj great
HOWLINGLY > HOWL
HOWLINGS > HOWL
HOWLROUND n condition, resulting in a howling noise, when sound from a loudspeaker is fed back into the microphone of a public-address or recording system
HOWLS > HOWL
HOWRE same as > HOUR
HOWRES > HOWRE
HOWS > HOW
HOWSO same as > HOWSOEVER
HOWSOEVER less common word for > HOWEVER
HOWTOWDIE n Scottish dish of boiled chicken with poached eggs and spinach
HOWZAT > HOW
HOWZIT informal word for > HELLO
HOX vb hamstring
HOXED > HOX
HOXES > HOX
HOXING > HOX
HOY interj cry used to attract someone's attention ▷ n freight barge ▷ vb drive animal with cry
HOYA n any of various E Asian or Australian plants
HOYAS > HOYA
HOYDEN n wild or boisterous girl ▷ vb behave like a hoyden
HOYDENED > HOYDEN
HOYDENING > HOYDEN
HOYDENISH > HOYDEN
HOYDENISM > HOYDEN
HOYDENS > HOYDEN
HOYED > HOY
HOYING > HOY
HOYLE n archer's mark used as a target
HOYLES > HOYLE
HOYS > HOY
HRYVNA n standard monetary unit of Ukraine, divided into 100 kopiykas
HRYVNAS > HRYVNA
HRYVNIA n money unit of Ukraine
HRYVNIAS > HRYVNIA
HRYVNYA same as > HRYVNA
HRYVNYAS > HRYVNYA

HUANACO same as
>GUANACO
HUANACOS >HUANACO
HUAQUERO n Central
American tomb robber
HUAQUEROS >HUAQUERO
HUARACHE n Mexican
sandal
HUARACHES >HUARACHE
HUARACHO same as
>HUARACHE
HUARACHOS >HUARACHO
HUB n centre of a wheel,
through which the axle
passes
HUBBIES >HUBBY
HUBBLY adj having an
irregular surface
HUBBUB n confused noise
of many voices
HUBBUBOO same as
>HUBBUB
HUBBUBOOS >HUBBUBOO
HUBBUBS >HUBBUB
HUBBY n husband
HUBCAP n metal disc that
fits on to and protects the
hub of a wheel, esp on a car
HUBCAPS >HUBCAP
HUBRIS n pride, arrogance
HUBRISES >HUBRIS
HUBRISTIC >HUBRIS
HUBS >HUB
HUCK same as >HUCKLE
HUCKABACK n coarse
absorbent linen or cotton
fabric used for towels and
informal shirts, etc
HUCKED >HUCK
HUCKERY adj ugly
HUCKING >HUCK
HUCKLE n hip or haunch
▷vb force out or arrest
roughly
HUCKLED >HUCKLE
HUCKLES >HUCKLE
HUCKLING >HUCKLE
HUCKS >HUCK
HUCKSTER n person using
aggressive methods of
selling ▷vb peddle
HUCKSTERS >HUCKSTER
HUCKSTERY >HUCKSTER
HUDDEN >HAUD
HUDDLE vb hunch (oneself)
through cold or fear ▷n
small group
HUDDLED >HUDDLE
HUDDLER >HUDDLE
HUDDLERS >HUDDLE
HUDDLES >HUDDLE
HUDDLING >HUDDLE
HUDDUP interj get up
HUDNA n truce or ceasefire
for a fixed duration
HUDNAS >HUDNA
HUDUD n set of laws and
punishments specified by
Allah in the Koran
HUDUDS >HUDUD
HUE n colour, shade
HUED adj having a hue or
colour as specified
HUELESS >HUE

HUER n pilchard fisherman
HUERS >HUER
HUES >HUE
HUFF n passing mood of
anger or resentment ▷vb
blow or puff heavily
HUFFED >HUFF
HUFFER >HUFFING
HUFFERS >HUFFING
HUFFIER >HUFF
HUFFIEST >HUFF
HUFFILY >HUFF
HUFFINESS >HUFF
HUFFING n practice of
inhaling toxic fumes from
glue and other household
products for their
intoxicating effects
HUFFINGS >HUFFING
HUFFISH >HUFF
HUFFISHLY >HUFF
HUFFKIN n type of muffin
HUFFKINS >HUFFKIN
HUFFS >HUFF
HUFFY >HUFF
HUG vb clasp tightly in the
arms, usu with affection
▷n tight or fond embrace
HUGE adj very big
HUGELY adv very much
HUGENESS >HUGE
HUGEOUS same as >HUGE
HUGEOUSLY >HUGEOUS
HUGER >HUGE
HUGEST >HUGE
HUGGABLE >HUG
HUGGED >HUG
HUGGER >HUG
HUGGERS >HUG
HUGGIER >HUGGY
HUGGIEST >HUGGY
HUGGING >HUG
HUGGY adj sensitive and
caring
HUGS >HUG
HUGY same as >HUGE
HUH interj exclamation of
derision, bewilderment, or
inquiry
HUHU n type of hairy New
Zealand beetle
HUHUS >HUHU
HUI n meeting of Māori
people
HUIA n extinct bird of New
Zealand, prized by early
Māoris for its distinctive tail
feathers
HUIAS >HUIA
HUIC interj in hunting, a call
to hounds
HUIPIL n Mayan woman's
blouse
HUIPILES >HUIPIL
HUIPILS >HUIPIL
HUIS >HUI
HUISACHE n American tree
HUISACHES >HUISACHE
HUISSIER n doorkeeper
HUISSIERS >HUISSIER
HUITAIN n verse of
eighteen lines
HUITAINS >HUITAIN
HULA n swaying Hawaiian

dance
HULAS >HULA
HULE same as >ULE
HULES >HULE
HULK n body of an
abandoned ship ▷vb move
clumsily
HULKED >HULK
HULKIER >HULKY
HULKIEST >HULKY
HULKING adj bulky,
unwieldy
HULKS >HULK
HULKY same as >HULKING
HULL n main body of a boat
▷vb remove the hulls from
HULLED >HULL
HULLER >HULL
HULLERS >HULL
HULLIER >HULLY
HULLIEST >HULLY
HULLING >HULL
HULLO same as >HELLO
HULLOA same as >HALLOA
HULLOAED >HULLOA
HULLOAING >HULLOA
HULLOAS >HULLOA
HULLOED >HULLO
HULLOES >HULLO
HULLOING >HULLO
HULLOO same as >HALLOO
HULLOOED >HULLOO
HULLOOING >HULLOO
HULLOOS >HULLOO
HULLOS >HULLO
HULLS >HULL
HULLY adj having husks
HUM vb make a low
continuous vibrating sound
▷n humming sound
HUMA n mythical bird
HUMAN adj of or typical of
people ▷n human being
HUMANE adj kind or merciful
HUMANELY >HUMANE
HUMANER >HUMANE
HUMANEST >HUMANE
HUMANHOOD n state of
being human
HUMANISE same as
>HUMANIZE
HUMANISED >HUMANISE
HUMANISER >HUMANISE
HUMANISES >HUMANISE
HUMANISM n belief in
human effort rather than
religion
HUMANISMS >HUMANISM
HUMANIST >HUMANISM
HUMANISTS >HUMANIST
HUMANITY n human race
HUMANIZE vb make
human or humane
HUMANIZED >HUMANIZE
HUMANIZER >HUMANIZE
HUMANIZES >HUMANIZE
HUMANKIND n human race
HUMANLIKE >HUMAN
HUMANLY adv by human
powers or means
HUMANNESS >HUMAN
HUMANOID adj resembling
a human being in
appearance ▷n (in science

fiction) a robot or creature
resembling a human being
HUMANOIDS >HUMANOID
HUMANS >HUMAN
HUMAS >HUMA
HUMATE n decomposed
plants used as fertilizer
HUMATES >HUMATE
HUMBLE adj conscious of
one's failings ▷vb cause to
feel humble, humiliate
HUMBLEBEE another name
for the >BUMBLEBEE
HUMBLED >HUMBLE
HUMBLER >HUMBLE
HUMBLERS >HUMBLE
HUMBLES >HUMBLE
HUMBLESSE n quality of
being humble
HUMBLEST >HUMBLE
HUMBLING >HUMBLE
HUMBLINGS >HUMBLE
HUMBLY >HUMBLE
HUMBUCKER n twin-coil
guitar pick-up
HUMBUG n hard striped
peppermint sweet ▷vb
cheat or deceive (someone)
HUMBUGGED >HUMBUG
HUMBUGGER >HUMBUG
HUMBUGS >HUMBUG
HUMBUZZ n type of beetle
HUMBUZZES >HUMBUZZ
HUMDINGER n excellent
person or thing
HUMDRUM adj ordinary, dull
▷n monotonous routine,
task, or concern
HUMDRUMS >HUMDRUM
HUMECT vb make moist
HUMECTANT adj producing
moisture ▷n substance
added to another
substance to keep it moist
HUMECTATE vb produce
moisture
HUMECTED >HUMECT
HUMECTING >HUMECT
HUMECTIVE >HUMECT
HUMECTS >HUMECT
HUMEFIED >HUMEFY
HUMEFIES >HUMEFY
HUMEFY same as >HUMIFY
HUMEFYING >HUMEFY
HUMERAL adj of or relating
to the humerus ▷n silk
shawl worn by a priest at
High Mass; humeral veil
HUMERALS >HUMERAL
HUMERI >HUMERUS
HUMERUS n bone from the
shoulder to the elbow
HUMF same as >HUMPH
HUMFED >HUMF
HUMFING >HUMF
HUMFS >HUMF
HUMHUM n Indian cotton
cloth
HUMHUMS >HUMHUM
HUMIC adj of, relating to,
derived from, or resembling
humus
HUMICOLE n any plant
that thrives on humus

HUMICOLES > HUMICOLE
HUMID *adj* damp and hot
HUMIDER > HUMID
HUMIDEST > HUMID
HUMIDEX *n* system of measuring discomfort showing the combined effect of humidity and temperature
HUMIDEXES > HUMIDEX
HUMIDICES > HUMIDEX
HUMIDIFY *vb* make the air in (a room) more humid or damp
HUMIDITY *n* dampness
HUMIDLY > HUMID
HUMIDNESS > HUMID
HUMIDOR *n* humid place or container for storing cigars, tobacco, etc
HUMIDORS > HUMIDOR
HUMIFIED > HUMIFY
HUMIFIES > HUMIFY
HUMIFY *vb* convert or be converted into humus
HUMIFYING > HUMIFY
HUMILIANT *adj* humiliating
HUMILIATE *vb* lower the dignity or hurt the pride of
HUMILITY *n* quality of being humble
HUMINT *n* human intelligence
HUMINTS > HUMINT
HUMITE *n* mineral containing magnesium
HUMITES > HUMITE
HUMITURE *n* measure of both humidity and temperature
HUMITURES > HUMITURE
HUMLIE *n* hornless cow
HUMLIES > HUMLIE
HUMMABLE > HUM
HUMMAUM *same as* > HAMMAM
HUMMAUMS > HUMMAUM
HUMMED > HUM
HUMMEL *adj* (of cattle) hornless ▷ *vb* remove horns from
HUMMELLED > HUMMEL
HUMMELLER > HUMMEL
HUMMELS > HUMMEL
HUMMER > HUM
HUMMERS > HUM
HUMMING > HUM
HUMMINGS > HUM
HUMMLE as in *hummle bonnet* type of Scottish cap
HUMMOCK *n* very small hill ▷ *vb* form into a hummock or hummocks
HUMMOCKED > HUMMOCK
HUMMOCKS > HUMMOCK
HUMMOCKY > HUMMOCK
HUMMUM *same as* > HAMMAM
HUMMUMS > HUMMUM
HUMMUS *n* creamy dip originating in the Middle East, made from puréed chickpeas
HUMMUSES > HUMMUS

HUMOGEN *n* type of fertilizer
HUMOGENS > HUMOGEN
HUMONGOUS *same as* > HUMUNGOUS
HUMOR *same as* > HUMOUR
HUMORAL *adj* denoting or relating to a type of immunity caused by free antibodies circulating in the blood
HUMORALLY > HUMORAL
HUMORED > HUMOR
HUMORESK *n* humorous musical composition
HUMORESKS > HUMORESK
HUMORFUL > HUMOR
HUMORING > HUMOR
HUMORIST *n* writer or entertainer who uses humour in his or her work
HUMORISTS > HUMORIST
HUMORLESS > HUMOR
HUMOROUS *adj* amusing, esp in a witty or clever way
HUMORS > HUMOR
HUMORSOME *adj* capricious
HUMOUR *n* ability to say or perceive things that are amusing ▷ *vb* be kind and indulgent to
HUMOURED > HUMOUR
HUMOURFUL > HUMOUR
HUMOURING > HUMOUR
HUMOURS > HUMOUR
HUMOUS *same as* > HUMUS
HUMP *n* raised piece of ground ▷ *vb* carry or heave
HUMPBACK *same as* > HUNCHBACK
HUMPBACKS > HUMPBACK
HUMPED > HUMP
HUMPEN *n* old German drinking glass
HUMPENS > HUMPEN
HUMPER > HUMP
HUMPERS > HUMP
HUMPH *interj* exclamation of annoyance or scepticism ▷ *vb* exclaim humph
HUMPHED > HUMPH
HUMPHING > HUMPH
HUMPHS > HUMPH
HUMPIER > HUMPY
HUMPIES > HUMPY
HUMPIEST > HUMPY
HUMPINESS > HUMPY
HUMPING > HUMP
HUMPLESS > HUMP
HUMPLIKE > HUMP
HUMPS > HUMP
HUMPTIES > HUMPTY
HUMPTY *n* low padded seat
HUMPY *adj* full of humps ▷ *n* primitive hut
HUMS > HUM
HUMSTRUM *n* medieval musical instrument
HUMSTRUMS > HUMSTRUM
HUMUNGOUS *adj* very large
HUMUS *n* decomposing vegetable and animal mould in the soil
HUMUSES > HUMUS

HUMUSY > HUMUS
HUMVEE *n* military vehicle
HUMVEES > HUMVEE
HUN *n* member of any of several Asiatic nomadic peoples speaking Mongoloid or Turkic languages
HUNCH *n* feeling or suspicion not based on facts ▷ *vb* draw (one's shoulders) up or together
HUNCHBACK *n* person with an abnormal curvature of the spine
HUNCHED > HUNCH
HUNCHES > HUNCH
HUNCHING > HUNCH
HUNDRED *n* ten times ten ▷ *adj* amounting to a hundred
HUNDREDER *n* inhabitant of a hundred
HUNDREDOR *same as* > HUNDREDER
HUNDREDS > HUNDRED
HUNDREDTH *adj* being the ordinal number of 100 in numbering or counting order, position, time, etc ▷ *n* one of 100 approximately equal parts of something
HUNG > HANG
HUNGAN *same as* > HOUNGAN
HUNGANS > HUNGAN
HUNGER *n* discomfort or weakness from lack of food ▷ *vb* want very much
HUNGERED > HUNGER
HUNGERFUL *adj* hungry
HUNGERING > HUNGER
HUNGERLY *adj* hungry
HUNGERS > HUNGER
HUNGOVER *adj* suffering from hangover
HUNGRIER > HUNGRY
HUNGRIEST > HUNGRY
HUNGRILY > HUNGRY
HUNGRY *adj* desiring food
HUNH *same as* > HUH
HUNK *n* large piece
HUNKER *vb* squat
HUNKERED > HUNKER
HUNKERING > HUNKER
HUNKERS *npl* haunches
HUNKEY *n* person of Hungarian descent
HUNKEYS > HUNKEY
HUNKIE *same as* > HUNKEY
HUNKIER > HUNKY
HUNKIES > HUNKY
HUNKIEST > HUNKY
HUNKS *n* crotchety old person
HUNKSES > HUNKS
HUNKY *adj* excellent
HUNNISH > HUN
HUNS > HUN
HUNT *vb* seek out and kill (wild animals) for food or sport ▷ *n* hunting
HUNTABLE > HUNT

HUNTAWAY *n* sheepdog trained to drive sheep by barking
HUNTAWAYS > HUNTAWAY
HUNTED *adj* harassed and worn
HUNTEDLY > HUNT
HUNTER *n* person or animal that hunts wild animals for food or sport
HUNTERS > HUNTER
HUNTING *n* pursuit and killing or capture of game and wild animals, regarded as a sport
HUNTINGS > HUNTING
HUNTRESS *same as* > HUNTER
HUNTS > HUNT
HUNTSMAN *n* man who hunts wild animals, esp foxes
HUNTSMEN > HUNTSMAN
HUP *vb* cry hup to get a horse to move
HUPIRO *in New Zealand English, same as* > STINKWOOD
HUPIROS > HUPIRO
HUPPAH *variant spelling of* > CHUPPAH
HUPPAHS > HUPPAH
HUPPED > HUP
HUPPING > HUP
HUPPOT > HUPPAH
HUPPOTH *same as* > HUPPOT
HUPS > HUP
HURCHEON *same as* > URCHIN
HURCHEONS > HURCHEON
HURDEN *same as* > HARDEN
HURDENS > HURDEN
HURDIES *npl* buttocks or haunches
HURDLE *n* light barrier for jumping over in some races ▷ *vb* jump over (something)
HURDLED > HURDLE
HURDLER > HURDLE
HURDLERS > HURDLE
HURDLES > HURDLE
HURDLING > HURDLE
HURDLINGS > HURDLE
HURDS *same as* > HARDS
HURL *vb* throw or utter forcefully ▷ *n* act or an instance of hurling
HURLBAT *same as* > WHIRLBAT
HURLBATS > HURLBAT
HURLED > HURL
HURLER > HURL
HURLERS > HURL
HURLEY *n* another word for the game of hurling
HURLEYS > HURLEY
HURLIES > HURLY
HURLING *n* Irish game like hockey
HURLINGS > HURLING
HURLS > HURL
HURLY *n* wheeled barrow
HURRA *same as* > HURRAH

HURRAED > HURRA
HURRAH interj exclamation of joy or applause ▷ n cheer of joy or victory ▷ vb shout "hurrah"
HURRAHED > HURRAH
HURRAHING > HURRAH
HURRAHS > HURRAH
HURRAING > HURRA
HURRAS > HURRA
HURRAY same as > HURRAH
HURRAYED > HURRAY
HURRAYING > HURRAY
HURRAYS > HURRAY
HURRICANE n very strong, often destructive, wind or storm
HURRICANO same as > HURRICANE
HURRIED adj done quickly or too quickly
HURRIEDLY > HURRIED
HURRIER > HURRY
HURRIERS > HURRY
HURRIES > HURRY
HURRY vb (cause to) move or act very quickly ▷ n doing something quickly or the need to do something quickly
HURRYING > HURRY
HURRYINGS > HURRY
HURST n wood
HURSTS > HURST
HURT vb cause physical or mental pain to ▷ n physical or mental pain ▷ adj injured or pained
HURTER > HURT
HURTERS > HURT
HURTFUL adj unkind
HURTFULLY > HURTFUL
HURTING > HURT
HURTLE vb move quickly or violently
HURTLED > HURTLE
HURTLES > HURTLE
HURTLESS adj uninjured
HURTLING > HURTLE
HURTS > HURT
HUSBAND n woman's partner in marriage ▷ vb use economically
HUSBANDED > HUSBAND
HUSBANDER > HUSBAND
HUSBANDLY > HUSBAND
HUSBANDRY n farming
HUSBANDS > HUSBAND
HUSH vb make or be silent ▷ n stillness or silence ▷ interj plea or demand for silence
HUSHABIED > HUSHABY
HUSHABIES > HUSHABY
HUSHABY interj used in quietening a baby or child to sleep ▷ n lullaby ▷ vb quieten to sleep
HUSHED > HUSH
HUSHEDLY > HUSH
HUSHER same as > USHER
HUSHERED > HUSHER
HUSHERING > HUSHER
HUSHERS > HUSHER

HUSHES > HUSH
HUSHFUL adj quiet
HUSHIER > HUSHY
HUSHIEST > HUSHY
HUSHING > HUSH
HUSHPUPPY n snack of deep-fried dough
HUSHY adj secret
HUSK n outer covering of certain seeds and fruits ▷ vb remove the husk from
HUSKED > HUSK
HUSKER > HUSK
HUSKERS > HUSK
HUSKIER > HUSKY
HUSKIES > HUSKY
HUSKIEST > HUSKY
HUSKILY > HUSKY
HUSKINESS > HUSKY
HUSKING > HUSK
HUSKINGS > HUSK
HUSKLIKE > HUSK
HUSKS > HUSK
HUSKY adj slightly hoarse ▷ n Arctic sledge dog with thick hair and a curled tail
HUSO n sturgeon
HUSOS > HUSO
HUSS n flesh of the European dogfish, when used as food
HUSSAR n lightly armed cavalry soldier
HUSSARS > HUSSAR
HUSSES > HUSS
HUSSIES > HUSSY
HUSSIF n sewing kit
HUSSIFS > HUSSIF
HUSSY n immodest or promiscuous woman
HUSTINGS npl political campaigns and speeches before an election
HUSTLE vb push about, jostle ▷ n lively activity or bustle
HUSTLED > HUSTLE
HUSTLER > HUSTLE
HUSTLERS > HUSTLE
HUSTLES > HUSTLE
HUSTLING > HUSTLE
HUSTLINGS > HUSTLE
HUSWIFE same as > HOUSEWIFE
HUSWIFES > HUSWIFE
HUSWIVES > HUSWIFE
HUT n small house, shelter, or shed
HUTCH n cage for pet rabbits etc ▷ vb store or keep in or as if in a hutch
HUTCHED > HUTCH
HUTCHES > HUTCH
HUTCHIE n groundsheet draped over an upright stick, used as a temporary shelter
HUTCHIES > HUTCHIE
HUTCHING > HUTCH
HUTIA n rodent of West Indies
HUTIAS > HUTIA
HUTLIKE > HUT
HUTMENT n number or

group of huts
HUTMENTS > HUTMENT
HUTS > HUT
HUTTED > HUT
HUTTING > HUT
HUTTINGS > HUT
HUTZPA same as > HUTZPAH
HUTZPAH variant spelling of > CHUTZPAH
HUTZPAHS > HUTZPAH
HUTZPAS > HUTZPA
HUZOOR n person of rank in India
HUZOORS > HUZOOR
HUZZA same as > HUZZAH
HUZZAED > HUZZA
HUZZAH archaic word for > HURRAH
HUZZAHED > HUZZAH
HUZZAHING > HUZZAH
HUZZAHS > HUZZAH
HUZZAING > HUZZA
HUZZAS > HUZZA
HUZZIES > HUZZY
HUZZY same as > HUSSY
HWAN another name for > WON
HWYL n emotional fervour, as in the recitation of poetry
HWYLS > HWYL
HYACINE same as > HYACINTH
HYACINES > HYACINE
HYACINTH n sweet-smelling spring flower that grows from a bulb
HYACINTHS > HYACINTH
HYAENA same as > HYENA
HYAENAS > HYAENA
HYAENIC > HYAENA
HYALIN n glassy translucent substance, such as occurs in certain degenerative skin conditions or in hyaline cartilage
HYALINE adj clear and translucent, with no fibres or granules ▷ n glassy transparent surface
HYALINES > HYALINE
HYALINISE same as > HYALINIZE
HYALINIZE vb give a glassy consistency to
HYALINS > HYALIN
HYALITE n clear and colourless variety of opal in globular form
HYALITES > HYALITE
HYALOGEN n insoluble substance in body structures
HYALOGENS > HYALOGEN
HYALOID adj clear and transparent ▷ n delicate transparent membrane enclosing the vitreous humour of the eye
HYALOIDS > HYALOID
HYALONEMA n species of sponge
HYBRID n offspring of two plants or animals of

different species ▷ adj of mixed origin
HYBRIDISE same as > HYBRIDIZE
HYBRIDISM > HYBRID
HYBRIDIST > HYBRID
HYBRIDITY > HYBRID
HYBRIDIZE vb produce or cause (species) to produce hybrids
HYBRIDOMA n hybrid cell formed by the fusion of two different types of cell, esp one capable of producing antibodies, but of limited lifespan, fused with an immortal tumour cell
HYBRIDOUS > HYBRID
HYBRIDS > HYBRID
HYBRIS same as > HUBRIS
HYBRISES > HYBRIS
HYBRISTIC > HYBRIS
HYDANTOIN n colourless odourless crystalline compound present in beet molasses and used in the manufacture of pharmaceuticals and synthetic resins
HYDATHODE n pore in plants, esp on the leaves, specialized for excreting water
HYDATID n cyst containing tapeworm larvae
HYDATIDS > HYDATID
HYDATOID adj watery
HYDRA n mythical many-headed water serpent
HYDRACID n acid, such as hydrochloric acid, that does not contain oxygen
HYDRACIDS > HYDRACID
HYDRAE > HYDRA
HYDRAEMIA n wateriness of blood
HYDRAGOG n drug that removes water
HYDRAGOGS > HYDRAGOG
HYDRANGEA n ornamental shrub with clusters of pink, blue, or white flowers
HYDRANT n outlet from a water main with a nozzle for a hose
HYDRANTH n polyp in a colony of hydrozoan coelenterates that is specialized for feeding rather than reproduction
HYDRANTHS > HYDRANTH
HYDRANTS > HYDRANT
HYDRAS > HYDRA
HYDRASE n enzyme that removes water
HYDRASES > HYDRASE
HYDRASTIS n any of various Japanese and E North American plants, such as goldenseal, having showy foliage and ornamental red fruits
HYDRATE n chemical compound of water with

another substance ▷ *vb* treat or impregnate with water

HYDRATED *adj* (of a compound) chemically bonded to water molecules

HYDRATES > HYDRATE

HYDRATING > HYDRATE

HYDRATION > HYDRATE

HYDRATOR > HYDRATE

HYDRATORS > HYDRATE

HYDRAULIC *adj* operated by pressure forced through a pipe by a liquid such as water or oil

HYDRAZIDE *n* any of a class of chemical compounds that result when hydrogen in hydrazine or any of its derivatives is replaced by an acid radical

HYDRAZINE *n* colourless basic liquid made from sodium hypochlorite and ammonia: a strong reducing agent, used chiefly as a rocket fuel

HYDRAZOIC as in *hydrazoic acid* colourless highly explosive liquid

HYDREMIA *same as* > HYDRAEMIA

HYDREMIAS > HYDREMIA

HYDRIA *n* (in ancient Greece and Rome) a large water jar

HYDRIAE > HYDRIA

HYDRIC *adj* of or containing hydrogen

HYDRID *same as* > HYDROID

HYDRIDE *n* compound of hydrogen with another element

HYDRIDES > HYDRIDE

HYDRIDS > HYDRID

HYDRILLA *n* aquatic plant used as an oxygenator in aquaria and pools

HYDRILLAS > HYDRILLA

HYDRIODIC as in *hydriodic acid* colourless or pale yellow aqueous solution of hydrogen iodide: a strong acid

HYDRO *n* hotel offering facilities for hydropathy ▷ *adj* electricity as supplied to a residence, business, etc

HYDROCAST *n* gathering of water samples for analysis

HYDROCELE *n* abnormal collection of fluid in any saclike space, esp around the testicles

HYDROFOIL *n* fast light boat with its hull raised out of the water on one or more pairs of fins

HYDROGEL *n* gel in which the liquid constituent is water

HYDROGELS > HYDROGEL

HYDROGEN *n* light

flammable colourless gas that combines with oxygen to form water

HYDROGENS > HYDROGEN

HYDROID *adj* of or relating to an order of colonial hydrozoan coelenterates that have the polyp phase dominant ▷ *n* hydroid colony or individual

HYDROIDS > HYDROID

HYDROLASE *n* enzyme, such as an esterase, that controls hydrolysis

HYDROLOGY *n* study of the distribution, conservation, and use of the water of the earth and its atmosphere

HYDROLYSE *vb* subject to or undergo hydrolysis

HYDROLYTE *n* substance subjected to hydrolysis

HYDROLYZE *same as* > HYDROLYSE

HYDROMA *same as* > HYGROMA

HYDROMAS > HYDROMA

HYDROMATA > HYDROMA

HYDROMEL *n* another word for 'mead' (the drink)

HYDROMELS > HYDROMEL

HYDRONAUT *n* person trained to operate deep submergence vessels

HYDRONIC *adj* using hot water in heating system

HYDRONIUM as in *hydronium ion* positive ion, formed by the attachment of a proton to a water molecule: occurs in solutions of acids and behaves like a hydrogen ion

HYDROPATH *n* exponent of treating disease using large quantities of water

HYDROPIC > HYDROPSY

HYDROPS *n* anaemia in a fetus

HYDROPSES > HYDROPS

HYDROPSY *same as* > DROPSY

HYDROPTIC > HYDROPSY

HYDROPULT *n* type of water pump

HYDROS > HYDRO

HYDROSERE *n* sere that begins in an aquatic environment

HYDROSKI *n* hydrofoil used on some seaplanes to provide extra lift when taking off

HYDROSKIS > HYDROSKI

HYDROSOL *n* sol that has water as its liquid phase

HYDROSOLS > HYDROSOL

HYDROSOMA *same as* > HYDROSOME

HYDROSOME *n* body of a colonial hydrozoon

HYDROSTAT *n* device that detects the presence of water as a prevention against drying out,

overflow, etc, esp one used as a warning in a steam boiler

HYDROUS *adj* containing water

HYDROVANE *n* vane on a seaplane conferring stability on water (a sponson) or facilitating take-off (a hydrofoil)

HYDROXIDE *n* compound containing a hydroxyl group or ion

HYDROXY *adj* (of a chemical compound) containing one or more hydroxyl groups

HYDROXYL *adj* of or containing the monovalent group -OH or the ion OH⁻ ▷ *n* of, consisting of, or containing the monovalent group -OH or the ion OH⁻

HYDROXYLS > HYDROXYL

HYDROZOA > HYDROZOON

HYDROZOAN *n* type of invertebrate of the class which includes the hydra and Portuguese man-of-war

HYDROZOON *same as* > HYDROZOON

HYDYNE *n* type of rocket fuel

HYDYNES > HYDYNE

HYE *same as* > HIE

HYED > HYE

HYEING > HYE

HYEN *same as* > HYENA

HYENA *n* scavenging doglike mammal of Africa and S Asia

HYENAS > HYENA

HYENIC > HYENA

HYENINE *adj* of hyenas

HYENOID *adj* of or like hyenas

HYENS > HYEN

HYES > HYE

HYETAL *adj* of or relating to rain, rainfall, or rainy regions

HYETOLOGY *n* study of rainfall

HYGEIST *same as* > HYGIENIST

HYGEISTS > HYGEIST

HYGIEIST *same as* > HYGIENIST

HYGIEISTS > HYGIEIST

HYGIENE *n* principles and practice of health and cleanliness

HYGIENES > HYGIENE

HYGIENIC *adj* promoting health or cleanliness

HYGIENICS *same as* > HYGIENICS

HYGIENIST *n* person skilled in the practice of hygiene

HYGRISTOR *n* electronic component the resistance of which varies with humidity

HYGRODEIK *n* type of

thermometer

HYGROLOGY *n* study of humidity of air

HYGROMA *n* swelling in the soft tissue that occurs over a joint, usually caused by repeated injury

HYGROMAS > HYGROMA

HYGROMATA > HYGROMA

HYGROPHIL *adj* moisture-loving

HYGROSTAT *n* a device for maintaining constant humidity

HYING > HIE

HYKE *same as* > HAIK

HYKES > HYKE

HYLA *n* type of tropical American tree frog

HYLAS > HYLA

HYLDING *same as* > HILDING

HYLDINGS > HYLDING

HYLE *n* wood

HYLEG *n* dominant planet when someone is born

HYLEGS > HYLEG

HYLES > HYLE

HYLIC *adj* solid

HYLICISM *n* materialism

HYLICISMS > HYLICISM

HYLICIST > HYLICISM

HYLICISTS > HYLICISM

HYLISM *same as* > HYLICISM

HYLISMS > HYLISM

HYLIST > HYLISM

HYLISTS > HYLISM

HYLOBATE *n* gibbon

HYLOBATES > HYLOBATE

HYLOIST *n* materialist

HYLOISTS > HYLOIST

HYLOPHYTE *n* plant that grows in woods

HYLOZOIC > HYLOZOISM

HYLOZOISM *n* philosophical doctrine that life is one of the properties of matter

HYLOZOIST > HYLOZOISM

HYMEN *n* membrane partly covering the opening of a girl's vagina, which breaks before puberty or at the first occurrence of sexual intercourse

HYMENAEAL *same as* > HYMENEAL

HYMENAEAN > HYMEN

HYMENAL > HYMEN

HYMENEAL *adj* of or relating to marriage ▷ *n* wedding song or poem

HYMENEALS > HYMENEAL

HYMENEAN > HYMEN

HYMENIA > HYMENIUM

HYMENIAL > HYMENIUM

HYMENIUM *n* (in basidiomycetous and ascomycetous fungi) a layer of cells some of which produce the spores

HYMENIUMS > HYMENIUM

HYMENS > HYMEN

HYMN n Christian song of praise sung to God or a saint ▷ vb express (praises, thanks, etc) by singing hymns

HYMNAL n book of hymns ▷ adj of, relating to, or characteristic of hymns

HYMNALS > HYMNAL

HYMNARIES > HYMNARY

HYMNARY same as > HYMNAL

HYMNBOOK n book containing the words and music of hymns

HYMNBOOKS > HYMNBOOK

HYMNED > HYMN

HYMNIC > HYMN

HYMNING > HYMN

HYMNIST n person who composes hymns

HYMNISTS > HYMNIST

HYMNLESS > HYMN

HYMNLIKE > HYMN

HYMNODIES > HYMNODY

HYMNODIST same as > HYMNIST

HYMNODY n composition or singing of hymns

HYMNOLOGY same as > HYMNODY

HYMNS > HYMN

HYNDE same as > HIND

HYNDES > HYNDE

HYOID adj of or relating to the hyoid bone ▷ n horseshoe-shaped bone that lies at the base of the tongue and above the thyroid cartilage

HYOIDAL adj of or relating to the hyoid bone

HYOIDEAN same as > HYOIDAL

HYOIDS > HYOID

HYOSCINE n a colourless viscous liquid alkaloid

HYOSCINES > HYOSCINE

HYP n short for hypotenuse

HYPALGIA n reduced ability to feel pain

HYPALGIAS > HYPALGIA

HYPALLAGE n figure of speech in which the natural relations of two words in a statement are interchanged, as in *the fire spread the wind*

HYPANTHIA n plural of hypanthium: cup-shaped receptacle of perigynous or epigynous flowers

HYPATE n string of lyre

HYPATES > HYPATE

HYPE n intensive or exaggerated publicity or sales promotion ▷ vb promote (a product) using intensive or exaggerated publicity

HYPED > HYPE

HYPER > HYPE

HYPERACID adj having excess acidity

HYPERARID adj extremely dry

HYPERBOLA n curve produced when a cone is cut by a plane at a steeper angle to its base than its side

HYPERBOLE n deliberate exaggeration for effect

HYPERCUBE n figure in a space of four or more dimensions having all its sides equal and all its angles right angles

HYPEREMIA n excessive blood in an organ or part

HYPEREMIC > HYPEREMIA

HYPERFINE as in *hyperfine structure* splitting of a spectral line of an atom or molecule into two or more closely spaced components as a result of interaction of the electrons with the magnetic moments of the nuclei

HYPERGAMY n custom that forbids a woman to marry a man of lower social status

HYPERGOL n type of fuel

HYPERGOLS > HYPERGOL

HYPERICIN n antidepressant and antiviral compound

HYPERICUM n herbaceous plant or shrub

HYPERLINK n link from a hypertext file that gives users instant access to related material in another file ▷ vb link (files) in this way

HYPERMART n very large supermarket

HYPERNOVA n exploding star that produces even more energy and light than a supernova

HYPERNYM n superordinate

HYPERNYMS > HYPERNYM

HYPERNYMY > HYPERNYM

HYPERON n any baryon that is not a nucleon

HYPERONS > HYPERON

HYPEROPE n person with hyperopia

HYPEROPES > HYPEROPE

HYPEROPIA n inability to see near objects clearly because the images received by the eye are focused behind the retina

HYPEROPIC > HYPEROPIA

HYPERPNEA n increase in breathing rate

HYPERPURE adj extremely pure

HYPERREAL adj involving or characterized by particularly realistic graphic representation ▷ n that which constitutes hyperreality

HYPERS > HYPE

HYPERTEXT n computer software and hardware that allows users to store and view text and move between related items easily

HYPES > HYPE

HYPESTER n person or organization that gives an idea or product intense publicity in order to promote it

HYPESTERS > HYPESTER

HYPETHRAL adj having no roof

HYPHA n any of the filaments that constitute the body (mycelium) of a fungus

HYPHAE > HYPHA

HYPHAL > HYPHA

HYPHEMIA n bleeding inside eye

HYPHEMIAS > HYPHEMIA

HYPHEN n punctuation mark (-) indicating that two words or syllables are connected ▷ vb hyphenate

HYPHENATE vb separate (words) with a hyphen

HYPHENED > HYPHEN

HYPHENIC > HYPHEN

HYPHENING > HYPHEN

HYPHENISE same as > HYPHENIZE

HYPHENISM > HYPHEN

HYPHENIZE same as > HYPHENATE

HYPHENS > HYPHEN

HYPHIES > HYPHY

HYPHY n type of hip-hop music

HYPING > HYPE

HYPINGS > HYPE

HYPINOSES > HYPINOSIS

HYPINOSIS n protein deficiency in blood

HYPNIC n sleeping drug

HYPNICS > HYPNIC

HYPNOGENY n hypnosis

HYPNOID adj of or relating to a state resembling sleep or hypnosis

HYPNOIDAL same as > HYPNOID

HYPNOLOGY n study of sleep and hypnosis

HYPNONE n sleeping drug

HYPNONES > HYPNONE

HYPNOSES > HYPNOSIS

HYPNOSIS n artificially induced state of relaxation in which the mind is more than usually receptive to suggestion

HYPNOTEE n person being hypnotized

HYPNOTEES > HYPNOTEE

HYPNOTIC adj of or (as if) producing hypnosis ▷ n drug that induces sleep

HYPNOTICS > HYPNOTIC

HYPNOTISE same as

> HYPNOTIZE

HYPNOTISM n inducing hypnosis in someone

HYPNOTIST n person skilled in the theory and practice of hypnosis

HYPNOTIZE vb induce hypnosis in (a person)

HYPNOTOID adj like hypnosis

HYPNUM n species of moss

HYPNUMS > HYPNUM

HYPO vb inject with a hypodermic syringe

HYPOACID adj abnormally acidic

HYPOBARIC adj below normal pressure

HYPOBLAST n inner layer of an embryo at an early stage of development that becomes the endoderm at gastrulation

HYPOBOLE n act of anticipating objection

HYPOBOLES > HYPOBOLE

HYPOCAUST n ancient Roman heating system in which hot air circulated under the floor and between double walls

HYPOCIST n type of juice

HYPOCISTS > HYPOCIST

HYPOCOTYL n part of an embryo plant between the cotyledons and the radicle

HYPOCRISY n (instance of) pretence of having standards or beliefs that are contrary to one's real character or actual behaviour

HYPOCRITE n person who pretends to be what he or she is not

HYPODERM n layer of thick-walled tissue in some plants

HYPODERMA n layer of skin tissue

HYPODERMS > HYPODERM

HYPOED > HYPO

HYPOGAEA > HYPOGAEUM

HYPOGAEAL > HYPOGAEUM

HYPOGAEAN > HYPOGAEUM

HYPOGAEUM same as > HYPOGEUM

HYPOGEA > HYPOGEUM

HYPOGEAL adj occurring or living below the surface of the ground

HYPOGEAN > HYPOGEUM

HYPOGENE adj formed, taking place, or originating beneath the surface of the earth

HYPOGENIC > HYPOGENE

HYPOGEOUS same as > HYPOGEAL

HYPOGEUM n underground vault, esp one used for burials

HYPOGYNY adj having the

gynoecium above the other floral parts

HYPOID as in *hypoid gear* gear having a tooth form generated by a hypocycloidal curve; used extensively in motor vehicle transmissions to withstand a high surface loading

HYPOING > HYPO

HYPOMANIA *n* abnormal condition of extreme excitement, milder than mania but characterized by great optimism and overactivity and often by reckless spending of money

HYPOMANIC > HYPOMANIA

HYPOMORPH *n* mutant gene

HYPONASTY *n* increased growth of the lower surface of a plant part, resulting in an upward bending of the part

HYPONEA *same as* > HYPOPNEA

HYPONEAS > HYPONEA

HYPONOIA *n* underlying meaning

HYPONOIAS > HYPONOIA

HYPONYM *n* word whose meaning is included in that of another word

HYPONYMS > HYPONYM

HYPONYMY > HYPONYM

HYPOPHYGE *another name for* > APOPHYGE

HYPOPLOID *adj* having or designating a chromosome number that is less than a multiple of the haploid number

HYPOPNEA *same as* > HYPOPNOEA

HYPOPNEAS > HYPOPNEA

HYPOPNEIC > HYPOPNEA

HYPOPNOEA *n* abnormally shallow breathing, usually accompanied by a decrease in the breathing rate

HYPOPYON *n* pus in eye

HYPOPYONS > HYPOPYON

HYPOS > HYPO

HYPOSTOME *n* invertebrate body part

HYPOSTYLE *adj* having a roof supported by columns

▷ *n* building constructed in this way

HYPOTAXES > HYPOTAXIS

HYPOTAXIS *n* subordination of one clause to another by a conjunction

HYPOTHEC *n* charge on property in favour of a creditor

HYPOTHECA *n* inner and younger layer of the cell wall of a diatom

HYPOTHECS > HYPOTHEC

HYPOTONIA *n* state of being hypnotized

HYPOTONIC *adj* (of muscles) lacking normal tone or tension

HYPOXEMIA *n* lack of oxygen in blood

HYPOXEMIC > HYPOXEMIA

HYPOXIA *n* deficiency in the amount of oxygen delivered to the body tissues

HYPOXIAS > HYPOXIA

HYPOXIC > HYPOXIA

HYPPED > HYP

HYPPING > HYP

HYPS > HYP

HYPURAL *adj* below the tail

HYRACES > HYRAX

HYRACOID *n* hyrax

HYRACOIDS > HYRACOID

HYRAX *n* type of hoofed rodent-like animal of Africa and Asia

HYRAXES > HYRAX

HYSON *n* Chinese green tea

HYSONS > HYSON

HYSSOP *n* sweet-smelling herb used in folk medicine

HYSSOPS > HYSSOP

HYSTERIA *n* state of uncontrolled excitement, anger, or panic

HYSTERIAS > HYSTERIA

HYSTERIC *adj* of or suggesting hysteria

HYSTERICS *npl* attack of hysteria

HYSTEROID *adj* resembling hysteria

HYTE *adj* insane

HYTHE *same as* > HITHE

HYTHES > HYTHE

h

Ii

IAMB *n* metrical foot of two syllables, a short one followed by a long one
IAMBI > IAMBUS
IAMBIC *adj* written in metrical units of one short and one long syllable ▷ *n* iambic foot, line, or stanza
IAMBICS > IAMBIC
IAMBIST *n* one who writes iambs
IAMBISTS > IAMBIST
IAMBS > IAMB
IAMBUS *same as* > IAMB
IAMBUSES > IAMBUS
IANTHINE *adj* violet
IATRIC *adj* relating to medicine or physicians
IATRICAL *same as* > IATRIC
IATROGENY *n* disease caused by medical intervention
IBADAH *n* following of Islamic beliefs and practices
IBADAT > IBADAH
IBERIS *n* plant with white or purple flowers
IBERISES > IBERIS
IBEX *n* wild goat with large backward-curving horns
IBEXES > IBEX
IBICES > IBEX
IBIDEM *adv* in the same place
IBIS *n* large wading bird with long legs
IBISES > IBIS
IBOGAINE *n* dopamine blocker
IBOGAINES > IBOGAINE
IBRIK *same as* > CEZVE
IBRIKS > IBRIK
IBUPROFEN *n* drug that relieves pain and reduces inflammation
ICE *n* water in the solid state, formed by freezing liquid water ▷ *vb* form or cause to form ice
ICEBALL *n* ball of ice
ICEBALLS > ICEBALL
ICEBERG *n* large floating mass of ice
ICEBERGS > ICEBERG
ICEBLINK *n* yellowish-white reflected glare in the sky over an ice field
ICEBLINKS > ICEBLINK
ICEBOAT *n* boat that

breaks up bodies of ice in water
ICEBOATER > ICEBOAT
ICEBOATS > ICEBOAT
ICEBOUND *adj* covered or made immobile by ice
ICEBOX *n* refrigerator
ICEBOXES > ICEBOX
ICECAP *n* mass of ice permanently covering an area
ICECAPPED *adj* having an icecap
ICECAPS > ICECAP
ICED *adj* covered with icing
ICEFALL *n* very steep part of a glacier that has deep crevasses and resembles a frozen waterfall
ICEFALLS > ICEFALL
ICEFIELD *n* very large flat expanse of ice floating in the sea; large ice floe
ICEFIELDS > ICEFIELD
ICEHOUSE *n* building for storing ice
ICEHOUSES > ICEHOUSE
ICEKHANA *n* motor race on a frozen lake
ICEKHANAS > ICEKHANA
ICELESS > ICE
ICELIKE > ICE
ICEMAKER *n* device for making ice
ICEMAKERS > ICEMAKER
ICEMAN *n* person who sells or delivers ice
ICEMEN > ICEMAN
ICEPACK *n* bag or folded cloth containing ice, applied to a part of the body, esp the head, to cool, reduce swelling, etc
ICEPACKS > ICEPACK
ICER *n* person who ices cakes
ICERS > ICER
ICES > ICE
ICESTONE *n* cryolite
ICESTONES > ICESTONE
ICEWINE *n* dessert wine made from grapes that have frozen before being harvested
ICEWINES > ICEWINE
ICH *archaic form of* > EKE
ICHABOD *interj* the glory has departed
ICHED > ICH
ICHES > ICH
ICHING > ICH

ICHNEUMON *n* greyish-brown mongoose
ICHNITE *n* trace fossil
ICHNITES > ICHNITE
ICHNOLITE *same as* > ICHNITE
ICHNOLOGY *n* study of trace fossils
ICHOR *n* fluid said to flow in the veins of the gods
ICHOROUS > ICHOR
ICHORS > ICHOR
ICHS > ICH
ICHTHIC *same as* > ICHTHYIC
ICHTHYIC *adj* of, relating to, or characteristic of fishes
ICHTHYOID *adj* resembling a fish ▷ *n* fishlike vertebrate
ICHTHYS *n* early Christian emblem
ICHTHYSES > ICHTHYS
ICICLE *n* tapering spike of ice hanging where water has dripped
ICICLED *adj* covered with icicles
ICICLES > ICICLE
ICIER > ICY
ICIEST > ICY
ICILY *adv* in an icy or reserved manner
ICINESS *n* condition of being icy or very cold
ICINESSES > ICINESS
ICING *n* mixture of sugar and water etc, used to cover and decorate cakes
ICINGS > ICING
ICK *interj* expression of disgust
ICKER *n* ear of corn
ICKERS > ICKER
ICKIER > ICKY
ICKIEST > ICKY
ICKILY > ICKY
ICKINESS > ICKY
ICKLE *ironically childish word for* > LITTLE
ICKLER > ICKLE
ICKLEST > ICKLE
ICKY *adj* sticky
ICON *n* picture of Christ or another religious figure, regarded as holy in the Orthodox Church
ICONES > ICON
ICONIC *adj* relating to, resembling, or having the

character of an icon
ICONICAL *same as* > ICONIC
ICONICITY > ICONIC
ICONIFIED > ICONIFY
ICONIFIES > ICONIFY
ICONIFY *vb* render as an icon
ICONISE *same as* > ICONIZE
ICONISED > ICONISE
ICONISES > ICONISE
ICONISING > ICONISE
ICONIZE *vb* render as an icon
ICONIZED > ICONIZE
ICONIZES > ICONIZE
ICONIZING > ICONIZE
ICONOLOGY *n* study or field of art history concerning icons
ICONOSTAS *n* a screen with doors and icons set in tiers, which separates the from the nave
ICONS > ICON
ICTAL > ICTUS
ICTERIC > ICTERUS
ICTERICAL > ICTERUS
ICTERICS > ICTERUS
ICTERID *n* bird of the oriole family
ICTERIDS > ICTERID
ICTERINE > ICTERID
ICTERUS *n* yellowing of plant leaves, caused by excessive cold or moisture
ICTERUSES > ICTERUS
ICTIC > ICTUS
ICTUS *n* metrical or rhythmic stress in verse feet, as contrasted with the stress accent on words
ICTUSES > ICTUS
ICY *adj* very cold
ID *n* mind's instinctive unconscious energies
IDANT *n* chromosome
IDANTS > IDANT
IDE *n* silver orfe fish
IDEA *n* plan or thought formed in the mind ▷ *vb* have or form an idea
IDEAED > IDEA
IDEAL *adj* most suitable ▷ *n* conception of something that is perfect
IDEALESS > IDEA
IDEALISE *same as* > IDEALIZE
IDEALISED > IDEALISE

IDEALISER > IDEALISE

IDEALISES > IDEALISE

IDEALISM n tendency to seek perfection in everything

IDEALISMS > IDEALISM

IDEALIST > IDEALISM

IDEALISTS > IDEALISM

IDEALITY > IDEAL

IDEALIZE vb regard or portray as perfect or nearly perfect

IDEALIZED > IDEALIZE

IDEALIZER > IDEALIZE

IDEALIZES > IDEALIZE

IDEALLESS > IDEAL

IDEALLY > IDEAL

IDEALNESS > IDEAL

IDEALOGUE corruption of > IDEOLOGUE

IDEALOGY corruption of > IDEOLOGY

IDEALS > IDEAL

IDEAS > IDEA

IDEATA > IDEATUM

IDEATE vb form or have an idea of

IDEATED > IDEATE

IDEATES > IDEATE

IDEATING > IDEATE

IDEATION > IDEATE

IDEATIONS > IDEATE

IDEATIVE > IDEATE

IDEATUM n objective reality with which human ideas are supposed to correspond

IDEE n idea

IDEES > IDEE

IDEM adj same: used to refer to an article, chapter, or book already quoted

IDENT n short visual image employed between television programmes that works as a logo to locate the viewer to the channel

IDENTIC adj (esp of opinions expressed by two or more governments) having the same wording or intention regarding another power

IDENTICAL adj exactly the same

IDENTIFY vb prove or recognize as being a certain person or thing

IDENTIKIT n trademark name for a set of transparencies of various typical facial characteristics that can be superimposed on one another to build up a picture of a person sought by the police

IDENTITY n state of being a specified person or thing

IDENTS > IDENT

IDEOGRAM n character or symbol that directly represents a concept or thing, rather than the

sounds that form its name

IDEOGRAMS > IDEOGRAM

IDEOGRAPH same as > IDEOGRAM

IDEOLOGIC > IDEOLOGY

IDEOLOGUE n ideologist

IDEOLOGY n body of ideas and beliefs of a group, nation, etc

IDEOMOTOR adj designating automatic muscular movements stimulated by ideas

IDEOPHONE n sound that represents a complete idea

IDEOPOLIS n city whose economy mainly consists of intellectual enterprises

IDES n (in the Ancient Roman calendar) the 15th of March, May, July, or October, or the 13th of other months

IDIOBLAST n plant cell that differs from those around it in the same tissue

IDIOCIES > IDIOCY

IDIOCY n utter stupidity

IDIOGRAM another name for > KARYOGRAM

IDIOGRAMS > IDIOGRAM

IDIOGRAPH n trademark

IDIOLECT n variety or form of a language used by an individual

IDIOLECTS > IDIOLECT

IDIOM n group of words which when used together have a different meaning from the words individually

IDIOMATIC > IDIOM

IDIOMS > IDIOM

IDIOPATHY n any disease of unknown cause

IDIOPHONE n percussion instrument, such as a cymbal or xylophone, made of naturally sonorous material

IDIOPLASM n germ plasm

IDIOT n foolish or stupid person

IDIOTCIES > IDIOTCY

IDIOTCY same as > IDIOCY

IDIOTIC adj of or resembling an idiot

IDIOTICAL same as > IDIOTIC

IDIOTICON n dictionary of dialect

IDIOTISH same as > IDIOTIC

IDIOTISM archaic word for > IDIOCY

IDIOTISMS > IDIOTISM

IDIOTS > IDIOT

IDIOTYPE n unique part of antibody

IDIOTYPES > IDIOTYPE

IDIOTYPIC > IDIOTYPE

IDLE adj not doing anything ⊳ vb spend (time) doing very little

IDLED > IDLE

IDLEHOOD > IDLE

IDLEHOODS > IDLE

IDLENESS > IDLE

IDLER n person who idles

IDLERS > IDLER

IDLES > IDLE

IDLESSE > IDLE

IDLESSES > IDLE

IDLEST > IDLE

IDLING > IDLE

IDLY > IDLE

IDOCRASE n green, brown, or yellow mineral

IDOCRASES > IDOCRASE

IDOL n object of excessive devotion

IDOLA > IDOLUM

IDOLATER > IDOLATRY

IDOLATERS > IDOLATRY

IDOLATOR > IDOLATRY

IDOLATORS > IDOLATRY

IDOLATRY n worship of idols

IDOLISE same as > IDOLIZE

IDOLISED > IDOLISE

IDOLISER > IDOLISE

IDOLISERS > IDOLISE

IDOLISES > IDOLISE

IDOLISING > IDOLISE

IDOLISM > IDOLIZE

IDOLISMS > IDOL

IDOLIST > IDOLIZE

IDOLISTS > IDOLIZE

IDOLIZE vb love or admire excessively

IDOLIZED > IDOLIZE

IDOLIZER > IDOLIZE

IDOLIZERS > IDOLIZE

IDOLIZES > IDOLIZE

IDOLIZING > IDOLIZE

IDOLON n mental image

IDOLS > IDOL

IDOLUM n mental picture

IDONEITY > IDONEOUS

IDONEOUS adj appropriate

IDS > ID

IDYL same as > IDYLL

IDYLIST same as > IDYLLIST

IDYLISTS > IDYLIST

IDYLL n scene or time of great peace and happiness

IDYLLIAN same as > IDYLLIC

IDYLLIC adj of or relating to an idyll

IDYLLIST n writer of idylls

IDYLLISTS > IDYLLIST

IDYLLS > IDYLL

IDYLS > IDYL

IF n uncertainty or doubt

IFF conj in logic, a shortened form of if and only if

IFFIER > IFFY

IFFIEST > IFFY

IFFINESS > IFFY

IFFY adj doubtful, uncertain

IFS > IF

IFTAR n meal eaten by Muslims to break their fast

after sunset every day during Ramadan

IFTARS > IFTAR

IGAD same as > EGAD

IGAPO n flooded forest

IGAPOS > IGAPO

IGARAPE n canoe route

IGARAPES > IGARAPE

IGG vb antagonize

IGGED > IGG

IGGING > IGG

IGGS > IGG

IGLOO n dome-shaped Inuit house made of snow and ice

IGLOOS > IGLOO

IGLU same as > IGLOO

IGLUS > IGLU

IGNARO n ignoramus

IGNAROES > IGNARO

IGNAROS > IGNARO

IGNATIA n dried seed

IGNATIAS > IGNATIA

IGNEOUS adj (of rock) formed as molten rock cools and hardens

IGNESCENT adj giving off sparks when struck, as a flint ⊳ n ignescent substance

IGNIFIED > IGNIFY

IGNIFIES > IGNIFY

IGNIFY vb turn into fire

IGNIFYING > IGNIFY

IGNITABLE > IGNITE

IGNITE vb catch fire or set fire to

IGNITED > IGNITE

IGNITER n person or thing that ignites

IGNITERS > IGNITER

IGNITES > IGNITE

IGNITIBLE > IGNITE

IGNITING > IGNITE

IGNITION n system that ignites the fuel-and-air mixture to start an engine

IGNITIONS > IGNITION

IGNITOR same as > IGNITER

IGNITORS > IGNITER

IGNITRON n mercury-arc rectifier controlled by a subsidiary electrode

IGNITRONS > IGNITRON

IGNOBLE adj dishonourable

IGNOBLER > IGNOBLE

IGNOBLEST > IGNOBLE

IGNOBLY > IGNOBLE

IGNOMIES > IGNOMY

IGNOMINY n humiliating disgrace

IGNOMY Shakespearean variant of > IGNOMINY

IGNORABLE > IGNORE

IGNORAMI > IGNORAMUS

IGNORAMUS n ignorant person

IGNORANCE n lack of knowledge or education

IGNORANT adj lacking knowledge ⊳ n ignorant person

IGNORANTS > IGNORANT

IGNORE vb refuse to notice, disregard deliberately ▷ n disregard

IGNORED > IGNORE

IGNORER > IGNORE

IGNORERS > IGNORE

IGNORES > IGNORE

IGNORING > IGNORE

IGUANA n large tropical American lizard

IGUANAS > IGUANA

IGUANIAN > IGUANA

IGUANIANS > IGUANA

IGUANID same as > IGUANA

IGUANIDS > IGUANID

IGUANODON n massive herbivorous long-tailed bipedal dinosaur

IHRAM n customary white robes worn by Muslim pilgrims to Mecca, symbolizing a sacred or consecrated state

IHRAMS > IHRAM

IJTIHAD n effort of a Muslim scholar to derive a legal ruling from the Koran

IJTIHADS > IJTIHAD

IKAN n (in Malaysia) fish used esp in names of cooked dishes

IKANS > IKAN

IKAT n method of creating patterns in fabric by tie-dyeing the yarn before weaving

IKATS > IKAT

IKEBANA n Japanese art of flower arrangement

IKEBANAS > IKEBANA

IKON same as > ICON

IKONS > IKON

ILEA > ILEUM

ILEAC adj of or relating to the ileum

ILEAL same as > ILEAC

ILEITIDES > ILEITIS

ILEITIS n inflammation of the ileum

ILEITISES > ILEITIS

ILEOSTOMY n surgical formation of a permanent opening through the abdominal wall into the ileum

ILEUM n lowest part of the small intestine

ILEUS n obstruction of the intestine, esp the ileum, by mechanical occlusion or as the result of distension of the bowel following loss of muscular action

ILEUSES > ILEUS

ILEX n any of a genus of trees or shrubs that includes holly

ILEXES > ILEX

ILIA > ILIUM

ILIAC adj of or relating to the ilium

ILIACUS n iliac

ILIACUSES > ILIACUS

ILIAD n epic poem

ILIADS > ILIAD

ILIAL > ILIUM

ILICES > ILEX

ILIUM n uppermost and widest of the three sections of the hipbone

ILK n type ▷ det each

ILKA same as > ILK

ILKADAY n every day

ILKADAYS > ILKADAY

ILKS > ILK

ILL adj not in good health ▷ n evil, harm ▷ adv badly

ILLAPSE vb slide in

ILLAPSED > ILLAPSE

ILLAPSES > ILLAPSE

ILLAPSING > ILLAPSE

ILLATION rare word for > INFERENCE

ILLATIONS > ILLATION

ILLATIVE adj of or relating to illation ▷ n illative case

ILLATIVES > ILLATIVE

ILLAWARRA n Australian breed of shorthorn dairy cattle

ILLEGAL adj against the law ▷ n person who has entered or attempted to enter a country illegally

ILLEGALLY > ILLEGAL

ILLEGALS > ILLEGAL

ILLEGIBLE adj unable to be read or deciphered

ILLEGIBLY > ILLEGIBLE

ILLER > ILL

ILLEST > ILL

ILLIAD n wink

ILLIADS > ILLIAD

ILLIBERAL adj narrow-minded, intolerant

ILLICIT adj illegal

ILLICITLY > ILLICIT

ILLIMITED adj infinite

ILLINIUM n type of radioactive element

ILLINIUMS > ILLINIUM

ILLIPE n Asian tree

ILLIPES > ILLIPE

ILLIQUID adj (of an asset) not easily convertible into cash

ILLISION n act of striking against

ILLISIONS > ILLISION

ILLITE n clay mineral of the mica group, found in shales and mudstones

ILLITES > ILLITE

ILLITIC > ILLITE

ILLNESS n disease or indisposition

ILLNESSES > ILLNESS

ILLOGIC n reasoning characterized by lack of logic

ILLOGICAL adj unreasonable

ILLOGICS > ILLOGIC

ILLS > ILL

ILLTH n condition of poverty or misery

ILLTHS > ILLTH

ILLUDE vb trick or deceive

ILLUDED > ILLUDE

ILLUDES > ILLUDE

ILLUDING > ILLUDE

ILLUME vb illuminate

ILLUMED > ILLUME

ILLUMES > ILLUME

ILLUMINE vb throw light in or into

ILLUMINED > ILLUMINE

ILLUMINER n illuminator

ILLUMINES > ILLUMINE

ILLUMING > ILLUME

ILLUPI same as > ILLIPE

ILLUPIS > ILLUPI

ILLUSION n deceptive appearance or belief

ILLUSIONS > ILLUSION

ILLUSIVE same as > ILLUSORY

ILLUSORY adj seeming to be true, but actually false

ILLUVIA > ILLUVIUM

ILLUVIAL > ILLUVIUM

ILLUVIATE vb deposit illuvium

ILLUVIUM n material, which includes colloids and mineral salts, that is washed down from one layer of soil to a lower layer

ILLUVIUMS > ILLUVIUM

ILLY adv badly

ILMENITE n black mineral found in igneous rocks as layered deposits and in veins

ILMENITES > ILMENITE

IMAGE n mental picture of someone or something ▷ vb picture in the mind

IMAGEABLE > IMAGE

IMAGED > IMAGE

IMAGELESS > IMAGE

IMAGER n device that produces images

IMAGERIES > IMAGERY

IMAGERS > IMAGER

IMAGERY n images collectively, esp in the arts

IMAGES > IMAGE

IMAGINAL adj of, relating to, or resembling an imago

IMAGINARY adj existing only in the imagination

IMAGINE vb form a mental image of ▷ sentence substitute exclamation of surprise

IMAGINED > IMAGINE

IMAGINEER n person skilled in devising or implementing creative ideas ▷ vb devise and implement (a creative idea)

IMAGINER > IMAGINE

IMAGINERS > IMAGINE

IMAGINES > IMAGO

IMAGING > IMAGE

IMAGINGS > IMAGE

IMAGINING > IMAGINE

IMAGINIST n imaginative person

IMAGISM n poetic movement in England and America between 1912 and 1917

IMAGISMS > IMAGISM

IMAGIST > IMAGISM

IMAGISTIC > IMAGISM

IMAGISTS > IMAGISM

IMAGO n sexually mature adult insect

IMAGOES > IMAGO

IMAGOS > IMAGO

IMAM n leader of prayers in a mosque

IMAMATE n region or territory governed by an imam

IMAMATES > IMAMATE

IMAMS > IMAM

IMARET n (in Turkey) a hospice for pilgrims or travellers

IMARETS > IMARET

IMARI n Japanese porcelain

IMARIS > IMARI

IMAUM same as > IMAM

IMAUMS > IMAUM

IMBALANCE n lack of balance or proportion

IMBALM same as > EMBALM

IMBALMED > IMBALM

IMBALMER > IMBALM

IMBALMERS > IMBALM

IMBALMING > IMBALM

IMBALMS > IMBALM

IMBAR vb bar in

IMBARK vb cover in bark

IMBARKED > IMBARK

IMBARKING > IMBARK

IMBARKS > IMBARK

IMBARRED > IMBAR

IMBARRING > IMBAR

IMBARS > IMBAR

IMBASE vb degrade

IMBASED > IMBASE

IMBASES > IMBASE

IMBASING > IMBASE

IMBATHE vb bathe

IMBATHED > IMBATHE

IMBATHES > IMBATHE

IMBATHING > IMBATHE

IMBECILE n stupid person ▷ adj stupid or senseless

IMBECILES > IMBECILE

IMBECILIC > IMBECILE

IMBED same as > EMBED

IMBEDDED > IMBED

IMBEDDING > IMBED

IMBEDS > IMBED

IMBIBE vb drink (alcoholic drinks)

IMBIBED > IMBIBE

IMBIBER > IMBIBE

IMBIBERS > IMBIBE

IMBIBES > IMBIBE

IMBIBING > IMBIBE

IMBITTER same as > EMBITTER

IMBITTERS > IMBITTER

IMBIZO n meeting, esp a gathering of the Zulu

people called by the king or a traditional leader
IMBIZOS > IMBIZO
IMBLAZE vb depict heraldically
IMBLAZED > IMBLAZE
IMBLAZES > IMBLAZE
IMBLAZING > IMBLAZE
IMBODIED > IMBODY
IMBODIES > IMBODY
IMBODY same as > EMBODY
IMBODYING > IMBODY
IMBOLDEN same as > EMBOLDEN
IMBOLDENS > IMBOLDEN
IMBORDER vb enclose in a border
IMBORDERS > IMBORDER
IMBOSK vb conceal
IMBOSKED > IMBOSK
IMBOSKING > IMBOSK
IMBOSKS > IMBOSK
IMBOSOM vb hold in one's heart
IMBOSOMED > IMBOSOM
IMBOSOMS > IMBOSOM
IMBOSS same as > EMBOSS
IMBOSSED > IMBOSS
IMBOSSES > IMBOSS
IMBOSSING > IMBOSS
IMBOWER vb enclose in a bower
IMBOWERED > IMBOWER
IMBOWERS > IMBOWER
IMBRANGLE vb entangle
IMBRAST Spenserian past participle of > EMBRACE
IMBREX n curved tile
IMBRICATE adj having tiles or slates that overlap ▷ vb decorate with a repeating pattern resembling scales or overlapping tiles
IMBRICES > IMBREX
IMBROGLIO n confusing and complicated situation
IMBROWN vb make brown
IMBROWNED > IMBROWN
IMBROWNS > IMBROWN
IMBRUE vb stain, esp with blood
IMBRUED > IMBRUE
IMBRUES > IMBRUE
IMBRUING > IMBRUE
IMBRUTE vb reduce to a bestial state
IMBRUTED > IMBRUTE
IMBRUTES > IMBRUTE
IMBRUTING > IMBRUTE
IMBUE vb fill or inspire with (ideals or principles)
IMBUED > IMBUE
IMBUEMENT > IMBUE
IMBUES > IMBUE
IMBUING > IMBUE
IMBURSE vb pay
IMBURSED > IMBURSE
IMBURSES > IMBURSE
IMBURSING > IMBURSE
IMID n immunomodulatory drug
IMIDAZOLE n white crystalline basic

heterocyclic compound
IMIDE n any of a class of organic compounds
IMIDES > IMIDE
IMIDIC > IMIDE
IMIDO > IMIDE
IMIDS > IMID
IMINAZOLE same as > IMIDAZOLE
IMINE n any of a class of organic compounds
IMINES > IMINE
IMINO > IMINE
IMINOUREA another name for > GUANIDINE
IMITABLE > IMITATE
IMITANCY n tendency to imitate
IMITANT same as > IMITATION
IMITANTS > IMITANT
IMITATE vb take as a model
IMITATED > IMITATE
IMITATES > IMITATE
IMITATING > IMITATE
IMITATION n copy of an original ▷ adj made to look like a material of superior quality
IMITATIVE adj imitating or tending to copy
IMITATOR > IMITATE
IMITATORS > IMITATE
IMMANACLE vb fetter
IMMANE adj monstrous
IMMANELY > IMMANE
IMMANENCE > IMMANENT
IMMANENCY > IMMANENT
IMMANENT adj present within and throughout something
IMMANITY > IMMANE
IMMANTLE vb cover with a mantle
IMMANTLED > IMMANTLE
IMMANTLES > IMMANTLE
IMMASK vb disguise
IMMASKED > IMMASK
IMMASKING > IMMASK
IMMASKS > IMMASK
IMMATURE n young animal ▷ adj not fully developed
IMMATURES > IMMATURE
IMMEDIACY > IMMEDIATE
IMMEDIATE adj occurring at once
IMMENSE adj extremely large
IMMENSELY > IMMENSE
IMMENSER > IMMENSE
IMMENSEST > IMMENSE
IMMENSITY n state or quality of being immense
IMMERGE archaic word for > IMMERSE
IMMERGED > IMMERGE
IMMERGES > IMMERGE
IMMERGING > IMMERGE
IMMERSE vb involve deeply, engross
IMMERSED adj sunk or submerged

IMMERSER > IMMERSE
IMMERSERS > IMMERSE
IMMERSES > IMMERSE
IMMERSING > IMMERSE
IMMERSION n form of baptism in which part or the whole of a person's body is submerged in the water
IMMERSIVE adj providing information or stimulation for a number of senses, not only sight and sound
IMMESH variant of > ENMESH
IMMESHED > IMMESH
IMMESHES > IMMESH
IMMESHING > IMMESH
IMMEW vb confine
IMMEWED > IMMEW
IMMEWING > IMMEW
IMMEWS > IMMEW
IMMIES > IMMY
IMMIGRANT n person who comes to a foreign country in order to settle there
IMMIGRATE vb come to a place or country of which one is not a native in order to settle there
IMMINENCE > IMMINENT
IMMINENCY > IMMINENT
IMMINENT adj about to happen
IMMINGLE vb blend or mix together
IMMINGLED > IMMINGLE
IMMINGLES > IMMINGLE
IMMINUTE adj reduced
IMMISSION n insertion
IMMIT vb insert
IMMITS > IMMIT
IMMITTED > IMMIT
IMMITTING > IMMIT
IMMIX vb mix in
IMMIXED > IMMIX
IMMIXES > IMMIX
IMMIXING > IMMIX
IMMIXTURE > IMMIX
IMMOBILE adj not moving
IMMODEST adj behaving in an indecent or improper manner
IMMODESTY > IMMODEST
IMMOLATE vb kill as a sacrifice
IMMOLATED > IMMOLATE
IMMOLATES > IMMOLATE
IMMOLATOR > IMMOLATE
IMMOMENT adj of no value
IMMORAL adj morally wrong, corrupt
IMMORALLY > IMMORAL
IMMORTAL adj living forever ▷ n person whose fame will last for all time
IMMORTALS > IMMORTAL
IMMOTILE adj (esp of living organisms or their parts) not capable of moving spontaneously and independently.
IMMOVABLE adj unable to be moved

IMMOVABLY > IMMOVABLE
IMMUNE adj protected against a specific disease ▷ n immune person or animal
IMMUNES > IMMUNE
IMMUNISE same as > IMMUNIZE
IMMUNISED > IMMUNISE
IMMUNISER > IMMUNISE
IMMUNISES > IMMUNISE
IMMUNITY n ability to resist disease
IMMUNIZE vb make immune to a disease
IMMUNIZED > IMMUNIZE
IMMUNIZER > IMMUNIZE
IMMUNIZES > IMMUNIZE
IMMUNOGEN n any substance that evokes an immune response
IMMURE vb imprison
IMMURED > IMMURE
IMMURES > IMMURE
IMMURING > IMMURE
IMMUTABLE adj unchangeable
IMMUTABLY > IMMUTABLE
IMMY n image-orthicon camera
IMP n (in folklore) mischievous small creature with magical powers ▷ vb insert (new feathers) into the stumps of broken feathers in order to repair the wing of a hawk or falcon
IMPACABLE adj incapable of being placated or pacified
IMPACT n strong effect ▷ vb have a strong effect on
IMPACTED > IMPACT
IMPACTER > IMPACT
IMPACTERS > IMPACT
IMPACTFUL > IMPACT
IMPACTING > IMPACT
IMPACTION > IMPACT
IMPACTITE n glassy rock formed in a meteor collision
IMPACTIVE adj of or relating to a physical impact
IMPACTOR > IMPACT
IMPACTORS > IMPACT
IMPACTS > IMPACT
IMPAINT vb paint
IMPAINTED > IMPAINT
IMPAINTS > IMPAINT
IMPAIR vb weaken or damage
IMPAIRED > IMPAIR
IMPAIRER > IMPAIR
IMPAIRERS > IMPAIR
IMPAIRING > IMPAIR
IMPAIRS > IMPAIR
IMPALA n southern African antelope
IMPALAS > IMPALA
IMPALE vb pierce with a sharp object

IMPALED > IMPALE
IMPALER > IMPALE
IMPALERS > IMPALE
IMPALES > IMPALE
IMPALING > IMPALE
IMPANATE adj embodied in bread
IMPANEL variant spelling (esp US) of > EMPANEL
IMPANELED > IMPANEL
IMPANELS > IMPANEL
IMPANNEL same as > IMPANEL
IMPANNELS > IMPANNEL
IMPARITY less common word for > DISPARITY
IMPARK vb make into a park
IMPARKED > IMPARK
IMPARKING > IMPARK
IMPARKS > IMPARK
IMPARL vb parley
IMPARLED > IMPARL
IMPARLING > IMPARL
IMPARLS > IMPARL
IMPART vb communicate (information)
IMPARTED > IMPART
IMPARTER > IMPART
IMPARTERS > IMPART
IMPARTIAL adj not favouring one side or the other
IMPARTING > IMPART
IMPARTS > IMPART
IMPASSE n situation in which progress is impossible
IMPASSES > IMPASSE
IMPASSION vb arouse the passions of
IMPASSIVE adj showing no emotion, calm
IMPASTE vb apply paint thickly to
IMPASTED > IMPASTE
IMPASTES > IMPASTE
IMPASTING > IMPASTE
IMPASTO n technique of applying paint thickly, so that brush marks are evident ▷ vb apply impasto
IMPASTOED > IMPASTO
IMPASTOS > IMPASTO
IMPATIENS n plant such as balsam, touch-me-not, busy Lizzie, and policeman's helmet
IMPATIENT adj irritable at any delay or difficulty
IMPAVE vb set in a pavement
IMPAVED > IMPAVE
IMPAVES > IMPAVE
IMPAVID adj fearless
IMPAVIDLY > IMPAVID
IMPAVING > IMPAVE
IMPAWN vb pawn
IMPAWNED > IMPAWN
IMPAWNING > IMPAWN
IMPAWNS > IMPAWN
IMPEACH vb charge with a serious crime against the state

IMPEACHED > IMPEACH
IMPEACHER > IMPEACH
IMPEACHES > IMPEACH
IMPEARL vb adorn with pearls
IMPEARLED > IMPEARL
IMPEARLS > IMPEARL
IMPECCANT adj not sinning
IMPED > IMP
IMPEDANCE n measure of the opposition to the flow of an alternating current
IMPEDE vb hinder in action or progress
IMPEDED > IMPEDE
IMPEDER > IMPEDE
IMPEDERS > IMPEDE
IMPEDES > IMPEDE
IMPEDING > IMPEDE
IMPEDOR n component, such as an inductor or resistor, that offers impedance
IMPEDORS > IMPEDOR
IMPEL vb push or force (someone) to do something
IMPELLED > IMPEL
IMPELLENT > IMPEL
IMPELLER n vaned rotating disc of a centrifugal pump, compressor, etc
IMPELLERS > IMPELLER
IMPELLING > IMPEL
IMPELLOR same as > IMPELLER
IMPELLORS > IMPELLOR
IMPELS > IMPEL
IMPEND vb (esp of something threatening) to be about to happen
IMPENDED > IMPEND
IMPENDENT > IMPEND
IMPENDING > IMPEND
IMPENDS > IMPEND
IMPENNATE adj (of birds) lacking true functional wings or feathers
IMPERATOR n (in imperial Rome) a title of the emperor
IMPERFECT adj having faults or mistakes ▷ n imperfect tense
IMPERIA > IMPERIUM
IMPERIAL adj of or like an empire or emperor ▷ n wine bottle holding the equivalent of eight normal bottles
IMPERIALS > IMPERIAL
IMPERIL vb put in danger
IMPERILED > IMPERIL
IMPERILS > IMPERIL
IMPERIOUS adj proud and domineering
IMPERIUM n (in ancient Rome) the supreme power, held esp by consuls and emperors, to command and administer in military, judicial, and civil affairs
IMPERIUMS > IMPERIUM
IMPETICOS vb put in a

pocket
IMPETIGO n contagious skin disease
IMPETIGOS > IMPETIGO
IMPETRATE vb supplicate or entreat for, esp by prayer
IMPETUOUS adj done or acting without thought, rash
IMPETUS n incentive, impulse
IMPETUSES > IMPETUS
IMPHEE n African sugar cane
IMPHEES > IMPHEE
IMPI n group of Zulu warriors
IMPIES > IMPI
IMPIETIES > IMPIETY
IMPIETY n lack of respect or religious reverence
IMPING > IMP
IMPINGE vb affect or restrict
IMPINGED > IMPINGE
IMPINGENT > IMPINGE
IMPINGER > IMPINGE
IMPINGERS > IMPINGE
IMPINGES > IMPINGE
IMPINGING > IMPINGE
IMPINGS > IMP
IMPIOUS adj showing a lack of respect or reverence
IMPIOUSLY > IMPIOUS
IMPIS > IMPI
IMPISH adj mischievous
IMPISHLY > IMPISH
IMPLANT n something put into someone's body, usu. by surgical operation ▷ vb put (something) into someone's body, usu. by surgical operation
IMPLANTED > IMPLANT
IMPLANTER > IMPLANT
IMPLANTS > IMPLANT
IMPLATE vb sheathe
IMPLATED > IMPLATE
IMPLATES > IMPLATE
IMPLATING > IMPLATE
IMPLEACH vb intertwine
IMPLEAD vb sue or prosecute
IMPLEADED > IMPLEAD
IMPLEADER > IMPLEAD
IMPLEADS > IMPLEAD
IMPLED > IMPLEAD
IMPLEDGE vb pledge
IMPLEDGED > IMPLEDGE
IMPLEDGES > IMPLEDGE
IMPLEMENT vb carry out (instructions etc) ▷ n tool, instrument
IMPLETE vb fill
IMPLETED > IMPLETE
IMPLETES > IMPLETE
IMPLETING > IMPLETE
IMPLETION > IMPLETE
IMPLEX n part of an arthropod
IMPLEXES > IMPLEX
IMPLEXION n complication
IMPLICATE vb show to be

involved, esp in a crime
IMPLICIT adj expressed indirectly
IMPLICITY > IMPLICIT
IMPLIED adj hinted at or suggested
IMPLIEDLY > IMPLIED
IMPLIES > IMPLY
IMPLODE vb collapse inwards
IMPLODED > IMPLODE
IMPLODENT n sound of an implosion
IMPLODES > IMPLODE
IMPLODING > IMPLODE
IMPLORE vb beg earnestly
IMPLORED > IMPLORE
IMPLORER > IMPLORE
IMPLORERS > IMPLORE
IMPLORES > IMPLORE
IMPLORING > IMPLORE
IMPLOSION n act or process of imploding
IMPLOSIVE n consonant pronounced in a particular way
IMPLUNGE vb submerge
IMPLUNGED > IMPLUNGE
IMPLUNGES > IMPLUNGE
IMPLUVIA > IMPLUVIUM
IMPLUVIUM n rain-filled water tank
IMPLY vb indicate by hinting, suggest
IMPLYING > IMPLY
IMPOCKET vb put in a pocket
IMPOCKETS > IMPOCKET
IMPOLDER vb make into a polder
IMPOLDERS > IMPOLDER
IMPOLICY n act or an instance of being unjudicious or impolitic
IMPOLITE adj showing bad manners
IMPOLITER > IMPOLITE
IMPOLITIC adj unwise or inadvisable
IMPONE vb impose
IMPONED > IMPONE
IMPONENT n person who imposes a duty, etc
IMPONENTS > IMPONENT
IMPONES > IMPONE
IMPONING > IMPONE
IMPOROUS adj not porous
IMPORT vb bring in (goods) from another country ▷ n something imported
IMPORTANT adj of great significance or value
IMPORTED > IMPORT
IMPORTER > IMPORT
IMPORTERS > IMPORT
IMPORTING > IMPORT
IMPORTS > IMPORT
IMPORTUNE vb harass with persistent requests
IMPOSABLE > IMPOSE
IMPOSE vb force the acceptance of
IMPOSED > IMPOSE
IMPOSER > IMPOSE

IMPOSERS > IMPOSE

IMPOSES > IMPOSE

IMPOSEX n imposition of male sexual characteristics on female gastropods, caused by pollutants

IMPOSEXES > IMPOSEX

IMPOSING adj grand, impressive

IMPOST n tax, esp a customs duty ▷ vb classify (imported goods) according to the duty payable on them

IMPOSTED > IMPOST

IMPOSTER > IMPOST

IMPOSTERS > IMPOST

IMPOSTING > IMPOST

IMPOSTOR n person who cheats or swindles by pretending to be someone else

IMPOSTORS > IMPOSTOR

IMPOSTS > IMPOST

IMPOSTUME archaic word for > ABSCESS

IMPOSTURE n deception, esp by pretending to be someone else

IMPOT n slang term for the act of imposing

IMPOTENCE > IMPOTENT

IMPOTENCY > IMPOTENT

IMPOTENT n one who is impotent ▷ adj powerless

IMPOTENTS > IMPOTENT

IMPOTS > IMPOT

IMPOUND vb take legal possession of, confiscate

IMPOUNDED > IMPOUND

IMPOUNDER > IMPOUND

IMPOUNDS > IMPOUND

IMPOWER less common spelling of > EMPOWER

IMPOWERED > IMPOWER

IMPOWERS > IMPOWER

IMPRECATE vb swear, curse, or blaspheme

IMPRECISE adj inexact or inaccurate

IMPREGN vb impregnate

IMPREGNED > IMPREGN

IMPREGNS > IMPREGN

IMPRESA n heraldic device

IMPRESARI n impresarios

IMPRESAS > IMPRESA

IMPRESE same as > IMPRESA

IMPRESES > IMPRESE

IMPRESS vb affect strongly, usu. favourably ▷ n impressing

IMPRESSE n heraldic device

IMPRESSED > IMPRESS

IMPRESSER > IMPRESS

IMPRESSES > IMPRESS

IMPREST n fund of cash from which a department or other unit pays incidental expenses, topped up periodically from central funds

IMPRESTS > IMPREST

IMPRIMIS adv in the first place

IMPRINT n mark made by printing or stamping ▷ vb produce (a mark) by printing or stamping

IMPRINTED > IMPRINT

IMPRINTER > IMPRINT

IMPRINTS > IMPRINT

IMPRISON vb put in prison

IMPRISONS > IMPRISON

IMPROBITY n dishonesty or wickedness

IMPROMPTU adj without planning or preparation ▷ adv in a spontaneous or improvised way ▷ n short piece of instrumental music resembling improvisation

IMPROPER adj indecent

IMPROV n improvisational comedy

IMPROVE vb make or become better

IMPROVED > IMPROVE

IMPROVER > IMPROVE

IMPROVERS > IMPROVE

IMPROVES > IMPROVE

IMPROVING > IMPROVE

IMPROVISE vb make use of whatever materials are available

IMPROVS > IMPROV

IMPRUDENT adj not sensible or wise

IMPS > IMP

IMPSONITE n asphaltite compound

IMPUDENCE n quality of being impudent

IMPUDENCY same as > IMPUDENCE

IMPUDENT adj cheeky, disrespectful

IMPUGN vb challenge the truth or validity of

IMPUGNED > IMPUGN

IMPUGNER > IMPUGN

IMPUGNERS > IMPUGN

IMPUGNING > IMPUGN

IMPUGNS > IMPUGN

IMPULSE vb give an impulse to ▷ n sudden urge to do something

IMPULSED > IMPULSE

IMPULSES > IMPULSE

IMPULSING > IMPULSE

IMPULSION n act of impelling or the state of being impelled

IMPULSIVE adj acting or done without careful consideration

IMPUNDULU n mythical bird associated with witchcraft, frequently manifested as the secretary bird

IMPUNITY n exemption or immunity from punishment or recrimination

IMPURE adj having dirty or unwanted substances mixed in

IMPURELY > IMPURE

IMPURER > IMPURE

IMPUREST > IMPURE

IMPURITY n impure element or thing

IMPURPLE vb colour purple

IMPURPLED > IMPURPLE

IMPURPLES > IMPURPLE

IMPUTABLE adj capable of being imputed

IMPUTABLY > IMPUTABLE

IMPUTE vb attribute responsibility to

IMPUTED > IMPUTE

IMPUTER > IMPUTE

IMPUTERS > IMPUTE

IMPUTES > IMPUTE

IMPUTING > IMPUTE

IMSHI interj go away!

IMSHY same as > IMSHI

IN prep indicating position inside, state or situation, etc ▷ adv indicating position inside, entry into, etc ▷ adj fashionable ▷ n way of approaching or befriending a person

INABILITY n lack of means or skill to do something

INACTION n act of doing nothing

INACTIONS > INACTION

INACTIVE adj idle

INAIDABLE adj beyond help

INAMORATA n woman with whom one is in love

INAMORATO n man with whom one is in love

INANE adj senseless, silly ▷ n something that is inane

INANELY > INANE

INANENESS > INANE

INANER > INANE

INANES > INANE

INANEST > INANE

INANGA n common type of New Zealand grass tree

INANGAS > INANGA

INANIMATE adj not living

INANITIES > INANITY

INANITION n exhaustion or weakness, as from lack of food

INANITY n lack of intelligence or imagination

INAPT adj not apt or fitting

INAPTLY > INAPT

INAPTNESS > INAPT

INARABLE adj not arable

INARCH vb graft (a plant) by uniting stock and scion while both are still growing independently

INARCHED > INARCH

INARCHES > INARCH

INARCHING > INARCH

INARM vb embrace

INARMED > INARM

INARMING > INARM

INARMS > INARM

INASMUCH as in inasmuch as, in view of the fact that

INAUDIBLE adj not loud enough to be heard

INAUDIBLY > INAUDIBLE

INAUGURAL adj of or for an inauguration ▷ n speech made at an inauguration

INAURATE adj gilded

INBEING n existence in something else

INBEINGS > INBEING

INBENT adj bent inwards

INBOARD adj (of a boat's engine) inside the hull ▷ adv within the sides of or towards the centre of a vessel or aircraft

INBOARDS same as > INBOARD

INBORN adj existing from birth, natural

INBOUND vb pass into the playing area from outside it ▷ adj coming in

INBOUNDED > INBOUND

INBOUNDS > INBOUND

INBOX n folder which stores in-coming email messages

INBOXES > INBOX

INBREAK n breaking in

INBREAKS > INBREAK

INBREATHE vb infuse or imbue

INBRED n inbred person or animal ▷ adj produced as a result of inbreeding

INBREDS > INBRED

INBREED vb breed from closely related individuals

INBREEDER > INBREED

INBREEDS > INBREED

INBRING vb bring in

INBRINGS > INBRING

INBROUGHT > INBRING

INBUILT adj present from the start

INBURNING adj burning within

INBURST n irruption

INBURSTS > INBURST

INBY adv into the house or an inner room ▷ adj located near or nearest to the house

INBYE adv near the house

INCAGE vb confine in or as in a cage

INCAGED > INCAGE

INCAGES > INCAGE

INCAGING > INCAGE

INCANT vb chant (a spell)

INCANTED > INCANT

INCANTING > INCANT

INCANTS > INCANT

INCAPABLE adj unable (to do something)

INCAPABLY > INCAPABLE

INCARNATE adj in human form ▷ vb give a bodily or concrete form to

INCASE *variant spelling of* > ENCASE

INCASED > INCASE

INCASES > INCASE

INCASING > INCASE

INCAUTION *n* act of not being cautious

INCAVE *vb* hide

INCAVED > INCAVE

INCAVES > INCAVE

INCAVI > INCAVO

INCAVING > INCAVE

INCAVO *n* incised part of a carving

INCEDE *vb* advance

INCEDED > INCEDE

INCEDES > INCEDE

INCEDING > INCEDE

INCENSE *vb* make very angry ▷ *n* substance that gives off a sweet perfume when burned

INCENSED > INCENSE

INCENSER *n* incense burner

INCENSERS > INCENSER

INCENSES > INCENSE

INCENSING > INCENSE

INCENSOR *n* incense burner

INCENSORS > INCENSOR

INCENSORY *less common name for* > CENSER

INCENT *vb* provide incentive

INCENTED > INCENT

INCENTER *same as* > INCENTRE

INCENTERS > INCENTER

INCENTING > INCENT

INCENTIVE *n* something that encourages effort or action ▷ *adj* encouraging greater effort

INCENTRE *n* centre of an inscribed circle

INCENTRES > INCENTRE

INCENTS > INCENT

INCEPT *vb* (of organisms) to ingest (food) ▷ *n* rudimentary organ

INCEPTED > INCEPT

INCEPTING > INCEPT

INCEPTION *n* beginning

INCEPTIVE *adj* beginning ▷ *n* type of verb

INCEPTOR > INCEPT

INCEPTORS > INCEPT

INCEPTS > INCEPT

INCERTAIN *archaic form of* > UNCERTAIN

INCESSANT *adj* never stopping

INCEST *n* sexual intercourse between two people too closely related to marry

INCESTS > INCEST

INCH *n* unit of length equal to one twelfth of a foot or 2.54 centimetres ▷ *vb* move slowly and gradually

INCHASE *same as* > ENCHASE

INCHASED > INCHASE

INCHASES > INCHASE

INCHASING > INCHASE

INCHED > INCH

INCHER *n* something measuring given amount of inches

INCHERS > INCHER

INCHES > INCH

INCHING > INCH

INCHMEAL *adv* gradually

INCHOATE *adj* just begun and not yet properly developed ▷ *vb* begin

INCHOATED > INCHOATE

INCHOATES > INCHOATE

INCHPIN *n* cervine sweetbread

INCHPINS > INCHPIN

INCHWORM *n* larva of a type of moth

INCHWORMS > INCHWORM

INCIDENCE *n* extent or frequency of occurrence

INCIDENT *n* something that happens ▷ *adj* related (to) or dependent (on)

INCIDENTS > INCIDENT

INCIPIENT *adj* just starting to appear or happen

INCIPIT *n* Latin introductory phrase

INCIPITS > INCIPIT

INCISAL *adj* relating to the cutting edge of incisors and cuspids

INCISE *vb* cut into with a sharp tool

INCISED > INCISE

INCISES > INCISE

INCISING > INCISE

INCISION *n* cut, esp one made during a surgical operation

INCISIONS > INCISION

INCISIVE *adj* direct and forceful

INCISOR *n* front tooth, used for biting into food

INCISORS > INCISOR

INCISORY > INCISOR

INCISURAL > INCISURE

INCISURE *n* incision or notch in an organ or part

INCISURES > INCISURE

INCITABLE > INCITE

INCITANT *n* something that incites

INCITANTS > INCITANT

INCITE *vb* stir up, provoke

INCITED > INCITE

INCITER > INCITE

INCITERS > INCITE

INCITES > INCITE

INCITING > INCITE

INCIVIL *archaic form of* > UNCIVIL

INCIVISM *n* neglect of a citizen's duties

INCIVISMS > INCIVISM

INCLASP *vb* clasp

INCLASPED > INCLASP

INCLASPS > INCLASP

INCLE *same as* > INKLE

INCLEMENT *adj* (of weather) stormy or severe

INCLES > INCLE

INCLINE *vb* lean, slope ▷ *n* slope

INCLINED *adj* having a disposition

INCLINER > INCLINE

INCLINERS > INCLINE

INCLINES > INCLINE

INCLINING > INCLINE

INCLIP *vb* embrace

INCLIPPED > INCLIP

INCLIPS > INCLIP

INCLOSE *less common spelling of* > ENCLOSE

INCLOSED > INCLOSE

INCLOSER > INCLOSE

INCLOSERS > INCLOSE

INCLOSES > INCLOSE

INCLOSING > INCLOSE

INCLOSURE > INCLOSE

INCLUDE *vb* have as part of the whole

INCLUDED *adj* (of the stamens or pistils of a flower) not protruding beyond the corolla

INCLUDES > INCLUDE

INCLUDING > INCLUDE

INCLUSION *n* including or being included

INCLUSIVE *adj* including everything (specified)

INCOG *n* incognito

INCOGNITA *n* female who is in disguise or unknown

INCOGNITO *adv* having adopted a false identity ▷ *n* false identity ▷ *adj* under an assumed name or appearance

INCOGS > INCOG

INCOME *n* amount of money earned from work, investments, etc

INCOMER *n* person who comes to live in a place in which he or she was not born

INCOMERS > INCOMER

INCOMES > INCOME

INCOMING *adj* coming in ▷ *n* act of coming in

INCOMINGS > INCOMING

INCOMMODE *vb* cause inconvenience to

INCOMPACT *adj* not compact

INCONDITE *adj* poorly constructed or composed

INCONIE *adj* fine or delicate

INCONNU *n* whitefish of Arctic waters

INCONNUE *n* unknown woman

INCONNUES > INCONNUE

INCONNUS > INCONNU

INCONY *adj* fine or delicate

INCORPSE *vb* incorporate

INCORPSED > INCORPSE

INCORPSES > INCORPSE

INCORRECT *adj* wrong

INCORRUPT *adj* free from corruption

INCREASE *vb* make or become greater in size, number, etc ▷ *n* rise in number, size, etc

INCREASED > INCREASE

INCREASER > INCREASE

INCREASES > INCREASE

INCREATE *adj* (esp of gods) never having been created

INCREMATE *vb* cremate

INCREMENT *n* increase in money or value, esp a regular salary increase

INCRETION *n* direct secretion into the bloodstream, esp of a hormone from an endocrine gland

INCRETORY > INCRETION

INCROSS *n* plant or animal produced by continued inbreeding ▷ *vb* inbreed or produce by inbreeding

INCROSSED > INCROSS

INCROSSES > INCROSS

INCRUST *same as* > ENCRUST

INCRUSTED > INCRUST

INCRUSTS > INCRUST

INCUBATE *vb* (of a bird) hatch (eggs) by sitting on them

INCUBATED > INCUBATE

INCUBATES > INCUBATE

INCUBATOR *n* heated enclosed apparatus for rearing premature babies

INCUBI > INCUBUS

INCUBOUS *adj* (of a liverwort) having the leaves arranged so that the upper margin of each leaf lies above the lower margin of the next leaf along

INCUBUS *n* (in folklore) demon believed to have sex with sleeping women

INCUBUSES > INCUBUS

INCUDAL > INCUS

INCUDATE > INCUS

INCUDES > INCUS

INCULCATE *vb* fix in someone's mind by constant repetition

INCULPATE *vb* cause (someone) to be blamed for a crime

INCULT *adj* (of land) uncultivated

INCUMBENT *n* person who holds a particular office or position ▷ *adj* morally binding as a duty

INCUMBER *less common spelling of* > ENCUMBER

INCUMBERS > INCUMBER

INCUNABLE *n* early printed book

INCUR *vb* cause (something unpleasant) to happen

INCURABLE adj not able to be cured ▷ n person with an incurable disease

INCURABLY > INCURABLE

INCURIOUS adj showing no curiosity or interest

INCURRED > INCUR

INCURRENT adj (of anatomical ducts, tubes, channels, etc) having an inward flow

INCURRING > INCUR

INCURS > INCUR

INCURSION n sudden brief invasion

INCURSIVE > INCURSION

INCURVATE vb curve or cause to curve inwards ▷ adj curved inwards

INCURVE vb curve or cause to curve inwards

INCURVED > INCURVE

INCURVES > INCURVE

INCURVING > INCURVE

INCURVITY > INCURVE

INCUS n central of the three small bones in the middle ear of mammals

INCUSE n design stamped or hammered onto a coin ▷ vb impress (a design) in a coin or to impress (a coin) with a design by hammering or stamping ▷ adj stamped or hammered onto a coin

INCUSED > INCUSE

INCUSES > INCUSE

INCUSING > INCUSE

INCUT adj cut or etched in

INDABA n (among native peoples of southern Africa) a meeting to discuss a serious topic

INDABAS > INDABA

INDAGATE vb investigate

INDAGATED > INDAGATE

INDAGATES > INDAGATE

INDAGATOR > INDAGATE

INDAMIN same as > INDAMINE

INDAMINE n organic base used in the production of the dye safranine

INDAMINES > INDAMINE

INDAMINS > INDAMIN

INDART vb dart in

INDARTED > INDART

INDARTING > INDART

INDARTS > INDART

INDEBTED adj owing gratitude for help or favours

INDECENCY n state or quality of being indecent

INDECENT adj morally or sexually offensive

INDECORUM n indecorous behaviour or speech

INDEED adv really, certainly ▷ interj expression of indignation or surprise

INDELIBLE adj impossible to erase or remove

INDELIBLY > INDELIBLE

INDEMNIFY vb secure against loss, damage, or liability

INDEMNITY n insurance against loss or damage

INDENE n colourless liquid hydrocarbon extracted from petroleum and coal tar and used in making synthetic resins

INDENES > INDENE

INDENT vb make a dent in

INDENTED > INDENT

INDENTER > INDENT

INDENTERS > INDENT

INDENTING > INDENT

INDENTION n space between a margin and the start of the line of text

INDENTOR > INDENT

INDENTORS > INDENT

INDENTS > INDENT

INDENTURE n contract, esp one binding an apprentice to his or her employer ▷ vb bind (an apprentice) by indenture

INDEVOUT adj not devout

INDEW same as > INDUE

INDEWED > INDEW

INDEWING > INDEW

INDEWS > INDEW

INDEX n alphabetical list of names or subjects dealt with in a book ▷ vb provide (a book) with an index

INDEXABLE > INDEX

INDEXAL > INDEX

INDEXED > INDEX

INDEXER > INDEX

INDEXERS > INDEX

INDEXES > INDEX

INDEXICAL adj arranged as or relating to an index or indexes ▷ n term whose reference depends on the context of utterance

INDEXING > INDEX

INDEXINGS > INDEX

INDEXLESS > INDEX

INDIA n code word for the letter I

INDIAS > INDIA

INDICAN n compound secreted in the urine, usually in the form of its potassium salt

INDICANS > INDICAN

INDICANT n something that indicates

INDICANTS > INDICANT

INDICATE vb be a sign or symptom of

INDICATED > INDICATE

INDICATES > INDICATE

INDICATOR n something acting as a sign or indication

INDICES plural of > INDEX

INDICIA > INDICIUM

INDICIAL > INDICIUM

INDICIAS > INDICIUM

INDICIUM n notice

INDICIUMS > INDICIUM

INDICT vb formally charge with a crime

INDICTED > INDICT

INDICTEE > INDICT

INDICTEES > INDICT

INDICTER > INDICT

INDICTERS > INDICT

INDICTING > INDICT

INDICTION n recurring fiscal period of 15 years, often used as a unit for dating events

INDICTOR > INDICT

INDICTORS > INDICT

INDICTS > INDICT

INDIE adj (of rock music) released by an independent record company ▷ n independent record company

INDIES > INDIE

INDIGEN same as > INDIGENE

INDIGENCE > INDIGENT

INDIGENCY > INDIGENT

INDIGENE n indigenous person, animal, or thing

INDIGENES > INDIGENE

INDIGENS > INDIGEN

INDIGENT adj extremely poor ▷ n impoverished person

INDIGENTS > INDIGENT

INDIGEST n undigested mass

INDIGESTS > INDIGEST

INDIGN adj undeserving

INDIGNANT adj feeling or showing indignation

INDIGNIFY vb treat in a humiliating manner

INDIGNITY n embarrassing or humiliating treatment

INDIGNLY > INDIGN

INDIGO adj deep violet-blue ▷ n dye of this colour

INDIGOES > INDIGO

INDIGOID adj of, concerned with, or resembling indigo or its blue colour ▷ n any of a number of synthetic dyes or pigments related in chemical structure to indigo

INDIGOIDS > INDIGOID

INDIGOS > INDIGO

INDIGOTIC > INDIGO

INDIGOTIN same as > INDIGO

INDINAVIR n drug used to treat AIDS

INDIRECT adj done or caused by someone or something else

INDIRUBIN n isomer of indigotin

INDISPOSE vb make unwilling or opposed

INDITE vb write

INDITED > INDITE

INDITER > INDITE

INDITERS > INDITE

INDITES > INDITE

INDITING > INDITE

INDIUM n soft silvery-white metallic element

INDIUMS > INDIUM

INDIVIDUA npl indivisible entities

INDOCIBLE same as > INDOCILE

INDOCILE adj difficult to discipline or instruct

INDOL same as > INDOLE

INDOLE n white or yellowish crystalline heterocyclic compound extracted from coal tar and used in perfumery, medicine, and as a flavouring agent

INDOLENCE > INDOLENT

INDOLENCY > INDOLENT

INDOLENT adj lazy

INDOLES > INDOLE

INDOLS > INDOL

INDOOR adj inside a building

INDOORS adj inside or into a building

INDORSE variant spelling of > ENDORSE

INDORSED > INDORSE

INDORSEE > INDORSE

INDORSEES > INDORSE

INDORSER > INDORSE

INDORSERS > INDORSE

INDORSES > INDORSE

INDORSING > INDORSE

INDORSOR > INDORSE

INDORSORS > INDORSE

INDOW archaic variant of > INDOW

INDOWED > INDOW

INDOWING > INDOW

INDOWS > INDOW

INDOXYL n yellow water-soluble crystalline compound occurring in woad as its glucoside and in urine as its ester

INDOXYLS > INDOXYL

INDRAFT same as > INDRAUGHT

INDRAFTS > INDRAFT

INDRAUGHT n act of drawing or pulling in

INDRAWN adj drawn or pulled in

INDRENCH vb submerge

INDRI same as > INDRIS

INDRIS n large Madagascan arboreal lemuroid primate

INDRISES > INDRIS

INDUBIOUS adj certain

INDUCE vb persuade or influence

INDUCED > INDUCE

INDUCER > INDUCE

INDUCERS > INDUCE

INDUCES > INDUCE

INDUCIAE n time limit for a defendant to appear in court

INDUCIBLE > INDUCE

INDUCING > INDUCE

INDUCT vb formally install (someone, esp a clergyman) in office

INDUCTED > INDUCT

INDUCTEE n military conscript

INDUCTEES > INDUCTEE

INDUCTILE adj not ductile, pliant, or yielding

INDUCTING > INDUCT

INDUCTION > INDUCT

INDUCTIVE adj of or using induction

INDUCTOR n device designed to create inductance in an electrical circuit

INDUCTORS > INDUCTOR

INDUCTS > INDUCT

INDUE variant spelling of > ENDUE

INDUED > INDUE

INDUES > INDUE

INDUING > INDUE

INDULGE vb allow oneself pleasure

INDULGED > INDULGE

INDULGENT adj kind or lenient, often to excess

INDULGER > INDULGE

INDULGERS > INDULGE

INDULGES > INDULGE

INDULGING > INDULGE

INDULIN same as > INDULINE

INDULINE n any of a class of blue dyes obtained from aniline and aminoazobenzene

INDULINES > INDULINE

INDULINS > INDULIN

INDULT n faculty granted by the Holy See allowing a specific deviation from the Church's common law

INDULTS > INDULT

INDUMENTA npl outer coverings of feather, fur, etc

INDUNA n (in South Africa) a Black African overseer in a factory, mine, etc

INDUNAS > INDUNA

INDURATE vb make or become hard or callous ▷ adj hardened, callous, or unfeeling

INDURATED > INDURATE

INDURATES > INDURATE

INDUSIA > INDUSIUM

INDUSIAL > INDUSIUM

INDUSIATE adj covered in indusia

INDUSIUM n membranous outgrowth on the undersurface of fern leaves that covers and protects the developing sporangia

INDUSTRY n manufacture of goods

INDUVIAE npl withered leaves

INDUVIAL > INDUVIAE

INDUVIATE > INDUVIAE

INDWELL vb (of a spirit, principle, etc) to inhabit

INDWELLER > INDWELL

INDWELLS > INDWELL

INDWELT > INDWELL

INEARTH poetic word for > BURY

INEARTHED > INEARTH

INEARTHS > INEARTH

INEBRIANT adj causing intoxication, esp drunkenness ▷ n something that inebriates

INEBRIATE adj (person who is) habitually drunk ▷ n person who is habitually drunk ▷ vb make drunk

INEBRIETY > INEBRIATE

INEBRIOUS adj drunk

INEDIBLE adj not fit to be eaten

INEDIBLY > INEDIBLE

INEDITA npl unpublished writings

INEDITED adj not edited

INEFFABLE adj too great for words

INEFFABLY > INEFFABLE

INELASTIC adj not elastic

INELEGANT adj lacking elegance or refinement

INEPT adj clumsy, lacking skill

INEPTER > INEPT

INEPTEST > INEPT

INEPTLY > INEPT

INEPTNESS > INEPT

INEQUABLE adj unfair

INEQUITY n injustice or unfairness

INERM adj without thorns

INERMOUS same as > INERM

INERRABLE adj not liable to error ▷ n person or thing that is incapable of error

INERRABLY > INERRABLE

INERRANCY > INERRABLE

INERRANT same as > INERRABLE

INERT n inert thing ▷ adj without the power of motion or resistance

INERTER > INERT

INERTEST > INERT

INERTIA n feeling of unwillingness to do anything

INERTIAE > INERTIA

INERTIAL > INERTIA

INERTIAS > INERTIA

INERTLY > INERT

INERTNESS > INERT

INERTS > INERT

INERUDITE adj not erudite

INESSIVE n grammatical case in Finnish

INESSIVES > INESSIVE

INEXACT adj not exact or accurate

INEXACTLY > INEXACT

INEXPERT n unskilled person ▷ adj lacking skill

INEXPERTS > INEXPERT

INFALL vb move towards a black hole, etc, under the influence of gravity

INFALLING > INFALL

INFALLS > INFALL

INFAME vb defame

INFAMED > INFAME

INFAMES > INFAME

INFAMIES > INFAMY

INFAMING > INFAME

INFAMISE same as > INFAMIZE

INFAMISED > INFAMISE

INFAMISES > INFAMISE

INFAMIZE vb make infamous

INFAMIZED > INFAMIZE

INFAMIZES > INFAMIZE

INFAMOUS adj well-known for something bad

INFAMY n state of being infamous

INFANCIES > INFANCY

INFANCY n early childhood

INFANT n very young child ▷ adj of, relating to, or designed for young children

INFANTA n (formerly) daughter of a king of Spain or Portugal

INFANTAS > INFANTA

INFANTE n (formerly) any son of a king of Spain or Portugal, except the heir to the throne

INFANTES > INFANTE

INFANTILE adj childish

INFANTINE adj infantile

INFANTRY n soldiers who fight on foot

INFANTS > INFANT

INFARCT n localized area of dead tissue (necrosis) resulting from obstruction of the blood supply to that part, esp by an embolus ▷ vb obstruct the blood supply to part of a body

INFARCTED > INFARCT

INFARCTS > INFARCT

INFARE vb enter

INFARES > INFARE

INFATUATE vb inspire or fill with an intense and unreasoning passion ▷ n person who is infatuated

INFAUNA n animals that live in ocean and river beds

INFAUNAE > INFAUNA

INFAUNAL > INFAUNA

INFAUNAS > INFAUNA

INFAUST adj unlucky

INFECT vb affect with a disease ▷ adj contaminated or polluted with or as if with a disease

INFECTANT adj causing infection

INFECTED > INFECT

INFECTER > INFECT

INFECTERS > INFECT

INFECTING > INFECT

INFECTION n infectious disease

INFECTIVE adj capable of causing infection

INFECTOR > INFECT

INFECTORS > INFECT

INFECTS > INFECT

INFECUND less common word for > INFERTILE

INFEFT vb give possession of heritable property

INFEFTED > INFEFT

INFEFTING > INFEFT

INFEFTS > INFEFT

INFELT adj heartfelt

INFEOFF same as > ENFEOFF

INFEOFFED > INFEOFF

INFEOFFS > INFEOFF

INFER vb work out from evidence

INFERABLE > INFER

INFERABLY > INFER

INFERE adv together

INFERENCE n act or process of reaching a conclusion by reasoning from evidence

INFERIAE npl offerings made to the spirits of the dead

INFERIBLE > INFER

INFERIOR adj lower in quality, position, or status ▷ n person of lower position or status

INFERIORS > INFERIOR

INFERNAL adj of hell

INFERNO n intense raging fire

INFERNOS > INFERNO

INFERRED > INFER

INFERRER > INFER

INFERRERS > INFER

INFERRING > INFER

INFERS > INFER

INFERTILE adj unable to produce offspring

INFEST vb inhabit or overrun in unpleasantly large numbers

INFESTANT n parasite

INFESTED > INFEST

INFESTER > INFEST

INFESTERS > INFEST

INFESTING > INFEST

INFESTS > INFEST

INFICETE adj not witty

INFIDEL n person with no religion ▷ adj of unbelievers or unbelief

INFIDELIC > INFIDEL

INFIDELS > INFIDEL

INFIELD n area of the field near the pitch

INFIELDER n player positioned in the infield

INFIELDS > INFIELD

INFIGHT *vb* box at close quarters
INFIGHTER > INFIGHT
INFIGHTS > INFIGHT
INFILL *vb* fill in ▷ *n* act of filling or closing gaps, etc, in something, such as a row of buildings
INFILLED > INFILL
INFILLING > INFILL
INFILLS > INFILL
INFIMA > INFIMUM
INFIMUM *n* greatest lower bound
INFIMUMS > INFIMUM
INFINITE *adj* without any limit or end ▷ *n* something without any limit or end
INFINITES > INFINITE
INFINITY *n* endless space, time, or number
INFIRM *vb* make infirm ▷ *adj* physically or mentally weak
INFIRMARY *n* hospital
INFIRMED > INFIRM
INFIRMER > INFIRM
INFIRMEST > INFIRM
INFIRMING > INFIRM
INFIRMITY *n* state of being infirm
INFIRMLY > INFIRM
INFIRMS > INFIRM
INFIX *vb* fix firmly in ▷ *n* affix inserted into the middle of a word
INFIXED > INFIX
INFIXES > INFIX
INFIXING > INFIX
INFIXION > INFIX
INFIXIONS > INFIX
INFLAME *vb* make angry or excited
INFLAMED > INFLAME
INFLAMER > INFLAME
INFLAMERS > INFLAME
INFLAMES > INFLAME
INFLAMING > INFLAME
INFLATE *vb* expand by filling with air or gas
INFLATED > INFLATE
INFLATER > INFLATE
INFLATERS > INFLATE
INFLATES > INFLATE
INFLATING > INFLATE
INFLATION *n* inflating
INFLATIVE *adj* causing inflation
INFLATOR > INFLATE
INFLATORS > INFLATE
INFLATUS *n* act of breathing in
INFLECT *vb* change (the voice) in tone or pitch
INFLECTED > INFLECT
INFLECTOR > INFLECT
INFLECTS > INFLECT
INFLEXED *adj* curved or bent inwards and downwards towards the axis
INFLEXION *n* modulation of the voice

INFLEXURE *same as* > INFLEXION
INFLICT *vb* impose (something unpleasant) on
INFLICTED > INFLICT
INFLICTER > INFLICT
INFLICTOR > INFLICT
INFLICTS > INFLICT
INFLIGHT *adj* provided during flight in an aircraft
INFLOW *n* something, such as liquid or gas, that flows in ▷ *vb* flow in
INFLOWING *same as* > INFLOW
INFLOWS > INFLOW
INFLUENCE *n* effect of one person or thing on another ▷ *vb* have an effect on
INFLUENT *adj* flowing in ▷ *n* something flowing in, esp a tributary
INFLUENTS > INFLUENT
INFLUENZA *n* contagious viral disease causing headaches, muscle pains, and fever
INFLUX *n* arrival or entry of many people or things
INFLUXES > INFLUX
INFLUXION *same as* > INFLUX
INFO *n* information
INFOBAHN *same as* > INTERNET
INFOBAHNS > INFOBAHN
INFOLD *variant spelling of* > ENFOLD
INFOLDED > INFOLD
INFOLDER > INFOLD
INFOLDERS > INFOLD
INFOLDING > INFOLD
INFOLDS > INFOLD
INFOMANIA *n* obsessive devotion to gathering information
INFORCE *same as* > ENFORCE
INFORCED > INFORCE
INFORCES > INFORCE
INFORCING > INFORCE
INFORM *vb* tell ▷ *adj* without shape
INFORMAL *adj* relaxed and friendly
INFORMANT *n* person who gives information
INFORMED > INFORM
INFORMER *n* person who informs to the police
INFORMERS > INFORMER
INFORMING > INFORM
INFORMS > INFORM
INFORTUNE *n* misfortune
INFOS > INFO
INFOTECH *n* information technology
INFOTECHS > INFOTECH
INFOUGHT > INFIGHT
INFRA *adv* (esp in textual annotation) below
INFRACT *vb* violate or break (a law, an agreement, etc)

INFRACTED > INFRACT
INFRACTOR > INFRACT
INFRACTS > INFRACT
INFRARED *adj* of or using rays below the red end of the visible spectrum ▷ *n* infrared part of the spectrum
INFRAREDS > INFRARED
INFRINGE *vb* break (a law or agreement)
INFRINGED > INFRINGE
INFRINGER > INFRINGE
INFRINGES > INFRINGE
INFRUGAL *adj* wasteful
INFULA *same as* > INFULAE
INFULAE *npl* two ribbons hanging from the back of a bishop's mitre
INFURIATE *vb* make very angry ▷ *adj* furious
INFUSCATE *adj* (esp of the wings of an insect) tinged with brown
INFUSE *vb* fill (with an emotion or quality)
INFUSED > INFUSE
INFUSER *n* any device used to make an infusion, esp a tea maker
INFUSERS > INFUSER
INFUSES > INFUSE
INFUSIBLE *adj* unable to be fused or melted
INFUSING > INFUSE
INFUSION *n* infusing
INFUSIONS > INFUSION
INFUSIVE > INFUSION
INFUSORIA *npl* tiny water-dwelling animals
INFUSORY *adj* containing infusoria
ING *n* meadow near a river
INGAN *Scots word for* > ONION
INGANS > INGAN
INGATE *n* entrance
INGATES > INGATE
INGATHER *vb* gather together or in (a harvest)
INGATHERS > INGATHER
INGENER *Shakespearean form of* > ENGINEER
INGENERS > INGENER
INGENIOUS *adj* showing cleverness and originality
INGENIUM *n* genius
INGENIUMS > INGENIUM
INGENU *n* artless or inexperienced boy or young man
INGENUE *n* artless or inexperienced girl or young woman
INGENUES > INGENUE
INGENUITY *n* cleverness at inventing things
INGENUOUS *adj* unsophisticated and trusting
INGENUS > INGENU
INGEST *vb* take (food or liquid) into the body
INGESTA *npl* nourishment

taken into the body through the mouth
INGESTED > INGEST
INGESTING > INGEST
INGESTION > INGEST
INGESTIVE > INGEST
INGESTS > INGEST
INGINE *n* genius
INGINES > INGINE
INGLE *n* fire in a room or a fireplace
INGLENEUK *same as* > INGLENOOK
INGLENOOK *n* corner by a fireplace
INGLES > INGLE
INGLOBE *vb* shape as a sphere
INGLOBED > INGLOBE
INGLOBES > INGLOBE
INGLOBING > INGLOBE
INGLUVIAL > INGLUVIES
INGLUVIES *n* bird's craw
INGO *n* a reveal
INGOES > INGO
INGOING *same as* > INGO
INGOINGS > INGO
INGOT *n* oblong block of cast metal ▷ *vb* shape (metal) into ingots
INGOTED > INGOT
INGOTING > INGOT
INGOTS > INGOT
INGRAFT *variant spelling of* > ENGRAFT
INGRAFTED > INGRAFT
INGRAFTS > INGRAFT
INGRAIN *vb* impress deeply on the mind or nature ▷ *adj* (of carpets) made of dyed yarn or of fibre that is dyed before being spun into yarn ▷ *n* carpet made from ingrained yarn
INGRAINED > INGRAIN
INGRAINER *n* person who ingrains
INGRAINS > INGRAIN
INGRAM *adj* ignorant
INGRATE *n* ungrateful person ▷ *adj* ungrateful
INGRATELY > INGRATE
INGRATES > INGRATE
INGRESS *n* entrance
INGRESSES > INGRESS
INGROOVE *vb* cut a groove into
INGROOVED > INGROOVE
INGROOVES > INGROOVE
INGROSS *archaic form of* > ENGROSS
INGROSSED > INGROSS
INGROSSES > INGROSS
INGROUND *adj* sunk into ground
INGROUP *n* highly cohesive and relatively closed social group
INGROUPS > INGROUP
INGROWING *adj* (of a toenail) growing abnormally into the flesh

i

INGROWN *adj* (esp of a toenail) grown abnormally into the flesh
INGROWTH *n* act of growing inwards
INGROWTHS > INGROWTH
INGRUM *adj* ignorant
INGS > ING
INGUINAL *adj* of or relating to the groin
INGULF *variant spelling of* > ENGULF
INGULFED > INGULF
INGULFING > INGULF
INGULFS > INGULF
INGULPH *archaic form of* > ENGULF
INGULPHED > INGULPH
INGULPHS > INGULPH
INHABIT *vb* live in
INHABITED > INHABIT
INHABITER *n* inhabitant
INHABITOR *n* inhabitant
INHABITS > INHABIT
INHALANT *n* medical preparation inhaled to help breathing problems ▷ *adj* inhaled for its soothing or therapeutic effect
INHALANTS > INHALANT
INHALATOR *n* device for converting drugs into a fine spray for inhaling
INHALE *vb* breathe in (air, smoke, etc)
INHALED > INHALE
INHALER *n* container for an inhalant
INHALERS > INHALER
INHALES > INHALE
INHALING > INHALE
INHARMONY *n* discord
INHAUL *n* line for hauling in a sail
INHAULER *same as* > INHAUL
INHAULERS > INHAULER
INHAULS > INHAUL
INHAUST *vb* drink in
INHAUSTED > INHAUST
INHAUSTS > INHAUST
INHEARSE *vb* bury
INHEARSED > INHEARSE
INHEARSES > INHEARSE
INHERCE *same as* > INHEARSE
INHERCED > INHERCE
INHERCES > INHERCE
INHERCING > INHERCE
INHERE *vb* be an inseparable part (of)
INHERED > INHERE
INHERENCE *n* state or condition of being inherent
INHERENCY *same as* > INHERENCE
INHERENT *adj* existing as an inseparable part
INHERES > INHERE
INHERING > INHERE
INHERIT *vb* receive (money etc) from someone who has died
INHERITED > INHERIT

INHERITOR > INHERIT
INHERITS > INHERIT
INHESION *less common word for* > INHERENCE
INHESIONS > INHESION
INHIBIN *n* peptide hormone
INHIBINS > INHIBIN
INHIBIT *vb* restrain (an impulse or desire)
INHIBITED > INHIBIT
INHIBITER *same as* > INHIBITOR
INHIBITOR *n* person or thing that inhibits
INHIBITS > INHIBIT
INHOLDER *n* inhabitant
INHOLDERS > INHOLDER
INHOLDING *n* privately owned land inside a federal reserve
INHOOP *vb* confine
INHOOPED > INHOOP
INHOOPING > INHOOP
INHOOPS > INHOOP
INHUMAN *adj* cruel or brutal
INHUMANE *same as* > INHUMAN
INHUMANLY > INHUMAN
INHUMATE *vb* bury
INHUMATED > INHUMATE
INHUMATES > INHUMATE
INHUME *vb* inter
INHUMED > INHUME
INHUMER > INHUME
INHUMERS > INHUME
INHUMES > INHUME
INHUMING > INHUME
INIA > INION
INIMICAL *adj* unfavourable or hostile
INION *n* most prominent point at the back of the head, used as a point of measurement in craniometry
INIONS > INION
INIQUITY *n* injustice or wickedness
INISLE *vb* put on or make into an island
INISLED > INISLE
INISLES > INISLE
INISLING > INISLE
INITIAL *adj* first, at the beginning ▷ *n* first letter, esp of a person's name ▷ *vb* sign with one's initials
INITIALED > INITIAL
INITIALLY > INITIAL
INITIALS > INITIAL
INITIATE *vb* begin or set going ▷ *n* recently initiated person ▷ *adj* initiated
INITIATED > INITIATE
INITIATES > INITIATE
INITIATOR *n* person or thing that initiates
INJECT *vb* put (a fluid) into the body with a syringe
INJECTANT *n* injected substance

INJECTED > INJECT
INJECTING > INJECT
INJECTION *n* fluid injected into the body, esp for medicinal purposes
INJECTIVE > INJECTION
INJECTOR *same as* > INJECT
INJECTORS > INJECT
INJECTS > INJECT
INJELLIED > INJELLY
INJELLIES > INJELLY
INJELLY *vb* place in jelly
INJERA *n* white Ethiopian flatbread, similar to a crepe
INJERAS > INJERA
INJOINT *vb* join
INJOINTED > INJOINT
INJOINTS > INJOINT
INJUNCT *vb* issue a legal injunction against (a person)
INJUNCTED > INJUNCT
INJUNCTS > INJUNCT
INJURABLE > INJURE
INJURE *vb* hurt physically or mentally
INJURED > INJURE
INJURER > INJURE
INJURERS > INJURE
INJURES > INJURE
INJURING > INJURE
INJURIOUS *adj* causing harm
INJURY *n* physical hurt
INJUSTICE *n* unfairness
INK *n* coloured liquid used for writing or printing ▷ *vb* mark in ink (something already marked in pencil)
INKBERRY *n* North American holly tree
INKBLOT *n* abstract patch of ink, one of ten commonly used in the Rorschach test
INKBLOTS > INKBLOT
INKED > INK
INKER > INK
INKERS > INK
INKHOLDER *same as* > INKHORN
INKHORN *n* (formerly) a small portable container for ink, usually made from horn
INKHORNS > INKHORN
INKHOSI *n* Zulu clan chief
INKHOSIS > INKHOSI
INKIER > INKY
INKIEST > INKY
INKINESS > INKY
INKING > INK
INKJET *adj* of a method of printing streams of electrically charged ink
INKLE *n* kind of linen tape used for trimmings ▷ *vb* to hint
INKLED > INKLE *vb*
INKLES > INKLE
INKLESS > INK
INKLIKE > INK

INKLING *n* slight idea or suspicion
INKLINGS > INKLING
INKOSI *same as* > INKHOSI
INKOSIS > INKOSI
INKPAD *n* ink-soaked pad used for rubber-stamping or fingerprinting
INKPADS > INKPAD
INKPOT *n* ink-bottle
INKPOTS > INKPOT
INKS > INK
INKSPOT *n* ink stain
INKSPOTS > INKSPOT
INKSTAND *n* stand or tray for holding writing tools and containers for ink
INKSTANDS > INKSTAND
INKSTONE *n* stone used in making ink
INKSTONES > INKSTONE
INKWELL *n* small container for ink, often fitted into the surface of a desk
INKWELLS > INKWELL
INKWOOD *n* type of tree
INKWOODS > INKWOOD
INKY *adj* dark or black
INLACE *variant spelling of* > ENLACE
INLACED > INLACE
INLACES > INLACE
INLACING > INLACE
INLAID > INLAY
INLAND *adv* in or towards the interior of a country, away from the sea ▷ *adj* of or in the interior of a country or region, away from a sea or border ▷ *n* interior of a country or region
INLANDER > INLAND
INLANDERS > INLAND
INLANDS > INLAND
INLAY *n* inlaid substance or pattern ▷ *vb* decorate (an article, esp of furniture) by inserting pieces of wood, ivory, or metal so that the surfaces are smooth and flat
INLAYER > INLAY
INLAYERS > INLAY
INLAYING > INLAY
INLAYINGS > INLAY
INLAYS > INLAY
INLET *n* narrow strip of water extending from the sea into the land ▷ *vb* insert or inlay
INLETS > INLET
INLETTING > INLET
INLIER *n* outcrop of rocks that is entirely surrounded by younger rocks
INLIERS > INLIER
INLOCK *vb* lock up
INLOCKED > INLOCK
INLOCKING > INLOCK
INLOCKS > INLOCK
INLY *adv* inwardly
INLYING *adj* situated within or inside

INMATE n person living in an institution such as a prison

INMATES > INMATE

INMESH variant spelling of > ENMESH

INMESHED > INMESH

INMESHES > INMESH

INMESHING > INMESH

INMIGRANT adj coming in from another area of the same country ▷ n inmigrant person or animal

INMOST adj innermost

INN n pub or small hotel, esp in the country ▷ vb stay at an inn

INNAGE n measurement from bottom of container to surface of liquid

INNAGES > INNAGE

INNARDS npl internal organs

INNATE adj being part of someone's nature, inborn

INNATELY > INNATE

INNATIVE adj native

INNED > INN

INNER adj happening or located inside ▷ n red innermost ring on a target

INNERLY > INNER

INNERMOST adj furthest inside

INNERNESS > INNER

INNERS > INNER

INNERSOLE same as > INSOLE

INNERVATE vb supply nerves to (a bodily organ or part)

INNERVE vb supply with nervous energy

INNERVED > INNERVE

INNERVES > INNERVE

INNERVING > INNERVE

INNERWEAR n underwear

INNING n division of cricket consisting of a turn at batting and a turn in the field for each side

INNINGS > INNING

INNIT interj isn't it

INNKEEPER n owner or manager of an inn

INNLESS adj without inns

INNOCENCE n quality or state of being innocent

INNOCENCY same as > INNOCENCE

INNOCENT adj not guilty of a crime ▷ n innocent person, esp a child

INNOCENTS > INNOCENT

INNOCUITY > INNOCUOUS

INNOCUOUS adj not harmful

INNOVATE vb introduce new ideas or methods

INNOVATED > INNOVATE

INNOVATES > INNOVATE

INNOVATOR > INNOVATE

INNOXIOUS adj not noxious

INNS > INN

INNUENDO n (remark making) an indirect reference to something rude or unpleasant

INNUENDOS > INNUENDO

INNYARD n courtyard of an inn

INNYARDS > INNYARD

INOCULA > INOCULUM

INOCULANT same as > INOCULUM

INOCULATE vb protect against disease by injecting with a vaccine

INOCULUM n substance used in giving an inoculation

INOCULUMS > INOCULUM

INODOROUS adj odourless

INOPINATE adj unexpected

INORB vb enclose in or as if in an orb

INORBED > INORB

INORBING > INORB

INORBS > INORB

INORGANIC adj not having the characteristics of living organisms

INORNATE adj simple

INOSINE n type of molecule making up cell

INOSINES > INOSINE

INOSITE same as > INOSITOL

INOSITES > INOSITE

INOSITOL n cyclic alcohol

INOSITOLS > INOSITOL

INOTROPIC adj affecting or controlling the contraction of muscles, esp those of the heart

INPATIENT n patient who stays in a hospital for treatment

INPAYMENT n money paid into a bank account

INPHASE adj in the same phase

INPOUR vb pour in

INPOURED > INPOUR

INPOURING > INPOUR

INPOURS > INPOUR

INPUT n resources put into a project etc ▷ vb enter (data) in a computer

INPUTS > INPUT

INPUTTED > INPUT

INPUTTER > INPUT

INPUTTERS > INPUT

INPUTTING > INPUT

INQILAB n (in India, Pakistan, etc) revolution

INQILABS > INQILAB

INQUERE Spenserian form of > INQUIRE

INQUERED > INQUERE

INQUERES > INQUERE

INQUERING > INQUERE

INQUEST n official inquiry into a sudden death

INQUESTS > INQUEST

INQUIET vb disturb

INQUIETED > INQUIET

INQUIETLY > INQUIET

INQUIETS > INQUIET

INQUILINE n animal that lives in close association with another animal without harming it ▷ adj of or living as an inquiline

INQUINATE vb corrupt

INQUIRE vb seek information or ask (about)

INQUIRED > INQUIRE

INQUIRER > INQUIRE

INQUIRERS > INQUIRE

INQUIRES > INQUIRE

INQUIRIES > INQUIRY

INQUIRING > INQUIRE

INQUIRY n question

INQUORATE adj without enough people present to make a quorum

INRO n Japanese seal-box

INROAD n invasion or hostile attack

INROADS > INROAD

INRUN n slope down which ski jumpers ski

INRUNS > INRUN

INRUSH n sudden and overwhelming inward flow

INRUSHES > INRUSH

INRUSHING same as > INRUSH

INS > IN

INSANE adj mentally ill

INSANELY > INSANE

INSANER > INSANE

INSANEST > INSANE

INSANIE n insanity

INSANIES > INSANIE

INSANITY n state of being insane

INSATIATE adj not able to be satisfied

INSATIETY n insatiability

INSCAPE n essential inner nature of a person, an object, etc

INSCAPES > INSCAPE

INSCIENCE n ignorance

INSCIENT adj ignorant

INSCONCE vb fortify

INSCONCED > INSCONCE

INSCONCES > INSCONCE

INSCRIBE vb write or carve words on

INSCRIBED > INSCRIBE

INSCRIBER > INSCRIBE

INSCRIBES > INSCRIBE

INSCROLL vb write on a scroll

INSCROLLS > INSCROLL

INSCULP vb engrave

INSCULPED > INSCULP

INSCULPS > INSCULP

INSCULPT adj engraved

INSEAM vb contain

INSEAMED > INSEAM

INSEAMING > INSEAM

INSEAMS > INSEAM

INSECT n small animal with six legs and usu. wings, such as an ant or fly

INSECTAN > INSECT

INSECTARY n place where insects are kept

INSECTEAN > INSECT

INSECTILE > INSECT

INSECTION n incision

INSECTS > INSECT

INSECURE adj anxious, not confident

INSEEM vb cover with grease

INSEEMED > INSEEM

INSEEMING > INSEEM

INSEEMS > INSEEM

INSELBERG n isolated rocky hill rising abruptly from a flat plain

INSENSATE adj without sensation, unconscious

INSERT vb put inside or include ▷ n something inserted

INSERTED adj (of a muscle) attached to the bone that it moves

INSERTER > INSERT

INSERTERS > INSERT

INSERTING > INSERT

INSERTION n act of inserting

INSERTS > INSERT

INSET n small picture inserted within a larger one ▷ vb place in or within ▷ adj decorated with something inserted

INSETS > INSET

INSETTED > INSET

INSETTER > INSET

INSETTERS > INSET

INSETTING > INSET

INSHALLAH sentence substitute if Allah wills it

INSHEATH vb sheathe

INSHEATHE vb sheathe

INSHEATHS > INSHEATH

INSHELL vb retreat, as into a shell

INSHELLED > INSHELL

INSHELLS > INSHELL

INSHELTER vb put in a shelter

INSHIP vb travel or send by ship

INSHIPPED > INSHIP

INSHIPS > INSHIP

INSHORE adj close to the shore ▷ adv towards the shore

INSHRINE variant spelling of > ENSHRINE

INSHRINED > INSHRINE

INSHRINES > INSHRINE

INSIDE prep in or to the interior of ▷ adj on or of the inside ▷ adv on, in, or to the inside, indoors ▷ n inner side, surface, or part

INSIDER n member of a group who has privileged knowledge about it

INSIDERS > INSIDER

INSIDES > INSIDE

INSIDIOUS adj subtle or unseen but dangerous

INSIGHT n deep understanding
INSIGHTS > INSIGHT
INSIGNE same as > INSIGNIA
INSIGNIA n badge or emblem of honour or office
INSIGNIAS > INSIGNIA
INSINCERE adj showing false feelings, not genuine
INSINEW vb connect or strengthen, as with sinews
INSINEWED > INSINEW
INSINEWS > INSINEW
INSINUATE vb suggest indirectly
INSIPID adj lacking interest, spirit, or flavour
INSIPIDLY > INSIPID
INSIPIENT adj lacking wisdom
INSIST vb demand or state firmly
INSISTED > INSIST
INSISTENT adj making persistent demands
INSISTER > INSIST
INSISTERS > INSIST
INSISTING > INSIST
INSISTS > INSIST
INSNARE less common spelling of > ENSNARE
INSNARED > INSNARE
INSNARER > INSNARE
INSNARERS > INSNARE
INSNARES > INSNARE
INSNARING > INSNARE
INSOFAR adv to the extent
INSOLATE vb expose to sunlight, as for bleaching
INSOLATED > INSOLATE
INSOLATES > INSOLATE
INSOLE n inner sole of a shoe or boot
INSOLENCE > INSOLENT
INSOLENT n insolent person ▷ adj rude and disrespectful
INSOLENTS > INSOLENT
INSOLES > INSOLE
INSOLUBLE adj incapable of being solved
INSOLUBLY > INSOLUBLE
INSOLVENT adj unable to pay one's debts ▷ n person who is insolvent
INSOMNIA n inability to sleep
INSOMNIAC adj exhibiting or causing insomnia ▷ n person experiencing insomnia
INSOMNIAS > INSOMNIA
INSOMUCH adv such an extent
INSOOTH adv indeed
INSOUL variant of > ENSOUL
INSOULED > INSOUL
INSOULING > INSOUL
INSOULS > INSOUL
INSOURCE vb subcontract work to a company under

the same general ownership
INSOURCED > INSOURCE
INSOURCES > INSOURCE
INSPAN vb harness (animals) to (a vehicle)
INSPANNED > INSPAN
INSPANS > INSPAN
INSPECT vb check closely or officially
INSPECTED > INSPECT
INSPECTOR n person who inspects
INSPECTS > INSPECT
INSPHERE variant spelling of > ENSPHERE
INSPHERED > INSPHERE
INSPHERES > INSPHERE
INSPIRE vb fill with enthusiasm, stimulate
INSPIRED adj brilliantly creative
INSPIRER > INSPIRE
INSPIRERS > INSPIRE
INSPIRES > INSPIRE
INSPIRING > INSPIRE
INSPIRIT vb fill with vigour
INSPIRITS > INSPIRIT
INSTABLE less common word for > UNSTABLE
INSTAL same as > INSTALL
INSTALL vb put in and prepare (equipment) for use
INSTALLED > INSTALL
INSTALLER > INSTALL
INSTALLS > INSTALL
INSTALS > INSTAL
INSTANCE n particular example ▷ vb mention as an example
INSTANCED > INSTANCE
INSTANCES > INSTANCE
INSTANCY n quality of being urgent or imminent
INSTANT n very brief time ▷ adj happening at once
INSTANTER adv without delay
INSTANTLY adv immediately
INSTANTS > INSTANT
INSTAR vb decorate with stars ▷ n stage in the development of an insect between any two moults
INSTARRED > INSTAR
INSTARS > INSTAR
INSTATE vb place in a position or office
INSTATED > INSTATE
INSTATES > INSTATE
INSTATING > INSTATE
INSTEAD adv as a replacement or substitute
INSTEP n part of the foot forming the arch between the ankle and toes
INSTEPS > INSTEP
INSTIGATE vb cause to happen
INSTIL vb introduce (an

idea etc) gradually into someone's mind
INSTILL same as > INSTIL
INSTILLED > INSTILL
INSTILLER > INSTIL
INSTILLS > INSTILL
INSTILS > INSTIL
INSTINCT n inborn tendency to behave in a certain way ▷ adj animated or impelled (by)
INSTINCTS > INSTINCT
INSTITUTE n organization set up for a specific purpose, esp research or teaching ▷ vb start or establish
INSTRESS vb create or sustain
INSTROKE n inward stroke
INSTROKES > INSTROKE
INSTRUCT vb order to do something
INSTRUCTS > INSTRUCT
INSUCKEN adj of a sucken
INSULA n pyramid-shaped area of the brain within each cerebral hemisphere beneath parts of the frontal and temporal lobes
INSULAE > INSULA
INSULANT n insulation
INSULANTS > INSULANT
INSULAR adj not open to new ideas, narrow-minded ▷ n islander
INSULARLY > INSULAR
INSULARS > INSULAR
INSULATE vb prevent or reduce the transfer of electricity, heat, or sound by surrounding or lining with a nonconducting material
INSULATED > INSULATE
INSULATES > INSULATE
INSULATOR n any material or device that insulates
INSULIN n hormone produced in the pancreas that controls the amount of sugar in the blood
INSULINS > INSULIN
INSULSE adj stupid
INSULSITY n stupidity
INSULT vb behave rudely to, offend ▷ n insulting remark or action
INSULTANT adj insulting
INSULTED > INSULT
INSULTER > INSULT
INSULTERS > INSULT
INSULTING > INSULT
INSULTS > INSULT
INSURABLE > INSURE
INSURANCE n agreement by which one makes regular payments to a company who pay an agreed sum if damage, loss, or death occurs
INSURANT n holder of an insurance policy

INSURANTS > INSURANT
INSURE vb protect by insurance
INSURED adj covered by insurance ▷ n person, persons, or organization covered by an insurance policy
INSUREDS > INSURED
INSURER n person or company that sells insurance
INSURERS > INSURER
INSURES > INSURE
INSURGENT adj in revolt against an established authority ▷ n person who takes part in a rebellion
INSURING > INSURE
INSWATHE vb bind or wrap
INSWATHED > INSWATHE
INSWATHES > INSWATHE
INSWEPT adj narrowed towards the front
INSWING n movement of a bowled ball from off to leg through the air
INSWINGER n ball bowled so as to move from off to leg through the air
INSWINGS > INSWING
INTACT adj not changed or damaged in any way
INTACTLY > INTACT
INTAGLI > INTAGLIO
INTAGLIO n (gem carved with) an engraved design
INTAGLIOS > INTAGLIO
INTAKE n amount or number taken in
INTAKES > INTAKE
INTARSIA n decorative or pictorial mosaic of inlaid wood or sometimes ivory of a style developed in the Italian Renaissance and used esp on wooden wall panels
INTARSIAS > INTARSIA
INTEGER n positive or negative whole number or zero
INTEGERS > INTEGER
INTEGRAL adj being an essential part of a whole ▷ n sum of a large number of very small quantities
INTEGRALS > INTEGRAL
INTEGRAND n mathematical function to be integrated
INTEGRANT adj part of a whole ▷ n integrant thing or part
INTEGRATE vb combine into a whole ▷ adj made up of parts
INTEGRIN n protein that acts as a signal receptor between cells
INTEGRINS > INTEGRIN
INTEGRITY n quality of having high moral principles
INTEL n US military

intelligence

INTELLECT n power of thinking and reasoning

INTELS > INTEL

INTENABLE adj untenable

INTEND vb propose or plan (to do something)

INTENDANT n provincial or colonial official of France, Spain, or Portugal

INTENDED adj planned or future ▷ n person whom one is to marry

INTENDEDS > INTENDED

INTENDER > INTEND

INTENDERS > INTEND

INTENDING > INTEND

INTENDS > INTEND

INTENIBLE adj incapable of holding

INTENSATE vb intensify

INTENSE adj of great strength or degree

INTENSELY > INTENSE

INTENSER > INTENSE

INTENSEST > INTENSE

INTENSIFY vb make or become more intense

INTENSION n set of characteristics or properties by which the referent or referents of a given word are determined

INTENSITY n state or quality of being intense

INTENSIVE adj using or needing concentrated effort or resources ▷ n intensifier or intensive pronoun or grammatical construction

INTENT n intention ▷ adj paying close attention

INTENTION n something intended

INTENTIVE adj intent

INTENTLY > INTENT

INTENTS > INTENT

INTER vb bury (a corpse)

INTERACT vb act on or in close relation with each other

INTERACTS > INTERACT

INTERAGE adj between different ages

INTERARCH vb have intersecting arches

INTERBANK adj conducted between or involving two or more banks

INTERBED vb lie between strata of different minerals

INTERBEDS > INTERBED

INTERBRED adj having been bred within a single family or strain so as to produce particular characteristics

INTERCEDE vb try to end a dispute between two people or groups

INTERCELL adj occurring between cells

INTERCEPT vb seize or stop in transit ▷ n point at

which two figures intersect

INTERCITY adj (in Britain) denoting a fast train or passenger rail service, esp between main towns

INTERCLAN adj occurring between clans

INTERCLUB adj of, relating to, or conducted between two or more clubs

INTERCOM n internal communication system with loudspeakers

INTERCOMS > INTERCOM

INTERCROP n crop grown between the rows of another crop ▷ vb grow (one crop) between the rows of (another)

INTERCUT another word for > CROSSCUT

INTERCUTS > INTERCUT

INTERDASH vb dash between

INTERDEAL vb intrigue or plot

INTERDICT n official prohibition or restraint ▷ vb prohibit or forbid

INTERDINE vb eat together

INTERESS vb interest

INTERESSE vb interest

INTEREST n desire to know or hear more about something ▷ vb arouse the interest of

INTERESTS > INTEREST

INTERFACE n area where two things interact or link ▷ vb connect or be connected with by interface

INTERFERE vb try to influence other people's affairs where one is not involved or wanted

INTERFILE vb place (one or more items) among other items in a file or arrangement

INTERFIRM adj occurring between companies

INTERFLOW vb flow together

INTERFOLD vb fold together

INTERFUSE vb mix or become mixed

INTERGANG adj occurring between gangs

INTERGREW > INTERGROW

INTERGROW vb grow among

INTERIM adj temporary, provisional, or intervening ▷ n intervening time ▷ adv meantime

INTERIMS > INTERIM

INTERIOR n inside ▷ adj inside, inner

INTERIORS > INTERIOR

INTERJECT vb make (a remark) suddenly or as an

interruption

INTERJOIN vb join together

INTERKNIT vb knit together

INTERKNOT vb knot together

INTERLACE vb join together as if by weaving

INTERLAID > INTERLAY

INTERLAP less common word for > OVERLAP

INTERLAPS > INTERLAP

INTERLARD vb insert in or occur throughout

INTERLAY vb insert (layers) between ▷ n material, such as paper, placed between a printing plate and its base

INTERLAYS > INTERLAY

INTERLEAF n extra leaf which is inserted

INTERLEND vb lend between libraries

INTERLENT > INTERLEND

INTERLINE vb write or print (matter) between the lines of (a text or book)

INTERLINK vb connect together

INTERLOAN n loan between one library and another

INTERLOCK vb join firmly together ▷ n device used to prevent a mechanism from operating independently or unsafely ▷ adj (of fabric) closely knitted

INTERLOOP vb loop together

INTERLOPE vb intrude

INTERLUDE n short rest or break in an activity or event

INTERMALE adj occurring between males

INTERMAT n patch of seabed devoid of vegetation

INTERMATS > INTERMAT

INTERMENT n burial

INTERMESH vb net together

INTERMIT vb suspend (activity) or (of activity) to be suspended temporarily or at intervals

INTERMITS > INTERMIT

INTERMIX vb mix together

INTERMONT adj located between mountains

INTERMURE vb wall in

INTERN vb imprison, esp during a war ▷ n trainee doctor in a hospital

INTERNAL adj of or on the inside ▷ n medical examination of the vagina, uterus, or rectum

INTERNALS > INTERNAL

INTERNE same as > INTERN

INTERNED > INTERN

INTERNEE n person who is interned

INTERNEES > INTERNEE

INTERNES > INTERNE

INTERNET n worldwide computer network

INTERNETS > INTERNET

INTERNING > INTERN

INTERNIST n physician who specializes in internal medicine

INTERNODE n part of a plant stem between two nodes

INTERNS > INTERN

INTERPAGE vb print (matter) on intervening pages

INTERPLAY n action and reaction of two things upon each other

INTERPLED adj having instituted a particular type of proceedings

INTERPONE vb interpose

INTERPOSE vb insert between or among things

INTERPRET vb explain the meaning of

INTERRACE adj between races

INTERRAIL vb travel on an international rail pass

INTERRED > INTER

INTERREX n person who governs during an interregnum

INTERRING > INTER

INTERROW adj occurring between rows

INTERRUPT vb break into (a conversation etc) ▷ n signal to initiate the stopping of the running of one computer program in order to run another

INTERS > INTER

INTERSECT vb (of roads) meet and cross

INTERSERT vb insert between

INTERSEX n condition of having characteristics intermediate between those of a male and a female

INTERTERM adj occurring between terms

INTERTEXT adj text seen as modifying another text in literary theory

INTERTIE n short roofing timber

INTERTIES > INTERTIE

INTERTILL vb cultivate between rows of crops

INTERUNIT adj occurring between units

INTERVAL n time between two particular moments or events

INTERVALE dialect form of > INTERVAL

INTERVALS > INTERVAL

INTERVEIN vb intersect

INTERVENE vb involve oneself in a situation, esp to prevent conflict

INTERVIEW n formal discussion, esp between a job-seeker and an employer ▷ vb conduct an interview with

INTERWAR adj of or happening in the period between World War I and World War II

INTERWEB same as > INTERNET

INTERWEBS > INTERWEB

INTERWIND vb wind together

INTERWORK vb interweave

INTERWOVE adj having been woven together

INTERZONE n area between two occupied zones

INTESTACY > INTESTATE

INTESTATE adj not having made a will ▷ n person who dies without having made a will

INTESTINE n lower part of the alimentary canal between the stomach and the anus

INTHRAL archaic form of > ENTHRAL

INTHRALL archaic form of > ENTHRAL

INTHRALLS > INTHRALL

INTHRALS > INTHRAL

INTHRONE archaic form of > ENTHRONE

INTHRONED > INTHRONE

INTHRONES > INTHRONE

INTI n former monetary unit of Peru

INTIFADA n Palestinian uprising against Israel in the West Bank and Gaza Strip

INTIFADAH same as > INTIFADA

INTIFADAS > INTIFADA

INTIFADEH same as > INTIFADA

INTIL Scot form of > INTO

INTIMA n innermost layer of an organ or part, esp of a blood vessel

INTIMACY n close or warm friendship

INTIMAE > INTIMA

INTIMAL > INTIMA

INTIMAS > INTIMA

INTIMATE adj having a close personal relationship ▷ n close friend ▷ vb hint at or suggest

INTIMATED > INTIMATE

INTIMATER > INTIMATE

INTIMATES > INTIMATE

INTIME adj intimate

INTIMISM n school of impressionist painting

INTIMISMS > INTIMISM

INTIMIST > INTIMISM

INTIMISTE > INTIMISM

INTIMISTS > INTIMISM

INTIMITY n intimacy

INTINE n inner wall of a pollen grain or a spore

INTINES > INTINE

INTIRE archaic form of > ENTIRE

INTIS > INTI

INTITLE archaic form of > ENTITLE

INTITLED > INTITLE

INTITLES > INTITLE

INTITLING > INTITLE

INTITULE vb (in Britain) to entitle (an act of parliament)

INTITULED > INTITULE

INTITULES > INTITULE

INTO prep indicating motion towards the centre, result of a change, division, etc

INTOED adj having inward-turning toes

INTOMB same as > ENTOMB

INTOMBED > INTOMB

INTOMBING > INTOMB

INTOMBS > INTOMB

INTONACO n wet plaster surface on which frescoes are painted

INTONACOS > INTONACO

INTONATE vb pronounce or articulate (continuous connected speech) with a characteristic rise and fall of the voice

INTONATED > INTONATE

INTONATES > INTONATE

INTONATOR > INTONATE

INTONE vb speak or recite in an unvarying tone of voice

INTONED > INTONE

INTONER > INTONE

INTONERS > INTONE

INTONES > INTONE

INTONING > INTONE

INTONINGS > INTONE

INTORSION n spiral twisting in plant stems or other parts

INTORT vb twist inward

INTORTED > INTORT

INTORTING > INTORT

INTORTION > INTORT

INTORTS > INTORT

INTOWN adj infield

INTRA prep within

INTRACITY same as > INTERCITY

INTRADA n prelude

INTRADAS > INTRADA

INTRADAY adj occurring within one day

INTRADOS n inner curve or surface of an arch or vault

INTRANET n internal network that makes use of Internet technology

INTRANETS > INTRANET

INTRANT n one who enters

INTRANTS > INTRANT

INTREAT archaic spelling of > ENTREAT

INTREATED > INTREAT

INTREATS > INTREAT

INTRENCH less common spelling of > ENTRENCH

INTREPID adj fearless, bold

INTRICACY > INTRICATE

INTRICATE adj involved or complicated

INTRIGANT n person who intrigues

INTRIGUE vb make interested or curious ▷ n secret plotting

INTRIGUED > INTRIGUE

INTRIGUER > INTRIGUE

INTRIGUES > INTRIGUE

INTRINCE adj intricate

INTRINSIC adj essential to the basic nature of something

INTRO n introduction

INTRODUCE vb present (someone) by name (to another person)

INTROFIED > INTROFY

INTROFIES > INTROFY

INTROFY vb increase the wetting properties

INTROIT n short prayer said or sung as the celebrant is entering the sanctuary to celebrate Mass

INTROITAL > INTROIT

INTROITS > INTROIT

INTROITUS n entrance to a body cavity

INTROJECT vb (esp of a child) to incorporate ideas of others, or (in fantasy) of objects

INTROLD variant of > ENTROLD

INTROMIT vb enter or insert or allow to enter or be inserted

INTROMITS > INTROMIT

INTRON n stretch of DNA that interrupts a gene and does not contribute to the specification of a protein

INTRONS > INTRON

INTRORSE adj turned inwards or towards the axis

INTROS > INTRO

INTROVERT n person concerned more with his or her thoughts and feelings than with the outside world ▷ adj shy and quiet ▷ vb turn (a hollow organ or part) inside out

INTRUDE vb come in or join in without being invited

INTRUDED > INTRUDE

INTRUDER n person who enters a place without permission

INTRUDERS > INTRUDER

INTRUDES > INTRUDE

INTRUDING > INTRUDE

INTRUSION n act of intruding

INTRUSIVE adj characterized by intrusion or tending to intrude

INTRUST same as > ENTRUST

INTRUSTED > INTRUST

INTRUSTS > INTRUST

INTUBATE vb insert a tube or cannula into (a hollow organ)

INTUBATED > INTUBATE

INTUBATES > INTUBATE

INTUIT vb know or discover by intuition

INTUITED > INTUIT

INTUITING > INTUIT

INTUITION n instinctive knowledge or insight without conscious reasoning

INTUITIVE adj of, possessing, or resulting from intuition

INTUITS > INTUIT

INTUMESCE vb swell or become swollen

INTURN n inward turn

INTURNED adj turned inward

INTURNS > INTURN

INTUSE n contusion

INTUSES > INTUSE

INTWINE less common spelling of > ENTWINE

INTWINED > INTWINE

INTWINES > INTWINE

INTWINING > INTWINE

INTWIST vb twist together

INTWISTED > INTWIST

INTWISTS > INTWIST

INUKSHUIT > INUKSHUK

INUKSHUK n stone used by Inuit people to mark a location

INUKSHUKS > INUKSHUK

INULA n plant of the elecampane genus

INULAS > INULA

INULASE n enzyme that hydrolyses inulin to fructose

INULASES > INULASE

INULIN n fructose polysaccharide present in the tubers and rhizomes of some plants

INULINS > INULIN

INUMBRATE vb shade

INUNCTION n application of an ointment to the skin, esp by rubbing

INUNDANT > INUNDATE

INUNDATE vb flood

INUNDATED > INUNDATE

INUNDATES > INUNDATE

INUNDATOR > INUNDATE

INURBANE adj not urbane

INURE vb cause to accept or become hardened to

INURED > INURE

INUREMENT > INURE

INURES > INURE

INURING > INURE

INURN vb place (esp cremated ashes) in an urn

INURNED > INURN

INURNING > INURN

INURNMENT > INURN

INURNS > INURN

INUSITATE adj out of use

INUST adj burnt in

INUSTION > INUST

INUSTIONS > INUST

INUTILE adj useless

INUTILELY > INUTILE

INUTILITY > INUTILE

INVADABLE > INVADE

INVADE vb enter (a country) by military force

INVADED > INVADE

INVADER > INVADE

INVADERS > INVADE

INVADES > INVADE

INVADING > INVADE

INVALID n disabled or chronically ill person ▷ vb dismiss from active service because of illness or injury ▷ adj having no legal force

INVALIDED > INVALID

INVALIDLY > INVALID

INVALIDS > INVALID

INVAR n alloy made from iron and nickel

INVARIANT n entity, quantity, etc, that is unaltered by a particular transformation of coordinates

INVARS > INVAR

INVASION n invading

INVASIONS > INVASION

INVASIVE adj of or relating to an invasion, intrusion, etc

INVEAGLE archaic form of > INVEIGLE

INVEAGLED > INVEAGLE

INVEAGLES > INVEAGLE

INVECKED same as > INVECTED

INVECTED adj bordered with small convex curves

INVECTIVE n abusive speech or writing ▷ adj characterized by or using abusive language, bitter sarcasm, etc

INVEIGH vb criticize strongly

INVEIGHED > INVEIGH

INVEIGHER > INVEIGH

INVEIGHS > INVEIGH

INVEIGLE vb coax by cunning or trickery

INVEIGLED > INVEIGLE

INVEIGLER > INVEIGLE

INVEIGLES > INVEIGLE

INVENIT sentence substitute (he or she) designed it: used formerly on objects such as pocket watches next to the designer's name

INVENT vb think up or create (something new)

INVENTED > INVENT

INVENTER same as > INVENTOR

INVENTERS > INVENTER

INVENTING > INVENT

INVENTION n something invented

INVENTIVE adj creative and resourceful

INVENTOR n person who invents, esp as a profession

INVENTORS > INVENTOR

INVENTORY n detailed list of goods or furnishings ▷ vb make a list of

INVENTS > INVENT

INVERITY n untruth

INVERNESS n type of cape

INVERSE vb make something opposite or contrary in effect ▷ adj reversed in effect, sequence, direction, etc ▷ n exact opposite

INVERSED > INVERSE

INVERSELY > INVERSE

INVERSES > INVERSE

INVERSING > INVERSE

INVERSION n act of inverting or state of being inverted

INVERSIVE > INVERSION

INVERT vb turn upside down or inside out ▷ n homosexual

INVERTASE n enzyme, occurring in the intestinal juice of animals and in yeasts

INVERTED > INVERT

INVERTER n any device for converting a direct current into an alternating current

INVERTERS > INVERTER

INVERTIN same as > INVERTASE

INVERTING > INVERT

INVERTINS > INVERTIN

INVERTOR same as > INVERTER

INVERTORS > INVERTOR

INVERTS > INVERT

INVEST vb spend (money, time, etc) on something with the expectation of profit

INVESTED > INVEST

INVESTING > INVEST

INVESTOR > INVEST

INVESTORS > INVEST

INVESTS > INVEST

INVEXED adj concave

INVIABLE adj not viable, esp financially

INVIABLY > INVIABLE

INVIDIOUS adj likely to cause resentment

INVIOLACY > INVIOLATE

INVIOLATE adj unharmed, unaffected

INVIOUS adj without paths or roads

INVIRILE adj unmanly

INVISCID adj not viscid

INVISIBLE adj not able to be seen ▷ n invisible item of trade

INVISIBLY > INVISIBLE

INVITAL adj not vital

INVITE vb request the company of ▷ n invitation

INVITED > INVITE

INVITEE n one who is invited

INVITEES > INVITEE

INVITER > INVITE

INVITERS > INVITE

INVITES > INVITE

INVITING adj tempting, attractive ▷ n old word for invitation

INVITINGS > INVITING

INVOCABLE > INVOKE

INVOCATE archaic word for > INVOKE

INVOCATED > INVOCATE

INVOCATES > INVOCATE

INVOCATOR > INVOCATE

INVOICE n (present with) a bill for goods or services supplied ▷ vb present (a customer) with an invoice

INVOICED > INVOICE

INVOICES > INVOICE

INVOICING > INVOICE

INVOKE vb put (a law or penalty) into operation

INVOKED > INVOKE

INVOKER > INVOKE

INVOKERS > INVOKE

INVOKES > INVOKE

INVOKING > INVOKE

INVOLUCEL n ring of bracts at the base of the florets of a compound umbel

INVOLUCRA n involucres

INVOLUCRE n ring of bracts at the base of an inflorescence in such plants as the composites

INVOLUTE adj complex, intricate, or involved ▷ n curve described by the free end of a thread as it is wound around another curve on the same plane ▷ vb become involute

INVOLUTED > INVOLUTE

INVOLUTES > INVOLUTE

INVOLVE vb include as a necessary part

INVOLVED > INVOLVE

INVOLVER > INVOLVE

INVOLVERS > INVOLVE

INVOLVES > INVOLVE

INVOLVING > INVOLVE

INWALL vb surround with a wall

INWALLED > INWALL

INWALLING > INWALL

INWALLS > INWALL

INWARD adj directed towards the middle ▷ adv towards the inside or middle ▷ n inward part

INWARDLY adv within the

private thoughts or feelings

INWARDS adv towards the inside or middle of something

INWEAVE vb weave together into or as if into a design, fabric, etc

INWEAVED > INWEAVE

INWEAVES > INWEAVE

INWEAVING > INWEAVE

INWICK vb perform a curling stroke in which the stone bounces off another stone

INWICKED > INWICK

INWICKING > INWICK

INWICKS > INWICK

INWIND vb wind or coil around

INWINDING > INWIND

INWINDS > INWIND

INWIT n conscience

INWITH adv within

INWITS > INWIT

INWORK vb work in

INWORKED > INWORK

INWORKING > INWORK

INWORKS > INWORK

INWORN adj worn in

INWOUND > INWIND

INWOVE > INWEAVE

INWOVEN > INWEAVE

INWRAP less common spelling of > ENWRAP

INWRAPPED > INWRAP

INWRAPS > INWRAP

INWREATHE same as > ENWREATHE

INWROUGHT adj worked or woven into material, esp decoratively

INYALA n antelope

INYALAS > INYALA

IO n type of moth

IODATE same as > IODIZE

IODATED > IODATE

IODATES > IODATE

IODATING > IODATE

IODATION > IODATE

IODATIONS > IODATE

IODIC adj of or containing iodine

IODID same as > IODIDE

IODIDE n compound containing an iodine atom, such as methyl iodide

IODIDES > IODIDE

IODIDS > IODID

IODIN same as > IODINE

IODINATE vb cause to combine with iodine

IODINATED > IODINATE

IODINATES > IODINATE

IODINE n bluish-black element used in medicine and photography

IODINES > IODINE

IODINS > IODIN

IODISE same as > IODIZE

IODISED > IODISE

IODISER > IODISE

IODISERS > IODISE

IODISES > IODISE

IODISING > IODISE

IODISM n poisoning induced by ingestion of iodine or its compounds
IODISMS > IODISM
IODIZE vb treat with iodine
IODIZED > IODIZE
IODIZER > IODIZE
IODIZERS > IODIZE
IODIZES > IODIZE
IODIZING > IODIZE
IODOFORM n yellow crystalline insoluble volatile solid
IODOFORMS > IODOFORM
IODOMETRY n procedure used in volumetric analysis for determining the quantity of substance present that contains iodine
IODOPHILE adj taking an intense iodine stain
IODOPHOR n substance in which iodine is combined with an agent that renders it soluble
IODOPHORS > IODOPHOR
IODOPSIN n violet light-sensitive pigment in the cones of the retina of the eye that is responsible for colour vision
IODOPSINS > IODOPSIN
IODOUS adj of or containing iodine, esp in the trivalent state
IODURET n iodide
IODURETS > IODURET
IODYRITE n silver iodide
IODYRITES > IODYRITE
IOLITE n grey or violet-blue dichroic mineral
IOLITES > IOLITE
ION n electrically charged atom
IONIC adj of or in the form of ions
IONICITY n ionic character
IONICS npl study of ions
IONISABLE > IONISE
IONISE same as > IONIZE
IONISED > IONISE
IONISER same as > IONIZER
IONISERS > IONISER
IONISES > IONISE
IONISING > IONISE
IONIUM n naturally occurring radioisotope of thorium
IONIUMS > IONIUM
IONIZABLE > IONIZE
IONIZE vb change into ions
IONIZED > IONIZE
IONIZER n person or thing that ionizes, esp an electrical device used within a room to refresh its atmosphere by restoring negative ions
IONIZERS > IONIZER
IONIZES > IONIZE

IONIZING > IONIZE
IONOGEN n compound that exists as ions when dissolved
IONOGENIC adj forming ions
IONOGENS > IONOGEN
IONOMER n thermoplastic with ionic bonding between polymer chains
IONOMERS > IONOMER
IONONE n yellowish liquid mixture of two isomers with an odour of violets
IONONES > IONONE
IONOPAUSE n transitional zone in the atmosphere between the ionosphere and the exosphere
IONOPHORE n chemical compound capable of forming a complex with an ion and transporting it through a biological membrane
IONOSONDE n instrument measuring ionization
IONOTROPY n reversible interconversion of a pair of organic isomers as a result of the migration of an ionic part of the molecule
IONS > ION
IOPANOIC as in iopanoic acid type of acid containing iodine
IOS > IO
IOTA n ninth letter in the Greek alphabet
IOTACISM n pronunciation tendency in Modern Greek
IOTACISMS > IOTACISM
IOTAS > IOTA
IPECAC n type of S American shrub
IPECACS > IPECAC
IPOMOEA n tropical or subtropical convolvulaceous plant
IPOMOEAS > IPOMOEA
IPPON n winning point awarded in a judo or karate competition
IPPONS > IPPON
IPRINDOLE n antidepressant
IRACUND adj easily angered
IRADE n written edict of a Muslim ruler
IRADES > IRADE
IRASCIBLE adj easily angered
IRASCIBLY > IRASCIBLE
IRATE adj very angry
IRATELY > IRATE
IRATENESS > IRATE
IRATER > IRATE
IRATEST > IRATE
IRE vb anger ▷ n anger
IRED > IRE
IREFUL > IRE
IREFULLY > IRE

IRELESS > IRE
IRENIC adj tending to conciliate or promote peace
IRENICAL same as > IRENIC
IRENICISM > IRENICS
IRENICON variant spelling of > EIRENICON
IRENICONS > IRENICON
IRENICS n that branch of theology that is concerned with unity between Christian sects and denominations
IRENOLOGY n study of peace
IRES > IRE
IRID n type of iris
IRIDAL > IRID
IRIDEAL > IRID
IRIDES > IRIS
IRIDIAL > IRID
IRIDIAN > IRID
IRIDIC adj of or containing iridium, esp in the tetravalent state
IRIDISE vb make iridescent
IRIDISED > IRIDISE
IRIDISES > IRIDISE
IRIDISING > IRIDISE
IRIDIUM n very hard corrosion-resistant metal
IRIDIUMS > IRIDIUM
IRIDIZE vb make iridescent
IRIDIZED > IRIDIZE
IRIDIZES > IRIDIZE
IRIDIZING > IRIDIZE
IRIDOCYTE n cell in the skin of fish that gives them iridescence
IRIDOLOGY n technique used in complementary medicine to diagnose illness by studying a patient's eyes
IRIDOTOMY n surgical incision into the iris, esp to create an artificial pupil
IRIDS > IRID
IRING > IRE
IRIS n coloured circular membrane of the eye containing the pupil ▷ vb display iridescence
IRISATE vb make iridescent
IRISATED > IRISATE
IRISATES > IRISATE
IRISATING > IRISATE
IRISATION > IRISATE
IRISCOPE n instrument that displays the prismatic colours
IRISCOPES > IRISCOPE
IRISED > IRIS
IRISES > IRIS
IRISING > IRIS
IRITIC > IRITIS
IRITIS n inflammation of the iris of the eye
IRITISES > IRITIS
IRK vb irritate, annoy

IRKED > IRK
IRKING > IRK
IRKS > IRK
IRKSOME adj irritating, annoying
IRKSOMELY > IRKSOME
IROKO n tropical African hardwood tree
IROKOS > IROKO
IRON n strong silvery-white metallic element, widely used for structural and engineering purposes ▷ adj made of iron ▷ vb smooth (clothes or fabric) with an iron
IRONBARK n Australian eucalyptus with hard rough bark
IRONBARKS > IRONBARK
IRONBOUND adj bound with iron
IRONCLAD adj covered or protected with iron ▷ n large wooden 19th-century warship with armoured plating
IRONCLADS > IRONCLAD
IRONE n fragrant liquid
IRONED > IRON
IRONER > IRON
IRONERS > IRON
IRONES > IRONE
IRONIC adj using irony
IRONICAL same as > IRONIC
IRONIER > IRONY
IRONIES > IRONY
IRONIEST > IRONY
IRONING n clothes to be ironed
IRONINGS > IRONING
IRONISE same as > IRONIZE
IRONISED > IRONISE
IRONISES > IRONISE
IRONISING > IRONISE
IRONIST > IRONIZE
IRONISTS > IRONIZE
IRONIZE vb use or indulge in irony
IRONIZED > IRONIZE
IRONIZES > IRONIZE
IRONIZING > IRONIZE
IRONLESS > IRON
IRONLIKE > IRON
IRONMAN n very strong man
IRONMEN > IRONMAN
IRONNESS > IRON
IRONS > IRON
IRONSIDE n person with great stamina or resistance
IRONSIDES > IRONSIDE
IRONSMITH adj blacksmith
IRONSTONE n rock consisting mainly of iron ore
IRONWARE n domestic articles made of iron
IRONWARES > IRONWARE
IRONWEED n plant with purplish leaves

IRONWEEDS > IRONWEED
IRONWOMAN n very strong woman
IRONWOMEN > IRONWOMAN
IRONWOOD n any of various trees, such as hornbeam, with exceptionally hard wood
IRONWOODS > IRONWOOD
IRONWORK n work done in iron, esp decorative work
IRONWORKS n building in which iron is smelted, cast, or wrought
IRONY n mildly sarcastic use of words to imply the opposite of what is said ▷ adj, resembling, or containing iron
IRRADIANT adj radiating light
IRRADIATE vb subject to or treat with radiation
IRREAL adj unreal
IRREALITY n unreality
IRREDENTA > IRRIDENTA
IRREGULAR adj not regular or even ▷ n soldier not in a regular army
IRRELATED adj irrelevant
IRRIDENTA n region that is ethnically or historically tied to one country, but which is ruled by another
IRRIGABLE > IRRIGATE
IRRIGABLY > IRRIGATE
IRRIGATE vb supply (land) with water by artificial channels or pipes
IRRIGATED > IRRIGATE
IRRIGATES > IRRIGATE
IRRIGATOR > IRRIGATE
IRRIGUOUS adj well-watered
IRRISION n mockery
IRRISIONS > IRRISION
IRRISORY adj mocking
IRRITABLE adj easily annoyed
IRRITABLY > IRRITABLE
IRRITANCY > IRRITANT
IRRITANT adj causing irritation ▷ n something that annoys or irritates
IRRITANTS > IRRITANT
IRRITATE vb annoy, anger
IRRITATED > IRRITATE
IRRITATES > IRRITATE
IRRITATOR > IRRITATE
IRRUPT vb enter forcibly or suddenly
IRRUPTED > IRRUPT
IRRUPTING > IRRUPT
IRRUPTION > IRRUPT
IRRUPTIVE adj irrupting or tending to irrupt
IRRUPTS > IRRUPT
IRUKANDJI n tiny but highly venomous Australian jellyfish
IS third person singular present tense of > BE

ISABEL n brown yellow colour
ISABELLA same as > ISABEL
ISABELLAS > ISABELLA
ISABELS > ISABEL
ISAGOGE n academic introduction to a specialized subject field or area of research
ISAGOGES > ISAGOGE
ISAGOGIC > ISAGOGICS
ISAGOGICS n introductory studies, esp in the history of the Bible
ISALLOBAR n line on a map connecting places with equal pressure changes
ISARITHM n line on a map connecting places with the same population density
ISARITHMS > ISARITHM
ISATIN n yellowish-red crystalline compound soluble in hot water, used for the preparation of vat dyes
ISATINE same as > ISATIN
ISATINES > ISATINE
ISATINIC > ISATIN
ISATINS > ISATIN
ISBA n log hut
ISBAS > ISBA
ISCHAEMIA n inadequate supply of blood to an organ or part, as from an obstructed blood flow
ISCHAEMIC > ISCHAEMIA
ISCHEMIA same as > ISCHAEMIA
ISCHEMIAS > ISCHEMIA
ISCHEMIC > ISCHAEMIA
ISCHIA > ISCHIUM
ISCHIADIC > ISCHIUM
ISCHIAL > ISCHIUM
ISCHIATIC > ISCHIUM
ISCHIUM n one of the three sections of the hipbone, situated below the ilium
ISCHURIA n retention of urine
ISCHURIAS > ISCHURIA
ISEIKONIA n seeing of same image in both eyes
ISEIKONIC > ISEIKONIA
ISENERGIC adj of equal energy
ISH n issue
ISHES > ISH
ISINGLASS n kind of gelatine obtained from some freshwater fish
ISIT sentence substitute expression used to seek confirmation of something or show one is listening
ISLAND n piece of land surrounded by water ▷ vb cause to become an island
ISLANDED > ISLAND

ISLANDER n person who lives on an island
ISLANDERS > ISLANDER
ISLANDING > ISLAND
ISLANDS > ISLAND
ISLE vb make an isle of ▷ n island
ISLED > ISLE
ISLELESS adj without islands
ISLEMAN n islander
ISLEMEN > ISLEMAN
ISLES > ISLE
ISLESMAN > ISLEMAN
ISLESMEN > ISLESMAN
ISLET n small island
ISLETED adj having islets
ISLETS > ISLET
ISLING > ISLE
ISLOMANIA n obsessional enthusiasm or partiality for islands
ISM n doctrine, system, or practice
ISMATIC adj following fashionable doctrines
ISMATICAL same as > ISMATIC
ISMS > ISM
ISNA vb is not
ISNAE same as > ISNA
ISO n short segment of film that can be replayed easily
ISOAMYL as in isoamyl acetate, colourless volatile compound used as a solvent for cellulose lacquers and as a flavouring
ISOAMYLS > ISOAMYL
ISOBAR n line on a map connecting places of equal atmospheric pressure
ISOBARE same as > ISOBAR
ISOBARES > ISOBARE
ISOBARIC adj having equal atmospheric pressure
ISOBARISM > ISOBAR
ISOBARS > ISOBAR
ISOBASE n line connecting points of equal land upheaval
ISOBASES > ISOBASE
ISOBATH n line on a map connecting points of equal underwater depth
ISOBATHIC > ISOBATH
ISOBATHS > ISOBATH
ISOBRONT n line connecting points of simultaneous storm development
ISOBRONTS > ISOBRONT
ISOBUTANE n form of butane
ISOBUTENE n isomer of butene
ISOBUTYL as in methyl isobutyl ketone colourless insoluble liquid ketone used as a solvent for organic compounds
ISOBUTYLS > ISOBUTYL
ISOCHASM n line

connecting points of equal aurorae frequency
ISOCHASMS > ISOCHASM
ISOCHEIM n line on a map connecting places with the same mean winter temperature
ISOCHEIMS > ISOCHEIM
ISOCHIMAL > ISOCHIME
ISOCHIME same as > ISOCHEIM
ISOCHIMES > ISOCHIME
ISOCHOR n line on a graph showing the variation of the temperature of a fluid with its pressure, when the volume is kept constant
ISOCHORE same as > ISOCHOR
ISOCHORES > ISOCHORE
ISOCHORIC > ISOCHOR
ISOCHORS > ISOCHOR
ISOCHRON n line on an isotope ratio diagram denoting a suite of rock or mineral samples all formed at the same time
ISOCHRONE n line on a map or diagram connecting places from which it takes the same time to travel to a certain point
ISOCHRONS > ISOCHRON
ISOCLINAL adj sloping in the same direction and at the same angle ▷ n imaginary line connecting points on the earth's surface having equal angles of dip
ISOCLINE same as > ISOCLINAL
ISOCLINES > ISOCLINE
ISOCLINIC same as > ISOCLINAL
ISOCRACY n form of government in which all people have equal powers
ISOCRATIC > ISOCRACY
ISOCRYMAL same as > ISOCRYME
ISOCRYME n line connecting points of equal winter temperature
ISOCRYMES > ISOCRYME
ISOCYANIC as in isocyanic acid, hypothetical acid known only in the form of its compounds
ISOCYCLIC adj containing a closed ring of atoms of the same kind, esp carbon atoms
ISODICA > ISODICON
ISODICON n short anthem
ISODOMA > ISODOMON
ISODOMON n masonry formed of uniform blocks, with courses are of equal height
ISODOMOUS > ISODOMON
ISODOMUM same as > ISODOMON

ISODONT n animal in which the teeth are of similar size

ISODONTAL same as > ISODONT

ISODONTS > ISODONT

ISODOSE n dose of radiation applied to a part of the body in radiotherapy that is equal to the dose applied to a different part

ISODOSES > ISODOSE

ISOENZYME same as > ISOZYME

ISOETES n quillwort

ISOFORM n protein similar in function but not form to another

ISOFORMS > ISOFORM

ISOGAMETE n gamete that is similar in size and form to the one with which it unites in fertilization

ISOGAMIC > ISOGAMY

ISOGAMIES > ISOGAMY

ISOGAMOUS > ISOGAMY

ISOGAMY n (in some algae and fungi) sexual fusion of gametes of similar size and form

ISOGENEIC same as > ISOGENIC

ISOGENIC same as > ISOGENOUS

ISOGENIES > ISOGENOUS

ISOGENOUS adj of similar origin, as parts derived from the same embryonic tissue

ISOGENY > ISOGENOUS

ISOGLOSS n line drawn on a map around the area in which a linguistic feature is to be found, such as a particular pronunciation of a given word

ISOGON n equiangular polygon

ISOGONAL same as > ISOGONIC

ISOGONALS > ISOGONAL

ISOGONE same as > ISOGONIC

ISOGONES > ISOGONE

ISOGONIC adj having, making, or involving equal angles ▷ n imaginary line connecting points on the earth's surface having equal magnetic declination

ISOGONICS > ISOGONIC

ISOGONIES > ISOGONIC

ISOGONS > ISOGON

ISOGONY > ISOGONIC

ISOGRAFT vb grafting tissue from a donor genetically identical to the recipient

ISOGRAFTS > ISOGRAFT

ISOGRAM same as > ISOPLETH

ISOGRAMS > ISOGRAM

ISOGRAPH n line connecting points of the same linguistic usage

ISOGRAPHS > ISOGRAPH

ISOGRIV n line connecting points of equal angular difference between magnetic north and grid north

ISOGRIVS > ISOGRIV

ISOHEL n line on a map connecting places with an equal period of sunshine

ISOHELS > ISOHEL

ISOHYDRIC adj having the same acidity or hydrogen-ion concentration

ISOHYET n line on a map connecting places having equal rainfall

ISOHYETAL > ISOHYET

ISOHYETS > ISOHYET

ISOKONT same as > ISOKONTAN

ISOKONTAN n alga whose zoophores have equal cilia

ISOKONTS > ISOKONT

ISOLABLE > ISOLATE

ISOLATE vb place apart or alone ▷ n isolated person or group

ISOLATED > ISOLATE

ISOLATES > ISOLATE

ISOLATING > ISOLATE

ISOLATION > ISOLATE

ISOLATIVE adj concerned with isolation

ISOLATOR > ISOLATE

ISOLATORS > ISOLATE

ISOLEAD n line on a ballistic graph

ISOLEADS > ISOLEAD

ISOLEX n isogloss marking off the area in which a particular item of vocabulary is found

ISOLEXES > ISOLEX

ISOLINE same as > ISOPLETH

ISOLINES > ISOLINE

ISOLOG > ISOLOGOUS

ISOLOGOUS adj (of two or more organic compounds) having a similar structure but containing different atoms of the same valency

ISOLOGS > ISOLOGOUS

ISOLOGUE > ISOLOGOUS

ISOLOGUES > ISOLOGOUS

ISOMER n substance whose molecules contain the same atoms as another but in a different arrangement

ISOMERASE n any enzyme that catalyses the conversion of one isomeric form of a compound to another

ISOMERE same as > ISOMER

ISOMERES > ISOMERE

ISOMERIC > ISOMER

ISOMERISE same as > ISOMERIZE

ISOMERISM n existence of two or more compounds having the same molecular formula but a different arrangement of atoms within the molecule

ISOMERIZE vb change or cause to change from one isomer to another

ISOMEROUS adj having an equal number of parts or markings

ISOMERS > ISOMER

ISOMETRIC adj relating to muscular contraction without shortening of the muscle ▷ n drawing made in this way

ISOMETRY n rigid motion of a plane or space such that the distance between any two points before and after this motion is unaltered

ISOMORPH n substance or organism that exhibits isomorphism

ISOMORPHS > ISOMORPH

ISONIAZID n soluble colourless crystalline compound used to treat tuberculosis

ISONOME n line on a chart connecting points of equal abundance values of a plant species sampled in different sections of an area

ISONOMES > ISONOME

ISONOMIC > ISONOMY

ISONOMIES > ISONOMY

ISONOMOUS > ISONOMY

ISONOMY n equality before the law of the citizens of a state

ISOOCTANE n colourless liquid alkane hydrocarbon produced from petroleum and used in standardizing petrol

ISOPACH n line on a map connecting points below which a particular rock stratum has the same thickness

ISOPACHS > ISOPACH

ISOPHONE n isogloss marking off an area in which a particular feature of pronunciation is found

ISOPHONES > ISOPHONE

ISOPHOTAL > ISOPHOTE

ISOPHOTE n line on a diagram or image of a galaxy, nebula, or other celestial object joining points of equal surface brightness

ISOPHOTES > ISOPHOTE

ISOPLETH n line on a map connecting places registering the same amount or ratio of some geographical or meteorological phenomenon or phenomena

ISOPLETHS > ISOPLETH

ISOPOD n type of crustacean including woodlice and pill bugs ▷ adj of this type of crustacean

ISOPODAN > ISOPOD

ISOPODANS > ISOPOD

ISOPODOUS > ISOPOD

ISOPODS > ISOPOD

ISOPOLITY n equality of political rights

ISOPRENE n colourless volatile liquid with a penetrating odour

ISOPRENES > ISOPRENE

ISOPROPYL n group of atoms

ISOPTERAN n termite

ISOPYCNAL n line on a map connecting points of equal atmospheric density

ISOPYCNIC same as > ISOPYCNAL

ISOS > ISO

ISOSCELES adj (of a triangle) having two sides of equal length

ISOSMOTIC same as > ISOTONIC

ISOSPIN n internal quantum number used in the classification of elementary particles

ISOSPINS > ISOSPIN

ISOSPORY n condition of having spores of only one kind

ISOSTACY n state of balance in earth's crust

ISOSTASY > ISOSTACY

ISOSTATIC > ISOSTASY

ISOSTERIC adj (of two different molecules) having the same number of atoms and the same number and configuration of valency electrons

ISOTACH n line on a map connecting points of equal wind speed

ISOTACHS > ISOTACH

ISOTACTIC adj (of a stereospecific polymer) having identical steric configurations of the groups on each asymmetric carbon atom on the chain

ISOTHERAL > ISOTHERE

ISOTHERE n line on a map linking places with the same mean summer temperature

ISOTHERES > ISOTHERE

ISOTHERM n line on a map connecting points of equal temperature

ISOTHERMS > ISOTHERM

ISOTONE n one of two or more atoms of different atomic number that contain the same number of neutrons

ISOTONES > ISOTONE

ISOTONIC adj (of two or more muscles) having

equal tension

ISOTOPE *n* one of two or more atoms with the same number of protons in the nucleus but a different number of neutrons

ISOTOPES > ISOTOPE

ISOTOPIC > ISOTOPE

ISOTOPIES > ISOTOPE

ISOTOPY > ISOTOPE

ISOTRON *n* device for separating small quantities of isotopes by ionizing them and separating the ions by a mass spectrometer

ISOTRONS > ISOTRON

ISOTROPIC *adj* having uniform physical properties, such as elasticity or conduction in all directions

ISOTROPY > ISOTROPIC

ISOTYPE *n* presentation of statistical information in a row of diagrams

ISOTYPES > ISOTYPE

ISOTYPIC > ISOTYPE

ISOZYME *n* any of a set of structural variants of an enzyme occurring in different tissues in a single species

ISOZYMES > ISOZYME

ISOZYMIC > ISOZYME

ISPAGHULA *n* dietary fibre derived from seed husks and used as a thickener or stabilizer in the food industry

ISSEI *n* first-generation Japanese immigrant

ISSEIS > ISSEI

ISSUABLE *adj* capable of issuing or being issued

ISSUABLY > ISSUABLE

ISSUANCE *n* act of issuing

ISSUANCES > ISSUANCE

ISSUANT *adj* emerging or issuing

ISSUE *n* topic of interest or discussion ▷ *vb* make (a statement etc) publicly

ISSUED > ISSUE

ISSUELESS > ISSUE

ISSUER > ISSUE

ISSUERS > ISSUE

ISSUES > ISSUE

ISSUING > ISSUE

ISTANA *n* (in Malaysia) a royal palace

ISTANAS > ISTANA

ISTHMI > ISTHMUS

ISTHMIAN *n* inhabitant of an isthmus ▷ *adj* relating to or situated in an isthmus

ISTHMIANS > ISTHMIAN

ISTHMIC > ISTHMUS

ISTHMOID > ISTHMUS

ISTHMUS *n* narrow strip of land connecting two areas of land

ISTHMUSES > ISTHMUS

ISTLE *n* fibre obtained from various tropical American agave and yucca trees used in making carpets, cord, etc

ISTLES > ISTLE

IT *pron* refers to a nonhuman, animal, plant, or inanimate object ▷ *n* player whose turn it is to catch the others in children's games

ITA *n* type of palm

ITACISM *n* pronunciation of the Greek letter eta as in Modern Greek

ITACISMS > ITACISM

ITACONIC as in *itaconic acid* , white colourless crystalline carboxylic acid

ITALIC *adj* (of printing type) sloping to the right ▷ *n* style of printing type modelled on this, chiefly used to indicate emphasis, a foreign word, etc

ITALICISE *same as* > ITALICIZE

ITALICIZE *vb* put in italics

ITALICS > ITALIC

ITAS > ITA

ITCH *n* skin irritation causing a desire to scratch ▷ *vb* have an itch

ITCHED > ITCH

ITCHES > ITCH

ITCHIER > ITCH

ITCHIEST > ITCH

ITCHILY > ITCH

ITCHINESS > ITCH

ITCHING > ITCH

ITCHINGS > ITCH

ITCHWEED *n* white hellebore

ITCHWEEDS > ITCHWEED

ITCHY > ITCH

ITEM *n* single thing in a list or collection ▷ *adv* likewise ▷ *vb* itemize

ITEMED > ITEM

ITEMING > ITEM

ITEMISE *same as* > ITEMIZE

ITEMISED > ITEMISE

ITEMISER > ITEMISE

ITEMISERS > ITEMISE

ITEMISES > ITEMISE

ITEMISING > ITEMISE

ITEMIZE *vb* make a list of

ITEMIZED > ITEMIZE

ITEMIZER > ITEMIZE

ITEMIZERS > ITEMIZE

ITEMIZES > ITEMIZE

ITEMIZING > ITEMIZE

ITEMS > ITEM

ITERANCE > ITERATE

ITERANCES > ITERATE

ITERANT > ITERATE

ITERATE *vb* repeat

ITERATED > ITERATE

ITERATES > ITERATE

ITERATING > ITERATE

ITERATION > ITERATE

ITERATIVE *adj* repetitious or frequent

ITERUM *adv* again

ITHER *Scot word for* > OTHER

ITINERACY *n* travelling from place to place

ITINERANT *adj* travelling from place to place ▷ *n* itinerant worker or other person

ITINERARY *n* detailed plan of a journey ▷ *adj* of or relating to travel or routes of travel

ITINERATE *vb* travel from place to place

ITS *pron* belonging to it ▷ *adj* of or belonging to it

ITSELF *pron* reflexive form of *it*

IURE *adv* by law

IVIED *adj* covered with ivy

IVIES > IVY

IVORIED > IVORY

IVORIES *npl* keys of a piano

IVORIST *n* worker in ivory

IVORISTS > IVORIST

IVORY *n* hard white bony substance forming the tusks of elephants ▷ *adj* yellowish-white

IVORYBILL *n* large American woodpecker

IVORYLIKE > IVORY

IVORYWOOD *n* yellowish-white wood of an Australian tree, used for engraving, inlaying, and turnery

IVRESSE *n* drunkenness

IVRESSES > IVRESSE

IVY *n* evergreen climbing plant

IVYLIKE > IVY

IWI *n* Māori tribe

IWIS *archaic word for* > CERTAINLY

IXIA *n* southern African plant of the iris family with showy ornamental funnel-shaped flowers

IXIAS > IXIA

IXODIASES > IXODIASIS

IXODIASIS *n* disease transmitted by ticks

IXODID *n* hard-bodied tick

IXODIDS > IXODID

IXORA *n* flowering shrub

IXORAS > IXORA

IXTLE *same as* > ISTLE

IXTLES > IXTLE

IZAR *n* long garment worn by Muslim women

IZARD *n* type of goat-antelope

IZARDS > IZARD

IZARS > IZAR

IZVESTIA *n* news

IZVESTIAS > IZVESTIA

IZVESTIYA *same as* > IZVESTIA

IZZARD *n* letter Z

IZZARDS > IZZARD

IZZAT *n* honour or prestige

IZZATS > IZZAT

i

Jj

JA interj yes ▷ sentence substitute yes
JAAP n S African offensive word for a simpleton or country bumpkin
JAAPS > JAAP
JAB vb poke sharply ▷ n quick punch or poke
JABBED > JAB
JABBER vb talk rapidly or incoherently ▷ n rapid or incoherent talk
JABBERED > JABBER
JABBERER > JABBER
JABBERERS > JABBER
JABBERING > JABBER
JABBERS > JABBER
JABBING > JAB
JABBINGLY > JAB
JABBLE vb ripple
JABBLED > JABBLE
JABBLES > JABBLE
JABBLING > JABBLE
JABERS interj Irish exclamation
JABIRU n large white-and-black Australian stork
JABIRUS > JABIRU
JABORANDI n any of several tropical American rutaceous shrubs
JABOT n frill or ruffle on the front of a blouse or shirt
JABOTS > JABOT
JABS > JAB
JACAL n Mexican daub hut
JACALES > JACAL
JACALS > JACAL
JACAMAR n tropical American bird with an iridescent plumage
JACAMARS > JACAMAR
JACANA n long-legged long-toed bird of tropical and subtropical marshy regions
JACANAS > JACANA
JACARANDA n tropical tree with sweet-smelling wood
JACARE another name for > CAYMAN
JACARES > JACARE
JACCHUS n small monkey
JACCHUSES > JACCHUS
JACENT adj lying
JACINTH another name for > HYACINTH
JACINTHE n hyacinth
JACINTHES > JACINTHE
JACINTHS > JACINTH

JACK n device for raising a motor vehicle or other heavy object ▷ vb lift or push (an object) with a jack
JACKAL n doglike wild animal of Africa and Asia ▷ vb behave like a jackal
JACKALLED > JACKAL
JACKALS > JACKAL
JACKAROO same as > JACKEROO
JACKAROOS > JACKAROO
JACKASS n fool
JACKASSES > JACKASS
JACKBOOT n high military boot ▷ vb oppress
JACKBOOTS > JACKBOOT
JACKDAW n black-and-grey Eurasian bird of the crow family
JACKDAWS > JACKDAW
JACKED > JACK
JACKEEN n slick self-assertive lower-class Dubliner
JACKEENS > JACKEEN
JACKER n labourer
JACKEROO n young male management trainee on a sheep or cattle station ▷ vb work as a jackeroo
JACKEROOS > JACKEROO
JACKERS > JACKER
JACKET n short coat ▷ vb put a jacket on (someone or something)
JACKETED > JACKET
JACKETING > JACKET
JACKETS > JACKET
JACKFISH n small pike fish
JACKFRUIT n tropical Asian tree
JACKIES > JACKY
JACKING > JACK
JACKINGS > JACK
JACKKNIFE vb (of an articulated truck) go out of control so that the trailer swings round at a sharp angle to the cab ▷ n large clasp knife
JACKLEG n unskilled worker
JACKLEGS > JACKLEG
JACKLIGHT same as > JACK
JACKMAN n retainer
JACKMEN > JACKMAN
JACKPLANE n large woodworking plane
JACKPOT n largest prize

that may be won in a game
JACKPOTS > JACKPOT
JACKROLL vb gang-rape
JACKROLLS > JACKROLL
JACKS n game in which metal, bone, or plastic pieces are thrown and then picked up between throws of a small ball
JACKSCREW n lifting device
JACKSHAFT n short length of shafting that transmits power from an engine or motor to a machine
JACKSIE n buttocks or anus
JACKSIES > JACKSIE
JACKSMELT n food fish of the North Pacific
JACKSMITH n smith who makes jacks
JACKSNIPE n small Eurasian short-billed snipe
JACKSTAY n metal rod, wire rope, or wooden batten to which an edge of a sail is fastened along a yard
JACKSTAYS > JACKSTAY
JACKSTONE n a small round pebble
JACKSTRAW n straw mannequin
JACKSY same as > JACKSIE
JACKY n offensive word for a native Australian
JACOBIN n variety of fancy pigeon with a hood of feathers swept up over and around the head
JACOBINS > JACOBIN
JACOBUS n English gold coin minted in the reign of James I
JACOBUSES > JACOBUS
JACONET n light cotton fabric used for clothing, bandages, etc
JACONETS > JACONET
JACQUARD n fabric in which the design is incorporated into the weave instead of being printed or dyed on
JACQUARDS > JACQUARD
JACQUERIE n peasant rising or revolt
JACTATION n act of boasting

JACULATE vb hurl
JACULATED > JACULATE
JACULATES > JACULATE
JACULATOR > JACULATE
JACUZZI n bath or pool equipped with a system of underwater jets
JACUZZIS > JACUZZI
JADE n ornamental semiprecious stone, usu dark green ▷ adj bluish-green ▷ vb exhaust or make exhausted from work or use
JADED adj tired and unenthusiastic
JADEDLY > JADED
JADEDNESS > JADED
JADEITE n usually green or white mineral, found in igneous and metamorphic rocks
JADEITES > JADEITE
JADELIKE > JADE
JADERIES > JADERY
JADERY n shrewishness
JADES > JADE
JADING > JADE
JADISH > JADE
JADISHLY > JADE
JADITIC > JADE
JAEGER n marksman in certain units of the German or Austrian armies
JAEGERS > JAEGER
JAFA n offensive name for a person from Auckland
JAFAS > JAFA
JAFFA n (in cricket) well-bowled ball that is practically unplayable
JAFFAS > JAFFA
JAG n period of uncontrolled indulgence in an activity ▷ vb cut unevenly
JAGA n guard ▷ vb guard or watch
JAGAED > JAGA
JAGAING > JAGA
JAGAS > JAGA
JAGER same as > JAEGER
JAGERS > JAGER
JAGG same as > JAG
JAGGARIES > JAGGARY
JAGGARY same as > JAGGERY
JAGGED > JAG
JAGGEDER > JAG
JAGGEDEST > JAG
JAGGEDLY > JAG

JAGGER n pedlar
JAGGERIES > JAGGERY
JAGGERS > JAGGER
JAGGERY n coarse brown sugar made in the East Indies from the sap of the date palm
JAGGHERY same as > JAGGERY
JAGGIER > JAGGY
JAGGIES > JAGGY
JAGGIEST > JAGGY
JAGGING > JAG
JAGGS > JAGG
JAGGY adj prickly ▷ n jagged computer image
JAGHIR n Indian regional governance
JAGHIRDAR n Indian regional governor
JAGHIRE n Indian regional governance
JAGHIRES > JAGHIRE
JAGHIRS > JAGHIR
JAGIR n Indian regional governance
JAGIRS > JAGIR
JAGLESS > JAG
JAGRA n Hindu festival
JAGRAS > JAGRA
JAGS > JAG
JAGUAR n large S American spotted cat
JAGUARS > JAGUAR
JAI interj victory (to)
JAIL n prison ▷ vb send to prison
JAILABLE > JAIL
JAILBAIT n young woman, or young women collectively, considered sexually attractive but below the age of consent
JAILBAITS > JAILBAIT
JAILBIRD n person who has often been in prison
JAILBIRDS > JAILBIRD
JAILBREAK n escape from jail
JAILED > JAIL
JAILER n person in charge of a jail
JAILERESS > JAILER
JAILERS > JAILER
JAILHOUSE n jail
JAILING > JAIL
JAILLESS > JAIL
JAILOR same as > JAILER
JAILORESS > JAILOR
JAILORS > JAILOR
JAILS > JAIL
JAK same as > JACK
JAKE adj slang word meaning all right
JAKES n human excrement
JAKESES > JAKES
JAKEY n derogatory Scots word for a homeless alcoholic
JAKEYS > JAKEY
JAKFRUIT same as > JACKFRUIT
JAKFRUITS > JAKFRUIT
JAKS > JACK

JALABIB n plural of jilbab
JALAP n Mexican convolvulaceous plant
JALAPENO n very hot type of green chilli pepper, used esp in Mexican cookery
JALAPENOS > JALAPENO
JALAPIC > JALAP
JALAPIN n purgative resin
JALAPINS > JALAPIN
JALAPS > JALAP
JALFREZI adj (in Indian cookery) stir-fried with green peppers, onions and green chillies
JALOP same as > JALAP
JALOPIES > JALOPY
JALOPPIES > JALOPPY
JALOPPY same as > JALOPY
JALOPS > JALOP
JALOPY n old car
JALOUSE vb suspect
JALOUSED > JALOUSE
JALOUSES > JALOUSE
JALOUSIE n window blind or shutter constructed from angled slats of wood, plastic, etc
JALOUSIED > JALOUSIE
JALOUSIES > JALOUSIE
JALOUSING > JALOUSE
JAM vb pack tightly into a place ▷ n fruit preserve or hold-up of traffic
JAMAAT n Islamic council
JAMAATS > JAMAAT
JAMADAR n Indian army officer
JAMADARS > JAMADAR
JAMB n side post of a door or window frame ▷ vb climb up a crack in rock
JAMBALAYA n Creole dish made of shrimps, ham, rice, onions, etc
JAMBART same as > GREAVE
JAMBARTS > JAMBART
JAMBE same as > JAMB
JAMBEAU another word for > GREAVE
JAMBEAUX > JAMBEAU
JAMBED > JAMB
JAMBEE n light cane
JAMBEES > JAMBEE
JAMBER same as > GREAVE
JAMBERS > JAMBER
JAMBES > JAMBE
JAMBEUX > JAMBEAU
JAMBIER n greave
JAMBIERS > JAMBIER
JAMBING > JAMB
JAMBIYA n curved dagger
JAMBIYAH same as > JAMBIYA
JAMBIYAHS > JAMBIYAH
JAMBIYAS > JAMBIYA
JAMBO sentence substitute E African salutation
JAMBOK same as > SJAMBOK
JAMBOKKED > JAMBOK
JAMBOKS > JAMBOK

JAMBOLAN n Asian tree
JAMBOLANA same as > JAMBOLAN
JAMBOLANS > JAMBOLAN
JAMBONE n type of play in the card game euchre
JAMBONES > JAMBONE
JAMBOOL same as > JAMBOLAN
JAMBOOLS > JAMBOOL
JAMBOREE n large gathering or celebration
JAMBOREES > JAMBOREE
JAMBS > JAMB
JAMBU same as > JAMBOLAN
JAMBUL same as > JAMBOLAN
JAMBULS > JAMBUL
JAMBUS > JAMBU
JAMDANI n patterned muslin
JAMDANIS > JAMDANI
JAMES n jemmy
JAMESES > JAMES
JAMJAR n container for preserves
JAMJARS > JAMJAR
JAMLIKE > JAM
JAMMABLE > JAM
JAMMED > JAM
JAMMER > JAM
JAMMERS > JAM
JAMMIER > JAMMY
JAMMIES informal word for > PYJAMAS
JAMMIEST > JAMMY
JAMMING > JAM
JAMMINGS > JAM
JAMMY adj lucky
JAMON n as in jamon serrano cured ham from Spain
JAMPACKED adj very crowded
JAMPAN n type of sedan chair used in India
JAMPANEE n jampan bearer
JAMPANEES > JAMPANEE
JAMPANI same as > JAMPANEE
JAMPANIS > JAMPANI
JAMPANS > JAMPAN
JAMPOT n container for preserves
JAMPOTS > JAMPOT
JAMS > JAM
JANE n girl or woman
JANES > JANE
JANGLE vb (cause to) make a harsh ringing noise ▷ n harsh ringing noise
JANGLED > JANGLE
JANGLER > JANGLE
JANGLERS > JANGLE
JANGLES > JANGLE
JANGLIER > JANGLY
JANGLIEST > JANGLY
JANGLING > JANGLE
JANGLINGS > JANGLE
JANGLY adj making a jangling sound
JANIFORM adj with two faces
JANISARY same as

> JANISSARY
JANISSARY n infantryman in the Turkish army, originally a member of the sovereign's personal guard, from the 14th to the early 19th century
JANITOR n caretaker of a school or other building
JANITORS > JANITOR
JANITRESS > JANITOR
JANITRIX > JANITOR
JANIZAR same as > JANISSARY
JANIZARS > JANIZAR
JANIZARY same as > JANISSARY
JANKER n device for transporting logs
JANKERS > JANKER
JANN n lesser jinn
JANNIES > JANNY
JANNOCK same as > JONNOCK
JANNOCKS > JANNOCK
JANNS > JANN
JANNY n janitor
JANSKY n unit of flux density used predominantly in radio and infrared astronomy
JANSKYS > JANSKY
JANTEE archaic version of > JAUNTY
JANTIER > JANTY
JANTIES > JANTY
JANTIEST > JANTY
JANTY n petty officer ▷ adj (in archaic usage) jaunty
JAP vb splash
JAPAN n very hard varnish, usu black ▷ vb cover with this varnish ▷ adj relating to or varnished with japan
JAPANISE same as > JAPANIZE
JAPANISED > JAPANISE
JAPANISES > JAPANISE
JAPANIZE vb make Japanese
JAPANIZED > JAPANIZE
JAPANIZES > JAPANIZE
JAPANNED > JAPAN
JAPANNER > JAPAN
JAPANNERS > JAPAN
JAPANNING > JAPAN
JAPANS > JAPAN
JAPE n joke or prank ▷ vb joke or jest (about)
JAPED > JAPE
JAPER > JAPE
JAPERIES > JAPE
JAPERS > JAPE
JAPERY > JAPE
JAPES > JAPE
JAPING > JAPE
JAPINGLY > JAPE
JAPINGS > JAPE
JAPONICA n shrub with red flowers
JAPONICAS > JAPONICA
JAPPED > JAP
JAPPING > JAP
JAPS > JAP

JAR n wide-mouthed container, usu round and made of glass ▷ vb have a disturbing or unpleasant effect
JARARACA n South American snake
JARARACAS > JARARACA
JARARAKA same as > JARARACA
JARARAKAS > JARARAKA
JARFUL same as > JAR
JARFULS > JARFUL
JARGON n specialized technical language of a particular subject ▷ vb use or speak in jargon
JARGONED > JARGON
JARGONEER n user of jargon
JARGONEL n pear
JARGONELS > JARGONEL
JARGONING > JARGON
JARGONISE same as > JARGONIZE
JARGONISH > JARGON
JARGONIST > JARGON
JARGONIZE vb render into jargon
JARGONS > JARGON
JARGONY > JARGON
JARGOON same as > JARGON
JARGOONS > JARGOON
JARHEAD n US Marine
JARHEADS > JARHEAD
JARINA n South American palm tree
JARINAS > JARINA
JARK n seal or pass
JARKMAN n forger of passes or licences
JARKMEN > JARKMAN
JARKS > JARK
JARL n Scandinavian chieftain or noble
JARLDOM > JARL
JARLDOMS > JARL
JARLS > JARL
JARLSBERG n Norwegian cheese
JAROOL n Indian tree
JAROOLS > JAROOL
JAROSITE n yellow to brown mineral
JAROSITES > JAROSITE
JAROVISE same as > JAROVIZE
JAROVISED > JAROVISE
JAROVISES > JAROVISE
JAROVIZE vb vernalize
JAROVIZED > JAROVIZE
JAROVIZES > JAROVIZE
JARP vb strike or smash, esp to break the shell of (an egg) at Easter
JARPED > JARP
JARPING > JARP
JARPS > JARP
JARRAH n Australian eucalypt yielding valuable timber
JARRAHS > JARRAH
JARRED > JAR

JARRING > JAR
JARRINGLY > JAR
JARRINGS > JAR
JARS > JAR
JARSFUL > JARFUL
JARTA n heart
JARTAS > JARTA
JARUL variant of > JAROOL
JARULS > JARUL
JARVEY n hackney coachman
JARVEYS > JARVEY
JARVIE same as > JARVEY
JARVIES > JARVIE
JASEY n wig
JASEYS > JASEY
JASIES > JASEY
JASMIN same as > JASMINE
JASMINE n shrub with sweet-smelling yellow or white flowers
JASMINES > JASMINE
JASMINS > JASMIN
JASMONATE n plant hormone that regulates growth
JASP another word for > JASPER
JASPE adj resembling jasper ▷ n subtly striped woven fabric
JASPER n red, yellow, dark green, or brown variety of quartz
JASPERISE same as > JASPERIZE
JASPERIZE vb turn into jasper
JASPEROUS > JASPER
JASPERS > JASPER
JASPERY > JASPER
JASPES > JASPE
JASPIDEAN > JASPER
JASPILITE n rock like jasper
JASPIS archaic word for > JASPER
JASPISES > JASPIS
JASPS > JASP
JASS obsolete variant of > JAZZ
JASSES > JASS
JASSID n leafhopper
JASSIDS > JASSID
JASY n wig
JATAKA n text describing the birth of Buddha
JATAKAS > JATAKA
JATO n jet-assisted takeoff
JATOS > JATO
JATROPHA n poisonous shrub of C America used primarily as a biofuel
JATROPHAS > JATROPHA
JAUK vb dawdle
JAUKED > JAUK
JAUKING > JAUK
JAUKS > JAUK
JAUNCE vb prance
JAUNCED > JAUNCE
JAUNCES > JAUNCE
JAUNCING > JAUNCE
JAUNDICE n disease

marked by yellowness of the skin ▷ vb distort (the judgment, etc) adversely
JAUNDICED > JAUNDICE
JAUNDICES > JAUNDICE
JAUNSE same as > JAUNCE
JAUNSED > JAUNSE
JAUNSES > JAUNSE
JAUNSING > JAUNSE
JAUNT n short journey for pleasure ▷ vb make such a journey
JAUNTED > JAUNT
JAUNTEE old spelling of > JAUNTY
JAUNTIE old spelling of > JAUNTY
JAUNTIER > JAUNTY
JAUNTIES > JAUNTY
JAUNTIEST > JAUNTY
JAUNTILY > JAUNTY
JAUNTING > JAUNT
JAUNTS > JAUNT
JAUNTY adj sprightly and cheerful ▷ n master-at-arms on a naval ship
JAUP same as > JARP
JAUPED > JAUP
JAUPING > JAUP
JAUPS > JAUP
JAVA n coffee or a variety of it
JAVAS > JAVA
JAVEL as in javel water aqueous solution containing sodium hypochlorite and some sodium chloride, used as a bleach and disinfectant
JAVELIN n light spear thrown in sports competitions ▷ vb spear with a javelin
JAVELINA n collared peccary
JAVELINAS > JAVELINA
JAVELINED > JAVELIN
JAVELINS > JAVELIN
JAVELS > JAVEL
JAW n one of the bones in which the teeth are set ▷ vb talk lengthily
JAWAN n (in India) a soldier
JAWANS > JAWAN
JAWARI n variety of sorghum
JAWARIS > JAWARI
JAWBATION n scolding
JAWBONE n lower jaw of a person or animal ▷ vb try to persuade or bring pressure to bear (on) by virtue of one's high office or position, esp in urging compliance with official policy
JAWBONED > JAWBONE
JAWBONER > JAWBONE
JAWBONERS > JAWBONE
JAWBONES > JAWBONE
JAWBONING > JAWBONE
JAWBOX n metal sink
JAWBOXES > JAWBOX
JAWED > JAW

JAWFALL n depression
JAWFALLS > JAWFALL
JAWHOLE n cesspit
JAWHOLES > JAWHOLE
JAWING > JAW
JAWINGS > JAW
JAWLESS > JAW
JAWLIKE > JAW
JAWLINE n outline of the jaw
JAWLINES > JAWLINE
JAWS > JAW
JAXIE same as > JACKSIE
JAXIES > JAXIE
JAXY same as > JACKSIE
JAY n bird with a pinkish body and blue-and-black wings
JAYBIRD n jay
JAYBIRDS > JAYBIRD
JAYCEE n member of a Junior Chamber of Commerce
JAYCEES > JAYCEE
JAYGEE n lieutenant junior grade in the US army
JAYGEES > JAYGEE
JAYHAWKER n Unionist guerrilla in US Civil War
JAYS > JAY
JAYVEE n junior varsity sports team
JAYVEES > JAYVEE
JAYWALK vb cross or walk in a street recklessly or illegally
JAYWALKED > JAYWALK
JAYWALKER > JAYWALK
JAYWALKS > JAYWALK
JAZERANT n coat of metal plates sewn onto cloth
JAZERANTS > JAZERANT
JAZIES > JAZY
JAZY n wig
JAZZ n kind of music with an exciting rhythm, usu involving improvisation ▷ vb play or dance to jazz music
JAZZBO n jazz musician or fan
JAZZBOS > JAZZBO
JAZZED > JAZZ
JAZZER > JAZZ
JAZZERS > JAZZ
JAZZES > JAZZ
JAZZIER > JAZZY
JAZZIEST > JAZZY
JAZZILY > JAZZY
JAZZINESS > JAZZY
JAZZING > JAZZ
JAZZLIKE > JAZZ
JAZZMAN > JAZZ
JAZZMEN > JAZZ
JAZZY adj flashy or showy
JEALOUS adj fearful of losing a partner or possession to a rival
JEALOUSE vb be jealous of
JEALOUSED > JEALOUSE
JEALOUSES > JEALOUSE
JEALOUSLY > JEALOUS
JEALOUSY n state of or an instance of feeling jealous

JEAN n tough twill-weave cotton fabric used for hard-wearing trousers, overalls, etc
JEANED adj wearing jeans
JEANETTE n light jean cloth
JEANETTES > JEANETTE
JEANS npl casual denim trousers
JEAT n jet
JEATS > JEAT
JEBEL n hill or mountain in an Arab country
JEBELS > JEBEL
JEDI n person claiming to live according to a philosophy based on that of the fictional Jedi, from the StarWars films
JEDIS > JEDI
JEE variant of > GEE
JEED > JEE
JEEING > JEE
JEEL vb make into jelly
JEELED > JEEL
JEELIE same as > JEELY
JEELIED > JEELY
JEELIEING > JEELIE
JEELIES > JEELY
JEELING > JEEL
JEELS > JEEL
JEELY n jelly ▷ vb make into jelly
JEELYING > JEELY
JEEP n small military four-wheel drive road vehicle ▷ vb travel in a jeep
JEEPED > JEEP
JEEPERS interj mild exclamation of surprise
JEEPING > JEEP
JEEPNEY n Filipino bus converted from a jeep
JEEPNEYS > JEEPNEY
JEEPS > JEEP
JEER vb scoff or deride ▷ n cry of derision
JEERED > JEER
JEERER > JEER
JEERERS > JEER
JEERING > JEER
JEERINGLY > JEER
JEERINGS > JEER
JEERS > JEER
JEES > JEE
JEEZ interj expression of surprise or irritation
JEFE n (in Spanish-speaking countries) a military or political leader
JEFES > JEFE
JEFF vb downsize or close down (an organization)
JEFFED > JEFF
JEFFING > JEFF
JEFFS > JEFF
JEHAD same as > JIHAD
JEHADEEN same as > JIHADEEN
JEHADI same as > JIHADI
JEHADIS > JEHADI
JEHADISM same as > JIHADISM

JEHADISMS > JEHADISM
JEHADIST > JEHADISM
JEHADISTS > JEHADISM
JEHADS > JEHAD
JEHU n fast driver
JEHUS > JEHU
JEJUNA > JEJUNUM
JEJUNAL > JEJUNUM
JEJUNE adj simple or naive
JEJUNELY > JEJUNE
JEJUNITY > JEJUNE
JEJUNUM n part of the small intestine between the duodenum and the ileum
JELAB same as > JELLABA
JELABS > JELAB
JELL vb form into a jelly-like substance
JELLABA n loose robe with a hood, worn by some Arab men
JELLABAH same as > JELLABA
JELLABAHS > JELLABAH
JELLABAS > JELLABA
JELLED > JELL
JELLIED > JELLY
JELLIES > JELLY
JELLIFIED > JELLIFY
JELLIFIES > JELLIFY
JELLIFY vb make into or become jelly
JELLING > JELL
JELLO n (in US English) fruit-flavoured clear dessert set with gelatine
JELLOS > JELLO
JELLS > JELL
JELLY n fruit-flavoured clear dessert set with gelatine ▷ vb jellify
JELLYBEAN n bean-shaped sweet with a brightly coloured coating around a gelatinous filling
JELLYFISH n small jelly-like sea animal
JELLYING > JELLY
JELLYLIKE > JELLY
JELLYROLL n type of cake
JELUTONG n Malaysian tree
JELUTONGS > JELUTONG
JEMADAR n native junior officer belonging to a locally raised regiment serving as mercenaries in India, esp with the British Army (until 1947)
JEMADARS > JEMADAR
JEMBE n hoe
JEMBES > JEMBE
JEMIDAR same as > JEMADAR
JEMIDARS > JEMIDAR
JEMIMA n boot with elastic sides
JEMIMAS > JEMIMA
JEMMIED > JEMMY
JEMMIER > JEMMY
JEMMIES > JEMMY
JEMMIEST > JEMMY
JEMMINESS > JEMMY

JEMMY n short steel crowbar used by burglars ▷ vb prise (something) open with a jemmy ▷ adj neat
JEMMYING > JEMMY
JENNET n female donkey or ass
JENNETING n early-season apple
JENNETS > JENNET
JENNIES > JENNY
JENNY same as > JENNET
JEOFAIL n oversight in legal pleading
JEOFAILS > JEOFAIL
JEON n Korean pancake
JEOPARD vb put in jeopardy
JEOPARDED > JEOPARD
JEOPARDER > JEOPARD
JEOPARDS > JEOPARD
JEOPARDY n danger ▷ vb put in jeopardy
JEQUERITY same as > JEQUIRITY
JEQUIRITY n seed of the Indian liquorice
JERBIL variant spelling of > GERBIL
JERBILS > JERBIL
JERBOA n small mouselike rodent with long hind legs
JERBOAS > JERBOA
JEREED same as > JERID
JEREEDS > JEREED
JEREMIAD n long mournful complaint
JEREMIADS > JEREMIAD
JEREPIGO n sweet fortified wine similar to port
JEREPIGOS > JEREPIGO
JERFALCON variant of > GYRFALCON
JERID n wooden javelin used in Muslim countries in military displays on horseback
JERIDS > JERID
JERK vb move or throw abruptly ▷ n sharp or abruptly stopped movement
JERKED > JERK
JERKER > JERK
JERKERS > JERK
JERKIER > JERKY
JERKIES > JERKY
JERKIEST > JERKY
JERKILY > JERKY
JERKIN n sleeveless jacket
JERKINESS > JERKY
JERKING > JERK
JERKINGLY > JERK
JERKINGS > JERK
JERKINS > JERKIN
JERKS > JERK
JERKWATER adj inferior and insignificant ▷ n railway locomotive
JERKY adj characterized by jerks ▷ n type of cured meat

JEROBOAM n wine bottle holding the equivalent of four normal bottles (approximately 104 ounces)
JEROBOAMS > JEROBOAM
JERQUE vb search for contraband
JERQUED > JERQUE
JERQUER > JERQUE
JERQUERS > JERQUE
JERQUES > JERQUE
JERQUING > JERQUE
JERQUINGS > JERQUE
JERREED variant spelling of > JERID
JERREEDS > JERREED
JERRICAN n five-gallon fuel can
JERRICANS > JERRICAN
JERRID n blunt javelin
JERRIDS > JERRID
JERRIES > JERRY
JERRY short for > JEROBOAM
JERRYCAN n flat-sided can used for storing or transporting liquids, esp motor fuel
JERRYCANS > JERRYCAN
JERSEY n knitted jumper
JERSEYED > JERSEY
JERSEYS > JERSEY
JESS n short leather strap, one end of which is permanently attached to the leg of a hawk or falcon while the other can be attached to a leash ▷ vb put jesses on (a hawk or falcon)
JESSAMIES > JESSAMY
JESSAMINE same as > JASMINE
JESSAMY n fop
JESSANT adj emerging
JESSE same as > JESS
JESSED > JESS
JESSERANT n coat of metal plates sewn onto cloth
JESSES > JESS
JESSIE n effeminate, weak, or cowardly boy or man
JESSIES > JESSIE
JESSING > JESS
JEST vb joke ▷ n something done or said for amusement
JESTBOOK n book of amusing stories
JESTBOOKS > JESTBOOK
JESTED > JEST
JESTEE n person about whom a joke is made
JESTEES > JESTEE
JESTER n professional clown at court
JESTERS > JESTER
JESTFUL > JEST
JESTING > JEST
JESTINGLY > JEST
JESTINGS > JEST
JESTS > JEST

j

JESUIT n offensive term for a person given to subtle and equivocating arguments
JESUITIC > JESUIT
JESUITISM > JESUIT
JESUITRY > JESUIT
JESUITS > JESUIT
JESUS n French paper size
JET n aircraft driven by jet propulsion ▷ vb fly by jet aircraft
JETBEAD n ornamental shrub
JETBEADS > JETBEAD
JETE n step in which the dancer springs from one leg and lands on the other
JETES > JETE
JETFOIL n type of hydrofoil that is propelled by water jets
JETFOILS > JETFOIL
JETLAG n tiredness caused by crossing timezones in jet flight
JETLAGS > JETLAG
JETLIKE > JET
JETLINER n commercial airliner powered by jet engines
JETLINERS > JETLINER
JETON n gambling chip
JETONS > JETON
JETPORT n airport for jet planes
JETPORTS > JETPORT
JETS > JET
JETSAM n goods thrown overboard to lighten a ship
JETSAMS > JETSAM
JETSOM same as > JETSAM
JETSOMS > JETSOM
JETSON archaic form of > JETSAM
JETSONS > JETSON
JETSTREAM n narrow belt of high-altitude winds moving east at high speeds)
JETTATURA n evil eye
JETTED > JET
JETTIED > JETTY
JETTIER > JETTY
JETTIES > JETTY
JETTIEST > JETTY
JETTINESS > JETTY
JETTING > JET
JETTISON vb abandon
JETTISONS > JETTISON
JETTON n counter or token, esp a chip used in such gambling games as roulette
JETTONS > JETTON
JETTY n small pier ▷ adj of or resembling jet, esp in colour or polish ▷ vb equip with a cantilevered floor
JETTYING > JETTY
JETWAY n tradename of a mobile elevated gangway connecting an aircraft to a departure gate, allowing passengers to board and disembark

JETWAYS > JETWAY
JEU n game
JEUNE adj young
JEUX > JEU
JEW vb obsolete offensive word for haggle ▷ n obsolete offensive word for a haggler
JEWED > JEW
JEWEL n precious or semiprecious stone ▷ vb fit or decorate with a jewel or jewels
JEWELED > JEWEL
JEWELER same as > JEWELLER
JEWELERS > JEWELER
JEWELFISH n beautifully coloured fish popular in aquaria
JEWELING > JEWEL
JEWELLED > JEWEL
JEWELLER n dealer in jewels
JEWELLERS > JEWELLER
JEWELLERY n objects decorated with precious stones
JEWELLIKE > JEWEL
JEWELLING > JEWEL
JEWELRIES > JEWELRY
JEWELRY same as > JEWELLERY
JEWELS > JEWEL
JEWELWEED n small bushy plant
JEWFISH n freshwater catfish
JEWFISHES > JEWFISH
JEWIE n jewfish
JEWIES > JEWIE
JEWING > JEW
JEWS > JEW
JEZAIL n Afghan musket
JEZAILS > JEZAIL
JEZEBEL n shameless or scheming woman
JEZEBELS > JEZEBEL
JHALA n Indian musical style
JHALAS > JHALA
JHATKA n slaughter of animals for food according to Sikh law
JHATKAS > JHATKA
JIAO n Chinese currency unit
JIAOS > JIAO
JIB same as > JIBE
JIBB same as > JIBE
JIBBA n long, loose coat worn by Muslim men
JIBBAH same as > JUBBAH
JIBBAHS > JIBBAH
JIBBAS > JIBBA
JIBBED > JIBB
JIBBER variant of > GIBBER
JIBBERED > JIBBER
JIBBERING > JIBBER
JIBBERS > JIBBER
JIBBING > JIBB
JIBBINGS > JIBB

JIBBONS npl spring onions
JIBBOOM n spar forming an extension of the bowsprit
JIBBOOMS > JIBBOOM
JIBBS > JIBB
JIBE vb taunt or jeer ▷ n insulting or taunting remark
JIBED > JIBE
JIBER > JIBE
JIBERS > JIBE
JIBES > JIBE
JIBING > JIBE
JIBINGLY > JIBE
JIBS > JIB
JICAMA n pale brown turnip with crisp sweet flesh, originating in Mexico
JICAMAS > JICAMA
JICKAJOG vb engage in sexual intercourse
JICKAJOGS > JICKAJOG
JIFF same as > JIFFY
JIFFIES > JIFFY
JIFFS > JIFF
JIFFY n very short period of time
JIG n type of lively dance ▷ vb dance a jig
JIGABOO n offensive term for a Black person
JIGABOOS > JIGABOO
JIGAJIG vb engage in sexual intercourse
JIGAJIGS > JIGAJIG
JIGAJOG variant of > JIGAJIG
JIGAJOGS > JIGAJOG
JIGAMAREE n thing
JIGGED > JIG
JIGGER n small whisky glass ▷ vb interfere or alter
JIGGERED > JIGGER
JIGGERING > JIGGER
JIGGERS > JIGGER
JIGGIER > JIGGY
JIGGIEST > JIGGY
JIGGING > JIG
JIGGINGS > JIG
JIGGISH > JIG
JIGGLE vb move up and down with short jerky movements ▷ n short jerky motion
JIGGLED > JIGGLE
JIGGLES > JIGGLE
JIGGLIER > JIGGLE
JIGGLIEST > JIGGLE
JIGGLING > JIGGLE
JIGGLY > JIGGLE
JIGGUMBOB n thing
JIGGY adj resembling a jig
JIGJIG variant of > JIGAJIG
JIGJIGGED > JIGJIG
JIGJIGS > JIGJIG
JIGLIKE > JIG
JIGOT same as > GIGOT
JIGOTS > JIGOT
JIGS > JIG
JIGSAW n picture cut into interlocking pieces, which the user tries to fit together

again ▷ vb cut with a jigsaw
JIGSAWED > JIGSAW
JIGSAWING > JIGSAW
JIGSAWN > JIGSAW
JIGSAWS > JIGSAW
JIHAD n Islamic holy war against unbelievers
JIHADEEN npl jihadists
JIHADI n person who takes part in a jihad
JIHADIS > JIHADI
JIHADISM n Islamic fundamentalist movement that favours the pursuit of jihads in defence of the Islamic faith
JIHADISMS > JIHADISM
JIHADIST > JIHADISM
JIHADISTS > JIHADISM
JIHADS > JIHAD
JILBAB n long robe worn by Muslim women
JILBABS > JILBAB
JILGIE n freshwater crayfish
JILGIES > JILGIE
JILL variant spelling of > GILL
JILLAROO n female jackeroo
JILLAROOS > JILLAROO
JILLET n wanton woman
JILLETS > JILLET
JILLFLIRT same as > JILLET
JILLION n extremely large number or amount
JILLIONS > JILLION
JILLIONTH > JILLION
JILLS > JILL
JILT vb leave or reject (one's lover) ▷ n woman who jilts a lover
JILTED > JILT
JILTER > JILT
JILTERS > JILT
JILTING > JILT
JILTS > JILT
JIMCRACK same as > GIMCRACK
JIMCRACKS > JIMCRACK
JIMINY interj expression of surprise
JIMJAM > JIMJAMS
JIMJAMS npl state of nervous tension, excitement, or anxiety
JIMMIE same as > JIMMY
JIMMIED > JIMMY
JIMMIES > JIMMY
JIMMINY interj expression of surprise
JIMMY same as > JEMMY
JIMMYING > JIMMY
JIMP adj handsome
JIMPER > JIMP
JIMPEST > JIMP
JIMPIER > JIMPY
JIMPIEST > JIMPY
JIMPLY adv neatly
JIMPNESS > JIMP
JIMPSON same as > JIMSON

JIMPY *adj* neat and tidy

JIMSON as in *jimson weed* type of poisonous plant with white flowers and shiny fruits

JIN *n* Chinese unit of weight

JINGAL *n* swivel-mounted gun

JINGALL *same as* > JINGAL

JINGALLS > JINGALL

JINGALS > JINGAL

JINGBANG *n* entirety of something

JINGBANGS > JINGBANG

JINGKO *same as* > GINGKO

JINGKOES > JINGKO

JINGLE *n* catchy verse or song used in a radio or television advert ▷ *vb* (cause to) make a gentle ringing sound

JINGLED > JINGLE

JINGLER > JINGLE

JINGLERS > JINGLE

JINGLES > JINGLE

JINGLET *n* sleigh-bell clapper

JINGLETS > JINGLET

JINGLIER > JINGLE

JINGLIEST > JINGLE

JINGLING > JINGLE

JINGLY > JINGLE

JINGO *n* loud and bellicose patriot; chauvinism

JINGOES > JINGO

JINGOISH > JINGO

JINGOISM *n* aggressive nationalism

JINGOISMS > JINGOISM

JINGOIST > JINGOISM

JINGOISTS > JINGOISM

JINJILI *n* type of sesame

JINJILIS > JINJILI

JINK *vb* move quickly or jerkily in order to dodge someone ▷ *n* jinking movement

JINKED > JINK

JINKER *n* vehicle for transporting timber, consisting of a tractor and two sets of wheels for supporting the logs ▷ *vb* carry or transport in a jinker

JINKERED > JINKER

JINKERING > JINKER

JINKERS > JINKER

JINKING > JINK

JINKS > JINK

JINN > JINNI

JINNE *interj* South African exclamation expressing surprise, admiration, shock, etc

JINNEE *same as* > JINNI

JINNI *n* spirit in Muslim mythology

JINNIS > JINNI

JINNS > JINNI

JINRIKSHA *same as* > RICKSHAW

JINS > JIN

JINX *n* person or thing bringing bad luck ▷ *vb* be or put a jinx on

JINXED > JINX

JINXES > JINX

JINXING > JINX

JIPIJAPA *n* palmlike Central and South American plant whose fanlike leaves are bleached for making panama hats

JIPIJAPAS > JIPIJAPA

JIPYAPA *same as* > JIPIJAPA

JIPYAPAS > JIPYAPA

JIRBLE *vb* pour carelessly

JIRBLED > JIRBLE

JIRBLES > JIRBLE

JIRBLING > JIRBLE

JIRD *n* gerbil

JIRDS > JIRD

JIRGA *n* Afghan council

JIRGAS > JIRGA

JIRKINET *n* bodice

JIRKINETS > JIRKINET

JIRRE *same as* > JINNE

JISM *slang word for* > SEMEN

JISMS > JISM

JISSOM *slang word for* > SEMEN

JISSOMS > JISSOM

JITNEY *n* small bus that carries passengers for a low price, originally five cents

JITNEYS > JITNEY

JITTER *vb* be anxious or nervous

JITTERBUG *n* fast jerky American dance that was popular in the 1940s ▷ *vb* dance the jitterbug

JITTERED > JITTER

JITTERIER > JITTERY

JITTERING > JITTER

JITTERS > JITTER

JITTERY *adj* nervous

JIUJITSU *variant spelling of* > JUJITSU

JIUJITSUS > JIUJITSU

JIUJUTSU *same as* > JUJITSU

JIUJUTSUS > JIUJUTSU

JIVE *n* lively dance of the 1940s and '50s ▷ *vb* dance the jive

JIVEASS *adj* misleading or phoney

JIVED > JIVE

JIVER > JIVE

JIVERS > JIVE

JIVES > JIVE

JIVEY > JIVE

JIVIER > JIVE

JIVIEST > JIVE

JIVING > JIVE

JIVY > JIVE

JIZ *n* wig

JIZZ *n* term for the total combination of characteristics that serve to identify a particular species of bird or plant

JIZZES > JIZZ

JNANA *n* type of yoga

JNANAS > JNANA

JO *n* Scots word for sweetheart

JOANNA *n* piano

JOANNAS > JOANNA

JOANNES *same as* > JOHANNES

JOANNESES > JOANNES

JOB *n* occupation or paid employment ▷ *vb* work at casual jobs

JOBATION *n* scolding

JOBATIONS > JOBATION

JOBBED > JOB

JOBBER *n* person who jobs

JOBBERIES > JOBBERY

JOBBERS > JOBBER

JOBBERY *n* practice of making private profit out of a public office

JOBBIE *n* piece of excrement

JOBBIES > JOBBIE

JOBBING *adj* doing individual jobs for payment ▷ *n* act of seeking work

JOBBINGS > JOBBING

JOBCENTRE *n* office where unemployed people can find out about job vacancies

JOBE *vb* scold

JOBED > JOBE

JOBERNOWL *n* stupid person

JOBES > JOBE

JOBHOLDER *n* person who has a job

JOBING > JOBE

JOBLESS *npl* unemployed people ▷ *adj* unemployed

JOBNAME *n* title of position

JOBNAMES > JOBNAME

JOBS > JOB

JOBSEEKER *n* person looking for employment

JOBSHARE *n* arrangement in which two or more people divide the duties and payment for one position between them, working at different times

JOBSHARES > JOBSHARE

JOBSWORTH *n* person in a position of minor authority who invokes the letter of the law in order to avoid any action requiring initiative, cooperation, etc

JOCK *n* athlete

JOCKETTE *n* female athlete

JOCKETTES > JOCKETTE

JOCKEY *n* person who rides horses in races, esp as a profession or for hire ▷ *vb* ride (a horse) in a race

JOCKEYED > JOCKEY

JOCKEYING > JOCKEY

JOCKEYISH > JOCKEY

JOCKEYISM *n* skills and practices of jockeys

JOCKEYS > JOCKEY

JOCKISH *adj* macho

JOCKO *n* chimpanzee

JOCKOS > JOCKO

JOCKS > JOCK

JOCKSTRAP *n* belt with a pouch to support the genitals, worn by male athletes

JOCKTELEG *n* clasp knife

JOCO *adj* relaxed

JOCOSE *adj* playful or humorous

JOCOSELY > JOCOSE

JOCOSITY > JOCOSE

JOCULAR *adj* fond of joking

JOCULARLY > JOCULAR

JOCULATOR *n* joker

JOCUND *adj* merry or cheerful

JOCUNDITY > JOCUND

JOCUNDLY > JOCUND

JODEL *same as* > YODEL

JODELLED > JODEL

JODELLING > JODEL

JODELS > JODEL

JODHPUR as in *jodhpur boots* ankle-length leather riding boots

JODHPURS *npl* riding breeches, loose-fitting around the hips and tight-fitting from the thighs to the ankles

JOE *same as* > JO

JOES > JOE

JOEY *n* young kangaroo

JOEYS > JOEY

JOG *vb* run at a gentle pace, esp for exercise ▷ *n* slow run

JOGGED > JOG

JOGGER *n* person who runs at a jog trot over some distance for exercise, usually regularly

JOGGERS > JOGGER

JOGGING > JOG

JOGGINGS > JOG

JOGGLE *vb* shake or move jerkily ▷ *n* act of joggling

JOGGLED > JOGGLE

JOGGLER > JOGGLE

JOGGLERS > JOGGLE

JOGGLES > JOGGLE

JOGGLING > JOGGLE

JOGPANTS *npl* trousers worn for jogging

JOGS > JOG

JOGTROT *n* easy bouncy gait, esp of a horse, midway between a walk and a trot

JOGTROTS > JOGTROT

JOHANNES *n* Portuguese gold coin minted in the early 18th century

JOHN *n* toilet

JOHNBOAT *n* small flat-bottomed boat

JOHNBOATS > JOHNBOAT

JOHNNIE *same as* > JOHNNY

JOHNNIES > JOHNNY

JOHNNY *n* chap

JOHNS > JOHN

JOHNSON *slang word for* > PENIS

j

JOHNSONS > JOHNSON
JOIN vb become a member (of) ▷ n place where two things are joined
JOINABLE > JOIN
JOINDER n act of joining, esp in legal contexts
JOINDERS > JOINDER
JOINED > JOIN
JOINER n maker of finished woodwork
JOINERIES > JOINERY
JOINERS > JOINER
JOINERY n joiner's work
JOINING > JOIN
JOININGS > JOIN
JOINS > JOIN
JOINT adj shared by two or more ▷ n place where bones meet but can move ▷ vb divide meat into joints
JOINTED adj having a joint or joints
JOINTEDLY > JOINTED
JOINTER n tool for pointing mortar joints, as in brickwork
JOINTERS > JOINTER
JOINTING > JOINT
JOINTINGS > JOINTING
JOINTLESS > JOINT
JOINTLY > JOINT
JOINTNESS > JOINT
JOINTRESS n woman entitled to a jointure
JOINTS > JOINT
JOINTURE n provision made by a husband for his wife by settling property upon her at marriage for her use after his death
JOINTURED > JOINTURE
JOINTURES > JOINTURE
JOINTWEED n American wild plant
JOINTWORM n larva of chalcid flies which form galls on the stems of cereal plants
JOIST n horizontal beam that helps support a floor or ceiling ▷ vb construct (a floor, roof, etc) with joists
JOISTED > JOIST
JOISTING > JOIST
JOISTS > JOIST
JOJOBA n shrub of SW North America whose seeds yield oil used in cosmetics
JOJOBAS > JOJOBA
JOKE n thing said or done to cause laughter ▷ vb make jokes
JOKED > JOKE
JOKER n person who jokes
JOKERS > JOKER
JOKES > JOKE
JOKESMITH n comedian
JOKESOME > JOKE
JOKESTER n person who makes jokes
JOKESTERS > JOKESTER
JOKEY adj intended as a joke

JOKIER > JOKEY
JOKIEST > JOKEY
JOKILY > JOKE
JOKINESS > JOKE
JOKING > JOKE
JOKINGLY > JOKE
JOKOL Shetland word for **>** YES
JOKY same as **>** JOKEY
JOL n party ▷ vb have a good time
JOLE vb knock
JOLED > JOLE
JOLES > JOLE
JOLING > JOLE
JOLIOTIUM n former name proposed for dubnium
JOLL variant of **>** JOLE
JOLLED > JOL
JOLLER n person who has a good time
JOLLERS > JOLLER
JOLLEY same as **>** JOLLY
JOLLEYER > JOLLEY
JOLLEYERS > JOLLEY
JOLLEYING > JOLLEY
JOLLEYS > JOLLEY
JOLLIED > JOLLY
JOLLIER n joker
JOLLIERS > JOLLIER
JOLLIES > JOLLY
JOLLIEST > JOLLY
JOLLIFIED > JOLLIFY
JOLLIFIES > JOLLIFY
JOLLIFY vb be or cause to be jolly
JOLLILY > JOLLY
JOLLIMENT > JOLLY
JOLLINESS > JOLLY
JOLLING > JOL
JOLLITIES > JOLLITY
JOLLITY n condition of being jolly
JOLLOP n cream or unguent
JOLLOPS > JOLLOP
JOLLS > JOLL
JOLLY adj full of good humour ▷ adv extremely ▷ vb try to make or keep (someone) cheerful ▷ n festivity or celebration
JOLLYBOAT n small boat used as a utility tender for a vessel
JOLLYER > JOLLY
JOLLYERS > JOLLY
JOLLYHEAD same as **>** JOLLITY
JOLLYING > JOLLY
JOLLYINGS > JOLLY
JOLS > JOL
JOLT n unpleasant surprise or shock ▷ vb surprise or shock
JOLTED > JOLT
JOLTER > JOLT
JOLTERS > JOLT
JOLTHEAD n fool
JOLTHEADS > JOLTHEAD
JOLTIER > JOLT
JOLTIEST > JOLT
JOLTILY > JOLT

JOLTING > JOLT
JOLTINGLY > JOLT
JOLTS > JOLT
JOLTY > JOLT
JOMO same as **>** ZO
JOMON n particular era in Japanese history
JOMOS > JOMO
JONCANOE n Jamaican ceremony
JONCANOES > JONCANOE
JONES vb desire
JONESED > JONES
JONESES > JONES
JONESING > JONES
JONG n friend, often used in direct address
JONGLEUR n (in medieval France) an itinerant minstrel
JONGLEURS > JONGLEUR
JONGS > JONG
JONNOCK adj genuine ▷ adv honestly
JONNYCAKE n type of flat bread
JONQUIL n fragrant narcissus
JONQUILS > JONQUIL
JONTIES > JONTY
JONTY vb petty officer
JOOK vb poke or puncture (the skin) ▷ n jab or the resulting wound
JOOKED > JOOK
JOOKERIES > JOOKERY
JOOKERY n mischief
JOOKING > JOOK
JOOKS > JOOK
JOR n movement in Indian music
JORAM same as **>** JORUM
JORAMS > JORAM
JORDAN n chamber pot
JORDANS > JORDAN
JORDELOO same as **>** GARDYLOO
JORDELOOS > JORDELOO
JORS > JOR
JORUM n large drinking bowl or vessel or its contents
JORUMS > JORUM
JOSEPH n woman's floor-length riding coat with a small cape, worn esp in the 18th century
JOSEPHS > JOSEPH
JOSH vb tease ▷ n teasing or bantering joke
JOSHED > JOSH
JOSHER > JOSH
JOSHERS > JOSH
JOSHES > JOSH
JOSHING > JOSH
JOSHINGLY > JOSH
JOSKIN n bumpkin
JOSKINS > JOSKIN
JOSS n Chinese deity worshipped in the form of an idol
JOSSER n simpleton
JOSSERS > JOSSER
JOSSES > JOSS

JOSTLE vb knock or push against ▷ n act of jostling
JOSTLED > JOSTLE
JOSTLER > JOSTLE
JOSTLERS > JOSTLE
JOSTLES > JOSTLE
JOSTLING > JOSTLE
JOSTLINGS > JOSTLE
JOT vb write briefly ▷ n very small amount
JOTA n Spanish dance with castanets in fast triple time, usually to a guitar and voice accompaniment
JOTAS > JOTA
JOTS > JOT
JOTTED > JOT
JOTTER n notebook
JOTTERS > JOTTER
JOTTIER > JOTTY
JOTTIEST > JOTTY
JOTTING > JOT
JOTTINGS > JOT
JOTTY > JOT
JOTUN n giant
JOTUNN same as **>** JOTUN
JOTUNNS > JOTUNN
JOTUNS > JOTUN
JOUAL n nonstandard variety of Canadian French
JOUALS > JOUAL
JOUGS npl iron ring, fastened by a chain to a wall, post, or tree, in which an offender was held by the neck
JOUISANCE n joy
JOUK vb duck or dodge ▷ n sudden evasive movement
JOUKED > JOUK
JOUKERIES > JOUKERY
JOUKERY same as **>** JOOKERY
JOUKING > JOUK
JOUKS > JOUK
JOULE n unit of work or energy ▷ vb knock
JOULED > JOULE
JOULES > JOULE
JOULING > JOULE
JOUNCE vb shake or jolt or cause to shake or jolt ▷ n jolting movement
JOUNCED > JOUNCE
JOUNCES > JOUNCE
JOUNCIER > JOUNCE
JOUNCIEST > JOUNCE
JOUNCING > JOUNCE
JOUNCY > JOUNCE
JOUR n day
JOURNAL n daily newspaper or magazine ▷ vb record in a journal
JOURNALED > JOURNAL
JOURNALS > JOURNAL
JOURNEY n act or process of travelling from one place to another ▷ vb travel
JOURNEYED > JOURNEY
JOURNEYER > JOURNEY
JOURNEYS > JOURNEY
JOURNO n journalist
JOURNOS > JOURNO
JOURS > JOUR

JOUST n combat with lances between two mounted knights ▷ vb fight on horseback using lances

JOUSTED > JOUST

JOUSTER > JOUST

JOUSTERS > JOUST

JOUSTING > JOUST

JOUSTS > JOUST

JOVIAL adj happy and cheerful

JOVIALITY > JOVIAL

JOVIALLY > JOVIAL

JOVIALTY same as > JOVIAL

JOW vb ring (a bell)

JOWAR n variety of sorghum

JOWARI same as > JOWAR

JOWARIS > JOWAR

JOWARS > JOWAR

JOWED > JOW

JOWING > JOW

JOWL n lower jaw ▷ vb knock

JOWLED > JOWL

JOWLER n dog with prominent jowls

JOWLERS > JOWLER

JOWLIER > JOWL

JOWLIEST > JOWL

JOWLINESS > JOWL

JOWLING > JOWL

JOWLS > JOWL

JOWLY > JOWL

JOWS > JOW

JOY n feeling of great delight or pleasure ▷ vb feel joy

JOYANCE n joyous feeling or festivity

JOYANCES > JOYANCE

JOYED > JOY

JOYFUL adj feeling or bringing great joy

JOYFULLER > JOYFUL

JOYFULLY > JOYFUL

JOYING > JOY

JOYLESS adj feeling or bringing no joy

JOYLESSLY > JOYLESS

JOYOUS adj extremely happy and enthusiastic

JOYOUSLY > JOYOUS

JOYPAD n computer games console consisting of buttons on a pad

JOYPADS > JOYPAD

JOYPOP vb take addictive drugs occasionally without becoming addicted

JOYPOPPED > JOYPOP

JOYPOPPER > JOYPOP

JOYPOPS > JOYPOP

JOYRIDDEN > JOYRIDE

JOYRIDE n drive in a car one has stolen ▷ vb take such a ride

JOYRIDER > JOYRIDE

JOYRIDERS > JOYRIDE

JOYRIDES > JOYRIDE

JOYRIDING > JOYRIDE

JOYRODE > JOYRIDE

JOYS > JOY

JOYSTICK n control device

for an aircraft or computer

JOYSTICKS > JOYSTICK

JUBA n lively African-American dance developed in the southern US

JUBAS > JUBA

JUBATE adj possessing a mane

JUBBAH n long loose outer garment with wide sleeves, worn by Muslim men and women, esp in India

JUBBAHS > JUBBAH

JUBE n gallery or loft over the rood screen in a church or cathedral

JUBES > JUBE

JUBHAH same as > JUBBAH

JUBHAHS > JUBHAH

JUBILANCE > JUBILANT

JUBILANCY > JUBILANT

JUBILANT adj feeling or expressing great joy

JUBILATE vb have or express great joy

JUBILATED > JUBILATE

JUBILATES > JUBILATE

JUBILE same as > JUBILEE

JUBILEE n special anniversary, esp 25th or 50th

JUBILEES > JUBILEE

JUBILES > JUBILE

JUCO n junior college in America

JUCOS > JUCO

JUD n large block of coal

JUDAS n peephole or a very small window in a door

JUDASES > JUDAS

JUDDER vb vibrate violently ▷ n violent vibration

JUDDERED > JUDDER

JUDDERING > JUDDER

JUDDERS > JUDDER

JUDDERY adj shaky

JUDGE n public official who tries cases and passes sentence in a court of law ▷ vb act as a judge

JUDGEABLE > JUDGE

JUDGED > JUDGE

JUDGELESS > JUDGE

JUDGELIKE > JUDGE

JUDGEMENT same as > JUDGMENT

JUDGER > JUDGE

JUDGERS > JUDGE

JUDGES > JUDGE

JUDGESHIP n position, office, or function of a judge

JUDGING > JUDGE

JUDGINGLY > JUDGE

JUDGMATIC adj judicious

JUDGMENT n opinion reached after careful thought

JUDGMENTS > JUDGMENT

JUDICABLE adj capable of being judged, esp in a court of law

JUDICATOR n person who

acts as a judge

JUDICIAL adj of or by a court or judge

JUDICIARY n system of courts and judges ▷ adj of or relating to courts of law, judgment, or judges

JUDICIOUS adj well-judged and sensible

JUDIES > JUDY

JUDO n sport in which two opponents try to throw each other to the ground

JUDOGI n white two-piece cotton costume worn during judo contests

JUDOGIS > JUDOGI

JUDOIST > JUDO

JUDOISTS > JUDO

JUDOKA n competitor or expert in judo

JUDOKAS > JUDOKA

JUDOS > JUDO

JUDS > JUD

JUDY n woman

JUG n container for liquids, with a handle and small spout ▷ vb stew or boil (meat, esp hare) in an earthenware container

JUGA > JUGUM

JUGAL adj of or relating to the zygomatic bone ▷ n cheekbone

JUGALS > JUGAL

JUGATE adj (esp of compound leaves) having parts arranged in pairs

JUGFUL same as > JUG

JUGFULS > JUGFUL

JUGGED > JUG

JUGGING > JUG

JUGGINGS > JUG

JUGGINS n silly person

JUGGLE vb throw and catch (several objects) so that most are in the air at the same time ▷ n act of juggling

JUGGLED > JUGGLE

JUGGLER n person who juggles, esp a professional entertainer

JUGGLERS > JUGGLER

JUGGLERY > JUGGLE

JUGGLES > JUGGLE

JUGGLING > JUGGLE

JUGGLINGS > JUGGLE

JUGHEAD n clumsy person

JUGHEADS > JUGHEAD

JUGLET n small jug

JUGLETS > JUGLET

JUGS > JUG

JUGSFUL > JUGFUL

JUGULA > JUGULUM

JUGULAR n one of three large veins of the neck that return blood from the head to the heart

JUGULARS > JUGULAR

JUGULATE vb check (a disease) by extreme measures or remedies

JUGULATED > JUGULATE

JUGULATES > JUGULATE

JUGULUM n lower throat

JUGUM n small process at the base of each forewing in certain insects by which the forewings are united to the hindwings during flight

JUGUMS > JUGUM

JUICE n liquid part of vegetables, fruit, or meat ▷ vb extract juice from fruits and vegetables

JUICED > JUICE

JUICEHEAD n alcoholic

JUICELESS > JUICE

JUICER n kitchen appliance, usually operated by electricity, for extracting juice from fruits and vegetables

JUICERS > JUICER

JUICES > JUICE

JUICIER > JUICY

JUICIEST > JUICY

JUICILY > JUICY

JUICINESS > JUICY

JUICING > JUICE

JUICY adj full of juice

JUJITSU n Japanese art of wrestling and self-defence

JUJITSUS > JUJITSU

JUJU n W African magic charm or fetish

JUJUBE n chewy sweet made of flavoured gelatine

JUJUBES > JUJUBE

JUJUISM > JUJU

JUJUISMS > JUJU

JUJUIST > JUJU

JUJUISTS > JUJU

JUJUS > JUJU

JUJUTSU same as > JUJITSU

JUJUTSUS > JUJUTSU

JUKE vb dance or play dance music

JUKEBOX n coin-operated machine on which records, CDs, or videos can be played

JUKEBOXES > JUKEBOX

JUKED > JUKE

JUKES > JUKE

JUKING > JUKE

JUKSKEI n game in which a peg is thrown over a fixed distance at a stake fixed into the ground

JUKSKEIS > JUKE

JUKU n Japanese martial art

JUKUS > JUKU

JULEP n sweet alcoholic drink

JULEPS > JULEP

JULIENNE adj (of vegetables or meat) cut into thin shreds ▷ n clear soup containing thinly shredded vegetables ▷ vb cut into thin pieces

JULIENNED > JULIENNE

JULIENNES > JULIENNE

JULIET n code word for the letter J

JULIETS > JULIET

JUMAR n clamp with a handle that can move freely up a rope on which it is clipped but locks when downward pressure is applied ▷ vb climb (up a fixed rope) using jumars
JUMARED > JUMAR
JUMARING > JUMAR
JUMARRED > JUMAR
JUMARRING > JUMAR
JUMARS > JUMAR
JUMART n mythical offspring of a bull and a mare
JUMARTS > JUMART
JUMBAL same as > JUMBLE
JUMBALS > JUMBAL
JUMBIE n Caribbean ghost
JUMBIES > JUMBIE
JUMBLE n confused heap or state ▷ vb mix in a disordered way
JUMBLED > JUMBLE
JUMBLER > JUMBLE
JUMBLERS > JUMBLE
JUMBLES > JUMBLE
JUMBLIER > JUMBLE
JUMBLIEST > JUMBLE
JUMBLING > JUMBLE
JUMBLY > JUMBLE
JUMBO adj very large ▷ n large jet airliner
JUMBOISE same as > JUMBOIZE
JUMBOISED > JUMBOISE
JUMBOISES > JUMBOISE
JUMBOIZE vb extend (a ship, esp a tanker) by cutting out the middle part and inserting a new larger part between the original bow and stern
JUMBOIZED > JUMBOIZE
JUMBOIZES > JUMBOIZE
JUMBOS > JUMBO
JUMBUCK n sheep
JUMBUCKS > JUMBUCK
JUMBY n Caribbean ghost
JUMELLE n paired objects
JUMELLES > JUMELLE
JUMP vb leap or spring into the air using the leg muscles ▷ n act of jumping
JUMPABLE > JUMP
JUMPED > JUMP
JUMPER n sweater or pullover
JUMPERS > JUMPER
JUMPIER > JUMPY
JUMPIEST > JUMPY
JUMPILY > JUMPY
JUMPINESS > JUMPY
JUMPING > JUMP
JUMPINGLY > JUMP
JUMPINGS > JUMP
JUMPOFF n extra round in a showjumping contest when two or more horses are equal first, the fastest round deciding the winner
JUMPOFFS > JUMPOFF
JUMPS > JUMP
JUMPSUIT n one-piece

garment of combined trousers and jacket or shirt
JUMPSUITS > JUMPSUIT
JUMPY adj nervous
JUN variant of > CHON
JUNCATE same as > JUNKET
JUNCATES > JUNCATE
JUNCO n North American bunting
JUNCOES > JUNCO
JUNCOS > JUNCO
JUNCTION n place where routes, railway lines, or roads meet
JUNCTIONS > JUNCTION
JUNCTURAL > JUNCTURE
JUNCTURE n point in time, esp a critical one
JUNCTURES > JUNCTURE
JUNCUS n type of rush
JUNCUSES > JUNCUS
JUNEATING n early-season apple
JUNGLE n tropical forest of dense tangled vegetation
JUNGLED adj covered with jungle
JUNGLEGYM n climbing frame for children
JUNGLES > JUNGLE
JUNGLI n uncultured person
JUNGLIER > JUNGLE
JUNGLIEST > JUNGLE
JUNGLIS > JUNGLI
JUNGLIST n jungle-music enthusiast
JUNGLISTS > JUNGLIST
JUNGLY > JUNGLE
JUNIOR adj of lower standing ▷ n junior person
JUNIORATE n preparatory course for candidates for religious orders
JUNIORITY n condition of being junior
JUNIORS > JUNIOR
JUNIPER n evergreen shrub with purple berries
JUNIPERS > JUNIPER
JUNK n discarded or useless objects ▷ vb discard as junk
JUNKANOO n Bahamian ceremony
JUNKANOOS > JUNKANOO
JUNKED > JUNK
JUNKER n (formerly) young German nobleman
JUNKERS > JUNKER
JUNKET n excursion by public officials paid for from public funds ▷ vb (of a public official, committee, etc) to go on a junket
JUNKETED > JUNKET
JUNKETEER > JUNKET
JUNKETER > JUNKET
JUNKETERS > JUNKET
JUNKETING > JUNKET
JUNKETS > JUNKET
JUNKETTED > JUNKET
JUNKETTER > JUNKET
JUNKIE n drug addict

JUNKIER > JUNKY
JUNKIES > JUNKY
JUNKIEST > JUNKY
JUNKINESS > JUNKY
JUNKING > JUNK
JUNKMAN n man who buys and sells discarded clothing, furniture, etc
JUNKMEN > JUNKMAN
JUNKS > JUNK
JUNKY n drug addict ▷ adj of low quality
JUNKYARD n place where junk is stored or collected for sale
JUNKYARDS > JUNKYARD
JUNTA n group of military officers holding power in a country, esp after a coup
JUNTAS > JUNTA
JUNTO same as > JUNTA
JUNTOS > JUNTO
JUPATI n type of palm tree
JUPATIS > JUPATI
JUPE n sleeveless jacket
JUPES > JUPE
JUPON n short close-fitting sleeveless padded garment, used in the late 14th and early 15th centuries with armour
JUPONS > JUPON
JURA > JUS
JURAL adj of or relating to law or to the administration of justice
JURALLY > JURAL
JURANT n person taking oath
JURANTS > JURANT
JURASSIC adj of, denoting, or formed in the second period of the Mesozoic era, between the Triassic and Cretaceous periods, lasting for 55 million years during which dinosaurs and ammonites flourished
JURAT n statement at the foot of an affidavit, naming the parties, stating when, where, and before whom it was sworn, etc
JURATORY adj of, relating to, or expressed in an oath
JURATS > JURAT
JURE adv by legal right
JUREL n edible fish found in warm American Atlantic waters
JURELS > JUREL
JURIDIC same as > JURIDICAL
JURIDICAL adj of law or the administration of justice
JURIED > JURY
JURIES > JURY
JURIST n expert in law
JURISTIC adj of or relating to jurists
JURISTS > JURIST
JUROR n member of a jury
JURORS > JUROR

JURY n group of people sworn to deliver a verdict in a court of law ▷ adj makeshift ▷ vb evaluate by jury
JURYING > JURY
JURYLESS > JURY
JURYMAN n member of a jury, esp a man
JURYMAST n replacement mast
JURYMASTS > JURYMAST
JURYMEN > JURYMAN
JURYWOMAN n female member of a jury
JURYWOMEN > JURYWOMAN
JUS n right, power, or authority
JUSSIVE n mood of verbs used for giving orders; imperative
JUSSIVES > JUSSIVE
JUST adv very recently ▷ adj fair or impartial in action or judgment ▷ vb joust
JUSTED > JUST
JUSTER > JUST
JUSTERS > JUST
JUSTEST > JUST
JUSTICE n quality of being just
JUSTICER n magistrate
JUSTICERS > JUSTICER
JUSTICES > JUSTICE
JUSTICIAR n chief political and legal officer from the time of William I to that of Henry III, who deputized for the king in his absence and presided over the kings' courts
JUSTIFIED > JUSTIFY
JUSTIFIER > JUSTIFY
JUSTIFIES > JUSTIFY
JUSTIFY vb prove right or reasonable
JUSTING > JOUST
JUSTLE less common word for > JOSTLE
JUSTLED > JUSTLE
JUSTLES > JUSTLE
JUSTLING > JUSTLE
JUSTLY > JUST
JUSTNESS > JUST
JUSTS same as > JOUST
JUT vb project or stick out ▷ n something that juts out
JUTE n plant fibre, used for rope, canvas, etc
JUTELIKE > JUTE
JUTES > JUTE
JUTS > JUT
JUTTED > JUT
JUTTIED > JUTTY
JUTTIES > JUTTY
JUTTING > JUT
JUTTINGLY > JUT
JUTTY vb project beyond
JUTTYING > JUTTY
JUVE same as > JUVENILE
JUVENAL variant spelling (esp US) of > JUVENILE

JUVENALS > JUVENAL
JUVENILE adj young ▷ n young person or child
JUVENILES > JUVENILE

JUVENILIA npl works produced in an author's youth
JUVES > JUVE

JUVIE n juvenile detention centre
JUVIES > JUVIE
JUXTAPOSE vb put side by side

JYMOLD adj having a hinge
JYNX n woodpecker
JYNXES > JYNX

Kk

KA n (in ancient Egypt) attendant spirit supposedly dwelling as a vital force in a man or statue ▷ vb (in archaic usage) help

KAAL adj naked

KAAMA n large African antelope with lyre-shaped horns

KAAMAS > KAAMA

KAAS n Dutch cabinet or wardrobe

KAB variant spelling of > CAB

KABAB same as > KEBAB

KABABBED > KABAB

KABABBING > KABAB

KABABS > KABAB

KABADDI n game in which players try to touch opposing players but avoid being captured by them

KABADDIS > KABADDI

KABAKA n any of the former rulers of the Baganda people of S Uganda

KABAKAS > KABAKA

KABALA same as > KABBALAH

KABALAS > KABALA

KABALISM > KABALA

KABALISMS > KABALA

KABALIST > KABALA

KABALISTS > KABALA

KABAR archaic form of > CABER

KABARS > KABAR

KABAYA n tunic

KABAYAS > KABAYA

KABBALA same as > KABBALAH

KABBALAH n ancient Jewish mystical tradition

KABBALAHS > KABBALAH

KABBALAS > KABBALAH

KABBALISM > KABBALAH

KABBALIST > KABBALAH

KABELE same as > KEBELE

KABELES > KABELE

KABELJOU n large fish that is an important food fish of South African waters

KABELJOUS > KABELJOU

KABELJOUW same as > KABELJOU

KABIKI n fruit tree found in India

KABIKIS > KABIKI

KABOB same as > KEBAB

KABOBBED > KABOB

KABOBBING > KABOB

KABOBS > KABOB

KABS > KAB

KABUKI n form of Japanese drama based on popular legends and characterized by elaborate costumes, stylized acting, and the use of male actors for all roles

KABUKIS > KABUKI

KACCHA n trousers worn traditionally by Sikhs

KACCHAS > KACCHA

KACHA adj crude

KACHAHRI n Indian courthouse

KACHAHRIS > KACHAHRI

KACHCHA same as > KACHA

KACHERI same as > KACHAHRI

KACHERIS > KACHERI

KACHINA n any of the supernatural beings believed by the Hopi Indians to be the ancestors of living humans

KACHINAS > KACHINA

KACK same as > CACK

KACKS > KACK

KADAITCHA n (in certain Central Australian Aboriginal tribes) man with the mission of avenging the death of a tribesman

KADDISH n ancient Jewish liturgical prayer

KADDISHES > KADDISH

KADDISHIM > KADDISH

KADE same as > KED

KADES > KADE

KADI variant spelling of > CADI

KADIS > KADI

KAE n dialect word for jackdaw or jay ▷ vb (in archaic usage) help

KAED > KAE

KAEING > KAE

KAES > KAE

KAF n letter of the Hebrew alphabet

KAFFIR n Southern African variety of sorghum, cultivated in dry regions for its grain and as fodder

KAFFIRS > KAFFIR

KAFFIYAH same as > KAFFIYEH

KAFFIYAHS > KAFFIYAH

KAFFIYEH same as > KEFFIYEH

KAFFIYEHS > KAFFIYEH

KAFILA n caravan

KAFILAS > KAFILA

KAFIR same as > KAFFIR

KAFIRS > KAFIR

KAFS > KAF

KAFTAN n long loose Eastern garment

KAFTANS > KAFTAN

KAGO n Japanese sedan chair

KAGOOL variant spelling of > CAGOULE

KAGOOLS > KAGOOL

KAGOS > KAGO

KAGOUL variant spelling of > CAGOULE

KAGOULE same as > KAGOUL

KAGOULES > KAGOULE

KAGOULS > KAGOUL

KAGU n crested nocturnal bird of New Caledonia with a red bill and greyish plumage

KAGUS > KAGU

KAHAL n Jewish community

KAHALS > KAHAL

KAHAWAI n food and game fish of New Zealand

KAHAWAIS > KAHAWAI

KAHIKATEA n tall New Zealand coniferous tree

KAHIKATOA n tall New Zealand coniferous tree

KAHUNA n Hawaiian priest, shaman, or expert

KAHUNAS > KAHUNA

KAI n food

KAIAK same as > KAYAK

KAIAKED > KAIAK

KAIAKING > KAIAK

KAIAKS > KAIAK

KAID n North African chieftan or leader

KAIDS > KAID

KAIE archaic form of > KEY

KAIES > KAIE

KAIF same as > KIF

KAIFS > KAIF

KAIK same as > KAINGA

KAIKA same as > KAINGA

KAIKAI n food

KAIKAIS > KAIKAI

KAIKAS > KAIKA

KAIKAWAKA n small pyramid-shaped New Zealand conifer

KAIKOMAKO n small New Zealand tree with white flowers and black fruit

KAIKS > KAIK

KAIL same as > KALE

KAILS > KAIL

KAILYAIRD same as > KALEYARD

KAILYARD same as > KALEYARD

KAILYARDS > KAILYARD

KAIM same as > KAME

KAIMAKAM n Turkish governor

KAIMAKAMS > KAIMAKAM

KAIMS > KAIM

KAIN variant spelling of > CAIN

KAING > KA

KAINGA n (in New Zealand) a Māori village or small settlement

KAINGAS > KAINGA

KAINIT same as > KAINITE

KAINITE n white mineral consisting of potassium chloride and magnesium sulphate: a fertilizer and source of potassium salts

KAINITES > KAINITE

KAINITS > KAINIT

KAINS > KAIN

KAIROMONE n substance secreted by animal

KAIS > KAI

KAISER n German or Austro-Hungarian emperor

KAISERDOM > KAISER

KAISERIN n empress

KAISERINS > KAISERIN

KAISERISM > KAISER

KAISERS > KAISER

KAIZEN n philosophy of continuous improvement of working practices that underlies total quality management and just-in-time business techniques

KAIZENS > KAIZEN

KAJAWAH n type of seat or panier used on a camel

KAJAWAHS > KAJAWAH

KAJEPUT n variety of Australian melaleuca

KAJEPUTS > KAJEPUT

KAK n South African slang word for faeces

KAKA n parrot of New Zealand

KAKAPO n ground-living nocturnal New Zealand parrot that resembles an owl

KAKAPOS > KAKAPO

KAKARIKI n green-feathered New Zealand parrot

KAKARIKIS > KAKARIKI

KAKAS > KAKA

KAKEMONO n Japanese paper or silk wall hanging, usually long and narrow, with a picture or inscription on it and a roller at the bottom

KAKEMONOS > KAKEMONO

KAKI n Asian persimmon tree

KAKIEMON n type of 17th century Japanese porcelain

KAKIEMONS > KAKIEMON

KAKIS > KAKI

KAKODYL variant spelling of > CACODYL

KAKODYLS > KAKODYL

KAKS > KAK

KAKURO n crossword-style puzzle with numbers

KAKUROS > KAKURO

KALAM n discussion and debate, especially relating to Islamic theology

KALAMATA as in kalamata olive aubergine-coloured Greek olive

KALAMATAS > KALAMATA

KALAMDAN n Persian box in which to keep pens

KALAMDANS > KALAMDAN

KALAMKARI n Indian cloth printing and printed Indian cloth

KALAMS > KALAM

KALANCHOE n tropical succulent plant having small brightly coloured flowers and dark shiny leaves

KALE n cabbage with crinkled leaves

KALENDAR variant form of > CALENDAR

KALENDARS > KALENDAR

KALENDS same as > CALENDS

KALES > KALE

KALEWIFE n Scots word for a female vegetable or cabbage seller

KALEWIVES > KALEWIFE

KALEYARD n vegetable garden

KALEYARDS > KALEYARD

KALI another name for > SALTWORT

KALIAN another name for > HOOKAH

KALIANS > KALIAN

KALIF variant spelling of > CALIPH

KALIFATE same as > CALIPHATE

KALIFATES > KALIFATE

KALIFS > KALIF

KALIMBA n musical instrument

KALIMBAS > KALIMBA

KALINITE n alum

KALINITES > KALINITE

KALIPH variant spelling of > CALIPH

KALIPHATE same as > CALIPHATE

KALIPHS > KALIPH

KALIS > KALI

KALIUM n Latin for potassium

KALIUMS > KALIUM

KALLIDIN n type of peptide

KALLIDINS > KALLIDIN

KALLITYPE n old printing process

KALMIA n N American evergreen ericaceous shrub with showy clusters of white or pink flowers

KALMIAS > KALMIA

KALONG n fruit bat

KALONGS > KALONG

KALOOKI n version of contract rummy popular in Jamaica

KALOOKIE same as > KALOOKI

KALOOKIES > KALOOKIE

KALOOKIS > KALOOKI

KALOTYPE variant spelling of > CALOTYPE

KALOTYPES > KALOTYPE

KALPA n (in Hindu cosmology) period in which the universe experiences a cycle of creation and destruction

KALPAC same as > CALPAC

KALPACS > KALPAC

KALPAK variant spelling of > CALPAC

KALPAKS > KALPAK

KALPAS > KALPA

KALPIS n Greek water jar

KALPISES > KALPIS

KALSOMINE variant of > CALCIMINE

KALUKI same as > KALOOKI

KALUKIS > KALUKI

KALUMPIT n type of Filipino fruit tree or its fruit

KALUMPITS > KALUMPIT

KALYPTRA n Greek veil

KALYPTRAS > KALYPTRA

KAM Shakespearean word for > CROOKED

KAMA n large African antelope with lyre-shaped horns

KAMAAINA n Hawaiian local

KAMAAINAS > KAMAAINA

KAMACITE n alloy of iron and nickel, occurring in meteorites

KAMACITES > KAMACITE

KAMAHI n tall New Zealand hardwood tree with pinkish flowers

KAMAHIS > KAMAHI

KAMALA n East Indian tree

KAMALAS > KAMALA

KAMAS > KAMA

KAME n irregular mound or ridge of gravel, sand, etc, deposited by water derived from melting glaciers

KAMEES > KAMEEZ

KAMEESES > KAMEES

KAMEEZ n long tunic worn in the Indian subcontinent, often with shalwar

KAMEEZES > KAMEEZ

KAMELA same as > KAMALA

KAMELAS > KAMELA

KAMERAD interj shout of surrender ▷ vb surrender

KAMERADED > KAMERAD

KAMERADS > KAMERAD

KAMES > KAME

KAMI n divine being or spiritual force in Shinto

KAMICHI n South American bird

KAMICHIS > KAMICHI

KAMIK n traditional Inuit boot made of caribou hide or sealskin

KAMIKAZE n (in World War II) Japanese pilot who performed a suicide mission ▷ adj (of an action) undertaken in the knowledge that it will kill or injure the person performing it

KAMIKAZES > KAMIKAZE

KAMIKS > KAMIK

KAMILA same as > KAMALA

KAMILAS > KAMILA

KAMIS same as > KAMEEZ

KAMISES > KAMIS

KAMME same as > KAM

KAMOKAMO n kind of marrow found in New Zealand

KAMOKAMOS > KAMOKAMO

KAMPONG n (in Malaysia) village

KAMPONGS > KAMPONG

KAMSEEN same as > KHAMSIN

KAMSEENS > KAMSEEN

KAMSIN same as > KAMSEEN

KAMSINS > KAMSIN

KANA n Japanese syllabary, which consists of two written varieties

KANAE n grey mullet

KANAES > KANAE

KANAKA n Australian word for any native of the South Pacific islands, esp (formerly) one abducted to work in Australia

KANAKAS > KANAKA

KANAMYCIN n type of antibiotic

KANAS > KANA

KANBAN n just-in-time manufacturing process in which the movements of materials through a process are recorded on specially designed cards

KANBANS > KANBAN

KANDIES > KANDY

KANDY same as > CANDIE

KANE n Hawaiian man or boy

KANEH n 6-cubit Hebrew measure

KANEHS > KANEH

KANES > KANE

KANG n Chinese heatable platform used for sleeping and sitting on

KANGA n piece of gaily decorated thin cotton cloth used as a garment by women in E Africa

KANGAROO n Australian marsupial which moves by jumping with its powerful hind legs ▷ vb (of a car) move forward or to cause (a car) to move forward with short sudden jerks, as a result of improper use of the clutch

KANGAROOS > KANGAROO

KANGAS > KANGA

KANGHA n comb traditionally worn by Sikhs as a symbol of their religious and cultural loyalty

KANGHAS > KANGHA

KANGS > KANG

KANJI n Japanese writing system using characters mainly derived from Chinese ideograms

KANJIS > KANJI

KANS n Indian wild sugar cane

KANSES > KANS

KANT archaic spelling of > CANT

KANTAR n unit of weight used in E Mediterranean countries, equivalent to 100 pounds or 45 kilograms but varying from place to place

KANTARS > KANTAR

KANTED > KANT

KANTELA same as > KANTELE

KANTELAS > KANTELA

KANTELE n Finnish stringed instrument

KANTELES > KANTELE

KANTEN same as > AGAR

KANTENS > KANTEN

KANTHA n Bengali embroidered quilt

KANTHAS > KANTHA

KANTIKOY vb dance ceremonially

KANTIKOYS > KANTIKOY

KANTING > KANT

KANTS > KANT

KANUKA n New Zealand myrtaceous tree

KANUKAS > KANUKA

KANZU n long garment, usually white, with long sleeves, worn by E African men

KANZUS > KANZU

k

KAOLIANG n any of various E Asian varieties of sorghum

KAOLIANGS > KAOLIANG

KAOLIN n fine white clay used to make porcelain and in some medicines

KAOLINE same as > KAOLIN

KAOLINES > KAOLINE

KAOLINIC > KAOLIN

KAOLINISE same as > KAOLINIZE

KAOLINITE n white or grey clay mineral consisting of hydrated aluminium silicate in triclinic crystalline form, the main constituent of kaolin

KAOLINIZE vb change into kaolin

KAOLINS > KAOLIN

KAON n meson that has a positive or negative charge and a rest mass of about 966 electron masses, or no charge and a rest mass of 974 electron masses

KAONIC > KAON

KAONS > KAON

KAPA n Hawaiian cloth made from beaten mulberry bark

KAPAS > KAPA

KAPH n 11th letter of the Hebrew alphabet

KAPHS > KAPH

KAPOK n fluffy fibre from a tropical tree, used to stuff cushions etc

KAPOKS > KAPOK

KAPPA n tenth letter in the Greek alphabet

KAPPAS > KAPPA

KAPUKA same as > BROADLEAF

KAPUKAS > KAPUKA

KAPUT adj ruined or broken

KAPUTT same as > KAPUT

KARA n steel bangle traditionally worn by Sikhs as a symbol of their religious and cultural loyalty

KARABINER n metal clip with a spring for attaching to a piton, belay, etc

KARAISM n beliefs and doctrines of a Jewish sect rejecting Rabbinism

KARAISMS > KARAISM

KARAIT same as > KRAIT

KARAITS > KRAIT

KARAKA n New Zealand tree

KARAKAS > KARAKA

KARAKIA n prayer

KARAKIAS > KARAKIA

KARAKUL n sheep of central Asia, the lambs of which have soft curled dark hair

KARAKULS > KARAKUL

KARAMU n small New Zealand tree with glossy leaves and orange fruit

KARAMUS > KARAMU

KARANGA n call or chant of welcome, sung by a female elder ▷ vb perform a karanga

KARANGAED > KARANGA

KARANGAS > KARANGA

KARAOKE n form of entertainment in which people sing over a prerecorded backing tape

KARAOKES > KARAOKE

KARAS > KARA

KARAT n measure of the proportion of gold in an alloy, expressed as the number of parts of gold in 24 parts of the alloy

KARATE n Japanese system of unarmed combat using blows with the feet, hands, elbows, and legs

KARATEIST same as > KARATEKA

KARATEKA n competitor or expert in karate

KARATEKAS > KARATEKA

KARATES > KARATE

KARATS > KARAT

KAREAREA n New Zealand falcon

KAREAREAS > KAREAREA

KARENGO n edible type of Pacific seaweed

KARENGOS > KARENGO

KARITE n shea tree

KARITES > KARITE

KARK variant spelling of > CARK

KARKED > KARK

KARKING > KARK

KARKS > KARK

KARMA n person's actions affecting his or her fate in the next reincarnation

KARMAS > KARMA

KARMIC > KARMA

KARN old word for > CAIRN

KARNS > KARN

KARO n small New Zealand tree or shrub with sweet-smelling brown flowers

KAROO n high arid plateau

KAROOS > KAROO

KARORO n large seagull with black feathers on its back

KAROROS > KARORO

KAROS > KARO

KAROSHI n (in Japan) death caused by overwork

KAROSHIS > KAROSHI

KAROSS n blanket made of animal skins sewn together

KAROSSES > KAROSS

KARRI n Australian eucalypt

KARRIS > KARRI

KARROO same as > KAROO

KARROOS > KARROO

KARSEY variant spelling of > KHAZI

KARSEYS > KARSEY

KARSIES > KARSY

KARST n denoting the characteristic scenery of a limestone region, including underground streams, gorges, etc

KARSTIC > KARST

KARSTIFY vb become karstic

KARSTS > KARST

KARSY variant spelling of > KHAZI

KART n light low-framed vehicle with small wheels and engine used for recreational racing

KARTER > KART

KARTERS > KART

KARTING > KART

KARTINGS > KART

KARTS > KART

KARYOGAMY n fusion of two gametic nuclei during fertilization

KARYOGRAM n diagram or photograph of the chromosomes of a cell, arranged in homologous pairs and in a numbered sequence

KARYOLOGY n study of cell nuclei, esp with reference to the number and shape of the chromosomes

KARYON n nucleus of a cell

KARYONS > KARYON

KARYOSOME n any of the dense aggregates of chromatin in the nucleus of a cell

KARYOTIN less common word for > CHROMATIN

KARYOTINS > KARYOTIN

KARYOTYPE n appearance of the chromosomes in a somatic cell of an individual or species, with reference to their number, size, shape, etc ▷ vb determine the karyotype of (a cell)

KARZIES > KARZY

KARZY variant spelling of > KHAZI

KAS > KA

KASBAH n citadel of any of various North African cities

KASBAHS > KASBAH

KASHA n dish originating in Eastern Europe, consisting of boiled or baked buckwheat

KASHAS > KASHA

KASHER vb make fit for use

KASHERED > KASHER

KASHERING > KASHER

KASHERS > KASHER

KASHMIR variant spelling of > CASHMERE

KASHMIRS > KASHMIR

KASHRUS same as > KASHRUTH

KASHRUSES > KASHRUS

KASHRUT same as > KASHRUTH

KASHRUTH n condition of being fit for ritual use in general

KASHRUTHS > KASHRUTH

KASHRUTS > KASHRUT

KASME interj (in Indian English) I swear

KAT same as > KHAT

KATA n exercise consisting of a sequence of the specific movements of a martial art, used in training and designed to show skill in technique

KATABASES > KATABASIS

KATABASIS n retreat of the Greek mercenaries of Cyrus the Younger, after his death at Cunaxa, from the Euphrates to the Black Sea in 401–400 BC under the leadership of Xenophon

KATABATIC adj (of winds) blowing downhill through having become denser with cooling, esp at night when heat is lost from the earth's surface

KATABOLIC same as > CATABOLIC

KATAKANA n one of the two systems of syllabic writing employed for the representation of Japanese, based on Chinese ideograms. It is used mainly for foreign or foreign-derived words

KATAKANAS > KATAKANA

KATAL n SI unit of catalytic activity

KATALS > KATAL

KATANA n Japanese samurai sword

KATANAS > KATANA

KATAS > KATA

KATCHINA variant spelling of > KACHINA

KATCHINAS > KATCHINA

KATCINA variant spelling of > KACHINA

KATCINAS > KATCINA

KATHAK n form of N Indian classical dancing that tells a story

KATHAKALI n form of dance drama of S India using mime and based on Hindu literature

KATHAKS > KATHAK

KATHARSES > KATHARSIS

KATHARSIS variant spelling of > CATHARSIS

KATHODAL > KATHODE

KATHODE variant spelling of > CATHODE

KATHODES > KATHODE

KATHODIC > KATHODE

KATI variant spelling of > CATTY

KATION variant spelling of > CATION

KATIONS > KATION

KATIPO n small poisonous

New Zealand spider
KATIPOS > KATIPO
KATIS > KATI
KATORGA n labour camp in Imperial Russia or the Soviet Union
KATORGAS > KATORGA
KATS > KAT
KATSURA n Asian tree
KATSURAS > KATSURA
KATTI variant spelling of > CATTY
KATTIS > KATTI
KATYDID n large green grasshopper of N America
KATYDIDS > KATYDID
KAUGH same as > KIAUGH
KAUGHS > KAUGH
KAUMATUA n senior member of a tribe
KAUMATUAS > KAUMATUA
KAUPAPA n strategy, policy, or cause
KAUPAPAS > KAUPAPA
KAURI n large NZ conifer that yields valuable timber and resin
KAURIES > KAURY
KAURIS > KAURI
KAURU n edible stem of the cabbage tree
KAURUS > KAURU
KAURY variant spelling of > KAURI
KAVA n Polynesian shrub
KAVAKAVA same as > KAVA
KAVAKAVAS > KAVAKAVA
KAVAL n type of flute played in the Balkans
KAVALS > KAVAL
KAVASS > KAVA
KAVASS n armed Turkish constable
KAVASSES > KAVASS
KAW variant spelling of > CAW
KAWA n protocol or etiquette, particularly in a Māori tribal meeting place
KAWAKAWA n aromatic shrub or small tree of New Zealand
KAWAKAWAS > KAWAKAWA
KAWAS > KAWA
KAWAU n New Zealand name for black shag
KAWAUS > KAWAU
KAWED > KAW
KAWING > KAW
KAWS > KAW
KAY n name of the letter K
KAYAK n Inuit canoe made of sealskins stretched over a frame ▷ vb travel by kayak
KAYAKED > KAYAK
KAYAKER > KAYAK
KAYAKERS > KAYAK
KAYAKING > KAYAK
KAYAKINGS > KAYAK
KAYAKS > KAYAK
KAYLE n one of a set of ninepins
KAYLES npl ninepins
KAYLIED adj (in British

slang) intoxicated or drunk
KAYO another term for > KNOCKOUT
KAYOED > KAYO
KAYOES > KAYO
KAYOING > KAYO
KAYOS > KAYO
KAYS > KAY
KAZACHKI same as > KAZACHOK
KAZACHOC n Ukrainian folk dance
KAZACHOCS > KAZACHOC
KAZACHOK n Russian folk dance in which the performer executes high kicks from a squatting position
KAZATSKI same as > KAZACHOK
KAZATSKY same as > KAZACHOK
KAZATZKA same as > KAZACHOK
KAZATZKAS > KAZACHOK
KAZI variant spelling of > KHAZI
KAZILLION same as > GAZILLION
KAZIS > KAZI
KAZOO n cigar-shaped metal musical instrument that produces a buzzing sound when the player hums into it
KAZOOS > KAZOO
KBAR n kilobar
KBARS > KBAR
KEA n large brownish-green parrot of NZ
KEAS > KEA
KEASAR archaic variant of > KAISER
KEASARS > KEASAR
KEAVIE n archaic or dialect word for a type of crab
KEAVIES > KEAVIE
KEB vb Scots word meaning miscarry or reject a lamb
KEBAB n dish of small pieces of meat grilled on skewers ▷ vb skewer
KEBABBED > KEBAB
KEBABBING > KEBAB
KEBABS > KEBAB
KEBAR n Scots word for beam or rafter
KEBARS > KEBAR
KEBBED > KEB
KEBBIE n Scots word for shepherd's crook
KEBBIES > KEBBIE
KEBBING > KEB
KEBBOCK n Scots word for a cheese
KEBBOCKS > CHEESE
KEBBUCK same as > KEBBOCK
KEBBUCKS > KEBBUCK
KEBELE n Ethiopian local council
KEBELES > KEBELE
KEBLAH same as > KIBLAH

KEBLAHS > KEBLAH
KEBOB same as > KEBAB
KEBOBBED > KEBOB
KEBOBBING > KEBOB
KEBOBS > KEBOB
KEBS > KEB
KECK vb retch or feel nausea
KECKED > KECK
KECKING > KECK
KECKLE Scots variant of > CACKLE
KECKLED > KECKLE
KECKLES > KECKLE
KECKLING > KECKLE
KECKLINGS > KECKLE
KECKS npl trousers
KECKSES > KECKS
KECKSIES > KECKSY
KECKSY n dialect word meaning hollow plant stalk
KED as in sheep ked sheep tick
KEDDAH same as > KHEDA
KEDDAHS > KEDDAH
KEDGE vb move (a ship) along by hauling in on the cable of a light anchor ▷ n light anchor used for kedging
KEDGED > KEDGE
KEDGER n small anchor
KEDGEREE n dish of fish with rice and eggs
KEDGEREES > KEDGEREE
KEDGERS > KEDGER
KEDGES > KEDGE
KEDGIER > KEDGY
KEDGIEST > KEDGY
KEDGING > KEDGE
KEDGY adj dialect word for happy or lively
KEDS > KED
KEECH n old word for lump of fat
KEECHES > KEECH
KEEF same as > KIF
KEEFS > KEEF
KEEK Scot word for > PEEP
KEEKED > KEEK
KEEKER > KEEK
KEEKERS > KEEK
KEEKING > KEEK
KEEKS > KEEK
KEEL n main lengthways timber or steel structure along the base of a ship ▷ vb mark with this stain
KEELAGE n fee charged by certain ports to allow a ship to dock
KEELAGES > KEELAGE
KEELBOAT n river boat with a shallow draught and a keel, used for freight and moved by towing, punting, or rowing
KEELBOATS > KEELBOAT
KEELED > KEEL
KEELER n bargeman
KEELERS > KEELER
KEELHALE same as > KEELHAUL
KEELHALED > KEELHALE
KEELHALES > KEELHALE

KEELHAUL vb reprimand (someone) harshly
KEELHAULS > KEELHAUL
KEELIE n kestrel
KEELIES > KEELIE
KEELING > KEEL
KEELINGS > KEEL
KEELIVINE Scots word for > PENCIL
KEELLESS > KEEL
KEELMAN n bargeman
KEELMEN > KEELMAN
KEELS > KEEL
KEELSON n lengthways beam fastened to the keel of a ship for strength
KEELSONS > KEELSON
KEELYVINE same as > KEELIVINE
KEEMA n (in Indian cookery) minced meat
KEEMAS > KEEMA
KEEN adj eager or enthusiastic ▷ vb wail over the dead ▷ n lament for the dead
KEENED > KEEN
KEENER > KEEN
KEENERS > KEEN
KEENEST > KEEN
KEENING > KEEN
KEENINGS > KEEN
KEENLY > KEEN
KEENNESS > KEEN
KEENO same as > KENO
KEENOS > KEENO
KEENS > KEEN
KEEP vb have or retain possession of ▷ n cost of food and everyday expenses
KEEPABLE > KEEP
KEEPER n person who looks after animals in a zoo
KEEPERS > KEEPER
KEEPING > KEEP
KEEPINGS > KEEP
KEEPNET n cylindrical net strung on wire hoops and sealed at one end, suspended in water by anglers to keep alive the fish they have caught
KEEPNETS > KEEPNET
KEEPS > KEEP
KEEPSAKE n gift treasured for the sake of the giver
KEEPSAKES > KEEPSAKE
KEEPSAKY > KEEPSAKE
KEESHOND n breed of dog of the spitz type with a shaggy greyish coat and tightly curled tail, originating in Holland
KEESHONDS > KEESHOND
KEESTER same as > KEISTER
KEESTERS > KEESTER
KEET short for > PARAKEET
KEETS > KEET
KEEVE n tub or vat
KEEVES > KEEVE
KEF same as > KIF

k

KEFFEL *dialect word for* > HORSE

KEFFELS > KEFFEL

KEFFIYAH *same as* > KAFFIYEH

KEFFIYAHS > KEFFIYAH

KEFFIYEH *n* cotton headdress worn by Arabs

KEFFIYEHS > KEFFIYEH

KEFIR *n* effervescent drink of the Caucasus made from fermented milk

KEFIRS > KEFIR

KEFS > KEF

KEFTEDES *n* Greek dish of meatballs cooked with herbs and onions

KEFUFFLE *same as* > KERFUFFLE

KEFUFFLED > KEFUFFLE

KEFUFFLES > KEFUFFLE

KEG *n* small metal beer barrel ▷ *vb* put in kegs

KEGELER *same as* > KEGLER

KEGELERS > KEGELER

KEGGED > KEG

KEGGER > KEG

KEGGERS > KEG

KEGGING > KEG

KEGLER *n* participant in a game of tenpin bowling

KEGLERS > KEGLER

KEGLING *n* bowling

KEGLINGS > KEGLING

KEGS > KEG

KEHUA *n* ghost or spirit

KEHUAS > KEHUA

KEIGHT > KETCH

KEIR *same as* > KIER

KEIREN *n* type of track cycling event

KEIRENS > KEIREN

KEIRETSU *n* group of Japanese businesses

KEIRETSUS > KEIRETSU

KEIRIN *n* cycling race originating in Japan

KEIRINS > KEIRIN

KEIRS > KEIR

KEISTER *n* rump

KEISTERS > KEISTER

KEITLOA *n* southern African black two-horned rhinoceros

KEITLOAS > KEITLOA

KEKENO *n* New Zealand fur seal

KEKENOS > KEKENO

KEKERENGU *n* Māori bug

KEKS *same as* > KECKS

KEKSYE *same as* > KEX

KEKSYES > KEKSYE

KELEP *n* large ant found in Central and South America

KELEPS > KELEP

KELIM *same as* > KILIM

KELIMS > KELIM

KELL *dialect word for* > HAIRNET

KELLAUT *same as* > KHILAT

KELLAUTS > KELLAUT

KELLIES > KELLY

KELLS > KELL

KELLY *n* part of a drill system

KELOID *n* hard smooth pinkish raised growth of scar tissue at the site of an injury, tending to occur more frequently in dark-skinned races

KELOIDAL > KELOID

KELOIDS > KELOID

KELP *n* large brown seaweed ▷ *vb* burn seaweed to make a type of ash used as a source for iodine and potash

KELPED > KELP

KELPER *n* Falkland Islander

KELPERS > KELPER

KELPIE *n* Australian sheepdog with a smooth coat and upright ears

KELPIES > KELPY

KELPING > KELP

KELPS > KELP

KELPY *same as* > KELPIE

KELSON *same as* > KEELSON

KELSONS > KELSON

KELT *n* salmon that has recently spawned

KELTER *same as* > KILTER

KELTERS > KELTER

KELTIE *variant spelling of* > KELTY

KELTIES > KELTY

KELTS > KELT

KELTY *n* old Scots word for an extra drink imposed on someone not thought to be drinking enough

KELVIN *n* SI unit of temperature

KELVINS > KELVIN

KEMB *old word for* > COMB

KEMBED > KEMB

KEMBING > KEMB

KEMBLA *n* small change

KEMBLAS > KEMBLA

KEMBO *same as* > KIMBO

KEMBOED > KEMBO

KEMBOING > KEMBO

KEMBOS > KEMBO

KEMBS > KEMB

KEMP *n* coarse hair or strand of hair, esp one in a fleece that resists dyeing ▷ *vb* dialect word meaning to compete or try to come first

KEMPED > KEMP

KEMPER > KEMP

KEMPERS > KEMP

KEMPIER > KEMPY

KEMPIEST > KEMPY

KEMPING > KEMP

KEMPINGS > KEMP

KEMPLE *n* variable Scottish measure for hay or straw

KEMPLES > KEMPLE

KEMPS > KEMP

KEMPT *adj* (of hair) tidy

KEMPY > KEMP

KEN *vb* know ▷ *n* range of knowledge or perception

KENAF *another name for* > AMBARY

KENAFS > KENAF

KENCH *n* bin for salting and preserving fish

KENCHES > KENCH

KENDO *n* Japanese sport of fencing using wooden staves

KENDOS > KENDO

KENNED > KEN

KENNEL *n* hutlike shelter for a dog ▷ *vb* put or go into a kennel

KENNELED > KENNEL

KENNELING > KENNEL

KENNELLED > KENNEL

KENNELMAN *n* man who works in a kennels

KENNELMEN > KENNELMAN

KENNELS > KENNEL

KENNER > KEN

KENNERS > KEN

KENNET *n* old word for a small hunting dog

KENNETS > KENNET

KENNETT *vb* spoil or destroy ruthlessly

KENNETTED > KENNETT

KENNETTS > KENNETT

KENNING > KEN

KENNINGS > KEN

KENO *n* game of chance similar to bingo

KENOS > KENO

KENOSES > KENOSIS

KENOSIS *n* Christ's voluntary renunciation of certain divine attributes, in order to identify himself with mankind

KENOSISES > KENOSIS

KENOTIC > KENOSIS

KENOTICS > KENOSIS

KENOTRON *n* signal-amplifying device

KENOTRONS > KENOTRON

KENS > KEN

KENSPECK *adj* Scots for easily seen or recognized

KENT *dialect word for* > PUNT

KENTE *n* brightly coloured handwoven cloth of Ghana, usually with some gold thread

KENTED > KENT

KENTES > KENTE

KENTIA *n* plant name formerly used to include palms now allotted to several different genera

KENTIAS > KENTIA

KENTING > KENT

KENTLEDGE *n* scrap metal used as ballast in a vessel

KENTS > KENT

KEP *vb* catch

KEPHALIC *variant spelling of* > CEPHALIC

KEPHALICS > KEPHALIC

KEPHALIN *same as* > CEPHALIN

KEPHALINS > KEPHALIN

KEPHIR *same as* > KEFIR

KEPHIRS > KEPHIR

KEPI *n* French military cap with a flat top and a horizontal peak

KEPIS > KEPI

KEPPED > KEP

KEPPEN > KEP

KEPPING > KEP

KEPPIT > KEP

KEPS > KEP

KEPT > KEEP

KERAMIC *rare variant of* > CERAMIC

KERAMICS *rare variant of* > CERAMICS

KERATIN *n* fibrous protein found in the hair and nails

KERATINS > KERATIN

KERATITIS *n* inflammation of the cornea

KERATOID *adj* resembling horn

KERATOMA *n* horny growth on the skin

KERATOMAS > KERATOMA

KERATOSE *adj* (esp of certain sponges) having a horny skeleton

KERATOSES > KERATOSIS

KERATOSIC > KERATOSE

KERATOSIS *n* any skin condition marked by a horny growth, such as a wart

KERATOTIC > KERATOSIS

KERB *n* edging to a footpath ▷ *vb* provide with or enclose with a kerb

KERBAYA *n* blouse worn by Malay women

KERBAYAS > KERBAYA

KERBED > KERB

KERBING *n* material used for a kerb

KERBINGS > KERBING

KERBS > KERB

KERBSIDE *n* edge of a pavement where it drops to the level of the road

KERBSIDES > KERBSIDE

KERBSTONE *n* one of a series of stones that form a kerb

KERCHIEF *n* piece of cloth worn over the head or round the neck

KERCHIEFS > KERCHIEF

KERCHOO *interj* atishoo

KEREL *n* chap or fellow

KERELS > KEREL

KERERU *n* New Zealand pigeon

KERERUS > KERERU

KERF *n* cut made by a saw, an axe, etc ▷ *vb* cut

KERFED > KERF

KERFING > KERF

KERFLOOEY *adv* into state of destruction or malfunction

KERFS > KERF

KERFUFFLE n commotion or disorder ▷ vb put into disorder or disarray

KERKIER > KERKY

KERKIEST > KERKY

KERKY adj stupid

KERMA n quotient of the sum of the initial kinetic energies of all the charged particles liberated by indirectly ionizing radiation in a volume element of a material divided by the mass of the volume element

KERMAS > KERMA

KERMES n dried bodies of female scale insects, used as a red dyestuff

KERMESITE n red antimony

KERMESS same as > KERMIS

KERMESSE same as > KERMIS

KERMESSES > KERMESSE

KERMIS n (formerly, esp in Holland and Northern Germany) annual country festival or carnival

KERMISES > KERMIS

KERN n part of the character on a piece of printer's type that projects beyond the body ▷ vb furnish (a typeface) with a kern

KERNE same as > KERN

KERNED > KERNE

KERNEL n seed of a nut, cereal, or fruit stone ▷ vb form kernels

KERNELED > KERNEL

KERNELING > KERNEL

KERNELLED > KERNEL

KERNELLY adj with or like kernels

KERNELS > KERNEL

KERNES > KERNE

KERNING n adjustment of space between the letters of words to improve the appearance of text matter

KERNINGS > KERNING

KERNISH adj of, belonging to, or resembling an armed foot soldier or peasant

KERNITE n light soft colourless or white mineral consisting of a hydrated sodium borate in monoclinic crystalline form: an important source of borax and other boron compounds

KERNITES > KERNITE

KERNS > KERN

KERO short for > KEROSENE

KEROGEN n solid organic material found in some rocks, such as oil shales, that produces hydrocarbons similar to petroleum when heated

KEROGENS > KEROGEN

KEROS > KERO

KEROSENE n liquid mixture distilled from petroleum and used as a fuel or solvent

KEROSENES > KEROSENE

KEROSINE same as > KEROSENE

KEROSINES > KEROSINE

KERPLUNK vb land noisily

KERPLUNKS > KERPLUNK

KERRIA n type of shrub with yellow flowers

KERRIAS > KERRIA

KERRIES > KERRY

KERRY n breed of dairy cattle

KERSEY n smooth woollen cloth used for overcoats, etc

KERSEYS > KERSEY

KERVE dialect word for > CARVE

KERVED > KERVE

KERVES > KERVE

KERVING > KERVE

KERYGMA n essential news of Jesus, as preached by the early Christians to elicit faith rather than to educate or instruct

KERYGMAS > KERYGMA

KERYGMATA > KERYGMA

KESAR old variant of > KAISER

KESARS > KESAR

KESH n beard and uncut hair, covered by the turban, traditionally worn by Sikhs as a symbol of their religious and cultural loyalty

KESHES > KESH

KEST old form of > CAST

KESTING > KEST

KESTREL n type of small falcon

KESTRELS > KESTREL

KESTS > KEST

KET n dialect word for carrion

KETA n type of salmon

KETAMINE n drug, chemically related to PCP, that is used in medicine as a general anaesthetic, being administered by injection

KETAMINES > KETAMINE

KETAS > KETA

KETCH n two-masted sailing vessel ▷ vb (in archaic usage) catch

KETCHES > KETCH

KETCHING > KETCH

KETCHUP n thick cold sauce, usu made of tomatoes

KETCHUPS > KETCHUP

KETE n basket woven from flax

KETENE n colourless irritating toxic gas used as an acetylating agent in organic synthesis

KETENES > KETENE

KETES > KETE

KETMIA as in bladder ketmia plant with pale yellow flowers and a bladder-like calyx

KETMIAS > KETMIA

KETO as in keto form form of tautomeric compounds when they are ketones rather than enol

KETOGENIC adj forming or able to stimulate the production of ketone bodies

KETOL n nitrogenous substance

KETOLS > KETOL

KETONE n type of organic solvent

KETONEMIA n excess of ketone bodies in the blood

KETONES > KETONE

KETONIC > KETONE

KETONURIA n presence of ketone bodies in the urine

KETOSE n any monosaccharide that contains a ketone group

KETOSES > KETOSIS

KETOSIS n high concentration of ketone bodies in the blood

KETOTIC > KETOSIS

KETOXIME n oxime formed by reaction between hydroxylamine and a ketone

KETOXIMES > KETOXIME

KETS > KET

KETTLE n container with a spout and handle used for boiling water

KETTLEFUL > KETTLE

KETTLES > KETTLE

KETUBAH n contract that states the obligations within Jewish marriage

KETUBAHS > KETUBAH

KETUBOT > KETUBAH

KETUBOTH > KETUBAH

KEVEL n strong bitt or bollard for securing heavy hawsers

KEVELS > KEVEL

KEVIL old variant of > KEVEL

KEVILS > KEVIL

KEWL nonstandard variant spelling of > COOL

KEWLER > KEWL

KEWLEST > KEWL

KEWPIE n type of brightly coloured doll, commonly given as a prize at carnival

KEWPIES > KEWPIE

KEX n any of several large hollow-stemmed umbelliferous plants, such as cow parsnip and chervil

KEXES > KEX

KEY n device for operating a lock by moving a bolt ▷ adj of great importance ▷ vb enter (text) using a keyboard

KEYBOARD n set of keys on a piano, computer, etc ▷ vb enter (text) using a keyboard

KEYBOARDS > KEYBOARD

KEYBUGLE n bugle with keys

KEYBUGLES > KEYBUGLE

KEYBUTTON n on a keyboard, an object which, when pressed, causes the letter, number, or symbol shown on it to be printed in a document

KEYCARD n card with an electronic strip or code on it that allows it to open a corresponding keycard-operated door

KEYCARDS > KEYCARD

KEYED > KEY

KEYHOLE n opening for inserting a key into a lock

KEYHOLES > KEYHOLE

KEYING > KEY

KEYINGS > KEY

KEYLESS > KEY

KEYLINE n outline image of something on artwork or plans to show where it is to be placed

KEYLINES > KEYLINE

KEYLOGGER n device or software application used for covertly recording and monitoring keystrokes made on a remote computer

KEYNOTE adj central or dominating ▷ n dominant idea of a speech etc ▷ vb deliver a keynote address to (a political convention, etc)

KEYNOTED > KEYNOTE

KEYNOTER n person delivering a keynote address

KEYNOTERS > KEYNOTER

KEYNOTES > KEYNOTE

KEYNOTING > KEYNOTE

KEYPAD n small panel with a set of buttons for operating a Teletext system, electronic calculator, etc

KEYPADS > KEYPAD

KEYPAL n person with whom one regularly exchanges emails for fun

KEYPALS > KEYPAL

KEYPUNCH n device having a keyboard that is operated manually to transfer data onto punched cards, paper tape, etc ▷ vb transfer (data) onto punched cards, paper tape, etc, by using a key punch

KEYRING adj of a type of computer drive

KEYS interj children's cry for truce or respite from the rules of a game

KEYSET n set of computer keys used for a particular purpose

KEYSETS > KEYSET

k

KEYSTER same as
> KEISTER
KEYSTERS > KEYSTER
KEYSTONE n most important part of a process, organization, etc ▷ vb project or provide with a distorted image
KEYSTONED > KEYSTONE
KEYSTONES > KEYSTONE
KEYSTROKE n single operation of the mechanism of a typewriter or keyboard-operated typesetting machine by the action of a key ▷ vb enter or cause to be recorded by pressing a key
KEYWAY n longitudinal slot cut into a component to accept a key that engages with a similar slot on a mating component to prevent relative motion of the two components
KEYWAYS > KEYWAY
KEYWORD n word or phrase that a computer will search for in order to locate the information or file that the computer user has requested
KEYWORDS > KEYWORD
KEYWORKER n public sector worker regarded as providing an essential service
KGOTLA n (in South African English) meeting place for village assemblies, court cases, and meetings of village leaders
KGOTLAS > KGOTLA
KHADDAR n cotton cloth of plain weave, produced in India
KHADDARS > KHADDAR
KHADI same as > KHADDAR
KHADIS > KHADI
KHAF n letter of the Hebrew alphabet
KHAFS > KHAF
KHAKI adj dull yellowish-brown ▷ n hard-wearing fabric of this colour used for military uniforms
KHAKILIKE > KHAKI
KHAKIS > KHAKI
KHALAT same as > KHILAT
KHALATS > KHALAT
KHALIF variant spelling of > CALIPH
KHALIFA same as > CALIPH
KHALIFAH same as > CALIPH
KHALIFAHS > KHALIFAH
KHALIFAS > KHALIFA
KHALIFAT same as > CALIPHATE
KHALIFATE same as > CALIPHATE
KHALIFATS > KHALIFAT
KHALIFS > KHALIF

KHAMSEEN same as > KHAMSIN
KHAMSEENS > KHAMSEEN
KHAMSIN n hot southerly wind blowing from about March to May, esp in Egypt
KHAMSINS > KHAMSIN
KHAN n title of respect in Afghanistan and central Asia
KHANATE n territory ruled by a khan
KHANATES > KHANATE
KHANDA n double-edged sword that appears as the emblem on the Sikh flag and is used in the Amrit ceremony to stir the amrit
KHANDAS > KHANDA
KHANGA same as > KANGA
KHANGAS > KHANGA
KHANJAR n type of dagger
KHANJARS > KHANJAR
KHANS > KHAN
KHANSAMA same as > KHANSAMAH
KHANSAMAH n Indian cook or other male servant
KHANSAMAS > KHANSAMA
KHANUM feminine form of > KHAN
KHANUMS > KHANUM
KHAPH n letter of the Hebrew alphabet
KHAPHS > KHAPH
KHARIF n (in Pakistan, India, etc) crop that is harvested at the beginning of winter
KHARIFS > KHARIF
KHAT n white-flowered evergreen shrub of Africa and Arabia whose leaves have narcotic properties
KHATS > KHAT
KHAYA n type of African tree
KHAYAL n kind of Indian classical vocal music
KHAYALS > KHAYAL
KHAYAS > KHAYA
KHAZEN same as > CHAZAN
KHAZENIM > KHAZEN
KHAZENS > KHAZEN
KHAZI n lavatory
KHAZIS > KHAZI
KHEDA n (in India, Myanmar, etc) enclosure into which wild elephants are driven to be captured
KHEDAH same as > KHEDA
KHEDAHS > KHEDAH
KHEDAS > KHEDA
KHEDIVA n khedive's wife
KHEDIVAL > KHEDIVE
KHEDIVAS > KHEDIVA
KHEDIVATE > KHEDIVE
KHEDIVE n viceroy of Egypt under Ottoman suzerainty
KHEDIVES > KHEDIVE
KHEDIVIAL > KHEDIVE
KHET n Thai district
KHETH same as > HETH
KHETHS > KHETH

KHETS > KHET
KHI n letter of the Greek alphabet
KHILAFAT same as > CALIPHATE
KHILAFATS > KHILAFAT
KHILAT n (in the Middle East) robe or other gift given to someone by a superior as a mark of honour
KHILATS > KHILAT
KHILIM same as > KILIM
KHILIMS > KHILIM
KHIMAR n type of headscarf worn by Muslim women
KHIMARS > KHIMAR
KHIRKAH n dervish's woollen or cotton outer garment
KHIRKAHS > KHIRKAH
KHIS > KHI
KHODJA same as > KHOJA
KHODJAS > KHODJA
KHOJA n teacher in a Muslim school
KHOJAS > KHOJA
KHOR n watercourse
KHORS > KHOR
KHOTBAH same as > KHUTBAH
KHOTBAHS > KHOTBAH
KHOTBEH same as > KHUTBAH
KHOTBEHS > KHOTBEH
KHOUM n Mauritanian monetary unit
KHOUMS > KHOUM
KHUD n Indian ravine
KHUDS > KHUD
KHURTA same as > KURTA
KHURTAS > KHURTA
KHUSKHUS n aromatic perennial Indian grass whose roots are woven into mats, fans, and baskets
KHUTBAH n sermon in a Mosque, especially on a Friday
KHUTBAHS > KHUTBAH
KI n vital energy
KIAAT n tropical African leguminous tree
KIAATS > KIAAT
KIANG n variety of wild ass that occurs in Tibet and surrounding regions
KIANGS > KIANG
KIAUGH n (in Scots) anxiety
KIAUGHS > KIAUGH
KIBBE n Middle Eastern dish made with minced meat and bulgur
KIBBEH same as > KIBBE
KIBBEHS > KIBBEH
KIBBES > KIBBE
KIBBI same as > KIBBE
KIBBIS > KIBBI
KIBBITZ same as > KIBITZ
KIBBITZED > KIBBITZ
KIBBITZER > KIBBITZ
KIBBITZES > KIBBITZ
KIBBLE n bucket used in

wells or in mining for hoisting ▷ vb grind into small pieces
KIBBLED > KIBBLE
KIBBLES > KIBBLE
KIBBLING > KIBBLE
KIBBUTZ n communal farm or factory in Israel
KIBBUTZIM > KIBBUTZ
KIBE n chilblain, esp an ulcerated one on the heel
KIBEI n someone of Japanese ancestry born in the US and educated in Japan
KIBEIS > KIBEI
KIBES > KIBE
KIBITKA n (in Russia) covered sledge or wagon
KIBITKAS > KIBITKA
KIBITZ vb interfere or offer unwanted advice, esp as a spectator at a card game
KIBITZED > KIBITZ
KIBITZER > KIBITZ
KIBITZERS > KIBITZ
KIBITZES > KIBITZ
KIBITZING > KIBITZ
KIBLA same as > KIBLAH
KIBLAH n direction of Mecca, to which Muslims turn in prayer, indicated in mosques by a niche (mihrab) in the wall
KIBLAHS > KIBLAH
KIBLAS > KIBLA
KIBOSH vb put a stop to
KIBOSHED > KIBOSH
KIBOSHES > KIBOSH
KIBOSHING > KIBOSH
KICK vb drive, push, or strike with the foot ▷ n thrust or blow with the foot
KICKABLE > KICK
KICKABOUT n informal game of soccer
KICKBACK n money paid illegally for favours done ▷ vb have a strong reaction
KICKBACKS > KICKBACK
KICKBALL n children's ball game or the large ball used in it
KICKBALLS > KICKBALL
KICKBOARD n type of float held on to by a swimmer when practising leg strokes
KICKBOX vb box with hands and feet
KICKBOXED > KICKBOX
KICKBOXER n someone who practises kickboxing, a martial art that resembles boxing but in which kicks are permitted
KICKBOXES > KICKBOX
KICKDOWN n method of changing gear in a car with automatic transmission, by fully depressing the accelerator
KICKDOWNS > KICKDOWN
KICKED > KICK
KICKER n person or thing

KICKERS > KICKER
KICKFLIP *n* type of skateboarding manoeuvre ▷ *vb* perform a kickflip in skateboarding
KICKFLIPS > KICKFLIP
KICKIER > KICKY
KICKIEST > KICKY
KICKING > KICK
KICKOFF *n* kick from the centre of the field that starts a game of football
KICKOFFS > KICKOFF
KICKOUT *n* (in basketball) instance of kicking the ball
KICKOUTS > KICKOUT
KICKS > KICK
KICKSHAW *n* valueless trinket
KICKSHAWS *same as* > KICKSHAW
KICKSTAND *n* short metal bar on a motorcycle, which when kicked into a vertical position holds the cycle upright when stationary
KICKSTART *vb* start by kicking pedal
KICKUP *n* fuss
KICKUPS > KICKUP
KICKY *adj* excitingly unusual and different
KID *n* child ▷ *vb* tease or deceive (someone) ▷ *adj* younger
KIDDED > KID
KIDDER > KID
KIDDERS > KID
KIDDIE *same as* > KIDDY
KIDDIED > KIDDY
KIDDIER *n* old word for a market trader
KIDDIERS > KIDDIER
KIDDIES > KIDDY
KIDDING > KID
KIDDINGLY > KID
KIDDISH > KID
KIDDLE *n* device, esp a barrier constructed of nets and stakes, for catching fish in a river or in the sea
KIDDLES > KIDDLE
KIDDO *n* very informal term of address for a young person
KIDDOES > KIDDO
KIDDOS > KIDDO
KIDDUSH *n* (in Judaism) special blessing said before a meal on sabbaths and festivals
KIDDUSHES > KIDDUSH
KIDDY *n* affectionate word for a child ▷ *vb* tease or deceive
KIDDYING > KIDDY
KIDDYWINK *n* humorous word for a child
KIDEL *same as* > KIDDLE
KIDELS > KIDEL
KIDGE *dialect word for* > LIVELY
KIDGIE *adj* dialect word for friendly and welcoming

KIDGIER > KIDGIE
KIDGIEST > KIDGIE
KIDGLOVE *adj* overdelicate or overrefined
KIDLET *n* humorous word for small child
KIDLETS > KIDLET
KIDLIKE > KID
KIDLING *n* young kid
KIDLINGS > KIDLING
KIDNAP *vb* seize and hold (a person) to ransom
KIDNAPED > KIDNAP
KIDNAPEE > KIDNAP
KIDNAPEES > KIDNAP
KIDNAPER > KIDNAP
KIDNAPERS > KIDNAP
KIDNAPING > KIDNAP
KIDNAPPED > KIDNAP
KIDNAPPEE > KIDNAP
KIDNAPPER > KIDNAP
KIDNAPS > KIDNAP
KIDNEY *n* either of the pair of organs that filter waste products from the blood to produce urine
KIDNEYS > KIDNEY
KIDOLOGY *n* practice of bluffing or deception in order to gain a psychological advantage over someone
KIDS > KID
KIDSKIN *n* soft smooth leather made from the hide of a young goat
KIDSKINS > KIDSKIN
KIDSTAKES *npl* pretence
KIDULT *n* adult who is interested in forms of entertainment such as computer games, television programmes, etc that are intended for children ▷ *adj* aimed at or suitable for kidults, or both children and adults
KIDULTS > KIDULT
KIDVID *n* informal word for children's video or television
KIDVIDS > KIDVID
KIEF *same as* > KIF
KIEFS > KIEF
KIEKIE *n* climbing bush plant of New Zealand
KIEKIES > KIEKIE
KIELBASA *n* Polish sausage
KIELBASAS > KIELBASA
KIELBASI *same as* > KIELBASA
KIELBASY *same as* > KIELBASA
KIER *n* vat in which cloth is bleached
KIERIE *n* South African cudgel
KIERIES > KIERIE
KIERS > KIER
KIESELGUR *n* type of mineral
KIESERITE *n* white mineral consisting of hydrated magnesium

sulphate
KIESTER *same as* > KEISTER
KIESTERS > KIESTER
KIEV *n* chicken breast filled with garlic butter and coated in breadcrumbs
KIEVE *same as* > KEEVE
KIEVES > KIEVE
KIEVS > KIEV
KIF *n* any drug or agent that when smoked is capable of producing a euphoric condition
KIFF *adj* South African slang for excellent
KIFS > KIF
KIGHT *n* archaic spelling of kite, the bird of prey
KIGHTS > KIGHT
KIKE *n* offensive word for a Jewish person
KIKES > KIKE
KIKOI *n* piece of cotton cloth with coloured bands, worn wrapped around the body
KIKOIS > KIKOI
KIKUMON *n* chrysanthemum emblem of the imperial family of Japan
KIKUMONS > KIKUMON
KIKUYU *n* type of grass
KIKUYUS > KIKUYU
KILD *old spelling of* > KILLED
KILDERKIN *n* obsolete unit of liquid capacity equal to 16 or 18 Imperial gallons or of dry capacity equal to 16 or 18 wine gallons
KILERG *n* 1000 ergs
KILERGS > KILERG
KILEY *same as* > KYLIE
KILEYS > KILEY
KILIM *n* pileless woven rug of intricate design made in the Middle East
KILIMS > KILIM
KILL *vb* cause the death of ▷ *n* act of killing
KILLABLE > KILL
KILLADAR *n* fort commander or governor
KILLADARS > KILLADAR
KILLAS *n* Cornish clay slate
KILLASES > KILLAS
KILLCOW *n* important person
KILLCOWS > KILLCOW
KILLCROP *n* ever-hungry baby, thought to be a fairy changeling
KILLCROPS > KILLCROP
KILLDEE *same as* > KILLDEER
KILLDEER *n* large brown-and-white North American plover with a noisy cry
KILLDEERS > KILLDEER
KILLDEES > KILLDEE
KILLED > KILL

KILLER *n* person or animal that kills, esp habitually
KILLERS > KILLER
KILLICK *n* small anchor, esp one made of a heavy stone
KILLICKS > KILLICK
KILLIE *same as* > KILLIFISH
KILLIES > KILLIE
KILLIFISH *n* any of various chiefly American minnow-like fishes
KILLING *adj* very tiring ▷ *n* sudden financial success
KILLINGLY > KILLING
KILLINGS > KILLING
KILLJOY *n* person who spoils others' pleasure
KILLJOYS > KILLJOY
KILLOCK *same as* > KILLICK
KILLOCKS > KILLOCK
KILLOGIE *n* sheltered place in front of a kiln
KILLOGIES > KILLOGIE
KILLS > KILL
KILLUT *same as* > KHILAT
KILLUTS > KILLUT
KILN *n* oven for baking, drying, or processing pottery, bricks, etc ▷ *vb* fire or process in a kiln
KILNED > KILN
KILNING > KILN
KILNS > KILN
KILO *n* code word for the letter k
KILOBAR *n* 1000 bars
KILOBARS > KILOBAR
KILOBASE *n* unit of measurement for DNA and RNA equal to 1000 base pairs
KILOBASES > KILOBASE
KILOBAUD *n* 1000 baud
KILOBAUDS > KILOBAUD
KILOBIT *n* 1024 bits
KILOBITS > KILOBIT
KILOBYTE *n* 1024 units of information
KILOBYTES > KILOBYTE
KILOCURIE *n* unit of thousand curies
KILOCYCLE *n* short for kilocycle per second: a former unit of frequency equal to 1 kilohertz
KILOGAUSS *n* 1000 gauss
KILOGRAM *n* one thousand grams
KILOGRAMS > KILOGRAM
KILOGRAY *n* 1000 gray
KILOGRAYS > KILOGRAY
KILOHERTZ *n* one thousand hertz
KILOJOULE *n* 1000 joules
KILOLITER *US spelling of* > KILOLITRE
KILOLITRE *n* 1000 litres
KILOMETER *same as* > KILOMETRE
KILOMETRE *n* one thousand metres

k

KILOMOLE n 1000 moles

KILOMOLES > KILOMOLE

KILOPOND n informal unit of gravitational force

KILOPONDS > KILOPOND

KILORAD n 1000 rads

KILORADS > KILORAD

KILOS > KILO

KILOTON n one thousand tons

KILOTONNE same as > KILOTON

KILOTONS > KILOTON

KILOVOLT n one thousand volts

KILOVOLTS > KILOVOLT

KILOWATT n one thousand watts

KILOWATTS > KILOWATT

KILP dialect form of > KELP

KILPS > KILP

KILT n knee-length pleated tartan skirt-like garment worn orig. by Scottish Highlanders ▷ vb put pleats in (cloth)

KILTED > KILT

KILTER n working order or alignment

KILTERS > KILTER

KILTIE n someone wearing a kilt

KILTIES > KILTIE

KILTING > KILT

KILTINGS > KILT

KILTLIKE > KILT

KILTS > KILT

KILTY same as > KILTIE

KIMBO vb place akimbo

KIMBOED > KIMBO

KIMBOING > KIMBO

KIMBOS > KIMBO

KIMCHEE same as > KIMCHI

KIMCHEES > KIMCHEE

KIMCHI n Korean dish made from fermented cabbage or other vegetables, garlic, and chillies

KIMCHIS > KIMCHI

KIMMER same as > CUMMER

KIMMERS > KIMMER

KIMONO n loose wide-sleeved Japanese robe, fastened with a sash

KIMONOED > KIMONO

KIMONOS > KIMONO

KIN n person's relatives collectively ▷ adj related by blood

KINA n standard monetary unit of Papua New Guinea, divided into 100 toea

KINAKINA same as > QUININE

KINAKINAS > KINAKINA

KINARA n African candle holder

KINARAS > KINARA

KINAS > KINA

KINASE n any enzyme that can convert an inactive zymogen to the corresponding enzyme

KINASES > KINASE

KINCHIN old slang word for > CHILD

KINCHINS > KINCHIN

KINCOB n fine silk fabric embroidered with threads of gold or silver, of a kind made in India

KINCOBS > KINCOB

KIND adj considerate, friendly, and helpful ▷ n class or group with common characteristics ▷ vb old word for beget or father

KINDA adv very informal shortening of kind of

KINDED > KIND

KINDER adj more kind ▷ n kindergarten or nursery school

KINDERS > KIND

KINDEST > KIND

KINDIE same as > KINDY

KINDIES > KINDY

KINDING > KIND

KINDLE vb set (a fire) alight

KINDLED > KINDLE

KINDLER > KINDLE

KINDLERS > KINDLE

KINDLES > KINDLE

KINDLESS adj heartless

KINDLIER > KINDLY

KINDLIEST > KINDLY

KINDLILY > KINDLY

KINDLING n dry wood or straw for starting fires

KINDLINGS > KINDLING

KINDLY adj having a warm-hearted nature ▷ adv in a considerate way

KINDNESS n quality of being kind

KINDRED adj having similar qualities ▷ n blood relationship

KINDREDS > KINDRED

KINDS > KIND

KINDY n kindergarten

KINE npl cows or cattle ▷ n Japanese pestle

KINEMA same as > CINEMA

KINEMAS > KINEMA

KINEMATIC adj of or relating to the study of the motion of bodies without reference to mass or force

KINES n > KINE

KINESCOPE n US name for a television tube ▷ vb record on film

KINESES > KINESIS

KINESIC adj of or relating to kinesics

KINESICS n study of the role of body movements, such as winking, shrugging, etc, in communication

KINESIS n nondirectional movement of an organism or cell in response to a stimulus, the rate of movement being dependent on the strength of the stimulus

KINETIC adj relating to or caused by motion

KINETICAL same as > KINETIC

KINETICS n branch of mechanics concerned with the study of bodies in motion

KINETIN n plant hormone

KINETINS > KINETIN

KINFOLK another word for > KINSFOLK

KINFOLKS > KINFOLK

KING n male ruler of a monarchy ▷ vb make king

KINGBIRD n any of several large American flycatchers

KINGBIRDS > KINGBIRD

KINGBOLT n pivot bolt that connects the body of a horse-drawn carriage to the front axle and provides the steering joint

KINGBOLTS > KINGBOLT

KINGCRAFT n art of ruling as a king, esp by diplomacy and cunning

KINGCUP n yellow-flowered plant

KINGCUPS > KINGCUP

KINGDOM n state ruled by a king or queen

KINGDOMED adj old word for with a kingdom

KINGDOMS > KINGDOM

KINGED > KING

KINGFISH n food and game fish occurring in warm American Atlantic coastal waters

KINGHOOD > KING

KINGHOODS > KING

KINGING > KING

KINGKLIP n edible eel-like marine fish of S Africa

KINGKLIPS > KINGKLIP

KINGLE n Scots word for a type of hard rock

KINGLES > KINGLE

KINGLESS > KING

KINGLET n king of a small or insignificant territory

KINGLETS > KINGLET

KINGLIER > KINGLY

KINGLIEST > KINGLY

KINGLIKE > KING

KINGLING n minor king

KINGLINGS > KINGLING

KINGLY adj appropriate to a king ▷ adv in a manner appropriate to a king

KINGMAKER n person who has control over appointments to positions of authority

KINGPIN n most important person in an organization

KINGPINS > KINGPIN

KINGPOST n vertical post connecting the apex of a triangular roof truss to the tie beam

KINGPOSTS > KINGPOST

KINGS > KING

KINGSHIP n position or authority of a king

KINGSHIPS > KINGSHIP

KINGSIDE n (in chess) side of the board on which a particular king is at the start of a game as opposed to the side the queen is on

KINGSIDES > KINGSIDE

KINGSNAKE n North American snake

KINGWOOD n hard fine-grained violet-tinted wood of a Brazilian leguminous tree

KINGWOODS > KINGWOOD

KININ n any of a group of polypeptides in the blood that cause dilation of the blood vessels and make smooth muscles contract

KININS > KININ

KINK n twist or bend in rope, wire, hair, etc ▷ vb form or cause to form a kink

KINKAJOU n arboreal fruit-eating mammal of Central and South America, with a long prehensile tail

KINKAJOUS > KINKAJOU

KINKED > KINK

KINKIER > KINKY

KINKIEST > KINKY

KINKILY > KINKY

KINKINESS > KINKY

KINKING > KINK

KINKLE n little kink

KINKLES > KINKLE

KINKS > KINK

KINKY adj given to unusual sexual practices

KINLESS adj without any relatives

KINO same as > KENO

KINONE n benzoquinone, a yellow crystalline water-soluble ketone used in the production of dyestuffs

KINONES > KINONE

KINOS > KINO

KINRED old form of > KINDRED

KINREDS > KINRED

KINS > KIN

KINSFOLK npl one's family or relatives

KINSFOLKS > KINSFOLK

KINSHIP n blood relationship

KINSHIPS > KINSHIP

KINSMAN n relative

KINSMEN > KINSMAN

KINSWOMAN > KINSMAN

KINSWOMEN > KINSMAN

KINTLEDGE same as > KENTLEDGE

KIORE n small brown rat native to New Zealand

KIORES > KIORE

KIOSK n small booth selling drinks, cigarettes, newspapers, etc

KIOSKS > KIOSK
KIP vb sleep ▷ n sleep or slumber
KIPE n dialect word for a basket for catching fish
KIPES > KIPE
KIPP uncommon variant of > KIP
KIPPA n skullcap worn by orthodox male Jews at all times and by others for prayer, esp a crocheted one worn by those with a specifically religious Zionist affiliation
KIPPAGE n Scots word for a state of anger or excitement
KIPPAGES > KIPPAGE
KIPPAS > KIPPA
KIPPED > KIP
KIPPEN > KEP
KIPPER n cleaned, salted, and smoked herring ▷ vb cure (a herring) by salting and smoking it
KIPPERED adj (of fish, esp herring) having been cleaned, salted, and smoked
KIPPERER > KIPPER
KIPPERERS > KIPPER
KIPPERING > KIPPER
KIPPERS > KIPPER
KIPPING > KIP
KIPPS > KIPP
KIPS > KIP
KIPSKIN same as > KIP
KIPSKINS > KIPSKIN
KIPUNJI n Tanzanian species of monkey
KIPUNJIS > KIPUNJI
KIR n drink made from dry white wine and cassis
KIRANA n small family-owned shop in India
KIRANAS > KIRANA
KIRBEH n leather bottle
KIRBEHS > KIRBEH
KIRBIGRIP n hairgrip
KIRBY as in kirby grip hairgrip consisting of a piece of wire bent back on itself and partly bent into ridges
KIRIGAMI n art, originally Japanese, of folding and cutting paper into decorative shapes
KIRIGAMIS > KIRIGAMI
KIRIMON n Japanese imperial crest
KIRIMONS > KIRIMON
KIRK Scot word for > CHURCH
KIRKED > KIRK
KIRKING > KIRK
KIRKINGS > KIRK
KIRKMAN n member or strong upholder of the Kirk
KIRKMEN > KIRKMAN
KIRKS > KIRK
KIRKTON n village or town with a parish church
KIRKTONS > KIRKTON

KIRKWARD adv towards the church
KIRKYAIRD same as > KIRKYARD
KIRKYARD n churchyard
KIRKYARDS > KIRKYARD
KIRMESS same as > KERMIS
KIRMESSES > KIRMESS
KIRN dialect word for > CHURN
KIRNED > KIRN
KIRNING > KIRN
KIRNS > KIRN
KIRPAN n short sword traditionally carried by Sikhs as a symbol of their religious and cultural loyalty
KIRPANS > KIRPAN
KIRRI n Hottentot stick
KIRRIS > KIRRI
KIRS > KIR
KIRSCH n cherry brandy
KIRSCHES > KIRSCH
KIRTAN n devotional singing, usually accompanied by musical instruments
KIRTANS > KIRTAN
KIRTLE n woman's skirt or dress ▷ vb dress with a kirtle
KIRTLED > KIRTLE
KIRTLES > KIRTLE
KIS > KI
KISAN n peasant or farmer
KISANS > KISAN
KISH n graphite formed on the surface of molten iron that contains a large amount of carbon
KISHES > KISH
KISHKA same as > KISHKE
KISHKAS > KISHKA
KISHKE n beef or fowl intestine or skin stuffed with flour, onion, etc, and boiled and roasted
KISHKES > KISHKE
KISMAT same as > KISMET
KISMATS > KISMAT
KISMET n fate or destiny
KISMETIC > KISMET
KISMETS > KISMET
KISS vb touch with the lips in affection or greeting ▷ n touch with the lips
KISSABLE > KISS
KISSABLY > KISS
KISSAGRAM n greetings service in which a messenger kisses the person celebrating
KISSED > KISS
KISSEL n Russian dessert of sweetened fruit purée thickened with arrowroot
KISSELS > KISSEL
KISSER n mouth or face
KISSERS > KISSER
KISSES > KISS
KISSIER > KISSY
KISSIEST > KISSY

KISSING > KISS
KISSINGS > KISSING
KISSOGRAM same as > KISSAGRAM
KISSY adj showing exaggerated affection, esp by frequent touching or kissing
KIST n large wooden chest ▷ vb place in a coffin
KISTED > KIST
KISTFUL > KIST
KISTFULS > KIST
KISTING > KIST
KISTS > KIST
KISTVAEN n stone tomb
KISTVAENS > KISTVAEN
KIT n outfit or equipment for a specific purpose ▷ vb fit or provide
KITBAG n bag for a soldier's or traveller's belongings
KITBAGS > KITBAG
KITCHEN n room used for cooking ▷ vb (in archaic usage) provide with food
KITCHENED > KITCHEN
KITCHENER n someone employed in kitchen work
KITCHENET n small kitchen or part of another room equipped for use as a kitchen
KITCHENS > KITCHEN
KITE n light frame covered with a thin material flown on a string in the wind ▷ vb soar and glide
KITEBOARD n board like a windsurfing board, towed by a large kite
KITED > KITE
KITELIKE > KITE
KITENGE n thick cotton cloth
KITENGES > KITENGE
KITER > KITE
KITERS > KITE
KITES > KITE
KITH n one's friends and acquaintances
KITHARA variant of > CITHARA
KITHARAS > KITHARA
KITHE same as > KYTHE
KITHED > KITHE
KITHES > KITHE
KITHING > KITHE
KITHS > KITH
KITING > KITE
KITINGS > KITE
KITLING dialect word for > KITTEN
KITLINGS > KITLING
KITS > KIT
KITSCH n art or literature with popular sentimental appeal ▷ n object or art that is tawdry, vulgarized, oversentimental or pretentious
KITSCHES > KITSCH
KITSCHIER > KITSCH
KITSCHIFY vb make kitsch

KITSCHILY > KITSCH
KITSCHY > KITSCH
KITSET n New Zealand word for a piece of furniture supplied in pieces for the purchaser to assemble
KITSETS > KITSET
KITTED > KIT
KITTEL n white garment worn for certain Jewish rituals or burial
KITTELS > KITTEL
KITTEN n young cat ▷ vb (of cats) give birth
KITTENED > KITTEN
KITTENING > KITTEN
KITTENISH adj lively and flirtatious
KITTENS > KITTEN
KITTENY > KITTEN
KITTIES > KITTY
KITTING > KIT
KITTIWAKE n type of seagull
KITTLE adj capricious and unpredictable ▷ vb be troublesome or puzzling to (someone)
KITTLED > KITTLE
KITTLER > KITTLE
KITTLES > KITTLE
KITTLEST > KITTLE
KITTLIER > KITTLY
KITTLIEST > KITTLY
KITTLING > KITTLE
KITTLY Scots word for > TICKLISH
KITTUL n type of palm from which jaggery sugar comes
KITTULS > KITTUL
KITTY n communal fund
KITUL same as > KITTUL
KITULS > KITUL
KIVA n large underground or partly underground room in a Pueblo Indian village, used chiefly for religious ceremonies
KIVAS > KIVA
KIWI n New Zealand flightless bird with a long beak and no tail
KIWIFRUIT n edible oval fruit of the kiwi plant
KIWIS > KIWI
KLANG n (in music) kind of tone
KLANGS > KLANG
KLAP vb slap or spank
KLAPPED > KLAP
KLAPPING > KLAP
KLAPS > KLAP
KLATCH n gathering, especially over coffee
KLATCHES > KLATCH
KLATSCH same as > KLATCH
KLATSCHES > KLATSCH
KLAVERN n local Ku Klux Klan group
KLAVERNS > KLAVERN
KLAVIER same as > CLAVIER**

k

KLAVIERS > KLAVIER

KLAXON n loud horn used on emergency vehicles as a warning signal ▷ vb hoot with a klaxon

KLAXONED > KLAXON

KLAXONING > KLAXON

KLAXONS > KLAXON

KLEAGLE n person with a particular rank in the Ku Klux Klan

KLEAGLES > KLEAGLE

KLEENEX n tradename for a kind of soft paper tissue, used esp as a handkerchief

KLEENEXES > KLEENEX

KLENDUSIC adj disease-resistant

KLEPHT n any of the Greeks who fled to the mountains after the 15th-century Turkish conquest of Greece and whose descendants survived as brigands into the 19th century

KLEPHTIC > KLEPHT

KLEPHTISM > KLEPHT

KLEPHTS > KLEPHT

KLEPTO n compulsive thief

KLEPTOS > KLEPTO

KLETT n lightweight climbing boot

KLETTS > KLETT

KLEZMER n Jewish folk musician, usually a member of a small band

KLEZMERS > KLEZMER

KLEZMORIM > KLEZMER

KLICK n kilometre

KLICKS > KLICK

KLIEG as in klieg light intense carbon-arc light used for illumination in producing films

KLIK US military slang word for > KILOMETRE

KLIKS > KLIK

KLINKER n type of brick used in paving

KLINKERS > KLINKER

KLINOSTAT n rotating and tilting plant holder for studying and experimenting with plant growth

KLIPDAS n rock hyrax

KLIPDASES > KLIPDAS

KLISTER n type of ski dressing for improving grip on snow

KLISTERS > KLISTER

KLONDIKE n rich source of something ▷ vb transfer (bulk loads of fish) to factory ships at sea for processing

KLONDIKED > KLONDIKE

KLONDIKER same as > KLONDYKER

KLONDIKES > KLONDIKE

KLONDYKE n rich source of something ▷ vb transfer (bulk loads of fish) to factory ships at sea for processing

KLONDYKED > KLONDYKE

KLONDYKER n East European factory ship

KLONDYKES > KLONDYKE

KLONG n type of canal in Thailand

KLONGS > KLONG

KLOOCH same as > KLOOCHMAN

KLOOCHES > KLOOCH

KLOOCHMAN n North American Indian woman

KLOOCHMEN > KLOOCHMAN

KLOOF n mountain pass or gorge

KLOOFS > KLOOF

KLOOTCH same as > KLOOCHMAN

KLOOTCHES > KLOOTCH

KLUDGE n untidy solution involving a variety of cobbled-together elements ▷ vb cobble something together

KLUDGED > KLUDGE

KLUDGES > KLUDGE

KLUDGEY > KLUDGE

KLUDGIER > KLUDGE

KLUDGIEST > KLUDGE

KLUDGING > KLUDGE

KLUDGY > KLUDGE

KLUGE same as > KLUDGE

KLUGED > KLUGE

KLUGES > KLUGE

KLUGING > KLUGE

KLUTZ n clumsy or stupid person

KLUTZES > KLUTZ

KLUTZIER > KLUTZ

KLUTZIEST > KLUTZ

KLUTZY > KLUTZ

KLYSTRON n electron tube for the amplification or generation of microwaves by means of velocity modulation

KLYSTRONS > KLYSTRON

KNACK n skilful way of doing something ▷ vb dialect word for crack or snap

KNACKED adj broken or worn out

KNACKER n buyer of old horses for killing ▷ vb exhaust

KNACKERED adj extremely tired

KNACKERS > KNACKER

KNACKERY n slaughterhouse for horses

KNACKIER > KNACKY

KNACKIEST > KNACKY

KNACKING > KNACK

KNACKISH adj old word meaning cunning or artful

KNACKS > KNACK

KNACKY adj old or dialect word for cunning or artful

KNAG n knot in wood

KNAGGIER > KNAGGY

KNAGGIEST > KNAGGY

KNAGGY adj knotty

KNAGS > KNAG

KNAIDEL same as > KNEIDEL

KNAIDLACH > KNAIDEL

KNAP n crest of a hill ▷ vb hit, hammer, or chip

KNAPPED > KNAP

KNAPPER > KNAP

KNAPPERS > KNAP

KNAPPING > KNAP

KNAPPLE old word for > NIBBLE

KNAPPLED > KNAPPLE

KNAPPLES > KNAPPLE

KNAPPLING > KNAPPLE

KNAPS > KNAP

KNAPSACK n soldier's or traveller's bag worn strapped on the back

KNAPSACKS > KNAPSACK

KNAPWEED n plant with purplish thistle-like flowers

KNAPWEEDS > KNAPWEED

KNAR old spelling of > GNAR

KNARL old spelling of > GNARL

KNARLIER > KNARLY

KNARLIEST > KNARLY

KNARLS > KNARL

KNARLY same as > GNARLY

KNARRED > KNAR

KNARRIER > KNAR

KNARRIEST > KNAR

KNARRING > KNAR

KNARRY > KNAR

KNARS > KNAR

KNAUR variant form of > KNUR

KNAURS > KNAUR

KNAVE n jack at cards

KNAVERIES > KNAVERY

KNAVERY n dishonest behaviour

KNAVES > KNAVE

KNAVESHIP n old Scottish legal term for the small proportion of milled grain due to the person doing the milling

KNAVISH > KNAVE

KNAVISHLY > KNAVE

KNAWE same as > KNAWEL

KNAWEL n type of Old World plant with heads of minute petal-less flowers

KNAWELS > KNAWEL

KNAWES > KNAWE

KNEAD vb work (dough) into a smooth mixture with the hands

KNEADABLE > KNEAD

KNEADED > KNEAD

KNEADER > KNEAD

KNEADERS > KNEAD

KNEADING > KNEAD

KNEADS > KNEAD

KNEE n joint between thigh and lower leg ▷ vb strike or push with the knee

KNEECAP nontechnical name for > PATELLA

KNEECAPS > KNEECAP

KNEED > KNEE

KNEEHOLE n space for the knees, esp under a desk

KNEEHOLES > KNEEHOLE

KNEEING > KNEE

KNEEJERK adj (of a reply or reaction) automatic and predictable

KNEEL vb fall or rest on one's knees ▷ n act or position of kneeling

KNEELED > KNEEL

KNEELER > KNEEL

KNEELERS > KNEEL

KNEELING > KNEEL

KNEELS > KNEEL

KNEEPAD n any of several types of protective covering for the knees

KNEEPADS > KNEEPAD

KNEEPAN another word for > PATELLA

KNEEPANS > KNEEPAN

KNEEPIECE n knee-shaped piece of timber in ship

KNEES > KNEE

KNEESIES n flirtatious touching of knees under table

KNEESOCK n type of sock that comes up to the knee

KNEESOCKS > KNEESOCK

KNEIDEL n (in Jewish cookery) small dumpling, usually served in chicken soup

KNEIDELS > KNEIDEL

KNEIDLACH > KNEIDEL

KNELL n sound of a bell, esp at a funeral or death ▷ vb ring a knell

KNELLED > KNELL

KNELLING > KNELL

KNELLS > KNELL

KNELT > KNEEL

KNESSET n parliament or assembly

KNESSETS > KNESSET

KNEVELL vb old Scots word meaning beat

KNEVELLED > KNEVELL

KNEVELLS > KNEVELL

KNEW > KNOW

KNICKER n woman's or girl's undergarment covering the lower trunk and having legs or legholes

KNICKERED > KNICKER

KNICKERS npl woman's or girl's undergarment covering the lower trunk and having legs or legholes

KNICKS npl knickers

KNIFE n cutting tool or weapon consisting of a sharp-edged blade with a handle ▷ vb cut or stab with a knife

KNIFED > KNIFE

KNIFELESS > KNIFE

KNIFELIKE > KNIFE

KNIFEMAN n man who is armed with a knife

KNIFEMEN > KNIFEMAN

KNIFER > KNIFE

KNIFEREST n support on

which a carving knife or carving fork is placed at the table

KNIFERS > KNIFE

KNIFES > KNIFE

KNIFING > KNIFE

KNIFINGS > KNIFE

KNIGHT *n* man who has been given a knighthood ▷ *vb* award a knighthood to

KNIGHTAGE *n* group of knights or knights collectively

KNIGHTED > KNIGHT

KNIGHTING > KNIGHT

KNIGHTLY *adj* of, resembling, or appropriate for a knight

KNIGHTS > KNIGHT

KNIPHOFIA *n* any of several perennial southern African flowering plants

KNISH *n* piece of dough stuffed with potato, meat, or some other filling and baked or fried

KNISHES > KNISH

KNIT *vb* make (a garment) by interlocking a series of loops in wool or other yarn ▷ *n* fabric made by knitting

KNITCH *dialect word for* > BUNDLE

KNITCHES > KNITCH

KNITS > KNIT

KNITTABLE > KNIT

KNITTED > KNIT

KNITTER > KNIT

KNITTERS > KNIT

KNITTING > KNIT

KNITTINGS > KNIT

KNITTLE *n* old word for string or cord

KNITTLES > KNITTLE

KNITWEAR *n* knitted clothes, such as sweaters

KNITWEARS > KNITWEAR

KNIVE *rare variant of* > KNIFE

KNIVED > KNIVE

KNIVES > KNIFE

KNIVING > KNIVE

KNOB *n* rounded projection, such as a switch on a radio ▷ *vb* supply with knobs

KNOBBED > KNOB

KNOBBER *n* two-year-old male deer

KNOBBERS > KNOBBER

KNOBBIER > KNOB

KNOBBIEST > KNOB

KNOBBING > KNOB

KNOBBLE *n* small knob ▷ *vb* dialect word meaning strike

KNOBBLED *same as* > KNOBBLY

KNOBBLES > KNOBBLE

KNOBBLIER > KNOBBLY

KNOBBLING > KNOBBLE

KNOBBLY *adj* covered with small bumps

KNOBBY > KNOB

KNOBHEAD *n* stupid person

KNOBHEADS > KNOBHEAD

KNOBLIKE > KNOB

KNOBS > KNOB

KNOBSTICK *n* stick with a round knob at the end, used as a club or missile by South African tribesmen

KNOCK *vb* give a blow or push to ▷ *n* blow or rap

KNOCKDOWN *adj* (of a price) very low

KNOCKED > KNOCK

KNOCKER *n* metal fitting for knocking on a door

KNOCKERS > KNOCKER

KNOCKING > KNOCK

KNOCKINGS > KNOCK

KNOCKLESS > KNOCK

KNOCKOFF *n* informal word for a cheap, often illegal, copy of something

KNOCKOFFS > KNOCKOFF

KNOCKOUT *n* blow that renders an opponent unconscious ▷ *vb* render (someone) unconscious

KNOCKOUTS > KNOCKOUT

KNOCKS > KNOCK

KNOLL *n* small rounded hill ▷ *vb* (in archaic or dialect usage) knell

KNOLLED > KNOLL

KNOLLER > KNOLL

KNOLLERS > KNOLL

KNOLLIER > KNOLL

KNOLLIEST > KNOLL

KNOLLING > KNOLL

KNOLLS > KNOLL

KNOLLY > KNOLL

KNOP *n* knob, esp an ornamental one

KNOPPED > KNOP

KNOPS > KNOP

KNOSP *n* budlike architectural feature

KNOSPS > KNOSP

KNOT *n* fastening made by looping and pulling tight strands of string, cord, or rope ▷ *vb* tie with or into a knot

KNOTGRASS *n* polygonaceous weedy plant whose small green flowers produce numerous seeds

KNOTHOLE *n* hole in a piece of wood where a knot has been

KNOTHOLES > KNOTHOLE

KNOTLESS > KNOT

KNOTLIKE > KNOT

KNOTS > KNOT

KNOTTED > KNOT

KNOTTER > KNOT

KNOTTERS > KNOT

KNOTTIER > KNOTTY

KNOTTIEST > KNOTTY

KNOTTILY > KNOTTY

KNOTTING > KNOT

KNOTTINGS > KNOT

KNOTTY *adj* full of knots

KNOTWEED *n* type of plant with small flowers and jointed stems

KNOTWEEDS > KNOTWEED

KNOTWORK *n* ornamentation consisting of a mass of intertwined and knotted cords

KNOTWORKS > KNOTWORK

KNOUT *n* stout whip used formerly in Russia as an instrument of punishment ▷ *vb* whip

KNOUTED > KNOUT

KNOUTING > KNOUT

KNOUTS > KNOUT

KNOW *vb* be or feel certain of the truth of (information etc)

KNOWABLE > KNOW

KNOWE *same as* > KNOLL

KNOWER > KNOW

KNOWERS > KNOW

KNOWES > KNOWE

KNOWHOW *n* ingenuity, knack, or skill

KNOWHOWS > KNOWHOW

KNOWING > KNOW

KNOWINGER > KNOW

KNOWINGLY > KNOW

KNOWINGS > KNOW

KNOWLEDGE *n* facts, feelings or experiences known by a person or group of people ▷ *vb* (in archaic usage) acknowledge

KNOWN > KNOW

KNOWNS > KNOW

KNOWS > KNOW

KNUB *dialect word for* > KNOB

KNUBBIER > KNUB

KNUBBIEST > KNUB

KNUBBLE *vb* dialect word for beat or pound using one's fists

KNUBBLED > KNUBBLE

KNUBBLES > KNUBBLE

KNUBBLIER > KNUBBLY

KNUBBLING > KNUBBLE

KNUBBLY *adj* having small lumps or protuberances

KNUBBY *adj* knub

KNUBS > KNUB

KNUCKLE *n* bone at the finger joint

KNUCKLED > KNUCKLE

KNUCKLER *n* type of throw in baseball

KNUCKLERS > KNUCKLER

KNUCKLES > KNUCKLE

KNUCKLIER > KNUCKLE

KNUCKLING > KNUCKLE

KNUCKLY > KNUCKLE

KNUR *n* knot or protuberance in a tree trunk or in wood

KNURL *n* small ridge, often one of a series ▷ *vb* impress with a series of fine ridges or serrations

KNURLED > KNURL

KNURLIER > KNURLY

KNURLIEST > KNURLY

KNURLING > KNURL

KNURLINGS > KNURL

KNURLS > KNURL

KNURLY *rare word for* > GNARLED

KNURR *same as* > KNUR

KNURRS > KNURR

KNURS > KNUR

KNUT *n* dandy

KNUTS > KNUT

KO *n* (in New Zealand) traditional digging tool

KOA *n* Hawaiian leguminous tree

KOALA *n* tree-dwelling Australian marsupial with dense grey fur

KOALAS > KOALA

KOAN *n* (in Zen Buddhism) problem or riddle that admits no logical solution

KOANS > KOAN

KOAP *n* (in Papua New Guinean slang) sexual intercourse

KOAPS > KOAP

KOAS > KOA

KOB *n* any of several waterbuck-like species of African antelope

KOBAN *n* old oval-shaped Japanese gold coin

KOBANG *same as* > KOBAN

KOBANGS > KOBANG

KOBANS > KOBAN

KOBO *n* Nigerian monetary unit, worth one hundredth of a naira

KOBOLD *n* mischievous household sprite

KOBOLDS > KOBOLD

KOBOS > KOBO

KOBS > KOB

KOCHIA *n* any of several plants whose foliage turns dark red in late summer

KOCHIAS > KOCHIA

KOEKOEA *n* long-tailed cuckoo of New Zealand

KOEKOEAS > KOEKOEA

KOEL *n* any of several parasitic cuckoos of S and SE Asia and Australia

KOELS > KOEL

KOFF *n* Dutch masted merchant vessel

KOFFS > KOFF

KOFTA *n* Indian dish of seasoned minced meat shaped into small balls and cooked

KOFTAS > KOFTA

KOFTGAR *n* (in India) person skilled in the art of inlaying steel with gold

KOFTGARI *n* ornamental Indian metalwork

KOFTGARIS > KOFTGARI

KOFTGARS > KOFTGAR

KOFTWORK *same as* > KOFTGARI

KOFTWORKS > KOFTWORK

KOGAL *n* (in Japan) teenage girl noted for her busy social life and trendy purchases

KOGALS > KOGAL

k

KOHA n gift or donation, esp of cash

KOHANIM > KOHEN

KOHAS > KOHA

KOHEKOHE n New Zealand tree with large glossy leaves and reddish wood

KOHEKOHES > KOHEKOHE

KOHEN n member of the Jewish priestly caste

KOHL n cosmetic powder used to darken the edges of the eyelids

KOHLRABI n type of cabbage with an edible stem

KOHLRABIS > KOHLRABI

KOHLS > KOHL

KOI n any of various ornamental forms of the common carp

KOINE n common language among speakers of different languages

KOINES > KOINE

KOIS > KOI

KOJI n Japanese steamed rice

KOJIS > KOJI

KOKA n former type of score in judo

KOKAKO n dark grey long-tailed wattled crow of New Zealand

KOKAKOS > KOKAKO

KOKANEE n freshwater salmon of lakes and rivers in W North America

KOKANEES > KOKANEE

KOKAS > KOKA

KOKER n Guyanese sluice

KOKERS > KOKER

KOKIRI n type of rough-skinned New Zealand triggerfish

KOKIRIS > KOKIRI

KOKOBEH adj (of certain fruit) having a rough skin

KOKOPU n any of several small freshwater fish of New Zealand

KOKOPUS > KOKOPU

KOKOWAI n type of clay used in decoration because of its red colour

KOKOWAIS > KOKOWAI

KOKRA n type of wood

KOKRAS > KOKRA

KOKUM n tropical tree

KOKUMS > KOKUM

KOLA as in kola nut caffeine-containing seed used in medicine and soft drinks

KOLACKY n sweet bun with a fruit, jam, or nut filling

KOLAS > KOLA

KOLBASI same as > KOLBASSI

KOLBASIS > KOLBASI

KOLBASSI n type of sausage

KOLBASSIS > KOLBASSI

KOLHOZ same as > KOLKHOZ

KOLHOZES > KOLHOZ

KOLHOZY same as > KOLKHOZ

KOLINSKI same as > KOLINSKY

KOLINSKY n Asian mink

KOLKHOS same as > KOLKHOZ

KOLKHOSES > KOLKHOS

KOLKHOSY > KOLKHOS

KOLKHOZ n (formerly) collective farm in the Soviet Union

KOLKHOZES > KOLKHOZ

KOLKHOZY > KOLKHOZ

KOLKOZ same as > KOLKHOZ

KOLKOZES > KOLKOZ

KOLKOZY > KOLKOZ

KOLO n Serbian folk dance in which a circle of people dance slowly around one or more dancers in the centre

KOLOS > KOLO

KOMATIK n sledge with wooden runners and crossbars bound with animal hides

KOMATIKS > KOMATIK

KOMBU n dark brown seaweed, the leaves of which are dried and used esp in Japanese cookery

KOMBUS > KOMBU

KOMISSAR same as > COMMISSAR

KOMISSARS > KOMISSAR

KOMITAJI n rebel or revolutionary

KOMITAJIS > KOMITAJI

KOMONDOR n large powerful dog of an ancient Hungarian breed, originally used for sheep herding

KOMONDORS > KOMONDOR

KON old word for > KNOW

KONAKI same as > KONEKE

KONAKIS > KONAKI

KONBU same as > KOMBU

KONBUS > KONBU

KOND > KON

KONDO n (in Uganda) thief or armed robber

KONDOS > KONDO

KONEKE n farm vehicle with runners in front and wheels at the rear

KONEKES > KONEKE

KONFYT n South African fruit preserve

KONFYTS > KONFYT

KONGONI n E African hartebeest

KONIMETER n device for measuring airborne dust concentration in which samples are obtained by sucking the air through a hole and allowing it to pass over a glass plate coated with grease on which the particles collect

KONINI n edible dark purple berry of the kotukutuku or tree fuchsia

KONINIS > KONINI

KONIOLOGY n study of atmospheric dust and its effects

KONISCOPE n device for detecting and measuring dust in the air

KONK same as > CONK

KONKED > KONK

KONKING > KONK

KONKS > KONK

KONNING > KON

KONS > KON

KOODOO same as > KUDU

KOODOOS > KOODOO

KOOK n eccentric person ▷ vb dialect word for vanish

KOOKED > KOOK

KOOKIE same as > KOOKY

KOOKIER > KOOKY

KOOKIEST > KOOKY

KOOKILY > KOOKY

KOOKINESS > KOOKY

KOOKING > KOOK

KOOKS > KOOK

KOOKY adj crazy, eccentric, or foolish

KOOLAH old form of > KOALA

KOOLAHS > KOOLAH

KOORI n Australian Aborigine

KOORIES > KOORI

KOORIS > KOORI

KOP n prominent isolated hill or mountain in southern Africa

KOPASETIC same as > COPACETIC

KOPECK n former Russian monetary unit, one hundredth of a rouble

KOPECKS > KOPECK

KOPEK same as > KOPECK

KOPEKS > KOPEK

KOPH n 19th letter in the Hebrew alphabet

KOPHS > KOPH

KOPIYKA n monetary unit of Ukraine, worth one hundredth of a hryvna

KOPIYKAS > KOPIYKA

KOPIYOK > KOPIYKA

KOPJE n small hill

KOPJES > KOPJE

KOPPA n consonantal letter in the Greek alphabet pronounced like kappa (K) with the point of articulation further back in the throat

KOPPAS > KOPPA

KOPPIE same as > KOPJE

KOPPIES > KOPPIE

KOPS > KOP

KOR n ancient Hebrew unit of capacity

KORA n West African instrument with twenty-one strings, combining features of the harp and the lute

KORAI > KORE

KORARI n native New Zealand flax plant

KORARIS > KORARI

KORAS > KORA

KORAT as in korat cat rare blue-grey breed of cat with brilliant green eyes

KORATS > KORAT

KORE n ancient Greek statue of a young woman wearing clothes

KORERO n talk or discussion ▷ vb speak or converse

KOREROED > KORERO

KOREROING > KORERO

KOREROS > KORERO

KORES > KORE

KORFBALL n game similar to basketball, in which each team consists of six men and six women

KORFBALLS > KORFBALL

KORIMAKO another name for > BELLBIRD

KORIMAKOS > KORIMAKO

KORKIR n variety of lichen used in dyeing

KORKIRS > KORKIR

KORMA n type of mild Indian dish consisting of meat or vegetables cooked in water, yoghurt, or cream

KORMAS > KORMA

KORO n elderly Māori man

KOROMIKO n flowering New Zealand shrub

KOROMIKOS > KOROMIKO

KORORA n small New Zealand penguin

KORORAS > KORORA

KOROS > KORO

KOROWAI n decorative woven cloak worn by a Māori chief

KOROWAIS > KOROWAI

KORS > KOR

KORU n stylized curved pattern used esp in carving

KORUN > KORUNA

KORUNA n standard monetary unit of the Czech Republic and Slovakia, divided into 100 hellers

KORUNAS > KORUNA

KORUNY > KORUNA

KORUS > KORU

KOS n Indian unit of distance having different values in different localities

KOSES > KOS

KOSHER adj conforming to Jewish religious law, esp (of food) to Jewish dietary law ▷ n kosher food ▷ vb prepare in accordance with Jewish dietary rules

KOSHERED > KOSHER

KOSHERING > KOSHER

KOSHERS > KOSHER

KOSMOS variant form of > COSMOS

KOSMOSES > KOSMOS

KOSS same as > KOS

KOSSES > KOSS

KOTARE n small greenish-blue kingfisher found in New Zealand,

Australia, and some Pacific islands to the north

KOTARES > KOTARE

KOTCH vb South African slang for vomit

KOTCHED > KOTCH

KOTCHES > KOTCH

KOTCHING > KOTCH

KOTO n Japanese stringed instrument, consisting of a rectangular wooden body over which are stretched silk strings, which are plucked with plectrums or a nail-like device

KOTOS > KOTO

KOTOW same as > KOWTOW

KOTOWED > KOTOW

KOTOWER > KOTOW

KOTOWERS > KOTOW

KOTOWING > KOTOW

KOTOWS > KOTOW

KOTTABOS > COTTABUS

KOTUKU n white heron with brilliant white plumage, black legs and yellow eyes and bill

KOTUKUS > KOTUKU

KOTWAL n senior police officer or magistrate in an Indian town

KOTWALS > KOTWAL

KOULAN same as > KULAN

KOULANS > KOULAN

KOUMIS same as > KUMISS

KOUMISES > KOUMIS

KOUMISS same as > KUMISS

KOUMISSES > KOUMISS

KOUMYS same as > KUMISS

KOUMYSES > KOUMYS

KOUMYSS same as > KUMISS

KOUMYSSES > KOUMYSS

KOUPREY n large wild SE Asian ox

KOUPREYS > KOUPREY

KOURA n New Zealand freshwater crayfish

KOURAS > KOURA

KOURBASH same as > KURBASH

KOUROI > KOUROS

KOUROS n ancient Greek statue of a young man

KOUSKOUS same as > COUSCOUS

KOUSSO n Abyssinian tree whose flowers have useful antiparasitic properties

KOUSSOS > KOUSSO

KOW old variant of > COW

KOWHAI n New Zealand tree with clusters of yellow flowers

KOWHAIS > KOWHAI

KOWS > KOW

KOWTOW vb be servile (towards) ▷ n act of kowtowing

KOWTOWED > KOWTOW

KOWTOWER > KOWTOW

KOWTOWERS > KOWTOW

KOWTOWING > KOWTOW

KOWTOWS > KOWTOW

KRAAL n S African village surrounded by a strong fence ▷ adj denoting or relating to the tribal aspects of the Black African way of life ▷ vb enclose (livestock) in a kraal

KRAALED > KRAAL

KRAALING > KRAAL

KRAALS > KRAAL

KRAB same as > KARABINER

KRABS > KRAB

KRAFT n strong wrapping paper, made from pulp processed with a sulphate solution

KRAFTS > KRAFT

KRAIT n brightly coloured venomous snake of S and SE Asia

KRAITS > KRAIT

KRAKEN n legendary sea monster

KRAKENS > KRAKEN

KRAKOWIAK n Polish dance

KRAMERIA another name for > RHATANY

KRAMERIAS > KRAMERIA

KRANG n dead whale from which the blubber has been removed

KRANGS > KRANG

KRANS n sheer rock face

KRANSES > KRANS

KRANTZ same as > KRANS

KRANTZES > KRANTZ

KRANZ same as > KRANS

KRANZES > KRANS

KRATER same as > CRATER

KRATERS > KRATER

KRAUT n sauerkraut

KRAUTS > KRAUT

KREASOTE same as > CREOSOTE

KREASOTED > KREASOTE

KREASOTES > KREASOTE

KREATINE same as > CREATINE

KREATINES > KREATINE

KREEP n lunar substance that is high in potassium, rare earth elements, and phosphorus

KREEPS > KREEP

KREESE same as > KRIS

KREESED > KREESE

KREESES > KREESE

KREESING > KREESE

KREMLIN n citadel of any Russian city

KREMLINS > KREMLIN

KRENG same as > KRANG

KRENGS > KRENG

KREOSOTE same as > CREOSOTE

KREOSOTED > KREOSOTE

KREOSOTES > KREOSOTE

KREPLACH npl small filled dough casings usually served in soup

KREPLECH same as > KREPLACH

KREUTZER n any of various former copper and silver coins of Germany or Austria

KREUTZERS > KREUTZER

KREUZER same as > KREUTZER

KREUZERS > KREUZER

KREWE n club taking part in New Orleans carnival parade

KREWES > KREWE

KRILL n small shrimplike sea creature

KRILLS > KRILL

KRIMMER n tightly curled light grey fur obtained from the skins of lambs from the Crimean region

KRIMMERS > KRIMMER

KRIS n Malayan and Indonesian stabbing or slashing knife with a scalloped edge ▷ vb stab or slash with a kris

KRISED > KRIS

KRISES > KRIS

KRISING > KRIS

KROMESKY n croquette consisting of a piece of bacon wrapped round minced meat or fish

KRONA n standard monetary unit of Sweden

KRONE n standard monetary unit of Norway and Denmark

KRONEN > KRONE

KRONER > KRONE

KRONOR > KRONA

KRONUR > KRONA

KROON n standard monetary unit of Estonia, divided into 100 senti

KROONI > KROON

KROONS > KROON

KRUBI n aroid plant with an unpleasant smell

KRUBIS > KRUBI

KRUBUT same as > KRUBI

KRUBUTS > KRUBUT

KRULLER variant spelling of > CRULLER

KRULLERS > KRULLER

KRUMHORN variant spelling of > CRUMHORN

KRUMHORNS > KRUMHORN

KRUMKAKE n Scandinavian biscuit

KRUMKAKES > KRUMKAKE

KRUMMHOLZ n zone of stunted wind-blown trees growing at high altitudes just above the timberline on tropical mountains

KRUMMHORN variant spelling of > CRUMHORN

KRUMPER > KRUMPING

KRUMPERS > KRUMPER

KRUMPING n type of dance in which participants wear face-paint and compete aggressively in lieu of violent conflict

KRUMPINGS > KRUMPING

KRUNK n style of hip-hop music

KRUNKED same as > CRUNKED

KRUNKS > KRUNK

KRYOLITE variant spelling of > CRYOLITE

KRYOLITES > KRYOLITE

KRYOLITH same as > CRYOLITE

KRYOLITHS > KRYOLITH

KRYOMETER same as > CRYOMETER

KRYPSES > KRYPSIS

KRYPSIS n idea that Christ made secret use of his divine attributes

KRYPTON n colourless gas present in the atmosphere and used in fluorescent lights

KRYPTONS > KRYPTON

KRYTRON n type of fast electronic gas-discharge switch, used as a trigger in nuclear weapons

KRYTRONS > KRYTRON

KSAR old form of > TSAR

KSARS > KSAR

k

KUCCHA same as > KACCHA

KUCCHAS > KUCCHA

KUCHCHA same as > KACHA

KUCHEN n breadlike cake containing apple, nuts, and sugar, originating from Germany

KUCHENS > KUCHEN

KUDLIK n Inuit soapstone seal-oil lamp

KUDLIKS > KUDLIK

KUDO variant of > KUDOS

KUDOS n fame or credit

KUDOSES > KUDOS

KUDU n African antelope with spiral horns

KUDUS > KUDU

KUDZU n hairy leguminous climbing plant of China and Japan, with trifoliate leaves and purple fragrant flowers

KUDZUS > KUDZU

KUE n name of the letter Q

KUEH n (in Malaysia) any cake of Malay, Chinese, or Indian origin

KUES > KUE

KUFI n cap for Muslim man

KUFIS > KUFI

KUFIYAH same as > KEFFIYEH

KUFIYAHS > KUFIYAH

KUGEL n baked pudding in traditional Jewish cooking

KUGELS > KUGEL

KUIA n Māori female elder or elderly woman

KUIAS > KUIA

KUKRI n heavy, curved knife used by Gurkhas

KUKRIS > KUKRI

KUKU n mussel

KUKUS > KUKU

KULA n ceremonial gift exchange practised among a group of islanders in the

W Pacific, used to establish relations between islands

KULAK n (formerly) property-owning Russian peasant

KULAKI > KULAK

KULAKS > KULAK

KULAN n Asiatic wild ass of the Russian steppes, probably a variety of kiang or onager

KULANS > KULAN

KULAS > KULA

KULBASA same as > KIELBASA

KULBASAS > KULBASA

KULFI n Indian dessert made by freezing milk which has been concentrated by boiling away some of the water in it, and flavoured with nuts and cardamom seeds

KULFIS > KULFI

KULTUR n German civilization

KULTURS > KULTUR

KUMARA n tropical root vegetable with yellow flesh

KUMARAHOU n New Zealand shrub

KUMARAS > KUMARA

KUMARI n (in Indian English) maiden

KUMARIS > KUMARI

KUMBALOI npl worry beads

KUMERA same as > KUMARA

KUMERAS > KUMERA

KUMIKUMI same as > KAMOKAMO

KUMIKUMIS > KUMIKUMI

KUMISS n drink made from fermented mare's or other milk, drunk by certain Asian tribes, esp in Russia or used for dietetic and medicinal purposes

KUMISSES > KUMISS

KUMITE n freestyle sparring or fighting

KUMITES > KUMITE

KUMMEL n German liqueur flavoured with aniseed and cumin

KUMMELS > KUMMEL

KUMQUAT n citrus fruit resembling a tiny orange

KUMQUATS > KUMQUAT

KUMYS same as > KUMISS

KUMYSES > KUMYS

KUNA n standard monetary unit of Croatia, divided into 100 lipa

KUNDALINI n (in yoga) life force that resides at the base of the spine

KUNE > KUNA

KUNEKUNE n a feral pig

KUNEKUNES > KUNEKUNE

KUNJOOS adj (in Indian English) mean or stingy

KUNKAR n type of limestone

KUNKARS > KUNKAR

KUNKUR same as > KUNKUR

KUNKURS > KUNKUR

KUNZITE n pink-coloured transparent variety of the mineral spodumene: a gemstone

KUNZITES > KUNZITE

KURBASH vb whip with a hide whip

KURBASHED > KURBASH

KURBASHES > KURBASH

KURFUFFLE same as > KERFUFFLE

KURGAN n Russian burial mound

KURGANS > KURGAN

KURI n mongrel dog

KURIS > KURI

KURRAJONG n Australian tree or shrub with tough fibrous bark

KURRE old variant of > CUR

KURRES > KURRE

KURSAAL n public room at a health resort

KURSAALS > KURSAAL

KURTA n long loose garment like a shirt without a collar worn in India

KURTAS > KURTA

KURTOSES > KURTOSIS

KURTOSIS n measure of the concentration of a distribution around its mean

KURU n degenerative disease of the nervous system, restricted to certain tribes in New Guinea, marked by loss of muscular control and thought to be caused by a slow virus

KURUS > KURU

KURVEY vb (in old South African English) transport goods by ox cart

KURVEYED > KURVEY

KURVEYING > KURVEY

KURVEYOR > KURVEY

KURVEYORS > KURVEY

KURVEYS > KURVEY

KUSSO variant spelling of > KOUSSO

KUSSOS > KUSSO

KUTA n (in Indian English) male dog

KUTAS > KUTA

KUTCH same as > CATECHU

KUTCHA adj makeshift or not solid

KUTCHES > KUTCH

KUTI n (in Indian English) female dog or bitch

KUTIS > KUTI

KUTU n body louse

KUTUS > KUTU

KUVASZ n breed of dog from Hungary

KUVASZOK > KUVASZ

KUZU same as > KUDZU

KUZUS > KUZU

KVAS same as > KVASS

KVASES > KVAS

KVASS n alcoholic drink of low strength made in Russia and E Europe from cereals and stale bread

KVASSES > KVASS

KVELL vb US word meaning be happy

KVELLED > KVELL

KVELLING > KVELL

KVELLS > KVELL

KVETCH vb complain or grumble

KVETCHED > KVETCH

KVETCHER > KVETCH

KVETCHERS > KVETCH

KVETCHES > KVETCH

KVETCHIER > KVETCHY

KVETCHILY > KVETCHY

KVETCHING > KVETCH

KVETCHY adj tending to grumble or complain

KWACHA n standard monetary unit of Zambia, divided into 100 ngwee

KWACHAS > KWACHA

KWAITO n type of South African pop music with lyrics spoken over an instrumental backing usually consisting of slowed-down house music layered with African percussion and melodies

KWAITOS > KWAITO

KWANZA n standard monetary unit of Angola, divided into 100 lwei

KWANZAS > KWANZA

KWELA n type of pop music popular among the Black communities of South Africa

KWELAS > KWELA

KY npl Scots word for cows

KYACK n type of panier

KYACKS > KYACK

KYAK same as > KAYAK

KYAKS > KYAK

KYANG same as > KIANG

KYANGS > KYANG

KYANISE same as > KYANIZE

KYANISED > KYANISE

KYANISES > KYANISE

KYANISING > KYANISE

KYANITE n grey, green, or blue mineral consisting of aluminium silicate in triclinic crystalline form

KYANITES > KYANITE

KYANITIC > KYANITE

KYANIZE vb treat (timber) with corrosive sublimate to make it resistant to decay

KYANIZED > KYANIZE

KYANIZES > KYANIZE

KYANIZING > KYANIZE

KYAR same as > COIR

KYARS > KYAR

KYAT n standard monetary unit of Myanmar, divided into 100 pyas

KYATS > KYAT

KYBO n temporary lavatory constructed for use when camping

KYBOS > KYBO

KYBOSH same as > KIBOSH

KYBOSHED > KYBOSH

KYBOSHES > KYBOSH

KYBOSHING > KYBOSH

KYDST > KYTHE

KYE n Korean fundraising meeting

KYES > KYE

KYLE n narrow strait or channel

KYLES > KYLE

KYLICES > KYLIX

KYLIE n boomerang that is flat on one side and convex on the other

KYLIES > KYLIE

KYLIKES > KYLIX

KYLIN n (in Chinese art) mythical animal of composite form

KYLINS > KYLIN

KYLIX n shallow two-handled drinking vessel used in ancient Greece

KYLLOSES > KYLLOSIS

KYLLOSIS n club foot

KYLOE n breed of small long-horned long-haired beef cattle from NW Scotland

KYLOES > KYLOE

KYMOGRAM n image or other visual record created by a kymograph

KYMOGRAMS > KYMOGRAM

KYMOGRAPH n rotatable drum for holding paper on which a tracking stylus continuously records variations in blood pressure, respiratory movements, etc

KYND old variant of > KIND

KYNDE old variant of > KIND

KYNDED > KYND

KYNDES > KYNDE

KYNDING > KYND

KYNDS > KYND

KYNE npl archaic word for cows

KYOGEN n type of Japanese drama

KYOGENS > KYOGEN

KYPE n hook on the lower jaw of a mature male salmon

KYPES > KYPE

KYPHOSES > KYPHOSIS

KYPHOSIS n backward curvature of the thoracic spine

KYPHOTIC > KYPHOSIS

KYRIE n type of prayer

KYRIELLE n verse form of French origin characterized by repeated lines or words

KYRIELLES > KYRIELLE

KYRIES > KYRIE

KYTE n belly

KYTES > KYTE

KYTHE vb appear

KYTHED > KYTHE
KYTHES > KYTHE
KYTHING > KYTHE
KYU *n* (in judo) one of the
five student grades for
inexperienced competitors
KYUS > KYU

k

Ll

LA n exclamation of surprise or emphasis

LAAGER n (in Africa) a camp defended by a circular formation of wagons ▷ vb form (wagons) into a laager

LAAGERED > LAAGER

LAAGERING > LAAGER

LAAGERS > LAAGER

LAARI same as **>** LARI

LAARIS > LAARI

LAB n laboratory

LABARA > LABARUM

LABARUM n standard or banner carried in Christian religious processions

LABARUMS > LABARUM

LABDA same as **>** LAMBDA

LABDACISM n excessive use or idiosyncratic pronunciation of (l)

LABDANUM n dark resinous juice obtained from various rockroses

LABDANUMS > LABDANUM

LABDAS > LABDA

LABEL n piece of card or other material fixed to an object to show its ownership, destination, etc ▷ vb give a label to

LABELABLE > LABEL

LABELED > LABEL

LABELER > LABEL

LABELERS > LABEL

LABELING > LABEL

LABELLA > LABELLUM

LABELLATE > LABELLUM

LABELLED > LABEL

LABELLER > LABEL

LABELLERS > LABEL

LABELLING > LABEL

LABELLIST n person who wears only clothes with fashionable brand names

LABELLOID > LABELLUM

LABELLUM n lip-like part of certain plants

LABELMATE n musician or singer who records for the same company as another

LABELS > LABEL

LABIA > LABIUM

LABIAL adj of the lips ▷ n speech sound that involves the lips

LABIALISE same as **>** LABIALIZE

LABIALISM **>** LABIALIZE

LABIALITY > LABIAL

LABIALIZE vb pronounce with articulation involving rounded lips

LABIALLY > LABIAL

LABIALS > LABIAL

LABIATE n any of a family of plants with square stems, aromatic leaves, and a two-lipped flower, such as mint or thyme ▷ adj of this family

LABIATED adj having a lip

LABIATES > LABIATE

LABILE adj (of a compound) prone to chemical change

LABILITY > LABILE

LABIS n cochlear

LABISES > LABIS

LABIUM n lip or liplike structure

LABLAB n twining leguminous plant

LABLABS > LABLAB

LABOR same as **>** LABOUR

LABORED same as **>** LABOURED

LABOREDLY > LABOURED

LABORER same as **>** LABOURER

LABORERS > LABORER

LABORING > LABOR

LABORIOUS adj involving great prolonged effort

LABORISM same as **>** LABOURISM

LABORISMS > LABORISM

LABORIST same as **>** LABOURIST

LABORISTS > LABORIST

LABORITE n adherent of the Labour party

LABORITES > LABORITE

LABORS > LABOR

LABOUR n physical work or exertion ▷ vb work hard

LABOURED adj uttered or done with difficulty

LABOURER n person who labours, esp someone doing manual work for wages

LABOURERS > LABOURER

LABOURING > LABOUR

LABOURISM n dominance of the working classes

LABOURIST n person who supports workers' rights

LABOURS > LABOUR

LABRA > LABRUM

LABRADOR n large retriever dog with a usu gold or black coat

LABRADORS > LABRADOR

LABRAL adj of or like a lip

LABRET n piece of bone, shell, etc

LABRETS > LABRET

LABRID same as **>** LABROID

LABRIDS > LABRID

LABROID n type of fish ▷ adj of or relating to such fish

LABROIDS > LABROID

LABROSE adj thick-lipped

LABRUM n lip or liplike part

LABRUMS > LABRUM

LABRUSCA n grape variety

LABRYS n type of axe

LABRYSES > LABRYS

LABS > LAB

LABURNUM n ornamental tree with yellow hanging flowers

LABURNUMS > LABURNUM

LABYRINTH n complicated network of passages

LAC same as **>** LAKH

LACCOLITE same as **>** LACCOLITH

LACCOLITH n dome-shaped body of igneous rock between two layers of older sedimentary rock

LACE n delicate loosely woven decorative fabric ▷ vb fasten with shoelaces, cords, etc

LACEBARK n small evergreen tree

LACEBARKS > LACEBARK

LACED > LACE

LACELESS > LACE

LACELIKE > LACE

LACER > LACE

LACERABLE > LACERATE

LACERANT adj painfully distressing

LACERATE vb tear (flesh) ▷ adj having edges that are jagged or torn

LACERATED > LACERATE

LACERATES > LACERATE

LACERS > LACE

LACERTIAN n type of reptile

LACERTID n type of lizard

LACERTIDS > LACERTID

LACERTINE adj relating to lacertid

LACES > LACE

LACET n braidwork

LACETS > LACET

LACEWING n any of various neuropterous insects

LACEWINGS > LACEWING

LACEWOOD n wood of sycamore tree

LACEWOODS > LACEWOOD

LACEWORK n work made from lace

LACEWORKS > LACEWORK

LACEY same as **>** LACY

LACHES n negligence or unreasonable delay in pursuing a legal remedy

LACHESES > LACHES

LACHRYMAL same as **>** LACRIMAL

LACIER > LACY

LACIEST > LACY

LACILY > LACY

LACINESS > LACY

LACING > LACE

LACINGS > LACE

LACINIA n narrow fringe on petal

LACINIAE > LACINIA

LACINIATE adj jagged

LACK n shortage or absence of something needed or wanted ▷ vb need or be short of (something)

LACKADAY another word for **>** ALAS

LACKED > LACK

LACKER variant spelling of **>** LACQUER

LACKERED > LACKER

LACKERING > LACKER

LACKERS > LACKER

LACKEY n servile follower ▷ vb act as a lackey (to)

LACKEYED > LACKEY

LACKEYING > LACKEY

LACKEYS > LACKEY

LACKING > LACK

LACKLAND n fool

LACKLANDS > LACKLAND

LACKS > LACK

LACMUS n old form of litmus

LACMUSES > LACMUS

LACONIC adj using only a few words, terse

LACONICAL same as **>** LACONIC

LACONISM n economy of expression

LACONISMS > LACONISM
LACQUER n hard varnish for wood or metal ▷ vb apply lacquer to
LACQUERED > LACQUER
LACQUERER > LACQUER
LACQUERS > LACQUER
LACQUEY same as > LACKEY
LACQUEYED > LACQUEY
LACQUEYS > LACQUEY
LACRIMAL adj of tears or the glands which produce them ▷ n bone near tear gland
LACRIMALS > LACRIMAL
LACRIMARY adj of or relating to tears or to the glands that secrete tears
LACRIMOSO adj tearful
LACROSSE n sport in which teams catch and throw a ball using long sticks with a pouched net at the end, in an attempt to score goals
LACROSSES > LACROSSE
LACRYMAL same as > LACRIMAL
LACRYMALS > LACRYMAL
LACS > LAC
LACTAM n any of a group of inner amides
LACTAMS > LACTAM
LACTARIAN n vegetarian who eats dairy products
LACTARY adj relating to milk
LACTASE n any of a group of enzymes that hydrolyse lactose to glucose and galactose
LACTASES > LACTASE
LACTATE vb (of mammals) to secrete milk ▷ n ester or salt of lactic acid
LACTATED > LACTATE
LACTATES > LACTATE
LACTATING > LACTATE
LACTATION n secretion of milk by female mammals to feed young
LACTEAL adj of or like milk ▷ n any of the lymphatic vessels that convey chyle from the small intestine to the blood
LACTEALLY > LACTEAL
LACTEALS > LACTEAL
LACTEAN another word for > LACTEOUS
LACTEOUS adj milky
LACTIC adj of or derived from milk
LACTIFIC adj yielding milk
LACTIVISM > LACTIVIST
LACTIVIST n person who advocates breast-feeding
LACTONE n any of a class of organic compounds
LACTONES > LACTONE
LACTONIC > LACTONE
LACTOSE n white

crystalline sugar found in milk
LACTOSES > LACTOSE
LACUNA n gap or missing part, esp in a document or series
LACUNAE > LACUNA
LACUNAL > LACUNA
LACUNAR n ceiling, soffit, or vault having coffers ▷ adj of, relating to, or containing a lacuna or lacunas
LACUNARIA > LACUNAR
LACUNARS > LACUNAR
LACUNARY > LACUNA
LACUNAS > LACUNA
LACUNATE > LACUNA
LACUNE n hiatus
LACUNES > LACUNE
LACUNOSE > LACUNA
LACY adj fine, like lace
LAD n boy or young man
LADANUM same as > LABDANUM
LADANUMS > LADANUM
LADDER n frame of two poles connected by horizontal steps used for climbing ▷ vb have or cause to have such a line of undone stitches
LADDERED > LADDER
LADDERING > LADDER
LADDERS > LADDER
LADDERY > LADDER
LADDIE n familiar term for a male, esp a young man
LADDIES > LADDIE
LADDISH adj informal word for behaving in a macho or immature manner
LADDISM n laddish attitudes and behaviour
LADDISMS > LADDISM
LADE vb put cargo on board (a ship) or (of a ship) to take on cargo ▷ n watercourse, esp a millstream
LADED > LADE
LADEN adj loaded ▷ vb load with cargo
LADENED > LADEN
LADENING > LADEN
LADENS > LADEN
LADER > LADE
LADERS > LADE
LADES > LADE
LADETTE n young woman whose social behaviour is similar to that of male adolescents or young men
LADETTES > LADETTE
LADHOOD > LAD
LADHOODS > LAD
LADIES n women's public toilet
LADIFIED > LADIFY
LADIFIES > LADIFY
LADIFY same as > LADYFY
LADIFYING > LADIFY
LADING > LADE
LADINGS > LADE

LADINO n Italian variety of white clover
LADINOS > LADINO
LADLE n spoon with a long handle and a large bowl, used for serving soup etc ▷ vb serve out
LADLED > LADLE
LADLEFUL > LADLE
LADLEFULS > LADLE
LADLER n person who serves with a ladle
LADLERS > LADLER
LADLES > LADLE
LADLING > LADLE
LADRON same as > LADRONE
LADRONE n thief
LADRONES > LADRONE
LADRONS > LADRON
LADS > LAD
LADY n woman regarded as having characteristics of good breeding or high rank ▷ adj female
LADYBIRD n small red beetle with black spots
LADYBIRDS > LADYBIRD
LADYBOY n transvestite or transsexual, esp one from the Far East
LADYBOYS > LADYBOY
LADYBUG same as > LADYBIRD
LADYBUGS > LADYBUG
LADYCOW another word for > LADYBIRD
LADYCOWS > LADYCOW
LADYFIED > LADYFY
LADYFIES > LADYFY
LADYFISH n type of game fish
LADYFLIES > LADYFLY
LADYFLY another word for > LADYBIRD
LADYFY vb make a lady of (someone)
LADYFYING > LADYFY
LADYHOOD > LADY
LADYHOODS > LADY
LADYISH > LADY
LADYISM > LADY
LADYISMS > LADY
LADYKIN n endearing form of lady
LADYKINS > LADYKIN
LADYLIKE adj polite and dignified
LADYLOVE n beloved woman
LADYLOVES > LADYLOVE
LADYPALM n small palm, grown indoors
LADYPALMS > LADYPALM
LADYSHIP n title of a peeress
LADYSHIPS > LADYSHIP
LAER another word for > LAAGER
LAERED > LAER
LAERING > LAER
LAERS > LAER
LAESIE old form of > LAZY
LAETARE n fourth Sunday

of Lent
LAETARES > LAETARE
LAETRILE n drug used to treat cancer
LAETRILES > LAETRILE
LAEVIGATE same as > LEVIGATE
LAEVO adj on the left
LAEVULIN n polysaccharide occurring in the tubers of certain helianthus plants
LAEVULINS > LAEVULIN
LAEVULOSE n fructose
LAG vb go too slowly, fall behind ▷ n delay between events
LAGAN n goods or wreckage on the sea bed, sometimes attached to a buoy to permit recovery
LAGANS > LAGAN
LAGENA n bottle with a narrow neck
LAGENAS > LAGENA
LAGEND same as > LAGAN
LAGENDS > LAGEND
LAGER n light-bodied beer ▷ vb ferment into lager
LAGERED > LAGER
LAGERING > LAGER
LAGERS > LAGER
LAGGARD n person who lags behind ▷ adj sluggish, slow, or dawdling
LAGGARDLY > LAGGARD
LAGGARDS > LAGGARD
LAGGED > LAG
LAGGEN n spar of a barrel
LAGGENS > LAGGEN
LAGGER n person who lags pipes
LAGGERS > LAGGER
LAGGIN same as > LAGGEN
LAGGING > LAG
LAGGINGLY > LAG
LAGGINGS > LAG
LAGGINS > LAGGIN
LAGNAPPE same as > LAGNIAPPE
LAGNAPPES > LAGNAPPE
LAGNIAPPE n small gift, esp one given to a customer who makes a purchase
LAGOMORPH n type of placental mammal of the order which includes rabbits and hares
LAGOON n body of water cut off from the open sea by coral reefs or sand bars
LAGOONAL > LAGOON
LAGOONS > LAGOON
LAGRIMOSO adj mournful
LAGS > LAG
LAGUNA n lagoon
LAGUNAS > LAGUNA
LAGUNE same as > LAGOON
LAGUNES > LAGUNE
LAH n (in tonic sol-fa) sixth degree of any major scale
LAHAR n landslide of volcanic debris and water
LAHARS > LAHAR

LAHS > LAH
LAIC adj laical ▷ n layman
LAICAL adj secular
LAICALLY > LAIC
LAICH n low-lying piece of land
LAICHS > LAICH
LAICISE same as > LAICIZE
LAICISED > LAICISE
LAICISES > LAICISE
LAICISING > LAICISE
LAICISM > LAIC
LAICISMS > LAIC
LAICITIES > LAICITY
LAICITY n state of being laical
LAICIZE vb withdraw clerical or ecclesiastical character or status from (an institution, building, etc)
LAICIZED > LAICIZE
LAICIZES > LAICIZE
LAICIZING > LAICIZE
LAICS > LAIC
LAID Scots form of > LOAD
LAIDED > LAID
LAIDING > LAID
LAIDLY adj very ugly
LAIDS > LAID
LAIGH adj low-lying ▷ n area of low-lying ground
LAIGHER > LAIGH
LAIGHEST > LAIGH
LAIGHS > LAIGH
LAIK vb play (a game, etc)
LAIKA n type of small dog
LAIKAS > LAIKA
LAIKED > LAIK
LAIKER > LAIK
LAIKERS > LAIK
LAIKING > LAIK
LAIKS > LAIK
LAIN > LIE
LAIPSE vb beat soundly
LAIPSED > LAIPSE
LAIPSES > LAIPSE
LAIPSING > LAIPSE
LAIR n resting place of an animal ▷ vb (esp of a wild animal) to retreat to or rest in a lair
LAIRAGE n accommodation for farm animals, esp at docks or markets
LAIRAGES > LAIRAGE
LAIRD n Scottish landowner
LAIRDLY adj pertaining to laird or lairds
LAIRDS > LAIRD
LAIRDSHIP n state of being laird
LAIRED > LAIR
LAIRIER > LAIRY
LAIRIEST > LAIRY
LAIRING > LAIR
LAIRISE same as > LAIRIZE
LAIRISED > LAIRISE
LAIRISES > LAIRISE
LAIRISING > LAIRISE

LAIRIZE vb show off
LAIRIZED > LAIRIZE
LAIRIZES > LAIRIZE
LAIRIZING > LAIRIZE
LAIRS > LAIR
LAIRY adj gaudy or flashy
LAISSE n type of rhyme scheme
LAISSES > LAISSE
LAITANCE n white film forming on drying concrete
LAITANCES > LAITANCE
LAITH Scots form of > LOATH
LAITHLY same as > LAIDLY
LAITIES > LAITY
LAITY n people who are not members of the clergy
LAKE n expanse of water entirely surrounded by land ▷ vb take time away from work
LAKEBED n bed of lake
LAKEBEDS > LAKEBED
LAKED > LAKE
LAKEFRONT n area at edge of lake
LAKELAND n countryside with a lot of lakes
LAKELANDS > LAKELAND
LAKELET n small lake
LAKELETS > LAKELET
LAKELIKE > LAKE
LAKEPORT n port on lake
LAKEPORTS > LAKEPORT
LAKER n cargo vessel used on lakes
LAKERS > LAKER
LAKES > LAKE
LAKESHORE n area at edge of lake
LAKESIDE n area at edge of lake
LAKESIDES > LAKESIDE
LAKH n (in India) 100 000, esp referring to this sum of rupees
LAKHS > LAKH
LAKIER > LAKY
LAKIEST > LAKY
LAKIN short form of > LADYKIN
LAKING > LAKE
LAKINGS > LAKE
LAKINS > LAKIN
LAKISH adj similar to poetry of Lake poets
LAKSA n (in Malaysia) a dish of Chinese origin consisting of rice noodles served in curry or hot soup
LAKSAS > LAKSA
LAKY adj of the reddish colour of the pigment lake
LALANG n coarse weedy Malaysian grass
LALANGS > LALANG
LALDIE n great gusto
LALDIES > LALDIE
LALDY same as > LALDIE
LALIQUE n type of ornamental glass
LALIQUES > LALIQUE

LALL vb make imperfect 'l' or 'r' sounds
LALLAN n literary version of the English spoken in Lowland Scotland
LALLAND same as > LALLAN
LALLANDS > LALLAND
LALLANS > LALLAN
LALLATION n defect of speech consisting of the pronunciation of 'r' as 'l'
LALLED > LALL
LALLING > LALL
LALLINGS > LALL
LALLS > LALL
LALLYGAG vb loiter aimlessly
LALLYGAGS > LALLYGAG
LAM vb attack vigorously
LAMA n Buddhist priest in Tibet or Mongolia
LAMAISTIC adj relating to the Mahayana form of Buddhism
LAMANTIN another word for > MANATEE
LAMANTINS > LAMANTIN
LAMAS > LAMA
LAMASERAI same as > LAMASERY
LAMASERY n monastery of lamas
LAMB n young sheep ▷ vb (of sheep) give birth to a lamb or lambs
LAMBADA n erotic Brazilian dance
LAMBADAS > LAMBADA
LAMBAST vb beat or thrash
LAMBASTE same as > LAMBAST
LAMBASTED > LAMBAST
LAMBASTES > LAMBASTE
LAMBASTS > LAMBAST
LAMBDA n 11th letter of the Greek alphabet
LAMBDAS > LAMBDA
LAMBDOID adj having the shape of the Greek letter lambda
LAMBED > LAMB
LAMBENCY > LAMBENT
LAMBENT adj (of a flame) flickering softly
LAMBENTLY > LAMBENT
LAMBER n person that attends to lambing ewes
LAMBERS > LAMBER
LAMBERT n cgs unit of illumination, equal to 1 lumen per square centimetre
LAMBERTS > LAMBERT
LAMBIE same as > LAMBKIN
LAMBIER > LAMBY
LAMBIES > LAMBIE
LAMBIEST > LAMBY
LAMBING n birth of lambs at the end of winter
LAMBINGS > LAMBING
LAMBITIVE n medicine taken by licking

LAMBKILL n N American dwarf shrub
LAMBKILLS > LAMBKILL
LAMBKIN n small or young lamb
LAMBKINS > LAMBKIN
LAMBLIKE > LAMB
LAMBLING n small lamb
LAMBLINGS > LAMBLING
LAMBOYS n skirt-like piece of armour made from metal strips
LAMBRUSCO n Italian sparkling wine
LAMBS > LAMB
LAMBSKIN n skin of a lamb, usually with the wool still on, used to make coats, slippers, etc
LAMBSKINS > LAMBSKIN
LAMBY adj lamb-like
LAME adj having an injured or disabled leg or foot ▷ vb make lame ▷ n fabric interwoven with gold or silver threads
LAMEBRAIN n stupid or slow-witted person
LAMED n 12th letter in the Hebrew alphabet
LAMEDH same as > LAMED
LAMEDHS > LAMEDH
LAMEDS > LAMED
LAMELLA n thin layer, plate, or membrane, esp any of the calcified layers of which bone is formed
LAMELLAE > LAMELLA
LAMELLAR > LAMELLA
LAMELLAS > LAMELLA
LAMELLATE > LAMELLA
LAMELLOID another word for > LAMELLA
LAMELLOSE > LAMELLA
LAMELY > LAME
LAMENESS > LAME
LAMENT vb feel or express sorrow (for) ▷ n passionate expression of grief
LAMENTED adj grieved for
LAMENTER > LAMENT
LAMENTERS > LAMENT
LAMENTING > LAMENT
LAMENTS > LAMENT
LAMER > LAME
LAMES > LAME
LAMEST > LAME
LAMETER Scots form of > LAMIGER
LAMETERS > LAMETER
LAMIA n one of a class of female monsters depicted with a snake's body and a woman's head and breasts
LAMIAE > LAMIA
LAMIAS > LAMIA
LAMIGER n disabled person
LAMIGERS > LAMIGER
LAMINA n thin plate, esp of bone or mineral
LAMINABLE > LAMINATE
LAMINAE > LAMINA
LAMINAL n consonant

articulated with blade of tongue

LAMINALS > LAMINAL

LAMINAR > LAMINA

LAMINARIA n type of brown seaweed

LAMINARIN n carbohydrate, consisting of repeated glucose units, that is the main storage product of brown algae

LAMINARY > LAMINA

LAMINAS > LAMINA

LAMINATE vb make (a sheet of material) by sticking together thin sheets ▷ n laminated sheet ▷ adj composed of lamina

LAMINATED adj composed of many layers stuck together

LAMINATES > LAMINATE

LAMINATOR > LAMINATE

LAMING > LAME

LAMINGTON n sponge cake coated with a sweet coating

LAMININ n type of protein

LAMININS > LAMININ

LAMINITIS n (in animals with hooves) inflammation of the tissue to which the hoof is attached

LAMINOSE > LAMINA

LAMINOUS > LAMINA

LAMISH adj rather lame

LAMISTER n fugitive

LAMISTERS > LAMISTER

LAMMED > LAM

LAMMER Scots word for > AMBER

LAMMERS > LAMMER

LAMMIE same as > LAMMY

LAMMIES > LAMMY

LAMMIGER same as > LAMIGER

LAMMIGERS > LAMMIGER

LAMMING > LAM

LAMMINGS > LAM

LAMMY n thick woollen jumper

LAMP n device which produces light from electricity, oil, or gas ▷ vb go quickly with long steps

LAMPAD n candlestick

LAMPADARY n person who lights the lamps in an Orthodox Greek Church

LAMPADIST n prize-winner in race run by young men with torches

LAMPADS > LAMPAD

LAMPAS n swelling of the mucous membrane of the hard palate of horses

LAMPASES > LAMPAS

LAMPASSE same as > LAMPAS

LAMPASSES > LAMPASSE

LAMPBLACK n fine black soot used as a pigment in paint and ink

LAMPBRUSH as in lampbrush chromosome type of chromosome

LAMPED > LAMP

LAMPER n lamprey

LAMPERN n migratory European lamprey

LAMPERNS > LAMPERN

LAMPERS > LAMPER

LAMPERSES > LAMPERS

LAMPHOLE n hole in ground for lowering lamp into sewer

LAMPHOLES > LAMPHOLE

LAMPING > LAMP

LAMPINGS > LAMP

LAMPION n oil-burning lamp

LAMPIONS > LAMPION

LAMPLIGHT n light produced by lamp

LAMPLIT adj lit by lamps

LAMPOON n humorous satire ridiculing someone ▷ vb satirize or ridicule

LAMPOONED > LAMPOON

LAMPOONER > LAMPOON

LAMPOONS > LAMPOON

LAMPPOST n post supporting a lamp in the street

LAMPPOSTS > LAMPPOST

LAMPREY n eel-like fish with a round sucking mouth

LAMPREYS > LAMPREY

LAMPS > LAMP

LAMPSHADE n shade used to reduce light shed by light bulb

LAMPSHELL n brachiopod

LAMPUKA same as > LAMPUKI

LAMPUKAS > LAMPUKA

LAMPUKI n type of fish

LAMPUKIS > LAMPUKI

LAMPYRID n firefly

LAMPYRIDS > LAMPYRID

LAMS > LAM

LAMSTER n fugitive

LAMSTERS > LAMSTER

LANA n wood from genipap tree

LANAI Hawaiian word for > VERANDA

LANAIS > LANAI

LANAS > LANA

LANATE adj having or consisting of a woolly covering of hairs

LANATED same as > LANATE

LANCE n long spear used by a mounted soldier ▷ vb pierce (a boil or abscess) with a lancet

LANCED > LANCE

LANCEGAY n kind of ancient spear

LANCEGAYS > LANCEGAY

LANCEJACK n lance corporal

LANCELET n type of marine invertebrate

LANCELETS > LANCELET

LANCEOLAR adj narrow and tapering to a point at each end

LANCER n formerly, cavalry soldier armed with a lance

LANCERS n quadrille for eight or sixteen couples

LANCES > LANCE

LANCET n pointed two-edged surgical knife

LANCETED adj having one or more lancet arches or windows

LANCETS > LANCET

LANCEWOOD n New Zealand tree with slender leaves

LANCH obsolete form of > LAUNCH

LANCHED > LANCH

LANCHES > LANCH

LANCHING > LANCH

LANCIERS npl type of dance

LANCIFORM adj in the form of a lance

LANCINATE adj (esp of pain) sharp or cutting

LANCING > LANCE

LAND n solid part of the earth's surface ▷ vb come or bring to earth after a flight, jump, or fall

LANDAMANN n chairman of the governing council in some Swiss cantons

LANDAU n four-wheeled carriage with two folding hoods

LANDAULET n small landau

LANDAUS > LANDAU

LANDBOARD n narrow board, with wheels larger than those on a skateboard, usually ridden while standing

LANDDAMNE vb Shakespearian word for make (a person's life) unbearable

LANDDROS n sheriff

LANDDROST n South African magistrate

LANDE n type of moorland in SW France

LANDED adj possessing or consisting of lands

LANDER n spacecraft designed to land on a planet or other body

LANDERS > LANDER

LANDES > LANDE

LANDFALL n ship's first landing after a voyage

LANDFALLS > LANDFALL

LANDFILL n disposing of rubbish by covering it with earth

LANDFILLS > LANDFILL

LANDFORCE n body of people trained for land warfare

LANDFORM n any natural feature of the earth's surface, such as valleys and mountains

LANDFORMS > LANDFORM

LANDGRAB n sudden attempt to establish ownership of or copyright on something in advance of competitors

LANDGRABS > LANDGRAB

LANDGRAVE n (from the 13th century to 1806) a count who ruled over a specified territory

LANDING n floor area at the top of a flight of stairs

LANDINGS > LANDING

LANDLADY n woman who owns and leases property

LANDLER n Austrian country dance in which couples spin and clap

LANDLERS > LANDLER

LANDLESS > LAND

LANDLINE n telecommunications cable laid over land

LANDLINES > LANDLINE

LANDLOPER n vagabond or vagrant

LANDLORD n person who rents out land, houses, etc

LANDLORDS > LANDLORD

LANDMAN n person who lives and works on land

LANDMARK n prominent object in or feature of a landscape

LANDMARKS > LANDMARK

LANDMASS n large continuous area of land

LANDMEN > LANDMAN

LANDMINE n type of bomb laid on or just under the surface of the ground ▷ vb lay (an area) with landmines

LANDMINED > LANDMINE vb

LANDMINES > LANDMINE

LANDOWNER n person who owns land

LANDRACE n white very long-bodied lop-eared breed of pork pig

LANDRACES > LANDRACE

LANDRAIL n type of bird

LANDRAILS > LANDRAIL

LANDS npl holdings in land

LANDSCAPE n extensive piece of inland scenery seen from one place ▷ vb improve natural features of (a piece of land) ▷ adj (of a publication or an illustration in a publication) of greater width than height

LANDSHARK n person who makes inordinate profits by buying and selling land

LANDSIDE n part of an airport farthest from the aircraft

LANDSIDES > LANDSIDE
LANDSKIP another word for > LANDSCAPE
LANDSKIPS > LANDSKIP
LANDSLEIT > LANDSMAN
LANDSLID > LANDSLIDE
LANDSLIDE vb cause land or rock to fall from hillside
LANDSLIP same as > LANDSLIDE
LANDSLIPS > LANDSLIP
LANDSMAN n person who works or lives on land, as distinguished from a seaman
LANDSMEN > LANDSMAN
LANDWARD same as > LANDWARDS
LANDWARDS adv towards land
LANDWIND n wind that comes from the land
LANDWINDS > LANDWIND
LANE n narrow road
LANELY Scots form of > LONELY
LANES > LANE
LANEWAY n lane
LANEWAYS > LANEWAY
LANG Scot word for > LONG
LANGAHA n type of Madagascan snake
LANGAHAS > LANGAHA
LANGAR n dining hall in a gurdwara
LANGARS > LANGAR
LANGER informal Irish word for > PENIS
LANGERED adj drunk
LANGERS > LANGER
LANGEST > LANG
LANGLAUF n cross-country skiing
LANGLAUFS > LANGLAUF
LANGLEY n unit of solar radiation
LANGLEYS > LANGLEY
LANGOUSTE n spiny lobster
LANGRAGE n shot consisting of scrap iron packed into a case, formerly used in naval warfare
LANGRAGES > LANGRAGE
LANGREL same as > LANGRAGE
LANGRELS > LANGREL
LANGRIDGE same as > LANGRAGE
LANGSHAN n breed of chicken
LANGSHANS > LANGSHAN
LANGSPEL n type of Scandinavian stringed instrument
LANGSPELS > LANGSPEL
LANGSPIEL same as > LANGSPEL
LANGSYNE adv long ago ▷ n times long past, esp those fondly remembered
LANGSYNES > LANGSYNE
LANGUAGE n system of sounds, symbols, etc for

communicating thought ▷ vb express in language
LANGUAGED > LANGUAGE
LANGUAGES > LANGUAGE
LANGUE n language considered as an abstract system or a social institution
LANGUED adj having a tongue
LANGUES > LANGUE
LANGUET n anything resembling a tongue in shape or function
LANGUETS > LANGUET
LANGUETTE same as > LANGUET
LANGUID adj lacking energy or enthusiasm
LANGUIDLY > LANGUID
LANGUISH vb suffer neglect or hardship
LANGUOR n state of dreamy relaxation
LANGUORS > LANGUOR
LANGUR n type of arboreal Old World monkey
LANGURS > LANGUR
LANIARD same as > LANYARD
LANIARDS > LANIARD
LANIARIES > LANIARY
LANIARY adj (esp of canine teeth) adapted for tearing ▷ n tooth adapted for tearing
LANITAL n fibre used in production of synthetic wool
LANITALS > LANITAL
LANK adj (of hair) straight and limp ▷ vb become or cause to become lank
LANKED > LANK
LANKER > LANK
LANKEST > LANK
LANKIER > LANKY
LANKIEST > LANKY
LANKILY > LANKY
LANKINESS > LANKY
LANKING > LANK
LANKLY > LANK
LANKNESS > LANK
LANKS > LANK
LANKY adj ungracefully tall and thin
LANNER n large falcon of Mediterranean regions, N Africa, and S Asia
LANNERET n male or tercel of the lanner falcon
LANNERETS > LANNERET
LANNERS > LANNER
LANOLATED > LANOLIN
LANOLIN n grease from sheep's wool used in ointments etc
LANOLINE same as > LANOLIN
LANOLINES > LANOLINE
LANOLINS > LANOLIN
LANOSE same as > LANATE
LANOSITY > LANOSE
LANT n stale urine

LANTANA n shrub with orange or yellow flowers, considered a weed in Australia
LANTANAS > LANTANA
LANTERLOO n old card game
LANTERN n light in a transparent protective case ▷ vb supply with lantern
LANTERNED > LANTERN
LANTERNS > LANTERN
LANTHANON n one of a group of chemical elements
LANTHANUM n silvery-white metallic element
LANTHORN archaic word for > LANTERN
LANTHORNS > LANTHORN
LANTS > LANT
LANTSKIP another word for > LANDSCAPE
LANTSKIPS > LANTSKIP
LANUGO n layer of fine hairs, esp the covering of the human fetus before birth
LANUGOS > LANUGO
LANX n dish; plate
LANYARD n cord worn round the neck to hold a knife or whistle
LANYARDS > LANYARD
LAODICEAN adj indifferent, esp in religious matters ▷ n person having a lukewarm attitude towards religious matters
LAOGAI n forced labour camp in China
LAOGAIS > LAOGAI
LAP n part between the waist and knees of a person when sitting ▷ vb overtake an opponent so as to be one or more circuits ahead
LAPBOARD n flat board that can be used on the lap as a makeshift table or desk
LAPBOARDS > LAPBOARD
LAPDOG n small pet dog
LAPDOGS > LAPDOG
LAPEL n part of the front of a coat or jacket folded back towards the shoulders
LAPELED > LAPEL
LAPELLED > LAPEL
LAPELS > LAPEL
LAPFUL same as > LAP
LAPFULS > LAPFUL
LAPHELD adj (esp of a personal computer) small enough to be used on one's lap
LAPIDARY adj of or relating to stones ▷ n person who cuts, polishes, sets, or deals in gemstones
LAPIDATE vb pelt with stones
LAPIDATED > LAPIDATE
LAPIDATES > LAPIDATE
LAPIDEOUS adj having appearance or texture of

stone
LAPIDES > LAPIS
LAPIDIFIC adj transforming into stone
LAPIDIFY vb change into stone
LAPIDIST n cutter and engraver of precious stones
LAPIDISTS > LAPIDIST
LAPILLI > LAPILLUS
LAPILLUS n small piece of lava thrown from a volcano
LAPIN n castrated rabbit
LAPINS > LAPIN
LAPIS as in lapis lazuli brilliant blue mineral used as a gemstone
LAPISES > LAPIS
LAPJE same as > LAPPIE
LAPJES > LAPJE
LAPPED > LAP
LAPPEL same as > LAPEL
LAPPELS > LAPPEL
LAPPER n one that laps ▷ vb curdle
LAPPERED > LAPPER
LAPPERING > LAPPER
LAPPERS > LAPPER
LAPPET n small hanging flap or piece of lace
LAPPETED > LAPPET
LAPPETS > LAPPET
LAPPIE n rag
LAPPIES > LAPPIE
LAPPING > LAP
LAPPINGS > LAP
LAPS > LAP
LAPSABLE > LAPSE
LAPSANG n smoky-tasting Chinese tea
LAPSANGS > LAPSANG
LAPSE n temporary drop in a standard, esp through forgetfulness or carelessness ▷ vb drop in standard
LAPSED > LAPSE
LAPSER > LAPSE
LAPSERS > LAPSE
LAPSES > LAPSE
LAPSIBLE > LAPSE
LAPSING > LAPSE
LAPSTONE n device used by a cobbler on which leather is beaten
LAPSTONES > LAPSTONE
LAPSTRAKE n clinker-built boat
LAPSTREAK same as > LAPSTRAKE
LAPSUS n lapse or error
LAPTOP adj small enough to fit on a user's lap ▷ n computer small enough to fit on a user's lap
LAPTOPS > LAPTOP
LAPTRAY n tray with a cushioned underside, designed to rest in a person's lap while supporting reading material, etc
LAPTRAYS > LAPTRAY
LAPWING n plover with a

tuft of feathers on the head

LAPWINGS > LAPWING

LAPWORK *n* work with lapping edges

LAPWORKS > LAPWORK

LAQUEARIA *n* ceiling made of panels

LAR *n* boy or young man

LARBOARD *n* port (side of a ship)

LARBOARDS > LARBOARD

LARCENER > LARCENY

LARCENERS > LARCENY

LARCENIES > LARCENY

LARCENIST > LARCENY

LARCENOUS > LARCENY

LARCENY *n* theft

LARCH *n* deciduous coniferous tree

LARCHEN *adj* of larch

LARCHES > LARCH

LARD *n* soft white fat obtained from a pig ▷ *vb* insert strips of bacon in (meat) before cooking

LARDALITE *n* type of mineral

LARDED > LARD

LARDER *n* storeroom for food

LARDERER *n* person in charge of larder

LARDERERS > LARDERER

LARDERS > LARDER

LARDIER > LARDY

LARDIEST > LARDY

LARDING > LARD

LARDLIKE > LARD

LARDON *n* strip or cube of fat or bacon used in larding meat

LARDONS > LARDON

LARDOON *same as* > LARDON

LARDOONS > LARDOON

LARDS > LARD

LARDY *adj* fat

LARE *another word for* > LORE

LAREE *n* Asian fish-hook formerly used as currency

LAREES > LAREE

LARES > LARE

LARGANDO *adv* (music) growing slower and more marked

LARGE *adj* great in size, number, or extent ▷ *n* formerly, musical note of particular length

LARGELY *adv* principally

LARGEN *another word for* > ENLARGE

LARGENED > LARGEN

LARGENESS > LARGE

LARGENING > LARGEN

LARGENS > LARGEN

LARGER > LARGE

LARGES > LARGE

LARGESS *same as* > LARGESSE

LARGESSE *n* generous giving, esp of money

LARGESSES > LARGESSE

LARGEST > LARGE

LARGHETTO *adv* be performed moderately slowly ▷ *n* piece or passage to be performed in this way

LARGISH *adj* fairly large

LARGITION *n* act of being generous

LARGO *adv* in a slow and dignified manner ▷ *n* piece or passage to be performed in a slow and stately manner

LARGOS > LARGO

LARI *n* standard monetary unit of Georgia, divided into 100 tetri

LARIAT *n* lasso ▷ *vb* tether with lariat

LARIATED > LARIAT

LARIATING > LARIAT

LARIATS > LARIAT

LARINE *adj* of, relating to, or resembling a gull

LARIS > LARI

LARK *n* small brown songbird, skylark ▷ *vb* have a good time by frolicking

LARKED > LARK

LARKER > LARK

LARKERS > LARK

LARKIER > LARKY

LARKIEST > LARKY

LARKINESS > LARKY

LARKING > LARK

LARKISH > LARK

LARKS > LARK

LARKSOME *adj* mischievous

LARKSPUR *n* plant with spikes of blue, pink, or white flowers with spurs

LARKSPURS > LARKSPUR

LARKY *adj* frolicsome or mischievous

LARMIER *n* pouch under lower eyelid of deer

LARMIERS > LARMIER

LARN *vb* learn

LARNAKES > LARNAX

LARNAX *n* coffin made of terracotta

LARNED > LARN

LARNEY *n* white person ▷ *adj* (of clothes) smart

LARNEYS > LARNEY

LARNIER > LARNEY

LARNIEST > LARNEY

LARNING > LARN

LARNS > LARN

LAROID *adj* relating to Larus genus of gull family

LARRIGAN *n* knee-high oiled leather moccasin boot worn by trappers, etc

LARRIGANS > LARRIGAN

LARRIKIN *n* mischievous or unruly person

LARRIKINS > LARRIKIN

LARRUP *vb* beat or flog

LARRUPED > LARRUP

LARRUPER > LARRUP

LARRUPERS > LARRUP

LARRUPING > LARRUP

LARRUPS > LARRUP

LARS > LAR

LARUM *archaic word for* > ALARM

LARUMS > LARUM

LARVA *n* insect in an immature stage, often resembling a worm

LARVAE > LARVA

LARVAL > LARVA

LARVAS > LARVA

LARVATE *adj* masked; concealed

LARVATED *same as* > LARVATE

LARVICIDE *n* chemical used for killing larvae

LARVIFORM *adj* in the form of a larva

LARVIKITE *n* type of mineral

LARYNGAL *adj* laryngeal ▷ *n* sound articulated in the larynx

LARYNGALS > LARYNGAL

LARYNGEAL *adj* of or relating to the larynx

LARYNGES > LARYNX

LARYNX *n* part of the throat containing the vocal cords

LARYNXES > LARYNX

LAS > LA

LASAGNA *same as* > LASAGNE

LASAGNAS > LASAGNA

LASAGNE *n* pasta in wide flat sheets

LASAGNES > LASAGNE

LASCAR *n* East Indian seaman

LASCARS > LASCAR

LASE *vb* (of a substance, such as carbon dioxide or ruby) to be capable of acting as a laser

LASED > LASE

LASER *n* device that produces a very narrow intense beam of light, used for cutting very hard materials and in surgery etc

LASERDISC *n* disk similar in size to a long-playing record, on which data is stored in pits in a similar way to data storage on a compact disk

LASERDISK *same as* > LASERDISC

LASERS > LASER

LASERWORT *n* type of plant

LASES > LASE

LASH *n* eyelash ▷ *vb* hit with a whip

LASHED > LASH

LASHER > LASH

LASHERS > LASH

LASHES > LASH

LASHING > LASH

LASHINGLY > LASH

LASHINGS *npl* great amount of

LASHINS *variant of* > LASHINGS

LASHKAR *n* troop of Indian men with weapons

LASHKARS > LASHKAR

LASING > LASE

LASINGS > LASE

LASKET *n* loop at the foot of a sail onto which an extra sail may be fastened

LASKETS > LASKET

LASQUE *n* flat-cut diamond

LASQUES > LASQUE

LASS *n* girl

LASSES > LASS

LASSI *n* cold drink made with yoghurt or buttermilk and flavoured with sugar, salt, or a mild spice

LASSIE *n* little lass

LASSIES > LASSIE

LASSIS > LASSI

LASSITUDE *n* physical or mental weariness

LASSLORN *adj* abandoned by a young girl

LASSO *n* rope with a noose for catching cattle and horses ▷ *vb* catch with a lasso

LASSOCK *another word for* > LASS

LASSOCKS > LASSOCK

LASSOED > LASSO

LASSOER > LASSO

LASSOERS > LASSO

LASSOES > LASSO

LASSOING > LASSO

LASSOS > LASSO

LASSU *n* slow part of csárdás folk dance

LASSUS > LASSU

LAST *adv* coming at the end or after all others ▷ *adj* only remaining ▷ *n* last person or thing ▷ *vb* continue

LASTAGE *n* space for storing goods in ship

LASTAGES > LASTAGE

LASTBORN *n* last child to be born

LASTBORNS > LASTBORN

LASTED > LAST

LASTER > LAST

LASTERS > LAST

LASTING *adj* existing or remaining effective for a long time ▷ *n* strong durable closely woven fabric used for shoe uppers, etc

LASTINGLY > LASTING

LASTINGS > LASTING

LASTLY *adv* at the end or at the last point

LASTS > LAST

LAT *n* former coin of Latvia

LATAH *n* psychological condition in which a traumatized individual becomes anxious and suggestible

LATAHS > LATAH

LATAKIA *n* type of Turkish tobacco

LATAKIAS > LATAKIA

LATCH n fastening for a door with a bar and lever ▷ vb fasten with a latch

LATCHED > LATCH

LATCHES > LATCH

LATCHET n shoe fastening, such as a thong or lace

LATCHETS > LATCHET

LATCHING > LATCH

LATCHKEY n key for an outside door or gate, esp one that lifts a latch

LATCHKEYS > LATCHKEY

LATE adj after the normal or expected time ▷ adv after the normal or expected time

LATECOMER n person or thing that comes late

LATED archaic word for > BELATED

LATEEN adj denoting a rig with a triangular sail bent to a yard hoisted to the head of a low mast

LATEENER n lateen-rigged ship

LATEENERS > LATEEN

LATEENS > LATEEN

LATELY adv in recent times

LATEN vb become or cause to become late

LATENCE > LATENCE

LATENCES > LATENCE

LATENCIES > LATENT

LATENCY > LATENT

LATENED > LATEN

LATENESS > LATE

LATENING > LATEN

LATENS > LATEN

LATENT adj hidden and not yet developed ▷ n fingerprint that is not visible to the eye

LATENTLY > LATENT

LATENTS > LATENT

LATER adv afterwards

LATERAD adv towards the side

LATERAL adj of or relating to the side or sides ▷ n lateral object, part, passage, or movement ▷ vb pass laterally

LATERALED > LATERAL

LATERALLY > LATERAL

LATERALS > LATERAL

LATERBORN adj born later ▷ n one born later

LATERISE same as > LATERIZE

LATERISED > LATERISE

LATERISES > LATERISE

LATERITE n any of a group of deposits consisting of residual insoluble ferric and aluminium oxides

LATERITES > LATERITE

LATERITIC > LATERITE

LATERIZE vb develop into a laterite

LATERIZED > LATERIZE

LATERIZES > LATERIZE

LATESCENT n becoming latent

LATEST n the most recent news, fashion, etc

LATESTS > LATEST

LATEWAKE n vigil held over corpse

LATEWAKES > LATEWAKE

LATEWOOD n wood formed later in tree's growing season

LATEWOODS > LATEWOOD

LATEX n milky fluid found in some plants, esp the rubber tree, used in making rubber

LATEXES > LATEX

LATH n thin strip of wood used to support plaster, tiles, etc ▷ vb attach laths to (a ceiling, roof, floor, etc)

LATHE n machine for turning wood or metal while it is being shaped ▷ vb shape, bore, or cut a screw thread in or on (a workpiece) on a lathe

LATHED > LATHE

LATHEE same as > LATHI

LATHEES > LATHEE

LATHEN adj covered with laths

LATHER n froth of soap and water ▷ vb make frothy

LATHERED > LATHER

LATHERER > LATHER

LATHERERS > LATHER

LATHERIER > LATHER

LATHERING > LATHER

LATHERS > LATHER

LATHERY > LATHER

LATHES > LATHE

LATHI n long heavy wooden stick used as a weapon in India, esp by the police

LATHIER > LATHY

LATHIEST > LATHY

LATHING > LATHE

LATHINGS > LATHE

LATHIS > LATHI

LATHLIKE > LATH

LATHS > LATH

LATHWORK n work made of laths

LATHWORKS > LATHWORK

LATHY adj resembling a lath, esp in being tall and thin

LATHYRISM n neurological disease often resulting in weakness and paralysis of the legs

LATHYRUS n genus of climbing plant

LATI > LAT

LATICES > LATEX

LATICIFER n cell or group of cells in a plant that contains latex

LATICLAVE n broad stripe on Roman senator's tunic

LATIFONDI npl large agricultural estates in ancient Rome

LATIGO n strap on horse's saddle

LATIGOES > LATIGO

LATIGOS > LATIGO

LATILLA n stick making up part of ceiling

LATILLAS > LATILLA

LATIMERIA n type of coelacanth fish

LATINA n female inhabitant of the US who is of Latin American origin

LATINAS > LATINA

LATINISE same as > LATINIZE

LATINISED > LATINISE

LATINISES > LATINISE

LATINITY n facility in the use of Latin

LATINIZE vb translate into Latin

LATINIZED > LATINIZE

LATINIZES > LATINIZE

LATINO n male inhabitant of the US who is of Latin American origin

LATINOS > LATINO

LATISH adv rather late ▷ adj rather late

LATITANCY > LATITANT

LATITANT adj concealed

LATITAT n writ presuming that person accused was hiding

LATITATS > LATITAT

LATITUDE n angular distance measured in degrees N or S of the equator

LATITUDES > LATITUDE

LATKE n crispy Jewish pancake

LATKES > LATKE

LATOSOL n type of deep, well-drained soil

LATOSOLIC > LATOSOL

LATOSOLS > LATOSOL

LATRANT adj barking

LATRATION n instance of barking

LATRIA n adoration that may be offered to God alone

LATRIAS > LATRIA

LATRINE n toilet in a barracks or camp

LATRINES > LATRINE

LATROCINY n banditry

LATRON n bandit

LATRONS > LATRON

LATS > LAT

LATTE n coffee made with hot milk

LATTEN n metal or alloy, esp brass, made in thin sheets

LATTENS > LATTEN

LATTER adj second of two

LATTERLY adv recently

LATTES > LATTE

LATTICE n framework of intersecting strips of wood, metal, etc ▷ vb make, adorn, or supply with a lattice

LATTICED > LATTICE

LATTICES > LATTICE

LATTICING > LATTICE

LATTICINI > LATTICINO

LATTICINO n type of Italian glass

LATTIN n brass alloy beaten into a thin sheet

LATTINS > LATTIN

LATU > LAT

LAUAN n type of wood used in furniture-making

LAUANS > LAUAN

LAUCH Scots form of > LAUGH

LAUCHING > LAUCH

LAUCHS > LAUCH

LAUD vb praise or glorify ▷ n praise or glorification

LAUDABLE adj praiseworthy

LAUDABLY > LAUDABLE

LAUDANUM n opium-based sedative

LAUDANUMS > LAUDANUM

LAUDATION formal word for > PRAISE

LAUDATIVE same as > LAUDATORY

LAUDATOR n one who praises highly

LAUDATORS > LAUDATOR

LAUDATORY adj praising or glorifying

LAUDED > LAUD

LAUDER > LAUD

LAUDERS > LAUD

LAUDING > LAUD

LAUDS n traditional morning prayer of the Western Church, constituting with matins the first of the seven canonical hours

LAUF n run in bobsleighing

LAUFS > LAUF

LAUGH vb make inarticulate sounds with the voice expressing amusement, merriment, or scorn ▷ n act or instance of laughing

LAUGHABLE adj ridiculously inadequate

LAUGHABLY > LAUGHABLE

LAUGHED > LAUGH

LAUGHER > LAUGH

LAUGHERS > LAUGH

LAUGHFUL > LAUGH

LAUGHIER > LAUGHY

LAUGHIEST > LAUGHY

LAUGHING > LAUGH

LAUGHINGS > LAUGH

LAUGHLINE n funny line in dialogue

LAUGHS > LAUGH

LAUGHSOME adj causing laughter

LAUGHTER n sound or action of laughing

LAUGHTERS > LAUGHTER

LAUGHY adj tending to laugh a lot

LAUNCE old form of > LANCE

LAUNCED > LAUNCE

LAUNCES > LAUNCE

LAUNCH vb put (a ship or boat) into the water, esp for the first time ▷ n launching

LAUNCHED > LAUNCH

LAUNCHER n any installation, vehicle, or other device for launching rockets, missiles, or other projectiles

LAUNCHERS > LAUNCHER

LAUNCHES > LAUNCH

LAUNCHING > LAUNCH

LAUNCHPAD n platform from which a spacecraft is launched

LAUNCING > LAUNCE

LAUND n open grassy space

LAUNDER vb wash and iron (clothes and linen) ▷ n water trough, esp one used for washing ore in mining

LAUNDERED > LAUNDER

LAUNDERER > LAUNDER

LAUNDERS > LAUNDER

LAUNDRESS n woman who launders clothes, sheets, etc, for a living

LAUNDRIES > LAUNDRY

LAUNDRY n clothes etc for washing or which have recently been washed

LAUNDS > LAUND

LAURA n group of monastic cells

LAURAE > LAURA

LAURAS > LAURA

LAUREATE adj crowned with laurel leaves as a sign of honour ▷ n person honoured with an award for art or science ▷ vb crown with laurel

LAUREATED > LAUREATE

LAUREATES > LAUREATE

LAUREL n glossy-leaved shrub, bay tree ▷ vb crown with laurel

LAURELED > LAUREL

LAURELING > LAUREL

LAURELLED > LAUREL

LAURELS > LAUREL

LAURIC as in lauric acid dodecanoic acid

LAURYL as in lauryl alcohol crystalline solid used to make detergents

LAURYLS > LAURYL

LAUWINE n avalanche

LAUWINES > LAUWINE

LAV short for > LAVATORY

LAVA n molten rock thrown out by volcanoes, which hardens as it cools

LAVABO n ritual washing of the celebrant's hands after the offertory at Mass

LAVABOES > LAVABO

LAVABOS > LAVABO

LAVAFORM n in form of lava

LAVAGE n washing out of a hollow organ by flushing with water

LAVAGES > LAVAGE

LAVALAVA n draped skirtlike garment worn by Polynesians

LAVALAVAS > LAVALAVA

LAVALIER n decorative pendant worn on chain

LAVALIERE same as > LAVALIER

LAVALIERES > LAVALIER

LAVALIKE > LAVA

LAVANDIN n hybrid of two varieties of the lavender plant

LAVANDINS > LAVANDIN

LAVAS > LAVA

LAVASH n Armenian flat bread

LAVASHES > LAVASH

LAVATERA n type of plant closely resembling the mallow

LAVATERAS > LAVATERA

LAVATION n act or process of washing

LAVATIONS > LAVATION

LAVATORY n toilet

LAVE archaic word for > WASH

LAVED > LAVE

LAVEER vb (in sailing) tack

LAVEERED > LAVEER

LAVEERING > LAVEER

LAVEERS > LAVEER

LAVEMENT n washing with injections of water

LAVEMENTS > LAVEMENT

LAVENDER n shrub with fragrant flowers ▷ adj bluish-purple

LAVENDERS > LAVENDER

LAVER n large basin of water used by priests for ritual ablutions

LAVEROCK Scot and northern English dialect word for > SKYLARK

LAVEROCKS > LAVEROCK

LAVERS > LAVER

LAVES > LAVE

LAVING > LAVE

LAVISH adj great in quantity or richness ▷ vb give or spend generously

LAVISHED > LAVISH

LAVISHER > LAVISH

LAVISHERS > LAVISH

LAVISHES > LAVISH

LAVISHEST > LAVISH

LAVISHING > LAVISH

LAVISHLY > LAVISH

LAVOLT same as > LAVOLTA

LAVOLTA n Italian dance of the 16th and 17th centuries ▷ vb dance the lavolta

LAVOLTAED > LAVOLTA

LAVOLTAS > LAVOLTA

LAVOLTED > LAVOLT

LAVOLTING > LAVOLT

LAVOLTS > LAVOLT

LAVRA same as > LAURA

LAVRAS > LAVRA

LAVROCK same as > LAVEROCK

LAVROCKS > LAVROCK

LAVS > LAV

LAVVIES > LAVVY

LAVVY n lavatory

LAW n rule binding on a community ▷ vb prosecute ▷ adj (in archaic usage) low

LAWBOOK n book on subject of law

LAWBOOKS > LAWBOOK

LAWCOURT n court of law

LAWCOURTS > LAWCOURT

LAWED > LAW

LAWER > LAW

LAWEST > LAW

LAWFARE n use of the law by a country against its enemies

LAWFARES > LAWFARE

LAWFUL adj allowed by law

LAWFULLY > LAWFUL

LAWGIVER n giver of a code of laws

LAWGIVERS > LAWGIVER

LAWGIVING > LAWGIVER

LAWIN n bill or reckoning

LAWINE n avalanche

LAWINES > LAWINE

LAWING same as > LAWIN

LAWINGS > LAWING

LAWINS > LAWIN

LAWK interj used to show surprise

LAWKS same as > LAWK

LAWLAND same as > LOWLAND

LAWLANDS > LAWLAND

LAWLESS adj breaking the law, esp in a violent way

LAWLESSLY > LAWLESS

LAWLIKE > LAW

LAWMAKER same as > LAWGIVER

LAWMAKERS > LAWMAKER

LAWMAKING n process of legislating

LAWMAN n officer of the law, such as a policeman or sheriff

LAWMEN > LAWMAN

LAWMONGER n inferior lawyer

LAWN n area of tended and mown grass

LAWNED adj having a lawn

LAWNIER > LAWN

LAWNIEST > LAWN

LAWNMOWER n machine for cutting grass on lawns

LAWNS > LAWN

LAWNY > LAWN

LAWS > LAW

LAWSUIT n court case brought by one person or group against another

LAWSUITS > LAWSUIT

LAWYER n professionally qualified legal expert ▷ vb act as lawyer

LAWYERED > LAWYER

LAWYERING > LAWYER

LAWYERLY > LAWYER

LAWYERS > LAWYER

LAX adj not strict ▷ n laxative

LAXATION n act of making lax or the state of being lax

LAXATIONS > LAXATION

LAXATIVE adj (medicine) inducing the emptying of the bowels ▷ n medicine that induces the emptying of the bowels

LAXATIVES > LAXATIVE

LAXATOR n muscle that loosens body part

LAXATORS > LAXATOR

LAXER > LAX

LAXES > LAX

LAXEST > LAX

LAXISM > LAXIST

LAXISMS > LAXIST

LAXIST n lenient or tolerant person

LAXISTS > LAXIST

LAXITIES > LAX

LAXITY > LAX

LAXLY > LAX

LAXNESS > LAX

LAXNESSES > LAX

LAY > LIE

LAYABOUT n lazy person ▷ vb hit out with violent and repeated blows in all directions

LAYABOUTS > LAYABOUT

LAYAWAY n merchandise reserved for future delivery

LAYAWAYS > LAYAWAY

LAYBACK n technique for climbing cracks by pulling on one side of the crack with the hands and pressing on the other with the feet ▷ vb in climbing, use layback technique

LAYBACKED > LAYBACK

LAYBACKS > LAYBACK

LAYDEEZ npl jocular spelling of ladies, as pronounced in a mid-Atlantic accent

LAYED > LAY

LAYER n single thickness of some substance, as a cover or coating on a surface ▷ vb form a layer

LAYERAGE n covering stem or branch with soil to encourage new roots

LAYERAGES > LAYERAGE

LAYERED > LAYER

LAYERING n method of propagation that induces a shoot or branch to take root while it is still attached to the parent plant

LAYERINGS > LAYERING

LAYERS > LAYER

LAYETTE n clothes for a newborn baby

LAYETTES > LAYETTE

LAYIN n basketball score made by dropping ball into basket

LAYING > LAY

LAYINGS > LAY

LAYINS > LAYIN

LAYLOCK old form of > LILAC

LAYLOCKS > LAYLOCK
LAYMAN n person who is not a member of the clergy
LAYMEN > LAYMAN
LAYOFF n act of suspending employees
LAYOFFS > LAYOFF
LAYOUT n arrangement, esp of matter for printing or of a building
LAYOUTS > LAYOUT
LAYOVER n break in a journey
LAYOVERS > LAYOVER
LAYPEOPLE > LAYPERSON
LAYPERSON n person who is not a member of the clergy
LAYS > LIE
LAYSHAFT n auxiliary shaft in a gearbox
LAYSHAFTS > LAYSHAFT
LAYSTALL n place where waste is deposited
LAYSTALLS > LAYSTALL
LAYTIME n time allowed for loading cargo
LAYTIMES > LAYTIME
LAYUP n period of incapacity through illness
LAYUPS > LAYUP
LAYWOMAN n woman who is not a member of the clergy
LAYWOMEN > LAYWOMAN
LAZAR archaic word for > LEPER
LAZARET same as > LAZARETTO
LAZARETS > LAZARET
LAZARETTE same as > LAZARETTO
LAZARETTO n small locker at the stern of a boat or a storeroom between decks of a ship
LAZARS > LAZAR
LAZE vb be idle or lazy ▷ n time spent lazing
LAZED > LAZE
LAZES > LAZE
LAZIED > LAZY
LAZIER > LAZY
LAZIES > LAZY
LAZIEST > LAZY
LAZILY > LAZY
LAZINESS > LAZY
LAZING > LAZE
LAZO another word for > LASSO
LAZOED > LAZO
LAZOES > LAZO
LAZOING > LAZO
LAZOS > LAZO
LAZULI n lapis lazuli
LAZULIS > LAZULI
LAZULITE n blue mineral, consisting of hydrated magnesium iron phosphate, occurring in metamorphic rocks
LAZULITES > LAZULITE
LAZURITE n rare blue

mineral consisting of a sodium-calcium-aluminium silicate
LAZURITES > LAZURITE
LAZY vb laze ▷ adj not inclined to work or exert oneself
LAZYBONES n lazy person
LAZYING > LAZY
LAZYISH > LAZY
LAZZARONE n Italian street beggar
LAZZARONI > LAZZARONE
LAZZI > LAZZO
LAZZO n comic routine in the commedia dell'arte
LEA n meadow
LEACH vb remove or be removed from a substance by a liquid passing through it ▷ n act or process of leaching
LEACHABLE > LEACH
LEACHATE n water that carries salts dissolved out of materials through which it has percolated
LEACHATES > LEACHATE
LEACHED > LEACH
LEACHER > LEACH
LEACHERS > LEACH
LEACHES > LEACH
LEACHIER > LEACHY
LEACHIEST > LEACHY
LEACHING > LEACH
LEACHINGS > LEACH
LEACHOUR old form of > LECHER
LEACHOURS > LEACHOUR
LEACHY adj porous
LEAD vb guide or conduct ▷ n first or most prominent place ▷ adj acting as a leader or lead
LEADED adj (of windows) made from many small panes of glass held together by lead strips
LEADEN adj heavy or sluggish ▷ vb become or cause to become leaden
LEADENED > LEADEN
LEADENING > LEADEN
LEADENLY > LEADEN
LEADENS > LEADEN
LEADER n person who leads
LEADERENE n strong female leader
LEADERS > LEADER
LEADIER > LEADY
LEADIEST > LEADY
LEADING > LEAD
LEADINGLY > LEAD
LEADINGS > LEAD
LEADLESS adj without lead
LEADMAN n man who leads
LEADMEN > LEADMAN
LEADOFF n initial move or action
LEADOFFS > LEADOFF
LEADPLANT n N American

shrub
LEADS > LEAD
LEADSCREW n threaded rod in a lathe
LEADSMAN n sailor who takes soundings with a lead line
LEADSMEN > LEADSMAN
LEADWORK n maintenance work involving lead pipes, etc
LEADWORKS > LEADWORK
LEADWORT n type of tropical or subtropical shrub with red, blue, or white flowers
LEADWORTS > LEADWORT
LEADY adj like lead
LEAF n flat usu green blade attached to the stem of a plant ▷ vb turn (pages) cursorily
LEAFAGE n leaves of plants
LEAFAGES > LEAFAGE
LEAFBUD n bud producing leaves rather than flowers
LEAFBUDS > LEAFBUD
LEAFED > LEAF
LEAFERIES > LEAFERY
LEAFERY n foliage
LEAFIER > LEAFY
LEAFIEST > LEAFY
LEAFINESS > LEAFY
LEAFING > LEAF
LEAFLESS > LEAF
LEAFLET n sheet of printed matter for distribution ▷ vb distribute leaflets (to)
LEAFLETED > LEAFLET
LEAFLETER > LEAFLET
LEAFLETS > LEAFLET
LEAFLIKE > LEAF
LEAFS > LEAF
LEAFSTALK n stalk attaching a leaf to a stem or branch
LEAFWORM n cotton plant pest
LEAFWORMS > LEAFWORM
LEAFY adj covered with leaves
LEAGUE n association promoting the interests of its members
LEAGUED > LEAGUE
LEAGUER vb harass; beset ▷ n encampment, esp of besiegers
LEAGUERED > LEAGUER
LEAGUERS > LEAGUER
LEAGUES > LEAGUE
LEAGUING > LEAGUE
LEAK n hole or defect that allows the escape or entrance of liquid, gas, radiation, etc ▷ vb let liquid etc in or out
LEAKAGE n act or instance of leaking
LEAKAGES > LEAKAGE
LEAKED > LEAK
LEAKER > LEAK
LEAKERS > LEAK

LEAKIER > LEAKY
LEAKIEST > LEAKY
LEAKILY > LEAKY
LEAKINESS > LEAKY
LEAKING > LEAK
LEAKLESS > LEAK
LEAKPROOF adj not likely to leak
LEAKS > LEAK
LEAKY adj leaking or tending to leak
LEAL adj loyal
LEALER > LEAL
LEALEST > LEAL
LEALLY > LEAL
LEALTIES > LEAL
LEALTY > LEAL
LEAM vb shine
LEAMED > LEAM
LEAMING > LEAM
LEAMS vb LEAM
LEAN vb rest (against) ▷ adj thin but healthy-looking ▷ n lean part of meat
LEANED > LEAN
LEANER > LEAN
LEANERS > LEAN
LEANEST > LEAN
LEANING > LEAN
LEANINGS > LEAN
LEANLY > LEAN
LEANNESS > LEAN
LEANS > LEAN
LEANT > LEAN
LEANY old form of > LEAN
LEAP vb make a sudden powerful jump ▷ n sudden powerful jump
LEAPED > LEAP
LEAPER > LEAP
LEAPEROUS old form of > LEPROUS
LEAPERS > LEAP
LEAPFROG n game in which a player vaults over another bending down ▷ vb play leapfrog
LEAPFROGS > LEAPFROG
LEAPING > LEAP
LEAPOROUS old form of > LEPROUS
LEAPROUS old form of > LEPROUS
LEAPS > LEAP
LEAPT > LEAP
LEAR vb instruct
LEARE same as > LEAR
LEARED > LEAR
LEARES > LEARE
LEARIER > LEARY
LEARIEST > LEARY
LEARINESS > LEARY
LEARING > LEAR
LEARN vb gain skill or knowledge by study, practice, or teaching
LEARNABLE > LEARN
LEARNED > LEARN
LEARNEDLY > LEARN
LEARNER n someone who is learning something
LEARNERS > LEARNER
LEARNING > LEARN
LEARNINGS > LEARN

LEARNS > LEARN

LEARNT > LEARN

LEARS > LEAR

LEARY same as > LEERY

LEAS > LEA

LEASABLE > LEASE

LEASE n contract by which land or property is rented for a stated time by the owner to a tenant ▷ vb let or rent by lease

LEASEBACK n property transaction in which the buyer leases the property to the seller

LEASED > LEASE

LEASEHOLD adj (land or property) held on lease ▷ n land or property held under a lease

LEASER > LEASE

LEASERS > LEASE

LEASES > LEASE

LEASH n lead for a dog ▷ vb control by a leash

LEASHED > LEASH

LEASHES > LEASH

LEASHING > LEASH

LEASING > LEASE

LEASINGS > LEASE

LEASOW vb pasture

LEASOWE same as > LEASOW

LEASOWED > LEASOW

LEASOWES > LEASOWE

LEASOWING > LEASOW

LEASOWS > LEASOW

LEAST n smallest amount ▷ adj smallest ▷ n smallest one ▷ adv in the smallest degree

LEASTS > LEAST

LEASTWAYS adv at least

LEASTWISE same as > LEASTWAYS

LEASURE old form of > LEISURE

LEASURES > LEASURE

LEAT n trench or ditch that conveys water to a mill wheel

LEATHER n material made from specially treated animal skins ▷ adj made of leather ▷ vb beat or thrash

LEATHERED > LEATHER

LEATHERN adj made of or resembling leather

LEATHERS > LEATHER

LEATHERY adj like leather, tough

LEATS > LEAT

LEAVE vb go away from ▷ n permission to be absent from work or duty

LEAVED adj with leaves

LEAVEN n substance that causes dough to rise ▷ vb raise with leaven

LEAVENED > LEAVEN

LEAVENING > LEAVEN

LEAVENOUS adj containing leaven

LEAVENS > LEAVEN

LEAVER > LEAVE

LEAVERS > LEAVE

LEAVES > LEAF

LEAVIER > LEAVY

LEAVIEST > LEAVY

LEAVING > LEAVE

LEAVINGS npl something remaining, such as refuse

LEAVY same as > LEAFY

LEAZE same as > LEASE

LEAZES > LEAZE

LEBBEK n type of timber tree

LEBBEKS > LEBBEK

LEBEN n semiliquid food made from curdled milk in N Africa and the Levant

LEBENS > LEBEN

LEBKUCHEN n biscuit, originating from Germany, usually containing honey, spices, etc

LECANORA n type of lichen

LECANORAS > LECANORA

LECCIES > LECCY

LECCY n electricity

LECH vb behave lecherously (towards) ▷ n lecherous act or indulgence

LECHAIM interj drinking toast ▷ n small drink with which to toast something or someone

LECHAIMS > LECHAIM

LECHAYIM same as > LECHAIM

LECHAYIMS > LECHAYIM

LECHED > LECH

LECHER n man who has or shows excessive sexual desire ▷ vb behave lecherously

LECHERED > LECHER

LECHERIES > LECHERY

LECHERING > LECHER

LECHEROUS adj (of a man) having or showing excessive sexual desire

LECHERS > LECHER

LECHERY n unrestrained and promiscuous sexuality

LECHES > LECH

LECHING > LECH

LECHWE n African antelope

LECHWES > LECHWE

LECITHIN n yellow-brown compound found in plant and animal tissues

LECITHINS > LECITHIN

LECTERN n sloping reading desk, esp in a church

LECTERNS > LECTERN

LECTIN n type of protein possessing high affinity for a specific sugar

LECTINS > LECTIN

LECTION n variant reading of a passage in a particular copy or edition of a text

LECTIONS > LECTION

LECTOR n lecturer or reader in certain universities

LECTORATE > LECTOR

LECTORS > LECTOR

LECTOTYPE n specimen designated by author after the publication of a species name

LECTRESS n female reader

LECTURE n informative talk to an audience on a subject ▷ vb give a talk

LECTURED > LECTURE

LECTURER n person who lectures, esp in a university or college

LECTURERS > LECTURER

LECTURES > LECTURE

LECTURING > LECTURE

LECTURN old form of > LECTERN

LECTURNS > LECTURN

LECYTHI > LECYTHUS

LECYTHIS n genus of very tall trees

LECYTHUS n (in ancient Greece) a vase with a narrow neck

LED > LEAD

LEDDEN n language; speech

LEDDENS > LEDDEN

LEDGE n narrow shelf sticking out from a wall

LEDGED > LEDGE

LEDGER n book of debit and credit accounts of a firm ▷ vb fish using a wire trace that allows the bait to float freely while the weight sinks

LEDGERED > LEDGER

LEDGERING > LEDGER

LEDGERS > LEDGER

LEDGES > LEDGE

LEDGIER > LEDGE

LEDGIEST > LEDGE

LEDGY > LEDGE

LEDUM n evergreen shrub

LEDUMS > LEDUM

LEE n sheltered side ▷ vb (Scots) lie

LEEAR Scots form of > LIAR

LEEARS > LEEAR

LEEBOARD n one of two paddle-like boards that can be lowered along the lee side of a vessel to reduce sideways drift

LEEBOARDS > LEEBOARD

LEECH n species of bloodsucking worm ▷ vb use leeches to suck the blood of

LEECHDOM n remedy

LEECHDOMS > LEECHDOM

LEECHED > LEECH

LEECHEE same as > LITCHI

LEECHEES > LEECHEE

LEECHES > LEECH

LEECHING > LEECH

LEECHLIKE > LEECH

LEED > LEE

LEEING > LEE

LEEK n vegetable of the onion family with a long bulb and thick stem

LEEKS > LEEK

LEEP vb boil; scald

LEEPED > LEEP

LEEPING > LEEP

LEEPS > LEEP

LEER vb look or grin at in a sneering or suggestive manner ▷ n sneering or suggestive look or grin

LEERED > LEER

LEERIER > LEERY

LEERIEST > LEERY

LEERILY > LEERY

LEERINESS > LEERY

LEERING > LEER

LEERINGLY > LEER

LEERINGS > LEER

LEERS > LEER

LEERY adj suspicious or wary (of)

LEES npl sediment of wine

LEESE old form of > LOOSE

LEESES > LEESE

LEESING > LEESE

LEET n list of candidates for an office

LEETLE form of > LITTLE

LEETS > LEET

LEETSPEAK n jargon used by some internet groups

LEEWARD n lee side ▷ adv towards this side ▷ adj of, in, or moving in the direction towards which the wind blows

LEEWARDLY > LEEWARD

LEEWARDS adv towards the lee side

LEEWAY n room for free movement within limits

LEEWAYS > LEEWAY

LEEZE as in leeze me Scots for lief is me, an expression of affection

LEFT adj on the opposite side from right ▷ n left side

LEFTE old past tense of > LIFT

LEFTER > LEFT

LEFTEST > LEFT

LEFTIE same as > LEFTY

LEFTIES > LEFTY

LEFTISH > LEFT

LEFTISM > LEFTIST

LEFTISMS > LEFTIST

LEFTIST adj (person) of the political left ▷ n person who supports the political left

LEFTISTS > LEFTIST

LEFTMOST > LEFT

LEFTMOSTS > LEFT

LEFTOVER n unused portion of food or material ▷ adj left as an unused portion

LEFTOVERS > LEFTOVER

LEFTS > LEFT

LEFTWARD same as > LEFTWARDS

LEFTWARDS adv towards or on the left

LEFTWING adj of or relating to the leftist faction of a party, etc

LEFTY n left-winger

LEG n one of the limbs on which a person or animal walks, runs, or stands

LEGACIES > LEGACY

LEGACY n thing left in a will

LEGAL adj established or permitted by law ▷ n legal expert

LEGALESE n conventional language in which legal documents are written

LEGALESES > LEGALESE

LEGALISE same as > LEGALIZE

LEGALISED > LEGALISE

LEGALISER > LEGALISE

LEGALISES > LEGALISE

LEGALISM n strict adherence to the letter of the law

LEGALISMS > LEGALISM

LEGALIST > LEGALISM

LEGALISTS > LEGALISM

LEGALITY n state or quality of being legal or lawful

LEGALIZE vb make legal

LEGALIZED > LEGALIZE

LEGALIZER > LEGALIZE

LEGALIZES > LEGALIZE

LEGALLY > LEGAL

LEGALS > LEGAL

LEGATARY n legatee

LEGATE n messenger or representative, esp from the Pope ▷ vb leave as legacy

LEGATED > LEGATE

LEGATEE n recipient of a legacy

LEGATEES > LEGATEE

LEGATES > LEGATE

LEGATINE > LEGATE

LEGATING > LEGATE

LEGATION n diplomatic minister and his staff

LEGATIONS > LEGATION

LEGATO adv (piece to be played) smoothly ▷ n style of playing with no gaps between notes

LEGATOR n person who gives a legacy or makes a bequest

LEGATORS > LEGATOR

LEGATOS > LEGATO

LEGEND n traditional story or myth

LEGENDARY adj famous

LEGENDISE same as > LEGENDIZE

LEGENDIST n writer of legends

LEGENDIZE vb make into legend

LEGENDRY > LEGEND

LEGENDS > LEGEND

LEGER variant of > LEDGER

LEGERING > LEGER

LEGERINGS > LEGER

LEGERITY n agility

LEGERS > LEGER

LEGES > LEX

LEGGE vb lighten or lessen

LEGGED > LEG

LEGGER n man who moves barge through tunnel using legs

LEGGERS > LEGGER

LEGGES > LEGGE

LEGGIE n (in Cricket) leg spin bowler

LEGGIER > LEGGY

LEGGIES > LEGGIE

LEGGIEST > LEGGY

LEGGIN same as > LEGGING

LEGGINESS > LEGGY

LEGGING n extra outer covering for the lower leg

LEGGINGED > LEGGING

LEGGINGS > LEGGING

LEGGINS > LEGGIN

LEGGISM n blacklegging

LEGGISMS > LEGGISM

LEGGY adj having long legs

LEGHORN n type of Italian wheat straw that is woven into hats

LEGHORNS > LEGHORN

LEGIBLE adj easily read

LEGIBLY > LEGIBLE

LEGION n large military force ▷ adj very large or numerous

LEGIONARY adj of or relating to a legion ▷ n soldier belonging to a legion

LEGIONED adj arranged in legions

LEGIONS > LEGION

LEGISLATE vb make laws

LEGIST n person versed in the law

LEGISTS > LEGIST

LEGIT n legitimate or professionally respectable drama ▷ adj legitimate

LEGITIM n amount of inheritance due to children from father

LEGITIMS > LEGITIM

LEGITS > LEGIT

LEGLAN same as > LEGLIN

LEGLANS > LEGLAN

LEGLEN same as > LEGLIN

LEGLENS > LEGLEN

LEGLESS adj without legs

LEGLET n jewellery worn around the leg

LEGLETS > LEGLET

LEGLIKE > LEG

LEGLIN n milk-pail

LEGLINS > LEGLIN

LEGMAN n newsman who reports on news stories from the scene of action or original source

LEGMEN > LEGMAN

LEGONG n Indonesian dance

LEGONGS > LEGONG

LEGROOM n space to move one's legs comfortably, as in a car

LEGROOMS > LEGROOM

LEGS > LEG

LEGSIDE n part of a cricket field to the left of a right-handed batsman as he faces the bowler

LEGSIDES > LEGSIDE

LEGUAAN n large S African lizard

LEGUAANS > LEGUAAN

LEGUAN same as > LEGUAAN

LEGUANS > LEGUAN

LEGUME n pod of a plant of the pea or bean family

LEGUMES > LEGUME

LEGUMIN n protein obtained mainly from the seeds of leguminous plants

LEGUMINS > LEGUMIN

LEGWARMER n one of a pair of garments resembling stockings without feet

LEGWEAR n clothing worn on the legs

LEGWEARS > LEGWEAR

LEGWORK n work that involves travelling on foot or as if on foot

LEGWORKS > LEGWORK

LEHAIM same as > LECHAIM

LEHAIMS > LEHAIM

LEHAYIM same as > LEHAIM

LEHAYIMS > LEHAYIM

LEHR n long tunnel-shaped oven used for annealing glass

LEHRJAHRE n apprenticeship

LEHRS > LEHR

LEHUA n flower of Hawaii

LEHUAS > LEHUA

LEI > LEU

LEIDGER same as > LEDGER

LEIDGERS > LEIDGER

LEIGER same as > LEDGER

LEIGERS > LEIGER

LEIOMYOMA same as > FIBROID

LEIPOA n Australian bird

LEIPOAS > LEIPOA

LEIR same as > LEAR

LEIRED > LEIR

LEIRING > LEIR

LEIRS > LEIR

LEIS > LEU

LEISH adj agile

LEISHER > LEISH

LEISHEST > LEISH

LEISLER n small bat

LEISLERS > LEISLER

LEISTER n spear with three or more prongs for spearing fish, esp salmon ▷ vb spear (a fish) with a leister

LEISTERED > LEISTER

LEISTERS > LEISTER

LEISURE n time for relaxation or hobbies ▷ vb have leisure

LEISURED > LEISURE

LEISURELY adj deliberate, unhurried ▷ adv slowly

LEISURES > LEISURE

LEISURING > LEISURE

LEITMOTIF n recurring theme associated with a person, situation, or thought

LEITMOTIV same as > LEITMOTIF

LEK n area where birds gather for sexual display and courtship ▷ vb (of birds) gather at lek

LEKE old form of > LEAK

LEKGOTLA n meeting place for village assemblies, court cases, and meetings of village leaders

LEKGOTLAS > LEKGOTLA

LEKKED > LEK

LEKKER adj attractive or nice

LEKKING > LEK

LEKKINGS > LEK

LEKS > LEK

LEKU > LEK

LEKVAR n prune or apricot pie filling

LEKVARS > LEKVAR

LEKYTHI > LEKYTHOS

LEKYTHOI > LEKYTHOS

LEKYTHOS n Greek flask

LEKYTHUS same as > LEKYTHOS

LEMAN n beloved

LEMANS > LEMAN

LEME same as > LEAM

LEMED > LEME

LEMEL n metal filings

LEMELS > LEMEL

LEMES > LEME

LEMING > LEME

LEMMA n subsidiary proposition, proved for use in the proof of another proposition

LEMMAS > LEMMA

LEMMATA > LEMMA

LEMMATISE same as > LEMMATIZE

LEMMATIZE vb group together the inflected forms of (a word) for analysis as a single item

LEMMING n rodent of arctic regions, reputed to run into the sea and drown during mass migrations

LEMMINGS > LEMMING

LEMNISCAL adj relating to a type of closed plane curve

LEMNISCI > LEMNISCUS

LEMNISCUS technical name for > FILLET

LEMON n yellow oval fruit that grows on trees ▷ adj pale-yellow ▷ vb flavour with lemon

LEMONADE n lemon-flavoured soft drink, often fizzy

LEMONADES > LEMONADE

LEMONED > LEMON
LEMONFISH n type of game fish
LEMONIER > LEMONY
LEMONIEST > LEMONY
LEMONING > LEMON
LEMONISH > LEMON
LEMONLIKE > LEMON
LEMONS > LEMON
LEMONWOOD n small tree of New Zealand
LEMONY adj having or resembling the taste or colour of a lemon
LEMPIRA n standard monetary unit of Honduras, divided into 100 centavos
LEMPIRAS > LEMPIRA
LEMUR n nocturnal animal like a small monkey, found in Madagascar
LEMURES npl spirits of the dead
LEMURIAN same as > LEMUROID
LEMURIANS > LEMURIAN
LEMURINE same as > LEMUROID
LEMURINES > LEMURINE
LEMURLIKE > LEMUR
LEMUROID adj of, relating to, or belonging to the superfamily which includes the lemurs and indrises ▷ n animal that resembles or is closely related to a lemur
LEMUROIDS > LEMUROID
LEMURS > LEMUR
LEND vb give the temporary use of
LENDABLE > LEND
LENDER > LEND
LENDERS > LEND
LENDING > LEND
LENDINGS > LEND
LENDS > LEND
LENES > LENIS
LENG vb linger ▷ adj long
LENGED > LENG
LENGER > LENG
LENGEST > LENG
LENGING > LENG
LENGS > LENG
LENGTH n extent or measurement from end to end
LENGTHEN vb make or become longer
LENGTHENS > LENGTHEN
LENGTHFUL > LENGTH
LENGTHIER > LENGTHY
LENGTHILY > LENGTHY
LENGTHMAN n person whose job it is to maintain a particular length of road or railway line
LENGTHMEN > LENGTHMAN
LENGTHS > LENGTH
LENGTHY adj very long or tiresome
LENIENCE > LENIENT
LENIENCES > LENIENT

LENIENCY > LENIENT
LENIENT adj tolerant, not strict or severe ▷ n lenient person
LENIENTLY > LENIENT
LENIENTS > LENIENT
LENIFIED > LENIFY
LENIFIES > LENIFY
LENIFY vb make lenient
LENIFYING > LENIFY
LENIS adj (of a consonant) pronounced with little muscular tension ▷ n consonant pronounced like this
LENITE vb undergo lenition
LENITED > LENITE
LENITES > LENITE
LENITIES > LENITY
LENITING > LENITE
LENITION n weakening of consonant sound
LENITIONS > LENITION
LENITIVE adj soothing or alleviating of pain or distress ▷ n lenitive drug
LENITIVES > LENITIVE
LENITY n mercy or clemency
LENO n (in textiles) a weave in which the warp yarns are twisted together in pairs between the weft or filling yarns
LENOS > LENO
LENS n piece of glass or similar material with one or both sides curved, used to bring together or spread light rays in cameras, spectacles, telescopes, etc
LENSE same as > LENS
LENSED adj incorporating a lens
LENSES > LENS
LENSING n materials which colour and diffuse light
LENSLESS > LENS
LENSMAN n camera operator
LENSMEN > LENSMAN
LENT > LEND
LENTANDO adv slowing down
LENTEN adj of or relating to Lent
LENTI > LENTO
LENTIC adj of, relating to, or inhabiting still water
LENTICEL n any of numerous pores in the stem of a woody plant
LENTICELS > LENTICEL
LENTICLE n lens-shaped layer of mineral or rock embedded in a matrix of different constitution
LENTICLES > LENTICLE
LENTICULE n small lentil
LENTIFORM adj shaped like a biconvex lens
LENTIGO technical name for a > FRECKLE

LENTIL n edible seed of a leguminous Asian plant
LENTILS > LENTIL
LENTISC same as > LENTISK
LENTISCS > LENTISC
LENTISK n mastic tree
LENTISKS > LENTISK
LENTO adv slowly ▷ n movement or passage performed slowly
LENTOID adj lentiform ▷ n lentiform object
LENTOIDS > LENTOID
LENTOR n lethargy
LENTORS > LENTOR
LENTOS > LENTO
LENTOUS adj lethargic
LENVOY another word for > ENVOY
LENVOYS > LENVOY
LEONE n standard monetary unit of Sierra Leone, divided into 100 cents
LEONES > LEONE
LEONINE adj like a lion
LEOPARD n large spotted carnivorous animal of the cat family
LEOPARDS > LEOPARD
LEOTARD n tight-fitting garment covering the upper body, worn for dancing or exercise
LEOTARDED adj wearing a leotard
LEOTARDS > LEOTARD
LEP dialect word for > LEAP
LEPER n person suffering from leprosy
LEPERS > LEPER
LEPID adj amusing
LEPIDOTE adj covered with scales, scaly leaves, or spots ▷ n lepidote person, creature, or thing
LEPIDOTES > LEPIDOTE
LEPORID adj of, relating to, or belonging to the family of mammals that includes rabbits and hares ▷ n any animal belonging to this family
LEPORIDAE > LEPORID
LEPORIDS > LEPORID
LEPORINE adj of, relating to, or resembling a hare
LEPPED > LEP
LEPPING > LEP
LEPRA n leprosy
LEPRAS > LEPRA
LEPROSE adj having or denoting a whitish scurfy surface
LEPROSERY n hospital for leprosy sufferers
LEPROSIES > LEPROSY
LEPROSITY n state of being leprous
LEPROSY n disease attacking the nerves and skin, resulting in loss of feeling in the affected parts

LEPROTIC adj relating to leprosy
LEPROUS adj having leprosy
LEPROUSLY > LEPROUS
LEPS > LEP
LEPT > LEAP
LEPTA > LEPTON
LEPTIN n protein, produced by fat cells in the body, that acts on the brain to regulate the amount of additional fat laid down in the body
LEPTINS > LEPTIN
LEPTOME n tissue of plant conducting food
LEPTOMES > LEPTOME
LEPTON n any of a group of elementary particles with weak interactions
LEPTONIC > LEPTON
LEPTONS > LEPTON
LEPTOPHOS n type of pesticide
LEPTOSOME n person with a small bodily frame and a slender physique
LEPTOTENE n (in reproduction) early stage in cell division
LEQUEAR same as > LACUNAR
LEQUEARS > LEQUEAR
LERE same as > LEAR
LERED > LERE
LERES > LERE
LERING > LERE
LERP n crystallized honeydew
LERPS > LERP
LES short form of > LESBIAN
LESBIAN n homosexual woman ▷ adj of homosexual women
LESBIANS > LESBIAN
LESBIC adj relating to lesbians
LESBO n lesbian
LESBOS > LESBO
LESES > LES
LESION n structural change in an organ of the body caused by illness or injury ▷ vb cause lesions
LESIONED > LESION
LESIONING > LESION
LESIONS > LESION
LESPEDEZA n bush clover
LESS n smaller amount ▷ adj smaller in extent, degree, or duration ▷ pron smaller part or quantity ▷ adv smaller extent or degree ▷ prep after deducting, minus
LESSEE n person to whom a lease is granted
LESSEES > LESSEE
LESSEN vb make or become smaller or not as much
LESSENED > LESSEN
LESSENING > LESSEN
LESSENS > LESSEN

LESSER *adj* not as great in quantity, size, or worth
LESSES > LESS
LESSON *n* class or single period of instruction in a subject ▷ *vb* censure or punish
LESSONED > LESSON
LESSONING > LESSON
LESSONS > LESSON
LESSOR *n* person who grants a lease of property
LESSORS > LESSOR
LEST *conj* so as to prevent any possibility that ▷ *vb* listen
LESTED > LEST
LESTING > LEST
LESTS > LEST
LET *n* act of letting property ▷ *vb* obstruct
LETCH *same as* > LECH
LETCHED > LETCH
LETCHES > LETCH
LETCHING > LETCH
LETCHINGS > LETCH
LETDOWN *n* disappointment
LETDOWNS > LETDOWN
LETHAL *adj* deadly ▷ *n* weapon, etc capable of causing death
LETHALITY > LETHAL
LETHALLY > LETHAL
LETHALS > LETHAL
LETHARGIC > LETHARGY
LETHARGY *n* sluggishness or dullness
LETHE *n* forgetfulness
LETHEAN > LETHE
LETHEE *n* life-blood
LETHEES > LETHEE
LETHES > LETHE
LETHIED *adj* forgetful
LETS > LET
LETTABLE > LET
LETTED > LET
LETTER *n* written message, usu sent by post ▷ *vb* inscribe letters on
LETTERBOX *n* slot through which letters are delivered into a building
LETTERED *adj* learned
LETTERER > LETTER
LETTERERS > LETTER
LETTERING *n* act, art, or technique of inscribing letters on to something
LETTERMAN *n* successful college sportsman
LETTERMEN > LETTERMAN
LETTERN *another word for* > LECTERN
LETTERNS > LETTERN
LETTERS *npl* literary knowledge or ability
LETTERSET *n* method of rotary printing in which ink is transferred from raised surfaces to paper via a rubber-covered cylinder
LETTING > LET

LETTINGS > LET
LETTRE *n* letter
LETTRES > LETTRE
LETTUCE *n* plant with large green leaves used in salads
LETTUCES > LETTUCE
LETUP *n* lessening or abatement
LETUPS > LETUP
LEU *n* standard monetary unit of Romania and Moldova, divided into 100 bani
LEUCAEMIA *same as* > LEUKAEMIA
LEUCAEMIC > LEUCAEMIA
LEUCEMIA *same as* > LEUKAEMIA
LEUCEMIAS > LEUCEMIA
LEUCEMIC > LEUCEMIA
LEUCH > LAUCH
LEUCHEN > LAUCH
LEUCIN *same as* > LEUCINE
LEUCINE *n* essential amino acid found in many proteins
LEUCINES > LEUCINE
LEUCINS > LEUCIN
LEUCISTIC *adj* having reduced pigmentation in the skin but normally-coloured eyes
LEUCITE *n* grey or white mineral consisting of potassium aluminium silicate
LEUCITES > LEUCITE
LEUCITIC > LEUCITE
LEUCO *as in leuco base* colourless compound formed by reducing a dye
LEUCOCYTE *n* white blood cell
LEUCOMA *n* white opaque scar of the cornea
LEUCOMAS > LEUCOMA
LEUCOSIN *n* albumin in cereal grains
LEUCOSINS > LEUCOSIN
LEUCOTOME *n* needle used in leucotomy
LEUCOTOMY *n* surgical operation of cutting some of the nerve fibres in the frontal lobes of the brain
LEUD *Scots word for* > BREADTH
LEUDES > LEUD
LEUDS > LEUD
LEUGH > LAUCH
LEUGHEN > LAUCH
LEUKAEMIA *n* disease caused by uncontrolled overproduction of white blood cells
LEUKEMIA *same as* > LEUKAEMIA
LEUKEMIAS > LEUKEMIA
LEUKEMIC > LEUKEMIA
LEUKEMICS > LEUKEMIA
LEUKEMOID *adj* resembling leukaemia

LEUKOCYTE *same as* > LEUCOCYTE
LEUKOMA *same as* > LEUCOMA
LEUKOMAS > LEUKOMA
LEUKON *n* white blood cell count
LEUKONS > LEUKON
LEUKOSES > LEUKOSIS
LEUKOSIS *n* abnormal growth of white blood cells
LEUKOTIC > LEUKOSIS
LEUKOTOMY *n* lobotomy
LEV *n* standard monetary unit of Bulgaria, divided into 100 stotinki
LEVA > LEV
LEVANT *n* type of leather made from the skins of goats, sheep, or seals ▷ *vb* bolt or abscond, esp to avoid paying debts
LEVANTED > LEVANT
LEVANTER *n* easterly wind in the W Mediterranean area, esp in the late summer
LEVANTERS > LEVANTER
LEVANTINE *n* cloth of twilled silk
LEVANTING > LEVANT
LEVANTS > LEVANT
LEVATOR *n* any of various muscles that raise a part of the body
LEVATORES > LEVATOR
LEVATORS > LEVATOR
LEVE *adj* darling ▷ *adv* gladly
LEVEE *n* natural or artificial river embankment ▷ *vb* go to the reception of
LEVEED > LEVEE
LEVEEING > LEVEE
LEVEES > LEVEE
LEVEL *adj* horizontal ▷ *vb* make even or horizontal ▷ *n* horizontal line or surface
LEVELED > LEVEL
LEVELER *same as* > LEVELLER
LEVELERS > LEVELER
LEVELING > LEVEL
LEVELLED > LEVEL
LEVELLER *n* person or thing that levels
LEVELLERS > LEVELLER
LEVELLEST > LEVEL
LEVELLING > LEVEL
LEVELLY > LEVEL
LEVELNESS > LEVEL
LEVELS > LEVEL
LEVER *n* handle used to operate machinery ▷ *vb* prise or move with a lever
LEVERAGE *n* action or power of a lever ▷ *vb* borrow capital required
LEVERAGED > LEVERAGE
LEVERAGES > LEVERAGE
LEVERED > LEVER
LEVERET *n* young hare
LEVERETS > LEVERET

LEVERING > LEVER
LEVERS > LEVER
LEVES > LEVE
LEVIABLE *adj* (of taxes, tariffs, etc) liable to be levied
LEVIATHAN *n* sea monster
LEVIED > LEVY
LEVIER > LEVY
LEVIERS > LEVY
LEVIES > LEVY
LEVIGABLE > LEVIGATE
LEVIGATE *vb* grind into a fine powder or a smooth paste ▷ *adj* having a smooth polished surface
LEVIGATED > LEVIGATE
LEVIGATES > LEVIGATE
LEVIGATOR > LEVIGATE
LEVIN *archaic word for* > LIGHTNING
LEVINS > LEVIN
LEVIRATE *n* practice, required by Old Testament law, of marrying the widow of one's brother
LEVIRATES > LEVIRATE
LEVIRATIC > LEVIRATE
LEVIS *n* jeans
LEVITATE *vb* rise or cause to rise into the air
LEVITATED > LEVITATE
LEVITATES > LEVITATE
LEVITATOR > LEVITATE
LEVITE *n* Christian clergyman
LEVITES > LEVITE
LEVITIC > LEVITE
LEVITICAL > LEVITE
LEVITIES > LEVITY
LEVITY *n* inclination to make a joke of serious matters
LEVO *adj* anticlockwise
LEVODOPA *n* substance occurring naturally in the bopy and used to treat Parkinson's disease
LEVODOPAS > LEVODOPA
LEVOGYRE *n* counterclockwise spiral
LEVULIN *n* substance obtained from certain bulbs
LEVULINS > LEVULIN
LEVULOSE *n* fructose
LEVULOSES > LEVULOSE
LEVY *vb* impose and collect (a tax) ▷ *n* imposition or collection of taxes
LEVYING > LEVY
LEW *adj* tepid
LEWD *adj* lustful or indecent
LEWDER > LEWD
LEWDEST > LEWD
LEWDLY > LEWD
LEWDNESS > LEWD
LEWDSBIES > LEWDSBY
LEWDSBY *another word for* > LEWDSTER
LEWDSTER *n* lewd person
LEWDSTERS > LEWDSTER
LEWIS *n* lifting device for heavy stone or concrete blocks

LEWISES > LEWIS
LEWISIA n type of herb
LEWISIAS > LEWISIA
LEWISITE n colourless oily poisonous liquid
LEWISITES > LEWISITE
LEWISSON same as > LEWIS
LEWISSONS > LEWISSON
LEX n system or body of laws
LEXEME n minimal meaningful unit of language, the meaning of which cannot be understood from that of its component morphemes
LEXEMES > LEXEME
LEXEMIC > LEXEME
LEXES > LEX
LEXICA > LEXICON
LEXICAL adj relating to the vocabulary of a language
LEXICALLY > LEXICAL
LEXICON n dictionary
LEXICONS > LEXICON
LEXIGRAM n figure or symbol that represents a word
LEXIGRAMS > LEXIGRAM
LEXIS n totality of vocabulary items in a language, including all forms having lexical meaning or grammatical function
LEXISES > LEXIS
LEY n land temporarily under grass
LEYLANDI same as > LEYLANDII
LEYLANDII n type of fast-growing cypress tree
LEYLANDIS > LEYLANDI
LEYS > LEY
LEZ short form of > LESBIAN
LEZES > LEZ
LEZZ short form of > LESBIAN
LEZZA same as > LEZZIE
LEZZAS > LEZZA
LEZZES > LEZZ
LEZZIE n lesbian
LEZZIES > LEZZIE
LEZZY short form of > LESBIAN
LI n Chinese measurement of distance
LIABILITY n hindrance or disadvantage
LIABLE adj legally obliged or responsible
LIAISE vb establish and maintain communication (with)
LIAISED > LIAISE
LIAISES > LIAISE
LIAISING > LIAISE
LIAISON n communication and contact between groups
LIAISONS > LIAISON
LIANA n climbing plant in tropical forests

LIANAS > LIANA
LIANE same as > LIANA
LIANES > LIANE
LIANG n Chinese unit of weight
LIANGS > LIANG
LIANOID > LIANA
LIAR n person who tells lies
LIARD adj grey ▷ n former small coin of various European countries
LIARDS > LIARD
LIARS > LIAR
LIART Scots form of > LIARD
LIAS n lowest series of rocks of the Jurassic system
LIASES > LIAS
LIATRIS n type of North American plant with small white flowers
LIATRISES > LIATRIS
LIB n informal, sometimes derogatory word for liberation ▷ vb geld
LIBANT adj touching lightly
LIBATE vb offer as gift to the gods
LIBATED > LIBATE
LIBATES > LIBATE
LIBATING > LIBATE
LIBATION n drink poured as an offering to the gods
LIBATIONS > LIBATION
LIBATORY > LIBATE
LIBBARD another word for > LEOPARD
LIBBARDS > LIBBARD
LIBBED > LIB
LIBBER n liberationist
LIBBERS > LIBBER
LIBBING > LIB
LIBECCHIO same as > LIBECCIO
LIBECCIO n strong westerly or southwesterly wind blowing onto the W coast of Corsica
LIBECCIOS > LIBECCIO
LIBEL n published statement falsely damaging a person's reputation ▷ vb falsely damage the reputation of (someone)
LIBELANT same as > LIBELLANT
LIBELANTS > LIBELANT
LIBELED > LIBEL
LIBELEE same as > LIBELLEE
LIBELEES > LIBELEE
LIBELER > LIBEL
LIBELERS > LIBEL
LIBELING > LIBEL
LIBELINGS > LIBEL
LIBELIST > LIBEL
LIBELISTS > LIBEL
LIBELLANT n party who brings an action in the ecclesiastical courts by presenting a libel

LIBELLED > LIBEL
LIBELLEE n person against whom a libel has been filed in an ecclesiastical court
LIBELLEES > LIBELLEE
LIBELLER > LIBEL
LIBELLERS > LIBEL
LIBELLING > LIBEL
LIBELLOUS > LIBEL
LIBELOUS > LIBEL
LIBELS > LIBEL
LIBER n tome or book
LIBERAL adj having social and political views that favour progress and reform ▷ n person who has liberal ideas or opinions
LIBERALLY > LIBERAL
LIBERALS > LIBERAL
LIBERATE vb set free
LIBERATED adj not bound by traditional sexual and social roles
LIBERATES > LIBERATE
LIBERATOR > LIBERATE
LIBERO another name for > SWEEPER
LIBEROS > LIBERO
LIBERS > LIBER
LIBERTIES > LIBERTY
LIBERTINE n morally dissolute person ▷ adj promiscuous and unscrupulous
LIBERTY n freedom
LIBIDINAL > LIBIDO
LIBIDO n psychic energy
LIBIDOS > LIBIDO
LIBKEN n lodging
LIBKENS > LIBKEN
LIBLAB n 19th century British liberal
LIBLABS > LIBLAB
LIBRA n ancient Roman unit of weight corresponding to 1 pound, but equal to about 12 ounces
LIBRAE > LIBRA
LIBRAIRE n bookseller
LIBRAIRES > LIBRAIRE
LIBRAIRIE n bookshop
LIBRARIAN n keeper of or worker in a library
LIBRARIES > LIBRARY
LIBRARY n room or building where books are kept
LIBRAS > LIBRA
LIBRATE vb oscillate or waver
LIBRATED > LIBRATE
LIBRATES > LIBRATE
LIBRATING > LIBRATE
LIBRATION n act or an instance of oscillating
LIBRATORY > LIBRATE
LIBRETTI > LIBRETTO
LIBRETTO n words of an opera
LIBRETTOS > LIBRETTO
LIBRI > LIBER
LIBRIFORM adj (of a fibre

of woody tissue) elongated and having a pitted thickened cell wall
LIBS > LIB
LICE > LOUSE
LICENCE n document giving official permission to do something ▷ vb (in the US) give permission to
LICENCED > LICENCE
LICENCEE same as > LICENSEE
LICENCEES > LICENCEE
LICENCER > LICENCE
LICENCERS > LICENCE
LICENCES > LICENCE
LICENCING > LICENCE
LICENSE vb grant or give a licence for
LICENSED > LICENSE
LICENSEE n holder of a licence, esp to sell alcohol
LICENSEES > LICENSEE
LICENSER > LICENSE
LICENSERS > LICENSE
LICENSES > LICENSE
LICENSING > LICENSE
LICENSOR > LICENSE
LICENSORS > LICENSE
LICENSURE n act of conferring licence
LICENTE adj permitted; allowed
LICH n dead body
LICHANOS n note played using forefinger
LICHEE same as > LITCHI
LICHEES > LICHEE
LICHEN n small flowerless plant forming a crust on rocks, trees, etc ▷ vb cover with lichen
LICHENED > LICHEN
LICHENIN n complex polysaccharide occurring in certain species of moss
LICHENING > LICHEN
LICHENINS > LICHENIN
LICHENISM n an association of fungus and alga as lichen
LICHENIST n person who studies lichens
LICHENOID > LICHEN
LICHENOSE > LICHEN
LICHENOUS > LICHEN
LICHENS > LICHEN
LICHES > LICH
LICHGATE n roofed gate to a churchyard
LICHGATES > LICHGATE
LICHI same as > LITCHI
LICHIS > LICHI
LICHT Scot word for > LIGHT
LICHTED > LICHT
LICHTER > LICHT
LICHTEST > LICHT
LICHTING > LICHT
LICHTLIED > LICHTLY
LICHTLIES > LICHTLY
LICHTLY vb treat discourteously
LICHTS > LICHT

LICHWAKE n night vigil over a dead body

LICHWAKES > LICHWAKE

LICHWAY n path used to carry coffin into church

LICHWAYS > LICHWAY

LICIT adj lawful, permitted

LICITLY > LICIT

LICITNESS > LICIT

LICK vb pass the tongue over ▷ n licking

LICKED > LICK

LICKER > LICK

LICKERISH adj lecherous or lustful

LICKERS > LICK

LICKING n beating

LICKINGS > LICKING

LICKPENNY n something that uses up large amounts of money

LICKS > LICK

LICKSPIT n flattering or servile person

LICKSPITS > LICKSPIT

LICORICE same as > LIQUORICE

LICORICES > LICORICE

LICTOR n one of a group of ancient Roman officials

LICTORIAN > LICTOR

LICTORS > LICTOR

LID n movable cover

LIDAR n radar-type instrument

LIDARS > LIDAR

LIDDED > LID

LIDDING n lids

LIDGER variant form of > LEDGER

LIDGERS > LEDGER

LIDLESS adj having no lid or top

LIDO n open-air centre for swimming and water sports

LIDOCAINE n powerful local anaesthetic administered by injection

LIDOS > LIDO

LIDS > LID

LIE vb make a deliberately false statement ▷ n deliberate falsehood

LIED n setting for solo voice and piano of a poem

LIEDER > LIED

LIEF adv gladly ▷ adj ready ▷ n beloved person

LIEFER > LIEF

LIEFEST > LIEF

LIEFLY > LIEF

LIEFS > LIEF

LIEGE adj bound to give or receive feudal service ▷ n lord

LIEGEDOM > LIEGE

LIEGEDOMS > LIEGE

LIEGELESS > LIEGE

LIEGEMAN n (formerly) the subject of a sovereign or feudal lord

LIEGEMEN > LIEGEMAN

LIEGER same as > LEDGER

LIEGERS > LIEGER

LIEGES > LIEGE

LIEN n right to hold another's property until a debt is paid

LIENABLE adj that can be subject of a lien

LIENAL adj of or relating to the spleen

LIENS > LIEN

LIENTERIC > LIENTERY

LIENTERY n passage of undigested food in the faeces

LIER n person who lies down

LIERNE n short secondary rib that connects the intersections of the primary ribs, esp as used in Gothic vaulting

LIERNES > LIERNE

LIERS > LIER

LIES > LIE

LIEU n stead

LIEUS > LIEU

LIEVE same as > LEVE

LIEVER > LIEVE

LIEVES > LIEVE

LIEVEST > LIEVE

LIFE n state of living beings, characterized by growth, reproduction, and response to stimuli

LIFEBELT n ring filled with air, used to keep a person afloat when in danger of drowning

LIFEBELTS > LIFEBELT

LIFEBLOOD n blood vital to life

LIFEBOAT n boat used for rescuing people at sea

LIFEBOATS > LIFEBOAT

LIFEBUOY n any of various kinds of buoyant device for keeping people afloat

LIFEBUOYS > LIFEBUOY

LIFECARE n care of person's health and welfare

LIFECARES > LIFECARE

LIFEFUL adj full of life

LIFEGUARD n person who saves people from drowning ▷ vb work as lifeguard

LIFEHACK n action that simplifies a task or reduces frustration in everyday life

LIFEHACKS > LIFEHACK

LIFEHOLD adj (of land) held while one is alive

LIFELESS adj dead

LIFELIKE adj closely resembling or representing life

LIFELINE n means of contact or support

LIFELINES > LIFELINE

LIFELONG adj lasting all of a person's life

LIFER n prisoner sentenced to imprisonment for life

LIFERS > LIFER

LIFES as in still lifes paintings or drawings of inanimate objects

LIFESAVER n saver of a person's life

LIFESOME adj full of life

LIFESPAN n period of time during which a person or animal may be expected to live

LIFESPANS > LIFESPAN

LIFESTYLE n particular attitudes, habits, etc ▷ adj suggestive of a fashionable or desirable lifestyle

LIFETIME n length of time a person is alive

LIFETIMES > LIFETIME

LIFEWAY n way of life

LIFEWAYS > LIFEWAY

LIFEWORK n work to which a person has devoted their life

LIFEWORKS > LIFEWORK

LIFEWORLD n way individual experiences world

LIFT vb move upwards in position, status, volume, etc ▷ n cage raised and lowered in a vertical shaft to transport people or goods

LIFTABLE > LIFT

LIFTBACK n hatchback

LIFTBACKS > LIFTBACK

LIFTBOY n person who operates a lift, esp in large public or commercial buildings and hotels

LIFTBOYS > LIFTBOY

LIFTED > LIFT

LIFTER > LIFT

LIFTERS > LIFT

LIFTGATE n rear opening of hatchback

LIFTGATES > LIFTGATE

LIFTING > LIFT

LIFTMAN same as > LIFTBOY

LIFTMEN > LIFTMAN

LIFTOFF n moment a rocket leaves the ground ▷ vb (of a rocket) to leave its launch pad

LIFTOFFS > LIFTOFF

LIFTS > LIFT

LIFULL obsolete form of > LIFEFUL

LIG n (esp in the media) a function with free entertainment and refreshments ▷ vb attend such a function

LIGAMENT n band of tissue joining bones

LIGAMENTS > LIGAMENT

LIGAN same as > LAGAN

LIGAND n atom, molecule, radical, or ion forming a complex with a central atom

LIGANDS > LIGAND

LIGANS > LIGAN

LIGASE n any of a class of enzymes

LIGASES > LIGASE

LIGATE vb tie up or constrict (something) with a ligature

LIGATED > LIGATE

LIGATES > LIGATE

LIGATING > LIGATE

LIGATION > LIGATE

LIGATIONS > LIGATE

LIGATIVE > LIGATE

LIGATURE n link, bond, or tie ▷ vb bind with a ligature

LIGATURED > LIGATURE

LIGATURES > LIGATURE

LIGER n hybrid offspring of a female tiger and a male lion

LIGERS > LIGER

LIGGE obsolete form of > LIE

LIGGED > LIG

LIGGER > LIG

LIGGERS > LIG

LIGGES > LIGGE

LIGGING > LIG

LIGGINGS > LIG

LIGHT n electromagnetic radiation by which things are visible ▷ adj bright ▷ vb ignite ▷ adv with little equipment or luggage

LIGHTBULB n glass bulb containing gas that emits light when a current is passed through it

LIGHTED > LIGHT

LIGHTEN vb make less dark

LIGHTENED > LIGHTEN

LIGHTENER > LIGHTEN

LIGHTENS > LIGHTEN

LIGHTER n device for lighting cigarettes etc ▷ vb convey in a type of flat-bottomed barge

LIGHTERED > LIGHTER

LIGHTERS > LIGHTER

LIGHTEST > LIGHT

LIGHTFACE n weight of type in printing

LIGHTFAST adj (of a dye) unaffected by light

LIGHTFUL adj full of light

LIGHTING > LIGHT

LIGHTINGS > LIGHT

LIGHTISH > LIGHT

LIGHTLESS > LIGHT

LIGHTLIED > LIGHTLY

LIGHTLIES > LIGHTLY

LIGHTLY adv in a light way ▷ vb belittle

LIGHTNESS n quality of being light

LIGHTNING n visible discharge of electricity in the atmosphere ▷ adj fast and sudden

LIGHTS > LIGHT

LIGHTSHIP n moored ship used as a lighthouse

LIGHTSOME adj lighthearted

LIGHTWAVE adj using light waves

LIGHTWOOD n Australian acacia

LIGNAGE another word for > LINEAGE

LIGNAGES > LIGNAGE

LIGNALOES another name for > EAGLEWOOD

LIGNAN n beneficial substance found in plants

LIGNANS > LIGNAN

LIGNE n unit of measurement

LIGNEOUS adj of or like wood

LIGNES > LIGNE

LIGNICOLE adj growing or living in wood

LIGNIFIED > LIGNIFY

LIGNIFIES > LIGNIFY

LIGNIFORM adj having the appearance of wood

LIGNIFY vb make or become woody as a result of the deposition of lignin in the cell walls

LIGNIN n complex polymer occurring in certain plant cell walls making the plant rigid

LIGNINS > LIGNIN

LIGNITE n woody textured rock used as fuel

LIGNITES > LIGNITE

LIGNITIC > LIGNITE

LIGNOSE n explosive compound

LIGNOSES > LIGNOSE

LIGNUM n wood

LIGNUMS > LIGNUM

LIGROIN n volatile fraction of petroleum that is used as a solvent

LIGROINE same as > LIGROIN

LIGROINES > LIGROINE

LIGROINS > LIGROIN

LIGS > LIG

LIGULA same as > LIGULE

LIGULAE > LIGULA

LIGULAR > LIGULA

LIGULAS > LIGULA

LIGULATE adj having the shape of a strap

LIGULATED same as > LIGULATE

LIGULE n membranous outgrowth at the junction between the leaf blade and sheath in many grasses and sedges

LIGULES > LIGULE

LIGULOID > LIGULA

LIGURE n any of the 12 precious stones used in the breastplates of high priests

LIGURES > LIGURE

LIKABLE adj easy to like

LIKABLY > LIKABLE

LIKE adj similar ▷ vb find enjoyable ▷ n favourable feeling, desire, or preference

LIKEABLE same as > LIKABLE

LIKEABLY same as

> LIKABLY

LIKED > LIKE

LIKELIER > LIKELY

LIKELIEST > LIKELY

LIKELY adj tending or inclined ▷ adv probably

LIKEN vb compare

LIKENED > LIKEN

LIKENESS n resemblance

LIKENING > LIKEN

LIKENS > LIKEN

LIKER > LIKE

LIKERS > LIKE

LIKES > LIKE

LIKEST > LIKE

LIKEWAKE same as > LYKEWAKE

LIKEWAKES > LIKEWAKE

LIKEWALK same as > LYKEWAKE

LIKEWALKS > LIKEWALK

LIKEWISE adv similarly

LIKIN n historically, Chinese tax

LIKING n fondness

LIKINGS > LIKING

LIKINS > LIKIN

LIKUTA n (formerly) a coin used in Zaire

LILAC n shrub with pale mauve or white flowers ▷ adj light-purple

LILACS > LILAC

LILANGENI n standard monetary unit of Swaziland, divided into 100 cents

LILIED adj decorated with lilies

LILIES > LILY

LILL obsolete form of > LOLL

LILLED > LILL

LILLING > LILL

LILLIPUT adj tiny ▷ n tiny person or being

LILLIPUTS > LILLIPUT

LILLS > LILL

LILO n trademark for a type of inflatable plastic mattress

LILOS > LILO

LILT n pleasing musical quality in speaking ▷ vb speak with a lilt

LILTED > LILT

LILTING > LILT

LILTINGLY > LILT

LILTS > LILT

LILY n plant which grows from a bulb and has large, often white, flowers

LILYLIKE adj resembling a lily

LIMA n type of edible bean

LIMACEL n small shell inside some kinds of slug

LIMACELS > LIMACEL

LIMACEOUS adj relating to the slug

LIMACES > LIMAX

LIMACINE adj relating to slugs

LIMACON n heart-shaped curve

LIMACONS > LIMACON

LIMAIL same as > LEMEL

LIMAILS > LIMAIL

LIMAN n lagoon

LIMANS > LIMAN

LIMAS > LIMA

LIMATION n polishing

LIMATIONS > LIMATION

LIMAX n slug

LIMB n arm, leg, or wing ▷ vb dismember

LIMBA n type of African tree

LIMBAS > LIMBA

LIMBATE adj having an edge or border of a different colour from the rest

LIMBEC obsolete form of > ALEMBIC

LIMBECK obsolete form of > ALEMBIC

LIMBECKS > LIMBECK

LIMBECS > LIMBEC

LIMBED > LIMB

LIMBER vb loosen stiff muscles by exercising ▷ adj pliant or supple ▷ n part of a gun carriage, consisting of an axle, pole, and two wheels

LIMBERED > LIMBER

LIMBERER > LIMBER

LIMBEREST > LIMBER

LIMBERING > LIMBER

LIMBERLY > LIMBER

LIMBERS > LIMBER

LIMBI > LIMBUS

LIMBIC > LIMBUS

LIMBIER > LIMBY

LIMBIEST > LIMBY

LIMBING > LIMB

LIMBLESS > LIMB

LIMBMEAL adv piece by piece

LIMBO n supposed region intermediate between Heaven and Hell for the unbaptized

LIMBOS > LIMBO

LIMBOUS adj with overlapping edges

LIMBS > LIMB

LIMBUS n border

LIMBUSES > LIMBUS

LIMBY adj with long legs, stem, branches, etc

LIME n calcium compound used as a fertilizer or in making cement ▷ vb spread a calcium compound upon (land) ▷ adj having the flavour of lime fruit

LIMEADE n drink made from sweetened lime juice and plain or carbonated water

LIMEADES > LIMEADE

LIMED > LIME

LIMEKILN n kiln in which calcium carbonate is burned to produce quicklime

LIMEKILNS > LIMEKILN

LIMELESS > LIME

LIMELIGHT n glare of publicity ▷ vb illuminate with limelight

LIMELIT > LIMELIGHT

LIMEN another term for > THRESHOLD

LIMENS > LIMEN

LIMEPIT n pit containing lime in which hides are placed to remove the hair

LIMEPITS > LIMEPIT

LIMERICK n humorous verse of five lines

LIMERICKS > LIMERICK

LIMES n fortified boundary of the Roman Empire

LIMESCALE n flaky deposit left in containers such as kettles by the action of heat on water containing calcium salts

LIMESTONE n sedimentary rock used in building

LIMEWASH n mixture of lime and water used to whitewash walls, ceilings, etc

LIMEWATER n clear colourless solution of calcium hydroxide in water

LIMEY n British person ▷ adj British

LIMEYS > LIMEY

LIMIER > LIMY

LIMIEST > LIMY

LIMINA > LIMEN

LIMINAL adj relating to the point (or threshold) beyond which a sensation becomes too faint to be experienced

LIMINESS > LIMY

LIMING > LIME

LIMINGS > LIME

LIMIT n ultimate extent, degree, or amount of something ▷ vb restrict or confine

LIMITABLE > LIMIT

LIMITARY adj of, involving, or serving as a limit

LIMITED adj having a limit ▷ n limited train, bus, etc

LIMITEDLY > LIMITED

LIMITEDS > LIMITED

LIMITER n electronic circuit that produces an output signal whose positive or negative amplitude, or both, is limited to some predetermined value above which the peaks become flattened

LIMITERS > LIMITER

LIMITES > LIMES

LIMITING > LIMIT

LIMITINGS > LIMIT

LIMITLESS > LIMIT

LIMITS > LIMIT

LIMMA n semitone

LIMMAS > LIMMA

LIMMER n scoundrel
LIMMERS > LIMMER
LIMN vb represent in drawing or painting
LIMNAEID n type of snail
LIMNAEIDS > LIMNAEID
LIMNED > LIMN
LIMNER > LIMN
LIMNERS > LIMN
LIMNETIC adj of, relating to, or inhabiting the open water of lakes down to the depth of light penetration
LIMNIC adj relating to lakes
LIMNING > LIMN
LIMNOLOGY n study of bodies of fresh water with reference to their plant and animal life, physical properties, geographical features, etc
LIMNS > LIMN
LIMO short for > LIMOUSINE
LIMONENE n liquid optically active terpene with a lemon-like odour
LIMONENES > LIMONENE
LIMONITE n common brown, black, or yellow amorphous secondary mineral
LIMONITES > LIMONITE
LIMONITIC > LIMONITE
LIMOS > LIMO
LIMOSES > LIMOSIS
LIMOSIS n excessive hunger
LIMOUS adj muddy
LIMOUSINE n large luxurious car
LIMP vb walk with an uneven step ▷ n limping walk ▷ adj without firmness or stiffness
LIMPA n type of rye bread
LIMPAS > LIMPA
LIMPED > LIMP
LIMPER > LIMP
LIMPERS > LIMP
LIMPEST > LIMP
LIMPET n shellfish which sticks tightly to rocks ▷ adj denoting certain weapons that are magnetically attached to their targets and resist removal
LIMPETS > LIMPET
LIMPID adj clear or transparent
LIMPIDITY > LIMPID
LIMPIDLY > LIMPID
LIMPING > LIMP
LIMPINGLY > LIMP
LIMPINGS > LIMP
LIMPKIN n rail-like wading bird
LIMPKINS > LIMPKIN
LIMPLY > LIMP
LIMPNESS > LIMP
LIMPS > LIMP
LIMPSEY same as > LIMPSY
LIMPSIER > LIMPSY

LIMPSIEST > LIMPSY
LIMPSY adj limp
LIMULI > LIMULUS
LIMULOID n type of crab
LIMULOIDS > LIMULOID
LIMULUS n type of horseshoe crab
LIMULUSES > LIMULUS
LIMY adj of, like, or smeared with birdlime
LIN vb cease
LINABLE > LINE
LINAC n linear accelerator
LINACS > LINAC
LINAGE n number of lines in written or printed matter
LINAGES > LINAGE
LINALOL same as > LINALOOL
LINALOLS > LINALOL
LINALOOL n optically active colourless fragrant liquid
LINALOOLS > LINALOOL
LINCH n ledge
LINCHES > LINCH
LINCHET another word for > LINCH
LINCHETS > LINCHET
LINCHPIN n pin to hold a wheel on its axle
LINCHPINS > LINCHPIN
LINCRUSTA n type of wallpaper having a hard embossed surface
LINCTURE n medicine taken by licking
LINCTURES > LINCTURE
LINCTUS n syrupy cough medicine
LINCTUSES > LINCTUS
LIND variant of > LINDEN
LINDANE n white poisonous crystalline powder
LINDANES > LINDANE
LINDEN n large tree with heart-shaped leaves and fragrant yellowish flowers
LINDENS > LINDEN
LINDIES > LINDY
LINDS > LIND
LINDWORM n wingless serpent-like dragon
LINDWORMS > LINDWORM
LINDY n lively dance
LINE n long narrow mark ▷ vb mark with lines
LINEABLE > LINE
LINEAGE n descent from an ancestor
LINEAGES > LINEAGE
LINEAL adj in direct line of descent
LINEALITY > LINEAL
LINEALLY > LINEAL
LINEAMENT n facial feature
LINEAR adj of or in lines
LINEARISE same as > LINEARIZE
LINEARITY > LINEAR
LINEARIZE vb make linear

LINEARLY > LINEAR
LINEATE adj marked with lines
LINEATED same as > LINEATE
LINEATION n act of marking with lines
LINEBRED adj having an ancestor that is common to sire and dam
LINECUT n method of relief printing
LINECUTS > LINECUT
LINED > LINE
LINELESS > LINE
LINELIKE > LINE
LINEMAN same as > LINESMAN
LINEMEN > LINEMAN
LINEN n cloth or thread made from flax
LINENS > LINEN
LINENY > LINEN
LINEOLATE adj marked with very fine parallel lines
LINER n large passenger ship or aircraft
LINERLESS adj having no lining
LINERS > LINER
LINES > LINE
LINESMAN n (in some sports) an official who helps the referee or umpire
LINESMEN > LINESMAN
LINEUP n row or arrangement of people or things
LINEUPS > LINEUP
LINEY > LINE
LING n slender food fish
LINGA same as > LINGAM
LINGAM n (in Sanskrit grammar) the masculine gender
LINGAMS > LINGAM
LINGAS > LINGA
LINGBERRY same as > COWBERRY
LINGCOD n type of food fish
LINGCODS > LINGCOD
LINGEL n strong shoemaker's thread
LINGELS > LINGEL
LINGER vb delay or prolong departure
LINGERED > LINGER
LINGERER > LINGER
LINGERERS > LINGER
LINGERIE n women's underwear or nightwear
LINGERIES > LINGERIE
LINGERING > LINGER
LINGERS > LINGER
LINGIER > LINGY
LINGIEST > LINGY
LINGLE same as > LINGEL
LINGLES > LINGLE
LINGO n foreign or unfamiliar language or jargon
LINGOES > LINGO
LINGOT n ingot

LINGOTS > LINGOT
LINGS > LING
LINGSTER n person able to communicate with aliens
LINGSTERS > LINGSTER
LINGUA n any tongue-like structure
LINGUAE > LINGUA
LINGUAL adj of the tongue ▷ n lingual consonant, such as Scots (r)
LINGUALLY > LINGUAL
LINGUALS > LINGUAL
LINGUAS > LINGUA
LINGUICA n Portuguese sausage
LINGUICAS > LINGUICA
LINGUINE n kind of pasta in the shape of thin flat strands
LINGUINES > LINGUINE
LINGUINI same as > LINGUINE
LINGUINIS > LINGUINI
LINGUISA same as > LINGUICA
LINGUISAS > LINGUISA
LINGUIST n person skilled in foreign languages
LINGUISTS > LINGUIST
LINGULA n small tongue
LINGULAE > LINGULA
LINGULAR > LINGULA
LINGULAS > LINGULA
LINGULATE adj shaped like a tongue
LINGY adj heather-covered
LINHAY n farm building with an open front
LINHAYS > LINHAY
LINIER > LINE
LINIEST > LINE
LINIMENT n medicated liquid rubbed on the skin to relieve pain or stiffness
LINIMENTS > LINIMENT
LININ n network of viscous material in the nucleus of a cell that connects the chromatin granules
LINING n layer of cloth attached to the inside of a garment etc
LININGS > LINING
LININS > LININ
LINISH vb polish metal
LINISHED > LINISH
LINISHER > LINISH
LINISHERS > LINISH
LINISHES > LINISH
LINISHING > LINISH
LINK n any of the rings forming a chain ▷ vb connect with or as if with links
LINKABLE > LINK
LINKAGE n act of linking or the state of being linked
LINKAGES > LINKAGE
LINKBOY n (formerly) a boy who carried a torch for pedestrians in dark streets
LINKBOYS > LINKBOY

LINKED > LINK

LINKER *n* person or thing that links

LINKERS > LINKER

LINKIER > LINKY

LINKIEST > LINKY

LINKING > LINK

LINKMAN *same as* > LINKBOY

LINKMEN > LINKMAN

LINKROT *n* state or condition of having expired hyperlinks on a website

LINKROTS > LINKROT

LINKS > LINK

LINKSLAND *n* land near sea used for golf

LINKSMAN *same as* > LINKBOY

LINKSMEN > LINKSMAN

LINKSPAN *n* hinged bridge on a quay, used to move vehicles on or off a vessel

LINKSPANS > LINKSPAN

LINKSTER *n* interpreter

LINKSTERS > LINKSTER

LINKUP *n* establishing of a connection or union between objects, groups, organizations, etc

LINKUPS > LINKUP

LINKWORK *n* something made up of links

LINKWORKS > LINKWORK

LINKY *adj* (of countryside) consisting of links

LINN *n* waterfall or a pool at the foot of it

LINNED > LIN

LINNET *n* songbird of the finch family

LINNETS > LINNET

LINNEY *same as* > LINHAY

LINNEYS > LINNEY

LINNIES > LINNY

LINNING > LIN

LINNS > LINN

LINNY *same as* > LINHAY

LINO *same as* > LINOLEUM

LINOCUT *n* design cut in relief in linoleum mounted on a block of wood

LINOCUTS > LINOCUT

LINOLEATE *n* ester or salt of linoleic acid

LINOLEIC as in *linoleic acid* colourless oily essential fatty acid found in linseed

LINOLENIC as in *linolenic acid* colourless unsaturated essential fatty acid

LINOLEUM *n* type of floor covering

LINOLEUMS > LINOLEUM

LINOS > LINO

LINOTYPE *n* line of metal type produced by machine ▷ *vb* set as line of type

LINOTYPED > LINOTYPE

LINOTYPER > LINOTYPE

LINOTYPES > LINOTYPE

LINS > LIN

LINSANG *n* any of several forest-dwelling viverrine mammals

LINSANGS > LINSANG

LINSEED *n* seed of the flax plant

LINSEEDS > LINSEED

LINSEY *n* type of cloth

LINSEYS > LINSEY

LINSTOCK *n* long staff holding a lighted match, formerly used to fire a cannon

LINSTOCKS > LINSTOCK

LINT *n* shreds of fibre, etc ▷ *vb* shed or remove lint

LINTED *adj* having lint

LINTEL *n* horizontal beam at the top of a door or window

LINTELLED *adj* having a lintel

LINTELS > LINTEL

LINTER *n* machine for stripping the short fibres of ginned cotton seeds

LINTERS > LINTER

LINTIE *Scot word for* > LINNET

LINTIER > LINT

LINTIES > LINTIE

LINTIEST > LINT

LINTING > LINT

LINTLESS > LINT

LINTOL *same as* > LINTEL

LINTOLS > LINTEL

LINTS > LINT

LINTSEED *same as* > LINSEED

LINTSEEDS > LINTSEED

LINTSTOCK *same as* > LINSTOCK

LINTWHITE *n* linnet

LINTY > LINT

LINUM *n* type of plant of temperate regions

LINUMS > LINUM

LINURON *n* type of herbicide

LINURONS > LINURON

LINUX *n* nonproprietary computer operating system suitable for use on personal computers

LINUXES > LINUX

LINY > LINE

LION *n* large animal of the cat family, the male of which has a shaggy mane

LIONCEL *n* (heraldry) small lion

LIONCELLE *same as* > LIONCEL

LIONCELS > LIONCEL

LIONEL *same as* > LIONCEL

LIONELS > LIONEL

LIONESS *n* female lion

LIONESSES > LIONESS

LIONET *n* young lion

LIONETS > LIONET

LIONFISH *n* any of various scorpion fishes of the Pacific

LIONHEAD *n* small breed of rabbit with long fur around the face

LIONHEADS > LIONHEAD

LIONISE *same as* > LIONIZE

LIONISED > LIONISE

LIONISER > LIONISE

LIONISERS > LIONISE

LIONISES > LIONISE

LIONISING > LIONISE

LIONISM *n* lion-like appearance of leprosy

LIONISMS > LIONISM

LIONIZE *vb* treat as a celebrity

LIONIZED > LIONIZE

LIONIZER > LIONIZE

LIONIZERS > LIONIZE

LIONIZES > LIONIZE

LIONIZING > LIONIZE

LIONLIKE > LION

LIONLY > LION

LIONS > LION

LIP *n* either of the fleshy edges of the mouth ▷ *vb* touch with the lips

LIPA *n* monetary unit of Croatia worth one hundredth of a kuna

LIPAEMIA *n* abnormally large amount of fat in the blood

LIPAEMIAS > LIPAEMIA

LIPARITE *n* type of igneous rock

LIPARITES > LIPARITE

LIPAS > LIPA

LIPASE *n* any of a group of enzymes that digest fat

LIPASES > LIPASE

LIPE > LIPA

LIPECTOMY *n* surgical operation to remove fat

LIPEMIA *same as* > LIPAEMIA

LIPEMIAS > LIPEMIA

LIPID *n* any of a group of organic compounds including fats, oils, waxes, and sterols

LIPIDE *same as* > LIPID

LIPIDES > LIPIDE

LIPIDIC > LIPID

LIPIDS > LIPID

LIPIN *n* family of nuclear proteins

LIPINS > LIPIN

LIPLESS > LIP

LIPLIKE > LIP

LIPO *n* liposuction

LIPOCYTE *n* fat-storing cell

LIPOCYTES > LIPOCYTE

LIPOGRAM *n* piece of writing in which all words containing a particular letter have been deliberately omitted

LIPOGRAMS > LIPOGRAM

LIPOIC as in *lipoic acid* sulphur-containing fatty acid

LIPOID *n* fatlike substance, such as wax

LIPOIDAL > LIPOID

LIPOIDS > LIPOID

LIPOLITIC *same as* > LIPOLYTIC

LIPOLYSES > LIPOLYSIS

LIPOLYSIS *n* hydrolysis of fats resulting in the production of carboxylic acids and glycerol

LIPOLYTIC *adj* fat-burning

LIPOMA *n* benign tumour composed of fatty tissue

LIPOMAS > LIPOMA

LIPOMATA > LIPOMA

LIPOPLAST *n* small particle in plant cytoplasm, esp that of seeds, in which fat is stored

LIPOS > LIPO

LIPOSOMAL > LIPOSOME

LIPOSOME *n* particle formed by lipids

LIPOSOMES > LIPOSOME

LIPOSUCK *vb* subject to liposuction

LIPOSUCKS > LIPOSUCK

LIPOTROPY *n* breaking down of fat in body

LIPPED > LIP

LIPPEN *vb* trust

LIPPENED > LIPPEN

LIPPENING > LIPPEN

LIPPENS > LIPPEN

LIPPER *Scots word for* > RIPPLE

LIPPERED > LIPPER

LIPPERING > LIPPER

LIPPERS > LIPPER

LIPPIE *variant of* > LIPPY

LIPPIER > LIPPY

LIPPIES > LIPPIE

LIPPIEST > LIPPY

LIPPINESS > LIPPY

LIPPING > LIP

LIPPINGS > LIP

LIPPITUDE *n* state of having bleary eyes

LIPPY *adj* insolent or cheeky ▷ *n* lipstick

LIPREAD *vb* follow what someone says by watching their lips

LIPREADER > LIPREAD

LIPREADS > LIPREAD

LIPS > LIP

LIPSALVE *n* substance used to prevent or relieve chapped lips

LIPSALVES > LIPSALVE

LIPSTICK *n* cosmetic in stick form, for colouring the lips ▷ *vb* put lipstick on

LIPSTICKS > LIPSTICK

LIPURIA *n* presence of fat in the urine

LIPURIAS > LIPURIA

LIQUABLE *adj* that can be melted

LIQUATE *vb* separate one component of (an alloy, impure metal, or ore) by heating so that the more fusible part melts

LIQUATED > LIQUATE
LIQUATES > LIQUATE
LIQUATING > LIQUATE
LIQUATION > LIQUATE
LIQUEFIED > LIQUEFY
LIQUEFIER > LIQUEFY
LIQUEFIES > LIQUEFY
LIQUEFY vb make or become liquid
LIQUESCE vb become liquid
LIQUESCED > LIQUESCE
LIQUESCES > LIQUESCE
LIQUEUR n flavoured and sweetened alcoholic spirit ▷ vb flavour with liqueur
LIQUEURED > LIQUEUR
LIQUEURS > LIQUEUR
LIQUID n substance in a physical state which can change shape but not size ▷ adj of or being a liquid
LIQUIDATE vb pay (a debt)
LIQUIDISE same as > LIQUIDIZE
LIQUIDITY n state of being able to meet financial obligations
LIQUIDIZE vb make or become liquid
LIQUIDLY > LIQUID
LIQUIDS > LIQUID
LIQUIDUS n line on graph above which a substance is in liquid form
LIQUIFIED > LIQUIFY
LIQUIFIES > LIQUIFY
LIQUIFY same as > LIQUEFY
LIQUOR n alcoholic drink, esp spirits ▷ vb steep (malt) in warm water to form wort in brewing
LIQUORED > LIQUOR
LIQUORICE n black substance used in medicine and as a sweet
LIQUORING > LIQUOR
LIQUORISH same as > LICKERISH
LIQUORS > LIQUOR
LIRA n monetary unit of Turkey, Malta, and formerly of Italy
LIRAS > LIRA
LIRE > LIRA
LIRI > LIRA
LIRIOPE n grasslike plant
LIRIOPES > LIRIOPE
LIRIPIPE n tip of a graduate's hood
LIRIPIPES > LIRIPIPE
LIRIPOOP same as > LIRIPIPE
LIRIPOOPS > LIRIPOOP
LIRK vb wrinkle
LIRKED > LIRK
LIRKING > LIRK
LIRKS > LIRK
LIROT > LIRA
LIROTH > LIRA
LIS n fleur-de-lis
LISENTE > SENTE

LISK Yorkshire dialect for > GROIN
LISKS > LISK
LISLE n strong fine cotton thread or fabric
LISLES > LISLE
LISP n speech defect in which s and z are pronounced th ▷ vb speak or utter with a lisp
LISPED > LISP
LISPER > LISP
LISPERS > LISP
LISPING > LISP
LISPINGLY > LISP
LISPINGS > LISP
LISPOUND n unit of weight
LISPOUNDS > LISPOUND
LISPS > LISP
LISPUND same as > LISPOUND
LISPUNDS > LISPUND
LISSES > LIS
LISSOM adj supple, agile
LISSOME same as > LISSOM
LISSOMELY > LISSOM
LISSOMLY > LISSOM
LIST n item-by-item record of names or things, usu written one below another ▷ vb make a list of
LISTABLE > LIST
LISTED > LIST
LISTEE n person on list
LISTEES > LISTEE
LISTEL another name for > FILLET
LISTELS > LISTEL
LISTEN vb concentrate on hearing something
LISTENED > LISTEN
LISTENER > LISTEN
LISTENERS > LISTEN
LISTENING > LISTEN
LISTENS > LISTEN
LISTER n plough with a double mouldboard designed to throw soil to either side of a central furrow
LISTERIA n type of rodlike Gram-positive bacterium
LISTERIAL > LISTERIA
LISTERIAS > LISTERIA
LISTERS > LISTER
LISTETH > LIST
LISTFUL adj paying attention
LISTING n list or an entry in a list
LISTINGS > LISTING
LISTLESS adj lacking interest or energy
LISTS npl field of combat in a tournament
LISTSERV n service on the internet that provides an electronic mailing to subscribers with similar interests
LISTSERVS > LISTSERV
LIT n archaic word for dye

or colouring
LITAI > LITAS
LITANIES > LITANY
LITANY n prayer with responses from the congregation
LITAS n standard monetary unit of Lithuania, divided into 100 centai
LITCHI n Chinese sapindaceous tree cultivated for its round edible fruits
LITCHIS > LITCHI
LITE same as > LIGHT
LITED > LIGHT
LITENESS > LITE
LITER same as > LITRE
LITERACY n ability to read and write
LITERAL adj according to the explicit meaning of a word or text, not figurative ▷ n misprint or misspelling in a text
LITERALLY adv in a literal manner
LITERALS > LITERAL
LITERARY adj of or knowledgeable about literature
LITERATE adj able to read and write ▷ n literate person
LITERATES > LITERATE
LITERATI npl literary people
LITERATIM adv letter for letter
LITERATO > LITERATI
LITERATOR n professional writer
LITERATUS > LITERATI
LITEROSE adj affectedly literary
LITERS > LITER
LITES > LITE
LITH n limb or joint
LITHARGE n lead monoxide
LITHARGES > LITHARGE
LITHATE n salt of uric acid
LITHATES > LITHATE
LITHE adj flexible or supple, pliant ▷ vb listen
LITHED > LITHE
LITHELY > LITHE
LITHEMIA n gout
LITHEMIAS > LITHEMIA
LITHEMIC > LITHEMIA
LITHENESS > LITHE
LITHER > LITHE
LITHERLY adj crafty; cunning
LITHES > LITHE
LITHESOME less common word for > LISSOM
LITHEST > LITHE
LITHIA n lithium present in mineral waters as lithium salts
LITHIAS > LITHIA
LITHIASES > LITHIASIS

LITHIASIS n formation of a calculus
LITHIC adj of, relating to, or composed of stone
LITHIFIED > LITHIFY
LITHIFIES > LITHIFY
LITHIFY vb turn into rock
LITHING > LITHO
LITHISTID n type of sponge
LITHITE n part of cell with sensory element
LITHITES > LITHITE
LITHIUM n chemical element, the lightest known metal
LITHIUMS > LITHIUM
LITHO n lithography ▷ vb print using lithography
LITHOCYST n sac containing otoliths
LITHOED > LITHO
LITHOID adj resembling stone or rock
LITHOIDAL same as > LITHOID
LITHOING > LITHO
LITHOLOGY n physical characteristics of a rock
LITHOPONE n white pigment consisting of a mixture of zinc sulphide, zinc oxide, and barium sulphate
LITHOPS n fleshy-leaved plant
LITHOS > LITHO
LITHOSOL n type of azonal soil consisting chiefly of unweathered or partly weathered rock fragments
LITHOSOLS > LITHOSOL
LITHOTOME n instrument used in lithotomy operation
LITHOTOMY n surgical removal of a calculus, esp one in the urinary bladder
LITHS > LITH
LITIGABLE adj that may be the subject of litigation
LITIGANT n person involved in a lawsuit ▷ adj engaged in litigation
LITIGANTS > LITIGANT
LITIGATE vb bring or contest a law suit
LITIGATED > LITIGATE
LITIGATES > LITIGATE
LITIGATOR > LITIGATE
LITIGIOUS adj frequently going to law
LITING > LITE
LITMUS n blue dye turned red by acids and restored to blue by alkalis
LITMUSES > LITMUS
LITORAL same as > LITTORAL
LITOTES n ironical understatement used for effect
LITOTIC > LITOTES
LITRE n unit of liquid measure equal to 1000

cubic centimetres or 1.76 pints

LITREAGE n volume in litres

LITREAGES > LITREAGE

LITRES > LITRE

LITS > LIT

LITTEN adj lighted

LITTER n untidy rubbish dropped in public places ▷ vb strew with litter

LITTERBAG n bag for putting rubbish in

LITTERBUG n person who tends to drop rubbish in public places

LITTERED > LITTER

LITTERER n one who litters

LITTERERS > LITTERER

LITTERING > LITTER

LITTERS > LITTER

LITTERY adj covered in litter

LITTLE adj small or smaller than average ▷ adv not a lot ▷ n small amount, extent, or duration

LITTLER > LITTLE

LITTLES > LITTLE

LITTLEST > LITTLE

LITTLIE n young child

LITTLIES > LITTLIE

LITTLIN same as > LITTLING

LITTLING n child

LITTLINGS > LITTLING

LITTLINS > LITTLIN

LITTLISH adj rather small

LITTORAL adj of or by the seashore ▷ n coastal district

LITTORALS > LITTORAL

LITU > LITAS

LITURGIC > LITURGY

LITURGICS n study of liturgies

LITURGIES > LITURGY

LITURGISM > LITURGIST

LITURGIST n student or composer of liturgical forms

LITURGY n prescribed form of public worship

LITUUS n type of curved trumpet

LITUUSES > LITUUS

LIVABLE adj tolerable or pleasant to live (with)

LIVE vb be alive ▷ adj living, alive ▷ adv in the form of a live performance

LIVEABLE same as > LIVABLE

LIVED > LIVE

LIVEDO n reddish discoloured patch on the skin

LIVEDOS > LIVEDO

LIVELIER > LIVELY

LIVELIEST > LIVELY

LIVELILY > LIVELY

LIVELOD n livelihood

LIVELODS > LIVELOD

LIVELONG adj long or seemingly long

LIVELONGS > LIVELONG

LIVELOOD n livelihood

LIVELOODS > LIVELOOD

LIVELY adj full of life or vigour

LIVEN vb make or become lively

LIVENED > LIVEN

LIVENER > LIVEN

LIVENERS > LIVEN

LIVENESS n state of being alive

LIVENING > LIVEN

LIVENS > LIVEN

LIVER n person who lives in a specified way

LIVERED adj having liver

LIVERIED adj wearing livery

LIVERIES > LIVERY

LIVERING n process of liquid becoming lumpy

LIVERISH adj having a disorder of the liver

LIVERLEAF n woodland plant

LIVERLESS > LIVER

LIVERS > LIVER

LIVERWORT n plant resembling seaweed or leafy moss

LIVERY n distinctive dress, esp of a servant or servants ▷ adj of or resembling liver

LIVERYMAN n member of a livery company

LIVERYMEN > LIVERYMAN

LIVES > LIFE

LIVEST > LIVE

LIVESTOCK n farm animals

LIVETRAP n box constructed to trap an animal without injuring it

LIVETRAPS > LIVETRAP

LIVEWARE n programmers, systems analysts, operating staff, and other personnel working in a computer system

LIVEWARES > LIVEWARE

LIVEYER n (in Newfoundland) a full-time resident

LIVEYERE same as > LIVEYER

LIVEYERES > LIVEYERE

LIVEYERS > LIVEYER

LIVID adj angry or furious

LIVIDER > LIVID

LIVIDEST > LIVID

LIVIDITY n state of being livid

LIVIDLY > LIVID

LIVIDNESS > LIVID

LIVIER same as > LIVEYER

LIVIERS > LIVIER

LIVING adj possessing life, not dead or inanimate ▷ n

condition of being alive

LIVINGLY > LIVING

LIVINGS > LIVING

LIVOR another word for > LIVIDITY

LIVORS > LIVOR

LIVRAISON n one of the numbers of a book published in parts

LIVRE n former French unit of money of account, equal to 1 pound of silver

LIVRES > LIVRE

LIVYER same as > LIVEYER

LIVYERS > LIVYER

LIXIVIA > LIXIVIUM

LIXIVIAL > LIXIVIATE

LIXIVIATE less common word for > LEACH

LIXIVIOUS > LIXIVIUM

LIXIVIUM n alkaline solution obtained by leaching wood ash with water

LIXIVIUMS > LIXIVIUM

LIZARD n four-footed reptile with a long body and tail

LIZARDS > LIZARD

LIZZIE as in tin lizzie an old or decrepit car

LIZZIES > LIZZIE

LLAMA n woolly animal of the camel family used as a beast of burden in S America

LLAMAS > LLAMA

LLANERO n native of llanos

LLANEROS > LLANERO

LLANO n extensive grassy treeless plain, esp in South America

LLANOS > LLANO

LO interj look!

LOACH n carplike freshwater fish

LOACHES > LOACH

LOAD n burden or weight ▷ vb put a load on or into

LOADED adj (of a question) containing a hidden trap or implication

LOADEN vb load

LOADENED > LOADEN

LOADENING > LOADEN

LOADENS > LOADEN

LOADER n person who loads a gun or other firearm

LOADERS > LOADER

LOADING n load or burden

LOADINGS > LOADING

LOADS npl lots or a lot

LOADSPACE n area in a motor vehicle where a load can be carried

LOADSTAR same as > LODESTAR

LOADSTARS > LOADSTAR

LOADSTONE same as > LODESTONE

LOAF n shaped mass of baked bread ▷ vb idle, loiter

LOAFED > LOAF

LOAFER n person who avoids work

LOAFERISH > LOAFER

LOAFERS > LOAFER

LOAFING > LOAF

LOAFINGS > LOAF

LOAFS > LOAF

LOAM n fertile soil ▷ vb cover, treat, or fill with loam

LOAMED > LOAM

LOAMIER > LOAM

LOAMIEST > LOAM

LOAMINESS > LOAM

LOAMING > LOAM

LOAMLESS > LOAM

LOAMS > LOAM

LOAMY > LOAM

LOAN n money lent at interest ▷ vb lend

LOANABLE > LOAN

LOANBACK n facility by which an individual can borrow from his or her pension fund ▷ vb make use of this facility

LOANBACKS > LOANBACK

LOANED > LOAN

LOANEE n sportsperson who is loaned from one organization to another

LOANEES > LOANEE

LOANER > LOAN

LOANERS > LOAN

LOANING > LOAN

LOANINGS > LOANING

LOANS > LOAN

LOANSHIFT n adaptation of word from one language by another

LOANWORD n word adopted from one language into another

LOANWORDS > LOANWORD

LOAST > LOOSE

LOATH adj unwilling or reluctant (to)

LOATHE vb hate, be disgusted by

LOATHED > LOATHE

LOATHER > LOATHE

LOATHERS > LOATHE

LOATHES > LOATHE

LOATHEST > LOATH

LOATHFUL adj causing loathing

LOATHING n strong disgust

LOATHINGS > LOATHING

LOATHLY adv with reluctance

LOATHNESS > LOATH

LOATHSOME adj causing loathing

LOATHY obsolete form of > LOATHSOME

LOAVE vb make into the form of a loaf

LOAVED > LOAVE

LOAVES > LOAF

LOAVING > LOAVE

LOB n ball struck or thrown in a high arc ▷ vb strike or throw (a ball) in a high arc

LOBAR adj of or affecting a lobe

LOBATE adj with or like lobes

LOBATED same as > LOBATE

LOBATELY > LOBATE

LOBATION n division into lobes

LOBATIONS > LOBATION

LOBBED > LOB

LOBBER n one who lobs

LOBBERS > LOBBER

LOBBIED > LOBBY

LOBBIES > LOBBY

LOBBING > LOB

LOBBY n corridor into which rooms open ⊳ vb try to influence (legislators) in the formulation of policy

LOBBYER > LOBBY

LOBBYERS > LOBBY

LOBBYGOW n errand boy

LOBBYGOWS > LOBBYGOW

LOBBYING > LOBBY

LOBBYINGS > LOBBY

LOBBYISM > LOBBYIST

LOBBYISMS > LOBBYIST

LOBBYIST n person who lobbies on behalf of a particular interest

LOBBYISTS > LOBBYIST

LOBE n rounded projection

LOBECTOMY n surgical removal of a lobe from any organ or gland in the body

LOBED > LOBE

LOBEFIN n type of fish

LOBEFINS > LOBEFIN

LOBELESS adj having no lobes

LOBELET n small lobe

LOBELETS > LOBELET

LOBELIA n garden plant with blue, red, or white flowers

LOBELIAS > LOBELIA

LOBELINE n crystalline alkaloid extracted from the seeds of the Indian tobacco plant

LOBELINES > LOBELINE

LOBES > LOBE

LOBI > LOBUS

LOBING n formation of lobes

LOBINGS > LOBING

LOBIPED adj with lobed toes

LOBLOLLY n southern US pine tree

LOBO n timber wolf

LOBOLA n (in African custom) price paid by a bridegroom's family to his bride's family

LOBOLAS > LOBOLA

LOBOLO same as > LOBOLA

LOBOLOS > LOBOLO

LOBOS > LOBO

LOBOSE another word for > LOBATE

LOBOTOMY n surgical incision into a lobe of the

brain to treat mental disorders

LOBS > LOB

LOBSCOUSE n sailor's stew of meat, vegetables, and hardtack

LOBSTER n shellfish with a long tail and claws, which turns red when boiled ⊳ vb fish for lobsters

LOBSTERED > LOBSTER

LOBSTERER n person who catches lobsters

LOBSTERS > LOBSTER

LOBSTICK n tree used as landmark

LOBSTICKS > LOBSTICK

LOBULAR > LOBULE

LOBULARLY > LOBULE

LOBULATE > LOBULE

LOBULATED > LOBULE

LOBULE n small lobe or a subdivision of a lobe

LOBULES > LOBULE

LOBULI > LOBULUS

LOBULOSE > LOBULE

LOBULUS n small lobe

LOBUS n lobe

LOBWORM same as > LUGWORM

LOBWORMS > LOBWORM

LOCA > LOCUS

LOCAL adj of or existing in a particular place ⊳ n person belonging to a particular district

LOCALE n scene of an event

LOCALES > LOCALE

LOCALISE same as > LOCALIZE

LOCALISED > LOCALISE

LOCALISER > LOCALISE

LOCALISES > LOCALISE

LOCALISM n pronunciation, phrase, etc, peculiar to a particular locality

LOCALISMS > LOCALISM

LOCALIST > LOCALISM

LOCALISTS > LOCALISM

LOCALITE n resident of an area

LOCALITES > LOCALITE

LOCALITY n neighbourhood or area

LOCALIZE vb restrict to a particular place

LOCALIZED > LOCALIZE

LOCALIZER > LOCALIZE

LOCALIZES > LOCALIZE

LOCALLY adv within a particular area or place

LOCALNESS > LOCAL

LOCALS > LOCAL

LOCATABLE > LOCATE

LOCATE vb discover the whereabouts of

LOCATED > LOCATE

LOCATER > LOCATE

LOCATERS > LOCATE

LOCATES > LOCATE

LOCATING > LOCATE

LOCATION n site or position

LOCATIONS > LOCATION

LOCATIVE adj (of a word or phrase) indicating place or direction ⊳ n locative case

LOCATIVES > LOCATIVE

LOCATOR n part of index that indicates where to look for information

LOCATORS > LOCATOR

LOCELLATE adj split into secondary cells

LOCH n lake

LOCHAN n small inland loch

LOCHANS > LOCHAN

LOCHIA n vaginal discharge of cellular debris, mucus, and blood following childbirth

LOCHIAL > LOCHIA

LOCHS > LOCH

LOCI > LOCUS

LOCK n appliance for fastening a door, case, etc ⊳ vb fasten or become fastened securely

LOCKABLE > LOCK

LOCKAGE n system of locks in a canal

LOCKAGES > LOCKAGE

LOCKAWAY n investment intended to be held for a relatively long time

LOCKAWAYS > LOCKAWAY

LOCKBOX n system of collecting funds from companies by banks

LOCKBOXES > LOCKBOX

LOCKDOWN n device used to secure equipment, etc

LOCKDOWNS > LOCKDOWN

LOCKED > LOCK

LOCKER n small cupboard with a lock

LOCKERS > LOCKER

LOCKET n small hinged pendant for a portrait etc

LOCKETS > LOCKET

LOCKFAST adj securely fastened with a lock

LOCKFUL n sufficient to fill a canal lock

LOCKFULS > LOCKFUL

LOCKHOUSE n house of lock-keeper

LOCKING > LOCK

LOCKINGS > LOCK

LOCKJAW n tetanus

LOCKJAWS > LOCKJAW

LOCKLESS adj having no lock

LOCKMAKER n maker of locks

LOCKMAN n lock-keeper

LOCKMEN > LOCKMAN

LOCKNUT n supplementary nut screwed down upon a primary nut to prevent it from shaking loose

LOCKNUTS > LOCKNUT

LOCKOUT n closing of a workplace by an employer to force workers to accept terms

LOCKOUTS > LOCKOUT

LOCKPICK another word for > PICKLOCK

LOCKPICKS > LOCKPICK

LOCKRAM n type of linen cloth

LOCKRAMS > LOCKRAM

LOCKS > LOCK

LOCKSET n hardware used to lock door

LOCKSETS > LOCKSET

LOCKSMAN same as > LOCKMAN

LOCKSMEN > LOCKSMAN

LOCKSMITH n person who makes and mends locks

LOCKSTEP n method of marching in step as closely as possible

LOCKSTEPS > LOCKSTEP

LOCKUP n prison

LOCKUPS > LOCKUP

LOCO n locomotive ⊳ adj insane ⊳ vb poison with locoweed

LOCOED > LOCO

LOCOES > LOCO

LOCOFOCO n match

LOCOFOCOS > LOCOFOCO

LOCOING > LOCO

LOCOISM n disease of cattle, sheep, and horses caused by eating locoweed

LOCOISMS > LOCOISM

LOCOMAN n railwayman, esp an engine-driver

LOCOMEN > LOCOMAN

LOCOMOTE vb move from one place to another

LOCOMOTED > LOCOMOTE

LOCOMOTES > LOCOMOTE

LOCOMOTOR adj of or relating to locomotion

LOCOPLANT another word for > LOCOWEED

LOCOS > LOCO

LOCOWEED n any of several perennial leguminous plants

LOCOWEEDS > LOCOWEED

LOCULAR adj divided into compartments by septa

LOCULATE same as > LOCULAR

LOCULATED same as > LOCULATE

LOCULE n any of the chambers of an ovary or anther

LOCULED adj having locules

LOCULES > LOCULE

LOCULI > LOCULUS

LOCULUS same as > LOCULE

LOCUM n temporary stand-in for a doctor or clergyman

LOCUMS > LOCUM

LOCUPLETE adj well-stored

LOCUS n area or place where something happens

LOCUST n destructive insect that flies in swarms and eats crops ⊳ vb ravage,

as locusts
LOCUSTA n flower cluster unit in grasses
LOCUSTAE > LOCUSTA
LOCUSTAL > LOCUSTA
LOCUSTED > LOCUST
LOCUSTING > LOCUST
LOCUSTS > LOCUST
LOCUTION n manner or style of speech
LOCUTIONS > LOCUTION
LOCUTORY adj room intended for conversation
LOD n type of logarithm
LODE n vein of ore
LODEN n thick heavy waterproof woollen cloth with a short pile, used to make garments, esp coats
LODENS > LODEN
LODES > LODE
LODESMAN n pilot
LODESMEN > LODESMAN
LODESTAR n star used in navigation or astronomy as a point of reference
LODESTARS > LODESTAR
LODESTONE n magnetic iron ore
LODGE n gatekeeper's house ▷ vb live in another's house at a fixed charge
LODGEABLE > LODGE
LODGED > LODGE
LODGEMENT same as > LODGMENT
LODGEPOLE n type of pine tree
LODGER n person who pays rent in return for accommodation in someone else's home
LODGERS > LODGER
LODGES > LODGE
LODGING n temporary residence
LODGINGS npl rented room or rooms in which to live, esp in another person's house
LODGMENT n act of lodging or the state of being lodged
LODGMENTS > LODGMENT
LODICULA n delicate scale in grass
LODICULAE > LODICULA
LODICULE n any of two or three minute scales at the base of the ovary in grass flowers that represent the corolla
LODICULES > LODICULE
LODS > LOD
LOERIE same as > LOURIE
LOERIES > LOERIE
LOESS n fine-grained soil, found mainly in river valleys, originally deposited by the wind
LOESSAL > LOESS
LOESSES > LOESS
LOESSIAL > LOESS
LOESSIC adj relating to or consisting of loess
LOFT n space between the

top storey and roof of a building ▷ vb strike, throw, or kick (a ball) high into the air
LOFTED > LOFT
LOFTER n type of golf club
LOFTERS > LOFTER
LOFTIER > LOFTY
LOFTIEST > LOFTY
LOFTILY > LOFTY
LOFTINESS > LOFTY
LOFTING > LOFT
LOFTLESS > LOFT
LOFTLIKE > LOFT
LOFTS > LOFT
LOFTSMAN n person who reproduces in actual size a draughtsman's design for a ship or an aircraft
LOFTSMEN > LOFTSMAN
LOFTY adj of great height
LOG n portion of a felled tree stripped of branches ▷ vb saw logs from a tree
LOGAN another name for > BOGAN
LOGANIA n type of Australian plant
LOGANIAS > LOGANIA
LOGANS > LOGAN
LOGAOEDIC adj of or relating to verse in which mixed metres are combined within a single line to give the effect of prose ▷ n line or verse of this kind
LOGARITHM n one of a series of arithmetical functions used to make certain calculations easier
LOGBOARD n board used for logging a ship's records
LOGBOARDS > LOGBOARD
LOGBOOK n book recording the details about a car or a ship's journeys
LOGBOOKS > LOGBOOK
LOGE n small enclosure or box in a theatre or opera house
LOGES > LOGE
LOGGAT n small piece of wood
LOGGATS > LOGGAT
LOGGED > LOG
LOGGER n tractor or crane for handling logs
LOGGERS > LOGGER
LOGGETS n old-fashioned game played with sticks
LOGGIA n covered gallery at the side of a building
LOGGIAS > LOGGIA
LOGGIE > LOGGIA
LOGGIER > LOGGY
LOGGIEST > LOGGY
LOGGING > LOG
LOGGINGS > LOG
LOGGISH > LOG
LOGGY adj slow, sluggish, or listless
LOGIA > LOGION
LOGIC n philosophy of reasoning
LOGICAL adj of logic

LOGICALLY > LOGICAL
LOGICIAN n person who specializes in or is skilled at logic
LOGICIANS > LOGICIAN
LOGICISE same as > LOGICIZE
LOGICISED > LOGICISE
LOGICISES > LOGICISE
LOGICISM n philosophical theory that all of mathematics can be deduced from logic
LOGICISMS > LOGICISM
LOGICIST > LOGICISM
LOGICISTS > LOGICISM
LOGICIZE vb present reasons for or against
LOGICIZED > LOGICIZE
LOGICIZES > LOGICIZE
LOGICLESS > LOGIC
LOGICS > LOGIC
LOGIE n fire-place of a kiln
LOGIER > LOGY
LOGIES > LOGIE
LOGIEST > LOGY
LOGILY > LOGY
LOGIN n process by which a computer user logs on
LOGINESS > LOGY
LOGINS > LOGIN
LOGION n saying of Christ regarded as authentic
LOGIONS > LOGION
LOGISTIC n uninterpreted calculus or system of symbolic logic ▷ adj (of a curve) having a particular form of equation
LOGISTICS n detailed planning and organization of a large, esp military, operation
LOGJAM n blockage caused by the crowding together of a number of logs floating in a river ▷ vb cause a logjam
LOGJAMMED > LOGJAM
LOGJAMS > LOGJAM
LOGJUICE n poor quality port wine
LOGJUICES > LOGJUICE
LOGLINE n synopsis of screenplay
LOGLINES > LOGLINE
LOGLOG n logarithm of a logarithm (in equations, etc)
LOGLOGS > LOGLOG
LOGNORMAL adj (maths) having a natural logarithm with normal distribution
LOGO same as > LOGOTYPE
LOGOFF n process by which a computer user logs out
LOGOFFS > LOGOFF
LOGOGRAM n single symbol representing an entire morpheme, word, or phrase
LOGOGRAMS > LOGOGRAM
LOGOGRAPH same as > LOGOGRAM
LOGOGRIPH n word

puzzle, esp one based on recombination of the letters of a word
LOGOI > LOGOS
LOGOMACH n one who argues over words
LOGOMACHS > LOGOMACH
LOGOMACHY n argument about words or the meaning of words
LOGON variant of > LOGIN
LOGONS > LOGON
LOGOPEDIC adj of or relating to speech therapy
LOGOPHILE n one who loves words
LOGORRHEA n excessive or uncontrollable talkativeness
LOGOS n reason or the rational principle expressed in words and things, argument, or justification
LOGOTHETE n officer of Byzantine empire
LOGOTYPE n piece of type with several uncombined characters cast on it
LOGOTYPES > LOGOTYPE
LOGOTYPY > LOGOTYPE
LOGOUT variant of > LOGOFF
LOGOUTS > LOGOUT
LOGROLL vb use logrolling in order to procure the passage of (legislation)
LOGROLLED > LOGROLL
LOGROLLER > LOGROLL
LOGROLLS > LOGROLL
LOGS > LOG
LOGWAY another name for > GANGWAY
LOGWAYS > LOGWAY
LOGWOOD n leguminous tree of the Caribbean and Central America
LOGWOODS > LOGWOOD
LOGY adj dull or listless
LOHAN another word for > ARHAT
LOHANS > LOHAN
LOID vb open (a lock) using a celluloid strip
LOIDED > LOID
LOIDING > LOID
LOIDS > LOID
LOIN n part of the body between the ribs and the hips
LOINCLOTH n piece of cloth covering the loins only
LOINS npl hips and the inner surface of the legs where they join the body
LOIPE n cross-country skiing track
LOIPEN > LOIPE
LOIR n large dormouse
LOIRS > LOIR
LOITER vb stand or wait aimlessly or idly
LOITERED > LOITER
LOITERER > LOITER
LOITERERS > LOITER

LOITERING > LOITER

LOITERS > LOITER

LOKE n track

LOKES > LOKE

LOKSHEN npl noodles

LOLIGO n type of squid

LOLIGOS > LOLIGO

LOLIUM n type of grass

LOLIUMS > LOLIUM

LOLL vb lounge lazily ▷ n act or instance of lolling

LOLLED > LOLL

LOLLER > LOLL

LOLLERS > LOLL

LOLLIES > LOLLY

LOLLING > LOLL

LOLLINGLY > LOLL

LOLLIPOP n boiled sweet on a small wooden stick

LOLLIPOPS > LOLLIPOP

LOLLOP vb move clumsily

LOLLOPED > LOLLOP

LOLLOPING > LOLLOP

LOLLOPS > LOLLOP

LOLLOPY > LOLLOP

LOLLS > LOLL

LOLLY n lollipop or ice lolly

LOLLYGAG same as > LALLYGAG

LOLLYGAGS > LOLLYGAG

LOLLYPOP same as > LOLLIPOP

LOLLYPOPS > LOLLYPOP

LOLOG same as > LOGLOG

LOLOGS > LOLOG

LOMA n lobe

LOMAS > LOMA

LOMATA > LOMA

LOME vb cover with lome

LOMED > LOME

LOMEIN n Chinese dish

LOMEINS > LOMEIN

LOMENT n pod of certain leguminous plants

LOMENTA > LOMENTUM

LOMENTS > LOMENT

LOMENTUM same as > LOMENT

LOMENTUMS > LOMENTUM

LOMES > LOME

LOMING > LOME

LOMPISH another word for > LUMPISH

LONE adj solitary

LONELIER > LONELY

LONELIEST > LONELY

LONELILY > LONELY

LONELY adj sad because alone

LONENESS > LONE

LONER n person who prefers to be alone

LONERS > LONER

LONESOME adj lonely ▷ n own

LONESOMES > LONESOME

LONG adj having length, esp great length, in space or time ▷ adv for a certain time ▷ vb have a strong desire (for)

LONGA n long note

LONGAEVAL adj long-lived

LONGAN n sapindaceous tree of tropical and subtropical Asia

LONGANS > LONGAN

LONGAS > LONGA

LONGBOARD n type of surfboard

LONGBOAT n largest boat carried on a ship

LONGBOATS > LONGBOAT

LONGBOW n large powerful bow

LONGBOWS > LONGBOW

LONGCASE as in longcase clock grandfather clock

LONGCLOTH n fine plain-weave cotton cloth made in long strips

LONGE n rope used in training a horse ▷ vb train using a longe

LONGED > LONG

LONGEING > LONGE

LONGER n line of barrels on a ship

LONGERON n main longitudinal structural member of an aircraft

LONGERONS > LONGERON

LONGERS > LONGER

LONGES > LONGE

LONGEST > LONG

LONGEVAL another word for > LONGAEVAL

LONGEVITY n long life

LONGEVOUS > LONGEVITY

LONGHAIR n cat with long hair

LONGHAIRS > LONGHAIR

LONGHAND n ordinary writing, not shorthand or typing

LONGHANDS > LONGHAND

LONGHEAD n person with long head

LONGHEADS > LONGHEAD

LONGHORN n British breed of beef cattle with long curved horns

LONGHORNS > LONGHORN

LONGHOUSE n long communal dwelling of Native American peoples

LONGICORN n type of beetle with long antennae

LONGIES n long johns

LONGING n yearning ▷ adj having or showing desire

LONGINGLY > LONGING

LONGINGS > LONGING

LONGISH adj rather long

LONGITUDE n distance east or west from a standard meridian

LONGJUMP n jumping contest decided by length

LONGJUMPS > LONGJUMP

LONGLEAF n North American pine tree

LONGLINE n (tennis) straight stroke played down court

LONGLINES > LONGLINE

LONGLIST n initial list from which a shortlist is selected ▷ vb include (eg a candidate) on a longlist

LONGLISTS > LONGLIST

LONGLY > LONG

LONGNECK n US, Canadian and Australian word for a 330-ml beer bottle with a long narrow neck

LONGNECKS > LONGNECK

LONGNESS > LONG

LONGS npl full-length trousers

LONGSHIP n narrow open boat with oars and a square sail, used by the Vikings

LONGSHIPS > LONGSHIP

LONGSHORE adj situated on, relating to, or along the shore

LONGSOME adj slow; boring

LONGSPUR n any of various Arctic and North American buntings

LONGSPURS > LONGSPUR

LONGTIME adj of long standing

LONGUEUR n period of boredom or dullness

LONGUEURS > LONGUEUR

LONGWALL n long face in coal mine

LONGWALLS > LONGWALL

LONGWAYS adv lengthways

LONGWISE same as > LONGWAYS

LONGWORM as in sea longworm kind of marine worm

LONGWORMS > LONGWORM

LONICERA n honeysuckle

LONICERAS > LONICERA

LOO n informal word meaning lavatory ▷ vb Scots word meaning love

LOOBIER > LOOBY

LOOBIES > LOOBY

LOOBIEST > LOOBY

LOOBILY > LOOBY

LOOBY adj foolish ▷ n foolish or stupid person

LOOED > LOO

LOOEY n lieutenant

LOOEYS > LOOEY

LOOF n part of ship's side

LOOFA same as > LOOFAH

LOOFAH n sponge made from the dried pod of a gourd

LOOFAHS > LOOFAH

LOOFAS > LOOFA

LOOFFUL n handful

LOOFFULS > LOOFFUL

LOOFS > LOOF

LOOIE same as > LOOEY

LOOIES > LOOIE

LOOING > LOO

LOOK vb direct the eyes or attention (towards) ▷ n instance of looking

LOOKALIKE n person who is the double of another

LOOKDOWN n way paper appears when looked at under reflected light

LOOKDOWNS > LOOKDOWN

LOOKED > LOOK

LOOKER n person who looks

LOOKERS > LOOKER

LOOKING > LOOK

LOOKISM n discrimination against a person on the grounds of physical appearance

LOOKISMS > LOOKISM

LOOKIST > LOOKISM

LOOKISTS > LOOKISM

LOOKOUT n act of watching for danger or for an opportunity ▷ vb be careful

LOOKOUTS > LOOKOUT

LOOKOVER n inspection, esp a brief one

LOOKOVERS > LOOKOVER

LOOKS > LOOK

LOOKSISM same as > LOOKISM

LOOKSISMS > LOOKSISM

LOOKUP n act of looking up information, esp on the internet

LOOKUPS > LOOKUP

LOOM n machine for weaving cloth ▷ vb appear dimly

LOOMED > LOOM

LOOMING > LOOM

LOOMS > LOOM

LOON n diving bird

LOONEY same as > LOONY

LOONEYS > LOONY

LOONIE n Canadian dollar coin with a loon bird on one of its faces

LOONIER > LOONY

LOONIES > LOONY

LOONIEST > LOONY

LOONILY > LOONY

LOONINESS > LOONY

LOONING n cry of the loon

LOONINGS > LOONING

LOONS > LOON

LOONY adj foolish or insane ▷ n foolish or insane person

LOOP n rounded shape made by a curved line or rope crossing itself ▷ vb form or fasten with a loop

LOOPED > LOOP

LOOPER n person or thing that loops or makes loops

LOOPERS > LOOPER

LOOPHOLE n means of evading a rule without breaking it ▷ vb provide with loopholes

LOOPHOLED > LOOPHOLE

LOOPHOLES > LOOPHOLE

LOOPIER > LOOPY

LOOPIEST > LOOPY

LOOPILY > LOOPY

LOOPINESS > LOOPY

LOOPING > LOOP

LOOPINGS > LOOP

LOOPS > LOOP

LOOPY adj slightly mad or crazy

LOOR > LIEF
LOORD *obsolete word for* > LOUT
LOORDS > LOORD
LOOS > LOO
LOOSE *adj* not tight, fastened, fixed, or tense ▷ *adv* in a loose manner ▷ *vb* free
LOOSEBOX *n* enclosed stall with a door in which an animal can be kept
LOOSED > LOOSE
LOOSELY > LOOSE
LOOSEN *vb* make loose
LOOSENED > LOOSEN
LOOSENER > LOOSEN
LOOSENERS > LOOSEN
LOOSENESS > LOOSE
LOOSENING > LOOSEN
LOOSENS > LOOSEN
LOOSER > LOOSE
LOOSES > LOOSE
LOOSEST > LOOSE
LOOSIE *n* informal word for loose forward
LOOSIES *npl* cigarettes sold individually
LOOSING *n* celebration of one's 21st birthday
LOOSINGS > LOOSING
LOOT *vb* pillage ▷ *n* goods stolen during pillaging
LOOTED > LOOT
LOOTEN *Scots past form of* > LET
LOOTER > LOOT
LOOTERS > LOOT
LOOTING > LOOT
LOOTINGS > LOOT
LOOTS > LOOT
LOOVES > LOOF
LOP *vb* cut away (twigs and branches) ▷ *n* part or parts lopped off, as from a tree
LOPE *vb* run with long easy strides ▷ *n* loping stride
LOPED > LOPE
LOPER > LOPE
LOPERS > LOPE
LOPES > LOPE
LOPGRASS *n* smooth-bladed grass
LOPHODONT *adj* (of teeth) having elongated ridges
LOPING > LOPE
LOPOLITH *n* saucer- or lens-shaped body of intrusive igneous rock
LOPOLITHS > LOPOLITH
LOPPED > LOP
LOPPER *n* tool for lopping ▷ *vb* curdle
LOPPERED > LOPPER
LOPPERING > LOPPER
LOPPERS > LOPPER
LOPPIER > LOPPY
LOPPIES > LOPPY
LOPPIEST > LOPPY
LOPPING > LOP
LOPPINGS > LOP
LOPPY *adj* floppy ▷ *n* man employed to do maintenance tasks on a ranch

LOPS > LOP
LOPSIDED *adj* greater in height, weight, or size on one side
LOPSTICK *variant of* > LOBSTICK
LOPSTICKS > LOPSTICK
LOQUACITY *n* tendency to talk a great deal
LOQUAT *n* ornamental evergreen rosaceous tree
LOQUATS > LOQUAT
LOQUITUR *n* stage direction meaning *he or she speaks*
LOR *interj* exclamation of surprise or dismay
LORAL *adj* of part of side of bird's head
LORAN *n* radio navigation system operating over long distances
LORANS > LORAN
LORATE *adj* like a strap
LORAZEPAM *n* type of tranquillizer
LORCHA *n* junk-rigged vessel
LORCHAS > LORCHA
LORD *n* person with power over others, such as a monarch or master ▷ *vb* act in a superior manner
LORDED > LORD
LORDING *n* gentleman
LORDINGS > LORDING
LORDKIN *n* little lord
LORDKINS > LORDKIN
LORDLESS > LORD
LORDLIER > LORDLY
LORDLIEST > LORDLY
LORDLIKE > LORD
LORDLING *n* young lord
LORDLINGS > LORDLING
LORDLY *adj* imperious, proud ▷ *adv* in the manner of a lord
LORDOMA *same as* > LORDOSIS
LORDOMAS > LORDOMA
LORDOSES > LORDOSIS
LORDOSIS *n* forward curvature of the lumbar spine
LORDOTIC > LORDOSIS
LORDS > LORD
LORDSHIP *n* position or authority of a lord
LORDSHIPS > LORDSHIP
LORDY *interj* exclamation of surprise or dismay
LORE *n* body of traditions on a subject
LOREAL *adj* concerning or relating to lore
LOREL *another word for* > LOSEL
LORELS > LOREL
LORES > LORE
LORETTE *n* concubine
LORETTES > LORETTE
LORGNETTE *n* pair of spectacles mounted on a

long handle
LORGNON *n* monocle or pair of spectacles
LORGNONS > LORGNON
LORIC > LORICA
LORICA *n* hard outer covering of rotifers, ciliate protozoans, and similar organisms
LORICAE > LORICA
LORICATE > LORICA
LORICATED > LORICA
LORICATES > LORICA
LORICS > LORICA
LORIES > LORY
LORIKEET *n* small brightly coloured Australian parrot
LORIKEETS > LORIKEET
LORIMER *n* (formerly) a person who made bits, spurs, and other small metal objects
LORIMERS > LORIMER
LORINER *same as* > LORIMER
LORINERS > LORINER
LORING *n* teaching
LORINGS > LORING
LORIOT *n* golden oriole (bird)
LORIOTS > LORIOT
LORIS *n* any of several omnivorous nocturnal slow-moving prosimian primates
LORISES > LORIS
LORN *adj* forsaken or wretched
LORNNESS > LORN
LORRELL *obsolete word for* > LOSEL
LORRELLS > LORRELL
LORRIES > LORRY
LORRY *n* large vehicle for transporting loads by road
LORY *n* any of various small brightly coloured parrots of Australia and Indonesia
LOS *n* approval
LOSABLE > LOOSE
LOSE *vb* part with or come to be without
LOSED > LOSE
LOSEL *n* worthless person ▷ *adj* (of a person) worthless, useless, or wasteful
LOSELS > LOSEL
LOSEN > LOOSE
LOSER *n* person or thing that loses
LOSERS > LOSER
LOSES > LOOSE
LOSH *interj* lord
LOSING > LOSE
LOSINGLY > LOSE
LOSINGS *npl* losses, esp money lost in gambling
LOSLYF *n* South African slang for a promiscuous female
LOSLYFS > LOSLYF
LOSS *n* losing
LOSSES > LOSS

LOSSIER > LOSSY
LOSSIEST > LOSSY
LOSSLESS > LOSS
LOSSMAKER *n* organization, industry, or enterprise that consistently fails to make a profit
LOSSY *adj* (of a dielectric material, transmission line, etc) designed to have a high attenuation
LOST *adj* missing
LOSTNESS > LOST
LOT *pron* great number ▷ *n* collection of people or things ▷ *vb* draw lots for
LOTA *n* globular water container, usually of brass, used in India, Myanmar, etc
LOTAH *same as* > LOTA
LOTAHS > LOTAH
LOTAS > LOTA
LOTE *another word for* > LOTUS
LOTES > LOTE
LOTH *same as* > LOATH
LOTHARIO *n* rake, libertine, or seducer
LOTHARIOS > LOTHARIO
LOTHEFULL *obsolete form of* > LOATHFUL
LOTHER > LOTH
LOTHEST > LOTH
LOTHFULL *obsolete form of* > LOATHFUL
LOTHNESS > LOTH
LOTHSOME *same as* > LOATHSOME
LOTI *n* standard monetary unit of Lesotho, divided into 100 lisente
LOTIC *adj* of, relating to, or designating natural communities living in rapidly flowing water
LOTION *n* medical or cosmetic liquid for use on the skin
LOTIONS > LOTION
LOTO *same as* > LOTTO
LOTOS *same as* > LOTUS
LOTOSES > LOTOS
LOTS > LOT
LOTTE *n* type of fish
LOTTED > LOT
LOTTER *n* someone who works an allotment
LOTTERIES > LOTTERY
LOTTERS > LOTTER
LOTTERY *n* method of raising money by selling tickets that win prizes by chance
LOTTES > LOTTE
LOTTING > LOT
LOTTO *n* game of chance like bingo
LOTTOS > LOTTO
LOTUS *n* legendary plant whose fruit induces forgetfulness
LOTUSES > LOTUS
LOTUSLAND *n* idyllic place of contentment

LOU Scot word for ➤ LOVE
LOUCHE adj shifty or disreputable
LOUCHELY ➤ LOUCHE
LOUCHER ➤ LOUCHE
LOUCHEST ➤ LOUCHE
LOUD adj relatively great in volume
LOUDEN vb make or become louder
LOUDENED ➤ LOUDEN
LOUDENING ➤ LOUDEN
LOUDENS ➤ LOUDEN
LOUDER ➤ LOUD
LOUDEST ➤ LOUD
LOUDISH adj fairly loud
LOUDLIER ➤ LOUD
LOUDLIEST ➤ LOUD
LOUDLY ➤ LOUD
LOUDMOUTH n person who talks too much, esp in a boastful or indiscreet way
LOUDNESS ➤ LOUD
LOUED ➤ LOU
LOUGH n loch
LOUGHS ➤ LOUGH
LOUIE same as ➤ LOOEY
LOUIES ➤ LOUIE
LOUING ➤ LOU
LOUIS n former French gold coin
LOUMA n weekly market in rural areas of developing countries
LOUMAS ➤ LOUMA
LOUN same as ➤ LOWN
LOUND same as ➤ LOUN
LOUNDED ➤ LOUND
LOUNDER vb beat severely
LOUNDERED ➤ LOUNDER
LOUNDERS ➤ LOUNDER
LOUNDING ➤ LOUND
LOUNDS ➤ LOUND
LOUNED ➤ LOUN
LOUNGE n living room in a private house ▷ vb sit, lie, or stand in a relaxed manner
LOUNGED ➤ LOUNGE
LOUNGER n comfortable sometimes adjustable couch or extending chair designed for someone to relax on
LOUNGERS ➤ LOUNGER
LOUNGES ➤ LOUNGE
LOUNGEY n suggestive of a lounge bar or easy-listening music
LOUNGIER ➤ LOUNGEY
LOUNGIEST ➤ LOUNGEY
LOUNGING ➤ LOUNGE
LOUNGINGS ➤ LOUNGE
LOUNGY adj casual; relaxed
LOUNING ➤ LOUN
LOUNS ➤ LOUN
LOUP Scot word for ➤ LEAP
LOUPE n magnifying glass used by jewellers, horologists, etc
LOUPED ➤ LOUP
LOUPEN ➤ LOUP
LOUPES ➤ LOUPE
LOUPING ➤ LOUP

LOUPIT ➤ LOUP
LOUPS ➤ LOUP
LOUR vb (esp of the sky, weather, etc) to be overcast, dark, and menacing ▷ n menacing scowl or appearance
LOURE n slow, former French dance
LOURED ➤ LOUR
LOURES ➤ LOURE
LOURIE n type of African bird with either crimson or grey plumage
LOURIER ➤ LOURY
LOURIES ➤ LOURIE
LOURIEST ➤ LOURY
LOURING ➤ LOUR
LOURINGLY ➤ LOUR
LOURINGS ➤ LOUR
LOURS ➤ LOUR
LOURY adj sombre
LOUS ➤ LOU
LOUSE n wingless parasitic insect ▷ vb ruin or spoil
LOUSED ➤ LOUSE
LOUSER n mean nasty person
LOUSERS ➤ LOUSER
LOUSES ➤ LOUSE
LOUSEWORT n any of various N temperate scrophulariaceous plants
LOUSIER ➤ LOUSY
LOUSIEST ➤ LOUSY
LOUSILY ➤ LOUSY
LOUSINESS ➤ LOUSY
LOUSING ➤ LOUSE
LOUSY adj mean or unpleasant
LOUT n crude, oafish, or aggressive person ▷ vb bow or stoop
LOUTED ➤ LOUT
LOUTING ➤ LOUT
LOUTISH adj characteristic of a lout
LOUTISHLY ➤ LOUTISH
LOUTS ➤ LOUT
LOUVAR n large silvery whalelike scombroid fish
LOUVARS ➤ LOUVAR
LOUVER same as ➤ LOUVRE
LOUVERED same as ➤ LOUVRED
LOUVERS ➤ LOUVER
LOUVRE n one of a set of parallel slats slanted to admit air but not rain
LOUVRED adj (of a window, door, etc) having louvres
LOUVRES ➤ LOUVRE
LOVABLE adj attracting or deserving affection
LOVABLY ➤ LOVABLE
LOVAGE n European plant used for flavouring food
LOVAGES ➤ LOVAGE
LOVAT n yellowish-green or bluish-green mixture, esp in tweeds or woollens
LOVATS ➤ LOVAT
LOVE vb have a great affection for ▷ n great

affection
LOVEABLE same as ➤ LOVABLE
LOVEABLY ➤ LOVABLE
LOVEBIRD n small parrot
LOVEBIRDS ➤ LOVEBIRD
LOVEBITE n temporary red mark left on a person's skin by someone biting or sucking it
LOVEBITES ➤ LOVEBITE
LOVEBUG n small US flying insect
LOVEBUGS ➤ LOVEBUG
LOVED ➤ LOVE
LOVEFEST n event when people talk about loving one another
LOVEFESTS ➤ LOVEFEST
LOVELESS adj without love
LOVELIER ➤ LOVELY
LOVELIES ➤ LOVELY
LOVELIEST ➤ LOVELY
LOVELIGHT n brightness of eyes of one in love
LOVELILY ➤ LOVELY
LOVELOCK n long lock of hair worn on the forehead
LOVELOCKS ➤ LOVELOCK
LOVELORN adj miserable because of unhappiness in love
LOVELY adj very attractive ▷ n attractive woman
LOVEMAKER n one involved in lovemaking
LOVER n person having a sexual relationship outside marriage
LOVERED adj having a lover
LOVERLESS ➤ LOVER
LOVERLY adj loverlike
LOVERS ➤ LOVE
LOVES ➤ LOVE
LOVESEAT n armchair for two people
LOVESEATS ➤ LOVESEAT
LOVESICK adj pining or languishing because of love
LOVESOME adj full of love
LOVEVINE n leafless parasitic vine
LOVEVINES ➤ LOVEVINE
LOVEY another word for ➤ LOVE
LOVEYS ➤ LOVEY
LOVING adj affectionate, tender
LOVINGLY ➤ LOVING
LOVINGS ➤ LOVING
LOW adj not tall, high, or elevated ▷ adv in or to a low position, level, or degree ▷ n low position, level, or degree ▷ vb moo
LOWAN n type of Australian bird
LOWANS ➤ LOWAN
LOWBALL vb deliberately under-charge
LOWBALLED ➤ LOWBALL
LOWBALLS ➤ LOWBALL
LOWBORN adj of ignoble or

common parentage
LOWBOY n table fitted with drawers
LOWBOYS ➤ LOWBOY
LOWBRED same as ➤ LOWBORN
LOWBROW adj with nonintellectual tastes and interests ▷ n person with uncultivated or nonintellectual tastes
LOWBROWED ➤ LOWBROW
LOWBROWS ➤ LOWBROW
LOWDOWN n inside information
LOWDOWNS ➤ LOWDOWN
LOWE variant of ➤ LOW
LOWED ➤ LOW
LOWER adj below one or more other things ▷ vb cause or allow to move down
LOWERABLE ➤ LOWER
LOWERCASE n small letters ▷ adj non-capitalized
LOWERED ➤ LOWER
LOWERIER ➤ LOWERY
LOWERIEST ➤ LOWERY
LOWERING ➤ LOWER
LOWERINGS ➤ LOWER
LOWERMOST adj lowest
LOWERS ➤ LOWER
LOWERY adj sombre
LOWES ➤ LOWE
LOWEST ➤ LOW
LOWING ➤ LOW
LOWINGS ➤ LOW
LOWISH ➤ LOW
LOWLAND n low-lying country ▷ adj of a lowland or lowlands
LOWLANDER ➤ LOWLAND
LOWLANDS ➤ LOWLAND
LOWLIER ➤ LOWLY
LOWLIEST ➤ LOWLY
LOWLIFE n member or members of the underworld
LOWLIFER ➤ LOWLIFE
LOWLIFERS ➤ LOWLIFE
LOWLIFES ➤ LOWLIFE
LOWLIGHT n unenjoyable or unpleasant part of an event
LOWLIGHTS ➤ LOWLIGHT
LOWLIHEAD n state of being humble
LOWLILY ➤ LOWLY
LOWLINESS ➤ LOWLY
LOWLIVES ➤ LOWLIFE
LOWLY adj modest, humble ▷ adv in a low or lowly manner
LOWN vb calm
LOWND same as ➤ LOWN
LOWNDED ➤ LOWND
LOWNDING ➤ LOWND
LOWNDS ➤ LOWND
LOWNE same as ➤ LOON
LOWNED ➤ LOWN
LOWNES ➤ LOWNE
LOWNESS ➤ LOW
LOWNESSES ➤ LOW
LOWNING ➤ LOWN

LOWNS > LOWN

LOWP same as > LOUP

LOWPED > LOWP

LOWPING > LOWP

LOWPS > LOWP

LOWRIDER n car with body close to ground

LOWRIDERS > LOWRIDER

LOWRIE another name for > LORY

LOWRIES > LOWRY

LOWRY another name for > LORY

LOWS > LOW

LOWSE vb release or loose ▷ adj loose

LOWSED > LOWSE

LOWSENING same as > LOOSING

LOWSER > LOWSE

LOWSES > LOWSE

LOWSEST > LOWSE

LOWSING > LOWSE

LOWSIT > LOWSE

LOWT same as > LOUT

LOWTED > LOWT

LOWTING > LOWT

LOWTS > LOWT

LOWVELD n low ground in S Africa

LOWVELDS > LOWVELD

LOX vb load fuel tanks of spacecraft with liquid oxygen ▷ n kind of smoked salmon

LOXED > LOX

LOXES > LOX

LOXING > LOX

LOXODROME n line on globe crossing all meridians at same angle

LOXODROMY n technique of navigating using rhumb lines

LOXYGEN n liquid oxygen

LOXYGENS > LOXYGEN

LOY n narrow spade with a single footrest

LOYAL adj faithful to one's friends, country, or government

LOYALER > LOYAL

LOYALEST > LOYAL

LOYALISM > LOYALIST

LOYALISMS > LOYALIST

LOYALIST n patriotic supporter of the sovereign or government

LOYALISTS > LOYALIST

LOYALLER > LOYAL

LOYALLEST > LOYAL

LOYALLY > LOYAL

LOYALNESS > LOYAL

LOYALTIES > LOYALTY

LOYALTY n quality of being loyal

LOYS > LOY

LOZELL obsolete form of > LOSEL

LOZELLS > LOZELL

LOZEN n window pane

LOZENGE n medicated tablet held in the mouth until it dissolves

LOZENGED adj decorated with lozenges

LOZENGES > LOZENGE

LOZENGY adj divided by diagonal lines to form a lattice

LOZENS > LOZEN

LUACH n calendar that shows the dates of festivals and, usually, the times of start and finish of the Sabbath

LUAU n feast of Hawaiian food

LUAUS > LUAU

LUBBARD same as > LUBBER

LUBBARDS > LUBBARD

LUBBER n big, awkward, or stupid person

LUBBERLY > LUBBER

LUBBERS > LUBBER

LUBE n lubricating oil ▷ vb lubricate with oil

LUBED > LUBE

LUBES > LUBE

LUBFISH n type of fish

LUBFISHES > LUBFISH

LUBING > LUBE

LUBRA n Aboriginal woman

LUBRAS > LUBRA

LUBRIC adj slippery

LUBRICAL same as > LUBRIC

LUBRICANT n lubricating substance, such as oil ▷ adj serving to lubricate

LUBRICATE vb oil or grease to lessen friction

LUBRICITY n lewdness or salaciousness

LUBRICOUS adj lewd or lascivious

LUCARNE n type of dormer window

LUCARNES > LUCARNE

LUCE another name for > PIKE

LUCENCE > LUCENT

LUCENCES > LUCENT

LUCENCIES > LUCENT

LUCENCY > LUCENT

LUCENT adj brilliant, shining, or translucent

LUCENTLY > LUCENT

LUCERN same as > LUCERNE

LUCERNE n alfalfa

LUCERNES > LUCERNE

LUCERNS > LUCERN

LUCES > LUCE

LUCHOT > LUACH

LUCHOTH > LUACH

LUCID adj clear and easily understood

LUCIDER > LUCID

LUCIDEST > LUCID

LUCIDITY > LUCID

LUCIDLY > LUCID

LUCIDNESS > LUCID

LUCIFER n friction match

LUCIFERIN n substance occurring in bioluminescent organisms, such as glow-worms and fireflies

LUCIFERS > LUCIFER

LUCIGEN n lamp burning oil mixed with hot air

LUCIGENS > LUCIGEN

LUCITE n brand name of a type of transparent acrylic-based plastic

LUCITES > LUCITE

LUCK n fortune, good or bad ▷ vb have good fortune

LUCKED > LUCK

LUCKEN adj shut

LUCKIE same as > LUCKY

LUCKIER > LUCKY

LUCKIES > LUCKIE

LUCKIEST > LUCKY

LUCKILY > LUCKY

LUCKINESS > LUCKY

LUCKING > LUCK

LUCKLESS adj having bad luck

LUCKPENNY n coin kept for luck

LUCKS > LUCK

LUCKY adj having or bringing good luck ▷ n old woman

LUCRATIVE adj very profitable

LUCRE n money or wealth

LUCRES > LUCRE

LUCTATION n effort; struggle

LUCUBRATE vb write or study, esp at night

LUCULENT adj easily understood

LUCUMA n type of S American tree

LUCUMAS > LUCUMA

LUCUMO n Etruscan king

LUCUMONES > LUCUMO

LUCUMOS > LUCUMO

LUD n lord ▷ interj exclamation of dismay or surprise

LUDE n slang word for drug for relieving anxiety

LUDERICK n Australian fish, usu black or dark brown in colour

LUDERICKS > LUDERICK

LUDES > LUDE

LUDIC adj playful

LUDICALLY > LUDIC

LUDICROUS adj absurd or ridiculous

LUDO n game played with dice and counters on a board

LUDOS > LUDO

LUDS > LUD

LUDSHIP > LUD

LUDSHIPS > LUD

LUES n any venereal disease

LUETIC > LUES

LUETICS > LUES

LUFF vb sail (a ship) towards the wind ▷ n leading edge of a fore-and-aft sail

LUFFA same as > LOOFAH

LUFFAS > LUFFA

LUFFED > LUFF

LUFFING > LUFF

LUFFS > LUFF

LUG vb carry or drag with great effort ▷ n projection serving as a handle

LUGE n racing toboggan on which riders lie on their backs, descending feet first ▷ vb ride on a luge

LUGED > LUGE

LUGEING > LUGE

LUGEINGS > LUGE

LUGER n tradename for a type of German automatic pistol

LUGERS > LUGER

LUGES > LUGE

LUGGABLE n unwieldy portable computer

LUGGABLES > LUGGABLE

LUGGAGE n suitcases, bags, etc

LUGGAGES > LUGGAGE

LUGGED > LUG

LUGGER n small working boat with an oblong sail

LUGGERS > LUGGER

LUGGIE n wooden bowl with handles

LUGGIES > LUGGIE

LUGGING > LUG

LUGHOLE informal word for > EAR

LUGHOLES > LUGHOLE

LUGING > LUGE

LUGINGS > LUGE

LUGS > LUG

LUGSAIL n four-sided sail bent and hoisted on a yard

LUGSAILS > LUGSAIL

LUGWORM n large worm used as bait

LUGWORMS > LUGWORM

LUIT Scots past form of > LET

LUITEN > LET

LUKE variant of > LUKEWARM

LUKEWARM adj moderately warm, tepid

LULIBUB obsolete form of > LOLLIPOP

LULIBUBS > LULIBUB

LULL vb soothe (someone) by soft sounds or motions ▷ n brief time of quiet in a storm etc

LULLABIED > LULLABY

LULLABIES > LULLABY

LULLABY n quiet song to send a child to sleep ▷ vb quiet or soothe with or as if with a lullaby

LULLED > LULL

LULLER > LULL

LULLERS > LULL

LULLING > LULL

LULLS > LULL

LULU n person or thing considered to be outstanding in size, appearance, etc

LULUS > LULU

LUM *n* chimney
LUMA *n* a monetary unit of Armenia worth one hundredth of a dram
LUMAS > LUMA
LUMBAGO *n* pain in the lower back
LUMBAGOS > LUMBAGO
LUMBANG *n* type of tree
LUMBANGS > LUMBANG
LUMBAR *adj* of the part of the body between the lowest ribs and the hipbones ▷ *n* old-fashioned kind of ship
LUMBARS > LUMBAR
LUMBER *n* unwanted disused household articles ▷ *vb* burden with something unpleasant
LUMBERED > LUMBER
LUMBERER > LUMBER
LUMBERERS > LUMBER
LUMBERING *n* business or trade of cutting, transporting, preparing, or selling timber ▷ *adj* awkward in movement
LUMBERLY *adj* heavy; clumsy
LUMBERMAN *n* person whose work involves felling trees
LUMBERMEN > LUMBERMAN
LUMBERS > LUMBER
LUMBRICAL *adj* relating to any of the four wormlike muscles in the hand or foot
LUMBRICI > LUMBRICUS
LUMBRICUS *n* type of worm
LUMEN *n* derived SI unit of luminous flux
LUMENAL > LUMEN
LUMENS > LUMEN
LUMINA > LUMEN
LUMINAIRE *n* light fixture
LUMINAL > LUMEN
LUMINANCE *n* state or quality of radiating or reflecting light
LUMINANT *n* something used to give light
LUMINANTS > LUMINANT
LUMINARIA *n* type of candle
LUMINARY *n* famous person ▷ *adj* of, involving, or characterized by light or enlightenment
LUMINE *vb* illuminate
LUMINED > LUMINE
LUMINES > LUMINE
LUMINESCE *vb* exhibit luminescence
LUMINING > LUMINE
LUMINISM *n* US artistic movement
LUMINISMS > LUMINISM
LUMINIST > LUMINISM
LUMINISTS > LUMINISM
LUMINOUS *adj* reflecting or giving off light

LUMME *interj* exclamation of surprise or dismay
LUMMIER > LUMMY
LUMMIEST > LUMMY
LUMMOX *n* clumsy or stupid person
LUMMOXES > LUMMOX
LUMMY *interj* exclamation of surprise ▷ *adj* excellent
LUMP *n* shapeless piece or mass ▷ *vb* consider as a single group
LUMPED > LUMP
LUMPEN *adj* stupid or unthinking ▷ *n* member of underclass
LUMPENLY > LUMPEN
LUMPENS > LUMPEN
LUMPER *n* stevedore
LUMPERS > LUMPER
LUMPFISH *n* North Atlantic scorpaenoid fish
LUMPIER > LUMPY
LUMPIEST > LUMPY
LUMPILY > LUMPY
LUMPINESS > LUMPY
LUMPING > LUMP
LUMPINGLY > LUMP
LUMPISH *adj* stupid or clumsy
LUMPISHLY > LUMPISH
LUMPKIN *n* lout
LUMPKINS > LUMPKIN
LUMPS > LUMP
LUMPY *adj* full of or having lumps
LUMS > LUM
LUNA *n* type of large American moth
LUNACIES > LUNACY
LUNACY *n* foolishness
LUNANAUT *same as* > LUNARNAUT
LUNANAUTS > LUNANAUT
LUNAR *adj* relating to the moon ▷ *n* lunar distance
LUNARIAN *n* inhabitant of the moon
LUNARIANS > LUNARIAN
LUNARIES > LUNARY
LUNARIST *n* one believing the moon influences weather
LUNARISTS > LUNARIST
LUNARNAUT *n* astronaut who travels to moon
LUNARS > LUNAR
LUNARY *n* moonwort herb
LUNAS > LUNA
LUNATE *adj* shaped like a crescent ▷ *n* crescent-shaped bone forming part of the wrist
LUNATED *variant of* > LUNATE
LUNATELY > LUNATE
LUNATES > LUNATE
LUNATIC *adj* foolish and irresponsible ▷ *n* foolish or annoying person
LUNATICAL *variant of* > LUNATIC
LUNATICS > LUNATIC
LUNATION *See* > MONTH

LUNATIONS > LUNATION
LUNCH *n* meal taken in the middle of the day ▷ *vb* eat lunch
LUNCHBOX *n* container for carrying a packed lunch
LUNCHED > LUNCH
LUNCHEON *n* formal lunch
LUNCHEONS > LUNCHEON
LUNCHER > LUNCH
LUNCHERS > LUNCH
LUNCHES > LUNCH
LUNCHING > LUNCH
LUNCHMEAT *n* mixture of meat and cereal
LUNCHROOM *n* room where lunch is served or people may eat lunches they bring
LUNCHTIME *n* time at which lunch is usually eaten
LUNE *same as* > LUNETTE
LUNES > LUNE
LUNET *n* small moon or satellite
LUNETS > LUNET
LUNETTE *n* anything that is shaped like a crescent
LUNETTES > LUNETTE
LUNG *n* organ that allows an animal or bird to breathe air
LUNGAN *same as* > LONGAN
LUNGANS > LUNGAN
LUNGE *n* sudden forward motion ▷ *vb* move with or make a lunge
LUNGED > LUNGE
LUNGEE *same as* > LUNGI
LUNGEES > LUNGEE
LUNGER > LUNGE
LUNGERS > LUNGE
LUNGES > LUNGE
LUNGEING > LUNGE
LUNGFISH *n* freshwater bony fish with an air-breathing lung
LUNGFUL > LUNG
LUNGFULS > LUNG
LUNGI *n* long piece of cotton cloth worn as a loincloth, sash, or turban by Indian men or as a skirt
LUNGIE *n* guillemot
LUNGIES > LUNGIE
LUNGING > LUNGE
LUNGIS > LUNGI
LUNGLESS *adj* having no lungs
LUNGS > LUNG
LUNGWORM *n* type of parasitic worm occurring in the lungs of mammals
LUNGWORMS > LUNGWORM
LUNGWORT *n* Eurasian plant with spotted leaves and clusters of blue or purple flowers, formerly used to treat lung diseases
LUNGWORTS > LUNGWORT
LUNGYI *same as* > LUNGI
LUNGYIS > LUNGYI
LUNIER > LUNY
LUNIES > LUNY

LUNIEST > LUNY
LUNINESS > LUNY
LUNISOLAR *adj* resulting from or based on the combined gravitational attraction of the sun and moon
LUNITIDAL *adj* of or relating to tidal phenomena as produced by the moon
LUNK *n* awkward, heavy, or stupid person
LUNKER *n* very large fish, esp bass
LUNKERS > LUNKER
LUNKHEAD *n* stupid person
LUNKHEADS > LUNKHEAD
LUNKS > LUNK
LUNT *vb* produce smoke
LUNTED > LUNT
LUNTING > LUNT
LUNTS > LUNT
LUNULA *n* white crescent-shaped area at the base of the human fingernail
LUNULAE > LUNULA
LUNULAR *same as* > LUNULATE
LUNULATE *adj* having markings shaped like crescents
LUNULATED *same as* > LUNULATE
LUNULE *same as* > LUNULA
LUNULES > LUNULE
LUNY *same as* > LOONY
LUNYIE *same as* > LUNGIE
LUNYIES > LUNYIE
LUPANAR *n* brothel
LUPANARS > LUPANAR
LUPIN *n* garden plant with tall spikes of flowers
LUPINE *adj* like a wolf ▷ *n* lupin
LUPINES > LUPINE
LUPINS > LUPIN
LUPOID *adj* suffering from lupus
LUPOUS *adj* relating to lupus
LUPPEN *Scots past form of* > LEAP
LUPULIN *n* resinous powder extracted from the female flowers of the hop plant
LUPULINE *adj* relating to lupulin
LUPULINIC *same as* > LUPULINE
LUPULINS > LUPULIN
LUPUS *n* ulcerous skin disease
LUPUSES > LUPUS
LUR *n* large bronze musical horn found in Danish peat bogs
LURCH *vb* tilt or lean suddenly to one side ▷ *n* lurching movement
LURCHED > LURCH
LURCHER *n* crossbred dog trained to hunt silently

LURCHERS > LURCHER

LURCHES > LURCH

LURCHING > LURCH

LURDAN n stupid or dull person ▷ adj dull or stupid

LURDANE same as > LURDAN

LURDANES > LURDANE

LURDANS > LURDAN

LURDEN same as > LURDAN

LURDENS > LURDEN

LURE vb tempt or attract by the promise of reward ▷ n person or thing that lures

LURED > LURE

LURER > LURE

LURERS > LURE

LURES > LURE

LUREX n thin glittery thread

LUREXES > LUREX

LURGI same as > LURGY

LURGIES > LURGY

LURGIS > LURGI

LURGY n any undetermined illness

LURID adj vivid in shocking detail, sensational

LURIDER > LURID

LURIDEST > LURID

LURIDLY > LURID

LURIDNESS > LURID

LURING > LURE

LURINGLY > LURE

LURINGS > LURING

LURK vb lie hidden or move stealthily, esp for sinister purposes

LURKED > LURK

LURKER > LURK

LURKERS > LURK

LURKING adj lingering but almost unacknowledged

LURKINGLY > LURKING

LURKINGS > LURKING

LURKS > LURK

LURRIES > LURRY

LURRY n confused jumble

LURS > LUR

LURVE n love

LURVES > LURVE

LUSCIOUS adj extremely pleasurable to taste or smell

LUSER n user of a computer system, as considered by a systems administrator or other member of a technical support team

LUSERS > LUSER

LUSH adj (of grass etc) growing thickly and healthily ▷ n alcoholic ▷ vb drink (alcohol) to excess

LUSHED > LUSH

LUSHER adj more lush ▷ n drunkard

LUSHERS > LUSHER

LUSHES > LUSH

LUSHEST > LUSH

LUSHIER > LUSHY

LUSHIEST > LUSHY

LUSHING > LUSH

LUSHLY > LUSH

LUSHNESS > LUSH

LUSHY adj slightly intoxicated

LUSK vb lounge around

LUSKED > LUSK

LUSKING > LUSK

LUSKISH adj lazy

LUSKS > LUSK

LUST n strong sexual desire ▷ vb have passionate desire (for)

LUSTED > LUST

LUSTER same as > LUSTRE

LUSTERED > LUSTER

LUSTERING > LUSTER

LUSTERS > LUSTER

LUSTFUL adj driven by lust

LUSTFULLY > LUSTFUL

LUSTICK obsolete word for > LUSTY

LUSTIER > LUSTY

LUSTIEST > LUSTY

LUSTIHEAD n vigour

LUSTIHOOD n vigour

LUSTILY > LUSTY

LUSTINESS > LUSTY

LUSTING > LUST

LUSTIQUE obsolete word for > LUSTY

LUSTLESS > LUST

LUSTRA > LUSTRUM

LUSTRAL adj of or relating to a ceremony of purification

LUSTRATE vb purify by means of religious rituals or ceremonies

LUSTRATED > LUSTRATE

LUSTRATES > LUSTRATE

LUSTRE n gloss, sheen ▷ vb make, be, or become lustrous

LUSTRED > LUSTRE

LUSTRES > LUSTRE

LUSTRINE same as > LUSTRING

LUSTRING n glossy silk cloth, formerly used for clothing, upholstery, etc

LUSTRINGS > LUSTRING

LUSTROUS > LUSTRE

LUSTRUM n period of five years

LUSTRUMS > LUSTRUM

LUSTS > LUST

LUSTY adj vigorous, healthy

LUSUS n freak, mutant, or monster

LUSUSES > LUSUS

LUTANIST same as > LUTENIST

LUTANISTS > LUTANIST

LUTE n ancient guitar-like musical instrument with a body shaped like a half pear ▷ vb seal (a joint or surface) with a mixture of cement and clay

LUTEA adj yellow

LUTEAL adj relating to or characterized by the development of the corpus luteum

LUTECIUM same as > LUTETIUM

LUTECIUMS > LUTECIUM

LUTED > LUTE

LUTEFISK n Scandinavian fish dish

LUTEFISKS > LUTEFISK

LUTEIN n xanthophyll pigment that has a light-absorbing function in photosynthesis

LUTEINISE same as > LUTEINIZE

LUTEINIZE vb develop into part of corpus luteum

LUTEINS > LUTEIN

LUTENIST n person who plays the lute

LUTENISTS > LUTENIST

LUTEOLIN n yellow crystalline compound found in many plants

LUTEOLINS > LUTEOLIN

LUTEOLOUS > LUTEOLIN

LUTEOUS adj of a light to moderate greenish-yellow colour

LUTER n lute player

LUTERS > LUTER

LUTES > LUTE

LUTESCENT adj yellowish in colour

LUTETIUM n silvery-white metallic element

LUTETIUMS > LUTETIUM

LUTEUM adj yellow

LUTFISK same as > LUTEFISK

LUTFISKS > LUTFISK

LUTHERN another name for > DORMER

LUTHERNS > LUTHERN

LUTHIER n lute-maker

LUTHIERS > LUTHIER

LUTING n mixture of cement and clay

LUTINGS > LUTING

LUTIST same as > LUTENIST

LUTISTS > LUTIST

LUTITE another name for > PELITE

LUTITES > LUTITE

LUTTEN > LOOT

LUTZ n jump in which the skater takes off from the back outside edge of one skate, makes one, two, or three turns in the air, and lands on the back outside edge of the other skate

LUTZES > LUTZ

LUV n love

LUVS > LOVE

LUVVIE n person who is involved in acting or the theatre

LUVVIEDOM n theatrical world

LUVVIES > LUVVY

LUVVY same as > LUVVIE

LUX n unit of illumination

LUXATE vb put (a shoulder, knee, etc) out of joint

LUXATED > LUXATE

LUXATES > LUXATE

LUXATING > LUXATE

LUXATION > LUXATE

LUXATIONS > LUXATE

LUXE as in de luxe rich, elegant, or sumptuous

LUXES > LUXE

LUXMETER n device for measuring light

LUXMETERS > LUXMETER

LUXURIANT adj rich and abundant

LUXURIATE vb take self-indulgent pleasure (in)

LUXURIES > LUXURY

LUXURIOUS adj full of luxury, sumptuous

LUXURIST n lover of luxury

LUXURISTS > LUXURIST

LUXURY n enjoyment of rich, very comfortable living ▷ adj of or providing luxury

LUZ n supposedly indestructible bone of the human body

LUZERN n alfalfa

LUZERNS > LUZERN

LUZZES > LUZ

LWEI n Angolan monetary unit

LWEIS > LWEI

LYAM n leash

LYAMS > LYAM

LYARD same as > LIARD

LYART same as > LIARD

LYASE n any enzyme that catalyses the separation of two parts of a molecule

LYASES > LYASE

LYCAENID n type of butterfly

LYCAENIDS > LYCAENID

LYCEA > LYCEUM

LYCEE n secondary school

LYCEES > LYCEE

LYCEUM n public building for events such as concerts and lectures

LYCEUMS > LYCEUM

LYCH same as > LICH

LYCHEE same as > LITCHI

LYCHEES > LYCHEE

LYCHES > LYCH

LYCHGATE same as > LICHGATE

LYCHGATES > LYCHGATE

LYCHNIS n type of plant with red, pink, or white five-petalled flowers

LYCHNISES > LYCHNIS

LYCOPENE n red pigment

LYCOPENES > LYCOPENE

LYCOPOD n type of moss

LYCOPODS > LYCOPOD

LYCRA n tradename for a type of synthetic elastic fabric and fibre used for tight-fitting garments, such as swimming costumes

LYCRAS > LYCRA

LYDDITE n explosive consisting chiefly of fused picric acid
LYDDITES > LYDDITE
LYE n caustic solution obtained by leaching wood ash
LYES > LYE
LYFULL obsolete form of > LIFEFUL
LYING > LIE
LYINGLY > LIE
LYINGS > LIE
LYKEWAKE n watch held over a dead person, often with festivities
LYKEWAKES > LYKEWAKE
LYKEWALK variant of > LYKEWAKE
LYKEWALKS > LYKEWALK
LYM obsolete form of > LYAM
LYME as in lyme grass type of perennial dune grass
LYMES > LYME
LYMITER same as > LIMITER
LYMITERS > LIMITER
LYMPH n colourless bodily fluid consisting mainly of white blood cells
LYMPHAD n ancient rowing boat
LYMPHADS > LYMPHAD
LYMPHATIC adj of, relating to, or containing lymph ▷ n lymphatic vessel
LYMPHOID adj of or resembling lymph, or relating to the lymphatic system
LYMPHOMA n any form of cancer of the lymph nodes
LYMPHOMAS > LYMPHOMA
LYMPHS n lymph
LYMS > LYM
LYNAGE obsolete form of > LINEAGE
LYNAGES > LYNAGE
LYNCEAN adj of or resembling a lynx
LYNCH vb put to death without a trial
LYNCHED > LYNCH
LYNCHER > LYNCH

LYNCHERS > LYNCH
LYNCHES > LYNCH
LYNCHET n terrace or ridge formed in prehistoric or medieval times by ploughing a hillside
LYNCHETS > LYNCHET
LYNCHING > LYNCH
LYNCHINGS > LYNCH
LYNCHPIN same as > LINCHPIN
LYNCHPINS > LYNCHPIN
LYNE n flax
LYNES > LYNE
LYNX n animal of the cat family with tufted ears and a short tail
LYNXES > LYNX
LYNXLIKE > LYNX
LYOLYSES > LYOLYSIS
LYOLYSIS n formation of an acid and a base from the interaction of a salt with a solvent
LYOMEROUS adj relating to Lyomeri fish
LYONNAISE adj (of food) cooked or garnished with onions, usually fried
LYOPHIL same as > LYOPHILIC
LYOPHILE same as > LYOPHILIC
LYOPHILED adj lyophiliized
LYOPHILIC adj (of a colloid) having a dispersed phase with a high affinity for the continuous phase
LYOPHOBE same as > LYOPHOBIC
LYOPHOBIC adj (of a colloid) having a dispersed phase with little or no affinity for the continuous phase
LYRA as in lyra viol lutelike musical instrument of the 16th and 17th centuries
LYRATE adj shaped like a lyre
LYRATED same as > LYRATE
LYRATELY > LYRATE

LYRE n ancient musical instrument like a U-shaped harp
LYREBIRD n Australian bird, the male of which spreads its tail into the shape of a lyre
LYREBIRDS > LYREBIRD
LYRES > LYRE
LYRIC adj (of poetry) expressing personal emotion in songlike style ▷ n short poem in a songlike style
LYRICAL same as > LYRIC
LYRICALLY > LYRIC
LYRICISE same as > LYRICIZE
LYRICISED > LYRICISE
LYRICISES > LYRICISE
LYRICISM n quality or style of lyric poetry
LYRICISMS > LYRICISM
LYRICIST n person who writes the words of songs or musicals
LYRICISTS > LYRICIST
LYRICIZE vb write lyrics
LYRICIZED > LYRICIZE
LYRICIZES > LYRICIZE
LYRICON n wind synthesizer
LYRICONS > LYRICON
LYRICS > LYRIC
LYRIFORM adj lyre-shaped
LYRISM n art or technique of playing the lyre
LYRISMS > LYRISM
LYRIST same as > LYRICIST
LYRISTS > LYRIST
LYSATE n material formed by lysis
LYSATES > LYSATE
LYSE vb undergo or cause to undergo lysis
LYSED > LYSE
LYSERGIC as in lysergic acid crystalline compound used in medical research
LYSERGIDE n LSD
LYSES > LYSIS
LYSIGENIC adj caused by breaking down of cells

LYSIMETER n instrument for determining solubility, esp the amount of water-soluble matter in soil
LYSIN n any of a group of antibodies that cause dissolution of cells against which they are directed
LYSINE n essential amino acid that occurs in proteins
LYSINES > LYSINE
LYSING > LYSE
LYSINS > LYSIN
LYSIS n destruction or dissolution of cells by the action of a particular lysin
LYSOGEN n lysis-inducing agent
LYSOGENIC > LYSOGEN
LYSOGENS > LYSOGEN
LYSOGENY > LYSOGEN
LYSOL n tradename for a solution used as an antiseptic and disinfectant
LYSOLS > LYSOL
LYSOSOMAL > LYSOSOME
LYSOSOME n any of numerous small particles that are present in the cytoplasm of most cells
LYSOSOMES > LYSOSOME
LYSOZYME n enzyme occurring in tears, certain body tissues, and egg white
LYSOZYMES > LYSOZYME
LYSSA less common word for > RABIES
LYSSAS > LYSSA
LYTE vb dismount
LYTED > LYTE
LYTES > LYTE
LYTHE n type of fish
LYTHES > LYTHE
LYTIC adj relating to, causing, or resulting from lysis
LYTICALLY > LYTIC
LYTING > LYTE
LYTTA n rodlike mass of cartilage beneath the tongue in the dog and other carnivores
LYTTAE > LYTTA
LYTTAS > LYTTA

Mm

MA *n* mother
MAA *vb* (of goats) bleat
MAAED > MAA
MAAING > MAA
MAAR *n* coneless volcanic crater that has been formed by a single explosion
MAARE > MAAR
MAARS > MAAR
MAAS *n* thick soured milk
MAASES > MAAS
MAATJES *n* pickled herring
MABE *n* type of pearl
MABELA *n* ground kaffir corn used for making porridge
MABELAS > MABELAS
MABES > MABE
MAC *n* macintosh
MACABER *same as* > MACABRE
MACABRE *adj* strange and horrible, gruesome
MACABRELY > MACABRE
MACACO *n* type of lemur
MACACOS > MACACO
MACADAM *n* road surface of pressed layers of small broken stones
MACADAMIA *n* Australian tree with edible nuts
MACADAMS > MACADAM
MACAHUBA *n* South American palm tree
MACAHUBAS > MACAHUBA
MACALLUM *n* ice cream with raspberry sauce
MACALLUMS > MACALLUM
MACAQUE *n* monkey of Asia and Africa with cheek pouches and either a short tail or no tail
MACAQUES > MACAQUE
MACARISE *vb* congratulate
MACARISED > MACARISE
MACARISES > MACARISE
MACARISM *n* blessing
MACARISMS > MACARISM
MACARIZE *same as* > MACARISE
MACARIZED > MACARIZE
MACARIZES > MACARIZE
MACARONI *n* pasta in short tube shapes
MACARONIC *adj* (of verse) characterized by a mixture of vernacular words jumbled together with Latin words or Latinized

words or with words from one or more other foreign languages ▷ *n* macaronic verse
MACARONIS > MACARONI
MACAROON *n* small biscuit or cake made with ground almonds
MACAROONS > MACAROON
MACASSAR *n* oily preparation formerly put on the hair to make it smooth and shiny
MACASSARS > MACASSAR
MACAW *n* large tropical American parrot
MACAWS > MACAW
MACCABAW *same as* > MACCABOY
MACCABAWS > MACCABAW
MACCABOY *n* dark rose-scented snuff
MACCABOYS > MACCABOY
MACCARONI *same as* > MACARONI
MACCHIA *n* thicket in Italy
MACCHIATO *n* espresso coffee served with a dash of hot or cold milk
MACCHIE > MACCHIA
MACCOBOY *same as* > MACCABOY
MACCOBOYS > MACCOBOY
MACE *n* club, usually having a spiked metal head, used esp in the Middle Ages ▷ *vb* use a mace
MACED > MACE
MACEDOINE *n* hot or cold mixture of diced vegetables
MACER *n* macebearer, esp (in Scotland) an official who acts as usher in a court of law
MACERAL *n* any of the organic units that constitute coal: equivalent to any of the mineral constituents of a rock
MACERALS > MACERAL
MACERATE *vb* soften by soaking
MACERATED > MACERATE
MACERATER > MACERATE
MACERATES > MACERATE
MACERATOR > MACERATE
MACERS > MACER
MACES > MACE
MACH *n* ratio of the speed of a body in a particular medium to the speed of

sound in that medium
MACHAIR *n* (in the western Highlands of Scotland) a strip of sandy, grassy, often lime-rich land just above the high-water mark at a sandy shore: used as grazing or arable land
MACHAIRS > MACHAIR
MACHAN *n* (in India) a raised platform used in tiger hunting
MACHANS > MACHAN
MACHE *n* papier-mâché
MACHER *n* important or influential person: often used ironically
MACHERS > MACHER
MACHES > MACHE
MACHETE *n* broad heavy knife used for cutting or as a weapon
MACHETES > MACHETE
MACHI as in *machi chips* in Indian English, fish and chips
MACHINATE *vb* contrive, plan, or devise (schemes, plots, etc)
MACHINE *n* apparatus, usu. powered by electricity, designed to perform a particular task ▷ *vb* make or produce by machine
MACHINED > MACHINE
MACHINERY *n* machines or machine parts collectively
MACHINES > MACHINE
MACHINIMA *n* use of real-time 3-D graphics to generate computer animation
MACHINING > MACHINE
MACHINIST *n* person who operates a machine
MACHISMO *n* exaggerated or strong masculinity
MACHISMOS > MACHISMO
MACHMETER *n* instrument for measuring the Mach number of an aircraft in flight
MACHO *adj* strongly or exaggeratedly masculine ▷ *n* strong or exaggerated masculinity
MACHOISM > MACHO
MACHOISMS > MACHO
MACHOS > MACHO
MACHREE *n* Irish form of address meaning my dear

MACHREES > MACHREE
MACHS > MACH
MACHZOR *n* Jewish prayer book containing prescribed holiday rituals
MACHZORIM > MACHZOR
MACHZORS > MACHZOR
MACING > MACE
MACINTOSH *n* waterproof raincoat
MACK *same as* > MAC
MACKEREL *n* edible sea fish
MACKERELS > MACKEREL
MACKINAW *n* thick short double-breasted plaid coat
MACKINAWS > MACKINAW
MACKLE *n* double or blurred impression caused by shifting paper or type ▷ *vb* mend hurriedly or in a makeshift way
MACKLED > MACKLE
MACKLES > MACKLE
MACKLING > MACKLE
MACKS > MACK
MACLE *n* crystal consisting of two parts
MACLED > MACLE
MACLES > MACLE
MACON *n* red or white wine from the Mâcon area, heavier than the other burgundies
MACONS > MACON
MACOYA *n* South American tree
MACOYAS > MACOYA
MACRAME *n* ornamental work of knotted cord
MACRAMES > MACRAME
MACRAMI *same as* > MACRAME
MACRAMIS > MACRAMI
MACRO *n* close-up lens
MACROBIAN *adj* long-lived
MACROCODE *n* computer instruction that triggers many other instructions
MACROCOPY *n* enlargement of printed material for easier reading
MACROCOSM *n* universe
MACROCYST *n* unusually large cyst
MACROCYTE *n* abnormally large red blood cell
MACRODOME *n* dome shape in crystal structure
MACRODONT *adj* having large teeth

MACROGLIA n one of the two types of non-nervous tissue (glia) found in the central nervous system: includes astrocytes

MACROLIDE n type of antibiotic drug

MACROLOGY n verbose but meaningless talk

MACROMERE n any of the large yolk-filled cells formed by unequal cleavage of a fertilized ovum

MACROMOLE n large chemistry mole

MACRON n mark placed over a letter to represent a long vowel

MACRONS > MACRON

MACROPOD n member of kangaroo family

MACROPODS > MACROPOD

MACROPSIA n condition of seeing everything in the field of view as larger than it really is, which can occur in diseases of the retina or in some brain disorders

MACROS > MACRO

MACROTOUS adj having large ears

MACRURAL > MACRURAN

MACRURAN n type of decapod crustacean of the group which includes the lobsters, prawns, and crayfish

MACRURANS > MACRURAN

MACRUROID > MACRURAN

MACRUROUS > MACRURAN

MACS > MAC

MACTATION n sacrificial killing

MACULA n small spot or area of distinct colour, such as a freckle

MACULAE > MACULA

MACULAR > MACULA

MACULAS > MACULA

MACULATE vb spot, stain, or pollute ▷ adj spotted or polluted

MACULATED > MACULATE

MACULATES > MACULATE

MACULE same as > MACKLE

MACULED > MACULE

MACULES > MACULE

MACULING > MACULE

MACULOSE adj having spots

MACUMBA n religious cult in Brazil that combines Christian and voodoo elements

MACUMBAS > MACUMBA

MAD adj mentally deranged, insane ▷ vb make mad

MADAFU n coconut milk

MADAFUS > MADAFU

MADAM n polite term of address for a woman ▷ vb call someone madam

MADAME n French title equivalent to Mrs

MADAMED > MADAM

MADAMES > MADAME

MADAMING > MADAM

MADAMS > MADAM

MADAROSES > MADAROSIS

MADAROSIS n abnormal loss of eyebrows or eyelashes

MADBRAIN adj insane

MADCAP adj foolish or reckless ▷ n impulsive or reckless person

MADCAPS > MADCAP

MADDED > MAD

MADDEN vb infuriate or irritate

MADDENED > MADDEN

MADDENING adj serving to send mad

MADDENS > MADDEN

MADDER n type of rose

MADDERS > MADDER

MADDEST > MAD

MADDING > MAD

MADDINGLY > MAD

MADDISH > MAD

MADDOCK same as > MATTOCK

MADDOCKS > MADDOCK

MADE > MAKE

MADEFIED > MADEFY

MADEFIES > MADEFY

MADEFY vb make moist

MADEFYING > MADEFY

MADEIRA n kind of rich sponge cake

MADEIRAS > MADEIRA

MADELEINE n small fancy sponge cake

MADERISE vb become reddish

MADERISED > MADERISE

MADERISES > MADERISE

MADERIZE same as > MADERISE

MADERIZED > MADERIZE

MADERIZES > MADERIZE

MADGE n type of hammer

MADGES > MADGE

MADHOUSE n place filled with uproar or confusion

MADHOUSES > MADHOUSE

MADID adj wet

MADISON n type of cycle relay race

MADISONS > MADISON

MADLING n insane person

MADLINGS > MADLING

MADLY adv with great speed and energy

MADMAN n person who is insane

MADMEN > MADMAN

MADNESS n insanity

MADNESSES > MADNESS

MADONNA n picture or statue of the Virgin Mary

MADONNAS > MADONNA

MADOQUA n Ethiopian antelope

MADOQUAS > MADOQUA

MADRAS n medium-hot curry

MADRASA same as > MADRASAH

MADRASAH n educational institution, particularly for Islamic religious instruction

MADRASAHS > MADRASAH

MADRASAS > MADRASA

MADRASES > MADRAS

MADRASSA same as > MADRASAH

MADRASSAH same as > MADRASAH

MADRASSAS > MADRASSA

MADRE Spanish word for > MOTHER

MADREPORE n type of coral which often occurs in tropical seas and forms large coral reefs

MADRES > MADRE

MADRIGAL n 16th-17th-century part song for unaccompanied voices

MADRIGALS > MADRIGAL

MADRILENE n cold consommé flavoured with tomato juice

MADRONA n N American evergreen tree or shrub with white flowers and red berry-like fruits

MADRONAS > MADRONA

MADRONE same as > MADRONA

MADRONES > MADRONE

MADRONO same as > MADRONA

MADRONOS > MADRONO

MADS > MAD

MADTOM n species of catfish

MADTOMS > MADTOM

MADURO adj (of cigars) dark and strong ▷ n cigar of this type

MADUROS > MADURO

MADWOMAN n woman who is insane, esp one who behaves violently

MADWOMEN > MADWOMAN

MADWORT n low-growing Eurasian plant with small blue flowers

MADWORTS > MADWORT

MADZOON same as > MATZOON

MADZOONS > MADZOON

MAE adj more

MAELID n mythical spirit of apple

MAELIDS > MAELID

MAELSTROM n great whirlpool

MAENAD n female disciple of Dionysus, the Greek god of wine

MAENADES > MAENAD

MAENADIC > MAENAD

MAENADISM > MAENAD

MAENADS > MAENAD

MAERL n type of red coralline algae

MAERLS > MAERL

MAES > MAE

MAESTOSO adv be performed majestically ▷ n piece or passage directed to be played in this way

MAESTOSOS > MAESTOSO

MAESTRI > MAESTRO

MAESTRO n outstanding musician or conductor

MAESTROS > MAESTRO

MAFFIA same as > MAFIA

MAFFIAS > MAFFIA

MAFFICK vb celebrate extravagantly and publicly

MAFFICKED > MAFFICK

MAFFICKER > MAFFICK

MAFFICKS > MAFFICK

MAFFLED adj baffled

MAFFLIN n half-witted person

MAFFLING same as > MAFFLIN

MAFFLINGS > MAFFLING

MAFFLINS > MAFFLIN

MAFIA n international secret organization founded in Sicily, probably in opposition to tyranny. It developed into a criminal organization and in the late 19th century was carried to the US by Italian immigrants

MAFIAS > MAFIA

MAFIC n collective term for minerals present in igneous rock

MAFICS > MAFIC

MAFIOSI > MAFIOSO

MAFIOSO n member of the Mafia

MAFIOSOS > MAFIOSO

MAFTED adj suffering under oppressive heat

MAFTIR n final section of the weekly Torah reading

MAFTIRS > MAFTIR

MAG vb talk ▷ n talk

MAGAININ n any of a series of related substances with antibacterial properties, derived from the skins of frogs

MAGAININS > MAGAININ

MAGALOG same as > MAGALOGUE

MAGALOGS > MAGALOG

MAGALOGUE n combination of a magazine and a catalogue

MAGAZINE n periodical publication with articles by different writers

MAGAZINES > MAGAZINE

MAGDALEN n reformed prostitute

MAGDALENE same as > MAGDALEN

MAGDALENS > MAGDALEN

MAGE archaic word for > MAGICIAN

MAGENTA adj deep purplish-red ▷ n deep purplish red that is the complementary colour of green and, with yellow and cyan, forms a set of primary colours

MAGENTAS >MAGENTA
MAGES >MAGE
MAGESHIP >MAGE
MAGESHIPS >MAGE
MAGG same as >MAG
MAGGED >MAG
MAGGIE n magpie
MAGGIES >MAGGIE
MAGGING >MAG
MAGGOT n larva of an insect
MAGGOTIER >MAGGOTY
MAGGOTS >MAGGOT
MAGGOTY adj relating to, resembling, or ridden with maggots
MAGGS >MAGG
MAGI >MAGUS
MAGIAN >MAGUS
MAGIANISM >MAGUS
MAGIANS >MAGUS
MAGIC n supposed art of invoking supernatural powers to influence events ▷ vb to transform or produce by or as if by magic ▷ adj of, using, or like magic
MAGICAL >MAGIC
MAGICALLY >MAGIC
MAGICIAN n conjuror
MAGICIANS >MAGICIAN
MAGICKED >MAGIC
MAGICKING >MAGIC
MAGICS >MAGIC
MAGILP same as >MEGILP
MAGILPS >MAGILP
MAGISM >MAGUS
MAGISMS >MAGUS
MAGISTER n person entitled to teach in medieval university
MAGISTERS >MAGISTER
MAGISTERY n agency or substance, such as the philosopher's stone, believed to transmute other substances
MAGISTRAL adj of, relating to, or characteristic of a master ▷ n fortification in a determining position
MAGLEV n type of high-speed train that runs on magnets supported by a magnetic field generated around the track
MAGLEVS >MAGLEV
MAGMA n molten rock inside the earth's crust
MAGMAS >MAGMA
MAGMATA >MAGMA
MAGMATIC >MAGMA
MAGMATISM >MAGMA
MAGNALIUM n alloy of magnesium and aluminium
MAGNATE n influential or wealthy person, esp in industry
MAGNATES >MAGNATE
MAGNES n magnetic iron ore
MAGNESES >MAGNES
MAGNESIA n white

tasteless substance used as an antacid and a laxative
MAGNESIAL >MAGNESIA
MAGNESIAN >MAGNESIA
MAGNESIAS >MAGNESIA
MAGNESIC >MAGNESIA
MAGNESITE n white, colourless, or lightly tinted mineral
MAGNESIUM n silvery-white metallic element
MAGNET n piece of iron or steel capable of attracting iron and pointing north when suspended
MAGNETAR n type of neutron star that has a very intense magnetic field, over 1000 times greater than that of a pulsar
MAGNETARS >MAGNETAR
MAGNETIC adj having the properties of a magnet
MAGNETICS n branch of physics concerned with magnetism
MAGNETISE same as >MAGNETIZE
MAGNETISM n magnetic property
MAGNETIST >MAGNETISM
MAGNETITE n black magnetizable mineral that is an important source of iron
MAGNETIZE vb make into a magnet
MAGNETO n apparatus for ignition in an internal-combustion engine
MAGNETON n unit of magnetic moment
MAGNETONS >MAGNETON
MAGNETOS >MAGNETO
MAGNETRON n electronic valve used with a magnetic field to generate microwave oscillations, used. esp in radar
MAGNETS >MAGNET
MAGNIFIC adj magnificent, grandiose, or pompous
MAGNIFICO n magnate
MAGNIFIED >MAGNIFY
MAGNIFIER >MAGNIFY
MAGNIFIES >MAGNIFY
MAGNIFY vb increase in apparent size, as with a lens
MAGNITUDE n relative importance or size
MAGNOLIA n shrub or tree with showy white or pink flowers
MAGNOLIAS >MAGNOLIA
MAGNON n short for Cro-Magnon
MAGNONS >MAGNON
MAGNOX n alloy composed mainly of magnesium, used in fuel elements of some nuclear reactors

MAGNOXES >MAGNOX
MAGNUM n large wine bottle holding about 1.5 litres
MAGNUMS >MAGNUM
MAGNUS as in magnus hitch knot similar to a clove hitch but having one more turn
MAGOT n Chinese or Japanese figurine in a crouching position, usually grotesque
MAGOTS >MAGOT
MAGPIE n black-and-white bird
MAGPIES >MAGPIE
MAGS >MAG
MAGSMAN n raconteur
MAGSMEN >MAGSMAN
MAGUEY n tropical American agave plant
MAGUEYS >MAGUEY
MAGUS n Zoroastrian priest of the ancient Medes and Persians
MAGYAR adj of or relating to a style of sleeve cut in one piece with the bodice
MAHA as in maha yoga form of yoga
MAHARAJA same as >MAHARAJAH
MAHARAJAH n former title of some Indian princes
MAHARAJAS >MAHARAJA
MAHARANEE same as >MAHARANI
MAHARANI n wife of a maharaja
MAHARANIS >MAHARANI
MAHARISHI n Hindu religious teacher or mystic
MAHATMA n person revered for holiness and wisdom
MAHATMAS >MAHATMA
MAHEWU n (in South Africa) fermented liquid mealie-meal porridge, used as a stimulant, esp by Black Africans
MAHEWUS >MAHEWU
MAHIMAHI n Pacific fish
MAHIMAHIS >MAHIMAHI
MAHJONG n game of Chinese origin, usually played by four people, in which tiles bearing various designs are drawn and discarded until one player has an entire hand of winning combinations
MAHJONGG same as >MAHJONG
MAHJONGGS >MAHJONGG
MAHJONGS >MAHJONG
MAHLSTICK same as >MAULSTICK
MAHMAL n litter used in Muslim ceremony
MAHMALS >MAHMAL
MAHOE n New Zealand tree
MAHOES >MAHOE
MAHOGANY n hard reddish-brown wood of several tropical trees ▷ adj reddish-brown

MAHONIA n Asian and American evergreen shrub cultivated for its ornamental spiny leaves and clusters of small yellow flowers
MAHONIAS >MAHONIA
MAHOUT n (in India and the East Indies) elephant driver or keeper
MAHOUTS >MAHOUT
MAHSEER n large freshwater Indian fish
MAHSEERS >MAHSEER
MAHSIR same as >MAHSEER
MAHSIRS >MAHSIR
MAHUA n Indian tree
MAHUANG n herbal medicine from shrub
MAHUANGS >MAHUANG
MAHUAS >MAHUA
MAHWA same as >MAHUA
MAHWAS >MAHWA
MAHZOR same as >MACHZOR
MAHZORIM >MAHZOR
MAHZORS >MAHZOR
MAIASAUR same as >MAIASAURA
MAIASAURA n species of dinosaur
MAIASAURS >MAIASAUR
MAID n female servant ▷ vb work as maid
MAIDAN n (in Pakistan, India, etc) an open space used for meetings, sports, etc
MAIDANS >MAIDAN
MAIDED >MAID
MAIDEN n young unmarried woman ▷ adj unmarried
MAIDENISH >MAIDEN
MAIDENLY adj modest
MAIDENS >MAIDEN
MAIDHOOD >MAID
MAIDHOODS >MAID
MAIDING >MAID
MAIDISH >MAID
MAIDISM n pellagra
MAIDISMS >MAIDISM
MAIDLESS >MAID
MAIDS >MAID
MAIEUTIC adj of or relating to the Socratic method of eliciting knowledge by a series of questions and answers
MAIEUTICS n Socratic method
MAIGRE adj not containing flesh, and so permissible as food on days of religious abstinence ▷ n species of fish
MAIGRES >MAIGRE
MAIHEM same as >MAYHEM
MAIHEMS >MAIHEM
MAIK n old halfpenny
MAIKO n apprentice geisha
MAIKOS >MAIKO**

m

MAIKS >MAIK
MAIL n letters and packages transported and delivered by the post office ▷vb send by mail
MAILABLE >MAIL
MAILBAG n large bag for transporting or delivering mail
MAILBAGS >MAILBAG
MAILBOX n box into which letters and parcels are delivered
MAILBOXES >MAILBOX
MAILCAR same as >MAILCOACH
MAILCARS >MAILCAR
MAILCOACH n railway coach specially constructed for the transportation of mail
MAILE n halfpenny
MAILED >MAIL
MAILER n person who addresses or mails letters, etc
MAILERS >MAILER
MAILES >MAILE
MAILGRAM n telegram
MAILGRAMS >MAILGRAM
MAILING >MAIL
MAILINGS >MAILING
MAILL n Scots word meaning rent
MAILLESS >MAIL
MAILLOT n tights worn for ballet, gymnastics, etc
MAILLOTS >MAILLOT
MAILLS >MAILL
MAILMAN n postman
MAILMEN >MAILMAN
MAILMERGE n computer program for sending mass mailings
MAILPOUCH same as >MAILBAG
MAILROOM n room where mail to and from building is dealt with
MAILROOMS >MAILROOM
MAILS >MAIL
MAILSACK same as >MAILBAG
MAILSACKS >MAILSACK
MAILSHOT n posting of advertising material to many selected people at once
MAILSHOTS >MAILSHOT
MAILVAN n vehicle used to transport post
MAILVANS >MAILVAN
MAIM vb cripple or mutilate ▷n injury or defect
MAIMED >MAIM
MAIMER >MAIM
MAIMERS >MAIM
MAIMING >MAIM
MAIMINGS >MAIM
MAIMS >MAIM
MAIN adj chief or principal ▷n principal pipe or line carrying water, gas, or electricity ▷vb lower sails
MAINBOOM n spar for

mainsail
MAINBOOMS >MAINBOOM
MAINBRACE n brace attached to the mainyard
MAINDOOR n door from street into house
MAINDOORS >MAINDOOR
MAINED >MAIN
MAINER >MAIN
MAINEST >MAIN
MAINFRAME adj denoting a high-speed general-purpose computer ▷n high-speed general-purpose computer, with a large store capacity
MAINING >MAIN
MAINLAND n stretch of land which forms the main part of a country
MAINLANDS >MAINLAND
MAINLINE n the trunk route between two points, usually fed by branch lines ▷vb to inject a drug into a vein ▷adj having an important position, esp having responsibility for the main areas of activity
MAINLINED >MAINLINE
MAINLINER >MAINLINE
MAINLINES >MAINLINE
MAINLY adv for the most part, chiefly
MAINMAST n chief mast of a ship
MAINMASTS >MAINMAST
MAINOR n act of doing something
MAINORS >MAINOR
MAINOUR same as >MAINOR
MAINOURS >MAINOUR
MAINPRISE n former legal surety
MAINS >MAIN
MAINSAIL n largest sail on a mainmast
MAINSAILS >MAINSAIL
MAINSHEET n line used to control the angle of the mainsail to the wind
MAINSTAY n chief support
MAINSTAYS >MAINSTAY
MAINTAIN vb continue or keep in existence
MAINTAINS >MAINTAIN
MAINTOP n top or platform at the head of the mainmast
MAINTOPS >MAINTOP
MAINYARD n yard for a square mainsail
MAINYARDS >MAINYARD
MAIOLICA same as >MAJOLICA
MAIOLICAS >MAIOLICA
MAIR Scots form of >MORE
MAIRE n New Zealand tree
MAIREHAU n small aromatic shrub of New Zealand
MAIREHAUS >MAIREHAU
MAIRES >MAIRE
MAIRS >MAIR

MAISE n measure of herring
MAISES >MAISE
MAIST Scot word for >MOST
MAISTER Scots word for >MASTER
MAISTERED >MAISTER
MAISTERS >MAISTER
MAISTRIES >MAISTER
MAISTRING >MAISTER
MAISTRY >MAISTER
MAISTS >MAIST
MAIZE n type of corn with spikes of yellow grains
MAIZES >MAIZE
MAJAGUA same as >MAHOE
MAJAGUAS >MAJAGUA
MAJESTIC adj beautiful, dignified, and impressive
MAJESTIES >MAJESTY
MAJESTY n stateliness or grandeur
MAJLIS n (in various N African and Middle Eastern countries) an assembly; council
MAJLISES >MAJLIS
MAJOLICA n type of ornamented Italian pottery
MAJOLICAS >MAJOLICA
MAJOR adj greater in number, quality, or extent ▷n middle-ranking army officer ▷vb do one's principal study in (a particular subject)
MAJORAT n estate, the right to which is that of the first born child of a family
MAJORATS >MAJORAT
MAJORDOMO n chief steward or butler of a great household
MAJORED >MAJOR
MAJORETTE n one of a group of girls who practise formation marching and baton twirling
MAJORING >MAJOR
MAJORITY n greater number
MAJORLY adv very
MAJORS >MAJOR
MAJORSHIP >MAJOR
MAJUSCULE n large letter, either capital or uncial, used in printing or writing ▷adj relating to, printed, or written in such letters
MAK Scot word for >MAKE
MAKABLE >MAKE
MAKAR same as >MAKER
MAKARS >MAKAR
MAKE vb create, construct, or establish ▷n brand, type, or style
MAKEABLE >MAKE
MAKEBATE n troublemaker
MAKEBATES >MAKEBATE
MAKEFAST n strong support to which a vessel is secured
MAKEFASTS >MAKEFAST
MAKELESS >MAKE
MAKEOVER vb to transfer

the title or possession of (property, etc) ▷n a series of alterations, including beauty treatments and new clothes, intended to make a noticeable improvement in a person's appearance
MAKEOVERS >MAKEOVER
MAKER n person or company that makes something
MAKEREADY n process of preparing the forme and the cylinder or platen packing to achieve the correct impression all over the forme
MAKERS >MAKER
MAKES >MAKE
MAKESHIFT adj serving as a temporary substitute ▷n something serving in this capacity
MAKEUP n cosmetics, such as powder, lipstick, etc, applied to the face to improve its appearance ▷vb devise, construct, or compose, sometimes with the intent to deceive
MAKEUPS >MAKEUP
MAKI n in Japanese cuisine, rice and other ingredients wrapped in a short seaweed roll
MAKIMONO n Japanese scroll
MAKIMONOS >MAKIMONO
MAKING >MAKE
MAKINGS npl potentials, qualities, or materials
MAKIS >MAKI
MAKO n powerful shark of the Atlantic and Pacific Oceans
MAKOS >MAKO
MAKS >MAK
MAKUTA plural of > LIKUTA
MAKUTU n Polynesian witchcraft ▷vb cast a spell on
MAKUTUED >MAKUTU
MAKUTUING >MAKUTU
MAKUTUS >MAKUTU
MAL n illness
MALA n string of beads or knots, used in praying and meditating
MALACCA n stem of the rattan palm
MALACCAS >MALACCA
MALACHITE n green mineral
MALACIA n pathological softening of an organ or tissue, such as bone
MALACIAS >MALACIA
MALADIES >MALADY
MALADROIT adj clumsy or awkward
MALADY n disease or illness
MALAGUENA n Spanish dance similar to the fandango

MALAISE n something wrong which affects a section of society or area of activity

MALAISES > MALAISE

MALAM same as > MALLAM

MALAMS > MALAM

MALAMUTE n Alaskan sled dog of the spitz type, having a dense usually greyish coat

MALAMUTES > MALAMUTE

MALANDER same as > MALANDERS

MALANDERS npl disease of horses characterized by an eczematous inflammation behind the knee

MALANGA same as > COCOYAM

MALANGAS > MALANGA

MALAPERT adj saucy or impudent ▷ n saucy or impudent person

MALAPERTS > MALAPERT

MALAPROP n word unintentionally confused with one of similar sound, esp when creating a ridiculous effect

MALAPROPS > MALAPROP

MALAR n cheekbone ▷ adj of or relating to the cheek or cheekbone

MALARIA n infectious disease caused by the bite of some mosquitoes

MALARIAL > MALARIA

MALARIAN > MALARIA

MALARIAS > MALARIA

MALARIOUS > MALARIA

MALARKEY n nonsense or rubbish

MALARKEYS > MALARKEY

MALARKIES > MALARKY

MALARKY same as > MALARKEY

MALAROMA n bad smell

MALAROMAS > MALAROMA

MALARS > MALAR

MALAS > MALA

MALATE n any salt or ester of malic acid

MALATES > MALATE

MALATHION n yellow organophosphorus insecticide used as a dust or mist for the control of house flies and garden pests

MALAX vb soften

MALAXAGE > MALAX

MALAXAGES > MALAX

MALAXATE same as > MALAX

MALAXATED > MALAXATE

MALAXATES > MALAXATE

MALAXATOR n machine for kneading or grinding

MALAXED > MALAX

MALAXES > MALAX

MALAXING > MALAX

MALE adj of the sex which can fertilize female reproductive cells ▷ n male

person or animal

MALEATE n any salt or ester of maleic acid

MALEATES > MALEATE

MALEDICT vb utter a curse against ▷ adj cursed or detestable

MALEDICTS > MALEDICT

MALEFFECT n bad effect

MALEFIC adj causing evil

MALEFICE n wicked deed

MALEFICES > MALEFICE

MALEIC as in maleic acid colourless soluble crystalline substance used to synthesize other compounds

MALEMIUT same as > MALAMUTE

MALEMIUTS > MALEMIUT

MALEMUTE same as > MALAMUTE

MALEMUTES > MALEMUTE

MALENESS > MALE

MALENGINE n wicked plan

MALES > MALE

MALFED adj having malfunctioned

MALFORMED adj deformed

MALGRADO prep in spite of

MALGRE same as > MAUGRE

MALGRED > MALGRE

MALGRES > MALGRE

MALGRING > MALGRE

MALI n member of an Indian caste

MALIBU as in malibu board lightweight surfboard

MALIC as in malic acid colourless crystalline compound occurring in apples and other fruit

MALICE n desire to cause harm to others ▷ vb wish harm to

MALICED > MALICE

MALICES > MALICE

MALICHO n mischief

MALICHOS > MALICHO

MALICING > MALICE

MALICIOUS adj characterized by malice

MALIGN vb slander or defame ▷ adj evil in influence or effect

MALIGNANT adj seeking to harm others

MALIGNED > MALIGN

MALIGNER > MALIGN

MALIGNERS > MALIGN

MALIGNING > MALIGN

MALIGNITY n evil disposition

MALIGNLY > MALIGN

MALIGNS > MALIGN

MALIHINI n (in Hawaii) a foreigner or stranger

MALIHINIS > MALIHINI

MALIK n person of authority in India

MALIKS > MALIK

MALINE n stiff net

MALINES > MALINE

MALINGER vb feign illness

to avoid work

MALINGERS > MALINGER

MALINGERY > MALINGER

MALIS > MALI

MALISM n belief that evil dominates world

MALISMS > MALISM

MALISON archaic or poetic word for > CURSE

MALISONS > MALISON

MALIST > MALISM

MALKIN archaic or dialect name for a > CAT

MALKINS > MALKIN

MALL n street or shopping area closed to vehicles ▷ vb maul

MALLAM n (in Islamic W Africa) a man learned in Koranic studies

MALLAMS > MALLAM

MALLANDER same as > MALANDERS

MALLARD n wild duck

MALLARDS > MALLARD

MALLCORE n type of rock music combining heavy metal and hip-hop

MALLCORES > MALLCORE

MALLEABLE adj capable of being hammered or pressed into shape

MALLEABLY > MALLEABLE

MALLEATE vb hammer

MALLEATED > MALLEATE

MALLEATES > MALLEATE

MALLECHO same as > MALICHO

MALLECHOS > MALLECHO

MALLED > MALL

MALLEE n low-growing eucalypt in dry regions

MALLEES > MALLEE

MALLEI > MALLEUS

MALLEMUCK n any of various sea birds, such as the albatross, fulmar, or shearwater

MALLENDER same as > MALANDERS

MALLEOLAR > MALLEOLUS

MALLEOLI > MALLEOLUS

MALLEOLUS n either of two rounded bony projections of the tibia and fibula on the sides of each ankle joint

MALLET n (wooden) hammer

MALLETS > MALLET

MALLEUS n outermost and largest of the three small bones in the middle ear of mammals

MALLEUSES > MALLEUS

MALLING > MALL

MALLINGS > MALL

MALLOW n plant with pink or purple flowers

MALLOWS > MALLOW

MALLS > MALL

MALM n soft greyish limestone that crumbles

easily

MALMAG n Asian monkey

MALMAGS > MALMAG

MALMIER > MALMY

MALMIEST > MALMY

MALMS > MALM

MALMSEY n sweet Madeira wine

MALMSEYS > MALMSEY

MALMSTONE same as > MALM

MALMY adj looking like malm

MALODOR same as > MALODOUR

MALODORS > MALODOR

MALODOUR n unpleasant smell

MALODOURS > MALODOUR

MALONATE n salt of malonic acid

MALONATES > MALONATE

MALONIC as in malonic acid colourless crystalline compound occurring in sugar beet

MALOTI plural of > LOTI

MALPIGHIA adj of a tropical shrub

MALPOSED adj in abnormal position

MALS > MAL

MALSTICK same as > MAULSTICK

MALSTICKS > MALSTICK

MALT n grain, such as barley, prepared for use in making beer or whisky ▷ vb make into or make with malt

MALTALENT n evil intention

MALTASE n enzyme that hydrolyses maltose and similar glucosides to glucose

MALTASES > MALTASE

MALTED > MALT

MALTEDS > MALT

MALTESE adj as in maltese cross cross-shaped part of a film projector

MALTHA n any of various naturally occurring mixtures of hydrocarbons, such as ozocerite

MALTHAS > MALTHA

MALTIER > MALTY

MALTIEST > MALTY

MALTINESS > MALTY

MALTING n building in which malt is made or stored

MALTINGS > MALTING

MALTMAN same as > MALTSTER

MALTMEN > MALTMAN

MALTOL n food additive

MALTOLS > MALTOL

MALTOSE n sugar formed by the action of enzymes on starch

MALTOSES > MALTOSE

MALTREAT vb treat badly

MALTREATS > MALTREAT

m

MALTS >MALT
MALTSTER n person who makes or deals in malt
MALTSTERS >MALTSTER
MALTWORM n heavy drinker
MALTWORMS >MALTWORM
MALTY adj of, like, or containing malt
MALVA n mallow plant
MALVAS >MALVA
MALVASIA n type of grape used to make malmsey
MALVASIAN >MALVASIA
MALVASIAS >MALVASIA
MALVESIE same as >MALMSEY
MALVESIES >MALVESIE
MALVOISIE n amber dessert wine made in France, similar to malmsey
MALWA n Ugandan drink brewed from millet
MALWARE n computer program designed to cause damage or disruption to a system
MALWARES >MALWARE
MALWAS >MALWA
MAM same as >MOTHER
MAMA n mother
MAMAGUY vb deceive or tease, either in jest or by deceitful flattery ▷ n instance of such deception or flattery
MAMAGUYED >MAMAGUY
MAMAGUYS >MAMAGUY
MAMAKAU same as >MAMAKU
MAMAKAUS >MAMAKAU
MAMAKO same as >MAMAKU
MAMAKOS >MAMAKO
MAMAKU n tall edible New Zealand tree fern
MAMAKUS >MAMAKU
MAMALIGA same as >POLENTA
MAMALIGAS >MAMALIGA
MAMAS >MAMA
MAMBA n deadly S African snake
MAMBAS >MAMBA
MAMBO n Latin American dance resembling the rumba ▷ vb perform this dance
MAMBOED >MAMBO
MAMBOES >MAMBO
MAMBOING >MAMBO
MAMBOS >MAMBO
MAMEE same as >MAMEY
MAMEES >MAMEE
MAMELON n small rounded hillock
MAMELONS >MAMELON
MAMELUCO n Brazilian of mixed European and South American descent
MAMELUCOS >MAMELUCO
MAMELUKE n member of a military class, originally of Turkish slaves, ruling in Egypt from about 1250 to 1517 and remaining powerful until crushed in 1811

MAMELUKES >MAMELUKE
MAMEY n tropical tree
MAMEYES >MAMEY
MAMEYS >MAMEY
MAMIE n tropical tree
MAMIES >MAMIE
MAMILLA n nipple or teat
MAMILLAE >MAMILLA
MAMILLAR adj of breast
MAMILLARY >MAMILLA
MAMILLATE adj having nipples or nipple-like protuberances
MAMLUK same as >MAMELUKE
MAMLUKS >MAMLUK
MAMMA n buxom and voluptuous woman
MAMMAE >MAMMA
MAMMAL n animal of the type that suckles its young
MAMMALIAN >MAMMAL
MAMMALITY >MAMMAL
MAMMALOGY n branch of zoology concerned with the study of mammals
MAMMALS >MAMMAL
MAMMARY adj of the breasts or milk-producing glands
MAMMAS >MAMMA
MAMMATE adj having breasts
MAMMATI >MAMMATUS
MAMMATUS n breast-shaped cloud
MAMMEE same as >MAMEY
MAMMEES >MAMMEE
MAMMER vb hesitate
MAMMERED >MAMMER
MAMMERING >MAMMER
MAMMERS >MAMMER
MAMMET same as >MAUMET
MAMMETRY n worship of idols
MAMMETS >MAMMET
MAMMEY same as >MAMEY
MAMMEYS >MAMMEY
MAMMIE same as >MAMMY
MAMMIES >MAMMY
MAMMIFER same as >MAMMAL
MAMMIFERS >MAMMIFER
MAMMIFORM adj in form of breast
MAMMILLA same as >MAMILLA
MAMMILLAE >MAMMILLA
MAMMITIS same as >MASTITIS
MAMMOCK n fragment ▷ vb tear or shred
MAMMOCKED >MAMMOCK
MAMMOCKS >MAMMOCK
MAMMOGRAM n xray to examine the breasts in early detection of cancer
MAMMON n wealth regarded as a source of evil
MAMMONISH >MAMMON
MAMMONISM >MAMMON
MAMMONIST >MAMMON
MAMMONITE >MAMMON
MAMMONS >MAMMON

MAMMOTH n extinct elephant-like mammal ▷ adj colossal
MAMMOTHS >MAMMOTH
MAMMY n Black woman employed as a nurse or servant to a White family
MAMPARA n foolish person, idiot
MAMPARAS >MAMPARA
MAMPOER n home-distilled brandy made from peaches, prickly pears, etc
MAMPOERS >MAMPOER
MAMS >MAM
MAMSELLE n mademoiselle
MAMSELLES >MAMSELLE
MAMZER n child of an incestuous or adulterous union
MAMZERIM >MAMZER
MAMZERS >MAMZER
MAN n adult male ▷ vb supply with sufficient people for operation or defence
MANA n authority, influence
MANACLE vb handcuff or fetter ▷ n metal ring or chain put round the wrists or ankles, used to restrict the movements of a prisoner or convict
MANACLED >MANACLE
MANACLES >MANACLE
MANACLING >MANACLE
MANAGE vb succeed in doing
MANAGED >MANAGE
MANAGER n person in charge of a business, institution, actor, sports team, etc
MANAGERS >MANAGER
MANAGES >MANAGE
MANAGING adj having administrative control or authority
MANAIA n common figure in Māori carving consisting of a human body and a bird-like head
MANAIAS >MANAIA
MANAKIN same as >MANIKIN
MANAKINS >MANAKIN
MANANA n tomorrow ▷ adv tomorrow
MANANAS >MANANA
MANAS >MANA
MANAT n standard monetary unit of Azerbaijan, divided into 100 gopik
MANATEE n large tropical plant-eating aquatic mammal
MANATEES >MANATEE
MANATI same as >MANATEE
MANATIS >MANATI
MANATOID >MANATEE
MANATS >MANAT
MANATU n large flowering

deciduous New Zealand tree
MANATUS >MANATU
MANAWA in New Zealand, same as >MANGROVE
MANAWAS >MANAWA
MANCALA n African and Asian board game
MANCALAS >MANCALA
MANCANDO adv musical direction meaning fading away
MANCHE n long sleeve
MANCHES >MANCHE
MANCHET n type of bread
MANCHETS >MANCHET
MANCIPATE vb make legal transfer in ancient Rome
MANCIPLE n steward who buys provisions, esp in a college, Inn of Court, or monastery
MANCIPLES >MANCIPLE
MANCUS n former English coin
MANCUSES >MANCUS
MAND >MAN
MANDALA n circular design symbolizing the universe
MANDALAS >MANDALA
MANDALIC >MANDALA
MANDAMUS n formerly a writ from, now an order of, a superior court commanding an inferior tribunal, public official, corporation, etc, to carry out a public duty
MANDARIN n high-ranking government official
MANDARINE same as >MANDARIN
MANDARINS >MANDARIN
MANDATARY same as >MANDATORY
MANDATE n official or authoritative command ▷ vb give authority to
MANDATED >MANDATE
MANDATES >MANDATE
MANDATING >MANDATE
MANDATOR >MANDATE
MANDATORS >MANDATE
MANDATORY adj compulsory ▷ n person or state holding a mandate
MANDI n (in India) a big market
MANDIBLE n lower jawbone or jawlike part
MANDIBLES >MANDIBLE
MANDILION same as >MANDYLION
MANDIOC same as >MANIOC
MANDIOCA same as >MANIOC
MANDIOCAS >MANDIOCA
MANDIOCCA same as >MANIOC
MANDIOCS >MANDIOC
MANDIR n Hindu or Jain temple
MANDIRA same as >MANDIR

MANDIRAS >MANDIRA

MANDIRS >MANDIR

MANDIS >MANDI

MANDOLA n early type of mandolin

MANDOLAS >MANDOLA

MANDOLIN n musical instrument with four pairs of strings

MANDOLINE same as >MANDOLIN

MANDOLINS >MANDOLIN

MANDOM n mankind

MANDOMS >MANDOM

MANDORA n ancestor of mandolin

MANDORAS >MANDORA

MANDORLA n (in painting, sculpture, etc) an almond-shaped area of light, usually surrounding the resurrected Christ or the Virgin at the Assumption

MANDORLAS >MANDORLA

MANDRAKE n plant with a forked root, formerly used as a narcotic

MANDRAKES >MANDRAKE

MANDREL n shaft on which work is held in a lathe

MANDRELS >MANDREL

MANDRIL same as >MANDREL

MANDRILL n large blue-faced baboon

MANDRILLS >MANDRILL

MANDRILS >MANDRIL

MANDUCATE vb eat or chew

MANDYLION n loose garment formerly worn over armour

MANE n long hair on the neck of a horse, lion, etc

MANED >MANE

MANEGE n art of training horses and riders ▷ vb train horse

MANEGED >MANEGE

MANEGES >MANEGE

MANEGING >MANEGE

MANEH same as >MINA

MANEHS >MANEH

MANELESS >MANE

MANENT >MANET

MANES npl spirits of the dead, often revered as minor deities

MANET vb theatre direction, remain on stage

MANEUVER same as >MANOEUVRE

MANEUVERS >MANEUVER

MANFUL adj determined and brave

MANFULLY >MANFUL

MANG vb speak

MANGA n type of Japanese comic book with an adult theme

MANGABEY n large Old World monkey of central Africa, with long limbs and tail and white upper eyelids

MANGABEYS >MANGABEY

MANGABIES >MANGABY

MANGABY same as >MANGABEY

MANGAL n Turkish brazier

MANGALS >MANGAL

MANGANATE n salt of manganic acid

MANGANESE n brittle greyish-white metallic element

MANGANIC adj of or containing manganese in the trivalent state

MANGANIN n copper-based alloy

MANGANINS >MANGANIN

MANGANITE n blackish mineral

MANGANOUS adj of or containing manganese in the divalent state

MANGAS >MANGA

MANGE n skin disease of domestic animals

MANGEAO n small New Zealand tree with glossy leaves

MANGEAOS >MANGEAO

MANGED >MANG

MANGEL n Eurasian variety of the beet plant with a large yellowish root, cultivated as a cattle food

MANGELS >MANGEL

MANGER n eating trough in a stable or barn

MANGERS >MANGER

MANGES >MANGE

MANGETOUT n variety of pea with an edible pod

MANGEY same as >MANGY

MANGIER >MANGY

MANGIEST >MANGY

MANGILY >MANGY

MANGINESS >MANGY

MANGING >MANG

MANGLE vb destroy by crushing and twisting ▷ n machine with rollers for squeezing water from washed clothes

MANGLED >MANGLE

MANGLER >MANGLE

MANGLERS >MANGLE

MANGLES >MANGLE

MANGLING >MANGLE

MANGO n tropical fruit with sweet juicy yellow flesh

MANGOES >MANGO

MANGOLD n type of root vegetable

MANGOLDS >MANGOLD

MANGONEL n war engine for hurling stones

MANGONELS >MANGONEL

MANGOS >MANGO

MANGOSTAN n East Indian tree with thick leathery leaves and edible fruit

MANGOUSTE same as >MONGOOSE

MANGROVE n tropical tree with exposed roots, which grows beside water

MANGROVES >MANGROVE

MANGS >MANG

MANGULATE vb bend or twist out of shape

MANGY adj having mange

MANHANDLE vb treat roughly

MANHATTAN n mixed drink consisting of four parts whisky, one part vermouth, and a dash of bitters

MANHOLE n hole with a cover, through which a person can enter a drain or sewer

MANHOLES >MANHOLE

MANHOOD n state or quality of being a man or being manly

MANHOODS >MANHOOD

MANHUNT n organized search, usu. by police, for a wanted man or a fugitive

MANHUNTER >MANHUNT

MANHUNTS >MANHUNT

MANI n place to pray

MANIA n extreme enthusiasm

MANIAC n mad person

MANIACAL adj affected with or characteristic of mania

MANIACS >MANIAC

MANIAS >MANIA

MANIC adj extremely excited or energetic ▷ n person afflicted with mania

MANICALLY >MANIC

MANICOTTI npl large tubular noodles, usually stuffed with ricotta cheese and baked in a tomato sauce

MANICS >MANIC

MANICURE n cosmetic care of the fingernails and hands ▷ vb care for (the fingernails and hands) in this way

MANICURED >MANICURE

MANICURES >MANICURE

MANIES >MANY

MANIFEST adj easily noticed, obvious ▷ vb show plainly ▷ n list of cargo or passengers for customs

MANIFESTO n declaration of policy as issued by a political party ▷ vb issued manifesto

MANIFESTS >MANIFEST

MANIFOLD adj numerous and varied ▷ n pipe with several outlets, esp in an internal-combustion engine ▷ vb duplicate (a page, book, etc)

MANIFOLDS >MANIFOLD

MANIFORM adj like hand

MANIHOC variation of >MANIOC

MANIHOCS >MANIHOC

MANIHOT n tropical American plant

MANIHOTS >MANIHOT

MANIKIN n little man or dwarf

MANIKINS >MANIKIN

MANILA n strong brown paper used for envelopes

MANILAS >MANILA

MANILLA n early currency in W Africa in the form of a small bracelet

MANILLAS >MANILLA

MANILLE n (in ombre and quadrille) the second best trump

MANILLES >MANILLE

MANIOC same as >CASSAVA

MANIOCA same as >MANIOC

MANIOCAS >MANIOCA

MANIOCS >MANIOC

MANIPLE n (in ancient Rome) a unit of 120 to 200 foot soldiers

MANIPLES >MANIPLE

MANIPLIES same as >MANYPLIES

MANIPULAR adj of or relating to an ancient Roman maniple

MANIS n pangolin

MANITO same as >MANITOU

MANITOS >MANITO

MANITOU n (among the Algonquian Indians) a deified spirit or force

MANITOUS >MANITOU

MANITU same as >MANITOU

MANITUS >MANITU

MANJACK n single individual

MANJACKS >MANJACK

MANKIER >MANKY

MANKIEST >MANKY

MANKIND n human beings collectively

MANKINDS >MANKIND

MANKINI n a revealing man's swimming costume

MANKINIS >MANKINI

MANKY adj worthless, rotten, or in bad taste

MANLESS >MAN

MANLIER >MANLY

MANLIEST >MANLY

MANLIKE adj resembling or befitting a man

MANLIKELY >MANLIKE

MANLILY >MANLY

MANLINESS >MANLY

MANLY adj (possessing qualities) appropriate to a man

MANMADE adj made or produced by man

MANNA n miraculous food which sustained the Israelites in the wilderness

MANNAN n drug derived from mannose

MANNANS >MANNAN

MANNAS >MANNA

MANNED >MAN

m

MANNEQUIN n woman who models clothes at a fashion show

MANNER n way a thing happens or is done

MANNERED adj affected

MANNERISM n person's distinctive habit or trait

MANNERIST >MANNERISM

MANNERLY adj having good manners, polite ▷ adv with good manners

MANNERS npl person's social conduct viewed in the light of whether it is regarded as polite or acceptable or not

MANNIKIN same as >MANIKIN

MANNIKINS >MANNIKIN

MANNING >MAN

MANNISH adj (of a woman) like a man

MANNISHLY >MANNISH

MANNITE same as >MANNITOL

MANNITES >MANNITE

MANNITIC >MANNITOL

MANNITOL n white crystalline water-soluble sweet-tasting alcohol

MANNITOLS >MANNITOL

MANNOSE n hexose sugar

MANNOSES >MANNOSE

MANO n stone for grinding grain

MANOAO n New Zealand shrub

MANOAOS >MANOAO

MANOEUVRE n skilful movement ▷ vb manipulate or contrive skilfully or cunningly

MANOMETER n instrument for comparing pressures

MANOMETRY >MANOMETER

MANOR n large country house and its lands

MANORIAL >MANOR

MANORS >MANOR

MANOS >MANO

MANOSCOPY n measurement of the densities of gases

MANPACK n load carried by one person

MANPACKS >MANPACK

MANPOWER n available number of workers

MANPOWERS >MANPOWER

MANQUE adj would-be

MANRED n homage

MANREDS >MANRED

MANRENT same as >MANRED

MANRENTS >MANRENT

MANRIDER n train carrying miners in coal mine

MANRIDERS >MANRIDER

MANRIDING adj carrying people rather than goods

MANROPE n rope railing

MANROPES >MANROPE

MANS >MAN

MANSARD n roof with two slopes on both sides and both ends, the lower slopes being steeper than the upper

MANSARDED adj having mansard roof

MANSARDS >MANSARD

MANSE n house provided for a minister in some religious denominations

MANSES >MANSE

MANSHIFT n work done by one person in one shift

MANSHIFTS >MANSHIFT

MANSION n large house

MANSIONS >MANSION

MANSLAYER n person who kills man

MANSONRY n mansions collectively

MANSUETE adj gentle

MANSWORN adj perjured

MANTA n type of large ray with very wide winglike pectoral fins

MANTAS >MANTA

MANTEAU n cloak or mantle

MANTEAUS >MANTEAU

MANTEAUX >MANTEAU

MANTEEL n cloak

MANTEELS >MANTEEL

MANTEL n structure round a fireplace ▷ vb construct a mantel

MANTELET n woman's short mantle, often lace-trimmed, worn in the mid-19th century

MANTELETS >MANTELET

MANTELS >MANTEL

MANTES >MANTIS

MANTIC adj of or relating to divination and prophecy

MANTICORA same as >MANTICORE

MANTICORE n mythical monster with body of lion and human head

MANTID same as >MANTIS

MANTIDS >MANTID

MANTIES >MANTY

MANTILLA n (in Spain) a lace scarf covering a woman's head and shoulders

MANTILLAS >MANTILLA

MANTIS n carnivorous insect like a grasshopper

MANTISES >MANTIS

MANTISSA n part of a common logarithm consisting of the decimal point and the figures following it

MANTISSAS >MANTISSA

MANTLE same as >MANTEL

MANTLED >MANTLE

MANTLES >MANTLE

MANTLET same as >MANTELET

MANTLETS >MANTLET

MANTLING n drapery or scrollwork around a shield

MANTLINGS >MANTLING

MANTO same as >MANTEAU

MANTOES >MANTO

MANTOS >MANTO

MANTRA n any sacred word or syllable used as an object of concentration

MANTRAM same as >MANTRA

MANTRAMS >MANTRAM

MANTRAP n snare for catching people, esp trespassers

MANTRAPS >MANTRAP

MANTRAS >MANTRA

MANTRIC >MANTRA

MANTUA n loose gown of the 17th and 18th centuries, worn open in front to show the underskirt

MANTUAS >MANTUA

MANTY Scots variant of >MANTUA

MANUAL adj of or done with the hands ▷ n handbook

MANUALLY >MANUAL

MANUALS >MANUAL

MANUARY same as >MANUAL

MANUBRIA >MANUBRIUM

MANUBRIAL >MANUBRIUM

MANUBRIUM n any handle-shaped part, esp the upper part of the sternum

MANUHIRI n visitor to a Māori marae

MANUHIRIS >MANUHIRI

MANUKA n New Zealand tree with strong elastic wood and aromatic leaves

MANUKAS >MANUKA

MANUL n Asian wildcat

MANULS >MANUL

MANUMEA n pigeon of Samoa

MANUMEAS >MANUMEA

MANUMIT vb free from slavery

MANUMITS >MANUMIT

MANURANCE n cultivation of land

MANURE n animal excrement used as a fertilizer ▷ vb fertilize (land) with this

MANURED >MANURE

MANURER >MANURE

MANURERS >MANURE

MANURES >MANURE

MANURIAL >MANURE

MANURING >MANURE

MANURINGS >MANURE

MANUS n wrist and hand

MANWARD adv towards humankind

MANWARDS same as >MANWARD

MANWISE adv in human way

MANY adj numerous ▷ n large number

MANYATA same as >MANYATTA

MANYATAS >MANYATA

MANYATTA n settlement of Masai people

MANYATTAS >MANYATTA

MANYFOLD adj many in number

MANYPLIES n third component of the stomach of ruminants

MANZANITA n Californian plant

MANZELLO n instrument like saxophone

MANZELLOS >MANZELLO

MAOMAO n fish of New Zealand seas

MAOMAOS >MAOMAO

MAORMOR same as >MORMAOR

MAORMORS >MAORMOR

MAP n representation of the earth's surface or some part of it, showing geographical features ▷ vb make a map of

MAPAU n small New Zealand tree with reddish bark, aromatic leaves, and dark berries

MAPAUS >MAPAU

MAPLE n tree with broad leaves, a variety of which yields sugar

MAPLELIKE >MAPLE

MAPLES >MAPLE

MAPLESS >MAP

MAPLIKE >MAP

MAPMAKER n person who draws maps

MAPMAKERS >MAPMAKER

MAPMAKING >MAPMAKER

MAPPABLE >MAP

MAPPED >MAP

MAPPEMOND n map of world

MAPPER >MAP

MAPPERIES >MAPPERY

MAPPERS >MAP

MAPPERY n making of maps

MAPPING >MAP

MAPPINGS >MAP

MAPPIST >MAP

MAPPISTS >MAP

MAPS >MAP

MAPSTICK same as >MOPSTICK

MAPSTICKS >MAPSTICK

MAPWISE adv like map

MAQUETTE n sculptor's small preliminary model or sketch

MAQUETTES >MAQUETTE

MAQUI n Chilean shrub

MAQUILA n US-owned factory in Mexico

MAQUILAS >MAQUILA

MAQUIS n French underground movement that fought against the German occupying forces in World War II

MAQUISARD n member of French maquis

MAR *vb* spoil or impair ⊳ *n* disfiguring mark

MARA *n* harelike S American rodent inhabiting the pampas of Argentina

MARABI *n* kind of music popular in S African townships in the 1930s

MARABIS >MARABI

MARABOU *n* large black-and-white African stork

MARABOUS >MARABOU

MARABOUT *n* Muslim holy man or hermit of North Africa

MARABOUTS >MARABOUT

MARABUNTA *n* any of several social wasps

MARACA *n* shaken percussion instrument made from a gourd containing dried seeds etc

MARACAS >MARACA

MARAE *n* enclosed space in front of a Māori meeting house

MARAES >MARAE

MARAGING as in *maraging steel* strong low-carbon steel containing nickel and small amounts of titanium, aluminium, and niobium, produced by transforming to a martensitic structure and heating at 500°C

MARAGINGS >MARAGING

MARAH *n* bitterness

MARAHS >MARAH

MARANATHA *n* member of Christian sect

MARANTA *n* tropical American plant, some species of which are grown as pot plants for their showy variegated leaves

MARANTAS >MARANTA

MARARI *n* eel-like blennoid food fish

MARARIS >MARARI

MARAS >MARA

MARASCA *n* European cherry tree with red acid-tasting fruit from which maraschino is made

MARASCAS >MARASCA

MARASMIC >MARASMUS

MARASMOID >MARASMUS

MARASMUS *n* general emaciation and wasting, esp of infants, thought to be associated with severe malnutrition or impaired utilization of nutrients

MARATHON *n* long-distance race of 26 miles 385 yards (42.195 kilometres) ⊳ *adj* of or relating to a race on foot of 26 miles 385 yards (42.195 kilometres)

MARATHONS >MARATHON

MARAUD *vb* wander or raid in search of plunder

MARAUDED >MARAUD

MARAUDER >MARAUD

MARAUDERS >MARAUD

MARAUDING *adj* wandering or raiding in search of plunder

MARAUDS >MARAUD

MARAVEDI *n* any of various Spanish coins of copper or gold

MARAVEDIS >MARAVEDI

MARBELISE *same as* >MARBELEIZE

MARBELIZE *same as* >MARBELEIZE

MARBLE *n* kind of limestone with a mottled appearance, which can be highly polished ⊳ *vb* mottle with variegated streaks in imitation of marble

MARBLED >MARBLE

MARBLEISE *same as* >MARBLEIZE

MARBLEIZE *vb* give a marble-like appearance to

MARBLER >MARBLE

MARBLERS >MARBLE

MARBLES *n* game in which marble balls are rolled at one another

MARBLIER >MARBLE

MARBLIEST >MARBLE

MARBLING *n* mottled effect or pattern resembling marble

MARBLINGS >MARBLING

MARBLY >MARBLE

MARC *n* remains of grapes or other fruit that have been pressed for wine-making

MARCASITE *n* crystals of iron pyrites, used in jewellery

MARCATO *adj* (of notes) heavily accented ⊳ *adv* with each note heavily accented ⊳ *n* a heavily accented note

MARCATOS >MARCATO

MARCEL *n* hairstyle characterized by repeated regular waves, popular in the 1920s ⊳ *vb* make such waves in (the hair) with special hot irons

MARCELLA *n* type of fabric

MARCELLAS >MARCELLA

MARCELLED >MARCEL

MARCELLER >MARCEL

MARCELS >MARCEL

MARCH *vb* walk with a military step ⊳ *n* action of marching

MARCHED >MARCH

MARCHEN *n* German story

MARCHER *n* person who marches

MARCHERS >MARCHER

MARCHES >MARCH

MARCHESA *n* (in Italy) the wife or widow of a marchese

MARCHESAS >MARCHESA

MARCHESE *n* (in Italy) a nobleman ranking below a prince and above a count

MARCHESI >MARCHESE

MARCHING >MARCH

MARCHLAND *n* border land

MARCHLIKE *adj* like march in rhythm

MARCHMAN *n* person living on border

MARCHMEN >MARCHMAN

MARCHPANE *same as* >MARZIPAN

MARCONI *vb* communicate by wireless

MARCONIED >MARCONI

MARCONIS >MARCONI

MARCS >MARC

MARD >MAR

MARDIED >MARDY

MARDIER >MARDY

MARDIES >MARDY

MARDIEST >MARDY

MARDY *adj* (of a child) spoilt ⊳ *vb* behave in mardy way

MARDYING >MARDY

MARE *n* female horse or zebra

MAREMMA *n* marshy unhealthy region near the shore, esp in Italy

MAREMMAS >MAREMMA

MAREMME >MAREMMA

MARENGO *adj* browned in oil and cooked with tomatoes, mushrooms, garlic, wine, etc

MARERO *n* member of a C American organized criminal gang

MAREROS >MARERO

MARES >MARE

MARESCHAL *same as* >MARSHAL

MARG *short for* >MARGARINE

MARGARIC *adj* of or resembling pearl

MARGARIN *n* ester of margaric acid

MARGARINE *n* butter substitute made from animal or vegetable fats

MARGARINS >MARGARIN

MARGARITA *n* mixed drink consisting of tequila and lemon juice

MARGARITE *n* pink pearly micaceous mineral

MARGAY *n* feline mammal of Central and S America with a dark-striped coat

MARGAYS >MARGAY

MARGE *n* margarine

MARGENT *same as* >MARGIN

MARGENTED >MARGENT

MARGENTS >MARGENT

MARGES >MARGE

MARGIN *n* edge or border ⊳ *vb* provide with a margin

MARGINAL *adj* insignificant, unimportant ⊳ *n* marginal constituency

MARGINALS >MARGINAL

MARGINATE *vb* provide with a margin or margins ⊳ *adj* having a margin of a distinct colour or form

MARGINED >MARGIN

MARGINING >MARGIN

MARGINS >MARGIN

MARGOSA *n* Indian tree

MARGOSAS >MARGOSA

MARGRAVE *n* (formerly) a German nobleman ranking above a count

MARGRAVES >MARGRAVE

MARGS >MARG

MARIA >MARE

MARIACHI *n* small ensemble of street musicians in Mexico

MARIACHIS >MARIACHI

MARIALITE *n* silicate mineral

MARID *n* spirit in Muslim mythology

MARIDS >MARID

MARIES >MARY

MARIGOLD *n* plant with yellow or orange flowers

MARIGOLDS >MARIGOLD

MARIGRAM *n* graphic record of the tide levels at a particular coastal station

MARIGRAMS >MARIGRAM

MARIGRAPH *n* gauge for recording the levels of the tides

MARIHUANA *same as* >MARIJUANA

MARIJUANA *n* dried flowers and leaves of the cannabis plant, used as a drug, esp in cigarettes

MARIMBA *n* Latin American percussion instrument resembling a xylophone

MARIMBAS >MARIMBA

MARIMBIST >MARIMBA

MARINA *n* harbour for yachts and other pleasure boats

MARINADE *n* seasoned liquid in which fish or meat is soaked before cooking

MARINADED >MARINADE

MARINADES >MARINADE

MARINARA *n* Italian pasta sauce

MARINARAS >MARINARA

MARINAS >MARINA

MARINATE *vb* soak in marinade

MARINATED >MARINATE

MARINATES >MARINATE

MARINE *adj* of the sea or shipping ⊳ *n* (esp in Britain and the US) soldier trained for land and sea combat

MARINER *n* sailor

MARINERA *n* folk dance of Peru

MARINERAS >MARINERA

MARINERS >MARINER

MARINES >MARINE

MARINIERE *adj* served in white wine and onion sauce

MARIPOSA *n* type of plant of the southwestern US

and Mexico, with brightly coloured tulip-like flowers

MARIPOSAS >MARIPOSA

MARISCHAL *Scots variant of* >MARSHAL

MARISH *n* marsh

MARISHES >MARISH

MARITAGE *n* right of a lord to choose the spouses of his wards

MARITAGES >MARITAGE

MARITAL *adj* relating to marriage

MARITALLY >MARITAL

MARITIME *adj* relating to shipping

MARJORAM *n* aromatic herb used for seasoning food and in salads

MARJORAMS >MARJORAM

MARK *n* line, dot, scar, etc visible on a surface ▷ *vb* make a mark on

MARKA *n* unit of currency introduced as an interim currency in Bosnia-Herzegovina

MARKAS >MARKA

MARKDOWN *n* price reduction ▷ *vb* reduce in price

MARKDOWNS >MARKDOWN

MARKED *adj* noticeable

MARKEDLY >MARKED

MARKER *n* object used to show the position of something

MARKERS >MARKER

MARKET *n* assembly or place for buying and selling ▷ *vb* offer or produce for sale

MARKETED >MARKET

MARKETEER *n* supporter of the European Union and of Britain's membership of it

MARKETER >MARKET

MARKETERS >MARKET

MARKETING *n* part of a business that controls the way that goods or services are sold

MARKETISE *same as* >MARKETIZE

MARKETIZE *vb* convert (a national economy) to a market economy

MARKETS >MARKET

MARKHOOR *same as* >MARKHOR

MARKHOORS >MARKHOOR

MARKHOR *n* large wild Himalayan goat with a reddish-brown coat and large spiralled horns

MARKHORS >MARKHOR

MARKING *n* arrangement of colours on an animal or plant

MARKINGS >MARKING

MARKKA *n* former standard monetary unit of Finland, divided into 100 penniä

MARKKAA >MARKKA

MARKKAS >MARKKA

MARKMAN *n* person owning land

MARKMEN >MARKMAN

MARKS >MARK

MARKSMAN *n* person skilled at shooting

MARKSMEN >MARKSMAN

MARKUP *n* percentage or amount added to the cost of a commodity to provide the seller with a profit and to cover overheads, costs, etc

MARKUPS >MARKUP

MARL *n* soil formed of clay and lime, used as fertilizer ▷ *vb* fertilize (land) with marl

MARLE *same as* >MARVEL

MARLED >MARL

MARLES >MARLE

MARLIER >MARLY

MARLIEST >MARLY

MARLIN *same as* >MARLINE

MARLINE *n* light rope, usually tarred, made of two strands laid left-handed

MARLINES >MARLINE

MARLING *same as* >MARLINE

MARLINGS >MARLING

MARLINS >MARLIN

MARLITE *n* type of marl that contains clay and calcium carbonate and is resistant to the decomposing action of air

MARLITES >MARLITE

MARLITIC >MARLITE

MARLS >MARL

MARLSTONE *same as* >MARLITE

MARLY *adj* marl-like

MARM *same as* >MADAM

MARMALADE *n* jam made from citrus fruits ▷ *adj* (of cats) streaked orange or yellow and brown

MARMALISE *vb* beat soundly or defeat utterly

MARMALIZE *same as* >MARMALISE

MARMARISE *same as* >MARMARIZE

MARMARIZE *vb* turn to marble

MARMELISE *same as* >MARMELIZE

MARMELIZE *vb* beat soundly

MARMEM *as in* marmem alloy type of alloy

MARMITE *n* large cooking pot

MARMITES >MARMITE

MARMOREAL *adj* of or like marble

MARMOREAN *same as* >MARMOREAL

MARMOSE *n* South American opossum

MARMOSES >MARMOSE

MARMOSET *n* small

bushy-tailed monkey

MARMOSETS >MARMOSET

MARMOT *n* burrowing rodent

MARMOTS >MARMOT

MARMS >MARM

MAROCAIN *n* fabric of ribbed crepe

MAROCAINS >MAROCAIN

MARON *n* freshwater crustacean

MARONS >MARON

MAROON *adj* reddish-purple ▷ *vb* abandon ashore, esp on an island ▷ *n* exploding firework or flare used as a warning signal

MAROONED >MAROON

MAROONER >MAROON

MAROONERS >MAROON

MAROONING >MAROON

MAROONS >MAROON

MAROQUIN *n* morocco leather

MAROQUINS >MAROQUIN

MAROR *n* Jewish ceremonial dish of bitter herbs

MARORS >MAROR

MARPLOT *n* person interfering with plot

MARPLOTS >MARPLOT

MARQUE *n* brand of product, esp of a car

MARQUEE *n* large tent used for a party or exhibition

MARQUEES >MARQUEE

MARQUES >MARQUE

MARQUESS *n* nobleman of the rank below a duke

MARQUETRY *n* ornamental inlaid work of wood

MARQUIS *n* (in some European countries) nobleman of the rank above a count

MARQUISE *same as* >MARQUEE

MARQUISES >MARQUISE

MARRAM *as in* marram grass any of several grasses of the genus that grow on sandy shores and can withstand drying

MARRAMS >MARRAM

MARRANO *n* Spanish or Portuguese Jew of the late Middle Ages who was converted to Christianity, esp one forcibly converted but secretly adhering to Judaism

MARRANOS >MARRANO

MARRED >MAR

MARRELS *same as* >MERILS

MARRER >MAR

MARRERS >MAR

MARRI *n* W Australian eucalyptus widely cultivated for its coloured flowers

MARRIAGE *n* state of being married

MARRIAGES >MARRIAGE

MARRIED >MARRY

MARRIEDS *npl* married people

MARRIER >MARRY

MARRIERS >MARRY

MARRIES >MARRY

MARRING >MAR

MARRIS >MARRI

MARRON *n* large edible sweet chestnut

MARRONS >MARRON

MARROW *n* fatty substance inside bones ▷ *vb* be mate to

MARROWED >MARROW

MARROWFAT *n* variety of large pea

MARROWING >MARROW

MARROWISH >MARROW

MARROWS >MARROW

MARROWSKY *n* spoonerism

MARROWY >MARROW

MARRUM *same as* >MARRAM

MARRUMS >MARRUM

MARRY *vb* take as a husband or wife ▷ *interj* exclamation of surprise or anger

MARRYING >MARRY

MARRYINGS >MARRY

MARS >MAR

MARSALA *n* dark sweet dessert wine made in Sicily

MARSALAS >MARSALA

MARSE *same as* >MASTER

MARSEILLE *n* strong cotton fabric with a raised pattern, used for bedspreads, etc

MARSES >MARSE

MARSH *n* low-lying wet land

MARSHAL *n* officer of the highest rank ▷ *vb* arrange in order

MARSHALCY >MARSHAL

MARSHALED >MARSHAL

MARSHALER >MARSHAL

MARSHALL *n* shortened form of Marshall Plan, programme of US economic aid for the reconstruction of post-World War II Europe (1948-52)

MARSHALLS >MARSHALL

MARSHALS >MARSHAL

MARSHBUCK *n* antelope of the central African swamplands, with spreading hoofs adapted to boggy ground

MARSHES >MARSH

MARSHIER >MARSHY

MARSHIEST >MARSHY

MARSHLAND *n* land consisting of marshes

MARSHLIKE >MARSH

MARSHWORT *n* type of creeping aquatic plant with small white flowers

MARSHY *adj* of, involving, or like a marsh

MARSPORT *n* spoilsport

MARSPORTS >MARSPORT

MARSQUAKE *n* Martian equivalent of earthquake

MARSUPIA > MARSUPIUM
MARSUPIAL n animal that carries its young in a pouch, such as a kangaroo ▷ adj of or like a marsupial
MARSUPIAN > MARSUPIAL
MARSUPIUM n external pouch in most female marsupials within which the newly born offspring are suckled and complete their development
MART n market ▷ vb sell or trade
MARTAGON n Eurasian lily plant cultivated for its mottled purplish-red flowers
MARTAGONS > MARTAGON
MARTED > MART
MARTEL n hammer-shaped weapon ▷ vb use such a weapon
MARTELLED > MARTEL
MARTELLO n small circular tower for coastal defence, formerly much used in Europe
MARTELLOS > MARTELLO
MARTELS > MARTEL
MARTEN n weasel-like animal
MARTENS > MARTEN
MARTEXT n preacher who makes many mistakes
MARTEXTS > MARTEXT
MARTIAL adj of war, warlike
MARTIALLY > MARTIAL
MARTIALS as in court martials military courts that try people subject to military law
MARTIAN n inhabitant of Mars
MARTIANS > MARTIAN
MARTIN n bird with a slightly forked tail
MARTINET n person who maintains strict discipline
MARTINETS > MARTINET
MARTING > MART
MARTINGAL n strap of a horse's harness
MARTINI n cocktail of vermouth and gin
MARTINIS > MARTINI
MARTINS > MARTIN
MARTLET n footless bird often found in coats of arms, standing for either a martin or a swallow
MARTLETS > MARTLET
MARTS > MART
MARTYR n person who dies or suffers for his or her beliefs ▷ vb make a martyr of
MARTYRDOM n sufferings or death of a martyr
MARTYRED > MARTYR
MARTYRIA > MARTYRIUM
MARTYRIES > MARTYRY
MARTYRING > MARTYR

MARTYRISE > MARTYR
MARTYRIUM same as > MARTYRY
MARTYRIZE > MARTYR
MARTYRLY > MARTYR
MARTYRS > MARTYR
MARTYRY n shrine or chapel erected in honour of a martyr
MARVEL vb be filled with wonder ▷ n wonderful thing
MARVELED > MARVEL
MARVELING > MARVEL
MARVELLED > MARVEL
MARVELOUS adj causing great wonder
MARVELS > MARVEL
MARVER vb roll molten glass on slab
MARVERED > MARVER
MARVERING > MARVER
MARVERS > MARVER
MARVIER > MARVY
MARVIEST > MARVY
MARVY shortened form of > MARVELOUS
MARXISANT adj sympathetic to Marxism
MARY n woman
MARYBUD n bud of marigold
MARYBUDS > MARYBUD
MARYJANE n slang for marijuana
MARYJANES > MARYJANE
MARZIPAN n paste of ground almonds, sugar, and egg whites ▷ modifier of or relating to the stratum of middle managers in a financial institution or other business
MARZIPANS > MARZIPAN
MAS > MA
MASA n Mexican maize dough
MASALA n mixture of spices ground into a paste ▷ adj spicy
MASALAS > MASALA
MASAS > MASA
MASCARA n cosmetic for darkening the eyelashes
MASCARAED adj wearing mascara
MASCARAS > MASCARA
MASCARON n in architecture, a face carved in stone or metal
MASCARONS n grotesque face used as decoration
MASCLE n charge consisting of a lozenge with a lozenge-shaped hole in the middle
MASCLED > MASCLE
MASCLES > MASCLE
MASCON n any of several lunar regions of high gravity
MASCONS > MASCON
MASCOT n person, animal,

or thing supposed to bring good luck
MASCOTS > MASCOT
MASCULINE adj relating to males
MASCULIST n advocate of rights of men)
MASCULY > MASCLE
MASE vb function as maser
MASED > MASE
MASER n device for amplifying microwaves
MASERS > MASER
MASES > MASE
MASH n soft pulpy mass ▷ vb crush into a soft mass
MASHALLAH interj what Allah wishes
MASHED > MASH
MASHER > MASH
MASHERS > MASH
MASHES > MASH
MASHGIACH n person who ensures adherence to kosher rules
MASHGIAH same as > MASHGIACH
MASHGIHIM > MASHGIACH
MASHIACH n messiah
MASHIACHS > MASHIACH
MASHIE n (formerly) a club, corresponding to the modern No. 5 or No. 6 iron, used for approach shots
MASHIER > MASHY
MASHIES > MASHIE
MASHIEST > MASHY
MASHING > MASH
MASHINGS > MASH
MASHLAM same as > MASLIN
MASHLAMS > MASHLAM
MASHLIM same as > MASLIN
MASHLIMS > MASHLIM
MASHLIN same as > MASLIN
MASHLINS > MASHLIN
MASHLOCH same as > MASLIN
MASHLOCHS > MASHLOCH
MASHLUM same as > MASLIN
MASHLUMS > MASHLUM
MASHMAN n brewery worker
MASHMEN > MASHMAN
MASHUA n South American plant
MASHUAS > MASHUA
MASHUP n piece of recorded or live music in which a producer or DJ blends together two or more tracks, often of contrasting genres
MASHUPS > MASHUP
MASHY adj like mash
MASING > MASE
MASJID same as > MOSQUE
MASJIDS > MASJID
MASK n covering for the face, as a disguise or

protection ▷ vb cover with a mask
MASKABLE > MASK
MASKED adj disguised or covered by or as if by a mask
MASKEG n North American bog
MASKEGS > MASKEG
MASKER n person who wears a mask or takes part in a masque
MASKERS > MASKER
MASKING n act or practice of masking
MASKINGS > MASKING
MASKLIKE > MASK
MASKS > MASK
MASLIN n mixture of wheat, rye or other grain
MASLINS > MASLIN
MASOCHISM n condition in which (sexual) pleasure is obtained from feeling pain or from being humiliated
MASOCHIST > MASOCHISM
MASON n person who works with stone ▷ vb construct or strengthen with masonry
MASONED > MASON
MASONIC adj of, characteristic of, or relating to Freemasons or Freemasonry
MASONING > MASON
MASONITE n tradename for a kind of dark brown hardboard used for partitions, lining, etc
MASONITES > MASONITE
MASONRIED adj built of masonry
MASONRIES > MASONRY
MASONRY n stonework
MASONS > MASON
MASOOLAH n Indian boat used in surf
MASOOLAHS > MASOOLAH
MASQUE n 16th-17th-century form of dramatic entertainment
MASQUER same as > MASKER
MASQUERS > MASQUER
MASQUES > MASQUE
MASS n coherent body of matter ▷ adj large-scale ▷ vb form into a mass
MASSA old fashioned variant of > MASTER
MASSACRE n indiscriminate killing of large numbers of people ▷ vb kill in large numbers
MASSACRED > MASSACRE
MASSACRER > MASSACRE
MASSACRES > MASSACRE
MASSAGE n rubbing and kneading of parts of the body to reduce pain or stiffness ▷ vb give a massage to
MASSAGED > MASSAGE
MASSAGER > MASSAGE

MASSAGERS >MASSAGE
MASSAGES >MASSAGE
MASSAGING >MASSAGE
MASSAGIST >MASSAGE
MASSAS >MASSA
MASSCULT n culture of masses
MASSCULTS >MASSCULT
MASSE n stroke made by hitting the cue ball off centre with the cue held nearly vertically, esp so as to make the ball move in a curve around another ball before hitting the object ball
MASSED >MASS
MASSEDLY >MASS
MASSES npl body of common people
MASSETER n muscle of the cheek used in moving the jaw, esp in chewing
MASSETERS >MASSETER
MASSEUR n person who gives massages
MASSEURS >MASSEUR
MASSEUSE n woman who gives massages, esp as a profession
MASSEUSES >MASSEUSE
MASSICOT n yellow earthy secondary mineral
MASSICOTS >MASSICOT
MASSIER >MASSY
MASSIEST >MASSY
MASSIF n connected group of mountains
MASSIFS >MASSIF
MASSINESS >MASSY
MASSING >MASS
MASSIVE adj large and heavy ▷ n group of friends or associates
MASSIVELY >MASSIVE
MASSIVES >MASSIVE
MASSLESS >MASS
MASSOOLA same as >MASOOLAH
MASSOOLAS >MASSOOLA
MASSTIGE n impression of exclusivity in mass-produced goods
MASSTIGES >MASSTIGE
MASSY literary word for >MASSIVE
MASSYMORE n underground prison
MAST n tall pole for supporting something, esp a ship's sails
MASTABA n mud-brick superstructure above tombs in ancient Egypt
MASTABAH same as >MASTABA
MASTABAHS >MASTABAH
MASTABAS >MASTABA
MASTED >MAST
MASTER n person in control, such as an employer or an owner of slaves or animals ▷ adj overall or controlling ▷ vb acquire knowledge of or

skill in ▷ modifier overall or controlling
MASTERATE n status of master
MASTERDOM >MASTER
MASTERED >MASTER
MASTERFUL adj domineering
MASTERIES >MASTERY
MASTERING >MASTER
MASTERLY adj showing great skill
MASTERS >MASTER
MASTERY n expertise
MASTFUL >MAST
MASTHEAD n head of a mast ▷ vb send (a sailor) to the masthead as a punishment
MASTHEADS >MASTHEAD
MASTHOUSE n place for storing masts
MASTIC n gum obtained from certain trees
MASTICATE vb chew
MASTICH same as >MASTIC
MASTICHE same as >MASTIC
MASTICHES >MASTICHE
MASTICHS >MASTICH
MASTICOT same as >MASSICOT
MASTICOTS >MASTICOT
MASTICS >MASTIC
MASTIER >MAST
MASTIEST >MAST
MASTIFF n large dog
MASTIFFS >MASTIFF
MASTING >MAST
MASTITIC >MASTITIS
MASTITIS n inflammation of a breast or udder
MASTIX n type of gum
MASTIXES >MASTIX
MASTLESS >MAST
MASTLIKE >MAST
MASTODON n extinct elephant-like mammal
MASTODONS >MASTODON
MASTODONT >MASTODON
MASTOID n projection of the bone behind the ear ▷ adj shaped like a nipple or breast
MASTOIDAL >MASTOID
MASTOIDS >MASTOID
MASTOPEXY n cosmetic surgery of breasts
MASTS >MAST
MASTY >MAST
MASU n Japanese salmon
MASULA same as >MASOOLAH
MASULAS >MASULA
MASURIUM n silver-grey metallic element
MASURIUMS >MASURIUM
MASUS >MASU
MAT n piece of fabric used as a floor covering or to protect a surface ▷ vb tangle or become tangled into a dense mass ▷ adj

having a dull, lustreless, or roughened surface
MATACHIN n dancer with sword
MATACHINA n feamale matachin
MATACHINI >MATACHIN
MATADOR n man who kills the bull in bullfights
MATADORA n female matador
MATADORAS >MATADORA
MATADORE n form of dominoes game
MATADORES >MATADORE
MATADORS >MATADOR
MATAGOURI n thorny bush of New Zealand that forms thickets in open country
MATAI n New Zealand tree, the wood of which is used for timber for building
MATAIS >MATAI
MATAMATA (in Malaysia) a former name for > POLICE
MATAMATAS >MATAMATA
MATAMBALA >TAMBALA
MATATA same as >FERNBIRD
MATATAS >MATATA
MATATU n type of shared taxi used in Kenya
MATATUS >MATATU
MATCH n contest in a game or sport ▷ vb be exactly like, equal to, or in harmony with
MATCHABLE >MATCH
MATCHBOOK n number of carboard matches attached in folder
MATCHBOX n small box for holding matches
MATCHED >MATCH
MATCHER >MATCH
MATCHERS >MATCH
MATCHES >MATCH
MATCHET same as >MACHETE
MATCHETS >MATCHET
MATCHING >MATCH
MATCHLESS adj unequalled
MATCHLOCK n obsolete type of gunlock igniting the powder by means of a slow match
MATCHMADE >MATCHMAKE
MATCHMAKE vb bring suitable people together for marriage
MATCHMARK n mark made on mating components of an engine, machine, etc, to ensure that the components are assembled in the correct relative positions ▷ vb stamp (an object) with matchmarks
MATCHPLAY adj of a golf scoring system relating to holes won and lost ▷ n (in golf) scoring system in which a point is earned for

each hole won
MATCHUP n sports match
MATCHUPS >MATCHUP
MATCHWOOD n small splinters
MATE n friend ▷ vb pair (animals) or (of animals) be paired for reproduction
MATED >MATE
MATELASSE adj (in textiles) having a raised design, as quilting
MATELESS >MATE
MATELOT n sailor
MATELOTE n fish served with a sauce of wine, onions, seasonings, and fish stock
MATELOTES >MATELOTE
MATELOTS >MATELOT
MATELOTTE same as >MATELOTE
MATER n mother: often used facetiously
MATERIAL n substance of which a thing is made ▷ adj of matter or substance
MATERIALS npl equipment necessary for a particular activity
MATERIEL n materials and equipment of an organization, esp of a military force
MATERIELS >MATERIEL
MATERNAL adj of a mother
MATERNITY n motherhood ▷ adj of or for pregnant women
MATERS >MATER
MATES >MATE
MATESHIP n comradeship of friends, usually male, viewed as an institution
MATESHIPS >MATESHIP
MATEY adj friendly or intimate ▷ n friend or fellow: usually used in direct address
MATEYNESS >MATEY
MATEYS >MATEY
MATFELLON n knapweed
MATFELON n knapweed
MATFELONS >MATFELON
MATGRASS n widespread perennial European grass with dense tufts of bristly leaves, characteristic of peaty moors
MATH same as >MATHS
MATHESES >MATHESIS
MATHESIS n learning or wisdom
MATHS same as >MATH
MATICO n Peruvian shrub
MATICOS >MATICO
MATIER >MATY
MATIES >MATY
MATIEST >MATY
MATILDA n bushman's swag
MATILDAS >MATILDA
MATILY >MATY
MATIN adj of or relating to matins

MATINAL same as > MATIN
MATINEE n afternoon performance in a theatre or cinema
MATINEES > MATINEE
MATINESS > MATY
MATING > MATE
MATINGS > MATE
MATINS npl early morning service in various Christian Churches
MATIPO n New Zealand shrub
MATIPOS > MATIPO
MATJES same as > MAATJES
MATLESS > MAT
MATLO same as > MATELOT
MATLOS > MATLO
MATLOW same as > MATELOT
MATLOWS > MATLOW
MATOKE n (in Uganda) the flesh of bananas, boiled and mashed as a food
MATOKES > MATOKE
MATOOKE same as > MATOKE
MATOOKES > MATOOKE
MATRASS n long-necked glass flask, used for distilling, dissolving substances, etc
MATRASSES > MATRASS
MATRES > MATER
MATRIARCH n female head of a tribe or family
MATRIC n matriculation
MATRICE same as > MATRIX
MATRICES > MATRIX
MATRICIDE n crime of killing one's mother
MATRICS > MATRIC
MATRICULA n register
MATRILINY n attention to descent of kinship through the female line
MATRIMONY n marriage
MATRIX n substance or situation in which something originates, takes form, or is enclosed
MATRIXES > MATRIX
MATRON n staid or dignified married woman
MATRONAGE n state of being a matron
MATRONAL > MATRON
MATRONISE same as > MATRONIZE
MATRONIZE vb make matronly
MATRONLY adj (of a woman) middle-aged and plump
MATRONS > MATRON
MATROSS n gunner's assistant
MATROSSES > MATROSS
MATS > MAT
MATSAH same as > MATZO
MATSAHS > MATSAH
MATSURI n Japanese religious ceremony

MATSURIS > MATSURI
MATSUTAKE n Japanese mushroom
MATT adj dull, not shiny
MATTAMORE n subterranean storehouse or dwelling
MATTE same as > MATT
MATTED > MAT
MATTEDLY > MAT
MATTER n substance of which something is made ▷ vb be of importance
MATTERED > MATTER
MATTERFUL > MATTER
MATTERING > MATTER
MATTERS > MATTER
MATTERY adj discharging pus
MATTES > MATTE
MATTIE n young herring
MATTIES > MATTIE
MATTIFIED > MATTIFY
MATTIFIES > MATTIFY
MATTIFY vb make (the skin of the face) less oily or shiny using cosmetics
MATTIN same as > MATIN
MATTING > MAT
MATTINGS > MAT
MATTINS same as > MATINS
MATTOCK n large pick with one of its blade ends flattened for loosening soil
MATTOCKS > MATTOCK
MATTOID n person displaying eccentric behaviour and mental characteristics that approach the psychotic
MATTOIDS > MATTOID
MATTRASS same as > MATRASS
MATTRESS n large stuffed flat case, often with springs, used on or as a bed
MATTS > MATT
MATURABLE > MATURE
MATURATE vb mature or bring to maturity
MATURATED > MATURATE
MATURATES > MATURATE
MATURE adj fully developed or grown-up ▷ vb make or become mature
MATURED > MATURE
MATURELY > MATURE
MATURER > MATURE
MATURERS > MATURE
MATURES > MATURE
MATUREST > MATURE
MATURING > MATURE
MATURITY n state of being mature
MATUTINAL adj of, occurring in, or during the morning
MATUTINE same as > MATUTINAL
MATWEED n grass found on moors
MATWEEDS > MATWEED
MATY same as > MATEY

MATZA same as > MATZO
MATZAH same as > MATZO
MATZAHS > MATZAH
MATZAS > MATZA
MATZO n large very thin biscuit of unleavened bread, traditionally eaten by Jews during Passover
MATZOH same as > MATZO
MATZOHS > MATZOH
MATZOON n fermented milk product similar to yogurt
MATZOONS > MATZOON
MATZOS > MATZO
MATZOT > MATZO
MATZOTH > MATZOH
MAUBIES > MAUBY
MAUBY n (in the E Caribbean) a bittersweet drink made from the bark of a rhamnaceous tree
MAUD n shawl or rug of grey wool plaid formerly worn in Scotland
MAUDLIN adj foolishly or tearfully sentimental
MAUDLINLY > MAUDLIN
MAUDS > MAUD
MAUGER same as > MAUGRE
MAUGRE prep in spite of ▷ vb behave spitefully towards
MAUGRED > MAUGRE
MAUGRES > MAUGRE
MAUGRING > MAUGRE
MAUL vb handle roughly ▷ n loose scrum
MAULED > MAUL
MAULER > MAUL
MAULERS npl hands
MAULGRE same as > MAUGRE
MAULGRED > MAULGRE
MAULGRES > MAULGRE
MAULGRING > MAULGRE
MAULING > MAUL
MAULS > MAUL
MAULSTICK n long stick used by artists to steady the hand holding the brush
MAULVI n expert in Islamic law
MAULVIS > MAULVI
MAUMET n false god
MAUMETRY > MAUMET
MAUMETS > MAUMET
MAUN dialect word for > MUST
MAUND n unit of weight used in Asia, esp India, having different values in different localities. A common value in India is 82 pounds or 37 kilograms ▷ vb beg
MAUNDED > MAUND
MAUNDER vb talk or act aimlessly or idly
MAUNDERED > MAUNDER
MAUNDERER > MAUNDER
MAUNDERS > MAUNDER
MAUNDIES > MAUNDY
MAUNDING > MAUND
MAUNDS > MAUND
MAUNDY n ceremonial washing of the feet of poor

persons in commemoration of Jesus' washing of his disciples' feet (John 13:4·34) re-enacted in some churches on Maundy Thursday
MAUNGIER > MAUNGY
MAUNGIEST > MAUNGY
MAUNGY adj (esp of a child) sulky, bad-tempered, or peevish
MAUNNA vb Scots term meaning must not
MAURI n soul
MAURIS > MAURI
MAUSOLEA > MAUSOLEUM
MAUSOLEAN > MAUSOLEUM
MAUSOLEUM n stately tomb
MAUT same as > MAHOUT
MAUTHER n girl
MAUTHERS > MAUTHER
MAUTS > MAUT
MAUVAIS adj bad
MAUVAISE feminine form of > MAUVAIS
MAUVE adj pale purple ▷ n any of various pale to moderate pinkish-purple or bluish-purple colours
MAUVEIN same as > MAUVEINE
MAUVEINE same as > MAUVE
MAUVEINES > MAUVEINE
MAUVEINS > MAUVEIN
MAUVER > MAUVE
MAUVES > MAUVE
MAUVEST > MAUVE
MAUVIN same as > MAUVEINE
MAUVINE same as > MAUVEINE
MAUVINES > MAUVINE
MAUVINS > MAUVIN
MAVEN n expert or connoisseur
MAVENS > MAVEN
MAVERICK adj independent and unorthodox (person) ▷ n person of independent or unorthodox views ▷ vb take illegally
MAVERICKS > MAVERICK
MAVIE n type of thrush
MAVIES > MAVIE
MAVIN same as > MAVEN
MAVINS > MAVIN
MAVIS n song thrush
MAVISES > MAVIS
MAVOURNIN n Irish form of address meaning my darling
MAW n animal's mouth, throat, or stomach ▷ vb eat or bite
MAWBOUND adj (of cattle) constipated
MAWED > MAW
MAWGER adj (of persons or animals) thin or lean
MAWING > MAW

m

MAWK n maggot
MAWKIER > MAWK
MAWKIEST > MAWK
MAWKIN n slovenly woman
MAWKINS > MAWKIN
MAWKISH adj foolishly sentimental
MAWKISHLY > MAWKISH
MAWKS > MAWK
MAWKY > MAWK
MAWMET same as > MAUMET
MAWMETRY > MAWMET
MAWMETS > MAWMET
MAWN > MAW
MAWPUS same as > MOPUS
MAWPUSES > MAWPUS
MAWR same as > MAUTHER
MAWRS > MAWR
MAWS > MAW
MAWSEED n poppy seed
MAWSEEDS > MAWSEED
MAWTHER same as > MAUTHER
MAWTHERS > MAWTHER
MAX vb reach the full extent
MAXED > MAX
MAXES > MAX
MAXI adj (of a garment) very long ▷ n type of large racing yacht
MAXICOAT n long coat
MAXICOATS > MAXICOAT
MAXILLA n upper jawbone of a vertebrate
MAXILLAE > MAXILLA
MAXILLAR > MAXILLA
MAXILLARY > MAXILLA
MAXILLAS > MAXILLA
MAXILLULA n jaw in crustacean
MAXIM n general truth or principle
MAXIMA > MAXIMUM
MAXIMAL adj maximum ▷ n maximum
MAXIMALLY > MAXIMAL
MAXIMALS > MAXIMAL
MAXIMIN n highest of a set of minimum values
MAXIMINS > MAXIMIN
MAXIMISE same as > MAXIMIZE
MAXIMISED > MAXIMISE
MAXIMISER > MAXIMISE
MAXIMISES > MAXIMISE
MAXIMIST > MAXIM
MAXIMISTS > MAXIM
MAXIMITE n type of explosive
MAXIMITES > MAXIMITE
MAXIMIZE vb increase to a maximum
MAXIMIZED > MAXIMIZE
MAXIMIZER > MAXIMIZE
MAXIMIZES > MAXIMIZE
MAXIMS > MAXIM
MAXIMUM n greatest possible (amount or number) ▷ adj of, being, or showing a maximum or maximums
MAXIMUMLY > MAXIMUM
MAXIMUMS > MAXIMUM
MAXIMUS n method rung

on twelve bells
MAXIMUSES > MAXIMUS
MAXING > MAX
MAXIS > MAXI
MAXIXE n Brazilian dance in duple time, a precursor of the tango
MAXIXES > MAXIXE
MAXWELL n cgs unit of magnetic flux
MAXWELLS > MAXWELL
MAY vb used as an auxiliary to express possibility, permission, opportunity, etc ▷ vb gather may
MAYA n illusion, esp the material world of the senses regarded as illusory
MAYAN > MAYA
MAYAPPLE n American plant
MAYAPPLES > MAYAPPLE
MAYAS > MAYA
MAYBE adv perhaps, possibly ▷ sentence substitute possibly
MAYBES > MAYBE
MAYBIRD n American songbird
MAYBIRDS > MAYBIRD
MAYBUSH n flowering shrub
MAYBUSHES > MAYBUSH
MAYDAY n international radiotelephone distress signal
MAYDAYS > MAYDAY
MAYED > MAY
MAYEST same as > MAYST
MAYFLIES > MAYFLY
MAYFLOWER n any of various plants that bloom in May
MAYFLY n short-lived aquatic insect
MAYHAP archaic word for > PERHAPS
MAYHAPPEN same as > MAYHAP
MAYHEM n violent destruction or confusion
MAYHEMS > MAYHEM
MAYING > MAY
MAYINGS > MAYING
MAYO n mayonnaise
MAYOR n head of a municipality
MAYORAL > MAYOR
MAYORALTY n (term of) office of a mayor
MAYORESS n mayor's wife
MAYORS > MAYOR
MAYORSHIP > MAYOR
MAYOS > MAYO
MAYPOLE n pole set up for dancing round on the first day of May to celebrate spring
MAYPOLES > MAYPOLE
MAYPOP n American wild flower
MAYPOPS > MAYPOP
MAYS > MAY
MAYST singular form of the

present tense of > MAY
MAYSTER same as > MASTER
MAYSTERS > MAYSTER
MAYVIN same as > MAVEN
MAYVINS > MAYVIN
MAYWEED n widespread Eurasian weedy plant, having evil-smelling leaves and daisy-like flower heads
MAYWEEDS > MAYWEED
MAZAEDIA > MAZAEDIUM
MAZAEDIUM n part of lichen
MAZARD same as > MAZER
MAZARDS > MAZARD
MAZARINE n blue colour
MAZARINES > MAZARINE
MAZE n complex network of paths or lines designed to puzzle
MAZED > MAZE
MAZEDLY adv in a bewildered way
MAZEDNESS n bewilderment
MAZEFUL > MAZE
MAZELIKE > MAZE
MAZELTOV interj congratulations
MAZEMENT > MAZE
MAZEMENTS > MAZE
MAZER n large hardwood drinking bowl
MAZERS > MAZER
MAZES > MAZE
MAZEY adj dizzy
MAZHBI n low-caste Sikh
MAZHBIS > MAZHBI
MAZIER > MAZY
MAZIEST > MAZY
MAZILY > MAZY
MAZINESS > MAZY
MAZING > MAZE
MAZOURKA same as > MAZURKA
MAZOURKAS > MAZOURKA
MAZOUT same as > MAZUT
MAZOUTS > MAZOUT
MAZUMA n money
MAZUMAS > MAZUMA
MAZURKA n lively Polish dance
MAZURKAS > MAZURKA
MAZUT n residue left after distillation of petrol
MAZUTS > MAZUT
MAZY adj of or like a maze
MAZZARD same as > MAZZARD
MAZZARDS > MAZZARD
MBAQANGA n style of Black popular music of urban South Africa
MBAQANGAS > MBAQANGA
MBIRA n African musical instrument consisting of tuned metal strips attached to a resonating box, which are plucked with the thumbs
MBIRAS > MBIRA
ME n (in tonic sol-fa) third degree of any major scale

▷ pron refers to the speaker or writer
MEACOCK n timid person
MEACOCKS > MEACOCK
MEAD n alcoholic drink made from honey
MEADOW n piece of grassland
MEADOWS > MEADOW
MEADOWY > MEADOW
MEADS > MEAD
MEAGER same as > MEAGRE
MEAGERLY > MEAGRE
MEAGRE adj scanty or insufficient ▷ n Mediterranean fish
MEAGRELY > MEAGRE
MEAGRER > MEAGRE
MEAGRES > MEAGRE
MEAGREST > MEAGRE
MEAL n occasion when food is served and eaten ▷ vb cover with meal
MEALED > MEAL
MEALER n person eating but not lodging at boarding house
MEALERS > MEALER
MEALIE n maize
MEALIER > MEALY
MEALIES South African word for > MAIZE
MEALIEST > MEALY
MEALINESS > MEALY
MEALING > MEAL
MEALLESS > MEAL
MEALS > MEAL
MEALTIME n time for meal
MEALTIMES > MEALTIME
MEALWORM n larva of various beetles which feeds on meal, flour, and similar stored foods
MEALWORMS > MEALWORM
MEALY adj resembling meal
MEALYBUG n plant-eating homopterous insect
MEALYBUGS > MEALYBUG
MEAN vb intend to convey or express ▷ adj miserly, ungenerous, or petty ▷ n middle point between two extremes
MEANDER vb follow a winding course ▷ n winding course
MEANDERED > MEANDER
MEANDERER > MEANDER
MEANDERS > MEANDER
MEANDRIAN > MEANDER
MEANDROUS > MEANDER
MEANE vb moan
MEANED > MEANE
MEANER > MEAN
MEANERS > MEAN
MEANES > MEANE
MEANEST > MEAN
MEANIE n unkind or miserly person
MEANIES > MEANY
MEANING n what something means
MEANINGLY > MEAN
MEANINGS > MEANING

MEANLY >MEAN
MEANNESS >MEAN
MEANS >MEAN
MEANT >MEAN
MEANTIME n intervening period ▷ adv meanwhile
MEANTIMES >MEANTIME
MEANWHILE adv during the intervening period
MEANY same as >MEANIE
MEARE same as >MERE
MEARES >MEARE
MEARING adj forming boundary
MEASE vb assuage
MEASED >MEASE
MEASES >MEASE
MEASING >MEASE
MEASLE vb infect with measles
MEASLED adj (of cattle, sheep, or pigs) infested with tapeworm larvae
MEASLES n infectious disease producing red spots
MEASLIER >MEASLY
MEASLIEST >MEASLY
MEASLING >MEASLE
MEASLY adj meagre
MEASURE n size or quantity ▷ vb determine the size or quantity of
MEASURED adj slow and steady
MEASURER >MEASURE
MEASURERS >MEASURE
MEASURES npl rock strata that contain a particular type of deposit
MEASURING adj used to measure quantities, esp in cooking
MEAT n animal flesh as food
MEATAL >MEATUS
MEATAXE n meat cleaver
MEATAXES >MEATAXE
MEATBALL n minced beef, shaped into a ball before cooking
MEATBALLS >MEATBALL
MEATED adj fattened
MEATH same as >MEAD
MEATHE same as >MEAD
MEATHEAD n stupid person
MEATHEADS >MEATHEAD
MEATHES >MEATHE
MEATHS >MEATH
MEATIER >MEATY
MEATIEST >MEATY
MEATILY >MEATY
MEATINESS >MEATY
MEATLESS >MEAT
MEATLOAF n chopped meat served in loaf-shaped mass
MEATMAN n meat seller
MEATMEN >MEATMAN
MEATS >MEAT
MEATSPACE n real physical world, as contrasted with the world of cyberspace
MEATUS n natural opening or channel, such as the canal leading from the

outer ear to the eardrum
MEATUSES >MEATUS
MEATY adj (tasting) of or like meat
MEAWES same as >MEWS
MEAZEL same as >MESEL
MEAZELS >MEAZEL
MEBOS n South African dried apricots
MEBOSES >MEBOS
MECCA n place that attracts many visitors
MECCAS >MECCA
MECHANIC n person skilled in repairing or operating machinery
MECHANICS n scientific study of motion and force
MECHANISE same as >MECHANIZE
MECHANISM n way a machine works
MECHANIST same as >MECHANIC
MECHANIZE vb equip with machinery
MECHITZA n screen in synagogue separating men and women
MECHITZAS >MECHITZA
MECHITZOT >MECHITZA
MECK same as >MAIK
MECKS >MECK
MECLIZINE n drug used to treat motion sickness
MECONATE n salt of meconic acid
MECONATES >MECONATE
MECONIC adj derived from poppies
MECONIN n substance found in opium
MECONINS >MECONIN
MECONIUM n dark green mucoid material that forms the first faeces of a newborn infant
MECONIUMS >MECONIUM
MED n doctor
MEDACCA n Japanese freshwater fish
MEDACCAS >MEDACCA
MEDAILLON n small round thin piece of food
MEDAKA same as >MEDACCA
MEDAKAS >MEDAKA
MEDAL n piece of metal with an inscription etc, given as a reward or memento ▷ vb honour with a medal
MEDALED >MEDAL
MEDALET n small medal
MEDALETS >MEDALET
MEDALING >MEDAL
MEDALIST same as >MEDALLIST
MEDALISTS >MEDALIST
MEDALLED >MEDAL
MEDALLIC >MEDAL
MEDALLING >MEDAL
MEDALLION n disc-shaped ornament worn on a chain round the neck

MEDALLIST n winner of a medal
MEDALPLAY n (in golf) scoring system in which the score is based on the total number of strokes taken
MEDALS >MEDAL
MEDCINAL same as >MEDICINAL
MEDDLE vb interfere annoyingly
MEDDLED >MEDDLE
MEDDLER >MEDDLE
MEDDLERS >MEDDLE
MEDDLES >MEDDLE
MEDDLING >MEDDLE
MEDDLINGS >MEDDLE
MEDEVAC n evacuation of casualties from forward areas to the nearest hospital or base ▷ vb transport (a wounded or sick person) to hospital by medevac
MEDEVACED >MEDEVAC
MEDEVACS >MEDEVAC
MEDFLIES >MEDFLY
MEDFLY n Mediterranean fruit fly
MEDIA n a medium of cultivation, conveyance, or expression
MEDIACIES >MEDIACY
MEDIACY n quality or state of being mediate
MEDIAD adj situated near the median line or plane of an organism
MEDIAE >MEDIUM
MEDIAEVAL adj of, relating to, or in the style of the Middle Ages ▷ n person living in medieval times
MEDIAL adj of or in the middle ▷ n speech sound between being fortis and lenis
MEDIALLY >MEDIAL
MEDIALS >MEDIAL
MEDIAN n middle (point or line) ▷ adj of, relating to, situated in, or directed towards the middle
MEDIANLY >MEDIAN
MEDIANS >MEDIAN
MEDIANT n third degree of a major or minor scale
MEDIANTS >MEDIANT
MEDIAS >MEDIUM
MEDIATE vb intervene in a dispute to bring about agreement ▷ adj occurring as a result of or dependent upon mediation
MEDIATED >MEDIATE
MEDIATELY >MEDIATE
MEDIATES >MEDIATE
MEDIATING >MEDIATE
MEDIATION n act of mediating
MEDIATISE same as >MEDIATIZE
MEDIATIVE >MEDIATE
MEDIATIZE vb annex (a state) to another state,

allowing the former ruler to retain his title and some authority
MEDIATOR >MEDIATE
MEDIATORS >MEDIATE
MEDIATORY >MEDIATE
MEDIATRIX n female mediator
MEDIC n doctor or medical student
MEDICABLE adj potentially able to be treated or cured medically
MEDICABLY >MEDICABLE
MEDICAID n health assistance programme financed by federal, state, and local taxes to help pay hospital and medical costs for persons of low income
MEDICAIDS >MEDICAID
MEDICAL adj of the science of medicine ▷ n medical examination
MEDICALLY >MEDICAL
MEDICALS >MEDICAL
MEDICANT n medicinal substance
MEDICANTS >MEDICANT
MEDICARE n (in the US) a federally sponsored health insurance programme for persons of 65 or older
MEDICARES >MEDICARE
MEDICATE vb treat with a medicinal substance
MEDICATED adj (of a patient) having been treated with a medicine or drug
MEDICATES >MEDICATE
MEDICIDE n suicide assisted by doctor
MEDICIDES >MEDICIDE
MEDICINAL adj having therapeutic properties ▷ n medicinal substance
MEDICINE n substance used to treat disease ▷ vb treat with medicine
MEDICINED >MEDICINE
MEDICINER n physician
MEDICINES >MEDICINE
MEDICK n type of small leguminous plant with yellow or purple flowers and trifoliate leaves
MEDICKS >MEDICK
MEDICO n doctor or medical student
MEDICOS >MEDICO
MEDICS >MEDIC
MEDIEVAL adj of the Middle Ages ▷ n person living in medieval times
MEDIEVALS >MEDIEVAL
MEDIGAP n private health insurance
MEDIGAPS >MEDIGAP
MEDII >MEDIUS
MEDINA n ancient quarter of any of various North African cities
MEDINAS >MEDINA

m

MEDIOCRE adj average in quality

MEDITATE vb reflect deeply, esp on spiritual matters

MEDITATED > MEDITATE

MEDITATES > MEDITATE

MEDITATOR > MEDITATE

MEDIUM adj midway between extremes, average ▷ n middle state, degree, or condition

MEDIUMS npl medium-dated gilt-edged securities

MEDIUS n middle finger

MEDIUSES > MEDIUS

MEDIVAC variant spelling of > MEDEVAC

MEDIVACED > MEDIVAC

MEDIVACS > MEDIVAC

MEDLAR n apple-like fruit of a small tree, eaten when it begins to decay

MEDLARS > MEDLAR

MEDLE same as > MEDDLE

MEDLED > MEDLE

MEDLES > MEDLE

MEDLEY n miscellaneous mixture ▷ adj of, being, or relating to a mixture or variety

MEDLEYS > MEDLEY

MEDLING > MEDLE

MEDRESA same as > MADRASAH

MEDRESAS > MEDRESA

MEDRESE same as > MADRASAH

MEDRESES > MEDRESE

MEDRESSEH same as > MADRASAH

MEDS > MED

MEDULLA n marrow, pith, or inner tissue

MEDULLAE > MEDULLA

MEDULLAR > MEDULLA

MEDULLARY > MEDULLA

MEDULLAS > MEDULLA

MEDULLATE adj having medulla

MEDUSA n jellyfish

MEDUSAE > MEDUSA

MEDUSAL > MEDUSA

MEDUSAN > MEDUSA

MEDUSANS > MEDUSA

MEDUSAS > MEDUSA

MEDUSOID same as > MEDUSA

MEDUSOIDS > MEDUSOID

MEE n Malaysian noodle dish

MEED n recompense

MEEDS > MEED

MEEK adj submissive or humble

MEEKEN vb make meek

MEEKENED > MEEKEN

MEEKENING > MEEKEN

MEEKENS > MEEKEN

MEEKER > MEEK

MEEKEST > MEEK

MEEKLY > MEEK

MEEKNESS > MEEK

MEEMIE n hysterical person

MEEMIES > MEEMIE

MEER same as > MERE

MEERCAT same as > MEERKAT

MEERCATS > MEERCAT

MEERED > MEER

MEERING > MEER

MEERKAT n S African mongoose

MEERKATS > MEERKAT

MEERS > MEER

MEES > MEE

MEET vb come together (with) ▷ n meeting, esp a sports meeting ▷ adj fit or suitable

MEETER > MEET

MEETERS > MEET

MEETEST > MEET

MEETING > MEET

MEETINGS > MEET

MEETLY > MEET

MEETNESS n properness

MEETS > MEET

MEFF dialect word for > TRAMP

MEFFS > MEFF

MEG short for > MEGABYTE

MEGA adj extremely good, great, or successful

MEGABAR n unit of million bars

MEGABARS > MEGABAR

MEGABIT n one million bits

MEGABITS > MEGABIT

MEGABUCK n million dollars

MEGABUCKS > MEGABUCK

MEGABYTE n 2^{20} or 1 048 576 bytes

MEGABYTES > MEGABYTE

MEGACITY n city with over 10 million inhabitants

MEGACURIE n unit of million curies

MEGACYCLE same as > MEGAHERTZ

MEGADEAL n very good deal

MEGADEALS > MEGADEAL

MEGADEATH n death of a million people, esp in a nuclear war or attack

MEGADOSE n very large dose, as of a medicine, vitamin, etc

MEGADOSES > MEGADOSE

MEGADYNE n unit of million dynes

MEGADYNES > MEGADYNE

MEGAFARAD n unit of million farads

MEGAFAUNA n component of the fauna of a region or period that comprises the larger terrestrial animals

MEGAFLOP n measure of processing speed, consisting of a million floating-point operations a second

MEGAFLOPS > MEGAFLOP

MEGAFLORA n plants large enough to be seen by naked eye

MEGAFOG n amplified fog signal

MEGAFOGS > MEGAFOG

MEGAGAUSS n unit of million gauss

MEGAHERTZ n one million hertz

MEGAHIT n great success

MEGAHITS > MEGAHIT

MEGAJOULE n unit of million joules

MEGALITH n great stone, esp as part of a prehistoric monument

MEGALITHS > MEGALITH

MEGALITRE n one million litres

MEGALOPIC adj having large eyes

MEGALOPS n crab in larval stage

MEGAPHONE n cone-shaped instrument used to amplify the voice ▷ vb speak through megaphone

MEGAPHYLL n relatively large type of leaf produced by ferns and seed plants

MEGAPIXEL n one million pixels

MEGAPLEX n cinema complex containing a large number of separate screens, and usually a restaurant or bar

MEGAPOD same as > MEGAPODE

MEGAPODE n bird of Australia, New Guinea, and adjacent islands

MEGAPODES > MEGAPODE

MEGAPODS > MEGAPOD

MEGARA > MEGARON

MEGARAD n unit of million rads

MEGARADS > MEGARAD

MEGARON n tripartite rectangular room containing a central hearth surrounded by four pillars, found in Bronze Age Greece and Asia Minor

MEGARONS > MEGARON

MEGASCOPE n type of image projector

MEGASPORE n larger of the two types of spore produced by some spore-bearing plants, which develops into the female gametophyte

MEGASS another name for > BAGASSE

MEGASSE same as > MEGASS

MEGASSES > MEGASS

MEGASTAR n very well-known personality in the entertainment business

MEGASTARS > MEGASTAR

MEGASTORE n very large store

MEGATHERE n type of gigantic extinct American sloth common in late Cenozoic times

MEGATON n explosive power equal to that of one million tons of TNT

MEGATONIC > MEGATON

MEGATONS > MEGATON

MEGAVOLT n one million volts

MEGAVOLTS > MEGAVOLT

MEGAWATT n one million watts

MEGAWATTS > MEGAWATT

MEGILLA same as > MEGILLAH

MEGILLAH n scroll of the Book of Esther, read on the festival of Purim

MEGILLAHS > MEGILLAH

MEGILLAS > MEGILLA

MEGILLOTH > MEGILLAH

MEGILP n oil-painting medium of linseed oil mixed with mastic varnish or turpentine

MEGILPH same as > MEGILP

MEGILPHS > MEGILPH

MEGILPS > MEGILP

MEGOHM n one million ohms

MEGOHMS > MEGOHM

MEGRIM n caprice

MEGRIMS n fit of depression

MEGS > MEG

MEH interj expression of indifference or boredom

MEHNDI n (esp in India) the practice of painting designs on the hands, feet, etc using henna

MEHNDIS > MEHNDI

MEIBOMIAN as in meibomian gland any of the small sebaceous glands in the eyelid, beneath the conjunctiva

MEIKLE adj Scots word meaning large

MEIN Scots word for > MOAN

MEINED > MEIN

MEINEY same as > MEINY

MEINEYS > MEINEY

MEINIE same as > MEINY

MEINIES > MEINY

MEINING > MEIN

MEINS > MEIN

MEINT same as > MING

MEINY n retinue or household

MEIOCYTE n cell that divides by meiosis to produce four haploid spores

MEIOCYTES > MEIOCYTE

MEIOFAUNA n component of the fauna of a sea or lake bed comprising small (but not microscopic) animals, such as tiny worms and crustaceans

MEIONITE n mineral containing silica

MEIONITES > MEIONITE

MEIOSES >MEIOSIS

MEIOSIS n type of cell division in which reproductive cells are produced, each containing half the chromosome number of the parent nucleus

MEIOSPORE n haploid spore

MEIOTIC >MEIOSIS

MEISHI n business card in Japan

MEISHIS >MEISHI

MEISTER n person who excels at a particular activity

MEISTERS >MEISTER

MEITH n landmark

MEITHS >MEITH

MEJLIS same as >MAJLIS

MEJLISES >MEJLIS

MEKKA same as >MECCA

MEKKAS >MEKKA

MEKOMETER n device for measuring distance

MEL n pure form of honey formerly used in pharmaceutical products

MELA n Asian cultural or religious fair or festival

MELALEUCA n Australian shrub or tree with a white trunk and black branches

MELAMDIM >MELAMED

MELAMED n Hebrew teacher

MELAMINE n colourless crystalline compound used in making synthetic resins

MELAMINES >MELAMINE

MELAMPODE n poisonous plant

MELANGE n mixture

MELANGES >MELANGE

MELANIAN n freshwater mollusc

MELANIC adj relating to melanism or melanosis ▷ n darker form of creature

MELANICS >MELANIC

MELANIN n dark pigment found in the hair, skin, and eyes of humans and animals

MELANINS >MELANIN

MELANISE same as >MELANIZE

MELANISED >MELANISE

MELANISES >MELANISE

MELANISM same as >MELANOSIS

MELANISMS >MELANISM

MELANIST >MELANISM

MELANISTS >MELANISM

MELANITE n black variety of andradite garnet

MELANITES >MELANITE

MELANITIC >MELANITE

MELANIZE vb turn into melanin

MELANIZED >MELANIZE

MELANIZES >MELANIZE

MELANO n person with abnormally dark skin

MELANOID adj resembling melanin ▷ n dark substance formed in skin

MELANOIDS >MELANOID

MELANOMA n tumour composed of dark-coloured cells, occurring in some skin cancers

MELANOMAS >MELANOMA

MELANOS >MELANO

MELANOSES >MELANOSIS

MELANOSIS n skin condition characterized by excessive deposits of melanin

MELANOTIC >MELANOSIS

MELANOUS adj having a dark complexion and black hair

MELANURIA n presence of melanin in urine

MELANURIC >MELANURIA

MELAPHYRE n type of weathered amygdaloidal basalt or andesite

MELAS >MELA

MELASTOME n tropical flowering plant

MELATONIN n hormone-like secretion of the pineal gland, causing skin colour changes in some animals and thought to be involved in reproductive function

MELBA adj relating to a type of dessert sauce or toast

MELD vb merge or blend ▷ n act of melding

MELDED >MELD

MELDER >MELD

MELDERS >MELD

MELDING >MELD

MELDS >MELD

MELEE n noisy confused fight or crowd

MELEES >MELEE

MELENA n excrement or vomit stained by blood

MELENAS >MELENA

MELIC adj (of poetry, esp ancient Greek lyric poems) intended to be sung ▷ n type of grass

MELICK n either of two pale green perennial grasses

MELICKS >MELICK

MELICS >MELIC

MELIK same as >MALIK

MELIKS >MELIK

MELILITE n mineral containing calcium

MELILITES >MELILITE

MELILOT n Old World leguminous plant with narrow clusters of small white or yellow fragrant flowers

MELILOTS >MELILOT

MELINITE n high explosive made from picric acid

MELINITES >MELINITE

MELIORATE vb improve

MELIORISM n notion that the world can be improved by human effort

MELIORIST >MELIORISM

MELIORITY n improved state

MELISMA n expressive vocal phrase or passage consisting of several notes sung to one syllable

MELISMAS >MELISMA

MELISMATA >MELISMA

MELITTIN n main toxic component in bee venom

MELITTINS >MELITTIN

MELL vb mix

MELLAY same as >MELEE

MELLAYS >MELLAY

MELLED >MELL

MELLIFIC adj forming or producing honey

MELLING >MELL

MELLITE n soft yellow mineral

MELLITES >MELLITE

MELLITIC >MELLITE

MELLOTRON n musical synthesizer

MELLOW adj soft, not harsh ▷ vb make or become mellow

MELLOWED >MELLOW

MELLOWER >MELLOW

MELLOWEST >MELLOW

MELLOWING >MELLOW

MELLOWLY >MELLOW

MELLOWS >MELLOW

MELLOWY same as >MELLOW

MELLS >MELL

MELOCOTON n variety of peach

MELODEON n small accordion

MELODEONS >MELODEON

MELODIA same as >MELODICA

MELODIAS >MELODIA

MELODIC adj of melody

MELODICA n type of flute

MELODICAS >MELODICA

MELODICS n study of melody

MELODIES >MELODY

MELODION same as >MELODEON

MELODIONS >MELODION

MELODIOUS adj pleasing to the ear

MELODISE same as >MELODIZE

MELODISED >MELODISE

MELODISER >MELODISE

MELODISES >MELODISE

MELODIST n composer of melodies

MELODISTS >MELODIST

MELODIZE vb provide with a melody

MELODIZED >MELODIZE

MELODIZER >MELODIZE

MELODIZES >MELODIZE

MELODRAMA n play full of extravagant action and emotion

MELODRAME same as >MELODRAMA

MELODY n series of musical notes which make a tune

MELOID n type of long-legged beetle of the family which includes the blister beetles and oil beetles

MELOIDS >MELOID

MELOMANIA n great enthusiasm for music

MELOMANIC >MELOMANIA

MELON n large round juicy fruit with a hard rind

MELONGENE n aubergine

MELONS >MELON

MELOXICAM n anti-inflammatory drug used to treat osteoarthritis

MELPHALAN n drug used to treat leukaemia

MELS >MEL

MELT vb (cause to) become liquid by heat ▷ n act or process of melting

MELTABLE >MELT

MELTAGE n process or result of melting or the amount melted

MELTAGES >MELTAGE

MELTDOWN n (in a nuclear reactor) melting of the fuel rods, with the possible release of radiation

MELTDOWNS >MELTDOWN

MELTED >MELT

MELTEMI n northerly wind in the northeast Mediterranean

MELTEMIS >MELTEMI

MELTER >MELT

MELTERS >MELT

MELTIER >MELTY

MELTIEST >MELTY

MELTING >MELT

MELTINGLY >MELT

MELTINGS >MELT

MELTITH n meal

MELTITHS >MELTITH

MELTON n heavy smooth woollen fabric with a short nap, used esp for overcoats

MELTONS >MELTON

MELTS >MELT

MELTWATER n melted snow or ice

MELTY adj tending to melt

MELUNGEON n any of a dark-skinned group of people of the Appalachians in E Tennessee, of mixed Indian, White, and Black ancestry

MEM n 13th letter in the Hebrew alphabet, transliterated as m

MEMBER n individual making up a body or society

m

▷ *adj* (of a (country or group) belonging to an organization or alliance

MEMBERED *adj* having members

MEMBERS >MEMBER

MEMBRAL *adj* of limbs

MEMBRANAL >MEMBRANE

MEMBRANE *n* thin flexible tissue in a plant or animal body

MEMBRANED *adj* having membrane

MEMBRANES >MEMBRANE

MEME *n* idea or element of social behaviour (passed on through generations in a culture, esp by imitation

MEMENTO *n* thing serving to remind, souvenir

MEMENTOES >MEMENTO

MEMENTOS >MEMENTO

MEMES >MEME

MEMETIC *adj* of or relating to a meme

MEMETICS *n* study of gentic transmission of culture

MEMO *n* memorandum

MEMOIR *n* biography or historical account based on personal knowledge

MEMOIRISM *n* writing of memoirs

MEMOIRIST
>MEMOIRISM

MEMOIRS *npl* collection of reminiscences about a period or series of events, written from personal experience

MEMORABLE *adj* worth remembering, noteworthy

MEMORABLY
>MEMORABLE

MEMORANDA *n* plural of memorandum: written statement of communications

MEMORIAL *n* something serving to commemorate a person or thing ▷ *adj* serving as a memorial

MEMORIALS >MEMORIAL

MEMORIES >MEMORY

MEMORISE *same as*
>MEMORIZE

MEMORISED >MEMORISE

MEMORISER >MEMORISE

MEMORISES >MEMORISE

MEMORITTER *adv* from memory

MEMORIZE *vb* commit to memory

MEMORIZED >MEMORIZE

MEMORIZER >MEMORIZE

MEMORIZES >MEMORIZE

MEMORY *n* ability to remember

MEMOS >MEMO

MEMS >MEM

MEMSAHIB *n* (formerly, in India) term of respect used for a European married woman

MEMSAHIBS >MEMSAHIB

MEN >MAN

MENACE *n* threat ▷ *vb* threaten, endanger

MENACED >MENACE

MENACER >MENACE

MENACERS >MENACE

MENACES >MENACE

MENACING >MENACE

MENAD *same as* >MAENAD

MENADIONE *n* yellow crystalline compound

MENADS >MENAD

MENAGE *old form of*
>MANAGE

MENAGED >MENAGE

MENAGERIE *n* collection of wild animals for exhibition

MENAGES >MENAGE

MENAGING >MENAGE

MENARCHE *n* first occurrence of menstruation in a woman's life

MENARCHES >MENARCHE

MENAZON *n* type of insecticide

MENAZONS >MENAZON

MEND *vb* repair or patch ▷ *n* mended area

MENDABLE >MEND

MENDACITY *n* (tendency to) untruthfulness

MENDED >MEND

MENDER >MEND

MENDERS >MEND

MENDICANT *adj* begging ▷ *n* beggar

MENDICITY
>MENDICANT

MENDIGO *n* Spanish beggar or vagrant

MENDIGOS >MENDIGO

MENDING *n* something to be mended, esp clothes

MENDINGS >MENDING

MENDS >MEND

MENE *Scots form of* >MOAN

MENED >MENE

MENEER *n* S African title of address

MENEERS >MENEER

MENES >MENE

MENFOLK *npl* men collectively, esp the men of a particular family

MENFOLKS *same as*
>MENFOLK

MENG *vb* mix

MENGE *same as* >MENG

MENGED >MENG

MENGES >MENGE

MENGING >MENG

MENGS >MENG

MENHADEN *n* marine N American fish, source of fishmeal, fertilizer, and oil

MENHADENS >MENHADEN

MENHIR *n* single upright prehistoric stone

MENHIRS >MENHIR

MENIAL *adj* involving boring work of low status ▷ *n* person with a menial job

MENIALLY >MENIAL

MENIALS >MENIAL

MENILITE *n* liver opal

MENILITES >MENILITE

MENING >MENE

MENINGEAL >MENINX

MENINGES >MENINX

MENINX *n* one of three membranes that envelop the brain and spinal cord

MENISCAL >MENISCUS

MENISCATE >MENISCUS

MENISCI >MENISCUS

MENISCOID >MENISCUS

MENISCUS *n* curved surface of a liquid

MENO *adv* (esp preceding a dynamic or tempo marking) to be played less quickly, less softly, etc

MENOLOGY *n* ecclesiastical calendar of the months

MENOMINEE *n* whitefish, found in N America and Siberia

MENOMINI *same as*
>MENOMINEE

MENOMINIS >MENOMINI

MENOPAUSE *n* time when a woman's menstrual cycle ceases

MENOPOLIS *n* informal word for an area with a high proportion of single men

MENOPOME *n* American salamander

MENOPOMES >MENOPOME

MENORAH *n* seven-branched candelabrum used as an emblem of Judaism

MENORAHS >MENORAH

MENORRHEA *n* normal bleeding in menstruation

MENSA *n* faint constellation in the S hemisphere lying between Hydrus and Volans and containing part of the Large Magellanic Cloud

MENSAE *n* star of the mensa constellation

MENSAL *adj* monthly

MENSAS >MENSA

MENSCH *n* decent person

MENSCHEN >MENSCH

MENSCHES >MENSCH

MENSCHY >MENSCH

MENSE *vb* grace

MENSED >MENSE

MENSEFUL *adj* gracious

MENSELESS *adj* graceless

MENSES *n* menstruation

MENSH *vb* mention

MENSHED >MENSH

MENSHEN *n* Chinese door god

MENSHES >MENSH

MENSHING >MENSH

MENSING >MENSE

MENSTRUA >MENSTRUUM

MENSTRUAL *adj* of or relating to menstruation

MENSTRUUM *n* solvent, esp one used in the preparation of a drug

MENSUAL *same as*
>MENSAL

MENSURAL *adj* of or involving measure

MENSWEAR *n* clothing for men

MENSWEARS >MENSWEAR

MENT *same as* >MING

MENTA >MENTUM

MENTAL *adj* of, in, or done by the mind

MENTALESE *n* picturing of concepts in mind without words

MENTALISM *n* doctrine that mind is the fundamental reality and that objects of knowledge exist only as aspects of the subject's consciousness

MENTALIST
>MENTALISM

MENTALITY *n* way of thinking

MENTALLY >MENTAL

MENTATION *n* process or result of mental activity

MENTEE *n* person trained by mentor

MENTEES >MENTEE

MENTHENE *n* liquid obtained from menthol

MENTHENES >MENTHENE

MENTHOL *n* organic compound found in peppermint, used medicinally

MENTHOLS >MENTHOL

MENTICIDE *n* destruction of person's mental independence

MENTION *vb* refer to briefly ▷ *n* brief reference to a person or thing

MENTIONED >MENTION

MENTIONER >MENTION

MENTIONS >MENTION

MENTO *n* Jamaican song

MENTOR *n* adviser or guide ▷ *vb* act as a mentor to (someone) ▷ *vb* act as mentor for

MENTORED >MENTOR

MENTORIAL >MENTOR

MENTORING *n* (in business) the practice of assigning a junior member of staff to the care of a more experienced person who assists him in his career

MENTORS >MENTOR

MENTOS >MENTO

MENTUM *n* chin

MENU *n* list of dishes to be served, or from which to order

MENUDO *n* Mexican soup

MENUDOS >MENUDO

MENUISIER *n* joiner

MENUS >MENU

MENYIE *same as* >MEINIE

MENYIES > MENYIE

MEOU same as **>** MEOW

MEOUED > MEOU

MEOUING > MEOU

MEOUS > MEOU

MEOW vb (of a cat) to make a characteristic crying sound ▷ interj imitation of this sound

MEOWED > MEOW

MEOWING > MEOW

MEOWS > MEOW

MEPACRINE n drug formerly widely used to treat malaria

MEPHITIC adj poisonous

MEPHITIS n foul-smelling discharge

MEPHITISM n poisoning

MERANTI n wood from any of several Malaysian trees

MERANTIS > MERANTI

MERBROMIN n green iridescent crystalline compound

MERC n mercenary

MERCAPTAN another name (not in technical usage) for **>** THIOL

MERCAPTO adj of a particular chemical group

MERCAT Scots word for **>** MARKET

MERCATS > MERCAT

MERCENARY adj influenced by greed ▷ n hired soldier

MERCER n dealer in textile fabrics and fine cloth

MERCERIES > MERCER

MERCERISE same as **>** MERCERIZE

MERCERIZE vb treat (cotton yarn) with an alkali to increase its strength and reception to dye and impart a lustrous silky appearance

MERCERS > MERCER

MERCERY > MERCER

MERCES > MERC

MERCH n merchandise

MERCHANT n person engaged in trade, wholesale trader ▷ adj of ships involved in commercial trade or their crews ▷ vb conduct trade in

MERCHANTS > MERCHANT

MERCHES > MERCH

MERCHET n (in feudal England) a fine paid by a tenant, esp a villein, to his lord for allowing the marriage of his daughter

MERCHETS > MERCHET

MERCHILD n mythical creature with upper body of child and lower body of fish

MERCIABLE adj merciful

MERCIES > MERCY

MERCIFIDE > MERCIFY

MERCIFIED > MERCIFY

MERCIFIES > MERCIFY

MERCIFUL adj compassionate

MERCIFY vb show mercy to

MERCILESS adj without mercy

MERCS > MERC

MERCURATE vb treat or mix with mercury

MERCURIAL adj lively, changeable ▷ n any salt of mercury for use as a medicine

MERCURIC adj of or containing mercury in the divalent state

MERCURIES > MERCURY

MERCURISE same as **>** MERCURATE

MERCURIZE same as **>** MERCURISE

MERCUROUS adj of or containing mercury in the monovalent state

MERCURY n silvery liquid metal

MERCY n compassionate treatment of an offender or enemy who is in one's power

MERDE French word for **>** EXCREMENT

MERDES > MERDE

MERE adj nothing more than ▷ n lake ▷ vb old form of survey

MERED adj forming a boundary

MEREL same as **>** MERIL

MERELL same as **>** MERIL

MERELLS same as **>** MERILS

MERELS > MERILS

MERELY adv only

MERENGUE n type of lively dance music originating in the Dominican Republic, which combines African and Spanish elements

MERENGUES > MERENGUE

MEREOLOGY n formal study of the logical properties of the relation of part and whole

MERER > MERE

MERES > MERE

MERESMAN n man who decides on boundaries

MERESMEN > MERESMAN

MEREST > MERE

MERESTONE n stone marking boundary

MERFOLK n mermaids and mermen

MERFOLKS > MERFOLK

MERGANSER n large crested diving duck

MERGE vb combine or blend

MERGED > MERGE

MERGEE n business taken over by merger

MERGEES > MERGEE

MERGENCE > MERGE

MERGENCES > MERGE

MERGER n combination of business firms into one

MERGERS > MERGER

MERGES > MERGE

MERGING > MERGE

MERGINGS > MERGE

MERI n Māori war club

MERICARP n part of plant fruit

MERICARPS > MERICARP

MERIDIAN n imaginary circle of the earth passing through both poles ▷ adj along or relating to a meridian

MERIDIANS > MERIDIAN

MERIL n counter used in merils

MERILS n old board game

MERIMAKE n merrymaking

MERIMAKES > MERIMAKE

MERING > MERE

MERINGS > MERING

MERINGUE n baked mixture of egg whites and sugar

MERINGUES > MERINGUE

MERINO n breed of sheep with fine soft wool

MERINOS > MERINO

MERIS > MERI

MERISES > MERISIS

MERISIS n growth by division of cells

MERISM n duplication of biological parts

MERISMS > MERISM

MERISTEM n plant tissue responsible for growth, whose cells divide and differentiate to form the tissues and organs of the plant

MERISTEMS > MERISTEM

MERISTIC adj of or relating to the number of organs or parts in an animal or plant body

MERIT n excellence or worth ▷ vb deserve

MERITED > MERIT

MERITING > MERIT

MERITLESS > MERIT

MERITS > MERIT

MERK n old Scots coin

MERKIN n artificial hairpiece for the pudendum

MERKINS > MERKIN

MERKS > MERK

MERL same as **>** MERLE

MERLE adj (of a dog, esp a collie) having a bluish-grey coat with speckles or streaks of black

MERLES > MERLE

MERLIN n small falcon

MERLING n whiting

MERLINGS > MERLING

MERLINS > MERLIN

MERLON n solid upright section in a crenellated battlement

MERLONS > MERLON

MERLOT n black grape grown in France and now throughout the wine-producing world,
used, often in a blend, for making wine

MERLOTS > MERLOT

MERLS > MERL

MERMAID n imaginary sea creature with the upper part of a woman and the lower part of a fish

MERMAIDEN same as **>** MERMAID

MERMAIDS > MERMAID

MERMAN n male counterpart of the mermaid

MERMEN > MERMAN

MEROCRINE adj (of the secretion of glands) characterized by formation of the product without undergoing disintegration

MEROGONY n development of embryo from part of ovum

MEROISTIC adj producing yolk and ova

MEROME same as **>** MEROSOME

MEROMES > MEROME

MERONYM n part of something used to refer to the whole

MERONYMS > MERONYM

MERONYMY > MERONYM

MEROPIA n partial blindness

MEROPIAS > MEROPIA

MEROPIC > MEROPIA

MEROPIDAN n bird of bee-eater family

MEROSOME n segment in body of worm

MEROSOMES > MEROSOME

MEROZOITE n any of the cells formed by fission of a schizont during the life cycle of sporozoan protozoans, such as the malaria parasite

MERPEOPLE same as **>** MERFOLK

MERRIER > MERRY

MERRIES > MERRY

MERRIEST > MERRY

MERRILY > MERRY

MERRIMENT n gaiety, fun, or mirth

MERRINESS > MERRY

MERRY adj cheerful or jolly ▷ n gean

MERRYMAN n jester

MERRYMEN > MERRYMAN

MERSALYL n salt of sodium

MERSALYLS > MERSALYL

MERSE n low level ground by a river or shore, often alluvial and fertile

MERSES > MERSE

MERSION n dipping in water

MERSIONS > MERSION

MERYCISM n rumination

MERYCISMS > MERYCISM

MES > ME

MESA n flat-topped hill found in arid regions

MESAIL n visor
MESAILS >MESAIL
MESAL same as >MESIAL
MESALLY >MESAL
MESARAIC adj of mesentery
MESARCH adj (of a xylem strand) having the first-formed xylem surrounded by that formed later, as in fern stems
MESAS >MESA
MESCAL n spineless globe-shaped cactus of Mexico and the SW of the USA
MESCALIN same as >MESCALINE
MESCALINE n hallucinogenic drug obtained from the tops of mescals
MESCALINS >MESCALIN
MESCALISM n addiction to mescal
MESCALS >MESCAL
MESCLUM same as >MESCLUN
MESCLUMS >MESCLUM
MESCLUN n type of green salad
MESCLUNS >MESCLUN
MESDAMES >MADAM
MESE n middle string on lyre
MESEEMED >MESEEMS
MESEEMETH same as >MESEEMS
MESEEMS vb it seems to me
MESEL n leper
MESELED adj afflicted by leprosy
MESELS >MESEL
MESENTERA same as >MIDGUTS
MESENTERY n double layer of peritoneum that is attached to the back wall of the abdominal cavity and supports most of the small intestine
MESES >MESE
MESETA n plateau in Spain
MESETAS >MESETA
MESH n network or net ▷ vb (of gear teeth) engage ▷ adj made from mesh
MESHED >MESH
MESHES >MESH
MESHIER >MESH
MESHIEST >MESH
MESHING >MESH
MESHINGS >MESH
MESHUGA adj crazy
MESHUGAAS n madness
MESHUGAH same as >MESHUGA
MESHUGAS adj crazy
MESHUGGA same as >MESHUGA
MESHUGGAH same as >MESHUGA
MESHUGGE same as >MESHUGA
MESHWORK n network
MESHWORKS >MESHWORK

MESHY >MESH
MESIAD adj relating to or situated at the middle or centre
MESIAL another word for >MEDIAL
MESIALLY >MESIAL
MESIAN same as >MESIAL
MESIC >MESON
MESICALLY >MESON
MESMERIC adj holding (someone) as if spellbound
MESMERISE same as >MESMERIZE
MESMERISM n hypnotic state induced by the operator's imposition of his will on that of the patient
MESMERIST >MESMERISM
MESMERIZE vb hold spellbound
MESNALTY n lands of a mesne lord
MESNE adj in Law, intermediate or intervening: used esp of any assignment of property before the last
MESNES >MESNE
MESOBLAST another name for >MESODERM
MESOCARP n middle layer of the pericarp of a fruit, such as the flesh of a peach
MESOCARPS >MESOCARP
MESOCRANY n medium skull breadth
MESODERM n middle germ layer of an animal embryo, giving rise to muscle, blood, bone, connective tissue, etc
MESODERMS >MESODERM
MESOGLEA n gelatinous material between the outer and inner cellular layers of jellyfish and other coelenterates
MESOGLEAL >MESOGLEA
MESOGLEAS >MESOGLEA
MESOGLOEA same as >MESOGLEA
MESOLITE n type of mineral
MESOLITES >MESOLITE
MESOMERE n cell in fertilized ovum
MESOMERES >MESOMERE
MESOMORPH n person with a muscular body build: said to be correlated with somatotonia
MESON n elementary atomic particle
MESONIC >MESON
MESONS >MESON
MESOPAUSE n zone of minimum temperature between the mesosphere and the thermosphere
MESOPHILE n ideal growth temperature of 20-45 degrees

MESOPHYL same as >MESOPHYLL
MESOPHYLL n soft chlorophyll-containing tissue of a leaf between the upper and lower layers of epidermis: involved in photosynthesis
MESOPHYLS >MESOPHYL
MESOPHYTE n any plant that grows in surroundings receiving an average supply of water
MESOSCALE adj of weather phenomena of medium duration
MESOSOME n part of bacterial cell
MESOSOMES >MESOSOME
MESOTRON same as >MESON
MESOTRONS >MESOTRON
MESOZOAN n type of parasite
MESOZOANS >MESOZOAN
MESOZOIC adj of, denoting, or relating to an era of geological time
MESPRISE same as >MISPRISE
MESPRISES >MESPRISE
MESPRIZE same as >MISPRISE
MESPRIZES >MESPRIZE
MESQUIN adj mean
MESQUINE same as >MESQUIN
MESQUIT same as >MESQUITE
MESQUITE n small tree whose sugary pods are used as animal fodder
MESQUITES >MESQUITE
MESQUITS >MESQUIT
MESS n untidy or dirty confusion ▷ vb muddle or dirty
MESSAGE n communication sent ▷ vb send as a message
MESSAGED >MESSAGE
MESSAGES >MESSAGE
MESSAGING n sending and receving of messages
MESSALINE n light lustrous twilled-silk fabric
MESSAN Scots word for >DOG
MESSANS >MESSAN
MESSED >MESS
MESSENGER n bearer of a message ▷ vb send by messenger
MESSES >MESS
MESSIAH n exceptional or hoped for liberator of a country or people
MESSIAHS >MESSIAH
MESSIANIC adj of or relating to the Messiah, his awaited deliverance of the Jews, or the new age of peace expected to follow this
MESSIAS same as >MESSIAH

MESSIASES >MESSIAS
MESSIER >MESSY
MESSIEST >MESSY
MESSIEURS >MONSIEUR
MESSILY >MESSY
MESSINESS >MESSY
MESSING >MESS
MESSMAN n sailor working in ship's mess
MESSMATE n person with whom one shares meals in a mess, esp in the army
MESSMATES >MESSMATE
MESSMEN >MESSMAN
MESSUAGE n dwelling house together with its outbuildings, curtilage, and the adjacent land appropriated to its use
MESSUAGES >MESSUAGE
MESSY adj dirty, confused, or untidy
MESTEE same as >MUSTEE
MESTEES >MESTEE
MESTER n master: used as a term of address for a man who is the head of a house
MESTERS >MESTER
MESTESO n Spanish music genre
MESTESOES >MESTESO
MESTESOS >MESTESO
MESTINO n person of mixed race
MESTINOES >MESTINO
MESTINOS >MESTINO
MESTIZA >MESTIZO
MESTIZAS >MESTIZO
MESTIZO n person of mixed parentage, esp the offspring of a Spanish American and an American Indian
MESTIZOES >MESTIZO
MESTIZOS >MESTIZO
MESTO adj sad
MESTOM same as >MESTOME
MESTOME n conducting tissue associated with parenchyma
MESTOMES >MESTOME
MESTOMS >MESTOM
MESTRANOL n synthetic oestrogen
MET n meteorology
META adj in a self-parodying style
METABASES >METABASIS
METABASIS n change
METABATIC >METABASIS
METABOLIC adj of or related to the sum total of the chemical processes that occurs in living organisms, resulting in growth, production of energy, elimination of waste material, etc
METABOLY n ability of some cells, esp protozoans, to alter their shape

METACARPI n skeleton of the hand between the wrist and the fingers

METADATA npl data which accompanies digital data and provides underlying information but is not visible to the end user

METAFILE n (in computing) file format that can hold other types of file

METAFILES > METAFILE

METAGE n official measuring of weight or contents

METAGENIC adj of or relating to the production within the life cycle of an organism of alternating asexual and sexual reproductive forms

METAGES > METAGE

METAIRIE n area of land on which farmer pays rent in kind

METAIRIES > METAIRIE

METAL n chemical element, such as iron or copper, that is malleable and capable of conducting heat and electricity ▷ adj made of metal ▷ vb fit or cover with metal

METALED > METAL

METALHEAD n fan of heavy metal music

METALING > METAL

METALISE same as > METALLIZE

METALISED > METALISE

METALISES > METALISE

METALIST same as > METALLIST

METALISTS > METALIST

METALIZE same as > METALLIZE

METALIZED > METALIZE

METALIZES > METALIZE

METALLED > METAL

METALLIC adj of or consisting of metal ▷ n something metallic

METALLICS > METALLIC

METALLIKE > METAL

METALLINE adj of, resembling, or relating to metals

METALLING > METAL

METALLISE same as > METALLIZE

METALLIST n person who works with metals

METALLIZE vb make metallic or to coat or treat with metal

METALLOID n nonmetallic element, such as arsenic or silicon, that has some of the properties of a metal ▷ adj of or being a metalloid

METALLY adj like metal

METALMARK n variety of butterfly

METALS > METAL

METALWARE n items made of metal

METALWORK n craft of making objects from metal

METAMALE n sterile male organism, esp a fruit fly that has one X chromosome and three sets of autosomes

METAMALES > METAMALE

METAMER n any of two or more isomeric compounds exhibiting metamerism

METAMERAL > METAMERE

METAMERE n one of the similar body segments into which earthworms, crayfish, and similar animals are divided longitudinally

METAMERES > METAMERE

METAMERIC adj divided into or consisting of metameres

METAMERS > METAMER

METAMICT adj of or denoting the amorphous state of a substance that has lost its crystalline structure as a result of the radioactivity of uranium or thorium within it

METANOIA n repentance

METANOIAS > METANOIA

METAPELET n foster mother

METAPHASE n second stage of mitosis during which the condensed chromosomes attach to the centre of the spindle

METAPHOR n figure of speech in which a term is applied to something it does not literally denote in order to imply a resemblance

METAPHORS > METAPHOR

METAPLASM n nonliving constituents, such as starch and pigment granules, of the cytoplasm of a cell

METAPLOT > METAPELET

METARCHON n nontoxic substance, such as a chemical to mask pheromones, that reduces the persistence of a pest

METASOMA n posterior part of an arachnid's abdomen (opisthosoma) that never carries appendages

METASOMAS > METASOMA

METATAG n element of HTML describing the contents of a web page and used by search engines to index pages by subject

METATAGS > METATAG

METATARSI npl skeleton of human foot between toes and tarsus

METATE n stone for grinding grain on

METATES > METATE

METAVERSE n virtual universe, eg one of a computer or role-playing game

METAXYLEM n xylem tissue that consists of rigid thick-walled cells and occurs in parts of the plant that have finished growing

METAYAGE n farming in which rent is paid in kind

METAYAGES > METAYAGE

METAYER n farmer who pays rent in kind

METAYERS > METAYER

METAZOA > METAZOAN

METAZOAL > METAZOAN

METAZOAN n any animal having a body composed of many cells: includes all animals except sponges and protozoans ▷ adj of the metazoans

METAZOANS > METAZOAN

METAZOIC adj relating to the group of muticellular animals that includes all animals except sponges

METAZOON same as > METAZOAN

METCAST n weather forecast

METCASTS > METCAST

METE vb deal out as punishment ▷ n (to) measure

METED > METE

METEOR n small fast-moving heavenly body, visible as a streak of incandescence if it enters the earth's atmosphere

METEORIC adj of a meteor

METEORISM n distension of the abdomen

METEORIST n person who studies meteors

METEORITE n meteor that has fallen to earth

METEOROID n any of the small celestial bodies that are thought to orbit the sun. When they enter the earth's atmosphere, they become visible as meteors

METEOROUS > METEOR

METEORS > METEOR

METEPA n type of pesticide

METEPAS > METEPA

METER same as > METRE

METERAGE n act of measuring

METERAGES > METERAGE

METERED > METER

METERING > METER

METERS > METER

METES > METE

METESTICK n measuring rod

METESTRUS n period in the oestrous cycle following oestrus, characterized by lack of sexual activity

METEWAND same as > METESTICK

METEWANDS > METEWAND

METEYARD same as > METESTICK

METEYARDS > METEYARD

METFORMIN n drug used to treat diabetes

METH n variety of amphetamine

METHADON same as > METHADONE

METHADONE n drug similar to morphine, sometimes prescribed as a heroin substitute

METHADONS > METHADON

METHANAL n colourless poisonous irritating gas with a pungent characteristic odour, made by the oxidation of methanol and used as formalin and in the manufacture of synthetic resins

METHANALS > METHANAL

METHANE n colourless inflammable gas

METHANES > METHANE

METHANOIC as in methanoic acid systematic name for formic acid

METHANOL n colourless poisonous liquid used as a solvent and fuel

METHANOLS > METHANOL

METHEGLIN n (esp formerly) spiced or medicated mead

METHINK same as > METHINKS

METHINKS vb it seems to me

METHO n methylated spirits

METHOD n way or manner

METHODIC same as > METHOD

METHODISE same as > METHODIZE

METHODISM n system and practices of the Methodist Church, developed by the English preacher John Wesley (1703-91) and his followers

METHODIST > METHODISM

METHODIZE vb organize according to a method

METHODS > METHOD

METHOS > METHO

METHOUGHT > METHINKS

METHOXIDE n saltlike compound in which the hydrogen atom in the hydroxyl group of methanol has been replaced by a metal atom, usually an alkali metal atom as in sodium methoxide, $NaOCH_3$

METHOXY n steroid drug

METHOXYL n chemical compound of methyl and hydroxyl

METHS n methylated spirits

m

METHYL n compound containing a saturated hydrocarbon group of atoms

METHYLAL n colourless volatile flammable liquid

METHYLALS >METHYLAL

METHYLASE n enzyme

METHYLATE vb mix with methanol

METHYLENE adj of, consisting of, or containing the divalent group of atoms =CH₂

METHYLIC >METHYL

METHYLS >METHYL

METHYSES >METHYSIS

METHYSIS n drunkenness

METHYSTIC adj intoxicating

METIC n (in ancient Greece) an alien having some rights of citizenship in the city in which he lives

METICALS >METICAL

METICAL n money unit in Mozambique

METICALS >METICAL

METICS >METIC

METIER n profession or trade

METIERS >METIER

METIF n person of mixed race

METIFS >METIF

METING >METE

METIS n person of mixed parentage

METISSE >METIS

METISSES >METIS

METOL n colourless soluble organic substance used, (in the form of its sulphate, as a photographic developer

METOLS >METOL

METONYM n word used in a metonymy

METONYMIC >METONYMY

METONYMS >METONYMY

METONYMY n figure of speech in which one thing is replaced by another associated with it

METOPAE >METOPE

METOPE n square space between two triglyphs in a Doric frieze

METOPES >METOPE

METOPIC adj of or relating to the forehead

METOPISM n congenital disfigurement of forehead

METOPISMS >METOPISM

METOPON n painkilling drug

METOPONS >METOPON

METOPRYL n type of anaesthetic

METOPRYLS >METOPRYL

METRALGIA n pain in the uterus

METRAZOL n drug used to improve blood circulation

METRAZOLS >METRAZOL

METRE n basic unit of length equal to about 1.094 yards (100 centimetres) ▷ vb express in poetry

METRED >METRE

METRES >METRE

METRIC adj of the decimal system of weights and measures based on the metre

METRICAL adj of measurement

METRICATE vb convert a measuring system or instrument to metric units

METRICIAN n writer of metrical verse

METRICISE vb study metre of poetry

METRICISM >METRICISE

METRICIST same as >METRICIAN

METRICIZE same as >METRICISE

METRICS n art of using poetic metre

METRIFIED >METRIFY

METRIFIER >METRIFY

METRIFIES >METRIFY

METRIFY vb render into poetic metre

METRING >METRE

METRIST n person skilled in the use of poetic metre

METRISTS >METRIST

METRITIS n inflammation of the uterus

METRO n underground railway system, esp in Paris

METROLOGY n science of weights and measures

METRONOME n instrument which marks musical time by means of a ticking pendulum

METROPLEX n large urban area

METROS >METRO

METS >MET

METTLE n courage or spirit

METTLED adj spirited, courageous, or valiant

METTLES >METTLE

METUMP n band for carrying a load or burden

METUMPS >METUMP

MEU another name for >SPIGNEL

MEUNIERE adj (of fish) dredged with flour, fried in butter, and served with butter, lemon juice, and parsley

MEUS >MEU

MEUSE n gap (in fence, wall etc) through which an animal passed ▷ vb go through this gap

MEUSED >MEUSE

MEUSES >MEUSE

MEUSING >MEUSE

MEVE same as >MOVE

MEVED >MEVE

MEVES >MEVE

MEVING >MEVE

MEVROU n S African title of address

MEVROUS >MEVROU

MEW n cry of a cat ▷ vb utter this cry

MEWED >MEW

MEWING >MEW

MEWL vb (esp of a baby) to cry weakly ▷ n weak or whimpering cry

MEWLED >MEWL

MEWLER >MEWL

MEWLERS >MEWL

MEWLING >MEWL

MEWLS >MEWL

MEWS same as >MEUSE

MEWSED >MEWS

MEWSES >MEWS

MEWSING >MEWS

MEYNT >MING

MEZAIL same as >MESAIL

MEZAILS >MEZAIL

MEZCAL variant spelling of >MESCAL

MEZCALINE variant spelling of >MESCALINE

MEZCALS >MEZCAL

MEZE n type of hors d'oeuvre eaten esp with an apéritif or other drink in Greece and the Near (East

MEZEREON same as >MEZEREUM

MEZEREONS >MEZEREON

MEZEREUM n dried bark of certain shrubs, formerly used to treat arthritis

MEZEREUMS >MEZEREUM

MEZES >MEZE

MEZQUIT same as >MESQUITE

MEZQUITE same as >MESQUITE

MEZQUITES >MEZQUITE

MEZQUITS >MEZQUIT

MEZUZA same as >MEZUZAH

MEZUZAH n piece of parchment inscribed with biblical passages and fixed to the doorpost of the rooms of a Jewish house

MEZUZAHS >MEZUZAH

MEZUZAS >MEZUZA

MEZUZOT >MEZUZAH

MEZUZOTH >MEZUZAH

MEZZ same as >MEZZANINE

MEZZALUNA n half-moon shaped kitchen chopper

MEZZANINE n intermediate storey, esp between the ground and first floor ▷ adj of or relating to an intermediate stage in a financial process

MEZZE same as >MEZE

MEZZES >MEZZE

MEZZO adv moderately

MEZZOS >MEZZO

MEZZOTINT n method of engraving by scraping the roughened surface of a metal plate ▷ vb engrave (a copper plate) in this fashion

MGANGA n witch doctor

MGANGAS >MGANGA

MHO former name for >SIEMENS

MHORR n African gazelle

MHORRS >MHORR

MHOS >MHO

MI n (in tonic sol-fa) the third degree of any major scale

MIAOU same as >MEOW

MIAOUED >MIAOU

MIAOUING >MIAOU

MIAOUS >MIAOU

MIAOW same as >MEOW

MIAOWED >MIAOW

MIAOWING >MIAOW

MIAOWS >MIAOW

MIASM same as >MIASMA

MIASMA n unwholesome or foreboding atmosphere

MIASMAL >MIASMA

MIASMAS >MIASMA

MIASMATA >MIASMA

MIASMATIC >MIASMA

MIASMIC >MIASMA

MIASMOUS >MIASMA

MIASMS >MIASM

MIAUL same as >MEOW

MIAULED >MIAUL

MIAULING >MIAUL

MIAULS >MIAUL

MIB n marble used in games

MIBS >MIB

MIBUNA n type of Japanese leafy vegetable

MIBUNAS >MIBUNA

MIC n microphone

MICA n glasslike mineral used as an electrical insulator

MICACEOUS >MICA

MICAS >MICA

MICATE vb add mica to

MICATED >MICATE

MICATES >MICATE

MICATING >MICATE

MICAWBER n person who idles and trusts to fortune

MICAWBERS >MICAWBER

MICE >MOUSE

MICELL same as >MICELLE

MICELLA same as >MICELLE

MICELLAE >MICELLA

MICELLAR >MICELLE

MICELLAS >MICELLA

MICELLE n charged aggregate of molecules of colloidal size in a solution

MICELLES >MICELLE

MICELLS >MICELL

MICH same as >MITCH

MICHAEL as in take the michael teasing

MICHAELS >MICHAEL

MICHE same as >MICH

MICHED >MICH

MICHER >MICH

MICHERS >MICH

MICHES >MICH

MICHIGAN US name for >NEWMARKET

MICHIGANS >MICHIGAN

MICHING >MICH

MICHINGS >MICH

MICHT n Scots word for might

MICHTS >MICHT

MICK n derogatory term for an Irish person

MICKERIES >MICKERY

MICKERY n waterhole, esp in a dry riverbed

MICKEY n young bull, esp one that is wild and unbranded ▷ vb drug person's drink

MICKEYED >MICKEY

MICKEYING >MICKEY

MICKEYS >MICKEY

MICKIES >MICKY

MICKLE adj large or abundant ▷ adv much ▷ n great amount

MICKLER >MICKLE

MICKLES >MICKLE

MICKLEST >MICKLE

MICKS >MICK

MICKY same as >MICKEY

MICO n marmoset

MICOS >MICO

MICRA >MICRON

MICRIFIED >MICRIFY

MICRIFIES >MICRIFY

MICRIFY vb make very small

MICRO n small computer

MICROBAR n millionth of bar of pressure

MICROBARS >MICROBAR

MICROBE n minute organism, esp one causing disease

MICROBEAM n X-ray machine with narrow focussed beam

MICROBES >MICROBE

MICROBIAL >MICROBE

MICROBIAN >MICROBE

MICROBIC >MICROBE

MICROBLOG vb contribute to a blog which limits the length of individual postings

MICROBREW n beer made in small brewery

MICROBUS n small bus

MICROCAP adj (of investments) involving very small amounts of capital

MICROCAR n small car

MICROCARD n card containing microprint

MICROCARS >MICROCAR

MICROCHIP n small wafer of silicon containing electronic circuits ▷ vb implant (an animal) with a microchip tag for purposes of identification

MICROCODE n set of computer instructions

MICROCOPY n greatly reduced photographic copy of a printed page, drawing, etc, on microfilm or microfiche

MICROCOSM n miniature

representation of something

MICROCYTE n unusually small red blood cell

MICRODONT adj having unusually small teeth

MICRODOT n photographic copy of a document reduced to pinhead size

MICRODOTS >MICRODOT

MICROFILM n miniaturized recording of books or documents on a roll of film ▷ vb photograph a page or document on microfilm

MICROFORM n method of storing symbolic information by using photographic reduction techniques, such as microfilm, microfiche, etc

MICROGLIA n one of the two types of non-nervous tissue (glia) found in the central nervous system, having macrophage activity

MICROGRAM n photograph or drawing of an object as viewed through a microscope

MICROHM n millionth of ohm

MICROHMS >MICROHM

MICROINCH n millionth of inch

MICROJET n light jet-propelled aircraft

MICROJETS >MICROJET

MICROLITE n small private aircraft carrying no more than two people, with an empty weight of not more than 150 kg and a wing area not less than 10 square metres: used in pleasure flying and racing

MICROLITH n small Mesolithic flint tool which was made from a blade and formed part of hafted tools

MICROLOAN n very small loan

MICROLOGY n study of microscopic things

MICROLUX n millionth of a lux

MICROMERE n any of the small cells formed by unequal cleavage of a fertilized ovum

MICROMESH n very fine mesh

MICROMHO n millionth of mho

MICROMHOS >MICROMHO

MICROMINI n very short skirt

MICROMOLE n millionth of mole

MICRON n unit of length equal to 10^{-6} metre

MICRONISE same as >MICRONIZE

MICRONIZE vb break

down to very small particles

MICRONS >MICRON

MICROPORE n very small pore

MICROPSIA n defect of vision in which objects appear to be smaller than they appear to a person with normal vision

MICROPUMP n small pump inserted in skin to automatically deliver medicine

MICROPYLE n small opening in the integuments of a plant ovule through which the male gametes pass

MICROS >MICRO

MICROSITE n website that is intended for a specific limited purpose and is often temporary

MICROSOME n any of the small particles consisting of ribosomes and fragments of attached endoplasmic reticulum that can be isolated from cells by centrifugal action

MICROTOME n instrument used for cutting thin sections, esp of biological material, for microscopical examination

MICROTOMY n cutting of sections with a microtome

MICROTONE n any musical interval smaller than a semitone

MICROVOLT n millionth of volt

MICROWATT n millionth of watt

MICROWAVE n electromagnetic wave with a wavelength of a few centimetres, used in radar and cooking ▷ vb cook in a microwave oven

MICROWIRE n very fine wire

MICRURGY n manipulation and examination of single cells under a microscope

MICS >MIC

MICTION n urination

MICTIONS >MICTION

MICTURATE vb urinate

MID adj intermediate, middle ▷ n middle ▷ prep amid

MIDAIR n some point above ground level, in the air

MIDAIRS >MIDAIR

MIDBAND adj (of a telecommunication transmission technique) using a range of frequencies between narrowband and broadband

MIDBRAIN n part of the brain that develops from

the middle portion of the embryonic neural tube

MIDBRAINS >MIDBRAIN

MIDCAP adj (of investments) involving medium-sized amounts of capital

MIDCOURSE adj in middle of course

MIDCULT n middlebrow culture

MIDCULTS >MIDCULT

MIDDAY n noon

MIDDAYS >MIDDAY

MIDDEN n dunghill or rubbish heap

MIDDENS >MIDDEN

MIDDEST adj in middle

MIDDIE n glass or bottle containing 285ml of beer

MIDDIES >MIDDY

MIDDLE adj equidistant from two extremes ▷ n middle point or part ▷ vb place in the middle

MIDDLED >MIDDLE

MIDDLEMAN n trader who buys from the producer and sells to the consumer

MIDDLEMEN >MIDDLEMAN

MIDDLER n pupil in middle years at school

MIDDLERS >MIDDLER

MIDDLES >MIDDLE

MIDDLING adj mediocre ▷ adv moderately

MIDDLINGS npl poorer or coarser part of flour or other products

MIDDORSAL adj in middle or back

MIDDY n middle-sized glass of beer

MIDFIELD n area between the two opposing defences

MIDFIELDS >MIDFIELD

MIDGE n small mosquito-like insect

MIDGES >MIDGE

MIDGET n very small person or thing ▷ adj much smaller than normal

MIDGETS >MIDGET

MIDGIE n informal word for a small winged biting insect such as the midge or sandfly

MIDGIER >MIDGE

MIDGIES >MIDGIE

MIDGIEST >MIDGE

MIDGUT n middle part of the digestive tract of vertebrates, including the small intestine

MIDGUTS >MIDGUT

MIDGY >MIDGE

MIDI adj (of a skirt, coat, etc) reaching to below the knee or midcalf ▷ n a skirt, coat, etc reaching to below the knee or midcalf

MIDINETTE n Parisian seamstress or salesgirl in a clothes shop

MIDIRON n club, usually a No. 5, 6, or 7 iron, used for medium-length approach shots

MIDIRONS >MIDIRON

MIDIS >MIDI

MIDISKIRT n skirt of medium length

MIDLAND n middle part of a country

MIDLANDER n person living in the midlands

MIDLANDS >MIDLAND

MIDLEG n middle of leg

MIDLEGS >MIDLEG

MIDLIFE n middle age
▷ modifier as in midlife crisis crisis that may be experienced in middle age involving frustration, panic, and feelings of pointlessness, sometimes resulting in radical and often ill-advised changes of lifestyle

MIDLIFER n middle-aged person

MIDLIFERS >MIDLIFER

MIDLINE n line at middle of something

MIDLINES >MIDLINE

MIDLIST n books in publisher's range that sell reasonably well

MIDLISTS >MIDLIST

MIDLIVES >MIDLIFE

MIDMONTH n middle of month

MIDMONTHS >MIDMONTH

MIDMOST adv in the middle or midst ▷ n the middle or midst

MIDMOSTS >MIDMOST

MIDNIGHT n twelve o'clock at night

MIDNIGHTS >MIDNIGHT

MIDNOON n noon

MIDNOONS >MIDNOON

MIDPOINT n point on a line equally distant from either end

MIDPOINTS >MIDPOINT

MIDRANGE n part of loudspeaker

MIDRANGES >MIDRANGE

MIDRASH n homily on a scriptural passage derived by traditional Jewish exegetical methods and consisting usually of embellishment of the scriptural narrative

MIDRASHIC >MIDRASH

MIDRASHIM >MIDRASH

MIDRASHOT >MIDRASH

MIDRIB n main vein of a leaf, running down the centre of the blade

MIDRIBS >MIDRIB

MIDRIFF n middle part of the body

MIDRIFFS >MIDRIFF

MIDS >MID

MIDSHIP adj in, of, or relating to the middle of a vessel ▷ n middle of a vessel

MIDSHIPS See >AMIDSHIPS

MIDSIZE adj medium-sized

MIDSIZED same as >MIDSIZE

MIDSOLE n layer between the inner and the outer sole of a shoe, contoured for absorbing shock

MIDSOLES >MIDSOLE

MIDSPACE n area in middle of space

MIDSPACES >MIDSPACE

MIDST See >AMID

MIDSTORY n level of forest trees between smallest and tallest

MIDSTREAM n middle of a stream or river ▷ adj in or towards the middle of a stream or river

MIDSTS >MIDST

MIDSUMMER n middle of summer

MIDTERM n middle of a term in a school, university, etc

MIDTERMS >MIDTERM

MIDTOWN n centre of a town

MIDTOWNS >MIDTOWN

MIDWATCH n naval watch period beginning at midnight

MIDWAY adv halfway ▷ adj in or at the middle of the distance ▷ n place in a fair, carnival, etc, where sideshows are located

MIDWAYS >MIDWAY

MIDWEEK n middle of the week

MIDWEEKLY >MIDWEEK

MIDWEEKS >MIDWEEK

MIDWIFE n trained person who assists at childbirth ▷ vb act as midwife

MIDWIFED >MIDWIFE

MIDWIFERY n art or practice of a midwife

MIDWIFES >MIDWIFE

MIDWIFING >MIDWIFE

MIDWINTER n middle or depth of winter

MIDWIVE vb act as midwife

MIDWIVED >MIDWIVE

MIDWIVES >MIDWIVE

MIDWIVING >MIDWIVE

MIDYEAR n middle of the year

MIDYEARS >MIDYEAR

MIELIE same as >MEALIE

MIELIES >MIELIE

MIEN n person's bearing, demeanour, or appearance

MIENS >MIEN

MIEVE same as >MOVE

MIEVED >MIEVE

MIEVES >MIEVE

MIEVING >MIEVE

MIFF vb take offence or offend ▷ n petulant mood

MIFFED >MIFF

MIFFIER >MIFFY

MIFFIEST >MIFFY

MIFFILY >MIFFY

MIFFINESS >MIFFY

MIFFING >MIFF

MIFFS >MIFF

MIFFY adj easily upset

MIFTY same as >MIFFY

MIG n marble used in games

MIGG same as >MIG

MIGGLE n US word for playing marble

MIGGLES >MIGGLE

MIGGS >MIGG

MIGHT >MAY

MIGHTEST >MAY

MIGHTFUL same as >MIGHTY

MIGHTIER >MIGHTY

MIGHTIEST >MIGHTY

MIGHTILY adv great extent, amount, or degree

MIGHTS >MAY

MIGHTST >MAY

MIGHTY adj powerful ▷ adv very

MIGMATITE n composite rock body containing two types of rock (esp igneous and metamorphic rock) that have interacted with each other but are nevertheless still distinguishable

MIGNON adj small and pretty ▷ n tender boneless cut of meat

MIGNONNE >MIGNON

MIGNONNES >MIGNON

MIGNONS >MIGNON

MIGRAINE n severe headache, often with nausea and visual disturbances

MIGRAINES >MIGRAINE

MIGRANT n person or animal that moves from one place to another ▷ adj moving from one place to another

MIGRANTS >MIGRANT

MIGRATE vb move from one place to settle in another

MIGRATED >MIGRATE

MIGRATES >MIGRATE

MIGRATING >MIGRATE

MIGRATION n act or an instance of migrating

MIGRATOR >MIGRATE

MIGRATORS >MIGRATE

MIGRATORY adj (of an animal) migrating every year

MIGS >MIG

MIHA n young fern frond which has not yet opened

MIHAS >MIHA

MIHI n Māori ceremonial greeting ▷ vb greet

MIHIED >MIHI

MIHIING >MIHI

MIHIS >MIHI

MIHRAB n niche in a mosque showing the direction of Mecca

MIHRABS >MIHRAB

MIJNHEER same as >MYNHEER

MIJNHEERS >MIJNHEER

MIKADO n Japanese emperor

MIKADOS >MIKADO

MIKE n microphone

MIKED >MIKE

MIKES >MIKE

MIKING >MIKE

MIKRA >MIKRON

MIKRON same as >MICRON

MIKRONS >MIKRON

MIKVAH n pool used esp by women for ritual purification after their monthly period

MIKVAHS >MIKVAH

MIKVEH same as >MIKVAH

MIKVEHS >MIKVEH

MIKVOS >MIKVEH

MIKVOT >MIKVEH

MIKVOTH >MIKVAH

MIL n unit of length equal to one thousandth of an inch

MILADI same as >MILADY

MILADIES >MILADY

MILADIS >MILADI

MILADY n (formerly) a continental title for an English gentlewoman

MILAGE same as >MILEAGE

MILAGES >MILAGE

MILCH adj (of a cow) giving milk

MILCHIG same as >MILCHIK

MILCHIK adj containing or used in the preparation of milk products and so not to be used with meat products

MILD adj not strongly flavoured ▷ n dark beer flavoured with fewer hops than bitter ▷ vb become gentle

MILDED >MILD

MILDEN vb make or become mild or milder

MILDENED >MILDEN

MILDENING >MILDEN

MILDENS >MILDEN

MILDER >MILD

MILDEST >MILD

MILDEW same as >MOULD

MILDEWED >MILDEW

MILDEWING >MILDEW

MILDEWS >MILDEW

MILDEWY >MILDEW

MILDING >MILD

MILDLY >MILD

MILDNESS >MILD

MILDS >MILD

MILE n unit of length equal to 1760 yards or 1.609 kilometres

MILEAGE n distance

travelled in miles

MILEAGES >MILEAGE

MILEPOST n signpost that shows the distance in miles to or from a place

MILEPOSTS >MILEPOST

MILER n athlete, horse, etc, that specializes in races of one mile

MILERS >MILER

MILES >MILE

MILESIAN adj Irish

MILESIMO n Spanish word meaning thousandth

MILESIMOS >MILESIMO

MILESTONE same as >MILEPOST

MILF n sexually attractive older woman

MILFOIL same as > YARROW

MILFOILS >MILFOIL

MILFS >MILF

MILIA >MILIUM

MILIARIA n acute itching eruption of the skin, caused by blockage of the sweat glands

MILIARIAL >MILIARIA

MILIARIAS >MILIARIA

MILIARY adj resembling or relating to millet seeds

MILIEU n environment or surroundings

MILIEUS >MILIEU

MILIEUX >MILIEU

MILITANCE >MILITANT

MILITANCY >MILITANT

MILITANT adj aggressive or vigorous in support of a cause ▷ n militant person

MILITANTS >MILITANT

MILITAR same as >MILITARY

MILITARIA npl items of military interest, such as weapons, uniforms, medals, etc, esp from the past

MILITARY adj of or for soldiers, armies, or war ▷ n armed services

MILITATE vb have a strong influence or effect

MILITATED >MILITATE

MILITATES >MILITATE

MILITIA n military force of trained citizens for use in emergency only

MILITIAS >MILITIA

MILIUM n pimple

MILK n white fluid produced by female mammals to feed their young ▷ vb draw milk from

MILKED >MILK

MILKEN adj of or like milk

MILKER n cow, goat, etc, that yields milk, esp of a specified quality or amount

MILKERS >MILKER

MILKFISH n type of large silvery tropical food and game fish

MILKIER >MILKY

MILKIEST >MILKY

MILKILY >MILKY

MILKINESS >MILKY

MILKING >MILK

MILKINGS >MILKING

MILKLESS >MILK

MILKLIKE >MILK

MILKMAID n (esp in former times) woman who milks cows

MILKMAIDS >MILKMAID

MILKMAN n man who delivers milk to people's houses

MILKMEN >MILKMAN

MILKO informal name for >MILKMAN

MILKOS >MILKO

MILKS >MILK

MILKSHAKE n drink of flavoured milk

MILKSHED n area where milk is produced

MILKSHEDS >MILKSHED

MILKSOP n feeble man

MILKSOPPY >MILKSOP

MILKSOPS >MILKSOP

MILKTOAST n meek, submissive, or timid person

MILKWEED n monarch butterfly

MILKWEEDS >MILKWEED

MILKWOOD n tree producing latex

MILKWOODS >MILKWOOD

MILKWORT n type of plant with small blue, pink, or white flowers, formerly believed to increase milk production in cows

MILKWORTS >MILKWORT

MILKY adj of or like milk

MILL n factory ▷ vb grind, press, or process in or as if in a mill

MILLABLE >MILL

MILLAGE adj American tax rate calculated in thousandths per dollar

MILLAGES >MILLAGE

MILLBOARD n strong pasteboard, used esp in book covers

MILLCAKE n food for livestock

MILLCAKES >MILLCAKE

MILLDAM n dam built in a stream to raise the water level sufficiently for it to turn a millwheel

MILLDAMS >MILLDAM

MILLE French word for >THOUSAND

MILLED adj crushed or ground in a mill

MILLENARY adj of or relating to a thousand or to a thousand years ▷ n adherent of millenarianism

MILLENNIA n plural of millennium: period or cycle of one thousand years

MILLEPED same as >MILLEPEDE

MILLEPEDE same as >MILLIPEDE

MILLEPEDS >MILLEPED

MILLEPORE n type of tropical colonial coral-like hydrozoan

MILLER n person who works in a mill

MILLERITE n yellow mineral consisting of nickel sulphide

MILLERS >MILLER

MILLES >MILLE

MILLET n type of cereal grass

MILLETS >MILLET

MILLHAND n person who works in a mill

MILLHANDS >MILLHAND

MILLHOUSE n house attached to mill

MILLIARD n one thousand millions

MILLIARDS >MILLIARD

MILLIARE n ancient Roman unit of distance

MILLIARES >MILLIARE

MILLIARY adj relating to or marking a distance equal to an ancient Roman mile of a thousand paces

MILLIBAR n unit of atmospheric pressure

MILLIBARS >MILLIBAR

MILLIE n derogatory name for a young working-class woman

MILLIEME n Tunisian monetary unit worth one thousandth of a dinar

MILLIEMES >MILLIEME

MILLIER n metric weight of million grams

MILLIERS >MILLIER

MILLIES >MILLIE

MILLIGAL n unit of gravity

MILLIGALS >MILLIGAL

MILLIGRAM n thousandth part of a gram

MILLILUX n thousandth of lux

MILLIME same as >MILLIEME

MILLIMES >MILLIME

MILLIMHO n thousandth of mho

MILLIMHOS >MILLIMHO

MILLIMOLE n thousandth of mole

MILLINE n measurement of advertising space

MILLINER n maker or seller of women's hats

MILLINERS >MILLINER

MILLINERY n hats, trimmings, etc, sold by a milliner

MILLINES >MILLINE

MILLING n act or process of grinding, cutting, pressing, or crushing in a mill

MILLINGS >MILLING

MILLIOHM n thousandth of ohm

MILLIOHMS >MILLIOHM

>MILLIPEDE

MILLEPEDS >MILLEPED

MILLEPORE n type of tropical colonial coral-like hydrozoan

MILLION n one thousand thousands

MILLIONS >MILLION

MILLIONTH n one of 1000 000 approximately equal parts of something ▷ adj being the ordinal number of 1 000 000 in numbering or counting order, etc

MILLIPED same as >MILLIPEDE

MILLIPEDE n small animal with a jointed body and many pairs of legs

MILLIPEDS >MILLIPED

MILLIREM n unit of radiation

MILLIREMS >MILLIREM

MILLIVOLT n thousandth of volt

MILLIWATT n thousandth of watt

MILLOCRAT n member of a government of millowners

MILLPOND n pool which provides water to turn a millwheel

MILLPONDS >MILLPOND

MILLRACE n current of water that turns a millwheel

MILLRACES >MILLRACE

MILLRIND n iron support fitted across an upper millstone

MILLRINDS >MILLRIND

MILLRUN same as >MILLRACE

MILLRUNS >MILLRUN

MILLS >MILL

MILLSCALE n scale on metal being heated

MILLSTONE n flat circular stone for grinding corn

MILLTAIL n channel carrying water away from mill

MILLTAILS >MILLTAIL

MILLWHEEL n waterwheel that drives a mill

MILLWORK n work done in a mill

MILLWORKS >MILLWORK

MILNEB n type of pesticide

MILNEBS >MILNEB

MILO n any of various early-growing cultivated varieties of sorghum with heads of yellow or pinkish seeds resembling millet

MILOMETER n device that records the number of miles that a bicycle or motor vehicle has travelled

MILOR same as >MILORD

MILORD n (formerly) a continental title used for an English gentleman

MILORDS >MILORD

MILORS >MILOR

MILOS >MILO

MILPA n form of subsistence agriculture in Mexico

MILPAS >MILPA

MILREIS n former monetary unit of Portugal and Brazil, divided into 1000 reis

MILS >MIL

MILSEY n milk strainer

MILSEYS >MILSEY

MILT n sperm of fish ▷ vb fertilize (the roe of a female fish) with milt, esp artificially

MILTED >MILT

MILTER n male fish that is mature and ready to breed

MILTERS >MILTER

MILTIER >MILTY

MILTIEST >MILTY

MILTING >MILT

MILTONIA n tropical American orchid

MILTONIAS >MILTONIA

MILTS >MILT

MILTY adj full of milt

MILTZ same as >MILT

MILTZES >MILTZ

MILVINE adj of kites and related birds

MIM adj prim, modest, or demure

MIMBAR n pulpit in mosque

MIMBARS >MIMBAR

MIME n acting without the use of words ▷ vb act in mime

MIMED >MIME

MIMEO vb mimeograph

MIMEOED >MIMEO

MIMEOING >MIMEO

MIMEOS >MIMEO

MIMER >MIME

MIMERS >MIME

MIMES >MIME

MIMESES >MIMESIS

MIMESIS n imitative representation of nature or human behaviour

MIMESISES >MIMESIS

MIMESTER >MIME

MIMESTERS >MIME

MIMETIC adj imitating or representing something

MIMETICAL >MIMETIC

MIMETITE n rare secondary mineral

MIMETITES >MIMETITE

MIMIC vb imitate (a person or manner), esp for satirical effect ▷ n person or animal that is good at mimicking ▷ adj of, relating to, or using mimicry

MIMICAL >MIMIC

MIMICKED >MIMIC

MIMICKER >MIMIC

MIMICKERS >MIMIC

MIMICKING >MIMIC

MIMICRIES >MIMICRY

MIMICRY n act or art of copying or imitating closely

MIMICS >MIMIC

MIMING >MIME

MIMIVIRUS n type of large virus

MIMMER >MIM

MIMMEST >MIM

MIMMICK same as >MINNICK

MIMMICKED >MIMMICK

MIMMICKS >MIMMICK

MIMOSA n shrub with fluffy yellow flowers and sensitive leaves

MIMOSAE >MIMOSA

MIMOSAS >MIMOSA

MIMSEY same as >MIMSY

MIMSIER >MIMSY

MIMSIEST >MIMSY

MIMSY adj prim, underwhelming, and ineffectual

MIMULUS n plants cultivated for their yellow or red flowers

MIMULUSES >MIMULUS

MINA n ancient unit of weight and money, used in Asia Minor, equal to one sixtieth of a talent

MINABLE >MINE

MINACIOUS adj threatening

MINACITY >MINACIOUS

MINAE >MINA

MINAR n tower

MINARET n tall slender tower of a mosque

MINARETED >MINARET

MINARETS >MINARET

MINARS >MINAR

MINAS >MINA

MINATORY adj threatening or menacing

MINBAR same as >MIMBAR

MINBARS >MINBAR

MINCE vb cut or grind into very small pieces ▷ n minced meat

MINCED >MINCE

MINCEMEAT n sweet mixture of dried fruit and spices

MINCER n machine for mincing meat

MINCERS >MINCER

MINCES >MINCE

MINCEUR adj (of food) low-fat

MINCIER >MINCY

MINCIEST >MINCY

MINCING adj affected in manner

MINCINGLY >MINCING

MINCY adj effeminate

MIND n thinking faculties ▷ vb take offence at

MINDED adj having an inclination as specified

MINDER n aide or bodyguard

MINDERS >MINDER

MINDFUCK n taboo term for deliberate infliction of psychological damage

MINDFUCKS >MINDFUCK

MINDFUL adj heedful

MINDFULLY >MINDFUL

MINDING >MIND

MINDINGS >MIND

MINDLESS adj stupid

MINDS >MIND

MINDSET n ideas and attitudes with which a person approaches a situation, esp when these are seen as being difficult to alter

MINDSETS >MINDSET

MINDSHARE n level of awareness in the minds of consumers that a particular product commands

MINE pron belonging to me ▷ n deep hole for digging out coal, ores, etc ▷ vb dig for minerals

MINEABLE >MINE

MINED >MINE

MINEFIELD n area of land or water containing mines

MINELAYER n warship or aircraft for carrying and laying mines

MINEOLA same as >MINNEOLA

MINEOLAS >MINEOLA

MINER n person who works in a mine

MINERAL n naturally occurring inorganic substance, such as metal ▷ adj of, containing, or like minerals

MINERALS >MINERAL

MINERS >MINER

MINES >MINE

MINESHAFT n vertical entrance into mine

MINESTONE n ore

MINETTE n type of rock

MINETTES >MINETTE

MINEVER same as >MINIVER

MINEVERS >MINEVER

MING vb mix

MINGE n taboo word fore female genitals

MINGED >MING

MINGER n unattractive person

MINGERS >MINGER

MINGES >MINGE

MINGIER >MINGY

MINGIEST >MINGY

MINGINESS >MINGY

MINGING adj unattractive or unpleasant

MINGLE vb mix or blend

MINGLED >MINGLE

MINGLER >MINGLE

MINGLERS >MINGLE

MINGLES >MINGLE

MINGLING >MINGLE

MINGLINGS >MINGLE

MINGS >MING

MINGY adj miserly

MINI same as >MINIDRESS

MINIATE vb paint with minium

MINIATED >MINIATE

MINIATES >MINIATE

MINIATING >MINIATE

MINIATION >MINIATE

MINIATURE n small portrait, model, or copy ▷ adj small-scale ▷ vb reproduce in miniature

MINIBAR n selection of drinks and confectionery provided in a hotel room

MINIBARS >MINIBAR

MINIBIKE n light motorcycle

MINIBIKER >MINIBIKE

MINIBIKES >MINIBIKE

MINIBREAK n short holiday

MINIBUS n small bus

MINIBUSES >MINIBUS

MINICAB n ordinary car used as a taxi

MINICABS >MINICAB

MINICAM n portable television camera

MINICAMP n period spent together in isolation by sports team

MINICAMPS >MINICAMP

MINICAMS >MINICAM

MINICAR n small car

MINICARS >MINICAR

MINICOM n device used by deaf and hard-of-hearing people, allowing typed telephone messages to be sent and received

MINICOMS >MINICOM

MINIDISC n small recordable compact disc

MINIDISCS >MINIDISC

MINIDISH n small parabolic aerial for reception or transmission to a communications satellite

MINIDISK same as >MINIDISC

MINIDISKS >MINIDISK

MINIDRESS n very short dress, at least four inches above the knee

MINIER >MINY

MINIEST >MINY

MINIFIED >MINIFY

MINIFIES >MINIFY

MINIFY vb minimize or lessen the size or importance of (something)

MINIFYING >MINIFY

MINIKIN n small, dainty, or affected person or thing ▷ adj dainty, prim, or affected

MINIKINS >MINIKIN

MINILAB n equipment for processing photographic film

MINILABS >MINILAB

MINIM n note half the length of a semibreve ▷ adj very small

MINIMA >MINIMUM

MINIMAL adj minimum ▷ n small surfboard

MINIMALLY >MINIMAL

MINIMALS >MINIMAL

MINIMART n convenience store

MINIMARTS > MINIMART

MINIMAX n lowest of a set of maximum values ▷ vb make maximum as low as possible

MINIMAXED > MINIMAX

MINIMAXES > MINIMAX

MINIMENT same as > MUNIMENT

MINIMENTS > MINIMENT

MINIMILL n small mill

MINIMILLS > MINIMILL

MINIMISE same as > MINIMIZE

MINIMISED > MINIMISE

MINIMISER > MINIMIZE

MINIMISES > MINIMISE

MINIMISM n desire to reduce to minimum

MINIMISMS > MINIMISM

MINIMIST > MINIMISM

MINIMISTS > MINIMISM

MINIMIZE vb reduce to a minimum

MINIMIZED > MINIMIZE

MINIMIZER > MINIMIZE

MINIMIZES > MINIMIZE

MINIMOTO n reduced-size replica motorcycle used for racing

MINIMOTOS > MINIMOTO

MINIMS > MINIM

MINIMUM n least possible (amount or number) ▷ adj of, being, or showing a minimum or minimums

MINIMUMS > MINIMUM

MINIMUS adj youngest: sometimes used after the surname of a schoolboy having elder brothers at the same school

MINIMUSES > MINIMUS

MINING n act, process, or industry of extracting coal or ores from the earth

MININGS > MINING

MINION n servile assistant ▷ adj dainty, pretty, or elegant

MINIONS > MINION

MINIPARK n small park

MINIPARKS > MINIPARK

MINIPILL n low-dose oral contraceptive containing a progestogen only

MINIPILLS > MINIPILL

MINIRUGBY n version of rugby with fewer players

MINIS > MINI

MINISCULE same as > MINUSCULE

MINISH vb diminish

MINISHED > MINISH

MINISHES > MINISH

MINISHING > MINISH

MINISKI n short ski

MINISKIRT n very short skirt

MINISKIS > MINISKI

MINISTATE n small independent state

MINISTER n head of a government department ▷ vb attend to the needs of

MINISTERS > MINISTER

MINISTRY n profession or duties of a clergyman

MINITOWER n computer in small vertical cabinet

MINITRACK n satellite tracking system

MINIUM n bright red poisonous insoluble oxide of lead usually obtained as a powder by heating litharge in air

MINIUMS > MINIUM

MINIVAN n small van, esp one with seats in the back for carrying passengers

MINIVANS > MINIVAN

MINIVER n white fur, used in ceremonial costumes

MINIVERS > MINIVER

MINIVET n brightly coloured tropical Asian cuckoo shrike

MINIVETS > MINIVET

MINK n stoatlike animal

MINKE as in minke whale type of small whalebone whale or rorqual

MINKES > MINKE

MINKS > MINK

MINNEOLA n juicy citrus fruit that is a cross between a tangerine and a grapefruit

MINNEOLAS > MINNEOLA

MINNICK vb behave in fussy way

MINNICKED > MINNICK

MINNICKS > MINNICK

MINNIE n mother

MINNIES > MINNIE

MINNOCK same as > MINNICK

MINNOCKED > MINNOCK

MINNOCKS > MINNOCK

MINNOW n small freshwater fish

MINNOWS > MINNOW

MINNY same as > MINNIE

MINO same as > MYNAH

MINOR adj lesser ▷ n person regarded legally as a child ▷ vb take a minor

MINORCA n breed of light domestic fowl with glossy white, black, or blue plumage

MINORCAS > MINORCA

MINORED > MINOR

MINORING > MINOR

MINORITY n lesser number

MINORS > MINOR

MINORSHIP > MINOR

MINOS > MINO

MINOTAUR as in minotaur beetle a kind of dung-beetle

MINOXIDIL n drug used to counter baldness

MINSHUKU n guesthouse in Japan

MINSHUKUS > MINSHUKU

MINSTER n cathedral or large church

MINSTERS > MINSTER

MINSTREL n medieval singer or musician

MINSTRELS > MINSTREL

MINT n plant with aromatic leaves used for seasoning and flavouring ▷ vb make (coins)

MINTAGE n process of minting

MINTAGES > MINTAGE

MINTED > MINT

MINTER > MINT

MINTERS > MINT

MINTIER > MINT

MINTIEST > MINT

MINTING > MINT

MINTS > MINT

MINTY > MINT

MINUEND n number from which another number is to be subtracted

MINUENDS > MINUEND

MINUET n stately dance

MINUETS > MINUET

MINUS adj indicating subtraction ▷ n sign (-) denoting subtraction or a number less than zero ▷ prep reduced by the subtraction of

MINUSCULE adj very small ▷ n lower-case letter

MINUSES > MINUS

MINUTE n 60th part of an hour or degree ▷ vb record in the minutes ▷ adj very small

MINUTED > MINUTE

MINUTELY adv in great detail ▷ adj occurring every minute

MINUTEMAN n (in the War of American Independence) colonial militiaman who promised to be ready to fight at one minute's notice

MINUTEMEN > MINUTEMAN

MINUTER > MINUTE

MINUTES npl official record of the proceedings of a meeting or conference

MINUTEST > MINUTE

MINUTIA singular noun of > MINUTIAE

MINUTIAE npl trifling or precise details

MINUTIAL > MINUTIAE

MINUTING > MINUTE

MINUTIOSE > MINUTIAE

MINX n bold or flirtatious girl

MINXES > MINX

MINXISH > MINX

MINY adj of or like mines

MINYAN n number of persons required by Jewish law to be present for a religious service, namely, at least ten males over thirteen years of age

MINYANIM > MINYAN

MINYANS > MINYAN

MIOCENE adj of, denoting, or formed in the fourth epoch of the Tertiary period, between the Oligocene and Pliocene epochs, which lasted for 19 million years

MIOMBO n (in E Africa) a dry wooded area with sparse deciduous growth

MIOMBOS > MIOMBO

MIOSES > MIOSIS

MIOSIS n excessive contraction of the pupil of the eye, as in response to drugs

MIOTIC > MIOSIS

MIOTICS > MIOSIS

MIPS n million instructions per second: a unit used to express the speed of a computer's central processing unit

MIQUELET n type of lock on old firearm

MIQUELETS > MIQUELET

MIR n peasant commune in prerevolutionary Russia

MIRABELLE n small sweet yellow-orange fruit that is a variety of greengage

MIRABILIA n wonders

MIRABILIS n tropical American plant

MIRABLE adj wonderful

MIRACIDIA n plural form of singular miracidium: flat ciliated larva of flukes that hatches from the egg and gives rise asexually to other larval forms

MIRACLE n wonderful supernatural event

MIRACLES > MIRACLE

MIRADOR n window, balcony, or turret

MIRADORS > MIRADOR

MIRAGE n optical illusion, esp one caused by hot air

MIRAGES > MIRAGE

MIRANDISE same as > MIRANDIZE

MIRANDIZE vb (in USA) inform arrested person of rights

MIRBANE n substance used in perfumes

MIRBANES > MIRBANE

MIRCHI Indian English word for > HOT

MIRE n swampy ground ▷ vb sink or be stuck in a mire

MIRED > MIRE

MIREPOIX n mixture of sautéed root vegetables used as a base for braising meat or for various sauces

MIRES > MIRE

MIREX n type of insecticide

MIREXES > MIREX

MIRI > MIR

MIRIER > MIRE

MIRIEST > MIRE

MIRIFIC *adj* achieving wonderful things
MIRIFICAL *same as* >MIRIFIC
MIRIN *n* Japanese rice wine
MIRINESS >MIRE
MIRING >MIRE
MIRINS >MIRIN
MIRITI *n* South American palm
MIRITIS >MIRITI
MIRK *same as* >MURK
MIRKER >MIRK
MIRKEST >MIRK
MIRKIER >MIRK
MIRKIEST >MURKY
MIRKILY >MIRK
MIRKINESS >MIRK
MIRKS >MIRK
MIRKY >MIRK
MIRLIER >MIRLY
MIRLIEST >MIRLY
MIRLIGOES *n* dizzy feeling
MIRLITON *another name* (chiefly US) for >CHAYOTE
MIRLITONS >MIRLITON
MIRLY *same as* >MARLY
MIRO *n* tall New Zealand tree
MIROMIRO *n* small New Zealand bird
MIROMIROS >MIROMIRO
MIROS >MIRO
MIRROR *n* coated glass surface for reflecting images ▷ *vb* reflect in or as if in a mirror
MIRRORED >MIRROR
MIRRORING >MIRROR
MIRRORS >MIRROR
MIRS >MIR
MIRTH *n* laughter, merriment, or gaiety
MIRTHFUL >MIRTH
MIRTHLESS >MIRTH
MIRTHS >MIRTH
MIRV *n* missile that has several warheads, each one being directed to different enemy targets ▷ *vb* arm with mirvs
MIRVED >MIRV
MIRVING >MIRV
MIRVS >MIRV
MIRY >MIRE
MIRZA *n* title of respect placed before the surname of an official, scholar, or other distinguished man
MIRZAS >MIRZA
MIS >MI
MISACT *vb* act wrongly
MISACTED >MISACT
MISACTING >MISACT
MISACTS >MISACT
MISADAPT *vb* adapt badly
MISADAPTS >MISADAPT
MISADD *vb* add badly
MISADDED >MISADD
MISADDING >MISADD
MISADDS >MISADD
MISADJUST *vb* adjust wrongly
MISADVICE *n* bad advice

MISADVISE *vb* give bad advice to
MISAGENT *n* bad agent
MISAGENTS >MISAGENT
MISAIM *vb* aim badly
MISAIMED >MISAIM
MISAIMING >MISAIM
MISAIMS >MISAIM
MISALIGN *vb* align badly
MISALIGNS >MISALIGN
MISALLEGE *vb* allege wrongly
MISALLIED >MISALLY
MISALLIES >MISALLY
MISALLOT *vb* allot wrongly
MISALLOTS >MISALLOT
MISALLY *vb* form unsuitable alliance
MISALTER *vb* alter wrongly
MISALTERS >MISALTER
MISANDRY *n* hatred of men
MISAPPLY *vb* use something for a purpose for which it is not intended or is not suited
MISARRAY *n* disarray
MISARRAYS >MISARRAY
MISASSAY *vb* assay wrongly
MISASSAYS >MISASSAY
MISASSIGN *vb* assign wrongly
MISATE >MISEAT
MISATONE *vb* atone wrongly
MISATONED >MISATONE
MISATONES >MISATONE
MISAUNTER *n* misadventure
MISAVER *vb* claim wrongly
MISAVERS >MISAVER
MISAVISED *adj* badly advised
MISAWARD *vb* award wrongly
MISAWARDS >MISAWARD
MISBECAME >MISBECOME
MISBECOME *vb* be unbecoming to or unsuitable for
MISBEGAN >MISBEGIN
MISBEGIN *vb* begin badly
MISBEGINS >MISBEGIN
MISBEGOT *adj* illegitimate
MISBEGUN >MISBEGIN
MISBEHAVE *vb* behave badly
MISBELIEF *n* false or unorthodox belief
MISBESEEM *vb* be unsuitable for
MISBESTOW *vb* bestow wrongly
MISBIAS *vb* prejudice wrongly
MISBIASED >MISBIAS
MISBIASES >MISBIAS
MISBILL *vb* present inaccurate bill
MISBILLED >MISBILL
MISBILLS >MISBILL

MISBIND *vb* bind wrongly
MISBINDS >MISBIND
MISBIRTH *n* abortion
MISBIRTHS >MISBIRTH
MISBORN *adj* abortive
MISBOUND >MISBIND
MISBRAND *vb* put misleading label on
MISBRANDS >MISBRAND
MISBUILD *vb* build badly
MISBUILDS >MISBUILD
MISBUILT >MISBUILD
MISBUTTON *vb* button wrongly
MISCALL *vb* call by the wrong name
MISCALLED >MISCALL
MISCALLER >MISCALL
MISCALLS >MISCALL
MISCARRY *vb* have a miscarriage
MISCAST *vb* cast (a role or actor) in (a play or film) inappropriately
MISCASTS >MISCAST
MISCEGEN *n* person of mixed race
MISCEGENE *same as* >MISCEGEN
MISCEGENS >MISCEGEN
MISCEGINE *same as* >MISCEGEN
MISCH *as in misch metal* alloy of cerium and other rare earth metals, used esp as a flint in cigarette lighters
MISCHANCE *n* unlucky event
MISCHANCY *adj* unlucky
MISCHARGE *vb* charge wrongly
MISCHIEF *n* annoying but not malicious behaviour
MISCHIEFS >MISCHIEF
MISCHOICE *n* bad choice
MISCHOOSE *vb* make bad choice
MISCHOSE >MISCHOOSE
MISCHOSEN >MISCHOOSE
MISCIBLE *adj* able to be mixed
MISCITE *vb* cite wrongly
MISCITED >MISCITE
MISCITES >MISCITE
MISCITING >MISCITE
MISCLAIM *vb* claim wrongly
MISCLAIMS >MISCLAIM
MISCLASS *adj* class badly
MISCODE *vb* code wrongly
MISCODED >MISCODE
MISCODES >MISCODE
MISCODING >MISCODE
MISCOIN *vb* coin wrongly
MISCOINED >MISCOIN
MISCOINS >MISCOIN
MISCOLOR *same as* >MISCOLOUR
MISCOLORS >MISCOLOR
MISCOLOUR *vb* give wrong colour to
MISCOOK *vb* cook badly

MISCOOKED >MISCOOK
MISCOOKS >MISCOOK
MISCOPIED >MISCOPY
MISCOPIES >MISCOPY
MISCOPY *vb* copy badly
MISCOUNT *vb* count or calculate incorrectly ▷ *n* false count or calculation
MISCOUNTS >MISCOUNT
MISCREANT *n* wrongdoer ▷ *adj* evil or villainous
MISCREATE *vb* create (something) badly or incorrectly ▷ *adj* badly or unnaturally formed or made
MISCREDIT *vb* disbelieve
MISCREED *n* false creed
MISCREEDS >MISCREED
MISCUE *n* faulty stroke in which the cue tip slips off the cue ball or misses it altogether ▷ *vb* make a miscue
MISCUED >MISCUE
MISCUEING >MISCUE
MISCUES >MISCUE
MISCUING >MISCUE
MISCUT *n* cut wrongly
MISCUTS >MISCUT
MISDATE *vb* date (a letter, event, etc) wrongly
MISDATED >MISDATE
MISDATES >MISDATE
MISDATING >MISDATE
MISDEAL *vb* deal out cards incorrectly ▷ *n* faulty deal
MISDEALER >MISDEAL
MISDEALS >MISDEAL
MISDEALT >MISDEAL
MISDEED *n* wrongful act
MISDEEDS >MISDEED
MISDEEM *vb* form bad opinion of
MISDEEMED >MISDEEM
MISDEEMS >MISDEEM
MISDEFINE *vb* define badly
MISDEMEAN *rare word for* >MISBEHAVE
MISDEMPT >MISDEEM
MISDESERT *n* quality of being undeserving
MISDIAL *vb* dial telephone number incorrectly
MISDIALED >MISDIAL
MISDIALS >MISDIAL
MISDID >MISDO
MISDIET *n* wrong diet
MISDIETS >MISDIET
MISDIGHT *adj* done badly
MISDIRECT *vb* give (someone) wrong directions or instructions
MISDIVIDE *vb* divide wrongly
MISDO *vb* do badly or wrongly
MISDOER >MISDO
MISDOERS >MISDO
MISDOES >MISDO
MISDOING >MISDO
MISDOINGS >MISDO
MISDONE *adj* done badly

MISDONNE same as >MISDONE

MISDOUBT archaic word for >DOUBT

MISDOUBTS >MISDOUBT

MISDRAW vb draw poorly

MISDRAWN >MISDRAW

MISDRAWS >MISDRAW

MISDREAD n fear of approaching evil

MISDREADS >MISDREAD

MISDREW >MISDRAW

MISDRIVE vb drive badly

MISDRIVEN >MISDRIVE

MISDRIVES >MISDRIVE

MISDROVE >MISDRIVE

MISE n issue in the obsolete writ of right

MISEASE n unease

MISEASES >MISEASE

MISEAT vb eat unhealthy food

MISEATEN >MISEAT

MISEATING >MISEAT

MISEATS >MISEAT

MISEDIT vb edit badly

MISEDITED >MISEDIT

MISEDITS >MISEDIT

MISEMPLOY vb employ badly

MISENROL vb enrol wrongly

MISENROLL same as >MISENROL

MISENROLS >MISENROL

MISENTER vb enter wrongly

MISENTERS >MISENTER

MISENTRY n wrong or mistaken entry

MISER n person who hoards money and hates spending it

MISERABLE adj very unhappy, wretched ▷ n wretched person

MISERABLY >MISERABLE

MISERE n call in solo whist and other card games declaring a hand that will win no tricks

MISERERE n type of psalm

MISERERES >MISERERE

MISERES >MISERE

MISERIES >MISERY

MISERLIER >MISERLY

MISERLY adj of or resembling a miser

MISERS >MISER

MISERY n great unhappiness

MISES >MISE

MISESTEEM n lack of respect

MISEVENT n mishap

MISEVENTS >MISEVENT

MISFAITH n distrust

MISFAITHS >MISFAITH

MISFALL vb happen as piece of bad luck

MISFALLEN >MISFALL

MISFALLS >MISFALL

MISFALNE >MISFALL

MISFARE vb get on badly

MISFARED >MISFARE

MISFARES >MISFARE

MISFARING >MISFARE

MISFEASOR n someone who carries out the improper performance of an act that is lawful in itself

MISFED >MISFEED

MISFEED vb feed wrongly

MISFEEDS >MISFEED

MISFEIGN vb feign with evil motive

MISFEIGNS >MISFEIGN

MISFELL >MISFALL

MISFIELD vb fail to field properly

MISFIELDS >MISFIELD

MISFILE vb file (papers, records, etc) wrongly

MISFILED >MISFILE

MISFILES >MISFILE

MISFILING >MISFILE

MISFIRE vb (of a firearm or engine) fail to fire correctly ▷ n act or an instance of misfiring

MISFIRED >MISFIRE

MISFIRES >MISFIRE

MISFIRING >MISFIRE

MISFIT n person not suited to his or her social environment ▷ vb fail to fit or be fitted

MISFITS >MISFIT

MISFITTED >MISFIT

MISFOCUS n wrong or poor focus

MISFORM vb form badly

MISFORMED >MISFORM

MISFORMS >MISFORM

MISFRAME vb frame wrongly

MISFRAMED >MISFRAME

MISFRAMES >MISFRAME

MISGAUGE vb gauge badly

MISGAUGED >MISGAUGE

MISGAUGES >MISGAUGE

MISGAVE >MISGIVE

MISGIVE vb make or be apprehensive or suspicious

MISGIVEN >MISGIVE

MISGIVES >MISGIVE

MISGIVING n feeling of fear or doubt

MISGO vb go wrong way

MISGOES >MISGO

MISGOING >MISGO

MISGONE >MISGO

MISGOTTEN adj obtained dishonestly

MISGOVERN vb govern badly

MISGRADE vb grade wrongly

MISGRADED >MISGRADE

MISGRADES >MISGRADE

MISGRAFF adj badly done

MISGRAFT vb graft wrongly

MISGRAFTS >MISGRAFT

MISGREW >MISGROW

MISGROW vb grow in unsuitable way

MISGROWN >MISGROW

MISGROWS >MISGROW

MISGROWTH >MISGROW

MISGUESS vb guess wrongly

MISGUGGLE vb handle incompetently

MISGUIDE vb guide or direct wrongly or badly

MISGUIDED adj mistaken or unwise

MISGUIDER >MISGUIDE

MISGUIDES >MISGUIDE

MISHANDLE vb handle badly or inefficiently

MISHANTER n misfortune

MISHAP n minor accident ▷ vb happen as bad luck

MISHAPPED >MISHAP

MISHAPPEN vb happen as bad luck

MISHAPS >MISHAP

MISHAPT same as >MISSHAPEN

MISHEAR vb hear (what someone says) wrongly

MISHEARD >MISHEAR

MISHEARS >MISHEAR

MISHEGAAS same as >MESHUGAAS

MISHEGOSS same as >MESHUGAAS

MISHIT n faulty shot, kick, or stroke ▷ vb hit or kick a ball with a faulty stroke

MISHITS >MISHIT

MISHMASH n confused collection or mixture

MISHMEE n root of Asian plant

MISHMEES >MISHMEE

MISHMI n evergreen perennial plant

MISHMIS >MISHMI

MISHMOSH same as >MISHMASH

MISINFER vb infer wrongly

MISINFERS >MISINFER

MISINFORM vb give incorrect information to

MISINTEND vb intend to harm

MISINTER vb bury wrongly

MISINTERS >MISINTER

MISJOIN vb join badly

MISJOINED >MISJOIN

MISJOINS >MISJOIN

MISJUDGE vb judge wrongly or unfairly

MISJUDGED >MISJUDGE

MISJUDGER >MISJUDGE

MISJUDGES >MISJUDGE

MISKAL n unit of weight in Iran

MISKALS >MISKAL

MISKEEP vb keep wrongly

MISKEEPS >MISKEEP

MISKEN vb be unaware of

MISKENNED >MISKEN

MISKENS >MISKEN

MISKENT >MISKEN

MISKEPT >MISKEEP

MISKEY vb key wrongly

MISKEYED >MISKEY

MISKEYING >MISKEY

MISKEYS >MISKEY

MISKICK vb fail to kick properly

MISKICKED >MISKICK

MISKICKS >MISKICK

MISKNEW vb >MISKNOW

MISKNOW vb have wrong idea about

MISKNOWN >MISKNOW

MISKNOWS >MISKNOW

MISLABEL vb label badly

MISLABELS >MISLABEL

MISLABOR vb labour wrongly

MISLABORS >MISLABOR

MISLAID >MISLAY

MISLAIN >MISLAY

MISLAY vb lose (something) temporarily

MISLAYER >MISLAY

MISLAYERS >MISLAY

MISLAYING >MISLAY

MISLAYS >MISLAY

MISLEAD vb give false or confusing information to

MISLEADER >MISLEAD

MISLEADS >MISLEAD

MISLEARED adj badly brought up

MISLEARN vb learn wrongly

MISLEARNS >MISLEARN

MISLEARNT >MISLEARN

MISLED >MISLEAD

MISLEEKE same as >MISLIKE

MISLEEKED >MISLEEKE

MISLEEKES >MISLEEKE

MISLETOE same as >MISTLETOE

MISLETOES >MISLETOE

MISLIE vb lie wrongly

MISLIES >MISLIE

MISLIGHT vb use light to lead astray

MISLIGHTS >MISLIGHT

MISLIKE vb dislike ▷ n dislike or aversion

MISLIKED >MISLIKE

MISLIKER >MISLIKE

MISLIKERS >MISLIKE

MISLIKES >MISLIKE

MISLIKING >MISLIKE

MISLIPPEN vb distrust

MISLIT >MISLIGHT

MISLIVE vb live wickedly

MISLIVED >MISLIVE

MISLIVES >MISLIVE

MISLIVING >MISLIVE

MISLOCATE vb put in wrong place

MISLODGE vb lodge wrongly

MISLODGED >MISLODGE

MISLODGES >MISLODGE

MISLUCK vb have bad luck

MISLUCKED >MISLUCK

MISLUCKS >MISLUCK

MISLYING >MISLIE

MISMADE >MISMAKE

MISMAKE vb make badly

MISMAKES >MISMAKE
MISMAKING >MISMAKE
MISMANAGE *vb* organize or run (something) badly
MISMARK *vb* mark wrongly
MISMARKED >MISMARK
MISMARKS >MISMARK
MISMARRY *vb* make unsuitable marriage
MISMATCH *vb* form an unsuitable partner, opponent, or set ▷ *n* unsuitable match
MISMATE *vb* mate wrongly
MISMATED >MISMATE
MISMATES >MISMATE
MISMATING >MISMATE
MISMEET *vb* fail to meet
MISMEETS >MISMEET
MISMET >MISMEET
MISMETRE *vb* fail to follow metre of poem
MISMETRED >MISMETRE
MISMETRES >MISMETRE
MISMOVE *vb* move badly
MISMOVED >MISMOVE
MISMOVES >MISMOVE
MISMOVING >MISMOVE
MISNAME *vb* name badly
MISNAMED >MISNAME
MISNAMES >MISNAME
MISNAMING >MISNAME
MISNOMER *n* incorrect or unsuitable name ▷ *vb* apply misnomer to
MISNOMERS >MISNOMER
MISNUMBER *vb* number wrongly
MISO *n* thick brown salty paste made from soya beans, used to flavour savoury dishes, esp soups
MISOCLERE *adj* hostile to clergy
MISOGAMIC >MISOGAMY
MISOGAMY *n* hatred of marriage
MISOGYNIC >MISOGYNY
MISOGYNY *n* hatred of women
MISOLOGY *n* hatred of reasoning or reasoned argument
MISONEISM *n* hatred of anything new
MISONEIST >MISONEISM
MISORDER *vb* order badly
MISORDERS >MISORDER
MISORIENT *vb* orient incorrectly
MISOS >MISO
MISPAGE *vb* page wrongly
MISPAGED >MISPAGE
MISPAGES >MISPAGE
MISPAGING >MISPAGE
MISPAINT *vb* paint badly or wrongly
MISPAINTS >MISPAINT
MISPARSE *vb* parse wrongly
MISPARSED >MISPARSE
MISPARSES >MISPARSE
MISPART *vb* part wrongly

MISPARTED >MISPART
MISPARTS >MISPART
MISPATCH *vb* patch wrongly
MISPEN *vb* write wrongly
MISPENNED >MISPEN
MISPENS >MISPEN
MISPHRASE *vb* phrase badly
MISPICKEL *n* white or grey metallic mineral consisting of a sulphide of iron and arsenic that forms monoclinic crystals with an orthorhombic shape: an ore of arsenic
MISPLACE *vb* mislay
MISPLACED *adj* (of an emotion or action) directed towards a person or thing that does not deserve it
MISPLACES >MISPLACE
MISPLAN *vb* plan badly or wrongly
MISPLANS >MISPLAN
MISPLANT *vb* plant badly or wrongly
MISPLANTS >MISPLANT
MISPLAY *vb* play badly or wrongly in games or sports ▷ *n* wrong or unskilful play
MISPLAYED >MISPLAY
MISPLAYS >MISPLAY
MISPLEAD *vb* plead incorrectly
MISPLEADS >MISPLEAD
MISPLEASE *vb* displease
MISPLED >MISPLEAD
MISPOINT *vb* punctuate badly
MISPOINTS >MISPOINT
MISPOISE *n* lack of poise ▷ *vb* lack poise
MISPOISED >MISPOISE
MISPOISES >MISPOISE
MISPRAISE *vb* fail to praise properly
MISPRICE *vb* give wrong price to
MISPRICED >MISPRICE
MISPRICES >MISPRICE
MISPRINT *n* printing error ▷ *vb* print a letter incorrectly
MISPRINTS >MISPRINT
MISPRISE *same as* >MISPRIZE
MISPRISED >MISPRISE
MISPRISES >MISPRISE
MISPRIZE *vb* fail to appreciate the value of
MISPRIZED >MISPRIZE
MISPRIZER >MISPRIZE
MISPRIZES >MISPRIZE
MISPROUD *adj* undeservedly proud
MISQUOTE *vb* quote inaccurately
MISQUOTED >MISQUOTE
MISQUOTER >MISQUOTE
MISQUOTES >MISQUOTE
MISRAISE *vb* raise wrongly or excessively
MISRAISED >MISRAISE

MISRAISES >MISRAISE
MISRATE *vb* rate wrongly
MISRATED >MISRATE
MISRATES >MISRATE
MISRATING >MISRATE
MISREAD *vb* misinterpret (a situation etc)
MISREADS >MISREAD
MISRECKON *vb* reckon wrongly
MISRECORD *vb* record wrongly
MISREFER *vb* refer wrongly
MISREFERS >MISREFER
MISREGARD *n* lack of attention
MISRELATE *vb* relate badly
MISRELIED >MISRELY
MISRELIES >MISRELY
MISRELY *vb* rely wrongly
MISRENDER *vb* render wrongly
MISREPORT *vb* report falsely or inaccurately ▷ *n* inaccurate or false report
MISRHYMED *adj* badly rhymed
MISROUTE *vb* send wrong way
MISROUTED >MISROUTE
MISROUTES >MISROUTE
MISRULE *vb* govern inefficiently or unjustly ▷ *n* inefficient or unjust government
MISRULED >MISRULE
MISRULES >MISRULE
MISRULING >MISRULE
MISS *vb* fail to notice, hear, hit, reach, find, or catch ▷ *n* fact or instance of missing
MISSA *n* Roman Catholic mass
MISSABLE >MISS
MISSAE >MISSA
MISSAID >MISSAY
MISSAL *n* book containing the prayers and rites of the Mass
MISSALS >MISSAL
MISSAW >MISSEE
MISSAY *vb* say wrongly
MISSAYING >MISSAY
MISSAYS >MISSAY
MISSEAT *vb* seat wrongly
MISSEATED >MISSEAT
MISSEATS >MISSEAT
MISSED >MISS
MISSEE *vb* see wrongly
MISSEEING >MISSEE
MISSEEM *vb* be unsuitable for
MISSEEMED >MISSEEM
MISSEEMS >MISSEEM
MISSEEN >MISSEE
MISSEES >MISSEE
MISSEL as in *missel thrush* large brown thrush with a brown back and spotted breast, noted for feeding on mistletoe berries
MISSELL *vb* sell (a product,

esp a financial one) misleadingly
MISSELLS >MISSELL
MISSELS >MISSEL
MISSEND *vb* send wrongly
MISSENDS >MISSEND
MISSENSE *n* type of genetic mutation
MISSENSES >MISSENSE
MISSENT >MISSEND
MISSES >MISS
MISSET *vb* set wrongly
MISSETS >MISSET
MISSHAPE *vb* shape badly ▷ *n* something that is badly shaped
MISSHAPED >MISSHAPE
MISSHAPEN *adj* badly shaped, deformed
MISSHAPER >MISSHAPE
MISSHAPES >MISSHAPE
MISSHOD *adj* badly shod
MISSHOOD *n* state of being unmarried woman
MISSHOODS >MISSHOOD
MISSIER >MISSY
MISSIES >MISSY
MISSIEST >MISSY
MISSILE *n* rocket with an exploding warhead, used as a weapon
MISSILEER *n* serviceman or servicewoman who is responsible for firing missiles
MISSILERY *n* missiles collectively
MISSILES >MISSILE
MISSILRY *same as* >MISSILERY
MISSING *adj* lost or absent
MISSINGLY >MISSING
MISSION *n* specific task or duty ▷ *vb* direct a mission to or establish a mission in (a given region)
MISSIONAL *adj* emphasizing preaching of gospel
MISSIONED >MISSION
MISSIONER *n* person heading a parochial mission in a Christian country
MISSIONS >MISSION
MISSIS *same as* >MISSUS
MISSISES >MISSIS
MISSISH *adj* like schoolgirl
MISSIVE *n* letter ▷ *adj* sent or intended to be sent
MISSIVES >MISSIVE
MISSOLD >MISSELL
MISSORT *vb* sort wrongly
MISSORTED >MISSORT
MISSORTS >MISSORT
MISSOUND *vb* sound wrongly
MISSOUNDS >MISSOUND
MISSOUT *n* someone who has been overlooked
MISSOUTS >MISSOUT
MISSPACE *vb* space out wrongly

MISSPACED >MISSPACE
MISSPACES >MISSPACE
MISSPEAK vb speak wrongly
MISSPEAKS >MISSPEAK
MISSPELL vb spell (a word) wrongly
MISSPELLS >MISSPELL
MISSPELT >MISSPELL
MISSPEND vb waste or spend unwisely
MISSPENDS >MISSPEND
MISSPENT >MISSPEND
MISSPOKE >MISSPEAK
MISSPOKEN >MISSPEAK
MISSTAMP vb stamp badly
MISSTAMPS >MISSTAMP
MISSTART vb start wrongly
MISSTARTS >MISSTART
MISSTATE vb state incorrectly
MISSTATED >MISSTATE
MISSTATES >MISSTATE
MISSTEER vb steer badly
MISSTEERS >MISSTEER
MISSTEP n false step ▷ vb take false step
MISSTEPS >MISSTEP
MISSTOP vb stop wrongly
MISSTOPS >MISSTOP
MISSTRIKE vb fail to strike properly
MISSTRUCK >MISSTRIKE
MISSTYLE vb call by wrong name
MISSTYLED >MISSTYLE
MISSTYLES >MISSTYLE
MISSUIT vb be unsuitable for
MISSUITED >MISSUIT
MISSUITS >MISSUIT
MISSUS n one's wife or the wife of the person addressed or referred to
MISSUSES >MISSUS
MISSY n affectionate or disparaging form of address to a girl ▷ adj missish
MIST n thin fog ▷ vb cover or be covered with mist
MISTAKE n error or blunder ▷ vb misunderstand
MISTAKEN adj wrong in judgment or opinion
MISTAKER >MISTAKE
MISTAKERS >MISTAKE
MISTAKES >MISTAKE
MISTAKING >MISTAKE
MISTAL n cow shed
MISTALS >MISTAL
MISTAUGHT >MISTEACH
MISTBOW same as >FOGBOW
MISTBOWS >MISTBOW
MISTEACH vb teach badly
MISTED >MIST
MISTELL vb tell wrongly
MISTELLS >MISTELL
MISTEMPER vb make disordered
MISTEND vb tend wrongly

MISTENDED >MISTEND
MISTENDS >MISTEND
MISTER n informal form of address for a man ▷ vb call (someone) mister
MISTERED >MISTER
MISTERIES >MISTERY
MISTERING >MISTER
MISTERM vb term badly
MISTERMED >MISTERM
MISTERMS >MISTERM
MISTERS >MISTER
MISTERY same as >MYSTERY
MISTEUK Scots variant of >MISTOOK
MISTFUL >MIST
MISTHINK vb have poor opinion of
MISTHINKS >MISTHINK
MISTHREW >MISTHROW
MISTHROW vb fail to throw properly
MISTHROWN >MISTHROW
MISTHROWS >MISTHROW
MISTICO n small Mediterranean sailing ship
MISTICOS >MISTICO
MISTIER >MISTY
MISTIEST >MISTY
MISTIGRIS n joker or a blank card used as a wild card in a variety of draw poker
MISTILY >MISTY
MISTIME vb do (something) at the wrong time
MISTIMED >MISTIME
MISTIMES >MISTIME
MISTIMING >MISTIME
MISTINESS >MISTY
MISTING n application of a fake suntan by spray
MISTINGS >MISTING
MISTITLE vb name badly
MISTITLED >MISTITLE
MISTITLES >MISTITLE
MISTLE same as >MIZZLE
MISTLED >MISTLE
MISTLES >MISTLE
MISTLETOE n evergreen plant with white berries growing as a parasite on trees
MISTLING >MISTLE
MISTOLD >MISTELL
MISTOOK past tense of >MISTAKE
MISTOUCH vb fail to touch properly
MISTRACE vb trace wrongly
MISTRACED >MISTRACE
MISTRACES >MISTRACE
MISTRAIN vb train wrongly
MISTRAINS >MISTRAIN
MISTRAL n strong dry northerly wind of S France
MISTRALS >MISTRAL
MISTREAT vb treat (a person or animal) badly
MISTREATS >MISTREAT

MISTRESS n woman who has a continuing sexual relationship with a married man ▷ vb make into mistress
MISTRIAL n trial made void because of some error
MISTRIALS >MISTRIAL
MISTRUST vb have doubts or suspicions about ▷ n lack of trust
MISTRUSTS >MISTRUST
MISTRUTH n something untrue
MISTRUTHS >MISTRUTH
MISTRYST vb fail to keep appointment with
MISTRYSTS >MISTRYST
MISTS >MIST
MISTUNE vb fail to tune properly
MISTUNED >MISTUNE
MISTUNES >MISTUNE
MISTUNING >MISTUNE
MISTUTOR vb instruct badly
MISTUTORS >MISTUTOR
MISTY adj full of mist
MISTYPE vb type badly
MISTYPED >MISTYPE
MISTYPES >MISTYPE
MISTYPING >MISTYPE
MISUNION n wrong or bad union
MISUNIONS >MISUNION
MISUSAGE >MISUSE
MISUSAGES >MISUSE
MISUSE n incorrect, improper, or careless use ▷ vb use wrongly
MISUSED >MISUSE
MISUSER n abuse of some right, privilege, office, etc, such as one that may lead to its forfeiture
MISUSERS >MISUSER
MISUSES >MISUSE
MISUSING >MISUSE
MISUST >MISUSE
MISVALUE vb value badly
MISVALUED >MISVALUE
MISVALUES >MISVALUE
MISWEEN vb assess wrongly
MISWEENED >MISWEEN
MISWEENS >MISWEEN
MISWEND vb become lost
MISWENDS >MISWEND
MISWENT >MISWEND
MISWORD vb word badly
MISWORDED >MISWORD
MISWORDS >MISWORD
MISWRIT >MISWRITE
MISWRITE vb write badly
MISWRITES >MISWRITE
MISWROTE >MISWRITE
MISYOKE vb join wrongly
MISYOKED >MISYOKE
MISYOKES >MISYOKE
MISYOKING >MISYOKE
MITCH vb play truant from school
MITCHED >MITCH
MITCHES >MITCH

MITCHING >MITCH
MITE n very small spider-like animal
MITER same as >MITRE
MITERED >MITER
MITERER >MITER
MITERERS >MITER
MITERING >MITER
MITERS >MITER
MITERWORT same as >MITREWORT
MITES >MITE
MITHER vb fuss over or moan about something
MITHERED >MITHER
MITHERING >MITHER
MITHERS >MITHER
MITICIDAL >MITICIDE
MITICIDE n any drug or agent that destroys mites
MITICIDES >MITICIDE
MITIER >MITY
MITIEST >MITY
MITIGABLE >MITIGATE
MITIGANT adj acting to mitigate
MITIGATE vb make less severe
MITIGATED >MITIGATE
MITIGATES >MITIGATE
MITIGATOR >MITIGATE
MITIS n malleable iron, fluid enough for casting, made by adding a small amount of aluminium to wrought iron
MITISES >MITIS
MITOGEN n any agent that induces mitosis
MITOGENIC >MITOGEN
MITOGENS >MITOGEN
MITOMYCIN n
MITOSES >MITOSIS
MITOSIS n type of cell division in which the nucleus divides into two nuclei which each contain the same number of chromosomes as the original nucleus
MITOTIC >MITOSIS
MITRAILLE n hail of bullets
MITRAL adj of or like a mitre
MITRE n bishop's pointed headdress. ▷ vb join with a mitre joint
MITRED >MITRE
MITRES >MITRE
MITREWORT n Asian and N American plant with clusters of small white flowers and capsules resembling a bishop's mitre
MITRIFORM adj shaped like mitre
MITRING >MITRE
MITSVAH same as >MITZVAH
MITSVAHS >MITSVAH
MITSVOTH >MITSVAH
MITT same as >MITTEN

MITTEN n glove with one section for the thumb and one for the four fingers together

MITTENED adj wearing mittens

MITTENS >MITTEN

MITTIMUS n warrant of commitment to prison or a command to a jailer directing him to hold someone in prison

MITTS >MITT

MITUMBA n used clothes imported for sale in African countries

MITUMBAS >MITUMBA

MITY adj having mites

MITZVAH n commandment or precept, esp one found in the Bible

MITZVAHS >MITZVAH

MITZVOTH >MITZVAH

MIURUS n type of rhythm in poetry

MIURUSES >MIURUS

MIX vb combine or blend into one mass ▷ n mixture

MIXABLE >MIX

MIXDOWN n (in sound recording) the transfer of a multitrack master mix to two-track stereo tape

MIXDOWNS >MIXDOWN

MIXED adj formed or blended together by mixing

MIXEDLY >MIXED

MIXEDNESS >MIXED

MIXEN n dunghill

MIXENS >MIXEN

MIXER n kitchen appliance used for mixing foods

MIXERS >MIXER

MIXES >MIX

MIXIBLE >MIX

MIXIER >MIX

MIXIEST >MIX

MIXING >MIX

MIXMASTER n disc jockey

MIXOLOGY n art of mixing cocktails

MIXT >MIX

MIXTE adj of or denoting a type of bicycle frame, usually for women, in which angled twin lateral tubes run back to the rear axle

MIXTION n amber-based mixture used in making gold leaf

MIXTIONS >MIXTION

MIXTURE n something mixed

MIXTURES >MIXTURE

MIXUP n something that is mixed up

MIXUPS >MIXUP

MIXY adj mixed

MIZ shortened form of >MISERY

MIZEN same as >MIZZEN

MIZENMAST n (on a yawl, ketch, or dandy) the after mast

MIZENS >MIZEN

MIZMAZE n maze

MIZMAZES >MIZMAZE

MIZUNA n Japanese variety of lettuce having crisp green leaves

MIZUNAS >MIZUNA

MIZZ same as >MIZ

MIZZEN n sail set on a mizzenmast ▷ adj of or relating to any kind of gear used with a mizzenmast

MIZZENS >MIZZEN

MIZZES >MIZ

MIZZLE vb decamp

MIZZLED >MIZZLE

MIZZLES >MIZZLE

MIZZLIER >MIZZLE

MIZZLIEST >MIZZLE

MIZZLING >MIZZLE

MIZZLINGS >MIZZLE

MIZZLY >MIZZLE

MIZZONITE n mineral containing sodium

MIZZY as in mizzy maze dialect expression meaning state of confusion

MM interj expression of enjoyment of taste or smell

MNA same as >MINA

MNAS >MNA

MNEME n ability to retain memory

MNEMES >MNEME

MNEMIC >MNEME

MNEMON n unit of memory

MNEMONIC adj intended to help the memory ▷ n something, for instance a verse, intended to help the memory

MNEMONICS n art or practice of improving of or aiding the memory

MNEMONIST >MNEMONICS

MNEMONS >MNEMON

MO n moment

MOA n large extinct flightless New Zealand bird

MOAI n any of the gigantic carved stone figures found on Easter Island (Rapa Nui)

MOAN n low cry of pain ▷ vb make or utter with a moan

MOANED >MOAN

MOANER >MOAN

MOANERS >MOAN

MOANFUL >MOAN

MOANFULLY >MOAN

MOANING >MOAN

MOANINGLY >MOAN

MOANINGS >MOAN

MOANS >MOAN

MOAS >MOA

MOAT n deep wide ditch, esp round a castle ▷ vb surround with or as if with a moat

MOATED >MOAT

MOATING >MOAT

MOATLIKE >MOAT

MOATS >MOAT

MOB n disorderly crowd ▷ vb surround in a mob to acclaim or attack

MOBBED >MOB

MOBBER >MOB

MOBBERS >MOB

MOBBIE same as >MOBBY

MOBBIES >MOBBY

MOBBING >MOB

MOBBINGS >MOB

MOBBISH >MOB

MOBBISHLY >MOB

MOBBISM n behaviour as mob

MOBBISMS >MOBBISM

MOBBLE same as >MOBLE

MOBBLED >MOBBLE

MOBBLES >MOBBLE

MOBBLING >MOBBLE

MOBBY n West Indian drink

MOBCAP n woman's 18th-century cotton cap with a pouched crown

MOBCAPS >MOBCAP

MOBCAST v create and upload a podcast directly from a mobile phone

MOBCASTED >MOBCAST

MOBCASTS >MOBCAST

MOBE n mobile phone

MOBEY same as >MOBY

MOBEYS >MOBEY

MOBIE n mobile phone

MOBIES >MOBY

MOBILE adj able to move ▷ n hanging structure designed to move in air currents

MOBILES >MOBILE

MOBILISE same as >MOBILIZE

MOBILISED >MOBILISE

MOBILISER >MOBILISE

MOBILISES >MOBILISE

MOBILITY n ability to move physically

MOBILIZE vb (of the armed services) prepare for active service

MOBILIZED >MOBILIZE

MOBILIZER >MOBILIZE

MOBILIZES >MOBILIZE

MOBLE vb muffle

MOBLED >MOBLE

MOBLES >MOBLE

MOBLING >MOBLE

MOBLOG n chronicle, which may be shared with others, of someone's thoughts and experiences recorded in the form of mobile phone calls, text messages, and photographs

MOBLOGGER >MOBLOG

MOBLOGS >MOBLOG

MOBOCRACY n rule or domination by a mob

MOBOCRAT >MOBOCRACY

MOBOCRATS >MOBOCRACY

MOBS >MOB

MOBSMAN n person in mob

MOBSMEN >MOBSMAN

MOBSTER n member of a criminal organization

MOBSTERS >MOBSTER

MOBY n mobile phone

MOC shortening of >MOCCASIN

MOCCASIN same as >MOCCASIN

MOCCASINS >MOCCASIN

MOCCASIN n soft leather shoe

MOCCASINS >MOCCASIN

MOCCIES npl informal Australian word for moccasins

MOCH n spell of humid weather

MOCHA n kind of strong dark coffee

MOCHAS >MOCHA

MOCHELL same as >MUCH

MOCHELLS >MOCHELL

MOCHIE adj damp or humid

MOCHIER >MOCHIE

MOCHIEST >MOCHIE

MOCHILA n South American shoulder bag

MOCHILAS >MOCHILA

MOCHINESS >MOCHIE

MOCHS >MOCH

MOCHY same as >MOCHIE

MOCK vb make fun of ▷ adj sham or imitation ▷ n act of mocking

MOCKABLE >MOCK

MOCKADO n imitation velvet

MOCKADOES >MOCKADO

MOCKAGE same as >MOCKERY

MOCKAGES >MOCKAGE

MOCKED >MOCK

MOCKER vb dress up

MOCKERED >MOCKER

MOCKERIES >MOCKERY

MOCKERING >MOCKER

MOCKERNUT n type of smooth-barked hickory with fragrant foliage that turns bright yellow in autumn

MOCKERS >MOCKER

MOCKERY n derision

MOCKING >MOCK

MOCKINGLY >MOCK

MOCKINGS >MOCK

MOCKNEY n person who affects a cockney accent ▷ adj denoting an affected cockney accent or a person who has one

MOCKNEYS >MOCKNEY

MOCKS >MOCK

MOCKTAIL n cocktail without alcohol

MOCKTAILS >MOCKTAIL

MOCKUP n working full-scale model of a machine, apparatus, etc, for testing, research, etc

MOCKUPS >MOCKUP

MOCOCK n Native American birchbark container

MOCOCKS >MOCOCK

MOCS >MOC

MOCUCK same as > MOCOCK
MOCUCKS > MOCUCK
MOCUDDUM same as > MUQADDAM
MOCUDDUMS > MOCUDDUM
MOD n member of a group of young people, orig. in the mid-1960s, who were very clothes-conscious and rode motor scooters ▷ vb modify (a piece of software or hardware)
MODAFINIL n type of drug used as a stimulant
MODAL adj of or relating to mode or manner ▷ n modal word
MODALISM n type of Christian doctrine
MODALISMS > MODALISM
MODALIST > MODALISM
MODALISTS > MODALISM
MODALITY n condition of being modal
MODALLY > MODAL
MODALS > MODAL
MODDED > MOD
MODDER n person who modifies a piece of hardware or software
MODDERS > MODDER
MODDING n practice of modifying a car to alter its appearance or performance
MODDINGS > MODDING
MODE n method or manner
MODEL n (miniature) representation ▷ adj excellent or perfect ▷ vb make a model of
MODELED > MODEL
MODELER > MODEL
MODELERS > MODEL
MODELING same as > MODELLING
MODELINGS > MODELING
MODELIST n person who constructs models
MODELISTS > MODELIST
MODELLED > MODEL
MODELLER > MODEL
MODELLERS > MODEL
MODELLI > MODELLO
MODELLING n act or an instance of making a model
MODELLO n artist's preliminary sketch or model
MODELLOS > MODELLO
MODELS > MODEL
MODEM n device for connecting two computers by a telephone line ▷ vb send or receive by modem
MODEMED > MODEM
MODEMING > MODEM
MODEMS > MODEM
MODENA n popular variety of domestic fancy pigeon originating in Modena
MODENAS > MODENA
MODER n intermediate layer in humus
MODERATE adj not extreme

▷ n person of moderate views ▷ vb make or become less violent or extreme
MODERATED > MODERATE
MODERATES > MODERATE
MODERATO adv at a moderate speed ▷ n moderato piece
MODERATOR n (Presbyterian Church) minister appointed to preside over a Church court, general assembly, etc
MODERATOS > MODERATO
MODERN adj of present or recent times ▷ n contemporary person
MODERNE n the style of architecture and design, prevalent in Europe and the US in the late 1920s and 1930s, typified by the use of straight lines, tubular chromed steel frames, contrasting inlaid woods, etc ▷ adj of or relating to this style of architecture and design
MODERNER > MODERN
MODERNES > MODERNE
MODERNEST > MODERN
MODERNISE same as > MODERNIZE
MODERNISM n (support of) modern tendencies, thoughts, or styles
MODERNIST > MODERNISM
MODERNITY n quality or state of being modern
MODERNIZE vb bring up to date
MODERNLY > MODERN
MODERNS > MODERN
MODERS > MODER
MODES > MODE
MODEST adj not vain or boastful
MODESTER > MODEST
MODESTEST > MODEST
MODESTIES > MODESTY
MODESTLY > MODEST
MODESTY n quality or condition of being modest
MODGE vb do shoddily
MODGED > MODGE
MODGES > MODGE
MODGING > MODGE
MODI > MODUS
MODICA > MODICUM
MODICUM n small quantity
MODICUMS > MODICUM
MODIFIED > MODIFY
MODIFIER n word that qualifies the sense of another
MODIFIERS > MODIFIER
MODIFIES > MODIFY
MODIFY vb change slightly
MODIFYING > MODIFY
MODII > MODIUS
MODILLION n one of a set of ornamental brackets

under a cornice, esp as used in the Corinthian order
MODIOLAR > MODIOLUS
MODIOLI > MODIOLUS
MODIOLUS n central bony pillar of the cochlea
MODISH adj in fashion
MODISHLY > MODISH
MODIST n follower of fashion
MODISTE n fashionable dressmaker or milliner
MODISTES > MODISTE
MODISTS > MODIST
MODIUS n ancient Roman quantity measure
MODIWORT Scots variant of > MOULDWARP
MODIWORTS > MODIWORT
MODS > MOD
MODULAR adj of, consisting of, or resembling a module or modulus ▷ n thing comprised of modules
MODULARLY > MODULAR
MODULARS > MODULAR
MODULATE vb vary in tone
MODULATED > MODULATE
MODULATES > MODULATE
MODULATOR > MODULATE
MODULE n self-contained unit, section, or component with a specific function
MODULES > MODULE
MODULI > MODULUS
MODULO adv with reference to modulus
MODULUS n coefficient expressing a specified property, for instance elasticity, of a specified substance
MODUS n way of doing something
MOE adv more ▷ n a wry face
MOELLON n rubble
MOELLONS > MOELLON
MOER n in South Africa, slang word for the womb ▷ vb in South Africa, attack (someone or something) violently
MOERED > MOER
MOERING > MOER
MOERS > MOER
MOES > MOE
MOFETTE n opening in a region of nearly extinct volcanic activity, through which carbon dioxide, nitrogen, and other gases pass
MOFETTES > MOFETTE
MOFFETTE same as > MOFETTE
MOFFETTES > MOFFETTE
MOFFIE n homosexual ▷ adj homosexual
MOFFIES > MOFFIE
MOFO n offensive term, a shortened form of motherfucker
MOFOS > MOFO
MOFUSSIL n provincial

area in India
MOFUSSILS > MOFUSSIL
MOG vb go away
MOGGAN n stocking without foot
MOGGANS > MOGGAN
MOGGED > MOG
MOGGIE same as > MOGGY
MOGGIES > MOGGY
MOGGING > MOG
MOGGY n cat
MOGHUL same as > MOGUL
MOGHULS > MOGHUL
MOGS > MOG
MOGUL n important or powerful person
MOGULED adj having moguls
MOGULS > MOGUL
MOHAIR n fine hair of the Angora goat
MOHAIRS > MOHAIR
MOHALIM same as > MOHELIM
MOHAWK n half turn from either edge of either skate to the corresponding edge of the other skate
MOHAWKS > MOHAWK
MOHEL n man qualified to conduct circumcisions
MOHELIM > MOHEL
MOHELS > MOHEL
MOHICAN n punk hairstyle
MOHICANS > MOHICAN
MOHR same as > MHORR
MOHRS > MOHR
MOHUA n small New Zealand bird with a yellow head and breast
MOHUAS > MOHUA
MOHUR n former Indian gold coin worth 15 rupees
MOHURS > MOHUR
MOI > ME
MOIDER same as > MOITHER
MOIDERED > MOIDER
MOIDERING > MOIDER
MOIDERS > MOIDER
MOIDORE n former Portuguese gold coin
MOIDORES > MOIDORE
MOIETIES > MOIETY
MOIETY n half
MOIL vb moisten or soil or become moist, soiled, etc ▷ n toil
MOILED > MOIL
MOILER > MOIL
MOILERS > MOIL
MOILING > MOIL
MOILINGLY > MOIL
MOILS > MOIL
MOINEAU n small fortification
MOINEAUS > MOINEAU
MOIRA n fate
MOIRAI > MOIRA
MOIRE adj having a watered or wavelike pattern ▷ n any fabric that has such a pattern
MOIRES > MOIRE**

MOISER n informer
MOISERS > MOISER
MOIST adj slightly wet ▷ vb moisten
MOISTED > MOIST
MOISTEN vb make or become moist
MOISTENED > MOISTEN
MOISTENER > MOISTEN
MOISTENS > MOISTEN
MOISTER > MOIST
MOISTEST > MOIST
MOISTFUL adj full of moisture
MOISTIFY vb moisten
MOISTING > MOIST
MOISTLY > MOIST
MOISTNESS > MOIST
MOISTS > MOIST
MOISTURE n liquid diffused as vapour or condensed in drops
MOISTURES > MOISTURE
MOIT same as > MOTE
MOITHER vb bother or bewilder
MOITHERED > MOITHER
MOITHERS > MOITHER
MOITS > MOIT
MOJARRA n tropical American sea fish
MOJARRAS > MOJARRA
MOJITO n cocktail consisting of rum, lime, mint, and soda water
MOJITOS > MOJITO
MOJO n charm or magic spell
MOJOES > MOJO
MOJOS > MOJO
MOKADDAM same as > MUQADDAM
MOKADDAMS > MOKADDAM
MOKE n donkey
MOKES > MOKE
MOKI n edible sea fish of New Zealand
MOKIHI n Māori raft
MOKIHIS > MOKIHI
MOKIS > MOKI
MOKO n Māori tattoo or tattoo pattern
MOKOMOKO n type of skink found in New Zealand
MOKOMOKOS > MOKOMOKO
MOKOPUNA n grandchild or young person
MOKOPUNAS > MOKOPUNA
MOKORO n (in Botswana) the traditional dugout canoe of the people of the Okavango Delta
MOKOROS > MOKORO
MOKOS > MOKO
MOKSHA n freedom from the endless cycle of transmigration into a state of bliss
MOKSHAS > MOKSHA
MOL n the SI unit mole
MOLA another name for > SUNFISH
MOLAL adj of or consisting of a solution containing

one mole of solute per thousand grams of solvent
MOLALITY n (not in technical usage) a measure of concentration equal to the number of moles of solute in a thousand grams of solvent
MOLAR n large back tooth used for grinding ▷ adj of any of these teeth
MOLARITY n concentration
MOLARS > MOLAR
MOLAS > MOLA
MOLASSE n soft sediment produced by the erosion of mountain ranges after the final phase of mountain building
MOLASSES n dark syrup, a by-product of sugar refining
MOLD same as > MOULD
MOLDABLE > MOLD
MOLDAVITE n green tektite found in the Czech Republic, thought to be the product of an ancient meteorite impact in Germany
MOLDBOARD n curved blade of a plough
MOLDED > MOLD
MOLDER same as > MOULDER
MOLDERED > MOLDER
MOLDERING > MOLDER
MOLDERS > MOLDER
MOLDIER > MOLDY
MOLDIEST > MOLDY
MOLDINESS > MOLDY
MOLDING same as > MOULDING
MOLDINGS > MOLDING
MOLDS > MOLD
MOLDWARP same as > MOULDWARP
MOLDWARPS > MOLDWARP
MOLDY same as > MOULDY
MOLE n small dark raised spot on the skin
MOLECAST n molehill
MOLECASTS > MOLECAST
MOLECULAR adj of or relating to molecules
MOLECULE n simplest freely existing chemical unit, composed of two or more atoms
MOLECULES > MOLECULE
MOLEHILL n small mound of earth thrown up by a burrowing mole
MOLEHILLS > MOLEHILL
MOLES > MOLE
MOLESKIN n dark grey dense velvety pelt of a mole, used as a fur
MOLESKINS npl clothing of moleskin
MOLEST vb interfere with sexually
MOLESTED > MOLEST
MOLESTER > MOLEST

MOLESTERS > MOLEST
MOLESTFUL adj molesting
MOLESTING > MOLEST
MOLESTS > MOLEST
MOLIES > MOLY
MOLIMEN n effort needed to perform bodily function
MOLIMENS > MOLIMEN
MOLINE adj (of a cross) having arms of equal length, forked and curved back at the ends ▷ n moline cross
MOLINES > MOLINE
MOLINET n stick for whipping chocolate
MOLINETS > MOLINET
MOLL n gangster's female accomplice
MOLLA same as > MOLLAH
MOLLAH same as > MULLAH
MOLLAHS > MOLLAH
MOLLAS > MOLLA
MOLLIE same as > MOLLY
MOLLIES > MOLLY
MOLLIFIED > MOLLIFY
MOLLIFIER > MOLLIFY
MOLLIFIES > MOLLIFY
MOLLIFY vb pacify or soothe
MOLLITIES n softness
MOLLS > MOLL
MOLLUSC n soft-bodied, usu. hard-shelled, animal, such as a snail or oyster
MOLLUSCA n molluscs collectively
MOLLUSCAN > MOLLUSC
MOLLUSCS > MOLLUSC
MOLLUSCUM n viral skin infection
MOLLUSK same as > MOLLUSC
MOLLUSKAN > MOLLUSK
MOLLUSKS > MOLLUSK
MOLLY n brightly coloured tropical or subtropical American freshwater fish
MOLLYHAWK n juvenile of the southern black-backed gull
MOLLYMAWK informal name for > MALLEMUCK
MOLOCH n spiny Australian desert-living lizard that feeds on ants
MOLOCHISE vb sacrifice to deity
MOLOCHIZE same as > MOLOCHISE
MOLOCHS > MOLOCH
MOLOSSI > MOLOSSUS
MOLOSSUS n division of metre in poetry
MOLS > MOL
MOLT same as > MOULT
MOLTED > MOLT
MOLTEN > MELT
MOLTENLY > MELT
MOLTER > MOLT
MOLTERS > MOLT
MOLTING > MOLT
MOLTO adv very
MOLTS > MOLT

MOLY n magic herb given by Hermes to Odysseus to nullify the spells of Circe
MOLYBDATE n salt or ester of a molybdic acid
MOLYBDIC adj of or containing molybdenum in the trivalent or hexavalent state
MOLYBDOUS adj of or containing molybdenum, esp in a low valence state
MOM same as > MOTHER
MOME n fool
MOMENT n short space of time
MOMENTA > MOMENTUM
MOMENTANY same as > MOMENTARY
MOMENTARY adj lasting only a moment
MOMENTLY same as > MOMENT
MOMENTO same as > MEMENTO
MOMENTOES > MOMENTO
MOMENTOS > MOMENTO
MOMENTOUS adj of great significance
MOMENTS > MOMENT
MOMENTUM n impetus to go forward, develop, or get stronger
MOMENTUMS > MOMENTUM
MOMES > MOME
MOMI same as > MOM
MOMISM n excessive domination of a child by his or her mother
MOMISMS > MOMISM
MOMMA same as > MAMMA
MOMMAS > MOMMA
MOMMET same as > MAMMET
MOMMETS > MOMMET
MOMMIES > MOMMY
MOMMY same as > MOM
MOMS > MOM
MOMSER same as > MOMZER
MOMSERS > MOMSER
MOMUS n person who ridicules
MOMUSES > MOMUS
MOMZER same as > MAMZER
MOMZERIM > MOMZER
MOMZERS > MOMZER
MON dialect variant of > MAN
MONA n W African guenon monkey with dark fur on the back and white or yellow underparts
MONACHAL less common word for > MONASTIC
MONACHISM > MONACHAL
MONACHIST > MONACHAL
MONACID same as > MONOACID
MONACIDIC same as > MONOACID
MONACIDS > MONOACID
MONACT adj (of sponge) with single-spiked structures in skeleton
MONACTINE > MONACT
MONAD n any fundamental

singular metaphysical entity

MONADAL > MONAD

MONADES > MONAS

MONADIC *adj* being or relating to a monad

MONADICAL > MONAD

MONADISM *n* (esp in the writings of Gottfried Leibnitz, the German rationalist philosopher and mathematician (1646-1716)) the philosophical doctrine that monads are the ultimate units of reality

MONADISMS > MONADISM

MONADNOCK *n* residual hill that consists of hard rock in an otherwise eroded area

MONADS > MONAD

MONAL *n* S Asian pheasant, the male of which has a brilliantly coloured plumage

MONALS > MONAL

MONANDRY *n* preference of only one male sexual partner over a period of time

MONARCH *n* sovereign ruler of a state

MONARCHAL > MONARCH

MONARCHIC > MONARCH

MONARCHS > MONARCH

MONARCHY *n* government by or a state ruled by a sovereign

MONARDA *n* mintlike N American plant

MONARDAS > MONARDA

MONAS *same as* > MONAD

MONASES > MONAS

MONASTERY *n* residence of a community of monks

MONASTIC *adj* of monks, nuns, or monasteries ▷ *n* person who is committed to this way of life, esp a monk

MONASTICS > MONASTIC

MONATOMIC *adj* consisting of single atoms

MONAUL *same as* > MONAL

MONAULS > MONAUL

MONAURAL *adj* relating to, having, or hearing with only one ear

MONAXIAL *another word for* > UNIAXIAL

MONAXON *n* type of sponge

MONAXONIC > MONAXON

MONAXONS > MONAXON

MONAZITE *n* yellow to reddish-brown mineral consisting of a phosphate of thorium, cerium, and lanthanum in monoclinic crystalline form

MONAZITES > MONAZITE

MONDAIN *n* man who moves in fashionable society ▷ *adj* characteristic of fashionable society

MONDAINE *n* woman who moves in fashionable

society ▷ *adj* characteristic of fashionable society

MONDAINES > MONDAINE

MONDAINS > MONDAIN

MONDE *n* French word meaning world or society

MONDES > MONDE

MONDIAL *adj* of or involving the whole world

MONDO *n* Buddhist questioning technique

MONDOS > MONDO

MONECIAN *same as* > MONECIOUS

MONECIOUS *adj* (of some flowering plants) having the male and female reproductive organs in separate flowers on the same plant

MONELLIN *n* sweet protein

MONELLINS > MONELLIN

MONEME *less common word for* > MORPHEME

MONEMES > MONEME

MONER *n* hypothetical simple organism

MONERA > MONER

MONERAN *n* type of bacterium

MONERANS > MONERAN

MONERGISM *n* Christian doctrine on spiritual regeneration

MONERON *same as* > MONER

MONETARY *adj* of money or currency

MONETH *same as* > MONTH

MONETHS > MONETH

MONETISE *same as* > MONETIZE

MONETISED > MONETISE

MONETISES > MONETISE

MONETIZE *vb* establish as the legal tender of a country

MONETIZED > MONETIZE

MONETIZES > MONETIZE

MONEY *n* medium of exchange, coins or banknotes

MONEYBAG *n* bag for money

MONEYBAGS *n* very rich person

MONEYED *adj* rich

MONEYER *n* person who coins money

MONEYERS > MONEYER

MONEYLESS > MONEY

MONEYMAN *n* person supplying money

MONEYMEN > MONEYMAN

MONEYS > MONEY

MONEYWORT *n* European and N American creeping plant with round leaves and yellow flowers

MONG *n* stupid or foolish person

MONGCORN *same as* > MASLIN

MONGCORNS > MONGCORN

MONGED *adj* under the influence of drugs

MONGEESE > MONGOOSE

MONGER *n* trader or dealer ▷ *vb* deal in

MONGERED > MONGER

MONGERIES > MONGER

MONGERING > MONGER

MONGERS > MONGER

MONGERY > MONGER

MONGO *same as* > MUNGO

MONGOE *same as* > MONGO

MONGOES > MONGOE

MONGOL *adj* offensive word for a person affected by Down's syndrome

MONGOLIAN *adj* offensive term meaning affected by Down's syndrome

MONGOLISM > MONGOL

MONGOLOID *adj* offensive term meaning characterized by Down's syndrome ▷ *n* offensive word for a person affected by Down's syndrome

MONGOLS > MONGOL

MONGOOSE *n* stoatlike mammal of Asia and Africa that kills snakes

MONGOOSES > MONGOOSE

MONGOS > MONGO

MONGREL *n* animal, esp a dog, of mixed breed ▷ *adj* of mixed breed or origin

MONGRELLY > MONGREL

MONGRELS > MONGREL

MONGS > MONG

MONGST *short for* > AMONGST

MONIAL *n* mullion

MONIALS > MONIAL

MONICKER *same as* > MONIKER

MONICKERS > MONICKER

MONIE *Scots word for* > MANY

MONIED *same as* > MONEYED

MONIES > MONEY

MONIKER *n* person's name or nickname

MONIKERS > MONIKER

MONILIA *n* type of fungus

MONILIAL *adj* denoting a thrush infection caused by a fungus

MONILIAS > MONILIA

MONIMENT *same as* > MONUMENT

MONIMENTS > MONIMENT

MONIPLIES *same as* > MANYPLIES

MONISH *same as* > ADMONISH

MONISHED > MONISH

MONISHES > MONISH

MONISHING > MONISH

MONISM *n* doctrine that reality consists of only one basic substance or element, such as mind or matter

MONISMS > MONISM

MONIST > MONISM

MONISTIC > MONISM

MONISTS > MONISM

MONITIONS > MONITION

MONITIVE *adj* reproving

MONITOR *n* person or device that checks, controls, warns, or keeps a record of something ▷ *vb* watch and check on

MONITORED > MONITOR

MONITORS > MONITOR

MONITORY *adj* acting as or giving a warning ▷ *n* letter containing a monition

MONITRESS > MONITOR

MONK *n* member of an all-male religious community bound by vows

MONKERIES > MONKERY

MONKERY *n* derogatory word for monastic life or practices

MONKEY *n* long-tailed primate ▷ *vb* meddle or fool

MONKEYED > MONKEY

MONKEYING > MONKEY

MONKEYISH > MONKEY

MONKEYISM *n* practice of behaving like monkey

MONKEYPOD *n* Central American tree

MONKEYPOT *n* type of tropical tree

MONKEYS > MONKEY

MONKFISH *n* type of fish

MONKHOOD *n* condition of being a monk

MONKHOODS > MONKHOOD

MONKISH *adj* of, relating to, or resembling a monk or monks

MONKISHLY > MONKISH

MONKS > MONK

MONKSHOOD *n* poisonous plant with hooded flowers

MONO *n* monophonic sound

MONOACID *adj* a base which is capable of reacting with only one molecule of a monobasic acid

MONOACIDS > MONOACID

MONOAMINE *n* substance, such as adrenaline, noradrenaline, or serotonin, that contains a single amine group

MONOAO *n* New Zealand plant with rigid leaves

MONOAOS > MONOAO

MONOBASIC *adj* (of an acid, such as hydrogen chloride) having only one replaceable hydrogen atom per molecule

MONOBROW *n* appearance of a single eyebrow as a result of the eyebrows joining above a person's nose

MONOBROWS > MONOBROW

MONOCARP *n* plant that is monocarpic

MONOCARPS > MONOCARP

MONOCEROS n faint constellation on the celestial equator crossed by the Milky Way and lying close to Orion and Canis Major

MONOCHORD n instrument employed in acoustic analysis or investigation, consisting usually of one string stretched over a resonator of wood

MONOCLE n eyeglass for one eye only

MONOCLED >MONOCLE

MONOCLES >MONOCLE

MONOCLINE n fold in stratified rocks in which the strata are inclined in the same direction from the horizontal

MONOCOQUE n vehicle body moulded from a single piece of material with no separate load-bearing parts ▷ adj of or relating to the design characteristic of a monocoque

MONOCOT n type of flowering plant with a single embryonic seed leaf, such as grasses, lilies, palms, and orchids

MONOCOTS >MONOCOT

MONOCOTYL same as >MONOCOT

MONOCRACY n government by one person

MONOCRAT >MONOCRACY

MONOCRATS >MONOCRACY

MONOCULAR adj having or for one eye only ▷ n device for use with one eye, such as a field glass

MONOCYCLE another name for >UNICYCLE

MONOCYTE n large phagocytic leucocyte with a spherical nucleus and clear cytoplasm

MONOCYTES >MONOCYTE

MONOCYTIC >MONOCYTE

MONODIC >MONODY

MONODICAL >MONODY

MONODIES >MONODY

MONODIST >MONODY

MONODISTS >MONODY

MONODONT adj (of certain animals, esp the male narwhal) having a single tooth throughout life

MONODRAMA n play or other dramatic piece for a single performer

MONODY n (in Greek tragedy) an ode sung by a single actor

MONOECIES >MONOECY

MONOECISM n being both male and female

MONOECY same as >MONOECISM

MONOESTER n type of ester

MONOFIL n synthetic thread or yarn composed of a single strand rather than twisted fibres

MONOFILS >MONOFIL

MONOFUEL n single type of fuel

MONOFUELS >MONOFUEL

MONOGAMIC >MONOGAMY

MONOGAMY n custom of being married to one person at a time

MONOGENIC adj of or relating to an inherited character difference that is controlled by a single gene

MONOGENY n the hypothetical descent of all organisms from a single cell or organism

MONOGERM adj containing single seed

MONOGLOT n person speaking only one language

MONOGLOTS >MONOGLOT

MONOGONY n asexual reproduction

MONOGRAM n design of combined letters, esp a person's initials ▷ vb decorate (clothing, stationery, etc) with a monogram

MONOGRAMS >MONOGRAM

MONOGRAPH n book or paper on a single subject ▷ vb write a monograph on

MONOGYNY n custom of having only one female sexual partner over a period of time

MONOHULL n sailing vessel with a single hull

MONOHULLS >MONOHULL

MONOICOUS adj (of some flowering plants) having the male and female reproductive organs in separate flowers on the same plant

MONOKINE n type of protein

MONOKINES >MONOKINE

MONOKINI n bottom half of bikini

MONOKINIS >MONOKINI

MONOLATER >MONOLATRY

MONOLATRY n exclusive worship of one god without excluding the existence of others

MONOLAYER n single layer of atoms or molecules adsorbed on a surface

MONOLINE adj as in monoline insurer insurer who pays the principal and interest on a bond in the event of a default

MONOLITH n large upright block of stone

MONOLITHS >MONOLITH

MONOLOG same as >MONOLOGUE

MONOLOGIC >MONOLOGUE

MONOLOGS >MONOLOG

MONOLOGUE n long speech by one person

MONOLOGY >MONOLOGUE

MONOMACHY n combat between two individuals

MONOMANIA n obsession with one thing

MONOMARK n series of letters or figures to identify goods, personal articles, etc

MONOMARKS >MONOMARK

MONOMER n compound whose molecules can join together to form a polymer

MONOMERIC >MONOMER

MONOMERS >MONOMER

MONOMETER n line of verse consisting of one metrical foot

MONOMIAL n expression consisting of a single term, such as $5ax$ ▷ adj consisting of a single algebraic term

MONOMIALS >MONOMIAL

MONOMODE adj denoting or relating to a type of optical fibre with a core less than 10 micrometres in diameter

MONONYM n person who is famous enough to be known only by one name, usually the first name

MONONYMS >MONONYM

MONOPHAGY n feeding on only one type of food

MONOPHASE adj having single alternating electric current

MONOPHONY >MONO

MONOPHYLY n group of ancestor and all descendants

MONOPITCH adj (of roof) having only one slope

MONOPLANE n aeroplane with one pair of wings

MONOPLOID less common word for >HAPLOID

MONOPOD same as >MONOPODE

MONOPODE n member of a legendary one-legged race of Africa

MONOPODES >MONOPODE

MONOPODIA n plural of monopodium: the main axis of growth in the pine tree and similar plants: the main stem, which elongates from the tip and gives rise to lateral branches

MONOPODS >MONOPOD

MONOPODY n single-foot measure in poetry

MONOPOLE n magnetic pole considered in isolation

MONOPOLES >MONOPOLE

MONOPOLY n exclusive possession of or right to do something

MONOPSONY n situation in which the entire market

demand for a product or service consists of only one buyer

MONOPTERA n plural of monopteron: circular classical building, esp a temple, that has a single ring of columns surrounding it

MONOPTOTE n word with only one form

MONOPULSE n radar transmitting single pulse only

MONORAIL n single-rail railway

MONORAILS >MONORAIL

MONORCHID adj having only one testicle ▷ n animal or person with only one testicle

MONORHINE adj having single nostril

MONORHYME n poem in which all lines rhyme

MONOS >MONO

MONOSEMY n fact of having only a single meaning

MONOSES >MONOSIS

MONOSIES >MONOSY

MONOSIS n abnormal separation

MONOSKI n wide ski on which the skier stands with both feet ▷ vb ski on a monoski

MONOSKIED >MONOSKI

MONOSKIER >MONOSKI

MONOSKIS >MONOSKI

MONOSOME n unpaired chromosome, esp an X-chromosome in an otherwise diploid cell

MONOSOMES >MONOSOME

MONOSOMIC >MONOSOME

MONOSOMY n condition with missing pair of chromosomes

MONOSTELE n type of plant tissue

MONOSTELY >MONOSTELE

MONOSTICH n poem of a single line

MONOSTOME adj having only one mouth, pore, or similar opening

MONOSTYLE adj having single shaft

MONOSY same as >MONOSIS

MONOTASK vb perform only one task at a time

MONOTASKS >MONOTASK

MONOTINT n black-and-white photograph or transparency

MONOTINTS >MONOTINT

MONOTONE n unvaried pitch in speech or sound ▷ adj unvarying ▷ vb speak in monotone

MONOTONED >MONOTONE

MONOTONES >MONOTONE

MONOTONIC same as
>MONOTONE

MONOTONY n wearisome
routine, dullness

MONOTREME n type of
primitive egg-laying
toothless mammal of
Australia and New Guinea

MONOTROCH n
wheelbarrow

MONOTYPE n single print
made from a metal or glass
plate on which a picture
has been painted

MONOTYPES >MONOTYPE

MONOTYPIC adj (of a genus
or species) consisting of
only one type of animal or
plant

MONOVULAR adj of single
ovum

MONOXIDE n oxide that
contains one oxygen atom
per molecule

MONOXIDES >MONOXIDE

MONOXYLON n canoe made
from one log

MONS >MON

MONSIEUR n French title of
address equivalent to sir or
Mr

MONSIGNOR n
ecclesiastical title attached
to certain offices or
distinctions usually
bestowed by the Pope

MONSOON n seasonal wind
of SE Asia

MONSOONAL >MONSOON

MONSOONS >MONSOON

MONSTER n imaginary, usu.
frightening, beast ▷ adj
huge ▷ vb criticize (a
person or group) severely

MONSTERA n type of
tropical climbing plant,
sometimes grown as a
greenhouse or pot plant for
its unusual leathery
perforated leaves

MONSTERAS >MONSTERA

MONSTERED >MONSTER

MONSTERS >MONSTER

MONSTROUS adj unnatural
or ugly

MONTADALE n breed of
sheep

MONTAGE n (making of) a
picture composed from
pieces of others ▷ vb make
as montage

MONTAGED >MONTAGE

MONTAGES >MONTAGE

MONTAGING >MONTAGE

MONTAN as in montan wax
hard wax obtained from
lignite and peat used in
polishes and candles

MONTANE n area of
mountain dominated by
vegetation ▷ adj of or
inhabiting mountainous
regions

MONTANES >MONTANE

MONTANT n vertical part in

woodwork

MONTANTO n rising blow

MONTANTOS >MONTANTO

MONTANTS >MONTANT

MONTARIA n Brazilian
canoe

MONTARIAS >MONTARIA

MONTE n gambling card
game of Spanish origin

MONTEITH n large
ornamental bowl, usually
of silver, for cooling
wineglasses, which are
suspended from the
notched rim

MONTEITHS >MONTEITH

MONTEM n former
money-raising practice at
Eton school

MONTEMS >MONTEM

MONTERO n round cap with
a flap at the back worn by
hunters, esp in Spain in the
17th and 18th centuries

MONTEROS >MONTERO

MONTES >MONTE

MONTH n one of the twelve
divisions of the calendar
year

MONTHLIES >MONTHLY

MONTHLING n month-old
child

MONTHLONG adj lasting all
month

MONTHLY adj happening or
payable once a month
▷ adv once a month ▷ n
monthly magazine

MONTHS >MONTH

MONTICLE same as
>MONTICULE

MONTICLES >MONTICLE

MONTICULE n small hill or
mound, such as a
secondary volcanic cone

MONTIES >MONTY

MONTRE n pipes of organ

MONTRES >MONTRE

MONTURE n mount or
frame

MONTURES >MONTURE

MONTY n complete form of
something

MONUMENT n something,
esp a building or statue,
that commemorates
something

MONUMENTS >MONUMENT

MONURON n type of
weedkiller

MONURONS >MONURON

MONY Scot word for >MANY

MONYPLIES same as
>MANYPLIES

MONZONITE n
coarse-grained plutonic
igneous rock consisting of
equal amounts of
plagioclase and orthoclase
feldspar, with
ferromagnesian minerals

MOO n long deep cry of a cow
▷ vb make this noise ▷ interj
instance or imitation of this
sound

MOOBS n overdeveloped
breasts on a man, caused
by excess weight or lack of
exercise

MOOCH vb loiter about
aimlessly

MOOCHED >MOOCH

MOOCHER >MOOCH

MOOCHERS >MOOCH

MOOCHES >MOOCH

MOOCHING >MOOCH

MOOD n temporary (gloomy)
state of mind

MOODIED >MOODY

MOODIER >MOODY

MOODIES >MOODY

MOODIEST >MOODY

MOODILY >MOODY

MOODINESS >MOODY

MOODS >MOOD

MOODY adj sullen or gloomy
▷ vb flatter

MOODYING >MOODY

MOOED >MOO

MOOI adj pleasing or nice

MOOING >MOO

MOOK n person regarded
with contempt, esp a
stupid person

MOOKS >MOOK

MOOKTAR same as
>MUKHTAR

MOOKTARS >MOOKTAR

MOOL same as >MOULD

MOOLA same as >MOOLAH

MOOLAH slang word for
>MONEY

MOOLAHS >MOOLAH

MOOLAS >MOOLA

MOOLED >MOOL

MOOLEY same as >MOOLY

MOOLEYS >MOOLEY

MOOLI n type of large white
radish

MOOLIES >MOOLY

MOOLING >MOOL

MOOLIS >MOOLI

MOOLOO n person from the
Waikato

MOOLOOS >MOOLOO

MOOLS >MOOL

MOOLVI same as
>MOOLVIE

MOOLVIE n (esp in India) a
Muslim doctor of the law,
teacher, or learned man
also used as a title of
respect

MOOLVIES >MOOLVIE

MOOLVIS >MOOLVI

MOOLY same as >MULEY

MOON n natural satellite of
the earth ▷ vb be idle in a
listless or dreamy way

MOONBEAM n ray of
moonlight

MOONBEAMS >MOONBEAM

MOONBLIND adj (in
horses), having a disorder
which causes inflammation
of the eyes and sometimes
blindness

MOONBOW n rainbow made
by moonlight

MOONBOWS >MOONBOW

MOONCAKE n type of round
Chinese cake

MOONCAKES >MOONCAKE

MOONCALF n born fool

MOONCHILD n someone
who is born under the
Cancer star sign

MOONDUST n dust on
surface of moon

MOONDUSTS >MOONDUST

MOONED adj decorated with
a moon

MOONER >MOON

MOONERS >MOON

MOONEYE n N American
large-eyed freshwater fish

MOONEYES >MOONEYE

MOONFACE n big round
face ▷ vb have a moon face

MOONFACED >MOONFACE

MOONFACES >MOONFACE

MOONFISH n any of several
deep-bodied silvery
carangid fishes, occurring
in warm and tropical
American coastal waters

MOONG as in moong bean
kind of bean

MOONIER >MOONY

MOONIES >MOONY

MOONIEST >MOONY

MOONILY >MOONY

MOONINESS >MOONY

MOONING >MOON

MOONISH >MOON

MOONISHLY >MOON

MOONLESS >MOON

MOONLET n small moon

MOONLETS >MOONLET

MOONLIGHT n light from
the moon ▷ adj illuminated
by the moon ▷ vb work at a
secondary job, esp illegally

MOONLIKE >MOON

MOONLIT adj illuminated
by the moon

MOONPHASE n phase of
moon

MOONPORT n place from
which flights leave for moon

MOONPORTS >MOONPORT

MOONQUAKE n light tremor
of the moon, detected on
the moon's surface

MOONRAKER n small
square sail set above a
skysail

MOONRISE n moment
when the moon appears
above the horizon

MOONRISES >MOONRISE

MOONROCK n rock from
moon

MOONROCKS >MOONROCK

MOONROOF same as
>SUNROOF

MOONROOFS >MOONROOF

MOONS >MOON

MOONSAIL n small sail
high on mast

MOONSAILS >MOONSAIL

MOONSCAPE n surface of
the moon or a picture or
model of it

MOONSEED n type of climbing plant with red or black fruits and crescent-shaped or ring-shaped seeds

MOONSEEDS > MOONSEED

MOONSET n moment when the moon disappears below the horizon

MOONSETS > MOONSET

MOONSHEE same as > MUNSHI

MOONSHEES > MOONSHEE

MOONSHINE same as > MOONLIGHT

MOONSHINY > MOONSHINE

MOONSHOT n launching of a spacecraft to the moon

MOONSHOTS > MOONSHOT

MOONSTONE n translucent semiprecious stone

MOONWALK n instance of walking on moon

MOONWALKS > MOONWALK

MOONWARD adj towards moon

MOONWARDS adv towards moon

MOONWORT n type of fern with crescent-shaped leaflets

MOONWORTS > MOONWORT

MOONY adj dreamy or listless ▷ n crazy or foolish person

MOOP same as > MOUP

MOOPED > MOOP

MOOPING > MOOP

MOOPS > MOOP

MOOR n tract of open uncultivated ground covered with grass and heather ▷ vb secure (a ship) with ropes etc

MOORAGE n place for mooring a vessel

MOORAGES > MOORAGE

MOORBURN n practice of burning off old growth on a heather moor to encourage new growth for grazing

MOORBURNS > MOORBURN

MOORCOCK n male of the red grouse

MOORCOCKS > MOORCOCK

MOORED > MOOR

MOORFOWL n red grouse

MOORFOWLS > MOORFOWL

MOORHEN n small black water bird

MOORHENS > MOORHEN

MOORIER > MOOR

MOORIEST > MOOR

MOORILL n disease of cattle on moors

MOORILLS > MOORILL

MOORING n place for mooring a ship

MOORINGS npl ropes and anchors used in mooring a vessel

MOORISH adj of or relating to the Moor people of North Africa

MOORLAND n area of moor

MOORLANDS > MOORLAND

MOORLOG n rotted wood below surface of moor

MOORLOGS > MOORLOG

MOORMAN n person living on moor

MOORMEN > MOORMAN

MOORS > MOOR

MOORVA same as > MURVA

MOORVAS > MOORVA

MOORWORT n low-growing pink-flowered shrub that grows in peaty bogs

MOORWORTS > MOORWORT

MOORY > MOOR

MOOS > MOO

MOOSE n large N American deer

MOOSEBIRD n North American jay

MOOSEWOOD n North American tree

MOOSEYARD n place where moose spend winter

MOOT adj debatable ▷ vb bring up for discussion ▷ n (in Anglo-Saxon England) a local administrative assembly

MOOTABLE > MOOT

MOOTED > MOOT

MOOTER > MOOT

MOOTERS > MOOT

MOOTEST > MOOT

MOOTING > MOOT

MOOTINGS > MOOT

MOOTMAN n person taking part in moot

MOOTMEN > MOOTMAN

MOOTNESS > MOOT

MOOTS > MOOT

MOOVE same as > MOVE

MOOVED > MOOVE

MOOVES > MOOVE

MOOVING > MOOVE

MOP n long stick with twists of cotton or a sponge on the end, used for cleaning ▷ vb clean or soak up with or as if with a mop

MOPANE same as > MOPANI

MOPANES > MOPANE

MOPANI n S African tree that is highly resistant to drought and produces very hard wood

MOPANIS > MOPANI

MOPBOARD n wooden border fixed round the base of an interior wall

MOPBOARDS > MOPBOARD

MOPE vb be gloomy and apathetic ▷ n gloomy person

MOPED n light motorized cycle

MOPEDS > MOPED

MOPEHAWK same as > MOPOKE

MOPEHAWKS > MOPEHAWK

MOPER > MOPE

MOPERIES > MOPERY

MOPERS > MOPE

MOPERY n gloominess

MOPES > MOPE

MOPEY > MOPE

MOPHEAD n person with shaggy hair

MOPHEADS > MOPHEAD

MOPIER > MOPE

MOPIEST > MOPE

MOPILY > MOPY

MOPINESS > MOPE

MOPING > MOPE

MOPINGLY > MOPE

MOPISH > MOPE

MOPISHLY > MOPE

MOPOKE n species of owl

MOPOKES > MOPOKE

MOPPED > MOP

MOPPER > MOP

MOPPERS > MOP

MOPPET same as > POPPET

MOPPETS > MOPPET

MOPPIER > MOPPY

MOPPIEST > MOPPY

MOPPING > MOP

MOPPY adj drunk

MOPS > MOP

MOPSIES > MOPSY

MOPSTICK n mop handle

MOPSTICKS > MOPSTICK

MOPSY n untidy or dowdy person

MOPUS n person who mopes

MOPUSES > MOPUS

MOPY > MOPE

MOQUETTE n thick velvety fabric used for carpets and upholstery

MOQUETTES > MOQUETTE

MOR n layer of acidic humus formed in cool moist areas where decomposition is slow

MORA n quantity of a short syllable in verse

MORACEOUS adj relating to a mostly tropical and subtropical family of trees and shrubs which includes the mulberry, fig, and breadfruit

MORAE > MORA

MORAINAL > MORAINE

MORAINE n accumulated mass of debris deposited by a glacier

MORAINES > MORAINE

MORAINIC > MORAINE

MORAL adj concerned with right and wrong conduct ▷ n lesson to be obtained from a story or event ▷ vb moralize

MORALE n degree of confidence or hope of a person or group

MORALES > MORALE

MORALISE same as > MORALIZE

MORALISED > MORALISE

MORALISER > MORALISE

MORALISES > MORALISE

MORALISM n habit or practice of moralizing

MORALISMS > MORALISM

MORALIST n person with a strong sense of right and wrong

MORALISTS > MORALIST

MORALITY n good moral conduct

MORALIZE vb make moral pronouncements

MORALIZED > MORALIZE

MORALIZER > MORALIZE

MORALIZES > MORALIZE

MORALL same as > MURAL

MORALLED > MORALL

MORALLER > MORAL

MORALLERS > MORAL

MORALLING > MORALL

MORALLS > MORALL

MORALLY > MORAL

MORALS > MORAL

MORAS > MORA

MORASS n marsh

MORASSES > MORASS

MORASSY > MORASS

MORAT n drink containing mulberry juice

MORATORIA n plural form of singular moratorium: legally authorized postponement of the fulfilment of an obligation

MORATORY > MORATORIA

MORATS > MORAT

MORAY n large voracious eel

MORAYS > MORAY

MORBID adj unduly interested in death or unpleasant events

MORBIDER > MORBID

MORBIDEST > MORBID

MORBIDITY n state of being morbid

MORBIDLY > MORBID

MORBIFIC adj causing disease

MORBILLI same as > MEASLES

MORBUS n disease

MORBUSES > MORBUS

MORCEAU n fragment or morsel

MORCEAUX > MORCEAU

MORCHA n (in India) a hostile demonstration against the government

MORCHAS > MORCHA

MORDACITY n quality of sarcasm

MORDANCY > MORDANT

MORDANT adj sarcastic or scathing ▷ n substance used to fix dyes ▷ vb treat (a fabric, yarn, etc) with a mordant

MORDANTED > MORDANT

MORDANTLY > MORDANT

MORDANTS > MORDANT

MORDENT n melodic ornament consisting of the rapid alternation of a note with a note one degree lower than it

MORDENTS > MORDENT

MORE adj greater in amount

or degree ▷ *adv* greater extent ▷ *pron* greater or additional amount or number

MOREEN *n* heavy, usually watered, fabric of wool or wool and cotton, used esp in furnishing

MOREENS >MOREEN

MOREISH *adj* (of food) causing a desire for more

MOREL *n* edible mushroom with a pitted cap

MORELLE *n* nightshade

MORELLES >MORELLE

MORELLO *n* variety of small very dark sour cherry

MORELLOS >MORELLO

MORELS >MOREL

MORENDO *adv* (in music) dying away

MORENESS >MORE

MOREOVER *adv* in addition to what has already been said

MOREPORK *same as* >MOPOKE

MOREPORKS >MOREPORK

MORES *npl* customs and conventions embodying the fundamental values of a community

MORESQUE *adj* (esp of decoration and architecture) of Moorish style ▷ *n* Moorish design or decoration

MORESQUES >MORESQUE

MORGAN *n* American breed of small compact saddle horse

MORGANITE *n* pink variety of beryl, used as a gemstone

MORGANS >MORGAN

MORGAY *n* small dogfish

MORGAYS >MORGAY

MORGEN *n* South African unit of area, equal to about two acres or 0.8 hectare

MORGENS >MORGEN

MORGUE *same as* >MORTUARY

MORGUES >MORGUE

MORIA *n* folly

MORIAS >MORIA

MORIBUND *adj* without force or vitality

MORICHE *same as* >MIRITI

MORICHES >MORICHE

MORION *n* 16th-century helmet with a brim and wide comb

MORIONS >MORION

MORISCO *n* a morris dance

MORISCOES >MORISCO

MORISCOS >MORISCO

MORISH *same as* >MOREISH

MORKIN *n* animal dying in accident

MORKINS >MORKIN

MORLING *n* sheep killed by disease

MORLINGS >MORLING

MORMAOR *n* former high-ranking Scottish nobleman

MORMAORS >MORMAOR

MORN *n* morning

MORNAY *adj* served with a cheese sauce

MORNAYS >MORNAY

MORNE *same as* >MOURN

MORNED >MORNE

MORNES >MORNE

MORNING *n* part of the day before noon

MORNINGS >MORNING

MORNS >MORN

MOROCCO *n* goatskin leather

MOROCCOS >MOROCCO

MORON *n* foolish or stupid person

MORONIC >MORON

MORONISM >MORON

MORONISMS >MORON

MORONITY >MORON

MORONS >MORON

MOROSE *adj* sullen or moody

MOROSELY >MOROSE

MOROSER >MOROSE

MOROSEST >MOROSE

MOROSITY >MOROSE

MORPH *n* phonological representation of a morpheme ▷ *vb* undergo or cause to undergo morphing

MORPHEAN *adj* of or relating to Morpheus, the god of sleep and dreams

MORPHED >MORPH

MORPHEME *n* speech element having a meaning or grammatical function that cannot be subdivided into further such elements

MORPHEMES >MORPHEME

MORPHEMIC >MORPHEME

MORPHETIC *same as* >MORPHEAN

MORPHEW *n* blemish on skin

MORPHEWS >MORPHEW

MORPHIA *same as* >MORPHINE

MORPHIAS >MORPHIA

MORPHIC *as in morphic resonance* idea that, through a telepathic effect or sympathetic vibration, an event or act can lead to similar events or acts in the future or an idea conceived in one mind can then arise in another

MORPHIN *variant form of* >MORPHINE

MORPHINE *n* drug extracted from opium, used as an anaesthetic and sedative

MORPHINES >MORPHINE

MORPHING *n* computer technique used for graphics and in films, in which one image is gradually transformed into another

image without individual changes being noticeable in the process

MORPHINGS >MORPHING

MORPHINIC >MORPHINE

MORPHINS >MORPHINE

MORPHO *n* type of butterfly

MORPHOGEN *n* chemical in body that influences growth

MORPHOS >MORPHO

MORPHOSES >MORPHOSIS

MORPHOSIS *n* development in an organism or its parts characterized by structural change

MORPHOTIC >MORPHOSIS

MORPHS >MORPH

MORRA *same as* >MORA

MORRAS >MORRA

MORRELL *n* tall SW Australian eucalyptus with pointed buds

MORRELLS >MORRELL

MORRHUA *n* cod

MORRHUAS >MORRHUA

MORRICE *same as* >MORRIS

MORRICES >MORRICE

MORRION *same as* >MORION

MORRIONS >MORRION

MORRIS *vb* perform morris dance

MORRISED >MORRIS

MORRISES >MORRIS

MORRISING >MORRIS

MORRO *n* rounded hill or promontory

MORROS >MORRO

MORROW *n* next day

MORROWS >MORROW

MORS >MOR

MORSAL >MORSURE

MORSE *n* clasp or fastening on a cope

MORSEL *n* small piece, esp of food ▷ *vb* divide into morsels

MORSELED >MORSEL

MORSELING >MORSEL

MORSELLED >MORSEL

MORSELS >MORSEL

MORSES >MORSE

MORSURE *n* bite

MORSURES >MORSURE

MORT *n* call blown on a hunting horn to signify the death of the animal hunted

MORTAL *adj* subject to death ▷ *n* human being

MORTALISE *same as* >MORTALIZE

MORTALITY *n* state of being mortal

MORTALIZE *vb* make mortal

MORTALLY >MORTAL

MORTALS >MORTAL

MORTAR *n* small cannon with a short range ▷ *vb* fire

on with mortars

MORTARED >MORTAR

MORTARING >MORTAR

MORTARMAN *n* person firing mortar

MORTARMEN >MORTAR

MORTARS >MORTAR

MORTARY *adj* of or like mortar

MORTBELL *n* bell rung for funeral

MORTBELLS >MORTBELL

MORTCLOTH *n* cloth spread over coffin

MORTGAGE *n* conditional pledging of property, esp a house, as security for the repayment of a loan ▷ *vb* pledge (property) as security thus ▷ *adj* of or relating to a mortgage

MORTGAGED >MORTGAGE

MORTGAGEE *n* creditor in a mortgage

MORTGAGER *same as* >MORTGAGOR

MORTGAGES >MORTGAGE

MORTGAGOR *n* debtor in a mortgage

MORTICE *same as* >MORTISE

MORTICED >MORTICE

MORTICER >MORTICE

MORTICERS >MORTICE

MORTICES >MORTICE

MORTICIAN *n* undertaker

MORTICING >MORTICE

MORTIFIC *adj* causing death

MORTIFIED >MORTIFY

MORTIFIER >MORTIFY

MORTIFIES >MORTIFY

MORTIFY *vb* humiliate

MORTISE *n* slot or recess, usually rectangular, cut into a piece of wood, stone, etc, to receive a matching projection (tenon) of another piece, or a mortise lock ▷ *vb* cut a slot or recess in (a piece of wood, stone, etc)

MORTISED >MORTISE

MORTISER >MORTISE

MORTISERS >MORTISE

MORTISES >MORTISE

MORTISING >MORTISE

MORTLING *n* corpse

MORTLINGS >MORTLING

MORTMAIN *n* state or condition of lands, buildings, etc, held inalienably, as by an ecclesiastical or other corporation

MORTMAINS >MORTMAIN

MORTS >MORT

MORTSAFE *n* heavy iron cage or grille placed over the grave of a newly deceased person during the 19th century in order to deter body snatchers

MORTSAFES >MORTSAFE

MORTUARY n building where corpses are kept before burial or cremation ▷ adj of or relating to death or burial

MORULA n solid ball of cells resulting from cleavage of a fertilized ovum

MORULAE > MORULA

MORULAR > MORULA

MORULAS > MORULA

MORWONG n food fish of Australasian coastal waters

MORWONGS > MORWONG

MORYAH interj exclamation of annoyance, disbelief, etc

MOS > MO

MOSAIC n design or decoration using small pieces of coloured stone or glass

MOSAICISM n occurrence of different types of tissue side by side

MOSAICIST > MOSAIC

MOSAICKED adj arranged in mosaic form

MOSAICS > MOSAIC

MOSASAUR n type of extinct Cretaceous giant marine lizard, typically with paddle-like limbs

MOSASAURI > MOSASAUR

MOSASAURS > MOSASAUR

MOSCHATE n odour like musk

MOSCHATEL n small N temperate plant with greenish-white musk-scented flowers

MOSE vb have glanders

MOSED > MOSE

MOSELLE n German white wine from the Moselle valley

MOSELLES > MOSELLE

MOSES > MOSE

MOSEY vb walk in a leisurely manner

MOSEYED > MOSEY

MOSEYING > MOSEY

MOSEYS > MOSEY

MOSH n type of dance, performed to loud rock music, in which people throw themselves about in a frantic and violent manner ▷ vb dance in this manner

MOSHAV n cooperative settlement in Israel, consisting of a number of small farms

MOSHAVIM > MOSHAV

MOSHED > MOSH

MOSHER > MOSH

MOSHERS > MOSH

MOSHES > MOSH

MOSHING > MOSH

MOSHINGS > MOSH

MOSING > MOSE

MOSK same as > MOSQUE

MOSKONFYT n South African grape syrup

MOSKS > MOSK

MOSLINGS n shavings from animal skin being prepared

MOSQUE n Muslim temple

MOSQUES > MOSQUE

MOSQUITO n blood-sucking flying insect

MOSQUITOS > MOSQUITO

MOSS n small flowerless plant growing in masses on moist surfaces ▷ vb gather moss

MOSSBACK n old turtle, shellfish, etc, that has a growth of algae on its back

MOSSBACKS > MOSSBACK

MOSSED > MOSS

MOSSER > MOSS

MOSSERS > MOSS

MOSSES > MOSS

MOSSGROWN adj covered in moss

MOSSIE n common sparrow

MOSSIER > MOSS

MOSSIES > MOSSIE

MOSSIEST > MOSS

MOSSINESS > MOSS

MOSSING > MOSS

MOSSLAND n land covered in peat

MOSSLANDS > MOSSLAND

MOSSLIKE > MOSS

MOSSO adv to be performed with rapidity

MOSSPLANT n individual plant in moss

MOSSY > MOSS

MOST n greatest number or degree ▷ adj greatest in number or degree ▷ adv in the greatest degree

MOSTE > MOTE

MOSTEST > MOST

MOSTESTS > MOST

MOSTLY adv for the most part, generally

MOSTS > MOST

MOSTWHAT adv mostly

MOT n girl or young woman, esp one's girlfriend

MOTE n tiny speck ▷ vb may or might

MOTED adj containing motes

MOTEL n roadside hotel for motorists

MOTELIER n person running motel

MOTELIERS > MOTELIER

MOTELS > MOTEL

MOTEN > MOTE

MOTES > MOTE

MOTET n short sacred choral song

MOTETS > MOTET

MOTETT same as > MOTET

MOTETTIST > MOTET

MOTETTS > MOTET

MOTEY adj containing motes

MOTH n nocturnal insect like a butterfly

MOTHBALL n small ball of camphor or naphthalene used to repel moths from stored clothes ▷ vb store (something operational) for future use

MOTHBALLS > MOTHBALL

MOTHED adj damaged by moths

MOTHER n female parent ▷ adj native or inborn ▷ vb look after as a mother

MOTHERED > MOTHER

MOTHERESE n simplified and repetitive type of speech, with exaggerated intonation and rhythm, often used by adults when speaking to babies

MOTHERING > MOTHER

MOTHERLY adj of or resembling a mother, esp in warmth, or protectiveness

MOTHERS > MOTHER

MOTHERY > MOTHER

MOTHIER > MOTHY

MOTHIEST > MOTHY

MOTHLIKE > MOTH

MOTHPROOF adj (esp of clothes) chemically treated so as to repel clothes moths ▷ vb make mothproof

MOTHS > MOTH

MOTHY adj ragged

MOTI n derogatory Indian English word for a fat woman or girl

MOTIER > MOTEY

MOTIEST > MOTEY

MOTIF n (recurring) theme or design

MOTIFIC adj causing motion

MOTIFS > MOTIF

MOTILE adj capable of independent movement ▷ n person whose mental imagery strongly reflects movement, esp his own

MOTILES > MOTILE

MOTILITY > MOTILE

MOTION n process, action, or way of moving ▷ vb direct (someone) by gesture

MOTIONAL > MOTION

MOTIONED > MOTION

MOTIONER > MOTION

MOTIONERS > MOTION

MOTIONING > MOTION

MOTIONIST n person proposing many motions

MOTIONS > MOTION

MOTIS > MOTI

MOTIVATE vb give incentive to

MOTIVATED > MOTIVATE

MOTIVATES > MOTIVATE

MOTIVATOR > MOTIVATE

MOTIVE n reason for a course of action ▷ adj causing motion ▷ vb motivate

MOTIVED > MOTIVE

MOTIVES > MOTIVE

MOTIVIC adj of musical motif

MOTIVING > MOTIVE

MOTIVITY n power of moving or of initiating motion

MOTLEY adj miscellaneous ▷ n costume of a jester

MOTLEYER > MOTLEY

MOTLEYEST > MOTLEY

MOTLEYS > MOTLEY

MOTLIER > MOTLEY

MOTLIEST > MOTLEY

MOTMOT n tropical American bird with a long tail and blue and brownish-green plumage

MOTMOTS > MOTMOT

MOTOCROSS n motorcycle race over a rough course

MOTOR n engine, esp of a vehicle ▷ vb travel by car ▷ adj of or relating to cars and other vehicles powered by petrol or diesel engines

MOTORABLE adj (of a road) suitable for use by motor vehicles

MOTORAIL n transport of cars by train

MOTORAILS > MOTORAIL

MOTORBIKE n motorcycle

MOTORBOAT n any boat powered by a motor

MOTORBUS n bus driven by an internal-combustion engine

MOTORCADE n procession of cars carrying important people

MOTORCAR n self-propelled electric railway car

MOTORCARS > MOTORCAR

MOTORDOM n world of motor cars

MOTORDOMS > MOTORDOM

MOTORED > MOTOR

MOTORHOME n large motor vehicle with living quarters behind the driver's compartment

MOTORIAL > MOTOR

MOTORIC > MOTOR

MOTORING > MOTOR

MOTORINGS > MOTOR

MOTORISE same as > MOTORIZE

MOTORISED > MOTORISE

MOTORISES > MOTORISE

MOTORIST n driver of a car

MOTORISTS > MOTORIST

MOTORIUM n area of nervous system involved in movement

MOTORIUMS > MOTORIUM

MOTORIZE vb equip with a motor

MOTORIZED > MOTORIZE

MOTORIZES > MOTORIZE

MOTORLESS > MOTOR

MOTORMAN n driver of an electric train

MOTORMEN > MOTORMAN

MOTORS > MOTOR

MOTORSHIP n ship with motor

MOTORWAY n main road for fast-moving traffic

MOTORWAYS > MOTORWAY

MOTORY > MOTOR

MOTOSCAFI > MOTOSCAFO

MOTOSCAFO n motorboat

MOTS > MOT

MOTSER n large sum of money, esp a gambling win

MOTSERS > MOTSER

MOTT n clump of trees

MOTTE n mound on which a castle was built

MOTTES > MOTTE

MOTTIER > MOTTY

MOTTIES > MOTTY

MOTTIEST > MOTTY

MOTTLE vb colour with streaks or blotches of different shades ▷ n mottled appearance, as of the surface of marble

MOTTLED > MOTTLE

MOTTLER n paintbrush for mottled effects

MOTTLERS > MOTTLER

MOTTLES > MOTTLE

MOTTLING > MOTTLE

MOTTLINGS > MOTTLE

MOTTO n saying expressing an ideal or rule of conduct

MOTTOED adj having motto

MOTTOES > MOTTO

MOTTOS > MOTTO

MOTTS > MOTT

MOTTY n target at which coins are aimed in pitch-and-toss ▷ adj containing motes

MOTU n derogatory Indian English word for a fat man or boy

MOTUCA n Brazilian fly

MOTUCAS > MOTUCA

MOTUS > MOTU

MOTZA same as > MOTSER

MOTZAS > MOTZA

MOU Scots word for > MOUTH

MOUCH same as > MOOCH

MOUCHARD n police informer

MOUCHARDS > MOUCHARD

MOUCHED > MOUCH

MOUCHER > MOUCH

MOUCHERS > MOUCH

MOUCHES > MOUCH

MOUCHING > MOUCH

MOUCHOIR n handkerchief

MOUCHOIRS > MOUCHOIR

MOUDIWART same as > MOULDWARP

MOUDIWORT same as > MOULDWARP

MOUE n disdainful or pouting look

MOUES > MOUE

MOUFFLON same as > MOUFLON

MOUFFLONS > MOUFFLON

MOUFLON n wild short-fleeced mountain sheep of Corsica and Sardinia

MOUFLONS > MOUFLON

MOUGHT > MOTE

MOUILLE adj palatalized, as in the sounds represented by Spanish ll or ñ

MOUJIK same as > MUZHIK

MOUJIKS > MOUJIK

MOULAGE n mould making

MOULAGES > MOULAGE

MOULD n hollow container in which metal etc is cast ▷ vb shape

MOULDABLE > MOULD

MOULDED > MOULD

MOULDER vb decay into dust ▷ n person who moulds or makes moulds

MOULDERED > MOULDER

MOULDERS > MOULDER

MOULDIER > MOULDY

MOULDIEST > MOULDY

MOULDING n moulded ornamental edging

MOULDINGS > MOULDING

MOULDS > MOULD

MOULDWARP archaic or dialect name for a > MOLE

MOULDY adj stale or musty

MOULIN n vertical shaft in a glacier, maintained by a constant descending stream of water and debris

MOULINET n device for bending crossbow

MOULINETS > MOULINET

MOULINS > MOULIN

MOULS Scots word for > MOULD

MOULT vb shed feathers, hair, or skin to make way for new growth ▷ n process of moulting

MOULTED > MOULT

MOULTEN adj having moulted

MOULTER > MOULT

MOULTERS > MOULT

MOULTING > MOULT

MOULTINGS > MOULT

MOULTS > MOULT

MOUND n heap, esp of earth or stones ▷ vb gather into a mound

MOUNDBIRD n Australian bird laying eggs in mounds

MOUNDED > MOUND

MOUNDING > MOUND

MOUNDS > MOUND

MOUNSEER same as > MONSIEUR

MOUNSEERS > MOUNSEER

MOUNT vb climb or ascend ▷ n backing or support on which something is fixed

MOUNTABLE > MOUNT

MOUNTAIN n hill of great size ▷ adj, found on, or for use on a mountain or mountains

MOUNTAINS > MOUNTAIN

MOUNTAINY > MOUNTAIN

MOUNTANT n adhesive for mounting pictures

MOUNTANTS > MOUNTANT

MOUNTED adj riding horses

MOUNTER > MOUNT

MOUNTERS > MOUNT

MOUNTING same as > MOUNT

MOUNTINGS > MOUNTING

MOUNTS > MOUNT

MOUP n nibble

MOUPED > MOUP

MOUPING > MOUP

MOUPS > MOUP

MOURN vb feel or express sorrow for (a dead person or lost thing)

MOURNED > MOURN

MOURNER n person attending a funeral

MOURNERS > MOURNER

MOURNFUL adj sad or dismal

MOURNING n grieving ▷ adj of or relating to mourning

MOURNINGS > MOURNING

MOURNIVAL n card game

MOURNS > MOURN

MOUS > MOU

MOUSAKA same as > MOUSSAKA

MOUSAKAS > MOUSAKA

MOUSE n small long-tailed rodent ▷ vb stalk and catch mice

MOUSEBIRD another name for > COLY

MOUSED > MOUSE

MOUSEKIN n little mouse

MOUSEKINS > MOUSEKIN

MOUSELIKE > MOUSE

MOUSEMAT n piece of material on which a computer mouse is moved

MOUSEMATS > MOUSEMAT

MOUSEOVER n on a web page, any item that changes or pops up when the pointer of a mouse moves over it

MOUSEPAD n pad for computer mouse

MOUSEPADS > MOUSEPAD

MOUSER n cat used to catch mice

MOUSERIES > MOUSERY

MOUSERS > MOUSER

MOUSERY n place infested with mice

MOUSES > MOUSE

MOUSETAIL n N temperate plant with tail-like flower spikes

MOUSETRAP n spring-loaded trap for killing mice

MOUSEY same as > MOUSY

MOUSIE n little mouse

MOUSIER > MOUSY

MOUSIES > MOUSIE

MOUSIEST > MOUSY

MOUSILY > MOUSY

MOUSINESS > MOUSY

MOUSING n lashing, shackle, etc, for closing off a hook to prevent a load from slipping off

MOUSINGS > MOUSING

MOUSLE vb handle roughly

MOUSLED > MOUSLE

MOUSLES > MOUSLE

MOUSLING > MOUSLE

MOUSME n Japanese girl

MOUSMEE same as > MOUSME

MOUSMEES > MOUSMEE

MOUSMES > MOUSME

MOUSSAKA n dish made with meat, aubergines, and tomatoes, topped with cheese sauce

MOUSSAKAS > MOUSSAKA

MOUSSE n dish of flavoured cream whipped and set ▷ vb apply mousse to

MOUSSED > MOUSSE

MOUSSES > MOUSSE

MOUSSING > MOUSSE

MOUST same as > MUST

MOUSTACHE n hair on the upper lip

MOUSTED > MOUST

MOUSTING > MOUST

MOUSTS > MOUST

MOUSY adj like a mouse, esp in hair colour

MOUTAN n variety of peony

MOUTANS > MOUTAN

MOUTER same as > MULTURE

MOUTERED > MOUTER

MOUTERER > MOUTER

MOUTERERS > MOUTER

MOUTERING > MOUTER

MOUTERS > MOUTER

MOUTH n opening in the head for eating and issuing sounds ▷ vb form (words) with the lips without speaking

MOUTHABLE adj able to be recited

MOUTHED > MOUTH

MOUTHER > MOUTH

MOUTHERS > MOUTH

MOUTHFEEL n texture of a substance as it is perceived in the mouth

MOUTHFUL n amount of food or drink put into the mouth at any one time when eating or drinking

MOUTHFULS > MOUTHFUL

MOUTHIER > MOUTHY

MOUTHIEST > MOUTHY

MOUTHILY > MOUTHY

MOUTHING > MOUTH

MOUTHLESS > MOUTH

MOUTHLIKE > MOUTH

MOUTHPART n any of the paired appendages in arthropods that surround the mouth and are specialized for feeding

MOUTHS > MOUTH

MOUTHWASH n medicated liquid for gargling and cleansing the mouth

MOUTHY *adj* bombastic

MOUTON *n* sheepskin processed to resemble the fur of another animal, esp beaver or seal

MOUTONNEE *adj* rounded by action of glacier

MOUTONS > MOUTON

MOVABLE *adj* able to be moved or rearranged ▷ *n* movable article, esp a piece of furniture

MOVABLES > MOVABLE

MOVABLY > MOVABLE

MOVE *vb* change in place or position ▷ *n* moving

MOVEABLE *same as* > MOVABLE

MOVEABLES > MOVEABLE

MOVEABLY > MOVEABLE

MOVED > MOVE

MOVELESS *adj* immobile

MOVEMENT *n* action or process of moving

MOVEMENTS > MOVEMENT

MOVER *n* person or animal that moves in a particular way

MOVERS > MOVER

MOVES > MOVE

MOVIE *n* cinema film

MOVIEDOM *n* world of cinema

MOVIEDOMS > MOVIEDOM

MOVIEGOER *n* person who goes to cinema

MOVIELAND *same as* > MOVIEDOM

MOVIEOKE *n* entertainment in which people act out well-known scenes from movies that are silently playing in the background

MOVIEOKES > MOVIEOKE

MOVIEOLA *same as* > MOVIOLA

MOVIEOLAS > MOVIEOLA

MOVIES > MOVIE

MOVING *adj* arousing or touching the emotions

MOVINGLY > MOVING

MOVIOLA *n* viewing machine used in cutting and editing film

MOVIOLAS > MOVIOLA

MOW *vb* cut (grass or crops) ▷ *n* part of a barn where hay, straw, etc, is stored

MOWA *same as* > MAHUA

MOWAS > MOWA

MOWBURN *vb* heat up in mow

MOWBURNED > MOWBURN

MOWBURNS > MOWBURN

MOWBURNT *adj* (of hay, straw, etc) damaged by overheating in a mow

MOWDIE *Scot words for* > MOLE

MOWDIES > MOWDIE

MOWED > MOW

MOWER > MOW

MOWERS > MOW

MOWING > MOW

MOWINGS > MOW

MOWN > MOW

MOWRA *same as* > MAHUA

MOWRAS > MOWRA

MOWS > MOW

MOXA *n* downy material obtained from various plants and used in Oriental medicine by being burned on the skin as a cauterizing agent or counterirritant for the skin

MOXAS > MOXA

MOXIE *n* courage, nerve, or vigour

MOXIES > MOXIE

MOY *n* coin

MOYA *n* mud emitted from a volcano

MOYAS > MOYA

MOYITIES > MOIETY

MOYITY *same as* > MOIETY

MOYL *same as* > MOYLE

MOYLE *vb* toil

MOYLED > MOYLE

MOYLES > MOYLE

MOYLING > MOYLE

MOYLS > MOYL

MOYS > MOY

MOZ *n* hex

MOZE *vb* give nap to

MOZED > MOZE

MOZES > MOZE

MOZETTA *same as* > MOZZETTA

MOZETTAS > MOZETTA

MOZETTE > MOZETTA

MOZING > MOZE

MOZO *n* porter in southwest USA

MOZOS > MOZO

MOZZ *same as* > MOZ

MOZZES > MOZZ

MOZZETTA *n* short hooded cape worn by the pope, cardinals, etc

MOZZETTAS > MOZZETTA

MOZZETTE > MOZZETTA

MOZZIE *same as* > MOSSIE

MOZZIES > MOZZIE

MOZZLE *n* luck

MOZZLES > MOZZLE

MPRET *n* former Albanian ruler

MPRETS > MPRET

MRIDAMGAM *same as* > MRIDANG

MRIDANG *n* drum used in Indian music

MRIDANGA *same as* > MRIDANG

MRIDANGAM *same as* > MRIDANG

MRIDANGAS > MRIDANGA

MRIDANGS > MRIDANG

MU *n* 12th letter in the Greek alphabet, a consonant, transliterated as m

MUCATE *n* salt of mucic acid

MUCATES > MUCATE

MUCH *adj* large amount or degree of ▷ *n* large amount or degree ▷ *adv* great degree

MUCHACHA *n* (in Spain etc) young woman or female servant

MUCHACHAS > MUCHACHA

MUCHACHO *n* young man

MUCHACHOS > MUCHACHO

MUCHEL *same as* > MUCH

MUCHELL *same as* > MUCH

MUCHELLS > MUCHELL

MUCHELS > MUCHEL

MUCHES > MUCH

MUCHLY > MUCH

MUCHNESS *n* magnitude

MUCHO *adv* Spanish for very

MUCIC as in *mucic acid* colourless crystalline solid carboxylic acid found in milk sugar and used in the manufacture of pyrrole

MUCID *adj* mouldy, musty, or slimy

MUCIDITY > MUCID

MUCIDNESS > MUCID

MUCIGEN *n* substance present in mucous cells that is converted into mucin

MUCIGENS > MUCIGEN

MUCILAGE *n* gum or glue

MUCILAGES > MUCILAGE

MUCIN *n* any of a group of nitrogenous mucoproteins occurring in saliva, skin, tendon, etc, that produce a very viscous solution in water

MUCINOGEN *n* substance forming mucin

MUCINOID *adj* of or like mucin

MUCINOUS > MUCIN

MUCINS > MUCIN

MUCK *n* dirt, filth

MUCKAMUCK *n* food ▷ *vb* consume food

MUCKED > MUCK

MUCKENDER *n* handkerchief

MUCKER *n* person who shifts broken rock or waste ▷ *vb* hoard

MUCKERED > MUCKER

MUCKERING > MUCKER

MUCKERISH > MUCKER

MUCKERS > MUCKER

MUCKHEAP *n* dunghill

MUCKHEAPS > MUCKHEAP

MUCKIER > MUCKY

MUCKIEST > MUCKY

MUCKILY > MUCKY

MUCKINESS > MUCKY

MUCKING > MUCK

MUCKLE *same as* > MICKLE

MUCKLES > MUCKLE

MUCKLUCK *same as* > MUKLUK

MUCKLUCKS > MUCKLUCK

MUCKRAKE *n* agricultural rake for spreading manure ▷ *vb* seek out and expose scandal, esp concerning public figures

MUCKRAKED > MUCKRAKE

MUCKRAKER > MUCKRAKE

MUCKRAKES > MUCKRAKE

MUCKS > MUCK

MUCKSWEAT *n* profuse sweat

MUCKWORM *n* any larva or worm that lives in mud

MUCKWORMS > MUCKWORM

MUCKY *adj* dirty or muddy

MUCKYMUCK *n* person who is or appears to be very important

MUCLUC *same as* > MUKLUK

MUCLUCS > MUCLUC

MUCOID *adj* of the nature of or resembling mucin ▷ *n* substance like mucin

MUCOIDAL *same as* > MUCOID

MUCOIDS > MUCOID

MUCOLYTIC *adj* breaking down mucus

MUCOR *n* type of fungus which comprises many common moulds

MUCORS > MUCOR

MUCOSA *n* mucous membrane; mucus-secreting membrane that lines body cavities or passages that are open to the external environment

MUCOSAE > MUCOSA

MUCOSAL > MUCOSA

MUCOSAS > MUCOSA

MUCOSE *same as* > MUCOUS

MUCOSITY > MUCOUS

MUCOUS *adj* of, resembling, or secreting mucus

MUCRO *n* short pointed projection from certain parts or organs, as from the tip of a leaf

MUCRONATE *adj* terminating in a sharp point

MUCRONES > MUCRO

MUCROS > MUCRO

MUCULENT *adj* like mucus

MUCUS *n* slimy secretion of the mucous membranes

MUCUSES > MUCUS

MUD *n* wet soft earth ▷ *vb* cover in mud

MUDBATH *n* medicinal bath in heated mud

MUDBATHS > MUDBATH

MUDBUG *n* crayfish

MUDBUGS > MUDBUG

MUDCAP *vb* use explosive charge in blasting

MUDCAPPED > MUDCAP

MUDCAPS > MUDCAP

MUDCAT *n* any of several large North American catfish living in muddy rivers, esp in the Mississippi valley

MUDCATS > MUDCAT

MUDDED > MUD

MUDDER *n* horse that runs well in mud

MUDDERS > MUDDER

MUDDIED > MUDDY

MUDDIER > MUDDY

MUDDIES > MUDDY

MUDDIEST > MUDDY
MUDDILY > MUDDY
MUDDINESS > MUDDY
MUDDING > MUD
MUDDLE vb confuse ▷ n state of confusion
MUDDLED > MUDDLE
MUDDLER n person who muddles or muddles through
MUDDLERS > MUDDLER
MUDDLES > MUDDLE
MUDDLIER > MUDDLE
MUDDLIEST > MUDDLE
MUDDLING > MUDDLE
MUDDLINGS > MUDDLE
MUDDLY > MUDDLE
MUDDY adj covered or filled with mud ▷ vb make muddy
MUDDYING > MUDDY
MUDEJAR n Spanish Moor, esp one permitted to stay in Spain after the Christian reconquest ▷ adj of or relating to a style of architecture orginated by Mudéjares
MUDEJARES > MUDEJAR
MUDEYE n larva of the dragonfly, commonly used as a fishing bait
MUDEYES > MUDEYE
MUDFISH n any of various fishes, such as the bowfin and cichlids, that live at or frequent the muddy bottoms of rivers, lakes, etc
MUDFISHES > MUDFISH
MUDFLAP n flap above wheel to deflect mud
MUDFLAPS > MUDFLAP
MUDFLAT n tract of low muddy land, esp near an estuary, that is covered at high tide and exposed at low tide
MUDFLATS > MUDFLAT
MUDFLOW n flow of soil or fine-grained sediment mixed with water down a steep unstable slope
MUDFLOWS > MUDFLOW
MUDGE vb speak vaguely
MUDGED > MUDGE
MUDGER > MUDGE
MUDGERS > MUDGE
MUDGES > MUDGE
MUDGING > MUDGE
MUDGUARD n cover over a wheel to prevent mud or water being thrown up by it
MUDGUARDS > MUDGUARD
MUDHEN n water bird living in muddy place
MUDHENS > MUDHEN
MUDHOLE n hole with mud at bottom
MUDHOLES > MUDHOLE
MUDHOOK n anchor
MUDHOOKS > MUDHOOK
MUDHOPPER n type of amphibious fish found on mud flats and in mangrove swamps

MUDIR n local governor
MUDIRIA n province of mudir
MUDIRIAS > MUDIRIA
MUDIRIEH same as > MUDIRIA
MUDIRIEHS > MUDIRIEH
MUDIRS > MUDIR
MUDLARK n street urchin ▷ vb play in mud
MUDLARKED > MUDLARK
MUDLARKS > MUDLARK
MUDLOGGER n person checking mud for traces of oil
MUDPACK n cosmetic paste applied to the face to improve the complexion
MUDPACKS > MUDPACK
MUDPUPPY n aquatic North American salamander of the genus with red feathery external gills and other persistent larval features
MUDRA n any of various ritual hand movements in Hindu religious dancing
MUDRAS > MUDRA
MUDROCK n type of sedimentary rock
MUDROCKS > MUDROCK
MUDROOM n room where muddy shoes may be left
MUDROOMS > MUDROOM
MUDS > MUD
MUDSCOW n boat for travelling over mudflats
MUDSCOWS > MUDSCOW
MUDSILL n support for building at or below ground
MUDSILLS > MUDSILL
MUDSLIDE n landslide of mud
MUDSLIDES > MUDSLIDE
MUDSTONE n dark grey clay rock similar to shale but with the lamination less well developed
MUDSTONES > MUDSTONE
MUDWORT n plant growing in mud
MUDWORTS > MUDWORT
MUEDDIN same as > MUEZZIN
MUEDDINS > MUEDDIN
MUENSTER n whitish-yellow semihard whole milk cheese, often flavoured with caraway or aniseed
MUENSTERS > MUENSTER
MUESLI n mixture of grain, nuts, and dried fruit, eaten with milk
MUESLIS > MUESLI
MUEZZIN n official who summons Muslims to prayer
MUEZZINS > MUEZZIN
MUFF n tube-shaped covering to keep the hands warm ▷ vb bungle (an action)
MUFFED > MUFF

MUFFETTEE n small muff worn over the wrist
MUFFIN n light round flat yeast cake
MUFFINEER n muffin dish
MUFFING > MUFF
MUFFINS > MUFFIN
MUFFISH > MUFF
MUFFLE vb wrap up for warmth or to deaden sound ▷ n something that muffles
MUFFLED > MUFFLE
MUFFLER n scarf
MUFFLERED adj with muffler
MUFFLERS > MUFFLER
MUFFLES > MUFFLE
MUFFLING > MUFFLE
MUFFS > MUFF
MUFLON same as > MOUFFLON
MUFLONS > MUFLON
MUFTI n civilian clothes worn by a person who usually wears a uniform
MUFTIS > MUFTI
MUG n large drinking cup ▷ vb attack in order to rob
MUGEARITE n crystalline rock
MUGFUL same as > MUG
MUGFULS > MUGFUL
MUGG same as > MUG
MUGGA n Australian eucalyptus tree with dark bark and pink flowers
MUGGAR same as > MUGGER
MUGGARS > MUGGAR
MUGGAS > MUGGA
MUGGED > MUG
MUGGEE n mugged person
MUGGEES > MUGGEE
MUGGER n person who commits robbery with violence, esp in the street
MUGGERS > MUGGER
MUGGIER > MUGGY
MUGGIEST > MUGGY
MUGGILY > MUGGY
MUGGINESS > MUGGY
MUGGING > MUG
MUGGINGS > MUG
MUGGINS n stupid or gullible person
MUGGINSES > MUGGINS
MUGGISH same as > MUGGY
MUGGS > MUG
MUGGUR same as > MUGGER
MUGGURS > MUGGUR
MUGGY adj (of weather) damp and stifling
MUGHAL same as > MOGUL
MUGHALS > MUGHAL
MUGS > MUG
MUGSHOT n police photograph of person's face
MUGSHOTS > MUGSHOT
MUGWORT n N temperate herbaceous plant with aromatic leaves and clusters of small greenish-white flowers

MUGWORTS > MUGWORT
MUGWUMP n neutral or independent person, esp in politics
MUGWUMPS > MUGWUMP
MUHLIES > MUHLY
MUHLY n American grass
MUID n former French measure of capacity
MUIDS > MUID
MUIL same as > MULE
MUILS > MUIL
MUIR same as > MOOR
MUIRBURN same as > MOORBURN
MUIRBURNS > MUIRBURN
MUIRS > MUIR
MUIST same as > MUST
MUISTED > MUIST
MUISTING > MUIST
MUISTS > MUIST
MUJAHEDIN n Muslim guerrilla
MUJAHIDIN same as > MUJAHEDIN
MUJIK same as > MUZHIK
MUJIKS > MUJIK
MUKHTAR n lawyer in India
MUKHTARS > MUKHTAR
MUKLUK n soft boot, usually of sealskin, worn in the American Arctic
MUKLUKS > MUKLUK
MUKTUK n thin outer skin of the beluga, used as food
MUKTUKS > MUKTUK
MULATTA n female mulatto
MULATTAS > MULATTA
MULATTO n child of one Black and one White parent ▷ adj of a light brown colour
MULATTOES > MULATTO
MULATTOS > MULATTO
MULBERRY n tree whose leaves are used to feed silkworms ▷ adj dark purple
MULCH n mixture of wet straw, leaves, etc, used to protect the roots of plants ▷ vb cover (land) with mulch
MULCHED > MULCH
MULCHES > MULCH
MULCHING > MULCH
MULCT vb cheat or defraud ▷ n fine or penalty
MULCTED > MULCT
MULCTING > MULCT
MULCTS > MULCT
MULE n offspring of a horse and a donkey ▷ vb strike coin with different die on each side
MULED > MULE
MULES vb surgically remove folds of skin from a sheep
MULESED > MULES
MULESES > MULES
MULESING > MULES
MULESINGS > MULESING
MULETA n small cape attached to a stick used by

the matador during the final stages of a bullfight

MULETAS >MULETA

MULETEER n mule driver

MULETEERS >MULETEER

MULEY adj (of cattle) having no horns ▷ n any hornless cow

MULEYS >MULEY

MULGA n Australian acacia shrub growing in desert regions

MULGAS >MULGA

MULING >MULE

MULISH adj obstinate

MULISHLY >MULISH

MULL vb think (over) or ponder ▷ n promontory or headland

MULLA same as >MULLAH

MULLAH n Muslim scholar, teacher, or religious leader

MULLAHED same as >MULLERED

MULLAHING same as >MULLERING

MULLAHISM n rule by mullahs

MULLAHS >MULLAH

MULLARKY same as >MALARKEY

MULLAS >MULLA

MULLED >MULL

MULLEIN n type of European plant

MULLEINS >MULLEIN

MULLEN same as >MULLEIN

MULLENS >MULLEN

MULLER n flat heavy implement of stone or iron used to grind material against a slab of stone ▷ vb beat up or defeat thoroughly

MULLERED adj drunk

MULLERING >MULLER

MULLERS >MULLER

MULLET n edible sea fish

MULLETS >MULLET

MULLEY same as >MULEY

MULLEYS >MULLEY

MULLIGAN n stew made from odds and ends of food

MULLIGANS >MULLIGAN

MULLING >MULL

MULLION n vertical dividing bar in a window ▷ vb furnish (a window, screen, etc) with mullions

MULLIONED >MULLION

MULLIONS >MULLION

MULLITE n colourless mineral

MULLITES >MULLITE

MULLOCK n waste material from a mine

MULLOCKS >MULLOCK

MULLOCKY >MULLOCK

MULLOWAY n large Australian sea fish, valued for sport and food

MULLOWAYS >MULLOWAY

MULLS >MULL

MULMUL n muslin

MULMULL same as >MULMUL

MULMULLS >MULMULL

MULMULS >MULMUL

MULSE n drink containing honey

MULSES >MULSE

MULSH same as >MULCH

MULSHED >MULSH

MULSHES >MULSH

MULSHING >MULSH

MULTEITY n manifoldness

MULTIAGE adj involving different age groups

MULTIATOM adj involving many atoms

MULTIBAND adj involving more than one waveband

MULTIBANK adj involving more than one bank

MULTICAR adj involving several cars

MULTICAST n broadcast from one source simultaneously to several receivers on a network

MULTICELL adj involving many cells

MULTICIDE n mass murder

MULTICITY adj involving more than one city

MULTICOPY adj involving many copies

MULTIDAY adj involving more than one day

MULTIDISC adj involving more than one disc

MULTIDRUG adj involving more than one drug

MULTIFID adj having or divided into many lobes or similar segments

MULTIFIL n fibre made up of many filaments

MULTIFILS >MULTIFIL

MULTIFOIL n ornamental design having a large number of foils

MULTIFOLD adj many times doubled

MULTIFORM adj having many shapes or forms

MULTIGERM adj (of plants) having the ability to multiply germinate

MULTIGRID adj involving several grids

MULTIGYM n exercise apparatus incorporating a variety of weights, used for toning the muscles

MULTIGYMS >MULTIGYM

MULTIHUED adj having many colours

MULTIHULL n sailing vessel with two or more hulls

MULTIJET adj involving more than one jet

MULTILANE adj having several lanes

MULTILINE adj involving several lines

MULTILOBE adj having more than one lobe

MULTIMODE adj involving several modes

MULTIPACK n form of packaging of foodstuffs, etc, that contains several units and is offered at a price below that of the equivalent number of units

MULTIPAGE adj involving many pages

MULTIPARA n woman who has given birth to more than one viable fetus or living child

MULTIPART adj involving many parts

MULTIPATH adj relating to television or radio signals that travel by more than one route from a transmitter and arrive at slightly different times, causing ghost images or audio distortion

MULTIPED adj having many feet ▷ n insect or animal having many feet

MULTIPEDE same as >MULTIPED

MULTIPEDS >MULTIPED

MULTIPION adj involving many pions

MULTIPLE adj having many parts ▷ n quantity which contains another an exact number of times

MULTIPLES >MULTIPLE

MULTIPLET n set of closely spaced lines in a spectrum, resulting from small differences between the energy levels of atoms or molecules

MULTIPLEX n purpose-built complex containing several cinemas and usu. restaurants and bars ▷ adj having many elements, complex ▷ vb send (messages or signals) or (of messages or signals) be sent by multiplex

MULTIPLY vb increase in number or degree

MULTIPOLE adj involving more than one pole

MULTIPORT adj involving more than one port

MULTIROLE adj having a number of roles, functions, etc

MULTIROOM adj having many rooms

MULTISITE adj involving more than one site

MULTISIZE adj involving more than size

MULTISTEP adj involving several steps

MULTITASK vb work at several different tasks simultaneously

MULTITON adj weighing several tons

MULTITONE adj involving more than one tone

MULTITOOL n device containing various tools attached to one handle

MULTITUDE n great number

MULTIUNIT adj involving more than one unit

MULTIUSE adj suitable for more than one use

MULTIUSER >MULTIUSE

MULTIWALL adj involving several layers

MULTIYEAR adj involving more than one year

MULTUM n substance used in brewing

MULTUMS >MULTUM

MULTURE n fee formerly paid to a miller for grinding grain ▷ vb take multure

MULTURED >MULTURE

MULTURER >MULTURE

MULTURERS >MULTURE

MULTURES >MULTURE

MULTURING >MULTURE

MUM n mother ▷ vb act in a mummer's play

MUMBLE vb speak indistinctly, mutter ▷ n indistinct utterance

MUMBLED >MUMBLE

MUMBLER >MUMBLE

MUMBLERS >MUMBLE

MUMBLES >MUMBLE

MUMBLIER >MUMBLY

MUMBLIEST >MUMBLY

MUMBLING >MUMBLE

MUMBLINGS >MUMBLE

MUMBLY >MUMBLE

MUMCHANCE adj silent

MUMM same as >MUM

MUMMED >MUM

MUMMER n actor in a traditional English folk play or mime

MUMMERIES >MUMMERY

MUMMERS >MUMMER

MUMMERY n performance by mummers

MUMMIA n mummified flesh used as medicine

MUMMIAS >MUMMIA

MUMMICHOG n small American fish

MUMMIED >MUMMY

MUMMIES >MUMMY

MUMMIFIED >MUMMIFY

MUMMIFIES >MUMMIFY

MUMMIFORM adj like mummy

MUMMIFY vb preserve the body of (a human or animal) as a mummy

MUMMING >MUM

MUMMINGS >MUM

MUMMOCK same as >MAMMOCK

MUMMOCKS >MUMMOCK

MUMMS >MUMM

MUMMY n body embalmed and wrapped for burial in ancient Egypt ▷ vb

mummify
MUMMYING > MUMMY
MUMP vb be silent
MUMPED > MUMP
MUMPER > MUMP
MUMPERS > MUMP
MUMPING > MUMP
MUMPISH > MUMPS
MUMPISHLY > MUMPS
MUMPS n infectious disease with swelling in the glands of the neck
MUMPSIMUS n opinion held obstinately
MUMS > MUM
MUMSIER > MUMSY
MUMSIEST > MUMSY
MUMSY adj out of fashion
MUMU n oven in Papua New Guinea
MUMUS > MUMU
MUN same as **>** MAUN
MUNCH vb chew noisily and steadily
MUNCHABLE > MUNCH
MUNCHED > MUNCH
MUNCHER > MUNCH
MUNCHERS > MUNCH
MUNCHES > MUNCH
MUNCHIES npl craving for food, induced by alcohol or drugs
MUNCHING > MUNCH
MUNCHKIN n undersized person or a child, esp an appealing one
MUNCHKINS > MUNCHKIN
MUNDANE adj everyday
MUNDANELY > MUNDANE
MUNDANER > MUNDANE
MUNDANEST > MUNDANE
MUNDANITY > MUNDANE
MUNDIC n iron pyrites
MUNDICS > MUNDIC
MUNDIFIED > MUNDIFY
MUNDIFIES > MUNDIFY
MUNDIFY vb cleanse
MUNDUNGO n tripe in Spain
MUNDUNGOS > MUNDUNGO
MUNDUNGUS n smelly tobacco
MUNG vb process (computer data)
MUNGA n army canteen
MUNGAS > MUNGA
MUNGCORN n maslin
MUNGCORNS > MUNGCORN
MUNGE vb modify a password into an unguessable state
MUNGED > MUNG
MUNGES > MUNG
MUNGING > MUNG
MUNGO n cheap felted fabric made from waste wool
MUNGOES > MUNGO
MUNGOOSE same as **>** MONGOOSE
MUNGOOSES > MUNGOOSE
MUNGOS > MUNGO
MUNGS > MUNG
MUNI n municipal radio broadcast
MUNICIPAL adj relating to

a city or town
MUNIFIED > MUNIFY
MUNIFIES > MUNIFY
MUNIFY vb fortify
MUNIFYING > MUNIFY
MUNIMENT n means of defence
MUNIMENTS npl title deeds or similar documents
MUNIS > MUNI
MUNITE vb strengthen
MUNITED > MUNITE
MUNITES > MUNITE
MUNITING > MUNITE
MUNITION vb supply with munitions
MUNITIONS npl military stores
MUNNION archaic word for **>** MULLION
MUNNIONS > MUNNION
MUNS > MUN
MUNSHI n secretary in India
MUNSHIS > MUNSHI
MUNSTER variant of **>** MUENSTER
MUNSTERS > MUNSTER
MUNT n derogatory word for a Black African
MUNTER n unattractive person
MUNTERS > MUNTER
MUNTIN n supporting or strengthening bar for a glass window, door, etc
MUNTING same as **>** MUNTIN
MUNTINGS > MUNTING
MUNTINS > MUNTIN
MUNTJAC n small Asian deer of the genus typically with a chestnut-brown coat, small antlers, and a barklike cry
MUNTJACS > MUNTJAC
MUNTJAK same as **>** MUNTJAC
MUNTJAKS > MUNTJAK
MUNTRIE n Australian shrub with green-red edible berries
MUNTRIES > MUNTRIE
MUNTS > MUNT
MUNTU same as **>** MUNT
MUNTUS > MUNTU
MUON n positive or negative elementary particle with a mass 207 times that of an electron
MUONIC > MUON
MUONIUM n form of hydrogen
MUONIUMS > MUONIUM
MUONS > MUON
MUPPET n stupid person
MUPPETS > MUPPET
MUQADDAM n person of authority in India
MUQADDAMS > MUQADDAM
MURA n group of people living together in Japanese countryside
MURAENA n moray eel
MURAENAS > MURAENA

MURAENID n eel of moray family
MURAENIDS > MURAENID
MURAGE n tax levied for the construction or maintenance of town walls
MURAGES > MURAGE
MURAL n painting on a wall **▷** adj of or relating to a wall
MURALED same as **>** MURALLED
MURALIST > MURAL
MURALISTS > MURAL
MURALLED adj decorated with mural
MURALS > MURAL
MURAS > MURA
MURDABAD interj down with
MURDER n unlawful intentional killing of a human being **▷** vb kill in this way
MURDERED > MURDER
MURDEREE n murder victim
MURDEREES > MURDEREE
MURDERER > MURDER
MURDERERS > MURDER
MURDERESS > MURDER
MURDERING > MURDER
MURDEROUS adj intending, capable of, or guilty of murder
MURDERS > MURDER
MURE archaic or literary word for **>** IMMURE
MURED > MURE
MUREIN n polymer found in cells
MUREINS > MUREIN
MURENA same as **>** MURAENA
MURENAS > MURENA
MURES > MURE
MUREX n type of spiny-shelled marine gastropod formerly used as a source of the dye Tyrian purple
MUREXES > MUREX
MURGEON vb grimace at
MURGEONED > MURGEON
MURGEONS > MURGEON
MURIATE obsolete name for a **>** CHLORIDE
MURIATED > MURIATE
MURIATES > MURIATE
MURIATIC as in muriatic acid former name for a strong acid used in many industrial processes
MURICATE adj having a surface roughened by numerous short points
MURICATED same as **>** MURICATE
MURICES > MUREX
MURID n animal of mouse family
MURIDS > MURID
MURIFORM adj like mouse
MURINE n type of animal belonging to the Old World family of rodents that

includes rats and mice
MURINES > MURINE
MURING > MURE
MURK n thick darkness **▷** adj dark or gloomy
MURKER > MURK
MURKEST > MURK
MURKIER > MURKY
MURKIEST > MURKY
MURKILY > MURKY
MURKINESS > MURKY
MURKISH > MURK
MURKLY > MURK
MURKS > MURK
MURKSOME > MURK
MURKY adj dark or gloomy
MURL vb crumble
MURLAIN n type of basket
MURLAINS > MURLAIN
MURLAN same as **>** MURLAIN
MURLANS > MURLAIN
MURLED > MURL
MURLIER > MURL
MURLIEST > MURL
MURLIN same as **>** MURLAIN
MURLING > MURL
MURLINS > MURLIN
MURLS > MURL
MURLY > MURL
MURMUR vb speak or say in a quiet indistinct way **▷** n continuous low indistinct sound
MURMURED > MURMUR
MURMURER > MURMUR
MURMURERS > MURMUR
MURMURING > MURMUR
MURMUROUS > MURMUR
MURMURS > MURMUR
MURPHIES > MURPHY
MURPHY dialect or informal word for **>** POTATO
MURR n former name for a cold
MURRA same as **>** MURRHINE
MURRAGH n type of large caddis fly
MURRAGHS > MURRAGH
MURRAIN n cattle plague
MURRAINED > MURRAIN
MURRAINS > MURRAIN
MURRAM n type of gravel
MURRAMS > MURRAM
MURRAS > MURRA
MURRAY n large Australian freshwater fish
MURRAYS > MURRAY
MURRE n type of guillemot
MURREE n native Australian
MURREES > MURREE
MURRELET n type of small diving bird related to the auks
MURRELETS > MURRELET
MURREN same as **>** MURRAIN
MURRENS > MURREN
MURRES > MURRE
MURREY adj mulberry colour
MURREYS > MURREY
MURRHA same as **>** MURRA

MURRHAS > MURRHA
MURRHINE adj of or relating to an unknown substance used in ancient Rome to make vases, cups, etc ▷ n substance so used
MURRHINES > MURRHINE
MURRI same as > MURREE
MURRIES > MURRY
MURRIN same as > MURRAIN
MURRINE same as > MURRHINE
MURRINES > MURRINE
MURRINS > MURRIN
MURRION same as > MURRAIN
MURRIONS > MURRION
MURRIS > MURRI
MURRS > MURR
MURRY same as > MORAY
MURTHER same as > MURDER
MURTHERED > MURTHER
MURTHERER > MURTHER
MURTHERS > MURTHER
MURTI n image of a deity, which itself is considered divine once consecrated
MURTIS > MURTI
MURVA n type of hemp
MURVAS > MURVA
MUS > MU
MUSACEOUS adj of, relating to, a family of tropical flowering plants with large leaves and clusters of elongated berry fruits: includes the banana, edible plantain, and Manila hemp
MUSANG n catlike animal of Malaysia
MUSANGS > MUSANG
MUSAR n rabbinic literature concerned with ethics, right conduct, etc
MUSARS > MUSAR
MUSCA n small constellation in the S hemisphere lying between the Southern Cross and Chamaeleon
MUSCADEL same as > MUSCATEL
MUSCADELS > MUSCADEL
MUSCADET n white grape, grown esp in the Loire valley, used for making wine
MUSCADETS > MUSCADET
MUSCADIN n Parisian dandy
MUSCADINE n woody climbing plant of the southeastern US
MUSCADINS > MUSCADIN
MUSCAE > MUSCA
MUSCARINE n poisonous alkaloid occurring in certain mushrooms
MUSCAT same as > MUSCATEL
MUSCATEL n rich sweet

wine made from muscat grapes
MUSCATELS > MUSCATEL
MUSCATS > MUSCAT
MUSCAVADO same as > MUSCOVADO
MUSCID n type of fly of the family which includes the housefly and tsetse fly
MUSCIDS > MUSCID
MUSCLE n tissue in the body which produces movement by contracting ▷ vb force one's way (in)
MUSCLED > MUSCLE
MUSCLEMAN n man with highly developed muscles
MUSCLEMEN > MUSCLEMAN
MUSCLES > MUSCLE
MUSCLIER > MUSCLE
MUSCLIEST > MUSCLE
MUSCLING > MUSCLE
MUSCLINGS > MUSCLE
MUSCLY > MUSCLE
MUSCOID adj of family of plants
MUSCOLOGY n branch of botany
MUSCONE same as > MUSKONE
MUSCONES > MUSCONE
MUSCOSE adj like moss
MUSCOVADO n raw sugar obtained from the juice of sugar cane by evaporating the molasses
MUSCOVITE n pale brown, or green, or colourless mineral of the mica group
MUSCOVY as in muscovy duck a kind of duck
MUSCULAR adj with well-developed muscles
MUSCULOUS adj muscular
MUSE vb ponder quietly ▷ n state of abstraction
MUSED > MUSE
MUSEFUL > MUSE
MUSEFULLY > MUSE
MUSEOLOGY n science of museum organization
MUSER > MUSE
MUSERS > MUSE
MUSES > MUSE
MUSET same as > MUSIT
MUSETS > MUSET
MUSETTE n type of bagpipe with a bellows popular in France during the 17th and 18th centuries
MUSETTES > MUSETTE
MUSEUM n building where natural, artistic, historical, or scientific objects are exhibited and preserved
MUSEUMS > MUSEUM
MUSH n soft pulpy mass ▷ interj order to dogs in a sled team to start up or go faster ▷ vb travel by or drive a dogsled
MUSHA interj Irish exclamation of surprise
MUSHED > MUSH

MUSHER > MUSH
MUSHERS > MUSH
MUSHES > MUSH
MUSHIER > MUSHY
MUSHIEST > MUSHY
MUSHILY > MUSHY
MUSHINESS > MUSHY
MUSHING > MUSH
MUSHMOUTH n person speaking indistinctly
MUSHROOM n edible fungus with a stem and cap ▷ vb grow rapidly
MUSHROOMS > MUSHROOM
MUSHY adj soft and pulpy
MUSIC n art form using a melodious and harmonious combination of notes ▷ vb play music
MUSICAL adj of or like music ▷ n play or film with songs and dancing
MUSICALE n party or social evening with a musical programme
MUSICALES > MUSICALE
MUSICALLY > MUSICAL
MUSICALS > MUSICAL
MUSICIAN n person who plays or composes music, esp as a profession
MUSICIANS > MUSICIAN
MUSICK same as > MUSIC
MUSICKED > MUSIC
MUSICKER > MUSIC
MUSICKERS > MUSIC
MUSICKING > MUSIC
MUSICKS > MUSICK
MUSICLESS > MUSIC
MUSICS > MUSIC
MUSIMON same as > MOUFFLON
MUSIMONS > MUSIMON
MUSING > MUSE
MUSINGLY > MUSE
MUSINGS > MUSE
MUSIT n gap in fence
MUSITS > MUSIT
MUSIVE adj mosaic
MUSJID same as > MASJID
MUSJIDS > MUSJID
MUSK n scent obtained from a gland of the musk deer or produced synthetically ▷ vb perfume with musk
MUSKED > MUSK
MUSKEG n area of undrained boggy land
MUSKEGS > MUSKEG
MUSKET n long-barrelled gun
MUSKETEER n (formerly) a soldier armed with a musket
MUSKETOON n small musket
MUSKETRY n (use of) muskets
MUSKETS > MUSKET
MUSKIE n large North American freshwater game fish
MUSKIER > MUSKIE
MUSKIES > MUSKIE

MUSKIEST > MUSKIE
MUSKILY > MUSKY
MUSKINESS > MUSKY
MUSKING > MUSK
MUSKIT same as > MESQUITE
MUSKITS > MUSKIT
MUSKLE same as > MUSSEL
MUSKLES > MUSKLE
MUSKMELON n any of several varieties of melon, such as the cantaloupe and honeydew
MUSKONE n substance in musk
MUSKONES > MUSKONE
MUSKOX n large Canadian mammal
MUSKOXEN > MUSKOX
MUSKRAT n N American beaver-like rodent
MUSKRATS > MUSKRAT
MUSKROOT same as > MOSCHATEL
MUSKROOTS > MUSKROOT
MUSKS > MUSK
MUSKY same as > MUSKIE
MUSLIN n fine cotton fabric
MUSLINED adj wearing muslin
MUSLINET n coarse muslin
MUSLINETS > MUSLINET
MUSLINS > MUSLIN
MUSMON same as > MUSIMON
MUSMONS > MUSMON
MUSO n musician, esp a pop musician, regarded as being overconcerned with technique rather than musical content or expression
MUSOS > MUSO
MUSPIKE n Canadian freshwater fish
MUSPIKES > MUSPIKE
MUSQUASH same as > MUSKRAT
MUSROL n part of bridle
MUSROLS > MUSROL
MUSS vb make untidy ▷ n state of disorder
MUSSE same as > MUSS
MUSSED > MUSS
MUSSEL n edible shellfish with a dark hinged shell
MUSSELLED adj poisoned through eating bad mussels
MUSSELS > MUSSEL
MUSSES > MUSS
MUSSIER > MUSSY
MUSSIEST > MUSSY
MUSSILY > MUSSY
MUSSINESS > MUSSY
MUSSING > MUSS
MUSSITATE vb mutter
MUSSY adj untidy or disordered
MUST vb used as an auxiliary to express obligation, certainty, or resolution ▷ n essential or necessary thing ▷ vb powder

MUSTACHE same as > MOUSTACHE

MUSTACHED > MUSTACHE

MUSTACHES > MUSTACHE

MUSTACHIO n moustache, esp a bushy or elaborate one

MUSTANG n wild horse of SW USA

MUSTANGS > MUSTANG

MUSTARD n paste made from the powdered seeds of a plant, used as a condiment ▷ adj brownish-yellow

MUSTARDS > MUSTARD

MUSTARDY > MUSTARD

MUSTED > MUST

MUSTEE n offspring of a White and a quadroon

MUSTEES > MUSTEE

MUSTELID n member of weasel family

MUSTELIDS > MUSTELID

MUSTELINE n type of predatory mammal of the family which includes weasels, ferrets, polecats, badgers, and otters

MUSTER vb summon up (strength, energy, or support) ▷ n assembly of military personnel

MUSTERED > MUSTER

MUSTERER > MUSTER

MUSTERERS > MUSTER

MUSTERING > MUSTER

MUSTERS > MUSTER

MUSTH n state of frenzied sexual excitement in the males of certain large mammals, esp elephants, associated with discharge from a gland between the ear and eye

MUSTHS > MUSTH

MUSTIER > MUSTY

MUSTIEST > MUSTY

MUSTILY > MUSTY

MUSTINESS > MUSTY

MUSTING > MUST

MUSTS > MUST

MUSTY adj smelling mouldy and stale

MUT another word for > EM

MUTABLE adj liable to change

MUTABLY > MUTABLE

MUTAGEN n any substance that can induce genetic mutation

MUTAGENIC > MUTAGEN

MUTAGENS > MUTAGEN

MUTANDA > MUTANDUM

MUTANDUM n something to be changed

MUTANT n mutated animal, plant, etc ▷ adj of or resulting from mutation

MUTANTS > MUTANT

MUTASE n type of enzyme

MUTASES > MUTASE

MUTATE vb (cause to) undergo mutation

MUTATED > MUTATE

MUTATES > MUTATE

MUTATING > MUTATE

MUTATION same as > MUTANT

MUTATIONS > MUTATION

MUTATIVE > MUTATE

MUTATORY adj subject to change

MUTCH n close-fitting linen cap formerly worn by women and children in Scotland ▷ vb cadge

MUTCHED > MUTCH

MUTCHES > MUTCH

MUTCHING > MUTCH

MUTCHKIN n Scottish unit of liquid measure equal to slightly less than one pint

MUTCHKINS > MUTCHKIN

MUTE adj silent ▷ n person who is unable to speak ▷ vb reduce the volume or soften the tone of a musical instrument by means of a mute or soft pedal

MUTED adj (of sound or colour) softened

MUTEDLY > MUTED

MUTELY > MUTE

MUTENESS > MUTE

MUTER > MUTE

MUTES > MUTE

MUTEST > MUTE

MUTHA n taboo slang word derived from motherfucker

MUTHAS > MUTHA

MUTI n medicine, esp herbal medicine

MUTICATE same as > MUTICOUS

MUTICOUS adj lacking an awn, spine, or point

MUTILATE vb deprive of a limb or other part

MUTILATED > MUTILATE

MUTILATES > MUTILATE

MUTILATOR > MUTILATE

MUTINE vb mutiny

MUTINED > MUTINE

MUTINEER n person who mutinies

MUTINEERS > MUTINEER

MUTINES > MUTINE

MUTING > MUTE

MUTINIED > MUTINY

MUTINIES > MUTINY

MUTINING > MUTINE

MUTINOUS adj openly rebellious

MUTINY n rebellion against authority, esp by soldiers or sailors ▷ vb commit mutiny

MUTINYING > MUTINY

MUTIS > MUTI

MUTISM n state of being mute

MUTISMS > MUTISM

MUTON n part of gene

MUTONS > MUTON

MUTOSCOPE n early form of cine camera

MUTS > MUT

MUTT n mongrel dog

MUTTER vb utter or speak indistinctly ▷ n muttered sound or grumble

MUTTERED > MUTTER

MUTTERER > MUTTER

MUTTERERS > MUTTER

MUTTERING > MUTTER

MUTTERS > MUTTER

MUTTON n flesh of sheep, used as food

MUTTONS > MUTTON

MUTTONY > MUTTON

MUTTS > MUTT

MUTUAL adj felt or expressed by each of two people about the other ▷ n mutual company

MUTUALISE same as > MUTUALIZE

MUTUALISM another name for > SYMBIOSIS

MUTUALIST > MUTUALISM

MUTUALITY > MUTUAL

MUTUALIZE vb make or become mutual

MUTUALLY > MUTUAL

MUTUALS > MUTUAL

MUTUCA same as > MOTUCA

MUTUCAS > MUTUCA

MUTUEL n system of betting in which those who have bet on the winners of a race share in the total amount wagered less a percentage for the management

MUTUELS > MUTUEL

MUTULAR > MUTULE

MUTULE n one of a set of flat blocks below the corona of a Doric cornice

MUTULES > MUTULE

MUTUUM n contract for loan of goods

MUTUUMS > MUTUUM

MUUMUU n loose brightly-coloured dress worn by women in Hawaii

MUUMUUS > MUUMUU

MUX vb spoil

MUXED > MUX

MUXES > MUX

MUXING > MUX

MUZAKY adj having a bland sound

MUZHIK n Russian peasant, esp under the tsars

MUZHIKS > MUZHIK

MUZJIK same as > MUZHIK

MUZJIKS > MUZJIK

MUZZ vb make (something) muzzy

MUZZED > MUZZ

MUZZES > MUZZ

MUZZIER > MUZZY

MUZZIEST > MUZZY

MUZZILY > MUZZY

MUZZINESS > MUZZY

MUZZING > MUZZ

MUZZLE n animal's mouth and nose ▷ vb prevent from being heard or noticed

MUZZLED > MUZZLE

MUZZLER > MUZZLE

MUZZLERS > MUZZLE

MUZZLES > MUZZLE

MUZZLING > MUZZLE

MUZZY adj confused or muddled

MVULE n tropical African tree

MVULES > MVULE

MWAH interj representation of the sound of a kiss

MWALIMU n teacher

MWALIMUS > MWALIMU

MY adj belonging to me ▷ interj exclamation of surprise or awe ▷ det of, belonging to, or associated with the speaker or writer (me)

MYAL > MYALISM

MYALGIA n pain in a muscle or a group of muscles

MYALGIAS > MYALGIA

MYALGIC > MYALGIA

MYALISM n kind of witchcraft, similar to obi, practised esp in the Caribbean

MYALISMS > MYALISM

MYALIST > MYALISM

MYALISTS > MYALISM

MYALL n Australian acacia with hard scented wood

MYALLS > MYALL

MYASES > MYASIS

MYASIS same as > MYIASIS

MYC n oncogene that aids the growth of tumorous cells

MYCELE n microscopic spike-like structure in mucus

MYCELES > MYCELE

MYCELIA > MYCELIUM

MYCELIAL > MYCELIUM

MYCELIAN > MYCELIUM

MYCELIUM n mass forming the body of a fungus

MYCELLA n blue-veined Danish cream cheese, less strongly flavoured than Danish blue

MYCELLAS > MYCELLA

MYCELOID > MYCELIUM

MYCETES n fungus

MYCETOMA n chronic fungal infection, esp of the foot, characterized by swelling, usually resulting from a wound

MYCETOMAS > MYCETOMA

MYCOBIONT n fungal constituent of a lichen

MYCOFLORA n all fungus growing in particular place

MYCOLOGIC > MYCOLOGY

MYCOLOGY n study of fungi

MYCOPHAGY n eating of mushrooms

MYCOPHILE n person who likes eating mushrooms

MYCORHIZA n association of a fungus and a plant in which the fungus lives within or on the outside of the plant's roots forming a symbiotic or parasitic relationship

MYCOSES >MYCOSIS

MYCOSIS *n* any infection or disease caused by fungus

MYCOTIC >MYCOSIS

MYCOTOXIN *n* any of various toxic substances produced by fungi some of which may affect food and others of which are alleged to have been used in warfare

MYCOVIRUS *n* virus attacking fungi

MYCS >MYC

MYDRIASES >MYDRIASIS

MYDRIASIS *n* abnormal dilation of the pupil of the eye, produced by drugs, coma, etc

MYDRIATIC *adj* relating to or causing mydriasis ▷ *n* mydriatic drug

MYELIN *n* white tissue forming an insulating sheath around certain nerve fibres

MYELINE *same as* >MYELIN

MYELINES >MYELINE

MYELINIC >MYELIN

MYELINS >MYELIN

MYELITIS *n* inflammation of the spinal cord or of the bone marrow

MYELOCYTE *n* immature granulocyte, normally occurring in the bone marrow but detected in the blood in certain diseases

MYELOGRAM *n* X-ray of the spinal cord, after injection with a radio-opaque medium

MYELOID *adj* of or relating to the spinal cord or the bone marrow

MYELOMA *n* tumour of the bone marrow

MYELOMAS >MYELOMA

MYELOMATA >MYELOMA

MYELON *n* spinal cord

MYELONS >MYELON

MYGALE *n* large American spider

MYGALES >MYGALE

MYIASES >MYIASIS

MYIASIS *n* infestation of the body by the larvae of flies

MYIOPHILY *same as* >MYOPHILY

MYLAR *n* tradename for a kind of strong polyester film

MYLARS >MYLAR

MYLODON *n* prehistoric giant sloth

MYLODONS >MYLODON

MYLODONT *same as* >MYLODON

MYLODONTS >MYLODONT

MYLOHYOID *n* muscle in neck

MYLONITE *n* fine-grained metamorphic rock, often showing banding and micaceous fracture, formed by the crushing, grinding, or rolling of the original structure

MYLONITES >MYLONITE

MYLONITIC >MYLONITE

MYNA *same as* >MYNAH

MYNAH *n* tropical Asian starling which can mimic human speech

MYNAHS >MYNAH

MYNAS >MYNA

MYNHEER *n* Dutch title of address

MYNHEERS >MYNHEER

MYOBLAST *n* cell from which muscle develops

MYOBLASTS >MYOBLAST

MYOCARDIA *npl* muscular tissues of the heart

MYOCLONIC >MYOCLONUS

MYOCLONUS *n* sudden involuntary muscle contraction

MYOFIBRIL *n* type of cell in muscle

MYOGEN *n* albumin found in muscle

MYOGENIC *adj* originating in or forming muscle tissue

MYOGENS >MYOGEN

MYOGLOBIN *n* protein that is the main oxygen-carrier of muscle

MYOGRAM *n* tracings of muscular contractions

MYOGRAMS >MYOGRAM

MYOGRAPH *n* instrument for recording tracings of muscular contractions

MYOGRAPHS >MYOGRAPH

MYOGRAPHY >MYOGRAPH

MYOID *adj* like muscle

MYOLOGIC >MYOLOGY

MYOLOGIES >MYOLOGY

MYOLOGIST >MYOLOGY

MYOLOGY *n* branch of medical science concerned with the structure and diseases of muscles

MYOMA *n* benign tumour composed of muscle tissue

MYOMANCY *n* divination through observing mice

MYOMANTIC >MYOMANCY

MYOMAS >MYOMA

MYOMATA >MYOMA

MYOMATOUS >MYOMA

MYONEURAL *adj* involving muscle and nerve

MYOPATHIC >MYOPATHY

MYOPATHY *n* any disease affecting muscles or muscle tissue

MYOPE *n* any person afflicted with myopia

MYOPES >MYOPE

MYOPHILY *n* pollination of

plants by flies

MYOPIA *n* short-sightedness

MYOPIAS >MYOPIA

MYOPIC *n* shortsighted person

MYOPICS >MYOPIC

MYOPIES >MYOPY

MYOPS *same as* >MYOPE

MYOPSES >MYOPS

MYOPY *same as* >MYOPIA

MYOSCOPE *n* electrical instrument for stimulating muscles

MYOSCOPES >MYOSCOPE

MYOSES >MYOSIS

MYOSIN *n* chief protein of muscle that interacts with actin to form actomyosin during muscle contraction

MYOSINS >MYOSIN

MYOSIS *same as* >MIOSIS

MYOSITIS *n* inflammation of muscle

MYOSOTE *same as* >MYOSOTIS

MYOSOTES >MYOSOTE

MYOSOTIS *n* type of hairy-leaved flowering plant, such as the forget-me-not

MYOSTATIN *n* protein that inhibits muscle tissue growth

MYOTIC >MIOSIS

MYOTICS >MIOSIS

MYOTOME *n* any segment of embryonic mesoderm that develops into skeletal muscle in the adult

MYOTOMES >MYOTOME

MYOTONIA *n* lack of muscle tone, frequently including muscle spasm or rigidity

MYOTONIAS >MYOTONIA

MYOTONIC >MYOTONIA

MYOTUBE *n* cylindrical cell in muscle

MYOTUBES >MYOTUBE

MYRBANE *same as* >MIRBANE

MYRBANES >MYRBANE

MYRIAD *adj* innumerable ▷ *n* large indefinite number

MYRIADS >MYRIAD

MYRIADTH >MYRIAD

MYRIADTHS >MYRIAD

MYRIAPOD *n* type of invertebrate with a long segmented body and many legs, such as a centipede

MYRIAPODS >MYRIAPOD

MYRICA *n* dried root bark of the wax myrtle, used as a tonic and to treat diarrhoea

MYRICAS >MYRICA

MYRINGA *n* eardrum

MYRINGAS >MYRINGA

MYRIOPOD *same as* >MYRIAPOD

MYRIOPODS >MYRIOPOD

MYRIORAMA *n* picture made up of different parts

MYRISTIC *adj* of nutmeg plant family

MYRMECOID *adj* like ant

MYRMIDON *n* follower or henchman

MYRMIDONS >MYRMIDON

MYROBALAN *n* dried plumlike fruit of various tropical trees, used in dyeing, tanning, ink, and medicine

MYRRH *n* aromatic gum used in perfume, incense, and medicine

MYRRHIC >MYRRH

MYRRHINE >MURRA

MYRRHOL *n* oil of myrrh

MYRRHOLS >MYRRHOL

MYRRHS >MYRRH

MYRTLE *n* flowering evergreen shrub

MYRTLES >MYRTLE

MYSELF *pron* reflexive form of I or me

MYSID *n* small shrimplike crustacean

MYSIDS >MYSID

MYSOST *n* Norwegian cheese

MYSOSTS >MYSOST

MYSPACE *vb* search for (someone) on the MySpace website

MYSPACED >MYSPACE

MYSPACES >MYSPACE

MYSPACING >MYSPACE

MYSTAGOG *n* person instructing others in religious mysteries

MYSTAGOGS >MYSTAGOG

MYSTAGOGY *n* instruction of those who are preparing for initiation into the mysteries

MYSTERIES >MYSTERY

MYSTERY *n* strange or inexplicable event or phenomenon

MYSTIC *n* person who seeks spiritual knowledge ▷ *adj* mystical

MYSTICAL *adj* having a spiritual or religious significance beyond human understanding

MYSTICETE *n* species of whale

MYSTICISM *n* belief in or experience of a reality beyond normal human understanding or experience

MYSTICLY >MYSTIC

MYSTICS >MYSTIC

MYSTIFIED >MYSTIFY

MYSTIFIER >MYSTIFY

MYSTIFIES >MYSTIFY

MYSTIFY *vb* bewilder or puzzle

MYSTIQUE *n* aura of mystery or power

MYSTIQUES >MYSTIQUE

MYTH *n* tale with supernatural characters, usu. of how the world and mankind began

MYTHI >MYTHUS

MYTHIC *same as*
>MYTHICAL
MYTHICAL *adj* of or
relating to myth
MYTHICISE *same as*
>MYTHICIZE
MYTHICISM *n* theory that
explains miracles as myths
MYTHICIST
>MYTHICIZE
MYTHICIZE *vb* make into
or treat as a myth
MYTHIER >MYTHY
MYTHIEST >MYTHY
MYTHISE *same as*
>MYTHIZE
MYTHISED >MYTHISE
MYTHISES >MYTHISE
MYTHISING >MYTHISE
MYTHISM *same as*
>MYTHICISM
MYTHISMS >MYTHISM
MYTHIST >MYTHISM
MYTHISTS >MYTHISM

MYTHIZE *same as*
>MYTHICIZE
MYTHIZED >MYTHIZE
MYTHIZES >MYTHIZE
MYTHIZING >MYTHIZE
MYTHMAKER *n* person who
creates myth
MYTHOI >MYTHOS
MYTHOLOGY *n* myths
collectively
MYTHOMANE *n* obsession
with lying, exaggerating, or
relating incredible
imaginary adventures as if
they had really happened
MYTHOPEIC *adj* of myths
MYTHOPOET *n* poet writing
on mythical theme
MYTHOS *n* complex of
beliefs, values, attitudes,
etc, characteristic of a
specific group or society
MYTHS >MYTH
MYTHUS *same as* >MYTHOS

MYTHY *adj* of or like myth
MYTILOID *adj* like mussel
MYXAMEBA *same as*
>MYXAMOEBA
MYXAMEBAE >MYXAMEBA
MYXAMEBAS >MYXAMEBA
MYXAMOEBA *n* cell
produced by spore
MYXEDEMA *same as*
>MYXOEDEMA
MYXEDEMAS >MYXEDEMA
MYXEDEMIC
>MYXOEDEMA
MYXO *n* infectious and
usually fatal viral disease of
rabbits characterized by
swelling of the mucous
membranes and formation
of skin tumours
MYXOCYTE *n* cell in
mucous tissue
MYXOCYTES >MYXOCYTE
MYXOEDEMA *n* disease
caused by an underactive

thyroid gland,
characterized by puffy eyes,
face, and hands, and
mental sluggishness
MYXOID *adj* containing
mucus
MYXOMA *n* tumour
composed of mucous
connective tissue, usually
situated in subcutaneous
tissue
MYXOMAS >MYXOMA
MYXOMATA >MYXOMA
MYXOS >MYXO
MYXOVIRAL
>MYXOVIRUS
MYXOVIRUS *n* any of a
group of viruses that cause
influenza, mumps, and
certain other diseases
MZEE *n* old person ▷ *adj*
advanced in years
MZEES >MZEE
MZUNGU *n* White person
MZUNGUS >MZUNGU

Nn

NA *same as* > NAE
NAAM *same as* > NAM
NAAMS > NAAM
NAAN *n* slightly leavened flat Indian bread
NAANS > NAAN
NAARTJE *same as* > NAARTJIE
NAARTJES > NAARTJE
NAARTJIE *n* tangerine
NAARTJIES > NAARTJIE
NAB *vb* arrest (someone)
NABBED > NAB
NABBER *n* thief
NABBERS > NABBER
NABBING > NAB
NABE *n* Japanese hotpot
NABES > NABE
NABIS *n* Parisian art movement
NABK *n* edible berry
NABKS > NABK
NABLA *another name for* > DEL
NABLAS > NABLA
NABOB *same as* > NAWAB
NABOBERY > NABOB
NABOBESS *n* rich, powerful, or important woman
NABOBISH > NABOB
NABOBISM > NABOB
NABOBISMS > NABOB
NABOBS > NABOB
NABS > NAB
NACARAT *n* red-orange colour
NACARATS > NACARAT
NACELLE *n* streamlined enclosure on an aircraft, esp one housing an engine
NACELLES > NACELLE
NACH *n* Indian dance
NACHAS *n* pleasure
NACHE *n* rump
NACHES > NACHE
NACHO *n* snack of a piece of tortilla topped with cheese, peppers, etc
NACHOS > NACHO
NACHTMAAL *same as* > NAGMAAL
NACKET *n* light lunch, snack
NACKETS > NACKET
NACRE *n* mother of pearl
NACRED > NACRE
NACREOUS *adj* relating to or consisting of mother-of-pearl

NACRES > NACRE
NACRITE *n* mineral
NACRITES > NACRITE
NACROUS > NACRE
NADA *n* nothing
NADAS > NADA
NADIR *n* point in the sky opposite the zenith
NADIRAL > NADIR
NADIRS > NADIR
NADORS *n* thirst brought on by excessive consumption of alcohol
NADS *npl* testicles
NAE *Scot word for* > NO
NAEBODIES > NAEBODY
NAEBODY *Scots variant of* > NOBODY
NAETHING *Scots variant of* > NOTHING
NAETHINGS > NAETHING
NAEVE *n* birthmark
NAEVES > NAEVUS
NAEVI > NAEVUS
NAEVOID > NAEVUS
NAEVUS *n* birthmark or mole
NAFF *adj* lacking quality or taste ▷ *vb* go away
NAFFED > NAFF
NAFFER > NAFF
NAFFEST > NAFF
NAFFING > NAFF
NAFFLY > NAFF
NAFFNESS > NAFF
NAFFS > NAFF
NAG *vb* scold or find fault constantly ▷ *n* person who nags
NAGA *n* cobra
NAGANA *n* disease of all domesticated animals of central and southern Africa
NAGANAS > NAGANA
NAGAPIE *n* bushbaby
NAGAPIES > NAGAPIE
NAGARI *n* set of scripts used as the writing systems for several languages of India
NAGARIS > NAGARI
NAGAS > NAGA
NAGGED > NAG
NAGGER > NAG
NAGGERS > NAG
NAGGIER > NAG
NAGGIEST > NAG
NAGGING > NAG
NAGGINGLY > NAG
NAGGINGS > NAGGING

NAGGY > NAG
NAGMAAL *n* Communion
NAGMAALS > NAGMAAL
NAGOR *another name for* > REEDBUCK
NAGORS > NAGOR
NAGS > NAG
NAH *same as* > NO
NAHAL *n* agricultural settlement run by an Israeli military youth organization
NAHALS > NAHAL
NAIAD *n* nymph living in a lake or river
NAIADES > NAIAD
NAIADS > NAIAD
NAIANT *adj* swimming
NAIF *less common word for* > NAIVE
NAIFER > NAIF
NAIFEST > NAIF
NAIFLY > NAIVE
NAIFNESS > NAIVE
NAIFS > NAIF
NAIK *n* chief
NAIKS > NAIK
NAIL *n* pointed piece of metal with a head, hit with a hammer to join two objects together ▷ *vb* attach (something) with nails
NAILBITER *n* person who bites his or her nails
NAILBRUSH *n* small stiff-bristled brush for cleaning the fingernails
NAILED > NAIL
NAILER > NAIL
NAILERIES > NAILERY
NAILERS > NAIL
NAILERY *n* nail factory
NAILFILE *n* small metal file used to shape and smooth the nails
NAILFILES > NAILFILE
NAILFOLD *n* skin at base of fingernail
NAILFOLDS > NAILFOLD
NAILHEAD *n* decorative device, as on tooled leather, resembling the round head of a nail
NAILHEADS > NAILHEAD
NAILING > NAIL
NAILINGS > NAIL
NAILLESS > NAIL
NAILS > NAIL
NAILSET *n* punch for driving the head of a nail below the surrounding

surface
NAILSETS > NAILSET
NAIN *adj* own
NAINSELL *n* own self
NAINSELLS > NAINSELL
NAINSOOK *n* light soft plain-weave cotton fabric, used esp for babies' wear
NAINSOOKS > NAINSOOK
NAIRA *n* standard monetary unit of Nigeria, divided into 100 kobo
NAIRAS > NAIRA
NAIRU *n* Non-Accelerating Inflation Rate of Unemployment
NAIRUS > NAIRU
NAISSANCE *French for* > BIRTH
NAISSANT *adj* (of a beast) having only the forepart shown above a horizontal division of a shield
NAIVE *adj* innocent and gullible ▷ *n* person who is naive, esp in artistic style
NAIVELY > NAIVE
NAIVENESS > NAIVE
NAIVER > NAIVE
NAIVES > NAIVE
NAIVEST > NAIVE
NAIVETE *variant of* > NAIVETY
NAIVETES > NAIVETE
NAIVETIES > NAIVETY
NAIVETY *n* state or quality of being naive
NAIVIST > NAIVE
NAKED *adj* without clothes
NAKEDER > NAKED
NAKEDEST > NAKED
NAKEDLY > NAKED
NAKEDNESS > NAKED
NAKER *n* one of a pair of small kettledrums used in medieval music
NAKERS > NAKER
NAKFA *n* standard currency unit of Eritrea
NAKFAS > NAKFA
NALA *n* ravine
NALAS > NALA
NALED *n* type of insecticide
NALEDS > NALED
NALIDIXIC *as in nalidixic acid* type of acid
NALLA *n* ravine
NALLAH *same as* > NALLA
NALLAHS > NALLAH
NALLAS > NALLA
NALOXONE *n* chemical

substance that counteracts the effects of opiates by binding to opiate receptors on cells

NALOXONES > NALOXONE

NAM n distraint

NAMABLE > NAME

NAMASKAR n salutation used in India

NAMASKARS > NAMASKAR

NAMASTE n Indian greeting

NAMASTES > NAMASTE

NAMAYCUSH n North American freshwater fish

NAME n word by which a person or thing is known ▷ vb give a name to

NAMEABLE > NAME

NAMECHECK vb mention (someone) by name ▷ n mention of someone's name, for example on a radio programme

NAMED > NAME

NAMELESS adj without a name

NAMELY adv that is to say

NAMEPLATE n small sign on or by a door giving the occupant's name and, sometimes, profession

NAMER > NAME

NAMERS > NAME

NAMES > NAME

NAMESAKE n person with the same name as another

NAMESAKES > NAMESAKE

NAMETAG n identification badge

NAMETAGS > NAMETAG

NAMETAPE n narrow cloth tape bearing the owner's name and attached to an article

NAMETAPES > NAMETAPE

NAMING > NAME

NAMINGS > NAME

NAMMA as in namma hole Australian word for a natural well in rock

NAMS > NAM

NAMU n black New Zealand sandfly

NAMUS > NAMU

NAN n grandmother

NANA same as > NAN

NANAS > NANA

NANCE n homosexual man

NANCES > NANCE

NANCIES > NANCY

NANCIFIED adj effeminate

NANCY n effeminate or homosexual boy or man

NANDIN n type of shrub

NANDINA n type of shrub

NANDINAS > NANDINA

NANDINE n African palm civet

NANDINES > NANDINE

NANDINS > NANDIN

NANDOO > NANDU

NANDOOS > NANDOO

NANDU n type of ostrich

NANDUS > NANDU

NANE Scot word for > NONE

NANG adj excellent; cool

NANISM n dwarfism

NANISMS > NANISM

NANITE n microscopically small machine or robot

NANITES > NANITE

NANKEEN n hard-wearing buff-coloured cotton fabric

NANKEENS > NANKEEN

NANKIN same as > NANKEEN

NANKINS > NANKIN

NANNA same as > NAN

NANNAS > NANNA

NANNIE same as > NANNY

NANNIED > NANNY

NANNIES > NANNY

NANNY n woman whose job is looking after young children ▷ vb be too protective towards

NANNYGAI n edible sea fish of Australia which is red in colour and has large prominent eyes

NANNYGAIS > NANNYGAI

NANNYING > NANNY

NANNYISH > NANNY

NANOBE n microbe that is smaller than the smallest known bacterium

NANOBES > NANOBE

NANOBOT n microscopically small robot

NANOBOTS > NANOBOT

NANODOT n microscopic cluster of several hundred nickel atoms used to store large amounts of data in a computer chip

NANODOTS > NANODOT

NANOGRAM n unit of measurement

NANOGRAMS > NANOGRAM

NANOMETER same as > NANOMETRE

NANOMETRE n one thousand-millionth of a metre

NANOOK n polar bear

NANOOKS > NANOOK

NANOPORE n microscopically small pore in an electrically insulating membrane

NANOPORES > NANOPORE

NANOSCALE adj on very small scale

NANOTECH n technology of very small objects

NANOTECHS > NANOTECH

NANOTESLA n unit of measurement

NANOTUBE n cylindrical molecule of carbon

NANOTUBES > NANOTUBE

NANOWATT n unit of measurement

NANOWATTS > NANOWATT

NANOWIRE n microscopically thin wire

NANOWIRES > NANOWIRE

NANOWORLD n world at a

microscopic level, as dealt with by nanotechnology

NANS > NAN

NANUA same as > MOKI

NANUAS > NANUA

NAOI > NAOS

NAOS n ancient classical temple

NAOSES > NAOS

NAP n short sleep ▷ vb have a short sleep

NAPA n type of leather

NAPALM n highly inflammable jellied petrol, used in bombs ▷ vb attack (people or places) with napalm

NAPALMED > NAPALM

NAPALMING > NAPALM

NAPALMS > NAPALM

NAPAS > NAPA

NAPE n back of the neck ▷ vb attack with napalm

NAPED > NAPE

NAPERIES > NAPERY

NAPERY n household linen, esp table linen

NAPES > NAPE

NAPHTHA n liquid mixture distilled from coal tar or petroleum, used as a solvent and in petrol

NAPHTHAS > NAPHTHA

NAPHTHENE n any of a class of cycloalkanes found in petroleum

NAPHTHOL n white crystalline solid used in dyes

NAPHTHOLS > NAPHTHOL

NAPHTHOUS > NAPHTHA

NAPHTHYL n of, consisting of, or containing either of two forms of the monovalent group $C_{10}H_7$

NAPHTHYLS > NAPHTHYL

NAPHTOL same as > NAPHTHOL

NAPHTOLS > NAPHTOL

NAPIFORM adj shaped like a turnip)

NAPING > NAPE

NAPKIN same as > NAPPY

NAPKINS > NAPKIN

NAPLESS adj threadbare

NAPOLEON n former French gold coin worth 20 francs

NAPOLEONS > NAPOLEON

NAPOO vb kill

NAPOOED > NAPOO

NAPOOING > NAPOO

NAPOOS > NAPOO

NAPPA n soft leather, used in gloves and clothes, made from sheepskin, lambskin, or kid

NAPPAS > NAPPA

NAPPE n large sheet or mass of rock that has been thrust from its original position by earth movements

NAPPED > NAP

NAPPER n person or thing that raises the nap on cloth

NAPPERS > NAPPER

NAPPES > NAPPE

NAPPIE same as > NAPPY

NAPPIER > NAPPY

NAPPIES > NAPPY

NAPPIEST > NAPPY

NAPPINESS > NAPPY

NAPPING > NAP

NAPPY n piece of absorbent material fastened round a baby's lower torso to absorb urine and faeces ▷ adj having a nap

NAPRON same as > APRON

NAPRONS > NAPRON

NAPROXEN n pain-killing drug

NAPROXENS > NAPROXEN

NAPS > NAP

NARAS same as > NARRAS

NARASES > NARAS

NARC n narcotics agent

NARCEEN same as > NARCEINE

NARCEENS > NARCEEN

NARCEIN same as > NARCEINE

NARCEINE n narcotic alkaloid that occurs in opium

NARCEINES > NARCEINE

NARCEINS > NARCEIN

NARCISM n exceptional admiration for oneself

NARCISMS > NARCISM

NARCISSI > NARCISSUS

NARCISSUS n yellow, orange, or white flower related to the daffodil

NARCIST n narcissist

NARCISTIC adj excessively admiring of oneself

NARCISTS > NARCIST

NARCO n officer working in the area of anti-drug operations

NARCOMA n coma caused by intake of narcotic drugs

NARCOMAS > NARCOMA

NARCOMATA > NARCOMA

NARCOS n drug smugglers

NARCOSE same as > NARCOSIS

NARCOSES > NARCOSIS

NARCOSIS n effect of a narcotic

NARCOTIC adj of a drug, such as morphine or opium, which produces numbness and drowsiness, used medicinally but addictive ▷ n such a drug

NARCOTICS > NARCOTIC

NARCOTINE n type of drug

NARCOTISE same as > NARCOTIZE

NARCOTISM n stupor or addiction induced by narcotic drugs

NARCOTIST n person affected by narcotics

NARCOTIZE vb place under the influence of a narcotic drug

NARCS > NARC
NARD *n* any of several plants whose aromatic roots were formerly used in medicine ▷ *vb* anoint with nard oil
NARDED > NARD
NARDINE > NARD
NARDING > NARD
NARDOO *n* any of certain cloverlike ferns which grow in swampy areas
NARDOOS > NARDOO
NARDS > NARD
NARE *n* nostril
NARES *npl* nostrils
NARGHILE another name for > HOOKAH
NARGHILES > NARGHILE
NARGHILLY same as > NARGHILE
NARGHILY same as > NARGHILE
NARGILE same as > NARGHILE
NARGILEH same as > NARGHILE
NARGILEHS > NARGILEH
NARGILES > NARGILE
NARGILIES > NARGILE
NARGILY same as > NARGHILE
NARGUILEH *n* hookah
NARIAL *adj* of or relating to the nares
NARIC > NARE
NARICORN *n* bird's nostril
NARICORNS > NARICORN
NARINE same as > NARIAL
NARIS > NARES
NARK *vb* annoy ▷ *n* informer or spy
NARKED > NARK
NARKIER > NARKY
NARKIEST > NARKY
NARKING > NARK
NARKS > NARK
NARKY *adj* irritable or complaining
NARQUOIS *adj* malicious
NARRAS *n* type of shrub
NARRASES > NARRAS
NARRATE *vb* tell (a story)
NARRATED > NARRATE
NARRATER same as > NARRATOR
NARRATERS > NARRATER
NARRATES > NARRATE
NARRATING > NARRATE
NARRATION *n* narrating
NARRATIVE *n* account, story ▷ *adj* telling a story
NARRATOR *n* person who tells a story or gives an account of something
NARRATORS > NARRATOR
NARRATORY > NARRATIVE
NARRE *adj* nearer
NARROW *adj* small in breadth in comparison to length ▷ *vb* make or become narrow
NARROWED > NARROW
NARROWER > NARROW

NARROWEST > NARROW
NARROWING > NARROW
NARROWISH > NARROW
NARROWLY > NARROW
NARROWS *npl* narrow part of a strait, river, or current
NARTHEX *n* portico at the west end of a basilica or church
NARTHEXES > NARTHEX
NARTJIE same as > NAARTJIE
NARTJIES > NARTJIE
NARWAL same as > NARWHAL
NARWALS > NARWAL
NARWHAL *n* arctic whale with a long spiral tusk
NARWHALE same as > NARWHAL
NARWHALES > NARWHALE
NARWHALS > NARWHAL
NARY *adv* not
NAS has not
NASAL *adj* of the nose ▷ *n* nasal speech sound, such as English *m*, *n*, or *ng*
NASALISE same as > NASALIZE
NASALISED > NASALISE
NASALISES > NASALISE
NASALISM *n* nasal pronunciation
NASALISMS > NASALISM
NASALITY > NASAL
NASALIZE *vb* pronounce nasally
NASALIZED > NASALIZE
NASALIZES > NASALIZE
NASALLY > NASAL
NASALS > NASAL
NASARD *n* organ stop
NASARDS > NASARD
NASCENCE > NASCENT
NASCENCES > NASCENT
NASCENCY > NASCENT
NASCENT *adj* starting to grow or develop
NASEBERRY another name for > SAPODILLA
NASHGAB *n* chatter
NASHGABS > NASHGAB
NASHI *n* fruit of the Japanese pear
NASHIS > NASHI
NASIAL > NASION
NASION *n* craniometric point where the top of the nose meets the ridge of the forehead
NASIONS > NASION
NASSELLA as in *nassella tussock* type of tussock grass
NASTALIK *n* type of script
NASTALIKS > NASTALIK
NASTIC *adj* (of movement of plants) independent of the direction of the external stimulus
NASTIER > NASTY
NASTIES > NASTY
NASTIEST > NASTY
NASTILY > NASTY

NASTINESS > NASTY
NASTY *adj* unpleasant ▷ *n* something unpleasant
NASUTE *n* type of termite
NASUTES > NASUTE
NAT *n* supporter of nationalism
NATAL *adj* of or relating to birth
NATALITY *n* birth rate in a given place
NATANT *adj* (of aquatic plants) floating on the water
NATANTLY *adv* in a floating manner
NATATION *n* swimming
NATATIONS > NATATION
NATATORIA *npl* indoor swimming pools
NATATORY *adj* of or relating to swimming
NATCH sentence substitute naturally ▷ *n* notch
NATCHES > NATCH
NATES *npl* buttocks
NATHELESS *prep* notwithstanding
NATHEMO same as > NATHEMORE
NATHEMORE *adv* nevermore
NATHLESS same as > NATHELESS
NATIFORM *adj* resembling buttocks
NATION *n* people of one or more cultures or races organized as a single state
NATIONAL *adj* of or serving a nation as a whole ▷ *n* citizen of a nation
NATIONALS > NATIONAL
NATIONS > NATION
NATIS > NATES
NATIVE *adj* relating to a place where a person was born ▷ *n* person born in a specified place
NATIVELY > NATIVE
NATIVES > NATIVE
NATIVISM *n* policy of favouring the natives of a country over the immigrants
NATIVISMS > NATIVISM
NATIVIST > NATIVISM
NATIVISTS > NATIVISM
NATIVITY *n* birth or origin
NATRIUM obsolete name for > SODIUM
NATRIUMS > NATRIUM
NATROLITE *n* colourless, white, or yellow zeolite mineral
NATRON *n* whitish or yellow mineral
NATRONS > NATRON
NATS > NAT
NATTER *vb* talk idly or chatter ▷ *n* long idle chat
NATTERED > NATTER
NATTERER > NATTER
NATTERERS > NATTER
NATTERING > NATTER

NATTERS > NATTER
NATTERY *adj* irritable
NATTIER > NATTY
NATTIEST > NATTY
NATTILY > NATTY
NATTINESS > NATTY
NATTY *adj* smart and spruce
NATURA *n* nature
NATURAE > NATURA
NATURAL *adj* normal or to be expected ▷ *n* person with an inborn talent or skill
NATURALLY > NATURAL
NATURALS > NATURAL
NATURE *n* whole system of the existence, forces, and events of the physical world that are not controlled by human beings
NATURED *adj* having a certain disposition
NATURES > NATURE
NATURING *adj* creative
NATURISM *n* nudism
NATURISMS > NATURISM
NATURIST > NATURISM
NATURISTS > NATURISM
NAUCH same as > NAUTCH
NAUCHES > NAUCH
NAUGAHYDE *n* type of vinyl-coated fabric
NAUGHT *n* nothing ▷ *adv* not at all
NAUGHTIER > NAUGHTY
NAUGHTIES > NAUGHTY
NAUGHTILY > NAUGHTY
NAUGHTS > NAUGHT
NAUGHTY *adj* disobedient or mischievous ▷ *n* act of sexual intercourse
NAUMACHIA *n* mock sea fight performed as an entertainment
NAUMACHY same as > NAUMACHIA
NAUNT *n* aunt
NAUNTS > NAUNT
NAUPLIAL > NAUPLIUS
NAUPLII > NAUPLIUS
NAUPLIOID > NAUPLIUS
NAUPLIUS *n* larva of many crustaceans
NAUSEA *n* feeling of being about to vomit
NAUSEANT *n* substance inducing nausea
NAUSEANTS > NAUSEANT
NAUSEAS > NAUSEA
NAUSEATE *vb* make (someone) feel sick
NAUSEATED > NAUSEATE
NAUSEATES > NAUSEATE
NAUSEOUS *adj* as if about to vomit
NAUTCH *n* intricate traditional Indian dance performed by professional dancing girls
NAUTCHES > NAUTCH
NAUTIC same as > NAUTICAL
NAUTICAL *adj* of the sea or ships

NAUTICS > NAUTIC
NAUTILI > NAUTILUS
NAUTILOID n type of mollusc ▷ adj of this type of mollusc
NAUTILUS n shellfish with many tentacles
NAVAID n navigational aid
NAVAIDS > NAVAID
NAVAL adj of or relating to a navy or ships
NAVALISM n domination of naval interests
NAVALISMS > NAVALISM
NAVALLY > NAVAL
NAVAR n system of air navigation
NAVARCH n admiral
NAVARCHS > NAVARCH
NAVARCHY n navarch's term of office
NAVARHO n aircraft navigation system
NAVARHOS > NAVARHO
NAVARIN n stew of mutton or lamb with root vegetables
NAVARINS > NAVARIN
NAVARS > NAVAR
NAVE n long central part of a church
NAVEL n hollow in the middle of the abdomen where the umbilical cord was attached
NAVELS > NAVEL
NAVELWORT another name for > PENNYWORT
NAVES > NAVE
NAVETTE n gem cut
NAVETTES > NAVETTE
NAVEW another name for > TURNIP
NAVEWS > NAVEW
NAVICERT n certificate specifying the contents of a neutral ship's cargo
NAVICERTS > NAVICERT
NAVICULA n incense holder
NAVICULAR adj shaped like a boat ▷ n small boat-shaped bone of the wrist or foot
NAVICULAS > NAVICULA
NAVIES > NAVY
NAVIGABLE adj wide, deep, or safe enough to be sailed through
NAVIGABLY > NAVIGABLE
NAVIGATE vb direct or plot the path or position of a ship, aircraft, or car
NAVIGATED > NAVIGATE
NAVIGATES > NAVIGATE
NAVIGATOR n person who is skilled in or performs navigation, esp on a ship or aircraft
NAVVIED > NAVVY
NAVVIES > NAVVY
NAVVY n labourer employed on a road or a building site ▷ vb work as a navvy

NAVVYING > NAVVY
NAVY n branch of a country's armed services comprising warships with their crews and organization ▷ adj navy-blue
NAW same as > NO
NAWAB n (formerly) a Muslim ruler or powerful landowner in India
NAWABS > NAWAB
NAY interj no ▷ n person who votes against a motion ▷ adv used for emphasis ▷ sentence substitute no
NAYS > NAY
NAYSAID > NAYSAY
NAYSAY vb say no
NAYSAYER n refuser
NAYSAYERS > NAYSAYER
NAYSAYING > NAYSAY
NAYSAYS > NAYSAY
NAYTHLES same as > NATHELESS
NAYWARD n towards denial
NAYWARDS same as > NAYWARD
NAYWORD n proverb
NAYWORDS > NAYWORD
NAZE n flat marshy headland
NAZES > NAZE
NAZI n person who thinks or acts in a brutal or dictatorial way
NAZIFIED > NAZIFY
NAZIFIES > NAZIFY
NAZIFY vb make nazi in character
NAZIFYING > NAZIFY
NAZIR n Muslim official
NAZIRS > NAZIR
NAZIS > NAZI
NE conj nor
NEAFE same as > NIEVE
NEAFES > NEAFE
NEAFFE same as > NIEVE
NEAFFES > NEAFFE
NEAL same as > ANNEAL
NEALED > NEAL
NEALING > NEAL
NEALS > NEAL
NEANIC adj of or relating to the early stages in the life cycle of an organism
NEAP adj of, relating to, or constituting a neap tide ▷ vb be grounded by a neap tide
NEAPED > NEAP
NEAPING > NEAP
NEAPS > NEAP
NEAR adj indicating a place or time not far away ▷ vb draw close (to) ▷ prep at or to a place or time not far away from ▷ adv at or to a place or time not far away ▷ n left side of a horse or vehicle
NEARBY adj not far away ▷ adv close at hand

NEARED > NEAR
NEARER > NEAR
NEAREST > NEAR
NEARING > NEAR
NEARLIER > NEARLY
NEARLIEST > NEARLY
NEARLY adv almost
NEARNESS > NEAR
NEARS > NEAR
NEARSHORE n area of coastline water
NEARSIDE n side of a vehicle that is nearer the kerb
NEARSIDES > NEARSIDE
NEAT adj tidy and clean ▷ n domestic bovine animal
NEATEN vb make neat
NEATENED > NEATEN
NEATENING > NEATEN
NEATENS > NEATEN
NEATER > NEAT
NEATEST > NEAT
NEATH short for > BENEATH
NEATHERD n cowherd
NEATHERDS > NEATHERD
NEATLY > NEAT
NEATNESS > NEAT
NEATNIK n very neat and tidy person
NEATNIKS > NEATNIK
NEATS > NEAT
NEB n beak of a bird or the nose of an animal ▷ vb look around nosily
NEBBED > NEB
NEBBICH same as > NEBBISH
NEBBICHS > NEBBICH
NEBBING > NEB
NEBBISH n unfortunate simpleton
NEBBISHE same as > NEBBISH
NEBBISHER same as > NEBBISH
NEBBISHES > NEBBISH
NEBBISHY > NEBBISH
NEBBUK n type of shrub
NEBBUKS > NEBBUK
NEBECK same as > NEBBUK
NEBECKS > NEBECK
NEBEK same as > NEBBUK
NEBEKS > NEBEK
NEBEL n Hebrew musical instrument
NEBELS > NEBEL
NEBENKERN n component of insect sperm
NEBISH same as > NEBBISH
NEBISHES > NEBISH
NEBRIS n fawn-skin
NEBRISES > NEBRIS
NEBS > NEB
NEBULA n hazy cloud of particles and gases
NEBULAE > NEBULA
NEBULAR > NEBULA
NEBULAS > NEBULA
NEBULE n cloud
NEBULES > NEBULE
NEBULISE same as > NEBULIZE

NEBULISED > NEBULISE
NEBULISER same as > NEBULIZER
NEBULISES > NEBULISE
NEBULIUM n element
NEBULIUMS > NEBULIUM
NEBULIZE vb turn (a liquid) into a fine spray
NEBULIZED > NEBULIZE
NEBULIZER n device which turns a drug from a liquid into a fine spray which can be inhaled
NEBULIZES > NEBULIZE
NEBULOSE same as > NEBULOUS
NEBULOUS adj vague and unclear
NEBULY adj wavy
NECESSARY adj needed to obtain the desired result
NECESSITY n circumstances that inevitably require a certain result
NECK n part of the body joining the head to the shoulders ▷ vb kiss and cuddle
NECKATEE n piece of ornamental cloth worn around the neck
NECKATEES > NECKATEE
NECKBAND n band around the neck of a garment
NECKBANDS > NECKBAND
NECKBEEF n cheap cattle flesh
NECKBEEFS > NECKBEEF
NECKCLOTH n large ornamental usually white cravat worn formerly by men
NECKED > NECK
NECKER > NECK
NECKERS > NECK
NECKGEAR n any neck covering
NECKGEARS > NECKGEAR
NECKING n activity of kissing and embracing passionately
NECKINGS > NECKING
NECKLACE n decorative piece of jewellery worn around the neck ▷ vb kill (someone) by placing a burning tyre round his or her neck
NECKLACED > NECKLACE
NECKLACES > NECKLACE
NECKLESS > NECK
NECKLET n ornament worn round the neck
NECKLETS > NECKLET
NECKLIKE > NECK
NECKLINE n shape or position of the upper edge of a dress or top
NECKLINES > NECKLINE
NECKPIECE n piece of fur, cloth, etc, worn around the neck or neckline
NECKS > NECK
NECKTIE same as > TIE

n

NECKTIES > NECKTIE

NECKVERSE *n* verse read to prove clergy membership

NECKWEAR *n* articles of clothing, such as ties, scarves, etc, worn around the neck

NECKWEARS > NECKWEAR

NECKWEED *n* type of plant

NECKWEEDS > NECKWEED

NECROLOGY *n* list of people recently dead

NECROPHIL *n* person who is sexually attracted to dead bodies

NECROPOLI *npl* burial sites or cemeteries

NECROPSY *n* postmortem examination ▷ *vb* carry out a necropsy

NECROSE *vb* cause or undergo necrosis

NECROSED > NECROSE

NECROSES > NECROSE

NECROSING > NECROSE

NECROSIS *n* death of cells in the body

NECROTIC > NECROSIS

NECROTISE *same as* > NECROTIZE

NECROTIZE *vb* undergo necrosis

NECROTOMY *n* dissection of a dead body

NECTAR *n* sweet liquid collected from flowers by bees

NECTAREAL > NECTAR

NECTAREAN > NECTAR

NECTARED *adj* filled with nectar

NECTARIAL > NECTARY

NECTARIED *adj* having nectaries

NECTARIES > NECTARY

NECTARINE *n* smooth-skinned peach

NECTAROUS > NECTAR

NECTARS > NECTAR

NECTARY *n* any of various glandular structures secreting nectar in a plant

NED *n* derogatory name for an adolescent hooligan

NEDDIER > NEDDY

NEDDIES > NEDDY

NEDDIEST > NEDDY

NEDDISH > NEDDY

NEDDY *n* donkey ▷ *adj* of or relating to neds

NEDETTE *n* derogatory name for a female adolescent hooligan

NEDETTES > NEDETTE

NEDS > NED

NEE *prep* indicating the maiden name of a married woman ▷ *adj* indicating the maiden name of a married woman

NEED *vb* require or be in want of ▷ *n* condition of lacking something

NEEDED > NEED

NEEDER > NEED

NEEDERS > NEED

NEEDFIRE *n* beacon

NEEDFIRES > NEEDFIRE

NEEDFUL *adj* necessary or required

NEEDFULLY > NEEDFUL

NEEDFULS *n* must-haves

NEEDIER > NEEDY

NEEDIEST > NEEDY

NEEDILY > NEEDY

NEEDINESS *n* state of being needy

NEEDING > NEED

NEEDLE *n* thin pointed piece of metal with an eye through which thread is passed for sewing ▷ *vb* goad or provoke

NEEDLED > NEEDLE

NEEDLEFUL *n* length of thread cut for use in a needle

NEEDLER *n* needle maker

NEEDLERS > NEEDLER

NEEDLES > NEEDLE

NEEDLESS *adj* unnecessary

NEEDLIER > NEEDLE

NEEDLIEST > NEEDLE

NEEDLING > NEEDLE

NEEDLINGS > NEEDLE

NEEDLY > NEEDLE

NEEDMENT > NEED

NEEDMENTS > NEED

NEEDS *adv* necessarily ▷ *npl* what is required

NEEDY *adj* poor, in need of financial support

NEELD *same as* > NEEDLE

NEELDS > NEELD

NEELE *same as* > NEEDLE

NEELES > NEELE

NEEM *n* type of large Indian tree

NEEMB *same as* > NEEM

NEEMBS > NEEMB

NEEMS > NEEM

NEEP *dialect name for* > TURNIP

NEEPS > NEEP

NEESBERRY *same as* > NASEBERRY

NEESE *same as* > NEEZE

NEESED > NEESE

NEESES > NEESE

NEESING > NEESE

NEEZE *vb* sneeze

NEEZED > NEEZE

NEEZES > NEEZE

NEEZING > NEEZE

NEF *n* church nave

NEFANDOUS *adj* unmentionable

NEFARIOUS *adj* wicked

NEFAST *adj* wicked

NEFS > NEF

NEG *n* photographic negative

NEGATE *vb* invalidate

NEGATED > NEGATE

NEGATER > NEGATE

NEGATERS > NEGATE

NEGATES > NEGATE

NEGATING > NEGATE

NEGATION *n* opposite or absence of something

NEGATIONS > NEGATION

NEGATIVE *adj* expressing a denial or refusal ▷ *n* negative word or statement

NEGATIVED > NEGATIVE

NEGATIVES > NEGATIVE

NEGATON *same as* > NEGATRON

NEGATONS > NEGATON

NEGATOR > NEGATE

NEGATORS > NEGATE

NEGATORY > NEGATION

NEGATRON *obsolete word for* > ELECTRON

NEGATRONS > NEGATRON

NEGLECT *vb* take no care of ▷ *n* neglecting or being neglected

NEGLECTED > NEGLECT

NEGLECTER > NEGLECT

NEGLECTOR > NEGLECT

NEGLECTS > NEGLECT

NEGLIGE *variant of* > NEGLIGEE

NEGLIGEE *n* woman's lightweight usu. lace-trimmed dressing gown

NEGLIGEES > NEGLIGEE

NEGLIGENT *adj* habitually neglecting duties, responsibilities, etc

NEGLIGES > NEGLIGE

NEGOCIANT *n* wine merchant

NEGOTIANT *n* person, nation, organization, etc, involved in a negotiation

NEGOTIATE *vb* discuss in order to reach (an agreement)

NEGRESS *n* old-fashioned offensive name for a Black woman

NEGRESSES > NEGRESS

NEGRITUDE *n* fact of being a Negro

NEGRO *n* old-fashioned offensive name for a Black man

NEGROES > NEGRO

NEGROHEAD *n* type of rubber

NEGROID *n* member of one of the major racial groups of mankind, which is characterized by brown-black skin and tightly-curled hair

NEGROIDAL > NEGROID

NEGROIDS > NEGROID

NEGROISM > NEGRO

NEGROISMS > NEGRO

NEGRONI *n* type of cocktail

NEGRONIS > NEGRONI

NEGROPHIL *n* person who admires Black people and their culture

NEGS > NEG

NEGUS *n* hot drink of port and lemon juice, usually

spiced and sweetened

NEGUSES > NEGUS

NEIF *same as* > NIEVE

NEIFS > NEIF

NEIGH *n* loud high-pitched sound made by a horse ▷ *vb* make this sound

NEIGHBOR *same as* > NEIGHBOUR

NEIGHBORS > NEIGHBOR

NEIGHBOUR *n* person who lives or is situated near another ▷ *vb* be or live close (to a person or thing)

NEIGHED > NEIGH

NEIGHING > NEIGH

NEIGHS > NEIGH

NEINEI *n* type of plant

NEINEIS > NEINEI

NEIST *Scots variant of* > NEXT

NEITHER *pron* not one nor the other ▷ *adj* not one nor the other (of two)

NEIVE *same as* > NIEVE

NEIVES > NEIVE

NEK *n* mountain pass

NEKS > NEK

NEKTON *n* population of free-swimming animals that inhabits the middle depths of a sea or lake

NEKTONIC > NEKTON

NEKTONS > NEKTON

NELIES *same as* > NELIS

NELIS *n* type of pear

NELLIE *n* effeminate man

NELLIES > NELLIE

NELLY as in *not on your nelly* not under any circumstances

NELSON *n* type of wrestling hold

NELSONS > NELSON

NELUMBIUM *same as* > NELUMBO

NELUMBO *n* type of aquatic plant

NELUMBOS > NELUMBO

NEMA *n* filament

NEMAS > NEMA

NEMATIC *adj* (of a substance) existing in or having a mesomorphic state in which a linear orientation of the molecules causes anisotropic properties

NEMATODE *n* slender cylindrical unsegmented worm

NEMATODES > NEMATODE

NEMATOID > NEMATODE

NEMERTEAN *n* type of ribbon-like marine worm ▷ *adj* of this worm

NEMERTIAN *same as* > NEMERTEAN

NEMERTINE *same as* > NEMERTEAN

NEMESES > NEMESIS

NEMESIA *n* type of southern African plant

NEMESIAS > NEMESIA

NEMESIS *n* retribution or

vengeance

NEMN vb name

NEMNED > NEMN

NEMNING > NEMN

NEMNS > NEMN

NEMOPHILA n any of a genus of low-growing hairy annual plants

NEMORAL adj of a wood

NEMOROUS adj woody

NEMPT adj named

NENE n rare black-and-grey short-winged Hawaiian goose

NENES > NENE

NENNIGAI same as > NANNYGAI

NENNIGAIS > NENNIGAI

NENUPHAR n type of water lily

NENUPHARS > NENUPHAR

NEOBLAST n worm cell

NEOBLASTS > NEOBLAST

NEOCON n supporter of conservative politics

NEOCONS > NEOCON

NEOCORTEX n part of the brain

NEODYMIUM n silvery-white metallic element of lanthanide series

NEOGENE adj of, denoting, or formed during the Miocene and Pliocene epochs

NEOGOTHIC n style of architecture popular in Britain in the 18th and 19th centuries

NEOLITH n Neolithic stone implement

NEOLITHIC adj relating to the Neolithic period

NEOLITHS > NEOLITH

NEOLOGIAN > NEOLOGY

NEOLOGIC > NEOLOGISM

NEOLOGIES > NEOLOGY

NEOLOGISE same as > NEOLOGIZE

NEOLOGISM n newly-coined word or an established word used in a new sense

NEOLOGIST > NEOLOGISM

NEOLOGIZE vb invent or use neologisms

NEOLOGY same as > NEOLOGISM

NEOMORPH n genetic component

NEOMORPHS > NEOMORPH

NEOMYCIN n type of antibiotic obtained from a bacterium

NEOMYCINS > NEOMYCIN

NEON n colourless odourless gaseous element used in illuminated signs and lights ▷ adj of or illuminated by neon

NEONATAL adj relating to the first few weeks of a baby's life

NEONATE n newborn child, esp in the first week of life and up to four weeks old

NEONATES > NEONATE

NEONED adj lit with neon

NEONOMIAN n Christian religious belief

NEONS > NEON

NEOPAGAN n advocate of the revival of paganism

NEOPAGANS > NEOPAGAN

NEOPHILE n person who welcomes new things

NEOPHILES > NEOPHILE

NEOPHILIA n tendency to like anything new

NEOPHOBE > NEOPHOBIA

NEOPHOBES > NEOPHOBIA

NEOPHOBIA n tendency to dislike anything new

NEOPHOBIC > NEOPHOBIA

NEOPHYTE n beginner or novice

NEOPHYTES > NEOPHYTE

NEOPHYTIC > NEOPHYTE

NEOPILINA n type of mollusc

NEOPLASIA n abnormal growth of tissue

NEOPLASM n any abnormal new growth of tissue

NEOPLASMS > NEOPLASM

NEOPLASTY n surgical formation of new tissue structures or repair of damaged structures

NEOPRENE n synthetic rubber used in waterproof products

NEOPRENES > NEOPRENE

NEOSOUL n type of popular music combining soul with other genres

NEOSOULS > NEOSOUL

NEOTEINIA n state of prolonged immaturity

NEOTENIC > NEOTENY

NEOTENIES > NEOTENY

NEOTENOUS > NEOTENY

NEOTENY n persistence of larval or fetal features in the adult form of an animal

NEOTERIC adj belonging to a new fashion or trend ▷ n new writer or philosopher

NEOTERICS > NEOTERIC

NEOTERISE same as > NEOTERIZE

NEOTERISM > NEOTERIC

NEOTERIST > NEOTERIC

NEOTERIZE vb introduce new things

NEOTOXIN n harmful agent

NEOTOXINS > NEOTOXIN

NEOTROPIC adj of tropical America

NEOTYPE n specimen selected to replace a type specimen that has been lost or destroyed

NEOTYPES > NEOTYPE

NEP n catmint

NEPENTHE n drug that ancient writers referred to as a means of forgetting grief or trouble

NEPENTHES > NEPENTHE

NEPER n unit expressing the ratio of two quantities

NEPERS > NEPER

NEPETA same as > CATMINT

NEPETAS > NEPETA

NEPHALISM n teetotalism

NEPHALIST > NEPHALISM

NEPHELINE n whitish mineral

NEPHELITE same as > NEPHELINE

NEPHEW n son of one's sister or brother

NEPHEWS > NEPHEW

NEPHOGRAM n photograph of a cloud

NEPHOLOGY n study of clouds

NEPHRALGY n pain in a kidney

NEPHRIC adj renal

NEPHRIDIA npl simple excretory organs of many invertebrates

NEPHRISM n chronic kidney disease

NEPHRISMS > NEPHRISM

NEPHRITE n tough fibrous amphibole mineral

NEPHRITES > NEPHRITE

NEPHRITIC adj of or relating to the kidneys

NEPHRITIS n inflammation of a kidney

NEPHROID adj kidney-shaped

NEPHRON n minute urine-secreting tubule in the kidney

NEPHRONS > NEPHRON

NEPHROSES > NEPHROSIS

NEPHROSIS n any noninflammatory degenerative kidney disease

NEPHROTIC > NEPHROSIS

NEPIONIC adj of or relating to the juvenile period in the life cycle of an organism

NEPIT n a unit of information equal to 1.44 bits

NEPITS > NEPIT

NEPOTIC > NEPOTISM

NEPOTISM n favouritism in business shown to relatives and friends

NEPOTISMS > NEPOTISM

NEPOTIST > NEPOTISM

NEPOTISTS > NEPOTISM

NEPS > NEP

NEPTUNIUM n synthetic radioactive metallic element

NERAL n isomer of citral

NERALS > NERAL

NERD n boring person obsessed with a particular subject

NERDIC same as > GEEKSPEAK

NERDICS > NERDIC

NERDIER > NERD

NERDIEST > NERD

NERDINESS > NERD

NERDISH > NERD

NERDS > NERD

NERDY > NERD

NEREID n sea nymph in Greek mythology

NEREIDES > NEREID

NEREIDS > NEREID

NEREIS n type of marine worm

NERINE n type of S African plant related to the amaryllis

NERINES > NERINE

NERITE n type of sea snail

NERITES > NERITE

NERITIC adj of or formed in the region of shallow seas near a coastline

NERK n fool

NERKA n type of salmon

NERKAS > NERKA

NERKS > NERK

NEROL n scented liquid

NEROLI n brown oil used in perfumery

NEROLIS > NEROLI

NEROLS > NEROL

NERTS interj nuts

NERTZ same as > NERTS

NERVAL > NERVE

NERVATE adj (of leaves) with veins

NERVATION less common word for > VENATION

NERVATURE same as > NERVATION

NERVE n cordlike bundle of fibres that conducts impulses between the brain and other parts of the body ▷ vb give courage to oneself

NERVED > NERVE

NERVELESS adj numb, without feeling

NERVELET n small nerve

NERVELETS > NERVELET

NERVER > NERVE

NERVERS > NERVE

NERVIER > NERVY

NERVIEST > NERVY

NERVILY > NERVY

NERVINE adj having a soothing or calming effect upon the nerves ▷ n nervine drug or agent

NERVINES > NERVINE

NERVINESS > NERVY

NERVING > NERVE

NERVINGS > NERVE

NERVOSITY n nervousness

n

NERVOUS adj apprehensive or worried

NERVOUSLY > NERVOUS

NERVULAR > NERVULE

NERVULE n small vein

NERVULES > NERVULE

NERVURE n any of the stiff rods that form the supporting framework of an insect's wing

NERVURES > NERVURE

NERVY adj excitable or nervous

NESCIENCE formal or literary word for > IGNORANCE

NESCIENT > NESCIENCE

NESCIENTS > NESCIENCE

NESH adj sensitive to the cold

NESHER > NESH

NESHEST > NESH

NESHNESS > NESH

NESS n headland, cape

NESSES > NESS

NEST n place or structure in which birds or certain animals lay eggs or give birth to young ▷ vb make or inhabit a nest

NESTABLE > NEST

NESTED > NEST

NESTER > NEST

NESTERS > NEST

NESTFUL > NEST

NESTFULS > NEST

NESTING > NEST

NESTINGS > NEST

NESTLE vb snuggle

NESTLED > NESTLE

NESTLER > NESTLE

NESTLERS > NESTLE

NESTLES > NESTLE

NESTLIKE > NEST

NESTLING n bird too young to leave the nest

NESTLINGS > NESTLING

NESTOR n wise old man

NESTORS > NESTOR

NESTS > NEST

NET n fabric of meshes of string, thread, or wire with many openings ▷ vb catch (a fish or animal) in a net ▷ adj left after all deductions

NETBALL n team game in which a ball has to be thrown through a net hanging from a ring at the top of a pole

NETBALLER > NETBALL

NETBALLS > NETBALL

NETE n lyre string

NETES > NETE

NETFUL > NET

NETFULS > NET

NETHEAD n person who is enthusiastic about or an expert on the internet

NETHEADS > NETHEAD

NETHELESS same as > NATHELESS

NETHER adj lower

NETIZEN n person who regularly uses the internet

NETIZENS > NETIZEN

NETLESS > NET

NETLIKE > NET

NETMINDER n goalkeeper

NETOP n friend

NETOPS > NETOP

NETROOT n political activist who promotes a cause via the internet

NETROOTS > NETROOT

NETS > NET

NETSPEAK n jargon, abbreviations, and emoticons typically used by frequent internet users

NETSPEAKS > NETSPEAK

NETSUKE n (in Japan) a carved toggle worn dangling from the waist

NETSUKES > NETSUKE

NETT same as > NET

NETTABLE > NETT

NETTED > NET

NETTER n person that makes nets

NETTERS > NETTER

NETTIE n habitual and enthusiastic user of the internet

NETTIER > NET

NETTIES > NETTY

NETTIEST > NET

NETTING > NET

NETTINGS > NET

NETTLE n plant with stinging hairs on the leaves ▷ vb bother or irritate

NETTLED > NETTLE

NETTLER > NETTLE

NETTLERS > NETTLE

NETTLES > NETTLE

NETTLIER > NETTLE

NETTLIEST > NETTLE

NETTLING > NETTLE

NETTLY > NETTLE

NETTS > NETT

NETTY n lavatory, originally an earth closet

NETWORK n system of intersecting lines, roads, etc ▷ vb broadcast (a programme) over a network

NETWORKED > NETWORK

NETWORKER n person who forms business contacts through informal social meetings

NETWORKS > NETWORK

NEUK Scot word for > NOOK

NEUKS > NEUK

NEUM same as > NEUME

NEUMATIC > NEUME

NEUME n one of a series of notational symbols used before the 14th century

NEUMES > NEUME

NEUMIC > NEUME

NEUMS > NEUM

NEURAL adj of a nerve or the nervous system

NEURALGIA n severe pain along a nerve

NEURALGIC > NEURALGIA

NEURALLY > NEURAL

NEURATION n arrangement of veins

NEURAXON n biological cell component

NEURAXONS > NEURAXON

NEURILITY n properties of the nerves

NEURINE n poisonous alkaloid

NEURINES > NEURINE

NEURISM n nerve force

NEURISMS > NEURISM

NEURITE n biological cell component

NEURITES > NEURITE

NEURITIC > NEURITIS

NEURITICS > NEURITIS

NEURITIS n inflammation of a nerve or nerves

NEUROCHIP n semiconductor chip designed for use in an electronic neural network

NEUROCOEL n cavity in brain

NEUROGLIA another name for > GLIA

NEUROGRAM same as > ENGRAM

NEUROID adj nervelike

NEUROLOGY n scientific study of the nervous system

NEUROMA n any tumour composed of nerve tissue

NEUROMAS > NEUROMA

NEUROMAST n sensory cell in fish

NEUROMATA > NEUROMA

NEURON same as > NEURONE

NEURONAL > NEURONE

NEURONE n cell specialized to conduct nerve impulses

NEURONES > NEURONE

NEURONIC > NEURONE

NEURONS > NEURON

NEUROPATH n person suffering from or predisposed to a disorder of the nervous system

NEUROPIL n dense network of neurons and glia in the central nervous system

NEUROPILS > NEUROPIL

NEUROSAL > NEUROSIS

NEUROSES > NEUROSIS

NEUROSIS n mental disorder producing hysteria, anxiety, depression, or obsessive behaviour

NEUROTIC adj emotionally unstable ▷ n neurotic person

NEUROTICS > NEUROTIC

NEUROTOMY n surgical cutting of a nerve, esp to relieve intractable pain

NEURULA n stage of embryonic development

NEURULAE > NEURULA

NEURULAR > NEURULA

NEURULAS > NEURULA

NEUSTIC > NEUSTON

NEUSTON n organisms, similar to plankton, that float on the surface film of open water

NEUSTONIC > NEUSTON

NEUSTONS > NEUSTON

NEUTER adj belonging to a particular class of grammatical inflections in some languages ▷ vb castrate (an animal) ▷ n neuter gender

NEUTERED > NEUTER

NEUTERING > NEUTER

NEUTERS > NEUTER

NEUTRAL adj taking neither side in a war or dispute ▷ n neutral person or nation

NEUTRALLY > NEUTRAL

NEUTRALS > NEUTRAL

NEUTRETTO n neutrino associated with the muon

NEUTRINO n elementary particle with no mass or electrical charge

NEUTRINOS > NEUTRINO

NEUTRON n electrically neutral elementary particle of about the same mass as a proton

NEUTRONIC > NEUTRON

NEUTRONS > NEUTRON

NEVE n mass of porous ice, formed from snow, that has not yet become frozen into glacier ice

NEVEL vb beat with the fists

NEVELLED > NEVEL

NEVELLING > NEVEL

NEVELS > NEVEL

NEVER adv at no time ▷ sentence substitute at no time ▷ interj surely not!

NEVERMIND n difference

NEVERMORE adv never again

NEVES > NEVE

NEVI > NEVUS

NEVOID > NAEVUS

NEVUS same as > NAEVUS

NEW adj not existing before ▷ adv recently ▷ vb make new

NEWBIE n person new to a job, club, etc

NEWBIES > NEWBIE

NEWBORN adj recently or just born ▷ n newborn baby

NEWBORNS > NEWBORN

NEWCOME > NEWCOMER

NEWCOMER n recent arrival or participant

NEWCOMERS > NEWCOMER

NEWED > NEW

NEWEL n post at the top or bottom of a flight of stairs

NEWELL *n* new thing
NEWELLED > NEWEL
NEWELLS > NEWELL
NEWELS > NEWEL
NEWER > NEW
NEWEST > NEW
NEWFANGLE *adj* newly come into existence or fashion
NEWFOUND *adj* newly or recently discovered
NEWIE *n* fresh idea or thing
NEWIES > NEWIE
NEWING > NEW
NEWISH *adj* fairly new
NEWISHLY > NEWISH
NEWLY *adv* recently
NEWLYWED *n* recently married person
NEWLYWEDS > NEWLYWED
NEWMARKET *n* double-breasted waisted coat with a full skirt
NEWMOWN *adj* freshly cut
NEWNESS > NEW
NEWNESSES > NEW
NEWS *n* important or interesting new happenings ▷ *vb* report
NEWSAGENT *n* shopkeeper who sells newspapers and magazines
NEWSBEAT *n* particular area of news reporting
NEWSBEATS > NEWSBEAT
NEWSBOY *n* boy who sells or delivers newspapers
NEWSBOYS > NEWSBOY
NEWSBREAK *n* newsflash
NEWSCAST *n* radio or television broadcast of the news
NEWSCASTS > NEWSCAST
NEWSDESK *n* news gathering and reporting department
NEWSDESKS > NEWSDESK
NEWSED > NEWS
NEWSES > NEWS
NEWSFLASH *n* brief important news item, which interrupts a radio or television programme
NEWSGIRL *n* female newsreader or reporter
NEWSGIRLS > NEWSGIRL
NEWSGROUP *n* forum where subscribers exchange information about a specific subject by e-mail
NEWSHAWK *n* newspaper reporter
NEWSHAWKS > NEWSHAWK
NEWSHOUND *same as* > NEWSHAWK
NEWSIE *same as* > NEWSY
NEWSIER > NEWSY
NEWSIES > NEWSIE
NEWSIEST > NEWSY
NEWSINESS > NEWSY
NEWSING > NEWS
NEWSLESS > NEWS

NEWSMAKER *n* person whose activities are reported in news
NEWSMAN *n* male newsreader or reporter
NEWSMEN > NEWSMAN
NEWSPAPER *n* weekly or daily publication containing news ▷ *vb* do newspaper related work
NEWSPEAK *n* language of politicians and officials regarded as deliberately ambiguous and misleading
NEWSPEAKS > NEWSPEAK
NEWSPRINT *n* inexpensive paper used for newspapers
NEWSREEL *n* short film giving news
NEWSREELS > NEWSREEL
NEWSROOM *n* room where news is received and prepared for publication or broadcasting
NEWSROOMS > NEWSROOM
NEWSSTAND *n* portable stand from which newspapers are sold
NEWSTRADE *n* newspaper retail
NEWSWIRE *n* electronic means of delivering up-to-the-minute news
NEWSWIRES > NEWSWIRE
NEWSWOMAN *n* female newsreader or reporter
NEWSWOMEN > NEWSWOMAN
NEWSY *adj* full of news ▷ *n* newsagent
NEWT *n* small amphibious creature with a long slender body and tail
NEWTON *n* unit of force
NEWTONS > NEWTON
NEWTS > NEWT
NEWWAVER *n* member of new wave
NEWWAVERS > NEWWAVER
NEXT *adv* immediately following ▷ *n* next person or thing
NEXTDOOR *adj* in or at the adjacent house or building
NEXTLY > NEXT
NEXTNESS > NEXT
NEXTS > NEXT
NEXUS *n* connection or link
NEXUSES > NEXUS
NGAI *n* clan or tribe
NGAIO *n* small New Zealand tree
NGAIOS > NGAIO
NGANA *same as* > NAGANA
NGANAS > NGANA
NGARARA *n* lizard found in New Zealand
NGARARAS > NGARARA
NGATI *n* (occurring as part of the tribe name) a tribe or clan
NGATIS > NGATI
NGOMA *n* type of drum
NGOMAS > NGOMA
NGULTRUM *n* standard

monetary unit of Bhutan, divided into 100 chetrum
NGULTRUMS > NGULTRUM
NGWEE *n* Zambian monetary unit worth one hundredth of a kwacha
NHANDU *n* type of spider
NHANDUS > NHANDU
NIACIN *n* vitamin of the B complex that occurs in milk, liver, and yeast
NIACINS > NIACIN
NIAISERIE *n* simplicity
NIALAMIDE *n* type of drug
NIB *n* writing point of a pen ▷ *vb* provide with a nib
NIBBED > NIB
NIBBING > NIB
NIBBLE *vb* take little bites (of) ▷ *n* little bite
NIBBLED > NIBBLE
NIBBLER *n* person, animal, or thing that nibbles
NIBBLERS > NIBBLER
NIBBLES > NIBBLE
NIBBLING > NIBBLE
NIBBLINGS > NIBBLE
NIBLICK *n* (formerly) a club, a No. 9 iron, giving a great deal of lift
NIBLICKS > NIBLICK
NIBLIKE > NIB
NIBS > NIB
NICAD *n* rechargeable dry-cell battery
NICADS > NICAD
NICCOLITE *n* copper-coloured mineral
NICE *adj* pleasant
NICEISH > NICE
NICELY > NICE
NICENESS > NICE
NICER > NICE
NICEST > NICE
NICETIES > NICETY
NICETY *n* subtle point
NICHE *n* hollow area in a wall ▷ *adj* of or aimed at a specialist group or market ▷ *vb* place (a statue) in a niche
NICHED > NICHE
NICHER *vb* snigger
NICHERED > NICHER
NICHERING > NICHER
NICHERS > NICHER
NICHES > NICHE
NICHING > NICHE
NICHT *Scot word for* > NIGHT
NICHTS > NICHT
NICISH > NICE
NICK *vb* make a small cut in ▷ *n* small cut
NICKAR *n* hard seed
NICKARS > NICKAR
NICKED > NICK
NICKEL *n* silvery-white metal often used in alloys ▷ *vb* plate with nickel
NICKELED > NICKEL
NICKELIC *adj* of or containing metallic nickel
NICKELINE *another name*

for > NICCOLITE
NICKELING > NICKEL
NICKELISE *same as* > NICKELIZE
NICKELIZE *vb* treat with nickel
NICKELLED > NICKEL
NICKELOUS *adj* of or containing nickel, esp in the divalent state
NICKELS > NICKEL
NICKER *n* pound sterling ▷ *vb* (of a horse) to neigh softly
NICKERED > NICKER
NICKERING > NICKER
NICKERS > NICKER
NICKING > NICK
NICKLE *same as* > NICKEL
NICKLED > NICKLE
NICKLES > NICKLE
NICKLING > NICKLE
NICKNACK *n* cheap ornament or trinket
NICKNACKS > NICKNACK
NICKNAME *n* familiar name given to a person or place ▷ *vb* call by a nickname
NICKNAMED > NICKNAME
NICKNAMER > NICKNAME
NICKNAMES > NICKNAME
NICKPOINT *n* break in the slope of a river caused by renewed erosion
NICKS > NICK
NICKSTICK *n* tally
NICKUM *n* mischievous person
NICKUMS > NICKUM
NICOISE *adj* prepared with tomatoes, black olives, garlic and anchovies
NICOL *n* device for producing plane-polarized light
NICOLS > NICOL
NICOMPOOP *n* stupid person
NICOTIAN *n* tobacco user
NICOTIANA *n* American and Australian plant such as tobacco, with white, yellow, or purple fragrant flowers
NICOTIANS > NICOTIAN
NICOTIN *same as* > NICOTINE
NICOTINE *n* poisonous substance found in tobacco
NICOTINED > NICOTINE
NICOTINES > NICOTINE
NICOTINIC > NICOTINE
NICOTINS *same as* > NICOTIN
NICTATE *same as* > NICTITATE
NICTATED > NICTATE
NICTATES > NICTATE
NICTATING > NICTATE
NICTATION *n* act of blinking
NICTITANT *adj* blinking
NICTITATE *vb* blink
NID *same as* > NIDE

n

NIDAL > NIDUS
NIDAMENTA npl egg capsules
NIDATE vb undergo nidation
NIDATED > NIDATE
NIDATES > NIDATE
NIDATING > NIDATE
NIDATION n implantation
NIDATIONS > NIDATION
NIDDERING n coward ▷ adj cowardly
NIDDICK n nape of the neck
NIDDICKS > NIDDICK
NIDE vb nest
NIDED > NIDE
NIDERING same as > NIDDERING
NIDERINGS > NIDERING
NIDERLING same as > NIDDERING
NIDES > NIDE
NIDGET n fool
NIDGETS > NIDGET
NIDI > NIDUS
NIDIFIED > NIDIFY
NIDIFIES > NIDIFY
NIDIFY vb (of a bird) to make or build a nest
NIDIFYING > NIDIFY
NIDING n coward
NIDINGS > NIDING
NIDOR n cooking smell
NIDOROUS > NIDOR
NIDORS > NIDOR
NIDS > NID
NIDUS n nest in which insects or spiders deposit their eggs
NIDUSES > NIDUS
NIE archaic spelling of > NIGH
NIECE n daughter of one's sister or brother
NIECES > NIECE
NIED > NIE
NIEF same as > NIEVE
NIEFS > NIEF
NIELLATED > NIELLO
NIELLI > NIELLO
NIELLIST > NIELLO
NIELLISTS > NIELLO
NIELLO n black compound of sulphur and silver, lead, or copper ▷ vb decorate or treat with niello
NIELLOED > NIELLO
NIELLOING > NIELLO
NIELLOS > NIELLO
NIES > NIE
NIEVE n closed hand
NIEVEFUL > NIEVE
NIEVEFULS > NIEVE
NIEVES > NIEVE
NIFE n earth's core, thought to be composed of nickel and iron
NIFES > NIFE
NIFF n stink ▷ vb stink
NIFFED > NIFF
NIFFER vb barter
NIFFERED > NIFFER
NIFFERING > NIFFER

NIFFERS > NIFFER
NIFFIER > NIFF
NIFFIEST > NIFF
NIFFING > NIFF
NIFFNAFF vb trifle
NIFFNAFFS > NIFFNAFF
NIFFS > NIFF
NIFFY > NIFF
NIFTIER > NIFTY
NIFTIES > NIFTY
NIFTIEST > NIFTY
NIFTILY > NIFTY
NIFTINESS > NIFTY
NIFTY adj neat or smart ▷ n nifty thing
NIGELLA n type of plant the Mediterranean and W Asia
NIGELLAS > NIGELLA
NIGER n obsolete offensive term for a Black person
NIGERS > NIGER
NIGGARD n stingy person ▷ adj miserly ▷ vb act in a niggardly way
NIGGARDED > NIGGARD
NIGGARDLY adj stingy ▷ adv stingily
NIGGARDS > NIGGARD
NIGGER n offensive name for a Black person ▷ vb burn
NIGGERDOM > NIGGER
NIGGERED > NIGGER
NIGGERING > NIGGER
NIGGERISH > NIGGER
NIGGERISM n offensive name for an idiom supposedly characteristic of Black people
NIGGERS > NIGGER
NIGGERY > NIGGER
NIGGLE vb worry slightly ▷ n small worry or doubt
NIGGLED > NIGGLE
NIGGLER > NIGGLE
NIGGLERS > NIGGLE
NIGGLES > NIGGLE
NIGGLIER > NIGGLE
NIGGLIEST > NIGGLE
NIGGLING adj petty ▷ n act or instance of niggling
NIGGLINGS > NIGGLING
NIGGLY > NIGGLE
NIGH prep near ▷ adv nearly ▷ adj near ▷ vb approach
NIGHED > NIGH
NIGHER > NIGH
NIGHEST > NIGH
NIGHING > NIGH
NIGHLY > NIGH
NIGHNESS > NIGH
NIGHS > NIGH
NIGHT n time of darkness between sunset and sunrise ▷ adj of, occurring, or working at night
NIGHTBIRD same as > NIGHTHAWK
NIGHTCAP n drink taken just before bedtime
NIGHTCAPS > NIGHTCAP
NIGHTCLUB n establishment for dancing,

music, etc, open late at night ▷ vb go to nightclubs
NIGHTED adj darkened
NIGHTFALL n approach of darkness
NIGHTFIRE n fire burned at night
NIGHTGEAR n nightclothes
NIGHTGLOW n faint light from the upper atmosphere in the night sky, esp in low latitudes
NIGHTGOWN n loose dress worn in bed by women
NIGHTHAWK n type of American nightjar
NIGHTIE same as > NIGHTGOWN
NIGHTIES > NIGHTY
NIGHTJAR n nocturnal bird with a harsh cry
NIGHTJARS > NIGHTJAR
NIGHTLESS > NIGHT
NIGHTLIFE n entertainment and social activities available at night in a town or city
NIGHTLIKE > NIGHT
NIGHTLONG adv throughout the night
NIGHTLY adv (happening) each night ▷ adj happening each night
NIGHTMARE n very bad dream
NIGHTMARY > NIGHTMARE
NIGHTS adv at night or on most nights
NIGHTSIDE n dark side
NIGHTSPOT n nightclub
NIGHTTIDE same as > NIGHTTIME
NIGHTTIME n time from sunset to sunrise
NIGHTWARD > NIGHT
NIGHTWEAR n apparel worn in bed or before retiring to bed
NIGHTY same as > NIGHTIE
NIGIRI n small oval block of cold rice, wasabi and fish, sometimes held together by a seaweed band
NIGIRIS > NIGIRI
NIGRICANT adj black
NIGRIFIED > NIGRIFY
NIGRIFIES > NIGRIFY
NIGRIFY vb blacken
NIGRITUDE n blackness
NIGROSIN same as > NIGROSINE
NIGROSINE n type of black pigment and dye used in inks and shoe polishes
NIGROSINS > NIGROSIN
NIHIL n nil
NIHILISM n rejection of all established authority and institutions
NIHILISMS > NIHILISM
NIHILIST > NIHILISM

NIHILISTS > NIHILISM
NIHILITY n state or condition of being nothing
NIHILS > NIHIL
NIHONGA n Japanese form of painting
NIHONGAS > NIHONGA
NIKAB same as > NIQAB
NIKABS > NIKAB
NIKAH n Islamic marriage contract
NIKAHS > NIKAH
NIKAU n palm tree native to New Zealand
NIKAUS > NIKAU
NIL n nothing, zero
NILGAI n large Indian antelope
NILGAIS > NILGAI
NILGAU same as > NILGHAU
NILGAUS > NILGAU
NILGHAI same as > NILGAI
NILGHAIS > NILGHAI
NILGHAU same as > NILGAI
NILGHAUS > NILGHAU
NILL vb be unwilling
NILLED > NILL
NILLING > NILL
NILLS > NILL
NILPOTENT n mathematical term
NILS > NIL
NIM n game in which two players alternately remove one or more small items from one of several rows or piles ▷ vb steal
NIMB n halo
NIMBED > NIMB
NIMBI > NIMBUS
NIMBLE adj agile and quick
NIMBLER > NIMBLE
NIMBLESSE > NIMBLE
NIMBLEST > NIMBLE
NIMBLEWIT n alert, bright, and clever person
NIMBLY > NIMBLE
NIMBS > NIMB
NIMBUS n dark grey rain cloud
NIMBUSED > NIMBUS
NIMBUSES > NIMBUS
NIMBYISM n practice of objecting to something that will affect one or take place in one's locality
NIMBYISMS > NIMBYISM
NIMBYNESS same as > NIMBYISM
NIMIETIES > NIMIETY
NIMIETY rare word for > EXCESS
NIMIOUS > NIMIETY
NIMMED > NIM
NIMMER > NIM
NIMMERS > NIM
NIMMING > NIM
NIMONIC as in nimonic alloy type of nickel-based alloy used at high temperature
NIMPS adj easy

NIMROD n hunter
NIMRODS > NIMROD
NIMS > NIM
NINCOM same as
> NICOMPOOP
NINCOMS > NINCOM
NINCUM same as
> NICOMPOOP
NINCUMS > NINCUM
NINE n one more than eight
NINEBARK n North
American shrub
NINEBARKS > NINEBARK
NINEFOLD adj having nine
times as many or as much
▷ adv by nine times as
much or as many
NINEHOLES n type of
game
NINEPENCE n coin worth
nine pennies
NINEPENNY same as
> NINEPENCE
NINEPIN n skittle used in
ninepins
NINEPINS n game of
skittles
NINES > NINE
NINESCORE n product of
nine times twenty
NINETEEN n ten and nine
NINETEENS > NINETEEN
NINETIES > NINETY
NINETIETH adj being the
ordinal number of ninety in
numbering order ▷ n one of
90 approximately equal
parts of something
NINETY n ten times nine
▷ det amounting to ninety
NINHYDRIN n chemical
reagent used for the
detection and analysis of
primary amines
NINJA n person skilled in
ninjutsu
NINJAS > NINJA
NINJITSU same as
> NINJUTSU
NINJITSUS > NINJITSU
NINJUTSU n Japanese
martial art
NINJUTSUS > NINJUTSU
NINNIES > NINNY
NINNY n stupid person
NINNYISH > NINNY
NINON n fine strong silky
fabric
NINONS > NINON
NINTH n (of) number nine
in a series ▷ adj coming
after the eighth in counting
order, position, time, etc
▷ adv after the eighth
person, position, event, etc
NINTHLY same as > NINTH
NINTHS > NINTH
NIOBATE n type of salt
crystal
NIOBATES > NIOBATE
NIOBIC adj of or
containing niobium in the
pentavalent state
NIOBITE another name for
> COLUMBITE

NIOBITES > NIOBITE
NIOBIUM n white
superconductive metallic
element
NIOBIUMS > NIOBIUM
NIOBOUS adj of or
containing niobium in the
trivalent state
NIP vb hurry ▷ n pinch or
light bite
NIPA n palm tree of S and
SE Asia
NIPAS > NIPA
NIPCHEESE n ship's purser
NIPPED > NIP
NIPPER n small child ▷ vb
secure with rope
NIPPERED > NIPPER
NIPPERING > NIPPER
NIPPERKIN n small
quantity of alcohol
NIPPERS npl instrument
or tool for snipping,
pinching, or squeezing
NIPPIER > NIPPY
NIPPIEST > NIPPY
NIPPILY > NIPPY
NIPPINESS > NIPPY
NIPPING > NIP
NIPPINGLY > NIP
NIPPLE n projection in the
centre of a breast ▷ vb
provide with a nipple
NIPPLED > NIPPLE
NIPPLES > NIPPLE
NIPPLING > NIPPLE
NIPPY adj frosty or chilly
NIPS > NIP
NIPTER n type of religious
ceremony
NIPTERS > NIPTER
NIQAB n type of veil worn
by some Muslim women
NIQABS > NIQAB
NIRAMIAI n sumo
wrestling procedure
NIRAMIAIS > NIRAMIAI
NIRL vb shrivel
NIRLED > NIRL
NIRLIE variant of > NIRLY
NIRLIER > NIRLY
NIRLIEST > NIRLY
NIRLING > NIRL
NIRLIT > NIRL
NIRLS > NIRL
NIRLY adj shrivelled
NIRVANA n absolute
spiritual enlightenment
and bliss
NIRVANAS > NIRVANA
NIRVANIC > NIRVANA
NIS n friendly goblin
NISBERRY same as
> NASEBERRY
NISEI n native-born
citizen of the US or Canada
whose parents were
Japanese immigrants
NISEIS > NISEI
NISGUL n smallest and
weakest bird in a brood of
chickens
NISGULS > NISGUL
NISH n nothing

NISHES > NISH
NISI adj (of a court order)
coming into effect on a
specified date
NISSE same as > NIS
NISSES > NISSE
NISUS n impulse towards
or striving after a goal
NIT n egg or larva of a louse
NITCHIE n offensive term
for a Native American
person
NITCHIES > NITCHIE
NITE variant of > NIGHT
NITER same as > NITRE
NITERIE n nightclub
NITERIES > NITERIE
NITERS > NITER
NITERY > NITER
NITES > NITE
NITHER vb shiver
NITHERED > NITHER
NITHERING > NITHER
NITHERS > NITHER
NITHING n coward
NITHINGS > NITHING
NITID adj bright
NITINOL n metal alloy
NITINOLS > NITINOL
NITON less common name for
> RADON
NITONS > NITON
NITPICK vb criticize
unnecessarily
NITPICKED > NITPICK
NITPICKER > NITPICK
NITPICKS > NITPICK
NITPICKY > NITPICK
NITRAMINE another name
for > TETRYL
NITRATE n compound of
nitric acid, used as a
fertilizer ▷ vb treat with
nitric acid or a nitrate
NITRATED > NITRATE
NITRATES > NITRATE
NITRATINE n type of
mineral
NITRATING > NITRATE
NITRATION > NITRATE
NITRATOR > NITRATE
NITRATORS > NITRATE
NITRE n potassium nitrate
NITRES > NITRE
NITRIC adj of or
containing nitrogen
NITRID same as
> NITRIDE
NITRIDE n compound of
nitrogen with a more
electropositive element
▷ vb make into a nitride
NITRIDED > NITRIDE
NITRIDES > NITRIDE
NITRIDING > NITRIDE
NITRIDS > NITRID
NITRIFIED > NITRIFY
NITRIFIER > NITRIFY
NITRIFIES > NITRIFY
NITRIFY vb treat (a
substance) or cause (a
substance) to react with
nitrogen
NITRIL same as

> NITRILE
NITRILE n any one of a
particular class of organic
compounds
NITRILES > NITRILE
NITRILS > NITRIL
NITRITE n salt or ester of
nitrous acid
NITRITES > NITRITE
NITRO n nitroglycerine
NITROGEN n colourless
odourless gas that forms
four fifths of the air
NITROGENS > NITROGEN
NITROLIC adj pertaining
to a group of acids
NITROS > NITRO
NITROSO adj of a particular
monovalent group
NITROSYL another word for
> NITROSO
NITROSYLS > NITROSYL
NITROUS adj derived from
or containing nitrogen in a
low valency state
NITROX n mixture of
nitrogen and oxygen used
in diving instead of air
NITROXES > NITROX
NITROXYL n type of
chemical
NITROXYLS > NITROXYL
NITRY adj nitrous
NITRYL n chemical
compound
NITRYLS > NITRYL
NITS > NIT
NITTIER > NITTY
NITTIEST > NITTY
NITTY adj infested with
nits
NITWIT n stupid person
NITWITS > NITWIT
NITWITTED > NITWIT
NIVAL adj of or growing in
or under snow
NIVATION n weathering
of rock around a patch of
snow by alternate freezing
and thawing
NIVATIONS > NIVATION
NIVEOUS adj resembling
snow, esp in colour
NIX sentence substitute be
careful! watch out! ▷ n
rejection or refusal ▷ vb
veto, deny, reject, or forbid
(plans, suggestions, etc)
NIXE n water sprite
NIXED > NIX
NIXER n spare-time job
NIXERS > NIXER
NIXES > NIX
NIXIE n female water
sprite, usually unfriendly to
humans
NIXIES > NIXIE
NIXING > NIX
NIXY same as > NIXIE
NIZAM n (formerly) a
Turkish regular soldier
NIZAMATE n territory of
the nizam
NIZAMATES > NIZAMATE

NIZAMS > NIZAM

NKOSI n term of address to a superior

NKOSIS > NKOSI

NO interj expresses denial, disagreement, or refusal ▷ adj not any, not a ▷ adv not at all ▷ n answer or vote of 'no'

NOAH n shark

NOAHS > NOAH

NOB n person of wealth or social distinction

NOBBIER > NOB

NOBBIEST > NOB

NOBBILY > NOB

NOBBINESS > NOB

NOBBLE vb attract the attention of (someone) in order to talk to him or her

NOBBLED > NOBBLE

NOBBLER > NOBBLE

NOBBLERS > NOBBLE

NOBBLES > NOBBLE

NOBBLING > NOBBLE

NOBBUT adv nothing but

NOBBY > NOB

NOBELIUM n artificially-produced radioactive element

NOBELIUMS > NOBELIUM

NOBILESSE same as **>** NOBLESSE

NOBILIARY adj of or relating to the nobility

NOBILITY n quality of being noble

NOBLE adj showing or having high moral qualities ▷ n member of the nobility

NOBLEMAN n person of noble rank

NOBLEMEN > NOBLEMAN

NOBLENESS > NOBLE

NOBLER > NOBLE

NOBLES > NOBLE

NOBLESSE n noble birth or condition

NOBLESSES > NOBLESSE

NOBLEST > NOBLE

NOBLY > NOBLE

NOBODIES > NOBODY

NOBODY pron no person ▷ n person of no importance

NOBS > NOB

NOCAKE n Indian meal made from dried corn

NOCAKES > NOCAKE

NOCENT n guilty person

NOCENTLY > NOCENT

NOCENTS > NOCENT

NOCHEL same as **>** NOTCHEL

NOCHELED same as **>** NOTCHELED

NOCHELING n refusal to pay another person's debts

NOCHELLED > NOCHEL

NOCHELS > NOCHEL

NOCK n notch on an arrow or a bow for the bowstring ▷ vb fit (an arrow) on a bowstring

NOCKED > NOCK

NOCKET same as **>** NACKET

NOCKETS > NOCKET

NOCKING > NOCK

NOCKS > NOCK

NOCTILIO n type of bat

NOCTILIOS > NOCTILIO

NOCTILUCA n type of bioluminescent unicellular marine organism

NOCTUA n type of moth

NOCTUARY n nightly journal

NOCTUAS > NOCTUA

NOCTUID n type of nocturnal moth ▷ adj of or relating to this type of moth

NOCTUIDS > NOCTUID

NOCTULE n any of several large Old World insectivorous bats

NOCTULES > NOCTULE

NOCTUOID > NOCTUA

NOCTURIA n excessive urination during the night

NOCTURIAS > NOCTURIA

NOCTURN n any of the main sections of the office of matins

NOCTURNAL adj of the night ▷ n something active at night

NOCTURNE n short dreamy piece of music

NOCTURNES > NOCTURNE

NOCTURNS > NOCTURN

NOCUOUS adj harmful

NOCUOUSLY > NOCUOUS

NOD vb lower and raise (one's head) briefly in agreement or greeting ▷ n act of nodding

NODAL adj of or like a node

NODALISE same as **>** NODALIZE

NODALISED same as **>** NODALISE

NODALISES same as **>** NODALISE

NODALITY > NODAL

NODALIZE vb make something nodal

NODALIZED > NODALIZE

NODALIZES > NODALIZE

NODALLY > NODAL

NODATED adj knotted

NODATION n knottiness

NODATIONS > NODATION

NODDED > NOD

NODDER > NOD

NODDERS > NOD

NODDIER > NODDY

NODDIES > NODDY

NODDIEST > NODDY

NODDING > NOD

NODDINGLY > NOD

NODDINGS > NOD

NODDLE n head ▷ vb nod (the head), as through drowsiness

NODDLED > NODDLE

NODDLES > NODDLE

NODDLING > NODDLE

NODDY n tropical tern with a dark plumage ▷ adj very easy to use or understand

NODE n point on a plant stem from which leaves grow

NODES > NODE

NODI > NODUS

NODICAL adj of or relating to the nodes of a celestial body, esp of the moon

NODOSE adj having nodes or knotlike swellings

NODOSITY > NODOSE

NODOUS same as **>** NODOSE

NODS > NOD

NODULAR > NODULE

NODULATED > NODULE

NODULE n small knot or lump

NODULED > NODULE

NODULES > NODULE

NODULOSE > NODULE

NODULOUS > NODULE

NODUS n problematic idea, situation, etc

NOEL n Christmas

NOELS > NOEL

NOES > NO

NOESES > NOESIS

NOESIS n exercise of reason, esp in the apprehension of universal forms

NOESISES > NOESIS

NOETIC adj of or relating to the mind, esp to its rational and intellectual faculties

NOG same as **>** NOGGING

NOGAKU n Japanese style of drama

NOGG same as **>** NOG

NOGGED adj built with timber and brick

NOGGIN n head

NOGGING n short horizontal timber member used between the studs of a framed partition

NOGGINGS > NOGGING

NOGGINS > NOGGIN

NOGGS > NOGG

NOGS > NOG

NOH n stylized classic drama of Japan

NOHOW adv under any conditions

NOHOWISH > NOHOW

NOIL n short or knotted fibres that are separated from the long fibres by combing

NOILIER > NOILY

NOILIEST > NOILY

NOILS > NOIL

NOILY > NOIL

NOINT vb anoint

NOINTED > NOINT

NOINTER n mischievous child

NOINTERS > NOINTER

NOINTING > NOINT

NOINTS > NOINT

NOIR adj (of a film) showing characteristics of a film noir,

in plot or style ▷ n film noir

NOIRISH > NOIR

NOIRS > NOIR

NOISE n sound, usu. a loud or disturbing one

NOISED > NOISE

NOISEFUL > NOISE

NOISELESS adj making little or no sound

NOISENIK n rock musician who performs loud harsh music

NOISENIKS > NOISENIK

NOISES > NOISE

NOISETTE n hazelnut chocolate ▷ adj flavoured or made with hazelnuts

NOISETTES > NOISETTE

NOISIER > NOISY

NOISIEST > NOISY

NOISILY > NOISY

NOISINESS > NOISY

NOISING > NOISE

NOISOME adj (of smells) offensive

NOISOMELY > NOISOME

NOISY adj making a lot of noise

NOLE same as **>** NOLL

NOLES > NOLE

NOLITION n unwillingness

NOLITIONS > NOLITION

NOLL n head

NOLLS > NOLL

NOLO as in nolo contendere plea indicating that the defendant does not wish to contest the case

NOLOS > NOLO

NOM n name

NOMA n gangrenous inflammation of the mouth, esp one affecting malnourished children

NOMAD n member of a tribe with no fixed dwelling place, wanderer

NOMADE same as **>** NOMAD

NOMADES > NOMADE

NOMADIC adj relating to or characteristic of nomads or their way of life

NOMADIES > NOMADY

NOMADISE same as **>** NOMADIZE

NOMADISED > NOMADISE

NOMADISES > NOMADISE

NOMADISM > NOMAD

NOMADISMS > NOMAD

NOMADIZE vb live as nomads

NOMADIZED > NOMADIZE

NOMADIZES > NOMADIZE

NOMADS > NOMAD

NOMADY n practice of living like nomads

NOMARCH n head of an ancient Egyptian nome

NOMARCHS > NOMARCH

NOMARCHY n any of the provinces of modern Greece

NOMAS > NOMA

NOMBLES *variant spelling of* >NUMBLES

NOMBRIL *n* point on a shield between the fesse point and the lowest point

NOMBRILS >NOMBRIL

NOME *n* any of the former provinces of modern Greece

NOMEN *n* ancient Roman's second name, designating his gens or clan

NOMES >NOME

NOMIC *adj* normal or habitual

NOMINA >NOMEN

NOMINABLE >NOMINATE

NOMINAL *adj* in name only ▷ *n* nominal element

NOMINALLY >NOMINAL

NOMINALS >NOMINAL

NOMINATE *vb* suggest as a candidate ▷ *adj* having a particular name

NOMINATED >NOMINATE

NOMINATES >NOMINATE

NOMINATOR >NOMINATE

NOMINEE *n* candidate

NOMINEES >NOMINEE

NOMISM *n* adherence to a law or laws as a primary exercise of religion

NOMISMS >NOMISM

NOMISTIC >NOMISM

NOMOCRACY *n* government based on the rule of law rather than arbitrary will, terror, etc

NOMOGENY *n* law of life originating as a natural process

NOMOGRAM *n* arrangement of two linear or logarithmic scales

NOMOGRAMS >NOMOGRAM

NOMOGRAPH *same as* >NOMOGRAM

NOMOI >NOMOS

NOMOLOGIC >NOMOLOGY

NOMOLOGY *n* science of law and law-making

NOMOS *n* convention

NOMOTHETE *n* legislator

NOMS >NOM

NON *adv* not

NONA *n* sleeping sickness

NONACID *adj* not acid ▷ *n* nonacid substance

NONACIDIC *adj* not acidic

NONACIDS >NONACID

NONACTING *adj* not acting

NONACTION *n* not action

NONACTIVE *adj* not active

NONACTOR *n* person who is not an actor

NONACTORS >NONACTOR

NONADDICT *n* person who is not an addict

NONADULT *n* person who is not an adult

NONADULTS >NONADULT

NONAGE *n* state of being under full legal age for various actions

NONAGED >NONAGE

NONAGES >NONAGE

NONAGON *n* geometric figure with nine sides

NONAGONAL >NONAGON

NONAGONS >NONAGON

NONANE *n* type of chemical compound

NONANES >NONANE

NONANIMAL *adj* not animal

NONANOIC as in *nonanoic acid* colourless oily fatty acid with a rancid odour

NONANSWER *n* unsatisfactory reply

NONARABLE *adj* not arable

NONART *n* something that does not constitute art

NONARTIST *n* person who is not an artist

NONARTS >NONART

NONARY *adj* based on the number nine

NONAS >NONES

NONATOMIC *adj* not atomic

NONAUTHOR *n* person who is not the author

NONBANK *n* business or institution that is not a bank but provides similar services

NONBANKS >NONBANK

NONBASIC *adj* not basic

NONBEING *n* philosophical problem relating to the question of existence

NONBEINGS >NONBEING

NONBELIEF *n* state of not believing

NONBINARY *adj* not binary

NONBITING *adj* not biting

NONBLACK *n* person or thing that is not black

NONBLACKS >NONBLACK

NONBODIES >NONBODY

NONBODY *n* nonphysical nature of a person

NONBONDED *adj* not bonded

NONBOOK *n* book with little substance

NONBOOKS >NONBOOK

NONBRAND *adj* not produced by a well-known company

NONBUYING *adj* not buying

NONCAKING *adj* not liable to cake

NONCAMPUS *adj* not on campus

NONCAREER *adj* not career-related

NONCASH *adj* other than cash

NONCASUAL *adj* not casual

NONCAUSAL *adj* not causal

NONCE *n* present time or occasion

NONCEREAL *adj* not cereal

NONCES >NONCE

NONCHURCH *adj* not related to the church

NONCLASS *n* lack of class

NONCLING *adj* not liable to stick

NONCODING *adj* (of DNA) not containing instructions for making protein

NONCOITAL *adj* not involving sexual intercourse

NONCOKING *adj* not liable to coke

NONCOLA *n* soft drink other than cola

NONCOLAS >NONCOLA

NONCOLOR *n* achromatic colour such as black or white

NONCOLORS >NONCOLOR

NONCOM *n* person not involved in combat

NONCOMBAT *adj* not involved in combat

NONCOMS >NONCOM

NONCONCUR *vb* disagree

NONCORE *adj* not central or essential

NONCOUNTY *adj* not controlled or run by a county

NONCREDIT *adj* relating to an educational course not providing a credit towards a degree

NONCRIME *n* incident that is not a crime

NONCRIMES >NONCRIME

NONCRISES >NONCRISIS

NONCRISIS *n* situation that is not a crisis

NONCYCLIC *adj* not cyclic

NONDAIRY *adj* not containing dairy products

NONDANCE *n* series of movements that do not constitute a dance

NONDANCER *n* person who is not a dancer

NONDANCES >NONDANCE

NONDEGREE *adj* not leading to a degree

NONDEMAND *adj* not involving demand

NONDESERT *adj* not belonging to the desert

NONDOCTOR *n* person who is not a doctor

NONDOLLAR *adj* not involving the dollar

NONDRIP *adj* (of paint) specially formulated to minimize dripping during application

NONDRIVER *n* person who does not drive

NONDRUG *adj* not involving the use of drugs

NONDRYING *adj* not drying

NONE *pron* not any

NONEDIBLE *n* not edible

NONEGO *n* everything that is outside one's conscious self, such as one's environment

NONEGOS >NONEGO

NONELECT *n* person not chosen

NONELITE *adj* not elite

NONEMPTY *adj* mathematical term

NONENDING *adj* not ending

NONENERGY *adj* without energy

NONENTITY *n* insignificant person or thing

NONENTRY *n* failure to enter

NONEQUAL *adj* not equal ▷ *n* person who is not the equal of another person

NONEQUALS >NONEQUAL

NONEROTIC *adj* not erotic

NONES *n* (in the Roman calendar) the ninth day before the ides of each month

NONESUCH *n* matchless person or thing

NONET *n* piece of music composed for a group of nine instruments

NONETHNIC *n* not ethnic

NONETS >NONET

NONETTE *same as* >NONET

NONETTES >NONETTE

NONETTI *same as* >NONET

NONETTO *same as* >NONET

NONETTOS >NONETTO

NONEVENT *n* disappointing or insignificant occurrence

NONEVENTS >NONEVENT

NONEXEMPT *adj* not exempt

NONEXOTIC *adj* not exotic

NONEXPERT *n* person who is not an expert

NONEXTANT *adj* no longer in existence

NONFACT *n* event or thing not provable

NONFACTOR *n* something that is not a factor

NONFACTS >NONFACT

NONFADING *adj* colourfast

NONFAMILY *n* household that does not consist of a family

NONFAN *n* person who is not a fan

NONFANS >NONFAN

NONFARM *adj* not connected with a farm

NONFARMER *n* person who is not a farmer

NONFAT *adj* fat free

NONFATAL *adj* not resulting in or capable of causing death

NONFATTY *adj* not fatty

NONFEUDAL *adj* not feudal

NONFILIAL *adj* not involving parent-child relationship

NONFINAL *adj* not final

NONFINITE *adj* not finite

NONFISCAL *adj* not involving government funds

n

NONFLUID adj not fluid ▷ n something that is not a fluid

NONFLUIDS > NONFLUID

NONFLYING adj not capable of flying

NONFOCAL adj not focal

NONFOOD n item that is not food

NONFORMAL adj not formal

NONFOSSIL adj not consisting of fossils

NONFROZEN adj not frozen

NONFUEL adj not relating to fuel

NONFUNDED adj not receiving funding

NONG n stupid or incompetent person

NONGAME adj not pursued for competitive sport purposes

NONGAY n person who is not gay

NONGAYS > NONGAY

NONGHETTO adj not belonging to the ghetto

NONGLARE adj not causing glare ▷ n any of various nonglare materials

NONGLARES > NONGLARE

NONGLAZED adj not glazed

NONGLOSSY adj not glossy

NONGOLFER n person who is not a golfer

NONGRADED adj not graded

NONGREASY adj not greasy

NONGREEN adj not green

NONGROWTH n failure to grow

NONGS > NONG

NONGUEST n person who is not a guest

NONGUESTS > NONGUEST

NONGUILT n state of being innocent

NONGUILTS > NONGUILT

NONHARDY adj fragile

NONHEME adj of dietary iron, obtained from vegetable foods

NONHERO n person who is not a hero

NONHEROES > NONHERO

NONHEROIC adj not heroic

NONHOME adj not of the home

NONHUMAN n something not human

NONHUMANS > NONHUMAN

NONHUNTER n person or thing that does not hunt

NONI n type of tree of SE Asia and the Pacific islands whose fruit provides a possibly health-promoting juice

NONIDEAL adj not ideal

NONILLION n (in Britain, France, and Germany) the number represented as one followed by 54 zeros

NONIMAGE n person who is not a celebrity

NONIMAGES > NONIMAGE

NONIMMUNE adj not immune

NONIMPACT adj not involving impact

NONINERT adj not inert

NONINJURY adj not involving injury

NONINSECT n animal that is not an insect

NONIONIC adj not ionic

NONIRON adj not requiring ironing

NONIS > NONI

NONISSUE n matter of little importance

NONISSUES > NONISSUE

NONJOINER n person who does not join (an organisation, etc)

NONJURIES > NONJURY

NONJURING adj refusing the oath of allegiance

NONJUROR n person who refuses to take an oath, as of allegiance

NONJURORS > NONJUROR

NONJURY n trial without a jury

NONKOSHER adj not kosher

NONLABOR adj not concerned with labour

NONLAWYER n person who is not a lawyer

NONLEADED adj not leaded

NONLEAFY adj not leafy

NONLEAGUE adj not belonging to a league

NONLEGAL adj not legal

NONLEGUME n not a pod of the pea or bean family

NONLETHAL adj not resulting in or capable of causing death

NONLEVEL adj not level

NONLIABLE adj not liable

NONLIFE n matter which is not living

NONLINEAL same as > NONLINEAR

NONLINEAR adj not of, in, along, or relating to a line

NONLIQUID n substance which is not liquid

NONLIVES > NONLIFE

NONLIVING adj not living

NONLOCAL adj not of, affecting, or confined to a limited area or part ▷ n person who is not local to an area

NONLOCALS > NONLOCAL

NONLOVING adj not loving

NONLOYAL adj not loyal

NONLYRIC adj without lyrics

NONMAJOR n student who is not majoring in a specified subject

NONMAJORS > NONMAJOR

NONMAN n being that is not a man

NONMANUAL adj not manual

NONMARKET adj not relating to markets

NONMATURE adj not mature

NONMEAT n not containing meat

NONMEMBER n person who is not a member of a particular club or organization

NONMEN > NONMAN

NONMENTAL adj not mental

NONMETAL n chemical element that forms acidic oxides and is a poor conductor of heat and electricity

NONMETALS > NONMETAL

NONMETRIC adj not metric

NONMETRO adj not metropolitan

NONMOBILE adj not mobile

NONMODAL adj not modal

NONMODERN adj not modern

NONMONEY adj not involving money

NONMORAL adj not involving morality

NONMORTAL adj not fatal

NONMOTILE adj not capable of movement

NONMOVING adj not moving

NONMUSIC n (unpleasant) noise

NONMUSICS > NONMUSIC

NONMUTANT n person or thing that is not mutated

NONMUTUAL adj not mutual

NONNASAL adj not nasal

NONNATIVE adj not native ▷ n person who is not native to a place

NONNAVAL adj not belonging to the navy

NONNEURAL adj not neural

NONNEWS adj not concerned with news

NONNIES > NONNY

NONNOBLE adj not noble

NONNORMAL adj not normal

NONNOVEL n literary work that is not a novel

NONNOVELS > NONNOVEL

NONNY n meaningless word

NONOBESE adj not obese

NONOHMIC adj not having electrical resistance

NONOILY adj not oily

NONORAL adj not oral

NONORALLY > NONORAL

NONOWNER n person who is not an owner

NONOWNERS > NONOWNER

NONPAGAN n person who is not a pagan

NONPAGANS > NONPAGAN

NONPAID adj without payment

NONPAPAL adj not of the pope

NONPAPIST adj not papist

NONPAR adj nonparticipating

NONPAREIL n person or thing that is unsurpassed ▷ adj having no match or equal

NONPARENT n person who is not a parent

NONPARITY n state of not being equal

NONPAROUS adj never having given birth

NONPARTY adj not connected with a political party

NONPAST n grammatical term

NONPASTS > NONPAST

NONPAYING adj (of guests, customers, etc) not expected or requested to pay

NONPEAK n period of low demand

NONPERSON n person regarded as nonexistent or unimportant

NONPLANAR adj not planar

NONPLAY n social behaviour that is not classed as play

NONPLAYER n person not playing

NONPLAYS > NONPLAY

NONPLIANT adj not pliant

NONPLUS vb put at a loss ▷ n state of utter perplexity prohibiting action or speech

NONPLUSED > NONPLUS

NONPLUSES > NONPLUS

NONPOETIC adj not poetic

NONPOINT adj without a specific site

NONPOLAR adj not polar

NONPOLICE adj not related to the police

NONPOOR adj not poor

NONPOROUS adj not permeable to water, air, or other fluids

NONPOSTAL adj not postal

NONPRINT adj published in a format other than print on paper

NONPROFIT n organization that is not intended to make a profit

NONPROS vb enter a judgment of non prosequitur against a plaintiff

NONPROVEN adj not tried and tested

NONPUBLIC adj not public

NONQUOTA adj not included in a quota

NONRACIAL adj not related to racial factors or discrimination

NONRANDOM adj not random

NONRATED adj not rated

NONREADER *n* person who does not or cannot read
NONRETURN *adj* denoting a mechanism that permits flow in a pipe in one direction only
NONRHOTIC *adj* denoting or speaking a dialect of English in which preconsonantal *r*s are not pronounced
NONRIGID *adj* not rigid
NONRIOTER *n* person who does not participate in a riot
NONRIVAL *n* person or thing not competing for success
NONRIVALS > NONRIVAL
NONROYAL *adj* not royal
NONRUBBER *adj* not containing rubber
NONRULING *adj* not ruling
NONRURAL *adj* not rural
NONSACRED *adj* not sacred
NONSALINE *adj* not containing salt
NONSCHOOL *adj* not relating to school
NONSECRET *adj* not sacred
NONSECURE *adj* not secure
NONSELF *n* foreign molecule in the body
NONSELVES > NONSELF
NONSENSE *n* something that has or makes no sense ▷ *interj* exclamation of disagreement
NONSENSES > NONSENSE
NONSERIAL *adj* not serial
NONSEXIST *adj* not discriminating on the basis of sex, esp not against women
NONSEXUAL *adj* not of, relating to, or characterized by sex or sexuality
NONSHRINK *adj* not likely to shrink
NONSIGNER *n* person who cannot use sign language
NONSKATER *n* person who does not skate
NONSKED *n* non-scheduled aeroplane
NONSKEDS > NONSKED
NONSKID *adj* designed to reduce skidding
NONSKIER *n* person who does not ski
NONSKIERS > NONSKIER
NONSLIP *adj* designed to prevent slipping
NONSMOKER *n* person who does not smoke
NONSOCIAL *adj* not social
NONSOLAR *adj* not related to the sun
NONSOLID *n* substance that is not a solid
NONSOLIDS > NONSOLID
NONSPEECH *adj* not involving speech
NONSTAPLE *adj* not staple

NONSTATIC *adj* not static
NONSTEADY *adj* not steady
NONSTICK *adj* coated with a substance that food will not stick to when cooked
NONSTICKY *adj* not sticky
NONSTOP *adv* without a stop ▷ *adj* without a stop ▷ *n* nonstop flight
NONSTOPS > NONSTOP
NONSTORY *n* story of little substance or importance
NONSTYLE *n* style that cannot be identified
NONSTYLES > NONSTYLE
NONSUCH *same as* > NONESUCH
NONSUCHES > NONSUCH
NONSUGAR *n* substance that is not a sugar
NONSUGARS > NONSUGAR
NONSUIT *n* order of a judge dismissing a suit when the plaintiff fails to show a good cause of action or to produce any evidence ▷ *vb* order the dismissal of the suit of (a person)
NONSUITED > NONSUIT
NONSUITS > NONSUIT
NONSYSTEM *adj* having no system
NONTALKER *n* person who does not talk
NONTARGET *adj* not being a target
NONTARIFF *adj* without tariff
NONTAX *n* tax that has little real effect
NONTAXES > NONTAX
NONTHEIST *n* person who believes the existence or non-existence of God is irrelevant
NONTIDAL *adj* not having a tide
NONTITLE *adj* without title
NONTONAL *adj* not written in a key
NONTONIC *adj* not tonic
NONTOXIC *adj* not poisonous
NONTRAGIC *adj* not tragic
NONTRIBAL *adj* not tribal
NONTRUMP *adj* not of the trump suit
NONTRUTH *same as* > UNTRUTH
NONTRUTHS > NONTRUTH
NONUNION *adj* (of a company) not employing trade union members ▷ *n* failure of broken bones or bone fragments to heal
NONUNIONS > NONUNION
NONUNIQUE *adj* not unique
NONUPLE *adj* ninefold ▷ *n* ninefold number
NONUPLES > NONUPLE
NONUPLET *n* child born in a multiple birth of nine siblings

NONUPLETS > NONUPLET
NONURBAN *adj* rural
NONURGENT *adj* not urgent
NONUSABLE *adj* not usable
NONUSE *n* failure to use
NONUSER > NONUSE
NONUSERS > NONUSE
NONUSES > NONUSE
NONUSING > NONUSE
NONVACANT *adj* not vacant
NONVALID *adj* not valid
NONVECTOR *n* quantity without size and direction
NONVENOUS *adj* not venous
NONVERBAL *adj* not involving the use of language
NONVESTED *adj* not vested
NONVIABLE *adj* not viable
NONVIEWER *n* person who does not watch (television)
NONVIRAL *adj* not caused by a virus
NONVIRGIN *n* person who is not a virgin
NONVIRILE *adj* not virile
NONVISUAL *adj* not visual
NONVITAL *adj* not vital
NONVOCAL *n* music track without singing
NONVOCALS > NONVOCAL
NONVOTER *n* person who does not vote
NONVOTERS > NONVOTER
NONVOTING *adj* (of shares in a company) not entitling the owner to vote at company meetings
NONWAGE *adj* not part of wages
NONWAR *n* state of nonviolence
NONWARS > NONWAR
NONWHITE *n* person who is not white
NONWHITES > NONWHITE
NONWINGED *adj* without wings
NONWOODY *adj* not woody
NONWOOL *adj* not wool
NONWORD *n* series of letters not recognised as a word
NONWORDS > NONWORD
NONWORK *adj* not involving work
NONWORKER *n* person who does not work
NONWOVEN *n* material made by a method other than weaving
NONWOVENS > NONWOVEN
NONWRITER *n* person who is not a writer
NONYL *n* type of chemical
NONYLS > NONYL
NONZERO *adj* not equal to zero
NOO *n* type of Japanese musical drama
NOOB *same as* > NEWBIE
NOOBS > NOOB
NOODGE *vb* annoy persistently

NOODGED > NOODGE
NOODGES > NOODGE
NOODGING > NOODGE
NOODLE *n* simpleton ▷ *vb* improvise aimlessly on a musical instrument
NOODLED > NOODLE
NOODLEDOM *n* state of being a simpleton
NOODLES > NOODLE
NOODLING *n* aimless musical improvisation
NOODLINGS > NOODLING
NOOGIE *n* act of inflicting pain by rubbing someone's head hard
NOOGIES > NOOGIE
NOOIT *interj* South African exclamation of pleased or shocked surprise
NOOK *n* corner or recess
NOOKIE *same as* > NOOKY
NOOKIER > NOOKY
NOOKIES > NOOKIE
NOOKIEST > NOOKY
NOOKLIKE > NOOK
NOOKS > NOOK
NOOKY *n* sexual intercourse ▷ *adj* resembling a nook
NOOLOGIES > NOOLOGY
NOOLOGY *n* study of intuition
NOOMETRY *n* mind measurement
NOON *n* twelve o'clock midday ▷ *vb* take a rest at noon
NOONDAY *adj* happening at noon ▷ *n* middle of the day
NOONDAYS > NOONDAY
NOONED > NOON
NOONER *n* sexual encounter during a lunch hour
NOONERS > NOONER
NOONING *n* midday break for rest or food
NOONINGS > NOONING
NOONS > NOON
NOONTIDE *same as* > NOONTIME
NOONTIDES > NOONTIDE
NOONTIME *n* middle of the day
NOONTIMES > NOONTIME
NOOP *n* point of the elbow
NOOPS > NOOP
NOOSE *n* loop in the end of a rope, tied with a slipknot
NOOSED > NOOSE
NOOSER *n* person who uses a noose
NOOSERS > NOOSER
NOOSES > NOOSE
NOOSING > NOOSE
NOOSPHERE *n* sphere of human thought
NOOTROPIC *adj* acting on mind
NOPAL *n* type of cactus
NOPALES > NOPAL
NOPALITO *n* small cactus
NOPALITOS > NOPALITO
NOPALS > NOPAL
NOPE *interj* no

NOPLACE same as
> NOWHERE
NOR prep and not
NORDIC adj of
competitions in
cross-country racing and
ski-jumping
NORI n edible seaweed
often used in Japanese
cookery, esp for wrapping
sushi or rice balls
NORIA n water wheel with
buckets attached to its rim
for raising water from a
stream into irrigation
canals
NORIAS > NORIA
NORIMON n Japanese
passenger vehicle
NORIMONS > NORIMON
NORIS > NORI
NORITE n variety of gabbro
composed mainly of
hypersthene and
labradorite feldspar
NORITES > NORITE
NORITIC > NORITE
NORK n female breast
NORKS > NORK
NORLAND n north part of a
country or the earth
NORLANDS > NORLAND
NORM n standard that is
regarded as normal
NORMA n norm or standard
NORMAL adj usual, regular,
or typical ⊳ n usual or
regular state, degree or
form
NORMALCY > NORMAL
NORMALISE same as
> NORMALIZE
NORMALITY > NORMAL
NORMALIZE vb make or
become normal
NORMALLY adv as a rule
NORMALS > NORMAL
NORMAN n post used for
winding on a ship
NORMANDE n type of cattle
NORMANS > NORMAN
NORMAS > NORMA
NORMATIVE adj of or
setting a norm or standard
NORMED n mathematical
term
NORMLESS adj without a
norm
NORMS > NORM
NOROVIRUS n virus that
causes gastroenteritis
NORSEL vb fit with short
lines for fastening hooks
NORSELLED > NORSEL
NORSELLER > NORSEL
NORSELS > NORSEL
NORTENA same as
> NORTENO
NORTENAS > NORTENA
NORTENO n type of
Mexican music
NORTENOS > NORTENO
NORTH n direction towards
the North Pole, opposite
south ⊳ adj or in the north

⊳ adv in, to, or towards the
north ⊳ vb move north
NORTHEAST adv (in or to)
direction between north
and east ⊳ n point of the
compass or direction
midway between north
and east ⊳ adj of or
denoting the northeastern
part of a specified country,
area, etc
NORTHED > NORTH
NORTHER n wind or storm
from the north ⊳ vb move
north
NORTHERED > NORTHER
NORTHERLY adj of or in the
north ⊳ adv towards the
north ⊳ n wind from the
north
NORTHERN adj situated in
or towards the north ⊳ n
person from the north
NORTHERNS > NORTHERN
NORTHERS > NORTHER
NORTHING n movement or
distance covered in a
northerly direction
NORTHINGS > NORTHING
NORTHLAND n lands that
are far to the north
NORTHMOST adj situated
furthest north
NORTHS > NORTH
NORTHWARD adv towards
the north
NORTHWEST adv (in or to)
direction between north
and west ⊳ n point of the
compass or direction
midway between north
and west ⊳ adj of or
denoting the northwestern
part of a specified country,
area, etc
NORWARD same as
> NORTHWARD
NORWARDS same as
> NORWARD
NOS > NO
NOSE n organ of smell, used
also in breathing ⊳ vb move
forward slowly and
carefully
NOSEAN n type of mineral
NOSEANS > NOSEAN
NOSEBAG n bag containing
feed fastened round a
horse's head
NOSEBAGS > NOSEBAG
NOSEBAND n part of a
horse's bridle that goes
around the nose
NOSEBANDS > NOSEBAND
NOSEBLEED n bleeding
from the nose
NOSED > NOSE
NOSEDIVE vb (of an
aircraft) plunge suddenly
with the nose pointing
downwards
NOSEDIVED > NOSEDIVE
NOSEDIVES > NOSEDIVE
NOSEDOVE > NOSEDIVE
NOSEGAY n small bunch of

flowers
NOSEGAYS > NOSEGAY
NOSEGUARD n position in
American football
NOSELESS > NOSE
NOSELIKE > NOSE
NOSELITE same as
> NOSEAN
NOSELITES > NOSELITE
NOSEPIECE same as
> NOSEBAND
NOSER n strong headwind
NOSERS > NOSER
NOSES > NOSE
NOSEWHEEL n wheel fitted
under the nose of an
aircraft
NOSEY adj prying or
inquisitive ⊳ n nosey
person
NOSEYS > NOSEY
NOSH n food ⊳ vb eat
NOSHED > NOSH
NOSHER > NOSH
NOSHERIE same as
> NOSHERY
NOSHERIES > NOSHERIE
NOSHERS > NOSH
NOSHERY n restaurant or
other place where food is
served
NOSHES > NOSH
NOSHING > NOSH
NOSIER > NOSY
NOSIES > NOSY
NOSIEST > NOSY
NOSILY > NOSY
NOSINESS > NOSY
NOSING n edge of a step or
stair tread that projects
beyond the riser
NOSINGS > NOSING
NOSODE n homeopathic
remedy
NOSODES > NOSODE
NOSOLOGIC > NOSOLOGY
NOSOLOGY n branch of
medicine concerned with
the classification of
diseases
NOSTALGIA n sentimental
longing for the past
NOSTALGIC adj of or
characterized by nostalgia
⊳ n person who indulges in
nostalgia
NOSTOC n type of
bacterium occurring in
moist places
NOSTOCS > NOSTOC
NOSTOI > NOSTOS
NOSTOLOGY n scientific
study of ageing
NOSTOS n story of a return
home
NOSTRIL n one of the two
openings at the end of the
nose
NOSTRILS > NOSTRIL
NOSTRO as in nostro account
bank account conducted by
a British bank with a
foreign bank
NOSTRUM n quack
medicine

NOSTRUMS > NOSTRUM
NOSY adj prying or
inquisitive
NOT adv expressing
negation, refusal, or denial
NOTA > NOTUM
NOTABILIA n things
worthy of notice
NOTABLE adj worthy of
being noted, remarkable
⊳ n person of distinction
NOTABLES > NOTABLE
NOTABLY adv particularly
or especially
NOTAEUM n back of a bird's
body
NOTAEUMS > NOTAEUM
NOTAIRE n (in France)
notary
NOTAIRES > NOTAIRE
NOTAL > NOTUM
NOTANDA > NOTANDUM
NOTANDUM n notable fact
NOTAPHILY n study of
paper money
NOTARIAL > NOTARY
NOTARIES > NOTARY
NOTARISE same as
> NOTARIZE
NOTARISED > NOTARISE
NOTARISES > NOTARISE
NOTARIZE vb attest to or
authenticate (a document,
contract, etc), as a notary
NOTARIZED > NOTARIZE
NOTARIZES > NOTARIZE
NOTARY n person
authorized to witness the
signing of legal documents
NOTATE vb write (esp
music) in notation
NOTATED > NOTATE
NOTATES > NOTATE
NOTATING > NOTATE
NOTATION n
representation of numbers
or quantities in a system by
a series of symbols
NOTATIONS > NOTATION
NOTCH n V-shaped cut ⊳ vb
make a notch in
NOTCHBACK n type of car
NOTCHED > NOTCH
NOTCHEL vb refuse to pay
another person's debts
NOTCHELED > NOTCHEL
NOTCHELS > NOTCHEL
NOTCHER n person who
cuts notches
NOTCHERS > NOTCHER
NOTCHES > NOTCH
NOTCHIER > NOTCHY
NOTCHIEST > NOTCHY
NOTCHING > NOTCH
NOTCHINGS > NOTCH
NOTCHY adj (of a motor
vehicle gear mechanism)
requiring careful
gear-changing
NOTE n short letter ⊳ vb
notice, pay attention to
NOTEBOOK n book for
writing in
NOTEBOOKS > NOTEBOOK

NOTECARD n greetings card with space to write note

NOTECARDS > NOTECARD

NOTECASE same as > WALLET

NOTECASES > NOTECASE

NOTED adj well-known

NOTEDLY > NOTED

NOTEDNESS > NOTED

NOTELESS > NOTE

NOTELET n small folded card with a design on the front, used for writing informal letters

NOTELETS > NOTELET

NOTEPAD n number of sheets of paper fastened together along one edge

NOTEPADS > NOTEPAD

NOTEPAPER n paper used for writing letters

NOTER n person who takes notes

NOTERS > NOTER

NOTES npl short descriptive or summarized jottings taken down for future reference

NOTHER same as > OTHER

NOTHING pron not anything ▷ adv not at all ▷ n person or thing of no importance

NOTHINGS > NOTHING

NOTICE n observation or attention ▷ vb observe, become aware of

NOTICED > NOTICE

NOTICER n person who takes notice

NOTICERS > NOTICER

NOTICES > NOTICE

NOTICING > NOTICE

NOTIFIED > NOTIFY

NOTIFIER > NOTIFY

NOTIFIERS > NOTIFY

NOTIFIES > NOTIFY

NOTIFY vb inform

NOTIFYING > NOTIFY

NOTING > NOTE

NOTION n idea or opinion

NOTIONAL adj speculative, imaginary, or unreal

NOTIONIST n person whose opinions are merely notions

NOTIONS npl pins, cotton, ribbon, and similar wares used for sewing

NOTITIA n register or list, esp of ecclesiastical districts

NOTITIAE > NOTITIA

NOTITIAS > NOTITIA

NOTOCHORD n fibrous longitudinal rod in all embryo and some adult chordate animals

NOTORIETY > NOTORIOUS

NOTORIOUS adj well known for something bad

NOTORNIS n rare flightless rail of New Zealand

NOTOUR adj notorious

NOTT same as > NOT

NOTTURNI > NOTTURNO

NOTTURNO n piece of music

NOTUM n cuticular plate covering the dorsal surface of a thoracic segment of an insect

NOUGAT n chewy sweet containing nuts and fruit

NOUGATINE n type of brown nougat with a firm texture

NOUGATS > NOUGAT

NOUGHT n figure o

NOUGHTIES npl decade from 2000 to 2009

NOUGHTS > NOUGHT

NOUL same as > NOLL

NOULD vb would not

NOULDE same as > NOULD

NOULE same as > NOLL

NOULES > NOULE

NOULS > NOUL

NOUMENA > NOUMENON

NOUMENAL > NOUMENON

NOUMENON n (in the philosophy of Kant) a thing as it is in itself, incapable of being known, but only inferred from the nature of experience

NOUN n word that refers to a person, place, or thing

NOUNAL > NOUN

NOUNALLY > NOUN

NOUNIER > NOUNY

NOUNIEST > NOUNY

NOUNLESS > NOUN

NOUNS > NOUN

NOUNY adj nounlike

NOUP n steep headland

NOUPS > NOUP

NOURICE n nurse

NOURICES > NOURICE

NOURISH vb feed

NOURISHED > NOURISH

NOURISHER > NOURISH

NOURISHES > NOURISH

NOURITURE n nourishment

NOURSLE vb nurse

NOURSLED > NOURSLE

NOURSLES > NOURSLE

NOURSLING > NOURSLE

NOUS n common sense

NOUSELL vb foster

NOUSELLED > NOUSELL

NOUSELLS > NOUSELL

NOUSES > NOUS

NOUSLE vb nuzzle

NOUSLED > NOUSLE

NOUSLES > NOUSLE

NOUSLING > NOUSLE

NOUT same as > NOUGHT

NOUVEAU adj having recently become the thing specified

NOUVEAUX same as > NOUVEAU

NOUVELLE n long short story

NOUVELLES > NOUVELLE

NOVA n star that suddenly becomes brighter and then gradually decreases to its original brightness

NOVAE > NOVA

NOVALIA n newly reclaimed land

NOVALIKE adj resembling a nova

NOVAS > NOVA

NOVATE vb substitute one thing (esp a legal contract) in place of another

NOVATED as in novated lease Australian system of employer-aided car purchase

NOVATES > NOVATE

NOVATING > NOVATE

NOVATION n substitution of a new obligation for an old one by mutual agreement between the parties

NOVATIONS > NOVATION

NOVEL n long fictitious story in book form ▷ adj fresh, new, or original

NOVELDOM n realm of fiction

NOVELDOMS > NOVELDOM

NOVELESE n style of writing characteristic of poor novels

NOVELESES > NOVELESE

NOVELETTE n short novel, esp one regarded as trivial or sentimental

NOVELISE same as > NOVELIZE

NOVELISED > NOVELISE

NOVELISER n person who novelizes

NOVELISES > NOVELISE

NOVELISH adj resembling a novel

NOVELISM n innovation

NOVELISMS > NOVELISM

NOVELIST n writer of novels

NOVELISTS > NOVELIST

NOVELIZE vb convert (a true story, film, etc) into a novel

NOVELIZED > NOVELIZE

NOVELIZER n person who novelizes

NOVELIZES > NOVELIZE

NOVELLA n short novel

NOVELLAE > NOVELLA

NOVELLAS > NOVELLA

NOVELLE > NOVELLA

NOVELLY > NOVEL

NOVELS > NOVEL

NOVELTIES > NOVELTY

NOVELTY n newness

NOVEMBER n code word for the letter N

NOVEMBERS > NOVEMBER

NOVENA n set of prayers or services on nine consecutive days

NOVENAE > NOVENA

NOVENARY n set of nine

NOVENAS > NOVENA

NOVENNIAL adj recurring every ninth year

NOVERCAL adj stepmotherly

NOVERINT n writ

NOVERINTS > NOVERINT

NOVICE n beginner

NOVICES > NOVICE

NOVICIATE same as > NOVITIATE

NOVITIATE n period of being a novice

NOVITIES > NOVITY

NOVITY n novelty

NOVOCAINE n tradename of a painkilling substance used as a local anaesthetic

NOVODAMUS n type of charter

NOVUM n game played with dice

NOVUMS > NOVUM

NOW adv at or for the present time

NOWADAYS adv in these times

NOWAY adv in no manner ▷ sentence substitute used to make an emphatic refusal, denial etc

NOWAYS same as > NOWAY

NOWED adj knotted

NOWHENCE adv from no place

NOWHERE adv not anywhere ▷ n nonexistent or insignicant place

NOWHERES > NOWHERE

NOWHITHER adv no place

NOWISE another word for > NOWAY

NOWL n crown of the head

NOWLS > NOWL

NOWN same as > OWN

NOWNESS > NOWN

NOWNESSES > NOWN

NOWS > NOW

NOWT n nothing

NOWTIER > NOWTY

NOWTIEST > NOWTY

NOWTS > NOWT

NOWTY adj bad-tempered

NOWY adj having a small projection at the centre (of a cross)

NOX n nitrogen oxide

NOXAL adj relating to damage done by something belonging to another

NOXES > NOX

NOXIOUS adj poisonous or harmful

NOXIOUSLY > NOXIOUS

NOY vb harrass

NOYADE n execution by drowning

NOYADES > NOYADE

NOYANCE n nuisance

NOYANCES > NOYANCE

NOYAU n liqueur made from brandy flavoured with nut kernels

NOYAUS > NOYAU

n

NOYED > NOY

NOYES *archaic form of* > NOISE

NOYESES > NOYES

NOYING > NOY

NOYOUS > NOY

NOYS > NOY

NOYSOME > NOY

NOZZER *n* new recruit (in the Navy)

NOZZERS > NOZZER

NOZZLE *n* projecting spout through which fluid is discharged

NOZZLES > NOZZLE

NTH *adj* of an unspecified number

NU *n* 13th letter in the Greek alphabet

NUANCE *n* subtle difference in colour, meaning, or tone ▷ *vb* give subtle differences to

NUANCED > NUANCE

NUANCES > NUANCE

NUANCING > NUANCE

NUB *n* point or gist (of a story etc) ▷ *vb* hang from the gallows

NUBBED > NUB

NUBBIER > NUBBY

NUBBIEST > NUBBY

NUBBIN *n* something small or undeveloped, esp a fruit or ear of corn

NUBBINESS > NUBBY

NUBBING > NUB

NUBBINS > NUBBIN

NUBBLE *n* small lump

NUBBLED > NUBBLE

NUBBLES > NUBBLE

NUBBLIER > NUBBLE

NUBBLIEST > NUBBLE

NUBBLING > NUBBLE

NUBBLY > NUBBLE

NUBBY *adj* having small lumps or protuberances

NUBECULA *n* small irregular galaxy near the S celestial pole

NUBECULAE > NUBECULA

NUBIA *n* fleecy scarf for the head, worn by women

NUBIAS > NUBIA

NUBIFORM *adj* cloudlike

NUBILE *adj* sexually attractive

NUBILITY > NUBILE

NUBILOSE *same as* > NUBILOUS

NUBILOUS *adj* cloudy

NUBS > NUB

NUBUCK *n* type of leather with a velvety finish

NUBUCKS > NUBUCK

NUCELLAR > NUCELLUS

NUCELLI > NUCELLUS

NUCELLUS *n* central part of a plant ovule containing the embryo sac

NUCHA *n* back or nape of the neck

NUCHAE > NUCHA

NUCHAL *n* scale on a reptile's neck

NUCHALS > NUCHAL

NUCLEAL > NUCLEUS

NUCLEAR *adj* of nuclear weapons or energy

NUCLEASE *n* any of a group of enzymes that hydrolyse nucleic acids to simple nucleotides

NUCLEASES > NUCLEASE

NUCLEATE *adj* having a nucleus ▷ *vb* form a nucleus

NUCLEATED > NUCLEATE

NUCLEATES > NUCLEATE

NUCLEATOR > NUCLEATE

NUCLEI > NUCLEUS

NUCLEIC as in *nucleic acid* type of complex compound that is a vital constituent of living cells

NUCLEIDE *same as* > NUCLIDE

NUCLEIDES > NUCLEIDE

NUCLEIN *n* any of a group of proteins that occur in the nuclei of living cells

NUCLEINIC > NUCLEIN

NUCLEINS > NUCLEIN

NUCLEOID *n* component of a bacterium

NUCLEOIDS > NUCLEOID

NUCLEOLAR > NUCLEOLUS

NUCLEOLE *variant of* > NUCLEOLUS

NUCLEOLES > NUCLEOLE

NUCLEOLI > NUCLEOLUS

NUCLEOLUS *n* small rounded body within a resting nucleus that contains RNA and proteins

NUCLEON *n* proton or neutron

NUCLEONIC *adj* relating to the branch of physics concerned with the applications of nuclear energy

NUCLEONS > NUCLEON

NUCLEUS *n* centre, esp of an atom or cell

NUCLEUSES > NUCLEUS

NUCLIDE *n* species of atom characterized by its atomic number and its mass number

NUCLIDES > NUCLIDE

NUCLIDIC > NUCLIDE

NUCULE *n* small seed

NUCULES > NUCULE

NUDATION *n* act of stripping

NUDATIONS > NUDATION

NUDDIES > NUDDY

NUDDY as in *in the nuddy* in the nude

NUDE *adj* naked ▷ *n* naked figure in painting, sculpture, or photography

NUDELY > NUDE

NUDENESS > NUDE

NUDER > NUDE

NUDES > NUDE

NUDEST > NUDE

NUDGE *vb* push gently, esp with the elbow ▷ *n* gentle push or touch

NUDGED > NUDGE

NUDGER > NUDGE

NUDGERS > NUDGE

NUDGES > NUDGE

NUDGING > NUDGE

NUDICAUL *adj* (of plants) having stems without leaves

NUDIE *n* film, show, or magazine depicting nudity

NUDIES > NUDIE

NUDISM *n* practice of not wearing clothes

NUDISMS > NUDISM

NUDIST > NUDISM

NUDISTS > NUDISM

NUDITIES > NUDITY

NUDITY *n* state or fact of being nude

NUDNICK *same as* > NUDNIK

NUDNICKS > NUDNICK

NUDNIK *n* boring person

NUDNIKS > NUDNIK

NUDZH *same as* > NUDGE

NUDZHED > NUDZH

NUDZHES > NUDZH

NUDZHING > NUDZH

NUFF *slang form of* > ENOUGH

NUFFIN *slang form of* > NOTHING

NUFFINS > NUFFIN

NUFFS > NUFF

NUGAE *n* jests

NUGATORY *adj* of little value

NUGGAR *n* sailing boat used to carry cargo on the Nile

NUGGARS > NUGGAR

NUGGET *n* small lump of gold in its natural state ▷ *vb* polish footwear

NUGGETED > NUGGET

NUGGETING > NUGGET

NUGGETS > NUGGET

NUGGETTED > NUGGET

NUGGETY *adj* of or resembling a nugget

NUISANCE *n* something or someone that causes annoyance or bother ▷ *adj* causing annoyance or bother

NUISANCER *n* person or thing causing a nuisance

NUISANCES > NUISANCE

NUKE *vb* attack with nuclear weapons ▷ *n* nuclear weapon

NUKED > NUKE

NUKES > NUKE

NUKING > NUKE

NULL *adj* without legal force ▷ *vb* make negative

NULLA *same as* > NULLAH

NULLAH *n* stream or drain

NULLAHS > NULLAH

NULLAS > NULLA

NULLED > NULL

NULLIFIED > NULLIFY

NULLIFIER > NULLIFY

NULLIFIES > NULLIFY

NULLIFY *vb* make ineffective

NULLING *n* knurling

NULLINGS > NULLING

NULLIPARA *n* woman who has never borne a child

NULLIPORE *n* any of several red seaweeds

NULLITIES > NULLITY

NULLITY *n* state of being null

NULLNESS > NULL

NULLS > NULL

NUMB *adj* without feeling, as through cold, shock, or fear ▷ *vb* make numb

NUMBAT *n* small Australian marsupial with a long snout and tongue

NUMBATS > NUMBAT

NUMBED > NUMB

NUMBER *n* sum or quantity ▷ *vb* count

NUMBERED > NUMBER

NUMBERER *n* person who numbers

NUMBERERS > NUMBERER

NUMBERING > NUMBER

NUMBERS > NUMBER

NUMBEST > NUMB

NUMBFISH *n* any of several electric ray fish

NUMBING > NUMB

NUMBINGLY > NUMB

NUMBLES *npl* heart, lungs, liver, etc, of a deer or other animal, cooked for food

NUMBLY > NUMB

NUMBNESS > NUMB

NUMBS > NUMB

NUMBSKULL *n* stupid person

NUMCHUCK *same as* > NUNCHAKU

NUMCHUCKS > NUMCHUCK

NUMDAH *n* coarse felt made esp in India

NUMDAHS > NUMDAH

NUMEN *n* (esp in ancient Roman religion) a deity or spirit presiding over a thing or place

NUMERABLE *adj* able to be numbered or counted

NUMERABLY > NUMERABLE

NUMERACY *n* ability to use numbers, esp in arithmetical operations

NUMERAIRE *n* unit in which prices are measured

NUMERAL *n* word or symbol used to express a sum or quantity ▷ *adj* of, consisting of, or denoting a number

NUMERALLY > NUMERAL

NUMERALS > NUMERAL

NUMERARY *adj* of or relating to numbers

NUMERATE *adj* able to do basic arithmetic ▷ *vb* read (a numerical expression)

NUMERATED > NUMERATE

NUMERATES > NUMERATE

NUMERATOR *n* number above the line in a fraction

NUMERIC *n* number or numeral

NUMERICAL *adj* measured or expressed in numbers

NUMERICS > NUMERIC

NUMEROUS *adj* existing or happening in large numbers

NUMINA *plural of* > NUMEN

NUMINOUS *adj* arousing religious or spiritual emotions ▷ *n* something that arouses religious or spiritual emotions

NUMMARY *adj* of or relating to coins

NUMMULAR *adj* shaped like a coin

NUMMULARY > NUMMULAR

NUMMULINE > NUMMULAR

NUMMULITE *n* type of large fossil protozoan

NUMNAH *same as* > NUMDAH

NUMNAHS > NUMNAH

NUMPTIES > NUMPTY

NUMPTY *n* stupid person

NUMSKULL *same as* > NUMBSKULL

NUMSKULLS > NUMSKULL

NUN *n* female member of a religious order

NUNATAK *n* isolated mountain peak projecting through the surface of surrounding glacial ice

NUNATAKER > NUNATAK

NUNATAKS > NUNATAK

NUNCHAKU *n* rice flail used as a weapon

NUNCHAKUS > NUNCHAKU

NUNCHEON *n* light snack

NUNCHEONS > NUNCHEON

NUNCHUCKS *same as* > NUNCHAKUS

NUNCIO *n* pope's ambassador

NUNCIOS > NUNCIO

NUNCLE *archaic or dialect word for* > UNCLE

NUNCLES > NUNCLE

NUNCUPATE *vb* declare publicly

NUNDINAL > NUNDINE

NUNDINE *n* market day

NUNDINES > NUNDINE

NUNHOOD *n* condition, practice, or character of a nun

NUNHOODS > NUNHOOD

NUNLIKE > NUN

NUNNATION *n* pronunciation of n at the end of words

NUNNERIES > NUNNERY

NUNNERY *n* convent

NUNNISH > NUN

NUNNY as in *nunny bag* small sealskin haversack used in Canada

NUNS > NUN

NUNSHIP > NUN

NUNSHIPS > NUN

NUPTIAL *adj* relating to marriage

NUPTIALLY > NUPTIAL

NUPTIALS *npl* wedding

NUR *n* wooden ball

NURAGHE *n* Sardinian round tower

NURAGHI > NURAGHE

NURAGHIC > NURAGHE

NURD *same as* > NERD

NURDIER > NERD

NURDIEST > NERD

NURDISH > NERD

NURDLE *vb* score runs in cricket by deflecting the ball rather than striking it hard

NURDLED > NURDLE

NURDLES > NURDLE

NURDLING > NURDLE

NURDS > NURD

NURDY > NURD

NURHAG *n* Sardinian round tower

NURHAGS > NURHAG

NURL *variant of* > KNURL

NURLED > NURL

NURLING > NURL

NURLS > NURL

NURR *n* wooden ball

NURRS > NURR

NURS > NUR

NURSE *n* person employed to look after sick people, usu. in a hospital ▷ *vb* look after (a sick person)

NURSED > NURSE

NURSELIKE > NURSE

NURSELING *same as* > NURSLING

NURSEMAID *n* woman employed to look after children

NURSER *n* person who treats something carefully

NURSERIES > NURSERY

NURSERS > NURSER

NURSERY *n* room where children sleep or play

NURSES > NURSE

NURSING *n* practice or profession of caring for the sick and injured

NURSINGS > NURSING

NURSLE *vb* nuzzle

NURSLED > NURSLE

NURSLES > NURSLE

NURSLING *n* child or young animal that is being suckled, nursed, or fostered

NURSLINGS > NURSLING

NURTURAL > NURTURE

NURTURANT > NURTURE

NURTURE *n* act or process of promoting the development of a child or young person ▷ *vb* promote or encourage the development of

NURTURED > NURTURE

NURTURER > NURTURE

NURTURERS > NURTURE

NURTURES > NURTURE

NURTURING > NURTURE

NUS > NU

NUT *n* fruit consisting of a hard shell and a kernel ▷ *vb* to gather nuts

NUTANT *adj* having the apex hanging down

NUTARIAN *n* person whose diet is based around nuts

NUTARIANS > NUTARIAN

NUTATE *vb* nod

NUTATED > NUTATE

NUTATES > NUTATE

NUTATING > NUTATE

NUTATION *n* periodic variation in the precession of the earth's axis

NUTATIONS > NUTATION

NUTBROWN *adj* of a brownish colour, esp a reddish-brown

NUTBUTTER *n* ground nuts blended with butter

NUTCASE *n* insane person

NUTCASES > NUTCASE

NUTGALL *n* nut-shaped gall caused by gall wasps on the oak and other trees

NUTGALLS > NUTGALL

NUTGRASS *n* type of plant

NUTHATCH *n* small songbird

NUTHOUSE *n* mental hospital or asylum

NUTHOUSES > NUTHOUSE

NUTJOB *n* crazy person

NUTJOBBER *n* nuthatch

NUTJOBS > NUTJOB

NUTLET *n* any of the one-seeded portions of a fruit that fragments when mature

NUTLETS > NUTLET

NUTLIKE > NUT

NUTMEAL *n* type of grain

NUTMEALS > NUTMEAL

NUTMEAT *n* kernel of a nut

NUTMEATS > NUTMEAT

NUTMEG *n* spice made from the seed of a tropical tree ▷ *vb* kick or hit the ball between the legs of (an opposing player)

NUTMEGGED > NUTMEG

NUTMEGGY > NUTMEG

NUTMEGS > NUTMEG

NUTPECKER *n* nuthatch

NUTPICK *n* tool used to dig the meat from nuts

NUTPICKS > NUTPICK

NUTRIA *n* fur of the coypu

NUTRIAS > NUTRIA

NUTRIENT *n* substance that provides nourishment ▷ *adj* providing nourishment

NUTRIENTS > NUTRIENT

NUTRIMENT *n* food or nourishment required by all living things to grow and stay healthy

NUTRITION *n* process of taking in and absorbing nutrients

NUTRITIVE *adj* of nutrition ▷ *n* nutritious food

NUTS > NUT

NUTSEDGE *same as* > NUTGRASS

NUTSEDGES > NUTSEDGE

NUTSHELL *n* shell around the kernel of a nut

NUTSHELLS > NUTSHELL

NUTSIER > NUTSY

NUTSIEST > NUTSY

NUTSO *adj* insane

NUTSY *adj* lunatic

NUTTED > NUT

NUTTER *n* insane person

NUTTERIES > NUTTERY

NUTTERS > NUTTER

NUTTERY *n* place where nut trees grow

NUTTIER > NUTTY

NUTTIEST > NUTTY

NUTTILY > NUTTY

NUTTINESS > NUTTY

NUTTING *n* act of gathering nuts

NUTTINGS > NUTTING

NUTTY *adj* containing or resembling nuts

NUTWOOD *n* any of various nut-bearing trees, such as walnut

NUTWOODS > NUTWOOD

NUZZER *n* present given to a superior in India

NUZZERS > NUZZER

NUZZLE *vb* push or rub gently with the nose or snout

NUZZLED > NUZZLE

NUZZLER *n* person or thing that nuzzles

NUZZLERS > NUZZLER

NUZZLES > NUZZLE

NUZZLING > NUZZLE

NY *same as* > NIGH

NYAFF *n* small or contemptible person ▷ *vb* yelp like a small dog

NYAFFED > NYAFF

NYAFFING > NYAFF

NYAFFS > NYAFF

NYALA *n* spiral-horned southern African antelope

NYALAS > NYALA

NYANZA *n* (in E Africa) a lake

NYANZAS > NYANZA

NYAS *n* young hawk

NYASES > NYAS

NYBBLE *n* small byte

NYBBLES > NYBBLE

NYCTALOPS *n* person or thing with night-vision

NYE *n* flock of pheasants ▷ *vb* near

NYED > NYE

NYES > NYE

NYING > NYE

NYLGHAI *same as* > NILGAI

NYLGHAIS > NYLGHAI

NYLGHAU *same as* > NILGAI

n

NYLGHAUS > NYLGHAU

NYLON *n* synthetic material used for clothing etc

NYLONS *npl* stockings made of nylon

NYMPH *n* mythical spirit of nature, represented as a beautiful young woman

NYMPHA *n* either one of the labia minora

NYMPHAE > NYMPHA

NYMPHAEA *n* water lily

NYMPHAEUM *n* shrine of the nymphs

NYMPHAL > NYMPH

NYMPHALID *n* butterfly of the family that includes the fritillaries and red admirals ⊳ *adj* of this family of butterflies

NYMPHEAN > NYMPH

NYMPHET *n* sexually precocious young girl

NYMPHETIC > NYMPHET

NYMPHETS > NYMPHET

NYMPHETTE *same as* > NYMPHET

NYMPHIC > NYMPH

NYMPHICAL > NYMPH

NYMPHISH > NYMPH

NYMPHLIKE > NYMPH

NYMPHLY > NYMPH

NYMPHO *n* nymphomaniac

NYMPHOS > NYMPHO

NYMPHS > NYMPH

NYS > NY

NYSSA *n* type of tree

NYSSAS > NYSSA

NYSTAGMIC > NYSTAGMUS

NYSTAGMUS *n* involuntary movement of the eye comprising a smooth drift followed by a flick back

NYSTATIN *n* type of antibiotic obtained from a bacterium

NYSTATINS > NYSTATIN

n

Oo

OAF *n* stupid or clumsy person
OAFISH > OAF
OAFISHLY > OAF
OAFS > OAF
OAK *n* deciduous forest tree
OAKED *adj* relating to wine that is stored for a time in oak barrels prior to bottling
OAKEN *adj* made of the wood of the oak
OAKENSHAW *n* small forest of oaks
OAKER *same as* > OCHRE
OAKERS > OAKER
OAKIER > OAKY
OAKIES > OAKY
OAKIEST > OAKY
OAKLIKE > OAK
OAKLING *n* young oak
OAKLINGS > OAKLING
OAKMOSS *n* type of lichen
OAKMOSSES > OAKMOSS
OAKS > OAK
OAKUM *n* fibre obtained by unravelling old rope
OAKUMS > OAKUM
OAKY *adj* hard like the wood of an oak ▷ *n* ice cream
OANSHAGH *n* foolish girl or woman
OANSHAGHS > OANSHAGH
OAR *n* pole with a broad blade, used for rowing a boat ▷ *vb* propel with oars
OARAGE *n* use or number of oars
OARAGES > OARAGE
OARED *adj* equipped with oars
OARFISH *n* very long ribbonfish with long slender ventral fins
OARFISHES > OARFISH
OARIER > OARY
OARIEST > OARY
OARING > OAR
OARLESS > OAR
OARLIKE > OAR
OARLOCK *n* swivelling device attached to the gunwale of a boat that holds an oar in place
OARLOCKS > OARLOCK
OARS > OAR
OARSMAN *n* person who rows
OARSMEN > OARSMAN
OARSWOMAN *n* female oarsman
OARSWOMEN
> OARSWOMAN
OARWEED *n* type of brown seaweed
OARWEEDS > OARWEED
OARY *adj* of or like an oar
OASES > OASIS
OASIS *n* fertile area in a desert
OAST *n* oven for drying hops
OASTHOUSE *n* building with kilns for drying hops
OASTS > OAST
OAT *n* hard cereal grown as food
OATCAKE *n* thin flat biscuit of oatmeal
OATCAKES > OATCAKE
OATEN *adj* made of oats or oat straw
OATER *n* film about the American Wild West
OATERS > OATER
OATH *n* solemn promise, esp to be truthful in court
OATHABLE *adj* able to take an oath
OATHS > OATH
OATIER > OATY
OATIEST > OATY
OATLIKE > OAT
OATMEAL *n* coarse flour made from oats ▷ *adj* pale brownish-cream
OATMEALS > OATMEAL
OATS > OAT
OATY *adj* of, like, or containing oats
OAVES > OAF
OB *n* expression of opposition
OBA *n* (in W Africa) a Yoruba chief or ruler
OBANG *n* former Japanese coin
OBANGS > OBANG
OBAS > OBA
OBBLIGATI
> OBBLIGATO
OBBLIGATO *n* essential part or accompaniment ▷ *adj* not to be omitted in performance
OBCONIC *adj* (of a fruit or similar part) shaped like a cone and attached at the pointed end
OBCONICAL *same as*
> OBCONIC
OBCORDATE *adj* heart-shaped and attached at the pointed end

OBDURACY > OBDURATE
OBDURATE *adj* hardhearted or stubborn ▷ *vb* make obdurate
OBDURATED > OBDURATE
OBDURATES > OBDURATE
OBDURE *vb* make obdurate
OBDURED > OBDURE
OBDURES > OBDURE
OBDURING > OBDURE
OBE *n* ancient Laconian village
OBEAH *vb* cast spell on
OBEAHED > OBEAH
OBEAHING > OBEAH
OBEAHISM > OBEAH
OBEAHISMS > OBEAH
OBEAHS > OBEAH
OBECHE *n* African tree
OBECHES > OBECHE
OBEDIENCE *n* condition or quality of being obedient
OBEDIENT *adj* obeying or willing to obey
OBEISANCE *n* attitude of respect
OBEISANT > OBEISANCE
OBEISM *n* belief in obeah
OBEISMS > OBEISM
OBELI > OBELUS
OBELIA *n* type of jellyfish
OBELIAS > OBELIA
OBELION *n* area of skull
OBELISCAL > OBELISK
OBELISE *same as*
> OBELIZE
OBELISED > OBELISE
OBELISES > OBELISE
OBELISING > OBELISE
OBELISK *n* four-sided stone column tapering to a pyramid at the top
OBELISKS > OBELISK
OBELISM *n* practice of marking passages in text
OBELISMS > OBELISM
OBELIZE *vb* mark (a word or passage) with an obelus
OBELIZED > OBELIZE
OBELIZES > OBELIZE
OBELIZING > OBELIZE
OBELUS *n* mark used in editions of ancient documents to indicate spurious words or passages
OBENTO *n* Japanese lunch box
OBENTOS > OBENTO
OBES > OBE
OBESE *adj* very fat

OBESELY > OBESE
OBESENESS > OBESE
OBESER > OBESE
OBESEST > OBESE
OBESITIES > OBESE
OBESITY > OBESE
OBEY *vb* carry out instructions or orders
OBEYABLE > OBEY
OBEYED > OBEY
OBEYER > OBEY
OBEYERS > OBEY
OBEYING > OBEY
OBEYS > OBEY
OBFUSCATE *vb* make (something) confusing
OBI *n* broad sash tied in a large flat bow at the back, worn by Japanese women and children ▷ *vb* bewitch
OBIA *same as* > OBEAH
OBIAS > OBIA
OBIED > OBI
OBIING > OBI
OBIISM > OBI
OBIISMS > OBI
OBIIT *vb* died
OBIS > OBI
OBIT *n* memorial service
OBITAL *adj* of obits
OBITER *adv* by the way
OBITS > OBIT
OBITUAL *adj* of obits
OBITUARY *n* announcement of someone's death, esp in a newspaper
OBJECT *n* physical thing ▷ *vb* express disapproval
OBJECTED > OBJECT
OBJECTIFY *vb* represent concretely
OBJECTING > OBJECT
OBJECTION *n* expression or feeling of opposition or disapproval
OBJECTIVE *n* aim or purpose ▷ *adj* not biased
OBJECTOR > OBJECT
OBJECTORS > OBJECT
OBJECTS > OBJECT
OBJET *n* object
OBJETS > OBJET
OBJURE *vb* put on oath
OBJURED > OBJURE
OBJURES > OBJURE
OBJURGATE *vb* scold or reprimand
OBJURING > OBJURE
OBLAST *n* administrative

division of the constituent republics of Russia

OBLASTI > OBLAST

OBLASTS > OBLAST

OBLATE adj (of a sphere) flattened at the poles ▷ n person dedicated to a monastic or religious life

OBLATELY > OBLATE

OBLATES > OBLATE

OBLATION n religious offering

OBLATIONS > OBLATION

OBLATORY > OBLATION

OBLIGABLE > OBLIGATE

OBLIGANT n person promising to pay a sum

OBLIGANTS > OBLIGANT

OBLIGATE vb compel, constrain, or oblige morally or legally ▷ adj compelled, bound, or restricted

OBLIGATED > OBLIGATE

OBLIGATES > OBLIGATE

OBLIGATI > OBLIGATO

OBLIGATO same as > OBBLIGATO

OBLIGATOR > OBLIGATE

OBLIGATOS > OBLIGATO

OBLIGE vb compel (someone) morally or by law to do something

OBLIGED > OBLIGE

OBLIGEE n person in whose favour an obligation, contract, or bond is created

OBLIGEES > OBLIGEE

OBLIGER > OBLIGE

OBLIGERS > OBLIGE

OBLIGES > OBLIGE

OBLIGING adj ready to help other people

OBLIGOR n person who binds himself by contract to perform some obligation

OBLIGORS > OBLIGOR

OBLIQUE adj slanting ▷ n symbol (/) ▷ vb take or have an oblique direction

OBLIQUED > OBLIQUE

OBLIQUELY > OBLIQUE

OBLIQUER > OBLIQUE

OBLIQUES > OBLIQUE

OBLIQUEST > OBLIQUE

OBLIQUID adj oblique

OBLIQUING > OBLIQUE

OBLIQUITY n state or condition of being oblique

OBLIVION n state of being forgotten

OBLIVIONS > OBLIVION

OBLIVIOUS adj unaware

OBLONG adj having two long sides, two short sides, and four right angles ▷ n oblong figure

OBLONGLY > OBLONG

OBLONGS > OBLONG

OBLOQUIAL > OBLOQUY

OBLOQUIES > OBLOQUY

OBLOQUY n verbal abuse

OBNOXIOUS adj offensive

OBO n ship carrying oil and ore

OBOE n double-reeded woodwind instrument

OBOES > OBOE

OBOIST > OBOE

OBOISTS > OBOE

OBOL same as > OBOLUS

OBOLARY adj very poor

OBOLE n former weight unit in pharmacy

OBOLES > OBOLE

OBOLI > OBOLUS

OBOLS > OBOL

OBOLUS n modern Greek unit of weight equal to one tenth of a gram

OBOS > OBO

OBOVATE adj (of a leaf) shaped like the longitudinal section of an egg with the narrower end at the base

OBOVATELY > OBOVATE

OBOVOID adj (of a fruit) egg-shaped with the narrower end at the base

OBREPTION n obtaining of something by giving false information

OBS > OB

OBSCENE adj portraying sex offensively

OBSCENELY > OBSCENE

OBSCENER > OBSCENE

OBSCENEST > OBSCENE

OBSCENITY n state or quality of being obscene

OBSCURANT n opposer of reform and enlightenment ▷ adj of or relating to an obscurant

OBSCURE adj not well known ▷ vb make (something) obscure

OBSCURED > OBSCURE

OBSCURELY > OBSCURE

OBSCURER > OBSCURE

OBSCURERS > OBSCURE

OBSCURES > OBSCURE

OBSCUREST > OBSCURE

OBSCURING > OBSCURE

OBSCURITY n state or quality of being obscure

OBSECRATE rare word for > BESEECH

OBSEQUENT adj (of a river) flowing into a subsequent stream in the opposite direction to the original slope of the land

OBSEQUIAL > OBSEQUIES

OBSEQUIE same as > OBSEQUY

OBSEQUIES npl funeral rites

OBSEQUY singular of > OBSEQUIES

OBSERVANT adj quick to notice things

OBSERVE vb see or notice

OBSERVED > OBSERVE

OBSERVER n person who observes, esp one who watches someone or

something carefully

OBSERVERS > OBSERVER

OBSERVES > OBSERVE

OBSERVING > OBSERVE

OBSESS vb preoccupy (someone) compulsively

OBSESSED > OBSESS

OBSESSES > OBSESS

OBSESSING > OBSESS

OBSESSION n something that preoccupies a person to the exclusion of other things

OBSESSIVE adj motivated by a persistent overriding idea or impulse ▷ n person subject to obsession

OBSESSOR > OBSESS

OBSESSORS > OBSESS

OBSIDIAN n dark glassy volcanic rock

OBSIDIANS > OBSIDIAN

OBSIGN vb confirm

OBSIGNATE same as > OBSIGN

OBSIGNED > OBSIGN

OBSIGNING > OBSIGN

OBSIGNS > OBSIGN

OBSOLESCE vb become obsolete

OBSOLETE adj no longer in use ▷ vb make obsolete

OBSOLETED > OBSOLETE

OBSOLETES > OBSOLETE

OBSTACLE n something that makes progress difficult

OBSTACLES > OBSTACLE

OBSTETRIC adj of or relating to childbirth

OBSTINACY n state or quality of being obstinate

OBSTINATE adj stubborn

OBSTRUCT vb block with an obstacle

OBSTRUCTS > OBSTRUCT

OBSTRUENT adj causing obstruction, esp of the intestinal tract ▷ n anything that causes obstruction

OBTAIN vb acquire intentionally

OBTAINED > OBTAIN

OBTAINER > OBTAIN

OBTAINERS > OBTAIN

OBTAINING > OBTAIN

OBTAINS > OBTAIN

OBTECT adj (of a pupa) encased in a hardened secretion

OBTECTED same as > OBTECT

OBTEMPER vb comply (with)

OBTEMPERS > OBTEMPER

OBTEND vb put forward

OBTENDED > OBTEND

OBTENDING > OBTEND

OBTENDS > OBTEND

OBTENTION n act of obtaining

OBTEST vb beg (someone) earnestly

OBTESTED > OBTEST

OBTESTING > OBTEST

OBTESTS > OBTEST

OBTRUDE vb push oneself or one's ideas on others

OBTRUDED > OBTRUDE

OBTRUDER > OBTRUDE

OBTRUDERS > OBTRUDE

OBTRUDES > OBTRUDE

OBTRUDING > OBTRUDE

OBTRUSION > OBTRUDE

OBTRUSIVE adj unpleasantly noticeable

OBTUND vb deaden or dull

OBTUNDED > OBTUND

OBTUNDENT > OBTUND

OBTUNDING > OBTUND

OBTUNDITY n semi-conscious state

OBTUNDS > OBTUND

OBTURATE vb stop up (an opening, esp the breech of a gun)

OBTURATED > OBTURATE

OBTURATES > OBTURATE

OBTURATOR > OBTURATE

OBTUSE adj mentally slow

OBTUSELY > OBTUSE

OBTUSER > OBTUSE

OBTUSEST > OBTUSE

OBTUSITY > OBTUSE

OBUMBRATE vb overshadow

OBVENTION n incidental expense

OBVERSE n opposite way of looking at an idea ▷ adj facing or turned towards the observer

OBVERSELY > OBVERSE

OBVERSES > OBVERSE

OBVERSION > OBVERT

OBVERT vb deduce the obverse of (a proposition)

OBVERTED > OBVERT

OBVERTING > OBVERT

OBVERTS > OBVERT

OBVIABLE > OBVIATE

OBVIATE vb make unnecessary

OBVIATED > OBVIATE

OBVIATES > OBVIATE

OBVIATING > OBVIATE

OBVIATION > OBVIATE

OBVIATOR > OBVIATE

OBVIATORS > OBVIATE

OBVIOUS adj easy to see or understand, evident

OBVIOUSLY adv in a way that is easy to see or understand

OBVOLUTE adj (of leaves or petals in the bud) folded so that the margins overlap each other

OBVOLUTED same as > OBVOLUTE

OBVOLVENT adj curving around something

OCA n any of various South American herbaceous plants

OCARINA n small oval wind instrument

OCARINAS > OCARINA

OCAS > OCA

OCCAM n computer programming language

OCCAMIES > OCCAMY

OCCAMS > OCCAM

OCCAMY n type of alloy

OCCASION n time at which a particular thing happens ▷ vb cause

OCCASIONS npl needs

OCCIDENT literary or formal word for > WEST

OCCIDENTS > OCCIDENT

OCCIES > OCCY

OCCIPITA > OCCIPUT

OCCIPITAL adj of or relating to the back of the head or skull

OCCIPUT n back of the head

OCCIPUTS > OCCIPUT

OCCLUDE vb obstruct

OCCLUDED > OCCLUDE

OCCLUDENT > OCCLUDE

OCCLUDER > OCCLUDE

OCCLUDERS > OCCLUDE

OCCLUDES > OCCLUDE

OCCLUDING > OCCLUDE

OCCLUSAL > OCCLUSION

OCCLUSION n act or process of occluding or the state of being occluded

OCCLUSIVE adj of or relating to the act of occlusion ▷ n occlusive speech sound

OCCLUSOR n muscle for closing opening

OCCLUSORS > OCCLUSOR

OCCULT adj relating to the supernatural ▷ vb (of a celestial body) to hide (another celestial body) from view

OCCULTED > OCCULT

OCCULTER n something that obscures

OCCULTERS > OCCULTER

OCCULTING > OCCULT

OCCULTISM n belief in and the study and practice of magic, astrology, etc

OCCULTIST > OCCULTISM

OCCULTLY > OCCULT

OCCULTS > OCCULT

OCCUPANCE same as > OCCUPANCY

OCCUPANCY n (length of) a person's stay in a specified place

OCCUPANT n person occupying a specified place

OCCUPANTS > OCCUPANT

OCCUPATE same as > OCCUPY

OCCUPATED > OCCUPATE

OCCUPATES > OCCUPATE

OCCUPIED > OCCUPY

OCCUPIER n person who lives in a particular house, whether as owner or tenant

OCCUPIERS > OCCUPIER

OCCUPIES > OCCUPY

OCCUPY vb live or work in (a building)

OCCUPYING > OCCUPY

OCCUR vb happen

OCCURRED > OCCUR

OCCURRENT adj (of a property) relating to some observable feature of its bearer

OCCURRING > OCCUR

OCCURS > OCCUR

OCCY as in all over the occy dialect expression meaning in every direction

OCEAN n vast area of sea between continents

OCEANARIA npl large saltwater aquaria for marine life

OCEANAUT n undersea explorer

OCEANAUTS > OCEANAUT

OCEANIC adj of or relating to the ocean

OCEANID n ocean nymph in Greek mythology

OCEANIDES > OCEANID

OCEANIDS > OCEANID

OCEANS > OCEAN

OCELLAR > OCELLUS

OCELLATE > OCELLUS

OCELLATED > OCELLUS

OCELLI > OCELLUS

OCELLUS n simple eye of insects and some other invertebrates

OCELOID adj of or like an ocelot

OCELOT n American wild cat with a spotted coat

OCELOTS > OCELOT

OCH interj expression of surprise, annoyance, or disagreement

OCHE n (in darts) mark on the floor behind which a player must stand

OCHER same as > OCHRE

OCHERED > OCHER

OCHERING > OCHER

OCHEROUS > OCHER

OCHERS > OCHER

OCHERY > OCHER

OCHES > OCHE

OCHIDORE n type of crab

OCHIDORES > OCHIDORE

OCHLOCRAT n supporter of rule by the mob

OCHONE interj expression of sorrow or regret

OCHRE n brownish-yellow earth ▷ adj moderate yellow-orange to orange ▷ vb colour with ochre

OCHREA n cup-shaped structure that sheathes the stems of certain plants

OCHREAE > OCHREA

OCHREATE same as > OCHREATE

OCHRED > OCHRE

OCHREOUS > OCHRE

OCHRES > OCHRE

OCHREY > OCHRE

OCHRING > OCHRE

OCHROID > OCHRE

OCHROUS > OCHRE

OCHRY > OCHRE

OCICAT n breed of large short-haired cat with a spotted coat

OCICATS > OCICAT

OCKER n uncultivated or boorish Australian

OCKERISM n Australian boorishness

OCKERISMS > OCKERISM

OCKERS > OCKER

OCKODOLS npl one's feet when wearing boots

OCOTILLO n cactus-like tree

OCOTILLOS > OCOTILLO

OCREA same as > OCHREA

OCREAE > OCREA

OCREATE adj possessing an ocrea

OCTA same as > OKTA

OCTACHORD n eight-stringed musical instrument

OCTAD n group or series of eight

OCTADIC > OCTAD

OCTADS > OCTAD

OCTAGON n geometric figure with eight sides

OCTAGONAL adj having eight sides and eight angles

OCTAGONS > OCTAGON

OCTAHEDRA npl solid eight-sided figures; octahedrons

OCTAL n number system with a base 8

OCTALS > OCTAL

OCTAMETER n verse line consisting of eight metrical feet

OCTAN n illness that occurs weekly

OCTANE n hydrocarbon found in petrol

OCTANES > OCTANE

OCTANGLE same as > OCTAGON

OCTANGLES > OCTANGLE

OCTANOL n alcohol containing eight carbon atoms

OCTANOLS > OCTANOL

OCTANS > OCTAN

OCTANT n any of the eight parts into which the three planes containing the Cartesian coordinate axes divide space

OCTANTAL > OCTANT

OCTANTS > OCTANT

OCTAPLA n book with eight texts

OCTAPLAS > OCTAPLA

OCTAPLOID adj having eight parts

OCTAPODIC > OCTAPODY

OCTAPODY n line of verse with eight metrical feet

OCTARCHY n government

by eight rulers

OCTAROON same as > OCTOROON

OCTAROONS > OCTAROON

OCTAS > OCTA

OCTASTICH n verse of eight lines

OCTASTYLE adj (of building) having eight columns

OCTAVAL > OCTAVE

OCTAVE n (interval between the first and) eighth note of a scale ▷ adj consisting of eight parts

OCTAVES > OCTAVE

OCTAVO n book size in which the sheets are folded into eight leaves

OCTAVOS > OCTAVO

OCTENNIAL adj occurring every eight years

OCTET n group of eight performers

OCTETS > OCTET

OCTETT same as > OCTET

OCTETTE same as > OCTET

OCTETTES > OCTETTE

OCTETTS > OCTETT

OCTILLION n (in Britain and Germany) the number represented as one followed by 48 zeros

OCTOFID adj divided into eight

OCTOHEDRA same as > OCTAHEDRA

OCTONARII npl lines with eight feet

OCTONARY adj relating to or based on the number eight ▷ n stanza of eight lines

OCTOPI > OCTOPUS

OCTOPLOID same as > OCTAPLOID

OCTOPOD n type of mollusc ▷ adj of these molluscs

OCTOPODAN > OCTOPOD

OCTOPODES > OCTOPOD

OCTOPODS > OCTOPOD

OCTOPOID adj of or like an octopus

OCTOPUS n sea creature with a soft body and eight tentacles

OCTOPUSES > OCTOPUS

OCTOPUSH n hockey-like game played underwater

OCTOROON n person having one quadroon and one White parent

OCTOROONS > OCTOROON

OCTOSTYLE same as > OCTASTYLE

OCTOTHORP n type of symbol in printing

OCTROI n duty on various goods brought into certain European towns

OCTROIS > OCTROI

OCTUOR n octet

OCTUORS > OCTUOR

OCTUPLE n quantity or number eight times as

great as another ▷ *adj* eight times as much or as many ▷ *vb* multiply by eight
OCTUPLED > OCTUPLE
OCTUPLES > OCTUPLE
OCTUPLET *n* one of eight offspring from one birth
OCTUPLETS > OCTUPLET
OCTUPLEX *n* something made up of eight parts
OCTUPLING > OCTUPLE
OCTUPLY *adv* by eight times
OCTYL *n* group of atoms
OCTYLS > OCTYL
OCULAR *adj* relating to the eyes or sight ▷ *n* lens in an optical instrument
OCULARIST *n* person who makes artificial eyes
OCULARLY > OCULAR
OCULARS > OCULAR
OCULATE *adj* possessing eyes
OCULATED *same as* > OCULATE
OCULI > OCULUS
OCULIST *n* ophthalmologist
OCULISTS > OCULIST
OCULUS *n* round window
OD *n* hypothetical force formerly thought to be responsible for many natural phenomena
ODA *n* room in a harem
ODAH *same as* > ODA
ODAHS > ODAH
ODAL *same as* > UDAL
ODALIQUE *same as* > ODALISQUE
ODALIQUES > ODALIQUE
ODALISK *same as* > ODALISQUE
ODALISKS > ODALISK
ODALISQUE *n* female slave in a harem
ODALLER > ODAL
ODALLERS > ODAL
ODALS > ODAL
ODAS > ODA
ODD *adj* unusual
ODDBALL *n* eccentric person ▷ *adj* strange or peculiar
ODDBALLS > ODDBALL
ODDER > ODD
ODDEST > ODD
ODDISH > ODD
ODDITIES > ODDITY
ODDITY *n* odd person or thing
ODDLY > ODD
ODDMENT *n* odd piece or thing
ODDMENTS > ODDMENT
ODDNESS > ODD
ODDNESSES > ODD
ODDS *npl* (ratio showing) the probability of something happening
ODDSMAKER *n* person setting odds in betting

ODDSMAN *n* umpire
ODDSMEN > ODDSMAN
ODE *n* lyric poem, usu addressed to a particular subject
ODEA > ODEUM
ODEON *same as* > ODEUM
ODEONS > ODEON
ODES > ODE
ODEUM *n* (esp in ancient Greece and Rome) a building for musical performances
ODEUMS > ODEUM
ODIC > OD
ODIFEROUS *adj* having odour
ODIOUS *adj* offensive
ODIOUSLY > ODIOUS
ODISM > OD
ODISMS > OD
ODIST > OD
ODISTS > OD
ODIUM *n* widespread dislike
ODIUMS > ODIUM
ODOGRAPH *same as* > ODOMETER
ODOGRAPHS > ODOGRAPH
ODOMETER *n* device that records the number of miles that a bicycle or motor vehicle has travelled
ODOMETERS > ODOMETER
ODOMETRY > ODOMETER
ODONATE *n* dragonfly or related insect
ODONATES > ODONATE
ODONATIST *n* dragonfly expert
ODONTALGY *n* toothache
ODONTIC *adj* of teeth
ODONTIST *n* dentist
ODONTISTS > ODONTIST
ODONTOID *adj* toothlike ▷ *n* bone in the spine
ODONTOIDS > ODONTOID
ODONTOMA *n* tumour near teeth
ODONTOMAS > ODONTOMA
ODOR *same as* > ODOUR
ODORANT *n* something with a strong smell
ODORANTS > ODORANT
ODORATE *adj* having a strong smell
ODORED *same as* > ODOURED
ODORFUL *same as* > ODOURFUL
ODORISE *same as* > ODORIZE
ODORISED > ODORISE
ODORISES > ODORISE
ODORISING > ODORISE
ODORIZE *vb* give an odour to
ODORIZED > ODORIZE
ODORIZES > ODORIZE
ODORIZING > ODORIZE
ODORLESS > ODOR
ODOROUS *adj* having or emitting a characteristic smell or odour

ODOROUSLY > ODOROUS
ODORS > ODOR
ODOUR *n* particular smell
ODOURED *adj* having odour
ODOURFUL *adj* full of odour
ODOURLESS > ODOUR
ODOURS > ODOUR
ODS > OD
ODSO *n* cry of suprise
ODYL *same as* > OD
ODYLE *same as* > OD
ODYLES > ODYLE
ODYLISM > ODYL
ODYLISMS > ODYL
ODYLS > ODYL
ODYSSEY *n* long eventful journey
ODYSSEYS > ODYSSEY
ODZOOKS *interj* cry of surprise
OE *n* grandchild
OECIST *n* colony founder
OECISTS > OECIST
OECOLOGIC *same as* > ECOLOGIC
OECOLOGY *less common spelling of* > ECOLOGY
OECUMENIC *variant of* > ECUMENIC
OEDEMA *n* abnormal swelling
OEDEMAS > OEDEMA
OEDEMATA > OEDEMA
OEDIPAL *adj* relating to an Oedipus complex, whereby a male child wants to replace his father
OEDIPALLY > OEDIPAL
OEDIPEAN *same as* > OEDIPAL
OEDOMETER *n* instrument for measuring the consolidation of a soil specimen under pressure
OEILLADE *n* amorous or suggestive glance
OEILLADES > OEILLADE
OENANTHIC *adj* smelling of or like wine
OENOLOGY *n* study of wine
OENOMANCY *n* divination by studying the colour of wine
OENOMANIA *n* craving for wine
OENOMEL *n* drink made of wine and honey
OENOMELS > OENOMEL
OENOMETER *n* device for measuring the strength of wine
OENOPHIL *same as* > OENOPHILE
OENOPHILE *n* lover or connoisseur of wines
OENOPHILS > OENOPHIL
OENOPHILY *n* love of wine
OENOTHERA *n* type of American plant with yellow flowers that open in the evening
OERLIKON *n* type of cannon
OERLIKONS > OERLIKON

OERSTED *n* cgs unit of magnetic field strength
OERSTEDS > OERSTED
OES > OE
OESOPHAGI *npl* gullets
OESTRAL > OESTRUS
OESTRIN *obsolete term for* > OESTROGEN
OESTRINS > OESTRIN
OESTRIOL *n* weak oestrogenic hormone secreted by the mammalian ovary
OESTRIOLS > OESTRIOL
OESTROGEN *n* female hormone that controls the reproductive cycle
OESTRONE *n* weak oestrogenic hormone secreted by the mammalian ovary
OESTRONES > OESTRONE
OESTROUS > OESTRUS
OESTRUM *same as* > OESTRUS
OESTRUMS > OESTRUM
OESTRUS *n* regularly occurring period of fertility and sexual receptivity in most female mammals
OESTRUSES > OESTRUS
OEUVRE *n* work of art, literature, music, etc
OEUVRES > OEUVRE
OF *prep* belonging to
OFAY *n* derogatory term for a White person
OFAYS > OFAY
OFF *prep* away from ▷ *adv* away ▷ *adj* not operating ▷ *n* side of the field to which the batsman's feet point ▷ *vb* kill
OFFAL *n* edible organs of an animal, such as liver or kidneys
OFFALS > OFFAL
OFFBEAT *adj* unusual or eccentric ▷ *n* any of the normally unaccented beats in a bar
OFFBEATS > OFFBEAT
OFFCAST *n* cast-off
OFFCASTS > OFFCAST
OFFCUT *n* piece remaining after the required parts have been cut out
OFFCUTS > OFFCUT
OFFED > OFF
OFFENCE *n* (cause of) hurt feelings or annoyance
OFFENCES > OFFENCE
OFFEND *vb* hurt the feelings of, insult
OFFENDED > OFFEND
OFFENDER > OFFEND
OFFENDERS > OFFEND
OFFENDING > OFFEND
OFFENDS > OFFEND
OFFENSE *same as* > OFFENCE
OFFENSES > OFFENSE
OFFENSIVE *adj* disagreeable ▷ *n* position or action of attack

OFFER *vb* present (something) for acceptance or rejection ▷ *n* something offered
OFFERABLE > OFFER
OFFERED > OFFER
OFFEREE *n* person to whom an offer is made
OFFEREES > OFFEREE
OFFERER > OFFER
OFFERERS > OFFER
OFFERING *n* thing offered
OFFERINGS > OFFERING
OFFEROR > OFFER
OFFERORS > OFFER
OFFERS > OFFER
OFFERTORY *n* offering of the bread and wine for Communion
OFFHAND *adj* casual, curt ▷ *adv* without preparation
OFFHANDED *adj* without care oe consideration
OFFICE *n* room or building where people work at desks
OFFICER *n* person in authority in the armed services ▷ *vb* furnish with officers
OFFICERED > OFFICER
OFFICERS > OFFICER
OFFICES > OFFICE
OFFICIAL *adj* of a position of authority ▷ *n* person who holds a position of authority
OFFICIALS > OFFICIAL
OFFICIANT *n* person who presides and officiates at a religious ceremony
OFFICIARY *n* body of officials ▷ *adj* of, relating to, or derived from office
OFFICIATE *vb* act in an official role
OFFICINAL *adj* (of pharmaceutical products) available without prescription ▷ *n* officinal preparation or plant
OFFICIOUS *adj* interfering unnecessarily
OFFIE *n* off-licence
OFFIES > OFFIE
OFFING *n* area of the sea visible from the shore
OFFINGS > OFFING
OFFISH *adj* aloof or distant in manner
OFFISHLY > OFFISH
OFFKEY *adj* out of tune
OFFLINE *adj* disconnected from a computer or the internet
OFFLOAD *vb* pass responsibility for (something unpleasant) to someone else
OFFLOADED > OFFLOAD
OFFLOADS > OFFLOAD
OFFPEAK *adj* relating to times outside periods of intensive use
OFFPRINT *n* separate reprint of an article that

originally appeared in a larger publication ▷ *vb* reprint (an article taken from a larger publication) separately
OFFPRINTS > OFFPRINT
OFFPUT *n* act of putting off
OFFPUTS > OFFPUT
OFFRAMP *n* road allowing traffic to leave a motorway
OFFRAMPS > OFFRAMP
OFFS > OFF
OFFSADDLE *vb* unsaddle
OFFSCREEN *adj* unseen by film viewers
OFFSCUM *n* scum
OFFSCUMS > OFFSCUM
OFFSEASON *n* period of little trade in a business
OFFSET *vb* cancel out, compensate for ▷ *n* printing method in which the impression is made onto a surface which transfers it to the paper
OFFSETS > OFFSET
OFFSHOOT *n* something developed from something else
OFFSHOOTS > OFFSHOOT
OFFSHORE *adv* away from or at some distance from the shore ▷ *adj* sited or conducted at sea ▷ *n* company operating abroad where the tax system is more advantageous than at home ▷ *vb* transfer (work) to another country where wages are lower
OFFSHORED > OFFSHORE
OFFSHORES > OFFSHORE
OFFSIDE *adv* (positioned) illegally ahead of the ball ▷ *n* side of a vehicle nearest the centre of the road
OFFSIDER *n* partner or assistant
OFFSIDERS > OFFSIDER
OFFSIDES > OFFSIDE
OFFSPRING *n* child
OFFSTAGE *adv* out of the view of the audience ▷ *n* something that happens offstage
OFFSTAGES > OFFSTAGE
OFFTAKE *n* act of taking off
OFFTAKES > OFFTAKE
OFFTRACK *adj* not at a racetrack
OFFY *same as* > OFFIE
OFLAG *n* German prisoner-of-war camp for officers in World War II
OFLAGS > OFLAG
OFT *adv* often
OFTEN *adv* frequently, much of the time
OFTENER > OFTEN
OFTENEST > OFTEN
OFTENNESS > OFTEN
OFTER > OFT
OFTEST > OFT
OFTTIMES *same as* > OFTEN

OGAM *same as* > OGHAM
OGAMIC > OGAM
OGAMS > OGAM
OGDOAD *n* group of eight
OGDOADS > OGDOAD
OGEE *n* moulding having a cross section in the form of a letter S
OGEED *adj* (of an arch or moulding) having an ogee
OGEES > OGEE
OGGIN *n* sea
OGGINS > OGGIN
OGHAM *n* ancient alphabetical writing system used by the Celts in Britain and Ireland
OGHAMIC > OGHAM
OGHAMIST > OGHAM
OGHAMISTS > OGHAM
OGHAMS > OGHAM
OGIVAL > OGIVE
OGIVE *n* diagonal rib or groin of a Gothic vault
OGIVES > OGIVE
OGLE *vb* stare at (someone) lustfully ▷ *n* flirtatious or lewd look
OGLED > OGLE
OGLER > OGLE
OGLERS > OGLE
OGLES > OGLE
OGLING > OGLE
OGLINGS > OGLE
OGMIC > OGAM
OGRE *n* giant that eats human flesh
OGREISH > OGRE
OGREISHLY > OGRE
OGREISM > OGRE
OGREISMS > OGRE
OGRES > OGRE
OGRESS > OGRE
OGRESSES > OGRE
OGRISH > OGRE
OGRISHLY > OGRE
OGRISM > OGRE
OGRISMS > OGRE
OH *interj* exclamation of surprise, pain, etc ▷ *vb* say oh
OHED > OH
OHIA *n* Hawaiian plant
OHIAS > OHIA
OHING > OH
OHM *n* unit of electrical resistance
OHMAGE *n* electrical resistance in ohms
OHMAGES > OHMAGE
OHMIC *adj* of or relating to a circuit element
OHMICALLY > OHMIC
OHMMETER *n* instrument for measuring electrical resistance
OHMMETERS > OHMMETER
OHMS > OHM
OHO *n* exclamation expressing surprise, exultation, or derision
OHONE *same as* > OCHONE
OHS > OH
OI *interj* shout to attract

attention ▷ *n* grey-faced petrel
OIDIA > OIDIUM
OIDIOID > OIDIUM
OIDIUM *n* type of fungal spore
OIK *n* person regarded as inferior because ignorant or lower-class
OIKIST *same as* > OECIST
OIKISTS > OIKIST
OIKS > OIK
OIL *n* viscous liquid, insoluble in water and usu flammable ▷ *vb* lubricate (a machine) with oil
OILBIRD *n* type of nocturnal gregarious cave-dwelling bird
OILBIRDS > OILBIRD
OILCAMP *n* camp for oilworkers
OILCAMPS > OILCAMP
OILCAN *n* container with a long nozzle for applying oil to machinery
OILCANS > OILCAN
OILCLOTH *n* waterproof material
OILCLOTHS > OILCLOTH
OILCUP *n* cup-shaped oil reservoir in a machine providing continuous lubrication for a bearing
OILCUPS > OILCUP
OILED > OIL
OILER *n* person, device, etc, that lubricates or supplies oil
OILERIES > OILERY
OILERS > OILER
OILERY *n* oil business
OILFIELD *n* area containing oil reserves
OILFIELDS > OILFIELD
OILFIRED *adj* using oil as fuel
OILGAS *n* gaseous mixture of hydrocarbons used as a fuel
OILGASES > OILGAS
OILHOLE *n* hole for oil
OILHOLES > OILHOLE
OILIER > OILY
OILIEST > OILY
OILILY > OILY
OILINESS > OILY
OILING > OIL
OILLET *same as* > EYELET
OILLETS > OILLET
OILMAN *n* person who owns or operates oil wells
OILMEN > OILMAN
OILNUT *n* nut from which oil is extracted
OILNUTS > OILNUT
OILPAPER *n* oiled paper
OILPAPERS > OILPAPER
OILPROOF *adj* resistant to oil
OILS > OIL
OILSEED *n* seed from which oil is extracted
OILSEEDS > OILSEED

O

OILSKIN n (garment made from) waterproof material

OILSKINS > OILSKIN

OILSTONE n stone with a fine grain lubricated with oil and used for sharpening cutting tools

OILSTONES > OILSTONE

OILTIGHT adj not allowing oil through

OILWAY n channel for oil

OILWAYS > OILWAY

OILY adj soaked or covered with oil

OINK n grunt of a pig or an imitation of this ▷ interj imitation or representation of the grunt of a pig ▷ vb make noise of pig

OINKED > OINK

OINKING > OINK

OINKS > OINK

OINOLOGY same as > OENOLOGY

OINOMEL same as > OENOMEL

OINOMELS > OINOMEL

OINT vb anoint

OINTED > OINT

OINTING > OINT

OINTMENT n greasy substance used for healing skin or as a cosmetic

OINTMENTS > OINTMENT

OINTS > OINT

OIS > OI

OITICICA n South American tree

OITICICAS > OITICICA

OJIME n Japanese bead used to secure cords

OJIMES > OJIME

OKA n unit of weight used in Turkey

OKAPI n African animal related to the giraffe but with a shorter neck

OKAPIS > OKAPI

OKAS > OKA

OKAY adj satisfactory ▷ vb approve or endorse ▷ n approval or agreement ▷ interj expression of approval

OKAYED > OKAY

OKAYING > OKAY

OKAYS > OKAY

OKE same as > OKA

OKEH variant of > OKAY

OKEHS > OKEH

OKES > OKE

OKEYDOKE variant of > OKAY

OKEYDOKEY variant of > OKAY

OKIMONO n Japanese ornamental item

OKIMONOS > OKIMONO

OKRA n tropical plant with edible green pods

OKRAS > OKRA

OKTA n unit used in meteorology to measure cloud cover

OKTAS > OKTA

OLD adj having lived or existed for a long time ▷ n earlier or past time

OLDE adj old-world or quaint, used facetiously

OLDEN adj old ▷ vb grow old

OLDENED > OLDEN

OLDENING > OLDEN

OLDENS > OLDEN

OLDER adj having lived or existed longer

OLDEST > OLD

OLDIE n old but popular song or film

OLDIES > OLDIE

OLDISH > OLD

OLDNESS > OLD

OLDNESSES > OLD

OLDS > OLD

OLDSQUAW n type of long-tailed sea duck

OLDSQUAWS > OLDSQUAW

OLDSTER n older person

OLDSTERS > OLDSTER

OLDSTYLE n printing type style

OLDSTYLES > OLDSTYLE

OLDWIFE n any of various fishes, esp the menhaden or the alewife

OLDWIVES > OLDWIFE

OLDY same as > OLDIE

OLE interj exclamation of approval or encouragement customary at bullfights ▷ n cry of olé

OLEA > OLEUM

OLEACEOUS adj relating to a family of trees and shrubs, including the ash, jasmine, and olive

OLEANDER n Mediterranean flowering evergreen shrub

OLEANDERS > OLEANDER

OLEARIA n daisy bush

OLEARIAS > OLEARIA

OLEASTER n type of shrub with silver-white twigs and yellow flowers

OLEASTERS > OLEASTER

OLEATE n any salt or ester of oleic acid

OLEATES > OLEATE

OLECRANAL > OLECRANON

OLECRANON n bony projection of the ulna behind the elbow joint

OLEFIANT adj forming oil

OLEFIN same as > OLEFINE

OLEFINE another name for > ALKENE

OLEFINES > OLEFINE

OLEFINIC > OLEFINE

OLEFINS > OLEFIN

OLEIC as in oleic acid colourless oily liquid used in making soap

OLEIN another name for > TRIOLEIN

OLEINE same as > OLEIN

OLEINES > OLEINE

OLEINS > OLEIN

OLENT adj having smell

OLEO as in oleo oil oil extracted from beef fat

OLEOGRAPH n chromolithograph printed in oil colours to imitate the appearance of an oil painting

OLEORESIN n semisolid mixture of a resin and essential oil

OLEOS > OLEO

OLES > OLE

OLESTRA n trademark term for an artificial fat

OLESTRAS > OLESTRA

OLEUM n type of sulphuric acid

OLEUMS > OLEUM

OLFACT vb smell something

OLFACTED > OLFACT

OLFACTING > OLFACT

OLFACTION n sense of smell

OLFACTIVE adj of sense of smell

OLFACTORY adj relating to the sense of smell ▷ n organ or nerve concerned with the sense of smell

OLFACTS > OLFACT

OLIBANUM n frankincense

OLIBANUMS > OLIBANUM

OLICOOK n doughnut

OLICOOKS > OLICOOK

OLID adj foul-smelling

OLIGAEMIA n reduction in the volume of the blood, as occurs after haemorrhage

OLIGAEMIC > OLIGAEMIA

OLIGARCH n member of an oligarchy

OLIGARCHS > OLIGARCH

OLIGARCHY n government by a small group of people

OLIGEMIA same as > OLIGAEMIA

OLIGEMIAS > OLIGEMIA

OLIGEMIC > OLIGAEMIA

OLIGIST n type of iron ore

OLIGISTS > OLIGIST

OLIGOCENE adj belonging to geological time period

OLIGOGENE n type of gene

OLIGOMER n compound of relatively low molecular weight containing up to five monomer units

OLIGOMERS > OLIGOMER

OLIGOPOLY n market situation in which control over the supply of a commodity is held by a small number of producers

OLIGURIA n excretion of an abnormally small volume of urine

OLIGURIAS > OLIGURIA

OLIGURIC adj relating to oliguria

OLINGO n South American mammal

OLINGOS > OLINGO

OLIO n dish of many different ingredients

OLIOS > OLIO

OLIPHANT archaic variant of > ELEPHANT

OLIPHANTS > OLIPHANT

OLITORIES > OLITORY

OLITORY n kitchen garden

OLIVARY adj shaped like an olive

OLIVE n small green or black fruit used as food or pressed for its oil ▷ adj greyish-green

OLIVENITE n green to black rare secondary mineral

OLIVER as in Bath oliver type of unsweetened biscuit

OLIVERS > OLIVER

OLIVES > OLIVE

OLIVET n button shaped like olive

OLIVETS > OLIVET

OLIVINE n olive-green mineral of the olivine group

OLIVINES > OLIVINE

OLIVINIC adj containing olivine

OLLA n cooking pot

OLLAMH n old Irish term for a wise man

OLLAMHS > OLLAMH

OLLAS > OLLA

OLLAV same as > OLLAMH

OLLAVS > OLLAV

OLLER n waste ground

OLLERS > OLLER

OLLIE n (in skateboarding and snowboarding) a jump into the air executed by stamping on the tail of the board

OLLIES > OLLIE

OLM n pale blind eel-like salamander

OLMS > OLM

OLOGIES > OLOGY

OLOGIST n scientist

OLOGISTS > OLOGIST

OLOGOAN vb complain loudly without reason

OLOGOANED > OLOGOAN

OLOGOANS > OLOGOAN

OLOGY n science or other branch of knowledge

OLOLIUQUI n medicinal plant used by the Aztecs

OLOROSO n golden-coloured sweet sherry

OLOROSOS > OLOROSO

OLPAE > OLPE

OLPE n ancient Greek jug

OLPES > OLPE

OLYCOOK same as > OLYKOEK

OLYCOOKS > OLYCOOK

OLYKOEK n American type of doughnut

OLYKOEKS > OLYKOEK

OLYMPIAD n staging of the modern Olympic Games
OLYMPIADS > OLYMPIAD
OLYMPICS npl modern revival of the ancient Greek games, featuring sporting contests
OM n sacred syllable in Hinduism
OMADHAUN n foolish man or boy
OMADHAUNS > OMADHAUN
OMASA > OMASUM
OMASAL > OMASUM
OMASUM n compartment in the stomach of a ruminant animal
OMBER same as > OMBRE
OMBERS > OMBER
OMBRE n 18th-century card game
OMBRELLA old form of > UMBRELLA
OMBRELLAS > OMBRELLA
OMBRES > OMBRE
OMBROPHIL n plant flourishing in rainy conditions
OMBU n South American tree
OMBUDSMAN n official who investigates complaints against government organizations
OMBUDSMEN > OMBUDSMAN
OMBUS > OMBU
OMEGA n last letter in the Greek alphabet
OMEGAS > OMEGA
OMELET same as > OMELETTE
OMELETS > OMELET
OMELETTE n dish of eggs beaten and fried
OMELETTES > OMELETTE
OMEN n happening or object thought to foretell success or misfortune ▷ vb portend
OMENED > OMEN
OMENING > OMEN
OMENS > OMEN
OMENTA > OMENTUM
OMENTAL > OMENTUM
OMENTUM n double fold of the peritoneum connecting the stomach with other abdominal organs
OMENTUMS > OMENTUM
OMER n ancient Hebrew unit of dry measure equal to one tenth of an ephah
OMERS > OMER
OMERTA n conspiracy of silence
OMERTAS > OMERTA
OMICRON n 15th letter in the Greek alphabet
OMICRONS > OMICRON
OMIGOD interj exclamation of surprise, pleasure, dismay, etc
OMIKRON same as > OMICRON
OMIKRONS > OMIKRON

OMINOUS adj worrying, seeming to foretell misfortune
OMINOUSLY > OMINOUS
OMISSIBLE > OMIT
OMISSION n something that has been left out or passed over
OMISSIONS > OMISSION
OMISSIVE > OMISSION
OMIT vb leave out
OMITS > OMIT
OMITTANCE n omission
OMITTED > OMIT
OMITTER > OMIT
OMITTERS > OMIT
OMITTING > OMIT
OMLAH n staff team in India
OMLAHS > OMLAH
OMMATEA > OMMATEUM
OMMATEUM n insect eye
OMMATIDIA npl cone-shaped parts of the eyes of some arthropods
OMNEITIES > OMNEITY
OMNEITY n state of being all
OMNIANA n miscellaneous collection
OMNIARCH n ruler of everything
OMNIARCHS > OMNIARCH
OMNIBUS n several books or TV or radio programmes made into one ▷ adj consisting of or dealing with several different things at once
OMNIBUSES > OMNIBUS
OMNIETIES > OMNIETY
OMNIETY same as > OMNEITY
OMNIFIC adj creating all things
OMNIFIED > OMNIFY
OMNIFIES > OMNIFY
OMNIFORM adj of all forms
OMNIFY vb make something universal
OMNIFYING > OMNIFY
OMNIMODE adj of all functions
OMNIRANGE n very-high-frequency ground radio navigational system
OMNIUM n total value
OMNIUMS > OMNIUM
OMNIVORA n group of omnivorous mammals
OMNIVORE n omnivorous animal
OMNIVORES > OMNIVORE
OMNIVORY n state of being omnivorous
OMOHYOID n muscle in shoulder
OMOHYOIDS > OMOHYOID
OMOPHAGIA n eating of raw food, esp meat
OMOPHAGIC > OMOPHAGIA
OMOPHAGY same as > OMOPHAGIA

OMOPHORIA npl stole-like bands worn by some bishops
OMOPLATE n shoulder blade
OMOPLATES > OMOPLATE
OMOV n one member one vote: a voting system in which each voter has one vote to cast
OMOVS > OMOV
OMPHACITE n type of mineral
OMPHALI > OMPHALOS
OMPHALIC > OMPHALOS
OMPHALOID adj like navel
OMPHALOS n (in the ancient world) a sacred conical object, esp a stone
OMRAH n Muslim noble
OMRAHS > OMRAH
OMS > OM
ON prep indicating position above, attachment, closeness, etc ▷ adv in operation ▷ adj operating ▷ n side of the field on which the batsman stands ▷ vb go on
ONAGER n wild ass of Persia
ONAGERS > ONAGER
ONAGRI > ONAGER
ONANISM n withdrawal in sexual intercourse before ejaculation
ONANISMS > ONANISM
ONANIST > ONANISM
ONANISTIC > ONANISM
ONANISTS > ONANISM
ONBEAT n first and third beats in a bar of four-four time
ONBEATS > ONBEAT
ONBOARD adj on a ship or other craft
ONCE adv on one occasion ▷ n one occasion
ONCER n (formerly) a one-pound note
ONCERS > ONCER
ONCES > ONCE
ONCET dialect form of > ONCE
ONCIDIUM n American orchid
ONCIDIUMS > ONCIDIUM
ONCOGEN n substance causing tumours to form
ONCOGENE n gene that can cause cancer when abnormally activated
ONCOGENES > ONCOGENE
ONCOGENIC adj causing the formation of a tumour
ONCOGENS > ONCOGEN
ONCOLOGIC > ONCOLOGY
ONCOLOGY n branch of medicine concerned with the study, classification, and treatment of tumours
ONCOLYSES > ONCOLYSIS
ONCOLYSIS n destruction of tumours
ONCOLYTIC adj destroying tumours

ONCOME n act of coming on
ONCOMES > ONCOME
ONCOMETER n instrument for measuring body organs
ONCOMING adj approaching from the front ▷ n approach or onset
ONCOMINGS > ONCOMING
ONCOST same as > OVERHEADS
ONCOSTMAN n miner paid daily
ONCOSTMEN > ONCOSTMAN
ONCOSTS > ONCOST
ONCOTOMY n surgical cutting of a tumour
ONCOVIRUS n virus causing cancer
ONCUS same as > ONKUS
ONDATRA same as > MUSQUASH
ONDATRAS > ONDATRA
ONDINE same as > UNDINE
ONDINES > ONDINE
ONDING Scots word for > ONSET
ONDINGS > ONDING
ONDOGRAM n record made by ondograph
ONDOGRAMS > ONDOGRAM
ONDOGRAPH n instrument for producing a graphical recording of an alternating current
ONE adj single, lone ▷ n number or figure 1 ▷ pron any person
ONEFOLD adj simple
ONEIRIC adj of or relating to dreams
ONELY same as > ONLY
ONENESS n unity
ONENESSES > ONENESS
ONER n single continuous action
ONERIER > ONERY
ONERIEST > ONERY
ONEROUS adj (of a task) difficult to carry out
ONEROUSLY > ONEROUS
ONERS > ONER
ONERY same as > ORNERY
ONES > ONE
ONESELF pron reflexive form of one
ONETIME adj at some time in the past
ONEYER old form of > ONE
ONEYERS > ONEYER
ONEYRE same as > ONEYER
ONEYRES > ONEYRE
ONFALL n attack or onset
ONFALLS > ONFALL
ONFLOW n flowing on
ONFLOWS > ONFLOW
ONGAONGA n New Zealand nettle with a severe or fatal sting
ONGAONGAS > ONGAONGA
ONGOING adj in progress, continuing
ONGOINGS npl things that are happening

O

ONIE variant spelling of > ONY

ONION n strongly flavoured edible bulb ▷ vb add onion to

ONIONED > ONION

ONIONIER > ONION

ONIONIEST > ONION

ONIONING > ONION

ONIONS > ONION

ONIONSKIN n glazed translucent paper

ONIONY > ONION

ONIRIC same as > ONEIRIC

ONISCOID adj of or like woodlice

ONIUM as in onium compound type of chemical salt

ONIUMS > ONIUM

ONKUS adj bad

ONLAY n artificial veneer for a tooth

ONLAYS > ONLAY

ONLIEST same as > ONLY

ONLINE adj connected to a computer or the internet

ONLINER n person who uses the internet regularly

ONLINERS > ONLINER

ONLOAD vb load files on to a computer

ONLOADED > ONLOAD

ONLOADING > ONLOAD

ONLOADS > ONLOAD

ONLOOKER n person who watches without taking part

ONLOOKERS > ONLOOKER

ONLOOKING > ONLOOKER

ONLY adj alone of its kind ▷ adv exclusively

ONNED > ON

ONNING > ON

ONO n Hawaiian fish

ONOMASTIC adj of or relating to proper names

ONOS > ONO

ONRUSH n forceful forward rush or flow

ONRUSHES > ONRUSH

ONRUSHING adj approaching quickly

ONS > ON

ONSCREEN adj appearing on screen

ONSET n beginning

ONSETS > ONSET

ONSETTER n attacker

ONSETTERS > ONSET

ONSETTING n attack

ONSHORE adv towards the land

ONSHORING n practice of employing white-collar workers from abroad

ONSIDE adv (of a player in various sports) in a legal position ▷ adj taking one's part or side ▷ n part of cricket field where a batsman stands

ONSIDES > ONSIDE

ONSLAUGHT n violent attack

ONST same as > ONCE

ONSTAGE adj visible by audience

ONSTEAD Scots word for > FARMSTEAD

ONSTEADS > ONSTEAD

ONSTREAM adj in operation

ONTIC adj having real existence

ONTICALLY > ONTIC

ONTO prep a position on

ONTOGENIC > ONTOGENY

ONTOGENY n entire sequence of events involved in the development of an individual organism

ONTOLOGIC > ONTOLOGY

ONTOLOGY n branch of philosophy concerned with existence

ONUS n responsibility or burden

ONUSES > ONUS

ONWARD same as > ONWARDS

ONWARDLY > ONWARD

ONWARDS adv at or towards a point or position ahead, in advance, etc

ONY Scots word for > ANY

ONYCHA n part of mollusc

ONYCHAS > ONYCHA

ONYCHIA n inflammation of the nails or claws of animals

ONYCHIAS > ONYCHIA

ONYCHITE n type of stone

ONYCHITES > ONYCHITE

ONYCHITIS n inflammation of nails

ONYCHIUM n part of insect foot

ONYCHIUMS > ONYCHIUM

ONYMOUS adj (of a book) bearing its author's name

ONYX n type of quartz with coloured layers

ONYXES > ONYX

OO Scots word for > WOOL

OOBIT n hairy caterpillar

OOBITS > OOBIT

OOCYST n type of zygote

OOCYSTS > OOCYST

OOCYTE n immature female germ cell that gives rise to an ovum

OOCYTES > OOCYTE

OODLES npl great quantities

OODLINS same as > OODLES

OOF n money

OOFIER > OOF

OOFIEST > OOF

OOFS > OOF

OOFTISH n money

OOFTISHES > OOFTISH

OOFY > OOF

OOGAMETE n female gamete

OOGAMETES > OOGAMETE

OOGAMIES > OOGAMY

OOGAMOUS > OOGAMY

OOGAMY n sexual reproduction involving a small motile male gamete and a large much less motile female gamete

OOGENESES > OOGENESIS

OOGENESIS n formation and maturation of ova from undifferentiated cells in the ovary

OOGENETIC > OOGENESIS

OOGENIES > OOGENY

OOGENY same as > OOGENESIS

OOGONIA > OOGONIUM

OOGONIAL > OOGONIUM

OOGONIUM n immature female germ cell forming oocytes by repeated divisions

OOGONIUMS > OOGONIUM

OOH interj exclamation of surprise, pleasure, pain, etc ▷ vb say ooh

OOHED > OOH

OOHING > OOH

OOHS > OOH

OOIDAL adj shaped like egg

OOLACHAN same as > EULACHON

OOLACHANS > OOLACHAN

OOLAKAN same as > EULACHON

OOLAKANS > OOLAKAN

OOLITE n limestone made up of tiny grains of calcium carbonate

OOLITES > OOLITE

OOLITH n any of the tiny spherical grains of sedimentary rock of which oolite is composed

OOLITHS > OOLITH

OOLITIC > OOLITE

OOLOGIC > OOLOGY

OOLOGICAL > OOLOGY

OOLOGIES > OOLOGY

OOLOGIST > OOLOGY

OOLOGISTS > OOLOGY

OOLOGY n branch of ornithology concerned with the study of birds' eggs

OOLONG n kind of dark tea that is partly fermented before being dried

OOLONGS > OOLONG

OOM n title of respect used to refer to an elderly man

OOMIAC same as > UMIAK

OOMIACK same as > UMIAK

OOMIACKS > OOMIACK

OOMIACS > OOMIAC

OOMIAK same as > UMIAK

OOMIAKS > OOMIAK

OOMPAH n representation of the sound made by a deep brass instrument ▷ vb make the noise of a brass instrument

OOMPAHED > OOMPAH

OOMPAHING > OOMPAH

OOMPAHS > OOMPAH

OOMPH n enthusiasm, vigour, or energy

OOMPHS > OOMPH

OOMS > OOM

OOMYCETE n organism formerly classified as fungi

OOMYCETES > OOMYCETE

OON Scots word for > OVEN

OONS > OON

OONT n camel

OONTS > OONT

OOP vb Scots word meaning to bind

OOPED > OOP

OOPHORON n ovary

OOPHORONS > OOPHORON

OOPHYTE n gametophyte in mosses, liverworts, and ferns

OOPHYTES > OOPHYTE

OOPHYTIC > OOPHYTE

OOPING > OOP

OOPS interj exclamation of surprise or apology

OOR Scots form of > OUR

OORALI n member of Indian people

OORALIS > OORALI

OORIAL n Himalayan sheep

OORIALS > OORIAL

OORIE adj Scots word meaning shabby

OORIER > OORIE

OORIEST > OORIE

OOS > OO

OOSE n dust

OOSES > OOSE

OOSIER > OOSE

OOSIEST > OOSE

OOSPERM n fertilized ovum

OOSPERMS > OOSPERM

OOSPHERE n large female gamete produced in the oogonia of algae and fungi

OOSPHERES > OOSPHERE

OOSPORE n thick-walled sexual spore that develops from a fertilized oosphere

OOSPORES > OOSPORE

OOSPORIC > OOSPORE

OOSPOROUS > OOSPORE

OOSY > OOSE

OOT Scots word for > OUT

OOTHECA n capsule containing eggs that is produced by some insects and molluscs

OOTHECAE > OOTHECA

OOTHECAL > OOTHECA

OOTID n immature female gamete that develops into an ovum

OOTIDS > OOTID

OOTS > OOT

OOZE vb flow slowly ▷ n sluggish flow

OOZED > OOZE

OOZES > OOZE

OOZIER > OOZY

OOZIEST > OOZY

OOZILY > OOZY

OOZINESS > OOZY

OOZING > OOZE
OOZY adj moist or dripping
OP n operation
OPACIFIED > OPACIFY
OPACIFIER > OPACIFY
OPACIFIES > OPACIFY
OPACIFY vb become or make opaque
OPACITIES > OPACITY
OPACITY n state or quality of being opaque
OPACOUS same as > OPAQUE
OPAH n large soft-finned deep-sea fish
OPAHS > OPAH
OPAL n iridescent precious stone
OPALED adj made like opal
OPALESCE vb exhibit a milky iridescence
OPALESCED > OPALESCE
OPALESCES > OPALESCE
OPALINE adj opalescent ▷ n opaque or semiopaque whitish glass
OPALINES > OPALINE
OPALISED same as > OPALIZED
OPALIZED adj made into opal
OPALS > OPAL
OPAQUE adj not able to be seen through, not transparent ▷ n opaque pigment used to block out particular areas on a negative ▷ vb make opaque
OPAQUED > OPAQUE
OPAQUELY > OPAQUE
OPAQUER > OPAQUE
OPAQUES > OPAQUE
OPAQUEST > OPAQUE
OPAQUING > OPAQUE
OPCODE n computer code containing operating instructions
OPCODES > OPCODE
OPE archaic or poetic word for > OPEN
OPED > OPE
OPEN adj not closed ▷ vb (cause to) become open ▷ n competition which all may enter
OPENABLE > OPEN
OPENCAST as in opencast mining mining by excavating from the surface
OPENED > OPEN
OPENER n tool for opening cans and bottles
OPENERS > OPENER
OPENEST > OPEN
OPENING n beginning ▷ adj first
OPENINGS > OPENING
OPENLY > OPEN
OPENNESS > OPEN
OPENS > OPEN
OPENSIDE n in rugby, flanker who plays on the open side of the scrum

OPENSIDES > OPENSIDE
OPENWORK n ornamental work, as of metal or embroidery, having a pattern of openings or holes
OPENWORKS > OPENWORK
OPEPE n African tree
OPEPES > OPEPE
OPERA n drama in which the text is sung to an orchestral accompaniment
OPERABLE adj capable of being treated by a surgical operation
OPERABLY > OPERABLE
OPERAGOER n person who goes to operas
OPERAND n quantity, variable, or function upon which an operation is performed
OPERANDS > OPERAND
OPERANT adj producing effects ▷ n person or thing that operates
OPERANTLY > OPERANT
OPERANTS > OPERANT
OPERAS > OPERA
OPERATE vb (cause to) work
OPERATED > OPERATE
OPERATES > OPERATE
OPERATIC adj of or relating to opera
OPERATICS n performance of operas
OPERATING > OPERATE
OPERATION n method or procedure of working
OPERATISE same as > OPERATIZE
OPERATIVE adj working ▷ n worker with a special skill
OPERATIZE vb turn (a play, novel, etc) into an opera
OPERATOR n person who operates a machine or instrument
OPERATORS > OPERATOR
OPERCELE same as > OPERCULE
OPERCELES > OPERCELE
OPERCULA > OPERCULUM
OPERCULAR > OPERCULUM
OPERCULE n gill cover
OPERCULES > OPERCULE
OPERCULUM n covering flap or lidlike structure in animals or plants
OPERETTA n light-hearted comic opera
OPERETTAS > OPERETTA
OPERON n group of adjacent genes in bacteria functioning as a unit
OPERONS > OPERON
OPEROSE adj laborious
OPEROSELY > OPEROSE
OPEROSITY > OPEROSE
OPES > OPE
OPGEFOK adj South African

taboo slang for damaged or bungled
OPHIDIAN n reptile of the suborder which comprises the snakes
OPHIDIANS > OPHIDIAN
OPHIOLITE n type of mineral
OPHIOLOGY n branch of zoology that is concerned with the study of snakes
OPHITE n any of several greenish mottled rocks
OPHITES > OPHITE
OPHITIC adj having small elongated feldspar crystals enclosed
OPHIURA n sea creature like a starfish
OPHIURAN same as > OPHIURA
OPHIURANS > OPHIURAN
OPHIURAS > OPHIURA
OPHIURID same as > OPHIURA
OPHIURIDS > OPHIURID
OPHIUROID adj of or like ophiura
OPIATE n narcotic drug containing opium ▷ adj containing or consisting of opium ▷ vb treat with an opiate
OPIATED > OPIATE
OPIATES > OPIATE
OPIATING > OPIATE
OPIFICER n craftsman
OPIFICERS > OPIFICER
OPINABLE adj thinkable
OPINE vb express an opinion
OPINED > OPINE
OPINES > OPINE
OPING > OPE
OPINICUS n mythical monster
OPINING > OPINE
OPINION n personal belief or judgment
OPINIONED adj having strong opinions
OPINIONS > OPINION
OPIOID n substance that resembles morphine in its physiological or pharmacological effect
OPIOIDS > OPIOID
OPIUM n addictive narcotic drug made from poppy seeds
OPIUMISM n addiction to opium
OPIUMISMS > OPIUMISM
OPIUMS > OPIUM
OPOBALSAM n soothing ointment
OPODELDOC n medical ointment
OPOPANAX n medical resin from plant
OPORICE n former medicine made from fruit
OPORICES > OPORICE
OPOSSUM n small marsupial of America or

Australasia
OPOSSUMS > OPOSSUM
OPPIDAN adj of a town ▷ n person living in a town
OPPIDANS > OPPIDAN
OPPILANT > OPPILATE
OPPILATE vb block (the pores, bowels, etc)
OPPILATED > OPPILATE
OPPILATES > OPPILATE
OPPO n counterpart in another organization
OPPONENCY > OPPONENT
OPPONENT n person one is working against in a contest, battle, or argument ▷ adj opposite, as in position
OPPONENTS > OPPONENT
OPPORTUNE adj happening at a suitable time
OPPOS > OPPO
OPPOSABLE adj (of the thumb) capable of touching the tip of all the other fingers
OPPOSABLY > OPPOSABLE
OPPOSE vb work against
OPPOSED > OPPOSE
OPPOSER > OPPOSE
OPPOSERS > OPPOSE
OPPOSES > OPPOSE
OPPOSING > OPPOSE
OPPOSITE adj situated on the other side ▷ n person or thing that is opposite ▷ prep facing ▷ adv on the other side
OPPOSITES > OPPOSITE
OPPRESS vb control by cruelty or force
OPPRESSED > OPPRESS
OPPRESSES > OPPRESS
OPPRESSOR > OPPRESS
OPPUGN vb call into question
OPPUGNANT adj combative, antagonistic, or contrary
OPPUGNED > OPPUGN
OPPUGNER > OPPUGN
OPPUGNERS > OPPUGN
OPPUGNING > OPPUGN
OPPUGNS > OPPUGN
OPS > OP
OPSIMATH n person who learns late in life
OPSIMATHS > OPSIMATH
OPSIMATHY > OPSIMATH
OPSIN n type of protein
OPSINS > OPSIN
OPSOMANIA n extreme enthusiasm for a particular food
OPSONIC > OPSONIN
OPSONIFY same as > OPSONIZE
OPSONIN n constituent of blood serum
OPSONINS > OPSONIN
OPSONISE same as > OPSONIZE

OPSONISED > OPSONISE
OPSONISES > OPSONISE
OPSONIUM n relish eaten with bread
OPSONIUMS > OPSONIUM
OPSONIZE vb subject (bacteria) to the action of opsonins
OPSONIZED > OPSONIZE
OPSONIZES > OPSONIZE
OPT vb show a preference, choose
OPTANT n person who opts
OPTANTS > OPTANT
OPTATIVE adj indicating or expressing choice, preference, or wish ⊳ n optative mood
OPTATIVES > OPTATIVE
OPTED > OPT
OPTER > OPT
OPTERS > OPT
OPTIC adj relating to the eyes or sight
OPTICAL adj of or involving light or optics
OPTICALLY > OPTICAL
OPTICIAN n person qualified to prescribe glasses
OPTICIANS > OPTICIAN
OPTICIST n optics expert
OPTICISTS > OPTICIST
OPTICS n science of sight and light
OPTIMA > OPTIMUM
OPTIMAL adj best or most favourable
OPTIMALLY > OPTIMAL
OPTIMATE n Roman aristocrat
OPTIMATES > OPTIMATE
OPTIME n mathematics student at Cambridge University
OPTIMES > OPTIME
OPTIMISE same as > OPTIMIZE
OPTIMISED > OPTIMISE
OPTIMISER > OPTIMISE
OPTIMISES > OPTIMISE
OPTIMISM n tendency to take the most hopeful view
OPTIMISMS > OPTIMISM
OPTIMIST > OPTIMISM
OPTIMISTS > OPTIMISM
OPTIMIZE vb make the most of
OPTIMIZED > OPTIMIZE
OPTIMIZER > OPTIMIZE
OPTIMIZES > OPTIMIZE
OPTIMUM n best possible conditions ⊳ adj most favourable
OPTIMUMS > OPTIMUM
OPTING > OPT
OPTION n choice ⊳ vb obtain an option on
OPTIONAL adj possible but not compulsory ⊳ n optional thing
OPTIONALS > OPTIONAL
OPTIONED > OPTION
OPTIONEE n holder of a financial option

OPTIONEES > OPTIONEE
OPTIONING > OPTION
OPTIONS > OPTION
OPTOLOGY n science of sight
OPTOMETER n any of various instruments for measuring the refractive power of the eye
OPTOMETRY n science or practice of testing visual acuity and prescribing corrective lenses
OPTOPHONE n device for blind people that converts printed words into sounds
OPTRONICS n science of electronic and light signals
OPTS > OPT
OPULENCE > OPULENT
OPULENCES > OPULENT
OPULENCY > OPULENT
OPULENT adj having or indicating wealth
OPULENTLY > OPULENT
OPULUS n flowering shrub
OPULUSES > OPULUS
OPUNTIA n type of cactus
OPUNTIAS > OPUNTIA
OPUS n artistic creation, esp a musical work
OPUSCLE same as > OPUSCULE
OPUSCLES > OPUSCLE
OPUSCULA > OPUSCULUM
OPUSCULAR > OPUSCULE
OPUSCULE n small or insignificant artistic work
OPUSCULES > OPUSCULE
OPUSCULUM same as > OPUSCULE
OPUSES > OPUS
OQUASSA n American trout
OQUASSAS > OQUASSA
OR prep before ⊳ adj of the metal gold ⊳ n gold
ORA > OS
ORACH same as > ORACHE
ORACHE n type of plant
ORACHES > ORACHE
ORACIES > ORACY
ORACLE n shrine of an ancient god ⊳ vb utter as an oracle
ORACLED > ORACLE
ORACLES > ORACLE
ORACLING > ORACLE
ORACULAR adj of or like an oracle
ORACULOUS adj of an oracle
ORACY n capacity to express oneself in and understand speech
ORAD adv towards the mouth
ORAGIOUS adj stormy
ORAL adj spoken ⊳ n spoken examination
ORALISM n oral method of communicating with deaf people
ORALISMS > ORALISM

ORALIST > ORALISM
ORALISTS > ORALISM
ORALITIES > ORALITY
ORALITY n state of being oral
ORALLY > ORAL
ORALS > ORAL
ORANG n orangutan
ORANGE n reddish-yellow citrus fruit ⊳ adj reddish-yellow
ORANGEADE n orange-flavoured, usu fizzy drink
ORANGER > ORANGE
ORANGERIE archaic variant of > ORANGERY
ORANGERY n greenhouse for growing orange trees
ORANGES > ORANGE
ORANGEST > ORANGE
ORANGEY > ORANGE
ORANGIER > ORANGE
ORANGIEST > ORANGE
ORANGISH > ORANGE
ORANGS > ORANG
ORANGUTAN n large ape with shaggy reddish-brown hair
ORANGY > ORANGE
ORANT n artistic representation of worshipper
ORANTS > ORANT
ORARIA > ORARIUM
ORARIAN n person who lives on the coast
ORARIANS > ORARIAN
ORARION n garment worn by Greek clergyman
ORARIONS > ORARION
ORARIUM n handkerchief
ORARIUMS > ORARIUM
ORATE vb make or give an oration
ORATED > ORATE
ORATES > ORATE
ORATING > ORATE
ORATION n formal speech
ORATIONS > ORATION
ORATOR n skilful public speaker
ORATORIAL adj of oratory
ORATORIAN n clergyman of a particular type of church
ORATORIES > ORATORY
ORATORIO n musical composition for choir and orchestra
ORATORIOS > ORATORIO
ORATORS > ORATOR
ORATORY n art of making speeches
ORATRESS n female orator
ORATRICES > ORATRIX
ORATRIX n female orator
ORATRIXES > ORATRIX
ORB n ceremonial decorated sphere with a cross on top, carried by a monarch ⊳ vb make or become circular or spherical
ORBED > ORB

ORBICULAR adj circular or spherical
ORBIER > ORBY
ORBIEST > ORBY
ORBING > ORB
ORBIT n curved path of a planet, satellite, or spacecraft around another body ⊳ vb move in an orbit around
ORBITA same as > ORBIT
ORBITAL adj of or denoting an orbit ⊳ n region surrounding an atomic nucleus
ORBITALLY > ORBITAL
ORBITALS > ORBITAL
ORBITAS > ORBITA
ORBITED > ORBIT
ORBITER n spacecraft or satellite designed to orbit a planet without landing on it
ORBITERS > ORBITER
ORBITIES > ORBITY
ORBITING > ORBIT
ORBITS > ORBIT
ORBITY n bereavement
ORBLESS > ORB
ORBS > ORB
ORBY adj orb-shaped
ORC n any of various whales, such as the killer and grampus
ORCA n killer whale
ORCAS > ORCA
ORCEIN n brown crystalline material
ORCEINS > ORCEIN
ORCHARD n area where fruit trees are grown
ORCHARDS > ORCHARD
ORCHAT same as > ORCHARD
ORCHATS > ORCHAT
ORCHEL same as > ORCHIL
ORCHELLA same as > ORCHIL
ORCHELLAS > ORCHELLA
ORCHELS > ORCHEL
ORCHESES > ORCHESIS
ORCHESIS n art of dance
ORCHESTIC adj of dance
ORCHESTRA n large group of musicians, esp playing a variety of instruments
ORCHID n plant with flowers that have unusual lip-shaped petals
ORCHIDIST n orchid grower
ORCHIDS > ORCHID
ORCHIL n any of various lichens
ORCHILLA same as > ORCHIL
ORCHILLAS > ORCHILLA
ORCHILS > ORCHIL
ORCHIS n type of orchid
ORCHISES > ORCHIS
ORCHITIC > ORCHITIS
ORCHITIS n inflammation of one or both testicles
ORCIN same as > ORCINOL

ORCINE same as
> ORCINOL
ORCINES > ORCINE
ORCINOL n colourless
crystalline water-soluble
solid
ORCINOLS > ORCINOL
ORCINS > ORCIN
ORCS > ORC
ORD n pointed weapon
ORDAIN vb make
(someone) a member of the
clergy
ORDAINED > ORDAIN
ORDAINER > ORDAIN
ORDAINERS > ORDAIN
ORDAINING > ORDAIN
ORDAINS > ORDAIN
ORDALIAN adj of an ordeal
ORDALIUM same as
> ORDEAL
ORDALIUMS > ORDALIUM
ORDEAL n painful or
difficult experience
ORDEALS > ORDEAL
ORDER n instruction to be
carried out ▷ vb give an
instruction to
ORDERABLE > ORDER
ORDERED > ORDER
ORDERER > ORDER
ORDERERS > ORDER
ORDERING > ORDER
ORDERINGS > ORDER
ORDERLESS > ORDER
ORDERLIES > ORDERLY
ORDERLY adj well-
organized ▷ n hospital
attendant ▷ adv according
to custom or rule
ORDERS > ORDER
ORDINAIRE adj ordinary
ORDINAL adj denoting a
certain position in a
sequence of numbers ▷ n
book containing the forms
of services for the
ordination of ministers
ORDINALLY > ORDINAL
ORDINALS > ORDINAL
ORDINANCE n official rule
or order
ORDINAND n candidate for
ordination
ORDINANDS > ORDINAND
ORDINANT n person who
ordains
ORDINANTS > ORDINANT
ORDINAR Scots word for
> ORDINARY
ORDINARS > ORDINAR
ORDINARY adj usual or
normal
ORDINATE n vertical
coordinate of a point in a
two-dimensional system of
coordinates ▷ vb ordain
ORDINATED > ORDINATE
ORDINATES > ORDINATE
ORDINEE n person being
ordained
ORDINEES > ORDINEE
ORDINES > ORDO
ORDNANCE n weapons and

military supplies
ORDNANCES > ORDNANCE
ORDO n religious order
ORDOS > ORDO
ORDS > ORD
ORDURE n excrement
ORDURES > ORDURE
ORDUROUS > ORDURE
ORE n (rock containing) a
mineral which yields metal
OREAD n mountain nymph
OREADES > OREAD
OREADS > OREAD
ORECTIC adj of or relating
to the desires
ORECTIVE > OREXIS
OREGANO n sweet-smelling
herb used in cooking
OREGANOS > OREGANO
OREIDE same as > OROIDE
OREIDES > OREIDE
OREODONT n extinct
prehistoric mammal
OREODONTS > OREODONT
OREOLOGY same as
> OROLOGY
OREPEARCH same as
> OVERPERCH
ORES > ORE
ORESTUNCK
> OVERSTINK
OREWEED n seaweed
OREWEEDS > OREWEED
OREXIN n hormone that
promotes wakefulness and
stimulates the appetite
OREXINS > OREXIN
OREXIS n appetite
OREXISES > OREXIS
ORF n infectious disease of
sheep and sometimes
goats and cattle
ORFE n small slender
European fish
ORFES > ORFE
ORFRAY same as
> ORPHREY
ORFRAYS > ORFRAY
ORFS > ORF
ORGAN n part of an animal
or plant that has a
particular function
ORGANA > ORGANON
ORGANDIE n fine cotton
fabric
ORGANDIES > ORGANDY
ORGANDY same as
> ORGANDIE
ORGANELLE n structural
and functional unit in a cell
ORGANIC adj of or
produced from animals or
plants ▷ n substance that
is derived from animal or
vegetable matter
ORGANICAL same as
> ORGANIC
ORGANICS > ORGANIC
ORGANISE same as
> ORGANIZE
ORGANISED same as
> ORGANIZED
ORGANISER same as
> ORGANIZER

ORGANISES > ORGANISE
ORGANISM n any living
animal or plant
ORGANISMS > ORGANISM
ORGANIST n organ player
ORGANISTS > ORGANIST
ORGANITY same as
> ORGANISM
ORGANIZE vb make
arrangements for
ORGANIZED > ORGANIZE
ORGANIZER n person who
organizes or is capable of
organizing
ORGANIZES > ORGANIZE
ORGANON n system of
logical or scientific rules,
esp that of Aristotle
ORGANONS > ORGANON
ORGANOSOL n resin-based
coating
ORGANOTIN adj of an
organic compound used as
a pesticide
ORGANS > ORGAN
ORGANUM same as
> ORGANON
ORGANUMS > ORGANUM
ORGANZA n thin stiff fabric
of silk, cotton, or synthetic
fibre
ORGANZAS > ORGANZA
ORGANZINE n strong
thread made of twisted
strands of raw silk
ORGASM n most intense
point of sexual pleasure
▷ vb experience orgasm
ORGASMED > ORGASM
ORGASMIC > ORGASM
ORGASMING > ORGASM
ORGASMS > ORGASM
ORGASTIC > ORGASM
ORGEAT n drink made from
barley or almonds, and
orange flower water
ORGEATS > ORGEAT
ORGIA same as > ORGY
ORGIAC > ORGY
ORGIAS > ORGIA
ORGIAST n participant in
orgy
ORGIASTIC > ORGY
ORGIASTS > ORGIAST
ORGIC > ORGY
ORGIES > ORGY
ORGILLOUS same as
> ORGULOUS
ORGONE n substance
claimed to be needed in
people for sexual activity
and mental health
ORGONES > ORGONE
ORGUE n number of stakes
lashed together
ORGUES > ORGUE
ORGULOUS adj proud
ORGY n party involving
promiscuous sexual
activity
ORIBATID n type of mite
ORIBATIDS > ORIBATID
ORIBI n small African
antelope

ORIBIS > ORIBI
ORICALCHE same as
> ORICHALC
ORICHALC n type of alloy
ORICHALCS > ORICHALC
ORIEL n type of bay
window
ORIELLED adj having an
oriel
ORIELS > ORIEL
ORIENCIES > ORIENCY
ORIENCY n state of being
orient
ORIENT vb position
(oneself) according to one's
surroundings ▷ n eastern
sky or the dawn ▷ adj
eastern
ORIENTAL adj eastern ▷ n
native of the orient
ORIENTALS > ORIENTAL
ORIENTATE vb position
(oneself) according to one's
surroundings
ORIENTED > ORIENT
ORIENTEER vb take part in
orienteering ▷ n person
who takes part in
orienteering
ORIENTER > ORIENT
ORIENTERS > ORIENT
ORIENTING > ORIENT
ORIENTS > ORIENT
ORIFEX same as
> ORIFICE
ORIFEXES > ORIFEX
ORIFICE n opening
or hole
ORIFICES > ORIFICE
ORIFICIAL > ORIFICE
ORIFLAMME n scarlet flag
adopted as the national
banner of France in the
Middle Ages
ORIGAMI n Japanese
decorative art of paper
folding
ORIGAMIS > ORIGAMI
ORIGAN another name for
> MARJORAM
ORIGANE same as
> ORIGAN
ORIGANES > ORIGANE
ORIGANS > ORIGAN
ORIGANUM n type of
aromatic plant
ORIGANUMS > ORIGANUM
ORIGIN n point from which
something develops
ORIGINAL adj first or
earliest ▷ n first version,
from which others are
copied
ORIGINALS > ORIGINAL
ORIGINATE vb come or
bring into existence
ORIGINS > ORIGIN
ORIHOU n small New
Zealand tree
ORIHOUS > ORIHOU
ORILLION n part of
bastion
ORILLIONS > ORILLION
ORINASAL adj pronounced
with simultaneous oral and

nasal articulation ▷ *n* orinasal speech sound

ORINASALS > ORINASAL

ORIOLE *n* tropical or American songbird

ORIOLES > ORIOLE

ORISHA *n* any of the minor gods or spirits of traditional Yoruba religion

ORISHAS > ORISHA

ORISON *another word for* > PRAYER

ORISONS > ORISON

ORIXA *same as* > ORISHA

ORIXAS > ORIXA

ORLE *n* border around a shield

ORLEANS *n* type of fabric

ORLEANSES > ORLEANS

ORLES > ORLE

ORLISTAT *n* drug used for slimming

ORLISTATS > ORLISTAT

ORLON *n* tradename for a crease-resistant acrylic fibre or fabric used for clothing, furnishings, etc

ORLONS > ORLON

ORLOP *n* (in a vessel with four or more decks) the lowest deck

ORLOPS > ORLOP

ORMER *n* edible marine mollusc

ORMERS > ORMER

ORMOLU *n* gold-coloured alloy used for decoration

ORMOLUS > ORMOLU

ORNAMENT *n* decorative object ▷ *vb* decorate

ORNAMENTS > ORNAMENT

ORNATE *adj* highly decorated, elaborate

ORNATELY > ORNATE

ORNATER > ORNATE

ORNATEST > ORNATE

ORNERIER > ORNERY

ORNERIEST > ORNERY

ORNERY *adj* stubborn or vile-tempered

ORNIS *less common word for* > AVIFAUNA

ORNISES > ORNIS

ORNITHES *n* birds in Greek myth

ORNITHIC *adj* of or relating to birds or a bird fauna

ORNITHINE *n* type of amino acid

ORNITHOID *adj* like bird

OROGEN *n* part of earth subject to orogeny

OROGENIC > OROGENY

OROGENIES > OROGENY

OROGENS > OROGEN

OROGENY *n* formation of mountain ranges by intense upward displacement of the earth's crust

OROGRAPHY *n* study or mapping of relief, esp of mountains

OROIDE *n* alloy containing

copper, tin, and other metals, used as imitation gold

OROIDES > OROIDE

OROLOGIES > OROLOGY

OROLOGIST > OROGRAPHY

OROLOGY *same as* > OROGRAPHY

OROMETER *n* aneroid barometer with an altitude scale

OROMETERS > OROMETER

ORONASAL *adj* of or relating to the mouth and nose

OROPESA *n* float used in minesweeping

OROPESAS > OROPESA

OROTUND *adj* (of the voice) resonant and booming

ORPHAN *n* child whose parents are dead ▷ *vb* deprive of parents

ORPHANAGE *n* children's home for orphans

ORPHANED > ORPHAN

ORPHANING > ORPHAN

ORPHANISM *n* state of being an orphan

ORPHANS > ORPHAN

ORPHARION *n* large lute in use during the 16th and 17th centuries

ORPHIC *adj* mystical or occult

ORPHICAL *same as* > ORPHIC

ORPHISM *n* style of abstract art

ORPHISMS > ORPHISM

ORPHREY *n* richly embroidered band or border

ORPHREYED *adj* emroidered with gold

ORPHREYS > ORPHREY

ORPIMENT *n* yellow mineral

ORPIMENTS > ORPIMENT

ORPIN *same as* > ORPINE

ORPINE *n* type of plant

ORPINES > ORPINE

ORPINS > ORPIN

ORRA *adj* odd or unmatched

ORRAMAN *n* man who does odd jobs

ORRAMEN > ORRAMAN

ORRERIES > ORRERY

ORRERY *n* mechanical model of the solar system

ORRICE *same as* > ORRIS

ORRICES > ORRICE

ORRIS *n* kind of iris

ORRISES > ORRIS

ORRISROOT *n* rhizome of a type of iris, used as perfume

ORS > OR

ORSEILLE *same as* > ORCHIL

ORSEILLES > ORSEILLE

ORSELLIC > ORSEILLE

ORT *n* fragment

ORTANIQUE *n* hybrid

between an orange and a tangerine

ORTHIAN *adj* having high pitch

ORTHICON *n* type of television camera tube

ORTHICONS > ORTHICON

ORTHO *n* type of photographic plate

ORTHOAXES > ORTHOAXIS

ORTHOAXIS *n* axis in a crystal

ORTHODOX *adj* conforming to established views

ORTHODOXY *n* orthodox belief or practice

ORTHOEPIC > ORTHOEPY

ORTHOEPY *n* study of correct or standard pronunciation

ORTHOPEDY *n* treatment of deformity

ORTHOPOD *n* surgeon

ORTHOPODS > ORTHOPOD

ORTHOPTER *n* type of aircraft propelled by flapping wings

ORTHOPTIC *adj* relating to normal binocular vision

ORTHOS > ORTHO

ORTHOSES > ORTHOSIS

ORTHOSIS *n* artificial or mechanical aid to support a weak part of the body

ORTHOTIC > ORTHOTICS

ORTHOTICS *n* use of artificial or mechanical aids to assist movement of weak joints or muscles

ORTHOTIST *n* person who is qualified to practise orthotics

ORTHOTONE *adj* (of a word) having an independent accent ▷ *n* independently accented word

ORTHROS *n* canonical hour in the Greek Church

ORTHROSES > ORTHROS

ORTOLAN *n* small European songbird eaten as a delicacy

ORTOLANS > ORTOLAN

ORTS *npl* scraps or leavings

ORVAL *n* plant of sage family

ORVALS > ORVAL

ORYX *n* large African antelope

ORYXES > ORYX

ORZO *n* pasta in small grain shapes

ORZOS > ORZO

OS *n* mouth or mouthlike part or opening

OSAR > OS

OSCAR *n* cash

OSCARS > OSCAR

OSCHEAL *adj* of scrotum

OSCILLATE *vb* swing back and forth

OSCINE *n* songbird ▷ *adj* of songbirds

OSCINES > OSCINE

OSCININE > OSCINE

OSCITANCE *same as* > OSCITANCY

OSCITANCY *n* state of being drowsy, lazy, or inattentive

OSCITANT > OSCITANCY

OSCITATE *vb* yawn

OSCITATED > OSCITATE

OSCITATES > OSCITATE

OSCULA > OSCULUM

OSCULANT *adj* possessing some of the characteristics of two different taxonomic groups

OSCULAR *adj* of or relating to an osculum

OSCULATE *vb* kiss

OSCULATED > OSCULATE

OSCULATES > OSCULATE

OSCULE *n* small mouth or opening

OSCULES > OSCULE

OSCULUM *n* mouthlike aperture

OSE *same as* > ESKER

OSES > OSE

OSETRA *n* type of caviar

OSETRAS > OSETRA

OSHAC *n* plant smelling of ammonia

OSHACS > OSHAC

OSIER *n* willow tree

OSIERED *adj* covered with osiers

OSIERIES > OSIERY

OSIERS > OSIER

OSIERY *n* work done with osiers

OSMATE *n* salt of osmic acid

OSMATES > OSMATE

OSMATIC *adj* relying on sense of smell

OSMETERIA *npl* glands in some caterpillars that secrete foul-smelling substances to deter predators

OSMIATE *same as* > OSMATE

OSMIATES > OSMIATE

OSMIC *adj* of or containing osmium in a high valence state

OSMICALLY > OSMIC

OSMICS *n* science of smell

OSMIOUS *same as* > OSMOUS

OSMIUM *n* heaviest known metallic element

OSMIUMS > OSMIUM

OSMOL *same as* > OSMOLE

OSMOLAL > OSMOLE

OSMOLAR *adj* containing one osmole per litre

OSMOLE *n* unit of osmotic pressure

OSMOLES > OSMOLE

OSMOLS > OSMOL

OSMOMETER *n* instrument for measuring osmotic pressure

OSMOMETRY > OSMOMETER

OSMOSE vb undergo or cause to undergo osmosis
OSMOSED >OSMOSE
OSMOSES >OSMOSE
OSMOSING >OSMOSE
OSMOSIS n movement of a liquid through a membrane from a lower to a higher concentration
OSMOTIC >OSMOSIS
OSMOUS adj of or containing osmium in a low valence state
OSMUND same as >OSMUNDA
OSMUNDA n type of fern
OSMUNDAS >OSMUNDA
OSMUNDINE n type of compost
OSMUNDS >OSMUND
OSNABURG n coarse plain-woven cotton used for sacks, furnishings, etc
OSNABURGS >OSNABURG
OSPREY n large fish-eating bird of prey
OSPREYS >OSPREY
OSSA >OS
OSSARIUM same as >OSSUARY
OSSARIUMS >OSSARIUM
OSSATURE n skeleton
OSSATURES >OSSATURE
OSSEIN n protein that forms the organic matrix of bone
OSSEINS >OSSEIN
OSSELET n growth on knee of horse
OSSELETS >OSSELET
OSSEOUS adj consisting of or like bone
OSSEOUSLY >OSSEOUS
OSSETER n sturgeon
OSSETERS >OSSETER
OSSETRA same as >OSETRA
OSSETRAS >OSSETRA
OSSIA conj (in music) or
OSSICLE n small bone, esp one of those in the middle ear
OSSICLES >OSSICLE
OSSICULAR >OSSICLE
OSSIFIC adj making something turn to bone
OSSIFIED adj converted into bone
OSSIFIER >OSSIFY
OSSIFIERS >OSSIFY
OSSIFIES >OSSIFY
OSSIFRAGA n large sea bird
OSSIFRAGE n osprey
OSSIFY vb (cause to) become bone, harden
OSSIFYING >OSSIFY
OSSOBUCO n Italian dish of veal shank and vegetables stewed in wine
OSSOBUCOS >OSSOBUCO
OSSUARIES >OSSUARY
OSSUARY n any container for the burial of human

bones, such as an urn or vault
OSTEAL adj of or relating to bone or to the skeleton
OSTEITIC >OSTEITIS
OSTEITIS n inflammation of a bone
OSTENSIVE adj directly showing or pointing out
OSTENSORY n (in the RC Church) receptacle for displaying the consecrated Host
OSTENT n appearance
OSTENTS >OSTENT
OSTEOCYTE n bone cell
OSTEODERM n bony area in skin
OSTEOGEN n material from which bone forms
OSTEOGENS >OSTEOGEN
OSTEOGENY n forming of bone
OSTEOID adj of or resembling bone ▷ n bony deposit
OSTEOIDS >OSTEOID
OSTEOLOGY n study of the structure and function of bones
OSTEOMA n benign tumour composed of bone or bonelike tissue
OSTEOMAS >OSTEOMA
OSTEOMATA >OSTEOMA
OSTEOPATH n person who practises osteopathy
OSTEOSES >OSTEOSIS
OSTEOSIS n forming of bony tissue
OSTEOTOME n surgical instrument for cutting bone, usually a special chisel
OSTEOTOMY n surgical cutting or dividing of bone
OSTIA >OSTIUM
OSTIAL >OSTIUM
OSTIARIES >OSTIARY
OSTIARY another word for >PORTER
OSTIATE adj having ostium
OSTINATI >OSTINATO
OSTINATO n persistently repeated phrase or rhythm
OSTINATOS >OSTINATO
OSTIOLAR >OSTIOLE
OSTIOLATE >OSTIOLE
OSTIOLE n pore in the reproductive bodies of certain algae and fungi through which spores pass
OSTIOLES >OSTIOLE
OSTIUM n any of the pores in sponges through which water enters the body
OSTLER n stableman at an inn
OSTLERESS n female ostler
OSTLERS >OSTLER
OSTMARK n currency of the former East Germany
OSTMARKS >OSTMARK

OSTOMATE n person with an ostomy
OSTOMATES >OSTOMATE
OSTOMIES >OSTOMY
OSTOMY n surgically made opening connecting organ to surface of body
OSTOSES >OSTOSIS
OSTOSIS n formation of bone
OSTOSISES >OSTOSIS
OSTRACA >OSTRACON
OSTRACEAN adj of oysters
OSTRACISE same as >OSTRACIZE
OSTRACISM >OSTRACIZE
OSTRACIZE vb exclude (a person) from a group
OSTRACOD n type of minute crustacean
OSTRACODE adj of ostracods
OSTRACODS >OSTRACOD
OSTRACON n (in ancient Greece) a potsherd used for ostracizing
OSTRAKA >OSTRAKON
OSTRAKON same as >OSTRACON
OSTREGER n keeper of hawks
OSTREGERS >OSTREGER
OSTRICH n large African bird that runs fast but cannot fly
OSTRICHES >OSTRICH
OTAKU n Japanese computer geeks
OTALGIA technical name for >EARACHE
OTALGIAS >OTALGIA
OTALGIC >OTALGIA
OTALGIES >OTALGY
OTALGY same as >OTALGIA
OTARIES >OTARY
OTARINE >OTARY
OTARY n seal with ears
OTHER adj remaining in a group of which one or some have been specified ▷ n other person or thing
OTHERNESS n quality of being different or distinct in appearance, character, etc
OTHERS >OTHER
OTHERWISE adv differently, in another way ▷ adj of an unexpected nature ▷ pron something different in outcome
OTIC adj of or relating to the ear
OTIOSE adj not useful
OTIOSELY >OTIOSE
OTIOSITY >OTIOSE
OTITIC >OTITIS
OTITIDES >OTITIS
OTITIS n inflammation of the ear
OTITISES >OTITIS
OTOCYST n embryonic structure in vertebrates

that develops into the inner ear in the adult
OTOCYSTIC >OTOCYST
OTOCYSTS >OTOCYST
OTOLITH n granule of calcium carbonate in the inner ear of vertebrates
OTOLITHIC >OTOLITH
OTOLITHS >OTOLITH
OTOLOGIES >OTOLOGY
OTOLOGIST >OTOLOGY
OTOLOGY n branch of medicine concerned with the ear
OTOPLASTY n cosmetic surgery on ears
OTORRHOEA n discharge from the ears
OTOSCOPE another name for >AURISCOPE
OTOSCOPES >OTOSCOPE
OTOSCOPIC >OTOSCOPY
OTOSCOPY n examination of ear using otoscope
OTOTOXIC adj toxic to the ear
OTTAR variant of >ATTAR
OTTARS >OTTAR
OTTAVA n interval of an octave
OTTAVAS >OTTAVA
OTTAVINO n piccolo
OTTAVINOS >OTTAVINO
OTTER n small brown freshwater mammal that eats fish ▷ vb fish using an otter board
OTTERED >OTTER
OTTERING >OTTER
OTTERS >OTTER
OTTO another name for >ATTAR
OTTOMAN n storage chest with a padded lid for use as a seat
OTTOMANS >OTTOMAN
OTTOS >OTTO
OTTRELITE n type of mineral
OU n man, bloke, or chap
OUABAIN n poisonous white crystalline glycoside
OUABAINS >OUABAIN
OUAKARI n South American monkey
OUAKARIS >OUAKARI
OUBAAS n man in authority
OUBAASES >OUBAAS
OUBIT n hairy caterpillar
OUBITS >OUBIT
OUBLIETTE n dungeon entered only by a trapdoor
OUCH interj exclamation of sudden pain ▷ n brooch or clasp set with gems ▷ vb say ouch
OUCHED >OUCH
OUCHES >OUCH
OUCHING >OUCH
OUCHT Scots word for >ANYTHING
OUCHTS >OUCHT
OUD n Arabic stringed musical instrument

resembling a lute or mandolin

OUDS > OUD

OUENS > OU

OUGHLIED > OUGHLY

OUGHLIES > OUGHLY

OUGHLY *variant of >* UGLY

OUGHLYING > OUGHLY

OUGHT *vb* have an obligation ▷ *n* zero

OUGHTED > OUGHT

OUGHTING > OUGHT

OUGHTNESS *n* state of being right

OUGHTS > OUGHT

OUGLIE *variant of >* UGLY

OUGLIED > OUGLIE

OUGLIEING > OUGLIE

OUGLIES > OUGLIE

OUGUIYA *n* standard monetary unit of Mauritania

OUGUIYAS > OUGUIYA

OUIJA *n* tradename for a board through which spirits supposedly answer questions

OUIJAS > OUIJA

OUISTITI *n* marmoset

OUISTITIS > OUISTITI

OUK *Scots word for >* WEEK

OUKS > OUK

OULACHON *same as >* EULACHON

OULACHONS > OULACHON

OULAKAN *same as >* EULACHON

OULAKANS > OULAKAN

OULD *Scots or Irish form of >* OLD

OULDER > OULD

OULDEST > OULD

OULK *Scots form of >* WEEK

OULKS > OULK

OULONG *same as >* OOLONG

OULONGS > OULONG

OUMA *n* grandmother, often as a title with a surname

OUMAS > OUMA

OUNCE *n* unit of weight equal to one sixteenth of a pound

OUNCES > OUNCE

OUNDY *adj* wavy

OUP *same as >* OOP

OUPA *n* grandfather, often as a title with a surname

OUPAS > OUPA

OUPED > OUP

OUPH *same as >* OAF

OUPHE *same as >* OAF

OUPHES > OUPHE

OUPHS > OUPH

OUPING > OUP

OUPS > OUP

OUR *adj* belonging to us ▷ *det* of, belonging to, or associated in some way with us

OURALI *n* plant from which curare comes

OURALIS > OURALI

OURANG *same as >* ORANG

OURANGS > OURANG

OURARI *same as >* OURALI

OURARIS > OURARI

OUREBI *same as >* ORIBI

OUREBIS > OUREBI

OURIE *same as >* OORIE

OURIER > OURIE

OURIEST > OURIE

OURN *dialect form of >* OUR

OUROBOROS *n* mythical serpent

OUROLOGY *same as >* UROLOGY

OUROSCOPY *same as >* UROSCOPY

OURS *pron* thing(s) belonging to us

OURSELF *pron* formal word for *myself* used by monarchs

OURSELVES *pron* reflexive form of *we* or *us*

OUS > OU

OUSEL *same as >* OUZEL

OUSELS > OUSEL

OUST *vb* force (someone) out, expel

OUSTED > OUST

OUSTER *n* act or instance of forcing someone out of a position

OUSTERS > OUSTER

OUSTING > OUST

OUSTITI *n* device for opening locked door

OUSTITIS > OUSTITI

OUSTS > OUST

OUT *adj* denoting movement or distance away from ▷ *vb* name (a public figure) as being homosexual

OUTACT *vb* surpass in acting

OUTACTED > OUTACT

OUTACTING > OUTACT

OUTACTS > OUTACT

OUTADD *vb* beat or surpass at adding

OUTADDED > OUTADD

OUTADDING > OUTADD

OUTADDS > OUTADD

OUTAGE *n* period of power failure

OUTAGES > OUTAGE

OUTARGUE *vb* defeat in argument

OUTARGUED > OUTARGUE

OUTARGUES > OUTARGUE

OUTASIGHT *adj* excellent or wonderful

OUTASK *vb* declare wedding banns

OUTASKED > OUTASK

OUTASKING > OUTASK

OUTASKS > OUTASK

OUTATE > OUTEAT

OUTBACK *n* remote bush country of Australia

OUTBACKER > OUTBACK

OUTBACKS > OUTBACK

OUTBAKE *vb* bake more or better than

OUTBAKED > OUTBAKE

OUTBAKES > OUTBAKE

OUTBAKING > OUTBAKE

OUTBAR *vb* keep out

OUTBARK *vb* bark more or louder than

OUTBARKED > OUTBARK

OUTBARKS > OUTBARK

OUTBARRED > OUTBAR

OUTBARS > OUTBAR

OUTBAWL *vb* bawl more or louder than

OUTBAWLED > OUTBAWL

OUTBAWLS > OUTBAWL

OUTBEAM *vb* beam more or brighter than

OUTBEAMED > OUTBEAM

OUTBEAMS > OUTBEAM

OUTBEG *vb* beg more or better than

OUTBEGGED > OUTBEG

OUTBEGS > OUTBEG

OUTBID *vb* offer a higher price than

OUTBIDDEN > OUTBID

OUTBIDDER > OUTBID

OUTBIDS > OUTBID

OUTBITCH *vb* bitch more or better than

OUTBLAZE *vb* blaze more or hotter than

OUTBLAZED > OUTBLAZE

OUTBLAZES > OUTBLAZE

OUTBLEAT *vb* bleat more or louder than

OUTBLEATS > OUTBLEAT

OUTBLESS *vb* bless more than

OUTBLOOM *vb* bloom more or better than

OUTBLOOMS > OUTBLOOM

OUTBLUFF *vb* surpass in bluffing

OUTBLUFFS > OUTBLUFF

OUTBLUSH *vb* blush more than

OUTBOARD *adj* (of a boat's engine) portable, with its own propeller ▷ *adv* away from the centre line of a vessel or aircraft ▷ *n* outboard motor

OUTBOARDS > OUTBOARD

OUTBOAST *vb* surpass in boasting

OUTBOASTS > OUTBOAST

OUTBOUGHT > OUTBUY

OUTBOUND *adj* going out

OUTBOUNDS *n* boundaries

OUTBOX *vb* surpass in boxing

OUTBOXED > OUTBOX

OUTBOXES > OUTBOX

OUTBOXING > OUTBOX

OUTBRAG *vb* brag more or better than

OUTBRAGS > OUTBRAG

OUTBRAVE *vb* surpass in bravery

OUTBRAVED > OUTBRAVE

OUTBRAVES > OUTBRAVE

OUTBRAWL *vb* defeat in a brawl

OUTBRAWLS > OUTBRAWL

OUTBRAZEN *vb* be more brazen than

OUTBREAK *n* sudden occurrence (of something unpleasant) ▷ *vb* break out

OUTBREAKS > OUTBREAK

OUTBRED > OUTBREED

OUTBREED *vb* produce offspring through sexual relations outside a particular family or tribe

OUTBREEDS > OUTBREED

OUTBRIBE *vb* bribe more than

OUTBRIBED > OUTBRIBE

OUTBRIBES > OUTBRIBE

OUTBROKE > OUTBREAK

OUTBROKEN > OUTBREAK

OUTBUILD *vb* exceed in building

OUTBUILDS > OUTBUILD

OUTBUILT > OUTBUILD

OUTBULGE *vb* bulge outwards

OUTBULGED > OUTBULGE

OUTBULGES > OUTBULGE

OUTBULK *vb* exceed in bulk

OUTBULKED > OUTBULK

OUTBULKS > OUTBULK

OUTBULLY *vb* exceed in bullying

OUTBURN *vb* burn longer or brighter than

OUTBURNED > OUTBURN

OUTBURNS > OUTBURN

OUTBURNT > OUTBURN

OUTBURST *n* sudden expression of emotion ▷ *vb* burst out

OUTBURSTS > OUTBURST

OUTBUY *vb* buy more than

OUTBUYING > OUTBUY

OUTBUYS > OUTBUY

OUTBY *adv* outside

OUTBYE *same as >* OUTBY

OUTCALL *n* visit to customer's home by professional

OUTCALLS > OUTCALL

OUTCAPER *vb* exceed in capering

OUTCAPERS > OUTCAPER

OUTCAST *n* person rejected by a particular group ▷ *adj* rejected, abandoned, or discarded

OUTCASTE *n* person who has been expelled from a caste ▷ *vb* cause (someone) to lose his caste

OUTCASTED > OUTCASTE

OUTCASTES > OUTCASTE

OUTCASTS > OUTCAST

OUTCATCH *vb* catch more than

OUTCAUGHT > OUTCATCH

OUTCAVIL *vb* exceed in cavilling

OUTCAVILS > OUTCAVIL

OUTCHARGE *vb* charge more than

OUTCHARM *vb* exceed in charming

OUTCHARMS > OUTCHARM

OUTCHEAT *vb* exceed in cheating

OUTCHEATS > OUTCHEAT

OUTCHID > OUTCHIDE
OUTCHIDE *vb* exceed in chiding
OUTCHIDED > OUTCHIDE
OUTCHIDES > OUTCHIDE
OUTCITIES > OUTCITY
OUTCITY *n* anywhere outside a city's confines
OUTCLASS *vb* surpass in quality
OUTCLIMB *vb* exceed in climbing
OUTCLIMBS > OUTCLIMB
OUTCLOMB > OUTCLIMB
OUTCOACH *vb* exceed in coaching
OUTCOME *n* result
OUTCOMES > OUTCOME
OUTCOOK *vb* cook more or better than
OUTCOOKED > OUTCOOK
OUTCOOKS > OUTCOOK
OUTCOUNT *vb* exceed in counting
OUTCOUNTS > OUTCOUNT
OUTCRAFTY *vb* be craftier than
OUTCRAWL *vb* crawl further or faster than
OUTCRAWLS > OUTCRAWL
OUTCRIED > OUTCRY
OUTCRIES > OUTCRY
OUTCROP *n* part of a rock formation that sticks out of the earth ▷ *vb* (of rock strata) to protrude through the surface of the earth
OUTCROPS > OUTCROP
OUTCROSS *vb* breed (animals or plants of the same breed but different strains) ▷ *n* animal or plant produced as a result of outcrossing
OUTCROW *vb* exceed in crowing
OUTCROWD *vb* have more crowd than
OUTCROWDS > OUTCROWD
OUTCROWED > OUTCROW
OUTCROWS > OUTCROW
OUTCRY *n* vehement or widespread protest ▷ *vb* cry louder or make more noise than (someone or something)
OUTCRYING > OUTCRY
OUTCURSE *vb* exceed in cursing
OUTCURSED > OUTCURSE
OUTCURSES > OUTCURSE
OUTCURVE *n* baseball thrown to curve away from batter
OUTCURVES > OUTCURVE
OUTDANCE *vb* surpass in dancing
OUTDANCED > OUTDANCE
OUTDANCES > OUTDANCE
OUTDARE *vb* be more brave than
OUTDARED > OUTDARE
OUTDARES > OUTDARE
OUTDARING > OUTDARE
OUTDATE *vb* make or

become old-fashioned or obsolete
OUTDATED *adj* old-fashioned
OUTDATES > OUTDATE
OUTDATING > OUTDATE
OUTDAZZLE *vb* exceed in dazzling
OUTDEBATE *vb* exceed in debate
OUTDESIGN *vb* exceed in designing
OUTDID > OUTDO
OUTDO *vb* surpass in performance
OUTDODGE *vb* surpass in dodging
OUTDODGED > OUTDODGE
OUTDODGES > OUTDODGE
OUTDOER > OUTDO
OUTDOERS > OUTDO
OUTDOES > OUTDO
OUTDOING > OUTDO
OUTDONE > OUTDO
OUTDOOR *adj* taking place, existing, or intended for use in the open air
OUTDOORS *adv* in(to) the open air ▷ *n* open air
OUTDOORSY *adj* taking part in activities relating to the outdoors
OUTDRAG *vb* beat in drag race
OUTDRAGS > OUTDRAG
OUTDRANK > OUTDRINK
OUTDRAW *vb* draw (a gun) faster than
OUTDRAWN > OUTDRAW
OUTDRAWS > OUTDRAW
OUTDREAM *vb* exceed in dreaming
OUTDREAMS > OUTDREAM
OUTDREAMT > OUTDREAM
OUTDRESS *vb* dress better than
OUTDREW > OUTDRAW
OUTDRINK *vb* drink more than
OUTDRINKS > OUTDRINK
OUTDRIVE *vb* exceed in driving
OUTDRIVEN > OUTDRIVE
OUTDRIVES > OUTDRIVE
OUTDROP *same as* **>** OUTCROP
OUTDROPS > OUTDROP
OUTDROVE > OUTDRIVE
OUTDRUNK > OUTDRINK
OUTDUEL *vb* defeat in duel
OUTDUELED > OUTDUEL
OUTDUELS > OUTDUEL
OUTDURE *vb* last longer than
OUTDURED > OUTDURE
OUTDURES > OUTDURE
OUTDURING > OUTDURE
OUTDWELL *vb* live outside something
OUTDWELLS > OUTDWELL
OUTDWELT > OUTDWELL
OUTEARN *vb* earn more than
OUTEARNED > OUTEARN

OUTEARNS > OUTEARN
OUTEAT *vb* eat more than
OUTEATEN > OUTEAT
OUTEATING > OUTEAT
OUTEATS > OUTEAT
OUTECHO *vb* echo more than
OUTECHOED > OUTECHO
OUTECHOES > OUTECHO
OUTED > OUT
OUTEDGE *n* furthest limit
OUTEDGES > OUTEDGE
OUTER *adj* on the outside ▷ *n* white outermost ring on a target
OUTERCOAT *same as* **>** OVERCOAT
OUTERMOST *adj* furthest out
OUTERS > OUTER
OUTERWEAR *n* clothes worn on top of other clothes
OUTFABLE *vb* exceed in creating fables
OUTFABLED > OUTFABLE
OUTFABLES > OUTFABLE
OUTFACE *vb* subdue or disconcert (someone) by staring
OUTFACED > OUTFACE
OUTFACES > OUTFACE
OUTFACING > OUTFACE
OUTFALL *n* mouth of a river or drain
OUTFALLS > OUTFALL
OUTFAST *vb* fast longer than
OUTFASTED > OUTFAST
OUTFASTS > OUTFAST
OUTFAWN *vb* exceed in fawning
OUTFAWNED > OUTFAWN
OUTFAWNS > OUTFAWN
OUTFEAST *vb* exceed in feasting
OUTFEASTS > OUTFEAST
OUTFEEL *vb* exceed in feeling
OUTFEELS > OUTFEEL
OUTFELT > OUTFEEL
OUTFENCE *vb* surpass at fencing
OUTFENCED > OUTFENCE
OUTFENCES > OUTFENCE
OUTFIELD *n* area far from the pitch
OUTFIELDS > OUTFIELD
OUTFIGHT *vb* surpass in fighting
OUTFIGHTS > OUTFIGHT
OUTFIGURE *same as* **>** OUTTHINK
OUTFIND *vb* exceed in finding
OUTFINDS > OUTFIND
OUTFIRE *vb* exceed in firing
OUTFIRED > OUTFIRE
OUTFIRES > OUTFIRE
OUTFIRING > OUTFIRE
OUTFISH *vb* catch more fish than
OUTFISHED > OUTFISH

OUTFISHES > OUTFISH
OUTFIT *n* matching set of clothes ▷ *vb* furnish or be furnished with an outfit, equipment, etc
OUTFITS > OUTFIT
OUTFITTED > OUTFIT
OUTFITTER *n* supplier of men's clothes
OUTFLANK *vb* get round the side of (an enemy army)
OUTFLANKS > OUTFLANK
OUTFLASH *vb* be flashier than
OUTFLEW > OUTFLY
OUTFLIES > OUTFLY
OUTFLING *n* cutting remark
OUTFLINGS > OUTFLING
OUTFLOAT *vb* surpass at floating
OUTFLOATS > OUTFLOAT
OUTFLOW *n* anything that flows out, such as liquid or money ▷ *vb* flow faster than
OUTFLOWED > OUTFLOW
OUTFLOWN > OUTFLY
OUTFLOWS > OUTFLOW
OUTFLUSH *n* burst of light
OUTFLY *vb* fly better or faster than
OUTFLYING > OUTFLY
OUTFOOL *vb* be more foolish than
OUTFOOLED > OUTFOOL
OUTFOOLS > OUTFOOL
OUTFOOT *vb* (of a boat) to go faster than (another boat)
OUTFOOTED > OUTFOOT
OUTFOOTS > OUTFOOT
OUTFOUGHT > OUTFIGHT
OUTFOUND > OUTFIND
OUTFOX *vb* defeat or foil (someone) by being more cunning
OUTFOXED > OUTFOX
OUTFOXES > OUTFOX
OUTFOXING > OUTFOX
OUTFROWN *vb* dominate by frowning more than
OUTFROWNS > OUTFROWN
OUTFUMBLE *vb* exceed in fumbling
OUTGAIN *vb* gain more than
OUTGAINED > OUTGAIN
OUTGAINS > OUTGAIN
OUTGALLOP *vb* gallop faster than
OUTGAMBLE *vb* defeat at gambling
OUTGAS *vb* undergo the removal of adsorbed or absorbed gas from solids
OUTGASES > OUTGAS
OUTGASSED > OUTGAS
OUTGASSES > OUTGAS
OUTGATE *n* way out
OUTGATES > OUTGATE
OUTGAVE > OUTGIVE
OUTGAZE *vb* gaze beyond
OUTGAZED > OUTGAZE

OUTGAZES > OUTGAZE
OUTGAZING > OUTGAZE
OUTGIVE vb exceed in giving
OUTGIVEN > OUTGIVE
OUTGIVES > OUTGIVE
OUTGIVING > OUTGIVE
OUTGLARE vb exceed in glaring
OUTGLARED > OUTGLARE
OUTGLARES > OUTGLARE
OUTGLEAM vb gleam more than
OUTGLEAMS > OUTGLEAM
OUTGLOW vb glow more than
OUTGLOWED > OUTGLOW
OUTGLOWS > OUTGLOW
OUTGNAW vb exceed in gnawing
OUTGNAWED > OUTGNAW
OUTGNAWN > OUTGNAW
OUTGNAWS > OUTGNAW
OUTGO vb exceed or outstrip ▷ n cost
OUTGOER > OUTGO
OUTGOERS > OUTGO
OUTGOES > OUTGO
OUTGOING adj leaving ▷ n act of going out
OUTGOINGS npl expenses
OUTGONE > OUTGO
OUTGREW > OUTGROW
OUTGRIN vb exceed in grinning
OUTGRINS > OUTGRIN
OUTGROSS vb earn more than
OUTGROUP n group of people outside one's own group of people
OUTGROUPS > OUTGROUP
OUTGROW vb become too large or too old for
OUTGROWN > OUTGROW
OUTGROWS > OUTGROW
OUTGROWTH n natural development
OUTGUARD n guard furthest away from main party
OUTGUARDS > OUTGUARD
OUTGUESS vb surpass in guessing
OUTGUIDE n folder in filing system ▷ vb beat or surpass at guiding
OUTGUIDED > OUTGUIDE
OUTGUIDES > OUTGUIDE
OUTGUN vb surpass in fire power
OUTGUNNED > OUTGUN
OUTGUNS > OUTGUN
OUTGUSH vb gush out
OUTGUSHED > OUTGUSH
OUTGUSHES > OUTGUSH
OUTHANDLE vb handle better than
OUTHAUL n line or cable for tightening the foot of a sail
OUTHAULER same as > OUTHAUL
OUTHAULS > OUTHAUL

OUTHEAR vb exceed in hearing
OUTHEARD > OUTHEAR
OUTHEARS > OUTHEAR
OUTHER same as > OTHER
OUTHIRE vb hire out
OUTHIRED > OUTHIRE
OUTHIRES > OUTHIRE
OUTHIRING > OUTHIRE
OUTHIT vb hit something further than (someone else)
OUTHITS > OUTHIT
OUTHOMER vb score more home runs than
OUTHOMERS > OUTHOMER
OUTHOUSE n building near a main building
OUTHOUSES > OUTHOUSE
OUTHOWL vb exceed in howling
OUTHOWLED > OUTHOWL
OUTHOWLS > OUTHOWL
OUTHUMOR vb exceed in humouring
OUTHUMORS > OUTHUMOR
OUTHUNT vb exceed in hunting
OUTHUNTED > OUTHUNT
OUTHUNTS > OUTHUNT
OUTHUSTLE vb be more competitive than
OUTHYRE same as > OUTHIRE
OUTHYRED > OUTHYRE
OUTHYRES > OUTHYRE
OUTHYRING > OUTHYRE
OUTING n leisure trip
OUTINGS > OUTING
OUTJEST vb exceed in jesting
OUTJESTED > OUTJEST
OUTJESTS > OUTJEST
OUTJET n projecting part
OUTJETS > OUTJET
OUTJINX vb exceed in jinxing
OUTJINXED > OUTJINX
OUTJINXES > OUTJINX
OUTJOCKEY vb outwit by deception
OUTJUGGLE vb surpass at juggling
OUTJUMP vb jump higher or farther than
OUTJUMPED > OUTJUMP
OUTJUMPS > OUTJUMP
OUTJUT vb jut out ▷ n projecting part
OUTJUTS > OUTJUT
OUTJUTTED > OUTJUT
OUTKEEP vb beat or surpass at keeping
OUTKEEPS > OUTKEEP
OUTKEPT > OUTKEEP
OUTKICK vb exceed in kicking
OUTKICKED > OUTKICK
OUTKICKS > OUTKICK
OUTKILL vb exceed in killing
OUTKILLED > OUTKILL
OUTKILLS > OUTKILL
OUTKISS vb exceed in

kissing
OUTKISSED > OUTKISS
OUTKISSES > OUTKISS
OUTLAID > OUTLAY
OUTLAIN > OUTLAY
OUTLAND adj outlying or distant ▷ n outlying areas of a country or region
OUTLANDER n foreigner or stranger
OUTLANDS > OUTLAND
OUTLASH n sudden attack
OUTLASHES > OUTLASH
OUTLAST vb last longer than
OUTLASTED > OUTLAST
OUTLASTS > OUTLAST
OUTLAUGH vb laugh longer or louder than
OUTLAUGHS > OUTLAUGH
OUTLAUNCE same as > OUTLAUNCH
OUTLAUNCH vb send out
OUTLAW n criminal deprived of legal protection, bandit ▷ vb make illegal
OUTLAWED > OUTLAW
OUTLAWING > OUTLAW
OUTLAWRY n act of outlawing or the state of being outlawed
OUTLAWS > OUTLAW
OUTLAY n expenditure ▷ vb spend (money)
OUTLAYING > OUTLAY
OUTLAYS > OUTLAY
OUTLEAD vb be better leader than
OUTLEADS > OUTLEAD
OUTLEAP vb leap higher or farther than
OUTLEAPED > OUTLEAP
OUTLEAPT > OUTLEAP
OUTLEARN vb exceed in learning
OUTLEARNS > OUTLEARN
OUTLEARNT > OUTLEARN
OUTLED > OUTLEAD
OUTLER n farm animal kept out of doors
OUTLERS > OUTLER
OUTLET n means of expressing emotion
OUTLETS > OUTLET
OUTLIE vb lie outside a particular place
OUTLIED > OUTLIE
OUTLIER n outcrop of rocks that is entirely surrounded by older rocks
OUTLIERS > OUTLIER
OUTLIES > OUTLIE
OUTLINE n short general explanation ▷ vb summarize
OUTLINEAR > OUTLINE
OUTLINED > OUTLINE
OUTLINER > OUTLINE
OUTLINERS > OUTLINE
OUTLINES > OUTLINE
OUTLINING > OUTLINE
OUTLIVE vb live longer

than
OUTLIVED > OUTLIVE
OUTLIVER > OUTLIVE
OUTLIVERS > OUTLIVE
OUTLIVES > OUTLIVE
OUTLIVING > OUTLIVE
OUTLOOK n attitude ▷ vb look out
OUTLOOKED > OUTLOOK
OUTLOOKS > OUTLOOK
OUTLOVE vb exceed in loving
OUTLOVED > OUTLOVE
OUTLOVES > OUTLOVE
OUTLOVING > OUTLOVE
OUTLUSTRE vb outshine
OUTLYING adj distant from the main area
OUTMAN vb surpass in manpower
OUTMANNED > OUTMAN
OUTMANS > OUTMAN
OUTMANTLE vb be better dressed than
OUTMARCH vb exceed in marching
OUTMASTER vb surpass
OUTMATCH vb surpass or outdo (someone)
OUTMODE vb make unfashionable
OUTMODED adj no longer fashionable or accepted
OUTMODES > OUTMODE
OUTMODING > OUTMODE
OUTMOST another word for > OUTERMOST
OUTMOVE vb move faster or better than
OUTMOVED > OUTMOVE
OUTMOVES > OUTMOVE
OUTMOVING > OUTMOVE
OUTMUSCLE vb dominate by physical strength
OUTNAME vb be more notorious than
OUTNAMED > OUTNAME
OUTNAMES > OUTNAME
OUTNAMING > OUTNAME
OUTNESS n state or quality of being external
OUTNESSES > OUTNESS
OUTNIGHT vb refer to night more often than
OUTNIGHTS > OUTNIGHT
OUTNUMBER vb exceed in number
OUTOFFICE n outbuilding
OUTPACE vb go faster than (someone)
OUTPACED > OUTPACE
OUTPACES > OUTPACE
OUTPACING > OUTPACE
OUTPAINT vb exceed in painting
OUTPAINTS > OUTPAINT
OUTPART n remote region
OUTPARTS > OUTPART
OUTPASS vb exceed in passing
OUTPASSED > OUTPASS
OUTPASSES > OUTPASS
OUTPEEP vb peep out
OUTPEEPED > OUTPEEP

OUTPEEPS > OUTPEEP

OUTPEER vb surpass

OUTPEERED > OUTPEER

OUTPEERS > OUTPEER

OUTPEOPLE vb rid a country of its people

OUTPITCH vb exceed in pitching

OUTPITIED > OUTPITY

OUTPITIES > OUTPITY

OUTPITY vb exceed in pitying

OUTPLACE vb find job for ex-employee

OUTPLACED > OUTPLACE

OUTPLACER > OUTPLACE

OUTPLACES > OUTPLACE

OUTPLAN vb exceed in planning

OUTPLANS > OUTPLAN

OUTPLAY vb perform better than one's opponent in a sport or game

OUTPLAYED > OUTPLAY

OUTPLAYS > OUTPLAY

OUTPLOD vb exceed in plodding

OUTPLODS > OUTPLOD

OUTPLOT vb exceed in plotting

OUTPLOTS > OUTPLOT

OUTPOINT vb score more points than

OUTPOINTS > OUTPOINT

OUTPOLL vb win more votes than

OUTPOLLED > OUTPOLL

OUTPOLLS > OUTPOLL

OUTPORT n isolated fishing village, esp in Newfoundland

OUTPORTER n inhabitant or native of a Newfoundland outport

OUTPORTS > OUTPORT

OUTPOST n outlying settlement

OUTPOSTS > OUTPOST

OUTPOUR n act of flowing or pouring out ▷ vb pour or cause to pour out freely or rapidly

OUTPOURED > OUTPOUR

OUTPOURER > OUTPOUR

OUTPOURS > OUTPOUR

OUTPOWER vb have more power than

OUTPOWERS > OUTPOWER

OUTPRAY vb exceed in praying

OUTPRAYED > OUTPRAY

OUTPRAYS > OUTPRAY

OUTPREACH vb outdo in preaching

OUTPREEN vb exceed in preening

OUTPREENS > OUTPREEN

OUTPRESS vb exceed in pressing

OUTPRICE vb sell at better price than

OUTPRICED > OUTPRICE

OUTPRICES > OUTPRICE

OUTPRIZE vb prize more

OUTPRIZED > OUTPRIZE

OUTPRIZES > OUTPRIZE

OUTPULL vb exceed in pulling

OUTPULLED > OUTPULL

OUTPULLS > OUTPULL

OUTPUNCH vb punch better than

OUTPUPIL n student sent to a different school to the one he or she would normally attend

OUTPUPILS > OUTPUPIL

OUTPURSUE vb pursue farther than

OUTPUSH vb exceed in pushing

OUTPUSHED > OUTPUSH

OUTPUSHES > OUTPUSH

OUTPUT n amount produced ▷ vb produce (data) at the end of a process

OUTPUTS > OUTPUT

OUTPUTTED > OUTPUT

OUTQUOTE vb exceed in quoting

OUTQUOTED > OUTQUOTE

OUTQUOTES > OUTQUOTE

OUTRACE vb surpass in racing

OUTRACED > OUTRACE

OUTRACES > OUTRACE

OUTRACING > OUTRACE

OUTRAGE n great moral indignation ▷ vb offend morally

OUTRAGED > OUTRAGE

OUTRAGES > OUTRAGE

OUTRAGING > OUTRAGE

OUTRAISE vb raise more money than

OUTRAISED > OUTRAISE

OUTRAISES > OUTRAISE

OUTRAN > OUTRUN

OUTRANCE n furthest extreme

OUTRANCES > OUTRANCE

OUTRANG > OUTRING

OUTRANGE vb have a greater range than

OUTRANGED > OUTRANGE

OUTRANGES > OUTRANGE

OUTRANK vb be of higher rank than (someone)

OUTRANKED > OUTRANK

OUTRANKS > OUTRANK

OUTRATE vb offer better rate than

OUTRATED > OUTRATE

OUTRATES > OUTRATE

OUTRATING > OUTRATE

OUTRAVE vb outdo in raving

OUTRAVED > OUTRAVE

OUTRAVES > OUTRAVE

OUTRAVING > OUTRAVE

OUTRE adj shockingly eccentric

OUTREACH vb surpass in reach ▷ n act or process of reaching out

OUTREAD vb outdo in reading

OUTREADS > OUTREAD

OUTREASON vb surpass in reasoning

OUTRECKON vb surpass in reckoning

OUTRED vb be redder than

OUTREDDED > OUTRED

OUTREDDEN same as > OUTRED

OUTREDS > OUTRED

OUTREIGN vb reign for longer than

OUTREIGNS > OUTREIGN

OUTRELIEF n aid given outdoors

OUTREMER n land overseas

OUTREMERS > OUTREMER

OUTRIDDEN > OUTRIDE

OUTRIDE vb outdo by riding faster, farther, or better than ▷ n extra unstressed syllable within a metrical foot

OUTRIDER n motorcyclist acting as an escort

OUTRIDERS > OUTRIDER

OUTRIDES > OUTRIDE

OUTRIDING > OUTRIDE

OUTRIG vb supply with outfit

OUTRIGGED > OUTRIG

OUTRIGGER n stabilizing frame projecting from a boat

OUTRIGHT adv absolute(ly) ▷ adj complete

OUTRIGS > OUTRIG

OUTRING vb exceed in ringing

OUTRINGS > OUTRING

OUTRIVAL vb surpass

OUTRIVALS > OUTRIVAL

OUTRO n instrumental passage that concludes a piece of music

OUTROAR vb roar louder than

OUTROARED > OUTROAR

OUTROARS > OUTROAR

OUTROCK vb outdo in rocking

OUTROCKED > OUTROCK

OUTROCKS > OUTROCK

OUTRODE > OUTRIDE

OUTROLL vb exceed in rolling

OUTROLLED > OUTROLL

OUTROLLS > OUTROLL

OUTROOP n auction

OUTROOPER > OUTROOP

OUTROOPS > OUTROOP

OUTROOT vb root out

OUTROOTED > OUTROOT

OUTROOTS > OUTROOT

OUTROPE same as > OUTROOP

OUTROPER > OUTROPE

OUTROPERS > OUTROPE

OUTROPES > OUTROPE

OUTROS > OUTRO

OUTROW vb outdo in rowing

OUTROWED > OUTROW

OUTROWING > OUTROW

OUTROWS > OUTROW

OUTRUN vb run faster than

OUTRUNG > OUTRING

OUTRUNNER n attendant who runs in front of a carriage, etc

OUTRUNS > OUTRUN

OUTRUSH n flowing or rushing out ▷ vb rush out

OUTRUSHED > OUTRUSH

OUTRUSHES > OUTRUSH

OUTS > OUT

OUTSAID > OUTSAY

OUTSAIL vb sail better than

OUTSAILED > OUTSAIL

OUTSAILS > OUTSAIL

OUTSANG > OUTSING

OUTSAT > OUTSIT

OUTSAVOR vb exceed in savouring

OUTSAVORS > OUTSAVOR

OUTSAW > OUTSEE

OUTSAY vb say something out loud

OUTSAYING > OUTSAY

OUTSAYS > OUTSAY

OUTSCHEME vb outdo in scheming

OUTSCOLD vb outdo in scolding

OUTSCOLDS > OUTSCOLD

OUTSCOOP vb outdo in achieving scoops

OUTSCOOPS > OUTSCOOP

OUTSCORE vb score more than

OUTSCORED > OUTSCORE

OUTSCORES > OUTSCORE

OUTSCORN vb defy with scorn

OUTSCORNS > OUTSCORN

OUTSCREAM vb scream louder than

OUTSEE vb exceed in seeing

OUTSEEING > OUTSEE

OUTSEEN > OUTSEE

OUTSEES > OUTSEE

OUTSELL vb be sold in greater quantities than

OUTSELLS > OUTSELL

OUTSERT another word for > WRAPROUND

OUTSERTS > OUTSERT

OUTSERVE vb serve better at tennis than

OUTSERVED > OUTSERVE

OUTSERVES > OUTSERVE

OUTSET n beginning

OUTSETS > OUTSET

OUTSHAME vb greatly shame

OUTSHAMED > OUTSHAME

OUTSHAMES > OUTSHAME

OUTSHINE vb surpass (someone) in excellence

OUTSHINED > OUTSHINE

OUTSHINES > OUTSHINE

OUTSHONE > OUTSHINE

OUTSHOOT vb surpass or excel in shooting ▷ n thing that projects or shoots out

OUTSHOOTS > OUTSHOOT

OUTSHOT n projecting part

OUTSHOTS > OUTSHOT
OUTSHOUT vb shout louder than
OUTSHOUTS > OUTSHOUT
OUTSIDE adv indicating movement to or position on the exterior ▷ adj unlikely ▷ n external area or surface
OUTSIDER n person outside a specific group
OUTSIDERS > OUTSIDER
OUTSIDES > OUTSIDE
OUTSIGHT n power of seeing
OUTSIGHTS > OUTSIGHT
OUTSIN vb sin more than
OUTSING vb sing better or louder than
OUTSINGS > OUTSING
OUTSINNED > OUTSIN
OUTSINS > OUTSIN
OUTSIT vb sit longer than
OUTSITS > OUTSIT
OUTSIZE adj larger than normal ▷ n outsize garment
OUTSIZED same as > OUTSIZE
OUTSIZES > OUTSIZE
OUTSKATE vb skate better than
OUTSKATED > OUTSKATE
OUTSKATES > OUTSKATE
OUTSKIRT singular of > OUTSKIRTS
OUTSKIRTS npl outer areas, esp of a town
OUTSLEEP vb sleep longer than
OUTSLEEPS > OUTSLEEP
OUTSLEPT > OUTSLEEP
OUTSLICK vb outsmart
OUTSLICKS > OUTSLICK
OUTSMART vb outwit
OUTSMARTS > OUTSMART
OUTSMELL vb surpass in smelling
OUTSMELLS > OUTSMELL
OUTSMELT > OUTSMELL
OUTSMILE vb outdo in smiling
OUTSMILED > OUTSMILE
OUTSMILES > OUTSMILE
OUTSMOKE vb smoke more than
OUTSMOKED > OUTSMOKE
OUTSMOKES > OUTSMOKE
OUTSNORE vb outdo in snoring
OUTSNORED > OUTSNORE
OUTSNORES > OUTSNORE
OUTSOAR vb fly higher than
OUTSOARED > OUTSOAR
OUTSOARS > OUTSOAR
OUTSOLD > OUTSELL
OUTSOLE n outermost sole of a shoe
OUTSOLES > OUTSOLE
OUTSOURCE vb subcontract (work) to another company
OUTSPAN vb relax
OUTSPANS > OUTSPAN

OUTSPEAK vb speak better or louder than
OUTSPEAKS > OUTSPEAK
OUTSPED > OUTSPEED
OUTSPEED vb go faster than
OUTSPEEDS > OUTSPEED
OUTSPELL vb exceed at spelling
OUTSPELLS > OUTSPELL
OUTSPELT > OUTSPELL
OUTSPEND vb spend more than
OUTSPENDS > OUTSPEND
OUTSPENT > OUTSPEND
OUTSPOKE > OUTSPEAK
OUTSPOKEN adj tending to say what one thinks
OUTSPORT vb sport in excess of
OUTSPORTS > OUTSPORT
OUTSPRANG > OUTSPRING
OUTSPREAD adj spread or stretched out as far as possible ▷ vb spread out or cause to spread out ▷ n spreading out
OUTSPRING vb spring out
OUTSPRINT vb run faster than (someone)
OUTSPRUNG > OUTSPRING
OUTSTAND vb be outstanding or excel
OUTSTANDS > OUTSTAND
OUTSTARE vb stare longer than
OUTSTARED > OUTSTARE
OUTSTARES > OUTSTARE
OUTSTART vb jump out ▷ n outset
OUTSTARTS > OUTSTART
OUTSTATE vb surpass in stating
OUTSTATED > OUTSTATE
OUTSTATES > OUTSTATE
OUTSTAY vb overstay
OUTSTAYED > OUTSTAY
OUTSTAYS > OUTSTAY
OUTSTEER vb steer better than
OUTSTEERS > OUTSTEER
OUTSTEP vb step farther than
OUTSTEPS > OUTSTEP
OUTSTOOD > OUTSTAND
OUTSTRAIN vb strain too much
OUTSTRIDE vb surpass in striding
OUTSTRIKE vb exceed in striking
OUTSTRIP vb surpass
OUTSTRIPS > OUTSTRIP
OUTSTRIVE vb strive harder than
OUTSTRODE > OUTSTRIDE
OUTSTROKE n outward stroke
OUTSTROVE > OUTSTRIVE
OUTSTRUCK

> OUTSTRIKE
OUTSTUDY vb outdo in studying
OUTSTUNT vb outdo in performing stunts
OUTSTUNTS > OUTSTUNT
OUTSULK vb outdo in sulking
OUTSULKED > OUTSULK
OUTSULKS > OUTSULK
OUTSUM vb add up to more than
OUTSUMMED > OUTSUM
OUTSUMS > OUTSUM
OUTSUNG > OUTSING
OUTSWAM > OUTSWIM
OUTSWARE > OUTSWEAR
OUTSWEAR vb swear more than
OUTSWEARS > OUTSWEAR
OUTSWEEP n outward movement of arms in swimming breaststroke
OUTSWEEPS > OUTSWEEP
OUTSWELL vb exceed in swelling
OUTSWELLS > OUTSWELL
OUTSWEPT adj curving outwards
OUTSWIM vb outdo in swimming
OUTSWIMS > OUTSWIM
OUTSWING n (in cricket) movement of a ball from leg to off through the air
OUTSWINGS > OUTSWING
OUTSWORE > OUTSWEAR
OUTSWORN > OUTSWEAR
OUTSWUM > OUTSWIM
OUTSWUNG adj made to curve outwards
OUTTAKE n unreleased take from a recording session, film, or TV programme ▷ vb take out
OUTTAKEN > OUTTAKE
OUTTAKES > OUTTAKE
OUTTAKING > OUTTAKE
OUTTALK vb talk more, longer, or louder than (someone)
OUTTALKED > OUTTALK
OUTTALKS > OUTTALK
OUTTASK vb assign task to staff outside organization
OUTTASKED > OUTTASK
OUTTASKS > OUTTASK
OUTTELL vb make known
OUTTELLS > OUTTELL
OUTTHANK vb outdo in thanking
OUTTHANKS > OUTTHANK
OUTTHIEVE vb surpass in stealing
OUTTHINK vb outdo in thinking
OUTTHINKS > OUTTHINK
OUTTHREW > OUTTHROW
OUTTHROB vb outdo in throbbing
OUTTHROBS > OUTTHROB
OUTTHROW vb throw better than
OUTTHROWN > OUTTHROW

OUTTHROWS > OUTTHROW
OUTTHRUST vb extend outwards
OUTTOLD > OUTTELL
OUTTONGUE vb speak louder than
OUTTOOK > OUTTAKE
OUTTOP vb rise higher than
OUTTOPPED > OUTTOP
OUTTOPS > OUTTOP
OUTTOWER vb tower over
OUTTOWERS > OUTTOWER
OUTTRADE vb surpass in trading
OUTTRADED > OUTTRADE
OUTTRADES > OUTTRADE
OUTTRAVEL vb oudo in travelling
OUTTRICK vb outdo in trickery
OUTTRICKS > OUTTRICK
OUTTROT vb exceed at trotting
OUTTROTS > OUTTROT
OUTTRUMP vb count for more than
OUTTRUMPS > OUTTRUMP
OUTTURN same as > OUTPUT
OUTTURNS > OUTTURN
OUTVALUE vb surpass in value
OUTVALUED > OUTVALUE
OUTVALUES > OUTVALUE
OUTVAUNT vb outdo in boasting
OUTVAUNTS > OUTVAUNT
OUTVENOM vb surpass in venomousness
OUTVENOMS > OUTVENOM
OUTVIE vb outdo in competition
OUTVIED > OUTVIE
OUTVIES > OUTVIE
OUTVOICE vb surpass in noise
OUTVOICED > OUTVOICE
OUTVOICES > OUTVOICE
OUTVOTE vb defeat by getting more votes than
OUTVOTED > OUTVOTE
OUTVOTER > OUTVOTE
OUTVOTERS > OUTVOTE
OUTVOTES > OUTVOTE
OUTVOTING > OUTVOTE
OUTVYING > OUTVIE
OUTWAIT vb wait longer than
OUTWAITED > OUTWAIT
OUTWAITS > OUTWAIT
OUTWALK vb walk farther or longer than
OUTWALKED > OUTWALK
OUTWALKS > OUTWALK
OUTWAR vb surpass or exceed in warfare
OUTWARD same as > OUTWARDS
OUTWARDLY adv in outward appearance
OUTWARDS adv towards the outside
OUTWARRED > OUTWAR
OUTWARS > OUTWAR

OUTWASH n mass of gravel carried and deposited by the water derived from melting glaciers
OUTWASHES > OUTWASH
OUTWASTE vb outdo in wasting
OUTWASTED > OUTWASTE
OUTWASTES > OUTWASTE
OUTWATCH vb surpass in watching
OUTWEAR vb use up or destroy by wearing
OUTWEARS > OUTWEAR
OUTWEARY vb exhaust
OUTWEED vb root out
OUTWEEDED > OUTWEED
OUTWEEDS > OUTWEED
OUTWEEP vb outdo in weeping
OUTWEEPS > OUTWEEP
OUTWEIGH vb be more important, significant, or influential than
OUTWEIGHS > OUTWEIGH
OUTWELL vb pour out
OUTWELLED > OUTWELL
OUTWELLS > OUTWELL
OUTWENT > OUTGO
OUTWEPT > OUTWEEP
OUTWHIRL vb surpass at whirling
OUTWHIRLS > OUTWHIRL
OUTWICK vb move one curling stone by striking with another
OUTWICKED > OUTWICK
OUTWICKS > OUTWICK
OUTWILE vb surpass in cunning
OUTWILED > OUTWILE
OUTWILES > OUTWILE
OUTWILING > OUTWILE
OUTWILL vb demonstrate stronger will than
OUTWILLED > OUTWILL
OUTWILLS > OUTWILL
OUTWIN vb get out of
OUTWIND vb unwind
OUTWINDED > OUTWIND
OUTWINDS > OUTWIND
OUTWING vb surpass in flying
OUTWINGED > OUTWING
OUTWINGS > OUTWING
OUTWINS > OUTWIN
OUTWISH vb surpass in wishing
OUTWISHED > OUTWISH
OUTWISHES > OUTWISH
OUTWIT vb get the better of (someone) by cunning
OUTWITH prep outside
OUTWITS > OUTWIT
OUTWITTED > OUTWIT
OUTWON > OUTWIN
OUTWORE > OUTWEAR
OUTWORK n defences which lie outside main defensive works ▷ vb work better, harder, etc, than
OUTWORKED > OUTWORK
OUTWORKER > OUTWORK
OUTWORKS > OUTWORK

OUTWORN adj no longer in use
OUTWORTH vb be more valuable than
OUTWORTHS > OUTWORTH
OUTWOUND > OUTWIND
OUTWREST vb extort
OUTWRESTS > OUTWREST
OUTWRIT > OUTWRITE
OUTWRITE vb outdo in writing
OUTWRITES > OUTWRITE
OUTWROTE > OUTWRITE
OUTYELL vb outdo in yelling
OUTYELLED > OUTYELL
OUTYELLS > OUTYELL
OUTYELP vb outdo in yelping
OUTYELPED > OUTYELP
OUTYELPS > OUTYELP
OUTYIELD vb yield more than
OUTYIELDS > OUTYIELD
OUVERT adj open
OUVERTE feminine form of > OUVERT
OUVRAGE n work
OUVRAGES > OUVRAGE
OUVRIER n worker
OUVRIERE feminine form of > OUVRIER
OUVRIERES > OUVRIERE
OUVRIERS > OUVRIER
OUZEL n type of bird
OUZELS > OUZEL
OUZO n strong aniseed-flavoured spirit from Greece
OUZOS > OUZO
OVA > OVUM
OVAL adj egg-shaped ▷ n anything that is oval in shape
OVALBUMIN n albumin in egg whites
OVALITIES > OVAL
OVALITY > OVAL
OVALLY > OVAL
OVALNESS > OVAL
OVALS > OVAL
OVARIAL > OVARY
OVARIAN > OVARY
OVARIES > OVARY
OVARIOLE n tube in insect ovary
OVARIOLES > OVARIOLE
OVARIOUS adj of eggs
OVARITIS n inflammation of an ovary
OVARY n female egg-producing organ
OVATE adj shaped like an egg ▷ vb give ovation
OVATED > OVATE
OVATELY > OVATE
OVATES > OVATE
OVATING > OVATE
OVATION n enthusiastic round of applause
OVATIONAL > OVATION
OVATIONS > OVATION
OVATOR > OVATE
OVATORS > OVATE

OVEL n mourner, esp during the first seven days after a death
OVELS > OVEL
OVEN n heated compartment or container for cooking or for drying or firing ceramics ▷ vb cook in an oven
OVENABLE adj (of food) suitable for cooking in an oven
OVENBIRD n type of small brownish South American bird
OVENBIRDS > OVENBIRD
OVENED > OVEN
OVENING > OVEN
OVENLIKE > OVEN
OVENPROOF adj able to be used in an oven
OVENS > OVEN
OVENWARE n heat-resistant dishes in which food can be both cooked and served
OVENWARES > OVENWARE
OVENWOOD n pieces of wood for burning in an oven
OVENWOODS > OVENWOOD
OVER adv indicating position on the top of, amount greater than, etc ▷ adj finished ▷ n (in cricket) series of six balls bowled from one end ▷ vb jump over
OVERABLE adj too able
OVERACT vb act in an exaggerated way
OVERACTED > OVERACT
OVERACTS > OVERACT
OVERACUTE adj too acute
OVERAGE adj beyond a specified age ▷ n amount beyond given limit
OVERAGED adj very old
OVERAGES > OVERAGE
OVERALERT adj abnormally alert
OVERALL adv in total ▷ n coat-shaped protective garment ▷ adj from one end to the other
OVERALLED adj wearing overalls
OVERALLS > OVERALL
OVERAPT adj tending excessively
OVERARCH vb form an arch over
OVERARM adv with the arm above the shoulder ▷ adj bowled, thrown, or performed with the arm raised above the shoulder ▷ vb throw (a ball) overarm
OVERARMED > OVERARM
OVERARMS > OVERARM
OVERATE > OVEREAT
OVERAWE vb affect (someone) with an overpowering sense of awe
OVERAWED > OVERAWE

OVERAWES > OVERAWE
OVERAWING > OVERAWE
OVERBAKE vb bake too long
OVERBAKED > OVERBAKE
OVERBAKES > OVERBAKE
OVERBANK n sediment deposited on the flood plain of a river
OVERBANKS > OVERBANK
OVERBEAR vb dominate or overcome
OVERBEARS > OVERBEAR
OVERBEAT vb beat too much
OVERBEATS > OVERBEAT
OVERBED adj fitting over bed
OVERBET vb bet too much
OVERBETS > OVERBET
OVERBID vb bid for more tricks than one can expect to win ▷ n bid higher than someone else's bid
OVERBIDS > OVERBID
OVERBIG adj too big
OVERBILL vb charge too much money
OVERBILLS > OVERBILL
OVERBITE n extension of the upper front teeth over the lower front teeth when the mouth is closed
OVERBITES > OVERBITE
OVERBLEW > OVERBLOW
OVERBLOW vb blow into (a wind instrument) with greater force than normal
OVERBLOWN adj excessive
OVERBLOWS > OVERBLOW
OVERBOARD adv from a boat into the water
OVERBOIL vb boil too much
OVERBOILS > OVERBOIL
OVERBOLD adj too bold
OVERBOOK vb accept too many bookings
OVERBOOKS > OVERBOOK
OVERBOOT n protective boot worn over an ordinary boot or shoe
OVERBOOTS > OVERBOOT
OVERBORE > OVERBEAR
OVERBORN > OVERBEAR
OVERBORNE > OVERBEAR
OVERBOUND vb jump over
OVERBRAKE vb brake too much
OVERBRED adj produced by too much selective breeding
OVERBREED vb produce by too much selective breeding
OVERBRIEF adj too brief
OVERBRIM vb overflow
OVERBRIMS > OVERBRIM
OVERBROAD adj not specific enough
OVERBROW vb hang over
OVERBROWS > OVERBROW
OVERBUILD vb build over or on top of

OVERBUILT
> OVERBUILD
OVERBULK vb loom large over
OVERBULKS > OVERBULK
OVERBURN vb copy information onto CD
OVERBURNS > OVERBURN
OVERBURNT > OVERBURN
OVERBUSY adj too busy ▷ vb make too busy
OVERBUY vb buy too much or too many
OVERBUYS > OVERBUY
OVERBY adv Scots expression meaning over the road or across the way
OVERCALL n bid higher than the preceding one ▷ vb bid higher than (an opponent)
OVERCALLS > OVERCALL
OVERCAME > OVERCOME
OVERCARRY vb carry too far or too many
OVERCAST adj (of the sky) covered by clouds ▷ vb make or become overclouded or gloomy ▷ n covering, as of clouds or mist
OVERCASTS > OVERCAST
OVERCATCH vb overtake
OVERCHEAP adj too cheap
OVERCHECK n thin leather strap attached to a horse's bit to keep its head up
OVERCHILL vb make too cold
OVERCIVIL adj too civil
OVERCLAD adj wearing too many clothes
OVERCLAIM vb claim too much
OVERCLASS n dominant group in society
OVERCLEAN adj too clean
OVERCLEAR adj too clear
OVERCLOCK vb modify a computer to run at greater speeds than originally intended
OVERCLOSE adj too close
OVERCLOUD vb make or become covered with clouds
OVERCLOY vb weary with excess
OVERCLOYS > OVERCLOY
OVERCLUB vb (in golf) use a club which causes the shot to go too far
OVERCLUBS > OVERCLUB
OVERCOACH vb coach too much
OVERCOAT n heavy coat
OVERCOATS > OVERCOAT
OVERCOLD adj too cold
OVERCOLOR vb colour too highly
OVERCOME vb gain control over after an effort
OVERCOMER > OVERCOME
OVERCOMES > OVERCOME
OVERCOOK vb spoil food by

cooking it for too long
OVERCOOKS > OVERCOOK
OVERCOOL vb cool too much
OVERCOOLS > OVERCOOL
OVERCOUNT vb outnumber
OVERCOVER vb cover up
OVERCOY adj too modest
OVERCRAM vb fill too full
OVERCRAMS > OVERCRAM
OVERCRAW same as > OVERCROW
OVERCRAWS > OVERCRAW
OVERCROP vb exhaust (land) by excessive cultivation
OVERCROPS > OVERCROP
OVERCROW vb crow over
OVERCROWD vb fill with more people or things than is desirable
OVERCROWS > OVERCROW
OVERCURE vb take curing process too far
OVERCURED > OVERCURE
OVERCURES > OVERCURE
OVERCUT vb cut too much
OVERCUTS > OVERCUT
OVERDARE vb dare too much
OVERDARED > OVERDARE
OVERDARES > OVERDARE
OVERDATED adj outdated
OVERDEAR adj too dear
OVERDECK n upper deck
OVERDECKS > OVERDECK
OVERDID > OVERDO
OVERDIGHT adj covered up
OVERDO vb do to excess
OVERDOER > OVERDO
OVERDOERS > OVERDO
OVERDOES > OVERDO
OVERDOG n person or side in an advantageous position
OVERDOGS > OVERDOG
OVERDOING > OVERDO
OVERDONE > OVERDO
OVERDOSE n excessive dose of a drug ▷ vb take an overdose
OVERDOSED > OVERDOSE
OVERDOSES > OVERDOSE
OVERDRAFT n overdrawing
OVERDRANK > OVERDRINK
OVERDRAW vb withdraw more money than is in (one's bank account)
OVERDRAWN > OVERDRAW
OVERDRAWS > OVERDRAW
OVERDRESS vb dress (oneself or another) too elaborately or finely ▷ n dress that may be worn over a jumper, blouse, etc
OVERDREW > OVERDRAW
OVERDRIED > OVERDRY
OVERDRIES > OVERDRY
OVERDRINK vb drink too much alcohol

OVERDRIVE n very high gear in a motor vehicle
OVERDROVE > OVERDRIVE
OVERDRUNK > OVERDRINK
OVERDRY vb dry too much
OVERDUB vb add (new sounds) to a tape so that the old and the new sounds can be heard ▷ n sound or series of sounds added by this method
OVERDUBS > OVERDUB
OVERDUE adj still due after the time allowed
OVERDUST vb dust too much
OVERDUSTS > OVERDUST
OVERDYE vb dye (a fabric, yarn, etc) excessively
OVERDYED > OVERDYE
OVERDYER > OVERDYE
OVERDYERS > OVERDYE
OVERDYES > OVERDYE
OVEREAGER adj excessively eager or keen
OVEREASY adj too easy
OVEREAT vb eat more than is necessary or healthy
OVEREATEN > OVEREAT
OVEREATER > OVEREAT
OVEREATS > OVEREAT
OVERED > OVER
OVEREDIT vb edit too much
OVEREDITS > OVEREDIT
OVEREGG vb exaggerate absurdly
OVEREGGED > OVEREGG
OVEREGGS > OVEREGG
OVEREMOTE vb emote too much
OVEREXERT vb exhaust or injure (oneself) by doing too much
OVEREYE vb survey
OVEREYED > OVEREYE
OVEREYES > OVEREYE
OVEREYING > OVEREYE
OVERFALL n turbulent stretch of water caused by marine currents over an underwater ridge
OVERFALLS > OVERFALL
OVERFAR adv too far
OVERFAST adj too fast
OVERFAT adj too fat
OVERFAVOR vb favour too much
OVERFEAR vb fear too much
OVERFEARS > OVERFEAR
OVERFED > OVERFEED
OVERFEED vb give (a person, plant, or animal) more food than is necessary or healthy
OVERFEEDS > OVERFEED
OVERFELL > OVERFALL
OVERFILL vb put more into (something) than there is room for
OVERFILLS > OVERFILL

OVERFINE adj too fine
OVERFISH vb fish too much
OVERFIT adj too fit
OVERFLEW > OVERFLY
OVERFLIES > OVERFLY
OVERFLOOD vb flood excessively
OVERFLOW vb flow over ▷ n something that overflows
OVERFLOWN > OVERFLY
OVERFLOWS > OVERFLOW
OVERFLUSH adj too flush
OVERFLY vb fly over (a territory) or past (a point)
OVERFOCUS vb focus too much
OVERFOLD n fold in which one or both limbs have been inclined more than 90° from their original orientation
OVERFOLDS > OVERFOLD
OVERFOND adj excessively keen (on)
OVERFOUL adj too foul
OVERFRANK adj too frank
OVERFREE adj too forward
OVERFULL adj excessively full
OVERFUND vb supply with too much money
OVERFUNDS > OVERFUND
OVERFUSSY adj too fussy
OVERGALL vb make sore all over
OVERGALLS > OVERGALL
OVERGANG vb dominate
OVERGANGS > OVERGANG
OVERGAVE > OVERGIVE
OVERGEAR vb cause (a company) to have too high a proportion of loan stock
OVERGEARS > OVERGEAR
OVERGET vb overtake
OVERGETS > OVERGET
OVERGILD vb gild too much
OVERGILDS > OVERGILD
OVERGILT > OVERGILD
OVERGIRD vb gird too tightly
OVERGIRDS > OVERGIRD
OVERGIRT > OVERGIRD
OVERGIVE vb give up
OVERGIVEN > OVERGIVE
OVERGIVES > OVERGIVE
OVERGLAD adj too glad
OVERGLAZE adj (of decoration or colours) applied to porcelain above the glaze
OVERGLOOM vb make gloomy
OVERGO vb go beyond
OVERGOAD vb goad too much
OVERGOADS > OVERGOAD
OVERGOES > OVERGO
OVERGOING > OVERGO
OVERGONE > OVERGO
OVERGORGE vb overeat
OVERGOT > OVERGET
OVERGRADE vb grade too highly

OVERGRAIN vb apply grainy texture to

OVERGRASS vb grow grass on top of

OVERGRAZE vb graze (land) too intensively

OVERGREAT adj too great

OVERGREEN vb cover with vegetation

OVERGREW > OVERGROW

OVERGROW vb grow over or across (an area, path, lawn, etc)

OVERGROWN > OVERGROW

OVERGROWS > OVERGROW

OVERHAILE vb pull over

OVERHAIR n outer coat of animal

OVERHAIRS > OVERHAIR

OVERHALE same as > OVERHAILE

OVERHALED > OVERHALE

OVERHALES > OVERHALE

OVERHAND adj thrown or performed with the hand raised above the shoulder ▷ adv with the hand above the shoulder ▷ vb sew with the thread passing over two edges in one direction

OVERHANDS > OVERHAND

OVERHANG vb project beyond something ▷ n overhanging part

OVERHANGS > OVERHANG

OVERHAPPY adj too happy

OVERHARD adj too hard

OVERHASTE n excessive haste

OVERHASTY > OVERHASTE

OVERHATE vb hate too much

OVERHATED > OVERHATE

OVERHATES > OVERHATE

OVERHAUL vb examine and repair ▷ n examination and repair

OVERHAULS > OVERHAUL

OVERHEAD adj above one's head ▷ adv over or above head height ▷ n stroke in racket games played from above head height

OVERHEADS npl general cost of maintaining a business

OVERHEAP vb supply too much

OVERHEAPS > OVERHEAP

OVERHEAR vb hear (a speaker or remark) unintentionally

OVERHEARD > OVERHEAR

OVERHEARS > OVERHEAR

OVERHEAT vb make or become excessively hot ▷ n condition of being overheated

OVERHEATS > OVERHEAT

OVERHELD > OVERHOLD

OVERHENT vb overtake

OVERHENTS > OVERHENT

OVERHIGH adj too high

OVERHIT vb hit too strongly

OVERHITS > OVERHIT

OVERHOLD vb value too highly

OVERHOLDS > OVERHOLD

OVERHOLY adj too holy

OVERHONOR vb honour too highly

OVERHOPE vb hope too much

OVERHOPED > OVERHOPE

OVERHOPES > OVERHOPE

OVERHOT adj too hot

OVERHUNG > OVERHANG

OVERHUNT vb hunt too much

OVERHUNTS > OVERHUNT

OVERHYPE vb hype too much

OVERHYPED > OVERHYPE

OVERHYPES > OVERHYPE

OVERIDLE adj too idle

OVERING > OVER

OVERINKED adj printed using too much ink

OVERISSUE vb issue (shares, banknotes, etc) in excess of demand or ability to pay ▷ n shares, banknotes, etc, thus issued

OVERJOY vb give great delight to

OVERJOYED adj extremely pleased

OVERJOYS > OVERJOY

OVERJUMP vb jump too far

OVERJUMPS > OVERJUMP

OVERJUST adj too just

OVERKEEN adj too keen

OVERKEEP vb keep too long

OVERKEEPS > OVERKEEP

OVERKEPT > OVERKEEP

OVERKEST same as > OVERCAST

OVERKILL n treatment that is greater than required

OVERKILLS > OVERKILL

OVERKIND adj too kind

OVERKING n supreme king

OVERKINGS > OVERKING

OVERKNEE adj reaching to above knee

OVERLABOR vb spend too much work on

OVERLADE vb overburden

OVERLADED > OVERLADE

OVERLADEN > OVERLADE

OVERLADES > OVERLADE

OVERLAID > OVERLAY

OVERLAIN > OVERLIE

OVERLAND adv by land ▷ vb drive (cattle or sheep) overland

OVERLANDS > OVERLAND

OVERLAP vb share part of the same space or period of time (as) ▷ n area overlapping

OVERLAPS > OVERLAP

OVERLARD vb cover with lard

OVERLARDS > OVERLARD

OVERLARGE adj excessively large

OVERLATE adj too late

OVERLAX adj too lax

OVERLAY vb cover with a thin layer ▷ n something that is laid over something else

OVERLAYS > OVERLAY

OVERLEAF adv on the back of the current page

OVERLEAP vb leap too far

OVERLEAPS > OVERLEAP

OVERLEAPT > OVERLEAP

OVERLEARN vb study too intensely

OVERLEND vb lend too much

OVERLENDS > OVERLEND

OVERLENT > OVERLEND

OVERLET vb let to too many

OVERLETS > OVERLET

OVERLEWD adj too lewd

OVERLIE vb lie on or cover (something or someone)

OVERLIER > OVERLIE

OVERLIERS > OVERLIE

OVERLIES > OVERLIE

OVERLIGHT vb illuminate too brightly

OVERLIT > OVERLIGHT

OVERLIVE vb live longer than (another person)

OVERLIVED > OVERLIVE

OVERLIVES > OVERLIVE

OVERLOAD vb put too large a load on or in ▷ n excessive load

OVERLOADS > OVERLOAD

OVERLOCK vb sew fabric with interlocking stitch

OVERLOCKS > OVERLOCK

OVERLONG adj too or excessively long

OVERLOOK vb fail to notice ▷ n high place affording a view

OVERLOOKS > OVERLOOK

OVERLORD n supreme lord or master

OVERLORDS > OVERLORD

OVERLOUD adj too loud

OVERLOVE vb love too much

OVERLOVED > OVERLOVE

OVERLOVES > OVERLOVE

OVERLUSH adj too lush

OVERLUSTY adj too lusty

OVERLY adv excessively

OVERLYING > OVERLIE

OVERMAN vb provide with too many staff ▷ n man who oversees others

OVERMANS > OVERMAN

OVERMANY adj too many

OVERMAST vb provide mast that is too big

OVERMASTS > OVERMAST

OVERMATCH vb be more than a match for ▷ n person superior in ability

OVERMEEK adj too meek

OVERMELT vb melt too much

OVERMELTS > OVERMELT

OVERMEN > OVERMAN

OVERMERRY adj very merry

OVERMILD adj too mild

OVERMILK vb milk too much

OVERMILKS > OVERMILK

OVERMINE vb mine too much

OVERMINED > OVERMINE

OVERMINES > OVERMINE

OVERMIX vb mix too much

OVERMIXED > OVERMIX

OVERMIXES > OVERMIX

OVERMOUNT vb surmount

OVERMUCH adj too much ▷ n excessive amount

OVERNAME vb repeat (someone's) name

OVERNAMED > OVERNAME

OVERNAMES > OVERNAME

OVERNEAR adj too near

OVERNEAT adj too neat

OVERNET vb cover with net

OVERNETS > OVERNET

OVERNEW adj too new

OVERNICE adj too fastidious, precise, etc

OVERNIGHT adv (taking place) during one night ▷ adj done in, occurring in, or lasting the night ▷ vb stay the night

OVERPACK vb pack too much

OVERPACKS > OVERPACK

OVERPAGE same as > OVERLEAF

OVERPAID > OVERPAY

OVERPAINT vb apply too much paint

OVERPART vb give an actor too difficult a role

OVERPARTS > OVERPART

OVERPASS vb pass over, through, or across

OVERPAST > OVERPASS

OVERPAY vb pay (someone) at too high a rate

OVERPAYS > OVERPAY

OVERPEDAL vb use piano pedal too much

OVERPEER vb look down over

OVERPEERS > OVERPEER

OVERPERCH vb fly up to perch on

OVERPERT adj too insolent

OVERPITCH vb bowl (a cricket ball) so that it pitches too close to the stumps

OVERPLAID n plaid in double layer

OVERPLAN vb plan excessively

OVERPLANS > OVERPLAN

OVERPLANT vb plant more than is necessary

OVERPLAST adj put above

OVERPLAY same as
> OVERACT

OVERPLAYS > OVERPLAY

OVERPLIED > OVERPLY

OVERPLIES > OVERPLY

OVERPLOT vb plot onto
existing graph or map

OVERPLOTS > OVERPLOT

OVERPLUS n surplus or
excess quantity

OVERPLY vb ply too much

OVERPOISE vb weigh
more than

OVERPOST vb hurry over

OVERPOSTS > OVERPOST

OVERPOWER vb subdue or
overcome (someone)

OVERPRESS vb oppress

OVERPRICE vb put too
high a price on

OVERPRINT vb print
(additional matter) onto
(something already
printed) ▷ n additional
matter printed onto
something already printed

OVERPRIZE vb prize too
highly

OVERPROOF adj
containing more alcohol
than standard spirit

OVERPROUD adj too proud

OVERPUMP vb pump too
much

OVERPUMPS > OVERPUMP

OVERQUICK adj too quick

OVERRACK vb strain too
much

OVERRACKS > OVERRACK

OVERRAKE vb rake over

OVERRAKED > OVERRAKE

OVERRAKES > OVERRAKE

OVERRAN > OVERRUN

OVERRANK adj too rank

OVERRASH adj too rash

OVERRATE vb have too
high an opinion of

OVERRATED > OVERRATE

OVERRATES > OVERRATE

OVERREACH vb defeat or
thwart (oneself) by
attempting to do or gain
too much

OVERREACT vb react more
strongly than is necessary

OVERREAD vb read over

OVERREADS > OVERREAD

OVERRED vb paint over in
red

OVERREDS > OVERRED

OVERREN same as
> OVERRUN

OVERRENS > OVERREN

OVERRICH adj (of food)
excessively flavoursome or
fatty

OVERRIDE vb overrule ▷ n
device or system that can
override an automatic
control

OVERRIDER > OVERRIDE

OVERRIDES > OVERRIDE

OVERRIFE adj too rife

OVERRIGID adj too rigid

OVERRIPE adj (of a fruit or
vegetable) so ripe that it
has started to decay

OVERRIPEN vb become
overripe

OVERROAST vb roast too
long

OVERRODE > OVERRIDE

OVERRUDE adj very rude

OVERRUFF vb defeat
trump card by playing
higher trump

OVERRUFFS > OVERRUFF

OVERRULE vb reverse the
decision of (a person with
less power)

OVERRULED > OVERRULE

OVERRULER > OVERRULE

OVERRULES > OVERRULE

OVERRUN vb conquer
rapidly ▷ n act or an
instance of overrunning

OVERRUNS > OVERRUN

OVERS > OVER

OVERSAD adj too sad

OVERSAIL vb project
beyond

OVERSAILS > OVERSAIL

OVERSALE n selling of
more than is available

OVERSALES > OVERSALE

OVERSALT vb put too
much salt in

OVERSALTS > OVERSALT

OVERSAUCE vb put too
much sauce on

OVERSAVE vb put too
much money in savings

OVERSAVED > OVERSAVE

OVERSAVES > OVERSAVE

OVERSAW > OVERSEE

OVERSCALE adj at higher
scale than standard

OVERSCORE vb cancel by
drawing a line or lines over
or through

OVERSEA same as
> OVERSEAS

OVERSEAS adj to, of, or
from a distant country
▷ adv across the sea ▷ n
foreign country or foreign
countries collectively

OVERSEE vb watch over
from a position of authority

OVERSEED vb plant too
much seed in

OVERSEEDS > OVERSEED

OVERSEEN > OVERSEE

OVERSEER n person who
oversees others, esp
workmen

OVERSEERS > OVERSEER

OVERSEES > OVERSEE

OVERSELL vb exaggerate
the merits or abilities of

OVERSELLS > OVERSELL

OVERSET vb disturb or
upset

OVERSETS > OVERSET

OVERSEW vb sew (two
edges) with stitches that
pass over them both

OVERSEWED > OVERSEW

OVERSEWN > OVERSEW

OVERSEWS > OVERSEW

OVERSEXED adj more
interested in sex than is
thought decent

OVERSHADE vb appear
more important than

OVERSHARP adj too sharp

OVERSHINE vb shine
down on

OVERSHIRT n shirt worn
over lighter clothes

OVERSHOE n protective
shoe worn over an ordinary
shoe

OVERSHOES > OVERSHOE

OVERSHONE
> OVERSHINE

OVERSHOOT vb go beyond
(a mark or target) ▷ n act or
instance of overshooting

OVERSHOT adj (of a water
wheel) driven by a flow of
water that passes over the
wheel ▷ n type of fishing
rod

OVERSHOTS > OVERSHOT

OVERSICK adj too sick

OVERSIDE adv over the
side (of a ship) ▷ n top side

OVERSIDES > OVERSIDE

OVERSIGHT n mistake
caused by not noticing
something

OVERSIZE adj larger than
the usual size ▷ n size
larger than the usual or
proper size

OVERSIZED same as
> OVERSIZE

OVERSIZES > OVERSIZE

OVERSKIP vb skip over

OVERSKIPS > OVERSKIP

OVERSKIRT n outer skirt,
esp one that reveals a
decorative underskirt

OVERSLEEP vb sleep
beyond the intended time

OVERSLEPT
> OVERSLEEP

OVERSLIP vb slip past

OVERSLIPS > OVERSLIP

OVERSLIPT > OVERSLIP

OVERSLOW adj too slow

OVERSMAN n overseer

OVERSMEN > OVERSMAN

OVERSMOKE vb smoke
something too much

OVERSOAK vb soak too
much

OVERSOAKS
> OVERSOAK

OVERSOFT adj too soft

OVERSOLD > OVERSELL

OVERSOON adv too soon

OVERSOUL n universal
divine essence

OVERSOULS > OVERSOUL

OVERSOW vb sow again
after first sowing

OVERSOWED > OVERSOW

OVERSOWN > OVERSOW

OVERSOWS > OVERSOW

OVERSPEND vb spend
more than one can afford
▷ n amount by which

someone or something is
overspent

OVERSPENT
> OVERSPEND

OVERSPICE vb add too
much spice to

OVERSPILL n rehousing
of people from crowded
cities in smaller towns ▷ vb
overflow

OVERSPILT
> OVERSPILL

OVERSPIN n forward
spinning motion

OVERSPINS > OVERSPIN

OVERSTAFF vb provide an
excessive number of staff
for (a factory, hotel, etc)

OVERSTAIN vb stain too
much

OVERSTAND vb remain
longer than

OVERSTANK
> OVERSTINK

OVERSTARE vb outstare

OVERSTATE vb state too
strongly

OVERSTAY vb stay beyond
the limit or duration of

OVERSTAYS > OVERSTAY

OVERSTEER vb (of a
vehicle) to turn more
sharply than is desirable or
anticipated

OVERSTEP vb go beyond (a
certain limit)

OVERSTEPS > OVERSTEP

OVERSTINK vb exceed in
stinking

OVERSTIR vb stir too
much

OVERSTIRS > OVERSTIR

OVERSTOCK vb hold or
supply (a commodity) in
excess of requirements

OVERSTOOD
> OVERSTAND

OVERSTORY n highest
level of trees in a rainforest

OVERSTREW vb scatter
over

OVERSTUDY vb study too
much

OVERSTUFF vb force too
much into

OVERSTUNK
> OVERSTINK

OVERSUDS vb produce too
much lather

OVERSUP vb sup too much

OVERSUPS > OVERSUP

OVERSURE adj too sure

OVERSWAM > OVERSWIM

OVERSWAY vb overrule

OVERSWAYS > OVERSWAY

OVERSWEAR vb swear
again

OVERSWEET adj too sweet

OVERSWELL vb overflow

OVERSWIM vb swim across

OVERSWIMS > OVERSWIM

OVERSWING vb swing too
much or too far

OVERSWORE
> OVERSWEAR

OVERSWORN
> OVERSWEAR

OVERSWUM > OVERSWIM

OVERSWUNG
> OVERSWING

OVERT adj open, not hidden

OVERTAKE vb move past (a vehicle or person) travelling in the same direction

OVERTAKEN > OVERTAKE

OVERTAKES > OVERTAKE

OVERTALK vb talk over

OVERTALKS > OVERTALK

OVERTAME adj too tame

OVERTART adj too bitter

OVERTASK vb impose too heavy a task upon

OVERTASKS > OVERTASK

OVERTAX vb put too great a strain on

OVERTAXED > OVERTAX

OVERTAXES > OVERTAX

OVERTEACH vb teach too much

OVERTEEM vb be too full of something

OVERTEEMS > OVERTEEM

OVERTHICK adj too thick

OVERTHIN adj too thin

OVERTHINK vb give too much thought to

OVERTHREW
> OVERTHROW

OVERTHROW vb defeat and replace ▷ n downfall, destruction

OVERTIGHT adj too tight

OVERTIME adv in addition to one's normal working hours ▷ n work at a regular job done in addition to regular working hours ▷ vb exceed the required time for (a photographic exposure)

OVERTIMED > OVERTIME

OVERTIMER > OVERTIME

OVERTIMES > OVERTIME

OVERTIMID adj too timid

OVERTIP vb give too much money as a tip

OVERTIPS > OVERTIP

OVERTIRE vb make too tired

OVERTIRED > OVERTIRE

OVERTIRES > OVERTIRE

OVERTLY > OVERT

OVERTNESS > OVERT

OVERTOIL vb work too hard

OVERTOILS > OVERTOIL

OVERTONE n additional meaning

OVERTONES > OVERTONE

OVERTOOK > OVERTAKE

OVERTOP vb exceed in height

OVERTOPS > OVERTOP

OVERTOWER vb tower above

OVERTRADE vb (of an enterprise) to trade in excess of working capital

OVERTRAIN vb train too much

OVERTREAT vb give too much medical treatment to

OVERTRICK n trick by which a player exceeds his contract

OVERTRIM vb trim too much

OVERTRIMS > OVERTRIM

OVERTRIP vb tread lightly over

OVERTRIPS > OVERTRIP

OVERTRUMP vb (in cards) play a trump higher than (one previously played to the trick)

OVERTRUST vb trust too much

OVERTURE n orchestral introduction ▷ vb make or present an overture to

OVERTURED > OVERTURE

OVERTURES > OVERTURE

OVERTURN vb turn upside down ▷ n act of overturning or the state of being overturned

OVERTURNS > OVERTURN

OVERTYPE vb type over existing text

OVERTYPED > OVERTYPE

OVERTYPES > OVERTYPE

OVERURGE vb urge too strongly

OVERURGED > OVERURGE

OVERURGES > OVERURGE

OVERUSE vb use excessively ▷ n excessive use

OVERUSED > OVERUSE

OVERUSES > OVERUSE

OVERUSING > OVERUSE

OVERVALUE vb regard (someone or something) as much more important than is the case

OVERVEIL vb cover over

OVERVEILS > OVERVEIL

OVERVIEW n general survey

OVERVIEWS > OVERVIEW

OVERVIVID adj too vivid

OVERVOTE vb vote more times than is allowed

OVERVOTED > OVERVOTE

OVERVOTES > OVERVOTE

OVERWARM vb make too warm

OVERWARMS > OVERWARM

OVERWARY adj excessively wary

OVERWASH n act of washing over something

OVERWATCH vb watch over

OVERWATER vb give too much water to

OVERWEAK adj too weak

OVERWEAR vb wear out

OVERWEARS > OVERWEAR

OVERWEARY vb make too tired

OVERWEEN vb think too highly of

OVERWEENS > OVERWEEN

OVERWEIGH vb exceed in weight

OVERWENT > OVERGO

OVERWET vb make too wet

OVERWETS > OVERWET

OVERWHELM vb overpower, esp emotionally

OVERWIDE adj too wide

OVERWILY adj too crafty

OVERWIND vb wind (a watch) beyond the proper limit

OVERWINDS > OVERWIND

OVERWING vb fly above

OVERWINGS > OVERWING

OVERWISE adj too wise

OVERWORD n repeated word or phrase

OVERWORDS > OVERWORD

OVERWORE > OVERWEAR

OVERWORK vb work too much ▷ n excessive work

OVERWORKS > OVERWORK

OVERWORN > OVERWEAR

OVERWOUND > OVERWIND

OVERWRAP vb cover with a wrapping

OVERWRAPS > OVERWRAP

OVERWREST vb strain too much

OVERWRITE vb write (something) in an excessively ornate or prolix style

OVERWROTE
> OVERWRITE

OVERYEAR vb keep for later year

OVERYEARS > OVERYEAR

OVERZEAL n excess of zeal

OVERZEALS > OVERZEAL

OVIBOS n type of ox

OVIBOSES > OVIBOS

OVIBOVINE > OVIBOS

OVICIDAL > OVICIDE

OVICIDE n killing of sheep

OVICIDES > OVICIDE

OVIDUCAL > OVIDUCT

OVIDUCT n tube through which eggs are conveyed from the ovary

OVIDUCTAL > OVIDUCT

OVIDUCTS > OVIDUCT

OVIFEROUS adj carrying or producing eggs or ova

OVIFORM adj shaped like an egg

OVIGEROUS same as
> OVIFEROUS

OVINE adj of or like a sheep ▷ n member of sheep family

OVINES > OVINE

OVIPARA n all oviparous animals

OVIPARITY
> OVIPAROUS

OVIPAROUS adj producing eggs that hatch outside the body of the mother

OVIPOSIT vb (of insects and fishes) to deposit eggs through an ovipositor

OVIPOSITS > OVIPOSIT

OVIRAPTOR n egg-eating dinosaur

OVISAC n capsule or sac, such as an ootheca, in which egg cells are produced

OVISACS > OVISAC

OVIST n person believing ovum contains all subsequent generations

OVISTS > OVIST

OVOID adj egg-shaped ▷ n something that is ovoid

OVOIDAL adj ovoid ▷ n something that is ovoid

OVOIDALS > OVOIDAL

OVOIDS > OVOID

OVOLI > OVOLO

OVOLO n convex moulding having a cross section in the form of a quarter of a circle or ellipse

OVOLOS > OVOLO

OVONIC adj using particular electronic storage batteries

OVONICS n science of ovonic equipment

OVOTESTES
> OVOTESTIS

OVOTESTIS n reproductive organ of snails

OVULAR > OVULE

OVULARY > OVULE

OVULATE vb produce or release an egg cell from an ovary

OVULATED > OVULATE

OVULATES > OVULATE

OVULATING > OVULATE

OVULATION > OVULATE

OVULATORY > OVULATE

OVULE n plant part that contains the egg cell and becomes the seed after fertilization

OVULES > OVULE

OVUM n unfertilized egg cell

OW interj exclamation of pain

OWCHE same as > OUCH

OWCHES > OWCHE

OWE vb be obliged to pay (a sum of money) to (a person)

OWED > OWE

OWELTIES > OWELTY

OWELTY n equality, esp in financial transactions

OWER Scots word for > OVER

OWERBY adv over there

OWERLOUP n Scots word meaning encroachment

OWERLOUPS > OWERLOUP

OWES > OWE

OWING > OWE

OWL n night bird of prey ▷ vb act like an owl

OWLED > OWL

OWLER vb smuggler

OWLERIES > OWLERY

OWLERS > OWLER

OWLERY n place where owls live

OWLET n young or nestling owl

o

OWLETS > OWLET
OWLIER > OWLY
OWLIEST > OWLY
OWLING > OWL
OWLISH adj like an owl
OWLISHLY > OWLISH
OWLLIKE > OWL
OWLS > OWL
OWLY same as > OWLISH
OWN adj used to emphasize possession ▷ pron thing(s) belonging to a particular person ▷ vb possess
OWNABLE adj able to be owned
OWNED > OWN
OWNER n person who owns
OWNERLESS > OWNER
OWNERS > OWNER
OWNERSHIP n state or fact of being an owner
OWNING > OWN
OWNS > OWN
OWRE same as > OWER
OWRECOME n chorus of song
OWRECOMES > OWRECOME
OWRELAY Scots form of > OVERLAY
OWRELAYS > OWRELAY
OWRES > OWRE
OWREWORD variant of > OVERWORD
OWREWORDS > OWREWORD
OWRIE same as > OORIE
OWRIER > OWRIE
OWRIEST > OWRIE
OWSE Scots form of > OX
OWSEN Scots word for > OXEN
OWT dialect word for > ANYTHING
OWTS > OWT
OX n castrated bull
OXACILLIN n antibiotic drug
OXALATE n salt or ester of oxalic acid ▷ vb treat with oxalate
OXALATED > OXALATE
OXALATES > OXALATE
OXALATING > OXALATE
OXALIC as in oxalic acid poisonous acid found in many plants
OXALIS n type of plant
OXALISES > OXALIS
OXAZEPAM n drug used to relieve anxiety
OXAZEPAMS > OXAZEPAM
OXAZINE n type of chemical compound
OXAZINES > OXAZINE
OXBLOOD n dark reddish-brown colour ▷ adj of this colour
OXBLOODS > OXBLOOD
OXBOW n U-shaped piece of wood fitted around the neck of a harnessed ox and attached to the yoke
OXBOWS > OXBOW
OXCART n cart pulled by ox
OXCARTS > OXCART
OXEN > OX

OXER n high fence
OXERS > OXER
OXES > OX
OXEYE n daisy-like flower
OXEYES > OXEYE
OXFORD n type of stout laced shoe with a low heel
OXFORDS > OXFORD
OXGANG n old measure of farmland
OXGANGS > OXGANG
OXGATE same as > OXGANG
OXGATES > OXGATE
OXHEAD n head of an ox
OXHEADS > OXHEAD
OXHEART n heart-shaped cherry
OXHEARTS > OXHEART
OXHIDE n leather made from the hide of an ox
OXHIDES > OXHIDE
OXID same as > OXIDE
OXIDABLE adj able to undergo oxidation
OXIDANT n substance that acts or is used as an oxidizing agent
OXIDANTS > OXIDANT
OXIDASE n any of a group of enzymes that bring about biological oxidation
OXIDASES > OXIDASE
OXIDASIC > OXIDASE
OXIDATE another word for > OXIDIZE
OXIDATED > OXIDATE
OXIDATES > OXIDATE
OXIDATING > OXIDATE
OXIDATION n oxidizing
OXIDATIVE > OXIDATION
OXIDE n compound of oxygen and one other element
OXIDES > OXIDE
OXIDIC > OXIDE
OXIDISE same as > OXIDIZE
OXIDISED > OXIDISE
OXIDISER same as > OXIDIZER
OXIDISERS > OXIDISER
OXIDISES > OXIDISE
OXIDISING > OXIDISE
OXIDIZE vb combine chemically with oxygen, as in burning or rusting
OXIDIZED > OXIDIZE
OXIDIZER same as > OXIDANT
OXIDIZERS > OXIDIZER
OXIDIZES > OXIDIZE
OXIDIZING > OXIDIZE
OXIDS > OXID
OXIES > OXY
OXIM same as > OXIME
OXIME n type of chemical compound
OXIMES > OXIME
OXIMETER n instrument for measuring oxygen in blood
OXIMETERS > OXIMETER
OXIMETRY > OXIMETER

OXIMS > OXIM
OXLAND same as > OXGANG
OXLANDS > OXLAND
OXLIKE > OX
OXLIP n type of woodland plant with small drooping pale yellow flowers
OXLIPS > OXLIP
OXO as in oxo acid acid that contains oxygen
OXONIUM as in oxonium compound type of salt derived from an organic ether
OXONIUMS > OXONIUM
OXPECKER n type of African starling
OXPECKERS > OXPECKER
OXSLIP same as > OXLIP
OXSLIPS > OXSLIP
OXTAIL n tail of an ox, used in soups and stews
OXTAILS > OXTAIL
OXTER n armpit ▷ vb grip under arm
OXTERED > OXTER
OXTERING > OXTER
OXTERS > OXTER
OXTONGUE n type of plant
OXTONGUES > OXTONGUE
OXY > OXO
OXYACID n any acid that contains oxygen
OXYACIDS > OXYACID
OXYCODONE as in oxycodone hydrochloride opiate drug used as a painkiller
OXYGEN n gaseous element essential to life and combustion
OXYGENASE n enzyme
OXYGENATE vb add oxygen to
OXYGENIC > OXYGEN
OXYGENISE variant of > OXYGENIZE
OXYGENIZE vb add oxygen to
OXYGENOUS > OXYGEN
OXYGENS > OXYGEN
OXYMEL n mixture of vinegar and honey
OXYMELS > OXYMEL
OXYMORA > OXYMORON
OXYMORON n figure of speech that combines two apparently contradictory ideas
OXYMORONS > OXYMORON
OXYNTIC adj of or denoting stomach cells that secrete acid
OXYPHIL n type of cell found in glands
OXYPHILE same as > OXYPHIL
OXYPHILES > OXYPHILE
OXYPHILIC > OXYPHILE
OXYPHILS > OXYPHIL
OXYSALT n any salt of an oxyacid
OXYSALTS > OXYSALT
OXYSOME n group of molecules

OXYSOMES > OXYSOME
OXYTOCIC adj accelerating childbirth by stimulating uterine contractions ▷ n oxytocic drug or agent
OXYTOCICS > OXYTOCIC
OXYTOCIN n hormone that stimulates the ejection of milk in mammals
OXYTOCINS > OXYTOCIN
OXYTONE adj having an accent on the final syllable ▷ n oxytone word
OXYTONES > OXYTONE
OXYTONIC adj (of a word) having the stress or acute accent on the last syllable
OY n grandchild
OYE same as > OY
OYER n (in the 13th century) an assize
OYERS > OYER
OYES same as > OYEZ
OYESES > OYES
OYESSES > OYES
OYEZ interj shouted three times by a public crier calling for attention before a proclamation ▷ n such a cry
OYEZES > OYEZ
OYS > OY
OYSTER n edible shellfish ▷ vb dredge for, gather, or raise oysters
OYSTERED > OYSTER
OYSTERER n person fishing for oysters
OYSTERERS > OYSTERER
OYSTERING > OYSTER
OYSTERMAN n person who gathers, cultivates, or sells oysters
OYSTERMEN > OYSTERMAN
OYSTERS > OYSTER
OYSTRIGE archaic variant of > OSTRICH
OYSTRIGES > OYSTRIGE
OZAENA n inflammation of nasal mucous membrane
OZAENAS > OZAENA
OZALID n method of duplicating writing or illustrations
OZALIDS > OZALID
OZEKI n sumo wrestling champion
OZEKIS > OZEKI
OZOCERITE n brown or greyish wax
OZOKERITE same as > OZOCERITE
OZONATE vb add ozone to
OZONATED > OZONATE
OZONATES > OZONATE
OZONATING > OZONATE
OZONATION > OZONATE
OZONE n strong-smelling form of oxygen
OZONES > OZONE
OZONIC > OZONE
OZONIDE n type of

unstable explosive
compound
OZONIDES > OZONIDE
OZONISE *same as*
  > OZONIZE

OZONISED > OZONISE
OZONISER > OZONISE
OZONISERS > OZONISE
OZONISES > OZONISE
OZONISING > OZONISE

OZONIZE *vb* convert
  (oxygen) into ozone
OZONIZED > OZONIZE
OZONIZER > OZONIZE
OZONIZERS > OZONIZE

OZONIZES > OZONIZE
OZONIZING > OZONIZE
OZONOUS > OZONE
OZZIE *n* hospital
OZZIES > OZZIE

o

Pp

PA n (formerly) fortified Māori settlement

PAAL n stake driven into the ground

PAALS > PAAL

PAAN n leaf of the betel tree

PAANS > PAAN

PABLUM same as > PABULUM

PABLUMS > PABLUM

PABOUCHE n soft shoe

PABOUCHES > PABOUCHE

PABULAR > PABULUM

PABULOUS > PABULUM

PABULUM n food

PABULUMS > PABULUM

PAC n soft shoe

PACA n large burrowing hystricomorph rodent of Central and South America

PACABLE adj easily appeased

PACAS > PACA

PACATION n act of making peace

PACATIONS > PACATION

PACE n single step in walking ▷ vb walk up and down, esp in anxiety ▷ prep with due respect to: used to express polite disagreement

PACED > PACE

PACEMAKER n electronic device surgically implanted in a person with heart disease to regulate the heartbeat

PACEMAN n (in cricket) fast bowler

PACEMEN > PACEMAN

PACER n horse trained to move at a special gait, esp for racing

PACERS > PACER

PACES > PACE

PACEWAY n racecourse for trotting and pacing

PACEWAYS > PACEWAY

PACEY adj fast-moving, quick, lively

PACHA same as > PASHA

PACHADOM n rank of pacha

PACHADOMS > PACHADOM

PACHAK n fragrant roots of Asian plant

PACHAKS > PACHAK

PACHALIC n jurisdiction of pasha

PACHALICS > PACHALIC

PACHAS > PACHA

PACHINKO n Japanese game similar to pinball

PACHINKOS > PACHINKO

PACHISI n Indian game somewhat resembling backgammon, played on a cruciform board using six cowries as dice

PACHISIS > PACHISI

PACHOULI same as > PATCHOULI

PACHOULIS > PACHOULI

PACHUCO n young Mexican living in the US, esp one of low social status who belongs to a street gang

PACHUCOS > PACHUCO

PACHYDERM n thick-skinned animal such as an elephant

PACHYTENE n third stage of the prophase of meiosis during which the chromosomes become shorter and thicker and divide into chromatids

PACIER > PACY

PACIEST > PACY

PACIFIC adj tending to bring peace

PACIFICAE npl medieval letters of introduction from the Church

PACIFICAL > PACIFIC

PACIFIED > PACIFY

PACIFIER n baby's dummy

PACIFIERS > PACIFIER

PACIFIES > PACIFY

PACIFISM n belief that violence of any kind is unjustifiable and that one should not participate in war

PACIFISMS > PACIFISM

PACIFIST n person who refuses on principle to take part in war ▷ adj advocating, relating to, or characterized by pacifism

PACIFISTS > PACIFIST

PACIFY vb soothe, calm

PACIFYING > PACIFY

PACING > PACE

PACK vb put (clothes etc) together in a suitcase or bag ▷ n bag carried on a person's or animal's back

PACKABLE > PACK

PACKAGE same as > PACKET

PACKAGED > PACKAGE

PACKAGER n independent firm specializing in design and production, as of illustrated books or television programmes which are sold to publishers or television companies as finished products

PACKAGERS > PACKAGER

PACKAGES > PACKAGE

PACKAGING n box or wrapping in which a product is offered for sale

PACKBOARD n frame for carrying goods

PACKCLOTH n cloth used for packing

PACKED adj completely filled

PACKER n person or company whose business is to pack goods, esp food

PACKERS > PACKER

PACKET n small container (and contents) ▷ vb wrap up in a packet or as a packet

PACKETED > PACKET

PACKETING > PACKET

PACKETS > PACKET

PACKFONG n Chinese alloy

PACKFONGS > PACKFONG

PACKFRAME n light metal frame with shoulder straps, used for carrying heavy or awkward loads

PACKHORSE n horse used for carrying goods

PACKING n material, such as paper or plastic, used to protect packed goods

PACKINGS > PACKING

PACKLY > PACK

PACKMAN n person carrying pack

PACKMEN > PACKMAN

PACKMULE n mule used to carry burdens

PACKMULES > PACKMULE

PACKNESS > PACK

PACKS > PACK

PACKSACK n bag carried strapped on the back or shoulder

PACKSACKS > PACKSACK

PACKSHEET n cover for pack

PACKSTAFF n staff for supporting pack

PACKWAX n neck ligament

PACKWAXES > PACKWAX

PACKWAY n path for pack animals

PACKWAYS > PACKWAY

PACO n S American mammal

PACOS > PACO

PACS > PAC

PACT n formal agreement

PACTA > PACTUM

PACTION vb concur with

PACTIONAL > PACTION

PACTIONED > PACTION

PACTIONS > PACTION

PACTS > PACT

PACTUM n pact

PACY same as > PACEY

PAD n piece of soft material used for protection, support, absorption of liquid, etc ▷ vb protect or fill with soft material

PADANG n (in Malaysia) playing field

PADANGS > PADANG

PADAUK n tropical African or Asian leguminous tree with reddish wood

PADAUKS > PADAUK

PADDED > PAD

PADDER n highwayman who robs on foot

PADDERS > PADDER

PADDIES > PADDY

PADDING > PAD

PADDINGS > PAD

PADDLE n short oar with a broad blade at one or each end ▷ vb move (a canoe etc) with a paddle

PADDLED > PADDLE

PADDLER > PADDLE

PADDLERS > PADDLE

PADDLES > PADDLE

PADDLING > PADDLE

PADDLINGS > PADDLE

PADDOCK n small field or enclosure for horses ▷ vb place (a horse) in a paddock

PADDOCKED > PADDOCK

PADDOCKS > PADDOCK

PADDY n fit of temper

PADDYWACK vb spank or smack

PADELLA n type of candle

PADELLAS > PADELLA

PADEMELON n small Australian wallaby

PADERERO same as > PATERERO

PADEREROS > PADERERO

PADI same as > PADDY

PADIS > PADI
PADISHAH *n* Iranian ruler
PADISHAHS > PADISHAH
PADKOS *n* snacks and provisions for a journey
PADLE *another name for* > LUMPFISH
PADLES > PADLE
PADLOCK *n* detachable lock with a hinged hoop fastened over a ring on the object to be secured ▷ *vb* fasten (something) with a padlock
PADLOCKED > PADLOCK
PADLOCKS > PADLOCK
PADMA *n* type of lotus
PADMAS > PADMA
PADNAG *n* ambling horse
PADNAGS > PADNAG
PADOUK *same as* > PADAUK
PADOUKS > PADOUK
PADRE *n* chaplain to the armed forces
PADRES > PADRE
PADRI > PADRE
PADRONE *n* owner or proprietor of an inn, esp in Italy
PADRONES > PADRONE
PADRONI > PADRONE
PADRONISM *n* system of work controlled by a padrone
PADS > PAD
PADSAW *n* small narrow saw used for cutting curves
PADSAWS > PADSAW
PADSHAH *same as* > PADISHAH
PADSHAHS > PADSHAH
PADUASOY *n* rich strong silk fabric used for hangings, vestments, etc
PADUASOYS > PADUASOY
PADYMELON *same as* > PADEMELON
PAEAN *n* song of triumph or thanksgiving
PAEANISM > PAEAN
PAEANISMS > PAEAN
PAEANS > PAEAN
PAEDERAST *same as* > PEDERAST
PAEDEUTIC *adj* of or relating to the study of teaching
PAEDIATRY *n* branch of medical science concerned with children and their diseases
PAEDO *n* paedophile
PAEDOLOGY *n* study of the character, growth, and development of children
PAEDOS > PAEDO
PAELLA *n* Spanish dish of rice, chicken, shellfish, and vegetables
PAELLAS > PAELLA
PAENULA *n* ancient Roman cloak
PAENULAE > PAENULA
PAENULAS > PAENULA
PAEON *n* metrical foot of

four syllables, with one long one and three short ones in any order
PAEONIC > PAEON
PAEONICS > PAEON
PAEONIES > PAEONY
PAEONS > PAEON
PAEONY *same as* > PEONY
PAESAN *n* fellow countryman
PAESANI > PAESANO
PAESANO *n* Italian-American man
PAESANOS > PAESANO
PAESANS > PAESAN
PAGAN *adj* not belonging to one of the world's main religions ▷ *n* pagan person
PAGANDOM > PAGAN
PAGANDOMS > PAGAN
PAGANISE *same as* > PAGANIZE
PAGANISED > PAGANISE
PAGANISER > PAGANISE
PAGANISES > PAGANISE
PAGANISH > PAGAN
PAGANISM > PAGAN
PAGANISMS > PAGAN
PAGANIST > PAGAN
PAGANISTS > PAGAN
PAGANIZE *vb* become pagan, render pagan, or convert to paganism
PAGANIZED > PAGANIZE
PAGANIZER > PAGANIZE
PAGANIZES > PAGANIZE
PAGANS > PAGAN
PAGE *n* (one side of) sheet of paper forming a book etc ▷ *vb* summon (someone) by bleeper or loudspeaker, in order to pass on a message
PAGEANT *n* parade or display of people in costume, usu illustrating a scene from history
PAGEANTRY *n* spectacular display or ceremony
PAGEANTS > PAGEANT
PAGEBOY *n* hairstyle in which the hair is smooth and the same medium length with the ends curled under
PAGEBOYS > PAGEBOY
PAGED > PAGE
PAGEFUL *n* amount (of text, etc) that a page will hold
PAGEFULS > PAGEFUL
PAGEHOOD *n* state of being a page
PAGEHOODS > PAGEHOOD
PAGER *n* small electronic device, capable of receiving short messages
PAGERS > PAGER
PAGES > PAGE
PAGEVIEW *n* electronic page of information displayed at the request of a user
PAGEVIEWS > PAGEVIEW
PAGINAL *adj* page-for-

page
PAGINATE *vb* number the pages of (a book, manuscript, etc) in sequence
PAGINATED > PAGINATE
PAGINATES > PAGINATE
PAGING > PAGE
PAGINGS > PAGE
PAGLE *same as* > PAIGLE
PAGLES > PAGLE
PAGOD *n* oriental idol
PAGODA *n* pyramid-shaped Asian temple or tower
PAGODAS > PAGODA
PAGODS > PAGOD
PAGRI *n* type of turban
PAGRIS > PAGRI
PAGURIAN *n* type of decapod crustacean of the family which includes the hermit crabs
PAGURIANS > PAGURIAN
PAGURID *same as* > PAGURIAN
PAGURIDS > PAGURID
PAH *same as* > PA
PAHAUTEA *same as* > KAIKAWAKA
PAHAUTEAS > PAHAUTEA
PAHLAVI *n* Iranian coin
PAHLAVIS > PAHLAVI
PAHOEHOE *n* hardened lava
PAHOEHOES > PAHOEHOE
PAHS > PAH
PAID > PAY
PAIDEUTIC *same as* > PAEDEUTIC
PAIDLE *Scots variant of* > PADDLE
PAIDLES > PAIDLE
PAIGLE *n* cowslip
PAIGLES > PAIGLE
PAIK *vb* thump or whack
PAIKED > PAIK
PAIKING > PAIK
PAIKS > PAIK
PAIL *n* bucket
PAILFUL *same as* > PAIL
PAILFULS > PAILFUL
PAILLARD *n* thin slice of meat
PAILLARDS > PAILLARD
PAILLASSE *same as* > PALLIASSE
PAILLETTE *n* sequin or spangle sewn onto a costume
PAILLON *n* thin leaf of metal
PAILLONS > PAILLON
PAILS > PAIL
PAILSFUL > PAILFUL
PAIN *n* physical or mental suffering ▷ *vb* cause (someone) mental or physical suffering
PAINCH *Scots variant of* > PAUNCH
PAINCHES > PAINCH
PAINED *adj* having or suggesting pain or distress
PAINFUL *adj* causing pain

or distress
PAINFULLY > PAINFUL
PAINIM *n* heathen or pagan
PAINIMS > PAINIM
PAINING > PAIN
PAINLESS *adj* not causing pain or distress
PAINS *npl* care or trouble
PAINT *n* coloured substance, spread on a surface with a brush or roller ▷ *vb* colour or coat with paint
PAINTABLE > PAINT
PAINTBALL *n* game in which teams of players simulate a military skirmish, shooting each other with paint pellets
PAINTBOX *n* box containing a tray of dry watercolour paints
PAINTED > PAINT
PAINTER *n* rope at the front of a boat, for tying it up
PAINTERLY *adj* having qualities peculiar to painting, esp the depiction of shapes by means of solid masses of colour, rather than by lines
PAINTERS > PAINTER
PAINTIER > PAINT
PAINTIEST > PAINT
PAINTING *n* picture produced by using paint
PAINTINGS > PAINTING
PAINTRESS *n* female painter
PAINTS > PAINT
PAINTURE *n* art of painting
PAINTURES > PAINTURE
PAINTWORK *n* covering of paint on parts of a vehicle, building, etc
PAINTY > PAINT
PAIOCK *obsolete word for* > PEACOCK
PAIOCKE *obsolete word for* > PEACOCK
PAIOCKES > PAIOCKE
PAIOCKS > PAIOCK
PAIR *n* set of two things matched for use together ▷ *vb* group or be grouped in twos
PAIRE *obsolete spelling of* > PAIR
PAIRED > PAIR
PAIRER > PAIR
PAIRES > PAIRE
PAIREST > PAIR
PAIRIAL *variant of* > PRIAL
PAIRIALS > PAIRIAL
PAIRING > PAIR
PAIRINGS > PAIR
PAIRS > PAIR
PAIRWISE *adv* in pairs
PAIS *n* country
PAISA *n* monetary unit of Bangladesh, Bhutan, India,

Nepal, and Pakistan worth one hundredth of a rupee

PAISAN n fellow countryman

PAISANA n female peasant

PAISANAS > PAISANA

PAISANO n friend

PAISANOS > PAISANO

PAISANS > PAISAN

PAISAS > PAISA

PAISE > PAISA

PAISLEY n pattern of small curving shapes with intricate detailing, usually printed in bright colours

PAISLEYS > PAISLEY

PAITRICK Scots word for > PARTRIDGE

PAITRICKS > PAITRICK

PAJAMA same as > PYJAMA

PAJAMAED adj wearing pajamas

PAJAMAS > PAJAMA

PAJOCK obsolete word for > PEACOCK

PAJOCKE obsolete word for > PEACOCK

PAJOCKES > PAJOCKE

PAJOCKS > PAJOCK

PAKAHI n acid land that is unsuitable for cultivation

PAKAHIS > PAKAHI

PAKAPOO n Chinese lottery with betting slips marked with Chinese characters

PAKAPOOS > PAKAPOO

PAKEHA n person of European descent, as distinct from a Māori

PAKEHAS > PAKEHA

PAKFONG same as > PACKFONG

PAKFONGS > PAKFONG

PAKIHI n area of swampy infertile land

PAKIHIS > PAKIHI

PAKKA variant of > PUKKA

PAKOKO n small freshwater fish

PAKOKOS > PAKOKO

PAKORA n Indian dish consisting of pieces of vegetable, chicken, etc, dipped in a spiced batter and deep-fried

PAKORAS > PAKORA

PAKTHONG n white alloy containing copper, zinc, and nickel

PAKTHONGS > PAKTHONG

PAKTONG same as > PAKTHONG

PAKTONGS > PAKTONG

PAL n friend ▷ vb associate as friends

PALABRA n word

PALABRAS > PALABRA

PALACE n residence of a king, bishop, etc

PALACED adj having palaces

PALACES > PALACE

PALADIN n knight who did battle for a monarch

PALADINS > PALADIN

PALAESTRA n (in ancient Greece or Rome) public place devoted to the training of athletes

PALAFITTE n prehistoric dwelling

PALAGI n (in Samoa) European

PALAGIS > PALAGI

PALAIS n dance hall

PALAMA n webbing on bird's feet

PALAMAE > PALAMA

PALAMATE > PALAMA

PALAMINO same as > PALOMINO

PALAMINOS > PALAMINO

PALAMPORE same as > PALEMPORE

PALANKEEN same as > PALANQUIN

PALANQUIN n (formerly, in the Orient) covered bed in which someone could be carried on the shoulders of four men

PALAPA n open-sided tropical building

PALAPAS > PALAPA

PALAS n East Indian tree

PALASES > PALAS

PALATABLE adj pleasant to taste

PALATABLY > PALATABLE

PALATAL adj of or relating to the palate ▷ n bony plate that forms the palate

PALATALLY > PALATAL

PALATALS > PALATAL

PALATE n roof of the mouth ▷ vb perceive by taste

PALATED > PALATE

PALATES > PALATE

PALATIAL adj like a palace, magnificent

PALATINE same as > PALATAL

PALATINES > PALATINE

PALATING > PALATE

PALAVER n time-wasting fuss ▷ vb (often used humorously) have a conference

PALAVERED > PALAVER

PALAVERER > PALAVER

PALAVERS > PALAVER

PALAY n type of rubber

PALAYS > PALAY

PALAZZI > PALAZZO

PALAZZO n Italian palace

PALAZZOS > PALAZZO

PALE adj light, whitish ▷ vb become pale ▷ n wooden or metal post used in fences

PALEA n inner of two bracts surrounding each floret in a grass spikelet

PALEAE > PALEA

PALEAL > PALEA

PALEATE adj having scales

PALEBUCK n small African antelope

PALEBUCKS > PALEBUCK

PALED > PALE

PALEFACE n offensive term for a White person, said to have been used by Native Americans of N America

PALEFACES > PALEFACE

PALELY > PALE

PALEMPORE n bed covering

PALENESS > PALE

PALEOCENE adj belonging to geological time period

PALEOGENE adj of early geological time period

PALEOLITH n Stone Age artefact

PALEOLOGY n study of prehistory

PALEOSOL n ancient soil horizon

PALEOSOLS > PALEOSOL

PALEOZOIC adj belonging to geological time period

PALER > PALE

PALES > PALE

PALEST > PALE

PALESTRA same as > PALAESTRA

PALESTRAE > PALESTRA

PALESTRAL > PALESTRA

PALESTRAS > PALESTRA

PALET n perpendicular band on escutcheon

PALETOT n loose outer garment

PALETOTS > PALETOT

PALETS > PALET

PALETTE n artist's flat board for mixing colours on

PALETTES > PALETTE

PALEWAYS same as > PALEWISE

PALEWISE adv by perpendicular lines

PALFREY n light saddle horse, esp ridden by women

PALFREYED > PALFREY

PALFREYS > PALFREY

PALIER > PALY

PALIEST > PALY

PALIFORM adj resembling coral

PALIKAR n Greek soldier in the war of independence against Turkey

PALIKARS > PALIKAR

PALILALIA n speech disorder in which a word or phrase is rapidly repeated

PALILLOGY n repetition of word or phrase

PALIMONY n alimony awarded to a nonmarried partner after the break-up of a long-term relationship

PALING n wooden or metal post used in fences

PALINGS > PALING

PALINKA n type of apricot brandy, originating in Central and Eastern Europe

PALINKAS > PALINKA

PALINODE n poem in which the poet recants something he has said in a former poem

PALINODES > PALINODE

PALINODY > PALINODE

PALINOPIA n visual disorder in which the patient perceives a prolonged afterimage

PALISADE n fence made of wooden posts driven into the ground ▷ vb enclose with a palisade

PALISADED > PALISADE

PALISADES > PALISADE

PALISADO same as > PALISADE

PALISH adj rather pale

PALKEE n covered Oriental litter

PALKEES > PALKEE

PALKI same as > PALKEE

PALKIS > PALKI

PALL n cloth spread over a coffin ▷ vb become boring

PALLA n ancient Roman cloak

PALLADIA > PALLADIUM

PALLADIC adj of or containing palladium in the trivalent or tetravalent state

PALLADIUM n silvery-white element of the platinum metal group

PALLADOUS adj of or containing palladium in the divalent state

PALLAE > PALLA

PALLAH n S African antelope

PALLAHS > PALLAH

PALLED > PALL

PALLET same as > PALETTE

PALLETED > PALLET

PALLETING > PALLET

PALLETISE same as > PALLETIZE

PALLETIZE vb stack or transport on a pallet or pallets

PALLETS > PALLET

PALLETTE n armpit plate of a suit of armour

PALLETTES > PALLETTE

PALLIA > PALLIUM

PALLIAL adj relating to cerebral cortex

PALLIARD n person who begs

PALLIARDS > PALLIARD

PALLIASSE n straw-filled mattress

PALLIATE vb lessen the severity of (something) without curing it

PALLIATED > PALLIATE

PALLIATES > PALLIATE

PALLIATOR > PALLIATE

PALLID adj pale, esp because ill or weak

PALLIDER > PALLID

PALLIDEST > PALLID

PALLIDITY > PALLID
PALLIDLY > PALLID
PALLIED > PALLY
PALLIER > PALLY
PALLIES > PALLY
PALLIEST > PALLY
PALLING > PALL
PALLIUM n garment worn by men in ancient Greece or Rome, made by draping a large rectangular cloth about the body
PALLIUMS > PALLIUM
PALLONE n Italian ball game
PALLONES > PALLONE
PALLOR n paleness of complexion, usually because of illness, shock, or fear
PALLORS > PALLOR
PALLS > PALL
PALLY adj on friendly terms ▷ vb as in pally up to become friends with
PALLYING > PALLY
PALM n inner surface of the hand ▷ vb conceal in or about the hand, as in sleight-of-hand tricks
PALMAR adj of or relating to the palm of the hand
PALMARIAN adj pre-eminent
PALMARY adj worthy of praise
PALMATE adj shaped like an open hand
PALMATED same as > PALMATE
PALMATELY > PALMATE
PALMATION n state of being palmate
PALMED > PALM
PALMER n (in Medieval Europe) pilgrim bearing a palm branch as a sign of his visit to the Holy Land
PALMERS > PALMER
PALMETTE n ornament or design resembling the palm leaf
PALMETTES > PALMETTE
PALMETTO n small palm tree with fan-shaped leaves
PALMETTOS > PALMETTO
PALMFUL n amount that can be held in the palm of a hand
PALMFULS > PALMFUL
PALMHOUSE n greenhouse for palms, etc
PALMIE n palmtop computer
PALMIER > PALMY
PALMIES > PALMIE
PALMIEST > PALMY
PALMIET n South African rush
PALMIETS > PALMIET
PALMING > PALM
PALMIPED n web-footed bird
PALMIPEDE same as > PALMIPED

PALMIPEDS > PALMIPED
PALMIST > PALMISTRY
PALMISTER n person telling fortunes by reading palms
PALMISTRY n fortune-telling from lines on the palm of the hand
PALMISTS > PALMISTRY
PALMITATE n any salt or ester of palmitic acid
PALMITIC as in palmitic acid white crystalline solid that is a saturated fatty acid
PALMITIN n colourless glyceride of palmitic acid
PALMITINS > PALMITIN
PALMLIKE > PALM
PALMS > PALM
PALMTOP adj small enough to be held in the hand ▷ n computer small enough to be held in the hand
PALMTOPS > PALMTOP
PALMY adj successful, prosperous and happy
PALMYRA n tall tropical Asian palm
PALMYRAS > PALMYRA
PALOLO n polychaete worm of the S Pacific Ocean
PALOLOS > PALOLO
PALOMINO n gold-coloured horse with a white mane and tail
PALOMINOS > PALOMINO
PALOOKA n stupid or clumsy boxer or other person
PALOOKAS > PALOOKA
PALOVERDE n thorny American shrub
PALP n either of a pair of sensory appendages that arise from the mouthparts of crustaceans and insects ▷ vb feel
PALPABLE adj obvious
PALPABLY > PALPABLE
PALPAL > PALP
PALPATE vb examine (an area of the body) by touching ▷ adj of, relating to, or possessing a palp or palps
PALPATED > PALPATE
PALPATES > PALPATE
PALPATING > PALPATE
PALPATION > PALPATE
PALPATOR n type of beetle
PALPATORS > PALPATOR
PALPATORY > PALPATE
PALPEBRA n eyelid
PALPEBRAE > PALPEBRA
PALPEBRAL adj of or relating to the eyelid
PALPEBRAS > PALPEBRA
PALPED > PALP
PALPI > PALPUS
PALPING > PALP
PALPITANT > PALPITATE
PALPITATE vb (of the heart) beat rapidly

PALPS > PALP
PALPUS same as > PALP
PALS > PAL
PALSGRAVE n German count palatine
PALSHIP n state of being pals
PALSHIPS > PALSHIP
PALSIED > PALSY
PALSIER > PALSY
PALSIES > PALSY
PALSIEST > PALSY
PALSTAFF variant of > PALSTAVE
PALSTAFFS > PALSTAFF
PALSTAVE n kind of celt, usually of bronze, made to fit into a split wooden handle rather than having a socket for the handle
PALSTAVES > PALSTAVE
PALSY n paralysis ▷ vb paralyse ▷ adj friendly
PALSYING > PALSY
PALSYLIKE > PALSY
PALTER vb act or talk insincerely
PALTERED > PALTER
PALTERER > PALTER
PALTERERS > PALTER
PALTERING > PALTER
PALTERS > PALTER
PALTRIER > PALTRY
PALTRIEST > PALTRY
PALTRILY > PALTRY
PALTRY adj insignificant
PALUDAL adj of, relating to, or produced by marshes
PALUDIC adj of malaria
PALUDINAL adj inhabiting swamps
PALUDINE adj relating to marsh
PALUDISM rare word for > MALARIA
PALUDISMS > PALUDISM
PALUDOSE adj growing or living in marshes
PALUDOUS adj marshy
PALUSTRAL adj marshy
PALY adj vertically striped
PAM n knave of clubs
PAMPA n grassland area
PAMPAS npl vast grassy plains in S America
PAMPASES > PAMPAS
PAMPEAN > PAMPAS
PAMPEANS > PAMPAS
PAMPER vb treat (someone) with great indulgence, spoil
PAMPERED > PAMPER
PAMPERER > PAMPER
PAMPERERS > PAMPER
PAMPERING > PAMPER
PAMPERO n dry cold wind in South America blowing across the pampas from the south or southwest
PAMPEROS > PAMPERO
PAMPERS > PAMPER
PAMPHLET n thin paper-covered booklet
PAMPHLETS > PAMPHLET

PAMPHREY n cabbage
PAMPHREYS > PAMPHREY
PAMPOEN n pumpkin
PAMPOENS > PAMPOEN
PAMPOOTIE n rawhide slipper worn by men in the Aran Islands
PAMS > PAM
PAN n wide long-handled metal container used in cooking ▷ vb sift gravel from (a river) in a pan to search for gold
PANACEA n remedy for all diseases or problems
PANACEAN > PANACEA
PANACEAS > PANACEA
PANACHAEA variant of > PANACEA
PANACHE n confident elegant style
PANACHES > PANACHE
PANADA n mixture of flour, water, etc, or of breadcrumbs soaked in milk, used as a thickening
PANADAS > PANADA
PANAMA n hat made of the plaited leaves of the jipijapa plant
PANAMAS > PANAMA
PANARIES > PANARY
PANARY n storehouse for bread
PANATELA same as > PANATELLA
PANATELAS > PANATELA
PANATELLA n long slender cigar
PANAX n genus of perennial herbs
PANAXES > PANAX
PANBROIL vb broil in a pan
PANBROILS > PANBROIL
PANCAKE n thin flat circle of fried batter ▷ vb cause (an aircraft) to make a pancake landing or (of an aircraft) to make a pancake landing
PANCAKED > PANCAKE
PANCAKES > PANCAKE
PANCAKING > PANCAKE
PANCE n pansy
PANCES > PANCE
PANCETTA n lightly spiced cured bacon from Italy
PANCETTAS > PANCETTA
PANCHAX n brightly coloured tropical Asian cyprinodont fish
PANCHAXES > PANCHAX
PANCHAYAT n village council in India
PANCHEON n shallow bowl
PANCHEONS > PANCHEON
PANCHION same as > PANCHEON
PANCHIONS > PANCHION
PANCOSMIC adj of every cosmos
PANCRATIA n wrestling and boxing contests
PANCRATIC > PANCRATIA

PANCREAS *n* large gland behind the stomach that produces insulin and helps digestion

PAND *n* valance

PANDA *n* large black-and-white bearlike mammal from China

PANDANI *n* tropical tree

PANDANUS *n* Old World tropical palmlike plant

PANDAR *vb* act as a pimp

PANDARED > PANDAR

PANDARING > PANDAR

PANDARS > PANDAR

PANDAS > PANDA

PANDATION *n* warping

PANDECT *n* treatise covering all aspects of a particular subject

PANDECTS > PANDECT

PANDEMIA *n* epidemic affecting everyone

PANDEMIAN *adj* sensual

PANDEMIAS > PANDEMIA

PANDEMIC *adj* (of a disease) occurring over a wide area ▷ *n* pandemic disease

PANDEMICS > PANDEMIC

PANDER *vb* indulge (a person his or her desires) ▷ *n* person who procures a sexual partner for someone

PANDERED > PANDER

PANDERER *n* person who procures a sexual partner for someone

PANDERERS > PANDERER

PANDERESS *n* female panderer

PANDERING > PANDER

PANDERISM > PANDER

PANDERLY > PANDER

PANDEROUS > PANDER

PANDERS > PANDER

PANDIED > PANDY

PANDIES > PANDY

PANDIT *same as* > PUNDIT

PANDITS > PANDIT

PANDOOR *same as* > PANDOUR

PANDOORS > PANDOOR

PANDORA *n* handsome red sea bream

PANDORAS > PANDORA

PANDORE *another word for* > BANDORE

PANDORES > PANDORE

PANDOUR *n* one of an 18th-century force of Croatian soldiers in the Austrian service, notorious for their brutality

PANDOURS > PANDOUR

PANDOWDY *n* deep-dish pie made from fruit, esp apples, with a cake topping

PANDS > PAND

PANDURA *n* ancient stringed instrument

PANDURAS > PANDURA

PANDURATE *adj* (of plant leaves) shaped like the body of a fiddle

PANDY *n* (in schools) stroke on the hand with a strap as a punishment ▷ *vb* punish with such strokes

PANDYING > PANDY

PANE *n* sheet of glass in a window or door ▷ *adj* (of fish, meat, etc) dipped or rolled in breadcrumbs before cooking

PANED > PANE

PANEER *n* soft white cheese, used in Indian cookery

PANEERS > PANEER

PANEGOISM *n* form of scepticism

PANEGYRIC *n* formal speech or piece of writing in praise of someone or something

PANEGYRY *n* panegyric

PANEITIES > PANEITY

PANEITY *n* state of being bread

PANEL *n* flat distinct section of a larger surface, for example in a door ▷ *vb* cover or decorate with panels ▷ *adj* of a group acting as a panel

PANELED > PANEL

PANELESS > PANE

PANELING *same as* > PANELLING

PANELINGS > PANELING

PANELISED *same as* > PANELIZED

PANELIST *same as* > PANELLIST

PANELISTS > PANELIST

PANELIZED *adj* made in sections for quick assembly

PANELLED > PANEL

PANELLING *n* panels collectively, esp on a wall

PANELLIST *n* member of a panel

PANELS > PANEL

PANES > PANE

PANETELA *same as* > PANATELA

PANETELAS > PANETELA

PANETELLA *n* long thin cigar

PANETTONE *n* kind of Italian spiced brioche containing sultanas

PANETTONI > PANETTONE

PANFISH *n* small food fish

PANFISHES > PANFISH

PANFRIED > PANFRY

PANFRIES > PANFRY

PANFRY *vb* fry in a pan

PANFRYING > PANFRY

PANFUL > PAN

PANFULS > PAN

PANG *n* sudden sharp feeling of pain or sadness ▷ *vb* cause pain

PANGA *n* broad heavy knife of E Africa, used as a tool or weapon

PANGAMIC > PANGAMY

PANGAMIES > PANGAMY

PANGAMY *n* unrestricted mating

PANGAS > PANGA

PANGED > PANG

PANGEN *same as* > PANGENE

PANGENE *n* hypothetical particle of protoplasm

PANGENES > PANGENE

PANGENS > PANGEN

PANGING > PANG

PANGLESS *adj* without pangs

PANGOLIN *n* animal of tropical countries with a scaly body and a long snout for eating ants and termites

PANGOLINS > PANGOLIN

PANGRAM *n* sentence incorporating all the letters of the alphabet

PANGRAMS > PANGRAM

PANGS > PANG

PANHANDLE *n* (in the US) narrow strip of land that projects from one state into another ▷ *vb* accost and beg from (passers-by), esp on the street

PANHUMAN *adj* relating to all humanity

PANIC *n* sudden overwhelming fear, often affecting a whole group of people ▷ *vb* feel or cause to feel panic ▷ *adj* of or resulting from such terror

PANICALLY > PANIC

PANICK *old word for* > PANIC

PANICKED > PANIC

PANICKIER > PANIC

PANICKING > PANIC

PANICKS > PANICK

PANICKY > PANIC

PANICLE *n* loose, irregularly branched cluster of flowers

PANICLED > PANICLE

PANICLES > PANICLE

PANICS > PANIC

PANICUM *n* type of grass

PANICUMS > PANICUM

PANIER *same as* > PANNIER

PANIERS > PANIER

PANIM *n* heathen or pagan

PANIMS > PANIM

PANING > PANE

PANINI > PANINO

PANINIS > PANINO

PANINO *n* Italian sandwich

PANISC *n* faun; attendant of Pan

PANISCS > PANISC

PANISK *same as* > PANISC

PANISKS > PANISK

PANJANDRA *n* pompous self-important officials of people of rank

PANKO *n* flaky breadcrumbs used as a coating in Japanese cookery

PANKOS > PANKO

PANLOGISM *n* metaphysics of Leibniz

PANMICTIC > PANMIXIA

PANMIXES > PANMIXIA

PANMIXIA *n* (in population genetics) random mating within an interbreeding population

PANMIXIAS > PANMIXIA

PANMIXIS *same as* > PANMIXIA

PANNAGE *n* pasturage for pigs, esp in a forest

PANNAGES > PANNAGE

PANNE *n* lightweight velvet fabric

PANNED > PAN

PANNELLED *adj* divided into panels

PANNER > PAN

PANNERS > PAN

PANNES > PANNE

PANNICK *old spelling of the noun* > PANIC

PANNICKS > PANNICK

PANNICLE *n* thin layer of body tissue

PANNICLES > PANNICLE

PANNIER *n* bag fixed on the back of a cycle

PANNIERED > PANNIER

PANNIERS > PANNIER

PANNIKEL *n* skull

PANNIKELL *same as* > PANNIKEL

PANNIKELS > PANNIKEL

PANNIKIN *n* small metal cup or pan

PANNIKINS > PANNIKIN

PANNING > PAN

PANNINGS > PAN

PANNOSE *adj* like felt

PANNUS *n* inflammatory fleshy lesion on the surface of the eye

PANNUSES > PANNUS

PANOCHA *n* coarse grade of sugar made in Mexico

PANOCHAS > PANOCHA

PANOCHE *n* type of dark sugar

PANOCHES > PANOCHE

PANOISTIC *adj* producing ova

PANOPLIED > PANOPLY

PANOPLIES > PANOPLY

PANOPLY *n* magnificent array

PANOPTIC *adj* taking in all parts, aspects, etc, in a single view

PANORAMA *n* wide unbroken view of a scene

PANORAMAS > PANORAMA

PANORAMIC > PANORAMA

PANPIPE *n* wind instrument

PANPIPES > PANPIPE

PANS > PAN

PANSEXUAL *n* person open to any sexual activity

PANSIED *adj* covered with pansies

PANSIES > PANSY

PANSOPHIC > PANSOPHY

PANSOPHY n universal knowledge

PANSPERMY n 19th-century evolutionary theory

PANSTICK n type of cosmetic in stick form

PANSTICKS > PANSTICK

PANSY n small garden flower with velvety purple, yellow, or white petals

PANT vb breathe quickly and noisily during or after exertion ▷ n act of panting

PANTABLE n soft shoe

PANTABLES > PANTABLE

PANTAGAMY n marriage to everyone

PANTALEON n percussion instrument

PANTALET same as > PANTALETS

PANTALETS npl long drawers, usually trimmed with ruffles, extending below the skirts

PANTALON n keyboard instrument

PANTALONE n Italian comic character

PANTALONS > PANTALON

PANTALOON n (in pantomime) absurd old man, the butt of the clown's tricks

PANTDRESS n dress with divided skirt

PANTED > PANT

PANTER n person who pants

PANTERS > PANTER

PANTHEISM n belief that God is present in everything

PANTHEIST > PANTHEISM

PANTHENOL n pantothenyl alcohol

PANTHEON n (in ancient Greece and Rome) temple built to honour all the gods

PANTHEONS > PANTHEON

PANTHER n leopard, esp a black one

PANTHERS > PANTHER

PANTIE same as > PANTY

PANTIES npl women's underpants

PANTIHOSE same as > PANTYHOSE

PANTILE n roofing tile with an S-shaped cross section ▷ vb tile roof with pantiles

PANTILED > PANTILE

PANTILES > PANTILE

PANTILING > PANTILE

PANTINE n pasteboard puppet

PANTINES > PANTINE

PANTING > PANT

PANTINGLY > PANT

PANTINGS > PANT

PANTLER n pantry servant

PANTLERS > PANTLER

PANTO same as > PANTOMIME

PANTOFFLE same as > PANTOFLE

PANTOFLE n kind of slipper

PANTOFLES > PANTOFLE

PANTOMIME n play based on a fairy tale, performed at Christmas time

PANTON n type of horseshoe

PANTONS > PANTON

PANTOS > PANTO

PANTOUFLE same as > PANTOFLE

PANTOUM n verse form

PANTOUMS > PANTOUM

PANTRIES > PANTRY

PANTROPIC adj found throughout tropics

PANTRY n small room or cupboard for storing food

PANTRYMAN n pantry servant

PANTRYMEN > PANTRYMAN

PANTS npl undergarment for the lower part of the body

PANTSUIT n woman's suit of a jacket or top and trousers

PANTSUITS > PANTSUIT

PANTUN n Malayan poetry

PANTUNS > PANTUN

PANTY n woman's undergarment

PANTYHOSE npl women's tights

PANZER n German tank

PANZERS > PANZER

PANZOOTIC n disease that affects all the animals in a geographical area

PAOLI > PAOLO

PAOLO n Italian silver coin

PAP n soft food for babies or invalids ▷ vb (of the paparazzi) to follow and photograph (a famous person) ▷ vb feed with pap

PAPA n father

PAPABLE adj suitable for papacy

PAPACIES > PAPACY

PAPACY n position or term of office of a pope

PAPADAM variant of > POPPADOM

PAPADAMS > PAPADAM

PAPADOM variant of > POPPADOM

PAPADOMS > PAPADOM

PAPADUM variant of > POPPADOM

PAPADUMS > PAPADUM

PAPAIN n proteolytic enzyme occurring in the unripe fruit of the papaya tree

PAPAINS > PAPAIN

PAPAL adj of the pope

PAPALISE same as > PAPALIZE

PAPALISED > PAPALISE

PAPALISES > PAPALISE

PAPALISM n papal system

PAPALISMS > PAPALISM

PAPALIST n supporter of a pope

PAPALISTS > PAPALIST

PAPALIZE vb make papal

PAPALIZED > PAPALIZE

PAPALIZES > PAPALIZE

PAPALLY > PAPAL

PAPARAZZI > PAPARAZZO

PAPARAZZO n photographer specializing in candid photographs of famous people

PAPAS > PAPA

PAPAUMA n New Zealand word for broadleaf

PAPAUMAS > PAPAUMA

PAPAW same as > PAPAYA

PAPAWS > PAPAW

PAPAYA n large sweet West Indian fruit

PAPAYAN > PAPAYA

PAPAYAS > PAPAYA

PAPE n spiritual father

PAPER n material made in sheets from wood pulp or other fibres ▷ vb cover (walls) with wallpaper

PAPERBACK n book with covers made of flexible card ▷ adj of a paperback or publication of paperbacks ▷ vb publish in paperback

PAPERBARK n Australian tree of swampy regions, with spear-shaped leaves and papery bark

PAPERBOY n boy employed to deliver newspapers to people's homes

PAPERBOYS > PAPERBOY

PAPERCLIP n bent wire clip for holding sheets of paper together

PAPERED > PAPER

PAPERER > PAPER

PAPERERS > PAPER

PAPERGIRL n girl employed to deliver newspapers to people's homes

PAPERIER > PAPERY

PAPERIEST > PAPERY

PAPERING > PAPER

PAPERINGS > PAPER

PAPERLESS adj of, relating to, or denoting a means of communication, record keeping, etc, esp electronic, that does not use paper

PAPERS > PAPER

PAPERWARE n printed matter

PAPERWORK n clerical work, such as writing reports and letters

PAPERY adj like paper, esp in thinness, flimsiness, or dryness

PAPES > PAPE

PAPETERIE n box or case for papers and other writing materials

PAPHIAN n prostitute

PAPHIANS > PAPHIAN

PAPILIO n butterfly

PAPILIOS > PAPILIO

PAPILLA n small projection of tissue at the base of a hair, tooth, or feather

PAPILLAE > PAPILLA

PAPILLAR > PAPILLA

PAPILLARY > PAPILLA

PAPILLATE > PAPILLA

PAPILLOMA n benign tumour derived from epithelial tissue and forming a rounded or lobulated mass

PAPILLON n breed of toy spaniel with large ears

PAPILLONS > PAPILLON

PAPILLOSE > PAPILLA

PAPILLOTE n paper frill around cutlets, etc

PAPILLOUS > PAPILLA

PAPILLULE n tubercle

PAPISH n Catholic

PAPISHER n derogatory term for a Roman Catholic

PAPISHERS > PAPISHER

PAPISHES > PAPISH

PAPISM n derogatory term for Roman Catholicism

PAPISMS > PAPISM

PAPIST n derogatory term for a Roman Catholic

PAPISTIC > PAPIST

PAPISTRY > PAPIST

PAPISTS > PAPIST

PAPOOSE n Native American child

PAPOOSES > PAPOOSE

PAPPADAM same as > POPPADOM

PAPPADAMS > PAPPADAM

PAPPADOM same as > POPPADOM

PAPPADOMS > PAPPADOM

PAPPED > PAP

PAPPI > PAPPUS

PAPPIER > PAPPY

PAPPIES > PAPPY

PAPPIEST > PAPPY

PAPPING > PAP

PAPPOOSE same as > PAPOOSE

PAPPOOSES > PAPPOOSE

PAPPOSE > PAPPUS

PAPPOUS > PAPPUS

PAPPUS n ring of fine feathery hairs surrounding the fruit in composite plants, such as the thistle

PAPPUSES > PAPPUS

PAPPY adj resembling pap

PAPRICA same as > PAPRIKA

PAPRICAS > PAPRICA

PAPRIKA n mild powdered seasoning made from red peppers

PAPRIKAS > PAPRIKA

PAPS > PAP
PAPULA same as > PAPULE
PAPULAE > PAPULA
PAPULAR > PAPULE
PAPULE n small solid usually round elevation of the skin
PAPULES > PAPULE
PAPULOSE > PAPULE
PAPULOUS > PAPULE
PAPYRAL > PAPYRUS
PAPYRI > PAPYRUS
PAPYRIAN > PAPYRUS
PAPYRINE > PAPYRUS
PAPYRUS n tall water plant
PAPYRUSES > PAPYRUS
PAR n usual or average condition ▷ vb play (a golf hole) in par
PARA n paratrooper
PARABASES > PARABASIS
PARABASIS n (in classical Greek comedy) address from the chorus to the audience
PARABEMA n architectural feature
PARABEN n carcinogenic ester
PARABENS > PARABEN
PARABLAST n yolk of an egg, such as a hen's egg, that undergoes meroblastic cleavage
PARABLE n story that illustrates a religious teaching ▷ vb write parable
PARABLED > PARABLE
PARABLES > PARABLE
PARABLING > PARABLE
PARABOLA n regular curve resembling the course of an object thrown forward and up
PARABOLAS > PARABOLA
PARABOLE n similitude
PARABOLES > PARABOLE
PARABOLIC adj of, relating to, or shaped like a parabola
PARABRAKE n parachute attached to the rear of a vehicle and opened to assist braking
PARACHOR n quantity constant over range of temperatures
PARACHORS > PARACHOR
PARACHUTE n large fabric canopy that slows the descent of a person or object from an aircraft ▷ vb land or drop by parachute
PARACLETE n mediator or advocate
PARACME n phase where fever lessens
PARACMES > PARACME
PARACRINE adj of signalling between biological cells
PARACUSES > PARACUSIS
PARACUSIS n hearing

disorder
PARADE n procession or march ▷ vb display or flaunt
PARADED > PARADE
PARADER > PARADE
PARADES > PARADE
PARADIGM n example or model
PARADIGMS > PARADIGM
PARADING > PARADE
PARADISAL adj of, relating to, or resembling paradise
PARADISE n heaven
PARADISES > PARADISE
PARADISIC > PARADISE
PARADOR n state-run hotel in Spain
PARADORES > PARADOR
PARADORS > PARADOR
PARADOS n bank behind a trench or other fortification, giving protection from being fired on from the rear
PARADOSES > PARADOS
PARADOX n person or thing made up of contradictory elements
PARADOXAL adj paradoxical
PARADOXER n proposer of paradox
PARADOXES > PARADOX
PARADOXY n state of being paradoxical
PARADROP n delivery of personnel or equipment from an aircraft by parachute
PARADROPS > PARADROP
PARAE n type of fish
PARAFFIN n liquid mixture distilled from petroleum and used as a fuel or solvent ▷ vb treat with paraffin or paraffin wax
PARAFFINE same as > PARAFFIN
PARAFFINS > PARAFFIN
PARAFFINY adj like paraffin
PARAFFLE n extravagant display
PARAFFLES > PARAFFLE
PARAFLE same as > PARAFFLE
PARAFLES > PARAFLE
PARAFOIL n airfoil used on a paraglider
PARAFOILS > PARAFOIL
PARAFORM n paraformaldehyde
PARAFORMS > PARAFORM
PARAGE n type of feudal land tenure
PARAGES > PARAGE
PARAGLIDE vb glide through the air on a special parachute
PARAGOGE n addition of a sound or a syllable to the end of a word, such as st in

amongst
PARAGOGES > PARAGOGE
PARAGOGIC > PARAGOGE
PARAGOGUE same as > PARAGOGE
PARAGON n model of perfection ▷ vb equal or surpass
PARAGONED > PARAGON
PARAGONS > PARAGON
PARAGRAM n pun
PARAGRAMS > PARAGRAM
PARAGRAPH n section of a piece of writing starting on a new line ▷ vb put (a piece of writing) into paragraphs
PARAKEET n small long-tailed parrot
PARAKEETS > PARAKEET
PARAKELIA n succulent herb with purple flowers that thrives in inland Australia
PARAKITE n series of linked kites
PARAKITES > PARAKITE
PARALALIA n any of various speech disorders, esp the production of a sound different from that intended
PARALEGAL n person trained to assist lawyers but not qualified to practise law ▷ adj of or designating such a person
PARALEXIA n disorder of the ability to read in which words and syllables are meaninglessly transposed
PARALEXIC > PARALEXIA
PARALLAX n apparent change in an object's position due to a change in the observer's position
PARALLEL adj separated by an equal distance at every point ▷ n line separated from another by an equal distance at every point ▷ vb correspond to
PARALLELS > PARALLEL
PARALOGIA n self-deception
PARALOGUE n either of a pair of genes derived from the same ancestral gene
PARALOGY n anatomical similarity
PARALYSE vb affect with paralysis
PARALYSED > PARALYSE
PARALYSER > PARALYSE
PARALYSES > PARALYSIS
PARALYSIS n inability to move or feel, because of damage to the nervous system
PARALYTIC adj affected with paralysis ▷ n person who is paralysed
PARALYZE same as > PARALYSE

PARALYZED > PARALYZE
PARALYZER > PARALYSE
PARALYZES > PARALYZE
PARAMATTA n lightweight twill-weave fabric of wool with silk or cotton
PARAMECIA n freshwater protozoans
PARAMEDIC n person working in support of the medical profession ▷ adj of or designating such a person
PARAMENT n ecclesiastical vestment or decorative hanging
PARAMENTA > PARAMENT
PARAMENTS > PARAMENT
PARAMESE n note in ancient Greek music
PARAMESES > PARAMESE
PARAMETER n limiting factor, boundary
PARAMO n high plateau in the Andes between the tree line and the permanent snow line
PARAMORPH n mineral that has undergone paramorphism
PARAMOS > PARAMO
PARAMOUNT adj of the greatest importance ▷ n supreme ruler
PARAMOUR n lover, esp of a person married to someone else
PARAMOURS > PARAMOUR
PARAMYLUM n starch-like substance
PARANETE n note in ancient Greek music
PARANETES > PARANETE
PARANG n short stout straight-edged knife used by the Dyaks of Borneo
PARANGS > PARANG
PARANOEA same as > PARANOIA
PARANOEAS > PARANOEA
PARANOEIC same as > PARANOIAC
PARANOIA n mental illness causing delusions of grandeur or persecution
PARANOIAC > PARANOIA
PARANOIAS > PARANOIA
PARANOIC > PARANOIA
PARANOICS > PARANOIA
PARANOID adj of, characterized by, or resembling paranoia ▷ n person who shows the behaviour patterns associated with paranoia
PARANOIDS > PARANOID
PARANYM n euphemism
PARANYMPH n bridesmaid or best man
PARANYMS > PARANYM
PARAPARA n small carnivorous New Zealand tree
PARAPARAS > PARAPARA
PARAPENTE n sport of

jumping off high mountains wearing skis and a light parachute

PARAPET n low wall or railing along the edge of a balcony or roof ▷ vb provide with a parapet

PARAPETED > PARAPET

PARAPETS > PARAPET

PARAPH n flourish after a signature, originally to prevent forgery ▷ vb embellish signature

PARAPHED > PARAPH

PARAPHING > PARAPH

PARAPHS > PARAPH

PARAPODIA n paired unjointed lateral appendages of polychaete worms

PARAQUAT n yellow extremely poisonous soluble solid used in solution as a weedkiller

PARAQUATS > PARAQUAT

PARAQUET n long-tailed parrot

PARAQUETS > PARAQUET

PARAQUITO n parakeet

PARARHYME n type of rhyme

PARAS > PARA

PARASAIL vb glide through air on parachute towed by boat

PARASAILS > PARASAIL

PARASANG n Persian unit of distance equal to about 5.5 km or 3.4 miles

PARASANGS > PARASANG

PARASCEVE n preparation

PARASHAH n section of the Torah read in the synagogue

PARASHAHS > PARASHAH

PARASHOT > PARASHAH

PARASHOTH > PARASHAH

PARASITE n animal or plant living in or on another

PARASITES > PARASITE

PARASITIC > PARASITE

PARASOL n umbrella-like sunshade

PARASOLED adj having a parasol

PARASOLS > PARASOL

PARATAXES > PARATAXIS

PARATAXIS n juxtaposition of clauses in a sentence without the use of a conjunction

PARATHA n (in Indian cookery) flat unleavened bread, resembling a small nan bread, that is fried on a griddle

PARATHAS > PARATHA

PARATHION n slightly water-soluble toxic oil, odourless and colourless when pure, used as an insecticide

PARATONIC adj (of a plant movement) occurring in

response to an external stimulus

PARATROOP n paratrooper

PARAVAIL adj lowest

PARAVANE n torpedo-shaped device towed from the bow of a vessel so that the cables will cut the anchors of any moored mines

PARAVANES > PARAVANE

PARAVANT adv in front

PARAVAUNT same as > PARAVANT

PARAWING n paraglider

PARAWINGS > PARAWING

PARAXIAL adj (of a light ray) parallel to the axis of an optical system

PARAZOA > PARAZOAN

PARAZOAN n sea sponge

PARAZOANS > PARAZOAN

PARAZOON n parasitic animal

PARBAKE vb partially bake

PARBAKED > PARBAKE

PARBAKES > PARBAKE

PARBAKING > PARBAKE

PARBOIL vb boil until partly cooked

PARBOILED > PARBOIL

PARBOILS > PARBOIL

PARBREAK vb vomit

PARBREAKS > PARBREAK

PARBUCKLE n rope sling for lifting or lowering a heavy cylindrical object, such as a cask or tree trunk ▷ vb raise or lower (an object) with such a sling

PARCEL n something wrapped up, package ▷ vb wrap up

PARCELED > PARCEL

PARCELING > PARCEL

PARCELLED > PARCEL

PARCELS > PARCEL

PARCENARY n joint heirship

PARCENER n person who takes an equal share with another or others

PARCENERS > PARCENER

PARCH vb make very hot and dry

PARCHED > PARCH

PARCHEDLY > PARCH

PARCHEESI n modern board game derived from the ancient game of pachisi

PARCHES > PARCH

PARCHESI same as > PARCHEESI

PARCHESIS > PARCHESI

PARCHING > PARCH

PARCHISI same as > PARCHEESI

PARCHISIS > PARCHISI

PARCHMENT n thick smooth writing material made from animal skin

PARCIMONY obsolete variant of > PARSIMONY

PARCLOSE n screen or railing in a church

separating off an altar, chapel, etc

PARCLOSES > PARCLOSE

PARD n leopard or panther

PARDAH same as > PURDAH

PARDAHS > PARDAH

PARDAL variant spelling of > PARDALE

PARDALE n leopard

PARDALES > PARDALE

PARDALIS n leopard

PARDALOTE n small Australian songbird

PARDALS > PARDAL

PARDED adj having spots

PARDEE adv certainly

PARDI same as > PARDEE

PARDIE same as > PARDEE

PARDINE adj spotted

PARDNER n friend or partner: used as a term of address

PARDNERS > PARDNER

PARDON vb forgive, excuse ▷ n forgiveness ▷ interj sorry ▷ sentence substitute sorry

PARDONED > PARDON

PARDONER n (before the Reformation) person licensed to sell ecclesiastical indulgences

PARDONERS > PARDONER

PARDONING > PARDON

PARDONS > PARDON

PARDS > PARD

PARDY same as > PARDEE

PARE vb cut off the skin or top layer of

PARECIOUS adj having the male and female reproductive organs at different levels on the same stem

PARECISM n state of having male and female organs close together

PARECISMS > PARECISM

PARED > PARE

PAREGORIC n medicine containing opium, benzoic acid, camphor or ammonia, and anise oil

PAREIRA n root of a South American menispermaceous climbing plant

PAREIRAS > PAREIRA

PARELLA n type of lichen

PARELLAS > PARELLA

PARELLE same as > PARELLA

PARELLES > PARELLE

PARENESES > PARENESIS

PARENESIS n exhortation

PARENT n father or mother ▷ vb raise offspring

PARENTAGE n ancestry or family

PARENTAL adj of or relating to a parent or parenthood

PARENTED > PARENT

PARENTING n activity of

bringing up children

PARENTS > PARENT

PAREO same as > PAREU

PAREOS > PAREU

PARER > PARE

PARERA n New Zealand duck with grey-edged brown feathers

PARERAS > PARERA

PARERGA > PARERGON

PARERGON n work that is not one's main employment

PARERS > PARE

PARES > PARE

PARESES > PARESIS

PARESIS n incomplete or slight paralysis of motor functions

PARETIC > PARESIS

PARETICS > PARESIS

PAREU n rectangle of fabric worn by Polynesians as a skirt or loincloth

PAREUS > PAREU

PAREV adj containing neither meat nor milk products and so fit for use with either meat or milk dishes

PAREVE same as > PAREV

PARFAIT n dessert consisting of layers of ice cream, fruit, and sauce, topped with whipped cream, and served in a tall glass

PARFAITS > PARFAIT

PARFLECHE n sheet of rawhide that has been dried after soaking in lye and water to remove the hair

PARFLESH same as > PARFLECHE

PARFOCAL adj with focal points in the same plane

PARGANA n Indian sub-district

PARGANAS > PARGANA

PARGASITE n dark green mineral

PARGE vb coat with plaster

PARGED > PARGE

PARGES > PARGE

PARGET n plaster, mortar, etc, used to line chimney flues or cover walls ▷ vb cover or decorate with parget

PARGETED > PARGET

PARGETER > PARGET

PARGETERS > PARGET

PARGETING same as > PARGET

PARGETS > PARGET

PARGETTED > PARGET

PARGETTER n plasterer

PARGING > PARGE

PARGINGS > PARGE

PARGO n sea bream

PARGOS > PARGO

PARGYLINE n monoamine oxidase inhibitor

PARHELIA > PARHELION

P

PARHELIC > PARHELION
PARHELION n one of several bright spots on the parhelic circle or solar halo
PARHYPATE n note in ancient Greek music
PARIAH n social outcast
PARIAHS > PARIAH
PARIAL n pair royal of playing cards
PARIALS > PARIAL
PARIAN n type of marble or porcelain
PARIANS > PARIAN
PARIES n wall of an organ or bodily cavity
PARIETAL adj of the walls of a body cavity such as the skull ▷ n parietal bone
PARIETALS > PARIETAL
PARIETES > PARIES
PARING n piece pared off
PARINGS > PARING
PARIS n type of herb
PARISCHAN variant of > PAROCHIN
PARISES > PARIS
PARISH n area that has its own church and a priest or pastor
PARISHAD n Indian assembly
PARISHADS > PARISHAD
PARISHEN n member of parish
PARISHENS > PARISHEN
PARISHES > PARISH
PARISON n unshaped mass of glass before it is moulded into its final form
PARISONS > PARISON
PARITIES > PARITY
PARITOR n official who summons witnesses
PARITORS > PARITOR
PARITY n equality or equivalence
PARK n area of open land for recreational use by the public ▷ vb stop and leave (a vehicle) temporarily
PARKA n large waterproof jacket with a hood
PARKADE n building used as a car park
PARKADES > PARKADE
PARKAS > PARKA
PARKED > PARK
PARKEE n Eskimo outer garment
PARKEES > PARKEE
PARKER > PARK
PARKERS > PARK
PARKETTE n small public car park
PARKETTES > PARKETTE
PARKI variant of > PARKA
PARKIE n park keeper
PARKIER > PARKY
PARKIES > PARKIE
PARKIEST > PARKY
PARKIN n moist spicy ginger cake usually containing oatmeal

PARKING > PARK
PARKINGS > PARK
PARKINS > PARKIN
PARKIS > PARKI
PARKISH adj like a park
PARKLAND n grassland with scattered trees
PARKLANDS > PARKLAND
PARKLIKE > PARK
PARKLY adj having many parks or resembling a park
PARKOUR n sport of running in urban areas performing gymnastics on manmade obstacles
PARKOURS > PARKOUR
PARKS > PARK
PARKWARD adv towards a park
PARKWARDS adv towards a park
PARKWAY n (in the US and Canada) wide road planted with trees, turf, etc
PARKWAYS > PARKWAY
PARKY adj (of the weather) chilly
PARLANCE n particular way of speaking, idiom
PARLANCES > PARLANCE
PARLANDO adv to be performed as though speaking
PARLANTE same as > PARLANDO
PARLAY vb stake (winnings from one bet) on a subsequent wager ▷ n bet in which winnings from one wager are staked on another, or a series of such bets
PARLAYED > PARLAY
PARLAYING > PARLAY
PARLAYS > PARLAY
PARLE vb speak
PARLED > PARLE
PARLEMENT n parliament
PARLES > PARLE
PARLEY n meeting between leaders or representatives of opposing forces to discuss terms ▷ vb have a parley
PARLEYED > PARLEY
PARLEYER > PARLEY
PARLEYERS > PARLEY
PARLEYING > PARLEY
PARLEYS > PARLEY
PARLEYVOO vb speak French ▷ n French language
PARLIES npl small Scottish biscuits
PARLING > PARLE
PARLOR same as > PARLOUR
PARLORS > PARLOR
PARLOUR n living room for receiving visitors
PARLOURS > PARLOUR
PARLOUS adj dire ▷ adv extremely
PARLOUSLY > PARLOUS
PARLY n short form of

parliament
PARMESAN n Italian hard cheese
PARMESANS > PARMESAN
PAROCHIAL adj narrow in outlook
PAROCHIN n old Scottish parish
PAROCHINE same as > PAROCHIN
PAROCHINS > PAROCHIN
PARODIC > PARODY
PARODICAL > PARODY
PARODIED > PARODY
PARODIES > PARODY
PARODIST > PARODY
PARODISTS > PARODY
PARODOI n path leading to Greek theatre
PARODOS n ode sung by Greek chorus
PARODY n exaggerated and amusing imitation of someone else's style ▷ vb make a parody of
PARODYING > PARODY
PAROEMIA n proverb
PAROEMIAC adj of proverbs
PAROEMIAL adj of proverbs
PAROEMIAS > PAROEMIA
PAROICOUS same as > PARECIOUS
PAROL n (formerly) pleadings in an action when presented by word of mouth ▷ adj (of a contract, lease, etc) made orally or in writing but not under seal
PAROLABLE > PAROLE
PAROLE n early freeing of a prisoner on condition that he or she behaves well ▷ vb put on parole
PAROLED > PAROLE
PAROLEE > PAROLE
PAROLEES > PAROLE
PAROLES > PAROLE
PAROLING > PAROLE
PAROLS > PAROL
PARONYM n cognate word
PARONYMIC > PARONYM
PARONYMS > PARONYM
PARONYMY > PARONYM
PAROQUET n small long-tailed parrot
PAROQUETS > PARROQUET
PARORE n type of fish found around Australia and New Zealand
PARORES > PARORE
PAROSMIA n any disorder of the sense of smell
PAROSMIAS > PAROSMIA
PAROTIC adj situated near the ear
PAROTID adj relating to or situated near the parotid gland ▷ n parotid gland
PAROTIDES > PAROTID
PAROTIDS > PAROTID
PAROTIS n parotid gland

PAROTITIC > PAROTITIS
PAROTITIS n inflammation of the parotid gland
PAROTOID n any of various warty poison glands on the head and back of certain toads and salamanders ▷ adj resembling a parotid gland
PAROTOIDS > PAROTOID
PAROUS adj having given birth
PAROUSIA n Second Coming
PAROUSIAS > PAROUSIA
PAROXYSM n uncontrollable outburst of rage, delight, etc
PAROXYSMS > PAROXYSM
PARP vb make a honking sound
PARPANE n parapet on bridge
PARPANES > PARPANE
PARPED > PARP
PARPEN same as > PARPEND
PARPEND same as > PERPEND
PARPENDS > PARPEND
PARPENS > PARPEN
PARPENT n parapet on bridge
PARPENTS > PARPENT
PARPING > PARP
PARPOINT n parapet on bridge
PARPOINTS > PARPOINT
PARPS > PARP
PARQUET n floor covering made of wooden blocks arranged in a geometric pattern ▷ vb cover with parquet
PARQUETED > PARQUET
PARQUETRY n pieces of wood arranged in a geometric pattern, used to cover floors
PARQUETS > PARQUET
PARR n salmon up to two years of age
PARRA n tourist or non-resident on a beach
PARRAKEET same as > PARAKEET
PARRAL same as > PARREL
PARRALS > PARRAL
PARRAS > PARRA
PARRED > PAR
PARREL n ring that holds the jaws of a boom to the mast but lets it slide up and down
PARRELS > PARREL
PARRHESIA n boldness of speech
PARRICIDE n crime of killing either of one's parents
PARRIDGE Scottish variant of > PORRIDGE
PARRIDGES > PARRIDGE

PARRIED > PARRY
PARRIER > PARRY
PARRIERS > PARRY
PARRIES > PARRY
PARRING > PAR
PARRITCH Scottish variant of > PORRIDGE
PARROCK vb put (an animal) in a small field
PARROCKED > PARROCK
PARROCKS > PARROCK
PARROKET n small long-tailed parrot
PARROKETS > PARROKET
PARROQUET n small long-tailed parrot
PARROT n tropical bird with a short hooked beak and an ability to imitate human speech ▷ vb repeat (someone else's words) without thinking
PARROTED > PARROT
PARROTER n person who repeats what is said
PARROTERS > PARROTER
PARROTING > PARROT
PARROTRY > PARROT
PARROTS > PARROT
PARROTY adj like a parrot; chattering
PARRS > PARR
PARRY vb ward off (an attack) ▷ n parrying
PARRYING > PARRY
PARS > PAR
PARSABLE > PARSE
PARSE vb analyse (a sentence) in terms of grammar
PARSEC n unit of astronomical distance
PARSECS > PARSEC
PARSED > PARSE
PARSER n program or part of a program that interprets input to a computer by recognizing key words or analysing sentence structure
PARSERS > PARSER
PARSES > PARSE
PARSIMONY n extreme caution in spending money
PARSING > PARSE
PARSINGS > PARSE
PARSLEY n herb used for seasoning and decorating food ▷ vb garnish with parsley
PARSLEYED > PARSLEY
PARSLEYS > PARSLEY
PARSLIED > PARSLEY
PARSNEP same as > PARSNIP
PARSNEPS > PARSNEP
PARSNIP n long tapering cream-coloured root vegetable
PARSNIPS > PARSNIP
PARSON n Anglican parish priest
PARSONAGE n parson's house
PARSONIC > PARSON

PARSONISH adj like a parson
PARSONS > PARSON
PART n one of the pieces that make up a whole ▷ vb divide or separate
PARTAKE vb take (food or drink)
PARTAKEN > PARTAKE
PARTAKER > PARTAKE
PARTAKERS > PARTAKE
PARTAKES > PARTAKE
PARTAKING > PARTAKE
PARTAN Scottish word for > CRAB
PARTANS > PARTAN
PARTED adj divided almost to the base
PARTER n thing that parts
PARTERRE n formally patterned flower garden
PARTERRES > PARTERRE
PARTERS > PARTER
PARTI n concept of architectural design
PARTIAL adj not complete ▷ n any of the component tones of a single musical sound, including both those that belong to the harmonic series of the sound and those that do not ▷ vb remove (a factor) from a set of statistics
PARTIALLY > PARTIAL
PARTIALS > PARTIAL
PARTIBLE adj (esp of property or an inheritance) divisible
PARTICLE n extremely small piece or amount
PARTICLES > PARTICLE
PARTIED > PARTY
PARTIER n person who parties
PARTIERS > PARTIER
PARTIES > PARTY
PARTIM adv in part
PARTING same as > PART
PARTINGS > PARTING
PARTIS > PARTI
PARTISAN n strong supporter of a party or group ▷ adj prejudiced or one-sided
PARTISANS > PARTISAN
PARTITA n type of suite
PARTITAS > PARTITA
PARTITE adj composed of or divided into a specified number of parts
PARTITION n screen or thin wall that divides a room ▷ vb divide with a partition
PARTITIVE adj (of a noun) referring to part of something ▷ n partitive word
PARTITURA n music score for several parts
PARTIZAN same as > PARTISAN
PARTIZANS > PARTIZAN
PARTLET n woman's

garment covering the neck and shoulders
PARTLETS > PARTLET
PARTLY adv not completely
PARTNER n either member of a couple in a relationship or activity ▷ vb be the partner of
PARTNERED > PARTNER
PARTNERS > PARTNER
PARTON n hypothetical elementary particle postulated as a constituent of neutrons and protons
PARTONS > PARTON
PARTOOK > PARTAKE
PARTRIDGE n game bird of the grouse family
PARTS npl abilities or talents
PARTURE n departure
PARTURES > PARTURE
PARTWAY adv some of the way
PARTWORK n series of magazines issued at weekly or monthly intervals, which are designed to be bound together to form a complete course or book
PARTWORKS > PARTWORK
PARTY n social gathering for pleasure ▷ vb celebrate, have fun ▷ adj (of a shield) divided vertically into two colours, metals, or furs
PARTYER n person who parties
PARTYERS > PARTYER
PARTYGOER n person who goes to party
PARTYING > PARTY
PARTYISM n devotion to political party
PARTYISMS > PARTYISM
PARULIDES > PARULIS
PARULIS another name for > GUMBOIL
PARULISES > PARULIS
PARURA same as > PARURE
PARURAS > PARURA
PARURE n set of jewels or other ornaments
PARURES > PARURE
PARURESES > PARURES
PARURESIS n phobia in which the sufferer cannot urinate in the presence of others
PARVE same as > PAREV
PARVENU n person newly risen to a position of power or wealth ▷ adj of or characteristic of a parvenu
PARVENUE n woman who, having risen socially or economically, is considered to be an upstart or to lack the appropriate refinement for her new position ▷ adj of or characteristic of a parvenue
PARVENUES > PARVENUE
PARVENUS > PARVENU
PARVIS n court or portico

in front of a building, esp a church
PARVISE same as > PARVIS
PARVISES > PARVISE
PARVO n disease of cattle and dogs
PARVOLIN n substance resulting from the putrefaction of flesh
PARVOLINE n liquid derived from coal tar
PARVOLINS > PARVOLIN
PARVOS > PARVO
PAS n dance step or movement, esp in ballet
PASCAL n unit of pressure
PASCALS > PASCAL
PASCHAL adj of the Passover or Easter ▷ n Passover or Easter
PASCHALS > PASCHAL
PASCUAL adj relating to pasture
PASE n movement of the cape or muleta by a matador to attract the bull's attention and guide its attack
PASEAR vb go for a rambling walk
PASEARED > PASEAR
PASEARING > PASEAR
PASEARS > PASEAR
PASELA same as > BONSELA
PASELAS > PASELA
PASEO n bullfighters' procession
PASEOS > PASEO
PASES > PASE
PASH n infatuation ▷ vb throw or be thrown and break or be broken to bits
PASHA n high official of the Ottoman Empire
PASHADOM n territory of a pasha
PASHADOMS > PASHADOM
PASHALIC same as > PASHALIK
PASHALICS > PASHALIC
PASHALIK n province or jurisdiction of a pasha
PASHALIKS > PASHALIK
PASHAS > PASHA
PASHED > PASH
PASHES > PASH
PASHIM same as > PASHM
PASHIMS > PASHM
PASHING > PASH
PASHKA n rich Russian dessert made of cottage cheese, cream, almonds, currants, etc
PASHKAS > PASHKA
PASHM n underfur of various Tibetan animals, esp goats, used for cashmere shawls
PASHMINA n type of cashmere scarf or shawl made from the underfur of Tibetan goats
PASHMINAS > PASHMINA

PASHMS > PASHM

PASODOBLE n fast modern ballroom dance

PASPALUM n type of grass with wide leaves

PASPALUMS > PASPALUM

PASPIES > PASPY

PASPY n piece of music in triple time

PASQUIL n abusive lampoon or satire ▷ vb ridicule with pasquil

PASQUILER n person who lampoons

PASQUILS > PASQUIL

PASS vb go by, past, or through ▷ n successful result in a test or examination

PASSABLE adj (just) acceptable

PASSABLY adv fairly

PASSADE n act of moving back and forth in the same place

PASSADES > PASSADE

PASSADO n forward thrust with sword

PASSADOS > PASSADO

PASSADOS > PASSADO

PASSAGE n channel or opening providing a way through ▷ vb move or cause to move at a passage

PASSAGED > PASSAGE

PASSAGER as in passager hawk young hawk or falcon caught while on migration

PASSAGES > PASSAGE

PASSAGING > PASSAGE

PASSALONG adj (of plants) easily propagated and given to others

PASSAMENT vb sew border on garment

PASSANT adj (of a beast) walking, with the right foreleg raised

PASSATA n sauce made from sieved tomatoes, often used in Italian cookery

PASSATAS > PASSATA

PASSBAND n band of frequencies that is transmitted with maximum efficiency through a circuit, filter, etc

PASSBANDS > PASSBAND

PASSBOOK n book issued by a bank or building society for keeping a record of deposits and withdrawals

PASSBOOKS > PASSBOOK

PASSE adj out-of-date

PASSED > PASS

PASSEE adj out of fashion

PASSEL n group or quantity of no fixed number

PASSELS > PASSEL

PASSEMENT vb sew border on garment

PASSENGER n person travelling in a vehicle driven by someone else

PASSEPIED n lively minuet of Breton origin

PASSER n person or thing that passes

PASSERBY n person that is passing or going by, esp on foot

PASSERINE adj belonging to the order of perching birds ▷ n any bird of this order

PASSERS > PASSER

PASSERSBY > PASSERBY

PASSES > PASS

PASSIBLE adj susceptible to emotion or suffering

PASSIBLY > PASSIBLE

PASSIM adv everywhere, throughout

PASSING adj brief or transitory ▷ n death

PASSINGLY > PASSING

PASSINGS > PASSING

PASSION n intense sexual love ▷ vb give passionate character to

PASSIONAL adj of, relating to, or due to passion or the passions ▷ n book recounting the sufferings of Christian martyrs or saints

PASSIONED > PASSION

PASSIONS > PASSION

PASSIVATE vb render (a metal) less susceptible to corrosion by coating the surface with a substance, such as an oxide

PASSIVE adj not playing an active part ▷ n passive form of a verb

PASSIVELY > PASSIVE

PASSIVES > PASSIVE

PASSIVISM n theory, belief, or practice of passive resistance

PASSIVIST > PASSIVISM

PASSIVITY > PASSIVE

PASSKEY n private key

PASSKEYS > PASSKEY

PASSLESS adj having no pass

PASSMAN n student who passes without honours

PASSMEN > PASSMAN

PASSMENT same as > PASSEMENT

PASSMENTS > PASSMENT

PASSOUT n (in ice hockey) pass by an attacking player from behind the opposition goal line

PASSOUTS > PASSOUT

PASSOVER n lamb eaten during Passover

PASSOVERS > PASSOVER

PASSPORT n official document of nationality granting permission to travel abroad

PASSPORTS > PASSPORT

PASSUS n (esp in medieval literature) division or section of a poem, story, etc

PASSUSES > PASSUS

PASSWORD n secret word or phrase that ensures admission

PASSWORDS > PASSWORD

PAST adj of the time before the present ▷ n period of time before the present ▷ adv ago ▷ prep beyond

PASTA n type of food, such as spaghetti, that is made in different shapes from flour and water

PASTALIKE > PASTA

PASTANCE n activity that passes time

PASTANCES > PASTANCE

PASTAS > PASTA

PASTE n moist soft mixture, such as toothpaste ▷ vb fasten with paste

PASTED > PASTE

PASTEDOWN n portion of endpaper pasted to cover of book

PASTEL n coloured chalk crayon for drawing ▷ adj pale and delicate in colour

PASTELIST > PASTEL

PASTELS > PASTEL

PASTER n person or thing that pastes

PASTERN n part of a horse's foot between the fetlock and the hoof

PASTERNS > PASTERN

PASTERS > PASTE

PASTES > PASTE

PASTEUP n assembly of typeset matter, illustrations, etc, pasted on a sheet of paper or board

PASTEUPS > PASTEUP

PASTICCI > PASTICCIO

PASTICCIO n art work borrowing various styles

PASTICHE n work of art that mixes styles or copies the style of another artist

PASTICHES > PASTICHE

PASTIE n decorative cover for nipple

PASTIER > PASTY

PASTIES > PASTY

PASTIEST > PASTY

PASTIL same as > PASTILLE

PASTILLE n small fruit-flavoured and sometimes medicated sweet

PASTILLES > PASTILLE

PASTILS > PASTIL

PASTILY > PASTY

PASTIME n activity that makes time pass pleasantly

PASTIMES > PASTIME

PASTINA n small pieces of pasta

PASTINAS > PASTINA

PASTINESS > PASTY

PASTING n heavy defeat

PASTINGS > PASTING

PASTIS n anise-flavoured alcoholic drink

PASTISES > PASTIS

PASTITSIO n Greek dish consisting of minced meat and macaroni topped with bechamel sauce

PASTITSO n Greek dish of baked pasta

PASTITSOS > PASTITSO

PASTLESS adj having no past

PASTNESS n quality of being past

PASTOR n member of the clergy in charge of a congregation ▷ vb act as a pastor

PASTORAL adj of or depicting country life ▷ n poem or picture portraying country life

PASTORALE n musical composition that suggests country life

PASTORALI > PASTORALE

PASTORALS > PASTORAL

PASTORATE n office or term of office of a pastor

PASTORED > PASTOR

PASTORING > PASTOR

PASTORIUM n residence of pastor

PASTORLY > PASTOR

PASTORS > PASTOR

PASTRAMI n highly seasoned smoked beef

PASTRAMIS > PASTRAMI

PASTRIES > PASTRY

PASTROMI same as > PASTRAMI

PASTROMIS > PASTROMI

PASTRY n baking dough made of flour, fat, and water

PASTS > PAST

PASTURAGE n business of grazing cattle

PASTURAL adj of pasture

PASTURE n grassy land for farm animals to graze on ▷ vb cause (livestock) to graze or (of livestock) to graze (a pasture)

PASTURED > PASTURE

PASTURER n person who tends cattle

PASTURERS > PASTURER

PASTURES > PASTURE

PASTURING > PASTURE

PASTY adj (of a complexion) pale and unhealthy ▷ n round of pastry folded over a savoury filling

PAT vb tap lightly ▷ n gentle tap or stroke ▷ adj quick, ready, or glib

PATACA n monetary unit of Macao

PATACAS > PATACA

PATAGIA > PATAGIUM

PATAGIAL > PATAGIUM

PATAGIUM n web of skin between the neck, limbs, and tail in bats and gliding mammals that functions as a wing

PATAKA n building on stilts, used for storing provisions

PATAKAS > PATAKA

PATAMAR n type of boat

PATAMARS > PATAMAR

PATBALL n game like squash but using hands instead of rackets

PATBALLS > PATBALL

PATCH n piece of material sewn on a garment ▷ vb mend with a patch

PATCHABLE > PATCH

PATCHED > PATCH

PATCHER > PATCH

PATCHERS > PATCH

PATCHERY n bungling work

PATCHES > PATCH

PATCHIER > PATCHY

PATCHIEST > PATCHY

PATCHILY > PATCHY

PATCHING > PATCH

PATCHINGS > PATCH

PATCHOCKE Spenserian word for > CLOWN

PATCHOULI n Asiatic tree, the leaves of which yield a heavy fragrant oil

PATCHOULY same as > PATCHOULI

PATCHWORK n needlework made of pieces of different materials sewn together

PATCHY adj of uneven quality or intensity

PATE n head

PATED > PATE

PATELLA n kneecap

PATELLAE > PATELLA

PATELLAR > PATELLA

PATELLAS > PATELLA

PATELLATE adj having the shape of a patella

PATEN n plate, usually made of silver or gold, used for the bread at Communion

PATENCIES > PATENCY

PATENCY n condition of being obvious

PATENS > PATEN

PATENT n document giving the exclusive right to make or sell an invention ▷ adj open to public inspection ▷ vb obtain a patent for

PATENTED > PATENT

PATENTEE n person, group, company, etc, that has been granted a patent

PATENTEES > PATENTEE

PATENTING > PATENT

PATENTLY adv obviously

PATENTOR n person who or official body that grants a patent or patents

PATENTORS > PATENTOR

PATENTS > PATENT

PATER n father

PATERA n shallow ancient Roman bowl

PATERAE > PATERA

PATERCOVE n fraudulent priest

PATERERO n type of cannon

PATEREROS > PATERERO

PATERNAL adj fatherly

PATERNITY n fact or state of being a father

PATERS > PATER

PATES > PATE

PATH n surfaced walk or track ▷ vb make a path

PATHED > PATH

PATHETIC adj causing feelings of pity or sadness ▷ npl pathetic sentiments ▷ n pathetic person

PATHETICS > PATHETIC

PATHIC n catamite ▷ adj of or relating to a catamite

PATHICS > PATHIC

PATHING > PATH

PATHLESS > PATH

PATHNAME n name of a file or directory together with its position in relation to other directories traced back in a line to the root

PATHNAMES > PATHNAME

PATHOGEN n thing that causes disease

PATHOGENE same as > PATHOGEN

PATHOGENS > PATHOGEN

PATHOGENY n origin, development, and resultant effects of a disease

PATHOLOGY n scientific study of diseases

PATHOS n power of arousing pity or sadness

PATHOSES > PATHOS

PATHS > PATH

PATHWAY n path

PATHWAYS > PATHWAY

PATIBLE adj endurable

PATIENCE n quality of being patient

PATIENCES > PATIENCE

PATIENT adj enduring difficulties or delays calmly ▷ n person receiving medical treatment ▷ vb make calm

PATIENTED > PATIENT

PATIENTER > PATIENT

PATIENTLY > PATIENT

PATIENTS > PATIENT

PATIKI n New Zealand sand flounder or dab

PATIKIS > PATIKI

PATIN same as > PATEN

PATINA n fine layer on a surface

PATINAE > PATINA

PATINAED adj having a patina

PATINAS > PATINA

PATINATE vb coat with patina

PATINATED > PATINATE

PATINATES > PATINATE

PATINE vb cover with patina

PATINED > PATINE

PATINES > PATINE

PATINING > PATINE

PATINISE same as > PATINIZE

PATINISED > PATINISE

PATINISES > PATINISE

PATINIZE vb coat with patina

PATINIZED > PATINIZE

PATINIZES > PATINIZE

PATINS > PATIN

PATIO n paved area adjoining a house

PATIOS > PATIO

PATISSIER n pastry chef

PATKA n head covering worn by Sikh men in place of or under a turban

PATKAS > PATKA

PATLY adv fitly

PATNESS n appropriateness

PATNESSES > PATNESS

PATOIS n regional dialect, esp of French

PATONCE adj (of cross) with limbs which broaden from centre

PATOOTIE n person's bottom

PATOOTIES > PATOOTIE

PATRIAL n (in Britain, formerly) person with a right by statute to live in the United Kingdom, and so not subject to immigration control

PATRIALS > PATRIAL

PATRIARCH n male head of a family or tribe

PATRIATE vb bring under the authority of an autonomous country

PATRIATED > PATRIATE

PATRIATES > PATRIATE

PATRICIAN n member of the nobility ▷ adj of noble birth

PATRICIDE n crime of killing one's father

PATRICK n former Irish coin

PATRICKS > PATRICK

PATRICO n fraudulent priest

PATRICOES > PATRICO

PATRILINY n tracing of family descent through males

PATRIMONY n property inherited from ancestors

PATRIOT n person who loves his or her country and supports its interests

PATRIOTIC > PATRIOT

PATRIOTS > PATRIOT

PATRISTIC adj of or relating to the Fathers of the Church, their writings, or the study of these

PATROL n regular circuit by

a guard ▷ vb go round on guard, or reconnoitring

PATROLLED > PATROL

PATROLLER > PATROL

PATROLMAN n man, esp a policeman, who patrols a certain area

PATROLMEN > PATROLMAN

PATROLOGY n study of the writings of the Fathers of the Church

PATROLS > PATROL

PATRON n person who gives financial support to charities, artists, etc

PATRONAGE n support given by a patron

PATRONAL > PATRONESS

PATRONESS n woman who sponsors or aids artists, charities, etc

PATRONISE same as > PATRONIZE

PATRONIZE vb treat in a condescending way

PATRONLY > PATRONESS

PATRONNE n woman who owns or manages a hotel, restaurant, or bar

PATRONNES > PATRONNE

PATRONS > PATRON

PATROON n Dutch land-holder in New Netherland and New York with manorial rights in the colonial era

PATROONS > PATROON

PATS > PAT

PATSIES > PATSY

PATSY n person who is easily cheated, victimized, etc

PATTAMAR n Indian courier

PATTAMARS > PATTAMAR

PATTE n band keeping belt in place

PATTED > PAT

PATTEE adj (of a cross) having triangular arms widening outwards

PATTEN n wooden clog or sandal on a raised wooden platform or metal ring ▷ vb wear pattens

PATTENED > PATTEN

PATTENING > PATTEN

PATTENS > PATTEN

PATTER vb make repeated soft tapping sounds ▷ n quick succession of taps

PATTERED > PATTER

PATTERER > PATTER

PATTERERS > PATTER

PATTERING > PATTER

PATTERN n arrangement of repeated parts or decorative designs ▷ vb model

PATTERNED > PATTERN

PATTERNS > PATTERN

PATTERS > PATTER

PATTES > PATTE

PATTIE same as > PATTY

PATTIES > PATTY

P

PATTING > PAT
PATTLE *dialect for* > PADDLE
PATTLES > PATTLE
PATTRESS *n* box for the space behind electrical sockets and switches
PATTY *n* small flattened cake of minced food
PATTYPAN *n* small round flattish squash
PATTYPANS > PATTYPAN
PATU *n* short Māori club, now used ceremonially
PATULENT *adj* spreading widely
PATULIN *n* toxic antibiotic
PATULINS > PATULIN
PATULOUS *adj* spreading widely or expanded
PATUS > PATU
PATUTUKI *n* blue cod
PATUTUKIS > PATUTUKI
PATY *adj* (of cross) having arms of equal length
PATZER *n* novice chess player
PATZERS > PATZER
PAUA *n* edible shellfish of New Zealand, which has a pearly shell used for jewellery
PAUAS > PAUA
PAUCAL *n* grammatical number occurring in some languages for words in contexts where a few of their referents are described or referred to ▷ *adj* relating to or inflected for this number
PAUCALS > PAUCAL
PAUCITIES > PAUCITY
PAUCITY *n* scarcity
PAUGHTIER > PAUGHTY
PAUGHTY *Scots word for* > HAUGHTY
PAUL *same as* > PAWL
PAULDRON *n* either of two metal plates worn with armour to protect the shoulders
PAULDRONS > PAULDRON
PAULIN *n* tarpaulin
PAULINS > PAULIN
PAULOWNIA *n* Japanese tree with large heart-shaped leaves and clusters of purplish or white flowers
PAULS > PAUL
PAUNCE *n* pansy
PAUNCES > PAUNCE
PAUNCH *n* protruding belly ▷ *vb* stab in the stomach
PAUNCHED > PAUNCH
PAUNCHES > PAUNCH
PAUNCHIER > PAUNCHY
PAUNCHING > PAUNCH
PAUNCHY *adj* having a protruding belly or abdomen
PAUPER *n* very poor person ▷ *vb* reduce to beggary
PAUPERED > PAUPER

PAUPERESS *n* female pauper
PAUPERING > PAUPER
PAUPERISE *same as* > PAUPERIZE
PAUPERISM > PAUPER
PAUPERIZE *vb* make a pauper of
PAUPERS > PAUPER
PAUPIETTE *n* rolled stuffed fish or meat
PAUROPOD *n* minute myriapod
PAUROPODS > PAUROPOD
PAUSAL > PAUSE
PAUSE *vb* stop for a time ▷ *n* stop or rest in speech or action
PAUSED > PAUSE
PAUSEFUL *adj* taking pauses
PAUSELESS *adj* without pauses
PAUSER > PAUSE
PAUSERS > PAUSE
PAUSES > PAUSE
PAUSING > PAUSE
PAUSINGLY *adv* with pauses
PAUSINGS > PAUSE
PAV *short for* > PAVLOVA
PAVAGE *n* tax towards paving streets, or the right to levy such a tax
PAVAGES > PAVAGE
PAVAN *same as* > PAVANE
PAVANE *n* slow and stately dance of the 16th and 17th centuries
PAVANES > PAVANE
PAVANS > PAVAN
PAVE *vb* form (a surface) with stone or brick ▷ *n* paved surface, esp an uneven one
PAVED > PAVE
PAVEED *adj* (of jewels) set close together
PAVEMENT *n* paved path for pedestrians ▷ *vb* provide with pavement
PAVEMENTS > PAVEMENT
PAVEN *same as* > PAVANE
PAVENS > PAVEN
PAVER > PAVE
PAVERS > PAVE
PAVES > PAVE
PAVID *adj* fearful
PAVILION *n* building on a playing field etc ▷ *vb* place or set in or as if in a pavilion
PAVILIONS > PAVILION
PAVILLON *n* bell of wind instrument
PAVILLONS > PAVILLON
PAVIN *same as* > PAVANE
PAVING *n* paved surface ▷ *adj* of or for a paved surface or pavement
PAVINGS > PAVING
PAVINS > PAVIN
PAVIOR *same as* > PAVIOUR
PAVIORS > PAVIOR

PAVIOUR *n* person who lays paving
PAVIOURS > PAVIOUR
PAVIS *n* large square shield, developed in the 15th century, at first portable but later heavy and set up in a permanent position
PAVISE *same as* > PAVIS
PAVISER *n* soldier holding pavise
PAVISERS > PAVISER
PAVISES > PAVISE
PAVISSE *same as* > PAVIS
PAVISSES > PAVISSE
PAVLOVA *n* meringue cake topped with whipped cream and fruit
PAVLOVAS > PAVLOVA
PAVONAZZO *n* white Italian marble
PAVONE *n* peacock
PAVONES > PAVONE
PAVONIAN *same as* > PAVONINE
PAVONINE *adj* of or resembling a peacock or the colours, design, or iridescence of a peacock's tail
PAVS > PAV
PAW *n* animal's foot with claws and pads ▷ *vb* scrape with the paw or hoof
PAWA *old word for* > PEACOCK
PAWAS > PAWA
PAWAW *vb* recite N American incantation
PAWAWED > PAWAW
PAWAWING > PAWAW
PAWAWS > PAWAW
PAWED > PAW
PAWER *n* person or animal that paws
PAWERS > PAWER
PAWING > PAW
PAWK *Scots word for* > TRICK
PAWKIER > PAWKY
PAWKIEST > PAWKY
PAWKILY > PAWKY
PAWKINESS > PAWKY
PAWKS > PAWK
PAWKY *adj* having or characterized by a dry wit
PAWL *n* pivoted lever shaped to engage with a ratchet to prevent motion in a particular direction
PAWLS > PAWL
PAWN *vb* deposit (an article) as security for money borrowed ▷ *n* chessman of the lowest value
PAWNABLE > PAWN
PAWNAGE > PAWN
PAWNAGES > PAWN
PAWNCE *old word for* > PANSY
PAWNCES > PAWNCE
PAWNED > PAWN
PAWNEE *n* one who accepts goods in pawn
PAWNEES > PAWNEE

PAWNER *n* one who pawns his or her possessions
PAWNERS > PAWNER
PAWNING > PAWN
PAWNOR *same as* > PAWNER
PAWNORS > PAWNOR
PAWNS > PAWN
PAWNSHOP *n* premises of a pawnbroker
PAWNSHOPS > PAWNSHOP
PAWPAW *same as* > PAPAW
PAWPAWS > PAWPAW
PAWS > PAW
PAX *n* kiss of peace ▷ *interj* call signalling a desire to end hostilities
PAXES > PAX
PAXIUBA *n* tropical tree
PAXIUBAS > PAXIUBA
PAXWAX *n* strong ligament in the neck of many mammals, which supports the head
PAXWAXES > PAXWAX
PAY *vb* give money etc in return for goods or services ▷ *n* wages or salary
PAYABLE *adj* due to be paid
PAYABLES *n* debts to be paid
PAYABLY > PAYABLE
PAYBACK *n* return on an investment
PAYBACKS > PAYBACK
PAYCHECK *n* payment for work done
PAYCHECKS > PAYCHECK
PAYDAY *n* day on which wages or salaries are paid
PAYDAYS > PAYDAY
PAYED > PAY
PAYEE *n* person to whom money is paid or due
PAYEES > PAYEE
PAYER *n* person who pays
PAYERS > PAYER
PAYFONE *US spelling of* > PAYPHONE
PAYFONES > PAYFONE
PAYGRADE *n* military rank
PAYGRADES > PAYGRADE
PAYING > PAY
PAYINGS > PAY
PAYLIST *n* list of people to be paid
PAYLISTS > PAYLIST
PAYLOAD *n* passengers or cargo of an aircraft
PAYLOADS > PAYLOAD
PAYMASTER *n* official responsible for the payment of wages and salaries
PAYMENT *n* act of paying
PAYMENTS > PAYMENT
PAYNIM *n* heathen or pagan
PAYNIMRY *n* state of being heathen
PAYNIMS > PAYNIM
PAYOFF *n* final settlement, esp in retribution
PAYOFFS > PAYOFF
PAYOLA *n* bribe to get

special treatment, esp to promote a commercial product

PAYOLAS > PAYOLA

PAYOR same as > PAYER

PAYORS > PAYOR

PAYOUT n sum of money paid out

PAYOUTS > PAYOUT

PAYPHONE n coin-operated telephone

PAYPHONES > PAYPHONE

PAYROLL n list of employees who receive regular pay

PAYROLLS > PAYROLL

PAYS > PAY

PAYSAGE n landscape

PAYSAGES > PAYSAGE

PAYSAGIST n painter of landscapes

PAYSD Spenserian form of > POISED

PAYSLIP n note of payment given to employee

PAYSLIPS > PAYSLIP

PAZAZZ same as > PIZZAZZ

PAZAZZES > PAZAZZ

PAZZAZZ same as > PIZZAZZ

PAZZAZZES > PAZZAZZ

PE n 17th letter of the Hebrew alphabet, transliterated as p

PEA n climbing plant with seeds growing in pods

PEABERRY n coffee berry containing one seed

PEACE n calm, quietness

PEACEABLE adj inclined towards peace

PEACEABLY > PEACEABLE

PEACED > PEACE

PEACEFUL adj not in a state of war or disagreement

PEACELESS adj without peace

PEACENIK n activist who opposes war

PEACENIKS > PEACENIK

PEACES > PEACE

PEACETIME n period without war

PEACH n soft juicy fruit with a stone and a downy skin ▷ adj pinkish-orange ▷ vb inform against an accomplice

PEACHBLOW n type of glaze on porcelain

PEACHED > PEACH

PEACHER > PEACH

PEACHERS > PEACH

PEACHES > PEACH

PEACHIER > PEACHY

PEACHIEST > PEACHY

PEACHILY > PEACHY

PEACHING > PEACH

PEACHY adj of or like a peach, esp in colour or texture

PEACING > PEACE

PEACOAT n woollen jacket

PEACOATS > PEACOAT

PEACOCK n large male bird with a brilliantly coloured fanlike tail ▷ vb display (oneself) proudly

PEACOCKED > PEACOCK

PEACOCKS > PEACOCK

PEACOCKY > PEACOCK

PEACOD same as > PEACOD

PEACODS > PEACOD

PEAFOWL n peacock or peahen

PEAFOWLS > PEAFOWL

PEAG n (formerly) money used by North American Indians, made of cylindrical shells strung or woven together

PEAGE same as > PEAG

PEAGES > PEAGE

PEAGS > PEAG

PEAHEN > PEACOCK

PEAHENS > PEACOCK

PEAK n pointed top, esp of a mountain ▷ vb form or reach a peak ▷ adj of or at the point of greatest demand

PEAKED adj having a peak

PEAKIER > PEAK

PEAKIEST > PEAK

PEAKING > PEAK

PEAKISH adj sickly

PEAKLESS > PEAK

PEAKLIKE > PEAK

PEAKS > PEAK

PEAKY > PEAK

PEAL n long loud echoing sound, esp of bells or thunder ▷ vb sound with a peal or peals

PEALED > PEAL

PEALIKE > PEA

PEALING > PEAL

PEALS > PEAL

PEAN same as > PEEN

PEANED > PEAN

PEANING > PEAN

PEANS > PEAN

PEANUT n pea-shaped nut that ripens underground

PEANUTS > PEANUT

PEAPOD n pod of the pea plant

PEAPODS > PEAPOD

PEAR n sweet juicy fruit with a narrow top and rounded base

PEARCE old spelling of > PIERCE

PEARCED > PEARCE

PEARCES > PEARCE

PEARCING > PEARCE

PEARE obsolete spelling of > PEAR

PEARES > PEARE

PEARL same as > PURL

PEARLASH n granular crystalline form of potassium carbonate

PEARLED > PEARL

PEARLER n person who dives for or trades in pearls

▷ adj excellent

PEARLERS > PEARLER

PEARLIER > PEARLY

PEARLIES > PEARLY

PEARLIEST > PEARLY

PEARLIN n type of lace used to trim clothes

PEARLING > PEARL

PEARLINGS > PEARL

PEARLINS n type of lace

PEARLISED same as > PEARLIZED

PEARLITE same as > PERLITE

PEARLITES > PEARLITE

PEARLITIC > PEARLITE

PEARLIZED adj having or given a pearly lustre

PEARLS > PEARL

PEARLWORT n plant with small white flowers that are spherical in bud

PEARLY adj resembling a pearl, esp in lustre ▷ n London costermonger who wears on ceremonial occasions a traditional dress of dark clothes covered with pearl buttons

PEARMAIN n any of several varieties of apple having a red skin

PEARMAINS > PEARMAIN

PEARS > PEAR

PEARST archaic variant of > PIERCED

PEART adj lively

PEARTER > PEART

PEARTEST > PEART

PEARTLY > PEART

PEARTNESS > PEART

PEARWOOD n wood from pear tree

PEARWOODS > PEARWOOD

PEAS > PEA

PEASANT n person working on the land, esp in poorer countries or in the past

PEASANTRY n peasants collectively

PEASANTS > PEASANT

PEASANTY adj having qualities ascribed to traditional country life or people

PEASCOD same as > COD

PEASCODS > PEASCOD

PEASE n archaic or dialect word for pea ▷ vb appease

PEASECOD n pod of a pea plant

PEASECODS > PEASECOD

PEASED > PEASE

PEASEN obsolete plural of > PEASE

PEASES > PEASE

PEASING > PEASE

PEASON obsolete plural of > PEASE

PEASOUPER n thick fog

PEAT n decayed vegetable material found in bogs, used as fertilizer or fuel

PEATARIES > PEATARY

PEATARY n area covered with peat

PEATERIES > PEATERY

PEATERY same as > PEATARY

PEATIER > PEAT

PEATIEST > PEAT

PEATLAND n area of land consisting of peat bogs, usually containing many species of flora and fauna

PEATLANDS > PEATLAND

PEATMAN n person who collects peat

PEATMEN > PEATMAN

PEATS > PEAT

PEATSHIP n ship carrying peat

PEATSHIPS > PEATSHIP

PEATY > PEAT

PEAVEY n wooden lever with a metal pointed end and a hinged hook, used for handling logs

PEAVEYS > PEAVEY

PEAVIES > PEAVEY

PEAVY same as > PEAVEY

PEAZE same as > PEASE

PEAZED > PEAZE

PEAZES > PEAZE

PEAZING > PEAZE

PEBA n type of armadillo

PEBAS > PEBA

PEBBLE n small roundish stone ▷ vb cover with pebbles

PEBBLED > PEBBLE

PEBBLES > PEBBLE

PEBBLIER > PEBBLE

PEBBLIEST > PEBBLE

PEBBLING n act of spraying the rink with drops of hot water to slow down the stone

PEBBLINGS > PEBBLING

PEBBLY > PEBBLE

PEBRINE n disease of silkworms

PEBRINES > PEBRINE

PEC n pectoral muscle

PECAN n edible nut of a N American tree

PECANS > PECAN

PECCABLE adj liable to sin

PECCANCY > PECCANT

PECCANT adj guilty of an offence

PECCANTLY > PECCANT

PECCARIES > PECCARY

PECCARY n piglike animal of American forests

PECCAVI n confession of guilt

PECCAVIS > PECCAVI

PECH Scottish word for > PANT

PECHAN Scots word for > STOMACH

PECHANS > PECHAN

PECHED > PECH

PECHING > PECH

PECHS > PECH

PECK vb strike or pick up

p

with the beak ▷ *n* pecking movement

PECKE *n* quarter of bushel

PECKED > PECK

PECKER *n* slang word for penis

PECKERS > PECKER

PECKES > PECKE

PECKIER > PECKY

PECKIEST > PECKY

PECKING peck

PECKINGS > PECK

PECKISH *adj* slightly hungry

PECKISHLY > PECKISH

PECKS > PECK

PECKY *adj* discoloured

PECORINI > PECORINO

PECORINO *n* Italian cheese made from ewes' milk

PECORINOS > PECORINO

PECS *npl* pectoral muscles

PECTASE *n* enzyme occurring in certain ripening fruits

PECTASES > PECTASE

PECTATE *n* salt or ester of pectic acid

PECTATES > PECTATE

PECTEN *n* comblike structure in the eye of birds and reptiles

PECTENS > PECTEN

PECTIC > PECTIN

PECTIN *n* substance in fruit that makes jam set

PECTINAL *adj* resembling a comb

PECTINATE *adj* shaped like a comb

PECTINEAL *adj* relating to pubic bone

PECTINES > PECTEN

PECTINOUS > PECTIN

PECTINS > PECTIN

PECTISE *same as* > PECTIZE

PECTISED > PECTISE

PECTISES > PECTISE

PECTISING > PECTISE

PECTIZE *vb* change into a jelly

PECTIZED > PECTIZE

PECTIZES > PECTIZE

PECTIZING > PECTIZE

PECTOLITE *n* silicate of lime and soda

PECTORAL *adj* of the chest or thorax ▷ *n* pectoral muscle or fin

PECTORALS > PECTORAL

PECTOSE *n* insoluble carbohydrate found in the cell walls of unripe fruit that is converted to pectin by enzymic processes

PECTOSES > PECTOSE

PECULATE *vb* embezzle (public money)

PECULATED > PECULATE

PECULATES > PECULATE

PECULATOR > PECULATE

PECULIA > PECULIUM

PECULIAR *adj* strange ▷ *n*

special sort, esp an accented letter

PECULIARS > PECULIAR

PECULIUM *n* property that a father or master allowed his child or slave to hold as his own

PECUNIARY *adj* relating to, or consisting of, money

PECUNIOUS *adj* having lots of money

PED *n* pannier

PEDAGOG *same as* > PEDAGOGUE

PEDAGOGIC > PEDAGOGUE

PEDAGOGS > PEDAGOG

PEDAGOGUE *n* schoolteacher, esp a pedantic one

PEDAGOGY *n* principles, practice, or profession of teaching

PEDAL *n* foot-operated lever used to control a vehicle or machine, or to modify the tone of a musical instrument ▷ *vb* propel (a bicycle) by using its pedals ▷ *adj* of or relating to the foot or the feet

PEDALED > PEDAL

PEDALER > PEDAL

PEDALERS > PEDAL

PEDALFER *n* type of zonal soil deficient in lime but containing deposits of aluminium and iron

PEDALFERS > PEDALFER

PEDALIER *n* pedal piano

PEDALIERS > PEDALIER

PEDALING > PEDAL

PEDALLED > PEDAL

PEDALLER *n* person who pedals

PEDALLERS > PEDALLER

PEDALLING > PEDAL

PEDALO *n* pleasure craft driven by pedal-operated paddle wheels

PEDALOES > PEDALO

PEDALOS > PEDALO

PEDALS > PEDAL

PEDANT *n* person who is excessively concerned with details and rules, esp in academic work

PEDANTIC *adj* of, relating to, or characterized by pedantry

PEDANTISE *same as* > PEDANTIZE

PEDANTISM > PEDANT

PEDANTIZE *vb* make pedantic comments

PEDANTRY *n* practice of being a pedant, esp in the minute observance of petty rules or details

PEDANTS > PEDANT

PEDATE *adj* (of a plant leaf) divided into several lobes arising at a common point, the lobes often being

stalked and the lateral lobes sometimes divided into smaller lobes

PEDATELY > PEDATE

PEDATIFID *adj* (of a plant leaf) pedately divided, with the divisions less deep than in a pedate leaf

PEDDER *old form of* > PEDLAR

PEDDERS > PEDDER

PEDDLE *vb* sell (goods) from door to door

PEDDLED > PEDDLE

PEDDLER *same as* > PEDLAR

PEDDLERS > PEDDLER

PEDDLERY *n* business of peddler

PEDDLES > PEDDLE

PEDDLING > PEDDLE

PEDDLINGS > PEDDLE

PEDERAST *n* man who has homosexual relations with boys

PEDERASTS > PEDERAST

PEDERASTY *n* homosexual relations between men and boys

PEDERERO *n* type of cannon

PEDEREROS > PEDERERO

PEDES > PES

PEDESES > PEDESIS

PEDESIS *n* random motion of small particles

PEDESTAL *n* base supporting a column, statue, etc

PEDESTALS > PEDESTAL

PEDETIC *adj* of feet

PEDIATRIC *adj* of or relating to the medical science of children and their diseases

PEDICAB *n* pedal-operated tricycle, available for hire, with an attached seat for one or two passengers

PEDICABS > PEDICAB

PEDICEL *n* stalk bearing a single flower of an inflorescence

PEDICELS > PEDICEL

PEDICLE *n* any small stalk

PEDICLED > PEDICLE

PEDICLES > PEDICLE

PEDICULAR *adj* relating to, infested with, or caused by lice

PEDICULI > PEDICULUS

PEDICULUS *n* wingless parasite

PEDICURE *n* medical or cosmetic treatment of the feet ▷ *vb* give a pedicure

PEDICURED > PEDICURE

PEDICURES > PEDICURE

PEDIFORM *adj* shaped like a foot

PEDIGREE *n* register of ancestors, esp of a purebred animal

PEDIGREED > PEDIGREE

PEDIGREES > PEDIGREE

PEDIMENT *n* triangular part over a door etc

PEDIMENTS > PEDIMENT

PEDIPALP *n* either member of the second pair of head appendages of arachnids

PEDIPALPI > PEDIPALP

PEDIPALPS > PEDIPALP

PEDLAR *n* person who sells goods from door to door

PEDLARIES > PEDLARY

PEDLARS > PEDLAR

PEDLARY *same as* > PEDLERY

PEDLER *same as* > PEDLAR

PEDLERIES > PEDLERY

PEDLERS > PEDLER

PEDLERY *n* business of pedler

PEDOCAL *n* type of zonal soil that is rich in lime and characteristic of relatively dry areas

PEDOCALIC > PEDOCAL

PEDOCALS > PEDOCAL

PEDOGENIC *adj* relating to soil

PEDOLOGIC > PEDOLOGY

PEDOLOGY *same as* > PAEDOLOGY

PEDOMETER *n* instrument which measures the distance walked

PEDOPHILE *n* person who is sexually attracted to children

PEDORTHIC *adj* (of footwear) designed to alleviate foot problems

PEDRAIL *n* device replacing wheel on rough surfaces

PEDRAILS > PEDRAIL

PEDRERO *n* type of cannon

PEDREROES > PEDRERO

PEDREROS > PEDRERO

PEDRO *n* card game

PEDROS > PEDRO

PEDS > PED

PEDUNCLE *same as* > PEDICEL

PEDUNCLED > PEDUNCLE

PEDUNCLES > PEDUNCLE

PEE *vb* urinate ▷ *n* urine

PEEBEEN *n* type of large evergreen

PEEBEENS > PEEBEEN

PEECE *obsolete variant of* > PIECE

PEECES > PEECE

PEED > PEE

PEEING > PEE

PEEK *n* peep or glance ▷ *vb* glance quickly or secretly

PEEKABO *same as* > PEEKABOO

PEEKABOO *n* game for young children, in which one person hides his face and suddenly reveals it and cries 'peekaboo' ▷ *adj* (of a garment) made of fabric that is almost transparent or patterned with small holes

PEEKABOOS > PEEKABOO
PEEKABOS > PEEKABO
PEEKAPOO *n* dog which is cross between Pekingese and poodle
PEEKAPOOS > PEEKAPOO
PEEKED > PEEK
PEEKING > PEEK
PEEKS > PEEK
PEEL *vb* remove the skin or rind of (a vegetable or fruit) ▷ *n* rind or skin
PEELABLE > PEEL
PEELED > PEEL
PEELER *n* special knife or mechanical device for peeling vegetables, fruit, etc
PEELERS > PEELER
PEELING *n* strip of skin, rind, bark, etc, that has been peeled off
PEELINGS > PEELING
PEELS > PEEL
PEEN *n* end of a hammer head opposite the striking face, often rounded or wedge-shaped ▷ *vb* strike with the peen of a hammer or with a stream of metal shot in order to bend or shape (a sheet of metal)
PEENED > PEEN
PEENGE *vb* complain
PEENGED > PEENGE
PEENGEING > PEENGE
PEENGES > PEENGE
PEENGING > PEENGE
PEENING > PEEN
PEENS > PEEN
PEEOY *n* homemade firework
PEEOYS > PEEOY
PEEP *vb* look slyly or quickly ▷ *n* peeping look
PEEPE *old spelling of >* PIP
PEEPED > PEEP
PEEPER *n* person who peeps
PEEPERS > PEEPER
PEEPES *archaic spelling of >* PEEPS
PEEPHOLE *n* small aperture, such as one in the door of a flat for observing callers before opening
PEEPHOLES > PEEPHOLE
PEEPING > PEEP
PEEPS > PEEP
PEEPSHOW *n* box containing a series of pictures that can be seen through a small hole
PEEPSHOWS > PEEPSHOW
PEEPUL *n* Indian moraceous tree
PEEPULS > PEEPUL
PEER *n* (in Britain) member of the nobility ▷ *vb* look closely and intently
PEERAGE *n* whole body of peers
PEERAGES > PEERAGE
PEERED > PEER
PEERESS *n* (in Britain)

woman holding the rank of a peer
PEERESSES > PEERESS
PEERIE *n* spinning top ▷ *adj* small
PEERIER > PEERIE
PEERIES > PEERIE
PEERIEST > PEERIE
PEERING > PEER
PEERLESS *adj* unequalled, unsurpassed
PEERS > PEER
PEERY *n* child's spinning top
PEES > PEE
PEESWEEP *n* early spring storm
PEESWEEPS > PEESWEEP
PEETWEET *n* spotted sandpiper
PEETWEETS > PEETWEET
PEEVE *vb* irritate or annoy ▷ *n* something that irritates
PEEVED > PEEVE
PEEVER *n* hopscotch
PEEVERS > PEEVER
PEEVES > PEEVE
PEEVING > PEEVE
PEEVISH *adj* fretful or irritable
PEEVISHLY > PEEVISH
PEEWEE *same as >* PEWEE
PEEWEES > PEEWEE
PEEWIT *same as >* LAPWING
PEEWITS > PEEWIT
PEG *n* pin or clip for joining, fastening, marking, etc ▷ *vb* fasten with pegs
PEGASUS *n* winged horse
PEGASUSES > PEGASUS
PEGBOARD *n* board with a pattern of holes into which small pegs can be fitted, used for playing certain games or keeping a score
PEGBOARDS > PEGBOARD
PEGBOX *n* part of stringed instrument that holds tuning pegs
PEGBOXES > PEGBOX
PEGGED > PEG
PEGGIES > PEGGY
PEGGING > PEG
PEGGINGS > PEG
PEGGY *n* type of small warbler
PEGH *variant of >* PECH
PEGHED > PEGH
PEGHING > PEGH
PEGHS > PEGH
PEGLEGGED *adj* having wooden leg
PEGLESS > PEG
PEGLIKE > PEG
PEGMATITE *n* exceptionally coarse-grained intrusive igneous rock
PEGS > PEG
PEH *same as >* PE
PEHS > PEH
PEIGNOIR *n* woman's

light dressing gown
PEIGNOIRS > PEIGNOIR
PEIN *same as >* PEEN
PEINCT *vb* paint
PEINCTED > PEINCT
PEINCTING > PEINCT
PEINCTS > PEINCT
PEINED > PEIN
PEINING > PEIN
PEINS > PEIN
PEIRASTIC *adj* experimental
PEISE *same as >* PEIZE
PEISED > PEISE
PEISES > PEISE
PEISHWA *n* Indian leader
PEISHWAH *same as >* PEISHWA
PEISHWAHS > PEISHWAH
PEISHWAS > PEISHWA
PEISING > PEISE
PEIZE *vb* weight or poise
PEIZED > PEIZE
PEIZES > PEIZE
PEIZING > PEIZE
PEJORATE *vb* change for the worse
PEJORATED > PEJORATE
PEJORATES > PEJORATE
PEKAN *n* large North American marten
PEKANS > PEKAN
PEKE *n* Pekingese dog
PEKEPOO *same as >* PEEKAPOO
PEKEPOOS > PEKEPOO
PEKES > PEKE
PEKIN *n* silk fabric
PEKINS > PEKIN
PEKOE *n* high-quality tea made from the downy tips of the young buds of the tea plant
PEKOES > PEKOE
PEL *n* pixel
PELA *n* insect living on wax
PELAGE *n* coat of a mammal, consisting of hair, wool, fur, etc
PELAGES > PELAGE
PELAGIAL *adj* of the open sea
PELAGIAN *adj* of or inhabiting the open sea ▷ *n* pelagic creature
PELAGIANS > PELAGIAN
PELAGIC *adj* of or relating to the open sea ▷ *n* any pelagic creature
PELAGICS > PELAGIC
PELAS > PELA
PELE *Spenserian variant of >* PEAL
PELECYPOD *another word for >* BIVALVE
PELERINE *n* woman's narrow cape with long pointed ends in front
PELERINES > PELERINE
PELES > PELE
PELF *n* money or wealth
PELFS > PELF
PELHAM *n* horse's bit for a

double bridle, less severe than a curb but more severe than a snaffle
PELHAMS > PELHAM
PELICAN *n* large water bird with a pouch beneath its bill for storing fish
PELICANS > PELICAN
PELISSE *n* cloak or loose coat which is usually fur-trimmed
PELISSES > PELISSE
PELITE *n* any argillaceous rock such as shale
PELITES > PELITE
PELITIC > PELITE
PELL *n* hide of an animal
PELLACH *same as >* PELLACK
PELLACHS > PELLACH
PELLACK *n* porpoise
PELLACKS > PELLACK
PELLAGRA *n* disease caused by lack of vitamin B
PELLAGRAS > PELLAGRA
PELLAGRIN *n* person who suffers from pellagra
PELLET *n* small ball of something ▷ *vb* strike with pellets
PELLETAL > PELLET
PELLETED > PELLET
PELLETIFY *vb* shape into pellets
PELLETING > PELLET
PELLETISE *vb* shape into pellets
PELLETIZE *vb* shape into pellets
PELLETS > PELLET
PELLICLE *n* thin skin or film
PELLICLES > PELLICLE
PELLITORY *n* urticaceous plant
PELLMELL *n* disorder
PELLMELLS > PELLMELL
PELLOCK *n* porpoise
PELLOCKS > PELLOCK
PELLS > PELL
PELLUCID *adj* very clear
PELLUM *n* dust
PELLUMS > PELLUM
PELMA *n* sole of the foot
PELMANISM *n* memory card game
PELMAS > PELMA
PELMATIC > PELMA
PELMET *n* ornamental drapery or board, concealing a curtain rail
PELMETS > PELMET
PELOID *n* mud used therapeutically
PELOIDS > PELOID
PELOLOGY *n* study of therapeutic uses of mud
PELON *adj* hairless
PELORIA *n* abnormal production of actinomorphic flowers in a plant of a species that usually produces zygomorphic flowers

p

PELORIAN > PELORIA

PELORIAS > PELORIA

PELORIC > PELORIA

PELORIES > PELORY

PELORISED *adj* affected by peloria

PELORISM *n* floral mutation

PELORISMS > PELORISM

PELORIZED *same as* > PELORISED

PELORUS *n* sighting device used in conjunction with a magnetic compass or a gyrocompass for measuring the relative bearings of observed points

PELORUSES > PELORUS

PELORY *n* floral mutation

PELOTA *n* game played by two players who use a basket strapped to their wrists or a wooden racket to propel a ball against a specially marked wall

PELOTAS > PELOTA

PELOTON *n* main field of riders in a road race

PELOTONS > PELOTON

PELS > PEL

PELT *vb* throw missiles at ▷ *n* skin of a fur-bearing animal

PELTA *n* small ancient shield

PELTAE > PELTA

PELTAS > PELTA

PELTAST *n* (in ancient Greece) lightly armed foot soldier

PELTASTS > PELTAST

PELTATE *adj* (of leaves) having the stalk attached to the centre of the lower surface

PELTATELY > PELTATE

PELTATION > PELTATE

PELTED > PELT

PELTER *vb* rain heavily

PELTERED > PELT

PELTERING > PELT

PELTERS > PELT

PELTING > PELT

PELTINGLY > PELT

PELTINGS > PELT

PELTLESS > PELT

PELTRIES > PELTRY

PELTRY *n* pelts of animals collectively

PELTS > PELT

PELVES > PELVIS

PELVIC *adj* of, near, or relating to the pelvis ▷ *n* pelvic bone

PELVICS > PELVIC

PELVIFORM *adj* shaped like pelvis

PELVIS *n* framework of bones at the base of the spine, to which the hips are attached

PELVISES > PELVIS

PEMBINA *n* type of cranberry

PEMBINAS > PEMBINA

PEMBROKE *n* small table

PEMBROKES > PEMBROKE

PEMICAN *same as* > PEMMICAN

PEMICANS > PEMICAN

PEMMICAN *n* small pressed cake of shredded dried meat, pounded into paste with fat and berries or dried fruits

PEMMICANS > PEMMICAN

PEMOLINE *n* mild stimulant

PEMOLINES > PEMOLINE

PEMPHIGUS *n* any of a group of blistering skin diseases

PEMPHIX *n* type of crustacean

PEMPHIXES > PEMPHIX

PEN *n* instrument for writing in ink ▷ *vb* write or compose

PENAL *adj* of or used in punishment

PENALISE *same as* > PENALIZE

PENALISED > PENALISE

PENALISES > PENALISE

PENALITY > PENAL

PENALIZE *vb* impose a penalty on

PENALIZED > PENALIZE

PENALIZES > PENALIZE

PENALLY > PENAL

PENALTIES > PENALTY

PENALTY *n* punishment for a crime or offence

PENANCE *n* voluntary self-punishment to make amends for wrongdoing ▷ *vb* (of ecclesiastical authorities) impose a penance upon (a sinner)

PENANCED > PENANCE

PENANCES > PENANCE

PENANCING > PENANCE

PENANG *variant of* > PINANG

PENANGS > PENANG

PENATES *npl* household gods

PENCE > PENNY

PENCEL *n* small pennon, originally one carried by a knight's squire

PENCELS > PENCEL

PENCES > PENNY

PENCHANT *n* inclination or liking

PENCHANTS > PENCHANT

PENCIL *n* thin cylindrical instrument containing graphite, for writing or drawing ▷ *vb* draw, write, or mark with a pencil

PENCILED > PENCIL

PENCILER > PENCIL

PENCILERS > PENCIL

PENCILING > PENCIL

PENCILLED > PENCIL

PENCILLER > PENCIL

PENCILS > PENCIL

PENCRAFT *n* skill in writing

PENCRAFTS > PENCRAFT

PEND *vb* await judgment or settlement ▷ *n* archway or vaulted passage

PENDANT *n* ornament worn on a chain round the neck

PENDANTLY > PENDANT

PENDANTS > PENDANT

PENDED > PEND

PENDENCY > PENDENT

PENDENT *adj* hanging ▷ *n* pendant

PENDENTLY > PENDENT

PENDENTS > PENDENT

PENDICLE *n* something dependent on another

PENDICLER *n* person who rents a croft

PENDICLES > PENDICLE

PENDING *prep* while waiting for ▷ *adj* not yet decided or settled

PENDRAGON *n* supreme war chief or leader of the ancient Britons

PENDS > PEND

PENDU *adj* in informal Indian English, culturally backward

PENDULAR *adj* pendulous

PENDULATE *vb* swing as pendulum

PENDULE *n* manoeuvre by which a climber on a rope from above swings in a pendulum-like series of movements to reach another line of ascent

PENDULES > PENDULE

PENDULINE *adj* building nests that hang down

PENDULOUS *adj* hanging, swinging

PENDULUM *same as* > PENDULE

PENDULUMS > PENDULUM

PENE *variant of* > PEEN

PENED > PENE

PENEPLAIN *n* relatively flat land surface produced by a long period of erosion

PENEPLANE *same as* > PENEPLAIN

PENES > PENIS

PENETRANT *adj* sharp ▷ *n* substance that lowers the surface tension of a liquid and thus causes it to penetrate or be absorbed more easily

PENETRATE *vb* find or force a way into or through

PENFOLD *same as* > PINFOLD

PENFOLDS > PENFOLD

PENFUL *n* contents of pen

PENFULS > PENFUL

PENGO *n* standard monetary unit of Hungary, replaced by the forint in 1946

PENGOS > PENGO

PENGUIN *n* flightless black-and-white sea bird of the southern hemisphere

PENGUINRY *n* breeding place of penguins

PENGUINS > PENGUIN

PENHOLDER *n* container for pens

PENI *old spelling of* > PENNY

PENIAL > PENIS

PENICIL *n* small pad for wounds

PENICILS > PENICIL

PENIE *old spelling of* > PENNY

PENIES > PENIE

PENILE *adj* of or relating to the penis

PENILL > PENILLION

PENILLION *npl* Welsh art or practice of singing poetry in counterpoint to a traditional melody played on the harp

PENING > PENE

PENINSULA *n* strip of land nearly surrounded by water

PENIS *n* organ of copulation and urination in male mammals

PENISES > PENIS

PENISTONE *n* coarse woollen cloth

PENITENCE > PENITENT

PENITENCY > PENITENT

PENITENT *adj* feeling sorry for having done wrong ▷ *n* someone who is penitent

PENITENTS > PENITENT

PENK *n* small fish

PENKNIFE *n* small knife with blade(s) that fold into the handle

PENKNIVES > PENKNIFE

PENKS > PENK

PENLIGHT *n* small thin flashlight

PENLIGHTS > PENLIGHT

PENLITE *same as* > PENLIGHT

PENLITES > PENLITE

PENMAN *n* person skilled in handwriting

PENMEN > PENMAN

PENNA *n* any large feather that has a vane and forms part of the main plumage of a bird

PENNAE > PENNA

PENNAL *n* first-year student of Protestant university

PENNALISM *n* menial choring at college

PENNALS > PENNAL

PENNAME *n* author's pseudonym

PENNAMES > PENNAME

PENNANT *same as* > PENDANT

PENNANTS > PENNANT

PENNATE *adj* having feathers, wings, or winglike structures

PENNATED *same as* > PENNATE

PENNATULA *n* sea pen

PENNE *n* pasta in the form

of short tubes
PENNED > PEN
PENNEECH *n* card game
PENNEECHS > PENNEECH
PENNEECK *same as*
> PENNEECH
PENNEECKS > PENNEECK
PENNER *n* person who
writes
PENNERS > PENNER
PENNES > PENNE
PENNI *n* former Finnish
monetary unit worth one
hundredth of a markka
PENNIA > PENNI
PENNIED *adj* having
money
PENNIES > PENNY
PENNIFORM *adj* shaped
like a feather
PENNILESS *adj* very poor
PENNILL *n* stanza in a
Welsh poem
PENNINE *n* mineral found
in the Pennine Alps
PENNINES > PENNINE
PENNING > PEN
PENNINITE *n*
bluish-green variety of
chlorite occurring in the
form of thick crystals
PENNIS > PENNI
PENNON *n* triangular or
tapering flag
PENNONCEL *n* small
narrow flag
PENNONED *n* equipped
with a pennon
PENNONS > PENNON
PENNY *n* British bronze coin
worth one hundredth of a
pound
PENNYBOY *n* employee
whose duties include
menial tasks, such as
running errands
PENNYBOYS > PENNYBOY
PENNYFEE *n* small
payment
PENNYFEES > PENNYFEE
PENNYLAND *n* old Scottish
division of land
PENNYWISE *adj* careful
with small amounts of
money
PENNYWORT *n* Eurasian
rock plant with
whitish-green tubular
flowers and rounded leaves
PENOCHE *n* type of fudge
PENOCHES > PENOCHE
PENOLOGY *n* study of
punishment and prison
management
PENONCEL *n* small narrow
flag
PENONCELS > PENONCEL
PENPOINT *n* tip of pen
PENPOINTS > PENPOINT
PENPUSHER *n* person
whose work involves a lot
of boring paperwork
PENS > PEN
PENSEE *n* thought put
down on paper

PENSEES > PENSEE
PENSEL *same as* > PENCEL
PENSELS > PENSEL
PENSIL *same as* > PENCEL
PENSILE *adj* designating
or building a hanging nest
PENSILITY > PENSILE
PENSILS > PENSIL
PENSION *n* regular
payment to people above a
certain age, retired
employees, widows, etc
▷ *vb* grant a pension to
PENSIONE *n* Italian
boarding house
PENSIONED > PENSION
PENSIONER *n* person
receiving a pension
PENSIONES > PENSIONE
PENSIONS > PENSION
PENSIVE *adj* deeply
thoughtful, often with a
tinge of sadness
PENSIVELY > PENSIVE
PENSTEMON *n* North
American flowering plant
with five stamens
PENSTER *n* writer
PENSTERS > PENSTER
PENSTOCK *n* conduit that
supplies water to a
hydroelectric power plant
PENSTOCKS > PENSTOCK
PENSUM *n* school exercise
PENSUMS > PENSUM
PENT *n* penthouse
PENTACLE *same as*
> PENTAGRAM
PENTACLES > PENTACLE
PENTACT *n* sponge spicule
with five rays
PENTACTS > PENTACT
PENTAD *n* group or series of
five
PENTADIC > PENTAD
PENTADS > PENTAD
PENTAGON *n* geometric
figure with five sides
PENTAGONS > PENTAGON
PENTAGRAM *n* five-pointed
star
PENTALOGY *n*
combination of five closely
related symptoms
PENTALPHA *n* five-pointed
star
PENTAMERY *n* state of
consisting of five parts
PENTANE *n* alkane
hydrocarbon with three
isomers
PENTANES > PENTANE
PENTANGLE *same as*
> PENTAGRAM
PENTANOIC *as in pentanoic
acid* colourless liquid
carboxylic acid
PENTANOL *n* colourless
oily liquid
PENTANOLS > PENTANOL
PENTAPODY *n* series or
measure of five feet
PENTARCH *n* member of
pentarchy
PENTARCHS > PENTARCH

PENTARCHY *n* government
by five rulers
PENTATHLA *n* pentathlons
PENTENE *n* colourless
flammable liquid alkene
with several straight-
chained isomeric forms
PENTENES > PENTENE
PENTHIA *n* child born fifth
PENTHIAS > PENTHIA
PENTHOUSE *n* flat built on
the roof or top floor of a
building
PENTICE *vb* accommodate
in a penthouse
PENTICED > PENTICE
PENTICES > PENTICE
PENTICING > PENTICE
PENTISE *same as*
> PENTICE
PENTISED > PENTISE
PENTISES > PENTISE
PENTISING > PENTISE
PENTITI > PENTITO
PENTITO *n* person
involved in organized crime
who offers information to
the police in return for
immunity from prosecution
PENTODE *n* electronic valve
having five electrodes: a
cathode, anode, and three
grids
PENTODES > PENTODE
PENTOMIC *adj* denoting or
relating to the subdivision
of an army division into five
battle groups, esp for
nuclear warfare
PENTOSAN *n*
polysaccharide occuring in
plants, humus, etc
PENTOSANE *same as*
> PENTOSAN
PENTOSANS > PENTOSAN
PENTOSE *n*
monosaccharide
containing five atoms of
carbon per molecule
PENTOSES > PENTOSE
PENTOSIDE *n* compound
containing sugar
PENTOXIDE *n* oxide of an
element with five atoms of
oxygen per molecule
PENTROOF *n* lean-to
PENTROOFS > PENTROOF
PENTS > PENT
PENTYL *n* one of a
particular chemical group
PENTYLENE *n* type of
chemical
PENTYLS > PENTYL
PENUCHE *same as*
> PANOCHA
PENUCHES > PENUCHE
PENUCHI *same as*
> PANOCHA
PENUCHIS > PENUCHI
PENUCHLE *same as*
> PINOCHLE
PENUCHLES > PENUCHLE
PENUCKLE *same as*
> PENUCHLE
PENUCKLES > PENUCKLE

PENULT *n* last syllable but
one in a word
PENULTIMA *same as*
> PENULT
PENULTS > PENULT
PENUMBRA *n* (in an eclipse)
partially shadowed region
which surrounds the full
shadow
PENUMBRAE > PENUMBRA
PENUMBRAL > PENUMBRA
PENUMBRAS > PENUMBRA
PENURIES > PENURY
PENURIOUS *adj* niggardly
with money
PENURY *n* extreme poverty
PENWOMAN *n* female
writer
PENWOMEN > PENWOMAN
PEON *n* Spanish-American
farm labourer or unskilled
worker
PEONAGE *n* state of being a
peon
PEONAGES > PEONAGE
PEONES > PEON
PEONIES > PEONY
PEONISM *same as*
> PEONAGE
PEONISMS > PEONISM
PEONS > PEON
PEONY *n* garden plant with
showy red, pink, or white
flowers
PEOPLE *npl* persons
generally ▷ *vb* provide with
inhabitants
PEOPLED > PEOPLE
PEOPLER *n* settler
PEOPLERS > PEOPLER
PEOPLES > PEOPLE
PEOPLING > PEOPLE
PEP *n* high spirits, energy,
or enthusiasm ▷ *vb* liven by
imbuing with new vigour
PEPERINO *n* type of
volcanic rock
PEPERINOS > PEPERINO
PEPEROMIA *n* plant from
tropical and subtropical
America with slightly fleshy
ornamental leaves
PEPERONI *same as*
> PEPPERONI
PEPERONIS
> PEPPERONI
PEPFUL *adj* full of vitality
PEPINO *n* purple-striped
yellow fruit
PEPINOS > PEPINO
PEPLA > PEPLUM
PEPLOS *n* (in ancient
Greece) top part of a
woman's attire, caught at
the shoulders and hanging
in folds to the waist
PEPLOSES > PEPLOS
PEPLUM *same as* > PEPLOS
PEPLUMED > PEPLUM
PEPLUMS > PEPLUM
PEPLUS *same as* > PEPLOS
PEPLUSES > PEPLUS
PEPO *n* fruit such as the
melon, squash, cucumber,
or pumpkin

P

PEPONIDA variant of > PEPO

PEPONIDAS > PEPO

PEPONIUM variant of > PEPO

PEPONIUMS > PEPONIUM

PEPOS > PEPO

PEPPED > PEP

PEPPER n sharp hot condiment made from the fruit of an East Indian climbing plant ▷ vb season with pepper

PEPPERBOX n container for pepper

PEPPERED > PEPPER

PEPPERER > PEPPER

PEPPERERS > PEPPER

PEPPERIER > PEPPERY

PEPPERING > PEPPER

PEPPERONI n dry sausage of pork and beef spiced with pepper

PEPPERS > PEPPER

PEPPERY adj tasting of pepper

PEPPIER > PEPPY

PEPPIEST > PEPPY

PEPPILY > PEPPY

PEPPINESS > PEPPY

PEPPING > PEP

PEPPY adj full of vitality

PEPS > PEP

PEPSIN n enzyme produced in the stomach, which, when activated by acid, breaks down proteins

PEPSINATE vb treat (a patient) with pepsin

PEPSINE same as > PEPSIN

PEPSINES > PEPSINE

PEPSINS > PEPSIN

PEPTALK n talk meant to inspire ▷ vb give a peptalk to

PEPTALKED > PEPTALK

PEPTALKS > PEPTALK

PEPTIC adj relating to digestion or the digestive juices ▷ n substance that aids digestion

PEPTICITY > PEPTIC

PEPTICS > PEPTIC

PEPTID variant of > PEPTIDE

PEPTIDASE n any of a group of proteolytic enzymes that hydrolyse peptides to amino acids

PEPTIDE n compound consisting of two or more amino acids linked by chemical bonding between the amino group of one and the carboxyl group of another

PEPTIDES > PEPTIDE

PEPTIDIC adj of peptides

PEPTIDS > PEPTID

PEPTISE same as > PEPTIZE

PEPTISED > PEPTISE

PEPTISER > PEPTISE

PEPTISERS > PEPTISE

PEPTISES > PEPTISE

PEPTISING > PEPTISE

PEPTIZE vb disperse (a substance) into a colloidal state, usually to form a sol

PEPTIZED > PEPTIZE

PEPTIZER > PEPTIZE

PEPTIZERS > PEPTIZE

PEPTIZES > PEPTIZE

PEPTIZING > PEPTIZE

PEPTONE n any of a group of compounds that form an intermediary group in the digestion of proteins to amino acids

PEPTONES > PEPTONE

PEPTONIC > PEPTONE

PEPTONISE same as > PEPTONIZE

PEPTONIZE vb hydrolyse (a protein) to peptones by enzymic action, esp by pepsin or pancreatic extract

PEQUISTE n in Canada, member or supporter of the Parti Québécois

PEQUISTES > PEQUISTE

PER prep for each

PERACID n acid, such as perchloric acid, in which the element forming the acid radical exhibits its highest valency

PERACIDS > PERACID

PERACUTE adj very acute

PERAEA > PERAEON

PERAEON same as > PEREION

PERAEONS > PERAEON

PERAEOPOD same as > PEREIOPOD

PERAI another name for > PIRANHA

PERAIS > PERAI

PERBORATE n salt derived, or apparently derived, from perboric acid

PERCALE n close-textured woven cotton fabric, plain or printed, used esp for sheets

PERCALES > PERCALE

PERCALINE n fine light cotton fabric, used esp for linings

PERCASE adv perchance

PERCE obsolete word for > PIERCE

PERCEABLE adj pierceable

PERCEANT adj piercing

PERCED > PERCE

PERCEIVE vb become aware of (something) through the senses

PERCEIVED > PERCEIVE

PERCEIVER > PERCEIVE

PERCEIVES > PERCEIVE

PERCEN > PERCE

PERCENT n percentage or proportion

PERCENTAL > PERCENT

PERCENTS > PERCENT

PERCEPT n concept that depends on recognition by the senses, such as sight, of some external object or phenomenon

PERCEPTS > PERCEPT

PERCES > PERCE

PERCH n resting place for a bird ▷ vb alight, rest, or place on or as if on a perch

PERCHANCE adv perhaps

PERCHED > PERCH

PERCHER > PERCH

PERCHERON n compact heavy breed of carthorse

PERCHERS > PERCH

PERCHERY n barn in which hens are allowed to move without restriction

PERCHES > PERCH

PERCHING > PERCH

PERCHINGS > PERCH

PERCIFORM adj of perch-like fishes

PERCINE adj of perches

PERCING > PERCE

PERCOCT adj well-cooked

PERCOID n type of spiny-finned teleost fish

PERCOIDS > PERCOID

PERCOLATE vb pass or filter through small holes ▷ n product of percolation

PERCOLIN n pain-relieving drug

PERCOLINS > PERCOLIN

PERCUSS vb strike sharply, rapidly, or suddenly

PERCUSSED > PERCUSS

PERCUSSES > PERCUSS

PERCUSSOR > PERCUSS

PERDENDO adj (of music) getting gradually quieter and slower

PERDIE adv certainly

PERDITION n spiritual ruin

PERDU adj (of a soldier) placed on hazardous sentry duty ▷ n soldier placed on hazardous sentry duty

PERDUE same as > PERDU

PERDUES > PERDUE

PERDURE vb last for long time

PERDURED > PERDURE

PERDURES > PERDURE

PERDURING > PERDURE

PERDUS > PERDU

PERDY adv certainly

PERE n addition to a French surname to specify the father rather than the son of the same name

PEREA > PEREON

PEREGAL adj equal ▷ n equal

PEREGALS > PEREGAL

PEREGRIN variant spelling of > PEREGRINE

PEREGRINE adj coming from abroad

PEREGRINS > PEREGRIN

PEREIA > PEREION

PEREION n thorax of some crustaceans

PEREIONS > PEREION

PEREIOPOD n appendage of the pereion

PEREIRA n bark of a South American apocynaceous tree

PEREIRAS > PEREIRA

PERENNATE vb (of plants) live from one growing season to another

PERENNIAL adj lasting through many years ▷ n plant lasting more than two years

PERENNITY n state of being perennial

PERENTIE n large dark-coloured Australian monitor lizard

PERENTIES > PERENTY

PERENTY same as > PERENTIE

PEREON same as > PEREION

PEREONS > PEREON

PEREOPOD same as > PEREIOPOD

PEREOPODS > PEREOPOD

PERES > PERE

PERFAY interj by my faith

PERFECT adj having all the essential elements ▷ n perfect tense ▷ vb improve

PERFECTA n bet on the order of the first and second in a race

PERFECTAS > PERFECTA

PERFECTED > PERFECT

PERFECTER same as > PERFECTOR

PERFECTI n ascetic group of elite Cathars

PERFECTLY adv completely, utterly, or absolutely

PERFECTO n large cigar that is tapered from both ends

PERFECTOR n person who completes or makes something perfect

PERFECTOS > PERFECTO

PERFECTS > PERFECT

PERFERVID adj extremely ardent, enthusiastic, or zealous

PERFERVOR n zealous person

PERFET obsolete variant of > PERFECT

PERFIDIES > PERFIDY

PERFIDY n perfidious act

PERFIN former name for > SPIF

PERFING n practice of taking early retirement, with financial compensation, from the police force

PERFINGS > PERFING

PERFINS > PERFIN

PERFORANS adj perforating or penetrating

PERFORANT adj perforating

PERFORATE *vb* make holes in ▷ *adj* pierced by small holes
PERFORCE *adv* of necessity
PERFORM *vb* carry out (an action)
PERFORMED > PERFORM
PERFORMER > PERFORM
PERFORMS > PERFORM
PERFUME *n* liquid cosmetic worn for its pleasant smell ▷ *vb* give a pleasant smell to
PERFUMED > PERFUME
PERFUMER *n* person who makes or sells perfume
PERFUMERS > PERFUMER
PERFUMERY *n* perfumes in general
PERFUMES > PERFUME
PERFUMIER *same as* > PERFUMER
PERFUMING > PERFUME
PERFUMY *adj* like perfume
PERFUSATE *n* fluid flowing through tissue or organ
PERFUSE *vb* permeate (a liquid, colour, etc) through or over (something)
PERFUSED > PERFUSE
PERFUSES > PERFUSE
PERFUSING > PERFUSE
PERFUSION > PERFUSE
PERFUSIVE > PERFUSE
PERGOLA *n* arch or framework of trellis supporting climbing plants
PERGOLAS > PERGOLA
PERGUNNAH *same as* > PARGANA
PERHAPS *adv* possibly, maybe ▷ *sentence substitute* it may happen, be so, etc ▷ *n* something that might have happened
PERHAPSES > PERHAPS
PERI *n* (in Persian folklore) one of a race of beautiful supernatural beings
PERIAGUA *n* dugout canoe
PERIAGUAS > PERIAGUA
PERIAKTOI > PERIAKTOS
PERIAKTOS *n* ancient device for changing theatre scenery
PERIANTH *n* outer part of a flower
PERIANTHS > PERIANTH
PERIAPSES > PERIAPSIS
PERIAPSIS *n* closest point to a central body reached by a body in orbit
PERIAPT *n* charm or amulet
PERIAPTS > PERIAPT
PERIBLAST *n* tissue surrounding blastoderm in meroblastic eggs
PERIBLEM *n* layer of meristematic tissue in stems and roots that gives rise to the cortex

PERIBLEMS > PERIBLEM
PERIBOLI > PERIBOLOS
PERIBOLOI > PERIBOLOS
PERIBOLOS *n* enclosed court surrounding ancient temple
PERIBOLUS *same as* > PERIBOLOS
PERICARP *n* part of a fruit enclosing the seed that develops from the wall of the ovary
PERICARPS > PERICARP
PERICLASE *n* mineral consisting of magnesium oxide in the form of isometric crystals or grains
PERICLINE *n* white translucent variety of albite in the form of elongated crystals
PERICON *n* Argentinian dance
PERICONES > PERICON
PERICOPAE > PERICOPE
PERICOPAL > PERICOPE
PERICOPE *n* selection from a book, esp a passage from the Bible read at religious services
PERICOPES > PERICOPE
PERICOPIC > PERICOPE
PERICYCLE *n* layer of plant tissue beneath the endodermis
PERIDERM *n* outer corky protective layer of woody stems and roots
PERIDERMS > PERIDERM
PERIDIA > PERIDIUM
PERIDIAL > PERIDIUM
PERIDINIA *n* genus of flagellate organisms
PERIDIUM *n* distinct outer layer of the spore-bearing organ in many fungi
PERIDIUMS > PERIDIUM
PERIDOT *n* pale green transparent gemstone
PERIDOTE *same as* > PERIDOT
PERIDOTES > PERIDOTE
PERIDOTIC > PERIDOT
PERIDOTS > PERIDOT
PERIDROME *n* space between the columns and inner room of a classical temple
PERIGEAL > PERIGEE
PERIGEAN > PERIGEE
PERIGEE *n* point in the orbit of the moon or a satellite that is nearest the earth
PERIGEES > PERIGEE
PERIGON *n* angle of 360°
PERIGONE *n* part enclosing the essential organs of a flower
PERIGONES > PERIGONE
PERIGONIA *n* perigones
PERIGONS > PERIGON
PERIGYNY *n* (of a flower) condition of having a

concave or flat receptacle with the gynoecium and other floral parts at the same level
PERIHELIA *n* points in the orbits of planets at which they are nearest the sun
PERIKARYA *n* parts of nerve cells that contain the nuclei
PERIL *n* great danger ▷ *vb* expose to danger
PERILED > PERIL
PERILING > PERIL
PERILLA *n* type of mint
PERILLAS > PERILLA
PERILLED > PERIL
PERILLING > PERIL
PERILOUS *adj* very hazardous or dangerous
PERILS > PERIL
PERILUNE *n* point in a lunar orbit when a spacecraft launched from the moon is nearest the moon
PERILUNES > PERILUNE
PERILYMPH *n* fluid filling the space between the membranous and bony labyrinths of the internal ear
PERIMETER *n* outer edge of an area
PERIMETRY > PERIMETER
PERIMORPH *n* mineral that encloses another mineral of a different type
PERIMYSIA *n* sheaths of fibrous connective tissue surrounding the primary bundles of muscle fibres
PERINAEUM *same as* > PERINEUM
PERINATAL *adj* of or in the weeks shortly before or after birth
PERINEA > PERINEUM
PERINEAL > PERINEUM
PERINEUM *n* region of the body between the anus and the genitals
PERINEUMS > PERINEUM
PERIOD *n* particular portion of time ▷ *adj* (of furniture, dress, a play, etc) dating from or in the style of an earlier time ▷ *vb* divide into periods
PERIODATE *n* any salt or ester of a periodic acid
PERIODED > PERIOD
PERIODIC *adj* recurring at intervals
PERIODID *n* kind of iodide
PERIODIDE *variant of* > PERIODID
PERIODIDS > PERIODID
PERIODING > PERIOD
PERIODISE *same as* > PERIODIZE
PERIODIZE *vb* divide (a portion of time) into periods

PERIODS > PERIOD
PERIOST *n* thick fibrous two-layered membrane covering the surface of bones
PERIOSTEA > PERIOSTS
PERIOSTS > PERIOST
PERIOTIC *adj* of or relating to the structures situated around the internal ear ▷ *n* periotic bone
PERIOTICS > PERIOTIC
PERIPATUS *n* wormlike arthropod with a segmented body and short unjointed limbs
PERIPETIA *n* abrupt turn of events or reversal of circumstances
PERIPETY *n* an abrupt turn of events or reversal of circumstances
PERIPHERY *n* boundary or edge
PERIPLASM *n* region inside wall of biological cell
PERIPLAST *n* nutritive and supporting tissue in animal organ
PERIPLUS *n* circumnavigation
PERIPROCT *n* tough membrane surrounding anus in echinoderms
PERIPTER *n* type of ancient temple
PERIPTERS > PERIPTER
PERIPTERY *n* region surrounding moving body
PERIQUE *n* strong highly-flavoured tobacco cured in its own juices and grown in Louisiana
PERIQUES > PERIQUE
PERIS > PERI
PERISARC *n* outer chitinous layer secreted by colonial hydrozoan coelenterates
PERISARCS > PERISARC
PERISCIAN *adj* person whose shadow moves round every point of compass during day
PERISCOPE *n* instrument used, esp in submarines, to give a view of objects on a different level
PERISH *vb* be destroyed or die
PERISHED *adj* (of a person, part of the body, etc) extremely cold
PERISHER *n* mischievous person
PERISHERS > PERISHER
PERISHES > PERISH
PERISHING *adj* very cold
PERISPERM *n* nutritive tissue surrounding the embryo in certain seeds, and developing from the nucellus of the ovule

p

PERISTOME n fringe of pointed teeth surrounding the opening of a moss capsule

PERISTYLE n colonnade that surrounds a court or building

PERITI > PERITUS

PERITONEA n thin translucent serous sacs that line the walls of abdominal cavities and cover the viscera

PERITRACK another name for > TAXIWAY

PERITRICH n ciliate protozoan in which the cilia are restricted to a spiral around the mouth

PERITUS n Catholic theology consultant

PERIWIG same as > PERUKE

PERIWIGS > PERIWIG

PERJINK adj prim or finicky

PERJURE vb render (oneself) guilty of perjury

PERJURED adj having sworn falsely

PERJURER > PERJURE

PERJURERS > PERJURE

PERJURES > PERJURE

PERJURIES > PERJURY

PERJURING > PERJURE

PERJUROUS > PERJURY

PERJURY n act or crime of lying while under oath in a court

PERK n incidental benefit gained from a job, such as a company car ▷ adj pert ▷ vb (of coffee) percolate

PERKED > PERK

PERKIER > PERKY

PERKIEST > PERKY

PERKILY > PERKY

PERKIN same as > PARKIN

PERKINESS > PERKY

PERKING > PERK

PERKINS > PERKIN

PERKISH adj perky

PERKS > PERK

PERKY adj lively or cheerful

PERLEMOEN n edible sea creature with a shell lined with mother of pearl

PERLITE n variety of obsidian consisting of masses of small pearly globules

PERLITES > PERLITE

PERLITIC > PERLITE

PERLOUS same as > PERILOUS

PERM n long-lasting curly hairstyle produced by treating the hair with chemicals ▷ vb give (hair) a perm

PERMALINK n permanent internet hyperlink

PERMALLOY n any of various alloys containing iron and nickel

PERMANENT adj lasting forever

PERMATAN n permanent tan, esp artificial

PERMATANS > PERMATAN

PERMEABLE adj able to be permeated, esp by liquid

PERMEABLY > PERMEABLE

PERMEANCE n act of permeating

PERMEANT > PERMEANCE

PERMEANTS > PERMEANCE

PERMEASE n carrier protein

PERMEASES > PERMEASE

PERMEATE vb pervade or pass through the whole of (something)

PERMEATED > PERMEATE

PERMEATES > PERMEATE

PERMEATOR > PERMEATE

PERMED > PERM

PERMIAN adj of, denoting, or formed in the last period of the Palaeozoic era

PERMIE n person, esp an office worker, employed by a firm on a permanent basis

PERMIES > PERMIE

PERMING > PERM

PERMIT vb give permission, allow ▷ n document giving permission to do something

PERMITS > PERMIT

PERMITTED > PERMIT

PERMITTEE n person given a permit

PERMITTER > PERMIT

PERMS > PERM

PERMUTATE vb alter the sequence or arrangement (of)

PERMUTE vb change the sequence of

PERMUTED > PERMUTE

PERMUTES > PERMUTE

PERMUTING > PERMUTE

PERN n type of buzzard

PERNANCY n receiving of rents

PERNIO n chilblain

PERNIONES > PERNIO

PERNOD n aniseed-flavoured aperitif from France

PERNODS > PERNOD

PERNS > PERN

PEROGI n type of Polish dumpling

PEROGIES > PEROGI

PERONE n fibula

PERONEAL adj of or relating to the fibula or the outer side of the leg

PERONES > PERONE

PERONEUS n lateral muscle of the leg

PERORAL adj administered through mouth

PERORALLY > PERORAL

PERORATE vb speak at

length, esp in a formal manner

PERORATED > PERORATE

PERORATES > PERORATE

PERORATOR > PERORATE

PEROVSKIA n Russian sage

PEROXID variant of > PEROXIDE

PEROXIDE n hydrogen peroxide used as a hair bleach ▷ adj bleached with or resembling peroxide ▷ vb bleach (the hair) with peroxide

PEROXIDED > PEROXIDE

PEROXIDES > PEROXIDE

PEROXIDIC > PEROXIDE

PEROXIDS > PEROXID

PEROXO n type of acid

PEROXY adj containing the peroxide group

PERP n informal US and Canadian word for someone who has committed a crime

PERPEND n large stone that passes through a wall from one side to the other ▷ vb ponder

PERPENDED > PERPEND

PERPENDS > PERPEND

PERPENT same as > PERPEND

PERPENTS > PERPENT

PERPETUAL adj lasting forever ▷ n (of a crop plant) continually producing edible parts

PERPLEX vb puzzle, bewilder

PERPLEXED > PERPLEX

PERPLEXER > PERPLEX

PERPLEXES > PERPLEX

PERPS > PERP

PERRADIAL adj situated around radii of radiate

PERRADII > PERRADIUS

PERRADIUS n primary tentacle of a polyp

PERRIER n short mortar

PERRIERS > PERRIER

PERRIES > PERRY

PERRON n external flight of steps, esp one at the front entrance of a building

PERRONS > PERRON

PERRUQUE old spelling of > PERUKE

PERRUQUES > PERRUQUE

PERRY n alcoholic drink made from fermented pears

PERSALT n any salt of a peracid

PERSALTS > PERSALT

PERSANT adj piercing

PERSAUNT adj piercing

PERSE old variant of > PIERCE

PERSECUTE vb treat cruelly because of race, religion, etc

PERSEITY n quality of having substance

independently of real objects

PERSELINE same as > PURSLANE

PERSES > PERSE

PERSEVERE vb keep making an effort despite difficulties

PERSICO same as > PERSICOT

PERSICOS > PERSICO

PERSICOT n cordial made from apricots

PERSICOTS > PERSICOT

PERSIENNE n printed calico

PERSIMMON n sweet red tropical fruit

PERSING > PERSE

PERSIST vb continue to be or happen, last

PERSISTED > PERSIST

PERSISTER > PERSIST

PERSISTS > PERSIST

PERSON n human being

PERSONA n someone's personality as presented to others

PERSONAE > PERSONA

PERSONAGE n important person

PERSONAL adj individual or private ▷ n item of movable property

PERSONALS > PERSONAL

PERSONAS > PERSONA

PERSONATE vb assume the identity of (another person) with intent to deceive ▷ adj (of the corollas of certain flowers) having two lips in the form of a face

PERSONIFY vb give human characteristics to

PERSONISE same as > PERSONIZE

PERSONIZE vb personify

PERSONNED adj manned

PERSONNEL n people employed in an organization

PERSONS > PERSON

PERSPEX n tradename for any of various clear acrylic resins, used chiefly as a substitute for glass

PERSPEXES > PERSPEX

PERSPIRE vb sweat

PERSPIRED > PERSPIRE

PERSPIRES > PERSPIRE

PERSPIRY adj perspiring

PERST adj perished

PERSUADE vb make (someone) do something by argument, charm, etc

PERSUADED > PERSUADE

PERSUADER > PERSUADE

PERSUADES > PERSUADE

PERSUE obsolete form of > PURSUE

PERSUED > PERSUE

PERSUES > PERSUE

PERSUING > PERSUE

PERSWADE obsolete form of

> PERSUADE
PERSWADED > PERSWADE
PERSWADES > PERSWADE
PERT *adj* saucy and cheeky
▷ *n* pert person
PERTAIN *vb* belong or be
relevant (to)
PERTAINED > PERTAIN
PERTAINS > PERTAIN
PERTAKE *obsolete form of*
> PARTAKE
PERTAKEN > PERTAKE
PERTAKES > PERTAKE
PERTAKING > PERTAKE
PERTER > PERT
PERTEST > PERT
PERTHITE *n* type of
feldspar
PERTHITES > PERTHITE
PERTHITIC > PERTHITE
PERTINENT *adj* relevant
PERTLY > PERT
PERTNESS > PERT
PERTOOK > PERTAKE
PERTS > PERT
PERTURB *vb* disturb greatly
PERTURBED > PERTURB
PERTURBER > PERTURB
PERTURBS > PERTURB
PERTUSATE *adj* pierced at
apex
PERTUSE *adj* having holes
PERTUSED *adj* having
holes
PERTUSION *n* punched
hole
PERTUSSAL
> PERTUSSIS
PERTUSSES
> PERTUSSIS
PERTUSSIS *n* whooping
cough
PERUKE *n* wig for men
worn in the 17th and 18th
centuries
PERUKED *adj* wearing wig
PERUKES > PERUKE
PERUSABLE > PERUSE
PERUSAL > PERUSE
PERUSALS > PERUSE
PERUSE *vb* read in a careful
or leisurely manner
PERUSED > PERUSE
PERUSER > PERUSE
PERUSERS > PERUSE
PERUSES > PERUSE
PERUSING > PERUSE
PERV *n* pervert ▷ *vb* give a
person an erotic look
PERVADE *vb* spread right
through (something)
PERVADED > PERVADE
PERVADER > PERVADE
PERVADERS > PERVADE
PERVADES > PERVADE
PERVADING > PERVADE
PERVASION > PERVADE
PERVASIVE *adj* pervading
or tending to pervade
PERVE *same as* > PERV
PERVED > PERV
PERVERSE *adj* deliberately
doing something different
from what is thought

normal or proper
PERVERSER > PERVERSE
PERVERT *vb* use or alter for
a wrong purpose ▷ *n*
person who practises
sexual perversion
PERVERTED *adj* deviating
greatly from what is
regarded as normal or right
PERVERTER > PERVERT
PERVERTS > PERVERT
PERVES > PERV
PERVIATE *vb* perforate or
burrow
PERVIATED > PERVIATE
PERVIATES > PERVIATE
PERVICACY *n* obstinacy
PERVIER > PERVY
PERVIEST > PERVY
PERVING > PERV
PERVIOUS *adj* able to be
penetrated, permeable
PERVS > PERV
PERVY *adj* perverted
PES *n* animal part
corresponding to the
human foot
PESADE *n* position in which
the horse stands on the
hind legs with the forelegs
in the air
PESADES > PESADE
PESANT *obsolete spelling of*
> PEASANT
PESANTE *adv* to be
performed clumsily
PESANTS > PESANT
PESAUNT *obsolete spelling of*
> PEASANT
PESAUNTS > PESAUNT
PESETA *n* former
monetary unit of Spain
PESETAS > PESETA
PESEWA *n* Ghanaian
monetary unit worth one
hundredth of a cedi
PESEWAS > PESEWA
PESHWA *same as*
> PEISHWA
PESHWAS > PESHWA
PESKIER > PESKY
PESKIEST > PESKY
PESKILY > PESKY
PESKINESS > PESKY
PESKY *adj* troublesome
PESO *n* monetary unit of
Argentina, Mexico, etc
PESOS > PESO
PESSARIES > PESSARY
PESSARY *n* appliance worn
in the vagina, either to
prevent conception or to
support the womb
PESSIMA *n* lowest point
PESSIMAL *adj* (of animal's
environment) least
favourable for survival
PESSIMISM *n* tendency to
expect the worst in all
things
PESSIMIST
> PESSIMISM
PESSIMUM *same as*
> PESSIMAL
PEST *n* annoying person

PESTER *vb* annoy or nag
continually
PESTERED > PESTER
PESTERER > PESTER
PESTERERS > PESTER
PESTERING > PESTER
PESTEROUS *adj* inclined to
annoy
PESTERS > PESTER
PESTFUL *adj* causing
annoyance
PESTHOLE *n* breeding
ground for disease
PESTHOLES > PESTHOLE
PESTHOUSE *n* hospital for
treating persons with
infectious diseases
PESTICIDE *n* chemical for
killing insect pests
PESTIER > PESTY
PESTIEST > PESTY
PESTILENT *adj* annoying,
troublesome
PESTLE *n* club-shaped
implement for grinding
things to powder in a
mortar ▷ *vb* pound (a
substance or object) with
or as if with a pestle
PESTLED > PESTLE
PESTLES > PESTLE
PESTLING > PESTLE
PESTO *n* sauce for pasta,
consisting of basil leaves,
pine nuts, garlic, oil, and
Parmesan cheese, all
crushed together
PESTOLOGY *n* study of
pests
PESTOS > PESTO
PESTS > PEST
PESTY *adj* persistently
annoying
PET *n* animal kept for
pleasure and
companionship ▷ *adj* kept
as a pet ▷ *vb* treat as a pet
PETABYTE *n* in computing,
10^{15} or 2^{50} bytes
PETABYTES > PETABYTE
PETAFLOP *n* (in
computing) unit of
processing speed
PETAFLOPS > PETAFLOP
PETAHERTZ *n* very large
unit of electrical frequency
PETAL *n* one of the brightly
coloured outer parts of a
flower
PETALED > PETAL
PETALINE > PETAL
PETALISM *n* ostracism in
ancient Syracuse
PETALISMS > PETALISM
PETALLED > PETAL
PETALLIKE > PETAL
PETALODIC > PETALODY
PETALODY *n* condition in
certain plants in which
stamens or other parts of
the flower assume the form
and function of petals
PETALOID *adj* resembling
a petal, esp in shape
PETALOUS *adj* bearing or

having petals
PETALS > PETAL
PETANQUE *n* game,
popular in France, in which
metal bowls are thrown to
land as near as possible to a
target ball
PETANQUES > PETANQUE
PETAR *obsolete variant of*
> PETARD
PETARA *n* clothes basket
PETARAS > PETARA
PETARD *n* device
containing explosives used
to breach a wall, doors, etc
PETARDS > PETARD
PETARIES > PETARY
PETARS > PETAR
PETARY *n* weapon for
hurling stones
PETASOS *same as*
> PETASUS
PETASOSES > PETASOS
PETASUS *n* broad-
brimmed hat worn by the
ancient Greeks
PETASUSES > PETASUS
PETAURINE *adj* similar to
a flying phalanger
PETAURIST *n* flying
phalanger
PETCHARY *n* type of
kingbird
PETCOCK *n* small valve for
checking the water level in
a steam boiler or draining
condensed steam from the
cylinder of a steam engine
PETCOCKS > PETCOCK
PETECHIA *n* minute
discoloured spot on the
surface of the skin or
mucous membrane,
caused by an underlying
ruptured blood vessel
PETECHIAE > PETECHIA
PETECHIAL > PETECHIA
PETER *vb* fall (off) in
volume, intensity, etc, and
finally cease ▷ *n* act of
petering
PETERED > PETER
PETERING > PETER
PETERMAN *n* burglar
skilled in safe-breaking
PETERMEN > PETERMAN
PETERS > PETER
PETERSHAM *n* thick corded
ribbon used to stiffen belts,
button bands, etc
PETHER *old variant of*
> PEDLAR
PETHERS > PETHER
PETHIDINE *n* white
crystalline water-soluble
drug used to relieve pain
PETILLANT *adj* (of wine)
slightly effervescent
PETIOLAR > PETIOLE
PETIOLATE *adj* (of a plant
or leaf) having a leafstalk
PETIOLE *n* stalk which
attaches a leaf to a plant
PETIOLED > PETIOLE
PETIOLES > PETIOLE

PETIOLULE n stalk of any of the leaflets making up a compound leaf

PETIT adj of little or lesser importance

PETITE adj (of a woman) small and dainty ▷ n clothing size for small women

PETITES > PETITE

PETITION n formal request, esp one signed by many people and presented to parliament ▷ vb present a petition to

PETITIONS > PETITION

PETITORY adj soliciting

PETNAP vb steal pet

PETNAPER > PETNAP

PETNAPERS > PETNAP

PETNAPING > PETNAP

PETNAPPED > PETNAP

PETNAPPER > PETNAP

PETNAPS > PETNAP

PETRALE n type of sole

PETRALES > PETRALE

PETRARIES > PETRARY

PETRARY n weapon for hurling stones

PETRE same as > SALTPETRE

PETREL n sea bird with a hooked bill and tubular nostrils

PETRELS > PETREL

PETRES > PETRE

PETRI as in petri dish shallow glass dish used for cultures of bacteria

PETRIFIC adj petrifying

PETRIFIED > PETRIFY

PETRIFIER > PETRIFY

PETRIFIES > PETRIFY

PETRIFY vb frighten severely

PETROGENY n origin of rocks

PETROGRAM n prehistoric rock painting

PETROL n flammable liquid obtained from petroleum, used as fuel in internal-combustion engines ▷ vb supply with petrol

PETROLAGE n addition of petrol (to a body of water) to get rid of mosquitoes

PETROLEUM n thick dark oil found underground

PETROLEUR n person using petrol to cause explosions

PETROLIC adj of, relating to, containing, or obtained from petroleum

PETROLLED > PETROL

PETROLOGY n study of the composition, origin, structure, and formation of rocks

PETROLS > PETROL

PETRONEL n firearm of large calibre used in the 16th and early 17th

centuries, esp by cavalry soldiers

PETRONELS > PETRONEL

PETROSAL adj of, relating to, or situated near the dense part of the temporal bone that surrounds the inner ear ▷ n petrosal bone

PETROSALS > PETROSAL

PETROUS adj denoting the dense part of the temporal bone that surrounds the inner ear

PETS > PET

PETSAI n Chinese cabbage

PETSAIS > PETSAI

PETTABLE > PET

PETTED > PET

PETTEDLY > PET

PETTER > PET

PETTERS > PET

PETTI > PETTO

PETTICOAT n woman's skirt-shaped undergarment

PETTIER > PETTY

PETTIES > PETTI

PETTIEST > PETTY

PETTIFOG vb quibble or fuss over details

PETTIFOGS > PETTIFOG

PETTILY > PETTY

PETTINESS > PETTY

PETTING > PET

PETTINGS > PET

PETTISH adj peevish or fretful

PETTISHLY > PETTISH

PETTITOES npl pig's trotters, esp when used as food

PETTLE vb pat animal

PETTLED > PETTLE

PETTLES > PETTLE

PETTLING > PETTLE

PETTO n breast of animal

PETTY adj unimportant, trivial

PETULANCE > PETULANT

PETULANCY > PETULANT

PETULANT adj childishly irritable or peevish

PETUNIA n garden plant with funnel-shaped flowers

PETUNIAS > PETUNIA

PETUNTSE n fusible feldspathic mineral used in hard-paste porcelain

PETUNTSES > PETUNTSE

PETUNTZE same as > PETUNTSE

PETUNTZES > PETUNTZE

PEW n fixed benchlike seat in a church

PEWEE n small N American flycatcher with a greenish-brown plumage

PEWEES > PEWEE

PEWHOLDER n renter of pew

PEWIT another name for > LAPWING

PEWITS > PEWIT

PEWS > PEW

PEWTER n greyish metal made of tin and lead

PEWTERER > PEWTER

PEWTERERS > PEWTER

PEWTERS > PEWTER

PEYOTE another name for > MESCAL

PEYOTES > PEYOTE

PEYOTISM n ritual use of peyote

PEYOTISMS > PEYOTISM

PEYOTIST n person who uses peyote

PEYOTISTS > PEYOTIST

PEYOTL same as > PEYOTE

PEYOTLS > PEYOTL

PEYSE vb weight or poise

PEYSED > PEYSE

PEYSES > PEYSE

PEYSING > PEYSE

PEYTRAL same as > PEYTREL

PEYTRALS > PEYTRAL

PEYTREL n breastplate of horse's armour

PEYTRELS > PEYTREL

PEZANT obsolete spelling of > PEASANT

PEZANTS > PEZANT

PEZIZOID adj having cup-like form

PFENNIG n former German monetary unit worth one hundredth of a mark

PFENNIGE > PFENNIG

PFENNIGS > PFENNIG

PFENNING old variant of > PFENNIG

PFENNINGS > PFENNING

PFFT interj sound indicating sudden disappearance of something

PFUI interj phooey

PHACELIA n plant grown for its large, deep blue bell flowers

PHACELIAS > PHACELIA

PHACOID adj lentil- or lens-shaped

PHACOIDAL same as > PHACOID

PHACOLITE n colourless variety of chabazite

PHACOLITH n lens-shaped igneous rock structure

PHAEIC adj (of animals) having dusky coloration

PHAEISM > PHAEIC

PHAEISMS > PHAEIC

PHAENOGAM n seed-bearing plant

PHAETON n light four-wheeled horse-drawn carriage with or without a top

PHAETONS > PHAETON

PHAGE n virus that is parasitic in a bacterium and multiplies within its host, which is destroyed when the new viruses are released

PHAGEDENA n rapidly spreading ulcer that

destroys tissues as it increases in size

PHAGES > PHAGE

PHAGOCYTE n cell or protozoan that engulfs particles, such as microorganisms

PHAGOSOME n part of biological cell

PHALANGAL > PHALANGE

PHALANGE another name for > PHALANX

PHALANGER same as > POSSUM

PHALANGES > PHALANX

PHALANGID n type of arachnid

PHALANX n closely grouped mass of people

PHALANXES > PHALANX

PHALAROPE n aquatic shore bird of northern oceans and lakes

PHALLI > PHALLUS

PHALLIC adj of or resembling a phallus

PHALLIN n poisonous substance from mushroom

PHALLINS > PHALLIN

PHALLISM n worship or veneration of the phallus

PHALLISMS > PHALLISM

PHALLIST n worshipper or venerator of the phallus

PHALLISTS > PHALLIST

PHALLOID adj resembling penis

PHALLUS n penis, esp as a symbol of reproductive power in primitive rites

PHALLUSES > PHALLUS

PHANG old variant spelling of > FANG

PHANGED > PHANG

PHANGING > PHANG

PHANGS > PHANG

PHANSIGAR n Indian assassin

PHANTASIM same as > PHANTASM

PHANTASM n unreal vision, illusion

PHANTASMA same as > PHANTASM

PHANTASMS > PHANTASM

PHANTAST same as > FANTAST

PHANTASTS > PHANTAST

PHANTASY same as > FANTASY

PHANTOM n ghost ▷ adj deceptive or unreal

PHANTOMS > PHANTOM

PHANTOMY adj of phantoms

PHANTOSME old spelling of > PHANTASM

PHARAOH n ancient Egyptian king

PHARAOHS > PHARAOH

PHARAONIC > PHARAOH

PHARE n beacon tower

PHARES > PHARE

PHARISAIC n righteously hypocritical

PHARISEE n self-righteous or hypocritical person

PHARISEES > PHARISEE

PHARM vb redirect (a website user) to another, bogus website for fraudulent purposes

PHARMA n pharmaceutical companies considered together as an industry

PHARMACY n preparation and dispensing of drugs and medicines

PHARMAS > PHARMA

PHARMED > PHARM

PHARMING n practice of rearing or growing genetically-modified animals or plants in order to develop pharmaceutical products

PHARMINGS > PHARMING

PHARMS > PHARM

PHAROS n lighthouse

PHAROSES > PHAROS

PHARYNGAL adj of, relating to, or situated in or near the pharynx

PHARYNGES > PHARYNX

PHARYNX n cavity forming the back part of the mouth

PHARYNXES > PHARYNX

PHASE n any distinct or characteristic stage in a development or chain of events ▷ vb arrange or carry out in stages or to coincide with something else

PHASEAL > PHASE

PHASED > PHASE

PHASEDOWN n gradual reduction

PHASELESS > PHASE

PHASEOLIN n anti-fungal substance from kidney bean

PHASEOUT n gradual reduction

PHASEOUTS > PHASEOUT

PHASES > PHASE

PHASIC > PHASE

PHASING n tonal sweep achieved by varying the phase relationship of two similar audio signals by mechanical or electronic means

PHASINGS > PHASING

PHASIS another word for > PHASE

PHASMID n stick insect or leaf insect

PHASMIDS > PHASMID

PHASOR n rotating vector representing a quantity, such as an alternating current or voltage, that varies sinusoidally

PHASORS > PHASOR

PHAT adj terrific

PHATIC adj (of speech, esp of conversational phrases) used to establish social contact and to express

sociability rather than specific meaning

PHATTER > PHAT

PHATTEST > PHAT

PHEASANT n game bird with bright plumage

PHEASANTS > PHEASANT

PHEAZAR old variant of > VIZIER

PHEAZARS > PHEAZAR

PHEER same as > FERE

PHEERE same as > FERE

PHEERES > PHEERE

PHEERS > PHEER

PHEESE vb worry

PHEESED > PHEESE

PHEESES > PHEESE

PHEESING > PHEESE

PHEEZE same as > PHEESE

PHEEZED > PHEEZE

PHEEZES > PHEEZE

PHEEZING > PHEEZE

PHELLEM technical name for > CORK

PHELLEMS > PHELLEM

PHELLOGEN n cork cambium

PHELLOID adj like cork

PHELONIA > PHELONION

PHELONION n vestment for an Orthodox priest

PHENACITE n colourless or white glassy mineral

PHENAKISM n deception

PHENAKITE same as > PHENACITE

PHENATE n ester or salt of phenol

PHENATES > PHENATE

PHENAZIN same as > PHENAZINE

PHENAZINE n yellow crystalline tricyclic compound

PHENAZINS > PHENAZIN

PHENE n genetically determined characteristic of organism

PHENES > PHENE

PHENETIC > PHENETICS

PHENETICS n system of classification based on similarities between organisms without regard to their evolutionary relationships

PHENETOL same as > PHENETOLE

PHENETOLE n colourless oily compound

PHENETOLS > PHENETOL

PHENGITE n type of alabaster

PHENGITES > PHENGITE

PHENIC adj of phenol

PHENIX same as > PHOENIX

PHENIXES > PHENIX

PHENOCOPY n noninheritable change in an organism that is caused by environmental influence during development but resembles the effects of a genetic mutation

PHENOGAM same as > PHAENOGAM

PHENOGAMS > PHENOGAM

PHENOL n chemical used in disinfectants and antiseptics

PHENOLATE vb treat or disinfect with phenol

PHENOLIC adj of, containing, or derived from phenol ▷ n derivative of phenol

PHENOLICS > PHENOLIC

PHENOLOGY n study of recurring phenomena, such as animal migration, esp as influenced by climatic conditions

PHENOLS > PHENOL

PHENOM n person or thing of outstanding abilities or qualities

PHENOMENA n phenomenons

PHENOMS > PHENOM

PHENOTYPE n physical form of an organism as determined by the interaction of its genetic make-up and its environment

PHENOXIDE n any of a class of salts of phenol

PHENOXY as in phenoxy resin any of a class of resins derived from polyhydroxy ethers

PHENYL n chemical substance

PHENYLENE n compound derived from benzene

PHENYLIC > PHENYL

PHENYLS > PHENYL

PHENYTOIN n anticonvulsant drug

PHEON n barbed iron head of dart

PHEONS > PHEON

PHERESES > PHERESIS

PHERESIS n specialized form of blood donation

PHEROMONE n chemical substance, secreted externally by certain animals, such as insects, affecting the behaviour or physiology of other animals of the same species

PHESE same as > PHEESE

PHESED > PHESE

PHESES > PHESE

PHESING > PHESE

PHEW interj exclamation of relief, surprise, etc

PHI n 21st letter in the Greek alphabet

PHIAL n small bottle for medicine etc ▷ vb put in phial

PHIALLED > PHIAL

PHIALLING > PHIAL

PHIALS > PHIAL

PHILABEG same as > FILIBEG

PHILABEGS > PHILABEG

PHILAMOT variant of > FILEMOT

PHILAMOTS > PHILAMOT

PHILANDER vb (of a man) flirt or have many casual love affairs with women

PHILATELY n stamp collecting

PHILHORSE n last horse in a team

PHILIBEG variant spelling of > FILIBEG

PHILIBEGS > PHILIBEG

PHILIPPIC n bitter or impassioned speech of denunciation, invective

PHILISTIA n domain of cultural philistine

PHILLABEG same as > FILIBEG

PHILLIBEG same as > FILIBEG

PHILOGYNY n fondness for women

PHILOLOGY n science of the structure and development of languages

PHILOMATH n lover of learning

PHILOMEL n nightingale

PHILOMELA same as > PHILOMEL

PHILOMELS > PHILOMEL

PHILOMOT n colour of dead leaf

PHILOMOTS > PHILOMOT

PHILOPENA n gift made as forfeit in game

PHILTER vb drink supposed to arouse love, desire, etc ▷ vb arouse sexual or romantic feelings by means of a philter

PHILTERED > PHILTER

PHILTERS > PHILTER

PHILTRA > PHILTRUM

PHILTRE n magic drink supposed to arouse love in the person who drinks it ▷ vb mix with love potion

PHILTRED > PHILTRE

PHILTRES > PHILTRE

PHILTRING > PHILTRE

PHILTRUM n indentation above the upper lip

PHIMOSES > PHIMOSIS

PHIMOSIS n abnormal tightness of the foreskin, preventing its being retracted over the tip of the penis

PHIMOTIC > PHIMOSIS

PHINNOCK variant spelling of > FINNOCK

PHINNOCKS > PHINNOCK

PHIS > PHI

PHISHING n use of fraudulent e-mails and lookalike websites to extract personal and financial details for criminal purposes

PHISHINGS > PHISHING

PHISNOMY n physiognomy

PHIZ n face or a facial expression
PHIZES > PHIZ
PHIZOG same as > PHIZ
PHIZOGS > PHIZOG
PHIZZES > PHIZ
PHLEBITIC > PHLEBITIS
PHLEBITIS n inflammation of a vein
PHLEGM n thick yellowish substance formed in the nose and throat during a cold
PHLEGMIER > PHLEGM
PHLEGMON n inflammatory mass that may progress to abscess
PHLEGMONS > PHLEGMON
PHLEGMS > PHLEGM
PHLEGMY > PHLEGM
PHLOEM n plant tissue that acts as a path for the distribution of food substances to all parts of the plant
PHLOEMS > PHLOEM
PHLOMIS n plant of Phlomis genus
PHLOMISES > PHLOMIS
PHLORIZIN n chemical found in root bark of fruit trees
PHLOX n flowering garden plant
PHLOXES > PHLOX
PHLYCTENA n small blister, vesicle, or pustule
PHO n Vietnamese noodle soup
PHOBIA n intense and unreasoning fear or dislike
PHOBIAS > PHOBIA
PHOBIC adj of, relating to, or arising from a phobia ▷ n person suffering from a phobia
PHOBICS > PHOBIC
PHOBISM n phobia
PHOBISMS > PHOBISM
PHOBIST > PHOBISM
PHOBISTS > PHOBISM
PHOCA n genus of seals
PHOCAE > PHOCA
PHOCAS > PHOCA
PHOCINE adj of, relating to, or resembling a seal
PHOCOMELY n congenital deformity resulting from prenatal interference with the development of the fetal limbs, characterized esp by short stubby hands or feet attached close to the body
PHOEBE n greyish-brown North American flycatcher
PHOEBES > PHOEBE
PHOEBUS n sun
PHOEBUSES > PHOEBUS
PHOENIX n legendary bird said to set fire to itself and rise anew from its ashes
PHOENIXES > PHOENIX
PHOH variant of > FOH

PHOLADES > PHOLAS
PHOLAS n type of bivalve mollusc
PHON n unit of loudness
PHONAL adj relating to voice
PHONATE vb articulate speech sounds, esp to cause the vocal cords to vibrate in the execution of a voiced speech sound
PHONATED > PHONATE
PHONATES > PHONATE
PHONATHON n telephone-based fund-raising campaign
PHONATING > PHONATE
PHONATION > PHONATE
PHONATORY > PHONATE
PHONE vb telephone ▷ n single uncomplicated speech sound
PHONECAM n digital camera incorporated in a mobile phone
PHONECAMS > PHONECAM
PHONECARD n card used to operate certain public telephones
PHONED > PHONE
PHONEME n one of the set of speech sounds in any given language that serve to distinguish one word from another
PHONEMES > PHONEME
PHONEMIC adj of or relating to the phoneme
PHONEMICS n classification and analysis of the phonemes of a language
PHONER n person making a telephone call
PHONERS > PHONER
PHONES > PHONE
PHONETIC adj of speech sounds
PHONETICS n science of speech sounds
PHONETISE same as > PHONETIZE
PHONETISM n phonetic writing
PHONETIST n person who advocates or uses a system of phonetic spelling
PHONETIZE vb represent by phonetic signs
PHONEY adj not genuine ▷ n phoney person or thing ▷ vb fake
PHONEYED > PHONEY
PHONEYING > PHONEY
PHONEYS > PHONEY
PHONIC > PHONICS
PHONICS n method of teaching people to read by training them to associate letters with their phonetic values
PHONIED > PHONY
PHONIER > PHONY
PHONIES > PHONY
PHONIEST > PHONY

PHONILY > PHONY
PHONINESS > PHONY
PHONING > PHONE
PHONMETER n instrument measuring sound levels
PHONO n phonograph
PHONOGRAM n any written symbol standing for a sound, syllable, morpheme, or word
PHONOLITE n fine-grained volcanic igneous rock consisting of alkaline feldspars and nepheline
PHONOLOGY n study of the speech sounds in a language
PHONON n quantum of vibrational energy in the acoustic vibrations of a crystal lattice
PHONONS > PHONON
PHONOPORE n device for conveying sound
PHONOS > PHONO
PHONOTYPE n letter or symbol representing a sound
PHONOTYPY n transcription of speech into phonetic symbols
PHONS > PHON
PHONY vb fake
PHONYING > PHONY
PHOOEY interj exclamation of scorn or contempt
PHORATE n type of insecticide
PHORATES > PHORATE
PHORESIES > PHORESY
PHORESY n association in which one animal clings to another to ensure movement from place to place, as some mites use some insects
PHORMINX n ancient Greek stringed instrument
PHORMIUM n New Zealand plant with leathery evergreen leaves and red or yellow flowers in panicles
PHORMIUMS > PHORMIUM
PHORONID n small wormlike marine animal
PHORONIDS > PHORONID
PHOS > PHO
PHOSGENE n poisonous gas used in warfare
PHOSGENES > PHOSGENE
PHOSPHATE n compound of phosphorus
PHOSPHENE n sensation of light caused by pressure on the eyelid of a closed eye or by other mechanical or electrical interference with the visual system
PHOSPHID same as > PHOSPHIDE
PHOSPHIDE n any compound of phosphorus with another element, esp a more electropositive element

PHOSPHIDS > PHOSPHID
PHOSPHIN same as > PHOSPHINE
PHOSPHINE n colourless flammable gas that is slightly soluble in water and has a strong fishy odour
PHOSPHINS > PHOSPHIN
PHOSPHITE n any salt or ester of phosphorous acid
PHOSPHOR n substance capable of emitting light when irradiated with particles of electromagnetic radiation
PHOSPHORE same as > PHOSPHOR
PHOSPHORI n plural of phosphorus
PHOSPHORS > PHOSPHOR
PHOSSY as in phossy jaw gangrenous condition of the lower jawbone caused by prolonged exposure to phosphorus fumes
PHOT n unit of illumination equal to one lumen per square centimetre
PHOTIC adj of or concerned with light
PHOTICS n science of light
PHOTINIA n genus of garden plants
PHOTINIAS > PHOTINIA
PHOTISM n sensation of light or colour caused by stimulus of another sense
PHOTISMS > PHOTISM
PHOTO n photograph ▷ vb take a photograph of
PHOTOCARD n identity card containing a photograph of the bearer
PHOTOCELL n cell which produces a current or voltage when exposed to light or other electromagnetic radiation
PHOTOCOPY n photographic reproduction ▷ vb make a photocopy of
PHOTOED > PHOTO
PHOTOFIT n method of combining photographs of facial features, hair, etc, into a composite picture of a face
PHOTOFITS > PHOTOFIT
PHOTOG n photograph
PHOTOGEN same as > PHOTOGENE
PHOTOGENE n afterimage
PHOTOGENS > PHOTOGEN
PHOTOGENY n photography
PHOTOGRAM n picture, usually abstract, produced on a photographic material without the use of a camera, as by placing an object on the material and exposing to light
PHOTOGS > PHOTOG
PHOTOING > PHOTO

PHOTOLYSE vb cause to undergo photolysis

PHOTOLYZE same as > PHOTOLYZE

PHOTOMAP n map constructed by adding grid lines, place names, etc, to one or more aerial photographs ▷ vb map (an area) using aerial photography

PHOTOMAPS > PHOTOMAP

PHOTOMASK n material on which etching pattern for integrated circuit is drawn

PHOTON n quantum of electromagnetic radiation energy, such as light, having both particle and wave behaviour

PHOTONIC > PHOTON

PHOTONICS n study and design of devices and systems, such as optical fibres, that depend on the transmission, modulation, or amplification of streams of photons

PHOTONS > PHOTON

PHOTOPHIL n light-seeking organism

PHOTOPIA n normal adaptation of the eye to light

PHOTOPIAS > PHOTOPIA

PHOTOPIC > PHOTOPIA

PHOTOPLAY n play filmed as movie

PHOTOPSIA n appearance of flashes due to retinal irritation

PHOTOPSY same as > PHOTOPSIA

PHOTOS > PHOTO

PHOTOSCAN n photographic scan

PHOTOSET vb set (type matter) by photosetting

PHOTOSETS > PHOTOSET

PHOTOSHOP vb edit or alter a picture digitally, usu with Adobe Photoshop

PHOTOSTAT n copy made by photocopying machine ▷ vb make a photostat copy (of)

PHOTOTAXY n movement of an entire organism in response to light

PHOTOTUBE n type of photocell in which radiation falling on a photocathode causes electrons to flow to an anode and thus produce an electric current

PHOTOTYPE n printing plate produced by photography ▷ vb reproduce (an illustration) using a phototype

PHOTOTYPY n process of producing phototypes

PHOTS > PHOT

PHPHT interj expressing irritation or reluctance

PHRASAL adj of, relating to, or composed of phrases

PHRASALLY > PHRASAL

PHRASE n group of words forming a unit of meaning, esp within a sentence ▷ vb express in words

PHRASED > PHRASE

PHRASEMAN n coiner of phrases

PHRASEMEN > PHRASEMAN

PHRASER > PHRASE

PHRASERS > PHRASE

PHRASES > PHRASE

PHRASIER > PHRASY

PHRASIEST > PHRASY

PHRASING n exact words used to say or write something

PHRASINGS > PHRASING

PHRASY adj containing phrases

PHRATRAL > PHRATRY

PHRATRIC > PHRATRY

PHRATRIES > PHRATRY

PHRATRY n group of people within a tribe who have a common ancestor

PHREAK vb hack into a telecommunications system

PHREAKED > PHREAK

PHREAKER > PHREAK

PHREAKERS > PHREAK

PHREAKING > PHREAK

PHREAKS > PHREAK

PHREATIC adj of or relating to ground water occurring below the water table

PHRENESES > PHRENESIS

PHRENESIS n mental confusion

PHRENETIC obsolete spelling of > FRENETIC

PHRENIC adj of or relating to the diaphragm ▷ n (a nerve, blood vessel, etc) located in the diaphragm

PHRENICS > PHRENIC

PHRENISM n belief in non-physical life force

PHRENISMS > PHRENISM

PHRENITIC > PHRENITIS

PHRENITIS n state of frenzy

PHRENSIED > PHRENSY

PHRENSIES > PHRENSY

PHRENSY obsolete spelling of > FRENZY

PHRENTICK obsolete spelling of > PHRENETIC

PHRYGANA another name for > GARIGUE

PHRYGANAS > PHRYGANA

PHT same as > PHPHT

PHTHALATE n salt or ester of phthalic acid

PHTHALEIN n any of a class of organic compounds obtained by the reaction of phthalic anhydride with a phenol and used in dyes

PHTHALIC as in phthalic anhydride white crystalline substance used mainly in producing dyestuffs

PHTHALIN n colourless compound formed by reduction of phthalein

PHTHALINS > PHTHALIN

PHTHISES > PHTHISIS

PHTHISIC adj relating to or affected with phthisis ▷ n person suffering from phthisis

PHTHISICS > PHTHISIC

PHTHISIS n any disease that causes wasting of the body, esp pulmonary tuberculosis

PHUT vb make muffled explosive sound

PHUTS > PHUT

PHUTTED > PHUT

PHUTTING > PHUT

PHWOAH > PHWOAR

PHWOAR interj expression of sexual interest or attraction

PHYCOCYAN n type of protein found in some algae

PHYCOLOGY n study of algae

PHYLA > PHYLUM

PHYLAE > PHYLE

PHYLAR > PHYLUM

PHYLARCH n chief of tribe

PHYLARCHS > PHYLARCH

PHYLARCHY > PHYLARCH

PHYLAXIS n protection against infection

PHYLE n tribe or clan of an ancient Greek people such as the Ionians

PHYLESES > PHYLESIS

PHYLESIS n evolutionary events that modify taxon without causing speciation

PHYLETIC adj of or relating to the evolution of a species or group of organisms

PHYLETICS n study of the evolution of species

PHYLIC > PHYLE

PHYLLARY n bract subtending flower head of composite plant

PHYLLID n leaf of a liverwort or moss

PHYLLIDS > PHYLLID

PHYLLITE n compact lustrous metamorphic rock, rich in mica, derived from a shale or other clay-rich rock

PHYLLITES > PHYLLITE

PHYLLITIC > PHYLLITE

PHYLLO variant of > FILO

PHYLLODE n flattened leafstalk that resembles and functions as a leaf

PHYLLODES > PHYLLODE

PHYLLODIA > PHYLLODE

PHYLLODY n abnormal development of leaves from parts of flower

PHYLLOID adj resembling a leaf ▷ n leaf-like organ

PHYLLOIDS > PHYLLOID

PHYLLOME n leaf or a leaflike organ

PHYLLOMES > PHYLLOME

PHYLLOMIC > PHYLLOME

PHYLLOPOD n crustacean with leaf-like appendages

PHYLLOS > PHYLLO

PHYLOGENY n sequence of events involved in the evolution of a species, genus, etc

PHYLON n tribe

PHYLUM n major taxonomic division of animals and plants that contains one or more classes

PHYSALIA n Portuguese man-of-war

PHYSALIAS > PHYSALIA

PHYSALIS n strawberry tomato

PHYSED n physical education

PHYSEDS > PHYSED

PHYSES > PHYSIS

PHYSETER n creature such as the sperm whale

PHYSETERS > PHYSETER

PHYSIATRY n treatment of injury by physical means

PHYSIC n medicine or drug, esp a cathartic or purge ▷ vb treat (a patient) with medicine

PHYSICAL adj of the body, as contrasted with the mind or spirit

PHYSICALS npl commodities that can be purchased and used, as opposed to those bought and sold in a futures market

PHYSICIAN n doctor of medicine

PHYSICISM n belief in the physical as opposed to the spiritual

PHYSICIST n person skilled in or studying physics

PHYSICKED > PHYSIC

PHYSICKY > PHYSIC

PHYSICS n science of the properties of matter and energy

PHYSIO n physiotherapy

PHYSIOS > PHYSIO

PHYSIQUE n person's bodily build and muscular development

PHYSIQUED adj having particular physique

PHYSIQUES > PHYSIQUE

PHYSIS n part of bone responsible for lengthening

PHYTANE n hydrocarbon found in some fossilised plant remains

PHYTANES > PHYTANE

PHYTIN n substance from plants used as an energy supplement

PHYTINS > PHYTIN

PHYTOGENY n branch of botany that is concerned with the detailed description of plants

PHYTOID adj resembling plant

PHYTOL n alcohol used to synthesize some vitamins

PHYTOLITH n microscopic particle in plants

PHYTOLOGY rare name for > BOTANY

PHYTOLS > PHYTOL

PHYTON n unit of plant structure, usually considered as the smallest part of the plant that is capable of growth when detached from the parent plant

PHYTONIC > PHYTON

PHYTONS > PHYTON

PHYTOSES > PHYTOSIS

PHYTOSIS n disease caused by vegetable parasite

PHYTOTOMY n dissection of plants

PHYTOTRON n building in which plants can be grown on a large scale, under controlled conditions

PI n sixteenth letter of the Greek alphabet ▷ vb spill and mix (set type) indiscriminately

PIA n innermost of the three membranes that cover the brain and the spinal cord

PIACEVOLE adv to be performed in playful manner

PIACULAR adj making expiation for a sacrilege

PIAFFE n passage done on the spot ▷ vb strut on the spot

PIAFFED > PIAFFE

PIAFFER > PIAFFE

PIAFFERS > PIAFFE

PIAFFES > PIAFFE

PIAFFING > PIAFFE

PIAL adj relating to pia mater

PIAN n contagious tropical skin disease

PIANETTE n small piano

PIANETTES > PIANETTE

PIANI > PIANO

PIANIC adj of piano

PIANINO n small upright piano

PIANINOS > PIANINO

PIANISM n technique, skill, or artistry in playing the piano

PIANISMS > PIANISM

PIANIST n person who plays the piano

PIANISTE variant of

> PIANIST

PIANISTES > PIANISTE

PIANISTIC > PIANISM

PIANISTS > PIANIST

PIANO n musical instrument with strings which are struck by hammers worked by a keyboard ▷ adv quietly

PIANOLIST n person who plays the Pianola

PIANOS > PIANO

PIANS > PIAN

PIARIST n member of a Roman religious order

PIARISTS > PIARIST

PIAS > PIA

PIASABA same as > PIASSAVA

PIASABAS > PIASABA

PIASAVA same as > PIASSAVA

PIASAVAS > PIASAVA

PIASSABA same as > PIASSAVA

PIASSABAS > PIASSABA

PIASSAVA n South American palm tree

PIASSAVAS > PIASSAVA

PIASTER same as > PIASTRE

PIASTERS > PIASTER

PIASTRE n standard monetary unit of South Vietnam, divided into 100 cents

PIASTRES > PIASTRE

PIAZZA n square or marketplace, esp in Italy

PIAZZAS > PIAZZA

PIAZZE > PIAZZA

PIAZZIAN > PIAZZA

PIBAL n method of measuring wind

PIBALS > PIBAL

PIBROCH n form of bagpipe music

PIBROCHS > PIBROCH

PIC n photograph or illustration

PICA n abnormal craving to ingest substances such as clay, dirt, and hair

PICACHO n pointed solitary mountain

PICACHOS > PICACHO

PICADILLO n Mexican dish

PICADOR n mounted bullfighter with a lance

PICADORES > PICADOR

PICADORS > PICADOR

PICAL adj relating to pica

PICAMAR n hydrocarbon extract of beechwood tar

PICAMARS > PICAMAR

PICANINNY n offensive term for a small Black or Aboriginal child

PICANTE adj spicy

PICARA n female adventurer

PICARAS > PICARA

PICARIAN n tree-haunting bird

PICARIANS > PICARIAN

PICARO n roguish adventurer

PICAROON n adventurer or rogue

PICAROONS > PICAROON

PICAROS > PICARO

PICAS > PICA

PICAYUNE adj of small value or importance ▷ n any coin of little value, such as a five-cent piece

PICAYUNES > PICAYUNE

PICCADILL n high stiff collar

PICCANIN n offensive word for a Black African child

PICCANINS > PICCANIN

PICCATA adj sautéed and served in a sauce containing lemon, butter, parsley and spices

PICCIES > PICCY

PICCOLO n small flute

PICCOLOS > PICCOLO

PICCY n picture or photograph

PICE n former Indian coin worth one sixty-fourth of a rupee

PICENE n type of hydrocarbon

PICENES > PICENE

PICEOUS adj of, relating to, or resembling pitch

PICHOLINE n variety of olive

PICHURIM n S American laurel tree

PICHURIMS > PICHURIM

PICIFORM adj relating to certain tree-haunting birds

PICINE adj relating to woodpeckers

PICK vb choose ▷ n choice

PICKABACK same as > PIGGYBACK

PICKABLE > PICK

PICKADIL same as > PICCADILL

PICKADILL same as > PICCADILL

PICKADILS > PICKADIL

PICKAPACK same as > PICKABACK

PICKAROON same as > PICAROON

PICKAX same as > PICKAXE

PICKAXE n large pick ▷ vb use a pickaxe on (earth, rocks, etc)

PICKAXED > PICKAXE

PICKAXES > PICKAXE

PICKAXING > PICKAXE

PICKBACK vb carry by piggyback

PICKBACKS > PICKBACK

PICKED > PICK

PICKEER vb make raid for booty

PICKEERED > PICKEER

PICKEERER > PICKEER

PICKEERS > PICKEER

PICKER n person or thing that picks, esp that gathers fruit, crops, etc

PICKEREL n North American freshwater game fish

PICKERELS > PICKEREL

PICKERIES > PICKERY

PICKERS > PICKER

PICKERY n petty theft

PICKET n person or group standing outside a workplace to deter would-be workers during a strike ▷ vb form a picket outside (a workplace)

PICKETED > PICKET

PICKETER > PICKET

PICKETERS > PICKET

PICKETING > PICKET

PICKETS > PICKET

PICKIER > PICKY

PICKIEST > PICKY

PICKILY > PICKY

PICKIN n small child

PICKINESS > PICKY

PICKING > PICK

PICKINGS npl money easily acquired

PICKINS > PICKIN

PICKLE n food preserved in vinegar or salt water ▷ vb preserve in vinegar or salt water

PICKLED adj (of food) preserved

PICKLER > PICKLE

PICKLERS > PICKLE

PICKLES > PICKLE

PICKLING > PICKLE

PICKLOCK n person who picks locks, esp one who gains unlawful access to premises by this means

PICKLOCKS > PICKLOCK

PICKMAW n type of gull

PICKMAWS > PICKMAW

PICKOFF n baseball play

PICKOFFS > PICKOFF

PICKPROOF adj (of a lock) unable to be picked

PICKS > PICK

PICKTHANK n flatterer

PICKUP n small truck with an open body and low sides

PICKUPS > PICKUP

PICKWICK n tool for raising the short wick of an oil lamp

PICKWICKS > PICKWICK

PICKY adj fussy

PICLORAM n type of herbicide

PICLORAMS > PICLORAM

PICNIC n informal meal out of doors ▷ vb have a picnic

PICNICKED > PICNIC

PICNICKER > PICNIC

PICNICKY > PICNIC

PICNICS > PICNIC

PICOCURIE n unit of radioactivity

PICOFARAD n unit of capacitance

PICOGRAM n trillionth of gram

PICOGRAMS > PICOGRAM

PICOLIN variant of > PICOLINE

PICOLINE n liquid derivative of pyridine found in bone oil and coal tar

PICOLINES > PICOLINE

PICOLINIC > PICOLINE

PICOLINS > PICOLIN

PICOMETER same as > PICOMETRE

PICOMETRE n trillionth fraction of metre

PICOMOLE n trillionth of a mole

PICOMOLES > PICOMOLE

PICONG n any teasing or satirical banter, originally a verbal duel in song

PICONGS > PICONG

PICOT n any of pattern of small loops, as on lace ▷ vb decorate material with small loops

PICOTE adj (of material) picoted

PICOTED > PICOT

PICOTEE n type of carnation having pale petals edged with a darker colour, usually red

PICOTEES > PICOTEE

PICOTING > PICOT

PICOTITE n dark-brown mineral

PICOTITES > PICOTITE

PICOTS > PICOT

PICOWAVE vb treat food with gamma waves

PICOWAVED > PICOWAVE

PICOWAVES > PICOWAVE

PICQUET vb provide early warning of attack

PICQUETED > PICQUET

PICQUETS > PICQUET

PICRA n powder of aloes and canella

PICRAS > PICRA

PICRATE n any salt or ester of picric acid, such as sodium picrate

PICRATED adj containing picrate

PICRATES > PICRATE

PICRIC as in picric acid toxic sparingly soluble crystalline yellow acid

PICRITE n coarse-grained ultrabasic igneous rock consisting of olivine and augite with small amounts of plagioclase feldspar

PICRITES > PICRITE

PICRITIC > PICRITE

PICS > PIC

PICTARNIE Scots word for > TERN

PICTOGRAM n picture or symbol standing for a word or group of words, as in written Chinese

PICTORIAL adj of or in painting or pictures ▷ n newspaper etc with many pictures

PICTURAL n picture

PICTURALS > PICTURAL

PICTURE n drawing or painting ▷ vb visualize, imagine

PICTURED > PICTURE

PICTURES > PICTURE

PICTURING > PICTURE

PICTURISE same as > PICTURIZE

PICTURIZE vb adorn with pictures

PICUL n unit of weight, used in China, Japan, and SE Asia

PICULET n small tropical woodpecker with a short tail

PICULETS > PICULET

PICULS > PICUL

PIDDLE vb urinate

PIDDLED > PIDDLE

PIDDLER > PIDDLE

PIDDLERS > PIDDLE

PIDDLIER > PIDDLY

PIDDLIEST > PIDDLY

PIDDLING adj small or unimportant

PIDDLY adj trivial

PIDDOCK n marine bivalve that bores into rock, clay, or wood

PIDDOCKS > PIDDOCK

PIDGEON variant of > PIDGIN

PIDGEONS > PIDGEON

PIDGIN n language, not a mother tongue, made up of elements of two or more other languages

PIDGINISE same as > PIDGINIZE

PIDGINIZE vb create pidgin language

PIDGINS > PIDGIN

PIE n dish of meat, fruit, etc baked in pastry

PIEBALD adj (horse) with irregular black-and-white markings ▷ n black-and-white horse

PIEBALDS > PIEBALD

PIECE n separate bit or part

PIECED > PIECE

PIECELESS > PIECE

PIECEMEAL adv bit by bit ▷ adj fragmentary or unsystematic

PIECEN vb join broken threads

PIECENED > PIECEN

PIECENER > PIECEN

PIECENERS > PIECEN

PIECENING > PIECEN

PIECENS > PIECEN

PIECER n person who mends, repairs, or joins something, esp broken threads on a loom

PIECERS > PIECER

PIECES > PIECE

PIECEWISE adv with respect to number of discrete pieces

PIECEWORK n work paid for according to the quantity produced

PIECING > PIECE

PIECINGS > PIECE

PIECRUST n pastry used for making pies

PIECRUSTS > PIECRUST

PIED > PI

PIEDFORT n coin thicker than normal

PIEDFORTS > PIEDFORT

PIEDISH n container for baking pies

PIEDISHES > PIEDISH

PIEDMONT adj (of glaciers, plains, etc) formed or situated at the foot of a mountain or mountain range ▷ n gentle slope leading from mountains to flat land

PIEDMONTS > PIEDMONT

PIEDNESS n state of being pied

PIEFORT same as > PIEDFORT

PIEFORTS > PIEFORT

PIEHOLE n person's mouth

PIEHOLES > PIEHOLE

PIEING > PIE

PIEMAN n seller of pies

PIEMEN > PIEMAN

PIEND n a salient angle

PIENDS > PIEND

PIEPLANT n rhubarb

PIEPLANTS > PIEPLANT

PIEPOWDER n former court for dealing with certain disputes

PIER n platform on stilts sticking out into the sea

PIERAGE n accommodation for ships at piers

PIERAGES > PIERAGE

PIERCE vb make a hole in or through with a sharp instrument

PIERCED > PIERCE

PIERCER > PIERCE

PIERCERS > PIERCE

PIERCES > PIERCE

PIERCING adj (of a sound) shrill and high-pitched ▷ n art or practice of piercing body parts for the insertion of jewellery

PIERCINGS > PIERCING

PIERHEAD n end of a pier farthest from the shore

PIERHEADS > PIERHEAD

PIERID n type of butterfly

PIERIDINE adj > PIERID

PIERIDS > PIERID

PIERIS n American or Asiatic shrub

PIERISES > PIERIS

PIEROGI n Polish dumpling

PIEROGIES > PIEROGI

PIERRETTE n female pierrot

PIERROT n clown or masquerader with a whitened face, white costume, and pointed hat

PIERROTS > PIERROT

PIERS > PIER

PIERST archaic spelling of > PIERCED

PIERT n small plant with small greenish flowers

PIERTS > PIERT

PIES > PIE

PIET n magpie

PIETA n sculpture, painting, or drawing of the dead Christ, supported by the Virgin Mary

PIETAS > PIETA

PIETIES > PIETY

PIETISM n exaggerated piety

PIETISMS > PIETISM

PIETIST > PIETISM

PIETISTIC > PIETISM

PIETISTS > PIETISM

PIETS > PIET

PIETY n deep devotion to God and religion

PIEZO adj piezoelectric

PIFFERARI > PIFFERARO

PIFFERARO n player of piffero

PIFFERO n small rustic flute

PIFFEROS > PIFFERO

PIFFLE n nonsense ▷ vb talk or behave feebly

PIFFLED > PIFFLE

PIFFLER n talker of nonsense

PIFFLERS > PIFFLER

PIFFLES > PIFFLE

PIFFLING adj worthless

PIG n animal kept and killed for pork, ham, and bacon ▷ vb eat greedily

PIGBOAT n submarine

PIGBOATS > PIGBOAT

PIGEON n bird with a heavy body and short legs, sometimes trained to carry messages ▷ vb pigeonhole

PIGEONED > PIGEON

PIGEONING > PIGEON

PIGEONITE n brownish mineral

PIGEONRY n loft for keeping pigeons

PIGEONS > PIGEON

PIGFACE n creeping succulent plant with bright-coloured flowers and red fruits

PIGFACES > PIGFACE

PIGFEED n food for pigs

PIGFEEDS > PIGFEED

PIGFISH n grunting fish of the North American Atlantic coast

PIGFISHES > PIGFISH

PIGGED > PIG
PIGGERIES > PIGGERY
PIGGERY n place for keeping and breeding pigs
PIGGIE same as > PIGGY
PIGGIER > PIGGY
PIGGIES > PIGGY
PIGGIEST > PIGGY
PIGGIN n small wooden bucket or tub
PIGGINESS > PIGGY
PIGGING > PIG
PIGGINGS > PIG
PIGGINS > PIGGIN
PIGGISH adj like a pig, esp in appetite or manners
PIGGISHLY > PIGGISH
PIGGY n child's word for a pig, esp a piglet ▷ adj like a pig, esp in appetite
PIGGYBACK n ride on someone's shoulders ▷ adv carried on someone's shoulders ▷ adj on the back and shoulders of another person ▷ vb give (a person) a piggyback on one's back and shoulders
PIGHEADED adj stupidly stubborn
PIGHT vb pierce
PIGHTED > PIGHT
PIGHTING > PIGHT
PIGHTLE n small enclosure
PIGHTLES > PIGHTLE
PIGHTS > PIGHT
PIGLET n young pig
PIGLETS > PIGLET
PIGLIKE > PIG
PIGLING n young pig
PIGLINGS > PIGLING
PIGMAEAN same as > PYGMAEAN
PIGMEAN same as > PYGMAEAN
PIGMEAT less common name for > PORK
PIGMEATS > PIGMEAT
PIGMENT n colouring matter, paint or dye ▷ vb colour with pigment
PIGMENTAL > PIGMENT
PIGMENTED > PIGMENT
PIGMENTS > PIGMENT
PIGMIES > PIGMY
PIGMOID adj of pygmies
PIGMY same as > PYGMY
PIGNERATE vb pledge or pawn
PIGNOLI same as > PIGNOLIA
PIGNOLIA n edible seed of nut pine
PIGNOLIAS > PIGNOLIA
PIGNOLIS > PIGNOLI
PIGNORA > PIGNUS
PIGNORATE same as > PIGNERATE
PIGNUS n pawn or pledge
PIGNUT n bitter nut of any of several North American hickory trees
PIGNUTS > PIGNUT
PIGOUT n binge

PIGOUTS > PIGOUT
PIGPEN same as > PIGSTY
PIGPENS > PIGPEN
PIGS > PIG
PIGSCONCE n foolish person
PIGSKIN n skin of the domestic pig ▷ adj made of pigskin
PIGSKINS > PIGSKIN
PIGSNEY same as > PIGSNY
PIGSNEYS > PIGSNEY
PIGSNIE same as > PIGSNY
PIGSNIES > PIGSNIE
PIGSNY n former pet name for girl
PIGSTICK vb (esp in India) hunt and spear wild boar, esp from horseback
PIGSTICKS > PIGSTICK
PIGSTIES > PIGSTY
PIGSTUCK > PIGSTICK
PIGSTY same as > PIGPEN
PIGSWILL n waste food or other edible matter fed to pigs
PIGSWILLS > PIGSWILL
PIGTAIL n plait of hair hanging from the back or either side of the head
PIGTAILED > PIGTAIL
PIGTAILS > PIGTAIL
PIGWASH n wet feed for pigs
PIGWASHES > PIGWASH
PIGWEED n coarse North American amaranthaceous weed
PIGWEEDS > PIGWEED
PIHOIHOI n variety of New Zealand pipit
PIHOIHOIS > PIHOIHOI
PIING > PI
PIKA n burrowing lagomorph mammal of mountainous regions of North America and Asia
PIKAKE n type of Asian vine
PIKAKES > PIKAKE
PIKAS > PIKA
PIKAU n pack, knapsack, or rucksack
PIKAUS > PIKAU
PIKE n large predatory freshwater fish ▷ vb stab or pierce using a pike ▷ adj (of the body position of a diver) bent at the hips but with the legs straight
PIKED > PIKE
PIKELET n small thick pancake
PIKELETS > PIKELET
PIKEMAN n (formerly) soldier armed with a pike
PIKEMEN > PIKEMAN
PIKEPERCH n pikelike freshwater teleost fish
PIKER n shirker
PIKERS > PIKER
PIKES > PIKE
PIKESTAFF n wooden

handle of a pike
PIKEY n in British English, derogatory word for gypsy or vagrant
PIKEYS > PIKEY
PIKI n bread made from blue cornmeal
PIKING > PIKE
PIKINGS > PIKE
PIKIS > PIKI
PIKUL same as > PICUL
PIKULS > PIKUL
PILA n pillar-like anatomical structure
PILAF same as > PILAU
PILAFF same as > PILAU
PILAFFS > PILAFF
PILAFS > PILAF
PILAO same as > PILAU
PILAOS > PILAO
PILAR adj relating to hair
PILASTER n square column, usu set in a wall
PILASTERS > PILASTER
PILAU n Middle Eastern dish of meat, fish, or poultry boiled with rice, spices, etc
PILAUS > PILAU
PILAW same as > PILAU
PILAWS > PILAW
PILCH n outer garment, originally one made of skin
PILCHARD n small edible sea fish of the herring family
PILCHARDS > PILCHARD
PILCHER n scabbard for sword
PILCHERS > PILCHER
PILCHES > PILCH
PILCORN n type if oat
PILCORNS > PILCORN
PILCROW n paragraph mark
PILCROWS > PILCROW
PILE n number of things lying on top of each other ▷ vb collect into a pile
PILEA n artillery or gunpowder plant, which releases a cloud of pollen when shaken
PILEAS > PILEA
PILEATE adj (of birds) having a crest
PILEATED same as > PILEATE
PILED > PILE
PILEI > PILEUS
PILELESS > PILE
PILEOUS adj hairy
PILER n placer of things on pile
PILERS > PILER
PILES npl swollen veins in the rectum, haemorrhoids
PILEUM n top of a bird's head from the base of the bill to the occiput
PILEUP n multiple collision of vehicles
PILEUPS > PILEUP
PILEUS n upper

cap-shaped part of a mushroom or similar spore-producing body
PILEWORK n construction built from heavy stakes or cylinders
PILEWORKS > PILEWORK
PILEWORT n any of several plants, such as lesser celandine, thought to be effective in treating piles
PILEWORTS > PILEWORT
PILFER vb steal in small quantities
PILFERAGE n act or practice of stealing small quantities or articles
PILFERED > PILFER
PILFERER > PILFER
PILFERERS > PILFER
PILFERIES > PILFERY
PILFERING > PILFER
PILFERS > PILFER
PILFERY n theft
PILGARLIC n bald head or a man with a bald head
PILGRIM n person who journeys to a holy place
PILGRIMER n one who undertakes a pilgrimage
PILGRIMS > PILGRIM
PILI n Philippine tree with edible seeds resembling almonds
PILIFORM adj resembling a long hair
PILING n act of driving piles
PILINGS > PILING
PILINUT n type of nut found in the Philippines
PILINUTS > PILINUT
PILIS > PILI
PILL n small ball of medicine swallowed whole ▷ vb peel or skin (something)
PILLAGE vb steal property by violence in war ▷ n violent seizure of goods, esp in war
PILLAGED > PILLAGE
PILLAGER > PILLAGE
PILLAGERS > PILLAGE
PILLAGES > PILLAGE
PILLAGING > PILLAGE
PILLAR n upright post, usu supporting a roof ▷ vb provide or support with pillars
PILLARED > PILLAR
PILLARING > PILLAR
PILLARIST n recluse who sat on high pillar
PILLARS > PILLAR
PILLAU same as > PILAU
PILLAUS > PILLAU
PILLBOX n small box for pills
PILLBOXES > PILLBOX
PILLED > PILL
PILLHEAD n person addicted to pills
PILLHEADS > PILLHEAD
PILLICOCK n penis

PILLIE n pilchard
PILLIES > PILLIE
PILLING > PILL
PILLINGS > PILL
PILLION n seat for a passenger behind the rider of a motorcycle ▷ adv on a pillion ▷ vb ride pillion
PILLIONED > PILLION
PILLIONS > PILLION
PILLOCK n stupid or annoying person
PILLOCKS > PILLOCK
PILLORIED > PILLORY
PILLORIES > PILLORY
PILLORISE same as > PILLORIZE
PILLORIZE vb put in pillory
PILLORY n frame with holes for the head and hands in which an offender was locked and exposed to public abuse ▷ vb ridicule publicly
PILLOW n stuffed cloth bag for supporting the head in bed ▷ vb rest as if on a pillow
PILLOWED > PILLOW
PILLOWING > PILLOW
PILLOWS > PILLOW
PILLOWY > PILLOW
PILLS > PILL
PILLWORM n worm that rolls up spirally
PILLWORMS > PILLWORM
PILLWORT n small Eurasian water fern
PILLWORTS > PILLWORT
PILOMOTOR adj causing movement of hairs
PILONIDAL adj of crease above buttocks
PILOSE adj covered with fine soft hairs
PILOSITY > PILOSE
PILOT n person qualified to fly an aircraft or spacecraft ▷ adj experimental and preliminary ▷ vb act as the pilot of
PILOTAGE n act of piloting an aircraft or ship
PILOTAGES > PILOTAGE
PILOTED > PILOT
PILOTFISH n fish that accompanies sharks
PILOTING n navigational handling of a ship near land using buoys, soundings, landmarks, etc, or the finding of a ship's position by such means
PILOTINGS > PILOTING
PILOTIS npl posts raising a building up from the ground
PILOTLESS > PILOT
PILOTMAN n railway worker who directs trains through hazardous stretches of track
PILOTMEN > PILOTMAN
PILOTS > PILOT

PILOUS same as > PILOSE
PILOW same as > PILAU
PILOWS > PILOW
PILSENER same as > PILSNER
PILSENERS > PILSENER
PILSNER n type of pale beer with a strong flavour of hops
PILSNERS > PILSNER
PILULA n pill
PILULAE > PILULA
PILULAR > PILULE
PILULAS > PILULA
PILULE n small pill
PILULES > PILULE
PILUM n ancient Roman javelin
PILUS > PILI
PILY adj like wool or pile
PIMA n type of cotton
PIMAS > PIMA
PIMENT n wine flavoured with spices
PIMENTO same as > PIMIENTO
PIMENTON n smoked chilli powder
PIMENTONS > PIMENTON
PIMENTOS > PIMENTO
PIMENTS > PIMENT
PIMIENTO n Spanish pepper with a red fruit used as a vegetable
PIMIENTOS > PIMIENTO
PIMP n man who gets customers for a prostitute in return for a share of his or her earnings ▷ vb act as a pimp
PIMPED > PIMP
PIMPERNEL n wild plant with small star-shaped flowers
PIMPING > PIMP
PIMPINGS > PIMPING
PIMPLE n small pus-filled spot on the skin
PIMPLED > PIMPLE
PIMPLES > PIMPLE
PIMPLIER > PIMPLE
PIMPLIEST > PIMPLE
PIMPLY > PIMPLE
PIMPS > PIMP
PIN n short thin piece of stiff wire with a point and head, for fastening things ▷ vb fasten with a pin
PINA n cone of silver amalgam
PINACEOUS adj relating to a family of conifers with needle-like leaves which includes the pine, spruce, fir, larch, and cedar
PINACOID n pair of opposite parallel faces of crystal
PINACOIDS > PINACOID
PINAFORE n apron
PINAFORED > PINAFORE
PINAFORES > PINAFORE
PINAKOID same as > PINACOID

PINAKOIDS > PINAKOID
PINANG n areca tree
PINANGS > PINANG
PINAS > PINA
PINASTER n Mediterranean pine tree
PINASTERS > PINASTER
PINATA n papier-mâché party decoration filled with sweets, hung up during parties, and struck with a stick until it breaks open
PINATAS > PINATA
PINBALL vb ricochet
PINBALLED > PINBALL
PINBALLS > PINBALL
PINBOARD n cork board for pinning notices, messages etc on
PINBOARDS > PINBOARD
PINBONE n part of sirloin
PINBONES > PINBONE
PINCASE n case for holding pins
PINCASES > PINCASE
PINCER vb grip with pincers
PINCERED > PINCER
PINCERING > PINCER
PINCERS npl tool consisting of two hinged arms, for gripping
PINCH vb squeeze between finger and thumb ▷ n act of pinching
PINCHBECK n alloy of zinc and copper, used as imitation gold ▷ adj sham or cheap
PINCHBUG n type of crab
PINCHBUGS > PINCHBUG
PINCHCOCK n clamp used to compress a flexible tube to control the flow of fluid through it
PINCHECK n small check woven into fabric
PINCHECKS > PINCHECK
PINCHED > PINCH
PINCHER > PINCH
PINCHERS > PINCH
PINCHES > PINCH
PINCHFIST n mean person
PINCHGUT n miserly person
PINCHGUTS > PINCHGUT
PINCHING > PINCH
PINCHINGS > PINCH
PINDAN n desert region of Western Australia
PINDANS > PINDAN
PINDAREE same as > PINDARI
PINDAREES > PINDAREE
PINDARI n former irregular Indian horseman
PINDARIS > PINDARI
PINDER n person who impounds
PINDERS > PINDER
PINDLING adj peevish or fractious
PINDOWN n wrestling

manoeuvre
PINDOWNS > PINDOWN
PINE n evergreen coniferous tree ▷ vb feel great longing (for)
PINEAL adj resembling a pine cone ▷ n pineal gland
PINEALS > PINEAL
PINEAPPLE n large tropical fruit with juicy yellow flesh and a hard skin
PINECONE n seed-producing structure of a pine tree
PINECONES > PINECONE
PINED > PINE
PINEDROPS n parasitic herb of pine trees
PINELAND n area covered with pine forest
PINELANDS > PINELAND
PINELIKE > PINE
PINENE n isomeric terpene found in many essential oils
PINENES > PINENE
PINERIES > PINERY
PINERY n place, esp a hothouse, where pineapples are grown
PINES > PINE
PINESAP n red herb of N America
PINESAPS > PINESAP
PINETA > PINETUM
PINETUM n area of land where pine trees and other conifers are grown
PINEWOOD n wood of pine trees
PINEWOODS > PINEWOOD
PINEY > PINE
PINFALL another name for > FALL
PINFALLS > PINFALL
PINFISH n small porgy of the SE North American coast of the Atlantic
PINFISHES > PINFISH
PINFOLD n pound for stray cattle ▷ vb gather or confine in or as if in a pinfold
PINFOLDED > PINFOLD
PINFOLDS > PINFOLD
PING n short high-pitched sound ▷ vb make such a noise
PINGED > PING
PINGER n device, esp a timer, that makes a pinging sound
PINGERS > PINGER
PINGING > PING
PINGLE vb enclose small area of ground
PINGLED > PINGLE
PINGLER > PINGLE
PINGLERS > PINGLE
PINGLES > PINGLE
PINGLING > PINGLE
PINGO n mound of earth or gravel formed through pressure from a layer of water trapped between newly frozen ice and

underlying permafrost in Arctic regions

PINGOES > PINGO

PINGOS > PINGO

PINGPONG n Australian football

PINGPONGS > PINGPONG

PINGRASS n weed with fernlike leaves

PINGS > PING

PINGUEFY vb become greasy or fat

PINGUID adj fatty, oily, or greasy

PINGUIN same as **>** PENGUIN

PINGUINS > PINGUIN

PINHEAD n head of a pin

PINHEADED adj stupid or silly

PINHEADS > PINHEAD

PINHOLE n small hole made with or as if with a pin

PINHOLES > PINHOLE

PINHOOKER n trader of young thoroughbred horses

PINIER > PINY

PINIES > PINY

PINIEST > PINY

PINING > PINE

PINION n bird's wing ▷ vb immobilize (someone) by tying or holding his or her arms

PINIONED > PINION

PINIONING > PINION

PINIONS > PINION

PINITE n greyish-green or brown mineral containing amorphous aluminium and potassium sulphates

PINITES > PINITE

PINITOL n compound found in pinewood

PINITOLS > PINITOL

PINK n pale reddish colour ▷ adj of the colour pink ▷ vb (of an engine) make a metallic noise because not working properly, knock

PINKED > PINK

PINKEN vb turn pink

PINKENED > PINKEN

PINKENING > PINKEN

PINKENS > PINKEN

PINKER n something that pinks

PINKERS > PINKER

PINKERTON n private detective

PINKEST > PINK

PINKEY n type of ship

PINKEYE n acute contagious inflammation of the conjunctiva of the eye

PINKEYES > PINKEYE

PINKEYS > PINKEY

PINKIE n little finger

PINKIER > PINKY

PINKIES > PINKIE

PINKIEST > PINKY

PINKINESS n quality of being pink

PINKING > PINK

PINKINGS > PINK

PINKISH > PINK

PINKLY > PINK

PINKNESS > PINK

PINKO n person regarded as mildly left-wing

PINKOES > PINKO

PINKOS > PINKO

PINKROOT n plant with red-and-yellow flowers and pink roots

PINKROOTS > PINKROOT

PINKS > PINK

PINKY adj of a pink colour

PINNA n external part of the ear

PINNACE n ship's boat

PINNACES > PINNACE

PINNACLE n highest point of fame or success ▷ vb set on or as if on a pinnacle

PINNACLED > PINNACLE

PINNACLES > PINNACLE

PINNAE > PINNA

PINNAL > PINNA

PINNAS > PINNA

PINNATE adj (of compound leaves) having leaflets growing opposite each other in pairs

PINNATED same as **>** PINNATE

PINNATELY > PINNATE

PINNATION > PINNATE

PINNED > PIN

PINNER n person or thing that pins

PINNERS > PINNER

PINNET n pinnacle

PINNETS > PINNET

PINNIE same as **>** PINNY

PINNIES > PINNIE

PINNING > PIN

PINNINGS > PIN

PINNIPED n aquatic placental mammal such as the seal, sea lion, walrus, etc

PINNIPEDE same as **>** PINNIPED

PINNIPEDS > PINNIPED

PINNOCK n small bird

PINNOCKS > PINNOCK

PINNOED adj held or bound by the arms

PINNULA same as **>** PINNULE

PINNULAE > PINNULA

PINNULAR > PINNULE

PINNULAS > PINNULA

PINNULATE > PINNULE

PINNULE n any of the lobes of a leaflet of a pinnate compound leaf, which is itself pinnately divided

PINNULES > PINNULE

PINNY informal or child's name for **>** PINAFORE

PINOCHLE n card game for two to four players similar to bezique

PINOCHLES > PINOCHLE

PINOCLE same as **>** PINOCHLE

PINOCLES > PINOCLE

PINOCYTIC adj of process of pinocytosis

PINOLE n (in the southwestern United States) flour made of parched ground corn, mesquite beans, sugar, etc

PINOLES > PINOLE

PINON n low-growing pine

PINONES > PINON

PINONS > PINON

PINOT n any of several grape varieties

PINOTAGE n variety of red wine grape

PINOTAGES > PINOTAGE

PINOTS > PINOT

PINPOINT vb locate or identify exactly ▷ adj exact ▷ n insignificant or trifling thing

PINPOINTS > PINPOINT

PINPRICK n small irritation or annoyance ▷ vb puncture with or as if with a pin

PINPRICKS > PINPRICK

PINS > PIN

PINSCHER n breed of dog

PINSCHERS > PINSCHER

PINSETTER n device that sets pins in bowling alley

PINSTRIPE n very narrow stripe in fabric

PINSWELL n small boil

PINSWELLS > PINSWELL

PINT n liquid measure, 1/8 gallon (.568 litre)

PINTA n pint of milk

PINTABLE n pinball machine

PINTABLES > PINTABLE

PINTADA same as **>** PINTADO

PINTADAS > PINTADA

PINTADERA n decorative stamp, usually made of clay, found in the Neolithic of the E Mediterranean and in many American cultures

PINTADO n species of seagoing petrel

PINTADOES > PINTADO

PINTADOS > PINTADO

PINTAIL n greyish-brown duck with a pointed tail

PINTAILED adj having tapered tail

PINTAILS > PINTAIL

PINTANO n tropical reef fish

PINTANOS > PINTANO

PINTAS > PINTA

PINTLE n pin or bolt forming the pivot of a hinge

PINTLES > PINTLE

PINTO adj marked with patches of white ▷ n pinto horse

PINTOES > PINTO

PINTOS > PINTO

PINTS > PINT

PINTSIZE same as **>** PINTSIZED

PINTSIZED adj very small

PINUP n picture of a sexually attractive person, esp when partially or totally undressed

PINUPS > PINUP

PINWALE n fabric with narrow ridges

PINWALES > PINWALE

PINWEED n herb with tiny flowers

PINWEEDS > PINWEED

PINWHEEL n cogwheel whose teeth are formed by small pins projecting either axially or radially from the rim of the wheel

PINWHEELS > PINWHEEL

PINWORK n (in needlepoint lace) fine raised stitches

PINWORKS > PINWORK

PINWORM n parasitic nematode worm

PINWORMS > PINWORM

PINWRENCH n wrench with a projection to fit a hole

PINXIT vb (he or she) painted (it): used formerly on paintings next to the artist's name

PINY variant of **>** PEONY

PINYIN n system of romanized spelling for the Chinese language

PINYON n low-growing pine

PINYONS > PINYON

PIOLET n type of ice axe

PIOLETS > PIOLET

PION n any of three subatomic particles which are classified as mesons

PIONED adj abounding in marsh marigolds

PIONEER n explorer or early settler of a new country ▷ vb be the pioneer or leader of

PIONEERED > PIONEER

PIONEERS > PIONEER

PIONER obsolete spelling of **>** PIONEER

PIONERS > PIONER

PIONEY same as **>** PEONY

PIONEYS > PIONEY

PIONIC > PION

PIONIES > PIONY

PIONING n work of pioneers

PIONINGS > PIONING

PIONS > PION

PIONY same as **>** PEONY

PIOPIO n New Zealand thrush, thought to be extinct

PIOPIOS > PIOPIO

PIOSITIES > PIOSITY

PIOSITY n grandiose display of piety

PIOTED adj pied

PIOUS adj deeply religious, devout

PIOUSLY > PIOUS

PIOUSNESS > PIOUS

PIOY variant of > PEEOY

PIOYE variant of > PEEOY

PIOYES > PIOYE

PIOYS > PIOY

PIP n small seed in a fruit ⊳ vb chirp

PIPA n tongueless S American toad that carries its young in pits in the skin of its back

PIPAGE n pipes collectively

PIPAGES > PIPAGE

PIPAL same as > PEEPUL

PIPALS > PIPAL

PIPAS > PIPA

PIPE n tube for conveying liquid or gas ⊳ vb play on a pipe

PIPEAGE same as > PIPAGE

PIPEAGES > PIPEAGE

PIPECLAY n fine white pure clay, used in tobacco pipes and pottery and to whiten leather and similar materials ⊳ vb whiten with pipeclay

PIPECLAYS > PIPECLAY

PIPED > PIPE

PIPEFISH n teleost fish with a long tubelike snout and an elongated body covered with bony plates

PIPEFUL > PIPE

PIPEFULS > PIPE

PIPELESS > PIPE

PIPELIKE > PIPE

PIPELINE n long pipe for transporting oil, water, etc

PIPELINED > PIPELINE

PIPELINES > PIPELINE

PIPER n player on a pipe or bagpipes

PIPERIC > PIPERINE

PIPERINE n crystalline insoluble alkaloid that is the active ingredient of pepper

PIPERINES > PIPERINE

PIPERONAL n white fragrant aldehyde used in flavourings, perfumery, and suntan lotions

PIPERS > PIPER

PIPES > PIPE

PIPESTEM n hollow stem of pipe

PIPESTEMS > PIPESTEM

PIPESTONE n variety of consolidated red clay used by American Indians to make tobacco pipes

PIPET same as > PIPETTE

PIPETS > PIPET

PIPETTE n slender glass tube used to transfer or measure fluids ⊳ vb transfer or measure out (a liquid) using a pipette

PIPETTED > PIPETTE

PIPETTES > PIPETTE

PIPETTING > PIPETTE

PIPEWORK n stops and flues on pipe organ

PIPEWORKS > PIPEWORK

PIPEWORT n perennial plant with a twisted flower stalk and a greenish-grey scaly flower head

PIPEWORTS > PIPEWORT

PIPI n edible mollusc often used as bait

PIPIER > PIPE

PIPIEST > PIPE

PIPINESS n material's suitability for use as pipe

PIPING n system of pipes

PIPINGLY > PIPING

PIPINGS > PIPING

PIPIS > PIPI

PIPISTREL n species of bat

PIPIT n small brownish songbird

PIPITS > PIPIT

PIPKIN same as > PIGGIN

PIPKINS > PIPKIN

PIPLESS > PIP

PIPPED > PIP

PIPPIER > PIPPY

PIPPIEST > PIPPY

PIPPIN n type of eating apple

PIPPING > PIP

PIPPINS > PIPPIN

PIPPY adj containing many pips

PIPS > PIP

PIPSQUEAK n insignificant or contemptible person

PIPUL n Indian fig tree

PIPULS > PIPUL

PIPY > PIPE

PIQUANCE same as > PIQUANT

PIQUANCES > PIQUANT

PIQUANCY > PIQUANT

PIQUANT adj having a pleasant spicy taste

PIQUANTLY > PIQUANT

PIQUE n feeling of hurt pride, baffled curiosity, or resentment ⊳ vb hurt the pride of

PIQUED > PIQUE

PIQUES > PIQUE

PIQUET n card game for two ⊳ vb play game of piquet

PIQUETED > PIQUET

PIQUETING > PIQUET

PIQUETS > PIQUET

PIQUILLO n variety of sweet red pepper

PIQUILLOS > PIQUILLO

PIQUING > PIQUE

PIR n Sufi master

PIRACETAM n drug used to treat muscle spasm

PIRACIES > PIRACY

PIRACY n robbery on the seas

PIRAGUA same as > PIROGUE

PIRAGUAS > PIRAGUA

PIRAI n large S American fish

PIRAIS > PIRAI

PIRANA same as > PIRANHA

PIRANAS > PIRANA

PIRANHA n small fierce freshwater fish of tropical America

PIRANHAS > PIRANHA

PIRARUCU n large S American food fish

PIRARUCUS > PIRARUCU

PIRATE n sea robber ⊳ vb sell or reproduce (artistic work etc) illegally

PIRATED > PIRATE

PIRATES > PIRATE

PIRATIC > PIRATE

PIRATICAL > PIRATE

PIRATING > PIRATE

PIRAYA same as > PIRAI

PIRAYAS > PIRAYA

PIRIFORM adj shaped like pear

PIRL n ripple in water

PIRLICUE same as > PURLICUE

PIRLICUED > PIRLICUE

PIRLICUES > PIRLICUE

PIRLS > PIRL

PIRN n reel or bobbin

PIRNIE n stripy nightcap

PIRNIES > PIRNIE

PIRNIT adj striped

PIRNS > PIRN

PIROG n large pie filled with meat, vegetables, etc

PIROGEN n turnovers made from kneaded dough

PIROGHI > PIROG

PIROGI > PIROG

PIROGIES > PIROG

PIROGUE n any of various kinds of dugout canoes

PIROGUES > PIROGUE

PIROJKI same as > PIROSHKI

PIROPLASM n parasite of red blood cells

PIROQUE same as > PIROGUE

PIROQUES > PIROQUE

PIROSHKI same as > PIROZHKI

PIROUETTE n spinning turn balanced on the toes of one foot ⊳ vb perform a pirouette

PIROZHKI > PIROZHOK

PIROZHOK n small triangular pastry filled with meat, vegetables, etc

PIRS > PIR

PIS > PI

PISCARIES > PISCARY

PISCARY n place where fishing takes place

PISCATOR n fisherman

PISCATORS > PISCATOR

PISCATORY adj of or relating to fish, fishing, or fishermen

PISCATRIX n female angler

PISCIFORM adj having form of fish

PISCINA n stone basin, with a drain, in a church or sacristy where water used at Mass is poured away

PISCINAE > PISCINA

PISCINAL > PISCINA

PISCINAS > PISCINA

PISCINE n pond or pool

PISCINES > PISCINE

PISCIVORE n eater of fish

PISCO n S American brandy

PISCOS > PISCO

PISE n rammed earth or clay used to make floors or walls

PISES > PISE

PISH interj exclamation of impatience or contempt ⊳ vb make this exclamation at (someone or something)

PISHED > PISH

PISHEOG same as > PISHOGUE

PISHEOGS > PISHEOG

PISHER n Yiddish term for small boy

PISHERS > PISHER

PISHES > PISH

PISHING > PISH

PISHOGE same as > PISHOGUE

PISHOGES > PISHOGE

PISHOGUE n sorcery

PISHOGUES > PISHOGUE

PISIFORM adj resembling a pea ⊳ n small pealike bone on the ulnar side of the carpus

PISIFORMS > PISIFORM

PISKIES > PISKY

PISKY n Cornish fairy

PISMIRE archaic or dialect word for > ANT

PISMIRES > PISMIRE

PISO n peso of the Philippines

PISOLITE n sedimentary rock

PISOLITES > PISOLITE

PISOLITH same as > PISOLITE

PISOLITHS > PISOLITH

PISOLITIC > PISOLITE

PISOS > PISO

PISS vb urinate ⊳ n act of urinating

PISSANT n insignificant person

PISSANTS > PISSANT

PISSED adj drunk

PISSER n someone or something that pisses

PISSERS > PISSER

PISSES > PISS

PISSHEAD n drunkard

PISSHEADS > PISSHEAD

PISSING > PISS

PISSOIR n public urinal, usu enclosed by a wall or screen

p

PISSOIRS > PISSOIR
PISTACHE n tree yielding pistachio nut
PISTACHES > PISTACHE
PISTACHIO n edible nut of a Mediterranean tree ▷ adj of a yellowish-green colour
PISTAREEN n Spanish coin, used in the US and the West Indies until the 18th century
PISTE n ski slope
PISTES > PISTE
PISTIL n seed-bearing part of a flower
PISTILS > PISTIL
PISTOL n short-barrelled handgun ▷ vb shoot with a pistol
PISTOLE n any of various gold coins of varying value, formerly used in Europe
PISTOLED > PISTOL
PISTOLEER n person, esp a soldier, who is armed with or fires a pistol
PISTOLERO n shooter of pistols
PISTOLES > PISTOLE
PISTOLET n small pistol
PISTOLETS > PISTOLET
PISTOLIER n shooter of pistols
PISTOLING > PISTOL
PISTOLLED > PISTOL
PISTOLS > PISTOL
PISTON n cylindrical part in an engine that slides to and fro in a cylinder
PISTONS > PISTON
PISTOU n French sauce
PISTOUS > PISTOU
PIT n deep hole in the ground ▷ vb mark with small dents or scars
PITA n any of several agave plants yielding a strong fibre
PITAHAYA n any giant cactus of Central America and the SW United States
PITAHAYAS > PITAHAYA
PITAPAT adv with quick light taps ▷ n such taps ▷ vb make quick light taps or beats
PITAPATS > PITAPAT
PITARA variant of > PETARA
PITARAH variant of > PETARA
PITARAHS > PITARAH
PITARAS > PITARA
PITAS > PITA
PITAYA same as > PITAHAYA
PITAYAS > PITAYA
PITCH vb throw, hurl ▷ n area marked out for playing sport
PITCHBEND n electronic device that enables a player to bend the pitch of a note being sounded on a synthesizer, usually with a

pitch wheel, strip, or lever
PITCHED > PITCH
PITCHER n large jug with a narrow neck
PITCHERS > PITCHER
PITCHES > PITCH
PITCHFORK n large long-handled fork for lifting hay ▷ vb thrust abruptly or violently
PITCHIER > PITCHY
PITCHIEST > PITCHY
PITCHILY > PITCHY
PITCHING > PITCH
PITCHINGS > PITCH
PITCHMAN n itinerant pedlar of small merchandise who operates from a stand at a fair, etc
PITCHMEN > PITCHMAN
PITCHOUT n type of baseball pitch
PITCHOUTS > PITCHOUT
PITCHPINE n large N American pine tree
PITCHPIPE n small one-note pipe used for tuning instruments
PITCHPOLE vb turn end over end
PITCHY adj full of or covered with pitch
PITEOUS adj arousing pity
PITEOUSLY > PITEOUS
PITFALL n hidden difficulty or danger
PITFALLS > PITFALL
PITH n soft white lining of the rind of oranges etc ▷ vb destroy the brain and spinal cord of (a laboratory animal) by piercing or severing
PITHBALL n type of conductor
PITHBALLS > PITHBALL
PITHEAD n top of a mine shaft and the buildings and hoisting gear around it
PITHEADS > PITHEAD
PITHECOID adj relating to apes
PITHED > PITH
PITHFUL > PITH
PITHIER > PITHY
PITHIEST > PITHY
PITHILY > PITHY
PITHINESS > PITHY
PITHING > PITH
PITHLESS > PITH
PITHLIKE > PITH
PITHOI > PITHOS
PITHOS n large ceramic container for oil or grain
PITHS > PITH
PITHY adj short and full of meaning
PITIABLE adj arousing or deserving pity or contempt
PITIABLY > PITIABLE
PITIED > PITY
PITIER > PITY
PITIERS > PITY
PITIES > PITY

PITIETH as in it pitieth me archaic inflection of 'pity'
PITIFUL adj arousing pity
PITIFULLY > PITIFUL
PITIKINS as in ods pitikins mild oath
PITILESS adj feeling no pity or mercy
PITMAN n coal miner ▷ n connecting rod (in a machine)
PITMANS > PITMAN
PITMEN > PITMAN
PITON n metal spike used in climbing to secure a rope
PITONS > PITON
PITPROP n support beam in mine shaft
PITPROPS > PITPROP
PITS > PIT
PITSAW n large saw formerly used for cutting logs into planks, operated by two men, one standing on top of the log and the other in a pit underneath it
PITSAWS > PITSAW
PITTA n small brightly coloured ground-dwelling tropical bird
PITTANCE n very small amount of money
PITTANCES > PITTANCE
PITTAS > PITTA
PITTED > PIT
PITTEN adj having been put
PITTER vb make pattering sound
PITTERED > PITTER
PITTERING > PITTER
PITTERS > PITTER
PITTING > PIT
PITTINGS > PIT
PITTITE n occupant of a theatre pit
PITTITES > PITTITE
PITUITA n thick nasal secretion
PITUITARY n gland at the base of the brain, that helps to control growth ▷ adj of or relating to the pituitary gland
PITUITAS > PITUITA
PITUITE n mucus
PITUITES > PITUITE
PITUITRIN n extract from pituitary gland
PITURI n Australian solanaceous shrub
PITURIS > PITURI
PITY n sympathy or sorrow for others' suffering ▷ vb feel pity for
PITYING > PITY
PITYINGLY > PITY
PITYROID adj resembling bran
PIU adv more (quickly, softly, etc)
PIUM n stinging insect
PIUMS > PIUM
PIUPIU n skirt made from the leaves of the New

Zealand flax, worn by Māoris on ceremonial occasions
PIUPIUS > PIUPIU
PIVOT n central shaft on which something turns ▷ vb provide with or turn on a pivot
PIVOTABLE > PIVOT
PIVOTAL adj of crucial importance
PIVOTALLY > PIVOTAL
PIVOTED > PIVOT
PIVOTER > PIVOT
PIVOTERS > PIVOT
PIVOTING > PIVOT
PIVOTINGS > PIVOT
PIVOTMAN n person in rank around whom others wheel
PIVOTMEN > PIVOTMAN
PIVOTS > PIVOT
PIX less common spelling of > PYX
PIXEL n any of a number of very small picture elements that make up a picture, as on a visual display unit
PIXELS > PIXEL
PIXES > PIX
PIXIE n (in folklore) fairy
PIXIEISH > PIXIE
PIXIES > PIXY
PIXILATED adj eccentric or whimsical
PIXINESS > PIXIE
PIXY same as > PIXIE
PIXYISH > PIXY
PIZAZZ same as > PIZZAZZ
PIZAZZES > PIZAZZ
PIZAZZY > PIZAZZ
PIZE vb strike (someone a blow)
PIZED > PIZE
PIZES > PIZE
PIZING > PIZE
PIZZA n flat disc of dough covered with a wide variety of savoury toppings and baked
PIZZAIOLA adj having a type of tomato sauce
PIZZALIKE > PIZZA
PIZZAS > PIZZA
PIZZAZ same as > PZAZZ
PIZZAZES > PIZZAZ
PIZZAZZ n attractive combination of energy and style
PIZZAZZES > PIZZAZZ
PIZZAZZY > PIZZAZZ
PIZZELLE n Italian sweet wafer
PIZZELLES > PIZZELLE
PIZZERIA n place where pizzas are made, sold, or eaten
PIZZERIAS > PIZZERIA
PIZZICATI > PIZZICATO
PIZZICATO adj played by plucking the string of a violin etc with the finger

▷ *adv* (in music for the violin family) to be plucked with the finger ▷ *n* style or technique of playing a normally bowed stringed instrument in this manner

PIZZLE *n* penis of an animal, esp a bull

PIZZLES > PIZZLE

PLAAS *n* farm

PLAASES > PLAAS

PLACABLE *adj* easily placated or appeased

PLACABLY > PLACABLE

PLACARD *n* notice that is carried or displayed in public ▷ *vb* attach placards to

PLACARDED > PLACARD

PLACARDS > PLACARD

PLACATE *vb* make (someone) stop feeling angry or upset

PLACATED > PLACATE

PLACATER > PLACATE

PLACATERS > PLACATE

PLACATES > PLACATE

PLACATING > PLACATE

PLACATION > PLACATE

PLACATIVE *same as* > PLACATORY

PLACATORY *adj* placating or intended to placate

PLACCAT *variant of* > PLACKET

PLACCATE *variant of* > PLACKET

PLACCATES > PLACCATE

PLACCATS > PLACCAT

PLACE *n* particular part of an area or space ▷ *vb* put in a particular place

PLACEABLE > PLACE

PLACEBO *n* sugar pill etc given to an unsuspecting patient instead of an active drug

PLACEBOES > PLACEBO

PLACEBOS > PLACEBO

PLACED > PLACE

PLACEKICK *n* (in football) kick in which the ball is placed in position before it is kicked ▷ *vb* take a placekick

PLACELESS *adj* not rooted in a specific place or community

PLACEMAN *n* person who holds a public office, esp for private profit and as a reward for political support

PLACEMEN > PLACEMAN

PLACEMENT *n* arrangement

PLACENTA *n* organ formed in the womb during pregnancy, providing nutrients for the fetus

PLACENTAE > PLACENTA

PLACENTAL *adj* (esp of animals) having a placenta

PLACENTAS > PLACENTA

PLACER *n* surface sediment containing

particles of gold or some other valuable mineral

PLACERS > PLACER

PLACES > PLACE

PLACET *n* vote or expression of assent by saying the word *placet*

PLACETS > PLACET

PLACID *adj* not easily excited or upset, calm

PLACIDER > PLACID

PLACIDEST > PLACID

PLACIDITY > PLACID

PLACIDLY > PLACID

PLACING *n* method of issuing securities to the public using an intermediary, such as a stockbroking firm

PLACINGS > PLACING

PLACIT *n* decree or dictum

PLACITA > PLACITUM

PLACITORY > PLACIT

PLACITS > PLACIT

PLACITUM *n* court or assembly in Middle Ages

PLACK *n* small former Scottish coin

PLACKET *n* opening at the waist of a dress or skirt for buttons or zips or for access to a pocket

PLACKETS > PLACKET

PLACKLESS *adj* lacking money

PLACKS > PLACK

PLACODERM *n* extinct bony-plated fishlike vertebrate

PLACOID *adj* platelike or flattened ▷ *n* fish with placoid scales

PLACOIDS > PLACOID

PLAFOND *n* ceiling, esp one having ornamentation

PLAFONDS > PLAFOND

PLAGAL *adj* (of a cadence) progressing from the subdominant to the tonic chord, as in the *Amen* of a hymn

PLAGE *n* bright patch in the sun's chromosphere

PLAGES > PLAGE

PLAGIARY *n* person who plagiarizes or a piece of plagiarism

PLAGIUM *n* crime of kidnapping

PLAGIUMS > PLAGIUM

PLAGUE *n* fast-spreading fatal disease ▷ *vb* trouble or annoy continually

PLAGUED > PLAGUE

PLAGUER > PLAGUE

PLAGUERS > PLAGUE

PLAGUES > PLAGUE

PLAGUEY *same as* > PLAGUY

PLAGUIER > PLAGUEY

PLAGUIEST > PLAGUEY

PLAGUILY > PLAGUY

PLAGUING > PLAGUE

PLAGUY *adj* disagreeable or vexing ▷ *adv* disagreeably

or annoyingly

PLAICE *n* edible European flatfish

PLAICES > PLAICE

PLAID *n* long piece of tartan cloth worn as part of Highland dress ▷ *vb* weave cloth into plaid

PLAIDED > PLAID

PLAIDING > PLAID

PLAIDINGS > PLAID

PLAIDMAN *n* wearer of plaid

PLAIDMEN > PLAIDMAN

PLAIDS > PLAID

PLAIN *adj* easy to see or understand ▷ *n* large stretch of level country ▷ *adv* clearly or simply ▷ *vb* complain

PLAINANT *n* plaintiff

PLAINANTS > PLAINANT

PLAINED > PLAIN

PLAINER > PLAIN

PLAINEST > PLAIN

PLAINFUL *adj* apt to complain

PLAINING > PLAIN

PLAININGS > PLAIN

PLAINISH > PLAIN

PLAINLY > PLAIN

PLAINNESS > PLAIN

PLAINS *npl* extensive tracts of level or almost level treeless countryside

PLAINSMAN *n* person who lives in a plains region, esp in the Great Plains of North America

PLAINSMEN > PLAINSMAN

PLAINSONG *n* unaccompanied singing, esp in a medieval church

PLAINT *n* complaint or lamentation

PLAINTEXT *n* (in telecommunications) message set in a directly readable form rather than in coded groups

PLAINTFUL *adj* complaining

PLAINTIFF *n* person who sues in a court of law

PLAINTIVE *adj* sad, mournful

PLAINTS > PLAINT

PLAINWORK *n* weaving

PLAISTER *n* plaster

PLAISTERS > PLAISTER

PLAIT *n* intertwined length of hair ▷ *vb* intertwine separate strands in a pattern

PLAITED > PLAIT

PLAITER > PLAIT

PLAITERS > PLAIT

PLAITING > PLAIT

PLAITINGS > PLAIT

PLAITS > PLAIT

PLAN *n* way thought out to do or achieve something ▷ *vb* arrange beforehand

PLANAR *adj* of or relating to a plane

PLANARIA *n* type of flatworm

PLANARIAN *n* type of flatworm

PLANARIAS > PLANARIA

PLANARITY > PLANAR

PLANATE *adj* having been flattened

PLANATION *n* erosion of a land surface until it is basically flat

PLANCH *vb* cover with planks

PLANCHE *same as* > PLANCH

PLANCHED > PLANCH

PLANCHES > PLANCH

PLANCHET *n* piece of metal ready to be stamped as a coin, medal, etc

PLANCHETS > PLANCHET

PLANCHING > PLANCH

PLANE *n* aeroplane ▷ *adj* perfectly flat or level ▷ *vb* glide or skim

PLANED > PLANE

PLANELOAD *n* amount or number carried by plane

PLANENESS > PLANE

PLANER *n* machine with a cutting tool that makes repeated horizontal strokes across the surface of a workpiece

PLANERS > PLANER

PLANES > PLANE

PLANESIDE *n* area next to aeroplane

PLANET *n* large body in space that revolves round the sun or another star

PLANETARY *adj* of or relating to a planet ▷ *n* train of planetary gears

PLANETIC > PLANET

PLANETOID *See* > ASTEROID

PLANETS > PLANET

PLANFORM *n* outline or silhouette of an object, esp an aircraft, as seen from above

PLANFORMS > PLANFORM

PLANGENCY > PLANGENT

PLANGENT *adj* (of sounds) mournful and resounding

PLANING > PLANE

PLANISH *vb* give a final finish to (metal) by hammering or rolling to produce a smooth surface

PLANISHED > PLANISH

PLANISHER > PLANISH

PLANISHES > PLANISH

PLANK *n* long flat piece of sawn timber ▷ *vb* cover or provide (an area) with planks

PLANKED > PLANK

PLANKING *n* number of planks

PLANKINGS > PLANKING

PLANKS > PLANK

p

PLANKTER n organism in plankton

PLANKTERS > PLANKTER

PLANKTON n minute animals and plants floating in the surface water of a sea or lake

PLANKTONS > PLANKTON

PLANLESS adj having no plan

PLANNED > PLAN

PLANNER n person who makes plans, esp for the development of a town, building, etc

PLANNERS > PLANNER

PLANNING > PLAN

PLANNINGS > PLAN

PLANOSOL n type of intrazonal soil of humid or subhumid uplands having a strongly leached upper layer overlying a clay hardpan

PLANOSOLS > PLANOSOL

PLANS > PLAN

PLANT n living organism that grows in the ground and has no power to move ▷ vb put in the ground to grow

PLANTA n sole of foot

PLANTABLE > PLANT

PLANTAE > PLANTA

PLANTAGE n plants

PLANTAGES > PLANTAGE

PLANTAIN n low-growing wild plant with broad leaves

PLANTAINS > PLANTAIN

PLANTAR adj of, relating to, or occurring on the sole of the foot or a corresponding part

PLANTAS > PLANTA

PLANTED > PLANT

PLANTER n owner of a plantation

PLANTERS > PLANTER

PLANTING > PLANT

PLANTINGS > PLANT

PLANTLESS > PLANT

PLANTLET n small plant

PLANTLETS > PLANTLET

PLANTLIKE > PLANT

PLANTLING n young plant

PLANTS > PLANT

PLANTSMAN n experienced gardener who specializes in collecting rare or interesting plants

PLANTSMEN > PLANTSMAN

PLANTULE n embryo in act of germination

PLANTULES > PLANTULE

PLANULA n ciliated free-swimming larva of hydrozoan coelenterates such as the hydra

PLANULAE > PLANULA

PLANULAR > PLANULA

PLANULATE adj flat

PLANULOID adj of planula

PLANURIA n expulsion of

urine from abnormal opening

PLANURIAS > PLANURIA

PLANURIES > PLANURY

PLANURY another name for > PLANURY

PLANXTIES > PLANXTY

PLANXTY n Celtic melody for harp

PLAP same as > PLOP

PLAPPED > PLAP

PLAPPING > PLAP

PLAPS > PLAP

PLAQUE n inscribed commemorative stone or metal plate

PLAQUES > PLAQUE

PLAQUETTE n small plaque

PLASH same as > PLEACH

PLASHED > PLASH

PLASHER n type of farm tool

PLASHERS > PLASHER

PLASHES > PLASH

PLASHET n small pond

PLASHETS > PLASHET

PLASHIER > PLASHY

PLASHIEST > PLASHY

PLASHING > PLASH

PLASHINGS > PLASH

PLASHY adj wet or marshy

PLASM same as > PLASMA

PLASMA n clear liquid part of blood

PLASMAGEL another name for > ECTOPLASM

PLASMAS > PLASMA

PLASMASOL another name for > ENDOPLASM

PLASMATIC > PLASMA

PLASMIC > PLASMA

PLASMID n small circle of bacterial DNA that is independent of the main bacterial chromosome

PLASMIDS > PLASMID

PLASMIN n proteolytic enzyme that causes fibrinolysis in blood clots

PLASMINS > PLASMIN

PLASMODIA n amoeboid masses of protoplasm, each containing many nuclei

PLASMOID n section of a plasma having a characteristic shape

PLASMOIDS > PLASMOID

PLASMON n sum total of plasmagenes in a cell

PLASMONS > PLASMON

PLASMS > PLASM

PLAST archaic past participle of > PLACE

PLASTE archaic past participle of > PLACE

PLASTER n mixture of lime, sand, etc for coating walls ▷ vb cover with plaster

PLASTERED adj drunk

PLASTERER > PLASTER

PLASTERS > PLASTER

PLASTERY > PLASTER

PLASTIC n synthetic material that can be moulded when soft but sets in a hard long-lasting shape ▷ adj made of plastic

PLASTICKY adj made of or resembling plastic

PLASTICLY > PLASTIC

PLASTICS > PLASTIC

PLASTID n any of various small particles in the cytoplasm of the cells of plants and some animals

PLASTIDS > PLASTID

PLASTIQUE n easily-moulded plastic explosive

PLASTISOL n suspension of resin particles convertible into solid plastic

PLASTRAL > PLASTRON

PLASTRON n bony plate forming the ventral part of the shell of a tortoise or turtle

PLASTRONS > PLASTRON

PLASTRUM variant of > PLASTRON

PLASTRUMS > PLASTRUM

PLAT n small area of ground

PLATAN n plane tree

PLATANE same as > PLATAN

PLATANES > PLATANE

PLATANNA n S African frog

PLATANNAS > PLATANNA

PLATANS > PLATAN

PLATBAND n border of flowers in garden

PLATBANDS > PLATBAND

PLATE n shallow dish for holding food ▷ vb cover with a thin coating of gold, silver, or other metal

PLATEASM n talking with mouth open too wide

PLATEASMS > PLATEASM

PLATEAU n area of level high land ▷ vb remain stable for a long period

PLATEAUED > PLATEAU

PLATEAUS > PLATEAU

PLATEAUX > PLATEAU

PLATED adj coated with a layer of metal

PLATEFUL same as > PLATE

PLATEFULS > PLATEFUL

PLATELET n minute particle occurring in blood of vertebrates and involved in clotting of blood

PLATELETS > PLATELET

PLATELIKE > PLATE

PLATEMAN n one of crew of steam train

PLATEMARK another name for > HALLMARK

PLATEMEN > PLATEMAN

PLATEN n roller of a typewriter, against which the paper is held

PLATENS > PLATEN

PLATER n person or thing that plates

PLATERS > PLATER

PLATES > PLATE

PLATESFUL > PLATEFUL

PLATFORM n raised floor

PLATFORMS > PLATFORM

PLATIER > PLATY

PLATIES > PLATY

PLATIEST > PLATY

PLATINA n alloy of platinum and several other metals, including palladium, osmium, and iridium

PLATINAS > PLATINA

PLATING n coating of metal

PLATINGS > PLATING

PLATINIC adj of or containing platinum, esp in the tetravalent state

PLATINISE same as > PLATINIZE

PLATINIZE vb coat with platinum

PLATINOID adj containing or resembling platinum

PLATINOUS adj of or containing platinum, esp in the divalent state

PLATINUM n valuable silvery-white metal

PLATINUMS > PLATINUM

PLATITUDE n remark that is true but not interesting or original

PLATONIC adj (of a relationship) friendly or affectionate but not sexual ▷ n platonic friend

PLATONICS > PLATONIC

PLATONISM n philosophy of Plato

PLATOON n smaller unit within a company of soldiers ▷ vb organise into platoons

PLATOONED > PLATOON

PLATOONS > PLATOON

PLATS > PLAT

PLATTED > PLAT

PLATTER n large dish

PLATTERS > PLATTER

PLATTING > PLAT

PLATTINGS > PLAT

PLATY adj of, relating to, or designating rocks the constituents of which occur in flaky layers ▷ n small brightly coloured freshwater cyprinodont fish

PLATYFISH same as > PLATY

PLATYPI > PLATYPUS

PLATYPUS n Australian egg-laying amphibious mammal, with dense fur, webbed feet, and a ducklike bill

PLATYS > PLATY

PLATYSMA n muscle located on side of neck

p

PLATYSMAS > PLATYSMA
PLAUDIT n expression of enthusiastic approval
PLAUDITE interj give a round of applause!
PLAUDITS > PLAUDIT
PLAUSIBLE adj apparently true or reasonable
PLAUSIBLY > PLAUSIBLE
PLAUSIVE adj expressing praise or approval
PLAUSTRAL adj relating to wagons
PLAY vb occupy oneself in (a game or recreation) ▷ n story performed on stage or broadcast
PLAYA n (in the US) temporary lake, or its dry often salty bed, in a desert basin
PLAYABLE > PLAY
PLAYACT vb pretend or make believe
PLAYACTED > PLAYACT
PLAYACTOR > PLAYACT
PLAYACTS > PLAYACT
PLAYAS > PLAYA
PLAYBACK n playing of a recording on magnetic tape ▷ vb listen to or watch (something recorded)
PLAYBACKS > PLAYBACK
PLAYBILL n poster or bill advertising a play
PLAYBILLS > PLAYBILL
PLAYBOOK n book containing a range of possible set plays
PLAYBOOKS > PLAYBOOK
PLAYBOY n rich man who lives only for pleasure
PLAYBOYS > PLAYBOY
PLAYDATE n gathering of children at house for play
PLAYDATES > PLAYDATE
PLAYDAY n day given to play
PLAYDAYS > PLAYDAY
PLAYDOUGH n soft modelling material used by children
PLAYDOWN same as > PLAYOFF
PLAYDOWNS > PLAYDOWN
PLAYED > PLAY
PLAYER n person who plays a game or sport
PLAYERS > PLAYER
PLAYFIELD n field for sports
PLAYFUL adj lively
PLAYFULLY > PLAYFUL
PLAYGIRL n rich woman devoted to pleasure
PLAYGIRLS > PLAYGIRL
PLAYGOER n person who goes often to the theatre
PLAYGOERS > PLAYGOER
PLAYGOING > PLAYGOER
PLAYGROUP n playschool
PLAYHOUSE n theatre
PLAYING > PLAY

PLAYLAND n playground
PLAYLANDS > PLAYLAND
PLAYLESS > PLAY
PLAYLET n short play
PLAYLETS > PLAYLET
PLAYLIKE > PLAY
PLAYLIST n list of records chosen for playing, such as on a radio station ▷ vb put (a song or record) on a playlist
PLAYLISTS > PLAYLIST
PLAYMAKER n player who creates scoring opportunities for his or her team-mates
PLAYMATE n companion in play
PLAYMATES > PLAYMATE
PLAYOFF n extra contest to decide the winner when two or more competitors are tied
PLAYOFFS > PLAYOFF
PLAYPEN n small portable enclosure in which a young child can safely be left to play
PLAYPENS > PLAYPEN
PLAYROOM n recreation room, esp for children
PLAYROOMS > PLAYROOM
PLAYS > PLAY
PLAYSLIP n form used to select numbers in a lottery draw
PLAYSLIPS > PLAYSLIP
PLAYSOME adj playful
PLAYSUIT n woman's or child's outfit, usually comprising shorts and a top
PLAYSUITS > PLAYSUIT
PLAYTHING n toy
PLAYTIME n time for play or recreation, such as a school break
PLAYTIMES > PLAYTIME
PLAYWEAR n clothes suitable for playing in
PLAZA n open space or square
PLAZAS > PLAZA
PLEA n serious or urgent request, entreaty ▷ vb entreat
PLEACH vb interlace the stems or boughs of (a tree or hedge)
PLEACHED > PLEACH
PLEACHES > PLEACH
PLEACHING > PLEACH
PLEAD vb ask urgently or with deep feeling
PLEADABLE > PLEAD
PLEADED > PLEAD
PLEADER > PLEAD
PLEADERS > PLEAD
PLEADING > PLEAD
PLEADINGS > PLEAD
PLEADS > PLEAD
PLEAED > PLEA
PLEAING > PLEA
PLEAS > PLEA
PLEASABLE > PLEASE

PLEASANCE n secluded part of a garden laid out with trees, walks, etc
PLEASANT adj pleasing, enjoyable
PLEASE vb give pleasure or satisfaction to ▷ adv polite word of request
PLEASED > PLEASE
PLEASEDLY > PLEASE
PLEASEMAN n person who courts favour
PLEASEMEN > PLEASEMAN
PLEASER > PLEASE
PLEASERS > PLEASE
PLEASES > PLEASE
PLEASETH obsolete inflection of > PLEASE
PLEASING adj giving pleasure or satisfaction ▷ n act of giving pleasure
PLEASINGS > PLEASING
PLEASURE n feeling of happiness and satisfaction ▷ vb give pleasure to or take pleasure (in)
PLEASURED > PLEASURE
PLEASURER > PLEASURE
PLEASURES > PLEASURE
PLEAT n fold made by doubling material back on itself ▷ vb arrange (material) in pleats
PLEATED > PLEAT
PLEATER n attachment on a sewing machine that makes pleats
PLEATERS > PLEATER
PLEATHER n synthetic leather
PLEATHERS > PLEATHER
PLEATING > PLEAT
PLEATLESS > PLEAT
PLEATS > PLEAT
PLEB n common vulgar person
PLEBBIER > PLEBBY
PLEBBIEST > PLEBBY
PLEBBY adj common or vulgar
PLEBE n member of the lowest class at the US Naval Academy or Military Academy
PLEBEAN old variant of > PLEBEIAN
PLEBEIAN adj of the lower social classes ▷ n member of the lower social classes
PLEBEIANS > PLEBEIAN
PLEBES > PLEBE
PLEBIFIED > PLEBIFY
PLEBIFIES > PLEBIFY
PLEBIFY vb make plebeian
PLEBS n common people
PLECTRA > PLECTRUM
PLECTRE variant of > PLECTRUM
PLECTRES > PLECTRE
PLECTRON same as > PLECTRUM
PLECTRONS > PLECTRON
PLECTRUM n small implement for plucking the

strings of a guitar etc
PLECTRUMS > PLECTRUM
PLED > PLEAD
PLEDGABLE > PLEDGE
PLEDGE n solemn promise ▷ vb promise solemnly
PLEDGED > PLEDGE
PLEDGEE n person to whom a pledge is given
PLEDGEES > PLEDGEE
PLEDGEOR same as > PLEDGOR
PLEDGEORS > PLEDGEOR
PLEDGER same as > PLEDGOR
PLEDGERS > PLEDGER
PLEDGES > PLEDGE
PLEDGET n small flattened pad of wool, cotton, etc, esp for use as a pressure bandage to be applied to wounds or sores
PLEDGETS > PLEDGET
PLEDGING > PLEDGE
PLEDGOR n person who gives or makes a pledge
PLEDGORS > PLEDGOR
PLEIAD n brilliant or talented group, esp one with seven members
PLEIADES > PLEIAD
PLEIADS > PLEIAD
PLEIOCENE variant spelling of > PLIOCENE
PLEIOMERY n state of having more than normal number
PLEIOTAXY n increase in whorls in flower
PLENA > PLENUM
PLENARIES > PLENARY
PLENARILY > PLENARY
PLENARTY n state of endowed church office when occupied
PLENARY adj (of a meeting) attended by all members ▷ n book of the gospels or epistles and homilies read at the Eucharist
PLENCH n tool combining wrench and pliers
PLENCHES > PLENCH
PLENILUNE n full moon
PLENIPO n plenipotentiary diplomat
PLENIPOES > PLENIPO
PLENIPOS > PLENIPO
PLENISH vb fill, stock, or resupply
PLENISHED > PLENISH
PLENISHER > PLENISH
PLENISHES > PLENISH
PLENISM n philosophical theory
PLENISMS > PLENISM
PLENIST > PLENISM
PLENISTS > PLENISM
PLENITUDE n completeness, abundance
PLENTEOUS adj plentiful
PLENTIES > PLENTY
PLENTIFUL adj existing in large amounts or numbers

PLENTY n large amount or number ▷ adj very many ▷ adv more than adequately

PLENUM n enclosure containing gas at a higher pressure than the surrounding environment

PLENUMS > PLENUM

PLEON n abdomen of crustacean

PLEONAL adj of the abdomen of a crustacean

PLEONASM n use of more words than necessary

PLEONASMS > PLEONASM

PLEONAST n person using more words than necessary

PLEONASTE n type of black mineral

PLEONASTS > PLEONAST

PLEONEXIA n greed

PLEONIC > PLEON

PLEONS > PLEON

PLEOPOD another name for > SWIMMERET

PLEOPODS > PLEOPOD

PLERION n filled-centre supernova remnant in which radiation is emitted by the centre as well as the shell

PLERIONS > PLERION

PLEROMA n abundance

PLEROMAS > PLEROMA

PLEROME n central column in growing stem or root

PLEROMES > PLEROME

PLESH n small pool

PLESHES > PLESH

PLESSOR same as > PLEXOR

PLESSORS > PLESSOR

PLETHORA n excess

PLETHORAS > PLETHORA

PLETHORIC > PLETHORA

PLEUCH same as > PLEUGH

PLEUCHED > PLEUCH

PLEUCHING > PLEUCH

PLEUCHS > PLEUCH

PLEUGH Scottish word for > PLOUGH

PLEUGHED > PLEUGH

PLEUGHING > PLEUGH

PLEUGHS > PLEUGH

PLEURA > PLEURON

PLEURAE > PLEURON

PLEURAL > PLEURON

PLEURAS > PLEURON

PLEURISY n inflammation of the membrane covering the lungs

PLEURITIC > PLEURISY

PLEURITIS n pleurisy

PLEURON n part of the cuticle of arthropods that covers the lateral surface of a body segment

PLEURONIA n combined disorder of pleurisy and pneumonia

PLEUSTON n mass of small organisms, esp algae, floating at the surface of shallow pools

PLEUSTONS > PLEUSTON

PLEW n (formerly in Canada) beaver skin used as a standard unit of value in the fur trade

PLEWS > PLEW

PLEX n shortening of multiplex

PLEXAL > PLEXUS

PLEXES > PLEX

PLEXIFORM adj like or having the form of a network or plexus

PLEXOR n small hammer with a rubber head for use in percussion of the chest and testing reflexes

PLEXORS > PLEXOR

PLEXURE n act of weaving together

PLEXURES > PLEXURE

PLEXUS n complex network of nerves or blood vessels

PLEXUSES > PLEXUS

PLIABLE adj easily bent

PLIABLY > PLIABLE

PLIANCIES > PLIANT

PLIANCY > PLIANT

PLIANT adj pliable

PLIANTLY > PLIANT

PLICA n folding over of parts, such as a fold of skin, muscle, peritoneum, etc

PLICAE > PLICA

PLICAL > PLICA

PLICATE adj having or arranged in parallel folds or ridges ▷ vb arrange into parallel folds

PLICATED > PLICATE

PLICATELY > PLICATE

PLICATES > PLICATE

PLICATING > PLICATE

PLICATION n act of folding or the condition of being folded or plicate

PLICATURE same as > PLICATION

PLIE n classic ballet practice posture with back erect and knees bent

PLIED > PLY

PLIER n person who plies a trade

PLIERS npl tool with hinged arms and jaws for gripping

PLIES > PLY

PLIGHT n difficult or dangerous situation

PLIGHTED > PLIGHT

PLIGHTER > PLIGHT

PLIGHTERS > PLIGHT

PLIGHTFUL > PLIGHT

PLIGHTING > PLIGHT

PLIGHTS > PLIGHT

PLIM vb swell with water

PLIMMED > PLIM

PLIMMING > PLIM

PLIMS > PLIM

PLIMSOL same as > PLIMSOLE

PLIMSOLE same as

> PLIMSOLL

PLIMSOLES > PLIMSOLE

PLIMSOLL n light rubber-soled canvas shoe worn for various sports

PLIMSOLLS > PLIMSOLL

PLIMSOLS > PLIMSOL

PLING n (in computer jargon) an exclamation mark

PLINGS > PLING

PLINK n short sharp often metallic sound as of a string on a musical instrument being plucked or a bullet striking metal ▷ vb make such a noise

PLINKED > PLINK

PLINKER > PLINK

PLINKERS > PLINK

PLINKIER > PLINKY

PLINKIEST > PLINKY

PLINKING > PLINK

PLINKINGS > PLINK

PLINKS > PLINK

PLINKY adj (of a sound) short, sharp, and often metallic

PLINTH n slab forming the base of a statue, column, etc

PLINTHS > PLINTH

PLIOCENE adj of the Pliocene geological time period

PLIOFILM n transparent plastic material

PLIOFILMS > PLIOFILM

PLIOSAUR n type of dinosaur

PLIOSAURS > PLIOSAUR

PLIOTRON n type of vacuum tube

PLIOTRONS > PLIOTRON

PLISKIE n practical joke

PLISKIES > PLISKIE

PLISKY same as

> PLISKIE

PLISSE n fabric with a wrinkled finish, achieved by treatment involving caustic soda

PLISSES > PLISSE

PLOAT vb thrash

PLOATED > PLOAT

PLOATING > PLOAT

PLOATS > PLOAT

PLOD vb walk with slow heavy steps ▷ n act of plodding

PLODDED > PLOD

PLODDER n person who plods, esp one who works in a slow and persevering but uninspired manner

PLODDERS > PLODDER

PLODDING > PLOD

PLODDINGS > PLOD

PLODGE vb wade in water, esp the sea ▷ n act of wading

PLODGED > PLODGE

PLODGES > PLODGE

PLODGING > PLODGE

PLODS > PLOD

PLOIDIES > PLOIDY

PLOIDY n number of copies of set of chromosomes in cell

PLONG obsolete variant of > PLUNGE

PLONGD > PLONG

PLONGE > PLUNGE

PLONGED > PLONGE

PLONGES > PLONGE

PLONGING > PLONGE

PLONGS > PLONG

PLONK vb put (something) down heavily and carelessly ▷ n cheap inferior wine ▷ interj exclamation imitative of this sound

PLONKED > PLONK

PLONKER n stupid person

PLONKERS > PLONKER

PLONKIER > PLONK

PLONKIEST > PLONK

PLONKING > PLONK

PLONKINGS > PLONK

PLONKO n alcoholic, esp one who drinks wine

PLONKOS > PLONKO

PLONKS > PLONK

PLONKY > PLONK

PLOOK same as > PLOUK

PLOOKIE same as

> PLOUKY

PLOOKIER > PLOUK

PLOOKIEST > PLOUK

PLOOKS > PLOOK

PLOOKY > PLOOK

PLOP n sound of an object falling into water without a splash ▷ vb make this sound ▷ interj exclamation imitative of this sound

PLOPPED > PLOP

PLOPPING > PLOP

PLOPS > PLOP

PLOSION n sound of an abrupt break or closure, esp the audible release of a stop

PLOSIONS > PLOSION

PLOSIVE adj pronounced with a sudden release of breath ▷ n plosive consonant

PLOSIVES > PLOSIVE

PLOT n secret plan to do something illegal or wrong ▷ vb plan secretly, conspire

PLOTFUL > PLOT

PLOTLESS > PLOT

PLOTLINE n literary or dramatic plot

PLOTLINES > PLOTLINE

PLOTS > PLOT

PLOTTAGE n land that makes up plot

PLOTTAGES > PLOTTAGE

PLOTTED > PLOT

PLOTTER same as

> PLOUTER

PLOTTERED > PLOTTER

PLOTTERS > PLOTTER

PLOTTIE n hot spiced drink

PLOTTIER > PLOTTY

PLOTTIES > PLOTTIE

PLOTTIEST > PLOTTY
PLOTTING > PLOT
PLOTTINGS > PLOT
PLOTTY adj intricately plotted
PLOTZ vb faint or collapse
PLOTZED > PLOTZ
PLOTZES > PLOTZ
PLOTZING > PLOTZ
PLOUGH n agricultural tool for turning over soil ▷ vb turn over (earth) with a plough
PLOUGHBOY n boy who guides the animals drawing a plough
PLOUGHED > PLOUGH
PLOUGHER > PLOUGH
PLOUGHERS > PLOUGH
PLOUGHING > PLOUGH
PLOUGHMAN n man who ploughs
PLOUGHMEN > PLOUGHMAN
PLOUGHS > PLOUGH
PLOUK n pimple
PLOUKIE > PLOUK
PLOUKIER > PLOUK
PLOUKIEST > PLOUK
PLOUKS > PLOUK
PLOUKY > PLOUK
PLOUTER same as > PLOWTER
PLOUTERED > PLOUTER
PLOUTERS > PLOUTER
PLOVER n shore bird with a straight bill and long pointed wings
PLOVERS > PLOVER
PLOVERY > PLOVER
PLOW same as > PLOUGH
PLOWABLE > PLOW
PLOWBACK n reinvestment of profits
PLOWBACKS > PLOWBACK
PLOWBOY same as > PLOUGHBOY
PLOWBOYS > PLOWBOY
PLOWED > PLOW
PLOWER > PLOW
PLOWERS > PLOW
PLOWHEAD n draught iron of plow
PLOWHEADS > PLOWHEAD
PLOWING > PLOW
PLOWLAND n land plowed
PLOWLANDS > PLOWLAND
PLOWMAN same as > PLOUGHMAN
PLOWMEN > PLOWMAN
PLOWS > PLOW
PLOWSHARE n horizontal pointed cutting blade of a mouldboard plow
PLOWSTAFF n one of the handles of a plow
PLOWTER vb work or play in water or mud ▷ n act of plowtering
PLOWTERED > PLOWTER
PLOWTERS > PLOWTER
PLOY n manoeuvre designed to gain an advantage ▷ vb form a

column from a line of troops
PLOYED > PLOY
PLOYING > PLOY
PLOYS > PLOY
PLU same as > PLEW
PLUCK vb pull or pick off ▷ n courage
PLUCKED > PLUCK
PLUCKER > PLUCK
PLUCKERS > PLUCK
PLUCKIER > PLUCKY
PLUCKIEST > PLUCKY
PLUCKILY > PLUCKY
PLUCKING > PLUCK
PLUCKS > PLUCK
PLUCKY adj brave
PLUE same as > PLEW
PLUES > PLUE
PLUFF vb expel in puffs
PLUFFED > PLUFF
PLUFFIER > PLUFF
PLUFFIEST > PLUFF
PLUFFING > PLUFF
PLUFFS > PLUFF
PLUFFY > PLUFF
PLUG n thing fitting into and filling a hole ▷ vb block or seal (a hole or gap) with a plug
PLUGBOARD n device with a large number of sockets in which electrical plugs can be inserted to form many different temporary circuits
PLUGGED > PLUG
PLUGGER > PLUG
PLUGGERS > PLUG
PLUGGING > PLUG
PLUGGINGS > PLUG
PLUGHOLE n hole, esp in a bath, basin, or sink, through which waste water drains and which can be closed with a plug
PLUGHOLES > PLUGHOLE
PLUGLESS > PLUG
PLUGOLA n plugging of products on television
PLUGOLAS > PLUGOLA
PLUGS > PLUG
PLUGUGLY n city tough; ruffian
PLUM n oval usu dark red fruit with a stone in the middle ▷ adj dark purplish-red
PLUMAGE n bird's feathers
PLUMAGED > PLUMAGE
PLUMAGES > PLUMAGE
PLUMATE adj of, relating to, or possessing one or more feathers or plumes
PLUMB vb understand (something obscure) ▷ adv exactly ▷ n weight, usually of lead, suspended at the end of a line and used to determine water depth or verticality
PLUMBABLE > PLUMB
PLUMBAGO n plant of warm regions with clusters of blue, white, or red

flowers
PLUMBAGOS > PLUMBAGO
PLUMBATE n compound formed from lead oxide
PLUMBATES > PLUMBATE
PLUMBED > PLUMB
PLUMBEOUS adj made of or relating to lead or resembling lead in colour
PLUMBER n person who fits and repairs pipes and fixtures for water and drainage systems
PLUMBERS > PLUMBER
PLUMBERY same as > PLUMBING
PLUMBIC adj of or containing lead in the tetravalent state
PLUMBING n pipes and fixtures used in water and drainage systems
PLUMBINGS > PLUMBING
PLUMBISM n chronic lead poisoning
PLUMBISMS > PLUMBISM
PLUMBITE n substance containing lead oxide
PLUMBITES > PLUMBITE
PLUMBLESS adj incapable of being sounded
PLUMBNESS > PLUMB
PLUMBOUS adj of or containing lead in the divalent state
PLUMBS > PLUMB
PLUMBUM n obsolete name for lead (the metal)
PLUMBUMS > PLUMBUM
PLUMCOT n hybrid of apricot and plum
PLUMCOTS > PLUMCOT
PLUMDAMAS n prune
PLUME n feather, esp one worn as an ornament ▷ vb adorn or decorate with feathers or plumes
PLUMED > PLUME
PLUMELESS > PLUME
PLUMELET n small plume
PLUMELETS > PLUMELET
PLUMELIKE > PLUME
PLUMERIA n tropical tree with candelabra-like branches
PLUMERIAS > PLUMERIA
PLUMERIES > PLUMERY
PLUMERY n plumes collectively
PLUMES > PLUME
PLUMIER > PLUMY
PLUMIEST > PLUMY
PLUMING > PLUME
PLUMIPED n bird with feathered feet
PLUMIPEDS > PLUMIPED
PLUMIST n person who makes plumes
PLUMISTS > PLUMIST
PLUMLIKE > PLUM
PLUMMER > PLUM
PLUMMEST > PLUM
PLUMMET vb plunge downward ▷ n weight on a

plumb line or fishing line
PLUMMETED > PLUMMET
PLUMMETS > PLUMMET
PLUMMIER > PLUMMY
PLUMMIEST > PLUMMY
PLUMMY adj of, full of, or like plums
PLUMOSE same as > PLUMATE
PLUMOSELY > PLUMOSE
PLUMOSITY > PLUMOSE
PLUMOUS adj having plumes or feathers
PLUMP adj moderately or attractively fat ▷ vb sit or fall heavily and suddenly ▷ n heavy abrupt fall or the sound of this ▷ adv suddenly or heavily
PLUMPED > PLUMP
PLUMPEN vb make or become plump
PLUMPENED > PLUMPEN
PLUMPENS > PLUMPEN
PLUMPER n pad carried in the mouth by actors to round out the cheeks
PLUMPERS > PLUMPER
PLUMPEST > PLUMP
PLUMPIE same as > PLUMPY
PLUMPIER > PLUMPY
PLUMPIEST > PLUMPY
PLUMPING > PLUMP
PLUMPISH adj on the plump side
PLUMPLY > PLUMP
PLUMPNESS > PLUMP
PLUMPS > PLUMP
PLUMPY adj plump
PLUMS > PLUM
PLUMULA n down feather
PLUMULAE > PLUMULA
PLUMULAR > PLUMULE
PLUMULATE adj covered with soft fine feathers
PLUMULE n embryonic shoot of seed-bearing plants
PLUMULES > PLUMULE
PLUMULOSE adj having hairs branching out like feathers
PLUMY adj like a feather
PLUNDER vb take by force, esp in time of war ▷ n things plundered, spoils
PLUNDERED > PLUNDER
PLUNDERER > PLUNDER
PLUNDERS > PLUNDER
PLUNGE vb put or throw forcibly or suddenly (into) ▷ n plunging dive
PLUNGED > PLUNGE
PLUNGER n rubber suction cup used to clear blocked pipes
PLUNGERS > PLUNGER
PLUNGES > PLUNGE
PLUNGING > PLUNGE
PLUNGINGS > PLUNGE
PLUNK vb pluck the strings of (a banjo etc) to produce a twanging sound ▷ n act or

sound of plunking ▷ *interj* exclamation imitative of the sound of something plunking ▷ *adv* exactly

PLUNKED > PLUNK

PLUNKER > PLUNK

PLUNKERS > PLUNK

PLUNKIER > PLUNKY

PLUNKIEST > PLUNKY

PLUNKING > PLUNK

PLUNKS > PLUNK

PLUNKY *adj* sounding like plucked banjo string

PLURAL *adj* of or consisting of more than one ▷ *n* word indicating more than one

PLURALISE *same as* > PLURALIZE

PLURALISM *n* existence and toleration of a variety of peoples, opinions, etc in a society

PLURALIST > PLURALISM

PLURALITY *n* state of being plural

PLURALIZE *vb* make or become plural

PLURALLY > PLURAL

PLURALS > PLURAL

PLURIPARA *n* woman who has borne more than one child

PLURISIE *same as* > PLEURISY

PLURISIES > PLURISIE

PLURRY *euphemism for* > BLOODY

PLUS *vb* make or become greater in value

PLUSAGE *same as* > PLUSSAGE

PLUSAGES > PLUSAGE

PLUSES > PLUS

PLUSH *n* fabric with long velvety pile ▷ *adj* luxurious

PLUSHER > PLUSH

PLUSHES > PLUSH

PLUSHEST > PLUSH

PLUSHIER > PLUSHY

PLUSHIEST > PLUSHY

PLUSHLY > PLUSHY

PLUSHNESS > PLUSH

PLUSHY *same as* > PLUSH

PLUSING > PLUS

PLUSSAGE *n* amount over and above another amount

PLUSSAGES > PLUSSAGE

PLUSSED > PLUS

PLUSSES > PLUS

PLUSSING > PLUS

PLUTEAL > PLUTEUS

PLUTEI > PLUTEUS

PLUTEUS *n* larva of sea urchin

PLUTEUSES > PLUTEUS

PLUTOCRAT *n* person who is powerful because of being very rich

PLUTOLOGY *n* study of wealth

PLUTON *n* any mass of igneous rock that has solidified below the surface of the earth

PLUTONIAN *adj* of or relating to the underworld

PLUTONIC *adj* (of igneous rocks) formed from molten rock that has cooled and solidified below the earth's surface

PLUTONISM *n* theory that the earth's crust was formed by volcanoes

PLUTONIUM *n* radioactive metallic element used esp in nuclear reactors and weapons

PLUTONOMY *n* economics

PLUTONS > PLUTON

PLUVIAL *adj* of or caused by the action of rain ▷ *n* of or relating to rainfall or precipitation

PLUVIALS > PLUVIAL

PLUVIAN *n* crocodile bird

PLUVIOSE *same as* > PLUVIOUS

PLUVIOUS *adj* of or relating to rain

PLUVIUS *as in pluvius insurance* insurance against rain

PLY *vb* work at (a job or trade) ▷ *n* thickness of wool, fabric, etc

PLYER *n* person who plies trade

PLYERS > PLYER

PLYING > PLY

PLYINGLY > PLY

PLYWOOD *n* board made of thin layers of wood glued together

PLYWOODS > PLYWOOD

PNEUMA *n* person's vital spirit, soul, or creative energy

PNEUMAS > PNEUMA

PNEUMATIC *adj* worked by or inflated with wind or air

PNEUMONIA *n* inflammation of the lungs

PNEUMONIC *adj* of, relating to, or affecting the lungs

PO *n* chamber pot

POA *n* type of grass

POACEOUS *adj* relating to the plant family which comprises grasses

POACH *vb* catch (animals) illegally on someone else's land

POACHABLE > POACH

POACHED > POACH

POACHER *n* person who catches animals illegally on someone else's land

POACHERS > POACHER

POACHES > POACH

POACHIER > POACHY

POACHIEST > POACHY

POACHING > POACH

POACHINGS > POACH

POACHY *adj* (of land) wet and soft

POAKA *n* type of stilt (bird) native to New Zealand

POAKAS > POAKA

POAKE *n* waste matter from tanning of hides

POAKES > POAKE

POAS > POA

POBLANO *n* variety of chilli pepper

POBLANOS > POBLANO

POBOY *n* New Orleans sandwich

POBOYS > POBOY

POCHARD *n* European diving duck

POCHARDS > POCHARD

POCHAY *n* post chaise: a closed horse-drawn four-wheeled coach

POCHAYS > POCHAY

POCHETTE *n* envelope-shaped handbag used by women and men

POCHETTES > POCHETTE

POCHOIR *n* print made from stencils

POCHOIRS > POCHOIR

POCK *n* pus-filled blister resulting from smallpox ▷ *vb* mark with scars

POCKARD *variant of* > POCHARD

POCKARDS > POCKARD

POCKED > POCK

POCKET *n* small bag sewn into clothing for carrying things ▷ *vb* put into one's pocket ▷ *adj* small

POCKETED > POCKET

POCKETER > POCKET

POCKETERS > POCKET

POCKETFUL *n* as much as a pocket will hold

POCKETING > POCKET

POCKETS > POCKET

POCKIER > POCK

POCKIES *npl* woollen mittens

POCKIEST > POCK

POCKILY > POCK

POCKING > POCK

POCKMANKY *n* portmanteau

POCKMARK *n* pitted scar left on the skin after the healing of a smallpox or similar pustule ▷ *vb* scar or pit (a surface) with pockmarks

POCKMARKS > POCKMARK

POCKPIT *n* mark left on skin after a pock has gone

POCKPITS > POCKPIT

POCKS > POCK

POCKY > POCK

POCO *adv* little

POCOSEN *same as* > POCOSIN

POCOSENS > POCOSEN

POCOSIN *n* swamp in US upland coastal region

POCOSINS > POCOSIN

POCOSON *same as* > POCOSIN

POCOSONS > POCOSON

POD *n* long narrow seed case of peas, beans, etc ▷ *vb* remove the pod from

PODAGRA *n* gout of the foot or big toe

PODAGRAL > PODAGRA

PODAGRAS > PODAGRA

PODAGRIC > PODAGRA

PODAGROUS > PODAGRA

PODAL *adj* relating to feet

PODALIC *adj* relating to feet

PODARGUS *n* bird of SE Asia and Australia

PODCAST *n* audio file similar to a radio broadcast, which can be downloaded and listened to on a computer or MP3 player ▷ *vb* make available in this format

PODCASTED > PODCAST

PODCASTER > PODCAST

PODCASTS > PODCAST

PODDED > POD

PODDIE *n* user of or enthusiast for the iPod, a portable digital music player

PODDIER > PODDY

PODDIES > PODDY

PODDIEST > PODDY

PODDING > POD

PODDLE *vb* move or travel in a leisurely manner

PODDLED > PODDLE

PODDLES > PODDLE

PODDLING > PODDLE

PODDY *n* handfed calf or lamb ▷ *adj* fat

PODESTA *n* (in modern Italy) subordinate magistrate in some towns

PODESTAS > PODESTA

PODEX *n* posterior

PODEXES > PODEX

PODGE *n* short chubby person

PODGES > PODGE

PODGIER > PODGY

PODGIEST > PODGY

PODGILY > PODGY

PODGINESS > PODGY

PODGY *adj* short and fat

PODIA > PODIUM

PODIAL > PODIUM

PODIATRIC > PODIATRY

PODIATRY *another word for* > CHIROPODY

PODITE *n* crustacean leg

PODITES > PODITE

PODITIC *adj* similar to the limb segment of an arthropod

PODIUM *n* small raised platform for a conductor or speaker

PODIUMS > PODIUM

PODLEY *n* young coalfish

PODLEYS > PODLEY

PODLIKE > POD

PODOCARP n stem supporting fruit
PODOCARPS > PODOCARP
PODOLOGY n study of feet
PODOMERE n segment of limb of arthropod
PODOMERES > PODOMERE
PODS > POD
PODSOL same as > PODZOL
PODSOLIC > PODZOL
PODSOLISE same as > PODZOLIZE
PODSOLIZE same as > PODZOLIZE
PODSOLS > PODSOL
PODZOL n type of soil characteristic of coniferous forest regions having a greyish-white colour in its upper leached layers
PODZOLIC > PODZOL
PODZOLISE same as > PODZOLIZE
PODZOLIZE vb make into or form a podzol
PODZOLS > PODZOL
POECHORE n dry region
POECHORES > POECHORE
POEM n imaginative piece of writing in rhythmic lines
POEMATIC adj of poetry
POEMS > POEM
POENOLOGY same as > PENOLOGY
POEP n emission of gas from the anus
POEPOL n South African slang for anus
POEPOLS > POEPOL
POEPS > POEP
POESIED > POESY
POESIES > POESY
POESY n poetry ▷ vb write poems
POESYING > POESY
POET n writer of poems
POETASTER n writer of inferior verse
POETASTRY > POETASTER
POETESS n female poet
POETESSES > POETESS
POETIC adj of or like poetry
POETICAL n poet
POETICALS > POETICAL
POETICISE same as > POETICIZE
POETICISM > POETICIZE
POETICIZE vb put into poetry or make poetic
POETICS n principles and forms of poetry or the study of these, esp as a form of literary criticism
POETICULE n inferior poet
POETISE same as > POETICIZE
POETISED > POETISE
POETISER > POETISE
POETISERS > POETISE
POETISES > POETISE
POETISING > POETISE

POETIZE same as > POETICIZE
POETIZED > POETIZE
POETIZER > POETIZE
POETIZERS > POETIZE
POETIZES > POETIZE
POETIZING > POETIZE
POETLESS > POET
POETLIKE > POET
POETRESSE old variant of > POETESS
POETRIES > POETRY
POETRY n poems
POETS > POET
POETSHIP n state of being poet
POETSHIPS > POETSHIP
POFFLE n small piece of land
POFFLES > POFFLE
POGEY n financial or other relief given to the unemployed by the government
POGEYS > POGEY
POGGE n European marine scorpaenoid fish
POGGES > POGGE
POGIES > POGY
POGO vb jump up and down in one spot, as in a punk dance of the 1970s
POGOED > POGO
POGOER > POGO
POGOERS > POGO
POGOING > POGO
POGONIA n orchid with pink or white fragrant flowers
POGONIAS > POGONIA
POGONIP n icy winter fog
POGONIPS > POGONIP
POGOS > POGO
POGROM n organized persecution and massacre ▷ vb carry out a pogrom
POGROMED > POGROM
POGROMING > POGROM
POGROMIST > POGROM
POGROMS > POGROM
POGY same as > POGEY
POH interj exclamation expressing contempt or disgust
POHIRI variant spelling of > POWHIRI
POHIRIS > POHIRI
POI n ball of woven flax swung rhythmically by Māori women during poi dances
POIGNADO old variant of > PONIARD
POIGNANCE > POIGNANT
POIGNANCY > POIGNANT
POIGNANT adj sharply painful to the feelings
POILU n infantryman in the French Army, esp one in the front lines in World War I
POILUS > POILU
POINADO old variant of > PONIARD
POINADOES > POINADO

POINCIANA n tropical leguminous tree with large orange or red flowers
POIND vb take (property of a debtor) in execution or by way of distress
POINDED > POIND
POINDER > POIND
POINDERS > POIND
POINDING > POIND
POINDINGS > POIND
POINDS > POIND
POINT n main idea in a discussion, argument, etc ▷ vb show the direction or position of something or draw attention to it by extending a finger or other pointed object towards it
POINTABLE > POINT
POINTE n tip of the toe
POINTED adj having a sharp end
POINTEDLY > POINTED
POINTEL n engraver's tool
POINTELLE n fabric design in form of chevrons
POINTELS > POINTEL
POINTER n helpful hint
POINTERS > POINTER
POINTES > POINTE
POINTIER > POINTY
POINTIEST > POINTY
POINTILLE n dotted lines and curves impressed on cover of book
POINTING n insertion of mortar between the joints in brickwork
POINTINGS > POINTING
POINTLESS adj meaningless, irrelevant
POINTMAN n soldier who walks at the front of an infantry patrol in combat
POINTMEN > POINTMAN
POINTS > POINT
POINTSMAN n person who operates railway points
POINTSMEN > POINTSMAN
POINTY adj having a sharp point or points
POIS > POI
POISE n calm dignified manner ▷ vb be balanced or suspended
POISED adj absolutely ready
POISER n balancing organ of some insects
POISERS > POISER
POISES > POISE
POISHA n monetary unit of Bangladesh
POISING > POISE
POISON n substance that kills or injures when swallowed or absorbed ▷ vb give poison to
POISONED > POISON
POISONER > POISON
POISONERS > POISON
POISONING n the act of giving poison to someone

POISONOUS adj of or like a poison
POISONS > POISON
POISSON n fish
POISSONS > POISSON
POTTIN variant spelling of > POTEEN
POTTINS > POITIN
POTTREL n breastplate of horse's armour
POTTRELS > POITREL
POITRINE n woman's bosom
POITRINES > POITRINE
POKABLE > POKE
POKAL n tall drinking cup
POKALS > POKAL
POKE vb jab or prod with one's finger, a stick, etc ▷ n poking
POKEBERRY same as > POKEWEED
POKED > POKE
POKEFUL n contents of small bag
POKEFULS > POKEFUL
POKELOGAN another name for > BOGAN
POKER n metal rod for stirring a fire
POKERISH adj stiff like poker
POKEROOT same as > POKEWEED
POKEROOTS > POKEROOT
POKERS > POKER
POKERWORK n art of producing pictures or designs on wood by burning it with a heated metal point
POKES > POKE
POKEWEED n tall North American plant that has small white flowers, juicy purple berries, and a poisonous purple root used medicinally
POKEWEEDS > POKEWEED
POKEY same as > POKIE
POKEYS > POKEY
POKIE n poker machine
POKIER > POKY
POKIES > POKY
POKIEST > POKY
POKILY > POKY
POKINESS > POKY
POKING > POKE
POKY adj small and cramped
POL n political campaigner
POLACCA same as > POLACRE
POLACCAS > POLACCA
POLACRE n three-masted sailing vessel used in the Mediterranean
POLACRES > POLACRE
POLAR adj of or near either of the earth's poles ▷ n type of line in geometry
POLARISE same as > POLARIZE
POLARISED > POLARISE

POLARISER *same as*
> POLARIZER

POLARISES > POLARISE

POLARITY *n* state of
having two directly
opposite tendencies or
opinions

POLARIZE *vb* form or
cause to form into groups
with directly opposite
views

POLARIZED > POLARIZE

POLARIZER *n* person or a
device that causes
polarization

POLARIZES > POLARIZE

POLARON *n* kind of electron

POLARONS > POLARON

POLARS > POLAR

POLDER *n* land reclaimed
from the sea, esp in the
Netherlands ▷ *vb* reclaim
land from the sea

POLDERED > POLDER

POLDERING > POLDER

POLDERS > POLDER

POLE *n* long rounded piece
of wood etc ▷ *vb* strike or
push with a pole

POLEAX *same as*
> POLEAXE

POLEAXE *vb* hit or stun
with a heavy blow ▷ *n* axe
formerly used in battle or
used by a butcher

POLEAXED > POLEAXE

POLEAXES > POLEAXE

POLEAXING > POLEAXE

POLECAT *n* small animal of
the weasel family

POLECATS > POLECAT

POLED > POLE

POLEIS > POLIS

POLELESS > POLE

POLEMARCH *n* (in ancient
Greece) civilian official,
originally a supreme
general

POLEMIC *n* fierce attack on
or defence of a particular
opinion, belief, etc ▷ *adj* of
or involving dispute or
controversy

POLEMICAL > POLEMIC

POLEMICS *n* art of
dispute

POLEMISE *same as*
> POLEMIZE

POLEMISED > POLEMISE

POLEMISES > POLEMISE

POLEMIST > POLEMIC

POLEMISTS > POLEMIC

POLEMIZE *vb* engage in
controversy

POLEMIZED > POLEMIZE

POLEMIZES > POLEMIZE

POLENTA *n* thick porridge
made in Italy, usually from
maize

POLENTAS > POLENTA

POLER *n* person or thing
that poles, esp a punter

POLERS > POLER

POLES > POLE

POLESTAR *n* guiding

principle, rule, standard,
etc

POLESTARS > POLESTAR

POLEWARD *adv* towards a
pole

POLEY *adj* (of cattle)
hornless or polled ▷ *n*
animal with horns removed

POLEYN *n* piece of armour
for protecting the knee

POLEYNS > POLEYN

POLEYS > POLEY

POLIANITE *n* manganese
dioxide occurring as hard
crystals

POLICE *n* organized force
in a state which keeps law
and order ▷ *vb* control or
watch over with police or a
similar body

POLICED > POLICE

POLICEMAN *n* member of
a police force

POLICEMEN
> POLICEMAN

POLICER *n* computer
device controlling use

POLICERS > POLICER

POLICES > POLICE

POLICIES > POLICY

POLICING > POLICE

POLICINGS > POLICE

POLICY *n* plan of action
adopted by a person,
group, or state

POLIES > POLY

POLING > POLE

POLINGS > POLE

POLIO *n* acute viral disease

POLIOS > POLIO

POLIS *n* ancient Greek
city-state

POLISES > POLIS

POLISH *vb* make smooth
and shiny by rubbing ▷ *n*
substance used for
polishing

POLISHED *adj*
accomplished

POLISHER > POLISH

POLISHERS > POLISH

POLISHES > POLISH

POLISHING > POLISH

POLITBURO *n* supreme
policy-making authority in
most communist countries

POLITE *adj* showing
consideration for others in
one's manners, speech, etc

POLITELY > POLITE

POLITER > POLITE

POLITESSE *n* formal or
genteel politeness

POLITEST > POLITE

POLITIC *adj* wise and
likely to prove
advantageous

POLITICAL *adj* of the
state, government, or
public administration

POLITICK *vb* engage in
politics

POLITICKS > POLITICK

POLITICLY > POLITIC

POLITICO *n* politician

POLITICOS > POLITICO

POLITICS *n* winning and
using of power to govern
society

POLITIES > POLITY

POLITIQUE *n*
16th-century French
moderate

POLITY *n* politically
organized state, church, or
society

POLJE *n* large elliptical
depression in karst regions,
sometimes containing a
marsh or small lake

POLJES > POLJE

POLK *vb* dance a polka

POLKA *n* lively 19th-century
dance ▷ *vb* dance a polka

POLKAED > POLKA

POLKAING > POLKA

POLKAS > POLKA

POLKED > POLK

POLKING > POLK

POLKS > POLK

POLL *n* questioning of a
random sample of people
to find out general opinion
▷ *vb* receive (votes)

POLLACK *n* food fish
related to the cod, found in
northern seas

POLLACKS > POLLACK

POLLAN *n* whitefish that
occurs in lakes in Northern
Ireland

POLLANS > POLLAN

POLLARD *n* animal that
has shed its horns or has
had them removed ▷ *vb* cut
off the top of (a tree) to
make it grow bushy

POLLARDED > POLLARD

POLLARDS > POLLARD

POLLAXE *same as*
> POLEAXE

POLLAXED > POLLAXE

POLLAXES > POLLAXE

POLLAXING > POLLAXE

POLLED *adj* (of animals, esp
cattle) having the horns cut
off or being naturally
hornless

POLLEE > POLL

POLLEES > POLL

POLLEN *n* fine dust
produced by flowers to
fertilize other flowers ▷ *vb*
collect pollen

POLLENATE *same as*
> POLLINATE

POLLENED > POLLEN

POLLENING > POLLEN

POLLENS > POLLEN

POLLENT *adj* strong

POLLER > POLL

POLLERS > POLL

POLLEX *n* first digit of the
forelimb of amphibians,
reptiles, birds, and
mammals, such as the
thumb of man and other
primates

POLLICAL > POLLEX

POLLICES > POLLEX

POLLICIE *obsolete spelling
of* > POLICY

POLLICIES > POLLICIE

POLLICY *obsolete spelling of*
> POLICY

POLLIES > POLLY

POLLINATE *vb* fertilize
with pollen

POLLING *n* casting or
registering of votes at an
election

POLLINGS > POLLING

POLLINIA > POLLINIUM

POLLINIC > POLLEN

POLLINISE *same as*
> POLLINIZE

POLLINIUM *n* mass of
cohering pollen grains,
produced by plants such as
orchids and transported as
a whole during pollination

POLLINIZE *same as*
> POLLINATE

POLLIST *n* one advocating
the use of polls

POLLISTS > POLLIST

POLLIWIG *same as*
> POLLIWOG

POLLIWIGS > POLLIWOG

POLLIWOG *n* sailor who
has not crossed the
equator

POLLIWOGS > POLLIWOG

POLLMAN *n* one passing a
degree without honours

POLLMEN > POLLMAN

POLLOCK *same as*
> POLLACK

POLLOCKS > POLLOCK

POLLS > POLL

POLLSTER *n* person who
conducts opinion polls

POLLSTERS > POLLSTER

POLLTAKER *n* person
conducting poll

POLLUCITE *n* colourless
rare mineral consisting of a
hydrated caesium
aluminium silicate

POLLUSION *n* comic
Shakespearian character's
version of "allusion"

POLLUTANT *n* something
that pollutes

POLLUTE *vb* contaminate
with something poisonous
or harmful

POLLUTED *adj* made
unclean or impure

POLLUTER > POLLUTE

POLLUTERS > POLLUTE

POLLUTES > POLLUTE

POLLUTING > POLLUTE

POLLUTION *n* act of
polluting or the state of
being polluted

POLLUTIVE *adj* causing
pollution

POLLY *n* politician

POLLYANNA *n* person who
is constantly or excessively
optimistic

POLLYWIG *same as*
> POLLIWOG

POLLYWIGS > POLLYWIG

POLLYWOG *same as*
> POLLIWOG
POLLYWOGS > POLLYWOG
POLO *n* game like hockey played by teams of players on horseback
POLOIDAL *adj* relating to a type of magnetic field
POLOIST *n* devotee of polo
POLOISTS > POLOIST
POLONAISE *n* old stately dance
POLONIE *same as*
> POLONY
POLONIES > POLONY
POLONISE *same as*
> POLONIZE
POLONISED > POLONISE
POLONISES > POLONISE
POLONISM > POLONISE
POLONISMS > POLONISE
POLONIUM *n* radioactive element that occurs in trace amounts in uranium ores
POLONIUMS > POLONIUM
POLONIZE *vb* make Polish
POLONIZED > POLONIZE
POLONIZES > POLONIZE
POLONY *n* bologna sausage
POLOS > POLO
POLS > POL
POLT *n* thump or blow ▷ *vb* strike
POLTED > POLT
POLTFEET > POLTFOOT
POLTFOOT *adj* having a club foot ▷ *n* club foot
POLTING > POLT
POLTROON *n* utter coward
POLTROONS > POLTROON
POLTS > POLT
POLVERINE *n* glassmakers' potash
POLY *n* polytechnic
POLYACID *adj* having two or more hydroxyl groups
POLYACT *adj* (of a sea creature) having many tentacles or limb-like protrusions
POLYADIC *adj* (of a relation, operation, etc) having several argument places
POLYAMIDE *n* synthetic polymeric material
POLYAMINE *n* compound containing two or more amine groups
POLYAMORY *n* practice of openly having more than one intimate relationship at a time
POLYANDRY *n* practice of having more than one husband at the same time
POLYANTHA *n* type of flower
POLYANTHI *n* hybrid garden primroses
POLYARCH *n* member of polyarchy
POLYARCHY *n* political system in which power is dispersed

POLYAXIAL *n* joint in which movement occurs in more than one axis
POLYAXON *n* nerve cell with multiple branches
POLYAXONS > POLYAXON
POLYBASIC *adj* (of an acid) having two or more replaceable hydrogen atoms per molecule
POLYBRID *n* hybrid plant with more than two parental groups
POLYBRIDS > POLYBRID
POLYCARPY *n* condition of being able to produce flowers and fruit several times in successive years or seasons
POLYCHETE *n* variety of worm
POLYCONIC as in *polyconic projection* type of projection used in making maps of large areas
POLYCOT *n* plant that has or appears to have more than two cotyledons
POLYCOTS > POLYCOT
POLYDEMIC *adj* growing in or inhabiting more than two regions
POLYENE *n* chemical compound containing a chain of alternating single and double carbon-carbon bonds
POLYENES > POLYENE
POLYENIC > POLYENE
POLYESTER *n* synthetic material used to make plastics and textile fibres
POLYGALA *n* herbaceous plant or small shrub
POLYGALAS > POLYGALA
POLYGAM *n* plant of the Polygamia class
POLYGAMIC > POLYGAMY
POLYGAMS > POLYGAM
POLYGAMY *n* practice of having more than one husband or wife at the same time
POLYGENE *n* any of a group of genes that each produce a small quantitative effect on a particular characteristic of the phenotype, such as height
POLYGENES > POLYGENE
POLYGENIC *adj* of, relating to, or controlled by polygenes
POLYGENY > POLYGENIC
POLYGLOT *adj* (person) able to speak or write several languages ▷ *n* person who can speak many languages
POLYGLOTS > POLYGLOT
POLYGLOTT *variant of*
> POLYGLOT
POLYGON *n* geometrical figure with three or more angles and sides

POLYGONAL > POLYGON
POLYGONS > POLYGON
POLYGONUM *n* plant with stems with knotlike joints and spikes of small white, green, or pink flowers
POLYGONY > POLYGON
POLYGRAPH *n* instrument for recording pulse rate and perspiration, used esp as a lie detector
POLYGYNY *n* practice of having more than one wife at the same time
POLYHEDRA *n* solid figures, each consisting of four or more plane faces
POLYIMIDE *n* type of polymer
POLYLEMMA *n* debate forcing choice between contradictory positions
POLYMASTY *n* condition in which more than two breasts are present
POLYMATH *n* person of great and varied learning
POLYMATHS > POLYMATH
POLYMATHY > POLYMATH
POLYMER *n* chemical compound with large molecules made of simple molecules of the same kind
POLYMERIC *adj* of or being a polymer
POLYMERS > POLYMER
POLYMERY > POLYMER
POLYMORPH *n* species of animal or plant that exhibits polymorphism
POLYMYXIN *n* polypeptide antibiotic
POLYNIA *same as*
> POLYNYA
POLYNIAS > POLYNIA
POLYNYA *n* stretch of open water surrounded by ice, esp near the mouths of large rivers, in arctic seas
POLYNYAS > POLYNYA
POLYNYI > POLYNYA
POLYOL *n* type of alcohol
POLYOLS > POLYOL
POLYOMA *n* type of tumour caused by virus
POLYOMAS > POLYOMA
POLYOMINO *n* polygon made from joining identical squares at their edges
POLYONYM *n* object with many names
POLYONYMS > POLYONYM
POLYONYMY > POLYONYM
POLYP *n* small simple sea creature with a hollow cylindrical body
POLYPARIA *n* polyparies
POLYPARY *n* common base and connecting tissue of a colony of coelenterate polyps, esp coral
POLYPE *variant of* > POLYP
POLYPED *same as*
> POLYPOD
POLYPEDS > POLYPED

POLYPES > POLYPE
POLYPHAGY *n* insatiable appetite
POLYPHASE *adj* (of an electrical system, circuit, or device) having, generating, or using two or more alternating voltages of the same frequency, the phases of which are cyclically displaced by fractions of a period
POLYPHON *n* musical instrument resembling a lute
POLYPHONE *n* letter or character with more than one phonetic value
POLYPHONS > POLYPHON
POLYPHONY *n* polyphonic style of composition or a piece of music using it
POLYPI > POLYPUS
POLYPIDE *n* polyp forming part of a colonial animal
POLYPIDES > POLYPIDE
POLYPIDOM *same as*
> POLYPARY
POLYPILL *n* proposed combined medication intended to reduce the likelihood of heart attacks and strokes
POLYPILLS > POLYPILL
POLYPINE *adj* of or relating to polyps
POLYPITE *same as*
> POLYPIDE
POLYPITES > POLYPITE
POLYPLOID *adj* (of cells, organisms, etc) having more than twice the basic (haploid) number of chromosomes ▷ *n* individual or cell of this type
POLYPNEA *n* rapid breathing
POLYPNEAS > POLYPNEA
POLYPNEIC > POLYPNEA
POLYPOD *adj* (esp of insect larvae) having many legs or similar appendages ▷ *n* animal of this type
POLYPODS > POLYPOD
POLYPODY *n* fern with deeply divided leaves and round naked sori
POLYPOID > POLYP
POLYPORE *n* type of fungi
POLYPORES > POLYPORE
POLYPOSES
> POLYPOSIS
POLYPOSIS *n* formation of many polyps
POLYPOUS > POLYP
POLYPS > POLYP
POLYPTYCH *n* altarpiece consisting of more than three panels, set with paintings or carvings, and usually hinged for folding
POLYPUS *same as* > POLYP
POLYPUSES > POLYPUS
POLYS > POLY

P

POLYSEME *n* word with many meanings

POLYSEMES > POLYSEME

POLYSEMIC > POLYSEME

POLYSEMY *n* existence of several meanings in a single word

POLYSOME *n* assemblage of ribosomes associated with a messenger RNA molecule

POLYSOMES > POLYSOME

POLYSOMIC *adj* of, relating to, or designating a basically diploid chromosome complement, in which some but not all the chromosomes are represented more than twice

POLYSOMY > POLYSOME

POLYSTYLE *adj* with many columns

POLYTENE *adj* denoting a type of giant-size chromosome

POLYTENY > POLYTENE

POLYTHENE *n* light plastic used for bags etc

POLYTONAL *adj* using more than two different tones or keys simultaneously

POLYTYPE *n* crystal occurring in more than one form

POLYTYPES > POLYTYPE

POLYTYPIC *adj* existing in, consisting of, or incorporating several different types or forms

POLYURIA *n* state or condition of discharging abnormally large quantities of urine, often accompanied by a need to urinate frequently

POLYURIAS > POLYURIA

POLYURIC > POLYURIA

POLYVINYL *n* designating a plastic or resin formed by polymerization of a vinyl derivative

POLYWATER *n* liquid formerly supposed to be polymeric form of water

POLYZOA *n* small mosslike aquatic creatures

POLYZOAN another word for > BRYOZOAN

POLYZOANS > POLYZOAN

POLYZOARY *n* colony of bryozoan animals

POLYZOIC *adj* (of certain colonial animals) having many zooids or similar polyps

POLYZONAL *adj* having many zones

POLYZOOID *adj* resembling a polyzoon

POLYZOON *n* individual zooid within polyzoan

POM same as > POMMY

POMACE *n* apple pulp left after pressing for juice

POMACEOUS *adj* of, relating to, or bearing pomes, such as the apple, pear, and quince trees

POMACES > POMACE

POMADE *n* perfumed oil put on the hair to make it smooth and shiny ⊳ *vb* put pomade on

POMADED > POMADE

POMADES > POMADE

POMADING > POMADE

POMANDER *n* mixture of sweet-smelling petals, herbs, etc

POMANDERS > POMANDER

POMATO *n* hybrid of tomato and potato

POMATOES > POMATO

POMATUM same as > POMADE

POMATUMS > POMATUM

POMBE *n* any alcoholic drink

POMBES > POMBE

POME *n* fleshy fruit of the apple and related plants, consisting of an enlarged receptacle enclosing the ovary and seeds

POMELO *n* edible yellow fruit, like a grapefruit, of a tropical tree

POMELOS > POMELO

POMEROY *n* bullet used to down airships

POMEROYS > POMEROY

POMES > POME

POMFRET *n* small black rounded liquorice sweet

POMFRETS > POMFRET

POMMEE *adj* (of cross) having end of each arm ending in disk

POMMEL same as > PUMMEL

POMMELE *adj* having a pommel

POMMELED > POMMEL

POMMELING > POMMEL

POMMELLED > POMMEL

POMMELS > POMMEL

POMMETTY *adj* having a pommel

POMMIE same as > POMMY

POMMIES > POMMY

POMMY *n* word used by Australians and New Zealanders for a British person

POMO *n* postmodernism

POMOERIUM *n* space around town within city walls

POMOLOGY *n* branch of horticulture that is concerned with the study and cultivation of fruit

POMOS > POMO

POMP *n* stately display or ceremony

POMPADOUR *n* early 18th-century hairstyle for women, having the front hair arranged over a pad to give it greater height and bulk

POMPANO *n* deep-bodied carangid food fish

POMPANOS > POMPANO

POMPELO *n* large Asian citrus fruit

POMPELOS > POMPELO

POMPEY *vb* mollycoddle

POMPEYED > POMPEY

POMPEYING > POMPEY

POMPEYS > POMPEY

POMPHOLYX *n* type of eczema

POMPIER *adj* slavishly conventional

POMPILID *n* spider-hunting wasp

POMPILIDS > POMPILID

POMPION *n* pumpkin

POMPIONS > POMPION

POMPOM *n* decorative ball of tufted wool, silk, etc

POMPOMS > POMPOM

POMPON same as > POMPOM

POMPONS > POMPON

POMPOON variant of > POMPOM

POMPOONS > POMPOON

POMPOSITY *n* vain or ostentatious display of dignity or importance

POMPOUS *adj* foolishly serious and grand, self-important

POMPOUSLY > POMPOUS

POMPS > POMP

POMROY variant of > POMEROY

POMROYS > POMROY

POMS > POM

POMWATER *n* kind of apple

POMWATERS > POMWATER

PONCE *n* derogatory word for an effeminate man ⊳ *vb* act stupidly or waste time

PONCEAU *n* scarlet red

PONCEAUS > PONCEAU

PONCEAUX > PONCEAU

PONCED > PONCE

PONCES > PONCE

PONCEY *adj* ostentatious, pretentious, or effeminate

PONCHO *n* loose circular cloak with a hole for the head

PONCHOED *adj* wearing poncho

PONCHOS > PONCHO

PONCIER > PONCEY

PONCIEST > PONCEY

PONCING > PONCE

PONCY same as > PONCEY

POND *n* small area of still water ⊳ *vb* hold back (flowing water)

PONDAGE *n* water held in reservoir

PONDAGES > PONDAGE

PONDED > POND

PONDER *vb* think thoroughly or deeply (about)

PONDERAL *adj* relating to weight

PONDERATE *vb* consider

PONDERED > PONDER

PONDERER > PONDER

PONDERERS > PONDER

PONDERING > PONDER

PONDEROSA *n* N American pine tree

PONDEROUS *adj* serious and dull

PONDERS > PONDER

PONDING > POND

PONDOK *n* (in southern Africa) crudely made house or shack

PONDOKKIE same as > PONDOK

PONDOKS > PONDOK

PONDS > POND

PONDWEED *n* plant that grows in ponds

PONDWEEDS > PONDWEED

PONE *n* bread made of maize

PONENT *adj* westerly

PONES > PONE

PONEY same as > PONY

PONEYS > PONEY

PONG *n* strong unpleasant smell ⊳ *vb* give off a strong unpleasant smell

PONGA *n* tall New Zealand tree fern with large leathery leaves

PONGAS > PONGA

PONGED > PONG

PONGEE *n* thin plain-weave silk fabric from China or India, left in its natural colour

PONGEES > PONGEE

PONGID *n* primate of the family which includes the gibbons and the great apes

PONGIDS > PONGID

PONGIER > PONG

PONGIEST > PONG

PONGING > PONG

PONGO *n* anthropoid ape, esp an orang-utan or (formerly) a gorilla

PONGOES > PONGO

PONGOS > PONGO

PONGS > PONG

PONGY > PONG

PONIARD *n* small slender dagger ⊳ *vb* stab with a poniard

PONIARDED > PONIARD

PONIARDS > PONIARD

PONIED > PONY

PONIES > PONY

PONK *n* evil spirit ⊳ *vb* stink

PONKED > PONK

PONKING > PONK

PONKS > PONK

PONS *n* bridge of connecting tissue

PONT *n* (in South Africa) river ferry, esp one that is guided by a cable from one bank to the other

PONTAGE *n* tax paid for repairing bridge

PONTAGES > PONTAGE

PONTAL *adj* of or relating to the pons

PONTES > PONS
PONTIANAC same as > PONTIANAK
PONTIANAK n (in Malay folklore) female vampire
PONTIC adj of or relating to the pons
PONTIE same as > PONTY
PONTIES > PONTY
PONTIFEX n (in ancient Rome) any of the senior members of the Pontifical College
PONTIFF n Pope
PONTIFFS > PONTIFF
PONTIFIC > PONTIFF
PONTIFICE n structure of bridge
PONTIFIED > PONTIFY
PONTIFIES > PONTIFY
PONTIFY vb speak or behave in a pompous or dogmatic manner
PONTIL same as > PUNTY
PONTILE adj relating to pons ▷ n metal bar used in glass-making
PONTILES > PONTILE
PONTILS > PONTIL
PONTINE adj of or relating to bridges
PONTLEVIS n horse rearing repeatedly
PONTON variant of > PONTOON
PONTONEER same as > PONTONIER
PONTONIER n person in charge of or involved in building a pontoon bridge
PONTONS > PONTON
PONTOON n floating platform supporting a temporary bridge ▷ vb cross a river using pontoons
PONTOONED > PONTOON
PONTOONER > PONTOON
PONTOONS > PONTOON
PONTS > PONT
PONTY n rod used for shaping molten glass
PONY n small horse ▷ vb settle bill or debt
PONYING > PONY
PONYSKIN n leather from pony hide
PONYSKINS > PONYSKIN
PONYTAIL n long hair tied in one bunch at the back of the head
PONYTAILS > PONYTAIL
PONZU n type of Japanese dipping sauce made from orange juice, sake, sugar, soy sauce, and red pepper
PONZUS > PONZU
POO vb defecate
POOCH n slang word for dog ▷ vb bulge or protrude
POOCHED > POOCH
POOCHES > POOCH
POOCHING > POOCH
POOD n unit of weight, used in Russia, equal to 36.1

pounds or 16.39 kilograms
POODLE n dog with curly hair often clipped fancifully
POODLES > POODLE
POODS > POOD
POOED > POO
POOF n derogatory word for a homosexual man
POOFIER > POOF
POOFIEST > POOF
POOFS > POOF
POOFTAH same as > POOFTER
POOFTAHS > POOFTAH
POOFTER n derogatory word for a man who is considered effeminate or homosexual
POOFTERS > POOFTER
POOFY > POOF
POOGYE n Hindu nose-flute
POOGYES > POOGYE
POOH interj exclamation of disdain, contempt, or disgust ▷ vb make such an exclamation
POOHED > POOH
POOHING > POOH
POOHS > POOH
POOING > POO
POOJA variant of > PUJA
POOJAH variant of > PUJA
POOJAHS > POOJAH
POOJAS > POOJA
POOK vb pluck
POOKA n malevolent Irish spirit
POOKAS > POOKA
POOKING > POOK
POOKIT > POOK
POOKS > POOK
POOL n small body of still water ▷ vb put in a common fund
POOLED > POOL
POOLER n person taking part in pool
POOLERS > POOLER
POOLHALL n room containing pool tables
POOLHALLS > POOLHALL
POOLING > POOL
POOLROOM n hall or establishment where pool, billiards, etc, are played
POOLROOMS > POOLROOM
POOLS npl organized nationwide principally postal gambling pool betting on the result of football matches
POOLSIDE n area surrounding swimming pool
POOLSIDES > POOLSIDE
POON n SE Asian tree with lightweight hard wood and shiny leathery leaves
POONAC n coconut residue
POONACS > POONAC
POONCE n derogatory word for a homosexual man ▷ vb behave effeminately
POONCED > POONCE

POONCES > POONCE
POONCING > POONCE
POONS > POON
POONTANG n taboo word for the female pudenda
POONTANGS > POONTANG
POOP n raised part at the back of a sailing ship ▷ vb (of a wave or sea) break over the stern of (a vessel)
POOPED > POOP
POOPER as in party pooper person whose behaviour or personality spoils other people's enjoyment
POOPERS > POOPER
POOPING > POOP
POOPS > POOP
POOR adj having little money and few possessions
POORER > POOR
POOREST > POOR
POORHOUSE n (formerly) publicly maintained institution offering accommodation to the poor
POORI n unleavened Indian bread
POORIS > POORI
POORISH > POOR
POORLIER > POORLY
POORLIEST > POORLY
POORLY adv in a poor manner ▷ adj not in good health
POORMOUTH vb complain about being poor
POORNESS > POOR
POORT n (in South Africa) steep narrow mountain pass, usually following a river or stream
POORTITH same as > PUIRTITH
POORTITHS > POORTITH
POORTS > POORT
POORWILL n bird of N America
POORWILLS > POORWILL
POOS > POO
POOT vb break wind
POOTED > POOT
POOTER > POOT
POOTERS > POOT
POOTING > POOT
POOTLE vb travel or go in a relaxed or leisurely manner
POOTLED > POOTLE
POOTLES > POOTLE
POOTLING > POOTLE
POOTS > POOT
POOVE same as > POOF
POOVERIES > POOVERY
POOVERY n derogatory word for homosexuality
POOVES > POOVE
POOVIER > POOVE
POOVIEST > POOVE
POOVY > POOVE
POP vb make or cause to make a small explosive sound ▷ n small explosive sound ▷ adj popular

POPADUM same as > POPPADOM
POPADUMS > POPPADUM
POPCORN n grains of maize heated until they puff up and burst
POPCORNS > POPCORN
POPE n bishop of Rome as head of the Roman Catholic Church
POPEDOM n office or dignity of a pope
POPEDOMS > POPEDOM
POPEHOOD > POPE
POPEHOODS > POPE
POPELESS > POPE
POPELIKE > POPE
POPELING n deputy or supporter of pope
POPELINGS > POPELING
POPERA n music drawing on opera or classical music and aiming for popular appeal
POPERAS > POPERA
POPERIES > POPERY
POPERIN n kind of pear
POPERINS > POPERIN
POPERY n derogatory word for Roman Catholicism
POPES > POPE
POPESEYE adj denoting a cut of steak
POPESHIP > POPE
POPESHIPS > POPE
POPETTE n young female fan or performer of pop music
POPETTES > POPETTE
POPEYED adj staring in astonishment
POPGUN n toy gun that fires a pellet or cork by means of compressed air
POPGUNS > POPGUN
POPINJAY n conceited, foppish, or overly talkative person
POPINJAYS > POPINJAY
POPISH adj derogatory word for Roman Catholic
POPISHLY > POPISH
POPJOY vb amuse oneself
POPJOYED > POPJOY
POPJOYING > POPJOY
POPJOYS > POPJOY
POPLAR n tall slender tree
POPLARS > POPLAR
POPLIN n ribbed cotton material
POPLINS > POPLIN
POPLITEAL adj of, relating to, or near the part of the leg behind the knee
POPLITEI > POPLITEUS
POPLITEUS n muscle in leg
POPLITIC same as > POPLITEAL
POPOVER n individual Yorkshire pudding, often served with roast beef
POPOVERS > POPOVER

P

POPPA same as > PAPA
POPPADOM n thin round crisp Indian bread
POPPADOMS > POPPADOM
POPPADUM same as > POPPADOM
POPPADUMS > POPPADUM
POPPAS > POPPA
POPPED > POP
POPPER n press stud
POPPERING n method of fishing
POPPERS > POPPER
POPPET n term of affection for a small child or sweetheart
POPPETS > POPPET
POPPIED adj covered with poppies
POPPIER > POPPY
POPPIES > POPPY
POPPIEST > POPPY
POPPING > POP
POPPISH adj like pop music
POPPIT n bead used to form necklace
POPPITS > POPPIT
POPPLE vb (of boiling water or a choppy sea) to heave or toss
POPPLED > POPPLE
POPPLES > POPPLE
POPPLIER > POPPLY
POPPLIEST > POPPLY
POPPLING > POPPLE
POPPLY adj covered in small bumps
POPPY n plant with a large red flower ▷ adj reddish-orange
POPPYCOCK n nonsense
POPPYHEAD n hard dry seed-containing capsule of a poppy
POPRIN same as > POPERIN
POPS > POP
POPSICLE n tradename for a kind of ice lolly
POPSICLES > POPSICLE
POPSIE same as > POPSY
POPSIES > POPSY
POPSOCK n women's knee-length nylon stocking
POPSOCKS > POPSOCK
POPSTER n pop star
POPSTERS > POPSTER
POPSTREL n young, attractive female pop star
POPSTRELS > POPSTREL
POPSY n attractive young woman
POPULACE n ordinary people
POPULACES > POPULACE
POPULAR adj widely liked and admired ▷ n cheap newspapers with mass circulation
POPULARLY adv by the public as a whole
POPULARS > POPULAR
POPULATE vb live in,

inhabit
POPULATED > POPULATE
POPULATES > POPULATE
POPULISM n political strategy based on a calculated appeal to the interests or prejudices of ordinary people
POPULISMS > POPULISM
POPULIST adj (person) appealing to the interests or prejudices of ordinary people ▷ n person, esp a politician, who appeals to the interests or prejudices of ordinary people
POPULISTS > POPULIST
POPULOUS adj densely populated
PORAE n large edible sea fish of New Zealand waters
PORAES > PORAE
PORAL adj relating to pores
PORANGI adj crazy
PORBEAGLE n kind of shark
PORCELAIN n fine china
PORCH n covered approach to the entrance of a building
PORCHES > PORCH
PORCHETTA n Italian boneless stuffed pork cut from a whole roast pig
PORCINE adj of or like a pig
PORCINI > PORCINO
PORCINIS > PORCINO
PORCINO n edible woodland fungus
PORCUPINE n animal covered with long pointed quills
PORCUPINY > PORCUPINE
PORE n tiny opening in the skin or in the surface of a plant ▷ vb make a close intent examination or study (of a book, map, etc)
PORED > PORE
PORER n person who pores
PORERS > PORE
PORES > PORE
PORGE vb cleanse (slaughtered animal) ceremonially
PORGED > PORGE
PORGES > PORGE
PORGIE same as > PORGY
PORGIES > PORGY
PORGING > PORGE
PORGY n any of various sparid fishes, many of which occur in American Atlantic waters
PORIER > PORY
PORIEST > PORY
PORIFER n type of invertebrate
PORIFERAL > PORIFERAN
PORIFERAN n invertebrate of the phylum which comprises the sponges

PORIFERS > PORIFER
PORINA n larva of a moth which causes damage to grassland
PORINAS > PORINA
PORINESS > PORY
PORING > PORE
PORISM n type of mathematical proposition, the meaning of which is now obscure
PORISMS > PORISM
PORISTIC > PORISM
PORK vb to eat ravenously ▷ n the flesh of pigs used as food
PORKED > PORK
PORKER n pig raised for food
PORKERS > PORKER
PORKIER > PORKY
PORKIES > PORKY
PORKIEST > PORKY
PORKINESS > PORKY
PORKING > PORK
PORKLING n pig
PORKLINGS > PORKLING
PORKPIE n hat with a round flat crown and a brim that can be turned up or down
PORKPIES > PORKPIE
PORKS > PORK
PORKWOOD n wood of small American tree
PORKWOODS > PORKWOOD
PORKY adj of or like pork ▷ n lie
PORLOCK vb interrupt or intrude at an awkward moment
PORLOCKED > PORLOCK
PORLOCKS > PORLOCK
PORN n pornography
PORNIER > PORNY
PORNIEST > PORNY
PORNO same as > PORN
PORNOS > PORNO
PORNS > PORN
PORNY adj pornographic
POROGAMIC > POROGAMY
POROGAMY n fertilization of seed plants
POROMERIC adj (of a plastic) permeable to water vapour ▷ n substance having this characteristic, esp one based on polyurethane and used in place of leather in making shoe uppers
POROSCOPE n instrument for assessing porosity
POROSCOPY > POROSCOPE
POROSE adj pierced with small pores
POROSES > POROSIS
POROSIS n porous condition of bones
POROSITY n state or condition of being porous
POROUS adj allowing liquid to pass through gradually
POROUSLY > POROUS

PORPESS n type of fish
PORPESSE same as > PORPOISE
PORPESSES > PORPESS
PORPHYRIA n hereditary disease of body metabolism, producing abdominal pain, mental confusion, etc
PORPHYRIC > PORPHYRIA
PORPHYRIN n any of a group of pigments occurring widely in animal and plant tissues and having a heterocyclic structure formed from four pyrrole rings linked by four methylene groups
PORPHYRIO n aquatic bird
PORPHYRY n reddish rock with large crystals in it
PORPOISE n fishlike sea mammal ▷ vb (of an aeroplane) nose-dive during landing
PORPOISED > PORPOISE
PORPOISES > PORPOISE
PORPORATE adj wearing purple
PORRECT adj extended forwards ▷ vb stretch forward
PORRECTED > PORRECT
PORRECTS > PORRECT
PORRENGER same as > PORRINGER
PORRIDGE n breakfast food made of oatmeal cooked in water or milk
PORRIDGES > PORRIDGE
PORRIDGY > PORRIDGE
PORRIGO n disease of the scalp
PORRIGOS > PORRIGO
PORRINGER n small dish, often with a handle, used esp formerly for soup or porridge
PORT same as > PORTHOLE
PORTA n aperture in an organ, such as the liver, esp one providing an opening for blood vessels
PORTABLE adj easily carried ▷ n article designed to be easily carried, such as a television or typewriter
PORTABLES > PORTABLE
PORTABLY > PORTABLE
PORTAGE n (route for) transporting boats and supplies overland between navigable waterways ▷ vb transport (boats and supplies) in this way
PORTAGED > PORTAGE
PORTAGES > PORTAGE
PORTAGING > PORTAGE
PORTAGUE n Portuguese gold coin
PORTAGUES > PORTAGUE
PORTAL n large imposing doorway or gate
PORTALED > PORTAL

PORTALS > PORTAL
PORTANCE n person's bearing
PORTANCES > PORTANCE
PORTAPACK n combined videotape recorder and camera
PORTAPAK same as > PORTAPACK
PORTAPAKS > PORTAPAK
PORTAS > PORTA
PORTASES variant of > PORTESSE
PORTATE adj diagonally athwart escutcheon
PORTATILE adj portable
PORTATIVE adj concerned with the act of carrying
PORTED > PORT
PORTEND vb be a sign of
PORTENDED > PORTEND
PORTENDS > PORTEND
PORTENT n sign of a future event
PORTENTS > PORTENT
PORTEOUS variant of > PORTESSE
PORTER n man who carries luggage ▷ vb carry luggage
PORTERAGE n work of carrying supplies, goods, etc, done by porters
PORTERED > PORTER
PORTERESS n female porter
PORTERING > PORTER
PORTERLY > PORTER
PORTERS > PORTER
PORTESS variant of > PORTESSE
PORTESSE n prayer book
PORTESSES > PORTESSE
PORTFIRE n (formerly) slow-burning fuse used for firing rockets and fireworks and, in mining, for igniting explosives
PORTFIRES > PORTFIRE
PORTFOLIO n (flat case for carrying) examples of an artist's work
PORTHOLE n small round window in a ship or aircraft
PORTHOLES > PORTHOLE
PORTHORS same as > PORTESSE
PORTHOS same as > PORTESSE
PORTHOSES > PORTHOS
PORTHOUSE n company producing port
PORTICO n porch or covered walkway with columns supporting the roof
PORTICOED > PORTICO
PORTICOES > PORTICO
PORTICOS > PORTICO
PORTIER > PORT
PORTIERE n curtain hung in a doorway
PORTIERED > PORTIERE
PORTIERES > PORTIERE
PORTIEST > PORT

PORTIGUE same as > PORTAGUE
PORTIGUES > PORTIGUE
PORTING > PORT
PORTION n part or share ▷ vb divide (something) into shares
PORTIONED > PORTION
PORTIONER > PORTION
PORTIONS > PORTION
PORTLAND n type of rose
PORTLANDS > PORTLAND
PORTLAST n gunwale of ship
PORTLASTS > PORTLAST
PORTLESS > PORT
PORTLIER > PORTLY
PORTLIEST > PORTLY
PORTLY adj rather fat
PORTMAN n inhabitant of port
PORTMEN > PORTMAN
PORTOISE same as > PORTLAST
PORTOISES > PORTOISE
PORTOLAN n book of sailing charts
PORTOLANI > PORTOLANO
PORTOLANO variant of > PORTOLAN
PORTOLANS > PORTOLAN
PORTOUS variant of > PORTESSE
PORTOUSES > PORTOUS
PORTRAIT n picture of a person ▷ adj (of a publication or an illustration in a publication) of greater height than width
PORTRAITS > PORTRAIT
PORTRAY vb describe or represent by artistic means, as in writing or film
PORTRAYAL > PORTRAY
PORTRAYED > PORTRAY
PORTRAYER > PORTRAY
PORTRAYS > PORTRAY
PORTREEVE n Saxon magistrate
PORTRESS n female porter, esp a doorkeeper
PORTS > PORT
PORTSIDE adj beside port
PORTULACA n tropical American plant with yellow, pink, or purple showy flowers
PORTULAN same as > PORTOLAN
PORTULANS > PORTULAN
PORTY adj like port
PORWIGGLE n tadpole
PORY adj containing pores
POS > PO
POSABLE > POSE
POSADA n inn in a Spanish-speaking country
POSADAS > POSADA
POSAUNE n organ chorus reed
POSAUNES > POSAUNE
POSE vb place in or take up

a particular position to be photographed or drawn ▷ n position while posing
POSEABLE adj able to be manipulated into poses
POSED > POSE
POSER n puzzling question
POSERISH same as > POSEY
POSERS > POSER
POSES > POSE
POSEUR n person who behaves in an affected way to impress others
POSEURS > POSEUR
POSEUSE n female poseur
POSEUSES > POSEUSE
POSEY adj (of a place) for, characteristic of, or full of posers
POSH adj smart, luxurious ▷ adv in a manner associated with the upper class ▷ vb make posh
POSHED > POSH
POSHER > POSH
POSHES > POSH
POSHEST > POSH
POSHING > POSH
POSHLY > POSH
POSHNESS > POSH
POSHO n corn meal
POSHOS > POSHO
POSHTEEN same as > POSTEEN
POSHTEENS > POSHTEEN
POSIER > POSY
POSIES > POSY
POSIEST > POSY
POSIGRADE adj producing positive thrust
POSING > POSE
POSINGLY > POSE
POSINGS > POSE
POSIT vb lay down as a basis for argument ▷ n fact, idea, etc, that is posited
POSITED > POSIT
POSITIF n (on older organs) manual controlling soft stops
POSITIFS > POSITIF
POSITING > POSIT
POSITION n place ▷ vb place
POSITIONS > POSITION
POSITIVE same as > PLUS
POSITIVER > POSITIVE
POSITIVES > POSITIVE
POSITON n part of chromosome
POSITONS > POSITON
POSITRON n particle with same mass as electron but positive charge
POSITRONS > POSITRON
POSITS > POSIT
POSNET n small basin or dish
POSNETS > POSNET
POSOLE n hominy
POSOLES > POSOLE
POSOLOGIC > POSOLOGY

POSOLOGY n branch of medicine concerned with the determination of appropriate doses of drugs or agents
POSS vb wash (clothes) by agitating them with a long rod, pole, etc
POSSE n group of men organized to maintain law and order
POSSED > POSS
POSSER n short stick used for stirring clothes in a washtub
POSSERS > POSSER
POSSES > POSSE
POSSESS vb have as one's property
POSSESSED adj owning or having
POSSESSES > POSSESS
POSSESSOR > POSSESS
POSSET n drink of hot milk curdled with ale, beer, etc, flavoured with spices, formerly used as a remedy for colds ▷ vb treat with a posset
POSSETED > POSSET
POSSETING > POSSET
POSSETS > POSSET
POSSIBLE adj able to exist, happen, or be done ▷ n person or thing that might be suitable for or chosen
POSSIBLER > POSSIBLE
POSSIBLES > POSSIBLE
POSSIBLY adv perhaps, not necessarily
POSSIE n place
POSSIES > POSSIE
POSSING > POSS
POSSUM vb pretend to be dead, asleep, ignorant, etc, to deceive an opponent
POSSUMED > POSSUM
POSSUMING > POSSUM
POSSUMS > POSSUM
POST n official system of delivering letters and parcels ▷ vb send by post
POSTAGE n charge for sending a letter or parcel by post
POSTAGES > POSTAGE
POSTAL adj of a Post Office or the mail-delivery service ▷ n postcard
POSTALLY > POSTAL
POSTALS > POSTAL
POSTANAL adj behind the anus
POSTAXIAL adj situated or occurring behind the axis of the body
POSTBAG n postman's bag
POSTBAGS > POSTBAG
POSTBASE adv (in linguistics) coming immediately after a base word
POSTBOX n box into which mail is put for collection by the postal service

POSTBOXES > POSTBOX
POSTBOY *n* man or boy who brings the post round to offices
POSTBOYS > POSTBOY
POSTBURN *adj* after injury from burns
POSTBUS *n* (in Britain, esp in rural districts) vehicle carrying the mail that also carries passengers
POSTBUSES > POSTBUS
POSTCARD *n* card for sending a message by post without an envelope
POSTCARDS > POSTCARD
POSTCAVA *n* inferior vena cava
POSTCAVAE > POSTCAVA
POSTCAVAL > POSTCAVA
POSTCAVAS > POSTCAVA
POSTCODE *n* system of letters and numbers used to aid the sorting of mail ▷ *vb* put a postcode on a letter
POSTCODED > POSTCODE
POSTCODES > POSTCODE
POSTCOUP *adj* after coup
POSTCRASH *adj* after a crash
POSTDATE *vb* write a date on (a cheque) that is later than the actual date
POSTDATED > POSTDATE
POSTDATES > POSTDATE
POSTDIVE *adj* following a dive
POSTDOC *n* postdoctoral degree
POSTDOCS > POSTDOC
POSTDRUG *adj* of time after drug has been taken
POSTED > POST
POSTEEN *n* Afghan leather jacket
POSTEENS > POSTEEN
POSTER *n* large picture or notice stuck on a wall ▷ *vb* cover with posters
POSTERED > POSTER
POSTERING > POSTER
POSTERIOR *n* buttocks ▷ *adj* behind, at the back of
POSTERITY *n* future generations, descendants
POSTERN *n* small back door or gate ▷ *adj* situated at the rear or the side
POSTERNS > POSTERN
POSTERS > POSTER
POSTFACE *n* note added to the end of a text
POSTFACES > POSTFACE
POSTFAULT *adj* after a fault
POSTFIRE *adj* of the period after a fire
POSTFIX *vb* add or append at the end of something
POSTFIXAL > POSTFIX
POSTFIXED > POSTFIX
POSTFIXES > POSTFIX
POSTFORM *vb* mould or shape (plastic) while it hot

from reheating
POSTFORMS > POSTFORM
POSTGAME *adj* of period after sports match
POSTGRAD *n* graduate taking further degree
POSTGRADS > POSTGRAD
POSTHASTE *adv* with great speed ▷ *n* great haste
POSTHEAT *n* industrial heating process
POSTHEATS > POSTHEAT
POSTHOLE *n* hole dug in ground to hold fence post
POSTHOLES > POSTHOLE
POSTHORSE *n* horse kept at an inn or posthouse for use by postriders or for hire to travellers
POSTHOUSE *n* house or inn where horses were kept for postriders or for hire to travellers
POSTICAL *adj* (of the position of plant parts) behind another part
POSTICHE *adj* (of architectural ornament) inappropriately applied ▷ *n* imitation, counterfeit, or substitute
POSTICHES > POSTICHE
POSTICOUS *same as* > POSTICAL
POSTIE *n* postman
POSTIES > POSTIE
POSTIL *n* commentary or marginal note, as in a Bible ▷ *vb* annotate (a biblical passage)
POSTILED > POSTIL
POSTILING > POSTIL
POSTILION *n* person riding one of a pair of horses drawing a carriage
POSTILLED > POSTIL
POSTILLER > POSTIL
POSTILS > POSTIL
POSTIN *variant of* > POSTEEN
POSTING *n* job to which someone is assigned by his or her employer which involves moving to a particular town or country
POSTINGS > POSTING
POSTINS > POSTIN
POSTIQUE *variant of* > POSTICHE
POSTIQUES > POSTIQUE
POSTLUDE *n* final or concluding piece or movement
POSTLUDES > POSTLUDE
POSTMAN *n* person who collects and delivers post
POSTMARK *n* official mark stamped on letters showing place and date of posting ▷ *vb* put such a mark on (mail)
POSTMARKS > POSTMARK
POSTMEN > POSTMAN
POSTNASAL *adj* situated at the back of the nose

POSTNATAL *adj* occurring after childbirth
POSTNATI *n* those born in Scotland after its union with England
POSTOP *n* person recovering from surgery
POSTOPS > POSTOP
POSTORAL *adj* situated at the back of the mouth
POSTPAID *adj* with the postage prepaid
POSTPONE *vb* put off to a later time
POSTPONED > POSTPONE
POSTPONER > POSTPONE
POSTPONES > POSTPONE
POSTPOSE *vb* place (word or phrase) after other constituents in sentence
POSTPOSED > POSTPOSE
POSTPOSES > POSTPOSE
POSTPUNK *adj* (of pop music) belonging to a style that followed punk rock
POSTRACE *adj* of the period after a race
POSTRIDER *n* (formerly) person who delivered post on horseback
POSTRIOT *adj* of the period after a riot
POSTS > POST
POSTSHOW *adj* of the period after a show
POSTSYNC *vb* add a sound recording to (and synchronize with) an existing video or film recording
POSTSYNCS > POSTSYNC
POSTTAX *adj* of the period after tax is paid
POSTTEEN *n* young adult
POSTTEENS > POSTTEEN
POSTTEST *n* test taken after a lesson
POSTTESTS > POSTTEST
POSTTRIAL *adj* of the period after a trial
POSTULANT *n* candidate for admission to a religious order
POSTULATA *n* things postulated
POSTULATE *vb* assume to be true as the basis of an argument or theory ▷ *n* something postulated
POSTURAL > POSTURE
POSTURE *n* position or way in which someone stands, walks, etc ▷ *vb* behave in an exaggerated way to get attention
POSTURED > POSTURE
POSTURER > POSTURE
POSTURERS > POSTURE
POSTURES > POSTURE
POSTURING > POSTURE
POSTURISE *same as* > POSTURIZE
POSTURIST > POSTURIZE
POSTURIZE *less common word for* > POSTURE

POSTVIRAL *as in postviral syndrome* debilitating condition occurring as a sequel to viral illness
POSTWAR *adj* occurring or existing after a war
POSTWOMAN *n* woman who carries and delivers mail as a profession
POSTWOMEN > POSTWOMAN
POSY *n* small bunch of flowers
POT *n* round deep container ▷ *vb* plant in a pot
POTABLE *adj* drinkable ▷ *n* something fit to drink
POTABLES > POTABLE
POTAE *n* hat
POTAES > POTAE
POTAGE *n* thick soup
POTAGER *n* small kitchen garden
POTAGERS > POTAGER
POTAGES > POTAGE
POTALE *n* residue from a grain distillery, used as animal feed
POTALES > POTALE
POTAMIC *adj* of or relating to rivers
POTASH *n* white powdery substance obtained from ashes and used as fertilizer ▷ *vb* treat with potash
POTASHED > POTASH
POTASHES > POTASH
POTASHING > POTASH
POTASS *abbreviated form of* > POTASSIUM
POTASSA *n* potassium oxide
POTASSAS > POTASSA
POTASSES > POTASS
POTASSIC > POTASSIUM
POTASSIUM *n* silvery metallic element
POTATION *n* act of drinking
POTATIONS > POTATION
POTATO *n* roundish starchy vegetable that grows underground
POTATOBUG *n* Colorado beetle
POTATOES > POTATO
POTATORY *adj* of, relating to, or given to drinking
POTBELLY *n* bulging belly
POTBOIL *vb* boil in a pot
POTBOILED > POTBOIL
POTBOILER *n* inferior work of art produced quickly to make money
POTBOILS > POTBOIL
POTBOUND *adj* (of plant) unable to grow because pot is too small
POTBOY *n* (esp formerly) youth or man employed at a public house to serve beer, etc
POTBOYS > POTBOY
POTCH *n* inferior quality

opal used in jewellery for mounting precious opals
POTCHE vb stab
POTCHED > POTCHE
POTCHER > POTCHE
POTCHERS > POTCHE
POTCHES > POTCH
POTCHING > POTCHE
POTE vb push
POTED > POTE
POTEEN n (in Ireland) illegally made alcoholic drink
POTEENS > POTEEN
POTENCE same as > POTENCY
POTENCES > POTENCE
POTENCIES > POTENCY
POTENCY n state or quality of being potent
POTENT adj having great power or influence ▷ n potentate or ruler
POTENTATE n ruler or monarch
POTENTIAL adj possible but not yet actual ▷ n ability or talent not yet fully used
POTENTISE same as > POTENTIZE
POTENTIZE vb make more potent
POTENTLY > POTENT
POTENTS > POTENT
POTES > POTE
POTFUL n amount held by a pot
POTFULS > POTFUL
POTGUN n pot-shaped mortar
POTGUNS > POTGUN
POTHEAD n habitual user of cannabis
POTHEADS > POTHEAD
POTHECARY n pharmacist
POTHEEN rare variant of > POTEEN
POTHEENS > POTHEEN
POTHER n fuss or commotion ▷ vb make or be troubled or upset
POTHERB n plant whose leaves, flowers, or stems are used in cooking
POTHERBS > POTHERB
POTHERED > POTHER
POTHERING > POTHER
POTHERS > POTHER
POTHERY adj stuffy
POTHOLDER n piece of material used to protect hands while lifting pot from oven
POTHOLE n hole in the surface of a road
POTHOLED > POTHOLE
POTHOLER > POTHOLING
POTHOLERS > POTHOLING
POTHOLES > POTHOLE
POTHOLING n sport of exploring underground caves

POTHOOK n S-shaped hook for suspending a pot over a fire
POTHOOKS > POTHOOK
POTHOS n climbing plant
POTHOUSE n (formerly) small tavern or pub
POTHOUSES > POTHOUSE
POTHUNTER n person who hunts for food or for profit without regard to the rules of sport
POTICARY obsolete spelling of > POTHECARY
POTICHE n tall vase or jar, as of porcelain, with a round or polygonal body that narrows towards the neck and a detached lid or cover
POTICHES > POTICHE
POTIN n bronze alloy with high tin content
POTING > POTE
POTINS > POTIN
POTION n dose of medicine or poison
POTIONS > POTION
POTJIE n 3-legged iron pot used for cooking
POTJIES > POTJIE
POTLACH same as > POTLATCH
POTLACHE same as > POTLATCH
POTLACHES > POTLACHE
POTLATCH n competitive ceremonial activity among certain North American Indians
POTLIKE > POT
POTLINE n row of electrolytic cells for reducing metals
POTLINES > POTLINE
POTLUCK n whatever food happens to be available without special preparation
POTLUCKS > POTLUCK
POTMAN same as > POTBOY
POTMEN > POTMAN
POTOMETER n apparatus that measures the rate of water uptake by a plant or plant part
POTOO n nocturnal tropical bird
POTOOS > POTOO
POTOROO n Australian leaping rodent
POTOROOS > POTOROO
POTPIE n meat and vegetable stew with a pie crust on top
POTPIES > POTPIE
POTPOURRI n fragrant mixture of dried flower petals
POTS > POT
POTSHARD same as > POTSHERD
POTSHARDS > POTSHARD
POTSHARE same as > POTSHERD

POTSHARES > POTSHARE
POTSHERD n broken fragment of pottery
POTSHERDS > POTSHERD
POTSHOP n public house
POTSHOPS > POTSHOP
POTSHOT n chance shot taken casually, hastily, or without careful aim
POTSHOTS > POTSHOT
POTSIE same as > POTSY
POTSIES > POTSY
POTSTONE n impure massive variety of soapstone, formerly used for making cooking vessels
POTSTONES > POTSTONE
POTSY n hopscotch
POTT old variant of > POT
POTTABLE adj (esp of a snooker ball) easily potted
POTTAGE n thick soup or stew
POTTAGES > POTTAGE
POTTED > POT
POTTEEN same as > POTEEN
POTTEENS > POTTEEN
POTTER same as > PUTTER
POTTERED > POTTER
POTTERER > POTTER
POTTERERS > POTTER
POTTERIES > POTTERY
POTTERING > POTTER
POTTERS > POTTER
POTTERY n articles made from baked clay
POTTIER > POTTY
POTTIES > POTTY
POTTIEST > POTTY
POTTINESS > POTTY
POTTING > POT
POTTINGAR same as > POTTINGER
POTTINGER n apothecary
POTTLE n liquid measure equal to half a gallon
POTTLES > POTTLE
POTTO n short-tailed prosimian primate
POTTOS > POTTO
POTTS > POTT
POTTY adj crazy or silly ▷ n bowl used by a small child as a toilet
POTWALLER n man entitled to the franchise before 1832 by virtue of possession of his own fireplace
POTZER same as > PATZER
POTZERS > POTZER
POUCH n small bag ▷ vb place in or as if in a pouch
POUCHED > POUCH
POUCHES > POUCH
POUCHFUL n amount a pouch will hold
POUCHFULS > POUCHFUL
POUCHIER > POUCH
POUCHIEST > POUCH
POUCHING > POUCH
POUCHY > POUCH

POUDER obsolete spelling of > POWDER
POUDERS > POUDER
POUDRE old spelling of > POWDER
POUDRES > POUDRE
POUF n large solid cushion used as a seat ▷ vb pile up hair into rolled puffs
POUFED > POUF
POUFF same as > POUF
POUFFE same as > POUF
POUFFED > POUFFE
POUFFES > POUFFE
POUFFIER > POUFFY
POUFFIEST > POUFFY
POUFFING > POUFFE
POUFS > POUF
POUFFY same as > POOFY
POUFING > POUF
POUFS > POUF
POUFTAH same as > POOFTER
POUFTAHS > POUFTAH
POUFTER same as > POOFTER
POUFTERS > POUFTER
POUK Scots variant of > POKE
POUKE n mischievous spirit
POUKES > POUKE
POUKING > POUK
POUKIT > POUK
POUKS > POUK
POULAINE n tapering toe of shoe
POULAINES > POULAINE
POULARD n hen that has been spayed for fattening
POULARDE same as > POULARD
POULARDES > POULARDE
POULARDS > POULARD
POULDER obsolete spelling of > POWDER
POULDERS > POULDER
POULDRE archaic spelling of > POWDER
POULDRES > POULDRE
POULDRON same as > PAULDRON
POULDRONS > POULDRON
POULE n fowl suitable for slow stewing
POULES > POULE
POULP n octopus
POULPE variant of > POULP
POULPES > POULPE
POULPS > POULP
POULT n young of a gallinaceous bird, esp of domestic fowl
POULTER n poultry dealer
POULTERER same as > POULTER
POULTERS > POULTER
POULTICE n moist dressing, often heated, applied to inflamed skin ▷ vb apply poultice to
POULTICED > POULTICE
POULTICES > POULTICE
POULTRIES > POULTRY
POULTRY n domestic fowls
POULTS > POULT

POUNCE vb spring upon suddenly to attack or capture ▷ n pouncing

POUNCED > POUNCE

POUNCER > POUNCE

POUNCERS > POUNCE

POUNCES > POUNCE

POUNCET n box with a perforated top used for perfume

POUNCETS > POUNCET

POUNCHING old variant of > PUNCHING

POUNCING > POUNCE

POUND n monetary unit of Britain and some other countries ▷ vb hit heavily and repeatedly

POUNDAGE n charge of so much per pound of weight or sterling

POUNDAGES > POUNDAGE

POUNDAL n fps unit of force

POUNDALS > POUNDAL

POUNDCAKE n cake containing a pound of each ingredient

POUNDED > POUND

POUNDER > POUND

POUNDERS > POUND

POUNDING > POUND

POUNDINGS > POUNDING

POUNDS > POUND

POUPE vb make sudden blowing sound

POUPED > POUPE

POUPES > POUPE

POUPING > POUPE

POUPT > POUPE

POUR vb flow or cause to flow out in a stream

POURABLE > POUR

POURBOIRE n tip or gratuity

POURED > POUR

POURER > POUR

POURERS > POUR

POURIE n jug

POURIES > POURIE

POURING > POUR

POURINGLY > POUR

POURINGS > POUR

POURPOINT n man's stuffed quilted doublet of a kind worn between the Middle Ages and the 17th century

POURS > POUR

POURSEW obsolete spelling of > PURSUE

POURSEWED > POURSEW

POURSEWS > POURSEW

POURSUE obsolete spelling of > PURSUE

POURSUED > PURSUE

POURSUES > PURSUE

POURSUING > PURSUE

POURSUIT same as > PURSUIT

POURSUITS > POURSUIT

POURTRAY obsolete spelling of > PORTRAY

POURTRAYD > PORTRAY

POURTRAYS > PORTRAY

POUSADA n traditional Portuguese hotel

POUSADAS > POUSADA

POUSOWDIE n Scottish stew made from sheep's head

POUSSE same as > PEASE

POUSSES > POUSSE

POUSSETTE n figure in country dancing in which couples hold hands and move up or down the set to change positions ▷ vb perform such a figure

POUSSIE old variant of > PUSSY

POUSSIES > POUSSIE

POUSSIN n young chicken reared for eating

POUSSINS > POUSSIN

POUT vb thrust out one's lips, look sulky ▷ n pouting look

POUTED > POUT

POUTER n pigeon that can puff out its crop

POUTERS > POUTER

POUTFUL adj tending to pout

POUTHER Scots variant of > POWDER

POUTHERED > POUTHER

POUTHERS > POUTHER

POUTIER > POUT

POUTIEST > POUT

POUTINE n dish of chipped potatoes topped with curd cheese and a tomato-based sauce

POUTINES > POUTINE

POUTING > POUT

POUTINGLY > POUT

POUTINGS > POUT

POUTS > POUT

POUTY > POUT

POVERTIES > POVERTY

POVERTY n state of being without enough food or money

POW interj exclamation to indicate that a collision or explosion has taken place ▷ n head or a head of hair

POWAN n type of freshwater whitefish occurring in some Scottish lakes

POWANS > POWAN

POWDER n substance in the form of tiny loose particles ▷ vb apply powder to

POWDERED > POWDER

POWDERER > POWDER

POWDERERS > POWDER

POWDERIER > POWDER

POWDERING > POWDER

POWDERS > POWDER

POWDERY > POWDER

POWELLISE > POWELLIZE

POWELLITE n type of mineral

POWELLIZE vb treat wood with a sugar solution

POWER n ability to do or act ▷ vb give or provide power to

POWERBOAT n fast powerful motorboat

POWERED > POWER

POWERFUL adj having great power or influence ▷ adv extremely

POWERING > POWER

POWERLESS adj without power or authority

POWERPLAY n behaviour intended to maximise person's power

POWERS > POWER

POWFAGGED adj exhausted

POWHIRI n Māori ceremony of welcome, esp to a marae

POWHIRIS > POWHIRI

POWIN n peacock

POWINS > POWIN

POWN variant of > POWIN

POWND obsolete spelling of > POUND

POWNDED > POWND

POWNDING > POWND

POWNDS > POWND

POWNEY old Scots spelling of > PONY

POWNEYS > POWNEY

POWNIE old Scots spelling of > PONY

POWNIES > POWNIE

POWNS > POWN

POWNY old Scots spelling of > PONY

POWRE obsolete spelling of > POWER

POWRED > POWRE

POWRES > POWRE

POWRING > POWRE

POWS > POW

POWSOWDY same as > POUSOWDIE

POWTER vb scrabble about

POWTERED > POWTER

POWTERING > POWTER

POWTERS > POWTER

POWWAW interj expression of disbelief or contempt

POWWOW n talk or conference ▷ vb hold a powwow

POWWOWED > POWWOW

POWWOWING > POWWOW

POWWOWS > POWWOW

POX n disease in which skin pustules form ▷ vb infect with pox

POXED > POX

POXES > POX

POXIER > POXY

POXIEST > POXY

POXING > POX

POXVIRUS n virus such as smallpox

POXY adj having or having had syphilis

POYNANT old variant of > POIGNANT

POYNT obsolete spelling of > POINT

POYNTED > POYNT

POYNTING > POYNT

POYNTS > POYNT

POYOU n type of armadillo

POYOUS > POYOU

POYSE obsolete variant of > POISE

POYSED > POYSE

POYSES > POYSE

POYSING > POYSE

POYSON obsolete spelling of > POISON

POYSONED > POYSON

POYSONING > POYSON

POYSONS > POYSON

POZ adj positive

POZOLE same as > POSOLE

POZOLES > POZOLE

POZZ adj positive

POZZIES > POZZY

POZZOLAN same as > POZZOLANA

POZZOLANA n type of porous volcanic ash

POZZOLANS > POZZOLAN

POZZY same as > POSSIE

PRAAM same as > PRAM

PRAAMS > PRAAM

PRABBLE variant of > BRABBLE

PRABBLES > PRABBLE

PRACHARAK n (in India) person appointed to propagate a cause through personal contact, meetings, public lectures, etc

PRACTIC adj practical ▷ n practice

PRACTICAL adj involving experience or actual use rather than theory ▷ n examination in which something has to be done or made

PRACTICE same as > PRACTISE

PRACTICED > PRACTICE

PRACTICER > PRACTICE

PRACTICES > PRACTICE

PRACTICK obsolete word for > PRACTICE

PRACTICKS > PRACTICK

PRACTICS > PRACTIC

PRACTICUM n course in which theory is put into practice

PRACTIQUE variant of > PRACTIC

PRACTISE vb do repeatedly so as to gain skill

PRACTISED > PRACTISE

PRACTISER > PRACTISE

PRACTISES > PRACTISE

PRACTIVE obsolete word for > ACTIVE

PRACTOLOL n type of drug

PRAD n horse

PRADS > PRAD

PRAEAMBLE same as > PREAMBLE

PRAECIPE n written request addressed to court

PRAECIPES > PRAECIPE

PRAECOCES n division of birds whose young are able to run when first hatched

p

PRAEDIAL adj of or relating to land, farming, etc ▷ n slave attached to a farm

PRAEDIALS > PRAEDIAL

PRAEFECT same as > PREFECT

PRAEFECTS > PRAEFECT

PRAELECT same as > PRAELECT

PRAELECTS > PRAELECT

PRAELUDIA n musical preludes

PRAENOMEN n ancient Roman's first or given name

PRAESES n Roman governor

PRAESIDIA n presidiums

PRAETOR n (in ancient Rome) senior magistrate ranking just below the consuls

PRAETORS > PRAETOR

PRAGMATIC adj concerned with practical consequences rather than theory

PRAHU same as > PROA

PRAHUS > PRAHU

PRAIRIE n large treeless area of grassland, esp in N America and Canada

PRAIRIED > PRAIRIE

PRAIRIES > PRAIRIE

PRAISE vb express approval or admiration of (someone or something) ▷ n something said or written to show approval or admiration

PRAISEACH n type of porridge

PRAISED > PRAISE

PRAISEFUL > PRAISE

PRAISER > PRAISE

PRAISERS > PRAISE

PRAISES > PRAISE

PRAISING > PRAISE

PRAISINGS > PRAISE

PRAJNA n wisdom or understanding considered as the goal of Buddhist contemplation

PRAJNAS > PRAJNA

PRALINE n sweet made of nuts and caramelized sugar

PRALINES > PRALINE

PRAM n four-wheeled carriage for a baby, pushed by hand

PRAMS > PRAM

PRANA n (in Oriental medicine, martial arts, etc) cosmic energy believed to come from the sun and connecting the elements of the universe

PRANAS > PRANA

PRANAYAMA n breath control in yoga

PRANCE vb walk with exaggerated bouncing steps ▷ n act of prancing

PRANCED > PRANCE

PRANCER > PRANCE

PRANCERS > PRANCE

PRANCES > PRANCE

PRANCING > PRANCE

PRANCINGS > PRANCE

PRANCK obsolete variant of > PRANK

PRANCKE obsolete variant of > PRANK

PRANCKED > PRANCK

PRANCKES > PRANCKE

PRANCKING > PRANCK

PRANCKS > PRANCK

PRANDIAL adj of or relating to a meal

PRANG n crash in a car or aircraft ▷ vb crash or damage (an aircraft or car)

PRANGED > PRANG

PRANGING > PRANG

PRANGS > PRANG

PRANK n mischievous trick ▷ vb dress or decorate showily or gaudily

PRANKED > PRANK

PRANKFUL > PRANK

PRANKIER > PRANK

PRANKIEST > PRANK

PRANKING > PRANK

PRANKINGS > PRANK

PRANKISH > PRANK

PRANKLE obsolete variant of > PRANCE

PRANKLED > PRANKLE

PRANKLES > PRANKLE

PRANKLING > PRANKLE

PRANKS > PRANK

PRANKSOME > PRANK

PRANKSTER n practical joker

PRANKY > PRANK

PRAO same as > PROA

PRAOS > PRAO

PRASE n light green translucent variety of chalcedony

PRASES > PRASE

PRAT n stupid person

PRATE vb talk idly and at length ▷ n chatter

PRATED > PRATE

PRATER > PRATE

PRATERS > PRATE

PRATES > PRATE

PRATFALL vb fall upon one's buttocks

PRATFALLS > PRATFALL

PRATFELL > PRATFALL

PRATIE n potato

PRATIES > PRATIE

PRATING > PRATE

PRATINGLY > PRATE

PRATINGS > PRATE

PRATIQUE n formal permission given to a vessel to use a foreign port upon satisfying the requirements of local health authorities

PRATIQUES > PRATIQUE

PRATS > PRAT

PRATT n buttocks ▷ vb hit on the buttocks

PRATTED > PRATT

PRATTING > PRATT

PRATTLE vb chatter in a childish or foolish way ▷ n childish or foolish talk

PRATTLED > PRATTLE

PRATTLER > PRATTLE

PRATTLERS > PRATTLE

PRATTLES > PRATTLE

PRATTLING > PRATTLE

PRATTS > PRATT

PRATY obsolete variant of > PRETTY

PRAU same as > PROA

PRAUNCE obsolete variant of > PRANCE

PRAUNCED > PRAUNCE

PRAUNCES > PRAUNCE

PRAUNCING > PRAUNCE

PRAUS > PRAU

PRAVITIES > PRAVITY

PRAVITY n moral degeneracy

PRAWLE n Shakespearian phonetic spelling of "brawl" meant to indicate that the speaker is Welsh

PRAWLES > PRAWLE

PRAWLIN variant of > PRALINE

PRAWLINS > PRAWLIN

PRAWN n edible shellfish like a large shrimp ▷ vb catch prawns

PRAWNED > PRAWN

PRAWNER > PRAWN

PRAWNERS > PRAWN

PRAWNING > PRAWN

PRAWNS > PRAWN

PRAXES > PRAXIS

PRAXIS n practice as opposed to theory

PRAXISES > PRAXIS

PRAY vb say prayers ▷ adv I beg you ▷ interj I beg you

PRAYED > PRAY

PRAYER n thanks or appeal addressed to one's God

PRAYERFUL adj inclined to or characterized by prayer

PRAYERS > PRAYER

PRAYING > PRAY

PRAYINGLY > PRAY

PRAYINGS > PRAY

PRAYS > PRAY

PRE prep before

PREABSORB vb absorb beforehand

PREACCUSE vb accuse beforehand

PREACE obsolete variant of > PRESS

PREACED > PREACE

PREACES > PREACE

PREACH vb give a talk on a religious theme as part of a church service

PREACHED > PREACH

PREACHER n person who preaches, esp in church

PREACHERS > PREACHER

PREACHES > PREACH

PREACHIER > PREACHY

PREACHIFY vb preach or moralize in a tedious manner

PREACHILY > PREACHY

PREACHING > PREACH

PREACHY adj inclined to or marked by preaching

PREACING > PREACE

PREACT vb act beforehand

PREACTED > PREACT

PREACTING > PREACT

PREACTS > PREACT

PREADAMIC adj of or relating to the belief that there were people on earth before Adam

PREADAPT vb adapt beforehand

PREADAPTS > PREADAPT

PREADJUST vb adjust beforehand

PREADMIT vb prepare patient prior to treatment

PREADMITS > PREADMIT

PREADOPT vb adopt in advance

PREADOPTS > PREADOPT

PREADULT n animal or person who has not reached adulthood

PREADULTS > PREADULT

PREAGED adj treated to appear older

PREALLOT vb allot beforehand

PREALLOTS > PREALLOT

PREALTER vb alter beforehand

PREALTERS > PREALTER

PREAMBLE n introductory part to something said or written ▷ vb write a preamble

PREAMBLED > PREAMBLE

PREAMBLES > PREAMBLE

PREAMP n electronic amplifier used to improve the signal-to-noise ratio of an electronic device

PREAMPS > PREAMP

PREANAL adj situated in front of anus

PREAPPLY vb apply beforehand

PREARM vb arm beforehand

PREARMED > PREARM

PREARMING > PREARM

PREARMS > PREARM

PREASE vb crowd or press

PREASED > PREASE

PREASES > PREASE

PREASING > PREASE

PREASSE obsolete spelling of > PRESS

PREASSED > PREASSE

PREASSES > PREASSE

PREASSIGN vb assign beforehand

PREASSING > PREASSE

PREASSURE vb assure beforehand

PREATOMIC adj before the atomic age

PREATTUNE vb attune beforehand

PREAUDIT n examination of contracts before a transaction

P

PREAUDITS > PREAUDIT

PREAVER *vb* aver in advance

PREAVERS > PREAVER

PREAXIAL *adj* situated or occurring in front of the axis of the body

PREBADE > PREBID

PREBAKE *vb* bake before further cooking

PREBAKED > PREBAKE

PREBAKES > PREBAKE

PREBAKING > PREBAKE

PREBASAL *adj* in front of a base

PREBATTLE *adj* of the period before a battle

PREBEND *n* allowance paid by a cathedral or collegiate church to a canon or member of the chapter

PREBENDAL > PREBEND

PREBENDS > PREBEND

PREBID *vb* bid beforehand

PREBIDDEN > PREBID

PREBIDS > PREBID

PREBILL *vb* issue an invoice before the service has been provided

PREBILLED > PREBILL

PREBILLS > PREBILL

PREBIND *vb* bind a book in a hard-wearing binding

PREBINDS > PREBIND

PREBIOTIC *adj* of the period before the existence of life on earth

PREBIRTH *n* period of life before birth

PREBIRTHS > PREBIRTH

PREBLESS *vb* bless a couple before they marry

PREBOARD *vb* board an aircraft before other passengers

PREBOARDS > PREBOARD

PREBOIL *vb* boil beforehand

PREBOILED > PREBOIL

PREBOILS > PREBOIL

PREBOOK *vb* book well in advance

PREBOOKED > PREBOOK

PREBOOKS > PREBOOK

PREBOOM *adj* of the period before an economic boom

PREBORN *adj* unborn

PREBOUGHT > PREBUY

PREBOUND > PREBIND

PREBUDGET *adj* before budget

PREBUILD *vb* build beforehand

PREBUILDS > PREBUILD

PREBUILT > PREBUILD

PREBUTTAL *n* prepared response to an anticipated criticism

PREBUY *vb* buy in advance

PREBUYING > PREBUY

PREBUYS > PREBUY

PRECANCEL *vb* cancel (postage stamps) before placing them on mail ▷ *n*

precancelled stamp

PRECANCER *n* condition that may develop into cancer

PRECAST *adj* (esp of concrete when employed as a structural element in building) cast in a particular form before being used ▷ *vb* cast (concrete) in a particular form before use

PRECASTS > PRECAST

PRECATIVE *same as* **>** PRECATORY

PRECATORY *adj* of, involving, or expressing entreaty

PRECAUDAL *adj* in front of the caudal fin

PRECAVA *n* superior vena cava

PRECAVAE > PRECAVA

PRECAVAL > PRECAVA

PRECEDE *vb* go or be before

PRECEDED > PRECEDE

PRECEDENT *n* previous case or occurrence regarded as an example to be followed ▷ *adj* preceding

PRECEDES > PRECEDE

PRECEDING *adj* going or coming before

PRECEESE *Scots variant of* **>** PRECISE

PRECENSOR *vb* censor (a film, play, book, etc) before its publication

PRECENT *vb* issue a command or law

PRECENTED > PRECENT

PRECENTOR *n* person who leads the singing in a church

PRECENTS > PRECENT

PRECEPIT *old word for* **>** PRECIPICE

PRECEPITS > PRECEPIT

PRECEPT *n* rule of behaviour

PRECEPTOR *n* instructor

PRECEPTS > PRECEPT

PRECES *npl* prayers

PRECESS *vb* undergo or cause to undergo precession

PRECESSED > PRECESS

PRECESSES > PRECESS

PRECHARGE *vb* charge beforehand

PRECHECK *vb* check beforehand

PRECHECKS > PRECHECK

PRECHILL *vb* chill beforehand

PRECHILLS > PRECHILL

PRECHOOSE *vb* choose in advance

PRECHOSE > PRECHOOSE

PRECHOSEN **>** PRECHOOSE

PRECIEUSE *n* pretentious female

PRECIEUX *n* pretentious

male

PRECINCT *n* area in a town closed to traffic

PRECINCTS *npl* surrounding region

PRECIOUS *adj* of great value and importance ▷ *adv* very

PRECIPE *n* type of legal document

PRECIPES > PRECIPE

PRECIPICE *n* very steep face of a cliff

PRECIS *n* short written summary of a longer piece ▷ *vb* make a precis of

PRECISE *adj* exact, accurate in every detail

PRECISED > PRECISE

PRECISELY *adv* in a precise manner

PRECISER > PRECISE

PRECISES > PRECIS

PRECISEST > PRECISE

PRECISIAN *n* punctilious observer of rules or forms, esp in the field of religion

PRECISING > PRECIS

PRECISION *n* quality of being precise ▷ *adj* accurate

PRECISIVE *adj* limiting by cutting off all that is unnecessary

PRECITED *adj* cited previously

PRECLEAN *vb* clean beforehand

PRECLEANS > PRECLEAN

PRECLEAR *vb* approve in advance

PRECLEARS > PRECLEAR

PRECLUDE *vb* make impossible to happen

PRECLUDED > PRECLUDE

PRECLUDES > PRECLUDE

PRECOCIAL *adj* (of the young of some species of birds after hatching) covered with down, having open eyes, and capable of leaving the nest within a few days of hatching ▷ *n* precocial bird

PRECOCITY *n* early maturing or development

PRECODE *vb* code beforehand

PRECODED > PRECODE

PRECODES > PRECODE

PRECODING > PRECODE

PRECOITAL *adj* before sex

PRECONISE *same as* **>** PRECONIZE

PRECONIZE *vb* announce or commend publicly

PRECOOK *vb* cook (food) beforehand

PRECOOKED > PRECOOK

PRECOOKER *n* device for preparing food before cooking

PRECOOKS > PRECOOK

PRECOOL *vb* cool in advance

PRECOOLED > PRECOOL

PRECOOLS > PRECOOL

PRECOUP *adj* of the period before a coup

PRECRASH *adj* of the period before a crash

PRECREASE *vb* provide with a crease in advance

PRECRISIS *adj* occurring before a crisis

PRECURE *vb* cure in advance

PRECURED > PRECURE

PRECURES > PRECURE

PRECURING > PRECURE

PRECURRER > PRECURSE

PRECURSE *n* forerunning

PRECURSES > PRECURSE

PRECURSOR *n* something that precedes and is a signal of something else, forerunner

PRECUT *vb* cut in advance

PRECUTS > PRECUT

PREDACITY *n* predatory nature

PREDATE *vb* occur at an earlier date than

PREDATED > PREDATE

PREDATES > PREDATE

PREDATING > PREDATE

PREDATION *n* relationship between two species of animal in a community, in which one (the predator) hunts, kills, and eats the other (the prey)

PREDATISM *n* state of preying on other animals

PREDATIVE > PREDATE

PREDATOR *n* predatory animal

PREDATORS > PREDATOR

PREDATORY *adj* habitually hunting and killing other animals for food

PREDAWN *n* period before dawn

PREDAWNS > PREDAWN

PREDEATH *n* period immediately before death

PREDEATHS > PREDEATH

PREDEBATE *adj* before a debate

PREDEDUCT *vb* deduct beforehand

PREDEFINE *vb* define in advance

PREDELLA *n* painting or sculpture or a series of small paintings or sculptures in a long narrow strip forming the lower edge of an altarpiece or the face of an altar step or platform

PREDELLAS > PREDELLA

PREDELLE > PREDELLA

PREDESIGN *vb* design beforehand

PREDEVOTE *adj* preordained

PREDIAL *same as* **>** PRAEDIAL

PREDIALS > PREDIAL

PREDICANT *same as* > PREDIKANT

PREDICATE *n* part of a sentence in which something is said about the subject ▷ *vb* declare or assert ▷ *adj* of or relating to something that has been predicated

PREDICT *vb* tell about in advance, prophesy

PREDICTED > PREDICT

PREDICTER > PREDICT

PREDICTOR *n* person or thing that predicts

PREDICTS > PREDICT

PREDIED > PREDY

PREDIES > PREDY

PREDIGEST *vb* treat (food) artificially to aid subsequent digestion in the body

PREDIKANT *n* minister in the Dutch Reformed Church in South Africa

PREDILECT *adj* chosen or preferred

PREDINNER *adj* of the period before dinner

PREDIVE *adj* happening before a dive

PREDOOM *vb* pronounce (someone or something's) doom beforehand

PREDOOMED > PREDOOM

PREDOOMS > PREDOOM

PREDRAFT *adj* before a draft

PREDRIED > PREDRY

PREDRIES > PREDRY

PREDRILL *vb* drill in advance

PREDRILLS > PREDRILL

PREDRY *vb* dry beforehand

PREDRYING > PREDRY

PREDUSK *n* period before dawn

PREDUSKS > PREDUSK

PREDY *vb* prepare for action

PREDYING > PREDY

PREE *vb* try or taste

PREED > PREE

PREEDIT *vb* edit beforehand

PREEDITED > PREEDIT

PREEDITS > PREEDIT

PREEING > PREE

PREELECT *vb* elect beforehand

PREELECTS > PREELECT

PREEMIE *n* premature infant

PREEMIES > PREEMIE

PREEMPT *vb* acquire in advance of or to the exclusion of others

PREEMPTED > PREEMPT

PREEMPTOR > PREEMPT

PREEMPTS > PREEMPT

PREEN *vb* (of a bird) clean or trim (feathers) with the beak ▷ *n* pin, esp a decorative one

PREENACT *vb* enact beforehand

PREENACTS > PREENACT

PREENED > PREEN

PREENER > PREEN

PREENERS > PREEN

PREENING > PREEN

PREENS > PREEN

PREERECT *vb* erect beforehand

PREERECTS > PREERECT

PREES > PREE

PREEVE *old form of* > PROVE

PREEVED > PREEVE

PREEVES > PREEVE

PREEVING > PREEVE

PREEXCITE *vb* stimulate in preparation

PREEXEMPT *vb* exempt beforehand

PREEXILIC *adj* prior to the Babylonian exile of the Jews

PREEXIST *vb* exist beforehand

PREEXISTS > PREEXIST

PREEXPOSE *vb* expose beforehand

PREFAB *n* prefabricated house ▷ *vb* manufacture sections of (building) in factory

PREFABBED > PREFAB

PREFABS > PREFAB

PREFACE *n* introduction to a book ▷ *vb* serve as an introduction to (a book, speech, etc)

PREFACED > PREFACE

PREFACER > PREFACE

PREFACERS > PREFACE

PREFACES > PREFACE

PREFACIAL *adj* anterior to face

PREFACING > PREFACE

PREFADE *vb* fade beforehand

PREFADED > PREFADE

PREFADES > PREFADE

PREFADING > PREFADE

PREFARD *vb* old form of preferred

PREFATORY *adj* concerning a preface

PREFECT *n* senior pupil in a school, with limited power over others

PREFECTS > PREFECT

PREFER *vb* like better

PREFERRED > PREFER

PREFERRER > PREFER

PREFERS > PREFER

PREFEUDAL *adj* of the period before the feudal era

PREFIGHT *adj* of the period before a boxing match

PREFIGURE *vb* represent or suggest in advance

PREFILE *vb* file beforehand

PREFILED > PREFILE

PREFILES > PREFILE

PREFILING > PREFILE

PREFILLED *adj* having been filled beforehand

PREFIRE *vb* fire beforehand

PREFIRED > PREFIRE

PREFIRES > PREFIRE

PREFIRING > PREFIRE

PREFIX *n* letter or group of letters put at the beginning of a word to make a new word, such as *un-* in *unhappy* ▷ *vb* put as an introduction or prefix (to)

PREFIXAL > PREFIX

PREFIXED > PREFIX

PREFIXES > PREFIX

PREFIXING > PREFIX

PREFIXION > PREFIX

PREFLAME *adj* of the period before combustion

PREFLIGHT *adj* of or relating to the period just prior to a plane taking off

PREFOCUS *vb* focus in advance

PREFORM *vb* form beforehand

PREFORMAT *vb* format in advance

PREFORMED > PREFORM

PREFORMS > PREFORM

PREFRANK *vb* frank in advance

PREFRANKS > PREFRANK

PREFREEZE *vb* freeze beforehand

PREFROZE > PREFREEZE

PREFROZEN > PREFREEZE

PREFUND *vb* pay for in advance

PREFUNDED > PREFUND

PREFUNDS > PREFUND

PREGAME *adj* of the period before a sports match ▷ *n* such a period

PREGAMES > PREGAME

PREGGERS *informal word for* > PREGNANT

PREGGIER > PREGGY

PREGGIEST > PREGGY

PREGGY *informal word for* > PREGNANT

PREGNABLE *adj* capable of being assailed or captured

PREGNANCE *obsolete word for* > PREGNANCY

PREGNANCY *n* state or condition of being pregnant

PREGNANT *adj* carrying a fetus in the womb

PREGROWTH *n* period before something begins to grow

PREGUIDE *vb* give guidance in advance

PREGUIDED > PREGUIDE

PREGUIDES > PREGUIDE

PREHALLUX *n* extra first toe

PREHANDLE *vb* handle beforehand

PREHARDEN *vb* harden beforehand

PREHEAT *vb* heat (an oven, grill, pan, etc) beforehand

PREHEATED > PREHEAT

PREHEATER > PREHEAT

PREHEATS > PREHEAT

PREHEND *vb* take hold of

PREHENDED > PREHEND

PREHENDS > PREHEND

PREHENSOR *n* part that grasps

PREHIRING *adj* relating to early hiring

PREHNITE *n* green mineral

PREHNITES > PREHNITE

PREHUMAN *n* hominid that predates man

PREHUMANS > PREHUMAN

PREIF *old form of* > PROOF

PREIFE *old form of* > PROOF

PREIFES > PREIFE

PREIFS > PREIF

PREIMPOSE *vb* impose beforehand

PREINFORM *vb* inform beforehand

PREINSERT *vb* insert beforehand

PREINVITE *vb* invite before others

PREJINK *variant of* > PERJINK

PREJUDGE *vb* judge beforehand without sufficient evidence

PREJUDGED > PREJUDGE

PREJUDGER > PREJUDGE

PREJUDGES > PREJUDGE

PREJUDICE *n* unreasonable or unfair dislike or preference ▷ *vb* cause (someone) to have a prejudice

PREJUDIZE *old form of* > PREJUDICE

PRELACIES > PRELACY

PRELACY *n* office or status of a prelate

PRELATE *n* bishop or other churchman of high rank

PRELATES > PRELATE

PRELATESS *n* female prelate

PRELATIAL > PRELATE

PRELATIC > PRELATE

PRELATIES > PRELATY

PRELATION *n* setting of one above another

PRELATISE *same as* > PRELATIZE

PRELATISH > PRELATE

PRELATISM *same as* > PRELACY

PRELATIST > PRELATISM

PRELATIZE *vb* exercise prelatical power

PRELATURE *same as* > PRELACY

PRELATY *n* prelacy

PRELAUNCH *adj* of the period before a launch

PRELAW *adj* before taking up study of law

PRELECT *vb* lecture or discourse in public

PRELECTED > PRELECT

p

PRELECTOR > PRELECT
PRELECTS > PRELECT
PRELEGAL adj of the period before the start of a law course
PRELIFE n life lived before one's life on earth
PRELIM n event which precedes another
PRELIMIT vb limit beforehand
PRELIMITS > PRELIMIT
PRELIMS npl pages of a book, such as the title page and contents, which come before the main text
PRELIVES > PRELIFE
PRELOAD vb load beforehand
PRELOADED > PRELOAD
PRELOADS > PRELOAD
PRELOCATE vb locate beforehand
PRELOVED adj previously owned or used
PRELUDE n introductory movement in music ▷ vb act as a prelude to (something)
PRELUDED > PRELUDE
PRELUDER > PRELUDE
PRELUDERS > PRELUDE
PRELUDES > PRELUDE
PRELUDI > PRELUDIO
PRELUDIAL > PRELUDE
PRELUDING > PRELUDE
PRELUDIO n musical prelude
PRELUNCH adj of the period before lunch
PRELUSION > PRELUDE
PRELUSIVE > PRELUDE
PRELUSORY > PRELUDE
PREM n informal word for a premature infant
PREMADE adj made in advance
PREMAN n a hominid
PREMARKET adj of the period before a product is available
PREMATURE adj happening or done before the normal or expected time
PREMEAL adj of the period before a meal
PREMED n premedical student
PREMEDIC same as > PREMED
PREMEDICS > PREMEDIC
PREMEDS > PREMED
PREMEET adj happening before a meet
PREMEN > PREMAN
PREMERGER adj of the period prior to a merger
PREMIA > PREMIUM
PREMIE same as > PREEMIE
PREMIER n prime minister ▷ adj chief, leading
PREMIERE n first performance of a play, film,

etc ▷ vb give, or (of a film, play, or opera) be, a premiere
PREMIERED > PREMIERE
PREMIERES > PREMIERE
PREMIERS > PREMIER
PREMIES > PREMIE
PREMISE n statement assumed to be true and used as the basis of reasoning ▷ vb state or assume (a proposition) as a premise in an argument, theory, etc
PREMISED > PREMISE
PREMISES > PREMISE
PREMISING > PREMISE
PREMISS same as > PREMISE
PREMISSED > PREMISS
PREMISSES > PREMISS
PREMIUM n additional sum of money, as on a wage or charge
PREMIUMS > PREMIUM
PREMIX vb mix beforehand
PREMIXED > PREMIX
PREMIXES > PREMIX
PREMIXING > PREMIX
PREMIXT > PREMIX
PREMODERN adj of the period before a modern era
PREMODIFY vb modify in advance
PREMOLAR n tooth between the canine and first molar in adult humans ▷ adj situated before a molar tooth
PREMOLARS > PREMOLAR
PREMOLD vb mold in advance
PREMOLDED > PREMOLD
PREMOLDS > PREMOLD
PREMOLT adj happening in the period before an animal molts
PREMONISH vb admonish beforehand
PREMORAL adj not governed by sense of right and wrong
PREMORSE adj appearing as though the end had been bitten off
PREMOSAIC adj of the period before Moses
PREMOTION n previous motion
PREMOVE vb prompt to action
PREMOVED > PREMOVE
PREMOVES > PREMOVE
PREMOVING > PREMOVE
PREMS > PREM
PREMUNE adj having immunity to a disease as a result of latent infection
PREMY variant of > PREEMIE
PRENAME n forename
PRENAMES > PRENAME
PRENASAL n bone in the front of the nose

PRENASALS > PRENASAL
PRENATAL adj before birth, during pregnancy ▷ n prenatal examination
PRENATALS > PRENATAL
PRENEED adj arranged in advance of eventual requirements
PRENOMEN less common spelling of > PRAENOMEN
PRENOMENS > PRENOMEN
PRENOMINA > PRENOMEN
PRENOON adj of the period before noon
PRENOTIFY vb notify in advance
PRENOTION n preconception
PRENT Scots variant of > PRINT
PRENTED > PRENT
PRENTICE vb bind as an apprentice
PRENTICED > PRENTICE
PRENTICES > PRENTICE
PRENTING > PRENT
PRENTS > PRENT
PRENUBILE adj of the period from birth to puberty
PRENUMBER vb number in advance
PRENUP n prenuptial agreement
PRENUPS > PRENUP
PRENZIE adj Shakespearian word, possibly a mistake, supposed by some to mean "princely"
PREOBTAIN vb obtain in advance
PREOCCUPY vb fill the thoughts or attention of (someone) to the exclusion of other things
PREOCULAR adj relating to the scale in front of the eye of a reptile or fish
PREON n (in particle physics) hypothetical subcomponent of a quark
PREONS > PREON
PREOP n patient being prepared for surgery
PREOPS > PREOP
PREOPTION n right of first choice
PREORAL adj situated in front of mouth
PREORDAIN vb ordain, decree, or appoint beforehand
PREORDER vb order in advance
PREORDERS > PREORDER
PREOWNED adj second-hand
PREP vb prepare
PREPACK vb pack in advance of sale
PREPACKED adj sold already wrapped
PREPACKS > PREPACK
PREPAID > PREPAY

PREPARE vb make or get ready
PREPARED > PREPARE
PREPARER > PREPARE
PREPARERS > PREPARE
PREPARES > PREPARE
PREPARING > PREPARE
PREPASTE vb paste in advance
PREPASTED > PREPASTE
PREPASTES > PREPASTE
PREPAVE vb pave beforehand
PREPAVED > PREPAVE
PREPAVES > PREPAVE
PREPAVING > PREPAVE
PREPAY vb pay for in advance
PREPAYING > PREPAY
PREPAYS > PREPAY
PREPENSE adj (usually in legal contexts) arranged in advance ▷ vb consider beforehand
PREPENSED > PREPENSE
PREPENSES > PREPENSE
PREPILL adj of the period before the contraceptive pill became available
PREPLACE vb place in advance
PREPLACED > PREPLACE
PREPLACES > PREPLACE
PREPLAN vb plan beforehand
PREPLANS > PREPLAN
PREPLANT adj planted in advance
PREPOLLEX n additional digit on thumb of some animals
PREPONE vb bring forward to an earlier time
PREPONED > PREPONE
PREPONES > PREPONE
PREPONING > PREPONE
PREPOSE vb place before
PREPOSED > PREPOSE
PREPOSES > PREPOSE
PREPOSING > PREPOSE
PREPOSTOR n prefect in certain public shcools
PREPOTENT adj greater in power, force, or influence
PREPPED > PREP
PREPPIE same as > PREPPY
PREPPIER > PREPPY
PREPPIES > PREPPY
PREPPIEST > PREPPY
PREPPILY > PREPPY
PREPPING > PREP
PREPPY adj characteristic of or denoting a fashion style of neat, understated, and often expensive clothes ▷ n person exhibiting such style
PREPREG n material already impregnated with synthetic resin
PREPREGS > PREPREG
PREPRESS adj before printing

PREPRICE vb price in advance

PREPRICED > PREPRICE

PREPRICES > PREPRICE

PREPRINT vb print in advance

PREPRINTS > PREPRINT

PREPS > PREP

PREPUBES > PREPUBIS

PREPUBIS n animal hip bone

PREPUCE n foreskin

PREPUCES > PREPUCE

PREPUEBLO adj belonging to the period before the Pueblo Indians

PREPUNCH vb pierce with holes in advance

PREPUPA n insect in stage of life before pupa

PREPUPAE > PREPUPA

PREPUPAL adj of the period between the larval and pupal stages

PREPUPAS > PREPUPA

PREPUTIAL > PREPUCE

PREQUEL n film or book about an earlier stage of a story or a character's life, released because the later part of it has already been successful

PREQUELS > PREQUEL

PRERACE adj of the period before a race

PRERADIO adj before the invention of radio

PRERECORD vb record (music or a programme) in advance so that it can be played or broadcast later

PRERECTAL adj in front of the rectum

PREREFORM adj before reform

PRERENAL adj anterior to kidney

PRERETURN adj of the period before return

PREREVIEW adj of the period before review

PRERINSE vb treat before rinsing

PRERINSED > PRERINSE

PRERINSES > PRERINSE

PRERIOT adj of the period before a riot

PREROCK adj of the era before rock music

PRERUPT adj abrupt

PRESA n sign or symbol used in a canon, round, etc, to indicate the entry of each part

PRESAGE vb be a sign or warning of ▷ n omen

PRESAGED > PRESAGE

PRESAGER > PRESAGE

PRESAGERS > PRESAGE

PRESAGES > PRESAGE

PRESAGING > PRESAGE

PRESALE n practice of arranging the sale of a product before it is available

PRESALES > PRESALE

PRESBYOPE n person with presbyopy

PRESBYOPY n diminishing ability of the eye to focus

PRESBYTE n person with presbyopy

PRESBYTER n (in some episcopal Churches) official with administrative and priestly duties

PRESBYTES > PRESBYTE

PRESBYTIC > PRESBYTE

PRESCHOOL adj of or for children below the age of five

PRESCIENT adj having knowledge of events before they take place

PRESCIND vb withdraw attention (from something)

PRESCINDS > PRESCIND

PRESCIOUS adj prescient

PRESCORE vb record (the score of a film) before shooting

PRESCORED > PRESCORE

PRESCORES > PRESCORE

PRESCREEN vb screen in advance

PRESCRIBE vb recommend the use of (a medicine)

PRESCRIPT n something laid down or prescribed ▷ adj prescribed as a rule

PRESCUTA > PRESCUTUM

PRESCUTUM n part of an insect's thorax

PRESE > PRESA

PRESEASON n period before the start of a sport season

PRESELECT vb select beforehand

PRESELL vb promote (a product, entertainment, etc) with publicity in advance of its appearance

PRESELLS > PRESELL

PRESENCE n fact of being in a specified place

PRESENCES > PRESENCE

PRESENILE adj occurring before the onset of old age

PRESENT adj being in a specified place ▷ n present time or tense ▷ vb introduce formally or publicly

PRESENTED > PRESENT

PRESENTEE n person who is presented, as at court

PRESENTER n person introducing a TV or radio show

PRESENTLY adv soon

PRESENTS npl used in a deed or document to refer to itself

PRESERVE vb keep from being damaged, changed, or ended ▷ n area of interest restricted to a

particular person or group

PRESERVED > PRESERVE

PRESERVER > PRESERVE

PRESERVES > PRESERVE

PRESES variant of > PRAESES

PRESET vb set the timer on a piece of equipment so that it starts to work at a specific time ▷ adj (of equipment) with the controls set in advance ▷ n control, such as a variable resistor, that is not as accessible as the main controls and is used to set initial conditions

PRESETS > PRESET

PRESETTLE vb settle beforehand

PRESHAPE vb shape beforehand

PRESHAPED > PRESHAPE

PRESHAPES > PRESHAPE

PRESHIP vb ship in advance

PRESHIPS > PRESHIP

PRESHOW vb show in advance

PRESHOWED > PRESHOW

PRESHOWN > PRESHOW

PRESHOWS > PRESHOW

PRESHRANK > PRESHRINK

PRESHRINK vb subject to a shrinking process so that further shrinkage will not occur

PRESHRUNK > PRESHRINK

PRESIDE vb be in charge, esp of a meeting

PRESIDED > PRESIDE

PRESIDENT n head of state in many countries

PRESIDER > PRESIDE

PRESIDERS > PRESIDE

PRESIDES > PRESIDE

PRESIDIA > PRESIDIUM

PRESIDIAL adj presidential

PRESIDING > PRESIDE

PRESIDIO n military post or establishment, esp in countries under Spanish control

PRESIDIOS > PRESIDIO

PRESIDIUM n (in Communist countries) permanent administrative committee

PRESIFT vb sift beforehand

PRESIFTED > PRESIFT

PRESIFTS > PRESIFT

PRESIGNAL vb signal in advance

PRESLEEP adj of the period before sleep

PRESLICE vb slice in advance

PRESLICED > PRESLICE

PRESLICES > PRESLICE

PRESOAK vb soak beforehand

PRESOAKED > PRESOAK

PRESOAKS > PRESOAK

PRESOLD > PRESELL

PRESOLVE vb solve beforehand

PRESOLVED > PRESOLVE

PRESOLVES > PRESOLVE

PRESONG adj of the period before a song is sung

PRESORT vb sort in advance

PRESORTED > PRESORT

PRESORTS > PRESORT

PRESPLIT adj of the period prior to a split

PRESS vb apply force or weight to ▷ n printing machine

PRESSED > PRESS

PRESSER > PRESS

PRESSERS > PRESS

PRESSES > PRESS

PRESSFAT n wine vat

PRESSFATS > PRESSFAT

PRESSFUL > PRESS

PRESSFULS > PRESS

PRESSGANG n squad of sailors forcing others into navy

PRESSIE informal word for > PRESENT

PRESSIES > PRESSIE

PRESSING adj urgent ▷ n large number of gramophone records produced at one time

PRESSINGS > PRESSING

PRESSION n act of pressing

PRESSIONS > PRESSION

PRESSMAN n person who works for the press

PRESSMARK n location mark on a book indicating a specific bookcase

PRESSMEN > PRESSMAN

PRESSOR n something that produces an increase in blood pressure

PRESSORS > PRESSOR

PRESSROOM n room in a printing establishment that houses the printing presses

PRESSRUN n number of books printed at one time

PRESSRUNS > PRESSRUN

PRESSURE n force produced by pressing ▷ vb persuade forcefully

PRESSURED > PRESSURE

PRESSURES > PRESSURE

PRESSWORK n operation of a printing press

PREST adj prepared for action or use ▷ n loan of money ▷ vb give as a loan

PRESTAMP vb stamp in advance

PRESTAMPS > PRESTAMP

PRESTED > PREST

PRESTER > PREST

PRESTERNA adj anterior to sternum

PRESTERS > PREST

PRESTIGE n high status or respect resulting from success or achievements

PRESTIGES > PRESTIGE

PRESTING > PREST

PRESTO adv very quickly ▷ n passage to be played very quickly

PRESTORE vb store in advance

PRESTORED > PRESTORE

PRESTORES > PRESTORE

PRESTOS > PRESTO

PRESTRESS vb apply tensile stress to (the steel cables, wires, etc, of a precast concrete part) before the load is applied

PRESTRIKE adj of the period before a strike

PRESTS > PREST

PRESUME vb suppose to be the case

PRESUMED > PRESUME

PRESUMER > PRESUME

PRESUMERS > PRESUME

PRESUMES > PRESUME

PRESUMING > PRESUME

PRESUMMIT n meeting held prior to a summit

PRESURVEY vb survey in advance

PRETAPE vb tape in advance

PRETAPED > PRETAPE

PRETAPES > PRETAPE

PRETAPING > PRETAPE

PRETASTE vb taste in advance

PRETASTED > PRETASTE

PRETASTES > PRETASTE

PRETAX adj before tax

PRETEEN n boy or girl approaching his or her teens

PRETEENS > PRETEEN

PRETELL vb predict

PRETELLS > PRETELL

PRETENCE n behaviour intended to deceive, pretending

PRETENCES > PRETENCE

PRETEND vb claim or give the appearance of (something untrue) to deceive or in play ▷ adj fanciful

PRETENDED > PRETEND

PRETENDER n person who makes a false or disputed claim to a position of power

PRETENDS > PRETEND

PRETENSE same as > PRETENCE

PRETENSES > PRETENSE

PRETERIST n person interested in past

PRETERIT same as > PRETERITE

PRETERITE n past tense of verbs, such as jumped, swam ▷ adj expressing such a past tense

PRETERITS > PRETERIT

PRETERM n premature

baby

PRETERMIT vb overlook intentionally

PRETERMS > PRETERM

PRETEST vb test (something) before presenting it to its intended public or client ▷ n act or instance of pretesting

PRETESTED > PRETEST

PRETESTS > PRETEST

PRETEXT n false reason given to hide the real one ▷ vb get personal information under false pretences

PRETEXTED > PRETEXT

PRETEXTS > PRETEXT

PRETOLD > PRETELL

PRETONIC adj denoting or relating to the syllable before the one bearing the primary stress in a word

PRETOR same as > PRAETOR

PRETORIAL > PRETOR

PRETORIAN n person with the rank of praetor

PRETORS > PRETOR

PRETRAIN vb train in advance

PRETRAINS > PRETRAIN

PRETRAVEL adj of the period before travel

PRETREAT vb treat in advance

PRETREATS > PRETREAT

PRETRIAL n hearing prior to a trial

PRETRIALS > PRETRIAL

PRETRIM vb trim in advance

PRETRIMS > PRETRIM

PRETTIED > PRETTY

PRETTIER > PRETTY

PRETTIES > PRETTY

PRETTIEST > PRETTY

PRETTIFY vb make pretty

PRETTILY > PRETTY

PRETTY adj pleasing to look at ▷ adv fairly, moderately ▷ vb pretty

PRETTYING > PRETTY

PRETTYISH adj quite pretty

PRETTYISM n affectedly pretty style

PRETYPE vb type in advance

PRETYPED > PRETYPE

PRETYPES > PRETYPE

PRETYPING > PRETYPE

PRETZEL n brittle salted biscuit

PRETZELS > PRETZEL

PREUNION n early form of trade union

PREUNIONS > PREUNION

PREUNITE vb unite in advance

PREUNITED > PREUNITE

PREUNITES > PREUNITE

PREVAIL vb gain mastery

PREVAILED > PREVAIL

PREVAILER > PREVAIL

PREVAILS > PREVAIL

PREVALENT adj widespread, common

PREVALUE vb value beforehand

PREVALUED > PREVALUE

PREVALUES > PREVALUE

PREVE vb prove

PREVED > PREVE

PREVENE vb come before

PREVENED > PREVENE

PREVENES > PREVENE

PREVENING > PREVENE

PREVENT vb keep from happening or doing

PREVENTED > PREVENT

PREVENTER n person or thing that prevents

PREVENTS > PREVENT

PREVERB n particle preceding root of verb

PREVERBAL > PREVERB

PREVERBS > PREVERB

PREVES > PREVE

PREVIABLE adj not yet viable

PREVIEW n advance showing of a film or exhibition before it is shown to the public ▷ vb view in advance

PREVIEWED > PREVIEW

PREVIEWER > PREVIEW

PREVIEWS > PREVIEW

PREVING > PREVE

PREVIOUS adj coming or happening before

PREVISE vb predict or foresee

PREVISED > PREVISE

PREVISES > PREVISE

PREVISING > PREVISE

PREVISION n act or power of foreseeing

PREVISIT vb visit beforehand

PREVISITS > PREVISIT

PREVISOR > PREVISE

PREVISORS > PREVISE

PREVUE same as > PREVIEW

PREVUED > PREVUE

PREVUES > PREVUE

PREVUING > PREVUE

PREWAR adj relating to the period before a war, esp before World War I or II

PREWARM vb warm beforehand

PREWARMED > PREWARM

PREWARMS > PREWARM

PREWARN vb warn in advance

PREWARNED > PREWARN

PREWARNS > PREWARN

PREWASH vb give a preliminary wash to (clothes), esp in a washing machine ▷ n preliminary wash, esp in a washing machine

PREWASHED > PREWASH

PREWASHES > PREWASH

PREWEIGH vb weigh beforehand

PREWEIGHS > PREWEIGH

PREWIRE vb wire beforehand

PREWIRED > PREWIRE

PREWIRES > PREWIRE

PREWIRING > PREWIRE

PREWORK vb work in advance

PREWORKED > PREWORK

PREWORKS > PREWORK

PREWORN adj (of clothes) second-hand

PREWRAP vb wrap in advance

PREWRAPS > PREWRAP

PREWYN obsolete spelling of > PRUNE

PREWYNS > PREWYN

PREX same as > PREXY

PREXES > PREX

PREXIES > PREXY

PREXY n US college president

PREY n animal hunted and killed for food by another animal ▷ vb hunt or seize food by killing other animals

PREYED > PREY

PREYER > PREY

PREYERS > PREY

PREYFUL adj rich in prey

PREYING > PREY

PREYS > PREY

PREZ n president

PREZES > PREZ

PREZZIE same as > PRESSIE

PREZZIES > PREZZIE

PRIAL n pair royal of cards

PRIALS > PRIAL

PRIAPEAN same as > PRIAPIC

PRIAPI > PRIAPUS

PRIAPIC adj phallic

PRIAPISM n prolonged painful erection of the penis, caused by neurological disorders, obstruction of the penile blood vessels, etc

PRIAPISMS > PRIAPISM

PRIAPUS n representation of the penis

PRIAPUSES > PRIAPUS

PRIBBLE variant of > PRABBLE

PRIBBLES > PRIBBLE

PRICE n amount of money for which a thing is bought or sold ▷ vb fix or ask the price of

PRICEABLE > PRICE

PRICED > PRICE

PRICELESS adj very valuable

PRICER > PRICE

PRICERS > PRICE

PRICES > PRICE

PRICEY adj expensive

PRICIER > PRICY

PRICIEST > PRICY

PRICILY > PRICEY
PRICINESS > PRICEY
PRICING > PRICE
PRICINGS > PRICE
PRICK *vb* pierce lightly with a sharp point ▷ *n* sudden sharp pain caused by pricking
PRICKED > PRICK
PRICKER *n* person or thing that pricks
PRICKERS > PRICKER
PRICKET *n* male deer in the second year of life having unbranched antlers
PRICKETS > PRICKET
PRICKIER > PRICKY
PRICKIEST > PRICKY
PRICKING > PRICK
PRICKINGS > PRICK
PRICKLE *n* thorn or spike on a plant ▷ *vb* have a tingling or pricking sensation
PRICKLED > PRICKLE
PRICKLES > PRICKLE
PRICKLIER > PRICKLY
PRICKLING > PRICKLE
PRICKLY *adj* having prickles
PRICKS > PRICK
PRICKWOOD *n* shrub with wood used for skewers
PRICKY *adj* covered with pricks
PRICY *same as* > PRICEY
PRIDE *n* feeling of pleasure and satisfaction when one has done well
PRIDED > PRIDE
PRIDEFUL > PRIDE
PRIDELESS > PRIDE
PRIDES > PRIDE
PRIDIAN *adj* relating to yesterday
PRIDING > PRIDE
PRIED > PRY
PRIEDIEU *n* piece of furniture consisting of a low surface for kneeling upon and a narrow front surmounted by a rest for the elbows or for books, for use when praying
PRIEDIEUS > PRIEDIEU
PRIEDIEUX > PRIEDIEU
PRIEF *obsolete variant of* > PROOF
PRIEFE *obsolete variant of* > PROOF
PRIEFES > PRIEFE
PRIEFS > PRIEF
PRIER *n* person who pries
PRIERS > PRIER
PRIES > PRY
PRIEST *n* (in the Christian church) person who can administer the sacraments and preach ▷ *vb* make a priest
PRIESTED > PRIEST
PRIESTESS *n* female official who offers sacrifice on behalf of the people and peforms various other religious ceremonies
PRIESTING > PRIEST
PRIESTLY *adj* of, relating to, characteristic of, or befitting a priest
PRIESTS > PRIEST
PRIEVE *obsolete variant of* > PROOF
PRIEVED > PRIEVE
PRIEVES > PRIEVE
PRIEVING > PRIEVE
PRIG *n* self-righteous person who acts as if superior to others
PRIGGED > PRIG
PRIGGER *n* thief
PRIGGERS > PRIGGER
PRIGGERY > PRIG
PRIGGING > PRIG
PRIGGINGS > PRIG
PRIGGISH > PRIG
PRIGGISM > PRIG
PRIGGISMS > PRIG
PRIGS > PRIG
PRILL *vb* convert (a material) into a granular free-flowing form ▷ *n* prilled material
PRILLED > PRILL
PRILLING > PRILL
PRILLS > PRILL
PRIM *adj* formal, proper, and rather prudish ▷ *vb* make prim
PRIMA *same as* > PRIMO
PRIMACIES > PRIMACY
PRIMACY *n* state of being first in rank, grade, etc
PRIMAEVAL *same as* > PRIMEVAL
PRIMAGE *n* tax added to customs duty
PRIMAGES > PRIMAGE
PRIMAL *adj* of basic causes or origins
PRIMALITY *n* state of being prime
PRIMALLY > PRIMAL
PRIMARIES > PRIMARY
PRIMARILY *adv* chiefly or mainly
PRIMARY *adj* chief, most important ▷ *n* person or thing that is first in position, time, or importance
PRIMAS > PRIMA
PRIMATAL *n* primate
PRIMATALS > PRIMATAL
PRIMATE *n* member of an order of mammals including monkeys and humans
PRIMATES > PRIMATE
PRIMATIAL > PRIMATE
PRIMATIC > PRIMATE
PRIMAVERA *n* springtime
PRIME *adj* main, most important ▷ *n* time when someone is at his or her best or most vigorous ▷ *vb* give (someone) information in advance to prepare them for something

PRIMED > PRIME
PRIMELY > PRIME
PRIMENESS > PRIME
PRIMER *n* special paint applied to bare wood etc before the main paint
PRIMERO *n* 16th- and 17th-century card game
PRIMEROS > PRIMERO
PRIMERS > PRIMER
PRIMES > PRIME
PRIMETIME *adj* occurring during or designed for prime time
PRIMEUR *n* anything (esp fruit) produced early
PRIMEURS > PRIMEUR
PRIMEVAL *adj* of the earliest age of the world
PRIMI > PRIMO
PRIMINE *n* integument surrounding an ovule or the outer of two such integuments
PRIMINES > PRIMINE
PRIMING *same as* > PRIMER
PRIMINGS > PRIMING
PRIMIPARA *n* woman who has borne only one child
PRIMITIAE *npl* first fruits of the season
PRIMITIAL > PRIMITIAE
PRIMITIAS > PRIMITIAE
PRIMITIVE *adj* of an early simple stage of development ▷ *n* primitive person or thing
PRIMLY > PRIM
PRIMMED > PRIM
PRIMMER > PRIM
PRIMMERS > PRIM
PRIMMEST > PRIM
PRIMMING > PRIM
PRIMNESS > PRIM
PRIMO *n* upper or right-hand part in a piano duet
PRIMORDIA *n* organs or parts in the earliest stage of development
PRIMOS > PRIMO
PRIMP *vb* tidy (one's hair or clothes) fussily
PRIMPED > PRIMP
PRIMPING > PRIMP
PRIMPS > PRIMP
PRIMROSE *n* pale yellow spring flower ▷ *adj* pale yellow
PRIMROSED > PRIMROSE
PRIMROSES > PRIMROSE
PRIMROSY > PRIMROSE
PRIMS > PRIM
PRIMSIE *Scots variant of* > PRIM
PRIMSIER > PRIMSIE
PRIMSIEST > PRIMSIE
PRIMULA *n* type of primrose with brightly coloured flowers
PRIMULAS > PRIMULA

PRIMULINE *n* type of dye
PRIMUS *n* presiding bishop in the Synod
PRIMUSES > PRIMUS
PRIMY *adj* prime
PRINCE *vb* act the prince
PRINCED > PRINCE
PRINCEDOM *n* dignity, rank, or position of a prince
PRINCEKIN *n* young prince
PRINCELET *n* petty or minor prince
PRINCELY *adj* of or like a prince ▷ *adv* in a princely manner
PRINCES > PRINCE
PRINCESS *n* female member of a royal family, esp the daughter of the king or queen
PRINCESSE *same as* > PRINCESS
PRINCING > PRINCE
PRINCIPAL *adj* main, most important ▷ *n* head of a school or college
PRINCIPE *n* prince
PRINCIPI > PRINCIPE
PRINCIPIA *n* principles
PRINCIPLE *n* moral rule guiding behaviour
PRINCOCK *same as* > PRINCOX
PRINCOCKS > PRINCOCK
PRINCOX *n* pert youth
PRINCOXES > PRINCOX
PRINK *vb* dress (oneself) finely
PRINKED > PRINK
PRINKER > PRINK
PRINKERS > PRINK
PRINKING > PRINK
PRINKS > PRINK
PRINT *vb* reproduce (a newspaper, book, etc) in large quantities by mechanical or electronic means ▷ *n* printed words etc
PRINTABLE *adj* capable of being printed or of producing a print
PRINTED > PRINT
PRINTER *n* person or company engaged in printing
PRINTERS > PRINTER
PRINTERY *n* establishment in which printing is carried out
PRINTHEAD *n* component in a printer that forms a printed character
PRINTING *n* process of producing printed matter
PRINTINGS > PRINTING
PRINTLESS > PRINT
PRINTOUT *n* printed information produced by a computer output device
PRINTOUTS > PRINTOUT
PRINTS > PRINT
PRION *n* dovelike petrel with a serrated bill**

P

PRIONS > PRION
PRIOR adj earlier ▷ n head monk in a priory
PRIORATE n office, status, or term of office of a prior
PRIORATES > PRIORATE
PRIORESS n deputy head nun in a convent
PRIORIES > PRIORY
PRIORITY n most important thing that must be dealt with first
PRIORLY > PRIOR
PRIORS > PRIOR
PRIORSHIP n office of prior
PRIORY n place where certain orders of monks or nuns live
PRISAGE n customs duty levied until 1809 upon wine imported into England
PRISAGES > PRISAGE
PRISE same as > PRY
PRISED > PRISE
PRISER > PRISE
PRISERE n primary sere or succession from bare ground to the community climax
PRISERES > PRISERE
PRISERS > PRISE
PRISES > PRISE
PRISING > PRISE
PRISM n transparent block usu with triangular ends and rectangular sides, used to disperse light into a spectrum or refract it in optical instruments
PRISMATIC adj of or shaped like a prism
PRISMOID n prismatoid having an equal number of vertices in each of the two parallel planes and whose sides are trapeziums or parallelograms
PRISMOIDS > PRISMOID
PRISMS > PRISM
PRISMY > PRISM
PRISON n building where criminals and accused people are held ▷ vb imprison
PRISONED > PRISON
PRISONER n person held captive
PRISONERS > PRISONER
PRISONING > PRISON
PRISONOUS > PRISON
PRISONS > PRISON
PRISS n prissy person ▷ vb act prissily
PRISSED > PRISS
PRISSES > PRISS
PRISSIER > PRISSY
PRISSIES > PRISSY
PRISSIEST > PRISSY
PRISSILY > PRISSY
PRISSING > PRISS
PRISSY adj prim, correct, and easily shocked ▷ n prissy person
PRISTANE n colourless combustible liquid
PRISTANES > PRISTANE
PRISTINE adj clean, new, and unused
PRITHEE interj pray thee
PRIVACIES > PRIVACY
PRIVACY n condition of being private
PRIVADO n close friend
PRIVADOES > PRIVADO
PRIVADOS > PRIVADO
PRIVATE adj for the use of one person or group only ▷ n soldier of the lowest rank
PRIVATEER n privately owned armed vessel authorized by the government to take part in a war ▷ vb competitor, esp in motor racing, who is privately financed rather than sponsored by a manufacturer
PRIVATELY > PRIVATE
PRIVATER > PRIVATE
PRIVATES > PRIVATE
PRIVATEST > PRIVATE
PRIVATION n loss or lack of the necessities of life
PRIVATISE same as > PRIVATIZE
PRIVATISM n lack of concern for public life
PRIVATIST > PRIVATISM
PRIVATIVE adj causing privation
PRIVATIZE vb sell (a publicly owned company) to individuals or a private company
PRIVET n bushy evergreen shrub used for hedges
PRIVETS > PRIVET
PRIVIER > PRIVY
PRIVIES > PRIVY
PRIVIEST > PRIVY
PRIVILEGE n advantage or favour that only some people have ▷ vb bestow a privilege or privileges upon
PRIVILY adv in a secret way
PRIVITIES > PRIVITY
PRIVITY n legally recognized relationship existing between two parties, such as that between lessor and lessee and between the parties to a contract
PRIVY adj sharing knowledge of something secret ▷ n toilet, esp an outside one
PRIZABLE adj of worth
PRIZE n reward given for success in a competition etc ▷ adj winning or likely to win a prize ▷ vb value highly
PRIZED > PRIZE
PRIZEMAN n winner of prize

PRIZEMEN > PRIZEMAN
PRIZER n contender for prize
PRIZERS > PRIZER
PRIZES > PRIZE
PRIZING > PRIZE
PRO prep in favour of ▷ n professional ▷ adv in favour of a motion etc
PROA n any of several kinds of canoe-like boats used in the South Pacific, esp one equipped with an outrigger and sails
PROACTION n action that initiates change as opposed to reaction to events
PROACTIVE adj tending to initiate change rather than reacting to events
PROAS > PROA
PROB n problem
PROBABLE adj likely to happen or be true ▷ n person who is likely to be chosen for a team, event, etc
PROBABLES > PROBABLE
PROBABLY adv in all likelihood ▷ sentence substitute I believe such a thing or situation may be the case
PROBALL adj believable
PROBAND n first patient to be investigated in a family study, to whom all relationships are referred
PROBANDS > PROBAND
PROBANG n long flexible rod, often with a small sponge at one end, for inserting into the oesophagus, as to apply medication
PROBANGS > PROBANG
PROBATE n process of proving the validity of a will ▷ vb establish officially the authenticity and validity of (a will)
PROBATED > PROBATE
PROBATES > PROBATE
PROBATING > PROBATE
PROBATION n system of dealing with law-breakers, esp juvenile ones, by placing them under supervision
PROBATIVE adj serving to test or designed for testing
PROBATORY same as > PROBATIVE
PROBE vb search into or examine closely ▷ n surgical instrument used to examine a wound, cavity, etc
PROBEABLE > PROBE
PROBED > PROBE
PROBER > PROBE
PROBERS > PROBE
PROBES > PROBE

PROBING > PROBE
PROBINGLY > PROBE
PROBIOTIC n bacterium that protects the body from harmful bacteria
PROBIT n statistical measurement
PROBITIES > PROBITY
PROBITS > PROBIT
PROBITY n honesty, integrity
PROBLEM n something difficult to deal with or solve ▷ adj of a literary work that deals with difficult moral questions
PROBLEMS > PROBLEM
PROBOSCIS n long trunk or snout
PROBS > PROB
PROCACITY n insolence
PROCAINE n colourless or white crystalline water-soluble substance
PROCAINES > PROCAINE
PROCAMBIA n plant part in stem and root
PROCARP n female reproductive organ in red algae
PROCARPS > PROCARP
PROCARYON same as > PROKARYON
PROCEDURE n way of doing something, esp the correct or usual one
PROCEED vb start or continue doing
PROCEEDED > PROCEED
PROCEEDER > PROCEED
PROCEEDS npl money obtained from an event or activity
PROCERITY n tallness
PROCESS n series of actions or changes ▷ vb handle or prepare by a special method of manufacture
PROCESSED > PROCESS
PROCESSER same as > PROCESSOR
PROCESSES > PROCESS
PROCESSOR n person or thing that carries out a process
PROCHAIN variant of > PROCHEIN
PROCHEIN adj next or nearest
PROCHOICE adj in favour of women's right to abortion
PROCHURCH adj favourable to church
PROCIDENT adj relating to prolapsus
PROCINCT n state of preparedness
PROCINCTS > PROCINCT
PROCLAIM vb declare publicly
PROCLAIMS > PROCLAIM
PROCLISES > PROCLITIC**

PROCLISIS
> PROCLITIC
PROCLITIC *adj* relating to or denoting a monosyllabic word or form having no stress or accent and pronounced as a prefix of the following word, as in English 't for it in 'twas ▷ *n* proclitic word or form
PROCLIVE *adj* prone
PROCONSUL *n* administrator or governor of a colony, occupied territory, or other dependency
PROCREANT
> PROCREATE
PROCREATE *vb* produce offspring
PROCTAL *adj* relating to the rectum
PROCTITIS *n* inflammation of the rectum
PROCTODEA *npl* parts of the anus
PROCTOR *n* member of the staff of certain universities having duties including the enforcement of discipline ▷ *vb* invigilate (an examination)
PROCTORED > PROCTOR
PROCTORS > PROCTOR
PROCURACY *n* office of a procurator
PROCURAL > PROCURE
PROCURALS > PROCURE
PROCURE *vb* get, provide
PROCURED > PROCURE
PROCURER *n* person who obtains people to act as prostitutes
PROCURERS > PROCURER
PROCURES > PROCURE
PROCURESS *same as*
> PROCURER
PROCUREUR *n* law officer in Guernsey
PROCURING > PROCURE
PROCYONID *n* animal of the raccoon family
PROD *vb* poke with something pointed ▷ *n* prodding
PRODDED > PROD
PRODDER > PROD
PRODDERS > PROD
PRODDING > PROD
PRODIGAL *adj* recklessly extravagant, wasteful ▷ *n* person who spends lavishly or squanders money
PRODIGALS > PRODIGAL
PRODIGIES > PRODIGY
PRODIGY *n* person with some marvellous talent
PRODITOR *n* traitor
PRODITORS > PRODITOR
PRODITORY > PRODITOR
PRODNOSE *vb* make uninvited inquiries (about someone else's business, for example)

PRODNOSED > PRODNOSE
PRODNOSES > PRODNOSE
PRODROMAL > PRODROME
PRODROME *n* any symptom that signals the impending onset of a disease
PRODROMES > PRODROME
PRODROMI > PRODROME
PRODROMIC > PRODROME
PRODROMUS *same as*
> PRODROME
PRODRUG *n* compound that is itself biologically inactive but is metabolized in the body to produce an active therapeutic drug
PRODRUGS > PRODRUG
PRODS > PROD
PRODUCE *vb* bring into existence ▷ *n* food grown for sale
PRODUCED > PRODUCE
PRODUCER *n* person with control over the making of a film, record, etc
PRODUCERS > PRODUCER
PRODUCES > PRODUCE
PRODUCING > PRODUCE
PRODUCT *n* something produced
PRODUCTS > PRODUCT
PROEM *n* introduction or preface
PROEMBRYO *n* stage prior to embryo in plants
PROEMIAL > PROEM
PROEMS > PROEM
PROENZYME *n* inactive form of an enzyme
PROESTRUS *n* period in the estrous cycle that immediately precedes estrus
PROETTE *n* female golfing professional
PROETTES > PROETTE
PROF *short for*
> PROFESSOR
PROFACE *interj* much good may it do you
PROFAMILY *adj* in favour of family
PROFANE *adj* showing disrespect for religion or holy things ▷ *vb* treat (something sacred) irreverently, desecrate
PROFANED > PROFANE
PROFANELY > PROFANE
PROFANER > PROFANE
PROFANERS > PROFANE
PROFANES > PROFANE
PROFANING > PROFANE
PROFANITY *n* profane talk or behaviour, blasphemy
PROFESS *vb* state or claim (something as true), sometimes falsely
PROFESSED *adj* supposed
PROFESSES > PROFESS
PROFESSOR *n* teacher of the highest rank in a university
PROFFER *vb* offer ▷ *n* act of proffering

PROFFERED > PROFFER
PROFFERER > PROFFER
PROFFERS > PROFFER
PROFILE *n* outline, esp of the face, as seen from the side ▷ *vb* draw, write, or make a profile of
PROFILED > PROFILE
PROFILER *n* person or device that creates a profile, esp someone with psychological training who assists police investigations by identifying the likely characteristics of the perpetrator of a particular crime
PROFILERS > PROFILER
PROFILES > PROFILE
PROFILING > PROFILE
PROFILIST > PROFILE
PROFIT *n* money gained ▷ *vb* gain or benefit
PROFITED > PROFIT
PROFITEER *n* person who makes excessive profits at the expense of the public ▷ *vb* make excessive profits
PROFITER > PROFIT
PROFITERS > PROFIT
PROFITING > PROFIT
PROFITS > PROFIT
PROFLUENT *adj* flowing smoothly or abundantly
PROFORMA *n* invoice issued before an order is placed or before the goods are delivered giving all the details and the cost of the goods
PROFOUND *adj* showing or needing great knowledge ▷ *n* great depth
PROFOUNDS > PROFOUND
PROFS > PROF
PROFUSE *adj* plentiful
PROFUSELY > PROFUSE
PROFUSER > PROFUSE
PROFUSERS > PROFUSE
PROFUSION > PROFUSE
PROFUSIVE *same as*
> PROFUSE
PROG *vb* prowl about for or as if for food or plunder ▷ *n* food obtained by begging
PROGENIES > PROGENY
PROGENY *n* children
PROGERIA *n* premature old age, a rare condition occurring in children and characterized by small stature, absent or greying hair, wrinkled skin, and other signs of old age
PROGERIAS > PROGERIA
PROGESTIN *n* type of steroid hormone
PROGGED > PROG
PROGGER *n* fan of progressive rock
PROGGERS > PROGGER
PROGGING > PROG
PROGGINS *n* proctor
PROGNOSE *vb* predict

course of disease
PROGNOSED > PROGNOSE
PROGNOSES
> PROGNOSIS
PROGNOSIS *n* doctor's forecast about the progress of an illness
PROGRADE *vb* (of beach) advance towards sea
PROGRADED > PROGRADE
PROGRADES > PROGRADE
PROGRAM *same as*
> PROGRAMME
PROGRAMED > PROGRAM
PROGRAMER *n* US spelling of programmer
PROGRAMME *same as*
> PROGRAM
PROGRAMS > PROGRAM
PROGRESS *n* improvement, development ▷ *vb* become more advanced or skilful
PROGS > PROG
PROGUN *adj* in favour of public owning firearms
PROHIBIT *vb* forbid or prevent from happening
PROHIBITS > PROHIBIT
PROIGN *same as* > PROIN
PROIGNED > PROIGN
PROIGNING > PROIGN
PROIGNS > PROIGN
PROIN *vb* trim or prune
PROINE *same as* > PROIN
PROINED > PROIN
PROINES > PROINE
PROINING > PROIN
PROINS > PROIN
PROJECT *n* planned scheme to do or examine something over a period ▷ *vb* make a forecast based on known data
PROJECTED > PROJECT
PROJECTOR *n* apparatus for projecting photographic images, films, or slides on a screen
PROJECTS > PROJECT
PROJET *n* draft of a proposed treaty
PROJETS > PROJET
PROKARYON *n* nucleus of a prokaryote
PROKARYOT *n* any organism having cells in each of which the genetic material is in a single DNA chain, not enclosed in a nucleus
PROKE *vb* thrust or poke
PROKED > PROKE
PROKER > PROKE
PROKERS > PROKE
PROKES > PROKE
PROKING > PROKE
PROLABOR *adj* favouring the Labor party
PROLACTIN *n* gonadotrophic hormone secreted by the anterior lobe of the pituitary gland
PROLAMIN *same as*
> PROLAMINE

PROLAMINE n any of a group of simple plant proteins, including gliadin, hordein, and zein

PROLAMINS > PROLAMIN

PROLAN n constituent of human pregnancy urine

PROLANS > PROLAN

PROLAPSE n slipping down of an internal organ of the body from its normal position ▷ vb (of an internal organ) slip from its normal position

PROLAPSED > PROLAPSE

PROLAPSES > PROLAPSE

PROLAPSUS same as > PROLAPSE

PROLATE adj having a polar diameter which is longer than the equatorial diameter ▷ vb pronounce or utter

PROLATED > PROLATE

PROLATELY > PROLATE

PROLATES > PROLATE

PROLATING > PROLATE

PROLATION > PROLATE

PROLATIVE > PROLATE

PROLE old form of > PROWL

PROLED > PROLE

PROLEG n any of the short paired unjointed appendages on each abdominal segment of a caterpillar and any of certain other insect larvae

PROLEGS > PROLEG

PROLEPSES > PROLEPSIS

PROLEPSIS n rhetorical device by which objections are anticipated and answered in advance

PROLEPTIC > PROLEPSIS

PROLER n prowler

PROLERS > PROLER

PROLES > PROLE

PROLETARY n member of the proletariat

PROLICIDE n killing of one's child

PROLIFIC adj very productive

PROLINE n nonessential amino acid that occurs in protein

PROLINES > PROLINE

PROLING > PROLE

PROLIX adj (of speech or a piece of writing) overlong and boring

PROLIXITY > PROLIX

PROLIXLY > PROLIX

PROLL vb prowl or search

PROLLED > PROLL

PROLLER > PROLL

PROLLERS > PROLL

PROLLING > PROLL

PROLLS > PROLL

PROLOG same as > PROLOGUE

PROLOGED > PROLOG

PROLOGING > PROLOG

PROLOGISE same as > PROLOGIZE

PROLOGIST n prologue writer

PROLOGIZE vb write a prologue

PROLOGS > PROLOG

PROLOGUE n introduction to a play or book ▷ vb introduce or preface with or as if with a prologue

PROLOGUED > PROLOGUE

PROLOGUES > PROLOGUE

PROLONG vb make (something) last longer

PROLONGE n (formerly) specially fitted rope used as part of the towing equipment of a gun carriage

PROLONGED > PROLONG

PROLONGER > PROLONG

PROLONGES > PROLONGE

PROLONGS > PROLONG

PROLUSION n preliminary written exercise

PROLUSORY > PROLUSION

PROM n formal dance held at a high school or college

PROMACHOS n defender or champion

PROMENADE n paved walkway along the seafront at a holiday resort ▷ vb take a leisurely walk

PROMETAL n type of cast iron

PROMETALS > PROMETAL

PROMETRIC adj in favour of the metric system

PROMINE n substance promoting cell growth

PROMINENT adj very noticeable

PROMINES > PROMINE

PROMISE vb say that one will definitely do or not do something ▷ n undertaking to do or not to do something

PROMISED > PROMISE

PROMISEE n person to whom a promise is made

PROMISEES > PROMISEE

PROMISER > PROMISE

PROMISERS > PROMISE

PROMISES > PROMISE

PROMISING adj likely to succeed or turn out well

PROMISOR n person who makes a promise

PROMISORS > PROMISOR

PROMISSOR n (in law) person who makes a promise

PROMMER n spectator at promenade concert

PROMMERS > PROMMER

PROMO vb promote (something)

PROMODERN adj in favour of the modern

PROMOED > PROMO

PROMOING > PROMO

PROMOS > PROMO

PROMOTE vb help to make (something) happen or increase

PROMOTED > PROMOTE

PROMOTER n person who organizes or finances an event etc

PROMOTERS > PROMOTER

PROMOTES > PROMOTE

PROMOTING > PROMOTE

PROMOTION > PROMOTE

PROMOTIVE adj tending to promote

PROMOTOR variant of > PROMOTER

PROMOTORS > PROMOTOR

PROMPT vb cause (an action) ▷ adj done without delay ▷ adv exactly ▷ n anything that serves to remind

PROMPTED > PROMPT

PROMPTER n person offstage who prompts actors

PROMPTERS > PROMPTER

PROMPTEST > PROMPT

PROMPTING > PROMPT

PROMPTLY > PROMPT

PROMPTS > PROMPT

PROMPTURE n prompting

PROMS > PROM

PROMULGE vb bring to public knowledge

PROMULGED > PROMULGE

PROMULGES > PROMULGE

PROMUSCES > PROMUSCIS

PROMUSCIS n proboscis of certain insects

PRONAOI > PRONAOS

PRONAOS n inner area of the portico of a classical temple

PRONATE vb turn (a limb, hand, or foot) so that the palm or sole is directed downwards

PRONATED > PRONATE

PRONATES > PRONATE

PRONATING > PRONATE

PRONATION > PRONATE

PRONATOR n any muscle whose contractions produce or affect pronation

PRONATORS > PRONATOR

PRONE n sermon

PRONELY > PRONE

PRONENESS > PRONE

PRONEPHRA n parts of the kidneys of lower vertebrates

PRONER > PRONE

PRONES > PRONE

PRONEST > PRONE

PRONEUR n flatterer

PRONEURS > PRONEUR

PRONG n one spike of a fork or similar instrument ▷ vb prick or spear with or as if with a prong

PRONGBUCK n horned N American ruminant

PRONGED > PRONG

PRONGHORN n ruminant mammal inhabiting rocky deserts of North America and having small branched horns

PRONGING > PRONG

PRONGS > PRONG

PRONK vb jump straight up

PRONKED > PRONK

PRONKING > PRONK

PRONKINGS > PRONKING

PRONKS > PRONK

PRONOTA > PRONOTUM

PRONOTAL > PRONOTUM

PRONOTUM n notum of the prothorax of an insect

PRONOUN n word, such as she or it, used to replace a noun

PRONOUNCE vb form the sounds of (words or letters), esp clearly or in a particular way

PRONOUNS > PRONOUN

PRONTO adv at once

PRONUCLEI n nuclei of mature ova or spermatozoa before fertilization

PRONUNCIO n papal ambassador

PROO interj (to a horse) stop!

PROOEMION n preface

PROOEMIUM n preface

PROOF n evidence that shows that something is true or has happened ▷ adj able to withstand ▷ vb take a proof from (type matter)

PROOFED > PROOF

PROOFER n reader of proofs

PROOFERS > PROOFER

PROOFING > PROOF

PROOFINGS > PROOF

PROOFLESS > PROOF

PROOFREAD vb read and correct (printer's proofs)

PROOFROOM n room for proofreading

PROOFS > PROOF

PROOTIC n bone in front of ear

PROOTICS > PROOTIC

PROP vb support (something) so that it stays upright or in place ▷ n pole, beam, etc used as a support

PROPAGATE vb spread (information and ideas)

PROPAGE vb propagate

PROPAGED > PROPAGE

PROPAGES > PROPAGE

PROPAGING > PROPAGE

PROPAGULA > PROPAGULE

PROPAGULE n plant part, such as a bud, that becomes detached from the rest of the plant and grows into a new plant

PROPALE vb publish (something)

PROPALED > PROPALE
PROPALES > PROPALE
PROPALING > PROPALE
PROPANE n flammable gas found in petroleum and used as a fuel
PROPANES > PROPANE
PROPANOIC as in *propanoic acid* colourless liquid carboxylic acid
PROPANOL n colourless alcohol
PROPANOLS > PROPANOL
PROPANONE n systematic name of acetone
PROPEL vb cause to move forward
PROPELLED > PROPEL
PROPELLER n revolving shaft with blades for driving a ship or aircraft
PROPELLOR same as > PROPELLER
PROPELS > PROPEL
PROPENAL n type of aldehyde used as a herbicide and tear gas
PROPENALS > PROPENAL
PROPEND vb be inclined or disposed
PROPENDED > PROPEND
PROPENDS > PROPEND
PROPENE n colourless gaseous alkene obtained by cracking petroleum
PROPENES > PROPENE
PROPENOIC as in *propenoic acid* systematic name of acrylic acid
PROPENOL n liquid used to make allylic alcohol
PROPENOLS > PROPENOL
PROPENSE adj inclining forward
PROPENYL n three-carbon radical
PROPER adj real or genuine ▷ n service or psalm regarded as appropriate to a specific day, season, etc
PROPERDIN n protein present in blood serum that, acting with complement, is involved in the destruction of alien cells, such as bacteria
PROPERER > PROPER
PROPEREST > PROPER
PROPERLY > PROPER
PROPERS > PROPER
PROPERTY same as > PROPRIUM
PROPHAGE n virus that exists in a bacterial cell and undergoes division with its host without destroying it
PROPHAGES > PROPHAGE
PROPHASE n first stage of mitosis, during which the nuclear membrane disappears and the nuclear material resolves itself into chromosomes
PROPHASES > PROPHASE
PROPHASIC > PROPHASE

PROPHECY n prediction
PROPHESY vb foretell
PROPHET n person supposedly chosen by God to spread His word
PROPHETIC adj foretelling what will happen
PROPHETS > PROPHET
PROPHYLL n leaf-shaped plant structure
PROPHYLLS > PROPHYLL
PROPINE vb to drink a toast to
PROPINED > PROPINE
PROPINES > PROPINE
PROPINING > PROPINE
PROPINED > PROPINE
PROPIONIC as in *propionic acid* former name for propanoic acid
PROPJET another name for > TURBOPROP
PROPJETS > PROPJET
PROPMAN n member of the stage crew in charge of the stage props
PROPMEN > PROPMAN
PROPODEON n part of an insect's thorax
PROPODEUM variant of > PROPODEON
PROPOLIS n greenish-brown resinous aromatic substance collected by bees from the buds of trees for use in the construction of hives
PROPONE vb propose or put forward, esp before a court
PROPONED > PROPONE
PROPONENT n person who argues in favour of something
PROPONES > PROPONE
PROPONING > PROPONE
PROPOSAL n act of proposing
PROPOSALS > PROPOSAL
PROPOSE vb put forward for consideration
PROPOSED > PROPOSE
PROPOSER > PROPOSE
PROPOSERS > PROPOSE
PROPOSES > PROPOSE
PROPOSING > PROPOSE
PROPOSITA n woman from whom a line of descent is traced
PROPOSITI n people from whom lines of descent are traced
PROPOUND vb put forward for consideration
PROPOUNDS > PROPOUND
PROPPANT n material used in the oil extraction process
PROPPANTS > PROPPANT
PROPPED > PROP
PROPPING > PROP
PROPRETOR n (in ancient Rome) citizen, esp an ex-praetor, granted a praetor's imperium, to be exercised outside Rome
PROPRIA > PROPRIUM
PROPRIETY n quality of

being appropriate or fitting
PROPRIUM n attribute that is not essential to a species but is common and peculiar to it
PROPS > PROP
PROPTOSES > PROPTOSIS
PROPTOSIS n forward displacement of an organ or part, such as the eyeball
PROPULSOR n propeller
PROPYL n of, consisting of, or containing the monovalent group of atoms C_3H_7-
PROPYLA > PROPYLON
PROPYLAEA n porticos, esp those that form the entrances to temples
PROPYLENE n gas found in petroleum and used to produce many organic compounds
PROPYLIC > PROPYL
PROPYLITE n altered andesite or similar rock containing calcite, chlorite, etc, produced by the action of hot water
PROPYLON n portico, esp one that forms the entrance to a temple
PROPYLONS > PROPYLON
PROPYLS > PROPYL
PRORATE vb divide, assess, or distribute (something) proportionately
PRORATED > PRORATE
PRORATES > PRORATE
PRORATING > PRORATE
PRORATION > PRORATE
PRORE n forward part of ship
PRORECTOR n official in German academia
PROREFORM adj in favour of or supporting reform, esp within politics
PRORES > PRORE
PROROGATE vb discontinue legislative meetings
PROROGUE vb suspend (parliament) without dissolving it
PROROGUED > PROROGUE
PROROGUES > PROROGUE
PROS > PRO
PROSAIC adj lacking imagination, dull
PROSAICAL same as > PROSAIC
PROSAISM n prosaic quality or style
PROSAISMS > PROSAISM
PROSAIST > PROSAISM
PROSAISTS > PROSAISM
PROSATEUR n writer of prose
PROSCENIA n arches or openings separating stages from auditoria together with the areas immediately in front of the arches

PROSCRIBE vb prohibit, outlaw
PROSCRIPT n proscription or prohibition
PROSE n ordinary speech or writing in contrast to poetry ▷ vb speak or write in a tedious style
PROSECCO n Italian sparkling white wine
PROSECCOS > PROSECCO
PROSECT vb dissect a cadaver for a public demonstration
PROSECTED > PROSECT
PROSECTOR n person who prepares or dissects anatomical subjects for demonstration
PROSECTS > PROSECT
PROSECUTE vb bring a criminal charge against
PROSED > PROSE
PROSELIKE > PROSE
PROSELYTE n recent convert
PROSEMAN n writer of prose
PROSEMEN > PROSEMAN
PROSER n writer of prose
PROSERS > PROSER
PROSES > PROSE
PROSEUCHA n place of prayer
PROSEUCHE n prayer
PROSIER > PROSY
PROSIEST > PROSY
PROSIFIED > PROSIFY
PROSIFIES > PROSIFY
PROSIFY vb write prose
PROSILY > PROSY
PROSIMIAN n primate of the primitive suborder which includes lemurs, lorises, and tarsiers
PROSINESS > PROSY
PROSING > PROSE
PROSINGS > PROSE
PROSIT interj good health! cheers!
PROSO n millet
PROSODIAL adj of prosody
PROSODIAN n writer of prose
PROSODIC > PROSODY
PROSODIES > PROSODY
PROSODIST > PROSODY
PROSODY n study of poetic metre and techniques
PROSOMA n head and thorax of an arachnid
PROSOMAL > PROSOMA
PROSOMAS > PROSOMA
PROSOMATA > PROSOMA
PROSOPON n (in Christianity) manifestation of any of the persons of the Trinity
PROSOPONS > PROSOPON
PROSOS > PROSO
PROSPECT n something anticipated ▷ vb explore, esp for gold
PROSPECTS > PROSPECT

PROSPER vb be successful

PROSPERED > PROSPER

PROSPERS > PROSPER

PROSS n prostitute

PROSSES > PROSS

PROSSIE n prostitute

PROSSIES > PROSSIE

PROST same as > PROSIT

PROSTATE n gland in male mammals that surrounds the neck of the bladder ▷ adj of or relating to the prostate gland

PROSTATES > PROSTATE

PROSTATIC same as > PROSTATE

PROSTERNA n sternums or thoraces of insects

PROSTIE n prostitute

PROSTIES > PROSTIE

PROSTOMIA n lobes at the head ends of earthworms and other annelids

PROSTRATE adj lying face downwards ▷ vb lie face downwards

PROSTYLE adj (of a building) having a row of columns in front, esp as in the portico of a Greek temple ▷ n prostyle building, portico, etc

PROSTYLES > PROSTYLE

PROSUMER n amateur user of electronic equipment suitable for professionals

PROSUMERS > PROSUMER

PROSY adj dull and long-winded

PROTAMIN same as > PROTAMINE

PROTAMINE n any of a group of basic simple proteins that occur, in association with nucleic acids, in the sperm of some fish

PROTAMINS > PROTAMIN

PROTANDRY n condition (in hermaphrodite plants) of maturing the anthers before the stigma

PROTANOPE n person with type of colour blindness

PROTASES > PROTASIS

PROTASIS n antecedent of a conditional statement

PROTATIC > PROTASIS

PROTEA n African shrub with showy flowers

PROTEAN adj constantly changing ▷ n creature that can change shape

PROTEANS > PROTEAN

PROTEAS > PROTEA

PROTEASE n any enzyme involved in proteolysis

PROTEASES > PROTEASE

PROTECT vb defend from trouble, harm, or loss

PROTECTED > PROTECT

PROTECTER same as > PROTECTOR

PROTECTOR n person or thing that protects

PROTECTS > PROTECT

PROTEGE n person who is protected and helped by another

PROTEGEE n woman or girl who is protected and helped by another

PROTEGEES > PROTEGEE

PROTEGES > PROTEGE

PROTEI > PROTEUS

PROTEID n protein

PROTEIDE variant of > PROTEID

PROTEIDES > PROTEIDE

PROTEIDS > PROTEID

PROTEIN n any of a group of complex organic compounds that are essential for life

PROTEINIC > PROTEIN

PROTEINS > PROTEIN

PROTEND vb hold out or stretch

PROTENDED > PROTEND

PROTENDS > PROTEND

PROTENSE n extension

PROTENSES > PROTENSE

PROTEOME n full complement of proteins that occur within a cell, tissue, or organism

PROTEOMES > PROTEOME

PROTEOMIC > PROTEOME

PROTEOSE n compounds formed during proteolysis that is less complex than metaproteins but more so than peptones

PROTEOSES > PROTEOSE

PROTEST n declaration or demonstration of objection ▷ vb object, disagree

PROTESTED > PROTEST

PROTESTER > PROTEST

PROTESTOR > PROTEST

PROTESTS > PROTEST

PROTEUS n aerobic bacterium

PROTEUSES > PROTEUS

PROTHALLI n small flat free-living gametophytes in ferns, club mosses etc

PROTHESES > PROTHESIS

PROTHESIS n process in the development of a language by which a phoneme or syllable is prefixed to a word to facilitate pronunciation

PROTHETIC > PROTHESIS

PROTHORAX n first segment of the thorax of an insect, which bears the first pair of walking legs

PROTHYL variant of > PROTYLE

PROTHYLS > PROTHYL

PROTIST n organism belonging to the kingdom which comprises protozoans, unicellular algae, and simple fungi

PROTISTAN > PROTIST

PROTISTIC > PROTIST

PROTISTS > PROTIST

PROTIUM n most common isotope of hydrogen

PROTIUMS > PROTIUM

PROTO as in proto team relates to a team of people trained to deal with underground rescues, etc

PROTOAVIS n bird-like fossil

PROTOCOL n rules of behaviour for formal occasions

PROTOCOLS > PROTOCOL

PROTODERM n outer primary meristem of a plant

PROTOGINE n type of granite

PROTOGYNY n (in hermaphrodite plants and animals) condition of producing female gametes before male ones

PROTON n positively charged particle in the nucleus of an atom

PROTONATE vb provide atom with proton

PROTONEMA n branched threadlike structure that grows from a moss spore and eventually develops into the moss plant

PROTONIC adj (of a solvent, such as water) able to donate hydrogen ions to solute molecules

PROTONS > PROTON

PROTOPOD n part of crustacean's leg

PROTOPODS > PROTOPOD

PROTORE n primary mineral deposit

PROTORES > PROTORE

PROTOSTAR n cloud of interstellar gas and dust that gradually collapses, forming a hot dense core, and evolves into a star once nuclear fusion can occur in the core

PROTOTYPE n original or model to be copied or developed

PROTOXID variant of > PROTOXIDE

PROTOXIDE n oxide of an element that contains the smallest amount of oxygen of any of its oxides

PROTOXIDS > PROTOXID

PROTOZOA > PROTOZOAN

PROTOZOAL > PROTOZOAN

PROTOZOAN n microscopic one-celled creature ▷ adj of or relating to protozoans

PROTOZOIC > PROTOZOAN

PROTOZOON same as > PROTOZOAN

PROTRACT vb lengthen or extend (a situation etc)

PROTRACTS > PROTRACT

PROTRADE adj in favour of trade

PROTRUDE vb stick out, project

PROTRUDED > PROTRUDE

PROTRUDES > PROTRUDE

PROTYL same as > PROTYLE

PROTYLE n hypothetical primitive substance from which the chemical elements were supposed to have been formed

PROTYLES > PROTYLE

PROTYLS > PROTYL

PROUD adj feeling pleasure and satisfaction

PROUDER > PROUD

PROUDEST > PROUD

PROUDFUL adj full of pride

PROUDISH adj rather proud

PROUDLY > PROUD

PROUDNESS > PROUD

PROUL variant of > PROWL

PROULED > PROUL

PROULER Scots variant of > PROWLER

PROULERS > PROULER

PROULING > PROUL

PROULS > PROUL

PROUNION adj in favour of or supporting the constitutional union between two or more countries

PROUSTITE n red mineral consisting of silver arsenic sulphide in hexagonal crystalline form

PROVABLE > PROVE

PROVABLY > PROVE

PROVAND n food

PROVANDS > PROVAND

PROVANT adj supplied with provisions

PROVE vb establish the validity of

PROVEABLE > PROVE

PROVEABLY > PROVEABLE

PROVED > PROVE

PROVEDOR variant of > PROVEDORE

PROVEDORE n purveyor

PROVEDORS > PROVEDOR

PROVEN > PROVE

PROVEND same as > PROVAND

PROVENDER n fodder

PROVENDS > PROVEND

PROVENLY > PROVE

PROVER > PROVE

PROVERB n short saying that expresses a truth or gives a warning ▷ vb utter or describe (something) in the form of a proverb

PROVERBED > PROVERB

PROVERBS > PROVERB

PROVERS > PROVE

PROVES > PROVE

PROVIANT variant of
> PROVAND

PROVIANTS > PROVIANT

PROVIDE vb make
available

PROVIDED > PROVIDE

PROVIDENT adj thrifty

PROVIDER > PROVIDE

PROVIDERS > PROVIDE

PROVIDES > PROVIDE

PROVIDING > PROVIDE

PROVIDOR variant of
> PROVEDORE

PROVIDORS > PROVIDOR

PROVINCE n area
governed as a unit of a
country or empire

PROVINCES > PROVINCE

PROVINE vb plant branch
of vine in ground for
propagation

PROVINED > PROVINE

PROVINES > PROVINE

PROVING > PROVE

PROVINGS > PROVE

PROVINING > PROVINE

PROVIRAL > PROVIRUS

PROVIRUS n inactive form
of a virus in a host cell

PROVISION n act of
supplying something ▷ vb
supply with food

PROVISO n condition,
stipulation

PROVISOES > PROVISO

PROVISOR n person who
receives provision

PROVISORS > PROVISOR

PROVISORY adj
containing a proviso

PROVISOS > PROVISO

PROVOCANT n
provocateur; one who
deliberately behaves
controversially to provoke
argument or other strong
reactions

PROVOKE vb deliberately
anger

PROVOKED > PROVOKE

PROVOKER > PROVOKE

PROVOKERS > PROVOKE

PROVOKES > PROVOKE

PROVOKING > PROVOKE

PROVOLONE n mellow,
pale yellow, soft, and
sometimes smoked cheese,
made of cow's milk: usually
moulded in the shape of a
pear

PROVOST n head of certain
university colleges in
Britain

PROVOSTRY n office of
provost

PROVOSTS > PROVOST

PROW n bow of a vessel ▷ adj
gallant

PROWAR adj in favour of or
supporting war

PROWER > PROW

PROWESS n superior skill or
ability

PROWESSED adj brave or
skilful

PROWESSES > PROWESS

PROWEST > PROW

PROWL vb move stealthily
around a place as if in
search of prey or plunder
▷ n prowling

PROWLED > PROWL

PROWLER > PROWL

PROWLERS > PROWL

PROWLING > PROWL

PROWLINGS > PROWL

PROWLS > PROWL

PROWS > PROW

PROXEMIC > PROXEMICS

PROXEMICS n study of
spatial interrelationships in
humans or in populations
of animals of the same
species

PROXIES > PROXY

PROXIMAL same as
> PROXIMATE

PROXIMATE adj next or
nearest in space or time

PROXIMITY n nearness in
space or time

PROXIMO adv in or during
the next or coming month

PROXY n person authorized
to act on behalf of someone
else

PROYN obsolete spelling of
> PRUNE

PROYNE obsolete spelling of
> PRUNE

PROYNED > PROYN

PROYNES > PROYNE

PROYNING > PROYN

PROYNS > PROYN

PROZYMITE n Christian
using leavened bread for
the Eucharist

PRUDE n person who is
excessively modest, prim,
or proper

PRUDENCE n caution in
practical affairs

PRUDENCES > PRUDENCE

PRUDENT adj cautious,
discreet, and sensible

PRUDENTLY > PRUDENT

PRUDERIES > PRUDE

PRUDERY > PRUDE

PRUDES > PRUDE

PRUDISH > PRUDE

PRUDISHLY > PRUDE

PRUH variant of > PROO

PRUINA n woolly white
covering on some lichens

PRUINAS > PRUINA

PRUINE obsolete spelling of
> PRUNE

PRUINES > PRUINE

PRUINOSE adj coated with
a powdery or waxy bloom

PRUNABLE > PRUNE

PRUNE n dried plum ▷ vb
cut off dead parts or
excessive branches from (a
tree or plant)

PRUNED > PRUNE

PRUNELLA n strong fabric,
esp a twill-weave worsted,
used for gowns and the
uppers of some shoes

PRUNELLAS > PRUNELLA

PRUNELLE same as
> PRUNELLA

PRUNELLES > PRUNELLE

PRUNELLO same as
> PRUNELLA

PRUNELLOS > PRUNELLO

PRUNER > PRUNE

PRUNERS > PRUNE

PRUNES > PRUNE

PRUNING > PRUNE

PRUNINGS > PRUNE

PRUNT n glass
ornamentation

PRUNTED > PRUNT

PRUNTS > PRUNT

PRUNUS n type of
ornamental tree or shrub

PRUNUSES > PRUNUS

PRURIENCE > PRURIENT

PRURIENCY n sexual
desire

PRURIENT adj excessively
interested in sexual
matters

PRURIGO n chronic
inflammatory disease of
the skin characterized by
the formation of papules
and intense itching

PRURIGOS > PRURIGO

PRURITIC > PRURITUS

PRURITUS n any intense
sensation of itching

PRUSIK n sliding knot that
locks under pressure and
can be used to form a loop
in which a climber can
place his or her foot in order
to stand or ascend a rope
▷ vb climb (up a standing
rope) using prusiks

PRUSIKED > PRUSIK

PRUSIKING > PRUSIK

PRUSIKS > PRUSIK

PRUSSIAN as in prussian
blue colour pigment,
discovered in Berlin

PRUSSIATE n any cyanide,
ferrocyanide, or
ferricyanide

PRUSSIC as in prussic acid
weakly acidic extremely
poisonous aqueous
solution of hydrogen
cyanide

PRUTA same as > PRUTAH

PRUTAH n former Israeli
coin

PRUTOT > PRUTAH

PRUTOTH > PRUTAH

PRY vb make an
impertinent or uninvited
inquiry into a private
matter ▷ n act of prying

PRYER same as > PRIER

PRYERS > PRYER

PRYING > PRY

PRYINGLY > PRY

PRYINGS > PRY

PRYS old variant of > PRICE

PRYSE old variant of
> PRICE

PRYSED > PRYSE

PRYSES > PRYSE

PRYSING > PRYSE

PRYTANEA > PRYTANEUM

PRYTANEUM n public hall
of a city in ancient Greece

PRYTHEE same as
> PRITHEE

PSALM n sacred song ▷ vb
sing a psalm

PSALMBOOK n book of
psalms

PSALMED > PSALM

PSALMIC > PSALM

PSALMING > PSALM

PSALMIST n writer of
psalms

PSALMISTS > PSALMIST

PSALMODIC > PSALMODY

PSALMODY n singing of
sacred music

PSALMS > PSALM

PSALTER n devotional or
liturgical book containing a
version of Psalms

PSALTERIA n omasums

PSALTERS > PSALTER

PSALTERY n ancient
instrument played by
plucking strings

PSALTRESS n woman
who sings psalms

PSALTRIES > PSALTRY

PSALTRY same as
> PSALTERY

PSAMMITE rare name for
> SANDSTONE

PSAMMITES > PSAMMITE

PSAMMITIC > PSAMMITE

PSAMMON n community of
microscopic life forms living
between grains of sand on
shores

PSAMMONS > PSAMMON

PSCHENT n ancient
Egyptian crown

PSCHENTS > PSCHENT

PSELLISM n stammering

PSELLISMS > PSELLISM

PSEPHISM n proposition
adopted by a majority vote

PSEPHISMS > PSEPHISM

PSEPHITE n any rock,
such as a breccia, that
consists of large fragments
embedded in a finer matrix

PSEPHITES > PSEPHITE

PSEPHITIC > PSEPHITE

PSEUD n pretentious
person

PSEUDAXES
> PSEUDAXIS

PSEUDAXIS another name
for > SYMPODIUM

PSEUDERY n pretentious
talk

PSEUDISH > PSEUD

PSEUDO n pretentious
person

PSEUDONYM n fictitious
name adopted esp by an
author

PSEUDOPOD n temporary
projection from the body of
a single-celled animal

PSEUDOS > PSEUDO

PSEUDS > PSEUD

p

PSHAW n exclamation of disgust, impatience, disbelief, etc ▷ vb make this exclamation

PSHAWED > PSHAW

PSHAWING > PSHAW

PSHAWS > PSHAW

PSI n 23rd letter of the Greek alphabet

PSILOCIN n hallucinogenic substance

PSILOCINS > PSILOCIN

PSILOSES > PSILOSIS

PSILOSIS n disease of the small intestine

PSILOTIC > PSILOSIS

PSION n type of elementary particle

PSIONIC > PSIONICS

PSIONICS n study of the practical use of psychic powers

PSIONS > PSION

PSIS > PSI

PSOAE > PSOAS

PSOAI > PSOAS

PSOAS n either of two muscles of the loins that aid in flexing and rotating the thigh

PSOASES > PSOAS

PSOATIC > PSOAS

PSOCID n tiny wingless insect

PSOCIDS > PSOCID

PSORA n itching skin complaint

PSORALEA n type of tropical and subtropical plant with curly leaves and white or purple flowers

PSORALEAS > PSORALEA

PSORALEN n treatment for some skin diseases

PSORALENS > PSORALEN

PSORAS > PSORA

PSORIASES > PSORIASIS

PSORIASIS n skin disease with reddish spots and patches covered with silvery scales

PSORIATIC > PSORIASIS

PSORIC > PSORA

PSST interj sound made to attract someone's attention, esp without others noticing

PST interj sound made to attract someone's attention

PSYCH vb psychoanalyse

PSYCHE same as > PSYCH

PSYCHED > PSYCH

PSYCHES > PSYCH

PSYCHIC adj having mental powers which cannot be explained by natural laws ▷ n person with psychic powers

PSYCHICAL > PSYCHIC

PSYCHICS > PSYCHIC

PSYCHING > PSYCH

PSYCHISM n belief in a universal soul

PSYCHISMS > PSYCHISM

PSYCHIST > PSYCHISM

PSYCHISTS > PSYCHISM

PSYCHO n psychopath

PSYCHOGAS n gas with a mind-altering effect

PSYCHOID n name for an animal's innate impetus to perform actions

PSYCHOIDS > PSYCHOID

PSYCHOS > PSYCHO

PSYCHOSES > PSYCHOSIS

PSYCHOSIS n severe mental disorder in which the sufferer's contact with reality becomes distorted

PSYCHOTIC adj of, relating to, or characterized by psychosis ▷ n person suffering from psychosis

PSYCHS > PSYCH

PSYLLA same as > PSYLLID

PSYLLAS > PSYLLA

PSYLLID n type of insect of the family which comprises the jumping plant lice

PSYLLIDS > PSYLLID

PSYLLIUM n grain, the husks of which are used medicinally as a laxative and to reduce blood cholesterol levels

PSYLLIUMS > PSYLLIUM

PSYOP n psychological operation

PSYOPS > PSYOP

PSYWAR n psychological warfare

PSYWARS > PSYWAR

PTARMIC n material that causes sneezing

PTARMICS > PTARMIC

PTARMIGAN n bird of the grouse family which turns white in winter

PTERIA > PTERION

PTERIDINE n yellow crystalline base

PTERIN n compound such as folic acid

PTERINS > PTERIN

PTERION n point on the side of the skull where a number of bones meet

PTEROIC as in pteroic acid a kind of acid found in spinach

PTEROPOD n small marine gastropod mollusc in which the foot is expanded into two winglike lobes for swimming and the shell is absent or thin-walled

PTEROPODS > PTEROPOD

PTEROSAUR n extinct flying reptile

PTERYGIA > PTERYGIUM

PTERYGIAL adj of or relating to a fin or wing

PTERYGIUM n abnormal tissue over corner of eye

PTERYGOID n either of two long bony plates extending downwards from each side of the sphenoid bone within the skull

PTERYLA n any of the tracts of skin that bear contour feathers, arranged in lines along the body of a bird

PTERYLAE > PTERYLA

PTILOSES > PTILOSIS

PTILOSIS n falling out of eye lashes

PTISAN n grape juice drained off without pressure

PTISANS > PTISAN

PTOMAIN same as > PTOMAINE

PTOMAINE n any of a group of poisonous alkaloids found in decaying matter

PTOMAINES > PTOMAINE

PTOMAINIC > PTOMAINE

PTOMAINS > PTOMAIN

PTOOEY interj imitation of the sound of spitting

PTOSES > PTOSIS

PTOSIS n prolapse or drooping of a part, esp the eyelid

PTOTIC > PTOSIS

PTUI same as > PTOOEY

PTYALIN n amylase secreted in the saliva of man and other animals

PTYALINS > PTYALIN

PTYALISE same as > PTYALIZE

PTYALISED > PTYALISE

PTYALISES > PTYALISE

PTYALISM n excessive secretion of saliva

PTYALISMS > PTYALISM

PTYALIZE vb expel saliva from the mouth

PTYALIZED > PTYALIZE

PTYALIZES > PTYALIZE

PTYXES > PTYXIS

PTYXIS n folding of a leaf in a bud

PTYXISES > PTYXIS

PUB n building with a bar licensed to sell alcoholic drinks ▷ vb visit a pub or pubs

PUBBED > PUB

PUBBING > PUB

PUBBINGS > PUBBING

PUBCO n company operating a chain of pubs

PUBCOS > PUBCO

PUBE n pubic hair

PUBERAL adj relating to puberty

PUBERTAL > PUBERTY

PUBERTIES > PUBERTY

PUBERTY n beginning of sexual maturity

PUBES > PUBE

PUBESCENT adj reaching or having reached puberty

PUBIC adj of the lower abdomen

PUBIS n one of the three sections of the hipbone that forms part of the pelvis

PUBISES > PUBIS

PUBLIC adj of or concerning the people as a whole ▷ n community, people in general

PUBLICAN n person who owns or runs a pub

PUBLICANS > PUBLICAN

PUBLICISE same as > PUBLICIZE

PUBLICIST n person, esp a press agent or journalist, who publicizes something

PUBLICITY n process or information used to arouse public attention

PUBLICIZE vb bring to public attention

PUBLICLY adv in a public manner

PUBLICS > PUBLIC

PUBLISH vb produce and issue (printed matter) for sale

PUBLISHED > PUBLISH

PUBLISHER n company or person that publishes books, periodicals, music, etc

PUBLISHES > PUBLISH

PUBS > PUB

PUCAN n traditional Connemara open sailing boat

PUCANS > PUCAN

PUCCOON n N American plant that yields a red dye

PUCCOONS > PUCCOON

PUCE adj purplish-brown ▷ n colour varying from deep red to dark purplish-brown

PUCELAGE n virginity

PUCELAGES > PUCELAGE

PUCELLE n maid or virgin

PUCELLES > PUCELLE

PUCER > PUCE

PUCES > PUCE

PUCEST > PUCE

PUCK n mischievous or evil spirit ▷ vb strike (the ball) in hurling

PUCKA same as > PUKKA

PUCKED > PUCK

PUCKER vb gather into wrinkles ▷ n wrinkle or crease

PUCKERED > PUCKER

PUCKERER > PUCKER

PUCKERERS > PUCKER

PUCKERIER > PUCKERY

PUCKERING > PUCKER

PUCKERS > PUCKER

PUCKERY adj (of wine) high in tannins

PUCKFIST n puffball

PUCKFISTS > PUCKFIST

PUCKING > PUCK

PUCKISH > PUCK

PUCKISHLY > PUCK
PUCKLE *n* early type of machine gun
PUCKLES > PUCKLE
PUCKOUT *n* (in hurling) free hit made by the goalkeeper
PUCKOUTS > PUCKOUT
PUCKS > PUCK
PUD *short for* > PUDDING
PUDDEN *dialect spelling of* > PUDDING
PUDDENING *n* rope fender on boat
PUDDENS > PUDDEN
PUDDER *vb* make bother or fuss
PUDDERED > PUDDER
PUDDERING > PUDDER
PUDDERS > PUDDER
PUDDIES > PUDDY
PUDDING *n* dessert, esp a cooked one served hot
PUDDINGS > PUDDING
PUDDINGY > PUDDING
PUDDLE *n* small pool of water, esp of rain ▷ *vb* make (clay etc) into puddle
PUDDLED > PUDDLE
PUDDLER > PUDDLE
PUDDLERS > PUDDLE
PUDDLES > PUDDLE
PUDDLIER > PUDDLE
PUDDLIEST > PUDDLE
PUDDLING *n* process for converting pig iron into wrought iron by heating it with ferric oxide in a furnace to oxidize the carbon
PUDDLINGS > PUDDLING
PUDDLY > PUDDLE
PUDDOCK *same as* > PADDOCK
PUDDOCKS > PUDDOCK
PUDDY *n* paw
PUDENCIES > PUDENCY
PUDENCY *n* modesty, shame, or prudishness
PUDENDA > PUDENDUM
PUDENDAL > PUDENDUM
PUDENDOUS *adj* shameful
PUDENDUM *n* human external genital organs collectively, esp of a female
PUDENT *adj* lacking in ostentation; humble
PUDGE *same as* > PODGE
PUDGES > PUDGE
PUDGIER > PUDGY
PUDGIEST > PUDGY
PUDGILY > PUDGY
PUDGINESS > PUDGY
PUDGY *adj* podgy
PUDIBUND *adj* prudish
PUDIC > PUDENDUM
PUDICITY *n* modesty
PUDOR *n* sense of shame
PUDORS > PUDOR
PUDS > PUD
PUDSEY *variant of* > PUDSY
PUDSIER > PUDSY
PUDSIEST > PUDSY
PUDSY *adj* plump
PUDU *n* diminutive Andean antelope with short straight horns and reddish-brown spotted coat
PUDUS > PUDU
PUEBLO *n* communal village, built by certain Indians of the southwestern US and parts of Latin America, consisting of one or more flat-roofed stone or adobe houses
PUEBLOS > PUEBLO
PUER *vb* steep hides in an alkaline substance from the dung of dogs
PUERED > PUER
PUERILE *adj* silly and childish
PUERILELY > PUERILE
PUERILISM *n* immature or childish behaviour by an adult
PUERILITY > PUERILE
PUERING > PUER
PUERPERA *n* woman who has recently given birth
PUERPERAE > PUERPERA
PUERPERAL *adj* concerning the period following childbirth
PUERPERIA *n* periods of around six weeks following childbirths when uteruses return to their normal size and shape
PUERS > PUER
PUFF *n* (sound of) short blast of breath, wind, etc ▷ *vb* blow or breathe in short quick draughts
PUFFBALL *n* ball-shaped fungus
PUFFBALLS > PUFFBALL
PUFFBIRD *n* brownish tropical American bird with a large head
PUFFBIRDS > PUFFBIRD
PUFFED > PUFF
PUFFER *n* person or thing that puffs
PUFFERIES > PUFFERY
PUFFERS > PUFFER
PUFFERY *n* exaggerated praise, esp in publicity or advertising
PUFFIER > PUFFY
PUFFIEST > PUFFY
PUFFILY > PUFFY
PUFFIN *n* black-and-white sea bird with a brightly-coloured beak
PUFFINESS > PUFFY
PUFFING > PUFF
PUFFINGLY > PUFF
PUFFINGS > PUFF
PUFFINS > PUFFIN
PUFFS > PUFF
PUFFY *adj* short of breath
PUFTALOON *n* Australian fried scone
PUG *n* small snub-nosed dog ▷ *vb* mix or knead (clay) with water to form a malleable mass or paste

PUGAREE *same as* > PUGGREE
PUGAREES > PUGAREE
PUGGAREE *same as* > PUGGREE
PUGGAREES > PUGGAREE
PUGGED > PUG
PUGGERIES > PUGGERY
PUGGERY *same as* > PUGGREE
PUGGIE *n* Scottish word for fruit machine
PUGGIER > PUGGY
PUGGIES > PUGGIE
PUGGIEST > PUGGY
PUGGINESS > PUGGY
PUGGING > PUG
PUGGINGS > PUG
PUGGISH > PUG
PUGGLE *vb* stir up by poking
PUGGLED > PUGGLE
PUGGLES > PUGGLE
PUGGLING > PUGGLE
PUGGREE *n* scarf, usually pleated, around the crown of some hats, esp sun helmets
PUGGREES > PUGGREE
PUGGRIES > PUGGRY
PUGGRY *same as* > PUGGREE
PUGGY *adj* sticky, claylike ▷ *n* term of endearment
PUGH *interj* exclamation of disgust
PUGIL *n* pinch or small handful
PUGILISM *n* art, practice, or profession of fighting with the fists
PUGILISMS > PUGILISM
PUGILIST > PUGILISM
PUGILISTS > PUGILISM
PUGILS > PUGIL
PUGMARK *n* trail of an animal
PUGMARKS > PUGMARK
PUGNACITY *n* readiness to fight
PUGREE *same as* > PUGGREE
PUGREES > PUGREE
PUGS > PUG
PUH *interj* exclamation expressing contempt or disgust
PUHA *n* sow thistle
PUHAS > PUHA
PUIR *Scottish word for* > POOR
PUIRER > PUIR
PUIREST > PUIR
PUIRTITH *n* poverty
PUIRTITHS > PUIRTITH
PUISNE *adj* (esp of a subordinate judge) of lower rank ▷ *n* judge of lower rank
PUISNES > PUISNE
PUISNY *adj* younger or inferior
PUISSANCE *n* showjumping competition that tests a horse's ability to jump large obstacles
PUISSANT *adj* powerful
PUISSAUNT *same as* > PUISSANT
PUJA *n* ritual in honour of the gods, performed either at home or in the mandir (temple)
PUJAH *same as* > PUJA
PUJAHS > PUJAH
PUJARI *n* Hindu priest
PUJARIS > PUJARI
PUJAS > PUJA
PUKA *in New Zealand English, same as* > BROADLEAF
PUKAS > PUKA
PUKATEA *n* aromatic New Zealand tree, valued for its high-quality timber
PUKATEAS > PUKATEA
PUKE *vb* vomit ▷ *n* act of vomiting
PUKED > PUKE
PUKEKO *n* brightly coloured New Zealand wading bird
PUKEKOS > PUKEKO
PUKER *n* person who vomits
PUKERS > PUKER
PUKES > PUKE
PUKEY *adj* of or like vomit
PUKIER > PUKEY
PUKIEST > PUKEY
PUKING > PUKE
PUKKA *adj* properly done, constructed, etc
PUKU *n* belly or stomach
PUKUS > PUKU
PUKY *same as* > PUKEY
PUL *n* Afghan monetary unit worth one hundredth of an afghani
PULA *n* standard monetary unit of Botswana, divided into 100 thebe
PULAO *same as* > PILAU
PULAOS > PULAO
PULAS > PULA
PULDRON *same as* > PAULDRON
PULDRONS > PULDRON
PULE *vb* whine or whimper
PULED > PULE
PULER > PULE
PULERS > PULE
PULES > PULE
PULI > PUL
PULICENE *adj* flea-ridden
PULICIDE *n* flea-killing substance
PULICIDES > PULICIDE
PULIER > PULY
PULIEST > PULY
PULIK > PUL
PULING > PULE
PULINGLY > PULE
PULINGS > PULE
PULIS > PUL
PULK *same as* > PULKA
PULKA *n* reindeer-drawn sleigh
PULKAS > PULKA
PULKHA *same as* > PULKA

PULKHAS > PULKHA

PULKS > PULK

PULL vb exert force on (an object) to move it towards the source of the force ▷ n act of pulling

PULLBACK n act of pulling back

PULLBACKS > PULLBACK

PULLED > PULL

PULLER > PULL

PULLERS > PULL

PULLET n young hen

PULLETS > PULLET

PULLEY n wheel with a grooved rim in which a belt, chain, or piece of rope runs in order to lift weights by a downward pull

PULLEYS > PULLEY

PULLI > PULLUS

PULLING > PULL

PULLMAN n luxurious railway coach, esp a sleeping car

PULLMANS > PULLMAN

PULLORUM as in *pullorum disease* acute serious bacterial disease of very young birds

PULLOUT n removable section of a magazine, etc

PULLOUTS > PULLOUT

PULLOVER n sweater that is pulled on over the head

PULLOVERS > PULLOVER

PULLS > PULL

PULLULATE vb (of animals, etc) breed rapidly or abundantly

PULLUP n exercise in which the body is raised up by the arms pulling on a horizontal bar fixed above the head

PULLUPS > PULLUP

PULLUS n technical term for a chick or young bird

PULMO n lung

PULMONARY adj of the lungs

PULMONATE adj having lungs or lung-like organs ▷ n any pulmonate mollusc

PULMONES > PULMO

PULMONIC adj of or relating to the lungs ▷ n person with lung disease

PULMONICS > PULMONIC

PULMOTOR n apparatus for pumping oxygen into the lungs during artificial respiration

PULMOTORS > PULMOTOR

PULP n soft wet substance made from crushed or beaten matter ▷ vb reduce to pulp

PULPAL > PULP

PULPALLY > PULP

PULPBOARD n board made from wood pulp

PULPED > PULP

PULPER > PULP

PULPERS > PULP

PULPIER > PULPY

PULPIEST > PULPY

PULPIFIED > PULPIFY

PULPIFIES > PULPIFY

PULPIFY vb reduce to pulp

PULPILY > PULPY

PULPINESS > PULPY

PULPING > PULP

PULPIT n raised platform for a preacher

PULPITAL > PULPIT

PULPITED > PULPIT

PULPITEER n deliverer of sermon

PULPITER n preacher

PULPITERS > PULPITER

PULPITRY n art of delivering sermons

PULPITS > PULPIT

PULPITUM n stone screen dividing nave and choir

PULPITUMS > PULPITUM

PULPLESS > PULP

PULPMILL n mill making raw material for paper

PULPMILLS > PULPMILL

PULPOUS n soft and yielding

PULPS > PULP

PULPSTONE n calcified mass in a tooth cavity

PULPWOOD n pine, spruce, or any other soft wood used to make paper

PULPWOODS > PULPWOOD

PULPY adj having a soft or soggy consistency

PULQUE n light alcoholic drink from Mexico made from the juice of various agave plants, esp the maguey

PULQUES > PULQUE

PULS > PUL

PULSANT adj vibrant

PULSAR n small dense star which emits regular bursts of radio waves

PULSARS > PULSAR

PULSATE vb throb, quiver

PULSATED > PULSATE

PULSATES > PULSATE

PULSATILE adj beating rhythmically

PULSATING > PULSATE

PULSATION n act of pulsating

PULSATIVE > PULSATE

PULSATOR n device that stimulates rhythmic motion of a body

PULSATORS > PULSATOR

PULSATORY adj of or relating to pulsation

PULSE n regular beating of blood through the arteries at each heartbeat ▷ vb beat, throb, or vibrate

PULSED > PULSE

PULSEJET n type of ramjet engine

PULSEJETS > PULSEJET

PULSELESS > PULSE

PULSER n thing that pulses

PULSERS > PULSER

PULSES > PULSE

PULSIDGE archaic word for > PULSE

PULSIDGES > PULSIDGE

PULSIFIC adj causing the pulse to increase

PULSING > PULSE

PULSION n act of driving forward

PULSIONS > PULSION

PULSOJET same as > PULSEJET

PULSOJETS > PULSOJET

PULTAN n native Indian regiment

PULTANS > PULTAN

PULTON same as > PULTAN

PULTONS > PULTON

PULTOON same as > PULTAN

PULTOONS > PULTOON

PULTUN same as > PULTAN

PULTUNS > PULTUN

PULTURE n food and drink claimed by foresters as their right from anyone within the limits of a given forest

PULTURES > PULTURE

PULU n substance from Hawaiian ferns, used for stuffing cushions, etc

PULUS > PULU

PULVER vb make into powder

PULVERED > PULVER

PULVERINE n ashes of the barilla plant

PULVERING > PULVER

PULVERISE same as > PULVERIZE

PULVERIZE vb reduce to fine pieces

PULVEROUS adj consisting of tiny particles

PULVERS > PULVER

PULVIL vb apply perfumed powder

PULVILIO n perfumed powder

PULVILIOS > PULVILIO

PULVILLAR adj like cushion

PULVILLE same as > PULVIL

PULVILLED > PULVIL

PULVILLES > PULVILLE

PULVILLI > PULVILLUS

PULVILLIO same as > PULVILIO

PULVILLUS n small pad between the claws at the end of an insect's leg

PULVILS > PULVIL

PULVINAR n part of the thalamus

PULVINARS > PULVINAR

PULVINATE adj (of a frieze) curved convexly

PULVINI > PULVINUS

PULVINULE n part of a leaf

PULVINUS n swelling at the base of a leafstalk

PULWAR n light Indian river boat

PULWARS > PULWAR

PULY adj whiny

PUMA n large American wild cat with a greyish-brown coat

PUMAS > PUMA

PUMELO same as > POMELO

PUMELOS > PUMELO

PUMICATE vb pound fruit with pumice to make juice

PUMICATED > PUMICATE

PUMICATES > PUMICATE

PUMICE n light porous stone used for scouring ▷ vb rub or polish with pumice

PUMICED > PUMICE

PUMICEOUS > PUMICE

PUMICER > PUMICE

PUMICERS > PUMICE

PUMICES > PUMICE

PUMICING > PUMICE

PUMICITE n fine-grained variety of pumice

PUMICITES > PUMICITE

PUMIE n small stone

PUMIES > PUMIE

PUMMEL vb strike repeatedly with or as if with the fists

PUMMELED > PUMMEL

PUMMELING > PUMMEL

PUMMELLED > PUMMEL

PUMMELO same as > POMELO

PUMMELOS > PUMMELO

PUMMELS > PUMMEL

PUMP n machine used to force a liquid or gas to move in a particular direction ▷ vb raise or drive with a pump

PUMPED > PUMP

PUMPER > PUMP

PUMPERS > PUMP

PUMPHOOD n cover for the upper wheel of a chain pump

PUMPHOODS > PUMPHOOD

PUMPING > PUMP

PUMPINGS > PUMPING

PUMPION archaic word for > PUMPKIN

PUMPIONS > PUMPION

PUMPKIN n large round fruit with an orange rind, soft flesh, and many seeds

PUMPKING n person involved in a web-based project who has temporary but exclusive authority to make changes to the master source code

PUMPKINGS > PUMPKING

PUMPKINS > PUMPKIN

PUMPLESS > PUMP

PUMPLIKE > PUMP

PUMPS > PUMP

PUMY adj large and round

PUN n use of words to exploit double meanings

for humorous effect ▷ *vb* make puns

PUNA *n* high cold dry plateau, esp in the Andes

PUNAANI *same as* > PUNANI

PUNAANY *same as* > PUNANI

PUNALUA *n* marriage between the sisters of one family to the brothers of another

PUNALUAN > PUNALUA

PUNALUAS > PUNALUA

PUNANI *n* vagina

PUNANY *same as* > PUNANI

PUNAS > PUNA

PUNCE *n* kick ▷ *vb* kick

PUNCED > PUNCE

PUNCES > PUNCE

PUNCH *vb* strike at with a clenched fist ▷ *n* blow with a clenched fist

PUNCHBAG *n* stuffed or inflated bag suspended by a flexible rod, that is punched for exercise, esp boxing training

PUNCHBAGS > PUNCHBAG

PUNCHBALL *n* stuffed or inflated ball supported by a flexible rod, that is punched for exercise, esp boxing training

PUNCHBOWL *n* large bowl for serving punch

PUNCHED > PUNCH

PUNCHEON *n* large cask of variable capacity, usually between 70 and 120 gallons

PUNCHEONS > PUNCHEON

PUNCHER > PUNCH

PUNCHERS > PUNCH

PUNCHES > PUNCH

PUNCHIER > PUNCHY

PUNCHIEST > PUNCHY

PUNCHILY > PUNCHY

PUNCHING > PUNCH

PUNCHLESS > PUNCH

PUNCHLINE *n* funny ending of a joke

PUNCHY *adj* forceful

PUNCING > PUNCE

PUNCTA > PUNCTUM

PUNCTATE *adj* having or marked with minute spots, holes, or depressions

PUNCTATED *same as* > PUNCTATE

PUNCTATOR *n* marker of points

PUNCTILIO *n* strict attention to minute points of etiquette

PUNCTO *n* tip of a fencing sword

PUNCTOS > PUNCTO

PUNCTUAL *adj* arriving or taking place at the correct time

PUNCTUATE *vb* put punctuation marks in

PUNCTULE *n* very small opening

PUNCTULES > PUNCTULE

PUNCTUM *n* tip or small point

PUNCTURE *n* small hole made by a sharp object, esp in a tyre ▷ *vb* pierce a hole in

PUNCTURED > PUNCTURE

PUNCTURER > PUNCTURE

PUNCTURES > PUNCTURE

PUNDIT *n* expert who speaks publicly on a subject

PUNDITIC *adj* of or relating to pundits

PUNDITRY *n* expressing of expert opinions

PUNDITS > PUNDIT

PUNDONOR *n* point of honour

PUNG *n* horse-drawn sleigh with a boxlike body on runners

PUNGA *variant spelling of* > PONGA

PUNGAS > PUNGA

PUNGENCE *n* pungency

PUNGENCES > PUNGENCE

PUNGENCY > PUNGENT

PUNGENT *adj* having a strong sharp bitter flavour

PUNGENTLY > PUNGENT

PUNGLE *vb* make payment

PUNGLED > PUNGLE

PUNGLES > PUNGLE

PUNGLING > PUNGLE

PUNGS > PUNG

PUNIER > PUNY

PUNIEST > PUNY

PUNILY > PUNY

PUNINESS > PUNY

PUNISH *vb* cause (someone) to suffer or undergo a penalty for some wrongdoing

PUNISHED > PUNISH

PUNISHER > PUNISH

PUNISHERS > PUNISH

PUNISHES > PUNISH

PUNISHING > PUNISH

PUNITION *n* punishment

PUNITIONS > PUNITION

PUNITIVE *adj* relating to punishment

PUNITORY *same as* > PUNITIVE

PUNJI *n* sharpened bamboo stick

PUNJIS > PUNJI

PUNK *n* anti-Establishment youth movement and style of rock music of the late 1970s ▷ *adj* relating to the punk youth movement of the late 1970s

PUNKA *n* fan made of a palm leaf or leaves

PUNKAH *same as* > PUNKA

PUNKAHS > PUNKAH

PUNKAS > PUNKA

PUNKER > PUNK

PUNKERS > PUNK

PUNKEST > PUNK

PUNKEY *n* small winged insect

PUNKEYS > PUNKEY

PUNKIE *same as* > PUNKEY

PUNKIER > PUNKY

PUNKIES > PUNKIE

PUNKIEST > PUNKY

PUNKIN *same as* > PUMPKIN

PUNKINESS > PUNKY

PUNKINS > PUNKIN

PUNKISH > PUNK

PUNKS > PUNK

PUNKY *adj* of punk music

PUNNED > PUN

PUNNER > PUN

PUNNERS > PUN

PUNNET *n* small basket for fruit

PUNNETS > PUNNET

PUNNIER > PUNNY

PUNNIEST > PUNNY

PUNNING > PUN

PUNNINGLY > PUN

PUNNINGS > PUN

PUNNY *adj* of puns

PUNS > PUN

PUNSTER *n* person who is fond of making puns

PUNSTERS > PUNSTER

PUNT *n* open flat-bottomed boat propelled by a pole ▷ *vb* travel in a punt

PUNTED > PUNT

PUNTEE *same as* > PUNTY

PUNTEES > PUNTEE

PUNTER *n* person who bets

PUNTERS > PUNTER

PUNTIES > PUNTY

PUNTING > PUNT

PUNTO *n* hit in fencing

PUNTOS > PUNTO

PUNTS > PUNT

PUNTSMAN *n* man in charge of a river punt

PUNTSMEN > PUNTSMAN

PUNTY *n* long iron rod used in the finishing process of glass-blowing

PUNY *adj* small and feeble

PUP *n* young of certain animals, such as dogs and seals ▷ *vb* (of dogs, seals, etc) to give birth to pups

PUPA *n* insect at the stage of development between a larva and an adult

PUPAE > PUPA

PUPAL > PUPA

PUPARIA > PUPARIUM

PUPARIAL > PUPARIUM

PUPARIUM *n* hard barrel-shaped case enclosing the pupae of the housefly and other dipterous insects

PUPAS > PUPA

PUPATE *vb* (of an insect larva) to develop into a pupa

PUPATED > PUPATE

PUPATES > PUPATE

PUPATING > PUPATE

PUPATION > PUPATE

PUPATIONS > PUPATE

PUPFISH *n* type of small fish

PUPFISHES > PUPFISH

PUPIL *n* person who is taught by a teacher

PUPILAGE *same as* > PUPILLAGE

PUPILAGES > PUPILAGE

PUPILAR > PUPIL

PUPILARY *same as* > PUPILLARY

PUPILLAGE *n* condition of being a pupil or duration for which one is a pupil

PUPILLAR > PUPIL

PUPILLARY *adj* of or relating to a pupil or a legal ward

PUPILLATE *adj* with a spot of a different colour in the middle

PUPILS > PUPIL

PUPILSHIP *n* state of being a pupil

PUPPED > PUP

PUPPET *n* small doll or figure moved by strings or by the operator's hand

PUPPETEER *n* person who operates puppets

PUPPETRY *n* art of making and manipulating puppets and presenting puppet shows

PUPPETS > PUPPET

PUPPIED > PUPPY

PUPPIES > PUPPY

PUPPING > PUP

PUPPODOM *same as* > POPPADOM

PUPPODOMS > PUPPODOM

PUPPY *n* young dog ▷ *vb* have puppies

PUPPYDOM *n* state of being a puppy

PUPPYDOMS > PUPPYDOM

PUPPYHOOD > PUPPY

PUPPYING > PUPPY

PUPPYISH > PUPPY

PUPPYISM *n* impudence

PUPPYISMS > PUPPYISM

PUPPYLIKE > PUPPY

PUPS > PUP

PUPU *n* Hawaiian dish

PUPUNHA *n* fruit of a type of palm tree

PUPUNHAS > PUPUNHA

PUPUS > PUPU

PUR *same as* > PURR

PURANA *n* any of a class of Sanskrit writings not included in the Vedas, characteristically recounting the birth and deeds of Hindu gods and the creation, destruction, or recreation of the universe

PURANAS > PURANA

PURANIC > PURANA

PURBLIND *adj* partly or nearly blind

PURCHASE *vb* obtain by payment ▷ *n* thing that is bought

PURCHASED > PURCHASE

PURCHASER > PURCHASE

PURCHASES > PURCHASE
PURDA same as > PURDAH
PURDAH n Muslim and Hindu custom of keeping women in seclusion, with clothing that conceals them completely when they go out
PURDAHED > PURDAH
PURDAHS > PURDAH
PURDAS > PURDA
PURDONIUM n type of coal scuttle having a slanted cover that is raised to open it, and an inner removable metal container for the coal
PURE adj unmixed, untainted ▷ vb make pure
PUREBLOOD n purebred animal
PUREBRED adj denoting a pure strain obtained through many generations of controlled breeding ▷ n purebred animal
PUREBREDS > PUREBRED
PURED > PURE
PUREE n smooth thick pulp of cooked and sieved fruit, vegetables, meat, or fish ▷ vb make (cooked foods) into a puree
PUREED > PUREE
PUREEING > PUREE
PUREES > PUREE
PURELY adv in a pure manner
PURENESS > PURE
PURER > PURE
PURES > PURE
PUREST > PURE
PURFLE n ruffled or curved ornamental band, as on clothing, furniture, etc ▷ vb decorate with such a band or bands
PURFLED > PURFLE
PURFLER > PURFLE
PURFLERS > PURFLE
PURFLES > PURFLE
PURFLING same as > PURFLE
PURFLINGS > PURFLING
PURFLY > PURFLE
PURGATION n act of purging or state of being purged
PURGATIVE adj (medicine) designed to cause defecation ▷ n medicine for emptying the bowels
PURGATORY n place or state of temporary suffering
PURGE vb rid (a thing or place) of (unwanted things or people) ▷ n purging
PURGEABLE > PURGE
PURGED > PURGE
PURGER > PURGE
PURGERS > PURGE
PURGES > PURGE
PURGING > PURGE
PURGINGS > PURGE
PURI n unleavened flaky

Indian bread, that is deep-fried in ghee and served hot
PURIFIED > PURIFY
PURIFIER n device or substance that frees something of extraneous, contaminating, or debasing matter
PURIFIERS > PURIFIER
PURIFIES > PURIFY
PURIFY vb make or become pure
PURIFYING > PURIFY
PURIN same as > PURINE
PURINE n colourless crystalline solid that can be prepared from uric acid
PURINES > PURINE
PURING > PURE
PURINS > PURIN
PURIRI n forest tree of New Zealand
PURIRIS > PURIRI
PURIS > PURI
PURISM n strict insistence on the correct usage or style, such as in grammar or art
PURISMS > PURISM
PURIST > PURISM
PURISTIC > PURISM
PURISTS > PURISM
PURITAN n person who follows strict moral or religious principles ▷ adj of or like a puritan
PURITANIC > PURITAN
PURITANS > PURITAN
PURITIES > PURITY
PURITY n state or quality of being pure
PURL n stitch made by knitting a plain stitch backwards ▷ vb knit in purl
PURLED > PURL
PURLER n headlong or spectacular fall
PURLERS > PURLER
PURLICUE vb finish a pen stroke with a flourish
PURLICUED > PURLICUE
PURLICUES > PURLICUE
PURLIEU n land on the edge of a royal forest
PURLIEUS > PURLIEU
PURLIN n horizontal beam that supports the rafters of a roof
PURLINE same as > PURLIN
PURLINES > PURLINE
PURLING > PURL
PURLINGS > PURL
PURLINS > PURLIN
PURLOIN vb steal
PURLOINED > PURLOIN
PURLOINER > PURLOIN
PURLOINS > PURLOIN
PURLS > PURL
PUROMYCIN n type of antibiotic
PURPIE old Scots word for > PURSLANE

PURPIES > PURPIE
PURPLE n colour between red and blue ▷ adj of a colour between red and blue ▷ vb make purple
PURPLED > PURPLE
PURPLER > PURPLE
PURPLES > PURPLE
PURPLEST > PURPLE
PURPLIER > PURPLE
PURPLIEST > PURPLE
PURPLING > PURPLE
PURPLISH > PURPLE
PURPLY > PURPLE
PURPORT vb claim (to be or do something) ▷ n apparent meaning, significance
PURPORTED adj alleged
PURPORTS > PURPORT
PURPOSE n reason for which something is done or exists
PURPOSED > PURPOSE
PURPOSELY adv intentionally
PURPOSES > PURPOSE
PURPOSING > PURPOSE
PURPOSIVE adj having or showing a definite intention
PURPURA n any of several blood diseases causing purplish spots or patches on the skin due to subcutaneous bleeding
PURPURAS > PURPURA
PURPURE n purple
PURPUREAL adj having a purple colour
PURPURES > PURPURE
PURPURIC > PURPURA
PURPURIN n red crystalline compound used as a stain for biological specimens
PURPURINS > PURPURIN
PURPY variant of > PURPIE
PURR vb (of cats) make low vibrant sound, usu when pleased ▷ n this sound
PURRED > PURR
PURRING > PURR
PURRINGLY > PURR
PURRINGS > PURR
PURRS > PURR
PURS > PUR
PURSE n small bag for money ▷ vb draw (one's lips) together into a small round shape
PURSED > PURSE
PURSEFUL n that which can be contained in purse
PURSEFULS > PURSEFUL
PURSELIKE > PURSE
PURSER n ship's officer who keeps the accounts
PURSERS > PURSER
PURSES > PURSE
PURSEW archaic spelling of > PURSUE
PURSEWED > PURSEW
PURSEWING > PURSEW
PURSEWS > PURSEW

PURSIER > PURSY
PURSIEST > PURSY
PURSILY > PURSY
PURSINESS > PURSY
PURSING > PURSE
PURSLAIN same as > PURSLANE
PURSLAINS > PURSLAIN
PURSLANE n type of weedy plant with small yellow flowers and fleshy leaves, used in salads and as a potherb
PURSLANES > PURSLANE
PURSUABLE > PURSUE
PURSUAL n act of pursuit
PURSUALS > PURSUAL
PURSUANCE n carrying out of an action or plan
PURSUANT adj in agreement or conformity
PURSUE vb chase
PURSUED > PURSUE
PURSUER > PURSUE
PURSUERS > PURSUE
PURSUES > PURSUE
PURSUING > PURSUE
PURSUINGS > PURSUE
PURSUIT n pursuing
PURSUITS > PURSUIT
PURSY adj short-winded
PURTIER > PURTY
PURTIEST > PURTY
PURTRAID > PURTRAYD
PURTRAYD adj archaic spelling of portrayed
PURTY adj pretty
PURULENCE > PURULENT
PURULENCY > PURULENT
PURULENT adj of or containing pus
PURVEY vb supply (provisions) ▷ n food and drink laid on at a wedding reception, etc
PURVEYED > PURVEY
PURVEYING > PURVEY
PURVEYOR n person, organization, etc, that supplies food and provisions
PURVEYORS > PURVEYOR
PURVEYS > PURVEY
PURVIEW n scope or range of activity or outlook
PURVIEWS > PURVIEW
PUS n yellowish matter produced by infected tissue
PUSES > PUS
PUSH vb move or try to move by steady force ▷ n act of pushing
PUSHBALL n game in which two teams try to push a heavy ball towards opposite goals
PUSHBALLS > PUSHBALL
PUSHBIKE n pedal-driven bicycle
PUSHBIKES > PUSHBIKE
PUSHCART n handcart, typically having two wheels and a canvas roof, used esp by street vendors

PUSHCARTS > PUSHCART
PUSHCHAIR n folding chair on wheels for a baby
PUSHDOWN n list in which the last item added is at the top
PUSHDOWNS > PUSHDOWN
PUSHED adj short of
PUSHER n person who sells illegal drugs
PUSHERS > PUSHER
PUSHES > PUSH
PUSHFUL > PUSH
PUSHFULLY > PUSH
PUSHIER > PUSHY
PUSHIEST > PUSHY
PUSHILY > PUSHY
PUSHINESS > PUSHY
PUSHING prep almost or nearly (a certain age, speed, etc) ▷ adj aggressively ambitious ▷ adv almost or nearly (a certain age, speed, etc)
PUSHINGLY > PUSHING
PUSHOVER n something easily achieved
PUSHOVERS > PUSHOVER
PUSHPIN n pin with a small ball-shaped head
PUSHPINS > PUSHPIN
PUSHPIT n safety rail at the stern of a boat
PUSHPITS > PUSHPIT
PUSHROD n metal rod transmitting the reciprocating motion that operates the valves of an internal-combustion engine having the camshaft in the crankcase
PUSHRODS > PUSHROD
PUSHUP n exercise in which the body is alternately raised from and lowered to the floor by the arms only, the trunk being kept straight with the toes and hands resting on the floor
PUSHUPS > PUSHUP
PUSHY adj too assertive or ambitious
PUSLE old spelling of > PUZZLE
PUSLED > PUSLE
PUSLES > PUSLE
PUSLEY same as > PURSLANE
PUSLEYS > PUSLEY
PUSLIKE > PUS
PUSLING > PUSLE
PUSS same as > PUSSY
PUSSEL n slatternly woman
PUSSELS > PUSSEL
PUSSER n naval purser
PUSSERS > PUSSER
PUSSES > PUSS
PUSSIER > PUSSY
PUSSIES > PUSSY
PUSSIEST > PUSSY
PUSSLEY n weedy trailing herb
PUSSLEYS > PUSSLEY
PUSSLIES > PUSSLY

PUSSLIKE > PUSS
PUSSLY variant of > PUSSLEY
PUSSY n cat ▷ adj containing or full of pus
PUSSYCAT same as > PUSSY
PUSSYCATS > PUSSYCAT
PUSSYFOOT vb behave too cautiously ▷ n person who pussyfoots
PUSSYTOES n type of low-growing plant
PUSTULANT adj causing the formation of pustules ▷ n agent causing such formation
PUSTULAR > PUSTULE
PUSTULATE vb form into pustules ▷ adj covered with pustules
PUSTULE n pimple containing pus
PUSTULED > PUSTULE
PUSTULES > PUSTULE
PUSTULOUS > PUSTULE
PUT vb cause to be (in a position, state, or place) ▷ n throw in putting the shot
PUTAMEN n hard endocarp or stone of fruits such as the peach, plum, and cherry
PUTAMINA > PUTAMEN
PUTATIVE adj reputed, supposed
PUTCHEON n trap for catching salmon
PUTCHEONS > PUTCHEON
PUTCHER n trap for catching salmon
PUTCHERS > PUTCHER
PUTCHOCK same as > PACHAK
PUTCHOCKS > PUTCHOCK
PUTCHUK same as > PACHAK
PUTCHUKS > PUTCHUK
PUTDOWN n snub or insult
PUTDOWNS > PUTDOWN
PUTEAL n enclosure around a well
PUTEALS > PUTEAL
PUTELI n (in India) type of boat
PUTELIS > PUTELI
PUTID adj having an unpleasant odour
PUTLOCK same as > PUTLOG
PUTLOCKS > PUTLOCK
PUTLOG n short horizontal beam that with others supports the floor planks of a scaffold
PUTLOGS > PUTLOG
PUTOFF n pretext or delay
PUTOFFS > PUTOFF
PUTOIS n brush to paint pottery
PUTON n hoax or piece of mockery
PUTONGHUA n Chinese language

PUTONS > PUTON
PUTOUT n baseball play in which the batter or runner is put out
PUTOUTS > PUTOUT
PUTREFIED > PUTREFY
PUTREFIER > PUTREFY
PUTREFIES > PUTREFY
PUTREFY vb rot and produce an offensive smell
PUTRID adj rotten and foul-smelling
PUTRIDER > PUTRID
PUTRIDEST > PUTRID
PUTRIDITY > PUTRID
PUTRIDLY > PUTRID
PUTS > PUT
PUTSCH n sudden violent attempt to remove a government from power
PUTSCHES > PUTSCH
PUTSCHIST n person taking part in putsch
PUTT n stroke on the putting green to roll the ball into or near the hole ▷ vb strike (the ball) in this way
PUTTED > PUTT
PUTTEE n (esp as part of a military uniform) strip of cloth worn wound around the leg from the ankle to the knee
PUTTEES > PUTTEE
PUTTEN old Scots past participle of > PUT
PUTTER n golf club for putting ▷ vb busy oneself in a desultory though agreeable manner
PUTTERED > PUTTER
PUTTERER > PUTTER
PUTTERERS > PUTTER
PUTTERING > PUTTER
PUTTERS > PUTTER
PUTTI > PUTTO
PUTTIE same as > PUTTEE
PUTTIED > PUTTY
PUTTIER n glazier
PUTTIERS > PUTTIER
PUTTIES > PUTTY
PUTTING > PUT
PUTTINGS > PUT
PUTTO n representation of a small boy, a cherub or cupid, esp in baroque painting or sculpture
PUTTOCK n type of bird of prey
PUTTOCKS > PUTTOCK
PUTTS > PUTT
PUTTY n stiff paste of whiting and linseed oil ▷ vb fill, fix, or coat with putty
PUTTYING > PUTTY
PUTTYLESS > PUTTY
PUTTYLIKE > PUTTY
PUTTYROOT n North American orchid
PUTURE n claim of foresters for food for men, horses, hawks, and hounds, within the bounds of the forest
PUTURES > PUTURE

PUTZ n despicable or stupid person ▷ vb waste time
PUTZED > PUTZ
PUTZES > PUTZ
PUTZING > PUTZ
PUY n small volcanic cone
PUYS > PUY
PUZEL same as > PUCELLE
PUZELS > PUZEL
PUZZEL n prostitute
PUZZELS > PUZZEL
PUZZLE vb perplex and confuse or be perplexed or confused ▷ n problem that cannot be easily solved
PUZZLED > PUZZLE
PUZZLEDLY > PUZZLE
PUZZLEDOM > PUZZLE
PUZZLER n person or thing that puzzles
PUZZLERS > PUZZLER
PUZZLES > PUZZLE
PUZZLING > PUZZLE
PUZZOLANA same as > POZZOLANA
PYA n monetary unit of Myanmar worth one hundredth of a kyat
PYAEMIA n blood poisoning with pus-forming microorganisms in the blood
PYAEMIAS > PYAEMIA
PYAEMIC > PYAEMIA
PYAS > PYA
PYAT n magpie ▷ adj pied
PYATS > PYAT
PYCNIC same as > PYKNIC
PYCNIDIA > PYCNIDIUM
PYCNIDIAL > PYCNIDIUM
PYCNIDIUM n small flask-shaped structure containing spores that occurs in ascomycetes and certain other fungi
PYCNITE n variety of topaz
PYCNITES > PYCNITE
PYCNON old word for > SEMITONE
PYCNONS > PYCNON
PYCNOSES > PYCNOSIS
PYCNOSIS n process of shrinking in a cell nucleus
PYCNOTIC > PYCNOSIS
PYE same as > PIE
PYEBALD same as > PIEBALD
PYEBALDS > PYEBALD
PYEING > PYE
PYELITIC > PYELITIS
PYELITIS n inflammation of the pelvis of the kidney
PYELOGRAM n film produced by pyelography
PYEMIA same as > PYAEMIA
PYEMIAS > PYEMIA
PYEMIC > PYAEMIA
PYENGADU variant of > PYINKADO
PYENGADUS > PYENGADU
PYES > PYE

P

PYET *same as* > PYAT

PYETS > PYET

PYGAL *n* rear part

PYGALS > PYGAL

PYGARG *n* type of horned mammal

PYGARGS > PYGARG

PYGIDIA > PYGIDIUM

PYGIDIAL > PYGIDIUM

PYGIDIUM *n* terminal segment, division, or other structure in certain annelids, arthropods, and other invertebrates

PYGIDIUMS > PYGIDIUM

PYGMAEAN > PYGMY

PYGMEAN > PYGMY

PYGMIES > PYGMY

PYGMOID *adj* of or like pygmies

PYGMY *n* something that is a very small example of its type ▷ *adj* very small

PYGMYISH > PYGMY

PYGMYISM > PYGMY

PYGMYISMS > PYGMY

PYGOSTYLE *n* vertebral bone in birds

PYIC *adj* relating to pus

PYIN *n* constituent of pus

PYINKADO *n* leguminous tree native to India and Myanmar

PYINKADOS > PYINKADO

PYINS > PYIN

PYJAMA *same as* > PYJAMAS

PYJAMAED > PYJAMAS

PYJAMAS *npl* loose-fitting trousers and top worn in bed

PYKNIC *adj* (of a physical type) characterized by a broad squat fleshy physique with a large chest and abdomen ▷ *n* person with this physical type

PYKNICS > PYKNIC

PYKNOSES > PYKNOSIS

PYKNOSIS *n* thickening of a cell

PYKNOSOME *n* stocky body type

PYKNOTIC > PYKNOSIS

PYLON *n* steel tower-like structure supporting electrical cables

PYLONS > PYLON

PYLORI > PYLORUS

PYLORIC > PYLORUS

PYLORUS *n* small circular opening at the base of the stomach through which partially digested food (chyme) passes to the duodenum

PYLORUSES > PYLORUS

PYNE *archaic variant of* > PINE

PYNED > PYNE

PYNES > PYNE

PYNING > PYNE

PYODERMA *n* any skin eruption characterized by pustules or the formation of pus

PYODERMAS > PYODERMA

PYODERMIC > PYODERMA

PYOGENIC *adj* of or relating to the formation of pus

PYOID *adj* resembling pus

PYONER *old variant of* > PIONEER

PYONERS > PYONER

PYONINGS *n* old term for the work of pioneers

PYORRHEA *same as* > PYORRHOEA

PYORRHEAL > PYORRHOEA

PYORRHEAS > PYORRHEA

PYORRHEIC > PYORRHOEA

PYORRHOEA *n* disease of the gums and tooth sockets which causes bleeding of the gums and the formation of pus

PYOSES > PYOSIS

PYOSIS *n* formation of pus

PYOT *same as* > PYAT

PYOTS > PYOT

PYRACANTH *n* type of thorny shrub

PYRAL > PYRE

PYRALID *n* tropical moth

PYRALIDID *same as* > PYRALID

PYRALIDS > PYRALID

PYRALIS *same as* > PYRALID

PYRALISES > PYRALIS

PYRAMID *n* solid figure with a flat base and triangular sides sloping upwards to a point ▷ *vb* build up or be arranged in the form of a pyramid

PYRAMIDAL > PYRAMID

PYRAMIDED > PYRAMID

PYRAMIDES > PYRAMIS

PYRAMIDIA *n* pyramidal apices of obelisks

PYRAMIDIC > PYRAMID

PYRAMIDON *n* type of pipe for an organ

PYRAMIDS > PYRAMID

PYRAMIS *n* pyramid-shaped structure

PYRAMISES > PYRAMIS

PYRAN *n* unsaturated heterocyclic compound having a ring containing five carbon atoms and one oxygen atom and two double bonds

PYRANOID > PYRAN

PYRANOSE *n* structure in many sugars

PYRANOSES > PYRANOSE

PYRANS > PYRAN

PYRAZOLE *n* crystalline soluble basic heterocyclic compound

PYRAZOLES > PYRAZOLE

PYRE *n* pile of wood for burning a corpse on

PYRENE *n* solid polynuclear aromatic hydrocarbon extracted from coal tar

PYRENEITE *n* dark mineral found in the Pyrenees

PYRENES > PYRENE

PYRENOID *n* any of various small protein granules that occur in certain algae, mosses, and protozoans and are involved in the synthesis of starch

PYRENOIDS > PYRENOID

PYRES > PYRE

PYRETHRIN *n* oily water-insoluble compound used as an insecticide

PYRETHRUM *n* Eurasian chrysanthemum with white, pink, red, or purple flowers

PYRETIC *adj* of, relating to, or characterized by fever

PYREX *n* tradename for any of a variety of borosilicate glasses that have low coefficients of expansion, making them suitable for heat-resistant glassware used in cookery and chemical apparatus

PYREXES > PYREX

PYREXIA *technical name for* > FEVER

PYREXIAL > PYREXIA

PYREXIAS > PYREXIA

PYREXIC > PYREXIA

PYRIC *adj* of or relating to burning

PYRIDIC > PYRIDINE

PYRIDINE *n* colourless hygroscopic liquid with a characteristic odour

PYRIDINES > PYRIDINE

PYRIDOXAL *n* naturally occurring derivative of pyridoxine that is a precursor of a coenzyme involved in several enzymic reactions

PYRIDOXIN *n* derivative of pyridine

PYRIFORM *adj* (esp of organs of the body) pear-shaped

PYRITE *n* yellow mineral consisting of iron sulphide in cubic crystalline form

PYRITES *same as* > PYRITE

PYRITIC > PYRITE

PYRITICAL > PYRITE

PYRITISE *same as* > PYRITIZE

PYRITISED > PYRITISE

PYRITISES > PYRITISE

PYRITIZE *vb* convert into pyrites

PYRITIZED > PYRITIZE

PYRITIZES > PYRITIZE

PYRITOUS > PYRITE

PYRO *n* pyromaniac

PYROCERAM *n* transparent ceramic material

PYROCLAST *n* piece of lava ejected from a volcano

PYROGEN *n* any of a group of substances that cause a rise in temperature in an animal body

PYROGENIC *adj* produced by or producing heat

PYROGENS > PYROGEN

PYROLA *n* evergreen perennial

PYROLAS > PYROLA

PYROLATER *n* worshipper of fire

PYROLATRY > PYROLATER

PYROLISE *same as* > PYROLIZE

PYROLISED > PYROLISE

PYROLISES > PYROLISE

PYROLIZE *vb* subject to pyrolysis

PYROLIZED > PYROLIZE

PYROLIZES > PYROLIZE

PYROLOGY *n* study of heat

PYROLYSE *vb* subject to pyrolysis

PYROLYSED > PYROLYSE

PYROLYSER > PYROLYSE

PYROLYSES > PYROLYSE

PYROLYSIS *n* application of heat to chemical compounds in order to cause decomposition

PYROLYTIC > PYROLYSIS

PYROLYZE *same as* > PYROLYSE

PYROLYZED > PYROLYZE

PYROLYZER > PYROLYZE

PYROLYZES > PYROLYZE

PYROMANCY *n* divination by fire or flames

PYROMANIA *n* uncontrollable urge to set things on fire

PYROMETER *n* instrument for measuring high temperatures

PYROMETRY > PYROMETER

PYRONE *n* type of heterocyclic compound

PYRONES > PYRONE

PYRONINE *n* red dye used as biological stain

PYRONINES > PYRONINE

PYROPE *n* deep yellowish-red garnet that consists of magnesium aluminium silicate and is used as a gemstone

PYROPES > PYROPE

PYROPHONE *n* musical instrument using hydrogen flames

PYROPUS *variant of* > PYROPE

PYROPUSES > PYROPUS

PYROS > PYRO

PYROSCOPE *n* instrument for measuring intensity of heat

PYROSES > PYROSIS

PYROSIS *technical name for* > HEARTBURN

PYROSISES > PYROSIS

PYROSOME *n* tube-shaped glowing marine creature

PYROSOMES > PYROSOME

PYROSTAT *n* device that activates an alarm or extinguisher in the event of a fire

PYROSTATS > PYROSTAT

PYROXENE *n* silicate mineral

PYROXENES > PYROXENE

PYROXENIC > PYROXENE

PYROXYLE *same as* > PYROXYLIN

PYROXYLES > PYROXYLE

PYROXYLIC > PYROXYLIN

PYROXYLIN *n* yellow substance obtained by nitrating cellulose with a mixture of nitric and sulphuric acids

PYRRHIC *n* metrical foot of two short or unstressed syllables ▷ *adj* of or relating to such a metrical foot

PYRRHICS > PYRRHIC

PYRRHOUS *adj* ruddy or reddish

PYRROL *same as* > PYRROLE

PYRROLE *n* colourless insoluble toxic liquid with a five-membered ring containing one nitrogen atom

PYRROLES > PYRROLE

PYRROLIC > PYRROLE

PYRROLS > PYRROL

PYRUVATE *n* ester or salt of pyruvic acid

PYRUVATES > PYRUVATE

PYRUVIC as in *pyruvic acid* colourless pleasant-smelling liquid

PYTHIUM *n* type of fungi

PYTHIUMS > PYTHIUM

PYTHON *n* large nonpoisonous snake that crushes its prey

PYTHONESS *n* woman, such as Apollo's priestess at Delphi, believed to be possessed by an oracular spirit

PYTHONIC > PYTHON

PYTHONS > PYTHON

PYURIA *n* any condition characterized by the presence of pus in the urine

PYURIAS > PYURIA

PYX *n* any receptacle for the Eucharistic Host ▷ *vb* put (something) in a pyx

PYXED > PYX

PYXES > PYX

PYXIDES > PYXIS

PYXIDIA > PYXIDIUM

PYXIDIUM *n* dry fruit of such plants as the plantain

PYXIE *n* creeping evergreen shrub of the eastern US with small white or pink star-shaped flowers

PYXIES > PYXIE

PYXING > PYX

PYXIS *same as* > PYXIDIUM

PZAZZ *same as* > PIZZAZZ

PZAZZES > PZAZZ

P

Qq

QABALA *same as*
> KABBALAH
QABALAH *same as*
> KABBALAH
QABALAHS > QABALAH
QABALAS > QABALA
QABALISM > QABALAH
QABALISMS > QABALAH
QABALIST > QABALAH
QABALISTS > QABALAH
QADI *variant spelling of*
> CADI
QADIS > QADI
QAID *n* chief
QAIDS > QAID
QAIMAQAM *n* Turkish
officer or official
QAIMAQAMS > QAIMAQAM
QALAMDAN *n* writing case
QALAMDANS > QALAMDAN
QANAT *n* underground
irrigation channel
QANATS > QANAT
QASIDA *n* Arabic verse
form
QASIDAS > QASIDA
QAT *variant spelling of*
> KHAT
QATS > QAT
QAWWAL *n* qawwali singer
QAWWALI *n* Islamic
religious song, esp in Asia
QAWWALIS > QAWWALI
QAWWALS > QAWWAL
QI *variant of* > KI
QIBLA *variant of* > KIBLAH
QIBLAS > QIBLA
QIGONG *n* system of
breathing and exercise
designed to benefit both
physical and mental health
QIGONGS > QIGONG
QIN *n* Chinese stringed
instrument related to the
zither
QINDAR *n* Albanian
monetary unit worth one
hundredth of a lek
QINDARKA > QINDAR
QINDARS > QINDAR
QINGHAOSU *n* Chinese
herb
QINS > QIN
QINTAR *same as* > QINDAR
QINTARKA > QINTAR
QINTARS > QINTAR
QIS > QI
QIVIUT *n* soft muskox
wool
QIVIUTS > QIVIUT

QOPH *variant of* > KOPH
QOPHS > QOPH
QORMA *variant spelling of*
> KORMA
QORMAS > QORMA
QUA *prep* in the capacity of
QUAALUDE *n*
methaqualone
QUAALUDES > QUAALUDE
QUACK *vb* (of a duck) utter a
harsh guttural sound ▷ *n*
an unqualified person who
claims medical knowledge
QUACKED > QUACK
QUACKER > QUACK
QUACKERS > QUACK
QUACKERY *n* activities or
methods of a quack
QUACKIER > QUACK
QUACKIEST > QUACK
QUACKING > QUACK
QUACKISH > QUACK
QUACKISM *same as*
> QUACKERY
QUACKISMS > QUACKISM
QUACKLE *same as* > QUACK
QUACKLED > QUACKLE
QUACKLES > QUACKLE
QUACKLING > QUACKLE
QUACKS > QUACK
QUACKY > QUACK
QUAD *n* quadrangle
QUADDED *adj* formed of
multiple quads
QUADDING *n* birdwatching
in a specified area
QUADPLAY *same as*
> FOURPLAY
QUADPLAYS > QUADPLAY
QUADPLEX *n* apartment
on four floors
QUADRANS *n* Roman coin
QUADRANT *n* quarter of a
circle
QUADRANTS > QUADRANT
QUADRAT *n* area of
vegetation, often one
square metre, marked out
for study of the plants in
the surrounding area
QUADRATE *n* cube or
square, or a square or
cubelike object ▷ *vb* make
square or rectangular ▷ *adj*
of or relating to this bone
QUADRATED > QUADRATE
QUADRATES > QUADRATE
QUADRATIC *n* equation in
which the variable is raised
to the power of two, but
nowhere raised to a higher

power ▷ *adj* of the second
power
QUADRATS > QUADRAT
QUADRATUS *n* type of
muscle
QUADRELLA *n* four
nominated horseraces in
which the punter bets on
selecting the four winners
QUADRIC *adj* having or
characterized by an
equation of the second
degree, usually in two or
three variables ▷ *n* quadric
curve, surface, or function
QUADRICEP *n* muscle in
thigh
QUADRICS > QUADRIC
QUADRIFID *adj* divided
into four lobes or other
parts
QUADRIGA *n* (in the
classical world) a
two-wheeled chariot
drawn by four horses
abreast
QUADRIGAE > QUADRIGA
QUADRIGAS > QUADRIGA
QUADRILLE *n* square
dance for four couples
QUADRIVIA *n* higher
divisions of the seven
liberal arts
QUADROON *n* an offensive
term for the offspring of a
mulatto and a white person
QUADROONS > QUADROON
QUADRUMAN *n* nonhuman
primate
QUADRUPED *n* any animal
with four legs ▷ *adj* having
four feet
QUADRUPLE *vb* multiply by
four ▷ *adj* four times as
much or as many ▷ *n*
quantity or number four
times as great as another
QUADRUPLY
> QUADRUPLE
QUADS > QUAD
QUAERE *n* query or
question ▷ *interj* ask or
inquire: used esp to
introduce a question ▷ *vb*
ask
QUAERED > QUAERE
QUAEREING > QUAERE
QUAERES > QUAERE
QUAERITUR *sentence
substitute* question is asked
QUAESITUM *n* object
sought

QUAESTOR *n* any of several
magistrates of ancient
Rome, usually a financial
administrator
QUAESTORS > QUAESTOR
QUAFF *vb* drink heartily or
in one draught
QUAFFABLE > QUAFF
QUAFFED > QUAFF
QUAFFER > QUAFF
QUAFFERS > QUAFF
QUAFFING > QUAFF
QUAFFS > QUAFF
QUAG *another word for*
> QUAGMIRE
QUAGGA *n* recently extinct
zebra, striped only on the
head and shoulders
QUAGGAS > QUAGGA
QUAGGIER > QUAGGY
QUAGGIEST > QUAGGY
QUAGGY *adj* resembling a
marsh or quagmire
QUAGMIRE *n* soft wet area
of land ▷ *vb* bog down
QUAGMIRED > QUAGMIRE
QUAGMIRES > QUAGMIRE
QUAGMIRY > QUAGMIRE
QUAGS > QUAG
QUAHAUG *same as*
> QUAHOG
QUAHAUGS > QUAHAUG
QUAHOG *n* edible clam
QUAHOGS > QUAHOG
QUAI *same as* > QUAY
QUAICH *n* small shallow
drinking cup, usually with
two handles
QUAICHES > QUAICH
QUAICHS > QUAICH
QUAIGH *same as* > QUAICH
QUAIGHS > QUAIGH
QUAIL *n* small game bird of
the partridge family ▷ *vb*
shrink back with fear
QUAILED > QUAIL
QUAILING > QUAIL
QUAILINGS > QUAIL
QUAILS > QUAIL
QUAINT *adj* attractively
unusual, esp in an
old-fashioned style
QUAINTER > QUAINT
QUAINTEST > QUAINT
QUAINTLY > QUAINT
QUAIR *n* book
QUAIRS > QUAIR
QUAIS > QUAI
QUAKE *vb* shake or tremble
with or as if with fear ▷ *n*
earthquake

QUAKED > QUAKE
QUAKER > QUAKE
QUAKERS > QUAKE
QUAKES > QUAKE
QUAKIER > QUAKY
QUAKIEST > QUAKY
QUAKILY > QUAKY
QUAKINESS > QUAKY
QUAKING > QUAKE
QUAKINGLY > QUAKE
QUAKINGS > QUAKE
QUAKY *adj* inclined to quake
QUALE *n* essential property or quality
QUALIA > QUALE
QUALIFIED > QUALIFY
QUALIFIER *n* person or thing that qualifies, esp a contestant in a competition who wins a preliminary heat or contest and so earns the right to take part in the next round
QUALIFIES > QUALIFY
QUALIFY *vb* provide or be provided with the abilities necessary for a task, office, or duty
QUALITIED *adj* possessing qualities
QUALITIES > QUALITY
QUALITY *n* degree or standard of excellence ▷ *adj* excellent or superior
QUALM *n* pang of conscience
QUALMIER > QUALM
QUALMIEST > QUALM
QUALMING *adj* having a qualm
QUALMISH > QUALM
QUALMLESS > QUALM
QUALMS > QUALM
QUALMY > QUALM
QUAMASH another name for **>** CAMASS
QUAMASHES > QUAMASH
QUANDANG same as **>** QUANDONG
QUANDANGS > QUANDANG
QUANDARY *n* difficult situation or dilemma
QUANDONG *n* small Australian tree with edible fruit and nuts used in preserves
QUANDONGS > QUANDONG
QUANGO *n* quasi-autonomous nongovernmental organization: any partly independent official body set up by a government
QUANGOS > QUANGO
QUANNET *n* flat file with handle at one end
QUANNETS > QUANNET
QUANT *n* long pole for propelling a boat, esp a punt, by pushing on the bottom of a river or lake ▷ *vb* propel (a boat) with a quant
QUANTA > QUANTUM

QUANTAL *adj* of or relating to a quantum or an entity that is quantized
QUANTALLY > QUANTAL
QUANTED > QUANT
QUANTIC *n* mathematical function
QUANTICAL > QUANTIC
QUANTICS > QUANTIC
QUANTIFY *vb* discover or express the quantity of
QUANTILE *n* element of a division
QUANTILES > QUANTILE
QUANTING > QUANT
QUANTISE same as **>** QUANTIZE
QUANTISED > QUANTISE
QUANTISER > QUANTISE
QUANTISES > QUANTISE
QUANTITY *n* specified or definite amount or number
QUANTIZE *vb* restrict (a physical quantity) to one of a set of values characterized by quantum numbers
QUANTIZED > QUANTIZE
QUANTIZER > QUANTIZE
QUANTIZES > QUANTIZE
QUANTONG same as **>** QUANDONG
QUANTONGS > QUANTONG
QUANTS > QUANT
QUANTUM *n* desired or required amount, esp a very small one ▷ *adj* of or designating a major breakthrough or sudden advance
QUANTUMS > QUANTUM
QUARE *adj* remarkable or strange
QUARENDEN *n* dark-red apple
QUARENDER same as **>** QUARENDEN
QUARER > QUARE
QUAREST > QUARE
QUARK *n* subatomic particle thought to be the fundamental unit of matter
QUARKS > QUARK
QUARREL *n* angry disagreement ▷ *vb* have a disagreement or dispute
QUARRELED > QUARREL
QUARRELER > QUARREL
QUARRELS > QUARREL
QUARRIAN *n* cockatiel of scrub and woodland regions of inland Australia
QUARRIANS > QUARRIAN
QUARRIED > QUARRY
QUARRIER another word for **>** QUARRYMAN
QUARRIERS > QUARRIER
QUARRIES > QUARRY
QUARRION same as **>** QUARRIAN
QUARRIONS > QUARRION
QUARRY *n* place where stone is dug from the surface of the earth ▷ *vb* extract (stone) from a

quarry
QUARRYING > QUARRY
QUARRYMAN *n* man who works in or manages a quarry
QUARRYMEN **>** QUARRYMAN
QUART *n* unit of liquid measure equal to two pints (1.136 litres)
QUARTAN *adj* (esp of a malarial fever) occurring every third day ▷ *n* quartan malaria
QUARTANS > QUARTAN
QUARTE *n* fourth of eight basic positions from which a parry or attack can be made in fencing
QUARTER *n* one of four equal parts of something ▷ *vb* divide into four equal parts ▷ *adj* being or consisting of one of four equal parts
QUARTERED *adj* (of a shield) divided into four sections, each having contrasting arms or having two sets of arms, each repeated in diagonally opposite corners
QUARTERER > QUARTER
QUARTERLY *adj* occurring, due, or issued at intervals of three months ▷ *n* magazine issued every three months ▷ *adv* once every three months
QUARTERN *n* fourth part of certain weights or measures, such as a peck or a pound
QUARTERNS > QUARTERN
QUARTERS *npl* accommodation, esp as provided for military personnel
QUARTES > QUARTE
QUARTET *n* group of four performers
QUARTETS > QUARTET
QUARTETT same as **>** QUARTET
QUARTETTE same as **>** QUARTET
QUARTETTI **>** QUARTETTO
QUARTETTO same as **>** QUARTET
QUARTETTS > QUARTETT
QUARTIC *n* biquadratic equation
QUARTICS > QUARTIC
QUARTIER *n* city district
QUARTIERS > QUARTIER
QUARTILE *n* one of three values of a variable dividing its distribution into four groups with equal frequencies ▷ *adj* of a quartile
QUARTILES > QUARTILE
QUARTO *n* book size in which the sheets are folded into four leaves

QUARTOS > QUARTO
QUARTS > QUART
QUARTZ *n* hard glossy mineral
QUARTZES > QUARTZ
QUARTZIER > QUARTZ
QUARTZITE *n* very hard metamorphic rock consisting of a mosaic of intergrown quartz crystals
QUARTZOSE > QUARTZ
QUARTZOUS > QUARTZ
QUARTZY > QUARTZ
QUASAR *n* extremely distant starlike object that emits powerful radio waves
QUASARS > QUASAR
QUASH *vb* annul or make void
QUASHED > QUASH
QUASHEE same as **>** QUASHIE
QUASHEES > QUASHEE
QUASHER > QUASH
QUASHERS > QUASH
QUASHES > QUASH
QUASHIE *n* in the Carribbean, an unsophisticated or gullible male Black peasant
QUASHIES > QUASHIE
QUASHING > QUASH
QUASI *adv* as if
QUASS variant of **>** KVASS
QUASSES > QUASS
QUASSIA *n* tropical American tree, the wood of which yields a substance used in insecticides
QUASSIAS > QUASSIA
QUASSIN *n* bitter crystalline substance
QUASSINS > QUASSIN
QUAT *n* spot
QUATCH *vb* move
QUATCHED > QUATCH
QUATCHES > QUATCH
QUATCHING > QUATCH
QUATE *n* fortune
QUATORZE *n* cards worth 14 points in piquet
QUATORZES > QUATORZE
QUATRAIN *n* stanza or poem of four lines
QUATRAINS > QUATRAIN
QUATRE *n* playing card with four pips
QUATRES > QUATRE
QUATS > QUAT
QUAVER *vb* (of a voice) quiver or tremble ▷ *n* note half the length of a crotchet
QUAVERED > QUAVER
QUAVERER > QUAVER
QUAVERERS > QUAVER
QUAVERIER > QUAVER
QUAVERING > QUAVER
QUAVERS > QUAVER
QUAVERY > QUAVER
QUAY *n* wharf built parallel to the shore
QUAYAGE *n* system of quays
QUAYAGES > QUAYAGE

QUAYD archaic past participle of > QUAIL
QUAYLIKE > QUAY
QUAYS > QUAY
QUAYSIDE n edge of a quay along the water
QUAYSIDES > QUAYSIDE
QUAZZIER > QUAZZY
QUAZZIEST > QUAZZY
QUAZZY adj unwell
QUBIT n quantum bit
QUBITS > QUBIT
QUBYTE n unit of eight qubits
QUBYTES > QUBYTE
QUEACH n thicket
QUEACHES > QUEACH
QUEACHIER > QUEACHY
QUEACHY adj unwell
QUEAN n boisterous, impudent, or disreputable woman
QUEANS > QUEAN
QUEASIER > QUEASY
QUEASIEST > QUEASY
QUEASILY > QUEASY
QUEASY adj having the feeling that one is about to vomit
QUEAZIER > QUEAZY
QUEAZIEST > QUEAZY
QUEAZY same as > QUEASY
QUEBEC n code word for the letter Q
QUEBECS > QUEBEC
QUEBRACHO n anacardiaceous South American tree
QUEECHIER > QUEECHY
QUEECHY same as > QUEACHY
QUEEN n female sovereign who is the official ruler or head of state ▷ vb flaunt one's homosexuality
QUEENCAKE n small light cake containing currants
QUEENDOM n territory, state, people, or community ruled over by a queen
QUEENDOMS > QUEENDOM
QUEENED > QUEEN
QUEENFISH n type of Californian marine fish
QUEENHOOD > QUEEN
QUEENIE n scallop
QUEENIER > QUEENY
QUEENIES > QUEENIE
QUEENIEST > QUEENY
QUEENING > QUEEN
QUEENINGS > QUEEN
QUEENITE n supporter of a queen
QUEENITES > QUEENITE
QUEENLESS > QUEEN
QUEENLET n queen of a small realm
QUEENLETS > QUEENLET
QUEENLIER > QUEENLY
QUEENLY adj resembling or appropriate to a queen ▷ adv in a manner appropriate to a queen

QUEENS > QUEEN
QUEENSHIP > QUEEN
QUEENSIDE n half of a chessboard in which the queen starts
QUEENY adj effeminate
QUEER adj not normal or usual ▷ n derogatory name for a homosexual person ▷ vb spoil or thwart
QUEERDOM n gay culture
QUEERDOMS > QUEERDOM
QUEERED > QUEER
QUEERER > QUEER
QUEEREST > QUEER
QUEERING > QUEER
QUEERISH > QUEER
QUEERITY > QUEER
QUEERLY > QUEER
QUEERNESS > QUEER
QUEERS > QUEER
QUEEST n wood pigeon
QUEESTS > QUEEST
QUEINT same as > QUAINT
QUELCH same as > SQUELCH
QUELCHED > QUELCH
QUELCHES > QUELCH
QUELCHING > QUELCH
QUELEA n East African weaver bird
QUELEAS > QUELEA
QUELL vb suppress
QUELLABLE > QUELL
QUELLED > QUELL
QUELLER > QUELL
QUELLERS > QUELL
QUELLING > QUELL
QUELLS > QUELL
QUEME vb please
QUEMED > QUEME
QUEMES > QUEME
QUEMING > QUEME
QUENA n Andean flute
QUENAS > QUENA
QUENCH vb satisfy (one's thirst)
QUENCHED > QUENCH
QUENCHER > QUENCH
QUENCHERS > QUENCH
QUENCHES > QUENCH
QUENCHING > QUENCH
QUENELLE n finely sieved mixture of cooked meat or fish, shaped into various forms and cooked in stock or fried as croquettes
QUENELLES > QUENELLE
QUEP interj expression of derision
QUERCETIC > QUERCETIN
QUERCETIN n yellow crystalline pigment found naturally in the rind and bark of many plants
QUERCETUM n group of oak trees
QUERCINE adj of or relating to oak trees
QUERCITIN same as > QUERCETIN
QUERIDA n sweetheart
QUERIDAS > QUERIDA

QUERIED > QUERY
QUERIER > QUERY
QUERIERS > QUERY
QUERIES > QUERY
QUERIMONY n complaint
QUERIST n person who makes inquiries or queries
QUERISTS > QUERIST
QUERN n stone hand mill for grinding corn
QUERNS > QUERN
QUERULOUS adj complaining or whining
QUERY n question, esp one raising doubt ▷ vb express uncertainty, doubt, or an objection concerning (something)
QUERYING > QUERY
QUERYINGS > QUERY
QUEST n long and difficult search ▷ vb go in search of
QUESTANT n one who quests
QUESTANTS > QUEST
QUESTED > QUEST
QUESTER > QUEST
QUESTERS > QUEST
QUESTING > QUEST
QUESTINGS > QUEST
QUESTION n form of words addressed to a person in order to obtain an answer ▷ vb put a question or questions to (a person)
QUESTIONS > QUESTION
QUESTOR same as > QUAESTOR
QUESTORS > QUESTOR
QUESTRIST n one who quests
QUESTS > QUEST
QUETCH vb move
QUETCHED > QUETCH
QUETCHES > QUETCH
QUETCHING > QUETCH
QUETHE vb say
QUETHES > QUETHE
QUETHING > QUETHE
QUETSCH n plum brandy
QUETSCHES > QUETSCH
QUETZAL n crested bird of Central and N South America
QUETZALES > QUETZAL
QUETZALS > QUETZAL
QUEUE n line of people or vehicles waiting for something ▷ vb form or remain in a line while waiting
QUEUED > QUEUE
QUEUEING > QUEUE
QUEUEINGS > QUEUE
QUEUER > QUEUE
QUEUERS > QUEUE
QUEUES > QUEUE
QUEUING > QUEUE
QUEUINGS > QUEUE
QUEY n young cow
QUEYN n girl
QUEYNIE same as > QUEYN
QUEYNIES > QUEYNIE
QUEYNS > QUEYN

QUEYS > QUEY
QUEZAL same as > QUETZAL
QUEZALES > QUEZAL
QUEZALS > QUEZAL
QUIBBLE vb make trivial objections ▷ n trivial objection
QUIBBLED > QUIBBLE
QUIBBLER > QUIBBLE
QUIBBLERS > QUIBBLE
QUIBBLES > QUIBBLE
QUIBBLING > QUIBBLE
QUIBLIN same as > QUIBBLE
QUIBLINS > QUIBLIN
QUICH vb move
QUICHE n savoury flan with an egg custard filling to which vegetables etc are added
QUICHED > QUICH
QUICHES > QUICHE
QUICHING > QUICH
QUICK adj speedy, fast ▷ n area of sensitive flesh under a nail ▷ adv in a rapid manner
QUICKBEAM n rowan tree
QUICKEN vb make or become faster ▷ n rowan tree
QUICKENED > QUICKEN
QUICKENER > QUICKEN
QUICKENS > QUICKEN
QUICKER > QUICK
QUICKEST > QUICK
QUICKIE n anything done or made hurriedly ▷ adj made or done rapidly
QUICKIES > QUICKIE
QUICKLIME n white solid used in the manufacture of glass and steel
QUICKLY > QUICK
QUICKNESS > QUICK
QUICKS > QUICK
QUICKSAND n deep mass of loose wet sand that sucks anything on top of it into it
QUICKSET adj (of plants or cuttings) planted so as to form a hedge ▷ n hedge composed of such plants
QUICKSETS > QUICKSET
QUICKSTEP n fast modern ballroom dance ▷ vb perform this dance
QUICKY n hastily arranged divorce
QUID n pound (sterling)
QUIDAM n specified person
QUIDAMS > QUIDAM
QUIDDANY n quince jelly
QUIDDIT same as > QUIDDITY
QUIDDITCH n imaginary game in which players fly on broomsticks
QUIDDITS > QUIDDIT
QUIDDITY n essential nature of something
QUIDDLE vb waste time
QUIDDLED > QUIDDLE

QUIDDLER > QUIDDLE

QUIDDLERS > QUIDDLE

QUIDDLES > QUIDDLE

QUIDDLING > QUIDDLE

QUIDNUNC n person eager to learn news and scandal

QUIDNUNCS > QUIDNUNC

QUIDS > QUID

QUIESCE vb quieten

QUIESCED > QUIETEN

QUIESCENT adj quiet, inactive, or dormant

QUIESCES > QUIESCE

QUIESCING > QUIESCE

QUIET adj with little noise ▷ n quietness ▷ vb make or become quiet

QUIETED > QUIET

QUIETEN vb make or become quiet

QUIETENED > QUIETEN

QUIETENER > QUIETEN

QUIETENS > QUIETEN

QUIETER > QUIET

QUIETERS > QUIET

QUIETEST > QUIET

QUIETING > QUIET

QUIETINGS > QUIET

QUIETISM n passivity and calmness of mind towards external events

QUIETISMS > QUIETISM

QUIETIST > QUIETISM

QUIETISTS > QUIETISM

QUIETIVE n sedative drug

QUIETIVES > QUIETIVE

QUIETLY > QUIET

QUIETNESS > QUIET

QUIETS > QUIET

QUIETSOME > QUIET

QUIETUDE n quietness, peace, or tranquillity

QUIETUDES > QUIETUDE

QUIETUS n release from life

QUIETUSES > QUIETUS

QUIFF n tuft of hair brushed up above the forehead

QUIFFS > QUIFF

QUIGHT vb quit

QUIGHTED > QUIGHT

QUIGHTING > QUIGHT

QUIGHTS > QUIGHT

QUILL n pen made from the feather of a bird's wing or tail ▷ vb wind (thread, yarn, etc) onto a spool or bobbin

QUILLAI another name for > SOAPBARK

QUILLAIA same as > QUILLAI

QUILLAIAS > QUILLAIA

QUILLAIS > QUILLAI

QUILLAJA same as > QUILLAI

QUILLAJAS > QUILLAJA

QUILLBACK n freshwater fish

QUILLED > QUILL

QUILLET n quibble or subtlety

QUILLETS > QUILLET

QUILLING n decorative craftwork in which material such as glass, fabric or paper is formed into small bands or rolls that form the basis of a design

QUILLINGS > QUILLING

QUILLMAN n clerk

QUILLMEN > QUILLMAN

QUILLON n either half of the extended crosspiece of a sword or dagger

QUILLONS > QUILLON

QUILLS > QUILL

QUILLWORK n embroidery using porcupine quills

QUILLWORT n aquatic tracheophyte plant with quill-like leaves

QUILT n padded covering for a bed ▷ vb stitch together two layers of (fabric) with padding between them

QUILTED > QUILT

QUILTER > QUILT

QUILTERS > QUILT

QUILTING n material used for making a quilt

QUILTINGS > QUILTING

QUILTS > QUILT

QUIM n taboo word for the female genitals

QUIMS > QUIM

QUIN short for > QUINTUPLET

QUINA n quinine

QUINARIES > QUINARY

QUINARY adj consisting of fives or by fives ▷ n set of five

QUINAS > QUINA

QUINATE adj arranged in or composed of five parts

QUINCE n acid-tasting pear-shaped fruit

QUINCES > QUINCE

QUINCHE vb move

QUINCHED > QUINCHE

QUINCHES > QUINCHE

QUINCHING > QUINCHE

QUINCUNX n group of five objects arranged in the shape of a rectangle with one at each corner and the fifth in the centre

QUINE variant of > QUEAN

QUINELA same as > QUINELLA

QUINELAS > QUINELA

QUINELLA n form of betting on a horse race in which the punter bets on selecting the first and second place-winners in any order

QUINELLAS > QUINELLA

QUINES > QUINE

QUINIC as in quinic acid white crystalline soluble optically active carboxylic acid

QUINIDINE n crystalline alkaloid drug

QUINIE n girl

QUINIELA same as > QUINELLA

QUINIELAS > QUINIELA

QUINIES > QUINIE

QUININ same as > QUININE

QUININA same as > QUININE

QUININAS > QUININA

QUININE n bitter drug used as a tonic and formerly to treat malaria

QUININES > QUININE

QUININS > QUININ

QUINNAT n Pacific salmon

QUINNATS > QUINNAT

QUINO same as > KENO

QUINOA n type of grain high in nutrients

QUINOAS > QUINOA

QUINOID same as > QUINONOID

QUINOIDAL > QUINOID

QUINOIDS > QUINOID

QUINOL n white crystalline soluble phenol used as a photographic developer

QUINOLIN same as > QUINOLINE

QUINOLINE n oily colourless insoluble basic heterocyclic compound

QUINOLINS > QUINOLIN

QUINOLONE n any of a group of synthetic antibiotics

QUINOLS > QUINOL

QUINONE n yellow crystalline water-soluble unsaturated ketone

QUINONES > QUINONE

QUINONOID adj of, resembling, or derived from quinone

QUINOS > QUINO

QUINQUINA same as > QUININE

QUINS > QUIN

QUINSIED > QUINSY

QUINSIES > QUINSY

QUINSY n inflammation of the throat or tonsils

QUINT same as > QUIN

QUINTA n Portuguese vineyard where grapes for wine or port are grown

QUINTAIN n post or target set up for tilting exercises for mounted knights or foot soldiers

QUINTAINS > QUINTAIN

QUINTAL n unit of weight equal to (esp in Britain) 112 pounds (50.85 kg) or (esp in US) 100 pounds (45.36 kg)

QUINTALS > QUINTAL

QUINTAN adj (of a fever) occurring every fourth day ▷ n quintan fever

QUINTANS > QUINTAN

QUINTAR n Albanian unit of currency

QUINTARS > QUINTAR

QUINTAS > QUINTA

QUINTE n fifth of eight

basic positions from which a parry or attack can be made in fencing

QUINTES > QUINTE

QUINTET n group of five performers

QUINTETS > QUINTET

QUINTETT same as > QUINTET

QUINTETTE same as > QUINTET

QUINTETTI > QUINTETTO

QUINTETTO same as > QUINTET

QUINTETTS > QUINTETT

QUINTIC adj of or relating to the fifth degree ▷ n mathematical function

QUINTICS > QUINTIC

QUINTILE n aspect of 72° between two heavenly bodies

QUINTILES > QUINTILE

QUINTIN same as > QUINTAIN

QUINTINS > QUINTIN

QUINTROON n person with one Black great-great-grandparent

QUINTS > QUINT

QUINTUPLE vb multiply by five ▷ adj five times as much or as many ▷ n quantity or number five times as great as another

QUINTUPLY > QUINTUPLE

QUINZE n card game with rules similar to those of vingt-et-un, except that the score aimed at is 15 rather than 21

QUINZES > QUINZE

QUIP n witty saying ▷ vb make a quip

QUIPO same as > QUIPU

QUIPOS > QUIPO

QUIPPED > QUIP

QUIPPER > QUIP

QUIPPERS > QUIP

QUIPPIER > QUIP

QUIPPIEST > QUIP

QUIPPING > QUIP

QUIPPISH > QUIP

QUIPPU same as > QUIPU

QUIPPUS > QUIPPU

QUIPPY > QUIP

QUIPS > QUIP

QUIPSTER n person inclined to make sarcastic or witty remarks

QUIPSTERS > QUIPSTER

QUIPU n device of the Incas of Peru used to record information, consisting of an arrangement of variously coloured and knotted cords attached to a base cord

QUIPUS > QUIPU

QUIRE n set of 24 or 25 sheets of paper ▷ vb arrange in quires

QUIRED > QUIRE

q

QUIRES > QUIRE
QUIRING > QUIRE
QUIRISTER *same as*
> CHORISTER
QUIRK *n* peculiarity of
character ▷ *vb* quip
QUIRKED > QUIRK
QUIRKIER > QUIRK
QUIRKIEST > QUIRK
QUIRKILY > QUIRK
QUIRKING > QUIRK
QUIRKISH > QUIRK
QUIRKS > QUIRK
QUIRKY > QUIRK
QUIRT *n* whip with a
leather thong at one end
▷ *vb* strike with a quirt
QUIRTED > QUIRT
QUIRTING > QUIRT
QUIRTS > QUIRT
QUISLING *n* traitor who
aids an occupying enemy
force
QUISLINGS > QUISLING
QUIST *n* wood pigeon
QUISTS > QUIST
QUIT *vb* stop (doing
something) ▷ *adj* free
(from)
QUITCH *vb* move
QUITCHED > QUITCH
QUITCHES > QUITCH
QUITCHING > QUITCH
QUITCLAIM *n* formal
renunciation of any claim
against a person or of a
right to land ▷ *vb* renounce
(a claim) formally
QUITE *archaic form of*
> QUIT
QUITTED > QUITE
QUITES > QUITE
QUITING > QUITE
QUITRENT *n* (formerly) a
rent payable by a freeholder
or copyholder to his lord
that released him from
liability to perform services
QUITRENTS > QUITRENT
QUITS > QUIT
QUITTAL *n* repayment of
an action with a similar
action
QUITTALS > QUITTAL
QUITTANCE *n* release from
debt or other obligation
QUITTED > QUIT

QUITTER *n* person who
lacks perseverance
QUITTERS > QUITTER
QUITTING > QUIT
QUITTOR *n* infection of the
cartilages on the side of a
horse's foot, characterized
by inflammation and the
formation of pus
QUITTORS > QUITTOR
QUIVER *vb* shake with a
tremulous movement ▷ *n*
shaking or trembling
QUIVERED > QUIVER
QUIVERER > QUIVER
QUIVERERS > QUIVER
QUIVERFUL *n* amount
that a quiver can hold
QUIVERIER > QUIVER
QUIVERING > QUIVER
QUIVERISH > QUIVER
QUIVERS > QUIVER
QUIVERY > QUIVER
QUIXOTE *n* impractical
idealist
QUIXOTES > QUIXOTE
QUIXOTIC *adj* romantic
and unrealistic
QUIXOTISM > QUIXOTIC
QUIXOTRY > QUIXOTE
QUIZ *n* entertainment in
which the knowledge of
the players is tested by a
series of questions ▷ *vb*
investigate by close
questioning
QUIZZED > QUIZ
QUIZZER > QUIZ
QUIZZERS > QUIZ
QUIZZERY > QUIZ
QUIZZES > QUIZ
QUIZZICAL *adj*
questioning and mocking
QUIZZIFY > QUIZ
QUIZZING > QUIZ
QUIZZINGS > QUIZ
QUOAD *adv* as far as
QUOD *n* jail ▷ *vb* say
QUODDED > QUOD
QUODDING > QUOD
QUODLIBET *n* light piece
of music based on two or
more popular tunes
QUODLIN *n* cooking apple
QUODLINS > QUODLIN
QUODS > QUOD
QUOHOG *n* edible clam

QUOHOGS > QUOHOG
QUOIF *vb* arrange (the hair)
QUOIFED > QUOIF
QUOIFING > QUOIF
QUOIFS > QUOIF
QUOIN *n* external corner of
a building ▷ *vb* wedge
QUOINED > QUOIN
QUOINING > QUOIN
QUOININGS > QUOINING
QUOINS > QUOIN
QUOIST *n* wood pigeon
QUOISTS > QUOIST
QUOIT *n* large ring used in
the game of quoits ▷ *vb*
throw as a quoit
QUOITED > QUOIT
QUOITER > QUOIT
QUOITERS > QUOIT
QUOITING > QUOIT
QUOITS *n* game in which
quoits are tossed at a stake
in the ground in attempts
to encircle it
QUOKKA *n* small Australian
wallaby
QUOKKAS > QUOKKA
QUOLL *n* Australian catlike
carnivorous marsupial
QUOLLS > QUOLL
QUOMODO *n* manner
QUOMODOS > QUOMODO
QUONDAM *adj* of an earlier
time
QUONK *vb* make an
accidental noise while
broadcasting
QUONKED > QUONK
QUONKING > QUONK
QUONKS > QUONK
QUOOKE *archaic past
participle of* > QUAKE
QUOP *vb* pulsate or throb
QUOPPED > QUOP
QUOPPING > QUOP
QUOPS > QUOP
QUORATE *adj* having or
being a quorum
QUORUM *n* minimum
number of people required
to be present at a meeting
before any transactions can
take place
QUORUMS > QUORUM
QUOTA *n* share that is due
from, due to, or allocated
to a group or person

QUOTABLE *adj* apt or
suitable for quotation
QUOTABLY > QUOTABLE
QUOTAS > QUOTA
QUOTATION *n* written or
spoken passage repeated
exactly in a later work,
speech, or conversation
QUOTATIVE *n* word
indicating quotation
QUOTE *vb* repeat (words)
exactly from (an earlier
work, speech, or
conversation) ▷ *n*
quotation ▷ *interj*
expression used
parenthetically to indicate
that the words that follow
it form a quotation
QUOTED > QUOTE
QUOTER > QUOTE
QUOTERS > QUOTE
QUOTES > QUOTE
QUOTH *vb* said
QUOTHA *interj* expression of
mild sarcasm, used in
picking up a word or phrase
used by someone else
QUOTIDIAN *adj* daily ▷ *n*
malarial fever
characterized by attacks
that recur daily
QUOTIENT *n* result of the
division of one number or
quantity by another
QUOTIENTS > QUOTIENT
QUOTING > QUOTE
QUOTITION *n* division by
repeated subtraction
QUOTUM *same as* > QUOTA
QUOTUMS > QUOTUM
QURSH *same as* > QURUSH
QURSHES > QURUSH
QURUSH *n* Saudi Arabian
currency unit
QURUSHES > QURUSH
QUYTE *same as* > QUIT
QUYTED > QUYTE
QUYTES > QUYTE
QUYTING > QUYTE
QWERTIES > QWERTY
QWERTY *n* standard
English-language
typewriter or computer
keyboard
QWERTYS > QWERTY

q

Rr

RABANNA n Madagascan woven raffia
RABANNAS > RABANNA
RABAT vb rotate so that the plane rotated coincides with another
RABATINE n type of collar
RABATINES > RABATINE
RABATMENT > RABAT
RABATO n wired or starched collar, often of intricate lace, that stood up at the back and sides: worn in the 17th century
RABATOES > RABATO
RABATOS > RABATO
RABATS > RABAT
RABATTE same as > RABAT
RABATTED > RABAT
RABATTES > RABATTE
RABATTING > RABAT
RABBET n recess, groove, or step, usually of rectangular section, cut into a surface or along the edge of a piece of timber to receive a mating piece ▷ vb cut or form a rabbet in (timber)
RABBETED > RABBET
RABBETING > RABBET
RABBETS > RABBET
RABBI n Jewish spiritual leader
RABBIES > RABBI
RABBIN same as > RABBI
RABBINATE n position, function, or tenure of office of a rabbi
RABBINIC adj of or relating to the rabbis, their teachings, writings, views, language, etc
RABBINICS n study of rabbinic literature of the post-Talmudic period
RABBINISM n teachings and traditions of the rabbis of the Talmudic period
RABBINIST
  > RABBINISM
RABBINITE
  > RABBINISM
RABBINS > RABBIN
RABBIS > RABBI
RABBIT n small burrowing mammal with long ears ▷ vb talk too much
RABBITED > RABBIT
RABBITER n person who traps and sells rabbits

RABBITERS > RABBITER
RABBITING n activity of hunting rabbits
RABBITO same as
  > RABBITOH
RABBITOH n (formerly) an itinerant seller of rabbits for eating
RABBITOHS > RABBITOH
RABBITOS > RABBITO
RABBITRY n place where tame rabbits are kept and bred
RABBITS > RABBIT
RABBITY adj rabbitlike
RABBLE n disorderly crowd of noisy people ▷ vb stir, mix, or skim (the molten charge) in a roasting furnace
RABBLED > RABBLE
RABBLER n iron tool or device for stirring, mixing, or skimming a molten charge in a roasting furnace
RABBLERS > RABBLER
RABBLES > RABBLE
RABBLING > RABBLE
RABBLINGS > RABBLE
RABBONI n very respectful Jewish title or form of address meaning my great master
RABBONIS > RABBONI
RABI n (in Pakistan, India, etc) a crop that is harvested at the end of winter
RABIC > RABIES
RABID adj fanatical
RABIDER > RABID
RABIDEST > RABID
RABIDITY > RABID
RABIDLY > RABID
RABIDNESS > RABID
RABIES n usu fatal viral disease transmitted by dogs and certain other animals
RABIETIC > RABIES
RABIS > RABI
RACA adj biblical word meaning worthless or empty-headed
RACAHOUT n acorn flour or drink made from it
RACAHOUTS > RACAHOUT
RACCAHOUT same as
  > RACAHOUT
RACCOON n small N American mammal with a long striped tail

RACCOONS > RACCOON
RACE n contest of speed ▷ vb compete with in a race
RACEABLE adj fit for racing
RACECARD n card or booklet at a race meeting with the times of the races, names of the runners, etc, printed on it
RACECARDS > RACECARD
RACED > RACE
RACEGOER n one who attends a race meeting, esp a habitual frequenter of race meetings
RACEGOERS > RACEGOER
RACEGOING > RACEGOER
RACEHORSE n horse specially bred for racing
RACEMATE n racemic compound
RACEMATES > RACEMATE
RACEME n cluster of flowers along a central stem, as in the foxglove
RACEMED adj with or in racemes
RACEMES > RACEME
RACEMIC adj of, concerned with, or being a mixture of equal amounts of enantiomers and consequently having no optical activity
RACEMISE same as
  > RACEMIZE
RACEMISED > RACEMISE
RACEMISES > RACEMISE
RACEMISM > RACEMIC
RACEMISMS > RACEMIC
RACEMIZE vb change or cause to change into a racemic mixture
RACEMIZED > RACEMIZE
RACEMIZES > RACEMIZE
RACEMOID adj resembling a raceme
RACEMOSE adj being or resembling a raceme
RACEMOUS same as
  > RACEMOSE
RACEPATH same as
  > RACETRACK
RACEPATHS > RACEPATH
RACER n person, animal, or machine that races
RACERS > RACER
RACES > RACE
RACETRACK n track for racing
RACEWALK vb race by

walking fast rather than running
RACEWALKS > RACEWALK
RACEWAY n racetrack, esp one for banger racing
RACEWAYS > RACEWAY
RACH n scent hound
RACHE same as > RACH
RACHES > RACH
RACHET same as
  > RATCHET
RACHETED > RACHET
RACHETING > RACHET
RACHETS > RACHET
RACHIAL > RACHIS
RACHIDES > RACHIS
RACHIDIAL > RACHIS
RACHIDIAN > RACHIS
RACHILLA n (in grasses) the short stem of a spikelet that bears the florets
RACHILLAE > RACHILLA
RACHILLAS > RACHILLA
RACHIS n main axis or stem of an inflorescence or compound leaf
RACHISES > RACHIS
RACHITIC > RACHITIS
RACHITIS another name for
  > RICKETS
RACIAL adj relating to the division of the human species into races
RACIALISE same as
  > RACIALIZE
RACIALISM same as
  > RACISM
RACIALIST
  > RACIALISM
RACIALIZE vb render racial in tone or content
RACIALLY > RACIAL
RACIATION n evolutionary development of races
RACIER > RACY
RACIEST > RACY
RACILY > RACY
RACINESS > RACY
RACING adj denoting or associated with horse races ▷ n practice of engaging horses (or sometimes greyhounds) in contests of speed
RACINGS > RACING
RACINO n combined racetrack and casino
RACINOS > RACINO
RACISM n hostile attitude or behaviour to members of

other races, based on a belief in the innate superiority of one's own race

RACISMS > RACISM

RACIST > RACISM

RACISTS > RACISM

RACK n framework for holding particular articles, such as coats or luggage ▷ vb cause great suffering to

RACKED > RACK

RACKER > RACK

RACKERS > RACK

RACKET n bat with strings stretched in an oval frame, used in tennis etc ▷ vb to strike with a racket

RACKETED > RACKET

RACKETEER n person making illegal profits ▷ vb operate a racket

RACKETER n someone making a racket

RACKETERS > RACKETER

RACKETIER > RACKETY

RACKETING > RACKET

RACKETRY n noise and commotion

RACKETS n ball game played in a paved walled court

RACKETT n early double-reeded wind instrument

RACKETTS > RACKETT

RACKETY adj involving noise, commotion and excitement

RACKFUL > RACK

RACKFULS > RACK

RACKING > RACK

RACKINGLY > RACK

RACKINGS > RACK

RACKLE adj dialect word meaning rash

RACKS > RACK

RACKWORK n mechanism with a rack and pinion

RACKWORKS > RACKWORK

RACLETTE n Swiss dish of melted cheese served on boiled potatoes

RACLETTES > RACLETTE

RACLOIR n scraper

RACLOIRS > RACLOIR

RACON n radar beacon

RACONS > RACON

RACONTEUR n skilled storyteller

RACOON same as > RACCOON

RACOONS > RACOON

RACQUET same as > RACKET n

RACQUETED > RACQUET

RACQUETS > RACQUET

RACY adj slightly shocking

RAD n former unit of absorbed ionizing radiation dose equivalent to an energy absorption per unit mass of 0.01 joule per kilogram of irradiated

material. 1 rad is equivalent to 0.01 gray ▷ vb fear ▷ adj slang term for great

RADAR n device for tracking distant objects by bouncing high-frequency radio pulses off them

RADARS > RADAR

RADDED > RAD

RADDER > RAD

RADDEST > RAD

RADDING > RAD

RADDLE same as > RUDDLE

RADDLED adj (of a person) unkempt or run-down in appearance

RADDLEMAN same as > RUDDLEMAN

RADDLEMEN > RADDLEMAN

RADDLES > RADDLE

RADDLING > RADDLE

RADDOCKE same as > RUDDOCK

RADDOCKES > RADDOCKE

RADE (in Scots dialect) past tense of > RIDE

RADGE adj angry or uncontrollable ▷ n person acting in such a way

RADGER > RADGE

RADGES > RADGE

RADGEST > RADGE

RADIABLE adj able to be x-rayed

RADIAL adj spreading out from a common central point ▷ n radial-ply tyre

RADIALE n bone in the wrist

RADIALIA > RADIALE

RADIALISE same as > RADIALIZE

RADIALITY > RADIAL

RADIALIZE vb arrange in a pattern of radii

RADIALLY > RADIAL

RADIALS > RADIAL

RADIAN n unit for measuring angles, equal to 57.296°

RADIANCE n quality or state of being radiant

RADIANCES > RADIANCE

RADIANCY same as > RADIANCE

RADIANS > RADIAN

RADIANT adj looking happy ▷ n point or object that emits radiation, esp the part of a heater that gives out heat

RADIANTLY > RADIANT

RADIANTS > RADIANT

RADIATA as in radiata pine type of pine tree

RADIATAS > RADIATA

RADIATE vb spread out from a centre ▷ adj having rays or a radial structure

RADIATED > RADIATE

RADIATELY > RADIATE

RADIATES > RADIATE

RADIATING > RADIATE

RADIATION n

transmission of energy from one body to another

RADIATIVE adj emitting or causing the emission of radiation

RADIATOR n arrangement of pipes containing hot water or steam to heat a room

RADIATORS > RADIATOR

RADIATORY same as > RADIATIVE

RADICAL adj fundamental ▷ n person advocating fundamental (political) change

RADICALLY adv thoroughly

RADICALS > RADICAL

RADICAND n number or quantity from which a root is to be extracted, usually preceded by a radical sign

RADICANDS > RADICAND

RADICANT adj forming roots from the stem

RADICATE vb root or cause to take root

RADICATED > RADICATE

RADICATES > RADICATE

RADICCHIO n Italian variety of chicory, with purple leaves streaked with white that are eaten raw in salads

RADICEL n very small root

RADICELS > RADICEL

RADICES > RADIX

RADICLE n small or developing root

RADICLES > RADICLE

RADICULAR adj root-related

RADICULE same as > RADICLE

RADICULES > RADICULE

RADII > RADIUS

RADIO n use of electromagnetic waves for broadcasting, communication, etc ▷ vb transmit (a message) by radio ▷ adj of, relating to, or using radio

RADIOED > RADIO

RADIOGOLD n radioactive isotope of gold

RADIOGRAM n image produced on a specially sensitized photographic film or plate by radiation, usually by X-rays or gamma rays

RADIOING > RADIO

RADIOLOGY n science of using x-rays in medicine

RADIOMAN n radio operator

RADIOMEN > RADIOMAN

RADIONICS n dowsing technique using a pendulum to detect the energy fields that are emitted by all forms of matter

RADIOS > RADIO

RADIOTHON n lengthy radio programme to raise charity funds, etc

RADISH n small hot-flavoured root vegetable eaten raw in salads

RADISHES > RADISH

RADIUM n radioactive metallic element

RADIUMS > RADIUM

RADIUS n (length of) a straight line from the centre to the circumference of a circle

RADIUSES > RADIUS

RADIX n any number that is the base of a number system or of a system of logarithms

RADIXES > RADIX

RADOME n protective housing for a radar antenna made from a material that is transparent to radio waves

RADOMES > RADOME

RADON n radioactive gaseous element

RADONS > RADON

RADS > RAD

RADULA n horny tooth-bearing strip on the tongue of molluscs that is used for rasping food

RADULAE > RADULA

RADULAR > RADULA

RADULAS > RADULA

RADULATE > RADULA

RADWASTE n radioactive wast

RADWASTES > RADWASTE

RAFALE n burst of artillery fire

RAFALES > RAFALE

RAFF n rubbish

RAFFIA n prepared palm fibre for weaving mats etc

RAFFIAS > RAFFIA

RAFFINATE n liquid left after a solute has been extracted by solvent extraction

RAFFINOSE n trisaccharide of fructose, glucose, and galactose that occurs in sugar beet, cotton seed, certain cereals, etc

RAFFISH adj slightly disreputable

RAFFISHLY > RAFFISH

RAFFLE n lottery with goods as prizes ▷ vb offer as a prize in a raffle

RAFFLED > RAFFLE

RAFFLER > RAFFLE

RAFFLERS > RAFFLE

RAFFLES > RAFFLE

RAFFLESIA n any of various tropical Asian parasitic leafless plants whose flowers smell of putrid meat and are

pollinated by carrion flies
RAFFLING > RAFFLE
RAFFS > RAFF
RAFT *n* floating platform of logs, planks, etc ▷ *vb* convey on or travel by raft, or make a raft from
RAFTED > RAFT
RAFTER *n* one of the main beams of a roof ▷ *vb* to fit with rafters
RAFTERED > RAFTER
RAFTERING > RAFTER
RAFTERS > RAFTER
RAFTING > RAFT
RAFTINGS > RAFT
RAFTMAN *same as* > RAFTSMAN
RAFTMEN > RAFTMAN
RAFTS > RAFT
RAFTSMAN *n* someone who does rafting
RAFTSMEN > RAFTSMAN
RAG *n* fragment of cloth ▷ *vb* tease ▷ *adj* (in British universities and colleges) of various events organized to raise money for charity
RAGA *n* any of several conventional patterns of melody and rhythm that form the basis for freely interpreted compositions. Each pattern is associated with different aspects of religious devotion
RAGAS > RAGA
RAGBAG *n* confused assortment, jumble
RAGBAGS > RAGBAG
RAGBOLT *n* bolt that has angled projections on it to prevent it working loose once it has been driven home
RAGBOLTS > RAGBOLT
RAGDE *archaic past form of* > RAGE
RAGE *n* violent anger or passion ▷ *vb* speak or act with fury
RAGED > RAGE
RAGEE *same as* > RAGI
RAGEES > RAGEE
RAGEFUL > RAGE
RAGER > RAGE
RAGERS > RAGE
RAGES > RAGE
RAGG *same as* > RAGSTONE
RAGGA *n* dance-oriented style of reggae
RAGGAS > RAGGA
RAGGED > RAG
RAGGEDER > RAG
RAGGEDEST > RAG
RAGGEDIER > RAGGEDY
RAGGEDLY > RAG
RAGGEDY *adj* somewhat ragged
RAGGEE *same as* > RAGI
RAGGEES > RAGGEE
RAGGERIES > RAGGERY
RAGGERY *n* rags
RAGGIER > RAGGY

RAGGIES > RAGGY
RAGGIEST > RAGGY
RAGGING > RAG
RAGGINGS > RAG
RAGGLE *n* thin groove cut in stone or brickwork, esp to hold the edge of a roof ▷ *vb* cut a raggle in
RAGGLED > RAGGLE
RAGGLES > RAGGLE
RAGGLING > RAGGLE
RAGGS > RAGG
RAGGY *adj* raglike ▷ *n* cereal grass cultivated in Africa and Asia for its edible grain
RAGHEAD *n* offensive term for an Arab person
RAGHEADS > RAGHEAD
RAGI *n* cereal grass cultivated in Africa and Asia for its edible grain
RAGING > RAGE
RAGINGLY > RAGE
RAGINGS > RAGE
RAGINI *n* Indian musical form related to a raga
RAGINIS > RAGINI
RAGIS > RAGI
RAGLAN *adj* (of a sleeve) joined to a garment by diagonal seams from the neck to the underarm ▷ *n* coat with sleeves that continue to the collar instead of having armhole seams
RAGLANS > RAGLAN
RAGMAN *n* rag-and-bone man
RAGMANS > RAGMAN
RAGMEN > RAGMAN
RAGMENT *n* statute, roll, or list
RAGMENTS > RAGMENT
RAGOUT *n* richly seasoned stew of meat and vegetables ▷ *vb* make into a ragout
RAGOUTED > RAGOUT
RAGOUTING > RAGOUT
RAGOUTS > RAGOUT
RAGPICKER *n* rag-and-bone man
RAGS > RAG
RAGSTONE *n* hard sandstone or limestone, esp when used for building
RAGSTONES > RAGSTONE
RAGTAG *n* disparaging term for common people
RAGTAGS > RAGTAG
RAGTIME *n* style of jazz piano music
RAGTIMER > RAGTIME
RAGTIMERS > RAGTIME
RAGTIMES > RAGTIME
RAGTOP *n* informal word for a car with a folding or removable roof
RAGTOPS > RAGTOP
RAGU *n* Italian meat and tomato sauce
RAGULED *same as* > RAGULY

RAGULY *adj* (in heraldry) having toothlike or stublike projections
RAGUS > RAGU
RAGWEED *n* any of several plants regarded as weeds, some of which produce a large amount of hay-fever-causing pollen
RAGWEEDS > RAGWEED
RAGWHEEL *n* toothed wheel
RAGWHEELS > RAGWHEEL
RAGWORK *n* weaving or needlework using rags
RAGWORKS > RAGWORK
RAGWORM *n* type of worm that lives chiefly in burrows in sand or mud
RAGWORMS > RAGWORM
RAGWORT *n* plant with ragged leaves and yellow flowers
RAGWORTS > RAGWORT
RAH *informal US word for* > CHEER
RAHED > RAH
RAHING > RAH
RAHS > RAH
RAHUI *n* Māori prohibition
RAHUIS > RAHUI
RAI *n* type of Algerian popular music based on traditional Algerian music influenced by modern Western pop
RAIA *same as* > RAYAH
RAIAS > RAIA
RAID *n* sudden surprise attack or search ▷ *vb* make a raid on
RAIDED > RAID
RAIDER > RAID
RAIDERS > RAID
RAIDING > RAID
RAIDINGS > RAID
RAIDS > RAID
RAIK *n* wander ▷ *vb* wander
RAIKED > RAIK
RAIKING > RAIK
RAIKS > RAIK
RAIL *n* horizontal bar, esp as part of a fence or track ▷ *vb* complain bitterly or loudly
RAILAGE *n* cost of transporting goods by rail
RAILAGES > RAILAGE
RAILBED *n* ballast layer supporting the sleepers of a railway track
RAILBEDS > RAILBED
RAILBIRD *n* racing aficionado
RAILBIRDS > RAILBIRD
RAILBUS *n* buslike vehicle for use on railway lines
RAILBUSES > RAILBUS
RAILCAR *n* passenger-carrying railway vehicle consisting of a single coach with its own power unit
RAILCARD *n* card which pensioners, young people,

etc can buy, entitling them to cheaper rail travel
RAILCARDS > RAILCARD
RAILCARS > RAILCAR
RAILE *archaic spelling of* > RAIL
RAILED > RAIL
RAILER > RAIL
RAILERS > RAIL
RAILES > RAILE
RAILHEAD *n* terminal of a railway
RAILHEADS > RAILHEAD
RAILING *n* fence made of rails supported by posts
RAILINGLY > RAIL
RAILINGS > RAILING
RAILLERY *n* teasing or joking
RAILLESS > RAIL
RAILLIES > RAILLY
RAILLY *old word for* > MOCK
RAILMAN *n* railway employee
RAILMEN > RAILMAN
RAILROAD *same as* > RAILWAY
RAILROADS > RAILROAD
RAILS > RAIL
RAILWAY *n* track of iron rails on which trains run
RAILWAYS > RAILWAY
RAILWOMAN *n* female railway employee
RAILWOMEN > RAILWOMAN
RAIMENT *n* clothing
RAIMENTS > RAIMENT
RAIN *n* water falling in drops from the clouds ▷ *vb* fall or pour down as rain
RAINBAND *n* dark band in the solar spectrum caused by water in the atmosphere
RAINBANDS > RAINBAND
RAINBIRD *n* a bird whose call is believed to be a sign of impending rain
RAINBIRDS > RAINBIRD
RAINBOW *n* arch of colours in the sky
RAINBOWED *adj* resembling or involving a rainbow
RAINBOWS > RAINBOW
RAINBOWY > RAINBOW
RAINCHECK *n* ticket stub allowing readmission to a game on a later date should bad weather prevent play
RAINCOAT *n* water-resistant overcoat
RAINCOATS > RAINCOAT
RAINDATE *n* US term for an alternative date in case of rain
RAINDATES > RAINDATE
RAINDROP *n* water droplet that falls from the sky when it is raining
RAINDROPS > RAINDROP
RAINE *archaic spelling of* > REIGN
RAINED > RAIN

RAINES > RAINE
RAINFALL n amount of rain
RAINFALLS > RAINFALL
RAINIER > RAINY
RAINIEST > RAINY
RAINILY > RAINY
RAININESS > RAINY
RAINING > RAIN
RAINLESS > RAIN
RAINMAKER n (among American Indians) a professional practitioner of ritual incantations or other actions intended to cause rain to fall
RAINOUT n radioactive fallout or atmospheric pollution carried to the earth by rain
RAINOUTS > RAINOUT
RAINPROOF adj (of garments, materials, buildings, etc) impermeable to rainwater ▷ vb make rainproof
RAINS > RAIN
RAINSPOUT n waterspout
RAINSTORM n storm with heavy rain
RAINTIGHT same as > RAINPROOF
RAINWASH n action of rain ▷ vb erode or wet as a result of rain
RAINWATER n water from rain
RAINWEAR n protective garments intended for use in wet weather
RAINWEARS > RAINWEAR
RAINY adj characterized by a large rainfall
RAIRD same as > REIRD
RAIRDS > RAIRD
RAIS > RAI
RAISABLE > RAISE
RAISE vb lift up ▷ n increase in pay
RAISEABLE > RAISE
RAISED > RAISE
RAISER > RAISE
RAISERS > RAISE
RAISES > RAISE
RAISIN n dried grape
RAISING n rule that moves a constituent from an embedded clause into the main clause
RAISINGS > RAISING
RAISINS > RAISIN
RAISINY > RAISIN
RAISONNE adj carefully thought out
RAIT same as > RET
RAITA n Indian dish of chopped cucumber, mint, etc, in yogurt, served with curries
RAITAS > RAITA
RAITED > RAIT
RAITING > RAIT
RAITS > RAIT
RAIYAT same as > RYOT
RAIYATS > RAIYAT

RAJ n (in India) government
RAJA same as > RAJAH
RAJAH n (in India, formerly) a ruler or landlord: sometimes used as a form of address or as a title preceding a name
RAJAHS > RAJAH
RAJAHSHIP > RAJAH
RAJAS > RAJA
RAJASHIP > RAJA
RAJASHIPS > RAJA
RAJES > RAJ
RAKE n tool with a long handle and a crosspiece with teeth, used for smoothing earth or gathering leaves, hay, etc ▷ vb gather or smooth with a rake
RAKED > RAKE
RAKEE same as > RAKI
RAKEES > RAKEE
RAKEHELL n dissolute man ▷ adj profligate
RAKEHELLS > RAKEHELL
RAKEHELLY adj profligate
RAKEOFF n share of profits, esp one that is illegal or given as a bribe
RAKEOFFS > RAKEOFF
RAKER n person who rakes
RAKERIES > RAKERY
RAKERS > RAKER
RAKERY n rakish behaviour
RAKES > RAKE
RAKESHAME n old word for someone shamefully dissolute
RAKI n strong spirit distilled in Turkey, the former Yugoslavia, etc, from grain, usually flavoured with aniseed or other aromatics
RAKIA n strong fruit-based alcoholic drink popular in the Balkans
RAKIAS > RAKIA
RAKIJA same as > RAKIA
RAKIJAS > RAKIJA
RAKING n offence committed when a player deliberately scrapes an opponent's leg, arm, etc with the studs of his or her boots
RAKINGS > RAKING
RAKIS > RAKI
RAKISH adj dashing or jaunty
RAKISHLY > RAKISH
RAKSHAS same as > RAKSHASA
RAKSHASA n Hindu demon
RAKSHASAS > RAKSHASA
RAKSHASES > RAKSHAS
RAKU n type of Japanese pottery
RAKUS > RAKU
RALE n abnormal coarse crackling sound heard on auscultation of the chest, usually caused by the accumulation of fluid in the lungs

RALES > RALE
RALLIED > RALLY
RALLIER > RALLY
RALLIERS > RALLY
RALLIES > RALLY
RALLIFORM adj of rail family of birds
RALLINE adj relating to a family of birds that includes the rails, crakes, and coots
RALLY n large gathering of people for a meeting ▷ vb bring or come together after dispersal or for a common cause
RALLYE US variant of > RALLY
RALLYES > RALLYE
RALLYING > RALLY
RALLYINGS > RALLY
RALLYIST > RALLY
RALLYISTS > RALLY
RALPH vb slang word meaning vomit
RALPHED > RALPH
RALPHING > RALPH
RALPHS > RALPH
RAM n male sheep ▷ vb strike against with force
RAMADA n outdoor eating area with roof but open sides
RAMADAS > RAMADA
RAMAKIN same as > RAMEKIN
RAMAKINS > RAMAKIN
RAMAL adj relating to a branch or branches
RAMATE adj with branches
RAMBLA n dried-up riverbed
RAMBLAS > RAMBLA
RAMBLE vb walk without a definite route ▷ n walk, esp in the country
RAMBLED > RAMBLE
RAMBLER n person who rambles
RAMBLERS > RAMBLER
RAMBLES > RAMBLE
RAMBLING adj large and irregularly shaped ▷ n activity of going for long walks in the country
RAMBLINGS > RAMBLING
RAMBUTAN n SE Asian tree that has bright red edible fruit
RAMBUTANS > RAMBUTAN
RAMCAT n dialect word for a male cat
RAMCATS > RAMCAT
RAMEAL same as > RAMAL
RAMEE same as > RAMIE
RAMEES > RAMEE
RAMEKIN n small ovenproof dish for a single serving of food
RAMEKINS > RAMEKIN
RAMEN n Japanese dish consisting of a clear broth containing thin white noodles and sometimes vegetables, meat, etc
RAMENS > RAMEN

RAMENTA > RAMENTUM
RAMENTUM n any of the thin brown scales that cover the stems and leaves of young ferns
RAMEOUS same as > RAMAL
RAMEQUIN same as > RAMEKIN
RAMEQUINS > RAMEQUIN
RAMET n any of the individuals in a group of clones
RAMETS > RAMET
RAMI same as > RAMIE
RAMIE n woody Asian shrub with broad leaves and a stem that yields a flaxlike fibre
RAMIES > RAMIE
RAMIFIED > RAMIFY
RAMIFIES > RAMIFY
RAMIFORM adj having a branchlike shape
RAMIFY vb become complex
RAMIFYING > RAMIFY
RAMILIE same as > RAMILLIE
RAMILIES > RAMILIE
RAMILLIE n wig with a plait at the back fashionable in the 18th century
RAMILLIES > RAMILLIE
RAMIN n swamp-growing tree found in Malaysia and Indonesia
RAMINS > RAMIN
RAMIS > RAMI
RAMJET n type of jet engine in which fuel is burned in a duct using air compressed by the forward speed of the aircraft
RAMJETS > RAMJET
RAMMED > RAM
RAMMEL n discarded or waste matter
RAMMELS > RAMMEL
RAMMER > RAM
RAMMERS > RAM
RAMMIER > RAMMISH
RAMMIES > RAMMISH
RAMMIEST > RAMMISH
RAMMING > RAM
RAMMISH adj like a ram, esp in being lustful or foul-smelling
RAMMISHLY > RAMMISH
RAMMLE n collection of items saved in case they become useful
RAMMLES > RAMMLE
RAMMY n noisy disturbance or free-for-all ▷ vb make a rammy
RAMONA same as > SAGEBRUSH
RAMONAS > RAMONA
RAMOSE adj having branches
RAMOSELY > RAMOSE
RAMOSITY > RAMOSE
RAMOUS same as > RAMOSE
RAMOUSLY > RAMOSE

RAMP n slope joining two level surfaces ▷ vb (esp of animals) to rush around in a wild excited manner

RAMPAGE vb dash about violently

RAMPAGED > RAMPAGE

RAMPAGER > RAMPAGE

RAMPAGERS > RAMPAGE

RAMPAGES > RAMPAGE

RAMPAGING > RAMPAGE

RAMPANCY > RAMPANT

RAMPANT adj growing or spreading uncontrollably

RAMPANTLY > RAMPANT

RAMPART n mound or wall for defence ▷ vb provide with a rampart

RAMPARTED > RAMPART

RAMPARTS > RAMPART

RAMPAUGE Scots variant of **>** RAMPAGE

RAMPAUGED > RAMPAUGE

RAMPAUGES > RAMPAUGE

RAMPED > RAMP

RAMPER > RAMP

RAMPERS > RAMP

RAMPICK same as **>** RAMPIKE

RAMPICKED > RAMPICK

RAMPICKS > RAMPICK

RAMPIKE n US or dialect word for a dead tree

RAMPIKES > RAMPIKE

RAMPING > RAMP

RAMPINGS > RAMP

RAMPION n European and Asian plant that has clusters of bluish flowers and an edible white tuberous root used in salads

RAMPIONS > RAMPION

RAMPIRE archaic variant of **>** RAMPART

RAMPIRED > RAMPIRE

RAMPIRES > RAMPIRE

RAMPOLE same as **>** RAMPIKE

RAMPOLES > RAMPOLE

RAMPS > RAMP

RAMPSMAN n mugger

RAMPSMEN > RAMPSMAN

RAMROD n long thin rod used for cleaning the barrel of a gun or forcing gunpowder into an old-fashioned gun ▷ adj (of someone's posture) very straight and upright ▷ vb drive

RAMRODDED > RAMROD

RAMRODS > RAMROD

RAMS > RAM

RAMSHORN as in ramshorn snail any of various freshwater snails

RAMSHORNS > RAMSHORN

RAMSON n type of garlic

RAMSONS > RAMSON

RAMSTAM adv headlong ▷ adj headlong

RAMTIL n African plant grown in India esp for its oil

RAMTILLA same as **>** RAMTIL

RAMTILLAS > RAMTILLA

RAMTILS > RAMTIL

RAMULAR adj relating to a branch or branches

RAMULI > RAMULUS

RAMULOSE adj (of the parts or organs of animals and plants) having many small branches

RAMULOUS same as **>** RAMULOSE

RAMULUS n small branch

RAMUS n barb of a bird's feather

RAN > RUN

RANA n genus of frogs

RANARIAN adj of or relating to frogs

RANARIUM n place for keeping frogs

RANARIUMS > RANARIUM

RANAS > RANA

RANCE Scots word for **>** PROP

RANCED > RANCE

RANCEL vb (in Shetland and Orkney) carry out a search

RANCELS > RANCEL

RANCES > RANCE

RANCH n large cattle farm in the American West ▷ vb run a ranch

RANCHED > RANCH

RANCHER n person who owns, manages, or works on a ranch

RANCHERIA n native American settlement or home of a rancher

RANCHERIE n (in British Columbia, Canada) a settlement of North American Indians, esp on a reserve

RANCHERO another word for **>** RANCHER

RANCHEROS > RANCHERO

RANCHERS > RANCHER

RANCHES > RANCH

RANCHING > RANCH

RANCHINGS > RANCH

RANCHLESS > RANCH

RANCHLIKE > RANCH

RANCHMAN n man who owns, manages, or works on a ranch

RANCHMEN > RANCHMAN

RANCHO n hut or group of huts for housing ranch workers

RANCHOS > RANCHO

RANCID adj (of butter, bacon, etc) stale and having an offensive smell

RANCIDER > RANCID

RANCIDEST > RANCID

RANCIDITY > RANCID

RANCIDLY > RANCID

RANCING > RANCE

RANCOR same as **>** RANCOUR

RANCORED > RANCOR

RANCOROUS > RANCOUR

RANCORS > RANCOR

RANCOUR n deep bitter hate

RANCOURED > RANCOUR

RANCOURS > RANCOUR

RAND n monetary unit of South Africa; leather strip on the heel of a shoe ▷ vb cut into rands

RANDAN n boat rowed by three people, in which the person in the middle uses two oars and the people fore and aft use one oar each

RANDANS > RANDAN

RANDED > RAND

RANDEM adv with three horses harnessed together as a team ▷ n carriage or team of horses so driven

RANDEMS > RANDEM

RANDIE same as **>** RANDY

RANDIER > RANDY

RANDIES > RANDY

RANDIEST > RANDY

RANDILY > RANDY

RANDINESS > RANDY

RANDING > RAND

RANDLORD n mining magnate during the 19th-century gold boom in Johannesburg

RANDLORDS > RANDLORD

RANDOM adj made or done by chance or without plan ▷ n (in mining) the course of a vein of ore

RANDOMISE same as **>** RANDOMIZE

RANDOMIZE vb set up (a selection process, sample, etc) in a deliberately random way in order to enhance the statistical validity of any results obtained

RANDOMLY > RANDOM

RANDOMS > RANDOM

RANDON old variant of **>** RANDOM

RANDONS > RANDON

RANDS > RAND

RANDY adj sexually aroused ▷ n rude or reckless person

RANEE same as **>** RANI

RANEES > RANEE

RANG > RING

RANGA n person with red hair

RANGAS > RANGA

RANGATIRA n Māori chief of either sex

RANGE n limits of effectiveness or variation ▷ vb vary between one point and another

RANGED > RANGE

RANGELAND n land that naturally produces forage plants suitable for grazing but where rainfall is too low or erratic for growing crops

RANGER n official in charge of a nature reserve etc

RANGERS > RANGER

RANGES > RANGE

RANGI n sky

RANGIER > RANGY

RANGIEST > RANGY

RANGILY > RANGY

RANGINESS > RANGY

RANGING > RANGE

RANGINGS > RANGE

RANGIORA n evergreen New Zealand shrub or small tree with large ovate leaves and small greenish-white flowers

RANGIORAS > RANGIORA

RANGIS > RANGI

RANGOLI n traditional Indian ground decoration using coloured sand or chalks

RANGOLIS > RANGOLI

RANGY adj having long slender limbs

RANI n wife or widow of a rajah

RANID n frog

RANIDS > RANID

RANIFORM adj froglike

RANINE adj relating to frogs

RANIS > RANI

RANK n relative place or position ▷ vb have a specific rank or position ▷ adj complete or absolute

RANKE archaic variant of **>** RANK

RANKED > RANK

RANKER n soldier in the ranks

RANKERS > RANKER

RANKES > RANKE

RANKEST > RANK

RANKING adj prominent ▷ n position on a scale

RANKINGS > RANKING

RANKISH adj old word meaning rather rank

RANKISM n discrimination against people on the grounds of rank

RANKISMS > RANKISM

RANKLE vb continue to cause resentment or bitterness

RANKLED > RANKLE

RANKLES > RANKLE

RANKLESS > RANK

RANKLING > RANKLE

RANKLY > RANK

RANKNESS > RANK

RANKS > RANK

RANKSHIFT n phenomenon in which a unit at one rank in the grammar has the function of a unit at a lower rank, as for example in the phrase the house on the corner, where the words on the corner shift down from the rank of group to the rank of word ▷ vb shift or be shifted from (one linguistic rank to another)

r

RANPIKE same as
> RAMPIKE
RANPIKES > RANPIKE
RANSACK vb search
thoroughly
RANSACKED > RANSACK
RANSACKER > RANSACK
RANSACKS > RANSACK
RANSEL same as > RANCEL
RANSELS > RANSEL
RANSHAKLE Scots word for
> RANSACK
RANSOM n money
demanded in return for the
release of someone who
has been kidnapped ▷ vb
pay money to obtain the
release of a captive
RANSOMED > RANSOM
RANSOMER > RANSOM
RANSOMERS > RANSOM
RANSOMING > RANSOM
RANSOMS > RANSOM
RANT vb talk in a loud and
excited way ▷ n loud
excited speech
RANTED > RANT
RANTER > RANT
RANTERISM > RANT
RANTERS > RANT
RANTING > RANT
RANTINGLY > RANT
RANTINGS > RANT
RANTIPOLE n reckless
person ▷ vb behave like a
rantipole
RANTS > RANT
RANULA n saliva-filled cyst
that develops under the
tongue
RANULAR adj of a cyst
under the tongue
RANULAS > RANULA
RANUNCULI npl plants of
the genus that includes the
buttercup, crowfoot,
spearwort, and lesser
celandine
RANZEL same as > RANCEL
RANZELMAN n (in Shetland
and Orkney) type of
constable
RANZELMEN
> RANZELMAN
RANZELS > RANZEL
RAOULIA n flowering plant
of New Zealand
RAOULIAS > RAOULIA
RAP vb hit with a sharp
quick blow ▷ n quick sharp
blow
RAPACIOUS adj greedy or
grasping
RAPACITY > RAPACIOUS
RAPE vb force to submit to
sexual intercourse ▷ n act
of raping
RAPED > RAPE
RAPER > RAPE
RAPERS > RAPE
RAPES > RAPE
RAPESEED n seed of the
oilseed rape plant
RAPESEEDS > RAPESEED
RAPHAE > RAPHE

RAPHANIA n type of
ergotism possibly resulting
from consumption of
radish seeds
RAPHANIAS > RAPHANIA
RAPHE n elongated ridge of
conducting tissue along
the side of certain seeds
RAPHES > RAPHE
RAPHIA same as > RAFFIA
RAPHIAS > RAPHIA
RAPHIDE n any of
numerous needle-shaped
crystals, usually of calcium
oxalate, that occur in many
plant cells as a metabolic
product
RAPHIDES > RAPHIDE
RAPHIS same as
> RAPHIDE
RAPID adj quick, swift
RAPIDER > RAPID
RAPIDEST > RAPID
RAPIDITY > RAPID
RAPIDLY > RAPID
RAPIDNESS > RAPID
RAPIDS npl part of a river
with a fast turbulent
current
RAPIER n fine-bladed
sword
RAPIERED adj carrying a
rapier
RAPIERS > RAPIER
RAPINE n pillage or
plundering
RAPINES > RAPINE
RAPING > RAPE
RAPINI npl type of leafy
vegetable
RAPIST n person who
commits rape
RAPISTS > RAPIST
RAPLOCH n Scots word for
homespun woollen
material ▷ adj Scots word
meaning coarse or
homemade
RAPLOCHS > RAPLOCH
RAPPAREE n Irish irregular
soldier of the late 17th
century
RAPPAREES > RAPPAREE
RAPPE n Arcadian dish of
grated potatoes and pork
or chicken
RAPPED > RAP
RAPPEE n moist English
snuff of the 18th and 19th
centuries
RAPPEES > RAPPEE
RAPPEL n (formerly) a
drumbeat to call soldiers to
arms ▷ vb abseil
RAPPELED > RAPPEL
RAPPELING > RAPPEL
RAPPELLED > RAPPEL
RAPPELS > RAPPEL
RAPPEN n Swiss coin equal
to one hundredth of a franc
RAPPER n something used
for rapping, such as a
knocker on a door
RAPPERS > RAPPER
RAPPES > RAPPE

RAPPING > RAP
RAPPINGS > RAP
RAPPINI same as
> RAPINI
RAPPORT n harmony or
agreement
RAPPORTS > RAPPORT
RAPS > RAP
RAPT adj engrossed or
spellbound
RAPTLY > RAPT
RAPTNESS > RAPT
RAPTOR n any bird of prey
RAPTORIAL adj (of the feet
of birds) adapted for seizing
prey
RAPTORS > RAPTOR
RAPTURE n ecstasy ▷ vb
entrance
RAPTURED > RAPTURE
RAPTURES > RAPTURE
RAPTURING > RAPTURE
RAPTURISE same as
> RAPTURIZE
RAPTURIST > RAPTURE
RAPTURIZE vb go into
ecstasies
RAPTUROUS adj
experiencing or
manifesting ecstatic joy or
delight
RARE adj uncommon ▷ vb
rear
RAREBIT as in Welsh rarebit
dish made from melted
cheese and sometimes milk
and seasonings and served
on toast
RAREBITS > RAREBIT
RARED > RARE
RAREE as in raree show
street show or carnival
RAREFIED adj highly
specialized, exalted
RAREFIER > RAREFY
RAREFIERS > RAREFY
RAREFIES > RAREFY
RAREFY vb make or
become rarer or less dense
RAREFYING > RAREFY
RARELY adv seldom
RARENESS > RARE
RARER > RARE
RARERIPE adj ripening
early ▷ n fruit or vegetable
that ripens early
RARERIPES > RARERIPE
RARES > RARE
RAREST > RARE
RARIFIED same as
> RAREFIED
RARIFIES > RARIFY
RARIFY same as > RAREFY
RARIFYING > RARIFY
RARING adj ready
RARITIES > RARITY
RARITY n something that
is valuable because it is
unusual
RARK as in rark up informal
New Zealand expression
meaning reprimand
severely
RARKED > RARK

RARKING > RARK
RARKS > RARK
RAS n headland
RASBORA n often brightly
coloured tropical fish
RASBORAS > RASBORA
RASCAILLE n rabble
RASCAL n rogue ▷ adj
belonging to the mob or
rabble
RASCALDOM > RASCAL
RASCALISM > RASCAL
RASCALITY n
mischievous, disreputable,
or dishonest character,
behaviour, or action
RASCALLY adj dishonest
or mean ▷ adv in a
dishonest or mean fashion
RASCALS > RASCAL
RASCASSE n any of various
fishes with venomous
spines on the dorsal and
anal fins
RASCASSES > RASCASSE
RASCHEL n type of loosely
knitted fabric
RASCHELS > RASCHEL
RASE same as > RAZE
RASED > RASE
RASER > RASE
RASERS > RASE
RASES > RASE
RASH adj hasty, reckless, or
incautious ▷ n eruption of
spots or patches on the skin
▷ vb (in old usage) cut
RASHED > RASH
RASHER n thin slice of
bacon
RASHERS > RASHER
RASHES > RASH
RASHEST > RASH
RASHIE n Australian word
for a shirt worn by surfers
as protection against
sunburn, heat rash, etc
RASHIES > RASHIE
RASHING > RASH
RASHLIKE > RASH
RASHLY > RASH
RASHNESS > RASH
RASING > RASE
RASMALAI n Indian
dessert made from cheese,
milk, and almonds
RASMALAIS > RASMALAI
RASORIAL adj (of birds
such as domestic poultry)
adapted for scratching the
ground for food
RASP n harsh grating noise
▷ vb speak in a grating
voice
RASPATORY n surgical
instrument for abrading
RASPBERRY n red juicy
edible berry
RASPED > RASP
RASPER > RASP
RASPERS > RASP
RASPIER > RASPY
RASPIEST > RASPY
RASPINESS > RASPY

RASPING adj (esp of a noise) harsh or grating

RASPINGLY > RASPING

RASPINGS npl browned breadcrumbs for coating fish and other foods before frying, baking, etc

RASPISH > RASP

RASPS > RASP

RASPY same as > RASPING

RASSE n small S Asian civet

RASSES > RASSE

RASSLE dialect variant of > WRESTLE

RASSLED > RASSLE

RASSLES > RASSLE

RASSLING > RASSLE

RAST archaic past form of > RACE

RASTA adj of a member of a particular Black religious movement

RASTAFARI n Black religious movement

RASTER n image consisting of rows of pixel information, such as a JPEG, GIF etc ▷ vb use web-based technology to turn a digital image into a large picture composed of a grid of black and white dots

RASTERED > RASTER

RASTERING > RASTER

RASTERISE same as > RASTERIZE

RASTERIZE vb (in computing) convert into pixels for screen output

RASTERS > RASTER

RASTRUM n pen for drawing the five lines of a musical stave simultaneously

RASTRUMS > RASTRUM

RASURE n scraping

RASURES > RASURE

RAT n small rodent ▷ vb inform (on)

RATA n New Zealand hard-wood forest tree with crimson flowers

RATABLE adj able to be rated or evaluated

RATABLES npl property that is liable to rates

RATABLY > RATABLE

RATAFEE same as > RATAFIA

RATAFEES > RATAFEE

RATAFIA n liqueur made from fruit

RATAFIAS > RATAFIA

RATAL n amount on which rates are assessed ▷ adj of or relating to rates (local taxation)

RATALS > RATAL

RATAN same as > RATTAN

RATANIES > RATANY

RATANS > RATAN

RATANY n flowering desert shrub

RATAPLAN n drumming sound ▷ vb drum

RATAPLANS > RATAPLAN

RATAS > RATA

RATATAT n sound of knocking on a door

RATATATS > RATATAT

RATBAG n eccentric, stupid, or unreliable person

RATBAGS > RATBAG

RATBITE as in ratbite fever acute infectious disease that can be caught from the bite of an infected rat

RATCH same as > RATCHET

RATCHED > RATCH

RATCHES > RATCH

RATCHET n set of teeth on a bar or wheel allowing motion in one direction only ▷ vb move using or as if using a ratchet system

RATCHETED > RATCHET

RATCHETS > RATCHET

RATCHING > RATCH

RATE n degree of speed or progress ▷ vb consider or value

RATEABLE same as > RATABLE

RATEABLY > RATEABLE

RATED > RATE

RATEEN same as > RATINE

RATEENS > RATEEN

RATEL n large African and S Asian musteline mammal

RATELS > RATEL

RATEMETER n device for counting and averaging the number of events in a given time

RATEPAYER n person who pays local rates on a building

RATER > RATE

RATERS > RATE

RATES npl (in some countries) a tax on property levied by a local authority

RATFINK n contemptible or undesirable person

RATFINKS > RATFINK

RATFISH n deep-sea fish with a whiplike tail

RATFISHES > RATFISH

RATH same as > RATHE

RATHA n (in India) a four-wheeled carriage drawn by horses or bullocks

RATHAS > RATHA

RATHE adj blossoming or ripening early in the season

RATHER adv some extent ▷ interj expression of strong affirmation ▷ sentence substitute expression of strong affirmation, often in answer to a question

RATHEREST adv archaic word equivalent to soonest

RATHERIPE same as > RATHRIPE

RATHERISH adv (in informal English) quite or fairly

RATHEST adv dialect or archaic word meaning soonest

RATHOLE n rat's hiding place or burrow

RATHOLES > RATHOLE

RATHOUSE n psychiatric hospital or asylum

RATHOUSES > RATHOUSE

RATHRIPE adj dialect word meaning mature or ripe ahead of time ▷ n variety of apple or other fruit that is quick to ripen

RATHRIPES > RATHRIPE

RATHS > RATH

RATICIDE n rat poison

RATICIDES > RATICIDE

RATIFIED > RATIFY

RATIFIER > RATIFY

RATIFIERS > RATIFY

RATIFIES > RATIFY

RATIFY vb give formal approval to

RATIFYING > RATIFY

RATINE n coarse loosely woven cloth

RATINES > RATINE

RATING n valuation or assessment

RATINGS > RATING

RATIO n relationship between two numbers or amounts expressed as a proportion

RATION n fixed allowance of food etc ▷ vb limit to a certain amount per person

RATIONAL adj reasonable, sensible ▷ n rational number

RATIONALE n reason for an action or decision

RATIONALS > RATIONAL

RATIONED > RATION

RATIONING > RATION

RATIONS npl fixed daily allowance of food, esp to military personnel or when supplies are limited

RATIOS > RATIO

RATITE adj (of flightless birds) having a breastbone that lacks a keel for the attachment of flight muscles ▷ n bird, such as an ostrich, kiwi, or rhea, that belongs to this group

RATITES > RATITE

RATLIKE > RAT

RATLIN same as > RATLINE

RATLINE n any of a series of light lines tied across the shrouds of a sailing vessel for climbing aloft

RATLINES > RATLINE

RATLING n young rat

RATLINGS > RATLING

RATLINS > RATLIN

RATO n rocket-assisted take-off

RATOO same as > RATU

RATOON n new shoot that grows from near the root or crown of crop plants, esp the sugar cane, after the old growth has been cut back ▷ vb propagate or cause to propagate by such a growth

RATOONED > RATOON

RATOONER n plant that spreads by ratooning

RATOONERS > RATOONER

RATOONING > RATOON

RATOONS > RATOON

RATOOS > RATOO

RATOS > RATO

RATPACK n members of the press who pursue celebrities and give wide coverage of their private lives

RATPACKS > RATPACK

RATPROOF adj impenetrable by rats

RATS > RAT

RATSBANE n rat poison, esp arsenic oxide

RATSBANES > RATSBANE

RATTAIL n type of fish

RATTAILED adj having tail like rat

RATTAILS > RATTAIL

RATTAN n climbing palm with jointed stems used for canes

RATTANS > RATTAN

RATTED > RAT

RATTEEN same as > RATINE

RATTEENS > RATTEEN

RATTEN vb sabotage or steal tools in order to disrupt the work of

RATTENED > RATTEN

RATTENER > RATTEN

RATTENERS > RATTEN

RATTENING > RATTEN

RATTENS > RATTEN

RATTER n dog or cat that catches and kills rats

RATTERIES > RATTERY

RATTERS > RATTER

RATTERY n rats' dwelling area

RATTIER > RATTY

RATTIEST > RATTY

RATTILY > RATTY

RATTINESS > RATTY

RATTING > RAT

RATTINGS > RAT

RATTISH adj of, resembling, or infested with rats

RATTLE vb give out a succession of short sharp sounds ▷ n short sharp sound

RATTLEBAG n rattle made out of a bag containing a variety of different things

RATTLEBOX n any of various tropical and subtropical leguminous plants that have inflated pods within which the seeds rattle

RATTLED > RATTLE

RATTLER n something that rattles

r

RATTLERS > RATTLER
RATTLES > RATTLE
RATTLIER > RATTLY
RATTLIEST > RATTLY
RATTLIN same as > RATLINE
RATTLINE same as > RATLINE
RATTLINES > RATTLINE
RATTLING adv exceptionally, very ▷ n succession of short sharp sounds
RATTLINGS > RATTLING
RATTLINS > RATTLIN
RATTLY adj having a rattle
RATTON n dialect word for a little rat
RATTONS > RATTON
RATTOON same as > RATOON
RATTOONED > RATTOON
RATTOONS > RATTOON
RATTRAP n device for catching rats
RATTRAPS > RATTRAP
RATTY adj bad-tempered, irritable
RATU n title used by Fijian chiefs or nobles
RATUS > RATU
RAUCID adj raucous
RAUCITIES > RAUCOUS
RAUCITY > RAUCOUS
RAUCLE adj Scots word for rough or tough
RAUCLER > RAUCLE
RAUCLEST > RAUCLE
RAUCOUS adj hoarse or harsh
RAUCOUSLY > RAUCOUS
RAUGHT archaic past form of > REACH
RAUN n fish roe or spawn
RAUNCH n lack of polish or refinement ▷ vb behave in a raunchy manner
RAUNCHED > RAUNCH
RAUNCHES > RAUNCH
RAUNCHIER > RAUNCHY
RAUNCHILY > RAUNCHY
RAUNCHING > RAUNCH
RAUNCHY adj earthy, sexy
RAUNGE archaic word for > RANGE
RAUNGED > RAUNGE
RAUNGES > RAUNGE
RAUNGING > RAUNGE
RAUNS > RAUN
RAUPATU n confiscation or seizure of land
RAUPATUS > RAUPATU
RAUPO n New Zealand bulrush
RAUPOS > RAUPO
RAURIKI n sow thistle, any of various plants with prickly leaves, milky juice and yellow heads
RAURIKIS > RAURIKI
RAUWOLFIA n tropical tree or shrub
RAV n Hebrew word for rabbi

RAVAGE vb cause extensive damage to ▷ n destructive action
RAVAGED > RAVAGE
RAVAGER > RAVAGE
RAVAGERS > RAVAGE
RAVAGES > RAVAGE
RAVAGING > RAVAGE
RAVE vb talk wildly or with enthusiasm ▷ n enthusiastically good review
RAVED > RAVE
RAVEL vb tangle or become entangled ▷ n tangle or complication
RAVELED > RAVEL
RAVELER > RAVEL
RAVELERS > RAVEL
RAVELIN n outwork having two embankments at a salient angle
RAVELING > RAVEL
RAVELINGS > RAVEL
RAVELINS > RAVELIN
RAVELLED > RAVEL
RAVELLER > RAVEL
RAVELLERS > RAVEL
RAVELLING > RAVEL
RAVELLY > RAVEL
RAVELMENT n ravel or tangle
RAVELS > RAVEL
RAVEN n black bird like a large crow ▷ adj (of hair) shiny black ▷ vb seize or seek (plunder, prey, etc)
RAVENED > RAVEN
RAVENER > RAVEN
RAVENERS > RAVEN
RAVENING adj (of animals) hungrily searching for prey
RAVENINGS npl rapacious behaviour and activities
RAVENLIKE > RAVEN
RAVENOUS adj very hungry
RAVENS > RAVEN
RAVER n person who leads a wild or uninhibited social life
RAVERS > RAVER
RAVES > RAVE
RAVIGOTE n rich white sauce with herbs and shallots
RAVIGOTES > RAVIGOTE
RAVIGOTTE n French salad sauce
RAVIN archaic spelling of > RAVEN
RAVINE n narrow steep-sided valley worn by a stream
RAVINED > RAVIN
RAVINES > RAVINE
RAVING adj delirious ▷ n frenzied, irrational, or wildly extravagant talk or utterances
RAVINGLY > RAVING
RAVINGS > RAVING
RAVINING > RAVIN
RAVINS > RAVIN
RAVIOLI n small squares

of pasta with a savoury filling
RAVIOLIS > RAVIOLI
RAVISH vb enrapture
RAVISHED > RAVISH
RAVISHER > RAVISH
RAVISHERS > RAVISH
RAVISHES > RAVISH
RAVISHING adj lovely or entrancing
RAVS > RAV
RAW adj uncooked ▷ n as in in the raw without clothes
RAWARU n New Zealand name for blue cod
RAWARUS > RAWARU
RAWBONE archaic variant of > RAWBONED
RAWBONED adj having a lean bony physique
RAWER > RAW
RAWEST > RAW
RAWHEAD n bogeyman
RAWHEADS > RAWHEAD
RAWHIDE n untanned hide ▷ vb whip
RAWHIDED > RAWHIDE
RAWHIDES > RAWHIDE
RAWHIDING > RAWHIDE
RAWIN n monitoring of winds in the upper atmosphere using radar and a balloon
RAWING (in dialect) same as > ROWEN
RAWINGS > RAWING
RAWINS > RAWIN
RAWISH > RAW
RAWLY > RAW
RAWMAISH n Irish word for foolish or exaggerated talk
RAWN (in dialect) same as > ROWEN
RAWNESS > RAW
RAWNESSES > RAW
RAWNS > RAWN
RAWS > RAW
RAX vb stretch or extend ▷ n act of stretching or straining
RAXED > RAX
RAXES > RAX
RAXING > RAX
RAY n single line or narrow beam of light ▷ vb (of an object) to emit (light) in rays or (of light) to issue in the form of rays
RAYA same as > RAYAH
RAYAH n (formerly) a non-Muslim subject of the Ottoman Empire
RAYAHS > RAYAH
RAYAS > RAYA
RAYED > RAY
RAYGRASS same as > RYEGRASS
RAYING > RAY
RAYLE archaic spelling of > RAIL
RAYLED > RAYLE
RAYLES > RAYLE
RAYLESS adj dark
RAYLESSLY > RAYLESS

RAYLET n small ray
RAYLETS > RAYLET
RAYLIKE adj resembling a ray
RAYLING > RAYLE
RAYNE archaic spelling of > REIGN
RAYNES > RAYNE
RAYON n (fabric made of) a synthetic fibre
RAYONS > RAYON
RAYS > RAY
RAZE vb destroy (buildings or a town) completely
RAZED > RAZE
RAZEE n sailing ship that has had its upper deck or decks removed ▷ vb remove the upper deck or decks of (a sailing ship)
RAZEED > RAZEE
RAZEEING > RAZEE
RAZEES > RAZEE
RAZER > RAZE
RAZERS > RAZE
RAZES > RAZE
RAZING > RAZE
RAZMATAZ n noisy or showy fuss or activity
RAZOO n imaginary coin
RAZOOS > RAZOO
RAZOR n sharp instrument for shaving ▷ vb cut or shave with a razor
RAZORABLE adj able to be shaved
RAZORBACK n another name for the common rorqual
RAZORBILL n sea bird of the North Atlantic with a stout sideways flattened bill
RAZORCLAM n type of mollusc with a long, narrow shell
RAZORED > RAZOR
RAZORFISH n type of mollusc with a long, narrow shell
RAZORING > RAZOR
RAZORS > RAZOR
RAZURE same as > RASURE
RAZURES > RAZURE
RAZZ vb make fun of
RAZZBERRY US variant of > RASPBERRY
RAZZED > RAZZ
RAZZES > RAZZ
RAZZIA n raid for plunder or slaves, esp one carried out by Moors in North Africa
RAZZIAS > RAZZIA
RAZZING > RAZZ
RAZZLE as in on the razzle celebration
RAZZLES > RAZZLE
RE prep concerning
REABSORB vb absorb again
REABSORBS > REABSORB
REACCEDE vb accede again
REACCEDED > REACCEDE
REACCEDES > REACCEDE

REACCENT vb accent again

REACCENTS > REACCENT

REACCEPT vb accept again

REACCEPTS > REACCEPT

REACCLAIM vb acclaim again

REACCUSE vb accuse again

REACCUSED > REACCUSE

REACCUSES > REACCUSE

REACH vb arrive at ▷ n distance that one can reach

REACHABLE > REACH

REACHED > REACH

REACHER > REACH

REACHERS > REACH

REACHES > REACH

REACHING > REACH

REACHLESS adj unreachable or unattainable

REACQUIRE vb get or gain (something) again which one has owned

REACT vb act in response (to)

REACTANCE n resistance to the flow of an alternating current caused by the inductance or capacitance of the circuit

REACTANT n substance that participates in a chemical reaction

REACTANTS > REACTANT

REACTED > REACT

REACTING > REACT

REACTION n physical or emotional response to a stimulus

REACTIONS > REACTION

REACTIVE adj chemically active

REACTOR n apparatus in which a nuclear reaction is maintained and controlled to produce nuclear energy

REACTORS > REACTOR

REACTS > REACT

REACTUATE vb activate again

READ vb look at and understand or take in (written or printed matter) ▷ n matter suitable for reading

READABLE adj enjoyable to read

READABLY > READABLE

READAPT vb adapt again

READAPTED > READAPT

READAPTS > READAPT

READD vb add again

READDED > READD

READDICT vb cause to become addicted again

READDICTS > READDICT

READDING > READD

READDRESS vb look at or discuss (an issue, situation, etc) from a new or different point of view

READDS > READD

READER n person who reads

READERLY adj pertaining

to or suitable for a reader

READERS > READER

READIED > READY

READIER > READY

READIES npl ready money

READIEST > READY

READILY adv promptly

READINESS n state of being ready or prepared

READING > READ

READINGS > READ

READJUST vb adapt to a new situation

READJUSTS > READJUST

README n document which accompanies computer files or software

READMIT vb let (a person, country, etc) back in to a place or organization

READMITS > READMIT

READOPT vb adopt again

READOPTED > READOPT

READOPTS > READOPT

READORN vb adorn again

READORNED > READORN

READORNS > READORN

READOUT n act of retrieving information from a computer memory or storage device

READOUTS > READOUT

READS > READ

READVANCE vb advance again

READVISE vb advise again

READVISED > READVISE

READVISES > READVISE

READY adj prepared for use or action ▷ vb prepare

READYING > READY

READYMADE adj made for purchase and immediate use by any customer

REAEDIFY vb rebuild

REAEDIFYE same as > REAEDIFY

REAFFIRM vb state again, confirm

REAFFIRMS > REAFFIRM

REAFFIX vb affix again

REAFFIXED > REAFFIX

REAFFIXES > REAFFIX

REAGENCY > REAGENT

REAGENT n chemical substance that reacts with another, used to detect the presence of the other

REAGENTS > REAGENT

REAGIN n type of antibody that is formed against an allergen and is attached to the cells of a tissue. The antigen-antibody reaction that occurs on subsequent contact with the allergen causes tissue damage, leading to the release of histamine and other substances responsible for an allergic reaction

REAGINIC > REAGIN

REAGINS > REAGIN

REAK same as > RECK

REAKED > REAK

REAKING > REAK

REAKS > REAK

REAL adj existing in fact ▷ n name of a former small Spanish or Spanish-American silver coin as well as of the standard monetary unit of Brazil

REALER > REAL

REALES > REAL

REALEST > REAL

REALGAR n rare orange-red soft mineral consisting of arsenic sulphide in monoclinic crystalline form

REALGARS > REALGAR

REALIA npl real-life facts and material used in teaching

REALIGN vb change or put back to a new or former place or position

REALIGNED > REALIGN

REALIGNS > REALIGN

REALISE same as > REALIZE

REALISED > REALISE

REALISER > REALISE

REALISERS > REALISE

REALISES > REALISE

REALISING > REALISE

REALISM n awareness or acceptance of things as they are

REALISMS > REALISM

REALIST n person who is aware of and accepts the physical universe, events, etc, as they are

REALISTIC adj seeing and accepting things as they really are, practical

REALISTS > REALIST

REALITIES > REALITY

REALITY n state of things as they are

REALIZE vb become aware of or grasp the significance of

REALIZED > REALIZE

REALIZER > REALIZE

REALIZERS > REALIZE

REALIZES > REALIZE

REALIZING > REALIZE

REALLIE old or dialect variant of > REALLY

REALLIED > REALLY

REALLIES > REALLY

REALLOT vb allot again

REALLOTS > REALLOT

REALLY adv very ▷ interj exclamation of dismay, doubt, or surprise ▷ vb (in archaic usage) rally

REALLYING > REALLY

REALM n kingdom

REALMLESS > REALM

REALMS > REALM

REALNESS > REAL

REALO n member of the German Green party with moderate views

REALOS > REALO

REALS > REAL

REALTER vb alter again

REALTERED > REALTER

REALTERS > REALTER

REALTIE n archaic word meaning sincerity

REALTIES > REALTY

REALTIME adj (of a data-processing system) constantly updating to reflect the latest changes in data

REALTONE n audio clip of an original recording, used as a mobile phone ringtone

REALTONES > REALTONE

REALTOR n estate agent

REALTORS > REALTOR

REALTY n immovable property

REAM n twenty quires of paper, generally 500 sheets ▷ vb enlarge (a hole) by use of a reamer

REAME archaic variant of > REALM

REAMED > REAM

REAMEND vb amend again

REAMENDED > REAMEND

REAMENDS > REAMEND

REAMER n steel tool with a cylindrical or tapered shank around which longitudinal teeth are ground, used for smoothing the bores of holes accurately to size

REAMERS > REAMER

REAMES > REAME

REAMIER > REAMY

REAMIEST > REAMY

REAMING > REAM

REAMS > REAM

REAMY Scots for > CREAMY

REAN same as > REEN

REANALYSE vb analyse again

REANALYZE US spelling of > REANALYSE

REANIMATE vb refresh or enliven (something) again

REANNEX vb annex again

REANNEXED > REANNEX

REANNEXES > REANNEX

REANOINT vb anoint again

REANOINTS > REANOINT

REANS > REAN

REANSWER vb answer again

REANSWERS > REANSWER

REAP vb cut and gather (a harvest)

REAPABLE > REAP

REAPED > REAP

REAPER n person who reaps or machine for reaping

REAPERS > REAPER

REAPHOOK n sickle

REAPHOOKS > REAPHOOK

REAPING > REAP

REAPPAREL vb clothe again

REAPPEAR vb appear again

REAPPEARS > REAPPEAR

REAPPLIED > REAPPLY
REAPPLIES > REAPPLY
REAPPLY vb put or spread (something) on again
REAPPOINT vb assign (a person, committee, etc) to a post or role again
REAPPROVE vb approve again
REAPS > REAP
REAR n back part ▷ vb care for and educate (children)
REARED > REAR
REARER > REAR
REARERS > REAR
REARGUARD n troops protecting the rear of an army
REARGUE vb argue again
REARGUED > REARGUE
REARGUES > REARGUE
REARGUING > REARGUE
REARHORSE n mantis
REARING > REAR
REARISE vb arise again
REARISEN > REARISE
REARISES > REARISE
REARISING > REARISE
REARLY old word for > EARLY
REARM vb arm again
REARMED > REARM
REARMICE > REARMOUSE
REARMING > REARM
REARMOST adj nearest the back
REARMOUSE same as > REREMOUSE
REARMS > REARM
REAROSE > REARISE
REAROUSAL > REAROUSE
REAROUSE vb arouse again
REAROUSED > REAROUSE
REAROUSES > REAROUSE
REARRANGE vb organize differently, alter
REARREST vb arrest again
REARRESTS > REARREST
REARS > REAR
REARWARD adj in the rear ▷ adv towards the rear ▷ n position in the rear, esp the rear division of a military formation
REARWARDS same as > REARWARD
REASCEND vb ascend again
REASCENDS > REASCEND
REASCENT n new ascent
REASCENTS > REASCENT
REASON n cause or motive ▷ vb think logically in forming conclusions
REASONED adj well thought out or well presented
REASONER > REASON
REASONERS > REASON
REASONING n process of drawing conclusions from facts or evidence
REASONS > REASON
REASSAIL vb assail again

REASSAILS > REASSAIL
REASSERT vb assert (rights, claims, etc) again
REASSERTS > REASSERT
REASSESS vb reconsider the value or importance of
REASSIGN vb move (personnel, resources, etc) to a new post, department, location, etc
REASSIGNS > REASSIGN
REASSORT vb assort again
REASSORTS > REASSORT
REASSUME vb assume again
REASSUMED > REASSUME
REASSUMES > REASSUME
REASSURE vb restore confidence to
REASSURED > REASSURE
REASSURER > REASSURE
REASSURES > REASSURE
REAST same as > REEST
REASTED > REAST
REASTIER > REASTY
REASTIEST > REASTY
REASTING > REAST
REASTS > REAST
REASTY adj (in dialect) rancid
REATA n lasso
REATAS > REATA
REATE n type of crowfoot
REATES > REATE
REATTACH vb attach again
REATTACK vb attack again
REATTACKS > REATTACK
REATTAIN vb attain again
REATTAINS > REATTAIN
REATTEMPT vb attempt again
REAVAIL vb avail again
REAVAILED > REAVAIL
REAVAILS > REAVAIL
REAVE vb carry off (property, prisoners, etc) by force
REAVED > REAVE
REAVER > REAVE
REAVERS > REAVE
REAVES > REAVE
REAVING > REAVE
REAVOW vb avow again
REAVOWED > REAVOW
REAVOWING > REAVOW
REAVOWS > REAVOW
REAWAKE vb awake again
REAWAKED > REAWAKE
REAWAKEN vb emerge or rouse from sleep
REAWAKENS > REAWAKEN
REAWAKES > REAWAKE
REAWAKING > REAWAKE
REAWOKE > REAWAKE
REAWOKEN > REAWAKE
REB n Confederate soldier in the American Civil War (1861–65)
REBACK vb provide with a new back, backing, or lining
REBACKED > REBACK
REBACKING > REBACK
REBACKS > REBACK

REBADGE vb relaunch (a product) under a new name, brand, or logo
REBADGED > REBADGE
REBADGES > REBADGE
REBADGING > REBADGE
REBAIT vb bait again
REBAITED > REBAIT
REBAITING > REBAIT
REBAITS > REBAIT
REBALANCE vb balance again
REBAPTISE same as > REBAPTIZE
REBAPTISM n new baptism
REBAPTIZE vb baptize again
REBAR n rod providing reinforcement in concrete structures
REBARS > REBAR
REBATABLE > REBATE
REBATE n discount or refund ▷ vb cut a rabbet in
REBATED > REBATE
REBATER > REBATE
REBATERS > REBATE
REBATES > REBATE
REBATING > REBATE
REBATO same as > RABATO
REBATOES > REBATO
REBATOS > REBATO
REBBE n individual's chosen spiritual mentor
REBBES > REBBE
REBBETZIN n wife of a rabbi
REBEC n medieval stringed instrument resembling the violin but having a lute-shaped body
REBECK same as > REBEC
REBECKS > REBECK
REBECS > REBEC
REBEGAN > REBEGIN
REBEGIN vb begin again
REBEGINS > REBEGIN
REBEGUN > REBEGIN
REBEL vb revolt against the ruling power ▷ n person who rebels ▷ adj rebelling
REBELDOM > REBEL
REBELDOMS > REBEL
REBELLED > REBEL
REBELLER > REBEL
REBELLERS > REBEL
REBELLING > REBEL
REBELLION n organized open resistance to authority
REBELLOW vb re-echo loudly
REBELLOWS > REBELLOW
REBELS > REBEL
REBID vb bid again
REBIDDEN > REBID
REBIDDING > REBID
REBIDS > REBID
REBILL vb bill again
REBILLED > REBILL
REBILLING > REBILL
REBILLS > REBILL
REBIND vb bind again

REBINDING > REBIND
REBINDS > REBIND
REBIRTH n revival or renaissance
REBIRTHER n person who has undergone rebirthing therapy
REBIRTHS > REBIRTH
REBIT > REBITE
REBITE vb (in printing) to give another application of acid in order to cause further cutting of a plate
REBITES > REBITE
REBITING > REBITE
REBITTEN > REBITE
REBLEND vb blend again
REBLENDED > REBLEND
REBLENDS > REBLEND
REBLENT same as > REBLEND
REBLOCHON n type of soft French cheese
REBLOOM vb bloom again
REBLOOMED > REBLOOM
REBLOOMS > REBLOOM
REBLOSSOM vb blossom again
REBOANT adj resounding or reverberating
REBOARD vb board again
REBOARDED > REBOARD
REBOARDS > REBOARD
REBOATION n repeated bellow
REBODIED > REBODY
REBODIES > REBODY
REBODY vb give a new body to
REBODYING > REBODY
REBOIL vb boil again
REBOILED > REBOIL
REBOILING > REBOIL
REBOILS > REBOIL
REBOOK vb book again
REBOOKED > REBOOK
REBOOKING > REBOOK
REBOOKS > REBOOK
REBOOT vb shut down and then restart (a computer system)
REBOOTED > REBOOT
REBOOTING > REBOOT
REBOOTS > REBOOT
REBOP same as > BEBOP
REBOPS > REBOP
REBORE n boring of a cylinder to restore its true shape ▷ vb carry out this process
REBORED > REBORE
REBORES > REBORE
REBORING > REBORE
REBORN adj active again after a period of inactivity
REBORROW vb borrow again
REBORROWS > REBORROW
REBOTTLE vb bottle again
REBOTTLED > REBOTTLE
REBOTTLES > REBOTTLE
REBOUGHT > REBUY
REBOUND vb spring back ▷ n act of rebounding

REBOUNDED > REBOUND
REBOUNDER > REBOUND
REBOUNDS > REBOUND
REBOZO n long wool or linen scarf covering the shoulders and head, worn by Latin American women
REBOZOS > REBOZO
REBRACE vb brace again
REBRACED > REBRACE
REBRACES > REBRACE
REBRACING > REBRACE
REBRANCH vb branch again
REBRAND vb change or update the image of (an organization or product)
REBRANDED > REBRAND
REBRANDS > REBRAND
REBRED > REBREED
REBREED vb breed again
REBREEDS > REBREED
REBS > REB
REBUFF vb reject or snub ▷ n blunt refusal, snub
REBUFFED > REBUFF
REBUFFING > REBUFF
REBUFFS > REBUFF
REBUILD vb build (a building or town) again, after severe damage
REBUILDED archaic past form of > REBUILD
REBUILDS > REBUILD
REBUILT > REBUILD
REBUKABLE > REBUKE
REBUKE vb scold sternly ▷ n stern scolding
REBUKED > REBUKE
REBUKEFUL > REBUKE
REBUKER > REBUKE
REBUKERS > REBUKE
REBUKES > REBUKE
REBUKING > REBUKE
REBURIAL > REBURY
REBURIALS > REBURY
REBURIED > REBURY
REBURIES > REBURY
REBURY vb bury again
REBURYING > REBURY
REBUS n puzzle consisting of pictures and symbols representing words or syllables
REBUSES > REBUS
REBUT vb prove that (a claim) is untrue
REBUTMENT > REBUT
REBUTS > REBUT
REBUTTAL > REBUT
REBUTTALS > REBUT
REBUTTED > REBUT
REBUTTER n defendant's pleading in reply to a claimant's surrejoinder
REBUTTERS > REBUTTER
REBUTTING > REBUT
REBUTTON vb button again
REBUTTONS > REBUTTON
REBUY vb buy again
REBUYING > REBUY
REBUYS > REBUY
REC n short for recreation
RECAL same as > RECALL

RECALESCE vb glow again
RECALL vb recollect or remember ▷ n ability to remember
RECALLED > RECALL
RECALLER > RECALL
RECALLERS > RECALL
RECALLING > RECALL
RECALLS > RECALL
RECALMENT > RECAL
RECALS > RECAL
RECAMIER n shade of pink
RECAMIERS > RECAMIER
RECANE vb cane again
RECANED > RECANE
RECANES > RECANE
RECANING > RECANE
RECANT vb withdraw (a statement or belief) publicly
RECANTED > RECANT
RECANTER > RECANT
RECANTERS > RECANT
RECANTING > RECANT
RECANTS > RECANT
RECAP vb recapitulate ▷ n recapitulation
RECAPPED > RECAP
RECAPPING > RECAP
RECAPS > RECAP
RECAPTION n process of taking back one's own wife, child, property, etc, without causing a breach of the peace
RECAPTOR > RECAPTURE
RECAPTORS > RECAPTURE
RECAPTURE vb experience again ▷ n act of recapturing
RECARPET vb replace one carpet with another
RECARPETS > RECARPET
RECARRIED > RECARRY
RECARRIES > RECARRY
RECARRY vb carry again
RECAST vb organize or set out in a different way
RECASTING > RECAST
RECASTS > RECAST
RECATALOG vb catalogue again
RECATCH vb catch again
RECATCHES > RECATCH
RECAUGHT > RECATCH
RECAUTION vb caution again
RECCE vb reconnoitre ▷ n reconnaissance
RECCED > RECCE
RECCEED > RECCE
RECCEING > RECCE
RECCES > RECCE
RECCIED > RECCY
RECCIES > RECCY
RECCO same as > RECCE
RECCOS > RECCO
RECCY same as > RECCE
RECCYING > RECCY
RECEDE vb move to a more distant place
RECEDED > RECEDE
RECEDES > RECEDE

RECEDING > RECEDE
RECEIPT n written acknowledgment of money or goods received ▷ vb acknowledge payment of (a bill), as by marking it
RECEIPTED > RECEIPT
RECEIPTOR n person who receipts
RECEIPTS > RECEIPT
RECEIVAL n act of receiving or state of being received
RECEIVALS > RECEIVAL
RECEIVE vb take, accept, or get
RECEIVED adj generally accepted
RECEIVER n part of telephone that is held to the ear
RECEIVERS > RECEIVER
RECEIVES > RECEIVE
RECEIVING > RECEIVE
RECEMENT vb cement again
RECEMENTS > RECEMENT
RECENCIES > RECENT
RECENCY > RECENT
RECENSE vb revise
RECENSED > RECENSE
RECENSES > RECENSE
RECENSING > RECENSE
RECENSION n critical revision of a literary work
RECENSOR vb censor again
RECENSORS > RECENSOR
RECENT adj having happened lately
RECENTER > RECENT
RECENTEST > RECENT
RECENTLY > RECENT
RECENTRE vb centre again
RECENTRED > RECENTRE
RECENTRES > RECENTRE
RECEPT n idea or image formed in the mind by repeated experience of a particular pattern of sensory stimulation
RECEPTION n area for receiving guests, clients, etc
RECEPTIVE adj willing to accept new ideas, suggestions, etc
RECEPTOR n sensory nerve ending that changes specific stimuli into nerve impulses
RECEPTORS > RECEPTOR
RECEPTS > RECEPT
RECERTIFY vb certify again
RECESS n niche or alcove ▷ vb place or set (something) in a recess
RECESSED > RECESS
RECESSES > RECESS
RECESSING > RECESS
RECESSION n period of economic difficulty when little is being bought or sold
RECESSIVE adj receding ▷ n recessive gene or

character
RECHANGE vb change again
RECHANGED > RECHANGE
RECHANGES > RECHANGE
RECHANNEL vb channel again
RECHARGE vb cause (a battery etc) to take in and store electricity again
RECHARGED > RECHARGE
RECHARGER > RECHARGE
RECHARGES > RECHARGE
RECHART vb chart again
RECHARTED > RECHART
RECHARTER vb charter again
RECHARTS > RECHART
RECHATE same as > RECHEAT
RECHATES > RECHATE
RECHAUFFE n warmed-up leftover food
RECHEAT n (in a hunt) sounding of the horn to call back the hounds ▷ vb sound the horn to call back the hounds
RECHEATED > RECHEAT
RECHEATS > RECHEAT
RECHECK vb check again
RECHECKED > RECHECK
RECHECKS > RECHECK
RECHERCHE adj refined or elegant
RECHEW vb chew again
RECHEWED > RECHEW
RECHEWING > RECHEW
RECHEWS > RECHEW
RECHIE adj smoky
RECHIP vb put a new chip into (a stolen mobile phone) so it can be reused
RECHIPPED > RECHIP
RECHIPS > RECHIP
RECHLESSE archaic form of > RECKLESS
RECHOOSE vb choose again
RECHOOSES > RECHOOSE
RECHOSE > RECHOOSE
RECHOSEN > RECHOOSE
RECIPE n directions for cooking a dish
RECIPES > RECIPE
RECIPIENT n person who receives something
RECIRCLE vb circle again
RECIRCLED > RECIRCLE
RECIRCLES > RECIRCLE
RECISION n act of cancelling or rescinding
RECISIONS > RECISION
RECIT n narrative
RECITABLE > RECITE
RECITAL n musical performance by a soloist or soloists
RECITALS > RECITAL
RECITE vb repeat (a poem, story, etc) aloud to an audience
RECITED > RECITE
RECITER > RECITE

RECITERS > RECITE
RECITES > RECITE
RECITING > RECITE
RECITS > RECIT
RECK vb mind or care about (something)
RECKAN adj strained, tormented, or twisted
RECKED > RECK
RECKING > RECK
RECKLESS adj heedless of danger
RECKLING dialect word for > RUNT
RECKLINGS > RECKLING
RECKON vb consider or think
RECKONED > RECKON
RECKONER n any of various devices or tables used to facilitate reckoning, esp a ready reckoner
RECKONERS > RECKONER
RECKONING n counting or calculating
RECKONS > RECKON
RECKS > RECK
RECLAD vb cover in a different substance
RECLADDED > RECLAD
RECLADS > RECLAD
RECLAIM vb regain possession of ▷ n act of reclaiming or state of being reclaimed
RECLAIMED > RECLAIM
RECLAIMER > RECLAIM
RECLAIMS > RECLAIM
RECLAME n public acclaim or attention
RECLAMES > RECLAME
RECLASP vb clasp again
RECLASPED > RECLASP
RECLASPS > RECLASP
RECLEAN vb clean again
RECLEANED > RECLEAN
RECLEANS > RECLEAN
RECLIMB vb climb again
RECLIMBED > RECLIMB
RECLIMBS > RECLIMB
RECLINATE adj (esp of a leaf or stem) naturally curved or bent backwards so that the upper part rests on the ground
RECLINE vb rest in a leaning position
RECLINED > RECLINE
RECLINER n type of armchair having a back that can be adjusted to slope at various angles and, usually, a leg rest
RECLINERS > RECLINER
RECLINES > RECLINE
RECLINING > RECLINE
RECLOSE vb close again
RECLOSED > RECLOSE
RECLOSES > RECLOSE
RECLOSING > RECLOSE
RECLOTHE vb clothe again
RECLOTHED > RECLOTHE
RECLOTHES > RECLOTHE
RECLUSE n person who

avoids other people ▷ adj solitary
RECLUSELY > RECLUSE
RECLUSES > RECLUSE
RECLUSION > RECLUSE
RECLUSIVE > RECLUSE
RECLUSORY n recluse's dwelling or cell
RECOAL vb supply or be supplied with fresh coal
RECOALED > RECOAL
RECOALING > RECOAL
RECOALS > RECOAL
RECOAT vb coat again
RECOATED > RECOAT
RECOATING > RECOAT
RECOATS > RECOAT
RECOCK vb cock again
RECOCKED > RECOCK
RECOCKING > RECOCK
RECOCKS > RECOCK
RECODE vb put into a new code
RECODED > RECODE
RECODES > RECODE
RECODIFY vb codify again
RECODING > RECODE
RECOGNISE same as > RECOGNIZE
RECOGNIZE vb identify as (a person or thing) already known
RECOIL vb jerk or spring back ▷ n backward jerk
RECOILED > RECOIL
RECOILER > RECOIL
RECOILERS > RECOIL
RECOILING > RECOIL
RECOILS > RECOIL
RECOIN vb coin again
RECOINAGE n new coinage
RECOINED > RECOIN
RECOINING > RECOIN
RECOINS > RECOIN
RECOLLECT vb call back to mind, remember
RECOLLET n member of a particular Franciscan order
RECOLLETS > RECOLLET
RECOLOR vb give a new colour to
RECOLORED > RECOLOR
RECOLORS > RECOLOR
RECOMB vb comb again
RECOMBED > RECOMB
RECOMBINE vb join together again
RECOMBING > RECOMB
RECOMBS > RECOMB
RECOMFORT archaic word for > COMFORT
RECOMMEND vb advise or counsel
RECOMMIT vb send (a bill) back to a committee for further consideration
RECOMMITS > RECOMMIT
RECOMPACT vb compact again
RECOMPILE vb compile again
RECOMPOSE vb restore to composure or calmness

RECOMPUTE vb compute again
RECON vb to make a preliminary survey
RECONCILE vb harmonize (conflicting beliefs etc)
RECONDITE adj difficult to understand
RECONDUCT vb conduct again
RECONFER vb confer again
RECONFERS > RECONFER
RECONFINE vb confine again
RECONFIRM vb confirm (an arrangement, agreement, etc) again
RECONNECT vb link or be linked together again
RECONNED > RECON
RECONNING > RECON
RECONQUER vb conquer again
RECONS > RECON
RECONSIGN vb consign again
RECONSOLE vb console again
RECONSULT vb consult again
RECONTACT vb contact again
RECONTOUR vb contour again
RECONVENE vb gather together again after an interval
RECONVERT vb change (something) back to a previous state or form
RECONVEY vb convey again
RECONVEYS > RECONVEY
RECONVICT vb convict again
RECOOK vb cook again
RECOOKED > RECOOK
RECOOKING > RECOOK
RECOOKS > RECOOK
RECOPIED > RECOPY
RECOPIES > RECOPY
RECOPY vb copy again
RECOPYING > RECOPY
RECORD n document or other thing that preserves information ▷ vb put in writing
RECORDED > RECORD
RECORDER n person or machine that records, esp a video, cassette, or tape recorder
RECORDERS > RECORDER
RECORDING n something, esp music, that has been recorded
RECORDIST n person that records
RECORDS > RECORD
RECORK vb cork again
RECORKED > RECORK
RECORKING > RECORK
RECORKS > RECORK
RECOUNT vb tell in detail
RECOUNTAL > RECOUNT

RECOUNTED > RECOUNT
RECOUNTER n narrator of a story
RECOUNTS > RECOUNT
RECOUP vb regain or make good (a loss)
RECOUPE vb (in law) keep back or withhold
RECOUPED > RECOUP
RECOUPING > RECOUP
RECOUPLE vb couple again
RECOUPLED > RECOUPLE
RECOUPLES > RECOUPLE
RECOUPS > RECOUP
RECOURE archaic variant of > RECOVER
RECOURED > RECOURE
RECOURES > RECOURE
RECOURING > RECOURE
RECOURSE archaic word for > RETURN
RECOURSED > RECOURSE
RECOURSES > RECOURSE
RECOVER vb become healthy again
RECOVERED > RECOVER
RECOVEREE n (in law) person found against in a recovery case
RECOVERER > RECOVER
RECOVEROR n (in law) person successfully demanding a right in a recovery case
RECOVERS > RECOVER
RECOVERY n act of recovering from sickness, a shock, or a setback
RECOWER archaic variant of > RECOVER
RECOWERED > RECOWER
RECOWERS > RECOWER
RECOYLE archaic spelling of > RECOIL
RECOYLED > RECOYLE
RECOYLES > RECOYLE
RECOYLING > RECOYLE
RECRATE vb crate again
RECRATED > RECRATE
RECRATES > RECRATE
RECRATING > RECRATE
RECREANCE > RECREANT
RECREANCY > RECREANT
RECREANT n disloyal or cowardly person ▷ adj cowardly
RECREANTS > RECREANT
RECREATE vb amuse (oneself or someone else)
RECREATED > RECREATE
RECREATES > RECREATE
RECREATOR > RECREATE
RECREMENT n any substance, such as bile, that is secreted from a part of the body and later reabsorbed instead of being excreted
RECROSS vb move or go across (something) again
RECROSSED > RECROSS
RECROSSES > RECROSS
RECROWN vb crown again
RECROWNED > RECROWN

RECROWNS > RECROWN
RECRUIT vb enlist (new soldiers, members, etc) ▷ n newly enlisted soldier
RECRUITAL n act of recruiting
RECRUITED > RECRUIT
RECRUITER > RECRUIT
RECRUITS > RECRUIT
RECS > REC
RECTA > RECTUM
RECTAL adj of the rectum
RECTALLY > RECTAL
RECTANGLE n oblong four-sided figure with four right angles
RECTI > RECTUS
RECTIFIED > RECTIFY
RECTIFIER n electronic device, such as a semiconductor diode or valve, that converts an alternating current to a direct current by suppression or inversion of alternate half cycles
RECTIFIES > RECTIFY
RECTIFY vb put right, correct
RECTION n (in grammar) the determination of the form of one word by another word
RECTIONS > RECTION
RECTITIC > RECTITIS
RECTITIS n inflammation of the rectum
RECTITUDE n moral correctness
RECTO n right-hand page of a book
RECTOCELE n protrusion or herniation of the rectum into the vagina
RECTOR n clergyman in charge of a parish
RECTORAL adj of or relating to God's rule or to a rector
RECTORATE > RECTOR
RECTORESS n female rector or the wife or widow of a rector
RECTORIAL adj of or relating to a rector ▷ n election of a rector
RECTORIES > RECTORY
RECTORS > RECTOR
RECTORY n rector's house
RECTOS > RECTO
RECTRESS same as > RECTORESS
RECTRICES > RECTRIX
RECTRIX n any of the large stiff feathers of a bird's tail, used in controlling the direction of flight
RECTUM n final section of the large intestine
RECTUMS > RECTUM
RECTUS n straight muscle, esp either of two muscles of the anterior abdominal wall
RECUILE archaic variant of

> RECOIL
RECUILED > RECUILE
RECUILES > RECUILE
RECUILING > RECUILE
RECULE archaic variant of > RECOIL
RECULED > RECULE
RECULES > RECULE
RECULING > RECULE
RECUMBENT adj lying down
RECUR vb happen again
RECURE vb archaic word for cure or recover
RECURED > RECURE
RECURES > RECURE
RECURING > RECURE
RECURRED > RECUR
RECURRENT adj happening or tending to happen again or repeatedly
RECURRING > RECUR
RECURS > RECUR
RECURSION n act or process of returning or running back
RECURSIVE > RECURSION
RECURVATE adj bent back
RECURVE vb curve or bend (something) back or down or (of something) to be so curved or bent
RECURVED > RECURVE
RECURVES > RECURVE
RECURVING > RECURVE
RECUSAL n withdrawal of a judge from a case
RECUSALS > RECUSAL
RECUSANCE > RECUSANT
RECUSANCY > RECUSANT
RECUSANT n Roman Catholic who did not attend the services of the Church of England ▷ adj (formerly, of Catholics) refusing to attend services of the Church of England
RECUSANTS > RECUSANT
RECUSE vb (in law) object to or withdraw (a judge)
RECUSED > RECUSE
RECUSES > RECUSE
RECUSING > RECUSE
RECUT vb cut again
RECUTS > RECUT
RECUTTING > RECUT
RECYCLATE n recyclable material
RECYCLE vb reprocess (used materials) for further use ▷ n repetition of a fixed sequence of events
RECYCLED > RECYCLE
RECYCLER > RECYCLE
RECYCLERS > RECYCLE
RECYCLES > RECYCLE
RECYCLING > RECYCLE
RECYCLIST > RECYCLE
RED adj of a colour varying from crimson to orange and seen in blood, fire, etc ▷ n red colour
REDACT vb compose or

draft (an edict, proclamation, etc)
REDACTED > REDACT
REDACTING > REDACT
REDACTION > REDACT
REDACTOR > REDACT
REDACTORS > REDACT
REDACTS > REDACT
REDAMAGE vb damage again
REDAMAGED > REDAMAGE
REDAMAGES > REDAMAGE
REDAN n fortification of two parapets at a salient angle
REDANS > REDAN
REDARGUE vb archaic word for disprove or refute
REDARGUED > REDARGUE
REDARGUES > REDARGUE
REDATE vb change date of
REDATED > REDATE
REDATES > REDATE
REDATING > REDATE
REDBACK n small venomous Australian spider
REDBACKS > REDBACK
REDBAIT vb harass those with leftwing leanings
REDBAITED > REDBAIT
REDBAITER n person who deliberately antagonizes communists
REDBAITS > REDBAIT
REDBAY n type of tree
REDBAYS > REDBAY
REDBELLY n any of various animals having red underparts, especially the char or the redbelly turtle
REDBIRD n type of bird, the male of which is distinguished by its bright red plumage and black wings
REDBIRDS > REDBIRD
REDBONE n type of American dog
REDBONES > REDBONE
REDBREAST n robin
REDBRICK adj (of a university in Britain) founded in the late 19th or early 20th century ▷ n denoting, relating to, or characteristic of a provincial British university of relatively recent foundation, esp as distinguished from Oxford and Cambridge
REDBRICKS > REDBRICK
REDBUD n American leguminous tree with heart-shaped leaves and small budlike pink flowers
REDBUDS > REDBUD
REDBUG another name for > CHIGGER
REDBUGS > REDBUG
REDCAP n military policeman
REDCAPS > REDCAP
REDCOAT n British soldier

REDCOATS > REDCOAT
REDD vb bring order to ▷ n act or an instance of redding
REDDED > REDD
REDDEN vb make or become red
REDDENDA > REDDENDUM
REDDENDO n (in Scotland) legal clause specifying what payment or duties are required in exchange for something
REDDENDOS > REDDENDO
REDDENDUM n legal clause specifying what shall be given in return for the granting of a lease
REDDENED > REDDEN
REDDENING > REDDEN
REDDENS > REDDEN
REDDER > REDD
REDDERS > REDD
REDDEST > RED
REDDIER > REDDY
REDDIEST > REDDY
REDDING > REDD
REDDINGS > REDD
REDDISH adj somewhat red
REDDISHLY > REDDISH
REDDLE same as > RUDDLE
REDDLED > REDDLE
REDDLEMAN same as > RUDDLEMAN
REDDLEMEN > REDDLEMAN
REDDLES > REDDLE
REDDLING > REDDLE
REDDS > REDD
REDDY adj reddish
REDE n advice or counsel ▷ vb advise
REDEAL vb deal again
REDEALING > REDEAL
REDEALS > REDEAL
REDEALT > REDEAL
REDEAR n variety of sunfish with a red flash above the gills
REDEARS > REDEAR
REDECIDE vb decide again
REDECIDED > REDECIDE
REDECIDES > REDECIDE
REDECRAFT n logic
REDED > REDE
REDEEM vb make up for
REDEEMED > REDEEM
REDEEMER > REDEEM
REDEEMERS > REDEEM
REDEEMING adj making up for faults or deficiencies
REDEEMS > REDEEM
REDEFEAT vb defeat again
REDEFEATS > REDEFEAT
REDEFECT vb defect back or again
REDEFECTS > REDEFECT
REDEFIED > REDEFY
REDEFIES > REDEFY
REDEFINE vb define (something) again or differently
REDEFINED > REDEFINE

r

REDEFINES > REDEFINE
REDEFY *vb* defy again
REDEFYING > REDEFY
REDELESS > REDE
REDELIVER *vb* deliver again
REDEMAND *vb* demand again
REDEMANDS > REDEMAND
REDENIED > REDENY
REDENIES > REDENY
REDENY *vb* deny again
REDENYING > REDENY
REDEPLOY *vb* assign to a new position or task
REDEPLOYS > REDEPLOY
REDEPOSIT *vb* deposit again
REDES > REDE
REDESCEND *vb* descend again
REDESIGN *vb* change the design of (something) ▷ *n* something that has been redesigned
REDESIGNS > REDESIGN
REDEVELOP *vb* rebuild or renovate (an area or building)
REDEYE *n* inferior whiskey
REDEYES > REDEYE
REDFIN *n* any of various small fishes with reddish fins that are popular aquarium fishes
REDFINS > REDFIN
REDFISH *n* male salmon that has recently spawned
REDFISHES > REDFISH
REDFOOT *n* fatal disease of newborn lambs of unknown cause in which the horny layers of the feet become separated, exposing the red laminae below
REDFOOTS > REDFOOT
REDHANDED *adj* in the act of doing something criminal, wrong, or shameful
REDHEAD *n* person with reddish hair
REDHEADED > REDHEAD
REDHEADS > REDHEAD
REDHORSE *n* type of fish
REDHORSES > REDHORSE
REDIA *n* parasitic larva of flukes that has simple locomotory organs, pharynx, and intestine and gives rise either to other rediae or to a different larva (the cercaria)
REDIAE > REDIA
REDIAL *vb* dial (a telephone number) again
REDIALED > REDIAL
REDIALING > REDIAL
REDIALLED > REDIAL
REDIALS > REDIAL
REDIAS > REDIA
REDICTATE *vb* dictate again

REDID > REDO
REDIGEST *vb* digest again
REDIGESTS > REDIGEST
REDIGRESS *vb* digress again
REDING > REDE
REDINGOTE *n* woman's coat with a close-fitting top and a full skirt
REDIP *vb* dip again
REDIPPED > REDIP
REDIPPING > REDIP
REDIPS > REDIP
REDIPT *archaic past form of* > REDIP
REDIRECT *vb* send in a new direction or course
REDIRECTS > REDIRECT
REDISCUSS *vb* discuss again
REDISPLAY *vb* display again
REDISPOSE *vb* dispose again
REDISTIL *vb* distil again
REDISTILL *US spelling of* > REDISTIL
REDISTILS > REDISTIL
REDIVIDE *vb* divide again
REDIVIDED > REDIVIDE
REDIVIDES > REDIVIDE
REDIVIVUS *adj* returned to life
REDIVORCE *vb* divorce again
REDLEG *n* derogatory term for poor White
REDLEGS > REDLEG
REDLINE *vb* (esp of a bank or group of banks) to refuse a loan to (a person or country) because of the presumed risks involved
REDLINED > REDLINE
REDLINER > REDLINE
REDLINERS > REDLINE
REDLINES > REDLINE
REDLINING > REDLINE
REDLY > RED
REDNECK *n* (in the southwestern US) derogatory term for a poor uneducated White farm worker ▷ *adj* reactionary and bigoted
REDNECKED *adj* with a red neck
REDNECKS > REDNECK
REDNESS > RED
REDNESSES > RED
REDO *vb* do over again in order to improve ▷ *n* instance of redoing something
REDOCK *vb* dock again
REDOCKED > REDOCK
REDOCKING > REDOCK
REDOCKS > REDOCK
REDOES > REDO
REDOING > REDO
REDOLENCE > REDOLENT
REDOLENCY > REDOLENT
REDOLENT *adj* reminiscent (of)

REDON *vb* don again
REDONE > REDO
REDONNED > REDON
REDONNING > REDON
REDONS > REDON
REDOS > REDO
REDOUBLE *vb* increase, multiply, or intensify ▷ *n* act of redoubling
REDOUBLED > REDOUBLE
REDOUBLER > REDOUBLE
REDOUBLES > REDOUBLE
REDOUBT *n* small fort defending a hilltop or pass ▷ *vb* fear
REDOUBTED > REDOUBT
REDOUBTS > REDOUBT
REDOUND *vb* cause advantage or disadvantage (to)
REDOUNDED > REDOUND
REDOUNDS > REDOUND
REDOUT *n* reddened vision and other symptoms caused by a rush of blood to the head in response to negative gravitational stresses
REDOUTS > REDOUT
REDOWA *n* Bohemian folk dance similar to the waltz
REDOWAS > REDOWA
REDOX *n* chemical reaction in which one substance is reduced and the other is oxidized
REDOXES > REDOX
REDPOLL *n* mostly grey-brown finch with a red crown and pink breast
REDPOLLS > REDPOLL
REDRAFT *vb* write a second copy of (a letter, proposal, essay, etc) ▷ *n* second draft
REDRAFTED > REDRAFT
REDRAFTS > REDRAFT
REDRAW *vb* draw or draw up (something) again or differently
REDRAWER > REDRAW
REDRAWERS > REDRAW
REDRAWING > REDRAW
REDRAWN > REDRAW
REDRAWS > REDRAW
REDREAM *vb* dream again
REDREAMED > REDREAM
REDREAMS > REDREAM
REDREAMT > REDREAM
REDRESS *vb* make amends for ▷ *n* compensation or amends
REDRESSAL *n* act of redressing
REDRESSED > REDRESS
REDRESSER > REDRESS
REDRESSES > REDRESS
REDRESSOR > REDRESS
REDREW > REDRAW
REDRIED > REDRY
REDRIES > REDRY
REDRILL *vb* drill again
REDRILLED > REDRILL
REDRILLS > REDRILL
REDRIVE *vb* drive again

REDRIVEN > REDRIVE
REDRIVES > REDRIVE
REDRIVING > REDRIVE
REDROOT *n* yellow-flowered bog plant of E North America whose roots yield a red dye
REDROOTS > REDROOT
REDROVE > REDRIVE
REDRY *vb* dry again
REDRYING > REDRY
REDS > RED
REDSEAR *same as* > REDSHORT
REDSHANK *n* large Eurasian sandpiper with red legs
REDSHANKS > REDSHANK
REDSHARE *n* red algae
REDSHIFT *n* shift in the lines of the spectrum of an astronomical object
REDSHIFTS > REDSHIFT
REDSHIRE *same as* > REDSHARE
REDSHIRT *vb* take a year out of a sports team
REDSHIRTS > REDSHIRT
REDSHORT *vb* become brittle at red-hot temperatures
REDSKIN *n* offensive term for Native American
REDSKINS > REDSKIN
REDSTART *n* European bird of the thrush family, the male of which has an orange-brown tail and breast
REDSTARTS > REDSTART
REDSTREAK *n* variety of apple
REDTAIL *n* variety of bird with red colouring on its tail
REDTAILS > REDTAIL
REDTOP *n* sensationalist tabloid newspaper
REDTOPS > REDTOP
REDUB *vb* fix or repair
REDUBBED > REDUB
REDUBBING > REDUB
REDUBS > REDUB
REDUCE *vb* bring down, lower
REDUCED > REDUCE
REDUCER *n* chemical solution used to lessen the density of a negative or print by oxidizing some of the blackened silver to soluble silver compounds
REDUCERS > REDUCER
REDUCES > REDUCE
REDUCIBLE > REDUCE
REDUCIBLY > REDUCE
REDUCING > REDUCE
REDUCTANT *n* reducing agent
REDUCTASE *n* any enzyme that catalyses a biochemical reduction reaction
REDUCTION *n* act of reducing

REDUCTIVE
> REDUCTION
REDUCTOR n apparatus in which substances can be reduced
REDUCTORS > REDUCTOR
REDUIT n fortified part from which a garrison may fight on once an enemy has taken outworks
REDUITS > REDUIT
REDUNDANT adj (of a worker) no longer needed
REDUVIID n type of bug of the family which includes the assassin bug and the wheel bug
REDUVIIDS > REDUVIID
REDUX adj brought back or returned
REDWARE another name for > KELP
REDWARES > REDWARE
REDWATER n tick-borne disease of cattle
REDWATERS > REDWATER
REDWING n small European thrush
REDWINGS > REDWING
REDWOOD n giant Californian conifer with reddish bark
REDWOODS > REDWOOD
REDYE vb dye again
REDYED > REDYE
REDYEING > REDYE
REDYES > REDYE
REE n Scots word for walled enclosure
REEARN vb earn again
REEARNED > REEARN
REEARNING > REEARN
REEARNS > REEARN
REEBOK same as > RHEBOK
REEBOKS > REEBOK
REECH vb (in dialect) smoke
REECHED > REECH
REECHES > REECH
REECHIE same as > REECHY
REECHIER > REECHY
REECHIEST > REECHY
REECHING > REECH
REECHO vb echo again
REECHOED > REECHO
REECHOES > REECHO
REECHOING > REECHO
REECHY adj (in dialect) smoky
REED n tall grass that grows in swamps and shallow water
REEDBED n area of wetland with reeds growing in it
REEDBEDS > REEDBED
REEDBIRD n any of several birds that frequent reed beds, esp (in the US and Canada) the bobolink
REEDBIRDS > REEDBIRD
REEDBUCK n buff-coloured African antelope with inward-curving horns
REEDBUCKS > REEDBUCK

REEDE obsolete variant of > RED
REEDED > REED
REEDEN adj of or consisting of reeds
REEDER n thatcher
REEDERS > REEDER
REEDES > REEDE
REEDIER > REEDY
REEDIEST > REEDY
REEDIFIED > REEDIFY
REEDIFIES > REEDIFY
REEDIFY vb edify again or rebuild
REEDILY > REEDY
REEDINESS > REEDY
REEDING n set of small semicircular architectural mouldings
REEDINGS > REEDING
REEDIT vb edit again
REEDITED > REEDIT
REEDITING > REEDIT
REEDITION n new edition
REEDITS > REEDIT
REEDLIKE adj resembling a reed
REEDLING n tawny titlike Eurasian songbird common in reed beds
REEDLINGS > REEDLING
REEDMAN n musician who plays a wind instrument that has a reed
REEDMEN > REEDMAN
REEDS > REED
REEDUCATE vb educate again
REEDY adj harsh and thin in tone
REEF n ridge of rock or coral near the surface of the sea ▷ vb roll up part of a sail
REEFABLE > REEF
REEFED > REEF
REEFER n short thick jacket worn esp by sailors
REEFERS > REEFER
REEFIER > REEFY
REEFIEST > REEFY
REEFING > REEF
REEFINGS > REEF
REEFS > REEF
REEFY adj with reefs
REEJECT vb eject again
REEJECTED > REEJECT
REEJECTS > REEJECT
REEK vb smell strongly ▷ n strong unpleasant smell
REEKED > REEK
REEKER > REEK
REEKERS > REEK
REEKIE same as > REEKY
REEKIER > REEK
REEKIEST > REEK
REEKING > REEK
REEKINGLY > REEK
REEKS > REEK
REEKY adj steamy or smoky
REEL n cylindrical object on which film, tape, thread, or wire is wound ▷ vb stagger, sway, or whirl
REELABLE > REEL

REELECT vb elect again
REELECTED > REELECT
REELECTS > REELECT
REELED > REEL
REELER > REEL
REELERS > REEL
REELEVATE vb elevate again
REELING > REEL
REELINGLY > REEL
REELINGS > REEL
REELMAN n (formerly) member of a beach life-saving team operating a winch
REELMEN > REELMAN
REELS > REEL
REEMBARK vb embark again
REEMBARKS > REEMBARK
REEMBODY vb embody again
REEMBRACE vb embrace again
REEMERGE vb emerge again
REEMERGED > REEMERGE
REEMERGES > REEMERGE
REEMIT vb emit again
REEMITS > REEMIT
REEMITTED > REEMIT
REEMPLOY vb employ again
REEMPLOYS > REEMPLOY
REEN n ditch, esp a drainage channel
REENACT vb enact again
REENACTED > REENACT
REENACTOR > REENACT
REENACTS > REENACT
REENDOW vb endow again
REENDOWED > REENDOW
REENDOWS > REENDOW
REENFORCE vb enforce again
REENGAGE vb engage again
REENGAGED > REENGAGE
REENGAGES > REENGAGE
REENGRAVE vb engrave again
REENJOY vb enjoy again
REENJOYED > REENJOY
REENJOYS > REENJOY
REENLARGE vb enlarge again
REENLIST vb enlist again
REENLISTS > REENLIST
REENROLL vb enrol again
REENROLLS > REENROLL
REENS > REEN
REENSLAVE vb enslave again
REENTER vb enter again
REENTERED > REENTER
REENTERS > REENTER
REENTRANT n reentering angle ▷ adj (of an angle) pointing inwards
REENTRIES > REENTRY
REENTRY n return of a spacecraft into the earth's atmosphere
REEQUIP vb equip again

REEQUIPS > REEQUIP
REERECT vb erect again
REERECTED > REERECT
REERECTS > REERECT
REES > REE
REEST vb (esp of horses) to be noisily uncooperative
REESTED > REEST
REESTIER > REESTY
REESTIEST > REESTY
REESTING > REEST
REESTS > REEST
REESTY same as > REASTY
REEVE n local representative of the king in a shire until the early 11th century ▷ vb pass (a rope or cable) through an eye or other narrow opening
REEVED > REEVE
REEVES > REEVE
REEVING > REEVE
REEVOKE vb evoke again
REEVOKED > REEVOKE
REEVOKES > REEVOKE
REEVOKING > REEVOKE
REEXAMINE vb examine again
REEXECUTE vb execute again
REEXHIBIT vb exhibit again
REEXPEL vb expel again
REEXPELS > REEXPEL
REEXPLAIN vb explain again
REEXPLORE vb explore again
REEXPORT vb export again
REEXPORTS > REEXPORT
REEXPOSE vb expose again
REEXPOSED > REEXPOSE
REEXPOSES > REEXPOSE
REEXPRESS vb express again
REF n referee in sport ▷ vb referee
REFACE vb repair or renew the facing of (a wall)
REFACED > REFACE
REFACES > REFACE
REFACING > REFACE
REFALL vb fall again
REFALLEN > REFALL
REFALLING > REFALL
REFALLS > REFALL
REFASHION vb give a new form to (something)
REFASTEN vb fasten again
REFASTENS > REFASTEN
REFECT vb archaic word for restore or refresh with food and drink
REFECTED > REFECT
REFECTING > REFECT
REFECTION n refreshment with food and drink
REFECTIVE > REFECT
REFECTORY n room for meals in a college etc
REFECTS > REFECT
REFED > REFEED
REFEED vb feed again
REFEEDING > REFEED

r

REFEEDS > REFEED
REFEEL *vb* feel again
REFEELING > REFEEL
REFEELS > REFEEL
REFEL *vb* refute
REFELL > REFALL
REFELLED > REFEL
REFELLING > REFEL
REFELS > REFEL
REFELT > REFEEL
REFENCE *vb* fence again
REFENCED > REFENCE
REFENCES > REFENCE
REFENCING > REFENCE
REFER *vb* allude (to)
REFERABLE > REFER
REFEREE *n* umpire in sports, esp soccer or boxing ▷ *vb* act as referee of
REFEREED > REFEREE
REFEREES > REFEREE
REFERENCE *n* act of referring
REFERENDA *npl* polls to determine the view of the electorate on something; referendums
REFERENT *n* object or idea to which a word or phrase refers
REFERENTS > REFERENT
REFERRAL > REFER
REFERRALS > REFER
REFERRED > REFER
REFERRER > REFER
REFERRERS > REFER
REFERRING > REFER
REFERS > REFER
REFFED > REF
REFFING > REF
REFFO *n* offensive name for a European refugee after World War II
REFFOS > REFFO
REFIGHT *vb* fight again ▷ *n* second or new fight
REFIGHTS > REFIGHT
REFIGURE *vb* figure again
REFIGURED > REFIGURE
REFIGURES > REFIGURE
REFILE *vb* file again
REFILED > REFILE
REFILES > REFILE
REFILING > REFILE
REFILL *vb* fill again ▷ *n* second or subsequent filling
REFILLED > REFILL
REFILLING > REFILL
REFILLS > REFILL
REFILM *vb* film again
REFILMED > REFILM
REFILMING > REFILM
REFILMS > REFILM
REFILTER *vb* filter again
REFILTERS > REFILTER
REFINABLE > REFINE
REFINANCE *vb* finance again
REFIND *vb* find again
REFINDING > REFIND
REFINDS > REFIND
REFINE *vb* purify
REFINED *adj* cultured or polite

REFINEDLY > REFINED
REFINER *n* person, device, or substance that removes impurities, sediment, or other unwanted matter from something
REFINERS > REFINER
REFINERY *n* place where sugar, oil, etc is refined
REFINES > REFINE
REFINING > REFINE
REFININGS > REFINE
REFINISH *vb* finish again
REFIRE *vb* fire again
REFIRED > REFIRE
REFIRES > REFIRE
REFIRING > REFIRE
REFIT *vb* make ready for use again by repairing or re-equipping ▷ *n* repair or re-equipping for further use
REFITMENT > REFIT
REFITS > REFIT
REFITTED > REFIT
REFITTING > REFIT
REFIX *vb* fix again
REFIXED > REFIX
REFIXES > REFIX
REFIXING > REFIX
REFLAG *vb* flag again
REFLAGGED > REFLAG
REFLAGS > REFLAG
REFLATE *vb* inflate or be inflated again
REFLATED > REFLATE
REFLATES > REFLATE
REFLATING > REFLATE
REFLATION *n* increase in the supply of money and credit designed to encourage economic activity
REFLECT *vb* throw back, esp rays of light, heat, etc
REFLECTED > REFLECT
REFLECTER *n* archaic word for a critic
REFLECTOR *n* polished surface for reflecting light etc
REFLECTS > REFLECT
REFLET *n* iridescent glow or lustre, as on ceramic ware
REFLETS > REFLET
REFLEW > REFLY
REFLEX *n* involuntary response to a stimulus or situation ▷ *adj* (of a muscular action) involuntary ▷ *vb* bend, turn, or reflect backwards
REFLEXED > REFLEX
REFLEXES > REFLEX
REFLEXING > REFLEX
REFLEXION *n* act of reflecting or the state of being reflected
REFLEXIVE *adj* denoting a pronoun that refers back to the subject of a sentence or clause ▷ *n* reflexive pronoun or verb

REFLEXLY > REFLEX
REFLIES > REFLY
REFLOAT *vb* float again
REFLOATED > REFLOAT
REFLOATS > REFLOAT
REFLOOD *vb* flood again
REFLOODED > REFLOOD
REFLOODS > REFLOOD
REFLOW *vb* flow again
REFLOWED > REFLOW
REFLOWER *vb* flower again
REFLOWERS > REFLOWER
REFLOWING > REFLOW
REFLOWN > REFLY
REFLOWS > REFLOW
REFLUENCE > REFLUENT
REFLUENT *adj* flowing back
REFLUX *vb* boil or be boiled in a vessel attached to a condenser, so that the vapour condenses and flows back into the vessel ▷ *n* act of refluxing
REFLUXED > REFLUX
REFLUXES > REFLUX
REFLUXING > REFLUX
REFLY *vb* fly again
REFLYING > REFLY
REFOCUS *vb* focus again or anew
REFOCUSED > REFOCUS
REFOCUSES > REFOCUS
REFOLD *vb* fold again
REFOLDED > REFOLD
REFOLDING > REFOLD
REFOLDS > REFOLD
REFOOT *vb* foot again
REFOOTED > REFOOT
REFOOTING > REFOOT
REFOOTS > REFOOT
REFOREST *vb* replant (an area that was formerly forested) with trees
REFORESTS > REFOREST
REFORGE *vb* forge again
REFORGED > REFORGE
REFORGES > REFORGE
REFORGING > REFORGE
REFORM *n* improvement ▷ *vb* improve
REFORMADE *archaic variant of* > REFORMADO
REFORMADO *n* formerly, an officer whose men have been disbanded
REFORMAT *vb* format again
REFORMATE *n* gas formed in certain processes
REFORMATS > REFORMAT
REFORMED > REFORM
REFORMER > REFORM
REFORMERS > REFORM
REFORMING > REFORM
REFORMISM *n* doctrine or movement advocating reform, esp political or religious reform, rather than advocating
REFORMIST > REFORMISM
REFORMS > REFORM
REFORTIFY *vb* fortify again or further

REFOUGHT > REFIGHT
REFOUND *vb* found again
REFOUNDED > REFOUND
REFOUNDER > REFOUND
REFOUNDS > REFOUND
REFRACT *vb* change the course of (light etc) passing from one medium to another
REFRACTED > REFRACT
REFRACTOR *n* object or material that refracts
REFRACTS > REFRACT
REFRAIN *n* frequently repeated part of a song ▷ *vb* abstain (from action)
REFRAINED > REFRAIN
REFRAINER > REFRAIN
REFRAINS > REFRAIN
REFRAME *vb* support or enclose (a picture, photograph, etc) in a new or different frame
REFRAMED > REFRAME
REFRAMES > REFRAME
REFRAMING > REFRAME
REFREEZE *vb* freeze or be frozen again after having defrosted
REFREEZES > REFREEZE
REFRESH *vb* revive or reinvigorate, as through food, drink, or rest
REFRESHED > REFRESH
REFRESHEN *vb* freshen again
REFRESHER *n* something that refreshes, such as a cold drink
REFRESHES > REFRESH
REFRIED > REFRY
REFRIES > REFRY
REFRINGE *formerly used to mean* > REFRACT
REFRINGED > REFRINGE
REFRINGES > REFRINGE
REFRONT *vb* put a new front on
REFRONTED > REFRONT
REFRONTS > REFRONT
REFROZE > REFREEZE
REFROZEN > REFREEZE
REFRY *vb* fry again
REFRYING > REFRY
REFS > REF
REFT > REAVE
REFUEL *vb* supply or be supplied with fresh fuel
REFUELED > REFUEL
REFUELING > REFUEL
REFUELLED > REFUEL
REFUELS > REFUEL
REFUGE *n* (source of) shelter or protection ▷ *vb* take refuge or give refuge to
REFUGED > REFUGE
REFUGEE *n* person who seeks refuge, esp in a foreign country
REFUGEES > REFUGEE
REFUGES > REFUGE
REFUGIA > REFUGIUM
REFUGING > REFUGE**

REFUGIUM n geographical region that has remained unaltered by a climatic change affecting surrounding regions and that therefore forms a haven for relict fauna and flora

REFULGENT adj shining, radiant

REFUND vb pay back ▷ n return of money

REFUNDED > REFUND

REFUNDER > REFUND

REFUNDERS > REFUND

REFUNDING > REFUND

REFUNDS > REFUND

REFURBISH vb renovate and brighten up

REFURNISH vb furnish again

REFUSABLE > REFUSE

REFUSAL n denial of anything demanded or offered

REFUSALS > REFUSAL

REFUSE vb decline, deny, or reject ▷ n rubbish or useless matter

REFUSED > REFUSE

REFUSENIK n person who refuses to obey a law or cooperate with the government because of strong beliefs

REFUSER > REFUSE

REFUSERS > REFUSE

REFUSES > REFUSE

REFUSING > REFUSE

REFUSION n new or further fusion

REFUSIONS > REFUSION

REFUSNIK same as > REFUSENIK

REFUSNIKS > REFUSNIK

REFUTABLE > REFUTE

REFUTABLY > REFUTE

REFUTAL n act or process of refuting

REFUTALS > REFUTAL

REFUTE vb disprove

REFUTED > REFUTE

REFUTER > REFUTE

REFUTERS > REFUTE

REFUTES > REFUTE

REFUTING > REFUTE

REG n large expanse of stony desert terrain

REGAIN vb get back or recover ▷ n process of getting something back, esp lost weight

REGAINED > REGAIN

REGAINER > REGAIN

REGAINERS > REGAIN

REGAINING > REGAIN

REGAINS > REGAIN

REGAL adj of or like a king or queen ▷ n portable organ equipped only with small reed pipes, popular from the 15th century and recently revived for modern performance

REGALE vb entertain (someone) with stories etc ▷ n feast

REGALED > REGALE

REGALER > REGALE

REGALERS > REGALE

REGALES > REGALE

REGALIA npl ceremonial emblems of royalty or high office

REGALIAN adj royal

REGALIAS > REGALIA

REGALING > REGALE

REGALISM n principle that the sovereign has supremacy in church affairs

REGALISMS > REGALISM

REGALIST > REGALISM

REGALISTS > REGALISM

REGALITY n state or condition of being royal

REGALLY > REGAL

REGALNESS > REGAL

REGALS > REGAL

REGAR same as > REGUR

REGARD vb consider ▷ n respect or esteem

REGARDANT adj (of a beast) shown looking backwards over its shoulder

REGARDED > REGARD

REGARDER > REGARD

REGARDERS > REGARD

REGARDFUL adj showing regard (for)

REGARDING prep on the subject of

REGARDS > REGARD

REGARS > REGAR

REGATHER vb gather again

REGATHERS > REGATHER

REGATTA n meeting for yacht or boat races

REGATTAS > REGATTA

REGAUGE vb gauge again

REGAUGED > REGAUGE

REGAUGES > REGAUGE

REGAUGING > REGAUGE

REGAVE > REGIVE

REGEAR vb readjust

REGEARED > REGEAR

REGEARING > REGEAR

REGEARS > REGEAR

REGELATE vb undergo or cause to undergo regelation

REGELATED > REGELATE

REGELATES > REGELATE

REGENCE old variant of > REGENCY

REGENCES > REGENCE

REGENCIES > REGENCY

REGENCY n status or period of office of a regent

REGENT n ruler of a kingdom during the absence, childhood, or illness of its monarch ▷ adj ruling as a regent

REGENTAL > REGENT

REGENTS > REGENT

REGES > REX

REGEST n archaic word for register

REGESTS > REGEST

REGGAE n style of Jamaican popular music with a strong beat

REGGAES > REGGAE

REGGAETON n popular music genre from Puerto Rico

REGGO same as > REGO

REGGOS > REGGO

REGICIDAL > REGICIDE

REGICIDE n killing of a king

REGICIDES > REGICIDE

REGIE n government-directed management or government monopoly

REGIES > REGIE

REGIFT vb give (a previously received gift) to someone else

REGIFTED > REGIFT

REGIFTING > REGIFT

REGIFTS > REGIFT

REGILD vb gild again

REGILDED > REGILD

REGILDING > REGILD

REGILDS > REGILD

REGILT archaic past form of > REGILD

REGIME n system of government

REGIMEN n prescribed system of diet etc

REGIMENS > REGIMEN

REGIMENT n organized body of troops as a unit of the army ▷ vb force discipline or order on, esp in a domineering manner

REGIMENTS > REGIMENT

REGIMES > REGIME

REGIMINAL adj regimen-related

REGINA n queen

REGINAE > REGINA

REGINAL adj queenly

REGINAS > REGINA

REGION n administrative division of a country

REGIONAL adj of, characteristic of, or limited to a region ▷ n regional heat of a competition

REGIONALS > REGIONAL

REGIONARY same as > REGIONAL

REGIONS > REGION

REGISSEUR n official in a dance company with varying duties, usually including directing productions

REGISTER n (book containing) an official list or record of things ▷ vb enter in a register or set down in writing

REGISTERS > REGISTER

REGISTRAR n keeper of official records

REGISTRY n place where official records are kept

REGIUS as in regius professor Crown-appointed holder of a university chair

REGIVE vb give again or back

REGIVEN > REGIVE

REGIVES > REGIVE

REGIVING > REGIVE

REGLAZE vb glaze again

REGLAZED > REGLAZE

REGLAZES > REGLAZE

REGLAZING > REGLAZE

REGLET n flat narrow architectural moulding

REGLETS > REGLET

REGLORIFY vb glorify again

REGLOSS vb gloss again or give a new gloss to

REGLOSSED > REGLOSS

REGLOSSES > REGLOSS

REGLOW vb glow again

REGLOWED > REGLOW

REGLOWING > REGLOW

REGLOWS > REGLOW

REGLUE vb glue again

REGLUED > REGLUE

REGLUES > REGLUE

REGLUING > REGLUE

REGMA n type of fruit with cells that break open and break away when ripe

REGMAKER n drink taken to relieve the symptoms of a hangover

REGMAKERS > REGMAKER

REGMATA > REGMA

REGNA > REGNUM

REGNAL adj of a sovereign, reign, or kingdom

REGNANCY > REGNANT

REGNANT adj reigning

REGNUM n reign or rule

REGO n registration of a motor vehicle

REGOLITH n layer of loose material covering the bedrock of the earth and moon, etc, comprising soil, sand, rock fragments, volcanic ash, glacial drift, etc

REGOLITHS > REGOLITH

REGORGE vb vomit up

REGORGED > REGORGE

REGORGES > REGORGE

REGORGING > REGORGE

REGOS > REGO

REGOSOL n type of azonal soil consisting of unconsolidated material derived from freshly deposited alluvium or sands

REGOSOLS > REGOSOL

REGRADE vb grade again

REGRADED > REGRADE

REGRADES > REGRADE

REGRADING > REGRADE

REGRAFT vb graft again

REGRAFTED > REGRAFT

REGRAFTS > REGRAFT

REGRANT vb grant again

REGRANTED > REGRANT

REGRANTS > REGRANT

REGRATE vb buy up (commodities) in advance

r

so as to raise their price for profitable resale

REGRATED > REGRATE

REGRATER > REGRATE

REGRATERS > REGRATE

REGRATES > REGRATE

REGRATING > REGRATE

REGRATOR > REGRATE

REGRATORS > REGRATE

REGREDE vb go back

REGREDED > REGREDE

REGREDES > REGREDE

REGREDING > REGREDE

REGREEN vb green again

REGREENED > REGREEN

REGREENS > REGREEN

REGREET vb greet again or return greetings of

REGREETED > REGREET

REGREETS > REGREET

REGRESS vb revert to a former worse condition ▷ n return to a former and worse condition

REGRESSED > REGRESS

REGRESSES > REGRESS

REGRESSOR > REGRESS

REGRET vb feel sorry about ▷ n feeling of repentance, guilt, or sorrow

REGRETFUL > REGRET

REGRETS > REGRET

REGRETTED > REGRET

REGRETTER > REGRET

REGREW > REGROW

REGRIND vb grind again

REGRINDS > REGRIND

REGROOM vb groom again

REGROOMED > REGROOM

REGROOMS > REGROOM

REGROOVE vb groove again

REGROOVED > REGROOVE

REGROOVES > REGROOVE

REGROUND > REGRIND

REGROUP vb reorganize (military forces) after an attack or a defeat

REGROUPED > REGROUP

REGROUPS > REGROUP

REGROW vb grow or be grown again after having been cut or having died or withered

REGROWING > REGROW

REGROWN > REGROW

REGROWS > REGROW

REGROWTH n growing back of hair, plants, etc

REGROWTHS > REGROWTH

REGS > REG

REGUERDON vb reward

REGULA n rule

REGULABLE adj able to be regulated

REGULAE > REGULA

REGULAR adj normal, customary, or usual ▷ n regular soldier

REGULARLY > REGULAR

REGULARS > REGULAR

REGULATE vb control, esp by rules

REGULATED > REGULATE

REGULATES > REGULATE

REGULATOR n device that automatically controls pressure, temperature, etc

REGULI > REGULUS

REGULINE > REGULUS

REGULISE variant spelling of > REGULIZE

REGULISED > REGULISE

REGULISES > REGULISE

REGULIZE vb turn into regulus

REGULIZED > REGULIZE

REGULIZES > REGULIZE

REGULO n any of a number of temperatures to which a gas oven may be set

REGULOS > REGULO

REGULUS n impure metal forming beneath the slag during the smelting of ores

REGULUSES > REGULUS

REGUR n black loamy Indian soil

REGURS > REGUR

REH n (in India) salty surface crust on the soil

REHAB vb help (addict, disabled person, prisoner, etc) to readapt to society or a new job ▷ n treatment or help given to an addict, disabled person, or prisoner, etc

REHABBED > REHAB

REHABBER > REHAB

REHABBERS > REHAB

REHABBING > REHAB

REHABS > REHAB

REHAMMER vb hammer again

REHAMMERS > REHAMMER

REHANDLE vb handle again

REHANDLED > REHANDLE

REHANDLES > REHANDLE

REHANG vb hang again

REHANGED > REHANG

REHANGING > REHANG

REHANGS > REHANG

REHARDEN vb harden again

REHARDENS > REHARDEN

REHASH vb rework or reuse ▷ n old ideas presented in a new form

REHASHED > REHASH

REHASHES > REHASH

REHASHING > REHASH

REHEAR vb hear again

REHEARD > REHEAR

REHEARING > REHEAR

REHEARS > REHEAR

REHEARSAL n preparatory practice session

REHEARSE vb practise (a play, concert, etc)

REHEARSED > REHEARSE

REHEARSER > REHEARSE

REHEARSES > REHEARSE

REHEAT vb heat or be heated again

REHEATED > REHEAT

REHEATER > REHEAT

REHEATERS > REHEAT

REHEATING > REHEAT

REHEATS > REHEAT

REHEEL vb put a new heel or new heels on

REHEELED > REHEEL

REHEELING > REHEEL

REHEELS > REHEEL

REHEM vb hem again

REHEMMED > REHEM

REHEMMING > REHEM

REHEMS > REHEM

REHINGE vb put a new hinge or new hinges on

REHINGED > REHINGE

REHINGES > REHINGE

REHINGING > REHINGE

REHIRE vb hire again

REHIRED > REHIRE

REHIRES > REHIRE

REHIRING > REHIRE

REHOBOAM n wine bottle holding the equivalent of six normal bottles (approximately 156 ounces)

REHOBOAMS > REHOBOAM

REHOME vb find a new home for (esp a pet)

REHOMED > REHOME

REHOMES > REHOME

REHOMING > REHOME

REHOUSE vb provide with a new (and better) home

REHOUSED > REHOUSE

REHOUSES > REHOUSE

REHOUSING > REHOUSE

REHS > REH

REHUNG > REHANG

REHYDRATE vb hydrate again

REI n name for a former Portuguese coin, more properly called a real

REIF n Scots word meaning robbery or plunder

REIFIED > REIFY

REIFIER > REIFY

REIFIERS > REIFY

REIFIES > REIFY

REIFS > REIF

REIFY vb consider or make (an abstract idea or concept) real or concrete

REIFYING > REIFY

REIGN n period of a sovereign's rule ▷ vb rule (a country)

REIGNED > REIGN

REIGNING > REIGN

REIGNITE vb catch fire or cause to catch fire again

REIGNITED > REIGNITE

REIGNITES > REIGNITE

REIGNS > REIGN

REIK Scots word for > SMOKE

REIKI n form of therapy in which the practitioner is believed to channel energy into the patient in order to encourage healing or restore wellbeing

REIKIS > REIKI

REIKS > REIK

REILLUME vb relight

REILLUMED > REILLUME

REILLUMES > REILLUME

REIMAGE vb image again

REIMAGED > REIMAGE

REIMAGES > REIMAGE

REIMAGINE vb imagine again

REIMAGING > REIMAGE

REIMBURSE vb refund, pay back

REIMMERSE vb immerse again

REIMPLANT vb implant again

REIMPORT vb import (goods manufactured from exported raw materials) ▷ n act of reimporting

REIMPORTS > REIMPORT

REIMPOSE vb establish previously imposed laws, controls, etc, again

REIMPOSED > REIMPOSE

REIMPOSES > REIMPOSE

REIN vb check or manage with reins

REINCITE vb incite again

REINCITED > REINCITE

REINCITES > REINCITE

REINCUR vb incur again

REINCURS > REINCUR

REINDEER n deer of arctic regions with large branched antlers

REINDEERS > REINDEER

REINDEX vb index again

REINDEXED > REINDEX

REINDEXES > REINDEX

REINDICT vb indict again

REINDICTS > REINDICT

REINDUCE vb induce again

REINDUCED > REINDUCE

REINDUCES > REINDUCE

REINDUCT vb induct again

REINDUCTS > REINDUCT

REINED > REIN

REINETTE n variety of apple

REINETTES > REINETTE

REINFECT vb infect or contaminate again

REINFECTS > REINFECT

REINFLAME vb inflame again

REINFLATE vb inflate again

REINFORCE vb give added emphasis to

REINFORM vb inform again

REINFORMS > REINFORM

REINFUND vb archaic word for pour in again

REINFUNDS > REINFUND

REINFUSE vb infuse again

REINFUSED > REINFUSE

REINFUSES > REINFUSE

REINHABIT vb inhabit again

REINING > REIN

REINJECT vb inject again

REINJECTS > REINJECT

REINJURE vb injure again

REINJURED > REINJURE

REINJURES > REINJURE

REINJURY n further injury

REINK *vb* ink again
REINKED > REINK
REINKING > REINK
REINKS > REINK
REINLESS > REIN
REINS *npl* narrow straps attached to a bit to guide a horse
REINSERT *vb* insert again
REINSERTS > REINSERT
REINSMAN *n* driver in a trotting race
REINSMEN > REINSMAN
REINSPECT *vb* inspect again
REINSPIRE *vb* inspire again
REINSTAL *same as* > REINSTALL
REINSTALL *vb* put in place and connect (machinery, equipment, etc) again
REINSTALS > REINSTAL
REINSTATE *vb* restore to a former position
REINSURE *vb* insure again
REINSURED > REINSURE
REINSURER > REINSURE
REINSURES > REINSURE
REINTER *vb* inter again
REINTERS > REINTER
REINVADE *vb* invade again
REINVADED > REINVADE
REINVADES > REINVADE
REINVENT *vb* replace (a product, etc) with an entirely new version
REINVENTS > REINVENT
REINVEST *vb* put back profits from a previous investment into the same enterprise
REINVESTS > REINVEST
REINVITE *vb* invite again
REINVITED > REINVITE
REINVITES > REINVITE
REINVOKE *vb* invoke again
REINVOKED > REINVOKE
REINVOKES > REINVOKE
REINVOLVE *vb* involve again
REIRD *Scots word for* > DIN
REIRDS > REIRD
REIS > REI
REISES > REI
REISSUE *n* book, record, etc, that is published or released again after being unavailable for a time ▷ *vb* publish or release (a book, record, etc) again after a period of unavailability
REISSUED > REISSUE
REISSUER > REISSUE
REISSUERS > REISSUE
REISSUES > REISSUE
REISSUING > REISSUE
REIST *same as* > REEST
REISTAFEL *same as* > RIJSTAFEL
REISTED > REIST
REISTING > REIST
REISTS > REIST
REITBOK *same as*

> REEDBUCK
REITBOKS > REITBOK
REITER *n* soldier in the German cavalry
REITERANT > REITERATE
REITERATE *vb* repeat again and again
REITERS > REITER
REIVE *vb* go on a plundering raid
REIVED > REIVE
REIVER > REIVE
REIVERS > REIVE
REIVES > REIVE
REIVING > REIVE
REJACKET *n* put a new jacket on
REJACKETS > REJACKET
REJECT *vb* refuse to accept or believe ▷ *n* person or thing rejected as not up to standard
REJECTED > REJECT
REJECTEE *n* someone who has been rejected
REJECTEES > REJECTEE
REJECTER > REJECT
REJECTERS > REJECT
REJECTING > REJECT
REJECTION > REJECT
REJECTIVE > REJECT
REJECTOR > REJECT
REJECTORS > REJECT
REJECTS > REJECT
REJIG *vb* re-equip (a factory or plant) ▷ *n* act or process of rejigging
REJIGGED > REJIG
REJIGGER > REJIG
REJIGGERS > REJIG
REJIGGING > REJIG
REJIGS > REJIG
REJOICE *vb* feel or express great happiness
REJOICED > REJOICE
REJOICER > REJOICE
REJOICERS > REJOICE
REJOICES > REJOICE
REJOICING > REJOICE
REJOIN *vb* join again
REJOINDER *n* answer, retort
REJOINED > REJOIN
REJOINING > REJOIN
REJOINS > REJOIN
REJON *n* bullfighting lance
REJONEO *n* bullfighting activity in which a mounted bullfighter spears the bull with lances
REJONEOS > REJONEO
REJONES > REJON
REJOURN *vb* archaic word meaning postpone or adjourn
REJOURNED > REJOURN
REJOURNS > REJOURN
REJUDGE *vb* judge again
REJUDGED > REJUDGE
REJUDGES > REJUDGE
REJUDGING > REJUDGE
REJUGGLE *vb* juggle again
REJUGGLED > REJUGGLE

REJUGGLES > REJUGGLE
REJUSTIFY *vb* justify again
REKE *same as* > RECK
REKED > REKE
REKES > REKE
REKEY *vb* key again
REKEYED > REKEY
REKEYING > REKEY
REKEYS > REKEY
REKINDLE *vb* arouse former emotions or interests
REKINDLED > REKINDLE
REKINDLES > REKINDLE
REKING > REKE
REKNIT *vb* knit again
REKNITS > REKNIT
REKNITTED > REKNIT
REKNOT *vb* knot again
REKNOTS > REKNOT
REKNOTTED > REKNOT
RELABEL *vb* label again
RELABELED > RELABEL
RELABELS > RELABEL
RELACE *vb* lace again
RELACED > RELACE
RELACES > RELACE
RELACHE *n* break
RELACHES > RELACHE
RELACING > RELACE
RELACQUER *vb* apply a new coat of lacquer to
RELAID > RELAY
RELAND *vb* land again
RELANDED > RELAND
RELANDING > RELAND
RELANDS > RELAND
RELAPSE *vb* fall back into bad habits, illness, etc ▷ *n* return of bad habits, illness, etc
RELAPSED > RELAPSE
RELAPSER > RELAPSE
RELAPSERS > RELAPSE
RELAPSES > RELAPSE
RELAPSING > RELAPSE
RELATA > RELATUM
RELATABLE > RELATE
RELATE *vb* establish a relation between
RELATED *adj* linked by kinship or marriage
RELATEDLY > RELATED
RELATER > RELATE
RELATERS > RELATE
RELATES > RELATE
RELATING > RELATE
RELATION *n* connection between things
RELATIONS *npl* social or political dealings between individuals or groups
RELATIVAL *adj* of or relating to a relative
RELATIVE *adj* true to a certain degree or extent ▷ *n* person connected by blood or marriage
RELATIVES > RELATIVE
RELATOR *n* person who relates a story
RELATORS > RELATOR
RELATUM *n* one of the

objects between which a relation is said to hold
RELAUNCH *vb* launch again ▷ *n* another launching, or something that is relaunched
RELAUNDER *vb* launder again
RELAX *vb* make or become looser, less tense, or less rigid
RELAXABLE > RELAX
RELAXANT *n* drug or agent that relaxes, esp one that relaxes tense muscles ▷ *adj* of, relating to, or tending to produce relaxation
RELAXANTS > RELAXANT
RELAXED > RELAX
RELAXEDLY > RELAX
RELAXER *n* person or thing that relaxes, esp a substance used to straighten curly hair
RELAXERS > RELAXER
RELAXES > RELAX
RELAXIN *n* mammalian polypeptide hormone secreted by the corpus luteum during pregnancy, which relaxes the pelvic ligaments
RELAXING > RELAX
RELAXINS > RELAXIN
RELAY *n* fresh set of people or animals relieving others ▷ *vb* pass on (a message)
RELAYED > RELAY
RELAYING > RELAY
RELAYS > RELAY
RELEARN *vb* learn (something previously known) again
RELEARNED > RELEARN
RELEARNS > RELEARN
RELEARNT > RELEARN
RELEASE *vb* set free ▷ *n* setting free
RELEASED > RELEASE
RELEASEE *n* someone to whom an estate is released or someone released from captivity
RELEASEES > RELEASEE
RELEASER > RELEASE
RELEASERS > RELEASE
RELEASES > RELEASE
RELEASING > RELEASE
RELEASOR *n* someone releasing an estate to someone else
RELEASORS > RELEASOR
RELEGABLE *adj* able to be relegated
RELEGATE *vb* put in a less important position
RELEGATED > RELEGATE
RELEGATES > RELEGATE
RELEND *vb* lend again
RELENDING > RELEND
RELENDS > RELEND
RELENT *vb* give up a harsh intention, become less severe
RELENTED > RELENT

r

RELENTING > RELENT
RELENTS > RELENT
RELET vb let again
RELETS > RELET
RELETTER vb redo lettering of
RELETTERS > RELETTER
RELETTING > RELET
RELEVANCE > RELEVANT
RELEVANCY > RELEVANT
RELEVANT adj do with the matter in hand
RELEVE n dance move in which heels are off the ground
RELEVES > RELEVE
RELIABLE adj able to be trusted, dependable ▷ n something or someone believed to be reliable
RELIABLES > RELIABLE
RELIABLY > RELIABLE
RELIANCE n dependence, confidence, or trust
RELIANCES > RELIANCE
RELIANT > RELIANCE
RELIANTLY > RELIANCE
RELIC n something that has survived from the past
RELICENSE vb license again
RELICS > RELIC
RELICT n relic
RELICTION n process by which sea water or fresh water recedes over time, changing the waterline and leaving land exposed
RELICTS > RELICT
RELIDE archaic past form of > RELY
RELIE archaic spelling of > RELY
RELIED > RELY
RELIEF n gladness at the end or removal of pain, distress, etc
RELIEFS > RELIEF
RELIER > RELY
RELIERS > RELY
RELIES > RELY
RELIEVE vb bring relief to
RELIEVED adj experiencing relief, esp from worry or anxiety
RELIEVER n person or thing that relieves
RELIEVERS > RELIEVER
RELIEVES > RELIEVE
RELIEVING > RELIEVE
RELIEVO same as > RELIEF
RELIEVOS > RELIEVO
RELIGHT vb ignite or cause to ignite again
RELIGHTED > RELIGHT
RELIGHTS > RELIGHT
RELIGIEUX n member of a monastic order or clerical body
RELIGION n system of belief in and worship of a supernatural power or god
RELIGIONS > RELIGION

RELIGIOSE adj affectedly or extremely pious
RELIGIOSO adj religious ▷ adv in a religious manner
RELIGIOUS adj of religion ▷ n monk or nun
RELINE vb line again or anew
RELINED > RELINE
RELINES > RELINE
RELINING > RELINE
RELINK vb link again
RELINKED > RELINK
RELINKING > RELINK
RELINKS > RELINK
RELIQUARY n case or shrine for holy relics
RELIQUE archaic spelling of > RELIC
RELIQUEFY vb liquefy again
RELIQUES > RELIQUE
RELIQUIAE npl fossil remains of animals or plants
RELISH vb enjoy, like very much ▷ n liking or enjoyment
RELISHED > RELISH
RELISHES > RELISH
RELISHING > RELISH
RELIST vb list again
RELISTED > RELIST
RELISTING > RELIST
RELISTS > RELIST
RELIT > RELIGHT
RELIVABLE > RELIVE
RELIVE vb experience (a sensation etc) again, esp in the imagination
RELIVED > RELIVE
RELIVER vb deliver up again
RELIVERED > RELIVER
RELIVERS > RELIVER
RELIVES > RELIVE
RELIVING > RELIVE
RELLENO n Mexican dish of stuffed vegetable
RELLENOS > RELLENO
RELLIE n relative
RELLIES npl relatives or relations
RELLISH (in music) variant of > RELISH
RELLISHED > RELLISH
RELLISHES > RELLISH
RELOAD vb put fresh ammunition into (a firearm)
RELOADED > RELOAD
RELOADER > RELOAD
RELOADERS > RELOAD
RELOADING > RELOAD
RELOADS > RELOAD
RELOAN vb loan again
RELOANED > RELOAN
RELOANING > RELOAN
RELOANS > RELOAN
RELOCATE vb move to a new place to live or work
RELOCATED > RELOCATE
RELOCATEE n someone who is relocated

RELOCATES > RELOCATE
RELOCATOR n program designed to transfer files from one computer to another
RELOCK vb lock again
RELOCKED > RELOCK
RELOCKING > RELOCK
RELOCKS > RELOCK
RELOOK vb look again
RELOOKED > RELOOK
RELOOKING > RELOOK
RELOOKS > RELOOK
RELUCENT adj bright
RELUCT vb struggle or rebel
RELUCTANT adj unwilling or disinclined
RELUCTATE vb be or appear reluctant
RELUCTED > RELUCT
RELUCTING > RELUCT
RELUCTS > RELUCT
RELUME vb light or brighten again
RELUMED > RELUME
RELUMES > RELUME
RELUMINE same as > RELUME
RELUMINED > RELUMINE
RELUMINES > RELUMINE
RELUMING > RELUME
RELY vb depend (on)
RELYING > RELY
REM n dose of ionizing radiation that produces the same effect in man as one roentgen of x- or gamma-radiation
REMADE n object that has been reconstructed from original materials
REMADES > REMADE
REMAIL vb mail again
REMAILED > REMAIL
REMAILING > REMAIL
REMAILS > REMAIL
REMAIN vb continue
REMAINDER n part which is left ▷ vb offer (copies of a poorly selling book) at reduced prices
REMAINED > REMAIN
REMAINING > REMAIN
REMAINS npl relics, esp of ancient buildings
REMAKE vb make again in a different way ▷ n new version of an old film
REMAKER > REMAKE
REMAKERS > REMAKE
REMAKES > REMAKE
REMAKING > REMAKE
REMAN vb man again or afresh
REMAND vb send back into custody or put on bail before trial
REMANDED > REMAND
REMANDING > REMAND
REMANDS > REMAND
REMANENCE n ability of a material to retain magnetization, equal to

the magnetic flux density of the material after the removal of the magnetizing field
REMANENCY archaic variant of > REMANENCE
REMANENT adj remaining or left over ▷ n archaic word meaning remainder
REMANENTS > REMANENT
REMANET n something left over
REMANETS > REMANET
REMANIE n fragments and fossils of older origin found in a more recent deposit
REMANIES > REMANIE
REMANNED > REMAN
REMANNING > REMAN
REMANS > REMAN
REMAP vb map again
REMAPPED > REMAP
REMAPPING > REMAP
REMAPS > REMAP
REMARK vb make a casual comment (on) ▷ n observation or comment
REMARKED > REMARK
REMARKER > REMARK
REMARKERS > REMARK
REMARKET vb market again
REMARKETS > REMARKET
REMARKING > REMARK
REMARKS > REMARK
REMARQUE n printing mark in the margin of a plate
REMARQUED adj having had a remarque put on
REMARQUES > REMARQUE
REMARRIED > REMARRY
REMARRIES > REMARRY
REMARRY vb marry again following a divorce or the death of one's previous husband or wife
REMASTER vb make a new master audio recording, now usually digital, from (an earlier recording), to produce compact discs or stereo records with improved sound reproduction
REMASTERS > REMASTER
REMATCH n second or return game or contest between two players ▷ vb match (two contestants) again
REMATCHED > REMATCH
REMATCHES > REMATCH
REMATE vb mate again ▷ n finishing pass in bullfighting
REMATED > REMATE
REMATES > REMATE
REMATING > REMATE
REMBLAI n earth used for an embankment or rampart
REMBLAIS > REMBLAI
REMBLE dialect word for > REMOVE
REMBLED > REMBLE**

REMBLES > REMBLE

REMBLING > REMBLE

REMEAD *archaic or dialect word for >* REMEDY

REMEADED > REMEAD

REMEADING > REMEAD

REMEADS > REMEAD

REMEASURE *vb* measure again

REMEDE *archaic or dialect word for >* REMEDY

REMEDED > REMEDE

REMEDES > REMEDE

REMEDIAL *adj* intended to correct a specific disability, handicap, etc

REMEDIAT *archaic word for >* REMEDIAL

REMEDIATE *archaic word for >* REMEDIAL

REMEDIED > REMEDY

REMEDIES > REMEDY

REMEDING > REMEDE

REMEDY *n* means of curing pain or disease ▷ *vb* put right

REMEDYING > REMEDY

REMEET *vb* meet again

REMEETING > REMEET

REMEETS > REMEET

REMEID *archaic or dialect word for >* REMEDY

REMEIDED > REMEID

REMEIDING > REMEID

REMEIDS > REMEID

REMELT *vb* melt again

REMELTED > REMELT

REMELTING > REMELT

REMELTS > REMELT

REMEMBER *vb* retain in or recall to one's memory

REMEMBERS > REMEMBER

REMEN *n* ancient Egyptian measurement unit

REMEND *vb* mend again

REMENDED > REMEND

REMENDING > REMEND

REMENDS > REMEND

REMENS > REMEN

REMERCIED > REMERCY

REMERCIES > REMERCY

REMERCY *vb* archaic word for thank

REMERGE *vb* merge again

REMERGED > REMERGE

REMERGES > REMERGE

REMERGING > REMERGE

REMET > REMEET

REMEX *n* any of the large flight feathers of a bird's wing

REMIGATE *vb* row

REMIGATED > REMIGATE

REMIGATES > REMIGATE

REMIGES > REMEX

REMIGIAL > REMEX

REMIGRATE *vb* migrate again

REMIND *vb* cause to remember

REMINDED > REMIND

REMINDER *n* something that recalls the past

REMINDERS > REMINDER

REMINDFUL *adj* serving to remind

REMINDING > REMIND

REMINDS > REMIND

REMINISCE *vb* talk or write of past times, experiences, etc

REMINT *vb* mint again

REMINTED > REMINT

REMINTING > REMINT

REMINTS > REMINT

REMISE *vb* give up or relinquish (a right, claim, etc) ▷ *n* second thrust made on the same lunge after the first has missed

REMISED > REMISE

REMISES > REMISE

REMISING > REMISE

REMISS *adj* negligent or careless

REMISSION *n* reduction in the length of a prison term

REMISSIVE > REMISSION

REMISSLY > REMISS

REMISSORY *adj* liable to or intended to gain remission

REMIT *vb* send (money) for goods, services, etc, esp by post ▷ *n* area of competence or authority

REMITMENT *n* archaic word for remittance or remission

REMITS > REMIT

REMITTAL > REMIT

REMITTALS > REMIT

REMITTED > REMIT

REMITTEE *n* recipient of a remittance

REMITTEES > REMITTEE

REMITTENT *adj* (of a disease) periodically less severe

REMITTER *n* person who remits

REMITTERS > REMITTER

REMITTING > REMIT

REMITTOR *same as >* REMITTER

REMITTORS > REMITTOR

REMIX *vb* change the relative prominence of each performer's part of (a recording) ▷ *n* remixed version of a recording

REMIXED > REMIX

REMIXES > REMIX

REMIXING > REMIX

REMIXT *informal past form of >* REMIX

REMIXTURE > REMIX

REMNANT *n* small piece, esp of fabric, left over ▷ *adj* remaining

REMNANTAL *adj* existing as remnant

REMNANTS > REMNANT

REMODEL *vb* give a different shape or form to ▷ *n* something that has been remodelled

REMODELED > REMODEL

REMODELER > REMODEL

REMODELS > REMODEL

REMODIFY *vb* modify again

REMOISTEN *vb* moisten again

REMOLADE *same as >* REMOULADE

REMOLADES > REMOLADE

REMOLD *US spelling of >* REMOULD

REMOLDED > REMOLD

REMOLDING > REMOLD

REMOLDS > REMOLD

REMONTANT *adj* (esp of cultivated roses) flowering more than once in a single season ▷ *n* rose having such a growth

REMONTOIR *n* any of various devices used in watches, clocks, etc, to compensate for errors arising from the changes in the force driving the escapement

REMORA *n* spiny-finned fish

REMORAS > REMORA

REMORID > REMORA

REMORSE *n* feeling of sorrow and regret for something one did

REMORSES > REMORSE

REMOTE *adj* far away, distant ▷ *n* (in informal usage) remote control

REMOTELY > REMOTE

REMOTER > REMOTE

REMOTES > REMOTE

REMOTEST > REMOTE

REMOTION *n* removal

REMOTIONS > REMOTION

REMOUD *Spenserian variant of >* REMOVED

REMOULADE *n* mayonnaise sauce flavoured with herbs, mustard, and capers, served with salads, cold meat, etc

REMOULD *vb* change completely ▷ *n* renovated tyre

REMOULDED > REMOULD

REMOULDS > REMOULD

REMOUNT *vb* get on (a horse, bicycle, etc) again ▷ *n* fresh horse, esp (formerly) to replace one killed or injured in battle

REMOUNTED > REMOUNT

REMOUNTS > REMOUNT

REMOVABLE > REMOVE

REMOVABLY > REMOVE

REMOVAL *n* removing, esp changing residence

REMOVALS > REMOVAL

REMOVE *vb* take away or off ▷ *n* degree of difference

REMOVED *adj* very different or distant

REMOVEDLY *adv* at a distance

REMOVER > REMOVE

REMOVERS > REMOVE

REMOVES > REMOVE

REMOVING > REMOVE

REMS > REM

REMUAGE *n* (in the making of sparkling wine) process of turning the bottles to let the sediment out

REMUAGES > REMUAGE

REMUDA *n* stock of horses enabling riders to change mounts

REMUDAS > REMUDA

REMUEUR *n* (in the making of sparkling wine) person carrying out remuage, or the turning of bottles

REMUEURS > REMUEUR

REMURMUR *vb* murmur again or murmur in reply

REMURMURS > REMURMUR

REN *archaic variant of >* RUN

RENAGUE *same as >* RENEGE

RENAGUED > RENAGUE

RENAGUES > RENAGUE

RENAGUING > RENAGUE

RENAIL *vb* nail again

RENAILED > RENAIL

RENAILING > RENAIL

RENAILS > RENAIL

RENAL *adj* of the kidneys

RENAME *vb* change the name of (someone or something)

RENAMED > RENAME

RENAMES > RENAME

RENAMING > RENAME

RENASCENT *adj* becoming active or vigorous again

RENATURE *vb* return to natural state

RENATURED > RENATURE

RENATURES > RENATURE

RENAY *vb* archaic word meaning renounce

RENAYED > RENAY

RENAYING > RENAY

RENAYS > RENAY

RENCONTRE *n* unexpected meeting

REND *vb* tear or wrench apart

RENDED > REND

RENDER *vb* cause to become ▷ *n* first thin coat of plaster applied to a surface

RENDERED > RENDER

RENDERER > RENDER

RENDERERS > RENDER

RENDERING *n* act or an instance of performing a play, piece of music, etc

RENDERS > RENDER

RENDIBLE > REND

RENDING > REND

RENDITION *n* performance ▷ *vb* subject someone to an extrajudiciary trial

RENDS > REND

RENDZINA *n* dark interzonal type of soil found in grassy or formerly grassy areas of moderate rainfall, esp on chalklands

RENDZINAS > RENDZINA

RENEGADE n person who deserts a cause ▷ vb become a renegade
RENEGADED > RENEGADE
RENEGADES > RENEGADE
RENEGADO archaic word for > RENEGADE
RENEGADOS > RENEGADO
RENEGATE old variant of > RENEGADE
RENEGATES > RENEGATE
RENEGE vb go back (on a promise etc)
RENEGED > RENEGE
RENEGER > RENEGE
RENEGERS > RENEGE
RENEGES > RENEGE
RENEGING > RENEGE
RENEGUE same as > RENEGE
RENEGUED > RENEGUE
RENEGUER > RENEGUE
RENEGUERS > RENEGUE
RENEGUES > RENEGUE
RENEGUING > RENEGUE
RENEST vb nest again or form a new nest
RENESTED > RENEST
RENESTING > RENEST
RENESTS > RENEST
RENEW vb begin again
RENEWABLE > RENEW
RENEWABLY > RENEW
RENEWAL n act of renewing or state of being renewed
RENEWALS > RENEWAL
RENEWED > RENEW
RENEWEDLY > RENEW
RENEWER > RENEW
RENEWERS > RENEW
RENEWING > RENEW
RENEWINGS > RENEW
RENEWS > RENEW
RENEY same as > RENAY
RENEYED > RENEY
RENEYING > RENEY
RENEYS > RENEY
RENFIERST adj archaic word for turned fierce
RENFORCE vb archaic word for reinforce
RENFORCED > RENFORCE
RENFORCES > RENFORCE
RENFORST > RENFORCE
RENGA n type of collaborative poetry found in Japan
RENGAS > RENGA
RENIED > RENY
RENIES > RENY
RENIFORM adj having the shape or profile of a kidney
RENIG same as > RENEGE
RENIGGED > RENIG
RENIGGING > RENIG
RENIGS > RENIG
RENIN n proteolytic enzyme secreted by the kidneys, which plays an important part in the maintenance of blood pressure
RENINS > RENIN
RENITENCE > RENITENT

RENITENCY > RENITENT
RENITENT adj reluctant
RENK adj unpleasant
RENKER > RENK
RENKEST > RENK
RENMINBI same as > YUAN
RENMINBIS > RENMINBI
RENNASE same as > RENNIN
RENNASES > RENNASE
RENNE archaic variant of > RUN
RENNED > REN
RENNES > RENNE
RENNET n substance for curdling milk to make cheese
RENNETS > RENNET
RENNIN n enzyme that occurs in gastric juice and is a constituent of rennet. It coagulates milk by converting caseinogen to casein
RENNING > REN
RENNINGS > REN
RENNINS > RENNIN
RENOGRAM n X-ray kidney image
RENOGRAMS > RENOGRAM
RENOTIFY vb notify again
RENOUNCE vb give up (a belief, habit, etc) voluntarily ▷ n failure to follow suit in a card game
RENOUNCED > RENOUNCE
RENOUNCER > RENOUNCE
RENOUNCES > RENOUNCE
RENOVATE vb restore to good condition
RENOVATED > RENOVATE
RENOVATES > RENOVATE
RENOVATOR > RENOVATE
RENOWN n widespread good reputation ▷ vb make famous
RENOWNED adj famous
RENOWNER n renown giver
RENOWNERS > RENOWNER
RENOWNING > RENOWN
RENOWNS > RENOWN
RENS > REN
RENT n payment made by a tenant to a landlord or owner of a property ▷ vb grant the right to use one's property for payment
RENTABLE > REND
RENTAL n sum payable as rent ▷ adj of or relating to rent
RENTALLER n (in Scots law) tenant with very favourable terms
RENTALS > RENTAL
RENTE n annual income from capital investment
RENTED > RENT
RENTER n person who lets his property in return for rent, esp a landlord
RENTERS > RENTER
RENTES > RENTE
RENTIER n person who

lives off unearned income such as rents or interest
RENTIERS > RENTIER
RENTING > RENT
RENTINGS > RENT
RENTS > RENT
RENUMBER vb number again or afresh
RENUMBERS > RENUMBER
RENVERSE vb archaic word meaning overturn
RENVERSED > RENVERSE
RENVERSES > RENVERSE
RENVERST > RENVERSE
RENVOI n referring of a dispute or other legal question to a jurisdiction other than that in which it arose
RENVOIS > RENVOI
RENVOY old variant of > RENVOI
RENVOYS > RENVOY
RENY same as > RENAY
RENYING > RENY
REO n a New Zealand language
REOBJECT vb object again
REOBJECTS > REOBJECT
REOBSERVE vb observe again
REOBTAIN vb obtain again
REOBTAINS > REOBTAIN
REOCCUPY vb occupy (a building, area, etc) again
REOCCUR vb happen, take place, or come about again
REOCCURS > REOCCUR
REOFFEND vb commit another offence
REOFFENDS > REOFFEND
REOFFER vb offer again
REOFFERED > REOFFER
REOFFERS > REOFFER
REOIL vb oil again
REOILED > REOIL
REOILING > REOIL
REOILS > REOIL
REOPEN vb open again after a period of being closed or suspended
REOPENED > REOPEN
REOPENER n clause in a legal document allowing for an issue to be revisited at a subsequent date
REOPENERS > REOPENER
REOPENING > REOPEN
REOPENS > REOPEN
REOPERATE vb operate again
REOPPOSE vb oppose again
REOPPOSED > REOPPOSE
REOPPOSES > REOPPOSE
REORDAIN vb ordain again
REORDAINS > REORDAIN
REORDER vb change the order of
REORDERED > REORDER
REORDERS > REORDER
REORIENT vb adjust or align (something) in a new or different way

REORIENTS > REORIENT
REOS > REO
REOUTFIT vb outfit again
REOUTFITS > REOUTFIT
REOVIRUS n type of virus
REOXIDISE same as > REOXIDIZE
REOXIDIZE vb oxidize again
REP n sales representative ▷ vb work as a representative
REPACIFY vb pacify again
REPACK vb place or arrange (articles) in (a container) again or in a different way
REPACKAGE vb wrap or put (something) in a package again
REPACKED > REPACK
REPACKING > REPACK
REPACKS > REPACK
REPAID > REPAY
REPAINT vb apply a new or fresh coat of paint
REPAINTED > REPAINT
REPAINTS > REPAINT
REPAIR vb restore to good condition, mend ▷ n act of repairing
REPAIRED > REPAIR
REPAIRER > REPAIR
REPAIRERS > REPAIR
REPAIRING > REPAIR
REPAIRMAN n man whose job it is to repair machines, appliances, etc
REPAIRMEN > REPAIRMAN
REPAIRS > REPAIR
REPAND adj having a wavy margin
REPANDLY > REPAND
REPANEL vb panel again or anew
REPANELED > REPANEL
REPANELS > REPANEL
REPAPER vb paper again or afresh
REPAPERED > REPAPER
REPAPERS > REPAPER
REPARABLE adj able to be repaired or remedied
REPARABLY > REPARABLE
REPARK vb park again
REPARKED > REPARK
REPARKING > REPARK
REPARKS > REPARK
REPARTEE n interchange of witty retorts ▷ vb retort
REPARTEED > REPARTEE
REPARTEES > REPARTEE
REPASS vb pass again
REPASSAGE n passage back or return
REPASSED > REPASS
REPASSES > REPASS
REPASSING > REPASS
REPAST n meal ▷ vb feed (on)
REPASTED > REPAST
REPASTING > REPAST
REPASTS > REPAST

REPASTURE old word for
> FOOD
REPATCH vb patch again
REPATCHED > REPATCH
REPATCHES > REPATCH
REPATTERN vb pattern
again
REPAVE vb pave again
REPAVED > REPAVE
REPAVES > REPAVE
REPAVING > REPAVE
REPAY vb pay back, refund
REPAYABLE > REPAY
REPAYING > REPAY
REPAYMENT > REPAY
REPAYS > REPAY
REPEAL vb cancel (a law)
officially ▷ n act of
repealing
REPEALED > REPEAL
REPEALER > REPEAL
REPEALERS > REPEAL
REPEALING > REPEAL
REPEALS > REPEAL
REPEAT vb say or do again
▷ n act or instance of
repeating
REPEATED adj done,
made, or said again and
again
REPEATER n firearm that
may be discharged many
times without reloading
REPEATERS > REPEATER
REPEATING > REPEAT
REPEATS > REPEAT
REPECHAGE n extra heat
or test providing second
chance to previous losers or
failing candidates
REPEG vb peg again
REPEGGED > REPEG
REPEGGING > REPEG
REPEGS > REPEG
REPEL vb be disgusting to
REPELLANT same as
> REPELLENT
REPELLED > REPEL
REPELLENT adj distasteful
▷ n something that repels,
esp a chemical to repel
insects
REPELLER > REPEL
REPELLERS > REPEL
REPELLING > REPEL
REPELS > REPEL
REPENT vb feel regret for (a
deed or omission) ▷ adj
lying or creeping along the
ground
REPENTANT adj
reproaching oneself for
one's past actions or sins
REPENTED > REPENT
REPENTER > REPENT
REPENTERS > REPENT
REPENTING > REPENT
REPENTS > REPENT
REPEOPLE vb people again
REPEOPLED > REPEOPLE
REPEOPLES > REPEOPLE
REPERCUSS vb have
repercussions
REPEREPE n New Zealand

word for the elephant fish,
a large fish of the
southwest Pacific with a
trunk-like snout
REPEREPES > REPEREPE
REPERK vb perk again
REPERKED > REPERK
REPERKING > REPERK
REPERKS > REPERK
REPERTORY n repertoire
REPERUSAL n fresh
perusal
REPERUSE vb peruse again
REPERUSED > REPERUSE
REPERUSES > REPERUSE
REPETEND n digit or series
of digits in a recurring
decimal that repeats itself
REPETENDS > REPETEND
REPHRASE vb express in
different words
REPHRASED > REPHRASE
REPHRASES > REPHRASE
REPIGMENT vb pigment
again
REPIN vb pin again
REPINE vb fret or complain
REPINED > REPINE
REPINER > REPINE
REPINERS > REPINE
REPINES > REPINE
REPINING > REPINE
REPININGS > REPINE
REPINNED > REPIN
REPINNING > REPIN
REPINS > REPIN
REPIQUE n score of 30
points made from the cards
held by a player before play
begins ▷ vb score a repique
against (someone)
REPIQUED > REPIQUE
REPIQUES > REPIQUE
REPIQUING > REPIQUE
REPLA > REPLUM
REPLACE vb substitute for
REPLACED > REPLACE
REPLACER > REPLACE
REPLACERS > REPLACE
REPLACES > REPLACE
REPLACING > REPLACE
REPLAN vb plan again
REPLANNED > REPLAN
REPLANS > REPLAN
REPLANT vb plant again
REPLANTED > REPLANT
REPLANTS > REPLANT
REPLASTER vb plaster
again
REPLATE vb plate again
REPLATED > REPLATE
REPLATES > REPLATE
REPLATING > REPLATE
REPLAY n immediate
reshowing on TV of an
incident in sport, esp in
slow motion ▷ vb play (a
match, recording, etc)
again
REPLAYED > REPLAY
REPLAYING > REPLAY
REPLAYS > REPLAY
REPLEAD vb plead again
REPLEADED > REPLEAD

REPLEADER n right to
plead again
REPLEADS > REPLEAD
REPLED > REPLEAD
REPLEDGE vb pledge again
REPLEDGED > REPLEDGE
REPLEDGES > REPLEDGE
REPLENISH vb fill up
again, resupply
REPLETE adj filled or
gorged ▷ vb fill again
REPLETED > REPLETE
REPLETELY > REPLETE
REPLETES > REPLETE
REPLETING > REPLETE
REPLETION n state or
condition of being replete
REPLEVIED > REPLEVY
REPLEVIES > REPLEVY
REPLEVIN n recovery of
goods unlawfully taken,
made subject to
establishing the validity of
the recovery in a legal
action and returning the
goods if the decision is
adverse
REPLEVINS > REPLEVIN
REPLEVY vb recover
possession of (goods) by
replevin
REPLICA n exact copy
REPLICANT n (in science
fiction) android
indistinguishable from a
human being
REPLICAS > REPLICA
REPLICASE n type of
enzyme
REPLICATE vb make or be
a copy of ▷ adj folded back
on itself
REPLICON n region of a
DNA molecule that is
replicated from a single
origin
REPLICONS > REPLICON
REPLIED > REPLY
REPLIER > REPLY
REPLIERS > REPLY
REPLIES > REPLY
REPLOT vb plot again
REPLOTS > REPLOT
REPLOTTED > REPLOT
REPLOW vb plow again
REPLOWED > REPLOW
REPLOWING > REPLOW
REPLOWS > REPLOW
REPLUM n internal
separating wall in some
fruits
REPLUMB vb plumb again
REPLUMBED > REPLUMB
REPLUMBS > REPLUMB
REPLUNGE vb plunge again
REPLUNGED > REPLUNGE
REPLUNGES > REPLUNGE
REPLY vb answer or
respond ▷ n answer or
response
REPLYING > REPLY
REPO n act of repossessing
REPOINT vb repair the
joints of (brickwork,

masonry, etc) with mortar
or cement
REPOINTED > REPOINT
REPOINTS > REPOINT
REPOLISH vb polish again
REPOLL vb poll again
REPOLLED > REPOLL
REPOLLING > REPOLL
REPOLLS > REPOLL
REPOMAN n informal word
for a man employed to
repossess goods in cases of
non-payment
REPOMEN > REPOMAN
REPONE vb restore
(someone) to his former
status, office, etc
REPONED > REPONE
REPONES > REPONE
REPONING > REPONE
REPORT vb give an account
of ▷ n account or
statement
REPORTAGE n act or
process of reporting news
or other events of general
interest
REPORTED > REPORT
REPORTER n person who
gathers news for a
newspaper, TV, etc
REPORTERS > REPORTER
REPORTING > REPORT
REPORTS > REPORT
REPOS > REPO
REPOSAL n repose
REPOSALL archaic spelling
of > REPOSAL
REPOSALLS > REPOSALL
REPOSALS > REPOSE
REPOSE n peace ▷ vb lie or
lay at rest
REPOSED > REPOSE
REPOSEDLY > REPOSE
REPOSEFUL > REPOSE
REPOSER > REPOSE
REPOSERS > REPOSE
REPOSES > REPOSE
REPOSING > REPOSE
REPOSIT vb put away,
deposit, or store up
REPOSITED > REPOSIT
REPOSITOR n any
instrument used for
correcting the position of
displaced organs or bones
REPOSITS > REPOSIT
REPOSSESS vb (of a
lender) take back property
from a customer who is
behind with payments
REPOST vb post again
REPOSTED > REPOST
REPOSTING > REPOST
REPOSTS > REPOST
REPOSURE old word for
> REPOSE
REPOSURES > REPOSURE
REPOT vb put (a house
plant) into a new usually
larger pot
REPOTS > REPOT
REPOTTED > REPOT
REPOTTING > REPOT

REPOUR *vb* pour back or again

REPOURED > REPOUR

REPOURING > REPOUR

REPOURS > REPOUR

REPOUSSE *adj* raised in relief, as a design on a thin piece of metal hammered through from the underside ▷ *n* design or surface made in this way

REPOUSSES > REPOUSSE

REPOWER *vb* put new engine in

REPOWERED > REPOWER

REPOWERS > REPOWER

REPP *same as* > REP

REPPED > REP

REPPING > REP

REPPINGS > REP

REPPS > REPP

REPREEVE *archaic spelling of* > REPRIEVE

REPREEVED > REPREEVE

REPREEVES > REPREEVE

REPREHEND *vb* find fault with

REPRESENT *vb* act as a delegate or substitute for

REPRESS *vb* keep (feelings) in check

REPRESSED *adj* (of a person) repressing feelings, instincts, desires, etc

REPRESSER > REPRESS

REPRESSES > REPRESS

REPRESSOR *n* protein synthesized under the control of a repressor gene, which has the capacity to bind to the operator gene and thereby shut off the expression of the structural genes of an operon

REPRICE *vb* price again

REPRICED > REPRICE

REPRICES > REPRICE

REPRICING > REPRICE

REPRIEFE *n* (in archaic usage) reproof

REPRIEFES > REPRIEFE

REPRIEVAL *old word for* > REPRIEVE

REPRIEVE *vb* postpone the execution of (a condemned person) ▷ *n* (document granting) postponement or cancellation of a punishment

REPRIEVED > REPRIEVE

REPRIEVER > REPRIEVE

REPRIEVES > REPRIEVE

REPRIMAND *vb* blame (someone) officially for a fault ▷ *n* official blame

REPRIME *vb* prime again

REPRIMED > REPRIME

REPRIMES > REPRIME

REPRIMING > REPRIME

REPRINT *vb* print further copies of (a book) ▷ *n* reprinted copy

REPRINTED > REPRINT

REPRINTER > REPRINT

REPRINTS > REPRINT

REPRISAL *n* retaliation

REPRISALS > REPRISAL

REPRISE *n* repeating of an earlier theme ▷ *vb* repeat an earlier theme

REPRISED > REPRISE

REPRISES > REPRISE

REPRISING > REPRISE

REPRIVE *archaic spelling of* > REPRIEVE

REPRIVED > REPRIVE

REPRIVES > REPRIVE

REPRIVING > REPRIVE

REPRIZE *archaic spelling of* > REPRISE

REPRIZED > REPRIZE

REPRIZES > REPRIZE

REPRIZING > REPRIZE

REPRO *n* imitation or facsimile of a work of art; reproduction

REPROACH *vb* blame, rebuke

REPROBACY > REPROBATE

REPROBATE *n* depraved or disreputable (person) ▷ *adj* morally unprincipled ▷ *vb* disapprove of

REPROBE *vb* probe again

REPROBED > REPROBE

REPROBES > REPROBE

REPROBING > REPROBE

REPROCESS *vb* treat or prepare (something) by a special method again

REPRODUCE *vb* produce a copy of

REPROGRAM *vb* program again

REPROOF *n* severe blaming of someone for a fault ▷ *vb* treat (a coat, jacket, etc) so as to renew its texture, waterproof qualities, etc

REPROOFED > REPROOF

REPROOFS > REPROOF

REPROS > REPRO

REPROVAL *same as* > REPROOF

REPROVALS > REPROVAL

REPROVE *vb* speak severely to (someone) about a fault

REPROVED > REPROVE

REPROVER > REPROVE

REPROVERS > REPROVE

REPROVES > REPROVE

REPROVING > REPROVE

REPRYVE *archaic spelling of* > REPRIEVE

REPRYVED > REPRYVE

REPRYVES > REPRYVE

REPRYVING > REPRYVE

REPS > REP

REPTANT *adj* creeping, crawling, or lying along the ground

REPTATION *n* creeping action

REPTILE *n* cold-blooded egg-laying vertebrate with horny scales or plates, such as a snake or tortoise ▷ *adj* creeping, crawling, or squirming

REPTILES > REPTILE

REPTILIA > REPTILIUM

REPTILIAN *adj* of, relating to, resembling, or characteristic of reptiles

REPTILIUM *n* place where live reptiles are kept for show

REPTILOID *adj* resembling a reptile

REPUBLIC *n* form of government in which the people or their elected representatives possess the supreme power

REPUBLICS > REPUBLIC

REPUBLISH *vb* publish again

REPUDIATE *vb* reject the authority or validity of

REPUGN *vb* oppose or conflict (with)

REPUGNANT *adj* offensive or distasteful

REPUGNED > REPUGN

REPUGNING > REPUGN

REPUGNS > REPUGN

REPULP *vb* pulp again

REPULPED > REPULP

REPULPING > REPULP

REPULPS > REPULP

REPULSE *vb* be disgusting to ▷ *n* driving back

REPULSED > REPULSE

REPULSER > REPULSE

REPULSERS > REPULSE

REPULSES > REPULSE

REPULSING > REPULSE

REPULSION *n* distaste or aversion

REPULSIVE *adj* loathsome, disgusting

REPUMP *vb* pump again

REPUMPED > REPUMP

REPUMPING > REPUMP

REPUMPS > REPUMP

REPUNIT *n* any number that consists entirely of the same repeated digits, such as 111 or 55,555

REPUNITS > REPUNIT

REPURE *vb* archaic word meaning make pure again

REPURED > REPURE

REPURES > REPURE

REPURIFY *vb* purify again

REPURING > REPURE

REPURPOSE *vb* find new purpose for

REPURSUE *vb* pursue again

REPURSUED > REPURSUE

REPURSUES > REPURSUE

REPUTABLE *adj* of good reputation, respectable

REPUTABLY > REPUTABLE

REPUTE *n* reputation ▷ *vb* consider (a person or thing) to be as specified

REPUTED *adj* supposed

REPUTEDLY *adv* according to general belief or supposition

REPUTES > REPUTE

REPUTING > REPUTE

REPUTINGS > REPUTE

REQUALIFY *vb* qualify again

REQUERE *archaic variant of* > REQUIRE

REQUERED > REQUERE

REQUERES > REQUERE

REQUERING > REQUERE

REQUEST *vb* ask ▷ *n* asking

REQUESTED > REQUEST

REQUESTER > REQUEST

REQUESTOR > REQUEST

REQUESTS > REQUEST

REQUICKEN *vb* quicken again

REQUIEM *n* Mass celebrated for the dead

REQUIEMS > REQUIEM

REQUIGHT *archaic spelling of* > REQUITE

REQUIGHTS > REQUIGHT

REQUIN *vb* type of shark

REQUINS > REQUIN

REQUIRE *vb* want or need

REQUIRED > REQUIRE

REQUIRER > REQUIRE

REQUIRERS > REQUIRE

REQUIRES > REQUIRE

REQUIRING > REQUIRE

REQUISITE *adj* necessary, essential ▷ *n* essential thing

REQUIT *vb* quit again

REQUITAL *n* act or an instance of requiting

REQUITALS > REQUITAL

REQUITE *vb* return to someone (the same treatment or feeling as received)

REQUITED > REQUITE

REQUITER > REQUITE

REQUITERS > REQUITE

REQUITES > REQUITE

REQUITING > REQUITE

REQUITS > REQUIT

REQUITTED > REQUIT

REQUOTE *vb* quote again

REQUOTED > REQUOTE

REQUOTES > REQUOTE

REQUOTING > REQUOTE

REQUOYLE *archaic spelling of* > RECOIL

REQUOYLED > REQUOYLE

REQUOYLES > REQUOYLE

RERACK *vb* rack again

RERACKED > RERACK

RERACKING > RERACK

RERACKS > RERACK

RERADIATE *vb* radiate again

RERAIL *vb* put back on a railway line

RERAILED > RERAIL

RERAILING *n* replacement of existing rails on a railway line

RERAILS > RERAIL

RERAISE *vb* raise again

RERAISED > RERAISE

RERAISES > RERAISE

RERAISING > RERAISE

RERAN > RERUN
REREAD vb read (something) again
REREADING > REREAD
REREADS > REREAD
REREBRACE n armour worn on the upper arm
RERECORD vb record again
RERECORDS > RERECORD
REREDOS n ornamental screen behind an altar
REREDOSES > REREDOS
REREDOSSE same as > REREDOS
RERELEASE vb release again
REREMAI n New Zealand word for the basking shark
REREMAIS > REREMAI
REREMICE > REREMOUSE
REREMIND vb remind again
REREMINDS > REREMIND
REREMOUSE n archaic or dialect word for 'bat' (the animal)
RERENT vb rent again
RERENTED > RERENT
RERENTING > RERENT
RERENTS > RERENT
REREPEAT vb repeat again
REREPEATS > REREPEAT
REREVIEW vb review again
REREVIEWS > REREVIEW
REREVISE vb revise again
REREVISED > REREVISE
REREVISES > REREVISE
REREWARD archaic spelling of > REARWARD
REREWARDS archaic spelling of > REARWARDS
RERIG vb rig again
RERIGGED > RERIG
RERIGGING > RERIG
RERIGS > RERIG
RERISE vb rise again
RERISEN > RERISE
RERISES > RERISE
RERISING > RERISE
REROLL vb roll again
REROLLED > REROLL
REROLLER > REROLL
REROLLERS > REROLL
REROLLING > REROLL
REROLLS > REROLL
REROOF vb put a new roof or roofs on
REROOFED > REROOF
REROOFING > REROOF
REROOFS > REROOF
REROSE > RERISE
REROUTE vb send or direct by a different route
REROUTED > REROUTE
REROUTES > REROUTE
REROUTING > REROUTE
RERUN n film or programme that is broadcast again, repeat ▷ vb put on (a film or programme) again
RERUNNING > RERUN
RERUNS > RERUN
RES informal word for > RESIDENCE

RESADDLE vb saddle again
RESADDLED > RESADDLE
RESADDLES > RESADDLE
RESAID > RESAY
RESAIL vb sail again
RESAILED > RESAIL
RESAILING > RESAIL
RESAILS > RESAIL
RESALABLE > RESALE
RESALE n selling of something purchased earlier
RESALES > RESALE
RESALGAR archaic variant of > REALGAR
RESALGARS > RESALGAR
RESALUTE vb salute back or again
RESALUTED > RESALUTE
RESALUTES > RESALUTE
RESAMPLE vb (in graphics or digital photography) change the size or resolution of
RESAMPLED > RESAMPLE
RESAMPLES > RESAMPLE
RESAT > RESIT
RESAW vb saw again
RESAWED > RESAW
RESAWING > RESAW
RESAWN > RESAW
RESAWS > RESAW
RESAY vb say again or in response
RESAYING > RESAY
RESAYS > RESAY
RESCALE vb resize
RESCALED > RESCALE
RESCALES > RESCALE
RESCALING > RESCALE
RESCHOOL vb retrain
RESCHOOLS > RESCHOOL
RESCIND vb annul or repeal
RESCINDED > RESCIND
RESCINDER > RESCIND
RESCINDS > RESCIND
RESCORE vb score afresh
RESCORED > RESCORE
RESCORES > RESCORE
RESCORING > RESCORE
RESCREEN vb screen again
RESCREENS > RESCREEN
RESCRIPT n (in ancient Rome) an ordinance taking the form of a reply by the emperor to a question on a point of law
RESCRIPTS > RESCRIPT
RESCUABLE > RESCUE
RESCUE vb deliver from danger or trouble, save ▷ n rescuing
RESCUED > RESCUE
RESCUER > RESCUE
RESCUERS > RESCUE
RESCUES > RESCUE
RESCUING > RESCUE
RESCULPT vb sculpt again
RESCULPTS > RESCULPT
RESEAL vb close or secure tightly again
RESEALED > RESEAL
RESEALING > RESEAL

RESEALS > RESEAL
RESEARCH n systematic investigation to discover facts or collect information ▷ vb carry out investigations
RESEASON vb season again
RESEASONS > RESEASON
RESEAT vb show (a person) to a new seat
RESEATED > RESEAT
RESEATING > RESEAT
RESEATS > RESEAT
RESEAU n mesh background to a lace or other pattern
RESEAUS > RESEAU
RESEAUX > RESEAU
RESECT vb cut out part of (a bone, an organ, or other structure or part)
RESECTED > RESECT
RESECTING > RESECT
RESECTION n excision of part of a bone, organ, or other part
RESECTS > RESECT
RESECURE vb secure again
RESECURED > RESECURE
RESECURES > RESECURE
RESEDA n plant that has small spikes of grey-green flowers ▷ adj of a greyish-green colour
RESEDAS > RESEDA
RESEE vb see again
RESEED vb form seed and reproduce naturally, forming a constant plant population
RESEEDED > RESEED
RESEEDING > RESEED
RESEEDS > RESEED
RESEEING > RESEE
RESEEK vb seek again
RESEEKING > RESEEK
RESEEKS > RESEEK
RESEEN > RESEE
RESEES > RESEE
RESEIZE vb seize again
RESEIZED > RESEIZE
RESEIZES > RESEIZE
RESEIZING > RESEIZE
RESEIZURE > RESEIZE
RESELECT vb choose (someone or something) again, esp to choose an existing office-holder as candidate for re-election
RESELECTS > RESELECT
RESELL vb sell (something) one has previously bought
RESELLER > RESELL
RESELLERS > RESELL
RESELLING > RESELL
RESELLS > RESELL
RESEMBLE vb be or look like
RESEMBLED > RESEMBLE
RESEMBLER > RESEMBLE
RESEMBLES > RESEMBLE
RESEND vb send again
RESENDING > RESEND
RESENDS > RESEND

RESENT vb feel bitter about
RESENTED > RESENT
RESENTER > RESENT
RESENTERS > RESENT
RESENTFUL adj feeling or characterized by resentment
RESENTING > RESENT
RESENTIVE archaic word for > RESENTFUL
RESENTS > RESENT
RESERPINE n insoluble alkaloid used medicinally to lower blood pressure and as a sedative
RESERVE vb set aside, keep for future use ▷ n something, esp money or troops, kept for emergencies
RESERVED adj not showing one's feelings, lacking friendliness
RESERVER > RESERVE
RESERVERS > RESERVE
RESERVES > RESERVE
RESERVICE vb service again
RESERVING > RESERVE
RESERVIST n member of a military reserve
RESERVOIR n natural or artificial lake storing water for community supplies
RESES > RES
RESET vb set again (a broken bone, matter in type, a gemstone, etc) ▷ n act or an instance of setting again
RESETS > RESET
RESETTED same as > RESET
RESETTER > RESET
RESETTERS > RESET
RESETTING > RESET
RESETTLE vb settle to live in a different place
RESETTLED > RESETTLE
RESETTLES > RESETTLE
RESEW vb sew again
RESEWED > RESEW
RESEWING > RESEW
RESEWN > RESEW
RESEWS > RESEW
RESH n 20th letter of the Hebrew alphabet
RESHAPE vb shape (something) again or differently
RESHAPED > RESHAPE
RESHAPER > RESHAPE
RESHAPERS > RESHAPE
RESHAPES > RESHAPE
RESHAPING > RESHAPE
RESHARPEN vb sharpen again
RESHAVE vb shave again
RESHAVED > RESHAVE
RESHAVEN > RESHAVE
RESHAVES > RESHAVE
RESHAVING > RESHAVE
RESHES > RESH
RESHINE vb shine again

RESHINED > RESHINE
RESHINES > RESHINE
RESHINGLE vb put new shingles on
RESHINING > RESHINE
RESHIP vb ship again
RESHIPPED > RESHIP
RESHIPPER > RESHIP
RESHIPS > RESHIP
RESHOD > RESHOE
RESHOE vb put a new shoe or shoes on
RESHOED > RESHOE
RESHOEING > RESHOE
RESHOES > RESHOE
RESHONE > RESHINE
RESHOOT vb shoot again
RESHOOTS > RESHOOT
RESHOT > RESHOOT
RESHOW vb show again
RESHOWED > RESHOW
RESHOWER vb have another shower
RESHOWERS > RESHOWER
RESHOWING > RESHOW
RESHOWN > RESHOW
RESHOWS > RESHOW
RESHUFFLE n reorganization ▷ vb reorganize
RESIANCE archaic word for > RESIDENCE
RESIANCES > RESIANCE
RESIANT archaic word for > RESIDENT
RESIANTS > RESIANT
RESID n residual oil left over from the petroleum distillation process
RESIDE vb dwell permanently
RESIDED > RESIDE
RESIDENCE n home or house
RESIDENCY n regular series of concerts by a band or singer at one venue
RESIDENT n person who lives in a place ▷ adj living in a place
RESIDENTS > RESIDENT
RESIDER > RESIDE
RESIDERS > RESIDE
RESIDES > RESIDE
RESIDING > RESIDE
RESIDS > RESID
RESIDUA > RESIDUUM
RESIDUAL adj of or being a remainder ▷ n something left over as a residue
RESIDUALS > RESIDUAL
RESIDUARY adj of, relating to, or constituting a residue
RESIDUE n what is left, remainder
RESIDUES > RESIDUE
RESIDUOUS adj residual
RESIDUUM n residue
RESIDUUMS > RESIDUUM
RESIFT vb sift again
RESIFTED > RESIFT
RESIFTING > RESIFT
RESIFTS > RESIFT

RESIGHT vb sight again
RESIGHTED > RESIGHT
RESIGHTS > RESIGHT
RESIGN vb give up office, a job, etc
RESIGNED adj content to endure
RESIGNER > RESIGN
RESIGNERS > RESIGN
RESIGNING > RESIGN
RESIGNS > RESIGN
RESILE vb spring or shrink back
RESILED > RESILE
RESILES > RESILE
RESILIENT adj (of a person) recovering quickly from a shock etc
RESILIN n substance found in insect bodies
RESILING > RESILE
RESILINS > RESILIN
RESILVER vb silver again
RESILVERS > RESILVER
RESIN n sticky substance from plants, esp pines ▷ vb treat or coat with resin
RESINATA n type of wine
RESINATAS > RESINATA
RESINATE vb impregnate with resin
RESINATED > RESINATE
RESINATES > RESINATE
RESINED > RESIN
RESINER n applier or collector of resin
RESINERS > RESINER
RESINIFY vb become or cause to be resinous
RESINING > RESIN
RESINISE variant spelling of > RESINIZE
RESINISED > RESINISE
RESINISES > RESINISE
RESINIZE vb apply resin to
RESINIZED > RESINIZE
RESINIZES > RESINIZE
RESINLIKE > RESIN
RESINOID adj resembling, characteristic of, or containing resin ▷ n any resinoid substance, esp a synthetic compound
RESINOIDS > RESINOID
RESINOSES > RESINOSIS
RESINOSIS n excessive resin loss in diseased or damaged conifers
RESINOUS > RESIN
RESINS > RESIN
RESINY adj resembling, containing or covered with resin
RESIST vb withstand or oppose ▷ n substance used to protect something, esp a coating that prevents corrosion
RESISTANT adj characterized by or showing resistance ▷ n person or thing that resists
RESISTED > RESIST

RESISTENT same as > RESISTANT
RESISTER > RESIST
RESISTERS > RESIST
RESISTING > RESIST
RESISTIVE adj exhibiting electrical resistance
RESISTOR n component of an electrical circuit producing resistance
RESISTORS > RESISTOR
RESISTS > RESIST
RESIT vb take (an exam) again ▷ n exam that has to be taken again
RESITE vb move to a different site
RESITED > RESITE
RESITES > RESITE
RESITING > RESITE
RESITS > RESIT
RESITTING > RESIT
RESITUATE vb situate elsewhere
RESIZE vb change size of
RESIZED > RESIZE
RESIZES > RESIZE
RESIZING > RESIZE
RESKETCH vb sketch again
RESKEW archaic spelling of > RESCUE
RESKEWED > RESKEW
RESKEWING > RESKEW
RESKEWS > RESKEW
RESKILL vb train (workers) to acquire new skills
RESKILLED > RESKILL
RESKILLS > RESKILL
RESKUE archaic spelling of > RESCUE
RESKUED > RESKUE
RESKUES > RESKUE
RESKUING > RESKUE
RESLATE vb slate again
RESLATED > RESLATE
RESLATES > RESLATE
RESLATING > RESLATE
RESMELT vb smelt again
RESMELTED > RESMELT
RESMELTS > RESMELT
RESMOOTH vb smooth again
RESMOOTHS > RESMOOTH
RESNATRON n tetrode used to generate high power at high frequencies
RESOAK vb soak again
RESOAKED > RESOAK
RESOAKING > RESOAK
RESOAKS > RESOAK
RESOD vb returf
RESODDED > RESOD
RESODDING > RESOD
RESODS > RESOD
RESOFTEN vb soften again
RESOFTENS > RESOFTEN
RESOJET n type of jet engine
RESOJETS > RESOJET
RESOLD > RESELL
RESOLDER vb solder again
RESOLDERS > RESOLDER
RESOLE vb put a new sole

or new soles on
RESOLED > RESOLE
RESOLES > RESOLE
RESOLING > RESOLE
RESOLUBLE adj able to be resolved
RESOLUTE adj firm in purpose ▷ n someone resolute
RESOLUTER > RESOLUTE
RESOLUTES > RESOLUTE
RESOLVE vb decide with an effort of will ▷ n absolute determination
RESOLVED adj determined
RESOLVENT adj serving to dissolve or separate something into its elements ▷ n something that resolves
RESOLVER > RESOLVE
RESOLVERS > RESOLVE
RESOLVES > RESOLVE
RESOLVING > RESOLVE
RESONANCE n echoing, esp with a deep sound
RESONANT adj resounding or re-echoing ▷ n type of unobstructed speech sound
RESONANTS > RESONANT
RESONATE vb resound or cause to resound
RESONATED > RESONATE
RESONATES > RESONATE
RESONATOR n any body or system that displays resonance, esp a tuned electrical circuit or a conducting cavity in which microwaves are generated by a resonant current
RESORB vb absorb again
RESORBED > RESORB
RESORBENT > RESORB
RESORBING > RESORB
RESORBS > RESORB
RESORCIN n substance used principally in dyeing
RESORCINS > RESORCIN
RESORT vb have recourse (to) for help etc ▷ n place for holidays
RESORTED > RESORT
RESORTER > RESORT
RESORTERS > RESORT
RESORTING > RESORT
RESORTS > RESORT
RESOUGHT > RESEEK
RESOUND vb echo or ring with sound
RESOUNDED > RESOUND
RESOUNDS > RESOUND
RESOURCE n thing resorted to for support ▷ vb provide funding or other resources for
RESOURCED > RESOURCE
RESOURCES > RESOURCE
RESOW vb sow again
RESOWED > RESOW
RESOWING > RESOW
RESOWN > RESOW
RESOWS > RESOW

r

RESPACE vb change the spacing of
RESPACED > RESPACE
RESPACES > RESPACE
RESPACING > RESPACE
RESPADE vb dig over
RESPADED > RESPADE
RESPADES > RESPADE
RESPADING > RESPADE
RESPEAK vb speak further
RESPEAKS > RESPEAK
RESPECIFY vb specify again
RESPECT n consideration ▷ vb treat with esteem
RESPECTED > RESPECT
RESPECTER n person who respects someone or something
RESPECTS > RESPECT
RESPELL vb spell again
RESPELLED > RESPELL
RESPELLS > RESPELL
RESPELT > RESPELL
RESPIRE vb breathe
RESPIRED > RESPIRE
RESPIRES > RESPIRE
RESPIRING > RESPIRE
RESPITE n pause, interval of rest ▷ vb grant a respite to
RESPITED > RESPITE
RESPITES > RESPITE
RESPITING > RESPITE
RESPLEND vb be resplendent
RESPLENDS > RESPLEND
RESPLICE vb splice again
RESPLICED > RESPLICE
RESPLICES > RESPLICE
RESPLIT vb split again
RESPLITS > RESPLIT
RESPOKE > RESPEAK
RESPOKEN > RESPEAK
RESPOND vb answer ▷ n pilaster or an engaged column that supports an arch or a lintel
RESPONDED > RESPOND
RESPONDER > RESPOND
RESPONDS > RESPOND
RESPONSA n that part of rabbinic literature concerned with written rulings in answer to questions
RESPONSE n answer
RESPONSER n radio or radar receiver used in conjunction with an interrogator to receive and display signals from a transponder
RESPONSES > RESPONSE
RESPONSOR same as > RESPONSER
RESPONSUM n written answer from a rabbinic authority to a question submitted
RESPOOL vb rewind onto spool
RESPOOLED > RESPOOL
RESPOOLS > RESPOOL

RESPOT vb (in billiards) replace on one of the spots
RESPOTS > RESPOT
RESPOTTED > RESPOT
RESPRANG > RESPRING
RESPRAY n new coat of paint applied to a car, van, etc ▷ vb spray (a car, wheels, etc) with a new coat of paint
RESPRAYED > RESPRAY
RESPRAYS > RESPRAY
RESPREAD vb spread again
RESPREADS > RESPREAD
RESPRING vb put new springs in
RESPRINGS > RESPRING
RESPROUT vb sprout again
RESPROUTS > RESPROUT
RESPRUNG > RESPRING
RESSALDAR n native cavalry commander in mixed Anglo-Indian army
REST n freedom from exertion etc ▷ vb take a rest
RESTABLE vb put in stable again or elsewhere
RESTABLED > RESTABLE
RESTABLES > RESTABLE
RESTACK vb stack again
RESTACKED > RESTACK
RESTACKS > RESTACK
RESTAFF vb staff again
RESTAFFED > RESTAFF
RESTAFFS > RESTAFF
RESTAGE vb produce or perform a new production of (a play)
RESTAGED > RESTAGE
RESTAGES > RESTAGE
RESTAGING > RESTAGE
RESTAMP vb stamp again
RESTAMPED > RESTAMP
RESTAMPS > RESTAMP
RESTART vb commence (something) or set (something) in motion again ▷ n act or an instance of starting again
RESTARTED > RESTART
RESTARTER > RESTART
RESTARTS > RESTART
RESTATE vb state or affirm (something) again or in a different way
RESTATED > RESTATE
RESTATES > RESTATE
RESTATING > RESTATE
RESTATION vb station elsewhere
RESTED > REST
RESTEM vb stem again
RESTEMMED > RESTEM
RESTEMS > RESTEM
RESTER > REST
RESTERS > REST
RESTFUL adj relaxing or soothing
RESTFULLY > RESTFUL
RESTIER > RESTY
RESTIEST > RESTY
RESTIFF same as > RESTIVE
RESTIFORM adj (esp of

bundles of nerve fibres) shaped like a cord or rope
RESTING > REST
RESTINGS > REST
RESTITCH vb stitch again
RESTITUTE vb restore
RESTIVE adj restless or impatient
RESTIVELY > RESTIVE
RESTLESS adj bored or dissatisfied
RESTO n restored antique, vintage car, etc
RESTOCK vb replenish stores or supplies
RESTOCKED > RESTOCK
RESTOCKS > RESTOCK
RESTOKE vb stoke again
RESTOKED > RESTOKE
RESTOKES > RESTOKE
RESTOKING > RESTOKE
RESTORAL n restoration
RESTORALS > RESTORAL
RESTORE vb return (a building, painting, etc) to its original condition
RESTORED > RESTORE
RESTORER > RESTORE
RESTORERS > RESTORE
RESTORES > RESTORE
RESTORING > RESTORE
RESTOS > RESTO
RESTRAIN vb hold (someone) back from action
RESTRAINS > RESTRAIN
RESTRAINT n something that restrains
RESTRESS vb stress again or differently
RESTRETCH vb stretch again
RESTRICT vb confine to certain limits
RESTRICTS > RESTRICT
RESTRIKE vb strike again
RESTRIKES > RESTRIKE
RESTRING vb string again or anew
RESTRINGE vb restrict
RESTRINGS > RESTRING
RESTRIVE vb strive again
RESTRIVEN > RESTRIVE
RESTRIVES > RESTRIVE
RESTROOM n room in a public building having lavatories, washing facilities, and sometimes couches
RESTROOMS > RESTROOM
RESTROVE > RESTRIVE
RESTRUCK > RESTRIKE
RESTRUNG > RESTRING
RESTS > REST
RESTUDIED > RESTUDY
RESTUDIES > RESTUDY
RESTUDY vb study again
RESTUFF vb put new stuffing in
RESTUFFED > RESTUFF
RESTUFFS > RESTUFF
RESTUMP vb Australian building term for provide with new stumps

RESTUMPED > RESTUMP
RESTUMPS > RESTUMP
RESTY adj restive
RESTYLE vb style again
RESTYLED > RESTYLE
RESTYLES > RESTYLE
RESTYLING > RESTYLE
RESUBJECT vb subject again
RESUBMIT vb submit again
RESUBMITS > RESUBMIT
RESULT n outcome or consequence ▷ vb be the outcome or consequence (of)
RESULTANT adj arising as a result ▷ n sum of two or more vectors, such as the force resulting from two or more forces acting on a single point
RESULTED > RESULT
RESULTFUL > RESULT
RESULTING > RESULT
RESULTS > RESULT
RESUMABLE > RESUME
RESUME vb begin again ▷ n summary
RESUMED > RESUME
RESUMER > RESUME
RESUMERS > RESUME
RESUMES > RESUME
RESUMING > RESUME
RESUMMON vb summon again
RESUMMONS > RESUMMON
RESUPINE adj lying on the back
RESUPPLY vb provide (with something) again
RESURFACE vb arise or occur again
RESURGE vb rise again from or as if from the dead
RESURGED > RESURGE
RESURGENT adj rising again, as to new life, vigour, etc
RESURGES > RESURGE
RESURGING > RESURGE
RESURRECT vb restore to life
RESURVEY vb survey again
RESURVEYS > RESURVEY
RESUSPEND vb put back into suspension
RESWALLOW vb swallow again
RET vb moisten or soak (flax, hemp, jute, etc) to promote bacterial action in order to facilitate separation of the fibres from the woody tissue by beating
RETABLE n ornamental screenlike structure above and behind an altar, esp one used as a setting for a religious picture or carving
RETABLES > RETABLE
RETACK vb tack again
RETACKED > RETACK
RETACKING > RETACK

r

RETACKLE vb tackle again
RETACKLED > RETACKLE
RETACKLES > RETACKLE
RETACKS > RETACK
RETAG vb tag again
RETAGGED > RETAG
RETAGGING > RETAG
RETAGS > RETAG
RETAIL n selling of goods individually or in small amounts to the public ▷ adj of or engaged in such selling ▷ adv by retail ▷ vb sell or be sold retail
RETAILED > RETAIL
RETAILER > RETAIL
RETAILERS > RETAIL
RETAILING > RETAIL
RETAILOR vb tailor afresh
RETAILORS > RETAILOR
RETAILS > RETAIL
RETAIN vb keep in one's possession
RETAINED > RETAIN
RETAINER n fee to retain someone's services
RETAINERS > RETAINER
RETAINING > RETAIN
RETAINS > RETAIN
RETAKE vb recapture ▷ n act of rephotographing a scene
RETAKEN > RETAKE
RETAKER > RETAKE
RETAKERS > RETAKE
RETAKES > RETAKE
RETAKING > RETAKE
RETAKINGS > RETAKE
RETALIATE vb repay an injury or wrong in kind
RETALLIED > RETALLY
RETALLIES > RETALLY
RETALLY vb count up again
RETAMA n type of shrub
RETAMAS > RETAMA
RETAPE vb tape again
RETAPED > RETAPE
RETAPES > RETAPE
RETAPING > RETAPE
RETARD vb delay or slow (progress or development) ▷ n offensive term for a retarded person
RETARDANT n substance that reduces the rate of a chemical reaction ▷ adj having a slowing effect
RETARDATE n person who is retarded
RETARDED adj underdeveloped, esp mentally
RETARDER n person or thing that retards
RETARDERS > RETARDER
RETARDING > RETARD
RETARDS > RETARD
RETARGET vb target afresh or differently
RETARGETS > RETARGET
RETASTE vb taste again
RETASTED > RETASTE
RETASTES > RETASTE

RETASTING > RETASTE
RETAUGHT > RETEACH
RETAX vb tax again
RETAXED > RETAX
RETAXES > RETAX
RETAXING > RETAX
RETCH vb try to vomit ▷ n involuntary spasm of the stomach
RETCHED > RETCH
RETCHES > RETCH
RETCHING > RETCH
RETCHLESS archaic variant of > RECKLESS
RETE n any network of nerves or blood vessels
RETEACH vb teach again
RETEACHES > RETEACH
RETEAM vb team up again
RETEAMED > RETEAM
RETEAMING > RETEAM
RETEAMS > RETEAM
RETEAR vb tear again
RETEARING > RETEAR
RETEARS > RETEAR
RETELL vb relate (a story, etc) again or differently
RETELLER > RETELL
RETELLERS > RETELL
RETELLING > RETELL
RETELLS > RETELL
RETEM n type of shrub
RETEMPER vb temper again
RETEMPERS > RETEMPER
RETEMS > RETEM
RETENE n yellow crystalline hydrocarbon found in tar oils from pine wood and in certain fossil resins
RETENES > RETENE
RETENTION n retaining
RETENTIVE adj capable of retaining or remembering
RETEST vb test (something) again or differently
RETESTED > RETEST
RETESTIFY vb testify again
RETESTING > RETEST
RETESTS > RETEST
RETEXTURE vb restore natural texture to
RETHINK vb consider again, esp with a view to changing one's tactics ▷ n act or an instance of thinking again
RETHINKER > RETHINK
RETHINKS > RETHINK
RETHOUGHT > RETHINK
RETHREAD vb thread again
RETHREADS > RETHREAD
RETIA > RETE
RETIAL > RETE
RETIARII > RETIARIUS
RETIARIUS n (in ancient Rome) a gladiator armed with a net and trident
RETIARY adj of, relating to, or resembling a net or web

RETICELLA n form of lace
RETICENCE > RETICENT
RETICENCY > RETICENT
RETICENT adj uncommunicative, reserved
RETICLE n network of fine lines, wires, etc, placed in the focal plane of an optical instrument to assist measurement of the size or position of objects under observation
RETICLES > RETICLE
RETICULA > RETICULUM
RETICULAR adj in the form of a network or having a network of parts
RETICULE same as > RETICLE
RETICULES > RETICULE
RETICULUM n any fine network, esp one in the body composed of cells, fibres, etc
RETIE vb tie again
RETIED > RETIE
RETIEING > RETIE
RETIES > RETIE
RETIFORM adj netlike
RETIGHTEN vb tighten again
RETILE vb put new tiles in or on
RETILED > RETILE
RETILES > RETILE
RETILING > RETILE
RETIME vb time again or alter time of
RETIMED > RETIME
RETIMES > RETIME
RETIMING > RETIME
RETINA n light-sensitive membrane at the back of the eye
RETINAE > RETINA
RETINAL adj of or relating to the retina ▷ n aldehyde form of the polyene retinol (vitamin A) that associates with the protein opsin to form the visual purple pigment rhodopsin
RETINALS > RETINAL
RETINAS > RETINA
RETINE n chemical found in body cells that slows cell growth and division
RETINENE n aldehyde form of the polyene retinol (vitamin A) that associates with the protein opsin to form the visual purple pigment rhodopsin
RETINENES > RETINENE
RETINES > RETINE
RETINITE n any of various resins of fossil origin, esp one derived from lignite
RETINITES > RETINITE
RETINITIS n inflammation of the retina
RETINOIC adj containing or derived from retinoid
RETINOID adj resinlike ▷ n

derivative of vitamin A
RETINOIDS > RETINOID
RETINOL n another name for vitamin A and rosin oil
RETINOLS > RETINOL
RETINT vb tint again or change tint of
RETINTED > RETINT
RETINTING > RETINT
RETINTS > RETINT
RETINUE n band of attendants
RETINUED > RETINUE
RETINUES > RETINUE
RETINULA n part of the compound eye in certain arthropods
RETINULAE > RETINULA
RETINULAR > RETINULA
RETINULAS > RETINULA
RETIRACY n (in US English) retirement
RETIRAL n act of retiring from office, one's work, etc
RETIRALS > RETIRAL
RETIRANT n (in US English) retired person
RETIRANTS > RETIRANT
RETIRE vb (cause to) give up office or work, esp through age
RETIRED adj having retired from work etc
RETIREDLY > RETIRED
RETIREE n person who has retired from work
RETIREES > RETIREE
RETIRER > RETIRE
RETIRERS > RETIRE
RETIRES > RETIRE
RETIRING adj shy
RETITLE vb give a new title to
RETITLED > RETITLE
RETITLES > RETITLE
RETITLING > RETITLE
RETOLD > RETELL
RETOOK > RETAKE
RETOOL vb replace, re-equip, or rearrange the tools in (a factory, etc)
RETOOLED > RETOOL
RETOOLING > RETOOL
RETOOLS > RETOOL
RETORE > RETEAR
RETORN > RETEAR
RETORSION n retaliatory action taken by a state whose citizens have been mistreated by a foreign power by treating the subjects of that power similarly
RETORT vb reply quickly, wittily, or angrily ▷ n quick, witty, or angry reply
RETORTED > RETORT
RETORTER > RETORT
RETORTERS > RETORT
RETORTING > RETORT
RETORTION n act of retorting
RETORTIVE > RETORT
RETORTS > RETORT

RETOTAL *vb* add up again
RETOTALED > RETOTAL
RETOTALS > RETOTAL
RETOUCH *vb* restore or improve by new touches, esp of paint ▷ *n* art or practice of retouching
RETOUCHED > RETOUCH
RETOUCHER > RETOUCH
RETOUCHES > RETOUCH
RETOUR *vb* (in Scottish law) to return as heir
RETOURED > RETOUR
RETOURING > RETOUR
RETOURS > RETOUR
RETRACE *vb* go back over (a route etc) again
RETRACED > RETRACE
RETRACER > RETRACE
RETRACERS > RETRACE
RETRACES > RETRACE
RETRACING > RETRACE
RETRACK *vb* track again
RETRACKED > RETRACK
RETRACKS > RETRACK
RETRACT *vb* withdraw (a statement etc)
RETRACTED > RETRACT
RETRACTOR *n* any of various muscles that retract an organ or part
RETRACTS > RETRACT
RETRAICT *archaic form of* > RETREAT
RETRAICTS > RETRAICT
RETRAIN *vb* train to do a new or different job
RETRAINED > RETRAIN
RETRAINEE > RETRAIN
RETRAINS > RETRAIN
RETRAIT *archaic form of* > RETREAT
RETRAITE *archaic form of* > RETREAT
RETRAITES > RETRAITE
RETRAITS > RETRAIT
RETRAITT *n* archaic word meaning portrait
RETRAITTS > RETRAITT
RETRAL *adj* at, near, or towards the back
RETRALLY > RETRAL
RETRATE *archaic form of* > RETREAT
RETRATED > RETRATE
RETRATES > RETRATE
RETRATING > RETRATE
RETREAD *n* remould ▷ *vb* remould tread again
RETREADED > RETREAD
RETREADS > RETREAD
RETREAT *vb* move back from a position, withdraw ▷ *n* act of or military signal for retiring or withdrawal
RETREATED > RETREAT
RETREATER > RETREAT
RETREATS > RETREAT
RETREE *n* imperfectly made paper
RETREES > RETREE
RETRENCH *vb* reduce expenditure, cut back
RETRIAL *n* second trial of

a case or defendant in a court of law
RETRIALS > RETRIAL
RETRIBUTE *vb* give back
RETRIED > RETRY
RETRIES > RETRY
RETRIEVAL *n* act or process of retrieving
RETRIEVE *vb* fetch back again ▷ *n* chance of being retrieved
RETRIEVED > RETRIEVE
RETRIEVER *n* dog trained to retrieve shot game
RETRIEVES > RETRIEVE
RETRIM *vb* trim again
RETRIMMED > RETRIM
RETRIMS > RETRIM
RETRO *adj* associated with or revived from the past
RETROACT *vb* act in opposition
RETROACTS > RETROACT
RETROCEDE *vb* give back
RETROD > RETREAD
RETRODDEN > RETREAD
RETRODICT *vb* make surmises about the past using information from the present
RETROFIRE *n* act of firing a retrorocket
RETROFIT *vb* equip (a vehicle, piece of equipment, etc) with new parts, safety devices, etc, after manufacture
RETROFITS > RETROFIT
RETROFLEX *adj* bent or curved backwards ▷ *vb* bend or turn backwards
RETROJECT *vb* throw backwards
RETRONYM *n* word coined for existing thing to distinguish it from new thing
RETRONYMS > RETRONYM
RETROPACK *n* system of retrorockets on a spacecraft
RETRORSE *adj* (esp of plant parts) pointing backwards or in a direction opposite to normal
RETROS > RETRO
RETROUSSE *adj* (of a nose) turned upwards
RETROVERT *vb* turn back
RETRY *vb* try again (a case already determined)
RETRYING > RETRY
RETS > RET
RETSINA *n* Greek wine flavoured with resin
RETSINAS > RETSINA
RETTED > RET
RETTERIES > RETTERY
RETTERY *n* flax-retting place
RETTING > RET
RETUND *vb* weaken or blunt
RETUNDED > RETUND
RETUNDING > RETUND
RETUNDS > RETUND

RETUNE *vb* tune (a musical instrument) differently or again
RETUNED > RETUNE
RETUNES > RETUNE
RETUNING > RETUNE
RETURF *vb* turf again
RETURFED > RETURF
RETURFING > RETURF
RETURFS > RETURF
RETURN *vb* go or come back ▷ *n* returning ▷ *adj* of or being a return
RETURNED > RETURN
RETURNEE *n* person who returns to his native country, esp after war service
RETURNEES > RETURNEE
RETURNER *n* person or thing that returns
RETURNERS > RETURNER
RETURNIK *n* someone returning or intending to return to their native land, especially when this is in the former Soviet Union
RETURNIKS > RETURNIK
RETURNING > RETURN
RETURNS > RETURN
RETUSE *adj* having a rounded apex and a central depression
RETWIST *vb* twist again
RETWISTED > RETWIST
RETWISTS > RETWIST
RETYING > RETIE
RETYPE *vb* type again
RETYPED > RETYPE
RETYPES > RETYPE
RETYPING > RETYPE
REUNIFIED > REUNIFY
REUNIFIES > REUNIFY
REUNIFY *vb* bring together again something previously divided
REUNION *n* meeting of people who have been apart
REUNIONS > REUNION
REUNITE *vb* bring or come together again after a separation
REUNITED > REUNITE
REUNITER > REUNITE
REUNITERS > REUNITE
REUNITES > REUNITE
REUNITING > REUNITE
REUPTAKE *vb* absorb again
REUPTAKES > REUPTAKE
REURGE *vb* urge again
REURGED > REURGE
REURGES > REURGE
REURGING > REURGE
REUSABLE *adj* able to be used more than once
REUSABLES *npl* products which can be used more than once
REUSE *vb* use again ▷ *n* act of using something again
REUSED > REUSE
REUSES > REUSE
REUSING > REUSE

REUTILISE *same as* > REUTILIZE
REUTILIZE *vb* utilize again
REUTTER *vb* utter again
REUTTERED > REUTTER
REUTTERS > REUTTER
REV *n* revolution (of an engine) ▷ *vb* increase the speed of revolution of (an engine)
REVALENTA *n* lentil flour
REVALUATE *same as* > REVALUE
REVALUE *vb* adjust the exchange value of (a currency) upwards
REVALUED > REVALUE
REVALUES > REVALUE
REVALUING > REVALUE
REVAMP *vb* renovate or restore ▷ *n* something that has been renovated or revamped
REVAMPED > REVAMP
REVAMPER > REVAMP
REVAMPERS > REVAMP
REVAMPING > REVAMP
REVAMPS > REVAMP
REVANCHE *n* revenge
REVANCHES > REVANCHE
REVARNISH *vb* varnish again
REVEAL *vb* make known ▷ *n* vertical side of an opening in a wall, esp the side of a window or door between the frame and the front of the wall
REVEALED > REVEAL
REVEALER > REVEAL
REVEALERS > REVEAL
REVEALING *adj* disclosing information that one did not know
REVEALS > REVEAL
REVEHENT *adj* (in anatomy) carrying back
REVEILLE *n* morning bugle call to waken soldiers
REVEILLES > REVEILLE
REVEL *vb* take pleasure (in) ▷ *n* occasion of noisy merrymaking
REVELATOR *n* revealer
REVELED > REVEL
REVELER > REVEL
REVELERS > REVEL
REVELING > REVEL
REVELLED > REVEL
REVELLER > REVEL
REVELLERS > REVEL
REVELLING > REVEL
REVELMENT > REVEL
REVELRIES > REVELRY
REVELROUS > REVELRY
REVELRY *n* festivity
REVELS > REVEL
REVENANT *n* something, esp a ghost, that returns
REVENANTS > REVENANT
REVENGE *n* retaliation for wrong done ▷ *vb* make retaliation for

r

REVENGED > REVENGE
REVENGER > REVENGE
REVENGERS > REVENGE
REVENGES > REVENGE
REVENGING > REVENGE
REVENGIVE > REVENGE
REVENUAL > REVENUE
REVENUE *n* income, esp of a state
REVENUED > REVENUE
REVENUER *n* revenue officer or cutter
REVENUERS > REVENUER
REVENUES > REVENUE
REVERABLE > REVERE
REVERB *n* electronic device that creates artificial acoustics ▷ *vb* reverberate
REVERBED > REVERB
REVERBING > REVERB
REVERBS > REVERB
REVERE *vb* be in awe of and respect greatly
REVERED > REVERE
REVERENCE *n* awe mingled with respect and esteem
REVEREND *adj* worthy of reverence ▷ *n* clergyman
REVERENDS > REVEREND
REVERENT *adj* showing reverence
REVERER > REVERE
REVERERS > REVERE
REVERES > REVERE
REVERIE *n* absent-minded daydream
REVERIES > REVERIE
REVERIFY *vb* verify again
REVERING > REVERE
REVERIST *n* someone given to reveries
REVERISTS > REVERIST
REVERS *n* turned back part of a garment, such as the lapel
REVERSAL *n* act or an instance of reversing
REVERSALS > REVERSAL
REVERSE *vb* turn upside down or the other way round ▷ *n* opposite ▷ *adj* opposite or contrary
REVERSED > REVERSE
REVERSELY > REVERSE
REVERSER > REVERSE
REVERSERS > REVERSE
REVERSES > REVERSE
REVERSI *n* game played on a draughtboard with 64 pieces, black on one side and white on the other. When pieces are captured they are turned over to join the capturing player's forces
REVERSING > REVERSE
REVERSION *n* return to a former state, practice, or belief
REVERSIS *n* type of card game
REVERSO *another name for* > VERSO

REVERSOS > REVERSO
REVERT *vb* return to a former state
REVERTANT *n* mutant that has reverted to an earlier form ▷ *adj* having mutated to an earlier form
REVERTED > REVERT
REVERTER > REVERT
REVERTERS > REVERT
REVERTING > REVERT
REVERTIVE > REVERT
REVERTS > REVERT
REVERY *same as* > REVERIE
REVEST *vb* restore (former power, authority, status, etc, to a person) or (of power, authority, etc) to be restored
REVESTED > REVEST
REVESTING > REVEST
REVESTRY *same as* > VESTRY
REVESTS > REVEST
REVET *vb* face (a wall or embankment) with stones
REVETMENT *n* facing of stones, sandbags, etc, to protect a wall, embankment, or earthworks
REVETS > REVET
REVETTED > REVET
REVETTING > REVET
REVEUR *n* daydreamer
REVEURS > REVEUR
REVEUSE *n* female daydreamer
REVEUSES > REVEUSE
REVIBRATE *vb* vibrate again
REVICTUAL *vb* victual again
REVIE *vb* archaic cards term meaning challenge by placing a larger stake
REVIED > REVIE
REVIES > REVIE
REVIEW *n* critical assessment of a book, concert, etc ▷ *vb* hold or write a review of
REVIEWAL *same as* > REVIEW
REVIEWALS > REVIEWAL
REVIEWED > REVIEW
REVIEWER > REVIEW
REVIEWERS > REVIEW
REVIEWING > REVIEW
REVIEWS > REVIEW
REVILE *vb* be abusively scornful of
REVILED > REVILE
REVILER > REVILE
REVILERS > REVILE
REVILES > REVILE
REVILING > REVILE
REVILINGS > REVILE
REVIOLATE *vb* violate again
REVISABLE > REVISE
REVISAL > REVISE
REVISALS > REVISE

REVISE *vb* change or alter ▷ *n* act, process, or result of revising
REVISED > REVISE
REVISER > REVISE
REVISERS > REVISE
REVISES > REVISE
REVISING > REVISE
REVISION *n* act of revising
REVISIONS > REVISION
REVISIT *vb* visit again
REVISITED > REVISIT
REVISITS > REVISIT
REVISOR > REVISE
REVISORS > REVISE
REVISORY *adj* of or having the power of revision
REVIVABLE > REVIVE
REVIVABLY > REVIVE
REVIVAL *n* reviving or renewal
REVIVALS > REVIVAL
REVIVE *vb* bring or come back to life, vigour, use, etc
REVIVED > REVIVE
REVIVER > REVIVE
REVIVERS > REVIVE
REVIVES > REVIVE
REVIVIFY *vb* give new life to
REVIVING > REVIVE
REVIVINGS > REVIVE
REVIVOR *n* means of reviving a lawsuit that has been suspended owing to the death or marriage of one of the parties
REVIVORS > REVIVOR
REVOCABLE *adj* capable of being revoked
REVOCABLY > REVOCABLE
REVOICE *vb* utter again
REVOICED > REVOICE
REVOICES > REVOICE
REVOICING > REVOICE
REVOKABLE *same as* > REVOCABLE
REVOKABLY > REVOCABLE
REVOKE *vb* cancel (a will, agreement, etc) ▷ *n* act of revoking
REVOKED > REVOKE
REVOKER > REVOKE
REVOKERS > REVOKE
REVOKES > REVOKE
REVOKING > REVOKE
REVOLT *n* uprising against authority ▷ *vb* rise in rebellion
REVOLTED > REVOLT
REVOLTER > REVOLT
REVOLTERS > REVOLT
REVOLTING *adj* disgusting, horrible
REVOLTS > REVOLT
REVOLUTE *adj* (esp of the margins of a leaf) rolled backwards and downwards
REVOLVE *vb* turn round, rotate ▷ *n* circular section of a stage that can be rotated by electric power to

provide a scene change
REVOLVED > REVOLVE
REVOLVER *n* repeating pistol
REVOLVERS > REVOLVER
REVOLVES > REVOLVE
REVOLVING *adj* denoting or relating to an engine, such as a radial aero engine, in which the cylinders revolve about a fixed shaft
REVOTE *vb* decide or grant again by a new vote
REVOTED > REVOTE
REVOTES > REVOTE
REVOTING > REVOTE
REVS > REV
REVUE *n* theatrical entertainment with topical sketches and songs
REVUES > REVUE
REVUIST > REVUE
REVUISTS > REVUE
REVULSED *adj* filled with disgust
REVULSION *n* strong disgust
REVULSIVE *adj* of or causing revulsion ▷ *n* counterirritant
REVVED > REV
REVVING > REV
REVYING > REVIE
REW *archaic spelling of* > RUE
REWAKE *vb* awaken again
REWAKED > REWAKE
REWAKEN *vb* awaken again
REWAKENED > REWAKEN
REWAKENS > REWAKEN
REWAKES > REWAKE
REWAKING > REWAKE
REWAN *archaic past form of* > REWIN
REWARD *n* something given in return for a service ▷ *vb* pay or give something to (someone) for a service, information, etc
REWARDED > REWARD
REWARDER > REWARD
REWARDERS > REWARD
REWARDFUL > REWARD
REWARDING *adj* giving personal satisfaction, worthwhile
REWARDS > REWARD
REWAREWA *n* New Zealand tree
REWAREWAS > REWAREWA
REWARM *vb* warm again
REWARMED > REWARM
REWARMING > REWARM
REWARMS > REWARM
REWASH *vb* wash again
REWASHED > REWASH
REWASHES > REWASH
REWASHING > REWASH
REWATER *vb* water again
REWATERED > REWATER
REWATERS > REWATER
REWAX *vb* wax again
REWAXED > REWAX
REWAXES > REWAX

REWAXING > REWAX
REWEAR vb wear again
REWEARING > REWEAR
REWEARS > REWEAR
REWEAVE vb weave again
REWEAVED > REWEAVE
REWEAVES > REWEAVE
REWEAVING > REWEAVE
REWED vb wed again
REWEDDED > REWED
REWEDDING > REWED
REWEDS > REWED
REWEIGH vb weigh again
REWEIGHED > REWEIGH
REWEIGHS > REWEIGH
REWELD vb weld again
REWELDED > REWELD
REWELDING > REWELD
REWELDS > REWELD
REWET vb wet again
REWETS > REWET
REWETTED > REWET
REWETTING > REWET
REWIDEN vb widen again
REWIDENED > REWIDEN
REWIDENS > REWIDEN
REWILDING n returing
land areas to a wild state
REWIN vb win again
REWIND vb wind again
REWINDED > REWIND
REWINDER > REWIND
REWINDERS > REWIND
REWINDING > REWIND
REWINDS > REWIND
REWINNING > REWIN
REWINS > REWIN
REWIRABLE > REWIRE
REWIRE vb provide (a
house, engine, etc) with
new wiring
REWIRED > REWIRE
REWIRES > REWIRE
REWIRING > REWIRE
REWOKE > REWAKE
REWOKEN > REWAKE
REWON > REWIN
REWORD vb alter the
wording of
REWORDED > REWORD
REWORDING > REWORD
REWORDS > REWORD
REWORE > REWEAR
REWORK vb improve or
bring up to date
REWORKED > REWORK
REWORKING > REWORK
REWORKS > REWORK
REWORN > REWEAR
REWOUND > REWIND
REWOVE > REWEAVE
REWOVEN > REWEAVE
REWRAP vb wrap again
REWRAPPED > REWRAP
REWRAPS > REWRAP
REWRAPT > REWRAP
REWRITE vb write again in
a different way ▷ n
something rewritten
REWRITER > REWRITE
REWRITERS > REWRITE
REWRITES > REWRITE
REWRITING > REWRITE

REWRITTEN > REWRITE
REWROTE > REWRITE
REWROUGHT > REWORK
REWS > REW
REWTH archaic variant of
> RUTH
REWTHS > REWTH
REX n king
REXES > REX
REXINE n tradename for a
form of artificial leather
REXINES > REXINE
REYNARD n fox
REYNARDS > REYNARD
REZ n informal word for an
instance of reserving;
reservation
REZERO vb reset to zero
REZEROED > REZERO
REZEROES > REZERO
REZEROING > REZERO
REZEROS > REZERO
REZONE vb zone again
REZONED > REZONE
REZONES > REZONE
REZONING > REZONE
REZZES > REZ
RHABDOID adj rod-shaped
▷ n rod-shaped structure
found in cells of some
plants and animals
RHABDOIDS > RHABDOID
RHABDOM n (in insect
anatomy) any of many
similar rodlike structures
found in the eye
RHABDOMAL > RHABDOM
RHABDOME same as
> RHABDOM
RHABDOMES > RHABDOME
RHABDOMS > RHABDOM
RHABDUS n sponge spicule
RHABDUSES > RHABDUS
RHACHIAL > RACHIS
RHACHIDES > RHACHIS
RHACHILLA same as
> RACHILLA
RHACHIS same as
> RACHIS
RHACHISES > RHACHIS
RHACHITIS same as
> RACHITIS
RHAGADES npl cracks
found in the skin
RHAMNOSE n type of plant
sugar
RHAMNOSES > RHAMNOSE
RHAMNUS n buckthorn
RHAMNUSES > RHAMNUS
RHAMPHOID adj beaklike
RHANJA n Indian English
word for a male lover
RHANJAS > RHANJA
RHAPHAE > RHAPHE
RHAPHE same as > RAPHE
RHAPHES > RHAPHE
RHAPHIDE same as
> RAPHIDE
RHAPHIDES > RHAPHIDE
RHAPHIS same as
> RAPHIDE
RHAPONTIC n rhubarb
RHAPSODE n (in ancient
Greece) professional reciter

of poetry
RHAPSODES > RHAPSODE
RHAPSODIC adj of or like a
rhapsody
RHAPSODY n freely
structured emotional piece
of music
RHATANIES > RHATANY
RHATANY n South
American leguminous
shrub
RHEA n S American
three-toed ostrich
RHEAS > RHEA
RHEBOK n woolly
brownish-grey southern
African antelope
RHEBOKS > RHEBOK
RHEMATIC adj of or
relating to word formation
RHEME n constituent of a
sentence that adds most
new information, in
addition to what has
already been said in the
discourse. The rheme is
usually, but not always,
associated with the subject
RHEMES > RHEME
RHENIUM n silvery-white
metallic element with a
high melting point
RHENIUMS > RHENIUM
RHEOBASE n minimum
nerve impulse required to
elicit a response from a
tissue
RHEOBASES > RHEOBASE
RHEOBASIC > RHEOBASE
RHEOCHORD n wire
inserted into an electrical
circuit to vary or regulate
the current
RHEOCORD same as
> RHEOCHORD
RHEOCORDS > RHEOCORD
RHEOLOGIC > RHEOLOGY
RHEOLOGY n branch of
physics concerned with the
flow and change of shape
of matter
RHEOMETER n instrument
for measuring the velocity
of the blood flow
RHEOMETRY
> RHEOMETER
RHEOPHIL adj liking
flowing water
RHEOPHILE n something
that likes flowing water
RHEOSTAT n instrument
for varying the resistance of
an electrical circuit
RHEOSTATS > RHEOSTAT
RHEOTAXES
> RHEOTAXIS
RHEOTAXIS n movement
of an organism towards or
away from a current of
water
RHEOTOME n interrupter
RHEOTOMES > RHEOTOME
RHEOTROPE n
electric-current-reversing
device

RHESUS n macaque
monkey
RHESUSES > RHESUS
RHETOR n teacher of
rhetoric
RHETORIC n art of
effective speaking or
writing
RHETORICS > RHETORIC
RHETORISE same as
> RHETORIZE
RHETORIZE vb make use
of rhetoric
RHETORS > RHETOR
RHEUM n watery discharge
from the eyes or nose
RHEUMATIC adj (person)
affected by rheumatism ▷ n
person suffering from
rheumatism
RHEUMATIZ n dialect word
meaning rheumatism, any
painful disorder of joints,
muscles, or connective
tissue
RHEUMED adj rheumy
RHEUMIC adj of or relating
to rheum
RHEUMIER > RHEUMY
RHEUMIEST > RHEUMY
RHEUMS > RHEUM
RHEUMY adj of the nature of
rheum
RHEXES > RHEXIS
RHEXIS n rupture
RHEXISES > RHEXIS
RHIES > RHY
RHIGOLENE n volatile
liquid obtained from
petroleum and used as a
local anaesthetic
RHIME old spelling of
> RHYME
RHIMES > RHIME
RHINAL adj of or relating to
the nose
RHINE n dialect word for a
ditch
RHINES > RHINE
RHINITIC > RHINITIS
RHINITIS n inflammation
of the mucous membrane
that lines the nose
RHINO n rhinoceros
RHINOCERI n
rhinoceroses
RHINOLITH n calculus
formed in the nose
RHINOLOGY n branch of
medical science concerned
with the nose and its
diseases
RHINOS > RHINO
RHIPIDATE adj shaped
like a fan
RHIPIDION n fan found in
Greek Orthodox churches
RHIPIDIUM n on a plant, a
fan-shaped arrangement of
flowers
RHIZIC adj of or relating to
the root of an equation
RHIZINE same as
> RHIZOID
RHIZINES > RHIZINE

r

RHIZOBIA > RHIZOBIUM
RHIZOBIAL
> RHIZOBIUM
RHIZOBIUM *n* type of rod-shaped bacterium typically occurring in the root nodules of leguminous plants
RHIZOCARP *n* plant that fruits underground or whose root remains intact while the leaves die off annually
RHIZOCAUL *n* rootlike stem
RHIZOID *n* any of various slender hairlike structures that function as roots in the gametophyte generation of mosses, ferns, and related plants
RHIZOIDAL > RHIZOID
RHIZOIDS > RHIZOID
RHIZOMA *same as* > RHIZOME
RHIZOMATA > RHIZOMA
RHIZOME *n* thick underground stem producing new plants
RHIZOMES > RHIZOME
RHIZOMIC > RHIZOME
RHIZOPI > RHIZOPUS
RHIZOPOD *n* type of protozoan of the phylum which includes the amoebas
RHIZOPODS > RHIZOPOD
RHIZOPUS *n* type of fungus
RHIZOTOMY *n* surgical incision into the roots of spinal nerves, esp for the relief of pain
RHO *n* 17th letter in the Greek alphabet, a consonant transliterated as r or rh
RHODAMIN *same as* > RHODAMINE
RHODAMINE *n* any one of a group of synthetic red or pink basic dyestuffs used for wool and silk. They are made from phthalic anhydride and aminophenols
RHODAMINS > RHODAMIN
RHODANATE *n* sulphocyanate
RHODANIC *adj* of or relating to sulphocyanic acid
RHODANISE *same as* > RHODANIZE
RHODANIZE *vb* plate with rhodium
RHODIC *adj* of or containing rhodium, esp in the tetravalent state
RHODIE *same as* > RHODY
RHODIES > RHODY
RHODINAL *n* substance with a lemon-like smell found esp in citronella and certain eucalyptus oils
RHODINALS > RHODINAL

RHODIUM *n* hard metallic element
RHODIUMS > RHODIUM
RHODOLITE *n* pale violet or red variety of garnet, used as a gemstone
RHODONITE *n* brownish translucent mineral
RHODOPSIN *n* red pigment in the rods of the retina in vertebrates. It is dissociated by light into retinene, the light energy being converted into nerve signals, and is re-formed in the dark
RHODORA *n* type of shrub
RHODORAS > RHODORA
RHODOUS *adj* of or containing rhodium (but proportionally more than a rhodic compound)
RHODY *n* rhododendron
RHOEADINE *n* alkaloid found in the poppy
RHOMB *same as* > RHOMBUS
RHOMBI > RHOMBUS
RHOMBIC *adj* relating to or having the shape of a rhombus
RHOMBICAL *same as* > RHOMBIC
RHOMBOI > RHOMBOS
RHOMBOID *n* parallelogram with adjacent sides of unequal length ▷ *adj* having such a shape
RHOMBOIDS > RHOMBOID
RHOMBOS *n* wooden slat attached to a thong that makes a roaring sound when the thong is whirled
RHOMBS > RHOMB
RHOMBUS *n* parallelogram with sides of equal length but no right angles, diamond-shaped figure
RHOMBUSES > RHOMBUS
RHONCHAL > RHONCHUS
RHONCHI > RHONCHUS
RHONCHIAL > RHONCHUS
RHONCHUS *n* rattling or whistling respiratory sound resembling snoring, caused by secretions in the trachea or bronchi
RHONE *same as* > RONE
RHONES > RHONE
RHOPALIC *adj* describes verse in which each successive word has one more syllable than the word before
RHOPALISM > RHOPALIC
RHOS > RHO
RHOTACISE *same as* > RHOTACIZE
RHOTACISM *n* excessive use or idiosyncratic pronunciation of r
RHOTACIST
> RHOTACISM
RHOTACIZE *vb* pronounce r excessively or

idiosyncratically
RHOTIC *adj* denoting or speaking a dialect of English in which postvocalic r s are pronounced
RHOTICITY > RHOTIC
RHUBARB *n* garden plant of which the fleshy stalks are cooked as fruit ▷ *interj* noise made by actors to simulate conversation, esp by repeating the word *rhubarb* ▷ *vb* simulate conversation in this way
RHUBARBED > RHUBARB
RHUBARBS > RHUBARB
RHUBARBY > RHUBARB
RHUMB as in *rhumb line* imaginary line on the surface of a sphere, such as the earth, that intersects all meridians at the same angle
RHUMBA *same as* > RUMBA
RHUMBAED > RHUMBA
RHUMBAING > RHUMBA
RHUMBAS > RHUMBA
RHUMBS > RHUMB
RHUS *n* genus of shrubs and small trees, several species of which are cultivated as ornamentals for their colourful autumn foliage
RHUSES > RHUS
RHY *archaic spelling of* > RYE
RHYME *n* sameness of the final sounds at the ends of lines of verse, or in words ▷ *vb* make a rhyme
RHYMED > RHYME
RHYMELESS > RHYME
RHYMER *same as* > RHYMESTER
RHYMERS > RHYMER
RHYMES > RHYME
RHYMESTER *n* mediocre poet
RHYMING > RHYME
RHYMIST > RHYME
RHYMISTS > RHYME
RHYNE *same as* > RHINE
RHYNES > RHYNE
RHYOLITE *n* fine-grained igneous rock consisting of quartz, feldspars, and mica or amphibole. It is the volcanic equivalent of granite
RHYOLITES > RHYOLITE
RHYOLITIC > RHYOLITE
RHYTA > RHYTON
RHYTHM *n* any regular movement or beat
RHYTHMAL *adj* rhythmic
RHYTHMED > RHYTHM
RHYTHMI > RHYTHMUS
RHYTHMIC *adj* of, relating to, or characterized by rhythm, as in movement or sound
RHYTHMICS *n* study of rhythmic movement
RHYTHMISE *same as* > RHYTHMIZE

RHYTHMIST *n* person who has a good sense of rhythm
RHYTHMIZE *vb* make rhythmic
RHYTHMS > RHYTHM
RHYTHMUS *n* rhythm
RHYTIDOME *n* bark
RHYTINA *n* type of sea cow
RHYTINAS > RHYTINA
RHYTON *n* (in ancient Greece) a horn-shaped drinking vessel with a hole in the pointed end through which to drink
RHYTONS > RHYTON
RIA *n* long narrow inlet of the seacoast, being a former valley that was submerged by a rise in the level of the sea. Rias are found esp on the coasts of SW Ireland and NW Spain
RIAD *n* traditional Moroccan house with an interior garden
RIADS > RIAD
RIAL *n* standard monetary unit of Iran
RIALS > RIAL
RIALTO *n* market or exchange
RIALTOS > RIALTO
RIANCIES > RIANT
RIANCY > RIANT
RIANT *adj* laughing
RIANTLY > RIANT
RIAS > RIA
RIATA *same as* > REATA
RIATAS > RIATA
RIB *n* one of the curved bones forming the framework of the upper part of the body ▷ *vb* provide or mark with ribs
RIBA *n* (in Islam) interest or usury, as forbidden by the Koran
RIBALD *adj* humorously or mockingly rude or obscene ▷ *n* ribald person
RIBALDLY > RIBALD
RIBALDRY *n* ribald language or behaviour
RIBALDS > RIBALD
RIBAND *n* ribbon awarded for some achievement
RIBANDS > RIBAND
RIBAS > RIBA
RIBATTUTA *n* (in music) type of trill
RIBAUD *archaic variant of* > RIBALD
RIBAUDRED *archaic variant of* > RIBALD
RIBAUDRY *archaic variant of* > RIBALDRY
RIBAUDS > RIBAUD
RIBAVIRIN *n* type of antiviral drug
RIBBAND *same as* > RIBAND
RIBBANDS > RIBBAND
RIBBED > RIB
RIBBER *n* someone who ribs

RIBBERS > RIBBER
RIBBIER > RIBBY
RIBBIEST > RIBBY
RIBBING > RIB
RIBBINGS > RIB
RIBBON n narrow band of fabric used for trimming, tying, etc ▷ vb adorn with a ribbon or ribbons
RIBBONED > RIBBON
RIBBONING > RIBBON
RIBBONRY n ribbons or ribbon work
RIBBONS > RIBBON
RIBBONY > RIBBON
RIBBY adj with noticeable ribs
RIBCAGE n bony structure of ribs enclosing the lungs
RIBCAGES > RIBCAGE
RIBES n genus of shrubs that includes currants
RIBEYE n beefsteak cut from the outer side of the rib section
RIBEYES > RIBEYE
RIBGRASS same as > RIBWORT
RIBIBE n rebeck
RIBIBES > RIBIBE
RIBIBLE same as > RIBIBE
RIBIBLES > RIBIBLE
RIBIER n variety of grape
RIBIERS > RIBIER
RIBLESS > RIB
RIBLET n small rib
RIBLETS > RIBLET
RIBLIKE > RIB
RIBOSE n pentose sugar that is an isomeric form of arabinose and that occurs in RNA and riboflavin
RIBOSES > RIBOSE
RIBOSOMAL > RIBOSOME
RIBOSOME n any of numerous minute particles in the cytoplasm of cells, either free or attached to the endoplasmic reticulum, that contain RNA and protein and are the site of protein synthesis
RIBOSOMES > RIBOSOME
RIBOZYMAL > RIBOZYME
RIBOZYME n RNA molecule capable of catalysing a chemical reaction, usually the cleavage of another RNA molecule
RIBOZYMES > RIBOZYME
RIBS > RIB
RIBSTON n variety of apple
RIBSTONE same as > RIBSTON
RIBSTONES > RIBSTONE
RIBSTONS > RIBSTON
RIBWORK n work or structure involving ribs
RIBWORKS > RIBWORK
RIBWORT n Eurasian plant with lancelike ribbed leaves and a dense spike of small white flowers

RIBWORTS > RIBWORT
RICE n cereal plant grown on wet ground in warm countries ▷ vb sieve (potatoes or other vegetables) to a coarse mashed consistency
RICEBIRD n any of various birds frequenting rice fields, esp the Java sparrow
RICEBIRDS > RICEBIRD
RICED > RICE
RICER n kitchen utensil with small holes through which cooked potatoes and similar soft foods are pressed to form a coarse mash
RICERCAR same as > RICERCARE
RICERCARE n elaborate polyphonic composition making extensive use of contrapuntal imitation and usually very slow in tempo
RICERCARI > RICERCARE
RICERCARS > RICERCAR
RICERCATA same as > RICERCARE
RICERS > RICER
RICES > RICE
RICEY adj resembling or containing rice
RICH adj owning a lot of money or property, wealthy ▷ vb (in archaic usage) enrich
RICHED > RICH
RICHEN vb enrich
RICHENED > RICHEN
RICHENING > RICHEN
RICHENS > RICHEN
RICHER > RICH
RICHES npl wealth
RICHESSE n wealth or richness
RICHESSES > RICHESSE
RICHEST > RICH
RICHING > RICH
RICHLY adv elaborately
RICHNESS n state or quality of being rich
RICHT adj, adv, n, vb right
RICHTED > RICHT
RICHTER > RICHT
RICHTEST > RICHT
RICHTING > RICHT
RICHTS > RICHT
RICHWEED n type of plant
RICHWEEDS > RICHWEED
RICIER > RICY
RICIEST > RICY
RICIN n highly toxic protein, a lectin, derived from castor-oil seeds: used in experimental cancer therapy
RICING > RICE
RICINS > RICIN
RICINUS n genus of plants
RICINUSES > RICINUS
RICK n stack of hay etc ▷ vb wrench or sprain (a joint)
RICKED > RICK

RICKER n young kauri tree of New Zealand
RICKERS > RICKER
RICKET n mistake
RICKETIER > RICKETY
RICKETILY > RICKETY
RICKETS n disease of children marked by softening of the bones, bow legs, etc, caused by vitamin D deficiency
RICKETTY same as > RICKETY
RICKETY adj shaky or unstable
RICKEY n cocktail consisting of gin or vodka, lime juice, and soda water, served iced
RICKEYS > RICKEY
RICKING > RICK
RICKLE n unsteady or shaky structure, esp a dilapidated building
RICKLES > RICKLE
RICKLY adj archaic word for run-down or rickety
RICKRACK n zigzag braid used for trimming
RICKRACKS > RICKRACK
RICKS > RICK
RICKSHA same as > RICKSHAW
RICKSHAS > RICKSHA
RICKSHAW n light two-wheeled man-drawn Asian vehicle
RICKSHAWS > RICKSHAW
RICKSTAND n platform on which to put a rick
RICKSTICK n tool used when making hayricks
RICKYARD n place where hayricks are put
RICKYARDS > RICKYARD
RICOCHET vb (of a bullet) rebound from a solid surface ▷ n such a rebound
RICOCHETS > RICOCHET
RICOTTA n soft white unsalted Italian cheese made from sheep's milk
RICOTTAS > RICOTTA
RICRAC same as > RICKRACK
RICRACS > RICRAC
RICTAL > RICTUS
RICTUS n gape or cleft of an open mouth or beak
RICTUSES > RICTUS
RICY same as > RICEY
RID vb clear or relieve (of)
RIDABLE > RIDE
RIDDANCE n act of getting rid of something undesirable or unpleasant
RIDDANCES > RIDDANCE
RIDDED > RID
RIDDEN > RIDE
RIDDER > RID
RIDDERS > RID
RIDDING > RID
RIDDLE n question made puzzling to test one's ingenuity ▷ vb speak in

riddles
RIDDLED > RIDDLE
RIDDLER > RIDDLE
RIDDLERS > RIDDLE
RIDDLES > RIDDLE
RIDDLING > RIDDLE
RIDDLINGS > RIDDLE
RIDE vb sit on and control or propel (a horse, bicycle, etc) ▷ n journey on a horse etc, or in a vehicle
RIDEABLE > RIDE
RIDENT adj laughing, smiling, or gay
RIDER n person who rides
RIDERED > RIDER
RIDERLESS > RIDER
RIDERS > RIDER
RIDERSHIP > RIDER
RIDES > RIDE
RIDGE n long narrow hill ▷ vb form into a ridge or ridges
RIDGEBACK as in Rhodesian ridgeback large short-haired breed of dog characterized by a ridge of hair growing along the back in the opposite direction to the rest of the coat
RIDGED > RIDGE
RIDGEL same as > RIDGELING
RIDGELIKE > RIDGE
RIDGELINE n ridge
RIDGELING n domestic male animal with one or both testicles undescended, esp a horse
RIDGELS > RIDGEL
RIDGEPOLE n timber along the ridge of a roof, to which the rafters are attached
RIDGER n plough used to form furrows and ridges
RIDGERS > RIDGER
RIDGES > RIDGE
RIDGETOP n summit of ridge
RIDGETOPS > RIDGETOP
RIDGETREE another name for > RIDGEPOLE
RIDGEWAY n road or track along a ridge, esp one of great antiquity
RIDGEWAYS > RIDGEWAY
RIDGIER > RIDGE
RIDGIEST > RIDGE
RIDGIL same as > RIDGELING
RIDGILS > RIDGIL
RIDGING > RIDGE
RIDGINGS > RIDGE
RIDGLING same as > RIDGELING
RIDGLINGS > RIDGLING
RIDGY > RIDGE
RIDICULE n treatment of a person or thing as ridiculous ▷ vb laugh at, make fun of
RIDICULED > RIDICULE
RIDICULER > RIDICULE

RIDICULES > RIDICULE

RIDING > RIDE

RIDINGS > RIDE

RIDLEY n marine turtle

RIDLEYS > RIDLEY

RIDOTTO n entertainment with music and dancing, often in masquerade: popular in 18th-century England

RIDOTTOS > RIDOTTO

RIDS > RID

RIEL n standard monetary unit of Cambodia, divided into 100 sen

RIELS > RIEL

RIEM n strip of hide

RIEMPIE n leather thong or lace used mainly to make chair seats

RIEMPIES > RIEMPIE

RIEMS > RIEM

RIESLING n type of white wine

RIESLINGS > RIESLING

RIEVE n archaic word for rob or plunder

RIEVER n archaic word for robber or plunderer

RIEVERS > RIEVER

RIEVES > RIEVE

RIEVING > RIEVE

RIF vb lay off

RIFAMPIN n drug used in the treatment of tuberculosis, meningitis, and leprosy

RIFAMPINS > RIFAMPIN

RIFAMYCIN n antibiotic

RIFE adj widespread or common

RIFELY > RIFE

RIFENESS > RIFE

RIFER > RIFE

RIFEST > RIFE

RIFF n short repeated melodic figure ▷ vb play or perform riffs in jazz or rock music

RIFFAGE n (in jazz or rock music) act or an instance of playing a short series of chords

RIFFAGES > RIFFAGE

RIFFED > RIFF

RIFFING > RIFF

RIFFLE vb flick through (pages etc) quickly ▷ n rapid in a stream

RIFFLED > RIFFLE

RIFFLER n file with a curved face for filing concave surfaces

RIFFLERS > RIFFLER

RIFFLES > RIFFLE

RIFFLING > RIFFLE

RIFFOLA n use of an abundance of dominant riffs

RIFFOLAS > RIFFOLA

RIFFRAFF n rabble, disreputable people

RIFFRAFFS > RIFFRAFF

RIFFS > RIFF

RIFLE n firearm with a long barrel ▷ vb cut spiral grooves inside the barrel of a gun

RIFLEBIRD n any of various birds of paradise

RIFLED > RIFLE

RIFLEMAN n person skilled in the use of a rifle, esp a soldier

RIFLEMEN > RIFLEMAN

RIFLER > RIFLE

RIFLERIES > RIFLERY

RIFLERS > RIFLE

RIFLERY n rifle shots

RIFLES > RIFLE

RIFLING n cutting of spiral grooves on the inside of a firearm's barrel

RIFLINGS > RIFLING

RIFLIP n genetic difference between two individuals

RIFLIPS > RIFLIP

RIFS > RIF

RIFT n break in friendly relations ▷ vb burst or cause to burst open

RIFTE archaic word for **>** RIFT

RIFTED > RIFT

RIFTIER > RIFT

RIFTIEST > RIFT

RIFTING > RIFT

RIFTLESS > RIFT

RIFTS > RIFT

RIFTY > RIFT

RIG vb arrange in a dishonest way ▷ n apparatus for drilling for oil and gas

RIGADOON n old Provençal couple dance, light and graceful, in lively duple time

RIGADOONS > RIGADOON

RIGATONI n macaroni in the form of short ridged often slightly curved pieces

RIGATONIS > RIGATONI

RIGAUDON same as **>** RIGADOON

RIGAUDONS > RIGAUDON

RIGG n type of fish

RIGGALD same as **>** RIDGELING

RIGGALDS > RIGGALD

RIGGED > RIG

RIGGER n workman who rigs vessels, etc

RIGGERS > RIGGER

RIGGING > RIG

RIGGINGS > RIG

RIGGISH adj dialect word meaning wanton

RIGGS > RIGG

RIGHT adj just ▷ adv correctly ▷ n claim, title, etc allowed or due ▷ vb bring or come back to a normal or correct state

RIGHTABLE adj capable of being righted

RIGHTABLY > RIGHTABLE

RIGHTED > RIGHT

RIGHTEN vb set right

RIGHTENED > RIGHTEN

RIGHTENS > RIGHTEN

RIGHTEOUS adj upright, godly, or virtuous

RIGHTER > RIGHT

RIGHTERS > RIGHT

RIGHTEST > RIGHT

RIGHTFUL adj in accordance with what is right

RIGHTIES > RIGHTY

RIGHTING > RIGHT

RIGHTINGS > RIGHT

RIGHTISH adj somewhat right, esp politically

RIGHTISM > RIGHTIST

RIGHTISMS > RIGHTIST

RIGHTIST adj (person) on the political right ▷ n supporter of the political right

RIGHTISTS > RIGHTIST

RIGHTLESS > RIGHT

RIGHTLY adv in accordance with the true facts or justice

RIGHTMOST > RIGHT

RIGHTNESS n state or quality of being right

RIGHTO n expression of agreement or compliance

RIGHTS > RIGHT

RIGHTSIZE vb restructure (an organization) to cut costs and improve effectiveness without ruthlessly downsizing

RIGHTWARD adj situated on or directed towards the right ▷ adv towards or on the right

RIGHTY n informal word for a right-winger

RIGID adj inflexible or strict ▷ adv completely or excessively ▷ n strict and unbending person

RIGIDER > RIGID

RIGIDEST > RIGID

RIGIDIFY vb make or become rigid

RIGIDISE same as **>** RIGIDIZE

RIGIDISED > RIGIDISE

RIGIDISES > RIGIDISE

RIGIDITY > RIGID

RIGIDIZE vb make or become rigid

RIGIDIZED > RIGIDIZE

RIGIDIZES > RIGIDIZE

RIGIDLY > RIGID

RIGIDNESS > RIGID

RIGIDS > RIGID

RIGLIN same as **>** RIDGELING

RIGLING same as **>** RIDGELING

RIGLINGS > RIGLING

RIGLINS > RIGLIN

RIGMAROLE n long complicated procedure

RIGOL n (in dialect) ditch or gutter

RIGOLL same as **>** RIGOL

RIGOLLS > RIGOLL

RIGOLS > RIGOL

RIGOR same as **>** RIGOUR

RIGORISM n strictness in judgment or conduct

RIGORISMS > RIGORISM

RIGORIST > RIGORISM

RIGORISTS > RIGORISM

RIGOROUS adj harsh, severe, or stern

RIGORS > RIGOR

RIGOUR n harshness, severity, or strictness

RIGOURS > RIGOUR

RIGOUT n person's clothing

RIGOUTS > RIGOUT

RIGS > RIG

RIGSDALER n any of various former Scandinavian or Dutch small silver coins

RIGWIDDIE n part of the carthorse's harness to which the shafts of the cart attach

RIGWOODIE same as **>** RIGWIDDIE

RIJSTAFEL n assortment of Indonesian rice dishes

RIKISHA same as **>** RICKSHAW

RIKISHAS > RIKISHA

RIKISHI n sumo wrestler

RIKSHAW same as **>** RICKSHAW

RIKSHAWS > RIKSHAW

RILE vb anger or annoy

RILED > RILE

RILES > RILE

RILEY adj cross or irritable

RILIER > RILEY

RILIEST > RILEY

RILIEVI > RILIEVO

RILIEVO same as **>** RELIEF

RILING > RILE

RILL n small stream ▷ vb trickle

RILLE same as **>** RILL

RILLED > RILL

RILLES > RILLE

RILLET n little rill

RILLETS > RILLET

RILLETTES npl potted meat

RILLING > RILL

RILLMARK n mark left by the trickle of a rill

RILLMARKS > RILLMARK

RILLS > RILL

RIM n edge or border ▷ vb put a rim on (a pot, cup, wheel, etc)

RIMA n long narrow opening

RIMAE > RIMA

RIMAYE n crevasse at the head of a glacier

RIMAYES > RIMAYE

RIME same as **>** RHYME

RIMED > RIME

RIMELESS > RHYME

RIMER same as
> RHYMESTER
RIMERS > RIMER
RIMES > RIME
RIMESTER same as
> RHYMESTER
RIMESTERS > RIMESTER
RIMFIRE adj (of a cartridge) having the primer in the rim of the base ⊳ n cartridge of this type
RIMFIRES > RIMFIRE
RIMIER > RIMY
RIMIEST > RIMY
RIMINESS > RIMY
RIMING > RIME
RIMLAND n area situated on the outer edges of a region
RIMLANDS > RIMLAND
RIMLESS > RIM
RIMMED > RIM
RIMMER n tool for shaping the edge of something
RIMMERS > RIMMER
RIMMING > RIM
RIMMINGS > RIM
RIMOSE adj (esp of plant parts) having the surface marked by a network of intersecting cracks
RIMOSELY > RIMOSE
RIMOSITY > RIMOSE
RIMOUS same as > RIMOSE
RIMPLE vb crease or wrinkle
RIMPLED > RIMPLE
RIMPLES > RIMPLE
RIMPLING > RIMPLE
RIMROCK n rock forming the boundaries of a sandy or gravelly alluvial deposit
RIMROCKS > RIMROCK
RIMS > RIM
RIMSHOT n deliberate simultaneous striking of skin and rim of drum
RIMSHOTS > RIMSHOT
RIMU n New Zealand tree whose wood is used for building and furniture
RIMUS > RIMU
RIMY adj coated with rime
RIN Scots variant of > RUN
RIND n tough outer coating of fruits, cheese, or bacon ⊳ vb take the bark off
RINDED > RIND
RINDIER > RINDY
RINDIEST > RINDY
RINDING > RIND
RINDLESS > RIND
RINDS > RIND
RINDY adj with a rind or rindlike skin
RINE archaic variant of
> RIND
RINES > RINE
RING vb give out a clear resonant sound, as a bell ⊳ n ringing
RINGBARK same as > RING
RINGBARKS > RINGBARK

RINGBIT n type of bit worn by a horse
RINGBITS > RINGBIT
RINGBOLT n bolt with a ring fitted through an eye attached to the bolt head
RINGBOLTS > RINGBOLT
RINGBONE n abnormal bony growth affecting the pastern of a horse, often causing lameness
RINGBONES > RINGBONE
RINGDOVE n large Eurasian pigeon with white patches on the wings and neck
RINGDOVES > RINGDOVE
RINGED > RING
RINGENT adj (of the corolla of plants such as the snapdragon) consisting of two distinct gaping lips
RINGER n person or thing apparently identical to another
RINGERS > RINGER
RINGETTE n team sport played on ice, using straight sticks to control a rubber ring
RINGETTES > RINGETTE
RINGGIT n standard monetary unit of Malaysia, divided into 100 sen
RINGGITS > RINGGIT
RINGHALS n variety of cobra
RINGING > RING
RINGINGLY > RING
RINGINGS > RING
RINGLESS > RING
RINGLET n curly lock of hair
RINGLETED > RINGLET
RINGLETS > RINGLET
RINGLIKE > RING
RINGMAN n (in dialect) ring finger
RINGMEN > RINGMAN
RINGNECK n any bird that has ringlike markings round its neck
RINGNECKS > RINGNECK
RINGS > RING
RINGSIDE n row of seats nearest a boxing or circus ring ⊳ adj providing a close uninterrupted view
RINGSIDER n someone with a ringside seat or position
RINGSIDES > RINGSIDE
RINGSTAND n stand for laboratory equipment
RINGSTER n member of a ring controlling a market in antiques, art treasures, etc
RINGSTERS > RINGSTER
RINGTAIL n possum with a curling tail used to grip branches while climbing
RINGTAILS > RINGTAIL
RINGTAW n game of marbles in which the aim is to knock other players'

marbles out of a ring
RINGTAWS > RINGTAW
RINGTONE n musical tune played by a mobile phone when a call is received
RINGTONES > RINGTONE
RINGTOSS n game in which participants try to throw hoops onto an upright stick
RINGWAY n bypass
RINGWAYS > RINGWAY
RINGWISE adj used to being in the ring and able to respond appropriately
RINGWOMB n complication at lambing resulting from failure of the cervix to open
RINGWOMBS > RINGWOMB
RINGWORK n circular earthwork
RINGWORKS > RINGWORK
RINGWORM n fungal skin disease in circular patches
RINGWORMS > RINGWORM
RINK n sheet of ice for skating or curling ⊳ vb skate on a rink
RINKED > RINK
RINKHALS n S African cobra that can spit venom
RINKING > RINK
RINKS > RINK
RINNING > RIN
RINS > RIN
RINSABLE > RINSE
RINSE vb remove soap from (washed clothes, hair, etc) by applying clean water ⊳ n rinsing
RINSEABLE > RINSE
RINSED > RINSE
RINSER > RINSE
RINSERS > RINSE
RINSES > RINSE
RINSIBLE > RINSE
RINSING > RINSE
RINSINGS > RINSE
RIOJA n red or white Spanish wine with a vanilla bouquet and flavour
RIOJAS > RIOJA
RIOT n disorderly unruly disturbance ⊳ vb take part in a riot
RIOTED > RIOT
RIOTER > RIOT
RIOTERS > RIOT
RIOTING > RIOT
RIOTINGS > RIOT
RIOTISE n archaic word for riotous behaviour and excess
RIOTISES > RIOTISE
RIOTIZE same as
> RIOTISE
RIOTIZES > RIOTISE
RIOTOUS adj unrestrained
RIOTOUSLY > RIOTOUS
RIOTRIES > RIOTRY
RIOTRY n riotous behaviour
RIOTS > RIOT
RIP vb tear violently ⊳ n

split or tear
RIPARIAL adj riparian
RIPARIAN adj of or on the banks of a river ⊳ n person who owns land on a river bank
RIPARIANS > RIPARIAN
RIPCORD n cord pulled to open a parachute
RIPCORDS > RIPCORD
RIPE adj ready to be reaped, eaten, etc ⊳ vb ripen
RIPECK same as
> RYEPECK
RIPECKS > RIPECK
RIPED > RIPE
RIPELY > RIPE
RIPEN vb grow ripe
RIPENED > RIPEN
RIPENER > RIPEN
RIPENERS > RIPEN
RIPENESS > RIPE
RIPENING > RIPEN
RIPENS > RIPEN
RIPER adj more ripe ⊳ n old Scots word meaning plunderer
RIPERS > RIPER
RIPES > RIPE
RIPEST > RIPE
RIPIENI > RIPIENO
RIPIENIST n orchestral member who is there to swell the sound rather than play solo
RIPIENO n (in baroque concertos and concerti grossi) the full orchestra, as opposed to the instrumental soloists
RIPIENOS > RIPIENO
RIPING > RIPE
RIPOFF n grossly overpriced article
RIPOFFS > RIPOFF
RIPOST same as
> RIPOSTE
RIPOSTE n verbal retort ⊳ vb make a riposte
RIPOSTED > RIPOSTE
RIPOSTES > RIPOSTE
RIPOSTING > RIPOSTE
RIPOSTS > RIPOST
RIPP n old Scots word for a handful of grain
RIPPABLE > RIP
RIPPED > RIP
RIPPER n person who rips
RIPPERS > RIPPER
RIPPIER n archaic word for fish seller
RIPPIERS > RIPPIER
RIPPING > RIP
RIPPINGLY > RIP
RIPPINGS > RIPPING
RIPPLE n slight wave or ruffling of a surface ⊳ vb flow or form into little waves (on)
RIPPLED > RIPPLE
RIPPLER > RIPPLE
RIPPLERS > RIPPLE
RIPPLES > RIPPLE

r

RIPPLET n tiny ripple
RIPPLETS > RIPPLET
RIPPLIER > RIPPLE
RIPPLIEST > RIPPLE
RIPPLING > RIPPLE
RIPPLINGS > RIPPLE
RIPPLY > RIPPLE
RIPPS > RIPP
RIPRAP vb deposit broken stones in or on
RIPRAPPED > RIPRAP
RIPRAPS > RIPRAP
RIPS > RIP
RIPSAW n handsaw for cutting along the grain of timber ▷ vb saw with a ripsaw
RIPSAWED > RIPSAW
RIPSAWING > RIPSAW
RIPSAWN > RIPSAW
RIPSAWS > RIPSAW
RIPSTOP n tear-resistant cloth
RIPSTOPS > RIPSTOP
RIPT archaic past form of > RIP
RIPTIDE n stretch of turbulent water in the sea, caused by the meeting of currents or abrupt changes in depth
RIPTIDES > RIPTIDE
RIRORIRO n small NZ bush bird that hatches the eggs of the shining cuckoo
RIRORIROS > RIRORIRO
RISALDAR n Indian cavalry officer
RISALDARS > RISALDAR
RISE vb get up from a lying, sitting, or kneeling position ▷ n rising
RISEN > RISE
RISER n person who rises, esp from bed
RISERS > RISER
RISES > RISE
RISHI n Indian seer or sage
RISHIS > RISHI
RISIBLE adj causing laughter, ridiculous
RISIBLES npl sense of humour
RISIBLY > RISIBLE
RISING > RISE
RISINGS > RISE
RISK n chance of disaster or loss ▷ vb act in spite of the possibility of (injury or loss)
RISKED > RISK
RISKER > RISK
RISKERS > RISK
RISKFUL > RISK
RISKIER > RISKY
RISKIEST > RISKY
RISKILY > RISKY
RISKINESS > RISKY
RISKING > RISK
RISKLESS > RISK
RISKS > RISK
RISKY adj full of risk, dangerous
RISOLUTO adj musical

term meaning firm and decisive ▷ adv firmly and decisively
RISORII > RISORIUS
RISORIUS n facial muscle responsible for smiling
RISOTTO n dish of rice cooked in stock with vegetables, meat, etc
RISOTTOS > RISOTTO
RISP vb Scots word meaning rasp
RISPED > RISP
RISPETTI > RISPETTO
RISPETTO n kind of folk song
RISPING > RISP
RISPINGS > RISP
RISPS > RISP
RISQUE n risk
RISQUES > RISQUE
RISSOLE n cake of minced meat, coated with breadcrumbs and fried
RISSOLES > RISSOLE
RISTRA n string of dried chilli peppers
RISTRAS > RISTRA
RISUS n involuntary grinning expression
RISUSES > RISUS
RIT vb Scots word for cut or slit
RITARD n (in music) a slowing down
RITARDS > RITARD
RITE n formal practice or custom, esp religious
RITELESS > RITE
RITENUTO adv held back momentarily ▷ n (in music) a slowing down
RITENUTOS > RITENUTO
RITES > RITE
RITONAVIR n drug used to treat HIV
RITORNEL n (in music) orchestral passage
RITORNELL same as > RITORNEL
RITORNELS > RITORNEL
RITS > RIT
RITT same as > RIT
RITTED > RIT
RITTER n knight or horseman
RITTERS > RITTER
RITTING > RIT
RITTS > RITT
RITUAL n prescribed order of rites ▷ adj concerning rites
RITUALISE same as > RITUALIZE
RITUALISM n exaggerated emphasis on the importance of rites and ceremonies
RITUALIST > RITUALISM
RITUALIZE vb engage in ritualism or devise rituals
RITUALLY > RITUAL
RITUALS > RITUAL

RITUXIMAB n drug used to treat non-Hodgkin's lymphoma
RITZ as in put on the ritz assume a superior air or make an ostentatious display
RITZES > RITZ
RITZIER > RITZY
RITZIEST > RITZY
RITZILY > RITZY
RITZINESS > RITZY
RITZY adj luxurious or elegant
RIVA n rock cleft
RIVAGE n bank, shore, or coast
RIVAGES > RIVAGE
RIVAL n person or thing that competes with or equals another for favour, success, etc ▷ adj in the position of a rival ▷ vb (try to) equal
RIVALED > RIVAL
RIVALESS n female rival
RIVALING > RIVAL
RIVALISE same as > RIVALIZE
RIVALISED > RIVALISE
RIVALISES > RIVALISE
RIVALITY > RIVAL
RIVALIZE vb become a rival
RIVALIZED > RIVALIZE
RIVALIZES > RIVALIZE
RIVALLED > RIVAL
RIVALLESS > RIVAL
RIVALLING > RIVAL
RIVALRIES > RIVALRY
RIVALROUS > RIVALRY
RIVALRY n keen competition
RIVALS > RIVAL
RIVALSHIP > RIVAL
RIVAS > RIVA
RIVE vb split asunder
RIVED > RIVE
RIVEL vb archaic word meaning wrinkle
RIVELLED > RIVEL
RIVELLING > RIVEL
RIVELS > RIVEL
RIVEN > RIVE
RIVER n large natural stream of water
RIVERAIN same as > RIPARIAN
RIVERAINS > RIVERAIN
RIVERBANK n bank of a river
RIVERBED n bed of a river
RIVERBEDS > RIVERBOAT
RIVERBOAT n boat, especially a barge, designed for use on rivers
RIVERED adj with a river or rivers
RIVERET n archaic word for rivulet or stream
RIVERETS > RIVERET
RIVERHEAD n source of river

RIVERINE same as > RIPARIAN
RIVERLESS > RIVER
RIVERLIKE adj resembling a river
RIVERMAN n boatman or man earning his living working on a river
RIVERMEN > RIVERMAN
RIVERS > RIVER
RIVERSIDE n area beside a river
RIVERWARD adj towards the river ▷ adv towards the river
RIVERWAY n river serving as a waterway
RIVERWAYS > RIVERWAY
RIVERWEED n type of plant found growing near rivers
RIVERY adj riverlike
RIVES > RIVE
RIVET n bolt for fastening metal plates, the end being put through holes and then beaten flat ▷ vb fasten with rivets
RIVETED > RIVET
RIVETER > RIVET
RIVETERS > RIVET
RIVETING > RIVET
RIVETINGS > RIVET
RIVETS > RIVET
RIVETTED > RIVET
RIVETTING > RIVET
RIVIERA n coastline resembling the Mediterranean Riviera
RIVIERAS > RIVIERA
RIVIERE n necklace of diamonds or other precious stones of which gradually increase in size up to a large centre stone
RIVIERES > RIVIERE
RIVING > RIVE
RIVLIN n Scots word for rawhide shoe
RIVLINS > RIVLIN
RIVO interj (in the past) an informal toast
RIVULET n small stream
RIVULETS > RIVULET
RIVULOSE adj having meandering lines
RIYAL n standard monetary unit of Qatar, divided into 100 dirhams
RIYALS > RIYAL
RIZ (in some dialects) past form of > RISE
RIZA n partial icon cover made from precious metal
RIZARD n redcurrant
RIZARDS > RIZARD
RIZAS > RIZA
RIZZAR n Scots word for red currant ▷ vb Scots word for sun-dry
RIZZARED > RIZZAR
RIZZARING > RIZZAR
RIZZARS > RIZZAR
RIZZART n Scots word for red currant

RIZZARTS > RIZZART
RIZZER same as **>** RIZZAR
RIZZERED > RIZZER
RIZZERING > RIZZER
RIZZERS > RIZZER
RIZZOR vb dry
RIZZORED > RIZZOR
RIZZORING > RIZZOR
RIZZORS > RIZZOR
ROACH n Eurasian freshwater fish ▷ vb clip (mane) short so that it stands upright
ROACHED adj arched convexly, as the back of certain breeds of dog, such as the whippet
ROACHES > ROACH
ROACHING > ROACH
ROAD n way prepared for passengers, vehicles, etc
ROADBED n material used to make a road
ROADBEDS > ROADBED
ROADBLOCK n barricade across a road to stop traffic for inspection etc
ROADCRAFT n skills and knowledge of a road user
ROADEO n competition in which drivers or other road users put their skills on the road to the test
ROADEOS > ROADEO
ROADHOUSE n pub or restaurant on a country road
ROADIE n person who transports and sets up equipment for a band
ROADIES > ROADIE
ROADING n road building
ROADINGS > ROADING
ROADKILL n remains of an animal or animals killed on the road by motor vehicles
ROADKILLS > ROADKILL
ROADLESS > ROAD
ROADMAN n someone involved in road repair or construction
ROADMEN > ROADMAN
ROADS > ROAD
ROADSHOW n radio show broadcast live from one of a number of places being visited by a touring disc jockey
ROADSHOWS > ROADSHOW
ROADSIDE n side of a road ▷ adj situated beside a road
ROADSIDES > ROADSIDE
ROADSMAN same as **>** ROADMAN
ROADSMEN > ROADSMAN
ROADSTEAD same as **>** ROAD
ROADSTER n open car with only two seats
ROADSTERS > ROADSTER
ROADWAY n part of a road used by vehicles
ROADWAYS > ROADWAY
ROADWORK n sports training by running along

roads
ROADWORKS npl repairs to a road, esp blocking part of the road
ROAM vb wander about ▷ n act of roaming
ROAMED > ROAM
ROAMER > ROAM
ROAMERS > ROAM
ROAMING > ROAM
ROAMINGS > ROAM
ROAMS > ROAM
ROAN adj (of a horse) having a brown or black coat sprinkled with white hairs ▷ n roan horse
ROANPIPE n drainpipe leading down from a gutter
ROANPIPES > ROANPIPE
ROANS > ROAN
ROAR vb make or utter a loud deep hoarse sound like that of a lion ▷ n such a sound
ROARED > ROAR
ROARER > ROAR
ROARERS > ROAR
ROARIE Scots word for **>** NOISY
ROARIER > ROARY
ROARIEST > ROARY
ROARING > ROAR
ROARINGLY > ROARING
ROARINGS > ROAR
ROARMING adj severe
ROARS > ROAR
ROARY adj roarlike or tending to roar
ROAST vb cook by dry heat, as in an oven ▷ n roasted joint of meat ▷ adj roasted
ROASTED > ROAST
ROASTER n person or thing that roasts
ROASTERS > ROASTER
ROASTING adj extremely hot ▷ n severe criticism or scolding
ROASTINGS > ROASTING
ROASTS > ROAST
ROATE archaic form of **>** ROTE
ROATED > ROATE
ROATES > ROATE
ROATING > ROATE
ROB vb steal from
ROBALO n tropical fish
ROBALOS > ROBALO
ROBAND n piece of marline used for fastening a sail to a spar
ROBANDS > ROBAND
ROBBED > ROB
ROBBER > ROB
ROBBERIES > ROBBERY
ROBBERS > ROB
ROBBERY n stealing of property from a person by using or threatening to use force
ROBBIN same as **>** ROBAND
ROBBING > ROB
ROBBINS > ROBBIN
ROBE n long loose outer

garment ▷ vb put a robe on
ROBED > ROBE
ROBES > ROBE
ROBIN n small brown bird with a red breast
ROBING > ROBE
ROBINGS > ROBE
ROBINIA n type of leguminous tree
ROBINIAS > ROBINIA
ROBINS > ROBIN
ROBLE n oak tree
ROBLES > ROBLE
ROBORANT adj tending to fortify or increase strength ▷ n drug or agent that increases strength
ROBORANTS > ROBORANT
ROBOT n automated machine, esp one performing functions in a human manner
ROBOTIC > ROBOT
ROBOTICS n science of designing and using robots
ROBOTISE same as **>** ROBOTIZE
ROBOTISED > ROBOTISE
ROBOTISES > ROBOTISE
ROBOTISM > ROBOT
ROBOTISMS > ROBOT
ROBOTIZE vb automate
ROBOTIZED > ROBOTIZE
ROBOTIZES > ROBOTIZE
ROBOTRIES > ROBOT
ROBOTRY > ROBOT
ROBOTS > ROBOT
ROBS > ROB
ROBURITE n flameless explosive
ROBURITES > ROBURITE
ROBUST adj very strong and healthy
ROBUSTA n species of coffee tree
ROBUSTAS > ROBUSTA
ROBUSTER > ROBUST
ROBUSTEST > ROBUST
ROBUSTLY > ROBUST
ROC n monstrous bird of Arabian mythology
ROCAILLE n decorative rock or shell work, esp as ornamentation in a rococo fountain, grotto, or interior
ROCAILLES > ROCAILLE
ROCAMBOLE n variety of sand leek whose garlic-like bulb is used for seasoning
ROCH same as **>** ROTCH
ROCHES > ROTCH
ROCHET n white surplice with tight sleeves, worn by bishops, abbots, and certain other Church dignitaries
ROCHETS > ROCHET
ROCK n hard mineral substance that makes up part of the earth's crust, stone ▷ vb (cause to) sway to and fro ▷ adj of or relating to rock music
ROCKABIES > ROCKABY

ROCKABLE > ROCK
ROCKABY same as **>** ROCKABYE
ROCKABYE n lullaby or rocking motion used with a baby during lullabies
ROCKABYES > ROCKABYE
ROCKAWAY n four-wheeled horse-drawn carriage, usually with two seats and a hard top
ROCKAWAYS > ROCKAWAY
ROCKBOUND adj hemmed in or encircled by rocks
ROCKED > ROCK
ROCKER n rocking chair
ROCKERIES > ROCKERY
ROCKERS > ROCKER
ROCKERY n mound of stones in a garden for rock plants
ROCKET n self-propelling device powered by the burning of explosive contents (used as a firework, weapon, etc) ▷ vb move fast, esp upwards, like a rocket
ROCKETED > ROCKET
ROCKETEER n engineer or scientist concerned with the design, operation, or launching of rockets
ROCKETER n bird that launches itself into the air like a rocket when flushed
ROCKETERS > ROCKETER
ROCKETING > ROCKET
ROCKETRY n science and technology of the design and operation of rockets
ROCKETS > ROCKET
ROCKFALL n instance of rocks breaking away and falling from an outcrop
ROCKFALLS > ROCKFALL
ROCKFISH n any of various fishes that live among rocks
ROCKHOUND n person interested in rocks and minerals
ROCKIER adj archaic or dialect word for rock pigeon
ROCKIERS > ROCKY
ROCKIEST > ROCKY
ROCKILY > ROCKY
ROCKINESS > ROCKY
ROCKING > ROCK
ROCKINGLY > ROCKING
ROCKINGS > ROCK
ROCKLAY same as **>** ROKELAY
ROCKLAYS > ROCKLAY
ROCKLESS > ROCK
ROCKLIKE > ROCK
ROCKLING n any of various small sea fishes having an elongated body and barbels around the mouth
ROCKLINGS > ROCKLING
ROCKOON n rocket carrying scientific equipment for studying the upper

atmosphere, fired from a balloon at high altitude

ROCKOONS > ROCKOON

ROCKROSE n any of various shrubs or herbaceous plants cultivated for their roselike flowers

ROCKROSES > ROCKROSE

ROCKS > ROCK

ROCKSHAFT n shaft that rotates backwards and forwards rather than continuously, esp one used in the valve gear of a steam engine

ROCKSLIDE n fall of rocks down hillside

ROCKWATER n water that comes out of rock

ROCKWEED n any of various seaweeds that grow on rocks exposed at low tide

ROCKWEEDS > ROCKWEED

ROCKWORK n structure made of rock

ROCKWORKS > ROCKWORK

ROCKY adj having many rocks

ROCOCO adj (of furniture, architecture, etc) having much elaborate decoration in an early 18th-century style ▷ n style of architecture and decoration that originated in France in the early 18th century, characterized by elaborate but graceful, light, ornamentation, often containing asymmetrical motifs

ROCOCOS > ROCOCO

ROCQUET n another name for the salad plant rocket

ROCQUETS > ROCQUET

ROCS > ROC

ROD n slender straight bar, stick ▷ vb clear with a rod

RODDED > ROD

RODDING > ROD

RODDINGS > ROD

RODE vb (of the male woodcock) to perform a display flight at dusk during the breeding season

RODED > RODE

RODENT n animal with teeth specialized for gnawing, such as a rat, mouse, or squirrel

RODENTS > RODENT

RODEO n display of skill by cowboys, such as bareback riding ▷ vb take part in a rodeo

RODEOED > RODEO

RODEOING > RODEO

RODEOS > RODEO

RODES > RODE

RODEWAY archaic spelling of **>** ROADWAY

RODEWAYS > RODEWAY

RODFISHER n angler

RODGERSIA n flowering plant

RODING > RODE

RODINGS > RODE

RODLESS > ROD

RODLIKE > ROD

RODMAN n someone who uses or fishes with a rod

RODMEN > RODMAN

RODS > ROD

RODSMAN same as **>** RODMAN

RODSMEN > RODSMAN

RODSTER n angler

RODSTERS > RODSTER

ROE n mass of roe in a fish, sometimes eaten as food

ROEBUCK n male of the roe deer

ROEBUCKS > ROEBUCK

ROED adj with roe inside

ROEMER n drinking glass, typically having an ovoid bowl on a short stem

ROEMERS > ROEMER

ROENTGEN n unit measuring a radiation dose

ROENTGENS > ROENTGEN

ROES > ROE

ROESTI same as **>** ROSTI

ROESTIS > ROESTI

ROESTONE same as **>** OOLITE

ROESTONES > ROESTONE

ROGALLO n flexible fabric delta wing, originally designed as a possible satellite retrieval vehicle but actually developed in the 1960s as the first successful hang-glider

ROGALLOS > ROGALLO

ROGATION n solemn supplication, esp in a form of ceremony prescribed by the Church

ROGATIONS > ROGATION

ROGATORY adj (esp in legal contexts) seeking or authorized to seek information

ROGER interj (used in signalling) message received ▷ vb (of a man) to copulate (with)

ROGERED > ROGER

ROGERING > ROGER

ROGERINGS > ROGER

ROGERS > ROGER

ROGNON n isolated rock outcrop on a glacier

ROGNONS > ROGNON

ROGUE n dishonest or unprincipled person ▷ adj (of a wild beast) having a savage temper and living apart from the herd ▷ vb rid (a field or crop) of plants that are inferior, diseased, or of an unwanted variety

ROGUED > ROGUE

ROGUEING > ROGUE

ROGUER n rogue

ROGUERIES > ROGUERY

ROGUERS > ROGUER

ROGUERY n dishonest or immoral behaviour

ROGUES > ROGUE

ROGUESHIP n being a rogue

ROGUING > ROGUE

ROGUISH adj dishonest or unprincipled

ROGUISHLY > ROGUISH

ROGUY same as **>** ROGUISH

ROIL vb make (a liquid) cloudy or turbid by stirring up dregs or sediment

ROILED > ROIL

ROILIER > ROILY

ROILIEST > ROILY

ROILING > ROIL

ROILS > ROIL

ROILY adj cloudy or muddy

ROIN same as **>** ROYNE

ROINED > ROIN

ROINING > ROIN

ROINISH same as **>** ROYNISH

ROINS > ROIN

ROIST archaic variant of **>** ROISTER

ROISTED > ROIST

ROISTER vb make merry noisily or boisterously

ROISTERED > ROISTER

ROISTERER > ROISTER

ROISTERS > ROISTER

ROISTING > ROIST

ROISTS > ROIST

ROJAK n (in Malaysia) a salad dish served in chilli sauce

ROJAKS > ROJAK

ROJI n Japanese tea garden or its path of stones

ROJIS > ROJI

ROK same as **>** ROC

ROKE vb (in dialect) steam or smoke

ROKED > ROKE

ROKELAY n type of cloak

ROKELAYS > ROKELAY

ROKER n variety of ray

ROKERS > ROKER

ROKES > ROKE

ROKIER > ROKY

ROKIEST > ROKY

ROKING > ROKE

ROKKAKU n hexagonal Japanese kite

ROKS > ROK

ROKY adj (in dialect) steamy or smoky

ROLAG n roll of carded wool ready for spinning

ROLAGS > ROLAG

ROLAMITE n type of bearing using two rollers and a moving flexible band

ROLAMITES > ROLAMITE

ROLE n task or function

ROLES > ROLE

ROLF vb massage following a particular technique

ROLFED > ROLF

ROLFER > ROLF

ROLFERS > ROLF

ROLFING > ROLF

ROLFINGS > ROLF

ROLFS > ROLF

ROLL vb move by turning over and over ▷ n act of rolling over or from side to side

ROLLABLE > ROLL

ROLLAWAY n mounted on rollers so as to be easily moved, esp to be stored away after use

ROLLAWAYS > ROLLAWAY

ROLLBACK n reduction to a previous price

ROLLBACKS > ROLLBACK

ROLLBAR n bar that reinforces the frame of a car, esp one used for racing, rallying, etc, to protect the driver if the car should turn over

ROLLBARS > ROLLBAR

ROLLED > ROLL

ROLLER n rotating cylinder used for smoothing or supporting a thing to be moved, spreading paint, etc

ROLLERS > ROLLER

ROLLICK vb behave in a carefree, frolicsome, or boisterous manner ▷ n boisterous or carefree escapade or event

ROLLICKED > ROLLICK

ROLLICKS > ROLLICK

ROLLICKY adj rollicking

ROLLING > ROLL

ROLLINGS > ROLL

ROLLMOP n herring fillet rolled round onion slices and pickled

ROLLMOPS > ROLLMOP

ROLLNECK adj (of a garment) having a high neck that is worn rolled over ▷ n rollneck sweater or other garment

ROLLNECKS > ROLLNECK

ROLLOCK same as **>** ROWLOCK

ROLLOCKS > ROLLOCK

ROLLOUT n presentation to the public of a new aircraft, product, etc; launch

ROLLOUTS > ROLLOUT

ROLLOVER n instance of a prize continuing in force for an additional period

ROLLOVERS > ROLLOVER

ROLLS > ROLL

ROLLTOP as in rolltop desk desk having a slatted wooden panel that can be pulled down over the writing surface when not in use

ROLLWAY n incline down which logs are rolled

ROLLWAYS > ROLLWAY

ROM n male gypsy

ROMA n gypsy

ROMAGE archaic variant of **>** RUMMAGE

ROMAGES > ROMAGE

ROMAIKA n Greek dance

ROMAIKAS > ROMAIKA

ROMAINE *n* usual US and Canadian name for 'cos' (lettuce)

ROMAINES > ROMAINE

ROMAJI *n* Roman alphabet as used to write Japanese

ROMAJIS > ROMAJI

ROMAL *same as* > RUMAL

ROMALS > ROMAL

ROMAN *adj* in or relating to the vertical style of printing type used for most printed matter ▷ *n* roman type

ROMANCE *n* love affair ▷ *vb* exaggerate or fantasize

ROMANCED > ROMANCE

ROMANCER > ROMANCE

ROMANCERS > ROMANCE

ROMANCES > ROMANCE

ROMANCING > ROMANCE

ROMANESCO *n* type of green cauliflower

ROMANISE *same as* > ROMANIZE

ROMANISED > ROMANISE

ROMANISES > ROMANISE

ROMANIZE *vb* impart a Roman Catholic character to (a ceremony, practice, etc)

ROMANIZED > ROMANIZE

ROMANIZES > ROMANIZE

ROMANO *n* hard light-coloured sharp-tasting cheese

ROMANOS > ROMANO

ROMANS > ROMAN

ROMANTIC *adj* of or dealing with love ▷ *n* romantic person or artist

ROMANTICS > ROMANTIC

ROMANZA *n* short instrumental piece of song-like character

ROMANZAS > ROMANZA

ROMAUNT *n* verse romance

ROMAUNTS > ROMAUNT

ROMCOM *n* film or television comedy based around the romantic relationships of the characters

ROMCOMS > ROMCOM

ROMELDALE *n* type of sheep

ROMEO *n* ardent male lover

ROMEOS > ROMEO

ROMNEYA *n* bushy type of poppy

ROMNEYAS > ROMNEYA

ROMP *vb* play wildly and joyfully ▷ *n* boisterous activity

ROMPED > ROMP

ROMPER *n* playful or boisterous child

ROMPERS *npl* child's overalls

ROMPING > ROMP

ROMPINGLY > ROMP

ROMPISH > ROMP

ROMPISHLY > ROMP

ROMPS > ROMP

ROMS > ROM

RONCADOR *n* any of several types of fish

RONCADORS > RONCADOR

RONDACHE *n* round shield

RONDACHES > RONDACHE

RONDAVEL *n* circular building, often thatched

RONDAVELS > RONDAVEL

RONDE *n* round dance

RONDEAU *n* poem consisting of 13 or 10 lines with the opening words of the first line used as a refrain

RONDEAUX > RONDEAU

RONDEL *n* rondeau consisting of three stanzas of 13 or 14 lines with a two-line refrain appearing twice or three times

RONDELET *n* brief rondeau, having five or seven lines and a refrain taken from the first line

RONDELETS > RONDELET

RONDELLE *n* type of bead

RONDELLES > RONDELLE

RONDELS > RONDEL

RONDES > RONDE

RONDINO *n* short rondo

RONDINOS > RONDINO

RONDO *n* piece of music with a leading theme continually returned to

RONDOS > RONDO

RONDURE *n* circle or curve

RONDURES > RONDURE

RONE *n* drainpipe or gutter for carrying rainwater from a roof

RONEO *vb* duplicate (a document) from a stencil ▷ *n* document reproduced by this process

RONEOED > RONEO

RONEOING > RONEO

RONEOS > RONEO

RONEPIPE *same as* > RONE

RONEPIPES > RONEPIPE

RONES > RONE

RONG *archaic past participle of* > RING

RONGGENG *n* Malay traditional dance

RONGGENGS > RONGGENG

RONIN *n* lordless samurai, esp one whose feudal lord had been deprived of his territory

RONINS > RONIN

RONION *same as* > RUNNION

RONIONS > RONION

RONNE *archaic form of* > RUN

RONNEL *n* type of pesticide

RONNELS > RONNEL

RONNIE *n* Dublin slang word for moustache

RONNIES > RONNIE

RONNING > RONNE

RONT *archaic variant of* > RUNT

RONTE *archaic variant of* > RUNT

RONTES > RONTE

RONTGEN *variant spelling of* > ROENTGEN

RONTGENS > RONTGEN

RONTS > RONT

RONYON *same as* > RUNNION

RONYONS > RUNNION

RONZ *n* rest of New Zealand

RONZER *n* New Zealand word for a New Zealander not from Auckland

RONZERS > RONZER

ROO *n* kangaroo

ROOD *n* Cross

ROODS > ROOD

ROOF *n* outside upper covering of a building, car, etc ▷ *vb* put a roof on

ROOFED > ROOF

ROOFER > ROOF

ROOFERS > ROOF

ROOFIE *n* tablet of sedative drug

ROOFIER > ROOFY

ROOFIES > ROOFIE

ROOFIEST > ROOFY

ROOFING *n* material used to build a roof

ROOFINGS > ROOFING

ROOFLESS > ROOF

ROOFLIKE > ROOF

ROOFLINE *n* uppermost edge of a roof

ROOFLINES > ROOFLINE

ROOFS > ROOF

ROOFSCAPE *n* view of the rooftops of a town, city, etc

ROOFTOP *n* outside part of the roof of a building

ROOFTOPS > ROOFTOP

ROOFTREE *same as* > RIDGEPOLE

ROOFTREES > ROOFTREE

ROOFY *adj* with roofs

ROOIBOS *n* tea prepared from the dried leaves of an African plant

ROOIKAT *n* South African lynx

ROOIKATS > ROOIKAT

ROOINEK *n* contemptuous name for an Englishman

ROOINEKS > ROOINEK

ROOK *n* Eurasian bird of the crow family ▷ *vb* swindle

ROOKED > ROOK

ROOKERIES > ROOKERY

ROOKERY *n* colony of rooks, penguins, or seals

ROOKIE *n* new recruit

ROOKIER > ROOKY

ROOKIES > ROOKIE

ROOKIEST > ROOKY

ROOKING > ROOK

ROOKISH > ROOK

ROOKS > ROOK

ROOKY *adj* abounding in rooks

ROOM *n* enclosed area in a building ▷ *vb* occupy or share a room

ROOMED > ROOM

ROOMER > ROOM

ROOMERS > ROOM

ROOMETTE *n* self-contained compartment in a railway sleeping car

ROOMETTES > ROOMETTE

ROOMFUL *n* number or quantity sufficient to fill a room

ROOMFULS > ROOMFUL

ROOMIE *n* roommate

ROOMIER > ROOMY

ROOMIES > ROOMIE

ROOMIEST > ROOMY

ROOMILY > ROOMY

ROOMINESS > ROOMY

ROOMING > ROOM

ROOMMATE *n* person with whom one shares a room or apartment

ROOMMATES > ROOMMATE

ROOMS > ROOM

ROOMSOME *adj* archaic word meaning roomy

ROOMY *adj* spacious

ROON *n* Scots word for shred or strip

ROONS > ROON

ROOP *same as* > ROUP

ROOPED > ROOP

ROOPIER > ROOPY

ROOPIEST > ROOPY

ROOPING > ROOP

ROOPIT *same as* > ROOPY

ROOPS > ROOP

ROOPY *adj* (in dialect) hoarse

ROORBACH *same as* > ROORBACK

ROORBACHS > ROORBACH

ROORBACK *n* false or distorted report or account, used to obtain political advantage

ROORBACKS > ROORBACK

ROOS > ROO

ROOSA *n* type of grass

ROOSAS > ROOSA

ROOSE *vb* flatter

ROOSED > ROOSE

ROOSER > ROOSE

ROOSERS > ROOSE

ROOSES > ROOSE

ROOSING > ROOSE

ROOST *n* perch for fowls ▷ *vb* perch

ROOSTED > ROOST

ROOSTER *n* domestic cock

ROOSTERS > ROOSTER

ROOSTING > ROOST

ROOSTS > ROOST

ROOT *n* part of a plant that grows down into the earth obtaining nourishment ▷ *vb* establish a root and start to grow

ROOTAGE *n* root system

ROOTAGES > ROOTAGE

ROOTBOUND *adj* (of a pot plant) having outgrown its pot, so that the roots are cramped and tangled

ROOTCAP *n* layer of cells at root tip

ROOTCAPS > ROOTCAP

ROOTED > ROOT

r

ROOTEDLY > ROOT
ROOTER > ROOT
ROOTERS > ROOT
ROOTHOLD > ROOT
ROOTHOLDS > ROOT
ROOTIER > ROOT
ROOTIES > ROOTY
ROOTIEST > ROOT
ROOTINESS > ROOT
ROOTING > ROOT
ROOTINGS > ROOT
ROOTKIT *n* set of programs used to gain unauthorized access to a computer system
ROOTKITS > ROOTKIT
ROOTLE *same as* > ROOT
ROOTLED > ROOTLE
ROOTLES > ROOTLE
ROOTLESS *adj* having no sense of belonging
ROOTLET *n* small root or branch of a root
ROOTLETS > ROOTLET
ROOTLIKE > ROOT
ROOTLING > ROOTLE
ROOTS *adj* (of popular music) going back to the origins of a style, esp in being unpretentious
ROOTSIER > ROOTS
ROOTSIEST > ROOTS
ROOTSTALK *same as* > RHIZOME
ROOTSTOCK *same as* > RHIZOME
ROOTSY > ROOTS
ROOTWORM *n* beetle larva feeding on roots
ROOTWORMS > ROOTWORM
ROOTY *adj* rootlike ▷ *n* (in military slang) bread
ROPABLE *adj* capable of being roped
ROPE *n* thick cord
ROPEABLE *same as* > ROPABLE
ROPED > ROPE
ROPELIKE > ROPE
ROPER *n* someone who makes ropes
ROPERIES > ROPERY
ROPERS > ROPER
ROPERY *n* place where ropes are made
ROPES > ROPE
ROPEWALK *n* long narrow usually covered path or shed where ropes are made
ROPEWALKS > ROPEWALK
ROPEWAY *n* type of aerial lift
ROPEWAYS > ROPEWAY
ROPEWORK *n* making, mending, or tying ropes
ROPEWORKS > ROPEWORK
ROPEY *adj* inferior or inadequate
ROPIER > ROPY
ROPIEST > ROPY
ROPILY > ROPEY
ROPINESS > ROPEY
ROPING > ROPE
ROPINGS > ROPE

ROPY *same as* > ROPEY
ROQUE *n* game developed from croquet, played on a hard surface with a resilient surrounding border from which the ball can rebound
ROQUES > ROQUE
ROQUET *vb* drive one's ball against (another person's ball) in order to be allowed to croquet ▷ *n* act of roqueting
ROQUETED > ROQUET
ROQUETING > ROQUET
ROQUETS > ROQUET
ROQUETTE *n* another name for the salad plant rocket
ROQUETTES > ROQUETTE
RORAL *archaic word for* > DEWY
RORE *archaic spelling of* > ROAR
RORES > RORE
RORIC *same as* > RORAL
RORID *same as* > RORAL
RORIE *same as* > ROARY
RORIER > RORY
RORIEST > RORY
RORQUAL *n* toothless whale with a dorsal fin
RORQUALS > RORQUAL
RORT *n* dishonest scheme ▷ *vb* take unfair advantage of something
RORTED > RORT
RORTER *n* small-scale confidence trickster
RORTERS > RORTER
RORTIER > RORT
RORTIEST > RORT
RORTING > RORT
RORTINGS > RORTING
RORTS > RORT
RORTY > RORT
RORY *adj* dewy
ROSACE *another name for* > ROSETTE
ROSACEA *n* chronic inflammatory disease causing the skin of the face to become abnormally flushed and sometimes pustular
ROSACEAS > ROSACEA
ROSACEOUS *adj* of or belonging to a family of plants typically having five-petalled flowers, which includes the rose, strawberry, and many fruit trees
ROSACES > ROSACE
ROSAKER *archaic word for* > REALGAR
ROSAKERS > ROSAKER
ROSALIA *n* melody which is repeated but at a higher pitch each time
ROSALIAS > ROSALIA
ROSANILIN *n* reddish-brown crystalline insoluble derivative of aniline used as a red dye
ROSARIA > ROSARIUM

ROSARIAN *n* person who cultivates roses, esp professionally
ROSARIANS > ROSARIAN
ROSARIES > ROSARY
ROSARIUM *n* rose garden
ROSARIUMS > ROSARIUM
ROSARY *n* series of prayers
ROSBIF *n* term used in France for an English person
ROSBIFS > ROSBIF
ROSCID *adj* dewy
ROSCOE *slang word for* > GUN
ROSCOES > ROSCOE
ROSE > RISE
ROSEAL *adj* rosy or roselike
ROSEATE *adj* rose-coloured
ROSEATELY > ROSEATE
ROSEBAY *as in* rosebay willowherb perennial plant with spikes of deep pink flowers
ROSEBAYS > ROSEBAY
ROSEBOWL *n* bowl for displaying roses or other flowers
ROSEBOWLS > ROSEBOWL
ROSEBUD *n* rose which has not yet fully opened
ROSEBUDS > ROSEBUD
ROSEBUSH *n* flowering shrub
ROSED > RISE
ROSEFINCH *n* any of various finches with pink patches
ROSEFISH *n* red food fish of North Atlantic coastal waters
ROSEHIP *n* berry-like fruit of a rose plant
ROSEHIPS > ROSEHIP
ROSELESS > RISE
ROSELIKE > RISE
ROSELLA *n* type of Australian parrot
ROSELLAS > ROSELLA
ROSELLE *n* Indian flowering plant
ROSELLES > ROSELLE
ROSEMARY *n* fragrant flowering shrub
ROSEOLA *n* feverish condition of young children that lasts for some five days during the last two of which the patient has a rose-coloured rash. It is caused by the human herpes virus
ROSEOLAR > ROSEOLA
ROSEOLAS > ROSEOLA
ROSERIES > ROSERY
ROSEROOT *n* Eurasian mountain plant
ROSEROOTS > ROSEROOT
ROSERY *n* bed or garden of roses
ROSES > RISE
ROSESLUG *n* one of various types of pest that feed on roses
ROSESLUGS > ROSESLUG

ROSET *n* Scots word meaning rosin ▷ *vb* rub rosin on
ROSETED > ROSET
ROSETING > ROSET
ROSETS > ROSET
ROSETTE *n* rose-shaped ornament, esp a circular bunch of ribbons
ROSETTED > ROSET
ROSETTES > ROSETTE
ROSETTING *n* abnormal leaf formation in a plant due to disease
ROSETTY > ROSET
ROSETY > ROSET
ROSEWATER *n* scented water used as a perfume and in cooking, made by the distillation of rose petals or by impregnation with oil of roses
ROSEWOOD *n* fragrant wood used to make furniture
ROSEWOODS > ROSEWOOD
ROSHI *n* teacher of Zen Buddhism
ROSHIS > ROSHI
ROSIED > ROSY
ROSIER *archaic word for* > ROSEBUSH
ROSIERE *archaic word for* > ROSEBUSH
ROSIERES > ROSIERE
ROSIERS > ROSIER
ROSIES > ROSY
ROSIEST > ROSY
ROSILY > ROSY
ROSIN *n* resin used for treating the bows of violins etc ▷ *vb* apply rosin to
ROSINATE *n* chemical compound
ROSINATES > ROSINATE
ROSINED > ROSIN
ROSINER *n* strong alcoholic drink
ROSINERS > ROSINER
ROSINESS > ROSY
ROSING > RISE
ROSINING > ROSIN
ROSINOL *n* yellowish fluorescent oily liquid obtained from certain resins, used in the manufacture of carbon black, varnishes, and lacquers
ROSINOLS > ROSINOL
ROSINOUS *adj* rosiny
ROSINS > ROSIN
ROSINWEED *n* N American plant with resinous juice, sticky foliage, and a strong smell
ROSINY > ROSIN
ROSIT *same as* > ROSET
ROSITED > ROSIT
ROSITING > ROSIT
ROSITS > ROSIT
ROSMARINE *archaic form of* > ROSEMARY
ROSOGLIO *same as* > ROSOLIO

r

ROSOGLIOS > ROSOGLIO
ROSOLIO *n* type of cordial
ROSOLIOS > ROSOLIO
ROSSER *n* bark-removing machine
ROSSERS > ROSSER
ROST *archaic spelling of* > ROAST
ROSTED > ROST
ROSTELLA > ROSTELLUM
ROSTELLAR > ROSTELLUM
ROSTELLUM *n* small beaklike process, such as the hooked projection from the top of the head in tapeworms or the outgrowth from the stigma of an orchid
ROSTER *n* list of people and their turns of duty ▷ *vb* place on a roster
ROSTERED > ROSTER
ROSTERING > ROSTER
ROSTERS > ROSTER
ROSTI *n* cheese-topped fried Swiss dish consisting of grated potato and, optionally, onion
ROSTING > ROST
ROSTIS > ROSTI
ROSTRA > ROSTRUM
ROSTRAL *adj* of or like a beak or snout
ROSTRALLY > ROSTRAL
ROSTRATE *adj* having a beak or beaklike process
ROSTRATED *same as* > ROSTRATE
ROSTRUM *n* platform or stage
ROSTRUMS > ROSTRUM
ROSTS > ROST
ROSULA *n* rosette
ROSULAS > ROSULA
ROSULATE *adj* in the form of a rose
ROSY *adj* pink-coloured ▷ *vb* redden or make pink
ROSYING > ROSY
ROT *vb* decompose or decay ▷ *n* decay
ROTA *n* list of people who take it in turn to do a particular task
ROTACHUTE *n* device serving the same purpose as a parachute, in which the canopy is replaced by freely revolving rotor blades, used for the delivery of stores or recovery of missiles
ROTAL *adj* of or relating to wheels or rotation
ROTAMETER *n* device for measuring the flow of a liquid
ROTAN *another name for* > RATTAN
ROTANS > ROTAN
ROTAPLANE *n* aircraft that derives its lift from freely revolving rotor blades
ROTARIES > ROTARY

ROTARY *adj* revolving ▷ *n* traffic roundabout
ROTAS > ROTA
ROTATABLE > ROTATE
ROTATE *vb* (cause to) move round a centre or on a pivot ▷ *adj* designating a corolla the united petals of which radiate from a central point like the spokes of a wheel
ROTATED > ROTATE
ROTATES > ROTATE
ROTATING *adj* revolving around a central axis, line, or point
ROTATION *n* act of rotating
ROTATIONS > ROTATION
ROTATIVE *same as* > ROTATORY
ROTATOR *n* person, device, or part that rotates or causes rotation
ROTATORES > ROTATOR
ROTATORS > ROTATOR
ROTATORY *adj* of, relating to, possessing, or causing rotation
ROTAVATE *same as* > ROTOVATE
ROTAVATED > ROTAVATE
ROTAVATES > ROTAVATE
ROTAVATOR *n* type of machine with rotating blades that will break up soil
ROTAVIRUS *n* any member of a genus of viruses that cause worldwide endemic infections. They occur in birds and mammals, cause diarrhoea in children, and are usually transmitted in food prepared with unwashed hands
ROTCH *n* little auk
ROTCHE *same as* > ROTCH
ROTCHES > ROTCH
ROTCHIE *same as* > ROTCH
ROTCHIES > ROTCHIE
ROTE *n* mechanical repetition ▷ *vb* learn by rote
ROTED > ROTE
ROTENONE *n* white odourless crystalline substance extracted from the roots of derris: a powerful insecticide
ROTENONES > ROTENONE
ROTES > ROTE
ROTGRASS *n* type of grass blamed for sheeprot
ROTGUT *n* alcoholic drink of inferior quality
ROTGUTS > ROTGUT
ROTHER *dialect word for* > OX
ROTHERS > ROTHER
ROTI *n* (in India and the Caribbean) a type of unleavened bread
ROTIFER *n* minute aquatic multicellular invertebrate
ROTIFERAL > ROTIFER
ROTIFERAN > ROTIFER

ROTIFERS > ROTIFER
ROTIFORM *adj* in the shape of a wheel
ROTING > ROTE
ROTIS > ROTI
ROTL *n* unit of weight used in Muslim countries, varying in value between about one and five pounds
ROTLS > ROTL
ROTO *n* printing process using a cylinder etched with many small recesses, from which ink is transferred to a moving web of paper, plastic, etc, in a rotary press
ROTOGRAPH *n* photograph made using a particular method ▷ *vb* photograph using this method
ROTOLO *n* (in Italian cuisine) a roll
ROTOLOS > ROTOLO
ROTON *n* quantum of vortex motion
ROTONS > ROTON
ROTOR *n* revolving portion of a dynamo, motor, or turbine
ROTORS > ROTOR
ROTOS > ROTO
ROTOSCOPE *n* projection device used for creating animated images out of live-action ones ▷ *vb* create animated images using a rotoscope
ROTOTILL *vb* break up the soil using a rototiller
ROTOTILLS > ROTOTILL
ROTOVATE *vb* break up (the surface of the earth, or an area of ground) using a rotavator
ROTOVATED > ROTOVATE
ROTOVATES > ROTOVATE
ROTOVATOR *same as* > ROTAVATOR
ROTS > ROT
ROTTAN *n* (in dialect) a rat
ROTTANS > ROTTAN
ROTTE *n* ancient stringed instrument
ROTTED > ROT
ROTTEN *adj* decaying ▷ *adv* extremely ▷ *n* (in dialect) a rat
ROTTENER > ROTTEN
ROTTENEST > ROTTEN
ROTTENLY > ROTTEN
ROTTENS > ROTTEN
ROTTER *n* despicable person
ROTTERS > ROTTER
ROTTES > ROTTE
ROTTING > ROT
ROTULA *n* kneecap
ROTULAE > ROTULA
ROTULAS > ROTULA
ROTUND *adj* round and plump ▷ *vb* make round
ROTUNDA *n* circular building or room, esp with a dome

ROTUNDAS > ROTUNDA
ROTUNDATE *adj* rounded
ROTUNDED > ROTUND
ROTUNDER > ROTUND
ROTUNDEST > ROTUND
ROTUNDING > ROTUND
ROTUNDITY > ROTUND
ROTUNDLY > ROTUND
ROTUNDS > ROTUND
ROTURIER *n* freeholder or ordinary person
ROTURIERS > ROTURIER
ROUBLE *n* monetary unit of Russia, Belarus, and Tajikistan
ROUBLES > ROUBLE
ROUCHE *same as* > RUCHE
ROUCHES > ROUCHE
ROUCOU *another name for* > ANNATTO
ROUCOUS > ROUCOU
ROUE *n* man given to immoral living
ROUEN *n* breed of duck
ROUENS > ROUEN
ROUES > ROUE
ROUGE *n* red cosmetic used to colour the cheeks ▷ *vb* apply rouge to
ROUGED > ROUGE
ROUGES > ROUGE
ROUGH *adj* uneven or irregular ▷ *vb* make rough ▷ *n* rough state or area
ROUGHAGE *n* indigestible constituents of food which aid digestion
ROUGHAGES > ROUGHAGE
ROUGHBACK *n* rough-skinned flatfish
ROUGHCAST *n* mixture of plaster and small stones for outside walls ▷ *vb* coat with this ▷ *adj* covered with or denoting roughcast
ROUGHDRY *vb* dry (clothes or linen) without smoothing
ROUGHED > ROUGH
ROUGHEN *vb* make or become rough
ROUGHENED > ROUGHEN
ROUGHENS > ROUGHEN
ROUGHER *n* person that does the rough preparatory work on something ▷ *adj* more rough
ROUGHERS > ROUGHER
ROUGHEST > ROUGH
ROUGHHEW *vb* cut or hew (timber, stone, etc) roughly without finishing the surface
ROUGHHEWN > ROUGHHEW
ROUGHHEWS > ROUGHHEW
ROUGHIE *n* small food fish found in southern and western Australian waters
ROUGHIES > ROUGHIE
ROUGHING > ROUGH
ROUGHISH *adj* somewhat rough
ROUGHLEG *n* any of several kinds of large hawk with feathered legs

r

ROUGHLEGS > ROUGHLEG

ROUGHLY *adv* without being exact or fully authenticated

ROUGHNECK *n* violent person

ROUGHNESS > ROUGH

ROUGHS > ROUGH

ROUGHSHOD *adj* (of a horse) shod with rough-bottomed shoes to prevent slidi

ROUGHT *archaic past form of* > REACH

ROUGHY *spelling variant of* > ROUGHIE

ROUGING > ROUGE

ROUILLE *n* kind of sauce

ROUILLES > ROUILLE

ROUL *archaic form of* > ROLL

ROULADE *n* slice of meat rolled, esp around a stuffing, and cooked

ROULADES > ROULADE

ROULE *archaic form of* > ROLL

ROULEAU *n* roll of paper containing coins

ROULEAUS > ROULEAU

ROULEAUX > ROULEAU

ROULES > ROULE

ROULETTE *n* gambling game played with a revolving wheel and a ball ▷ *vb* use a toothed wheel on (something), as in engraving, making stationery, etc

ROULETTED > ROULETTE

ROULETTES > ROULETTE

ROULS > ROUL

ROUM *archaic spelling of* > ROOM

ROUMING *n* pasture given for an animal

ROUMINGS > ROUMING

ROUMS > ROUM

ROUNCE *n* handle that is turned to move paper and plates on a printing press

ROUNCES > ROUNCE

ROUNCEVAL *n* giant or monster

ROUNCIES > ROUNCY

ROUNCY *archaic word for* > HORSE

ROUND *adj* spherical, cylindrical, circular, or curved ▷ *prep* indicating an encircling movement, presence on all sides, etc ▷ *vb* move round ▷ *n* round shape

ROUNDARCH *adj* with rounded arches

ROUNDBALL *n* form of basketball

ROUNDED *adj* round or curved

ROUNDEDLY > ROUNDED

ROUNDEL *same as* > ROUNDELAY

ROUNDELAY *n* simple song with a refrain

ROUNDELS > ROUNDEL

ROUNDER *n* run round all four bases after one hit in rounders

ROUNDERS *n* bat-and-ball team game

ROUNDEST > ROUND

ROUNDHAND *n* style of handwriting with large rounded curves

ROUNDHEEL *n* immoral woman

ROUNDING *n* process in which a number is approximated as the closest number that can be expressed using the number of bits or digits available

ROUNDINGS > ROUNDING

ROUNDISH *adj* somewhat round

ROUNDLE *same as* > ROUNDEL

ROUNDLES > ROUNDLE

ROUNDLET *n* small circle

ROUNDLETS > ROUNDLET

ROUNDLY *adv* thoroughly

ROUNDNESS > ROUND

ROUNDS > ROUND

ROUNDSMAN *n* person who makes rounds, as for inspection or to deliver goods

ROUNDSMEN > ROUNDSMAN

ROUNDTRIP *n* US term for return trip

ROUNDUP *n* act of gathering together livestock, people, facts, etc

ROUNDUPS > ROUNDUP

ROUNDURE *n* archaic word meaning roundness

ROUNDURES > ROUNDURE

ROUNDWOOD *n* small pieces of timber (about 5·15 cm, or 2·6 in.) in diameter

ROUNDWORM *n* worm that is a common intestinal parasite of man

ROUP *n* any of various chronic respiratory diseases of birds, esp poultry ▷ *vb* sell by auction

ROUPED > ROUP

ROUPET *adj* Scots word meaning hoarse or croaky

ROUPIER > ROUP

ROUPIEST > ROUP

ROUPILY > ROUP

ROUPING > ROUP

ROUPIT *same as* > ROUPET

ROUPS > ROUP

ROUPY > ROUP

ROUSANT *adj* (in heraldry) rising

ROUSE *same as* > REVEILLE

ROUSED > ROUSE

ROUSEMENT *n* stirring up

ROUSER *n* person or thing that rouses people, such as a stirring speech or compelling rock song

ROUSERS > ROUSER

ROUSES > ROUSE

ROUSING *adj* lively, vigorous

ROUSINGLY > ROUSING

ROUSSEAU *n* pemmican fried in its own fat

ROUSSEAUS > ROUSSEAU

ROUSSETTE *n* dogfish

ROUST *vb* rout or stir, as out of bed

ROUSTED > ROUST

ROUSTER *n* unskilled labourer on an oil rig

ROUSTERS > ROUSTER

ROUSTING > ROUST

ROUSTS > ROUST

ROUT *n* overwhelming defeat ▷ *vb* defeat and put to flight

ROUTE *n* roads taken to reach a destination ▷ *vb* send by a particular route

ROUTED > ROUTE

ROUTEING > ROUTE

ROUTEMAN *n* (in US English) delivery man or salesman doing a particular round

ROUTEMEN > ROUTEMAN

ROUTER *n* device that allows data to be moved efficiently between two points on a network

ROUTERS > ROUTER

ROUTES > ROUTE

ROUTEWAY *n* track, road, or waterway, etc, used as a route to somewhere

ROUTEWAYS > ROUTEWAY

ROUTH *n* abundance ▷ *adj* abundant

ROUTHIE *adj* abundant, plentiful, or well filled

ROUTHIER > ROUTHIE

ROUTHIEST > ROUTHIE

ROUTHS > ROUTH

ROUTINE *n* usual or regular method of procedure ▷ *adj* ordinary or regular

ROUTINEER *n* someone who believes in routine

ROUTINELY > ROUTINE

ROUTINES > ROUTINE

ROUTING > ROUT

ROUTINGS > ROUT

ROUTINISE *same as* > ROUTINIZE

ROUTINISM > ROUTINE

ROUTINIST > ROUTINE

ROUTINIZE *vb* make routine

ROUTOUS > ROUT

ROUTOUSLY > ROUT

ROUTS > ROUT

ROUX *n* fat and flour cooked together as a basis for sauces

ROVE > REEVE

ROVED > REEVE

ROVEN > REEVE

ROVER *n* wanderer, traveller

ROVERS > ROVER

ROVES > REEVE

ROVING > ROVE

ROVINGLY > ROVING

ROVINGS > ROVE

ROW *n* straight line of people or things ▷ *vb* propel (a boat) by oars

ROWABLE > ROW

ROWAN *n* tree producing bright red berries, mountain ash

ROWANS > ROWAN

ROWBOAT *n* small boat propelled by one or more pairs of oars

ROWBOATS > ROWBOAT

ROWDEDOW *same as* > ROWDYDOW

ROWDEDOWS > ROWDEDOW

ROWDIER > ROWDY

ROWDIES > ROWDY

ROWDIEST > ROWDY

ROWDILY > ROWDY

ROWDINESS > ROWDY

ROWDY *adj* disorderly, noisy, and rough ▷ *n* person like this

ROWDYDOW *n* hullabaloo

ROWDYDOWS > ROWDYDOW

ROWDYISH > ROWDY

ROWDYISM *n* rowdy behaviour or tendencies or a habitual pattern of rowdy behaviour

ROWDYISMS > ROWDYISM

ROWED > ROW

ROWEL *n* small spiked wheel on a spur ▷ *vb* goad (a horse) using a rowel

ROWELED > ROWEL

ROWELING > ROWEL

ROWELLED > ROWEL

ROWELLING > ROWEL

ROWELS > ROWEL

ROWEN *another word for* > AFTERMATH

ROWENS > ROWEN

ROWER > ROW

ROWERS > ROW

ROWING > ROW

ROWINGS > ROW

ROWLOCK *n* device on a boat that holds an oar in place

ROWLOCKS > ROWLOCK

ROWME *archaic variant of* > ROOM

ROWMES > ROWME

ROWND *archaic variant of* > ROUND

ROWNDED > ROWND

ROWNDELL *archaic variant of* > ROUNDEL

ROWNDELLS > ROWNDELL

ROWNDING > ROWND

ROWNDS > ROWND

ROWOVER *n* act of winning a rowing race unopposed, by rowing the course

ROWOVERS > ROWOVER

ROWS > ROW

ROWT *archaic variant of* > ROUT

ROWTED > ROWT

ROWTH *same as* > ROUTH

ROWTHS > ROWTH

ROWTING > ROWT
ROWTS > ROWT
ROYAL adj of, befitting, or supported by a king or queen ▷ n member of a royal family
ROYALET n minor king
ROYALETS > ROYALET
ROYALISE same as > ROYALIZE
ROYALISED > ROYALISE
ROYALISES > ROYALISE
ROYALISM > ROYALIST
ROYALISMS > ROYALIST
ROYALIST n supporter of monarchy ▷ adj of or relating to royalists
ROYALISTS > ROYALIST
ROYALIZE vb make royal
ROYALIZED > ROYALIZE
ROYALIZES > ROYALIZE
ROYALLER > ROYAL
ROYALLEST > ROYAL
ROYALLY > ROYAL
ROYALMAST n highest part of mast
ROYALS > ROYAL
ROYALTIES > ROYALTY
ROYALTY n royal people
ROYNE archaic word for > GNAW
ROYNED > ROYNE
ROYNES > ROYNE
ROYNING > ROYNE
ROYNISH archaic word for > MANGY
ROYST same as > ROIST
ROYSTED > ROYST
ROYSTER same as > ROISTER
ROYSTERED > ROYSTER
ROYSTERER > ROYSTER
ROYSTERS > ROISTER
ROYSTING > ROYST
ROYSTS > ROYST
ROZELLE same as > ROSELLE
ROZELLES > ROZELLE
ROZET same as > ROSET
ROZETED > ROZET
ROZETING > ROZET
ROZETS > ROZET
ROZIT same as > ROSET
ROZITED > ROZIT
ROZITING > ROZIT
ROZITS > ROZIT
ROZZER n policeman
ROZZERS > ROZZER
RUANA n woollen wrap resembling a poncho
RUANAS > RUANA
RUB vb apply pressure and friction to (something) with a circular or backwards-and-forwards movement ▷ n act of rubbing
RUBABOO n soup or stew made by boiling pemmican with, if available, flour and vegetables
RUBABOOS > RUBABOO
RUBACE same as > RUBASSE

RUBACES > RUBACE
RUBAI n verse form of Persian origin consisting of four-line stanzas
RUBAIYAT n (in Persian poetry) a verse form consisting of four-line stanzas
RUBASSE n type of quartz containing red haematite
RUBASSES > RUBASSE
RUBATI > RUBATO
RUBATO n (with) expressive flexibility of tempo ▷ adv be played with a flexible tempo
RUBATOS > RUBATO
RUBBABOO same as > RUBABOO
RUBBABOOS > RUBABOO
RUBBED > RUB
RUBBER n strong waterproof elastic material, orig. made from the dried sap of a tropical tree, now usu synthetic ▷ adj made of or producing rubber ▷ vb provide with rubber coating
RUBBERED > RUBBER
RUBBERIER > RUBBERY
RUBBERING > RUBBER
RUBBERISE same as > RUBBERIZE
RUBBERIZE vb coat or treat with rubber
RUBBERS > RUBBER
RUBBERY adj having the texture of or resembling rubber, esp in flexibility or toughness
RUBBET old Scots past form of > ROB
RUBBIDIES > RUBBIDY
RUBBIDY same as > RUBBITY
RUBBIES > RUBBY
RUBBING > RUB
RUBBINGS > RUB
RUBBISH n waste matter ▷ vb criticize
RUBBISHED > RUBBISH
RUBBISHES > RUBBISH
RUBBISHLY variant of > RUBBISHY
RUBBISHY adj worthless, of poor quality, or useless
RUBBIT old Scots past form of > ROB
RUBBITIES > RUBBITY
RUBBITY n pub
RUBBLE n fragments of broken stone, brick, etc ▷ vb turn into rubble
RUBBLED > RUBBLE
RUBBLES > RUBBLE
RUBBLIER > RUBBLE
RUBBLIEST > RUBBLE
RUBBLING > RUBBLE
RUBBLY > RUBBLE
RUBBOARD n board for scrubbing clothes on
RUBBOARDS > RUBBOARD
RUBBY n rubbing alcohol,

esp when mixed with cheap wine for drinking
RUBDOWN n act of drying or cleaning vigorously
RUBDOWNS > RUBDOWN
RUBE n unsophisticated countryman
RUBEFIED > RUBEFY
RUBEFIES > RUBEFY
RUBEFY vb make red, esp (of a counterirritant) to make the skin go red
RUBEFYING > RUBEFY
RUBEL n currency unit of Belarus
RUBELLA n mild contagious viral disease characterized by cough, sore throat, and skin rash
RUBELLAN n red-coloured mineral
RUBELLANS > RUBELLAN
RUBELLAS > RUBELLA
RUBELLITE n red transparent variety of tourmaline, used as a gemstone
RUBELS > RUBEL
RUBEOLA technical name for > MEASLES
RUBEOLAR > RUBEOLA
RUBEOLAS > RUBEOLA
RUBES > RUBE
RUBESCENT adj reddening
RUBICELLE n variety of spinel that is orange or yellow in colour
RUBICON n point of no return ▷ vb (in bezique) to beat before the loser has managed to gain as many as 1000 points
RUBICONED > RUBICON
RUBICONS > RUBICON
RUBICUND adj ruddy
RUBIDIC > RUBIDIUM
RUBIDIUM n soft highly reactive radioactive element
RUBIDIUMS > RUBIDIUM
RUBIED > RUBY
RUBIER > RUBY
RUBIES > RUBY
RUBIEST > RUBY
RUBIFIED > RUBIFY
RUBIFIES > RUBIFY
RUBIFY same as > RUBEFY
RUBIFYING > RUBIFY
RUBIGO old Scots word for > PENIS
RUBIGOS > RUBIGO
RUBIN archaic word for > RUBY
RUBINE archaic word for > RUBY
RUBINEOUS same as > RUBIOUS
RUBINES > RUBINE
RUBINS > RUBIN
RUBIOUS adj of the colour ruby
RUBLE same as > ROUBLE
RUBLES > RUBLE
RUBOFF n resulting effect

on something else; consequences
RUBOFFS > RUBOFF
RUBOUT n killing or elimination
RUBOUTS > RUBOUT
RUBRIC n set of rules for behaviour ▷ adj written, printed, or marked in red
RUBRICAL > RUBRIC
RUBRICATE vb print (a book or manuscript) with red titles, headings, etc
RUBRICIAN n authority on liturgical rubrics
RUBRICS > RUBRIC
RUBS > RUB
RUBSTONE n stone used for sharpening or smoothing, esp a whetstone
RUBSTONES > RUBSTONE
RUBUS n fruit-bearing genus of shrubs
RUBY n red precious gemstone ▷ adj deep red ▷ vb redden
RUBYING > RUBY
RUBYLIKE > RUBY
RUC same as > ROC
RUCHE n pleat or frill of lace etc as a decoration ▷ vb put a ruche on
RUCHED > RUCHE
RUCHES > RUCHE
RUCHING n material used for a ruche
RUCHINGS > RUCHING
RUCK n rough crowd of common people ▷ vb wrinkle or crease
RUCKED > RUCK
RUCKING > RUCK
RUCKLE another word for > RUCK
RUCKLED > RUCKLE
RUCKLES > RUCKLE
RUCKLING > RUCKLE
RUCKMAN n person who plays in the ruck
RUCKMEN > RUCKMAN
RUCKS > RUCK
RUCKSACK n large pack carried on the back
RUCKSACKS > RUCKSACK
RUCKSEAT n seat fixed to or forming part of a rucksack
RUCKSEATS > RUCKSEAT
RUCKUS n uproar
RUCKUSES > RUCKUS
RUCOLA n another name for the salad plant rocket
RUCOLAS > RUCOLA
RUCS > RUC
RUCTATION n archaic word meaning eructation or belch
RUCTION n uproar
RUCTIONS > RUCTION
RUCTIOUS adj tending or likely to cause ructions
RUD n red or redness ▷ vb redden

r

RUDACEOUS *adj* (of conglomerate, breccia, and similar rocks) composed of coarse-grained material

RUDAS *n* Scots word for a coarse, rude old woman

RUDASES > RUDAS

RUDBECKIA *n* N American plant cultivated for its showy flowers

RUDD *n* European freshwater fish

RUDDED > RUD

RUDDER *n* vertical hinged piece at the stern of a boat or at the rear of an aircraft, for steering

RUDDERS > RUDDER

RUDDIED > RUDDY

RUDDIER > RUDDY

RUDDIES > RUDDY

RUDDIEST > RUDDY

RUDDILY > RUDDY

RUDDINESS > RUDDY

RUDDING > RUD

RUDDLE *n* red ochre, used esp to mark sheep ▷ *vb* mark (sheep) with ruddle

RUDDLED > RUDDLE

RUDDLEMAN *n* ruddle dealer

RUDDLEMEN > RUDDLEMAN

RUDDLES > RUDDLE

RUDDLING > RUDDLE

RUDDOCK *dialect name for the* > ROBIN

RUDDOCKS > RUDDOCK

RUDDS > RUDD

RUDDY *adj* of a fresh healthy red colour ▷ *adv* bloody ▷ *vb* redden

RUDDYING > RUDDY

RUDE *archaic spelling of* > ROOD

RUDELY > RUDE

RUDENESS > RUDE

RUDER > RUDE

RUDERAL *n* plant that grows on waste ground ▷ *adj* growing in waste places

RUDERALS > RUDERAL

RUDERIES > RUDE

RUDERY > RUDE

RUDES > RUDE

RUDESBIES > RUDESBY

RUDESBY *n* archaic word for rude person

RUDEST > RUDE

RUDIE *n* member of a youth movement originating in the 1960s

RUDIES > RUDIE

RUDIMENT *n* first principles or elementary stages of a subject

RUDIMENTS > RUDIMENT

RUDISH *adj* somewhat rude

RUDS > RUD

RUE *vb* feel regret for ▷ *n* plant with evergreen bitter leaves

RUED > RUE

RUEDA *n* type of Cuban round dance

RUEDAS > RUEDA

RUEFUL *adj* regretful or sorry

RUEFULLY > RUEFUL

RUEING > RUE

RUEINGS > RUE

RUELLE *n* area between bed and wall, at one time used by French ladies of standing for receiving visitors

RUELLES > RUELLE

RUELLIA *n* genus of plants

RUELLIAS > RUELLIA

RUER > RUE

RUERS > RUE

RUES > RUE

RUFESCENT *adj* tinged with red or becoming red

RUFF *n* circular pleated, gathered, or fluted collar of lawn, muslin, etc, often starched or wired, worn by both men and women in the 16th and 17th centuries ▷ *vb* trump

RUFFE *n* European freshwater fish

RUFFED > RUFF

RUFFES > RUFFE

RUFFIAN *n* violent lawless person ▷ *vb* act like a ruffian

RUFFIANED > RUFFIAN

RUFFIANLY > RUFFIAN

RUFFIANS > RUFFIAN

RUFFIN *archaic name for* > RUFFE

RUFFING > RUFF

RUFFINS > RUFFIN

RUFFLE *vb* disturb the calm of ▷ *n* frill or pleat

RUFFLED > RUFFLE

RUFFLER *n* person or thing that ruffles

RUFFLERS > RUFFLER

RUFFLES > RUFFLE

RUFFLIER > RUFFLY

RUFFLIEST > RUFFLY

RUFFLIKE > RUFF

RUFFLING > RUFFLE

RUFFLINGS > RUFFLE

RUFFLY *adj* ruffled

RUFFS > RUFF

RUFIYAA *n* standard monetary unit of the Maldives, divided into 100 laari

RUFIYAAS > RUFIYAA

RUFOUS *adj* reddish-brown

RUG *n* small carpet ▷ *vb* (in dialect) tug

RUGA *n* fold, wrinkle, or crease

RUGAE > RUGA

RUGAL *adj* (in anatomy) with ridges or folds

RUGALACH *same as* > RUGELACH

RUGATE *same as* > RUGOSE

RUGBIES > RUGBY

RUGBY *n* form of football

played with an oval ball which may be handled by the players

RUGELACH *n* fruit and nut pastry shaped like a croissant

RUGGED *adj* rocky or steep

RUGGEDER > RUGGED

RUGGEDEST > RUGGED

RUGGEDISE *same as* > RUGGEDIZE

RUGGEDIZE *vb* make durable, as for military use

RUGGEDLY > RUGGED

RUGGELACH *same as* > RUGELACH

RUGGER *same as* > RUGBY

RUGGERS > RUGGER

RUGGIER > RUGGY

RUGGIEST > RUGGY

RUGGING > RUG

RUGGINGS > RUG

RUGGY *adj* (in dialect) rough or rugged

RUGLIKE > RUG

RUGOLA *n* another name for the salad plant rocket

RUGOLAS > RUGOLA

RUGOSA *n* any of various shrubs descended from a particular type of wild rose

RUGOSAS > RUGOSA

RUGOSE *adj* wrinkled

RUGOSELY > RUGOSE

RUGOSITY > RUGOSE

RUGOUS *same as* > RUGOSE

RUGS > RUG

RUGULOSE *adj* with little wrinkles

RUIN *vb* destroy or spoil completely ▷ *n* destruction or decay

RUINABLE > RUIN

RUINATE *vb* archaic word for bring or come to ruin

RUINATED > RUINATE

RUINATES > RUINATE

RUINATING > RUINATE

RUINATION *n* act of ruining

RUINED > RUIN

RUINER > RUIN

RUINERS > RUIN

RUING > RUE

RUINGS > RUE

RUINING > RUIN

RUININGS > RUIN

RUINOUS *adj* causing ruin

RUINOUSLY > RUINOUS

RUINS > RUIN

RUKH *same as* > ROC

RUKHS > RUKH

RULABLE > RULE

RULE *n* statement of what is allowed, for example in a game or procedure ▷ *vb* govern

RULED > RULE

RULELESS > RULE

RULER *n* person who governs ▷ *vb* punish by hitting with a ruler

RULERED > RULER

RULERING > RULER

RULERS > RULER

RULERSHIP > RULER

RULES > RULE

RULESSE *adj* archaic word meaning ruleless or without rules

RULIER > RULY

RULIEST > RULY

RULING *n* formal decision ▷ *adj* controlling or exercising authority

RULINGS > RULING

RULLION *n* Scots word for rawhide shoe

RULLIONS > RULLION

RULLOCK *same as* > ROWLOCK

RULLOCKS > RULLOCK

RULY *adj* orderly

RUM *n* alcoholic drink distilled from sugar cane ▷ *adj* odd, strange

RUMAKI *n* savoury of chicken liver and sliced water chestnut wrapped in bacon

RUMAKIS > RUMAKI

RUMAL *n* handkerchief or type of cloth

RUMALS > RUMAL

RUMBA *n* lively ballroom dance of Cuban origin ▷ *vb* dance the rumba

RUMBAED > RUMBA

RUMBAING > RUMBA

RUMBAS > RUMBA

RUMBELOW *n* nonsense word used in the refrain of certain sea shanties

RUMBELOWS > RUMBELOW

RUMBLE *vb* make a low continuous noise ▷ *n* deep resonant sound

RUMBLED > RUMBLE

RUMBLER > RUMBLE

RUMBLERS > RUMBLE

RUMBLES > RUMBLE

RUMBLIER > RUMBLY

RUMBLIEST > RUMBLY

RUMBLING > RUMBLE

RUMBLINGS > RUMBLE

RUMBLY *adj* rumbling or liable to rumble

RUMBO *n* rum-based cocktail

RUMBOS > RUMBO

RUME *archaic form of* > RHEUM

RUMEN *n* first compartment of the stomach of ruminants, behind the reticulum, in which food is partly digested before being regurgitated as cud

RUMENS > RUMEN

RUMES > RUME

RUMINA > RUMEN

RUMINAL > RUMEN

RUMINANT *n* cud-chewing (animal, such as a cow, sheep, or deer) ▷ *adj* of ruminants

RUMINANTS > RUMINANT

RUMINATE *vb* chew the cud

RUMINATED > RUMINATE

RUMINATES > RUMINATE

RUMINATOR > RUMINATE

RUMKIN n archaic term for a drinking vessel

RUMKINS > RUMKIN

RUMLY > RUM

RUMMAGE vb search untidily and at length ▷ n untidy search through a collection of things

RUMMAGED > RUMMAGE

RUMMAGER > RUMMAGE

RUMMAGERS > RUMMAGE

RUMMAGES > RUMMAGE

RUMMAGING > RUMMAGE

RUMMER > RUM

RUMMERS > RUM

RUMMEST > RUM

RUMMIER > RUMMY

RUMMIES > RUMMY

RUMMIEST > RUMMY

RUMMILY > RUMMY

RUMMINESS > RUMMY

RUMMISH adj rather strange, peculiar or odd

RUMMY n card game in which players try to collect sets or sequences ▷ adj of or like rum in taste or smell

RUMNESS > RUM

RUMNESSES > RUM

RUMOR same as > RUMOUR

RUMORED > RUMOR

RUMORING > RUMOR

RUMOROUS adj involving or containing rumours

RUMORS > RUMOR

RUMOUR n unproved statement ▷ vb pass around or circulate in the form of a rumour

RUMOURED > RUMOUR

RUMOURER n someone given to spreading rumours

RUMOURERS > RUMOURER

RUMOURING > RUMOUR

RUMOURS > RUMOUR

RUMP n buttocks ▷ vb turn back on

RUMPED > RUMP

RUMPIES > RUMPY

RUMPING > RUMP

RUMPLE vb make untidy, crumpled, or dishevelled ▷ n wrinkle, fold, or crèase

RUMPLED > RUMPLE

RUMPLES > RUMPLE

RUMPLESS > RUMP

RUMPLIER > RUMPLE

RUMPLIEST > RUMPLE

RUMPLING > RUMPLE

RUMPLY > RUMPLE

RUMPO n slang word for sexual intercourse

RUMPOS > RUMPO

RUMPS > RUMP

RUMPUS n noisy commotion

RUMPUSES > RUMPUS

RUMPY n tailless Manx cat ▷ adj with a large or noticeable rump

RUMRUNNER n alcohol smuggler

RUMS > RUM

RUN vb move with a more rapid gait than walking ▷ n act or spell of running

RUNABOUT n small car used for short journeys ▷ vb move busily from place to place

RUNABOUTS > RUNABOUT

RUNAGATE n vagabond, fugitive, or renegade

RUNAGATES > RUNAGATE

RUNANGA n Māori assembly or council

RUNANGAS > RUNANGA

RUNAROUND n deceitful or evasive treatment of a person

RUNAWAY n person or animal that runs away

RUNAWAYS > RUNAWAY

RUNBACK n (in tennis) the areas behind the baselines of the court

RUNBACKS > RUNBACK

RUNCH n another name for white charlock

RUNCHES > RUNCH

RUNCIBLE as in runcible spoon forklike utensil with two prongs and one sharp curved prong

RUNCINATE adj (of a leaf) having a saw-toothed margin with the teeth or lobes pointing backwards

RUND same as > ROON

RUNDALE n (formerly) the name given, esp in Ireland and earlier in Scotland, to the system of land tenure in which each land-holder had several strips of land that were not contiguous

RUNDALES > RUNDALE

RUNDLE n rung of a ladder

RUNDLED adj rounded

RUNDLES > RUNDLE

RUNDLET n liquid measure, generally about 15 gallons

RUNDLETS > RUNDLET

RUNDOWN adj tired; exhausted ▷ n brief review, résumé, or summary

RUNDOWNS > RUNDOWN

RUNDS > RUND

RUNE n any character of the earliest Germanic alphabet

RUNECRAFT n understanding of and skill working with runes

RUNED n with runes on

RUNELIKE adj resembling a rune or runes

RUNES > RUNE

RUNFLAT adj having a safety feature that prevents tyres becoming dangerous or liable to damage when flat

RUNFLATS > RUNFLAT

RUNG > RING

RUNGLESS > RING

RUNGS > RING

RUNIC > RUNE

RUNKLE vb (in dialect) crease or wrinkle

RUNKLED > RUNKLE

RUNKLES > RUNKLE

RUNKLING > RUNKLE

RUNLESS > RUN

RUNLET n cask for wine, beer, etc

RUNLETS > RUNLET

RUNNABLE > RUN

RUNNEL n small brook

RUNNELS > RUNNEL

RUNNER n competitor in a race

RUNNERS > RUNNER

RUNNET dialect word for > RENNET

RUNNETS > RUNNET

RUNNIER > RUNNY

RUNNIEST > RUNNY

RUNNINESS > RUNNY

RUNNING > RUN

RUNNINGLY > RUN

RUNNINGS > RUN

RUNNION n archaic pejorative term for a woman

RUNNIONS > RUNNION

RUNNY adj tending to flow

RUNOFF n extra race to decide the winner after a tie

RUNOFFS > RUNOFF

RUNOUT n dismissal of a batsman by running him out

RUNOUTS > RUNOUT

RUNOVER n incident in which someone is run over by a vehicle

RUNOVERS > RUNOVER

RUNRIG same as > RUNDALE

RUNRIGS > RUNRIG

RUNROUND same as > RUNAROUND

RUNROUNDS > RUNROUND

RUNS > RUN

RUNT n smallest animal in a litter

RUNTED adj stunted

RUNTIER > RUNT

RUNTIEST > RUNT

RUNTINESS > RUNT

RUNTISH > RUNT

RUNTISHLY > RUNT

RUNTS > RUNT

RUNTY > RUNT

RUNWAY n hard level roadway where aircraft take off and land

RUNWAYS > RUNWAY

RUPEE n monetary unit of India and Pakistan

RUPEES > RUPEE

RUPIA n type of skin eruption

RUPIAH n standard monetary unit of Indonesia, divided into 100 sen

RUPIAHS > RUPIAH

RUPIAS > RUPIA

RUPTURE n breaking, breach ▷ vb break, burst, or sever

RUPTURED > RUPTURE

RUPTURES > RUPTURE

RUPTURING > RUPTURE

RURAL adj in or of the countryside ▷ n country dweller

RURALISE same as > RURALIZE

RURALISED > RURALISE

RURALISES > RURALISE

RURALISM > RURAL

RURALISMS > RURAL

RURALIST > RURAL

RURALISTS > RURAL

RURALITE > RURAL

RURALITES > RURAL

RURALITY > RURAL

RURALIZE vb make rural in character, appearance, etc

RURALIZED > RURALIZE

RURALIZES > RURALIZE

RURALLY > RURAL

RURALNESS > RURAL

RURALS > RURAL

RURBAN adj part country, part urban

RURP n very small piton

RURPS > RURP

RURU another name for > MOPOKE

RURUS > RURU

RUSA n type of deer with a mane

RUSALKA n water nymph or spirit

RUSALKAS > RUSALKA

RUSAS > RUSA

RUSCUS n type of shrub

RUSCUSES > RUSCUS

RUSE n stratagem or trick

RUSES > RUSE

RUSH vb move or do very quickly ▷ n sudden quick or violent movement ▷ adj done with speed, hasty

RUSHED > RUSH

RUSHEE n someone interested in gaining fraternity or sorority membership

RUSHEES > RUSHEE

RUSHEN adj made of rushes

RUSHER > RUSH

RUSHERS > RUSH

RUSHES npl (in film-making) the initial prints of a scene or scenes before editing, usually prepared daily

RUSHIER > RUSHY

RUSHIEST > RUSHY

RUSHINESS > RUSHY

RUSHING > RUSH

RUSHINGS > RUSH

RUSHLIGHT n narrow candle, formerly in use, made of the pith of various types of rush dipped in tallow

RUSHLIKE > RUSH

RUSHY adj full of rushes
RUSINE adj of or relating to rusa deer
RUSK n hard brown crisp biscuit, used esp for feeding babies
RUSKS > RUSK
RUSMA n Turkish depilatory
RUSMAS > RUSMA
RUSSE as in charlotte russe cold dessert made from whipped cream, custard, etc, surrounded by sponge fingers
RUSSEL n type of woollen fabric
RUSSELS > RUSSEL
RUSSET adj reddish-brown ▷ n apple with rough reddish-brown skin ▷ vb become russet-coloured
RUSSETED > RUSSET
RUSSETING > RUSSET
RUSSETS > RUSSET
RUSSETY > RUSSET
RUSSIA n Russia leather
RUSSIAS > RUSSIA
RUSSIFIED > RUSSIFY
RUSSIFIES > RUSSIFY
RUSSIFY vb cause to become Russian in character
RUSSULA n type of fungus, typically of toadstool shape and often brightly coloured
RUSSULAE > RUSSULA
RUSSULAS > RUSSULA
RUST n reddish-brown coating formed on iron etc that has been exposed to moisture ▷ adj reddish-brown ▷ vb become coated with rust
RUSTABLE adj liable to rust
RUSTED > RUST
RUSTIC adj of or resembling country people ▷ n person from the country
RUSTICAL n rustic
RUSTICALS > RUSTICAL
RUSTICANA npl objects, such as agricultural

implements, garden furniture, etc, relating to the countryside or made in imitation of rustic styles
RUSTICATE vb banish temporarily from university as a punishment
RUSTICIAL made-up variant of > RUSTIC
RUSTICISE same as > RUSTICIZE
RUSTICISM > RUSTIC
RUSTICITY > RUSTIC
RUSTICIZE vb make rustic
RUSTICLY > RUSTIC
RUSTICS > RUSTIC
RUSTIER > RUSTY
RUSTIEST > RUSTY
RUSTILY > RUSTY
RUSTINESS > RUSTY
RUSTING > RUST
RUSTINGS > RUST
RUSTLE n (make) a low whispering sound ▷ vb steal (cattle)
RUSTLED > RUSTLE
RUSTLER n cattle thief
RUSTLERS > RUSTLER
RUSTLES > RUSTLE
RUSTLESS > RUST
RUSTLING > RUSTLE
RUSTLINGS > RUSTLE
RUSTPROOF adj treated against rusting
RUSTRE n (in heraldry) lozenge with a round hole in the middle showing the background colour
RUSTRED > RUSTRE
RUSTRES > RUSTRE
RUSTS > RUST
RUSTY adj coated with rust
RUT n furrow made by wheels ▷ vb be in a period of sexual excitability
RUTABAGA n Eurasian plant with a bulbous edible root which is used as a vegetable and as cattle fodder
RUTABAGAS > RUTABAGA
RUTACEOUS adj relating to a family of tropical and

temperate flowering plants which includes rue and citrus trees
RUTH n pity
RUTHENIC adj of or containing ruthenium, esp in a high valency state
RUTHENIUM n rare hard brittle white element
RUTHFUL adj full of or causing sorrow or pity
RUTHFULLY > RUTHFUL
RUTHLESS adj pitiless, merciless
RUTHS > RUTH
RUTILANT adj of a reddish colour or glow
RUTILATED adj (of minerals, esp quartz) containing needles of rutile
RUTILE n black, yellowish, or reddish-brown mineral
RUTILES > RUTILE
RUTIN n bioflavonoid found in various plants including rue
RUTINS > RUTIN
RUTS > RUT
RUTTED > RUT
RUTTER n (in history) type of cavalry soldier
RUTTERS > RUTTER
RUTTIER > RUTTY
RUTTIEST > RUTTY
RUTTILY > RUTTY
RUTTINESS > RUTTY
RUTTING > RUT
RUTTINGS > RUT
RUTTISH adj (of an animal) in a condition of rut
RUTTISHLY > RUTTISH
RUTTY adj full of ruts or holes
RYA n type of rug originating in Scandinavia
RYAL n one of several old coins
RYALS > RYAL
RYAS > RYA
RYBAT n polished stone piece forming the side of a window or door
RYBATS > RYBAT
RYBAUDRYE archaic variant

of > RIBALDRY
RYE n kind of grain used for fodder and bread
RYEBREAD n any of various breads made entirely or partly from rye flour, often with caraway seeds
RYEBREADS > RYEBREAD
RYEFLOUR n flour made from rye
RYEFLOURS > RYEFLOUR
RYEGRASS n type of grass native to Europe, N Africa, and Asia, widely cultivated as a forage crop
RYEPECK n punt-mooring pole
RYEPECKS > RYEPECK
RYES > RYE
RYFE archaic variant of > RIFE
RYKE Scots variant of > REACH
RYKED > RYKE
RYKES > RYKE
RYKING > RYKE
RYMME same as > RIM
RYMMED > RYMME
RYMMES > RYMME
RYMMING > RYMME
RYND n (in milling) crossbar piece forming part of the support structure of the upper millstone
RYNDS > RYND
RYOKAN n traditional Japanese inn
RYOKANS > RYOKAN
RYOT n (in India) a peasant or tenant farmer
RYOTS > RYOT
RYOTWARI n (in India) system of land tenure in which land taxes are paid to the state
RYOTWARIS > RYOTWARI
RYPE n ptarmigan
RYPECK same as > RYEPECK
RYPECKS > RYEPECK
RYPER > RYPE

Ss

SAAG n (in Indian cookery) spinach

SAAGS > SAAG

SAB n person engaged in direct action to prevent a targeted activity taking place ▷ vb take part in such action

SABADILLA n tropical American liliaceous plant

SABAL n variety of palm tree

SABALS > SABAL

SABATON n foot covering in suit of armour

SABATONS > SABATON

SABAYON n dessert or sweet sauce made with egg yolks, sugar, and wine beaten together over heat till thick

SABAYONS > SABAYON

SABBAT n midnight meeting of witches

SABBATH n period of rest

SABBATHS > SABBATH

SABBATIC n period of leave granted to university staff

SABBATICS > SABBATIC

SABBATINE adj of Saturday

SABBATISE same as > SABBATIZE

SABBATISM n sabbath observance

SABBATIZE vb observe as sabbath

SABBATS > SABBAT

SABBED > SAB

SABBING > SAB

SABBINGS > SABBING

SABE n very informal word meaning sense or savvy ▷ vb very informal word meaning know or savvy

SABED > SABE

SABEING > SABE

SABELLA n marine worm

SABELLAS > SABELLA

SABER same as > SABRE

SABERED > SABER

SABERING > SABER

SABERLIKE > SABER

SABERS > SABER

SABES > SABE

SABHA n set of Muslim prayer beads

SABHAS > SABHA

SABIN n unit of acoustic absorption equal to the absorption resulting from one square foot of a perfectly absorbing surface

SABINE variant of > SAVIN

SABINES > SABINE

SABINS > SABIN

SABIR n member of ancient Turkic people

SABIRS > SABIR

SABKHA n flat coastal plain with a salt crust, common in Arabia

SABKHAH n sabkha

SABKHAHS > SABKHAH

SABKHAS > SABKHA

SABKHAT n sabkha

SABKHATS > SABKHAT

SABLE n dark fur from a small weasel-like Arctic animal ▷ adj black

SABLED > SABLE

SABLEFISH n North American fish

SABLES > SABLE

SABLING > SABLE

SABOT n wooden shoe traditionally worn by peasants in France

SABOTAGE n intentional damage done to machinery, systems, etc ▷ vb damage intentionally

SABOTAGED > SABOTAGE

SABOTAGES > SABOTAGE

SABOTEUR n person who commits sabotage

SABOTEURS > SABOTEUR

SABOTIER n wearer of wooden clogs

SABOTIERS > SABOTIER

SABOTS > SABOT

SABRA n native-born Israeli Jew

SABRAS > SABRA

SABRE n curved cavalry sword ▷ vb injure or kill with a sabre

SABRED > SABRE

SABRES > SABRE

SABREUR n person wielding sabre

SABREURS > SABREUR

SABREWING n large type of hummingbird with long curved wings

SABRING > SABRE

SABS > SAB

SABULINE same as > SABULOUS

SABULOSE same as > SABULOUS

SABULOUS adj like sand in texture

SABURRA n granular deposit

SABURRAL > SABURRA

SABURRAS > SABURRA

SAC n pouchlike structure in an animal or plant

SACATON n coarse grass of the southwestern US and Mexico, grown for hay and pasture

SACATONS > SACATON

SACBUT n medieval trombone

SACBUTS > SACBUT

SACCADE n movement of the eye when it makes a sudden change of fixation, as in reading

SACCADES > SACCADE

SACCADIC > SACCADE

SACCATE adj in the form of a sac

SACCHARIC as in saccharic acid white soluble solid acid

SACCHARIN n artificial sweetener

SACCHARUM n cane sugar

SACCIFORM adj like a sac

SACCOI > SACCOS

SACCOS n bishop's garment in the Orthodox Church

SACCOSES > SACCOS

SACCULAR adj of or resembling a sac

SACCULATE adj of, relating to, or possessing a saccule, saccules, or a sacculus

SACCULE n small sac

SACCULES > SACCULE

SACCULI > SACCULUS

SACCULUS same as > SACCULE

SACELLA > SACELLUM

SACELLUM n tomb within a church

SACHEM same as > SAGAMORE

SACHEMDOM > SACHEM

SACHEMIC > SACHEM

SACHEMS > SACHEM

SACHET n small envelope or bag containing a single portion

SACHETED adj contained in a sachet

SACHETS > SACHET

SACK n large bag made of coarse material ▷ vb dismiss

SACKABLE adj of or denoting an offence, infraction of rules, etc, that is sufficiently serious to warrant dismissal from an employment

SACKAGE n act of sacking a place

SACKAGES > SACKAGE

SACKBUT n medieval form of trombone

SACKBUTS > SACKBUT

SACKCLOTH n coarse fabric used for sacks, formerly worn as a penance

SACKED > SACK

SACKER > SACK

SACKERS > SACK

SACKFUL > SACK

SACKFULS > SACKFUL

SACKING n rough woven material used for sacks

SACKINGS > SACKING

SACKLESS adj old word meaning innocent

SACKLIKE > SACK

SACKS > SACK

SACKSFUL > SACKFUL

SACLESS adj old word meaning unchallengeable

SACLIKE > SAC

SACQUE same as > SACK

SACQUES > SACQUE

SACRA > SACRUM

SACRAL adj of or associated with sacred rites ▷ n sacral vertebra

SACRALGIA n pain in sacrum

SACRALISE same as > SACRALIZE

SACRALITY n sacredness

SACRALIZE vb make sacred

SACRALS > SACRAL

SACRAMENT n ceremony of the Christian Church, esp Communion

SACRARIA > SACRARIUM

SACRARIAL > SACRARIUM

SACRARIUM n sanctuary of a church

SACRED adj holy

SACREDLY > SACRED

SACRIFICE n giving something up ▷ vb offer as a sacrifice

SACRIFIDE vb old form of sacrifice

SACRIFIED > SACRIFY

SACRIFIES > SACRIFY

SACRIFY vb old form of sacrifice

SACRILEGE n misuse or desecration of something sacred

SACRING n act or ritual of consecration, esp of the Eucharist or of a bishop

SACRINGS > SACRING

SACRIST same as > SACRISTAN

SACRISTAN n person in charge of the contents of a church

SACRISTS > SACRIST

SACRISTY n room in a church where sacred objects are kept

SACRUM n wedge-shaped bone at the base of the spine

SACRUMS > SACRUM

SACS > SAC

SAD adj sorrowful, unhappy ▷ vb New Zealand word meaning express sadness or displeasure strongly

SADDED > SAD

SADDEN vb make (someone) sad

SADDENED > SADDEN

SADDENING > SADDEN

SADDENS > SADDEN

SADDER > SAD

SADDEST > SAD

SADDHU same as > SADHU

SADDHUS > SADDHU

SADDIE same as > SADDO

SADDIES > SADDIE

SADDING > SAD

SADDISH > SAD

SADDLE n rider's seat on a horse or bicycle ▷ vb put a saddle on (a horse)

SADDLEBAG n pouch or small bag attached to the saddle of a horse, bicycle, or motorcycle

SADDLEBOW n pommel of a saddle

SADDLED > SADDLE

SADDLER n maker or seller of saddles

SADDLERS > SADDLER

SADDLERY n saddles and harness for horses collectively

SADDLES > SADDLE

SADDLING > SADDLE

SADDO vb make sad ▷ n socially inadequate or pathetic person

SADDOES > SADDO

SADDOS > SADDO

SADE same as > SADHE

SADES > SADE

SADHANA n one of a number of spiritual practices or disciplines which lead to perfection, these being contemplation,

asceticism, worship of a god, and correct living

SADHANAS > SADHANA

SADHE n 18th letter in the Hebrew alphabet

SADHES > SADHE

SADHU n Hindu wandering holy man

SADHUS > SADHU

SADI variant of > SADHE

SADIRON n heavy iron pointed at both ends, for pressing clothes

SADIRONS > SADIRON

SADIS > SADI

SADISM n gaining of (sexual) pleasure from inflicting pain

SADISMS > SADISM

SADIST > SADISM

SADISTIC > SADISM

SADISTS > SADISM

SADLY > SAD

SADNESS > SAD

SADNESSES > SAD

SADO variant of > CHADO

SADOS > SADO

SADS > SAD

SADZA n southern African porridge

SADZAS > SADZA

SAE Scot word for > SO

SAECULUM n age in astronomy

SAECULUMS > SAECULUM

SAETER n upland pasture in Norway

SAETERS > SAETER

SAFARI n expedition to hunt or observe wild animals, esp in Africa ▷ vb go on safari

SAFARIED > SAFARI

SAFARIING > SAFARI

SAFARIS > SAFARI

SAFARIST n person on safari

SAFARISTS > SAFARIST

SAFE adj secure, protected ▷ n strong lockable container ▷ vb make safe

SAFED > SAFE

SAFEGUARD vb protect ▷ n protection

SAFELIGHT n light that can be used in a room in which photographic material is handled, transmitting only those colours to which a particular type of film, plate, or paper is relatively insensitive

SAFELY > SAFE

SAFENESS > SAFE

SAFER > SAFE

SAFES > SAFE

SAFEST > SAFE

SAFETIED > SAFETY

SAFETIES > SAFETY

SAFETY n state of being safe ▷ vb make safe

SAFETYING > SAFETY

SAFETYMAN n defensive

player in American football

SAFETYMEN > SAFETYMAN

SAFFIAN n leather tanned with sumach and usually dyed a bright colour

SAFFIANS > SAFFIAN

SAFFLOWER n thistle-like plant with flowers used for dye and oil

SAFFRON n orange-coloured flavouring obtained from a crocus ▷ adj orange

SAFFRONED adj containing saffron

SAFFRONS > SAFFRON

SAFFRONY adj like saffron

SAFING > SAFE

SAFRANIN same as > SAFRANINE

SAFRANINE n any of a class of azine dyes, used for textiles and biological stains

SAFRANINS > SAFRANIN

SAFROL n oily liquid obtained from sassafras

SAFROLE n colourless or yellowish oily water-insoluble liquid

SAFROLES > SAFROLE

SAFROLS > SAFROL

SAFRONAL n oily liquid derived from saffron

SAFRONALS > SAFRONAL

SAFT Scot word for > SOFT

SAFTER > SAFT

SAFTEST > SAFT

SAG vb sink in the middle ▷ n droop

SAGA n legend of Norse heroes

SAGACIOUS adj wise

SAGACITY n foresight, discernment, or keen perception

SAGAMAN n person reciting Norse sagas

SAGAMEN > SAGAMAN

SAGAMORE n (among some Native Americans) a chief or eminent man

SAGAMORES > SAGAMORE

SAGANASH n Algonquian term for an Englishman

SAGAPENUM n resin formerly used as drug

SAGAS > SAGA

SAGATHIES > SAGATHY

SAGATHY n type of light fabric

SAGBUT n medieval trombone

SAGBUTS > SAGBUT

SAGE n very wise man ▷ adj wise

SAGEBRUSH n aromatic plant of West N America

SAGELY > SAGE

SAGENE n fishing net

SAGENES > SAGENE

SAGENESS > SAGE

SAGENITE n mineral found in crystal form

SAGENITES > SAGENITE

SAGENITIC > SAGENITE

SAGER > SAGE

SAGES > SAGE

SAGEST > SAGE

SAGGAR n clay box in which fragile ceramic wares are placed for protection during firing ▷ vb put in a saggar

SAGGARD n saggar

SAGGARDS > SAGGARD

SAGGARED > SAGGAR

SAGGARING > SAGGAR

SAGGARS > SAGGAR

SAGGED > SAG

SAGGER same as > SAGGAR

SAGGERED > SAGGER

SAGGERING > SAGGER

SAGGERS > SAGGER

SAGGIER > SAGGY

SAGGIEST > SAGGY

SAGGING > SAG

SAGGINGS > SAG

SAGGY adj tending to sag

SAGIER > SAGY

SAGIEST > SAGY

SAGINATE vb fatten livestock

SAGINATED > SAGINATE

SAGINATES > SAGINATE

SAGITTA n sine of an arc

SAGITTAL adj resembling an arrow

SAGITTARY n centaur

SAGITTAS > SAGITTA

SAGITTATE adj (esp of leaves) shaped like the head of an arrow

SAGO n starchy cereal from the powdered pith of the sago palm tree

SAGOIN n South American monkey

SAGOINS > SAGOIN

SAGOS > SAGO

SAGOUIN n South American monkey

SAGOUINS > SAGOUIN

SAGRADA as in cascara sagrada dried bark of the cascara buckthorn, used as a stimulant and laxative

SAGS > SAG

SAGUARO n giant cactus of desert regions of Arizona, S California, and Mexico

SAGUAROS > SAGUARO

SAGUIN n South American monkey

SAGUINS > SAGUIN

SAGUM n Roman soldier's cloak

SAGY adj like or containing sage

SAHEB same as > SAHIB

SAHEBS > SAHEB

SAHIB n Indian term of address placed after a man's name as a mark of respect

SAHIBA n respectful Indian term of address for woman

SAHIBAH n sahiba

SAHIBAHS > SAHIBAH
SAHIBAS > SAHIBA
SAHIBS > SAHIB
SAHIWAL *n* breed of cattle in India
SAHIWALS > SAHIWAL
SAHUARO *same as* > SAGUARO
SAHUAROS > SAHUARO
SAI *n* South American monkey
SAIBLING *n* freshwater fish
SAIBLINGS > SAIBLING
SAIC *n* boat of eastern Mediterranean
SAICE *same as* > SYCE
SAICES > SAICE
SAICK *n* boat of eastern Mediterranean
SAICKS > SAICK
SAICS > SAIC
SAID *same as* > SAYYID
SAIDEST > SAY
SAIDS > SAID
SAIDST > SAY
SAIGA *n* either of two antelopes of the plains of central Asia
SAIGAS > SAIGA
SAIKEI *n* Japanese ornamental miniature landscape
SAIKEIS > SAIKEI
SAIKLESS *old Scots word for* > INNOCENT
SAIL *n* sheet of fabric stretched to catch the wind for propelling a sailing boat ▷ *vb* travel by water
SAILABLE > SAIL
SAILBOARD *n* board with a mast and single sail, used for windsurfing
SAILBOAT *n* boat propelled chiefly by sail
SAILBOATS > SAILBOAT
SAILCLOTH *n* fabric for making sails
SAILED > SAIL
SAILER *n* vessel, esp one equipped with sails, with specified sailing characteristics
SAILERS > SAILER
SAILFISH *n* large tropical game fish, with a long sail-like fin on its back
SAILING *n* practice, art, or technique of sailing a vessel
SAILINGS > SAILING
SAILLESS > SAIL
SAILMAKER *n* person who makes sails
SAILOR *n* member of a ship's crew
SAILORING *n* activity of working as sailor
SAILORLY > SAILOR
SAILORS > SAILOR
SAILPLANE *n* high-performance glider
SAILROOM *n* space on ship for storing sails
SAILROOMS > SAILROOM

SAILS > SAIL
SAIM *Scots word for* > LARD
SAIMIN *n* Hawaiian dish of noodles
SAIMINS > SAIMIN
SAIMIRI *n* South American monkey
SAIMIRIS > SAIMIRI
SAIMS > SAIM
SAIN *vb* make the sign of the cross over so as to bless or protect from evil or sin
SAINE *vb* old form of say
SAINED > SAIN
SAINFOIN *n* Eurasian plant with pink flowers, widely grown as feed for grazing farm animals
SAINFOINS > SAINFOIN
SAINING > SAIN
SAINS > SAIN
SAINT *n* person venerated after death as specially holy ▷ *vb* canonize
SAINTDOM > SAINT
SAINTDOMS > SAINT
SAINTED *adj* formally recognized by a Christian Church as a saint
SAINTESS *n* female saint
SAINTFOIN *n* sainfoin
SAINTHOOD *n* state or character of being a saint
SAINTING > SAINT
SAINTISH > SAINT
SAINTISM *n* quality of being saint
SAINTISMS > SAINTISM
SAINTLESS > SAINT
SAINTLIER > SAINTLY
SAINTLIKE > SAINT
SAINTLILY > SAINTLY
SAINTLING *n* little saint
SAINTLY *adj* behaving in a very good, patient, or holy way
SAINTS > SAINT
SAINTSHIP > SAINT
SAIQUE *n* boat in eastern Mediterranean
SAIQUES > SAIQUE
SAIR *Scot word for* > SORE
SAIRED > SAIR
SAIRER > SAIR
SAIREST > SAIR
SAIRING > SAIR
SAIRS > SAIR
SAIS > SAI
SAIST > SAY
SAITH *form of the present tense (indicative mood) of* > SAY
SAITHE *n* dark-coloured food fish found in northern seas
SAITHES > SAITHE
SAITHS > SAITH
SAIYID *n* Muslim descended from Mohammed's grandson
SAIYIDS > SAIYID
SAJOU *n* South American monkey
SAJOUS > SAJOU

SAKAI *n* Malaysian aborigine
SAKAIS > SAKAI
SAKE *n* benefit
SAKER *n* large falcon of E Europe and central Asia
SAKERET *n* male saker
SAKERETS > SAKERET
SAKERS > SAKER
SAKES > SAKE
SAKI *same as* > SAKE
SAKIA *n* water wheel in Middle East
SAKIAS > SAKIA
SAKIEH *n* water wheel in Middle East
SAKIEHS > SAKIEH
SAKIS > SAKI
SAKIYEH *n* water wheel in Middle East
SAKIYEHS > SAKIYEH
SAKKOI > SAKKOS
SAKKOS *n* bishop's garment in Orthodox Church
SAKKOSES > SAKKOS
SAKSAUL *n* Asian tree
SAKSAULS > SAKSAUL
SAL *pharmacological term for* > SALT
SALAAM *n* low bow of greeting among Muslims ▷ *vb* make a salaam
SALAAMED > SALAAM
SALAAMING > SALAAM
SALAAMS > SALAAM
SALABLE *same as* > SALEABLE
SALABLY > SALEABLY
SALACIOUS *adj* excessively concerned with sex
SALACITY *n* excessive interest in sex
SALAD *n* dish of raw vegetables, eaten as a meal or part of a meal
SALADANG *n* variety of ox
SALADANGS > SALADANG
SALADE *same as* > SALLET
SALADES > SALADE
SALADING *n* ingredients for salad
SALADINGS > SALADING
SALADS > SALAD
SALAL *n* North American shrub
SALALS > SALAL
SALAMI *n* highly spiced sausage
SALAMIS > SALAMI
SALAMON *n* word used in old oaths
SALAMONS > SALAMON
SALANGANE *n* Asian swift
SALARIAT *n* salary-earning class
SALARIATS > SALARIAT
SALARIED *adj* earning or providing a salary
SALARIES > SALARY
SALARY *n* fixed regular payment, usu monthly, to an employee ▷ *vb* pay a salary to

SALARYING > SALARY
SALARYMAN *n* (in Japan) an office worker
SALARYMEN > SALARYMAN
SALBAND *n* coating of mineral
SALBANDS > SALBAND
SALCHOW *n* type of figure-skating jump
SALCHOWS > SALCHOW
SALE *n* exchange of goods for money
SALEABLE *adj* fit or likely to be sold
SALEABLY > SALEABLE
SALEP *n* dried ground starchy tubers of various orchids, used for food and formerly as drugs
SALEPS > SALEP
SALERATUS *n* sodium bicarbonate when used in baking powder
SALERING *n* enclosed area for livestock at market
SALERINGS > SALERING
SALEROOM *n* place where goods are sold by auction
SALEROOMS > SALEROOM
SALES > SALE
SALESGIRL *n* person who sells goods
SALESLADY *n* person who sells goods
SALESMAN *n* person who sells goods
SALESMEN > SALESMAN
SALESROOM *n* room in which merchandise on sale is displayed
SALET *same as* > SALLET
SALETS > SALET
SALEWD > SALUE
SALEYARD *n* area with pens for holding animals before auction
SALEYARDS > SALEYARD
SALFERN *n* plant of borage family
SALFERNS > SALFERN
SALIAUNCE *n* old word meaning onslaught
SALIC *adj* (of rocks and minerals) having a high content of silica and alumina
SALICES > SALIX
SALICET *n* soft-toned organ stop
SALICETA > SALICETUM
SALICETS > SALICET
SALICETUM *n* plantation of willows
SALICIN *n* colourless or white crystalline water-soluble glucoside
SALICINE *same as* > SALICIN
SALICINES > SALICINE
SALICINS > SALICIN
SALICYLIC *as in salicylic acid* white crystalline substance with a sweet taste and a bitter aftertaste

SALIENCE > SALIENT
SALIENCES > SALIENT
SALIENCY *n* quality of being prominent
SALIENT *adj* prominent, noticeable ▷ *n* projecting part of a front line
SALIENTLY > SALIENT
SALIENTS > SALIENT
SALIFIED > SALIFY
SALIFIES > SALIFY
SALIFY *vb* treat, mix with, or cause to combine with a salt
SALIFYING > SALIFY
SALIGOT *n* water chestnut
SALIGOTS > SALIGOT
SALIMETER *n* hydrometer for measuring salt in a solution
**SALIMETRY
>** SALIMETER
SALINA *n* salt marsh, lake, or spring
SALINAS > SALINA
SALINE *adj* containing salt ▷ *n* solution of sodium chloride and water
SALINES > SALINE
SALINISE *same as*
> SALINIZE
SALINISED > SALINISE
SALINISES > SALINISE
SALINITY > SALINE
SALINIZE *vb* treat with salt
SALINIZED > SALINIZE
SALINIZES > SALINIZE
SALIVA *n* liquid that forms in the mouth, spittle
SALIVAL > SALIVA
SALIVARY > SALIVA
SALIVAS > SALIVA
SALIVATE *vb* produce saliva
SALIVATED > SALIVATE
SALIVATES > SALIVATE
SALIVATOR > SALIVATE
SALIX *n* plant or tree of willow family
SALL *archaic form of*
> SHALL
SALLAD *old spelling of*
> SALAD
SALLADS > SALLAD
SALLAL *n* North American shrub
SALLALS > SALLAL
SALLE *n* hall
SALLEE *n* SE Australian eucalyptus with a pale grey bark
SALLEES > SALLEE
SALLES > SALLE
SALLET *n* light round helmet extending over the back of the neck
SALLETS > SALLET
SALLIED > SALLY
SALLIER > SALLY
SALLIERS > SALLY
SALLIES > SALLY
SALLOW *adj* of an unhealthy pale or yellowish colour

▷ *vb* make sallow ▷ *n* any of several small willow trees
SALLOWED > SALLOW
SALLOWER > SALLOW
SALLOWEST > SALLOW
SALLOWING > SALLOW
SALLOWISH > SALLOW
SALLOWLY > SALLOW
SALLOWS > SALLOW
SALLOWY > SALLOW
SALLY *n* violent excursion ▷ *vb* set or rush out
SALLYING > SALLY
SALLYPORT *n* opening in a fortified place from which troops may make a sally
SALMI *n* ragout of game stewed in a rich brown sauce
SALMIS *same as* **>** SALMI
SALMON *n* large fish with orange-pink flesh valued as food ▷ *adj* orange-pink
SALMONET *n* young salmon
SALMONETS > SALMONET
SALMONID *n* type of soft-finned fish of the family which includes the salmon
SALMONIDS > SALMONID
SALMONOID *adj* belonging to the order of soft-finned teleost fishes that includes the salmon, whitefish, grayling, and char ▷ *n* any of these fish
SALMONS > SALMON
SALMONY *adj* of or like a salmon
SALOL *n* white sparingly soluble crystalline compound with a slight aromatic odour, used as a preservative and to absorb light in sun-tan lotions, plastics, etc
SALOLS > SALOL
SALOMETER *n* instrument for measuring salt in solution
SALON *n* commercial premises of a hairdresser, beautician, etc
SALONS > SALON
SALOON *n* closed car with four or more seats
SALOONS > SALOON
SALOOP *n* infusion of aromatic herbs or other plant parts formerly used as a tonic or cure
SALOOPS > SALOOP
SALOP *variant of* **>** SALOOP
SALOPIAN > SALOOP
SALOPS > SALOOP
SALP *n* minute animal floating in sea
SALPA *n* any of various minute floating animals of warm oceans
SALPAE > SALPA
SALPAS > SALPA
SALPIAN *n* minute animal

floating in sea
SALPIANS > SALPIAN
SALPICON *n* mixture of chopped fish, meat, or vegetables in a sauce
SALPICONS > SALPICON
SALPID *n* minute animal floating in sea
SALPIDS > SALPID
SALPIFORM > SALPA
SALPINGES > SALPINX
SALPINX *n* Fallopian tube or Eustachian tube
SALPINXES > SALPINX
SALPS > SALP
SALS > SAL
SALSA *n* lively Puerto Rican dance ▷ *vb* dance the salsa
SALSAED > SALSA
SALSAING > SALSA
SALSAS > SALSA
SALSE *n* volcano expelling mud
SALSES > SALSE
SALSIFIES > SALSIFY
SALSIFY *n* Mediterranean plant with a long white edible root
SALSILLA *n* tropical American vine
SALSILLAS > SALSILLA
SALT *n* white crystalline substance used to season food ▷ *vb* season or preserve with salt
SALTANDO *n* staccato piece of violin playing
SALTANT *adj* (of an organism) differing from others of its species because of a saltation ▷ *n* saltant organism
SALTANTS > SALTANT
SALTATE *vb* go through saltation
SALTATED > SALTATE
SALTATES > SALTATE
SALTATING > SALTATE
SALTATION *n* abrupt variation in the appearance of an organism, usu caused by genetic mutation
SALTATO > saltando
SALTATORY *adj* specialized for jumping
SALTBOX *n* box for salt with a sloping lid
SALTBOXES > SALTBOX
SALTBUSH *n* shrub that grows in alkaline desert regions
SALTCAT *n* salty medicine for pigeons
SALTCATS > SALTCAT
SALTCHUCK *n* any body of salt water
SALTED *adj* seasoned, preserved, or treated with salt
SALTER *n* person who deals in or manufactures salt
SALTERN *n* place where salt is obtained from pools of evaporated sea water

SALTERNS > SALTERN
SALTERS > SALTER
SALTEST > SALT
SALTFISH *n* salted cod
SALTIE *n* saltwater crocodile
SALTIER > SALTIRE
SALTIERS > SALTIER
SALTIES > SALTIE
SALTIEST > SALTY
SALTILY > SALTY
SALTINE *n* salty biscuit
SALTINES > SALTINE
SALTINESS > SALTY
SALTING *n* area of low ground regularly inundated with salt water
SALTINGS > SALTING
SALTIRE *n* diagonal cross on a shield
SALTIRES > SALTIRE
SALTISH > SALT
SALTISHLY > SALT
SALTLESS > SALT
SALTLIKE > SALT
SALTLY > SALT
SALTNESS > SALT
SALTO *n* daring jump ▷ *vb* perform a daring jump
SALTOED > SALTO
SALTOING > SALTO
SALTOS > SALTO
SALTPAN *n* shallow basin containing salt, gypsum, etc, that was deposited from an evaporated salt lake
SALTPANS > SALTPAN
SALTPETER *same as*
> SALTPETRE
SALTPETRE *n* compound used in gunpowder and as a preservative
SALTS > SALT
SALTUS *n* break in the continuity of a sequence, esp the omission of a necessary step in a logical argument
SALTUSES > SALTUS
SALTWATER *adj* living in the sea
SALTWORK *n* place where salt is refined
SALTWORKS *n* place, building, or factory where salt is produced
SALTWORT *n* any of several chenopodiaceous plants with prickly leaves, striped stems, and small green flowers
SALTWORTS > SALTWORT
SALTY *adj* of, tasting of, or containing salt
SALUBRITY *n* quality of being favourable to health or wholesome
SALUE *vb* old word meaning salute
SALUED > SALUE
SALUES > SALUE
SALUING > SALUE
SALUKI *n* type of tall hound with a smooth coat

SALUKIS > SALUKI
SALURETIC n drug that increases secretion of salt in urine
SALUTARY adj producing a beneficial result
SALUTE n motion of the arm as a formal military sign of respect ▷ vb greet with a salute
SALUTED > SALUTE
SALUTER > SALUTE
SALUTERS > SALUTE
SALUTES > SALUTE
SALUTING > SALUTE
SALVABLE adj capable of or suitable for being saved or salvaged
SALVABLY > SALVABLE
SALVAGE n saving of a ship or other property from destruction ▷ vb save from destruction or waste
SALVAGED > SALVAGE
SALVAGEE n rope on sailing ship
SALVAGEES > SALVAGEE
SALVAGER > SALVAGE
SALVAGERS > SALVAGE
SALVAGES > SALVAGE
SALVAGING > SALVAGE
SALVARSAN n old medicine containing arsenic
SALVATION n fact or state of being saved from harm or the consequences of sin
SALVATORY n place for storing something safely
SALVE n healing or soothing ointment ▷ vb soothe or appease
SALVED > SALVE
SALVER same as > SALVOR
SALVERS > SALVER
SALVES > SALVE
SALVETE n Latin greeting
SALVETES > SALVETE
SALVIA n plant with blue or red flowers
SALVIAS > SALVIA
SALVIFIC adj acting to salve
SALVING > SALVE
SALVINGS > SALVE
SALVO n simultaneous discharge of guns etc ▷ vb attack with a salvo
SALVOED > SALVO
SALVOES > SALVO
SALVOING > SALVO
SALVOR n person instrumental in salvaging a vessel or its cargo
SALVORS > SALVOR
SALVOS > SALVO
SALWAR as in salwar kameez long tunic worn over a pair of baggy trousers, usually worn by women, esp in Pakistan
SALWARS > SALWAR
SAM vb collect
SAMA n Japanese title of respect

SAMAAN n South American tree
SAMAANS > SAMAAN
SAMADHI n state of deep meditative contemplation which leads to higher consciousness
SAMADHIS > SAMADHI
SAMAN n South American tree
SAMANS > SAMAN
SAMARA n dry indehiscent one-seeded fruit with a winglike extension to aid dispersal
SAMARAS > SAMARA
SAMARITAN n kindly person who helps another in distress
SAMARIUM n silvery metallic element
SAMARIUMS > SAMARIUM
SAMAS > SAMA
SAMBA n lively Brazilian dance ▷ vb perform such a dance
SAMBAED > SAMBA
SAMBAING > SAMBA
SAMBAL n Malaysian dish
SAMBALS > SAMBAL
SAMBAR n S Asian deer with three-tined antlers
SAMBARS > SAMBAR
SAMBAS > SAMBA
SAMBHAR n Indian dish
SAMBHARS > SAMBHAR
SAMBHUR n Asian deer
SAMBHURS > SAMBHUR
SAMBO n offensive word for a Black person
SAMBOS > SAMBO
SAMBUCA n Italian liqueur
SAMBUCAS > SAMBUCA
SAMBUKE n ancient Greek stringed instrument
SAMBUKES > SAMBUKE
SAMBUR same as > SAMBAR
SAMBURS > SAMBUR
SAME adj identical, not different, unchanged ▷ n something identical
SAMECH n letter in Hebrew alphabet
SAMECHS > SAMECH
SAMEK variant of > SAMEKH
SAMEKH n 15th letter in the Hebrew alphabet, transliterated as s
SAMEKHS > SAMEKH
SAMEKS > SAMEK
SAMEL adj of brick, not sufficiently fired
SAMELY adj the same
SAMEN old Scots form of > SAME
SAMENESS n state or quality of being the same
SAMES > SAME
SAMEY adj monotonous
SAMEYNESS n quality of being samey
SAMFOO n style of casual dress worn by Chinese women, consisting of a

waisted blouse and trousers
SAMFOOS > SAMFOO
SAMFU n Chinese female outfit
SAMFUS > SAMFU
SAMIEL same as > SIMOOM
SAMIELS > SAMIEL
SAMIER > SAMEY
SAMIEST > SAMEY
SAMISEN n Japanese plucked stringed instrument with a long neck, an unfretted fingerboard, and a rectangular soundbox
SAMISENS > SAMISEN
SAMITE n heavy fabric of silk, often woven with gold or silver threads, used in the Middle Ages for clothing
SAMITES > SAMITE
SAMITHI same as > SAMITI
SAMITHIS > SAMITHI
SAMITI n (in India) an association, esp one formed to organize political activity
SAMITIS > SAMITI
SAMIZDAT n (in the former Soviet Union) a system of secret printing and distribution of banned literature
SAMIZDATS > SAMIZDAT
SAMLET n young salmon
SAMLETS > SAMLET
SAMLOR n motor vehicle in Thailand
SAMLORS > SAMLOR
SAMMED > SAM
SAMMIES > SAMMY
SAMMING > SAM
SAMMY n (in South Africa) an Indian fruit and vegetable vendor who goes from house to house
SAMNITIS n poisonous plant mentioned by Spenser
SAMOSA n (in Indian cookery) a small fried triangular spiced meat or vegetable pasty
SAMOSAS > SAMOSA
SAMOVAR n Russian tea urn
SAMOVARS > SAMOVAR
SAMOYED n Siberian breed of dog of the spitz type, having a dense white or cream coat with a distinct ruff, and a tightly curled tail
SAMOYEDS > SAMOYED
SAMP n crushed maize used for porridge
SAMPAN n small boat with oars used in China
SAMPANS > SAMPAN
SAMPHIRE n plant found on rocks by the seashore
SAMPHIRES > SAMPHIRE
SAMPI n old Greek number character

SAMPIRE n samphire
SAMPIRES > SAMPIRE
SAMPIS > SAMPI
SAMPLE n part taken as representative of a whole ▷ vb take and test a sample of
SAMPLED > SAMPLE
SAMPLER n piece of embroidery showing the embroiderer's skill
SAMPLERS > SAMPLER
SAMPLERY n making of samplers
SAMPLES > SAMPLE
SAMPLING n process of selecting a random sample
SAMPLINGS > SAMPLING
SAMPS > SAMP
SAMS > SAM
SAMSARA n endless cycle of birth, death, and rebirth
SAMSARAS > SAMSARA
SAMSARIC adj relating to the eternal cycle of birth, suffering, death and rebirth in Indian religions
SAMSHOO n Chinese alcoholic drink
SAMSHOOS > SAMSHOO
SAMSHU n alcoholic drink from China that is made from fermented rice and resembles sake
SAMSHUS > SAMSHU
SAMURAI n member of an ancient Japanese warrior caste
SAMURAIS > SAMURAI
SAN n sanatorium
SANATIVE less common word for > CURATIVE
SANATORIA npl institutions for the care of chronically ill people
SANATORY adj healing
SANBENITO n yellow garment bearing a red cross, worn by penitent heretics in the Inquisition
SANCAI n glaze in Chinese pottery
SANCAIS > SANCAI
SANCHO n African stringed instrument
SANCHOS > SANCHO
SANCTA > SANCTUM
SANCTIFY vb make holy
SANCTION n permission, authorization ▷ vb allow, authorize
SANCTIONS > SANCTION
SANCTITY n sacredness, inviolability
SANCTUARY n holy place
SANCTUM n sacred place
SANCTUMS > SANCTUM
SAND n substance consisting of small grains of rock, esp on a beach or in a desert ▷ vb smooth with sandpaper
SANDABLE > SAND
SANDAL n light shoe consisting of a sole

S

attached by straps ▷ vb put sandals on

SANDALED > SANDAL

SANDALING > SANDAL

SANDALLED > SANDAL

SANDALS > SANDAL

SANDARAC n either of two coniferous trees having hard fragrant dark wood

SANDARACH same as > SANDARAC

SANDARACS > SANDARAC

SANDBAG n bag filled with sand, used as protection against gunfire or flood water ▷ vb protect with sandbags

SANDBAGS > SANDBAG

SANDBANK n bank of sand below the surface of a river or sea

SANDBANKS > SANDBANK

SANDBAR n ridge of sand in a river or sea, often exposed at low tide

SANDBARS > SANDBAR

SANDBLAST n (clean with) a jet of sand blown from a nozzle under pressure ▷ vb clean or decorate (a surface) with a sandblast

SANDBOX n container on a railway locomotive from which sand is released onto the rails to assist the traction

SANDBOXES > SANDBOX

SANDBOY as in happy as a sandboy very happy or high-spirited

SANDBOYS > SANDBOY

SANDBUR n variety of wild grass

SANDBURR n variety of wild grass

SANDBURRS > SANDBURR

SANDBURS > SANDBUR

SANDCRACK n crack in horse's hoof

SANDDAB n type of small Pacific flatfish

SANDDABS > SANDDAB

SANDED > SAND

SANDEK n man who holds a baby being circumcised

SANDEKS > SANDEK

SANDER n power tool for smoothing surfaces

SANDERS > SANDER

SANDERSES > SANDER

SANDFISH n burrowing Pacific fish

SANDFLIES > SANDFLY

SANDFLY n any of various small mothlike dipterous flies: the bloodsucking females transmit diseases including leishmaniasis

SANDGLASS less common word for > HOURGLASS

SANDHEAP n heap of sand

SANDHEAPS > SANDHEAP

SANDHI n modification of the form or sound of a word under the influence of an adjacent word

SANDHILL n hill of sand

SANDHILLS > SANDHILL

SANDHIS > SANDHI

SANDHOG n person who works in underground or underwater construction projects

SANDHOGS > SANDHOG

SANDIER > SANDY

SANDIEST > SANDY

SANDINESS > SANDY

SANDING > SAND

SANDINGS > SAND

SANDIVER n scum forming on molten glass

SANDIVERS > SANDIVER

SANDLESS > SAND

SANDLIKE > SAND

SANDLING n sand eel

SANDLINGS > SANDLING

SANDLOT n area of vacant ground used by children for playing baseball and other games

SANDLOTS > SANDLOT

SANDMAN n (in folklore) a magical person supposed to put children to sleep by sprinkling sand in their eyes

SANDMEN > SANDMAN

SANDPAPER n paper coated with sand for smoothing a surface ▷ vb smooth with sandpaper

SANDPEEP n small sandpiper

SANDPEEPS > SANDPEEP

SANDPILE n pile of sand

SANDPILES > SANDPILE

SANDPIPER n shore bird with a long bill and slender legs

SANDPIT n shallow pit or container holding sand for children to play in

SANDPITS > SANDPIT

SANDPUMP n pump for wet sand

SANDPUMPS > SANDPUMP

SANDS > SAND

SANDSHOE n light canvas shoe with a rubber sole

SANDSHOES > SANDSHOE

SANDSOAP n gritty general-purpose soap

SANDSOAPS > SANDSOAP

SANDSPOUT n sand sucked into air by whirlwind

SANDSPUR n American wild grass

SANDSPURS > SANDSPUR

SANDSTONE n rock composed of sand

SANDSTORM n desert wind that whips up clouds of sand

SANDWICH n two slices of bread with a layer of food between ▷ vb insert between two other things

SANDWORM n any of various polychaete worms that live in burrows on sandy shores, esp the lugworm

SANDWORMS > SANDWORM

SANDWORT n any of numerous caryophyllaceous plants which grow in dense tufts on sandy soil and have white or pink solitary flowers

SANDWORTS > SANDWORT

SANDY adj covered with sand

SANDYISH adj somewhat sandy or covered with sand

SANE adj of sound mind ▷ vb heal

SANED > SANE

SANELY > SANE

SANENESS > SANE

SANER > SANE

SANES > SANE

SANEST > SANE

SANG Scots word for > SONG

SANGA n Ethiopian ox

SANGAR n breastwork of stone or sods

SANGAREE n spiced drink similar to sangria

SANGAREES > SANGAREE

SANGARS > SANGAR

SANGAS > SANGA

SANGEET n Indian pre-wedding celebration

SANGEETS > SANGEET

SANGER n sandwich

SANGERS > SANGER

SANGFROID n composure or self-possession

SANGH n Indian union or association

SANGHA n Buddhist monastic order or community

SANGHAS > SANGHA

SANGHAT n fellowship or assembly, esp a local Sikh community or congregation

SANGHATS > SANGHAT

SANGHS > SANGH

SANGLIER n wild boar

SANGLIERS > SANGLIER

SANGO same as > SANGER

SANGOMA n witch doctor or herbalist

SANGOMAS > SANGOMA

SANGOS > SANGO

SANGRIA n Spanish drink of red wine and fruit

SANGRIAS > SANGRIA

SANGS > SANG

SANGUIFY vb turn into blood

SANGUINE adj cheerful, optimistic ▷ n red pencil containing ferric oxide, used in drawing

SANGUINED > SANGUINE

SANGUINES > SANGUINE

SANICLE n type of plant with clusters of small white flowers and oval fruits with hooked bristles

SANICLES > SANICLE

SANIDINE n alkali feldspar that is found in lavas

SANIDINES > SANIDINE

SANIES n thin greenish foul-smelling discharge from a wound, etc, containing pus and blood

SANIFIED > SANIFY

SANIFIES > SANIFY

SANIFY vb make healthy

SANIFYING > SANIFY

SANING > SANE

SANIOUS > SANIES

SANITARIA variant of > SANATORIA

SANITARY adj promoting health by getting rid of dirt and germs

SANITATE vb make sanitary

SANITATED > SANITATE

SANITATES > SANITATE

SANITIES > SANITY

SANITISE same as > SANITIZE

SANITISED > SANITISE

SANITISER > SANITISE

SANITISES > SANITISE

SANITIZE vb omit unpleasant details to make (news) more acceptable

SANITIZED > SANITIZE

SANITIZER > SANITIZE

SANITIZES > SANITIZE

SANITORIA variant of > SANATORIA

SANITY n state of having a normal healthy mind

SANJAK n (in the Turkish Empire) a subdivision of a vilayet

SANJAKS > SANJAK

SANK > SINK

SANKO n African stringed instrument

SANKOS > SANKO

SANNIE Scots word for > SANDSHOE

SANNIES > SANNIE

SANNOP n Native American married man

SANNOPS > SANNOP

SANNUP n Native American married man

SANNUPS > SANNUP

SANNYASI n Brahman who having attained the fourth and last stage of life as a beggar will not be reborn, but will instead be absorbed into the Universal Soul

SANNYASIN same as > SANNYASI

SANNYASIS > SANNYASI

SANPAN n sampan

SANPANS > SANPAN

SANPRO n sanitary-protection products, collectively

SANPROS > SANPRO

SANS archaic word for > WITHOUT

SANSA n African musical instrument

SANSAR n name of a wind that blows in Iran

SANSARS > SANSAR
SANSAS > SANSA
SANSEI *n* American whose parents were Japanese immigrants
SANSEIS > SANSEI
SANSERIF *n* style of printer's typeface
SANSERIFS > SANSERIF
SANT *n* devout person in India
SANTAL *n* sandalwood
SANTALIC *adj* of sandalwood
SANTALIN *n* substance giving sandalwood its colour
SANTALINS > SANTALIN
SANTALOL *n* liquid from sandalwood used in perfume
SANTALOLS > SANTALOL
SANTALS > SANTAL
SANTERA *n* priestess of santeria
SANTERAS > SANTERA
SANTERIA *n* Caribbean religious cult
SANTERIAS > SANTERIA
SANTERO *n* priest of santeria
SANTEROS > SANTERO
SANTIMI > SANTIMS
SANTIMS *n* money unit in Latvia
SANTIMU *same as* **>** SANTIMS
SANTIR *n* Middle Eastern stringed instrument
SANTIRS > SANTIR
SANTO *n* saint or representation of one
SANTOL *n* fruit from Southeast Asia
SANTOLINA *n* any plant of an evergreen Mediterranean genus grown for its silvery-grey felted foliage
SANTOLS > SANTOL
SANTON *n* French figurine
SANTONICA *n* oriental wormwood plant
SANTONIN *n* white crystalline soluble substance extracted from the dried flower heads of santonica
SANTONINS > SANTONIN
SANTONS > SANTON
SANTOOR *same as* **>** SANTIR
SANTOORS > SANTOOR
SANTOS > SANTO
SANTOUR *n* Middle Eastern stringed instrument
SANTOURS > SANTOUR
SANTS > SANT
SANTUR *n* Middle Eastern stringed instrument
SANTURS > SANTUR
SANYASI *same as* **>** SANNYASI
SANYASIS > SANNYASI
SAOLA *n* small, very rare

bovine mammal of Vietnam and Laos
SAOLAS > SAOLA
SAOUARI *n* tropical American tree
SAOUARIS > SAOUARI
SAP *n* moisture that circulates in plants **▷** *vb* undermine
SAPAJOU *n* capuchin monkey
SAPAJOUS > SAPAJOU
SAPAN *n* tropical tree
SAPANS > SAPAN
SAPANWOOD *n* small S Asian tree
SAPEGO *n* skin disease
SAPEGOES > SAPEGO
SAPELE *n* type of W African tree
SAPELES > SAPELE
SAPFUL *adj* full of sap
SAPHEAD *n* simpleton, idiot, or fool
SAPHEADED > SAPHEAD
SAPHEADS > SAPHEAD
SAPHENA *n* either of two large superficial veins of the legs
SAPHENAE > SAPHENA
SAPHENAS > SAPHENA
SAPHENOUS > SAPHENA
SAPID *adj* having a pleasant taste
SAPIDITY > SAPID
SAPIDLESS *adj* lacking flavour
SAPIDNESS > SAPID
SAPIENCE > SAPIENT
SAPIENCES > SAPIENT
SAPIENCY > SAPIENT
SAPIENS *adj* relating to or like modern human beings
SAPIENT *adj* wise, shrewd **▷** *n* wise person
SAPIENTLY > SAPIENT
SAPIENTS > SAPIENT
SAPLESS > SAP
SAPLING *n* young tree
SAPLINGS > SAPLING
SAPODILLA *n* large tropical American evergreen tree
SAPOGENIN *n* substance derived from saponin
SAPONARIA *See* **>** SOAPWORT
SAPONATED *adj* treated or combined with soap
SAPONIFY *vb* convert (a fat) into a soap by treatment with alkali
SAPONIN *n* any of a group of plant glycosides
SAPONINE *n* saponin
SAPONINES > SAPONINE
SAPONINS > SAPONIN
SAPONITE *n* type of clay mineral
SAPONITES > SAPONITE
SAPOR *n* quality in a substance that is perceived by the sense of taste
SAPORIFIC > SAPOR

SAPOROUS > SAPOR
SAPORS > SAPOR
SAPOTA *same as* **>** SAPODILLA
SAPOTAS > SAPOTA
SAPOTE *n* Central American tree
SAPOTES > SAPOTE
SAPOUR *variant of* SAPOR
SAPOURS > SAPOUR
SAPPAN *n* tropical tree
SAPPANS > SAPPAN
SAPPED > SAP
SAPPER *n* soldier in an engineering unit
SAPPERS > SAPPER
SAPPHIC *adj* lesbian **▷** *n* verse written in a particular form
SAPPHICS > SAPPHIC
SAPPHIRE *n* blue precious stone **▷** *adj* deep blue
SAPPHIRED *adj* blue-coloured
SAPPHIRES > SAPPHIRE
SAPPHISM *n* lesbianism
SAPPHISMS > SAPPHISM
SAPPHIST *n* lesbian
SAPPHISTS > SAPPHIST
SAPPIER > SAPPY
SAPPIEST > SAPPY
SAPPILY > SAPPY
SAPPINESS > SAPPY
SAPPING > SAP
SAPPLE *vb* Scots word meaning wash in water
SAPPLED > SAPPLE
SAPPLES > SAPPLE
SAPPLING > SAPPLE
SAPPY *adj* (of plants) full of sap
SAPRAEMIA *n* blood poisoning caused by toxins of putrefactive bacteria
SAPRAEMIC **>** SAPRAEMIA
SAPREMIA *American spelling of* **>** SAPRAEMIA
SAPREMIAS > SAPREMIA
SAPREMIC > SAPREMIA
SAPROBE *n* organism that lives on decaying organisms
SAPROBES > SAPROBE
SAPROBIAL > SAPROBE
SAPROBIC > SAPROBE
SAPROLITE *n* deposit of earth, etc, formed by decomposition of rocks that has remained in its original site
SAPROPEL *n* unconsolidated sludge consisting of the decomposed remains of aquatic organisms at the bottoms of lakes and oceans
SAPROPELS > SAPROPEL
SAPROZOIC *adj* (of animals or plants) feeding on dead organic matter
SAPS > SAP
SAPSAGO *n* hard greenish

Swiss cheese made with sour skimmed milk and coloured and flavoured with clover
SAPSAGOS > SAPSAGO
SAPSUCKER *n* either of two North American woodpeckers
SAPUCAIA *n* Brazilian tree
SAPUCAIAS > SAPUCAIA
SAPWOOD *n* soft wood, just beneath the bark in tree trunks, that consists of living tissue
SAPWOODS > SAPWOOD
SAR *n* marine fish **▷** *vb* Scots word meaning savour
SARABAND *same as* **>** SARABANDE
SARABANDE *n* slow stately Spanish dance
SARABANDS > SARABANDE
SARAFAN *n* Russian woman's cloak
SARAFANS > SARAFAN
SARAN *n* any one of a class of thermoplastic resins
SARANGI *n* stringed instrument of India played with a bow
SARANGIS > SARANGI
SARANS > SARAN
SARAPE *n* serape
SARAPES > SARAPE
SARBACANE *n* type of blowpipe
SARCASM *n* (use of) bitter or wounding ironic language
SARCASMS > SARCASM
SARCASTIC *adj* full of or showing sarcasm
SARCENET *n* fine soft silk fabric formerly from Italy and used for clothing, ribbons, etc
SARCENETS > SARCENET
SARCINA *n* type of bacterium
SARCINAE > SARCINA
SARCINAS > SARCINA
SARCOCARP *n* fleshy mesocarp of such fruits as the peach or plum
SARCODE *n* material making up living cell
SARCODES > SARCODE
SARCODIC > SARCODE
SARCOID *adj* of, relating to, or resembling flesh **▷** *n* tumour resembling a sarcoma
SARCOIDS > SARCOID
SARCOLOGY *n* study of flesh
SARCOMA *n* malignant tumour beginning in connective tissue
SARCOMAS > SARCOMA
SARCOMATA > SARCOMA
SARCOMERE *n* any of the units that together comprise skeletal muscle
SARCONET *n* type of silk
SARCONETS > SARCONET

S

SARCOPTIC *adj* relating to mange

SARCOSOME *n* energy-producing tissue in muscle

SARCOUS *adj* (of tissue) muscular or fleshy

SARD *n* orange, red, or brown variety of chalcedony, used as a gemstone

SARDANA *n* Catalan dance

SARDANAS > SARDANA

SARDAR *n* title used before the name of Sikh men

SARDARS > SARDAR

SARDEL *n* small fish

SARDELLE *n* small fish

SARDELLES > SARDELLE

SARDELS > SARDEL

SARDINE *n* small fish of the herring family, usu preserved tightly packed in tins ▷ *vb* cram together

SARDINED > SARDINE

SARDINES > SARDINE

SARDINING > SARDINE

SARDIUS *same as* > SARD

SARDIUSES > SARDIUS

SARDONIAN *adj* sardonic

SARDONIC *adj* mocking or scornful

SARDONYX *n* brown-and-white gemstone

SARDS > SARD

SARED > SAR

SAREE *same as* > SARI

SAREES > SAREE

SARGASSO *same as* > SARGASSUM

SARGASSOS > SARGASSO

SARGASSUM *n* type of floating seaweed

SARGE *n* sergeant

SARGES > SARGE

SARGO *same as* > SARGUS

SARGOS *variant of* > SARGUS

SARGOSES > SARGOS

SARGUS *n* species of sea fish

SARGUSES > SARGUS

SARI *n* long piece of cloth draped around the body and over one shoulder, worn by Hindu women

SARIN *n* chemical used in warfare as a lethal nerve gas producing asphyxia

SARING > SAR

SARINS > SARIN

SARIS > SARI

SARK *n* shirt or (formerly) chemise

SARKIER > SARKY

SARKIEST > SARKY

SARKILY > SARKY

SARKINESS *n* quality of being sarcastic

SARKING *n* flat planking supporting the roof cladding of a building

SARKINGS > SARKING

SARKS > SARK

SARKY *adj* sarcastic

SARMENT *n* thin twig

SARMENTA > SARMENTUM

SARMENTS > SARMENT

SARMENTUM *n* runner on plant

SARMIE *n* sandwich

SARMIES > SARMIE

SARNEY *n* sandwich

SARNEYS > SARNEY

SARNIE *n* sandwich

SARNIES > SARNIE

SAROD *n* Indian stringed musical instrument that may be played with a bow or plucked

SARODE *n* Indian stringed instrument

SARODES > SARODE

SARODIST *n* sarod player

SARODISTS > SARODIST

SARODS > SAROD

SARONG *n* long piece of cloth tucked around the waist or under the armpits, worn esp in Malaysia

SARONGS > SARONG

SARONIC > SAROS

SAROS *n* cycle of about 18 years 11 days in which eclipses of the sun and moon occur in the same sequence

SAROSES > SAROS

SARPANCH *n* head of a panchayat

SARRASIN *n* buckwheat

SARRASINS > SARRASIN

SARRAZIN *n* buckwheat

SARRAZINS > SARRAZIN

SARS > SAR

SARSAR *same as* > SANSAR

SARSARS > SARSAR

SARSDEN *n* sarsen

SARSDENS > SARSDEN

SARSEN *n* boulder of silicified sandstone found in large numbers in S England

SARSENET *same as* > SARCENET

SARSENETS > SARSENET

SARSENS > SARSEN

SARSNET *n* type of silk

SARSNETS > SARSNET

SARTOR *humorous or literary word for* > TAILOR

SARTORIAL *adj* of men's clothes or tailoring

SARTORIAN *adj* of tailoring

SARTORII > SARTORIUS

SARTORIUS *n* long ribbon-shaped muscle that aids in flexing the knee

SARTORS > SARTOR

SARUS *n* Indian bird of crane family

SARUSES > SARUS

SASARARA *n* scolding

SASARARAS > SASARARA

SASER *n* device for amplifying ultrasound, working on a similar principle to a laser

SASERS > SASER

SASH *n* decorative strip of cloth worn round the waist or over one shoulder ▷ *vb* furnish with a sash, sashes, or sash windows

SASHAY *vb* move or walk in a casual or a showy manner

SASHAYED > SASHAY

SASHAYING > SASHAY

SASHAYS > SASHAY

SASHED > SASH

SASHES > SASH

SASHIMI *n* Japanese dish of thin fillets of raw fish

SASHIMIS > SASHIMI

SASHING > SASH

SASHLESS > SASH

SASIN *another name for* > BLACKBUCK

SASINE *n* granting of legal possession of feudal property

SASINES > SASINE

SASINS > SASIN

SASKATOON *n* species of serviceberry of W Canada

SASQUATCH *n* (in Canadian folklore) hairy beast or manlike monster said to leave huge footprints

SASS *n* insolent or impudent talk or behaviour ▷ *vb* talk or answer back in such a way

SASSABIES > SASSABY

SASSABY *n* African antelope of grasslands and semideserts

SASSAFRAS *n* American tree with aromatic bark used medicinally

SASSARARA *n* scolding

SASSE *n* old word meaning canal lock

SASSED > SASS

SASSES > SASS

SASSIER > SASSY

SASSIES > SASSY

SASSIEST > SASSY

SASSILY > SASSY

SASSINESS > SASSY

SASSING > SASS

SASSOLIN *n* boric acid

SASSOLINS > SASSOLIN

SASSOLITE *n* boric acid

SASSWOOD *same as* > SASSY

SASSWOODS > SASSWOOD

SASSY *adj* insolent, impertinent ▷ *n* W African leguminous tree with poisonous bark

SASSYWOOD *n* trial by ordeal in Liberia

SASTRA *same as* > SHASTRA

SASTRAS > SASTRA

SASTRUGA *n* one of a series of ridges on snow-covered plains, caused by the action of wind laden with ice particles

SASTRUGI > SASTRUGA

SAT > SIT

SATAI *same as* > SATAY

SATAIS > SATAI

SATANG *n* monetary unit of Thailand worth one hundredth of a baht

SATANGS > SATANG

SATANIC *adj* of Satan

SATANICAL *same as* > SATANIC

SATANISM *n* worship of the devil

SATANISMS > SATANISM

SATANIST > SATANISM

SATANISTS > SATANIST

SATANITY *n* quality of being satanic

SATARA *n* type of cloth

SATARAS > SATARA

SATAY *n* Indonesian and Malaysian dish consisting of pieces of chicken, pork, etc, grilled on skewers and served with peanut sauce

SATAYS > SATAY

SATCHEL *n* bag, usu with a shoulder strap, for carrying books

SATCHELED *adj* carrying a satchel

SATCHELS > SATCHEL

SATE *vb* satisfy (a desire or appetite) fully

SATED > SATE

SATEDNESS > SATE

SATEEN *n* glossy linen or cotton fabric, woven in such a way that it resembles satin

SATEENS > SATEEN

SATELESS *adj* old word meaning insatiable

SATELLES *n* species of bacteria

SATELLITE *n* man-made device orbiting in space ▷ *adj* of or used in the transmission of television signals from a satellite to the home ▷ *vb* transmit by communications satellite

SATEM *adj* denoting or belonging to a particular group of Indo-European languages

SATES > SATE

SATI *n* Indian widow suicide

SATIABLE *adj* capable of being satiated

SATIABLY > SATIABLE

SATIATE *vb* provide with more than enough, so as to disgust

SATIATED > SATIATE

SATIATES > SATIATE

SATIATING > SATIATE

SATIATION > SATIATE

SATIETIES > SATIETY

SATIETY *n* feeling of having had too much

SATIN *n* silky fabric with a glossy surface on one side ▷ *adj* like satin in texture

S

▷ *vb* cover with satin
SATINED > SATIN
SATINET *n* thin or imitation satin
SATINETS > SATINET
SATINETTA *n* thin satin
SATINETTE *same as* > SATINET
SATING > SATE
SATINING > SATIN
SATINPOD *n* honesty (the plant)
SATINPODS > SATINPOD
SATINS > SATIN
SATINWOOD *n* tropical tree yielding hard wood
SATINY > SATIN
SATIRE *n* use of ridicule to expose vice or folly
SATIRES > SATIRE
SATIRIC *same as* > SATIRICAL
SATIRICAL *adj* of, relating to, or containing satire
SATIRISE *same as* > SATIRIZE
SATIRISED > SATIRISE
SATIRISER > SATIRISE
SATIRISES > SATIRISE
SATIRIST *n* writer of satire
SATIRISTS > SATIRIST
SATIRIZE *vb* ridicule by means of satire
SATIRIZED > SATIRIZE
SATIRIZER > SATIRIZE
SATIRIZES > SATIRIZE
SATIS > SATI
SATISFICE *vb* act in such a way as to satisfy the minimum requirements for achieving a particular result
SATISFIED > SATISFY
SATISFIER > SATISFY
SATISFIES > SATISFY
SATISFY *vb* please, content
SATIVE *adj* old word meaning cultivated
SATORI *n* state of sudden indescribable intuitive enlightenment
SATORIS > SATORI
SATRAP *n* (in ancient Persia) a provincial governor or subordinate ruler
SATRAPAL > SATRAP
SATRAPIES > SATRAPY
SATRAPS > SATRAP
SATRAPY *n* province, office, or period of rule of a satrap
SATSUMA *n* kind of small orange
SATSUMAS > SATSUMA
SATURABLE *adj* capable of being saturated
SATURANT *n* substance that causes a solution, etc, to be saturated ▷ *adj* (of a substance) causing saturation

SATURANTS > SATURANT
SATURATE *vb* soak thoroughly
SATURATED *adj* (of a solution or solvent) containing the maximum amount of solute that can normally be dissolved at a given temperature and pressure
SATURATER > SATURATE
SATURATES > SATURATE
SATURATOR > SATURATE
SATURNIC *adj* poisoned by lead
SATURNIID *n* type of mainly tropical moth, usu with large brightly coloured wings
SATURNINE *adj* gloomy in temperament or appearance
SATURNISM *n* lead poisoning
SATURNIST *n* old word meaning glum person
SATYR *n* woodland god, part man, part goat
SATYRA *n* female satyr
SATYRAL *n* mythical beast in heraldry
SATYRALS > SATYRAL
SATYRAS > SATYRA
SATYRESS *n* female satyr
SATYRIC > SATYR
SATYRICAL > SATYR
SATYRID *n* butterfly with typically brown or dark wings with paler markings
SATYRIDS > SATYRID
SATYRISK *n* small satyr
SATYRISKS > SATYRISK
SATYRLIKE > SATYR
SATYRS > SATYR
SAU *archaic past tense of* > SEE
SAUBA *n* South American ant
SAUBAS > SAUBA
SAUCE *n* liquid added to food to enhance flavour ▷ *vb* prepare (food) with sauce
SAUCEBOAT *n* gravy boat
SAUCEBOX *n* saucy person
SAUCED > SAUCE
SAUCELESS > SAUCE
SAUCEPAN *n* cooking pot with a long handle
SAUCEPANS > SAUCEPAN
SAUCEPOT *n* cooking pot with lid
SAUCEPOTS > SAUCEPOT
SAUCER *n* small round dish put under a cup
SAUCERFUL > SAUCER
SAUCERS > SAUCER
SAUCES > SAUCE
SAUCH *n* sallow or willow
SAUCHS > SAUCH
SAUCIER *n* chef who makes sauces
SAUCIERS > SAUCIER
SAUCIEST > SAUCY

SAUCILY > SAUCY
SAUCINESS > SAUCY
SAUCING > SAUCE
SAUCISSE *n* type of explosive fuse
SAUCISSES > SAUCISSE
SAUCISSON *n* type of explosive fuse
SAUCY *adj* impudent
SAUFGARD *old form of* > SAFEGUARD
SAUFGARDS > SAUFGARD
SAUGER *n* small North American pikeperch
SAUGERS > SAUGER
SAUGH *same as* > SAUCH
SAUGHS > SAUGH
SAUGHY *adj* Scots word meaning made of willow
SAUL *Scots word for* > SOUL
SAULGE *n* old word for sage plant
SAULGES > SAULGE
SAULIE *n* Scots word meaning professional mourner
SAULIES > SAULIE
SAULS > SAUL
SAULT *n* waterfall in Canada
SAULTS > SAULT
SAUNA *n* Finnish-style steam bath ▷ *vb* have a sauna
SAUNAED > SAUNA
SAUNAING > SAUNA
SAUNAS > SAUNA
SAUNT *Scots form of* > SAINT
SAUNTED > SAUNT
SAUNTER *vb* walk in a leisurely manner, stroll ▷ *n* leisurely walk
SAUNTERED > SAUNTER
SAUNTERER > SAUNTER
SAUNTERS > SAUNTER
SAUNTING > SAUNT
SAUNTS > SAUNT
SAUREL *n* type of mackerel
SAURELS > SAUREL
SAURIAN *n* lizard
SAURIANS > SAURIAN
SAURIES > SAURY
SAUROID *adj* like a lizard
SAUROPOD *n* type of herbivorous dinosaur including the brontosaurus and the diplodocus
SAUROPODS > SAUROPOD
SAURY *n* type of fish of tropical and temperate seas, having an elongated body and long toothed jaws
SAUSAGE *n* minced meat in an edible tube-shaped skin
SAUSAGES > SAUSAGE
SAUT *Scot word for* > SALT
SAUTE *vb* fry quickly in a little fat ▷ *n* dish of sautéed food ▷ *adj* sautéed until lightly brown
SAUTED > SAUT
SAUTEED > SAUTE
SAUTEEING > SAUTE

SAUTEING > SAUTE
SAUTERNE *n* sauternes
SAUTERNES *n* sweet white French wine
SAUTES > SAUTE
SAUTING > SAUT
SAUTOIR *n* long necklace or pendant
SAUTOIRE *variant of* > SAUTOIR
SAUTOIRES > SAUTOIRE
SAUTOIRS > SAUTOIR
SAUTS > SAUT
SAV *short for* > SAVELOY
SAVABLE > SAVE
SAVAGE *adj* wild, untamed ▷ *n* uncivilized person ▷ *vb* attack ferociously
SAVAGED > SAVAGE
SAVAGEDOM > SAVAGE
SAVAGELY > SAVAGE
SAVAGER > SAVAGE
SAVAGERY *n* viciousness and cruelty
SAVAGES > SAVAGE
SAVAGEST > SAVAGE
SAVAGING > SAVAGE
SAVAGISM > SAVAGE
SAVAGISMS > SAVAGE
SAVANNA *n* open grasslands, usually with scattered bushes or trees, characteristic of much of tropical Africa
SAVANNAH *same as* > SAVANNA
SAVANNAHS > SAVANNAH
SAVANNAS > SAVANNA
SAVANT *n* learned person
SAVANTE > SAVANT
SAVANTES > SAVANT
SAVANTS > SAVANT
SAVARIN *n* type of cake
SAVARINS > SAVARIN
SAVATE *n* form of boxing in which blows may be delivered with the feet as well as the hands
SAVATES > SAVATE
SAVE *vb* rescue or preserve from harm, protect ▷ *n* act of preventing a goal ▷ *prep* except
SAVEABLE > SAVE
SAVED > SAVE
SAVEGARD *vb* old word meaning protect
SAVEGARDS > SAVEGARD
SAVELOY *n* spicy smoked sausage
SAVELOYS > SAVELOY
SAVER > SAVE
SAVERS > SAVE
SAVES > SAVE
SAVEY *vb* understand
SAVEYED > SAVEY
SAVEYING > SAVEY
SAVEYS > SAVEY
SAVIN *n* small spreading juniper bush of Europe, N Asia, and North America
SAVINE *same as* > SAVIN
SAVINES > SAVINE
SAVING *n* economy ▷ *prep*

S

except ▷ *adj* tending to save or preserve
SAVINGLY > SAVING
SAVINGS > SAVING
SAVINS > SAVIN
SAVIOR *same as* > SAVIOUR
SAVIORS > SAVIOR
SAVIOUR *n* person who rescues another
SAVIOURS > SAVIOUR
SAVOR *same as* > SAVOUR
SAVORED > SAVOR
SAVORER > SAVOR
SAVORERS > SAVOR
SAVORIER > SAVORY
SAVORIES > SAVORY
SAVORIEST > SAVORY
SAVORILY > SAVORY
SAVORING > SAVOR
SAVORLESS > SAVOUR
SAVOROUS > SAVOUR
SAVORS > SAVOR
SAVORY *same as* > SAVOURY
SAVOUR *vb* enjoy, relish ▷ *n* characteristic taste or odour
SAVOURED > SAVOUR
SAVOURER > SAVOUR
SAVOURERS > SAVOUR
SAVOURIER > SAVOURY
SAVOURIES > SAVOURY
SAVOURILY > SAVOURY
SAVOURING > SAVOUR
SAVOURLY *adv* old word meaning refreshingly
SAVOURS > SAVOUR
SAVOURY *adj* salty or spicy ▷ *n* savoury dish served before or after a meal
SAVOY *n* variety of cabbage
SAVOYARD *n* person keenly interested in the operettas of Gilbert and Sullivan
SAVOYARDS > SAVOYARD
SAVOYS > SAVOY
SAVS > SAV
SAVVEY *vb* understand
SAVVEYED > SAVVEY
SAVVEYING > SAVVEY
SAVVEYS > SAVVEY
SAVVIED > SAVVY
SAVVIER > SAVVY
SAVVIES > SAVVY
SAVVIEST > SAVVY
SAVVILY > SAVVY
SAVVINESS > SAVVY
SAVVY *vb* understand ▷ *n* understanding, intelligence ▷ *adj* shrewd
SAVVYING > SAVVY
SAW *n* hand tool for cutting wood and metal ▷ *vb* cut with a saw
SAWAH *n* paddyfield
SAWAHS > SAWAH
SAWBILL *n* type of hummingbird
SAWBILLS > SAWBILL
SAWBLADE *n* blade of a saw
SAWBLADES > SAWBLADE
SAWBONES *n* surgeon or doctor

SAWBUCK *n* sawhorse, esp one having an X-shaped supporting structure
SAWBUCKS > SAWBUCK
SAWDER *n* flattery ▷ *vb* flatter
SAWDERED > SAWDER
SAWDERING > SAWDER
SAWDERS > SAWDER
SAWDUST *n* fine wood fragments made in sawing ▷ *vb* cover with sawdust
SAWDUSTED > SAWDUST
SAWDUSTS > SAWDUST
SAWDUSTY > SAWDUST
SAWED > SAW
SAWER > SAW
SAWERS > SAW
SAWFISH *n* fish with a long toothed snout
SAWFISHES > SAWFISH
SAWFLIES > SAWFLY
SAWFLY *n* any of various hymenopterous insects
SAWGRASS *n* type of sedge with serrated leaves
SAWHORSE *n* structure for supporting wood that is being sawn
SAWHORSES > SAWHORSE
SAWING > SAW
SAWINGS > SAW
SAWLIKE > SAW
SAWLOG *n* log suitable for sawing
SAWLOGS > SAWLOG
SAWMILL *n* mill where timber is sawn into planks
SAWMILLS > SAWMILL
SAWN *past participle of* > SAW
SAWNEY *n* derogatory word for a fool
SAWNEYS > SAWNEY
SAWPIT *n* pit above which a log is sawn into planks
SAWPITS > SAWPIT
SAWS > SAW
SAWSHARK *n* shark with long sawlike snout
SAWSHARKS > SAWSHARK
SAWTEETH > SAWTOOTH
SAWTIMBER *n* wood for sawing
SAWTOOTH *adj* (of a waveform) having an amplitude that varies linearly with time between two values
SAWYER *n* person who saws timber for a living
SAWYERS > SAWYER
SAX *same as* > SAXOPHONE
SAXATILE *adj* living among rocks
SAXAUL *n* Asian tree
SAXAULS > SAXAUL
SAXE *as in saxe blue* light greyish-blue colour
SAXES > SAX
SAXHORN *n* valved brass instrument used chiefly in brass and military bands
SAXHORNS > SAXHORN
SAXICOLE *variant of*

> SAXATILE
SAXIFRAGE *n* alpine rock plant with small flowers
SAXITOXIN *n* poison extracted from mollusc
SAXONIES > SAXONY
SAXONITE *n* igneous rock
SAXONITES > SAXONITE
SAXONY *n* fine 3-ply yarn used for knitting and weaving
SAXOPHONE *n* brass wind instrument with keys and a curved body
SAXTUBA *n* bass saxhorn
SAXTUBAS > SAXTUBA
SAY *vb* speak or utter ▷ *n* right or chance to speak
SAYABLE > SAY
SAYED *same as* > SAYYID
SAYEDS > SAYED
SAYER > SAY
SAYERS > SAY
SAYEST > SAY
SAYID *same as* > SAYYID
SAYIDS > SAYID
SAYING > SAY
SAYINGS > SAY
SAYNE > SAY
SAYON *n* type of tunic
SAYONARA *n* Japanese farewell
SAYONARAS > SAYONARA
SAYONS > SAYON
SAYS > SAY
SAYST > SAY
SAYYID *n* Muslim claiming descent from Mohammed's grandson Husain
SAYYIDS > SAYYID
SAZ *n* Middle Eastern stringed instrument
SAZERAC *n* mixed drink of whisky, Pernod, syrup, bitters, and lemon
SAZERACS > SAZERAC
SAZES > SAZ
SAZHEN *n* Russian measure of length
SAZHENS > SAZHEN
SAZZES > SAZ
SBIRRI > SBIRRO
SBIRRO *n* Italian police officer
SCAB *n* crust formed over a wound ▷ *vb* become covered with a scab
SCABBARD *n* sheath for a sword or dagger
SCABBARDS > SCABBARD
SCABBED > SCAB
SCABBIER > SCABBY
SCABBIEST > SCABBY
SCABBILY > SCABBY
SCABBING > SCAB
SCABBLE *vb* shape (stone) roughly
SCABBLED > SCABBLE
SCABBLES > SCABBLE
SCABBLING > SCABBLE
SCABBY *adj* covered with scabs
SCABIES *n* itchy skin disease

SCABIETIC > SCABIES
SCABIOSA *n* flowering plant
SCABIOSAS > SCABIOSA
SCABIOUS *n* plant with showy blue, red, or whitish dome-shaped flower heads ▷ *adj* having or covered with scabs
SCABLAND *n* barren rocky land
SCABLANDS *npl* type of terrain consisting of bare rock surfaces, with little or no soil cover and scanty vegetation
SCABLIKE > SCAB
SCABRID *adj* having a rough or scaly surface
SCABROUS *adj* rough and scaly
SCABS > SCAB
SCAD *n* any of various carangid fishes
SCADS *npl* large amount or number
SCAFF *n* Scots word meaning food
SCAFFIE *n* Scots word meaning street cleaner
SCAFFIES > SCAFFIE
SCAFFOLD *n* temporary platform for workmen ▷ *vb* provide with a scaffold
SCAFFOLDS > SCAFFOLD
SCAFFS > SCAFF
SCAG *n* tear in a garment or piece of cloth ▷ *vb* make a tear in (cloth)
SCAGGED > SCAG
SCAGGING > SCAG
SCAGLIA *n* type of limestone
SCAGLIAS > SCAGLIA
SCAGLIOLA *n* type of imitation marble made of glued gypsum
SCAGS > SCAG
SCAIL *n* Scots word meaning disperse
SCAILED > SCAIL
SCAILING > SCAIL
SCAILS > SCAIL
SCAITH *vb* old word meaning injure
SCAITHED > SCAITH
SCAITHING > SCAITH
SCAITHS > SCAITH
SCALA *n* passage inside the cochlea
SCALABLE *adj* capable of being scaled or climbed
SCALABLY > SCALABLE
SCALADE *short for*

> ESCALADE
SCALADES > SCALADE
SCALADO *same as*

> SCALADE
SCALADOS > SCALADO
SCALAE > SCALA
SCALAGE *n* percentage deducted from the price of goods liable to shrink or leak
SCALAGES > SCALAGE

SCALAR adj (variable quantity) having magnitude but no direction ▷ n quantity, such as time or temperature, that has magnitude but not direction
SCALARE another name for > ANGELFISH
SCALARES > SCALARE
SCALARS > SCALAR
SCALATION n way scales are arranged
SCALAWAG same as > SCALLYWAG
SCALAWAGS > SCALAWAG
SCALD same as > SKALD
SCALDED > SCALD
SCALDER > SCALD
SCALDERS > SCALD
SCALDFISH n small European flatfish
SCALDHEAD n diseased scalp
SCALDIC > SKALD
SCALDING > SCALD
SCALDINGS > SCALD
SCALDINI > SCALDINO
SCALDINO n Italian brazier
SCALDS > SCALD
SCALDSHIP n position of being Scandinavian poet
SCALE n one of the thin overlapping plates covering fishes and reptiles ▷ vb remove scales from
SCALEABLE same as > SCALABLE
SCALEABLY same as > SCALABLY
SCALED > SCALE
SCALELESS > SCALE
SCALELIKE > SCALE
SCALENE adj (of a triangle) with three unequal sides
SCALENI > SCALENUS
SCALENUS n any one of the three muscles situated on each side of the neck
SCALEPAN n part of scales holding weighed object
SCALEPANS > SCALEPAN
SCALER n person or thing that scales
SCALERS > SCALER
SCALES > SCALE
SCALETAIL n type of squirrel
SCALEUP n increase
SCALEUPS > SCALEUP
SCALEWORK n artistic representation of scales
SCALIER > SCALY
SCALIEST > SCALY
SCALINESS > SCALY
SCALING > SCALING
SCALINGS > SCALE
SCALL n disease of the scalp characterized by itching and scab formation
SCALLAWAG same as > SCALLYWAG
SCALLED > SCALL
SCALLIES > SCALLY

SCALLION same as > SHALLOT
SCALLIONS > SCALLION
SCALLOP n edible shellfish with two fan-shaped shells ▷ vb decorate (an edge) with scallops
SCALLOPED > SCALLOP
SCALLOPER > SCALLOP
SCALLOPS > SCALLOP
SCALLS > SCALL
SCALLY n rascal
SCALLYWAG n scamp, rascal
SCALOGRAM n scale for measuring opinion
SCALP n skin and hair on top of the head ▷ vb cut off the scalp of
SCALPED > SCALP
SCALPEL n small surgical knife
SCALPELS > SCALPEL
SCALPER > SCALP
SCALPERS > SCALP
SCALPING n process in which the top portion of a metal ingot is machined away before use
SCALPINGS > SCALPING
SCALPINS n small stones
SCALPLESS > SCALP
SCALPRUM n large scalpel
SCALPRUMS > SCALPRUM
SCALPS > SCALP
SCALY adj resembling or covered in scales
SCAM n dishonest scheme ▷ vb swindle (someone) by means of a trick
SCAMBLE vb scramble
SCAMBLED > SCAMBLE
SCAMBLER > SCAMBLE
SCAMBLERS > SCAMBLE
SCAMBLES > SCAMBLE
SCAMBLING > SCAMBLE
SCAMEL n Shakespearian word of uncertain meaning
SCAMELS > SCAMEL
SCAMMED > SCAM
SCAMMER n person who perpetrates a scam
SCAMMERS > SCAMMER
SCAMMING > SCAM
SCAMMONY n twining Asian convolvulus plant
SCAMP n mischievous child ▷ vb perform without care
SCAMPED > SCAMP
SCAMPER vb run about hurriedly or in play ▷ n scampering
SCAMPERED > SCAMP
SCAMPERER > SCAMPER
SCAMPERS > SCAMP
SCAMPI npl large prawns
SCAMPIES > SCAMPI
SCAMPING > SCAMP
SCAMPINGS > SCAMP
SCAMPIS > SCAMPI
SCAMPISH > SCAMP
SCAMPS > SCAMP
SCAMS > SCAM
SCAMSTER same as

> SCAMMER
SCAMSTERS > SCAMSTER
SCAMTO n argot of urban South African Blacks
SCAMTOS > SCAMTO
SCAN vb scrutinize carefully ▷ n scanning
SCAND > SCAN
SCANDAL n disgraceful action or event ▷ vb disgrace
SCANDALED > SCANDAL
SCANDALS > SCANDAL
SCANDENT adj (of plants) having a climbing habit
SCANDIA n scandium oxide
SCANDIAS > SCANDIA
SCANDIC adj of or containing scandium
SCANDIUM n rare silvery-white metallic element
SCANDIUMS > SCANDIUM
SCANNABLE > SCAN
SCANNED > SCAN
SCANNER n electronic device used for scanning
SCANNERS > SCANNER
SCANNING > SCAN
SCANNINGS > SCAN
SCANS > SCAN
SCANSION n metrical scanning of verse
SCANSIONS > SCANSION
SCANT adj barely sufficient, meagre ▷ vb limit in size or quantity ▷ adv scarcely
SCANTED > SCANT
SCANTER > SCANT
SCANTEST > SCANT
SCANTIER > SCANTY
SCANTIES n women's underwear
SCANTIEST > SCANTY
SCANTILY > SCANTY
SCANTING > SCANT
SCANTITY n quality of being scant
SCANTLE vb stint
SCANTLED > SCANTLE
SCANTLES > SCANTLE
SCANTLING n piece of sawn timber, such as a rafter, that has a small cross section
SCANTLY > SCANT
SCANTNESS > SCANT
SCANTS > SCANT
SCANTY adj barely sufficient or not sufficient
SCAPA variant of > SCARPER
SCAPAED > SCAPA
SCAPAING > SCAPA
SCAPAS > SCAPA
SCAPE n leafless stalk in plants that arises from a rosette of leaves and bears one or more flowers ▷ vb archaic word for escape
SCAPED > SCAPE
SCAPEGOAT n person made to bear the blame for

others ▷ vb make a scapegoat of
SCAPELESS adj allowing no escape
SCAPEMENT n escapement
SCAPES > SCAPE
SCAPHOID obsolete word for > NAVICULAR
SCAPHOIDS > SCAPHOID
SCAPHOPOD n type of marine mollusc of the class which includes tusk (or tooth) shells
SCAPI > SCAPUS
SCAPING > SCAPE
SCAPOLITE n any of a group of colourless, white, grey, or violet fluorescent minerals
SCAPOSE > SCAPE
SCAPPLE vb shape roughly
SCAPPLED > SCAPPLE
SCAPPLES > SCAPPLE
SCAPPLING > SCAPPLE
SCAPULA n shoulder blade
SCAPULAE > SCAPULA
SCAPULAR adj of the scapula ▷ n loose sleeveless garment worn by monks over their habits
SCAPULARS > SCAPULAR
SCAPULARY same as > SCAPULAR
SCAPULAS > SCAPULA
SCAPUS n flower stalk
SCAR n mark left by a healed wound ▷ vb mark or become marked with a scar
SCARAB n sacred beetle of ancient Egypt
SCARABAEI npl scarabs
SCARABEE n old word for scarab beetle
SCARABEES > SCARABEE
SCARABOID adj resembling a scarab beetle ▷ n beetle that resembles a scarab
SCARABS > SCARAB
SCARCE adj insufficient to meet demand
SCARCELY adv hardly at all
SCARCER > SCARCE
SCARCEST > SCARCE
SCARCITY n inadequate supply
SCARE vb frighten or be frightened ▷ n fright, sudden panic ▷ adj causing (needless) fear or alarm
SCARECROW n figure dressed in old clothes, set up to scare birds away from crops
SCARED > SCARE
SCAREDER > SCARE
SCAREDEST > SCARE
SCAREHEAD n newspaper headline intended to shock
SCARER > SCARE
SCARERS > SCARE
SCARES > SCARE
SCAREY adj frightening
SCARF n piece of material worn round the neck, head,

or shoulders ▷ *vb* join in
this way
SCARFED > SCARF
SCARFER > SCARF
SCARFERS > SCARF
SCARFING > SCARF
SCARFINGS > SCARF
SCARFISH *n* type of fish
SCARFPIN *n* decorative
pin securing scarf
SCARFPINS > SCARFPIN
SCARFS > SCARF
SCARFSKIN *n* outermost
layer of the skin
SCARFWISE *adv* like scarf
SCARIER > SCARY
SCARIEST > SCARY
SCARIFIED > SCARIFY
SCARIFIER > SCARIFY
SCARIFIES > SCARIFY
SCARIFY *vb* scratch or cut
slightly all over
SCARILY > SCARY
SCARINESS > SCARY
SCARING > SCARE
SCARIOSE *same as*
> SCARIOUS
SCARIOUS *adj* (of plant
parts) membranous, dry,
and brownish in colour
SCARLESS > SCAR
SCARLET *n* brilliant red
▷ *adj* bright red ▷ *vb* make
scarlet
SCARLETED > SCARLET
SCARLETS > SCARLET
SCARMOGE *n* old form of
skirmish
SCARMOGES > SCARMOGE
SCARP *n* steep slope ▷ *vb*
wear or cut so as to form a
steep slope
SCARPA *vb* run away
SCARPAED > SCARPA
SCARPAING > SCARPA
SCARPAS > SCARPA
SCARPED > SCARP
SCARPER *vb* run away ▷ *n*
hasty departure
SCARPERED > SCARPER
SCARPERS > SCARPER
SCARPETTI
> SCARPETTO
SCARPETTO *n* type of shoe
SCARPH *vb* join with scarf
joint
SCARPHED > SCARPH
SCARPHING > SCARPH
SCARPHS > SCARPH
SCARPINES *n* device for
torturing feet
SCARPING > SCARP
SCARPINGS > SCARP
SCARPS > SCARP
SCARRE *n* Shakespearian
word of unknown meaning
SCARRED > SCAR
SCARRES > SCARRE
SCARRIER > SCAR
SCARRIEST > SCAR
SCARRING > SCAR
SCARRINGS > SCAR
SCARRY > SCAR
SCARS > SCAR

SCART *vb* scratch or scrape
▷ *n* scratch or scrape
SCARTED > SCART
SCARTH *Scots word for*
> CORMORANT
SCARTHS > SCARTH
SCARTING > SCART
SCARTS > SCART
SCARVES > SCARF
SCARY *adj* frightening
SCAT *vb* go away ▷ *n* jazz
singing using improvised
vocal sounds instead of
words
SCATBACK *n* American
football player
SCATBACKS > SCATBACK
SCATCH *same as* > STILT
SCATCHES > SCATCH
SCATH *vb* old word
meaning injure
SCATHE *vb* attack with
severe criticism ▷ *n* harm
SCATHED > SCATHE
SCATHEFUL *adj* old word
meaning harmful
SCATHES > SCATHE
SCATHING *adj* harshly
critical
SCATHS > SCATH
SCATOLE *n* substance
found in coal
SCATOLES > SCATOLE
SCATOLOGY *n*
preoccupation with
obscenity, esp with
references to excrement
SCATS > SCAT
SCATT *n* old word meaning
tax ▷ *vb* tax
SCATTED > SCATT
SCATTER *vb* throw about
in various directions ▷ *n*
scattering
SCATTERED > SCATTER
SCATTERER > SCATTER
SCATTERS > SCATTER
SCATTERY *adj* dispersed
SCATTIER > SCATTY
SCATTIEST > SCATTY
SCATTILY > SCATTY
SCATTING > SCAT
SCATTINGS > SCAT
SCATTS > SCATT
SCATTY *adj* empty-headed
SCAUD *Scot word for*
> SCALD
SCAUDED > SCAUD
SCAUDING > SCAUD
SCAUDS > SCAUD
SCAUP *variant of* > SCALP
SCAUPED > SCAUP
SCAUPER *same as*
> SCORPER
SCAUPERS > SCAUPER
SCAUPING > SCAUP
SCAUPS > SCAUP
SCAUR *same as* > SCAR
SCAURED > SCAUR
SCAURIES > SCAURY
SCAURING > SCAUR
SCAURS > SCAUR
SCAURY *n* young seagull
SCAVAGE *n* old word

meaning toll
SCAVAGER > SCAVAGE
SCAVAGERS > SCAVAGE
SCAVAGES > SCAVAGE
SCAVENGE *vb* search for
(anything usable) among
discarded material
SCAVENGED > SCAVENGE
SCAVENGER *n* person who
scavenges
SCAVENGES > SCAVENGE
SCAW *n* headland
SCAWS > SCAW
SCAWTITE *n* mineral
containing calcium
SCAWTITES > SCAWTITE
SCAZON *n* metre in poetry
SCAZONS > SCAZON
SCAZONTES > SCAZON
SCAZONTIC > SCAZON
SCEAT *n* Anglo-Saxon coin
SCEATT *n* Anglo-Saxon
coin
SCEATTAS > SCEAT
SCEDULE *old spelling of*
> SCHEDULE
SCEDULED > SCEDULE
SCEDULES > SCEDULE
SCEDULING > SCEDULE
SCELERAT *n* villain
SCELERATE *n* villain
SCELERATS > SCELERAT
SCENA *n* scene in an opera,
usually longer than a single
aria
SCENARIES > SCENARY
SCENARIO *n* summary of
the plot of a play or film
SCENARIOS > SCENARIO
SCENARISE *same as*
> SCENARIZE
SCENARIST > SCENARIO
SCENARIZE *vb* create
scenario
SCENARY *n* scenery
SCENAS > SCENA
SCEND *vb* (of a vessel) to
surge upwards in a heavy
sea ▷ *n* upward heaving of
a vessel pitching
SCENDED > SCEND
SCENDING > SCEND
SCENDS > SCEND
SCENE *n* place of action of a
real or imaginary event ▷ *vb*
set in a scene
SCENED > SCENE
SCENEMAN *n* person
shifting stage scenery
SCENEMEN > SCENEMAN
SCENERIES > SCENERY
SCENERY *n* natural
features of a landscape
SCENES > SCENE
SCENESTER *n* person who
tries to fit into a particular
cultural scene
SCENIC *adj* picturesque
▷ *n* something scenic
SCENICAL > SCENE
SCENICS > SCENIC
SCENING > SCENE
SCENT *n* pleasant smell
▷ *vb* detect by smell

SCENTED > SCENT
SCENTFUL *adj* old word
meaning having scent
SCENTING > SCENT
SCENTINGS > SCENT
SCENTLESS > SCENT
SCENTS > SCENT
SCEPSIS *n* doubt
SCEPSISES > SCEPSIS
SCEPTER *same as*
> SCEPTRE
SCEPTERED > SCEPTER
SCEPTERS > SCEPTER
SCEPTIC *n* person who
habitually doubts generally
accepted beliefs ▷ *adj* of or
relating to sceptics
SCEPTICAL *adj* not
convinced that something
is true
SCEPTICS > SCEPTIC
SCEPTRAL *adj* royal
SCEPTRE *n* ornamental
rod symbolizing royal
power ▷ *vb* invest with
authority
SCEPTRED > SCEPTRE
SCEPTRES > SCEPTRE
SCEPTRING > SCEPTRE
SCEPTRY *adj* having
sceptre
SCERNE *vb* old word
meaning discern
SCERNED > SCERNE
SCERNES > SCERNE
SCERNING > SCERNE
SCHANSE *n* stones heaped
to shelter soldier in battle
SCHANSES > SCHANSE
SCHANTZE *n* stones
heaped to shelter soldier in
battle
SCHANTZES > SCHANTZE
SCHANZE *n* stones heaped
to shelter soldier in battle
SCHANZES > SCHANZE
SCHAPPE *n* yarn or fabric
made from waste silk
SCHAPPED > SCHAPPE
SCHAPPES > SCHAPPE
SCHAPSKA *n* cap worn by
lancer
SCHAPSKAS > SCHAPSKA
SCHATCHEN *same as*
> SHADCHAN
SCHAV *n* Polish soup
SCHAVS > SCHAV
SCHECHITA *n* slaughter of
animals according to
Jewish law
SCHEDULAR > SCHEDULE
SCHEDULE *n* plan of
procedure for a project ▷ *vb*
plan to occur at a certain
time
SCHEDULED *adj* arranged
or planned according to a
programme, timetable, etc
SCHEDULER > SCHEDULE
SCHEDULES > SCHEDULE
SCHEELITE *n* white,
brownish, or greenish
mineral
SCHELLIES > SCHELLY

SCHELLUM n Scots word meaning rascal
SCHELLUMS > SCHELLUM
SCHELLY n freshwater whitefish of the English Lake District
SCHELM n South African word meaning rascal
SCHELMS > SCHELM
SCHEMA n overall plan or diagram
SCHEMAS > SCHEMA
SCHEMATA > SCHEMA
SCHEMATIC adj presented as a plan or diagram ▷ n schematic diagram, esp of an electrical circuit
SCHEME n systematic plan ▷ vb plan in an underhand manner
SCHEMED > SCHEME
SCHEMER > SCHEME
SCHEMERS > SCHEME
SCHEMES > SCHEME
SCHEMIE n Scots derogatory word for a resident of a housing scheme
SCHEMIES > SCHEMIE
SCHEMING adj given to making plots ▷ n intrigues
SCHEMINGS > SCHEMING
SCHERZI > SCHERZO
SCHERZO n brisk lively piece of music
SCHERZOS > SCHERZO
SCHIAVONE n type of sword
SCHIEDAM n type of gin produced in the Netherlands
SCHIEDAMS > SCHIEDAM
SCHILLER n unusual iridescent or metallic lustre in some minerals
SCHILLERS > SCHILLER
SCHILLING n former monetary unit of Austria
SCHIMMEL n roan horse
SCHIMMELS > SCHIMMEL
SCHISM n (group resulting from) division in an organization
SCHISMA n musical term
SCHISMAS > SCHISMA
SCHISMS > SCHISM
SCHIST n crystalline rock which splits into layers
SCHISTOSE > SCHIST
SCHISTOUS > SCHIST
SCHISTS > SCHIST
SCHIZIER > SCHIZY
SCHIZIEST > SCHIZY
SCHIZO n derogatory term for a schizophrenic (person) ▷ adj schizophrenic
SCHIZOID adj abnormally introverted ▷ n schizoid person
SCHIZOIDS > SCHIZOID
SCHIZONT n cell formed from a trophozoite during the asexual stage of the life cycle of sporozoan protozoans

SCHIZONTS > SCHIZONT
SCHIZOPOD n any of various shrimplike crustaceans
SCHIZOS > SCHIZO
SCHIZY adj slang term meaning schizophrenic
SCHIZZIER > SCHIZZY
SCHIZZY adj slang term meaning schizophrenic
SCHLAGER n German duelling sword
SCHLAGERS > SCHLAGER
SCHLEMIEL n awkward or unlucky person whose endeavours usually fail
SCHLEMIHL same as > SCHLEMIEL
SCHLEP vb drag or lug (oneself or an object) with difficulty ▷ n stupid or clumsy person
SCHLEPP vb schlep
SCHLEPPED > SCHLEP
SCHLEPPER n incompetent person
SCHLEPPS > SCHLEPP
SCHLEPPY > SCHLEPP
SCHLEPS > SCHLEP
SCHLICH n finely crushed ore
SCHLICHS > SCHLICH
SCHLIERE n (in physics or geology) streak of different density or composition from surroundings
SCHLIEREN > SCHLIERE
SCHLIERIC > SCHLIERE
SCHLOCK n goods or produce of cheap or inferior quality ▷ adj cheap, inferior, or trashy
SCHLOCKER n thing of poor quality
SCHLOCKS > SCHLOCK
SCHLOCKY adj of poor quality
SCHLONG slang word for > PENIS
SCHLONGS > SCHLONG
SCHLOSS n castle
SCHLOSSES > SCHLOSS
SCHLUB n coarse or contemptible person
SCHLUBS > SCHLUB
SCHLUMP vb move in lazy way
SCHLUMPED > SCHLUMP
SCHLUMPS > SCHLUMP
SCHLUMPY > SCHLUMP
SCHMALTZ n excessive sentimentality
SCHMALTZY adj excessively sentimental
SCHMALZ same as > SCHMALTZ
SCHMALZES > SCHMALZ
SCHMALZY adj schmaltzy
SCHMATTE same as > SCHMUTTER
SCHMATTES > SCHMATTE
SCHMEAR n situation, matter, or affair ▷ vb spread or smear
SCHMEARED > SCHMEAR

SCHMEARS > SCHMEAR
SCHMECK n taste
SCHMECKS > SCHMECK
SCHMEER same as > SCHMEAR
SCHMEERED > SCHMEER
SCHMEERS > SCHMEER
SCHMELZ n ornamental glass
SCHMELZE variant of > SCHMELZ
SCHMELZES > SCHMELZ
SCHMICK adj (in Australia) excellent, elegant, or stylish
SCHMICKER > SCHMICK
SCHMO n dull, stupid, or boring person
SCHMOCK n stupid person
SCHMOCKS > SCHMOCK
SCHMOE n stupid person
SCHMOES > SCHMO
SCHMOOS variant of > SCHMOOSE
SCHMOOSE vb chat
SCHMOOSED > SCHMOOSE
SCHMOOSES > SCHMOOSE
SCHMOOZ n chat
SCHMOOZE vb chat or gossip ▷ n trivial conversation
SCHMOOZED > SCHMOOZE
SCHMOOZER > SCHMOOZE
SCHMOOZES > SCHMOOZE
SCHMOOZY > SCHMOOZE
SCHMOS > SCHMO
SCHMUCK n stupid or contemptible person
SCHMUCKS > SCHMUCK
SCHMUTTER n cloth or clothing
SCHNAPPER same as > SNAPPER
SCHNAPPS n strong alcoholic spirit
SCHNAPS same as > SCHNAPPS
SCHNAPSES > SCHNAPS
SCHNAUZER n wire-haired breed of dog of the terrier type, originally from Germany
SCHNECKE > SCHNECKEN
SCHNECKEN npl sweet spiral-shaped bread roll flavoured with cinnamon and nuts
SCHNELL adj German word meaning quick
SCHNITZEL n thin slice of meat, esp veal
SCHNOOK n stupid or gullible person
SCHNOOKS > SCHNOOK
SCHNORKEL less common variant of > SNORKEL
SCHNORR vb beg
SCHNORRED > SCHNORR
SCHNORRER n person who lives off the charity of others
SCHNORRS > SCHNORR
SCHNOZ n nose
SCHNOZES > SCHNOZ

SCHNOZZ n nose
SCHNOZZES > SCHNOZZ
SCHNOZZLE slang word for > NOSE
SCHOLAR n learned person
SCHOLARCH n head of school
SCHOLARLY > SCHOLAR
SCHOLARS > SCHOLAR
SCHOLIA > SCHOLIUM
SCHOLIAST n medieval annotator, esp of classical texts
SCHOLION n scholarly annotation
SCHOLIUM n commentary or annotation, esp on a classical text
SCHOLIUMS > SCHOLIUM
SCHOOL n place where children are taught or instruction is given in a subject ▷ vb educate or train
SCHOOLBAG n school pupil's bag
SCHOOLBOY n child attending school
SCHOOLDAY n day for going to school
SCHOOLE n old form of shoal
SCHOOLED > SCHOOL
SCHOOLERY n old word meaning something taught
SCHOOLES > SCHOOLE
SCHOOLIE n schoolteacher or a high-school student
SCHOOLIES > SCHOOLIE
SCHOOLING n education
SCHOOLKID n child who goes to school
SCHOOLMAN n scholar versed in the learning of the Schoolmen
SCHOOLMEN > SCHOOLMAN
SCHOOLS > SCHOOL
SCHOONER n sailing ship rigged fore-and-aft
SCHOONERS > SCHOONER
SCHORL n type of black tourmaline
SCHORLS > SCHORL
SCHOUT n council officer in Netherlands
SCHOUTS > SCHOUT
SCHRIK variant of > SKRIK
SCHRIKS > SCHRIK
SCHROD n young cod
SCHRODS > SCHROD
SCHTICK same as > SHTICK
SCHTICKS > SCHTICK
SCHTIK n schtick
SCHTIKS > SCHTIK
SCHTOOK n trouble
SCHTOOKS > SCHTOOK
SCHTOOM adj silent
SCHTUCK n trouble
SCHTUCKS > SCHTUCK
SCHTUM adj silent or dumb

S

SCHUIT n Dutch boat with flat bottom
SCHUITS > SCHUIT
SCHUL same as > SHUL
SCHULN > SCHUL
SCHULS > SCHUL
SCHUSS n straight high-speed downhill run ▷ vb perform a schuss
SCHUSSED > SCHUSS
SCHUSSER > SCHUSS
SCHUSSERS > SCHUSS
SCHUSSES > SCHUSS
SCHUSSING > SCHUSS
SCHUYT n Dutch boat with flat bottom
SCHUYTS > SCHUYT
SCHVARTZE n Yiddish word for black person
SCHWA n central vowel representing the sound that occurs in unstressed syllables in English
SCHWARTZE same as > SCHVARTZE
SCHWAS > SCHWA
SCIAENID adj of or relating to a family of mainly tropical and subtropical marine percoid fishes ▷ n any of these fish
SCIAENIDS > SCIAENID
SCIAENOID same as > SCIAENID
SCIAMACHY n fight with an imaginary enemy
SCIARID n small fly
SCIARIDS > SCIARID
SCIATIC adj of the hip ▷ n sciatic part of the body
SCIATICA n severe pain in the large nerve in the back of the leg
SCIATICAL > SCIATICA
SCIATICAS > SCIATICA
SCIATICS > SCIATIC
SCIENCE n systematic study and knowledge of natural or physical phenomena
SCIENCED adj old word meaning learned
SCIENCES > SCIENCE
SCIENT adj old word meaning scientific
SCIENTER adv knowingly
SCIENTIAL adj of or relating to science
SCIENTISE same as > SCIENTIZE
SCIENTISM n application of, or belief in, the scientific method
SCIENTIST n person who studies or practises a science
SCIENTIZE vb treat scientifically
SCILICET adv namely
SCILLA n a plant with small bell-shaped flowers
SCILLAS > SCILLA
SCIMETAR n scimitar
SCIMETARS > SCIMETAR
SCIMITAR n curved

oriental sword
SCIMITARS > SCIMITAR
SCIMITER n scimitar
SCIMITERS > SCIMITER
SCINCOID adj of, relating to, or resembling a skink ▷ n any animal, esp a lizard, resembling a skink
SCINCOIDS > SCINCOID
SCINTILLA n very small amount
SCIOLISM n practice of opinionating on subjects of which one has only superficial knowledge
SCIOLISMS > SCIOLISM
SCIOLIST > SCIOLISM
SCIOLISTS > SCIOLISM
SCIOLOUS > SCIOLISM
SCIOLTO adv musical direction meaning freely
SCIOMACHY same as > SCIAMACHY
SCIOMANCY n divination with the help of ghosts
SCION n descendant or heir
SCIONS > SCION
SCIOPHYTE n any plant that grows best in the shade
SCIOSOPHY n unscientific system of knowledge
SCIROC n hot Mediterranean wind
SCIROCCO n hot Mediterranean wind
SCIROCCOS > SCIROCCO
SCIROCS > SCIROC
SCIRRHI > SCIRRHUS
SCIRRHOID > SCIRRHUS
SCIRRHOUS adj of or resembling a scirrhus
SCIRRHUS n hard cancerous growth composed of fibrous tissues
SCISSEL n waste metal left over from sheet metal after discs have been punched out of it
SCISSELS > SCISSEL
SCISSIL n scissel
SCISSILE adj capable of being cut or divided
SCISSILS > SCISSIL
SCISSION n act or an instance of cutting, splitting, or dividing
SCISSIONS > SCISSION
SCISSOR vb cut (an object) with scissors
SCISSORED > SCISSOR
SCISSORER > SCISSOR
SCISSORS npl cutting instrument with two crossed pivoted blades
SCISSURE n longitudinal cleft
SCISSURES > SCISSURE
SCIURID n squirrel or related rodent
SCIURIDS > SCIURID
SCIURINE adj relating to a family of rodents that includes squirrels, marmots, and chipmunks

▷ n any sciurine animal
SCIURINES > SCIURINE
SCIUROID adj (of an animal) resembling a squirrel
SCLAFF vb cause (the club) to hit (the ground behind the ball) when making a stroke ▷ n sclaffing stroke or shot
SCLAFFED > SCLAFF
SCLAFFER > SCLAFF
SCLAFFERS > SCLAFF
SCLAFFING > SCLAFF
SCLAFFS > SCLAFF
SCLATE vb Scots word meaning slate
SCLATES > SCLATE
SCLAUNDER n old form of slander
SCLAVE n old form of slave
SCLAVES > SCLAVE
SCLERA n tough white substance that forms the outer covering of the eyeball
SCLERAE > SCLERA
SCLERAL > SCLERA
SCLERAS > SCLERA
SCLERE n supporting anatomical structure, esp a sponge spicule
SCLEREID n type of biological cell
SCLEREIDE n type of biological cell
SCLEREIDS > SCLEREID
SCLEREMA n condition in which body tissues harden
SCLEREMAS > SCLEREMA
SCLERES > SCLERE
SCLERITE n any of the hard chitinous plates that make up the exoskeleton of an arthropod
SCLERITES > SCLERITE
SCLERITIC > SCLERITE
SCLERITIS n inflammation of the sclera
SCLEROID adj (of organisms and their parts) hard or hardened
SCLEROMA n any small area of abnormally hard tissue, esp in a mucous membrane
SCLEROMAS > SCLEROMA
SCLEROSAL > SCLEROSIS
SCLEROSE vb affect with sclerosis
SCLEROSED adj hardened
SCLEROSES > SCLEROSIS
SCLEROSIS n abnormal hardening of body tissues
SCLEROTAL n bony area in sclerotic
SCLEROTIA npl masses of hyphae formed in certain fungi
SCLEROTIC same as > SCLERA
SCLEROTIN n protein in the cuticle of insects that

becomes hard and dark
SCLEROUS adj hard
SCLIFF n Scots word for small piece
SCLIFFS > SCLIFF
SCLIM vb Scots word meaning climb
SCLIMMED > SCLIM
SCLIMMING > SCLIM
SCLIMS > SCLIM
SCODIER > SCODY
SCODIEST > SCODY
SCODY adj unkempt
SCOFF vb express derision ▷ n mocking expression
SCOFFED > SCOFF
SCOFFER > SCOFF
SCOFFERS > SCOFF
SCOFFING > SCOFF
SCOFFINGS > SCOFF
SCOFFLAW n person who habitually flouts or violates the law
SCOFFLAWS > SCOFFLAW
SCOFFS > SCOFF
SCOG vb shelter
SCOGGED > SCOG
SCOGGING > SCOG
SCOGS > SCOG
SCOINSON n part of door or window frame
SCOINSONS > SCOINSON
SCOLD vb find fault with, reprimand ▷ n person who scolds
SCOLDABLE > SCOLD
SCOLDED > SCOLD
SCOLDER > SCOLD
SCOLDERS > SCOLD
SCOLDING > SCOLD
SCOLDINGS > SCOLD
SCOLDS > SCOLD
SCOLECES > SCOLEX
SCOLECID n variety of worm
SCOLECIDS > SCOLECID
SCOLECITE n white zeolite mineral
SCOLECOID adj like scolex
SCOLEX n headlike part of a tapeworm
SCOLIA > SCOLION
SCOLICES > SCOLEX
SCOLIOMA n condition with abnormal curvature of spine
SCOLIOMAS > SCOLIOMA
SCOLION n ancient Greek drinking song
SCOLIOSES > SCOLIOSIS
SCOLIOSIS n abnormal lateral curvature of the spine
SCOLIOTIC > SCOLIOSIS
SCOLLOP variant of > SCALLOP
SCOLLOPED > SCOLLOP
SCOLLOPS > SCOLLOP
SCOLYTID n type of beetle
SCOLYTIDS > SCOLYTID
SCOLYTOID n type of beetle

SCOMBRID n fish of mackerel family
SCOMBRIDS > SCOMBRID
SCOMBROID adj relating to a suborder of marine spiny-finned fishes ▷ n any fish belonging to this suborder
SCOMFISH vb Scots word meaning stifle
SCONCE n bracket on a wall for holding candles or lights ▷ vb challenge (a fellow student) on the grounds of a social misdemeanour to drink a large quantity of beer without stopping
SCONCED > SCONCE
SCONCES > SCONCE
SCONCHEON n part of door or window frame
SCONCING > SCONCE
SCONE n small plain cake baked in an oven or on a griddle
SCONES > SCONE
SCONTION n part of door or window frame
SCONTIONS > SCONTION
SCOOBIES > SCOOBY
SCOOBY n clue; notion
SCOOCH vb compress one's body into smaller space
SCOOCHED > SCOOCH
SCOOCHES > SCOOCH
SCOOCHING > SCOOCH
SCOOG vb shelter
SCOOGED > SCOOG
SCOOGING > SCOOG
SCOOGS > SCOOG
SCOOP n shovel-like tool for ladling or hollowing out ▷ vb take up or hollow out with or as if with a scoop
SCOOPABLE > SCOOP
SCOOPED > SCOOP
SCOOPER > SCOOP
SCOOPERS > SCOOP
SCOOPFUL > SCOOP
SCOOPFULS > SCOOP
SCOOPING > SCOOP
SCOOPINGS > SCOOP
SCOOPS > SCOOP
SCOOPSFUL > SCOOP
SCOOSH vb squirt ▷ n squirt or rush of liquid
SCOOSHED > SCOOSH
SCOOSHES > SCOOSH
SCOOSHING > SCOOSH
SCOOT vb leave or move quickly ▷ n act of scooting
SCOOTCH same as > SCOOCH
SCOOTCHED > SCOOTCH
SCOOTCHES > SCOOTCH
SCOOTED > SCOOT
SCOOTER n child's vehicle propelled by pushing on the ground with one foot
SCOOTERS > SCOOTER
SCOOTING > SCOOT
SCOOTS > SCOOT
SCOP n (in Anglo-Saxon England) a bard or minstrel

SCOPA n tuft of hairs on the abdomen or hind legs of bees, used for collecting pollen
SCOPAE > SCOPA
SCOPATE adj having tuft
SCOPE n opportunity for using abilities ▷ vb look at or examine carefully
SCOPED > SCOPE
SCOPELID n deep-sea fish
SCOPELIDS > SCOPELID
SCOPELOID n deep-sea fish
SCOPES > SCOPE
SCOPING > SCOPE
SCOPOLINE n soluble crystalline alkaloid
SCOPS > SCOP
SCOPULA n small tuft of dense hairs on the legs and chelicerae of some spiders
SCOPULAE > SCOPULA
SCOPULAS > SCOPULA
SCOPULATE > SCOPULA
SCORBUTIC adj of or having scurvy
SCORCH vb burn on the surface ▷ n slight burn
SCORCHED > SCORCH
SCORCHER n very hot day
SCORCHERS > SCORCHER
SCORCHES > SCORCH
SCORCHING > SCORCH
SCORDATO adj musical term meaning out of tune
SCORE n points gained in a game or competition ▷ vb gain (points) in a game
SCORECARD n card on which scores are recorded in games such as golf
SCORED > SCORE
SCORELESS adj without anyone scoring
SCORELINE n final score in game
SCOREPAD n pad for recording score in game
SCOREPADS > SCOREPAD
SCORER > SCORE
SCORERS > SCORE
SCORES > SCORE
SCORIA n mass of solidified lava containing many cavities
SCORIAC > SCORIA
SCORIAE > SCORIA
SCORIFIED > SCORIFY
SCORIFIER > SCORIFY
SCORIFIES > SCORIFY
SCORIFY vb remove (impurities) from metals by forming scoria
SCORING n act or practice of scoring
SCORINGS > SCORING
SCORIOUS > SCORIA
SCORN n open contempt ▷ vb despise
SCORNED > SCORN
SCORNER > SCORN
SCORNERS > SCORN
SCORNFUL > SCORN

SCORNING > SCORN
SCORNINGS > SCORN
SCORNS > SCORN
SCORODITE n mineral containing iron and aluminium
SCORPER n kind of fine chisel with a square or curved tip
SCORPERS > SCORPER
SCORPIOID adj of, relating to, or resembling scorpions
SCORPION n small lobster-shaped animal with a sting at the end of a jointed tail
SCORPIONS > SCORPION
SCORRENDO adj musical term meaning gliding
SCORSE vb exchange
SCORSED > SCORSE
SCORSER > SCORSE
SCORSERS > SCORSE
SCORSES > SCORSE
SCORSING > SCORSE
SCOT n payment or tax
SCOTCH vb put an end to ▷ n gash
SCOTCHED > SCOTCH
SCOTCHES > SCOTCH
SCOTCHING > SCOTCH
SCOTER n type of sea duck
SCOTERS > SCOTER
SCOTIA n deep concave moulding
SCOTIAS > SCOTIA
SCOTOMA n blind spot
SCOTOMAS > SCOTOMA
SCOTOMATA > SCOTOMA
SCOTOMIA n dizziness
SCOTOMIAS > SCOTOMIA
SCOTOMIES > SCOTOMY
SCOTOMY n dizziness
SCOTOPHIL adj liking darkness
SCOTOPIA n ability of the eye to adjust for night vision
SCOTOPIAS > SCOTOPIA
SCOTOPIC > SCOTOPIA
SCOTS > SCOT
SCOTTIE n type of small sturdy terrier
SCOTTIES > SCOTTIE
SCOUG vb shelter
SCOUGED > SCOUG
SCOUGING > SCOUG
SCOUGS > SCOUG
SCOUNDREL n cheat or deceiver
SCOUP vb Scots word meaning jump
SCOUPED > SCOUP
SCOUPING > SCOUP
SCOUPS > SCOUP
SCOUR vb clean or polish by rubbing with something rough ▷ n scouring
SCOURED > SCOUR
SCOURER > SCOUR
SCOURERS > SCOUR
SCOURGE n person or thing causing severe suffering

▷ vb cause severe suffering to
SCOURGED > SCOURGE
SCOURGER > SCOURGE
SCOURGERS > SCOURGE
SCOURGES > SCOURGE
SCOURGING > SCOURGE
SCOURIE n young seagull
SCOURIES > SCOURIE
SCOURING > SCOUR
SCOURINGS npl residue left after cleaning grain
SCOURS > SCOUR
SCOURSE vb exchange
SCOURSED > SCOURSE
SCOURSES > SCOURSE
SCOURSING > SCOURSE
SCOUSE n stew made from left-over meat
SCOUSER n inhabitant of Liverpool
SCOUSERS > SCOUSER
SCOUSES > SCOUSE
SCOUT n person sent out to reconnoitre ▷ vb act as a scout
SCOUTED > SCOUT
SCOUTER > SCOUT
SCOUTERS > SCOUT
SCOUTH n Scots word meaning plenty of scope
SCOUTHER vb Scots word meaning scorch
SCOUTHERS > SCOUTHER
SCOUTHERY > SCOUTHER
SCOUTHS > SCOUTH
SCOUTING > SCOUT
SCOUTINGS > SCOUT
SCOUTS > SCOUT
SCOW n unpowered barge used for carrying freight ▷ vb transport by scow
SCOWDER vb Scots word meaning scorch
SCOWDERED > SCOWDER
SCOWDERS > SCOWDER
SCOWED > SCOW
SCOWING > SCOW
SCOWL n (have) an angry or sullen expression ▷ vb have an angry or bad-tempered facial expression
SCOWLED > SCOWL
SCOWLER n person who scowls
SCOWLERS > SCOWLER
SCOWLING > SCOWL
SCOWLS > SCOWL
SCOWP vb Scots word meaning jump
SCOWPED > SCOWP
SCOWPING > SCOWP
SCOWPS > SCOWP
SCOWRER n old word meaning hooligan
SCOWRERS > SCOWRER
SCOWRIE n young seagull
SCOWRIES > SCOWRIE
SCOWS > SCOW
SCOWTH n Scots word meaning plenty of scope
SCOWTHER vb Scots word meaning scorch
SCOWTHERS > SCOWTHER

S

SCOWTHS > SCOWTH

SCOZZA n rowdy person, esp one who drinks a lot of alcohol

SCOZZAS > SCOZZA

SCRAB vb scratch

SCRABBED > SCRAB

SCRABBING > SCRAB

SCRABBLE vb scrape at with the hands, feet, or claws ▷ n board game in which words are formed by letter tiles

SCRABBLED > SCRABBLE

SCRABBLER > SCRABBLE

SCRABBLES > SCRABBLE

SCRABBLY adj covered with stunted trees

SCRABS > SCRAB

SCRAE Scots word for > SCREE

SCRAES > SCRAE

SCRAG n thin end of a neck of mutton ▷ vb wring the neck of

SCRAGGED > SCRAG

SCRAGGIER > SCRAGGY

SCRAGGILY > SCRAGGY

SCRAGGING > SCRAG

SCRAGGLY adj untidy or irregular

SCRAGGY adj thin, bony

SCRAGS > SCRAG

SCRAICH vb Scots word meaning scream

SCRAICHED > SCRAICH

SCRAICHS > SCRAICH

SCRAIGH vb Scots word meaning scream

SCRAIGHED > SCRAIGH

SCRAIGHS > SCRAIGH

SCRAM vb go away quickly ▷ n emergency shutdown of a nuclear reactor

SCRAMB vb scratch with nails or claws

SCRAMBED > SCRAMB

SCRAMBING > SCRAMB

SCRAMBLE vb climb or crawl hastily or awkwardly ▷ n scrambling

SCRAMBLED > SCRAMBLE

SCRAMBLER n electronic device that makes transmitted speech unintelligible

SCRAMBLES > SCRAMBLE

SCRAMBS > SCRAMB

SCRAMJET n type of jet engine

SCRAMJETS > SCRAMJET

SCRAMMED > SCRAM

SCRAMMING > SCRAM

SCRAMS > SCRAM

SCRAN n food

SCRANCH vb crunch

SCRANCHED > SCRANCH

SCRANCHES > SCRANCH

SCRANNEL adj thin ▷ n thin person or thing

SCRANNELS > SCRANNEL

SCRANNIER > SCRANNY

SCRANNY adj scrawny

SCRANS > SCRAN

SCRAP n small piece ▷ vb discard as useless

SCRAPABLE > SCRAPE

SCRAPBOOK n book with blank pages in which newspaper cuttings or pictures are stuck ▷ vb keep (cuttings etc) in a scrapbook

SCRAPE vb rub with something rough or sharp ▷ n act or sound of scraping

SCRAPED > SCRAPE

SCRAPEGUT n old word for fiddle player

SCRAPER > SCRAPE

SCRAPERS > SCRAPE

SCRAPES > SCRAPE

SCRAPHEAP n pile of discarded material

SCRAPIE n disease of sheep and goats

SCRAPIES > SCRAPIE

SCRAPING n act of scraping

SCRAPINGS > SCRAPING

SCRAPPAGE n act of scrapping

SCRAPPED > SCRAP

SCRAPPER n person who scraps

SCRAPPERS > SCRAPPER

SCRAPPIER > SCRAPPY

SCRAPPILY > SCRAPPY

SCRAPPING > SCRAP

SCRAPPLE n scraps of pork cooked with cornmeal and formed into a loaf

SCRAPPLES > SCRAPPLE

SCRAPPY adj fragmentary, disjointed

SCRAPS > SCRAP

SCRAPYARD n place for scrap metal

SCRAT vb scratch

SCRATCH vb mark or cut with claws, nails, or anything rough or sharp ▷ n wound, mark, or sound made by scratching ▷ adj put together at short notice

SCRATCHED > SCRATCH

SCRATCHER n person, animal, or thing that scratches

SCRATCHES n disease of horses characterized by dermatitis in the region of the fetlock

SCRATCHIE n scratchcard

SCRATCHY > SCRATCH

SCRATS > SCRAT

SCRATTED > SCRAT

SCRATTING > SCRAT

SCRATTLE vb dialect word meaning scratch

SCRATTLED > SCRATTLE

SCRATTLES > SCRATTLE

SCRAUCH vb squawk

SCRAUCHED > SCRAUCH

SCRAUCHS > SCRAUCH

SCRAUGH vb squawk

SCRAUGHED > SCRAUGH

SCRAUGHS > SCRAUGH

SCRAW n sod from the surface of a peat bog or from a field

SCRAWL vb write carelessly or hastily ▷ n scribbled writing

SCRAWLED > SCRAWL

SCRAWLER > SCRAWL

SCRAWLERS > SCRAWL

SCRAWLIER > SCRAWL

SCRAWLING > SCRAWL

SCRAWLS > SCRAWL

SCRAWLY > SCRAWL

SCRAWM vb dialect word meaning scratch

SCRAWMED > SCRAWM

SCRAWMING > SCRAWM

SCRAWMS > SCRAWM

SCRAWNIER > SCRAWNY

SCRAWNILY > SCRAWNY

SCRAWNY adj thin and bony

SCRAWP vb scratch (the skin) to relieve itching

SCRAWPED > SCRAWP

SCRAWPING > SCRAWP

SCRAWPS > SCRAWP

SCRAWS > SCRAW

SCRAY n tern

SCRAYE n tern

SCRAYES > SCRAYE

SCRAYS > SCRAY

SCREAK vb screech or creak ▷ n screech or creak

SCREAKED > SCREAK

SCREAKIER > SCREAK

SCREAKING > SCREAK

SCREAKS > SCREAK

SCREAKY > SCREAK

SCREAM vb utter a piercing cry, esp of fear or pain ▷ n shrill piercing cry

SCREAMED > SCREAM

SCREAMER n person or thing that screams

SCREAMERS > SCREAMER

SCREAMING > SCREAM

SCREAMO n type of emo music featuring screaming vocals

SCREAMOS > SCREAMO

SCREAMS > SCREAM

SCREE n slope of loose shifting stones

SCREECH n (utter) a shrill cry ▷ vb utter a shrill cry

SCREECHED > SCREECH

SCREECHER > SCREECH

SCREECHES > SCREECH

SCREECHY adj loud and shrill

SCREED n long tedious piece of writing ▷ vb rip

SCREEDED > SCREED

SCREEDER > SCREED

SCREEDERS > SCREED

SCREEDING > SCREED

SCREEDS > SCREED

SCREEN n surface of a television set, VDU, etc, on which an image is formed ▷ vb shelter or conceal with or as if with a screen

SCREENED > SCREEN

SCREENER > SCREEN

SCREENERS > SCREEN

SCREENFUL > SCREEN

SCREENIE n informal Australian word for screensaver

SCREENIES > SCREENIE

SCREENING > SCREEN

SCREENS > SCREEN

SCREES > SCREE

SCREET vb shed tears ▷ n act or sound of crying

SCREETED > SCREET

SCREETING > SCREET

SCREETS > SCREET

SCREEVE vb write

SCREEVED > SCREEVE

SCREEVER > SCREEVE

SCREEVERS > SCREEVE

SCREEVES > SCREEVE

SCREEVING > SCREEVE

SCREICH same as > SCREIGH

SCREICHED > SCREICH

SCREICHS > SCREICH

SCREIGH Scot word for > SCREECH

SCREIGHED > SCREIGH

SCREIGHS > SCREIGH

SCREW n metal pin with a spiral ridge along its length, twisted into materials to fasten them together ▷ vb turn (a screw)

SCREWABLE > SCREW

SCREWBALL n odd or eccentric person ▷ adj crazy or eccentric

SCREWBEAN n variety of mesquite

SCREWED adj fastened by a screw or screws

SCREWER > SCREW

SCREWERS > SCREW

SCREWIER > SCREWY

SCREWIEST > SCREWY

SCREWING > SCREW

SCREWINGS > SCREW

SCREWLIKE > SCREW

SCREWS > SCREW

SCREWTOP n lid with a threaded rim that is turned to close it securely

SCREWTOPS > SCREWTOP

SCREWUP n something done badly

SCREWUPS > SCREWUP

SCREWWORM n larva of a fly that develops beneath the skin of living mammals often causing illness or death

SCREWY adj crazy or eccentric

SCRIBABLE > SCRIBE

SCRIBAL > SCRIBE

SCRIBBLE vb write hastily or illegibly ▷ n something scribbled

SCRIBBLED > SCRIBBLE

SCRIBBLER n often derogatory term for a writer of poetry, novels, journalism, etc

SCRIBBLES > SCRIBBLE

SCRIBBLY > SCRIBBLE

SCRIBE n person who copies documents ▷ vb to score a line with a pointed instrument

SCRIBED > SCRIBE

SCRIBER n pointed steel tool used to score materials as a guide to cutting, etc

SCRIBERS > SCRIBER

SCRIBES > SCRIBE

SCRIBING > SCRIBE

SCRIBINGS > SCRIBE

SCRIBISM > SCRIBE

SCRIBISMS > SCRIBE

SCRIECH vb Scots word meaning screech

SCRIECHED > SCRIECH

SCRIECHS > SCRIECH

SCRIED > SCRY

SCRIENE n old form of screen

SCRIENES > SCRIENE

SCRIES > SCRY

SCRIEVE vb Scots word meaning write

SCRIEVED > SCRIEVE

SCRIEVES > SCRIEVE

SCRIEVING > SCRIEVE

SCRIGGLE vb wriggle

SCRIGGLED > SCRIGGLE

SCRIGGLES > SCRIGGLE

SCRIGGLY > SCRIGGLE

SCRIKE vb old word meaning shriek

SCRIKED > SCRIKE

SCRIKES > SCRIKE

SCRIKING > SCRIKE

SCRIM n open-weave muslin or hessian fabric, used in upholstery, lining, building

SCRIMMAGE n rough or disorderly struggle ▷ vb engage in a scrimmage

SCRIMP vb be very economical

SCRIMPED > SCRIMP

SCRIMPER > SCRIMP

SCRIMPERS > SCRIMP

SCRIMPIER > SCRIMP

SCRIMPILY > SCRIMP

SCRIMPING > SCRIMP

SCRIMPIT adj Scots word meaning ungenerous

SCRIMPLY adv sparingly

SCRIMPS > SCRIMP

SCRIMPY > SCRIMP

SCRIMS > SCRIM

SCRIMSHAW n art of decorating or carving shells, etc, done by sailors as a leisure activity ▷ vb produce scrimshaw (from)

SCRIMURE old word for > FENCER

SCRIMURES > SCRIMURE

SCRINE n old form of shrine

SCRINES > SCRINE

SCRIP n certificate representing a claim to stocks or shares

SCRIPPAGE n contents of scrip

SCRIPS > SCRIP

SCRIPT n text of a film, play, or TV programme ▷ vb write a script for

SCRIPTED > SCRIPT

SCRIPTER n person who writes scripts for films, play, or television dramas

SCRIPTERS > SCRIPTER

SCRIPTING > SCRIPT

SCRIPTORY adj of writing

SCRIPTS > SCRIPT

SCRIPTURE n sacred writings of a religion

SCRITCH vb screech

SCRITCHED > SCRITCH

SCRITCHES > SCRITCH

SCRIVE Scots word for > WRITE

SCRIVED > SCRIVE

SCRIVENER n person who writes out deeds, letters, etc

SCRIVES > SCRIVE

SCRIVING > SCRIVE

SCROBBLE vb record a person's music preferences in order to recommend similar music

SCROBBLED > SCROBBLE

SCROBBLES > SCROBBLE

SCROBE n groove

SCROBES > SCROBE

SCROD n young cod or haddock, esp one split and prepared for cooking

SCRODDLED adj made of scraps of pottery

SCRODS > SCROD

SCROFULA n tuberculosis of the lymphatic glands

SCROFULAS > SCROFULA

SCROG n Scots word meaning small tree

SCROGGIE adj having scrogs upon it

SCROGGIER > SCROGGIE

SCROGGIN n mixture of nuts and dried fruits

SCROGGINS > SCROGGIN

SCROGGY variant of > SCROGGIE

SCROGS > SCROG

SCROLL n roll of parchment or paper ▷ vb move (text) up or down on a VDU screen

SCROLLED > SCROLL

SCROLLER n person or thing that scrolls

SCROLLERS > SCROLLER

SCROLLING > SCROLL

SCROLLS > SCROLL

SCROME vb crawl or climb, esp using the hands to aid movement

SCROMED > SCROME

SCROMES > SCROME

SCROMING > SCROME

SCROOCH vb scratch (the skin) to relieve itching

SCROOCHED > SCROOCH

SCROOCHES > SCROOCH

SCROOGE variant of > SCROUGE

SCROOGED > SCROOGE

SCROOGES > SCROOGE

SCROOGING > SCROOGE

SCROOP vb emit a grating or creaking sound ▷ n such a sound

SCROOPED > SCROOP

SCROOPING > SCROOP

SCROOPS > SCROOP

SCROOTCH vb hunch up

SCRORP n deep scratch or weal

SCRORPS > SCRORP

SCROTA > SCROTUM

SCROTAL > SCROTUM

SCROTE n slang derogatory word meaning a worthless fellow

SCROTES > SCROTE

SCROTUM n pouch of skin containing the testicles

SCROTUMS > SCROTUM

SCROUGE vb crowd or press

SCROUGED > SCROUGE

SCROUGER n American word meaning whopper

SCROUGERS > SCROUGER

SCROUGES > SCROUGE

SCROUGING > SCROUGE

SCROUNGE vb get by cadging or begging

SCROUNGED > SCROUNGE

SCROUNGER > SCROUNGE

SCROUNGES > SCROUNGE

SCROUNGY adj shabby

SCROW n scroll

SCROWDGE vb squeeze

SCROWDGED > SCROWDGE

SCROWDGES > SCROWDGE

SCROWL vb old form of scroll

SCROWLE vb old form of scroll

SCROWLED > SCROWL

SCROWLES > SCROWLE

SCROWLING > SCROWL

SCROWLS > SCROWL

SCROWS > SCROW

SCROYLE n old word meaning wretch

SCROYLES > SCROYLE

SCRUB vb clean by rubbing, often with a hard brush and water ▷ n scrubbing ▷ adj stunted or inferior

SCRUBBED > SCRUB

SCRUBBER n woman who has many sexual partners

SCRUBBERS > SCRUBBER

SCRUBBIER > SCRUBBY

SCRUBBILY > SCRUBBY

SCRUBBING > SCRUB

SCRUBBY adj covered with scrub

SCRUBLAND n area of scrub vegetation

SCRUBS > SCRUB

SCRUFF same as > SCUM

SCRUFFIER > SCRUFFY

SCRUFFILY > SCRUFFY

SCRUFFS > SCRUFF

SCRUFFY adj unkempt or shabby

SCRUM n restarting of play in which opposing packs of forwards push against each other to gain possession of the ball ▷ vb form a scrum

SCRUMDOWN n forming of scrum in rugby

SCRUMMAGE same as > SCRUM

SCRUMMED > SCRUM

SCRUMMIE n informal word for a scrum half

SCRUMMIER > SCRUMMY

SCRUMMIES > SCRUMMIE

SCRUMMING > SCRUM

SCRUMMY adj delicious

SCRUMP vb steal (apples) from an orchard or garden

SCRUMPED > SCRUMP

SCRUMPIES > SCRUMPY

SCRUMPING > SCRUMP

SCRUMPLE vb crumple or crush

SCRUMPLED > SCRUMPLE

SCRUMPLES > SCRUMPLE

SCRUMPOX n skin infection spread among players in scrum

SCRUMPS > SCRUMP

SCRUMPY n rough dry cider

SCRUMS > SCRUM

SCRUNCH vb crumple or crunch or be crumpled or crunched ▷ n act or sound of scrunching

SCRUNCHED > SCRUNCH

SCRUNCHES > SCRUNCH

SCRUNCHIE n loop of elastic covered loosely with fabric, used to hold the hair in a ponytail

SCRUNCHY adj crunchy

SCRUNT n Scots word meaning stunted thing

SCRUNTIER > SCRUNT

SCRUNTS > SCRUNT

SCRUNTY > SCRUNT

SCRUPLE n doubt produced by one's conscience or morals ▷ vb have doubts on moral grounds

SCRUPLED > SCRUPLE

SCRUPLER > SCRUPLE

SCRUPLERS > SCRUPLE

SCRUPLES > SCRUPLE

SCRUPLING > SCRUPLE

SCRUTABLE adj open to or able to be understood by scrutiny

SCRUTATOR n person who examines or scrutinizes

SCRUTINY n close examination

SCRUTO n trapdoor on stage

SCRUTOIRE n writing desk

SCRUTOS > SCRUTO

SCRUZE vb old word meaning squeeze

SCRUZED > SCRUZE

SCRUZES > SCRUZE

SCRUZING > SCRUZE

S

SCRY vb divine, esp by crystal gazing

SCRYDE > SCRY

SCRYER > SCRY

SCRYERS > SCRY

SCRYING > SCRY

SCRYINGS > SCRY

SCRYNE n old form of shrine

SCRYNES > SCRYNE

SCUBA n apparatus used in skin diving, consisting of cylinders containing compressed air attached to a breathing apparatus ▷ vb dive using scuba equipment

SCUBAED > SCUBA

SCUBAING > SCUBA

SCUBAS > SCUBA

SCUCHIN n old form of scutcheon

SCUCHINS > SCUCHIN

SCUD vb move along swiftly ▷ n act of scudding

SCUDDALER n Scots word meaning leader of festivities

SCUDDED > SCUD

SCUDDER > SCUD

SCUDDERS > SCUD

SCUDDING > SCUD

SCUDDLE vb scuttle

SCUDDLED > SCUDDLE

SCUDDLES > SCUDDLE

SCUDDLING > SCUDDLE

SCUDI > SCUDO

SCUDLER n Scots word meaning leader of festivities

SCUDLERS > SCUDLER

SCUDO n any of several former Italian coins

SCUDS > SCUD

SCUFF vb drag (the feet) while walking ▷ n mark caused by scuffing

SCUFFED > SCUFF

SCUFFER n type of sandal

SCUFFERS > SCUFFER

SCUFFING > SCUFF

SCUFFLE vb fight in a disorderly manner ▷ n disorderly struggle

SCUFFLED > SCUFFLE

SCUFFLER > SCUFFLE

SCUFFLERS > SCUFFLE

SCUFFLES > SCUFFLE

SCUFFLING > SCUFFLE

SCUFFS > SCUFF

SCUFT n dialect word meaning nape of neck

SCUFTS > SCUFT

SCUG vb shelter

SCUGGED > SCUG

SCUGGING > SCUG

SCUGS > SCUG

SCUL n old form of school

SCULCH n rubbish

SCULCHES > SCULCH

SCULK vb old form of skulk

SCULKED > SCULK

SCULKER > SCULK

SCULKERS > SCULK

SCULKING > SCULK

SCULKS > SCULK

SCULL n small oar ▷ vb row (a boat) using sculls

SCULLE n old form of school

SCULLED > SCULL

SCULLER > SCULL

SCULLERS > SCULL

SCULLERY n small room where washing-up and other kitchen work is done

SCULLES > SCULLE

SCULLING > SCULL

SCULLINGS > SCULL

SCULLION n servant employed to do the hard work in a kitchen

SCULLIONS > SCULLION

SCULLS > SCULL

SCULP variant of > SCULPTURE

SCULPED > SCULP

SCULPIN n type of fish of the family which includes bullheads and sea scorpions

SCULPING > SCULP

SCULPINS > SCULPIN

SCULPS > SCULP

SCULPSIT (he or she) sculptured it: used formerly on sculptures next to a sculptor's name

SCULPT same as > SCULPTURE

SCULPTED > SCULPT

SCULPTING > SCULPT

SCULPTOR n person who makes sculptures

SCULPTORS > SCULPTOR

SCULPTS > SCULPT

SCULPTURE n art of making figures or designs in wood, stone, etc ▷ vb represent in sculpture

SCULS > SCUL

SCULTCH same as > SCULCH

SCULTCHES > SCULTCH

SCUM n impure or waste matter on the surface of a liquid ▷ vb remove scum from

SCUMBAG n offensive or despicable person

SCUMBAGS > SCUMBAG

SCUMBER vb old word meaning defecate

SCUMBERED > SCUMBER

SCUMBERS > SCUMBER

SCUMBLE vb soften or blend (an outline or colour) with a thin upper coat of opaque colour ▷ n upper layer of colour applied in this way

SCUMBLED > SCUMBLE

SCUMBLES > SCUMBLE

SCUMBLING > SCUMBLE

SCUMFISH vb Scots word meaning disgust

SCUMLESS > SCUM

SCUMLIKE > SCUM

SCUMMED > SCUM

SCUMMER > SCUM

SCUMMERS > SCUM

SCUMMIER > SCUMMY

SCUMMIEST > SCUMMY

SCUMMILY > SCUMMY

SCUMMING > SCUM

SCUMMINGS > SCUM

SCUMMY adj of, resembling, consisting of, or covered with scum

SCUMS > SCUM

SCUNCHEON n inner part of a door jamb or window frame

SCUNDERED adj Irish dialect word for embarrassed

SCUNGE vb borrow ▷ n dirty or worthless person

SCUNGED > SCUNGE

SCUNGES > SCUNGE

SCUNGIER > SCUNGY

SCUNGIEST > SCUNGY

SCUNGILLI n seafood dish of conch

SCUNGING > SCUNGE

SCUNGY adj sordid or dirty

SCUNNER vb feel aversion ▷ n strong aversion

SCUNNERED adj annoyed, discontented, or bored

SCUNNERS > SCUNNER

SCUP n common sparid fish of American coastal regions of the Atlantic

SCUPPAUG n sea fish

SCUPPAUGS > SCUPPAUG

SCUPPER vb defeat or ruin ▷ n drain in the side of a ship

SCUPPERED > SCUPPER

SCUPPERS > SCUPPER

SCUPS > SCUP

SCUR n small unattached growth of horn at the site of a normal horn in cattle

SCURF n flaky skin on the scalp

SCURFIER > SCURF

SCURFIEST > SCURF

SCURFS > SCURF

SCURFY > SCURF

SCURRED > SCUR

SCURRIED > SCURRY

SCURRIER n old word meaning scout

SCURRIERS > SCURRIER

SCURRIES > SCURRY

SCURRIL adj old word meaning vulgar

SCURRILE adj old word meaning vulgar

SCURRING > SCUR

SCURRIOUR n old word meaning scout

SCURRY vb move hastily ▷ n act or sound of scurrying

SCURRYING > SCURRY

SCURS > SCUR

SCURVIER > SCURVY

SCURVIES > SCURVY

SCURVIEST > SCURVY

SCURVILY > SCURVY

SCURVY n disease caused by lack of vitamin C ▷ adj mean and despicable

SCUSE shortened form of > EXCUSE

SCUSED > SCUSE

SCUSES > SCUSE

SCUSING > SCUSE

SCUT n short tail of the hare, rabbit, or deer

SCUTA > SCUTUM

SCUTAGE n payment sometimes exacted by a lord from his vassal in lieu of military service

SCUTAGES > SCUTAGE

SCUTAL > SCUTE

SCUTATE adj (of animals) having or covered with large bony or horny plates

SCUTATION > SCUTATE

SCUTCH vb separate the fibres from the woody part of (flax) by pounding ▷ n tool used for this

SCUTCHED > SCUTCH

SCUTCHEON same as > SHIELD

SCUTCHER same as > SCUTCH

SCUTCHERS > SCUTCHER

SCUTCHES > SCUTCH

SCUTCHING > SCUTCH

SCUTE n horny or chitinous plate that makes up part of the exoskeleton in armadillos, etc

SCUTELLA > SCUTELLUM

SCUTELLAR > SCUTELLUM

SCUTELLUM n last of three plates into which the notum of an insect's thorax is divided

SCUTES > SCUTE

SCUTIFORM adj (esp of plant parts) shaped like a shield

SCUTIGER n species of centipede

SCUTIGERS > SCUTIGER

SCUTS > SCUT

SCUTTER informal word for > SCURRY

SCUTTERED > SCUTTER

SCUTTERS > SCUTTER

SCUTTLE n fireside container for coal ▷ vb run with short quick steps

SCUTTLED > SCUTTLE

SCUTTLER > SCUTTLE

SCUTTLERS > SCUTTLE

SCUTTLES > SCUTTLE

SCUTTLING > SCUTTLE

SCUTUM n middle of three plates into which the notum of an insect's thorax is divided

SCUTWORK n menial or dull work

SCUTWORKS > SCUTWORK

SCUZZ n dirt

SCUZZBAG n disagreeable or disgusting person

SCUZZBAGS > SCUZZBAG

SCUZZBALL n despicable person
SCUZZES > SCUZZ
SCUZZIER > SCUZZY
SCUZZIEST > SCUZZY
SCUZZY adj unkempt, dirty, or squalid
SCYBALA > SCYBALUM
SCYBALOUS > SCYBALUM
SCYBALUM n hard faeces in stomach
SCYE n Scots word meaning sleeve-hole
SCYES > SCYE
SCYPHATE adj shaped like cup
SCYPHI > SCYPHUS
SCYPHUS n ancient Greek two-handled drinking cup without a footed base
SCYTALE n coded message in ancient Sparta
SCYTALES > SCYTALE
SCYTHE n long-handled tool with a curved blade for cutting grass ▷ vb cut with a scythe
SCYTHED > SCYTHE
SCYTHEMAN n scythe user
SCYTHEMEN > SCYTHEMAN
SCYTHER > SCYTHE
SCYTHERS > SCYTHE
SCYTHES > SCYTHE
SCYTHING > SCYTHE
SDAINE vb old form of disdain
SDAINED > SDAINE
SDAINES > SDAINE
SDAINING > SDAINE
SDAYN vb old form of disdain
SDAYNED > SDAYN
SDAYNING > SDAYN
SDAYNS > SDAYN
SDEIGN vb old form of disdain
SDEIGNE vb old form of disdain
SDEIGNED > SDEIGN
SDEIGNES > SDEIGNE
SDEIGNING > SDEIGNE
SDEIGNS > SDEIGN
SDEIN vb old form of disdain
SDEINED > SDEIN
SDEINING > SDEIN
SDEINS > SDEIN
SEA n mass of salt water covering three quarters of the earth's surface
SEABAG n canvas bag for holding a sailor's belongings
SEABAGS > SEABAG
SEABANK n sea shore
SEABANKS > SEABANK
SEABEACH n beach at seaside
SEABED n bottom of sea
SEABEDS > SEABED
SEABIRD n bird that lives on the sea
SEABIRDS > SEABIRD

SEABLITE n prostrate annual plant of the goosefoot family
SEABLITES > SEABLITE
SEABOARD n coast
SEABOARDS > SEABOARD
SEABOOT n sailor's waterproof boot
SEABOOTS > SEABOOT
SEABORNE adj carried on or by the sea
SEABOTTLE n type of seaweed
SEACOAST n land bordering on the sea
SEACOASTS > SEACOAST
SEACOCK n valve in the hull of a vessel below the water line for admitting sea water or for pumping out bilge water
SEACOCKS > SEACOCK
SEACRAFT n skill as sailor
SEACRAFTS > SEACRAFT
SEACUNNY n quartermaster on Indian ship
SEADOG another word for > FOGBOW
SEADOGS > SEADOG
SEADROME n aerodrome floating on sea
SEADROMES > SEADROME
SEAFARER n traveller who goes by sea
SEAFARERS > SEAFARER
SEAFARING adj working or travelling by sea ▷ n act of travelling by sea
SEAFLOOR n bottom of the sea
SEAFLOORS > SEAFLOOR
SEAFOLK n people who sail sea
SEAFOLKS > SEAFOLK
SEAFOOD n edible saltwater fish or shellfish
SEAFOODS > SEAFOOD
SEAFOWL n seabird
SEAFOWLS > SEAFOWL
SEAFRONT n built-up area facing the sea
SEAFRONTS > SEAFRONT
SEAGIRT adj surrounded by the sea
SEAGOING adj built for travelling on the sea
SEAGULL n gull
SEAGULLS > SEAGULL
SEAHAWK n skua
SEAHAWKS > SEAHAWK
SEAHOG n porpoise
SEAHOGS > SEAHOG
SEAHORSE n marine fish with a horselike head that swims upright
SEAHORSES > SEAHORSE
SEAHOUND n dogfish
SEAHOUNDS > SEAHOUND
SEAKALE n European coastal plant
SEAKALES > SEAKALE
SEAL n piece of wax, lead, etc with a special design

impressed upon it, attached to a letter or document as a mark of authentication ▷ vb close with or as if with a seal
SEALABLE > SEAL
SEALANT n any substance used for sealing
SEALANTS > SEALANT
SEALCH Scots word for > SEAL
SEALCHS > SEALCH
SEALED adj (of a road) having a hard surface
SEALER n person or thing that seals
SEALERIES > SEALERY
SEALERS > SEALER
SEALERY n occupation of hunting seals
SEALGH Scots word for > SEAL
SEALGHS > SEALGH
SEALIFT vb transport by ship
SEALIFTED > SEALIFT
SEALIFTS > SEALIFT
SEALINE n company running regular sailings
SEALINES > SEALINE
SEALING > SEAL
SEALINGS > SEAL
SEALLIKE adj resembling a seal
SEALPOINT n popular variety of Siamese cat
SEALS > SEAL
SEALSKIN n skin or prepared fur of a seal, used to make coats
SEALSKINS > SEALSKIN
SEALWAX n sealing wax
SEALWAXES > SEALWAX
SEALYHAM n type of short-legged terrier
SEALYHAMS > SEALYHAM
SEAM n line where two edges are joined, as by stitching ▷ vb mark with furrows or wrinkles
SEAMAID n mermaid
SEAMAIDS > SEAMAID
SEAMAN n sailor
SEAMANLY > SEAMAN
SEAMARK n aid to navigation, such as a conspicuous object on a shore used as a guide
SEAMARKS > SEAMARK
SEAME n old word meaning grease
SEAMED > SEAM
SEAMEN > SEAMAN
SEAMER n fast bowler who makes the ball bounce on its seam so that it will change direction
SEAMERS > SEAMER
SEAMES > SEAME
SEAMFREE adj having no seam
SEAMIER > SEAMY
SEAMIEST > SEAMY
SEAMINESS > SEAMY

SEAMING > SEAM
SEAMINGS > SEAMING
SEAMLESS adj (of a garment) without seams
SEAMLIKE > SEAM
SEAMOUNT n submarine mountain rising more than 1000 metres above the surrounding ocean floor
SEAMOUNTS > SEAMOUNT
SEAMS > SEAM
SEAMSET n tool for flattening seams in metal
SEAMSETS > SEAMSET
SEAMSTER n person who sews
SEAMSTERS > SEAMSTER
SEAMY adj sordid
SEAN vb fish with seine net
SEANCE n meeting at which spiritualists attempt to communicate with the dead
SEANCES > SEANCE
SEANED > SEAN
SEANING > SEAN
SEANNACHY n Highland genealogist, chronicler, or bard
SEANS > SEAN
SEAPIECE n artwork depicting sea
SEAPIECES > SEAPIECE
SEAPLANE n aircraft designed to take off from and land on water
SEAPLANES > SEAPLANE
SEAPORT n town or city with a harbour for boats and ships
SEAPORTS > SEAPORT
SEAQUAKE n agitation and disturbance of the sea caused by an earthquake at the sea bed
SEAQUAKES > SEAQUAKE
SEAQUARIA npl areas of salt water where sea animals are kept
SEAR vb scorch, burn the surface of ▷ n mark caused by searing ▷ adj dried up
SEARAT n pirate
SEARATS > SEARAT
SEARCE vb sift
SEARCED > SEARCE
SEARCES > SEARCE
SEARCH vb examine closely in order to find something ▷ n searching
SEARCHED > SEARCH
SEARCHER > SEARCH
SEARCHERS > SEARCH
SEARCHES > SEARCH
SEARCHING adj keen or thorough
SEARCING > SEARCE
SEARE adj old word meaning dry and withered
SEARED > SEAR
SEARER > SEAR
SEAREST > SEAR
SEARING > SEAR
SEARINGLY > SEAR

SEARINGS > SEAR

SEARNESS > SEAR

SEAROBIN n type of American gurnard

SEAROBINS > SEAROBIN

SEARS > SEAR

SEAS > SEA

SEASCAPE n picture of a scene at sea

SEASCAPES > SEASCAPE

SEASCOUT n member of seagoing scouts

SEASCOUTS > SEASCOUT

SEASE vb old form of seize

SEASED > SEASE

SEASES > SEASE

SEASHELL n empty shell of a mollusc

SEASHELLS > SEASHELL

SEASHORE n land bordering on the sea

SEASHORES > SEASHORE

SEASICK adj suffering from nausea caused by the motion of a ship

SEASICKER > SEASICK

SEASIDE n area, esp a holiday resort, on the coast

SEASIDES > SEASIDE

SEASING > SEASE

SEASON n one of four divisions of the year, each of which has characteristic weather conditions ▷ vb flavour with salt, herbs, etc

SEASONAL adj depending on or varying with the seasons ▷ n seasonal thing

SEASONALS > SEASONAL

SEASONED > SEASON

SEASONER > SEASON

SEASONERS > SEASON

SEASONING n salt, herbs, etc added to food to enhance flavour

SEASONS > SEASON

SEASPEAK n language used by sailors

SEASPEAKS > SEASPEAK

SEASTRAND n seashore

SEASURE n old form of seizure

SEASURES > SEASURE

SEAT n thing designed or used for sitting on ▷ vb cause to sit

SEATBACK n back of seat

SEATBACKS > SEATBACK

SEATBELT n safety belt in vehicle

SEATBELTS > SEATBELT

SEATED > SEAT

SEATER n person or thing that seats

SEATERS > SEATER

SEATING n supply or arrangement of seats ▷ adj of or relating to the provision of places to sit

SEATINGS > SEATING

SEATLESS > SEAT

SEATMATE n person sitting in next seat

SEATMATES > SEATMATE

SEATRAIN n ship that can carry train

SEATRAINS > SEATRAIN

SEATROUT n trout living in the sea

SEATROUTS > SEATROUT

SEATS > SEAT

SEATWORK n school work done at pupils' desks

SEATWORKS > SEATWORK

SEAWALL n wall built to prevent encroachment or erosion by the sea

SEAWALLS > SEAWALL

SEAWAN n shell beads, usually unstrung, used by certain North American Indians as money

SEAWANS > SEAWAN

SEAWANT n Native American name for silver coins

SEAWANTS > SEAWANT

SEAWARD same as > SEAWARDS

SEAWARDLY > SEAWARD

SEAWARDS adv towards the sea

SEAWARE n any of numerous large coarse seaweeds

SEAWARES > SEAWARE

SEAWATER n water from sea

SEAWATERS > SEAWATER

SEAWAY n waterway giving access to an inland port, navigable by ocean-going ships

SEAWAYS > SEAWAY

SEAWEED n plant growing in the sea

SEAWEEDS > SEAWEED

SEAWIFE n variety of sea fish

SEAWIVES > SEAWIFE

SEAWOMAN n mermaid

SEAWOMEN > SEAWOMAN

SEAWORM n marine worm

SEAWORMS > SEAWORM

SEAWORTHY adj (of a ship) in fit condition for a sea voyage

SEAZE vb old form of seize

SEAZED > SEAZE

SEAZES > SEAZE

SEAZING > SEAZE

SEBACEOUS adj of, like, or secreting fat or oil

SEBACIC adj derived from sebacic acid, a white crystalline acid

SEBASIC same as > SEBACIC

SEBATE n salt of sebacic acid

SEBATES > SEBATE

SEBESTEN n Asian tree

SEBESTENS > SEBESTEN

SEBIFIC adj producing fat

SEBORRHEA n skin disease in which excessive oil is secreted

SEBUM n oily substance

secreted by the sebaceous glands

SEBUMS > SEBUM

SEBUNDIES > SEBUNDY

SEBUNDY n irregular soldier in India

SEC same as > SECANT

SECALOSE n type of sugar

SECALOSES > SECALOSE

SECANT n (in trigonometry) the ratio of the length of the hypotenuse to the length of the adjacent side in a right-angled triangle

SECANTLY > SECANT

SECANTS > SECANT

SECATEUR n secateurs

SECATEURS npl small pruning shears

SECCO n wall painting done on dried plaster with tempera or pigments ground in limewater

SECCOS > SECCO

SECEDE vb withdraw formally from a political alliance or federation

SECEDED > SECEDE

SECEDER > SECEDE

SECEDERS > SECEDE

SECEDES > SECEDE

SECEDING > SECEDE

SECERN vb (of a gland or follicle) to secrete

SECERNED > SECERN

SECERNENT > SECERN

SECERNING > SECERN

SECERNS > SECERN

SECESH n secessionist in US Civil War

SECESHER n secessionist in US Civil War

SECESHERS > SECESHER

SECESHES > SECESH

SECESSION n act of seceding

SECH n hyperbolic secant

SECHS > SECH

SECKEL variant of > SECKLE

SECKELS > SECKEL

SECKLE n type of pear

SECKLES > SECKLE

SECLUDE vb keep (a person) from contact with others

SECLUDED adj private, sheltered

SECLUDES > SECLUDE

SECLUDING > SECLUDE

SECLUSION n state of being secluded

SECLUSIVE adj tending to seclude

SECO adj (of wine) dry

SECODONT n animal with cutting back teeth

SECODONTS > SECODONT

SECONAL n tradename for secobarbitol

SECONALS > SECONAL

SECOND adj coming directly after the first ▷ n person or

thing coming second ▷ vb express formal support for (a motion proposed in a meeting)

SECONDARY adj of less importance ▷ n person or thing that is secondary

SECONDE n second of eight positions from which a parry or attack can be made in fencing

SECONDED > SECOND

SECONDEE n person who is seconded

SECONDEES > SECONDEE

SECONDER > SECOND

SECONDERS > SECOND

SECONDES > SECONDE

SECONDI > SECONDO

SECONDING > SECOND

SECONDLY same as > SECOND

SECONDO n left-hand part in a piano duet

SECONDS > SECOND

SECPAR n distance unit in astronomy

SECPARS > SECPAR

SECRECIES > SECRECY

SECRECY n state of being secret

SECRET adj kept from the knowledge of others ▷ n something kept secret

SECRETA n secretions

SECRETAGE n use of mercury in treating furs

SECRETARY n person who deals with correspondence and general clerical work

SECRETE vb (of an organ, gland, etc) produce and release (a substance)

SECRETED > SECRETE

SECRETER > SECRETE

SECRETES > SECRETE

SECRETEST > SECRET

SECRETIN n peptic hormone secreted by the mucosae of the duodenum and jejunum

SECRETING > SECRETE

SECRETINS > SECRETIN

SECRETION n substance that is released from a cell, organ, or gland

SECRETIVE adj inclined to keep things secret

SECRETLY > SECRET

SECRETOR > SECRETE

SECRETORS > SECRETE

SECRETORY adj of, relating to, or producing a secretion

SECRETS > SECRET

SECS > SEC

SECT n often disparaging term for a subdivision of a religious or political group, esp one with extreme beliefs

SECTARIAL > SECT

SECTARIAN adj of a sect ▷ n member of a sect

SECTARIES > SECTARY

SECTARY n member of a sect

SECTATOR n member of sect

SECTATORS > SECTATOR

SECTILE adj able to be cut smoothly

SECTILITY > SECTILE

SECTION n part cut off ▷ vb cut or divide into sections

SECTIONAL adj concerned with a particular area or group within a country or community

SECTIONED > SECTION

SECTIONS > SECTION

SECTOR n part or subdivision ▷ vb divide into sectors

SECTORAL > SECTOR

SECTORED > SECTOR

SECTORIAL adj of or relating to a sector

SECTORING > SECTOR

SECTORISE same as > SECTORIZE

SECTORIZE vb split into sectors

SECTORS > SECTOR

SECTS > SECT

SECULAR adj worldly, as opposed to sacred ▷ n member of the secular clergy

SECULARLY > SECULAR

SECULARS > SECULAR

SECULUM n age in astronomy

SECULUMS > SECULUM

SECUND adj having or designating parts arranged on or turned to one side of the axis

SECUNDINE n one of the two integuments surrounding the ovule of a plant

SECUNDLY > SECUND

SECUNDUM adj according to

SECURABLE > SECURE

SECURANCE > SECURE

SECURE adj free from danger ▷ vb obtain

SECURED > SECURE

SECURELY > SECURE

SECURER > SECURE

SECURERS > SECURE

SECURES > SECURE

SECUREST > SECURE

SECURING > SECURE

SECURITAN n person believing they are secure

SECURITY n precautions against theft, espionage, or other danger

SED old spelling of > SAID

SEDAN same as > SALOON

SEDANS > SEDAN

SEDARIM > SEDER

SEDATE adj calm and dignified ▷ vb give a sedative drug to

SEDATED > SEDATE

SEDATELY > SEDATE

SEDATER > SEDATE

SEDATES > SEDATE

SEDATEST > SEDATE

SEDATING > SEDATE

SEDATION n state of calm, esp when brought about by sedatives

SEDATIONS > SEDATION

SEDATIVE adj having a soothing or calming effect ▷ n sedative drug

SEDATIVES > SEDATIVE

SEDENT adj seated

SEDENTARY adj done sitting down, involving little exercise

SEDER n Jewish ceremonial meal held on the first night or first two nights of Passover

SEDERS > SEDER

SEDERUNT n sitting of an ecclesiastical assembly, court, etc

SEDERUNTS > SEDERUNT

SEDES Latin word for > SEAT

SEDGE n coarse grasslike plant growing on wet ground

SEDGED adj having sedge

SEDGELAND n land covered with sedge

SEDGES > SEDGE

SEDGIER > SEDGE

SEDGIEST > SEDGE

SEDGY > SEDGE

SEDILE n seat for clergy in church

SEDILIA n group of three seats where the celebrant and ministers sit at certain points during High Mass

SEDILIUM n seat for clergy in church

SEDIMENT n matter which settles to the bottom of a liquid

SEDIMENTS > SEDIMENT

SEDITION n speech or action encouraging rebellion against the government

SEDITIONS > SEDITION

SEDITIOUS adj of, like, or causing sedition

SEDUCE vb persuade into sexual intercourse

SEDUCED > SEDUCE

SEDUCER n person who entices, allures, or seduces

SEDUCERS > SEDUCER

SEDUCES > SEDUCE

SEDUCIBLE > SEDUCE

SEDUCING > SEDUCE

SEDUCINGS > SEDUCE

SEDUCIVE adj seductive

SEDUCTION n act of seducing or the state of being seduced

SEDUCTIVE adj (of a woman) sexually attractive

SEDUCTOR n person who seduces

SEDUCTORS > SEDUCTOR

SEDULITY > SEDULOUS

SEDULOUS adj diligent or persevering

SEDUM n rock plant

SEDUMS > SEDUM

SEE vb perceive with the eyes or mind ▷ n diocese of a bishop

SEEABLE > SEE

SEECATCH n male seal in Aleutians

SEED n mature fertilized grain of a plant ▷ vb sow with seed

SEEDBED n area of soil prepared for the growing of seedlings before they are transplanted

SEEDBEDS > SEEDBED

SEEDBOX n part of plant that contains seeds

SEEDBOXES > SEEDBOX

SEEDCAKE n sweet cake flavoured with caraway seeds and lemon rind or essence

SEEDCAKES > SEEDCAKE

SEEDCASE n part of a fruit enclosing the seeds

SEEDCASES > SEEDCASE

SEEDEATER n bird feeding on seeds

SEEDED > SEED

SEEDER n person or thing that seeds

SEEDERS > SEEDER

SEEDIER > SEEDY

SEEDIEST > SEEDY

SEEDILY > SEEDY

SEEDINESS > SEEDY

SEEDING > SEED

SEEDINGS > SEED

SEEDLESS > SEED

SEEDLIKE > SEED

SEEDLING n young plant raised from a seed

SEEDLINGS > SEEDLING

SEEDLIP n basket holding seeds to be sown

SEEDLIPS > SEEDLIP

SEEDMAN n seller of seeds

SEEDMEN > SEEDMAN

SEEDNESS n old word meaning sowing of seeds

SEEDPOD n carpel enclosing the seeds of a flowering plant

SEEDPODS > SEEDPOD

SEEDS > SEED

SEEDSMAN n seller of seeds

SEEDSMEN > SEEDSMAN

SEEDSTOCK n livestock used for breeding

SEEDTIME n season when seeds are sown

SEEDTIMES > SEEDTIME

SEEDY adj shabby

SEEING > SEE

SEEINGS > SEE

SEEK vb try to find or obtain

SEEKER > SEEK

SEEKERS > SEEK

SEEKING > SEEK

SEEKS > SEEK

SEEL vb sew up the eyelids of (a hawk or falcon) so as to render it quiet and tame

SEELD adj old word meaning rare

SEELED > SEEL

SEELIE npl good benevolent fairies

SEELIER > SEELY

SEELIEST > SEELY

SEELING > SEEL

SEELINGS > SEEL

SEELS > SEEL

SEELY adj old word meaning happy

SEEM vb appear to be

SEEMED > SEEM

SEEMER > SEEM

SEEMERS > SEEM

SEEMING adj apparent but not real ▷ n outward or false appearance

SEEMINGLY adv in appearance but not necessarily in actuality

SEEMINGS > SEEMING

SEEMLESS adj old word meaning unseemly

SEEMLIER > SEEMLY

SEEMLIEST > SEEMLY

SEEMLIHED n old word meaning seemliness

SEEMLY adj proper or fitting ▷ adv properly or decorously

SEEMLYHED n old word meaning seemliness

SEEMS > SEEM

SEEN > SEE

SEEP vb trickle through slowly, ooze ▷ n small spring or place where water, oil, etc, has oozed through the ground

SEEPAGE n act or process of seeping

SEEPAGES > SEEPAGE

SEEPED > SEEP

SEEPIER > SEEPY

SEEPIEST > SEEPY

SEEPING > SEEP

SEEPS > SEEP

SEEPY adj tending to seep

SEER n person who sees

SEERESS > SEER

SEERESSES > SEER

SEERS > SEER

SEES > SEE

SEESAW n plank balanced in the middle so that two people seated on either end ride up and down alternately ▷ vb move up and down

SEESAWED > SEESAW

SEESAWING > SEESAW

SEESAWS > SEESAW

SEETHE vb be very agitated ▷ n act or state of seething

SEETHED > SEETHE

SEETHER > SEETHE

SEETHERS > SEETHE

SEETHES > SEETHE

S

SEETHING adj boiling or foaming as if boiling
SEETHINGS > SEETHING
SEEWING n suing
SEFER n scrolls of the Law
SEG n metal stud on shoe sole
SEGAR n cigar
SEGARS > SEGAR
SEGETAL adj (of weeds) growing amongst crops
SEGGAR n box in which pottery is baked
SEGGARS > SEGGAR
SEGHOL n pronunciation mark in Hebrew
SEGHOLATE n vowel sound in Hebrew
SEGHOLS > SEGHOL
SEGMENT n one of several sections into which something may be divided ▷ vb divide into segments
SEGMENTAL adj of, like, or having the form of a segment
SEGMENTED > SEGMENT
SEGMENTS > SEGMENT
SEGNI > SEGNO
SEGNO n sign at the beginning or end of a section directed to be repeated
SEGNOS > SEGNO
SEGO n American variety of lily
SEGOL variant of > SEGHOL
SEGOLATE variant of > SEGHOLATE
SEGOLATES > SEGOLATE
SEGOLS > SEGOL
SEGOS > SEGO
SEGREANT adj having raised wings in heraldry
SEGREGANT n organism different because of segregation
SEGREGATE vb set apart
SEGS > SEG
SEGUE vb proceed from one section or piece of music to another without a break ▷ n practice or an instance of playing music in this way
SEGUED > SEGUE
SEGUEING > SEGUE
SEGUES > SEGUE
SEHRI n meal eaten before sunrise by Muslims fasting during Ramadan
SEHRIS > SEHRI
SEI n type of rorqual
SEICENTO n 17th century with reference to Italian art and literature
SEICENTOS > SEICENTO
SEICHE n periodic oscillation of the surface of an enclosed or semienclosed body of water
SEICHES > SEICHE
SEIDEL n vessel for drinking beer
SEIDELS > SEIDEL

SEIF n long ridge of blown sand in a desert
SEIFS > SEIF
SEIGNEUR n feudal lord
SEIGNEURS > SEIGNEUR
SEIGNEURY n estate of a seigneur
SEIGNIOR n (in England) the lord of a seigniory
SEIGNIORS > SEIGNIOR
SEIGNIORY n (in England) the fee or manor of a seignior
SEIGNORAL adj relating to the quality of being a lord
SEIGNORY n lordship
SEIK Scot word for > SICK
SEIKER > SEIK
SEIKEST > SEIK
SEIL vb dialect word meaning strain
SEILED > SEIL
SEILING > SEIL
SEILS > SEIL
SEINE n large fishing net that hangs vertically from floats ▷ vb catch (fish) using this net
SEINED > SEINE
SEINER > SEINE
SEINERS > SEINE
SEINES > SEINE
SEINING > SEINE
SEININGS > SEINE
SEIR n fish of Indian seas
SEIRS > SEIR
SEIS > SEI
SEISABLE > SEISE
SEISE vb put into legal possession of (property, etc)
SEISED > SEISE
SEISER > SEISE
SEISERS > SEISE
SEISES > SEISE
SEISIN n feudal possession of an estate in land
SEISING > SEISE
SEISINGS > SEISE
SEISINS > SEISIN
SEISM n earthquake
SEISMAL adj of earthquakes
SEISMIC adj relating to earthquakes
SEISMICAL same as > SEISMIC
SEISMISM n occurrence of earthquakes
SEISMISMS > SEISMISM
SEISMS > SEISM
SEISOR n person who takes seisin
SEISORS > SEISOR
SEISURE n act of seisin
SEISURES > SEISURE
SEITAN same as > SEITEN
SEITANS > SEITAN
SEITEN n gluten from wheat
SEITENS > SEITEN
SEITIES > SEITY
SEITY n selfhood

SEIZABLE > SEIZE
SEIZE vb take hold of forcibly or quickly
SEIZED > SEIZE
SEIZER > SEIZE
SEIZERS > SEIZE
SEIZES > SEIZE
SEIZIN same as > SEISIN
SEIZING n binding used for holding together two ropes, two spars, etc, esp by lashing with a separate rope
SEIZINGS > SEIZING
SEIZINS > SEIZIN
SEIZOR n person who takes seisin
SEIZORS > SEIZOR
SEIZURE n sudden violent attack of an illness
SEIZURES > SEIZURE
SEJANT adj (of a beast) shown seated
SEJEANT same as > SEJANT
SEKOS n holy place
SEKOSES > SEKOS
SEKT n German sparkling wine
SEKTS > SEKT
SEL Scot word for > SELF
SELACHIAN adj relating to a large subclass of cartilaginous fishes including the sharks, rays, dogfish, and skates ▷ n any fish belonging to this subclass
SELADANG n Malaysian tapir
SELADANGS > SELADANG
SELAH n Hebrew word of unknown meaning occurring in the Old Testament psalms, and thought to be a musical direction
SELAHS > SELAH
SELAMLIK n men's quarters in Turkish house
SELAMLIKS > SELAMLIK
SELCOUTH adj old word meaning strange
SELD adj old word meaning rare
SELDOM adv not often, rarely
SELDOMLY > SELDOM
SELDSEEN adj old word meaning seldom seen
SELDSHOWN adj old word meaning seldom shown
SELE n old word meaning happiness
SELECT vb pick out or choose ▷ adj chosen in preference to others
SELECTA n disc jockey
SELECTAS > SELECTA
SELECTED > SELECT
SELECTEE n person who is selected, esp for military service
SELECTEES > SELECTEE
SELECTING > SELECT

SELECTION n selecting
SELECTIVE adj chosen or choosing carefully
SELECTLY > SELECT
SELECTMAN n any of the members of the local boards of most New England towns
SELECTMEN > SELECTMAN
SELECTOR n person or thing that selects
SELECTORS > SELECTOR
SELECTS > SELECT
SELENATE n any salt or ester formed by replacing one or both of the hydrogens of selenic acid with metal ions or organic groups
SELENATES > SELENATE
SELENIAN adj of the moon
SELENIC adj of or containing selenium, esp in the hexavalent state
SELENIDE n compound containing selenium
SELENIDES > SELENIDE
SELENIOUS adj of or containing selenium in the divalent or tetravalent state
SELENITE n colourless glassy variety of gypsum
SELENITES > SELENITE
SELENITIC > SELENITE
SELENIUM n nonmetallic element with photoelectric properties
SELENIUMS > SELENIUM
SELENOSES > SELENOSIS
SELENOSIS n poisoned condition caused by selenium
SELENOUS same as > SELENIOUS
SELES > SELE
SELF n distinct individuality or identity of a person or thing ▷ pron myself, yourself, himself, or herself ▷ vb reproduce by oneself
SELFDOM n selfhood
SELFDOMS > SELFDOM
SELFED > SELF
SELFHEAL n low-growing European herbaceous plant
SELFHEALS > SELFHEAL
SELFHOOD n state of having a distinct identity
SELFHOODS > SELFHOOD
SELFING > SELF
SELFINGS > SELF
SELFISH adj caring too much about oneself and not enough about others
SELFISHLY > SELFISH
SELFISM n emphasis on self
SELFISMS > SELFISM
SELFIST > SELFISM
SELFISTS > SELFISM
SELFLESS adj unselfish

SELFNESS n egotism
SELFS > SELF
SELFSAME adj very same
SELFWARD adj toward self
SELFWARDS adv towards self
SELICTAR n Turkish sword-bearer
SELICTARS > SELICTAR
SELKIE same as > SILKIE
SELKIES > SELKIE
SELL vb exchange (something) for money ▷ n manner of selling
SELLA n area of bone in body
SELLABLE > SELL
SELLAE > SELLA
SELLAS > SELLA
SELLE n old word meaning seat
SELLER n person who sells
SELLERS > SELLER
SELLES > SELLE
SELLING n the act of providing (e.g. goods or services) to customers in exchange for money
SELLINGS > SELLING
SELLOFF n act of selling cheaply
SELLOFFS > SELLOFF
SELLOTAPE n tradename for a type of transparent adhesive tape
SELLOUT n performance of a show etc for which all the tickets are sold
SELLOUTS > SELLOUT
SELLS > SELL
SELS > SEL
SELSYN same as > SYNCHRO
SELSYNS > SELSYN
SELTZER n natural effervescent water containing minerals
SELTZERS > SELTZER
SELVA n dense equatorial forest characterized by tall broad-leaved evergreen trees, lianas, etc
SELVAGE n edge of cloth, woven so as to prevent unravelling ▷ vb edge or border
SELVAGED > SELVAGE
SELVAGEE n rope used as strap
SELVAGEES > SELVAGEE
SELVAGES > SELVAGE
SELVAGING > SELVAGE
SELVAS > SELVA
SELVEDGE same as > SELVAGE
SELVEDGED > SELVEDGE
SELVEDGES > SELVEDGE
SELVES > SELF
SEMAINIER n chest of drawers
SEMANTEME same as > SEMEME
SEMANTIC adj relating to the meaning of words

SEMANTICS n study of linguistic meaning
SEMANTIDE n type of molecule
SEMANTRA > SEMANTRON
SEMANTRON n bar struck instead of bell in Orthodox church
SEMAPHORE n system of signalling by holding two flags in different positions to represent letters of the alphabet ▷ vb signal (information) by semaphore
SEMATIC adj (of the conspicuous coloration of certain animals) acting as a warning, esp to potential predators
SEMBLABLE adj resembling or similar ▷ n something that resembles another thing
SEMBLABLY > SEMBLABLE
SEMBLANCE n outward or superficial appearance
SEMBLANT n semblance
SEMBLANTS > SEMBLANT
SEMBLE vb seem
SEMBLED > SEMBLE
SEMBLES > SEMBLE
SEMBLING > SEMBLE
SEME adj dotted (with)
SEMEE variant of > SEME
SEMEED adj seme
SEMEIA > SEMEION
SEMEION n unit of metre in ancient poetry
SEMEIOTIC same as > SEMIOTIC
SEMEME n meaning of a morpheme
SEMEMES > SEMEME
SEMEMIC > SEMEME
SEMEN n sperm-carrying fluid produced by male animals
SEMENS > SEMEN
SEMES > SEME
SEMESTER n either of two divisions of the academic year
SEMESTERS > SEMESTER
SEMESTRAL > SEMESTER
SEMI n semidetached house
SEMIANGLE n half angle
SEMIARID adj denoting land that lies on the edges of a desert but has a slightly higher rainfall
SEMIBALD adj partly bald
SEMIBOLD adj denoting a weight of typeface between medium and bold face ▷ n semibold type
SEMIBOLDS > SEMIBOLD
SEMIBREVE n musical note four beats long
SEMIBULL n papal bull issued before coronation
SEMIBULLS > SEMIBULL
SEMICOLON n

punctuation mark (;)
SEMICOMA n condition similar to a coma
SEMICOMAS > SEMICOMA
SEMICURED adj partly cured
SEMIDEAF adj partly deaf
SEMIDEIFY vb treat almost as god
SEMIDOME n half-dome, esp one used to cover a semicircular apse
SEMIDOMED adj having semidome
SEMIDOMES > SEMIDOME
SEMIDRY adj partly dry
SEMIDWARF adj smaller than standard variety
SEMIE n historical name for a student in second year at a Scottish university
SEMIERECT adj partly erect
SEMIES > SEMIE
SEMIFINAL n match or round before the final
SEMIFIT adj not fully fit
SEMIFLUID adj having properties between those of a liquid and those of a solid ▷ n substance that has such properties because of high viscosity
SEMIGALA n characterized by quite a lot of celebration and fun
SEMIGLOSS adj (of paint) giving finish between matt and gloss
SEMIGROUP n type of set in mathematics
SEMIHARD adj partly hard
SEMIHIGH adj moderately high
SEMIHOBO n person looking almost like hobo
SEMIHOBOS > SEMIHOBO
SEMILLON n grape used to make wine
SEMILLONS > SEMILLON
SEMILOG adj semilogarithmic
SEMILUNAR adj shaped like a crescent or half-moon
SEMILUNE n half-moon shape
SEMILUNES > SEMILUNE
SEMIMAT adj semimatt
SEMIMATT adj with surface midway between matt and gloss
SEMIMATTE adj semimatt
SEMIMETAL n metal not fully malleable
SEMIMICRO adj using microwaves
SEMIMILD adj somewhat mild
SEMIMOIST adj slightly wet
SEMIMUTE adj having speech impairment through hearing loss
SEMINA > SEMEN
SEMINAL adj original and

influential
SEMINALLY > SEMINAL
SEMINAR n meeting of a group of students for discussion
SEMINARS > SEMINAR
SEMINARY n college for priests
SEMINATE vb sow
SEMINATED > SEMINATE
SEMINATES > SEMINATE
SEMINOMA n malignant tumour of the testicle
SEMINOMAD n person living partly nomadic life
SEMINOMAS > SEMINOMA
SEMINUDE adj partly nude
SEMIOLOGY same as > SEMIOTICS
SEMIOPEN adj half-open
SEMIOSES > SEMIOSIS
SEMIOSIS n action involving establishing relationship between signs
SEMIOTIC adj relating to signs and symbols, esp spoken or written signs
SEMIOTICS n study of human communications, esp signs and symbols
SEMIOVAL adj shaped like half of oval
SEMIPED n measure in poetic metre
SEMIPEDS > SEMIPED
SEMIPIOUS adj quite pious
SEMIPLUME n type of bird feather
SEMIPOLAR as in semipolar bond type of chemical bond
SEMIPRO n semiprofessional
SEMIPROS > SEMIPRO
SEMIRAW adj not fully cooked or processed
SEMIRIGID adj (of an airship) maintaining shape by means of a main supporting keel and internal gas pressure
SEMIROUND adj with one flat side and one round side ▷ n something semiround
SEMIRURAL adj partly rural
SEMIS > SEMI
SEMISES > SEMI
SEMISOFT adj partly soft
SEMISOLID adj having a viscosity and rigidity intermediate between that of a solid and a liquid ▷ n substance in this state
SEMISOLUS n advertisement that appears on the same page as another advertisement but not adjacent to it
SEMISTIFF adj partly stiff
SEMISWEET adj partly sweet
SEMITAR old spelling of > SCIMITAR
SEMITARS > SEMITAR

S

SEMITAUR old spelling of > SCIMITAR

SEMITAURS > SEMITAUR

SEMITIST n student of Semitic languages and culture

SEMITISTS > SEMITIST

SEMITONAL > SEMITONE

SEMITONE n smallest interval between two notes in Western music

SEMITONES > SEMITONE

SEMITONIC > SEMITONE

SEMITRUCK n articulated lorry

SEMIURBAN adj suburban

SEMIVOCAL adj of or relating to a semivowel

SEMIVOWEL n vowel-like sound that acts like a consonant, such as the sound in well

SEMIWATER as in semiwater gas a mixed gas of steam and air

SEMIWILD adj not fully domesticated

SEMIWORKS adj equipped to manufacture but not in great numbers

SEMMIT n vest

SEMMITS > SEMMIT

SEMOLINA n hard grains of wheat left after the milling of flour, used to make puddings and pasta

SEMOLINAS > SEMOLINA

SEMPER adv Latin word meaning always

SEMPLE adj Scots word meaning simple

SEMPLER > SEMPLE

SEMPLEST > SEMPLE

SEMPLICE adv be performed in a simple manner

SEMPRE adv (preceding a tempo or dynamic marking) always

SEMPSTER n person who sews

SEMPSTERS > SEMPSTER

SEMSEM n sesame

SEMSEMS > SEMSEM

SEMUNCIA n ancient Roman coin

SEMUNCIAE > SEMUNCIA

SEMUNCIAL > SEMUNCIA

SEMUNCIAS > SEMUNCIA

SEN n monetary unit of Brunei, Cambodia, Indonesia, Malaysia, and formerly of Japan

SENA n (in India) the army: used in the names of certain paramilitary political organizations

SENARIES > SENARY

SENARII > SENARIUS

SENARIUS n type of poem

SENARY adj of or relating to the number six

SENAS > SENA

SENATE n main governing body at some universities

SENATES > SENATE

SENATOR n member of a senate

SENATORS > SENATOR

SEND vb cause (a person or thing) to go to or be taken or transmitted to a place

SENDABLE > SEND

SENDAL n fine silk fabric used, esp in the Middle Ages, for ceremonial clothing, etc

SENDALS > SENDAL

SENDED vb old word meaning sent

SENDER > SEND

SENDERS > SEND

SENDING > SEND

SENDINGS > SEND

SENDOFF n demonstration of good wishes at a person's departure ▷ vb dispatch (something, such as a letter)

SENDOFFS > SENDOFF

SENDS > SEND

SENDUP n parody or imitation

SENDUPS > SENDUP

SENE n money unit in Samoa

SENECA variant of > SENEGA

SENECAS > SENECA

SENECIO n type of plant of the genus which includes groundsels and ragworts

SENECIOS > SENECIO

SENEGA n milkwort plant of the eastern US, with small white flowers

SENEGAS > SENEGA

SENES > SENE

SENESCENT adj growing old

SENESCHAL n steward of the household of a medieval prince or nobleman

SENGI n African shrew

SENGREEN n house leek

SENGREENS > SENGREEN

SENHOR n Portuguese term of address for man

SENHORA n Portuguese term of address for woman

SENHORAS > SENHORA

SENHORES > SENHOR

SENHORITA n Portuguese term of address for girl

SENHORS > SENHOR

SENILE adj mentally or physically weak because of old age ▷ n senile person

SENILELY > SENILE

SENILES > SENILE

SENILITY > SENILE

SENIOR adj superior in rank or standing ▷ n senior person

SENIORITY n state of being senior

SENIORS > SENIOR

SENITI n money unit in Tonga

SENNA n tropical plant

SENNACHIE n Gaelic storyteller

SENNAS > SENNA

SENNET n fanfare: used as a stage direction in Elizabethan drama

SENNETS > SENNET

SENNIGHT archaic word for > WEEK

SENNIGHTS > SENNIGHT

SENNIT n flat braided cordage used on ships

SENNITS > SENNIT

SENOPIA n shortsightedness in old age

SENOPIAS > SENOPIA

SENOR n Spanish term of address equivalent to sir or Mr

SENORA n Spanish term of address equivalent to madam or Mrs

SENORAS > SENORA

SENORES > SENOR

SENORITA n Spanish term of address equivalent to madam or Miss

SENORITAS > SENORITA

SENORS > SENOR

SENRYU n Japanese short poem

SENS > SEN

SENSA > SENSUM

SENSATE adj perceived by the senses ▷ vb make sensate

SENSATED > SENSATE

SENSATELY > SENSATE

SENSATES > SENSATE

SENSATING > SENSATE

SENSATION n ability to feel things physically

SENSE n any of the faculties of perception or feeling ▷ vb perceive

SENSED > SENSE

SENSEFUL adj full of sense

SENSEI n martial arts teacher

SENSEIS > SENSEI

SENSELESS adj foolish

SENSES > SENSE

SENSI same as > SENSEI

SENSIBLE adj having or showing good sense ▷ n sensible thing or person

SENSIBLER > SENSIBLE

SENSIBLES > SENSIBLE

SENSIBLY > SENSIBLE

SENSILE adj capable of feeling

SENSILLA > SENSILLUM

SENSILLAE > SENSILLUM

SENSILLUM n sense organ in insects

SENSING > SENSE

SENSINGS > SENSE

SENSIS > SENSI

SENSISM n theory that ideas spring from senses

SENSISMS > SENSISM

SENSIST > SENSISM

SENSISTS > SENSISM

SENSITISE same as > SENSITIZE

SENSITIVE adj easily hurt or offended

SENSITIZE vb make sensitive

SENSOR n device that detects or measures the presence of something, such as radiation

SENSORIA > SENSORIUM

SENSORIAL same as > SENSORY

SENSORILY > SENSORY

SENSORIUM n area of the brain considered responsible for receiving and integrating sensations from the outside world

SENSORS > SENSOR

SENSORY adj of the senses or sensation

SENSUAL adj giving pleasure to the body and senses rather than the mind

SENSUALLY > SENSUAL

SENSUM n sensation detached from the information it conveys and also from its source in the external world

SENSUOUS adj pleasing to the senses

SENT n former monetary unit of Estonia

SENTE n money unit in Lesotho

SENTED > SEND

SENTENCE n sequence of words capable of standing alone as a statement, question, or command ▷ vb pass sentence on (a convicted person)

SENTENCED > SENTENCE

SENTENCER > SENTENCE

SENTENCES > SENTENCE

SENTENTIA n opinion

SENTI > SENT

SENTIENCE n state or quality of being sentient

SENTIENCY same as > SENTIENCE

SENTIENT adj capable of feeling ▷ n sentient person or thing

SENTIENTS > SENTIENT

SENTIMENT n thought, opinion, or attitude

SENTIMO n money unit in Philippines

SENTIMOS > SENTIMO

SENTINEL n sentry ▷ vb guard as a sentinel

SENTINELS > SENTINEL

SENTING > SEND

SENTRIES > SENTRY

SENTRY n soldier on watch

SENTS > SENT

SENVIES > SENVY

SENVY n mustard

SENZA prep without

SEPAD vb suppose

SEPADDED > SEPAD
SEPADDING > SEPAD
SEPADS > SEPAD
SEPAL n leaflike division of the calyx of a flower
SEPALED > SEPAL
SEPALINE same as > SEPALOID
SEPALLED > SEPAL
SEPALODY n changing of flower part into sepal
SEPALOID adj (esp of petals) resembling a sepal in structure and function
SEPALOUS adj with sepals
SEPALS > SEPAL
SEPARABLE adj able to be separated
SEPARABLY > SEPARABLE
SEPARATA > SEPARATUM
SEPARATE vb act as a barrier between ▷ adj not the same, different ▷ n item of clothing that only covers half the body
SEPARATED > SEPARATE
SEPARATES > SEPARATE
SEPARATOR n person or thing that separates
SEPARATUM n separate printing of article from magazine
SEPHEN n stingray
SEPHENS > SEPHEN
SEPIA n reddish-brown pigment ▷ adj dark reddish-brown, like the colour of very old photographs
SEPIAS > SEPIA
SEPIC adj of sepia
SEPIMENT n hedge
SEPIMENTS > SEPIMENT
SEPIOLITE n meerschaum
SEPIOST n cuttlefish bone
SEPIOSTS > SEPIOST
SEPIUM n cuttlefish bone
SEPIUMS > SEPIUM
SEPMAG adj designating a film or television programme for which the sound is recorded on separate magnetic material and run in synchronism with the picture
SEPOY n (formerly) Indian soldier in the service of the British
SEPOYS > SEPOY
SEPPUKU n Japanese ritual suicide
SEPPUKUS > SEPPUKU
SEPS n species of lizard
SEPSES > SEPSIS
SEPSIS n poisoning caused by pus-forming bacteria
SEPT n clan, esp in Ireland or Scotland
SEPTA > SEPTUM
SEPTAGE n waste removed from septic tank

SEPTAGES > SEPTAGE
SEPTAL adj of or relating to a septum
SEPTARIA > SEPTARIUM
SEPTARIAN > SEPTARIUM
SEPTARIUM n mass of mineral substance having cracks filled with another mineral
SEPTATE adj divided by septa
SEPTATION n division by partitions
SEPTEMFID adj divided into seven
SEPTEMVIR n member of government of seven men
SEPTENARY adj of or relating to the number seven ▷ n number seven
SEPTENNIA npl cycles of seven years
SEPTET n group of seven performers
SEPTETS > SEPTET
SEPTETTE same as > SEPTET
SEPTETTES > SEPTETTE
SEPTIC adj (of a wound) infected ▷ n infected wound
SEPTICAL > SEPTIC
SEPTICITY > SEPTIC
SEPTICS > SEPTIC
SEPTIFORM adj acting as partition
SEPTIMAL adj of number seven
SEPTIME n seventh of eight basic positions from which a parry can be made in fencing
SEPTIMES > SEPTIME
SEPTIMOLE n group of seven musical notes
SEPTLEVA n gambling term from old card game
SEPTLEVAS > SEPTLEVA
SEPTS > SEPT
SEPTUM n dividing partition between two cavities in the body
SEPTUMS > SEPTUM
SEPTUOR n group of seven musicians
SEPTUORS > SEPTUOR
SEPTUPLE vb multiply by seven ▷ adj seven times as much or as many ▷ n quantity or number seven times as great as another
SEPTUPLED > SEPTUPLE
SEPTUPLES > SEPTUPLE
SEPTUPLET n group of seven notes played in a time value of six, eight, etc
SEPULCHER same as > SEPULCHRE
SEPULCHRE n tomb or burial vault ▷ vb bury in a sepulchre
SEPULTURE n act of placing in a sepulchre
SEQUACITY quality of

being pliant or controllable
SEQUEL n novel, play, or film that continues the story of an earlier one
SEQUELA n any abnormal bodily condition or disease related to or arising from a pre-existing disease
SEQUELAE > SEQUELA
SEQUELISE same as > SEQUELIZE
SEQUELIZE vb create sequel to
SEQUELS > SEQUEL
SEQUENCE n arrangement of two or more things in successive order ▷ vb arrange in a sequence
SEQUENCED > SEQUENCE
SEQUENCER n electronic device that determines the order in which a number of operations occur
SEQUENCES > SEQUENCE
SEQUENCY n number of changes in mathematical list
SEQUENT adj following in order or succession ▷ n something that follows
SEQUENTLY > SEQUENT
SEQUENTS > SEQUENT
SEQUESTER vb seclude
SEQUESTRA npl detached pieces of necrotic bone that often migrate to wounds
SEQUIN n small ornamental metal disc on a garment ▷ vb apply sequins
SEQUINED > SEQUIN
SEQUINING > SEQUIN
SEQUINNED > SEQUIN
SEQUINS > SEQUIN
SEQUITUR n conclusion that follows from the premises
SEQUITURS > SEQUITUR
SEQUOIA n giant Californian coniferous tree
SEQUOIAS > SEQUOIA
SER n unit of weight used in India, usually taken as one fortieth of a maund
SERA > SERUM
SERAC n pinnacle of ice among crevasses on a glacier, usually on a steep slope
SERACS > SERAC
SERAFILE n line of soldiers
SERAFILES > SERAFILE
SERAFIN n old silver coin of Goa
SERAFINS > SERAFIN
SERAGLIO n harem of a Muslim palace
SERAGLIOS > SERAGLIO
SERAI n (in the East) a caravanserai or inn
SERAIL same as > SERAGLIO
SERAILS > SERAIL
SERAIS > SERAI

SERAL > SERE
SERANG n native captain of a crew of sailors in the East Indies
SERANGS > SERANG
SERAPE n blanket-like shawl often of brightly-coloured wool worn by men in Latin America
SERAPES > SERAPE
SERAPH n member of the highest order of angels
SERAPHIC adj of or resembling a seraph
SERAPHIM > SERAPH
SERAPHIMS > SERAPH
SERAPHIN n angel
SERAPHINE n old keyboard instrument
SERAPHINS > SERAPHIN
SERAPHS > SERAPH
SERASKIER n Turkish military leader
SERDAB n secret chamber in an ancient Egyptian tomb
SERDABS > SERDAB
SERE adj dried up or withered ▷ n series of changes occurring in the ecological succession of a particular community ▷ vb sear
SERED > SERE
SEREIN n fine rain falling from a clear sky after sunset, esp in the tropics
SEREINS > SEREIN
SERENADE n music played or sung to a woman by a lover ▷ vb sing or play a serenade to (someone)
SERENADED > SERENADE
SERENADER > SERENADE
SERENADES > SERENADE
SERENATA n 18th-century cantata, often dramatic in form
SERENATAS > SERENATA
SERENATE n old form of serenade
SERENATES > SERENATE
SERENE adj calm, peaceful ▷ vb make serene
SERENED > SERENE
SERENELY > SERENE
SERENER > SERENE
SERENES > SERENE
SERENEST > SERENE
SERENING > SERENE
SERENITY n state or quality of being serene
SERER > SERE
SERES > SERE
SEREST > SERE
SERF n medieval farm labourer who could not leave the land he worked on
SERFAGE > SERF
SERFAGES > SERF
SERFDOM > SERF
SERFDOMS > SERF
SERFHOOD > SERF

S

SERFHOODS > SERF

SERFISH > SERF

SERFLIKE > SERF

SERFS > SERF

SERFSHIP > SERF

SERFSHIPS > SERF

SERGE *n* strong woollen fabric

SERGEANCY > SERGEANT

SERGEANT *n* noncommissioned officer in the army

SERGEANTS > SERGEANT

SERGEANTY *n* form of feudal tenure

SERGED *adj* with sewn seam

SERGER *n* sewing machine attachment for finishing seams

SERGERS > SERGER

SERGES > SERGE

SERGING *n* type of sewing

SERGINGS > SERGING

SERIAL *n* story or play produced in successive instalments ▷ *adj* of or forming a series

SERIALISE *same as* > SERIALIZE

SERIALISM *n* musical technique using a sequence of notes in a definite order

SERIALIST *n* writer of serials

SERIALITY > SERIAL

SERIALIZE *vb* publish or present as a serial

SERIALLY > SERIAL

SERIALS > SERIAL

SERIATE *adj* forming a series ▷ *vb* form into a series

SERIATED > SERIATE

SERIATELY > SERIATE

SERIATES > SERIATE

SERIATIM *adv* in a series

SERIATING > SERIATE

SERIATION > SERIATE

SERIC *adj* of silk

SERICEOUS *adj* covered with a layer of small silky hairs

SERICIN *n* gelatinous protein found on the fibres of raw silk

SERICINS > SERICIN

SERICITE *n* type of mica

SERICITES > SERICITE

SERICITIC > SERICITE

SERICON *n* solution used in alchemy

SERICONS > SERICON

SERIEMA *n* either of two cranelike South American birds

SERIEMAS > SERIEMA

SERIES *n* group or succession of related things, usu arranged in order

SERIF *n* small line at the extremities of a main stroke in a type character

SERIFED *adj* having serifs

SERIFFED *adj* having serifs

SERIFS > SERIF

SERIGRAPH *n* colour print made by an adaptation of the silk-screen process

SERIN *n* any of various small yellow-and-brown finches

SERINE *n* sweet-tasting amino acid

SERINES > SERINE

SERINETTE *n* barrel organ

SERING > SERE

SERINGA *n* any of several trees that yield rubber

SERINGAS > SERINGA

SERINS > SERIN

SERIOUS *adj* giving cause for concern

SERIOUSLY *adv* in a serious manner or to a serious degree

SERIPH *same as* > SERIF

SERIPHS > SERIPH

SERJEANCY *n* rank of sergeant

SERJEANT *same as* > SERGEANT

SERJEANTS > SERJEANT

SERJEANTY *n* type of feudal tenure

SERK *Scots word for* > SHIRT

SERKALI *n* government in Africa

SERKALIS > SERKALI

SERKS > SERK

SERMON *n* speech on a religious or moral subject by a clergyman in a church service ▷ *vb* deliver a sermon

SERMONED > SERMON

SERMONEER *n* preacher

SERMONER *variant of* > SERMONEER

SERMONERS > SERMONER

SERMONET *n* short sermon

SERMONETS > SERMONET

SERMONIC > SERMON

SERMONING > SERMON

SERMONISE *same as* > SERMONIZE

SERMONIZE *vb* make a long moralizing speech

SERMONS > SERMON

SEROGROUP *n* group of bacteria with a common antigen

SEROLOGIC > SEROLOGY

SEROLOGY *n* science concerned with serums

SERON *n* crate

SERONS > SERON

SEROON *n* crate

SEROONS > SEROON

SEROPUS *n* liquid consisting of serum and pus

SEROPUSES > SEROPUS

SEROSA *n* one of the thin membranes surrounding the embryo in an insect's egg

SEROSAE > SEROSA

SEROSAL > SEROSA

SEROSAS > SEROSA

SEROSITY > SEROUS

SEROTINAL *same as* > SEROTINE

SEROTINE *adj* produced, flowering, or developing late in the season ▷ *n* either of two insectivorous bats

SEROTINES > SEROTINE

SEROTINY *n* state of being serotinous

SEROTONIN *n* compound that occurs in the brain, intestines, and blood platelets and acts as a neurotransmitter

SEROTYPE *n* category into which material, usually a bacterium, is placed based on its serological activity ▷ *vb* class according to serotype

SEROTYPED > SEROTYPE

SEROTYPES > SEROTYPE

SEROTYPIC *adj* relating to a serotype

SEROUS *adj* of, containing, or like serum

SEROVAR *n* subdivision of species

SEROVARS > SEROVAR

SEROW *n* either of two antelopes of mountainous regions of S and SE Asia

SEROWS > SEROW

SERPENT *n* snake

SERPENTRY *n* serpents

SERPENTS > SERPENT

SERPIGO *n* any progressive skin eruption, such as ringworm or herpes

SERPIGOES > SERPIGO

SERPIGOS > SERPIGO

SERPULID *n* marine polychaete worm

SERPULIDS > SERPULID

SERPULITE *n* variety of fossil

SERR *vb* press close together

SERRA *n* sawlike part or organ

SERRAE > SERRA

SERRAN *n* species of fish

SERRANID *n* type of marine fish of the family which includes the sea bass and sea perch

SERRANIDS > SERRANID

SERRANO *n* type of Spanish ham

SERRANOID *same as* > SERRANID

SERRANOS > SERRANO

SERRANS > SERRAN

SERRAS > SERRA

SERRATE *adj* (of leaves) having a margin of forward pointing teeth ▷ *vb* make serrate

SERRATED *adj* having a notched or sawlike edge

SERRATES > SERRATE

SERRATI > SERRATUS

SERRATING > SERRATE

SERRATION *n* state or condition of being serrated

SERRATURE *same as* > SERRATION

SERRATUS *n* muscle in thorax

SERRE *vb* press close together

SERRED > SERRE

SERREFILE *n* file of soldiers

SERRES > SERRE

SERRICORN *n* with serrate antennae

SERRIED *adj* in close formation

SERRIEDLY > SERRIED

SERRIES > SERRY

SERRIFORM *adj* resembling a notched or sawlike edge

SERRING > SERRE

SERRS > SERR

SERRULATE *adj* (esp of leaves) minutely serrate

SERRY *vb* close together

SERRYING > SERRY

SERS > SER

SERUEWE *vb* old word meaning survey

SERUEWED > SERUEWE

SERUEWES > SERUEWE

SERUEWING > SERUEWE

SERUM *n* watery fluid left after blood has clotted

SERUMAL > SERUM

SERUMS > SERUM

SERVABLE > SERVE

SERVAL *n* feline African mammal

SERVALS > SERVAL

SERVANT *n* person employed to do household work for another ▷ *vb* work as a servant

SERVANTED > SERVANT

SERVANTRY *n* servants

SERVANTS > SERVANT

SERVE *vb* work for (a person, community, or cause) ▷ *n* act of serving the ball

SERVEABLE > SERVE

SERVED > SERVE

SERVER *n* player who serves in racket games

SERVERIES > SERVERY

SERVERS > SERVER

SERVERY *n* room from which food is served

SERVES > SERVE

SERVEWE *vb* old word meaning survey

SERVEWED > SERVEWE

SERVEWES > SERVEWE

SERVEWING > SERVEWE

SERVICE *n* serving ▷ *adj* serving the public rather than producing goods ▷ *vb* provide a service or services to

SERVICED > SERVICE

SERVICER > SERVICE
SERVICERS > SERVICE
SERVICES > SERVICE
SERVICING > SERVICE
SERVIENT *adj* subordinate
SERVIETTE *n* table napkin
SERVILE *adj* too eager to obey people, fawning ▷ *n* servile person
SERVILELY > SERVILE
SERVILES > SERVILE
SERVILISM *n* condition of being servile
SERVILITY > SERVILE
SERVING *n* portion of food
SERVINGS > SERVING
SERVITOR *n* servant or attendant
SERVITORS > SERVITOR
SERVITUDE *n* bondage or slavery
SERVLET *n* small program that runs on a web server often accessing databases in response to client input
SERVLETS > SERVLET
SERVO *n* servomechanism ▷ *adj* of a servomechanism
SERVOS > SERVO
SERVQUAL *n* provision of high-quality products by an organization backed by a high level of service for consumers
SERVQUALS > SERVQUAL
SESAME *n* plant cultivated for its seeds and oil, which are used in cooking
SESAMES > SESAME
SESAMOID *adj* of or relating to various small bones formed in tendons ▷ *n* sesamoid bone
SESAMOIDS > SESAMOID
SESE *interj* exclamation found in Shakespeare
SESELI *n* garden plant
SESELIS > SESELI
SESEY *interj* exclamation found in Shakespeare
SESH *short for >* SESSION
SESHES > SESH
SESS *n* old word meaning tax
SESSA *interj* exclamation found in Shakespeare
SESSES > SESS
SESSILE *adj* (of flowers or leaves) having no stalk
SESSILITY > SESSILE
SESSION *n* period spent in an activity
SESSIONAL > SESSION
SESSIONS *npl* sittings or a sitting of justice in court
SESSPOOL *n* cesspool
SESSPOOLS > SESSPOOL
SESTERCE *n* silver or, later, bronze coin of ancient Rome worth a quarter of a denarius
SESTERCES > SESTERCE
SESTERTIA *npl* ancient Roman money accounts

SESTERTII *npl* sesterces
SESTET *n* last six lines of a sonnet
SESTETS > SESTET
SESTETT *n* group of six
SESTETTE *n* group of six
SESTETTES > SESTETTE
SESTETTO *n* composition for six musicians
SESTETTOS > SESTETTO
SESTETTS > SESTETT
SESTINA *n* elaborate verse form of Italian origin
SESTINAS > SESTINA
SESTINE *n* poem of six lines
SESTINES > SESTINE
SESTON *n* type of plankton
SESTONS > SESTON
SET *vb* put in a specified position or state ▷ *n* setting or being set ▷ *adj* fixed or established beforehand
SETA *n* (in invertebrates and some plants) any bristle or bristle-like appendage
SETACEOUS > SETA
SETAE > SETA
SETAL > SETA
SETBACK *n* anything that delays progress
SETBACKS > SETBACK
SETENANT *n* pair of postage stamps of different values joined together
SETENANTS > SETENANT
SETIFORM *adj* shaped like a seta
SETLINE *n* any of various types of fishing line
SETLINES > SETLINE
SETNESS > SET
SETNESSES > SET
SETOFF *n* counterbalance
SETOFFS > SETOFF
SETON *n* surgical thread inserted below the skin
SETONS > SETON
SETOSE *adj* covered with setae
SETOUS > SETA
SETOUT *n* beginning or outset
SETOUTS > SETOUT
SETS > SET
SETSCREW *n* screw that fits into the boss or hub of a wheel, and prevents motion of the part relative to the shaft on which it is mounted
SETSCREWS > SETSCREW
SETT *n* badger's burrow
SETTEE *n* couch
SETTEES > SETTEE
SETTER *n* long-haired gun dog ▷ *vb* treat with a piece of setterwort
SETTERED > SETTER
SETTERING > SETTER
SETTERS > SETTER
SETTING > SET

SETTINGS > SET
SETTLE *vb* arrange or put in order ▷ *n* long wooden bench with high back and arms
SETTLED > SETTLE
SETTLER *n* colonist
SETTLERS > SETTLER
SETTLES > SETTLE
SETTLING > SETTLE
SETTLINGS *npl* any matter or substance that has settled at the bottom of a liquid
SETTLOR *n* person who settles property on someone
SETTLORS > SETTLOR
SETTS > SETT
SETUALE *n* valerian
SETUALES > SETUALE
SETULE *n* small bristle
SETULES > SETULE
SETULOSE > SETULE
SETULOUS > SETULE
SETUP *n* way in which anything is organized or arranged
SETUPS > SETUP
SETWALL *n* valerian
SETWALLS > SETWALL
SEVEN *n* one more than six ▷ *adj* amounting to seven ▷ *det* amounting to seven
SEVENFOLD *adj* having seven times as many or as much ▷ *adv* by seven times as many or as much
SEVENS *n* Rugby Union match or series of matches played with seven players on each side
SEVENTEEN *n* ten and seven ▷ *adj* amounting to seventeen ▷ *det* amounting to seventeen
SEVENTH *n* (of) number seven in a series ▷ *adj* coming after the sixth and before the eighth ▷ *adv* after the sixth person, position, event, etc
SEVENTHLY *same as* > SEVENTH
SEVENTHS > SEVENTH
SEVENTIES > SEVENTY
SEVENTY *n* ten times seven ▷ *adj* amounting to seventy ▷ *det* amounting to seventy
SEVER *vb* cut through or off
SEVERABLE *adj* able to be severed
SEVERAL *adj* some, a few ▷ *n* individual person
SEVERALLY *adv* separately
SEVERALS > SEVERAL
SEVERALTY *n* state of being several or separate
SEVERANCE *n* act of severing or state of being severed
SEVERE *adj* strict or harsh
SEVERED > SEVER
SEVERELY > SEVERE

SEVERER > SEVERE
SEVEREST > SEVERE
SEVERIES > SEVERY
SEVERING > SEVER
SEVERITY > SEVERE
SEVERS > SEVER
SEVERY *n* part of vaulted ceiling
SEVICHE *n* Mexican fish dish
SEVICHES > SEVICHE
SEVRUGA *n* species of sturgeon
SEVRUGAS > SEVRUGA
SEW *vb* join with thread repeatedly passed through with a needle
SEWABLE > SEW
SEWAGE *n* waste matter or excrement carried away in sewers
SEWAGES > SEWAGE
SEWAN *same as >* SEAWAN
SEWANS > SEWAN
SEWAR *n* Asian dagger
SEWARS > SEWAR
SEWED > SEW
SEWEL *n* scarecrow
SEWELLEL *n* mountain beaver
SEWELLELS > SEWELLEL
SEWELS > SEWEL
SEWEN *same as >* SEWIN
SEWENS > SEWEN
SEWER *n* drain to remove waste water and sewage ▷ *vb* provide with sewers
SEWERAGE *n* system of sewers
SEWERAGES > SEWERAGE
SEWERED > SEWER
SEWERING > SEWER
SEWERINGS > SEWER
SEWERLESS > SEWER
SEWERLIKE > SEWER
SEWERS > SEWER
SEWIN *n* sea trout
SEWING > SEW
SEWINGS > SEW
SEWINS > SEWIN
SEWN > SEW
SEWS > SEW
SEX *n* state of being male or female ▷ *vb* find out the sex of ▷ *adj* of sexual matters
SEXAHOLIC *n* person who is addicted to sex
SEXED *adj* having a specified degree of sexuality
SEXENNIAL *adj* occurring once every six years or over a period of six years ▷ *n* sixth anniversary
SEXER *n* person checking sex of chickens
SEXERCISE *n* sexual activity, regarded as a way of keeping fit
SEXERS > SEXER
SEXES > SEX
SEXFID *adj* split into six
SEXFOIL *n* flower with six petals or leaves**

S

SEXFOILS > SEXFOIL

SEXIER > SEXY

SEXIEST > SEXY

SEXILY > SEXY

SEXINESS > SEXY

SEXING > SEX

SEXINGS > SEXING

SEXISM n discrimination on the basis of a person's sex

SEXISMS > SEXISM

SEXIST > SEXISM

SEXISTS > SEXISM

SEXLESS adj neither male nor female

SEXLESSLY > SEXLESS

SEXLINKED adj (of a gene) found on a sex chromosome

SEXOLOGIC > SEXOLOGY

SEXOLOGY n study of sexual behaviour in human beings

SEXPERT n person who professes a knowledge of sexual matters .

SEXPERTS > SEXPERT

SEXPOT n person, esp a young woman, considered as being sexually very attractive

SEXPOTS > SEXPOT

SEXT n fourth of the seven canonical hours of the divine office or the prayers prescribed for it: originally the sixth hour of the day (noon)

SEXTAIN same as > SESTINA

SEXTAINS > SEXTAIN

SEXTAN adj (of a fever) marked by paroxysms that recur after an interval of five days

SEXTANS n Roman coin

SEXTANSES > SEXTANS

SEXTANT n navigator's instrument for measuring angles to calculate one's position

SEXTANTAL > SEXTANT

SEXTANTS > SEXTANT

SEXTARII > SEXTARIUS

SEXTARIUS n ancient Roman quantity measure

SEXTET n group of six performers

SEXTETS > SEXTET

SEXTETT n sextet

SEXTETTE same as > SEXTET

SEXTETTES > SEXTETTE

SEXTETTS > SEXTETT

SEXTILE n one of five values of a variable dividing its distribution into six groups with equal frequencies

SEXTILES > SEXTILE

SEXTO same as > SIXMO

SEXTOLET n group of six musical notes

SEXTOLETS > SEXTOLET

SEXTON n official in charge of a church and churchyard

SEXTONESS n female sexton

SEXTONS > SEXTON

SEXTOS > SEXTO

SEXTS > SEXT

SEXTUOR n sextet

SEXTUORS > SEXTUOR

SEXTUPLE vb multiply by six ▷ adj six times as much or as many ▷ n quantity or number six times as great as another

SEXTUPLED > SEXTUPLE

SEXTUPLES > SEXTUPLE

SEXTUPLET n one of six children born at one birth

SEXTUPLY > SEXTUPLE

SEXUAL adj of or characterized by sex

SEXUALISE same as > SEXUALIZE

SEXUALISM n emphasising of sexuality

SEXUALIST > SEXUALISM

SEXUALITY n state or quality of being sexual

SEXUALIZE vb make or become sexual or sexually aware

SEXUALLY > SEXUAL

SEXVALENT adj with valency of six

SEXY adj sexually exciting or attractive

SEY n Scots word meaning part of cow carcase

SEYEN n old form of scion

SEYENS > SEYEN

SEYS > SEY

SEYSURE n old form of seizure

SEYSURES > SEYSURE

SEZ vb informal spelling of 'says'

SFERICS same as > SPHERICS

SFORZANDI > SFORZANDO

SFORZANDO adv be played with strong initial attack ▷ n symbol written above a note, indicating this

SFORZATI > SFORZATO

SFORZATO same as > SFORZANDO

SFORZATOS > SFORZATO

SFUMATO n gradual transition between areas of different colour in painting

SFUMATOS > SFUMATO

SGRAFFITI > SGRAFFITO

SGRAFFITO n technique in mural or ceramic decoration in which the top layer of glaze is incised with a design to reveal parts of the ground

SH same as > SHILLING

SHA interj be quiet

SHABASH interj (in Indian English) bravo or well done

SHABBATOT npl Jewish sabbaths

SHABBIER > SHABBY

SHABBIEST > SHABBY

SHABBILY > SHABBY

SHABBLE n Scots word meaning old sword

SHABBLES > SHABBLE

SHABBY adj worn or dilapidated in appearance

SHABRACK n cavalryman's saddle cloth

SHABRACKS > SHABRACK

SHACK n rough hut ▷ vb evade (work or responsibility)

SHACKED > SHACK

SHACKING > SHACK

SHACKLE n metal ring for securing a person's wrists or ankles ▷ vb fasten with shackles

SHACKLED > SHACKLE

SHACKLER > SHACKLE

SHACKLERS > SHACKLE

SHACKLES > SHACKLE

SHACKLING > SHACKLE

SHACKO same as > SHAKO

SHACKOES > SHACKO

SHACKOS > SHACKO

SHACKS > SHACK

SHAD n herring-like fish

SHADBERRY n edible purplish berry of the shadbush

SHADBLOW n type of shrub

SHADBLOWS > SHADBLOW

SHADBUSH n type of N American tree or shrub

SHADCHAN n Jewish marriage broker

SHADCHANS > SHADCHAN

SHADDOCK another name for > POMELO

SHADDOCKS > SHADDOCK

SHADE n relative darkness ▷ vb screen from light

SHADED > SHADE

SHADELESS > SHADE

SHADER > SHADE

SHADERS > SHADE

SHADES npl gathering darkness at nightfall

SHADFLIES > SHADFLY

SHADFLY American name for > MAYFLY

SHADIER > SHADY

SHADIEST > SHADY

SHADILY > SHADY

SHADINESS > SHADY

SHADING n graded areas of tone indicating light and dark in a painting or drawing

SHADINGS > SHADING

SHADKHAN same as > SHADCHAN

SHADKHANS > SHADKHAN

SHADOOF n mechanism for raising water, esp as used in Egypt and the Near East

SHADOOFS > SHADOOF

SHADOW n dark shape cast on a surface when something stands between a light and the surface ▷ vb cast a shadow over

SHADOWBOX vb practise boxing against an imaginary opponent

SHADOWED > SHADOW

SHADOWER > SHADOW

SHADOWERS > SHADOW

SHADOWIER > SHADOWY

SHADOWILY > SHADOWY

SHADOWING > SHADOW

SHADOWS > SHADOW

SHADOWY adj (of a place) full of shadows

SHADRACH n lump of iron that has not been melted in the furnace

SHADRACHS > SHADRACH

SHADS > SHAD

SHADUF same as > SHADOOF

SHADUFS > SHADUF

SHADY adj situated in or giving shade

SHAFT n long narrow straight handle of a tool or weapon ▷ vb treat badly

SHAFTED > SHAFT

SHAFTER > SHAFT

SHAFTERS > SHAFT

SHAFTING n assembly of rotating shafts for transmitting power

SHAFTINGS > SHAFTING

SHAFTLESS > SHAFT

SHAFTS > SHAFT

SHAG n coarse shredded tobacco ▷ adj having a long pile ▷ vb have sexual intercourse with (a person)

SHAGBARK n North American hickory tree

SHAGBARKS > SHAGBARK

SHAGGABLE adj sexually attractive

SHAGGED > SHAG

SHAGGER n person who has sexual intercourse

SHAGGERS > SHAGGER

SHAGGIER > SHAGGY

SHAGGIEST > SHAGGY

SHAGGILY > SHAGGY

SHAGGING > SHAG

SHAGGY adj covered with rough hair or wool

SHAGPILE adj (of carpet) having long fibres

SHAGREEN n sharkskin

SHAGREENS > SHAGREEN

SHAGROON n nineteenth-century Australian settler in Canterbury

SHAGROONS > SHAGROON

SHAGS > SHAG

SHAH n formerly, ruler of Iran

SHAHADA n Islamic declaration of faith, repeated daily by Muslims

SHAHADAS > SHAHADA

SHAHDOM > SHAH

SHAHDOMS > SHAH

SHAHEED same as > SHAHID

SHAHEEDS > SHAHEED

SHAHID n Muslim martyr

SHAHIDS > SHAHID

SHAHS > SHAH

SHAHTOOSH n soft wool that comes from the protected Tibetan antelope

SHAIKH n sheikh

SHAIKHS > SHAIKH

SHAIRD n Scots word meaning shred

SHAIRDS > SHAIRD

SHAIRN Scots word for > DUNG

SHAIRNS > SHAIRN

SHAITAN n (in Muslim countries) an evil spirit

SHAITANS > SHAITAN

SHAKABLE > SHAKE

SHAKE vb move quickly up and down or back and forth ▷ n shaking

SHAKEABLE > SHAKE

SHAKED vb old form of shook

SHAKEDOWN n act of extortion

SHAKEN > SHAKE

SHAKEOUT n process of reducing the number of people in a workforce

SHAKEOUTS > SHAKEOUT

SHAKER n container in which drinks are mixed or from which powder is shaken

SHAKERS > SHAKER

SHAKES > SHAKE

SHAKEUP n radical reorganization

SHAKEUPS > SHAKEUP

SHAKIER > SHAKY

SHAKIEST > SHAKY

SHAKILY > SHAKY

SHAKINESS > SHAKY

SHAKING > SHAKE

SHAKINGS > SHAKE

SHAKO n tall cylindrical peaked military hat with a plume

SHAKOES > SHAKO

SHAKOS > SHAKO

SHAKT vb old form of shook

SHAKUDO n Japanese alloy of copper and gold

SHAKUDOS > SHAKUDO

SHAKY adj unsteady

SHALE n flaky sedimentary rock

SHALED > SHALE

SHALELIKE > SHALE

SHALES > SHALE

SHALEY > SHALE

SHALIER > SHALE

SHALIEST > SHALE

SHALING > SHALE

SHALL vb used as an auxiliary to make the future tense

SHALLI n type of fabric

SHALLIS > SHALLI

SHALLON n American

shrub

SHALLONS > SHALLON

SHALLOON n light twill-weave woollen fabric used chiefly for coat linings, etc

SHALLOONS > SHALLOON

SHALLOP n light boat used for rowing in shallow water

SHALLOPS > SHALLOP

SHALLOT n kind of small onion

SHALLOTS > SHALLOT

SHALLOW adj not deep ▷ n shallow place in a body of water ▷ vb make or become shallow

SHALLOWED > SHALLOW

SHALLOWER > SHALLOW

SHALLOWLY > SHALLOW

SHALLOWS > SHALLOW

SHALM n old woodwind instrument

SHALMS > SHALM

SHALOM n Jewish greeting meaning 'peace be with you'

SHALOMS > SHALOM

SHALOT n shallot

SHALOTS > SHALOT

SHALT singular form of the present tense (indicative mood) of > SHALL

SHALWAR n pair of loose-fitting trousers tapering to a narrow fit around the ankles, worn in the Indian subcontinent, often with a kameez

SHALWARS > SHALWAR

SHALY > SHALE

SHAM n thing or person that is not genuine ▷ adj not genuine ▷ vb fake, feign

SHAMA n Indian songbird

SHAMABLE > SHAME

SHAMABLY > SHAME

SHAMAL n hot northwesterly wind that blows across Iraq and the Persian Gulf

SHAMALS > SHAMAL

SHAMAN n priest of shamanism

SHAMANIC > SHAMAN

SHAMANISM n religion of northern Asia, based on a belief in good and evil spirits

SHAMANIST > SHAMANISM

SHAMANS > SHAMAN

SHAMAS > SHAMA

SHAMATEUR n sportsperson who is officially an amateur but accepts payment

SHAMBA n (in E Africa) any field used for growing crops

SHAMBAS > SHAMBA

SHAMBLE vb walk in a shuffling awkward way ▷ n awkward or shuffling walk

SHAMBLED > SHAMBLE

SHAMBLES n disorderly

event or place

SHAMBLIER > SHAMBLE

SHAMBLING > SHAMBLE

SHAMBLY > SHAMBLE

SHAMBOLIC adj completely disorganized

SHAME n painful emotion caused by awareness of having done something dishonourable or foolish ▷ vb cause to feel shame

SHAMEABLE > SHAME

SHAMEABLY > SHAME

SHAMED > SHAME

SHAMEFAST adj old form of shamefaced

SHAMEFUL adj causing or deserving shame

SHAMELESS adj with no sense of shame

SHAMER n cause of shame

SHAMERS > SHAME

SHAMES > SHAME

SHAMIANA n tent in India

SHAMIANAH n tent in India

SHAMIANAS > SHAMIANA

SHAMINA n wool blend of pashm and shahtoosh

SHAMINAS > SHAMINA

SHAMING > SHAME

SHAMISEN n Japanese stringed instrument

SHAMISENS > SHAMISEN

SHAMMAS same as > SHAMMES

SHAMMASH same as > SHAMMES

SHAMMASIM > SHAMMES

SHAMMED > SHAM

SHAMMER > SHAM

SHAMMERS > SHAM

SHAMMES n official acting as the beadle, sexton, and caretaker of a synagogue

SHAMMIED > SHAMMY

SHAMMIES > SHAMMY

SHAMMING > SHAM

SHAMMOS same as > SHAMMES

SHAMMOSIM > SHAMMES

SHAMMY n piece of chamois leather ▷ vb rub with a shammy

SHAMMYING > SHAMMY

SHAMOIS n chamois

SHAMOS same as > SHAMMES

SHAMOSIM > SHAMMES

SHAMOY n chamois ▷ vb rub with a shamoy

SHAMOYED > SHAMOY

SHAMOYING > SHAMOY

SHAMOYS > SHAMOY

SHAMPOO n liquid soap for washing hair, carpets, or upholstery ▷ vb wash with shampoo

SHAMPOOED > SHAMPOO

SHAMPOOER > SHAMPOO

SHAMPOOS > SHAMPOO

SHAMROCK n clover leaf, esp the Irish emblem

SHAMROCKS > SHAMROCK

SHAMS > SHAM

SHAMUS n police or private detective

SHAMUSES > SHAMUS

SHAN variant of > SHAND

SHANACHIE n Gaelic storyteller

SHAND n old word meaning fake coin

SHANDIES > SHANDY

SHANDRIES > SHANDRY

SHANDRY n light horse-drawn cart

SHANDS > SHAND

SHANDY n drink made of beer and lemonade

SHANGHAI vb force or trick (someone) into doing something ▷ n catapult

SHANGHAIS > SHANGHAI

SHANK n lower leg ▷ vb (of fruits, roots, etc) to show disease symptoms, esp discoloration

SHANKBONE n bone in lower leg

SHANKED > SHANK

SHANKING > SHANK

SHANKS > SHANK

SHANNIES > SHANNY

SHANNY n European blenny of rocky coastal waters

SHANS > SHAN

SHANTEY same as > SHANTY

SHANTEYS > SHANTEY

SHANTI n peace

SHANTIES > SHANTY

SHANTIH same as > SHANTI

SHANTIHS > SHANTIH

SHANTIS > SHANTI

SHANTUNG n soft Chinese silk with a knobbly surface

SHANTUNGS > SHANTUNG

SHANTY n shack or crude dwelling

SHANTYMAN n man living in shanty

SHANTYMEN > SHANTYMAN

SHAPABLE > SHAPE

SHAPE n outward form of an object ▷ vb form or mould

SHAPEABLE > SHAPE

SHAPED > SHAPE

SHAPELESS adj (of a person or object) lacking a pleasing shape

SHAPELIER > SHAPELY

SHAPELY adj having an attractive shape

SHAPEN vb old form of shaped

SHAPER > SHAPE

SHAPERS > SHAPE

SHAPES > SHAPE

SHAPEUP n system of hiring dockers for a day's work

SHAPEUPS > SHAPEUP

SHAPEWEAR n underwear that shapes body

SHAPING > SHAPE

S

SHAPINGS > SHAPE

SHAPS n leather over-trousers worn by cowboys

SHARABLE > SHARE

SHARD n broken piece of pottery or glass

SHARDED adj old word meaning hidden under dung

SHARDS > SHARD

SHARE n part of something that belongs to or is contributed by a person ▷ vb give or take a share of (something)

SHAREABLE > SHARE

SHARECROP vb cultivate (farmland) as a sharecropper

SHARED > SHARE

SHAREMAN n member of fishing-boat crew who shares profits

SHAREMEN > SHAREMAN

SHARER > SHARE

SHARERS > SHARE

SHARES > SHARE

SHARESMAN n member of fishing-boat crew who shares profits

SHARESMEN > SHARESMAN

SHAREWARE n software available to all users without the need for a licence

SHARIA n body of doctrines that regulate the lives of Muslims

SHARIAH same as > SHARIA

SHARIAHS > SHARIAH

SHARIAS > SHARIA

SHARIAT n Islamic religious law

SHARIATS > SHARIAT

SHARIF same as > SHERIF

SHARIFIAN > SHARIF

SHARIFS > SHARIF

SHARING > SHARE

SHARINGS > SHARE

SHARK n large usu predatory sea fish ▷ vb obtain (something) by cheating or deception

SHARKED > SHARK

SHARKER n shark hunter

SHARKERS > SHARKER

SHARKING > SHARK

SHARKINGS > SHARK

SHARKLIKE > SHARK

SHARKS > SHARK

SHARKSKIN n stiff glossy fabric

SHARN Scots word for > DUNG

SHARNIER > SHARN

SHARNIEST > SHARN

SHARNS > SHARN

SHARNY > SHARN

SHARON as in sharon fruit persimmon

SHARP adj having a keen cutting edge or fine point ▷ adv promptly ▷ n symbol

raising a note one semitone above natural pitch ▷ vb make sharp

SHARPED > SHARP

SHARPEN vb make or become sharp or sharper

SHARPENED > SHARPEN

SHARPENER > SHARPEN

SHARPENS > SHARPEN

SHARPER n person who cheats

SHARPERS > SHARPER

SHARPEST > SHARP

SHARPIE n member of a teenage group having short hair and distinctive clothes

SHARPIES > SHARPIE

SHARPING > SHARP

SHARPINGS > SHARP

SHARPISH adj fairly sharp ▷ adv promptly

SHARPLY > SHARP

SHARPNESS > SHARP

SHARPS > SHARP

SHARPY n swindler

SHASH vb old form of sash

SHASHED > SHASH

SHASHES > SHASH

SHASHING > SHASH

SHASHLICK same as > SHASHLIK

SHASHLIK n type of kebab

SHASHLIKS > SHASHLIK

SHASLIK n type of kebab

SHASLIKS > SHASLIK

SHASTER same as > SHASTRA

SHASTERS > SHASTER

SHASTRA n any of the sacred writings of Hinduism

SHASTRAS > SHASTRA

SHAT past tense and past participle of > SHIT

SHATOOSH same as > SHAHTOOSH

SHATTER vb break into pieces ▷ n fragment

SHATTERED adj completely exhausted

SHATTERER > SHATTER

SHATTERS > SHATTER

SHATTERY adj liable to shatter

SHAUCHLE vb Scots word meaning shuffle

SHAUCHLED > SHAUCHLE

SHAUCHLES > SHAUCHLE

SHAUCHLY > SHAUCHLE

SHAUGH n old word meaning small wood

SHAUGHS > SHAUGH

SHAUL vb old form of shawl

SHAULED > SHAUL

SHAULING > SHAUL

SHAULS > SHAUL

SHAVABLE > SHAVE

SHAVE vb remove (hair) from (the face, head, or body) with a razor or shaver ▷ n shaving

SHAVEABLE > SHAVE

SHAVED > SHAVE

SHAVELING n derogatory term for a priest or clergyman with a shaven head

SHAVEN adj closely shaved or tonsured

SHAVER n electric razor

SHAVERS > SHAVER

SHAVES > SHAUL

SHAVETAIL n American slang for second lieutenant

SHAVIE n Scots word meaning trick

SHAVIES > SHAVIE

SHAVING > SHAVE

SHAVINGS > SHAVE

SHAW n small wood ▷ vb show

SHAWED > SHAW

SHAWING > SHAW

SHAWL n piece of cloth worn over a woman's shoulders or wrapped around a baby ▷ vb cover with a shawl

SHAWLED > SHAWL

SHAWLEY n Irish word for woman wearing shawl

SHAWLEYS > SHAWLEY

SHAWLIE n disparaging term for a working-class woman who wears a shawl

SHAWLIES > SHAWLIE

SHAWLING > SHAWL

SHAWLINGS > SHAWL

SHAWLLESS > SHAWL

SHAWLS > SHAWL

SHAWM n medieval form of the oboe with a conical bore and flaring bell

SHAWMS > SHAWM

SHAWN variant of > SHAWM

SHAWS > SHAW

SHAY dialect word for > CHAISE

SHAYA n Indian plant

SHAYAS > SHAYA

SHAYS > SHAY

SHAZAM interj magic slogan

SHCHI n Russian cabbage soup

SHCHIS > SHCHI

SHE pron female person or animal previously mentioned ▷ n female person or animal

SHEA n tropical African tree

SHEADING n any of the six subdivisions of the Isle of Man

SHEADINGS > SHEADING

SHEAF n bundle of papers ▷ vb tie into a sheaf

SHEAFED > SHEAF

SHEAFIER > SHEAF

SHEAFIEST > SHEAF

SHEAFING > SHEAF

SHEAFLIKE > SHEAF

SHEAFS > SHEAF

SHEAFY > SHEAF

SHEAL vb old word meaning shell

SHEALED > SHEAL

SHEALING > SHEAL

SHEALINGS > SHEAL

SHEALS > SHEAL

SHEAR vb clip hair or wool from ▷ n breakage caused through strain or twisting

SHEARED > SHEAR

SHEARER > SHEAR

SHEARERS > SHEAR

SHEARING > SHEAR

SHEARINGS > SHEAR

SHEARLEG n one spar of shearlegs

SHEARLEGS same as > SHEERLEGS

SHEARLING n young sheep after its first shearing

SHEARMAN n person who trims cloth

SHEARMEN > SHEARMAN

SHEARS > SHEAR

SHEAS > SHEA

SHEATFISH n European catfish

SHEATH n close-fitting cover, esp for a knife or sword

SHEATHE vb put into a sheath

SHEATHED > SHEATHE

SHEATHER > SHEATHE

SHEATHERS > SHEATHE

SHEATHES > SHEATHE

SHEATHIER > SHEATHE

SHEATHING n any material used as an outer layer

SHEATHS > SHEATH

SHEATHY > SHEATHE

SHEAVE vb gather or bind into sheaves ▷ n wheel with a grooved rim, esp one used as a pulley

SHEAVED > SHEAVE

SHEAVES > SHEAF

SHEAVING > SHEAVE

SHEBANG n situation, matter, or affair

SHEBANGS > SHEBANG

SHEBEAN same as > SHEBEEN

SHEBEANS > SHEBEAN

SHEBEEN n place where alcohol is sold illegally ▷ vb run a shebeen

SHEBEENED > SHEBEEN

SHEBEENER > SHEBEEN

SHEBEENS > SHEBEEN

SHECHITA n Jewish method of killing animals for food

SHECHITAH same as > SHECHITA

SHECHITAS > SHECHITA

SHED n building used for storage or shelter or as a workshop ▷ vb get rid of

SHEDABLE > SHED

SHEDDABLE > SHED

SHEDDED > SHED

SHEDDER n person or thing that sheds

SHEDDERS > SHEDDER

SHEDDING > SHED

SHEDDINGS > SHED

SHEDFUL n quantity or amount contained in a shed
SHEDFULS > SHEDFUL
SHEDHAND n labourer working in a shearing shed
SHEDHANDS > SHEDHAND
SHEDLIKE > SHED
SHEDLOAD n very large amount or number
SHEDLOADS > SHEDLOAD
SHEDS > SHED
SHEEL vb old word meaning shell
SHEELED > SHEEL
SHEELING > SHEEL
SHEELS > SHEEL
SHEEN n glistening brightness on the surface of something ▷ adj shining and beautiful ▷ vb give a sheen to
SHEENED > SHEEN
SHEENEY n offensive word for Jew
SHEENEYS > SHEENEY
SHEENFUL > SHEEN
SHEENIE n offensive word for Jew
SHEENIER > SHEEN
SHEENIES > SHEENIE
SHEENIEST > SHEEN
SHEENING > SHEEN
SHEENS > SHEEN
SHEENY > SHEEN
SHEEP n ruminant animal bred for wool and meat
SHEEPCOT n sheepcote
SHEEPCOTE another word for > SHEEPFOLD
SHEEPCOTS > SHEEPCOT
SHEEPDOG n dog used for herding sheep
SHEEPDOGS > SHEEPDOG
SHEEPFOLD n pen or enclosure for sheep
SHEEPHEAD n species of fish
SHEEPIER > SHEEP
SHEEPIEST > SHEEP
SHEEPISH adj embarrassed because of feeling foolish
SHEEPLE npl informal derogatory word for people who follow the majority in matters of opinion, taste, etc
SHEEPLIKE > SHEEP
SHEEPMAN n person who keeps sheep
SHEEPMEN > SHEEPMAN
SHEEPO n person employed to bring sheep to the catching pen in a shearing shed
SHEEPOS > SHEEPO
SHEEPSKIN n skin of a sheep with the fleece still on, used for clothing or rugs
SHEEPWALK n tract of land for grazing sheep
SHEEPY > SHEEP
SHEER adj absolute,

complete ▷ adv steeply ▷ vb change course suddenly ▷ n any transparent fabric used for making garments
SHEERED > SHEER
SHEERER > SHEER
SHEEREST > SHEER
SHEERING > SHEER
SHEERLEG n one spar of sheerleg
SHEERLEGS n device for lifting heavy weights
SHEERLY > SHEER
SHEERNESS > SHEER
SHEERS > SHEER
SHEESH interj exclamation of surprise or annoyance
SHEESHA n Oriental water-pipe for smoking tobacco
SHEESHAS > SHEESHA
SHEET n large piece of cloth used as an inner bed cover ▷ vb provide with, cover, or wrap in a sheet
SHEETED > SHEET
SHEETER > SHEET
SHEETERS > SHEET
SHEETFED adj printing on separate sheets of paper
SHEETIER > SHEET
SHEETIEST > SHEET
SHEETING n material from which sheets are made
SHEETINGS > SHEETING
SHEETLESS > SHEET
SHEETLIKE > SHEET
SHEETROCK n brand name for plasterboard
SHEETS > SHEET
SHEETY > SHEET
SHEEVE n part of mine winding gear
SHEEVES > SHEEVE
SHEGETZ n offensive word for non-Jew
SHEHITA n slaughter of animal according to Jewish religious law
SHEHITAH n slaughter of animal according to Jewish religious law
SHEHITAHS > SHEHITAH
SHEHITAS > SHEHITA
SHEIK same as > SHEIKH
SHEIKDOM same as > SHEIKHDOM
SHEIKDOMS > SHEIKDOM
SHEIKH n Arab chief
SHEIKHA n chief wife of sheikh
SHEIKHAS > SHEIKHA
SHEIKHDOM n territory ruled by a sheikh
SHEIKHS > SHEIKH
SHEIKS > SHEIK
SHEILA n girl or woman
SHEILAS > SHEILA
SHEILING n hut used by shepherds
SHEILINGS > SHEILING
SHEITAN n Muslim demon
SHEITANS > SHEITAN

SHEKALIM > SHEKEL
SHEKEL n monetary unit of Israel
SHEKELIM > SHEKEL
SHEKELS > SHEKEL
SHELDDUCK n species of large duck
SHELDRAKE same as > SHELDUCK
SHELDUCK n large brightly coloured wild duck of Europe and Asia
SHELDUCKS > SHELDUCK
SHELF n board fixed horizontally for holding things ▷ vb put on a shelf
SHELFED > SHELF
SHELFFUL > SHELF
SHELFFULS > SHELF
SHELFIER > SHELF
SHELFIEST > SHELF
SHELFING > SHELF
SHELFLIKE > SHELF
SHELFROOM n space on shelf
SHELFS > SHELF
SHELFY > SHELF
SHELL n hard outer covering of an egg, nut, or certain animals ▷ vb take the shell from
SHELLAC n resin used in varnishes ▷ vb coat with shellac
SHELLACK vb shellac
SHELLACKS > SHELLAC
SHELLACS > SHELLAC
SHELLBACK n sailor who has crossed the equator
SHELLBARK same as > SHAGBARK
SHELLDUCK n shelduck
SHELLED > SHELL
SHELLER > SHELL
SHELLERS > SHELL
SHELLFIRE n firing of artillery shells
SHELLFISH n sea-living animal, esp one that can be eaten, with a shell
SHELLFUL > SHELL
SHELLFULS > SHELL
SHELLIER > SHELL
SHELLIEST > SHELL
SHELLING > SHELL
SHELLINGS > SHELL
SHELLS > SHELL
SHELLWORK n decoration with shells
SHELLY > SHELL
SHELTA n secret language used by some traveling people in Britain and Ireland
SHELTAS > SHELTA
SHELTER n structure providing protection from danger or the weather ▷ vb give shelter to
SHELTERED adj protected from wind and rain
SHELTERER > SHELTER
SHELTERS > SHELTER
SHELTERY > SHELTER

SHELTIE n small dog similar to a collie
SHELTIES > SHELTY
SHELTY same as > SHELTIE
SHELVE vb put aside or postpone
SHELVED > SHELVE
SHELVER > SHELVE
SHELVERS > SHELVE
SHELVES > SHELF
SHELVIER > SHELVY
SHELVIEST > SHELVY
SHELVING n (material for) shelves
SHELVINGS > SHELVING
SHELVY adj having shelves
SHEMALE n male who has acquired female physical characteristics through surgery
SHEMALES > SHEMALE
SHEMOZZLE n noisy confusion or dispute
SHEND vb put to shame
SHENDING > SHEND
SHENDS > SHEND
SHENT > SHEND
SHEOL n hell
SHEOLS > SHEOL
SHEPHERD n person who tends sheep ▷ vb guide or watch over (people)
SHEPHERDS > SHEPHERD
SHEQALIM n plural of sheqel
SHEQEL same as > SHEKEL
SHEQELS > SHEQEL
SHERANG n person in charge
SHERANGS > SHERANG
SHERBERT same as > SHERBET
SHERBERTS > SHERBET
SHERBET n fruit-flavoured fizzy powder
SHERBETS > SHERBET
SHERD same as > SHARD
SHERDS > SHERD
SHERE old spelling of > SHEER
SHEREEF same as > SHERIF
SHEREEFS > SHEREEF
SHERIA same as > SHARIA
SHERIAS > SHERIA
SHERIAT n Muslim religious law
SHERIATS > SHERIAT
SHERIF n descendant of Mohammed through his daughter Fatima
SHERIFF n (in the US) chief law enforcement officer of a county
SHERIFFS > SHERIFF
SHERIFIAN > SHERIF
SHERIFS > SHERIF
SHERLOCK n detective
SHERLOCKS > SHERLOCK
SHEROOT n cheroot
SHEROOTS > SHEROOT
SHERPA n official who assists at a summit meeting

S

SHERPAS > SHERPA
SHERRIES > SHERRY
SHERRIS n old form of sherry
SHERRISES > SHERRIS
SHERRY n pale or dark brown fortified wine
SHERWANI n long coat closed up to the neck, worn by men in India
SHERWANIS > SHERWANI
SHES > SHE
SHET vb old form of shut
SHETLAND n type of wool spun in the Shetland islands
SHETLANDS > SHETLAND
SHETS > SHET
SHETTING > SHET
SHEUCH n ditch or trough ▷ vb dig
SHEUCHED > SHEUCH
SHEUCHING > SHEUCH
SHEUCHS > SHEUCH
SHEUGH same as **>** SHEUCH
SHEUGHED > SHEUGH
SHEUGHING > SHEUGH
SHEUGHS > SHEUGH
SHEVA n mark in Hebrew writing
SHEVAS > SHEVA
SHEW archaic spelling of **>** SHOW
SHEWBREAD n loaves of bread placed every Sabbath on the table beside the altar of incense in the tabernacle of ancient Israel
SHEWED > SHEW
SHEWEL n old word meaning scarecrow
SHEWELS > SHEWEL
SHEWER > SHEW
SHEWERS > SHEW
SHEWING > SHEW
SHEWN > SHEW
SHEWS > SHEW
SHH interj sound made to ask for silence
SHIAI n judo contest
SHIAIS > SHIAI
SHIATSU n massage in which pressure is applied to the same points of the body as in acupuncture
SHIATSUS > SHIATSU
SHIATZU n shiatzu
SHIATZUS > SHIATZU
SHIBAH n Jewish period of mourning
SHIBAHS > SHIBAH
SHIBUICHI n Japanese alloy of copper and silver
SHICKER n alcoholic drink
SHICKERED adj drunk
SHICKERS > SHICKER
SHICKSA n non-Jewish girl
SHICKSAS > SHICKSA
SHIDDER n old word meaning female animal
SHIDDERS > SHIDDER
SHIDDUCH n arranged marriage
SHIED > SHY

SHIEL vb sheal
SHIELD n piece of armour carried on the arm to protect the body from blows or missiles ▷ vb protect
SHIELDED > SHIELD
SHIELDER > SHIELD
SHIELDERS > SHIELD
SHIELDING > SHIELD
SHIELDS > SHIELD
SHIELED > SHIEL
SHIELING n rough hut or shelter used by people tending cattle on high or remote ground
SHIELINGS > SHIELING
SHIELS > SHIEL
SHIER n horse that shies habitually
SHIERS > SHIER
SHIES > SHY
SHIEST > SHY
SHIFT vb move ▷ n shifting
SHIFTABLE > SHIFT
SHIFTED > SHIFT
SHIFTER > SHIFT
SHIFTERS > SHIFT
SHIFTIER > SHIFTY
SHIFTIEST > SHIFTY
SHIFTILY > SHIFTY
SHIFTING > SHIFT
SHIFTINGS > SHIFT
SHIFTLESS adj lacking in ambition or initiative
SHIFTS > SHIFT
SHIFTWORK n system of employment where an individual's normal hours of work are outside the period of normal day working
SHIFTY adj evasive or untrustworthy
SHIGELLA n type of rod-shaped Gram-negative bacterium
SHIGELLAE > SHIGELLA
SHIGELLAS > SHIGELLA
SHIITAKE n kind of mushroom widely used in Oriental cookery
SHIITAKES > SHIITAKE
SHIKAR n hunting, esp big-game hunting ▷ vb hunt (game, esp big game)
SHIKAREE same as **>** SHIKARI
SHIKAREES > SHIKAREE
SHIKARI n (in India) a hunter
SHIKARIS > SHIKARI
SHIKARRED > SHIKAR
SHIKARS > SHIKAR
SHIKKER n Yiddish term for drunk person
SHIKKERS > SHIKKER
SHIKSA n often derogatory term for a non-Jewish girl
SHIKSAS > SHIKSA
SHIKSE n non-Jewish girl
SHIKSEH same as **>** SHIKSE
SHIKSEHS > SHIKSEH
SHIKSES > SHIKSE

SHILINGI n money unit in Tanzania
SHILL n confidence trickster's assistant ▷ vb act as a shill
SHILLABER n keen customer
SHILLALA n short Irish clud or cudgel
SHILLALAH same as **>** SHILLALA
SHILLALAS > SHILLALA
SHILLED > SHILL
SHILLELAH same as **>** SHILLALA
SHILLING n former British coin
SHILLINGS > SHILLING
SHILLS > SHILL
SHILPIT adj puny
SHILY > SHY
SHIM n thin strip of material placed between two close surfaces to fill a gap ▷ vb fit or fill up with a shim
SHIMAAL n hot Middle Eastern wind
SHIMAALS > SHIMAAL
SHIMMED > SHIM
SHIMMER n (shine with) a faint unsteady light ▷ vb shine with a faint unsteady light
SHIMMERED > SHIMMER
SHIMMERS > SHIMMER
SHIMMERY adj shining with a glistening or tremulous light
SHIMMEY n chemise
SHIMMEYS > SHIMMEY
SHIMMIED > SHIMMY
SHIMMIES > SHIMMY
SHIMMING > SHIM
SHIMMY n American ragtime dance with much shaking of the hips and shoulders ▷ vb dance the shimmy
SHIMMYING > SHIMMY
SHIMOZZLE n predicament
SHIMS > SHIM
SHIN n front of the lower leg ▷ vb climb by using the hands or arms and legs
SHINBONE n tibia
SHINBONES > SHINBONE
SHINDIES > SHINDY
SHINDIG n noisy party
SHINDIGS > SHINDIG
SHINDY n quarrel or commotion
SHINDYS > SHINDY
SHINE vb give out or reflect light; cause to gleam ▷ n brightness or lustre
SHINED > SHINE
SHINELESS > SHINE
SHINER n black eye
SHINERS > SHINER
SHINES > SHINE
SHINESS > SHY
SHINESSES > SHY

SHINGLE n wooden roof tile ▷ vb cover (a roof) with shingles
SHINGLED > SHINGLE
SHINGLER > SHINGLE
SHINGLERS > SHINGLE
SHINGLES n disease causing a rash of small blisters along a nerve
SHINGLIER > SHINGLE
SHINGLING > SHINGLE
SHINGLY > SHINGLE
SHINGUARD n rigid piece of plastic to protect footballer's shin
SHINIER > SHINY
SHINIES > SHINY
SHINIEST > SHINY
SHINILY > SHINY
SHININESS > SHINY
SHINING > SHINE
SHININGLY > SHINE
SHINJU n (formerly, in Japan) a ritual double suicide of lovers
SHINJUS > SHINJU
SHINKIN n worthless person
SHINKINS > SHINKIN
SHINLEAF n wintergreen
SHINLEAFS > SHINLEAF
SHINNE n old form of chin
SHINNED > SHIN
SHINNERY n American oak tree
SHINNES > SHINNE
SHINNEY vb climb with hands and legs
SHINNEYED > SHINNEY
SHINNEYS > SHINNEY
SHINNIED > SHINNY
SHINNIES > SHINNY
SHINNING > SHIN
SHINNY same as **>** SHINTY
SHINNYING > SHINNY
SHINS > SHIN
SHINTIED > SHINTY
SHINTIES > SHINTY
SHINTY n game like hockey ▷ vb play shinty
SHINTYING > SHINTY
SHINY adj bright and polished
SHIP n large seagoing vessel ▷ vb send or transport by carrier, esp a ship
SHIPBOARD adj taking place or used aboard a ship
SHIPBORNE adj carried on ship
SHIPFUL n amount carried by ship
SHIPFULS > SHIPFUL
SHIPLAP n method of constructing ship hull
SHIPLAPS > SHIPLAP
SHIPLESS > SHIP
SHIPLOAD n quantity carried by a ship
SHIPLOADS > SHIPLOAD
SHIPMAN n master or captain of a ship
SHIPMATE n sailor serving

on the same ship as another
SHIPMATES > SHIPMATE
SHIPMEN > SHIPMAN
SHIPMENT n act of shipping cargo
SHIPMENTS > SHIPMENT
SHIPOWNER n person who owns or has shares in a ship or ships
SHIPPABLE > SHIP
SHIPPED > SHIP
SHIPPEN n dialect word for cattle shed
SHIPPENS > SHIPPEN
SHIPPER n person or company that ships
SHIPPERS > SHIPPER
SHIPPIE n prostitute who solicits at a port
SHIPPIES > SHIPPIE
SHIPPING > SHIP
SHIPPINGS > SHIP
SHIPPO n Japanese enamel work
SHIPPON n dialect word for cattle shed
SHIPPONS > SHIPPON
SHIPPOS > SHIPPO
SHIPPOUND n Baltic weight measure
SHIPS > SHIP
SHIPSHAPE adj orderly or neat ▷ adv in a neat and orderly manner
SHIPSIDE n part of wharf next to ship
SHIPSIDES > SHIPSIDE
SHIPWAY n structure on which a vessel is built, then launched
SHIPWAYS > SHIPWAY
SHIPWORM n type of wormlike marine bivalve mollusc
SHIPWORMS > SHIPWORM
SHIPWRECK n destruction of a ship through storm or collision ▷ vb cause to undergo shipwreck
SHIPYARD n place where ships are built
SHIPYARDS > SHIPYARD
SHIR n gathering in material
SHIRALEE n swag
SHIRALEES > SHIRALEE
SHIRE n county ▷ vb refresh or rest
SHIRED > SHIRE
SHIREMAN n sheriff
SHIREMEN > SHIREMAN
SHIRES > SHIRE
SHIRING > SHIRE
SHIRK vb avoid (duty or work) ▷ n person who shirks
SHIRKED > SHIRK
SHIRKER n
SHIRKERS > SHIRK
SHIRKING > SHIRK
SHIRKS > SHIRK
SHIRR vb gather (fabric) into two or more parallel

rows to decorate a dress, etc ▷ n series of gathered rows decorating a dress, blouse, etc
SHIRRA old Scots word for **>** SHERIFF
SHIRRALEE n swagman's bundle of possessions
SHIRRAS > SHIRRA
SHIRRED > SHIRR
SHIRRING > SHIRR
SHIRRINGS > SHIRR
SHIRRS > SHIRR
SHIRS > SHIR
SHIRT n garment for the upper part of the body ▷ vb put a shirt on
SHIRTBAND n neckband on shirt
SHIRTED > SHIRT
SHIRTIER > SHIRTY
SHIRTIEST > SHIRTY
SHIRTILY > SHIRTY
SHIRTING n fabric used in making men's shirts
SHIRTINGS > SHIRTING
SHIRTLESS > SHIRT
SHIRTS > SHIRT
SHIRTTAIL n part of a shirt that extends below the waist
SHIRTY adj bad-tempered or annoyed
SHISH as in shish kebab dish of meat and vegetables threaded onto skewers and grilled
SHISHA same as **>** HOOKAH
SHISHAS > SHISHA
SHISO n Asian plant with aromatic leaves that are used in cooking
SHISOS > SHISO
SHIST n schist
SHISTS > SHIST
SHIT vb defecate ▷ n excrement ▷ interj exclamation of anger or disgust
SHITAKE same as **>** SHIITAKE
SHITAKES > SHITAKE
SHITE same as **>** SHIT
SHITED > SHITE
SHITES > SHITE
SHITFACE n despicable person
SHITFACED adj drunk
SHITFACES > SHITFACE
SHITHEAD n fool
SHITHEADS > SHITHEAD
SHITHOLE n dirty place
SHITHOLES > SHITHOLE
SHITHOUSE n lavatory
SHITING > SHITE
SHITLESS adj very frightened
SHITLIST n list of hated things
SHITLISTS > SHITLIST
SHITLOAD n taboo slang for a lot
SHITLOADS > SHITLOAD
SHITS > SHIT

SHITTAH n tree mentioned in the Old Testament
SHITTAHS > SHITTAH
SHITTED > SHIT
SHITTIER > SHIT
SHITTIEST > SHIT
SHITTILY > SHIT
SHITTIM > SHITTAH
SHITTIMS > SHITTAH
SHITTING > SHIT
SHITTY > SHIT
SHITZU n breed of small dog with long, silky fur
SHITZUS > SHITZU
SHIUR n lesson in which a passage of the Talmud is studied together by a group of people
SHIURIM > SHIUR
SHIV variant spelling of **>** CHIV
SHIVA variant of **>** SHIVAH
SHIVAH n Jewish period of formal mourning
SHIVAHS > SHIVAH
SHIVAREE n discordant mock serenade to newlyweds, made with pans, kettles, etc
SHIVAREED > SHIVAREE
SHIVAREES > SHIVAREE
SHIVAS > SHIVA
SHIVE n flat cork or bung for wide-mouthed bottles
SHIVER vb tremble, as from cold or fear ▷ n shivering
SHIVERED > SHIVER
SHIVERER > SHIVER
SHIVERERS > SHIVER
SHIVERIER > SHIVERY
SHIVERING > SHIVER
SHIVERS > SHIVER
SHIVERY adj inclined to shiver or tremble
SHIVES > SHIVE
SHIVITI n Jewish decorative plaque with religious message
SHIVITIS > SHIVITI
SHIVOO n Australian word meaning rowdy party
SHIVOOS > SHIVOO
SHIVS > SHIV
SHIVVED > SHIV
SHIVVING > SHIV
SHKOTZIM n plural of shegetz
SHLEMIEHL Yiddish word for **>** FOOL
SHLEMIEL same as **>** SCHLEMIEL
SHLEMIELS > SHLEMIEL
SHLEP vb schlep
SHLEPP vb schlep
SHLEPPED > SHLEP
SHLEPPER > SHLEP
SHLEPPERS > SHLEP
SHLEPPING > SHLEP
SHLEPPS > SHLEPP
SHLEPS > SHLEP
SHLIMAZEL n unlucky person
SHLOCK n something of

poor quality
SHLOCKIER > SHLOCK
SHLOCKS > SHLOCK
SHLOCKY > SHLOCK
SHLOSHIM n period of thirty days' deep mourning following a death
SHLOSHIMS > SHLOSHIM
SHLUB same as **>** SCHLUB
SHLUBS > SHLUB
SHLUMP vb move in lazy way
SHLUMPED > SHLUMP
SHLUMPING > SHLUMP
SHLUMPS > SHLUMP
SHLUMPY > SHLUMP
SHMALTZ n schmaltz
SHMALTZES > SHMALTZ
SHMALTZY > SHMALTZ
SHMATTE n rag
SHMATTES > SHMATTE
SHMEAR n set of things
SHMEARS > SHMEAR
SHMEK n smell
SHMEKS > SHMEK
SHMO same as **>** SCHMO
SHMOCK n despicable person
SHMOCKS > SHMOCK
SHMOES > SHMO
SHMOOSE variant of **>** SCHMOOZE
SHMOOSED > SHMOOSE
SHMOOSES > SHMOOSE
SHMOOSING > SHMOOSE
SHMOOZE variant of **>** SCHMOOZE
SHMOOZED > SHMOOZE
SHMOOZER same as **>** SCHMOOZER
SHMOOZERS > SHMOOZER
SHMOOZES > SHMOOZE
SHMOOZIER > SHMOOZY
SHMOOZING > SHMOOZE
SHMOOZY adj talking casually, gossipy
SHMUCK n despicable person
SHMUCKS > SCHMUCK
SHNAPPS same as **>** SCHNAPPS
SHNAPS n schnaps
SHNOOK n stupid person
SHNOOKS > SHNOOK
SHNORRER same as **>** SCHNORRER
SHNORRERS > SHNORRER
SHOAL n large number of fish swimming together ▷ vb make or become shallow ▷ adj (of the draught of a vessel) drawing little water
SHOALED > SHOAL
SHOALER > SHOAL
SHOALEST > SHOAL
SHOALIER > SHOALY
SHOALIEST > SHOALY
SHOALING > SHOAL
SHOALINGS > SHOAL
SHOALNESS > SHOAL
SHOALS > SHOAL
SHOALWISE adv in a large group or in large groups

S

SHOALY adj shallow

SHOAT n piglet that has recently been weaned

SHOATS > SHOAT

SHOCHET n (in Judaism) a person who has been specially trained and licensed to slaughter animals and birds in accordance with the laws of shechita

SHOCHETIM > SHOCHET

SHOCHETS > SHOCHET

SHOCK vb horrify, disgust, or astonish ▷ n sudden violent emotional disturbance ▷ adj bushy

SHOCKABLE > SHOCK

SHOCKED > SHOCK

SHOCKER n person or thing that shocks or horrifies

SHOCKERS > SHOCKER

SHOCKING adj causing horror, disgust, or astonishment

SHOCKS > SHOCK

SHOD > SHOE

SHODDEN vb old form of shod

SHODDIER > SHODDY

SHODDIES > SHODDY

SHODDIEST > SHODDY

SHODDILY > SHODDY

SHODDY adj made or done badly ▷ n yarn or fabric made from wool waste or clippings

SHODER n skins used in making gold leaf

SHODERS > SHODER

SHOE n outer covering for the foot, ending below the ankle ▷ vb fit with a shoe or shoes

SHOEBILL n large wading bird of tropical E African swamps

SHOEBILLS > SHOEBILL

SHOEBLACK n (esp formerly) a person who shines boots and shoes

SHOEBOX n cardboard box for shoes

SHOEBOXES > SHOEBOX

SHOED > SHOE

SHOEHORN n smooth curved implement inserted at the heel of a shoe to ease the foot into it ▷ vb cram (people or things) into a very small space

SHOEHORNS > SHOEHORN

SHOEING > SHOE

SHOEINGS > SHOE

SHOELACE n cord for fastening shoes

SHOELACES > SHOELACE

SHOELESS > SHOE

SHOEMAKER n person who makes or repairs shoes or boots

SHOEPAC n waterproof boot

SHOEPACK n waterproof boot

SHOEPACKS > SHOEPACK

SHOEPACS > SHOEPAC

SHOER n person who shoes horses

SHOERS > SHOER

SHOES > SHOE

SHOESHINE n act or an instance of polishing a pair of shoes

SHOETREE n piece of metal, wood, or plastic inserted in a shoe to keep its shape

SHOETREES > SHOETREE

SHOFAR n ram's horn sounded in the synagogue daily during the month of Elul and repeatedly on Rosh Hashanah

SHOFARS > SHOFAR

SHOFROTH > SHOFAR

SHOG vb shake

SHOGGED > SHOG

SHOGGING > SHOG

SHOGGLE vb shake

SHOGGLED > SHOGGLE

SHOGGLES > SHOGGLE

SHOGGLIER > SHOGGLE

SHOGGLING > SHOGGLE

SHOGGLY > SHOGGLE

SHOGI n Japanese chess

SHOGIS > SHOGI

SHOGS > SHOG

SHOGUN n Japanese chief military commander

SHOGUNAL > SHOGUN

SHOGUNATE n office or rule of a shogun

SHOGUNS > SHOGUN

SHOJI n Japanese rice-paper screen in a sliding wooden frame

SHOJIS > SHOJI

SHOLA n Indian plant

SHOLAS > SHOLA

SHOLOM n Hebrew greeting

SHOLOMS > SHOLOM

SHONE > SHINE

SHONEEN n Irishman who imitates English ways

SHONEENS > SHONEEN

SHONKIER > SHONKY

SHONKIEST > SHONKY

SHONKY adj unreliable or unsound

SHOO interj go away! ▷ vb drive away as by saying 'shoo'

SHOOED > SHOO

SHOOFLIES > SHOOFLY

SHOOFLY as in shoofly pie US dessert similar to treacle tart

SHOOGIE vb Scots word meaning swing

SHOOGIED > SHOOGIE

SHOOGIES > SHOOGIE

SHOOGLE vb shake, sway, or rock back and forth ▷ n rocking motion

SHOOGLED > SHOOGLE

SHOOGLES > SHOOGLE

SHOOGLIER > SHOOGLE

SHOOGLING > SHOOGLE

SHOOGLY > SHOOGLE

SHOOING > SHOO

SHOOK n set of parts ready for assembly

SHOOKS > SHOOK

SHOOL dialect word for > SHOVEL

SHOOLE dialect word for > SHOVEL

SHOOLED > SHOOL

SHOOLES > SHOOLE

SHOOLING > SHOOL

SHOOLS > SHOOL

SHOON plural of > SHOE

SHOORA same as > SHURA

SHOORAS > SHOORA

SHOOS > SHOO

SHOOT vb hit, wound, or kill with a missile fired from a weapon ▷ n new branch or sprout of a plant

SHOOTABLE > SHOOT

SHOOTDOWN n act of shooting down aircraft

SHOOTER n person or thing that shoots

SHOOTERS > SHOOTER

SHOOTING > SHOOT

SHOOTINGS > SHOOT

SHOOTIST n person who shoots

SHOOTISTS > SHOOTIST

SHOOTOUT n conclusive gunfight

SHOOTOUTS > SHOOTOUT

SHOOTS > SHOOT

SHOP n place for sale of goods and services ▷ vb visit a shop or shops to buy goods

SHOPBOARD n shop counter

SHOPBOT n price-comparison website

SHOPBOTS > SHOPBOT

SHOPBOY n boy working in shop

SHOPBOYS > SHOPBOY

SHOPE n old form of shape

SHOPFRONT n area of shop facing street

SHOPFUL n amount stored in shop

SHOPFULS > SHOPFUL

SHOPGIRL n girl working in shop

SHOPGIRLS > SHOPGIRL

SHOPHAR same as > SHOFAR

SHOPHARS > SHOPHAR

SHOPHROTH > SHOPHAR

SHOPLIFT vb steal from shop

SHOPLIFTS > SHOPLIFT

SHOPMAN n man working in shop

SHOPMEN > SHOPMAN

SHOPPE old-fashioned spelling of > SHOP

SHOPPED > SHOP

SHOPPER n person who buys goods in a shop

SHOPPERS > SHOPPER

SHOPPES > SHOPPE

SHOPPIER > SHOPPY

SHOPPIEST > SHOPPY

SHOPPING > SHOP

SHOPPINGS > SHOP

SHOPPY adj of a shop

SHOPS > SHOP

SHOPTALK n conversation about one's work, carried on outside working hours

SHOPTALKS > SHOPTALK

SHOPWOMAN n woman working in a shop

SHOPWOMEN > SHOPWOMAN

SHOPWORN adj worn or faded from being displayed in a shop

SHORAN n short-range radar system

SHORANS > SHORAN

SHORE n edge of a sea or lake ▷ vb prop or support

SHOREBIRD n bird that lives close to the water

SHORED > SHORE

SHORELESS adj without a shore suitable for landing

SHORELINE n edge of a sea, lake, or wide river

SHOREMAN n person who lives on shore

SHOREMEN > SHOREMAN

SHORER > SHORE

SHORERS > SHORE

SHORES > SHORE

SHORESIDE n area at shore

SHORESMAN n fishing industry worker on shore

SHORESMEN > SHORESMAN

SHOREWARD adj near or facing the shore ▷ adv towards the shore

SHOREWEED n tufty aquatic perennial plant

SHORING > SHORE

SHORINGS > SHORE

SHORL n black mineral

SHORLS > SHORL

SHORN past participle of > SHEAR

SHORT adj not long ▷ adv abruptly ▷ n drink of spirits ▷ vb short-circuit

SHORTAGE n deficiency

SHORTAGES > SHORTAGE

SHORTARM adj (of a punch) with the arm bent

SHORTARSE n short person

SHORTCAKE n shortbread

SHORTCUT n route that is shorter than the usual one

SHORTCUTS > SHORTCUT

SHORTED > SHORT

SHORTEN vb make or become shorter

SHORTENED > SHORTEN

SHORTENER > SHORTEN

SHORTENS > SHORTEN

SHORTER > SHORT

SHORTEST > SHORT

SHORTFALL n deficit

SHORTGOWN n old Scots word meaning woman's jacket

SHORTHAIR n cat with short fur

SHORTHAND n system of rapid writing using symbols to represent words

SHORTHEAD n species of fish

SHORTHOLD as in shorthold tenancy letting of a dwelling for between one and five years at a fair rent

SHORTHORN n member of a breed of cattle with short horns

SHORTIA n American flowering plant

SHORTIAS > SHORTIA

SHORTIE n person or thing that is extremely short

SHORTIES > SHORTY

SHORTING > SHORT

SHORTISH > SHORT

SHORTLIST n list of suitable applicants for a job, etc

SHORTLY adv soon

SHORTNESS > SHORT

SHORTS npl trousers reaching the top of the thigh or partway to the knee

SHORTSTOP n fielding position to the left of second base viewed from home plate

SHORTWAVE n radio wave with a wavelength in the range 10-100 metres

SHORTY same as > SHORTIE

SHOT vb load with shot

SHOTE same as > SHOAT

SHOTES > SHOTE

SHOTFIRER n person detonating blasting charge

SHOTGUN n gun for firing a charge of shot at short range ▷ adj involving coercion or duress ▷ vb shoot or threaten with or as if with a shotgun

SHOTGUNS > SHOTGUN

SHOTHOLE n drilled hole in to which explosive is put for blasting

SHOTHOLES > SHOTHOLE

SHOTMAKER n sport player making good shots

SHOTPROOF adj able to withstand shot

SHOTS > SHOT

SHOTT n shallow temporary salt lake or marsh in the North African desert

SHOTTE n old form of shoat

SHOTTED > SHOT

SHOTTEN adj (of fish, esp herring) having recently spawned

SHOTTES > SHOTTE

SHOTTING > SHOT

SHOTTLE n small drawer

SHOTTLES > SHOTTLE

SHOTTS > SHOTT

SHOUGH n old word meaning lapdog

SHOUGHS > SHOUGH

SHOULD > SHALL

SHOULDER n part of the body to which an arm, foreleg, or wing is attached ▷ vb bear (a burden or responsibility)

SHOULDERS > SHOULDER

SHOULDEST same as > SHOULDST

SHOULDST form of the past tense of > SHALL

SHOUSE n toilet ▷ adj unwell or in poor spirits

SHOUSES > SHOUSE

SHOUT n loud cry ▷ vb cry out loudly

SHOUTED > SHOUT

SHOUTER > SHOUT

SHOUTERS > SHOUT

SHOUTHER Scots form of > SHOULDER

SHOUTHERS > SHOUTHER

SHOUTIER > SHOUTY

SHOUTIEST > SHOUTY

SHOUTING > SHOUT

SHOUTINGS > SHOUT

SHOUTLINE n line in advertisement made prominent to catch attention

SHOUTS > SHOUT

SHOUTY adj characterized by or involving shouting

SHOVE vb push roughly ▷ n rough push

SHOVED > SHOVE

SHOVEL n tool for lifting or moving loose material ▷ vb lift or move as with a shovel

SHOVELED > SHOVEL

SHOVELER n type of duck

SHOVELERS > SHOVELER

SHOVELFUL > SHOVEL

SHOVELING > SHOVEL

SHOVELLED > SHOVEL

SHOVELLER > SHOVEL

SHOVELS > SHOVEL

SHOVER > SHOVE

SHOVERS > SHOVE

SHOVES > SHOVE

SHOVING n act of pushing hard

SHOVINGS > SHOVING

SHOW vb make, be, or become noticeable or visible ▷ n public exhibition

SHOWABLE > SHOW

SHOWBIZ n entertainment industry including theatre, films, and TV

SHOWBIZZY > SHOWBIZ

SHOWBOAT n paddle-wheel river steamer with a theatre and a repertory company ▷ vb perform or behave in a showy and flamboyant way

SHOWBOATS > SHOWBOAT

SHOWBOX n box containing showman's material

SHOWBOXES > SHOWBOX

SHOWBREAD same as > SHEWBREAD

SHOWCASE n situation in which something is displayed to best advantage ▷ vb exhibit or display ▷ adj displayed or meriting display as in a showcase

SHOWCASED > SHOWCASE

SHOWCASES > SHOWCASE

SHOWD vb rock or sway to and fro ▷ n rocking motion

SHOWDED > SHOWD

SHOWDING > SHOWD

SHOWDOWN n confrontation that settles a dispute

SHOWDOWNS > SHOWDOWN

SHOWDS > SHOWD

SHOWED > SHOW

SHOWER n kind of bath in which a person stands while being sprayed with water ▷ vb wash in a shower

SHOWERED > SHOWER

SHOWERER > SHOWER

SHOWERERS > SHOWER

SHOWERFUL > SHOWER

SHOWERIER > SHOWER

SHOWERING > SHOWER

SHOWERS > SHOWER

SHOWERY > SHOWER

SHOWGHE n old word meaning lapdog

SHOWGHES > SHOWGHE

SHOWGIRL n girl who appears in shows, etc, esp as a singer or dancer

SHOWGIRLS > SHOWGIRL

SHOWIER > SHOWY

SHOWIEST > SHOWY

SHOWILY > SHOWY

SHOWINESS > SHOWY

SHOWING > SHOW

SHOWINGS > SHOW

SHOWJUMP vb take part in a showjumping competition

SHOWJUMPS > SHOWJUMP

SHOWMAN n man skilled at presenting anything spectacularly

SHOWMANLY > SHOWMAN

SHOWMEN > SHOWMAN

SHOWN > SHOW

SHOWOFF n person who makes a vain display of himself or herself

SHOWOFFS > SHOWOFF

SHOWPIECE n excellent specimen shown for display or as an example

SHOWPLACE n place visited for its beauty or interest

SHOWRING n area where animals are displayed for sale or competition

SHOWRINGS > SHOWRING

SHOWROOM n room in which goods for sale are on display

SHOWROOMS > SHOWROOM

SHOWS > SHOW

SHOWTIME n time when show begins

SHOWTIMES > SHOWTIME

SHOWY adj gaudy

SHOWYARD n yard where cattle are displayed

SHOWYARDS > SHOWYARD

SHOYU n Japanese variety of soy sauce

SHOYUS > SHOYU

SHRADDHA n Hindu offering to an ancestor

SHRADDHAS > SHRADDHA

SHRANK > SHRINK

SHRAPNEL n artillery shell filled with pellets which scatter on explosion

SHRAPNELS > SHRAPNEL

SHRED n long narrow strip torn from something ▷ vb tear to shreds

SHREDDED > SHRED

SHREDDER > SHRED

SHREDDERS > SHRED

SHREDDIER > SHRED

SHREDDING > SHRED

SHREDDY > SHRED

SHREDLESS > SHRED

SHREDS > SHRED

SHREEK old spelling of > SHRIEK

SHREEKED > SHREEK

SHREEKING > SHREEK

SHREEKS > SHREEK

SHREIK old spelling of > SHRIEK

SHREIKED > SHREIK

SHREIKING > SHREIK

SHREIKS > SHREIK

SHREW n small mouselike animal ▷ vb curse or damn

SHREWD adj clever and perceptive

SHREWDER > SHREWD

SHREWDEST > SHREWD

SHREWDIE n shrewd person

SHREWDIES > SHREWDIE

SHREWDLY > SHREWD

SHREWED > SHREW

SHREWING > SHREW

SHREWISH adj (esp of a woman) bad-tempered and nagging

SHREWLIKE > SHREW

SHREWMICE npl shrews

SHREWS > SHREW

SHRI n Indian title of respect

SHRIECH old spelling of > SHRIEK

SHRIECHED > SHRIECH

SHRIECHES > SHRIECH

SHRIEK n shrill cry ▷ vb utter (with) a shriek

SHRIEKED > SHRIEK

SHRIEKER > SHRIEK

SHRIEKERS > SHRIEK

SHRIEKIER > SHRIEK

SHRIEKING > SHRIEK

SHRIEKS > SHRIEK

SHRIEKY > SHRIEK

S

SHRIEVAL adj of or relating to a sheriff
SHRIEVE archaic word for > SHERIFF
SHRIEVED > SHRIEVE
SHRIEVES > SHRIEVE
SHRIEVING > SHRIEVE
SHRIFT n act or an instance of shriving or being shriven
SHRIFTS > SHRIFT
SHRIGHT n old word meaning shriek
SHRIGHTS > SHRIGHT
SHRIKE n songbird with a heavy hooked bill ▷ vb archaic word for shriek
SHRIKED > SHRIKE
SHRIKES > SHRIKE
SHRIKING > SHRIKE
SHRILL adj (of a sound) sharp and high-pitched ▷ vb utter shrilly
SHRILLED > SHRILL
SHRILLER > SHRILL
SHRILLEST > SHRILL
SHRILLIER > SHRILL
SHRILLING > SHRILL
SHRILLS > SHRILL
SHRILLY > SHRILL
SHRIMP n small edible shellfish ▷ vb fish for shrimps
SHRIMPED > SHRIMP
SHRIMPER > SHRIMP
SHRIMPERS > SHRIMP
SHRIMPIER > SHRIMP
SHRIMPING > SHRIMP
SHRIMPS > SHRIMP
SHRIMPY > SHRIMP
SHRINAL > SHRINE
SHRINE n place of worship associated with a sacred person or object ▷ vb enshrine
SHRINED > SHRINE
SHRINES > SHRINE
SHRINING > SHRINE
SHRINK vb become or make smaller ▷ n psychiatrist
SHRINKAGE n decrease in size, value, or weight
SHRINKER > SHRINK
SHRINKERS > SHRINK
SHRINKING > SHRINK
SHRINKS > SHRINK
SHRIS > SHRI
SHRITCH n old word meaning shriek
SHRITCHED > SHRITCH
SHRITCHES > SHRITCH
SHRIVE vb hear the confession of (a penitent)
SHRIVED > SHRIVE
SHRIVEL vb shrink and wither
SHRIVELED > SHRIVEL
SHRIVELS > SHRIVEL
SHRIVEN > SHRIVE
SHRIVER > SHRIVE
SHRIVERS > SHRIVE
SHRIVES > SHRIVE
SHRIVING > SHRIVE

SHRIVINGS > SHRIVE
SHROFF n (in China and Japan) expert employed to separate counterfeit money from the genuine ▷ vb test (money) and separate out the counterfeit and base
SHROFFAGE > SHROFF
SHROFFED > SHROFF
SHROFFING > SHROFF
SHROFFS > SHROFF
SHROOM n slang for magic mushroom ▷ vb take magic mushrooms
SHROOMED > SHROOM
SHROOMER > SHROOM
SHROOMERS > SHROOM
SHROOMING > SHROOM
SHROOMS > SHROOM
SHROUD n piece of cloth used to wrap a dead body ▷ vb conceal
SHROUDED > SHROUD
SHROUDIER > SHROUD
SHROUDING > SHROUD
SHROUDS > SHROUD
SHROUDY > SHROUD
SHROVE vb dialect word meaning to observe Shrove-tide
SHROVED > SHROVE
SHROVES > SHROVE
SHROVING > SHROVE
SHROW vb old form of shrew
SHROWD adj old form of shrewd
SHROWED > SHROW
SHROWING > SHROW
SHROWS > SHROW
SHRUB n woody plant smaller than a tree ▷ vb plant shrubs
SHRUBBED > SHRUB
SHRUBBERY n area planted with shrubs
SHRUBBIER > SHRUBBY
SHRUBBING > SHRUB
SHRUBBY adj consisting of, planted with, or abounding in shrubs
SHRUBLAND n land covered by shrubs
SHRUBLESS > SHRUB
SHRUBLIKE > SHRUB
SHRUBS > SHRUB
SHRUG vb raise and then drop (the shoulders) as a sign of indifference or doubt ▷ n shrugging
SHRUGGED > SHRUG
SHRUGGING > SHRUG
SHRUGS > SHRUG
SHRUNK > SHRINK
SHRUNKEN adj reduced in size
SHTCHI n Russian cabbage soup
SHTCHIS > SHTCHI
SHTETEL n Jewish community in Eastern Europe
SHTETELS > SHTETEL
SHTETL n (formerly) a

small Jewish community in Eastern Europe
SHTETLACH > SHTETL
SHTETLS > SHTETL
SHTICK n comedian's routine
SHTICKIER > SHTICK
SHTICKS > SHTICK
SHTICKY > SHTICK
SHTIK n shtick
SHTIKS > SHTIK
SHTOOK n trouble
SHTOOKS > SHTOOK
SHTOOM adj silent
SHTUCK n trouble
SHTUCKS > SHTUCK
SHTUM adj silent
SHTUMM adj silent
SHTUP vb have sex (with)
SHTUPPED > SHTUP
SHTUPPING > SHTUP
SHTUPS > SHTUP
SHUBUNKIN n type of goldfish
SHUCK n outer covering of something ▷ vb remove the shucks from
SHUCKED > SHUCK
SHUCKER > SHUCK
SHUCKERS > SHUCK
SHUCKING > SHUCK
SHUCKINGS > SHUCK
SHUCKS npl something of little value ▷ interj exclamation of disappointment, annoyance, etc
SHUDDER vb shake or tremble violently, esp with horror ▷ n shaking or trembling
SHUDDERED > SHUDDER
SHUDDERS > SHUDDER
SHUDDERY > SHUDDER
SHUFFLE vb walk without lifting the feet ▷ n shuffling
SHUFFLED > SHUFFLE
SHUFFLER > SHUFFLE
SHUFFLERS > SHUFFLE
SHUFFLES > SHUFFLE
SHUFFLING > SHUFFLE
SHUFTI same as > SHUFTY
SHUFTIES > SHUFTY
SHUFTIS > SHUFTI
SHUFTY n look
SHUGGIES > SHUGGY
SHUGGY n swing, as at a fairground
SHUL Yiddish word for > SYNAGOGUE
SHULE vb saunter
SHULED > SHULE
SHULES > SHULE
SHULING > SHULE
SHULN > SHUL
SHULS > SHUL
SHUN vb avoid
SHUNLESS adj old word meaning not to be shunned
SHUNNABLE > SHUN
SHUNNED > SHUN
SHUNNER > SHUN
SHUNNERS > SHUN
SHUNNING > SHUN

SHUNPIKE vb take side road to avoid toll at turnpike
SHUNPIKED > SHUNPIKE
SHUNPIKER > SHUNPIKE
SHUNPIKES > SHUNPIKE
SHUNS > SHUN
SHUNT vb move (objects or people) to a different position ▷ n shunting
SHUNTED > SHUNT
SHUNTER n small railway locomotive used for manoeuvring coaches
SHUNTERS > SHUNTER
SHUNTING > SHUNT
SHUNTINGS > SHUNT
SHUNTS > SHUNT
SHURA n consultative council or assembly
SHURAS > SHURA
SHURIKEN n Japanese weapon with blades or points, thrown by hand
SHURIKENS > SHURIKEN
SHUSH interj be quiet! ▷ vb quiet by saying 'shush'
SHUSHED > SHUSH
SHUSHER > SHUSH
SHUSHERS > SHUSH
SHUSHES > SHUSH
SHUSHING > SHUSH
SHUT vb bring together or fold, close
SHUTDOWN n closing of a factory, shop, or other business ▷ vb discontinue operations permanently
SHUTDOWNS > SHUTDOWN
SHUTE variant of > CHUTE
SHUTED > SHUTE
SHUTES > SHUTE
SHUTEYE n sleep
SHUTEYES > SHUTEYE
SHUTING > SHUTE
SHUTOFF n device that shuts something off, esp a machine control
SHUTOFFS > SHUTOFF
SHUTOUT n game in which the opposing team does not score ▷ vb keep out or exclude
SHUTOUTS > SHUTOUT
SHUTS > SHUT
SHUTTER n hinged doorlike cover for closing off a window ▷ vb close or equip with a shutter
SHUTTERED > SHUTTER
SHUTTERS > SHUTTER
SHUTTING > SHUT
SHUTTLE n bobbin-like device used in weaving ▷ vb move by or as if by a shuttle
SHUTTLED > SHUTTLE
SHUTTLER > SHUTTLE
SHUTTLERS > SHUTTLE
SHUTTLES > SHUTTLE
SHUTTLING > SHUTTLE
SHVARTZE same as > SCHVARTZE
SHVARTZES > SHVARTZE
SHWA same as > SCHWA

SHWANPAN *same as* > SWANPAN

SHWANPANS > SHWANPAN

SHWAS > SHWA

SHWESHWE *n* African cotton print fabric

SHWESHWES > SHWESHWE

SHY *adj* not at ease in company ▷ *vb* start back in fear ▷ *n* throw

SHYER > SHY

SHYERS > SHY

SHYEST > SHY

SHYING > SHY

SHYISH > SHY

SHYLOCK *vb* lend money at an exorbitant rate of interest

SHYLOCKED > SHYLOCK

SHYLOCKS > SHYLOCK

SHYLY > SHY

SHYNESS > SHY

SHYNESSES > SHY

SHYPOO *n* liquor of poor quality

SHYPOOS > SHYPOO

SHYSTER *n* person, esp a lawyer or politician, who uses discreditable or unethical methods

SHYSTERS > SHYSTER

SI *same as* > TE

SIAL *n* silicon-rich and aluminium-rich rocks of the earth's continental upper crust

SIALIC > SIAL

SIALID *n* species of fly

SIALIDAN > SIALID

SIALIDANS > SIALID

SIALIDS > SIALID

SIALOGRAM *n* X-ray of salivary gland

SIALOID *adj* resembling saliva

SIALOLITH *n* hard deposit formed in salivary gland

SIALON *n* type of ceramic

SIALONS > SIALON

SIALS > SIAL

SIAMANG *n* large black gibbon

SIAMANGS > SIAMANG

SIAMESE *variant of* > SIAMEZE

SIAMESED > SIAMESE

SIAMESES > SIAMESE

SIAMESING > SIAMESE

SIAMEZE *vb* join together

SIAMEZED > SIAMEZE

SIAMEZES > SIAMEZE

SIAMEZING > SIAMEZE

SIB *n* blood relative

SIBB *n* sib

SIBBS > SIBB

SIBILANCE > SIBILANT

SIBILANCY > SIBILANT

SIBILANT *adj* hissing ▷ *n* consonant pronounced with a hissing sound

SIBILANTS > SIBILANT

SIBILATE *vb* pronounce or utter (words or speech)

with a hissing sound

SIBILATED > SIBILATE

SIBILATES > SIBILATE

SIBILATOR > SIBILATE

SIBILOUS > SIBILANT

SIBLING *n* brother or sister

SIBLINGS > SIBLING

SIBS > SIB

SIBSHIP *n* group of children of the same parents

SIBSHIPS > SIBSHIP

SIBYL *n* (in ancient Greece and Rome) prophetess

SIBYLIC > SIBYL

SIBYLLIC > SIBYL

SIBYLLINE > SIBYL

SIBYLS > SIBYL

SIC *adv* thus ▷ *vb* attack

SICCAN *adj* Scots word meaning such

SICCAR *adj* sure

SICCATIVE *n* substance added to a liquid to promote drying

SICCED > SIC

SICCING > SIC

SICCITIES > SICCITY

SICCITY *n* dryness

SICE *same as* > SYCE

SICES > SICE

SICH *adj* old form of such

SICHT *Scot word for* > SIGHT

SICHTED > SICHT

SICHTING > SICHT

SICHTS > SICHT

SICILIANA *n* Sicilian dance

SICILIANE > SICILIANA

SICILIANO *n* old dance in six-beat or twelve-beat time

SICK *adj* vomiting or likely to vomit ▷ *n* vomit ▷ *vb* vomit

SICKBAY *n* room for the treatment of sick people, for example on a ship

SICKBAYS > SICKBAY

SICKBED *n* bed where sick person lies

SICKBEDS > SICKBED

SICKED > SICK

SICKEE *n* person off work through illness

SICKEES > SICKEE

SICKEN *vb* make nauseated or disgusted

SICKENED > SICKEN

SICKENER *n* something that induces sickness or nausea

SICKENERS > SICKENER

SICKENING *adj* causing horror or disgust

SICKENS > SICKEN

SICKER > SICK

SICKERLY *adv* Scots word meaning surely

SICKEST > SICK

SICKIE *n* day of sick leave

from work

SICKIES > SICKIE

SICKING > SICK

SICKISH > SICK

SICKISHLY > SICK

SICKLE *n* tool with a curved blade for cutting grass or grain ▷ *vb* cut with a sickle

SICKLED > SICKLE

SICKLEMAN *n* person reaping with sickle

SICKLEMEN > SICKLEMAN

SICKLEMIA *n* form of anaemia

SICKLEMIC > SICKLEMIA

SICKLES > SICKLE

SICKLIED > SICKLY

SICKLIER > SICKLY

SICKLIES > SICKLY

SICKLIEST > SICKLY

SICKLILY > SICKLY

SICKLING > SICKLE

SICKLY *adj* unhealthy, weak ▷ *adv* suggesting sickness ▷ *vb* make sickly

SICKLYING > SICKLY

SICKNESS *n* particular illness or disease

SICKNURSE *n* person nursing sick person

SICKO *n* person who is mentally disturbed or perverted ▷ *adj* perverted or in bad taste

SICKOS > SICKO

SICKOUT *n* form of industrial action in which all workers in a workplace report sick simultaneously

SICKOUTS > SICKOUT

SICKROOM *n* room to which a person who is ill is confined

SICKROOMS > SICKROOM

SICKS > SICK

SICLIKE *adj* Scots word meaning suchlike

SICS > SIC

SIDA *n* Australian hemp plant

SIDALCEA *n* type of perennial N American plant

SIDALCEAS > SIDALCEA

SIDAS > SIDA

SIDDHA *n* (in Hinduism) person who has achieved perfection

SIDDHAS > SIDDHA

SIDDHI *n* (in Hinduism) power attained with perfection

SIDDHIS > SIDDHI

SIDDHUISM *n* (in Indian English) any contrived metaphor or simile

SIDDUR *n* Jewish prayer book

SIDDURIM > SIDDUR

SIDDURS > SIDDUR

SIDE *n* line or surface that borders anything ▷ *adj* at or on the side

SIDEARM *n* weapon worn on belt

SIDEARMS > SIDEARM

SIDEBAND *n* frequency band either above or below the carrier frequency

SIDEBANDS > SIDEBAND

SIDEBAR *n* small newspaper article beside larger one

SIDEBARS > SIDEBAR

SIDEBOARD *n* piece of furniture for holding plates, cutlery, etc in a dining room

SIDEBONES *n* part of horse's hoof

SIDEBURNS *npl* man's side whiskers

SIDECAR *n* small passenger car on the side of a motorcycle

SIDECARS > SIDECAR

SIDECHECK *n* part of horse's harness

SIDED > SIDE

SIDEDNESS > SIDE

SIDEDRESS *vb* place fertilizer in the soil near the roots of a plant

SIDEHILL *n* side of hill

SIDEHILLS > SIDEHILL

SIDEKICK *n* close friend or associate

SIDEKICKS > SIDEKICK

SIDELIGHT *n* either of two small lights on the front of a vehicle

SIDELINE *n* subsidiary interest or source of income ▷ *vb* prevent (a player) from taking part in a game

SIDELINED > SIDELINE

SIDELINER > SIDELINE

SIDELINES *npl* area immediately outside the playing area, where substitute players sit

SIDELING *adj* to one side

SIDELOCK *n* long lock of hair on side of head

SIDELOCKS > SIDELOCK

SIDELONG *adj* sideways ▷ *adv* obliquely

SIDEMAN *n* member of a dance band or a jazz group other than the leader

SIDEMEN > SIDEMAN

SIDENOTE *n* note written in margin

SIDENOTES > SIDENOTE

SIDEPATH *n* minor path

SIDEPATHS > SIDEPATH

SIDEPIECE *n* part forming side of something

SIDER *n* one who sides with another

SIDERAL *adj* from the stars

SIDERATE *vb* strike violently

SIDERATED > SIDERATE

SIDERATES > SIDERATE

SIDEREAL *adj* of or determined with reference to the stars

S

SIDERITE n pale yellow to brownish-black mineral

SIDERITES > SIDERITE

SIDERITIC > SIDERITE

SIDEROAD n (esp in Ontario) a road going at right angles to concession roads

SIDEROADS > SIDEROAD

SIDEROSES > SIDEROSIS

SIDEROSIS n lung disease caused by breathing in fine particles of iron or other metallic dust

SIDEROTIC > SIDEROSIS

SIDERS > SIDER

SIDES > SIDE

SIDESHOOT n minor shoot growing on plant

SIDESHOW n entertainment offered along with the main show

SIDESHOWS > SIDESHOW

SIDESLIP same as > SLIP

SIDESLIPS > SIDESLIP

SIDESMAN n man elected to help the parish church warden

SIDESMEN > SIDESMAN

SIDESPIN n horizontal spin put on ball

SIDESPINS > SIDESPIN

SIDESTEP vb dodge (an issue) ▷ n movement to one side, such as in dancing or boxing

SIDESTEPS > SIDESTEP

SIDESWIPE n unexpected criticism of someone or something while discussing another subject ▷ vb make a sideswipe

SIDETRACK vb divert from the main topic ▷ n railway siding

SIDEWALK n paved path for pedestrians, at the side of a road

SIDEWALKS > SIDEWALK

SIDEWALL n either of the sides of a pneumatic tyre between the tread and the rim

SIDEWALLS > SIDEWALL

SIDEWARD adj directed or moving towards one side ▷ adv towards one side

SIDEWARDS adv towards one side

SIDEWAY variant of > SIDEWAYS

SIDEWAYS adv or from the side ▷ adj moving or directed to or from one side

SIDEWHEEL n one of the paddle wheels of a sidewheeler

SIDEWISE adv sideways

SIDH npl fairy people

SIDHA n (in Hinduism) person who has achieved perfection

SIDHAS > SIDHA

SIDHE npl inhabitants of fairyland

SIDING n short stretch of railway track on which trains are shunted from the main line

SIDINGS > SIDING

SIDLE vb walk in a furtive manner ▷ n sideways movement

SIDLED > SIDLE

SIDLER > SIDLE

SIDLERS > SIDLE

SIDLES > SIDLE

SIDLING > SIDLE

SIDLINGLY > SIDLE

SIECLE n century, period, or era

SIECLES > SIECLE

SIEGE n surrounding and blockading of a place ▷ vb lay siege to

SIEGED > SIEGE

SIEGER n person who besieges

SIEGERS > SIEGER

SIEGES > SIEGE

SIEGING > SIEGE

SIELD vb old word meaning given a ceiling

SIEMENS n SI unit of electrical conductance

SIEN n old word meaning scion

SIENITE n type of igneous rock

SIENITES > SIENITE

SIENNA n reddish- or yellowish-brown pigment made from natural earth

SIENNAS > SIENNA

SIENS > SIEN

SIENT n old word meaning scion

SIENTS > SIENT

SIEROZEM n type of soil

SIEROZEMS > SIEROZEM

SIERRA n range of mountains in Spain or America with jagged peaks

SIERRAN > SIERRA

SIERRAS > SIERRA

SIES interj in South Africa, an exclamation of disgust

SIESTA n afternoon nap, taken in hot countries

SIESTAS > SIESTA

SIETH n old form of scythe

SIETHS > SIETH

SIEUR n French word meaning lord

SIEURS > SIEUR

SIEVE n utensil with mesh through which a substance is sifted or strained ▷ vb sift or strain through a sieve

SIEVED > SIEVE

SIEVELIKE > SIEVE

SIEVERT n derived SI unit of dose equivalent, equal to 1 joule per kilogram

SIEVERTS > SIEVERT

SIEVES > SIEVE

SIEVING > SIEVE

SIF adj South African slang for disgusting

SIFAKA n either of two large rare arboreal lemuroid primates

SIFAKAS > SIFAKA

SIFFLE vb whistle

SIFFLED > SIFFLE

SIFFLES > SIFFLE

SIFFLEUR n male professional whistler

SIFFLEURS > SIFFLEUR

SIFFLEUSE n female professional whistler

SIFFLING > SIFFLE

SIFREI > SEFER

SIFT vb remove the coarser particles from a substance with a sieve

SIFTED > SIFT

SIFTER > SIFT

SIFTERS > SIFT

SIFTING > SIFT

SIFTINGLY > SIFT

SIFTINGS npl material or particles separated out by or as if by a sieve

SIFTS > SIFT

SIGANID n tropical fish

SIGANIDS > SIGANID

SIGH n long audible breath expressing sadness, tiredness, relief, or longing ▷ vb utter a sigh

SIGHED > SIGH

SIGHER > SIGH

SIGHERS > SIGH

SIGHFUL > SIGH

SIGHING > SIGH

SIGHINGLY > SIGH

SIGHLESS > SIGH

SIGHLIKE > SIGH

SIGHS > SIGH

SIGHT n ability to see ▷ vb catch sight of

SIGHTABLE > SIGHT

SIGHTED adj not blind

SIGHTER n any of six practice shots allowed to each competitor in a tournament

SIGHTERS > SIGHTER

SIGHTING > SIGHT

SIGHTINGS > SIGHT

SIGHTLESS adj blind

SIGHTLIER > SIGHTLY

SIGHTLINE n uninterrupted line of vision

SIGHTLY adj pleasing or attractive to see

SIGHTS > SIGHT

SIGHTSAW > SIGHTSEE

SIGHTSEE vb visit the famous or interesting sights of (a place)

SIGHTSEEN > SIGHTSEE

SIGHTSEER > SIGHTSEE

SIGHTSEES > SIGHTSEE

SIGHTSMAN n tourist guide

SIGHTSMEN > SIGHTSMAN

SIGIL n seal or signet

SIGILLARY > SIGIL

SIGILLATE adj closed with seal

SIGILS > SIGIL

SIGISBEI > SIGISBEO

SIGISBEO n male escort for a married woman

SIGLA n list of symbols used in a book

SIGLAS > SIGLA

SIGLOI > SIGLOS

SIGLOS n silver coin of ancient Persia worth one twentieth of a daric

SIGLUM n symbol used in book

SIGMA n 18th letter in the Greek alphabet

SIGMAS > SIGMA

SIGMATE adj shaped like the Greek letter sigma or the Roman S ▷ n sigmate thing ▷ vb add a sigma

SIGMATED > SIGMATE

SIGMATES > SIGMATE

SIGMATIC > SIGMATE

SIGMATING > SIGMATE

SIGMATION > SIGMATE

SIGMATISM n repetition of letter s

SIGMATRON n machine for generating X-rays

SIGMOID adj shaped like the letter S ▷ n S-shaped bend in the final portion of the large intestine

SIGMOIDAL variant of > SIGMOID

SIGMOIDS > SIGMOID

SIGN n indication of something not immediately or outwardly observable ▷ vb write (one's name) on (a document or letter) to show its authenticity or one's agreement

SIGNA npl symbols

SIGNABLE > SIGN

SIGNAGE n signs collectively, esp street signs or signs giving directions

SIGNAGES > SIGNAGE

SIGNAL n sign or gesture to convey information ▷ adj very important ▷ vb convey (information) by signal

SIGNALED > SIGNAL

SIGNALER > SIGNAL

SIGNALERS > SIGNAL

SIGNALING > SIGNAL

SIGNALISE same as > SIGNALIZE

SIGNALIZE vb make noteworthy or conspicuous

SIGNALLED > SIGNAL

SIGNALLER > SIGNAL

SIGNALLY adv conspicuously or especially

SIGNALMAN n railwayman in charge of signals and points

SIGNALMEN > SIGNALMAN

SIGNALS > SIGNAL

SIGNARIES > SIGNARY

SIGNARY *n* set of symbols

SIGNATORY *n* one of the parties who sign a document ▷ *adj* having signed a document or treaty

SIGNATURE *n* person's name written by himself or herself in signing something

SIGNBOARD *n* board carrying a sign or notice, often to advertise a business or product

SIGNED > SIGN

SIGNEE *n* person signing document

SIGNEES > SIGNEE

SIGNER *n* person who signs something

SIGNERS > SIGNER

SIGNET *n* small seal used to authenticate documents ▷ *vb* stamp or authenticate with a signet

SIGNETED > SIGNET

SIGNETING > SIGNET

SIGNETS > SIGNET

SIGNEUR *old spelling of* > SENIOR

SIGNEURIE *n* old word meaning seniority

SIGNIEUR *n* old word meaning lord

SIGNIEURS > SIGNIEUR

SIGNIFICS *n* study of meaning

SIGNIFIED > SIGNIFY

SIGNIFIER > SIGNIFY

SIGNIFIES > SIGNIFY

SIGNIFY *vb* indicate or suggest

SIGNING *n* system of communication using hand and arm movements, such as one used by deaf people

SIGNINGS > SIGNING

SIGNIOR *same as* > SIGNOR

SIGNIORI > SIGNIOR

SIGNIORS > SIGNIOR

SIGNIORY *n* old word meaning lordship

SIGNLESS > SIGN

SIGNOR *n* Italian term of address equivalent to *sir* or *Mr*

SIGNORA *n* Italian term of address equivalent to *madam* or *Mrs*

SIGNORAS > SIGNORA

SIGNORE *n* Italian man: a title of respect equivalent to *sir*

SIGNORES > SIGNORE

SIGNORI > SIGNORE

SIGNORIA *n* government of Italian city

SIGNORIAL > SIGNORIA

SIGNORIAS > SIGNORIA

SIGNORIES > SIGNORY

SIGNORINA *n* Italian term of address equivalent to *madam* or *Miss*

SIGNORINE

> SIGNORINA

SIGNORINI

> SIGNORINO

SIGNORINO *n* young gentleman

SIGNORS > SIGNOR

SIGNORY *same as* > SEIGNIORY

SIGNPOST *n* post bearing a sign that shows the way ▷ *vb* mark with signposts

SIGNPOSTS > SIGNPOST

SIGNS > SIGN

SIJO *n* Korean poem

SIJOS > SIJO

SIK *adj* excellent

SIKA *n* Japanese forest-dwelling deer

SIKAS > SIKA

SIKE *n* small stream

SIKER *adj* old spelling of *sicker*

SIKES > SIKE

SIKORSKY *n* type of helicopter

SILAGE *n* fodder crop harvested while green and partially fermented in a silo ▷ *vb* make silage

SILAGED > SILAGE

SILAGEING > SILAGE

SILAGES > SILAGE

SILAGING > SILAGE

SILANE *n* gas containing silicon

SILANES > SILANE

SILASTIC *n* tradename for a type of flexible silicone rubber

SILASTICS > SILASTIC

SILD *n* any of various small young herrings, esp when prepared and canned in Norway

SILDS > SILD

SILE *vb* pour with rain

SILED > SILE

SILEN *n* god of woodland

SILENCE *n* absence of noise or speech ▷ *vb* make silent

SILENCED *adj* (of a clergyman) forbidden to preach or perform his clerical functions

SILENCER *n* device to reduce the noise of an engine exhaust or gun

SILENCERS > SILENCER

SILENCES > SILENCE

SILENCING > SILENCE

SILENE *n* type of plant with mostly red or pink flowers, often grown as a garden plant

SILENES > SILENE

SILENI > SILENUS

SILENS > SILEN

SILENT *adj* tending to speak very little ▷ *n* silent film

SILENTER > SILENT

SILENTEST > SILENT

SILENTLY > SILENT

SILENTS > SILENT

SILENUS *n* woodland deity

SILER *n* strainer

SILERS > SILER

SILES > SILE

SILESIA *n* twill-weave fabric of cotton or other fibre

SILESIAS > SILESIA

SILEX *n* type of heat-resistant glass made from fused quartz

SILEXES > SILEX

SILICA *n* hard glossy mineral found as quartz and in sandstone

SILICAS > SILICA

SILICATE *n* compound of silicon, oxygen, and a metal

SILICATED > SILICATE

SILICATES > SILICATE

SILICEOUS *adj* of, relating to, or containing abundant silica

SILICIC *adj* of, concerned with, or containing silicon or an acid obtained from silicon

SILICIDE *n* any one of a class of binary compounds formed between silicon and certain metals

SILICIDES > SILICIDE

SILICIFY *vb* convert or be converted into silica

SILICIOUS *same as* > SILICEOUS

SILICIUM *rare name for* > SILICON

SILICIUMS > SILICIUM

SILICLE *same as* > SILICULA

SILICLES > SILICLE

SILICON *n* brittle nonmetallic element widely used in chemistry and industry ▷ *adj* denoting an area of a country that contains much high-technology industry

SILICONE *n* tough synthetic substance made from silicon and used in lubricants

SILICONES > SILICONE

SILICONS > SILICON

SILICOSES

> SILICOSIS

SILICOSIS *n* lung disease caused by inhaling silica dust

SILICOTIC *n* person suffering from silicosis

SILICULA *n* short broad siliqua, occurring in such cruciferous plants as honesty and shepherd's-purse

SILICULAE > SILICULA

SILICULAS > SILICULA

SILICULE *same as* > SILICULA

SILICULES > SILICULE

SILING > SILE

SILIQUA *n* long dry

dehiscent fruit of cruciferous plants such as the wallflower

SILIQUAE > SILIQUA

SILIQUAS > SILIQUA

SILIQUE *same as* > SILIQUA

SILIQUES > SILIQUE

SILIQUOSE > SILIQUA

SILIQUOUS > SILIQUA

SILK *n* fibre made by the larva of a certain moth ▷ *vb* (of maize) develop long hairlike styles

SILKALENE *same as* > SILKALINE

SILKALINE *n* fine smooth cotton fabric used for linings, etc

SILKED > SILK

SILKEN *adj* made of silk ▷ *vb* make like silk

SILKENED > SILKEN

SILKENING > SILKEN

SILKENS > SILKEN

SILKIE *n* Scots word for a seal

SILKIER > SILKY

SILKIES > SILKIE

SILKIEST > SILKY

SILKILY > SILKY

SILKINESS > SILKY

SILKING > SILK

SILKLIKE > SILK

SILKOLINE *n* material like silk

SILKS > SILK

SILKTAIL *n* waxwing

SILKTAILS > SILKTAIL

SILKWEED *another name for* > MILKWEED

SILKWEEDS > SILKWEED

SILKWORM *n* caterpillar that spins a cocoon of silk

SILKWORMS > SILKWORM

SILKY *adj* of or like silk

SILL *n* ledge at the bottom of a window or door

SILLABUB *same as* > SYLLABUB

SILLABUBS > SILLABUB

SILLADAR *n* Indian irregular cavalryman

SILLADARS > SILLADAR

SILLER *n* silver ▷ *adj* silver

SILLERS > SILLER

SILLIBUB *n* syllabub

SILLIBUBS > SILLIBUB

SILLIER > SILLY

SILLIES > SILLY

SILLIEST > SILLY

SILLILY > SILLY

SILLINESS > SILLY

SILLOCK *n* young coalfish

SILLOCKS > SILLOCK

SILLS > SILL

SILLY *adj* foolish ▷ *n* foolish person

SILO *n* pit or airtight tower for storing silage or grains ▷ *vb* put in a silo

SILOED > SILO

SILOING > SILO

SILOS > SILO

SILOXANE n any of a class of compounds containing alternate silicon and oxygen atoms

SILOXANES > SILOXANE

SILPHIA > SILPHIUM

SILPHIUM n American flowering wild plant

SILPHIUMS > SILPHIUM

SILT n mud deposited by moving water ▷ vb fill or be choked with silt

SILTATION > SILT

SILTED > SILT

SILTIER > SILT

SILTIEST > SILT

SILTING > SILT

SILTS > SILT

SILTSTONE n variety of fine sandstone formed from consolidated silt

SILTY > SILT

SILURIAN adj formed in the third period of the Palaeozoic

SILURID n type of freshwater fish of the family which includes catfish

SILURIDS > SILURID

SILURIST n member of ancient Silurian tribe

SILURISTS > SILURIST

SILUROID n freshwater fish

SILUROIDS > SILUROID

SILVA same as > SYLVA

SILVAE > SILVA

SILVAN same as > SYLVAN

SILVANS > SILVAN

SILVAS > SILVA

SILVATIC adj wild, not domestic

SILVER n white precious metal ▷ adj made of or of the colour of silver ▷ vb coat with silver

SILVERED > SILVER

SILVERER > SILVER

SILVERERS > SILVER

SILVEREYE n greenish-coloured songbird of Africa, Australia, New Zealand, and Asia

SILVERIER > SILVERY

SILVERING > SILVER

SILVERISE same as > SILVERIZE

SILVERIZE vb coat with silver

SILVERLY adv like silver

SILVERN adj silver

SILVERS > SILVER

SILVERY adj like silver

SILVEX n type of weedkiller

SILVEXES > SILVEX

SILVICAL adj of trees

SILVICS n study of trees

SILYMARIN n antioxidant found in milk thistle

SIM n computer game that simulates an activity such as flying or playing a sport

SIMA n silicon-rich and magnesium-rich rocks of the earth's oceanic crust

SIMAR variant spelling of > CYMAR

SIMAROUBA n tropical American tree with divided leaves and fleshy fruits

SIMARRE n woman's loose gown

SIMARRES > SIMARRE

SIMARS > SIMAR

SIMARUBA same as > SIMAROUBA

SIMARUBAS > SIMARUBA

SIMAS > SIMA

SIMATIC > SIMA

SIMAZINE n organic weedkiller

SIMAZINES > SIMAZINE

SIMBA E African word for > LION

SIMBAS > SIMBA

SIMI n East African sword

SIMIAL adj of apes

SIMIAN n a monkey or ape ▷ adj of or resembling a monkey or ape

SIMIANS > SIMIAN

SIMILAR adj alike but not identical

SIMILARLY > SIMILAR

SIMILE n figure of speech comparing one thing to another, using 'as' or 'like'

SIMILES > SIMILE

SIMILISE same as > SIMILIZE

SIMILISED > SIMILISE

SIMILISES > SIMILISE

SIMILIZE vb use similes

SIMILIZED > SIMILIZE

SIMILIZES > SIMILIZE

SIMILOR n alloy used in cheap jewellery

SIMILORS > SIMILOR

SIMIOID adj of apes

SIMIOUS adj of apes

SIMIS > SIMI

SIMITAR same as > SCIMITAR

SIMITARS > SIMITAR

SIMKIN word used in India for > CHAMPAGNE

SIMKINS > SIMKIN

SIMLIN n American variety of squash plant

SIMLINS > SIMLIN

SIMMER vb cook gently at just below boiling point ▷ n state of simmering

SIMMERED > SIMMER

SIMMERING > SIMMER

SIMMERS > SIMMER

SIMNEL as in simnel cake fruit cake with marzipan eaten at Easter

SIMNELS > SIMNEL

SIMOLEON n American slang for dollar

SIMOLEONS > SIMOLEON

SIMONIAC n person who is guilty of practising simony

SIMONIACS > SIMONIAC

SIMONIES > SIMONY

SIMONIOUS > SIMONY

SIMONISE same as > SIMONIZE

SIMONISED > SIMONISE

SIMONISES > SIMONISE

SIMONIST > SIMONY

SIMONISTS > SIMONY

SIMONIZE vb polish with wax

SIMONIZED > SIMONIZE

SIMONIZES > SIMONIZE

SIMONY n practice of buying or selling Church benefits such as pardons

SIMOOM n hot suffocating sand-laden desert wind

SIMOOMS > SIMOOM

SIMOON same as > SIMOOM

SIMOONS > SIMOON

SIMORG n bird in Persian myth

SIMORGS > SIMORG

SIMP short for > SIMPLETON

SIMPAI n Indonesian monkey

SIMPAIS > SIMPAI

SIMPATICO adj pleasant or congenial

SIMPER vb smile in a silly or affected way ▷ n simpering smile

SIMPERED > SIMPER

SIMPERER > SIMPER

SIMPERERS > SIMPER

SIMPERING > SIMPER

SIMPERS > SIMPER

SIMPKIN word used in India for > CHAMPAGNE

SIMPKINS > SIMPKIN

SIMPLE adj easy to understand or do ▷ n simpleton ▷ vb archaic word meaning to look for medicinal herbs

SIMPLED > SIMPLE

SIMPLER > SIMPLE

SIMPLERS > SIMPLE

SIMPLES > SIMPLE

SIMPLESSE n old word meaning simplicity

SIMPLEST > SIMPLE

SIMPLETON n foolish or half-witted person

SIMPLEX adj permitting the transmission of signals in only one direction in a radio circuit ▷ n simple not a compound word

SIMPLEXES > SIMPLEX

SIMPLICES > SIMPLEX

SIMPLICIA n species of moth

SIMPLIFY vb make less complicated

SIMPLING > SIMPLE

SIMPLINGS > SIMPLE

SIMPLISM n quality of being extremely naive

SIMPLISMS > SIMPLISM

SIMPLIST n old word meaning expert in herbal medicine

SIMPLISTE adj simplistic

SIMPLISTS > SIMPLIST

SIMPLY adv in a simple manner

SIMPS > SIMP

SIMS > SIM

SIMUL adj simultaneous ▷ n simultaneous broadcast

SIMULACRA npl representations of things

SIMULACRE n resemblance

SIMULANT adj simulating ▷ n simulant thing

SIMULANTS > SIMULANT

SIMULAR n person or thing that simulates or imitates ▷ adj fake

SIMULARS > SIMULAR

SIMULATE vb make a pretence of ▷ adj assumed or simulated

SIMULATED adj being an imitation of the genuine article, usually made from cheaper material

SIMULATES > SIMULATE

SIMULATOR n device that simulates specific conditions for the purposes of research or training

SIMULCAST vb broadcast (a programme) simultaneously on radio and television ▷ n programme broadcast in this way

SIMULIUM n tropical fly

SIMULIUMS > SIMULIUM

SIMULS > SIMUL

SIMURG n bird in Persian myth

SIMURGH n bird in Persian myth

SIMURGHS > SIMURGH

SIMURGS > SIMURG

SIN n offence or transgression ▷ vb commit a sin

SINAPISM n mixture of black mustard seeds and an adhesive, applied to the skin

SINAPISMS > SINAPISM

SINCE prep during the period of time after ▷ adv from that time

SINCERE adj without pretence or deceit

SINCERELY > SINCERE

SINCERER > SINCERE

SINCEREST > SINCERE

SINCERITY > SINCERE

SINCIPITA > SINCIPUT

SINCIPUT n forward upper part of the skull

SINCIPUTS > SINCIPUT

SIND variant of > SYNE

SINDED > SIND

SINDING > SIND

SINDINGS > SIND

SINDON n type of cloth

SINDONS > SINDON

SINDS > SIND

SINE same as > SYNE

SINECURE n paid job with minimal duties

SINECURES > SINECURE

SINED > SINE

SINES > SINE

SINEW n tough fibrous tissue joining muscle to bone ▷ vb make strong

SINEWED adj having sinews

SINEWIER > SINEWY

SINEWIEST > SINEWY

SINEWING > SINEW

SINEWLESS > SINEW

SINEWS > SINEW

SINEWY adj lean and muscular

SINFONIA n symphony orchestra

SINFONIAS > SINFONIA

SINFONIE > SINFONIA

SINFUL adj guilty of sin

SINFULLY > SINFUL

SING vb make musical sounds with the voice ▷ n act or performance of singing

SINGABLE > SING

SINGALONG n act of singing along with a performer

SINGE vb burn the surface of ▷ n superficial burn

SINGED > SINGE

SINGEING > SINGE

SINGER n person who sings, esp professionally

SINGERS > SINGER

SINGES > SINGE

SINGING > SING

SINGINGLY > SING

SINGINGS > SING

SINGLE adj one only ▷ n single thing ▷ vb pick out from others

SINGLED > SINGLE

SINGLEDOM n state of being unmarried or not involved in a long-term relationship

SINGLES npl match played with one person on each side

SINGLET n sleeveless vest

SINGLETON n only card of a particular suit held by a player

SINGLETS > SINGLET

SINGLING > SINGLE

SINGLINGS > SINGLE

SINGLY adv one at a time

SINGS > SING

SINGSONG n informal singing session ▷ adj (of the voice) repeatedly rising and falling in pitch

SINGSONGS > SINGSONG

SINGSONGY > SINGSONG

SINGSPIEL n type of German comic opera with spoken dialogue

SINGULAR adj (of a word or form) denoting one person or thing ▷ n

singular form of a word

SINGULARS > SINGULAR

SINGULARY adj (of an operator) monadic

SINGULT n old word meaning sob

SINGULTS > SINGULT

SINGULTUS technical name for > HICCUP

SINH n hyperbolic sine

SINHS > SINH

SINICAL > SINE

SINICISE same as > SINICIZE

SINICISED > SINICISE

SINICISES > SINICISE

SINICIZE vb make Chinese

SINICIZED > SINICIZE

SINICIZES > SINICIZE

SINING > SINE

SINISTER adj threatening or suggesting evil or harm

SINISTRAL adj of, relating to, or located on the left side, esp the left side of the body

SINK vb submerge (in liquid) ▷ n fixed basin with a water supply and drainage pipe

SINKABLE > SINK

SINKAGE n act of sinking or degree to which something sinks or has sunk

SINKAGES > SINKAGE

SINKER n weight for a fishing line

SINKERS > SINKER

SINKHOLE n depression in the ground surface, esp in limestone, where a surface stream disappears underground

SINKHOLES > SINKHOLE

SINKIER > SINKY

SINKIEST > SINKY

SINKING > SINK

SINKINGS > SINK

SINKS > SINK

SINKY adj giving underfoot

SINLESS adj free from sin or guilt

SINLESSLY > SINLESS

SINNED > SIN

SINNER n person that sins ▷ vb behave like a sinner

SINNERED > SINNER

SINNERING > SINNER

SINNERS > SIN

SINNET n braided rope

SINNETS > SINNET

SINNING > SIN

SINNINGIA n tropical flowering plant

SINOLOGUE > SINOLOGY

SINOLOGY n study of Chinese culture, etc

SINOPIA n pigment made from iron ore

SINOPIAS > SINOPIA

SINOPIE > SINOPIA

SINOPIS n pigment made

from iron ore

SINOPISES > SINOPIS

SINOPITE n iron ore

SINOPITES > SINOPITE

SINS > SIN

SINSYNE adv Scots word meaning since

SINTER n whitish porous incrustation that is deposited from hot springs ▷ vb form large particles from (metal powders or powdery ores) by heating or pressure

SINTERED > SINTER

SINTERING > SINTER

SINTERS > SINTER

SINTERY > SINTER

SINUATE vb wind

SINUATED same as > SINUATE

SINUATELY > SINUATE

SINUATES > SINUATE

SINUATING > SINUATE

SINUATION same as > SINUOSITY

SINUITIS variant of > SINUSITIS

SINUOSE adj sinuous

SINUOSITY n quality of being sinuous

SINUOUS adj full of turns or curves

SINUOUSLY > SINUOUS

SINUS n hollow space in a bone, esp an air passage opening into the nose

SINUSES > SINUS

SINUSITIS n inflammation of a sinus membrane

SINUSLIKE > SINUS

SINUSOID n any of the irregular terminal blood vessels that replace capillaries in certain organs ▷ adj resembling a sinus

SINUSOIDS > SINUSOID

SIP vb drink in small mouthfuls ▷ n amount sipped

SIPE vb soak

SIPED > SIPE

SIPES > SIPE

SIPHON n bent tube which uses air pressure to draw liquid from a container ▷ vb draw off thus

SIPHONAGE > SIPHON

SIPHONAL > SIPHON

SIPHONATE adj having a syphon

SIPHONED > SIPHON

SIPHONET n sucking tube on an aphid

SIPHONETS > SIPHONET

SIPHONIC > SIPHON

SIPHONING > SIPHON

SIPHONS > SIPHON

SIPHUNCLE n tube inside shellfish

SIPING > SIPE

SIPPED > SIP

SIPPER > SIP

SIPPERS > SIP

SIPPET n small piece of toast eaten with soup or gravy

SIPPETS > SIPPET

SIPPING > SIP

SIPPLE vb sip

SIPPLED > SIPPLE

SIPPLES > SIPPLE

SIPPLING > SIPPLE

SIPPY as in sippy cup infant's drinking cup with a tight-fitting lid and perforated spout

SIPS > SIP

SIR n polite term of address for a man ▷ vb call someone 'sir'

SIRCAR n government in India

SIRCARS > SIRCAR

SIRDAR same as > SARDAR

SIRDARS > SIRDAR

SIRE n male parent of a horse or other domestic animal ▷ vb father

SIRED > SIRE

SIREE emphasized form of > SIR

SIREES > SIREE

SIREN n device making a loud wailing noise as a warning

SIRENIAN n animal belonging to the order of aquatic herbivorous mammals that includes the dugong and manatee

SIRENIANS > SIRENIAN

SIRENIC > SIREN

SIRENISE variant of > SIRENIZE

SIRENISED > SIRENISE

SIRENISES > SIRENISE

SIRENIZE vb bewitch

SIRENIZED > SIRENIZE

SIRENIZES > SIRENIZE

SIRENS > SIREN

SIRES > SIRE

SIRGANG n Asian bird

SIRGANGS > SIRGANG

SIRI n betel

SIRIASES > SIRIASIS

SIRIASIS n sunstroke

SIRIH n betel

SIRIHS > SIRIH

SIRING > SIRE

SIRINGS > SIRING

SIRIS > SIRI

SIRKAR n government in India

SIRKARS > SIRKAR

SIRLOIN n prime cut of loin of beef

SIRLOINS > SIRLOIN

SIRNAME vb old form of surname

SIRNAMED > SIRNAME

SIRNAMES > SIRNAME

SIRNAMING > SIRNAME

SIROC n sirocco

SIROCCO n hot wind blowing from N Africa into S Europe

SIROCCOS > SIROCCO
SIROCS > SIROC
SIRONISE *same as*
> SIRONIZE
SIRONISED > SIRONISE
SIRONISES > SIRONISE
SIRONIZE *vb* treat (a woollen fabric) chemically to prevent it wrinkling after being washed
SIRONIZED > SIRONIZE
SIRONIZES > SIRONIZE
SIROSET *adj* of the chemical treatment of woollen fabrics to give a permanent-press effect
SIRRA *disrespectful form of* **>** SIR
SIRRAH *n* contemptuous term used in addressing a man or boy
SIRRAHS > SIRRAH
SIRRAS > SIRRA
SIRRED > SIR
SIRREE *n* form of 'sir' used for emphasis
SIRREES > SIRREE
SIRRING > SIR
SIRS > SIR
SIRTUIN *n* protein that regulates cell metabolism and ageing
SIRTUINS > SIRTUIN
SIRUP *same as* **>** SYRUP
SIRUPED > SIRUP
SIRUPIER > SIRUP
SIRUPIEST > SIRUP
SIRUPING > SIRUP
SIRUPS > SIRUP
SIRUPY > SIRUP
SIRVENTE *n* verse form employed by the troubadours of Provence to satirize political themes
SIRVENTES > SIRVENTE
SIS *n* sister
SISAL *n* (fibre of) plant used in making ropes
SISALS > SISAL
SISERARY *n* scolding
SISES > SIS
SISKIN *n* yellow-and-black finch
SISKINS > SISKIN
SISS *shortening of* **>** SISTER
SISSES > SISS
SISSIER > SISSY
SISSIES > SISSY
SISSIEST > SISSY
SISSIFIED > SISSY
SISSINESS > SISSY
SISSOO *n* Indian tree
SISSOOS > SISSOO
SISSY *n* weak or cowardly (person) ▷ *adj* effeminate, weak, or cowardly
SISSYISH > SISSY
SISSYNESS > SISSY
SIST *vb* Scottish law term meaning stop
SISTED > SIST
SISTER *n* girl or woman with the same parents as

another person ▷ *adj* closely related, similar ▷ *vb* be or be like a sister
SISTERED > SISTER
SISTERING > SISTER
SISTERLY *adj* of or like a sister
SISTERS > SISTER
SISTING > SIST
SISTRA > SISTRUM
SISTROID *adj* contained between the convex sides of two intersecting curves
SISTRUM *n* musical instrument of ancient Egypt consisting of a metal rattle
SISTRUMS > SISTRUM
SISTS > SIST
SIT *vb* rest one's body upright on the buttocks
SITAR *n* Indian stringed musical instrument
SITARIST > SITAR
SITARISTS > SITAR
SITARS > SITAR
SITATUNGA *another name for* **>** MARSHBUCK
SITCOM *n* situation comedy
SITCOMS > SITCOM
SITE *n* place where something is, was, or is intended to be located ▷ *vb* provide with a site
SITED > SITE
SITELLA *n* type of small generally black-and-white bird
SITELLAS > SITELLA
SITES > SITE
SITFAST *n* sore on a horse's back caused by rubbing of the saddle
SITFASTS > SITFAST
SITH *archaic word for* **>** SINCE
SITHE *vb* old form of scythe
SITHED > SITHE
SITHEE *interj* look here! listen!
SITHEN *adv* old word meaning since
SITHENCE *adv* old word meaning since
SITHENS *adv* old word meaning since
SITHES > SITHE
SITHING > SITHE
SITING > SITE
SITIOLOGY *n* study of diet and nutrition
SITKA *as in sitka spruce* tall North American spruce tree
SITKAMER *n* sitting room
SITKAMERS > SITKAMER
SITOLOGY *n* scientific study of food, diet, and nutrition
SITREP *n* military situation report
SITREPS > SITREP
SITS > SIT
SITTAR *n* sitar

SITTARS > SITTAR
SITTELLA *variant spelling of* **>** SITELLA
SITTELLAS > SITTELLA
SITTEN *adj* dialect word for in the saddle
SITTER *n* baby-sitter
SITTERS > SITTER
SITTINE *adj* of nuthatch bird family
SITTING > SIT
SITTINGS > SIT
SITUATE *vb* place ▷ *adj* (now used esp in legal contexts) situated
SITUATED > SITUATE
SITUATES > SITUATE
SITUATING > SITUATE
SITUATION *n* state of affairs
SITULA *n* bucket-shaped container, usually of metal or pottery and often richly decorated
SITULAE > SITULA
SITUP *n* exercise in which the body is brought into a sitting position from one lying on the back
SITUPS > SITUP
SITUS *n* position or location, esp the usual or right position of an organ or part of the body
SITUSES > SITUS
SITUTUNGA *n* African antelope
SITZ *as in sitz bath* bath in which the buttocks and hips are immersed in hot water
SITZKRIEG *n* period during a war in which both sides change positions very slowly or not at all
SITZMARK *n* depression in the snow where a skier has fallen
SITZMARKS > SITZMARK
SIVER *same as* **>** SYVER
SIVERS > SIVER
SIWASH *vb* (in the Pacific Northwest) to camp out with only natural shelter
SIWASHED > SIWASH
SIWASHES > SIWASH
SIWASHING > SIWASH
SIX *n* one more than five
SIXAIN *n* stanza or poem of six lines
SIXAINE *n* six-line stanza of poetry
SIXAINES > SIXAINE
SIXAINS > SIXAIN
SIXER *same as* **>** SIX
SIXERS > SIXER
SIXES > SIX
SIXFOLD *adj* having six times as many or as much ▷ *adv* by six times as many or as much
SIXMO *n* book size resulting from folding a sheet of paper into six leaves or twelve pages, each one

sixth the size of the sheet
SIXMOS > SIXMO
SIXPENCE *n* former British and Australian coin worth six pennies
SIXPENCES > SIXPENCE
SIXPENNY *adj* (of a nail) two inches in length
SIXSCORE *n* hundred and twenty
SIXSCORES > SIXSCORE
SIXTE *n* sixth of eight basic positions from which a parry or attack can be made in fencing
SIXTEEN *n* six and ten ▷ *adj* amounting to sixteen ▷ *det* amounting to sixteen
SIXTEENER *n* poem verse with sixteen syllables
SIXTEENMO *n* book size resulting from folding a sheet of paper into 16 leaves or 32 pages
SIXTEENS > SIXTEEN
SIXTEENTH *adj* coming after the fifteenth in numbering order ▷ *n* one of 16 equal or nearly equal parts of something
SIXTES > SIXTE
SIXTH *n* (of) number six in a series ▷ *adj* coming after the fifth and before the seventh in numbering order ▷ *adv* after the fifth person, position, etc
SIXTHLY *same as* **>** SIXTH
SIXTHS > SIXTH
SIXTIES > SIXTY
SIXTIETH *adj* being the ordinal number of sixty in numbering order ▷ *n* one of 60 approximately equal parts of something
SIXTIETHS > SIXTIETH
SIXTY *n* six times ten ▷ *adj* amounting to sixty
SIXTYISH > SIXTY
SIZABLE *adj* quite large
SIZABLY > SIZABLE
SIZAR *n* (at certain universities) an undergraduate receiving a maintenance grant from the college
SIZARS > SIZAR
SIZARSHIP > SIZAR
SIZE *n* dimensions, bigness ▷ *vb* arrange according to size
SIZEABLE *same as* **>** SIZABLE
SIZEABLY > SIZABLE
SIZED *adj* of a specified size
SIZEISM *n* discrimination on the basis of a person's size, esp against people considered to be overweight
SIZEISMS > SIZEISM
SIZEIST > SIZEISM
SIZEISTS > SIZEISM
SIZEL *n* scrap metal clippings

SIZELS > SIZEL

SIZER > SIZE

SIZERS > SIZE

SIZES > SIZE

SIZIER > SIZE

SIZIEST > SIZE

SIZINESS > SIZE

SIZING > SIZE

SIZINGS > SIZE

SIZISM n discrimination against people because of weight

SIZISMS > SIZISM

SIZIST > SIZISM

SIZISTS > SIZISM

SIZY > SIZE

SIZZLE vb make a hissing sound like frying fat ▷ n hissing sound

SIZZLED > SIZZLE

SIZZLER n something that sizzles

SIZZLERS > SIZZLER

SIZZLES > SIZZLE

SIZZLING adj extremely hot

SIZZLINGS > SIZZLING

SJAMBOK n whip or riding crop made of hide ▷ vb beat with a sjambok

SJAMBOKED > SJAMBOK

SJAMBOKS > SJAMBOK

SJOE interj South African exclamation of surprise, admiration, exhaustion, etc

SKA n type of West Indian pop music of the 1960s

SKAG same as > SCAG

SKAGS > SKAG

SKAIL vb Scots word meaning disperse

SKAILED > SKAIL

SKAILING > SKAIL

SKAILS > SKAIL

SKAITH vb Scots word meaning injure

SKAITHED > SKAITH

SKAITHING > SKAITH

SKAITHS > SKAITH

SKALD n (in ancient Scandinavia) a bard or minstrel

SKALDIC > SKALD

SKALDS > SKALD

SKALDSHIP > SKALD

SKANGER n Irish derogatory slang for a young working-class person who wears casual sports clothes

SKANGERS > SKANGER

SKANK n fast dance to reggae music ▷ vb perform this dance

SKANKED > SKANK

SKANKER > SKANK

SKANKERS > SKANK

SKANKIER > SKANKY

SKANKIEST > SKANKY

SKANKING > SKANK

SKANKINGS > SKANK

SKANKS > SKANK

SKANKY adj dirty or unattractive

SKART Scots word for > CORMORANT

SKARTH Scots word for > CORMORANT

SKARTHS > SKARTH

SKARTS > SKART

SKAS > SKA

SKAT n three-handed card game using 32 cards, popular in German-speaking communities

SKATE n boot with a steel blade or sets of wheels attached to the sole for gliding over ice or a hard surface ▷ vb glide on or as if on skates

SKATED > SKATE

SKATEPARK n place for skateboarding

SKATER n person who skates

SKATERS > SKATER

SKATES > SKATE

SKATING > SKATE

SKATINGS > SKATE

SKATOL n skatole

SKATOLE n white or brownish crystalline solid

SKATOLES > SKATOLE

SKATOLS > SKATOL

SKATS > SKAT

SKATT n dialect word meaning throw

SKATTS > SKATT

SKAW variant of > SCAW

SKAWS > SKAW

SKEAN n kind of double-edged dagger formerly used in Ireland and Scotland

SKEANE same as > SKEIN

SKEANES > SKEANE

SKEANS > SKEAN

SKEAR dialect form of > SCARE

SKEARED > SKEAR

SKEARIER > SKEARY

SKEARIEST > SKEARY

SKEARING > SKEAR

SKEARS > SKEAR

SKEARY dialect form of > SCARY

SKEDADDLE vb run off ▷ n hasty retreat

SKEE variant spelling of > SKI

SKEECHAN n old Scots type of beer

SKEECHANS > SKEECHAN

SKEED > SKEE

SKEEF adj, adv South African slang for at an oblique angle

SKEEING > SKEE

SKEELIER > SKEELY

SKEELIEST > SKEELY

SKEELY adj Scots word meaning skilful

SKEEN n type of ibex

SKEENS > SKEEN

SKEER dialect form of > SCARE

SKEERED > SKEER

SKEERIER > SKEERY

SKEERIEST > SKEERY

SKEERING > SKEER

SKEERS > SKEER

SKEERY dialect form of > SCARY

SKEES > SKEE

SKEESICKS American word meaning > ROGUE

SKEET n form of clay-pigeon shooting

SKEETER informal word for > MOSQUITO

SKEETERS > SKEETER

SKEETS > SKEET

SKEG n reinforcing brace between the after end of a keel and the rudderpost

SKEGG n skeg

SKEGGER n young salmon

SKEGGERS > SKEGGER

SKEGGS > SKEGG

SKEGS > SKEG

SKEIGH adj Scots word meaning shy

SKEIGHER > SKEIGH

SKEIGHEST > SKEIGH

SKEIN n yarn wound in a loose coil ▷ vb wind into a skein

SKEINED > SKEIN

SKEINING > SKEIN

SKEINS > SKEIN

SKELDER vb beg

SKELDERED > SKELDER

SKELDERS > SKELDER

SKELETAL > SKELETON

SKELETON n framework of bones inside a person's or animal's body ▷ adj reduced to a minimum

SKELETONS > SKELETON

SKELF n splinter of wood, esp when embedded accidentally in the skin

SKELFS > SKELF

SKELL n homeless person

SKELLIE adj skelly

SKELLIED > SKELLY

SKELLIER > SKELLY

SKELLIES > SKELLY

SKELLIEST > SKELLY

SKELLOCH n Scots word meaning scream

SKELLOCHS > SKELLOCH

SKELLS > SKELL

SKELLUM n rogue

SKELLUMS > SKELLUM

SKELLY n whitefish of certain lakes in the Lake District ▷ vb look sideways or squint ▷ adj cross-eyed

SKELLYING > SKELLY

SKELM n villain or crook

SKELMS > SKELM

SKELP vb slap ▷ n slap

SKELPED > SKELP

SKELPING > SKELP

SKELPINGS > SKELP

SKELPIT vb Scots word meaning skelped

SKELPS > SKELP

SKELTER vb scurry

SKELTERED > SKELTER

SKELTERS > SKELTER

SKELUM n Scots word meaning rascal

SKELUMS > SKELUM

SKEN vb squint or stare

SKENE n Scots word meaning dagger

SKENES > SKENE

SKENNED > SKEN

SKENNING > SKEN

SKENS > SKEN

SKEO n Scots dialect word meaning hut

SKEOS > SKEO

SKEP n beehive, esp one constructed of straw ▷ vb gather into a hive

SKEPFUL n amount skep will hold

SKEPFULS > SKEP

SKEPPED > SKEP

SKEPPING > SKEP

SKEPS > SKEP

SKEPSIS n doubt

SKEPSISES > SKEPSIS

SKEPTIC same as > SCEPTIC

SKEPTICAL > SKEPTIC

SKEPTICS > SKEPTIC

SKER vb scour

SKERRED > SKER

SKERRICK n small fragment or amount

SKERRICKS > SKERRICK

SKERRIES > SKERRY

SKERRING > SKER

SKERRY n rocky island or reef

SKERS > SKER

SKET vb splash (water)

SKETCH n rough drawing ▷ vb make a sketch (of)

SKETCHED > SKETCH

SKETCHER > SKETCH

SKETCHERS > SKETCH

SKETCHES > SKETCH

SKETCHIER > SKETCHY

SKETCHILY > SKETCHY

SKETCHING > SKETCH

SKETCHPAD n pad of paper for sketching

SKETCHY adj incomplete or inadequate

SKETS > SKET

SKETTED > SKET

SKETTING > SKET

SKEW vb make slanting or crooked ▷ adj slanting or crooked ▷ n slanting position

SKEWBACK n sloping surface on both sides of a segmental arch that takes the thrust

SKEWBACKS > SKEWBACK

SKEWBALD adj (horse) marked with patches of white and another colour ▷ n horse with this marking

SKEWBALDS > SKEWBALD

SKEWED > SKEW

SKEWER n pin to hold meat together during cooking ▷ vb fasten with a skewer
SKEWERED > SKEWER
SKEWERING > SKEWER
SKEWERS > SKEWER
SKEWEST > SKEW
SKEWING > SKEW
SKEWNESS n quality or condition of being skew
SKEWS > SKEW
SKEWWHIFF adj crooked or slanting
SKI n one of a pair of long runners fastened to boots for gliding over snow or water ▷ vb travel on skis
SKIABLE > SKI
SKIAGRAM n picture made from shadows
SKIAGRAMS > SKIAGRAM
SKIAGRAPH n skiagram
SKIAMACHY same as > SCIAMACHY
SKIASCOPE n medical instrument for examining the eye to detect errors of refraction
SKIASCOPY n retinoscopy
SKIATRON n type of cathode ray tube
SKIATRONS > SKIATRON
SKIBOB n vehicle made of two short skis for gliding down snow slopes
SKIBOBBED > SKIBOB
SKIBOBBER > SKIBOB
SKIBOBS > SKIBOB
SKID vb (of a moving vehicle) slide sideways uncontrollably ▷ n skidding
SKIDDED > SKID
SKIDDER > SKID
SKIDDERS > SKID
SKIDDIER > SKID
SKIDDIEST > SKID
SKIDDING > SKID
SKIDDOO vb go away quickly
SKIDDOOED > SKIDDOO
SKIDDOOS > SKIDDOO
SKIDDY > SKID
SKIDLID n crash helmet
SKIDLIDS > SKIDLID
SKIDOO n snowmobile ▷ vb travel on a skidoo
SKIDOOED > SKIDOO
SKIDOOING > SKIDOO
SKIDOOS > SKIDOO
SKIDPAN n area made slippery so that vehicle drivers can practise controlling skids
SKIDPANS > SKIDPAN
SKIDPROOF adj (of a road surface, tyre, etc) preventing or resistant to skidding
SKIDS > SKID
SKIDWAY n platform on which logs ready for sawing are piled
SKIDWAYS > SKIDWAY

SKIED > SKY
SKIER > SKI
SKIERS > SKI
SKIES > SKY
SKIEY adj of the sky
SKIEYER > SKIEY
SKIEYEST > SKIEY
SKIFF n small boat ▷ vb travel in a skiff
SKIFFED > SKIFF
SKIFFING > SKIFF
SKIFFLE n style of popular music of the 1950s, played chiefly on guitars and improvised percussion instruments ▷ vb play this style of music
SKIFFLED > SKIFFLE
SKIFFLES > SKIFFLE
SKIFFLESS > SKIFF
SKIFFLING > SKIFFLE
SKIFFS > SKIFF
SKIING > SKI
SKIINGS > SKI
SKIJORER > SKIJORING
SKIJORERS > SKIJORING
SKIJORING n sport in which a skier is pulled over snow or ice, usually by a horse
SKILFUL adj having or showing skill
SKILFULLY > SKILFUL
SKILL n special ability or expertise
SKILLED adj possessing or demonstrating accomplishment, skill, or special training
SKILLESS > SKILL
SKILLET n small frying pan or shallow cooking pot
SKILLETS > SKILLET
SKILLFUL same as > SKILFUL
SKILLIER > SKILLY
SKILLIES > SKILLY
SKILLIEST > SKILLY
SKILLING n former Scandinavian coin of low denomination
SKILLINGS > SKILLING
SKILLION n part of a building having a lower, esp sloping, roof
SKILLIONS > SKILLION
SKILLS > SKILL
SKILLY n thin soup or gruel ▷ adj skilled
SKIM vb remove floating matter from the surface of (a liquid) ▷ n act or process of skimming
SKIMBOARD n type of surfboard, shorter than standard and rounded at both ends ▷ vb surf on a skimboard
SKIMMED > SKIM
SKIMMER n person or thing that skims
SKIMMERS > SKIMMER
SKIMMIA n shrub of S and SE Asia grown for its

ornamental red berries and evergreen foliage
SKIMMIAS > SKIMMIA
SKIMMING > SKIM
SKIMMINGS npl material that is skimmed off a liquid
SKIMO n informal and offensive word for an Inuit
SKIMOBILE n motor vehicle with skis for travelling on snow
SKIMOS > SKIMO
SKIMP vb not invest enough time, money, material, etc
SKIMPED > SKIMP
SKIMPIER > SKIMPY
SKIMPIEST > SKIMPY
SKIMPILY > SKIMPY
SKIMPING > SKIMP
SKIMPS > SKIMP
SKIMPY adj scanty or insufficient
SKIMS > SKIM
SKIN n outer covering of the body ▷ vb remove the skin of
SKINCARE n use of cosmetics in taking care of skin
SKINCARES > SKINCARE
SKINFLICK n film containing much nudity and sex
SKINFLINT n miser
SKINFOOD n cosmetic cream for the skin
SKINFOODS > SKINFOOD
SKINFUL n sufficient alcoholic drink to make one drunk
SKINFULS > SKINFUL
SKINHEAD n youth with very short hair
SKINHEADS > SKINHEAD
SKINK n type of lizard with reduced limbs and smooth scales ▷ vb serve a drink
SKINKED > SKINK
SKINKER > SKINK
SKINKERS > SKINK
SKINKING > SKINK
SKINKS > SKINK
SKINLESS > SKIN
SKINLIKE > SKIN
SKINNED > SKIN
SKINNER n person who prepares or deals in animal skins
SKINNERS > SKINNER
SKINNIER > SKINNY
SKINNIES > SKINNY
SKINNIEST > SKINNY
SKINNING > SKIN
SKINNY adj thin ▷ n information
SKINS > SKIN
SKINT adj having no money
SKINTER > SKINT
SKINTEST > SKINT
SKINTIGHT adj fitting tightly over the body
SKIO n Scots dialect word

meaning hut
SKIORING n sport of being towed on skis by horse
SKIORINGS > SKIORING
SKIOS > SKIO
SKIP vb leap lightly from one foot to the other ▷ n skipping
SKIPJACK n important food fish of tropical seas
SKIPJACKS > SKIPJACK
SKIPLANE n aircraft fitted with skis to enable it to land on and take off from snow
SKIPLANES > SKIPLANE
SKIPPABLE > SKIP
SKIPPED > SKIP
SKIPPER vb captain ▷ n captain of a ship or aircraft
SKIPPERED > SKIPPER
SKIPPERS > SKIPPER
SKIPPET n small round box for preserving a document or seal
SKIPPETS > SKIPPET
SKIPPIER > SKIPPY
SKIPPIEST > SKIPPY
SKIPPING > SKIP
SKIPPINGS > SKIP
SKIPPY adj in high spirits
SKIPS > SKIP
SKIRL n sound of bagpipes ▷ vb (of bagpipes) to give out a shrill sound
SKIRLED > SKIRL
SKIRLING > SKIRL
SKIRLINGS > SKIRL
SKIRLS > SKIRL
SKIRMISH n brief or minor fight or argument ▷ vb take part in a skirmish
SKIRR vb move, run, or fly rapidly ▷ n whirring or grating sound, as of the wings of birds in flight
SKIRRED > SKIRR
SKIRRET n umbelliferous Old World plant
SKIRRETS > SKIRRET
SKIRRING > SKIRR
SKIRRS > SKIRR
SKIRT n woman's garment hanging from the waist ▷ vb border
SKIRTED > SKIRT
SKIRTER n man who skirts fleeces
SKIRTERS > SKIRTER
SKIRTING n border fixed round the base of an interior wall to protect it from kicks, dirt, etc
SKIRTINGS npl ragged edges trimmed from the fleece of a sheep
SKIRTLESS > SKIRT
SKIRTLIKE > SKIRT
SKIRTS > SKIRT
SKIS > SKI
SKIT n brief satirical sketch
SKITCH vb (of a dog) to attack
SKITCHED > SKITCH

SKITCHES > SKITCH
SKITCHING > SKITCH
SKITE n boast ▷ vb boast
SKITED > SKITE
SKITES > SKITE
SKITING > SKITE
SKITS > SKIT
SKITTER vb move or run rapidly or lightly
SKITTERED > SKITTER
SKITTERS > SKITTER
SKITTERY adj moving lightly and rapidly
SKITTISH adj playful or lively
SKITTLE n bottle-shaped object used as a target in some games ▷ vb play skittles
SKITTLED > SKITTLE
SKITTLES > SKITTLE
SKITTLING > SKITTLE
SKIVE vb evade work or responsibility
SKIVED > SKIVE
SKIVER n tanned outer layer split from a skin ▷ vb cut leather
SKIVERED > SKIVER
SKIVERING > SKIVER
SKIVERS > SKIVER
SKIVES > SKIVE
SKIVIE adj old Scots word meaning disarranged
SKIVIER > SKIVIE
SKIVIEST > SKIVIE
SKIVING > SKIVE
SKIVINGS > SKIVE
SKIVVIED > SKIVVY
SKIVVIES > SKIVVY
SKIVVY n female servant who does menial work ▷ vb work as a skivvy
SKIVVYING > SKIVVY
SKIVY > SKIVE
SKIWEAR n clothes for skiing in
SKLATE Scots word for > SLATE
SKLATED > SKLATE
SKLATES > SKLATE
SKLATING > SKLATE
SKLENT Scots word for > SLANT
SKLENTED > SKLENT
SKLENTING > SKLENT
SKLENTS > SKLENT
SKLIFF n Scots word meaning little piece
SKLIFFS > SKLIFF
SKLIM vb Scots word meaning climb
SKLIMMED > SKLIM
SKLIMMING > SKLIM
SKLIMS > SKLIM
SKOAL same as > SKOL
SKOALED > SKOAL
SKOALING > SKOAL
SKOALS > SKOAL
SKOFF vb eat greedily
SKOFFED > SKOFF
SKOFFING > SKOFF
SKOFFS > SKOFF
SKOKIAAN n (in South

Africa) a potent alcoholic beverage
SKOKIAANS > SKOKIAAN
SKOL sentence substitute good health! (a drinking toast) ▷ vb down (an alcoholic drink) in one go
SKOLIA > SKOLION
SKOLION n ancient Greek drinking song
SKOLLED > SKOL
SKOLLIE same as > SKOLLY
SKOLLIES > SKOLLY
SKOLLING > SKOL
SKOLLY n hooligan, usually one of a gang
SKOLS > SKOL
SKOOKUM adj strong or brave
SKOOL ironically illiterate or childish spelling of > SCHOOL
SKOOLS > SKOOL
SKOOSH vb Scots word meaning squirt
SKOOSHED > SKOOSH
SKOOSHES > SKOOSH
SKOOSHING > SKOOSH
SKORT n pair of shorts with a front panel that gives the appearance of a skirt
SKORTS > SKORT
SKOSH n little bit
SKOSHES > SKOSH
SKRAN n food
SKRANS > SKRAN
SKREEGH vb Scots word meaning screech
SKREEGHED > SKREEGH
SKREEGHS > SKREEGH
SKREEN n screen
SKREENS > SKREEN
SKREIGH vb Scots word meaning screech
SKREIGHED > SKREIGH
SKREIGHS > SKREIGH
SKRIECH vb Scots word meaning screech
SKRIECHED > SKRIECH
SKRIECHS > SKRIECH
SKRIED > SKRY
SKRIEGH vb Scots word meaning screech
SKRIEGHED > SKRIEGH
SKRIEGHS > SKRIEGH
SKRIES > SKRY
SKRIK n South African word meaning fright
SKRIKE vb cry
SKRIKED > SKRIKE
SKRIKES > SKRIKE
SKRIKING > SKRIKE
SKRIKS > SKRIK
SKRIMMAGE vb scrimmage
SKRIMP vb steal apples
SKRIMPED > SKRIMP
SKRIMPING > SKRIMP
SKRIMPS > SKRIMP
SKRONK n type of dissonant, grating popular music
SKRONKS > SKRONK
SKRUMP vb steal apples
SKRUMPED > SKRUMP

SKRUMPING > SKRUMP
SKRUMPS > SKRUMP
SKRY vb try to tell future
SKRYER > SKRY
SKRYERS > SKRY
SKRYING > SKRY
SKUA n large predatory gull
SKUAS > SKUA
SKUDLER n Scots word meaning leader of festivities
SKUDLERS > SKUDLER
SKUG vb shelter
SKUGGED > SKUG
SKUGGING > SKUG
SKUGS > SKUG
SKULK vb move stealthily ▷ n person who skulks
SKULKED > SKULK
SKULKER > SKULK
SKULKERS > SKULK
SKULKING > SKULK
SKULKINGS > SKULK
SKULKS > SKULK
SKULL n bony framework of the head ▷ vb strike on the head
SKULLCAP n close-fitting brimless cap
SKULLCAPS > SKULLCAP
SKULLED > SKULL
SKULLING > SKULL
SKULLS > SKULL
SKULPIN n North American fish
SKULPINS > SKULPIN
SKUMMER vb defecate
SKUMMERED > SKUMMER
SKUMMERS > SKUMMER
SKUNK n small black-and-white N American mammal which emits a foul-smelling fluid when attacked ▷ vb defeat overwhelmingly in a game
SKUNKBIRD n North American songbird
SKUNKED > SKUNK
SKUNKIER > SKUNK
SKUNKIEST > SKUNK
SKUNKING > SKUNK
SKUNKS > SKUNK
SKUNKWEED n low-growing fetid swamp plant of N America
SKUNKY > SKUNK
SKURRIED > SKURRY
SKURRIES > SKURRY
SKURRY vb scurry
SKURRYING > SKURRY
SKUTTLE vb scuttle
SKUTTLED > SKUTTLE
SKUTTLES > SKUTTLE
SKUTTLING > SKUTTLE
SKY n upper atmosphere as seen from the earth ▷ vb hit high in the air
SKYBOARD n small board used for skysurfing
SKYBOARDS > SKYBOARD
SKYBORN adj born in heaven
SKYBORNE adj flying through sky

SKYBOX n luxurious suite high up in the stand of a sports stadium
SKYBOXES > SKYBOX
SKYBRIDGE n covered, elevated bridge connecting two buildings
SKYCAP n luggage porter at American airport
SKYCAPS > SKYCAP
SKYCLAD adj naked
SKYDIVE vb take part in skydiving
SKYDIVED > SKYDIVE
SKYDIVER > SKYDIVE
SKYDIVERS > SKYDIVE
SKYDIVES > SKYDIVE
SKYDIVING n sport of jumping from an aircraft and performing manoeuvres before opening one's parachute
SKYDOVE > SKYDIVE
SKYED > SKY
SKYER n cricket ball hit up into air
SKYERS > SKYER
SKYEY adj of the sky
SKYF n South African slang for a cigarette or substance for smoking ▷ vb smoke a cigarette
SKYFED > SKYF
SKYFING > SKYF
SKYFS > SKYF
SKYHOME n Australian slang for a sub-penthouse flat in a tall building
SKYHOMES > SKYHOME
SKYHOOK n hook hung from helicopter
SKYHOOKS > SKYHOOK
SKYIER > SKYEY
SKYIEST > SKYEY
SKYING > SKY
SKYISH > SKY
SKYJACK vb hijack (an aircraft)
SKYJACKED > SKYJACK
SKYJACKER > SKYJACK
SKYJACKS > SKYJACK
SKYLAB n orbiting space station
SKYLABS > SKYLAB
SKYLARK n lark that sings while soaring at a great height ▷ vb play or frolic
SKYLARKED > SKYLARK
SKYLARKER > SKYLARK
SKYLARKS > SKYLARK
SKYLESS adj having no sky
SKYLIGHT n window in a roof or ceiling
SKYLIGHTS > SKYLIGHT
SKYLIKE > SKY
SKYLINE n outline of buildings, trees, etc against the sky
SKYLINES > SKYLINE
SKYLIT adj having skylight
SKYMAN n paratrooper
SKYMEN > SKYMAN
SKYPHOI > SKYPHOS

S

SKYPHOS n ancient Greek drinking cup
SKYR n Scandinavian cheese
SKYRE vb Scots word meaning shine
SKYRED > SKYRE
SKYRES > SKYRE
SKYRING > SKYRE
SKYRMION n (in theoretical physics) mathematical model used to model baryons
SKYRMIONS > SKYRMION
SKYROCKET vb rise very quickly
SKYRS > SKYR
SKYSAIL n square sail set above the royal on a square-rigger
SKYSAILS > SKYSAIL
SKYSCAPE n painting, drawing, photograph, etc, representing or depicting the sky
SKYSCAPES > SKYSCAPE
SKYSURF vb perform freefall aerobatics
SKYSURFED > SKYSURF
SKYSURFER n someone who performs stunts with a small board attached to his or her feet while in free fall
SKYSURFS > SKYSURF
SKYTE vb Scots word meaning slide
SKYTED > SKYTE
SKYTES > SKYTE
SKYTING > SKYTE
SKYWALK n tightrope walk at great height
SKYWALKS > SKYWALK
SKYWARD adj towards the sky ▷ adv towards the sky
SKYWARDS same as > SKYWARD
SKYWAY n air route
SKYWAYS > SKYWAY
SKYWRITE vb write message in sky with smoke from aircraft
SKYWRITER > SKYWRITE
SKYWRITES > SKYWRITE
SKYWROTE > SKYWRITE
SLAB n broad flat piece ▷ vb cut or make into a slab or slabs
SLABBED > SLAB
SLABBER vb dribble from the mouth
SLABBERED > SLABBER
SLABBERER > SLABBER
SLABBERS > SLABBER
SLABBERY > SLABBER
SLABBIER > SLAB
SLABBIEST > SLAB
SLABBING > SLAB
SLABBY > SLAB
SLABLIKE > SLAB
SLABS > SLAB
SLABSTONE n flagstone
SLACK same as > SLAKE
SLACKED > SLACK

SLACKEN vb make or become slack
SLACKENED > SLACKEN
SLACKENER > SLACKEN
SLACKENS > SLACKEN
SLACKER n person who evades work or duty
SLACKERS > SLACKER
SLACKEST > SLACK
SLACKING > SLACK
SLACKLY > SLACK
SLACKNESS > SLACK
SLACKS npl casual trousers
SLADANG n Malayan tapir
SLADANGS > SLADANG
SLADE n little valley
SLADES > SLADE
SLAE Scots word for > SLOE
SLAES > SLAE
SLAG n waste left after metal is smelted ▷ vb criticize
SLAGGED > SLAG
SLAGGIER > SLAG
SLAGGIEST > SLAG
SLAGGING > SLAG
SLAGGINGS > SLAG
SLAGGY > SLAG
SLAGS > SLAG
SLAID vb Scots word for 'slid'
SLAIN > SLAY
SLAINTE interj cheers!
SLAIRG Scots word for > SPREAD
SLAIRGED > SLAIRG
SLAIRGING > SLAIRG
SLAIRGS > SLAIRG
SLAISTER vb cover with a sloppy mess ▷ n sloppy mess
SLAISTERS > SLAISTER
SLAISTERY > SLAISTER
SLAKABLE > SLAKE
SLAKE vb satisfy (thirst or desire)
SLAKEABLE > SLAKE
SLAKED > SLAKE
SLAKELESS adj impossible to slake
SLAKER > SLAKE
SLAKERS > SLAKE
SLAKES > SLAKE
SLAKING > SLAKE
SLALOM n skiing or canoeing race over a winding course ▷ vb take part in a slalom
SLALOMED > SLALOM
SLALOMER > SLALOM
SLALOMERS > SLALOM
SLALOMING > SLALOM
SLALOMIST > SLALOM
SLALOMS > SLALOM
SLAM vb shut, put down, or hit violently and noisily ▷ n act or sound of slamming
SLAMDANCE vb dance aggressively, bumping into others
SLAMMAKIN n woman's loose dress
SLAMMED > SLAM
SLAMMER n prison

SLAMMERS > SLAMMER
SLAMMING > SLAM
SLAMMINGS > SLAM
SLAMS > SLAM
SLANDER n false and malicious statement about a person ▷ vb utter slander about
SLANDERED > SLANDER
SLANDERER > SLANDER
SLANDERS > SLANDER
SLANE n spade for cutting turf
SLANES > SLANE
SLANG n very informal language ▷ vb use insulting language to (someone)
SLANGED > SLANG
SLANGER n street vendor
SLANGERS > SLANGER
SLANGIER > SLANG
SLANGIEST > SLANG
SLANGILY > SLANG
SLANGING > SLANG
SLANGINGS > SLANG
SLANGISH > SLANG
SLANGS > SLANG
SLANGUAGE n language using slang
SLANGULAR adj of or using slang
SLANGY > SLANG
SLANK dialect word for > LANK
SLANT vb lean at an angle, slope ▷ n slope
SLANTED > SLANT
SLANTER same as > SLINTER
SLANTERS > SLANTER
SLANTIER > SLANTY
SLANTIEST > SLANTY
SLANTING > SLANT
SLANTLY > SLANT
SLANTS > SLANT
SLANTWAYS same as > SLANTWISE
SLANTWISE adj in a slanting or oblique direction
SLANTY adj slanting
SLAP n blow with the open hand or a flat object ▷ vb strike with the open hand or a flat object
SLAPDASH adj careless and hasty ▷ adv carelessly or hastily ▷ n slapdash activity or work ▷ vb do in a hurried and careless manner
SLAPHAPPY adj cheerfully irresponsible or careless
SLAPHEAD n derogatory term for a bald person
SLAPHEADS > SLAPHEAD
SLAPJACK n simple card game
SLAPJACKS > SLAPJACK
SLAPPED > SLAP
SLAPPER > SLAP
SLAPPERS > SLAP
SLAPPING n as in happy slapping filming random

acts of violence as a source of amusement
SLAPPINGS > SLAPPING
SLAPS > SLAP
SLAPSHOT n hard, fast, often wild, shot executed with a powerful downward swing
SLAPSHOTS > SLAPSHOT
SLAPSTICK n boisterous knockabout comedy
SLART vb spill (something)
SLARTED > SLART
SLARTING > SLART
SLARTS > SLART
SLASH vb cut with a sweeping stroke ▷ n sweeping stroke
SLASHED > SLASH
SLASHER n tool or tractor-drawn machine used for cutting scrub or undergrowth in the bush
SLASHERS > SLASHER
SLASHES > SLASH
SLASHFEST n film or computer game that features bloody killings involving blades
SLASHING adj aggressively critical ▷ n act of slashing
SLASHINGS > SLASHING
SLAT n narrow strip of wood or metal ▷ vb provide with slats
SLATCH n slack part of rope
SLATCHES > SLATCH
SLATE n rock which splits easily into thin layers ▷ vb cover with slates ▷ adj dark grey
SLATED > SLATE
SLATELIKE > SLATE
SLATER n person trained in laying roof slates
SLATERS > SLATER
SLATES > SLATE
SLATEY adj slightly mad
SLATHER vb spread quickly or lavishly
SLATHERED > SLATHER
SLATHERS > SLATHER
SLATIER > SLATY
SLATIEST > SLATY
SLATINESS > SLATY
SLATING n act or process of laying slates
SLATINGS > SLATING
SLATS > SLAT
SLATTED > SLAT
SLATTER vb be slovenly
SLATTERED > SLATTER
SLATTERN n slovenly woman
SLATTERNS > SLATTERN
SLATTERS > SLATTER
SLATTERY adj slovenly
SLATTING > SLAT
SLATTINGS > SLAT
SLATY adj consisting of or resembling slate
SLAUGHTER vb kill (animals) for food ▷ n slaughtering

SLAVE n person owned by another for whom he or she has to work ▷ vb work like a slave

SLAVED > SLAVE

SLAVER n person or ship engaged in the slave trade ▷ vb dribble saliva from the mouth

SLAVERED > SLAVER

SLAVERER > SLAVER

SLAVERERS > SLAVER

SLAVERIES > SLAVERY

SLAVERING > SLAVER

SLAVERS > SLAVER

SLAVERY n state or condition of being a slave

SLAVES > SLAVE

SLAVEY n female general servant

SLAVEYS > SLAVEY

SLAVING > SLAVE

SLAVISH adj of or like a slave

SLAVISHLY > SLAVISH

SLAVOCRAT n US slaveholder before the Civil War

SLAVOPHIL n person who admires the Slavs or their cultures

SLAW short for > COLESLAW

SLAWS > SLAW

SLAY vb kill

SLAYABLE > SLAY

SLAYED > SLAY

SLAYER > SLAY

SLAYERS > SLAY

SLAYING > SLAY

SLAYS > SLAY

SLEAVE n tangled thread ▷ vb disentangle (twisted thread, etc)

SLEAVED > SLEAVE

SLEAVES > SLEAVE

SLEAVING > SLEAVE

SLEAZE n behaviour in public life considered immoral, dishonest, or disreputable

SLEAZEBAG n disgusting person

SLEAZES > SLEAZE

SLEAZIER > SLEAZY

SLEAZIEST > SLEAZY

SLEAZILY > SLEAZY

SLEAZO n sleazy person

SLEAZOID n sleazy person

SLEAZOIDS > SLEAZOID

SLEAZY adj run-down or sordid

SLEB n celebrity

SLEBS > SLEB

SLED same as > SLEDGE

SLEDDED > SLED

SLEDDER > SLED

SLEDDERS > SLED

SLEDDING > SLED

SLEDDINGS > SLED

SLEDED > SLED

SLEDGE n carriage on runners for sliding on snow ▷ vb travel by sledge

SLEDGED > SLEDGE

SLEDGER > SLEDGE

SLEDGERS > SLEDGE

SLEDGES > SLEDGE

SLEDGING > SLEDGE

SLEDGINGS > SLEDGE

SLEDS > SLED

SLEE Scots word for > SLY

SLEECH n slippery mud

SLEECHES > SLEECH

SLEECHIER > SLEECH

SLEECHY > SLEECH

SLEEK adj glossy, smooth, and shiny ▷ vb make smooth and glossy, as by grooming, etc

SLEEKED > SLEEK

SLEEKEN vb make sleek

SLEEKENED > SLEEKEN

SLEEKENS > SLEEKEN

SLEEKER > SLEEK

SLEEKERS > SLEEK

SLEEKEST > SLEEK

SLEEKIER > SLEEK

SLEEKIEST > SLEEK

SLEEKING > SLEEK

SLEEKINGS > SLEEK

SLEEKIT adj smooth

SLEEKLY > SLEEK

SLEEKNESS > SLEEK

SLEEKS > SLEEK

SLEEKY > SLEEK

SLEEP n state of rest characterized by unconsciousness ▷ vb be in or as if in a state of sleep

SLEEPAWAY adj describing a type of camp for teenagers

SLEEPER n railway car fitted for sleeping in

SLEEPERS > SLEEPER

SLEEPERY Scots word for > SLEEPY

SLEEPIER > SLEEPY

SLEEPIEST > SLEEPY

SLEEPILY > SLEEPY

SLEEPING > SLEEP

SLEEPINGS > SLEEP

SLEEPLESS adj (of a night) one during which one does not sleep

SLEEPLIKE > SLEEP

SLEEPOUT n small building for sleeping in

SLEEPOUTS > SLEEPOUT

SLEEPOVER n occasion when a person stays overnight at a friend's house

SLEEPRY Scots word for > SLEEPY

SLEEPS > SLEEP

SLEEPSUIT n baby's sleeping garment

SLEEPWALK vb walk while asleep

SLEEPWEAR n clothes for sleeping in

SLEEPY adj needing sleep

SLEER > SLEE

SLEEST > SLEE

SLEET n rain and snow or hail falling together ▷ vb fall as sleet

SLEETED > SLEET

SLEETIER > SLEET

SLEETIEST > SLEET

SLEETING > SLEET

SLEETS > SLEET

SLEETY > SLEET

SLEEVE n part of a garment which covers the arm

SLEEVED > SLEEVE

SLEEVEEN n sly obsequious smooth-tongued person

SLEEVEENS > SLEEVEEN

SLEEVELET n protective covering for forearm

SLEEVER n old beer measure

SLEEVERS > SLEEVER

SLEEVES > SLEEVE

SLEEVING n tubular flexible insulation into which bare wire can be inserted

SLEEVINGS > SLEEVING

SLEEZIER > SLEEZY

SLEEZIEST > SLEEZY

SLEEZY adj sleazy

SLEIDED adj old word meaning separated

SLEIGH same as > SLEDGE

SLEIGHED > SLEIGH

SLEIGHER > SLEIGH

SLEIGHERS > SLEIGH

SLEIGHING > SLEIGH

SLEIGHS > SLEIGH

SLEIGHT n skill or cunning

SLEIGHTS > SLEIGHT

SLENDER adj slim

SLENDERER > SLENDER

SLENDERLY > SLENDER

SLENTER same as > SLINTER

SLENTERS > SLENTER

SLEPT > SLEEP

SLEUTH n detective ▷ vb track or follow

SLEUTHED > SLEUTH

SLEUTHING > SLEUTH

SLEUTHS > SLEUTH

SLEW vb twist sideways, esp awkwardly

SLEWED > SLEW

SLEWING > SLEW

SLEWS > SLEW

SLEY n weaver's tool for separating threads

SLEYS > SLEY

SLICE n thin flat piece cut from something ▷ vb cut into slices

SLICEABLE > SLICE

SLICED > SLICE

SLICER > SLICE

SLICERS > SLICE

SLICES > SLICE

SLICING > SLICE

SLICINGS > SLICE

SLICK adj persuasive and glib ▷ n patch of oil on water ▷ vb make smooth or sleek

SLICKED > SLICK

SLICKEN vb make smooth

SLICKENED > SLICKEN

SLICKENER > SLICKEN

SLICKENS > SLICKEN

SLICKER n sly or untrustworthy person

SLICKERED adj wearing a waterproof jacket

SLICKERS > SLICKER

SLICKEST > SLICK

SLICKING > SLICK

SLICKINGS > SLICK

SLICKLY > SLICK

SLICKNESS > SLICK

SLICKROCK n weathered and smooth sandstone or other rock

SLICKS > SLICK

SLICKSTER n dishonest person

SLID > SLIDE

SLIDABLE > SLIDE

SLIDDEN > SLIDE

SLIDDER vb slip

SLIDDERED > SLIDDER

SLIDDERS > SLIDDER

SLIDDERY adj slippery

SLIDE vb slip smoothly along (a surface) ▷ n sliding

SLIDED > SLIDE

SLIDER > SLIDE

SLIDERS > SLIDE

SLIDES > SLIDE

SLIDEWAY n sloping channel down which things are slid

SLIDEWAYS > SLIDEWAY

SLIDING > SLIDE

SLIDINGLY > SLIDE

SLIDINGS > SLIDE

SLIER > SLY

SLIEST > SLY

SLIEVE n Irish mountain

SLIEVES > SLIEVE

SLIGHT adj small in quantity or extent ▷ n snub ▷ vb insult (someone) by behaving rudely

SLIGHTED > SLIGHT

SLIGHTER > SLIGHT

SLIGHTERS > SLIGHT

SLIGHTEST > SLIGHT

SLIGHTING adj characteristic of a slight

SLIGHTISH > SLIGHT

SLIGHTLY adv in small measure or degree

SLIGHTS > SLIGHT

SLILY > SLY

SLIM adj not heavy or stout, thin ▷ vb make or become slim by diet and exercise

SLIMDOWN n instance of an organization cutting staff

SLIMDOWNS > SLIMDOWN

SLIME n unpleasant thick slippery substance ▷ vb cover with slime

SLIMEBALL n odious and contemptible person

SLIMED > SLIME

SLIMES > SLIME

SLIMIER > SLIMY

SLIMIEST > SLIMY

S

SLIMILY > SLIMY
SLIMINESS > SLIMY
SLIMING > SLIME
SLIMLINE adj slim
SLIMLY > SLIM
SLIMMED > SLIM
SLIMMER > SLIM
SLIMMERS > SLIM
SLIMMEST > SLIM
SLIMMING > SLIM
SLIMMINGS > SLIM
SLIMMISH > SLIM
SLIMNESS > SLIM
SLIMPSIER > SLIMPSY
SLIMPSY adj thin and
flimsy
SLIMS > SLIM
SLIMSIER > SLIMSY
SLIMSIEST > SLIMSY
SLIMSY adj frail
SLIMY adj of, like, or
covered with slime
SLING n bandage hung
from the neck to support
an injured hand or arm ▷ vb
throw
SLINGBACK n shoe with a
strap that goes around the
back of the heel
SLINGER > SLING
SLINGERS > SLING
SLINGING > SLING
SLINGS > SLING
SLINGSHOT n Y-shaped
implement with a loop of
elastic fastened to the ends
of the two prongs, used for
shooting small stones, etc
SLINK vb move furtively or
guiltily ▷ n animal, esp a
calf, born prematurely
SLINKED > SLINK
SLINKER > SLINK
SLINKERS > SLINK
SLINKIER > SLINKY
SLINKIEST > SLINKY
SLINKILY > SLINKY
SLINKING > SLINK
SLINKS > SLINK
SLINKSKIN n skin of
premature calf
SLINKWEED n plant
believed to make cow give
birth prematurely
SLINKY adj (of clothes)
figure-hugging
SLINTER n dodge, trick, or
stratagem
SLINTERS > SLINTER
SLIOTAR n ball used in
hurling
SLIOTARS > SLIOTAR
SLIP vb lose balance by
sliding ▷ n slipping
SLIPCASE n protective
case for a book that is open
at one end so that only the
spine of the book is visible
SLIPCASED adj having a
slipcase
SLIPCASES > SLIPCASE
SLIPCOVER n fitted but
easily removable cloth
cover for a chair, sofa, etc

SLIPDRESS n silky
sleeveless dress
SLIPE n wool removed
from the pelt of a
slaughtered sheep by
immersion in a chemical
bath ▷ vb remove skin
SLIPED > SLIPE
SLIPES > SLIPE
SLIPFORM n mould used in
building
SLIPFORMS > SLIPFORM
SLIPING > SLIPE
SLIPKNOT n knot tied so
that it will slip along the
rope round which it is made
SLIPKNOTS > SLIPKNOT
SLIPLESS > SLIP
SLIPNOOSE n noose made
with a slipknot, so that it
tightens when pulled
SLIPOUT n instance of
slipping out
SLIPOUTS > SLIPOUT
SLIPOVER adj of or
denoting a garment that
can be put on easily over
the head ▷ n such a
garment, esp a sleeveless
pullover
SLIPOVERS > SLIPOVER
SLIPPAGE n act or an
instance of slipping
SLIPPAGES > SLIPPAGE
SLIPPED > SLIP
SLIPPER n light shoe for
indoor wear ▷ vb hit or
beat with a slipper
SLIPPERED > SLIPPER
SLIPPERS > SLIPPER
SLIPPERY adj so smooth
or wet as to cause slipping
or be difficult to hold
SLIPPIER > SLIPPY
SLIPPIEST > SLIPPY
SLIPPILY > SLIPPY
SLIPPING > SLIP
SLIPPY adj slippery
SLIPRAIL n rail in a fence
that can be slipped out of
place to make an opening
SLIPRAILS > SLIPRAIL
SLIPS > SLIP
SLIPSHEET n sheet of
paper that is interleaved
between freshly printed
sheets
SLIPSHOD adj (of an
action) careless
SLIPSLOP n weak or
unappetizing food or drink
SLIPSLOPS > SLIPSLOP
SLIPSOLE n separate sole
on shoe
SLIPSOLES > SLIPSOLE
SLIPT vb old form of
slipped
SLIPUP n mistake or
mishap
SLIPUPS > SLIPUP
SLIPWARE n pottery that
has been decorated with
slip
SLIPWARES > SLIPWARE
SLIPWAY n launching

slope on which ships are
built or repaired
SLIPWAYS > SLIPWAY
SLISH n old word meaning
cut
SLISHES > SLISH
SLIT n long narrow cut or
opening ▷ vb make a long
straight cut in
SLITHER vb slide
unsteadily ▷ n slithering
movement
SLITHERED > SLITHER
SLITHERS > SLITHER
SLITHERY adj moving
with a slithering motion
SLITLESS > SLIT
SLITLIKE > SLIT
SLITS > SLIT
SLITTED > SLIT
SLITTER > SLIT
SLITTERS > SLIT
SLITTIER > SLIT
SLITTIEST > SLIT
SLITTING > SLIT
SLITTY > SLIT
SLIVE vb slip
SLIVED > SLIVE
SLIVEN > SLIVE
SLIVER n small thin piece
▷ vb cut into slivers
SLIVERED > SLIVER
SLIVERER > SLIVER
SLIVERERS > SLIVER
SLIVERING > SLIVER
SLIVERS > SLIVER
SLIVES > SLIVE
SLIVING > SLIVE
SLIVOVIC n plum brandy
SLIVOVICA n plum
brandy
SLIVOVITZ n plum
brandy from E Europe
SLIVOWITZ n plum
brandy
SLOAN n severe telling-off
SLOANS > SLOAN
SLOB n lazy and untidy
person
SLOBBER vb dribble or
drool ▷ n liquid or saliva
spilt from the mouth
SLOBBERED > SLOBBER
SLOBBERER > SLOBBER
SLOBBERS > SLOBBER
SLOBBERY > SLOBBER
SLOBBIER > SLOB
SLOBBIEST > SLOB
SLOBBISH > SLOB
SLOBBY > SLOB
SLOBLAND n muddy
ground
SLOBLANDS > SLOBLAND
SLOBS > SLOB
SLOCKEN vb Scots word
meaning slake
SLOCKENED > SLOCKEN
SLOCKENS > SLOCKEN
SLOE n sour blue-black fruit
SLOEBUSH n bush on
which sloes grow
SLOES > SLOE
SLOETHORN n sloe plant
SLOETREE n sloe plant

SLOETREES > SLOETREE
SLOG vb work hard and
steadily ▷ n long and
exhausting work or walk
SLOGAN n catchword or
phrase used in politics or
advertising
SLOGANEER n person who
coins or employs slogans
frequently ▷ vb coin or
employ slogans so as to
sway opinion
SLOGANISE same as
> SLOGANIZE
SLOGANIZE vb use slogans
SLOGANS > SLOGAN
SLOGGED > SLOG
SLOGGER > SLOG
SLOGGERS > SLOG
SLOGGING > SLOG
SLOGS > SLOG
SLOID n Swedish
woodwork
SLOIDS > SLOID
SLOJD n Swedish
woodwork
SLOJDS > SLOJD
SLOKEN vb Scots word
meaning slake
SLOKENED > SLOKEN
SLOKENING > SLOKEN
SLOKENS > SLOKEN
SLOMMOCK vb walk
assertively with a
hip-rolling gait
SLOMMOCKS > SLOMMOCK
SLOOM n slumber
SLOOMED > SLOOM
SLOOMIER > SLOOM
SLOOMIEST > SLOOM
SLOOMING > SLOOM
SLOOMS > SLOOM
SLOOMY > SLOOM
SLOOP n small
single-masted ship
SLOOPS > SLOOP
SLOOSH vb wash with
water
SLOOSHED > SLOOSH
SLOOSHES > SLOOSH
SLOOSHING > SLOOSH
SLOOT n ditch for irrigation
or drainage
SLOOTS > SLOOT
SLOP vb splash or spill ▷ n
spilt liquid
SLOPE vb slant ▷ n sloping
surface
SLOPED > SLOPE
SLOPER > SLOPE
SLOPERS > SLOPE
SLOPES > SLOPE
SLOPEWISE > SLOPE
SLOPIER > SLOPE
SLOPIEST > SLOPE
SLOPING > SLOPE
SLOPINGLY > SLOPE
SLOPPED > SLOP
SLOPPIER > SLOPPY
SLOPPIEST > SLOPPY
SLOPPILY > SLOPPY
SLOPPING > SLOP
SLOPPY adj careless or
untidy

SLOPS > SLOP
SLOPWORK n manufacture of cheap shoddy clothing or the clothes so produced
SLOPWORKS > SLOPWORK
SLOPY > SLOPE
SLORM vb wipe carelessly
SLORMED > SLORM
SLORMING > SLORM
SLORMS > SLORM
SLOSH vb pour carelessly ▷ n splashing sound
SLOSHED > SLOSH
SLOSHES > SLOSH
SLOSHIER > SLOSH
SLOSHIEST > SLOSH
SLOSHING > SLOSH
SLOSHINGS > SLOSH
SLOSHY > SLOSH
SLOT n narrow opening for inserting something ▷ vb make a slot or slots in
SLOTBACK n American football player
SLOTBACKS > SLOTBACK
SLOTH n slow-moving animal of tropical America ▷ vb be lazy
SLOTHED > SLOTH
SLOTHFUL adj lazy or idle
SLOTHING > SLOTH
SLOTHS > SLOTH
SLOTS > SLOT
SLOTTED > SLOT
SLOTTER > SLOT
SLOTTERS > SLOT
SLOTTING > SLOT
SLOUCH vb sit, stand, or move with a drooping posture ▷ n drooping posture
SLOUCHED > SLOUCH
SLOUCHER > SLOUCH
SLOUCHERS > SLOUCH
SLOUCHES > SLOUCH
SLOUCHIER > SLOUCHY
SLOUCHILY > SLOUCHY
SLOUCHING > SLOUCH
SLOUCHY adj slouching
SLOUGH n bog ▷ vb (of a snake) shed (its skin)
SLOUGHED > SLOUGH
SLOUGHI n N African breed of dog resembling a greyhound
SLOUGHIER > SLOUGH
SLOUGHING > SLOUGH
SLOUGHIS > SLOUGHI
SLOUGHS > SLOUGH
SLOUGHY > SLOUGH
SLOVE > SLIVE
SLOVEN n habitually dirty or untidy person
SLOVENLY adj dirty or untidy ▷ adv in a slovenly manner
SLOVENRY n quality of being slovenly
SLOVENS > SLOVEN
SLOW adj taking a longer time than is usual or expected ▷ adv slowly ▷ vb reduce the speed (of)
SLOWBACK n lazy person

SLOWBACKS > SLOWBACK
SLOWCOACH n person who moves or works slowly
SLOWDOWN n any slackening of pace
SLOWDOWNS > SLOWDOWN
SLOWED > SLOW
SLOWER > SLOW
SLOWEST > SLOW
SLOWING > SLOW
SLOWINGS > SLOW
SLOWISH > SLOW
SLOWLY > SLOW
SLOWNESS > SLOW
SLOWPOKE same as > SLOWCOACH
SLOWPOKES > SLOWPOKE
SLOWS > SLOW
SLOWWORM n small legless lizard
SLOWWORMS > SLOWWORM
SLOYD n Swedish woodwork
SLOYDS > SLOYD
SLUB n lump in yarn or fabric, often made intentionally to give a knobbly effect ▷ vb draw out and twist (a sliver of fibre) preparatory to spinning ▷ adj (of material) having an irregular appearance
SLUBB same as > SLUB
SLUBBED > SLUB
SLUBBER vb smear
SLUBBERED > SLUBBER
SLUBBERS > SLUBBER
SLUBBIER > SLUB
SLUBBIEST > SLUB
SLUBBING > SLUB
SLUBBINGS > SLUB
SLUBBS > SLUBB
SLUBBY > SLUB
SLUBS > SLUB
SLUDGE n thick mud ▷ vb to convert into sludge
SLUDGED > SLUDGE
SLUDGES > SLUDGE
SLUDGIER > SLUDGY
SLUDGIEST > SLUDGY
SLUDGING > SLUDGE
SLUDGY adj consisting of, containing, or like sludge
SLUE same as > SLEW
SLUED > SLUE
SLUEING > SLUE
SLUES > SLUE
SLUFF same as > SLOUGH
SLUFFED > SLUFF
SLUFFING > SLUFF
SLUFFS > SLUFF
SLUG n land snail with no shell ▷ vb hit hard
SLUGABED n person who remains in bed through laziness
SLUGABEDS > SLUGABED
SLUGFEST n fist fight
SLUGFESTS > SLUGFEST
SLUGGABED same as > SLUGABED
SLUGGARD n lazy person ▷ adj lazy

SLUGGARDS > SLUGGARD
SLUGGED > SLUG
SLUGGER n (esp in boxing, baseball, etc) a person who strikes hard
SLUGGERS > SLUGGER
SLUGGING > SLUG
SLUGGISH adj slow-moving, lacking energy
SLUGHORN same as > SLOGAN
SLUGHORNE same as > SLOGAN
SLUGHORNS > SLUGHORN
SLUGS > SLUG
SLUICE n channel that carries a rapid current of water ▷ vb drain water by means of a sluice
SLUICED > SLUICE
SLUICES > SLUICE
SLUICEWAY same as > SLUICE
SLUICIER > SLUICE
SLUICIEST > SLUICE
SLUICING > SLUICE
SLUICY > SLUICE
SLUING > SLUE
SLUIT n water channel in South Africa
SLUITS > SLUIT
SLUM n squalid overcrowded house or area ▷ vb temporarily and deliberately experience poorer places or conditions than usual
SLUMBER n sleep ▷ vb sleep
SLUMBERED > SLUMBER
SLUMBERER > SLUMBER
SLUMBERS > SLUMBER
SLUMBERY adj sleepy
SLUMBROUS adj sleepy
SLUMBRY same as > SLUMBERY
SLUMGUM n material left after wax is extracted from honeycomb
SLUMGUMS > SLUMGUM
SLUMISM n existence of slums
SLUMISMS > SLUMISM
SLUMLORD n absentee landlord of slum property, esp one who profiteers
SLUMLORDS > SLUMLORD
SLUMMED > SLUM
SLUMMER > SLUM
SLUMMERS > SLUM
SLUMMIER > SLUM
SLUMMIEST > SLUM
SLUMMING > SLUM
SLUMMINGS > SLUM
SLUMMOCK vb move slowly and heavily
SLUMMOCKS > SLUMMOCK
SLUMMY > SLUM
SLUMP vb (of prices or demand) decline suddenly ▷ n sudden decline in prices or demand
SLUMPED > SLUMP

SLUMPIER > SLUMPY
SLUMPIEST > SLUMPY
SLUMPING > SLUMP
SLUMPS > SLUMP
SLUMPY adj boggy
SLUMS > SLUM
SLUNG > SLING
SLUNGSHOT n weight attached to the end of a cord and used as a weapon
SLUNK > SLINK
SLUR vb pronounce or utter (words) indistinctly ▷ n slurring of words
SLURB n suburban slum
SLURBAN > SLURB
SLURBS > SLURB
SLURP vb eat or drink noisily ▷ n slurping sound
SLURPED > SLURP
SLURPER > SLURP
SLURPERS > SLURP
SLURPIER > SLURPY
SLURPIEST > SLURPY
SLURPING > SLURP
SLURPS > SLURP
SLURPY adj making a slurping noise
SLURRED > SLUR
SLURRIED > SLURRY
SLURRIES > SLURRY
SLURRING > SLUR
SLURRY n muddy liquid mixture ▷ vb spread slurry
SLURRYING > SLURRY
SLURS > SLUR
SLUSE same as > SLUICE
SLUSES > SLUICE
SLUSH n watery muddy substance ▷ vb make one's way through or as if through slush
SLUSHED > SLUSH
SLUSHES > SLUSH
SLUSHIER > SLUSHY
SLUSHIES > SLUSHY
SLUSHIEST > SLUSHY
SLUSHILY > SLUSHY
SLUSHING > SLUSH
SLUSHY adj of, resembling, or consisting of slush ▷ n unskilled kitchen assistant
SLUT n derogatory term for a dirty or immoral woman
SLUTCH n mud
SLUTCHES > SLUTCH
SLUTCHIER > SLUTCH
SLUTCHY > SLUTCH
SLUTS > SLUT
SLUTTERY n state of being slut
SLUTTIER > SLUT
SLUTTIEST > SLUT
SLUTTILY > SLUTTY
SLUTTISH > SLUT
SLUTTY > SLUT
SLY adj crafty
SLYBOOTS npl person who is sly
SLYER > SLY
SLYEST > SLY
SLYISH > SLY
SLYLY > SLY

SLYNESS > SLY
SLYNESSES > SLY
SLYPE n covered passageway in a church that connects the transept to the chapterhouse
SLYPES > SLYPE
SMA Scots word for **>** SMALL
SMAAK vb South African slang for like or love
SMAAKED > SMAAK
SMAAKING > SMAAK
SMAAKS > SMAAK
SMACK vb slap sharply ▷ n sharp slap ▷ adv squarely or directly
SMACKDOWN n severe beating or defeat
SMACKED > SMACK
SMACKER n loud kiss
SMACKERS > SMACKER
SMACKHEAD n person who is addicted to heroin
SMACKING adj brisk
SMACKINGS > SMACKING
SMACKS > SMACK
SMAIK n Scots word meaning rascal
SMAIKS > SMAIK
SMALL adj not large in size, number, or amount ▷ n narrow part of the lower back ▷ adv into small pieces ▷ vb make small
SMALLAGE n wild celery
SMALLAGES > SMALLAGE
SMALLBOY n steward's assistant or deputy steward in European households in W Africa
SMALLBOYS > SMALLBOY
SMALLED > SMALL
SMALLER > SMALL
SMALLEST > SMALL
SMALLING > SMALL
SMALLISH > SMALL
SMALLNESS > SMALL
SMALLPOX n contagious disease with blisters that leave scars
SMALLS > SMALL
SMALLSAT n small communications satellite
SMALLSATS > SMALLSAT
SMALLTIME adj unimportant
SMALM same as **>** SMARM
SMALMED > SMALM
SMALMILY > SMALMY
SMALMING > SMALM
SMALMS > SMALM
SMALMY same as **>** SMARMY
SMALT n type of silica glass coloured deep blue with cobalt oxide
SMALTI > SMALTO
SMALTINE n mineral containing cobalt
SMALTINES > SMALTINE
SMALTITE n silver-white to greyish mineral
SMALTITES > SMALTITE
SMALTO n coloured glass, etc, used in mosaics

SMALTOS > SMALTO
SMALTS > SMALT
SMARAGD n any green gemstone, such as the emerald
SMARAGDE same as **>** SMARAGD
SMARAGDES > SMARAGDE
SMARAGDS > SMARAGD
SMARM vb bring (oneself) into favour (with) ▷ n obsequious flattery
SMARMED > SMARM
SMARMIER > SMARMY
SMARMIEST > SMARMY
SMARMILY > SMARMY
SMARMING > SMARM
SMARMS > SMARM
SMARMY adj unpleasantly suave or flattering
SMART adj well-kept and neat ▷ vb feel or cause stinging pain ▷ n stinging pain ▷ adv in a smart manner
SMARTARSE n derogatory term for a clever person, esp one who parades his knowledge offensively
SMARTASS same as **>** SMARTARSE
SMARTED > SMART
SMARTEN vb make or become smart
SMARTENED > SMARTEN
SMARTENS > SMARTEN
SMARTER > SMART
SMARTEST > SMART
SMARTIE same as **>** SMARTY
SMARTIES > SMARTY
SMARTING > SMART
SMARTISH > SMART
SMARTLY > SMART
SMARTNESS > SMART
SMARTS npl know-how, intelligence, or wits
SMARTWEED n grass with acrid smell
SMARTY n would-be clever person
SMASH vb break violently and noisily ▷ n act or sound of smashing ▷ adv with a smash
SMASHABLE > SMASH
SMASHED adj completely intoxicated with alcohol
SMASHER n attractive person or thing
SMASHEROO n excellent person or thing
SMASHERS > SMASHER
SMASHES > SMASH
SMASHING adj excellent
SMASHINGS > SMASHING
SMASHUP n bad collision of cars
SMASHUPS > SMASHUP
SMATCH less common word for **>** SMACK
SMATCHED > SMATCH
SMATCHES > SMATCH
SMATCHING > SMATCH

SMATTER n smattering ▷ vb prattle
SMATTERED > SMATTER
SMATTERER > SMATTER
SMATTERS > SMATTER
SMAZE n smoky haze, less damp than fog
SMAZES > SMAZE
SMEAR vb spread with a greasy or sticky substance ▷ n dirty mark or smudge
SMEARCASE n American type of cottage cheese
SMEARED > SMEAR
SMEARER > SMEAR
SMEARERS > SMEAR
SMEARIER > SMEARY
SMEARIEST > SMEARY
SMEARILY > SMEARY
SMEARING > SMEAR
SMEARS > SMEAR
SMEARY adj smeared, dirty
SMEATH n duck
SMEATHS > SMEATH
SMECTIC adj (of a substance) existing in state in which the molecules are oriented in layers
SMECTITE n type of clay mineral
SMECTITES > SMECTITE
SMECTITIC > SMECTITE
SMEDDUM n any fine powder
SMEDDUMS > SMEDDUM
SMEE n duck
SMEECH Southwest English dialect form of **>** SMOKE
SMEECHED > SMEECH
SMEECHES > SMEECH
SMEECHING > SMEECH
SMEEK vb smoke
SMEEKED > SMEEK
SMEEKING > SMEEK
SMEEKS > SMEEK
SMEES > SMEE
SMEETH n duck
SMEETHS > SMEETH
SMEGMA n whitish sebaceous secretion that accumulates beneath the prepuce
SMEGMAS > SMEGMA
SMEIK same as **>** SMEKE
SMEIKED > SMEKED
SMEIKING same as **>** SMEKING
SMEIKS > SMEIK
SMEKE n smoke ▷ vb smoke
SMEKED > SMEKE
SMEKES > SMEKE
SMEKING > SMEKE
SMELL vb perceive (a scent or odour) by means of the nose ▷ n ability to perceive odours by the nose
SMELLABLE adj capable of being smelled
SMELLED > SMELL
SMELLER > SMELL
SMELLERS > SMELL
SMELLIER > SMELLY
SMELLIES npl pleasant-smelling products

such as perfumes, body lotions, bath salts, etc
SMELLIEST > SMELLY
SMELLING > SMELL
SMELLINGS > SMELL
SMELLS > SMELL
SMELLY adj having a nasty smell
SMELT vb extract metal from an ore
SMELTED > SMELL
SMELTER n industrial plant where smelting is carried out
SMELTERS > SMELTER
SMELTERY variant of **>** SMELTER
SMELTING > SMELL
SMELTINGS > SMELL
SMELTS > SMELL
SMERK same as **>** SMIRK
SMERKED > SMERK
SMERKING > SMERK
SMERKS > SMERK
SMEUSE n way through hedge
SMEUSES > SMEUSE
SMEW n duck of N Europe and Asia
SMEWS > SMEW
SMICKER vb look at someone amorously
SMICKERED > SMICKER
SMICKERS > SMICKER
SMICKET n smock
SMICKETS > SMICKET
SMICKLY adv amorously
SMIDDIED > SMIDDY
SMIDDIES > SMIDDY
SMIDDY Scots word for **>** SMITHY
SMIDDYING > SMIDDY
SMIDGE n very small amount or part
SMIDGEN n very small amount or part
SMIDGENS > SMIDGEN
SMIDGEON same as **>** SMIDGEN
SMIDGEONS > SMIDGEON
SMIDGES > SMIDGE
SMIDGIN same as **>** SMIDGEN
SMIDGINS > SMIDGIN
SMIERCASE same as **>** SMEARCASE
SMIGHT same as **>** SMITE
SMIGHTING > SMIGHT
SMIGHTS > SMIGHT
SMILAX n type of climbing shrub
SMILAXES > SMILAX
SMILE n turning up of the corners of the mouth to show pleasure or friendliness ▷ vb give a smile
SMILED > SMILE
SMILEFUL adj full of smiles
SMILELESS > SMILE
SMILER > SMILE
SMILERS > SMILE
SMILES > SMILE
SMILET n little smile

SMILETS > SMILET
SMILEY n symbol depicting a smile or other facial expression, used in e-mail ▷ adj cheerful
SMILEYS > SMILEY
SMILIER > SMILEY
SMILIEST > SMILEY
SMILING > SMILE
SMILINGLY > SMILE
SMILINGS > SMILE
SMILODON n extinct sabre-toothed tiger
SMILODONS > SMILODON
SMIR n drizzly rain ▷ vb drizzle lightly
SMIRCH n stain ▷ vb disgrace
SMIRCHED > SMIRCH
SMIRCHER > SMIRCH
SMIRCHERS > SMIRCH
SMIRCHES > SMIRCH
SMIRCHING > SMIRCH
SMIRK n smug smile ▷ vb give a smirk
SMIRKED > SMIRK
SMIRKER > SMIRK
SMIRKERS > SMIRK
SMIRKIER > SMIRK
SMIRKIEST > SMIRK
SMIRKILY > SMIRK
SMIRKING > SMIRK
SMIRKS > SMIRK
SMIRKY > SMIRK
SMIRR same as > SMIR
SMIRRED > SMIRR
SMIRRIER > SMIRR
SMIRRIEST > SMIRR
SMIRRING > SMIRR
SMIRRS > SMIRR
SMIRRY > SMIRR
SMIRS > SMIR
SMIRTING n flirting amongst those smoking outside a non-smoking office, pub, etc
SMIRTINGS > SMIRTING
SMIT > SMITE
SMITE vb strike hard
SMITER > SMITE
SMITERS > SMITE
SMITES > SMITE
SMITH n worker in metal ▷ vb work in metal
SMITHED > SMITH
SMITHERS npl little shattered pieces
SMITHERY n trade or craft of a blacksmith
SMITHIED > SMITHY
SMITHIES > SMITHY
SMITHING > SMITH
SMITHS > SMITH
SMITHY n blacksmith's workshop ▷ vb work as a smith
SMITHYING > SMITHY
SMITING > SMITE
SMITS > SMIT
SMITTED > SMIT
SMITTEN > SMITE
SMITTING > SMIT
SMITTLE adj infectious
SMOCK n loose overall ▷ vb

gather (material) by sewing in a honeycomb pattern
SMOCKED > SMOCK
SMOCKING n ornamental needlework used to gather material
SMOCKINGS > SMOCKING
SMOCKLIKE > SMOCK
SMOCKS > SMOCK
SMOG n mixture of smoke and fog
SMOGGIER > SMOG
SMOGGIEST > SMOG
SMOGGY > SMOG
SMOGLESS > SMOG
SMOGS > SMOG
SMOILE same as > SMILE
SMOILED > SMOILE
SMOILES > SMOILE
SMOILING > SMOILE
SMOKABLE > SMOKE
SMOKE n cloudy mass that rises from something burning ▷ vb give off smoke or treat with smoke
SMOKEABLE > SMOKE
SMOKEBOX n part of a steam engine or boiler
SMOKED > SMOKE
SMOKEHO same as > SMOKO
SMOKEHOOD n hood worn to keep out smoke
SMOKEHOS > SMOKEHO
SMOKEJACK n device formerly used for turning a roasting spit, operated by the movement of ascending gases in a chimney
SMOKELESS adj having or producing little or no smoke
SMOKELIKE > SMOKE
SMOKEPOT n device for producing smoke
SMOKEPOTS > SMOKEPOT
SMOKER n person who habitually smokes tobacco
SMOKERS > SMOKER
SMOKES > SMOKE
SMOKEY same as > SMOKY
SMOKIE n smoked haddock
SMOKIER > SMOKY
SMOKIES > SMOKY
SMOKIEST > SMOKY
SMOKILY > SMOKY
SMOKINESS > SMOKY
SMOKING > SMOKE
SMOKINGS > SMOKING
SMOKO n short break from work for tea or a cigarette
SMOKOS > SMOKO
SMOKY adj filled with or giving off smoke, sometimes excessively ▷ n haddock that has been smoked
SMOLDER same as > SMOULDER
SMOLDERED > SMOLDER
SMOLDERS > SMOLDER
SMOLT n young salmon at the stage when it migrates to the sea

SMOLTS > SMOLT
SMOOCH vb kiss and cuddle ▷ n smooching
SMOOCHED > SMOOCH
SMOOCHER > SMOOCH
SMOOCHERS > SMOOCH
SMOOCHES > SMOOCH
SMOOCHIER > SMOOCHY
SMOOCHING > SMOOCH
SMOOCHY adj romantic
SMOODGE same as > SMOOCH
SMOODGED > SMOODGE
SMOODGES > SMOODGE
SMOODGING > SMOODGE
SMOOGE same as > SMOOCH
SMOOGED > SMOOGE
SMOOGES > SMOOGE
SMOOGING > SMOOGE
SMOOR n Scots word meaning put out fire
SMOORED > SMOOR
SMOORING > SMOOR
SMOORS > SMOOR
SMOOSH vb paint to give softened look
SMOOSHED > SMOOSH
SMOOSHES > SMOOSH
SMOOSHING > SMOOSH
SMOOT vb work as printer
SMOOTED > SMOOT
SMOOTH adj even in surface, texture, or consistency ▷ vb make smooth ▷ adv in a smooth manner ▷ n smooth part of something
SMOOTHED > SMOOTH
SMOOTHEN vb make or become smooth
SMOOTHENS > SMOOTHEN
SMOOTHER > SMOOTH
SMOOTHERS > SMOOTH
SMOOTHES > SMOOTH
SMOOTHEST > SMOOTH
SMOOTHIE n slang, usu derogatory term for a charming but possibly insincere man
SMOOTHIES > SMOOTHY
SMOOTHING > SMOOTH
SMOOTHISH > SMOOTH
SMOOTHLY > SMOOTH
SMOOTHS > SMOOTH
SMOOTHY same as > SMOOTHIE
SMOOTING > SMOOT
SMOOTS > SMOOT
SMORBROD n Danish hors d'oeuvre
SMORBRODS > SMORBROD
SMORE same as > SMOOR
SMORED > SMORE
SMORES > SMORE
SMORING > SMORE
SMORZANDO adv musical instruction meaning fading away gradually
SMORZATO same as > SMORZANDO
SMOTE > SMITE
SMOTHER vb suffocate or stifle ▷ n anything, such as a cloud of smoke, that stifles

SMOTHERED > SMOTHER
SMOTHERER > SMOTHER
SMOTHERS > SMOTHER
SMOTHERY > SMOTHER
SMOUCH vb kiss
SMOUCHED > SMOUCH
SMOUCHES > SMOUCH
SMOUCHING > SMOUCH
SMOULDER vb burn slowly with smoke but no flame ▷ n dense smoke, as from a smouldering fire
SMOULDERS > SMOULDER
SMOULDRY adj smouldering
SMOUSE vb South African word meaning peddle
SMOUSED > SMOUSE
SMOUSER > SMOUSE
SMOUSERS > SMOUSE
SMOUSES > SMOUSE
SMOUSING > SMOUSE
SMOUT n child or undersized person ▷ vb creep or sneak
SMOUTED > SMOUT
SMOUTING > SMOUT
SMOUTS > SMOUT
SMOWT same as > SMOUT
SMOWTS > SMOWT
SMOYLE same as > SMILE
SMOYLED > SMOYLE
SMOYLES > SMOYLE
SMOYLING > SMOYLE
SMRITI n class of Hindu sacred literature derived from the Vedas
SMRITIS > SMRITI
SMUDGE vb make or become smeared or soiled ▷ n dirty mark
SMUDGED > SMUDGE
SMUDGEDLY > SMUDGE
SMUDGER > SMUDGE
SMUDGERS > SMUDGE
SMUDGES > SMUDGE
SMUDGIER > SMUDGY
SMUDGIEST > SMUDGY
SMUDGILY > SMUDGE
SMUDGING > SMUDGE
SMUDGINGS > SMUDGE
SMUDGY adj smeared, blurred, or soiled, or likely to become so
SMUG adj self-satisfied ▷ vb make neat
SMUGGED > SMUG
SMUGGER > SMUG
SMUGGERY n condition or an instance of being smug
SMUGGEST > SMUG
SMUGGING > SMUG
SMUGGLE vb import or export (goods) secretly and illegally
SMUGGLED > SMUGGLE
SMUGGLER > SMUGGLE
SMUGGLERS > SMUGGLE
SMUGGLES > SMUGGLE
SMUGGLING > SMUGGLE
SMUGLY > SMUG
SMUGNESS > SMUG
SMUGS > SMUG
SMUR same as > SMIR

S

SMURFING n intentionally flooding and overwhelming a computer network with messages by means of a program
SMURFINGS > SMURFING
SMURRED > SMUR
SMURRIER > SMUR
SMURRIEST > SMUR
SMURRING > SMUR
SMURRY > SMUR
SMURS > SMUR
SMUSH vb crush
SMUSHED > SMUSH
SMUSHES > SMUSH
SMUSHING > SMUSH
SMUT n obscene jokes, pictures, etc ▷ vb mark or become marked or smudged, as with soot
SMUTCH vb smudge ▷ n mark
SMUTCHED > SMUTCH
SMUTCHES > SMUTCH
SMUTCHIER > SMUTCH
SMUTCHING > SMUTCH
SMUTCHY > SMUTCH
SMUTS > SMUT
SMUTTED > SMUT
SMUTTIER > SMUT
SMUTTIEST > SMUT
SMUTTILY > SMUT
SMUTTING > SMUT
SMUTTY > SMUT
SMYTRIE n Scots word meaning collection
SMYTRIES > SMYTRIE
SNAB same as **>** SNOB
SNABBLE same as **>** SNAFFLE
SNABBLED > SNABBLE
SNABBLES > SNABBLE
SNABBLING > SNABBLE
SNABS > SNAB
SNACK n light quick meal ▷ vb eat a snack
SNACKED > SNACK
SNACKER > SNACK
SNACKERS > SNACK
SNACKETTE n snack bar
SNACKING > SNACK
SNACKS > SNACK
SNAFFLE n jointed bit for a horse ▷ vb steal
SNAFFLED > SNAFFLE
SNAFFLES > SNAFFLE
SNAFFLING > SNAFFLE
SNAFU n confusion or chaos regarded as the normal state ▷ adj confused or muddled up, as usual ▷ vb throw into chaos
SNAFUED > SNAFU
SNAFUING > SNAFU
SNAFUS > SNAFU
SNAG n difficulty or disadvantage ▷ vb catch or tear on a point
SNAGGED > SNAG
SNAGGIER > SNAGGY
SNAGGIEST > SNAGGY
SNAGGING > SNAG
SNAGGY adj having sharp protuberances

SNAGLIKE > SNAG
SNAGS > SNAG
SNAIL n slow-moving mollusc with a spiral shell ▷ vb move slowly
SNAILED > SNAIL
SNAILERY n place where snails are bred
SNAILFISH n sea snail
SNAILIER > SNAIL
SNAILIEST > SNAIL
SNAILING > SNAIL
SNAILLIKE adj resembling a snail
SNAILS > SNAIL
SNAILY > SNAIL
SNAKE n long thin scaly limbless reptile ▷ vb move in a winding course like a snake
SNAKEBIRD n darter bird
SNAKEBIT adj bitten by snake
SNAKEBITE n bite of a snake
SNAKED > SNAKE
SNAKEFISH n fish resembling snake
SNAKEHEAD n Chinese criminal involved in the illegal transport of Chinese citizens to other parts of the world
SNAKELIKE > SNAKE
SNAKEPIT n pit filled with snakes
SNAKEPITS > SNAKEPIT
SNAKEROOT n any of various North American plants
SNAKES > SNAKE
SNAKESKIN n skin of a snake, esp when made into a leather valued for handbags, shoes, etc
SNAKEWEED same as **>** SNAKEROOT
SNAKEWISE adv in snakelike way
SNAKEWOOD n South American tree
SNAKEY same as **>** SNAKY
SNAKIER > SNAKY
SNAKIEST > SNAKY
SNAKILY > SNAKY
SNAKINESS > SNAKY
SNAKING > SNAKE
SNAKISH > SNAKE
SNAKY adj twisted or winding
SNAP vb break suddenly ▷ n act or sound of snapping ▷ adj made on the spur of the moment ▷ adv with a snap
SNAPBACK n sudden rebound or change in direction
SNAPBACKS > SNAPBACK
SNAPHANCE n flintlock gun
SNAPLESS > SNAP
SNAPLINK n metal link used in mountaineering
SNAPLINKS > SNAPLINK

SNAPPABLE > SNAP
SNAPPED > SNAP
SNAPPER n food fish of Australia and New Zealand ▷ vb stumble
SNAPPERED > SNAPPER
SNAPPERS > SNAPPER
SNAPPIER > SNAPPY
SNAPPIEST > SNAPPY
SNAPPILY > SNAPPY
SNAPPING > SNAP
SNAPPINGS > SNAP
SNAPPISH same as **>** SNAPPY
SNAPPY adj irritable
SNAPS > SNAP
SNAPSHOT n informal photograph
SNAPSHOTS > SNAPSHOT
SNAPTIN n container for food
SNAPTINS > SNAPTIN
SNAPWEED n impatiens
SNAPWEEDS > SNAPWEED
SNAR same as **>** SNARL
SNARE n trap with a noose ▷ vb catch in or as if in a snare
SNARED > SNARE
SNARELESS > SNARE
SNARER > SNARE
SNARERS > SNARE
SNARES > SNARE
SNARF vb eat or drink greedily
SNARFED > SNARF
SNARFING > SNARF
SNARFS > SNARF
SNARIER > SNARE
SNARIEST > SNARE
SNARING > SNARE
SNARINGS > SNARE
SNARK n imaginary creature in Lewis Carroll's poetry
SNARKIER > SNARKY
SNARKIEST > SNARKY
SNARKILY > SNARKY
SNARKS > SNARK
SNARKY adj unpleasant and scornful
SNARL vb (of an animal) growl with bared teeth ▷ n act or sound of snarling
SNARLED > SNARL
SNARLER > SNARL
SNARLERS > SNARL
SNARLIER > SNARL
SNARLIEST > SNARL
SNARLING > SNARL
SNARLINGS > SNARL
SNARLS > SNARL
SNARLY > SNARL
SNARRED > SNAR
SNARRING > SNAR
SNARS > SNAR
SNARY > SNARE
SNASH n Scots word meaning speak cheekily
SNASHED > SNASH
SNASHES > SNASH
SNASHING > SNASH
SNASTE n candle wick
SNASTES > SNASTE

SNATCH vb seize or try to seize suddenly ▷ n snatching
SNATCHED > SNATCH
SNATCHER > SNATCH
SNATCHERS > SNATCH
SNATCHES > SNATCH
SNATCHIER > SNATCHY
SNATCHILY > SNATCHY
SNATCHING > SNATCH
SNATCHY adj disconnected or spasmodic
SNATH n handle of a scythe
SNATHE same as **>** SNATH
SNATHES > SNATHE
SNATHS > SNATH
SNAW Scots variant of **>** SNOW
SNAWED > SNAW
SNAWING > SNAW
SNAWS > SNAW
SNAZZIER > SNAZZY
SNAZZIEST > SNAZZY
SNAZZILY > SNAZZY
SNAZZY adj stylish and flashy
SNEAD n scythe handle
SNEADS > SNEAD
SNEAK vb move furtively ▷ n cowardly or underhand person ▷ adj without warning
SNEAKED > SNEAK
SNEAKER n soft shoe
SNEAKERED adj wearing sneakers
SNEAKERS npl canvas shoes with rubber soles
SNEAKEUP n sneaky person
SNEAKEUPS > SNEAKEUP
SNEAKIER > SNEAK
SNEAKIEST > SNEAK
SNEAKILY > SNEAK
SNEAKING adj slight but persistent
SNEAKISH adj typical of sneak
SNEAKS > SNEAK
SNEAKSBY n sneak
SNEAKY > SNEAK
SNEAP vb nip
SNEAPED > SNEAP
SNEAPING > SNEAP
SNEAPS > SNEAP
SNEATH same as **>** SNATH
SNEATHS > SNEATH
SNEB same as **>** SNIB
SNEBBE same as **>** SNUB
SNEBBED > SNEB
SNEBBES > SNEBBE
SNEBBING > SNEB
SNEBS > SNEB
SNECK n small squared stone used in a rubble wall to fill spaces between stones ▷ vb fasten (a latch)
SNECKED > SNECK
SNECKING > SNECK
SNECKS > SNECK
SNED vb prune or trim
SNEDDED > SNED
SNEDDING > SNED
SNEDS > SNED
SNEE vb cut

SNEED > SNEE
SNEEING > SNEE
SNEER n contemptuous expression or remark ▷ vb show contempt by a sneer
SNEERED > SNEER
SNEERER > SNEER
SNEERERS > SNEER
SNEERFUL > SNEER
SNEERIER > SNEERY
SNEERIEST > SNEERY
SNEERING > SNEER
SNEERINGS > SNEER
SNEERS > SNEER
SNEERY adj contemptuous or scornful
SNEES > SNEE
SNEESH n Scots word meaning pinch of snuff
SNEESHAN n Scots word meaning pinch of snuff
SNEESHANS > SNEESHAN
SNEESHES > SNEESH
SNEESHIN same as > SNEESHAN
SNEESHING same as > SNEESHAN
SNEESHINS > SNEESHIN
SNEEZE vb expel air from the nose suddenly, involuntarily, and noisily ▷ n act or sound of sneezing
SNEEZED > SNEEZE
SNEEZER > SNEEZE
SNEEZERS > SNEEZE
SNEEZES > SNEEZE
SNEEZIER > SNEEZE
SNEEZIEST > SNEEZE
SNEEZING > SNEEZE
SNEEZINGS > SNEEZE
SNEEZY > SNEEZE
SNELL adj biting ▷ vb attach hook to fishing line
SNELLED > SNELL
SNELLER > SNELL
SNELLEST > SNELL
SNELLING > SNELL
SNELLS > SNELL
SNELLY > SNELL
SNIB n catch of a door or window ▷ vb bolt or fasten (a door)
SNIBBED > SNIB
SNIBBING > SNIB
SNIBS > SNIB
SNICK n (make) a small cut or notch ▷ vb make a small cut or notch in (something)
SNICKED > SNICK
SNICKER same as > SNIGGER
SNICKERED > SNICKER
SNICKERER > SNICKER
SNICKERS > SNICKER
SNICKERY > SNICKER
SNICKET n passageway between walls or fences
SNICKETS > SNICKET
SNICKING > SNICK
SNICKS > SNICK
SNIDE adj critical in an unfair and nasty way ▷ n sham jewellery ▷ vb fill or load

SNIDED > SNIDE
SNIDELY > SNIDE
SNIDENESS > SNIDE
SNIDER > SNIDE
SNIDES > SNIDE
SNIDEST > SNIDE
SNIDEY same as > SNIDE
SNIDIER > SNIDEY
SNIDIEST > SNIDEY
SNIDING > SNIDE
SNIES > SNY
SNIFF vb inhale through the nose in short audible breaths ▷ n act or sound of sniffing
SNIFFABLE > SNIFF
SNIFFED > SNIFF
SNIFFER n device for detecting hidden substances such as drugs or explosives, esp by their odour
SNIFFERS > SNIFFER
SNIFFIER > SNIFFY
SNIFFIEST > SNIFFY
SNIFFILY > SNIFFY
SNIFFING > SNIFF
SNIFFINGS > SNIFF
SNIFFISH adj disdainful
SNIFFLE vb sniff repeatedly, as when suffering from a cold ▷ n slight cold
SNIFFLED > SNIFFLE
SNIFFLER > SNIFFLE
SNIFFLERS > SNIFFLE
SNIFFLES > SNIFFLE
SNIFFLIER > SNIFFLE
SNIFFLING > SNIFFLE
SNIFFLY > SNIFFLE
SNIFFS > SNIFF
SNIFFY adj contemptuous or scornful
SNIFT same as > SNIFF
SNIFTED > SNIFT
SNIFTER n small quantity of alcoholic drink ▷ vb sniff
SNIFTERED > SNIFTER
SNIFTERS > SNIFTER
SNIFTIER > SNIFTY
SNIFTIEST > SNIFTY
SNIFTING > SNIFT
SNIFTS > SNIFT
SNIFTY adj slang word meaning excellent
SNIG vb drag (a felled log) by a chain or cable
SNIGGED > SNIG
SNIGGER n a sly laugh ▷ vb laugh slyly
SNIGGERED > SNIGGER
SNIGGERER > SNIGGER
SNIGGERS > SNIGGER
SNIGGING > SNIG
SNIGGLE vb fish for eels by dangling or thrusting a baited hook into cavities ▷ n baited hook used for sniggling eels
SNIGGLED > SNIGGLE
SNIGGLER > SNIGGLE
SNIGGLERS > SNIGGLE
SNIGGLES > SNIGGLE
SNIGGLING > SNIGGLE

SNIGLET n invented word
SNIGLETS > SNIGLET
SNIGS > SNIG
SNIP vb cut in small quick strokes with scissors or shears ▷ n bargain ▷ interj representation of the sound of scissors or shears closing
SNIPE n wading bird with a long straight bill ▷ vb shoot at (a person) from cover
SNIPED > SNIPE
SNIPEFISH n type of fish of tropical and temperate seas, with a long snout and a single dorsal fin
SNIPELIKE > SNIPE
SNIPER n person who shoots at someone from cover
SNIPERS > SNIPER
SNIPES > SNIPE
SNIPIER > SNIPY
SNIPIEST > SNIPY
SNIPING > SNIPE
SNIPINGS > SNIPE
SNIPPED > SNIP
SNIPPER > SNIP
SNIPPERS > SNIP
SNIPPET n small piece
SNIPPETS > SNIPPET
SNIPPETY > SNIPPET
SNIPPIER > SNIPPY
SNIPPIEST > SNIPPY
SNIPPILY > SNIPPY
SNIPPING > SNIP
SNIPPINGS > SNIP
SNIPPY adj scrappy
SNIPS > SNIP
SNIPY adj like a snipe
SNIRT n Scots word meaning suppressed laugh
SNIRTLE vb Scots word meaning snicker
SNIRTLED > SNIRTLE
SNIRTLES > SNIRTLE
SNIRTLING > SNIRTLE
SNIRTS > SNIRT
SNIT n fit of temper
SNITCH vb act as an informer ▷ n informer
SNITCHED > SNITCH
SNITCHER > SNITCH
SNITCHERS > SNITCH
SNITCHES > SNITCH
SNITCHIER > SNITCHY
SNITCHING > SNITCH
SNITCHY adj bad-tempered or irritable
SNITS > SNIT
SNIVEL vb cry in a whining way ▷ n act of snivelling
SNIVELED > SNIVEL
SNIVELER > SNIVEL
SNIVELERS > SNIVEL
SNIVELING > SNIVEL
SNIVELLED > SNIVEL
SNIVELLER > SNIVEL
SNIVELLY > SNIVEL
SNIVELS > SNIVEL
SNOB n person who judges others by social rank
SNOBBERY > SNOB

SNOBBIER > SNOB
SNOBBIEST > SNOB
SNOBBILY > SNOB
SNOBBISH > SNOB
SNOBBISM > SNOB
SNOBBISMS > SNOB
SNOBBY > SNOB
SNOBLING n little snob
SNOBLINGS > SNOBLING
SNOBS > SNOB
SNOD vb Scots word meaning make tidy
SNODDED > SNOD
SNODDER > SNOD
SNODDEST > SNOD
SNODDING > SNOD
SNODDIT > SNOD
SNODS > SNOD
SNOEK n edible marine fish
SNOEKS > SNOEK
SNOEP adj mean or tight-fisted
SNOG vb kiss and cuddle ▷ n act of kissing and cuddling
SNOGGED > SNOG
SNOGGING > SNOG
SNOGS > SNOG
SNOKE same as > SNOOK
SNOKED > SNOKE
SNOKES > SNOKE
SNOKING > SNOKE
SNOOD n pouch, often of net, loosely holding a woman's hair at the back ▷ vb hold (the hair) in a snood
SNOODED > SNOOD
SNOODING > SNOOD
SNOODS > SNOOD
SNOOK n any of several large game fishes ▷ vb lurk
SNOOKED > SNOOK
SNOOKER n game played on a billiard table ▷ vb leave (a snooker opponent) in a position such that another ball blocks the target ball
SNOOKERED > SNOOKER
SNOOKERS > SNOOKER
SNOOKING > SNOOK
SNOOKS > SNOOK
SNOOL vb Scots word meaning dominate
SNOOLED > SNOOL
SNOOLING > SNOOL
SNOOLS > SNOOL
SNOOP vb pry ▷ n snooping
SNOOPED > SNOOP
SNOOPER n person who snoops
SNOOPERS > SNOOPER
SNOOPIER > SNOOP
SNOOPIEST > SNOOP
SNOOPILY > SNOOP
SNOOPING > SNOOP
SNOOPS > SNOOP
SNOOPY > SNOOP
SNOOT n nose ▷ vb look contemptuously at
SNOOTED > SNOOT
SNOOTFUL n enough alcohol to make someone drunk
SNOOTFULS > SNOOTFUL

S

SNOOTIER > SNOOTY
SNOOTIEST > SNOOTY
SNOOTILY > SNOOTY
SNOOTING > SNOOT
SNOOTS > SNOOT
SNOOTY *adj* haughty
SNOOZE *vb* take a brief light sleep ▷ *n* brief light sleep
SNOOZED > SNOOZE
SNOOZER > SNOOZE
SNOOZERS > SNOOZE
SNOOZES > SNOOZE
SNOOZIER > SNOOZE
SNOOZIEST > SNOOZE
SNOOZING > SNOOZE
SNOOZLE *vb* cuddle and sleep
SNOOZLED > SNOOZLE
SNOOZLES > SNOOZLE
SNOOZLING > SNOOZLE
SNOOZY > SNOOZE
SNORE *vb* make snorting sounds while sleeping ▷ *n* sound of snoring
SNORED > SNORE
SNORER > SNORE
SNORERS > SNORE
SNORES > SNORE
SNORING > SNORE
SNORINGS > SNORE
SNORKEL *n* tube allowing a swimmer to breathe while face down on the surface of the water ▷ *vb* swim using a snorkel
SNORKELED > SNORKEL
SNORKELER > SNORKEL
SNORKELS > SNORKEL
SNORT *vb* exhale noisily through the nostrils ▷ *n* act or sound of snorting
SNORTED > SNORT
SNORTER *n* person or animal that snorts
SNORTERS > SNORTER
SNORTIER > SNORT
SNORTIEST > SNORT
SNORTING > SNORT
SNORTINGS > SNORT
SNORTS > SNORT
SNORTY > SNORT
SNOT *n* mucus from the nose ▷ *vb* blow one's nose
SNOTRAG *n* handkerchief
SNOTRAGS > SNOTRAG
SNOTS > SNOT
SNOTTED > SNOT
SNOTTER *vb* breathe through obstructed nostrils
SNOTTERED > SNOTTER
SNOTTERS > SNOTTER
SNOTTERY *n* snot
SNOTTIE *n* midshipman
SNOTTIER > SNOTTY
SNOTTIES > SNOTTY
SNOTTIEST > SNOTTY
SNOTTILY > SNOTTY
SNOTTING > SNOT
SNOTTY *adj* covered with mucus from the nose
SNOUT *n* animal's projecting nose and jaws ▷ *vb* have or give a snout

SNOUTED > SNOUT
SNOUTIER > SNOUT
SNOUTIEST > SNOUT
SNOUTING > SNOUT
SNOUTISH > SNOUT
SNOUTLESS > SNOUT
SNOUTLIKE > SNOUT
SNOUTS > SNOUT
SNOUTY > SNOUT
SNOW *n* frozen vapour falling from the sky in flakes ▷ *vb* fall as or like snow
SNOWBALL *n* snow pressed into a ball for throwing ▷ *vb* increase rapidly
SNOWBALLS > SNOWBALL
SNOWBANK *n* bank of snow
SNOWBANKS > SNOWBANK
SNOWBELL *n* Asian shrub
SNOWBELLS > SNOWBELL
SNOWBELT *n* northern states of USA
SNOWBELTS > SNOWBELT
SNOWBERRY *n* shrub grown for its white berries
SNOWBIRD *n* person addicted to cocaine, or sometimes heroin
SNOWBIRDS > SNOWBIRD
SNOWBLINK *n* whitish glare in the sky reflected from snow
SNOWBOARD *n* board on which a person stands to slide across the snow
SNOWBOOT *n* boot for walking in snow
SNOWBOOTS > SNOWBOOT
SNOWBOUND *adj* shut in by snow
SNOWBRUSH *n* brush for clearing snow
SNOWBUSH *n* North American plant
SNOWCAP *n* cap of snow on top of a mountain
SNOWCAPS > SNOWCAP
SNOWCAT *n* tracked vehicle for travelling over snow
SNOWCATS > SNOWCAT
SNOWCLONE *n* reusable verbal formula
SNOWDOME *n* leisure centre with facilities for skiing, skating, etc
SNOWDOMES > SNOWDOME
SNOWDRIFT *n* bank of deep snow
SNOWDROP *n* small white bell-shaped spring flower
SNOWDROPS > SNOWDROP
SNOWED *adj* under the influence of narcotic drugs
SNOWFALL *n* fall of snow
SNOWFALLS > SNOWFALL
SNOWFIELD *n* large area of permanent snow
SNOWFLAKE *n* single crystal of snow
SNOWFLECK *n* snow bunting
SNOWFLICK *same as* > SNOWFLECK
SNOWGLOBE *n* transparent sphere filled with water

and white particles which resemble snow falling when shaken
SNOWIER > SNOWY
SNOWIEST > SNOWY
SNOWILY > SNOWY
SNOWINESS > SNOWY
SNOWING > SNOW
SNOWISH *adj* like snow
SNOWK *same as* > SNOOK
SNOWKED > SNOWK
SNOWKING > SNOWK
SNOWKS > SNOWK
SNOWLAND *n* area where snow lies
SNOWLANDS > SNOWLAND
SNOWLESS > SNOW
SNOWLIKE > SNOW
SNOWLINE *n* limit of permanent snow
SNOWLINES > SNOWLINE
SNOWMAKER *n* machine making artificial snow
SNOWMAN *n* figure shaped out of snow
SNOWMELT *n* melting of snow in spring
SNOWMELTS > SNOWMELT
SNOWMEN > SNOWMAN
SNOWMOLD *n* fungus growing on grass under snow
SNOWMOLDS > SNOWMOLD
SNOWPACK *n* body of hard-packed snow
SNOWPACKS > SNOWPACK
SNOWPLOW *n* implement or vehicle for clearing snow away
SNOWPLOWS > SNOWPLOW
SNOWS > SNOW
SNOWSCAPE *n* snow-covered landscape
SNOWSHED *n* shelter built over an exposed section of railway track to prevent its blockage by snow
SNOWSHEDS > SNOWSHED
SNOWSHOE *n* racket-shaped frame with a network of thongs stretched across it, worn on the feet to make walking on snow less difficult ▷ *vb* walk or go using snowshoes
SNOWSHOED > SNOWSHOE
SNOWSHOER > SNOWSHOE
SNOWSHOES > SNOWSHOE
SNOWSLIDE *n* snow avalanche
SNOWSLIP *n* small snow avalanche
SNOWSLIPS > SNOWSLIP
SNOWSTORM *n* storm with heavy snow
SNOWSUIT *n* one-piece winter outer garment for child
SNOWSUITS > SNOWSUIT
SNOWY *adj* covered with or abounding in snow
SNUB *vb* insult deliberately ▷ *n* deliberate insult ▷ *adj* (of a nose) short and blunt

SNUBBE *n* stub
SNUBBED > SNUB
SNUBBER > SNUB
SNUBBERS > SNUB
SNUBBES > SNUBBE
SNUBBIER > SNUB
SNUBBIEST > SNUB
SNUBBING > SNUB
SNUBBINGS > SNUB
SNUBBISH > SNUB
SNUBBY > SNUB
SNUBFIN *adj* as in *snubfin dolphin* Australian dolphin with a small dorsal fin
SNUBNESS > SNUB
SNUBS > SNUB
SNUCK *past tense and past participle of* > SNEAK
SNUDGE *vb* be miserly
SNUDGED > SNUDGE
SNUDGES > SNUDGE
SNUDGING > SNUDGE
SNUFF *n* powdered tobacco for sniffing up the nostrils ▷ *vb* extinguish (a candle)
SNUFFBOX *n* small container for holding snuff
SNUFFED > SNUFF
SNUFFER > SNUFF
SNUFFERS > SNUFF
SNUFFIER > SNUFFY
SNUFFIEST > SNUFFY
SNUFFILY > SNUFFY
SNUFFING > SNUFF
SNUFFINGS > SNUFF
SNUFFLE *vb* breathe noisily or with difficulty ▷ *n* act or the sound of snuffling
SNUFFLED > SNUFFLE
SNUFFLER > SNUFFLE
SNUFFLERS > SNUFFLE
SNUFFLES *same as* > SNIFFLES
SNUFFLIER > SNUFFLE
SNUFFLING > SNUFFLE
SNUFFLY > SNUFFLE
SNUFFS > SNUFF
SNUFFY *adj* of, relating to, or resembling snuff
SNUG *adj* warm and comfortable ▷ *n* (in Britain and Ireland) small room in a pub ▷ *vb* make or become comfortable and warm
SNUGGED > SNUG
SNUGGER > SNUG
SNUGGERIE *n* small bar in pub
SNUGGERY *n* cosy and comfortable place or room
SNUGGEST > SNUG
SNUGGIES *npl* specially warm underwear
SNUGGING > SNUG
SNUGGLE *vb* nestle into a person or thing for warmth or from affection ▷ *n* act of snuggling
SNUGGLED > SNUGGLE
SNUGGLES > SNUGGLE
SNUGGLING > SNUGGLE
SNUGLY > SNUG
SNUGNESS > SNUG

S

SNUGS > SNUG

SNUSH vb take snuff

SNUSHED > SNUSH

SNUSHES > SNUSH

SNUSHING > SNUSH

SNUZZLE vb root in ground

SNUZZLED > SNUZZLE

SNUZZLES > SNUZZLE

SNUZZLING > SNUZZLE

SNY same as > SNYE

SNYE n side channel of a river

SNYES > SNYE

SO adv such an extent ▷ interj exclamation of surprise, triumph, or realization

SOAK vb make wet ▷ n soaking

SOAKAGE n process or a period in which a permeable substance is soaked in a liquid

SOAKAGES > SOAKAGE

SOAKAWAY n pit filled with rubble, etc, into which rain or waste water drains

SOAKAWAYS > SOAKAWAY

SOAKED > SOAK

SOAKEN > SOAK

SOAKER > SOAK

SOAKERS > SOAK

SOAKING > SOAK

SOAKINGLY > SOAK

SOAKINGS > SOAK

SOAKS > SOAK

SOAP n compound of alkali and fat, used with water as a cleaning agent ▷ vb apply soap to

SOAPBARK n W South American rosaceous tree

SOAPBARKS > SOAPBARK

SOAPBERRY n any of various chiefly tropical American sapindaceous trees

SOAPBOX n crate used as a platform for speech-making ▷ vb deliver a speech from a soapbox

SOAPBOXED > SOAPBOX

SOAPBOXES > SOAPBOX

SOAPED > SOAP

SOAPER n soap opera

SOAPERS > SOAPER

SOAPIE n soap opera

SOAPIER > SOAPY

SOAPIES > SOAPIE

SOAPIEST > SOAPY

SOAPILY > SOAPY

SOAPINESS > SOAPY

SOAPING > SOAP

SOAPLAND n Japanese massage parlour and brothel

SOAPLANDS > SOAPLAND

SOAPLESS > SOAP

SOAPLIKE > SOAP

SOAPROOT n plant with roots used as soap substitute

SOAPROOTS > SOAPROOT

SOAPS > SOAP

SOAPSTONE n soft mineral used for making table tops and ornaments

SOAPSUDS npl foam or lather produced when soap is mixed with water

SOAPSUDSY > SOAPSUDS

SOAPWORT n Eurasian plant with clusters of fragrant pink or white flowers

SOAPWORTS > SOAPWORT

SOAPY adj covered with soap

SOAR vb rise or fly upwards ▷ n act of soaring

SOARAWAY adj exceedingly successful

SOARE n young hawk

SOARED > SOAR

SOARER > SOAR

SOARERS > SOAR

SOARES > SOARE

SOARING > SOAR

SOARINGLY > SOAR

SOARINGS > SOAR

SOARS > SOAR

SOAVE n dry white Italian wine

SOAVES > SOAVE

SOB vb weep with convulsive gasps ▷ n act or sound of sobbing

SOBA n (in Japanese cookery) noodles made from buckwheat flour

SOBAS > SOBA

SOBBED > SOB

SOBBER > SOB

SOBBERS > SOB

SOBBING > SOB

SOBBINGLY > SOB

SOBBINGS > SOB

SOBEIT conj provided that

SOBER adj not drunk ▷ vb make or become sober

SOBERED > SOBER

SOBERER > SOBER

SOBEREST > SOBER

SOBERING > SOBER

SOBERISE same as > SOBERIZE

SOBERISED > SOBERISE

SOBERISES > SOBERISE

SOBERIZE vb make sober

SOBERIZED > SOBERIZE

SOBERIZES > SOBERIZE

SOBERLY > SOBER

SOBERNESS > SOBER

SOBERS > SOBER

SOBFUL adj tearful

SOBOLE n creeping underground stem that produces roots and buds

SOBOLES > SOBOLE

SOBRIETY n state of being sober

SOBRIQUET n nickname

SOBS > SOB

SOC n feudal right to hold court

SOCA n mixture of soul and calypso music popular in the E Caribbean

SOCAGE n tenure of land by certain services, esp of agricultural nature

SOCAGER > SOCAGE

SOCAGERS > SOCAGE

SOCAGES > SOCAGE

SOCAS > SOCA

SOCCAGE same as > SOCAGE

SOCCAGES > SOCCAGE

SOCCER n football played by two teams of eleven kicking a spherical ball

SOCCERS > SOCCER

SOCIABLE adj friendly or companionable ▷ n type of open carriage with two seats facing each other

SOCIABLES > SOCIABLE

SOCIABLY > SOCIABLE

SOCIAL adj living in a community ▷ n informal gathering

SOCIALISE same as > SOCIALIZE

SOCIALISM n political system which advocates public ownership of industries, resources, and transport

SOCIALIST n supporter or advocate of socialism ▷ adj of or relating to socialism

SOCIALITE n member of fashionable society

SOCIALITY n tendency of groups and persons to develop social links and live in communities

SOCIALIZE vb meet others socially

SOCIALLY > SOCIAL

SOCIALS > SOCIAL

SOCIATE n associate

SOCIATES > SOCIATE

SOCIATION n plant community

SOCIATIVE adj of association

SOCIETAL adj of or relating to society, esp human society or social relations

SOCIETIES > SOCIETY

SOCIETY n human beings considered as a group

SOCIOGRAM n chart showing social relationships

SOCIOLECT n language spoken by particular social class

SOCIOLOGY n study of human societies

SOCIOPATH n person with a personality disorder characterized by a tendency to commit antisocial acts without any feelings of guilt

SOCK n knitted covering for the foot ▷ vb hit hard

SOCKED > SOCK

SOCKET n hole or recess

into which something fits ▷ vb furnish with or place into a socket

SOCKETED > SOCKET

SOCKETING > SOCKET

SOCKETS > SOCKET

SOCKETTE n sock not covering ankle

SOCKETTES > SOCKETTE

SOCKEYE n Pacific salmon with red flesh

SOCKEYES > SOCKEYE

SOCKING > SOCK

SOCKLESS > SOCK

SOCKMAN same as > SOCMAN

SOCKMEN > SOCKMAN

SOCKO adj excellent

SOCKS > SOCK

SOCLE another name for > PLINTH

SOCLES > SOCLE

SOCMAN n tenant holding land by socage

SOCMEN > SOCMAN

SOCS > SOC

SOD n (piece of) turf ▷ vb cover with sods

SODA n compound of sodium

SODAIC adj containing soda

SODAIN same as > SUDDEN

SODAINE same as > SUDDEN

SODALESS > SODA

SODALIST n member of sodality

SODALISTS > SODALIST

SODALITE n blue, grey, yellow, or colourless mineral

SODALITES > SODALITE

SODALITY n religious or charitable society

SODAMIDE n white crystalline compound used as a dehydrating agent

SODAMIDES > SODAMIDE

SODAS > SODA

SODBUSTER n farmer who grows crops

SODDED > SOD

SODDEN adj soaked ▷ vb make or become sodden

SODDENED > SODDEN

SODDENING > SODDEN

SODDENLY > SODDEN

SODDENS > SODDEN

SODDIER > SODDY

SODDIES > SODDY

SODDIEST > SODDY

SODDING > SOD

SODDY adj covered with turf

SODGER dialect variant of > SOLDIER

SODGERED > SODGER

SODGERING > SODGER

SODGERS > SODGER

SODIC adj containing sodium

SODICITY > SODIC

SODIUM n silvery-white metallic element

S

SODIUMS > SODIUM
SODOM n person who performs sodomy
SODOMIES > SODOMY
SODOMISE same as **>** SODOMIZE
SODOMISED > SODOMISE
SODOMISES > SODOMISE
SODOMIST > SODOMY
SODOMISTS > SODOMY
SODOMITE n person who practises sodomy
SODOMITES > SODOMITE
SODOMITIC > SODOMY
SODOMIZE vb be the active partner in anal intercourse
SODOMIZED > SODOMIZE
SODOMIZES > SODOMIZE
SODOMS > SODOM
SODOMY n anal intercourse
SODS > SOD
SOEVER adv in any way at all
SOFA n couch
SOFABED n sofa that converts into a bed
SOFABEDS > SOFABED
SOFAR n system for determining a position at sea
SOFARS > SOFAR
SOFAS > SOFA
SOFFIONI n holes in volcano that emit steam
SOFFIT n underside of a part of a building or a structural component
SOFFITS > SOFFIT
SOFT adj easy to shape or cut ▷ adv softly ▷ vb soften
SOFTA n Muslim student of divinity and jurisprudence, esp in Turkey
SOFTAS > SOFTA
SOFTBACK n paperback
SOFTBACKS > SOFTBACK
SOFTBALL n game similar to baseball, played using a larger softer ball
SOFTBALLS > SOFTBALL
SOFTBOUND adj having paperback binding
SOFTCORE adj describing pornography that is not explicit
SOFTCOVER n book with paper covers
SOFTED > SOFT
SOFTEN vb make or become soft or softer
SOFTENED > SOFTEN
SOFTENER n substance added to another substance to increase its softness
SOFTENERS > SOFTENER
SOFTENING > SOFTEN
SOFTENS > SOFTEN
SOFTER > SOFT
SOFTEST > SOFT
SOFTGOODS n clothing and soft furniture
SOFTHEAD n half-witted person

SOFTHEADS > SOFTHEAD
SOFTIE n person who is easily upset
SOFTIES > SOFTY
SOFTING > SOFT
SOFTISH > SOFT
SOFTLING n weakling
SOFTLINGS > SOFTLING
SOFTLY > SOFT
SOFTNESS n quality or an instance of being soft
SOFTS > SOFT
SOFTSHELL n crab or turtle with a soft shell
SOFTWARE n computer programs
SOFTWARES > SOFTWARE
SOFTWOOD n wood of a coniferous tree
SOFTWOODS > SOFTWOOD
SOFTY same as **>** SOFTIE
SOG vb soak
SOGER same as **>** SODGER
SOGERS > SOGER
SOGGED > SOG
SOGGIER > SOGGY
SOGGIEST > SOGGY
SOGGILY > SOGGY
SOGGINESS > SOGGY
SOGGING > SOG
SOGGINGS > SOG
SOGGY adj soaked
SOGS > SOG
SOH n (in tonic sol-fa) fifth degree of any major scale
SOHO interj exclamation announcing the sighting of a hare
SOHS > SOH
SOHUR same as **>** SUHUR
SOHURS > SOHUR
SOIGNE adj well-groomed, elegant
SOIGNEE variant of **>** SOIGNE
SOIL n top layer of earth ▷ vb make or become dirty
SOILAGE n green fodder, esp when freshly cut and fed to livestock in a confined area
SOILAGES > SOILAGE
SOILBORNE adj carried in soil
SOILED > SOIL
SOILIER > SOIL
SOILIEST > SOIL
SOILINESS > SOIL
SOILING > SOIL
SOILINGS > SOIL
SOILLESS > SOIL
SOILS > SOIL
SOILURE n act of soiling or the state of being soiled
SOILURES > SOILURE
SOILY > SOIL
SOIREE n evening party or gathering
SOIREES > SOIREE
SOJA same as **>** SOYA
SOJAS > SOJA
SOJOURN n temporary stay ▷ vb stay temporarily
SOJOURNED > SOJOURN

SOJOURNER > SOJOURN
SOJOURNS > SOJOURN
SOKAH same as **>** SOCA
SOKAHS > SOKAH
SOKAIYA n Japanese extortionist
SOKE n right to hold a local court
SOKEMAN same as **>** SOCMAN
SOKEMANRY n feudal tenure by socage
SOKEMEN > SOKEMAN
SOKEN n feudal district
SOKENS > SOKEN
SOKES > SOKE
SOKOL n Czech gymnastic association
SOKOLS > SOKOL
SOL n liquid colloidal solution
SOLA > SOLUM
SOLACE vb comfort in distress ▷ n comfort in misery or disappointment
SOLACED > SOLACE
SOLACER > SOLACE
SOLACERS > SOLACE
SOLACES > SOLACE
SOLACING > SOLACE
SOLACIOUS adj providing solace
SOLAH n Indian plant
SOLAHS > SOLAH
SOLAN archaic name for **>** GANNET
SOLAND n solan goose
SOLANDER n box for botanical specimens, maps, etc, made in the form of a book, the front cover being the lid
SOLANDERS > SOLANDER
SOLANDS > SOLAND
SOLANIN same as **>** SOLANINE
SOLANINE n poisonous alkaloid found in various solanaceous plants
SOLANINES > SOLANINE
SOLANINS > SOLANIN
SOLANO n hot wind in Spain
SOLANOS > SOLANO
SOLANS > SOLAN
SOLANUM n any plant of the mainly tropical genus that includes the potato, aubergine, and certain nightshades
SOLANUMS > SOLANUM
SOLAR adj of the sun
SOLARIA > SOLARIUM
SOLARISE same as **>** SOLARIZE
SOLARISED > SOLARISE
SOLARISES > SOLARISE
SOLARISM n explanation of myths in terms of the movements and influence of the sun
SOLARISMS > SOLARISM
SOLARIST > SOLARISM
SOLARISTS > SOLARISM
SOLARIUM n place with

beds and ultraviolet lights used for acquiring an artificial suntan
SOLARIUMS > SOLARIUM
SOLARIZE vb treat by exposure to the sun's rays
SOLARIZED > SOLARIZE
SOLARIZES > SOLARIZE
SOLARS > SOLUM
SOLAS > SOLA
SOLATE vb change from gel to liquid
SOLATED > SOLATE
SOLATES > SOLATE
SOLATIA > SOLATIUM
SOLATING > SOLATE
SOLATION n liquefaction of a gel
SOLATIONS > SOLATION
SOLATIUM n compensation awarded for injury to the feelings
SOLD n obsolete word for salary
SOLDADO n soldier
SOLDADOS > SOLDADO
SOLDAN archaic word for **>** SULTAN
SOLDANS > SOLDAN
SOLDE n wages
SOLDER n soft alloy used to join two metal surfaces ▷ vb join with solder
SOLDERED > SOLDER
SOLDERER > SOLDER
SOLDERERS > SOLDER
SOLDERING > SOLDER
SOLDERS > SOLDER
SOLDES > SOLDE
SOLDI > SOLDO
SOLDIER n member of an army ▷ vb serve in an army
SOLDIERED > SOLDIER
SOLDIERLY adj of or befitting a good soldier
SOLDIERS > SOLDIER
SOLDIERY n soldiers collectively
SOLDO n former Italian copper coin worth one twentieth of a lira
SOLDS > SOLD
SOLE adj one and only ▷ n underside of the foot ▷ vb provide (a shoe) with a sole
SOLECISE variant of **>** SOLECIZE
SOLECISED > SOLECISE
SOLECISES > SOLECISE
SOLECISM n minor grammatical mistake
SOLECISMS > SOLECISM
SOLECIST > SOLECISM
SOLECISTS > SOLECISM
SOLECIZE vb commit a solecism
SOLECIZED > SOLECIZE
SOLECIZES > SOLECIZE
SOLED > SOLE
SOLEI > SOLEUS
SOLEIN same as **>** SULLEN
SOLELESS > SOLE
SOLELY adv only, completely

SOLEMN *adj* serious, deeply sincere
SOLEMNER > SOLEMN
SOLEMNESS > SOLEMN
SOLEMNEST > SOLEMN
SOLEMNIFY *vb* make serious or grave
SOLEMNISE *same as* > SOLEMNIZE
SOLEMNITY *n* state or quality of being solemn
SOLEMNIZE *vb* celebrate or perform (a ceremony)
SOLEMNLY > SOLEMN
SOLENESS > SOLE
SOLENETTE *n* small European sole
SOLENODON *n* either of two rare shrewlike nocturnal mammals of the Caribbean
SOLENOID *n* coil of wire magnetized by passing a current through it
SOLENOIDS > SOLENOID
SOLEPLATE *n* joist forming the lowest member of a timber frame
SOLEPRINT *n* print of sole of foot
SOLER *same as* > SOLE
SOLERA *n* system for aging sherry and other fortified wines
SOLERAS > SOLERA
SOLERET *n* armour for foot
SOLERETS > SOLERET
SOLERS > SOLER
SOLES > SOLE
SOLEUS *n* muscle in calf of leg
SOLEUSES > SOLEUS
SOLFATARA *n* volcanic vent emitting only sulphurous gases and water vapour or sometimes hot mud
SOLFEGE *variant of* > SOLFEGGIO
SOLFEGES > SOLFEGE
SOLFEGGI > SOLFEGGIO
SOLFEGGIO *n* voice exercise in which runs, scales, etc, are sung to the same syllable or syllables
SOLFERINO *n* moderate purplish-red colour
SOLGEL *adj* changing between sol and gel
SOLI *adv* (of a piece or passage) to be performed by or with soloists
SOLICIT *vb* request
SOLICITED > SOLICIT
SOLICITOR *n* lawyer who advises clients and prepares documents and cases
SOLICITS > SOLICIT
SOLICITY *n* act of making a request
SOLID *adj* (of a substance) keeping its shape ▷ *n* three-dimensional shape

SOLIDAGO *n* chiefly American plant of the genus which includes the goldenrods
SOLIDAGOS > SOLIDAGO
SOLIDARE *n* old coin
SOLIDARES > SOLIDARE
SOLIDARY *adj* marked by unity of interests, responsibilities, etc
SOLIDATE *vb* consolidate
SOLIDATED > SOLIDATE
SOLIDATES > SOLIDATE
SOLIDER > SOLID
SOLIDEST > SOLID
SOLIDI > SOLIDUS
SOLIDIFY *vb* make or become solid or firm
SOLIDISH > SOLID
SOLIDISM *n* belief that diseases spring from damage to solid parts of body
SOLIDISMS > SOLIDISM
SOLIDIST > SOLIDISM
SOLIDISTS > SOLIDISM
SOLIDITY > SOLID
SOLIDLY > SOLID
SOLIDNESS > SOLID
SOLIDS > SOLID
SOLIDUM *n* part of pedestal
SOLIDUMS > SOLIDUM
SOLIDUS *same as* > SLASH
SOLILOQUY *n* speech made by a person while alone, esp in a play
SOLING > SOLE
SOLION *n* amplifier used in chemistry
SOLIONS > SOLION
SOLIPED *n* animal whose hooves are not cloven
SOLIPEDS > SOLIPED
SOLIPSISM *n* doctrine that the self is the only thing known to exist
SOLIPSIST > SOLIPSISM
SOLIQUID *n* semi-solid, semi-liquid solution
SOLIQUIDS > SOLIQUID
SOLITAIRE *n* game for one person played with pegs set in a board
SOLITARY *adj* alone, single ▷ *n* hermit
SOLITO *adv* musical instruction meaning play in usual manner
SOLITON *n* type of isolated particle-like wave
SOLITONS > SOLITON
SOLITUDE *n* state of being alone
SOLITUDES > SOLITUDE
SOLIVE *n* type of joist
SOLIVES > SOLIVE
SOLLAR *n* archaic word meaning attic
SOLLARS > SOLLAR
SOLLER *same as* > SOLLAR
SOLLERET *n* protective covering for the foot

consisting of riveted plates of armour
SOLLERETS > SOLLERET
SOLLERS > SOLLER
SOLLICKER *n* something very large
SOLO *n* music for one performer ▷ *adj* done alone ▷ *adv* by oneself, alone ▷ *vb* undertake a venture alone, esp to operate an aircraft alone or climb alone
SOLOED > SOLO
SOLOING > SOLO
SOLOIST *n* person who performs a solo
SOLOISTIC > SOLOIST
SOLOISTS > SOLOIST
SOLON *n* US congressman
SOLONCHAK *n* type of intrazonal soil of arid regions with a greyish surface crust
SOLONETS *same as* > SOLONETZ
SOLONETZ *n* type of intrazonal soil with a high saline content characterized by leaching
SOLONS > SOLON
SOLOS > SOLO
SOLPUGID *n* venomous arachnid
SOLPUGIDS > SOLPUGID
SOLS > SOL
SOLSTICE *n* either the shortest (in winter) or longest (in summer) day of the year
SOLSTICES > SOLSTICE
SOLUBLE *adj* able to be dissolved ▷ *n* soluble substance
SOLUBLES > SOLUBLE
SOLUBLY > SOLUBLE
SOLUM *n* upper layers of the soil profile, affected by climate and vegetation
SOLUMS > SOLUM
SOLUNAR *adj* relating to sun and moon
SOLUS *adj* alone
SOLUTAL *adj* relating to a solute
SOLUTE *n* substance in a solution that is dissolved ▷ *adj* loose or unattached
SOLUTES > SOLUTE
SOLUTION *n* answer to a problem
SOLUTIONS > SOLUTION
SOLUTIVE *adj* dissolving
SOLVABLE *adj* capable of being solved
SOLVATE *vb* undergo, cause to undergo, or partake in solvation
SOLVATED > SOLVATE
SOLVATES > SOLVATE
SOLVATING > SOLVATE
SOLVATION *n* type of chemical process
SOLVE *vb* find the answer to (a problem)
SOLVED > SOLVE

SOLVENCY *n* ability to pay all debts
SOLVENT *adj* having enough money to pay one's debts ▷ *n* liquid capable of dissolving other substances
SOLVENTLY > SOLVENT
SOLVENTS > SOLVENT
SOLVER > SOLVE
SOLVERS > SOLVE
SOLVES > SOLVE
SOLVING > SOLVE
SOM *n* currency of Kyrgyzstan and Uzbekistan
SOMA *n* body of an organism, esp an animal, as distinct from the germ cells
SOMAN *n* organophosphorus compound developed as a nerve gas in Germany during World War II
SOMANS > SOMAN
SOMAS > SOMA
SOMASCOPE *n* instrument for inspecting internal organs
SOMATA > SOMA
SOMATIC *adj* of the body, as distinct from the mind
SOMATISM *n* materialism
SOMATISMS > SOMATISM
SOMATIST > SOMATISM
SOMATISTS > SOMATISM
SOMBER *adj* (in the US) sombre ▷ *vb* (in the US) make sombre
SOMBERED > SOMBER
SOMBERER > SOMBER
SOMBEREST > SOMBER
SOMBERING > SOMBER
SOMBERLY > SOMBER
SOMBERS > SOMBER
SOMBRE *adj* dark, gloomy ▷ *vb* make sombre
SOMBRED > SOMBRE
SOMBRELY > SOMBRE
SOMBRER > SOMBRE
SOMBRERO *n* wide-brimmed Mexican hat
SOMBREROS > SOMBRERO
SOMBRES > SOMBRE
SOMBREST > SOMBRE
SOMBRING > SOMBRE
SOMBROUS > SOMBRE
SOME *adj* unknown or unspecified ▷ *pron* certain unknown or unspecified people or things ▷ *adv* approximately ▷ *det* (a) certain unknown or unspecified
SOMEBODY *pron* some person ▷ *n* important person
SOMEDAY *adv* at some unspecified time in the future
SOMEDEAL *adv* to some extent
SOMEDELE *same as* > SOMEDEAL
SOMEGATE *adv* Scots word meaning somehow

SOMEHOW adv in some unspecified way
SOMEONE pron somebody ▷ n significant or important person
SOMEONES > SOMEONE
SOMEPLACE adv in, at, or to some unspecified place or region
SOMERSET n somersault
SOMERSETS > SOMERSET
SOMETHING pron unknown or unspecified thing or amount ▷ n impressive or important person or thing
SOMETIME adv at some unspecified time ▷ adj former
SOMETIMES adv from time to time, now and then
SOMEWAY adv in some unspecified manner
SOMEWAYS same as > SOMEWAY
SOMEWHAT adv some extent, rather ▷ n vague amount
SOMEWHATS > SOMEWHAT
SOMEWHEN adv at some time
SOMEWHERE adv in, to, or at some unspecified or unknown place
SOMEWHILE adv sometimes
SOMEWHY adv for some reason
SOMEWISE adv in some way or to some degree
SOMITAL > SOMITE
SOMITE n any of a series of dorsal paired segments of mesoderm occurring along the notochord in vertebrate embryos
SOMITES > SOMITE
SOMITIC > SOMITE
SOMMELIER n wine steward in a restaurant or hotel
SOMNIAL adj of dreams
SOMNIATE vb dream
SOMNIATED > SOMNIATE
SOMNIATES > SOMNIATE
SOMNIFIC adj inducing sleep
SOMNOLENT adj drowsy
SOMONI n monetary unit of Tajikistan
SOMS > SOM
SOMY > SOM
SON n male offspring
SONANCE > SONANT
SONANCES > SONANT
SONANCIES > SONANT
SONANCY > SONANT
SONANT n voiced sound able to form a syllable or syllable nucleus ▷ adj denoting a voiced sound like this
SONANTAL > SONANT
SONANTIC > SONANT
SONANTS > SONANT

SONAR n device for detecting underwater objects by the reflection of sound waves
SONARMAN n sonar operator
SONARMEN > SONARMAN
SONARS > SONAR
SONATA n piece of music in several movements for one instrument with or without piano
SONATAS > SONATA
SONATINA n short sonata
SONATINAS > SONATINA
SONATINE same as > SONATINA
SONCE n Scots word meaning good luck
SONCES > SONCE
SONDAGE n deep trial trench for inspecting stratigraphy
SONDAGES > SONDAGE
SONDE n rocket, balloon, or probe used for observing in the upper atmosphere
SONDELI n Indian shrew
SONDELIS > SONDELI
SONDER n yacht category
SONDERS > SONDER
SONDES > SONDE
SONE n subjective unit of loudness
SONERI n Indian cloth of gold
SONERIS > SONERI
SONES > SONE
SONG n music for the voice
SONGBIRD n any bird with a musical call
SONGBIRDS > SONGBIRD
SONGBOOK n book of songs
SONGBOOKS > SONGBOOK
SONGCRAFT n art of songwriting
SONGFEST n event with many songs
SONGFESTS > SONGFEST
SONGFUL adj tuneful
SONGFULLY > SONGFUL
SONGKOK n (in Malaysia and Indonesia) a kind of oval brimless hat, resembling a skull
SONGKOKS > SONGKOK
SONGLESS > SONG
SONGLIKE > SONG
SONGMAN n singer
SONGMEN > SONGMAN
SONGOLOLO n kind of millipede
SONGS > SONG
SONGSMITH n person who writes songs
SONGSTER n singer
SONGSTERS > SONGSTER
SONHOOD > SON
SONHOODS > SON
SONIC adj of or producing sound
SONICALLY > SONIC
SONICATE vb subject to sound waves

SONICATED > SONICATE
SONICATES > SONICATE
SONICATOR > SONICATE
SONICS n study of mechanical vibrations in matter
SONLESS > SON
SONLIKE > SON
SONLY adj like a son
SONNE same as > SON
SONNES > SONNE
SONNET n fourteen-line poem with a fixed rhyme scheme ▷ vb compose sonnets
SONNETARY > SONNET
SONNETED > SONNET
SONNETEER n writer of sonnets
SONNETING > SONNET
SONNETISE same as > SONNETIZE
SONNETIZE vb write sonnets
SONNETS > SONNET
SONNETTED > SONNET
SONNIES > SONNY
SONNY n term of address to a boy
SONOBUOY n buoy equipped to detect underwater noises and transmit them by radio
SONOBUOYS > SONOBUOY
SONOGRAM n three-dimensional representation of a sound signal
SONOGRAMS > SONOGRAM
SONOGRAPH n device for scanning sound
SONOMETER same as > MONOCHORD
SONORANT n type of frictionless continuant or nasal
SONORANTS > SONORANT
SONORITY > SONOROUS
SONOROUS adj (of sound) deep or resonant
SONOVOX n device used to alter sound of human voice in music recordings
SONOVOXES > SONOVOX
SONS > SON
SONSE same as > SONCE
SONSES > SONSE
SONSHIP > SON
SONSHIPS > SON
SONSIE same as > SONSY
SONSIER > SONSY
SONSIEST > SONSY
SONSY adj plump
SONTAG n type of knitted women's cape
SONTAGS > SONTAG
SONTIES n Shakespearian oath
SOOCHONG same as > SOUCHONG
SOOCHONGS > SOOCHONG
SOOEY interj call used to summon pigs
SOOGEE vb clean ship using

a special solution
SOOGEED > SOOGEE
SOOGEEING > SOOGEE
SOOGEES > SOOGEE
SOOGIE same as > SOOGEE
SOOGIED > SOOGIE
SOOGIEING > SOOGIE
SOOGIES > SOOGIE
SOOJEY same as > SOOGEE
SOOJEYS > SOOJEY
SOOK n baby ▷ vb suck
SOOKED > SOOK
SOOKING > SOOK
SOOKS > SOOK
SOOL vb incite (a dog) to attack
SOOLE same as > SOOL
SOOLED > SOOL
SOOLES > SOOLE
SOOLING > SOOL
SOOLS > SOOL
SOOM Scots word for > SWIM
SOOMED > SOOM
SOOMING > SOOM
SOOMS > SOOM
SOON adv in a short time
SOONER adv rather ▷ n an idler or shirker
SOONERS > SOONER
SOONEST adv as soon as possible
SOOP Scots word for > SWEEP
SOOPED > SOOP
SOOPING > SOOP
SOOPINGS > SOOP
SOOPS > SOOP
SOOPSTAKE adv sweeping up all stakes
SOOT n black powder formed by the incomplete burning of an organic substance ▷ vb cover with soot
SOOTE n sweet
SOOTED > SOOT
SOOTERKIN n mythical black afterbirth of Dutch women that was believed to result from their warming themselves on stoves
SOOTES > SOOT
SOOTFLAKE n speck of soot
SOOTH n truth or reality ▷ adj true or real
SOOTHE vb make calm
SOOTHED > SOOTHE
SOOTHER vb flatter
SOOTHERED > SOOTHE
SOOTHERS > SOOTHE
SOOTHES > SOOTHE
SOOTHEST > SOOTH
SOOTHFAST adj truthful
SOOTHFUL adj truthful
SOOTHING adj having a calming, assuaging, or relieving effect
SOOTHINGS > SOOTHING
SOOTHLICH adv truly
SOOTHLY > SOOTH
SOOTHS > SOOTH
SOOTHSAID > SOOTHSAY

SOOTHSAY vb predict the future

SOOTHSAYS > SOOTHSAY

SOOTIER > SOOTY

SOOTIEST > SOOTY

SOOTILY > SOOTY

SOOTINESS > SOOTY

SOOTING > SOOT

SOOTLESS > SOOT

SOOTS > SOOT

SOOTY adj covered with soot

SOP n concession to pacify someone ▷ vb mop up or absorb (liquid)

SOPAPILLA n Mexican deep-fried pastry

SOPH shortened form of > SOPHOMORE

SOPHERIC > SOPHERIM

SOPHERIM n Jewish scribes

SOPHIES > SOPHY

SOPHISM n argument that seems reasonable but is actually false and misleading

SOPHISMS > SOPHISM

SOPHIST n person who uses clever but invalid arguments

SOPHISTER n (esp formerly) a second-year undergraduate at certain British universities

SOPHISTIC adj of or relating to sophists or sophistry

SOPHISTRY n clever but invalid argument

SOPHISTS > SOPHIST

SOPHOMORE n student in second year at college

SOPHS > SOPH

SOPHY n title of the Persian monarchs

SOPITE vb lull to sleep

SOPITED > SOPITE

SOPITES > SOPITE

SOPITING > SOPITE

SOPOR n abnormally deep sleep

SOPORIFIC adj causing sleep ▷ n drug that causes sleep

SOPOROSE adj sleepy

SOPOROUS same as > SOPOROSE

SOPORS > SOPOR

SOPPED > SOP

SOPPIER > SOPPY

SOPPIEST > SOPPY

SOPPILY > SOPPY

SOPPINESS > SOPPY

SOPPING > SOP

SOPPINGS > SOP

SOPPY adj oversentimental

SOPRA adv musical instruction meaning above

SOPRANI > SOPRANO

SOPRANINI > SOPRANINO

SOPRANINO n instrument with the highest possible pitch in a family of instruments

SOPRANIST n soprano

SOPRANO n singer with the highest female or boy's voice ▷ adj of a musical instrument that is the highest or second highest pitched in its family

SOPRANOS > SOPRANO

SOPS > SOP

SORA n North American rail with a yellow bill

SORAGE n first year in hawk's life

SORAGES > SORAGE

SORAL > SORUS

SORAS > SORA

SORB n any of various related trees, esp the mountain ash ▷ vb absorb or adsorb

SORBABLE > SORB

SORBARIA n Asian shrub

SORBARIAS > SORBARIA

SORBATE n salt of sorbic acid

SORBATES > SORBATE

SORBED > SORB

SORBENT > SORB

SORBENTS > SORB

SORBET same as > SHERBET

SORBETS > SORBET

SORBIC > SORB

SORBING > SORB

SORBITE n mineral found in steel

SORBITES > SORBITE

SORBITIC > SORBITE

SORBITISE same as > SORBITIZE

SORBITIZE vb turn metal into form containing sorbite

SORBITOL n white water-soluble crystalline alcohol with a sweet taste

SORBITOLS > SORBITOL

SORBO as in sorbo rubber spongy form of rubber

SORBOSE n sweet-tasting hexose sugar derived from the berries of the mountain ash

SORBOSES > SORBOSE

SORBS > SORB

SORBUS n rowan or related tree

SORBUSES > SORBUS

SORCERER n magician

SORCERERS > SORCERER

SORCERESS same as > SORCERER

SORCERIES > SORCERY

SORCEROUS > SORCERY

SORCERY n witchcraft or magic

SORD n flock of mallard ducks

SORDA n deaf woman

SORDES npl dark incrustations on the lips and teeth of patients with prolonged fever

SORDID adj dirty, squalid

SORDIDER > SORDID

SORDIDEST > SORDID

SORDIDLY > SORDID

SORDINE same as > SORDINO

SORDINES > SORDINE

SORDINI > SORDINO

SORDINO n mute for a stringed or brass musical instrument

SORDO n deaf man

SORDOR n sordidness

SORDORS > SORDOR

SORDS > SORD

SORE adj painful ▷ n painful area on the body ▷ adv greatly ▷ vb make sore

SORED > SORE

SOREDIA > SOREDIUM

SOREDIAL > SOREDIUM

SOREDIATE > SOREDIUM

SOREDIUM n organ of vegetative reproduction in lichens

SOREE same as > SORA

SOREES > SOREE

SOREHEAD n peevish or disgruntled person

SOREHEADS > SOREHEAD

SOREHON n old Irish feudal right

SOREHONS > SOREHON

SOREL variant of > SORREL

SORELL same as > SORREL

SORELLS > SORELL

SORELS > SOREL

SORELY adv greatly

SORENESS > SORE

SORER > SORE

SORES > SORE

SOREST > SORE

SOREX n shrew or related animal

SOREXES > SOREX

SORGHO same as > SORGO

SORGHOS > SORGHO

SORGHUM n kind of grass cultivated for grain

SORGHUMS > SORGHUM

SORGO n any of several varieties of sorghum that have watery sweet juice

SORGOS > SORGO

SORI > SORUS

SORICINE adj of or resembling a shrew

SORICOID same as > SORICINE

SORING > SORE

SORINGS > SORE

SORITES n polysyllogism in which the premises are arranged so that intermediate conclusions are omitted, being understood, and only the final conclusion is stated

SORITIC > SORITES

SORITICAL > SORITES

SORN vb obtain food, lodging, etc, from another person by presuming on his or her generosity

SORNED > SORN

SORNER > SORN

SORNERS > SORE

SORNING > SORN

SORNINGS > SORN

SORNS > SORN

SOROBAN n Japanese abacus

SOROBANS > SOROBAN

SOROCHE n altitude sickness

SOROCHES > SOROCHE

SORORAL adj of sister

SORORALLY > SORORAL

SORORATE n custom in some societies of a widower marrying his deceased wife's younger sister

SORORATES > SORORATE

SORORIAL same as > SORORAL

SORORISE same as > SORORIZE

SORORISED > SORORISE

SORORISES > SORORISE

SORORITY n society for female students

SORORIZE vb socialize in sisterly way

SORORIZED > SORORIZE

SORORIZES > SORORIZE

SOROSES > SOROSIS

SOROSIS n fleshy multiple fruit

SOROSISES > SOROSIS

SORPTION n process in which one substance takes up or holds another

SORPTIONS > SORPTION

SORPTIVE > SORPTION

SORRA Irish word for > SORROW

SORRAS > SORRA

SORREL n bitter-tasting plant

SORRELS > SORREL

SORRIER > SORRY

SORRIEST > SORRY

SORRILY > SORRY

SORRINESS > SORRY

SORROW n grief or sadness ▷ vb grieve

SORROWED > SORROW

SORROWER > SORROW

SORROWERS > SORROW

SORROWFUL > SORROW

SORROWING > SORROW

SORROWS > SORROW

SORRY adj feeling pity or regret ▷ interj exclamation expressing apology or asking someone to repeat what he or she has said

SORRYISH > SORRY

SORT n group all sharing certain qualities or characteristics ▷ vb arrange according to kind

SORTA adv phonetic representation of 'sort of'

SORTABLE > SORT

SORTABLY > SORT

SORTAL n type of logical or linguistic concept

S

SORTALS > SORTAL

SORTANCE n suitableness

SORTANCES > SORTANCE

SORTATION n act of sorting

SORTED interj exclamation of satisfaction, approval, etc ▷ adj possessing the desired recreational drugs

SORTER > SORT

SORTERS > SORT

SORTES n divination by opening book at random

SORTIE n relatively short return trip ▷ vb make a sortie

SORTIED > SORTIE

SORTIEING > SORTIE

SORTIES > SORTIE

SORTILEGE n act or practice of divination by drawing lots

SORTILEGY same as > SORTILEGE

SORTING > SORT

SORTINGS > SORT

SORTITION n act of casting lots

SORTMENT n assortment

SORTMENTS > SORTMENT

SORTS > SORT

SORUS n cluster of sporangia on the undersurface of certain fern leaves

SOS > SO

SOSATIE n skewer of curried meat pieces

SOSATIES > SOSATIE

SOSS vb make dirty or muddy

SOSSED > SOSS

SOSSES > SOSS

SOSSING > SOSS

SOSSINGS > SOSS

SOSTENUTI > SOSTENUTO

SOSTENUTO adv to be performed in a smooth sustained manner

SOT n habitual drunkard ▷ adv indeed: used to contradict a negative statement ▷ vb be a drunkard

SOTERIAL adj of salvation

SOTH archaic variant of > SOOTH

SOTHS > SOTH

SOTOL n American plant related to agave

SOTOLS > SOTOL

SOTS > SOT

SOTTED > SOT

SOTTEDLY > SOT

SOTTING > SOT

SOTTINGS > SOT

SOTTISH > SOT

SOTTISHLY > SOT

SOTTISIER n collection of jokes

SOU n former French coin

SOUARI n tree of tropical America

SOUARIS > SOUARI

SOUBISE n purée of onions mixed into a thick white sauce and served over eggs, fish, etc

SOUBISES > SOUBISE

SOUBRETTE n minor female role in comedy, often that of a pert maid

SOUCAR n Indian banker

SOUCARS > SOUCAR

SOUCE same as > SOUSE

SOUCED > SOUCE

SOUCES > SOUCE

SOUCHONG n black tea with large leaves

SOUCHONGS > SOUCHONG

SOUCING > SOUCE

SOUCT > SOUCE

SOUDAN obsolete variant of > SULTAN

SOUDANS > SOUDAN

SOUFFLE n light fluffy dish made with beaten egg whites and other ingredients ▷ adj made light and puffy, as by beating and cooking

SOUFFLED > SOUFFLE

SOUFFLEED > SOUFFLE

SOUFFLES > SOUFFLE

SOUGH vb (of the wind) make a sighing sound ▷ n soft continuous murmuring sound

SOUGHED > SOUGH

SOUGHING > SOUGH

SOUGHS > SOUGH

SOUGHT > SEEK

SOUK same as > SOOK

SOUKED > SOUK

SOUKING > SOUK

SOUKOUS n style of African popular music characterized by syncopated rhythms and intricate contrasting guitar melodies

SOUKOUSES > SOUKOUS

SOUKS > SOUK

SOUL n spiritual and immortal part of a human being

SOULDAN same as > SOLDAN

SOULDANS > SOULDAN

SOULDIER same as > SOLDIER

SOULDIERS > SOULDIER

SOULED adj having soul

SOULFUL adj full of emotion

SOULFULLY > SOULFUL

SOULLESS adj lacking human qualities, mechanical

SOULLIKE adj resembling a soul

SOULMATE n person with whom one has most affinity

SOULMATES > SOULMATE

SOULS > SOUL

SOUM vb decide how many animals can graze

particular pasture

SOUMED > SOUM

SOUMING > SOUM

SOUMINGS > SOUM

SOUMS > SOUM

SOUND n something heard, noise ▷ vb make or cause to make a sound ▷ adj in good condition ▷ adv soundly

SOUNDABLE > SOUND

SOUNDBITE n short pithy sentence or phrase extracted from a longer speech

SOUNDBOX n resonating chamber of the hollow body of a violin, guitar, etc

SOUNDCARD n component giving computer sound effects

SOUNDED > SOUND

SOUNDER n electromagnetic device formerly used in telegraphy to convert electric signals into audible sounds

SOUNDERS > SOUNDER

SOUNDEST > SOUND

SOUNDING adj resounding

SOUNDINGS > SOUNDING

SOUNDLESS adj extremely still or silent

SOUNDLY > SOUND

SOUNDMAN n sound recorder in television crew

SOUNDMEN > SOUNDMAN

SOUNDNESS > SOUND

SOUNDPOST n small post on guitars, violins, etc, that joins the front surface to the back and allows the whole body of the instrument to vibrate

SOUNDS > SOUND

SOUP n liquid food made from meat, vegetables, etc ▷ vb give soup to

SOUPCON n small amount

SOUPCONS > SOUPCON

SOUPED > SOUP

SOUPER n person dispensing soup

SOUPERS > SOUPER

SOUPFIN n Pacific requiem shark valued for its fins

SOUPFINS > SOUPFIN

SOUPIER > SOUPY

SOUPIEST > SOUPY

SOUPING > SOUP

SOUPLE same as > SUPPLE

SOUPLED > SOUPLE

SOUPLES > SOUPLE

SOUPLESS > SOUP

SOUPLIKE > SOUP

SOUPLING > SOUPLE

SOUPS > SOUP

SOUPSPOON n spoon for eating soup

SOUPY adj having the appearance or consistency of soup

SOUR adj sharp-tasting ▷ vb make or become sour

SOURBALL n tart-flavoured boiled sweet

SOURBALLS > SOURBALL

SOURCE n origin or starting point ▷ vb establish a supplier of (a product, etc)

SOURCED > SOURCE

SOURCEFUL adj offering useful things

SOURCES > SOURCE

SOURCING > SOURCE

SOURCINGS > SOURCE

SOURDINE n soft stop on an organ or harmonium

SOURDINES > SOURDINE

SOURDOUGH adj (of bread) made with fermented dough used as a leaven ▷ n (in Western US, Canada, and Alaska) an old-time prospector or pioneer

SOURED > SOUR

SOURER > SOUR

SOUREST > SOUR

SOURING > SOUR

SOURINGS > SOUR

SOURISH > SOUR

SOURISHLY > SOUR

SOURLY > SOUR

SOURNESS > SOUR

SOUROCK n Scots word for sorrel plant

SOUROCKS > SOUROCK

SOURPUSS n person who is always gloomy, pessimistic, or bitter

SOURS > SOUR

SOURSE same as > SOURCE

SOURSES > SOURSE

SOURSOP n small West Indian tree

SOURSOPS > SOURSOP

SOURVELD n grazing field with long coarse grass

SOURVELDS > SOURVELD

SOURWOOD n sorrel tree

SOURWOODS > SOURWOOD

SOUS > SOU

SOUSE vb plunge (something) into liquid ▷ n liquid used in pickling

SOUSED > SOUSE

SOUSES > SOUSE

SOUSING > SOUSE

SOUSINGS > SOUSE

SOUSLIK same as > SUSLIK

SOUSLIKS > SOUSLIK

SOUT same as > SOOT

SOUTACHE n narrow braid used as a decorative trimming

SOUTACHES > SOUTACHE

SOUTANE n Roman Catholic priest's cassock

SOUTANES > SOUTANE

SOUTAR same as > SOUTER

SOUTARS > SOUTAR

SOUTENEUR n pimp

SOUTER n shoemaker or cobbler

SOUTERLY > SOUTER

SOUTERS > SOUTER

SOUTH n direction towards the South Pole, opposite north ▷ adj or in the south

▷ *adv* in, to, or towards the south ▷ *vb* turn south

SOUTHEAST *adv* (in or to) direction between south and east ▷ *n* point of the compass or the direction midway between south and east ▷ *adj* of or denoting the southeastern part of a specified country, area, etc

SOUTHED > SOUTH

SOUTHER *n* strong wind or storm from the south ▷ *vb* turn south

SOUTHERED > SOUTHER

SOUTHERLY *adj* of or in the south ▷ *adv* towards the south ▷ *n* wind from the south

SOUTHERN *adj* situated in or towards the south ▷ *n* southerner

SOUTHERNS > SOUTHERN

SOUTHERS > SOUTHER

SOUTHING *n* movement, deviation, or distance covered in a southerly direction

SOUTHINGS > SOUTHING

SOUTHLAND *n* southern part of country

SOUTHMOST *adj* situated or occurring farthest south

SOUTHPAW *n* left-handed person, esp a boxer ▷ *adj* left-handed

SOUTHPAWS > SOUTHPAW

SOUTHRON *n* southerner

SOUTHRONS > SOUTHRON

SOUTHS > SOUTH

SOUTHSAID > SOUTHSAY

SOUTHSAY *same as* > SOOTHSAY

SOUTHSAYS > SOUTHSAY

SOUTHWARD *adv* towards the south

SOUTHWEST *adv* (in or to) direction between south and west ▷ *n* point of the compass or the direction midway between west and south ▷ *adj* of or denoting the southwestern part of a specified country, area, etc

SOUTIE *same as* > SOUTPIEL

SOUTIES > SOUTIE

SOUTPIEL *n* South African derogatory slang for an English-speaking South African

SOUTPIELS > SOUTPIEL

SOUTS > SOUT

SOUVENIR *n* keepsake, memento ▷ *vb* steal or keep (something, esp a small article) for one's own use

SOUVENIRS > SOUVENIR

SOUVLAKI *same as* > SOUVLAKIA

SOUVLAKIA *n* Greek dish of kebabs, esp made with lamb

SOUVLAKIS > SOUVLAKI

SOV *shortening of* > SOVEREIGN

SOVENANCE *n* memory

SOVEREIGN *n* king or queen ▷ *adj* (of a state) independent

SOVIET *n* formerly, elected council at various levels of government in the USSR ▷ *adj* of the former USSR

SOVIETIC > SOVIET

SOVIETISE *same as* > SOVIETIZE

SOVIETISM *n* principle or practice of government through soviets

SOVIETIST > SOVIETISM

SOVIETIZE *vb* bring (a country, person, etc) under Soviet control or influence

SOVIETS > SOVIET

SOVKHOZ *n* (in the former Soviet Union) a large mechanized farm owned by the state

SOVKHOZES > SOVKHOZ

SOVKHOZY > SOVKHOZ

SOVRAN *literary word for* > SOVEREIGN

SOVRANLY > SOVRAN

SOVRANS > SOVRAN

SOVRANTY > SOVRAN

SOVS > SOV

SOW *vb* scatter or plant (seed) in or on (the ground) ▷ *n* female adult pig

SOWABLE > SOW

SOWANS *same as* > SOWENS

SOWAR *n* Indian cavalryman

SOWARREE *n* Indian mounted escort

SOWARREES > SOWARREE

SOWARRIES > SOWARRY

SOWARRY *same as* > SOWARREE

SOWARS > SOWAR

SOWBACK *another name for* > HOGBACK

SOWBACKS > SOWBACK

SOWBELLY *n* salt pork from pig's belly

SOWBREAD *n* S European primulaceous plant

SOWBREADS > SOWBREAD

SOWCAR *same as* > SOUCAR

SOWCARS > SOWCAR

SOWCE *same as* > SOUSE

SOWCED > SOWCE

SOWCES > SOWCE

SOWCING > SOWCE

SOWDER *same as* > SAWDER

SOWDERS > SOWDER

SOWED > SOW

SOWENS *n* pudding made from oatmeal husks steeped and boiled

SOWER > SOW

SOWERS > SOW

SOWF *same as* > SOWTH

SOWFED > SOWF

SOWFF *same as* > SOWTH

SOWFFED > SOWFF

SOWFFING > SOWFF

SOWFFS > SOWFF

SOWFING > SOWF

SOWFS > SOWF

SOWING > SOW

SOWINGS > SOW

SOWL *same as* > SOLE

SOWLE *same as* > SOLE

SOWLED > SOWL

SOWLES > SOWLE

SOWLING > SOWL

SOWLS > SOWL

SOWM *same as* > SOUM

SOWMED > SOWM

SOWMING > SOWM

SOWMS > SOWM

SOWN > SOW

SOWND *vb* wield

SOWNDED > SOWND

SOWNDING > SOWND

SOWNDS > SOWND

SOWNE *same as* > SOUND

SOWNES > SOWNE

SOWP *n* spoonful

SOWPS > SOWP

SOWS > SOW

SOWSE *same as* > SOUSE

SOWSED > SOWSE

SOWSES > SOWSE

SOWSING > SOWSE

SOWSSE *same as* > SOUSE

SOWSSED > SOWSSE

SOWSSES > SOWSSE

SOWSSING > SOWSSE

SOWTER *same as* > SOUTER

SOWTERS > SOWTER

SOWTH *vb* Scots word meaning whistle

SOWTHED > SOWTH

SOWTHING > SOWTH

SOWTHS > SOWTH

SOX *npl* informal spelling of 'socks'

SOY as in *soy sauce* salty dark brown sauce made from soya beans, used in Chinese and Japanese cookery

SOYA *n* plant whose edible bean is used for food and as a source of oil

SOYAS > SOYA

SOYBEAN *n* soya bean

SOYBEANS > SOYBEAN

SOYLE *n* body

SOYLES > SOYLE

SOYMILK *n* milk substitute made from soya

SOYMILKS > SOYMILK

SOYS > SOY

SOYUZ *n* Russian spacecraft used to ferry crew to and from space stations

SOYUZES > SOYUZ

SOZ *interj* (slang) sorry

SOZIN *n* form of protein

SOZINE *same as* > SOZIN

SOZINES > SOZINE

SOZINS > SOZIN

SOZZLE *vb* make wet

SOZZLED *adj* drunk

SOZZLES > SOZZLE

SOZZLIER > SOZZLY

SOZZLIEST > SOZZLY

SOZZLING > SOZZLE

SOZZLY *adj* wet

SPA *n* resort with a mineral-water spring ▷ *vb* visit a spa

SPACE *n* unlimited expanse in which all objects exist and move ▷ *vb* place at intervals

SPACEBAND *n* device on a linecaster for evening up the spaces between words

SPACED > SPACE

SPACELAB *n* laboratory in space where scientific experiments are performed

SPACELABS > SPACELAB

SPACELESS *adj* having no limits in space

SPACEMAN *n* person who travels in space

SPACEMEN > SPACEMAN

SPACEPORT *n* base equipped to launch, maintain, and test spacecraft

SPACER *n* piece of material used to create or maintain a space between two things

SPACERS > SPACER

SPACES > SPACE

SPACESHIP *n* (in science fiction) a spacecraft used for travel between planets and galaxies

SPACESUIT *n* sealed pressurized suit worn by an astronaut

SPACEWALK *n* instance of floating and manoeuvring in space, outside but attached by a lifeline to a spacecraft ▷ *vb* float and manoeuvre in space while outside but attached to a spacecraft

SPACEWARD *adv* into space

SPACEY *adj* vague and dreamy, as if under the influence of drugs

SPACIAL *same as* > SPATIAL

SPACIALLY > SPACIAL

SPACIER > SPACEY

SPACIEST > SPACEY

SPACINESS > SPACEY

SPACING *n* arrangement of letters, words, etc, on a page in order to achieve legibility

SPACINGS > SPACING

SPACIOUS *adj* having a large capacity or area

SPACKLE *vb* fill holes in plaster

SPACKLED > SPACKLE

SPACKLES > SPACKLE

SPACKLING > SPACKLE

SPACY *same as* > SPACEY

SPADASSIN *n* swordsman

SPADE *n* tool for digging

SPADED > SPADE

SPADEFISH *n* type of spiny-finned food fish
SPADEFUL *n* amount spade will hold
SPADEFULS > SPADEFUL
SPADELIKE > SPADE
SPADEMAN *n* man who works with spade
SPADEMEN > SPADEMAN
SPADER > SPADE
SPADERS > SPADE
SPADES > SPADE
SPADESMAN *same as* **>** SPADEMAN
SPADESMEN > SPADEMAN
SPADEWORK *n* hard preparatory work
SPADGER *n* sparrow
SPADGERS > SPADGER
SPADICES > SPADIX
SPADILLE *n* (in ombre and quadrille) the ace of spades
SPADILLES > SPADILLE
SPADILLIO *same as* **>** SPADILLE
SPADILLO *same as* **>** SPADILLE
SPADILLOS > SPADILLO
SPADING > SPADE
SPADIX *n* spike of small flowers on a fleshy stem
SPADIXES > SPADIX
SPADO *n* neutered animal
SPADOES > SPADO
SPADONES > SPADO
SPADOS > SPADO
SPADROON *n* type of sword
SPADROONS > SPADROON
SPAE *vb* foretell (the future)
SPAED > SPAE
SPAEING > SPAE
SPAEINGS > SPAE
SPAEMAN *n* man who foretells future
SPAEMEN > SPAEMAN
SPAER > SPAE
SPAERS > SPAE
SPAES > SPAE
SPAETZLE *n* German noodle dish
SPAETZLES > SPAETZLE
SPAEWIFE *n* woman who can supposedly foretell the future
SPAEWIVES > SPAEWIFE
SPAG *vb* (of a cat) to scratch (a person) with the claws **▷** *n* Australian offensive slang for an Italian
SPAGERIC *same as* **>** SPAGYRIC
SPAGGED > SPAG
SPAGGING > SPAG
SPAGHETTI *n* pasta in the form of long strings
SPAGIRIC *same as* **>** SPAGYRIC
SPAGS > SPAG
SPAGYRIC *adj* of or relating to alchemy **▷** *n* alchemist
SPAGYRICS > SPAGYRIC
SPAGYRIST > SPAGYRIC
SPAHEE *same as* **>** SPAHI

SPAHEES > SPAHEE
SPAHI *n* (formerly) an irregular cavalryman in the Turkish armed forces
SPAHIS > SPAHI
SPAIL *Scots word for* **>** SPALL
SPAILS > SPAIL
SPAIN *variant of* **>** SPANE
SPAINED > SPAIN
SPAING > SPA
SPAINGS > SPA
SPAINING > SPAIN
SPAINS > SPAIN
SPAIRGE *Scots word for* **>** SPARGE
SPAIRGED > SPAIRGE
SPAIRGES > SPAIRGE
SPAIRGING > SPAIRGE
SPAIT *same as* **>** SPATE
SPAITS > SPAIT
SPAKE *past tense of* **>** SPEAK
SPALD *same as* **>** SPAULD
SPALDEEN *n* ball used in street game
SPALDEENS > SPALDEEN
SPALDS > SPALD
SPALE *Scots word for* **>** SPALL
SPALES > SPALE
SPALL *n* splinter or chip of ore, rock, or stone **▷** *vb* split or cause to split into such fragments
SPALLABLE > SPALL
SPALLE *same as* **>** SPAULD
SPALLED > SPALL
SPALLER > SPALL
SPALLERS > SPALL
SPALLES > SPALLE
SPALLING > SPALL
SPALLINGS > SPALL
SPALLS > SPALL
SPALPEEN *n* itinerant seasonal labourer
SPALPEENS > SPALPEEN
SPALT *vb* split
SPALTED > SPALT
SPALTING > SPALT
SPALTS > SPALT
SPAM *vb* send unsolicited e-mail simultaneously to a number of newsgroups on the internet **▷** *n* unsolicited electronic mail or text messages sent in this way
SPAMBOT *n* computer programme that identifies email addresses to send spam to
SPAMBOTS > SPAMBOT
SPAMMED > SPAM
SPAMMER > SPAM
SPAMMERS > SPAM
SPAMMIE *n* love bite
SPAMMIER > SPAMMY
SPAMMIES > SPAMMIE
SPAMMIEST > SPAMMY
SPAMMING > SPAM
SPAMMINGS > SPAM
SPAMMY *adj* bland
SPAMS > SPAM
SPAN *n* space between two points **▷** *vb* stretch or

extend across
SPANAEMIA *n* lack of red corpuscles in blood
SPANAEMIC **>** SPANAEMIA
SPANCEL *n* length of rope for hobbling an animal, esp a horse or cow **▷** *vb* hobble (an animal) with a loose rope
SPANCELED > SPANCEL
SPANCELS > SPANCEL
SPANDEX *n* type of synthetic stretch fabric made from polyurethane fibre
SPANDEXES > SPANDEX
SPANDREL *n* triangular surface bounded by the outer curve of an arch and the adjacent wall
SPANDRELS > SPANDREL
SPANDRIL *same as* **>** SPANDREL
SPANDRILS > SPANDRIL
SPANE *vb* Scots word meaning wean
SPANED > SPANE
SPANES > SPANE
SPANG *adv* exactly, firmly, or straight **▷** *vb* dash
SPANGED > SPANG
SPANGHEW *vb* throw in air
SPANGHEWS > SPANGHEW
SPANGING > SPANG
SPANGLE *n* small shiny metallic ornament **▷** *vb* decorate with spangles
SPANGLED > SPANGLE
SPANGLER > SPANGLE
SPANGLERS > SPANGLE
SPANGLES > SPANGLE
SPANGLET *n* little spangle
SPANGLETS > SPANGLET
SPANGLIER > SPANGLE
SPANGLING > SPANGLE
SPANGLY > SPANGLE
SPANGS > SPANG
SPANIEL *n* dog with long ears and silky hair
SPANIELS > SPANIEL
SPANING > SPANE
SPANK *vb* slap with the open hand, on the buttocks or legs **▷** *n* such a slap
SPANKED > SPANK
SPANKER *n* fore-and-aft sail or a mast that is aftermost in a sailing vessel
SPANKERS > SPANKER
SPANKING *adj* outstandingly fine or smart **▷** *n* series of spanks, usually as a punishment for children
SPANKINGS > SPANKING
SPANKS > SPANK
SPANLESS *adj* impossible to span
SPANNED > SPAN
SPANNER *n* tool for gripping and turning a nut or bolt
SPANNERS > SPANNER
SPANNING > SPAN

SPANS > SPAN
SPANSPEK *n* cantaloupe melon
SPANSPEKS > SPANSPEK
SPANSULE *n* modified-release capsule of a drug
SPANSULES > SPANSULE
SPANWORM *n* larva of a type of moth
SPANWORMS > SPANWORM
SPAR *n* pole used as a ship's mast, boom, or yard **▷** *vb* box or fight using light blows for practice
SPARABLE *n* small nail with no head, used for fixing the soles and heels of shoes
SPARABLES > SPARABLE
SPARAXIS *n* type of plant with dainty spikes of star-shaped purple, red, or orange flowers
SPARD > SPARE
SPARE *adj* extra **▷** *n* duplicate kept in case of damage or loss **▷** *vb* refrain from punishing or harming
SPAREABLE > SPARE
SPARED > SPARE
SPARELESS *adj* merciless
SPARELY > SPARE
SPARENESS > SPARE
SPARER > SPARE
SPARERIB *n* cut of pork ribs with most of the meat trimmed off
SPARERIBS > SPARERIB
SPARERS > SPARE
SPARES > SPARE
SPAREST > SPARE
SPARGE *vb* sprinkle or scatter (something)
SPARGED > SPARGE
SPARGER > SPARGE
SPARGERS > SPARGE
SPARGES > SPARGE
SPARGING > SPARGE
SPARID *n* type of marine percoid fish **▷** *adj* of or belonging to this family of fish
SPARIDS > SPARID
SPARING *adj* economical
SPARINGLY > SPARING
SPARK *n* fiery particle thrown out from a fire or caused by friction **▷** *vb* give off sparks
SPARKE *n* weapon
SPARKED > SPARK
SPARKER > SPARK
SPARKERS > SPARKE
SPARKIE *n* electrician
SPARKIER > SPARKY
SPARKIES > SPARKIE
SPARKIEST > SPARKY
SPARKILY > SPARKY
SPARKING > SPARK
SPARKISH > SPARK
SPARKLE *vb* glitter with many points of light **▷** *n* sparkling points of light

SPARKLED > SPARKLE
SPARKLER n hand-held firework that emits sparks
SPARKLERS > SPARKLER
SPARKLES > SPARKLE
SPARKLESS > SPARK
SPARKLET n little spark
SPARKLETS > SPARKLET
SPARKLIER > SPARKLY
SPARKLIES > SPARKLY
SPARKLING adj (of wine or mineral water) slightly fizzy
SPARKLY adj sparkling ▷ n sparkling thing
SPARKPLUG n device in an engine that ignites the fuel
SPARKS n electrician
SPARKY adj lively
SPARLIKE > SPAR
SPARLING n European smelt
SPARLINGS > SPARLING
SPAROID same as > SPARID
SPAROIDS > SPAROID
SPARRE same as > SPAR
SPARRED > SPAR
SPARRER > SPAR
SPARRERS > SPAR
SPARRES > SPARRE
SPARRIER > SPARRY
SPARRIEST > SPARRY
SPARRING > SPAR
SPARRINGS > SPAR
SPARROW n small brownish bird
SPARROWS > SPARROW
SPARRY adj (of minerals) containing, relating to, or resembling spar
SPARS > SPAR
SPARSE adj thinly scattered
SPARSEDLY > SPARSE
SPARSELY > SPARSE
SPARSER > SPARSE
SPARSEST > SPARSE
SPARSITY > SPARSE
SPART n esparto
SPARTAN adj strict and austere ▷ n disciplined or brave person
SPARTANS > SPARTAN
SPARTEINE n viscous oily alkaloid extracted from the broom plant and lupin seeds
SPARTERIE n things made from esparto
SPARTH n type of battle-axe
SPARTHE same as > SPARTH
SPARTHES > SPARTHE
SPARTHS > SPARTH
SPARTICLE n hypothetical elementary particle thought to have been produced in the Big Bang
SPARTINA n grass growing in salt marshes
SPARTINAS > SPARTINA
SPARTS > SPART

SPAS > SPA
SPASM n involuntary muscular contraction ▷ vb go into spasm
SPASMATIC > SPASM
SPASMED > SPASM
SPASMIC > SPASM
SPASMING > SPASM
SPASMODIC adj occurring in spasms
SPASMS > SPASM
SPASTIC n offensive slang for a person with cerebral palsy ▷ adj suffering from cerebral palsy
SPASTICS > SPASTIC
SPAT vb have a quarrel
SPATE n large number of things happening within a period of time
SPATES > SPATE
SPATFALL n mass of larvae on sea bed
SPATFALLS > SPATFALL
SPATHAL > SPATHE
SPATHE n large sheathlike leaf enclosing a flower cluster
SPATHED > SPATHE
SPATHES > SPATHE
SPATHIC adj (of minerals) resembling spar, esp in having good cleavage
SPATHOSE same as > SPATHIC
SPATIAL adj of or in space
SPATIALLY > SPATIAL
SPATLESE n type of German wine, usu white
SPATLESEN > SPATLESE
SPATLESES > SPATLESE
SPATS > SPAT
SPATTED > SPAT
SPATTEE n type of gaiter
SPATTEES > SPATTEE
SPATTER vb scatter or be scattered in drops over (something) ▷ n spattering sound
SPATTERED > SPATTER
SPATTERS > SPATTER
SPATTING > SPIT
SPATULA n utensil with a broad flat blade for spreading or stirring
SPATULAR > SPATULA
SPATULAS > SPATULA
SPATULATE adj shaped like a spatula
SPATULE n spatula
SPATULES > SPATULE
SPATZLE same as > SPAETZLE
SPATZLES > SPATZLE
SPAUL same as > SPAULD
SPAULD n shoulder
SPAULDS > SPAULD
SPAULS > SPAUL
SPAVIE Scots variant of > SPAVIN
SPAVIES > SPAVIE
SPAVIET adj Scots word meaning spavined
SPAVIN n enlargement of

the hock of a horse by a bony growth
SPAVINED adj affected with spavin
SPAVINS > SPAVIN
SPAW same as > SPA
SPAWL vb spit
SPAWLED > SPAWL
SPAWLING > SPAWL
SPAWLS > SPAWL
SPAWN n jelly-like mass of eggs of fish, frogs, or molluscs ▷ vb (of fish, frogs, or molluscs) lay eggs
SPAWNED > SPAWN
SPAWNER > SPAWN
SPAWNERS > SPAWN
SPAWNIER > SPAWNY
SPAWNIEST > SPAWNY
SPAWNING > SPAWN
SPAWNINGS > SPAWN
SPAWNS > SPAWN
SPAWNY adj like spawn
SPAWS > SPAW
SPAY vb remove the ovaries from (a female animal)
SPAYAD n male deer
SPAYADS > SPAYAD
SPAYD same as > SPAYAD
SPAYDS > SPAYD
SPAYED > SPAY
SPAYING > SPAY
SPAYS > SPAY
SPAZ vb offensive slang meaning lose self-control
SPAZA as in spaza shop South African slang for a small shop in a township
SPAZZ same as > SPAZ
SPAZZED > SPAZ
SPAZZES > SPAZ
SPAZZING > SPAZ
SPEAK vb say words, talk
SPEAKABLE > SPEAK
SPEAKEASY n place where alcoholic drink was sold illegally during Prohibition
SPEAKER n person who speaks, esp at a formal occasion
SPEAKERS > SPEAKER
SPEAKING > SPEAK
SPEAKINGS > SPEAK
SPEAKOUT n firm or brave statement of one's beliefs
SPEAKOUTS > SPEAKOUT
SPEAKS > SPEAK
SPEAL same as > SPULE
SPEALS > SPEAL
SPEAN same as > SPANE
SPEANED > SPEAN
SPEANING > SPEAN
SPEANS > SPEAN
SPEAR n weapon consisting of a long shaft with a sharp point ▷ vb pierce with or as if with a spear
SPEARED > SPEAR
SPEARER > SPEAR
SPEARERS > SPEAR
SPEARFISH another name for > MARLIN
SPEARGUN n device for

shooting spears underwater
SPEARGUNS > SPEARGUN
SPEARHEAD vb lead (an attack or campaign) ▷ n leading force in an attack or campaign
SPEARIER > SPEAR
SPEARIEST > SPEAR
SPEARING > SPEAR
SPEARLIKE > SPEAR
SPEARMAN n soldier armed with a spear
SPEARMEN > SPEARMAN
SPEARMINT n type of mint
SPEARS > SPEAR
SPEARWORT n any of several Eurasian ranunculaceous plants
SPEARY > SPEAR
SPEAT same as > SPATE
SPEATS > SPEAT
SPEC vb set specifications
SPECCED > SPEC
SPECCIES > SPECCY
SPECCING > SPEC
SPECCY n person wearing spectacles
SPECIAL adj distinguished from others of its kind ▷ n product, programme, etc which is only available at a certain time ▷ vb advertise and sell (an item) at a reduced price
SPECIALER > SPECIAL
SPECIALLY > SPECIAL
SPECIALS > SPECIAL
SPECIALTY n special interest or skill
SPECIATE vb form or develop into a new biological species
SPECIATED > SPECIATE
SPECIATES > SPECIATE
SPECIE n coins as distinct from paper money
SPECIES n group of plants or animals that are related closely enough to interbreed naturally
SPECIFIC adj particular, definite ▷ n drug used to treat a particular disease
SPECIFICS > SPECIFIC
SPECIFIED > SPECIFY
SPECIFIER > SPECIFY
SPECIFIES > SPECIFY
SPECIFY vb refer to or state specifically
SPECIMEN n individual or part typifying a whole
SPECIMENS > SPECIMEN
SPECIOUS adj apparently true, but actually false
SPECK n small spot or particle ▷ vb mark with specks or spots
SPECKED > SPECK
SPECKIER > SPECKY
SPECKIEST > SPECKY
SPECKING > SPECK
SPECKLE n small spot ▷ vb mark with speckles
SPECKLED > SPECKLE

S

SPECKLES > SPECKLE
SPECKLESS > SPECK
SPECKLING > SPECKLE
SPECKS > SPECK
SPECKY same as > SPECCY
SPECS npl spectacles
SPECTACLE n strange, interesting, or ridiculous sight
SPECTATE vb watch
SPECTATED > SPECTATE
SPECTATES > SPECTATE
SPECTATOR n person viewing anything, onlooker
SPECTER same as > SPECTRE
SPECTERS > SPECTER
SPECTRA > SPECTRUM
SPECTRAL adj of or like a spectre
SPECTRE n ghost
SPECTRES > SPECTRE
SPECTRIN n any one of a class of fibrous proteins found in the membranes of red blood cells
SPECTRINS > SPECTRIN
SPECTRUM n range of different colours, radio waves, etc in order of their wavelengths
SPECTRUMS > SPECTRUM
SPECULA > SPECULUM
SPECULAR adj of, relating to, or having the properties of a mirror
SPECULATE vb guess, conjecture
SPECULUM n medical instrument for examining body cavities
SPECULUMS > SPECULUM
SPED > SPEED
SPEECH n act, power, or manner of speaking ▷ vb make a speech
SPEECHED > SPEECH
SPEECHES > SPEECH
SPEECHFUL > SPEECH
SPEECHIFY vb make speeches, esp boringly
SPEECHING > SPEECH
SPEED n swiftness ▷ vb go quickly
SPEEDBALL n mixture of heroin with amphetamine or cocaine
SPEEDBOAT n light fast motorboat
SPEEDED > SPEED
SPEEDER > SPEED
SPEEDERS > SPEED
SPEEDFUL > SPEED
SPEEDIER > SPEEDY
SPEEDIEST > SPEEDY
SPEEDILY > SPEEDY
SPEEDING > SPEED
SPEEDINGS > SPEED
SPEEDLESS > SPEED
SPEEDO n speedometer
SPEEDOS > SPEEDO
SPEEDREAD vb read very quickly
SPEEDS > SPEED

SPEEDSTER n fast car, esp a sports model
SPEEDUP n acceleration
SPEEDUPS > SPEEDUP
SPEEDWAY n track for motorcycle racing
SPEEDWAYS > SPEEDWAY
SPEEDWELL n plant with small blue flowers
SPEEDY adj prompt
SPEEL n splinter of wood ▷ vb Scots word meaning climb
SPEELED > SPEEL
SPEELER > SPEEL
SPEELERS > SPEEL
SPEELING > SPEEL
SPEELS > SPEEL
SPEER same as > SPEIR
SPEERED > SPEER
SPEERING > SPEER
SPEERINGS > SPEER
SPEERS > SPEER
SPEIL dialect word for > CLIMB
SPEILED > SPEIL
SPEILING > SPEIL
SPEILS > SPEIL
SPEIR vb ask
SPEIRED > SPEIR
SPEIRING > SPEIR
SPEIRINGS > SPEIR
SPEIRS > SPEIR
SPEISE same as > SPEISS
SPEISES > SPEISE
SPEISS n arsenides and antimonides that form when ores containing arsenic or antimony are smelted
SPEISSES > SPEISS
SPEK n bacon, fat, or fatty pork used for larding venison or other game
SPEKBOOM n South African shrub
SPEKBOOMS > SPEKBOOM
SPEKS > SPEK
SPELAEAN adj of, found in, or inhabiting caves
SPELD vb Scots word meaning spread
SPELDED > SPELD
SPELDER same as > SPELD
SPELDERED > SPELDER
SPELDERS > SPELDER
SPELDIN n fish split and dried
SPELDING same as > SPELDIN
SPELDINGS > SPELDING
SPELDINS > SPELDIN
SPELDRIN same as > SPELDIN
SPELDRING same as > SPELDIN
SPELDRINS > SPELDRIN
SPELDS > SPELD
SPELEAN same as > SPELAEAN
SPELK n splinter of wood
SPELKS > SPELK
SPELL vb give in correct order the letters that form

(a word) ▷ n formula of words supposed to have magic power
SPELLABLE > SPELL
SPELLBIND vb cause to be spellbound
SPELLDOWN n spelling competition
SPELLED > SPELL
SPELLER n person who spells words in the manner specified
SPELLERS > SPELLER
SPELLFUL adj magical
SPELLICAN same as > SPILLIKIN
SPELLING > SPELL
SPELLINGS > SPELL
SPELLS > SPELL
SPELT > SPELL
SPELTER n impure zinc, usually containing about 3 per cent of lead and other impurities
SPELTERS > SPELTER
SPELTS > SPELL
SPELTZ n wheat variety
SPELTZES > SPELTZ
SPELUNK vb explore caves
SPELUNKED > SPELUNK
SPELUNKER n person whose hobby is the exploration and study of caves
SPELUNKS > SPELUNK
SPENCE n larder or pantry
SPENCER n short fitted coat or jacket
SPENCERS > SPENCER
SPENCES > SPENCE
SPEND vb pay out (money)
SPENDABLE > SPEND
SPENDALL n spendthrift
SPENDALLS > SPENDALL
SPENDER n person who spends money in a manner specified
SPENDERS > SPENDER
SPENDIER > SPENDY
SPENDIEST > SPENDY
SPENDING > SPEND
SPENDINGS > SPEND
SPENDS > SPEND
SPENDY adj expensive
SPENSE same as > SPENCE
SPENSES > SPENSE
SPENT > SPEND
SPEOS n (esp in ancient Egypt) a temple or tomb cut into a rock face
SPEOSES > SPEOS
SPERLING same as > SPARLING
SPERLINGS > SPERLING
SPERM n male reproductive cell released in semen during ejaculation
SPERMARIA npl spermaries
SPERMARY n any organ in which spermatozoa are produced, esp a testis
SPERMATIA npl male reproductive cells in red

algae and some fungi
SPERMATIC adj of or relating to spermatozoa
SPERMATID n any of four immature male gametes that are formed from a spermatocyte
SPERMIC same as > SPERMATIC
SPERMINE n colourless basic water-soluble amine that is found in semen, sputum, and animal tissues
SPERMINES > SPERMINE
SPERMOUS same as > SPERMATIC
SPERMS > SPERM
SPERRE vb bolt
SPERRED > SPERRE
SPERRES > SPERRE
SPERRING > SPERRE
SPERSE vb disperse
SPERSED > SPERSE
SPERSES > SPERSE
SPERSING > SPERSE
SPERST > SPERSE
SPERTHE same as > SPARTH
SPERTHES > SPERTHE
SPET same as > SPIT
SPETCH n piece of animal skin
SPETCHES > SPETCH
SPETS > SPET
SPETSNAZ n Soviet intelligence force
SPETTING > SPET
SPETZNAZ same as > SPETSNAZ
SPEUG n sparrow
SPEUGS > SPEUG
SPEW vb vomit ▷ n something ejected from the mouth
SPEWED > SPEW
SPEWER > SPEW
SPEWERS > SPEW
SPEWIER > SPEWY
SPEWIEST > SPEWY
SPEWINESS > SPEWY
SPEWING > SPEW
SPEWS > SPEW
SPEWY adj marshy
SPHACELUS n death of living tissue
SPHAER same as > SPHERE
SPHAERE same as > SPHERE
SPHAERES > SPHAERE
SPHAERITE n aluminium phosphate
SPHAERS > SPHAERE
SPHAGNOUS > SPHAGNUM
SPHAGNUM n moss found in bogs
SPHAGNUMS > SPHAGNUM
SPHAIREE n game resembling tennis played with wooden bats and a perforated plastic ball
SPHAIREES > SPHAIREE
SPHEAR same as > SPHERE
SPHEARE same as > SPHERE

SPHEARES > SPHEARE

SPHEARS > SPHEAR

SPHENDONE n ancient Greek headband

SPHENE n brown, yellow, green, or grey lustrous mineral

SPHENES > SPHENE

SPHENIC adj having the shape of a wedge

SPHENODON technical name for the > TUATARA

SPHENOID adj wedge-shaped ▷ n wedge-shaped thing

SPHENOIDS > SPHENOID

SPHERAL adj of or shaped like a sphere

SPHERE n perfectly round solid object ▷ vb surround or encircle

SPHERED > SPHERE

SPHERES > SPHERE

SPHERIC same as > SPHERICAL

SPHERICAL adj shaped like a sphere

SPHERICS n geometry and trigonometry of figures on the surface of a sphere

SPHERIER > SPHERY

SPHERIEST > SPHERY

SPHERING > SPHERE

SPHEROID n solid figure that is almost but not exactly a sphere

SPHEROIDS > SPHEROID

SPHERULAR > SPHERULE

SPHERULE n very small sphere or globule

SPHERULES > SPHERULE

SPHERY adj resembling a sphere

SPHINCTER n ring of muscle which controls the opening and closing of a hollow organ

SPHINGES > SPHINX

SPHINGID n hawk moth

SPHINGIDS > SPHINGID

SPHINX n one of the huge statues built by the ancient Egyptians, with the body of a lion and the head of a man

SPHINXES > SPHINX

SPHYGMIC adj of or relating to the pulse

SPHYGMOID adj resembling the pulse

SPHYGMUS n person's pulse

SPHYNX n breed of cat

SPHYNXES > SPHYNX

SPIAL n observation

SPIALS > SPIAL

SPIC n derogatory word for a Spanish-speaking person

SPICA n spiral bandage formed by a series of overlapping figure-of-eight turns

SPICAE > SPICA

SPICAS > SPICA

SPICATE adj having,

arranged in, or relating to spikes

SPICATED same as > SPICATE

SPICCATO n style of playing a bowed stringed instrument in which the bow bounces lightly off the strings ▷ adv be played in this manner

SPICCATOS > SPICCATO

SPICE n aromatic substance used as flavouring ▷ vb flavour with spices

SPICEBUSH n North American lauraceous shrub

SPICED > SPICE

SPICELESS > SPICE

SPICER > SPICE

SPICERIES > SPICERY

SPICERS > SPICE

SPICERY n spices collectively

SPICES > SPICE

SPICEY same as > SPICY

SPICIER > SPICY

SPICIEST > SPICY

SPICILEGE n anthology

SPICILY > SPICY

SPICINESS > SPICY

SPICING > SPICE

SPICK adj neat and clean ▷ n spic

SPICKER > SPICK

SPICKEST > SPICK

SPICKNEL same as > SPIGNEL

SPICKNELS > SPICKNEL

SPICKS > SPICK

SPICS > SPIC

SPICULA > SPICULUM

SPICULAE > SPICULUM

SPICULAR > SPICULUM

SPICULATE > SPICULE

SPICULE n small slender pointed structure or crystal

SPICULES > SPICULE

SPICULUM same as > SPICULE

SPICY adj flavoured with spices

SPIDE n Irish derogatory slang for a young working-class man who dresses in casual sports clothes

SPIDER n small eight-legged creature which spins a web to catch insects for food

SPIDERIER > SPIDERY

SPIDERISH > SPIDER

SPIDERMAN n person who erects the steel structure of a building

SPIDERMEN > SPIDERMAN

SPIDERS > SPIDER

SPIDERWEB n spider's web

SPIDERY adj thin and angular like a spider's legs

SPIDES > SPIDE

SPIE same as > SPY

SPIED > SPY

SPIEGEL n manganese-rich pig iron

SPIEGELS > SPIEGEL

SPIEL n speech made to persuade someone to do something ▷ vb deliver a prepared spiel

SPIELED > SPIEL

SPIELER > SPIEL

SPIELERS > SPIEL

SPIELING > SPIEL

SPIELS > SPIEL

SPIER variant of > SPEIR

SPIERED > SPIER

SPIERING > SPIER

SPIERS > SPIER

SPIES > SPY

SPIF n postage stamp perforated with the initials of a firm to avoid theft by employees

SPIFFED > SPIFF

SPIFF vb make smart

SPIFFIED > SPIFFY

SPIFFIER > SPIFFY

SPIFFIES > SPIFFY

SPIFFIEST > SPIFFY

SPIFFILY > SPIFFY

SPIFFING adj excellent

SPIFFS > SPIFF

SPIFFY adj smart ▷ n smart thing or person ▷ vb to smarten

SPIFFYING > SPIFFY

SPIFS > SPIF

SPIGHT same as > SPITE

SPIGHTED > SPIGHT

SPIGHTING > SPIGHT

SPIGHTS > SPIGHT

SPIGNEL n European umbelliferous plant

SPIGNELS > SPIGNEL

SPIGOT n stopper for, or tap fitted to, a cask

SPIGOTS > SPIGOT

SPIK same as > SPIC

SPIKE n sharp point ▷ vb put spikes on

SPIKED > SPIKE

SPIKEFISH n large sea fish

SPIKELET n unit of a grass inflorescence

SPIKELETS > SPIKELET

SPIKELIKE > SPIKE

SPIKENARD n fragrant Indian plant with rose-purple flowers

SPIKER > SPIKE

SPIKERIES > SPIKERY

SPIKERS > SPIKE

SPIKERY n High-Church Anglicanism

SPIKES > SPIKE

SPIKEY same as > SPIKY

SPIKIER > SPIKY

SPIKIEST > SPIKY

SPIKILY > SPIKY

SPIKINESS > SPIKY

SPIKING > SPIKE

SPIKS > SPIK

SPIKY adj resembling a spike

SPILE n heavy timber stake or pile ▷ vb provide or support with a spile

SPILED > SPILE

SPILES > SPILE

SPILIKIN same as > SPILLIKIN

SPILIKINS > SPILIKIN

SPILING > SPILE

SPILINGS > SPILE

SPILITE n type of igneous rock

SPILITES > SPILITE

SPILITIC > SPILITE

SPILL vb pour from or as if from a container ▷ n fall

SPILLABLE > SPILL

SPILLAGE n instance or the process of spilling

SPILLAGES > SPILLAGE

SPILLED > SPILL

SPILLER > SPILL

SPILLERS > SPILL

SPILLIKIN n thin strip of wood, cardboard, or plastic used in spillikins

SPILLING > SPILL

SPILLINGS > SPILL

SPILLOVER n act of spilling over

SPILLS > SPILL

SPILLWAY n channel that carries away surplus water, as from a dam

SPILLWAYS > SPILLWAY

SPILOSITE n form of slate

SPILT > SPILL

SPILTH n something spilled

SPILTHS > SPILTH

SPIM n unsolicited commercial communications received on a computer via an instant-messaging system

SPIMS > SPIM

SPIN vb revolve or cause to revolve rapidly ▷ n revolving motion

SPINA n spine

SPINACENE n type of vaccine

SPINACH n dark green leafy vegetable

SPINACHES > SPINACH

SPINACHY > SPINACH

SPINAE > SPINA

SPINAGE same as > SPINACH

SPINAGES > SPINAGE

SPINAL adj of the spine ▷ n anaesthetic administered in the spine

SPINALLY > SPINAL

SPINALS > SPINAL

SPINAR n fast-spinning star

SPINARS > SPINAR

SPINAS > SPINA

SPINATE adj having a spine

SPINDLE n rotating rod that acts as an axle ▷ vb

S

form into a spindle or equip with spindles

SPINDLED > SPINDLE

SPINDLER > SPINDLE

SPINDLERS > SPINDLE

SPINDLES > SPINDLE

SPINDLIER > SPINDLY

SPINDLING adj long and slender, esp disproportionately so ▷ n spindling person or thing

SPINDLY adj long, slender, and frail

SPINDRIFT n spray blown up from the sea

SPINE n backbone

SPINED > SPINE

SPINEL n any of a group of hard glassy minerals of variable colour

SPINELESS adj lacking courage

SPINELIKE > SPINE

SPINELLE same as > SPINEL

SPINELLES > SPINELLE

SPINELS > SPINEL

SPINES > SPINE

SPINET n small harpsichord

SPINETS > SPINET

SPINETTE same as > SPINET

SPINETTES > SPINETTE

SPINIER > SPINY

SPINIEST > SPINY

SPINIFEX n coarse spiny Australian grass

SPINIFORM adj like a thorn

SPININESS > SPINY

SPINK n finch

SPINKS > SPINK

SPINLESS > SPIN

SPINNAKER n large sail on a racing yacht

SPINNER n bowler who specializes in spinning the ball to make it change direction when it bounces or strikes the bat

SPINNERET n organ through which silk threads come out of a spider

SPINNERS > SPINNER

SPINNERY n spinning mill

SPINNET same as > SPINET

SPINNETS > SPINNET

SPINNEY n small wood

SPINNEYS > SPINNEY

SPINNIES > SPINNY

SPINNING > SPIN

SPINNINGS > SPIN

SPINNY same as > SPINNEY

SPINODE another name for > CUSP

SPINODES > SPINODE

SPINOFF n development derived incidentally from an existing enterprise

SPINOFFS > SPINOFF

SPINONE as in Italian

spinone wiry-coated gun dog

SPINONI > SPINONE

SPINOR n type of mathematical object

SPINORS > SPINOR

SPINOSE adj (esp of plants) bearing many spines

SPINOSELY > SPINOSE

SPINOSITY > SPINOSE

SPINOUS adj resembling a spine or thorn

SPINOUT n spinning skid that causes a car to run off the road

SPINOUTS > SPINOUT

SPINS > SPIN

SPINSTER n unmarried woman

SPINSTERS > SPINSTER

SPINTEXT n preacher

SPINTEXTS > SPINTEXT

SPINTO n lyrical singing voice

SPINTOS > SPINTO

SPINULA n small spine

SPINULAE > SPINULA

SPINULATE adj like a spine

SPINULE n very small spine, thorn, or prickle

SPINULES > SPINULE

SPINULOSE > SPINULE

SPINULOUS > SPINULE

SPINY adj covered with spines

SPIRACLE n small blowhole for breathing through, such as that of a whale

SPIRACLES > SPIRACLE

SPIRACULA npl spiracles

SPIRAEA n plant with small white or pink flowers

SPIRAEAS > SPIRAEA

SPIRAL n continuous curve formed by a point winding about a central axis to an ever-increasing distance from it ▷ vb move in a spiral ▷ adj having the form of a spiral

SPIRALED > SPIRAL

SPIRALING > SPIRAL

SPIRALISM n ascent in spiral structure

SPIRALIST > SPIRALISM

SPIRALITY > SPIRAL

SPIRALLED > SPIRAL

SPIRALLY > SPIRAL

SPIRALS > SPIRAL

SPIRANT n fricative consonant

SPIRANTS > SPIRANT

SPIRASTER n part of living sponge

SPIRATED adj twisted in spiral

SPIRATION n breathing

SPIRE n pointed part of a steeple ▷ vb assume the shape of a spire

SPIREA same as > SPIRAEA

SPIREAS > SPIREA

SPIRED > SPIRE

SPIRELESS > SPIRE

SPIRELET another name for > FLECHE

SPIRELETS > SPIRELET

SPIREM same as > SPIREME

SPIREME n tangled mass of chromatin threads into which the nucleus of a cell is resolved at the start of mitosis

SPIREMES > SPIREME

SPIREMS > SPIREM

SPIRES > SPIRE

SPIREWISE > SPIRE

SPIRIC n type of curve

SPIRICS > SPIRIC

SPIRIER > SPIRE

SPIRIEST > SPIRE

SPIRILLA > SPIRILLUM

SPIRILLAR > SPIRILLUM

SPIRILLUM n any bacterium having a curved or spirally twisted rodlike body

SPIRING > SPIRE

SPIRIT n nonphysical aspect of a person concerned with profound thoughts ▷ vb carry away mysteriously

SPIRITED adj lively

SPIRITFUL > SPIRIT

SPIRITING > SPIRIT

SPIRITISM n belief that the spirits of the dead can communicate with the living

SPIRITIST > SPIRITISM

SPIRITOSO adv to be played in a spirited or animated manner

SPIRITOUS adj high-spirited

SPIRITS > SPIRIT

SPIRITUAL adj relating to the spirit ▷ n type of religious folk song originating among Black slaves in America

SPIRITUEL adj having a refined and lively mind or wit

SPIRITUS n spirit

SPIRITTY adj spirited

SPIRLING same as > SPARLING

SPIRLINGS > SPIRLING

SPIROGRAM n record made by spirograph

SPIROGYRA n green freshwater plant that floats on the surface of ponds and ditches

SPIROID adj resembling a spiral or displaying a spiral form

SPIRT same as > SPURT

SPIRTED > SPIRT

SPIRTING > SPIRT

SPIRTLE same as > SPURTLE

SPIRTLES > SPIRTLE

SPIRTS > SPIRT

SPIRULA n tropical cephalopod mollusc

SPIRULAE > SPIRULA

SPIRULAS > SPIRULA

SPIRULINA n type of cyanobacterium processed as a source of nutrients

SPIRY > SPIRE

SPIT vb eject (saliva or food) from the mouth ▷ n saliva

SPITAL n hospital, esp for the needy sick

SPITALS > SPITAL

SPITBALL n small missile made from chewed paper

SPITBALLS > SPITBALL

SPITCHER adj doomed

SPITE n deliberate nastiness ▷ vb annoy or hurt from spite

SPITED > SPITE

SPITEFUL adj full of or motivated by spite

SPITES > SPITE

SPITFIRE n person with a fiery temper

SPITFIRES > SPITFIRE

SPITING > SPITE

SPITS > SPIT

SPITTED > SPIT

SPITTEN > SPIT

SPITTER > SPIT

SPITTERS > SPIT

SPITTING > SPIT

SPITTINGS > SPIT

SPITTLE n fluid produced in the mouth, saliva

SPITTLES > SPITTLE

SPITTOON n bowl to spit into

SPITTOONS > SPITTOON

SPITZ n stockily built dog with a pointed face, erect ears, and a tightly curled tail

SPITZES > SPITZ

SPIV n smartly dressed man who makes a living by shady dealings

SPIVS > SPIV

SPIVVERY n behaviour of spivs

SPIVVIER > SPIV

SPIVVIEST > SPIV

SPIVVY > SPIV

SPLAKE n type of hybrid trout bred by Canadian zoologists

SPLAKES > SPLAKE

SPLASH vb scatter liquid on (something) ▷ n splashing sound

SPLASHED > SPLASH

SPLASHER n anything used for protection against splashes

SPLASHERS > SPLASHER

SPLASHES > SPLASH

SPLASHIER > SPLASHY
SPLASHILY > SPLASHY
SPLASHING > SPLASH
SPLASHY *adj* having irregular marks
SPLAT *n* wet slapping sound ▷ *vb* make wet slapping sound
SPLATCH *vb* splash
SPLATCHED > SPLATCH
SPLATCHES > SPLATCH
SPLATS > SPLAT
SPLATTED > SPLAT
SPLATTER *n* splash ▷ *vb* splash (something or someone) with small blobs
SPLATTERS > SPLATTER
SPLATTING > SPLAT
SPLAY *vb* spread out, with ends spreading in different directions ▷ *adj* spread out ▷ *n* surface of a wall that forms an oblique angle to the main flat surfaces
SPLAYED > SPLAY
SPLAYFEET > SPLAYFOOT
SPLAYFOOT *n* foot of which the toes are spread out
SPLAYING > SPLAY
SPLAYS > SPLAY
SPLEEN *n* abdominal organ which filters bacteria from the blood
SPLEENFUL *adj* bad-tempered or irritable
SPLEENIER > SPLEEN
SPLEENISH > SPLEEN
SPLEENS > SPLEEN
SPLEENY > SPLEEN
SPLENDENT *adj* shining brightly
SPLENDID *adj* excellent
SPLENDOR *same as* > SPLENDOUR
SPLENDORS > SPLENDOR
SPLENDOUR *n* state or quality of being splendid
SPLENETIC *adj* spiteful or irritable ▷ *n* spiteful or irritable person
SPLENIA > SPLENIUM
SPLENIAL > SPLENIUS
SPLENIC *adj* of, relating to, or in the spleen
SPLENII > SPLENIUS
SPLENITIS *n* inflammation of the spleen
SPLENIUM *n* structure in brain
SPLENIUMS > SPLENIUM
SPLENIUS *n* either of two flat muscles situated at the back of the neck
SPLENT *same as* > SPLINT
SPLENTS > SPLENT
SPLEUCHAN *n* pouch for tobacco
SPLICE *vb* join by interweaving or overlapping ends
SPLICED > SPLICE
SPLICER > SPLICE
SPLICERS > SPLICE

SPLICES > SPLICE
SPLICING > SPLICE
SPLICINGS > SPLICING
SPLIFF *n* cannabis, used as a drug
SPLIFFS > SPLIFF
SPLINE *n* type of narrow key around a shaft that fits into a corresponding groove ▷ *vb* provide (a shaft, part, etc) with splines
SPLINED > SPLINE
SPLINES > SPLINE
SPLINING > SPLINE
SPLINT *n* rigid support for a broken bone ▷ *vb* apply a splint to (a broken arm, etc)
SPLINTED > SPLINT
SPLINTER *n* thin sharp piece broken off, esp from wood ▷ *vb* break into fragments
SPLINTERS > SPLINTER
SPLINTERY *adj* liable to produce or break into splinters
SPLINTING > SPLINT
SPLINTS > SPLINT
SPLISH *vb* splash
SPLISHED > SPLISH
SPLISHES > SPLISH
SPLISHING > SPLISH
SPLIT *vb* break into separate pieces ▷ *n* splitting
SPLITS > SPLIT
SPLITTED > SPLIT
SPLITTER > SPLIT
SPLITTERS > SPLIT
SPLITTING *n* a Freudian psychological defence mechanism
SPLITTISM *n* advocation of separatism from a larger body
SPLITTIST *n* person who advocates separatism from a larger body
SPLODGE *n* large uneven spot or stain ▷ *vb* mark (something) with a splodge or splodges
SPLODGED > SPLODGE
SPLODGES > SPLODGE
SPLODGIER > SPLODGE
SPLODGILY > SPLODGE
SPLODGING > SPLODGE
SPLODGY > SPLODGE
SPLOG *n* spam blog
SPLOGS > SPLOG
SPLOOSH *vb* splash or cause to splash about uncontrollably ▷ *n* instance or sound of splooshing
SPLOOSHED > SPLOOSH
SPLOOSHES > SPLOOSH
SPLORE *n* revel
SPLORES > SPLORE
SPLOSH *vb* scatter (liquid) vigorously about in blobs ▷ *n* instance or sound of sploshing
SPLOSHED > SPLOSH

SPLOSHES > SPLOSH
SPLOSHING > SPLOSH
SPLOTCH *vb* splash, daub
SPLOTCHED > SPLOTCH
SPLOTCHES > SPLOTCH
SPLOTCHY > SPLOTCH
SPLURGE *vb* spend money extravagantly ▷ *n* bout of extravagance
SPLURGED > SPLURGE
SPLURGER > SPLURGE
SPLURGERS > SPLURGE
SPLURGES > SPLURGE
SPLURGIER > SPLURGE
SPLURGING > SPLURGE
SPLURGY > SPLURGE
SPLUTTER *vb* utter with spitting or choking sounds ▷ *n* spluttering
SPLUTTERS > SPLUTTER
SPLUTTERY > SPLUTTER
SPOD *adj* boring, unattractive, or overstudious
SPODDIER > SPOD
SPODDIEST > SPOD
SPODDY > SPOD
SPODE *n* type of English china or porcelain
SPODES > SPODE
SPODIUM *n* black powder
SPODIUMS > SPODIUM
SPODOGRAM *n* ash from plant used in studying it
SPODOSOL *n* ashy soil
SPODOSOLS > SPODOSOL
SPODS > SPOD
SPODUMENE *n* greyish-white, green, or lilac pyroxene mineral
SPOFFISH *adj* officious
SPOFFY *same as* > SPOFFISH
SPOIL *vb* damage
SPOILABLE > SPOIL
SPOILAGE *n* amount of material that has been spoilt
SPOILAGES > SPOILAGE
SPOILED > SPOIL
SPOILER *n* device on an aircraft or car to increase drag
SPOILERS > SPOILER
SPOILFIVE *n* card game for two or more players with five cards each
SPOILFUL *adj* taking spoils
SPOILING > SPOIL
SPOILS > SPOIL
SPOILSMAN *n* person who shares in the spoils of office or advocates the spoils system
SPOILSMEN > SPOILSMAN
SPOILT > SPOIL
SPOKE *n* radial member of a wheel ▷ *vb* equip with spokes
SPOKED > SPOKE
SPOKEN > SPEAK
SPOKES > SPOKE

SPOKESMAN *n* person chosen to speak on behalf of a group
SPOKESMEN > SPOKESMAN
SPOKEWISE > SPEAK
SPOKING > SPOKE
SPOLIATE *less common word for* > DESPOIL
SPOLIATED > SPOLIATE
SPOLIATES > SPOLIATE
SPOLIATOR > SPOLIATE
SPONDAIC *adj* of, relating to, or consisting of spondees ▷ *n* spondaic line
SPONDAICS > SPONDAIC
SPONDEE *n* metrical foot of two long syllables
SPONDEES > SPONDEE
SPONDULIX *n* money
SPONDYL *n* vertebra
SPONDYLS > SPONDYL
SPONGE *n* sea animal with a porous absorbent skeleton ▷ *vb* wipe with a sponge
SPONGEBAG *n* small bag for holding toiletries when travelling
SPONGED > SPONGE
SPONGEOUS *adj* spongy
SPONGER *n* person who sponges on others
SPONGERS > SPONGER
SPONGES > SPONGE
SPONGIER > SPONGY
SPONGIEST > SPONGY
SPONGILY > SPONGY
SPONGIN *n* fibrous horny protein that forms the skeletal framework of the bath sponge and related sponges
SPONGING > SPONGE
SPONGINS > SPONGIN
SPONGIOSE > SPONGE
SPONGIOUS > SPONGE
SPONGOID > SPONGE
SPONGY *adj* of or resembling a sponge
SPONSAL *n* marriage
SPONSALIA *n* marriage ceremony
SPONSIBLE *adj* responsible
SPONSING *same as* > SPONSON
SPONSINGS > SPONSING
SPONSION *n* act or process of becoming surety
SPONSIONS > SPONSION
SPONSON *n* outboard support for a gun enabling it to fire fore and aft
SPONSONS > SPONSON
SPONSOR *n* person who promotes something ▷ *vb* act as a sponsor for
SPONSORED > SPONSOR
SPONSORS > SPONSOR
SPONTOON *n* form of halberd carried by some junior infantry officers in the 18th and 19th centuries
SPONTOONS > SPONTOON

S

SPOOF n mildly satirical parody ▷ vb fool (a person) with a trick or deception
SPOOFED > SPOOF
SPOOFER > SPOOF
SPOOFERS > SPOOF
SPOOFERY > SPOOFY
SPOOFIER > SPOOFY
SPOOFIEST > SPOOFY
SPOOFING > SPOOF
SPOOFINGS > SPOOF
SPOOFS > SPOOF
SPOOFY > SPOOF
SPOOK n ghost ▷ vb frighten
SPOOKED > SPOOK
SPOOKERY n spooky events
SPOOKIER > SPOOKY
SPOOKIEST > SPOOKY
SPOOKILY > SPOOKY
SPOOKING > SPOOK
SPOOKISH > SPOOK
SPOOKS > SPOOK
SPOOKY adj ghostly or eerie
SPOOL n cylinder round which something can be wound ▷ vb wind or be wound onto a spool or reel
SPOOLED > SPOOL
SPOOLER > SPOOL
SPOOLERS > SPOOL
SPOOLING > SPOOL
SPOOLINGS > SPOOL
SPOOLS > SPOOL
SPOOM vb sail fast before wind
SPOOMED > SPOOM
SPOOMING > SPOOM
SPOOMS > SPOOM
SPOON n shallow bowl attached to a handle for eating, stirring, or serving food ▷ vb lift with a spoon
SPOONBAIT n type of lure used in angling
SPOONBILL n wading bird of warm regions with a long flat bill
SPOONED > SPOON
SPOONEY same as > SPOONY
SPOONEYS > SPOONEY
SPOONFED adj having been given someone else's opinions
SPOONFUL n amount that a spoon is able to hold
SPOONFULS > SPOONFUL
SPOONHOOK n type of fishing lure
SPOONIER > SPOONY
SPOONIES > SPOONY
SPOONIEST > SPOONY
SPOONILY > SPOONY
SPOONING > SPOON
SPOONS > SPOON
SPOONSFUL > SPOONFUL
SPOONWAYS adv like spoons
SPOONWISE same as > SPOONWAYS
SPOONWORM n type of small marine worm with a spoonlike proboscis

SPOONY adj foolishly or stupidly amorous ▷ n fool or silly person, esp one in love
SPOOR n trail of an animal ▷ vb track (an animal) by following its trail
SPOORED > SPOOR
SPOORER > SPOOR
SPOORERS > SPOOR
SPOORING > SPOOR
SPOORS > SPOOR
SPOOT n razor shell
SPOOTS > SPOOT
SPORADIC adj intermittent, scattered
SPORAL > SPORE
SPORANGIA npl organs in fungi in which asexual spores are produced
SPORE n minute reproductive body of some plants ▷ vb produce, carry, or release spores
SPORED > SPORE
SPORES > SPORE
SPORICIDE n substance killing spores
SPORIDESM n group of spores
SPORIDIA > SPORIDIUM
SPORIDIAL > SPORIDIUM
SPORIDIUM n type of spore
SPORING > SPORE
SPORK n spoon-shaped piece of cutlery with tines like a fork
SPORKS > SPORK
SPOROCARP n specialized leaf branch in certain aquatic ferns that encloses the sori
SPOROCYST n thick-walled rounded structure produced by sporozoan protozoans
SPOROCYTE n diploid cell that divides by meiosis to produce four haploid spores
SPOROGENY n process of spore formation in plants and animals
SPOROGONY n process in sporozoans by which sporozoites are formed
SPOROID adj of or like a spore
SPOROPHYL n leaf in ferns that bears the sporangia
SPOROZOA n class of microscopic creature
SPOROZOAL > SPOROZOA
SPOROZOAN n type of parasitic protozoan
SPOROZOIC > SPOROZOA
SPOROZOON same as > SPOROZOAN
SPORRAN n pouch worn in front of a kilt
SPORRANS > SPORRAN
SPORT n activity for

pleasure, competition, or exercise ▷ vb wear proudly
SPORTABLE adj playful
SPORTANCE n playing
SPORTED > SPORT
SPORTER > SPORT
SPORTERS > SPORT
SPORTFUL > SPORT
SPORTIER > SPORTY
SPORTIES > SPORTY
SPORTIEST > SPORTY
SPORTIF adj sporty
SPORTILY > SPORTY
SPORTING adj of sport
SPORTIVE adj playful
SPORTLESS > SPORT
SPORTS adj of or used in sports ▷ n meeting held at a school or college for competitions in athletic events
SPORTSMAN n person who plays sports
SPORTSMEN > SPORTSMAN
SPORTY adj (of a person) interested in sport ▷ n young person who typically wears sportswear, is competitive about sport, and takes an interest in his or her fitness
SPORULAR > SPORULE
SPORULATE vb produce spores, esp by multiple fission
SPORULE n spore, esp a very small spore
SPORULES > SPORULE
SPOSH n slush
SPOSHES > SPOSH
SPOSHIER > SPOSH
SPOSHIEST > SPOSH
SPOSHY > SPOSH
SPOT n small mark on a surface ▷ vb notice
SPOTLESS adj absolutely clean
SPOTLIGHT n powerful light illuminating a small area ▷ vb draw attention to
SPOTLIT > SPOTLIGHT
SPOTS > SPOT
SPOTTABLE > SPOT
SPOTTED > SPOT
SPOTTER n person whose hobby is watching for and noting numbers or types of trains or planes
SPOTTERS > SPOTTER
SPOTTIE n young deer of up to three months of age
SPOTTIER > SPOTTY
SPOTTIES > SPOTTIE
SPOTTIEST > SPOTTY
SPOTTILY > SPOTTY
SPOTTING > SPOT
SPOTTINGS > SPOT
SPOTTY adj with spots
SPOUSAGE n marriage
SPOUSAGES > SPOUSAGE
SPOUSAL n marriage ceremony ▷ adj of or relating to marriage

SPOUSALLY > SPOUSAL
SPOUSALS > SPOUSAL
SPOUSE n husband or wife ▷ vb marry
SPOUSED > SPOUSE
SPOUSES > SPOUSE
SPOUSING > SPOUSE
SPOUT vb pour out in a stream or jet ▷ n projecting tube or lip for pouring liquids
SPOUTED > SPOUT
SPOUTER > SPOUT
SPOUTERS > SPOUT
SPOUTIER > SPOUT
SPOUTIEST > SPOUT
SPOUTING n rainwater downpipe on the outside of a building
SPOUTINGS > SPOUTING
SPOUTLESS > SPOUT
SPOUTS > SPOUT
SPOUTY > SPOUT
SPRACK adj vigorous
SPRACKLE vb clamber
SPRACKLED > SPRACKLE
SPRACKLES > SPRACKLE
SPRAD > SPREAD
SPRADDLE n disease of fowl preventing them from standing
SPRADDLED adj affected by spraddle
SPRADDLES > SPRADDLE
SPRAG n chock or steel bar used to prevent a vehicle from running backwards on an incline ▷ vb use sprag to prevent vehicle from moving
SPRAGGED > SPRAG
SPRAGGING > SPRAG
SPRAGS > SPRAG
SPRAID vb chapped
SPRAIN vb injure (a joint) by a sudden twist ▷ n such an injury
SPRAINED > SPRAIN
SPRAINING > SPRAIN
SPRAINS > SPRAIN
SPRAINT n piece of otter's dung
SPRAINTS > SPRAINT
SPRANG n branch
SPRANGLE vb sprawl
SPRANGLED > SPRANGLE
SPRANGLES > SPRANGLE
SPRANGS > SPRANG
SPRAT n small sea fish
SPRATS > SPRAT
SPRATTLE vb scramble
SPRATTLED > SPRATTLE
SPRATTLES > SPRATTLE
SPRAUCHLE same as > SPRACKLE
SPRAUNCY adj smart
SPRAWL vb lie or sit with the limbs spread out ▷ n part of a city that has spread untidily over a large area
SPRAWLED > SPRAWL
SPRAWLER > SPRAWL
SPRAWLERS > SPRAWL

S

SPRAWLIER > SPRAWL
SPRAWLING > SPRAWL
SPRAWLS > SPRAWL
SPRAWLY > SPRAWL
SPRAY *n* (device for producing) fine drops of liquid ▷ *vb* scatter in fine drops
SPRAYED > SPRAY
SPRAYER > SPRAY
SPRAYERS > SPRAY
SPRAYEY > SPRAY
SPRAYIER > SPRAY
SPRAYIEST > SPRAY
SPRAYING > SPRAY
SPRAYINGS > SPRAY
SPRAYS > SPRAY
SPREAD *vb* open out or be displayed to the fullest extent ▷ *n* spreading ▷ *adj* extended or stretched out, esp to the fullest extent
SPREADER *n* machine or device used for scattering bulk materials over a relatively wide area
SPREADERS > SPREADER
SPREADING > SPREAD
SPREADS > SPREAD
SPREAGH *n* cattle raid
SPREAGHS > SPREAGH
SPREATHE *vb* chap
SPREATHED *adj* sore
SPREATHES > SPREATHE
SPREAZE *same as* > SPREATHE
SPREAZED *same as* > SPREATHED
SPREAZES > SPREAZE
SPREAZING > SPREAZE
SPRECHERY *n* theft of cattle
SPRECKLED *adj* speckled
SPRED *same as* > SPREAD
SPREDD *same as* > SPREAD
SPREDDE *same as* > SPREAD
SPREDDEN > SPREDDE
SPREDDES > SPREDDE
SPREDDING > SPREDDE
SPREDDS > SPREDD
SPREDS > SPRED
SPREE *n* session of overindulgence, usu in drinking or spending money ▷ *vb* go on a spree
SPREED > SPREE
SPREEING > SPREE
SPREES > SPREE
SPREETHE *same as* > SPREATHE
SPREETHED > SPREETHE
SPREETHES > SPREETHE
SPREEZE *same as* > SPREATHE
SPREEZED > SPREEZE
SPREEZES > SPREEZE
SPREEZING > SPREEZE
SPREKELIA *n* bulbous plant grown for its striking crimson or white pendent flowers
SPRENT > SPRINKLE
SPREW *same as* > SPRUE

SPREWS > SPREW
SPRIER > SPRY
SPRIEST > SPRY
SPRIG *n* twig or shoot ▷ *vb* fasten or secure with sprigs
SPRIGGED > SPRIG
SPRIGGER > SPRIG
SPRIGGERS > SPRIG
SPRIGGIER > SPRIG
SPRIGGING > SPRIG
SPRIGGY > SPRIG
SPRIGHT *same as* > SPRITE
SPRIGHTED > SPRIGHT
SPRIGHTLY *adj* lively and brisk ▷ *adv* in a lively manner
SPRIGHTS > SPRIGHT
SPRIGS > SPRIG
SPRIGTAIL *n* species of duck
SPRING *vb* move suddenly upwards or forwards in a single motion, jump ▷ *n* season between winter and summer
SPRINGAL *n* young man
SPRINGALD *same as* > SPRINGAL
SPRINGALS > SPRINGAL
SPRINGBOK *n* S African antelope
SPRINGE *n* type of snare for catching small wild animals or birds ▷ *vb* set such a snare
SPRINGED > SPRINGE
SPRINGER *n* small spaniel
SPRINGERS > SPRINGER
SPRINGES > SPRINGE
SPRINGIER > SPRINGY
SPRINGILY > SPRINGY
SPRINGING > SPRING
SPRINGLE *same as* > SPRINGE
SPRINGLES > SPRINGE
SPRINGLET *n* small spring
SPRINGS > SPRING
SPRINGY *adj* elastic
SPRINKLE *vb* scatter (liquid or powder) in tiny drops or particles over (something) ▷ *n* act or an instance of sprinkling or a quantity that is sprinkled
SPRINKLED > SPRINKLE
SPRINKLER *n* device with small holes that is attached to a garden hose or watering can and used to spray water
SPRINKLES > SPRINKLE
SPRINT *n* short race run at top speed ▷ *vb* run a short distance at top speed
SPRINTED > SPRINT
SPRINTER > SPRINT
SPRINTERS > SPRINT
SPRINTING > SPRINT
SPRINTS > SPRINT
SPRIT *n* small spar set diagonally across a sail to extend it
SPRITE *n* elf

SPRITEFUL > SPRITE
SPRITELY *same as* > SPRIGHTLY
SPRITES > SPRITE
SPRITS > SPRIT
SPRITSAIL *n* sail extended by a sprit
SPRITZ *vb* spray liquid
SPRITZED > SPRITZ
SPRITZER *n* tall drink of wine and soda water
SPRITZERS > SPRITZER
SPRITZES > SPRITZ
SPRITZIG *adj* (of wine) sparkling ▷ *n* sparkling wine
SPRITZIGS > SPRITZIG
SPRITZING > SPRITZ
SPROCKET *n* wheel with teeth on the rim, that drives or is driven by a chain
SPROCKETS > SPROCKET
SPROD *n* young salmon
SPRODS > SPROD
SPROG *n* child
SPROGS > SPROG
SPRONG > SPRING
SPROUT *vb* put forth shoots ▷ *n* shoot
SPROUTED > SPROUT
SPROUTING > SPROUT
SPROUTS > SPROUT
SPRUCE *n* kind of fir ▷ *adj* neat and smart
SPRUCED > SPRUCE
SPRUCELY > SPRUCE
SPRUCER > SPRUCE
SPRUCES > SPRUCE
SPRUCEST > SPRUCE
SPRUCIER > SPRUCE
SPRUCIEST > SPRUCE
SPRUCING > SPRUCE
SPRUCY > SPRUCE
SPRUE *n* vertical channel in a mould through which plastic or molten metal is poured
SPRUES > SPRUE
SPRUG *n* sparrow
SPRUGS > SPRUG
SPRUIK *vb* speak in public (used esp of a showman or salesman)
SPRUIKED > SPRUIK
SPRUIKER > SPRUIK
SPRUIKERS > SPRUIK
SPRUIKING > SPRUIK
SPRUIKS > SPRUIK
SPRUITT *n* small tributary stream or watercourse
SPRUITS > SPRUITT
SPRUNG > SPRING
SPRUSH *Scots form of* > SPRUCE
SPRUSHED > SPRUSH
SPRUSHES > SPRUSH
SPRUSHING > SPRUSH
SPRY *adj* active or nimble
SPRYER > SPRY
SPRYEST > SPRY
SPRYLY > SPRY
SPRYNESS > SPRY
SPUD *n* potato ▷ *vb* remove (bark) or eradicate (weeds)

with a spud
SPUDDED > SPUD
SPUDDER *same as* > SPUD
SPUDDERS > SPUDDER
SPUDDIER > SPUDDY
SPUDDIEST > SPUDDY
SPUDDING > SPUD
SPUDDINGS > SPUD
SPUDDLE *n* feeble movement
SPUDDLES > SPUDDLE
SPUDDY *adj* short and fat
SPUDS > SPUD
SPUE *same as* > SPEW
SPUED > SPUE
SPUEING > SPUE
SPUER > SPUE
SPUERS > SPUE
SPUES > SPUE
SPUG *same as* > SPUGGY
SPUGGIES > SPUGGY
SPUGGY *n* house sparrow
SPUGS > SPUG
SPUILZIE *vb* plunder
SPUILZIED > SPUILZIE
SPUILZIES > SPUILZIE
SPUING > SPUE
SPULE *Scots word for* > SHOULDER
SPULES > SPULE
SPULYE *same as* > SPUILZIE
SPULYED > SPULYE
SPULYEING > SPULYE
SPULYES > SPULYE
SPULYIE *same as* > SPUILZIE
SPULYIED > SPULYIE
SPULYIES > SPULYIE
SPULZIE *same as* > SPUILZIE
SPULZIED > SPULZIE
SPULZIES > SPULZIE
SPUMANTE *n* Italian sparkling wine
SPUMANTES > SPUMANTE
SPUME *vb* froth ▷ *n* foam or froth on the sea
SPUMED > SPUMY
SPUMES > SPUME
SPUMIER > SPUMY
SPUMIEST > SPUMY
SPUMING > SPUME
SPUMONE *n* creamy Italian ice cream
SPUMONES > SPUMONE
SPUMONI *same as* > SPUMONE
SPUMONIS > SPUMONI
SPUMOUS > SPUME
SPUMY > SPUME
SPUN > SPIN
SPUNGE *same as* > SPONGE
SPUNGES > SPUNGE
SPUNK *n* courage, spirit ▷ *vb* catch fire
SPUNKED > SPUNK
SPUNKIE *n* will-o'-the-wisp
SPUNKIER > SPUNK
SPUNKIES > SPUNKIE
SPUNKIEST > SPUNK
SPUNKILY > SPUNK

S

SPUNKING > SPUNK
SPUNKS > SPUNK
SPUNKY > SPUNK
SPUNYARN n small stuff made from rope yarns twisted together
SPUNYARNS > SPUNYARN
SPUR n stimulus or incentive ▷ vb urge on, incite (someone)
SPURGALL vb prod with spur
SPURGALLS > SPURGALL
SPURGE n plant with milky sap
SPURGES > SPURGE
SPURIAE n type of bird feathers
SPURIOUS adj not genuine
SPURLESS > SPUR
SPURLING same as > SPARLING
SPURLINGS > SPURLING
SPURN vb reject with scorn ▷ n instance of spurning
SPURNE vb spur
SPURNED > SPURN
SPURNER > SPURN
SPURNERS > SPURN
SPURNES > SPURNE
SPURNING > SPURN
SPURNINGS > SPURN
SPURNS > SPURN
SPURRED > SPUR
SPURRER > SPUR
SPURRERS > SPUR
SPURREY n any of several low-growing European plants
SPURREYS > SPURREY
SPURRIER n maker of spurs
SPURRIERS > SPURRIER
SPURRIES > SPURRY
SPURRIEST > SPURRY
SPURRING > SPUR
SPURRINGS > SPUR
SPURRY n spurrey ▷ adj resembling a spur
SPURS > SPUR
SPURT vb gush or cause to gush out in a jet ▷ n short sudden burst of activity or speed
SPURTED > SPURT
SPURTER > SPURT
SPURTERS > SPURT
SPURTING > SPURT
SPURTLE n wooden spoon for stirring porridge
SPURTLES > SPURTLE
SPURTS > SPURT
SPURWAY n path used by riders
SPURWAYS > SPURWAY
SPUTA > SPUTUM
SPUTNIK n early Soviet artificial satellite
SPUTNIKS > SPUTNIK
SPUTTER n splutter ▷ vb splutter
SPUTTERED > SPUTTER
SPUTTERER > SPUTTER
SPUTTERS > SPUTTER

SPUTTERY > SPUTTER
SPUTUM n spittle, usu mixed with mucus
SPY n person employed to obtain secret information ▷ vb act as a spy
SPYAL n spy
SPYALS > SPYAL
SPYCAM n camera used for covert surveillance
SPYCAMS > SPYCAM
SPYGLASS n small telescope
SPYHOLE n small hole in a door, etc through which one may watch secretly
SPYHOLES > SPYHOLE
SPYING > SPY
SPYINGS > SPY
SPYMASTER n person who controls spy network
SPYPLANE n military aeroplane used to spy on enemy
SPYPLANES > SPYPLANE
SPYRE same as > SPIRE
SPYRES > SPYRE
SPYWARE n software installed via the internet on a computer without the user's knowledge and used to gain information about the user
SPYWARES > SPYWARE
SQUAB n young bird yet to leave the nest ▷ adj (of birds) recently hatched and still unfledged ▷ vb fall
SQUABASH vb crush
SQUABBED > SQUAB
SQUABBER > SQUAB
SQUABBEST > SQUAB
SQUABBIER > SQUAB
SQUABBING > SQUAB
SQUABBISH > SQUAB
SQUABBLE n (engage in) a petty or noisy quarrel ▷ vb quarrel over a small matter
SQUABBLED > SQUABBLE
SQUABBLER > SQUABBLE
SQUABBLES > SQUABBLE
SQUABBY > SQUAB
SQUABS > SQUAB
SQUACCO n S European heron
SQUACCOS > SQUACCO
SQUAD n small group of people working or training together ▷ vb set up squads
SQUADDED > SQUAD
SQUADDIE n private soldier
SQUADDIES > SQUADDY
SQUADDING > SQUAD
SQUADDY same as > SQUADDIE
SQUADRON n division of an air force, fleet, or cavalry regiment ▷ vb assign to squadrons
SQUADRONE n former Scottish political party
SQUADRONS > SQUADRON
SQUADS > SQUAD

SQUAIL vb throw sticks at
SQUAILED > SQUAIL
SQUAILER > SQUAIL
SQUAILERS > SQUAIL
SQUAILING > SQUAIL
SQUAILS > SQUAIL
SQUALENE n terpene first found in the liver of sharks
SQUALENES > SQUALENE
SQUALID adj dirty and unpleasant
SQUALIDER > SQUALID
SQUALIDLY > SQUALID
SQUALL n sudden strong wind ▷ vb cry noisily, yell
SQUALLED > SQUALL
SQUALLER > SQUALL
SQUALLERS > SQUALL
SQUALLIER > SQUALL
SQUALLING > SQUALL
SQUALLISH > SQUALL
SQUALLS > SQUALL
SQUALLY > SQUALL
SQUALOID adj of or like a shark
SQUALOR n disgusting dirt and filth
SQUALORS > SQUALOR
SQUAMA n scale or scalelike structure
SQUAMAE > SQUAMA
SQUAMATE > SQUAMA
SQUAMATES > SQUAMA
SQUAME same as > SQUAMA
SQUAMELLA n small scale
SQUAMES > SQUAME
SQUAMOSAL n thin platelike paired bone in the skull of vertebrates ▷ adj of or relating to this bone
SQUAMOSE same as > SQUAMOUS
SQUAMOUS adj (of epithelium) consisting of one or more layers of flat platelike cells
SQUAMULA same as > SQUAMELLA
SQUAMULAS > SQUAMULA
SQUAMULE same as > SQUAMELLA
SQUAMULES > SQUAMULE
SQUANDER vb waste (money or resources) ▷ n extravagance or dissipation
SQUANDERS > SQUANDER
SQUARE n geometric figure with four equal sides and four right angles ▷ adj square in shape ▷ vb multiply (a number) by itself ▷ adv squarely, directly
SQUARED > SQUARE
SQUARELY adv in a direct way
SQUARER > SQUARE
SQUARERS > SQUARE
SQUARES > SQUARE
SQUAREST > SQUARE
SQUARIAL n type of square dish for receiving satellite television

SQUARIALS > SQUARIAL
SQUARING > SQUARE
SQUARINGS > SQUARE
SQUARISH > SQUARE
SQUARK n hypothetical boson partner of a quark
SQUARKS > SQUARK
SQUARROSE adj having a rough surface
SQUARSON n clergyman who is also landowner
SQUARSONS > SQUARSON
SQUASH vb crush flat ▷ n sweet fruit drink diluted with water
SQUASHED > SQUASH
SQUASHER > SQUASH
SQUASHERS > SQUASH
SQUASHES > SQUASH
SQUASHIER > SQUASHY
SQUASHILY > SQUASHY
SQUASHING > SQUASH
SQUASHY adj soft and easily squashed
SQUAT vb crouch with the knees bent and the weight on the feet ▷ n place where squatters live ▷ adj short and broad
SQUATLY > SQUAT
SQUATNESS > SQUAT
SQUATS > SQUAT
SQUATTED > SQUAT
SQUATTER n illegal occupier of unused premises ▷ vb to splash along
SQUATTERS > SQUATTER
SQUATTEST > SQUAT
SQUATTIER > SQUATTY
SQUATTILY > SQUATTY
SQUATTING > SQUAT
SQUATTLE vb squat
SQUATTLED > SQUATTLE
SQUATTLES > SQUATTLE
SQUATTY adj short and broad
SQUAW n offensive term for a Native American woman
SQUAWBUSH n American shrub
SQUAWFISH n North American minnow
SQUAWK n loud harsh cry ▷ vb utter a squawk
SQUAWKED > SQUAWK
SQUAWKER > SQUAWK
SQUAWKERS > SQUAWK
SQUAWKIER > SQUAWK
SQUAWKING > SQUAWK
SQUAWKS > SQUAWK
SQUAWKY > SQUAWK
SQUAWMAN n offensive term for a White man married to a Native American woman
SQUAWMEN > SQUAWMAN
SQUAWROOT n North American parasitic plant
SQUAWS > SQUAW
SQUEAK n short shrill cry or sound ▷ vb make or utter a squeak
SQUEAKED > SQUEAK

SQUEAKER > SQUEAK
SQUEAKERS > SQUEAK
SQUEAKERY > SQUEAK
SQUEAKIER > SQUEAK
SQUEAKILY > SQUEAK
SQUEAKING > SQUEAK
SQUEAKS > SQUEAK
SQUEAKY > SQUEAK
SQUEAL n long shrill cry or sound ▷ vb make or utter a squeal
SQUEALED > SQUEAL
SQUEALER > SQUEAL
SQUEALERS > SQUEAL
SQUEALING > SQUEAL
SQUEALS > SQUEAL
SQUEAMISH adj easily sickened or shocked
SQUEEGEE n tool with a rubber blade for clearing water from a surface ▷ vb remove (water or other liquid) from (something) by use of a squeegee
SQUEEGEED > SQUEEGEE
SQUEEGEES > SQUEEGEE
SQUEEZE vb grip or press firmly ▷ n squeezing
SQUEEZED > SQUEEZE
SQUEEZER > SQUEEZE
SQUEEZERS > SQUEEZE
SQUEEZES > SQUEEZE
SQUEEZIER > SQUEEZE
SQUEEZING > SQUEEZE
SQUEEZY > SQUEEZE
SQUEG vb oscillate
SQUEGGED > SQUEG
SQUEGGER > SQUEG
SQUEGGERS > SQUEG
SQUEGGING > SQUEG
SQUEGS > SQUEG
SQUELCH vb make a wet sucking sound, as by walking through mud ▷ n squelching sound
SQUELCHED > SQUELCH
SQUELCHER > SQUELCH
SQUELCHES > SQUELCH
SQUELCHY > SQUELCH
SQUIB n small firework that hisses before exploding
SQUIBBED > SQUIB
SQUIBBING > SQUIB
SQUIBS > SQUIB
SQUID n sea creature with a long soft body and ten tentacles ▷ vb (of a parachute) to assume an elongated squidlike shape owing to excess air pressure
SQUIDDED > SQUID
SQUIDDING > SQUID
SQUIDGE vb squash
SQUIDGED > SQUIDGE
SQUIDGES > SQUIDGE
SQUIDGIER > SQUIDGE
SQUIDGING > SQUIDGE
SQUIDGY adj soft, moist, and squashy
SQUIDS > SQUID
SQUIER same as > SQUIRE
SQUIERS > SQUIER

SQUIFF same as > SQUIFFY
SQUIFFED same as > SQUIFFY
SQUIFFER n concertina
SQUIFFERS > SQUIFFER
SQUIFFIER > SQUIFFY
SQUIFFY adj slightly drunk
SQUIGGLE n wavy line ▷ vb wriggle
SQUIGGLED > SQUIGGLE
SQUIGGLER > SQUIGGLE
SQUIGGLES > SQUIGGLE
SQUIGGLY > SQUIGGLE
SQUILGEE same as > SQUEEGEE
SQUILGEED > SQUILGEE
SQUILGEES > SQUILGEE
SQUILL n Mediterranean plant of the lily family
SQUILLA n type of mantis shrimp
SQUILLAE > SQUILLA
SQUILLAS > SQUILLA
SQUILLION n extremely large but unspecified number, quantity, or amount
SQUILLS > SQUILL
SQUINANCY same as > QUINSY
SQUINCH n small arch across an internal corner of a tower, used to support a superstructure such as a spire ▷ vb squeeze
SQUINCHED > SQUINCH
SQUINCHES > SQUINCH
SQUINIED > SQUINY
SQUINIES > SQUINY
SQUINNIED > SQUINNY
SQUINNIER > SQUINNY
SQUINNIES > SQUINNY
SQUINNY vb squint ▷ adj squint
SQUINT vb have eyes which face in different directions ▷ n squinting condition of the eye ▷ adj crooked
SQUINTED > SQUINT
SQUINTER > SQUINT
SQUINTERS > SQUINT
SQUINTEST > SQUINT
SQUINTIER > SQUINT
SQUINTING > SQUINT
SQUINTS > SQUINT
SQUINTY > SQUINT
SQUINY same as > SQUINNY
SQUINYING > SQUINY
SQUIRAGE n body of squires
SQUIRAGES > SQUIRAGE
SQUIRALTY same as > SQUIRAGE
SQUIRARCH n person who believes in government by squires
SQUIRE n country gentleman, usu the main landowner in a community ▷ vb (of a man) escort (a woman)
SQUIREAGE same as

> SQUIRAGE
SQUIRED > SQUIRE
SQUIREDOM > SQUIRE
SQUIREEN n petty squire
SQUIREENS > SQUIREEN
SQUIRELY > SQUIRE
SQUIRES > SQUIRE
SQUIRESS n wife of squire
SQUIRING > SQUIRE
SQUIRISH > SQUIRE
SQUIRM vb wriggle, writhe ▷ n wriggling movement
SQUIRMED > SQUIRM
SQUIRMER > SQUIRM
SQUIRMERS > SQUIRM
SQUIRMIER > SQUIRMY
SQUIRMING > SQUIRM
SQUIRMS > SQUIRM
SQUIRMY adj moving with a wriggling motion
SQUIRR same as > SKIRR
SQUIRRED > SQUIRR
SQUIRREL n small bushy-tailed tree-living animal ▷ vb store for future use
SQUIRRELS > SQUIRREL
SQUIRRELY > SQUIRREL
SQUIRRING > SQUIRR
SQUIRRS > SQUIRR
SQUIRT vb force (a liquid) or (of a liquid) be forced out of a narrow opening ▷ n jet of liquid
SQUIRTED > SQUIRT
SQUIRTER > SQUIRT
SQUIRTERS > SQUIRT
SQUIRTING > SQUIRT
SQUIRTS > SQUIRT
SQUISH n (make) a soft squelching sound ▷ vb crush (something) with a soft squelching sound
SQUISHED > SQUISH
SQUISHES > SQUISH
SQUISHIER > SQUISHY
SQUISHING > SQUISH
SQUISHY adj soft and yielding to the touch
SQUIT n insignificant person
SQUITCH n couch grass
SQUITCHES > SQUITCH
SQUITS > SQUIT
SQUITTERS npl diarrhoea
SQUIZ n look or glance, esp an inquisitive one
SQUIZZES > SQUIZ
SQUOOSH vb squash
SQUOOSHED > SQUOOSH
SQUOOSHES > SQUOOSH
SQUOOSHY > SQUOOSH
SQUUSH same as > SQUOOSH
SQUUSHED > SQUUSH
SQUUSHES > SQUUSH
SQUUSHING > SQUUSH
SRADDHA n Hindu offering to ancestor
SRADDHAS > SRADDHA
SRADHA same as > SRADHA
SRADHAS > SRADHA
SRI n title of respect used when addressing a Hindu

SRIS > SRI
ST interj exclamation to attract attention
STAB vb pierce with something pointed ▷ n stabbing
STABBED > STAB
STABBER > STAB
STABBERS > STAB
STABBING > STAB
STABBINGS > STAB
STABILATE n preserved collection of tiny animals
STABILE n stationary abstract construction, usually of wire, metal, wood, etc ▷ adj fixed
STABILES > STABILE
STABILISE same as > STABILIZE
STABILITY n quality of being stable
STABILIZE vb make or become stable
STABLE n building in which horses are kept ▷ vb put or keep (a horse) in a stable ▷ adj firmly fixed or established
STABLEBOY n boy or man who works in a stable
STABLED > STABLE
STABLEMAN same as > STABLEBOY
STABLEMEN > STABLEMAN
STABLER n stable owner
STABLERS > STABLER
STABLES > STABLE
STABLEST > STABLE
STABLING n stable buildings or accommodation
STABLINGS > STABLING
STABLISH archaic variant of > ESTABLISH
STABLY > STABLE
STABS > STAB
STACATION same as > STAYCATION
STACCATI > STACCATO
STACCATO adv with the notes sharply separated ▷ adj consisting of short abrupt sounds ▷ n staccato note
STACCATOS > STACCATO
STACHYS n type of plant of the genus which includes lamb's ears and betony
STACHYSES > STACHYS
STACK n ordered pile ▷ vb pile in a stack
STACKABLE > STACK
STACKED > STACK
STACKER > STACK
STACKERS > STACK
STACKET n fence of wooden posts
STACKETS > STACKET
STACKING n arrangement of aircraft traffic in busy flight lanes
STACKINGS > STACKING
STACKLESS > STACK

S

STACKROOM n area of library where books are not on open shelves
STACKS > STACK
STACKUP n number of aircraft waiting to land
STACKUPS > STACKUP
STACKYARD n place where livestock are kept
STACTE n one of several sweet-smelling spices used in incense
STACTES > STACTE
STADDA n type of saw
STADDAS > STADDA
STADDLE n type of support or prop
STADDLES > STADDLE
STADE same as > STADIUM
STADES > STADE
STADIA n instrument used in surveying
STADIAL n stage in development of glacier
STADIALS > STADIAL
STADIAS > STADIA
STADIUM n sports arena with tiered seats for spectators
STADIUMS > STADIUM
STAFF n people employed in an organization ▷ vb supply with personnel
STAFFAGE n ornamentation in work of art
STAFFAGES > STAFFAGE
STAFFED > STAFF
STAFFER n member of staff, esp, in journalism, of editorial staff
STAFFERS > STAFFER
STAFFING > STAFF
STAFFMAN n person who holds the levelling staff when a survey is being made
STAFFMEN > STAFFMAN
STAFFROOM n common room for teachers
STAFFS > STAFF
STAG n adult male deer ▷ adv without a female escort ▷ vb apply for (shares in a new issue) with the intention of selling them for a quick profit
STAGE n step or period of development ▷ vb put (a play) on stage
STAGEABLE > STAGE
STAGED > STAGE
STAGEFUL n amount that can appear on stage
STAGEFULS > STAGEFUL
STAGEHAND n person who moves props and scenery on a stage
STAGELIKE > STAGE
STAGER n person of experience
STAGERIES > STAGERY
STAGERS > STAGER
STAGERY n theatrical effects or techniques

STAGES > STAGE
STAGETTE same as > BACHELORETTE
STAGETTES > STAGETTE
STAGEY same as > STAGY
STAGGARD n male red deer in the fourth year of life
STAGGARDS > STAGGARD
STAGGART same as > STAGGARD
STAGGARTS > STAGGART
STAGGED > STAG
STAGGER vb walk unsteadily ▷ n staggering
STAGGERED > STAGGER
STAGGERER > STAGGER
STAGGERS n disease of horses and other domestic animals that causes staggering
STAGGERY > STAGGER
STAGGIE n little stag
STAGGIER > STAG
STAGGIES > STAGGIE
STAGGIEST > STAG
STAGGING > STAG
STAGGY > STAG
STAGHORN as in staghorn fern type of fern with fronds that resemble antlers
STAGHORNS > STAGHORN
STAGHOUND n breed of hound similar in appearance to the foxhound but larger
STAGIER > STAGY
STAGIEST > STAGY
STAGILY > STAGY
STAGINESS > STAGY
STAGING n temporary support used in building
STAGINGS > STAGING
STAGNANCE > STAGNANT
STAGNANCY > STAGNANT
STAGNANT adj (of water or air) stale from not moving
STAGNATE vb be stagnant
STAGNATED > STAGNATE
STAGNATES > STAGNATE
STAGS > STAG
STAGY adj too theatrical or dramatic
STAID adj sedate, serious, and rather dull
STAIDER > STAID
STAIDEST > STAID
STAIDLY > STAID
STAIDNESS > STAID
STAIG Scots variant of > STAG
STAIGS > STAIG
STAIN vb discolour, mark ▷ n discoloration or mark
STAINABLE > STAIN
STAINED > STAIN
STAINER > STAIN
STAINERS > STAIN
STAINING > STAIN
STAININGS > STAIN
STAINLESS adj resistant to discoloration, esp discoloration resulting from corrosion ▷ n stainless steel

STAINS > STAIN
STAIR n one step in a flight of stairs
STAIRCASE n flight of stairs with a handrail or banisters ▷ vb buy other houses in same building
STAIRED adj having stairs
STAIRFOOT n place at foot of stairs
STAIRHEAD n top of a flight of stairs
STAIRLESS > STAIR
STAIRLIFT n wall-mounted lifting device to carry person up stairs
STAIRLIKE > STAIR
STAIRS npl flight of steps between floors, usu indoors
STAIRSTEP n one of the steps in a staircase
STAIRWAY n staircase
STAIRWAYS > STAIRWAY
STAIRWELL n vertical shaft in a building that contains a staircase
STAIRWISE adv by steps
STAIRWORK n unseen plotting
STAITH same as > STAITHE
STAITHE n wharf
STAITHES > STAITHE
STAITHS > STAITH
STAKE n pointed stick or post driven into the ground as a support or marker ▷ vb support or mark out with stakes
STAKED > STAKE
STAKEOUT n police surveillance of an area or house ▷ vb keep an area or house under surveillance
STAKEOUTS > STAKEOUT
STAKES > STAKE
STAKING > STAKE
STALACTIC adj relating to the masses of calcium carbonate hanging from the roofs of limestone caves
STALAG n German prisoner-of-war camp in World War II
STALAGMA n stalagmite
STALAGMAS > STALAGMA
STALAGS > STALAG
STALE adj not fresh ▷ vb make or become stale ▷ n urine of horses or cattle
STALED > STALE
STALELY > STALE
STALEMATE n (in chess) position in which any of a player's moves would put his king in check, resulting in a draw ▷ vb subject to a stalemate
STALENESS > STALE
STALER > STALE
STALES > STALE
STALEST > STALE
STALING > STALE

STALK n plant's stem ▷ vb follow or approach stealthily
STALKED > STALK
STALKER > STALK
STALKERS > STALK
STALKIER > STALKY
STALKIEST > STALKY
STALKILY > STALKY
STALKING > STALK
STALKINGS > STALK
STALKLESS > STALK
STALKLIKE > STALK
STALKO n idle gentleman
STALKOES > STALKO
STALKS > STALK
STALKY adj like a stalk
STALL n small stand for the display and sale of goods ▷ vb stop (a motor vehicle or engine) or (of a motor vehicle or engine) stop accidentally
STALLAGE n rent paid for market stall
STALLAGES > STALLAGE
STALLED > STALL
STALLING > STALL
STALLINGS > STALL
STALLION n uncastrated male horse
STALLIONS > STALLION
STALLMAN n keeper of a stall
STALLMEN > STALLMAN
STALLS > STALL
STALWART adj strong and sturdy ▷ n stalwart person
STALWARTS > STALWART
STALWORTH n stalwart person
STAMEN n pollen-producing part of a flower
STAMENED adj having stamen
STAMENS > STAMEN
STAMINA n enduring energy and strength
STAMINAL > STAMINA
STAMINAS > STAMINA
STAMINATE adj (of plants) having stamens, esp having stamens but no carpels
STAMINEAL adj having a stamen
STAMINODE n stamen that produces no pollen
STAMINODY n development of any of various plant organs into stamens
STAMINOID adj like a stamen
STAMMEL n coarse woollen cloth in former use for undergarments
STAMMELS > STAMMEL
STAMMER vb speak or say with involuntary pauses or repetition of syllables ▷ n tendency to stammer
STAMMERED > STAMMER
STAMMERER > STAMMER
STAMMERS > STAMMER

STAMNOI > STAMNOS
STAMNOS *n* ancient Greek jar
STAMP *n* piece of gummed paper stuck to an envelope or parcel to show that the postage has been paid ▷ *vb* bring (one's foot) down forcefully
STAMPED > STAMP
STAMPEDE *n* sudden rush of frightened animals or of a crowd ▷ *vb* (cause to) take part in a stampede
STAMPEDED > STAMPEDE
STAMPEDER > STAMPEDE
STAMPEDES > STAMPEDE
STAMPEDO *same as* > STAMPEDE
STAMPEDOS > STAMPEDO
STAMPER > STAMP
STAMPERS > STAMP
STAMPING > STAMP
STAMPINGS > STAMP
STAMPLESS > STAMP
STAMPS > STAMP
STANCE *n* attitude
STANCES > STANCE
STANCH *vb* stem the flow of (a liquid, esp blood) ▷ *adj* loyal and dependable
STANCHED > STANCH
STANCHEL *same as* > STANCHION
STANCHELS > STANCHEL
STANCHER > STANCH
STANCHERS > STANCH
STANCHES > STANCH
STANCHEST > STANCH
STANCHING > STANCH
STANCHION *n* upright bar used as a support ▷ *vb* provide or support with a stanchion or stanchions
STANCHLY > STANCH
STANCK *adj* faint
STAND *vb* be in, rise to, or place in an upright position ▷ *n* stall for the sale of goods
STANDARD *n* level of quality ▷ *adj* usual, regular, or average
STANDARDS > STANDARD
STANDAWAY *adj* erect
STANDBY *n* person or thing that is ready for use
STANDBYS > STANDBY
STANDDOWN *n* return to normal after alert
STANDEE *n* person who stands, esp when there are no vacant seats
STANDEES > STANDEE
STANDEN > STAND
STANDER > STAND
STANDERS > STAND
STANDFAST *n* reliable person or thing
STANDGALE *same as* > STANIEL
STANDING > STAND
STANDINGS > STAND
STANDISH *n* stand, usually

of metal, for pens, ink bottles, etc
STANDOFF *n* act or an instance of standing off or apart ▷ *vb* stay at a distance
STANDOFFS > STANDOFF
STANDOUT *n* distinctive or outstanding person or thing
STANDOUTS > STANDOUT
STANDOVER *n* threatening or intimidating act
STANDPAT *n* (in poker) refusal to change one's card
STANDPIPE *n* tap attached to a water main to provide a public water supply
STANDS > STAND
STANDUP *n* comedian who performs solo
STANDUPS > STANDUP
STANE *Scot word for* > STONE
STANED > STANE
STANES > STANE
STANG *vb* sting
STANGED > STANG
STANGING > STANG
STANGS > STANG
STANHOPE *n* light one-seater carriage with two or four wheels
STANHOPES > STANHOPE
STANIEL *n* kestrel
STANIELS > STANIEL
STANINE *n* scale of nine levels
STANINES > STANINE
STANING > STANE
STANK *vb* dam
STANKED > STINK
STANKING > STINK
STANKS > STINK
STANNARY *n* place or region where tin is mined or worked
STANNATE *n* salt of stannic acid
STANNATES > STANNATE
STANNATOR *n* member of old Cornish parliament
STANNEL *same as* > STANIEL
STANNELS > STANNEL
STANNIC *adj* of or containing tin, esp in the tetravalent state
STANNITE *n* grey metallic mineral
STANNITES > STANNITE
STANNOUS *adj* of or containing tin, esp in the divalent state
STANNUM *n* tin (the metal)
STANNUMS > STANNUM
STANOL *n* drug taken to prevent heart disease
STANOLS > STANOL
STANYEL *same as* > STANIEL
STANYELS > STANYEL
STANZA *n* verse of a poem

STANZAED > STANZA
STANZAIC > STANZA
STANZAS > STANZA
STANZE *same as* > STANZA
STANZES > STANZE
STANZO *same as* > STANZO
STANZOES > STANZO
STANZOS > STANZO
STAP *same as* > STOP
STAPEDES > STAPES
STAPEDIAL > STAPES
STAPEDII > STAPEDIUS
STAPEDIUS *n* muscle in stapes
STAPELIA *n* fleshy cactus-like leafless African plant
STAPELIAS > STAPELIA
STAPES *n* stirrup-shaped bone that is the innermost of three small bones in the middle ear of mammals
STAPH *n* staphylococcus
STAPHS > STAPH
STAPLE *n* U-shaped piece of metal used to fasten papers or secure things ▷ *vb* fasten with staples ▷ *adj* of prime importance, principal
STAPLED > STAPLE
STAPLER *n* small device for fastening papers together
STAPLERS > STAPLER
STAPLES > STAPLE
STAPLING *n* as in *stomach stapling* a surgical treatment for obesity
STAPLINGS > STAPLING
STAPPED > STAP
STAPPING > STAP
STAPPLE *same as* > STOPPLE
STAPPLES > STAPPLE
STAPS > STAP
STAR *n* hot gaseous mass in space, visible in the night sky as a point of light ▷ *vb* feature or be featured as a star ▷ *adj* leading, famous
STARAGEN *n* tarragon
STARAGENS > STARAGEN
STARBOARD *n* right-hand side of a ship, when facing forward ▷ *adj* of or on this side ▷ *vb* turn or be turned towards the starboard
STARBURST *n* pattern of rays or lines radiating from a light source
STARCH *n* carbohydrate forming the main food element in bread, potatoes, etc, and used mixed with water for stiffening fabric ▷ *vb* stiffen (fabric) with starch ▷ *adj* (of a person) formal
STARCHED > STARCH
STARCHER > STARCH
STARCHERS > STARCH
STARCHES > STARCH
STARCHIER > STARCHY
STARCHILY > STARCHY
STARCHING > STARCH

STARCHY *adj* containing starch
STARDOM *n* status of a star in the entertainment or sports world
STARDOMS > STARDOM
STARDRIFT *n* regular movement of stars
STARDUST *n* dusty material found between the stars
STARDUSTS > STARDUST
STARE *vb* look or gaze fixedly (at) ▷ *n* fixed gaze
STARED > STARE
STARER > STARE
STARERS > STARE
STARES > STARE
STARETS *n* Russian holy man
STARETSES > STARETS
STARETZ *same as* > STARETZ
STARETZES > STARETZ
STARFISH *n* star-shaped sea creature
STARFRUIT *n* tree with edible yellow fruit which is star-shaped on cross section
STARGAZE *vb* observe the stars
STARGAZED > STARGAZE
STARGAZER > STARGAZE
STARGAZES > STARGAZE
STARGAZEY as in *stargazey pie* Cornish fish pie
STARING > STARE
STARINGLY > STARE
STARINGS > STARE
STARK *adj* harsh, unpleasant, and plain ▷ *adv* completely ▷ *vb* stiffen
STARKED > STARK
STARKEN *vb* become or make stark
STARKENED > STARKEN
STARKENS > STARKEN
STARKER > STARK
STARKERS *adj* completely naked
STARKEST > STARK
STARKING > STARK
STARKLY > STARK
STARKNESS > STARK
STARKS > STARK
STARLESS > STAR
STARLET *n* young actress presented as a future star
STARLETS > STARLET
STARLIGHT *n* light that comes from the stars ▷ *adj* of or like starlight
STARLIKE > STAR
STARLING *n* songbird with glossy black speckled feathers
STARLINGS > STARLING
STARLIT *same as* > STARLIGHT
STARN *same as* > STERN
STARNED > STARN
STARNIE *n* Scots word for little star

STARNIES > STARNIE
STARNING > STARN
STARNOSE n American mole with starlike nose
STARNOSES > STARNOSE
STARNS > STARN
STAROSTA n headman of Russian village
STAROSTAS > STAROSTA
STAROSTY n estate of Polish nobleman
STARR n (in Judaism) release from a debt
STARRED > STAR
STARRIER > STARRY
STARRIEST > STARRY
STARRILY > STARRY
STARRING > STAR
STARRINGS > STARE
STARRS > STARR
STARRY adj full of or like stars
STARS > STAR
STARSHINE n starlight
STARSHIP n spacecraft in science fiction
STARSHIPS > STARSHIP
STARSPOT n dark patch on surface of star
STARSPOTS > STARSPOT
STARSTONE n precious stone reflecting light in starlike pattern
START vb take the first step, begin ▷ n first part of something
STARTED > START
STARTER n first course of a meal
STARTERS > STARTER
STARTFUL adj tending to start
STARTING > START
STARTINGS > START
STARTISH same as > STARTFUL
STARTLE vb slightly surprise or frighten
STARTLED > STARTLE
STARTLER > STARTLE
STARTLERS > STARTLE
STARTLES > STARTLE
STARTLING adj causing surprise or fear
STARTLISH adj easily startled
STARTLY same as > STARTLISH
STARTS > START
STARTSY > STARETS
STARTUP n business enterprise that has been launched recently
STARTUPS > STARTUP
STARVE vb die or suffer or cause to die or suffer from hunger
STARVED > STARVE
STARVER > STARVE
STARVERS > STARVE
STARVES > STARVE
STARVING > STARVE
STARVINGS > STARVE
STARWORT n plant with

star-shaped flowers
STARWORTS > STARWORT
STASES > STASIS
STASH vb store in a secret place ▷ n secret store
STASHED > STASH
STASHES > STASH
STASHIE same as > STUSHIE
STASHIES > STASHIE
STASHING > STASH
STASIDION n stall in Greek church
STASIMA > STASIMON
STASIMON n ode sung in Greek tragedy
STASIS n stagnation in the normal flow of bodily fluids, such as the blood or urine
STAT n statistic
STATABLE > STATE
STATAL adj of a federal state
STATANT adj (of an animal) in profile with all four feet on the ground
STATE n condition of a person or thing ▷ adj of or concerning the State ▷ vb express in words
STATEABLE > STATE
STATED adj (esp of a sum) determined by agreement
STATEDLY > STATED
STATEHOOD > STATE
STATELESS adj not belonging to any country
STATELET n small state
STATELETS > STATELET
STATELIER > STATELY
STATELILY > STATELY
STATELY adj dignified or grand ▷ adv in a stately manner
STATEMENT n something stated ▷ vb assess (a pupil) with regard to his or her special educational needs
STATER n any of various usually silver coins of ancient Greece
STATEROOM n private cabin on a ship
STATERS > STATER
STATES > STATE
STATESIDE adv of, in, to, or towards the US
STATESMAN n experienced and respected political leader
STATESMEN > STATESMAN
STATEWIDE adj throughout a state
STATIC adj stationary or inactive ▷ n crackling sound or speckled picture caused by interference in radio or television reception
STATICAL > STATIC
STATICE n plant name formerly used for both thrift and sea lavender
STATICES > STATICE

STATICKY > STATIC
STATICS n branch of mechanics dealing with the forces producing a state of equilibrium
STATIM adv right away
STATIN n type of drug that lowers the levels of low-density lipoproteins in the blood
STATING > STATE
STATINS > STATIN
STATION n place where trains stop for passengers ▷ vb assign (someone) to a particular place
STATIONAL > STATION
STATIONED > STATION
STATIONER n dealer in stationery
STATIONS > STATION
STATISM n theory or practice of concentrating economic and political power in the state
STATISMS > STATISM
STATIST n advocate of statism ▷ adj of, characteristic of, advocating, or relating to statism
STATISTIC n numerical fact collected and classified systematically
STATISTS > STATIST
STATIVE adj denoting a verb describing a state rather than an activity, act, or event ▷ n stative verb
STATIVES > STATIVE
STATOCYST n organ of balance in some invertebrates
STATOLITH n any of the granules of calcium carbonate occurring in a statocyst
STATOR n stationary part of a rotary machine or device, esp of a motor or generator
STATORS > STATOR
STATS > STAT
STATTO n person preoccupied with the facts and figures of a subject
STATTOS > STATTO
STATUA same as > STATUE
STATUARY n statues collectively ▷ adj of, relating to, or suitable for statues
STATUAS > STATUA
STATUE n large sculpture of a human or animal figure
STATUED adj decorated with or portrayed in a statue or statues
STATUES > STATUE
STATUETTE n small statue
STATURE n person's height
STATURED adj having stature
STATURES > STATURE
STATUS n social position

STATUSES > STATUS
STATUSY adj conferring or having status
STATUTE n written law
STATUTES > STATUTE
STATUTORY adj required or authorized by law
STAUMREL n stupid person
STAUMRELS > STAUMREL
STAUN Scot word for > STAND
STAUNCH same as > STANCH
STAUNCHED > STAUNCH
STAUNCHER > STAUNCH
STAUNCHES > STAUNCH
STAUNCHLY > STAUNCH
STAUNING > STAUN
STAUNS > STAUN
STAVE same as > STAFF
STAVED > STAVE
STAVES > STAVE
STAVING > STAVE
STAVUDINE n drug used to treat HIV
STAW Scots form of > STALL
STAWED > STAW
STAWING > STAW
STAWS > STAW
STAY vb remain in a place or condition ▷ n period of staying in a place
STAYAWAY n strike in South Africa
STAYAWAYS > STAYAWAY
STAYED > STAY
STAYER n person or thing that stays
STAYERS > STAYER
STAYING > STAY
STAYLESS adj with no stays or support
STAYMAKER n corset maker
STAYNE same as > STAIN
STAYNED > STAYNE
STAYNES > STAYNE
STAYNING > STAYNE
STAYRE same as > STAIR
STAYRES > STAYRE
STAYS npl old-fashioned corsets with bones in them
STAYSAIL n sail fastened on a stay
STAYSAILS > STAYSAIL
STEAD n place or function that should be taken by another ▷ vb help or benefit
STEADED > STEAD
STEADFAST adj firm, determined
STEADIED > STEADY
STEADIER > STEADY
STEADIERS > STEADY
STEADIES > STEADY
STEADIEST > STEADY
STEADILY > STEADY
STEADING n farmstead
STEADINGS > STEADING
STEADS > STEAD
STEADY adj not shaky or wavering ▷ vb make steady ▷ adv in a steady manner

STEADYING > STEADY
STEAK *n* thick slice of meat, esp beef
STEAKS > STEAK
STEAL *vb* take unlawfully or without permission
STEALABLE > STEAL
STEALAGE *n* theft
STEALAGES > STEALAGE
STEALE *n* handle
STEALED > STEAL
STEALER *n* person who steals something
STEALERS > STEALER
STEALES > STEALE
STEALING > STEAL
STEALINGS > STEAL
STEALS > STEAL
STEALT > STEAL
STEALTH *n* moving carefully and quietly ▷ *adj* (of technology) able to render an aircraft almost invisible to radar ▷ *vb* approach undetected
STEALTHED > STEALTH
STEALTHS > STEALTH
STEALTHY *adj* characterized by great caution, secrecy, etc
STEAM *n* vapour into which water changes when boiled ▷ *vb* give off steam
STEAMBOAT *n* boat powered by a steam engine
STEAMED > STEAM
STEAMER *n* steam-propelled ship ▷ *vb* travel by steamer
STEAMERED > STEAMER
STEAMERS > STEAMER
STEAMIE *n* public wash house
STEAMIER > STEAMY
STEAMIES > STEAMIE
STEAMIEST > STEAMY
STEAMILY > STEAMY
STEAMING *adj* very hot ▷ *n* robbery, esp of passengers in a railway carriage or bus, by a large gang of armed youths
STEAMINGS > STEAMING
STEAMROLL *vb* crush (opposition) by overpowering force
STEAMS > STEAM
STEAMSHIP *n* ship powered by steam engines
STEAMY *adj* full of steam
STEAN *n* earthenware vessel
STEANE *same as >* STEEN
STEANED > STEANE
STEANES > STEANE
STEANING > STEANE
STEANINGS > STEANE
STEANS > STEAN
STEAPSIN *n* pancreatic lipase
STEAPSINS > STEAPSIN
STEAR *same as >* STEER
STEARAGE *same as >* STEERAGE

STEARAGES > STEARAGE
STEARATE *n* any salt or ester of stearic acid
STEARATES > STEARATE
STEARD > STEAR
STEARE *same as >* STEER
STEARED > STEARE
STEARES > STEARE
STEARIC *adj* of or relating to suet or fat
STEARIN *n* colourless crystalline ester of glycerol and stearic acid
STEARINE *same as >* STEARIN
STEARINES > STEARINE
STEARING > STEAR
STEARINS > STEARIN
STEARS > STEAR
STEARSMAN *same as >* STEERSMAN
STEARSMEN > STEARSMAN
STEATITE *same as >* SOAPSTONE
STEATITES > STEATITE
STEATITIC > STEATITE
STEATOMA *n* tumour of sebaceous gland
STEATOMAS > STEATOMA
STEATOSES > STEATOSIS
STEATOSIS *n* abnormal accumulation of fat
STED *same as >* STEAD
STEDD *same as >* STEAD
STEDDE *same as >* STEAD
STEDDED > STED
STEDDES > STEDDE
STEDDIED > STEDDY
STEDDIES > STEDDY
STEDDING > STED
STEDDS > STEDD
STEDDY *same as >* STEADY
STEDDYING > STEDDY
STEDE *same as >* STEAD
STEDED > STEDE
STEDES > STEDE
STEDFAST *same as >* STEADFAST
STEDING > STEDE
STEDS > STED
STEED *same as >* STEAD
STEEDED > STEED
STEEDIED > STEEDY
STEEDIES > STEEDY
STEEDING > STEED
STEEDLIKE > STEED
STEEDS > STEED
STEEDY *same as >* STEADY
STEEDYING > STEEDY
STEEK *vb* Scots word meaning shut
STEEKED > STEEK
STEEKING > STEEK
STEEKIT > STEEK
STEEKS > STEEK
STEEL *n* hard malleable alloy of iron and carbon ▷ *vb* prepare (oneself) for something unpleasant
STEELBOW *n* material lent to tenant by landlord
STEELBOWS > STEELBOW

STEELD > STEEL
STEELED > STEEL
STEELHEAD *n* silvery North Pacific variety of the rainbow trout
STEELIE *n* steel ball bearing used as marble
STEELIER > STEEL
STEELIES > STEELIE
STEELIEST > STEELIE
STEELING > STEEL
STEELINGS > STEEL
STEELMAN *n* person working in steel industry
STEELMEN > STEELMAN
STEELS *npl* shares and bonds of steel companies
STEELWARE *n* things made of steel
STEELWORK *n* frame, foundation, building, or article made of steel
STEELY > STEEL
STEELYARD *n* portable balance consisting of a pivoted bar with two unequal arms
STEEM *variant of >* ESTEEM
STEEMED > STEEM
STEEMING > STEEM
STEEMS > STEEM
STEEN *vb* line with stone
STEENBOK *n* small antelope of central and southern Africa
STEENBOKS > STEENBOK
STEENBRAS *n* variety of sea bream
STEENBUCK *same as >* STEENBOK
STEENED > STEEN
STEENING > STEEN
STEENINGS > STEEN
STEENKIRK *n* type of cravat
STEENS > STEEN
STEEP *adj* sloping sharply ▷ *vb* soak or be soaked in liquid ▷ *n* instance or the process of steeping or the condition of being steeped
STEEPED > STEEP
STEEPEN *vb* become or cause (something) to become steep or steeper
STEEPENED > STEEPEN
STEEPENS > STEEPEN
STEEPER > STEEP
STEEPERS > STEEP
STEEPEST > STEEP
STEEPEUP *adj* very steep
STEEPIER > STEEPY
STEEPIEST > STEEPY
STEEPING > STEEP
STEEPISH > STEEP
STEEPLE *same as >* SPIRE
STEEPLED > STEEPLE
STEEPLES > STEEPLE
STEEPLING *adj* going up on a steep trajectory
STEEPLY > STEEP
STEEPNESS > STEEP
STEEPS > STEEP
STEEPUP *adj* very steep

STEEPY *same as >* STEEP
STEER *vb* direct the course of (a vehicle or ship) ▷ *n* castrated male ox
STEERABLE > STEER
STEERAGE *n* cheapest accommodation on a passenger ship
STEERAGES > STEERAGE
STEERED > STEER
STEERER > STEER
STEERERS > STEER
STEERIES > STEERY
STEERING > STEER
STEERINGS > STEER
STEERLING *n* young steer
STEERS > STEER
STEERSMAN *n* person who steers a vessel
STEERSMEN > STEERSMAN
STEERY *n* commotion
STEEVE *n* spar having a pulley block at one end, used for stowing cargo on a ship ▷ *vb* stow (cargo) securely in the hold of a ship
STEEVED > STEEVE
STEEVELY > STEEVE
STEEVER > STEEVE
STEEVES > STEEVE
STEEVEST > STEEVE
STEEVING > STEEVE
STEEVINGS > STEEVE
STEGNOSES > STEGNOSIS
STEGNOSIS *n* constriction of bodily pores
STEGNOTIC > STEGNOSIS
STEGODON *n* mammal of Pliocene to Pleistocene times, similar to the mastodon
STEGODONS > STEGODON
STEGODONT *same as >* STEGODON
STEGOMYIA *former name for >* AEDES
STEGOSAUR *n* quadrupedal herbivorous dinosaur
STEIL *same as >* STEAL
STEILS > STEIL
STEIN *same as >* STEEN
STEINBOCK *another name for >* IBEX
STEINBOK *same as >* STEENBOK
STEINBOKS > STEINBOK
STEINED > STEIN
STEINING > STEIN
STEININGS > STEIN
STEINKIRK *same as >* STEENKIRK
STEINS > STEIN
STELA *same as >* STELE
STELAE > STELE
STELAI > STELE
STELAR > STELE
STELE *n* upright stone slab or column decorated with figures or inscriptions

STELENE > STELE
STELES > STELE
STELIC > STELE
STELL n shelter for cattle or sheep built on moorland or hillsides ▷ vb position or place
STELLA n star or something star-shaped
STELLAR adj of stars
STELLAS > STELLA
STELLATE adj resembling a star in shape
STELLATED same as > STELLATE
STELLED > STELL
STELLERID n starfish
STELLIFY vb change or be changed into a star
STELLING > STELL
STELLIO n as in stellio lizard denoting type of lizard
STELLION n Mediterranean lizard
STELLIONS > STELLION
STELLITE n tradename for any of various alloys containing cobalt, chromium, carbon, tungsten, and molybdenum
STELLITES > STELLITE
STELLS > STELL
STELLULAR adj displaying or abounding in small stars
STEM vb stop (the flow of something) ▷ n main axis of a plant, which bears the leaves, axillary buds, and flowers
STEMBOK same as > STEENBOK
STEMBOKS > STEMBOK
STEMBUCK same as > STEENBOK
STEMBUCKS > STEMBUCK
STEME same as > STEAM
STEMED > STEME
STEMES > STEME
STEMHEAD n head of the stem of a vessel
STEMHEADS > STEMHEAD
STEMING > STEME
STEMLESS > STEM
STEMLET n little stem
STEMLETS > STEMLET
STEMLIKE > STEM
STEMMA n family tree
STEMMAS > STEMMA
STEMMATA > STEMMA
STEMMATIC > STEMMA
STEMME archaic variant of > STEM
STEMMED > STEM
STEMMER > STEM
STEMMERS > STEM
STEMMERY n tobacco factory
STEMMES > STEMME
STEMMIER > STEMMY
STEMMIEST > STEMMY
STEMMING > STEM
STEMMINGS > STEM

STEMMY adj (of wine) young and raw
STEMPEL n timber support
STEMPELS > STEMPEL
STEMPLE same as > STEMPEL
STEMPLES > STEMPLE
STEMS > STEM
STEMSON n curved timber scarfed into or bolted to the stem and keelson at the bow of a wooden vessel
STEMSONS > STEMSON
STEMWARE n collective term for glasses, goblets, etc, with stems
STEMWARES > STEMWARE
STEN vb stride
STENCH n foul smell ▷ vb cause to smell
STENCHED > STENCH
STENCHES > STENCH
STENCHFUL > STENCH
STENCHIER > STENCH
STENCHING > STENCH
STENCHY > STENCH
STENCIL n thin sheet with cut-out pattern through which ink or paint passes to form the pattern on the surface below ▷ vb make (a pattern) with a stencil
STENCILED > STENCIL
STENCILER > STENCIL
STENCILS > STENCIL
STEND vb Scots word meaning bound
STENDED > STEND
STENDING > STEND
STENDS > STEND
STENGAH same as > STINGER
STENGAHS > STENGAH
STENLOCK n fish of northern seas
STENLOCKS > STENLOCK
STENNED > STEN
STENNING > STEN
STENO n stenographer
STENOBATH n stenobathic organism
STENOKIES > STENOKY
STENOKOUS adj able to live in narrow range of environments
STENOKY n life and survival that is dependent on conditions remaining within a narrow range of variables
STENOPAIC adj having narrow opening
STENOS > STENO
STENOSED adj abnormally contracted
STENOSES > STENOSIS
STENOSIS n abnormal narrowing of a bodily canal or passage
STENOTIC > STENOSIS
STENOTYPE n machine with a keyboard for recording speeches in a phonetic shorthand
STENOTYPY n form of

shorthand in which alphabetic combinations are used to represent groups of sounds or short common words
STENS > STEN
STENT n surgical implant used to keep an artery open ▷ vb assess
STENTED > STENT
STENTING > STENT
STENTOR n person with an unusually loud voice
STENTORS > STENTOR
STENTOUR n tax assessor
STENTOURS > STENTOUR
STENTS > STENT
STEP vb move and set down the foot, as when walking ▷ n stepping
STEPBAIRN Scots word for > STEPCHILD
STEPCHILD n stepson or stepdaughter
STEPDAME n woman married to one's father
STEPDAMES > STEPDAME
STEPHANE n ancient Greek headdress
STEPHANES > STEPHANE
STEPLIKE > STEP
STEPNEY n spare wheel
STEPNEYS > STEPNEY
STEPOVER n (in football) instance of raising the foot over the ball as a feint
STEPOVERS > STEPOVER
STEPPE n extensive grassy plain usually without trees
STEPPED > STEP
STEPPER n person who or animal that steps, esp a horse or a dancer
STEPPERS > STEPPER
STEPPES > STEPPE
STEPPING > STEP
STEPS > STEP
STEPSON n son of one's husband or wife by an earlier relationship
STEPSONS > STEPSON
STEPSTOOL n stool able to be used as step
STEPT > STEP
STEPWISE adj arranged in the manner of or resembling steps ▷ adv with the form or appearance of steps
STERADIAN n SI unit of solid angle
STERCORAL adj relating to excrement
STERCULIA n dietary fibre used as a food stabilizer and denture adhesive
STERE n unit used to measure volumes of stacked timber
STEREO n stereophonic record player ▷ adj (of a sound system) using two or more separate microphones to feed two or more loudspeakers

through separate channels ▷ vb make stereophonic
STEREOED > STEREO
STEREOING > STEREO
STEREOME n tissue of a plant that provides mechanical support
STEREOMES > STEREOME
STEREOS > STEREO
STERES > STERE
STERIC adj of or caused by the spatial arrangement of atoms in a molecule
STERICAL same as > STERIC
STERIGMA n minute stalk bearing a spore or chain of spores in certain fungi
STERIGMAS > STERIGMA
STERILANT n any substance or agent used in sterilization
STERILE adj free from germs
STERILELY > STERILE
STERILISE same as > STERILIZE
STERILITY > STERILE
STERILIZE vb make sterile
STERLET n small sturgeon of seas and rivers in N Asia and E Europe
STERLETS > STERLET
STERLING n British money system ▷ adj genuine and reliable
STERLINGS > STERLING
STERN adj severe, strict ▷ n rear part of a ship ▷ vb row boat backward
STERNA > STERNUM
STERNAGE n sterns
STERNAGES > STERNAGE
STERNAL > STERNUM
STERNEBRA n part of breastbone
STERNED > STERN
STERNER > STERN
STERNEST > STERN
STERNFAST n rope for securing boat at stern
STERNING > STERN
STERNITE n part of arthropod
STERNITES > STERNITE
STERNITIC > STERNITE
STERNLY > STERN
STERNMOST adj farthest to the stern
STERNNESS > STERN
STERNPORT n opening in stern of ship
STERNPOST n main upright timber or structure at the stern of a vessel
STERNS > STERN
STERNSON n timber scarfed into or bolted to the sternpost and keelson at the stern of a wooden vessel
STERNSONS > STERNSON
STERNUM n long flat bone in the front of the body, to

which the collarbone and most of the ribs are attached

STERNUMS > STERNUM

STERNWARD *adv* towards the stern

STERNWAY *n* movement of a vessel sternforemost

STERNWAYS > STERNWAY

STEROID *n* organic compound containing a carbon ring system, such as many hormones

STEROIDAL > STEROID

STEROIDS > STEROID

STEROL *n* natural insoluble alcohol such as cholesterol and ergosterol

STEROLS > STEROL

STERTOR *n* laborious or noisy breathing caused by obstructed air passages

STERTORS > STERTOR

STERVE *same as* **>** STARVE

STERVED > STERVE

STERVES > STERVE

STERVING > STERVE

STET *interj* instruction to ignore an alteration previously made by a proofreader ▷ *vb* indicate to a printer that certain deleted matter is to be kept ▷ *n* word or mark indicating that certain deleted written matter is to be retained

STETS > STET

STETSON *n* cowboy hat

STETSONS > STETSON

STETTED > STET

STETTING > STET

STEVEDORE *n* person who loads and unloads ships ▷ *vb* load or unload (a ship, ship's cargo, etc)

STEVEN *n* voice

STEVENS > STEVEN

STEW *n* food cooked slowly in a closed pot ▷ *vb* cook slowly in a closed pot

STEWABLE > STEW

STEWARD *n* person who looks after passengers on a ship or aircraft ▷ *vb* act as a steward (of)

STEWARDED > STEWARD

STEWARDRY *n* office of steward

STEWARDS > STEWARD

STEWARTRY *variant of* **>** STEWARDRY

STEWBUM *n* drunkard

STEWBUMS > STEWBUM

STEWED *adj* (of food) cooked by stewing

STEWER > STEW

STEWERS > STEW

STEWIER > STEW

STEWIEST > STEW

STEWING > STEW

STEWINGS > STEW

STEWPAN *n* pan used for making stew

STEWPANS > STEWPAN

STEWPOND *n* fishpond

STEWPONDS > STEWPOND

STEWPOT *n* pot used for making stew

STEWPOTS > STEWPOT

STEWS > STEW

STEWY > STEW

STEY *adj* Scots word meaning steep

STEYER > STEY

STEYEST > STEY

STHENIA *n* abnormal strength

STHENIAS > STHENIA

STHENIC *adj* abounding in energy or bodily strength

STIBBLE *Scots form of* **>** STUBBLE

STIBBLER *n* horse allowed to eat stubble

STIBBLERS > STIBBLE

STIBBLES > STIBBLE

STIBIAL > STIBIUM

STIBINE *n* colourless slightly soluble poisonous gas

STIBINES > STIBINE

STIBIUM *obsolete name for* **>** ANTIMONY

STIBIUMS > STIBIUM

STIBNITE *n* soft greyish mineral

STIBNITES > STIBNITE

STICCADO *n* type of xylophone

STICCADOS > STICCADO

STICCATO *same as* **>** STICCADO

STICCATOS > STICCATO

STICH *n* line of poetry

STICHARIA *npl* priest's robes of the Greek Church

STICHERA > STICHERON

STICHERON *n* short hymn in Greek Church

STICHIC > STICH

STICHIDIA *npl* seaweed branches

STICHOI > STICHOS

STICHOS *n* line of poem

STICHS > STICH

STICK *n* long thin piece of wood ▷ *vb* push (a pointed object) into (something)

STICKABLE > STICK

STICKBALL *n* form of baseball played in street

STICKED > STICK

STICKER *n* adhesive label or sign ▷ *vb* put stickers on

STICKERED > STICKER

STICKERS > STICKER

STICKFUL > STICK

STICKFULS > STICK

STICKIED > STICKY

STICKIER > STICKY

STICKIES > STICKY

STICKIEST > STICKY

STICKILY > STICKY

STICKING > STICK

STICKINGS > STICK

STICKIT *Scots form of* **>** STUCK

STICKJAW *n* stodgy food

STICKJAWS > STICKJAW

STICKLE *vb* dispute stubbornly, esp about minor points

STICKLED > STICKLE

STICKLER *n* person who insists on something

STICKLERS > STICKLER

STICKLES > STICKLE

STICKLIKE > STICK

STICKLING > STICKLE

STICKMAN *n* human figure drawn in thin strokes

STICKMEN > STICKMAN

STICKOUT *n* conspicuous person or thing

STICKOUTS > STICKOUT

STICKPIN *n* tiepin

STICKPINS > STICKPIN

STICKS > STICK

STICKSEED *n* type of Eurasian and North American plant

STICKUM *n* adhesive

STICKUMS > STICKUM

STICKUP *n* robbery at gun-point

STICKUPS > STICKUP

STICKWEED *n* any of several plants that have clinging fruits or seeds, esp the ragweed

STICKWORK *n* use of stick in hockey

STICKY *adj* covered with an adhesive substance ▷ *vb* make sticky ▷ *n* inquisitive look or stare

STICKYING > STICKY

STICTION *n* frictional force to be overcome to set one object in motion when it is in contact with another

STICTIONS > STICTION

STIDDIE *same as* **>** STITHY

STIDDIED > STIDDIE

STIDDIES > STIDDIE

STIE *same as* **>** STY

STIED > STY

STIES > STY

STIEVE *same as* **>** STEEVE

STIEVELY > STIEVE

STIEVER > STIEVE

STIEVEST > STIEVE

STIFF *adj* not easily bent or moved ▷ *n* corpse ▷ *adv* completely or utterly ▷ *vb* fail completely

STIFFED > STIFF

STIFFEN *vb* make or become stiff

STIFFENED > STIFFEN

STIFFENER > STIFFEN

STIFFENS > STIFFEN

STIFFER > STIFF

STIFFEST > STIFF

STIFFIE *n* erection of the penis

STIFFIES > STIFFIE

STIFFING > STIFF

STIFFISH > STIFF

STIFFLY > STIFF

STIFFNESS > STIFF

STIFFS > STIFF

STIFFWARE *n* computer software that is hard to modify

STIFFY *n* erection of the penis

STIFLE *vb* suppress ▷ *n* joint in the hind leg of a horse, dog, etc, between the femur and tibia

STIFLED > STIFLE

STIFLER > STIFLE

STIFLERS > STIFLE

STIFLES > STIFLE

STIFLING *adj* uncomfortably hot and stuffy

STIFLINGS > STIFLING

STIGMA *n* mark of social disgrace

STIGMAL *adj* of part of insect wing

STIGMAS > STIGMA

STIGMATA > STIGMA

STIGMATIC *adj* relating to or having a stigma or stigmata ▷ *n* person marked with the stigmata

STIGME *n* dot in Greek punctuation

STIGMES > STIGME

STILB *n* unit of luminance equal to 1 candela per square centimetre.

STILBENE *n* colourless or slightly yellow crystalline hydrocarbon used in the manufacture of dyes

STILBENES > STILBENE

STILBITE *n* white or yellow zeolite mineral

STILBITES > STILBITE

STILBS > STILB

STILE *same as* **>** STYLE

STILED > STILE

STILES > STILE

STILET *same as* **>** STYLET

STILETS > STILET

STILETTO *n* high narrow heel on a woman's shoe ▷ *vb* stab with a stiletto

STILETTOS > STILETTO

STILING > STILE

STILL *adv* now or in the future as before ▷ *adj* motionless ▷ *n* calmness; apparatus for distillation ▷ *vb* make still

STILLAGE *n* frame or stand for keeping things off the ground, such as casks in a brewery

STILLAGES > STILLAGE

STILLBORN *adj* born dead ▷ *n* stillborn fetus or baby

STILLED > STILL

STILLER > STILL

STILLEST > STILL

STILLIER > STILLY

STILLIEST > STILLY

STILLING > STILL

STILLINGS > STILL

STILLION *n* stand for cask

STILLIONS > STILLION

S

STILLMAN n someone involved in the operation of a still
STILLMEN > STILLMAN
STILLNESS > STILL
STILLROOM n room in which distilling is carried out
STILLS > STILL
STILLY adv quietly or calmly ▷ adj still, quiet, or calm
STILT n either of a pair of long poles with footrests for walking raised from the ground ▷ vb raise or place on or as if on stilts
STILTBIRD n long-legged wading bird
STILTED adj stiff and formal in manner
STILTEDLY > STILTED
STILTER > STILT
STILTERS > STILT
STILTIER > STILT
STILTIEST > STILT
STILTING > STILT
STILTINGS > STILT
STILTISH > STILT
STILTS > STILT
STILTY > STILT
STIM n very small amount
STIME same as > STYME
STIMED > STIME
STIMES > STIME
STIMIE same as > STIMIE
STIMIED > STIMIE
STIMIES > STIMIE
STIMING > STIME
STIMS > STIM
STIMULANT n something, such as a drug, that acts as a stimulus ▷ adj stimulating
STIMULATE vb act as a stimulus (on)
STIMULI > STIMULUS
STIMULUS n something that rouses a person or thing to activity
STIMY same as > STYMIE
STIMYING > STIMY
STING vb (of certain animals or plants) wound by injecting with poison ▷ n wound or pain caused by or as if by stinging
STINGAREE popular name for > STINGRAY
STINGBULL n spiny fish
STINGED > STING
STINGER n person, plant, animal, etc, that stings or hurts
STINGERS > STINGER
STINGFISH same as > STINGBULL
STINGIER > STINGY
STINGIES > STINGY
STINGIEST > STINGY
STINGILY > STINGY
STINGING > STING
STINGINGS > STING
STINGLESS > STING

STINGO n strong alcohol
STINGOS > STINGO
STINGRAY n flatfish capable of inflicting painful wounds
STINGRAYS > STINGRAY
STINGS > STING
STINGY adj mean or miserly ▷ n stinging nettle
STINK n strong unpleasant smell ▷ vb give off a strong unpleasant smell
STINKARD n smelly person
STINKARDS > STINKARD
STINKBIRD same as > HOATZIN
STINKBUG n type of insect that releases an unpleasant odour
STINKBUGS > STINKBUG
STINKER n difficult or unpleasant person or thing
STINKEROO n bad or contemptible person or thing
STINKERS > STINKER
STINKHORN n type of fungus with an offensive odour
STINKIER > STINKY
STINKIEST > STINKY
STINKING > STINK
STINKO adj drunk
STINKPOT n person or thing that stinks
STINKPOTS > STINKPOT
STINKS > STINK
STINKWEED n plant that has a disagreeable smell when bruised
STINKWOOD n any of various trees having offensive-smelling wood
STINKY adj having a foul smell
STINT vb be miserly with (something) ▷ n allotted amount of work
STINTED > STINT
STINTEDLY > STINT
STINTER > STINT
STINTERS > STINT
STINTIER > STINT
STINTIEST > STINT
STINTING > STINT
STINTINGS > STINT
STINTLESS > STINT
STINTS > STINT
STINTY > STINT
STIPA n variety of grass
STIPAS > STIPA
STIPE n stalk in plants that bears reproductive structures
STIPED same as > STIPITATE
STIPEL n small paired leaflike structure at the base of certain leaflets
STIPELS > STIPEL
STIPEND n regular allowance or salary, esp that paid to a clergyman
STIPENDS > STIPEND

STIPES n second maxillary segment in insects and crustaceans
STIPIFORM > STIPES
STIPITATE adj possessing or borne on the end of a stipe
STIPITES > STIPES
STIPPLE vb paint, draw, or engrave using dots ▷ n technique of stippling or a picture produced by or using stippling
STIPPLED > STIPPLE
STIPPLER > STIPPLE
STIPPLERS > STIPPLE
STIPPLES > STIPPLE
STIPPLING > STIPPLE
STIPULAR > STIPULE
STIPULARY > STIPULE
STIPULATE vb specify as a condition of an agreement ▷ adj (of a plant) having stipules
STIPULE n small paired usually leaflike outgrowth occurring at the base of a leaf or its stalk
STIPULED > STIPULE
STIPULES > STIPULE
STIR vb mix up (a liquid) by moving a spoon etc around in it ▷ n stirring
STIRABOUT n kind of porridge orginally made in Ireland
STIRE same as > STEER
STIRED > STIRE
STIRES > STIRE
STIRING > STIRE
STIRK n heifer of 6 to 12 months old
STIRKS > STIRK
STIRLESS > STIR
STIRP same as > STIRPS
STIRPES > STIRPS
STIRPS n line of descendants from an ancestor
STIRRA same as > SIRRA
STIRRABLE > STIR
STIRRAH same as > SIRRAH
STIRRAHS > STIRRAH
STIRRAS > STIRRA
STIRRE same as > STEER
STIRRED > STIR
STIRRER n person who deliberately causes trouble
STIRRERS > STIRRER
STIRRES > STIRRE
STIRRING > STIR
STIRRINGS > STIR
STIRRUP n metal loop attached to a saddle for supporting a rider's foot
STIRRUPS > STIRRUP
STIRS > STIR
STISHIE same as > STUSHIE
STISHIES > STISHIE
STITCH n link made by drawing thread through material with a needle ▷ vb sew

STITCHED > STITCH
STITCHER > STITCH
STITCHERS > STITCH
STITCHERY n needlework, esp modern embroidery
STITCHES > STITCH
STITCHING > STITCH
STITHIED > STITHY
STITHIES > STITHY
STITHY n forge or anvil ▷ vb forge on an anvil
STITHYING > STITHY
STIVE vb stifle
STIVED > STIVE
STIVER n former Dutch coin worth one twentieth of a guilder
STIVERS > STIVER
STIVES > STIVE
STIVIER > STIVY
STIVIEST > STIVY
STIVING > STIVE
STIVY adj stuffy
STOA n covered walk that has a colonnade on one or both sides, esp as used in ancient Greece
STOAE > STOA
STOAI > STOA
STOAS > STOA
STOAT n small mammal of the weasel family, with brown fur that turns white in winter
STOATS > STOAT
STOB same as > STAB
STOBBED > STOB
STOBBING > STOB
STOBIE as in stobie pole steel and concrete pole for supporting electricity wires
STOBS > STOB
STOCCADO n fencing thrust
STOCCADOS > STOCCADO
STOCCATA same as > STOCCADO
STOCCATAS > STOCCATA
STOCIOUS same as > STOTIOUS
STOCK n total amount of goods available for sale in a shop ▷ adj kept in stock, standard ▷ vb keep for sale or future use
STOCKADE n enclosure or barrier made of stakes ▷ vb surround with a stockade
STOCKADED > STOCKADE
STOCKADES > STOCKADE
STOCKAGE n livestock put to graze on crops
STOCKAGES > STOCKAGE
STOCKCAR n car that has been strengthened for a form of racing in which the cars often collide
STOCKCARS > STOCKCAR
STOCKED > STOCK
STOCKER > STOCK
STOCKERS > STOCK
STOCKFISH n fish, such as cod or haddock, cured by

splitting and drying in the air

STOCKIER > STOCKY

STOCKIEST > STOCKY

STOCKILY > STOCKY

STOCKINET n machine-knitted elastic fabric

STOCKING n close-fitting covering for the foot and leg

STOCKINGS > STOCKING

STOCKISH adj stupid or dull

STOCKIST n dealer who stocks a particular product

STOCKISTS > STOCKIST

STOCKLESS > STOCK

STOCKLIST n list of items in stock

STOCKLOCK n lock that is enclosed in a wooden case

STOCKMAN n man engaged in the rearing or care of farm livestock, esp cattle

STOCKMEN > STOCKMAN

STOCKPILE vb store a large quantity of (something) for future use ▷ n accumulated store

STOCKPOT n pot in which stock for soup is made

STOCKPOTS > STOCKPOT

STOCKROOM n room in which a stock of goods is kept in a shop or factory

STOCKS npl instrument of punishment consisting of a heavy wooden frame with holes in which the feet, hands, or head of an offender were locked

STOCKTAKE vb take stock

STOCKTOOK > STOCKTAKE

STOCKWORK n group of veins in mine

STOCKY adj (of a person) broad and sturdy

STOCKYARD n yard where farm animals are sold

STODGE n heavy starchy food ▷ vb stuff (oneself or another) with food

STODGED > STODGE

STODGER n dull person

STODGERS > STODGER

STODGES > STODGE

STODGIER > STODGY

STODGIEST > STODGY

STODGILY > STODGY

STODGING > STODGE

STODGY adj (of food) heavy and starchy

STOEP n verandah

STOEPS > STOEP

STOGEY same as > STOGY

STOGEYS > STOGEY

STOGIE same as > STOGY

STOGIES > STOGY

STOGY n any long cylindrical inexpensive cigar

STOIC n person who suffers hardship without

showing his or her feelings ▷ adj suffering hardship without showing one's feelings

STOICAL adj suffering great difficulties without showing one's feelings

STOICALLY > STOICAL

STOICISM n indifference to pleasure and pain

STOICISMS > STOICISM

STOICS > STOIC

STOIT vb bounce

STOITED > STOIT

STOITER vb stagger

STOITERED > STOITER

STOITERS > STOITER

STOITING > STOIT

STOITS > STOIT

STOKE vb feed and tend (a fire or furnace)

STOKED adj very pleased

STOKEHOLD n hold for a ship's boilers

STOKEHOLE n hole in a furnace through which it is stoked

STOKER n person employed to tend a furnace on a ship or train powered by steam

STOKERS > STOKER

STOKES n cgs unit of kinematic viscosity

STOKESIA n American flowering plant

STOKESIAS > STOKESIA

STOKING > STOKE

STOKVEL n (in S Africa) informal savings pool or syndicate

STOKVELS > STOKVEL

STOLE n long scarf or shawl

STOLED adj wearing a stole

STOLEN > STEAL

STOLES > STOLE

STOLID adj showing little emotion or interest

STOLIDER > STOLID

STOLIDEST > STOLID

STOLIDITY > STOLID

STOLIDLY > STOLID

STOLLEN n rich sweet bread containing nuts, raisins, etc

STOLLENS > STOLLEN

STOLN > STEAL

STOLON n long horizontal stem that grows along the surface of the soil and propagates by producing roots and shoots at the nodes or tip

STOLONATE adj having a stolon

STOLONIC > STOLON

STOLONS > STOLON

STOLPORT n airport for short take-off aircraft

STOLPORTS > STOLPORT

STOMA n pore in a plant leaf that controls the passage of gases into and out of the plant

STOMACH n organ in the body which digests food

▷ vb put up with

STOMACHAL > STOMACH

STOMACHED > STOMACH

STOMACHER n decorative V-shaped panel of stiff material worn over the chest and stomach

STOMACHIC adj stimulating gastric activity ▷ n stomachic medicine

STOMACHS > STOMACH

STOMACHY adj having a large belly

STOMACK as in have a stomack (in E Africa) be pregnant

STOMACKS > STOMACK

STOMAL > STOMA

STOMAS > STOMA

STOMATA > STOMA

STOMATAL adj of, relating to, or possessing stomata or a stoma

STOMATE n opening on leaf through which water evaporates

STOMATES > STOMATE

STOMATIC adj of or relating to a mouth or mouthlike part

STOMATOUS same as > STOMATAL

STOMIA > STOMIUM

STOMIUM n part of the sporangium of ferns that ruptures to release the spores

STOMIUMS > STOMIUM

STOMODAEA > STOMODEUM

STOMODEA > STOMODEUM

STOMODEAL > STOMODEUM

STOMODEUM n oral cavity of a vertebrate embryo

STOMP vb tread heavily ▷ n rhythmic stamping jazz dance

STOMPED > STOMP

STOMPER n rock or jazz song with a particularly strong and danceable beat

STOMPERS > STOMPER

STOMPIE n cigarette butt

STOMPIES > STOMPIE

STOMPING > STOMP

STOMPS > STOMP

STONABLE > STONE

STOND same as > STAND

STONDS > STOND

STONE n material of which rocks are made ▷ vb throw stones at

STONEABLE > STONE

STONEBOAT n type of sleigh used for moving rocks from fields

STONECAST n short distance

STONECHAT n songbird that has black feathers and a reddish-brown breast

STONECROP n type of plant with fleshy leaves and red, yellow, or white

flowers

STONED adj under the influence of alcohol or drugs

STONEFISH n venomous tropical marine scorpaenid fish

STONEFLY n type of insect whose larvae are aquatic

STONEHAND n type of compositor

STONELESS > STONE

STONELIKE > STONE

STONEN adj of stone

STONER n device for removing stones from fruit

STONERAG n type of lichen

STONERAGS > STONERAG

STONERAW same as > STONERAG

STONERAWS > STONERAW

STONERN same as > STONEN

STONERS > STONER

STONES > STONE

STONESHOT n stone's throw

STONEWALL vb obstruct or hinder discussion

STONEWARE n hard kind of pottery fired at a very high temperature ▷ adj made of stoneware

STONEWASH vb wash with stones to give worn appearance

STONEWORK n part of a building made of stone

STONEWORT n any of various green algae which grow in brackish or fresh water

STONEY same as > STONY

STONG > STING

STONIED > STONY

STONIER > STONY

STONIES > STONY

STONIEST > STONY

STONILY > STONY

STONINESS > STONY

STONING > STONE

STONINGS > STONE

STONISH same as > ASTONISH

STONISHED > STONISH

STONISHES > STONISH

STONK vb bombard (soldiers, buildings, etc) with artillery ▷ n concentrated bombardment by artillery

STONKED > STONK

STONKER vb destroy

STONKERED adj completely exhausted or beaten

STONKERS > STONKER

STONKING > STONK

STONKS > STONK

STONN same as > STUN

STONNE same as > STUN

STONNED > STONNE

STONNES > STONNE

STONNING > STONN

STONNS > STONN

STONY *adj* of or like stone ▷ *vb* astonish

STONYING > STONY

STOOD > STAND

STOODEN > STAND

STOOGE *n* actor who feeds lines to a comedian or acts as the butt of his jokes ▷ *vb* act as a stooge

STOOGED > STOOGE

STOOGES > STOOGE

STOOGING > STOOGE

STOOK *n* number of sheaves set upright in a field to dry with their heads together ▷ *vb* set up (sheaves) in stooks

STOOKED > STOOK

STOOKER > STOOK

STOOKERS > STOOK

STOOKIE *n* stucco

STOOKIES > STOOKIE

STOOKING > STOOK

STOOKS > STOOK

STOOL *n* chair without arms or back ▷ *vb* (of a plant) send up shoots from the base of the stem

STOOLBALL *n* game resembling cricket played by girls

STOOLED > STOOL

STOOLIE *n* police informer

STOOLIES > STOOLIE

STOOLING > STOOL

STOOLS > STOOL

STOOP *vb* bend forward and downward

STOOPBALL *n* American street game

STOOPE *same as* > STOUP

STOOPED > STOOP

STOOPER > STOOP

STOOPERS > STOOP

STOOPES > STOOPE

STOOPING > STOOP

STOOPS > STOOP

STOOR *same as* > STOUR

STOORS > STOOR

STOOSHIE *same as* > STUSHIE

STOOSHIES > STOOSHIE

STOOZE *vb* borrow money at 0% interest rate on a credit card then invest it to make a profit

STOOZED > STOOZE

STOOZER *n* person who borrows money at 0% interest rate on a credit card then invests it to make a profit

STOOZERS > STOOZER

STOOZES > STOOZE

STOOZING > STOOZE

STOOZINGS > STOOZING

STOP *vb* cease or cause to cease from doing (something) ▷ *n* stopping or being stopped

STOPBANK *n* embankment to prevent flooding

STOPBANKS > STOPBANK

STOPCOCK *n* valve to control or stop the flow of fluid in a pipe

STOPCOCKS > STOPCOCK

STOPE *n* steplike excavation made in a mine to extract ore ▷ *vb* mine (ore, etc) by cutting stopes

STOPED > STOPE

STOPER *n* drill used in mining

STOPERS > STOPER

STOPES > STOPE

STOPGAP *n* temporary substitute

STOPGAPS > STOPGAP

STOPING *n* process by which country rock is broken up and engulfed by the upward movement of magma

STOPINGS > STOPING

STOPLESS > STOP

STOPLIGHT *n* red light on a traffic signal indicating that vehicles coming towards it should stop

STOPOFF *n* break in a journey

STOPOFFS > STOPOFF

STOPOVER *n* short break in a journey ▷ *vb* make a stopover

STOPOVERS > STOPOVER

STOPPABLE > STOP

STOPPAGE *n* act of stopping something or the state of being stopped

STOPPAGES > STOPPAGE

STOPPED > STOP

STOPPER *n* plug for closing a bottle etc ▷ *vb* close or fit with a stopper

STOPPERED > STOPPER

STOPPERS > STOPPER

STOPPING > STOP

STOPPINGS > STOP

STOPPLE *same as* > STOPPER

STOPPLED > STOPPLE

STOPPLES > STOPPLE

STOPPLING > STOPPLE

STOPS > STOP

STOPT > STOP

STOPWATCH *n* watch which can be stopped instantly for exact timing of a sporting event

STOPWORD *n* common word not used in computer search engines

STOPWORDS > STOPWORD

STORABLE > STORE

STORABLES > STORE

STORAGE *n* storing

STORAGES > STORAGE

STORAX *n* type of tree or shrub with drooping showy white flowers

STORAXES > STORAX

STORE *vb* collect and keep (things) for future use ▷ *n* shop

STORED > STORE

STOREMAN *n* man looking after storeroom

STOREMEN > STOREMAN

STORER > STORE

STOREROOM *n* room in which things are stored

STORERS > STORE

STORES *npl* supply or stock of food and other essentials for a journey

STORESHIP *n* ship carrying naval stores

STOREWIDE *adj* throughout stores

STOREY *n* floor or level of a building

STOREYED *adj* having a storey or storeys

STOREYS > STOREY

STORGE *n* affection

STORGES > STORGE

STORIATED *adj* decorated with flowers or animals

STORIED > STORY

STORIES > STORY

STORIETTE *n* short story

STORING > STORE

STORK *n* large wading bird

STORKS > STORK

STORM *n* violent weather with wind, rain, or snow ▷ *vb* attack or capture (a place) suddenly

STORMBIRD *n* petrel

STORMCOCK *n* mistle thrush

STORMED > STORM

STORMER *n* outstanding example of its kind

STORMERS > STORMER

STORMFUL > STORM

STORMIER > STORMY

STORMIEST > STORMY

STORMILY > STORMY

STORMING *adj* characterized by or displaying dynamism, speed, and energy

STORMINGS > STORM

STORMLESS > STORM

STORMLIKE > STORM

STORMS > STORM

STORMY *adj* characterized by storms

STORNELLI > STORNELLO

STORNELLO *n* type of Italian poem

STORY *n* narration of a chain of events ▷ *vb* decorate with scenes from history

STORYBOOK *n* book containing stories for children ▷ *adj* better or happier than in real life

STORYETTE *n* short story

STORYING > STORY

STORYINGS > STORY

STORYLINE *n* plot of a book, film, play, etc

STOSS *adj* (of the side of a hill) facing the onward flow of a glacier ▷ *n* hillside facing glacier flow

STOSSES > STOSS

STOT *n* bullock ▷ *vb* bounce or cause to bounce

STOTIN *n* monetary unit of Slovenia, worth one hundredth of a tolar

STOTINKA *n* monetary unit of Bulgaria, worth one hundredth of a lev

STOTINKI > STOTINKA

STOTINOV > STOTIN

STOTINS > STOTIN

STOTIOUS *adj* drunk

STOTS > STOT

STOTT *same as* > STOT

STOTTED > STOT

STOTTER *same as* > STOT

STOTTERED > STOTTER

STOTTERS > STOTTER

STOTTIE *n* wedge of bread cut from a flat round loaf that has been split and filled with meat, cheese, etc

STOTTIES > STOTTIE

STOTTING > STOT

STOTTS > STOTT

STOTTY *n* type of flat, round loaf made in NE England

STOUN *same as* > STUN

STOUND *n* short while ▷ *vb* ache

STOUNDED > STOUND

STOUNDING > STOUND

STOUNDS > STOUND

STOUNING > STOUN

STOUNS > STOUN

STOUP *n* small basin for holy water

STOUPS > STOUP

STOUR *n* turmoil or conflict

STOURE *same as* > STOUR

STOURES > STOURE

STOURIE *same as* > STOURY

STOURIER > STOURY

STOURIEST > STOURY

STOURS > STOUR

STOURY *adj* dusty

STOUSH *vb* hit or punch (someone) ▷ *n* fighting or violence

STOUSHED > STOUSH

STOUSHES > STOUSH

STOUSHIE *same as* > STUSHIE

STOUSHIES > STOUSHIE

STOUSHING > STOUSH

STOUT *adj* fat ▷ *n* strong dark beer

STOUTEN *vb* make or become stout

STOUTENED > STOUTEN

STOUTENS > STOUTEN

STOUTER > STOUT

STOUTEST > STOUT

STOUTH *n* Scots word meaning theft

STOUTHS > STOUTH

STOUTISH > STOUT

STOUTLY > STOUT

STOUTNESS > STOUT

STOUTS > STOUT

STOVAINE n anaesthetic drug
STOVAINES > STOVAINE
STOVE n apparatus for cooking or heating ▷ vb process (ceramics, metalwork, etc) by heating in a stove
STOVED > STOVE
STOVEPIPE n pipe that takes fumes and smoke away from a stove
STOVER n fodder
STOVERS > STOVER
STOVES > STOVE
STOVETOP US word for > HOB
STOVETOPS > STOVETOP
STOVIES npl potatoes stewed with onions
STOVING > STOVE
STOVINGS > STOVE
STOW vb pack or store
STOWABLE > STOVE
STOWAGE n space or charge for stowing goods
STOWAGES > STOWAGE
STOWAWAY n person who hides on a ship or aircraft in order to travel free ▷ vb travel in such a way
STOWAWAYS > STOWAWAY
STOWDOWN n packing of ship's hold
STOWDOWNS > STOWDOWN
STOWED > STOW
STOWER > STOW
STOWERS > STOW
STOWING > STOW
STOWINGS > STOW
STOWLINS adv stealthily
STOWN > STEAL
STOWND same as > STOUND
STOWNDED > STOWND
STOWNDING > STOWND
STOWNDS > STOWND
STOWNLINS same as > STOWLINS
STOWP same as > STOUP
STOWPS > STOWP
STOWRE same as > STOUR
STOWRES > STOWRE
STOWS > STOW
STRABISM n abnormal alignment of one or both eyes
STRABISMS > STRABISM
STRACK vb archaic past tense form of strike
STRAD n violin made by Stradivarius
STRADDLE vb have one leg or part on each side of (something) ▷ n act or position of straddling
STRADDLED > STRADDLE
STRADDLER > STRADDLE
STRADDLES > STRADDLE
STRADIOT n Venetian cavalryman
STRADIOTS > STRADIOT
STRADS > STRAD
STRAE Scots form of > STRAW

STRAES > STRAE
STRAFE vb attack (an enemy) with machine guns from the air ▷ n act or instance of strafing
STRAFED > STRAFE
STRAFER > STRAFE
STRAFERS > STRAFE
STRAFES > STRAFE
STRAFF same as > STRAFE
STRAFFED > STRAFF
STRAFFING > STRAFF
STRAFFS > STRAFF
STRAFING > STRAFE
STRAG n straggler
STRAGGLE vb go or spread in a rambling or irregular way
STRAGGLED > STRAGGLE
STRAGGLER > STRAGGLE
STRAGGLES > STRAGGLE
STRAGGLY > STRAGGLE
STRAGS > STRAG
STRAICHT Scots word for > STRAIGHT
STRAIGHT adj not curved or crooked ▷ adv in a straight line ▷ n straight part, esp of a racetrack ▷ vb tighten
STRAIGHTS > STRAIGHT
STRAIK Scots word for > STROKE
STRAIKED > STRAIK
STRAIKING > STRAIK
STRAIKS > STRAIK
STRAIN vb subject to mental tension ▷ n tension or tiredness
STRAINED adj not natural, forced
STRAINER n sieve
STRAINERS > STRAINER
STRAINING > STRAIN
STRAINS > STRAIN
STRAINT n pressure
STRAINTS > STRAINT
STRAIT n narrow channel connecting two areas of sea ▷ adj (of spaces, etc) affording little room ▷ vb tighten
STRAITED > STRAIT
STRAITEN vb embarrass or distress, esp financially
STRAITENS > STRAITEN
STRAITER > STRAIT
STRAITEST > STRAIT
STRAITING > STRAIT
STRAITLY > STRAIT
STRAITS > STRAIT
STRAK vb archaic past tense form of strike
STRAKE n curved metal plate forming part of the metal rim on a wooden wheel
STRAKED adj having a strake
STRAKES > STRAKE
STRAMACON same as > STRAMAZON
STRAMASH n uproar ▷ vb destroy

STRAMAZON n downward fencing stroke
STRAMMEL same as > STRUMMEL
STRAMMELS > STRAMMEL
STRAMONY n former asthma medicine made from the dried leaves and flowers of the thorn apple
STRAMP Scots variant of > TRAMP
STRAMPED > STRAMP
STRAMPING > STRAMP
STRAMPS > STRAMP
STRAND vb run aground ▷ n shore
STRANDED > STRAND
STRANDER > STRAND
STRANDERS > STRAND
STRANDING > STRAND
STRANDS > STRAND
STRANG dialect variant of > STRONG
STRANGE adj odd or unusual ▷ n odd or unfamiliar person or thing
STRANGELY > STRANGE
STRANGER n person who is not known or is new to a place or experience
STRANGERS > STRANGER
STRANGES > STRANGE
STRANGEST > STRANGE
STRANGLE vb kill by squeezing the throat
STRANGLED > STRANGLE
STRANGLER n person or thing that strangles
STRANGLES n acute bacterial disease of horses
STRANGURY n painful excretion of urine caused by muscular spasms of the urinary tract
STRAP n strip of flexible material for lifting or holding in place ▷ vb fasten with a strap or straps
STRAPHANG vb travel standing on public transport
STRAPHUNG > STRAPHANG
STRAPLESS adj (of women's clothes) without straps over the shoulders
STRAPLINE n subheading in a newspaper or magazine article or in any advertisement
STRAPPADO n system of torture in which a victim was hoisted by a rope tied to his wrists and then allowed to drop until his fall was suddenly checked by the rope ▷ vb subject to strappado
STRAPPED > STRAP
STRAPPER n strapping person
STRAPPERS > STRAPPER
STRAPPIER > STRAPPY
STRAPPING > STRAP
STRAPPY adj having straps

STRAPS > STRAP
STRAPWORT n plant with leaves like straps
STRASS another word for > PASTE
STRASSES > STRASS
STRATA > STRATUM
STRATAGEM n clever plan, trick
STRATAL > STRATUM
STRATAS > STRATUM
STRATEGIC adj advantageous
STRATEGY n overall plan
STRATH n flat river valley
STRATHS > STRATH
STRATI > STRATUS
STRATIFY vb form or be formed in layers or strata
STRATONIC adj of army
STRATOSE adj formed in strata
STRATOUS adj of stratus
STRATUM n layer, esp of rock
STRATUMS > STRATUM
STRATUS n grey layer cloud
STRAUCHT Scots word for > STRETCH
STRAUCHTS > STRAUCHT
STRAUGHT same as > STRAUCHT
STRAUGHTS > STRAUGHT
STRAUNGE same as > STRANGE
STRAVAGE same as > STRAVAIG
STRAVAGED > STRAVAGE
STRAVAGES > STRAVAGE
STRAVAIG vb wander aimlessly
STRAVAIGS > STRAVAIG
STRAW n dried stalks of grain ▷ vb spread around
STRAWED > STRAW
STRAWEN adj of straw
STRAWHAT adj of summer dramatic performance
STRAWIER > STRAWY
STRAWIEST > STRAWY
STRAWING > STRAW
STRAWLESS > STRAW
STRAWLIKE > STRAW
STRAWN > STREW
STRAWS > STRAW
STRAWWORM n aquatic larva of a caddis fly
STRAWY adj containing straw, or like straw in colour or texture
STRAY vb wander ▷ adj having strayed ▷ n stray animal
STRAYED > STRAY
STRAYER > STRAY
STRAYERS > STRAY
STRAYING > STRAY
STRAYINGS > STRAY
STRAYLING n stray
STRAYS > STRAY
STRAYVE vb wander aimlessly
STRAYVED > STRAYVE
STRAYVES > STRAYVE

S

STRAYVING > STRAYVE

STREAK n long band of contrasting colour or substance ▷ vb mark with streaks

STREAKED > STREAK

STREAKER > STREAK

STREAKERS > STREAK

STREAKIER > STREAKY

STREAKILY > STREAKY

STREAKING > STREAK

STREAKS > STREAK

STREAKY adj marked with streaks

STREAM n small river ▷ vb flow steadily

STREAMBED n bottom of stream

STREAMED > STREAM

STREAMER n strip of coloured paper that unrolls when tossed

STREAMERS > STREAMER

STREAMIER > STREAMY

STREAMING > STREAM

STREAMLET > STREAM

STREAMS > STREAM

STREAMY adj (of an area, land, etc) having many streams

STREEK Scots word for > STRETCH

STREEKED > STREEK

STREEKER > STREEK

STREEKERS > STREEK

STREEKING > STREEK

STREEKS > STREEK

STREEL n slovenly woman ▷ vb trail

STREELED > STREEL

STREELING > STREEL

STREELS > STREEL

STREET n public road, usu lined with buildings ▷ vb lay out a street or streets

STREETAGE n toll charged for using a street

STREETBOY n boy living on the street

STREETED > STREET

STREETFUL n amount of people or things street can hold

STREETIER > STREETY

STREETING > STREET

STREETS > STREET

STREETY adj of streets

STREIGHT same as > STRAIT

STREIGHTS > STREIGHT

STREIGNE same as > STRAIN

STREIGNED > STREIGNE

STREIGNES > STREIGNE

STRELITZ n former Russian soldier

STRELITZI > STRELITZ

STRENE same as > STRAIN

STRENES > STRENE

STRENGTH n quality of being strong

STRENGTHS > STRENGTH

STRENUITY > STRENUOUS

STRENUOUS adj requiring great energy or effort

STREP n streptococcus

STREPENT adj noisy

STREPS > STREP

STRESS n tension or strain ▷ vb emphasize

STRESSED > STRESS

STRESSES > STRESS

STRESSFUL > STRESS

STRESSING > STRESS

STRESSOR n event, experience, etc, that causes stress

STRESSORS > STRESSOR

STRETCH vb extend or be extended ▷ n stretching

STRETCHED > STRETCH

STRETCHER n frame covered with canvas, on which an injured person is carried ▷ vb transport (a sick or injured person) on a stretcher

STRETCHES > STRETCH

STRETCHY adj characterized by elasticity

STRETTA same as > STRETTO

STRETTAS > STRETTA

STRETTE > STRETTA

STRETTI > STRETTO

STRETTO n (in a fugue) the close overlapping of two parts or voices

STRETTOS > STRETTO

STREUSEL n crumbly topping for rich pastries

STREUSELS > STREUSEL

STREW vb scatter (things) over a surface

STREWAGE > STREW

STREWAGES > STREW

STREWED > STREW

STREWER > STREW

STREWERS > STREW

STREWING > STREW

STREWINGS > STREW

STREWMENT n strewing

STREWN > STREW

STREWS > STREW

STREWTH interj expression of surprise or alarm

STRIA n scratch or groove on the surface of a rock crystal

STRIAE > STRIA

STRIATA > STRIATUM

STRIATE adj marked with striae ▷ vb mark with striae

STRIATED adj having a pattern of scratches or grooves

STRIATES > STRIATE

STRIATING > STRIATE

STRIATION same as > STRIA

STRIATUM n part of brain

STRIATUMS > STRIATUM

STRIATURE n way something is striated

STRICH n screech owl

STRICHES > STRICH

STRICK n any bast fibres preparatory to being made into slivers

STRICKEN adj seriously affected by disease, grief, pain, etc

STRICKLE n board used for sweeping off excess material in a container ▷ vb level, form, or sharpen with a strickle

STRICKLED > STRICKLE

STRICKLES > STRICKLE

STRICKS > STRICK

STRICT adj stern or severe

STRICTER > STRICT

STRICTEST > STRICT

STRICTION n act of restricting

STRICTISH > STRICT

STRICTLY > STRICT

STRICTURE n severe criticism

STRIDDEN > STRIDE

STRIDDLE same as > STRADDLE

STRIDDLED > STRIDDLE

STRIDDLES > STRIDDLE

STRIDE vb walk with long steps ▷ n long step

STRIDENCE > STRIDENT

STRIDENCY > STRIDENT

STRIDENT adj loud and harsh

STRIDER > STRIDE

STRIDERS > STRIDE

STRIDES > STRIDE

STRIDING > STRIDE

STRIDLING adv astride

STRIDOR n high-pitched whistling sound made during respiration

STRIDORS > STRIDOR

STRIFE n conflict, quarrelling

STRIFEFUL > STRIFE

STRIFES > STRIFE

STRIFT n struggle

STRIFTS > STRIFT

STRIG vb remove stalk from

STRIGA same as > STRIA

STRIGAE > STRIGA

STRIGATE adj streaked

STRIGGED > STRIG

STRIGGING > STRIG

STRIGIL n curved blade used by the ancient Romans and Greeks to scrape the body after bathing

STRIGILS > STRIGIL

STRIGINE adj of or like owl

STRIGOSE adj bearing stiff hairs or bristles

STRIGS > STRIG

STRIKE vb cease work as a protest ▷ n stoppage of work as a protest

STRIKEOUT n dismissal in baseball due to three successive failures to hit the ball

STRIKER n striking worker

STRIKERS > STRIKER

STRIKES > STRIKE

STRIKING > STRIKE

STRIKINGS > STRIKE

STRIM vb cut (grass) using a strimmer

STRIMMED > STRIM

STRIMMING > STRIM

STRIMS > STRIM

STRING n thin cord used for tying ▷ vb provide with a string or strings

STRINGED adj (of a musical instrument) having strings that are plucked or played with a bow

STRINGENT adj strictly controlled or enforced

STRINGER n journalist retained by a newspaper to cover a particular town or area

STRINGERS > STRINGER

STRINGIER > STRINGY

STRINGILY > STRINGY

STRINGING > STRING

STRINGS > STRING

STRINGY adj like string

STRINKLE Scots variant of > SPRINKLE

STRINKLED > STRINKLE

STRINKLES > STRINKLE

STRIP vb take (the covering or clothes) off ▷ n act of stripping

STRIPE n long narrow band of contrasting colour or substance ▷ vb mark (something) with stripes

STRIPED adj marked or decorated with stripes

STRIPER n officer who has a stripe or stripes on his uniform, esp in the navy

STRIPERS > STRIPER

STRIPES > STRIPE

STRIPEY same as > STRIPY

STRIPIER > STRIPY

STRIPIEST > STRIPY

STRIPING > STRIPE

STRIPINGS > STRIPE

STRIPLING n youth

STRIPPED > STRIP

STRIPPER n person who performs a striptease

STRIPPERS > STRIPPER

STRIPPING > STRIP

STRIPS > STRIP

STRIPT > STRIP

STRIPY adj marked by or with stripes

STRIVE vb make a great effort

STRIVED > STRIVE

STRIVEN > STRIVE

STRIVER > STRIVE

STRIVERS > STRIVE

STRIVES > STRIVE

STRIVING > STRIVE

STRIVINGS > STRIVE

S

STROAM vb wander

STROAMED > STROAM

STROAMING > STROAM

STROAMS > STROAM

STROBE n high intensity flashing beam of light ▷ vb give the appearance of slow motion by using a strobe

STROBED > STROBE

STROBES > STROBE

STROBIC adj spinning or appearing to spin

STROBIL n scaly multiple fruit

STROBILA n body of a tapeworm, consisting of a string of similar segments

STROBILAE > STROBILA

STROBILAR > STROBILA

STROBILE same as > STROBILUS

STROBILES > STROBILE

STROBILI > STROBILUS

STROBILS > STROBIL

STROBILUS technical name for > CONE

STROBING > STROBE

STROBINGS > STROBE

STRODDLE same as > STRADDLE

STRODDLED > STRODDLE

STRODDLES > STRODDLE

STRODE > STRIDE

STRODLE same as > STRADDLE

STRODLED > STRODLE

STRODLES > STRODLE

STRODLING > STRODLE

STROKABLE adj appearing pleasant to stroke

STROKE vb touch or caress lightly with the hand ▷ n light touch or caress with the hand

STROKED > STROKE

STROKEN > STRIKE

STROKER > STROKE

STROKERS > STROKE

STROKES > STROKE

STROKING > STROKE

STROKINGS > STROKE

STROLL vb walk in a leisurely manner ▷ n leisurely walk

STROLLED > STROLL

STROLLER n chair-shaped carriage for a baby

STROLLERS > STROLLER

STROLLING > STROLL

STROLLS > STROLL

STROMA n gel-like matrix of chloroplasts and certain cells

STROMAL > STROMA

STROMATA > STROMA

STROMATIC > STROMA

STROMB n shellfish like a whelk

STROMBS > STROMB

STROMBUS same as > STROMB

STROND same as > STRAND

STRONDS > STROND

STRONG adj having physical power

STRONGARM adj involving physical force

STRONGBOX n box in which valuables are locked for safety

STRONGER > STRONG

STRONGEST > STRONG

STRONGISH > STRONG

STRONGLY > STRONG

STRONGMAN n performer, esp one in a circus, who performs feats of strength

STRONGMEN > STRONGMAN

STRONGYL same as > STRONGYLE

STRONGYLE n type of parasitic worm chiefly occurring in the intestines of horses

STRONGYLS > STRONGYL

STRONTIA > STRONTIUM

STRONTIAN n type of white mineral

STRONTIAS > STRONTIA

STRONTIC > STRONTIUM

STRONTIUM n silvery-white metallic element

STROOK > STRIKE

STROOKE n stroke

STROOKEN same as > STRICKEN

STROOKES > STROOKE

STROP n leather strap for sharpening razors ▷ vb sharpen (a razor, etc) on a strop

STROPHE n first of two movements made by a chorus during the performance of a choral ode

STROPHES > STROPHE

STROPHIC adj of, relating to, or employing a strophe or strophes

STROPHOID n type of curve on graph

STROPHULI npl skin inflammations seen primarily on small children

STROPPED > STROP

STROPPER > STROP

STROPPERS > STROP

STROPPIER > STROPPY

STROPPILY > STROPPY

STROPPING > STROP

STROPPY adj angry or awkward

STROPS > STROP

STROSSERS same as > TROUSERS

STROUD n coarse woollen fabric

STROUDING n woolly material for making strouds

STROUDS > STROUD

STROUP Scots word for > SPOUT

STROUPACH n cup of tea

STROUPAN same as > STROUPACH

STROUPANS > STROUPAN

STROUPS > STROUP

STROUT vb bulge

STROUTED > STROUT

STROUTING > STROUT

STROUTS > STROUT

STROVE > STRIVE

STROW archaic variant of > STREW

STROWED > STROW

STROWER > STROW

STROWERS > STROW

STROWING > STROW

STROWINGS > STROW

STROWN > STROW

STROWS > STROW

STROY archaic variant of > DESTROY

STROYED > STROY

STROYER > STROY

STROYERS > STROY

STROYING > STROY

STROYS > STROY

STRUCK > STRIKE

STRUCKEN same as > STRICKEN

STRUCTURE n complex construction ▷ vb give a structure to

STRUDEL n thin sheet of filled dough rolled up and baked, usu with an apple filling

STRUDELS > STRUDEL

STRUGGLE vb work, strive, or make one's way with difficulty ▷ n striving

STRUGGLED > STRUGGLE

STRUGGLER > STRUGGLE

STRUGGLES > STRUGGLE

STRUM vb play (a guitar or banjo) by sweeping the thumb or a plectrum across the strings

STRUMA n abnormal enlargement of the thyroid gland

STRUMAE > STRUMA

STRUMAS > STRUMA

STRUMATIC > STRUMA

STRUMITIS n inflammation of thyroid gland

STRUMMED > STRUM

STRUMMEL n straw

STRUMMELS > STRUMMEL

STRUMMER > STRUM

STRUMMERS > STRUM

STRUMMING > STRUM

STRUMOSE > STRUMA

STRUMOUS > STRUMA

STRUMPET n prostitute ▷ vb turn into a strumpet

STRUMPETS > STRUMPET

STRUMS > STRUM

STRUNG > STRING

STRUNT Scots word for > STRUT

STRUNTED > STRUNT

STRUNTING > STRUNT

STRUNTS > STRUNT

STRUT vb walk pompously, swagger ▷ n bar supporting a structure

STRUTS > STRUT

STRUTTED > STRUT

STRUTTER > STRUT

STRUTTERS > STRUT

STRUTTING > STRUT

STRYCHNIA n strychnine

STRYCHNIC adj of, relating to, or derived from strychnine

STUB n short piece left after use ▷ vb strike (the toe) painfully against an object

STUBBED > STUB

STUBBIE same as > STUBBY

STUBBIER > STUBBY

STUBBIES > STUBBY

STUBBIEST > STUBBY

STUBBILY > STUBBY

STUBBING > STUB

STUBBLE n short stalks of grain left in a field after reaping

STUBBLED adj having the stubs of stalks left after a crop has been cut and harvested

STUBBLES > STUBBLE

STUBBLIER > STUBBLE

STUBBLY > STUBBLE

STUBBORN adj refusing to agree or give in ▷ vb make stubborn

STUBBORNS > STUBBORN

STUBBY adj short and broad ▷ n small bottle of beer

STUBS > STUB

STUCCO n plaster used for coating or decorating walls ▷ vb apply stucco to (a building)

STUCCOED > STUCCO

STUCCOER > STUCCO

STUCCOERS > STUCCO

STUCCOES > STUCCO

STUCCOING > STUCCO

STUCCOS > STUCCO

STUCK n thrust

STUCKS > STUCK

STUD n small piece of metal attached to a surface for decoration ▷ vb set with studs

STUDBOOK n written record of the pedigree of a purebred stock, esp of racehorses

STUDBOOKS > STUDBOOK

STUDDED > STUD

STUDDEN > STAND

STUDDIE Scots word for > ANVIL

STUDDIES > STUDDIE

STUDDING > STUD

STUDDINGS > STUD

STUDDLE n post

STUDDLES > STUDDLE

STUDE vb past tense and past participle of staun (Scots form of stand)

STUDENT n person who studies a subject, esp at university

S

STUDENTRY n body of students

STUDENTS > STUDENT

STUDENTY adj informal, sometimes derogatory term denoting the characteristics believed typical of an undergraduate student

STUDFARM n farm where horses are bred

STUDFARMS > STUDFARM

STUDFISH n American minnow

STUDHORSE another word for > STALLION

STUDIED adj carefully practised

STUDIEDLY > STUDIED

STUDIER > STUDY

STUDIERS > STUDY

STUDIES > STUDY

STUDIO n workroom of an artist or photographer

STUDIOS > STUDIO

STUDIOUS adj fond of study

STUDLIER > STUDLY

STUDLIEST > STUDLY

STUDLY adj strong and virile

STUDS > STUD

STUDWORK n work decorated with studs

STUDWORKS > STUDWORK

STUDY vb be engaged in learning (a subject) ▷ n act or process of studying

STUDYING > STUDY

STUFF n substance or material ▷ vb pack, cram, or fill completely

STUFFED > STUFF

STUFFER > STUFF

STUFFERS > STUFF

STUFFIER > STUFFY

STUFFIEST > STUFFY

STUFFILY > STUFFY

STUFFING n seasoned mixture with which food is stuffed

STUFFINGS > STUFFING

STUFFLESS > STUFF

STUFFS > STUFF

STUFFY adj lacking fresh air

STUGGIER > STUGGY

STUGGIEST > STUGGY

STUGGY adj stout

STUIVER same as > STIVER

STUIVERS > STUIVER

STUKKEND adj South African slang for broken or wrecked

STULL n timber prop or platform in a stope

STULLS > STULL

STULM n shaft

STULMS > STULM

STULTIFY vb dull (the mind) by boring routine

STUM n partly fermented wine added to fermented

wine as a preservative ▷ vb preserve (wine) by adding stum

STUMBLE vb trip and nearly fall ▷ n stumbling

STUMBLED > STUMBLE

STUMBLER > STUMBLE

STUMBLERS > STUMBLE

STUMBLES > STUMBLE

STUMBLIER > STUMBLY

STUMBLING > STUMBLE

STUMBLY adj tending to stumble

STUMER n forgery or cheat

STUMERS > STUMER

STUMM same as > SHTOOM

STUMMED > STUM

STUMMEL n bowl of pipe

STUMMELS > STUMMEL

STUMMING > STUM

STUMP n base of a tree left when the main trunk has been cut away ▷ vb baffle

STUMPAGE n standing timber or its value

STUMPAGES > STUMPAGE

STUMPED > STUMP

STUMPER > STUMP

STUMPERS > STUMP

STUMPIER > STUMPY

STUMPIES > STUMPY

STUMPIEST > STUMPY

STUMPILY > STUMPY

STUMPING > STUMP

STUMPINGS > STUMPING

STUMPS > STUMP

STUMPWORK n type of embroidery featuring raised figures, padded with cotton wool or hair

STUMPY adj short and thick ▷ n stumpy thing

STUMS > STUM

STUN vb shock or overwhelm ▷ n state or effect of being stunned

STUNG > STING

STUNK > STINK

STUNKARD adj sulky

STUNNED > STUN

STUNNER n beautiful person or thing

STUNNERS > STUNNER

STUNNING > STUN

STUNNINGS > STUN

STUNS > STUN

STUNSAIL n type of light auxiliary sail

STUNSAILS > STUNSAIL

STUNT vb prevent or impede the growth of ▷ n acrobatic or dangerous action

STUNTED > STUNT

STUNTING > STUNT

STUNTMAN n person who performs dangerous acts in a film, etc in place of an actor

STUNTMEN > STUNTMAN

STUNTS > STUNT

STUPA n domed edifice housing Buddhist or Jain relics

STUPAS > STUPA

STUPE n hot damp cloth applied to the body to relieve pain ▷ vb treat with a stupe

STUPED > STUPE

STUPEFIED > STUPEFY

STUPEFIER > STUPEFY

STUPEFIES > STUPEFY

STUPEFY vb make insensitive or lethargic

STUPENT adj astonished

STUPES > STUPE

STUPID adj lacking intelligence ▷ n stupid person

STUPIDER > STUPID

STUPIDEST > STUPID

STUPIDITY n quality or state of being stupid

STUPIDLY > STUPID

STUPIDS > STUPID

STUPING > STUPE

STUPOR n dazed or unconscious state

STUPOROUS > STUPOR

STUPORS > STUPOR

STUPRATE vb ravish

STUPRATED > STUPRATE

STUPRATES > STUPRATE

STURDIED > STURDY

STURDIER > STURDY

STURDIES > STURDY

STURDIEST > STURDY

STURDILY > STURDY

STURDY adj healthy and robust ▷ n disease of sheep

STURE same as > STOOR

STURGEON n fish from which caviar is obtained

STURGEONS > STURGEON

STURMER n type of eating apple with pale green skin

STURMERS > STURMER

STURNINE > STURNUS

STURNOID > STURNUS

STURNUS n bird of starling family

STURNUSES > STURNUS

STURT vb bother

STURTED > STURT

STURTING > STURT

STURTS > STURT

STUSHIE n commotion, rumpus, or row

STUSHIES > STUSHIE

STUTTER vb speak with repetition of initial consonants ▷ n tendency to stutter

STUTTERED > STUTTER

STUTTERER > STUTTER

STUTTERS > STUTTER

STY vb climb

STYE n inflammation at the base of an eyelash

STYED > STYE

STYES > STYE

STYGIAN adj dark, gloomy, or hellish

STYING > STY

STYLAR > STYLUS

STYLATE adj having style

STYLE n shape or design ▷ vb shape or design

STYLEBOOK n book containing rules of punctuation, etc, for the use of writers, editors, and printers

STYLED > STYLE

STYLEE same as > STYLE

STYLEES > STYLEE

STYLELESS > STYLE

STYLER > STYLE

STYLERS > STYLE

STYLES > STYLE

STYLET n wire for insertion into a flexible cannula or catheter to maintain its rigidity during passage

STYLETS > STYLET

STYLI > STYLUS

STYLIE adj fashion-conscious

STYLIER > STYLIE

STYLIEST > STYLIE

STYLIFORM adj shaped like a stylus or bristle

STYLING > STYLE

STYLINGS > STYLE

STYLISE same as > STYLIZE

STYLISED > STYLISE

STYLISER > STYLISE

STYLISERS > STYLISE

STYLISES > STYLISE

STYLISH adj smart, elegant, and fashionable

STYLISHLY > STYLISH

STYLISING > STYLISE

STYLIST n hairdresser

STYLISTIC adj of literary or artistic style

STYLISTS > STYLIST

STYLITE n one of a class of recluses who in ancient times lived on the top of high pillars

STYLITES > STYLITE

STYLITIC > STYLITE

STYLITISM > STYLITE

STYLIZE vb cause to conform to an established stylistic form

STYLIZED > STYLIZE

STYLIZER > STYLIZE

STYLIZERS > STYLIZE

STYLIZES > STYLIZE

STYLIZING > STYLIZE

STYLO n type of fountain pen

STYLOBATE n continuous horizontal course of masonry that supports a colonnade

STYLOID adj resembling a stylus ▷ n spiny growth

STYLOIDS > STYLOID

STYLOLITE n any of the small striated columnar or irregular structures within the strata of some limestones

STYLOPES > STYLOPS

STYLOPISE same as > STYLOPIZE**

STYLOPIZE *vb* (of a stylops) to parasitize (a host)

STYLOPS *n* type of insect that lives as a parasite in other insects

STYLOS > STYLO

STYLUS *n* needle-like device on a record player that rests in the groove of the record and picks up the sound signals

STYLUSES > STYLUS

STYME *vb* peer

STYMED > STYME

STYMES > STYME

STYMIE *vb* hinder or thwart

STYMIED > STYMY

STYMIEING > STYMIE

STYMIES > STYMY

STYMING > STYME

STYMY *same as >* STYMIE

STYMYING > STYMY

STYPSIS *n* action, application, or use of a styptic

STYPSISES > STYPSIS

STYPTIC *adj* (drug) used to stop bleeding ▷ *n* styptic drug

STYPTICAL > STYPTIC

STYPTICS > STYPTIC

STYRAX *n* type of tropical or subtropical tree

STYRAXES > STYRAX

STYRE *same as >* STIR

STYRED > STYRE

STYRENE *n* colourless oily volatile flammable water-insoluble liquid

STYRENES > STYRENE

STYRES > STYRE

STYRING > STYRE

STYROFOAM *n* tradename for a light expanded polystyrene plastic

STYTE *vb* bounce

STYTED > STYTE

STYTES > STYTE

STYTING > STYTE

SUABILITY > SUABLE

SUABLE *adj* liable to be sued in a court

SUABLY > SUABLE

SUASIBLE > SUASION

SUASION *n* persuasion

SUASIONS > SUASION

SUASIVE > SUASION

SUASIVELY > SUASION

SUASORY > SUASION

SUAVE *adj* smooth and sophisticated in manner

SUAVELY > SUAVE

SUAVENESS > SUAVE

SUAVER > SUAVE

SUAVEST > SUAVE

SUAVITIES > SUAVE

SUAVITY > SUAVE

SUB *n* subeditor ▷ *vb* act as a substitute

SUBA *n* shepherd's cloak

SUBABBOT *n* abbot who is subordinate to

another abbot

SUBABBOTS > SUBABBOT

SUBACID *adj* (esp of some fruits) moderately acid or sour

SUBACIDLY > SUBACID

SUBACRID *adj* slightly acrid

SUBACT *vb* subdue

SUBACTED > SUBACT

SUBACTING > SUBACT

SUBACTION > SUBACT

SUBACTS > SUBACT

SUBACUTE *adj* intermediate between acute and chronic

SUBADAR *n* (formerly) the chief native officer of a company of Indian soldiers in the British service

SUBADARS > SUBADAR

SUBADULT *n* animal not quite at adult stage

SUBADULTS > SUBADULT

SUBAERIAL *adj* in open air

SUBAGENCY *n* agency employed by larger agency

SUBAGENT *n* agent who is subordinate to another agent

SUBAGENTS > SUBAGENT

SUBAH *same as >* SUBADAR

SUBAHDAR *same as >* SUBADAR

SUBAHDARS > SUBAHDAR

SUBAHDARY *n* office of subahdar

SUBAHS > SUBAH

SUBAHSHIP > SUBAH

SUBALAR *adj* below a wing

SUBALPINE *adj* situated in or relating to the regions at the foot of mountains

SUBALTERN *n* British army officer below the rank of captain ▷ *adj* of inferior position or rank

SUBAPICAL *adj* below an apex

SUBAQUA *adj* of or relating to underwater sport

SUBARCTIC *adj* of or relating to latitudes immediately south of the Arctic Circle

SUBAREA *n* area within a larger area

SUBAREAS > SUBAREA

SUBARID *adj* receiving slightly more rainfall than arid regions

SUBAS > SUBA

SUBASTRAL *adj* terrestrial

SUBATOM *n* part of an atom

SUBATOMIC *adj* of or being one of the particles which make up an atom

SUBATOMS > SUBATOM

SUBAUDIO *adj* (of sound) low frequency

SUBAURAL *adj* below the ear

SUBAXIAL *adj* below an axis of the body

SUBBASAL > SUBBASE

SUBBASE *same as >* SUBBASS

SUBBASES > SUBBASE

SUBBASIN *n* geographical basin within larger basin

SUBBASINS > SUBBASIN

SUBBASS *another name for >* BOURDON

SUBBASSES > SUBBASS

SUBBED > SUB

SUBBIE *n* subcontractor

SUBBIES > SUBBIE

SUBBING > SUB

SUBBINGS > SUB

SUBBLOCK *n* part of mathematical matrix

SUBBLOCKS > SUBBLOCK

SUBBRANCH *n* branch within another branch

SUBBREED *n* breed within a larger breed

SUBBREEDS > SUBBREED

SUBBUREAU *n* bureau subordinate to the main bureau

SUBBY *same as >* SUBBIE

SUBCANTOR *n* deputy to a cantor

SUBCASTE *n* subdivision of a caste

SUBCASTES > SUBCASTE

SUBCAUDAL *adj* below a tail

SUBCAUSE *n* factor less important than a cause

SUBCAUSES > SUBCAUSE

SUBCAVITY *n* cavity within a larger cavity

SUBCELL *n* cell within a larger cell

SUBCELLAR *n* cellar below another cellar

SUBCELLS > SUBCELL

SUBCENTER *n* secondary center

SUBCHASER *n* anti-submarine warship

SUBCHIEF *n* chief below the main chief

SUBCHIEFS > SUBCHIEF

SUBCHORD *n* part of a curve

SUBCHORDS > SUBCHORD

SUBCLAIM *n* claim that is part of a larger claim

SUBCLAIMS > SUBCLAIM

SUBCLAN *n* clan within a larger clan

SUBCLANS > SUBCLAN

SUBCLASS *n* principal subdivision of a class ▷ *vb* assign to a subclass

SUBCLAUSE *n* subordinate section of a larger clause in a document

SUBCLERK *n* clerk who is subordinate to another clerk

SUBCLERKS > SUBCLERK

SUBCLIMAX *n* community in which development has been arrested before climax has been attained

SUBCODE *n* computer tag identifying data

SUBCODES > SUBCODE

SUBCOLONY *n* colony established by existing colony

SUBCONSUL *n* assistant to a consul

SUBCOOL *vb* make colder

SUBCOOLED > SUBCOOL

SUBCOOLS > SUBCOOL

SUBCORTEX *n* matter of the brain situated beneath the cerebral cortex

SUBCOSTA *n* vein in insect wing

SUBCOSTAE > SUBCOSTA

SUBCOSTAL *adj* below the rib

SUBCOUNTY *n* division of a county

SUBCRUST *n* secondary crust below main crust

SUBCRUSTS > SUBCRUST

SUBCULT *n* cult within larger cult

SUBCULTS > SUBCULT

SUBCUTES > SUBCUTIS

SUBCUTIS *n* layer of tissue beneath outer skin

SUBDEACON *n* cleric who assists at High Mass

SUBDEALER *n* dealer who buys from other dealer

SUBDEAN *n* deputy of dean

SUBDEANS > SUBDEAN

SUBDEB *n* young woman who is not yet a debutante

SUBDEBS > SUBDEB

SUBDEPOT *n* depot within a larger depot

SUBDEPOTS > SUBDEPOT

SUBDEPUTY *n* assistant to a deputy

SUBDERMAL *adj* below the skin

SUBDEW *same as >* SUBDUE

SUBDEWED > SUBDEW

SUBDEWING > SUBDEW

SUBDEWS > SUBDEW

SUBDIVIDE *vb* divide (a part of something) into smaller parts

SUBDOLOUS *adj* clever

SUBDORSAL *adj* situated close to the back

SUBDUABLE > SUBDUE

SUBDUABLY > SUBDUE

SUBDUAL *n* SUBDUE

SUBDUALS > SUBDUE

SUBDUCE *vb* withdraw

SUBDUCED > SUBDUCE

SUBDUCES > SUBDUCE

SUBDUCING > SUBDUCE

SUBDUCT *vb* draw or turn (the eye, etc) downwards

SUBDUCTED > SUBDUCT

SUBDUCTS > SUBDUCT

SUBDUE *vb* overcome

SUBDUED *adj* cowed, passive, or shy

SUBDUEDLY > SUBDUED

SUBDUER > SUBDUE

SUBDUERS > SUBDUE

SUBDUES > SUBDUE

SUBDUING > SUBDUE

S

SUBDUPLE adj in proportion of one to two

SUBDURAL adj between the dura mater and the arachnoid

SUBDWARF n star smaller than a dwarf star

SUBDWARFS > SUBDWARF

SUBECHO n echo resonating more quietly than another echo

SUBECHOES > SUBECHO

SUBEDAR same as **>** SUBADAR

SUBEDARS > SUBEDAR

SUBEDIT vb edit and correct (written or printed material)

SUBEDITED > SUBEDIT

SUBEDITOR n person who checks and edits text for a newspaper or magazine

SUBEDITS > SUBEDIT

SUBENTIRE adj slightly indented

SUBENTRY n entry within another entry

SUBEPOCH n epoch within another epoch

SUBEPOCHS > SUBEPOCH

SUBEQUAL adj not quite equal

SUBER n cork

SUBERATE n salt of suberic acid

SUBERATES > SUBERATE

SUBERECT adj not quite erect

SUBEREOUS same as **>** SUBEROSE

SUBERIC same as **>** SUBEROSE

SUBERIN n fatty or waxy substance that is present in the walls of cork cells

SUBERINS > SUBERIN

SUBERISE same as **>** SUBERIZE

SUBERISED > SUBERISE

SUBERISES > SUBERISE

SUBERIZE vb impregnate (cell walls) with suberin during the formation of corky tissue

SUBERIZED > SUBERIZE

SUBERIZES > SUBERIZE

SUBEROSE adj relating to, resembling, or consisting of cork

SUBEROUS same as **>** SUBEROSE

SUBERS > SUBER

SUBFAMILY n taxonomic group that is a subdivision of a family

SUBFEU vb grant feu to vassal

SUBFEUED > SUBFEU

SUBFEUING > SUBFEU

SUBFEUS > SUBFEU

SUBFIELD n subdivision of a field

SUBFIELDS > SUBFIELD

SUBFILE n file within another file

SUBFILES > SUBFILE

SUBFIX n suffix

SUBFIXES > SUBFIX

SUBFLOOR n rough floor that forms a base for a finished floor

SUBFLOORS > SUBFLOOR

SUBFLUID adj viscous

SUBFOSSIL n something partly fossilized

SUBFRAME n frame on which car body is built

SUBFRAMES > SUBFRAME

SUBFUSC adj devoid of brightness or appeal ▷ n (at Oxford University) formal academic dress

SUBFUSCS > SUBFUSC

SUBFUSK same as **>** SUBFUSC

SUBFUSKS > SUBFUSK

SUBGENERA > SUBGENUS

SUBGENRE n genre within a larger genre

SUBGENRES > SUBGENRE

SUBGENUS n taxonomic group that is a subdivision of a genus but of higher rank than a species

SUBGOAL n secondary goal

SUBGOALS > SUBGOAL

SUBGRADE n ground beneath a roadway or pavement

SUBGRADES > SUBGRADE

SUBGRAPH n graph sharing vertices of other graph

SUBGRAPHS > SUBGRAPH

SUBGROUP n small group that is part of a larger group

SUBGROUPS > SUBGROUP

SUBGUM n Chinese dish

SUBGUMS > SUBGUM

SUBHA n string of beads used in praying and meditating

SUBHAS > SUBHA

SUBHEAD n heading of a subsection in a printed work

SUBHEADS > SUBHEAD

SUBHEDRAL adj with some characteristics of crystal

SUBHUMAN adj less than human

SUBHUMANS > SUBHUMAN

SUBHUMID adj not wet enough for trees to grow

SUBIDEA n secondary idea

SUBIDEAS > SUBIDEA

SUBIMAGO n first winged stage of the mayfly

SUBIMAGOS > SUBIMAGO

SUBINCISE vb perform subincision

SUBINDEX same as **>** SUBSCRIPT

SUBINFEUD vb grant by feudal tenant to further tenant

SUBITEM n item that is less important than another item

SUBITEMS > SUBITEM

SUBITISE same as **>** SUBITIZE

SUBITISED > SUBITISE

SUBITISES > SUBITISE

SUBITIZE vb perceive the number of (a group of items) at a glance and without counting

SUBITIZED > SUBITIZE

SUBITIZES > SUBITIZE

SUBITO adv (preceding or following a dynamic marking, etc) suddenly

SUBJACENT adj forming a foundation

SUBJECT n person or thing being dealt with or studied ▷ adj being under the rule of a monarch or government ▷ vb cause to undergo

SUBJECTED > SUBJECT

SUBJECTS > SUBJECT

SUBJOIN vb add or attach at the end of something spoken, written, etc

SUBJOINED > SUBJOIN

SUBJOINS > SUBJOIN

SUBJUGATE vb bring (a group of people) under one's control

SUBLATE vb deny

SUBLATED > SUBLATE

SUBLATES > SUBLATE

SUBLATING > SUBLATE

SUBLATION > SUBLATE

SUBLEASE n lease of property made by a person who is himself or herself a lessee or tenant of that property ▷ vb grant a sublease of (property)

SUBLEASED > SUBLEASE

SUBLEASES > SUBLEASE

SUBLESSEE > SUBLEASE

SUBLESSOR > SUBLEASE

SUBLET vb rent out (property rented from someone else) ▷ n sublease

SUBLETHAL adj not strong enough to kill

SUBLETS > SUBLET

SUBLETTER > SUBLET

SUBLEVEL n subdivision of a level

SUBLEVELS > SUBLEVEL

SUBLIMATE vb direct the energy of (a strong desire, esp a sexual one) into socially acceptable activities ▷ n material obtained when a substance is sublimed ▷ adj exalted or purified

SUBLIME adj of high moral, intellectual, or spiritual value ▷ vb change from a solid to a vapour without first melting

SUBLIMED > SUBLIME

SUBLIMELY > SUBLIME

SUBLIMER > SUBLIME

SUBLIMERS > SUBLIME

SUBLIMES > SUBLIME

SUBLIMEST > SUBLIME

SUBLIMING > SUBLIME

SUBLIMISE same as **>** SUBLIMIZE

SUBLIMIT n limit on a subcategory

SUBLIMITS > SUBLIMIT

SUBLIMITY > SUBLIME

SUBLIMIZE vb make sublime

SUBLINE n secondary headline

SUBLINEAR adj beneath a line

SUBLINES > SUBLINE

SUBLOT n subdivision of a lot

SUBLOTS > SUBLOT

SUBLUNAR same as **>** SUBLUNARY

SUBLUNARY adj situated between the moon and the earth

SUBLUNATE adj almost crescent-shaped

SUBLUXATE vb partially dislocate

SUBMAN n primitive form of human

SUBMARINE n vessel which can operate below the surface of the sea ▷ adj below the surface of the sea ▷ vb slide beneath seatbelt in car crash

SUBMARKET n specialized market within larger market

SUBMATRIX n part of matrix

SUBMEN > SUBMAN

SUBMENTA > SUBMENTUM

SUBMENTAL adj situated beneath the chin

SUBMENTUM n base of insect lip

SUBMENU n further list of options within computer menu

SUBMENUS > SUBMENU

SUBMERGE vb put or go below the surface of water or other liquid

SUBMERGED adj (of plants or plant parts) growing beneath the surface of the water

SUBMERGES > SUBMERGE

SUBMERSE same as **>** SUBMERGE

SUBMERSED same as **>** SUBMERGED

SUBMERSES > SUBMERSE

SUBMICRON n object only visible through powerful microscope

SUBMISS adj docile

SUBMISSLY adv submissively

SUBMIT vb surrender

SUBMITS > SUBMIT

SUBMITTAL > SUBMIT

SUBMITTED > SUBMIT

SUBMITTER > SUBMIT

SUBMUCOSA n connective tissue beneath a mucous membrane

SUBMUCOUS
> SUBMUCOSA
SUBNASAL *adj* beneath nose
SUBNET *n* part of network
SUBNETS > SUBNET
SUBNEURAL *adj* beneath a nerve centre
SUBNICHE *n* subdivision of a niche
SUBNICHES > SUBNICHE
SUBNIVEAL *adj* beneath the snow
SUBNIVEAN *same as* > SUBNIVEAL
SUBNODAL *adj* below the level of a node
SUBNORMAL *adj* less than normal, esp in intelligence ▷ *n* subnormal person
SUBNUCLEI *npl* plural of subnucleus, secondary nucleus
SUBOCEAN *adj* beneath the ocean
SUBOCTAVE *n* octave below another
SUBOCULAR *adj* below the eye
SUBOFFICE *n* office that is subordinate to another office
SUBOPTIC *adj* below the eye
SUBORAL *adj* not quite oral
SUBORDER *n* taxonomic group that is a subdivision of an order
SUBORDERS > SUBORDER
SUBORN *vb* bribe or incite (a person) to commit a wrongful act
SUBORNED > SUBORN
SUBORNER > SUBORN
SUBORNERS > SUBORN
SUBORNING > SUBORN
SUBORNS > SUBORN
SUBOSCINE *n* belonging to a subfamily of birds
SUBOVAL *adj* not quite oval
SUBOVATE *adj* almost egg-shaped
SUBOXIDE *n* oxide of an element containing less oxygen than the common oxide formed by the element
SUBOXIDES > SUBOXIDE
SUBPANEL *n* panel that is part of larger panel
SUBPANELS > SUBPANEL
SUBPAR *adj* not up to standard
SUBPART *n* part within another part
SUBPARTS > SUBPART
SUBPENA *same as* > SUBPOENA
SUBPENAED > SUBPENA
SUBPENAS > SUBPENA
SUBPERIOD *n* subdivision of time period
SUBPHASE *n* subdivision of phase
SUBPHASES > SUBPHASE

SUBPHYLA
> SUBPHYLUM
SUBPHYLAR
> SUBPHYLUM
SUBPHYLUM *n* taxonomic group that is a subdivision of a phylum
SUBPLOT *n* secondary plot in a novel, play, or film
SUBPLOTS > SUBPLOT
SUBPOENA *n* writ requiring a person to appear before a lawcourt ▷ *vb* summon (someone) with a subpoena
SUBPOENAS > SUBPOENA
SUBPOLAR *adj* not quite polar
SUBPOTENT *adj* not at full strength
SUBPRIME *n* loan made to a borrower with a poor credit rating
SUBPRIMES > SUBPRIME
SUBPRIOR *n* monk junior to a prior
SUBPRIORS > SUBPRIOR
SUBPUBIC *adj* beneath the pubic bone
SUBRACE *n* race of people considered to be inferior
SUBRACES > SUBRACE
SUBREGION *n* subdivision of a region, esp a zoogeographical or ecological region
SUBRENT *n* rent paid to renter who rents to another
SUBRENTS > SUBRENT
SUBRING *n* mathematical ring that is a subset of another ring
SUBRINGS > SUBRING
SUBROGATE *vb* put (one person or thing) in the place of another in respect of a right or claim
SUBRULE *n* rule within another rule
SUBRULES > SUBRULE
SUBS > SUB
SUBSACRAL *adj* below the sacrum
SUBSALE *n* sale carried out within the process of a larger sale
SUBSALES > SUBSALE
SUBSAMPLE *vb* take further sample from existing sample
SUBSCALE *n* scale within a scale
SUBSCALES > SUBSCALE
SUBSCHEMA *n* part of computer database used by an individual
SUBSCRIBE *vb* pay (a subscription)
SUBSCRIPT *adj* (character) printed below the line ▷ *n* subscript character
SUBSEA *adj* undersea
SUBSECIVE *adj* left over

SUBSECT *n* sect within a larger sect
SUBSECTOR *n* subdivision of sector
SUBSECTS > SUBSECT
SUBSELLIA *npl* ledges underneath the hinged seats in a church
SUBSENSE *n* definition that is division of wider definition
SUBSENSES > SUBSENSE
SUBSERE *n* secondary sere arising when the progress of a sere towards its climax has been interrupted
SUBSERES > SUBSERE
SUBSERIES *n* series within a larger series
SUBSERVE *vb* be helpful or useful to
SUBSERVED > SUBSERVE
SUBSERVES > SUBSERVE
SUBSET *n* mathematical set contained within a larger set
SUBSETS > SUBSET
SUBSHAFT *n* secondary shaft in mine
SUBSHAFTS > SUBSHAFT
SUBSHELL *n* part of a shell of an atom
SUBSHELLS > SUBSHELL
SUBSHRUB *n* small bushy plant that is woody except for the tips of the branches
SUBSHRUBS > SUBSHRUB
SUBSIDE *vb* become less intense
SUBSIDED > SUBSIDE
SUBSIDER > SUBSIDE
SUBSIDERS > SUBSIDE
SUBSIDES > SUBSIDE
SUBSIDIES > SUBSIDY
SUBSIDING > SUBSIDE
SUBSIDISE *same as* > SUBSIDIZE
SUBSIDIZE *vb* help financially
SUBSIDY *n* financial aid
SUBSIST *vb* manage to live
SUBSISTED > SUBSIST
SUBSISTER > SUBSIST
SUBSISTS > SUBSIST
SUBSITE *n* location within a website
SUBSITES > SUBSITE
SUBSIZAR *n* type of undergraduate at Cambridge
SUBSIZARS > SUBSIZAR
SUBSKILL *n* element of a wider skill
SUBSKILLS > SUBSKILL
SUBSOCIAL *adj* lacking a complex or definite social structure
SUBSOIL *n* earth just below the surface soil ▷ *vb* plough (land) to a depth below the normal ploughing level
SUBSOILED > SUBSOIL
SUBSOILER > SUBSOIL
SUBSOILS > SUBSOIL

SUBSOLAR *adj* (of a point on the earth) directly below the sun
SUBSONG *n* subdued form of birdsong modified from the full territorial song
SUBSONGS > SUBSONG
SUBSONIC *adj* moving at a speed less than that of sound
SUBSPACE *n* part of a mathematical matrix
SUBSPACES > SUBSPACE
SUBSTAGE *n* part of a microscope below the stage
SUBSTAGES > SUBSTAGE
SUBSTANCE *n* physical composition of something
SUBSTATE *n* subdivision of state
SUBSTATES > SUBSTATE
SUBSTRACT *same as* > SUBTRACT
SUBSTRATA *npl* layers lying underneath other layers
SUBSTRATE *n* substance upon which an enzyme acts
SUBSTRUCT *vb* build as a foundation
SUBSTYLAR > SUBSTYLE
SUBSTYLE *n* line on a dial
SUBSTYLES > SUBSTYLE
SUBSULTUS *n* abnormal twitching
SUBSUME *vb* include (an idea, case, etc) under a larger classification or group
SUBSUMED > SUBSUME
SUBSUMES > SUBSUME
SUBSUMING > SUBSUME
SUBSYSTEM *n* system operating within a larger system
SUBTACK *Scots word for* > SUBLEASE
SUBTACKS > SUBTACK
SUBTALAR *adj* beneath the ankle-bone
SUBTASK *n* task that is part of a larger task
SUBTASKS > SUBTASK
SUBTAXA > SUBTAXON
SUBTAXON *n* supplementary piece of identifying information in plant or animal scientific name
SUBTAXONS > SUBTAXON
SUBTEEN *n* young person who has not yet become a teenager
SUBTEENS > SUBTEEN
SUBTENANT *n* person who rents property from a tenant
SUBTEND *vb* be opposite (an angle or side)
SUBTENDED > SUBTEND
SUBTENDS > SUBTEND
SUBTENSE *n* line that subtends
SUBTENSES > SUBTENSE

S

SUBTENURE n tenancy given by other tenant

SUBTEST n test that is part of larger test

SUBTESTS > SUBTEST

SUBTEXT n underlying theme in a piece of writing

SUBTEXTS > SUBTEXT

SUBTHEME n secondary theme

SUBTHEMES > SUBTHEME

SUBTIDAL adj below the level of low tide

SUBTIL same as > SUBTLE

SUBTILE rare spelling of > SUBTLE

SUBTILELY > SUBTILE

SUBTILER > SUBTILE

SUBTILEST > SUBTILE

SUBTILIN n antibiotic drug

SUBTILINS > SUBTILIN

SUBTILISE same as > SUBTILIZE

SUBTILITY > SUBTILE

SUBTILIZE vb bring to a purer state

SUBTILTY > SUBTILE

SUBTITLE n secondary title of a book ▷ vb provide with a subtitle or subtitles

SUBTITLED > SUBTITLE

SUBTITLES > SUBTITLE

SUBTLE adj not immediately obvious

SUBTLER > SUBTLE

SUBTLEST > SUBTLE

SUBTLETY n fine distinction

SUBTLY > SUBTLE

SUBTONE n subdivision of a tone

SUBTONES > SUBTONE

SUBTONIC n seventh degree of a major or minor scale

SUBTONICS > SUBTONIC

SUBTOPIA n suburban development that encroaches on rural areas yet appears to offer the attractions of country life to suburban dwellers

SUBTOPIAN > SUBTOPIA

SUBTOPIAS > SUBTOPIA

SUBTOPIC n topic within a larger topic

SUBTOPICS > SUBTOPIC

SUBTORRID same as > SUBTROPIC

SUBTOTAL n total made up by a column of figures, forming part of the total made up by a larger column or group ▷ vb establish or work out a subtotal for (a column, group, etc)

SUBTOTALS > SUBTOTAL

SUBTRACT vb take (one number or quantity) from another

SUBTRACTS > SUBTRACT

SUBTREND n minor trend

SUBTRENDS > SUBTREND

SUBTRIBE n tribe within a larger tribe

SUBTRIBES > SUBTRIBE

SUBTRIST adj slightly sad

SUBTROPIC adj relating to the region lying between the tropics and the temperate lands

SUBTRUDE vb intrude stealthily

SUBTRUDED > SUBTRUDE

SUBTRUDES > SUBTRUDE

SUBTUNIC adj below membrane ▷ n garment worn under a tunic

SUBTUNICS > SUBTUNIC

SUBTYPE n secondary or subordinate type or genre

SUBTYPES > SUBTYPE

SUBUCULA n ancient Roman man's undergarment

SUBUCULAS > SUBUCULA

SUBULATE adj (esp of plant parts) tapering to a point

SUBUNIT n distinct part or component of something larger

SUBUNITS > SUBUNIT

SUBURB n residential area on the outskirts of a city

SUBURBAN adj mildly derogatory term for inhabiting a suburb ▷ n mildly derogatory term for a person who lives in a suburb

SUBURBANS > SUBURBAN

SUBURBED > SUBURB

SUBURBIA n suburbs and their inhabitants

SUBURBIAS > SUBURBIA

SUBURBS > SUBURB

SUBURSINE adj of a bear subspecies

SUBVASSAL n vassal of a vassal

SUBVENE vb happen in such a way as to be of assistance, esp in preventing something

SUBVENED > SUBVENE

SUBVENES > SUBVENE

SUBVENING > SUBVENE

SUBVERSAL > SUBVERT

SUBVERSE same as > SUBVERT

SUBVERSED > SUBVERSE

SUBVERSES > SUBVERSE

SUBVERST > SUBVERSE

SUBVERT vb overthrow the authority of

SUBVERTED > SUBVERT

SUBVERTER > SUBVERT

SUBVERTS > SUBVERT

SUBVICAR n assistant to a vicar

SUBVICARS > SUBVICAR

SUBVIRAL adj of, caused by, or denoting a part of the structure of a virus

SUBVIRUS n organism smaller than a virus

SUBVISUAL adj not visible to the naked eye

SUBVOCAL adj formed in mind without being spoken aloud

SUBWARDEN n assistant to a warden

SUBWAY n passage under a road or railway ▷ vb travel by subway

SUBWAYED > SUBWAY

SUBWAYING > SUBWAY

SUBWAYS > SUBWAY

SUBWOOFER n loudspeaker for very low tones

SUBWORLD n underworld

SUBWORLDS > SUBWORLD

SUBWRITER n person carrying out writing tasks for other writer

SUBZERO adj lower than zero

SUBZONAL > SUBZONE

SUBZONE n subdivision of a zone

SUBZONES > SUBZONE

SUCCADE n piece of candied fruit

SUCCADES > SUCCADE

SUCCAH same as > SUKKAH

SUCCAHS > SUCCAH

SUCCEDENT adj following

SUCCEED vb accomplish an aim

SUCCEEDED > SUCCEED

SUCCEEDER > SUCCEED

SUCCEEDS > SUCCEED

SUCCENTOR n deputy of the precentor of a cathedral that has retained its statutes from pre-Reformation days

SUCCES French word for > SUCCESS

SUCCESS n achievement of something attempted

SUCCESSES > SUCCESS

SUCCESSOR n person who succeeds someone in a position

SUCCI > SUCCUS

SUCCINATE n any salt or ester of succinic acid

SUCCINCT adj brief and clear

SUCCINIC adj of, relating to, or obtained from amber

SUCCINITE n type of amber

SUCCINYL n constituent of succinic acid

SUCCINYLS > SUCCINYL

SUCCISE adj ending abruptly, as if cut off

SUCCOR same as > SUCCOUR

SUCCORED > SUCCOR

SUCCORER > SUCCOR

SUCCORERS > SUCCOR

SUCCORIES > SUCCORY

SUCCORS > SUCCOR

SUCCORY another name for > CHICORY

SUCCOS same as > SUCCOTH

SUCCOSE > SUCCUS

SUCCOT same as > SUKKOTH

SUCCOTASH n mixture of cooked sweet corn kernels and lima beans, served as a vegetable

SUCCOTH variant of . > SUKKOTH

SUCCOUR n help in distress ▷ vb give aid to (someone in time of difficulty)

SUCCOURED > SUCCOUR

SUCCOURER > SUCCOUR

SUCCOURS > SUCCOUR

SUCCOUS > SUCCUS

SUCCUBA same as > SUCCUBUS

SUCCUBAE > SUCCUBA

SUCCUBAS > SUCCUBA

SUCCUBI > SUCCUBUS

SUCCUBINE > SUCCUBUS

SUCCUBOUS adj having the leaves arranged so that the upper margin of each leaf is covered by the lower margin of the next leaf along

SUCCUBUS n female demon believed to have sex with sleeping men

SUCCULENT adj juicy and delicious ▷ n succulent plant

SUCCUMB vb give way (to something overpowering)

SUCCUMBED > SUCCUMB

SUCCUMBER > SUCCUMB

SUCCUMBS > SUCCUMB

SUCCURSAL adj (esp of a religious establishment) subsidiary ▷ n subsidiary establishment

SUCCUS n fluid

SUCCUSS vb shake (a patient) to detect the sound of fluid in the thoracic or another bodily cavity

SUCCUSSED > SUCCUSS

SUCCUSSES > SUCCUSS

SUCH adj of the kind specified ▷ pron such things

SUCHLIKE pron such or similar things ▷ n such or similar things ▷ adj of such a kind

SUCHNESS > SUCH

SUCHWISE > SUCH

SUCK vb draw (liquid or air) into the mouth ▷ n sucking

SUCKED > SUCK

SUCKEN Scots word for > DISTRICT

SUCKENER n tenant

SUCKENERS > SUCKENER

SUCKENS > SUCKEN

SUCKER n person who is easily deceived or swindled ▷ vb strip off the suckers from (a plant)

SUCKERED > SUCKER

SUCKERING > SUCKER

SUCKERS > SUCKER

SUCKET same as > SUCCADE

SUCKETS > SUCKET

SUCKFISH n type of spiny-finned marine fish

SUCKHOLE n sycophant

SUCKHOLES > SUCKHOLE

SUCKIER > SUCKY

SUCKIEST > SUCKY

SUCKING adj not yet weaned

SUCKINGS > SUCKING

SUCKLE vb feed at the breast

SUCKLED > SUCKLE

SUCKLER > SUCKLE

SUCKLERS > SUCKLE

SUCKLES > SUCKLE

SUCKLESS > SUCK

SUCKLING n unweaned baby or young animal

SUCKLINGS > SUCKLING

SUCKS interj expression of disappointment

SUCKY adj despicable

SUCRALOSE n artificial sweetener

SUCRASE another name for > INVERTASE

SUCRASES > SUCRASE

SUCRE n former standard monetary unit of Ecuador

SUCRES > SUCRE

SUCRIER n small container for sugar at table

SUCRIERS > SUCRIER

SUCROSE same as > SUGAR

SUCROSES > SUCROSE

SUCTION n sucking ▷ vb subject to suction

SUCTIONAL > SUCTION

SUCTIONED > SUCTION

SUCTIONS > SUCTION

SUCTORIAL adj specialized for sucking or adhering

SUCTORIAN n microscopic creature

SUCURUJU n anaconda

SUCURUJUS > SUCURUJU

SUD singular of > SUDS

SUDAMEN n small cavity in the skin

SUDAMINA > SUDAMEN

SUDAMINAL > SUDAMEN

SUDARIA > SUDARIUM

SUDARIES > SUDARY

SUDARIUM n room in a Roman bathhouse where sweating is induced by heat

SUDARY same as > SUDARIUM

SUDATE vb sweat

SUDATED > SUDATE

SUDATES > SUDATE

SUDATING > SUDATE

SUDATION > SUDATE

SUDATIONS > SUDATE

SUDATORIA same as > SUDARIA

SUDATORY > SUDATORIUM

SUDD n floating masses of reeds and weeds that occur on the White Nile

SUDDEN adj done or occurring quickly and unexpectedly

SUDDENLY adv quickly and without warning

SUDDENS > SUDDEN

SUDDENTY n suddenness

SUDDER n supreme court in India

SUDDERS > SUDDER

SUDDS > SUDD

SUDOR technical name for > SWEAT

SUDORAL > SUDOR

SUDORIFIC adj (drug) causing sweating ▷ n drug that causes sweating

SUDOROUS > SUDOR

SUDORS > SUDOR

SUDS npl froth of soap and water, lather ▷ vb wash in suds

SUDSED > SUDS

SUDSER n soap opera

SUDSERS > SUDSER

SUDSES > SUDS

SUDSIER > SUDS

SUDSIEST > SUDS

SUDSING > SUDS

SUDSLESS > SUDS

SUDSY > SUDS

SUE vb start legal proceedings against

SUEABLE > SUE

SUED > SUE

SUEDE n leather with a velvety finish on one side ▷ vb give a suede finish to

SUEDED > SUEDE

SUEDES > SUEDE

SUEDETTE n imitation suede fabric

SUEDETTES > SUEDETTE

SUEDING > SUEDE

SUENT adj smooth

SUER > SUE

SUERS > SUE

SUES > SUE

SUET n hard fat obtained from sheep and cattle, used in cooking

SUETIER > SUET

SUETIEST > SUET

SUETS > SUET

SUETTIER > SUET

SUETTIEST > SUET

SUETTY > SUET

SUETY > SUET

SUFFARI same as > SAFARI

SUFFARIS > SUFFARI

SUFFECT adj additional

SUFFER vb undergo or be subjected to

SUFFERED > SUFFER

SUFFERER > SUFFER

SUFFERERS > SUFFER

SUFFERING n pain, misery, or loss experienced by a person who suffers

SUFFERS > SUFFER

SUFFETE n official in ancient Carthage

SUFFETES > SUFFETE

SUFFICE vb be enough for a purpose

SUFFICED > SUFFICE

SUFFICER > SUFFICE

SUFFICERS > SUFFICE

SUFFICES > SUFFICE

SUFFICING > SUFFICE

SUFFIX n letter or letters added to the end of a word to form another word ▷ vb add (a letter or letters) to the end of a word to form another word

SUFFIXAL > SUFFIX

SUFFIXED > SUFFIX

SUFFIXES > SUFFIX

SUFFIXING > SUFFIX

SUFFIXION > SUFFIX

SUFFLATE archaic word for > INFLATE

SUFFLATED > SUFFLATE

SUFFLATES > SUFFLATE

SUFFOCATE vb kill or be killed by deprivation of oxygen

SUFFRAGAN n bishop appointed to assist an archbishop ▷ adj (of any bishop of a diocese) subordinate to and assisting his superior archbishop

SUFFRAGE n right to vote in public elections

SUFFRAGES > SUFFRAGE

SUFFUSE vb spread through or over (something)

SUFFUSED > SUFFUSE

SUFFUSES > SUFFUSE

SUFFUSING > SUFFUSE

SUFFUSION > SUFFUSE

SUFFUSIVE > SUFFUSE

SUG vb sell a product while pretending to conduct market research

SUGAN n straw rope

SUGANS > SUGAN

SUGAR n sweet crystalline carbohydrate used to sweeten food and drinks ▷ vb sweeten or cover with sugar

SUGARALLY n liquorice

SUGARBUSH n area covered in sugar maple trees

SUGARCANE n coarse grass that yields sugar

SUGARCOAT vb cover with sugar

SUGARED adj made sweeter or more appealing with or as with sugar

SUGARER > SUGAR

SUGARERS > SUGAR

SUGARIEST > SUGARY

SUGARING n method of removing unwanted body hair

SUGARINGS > SUGARING

SUGARLESS > SUGAR

SUGARLIKE > SUGAR

SUGARLOAF n large conical mass of unrefined sugar

SUGARPLUM n crystallized plum

SUGARS > SUGAR

SUGARY adj of, like, or containing sugar

SUGGED > SUG

SUGGEST vb put forward (an idea) for consideration

SUGGESTED > SUGGEST

SUGGESTER > SUGGEST

SUGGESTS > SUGGEST

SUGGING n practice of selling products under the pretence of conducting market research

SUGGINGS > SUGGING

SUGH same as > SOUGH

SUGHED > SUGH

SUGHING > SUGH

SUGHS > SUGH

SUGO n Italian pasta sauce

SUGOS > SUGO

SUGS > SUG

SUHUR n meal eaten before sunrise by Muslims fasting during Ramadan

SUHURS > SUHUR

SUI adj of itself

SUICIDAL adj liable to commit suicide

SUICIDE n killing oneself intentionally ▷ vb commit suicide

SUICIDED > SUICIDE

SUICIDES > SUICIDE

SUICIDING > SUICIDE

SUID n pig or related animal

SUIDIAN > SUID

SUIDIANS > SUID

SUIDS > SUID

SUILLINE adj of or like a pig

SUING > SUE

SUINGS > SUE

SUINT n water-soluble substance found in the fleece of sheep

SUINTS > SUINT

SUIPLAP n South African slang for a drunkard

SUIPLAPS > SUIPLAP

SUIT n set of clothes designed to be worn together ▷ vb be appropriate for

SUITABLE adj appropriate or proper

SUITABLY > SUITABLE

SUITCASE n portable travelling case for clothing

SUITCASES > SUITCASE

SUITE n set of connected rooms in a hotel

SUITED > SUIT

SUITER n piece of luggage for carrying suits and dresses

SUITERS > SUITER

SUITES > SUITE

SUITING n fabric used for suits

S

SUITINGS > SUITING
SUITLIKE > SUIT
SUITOR n man who is courting a woman ▷ vb act as a suitor
SUITORED > SUITOR
SUITORING > SUITOR
SUITORS > SUITOR
SUITRESS n female suitor
SUITS > SUIT
SUIVANTE n lady's maid
SUIVANTES > SUIVANTE
SUIVEZ vb musical direction meaning follow
SUJEE same as > SOOGEE
SUJEES > SUJEE
SUK same as > SOUK
SUKH same as > SOUK
SUKHS > SUKH
SUKIYAKI n Japanese dish consisting of very thinly sliced beef, vegetables, and seasonings cooked together quickly
SUKIYAKIS > SUKIYAKI
SUKKAH n temporary structure with a roof of branches in which orthodox Jews eat and, if possible, sleep during the festival of Sukkoth
SUKKAHS > SUKKAH
SUKKOS same as > SUKKOTH
SUKKOT same as > SUKKOTH
SUKKOTH n eight-day Jewish harvest festival
SUKS > SUK
SUKUK n financial certificate conforming to Islam lending principles
SUKUKS > SUKUK
SULCAL > SULCUS
SULCALISE same as > SULCALIZE
SULCALIZE vb furrow
SULCATE adj marked with longitudinal parallel grooves
SULCATED same as > SULCATE
SULCATION > SULCATE
SULCI > SULCUS
SULCUS n linear groove, furrow, or slight depression
SULDAN same as > SULTAN
SULDANS > SULDAN
SULFA same as > SULPHA
SULFAS > SULFA
SULFATASE n type of enzyme
SULFATE same as > SULPHATE
SULFATED > SULFATE
SULFATES > SULFATE
SULFATIC adj relating to sulphate
SULFATING > SULFATE
SULFATION > SULFATE
SULFID same as > SULPHIDE
SULFIDE same as > SULPHIDE

SULFIDES > SULFIDE
SULFIDS > SULFID
SULFINYL same as > SULPHINYL
SULFINYLS > SULFINYL
SULFITE same as > SULPHITE
SULFITES > SULFITE
SULFITIC > SULFITE
SULFO same as > SULPHONIC
SULFONATE n salt or ester of sulphonic acid
SULFONE same as > SULPHONE
SULFONES > SULFONE
SULFONIC > SULFONE
SULFONIUM n one of a type of salts
SULFONYL same as > SULPHURYL
SULFONYLS > SULFONYL
SULFOXIDE n compound containing sulphur
SULFUR variant of > SULPHUR
SULFURATE vb treat with sulphur
SULFURED > SULFUR
SULFURET same as > SULPHURET
SULFURETS > SULFURET
SULFURIC > SULFUR
SULFURING > SULFUR
SULFURISE variant of > SULFURIZE
SULFURIZE vb combine or treat with sulphur
SULFUROUS adj resembling sulphur
SULFURS > SULFUR
SULFURY > SULFUR
SULFURYL same as > SULPHURYL
SULFURYLS > SULFURYL
SULK vb be silent and sullen because of resentment or bad temper ▷ n resentful or sullen mood
SULKED > SULK
SULKER same as > SULK
SULKERS > SULKER
SULKIER > SULKY
SULKIES > SULKY
SULKIEST > SULKY
SULKILY > SULKY
SULKINESS > SULKY
SULKING > SULK
SULKS > SULK
SULKY adj moody or silent because of anger or resentment ▷ n light two-wheeled vehicle for one person, usually drawn by one horse
SULLAGE n filth or waste, esp sewage
SULLAGES > SULLAGE
SULLEN adj unwilling to talk or be sociable ▷ n sullen mood
SULLENER > SULLEN
SULLENEST > SULLEN
SULLENLY > SULLEN

SULLENS > SULLEN
SULLIABLE > SULLY
SULLIED > SULLY
SULLIES > SULLY
SULLY vb ruin (someone's reputation) ▷ n stain
SULLYING > SULLY
SULPH n amphetamine sulphate
SULPHA n any of a group of sulphonamides that prevent the growth of bacteria
SULPHAS > SULPHA
SULPHATE n salt or ester of sulphuric acid ▷ vb treat with a sulphate or convert into a sulphate
SULPHATED > SULPHATE
SULPHATES > SULPHATE
SULPHATIC > SULPHATE
SULPHID same as > SULPHIDE
SULPHIDE n compound of sulphur with another element
SULPHIDES > SULPHIDE
SULPHIDS > SULPHID
SULPHINYL another term for > THIONYL
SULPHITE n salt or ester of sulphurous acid
SULPHITES > SULPHITE
SULPHITIC > SULPHITE
SULPHONE n type of organic compound
SULPHONES > SULPHONE
SULPHONIC as in sulphonic acid type of strong organic acid
SULPHONYL same as > SULPHURYL
SULPHS > SULPH
SULPHUR n pale yellow nonmetallic element ▷ vb treat with sulphur
SULPHURED > SULPHUR
SULPHURET vb treat or combine with sulphur
SULPHURIC > SULPHUR
SULPHURS > SULPHUR
SULPHURY > SULPHUR
SULPHURYL n particular chemical divalent group
SULTAN n sovereign of a Muslim country
SULTANA n kind of raisin
SULTANAS > SULTANA
SULTANATE n territory of a sultan
SULTANESS same as > SULTANA
SULTANIC > SULTAN
SULTANS > SULTAN
SULTRIER > SULTRY
SULTRIEST > SULTRY
SULTRILY > SULTRY
SULTRY adj (of weather or climate) hot and humid
SULU n type of sarong worn in Fiji
SULUS > SULU
SUM n result of addition, total ▷ vb add or form a

total of (something)
SUMAC same as > SUMACH
SUMACH n type of temperate or subtropical shrub or small tree
SUMACHS > SUMACH
SUMACS > SUMAC
SUMATRA n violent storm blowing from the direction of Sumatra
SUMATRAS > SUMATRA
SUMLESS adj uncountable
SUMMA n compendium of theology, philosophy, or canon law, or sometimes of all three together
SUMMABLE > SUM
SUMMAE > SUMMA
SUMMAND n number or quantity forming part of a sum
SUMMANDS > SUMMAND
SUMMAR Scots variant of > SUMMER
SUMMARIES > SUMMARY
SUMMARILY > SUMMARY
SUMMARISE same as > SUMMARIZE
SUMMARIST > SUMMARIZE
SUMMARIZE vb make or be a summary of (something)
SUMMARY n brief account giving the main points of something ▷ adj done quickly, without formalities
SUMMAS > SUMMA
SUMMAT pron something ▷ n impressive or important person or thing
SUMMATE vb add up
SUMMATED > SUMMATE
SUMMATES > SUMMATE
SUMMATING > SUMMATE
SUMMATION n summary
SUMMATIVE > SUMMATION
SUMMATS > SUMMAT
SUMMED > SUM
SUMMER n warmest season of the year, between spring and autumn ▷ vb spend the summer (at a place)
SUMMERED > SUMMER
SUMMERIER > SUMMER
SUMMERING > SUMMER
SUMMERLY > SUMMER
SUMMERS > SUMMER
SUMMERSET n somersault
SUMMERY > SUMMER
SUMMING > SUM
SUMMINGS > SUM
SUMMIST n writer of summae
SUMMISTS > SUMMIST
SUMMIT n top of a mountain or hill ▷ vb reach summit
SUMMITAL > SUMMIT
SUMMITED > SUMMIT
SUMMITEER n person who participates in a summit conference

SUMMITING > SUMMIT

SUMMITRY n practice of conducting international negotiations by summit conferences

SUMMITS > SUMMIT

SUMMON vb order (someone) to come

SUMMONED > SUMMON

SUMMONER > SUMMON

SUMMONERS > SUMMON

SUMMONING > SUMMON

SUMMONS n command summoning someone ▷ vb order (someone) to appear in court

SUMMONSED > SUMMONS

SUMMONSES > SUMMONS

SUMO n Japanese style of wrestling

SUMOIST > SUMO

SUMOISTS > SUMO

SUMOS > SUMO

SUMOTORI n sumo wrestler

SUMOTORIS > SUMOTORI

SUMP n container in an internal-combustion engine into which oil can drain

SUMPH n stupid person

SUMPHISH > SUMPH

SUMPHS > SUMPH

SUMPIT n Malay blowpipe

SUMPITAN same as > SUMPIT

SUMPITANS > SUMPITAN

SUMPITS > SUMPIT

SUMPS > SUMP

SUMPSIMUS n correct form of expression

SUMPTER n packhorse, mule, or other beast of burden

SUMPTERS > SUMPTER

SUMPTUARY adj controlling expenditure or extravagant use of resources

SUMPTUOUS adj lavish, magnificent

SUMPWEED n American weed

SUMPWEEDS > SUMPWEED

SUMS > SUM

SUMY npl the monetary units of Uzbekistan

SUN n star around which the earth and other planets revolve ▷ vb expose (oneself) to the sun's rays

SUNBACK adj (of dress) cut low at back

SUNBAKE vb sunbathe, esp in order to become tanned ▷ n period of sunbaking

SUNBAKED adj (esp of roads, etc) dried or cracked by the sun's heat

SUNBAKES > SUNBAKE

SUNBAKING > SUNBAKE

SUNBATH n exposure of the body to the sun to get a suntan

SUNBATHE vb lie in the sunshine in order to get a suntan

SUNBATHED > SUNBATHE

SUNBATHER > SUNBATHE

SUNBATHES > SUNBATHE

SUNBATHS > SUNBATH

SUNBEAM n ray of sun

SUNBEAMED > SUNBEAM

SUNBEAMS > SUNBEAM

SUNBEAMY > SUNBEAM

SUNBEAT adj exposed to sun

SUNBEATEN same as > SUNBEAT

SUNBED n machine for giving an artificial tan

SUNBEDS > SUNBED

SUNBELT n southern states of the US

SUNBELTS > SUNBELT

SUNBERRY n red fruit like the blackberry

SUNBIRD n type of small songbird with a bright plumage in the males

SUNBIRDS > SUNBIRD

SUNBLIND n blind that shades a room from the sun's glare

SUNBLINDS > SUNBLIND

SUNBLOCK n cream applied to the skin to protect it from the sun's rays

SUNBLOCKS > SUNBLOCK

SUNBONNET n hat that shades the face and neck from the sun

SUNBOW n bow of prismatic colours similar to a rainbow, produced when sunlight shines through spray

SUNBOWS > SUNBOW

SUNBRIGHT adj bright as the sun

SUNBURN n painful reddening of the skin caused by overexposure to the sun ▷ vb become sunburnt

SUNBURNED > SUNBURN

SUNBURNS > SUNBURN

SUNBURNT > SUNBURN

SUNBURST n burst of sunshine, as through a break in the clouds

SUNBURSTS > SUNBURST

SUNCHOKE n Jerusalem artichoke

SUNCHOKES > SUNCHOKE

SUNDAE n ice cream topped with fruit etc

SUNDAES > SUNDAE

SUNDARI n Indian tree

SUNDARIS > SUNDARI

SUNDECK n upper open deck on a passenger ship

SUNDECKS > SUNDECK

SUNDER vb break apart

SUNDERED > SUNDER

SUNDERER > SUNDER

SUNDERERS > SUNDER

SUNDERING > SUNDER

SUNDERS > SUNDER

SUNDEW n type of bog plant with leaves covered in sticky hairs that trap and digest insects

SUNDEWS > SUNDEW

SUNDIAL n device showing the time by means of a pointer that casts a shadow on a marked dial

SUNDIALS > SUNDIAL

SUNDOG n small rainbow or halo near the horizon

SUNDOGS > SUNDOG

SUNDOWN same as > SUNSET

SUNDOWNED > SUNDOWN

SUNDOWNER n tramp, esp one who seeks food and lodging at sundown when it is too late to work

SUNDOWNS > SUNDOWN

SUNDRA same as > SUNDARI

SUNDRAS > SUNDRA

SUNDRESS n dress for hot weather that exposes the shoulders, arms, and back, esp one with straps over the shoulders

SUNDRI same as > SUNDARI

SUNDRIES > SUNDRY

SUNDRILY > SUNDRY

SUNDRIS > SUNDRI

SUNDROPS n American primrose

SUNDRY adj several, various

SUNFAST adj not fading in sunlight

SUNFISH n large sea fish with a rounded body

SUNFISHES > SUNFISH

SUNFLOWER n tall plant with large golden flowers

SUNG > SING

SUNGAR same as > SANGAR

SUNGARS > SUNGAR

SUNGAZER n person who practices sungazing

SUNGAZERS > SUNGAZER

SUNGAZING n staring directly at the sun

SUNGLASS n convex lens used to focus the sun's rays and thus produce heat or ignition

SUNGLOW n pinkish glow often seen in the sky before sunrise or after sunset

SUNGLOWS > SUNGLOW

SUNGREBE another name for > FINFOOT

SUNGREBES > SUNGREBE

SUNHAT n hat that shades the face and neck from the sun

SUNHATS > SUNHAT

SUNI n S African dwarf antelope

SUNIS > SUNI

SUNK n bank or pad

SUNKEN adj unhealthily hollow

SUNKET n something good to eat

SUNKETS > SUNKET

SUNKIE n little stool

SUNKIES > SUNKIE

SUNKS > SUNK

SUNLAMP n lamp that generates ultraviolet rays

SUNLAMPS > SUNLAMP

SUNLAND n sunny area

SUNLANDS > SUNLAND

SUNLESS adj without sun or sunshine

SUNLESSLY > SUNLESS

SUNLIGHT n light that comes from the sun

SUNLIGHTS > SUNLIGHT

SUNLIKE > SUN

SUNLIT > SUNLIGHT

SUNN n leguminous plant of the East Indies, having yellow flowers

SUNNA n body of traditional Islamic law

SUNNAH same as > SUNNA

SUNNAHS > SUNNAH

SUNNAS > SUNNA

SUNNED > SUN

SUNNIER > SUNNY

SUNNIES npl pair of sunglasses

SUNNIEST > SUNNY

SUNNILY > SUNNY

SUNNINESS > SUNNY

SUNNING > SUN

SUNNS > SUNN

SUNNY adj full of or exposed to sunlight

SUNPORCH n porch for sunbathing on

SUNPROOF > SUN

SUNRAY n ray of light from the sun

SUNRAYS > SUNRAY

SUNRISE n daily appearance of the sun above the horizon

SUNRISES > SUNRISE

SUNRISING same as > SUNRISE

SUNROOF n panel in the roof of a car that opens to let in air

SUNROOFS > SUNROOF

SUNROOM n room or glass-enclosed porch designed to display beautiful views

SUNROOMS > SUNROOM

SUNS > SUN

SUNSCALD n sun damage on tomato plants

SUNSCALDS > SUNSCALD

SUNSCREEN n cream or lotion applied to exposed skin to protect it from the ultraviolet rays of the sun

SUNSEEKER n person looking for sunny weather

SUNSET n daily disappearance of the sun below the horizon

SUNSETS > SUNSET

SUNSHADE n anything used to shade people from the sun, such as a parasol or awning

S

SUNSHADES > SUNSHADE

SUNSHINE *n* light and warmth from the sun

SUNSHINES > SUNSHINE

SUNSHINY > SUNSHINE

SUNSPOT *n* dark patch appearing temporarily on the sun's surface

SUNSPOTS > SUNSPOT

SUNSTAR *n* type of starfish with up to 13 arms radiating from a central disc

SUNSTARS > SUNSTAR

SUNSTONE *n* type of translucent feldspar with reddish-gold speckles

SUNSTONES > SUNSTONE

SUNSTROKE *n* illness caused by prolonged exposure to intensely hot sunlight

SUNSTRUCK *adj* suffering from sunstroke

SUNSUIT *n* child's outfit consisting of a brief top and shorts or a short skirt

SUNSUITS > SUNSUIT

SUNTAN *n* browning of the skin caused by exposure to the sun

SUNTANNED > SUNTAN

SUNTANS > SUNTAN

SUNTRAP *n* very sunny sheltered place

SUNTRAPS > SUNTRAP

SUNUP *same as >* SUNRISE

SUNUPS > SUNUP

SUNWARD *same as >* SUNWARDS

SUNWARDS *adv* towards the sun

SUNWISE *adv* moving in the same direction as the sun

SUP *same as >* SUPINE

SUPAWN *same as >* SUPPAWN

SUPAWNS > SUPAWN

SUPE *n* superintendent

SUPER *adj* excellent ▷ *n* superannuation ▷ *interj* enthusiastic expression of approval or assent ▷ *vb* work as superintendent

SUPERABLE *adj* able to be surmounted or overcome

SUPERABLY > SUPERABLE

SUPERADD *vb* add (something) to something that has already been added

SUPERADDS > SUPERADD

SUPERATE *vb* overcome

SUPERATED > SUPERATE

SUPERATES > SUPERATE

SUPERATOM *n* cluster of atoms behaving like a single atom

SUPERB *adj* excellent, impressive, or splendid

SUPERBAD *adj* exceptionally bad

SUPERBANK *n* bank that owns other banks

SUPERBER > SUPERB

SUPERBEST > SUPERB

SUPERBIKE *n* high-performance motorcycle

SUPERBITY > SUPERB

SUPERBLY > SUPERB

SUPERBOLD *adj* exceptionally bold

SUPERBOMB *n* large bomb

SUPERBRAT *n* exceptionally unpleasant child

SUPERBUG *n* bacterium resistant to antibiotics

SUPERBUGS > SUPERBUG

SUPERCAR *n* very expensive fast or powerful car with a centrally located engine

SUPERCARS > SUPERCAR

SUPERCEDE *former variant of >* SUPERSEDE

SUPERCHIC *adj* highly chic

SUPERCITY *n* very large city

SUPERCLUB *n* large and important club

SUPERCOIL *vb* form a complex coil

SUPERCOLD *adj* very cold

SUPERCOOL *vb* cool or be cooled to a temperature below that at which freezing or crystallization should occur

SUPERCOP *n* high-ranking police officer

SUPERCOPS > SUPERCOP

SUPERCOW *n* dairy cow that produces a very high milk yield

SUPERCOWS > SUPERCOW

SUPERCUTE *adj* very cute

SUPERED > SUPER

SUPEREGO *n* that part of the unconscious mind that governs ideas about what is right and wrong

SUPEREGOS > SUPEREGO

SUPERETTE *n* small store or dairy laid out along the lines of a supermarket

SUPERFAN *n* very devoted fan

SUPERFANS > SUPERFAN

SUPERFARM *n* very large farm

SUPERFAST *adj* very fast

SUPERFINE *adj* of exceptional fineness or quality

SUPERFIRM *adj* very firm

SUPERFIT *adj* highly fit

SUPERFIX *n* lingustic feature distinguishing the meaning of one word that of another

SUPERFLUX *n* superfluity

SUPERFOOD *n* food thought to be beneficial to health

SUPERFUND *n* large fund

SUPERFUSE *vb* pour or be poured so as to cover something

SUPERGENE *n* cluster of genes

SUPERGLUE *n* extremely strong and quick-drying glue ▷ *vb* fix with superglue

SUPERGOOD *adj* very good

SUPERGUN *n* large powerful gun

SUPERGUNS > SUPERGUN

SUPERHEAT *vb* heat (a vapour, esp steam) to a temperature above its saturation point for a given pressure

SUPERHERO *n* any of various comic-strip characters with superhuman abilities or magical powers

SUPERHET *n* type of radio receiver

SUPERHETS > SUPERHET

SUPERHIGH *adj* extremely high

SUPERHIT *n* very popular hit

SUPERHITS > SUPERHIT

SUPERHIVE *n* upper part of beehive

SUPERHOT *adj* very hot

SUPERHYPE *n* exaggerated hype

SUPERING > SUPER

SUPERIOR *adj* greater in quality, quantity, or merit ▷ *n* person of greater rank or status

SUPERIORS > SUPERIOR

SUPERJET *n* supersonic aircraft

SUPERJETS > SUPERJET

SUPERJOCK *n* very athletic person

SUPERLAIN > SUPERLIE

SUPERLAY > SUPERLIE

SUPERLIE *vb* lie above

SUPERLIES > SUPERLIE

SUPERLOAD *n* variable weight on a structure

SUPERLONG *adj* very long

SUPERLOO *n* automated public toilet

SUPERLOOS > SUPERLOO

SUPERMALE *former name for >* METAMALE

SUPERMAN *n* man with great physical or mental powers

SUPERMART *n* large self-service store selling food and household supplies

SUPERMAX *n* jail or other facility having the very highest levels of security

SUPERMEN > SUPERMAN

SUPERMIND *n* very powerful brain

SUPERMINI *n* small car, usually a hatchback, that is economical to run but has a high level of performance

SUPERMOM *n* very capable and busy mother

SUPERMOMS > SUPERMOM

SUPERMOTO *n* form of motorcycle racing over part-tarmac and part-dirt circuits

SUPERNAL *adj* of or from the world of the divine

SUPERNATE *n* liquid lying above a sediment

SUPERNOVA *n* star that explodes and briefly becomes exceptionally bright

SUPERPIMP *n* pimp controlling many prostitutes

SUPERPLUS *n* surplus

SUPERPORT *n* large port

SUPERPOSE *vb* transpose (the coordinates of one geometric figure) to coincide with those of another

SUPERPRO *n* person regarded as a real professional

SUPERPROS > SUPERPRO

SUPERRACE *n* important race

SUPERREAL *adj* surreal

SUPERRICH *adj* exceptionally wealthy

SUPERROAD *n* very large road

SUPERS > SUPER

SUPERSAFE *adj* very safe

SUPERSALE *n* large sale

SUPERSALT *n* acid salt

SUPERSAUR *n* very large dinosaur

SUPERSEDE *vb* replace, supplant

SUPERSELL *vb* sell in very large numbers

SUPERSEX *n* sterile organism in which the ratio between the sex chromosomes is disturbed

SUPERSHOW *n* very impressive show

SUPERSIZE *vb* make larger

SUPERSOFT *adj* very soft

SUPERSOLD > SUPERSELL

SUPERSPY *n* highly accomplished spy

SUPERSTAR *n* very famous entertainer or sportsperson

SUPERSTUD *n* highly virile man

SUPERTAX *n* extra tax on incomes above a certain level

SUPERTHIN *adj* very thin

SUPERTRAM *n* type of tram with greater capacity and speed than conventional trams

SUPERVENE *vb* occur as an unexpected development

SUPERVISE *vb* watch over to direct or check

SUPERWAIF *n* very young and very thin supermodel
SUPERWAVE *n* large wave
SUPERWEED *n* hybrid plant that contains genes for herbicide resistance
SUPERWIDE *n* very wide lens
SUPERWIFE *n* highly accomplished wife
SUPES > SUPE
SUPINATE *vb* turn (the hand and forearm) so that the palm faces up or forwards
SUPINATED > SUPINATE
SUPINATES > SUPINATE
SUPINATOR *n* muscle of the forearm that can produce the motion of supination
SUPINE *adj* lying flat on one's back ▷ *n* noun form derived from a verb in Latin
SUPINELY > SUPINE
SUPINES > SUPINE
SUPLEX *n* wrestling hold in which a wrestler grasps his opponent round the waist from behind and carries him backwards
SUPLEXES > SUPLEX
SUPPAWN *n* kind of porridge
SUPPAWNS > SUPPAWN
SUPPEAGO *same as* > SERPIGO
SUPPED > SUP
SUPPER *n* light evening meal ▷ *vb* eat supper
SUPPERED > SUPPER
SUPPERING > SUPPER
SUPPERS > SUPPER
SUPPING > SUP
SUPPLANT *vb* take the place of, oust
SUPPLANTS > SUPPLANT
SUPPLE *adj* (of a person) moving and bending easily and gracefully ▷ *vb* make or become supple
SUPPLED > SUPPLE
SUPPLELY *same as* > SUPPLY
SUPPLER > SUPPLE
SUPPLES > SUPPLE
SUPPLEST > SUPPLE
SUPPLIAL *n* instance of supplying
SUPPLIALS > SUPPLIAL
SUPPLIANT *n* person who requests humbly
SUPPLICAT *n* university petition
SUPPLIED > SUPPLY
SUPPLIER > SUPPLY
SUPPLIERS > SUPPLY
SUPPLIES > SUPPLY
SUPPLING > SUPPLE
SUPPLY *vb* provide with something required ▷ *n* supplying ▷ *adj* acting as a temporary substitute ▷ *adv* in a supple manner
SUPPLYING > SUPPLY

SUPPORT *vb* bear the weight of ▷ *n* supporting
SUPPORTED > SUPPORT
SUPPORTER *n* person who supports a team, principle, etc
SUPPORTS > SUPPORT
SUPPOSAL *n* supposition
SUPPOSALS > SUPPOSAL
SUPPOSE *vb* presume to be true
SUPPOSED *adj* presumed to be true without proof, doubtful
SUPPOSER > SUPPOSE
SUPPOSERS > SUPPOSE
SUPPOSES > SUPPOSE
SUPPOSING > SUPPOSE
SUPPRESS *vb* put an end to
SUPPURATE *vb* (of a wound etc) produce pus
SUPRA *adv* above, esp referring to earlier parts of a book etc
SUPREMA > SUPREMUM
SUPREMACY *n* supreme power
SUPREME *adj* highest in authority, rank, or degree ▷ *n* rich velouté sauce made with a base of veal or chicken stock, with cream or egg yolks added
SUPREMELY > SUPREME
SUPREMER > SUPREME
SUPREMES > SUPREME
SUPREMEST > SUPREME
SUPREMITY *n* supremeness
SUPREMO *n* person in overall authority
SUPREMOS > SUPREMO
SUPREMUM *n* (in maths) smallest quantity greater than or equal to each of a set or subset
SUPREMUMS > SUPREMUM
SUPS > SUP
SUQ *same as* > SOUK
SUQS > SUQ
SUR *prep* above
SURA *n* any of the 114 chapters of the Koran
SURAH *n* twill-weave fabric of silk or rayon, used for dresses, blouses, etc
SURAHS > SURAH
SURAL *adj* of or relating to the calf of the leg
SURAMIN *n* drug used in treating sleeping sickness
SURAMINS > SURAMIN
SURANCE *same as* > ASSURANCE
SURANCES > SURANCE
SURAS > SURA
SURAT *n* (formerly) a cotton fabric from the Surat area of India
SURATS > SURAT
SURBAHAR *n* Indian string instrument
SURBAHARS > SURBAHAR
SURBASE *n* uppermost

part, such as a moulding, of a pedestal, base, or skirting
SURBASED *adj* having a surbase
SURBASES > SURBASE
SURBATE *vb* make feet sore through walking
SURBATED > SURBATE
SURBATES > SURBATE
SURBATING > SURBATE
SURBED *vb* put something on its edge
SURBEDDED > SURBED
SURBEDS > SURBED
SURBET > SURBATE
SURCEASE *n* cessation or intermission ▷ *vb* desist from (some action)
SURCEASED > SURCEASE
SURCEASES > SURCEASE
SURCHARGE *n* additional charge ▷ *vb* charge (someone) an additional sum or tax
SURCINGLE *n* girth for a horse which goes around the body, used esp with a racing saddle ▷ *vb* put a surcingle on or over (a horse)
SURCOAT *n* tunic worn by a knight over his armour during the Middle Ages
SURCOATS > SURCOAT
SURCULI > SURCULUS
SURCULOSE *adj* (of a plant) bearing suckers
SURCULUS *n* sucker on plant
SURD *n* number that cannot be expressed in whole numbers ▷ *adj* of or relating to a surd
SURDITIES > SURDITY
SURDITY *n* deafness
SURDS > SURD
SURE *adj* free from uncertainty or doubt ▷ *interj* certainly ▷ *vb* archaic form of sewer
SURED > SURE
SUREFIRE *adj* certain to succeed
SURELY *adv* it must be true that
SURENESS > SURE
SURER > SURE
SURES > SURE
SUREST > SURE
SURETIED > SURETY
SURETIES > SURETY
SURETY *n* person who takes responsibility for the fulfilment of another's obligation ▷ *vb* be surety for
SURETYING > SURETY
SURF *n* foam caused by waves breaking on the shore ▷ *vb* take part in surfing
SURFABLE > SURF
SURFACE *n* outside or top of an object ▷ *vb* become apparent

SURFACED > SURFACE
SURFACER > SURFACE
SURFACERS > SURFACE
SURFACES > SURFACE
SURFACING > SURFACE
SURFBIRD *n* American shore bird
SURFBIRDS > SURFBIRD
SURFBOARD *n* long smooth board used in surfing
SURFBOAT *n* boat with a high bow and stern and flotation chambers
SURFBOATS > SURFBOAT
SURFED > SURF
SURFEIT *n* excessive amount ▷ *vb* supply or feed excessively
SURFEITED > SURFEIT
SURFEITER > SURFEIT
SURFEITS > SURFEIT
SURFER > SURFING
SURFERS > SURFING
SURFFISH *n* fish of American coastal seas
SURFICIAL *adj* superficial
SURFIE *n* young person whose main interest is in surfing
SURFIER > SURF
SURFIES > SURFIE
SURFIEST > SURF
SURFING *n* sport of riding towards the shore on a surfboard on the crest of a wave
SURFINGS > SURFING
SURFLIKE > SURF
SURFMAN *n* sailor skilled in sailing through surf
SURFMEN > SURFMAN
SURFPERCH *n* type of marine fish of North American Pacific coastal waters
SURFRIDER > SURFING
SURFS > SURF
SURFSIDE *adj* next to the sea
SURFY > SURF
SURGE *n* sudden powerful increase ▷ *vb* increase suddenly
SURGED > SURGE
SURGEFUL > SURGE
SURGELESS > SURGE
SURGENT > SURGE
SURGEON *n* doctor who specializes in surgery
SURGEONCY *n* office, duties, or position of a surgeon, esp in the army or navy
SURGEONS > SURGEON
SURGER > SURGE
SURGERIES > SURGERY
SURGERS > SURGE
SURGERY *n* treatment in which the patient's body is cut open in order to treat the affected part
SURGES > SURGE

S

SURGICAL *adj* involving or used in surgery
SURGIER > SURGE
SURGIEST > SURGE
SURGING > SURGE
SURGINGS > SURGE
SURGY > SURGE
SURICATE *n* type of meerkat
SURICATES > SURICATE
SURIMI *n* blended seafood product made from precooked fish, restructured into stick shapes
SURIMIS > SURIMI
SURING > SURE
SURLIER > SURLY
SURLIEST > SURLY
SURLILY > SURLY
SURLINESS > SURLY
SURLOIN *same as*
> SIRLOIN
SURLOINS > SURLOIN
SURLY *adj* ill-tempered and rude
SURMASTER *n* deputy headmaster
SURMISAL > SURMISE
SURMISALS > SURMISE
SURMISE *n* guess, conjecture ▷ *vb* guess (something) from incomplete or uncertain evidence
SURMISED > SURMISE
SURMISER > SURMISE
SURMISERS > SURMISE
SURMISES > SURMISE
SURMISING > SURMISE
SURMOUNT *vb* overcome (a problem)
SURMOUNTS > SURMOUNT
SURMULLET *n* red mullet
SURNAME *n* family name ▷ *vb* furnish with or call by a surname
SURNAMED > SURNAME
SURNAMER > SURNAME
SURNAMERS > SURNAME
SURNAMES > SURNAME
SURNAMING > SURNAME
SURPASS *vb* be greater than or superior to
SURPASSED > SURPASS
SURPASSER > SURPASS
SURPASSES > SURPASS
SURPLICE *n* loose white robe worn by clergymen and choristers
SURPLICED > SURPLICE
SURPLICES > SURPLICE
SURPLUS *n* amount left over in excess of what is required ▷ *adj* extra ▷ *vb* be left over in excess of what is required
SURPLUSED > SURPLUS
SURPLUSES > SURPLUS
SURPRINT *vb* print (additional matter) over something already printed ▷ *n* marks, printed matter, etc, that have been

surprinted
SURPRINTS > SURPRINT
SURPRISAL > SURPRISE
SURPRISE *n* unexpected event ▷ *vb* cause to feel amazement or wonder
SURPRISED > SURPRISE
SURPRISER > SURPRISE
SURPRISES > SURPRISE
SURPRIZE *same as*
> SURPRISE
SURPRIZED > SURPRIZE
SURPRIZES > SURPRIZE
SURQUEDRY *n* arrogance
SURQUEDY *same as*
> SURQUEDRY
SURRA *n* tropical febrile disease of animals
SURRAS > SURRA
SURREAL *adj* bizarre ▷ *n* atmosphere or qualities evoked by surrealism
SURREALLY > SURREAL
SURREALS > SURREAL
SURREBUT *vb* give evidence to support the surrebutter
SURREBUTS > SURREBUT
SURREINED *adj* (of horse) ridden too much
SURREJOIN *vb* reply to legal rejoinder
SURRENDER *vb* give oneself up ▷ *n* surrendering
SURRENDRY *same as*
> SURRENDER
SURREY *n* light four-wheeled horse-drawn carriage having two or four seats
SURREYS > SURREY
SURROGACY
> SURROGATE
SURROGATE *n* substitute ▷ *adj* acting as a substitute ▷ *vb* put in another's position as a deputy, substitute, etc
SURROUND *vb* be, come, or place all around (a person or thing) ▷ *n* border or edging
SURROUNDS > SURROUND
SURROYAL *n* high point on stag's horns
SURROYALS > SURROYAL
SURTAX *n* extra tax on incomes above a certain level ▷ *vb* assess for liability to surtax
SURTAXED > SURTAX
SURTAXES > SURTAX
SURTAXING > SURTAX
SURTITLE *singular of*
> SURTITLE
SURTITLES *npl* brief translations of the text of an opera or play projected above the stage
SURTOUT *n* man's overcoat resembling a frock coat, popular in the late 19th century
SURTOUTS > SURTOUT
SURUCUCU *n* South

American snake
SURUCUCUS > SURUCUCU
SURVEIL *same as*
> SURVEILLE
SURVEILED > SURVEIL
SURVEILLE *vb* observe closely
SURVEILS > SURVEIL
SURVEY *vb* view or consider in a general way ▷ *n* surveying
SURVEYAL > SURVEY
SURVEYALS > SURVEY
SURVEYED > SURVEY
SURVEYING *n* practice of measuring altitudes, angles, and distances on the land surface so that they can be accurately plotted on a map
SURVEYOR *n* person whose occupation is to survey land or buildings
SURVEYORS > SURVEYOR
SURVEYS > SURVEY
SURVIEW *vb* survey
SURVIEWED > SURVIEW
SURVIEWS > SURVIEW
SURVIVAL *n* condition of having survived ▷ *adj* of, relating to, or assisting the act of surviving
SURVIVALS > SURVIVAL
SURVIVE *vb* continue to live or exist after (a difficult experience)
SURVIVED > SURVIVE
SURVIVER *same as*
> SURVIVOR
SURVIVERS > SURVIVER
SURVIVES > SURVIVE
SURVIVING > SURVIVE
SURVIVOR *n* person or thing that survives
SURVIVORS > SURVIVOR
SUS *same as* > SUSS
SUSCEPTOR *n* sponsor
SUSCITATE *vb* excite
SUSES > SUS
SUSHI *n* Japanese dish of small cakes of cold rice with a topping of raw fish
SUSHIS > SUSHI
SUSLIK *n* central Eurasian ground squirrel
SUSLIKS > SUSLIK
SUSPECT *vb* believe (someone) to be guilty without having any proof ▷ *adj* not to be trusted ▷ *n* person who is suspected
SUSPECTED > SUSPECT
SUSPECTER > SUSPECT
SUSPECTS > SUSPECT
SUSPENCE *same as*
> SUSPENSE
SUSPEND *vb* hang from a high place
SUSPENDED > SUSPEND
SUSPENDER *n* elastic strap for holding up women's stockings
SUSPENDS > SUSPEND
SUSPENS *same as*
> SUSPENSE

SUSPENSE *n* state of uncertainty while awaiting news, an event, etc
SUSPENSER *n* film that creates a feeling of suspense
SUSPENSES > SUSPENSE
SUSPENSOR *n* ligament or muscle that holds a part in position
SUSPICION *n* feeling of not trusting a person or thing
SUSPIRE *vb* sigh or utter with a sigh
SUSPIRED > SUSPIRE
SUSPIRES > SUSPIRE
SUSPIRING > SUSPIRE
SUSS *vb* attempt to work out (a situation, etc), using one's intuition ▷ *n* sharpness of mind
SUSSED > SUSS
SUSSES > SUSS
SUSSING > SUSS
SUSTAIN *vb* maintain or prolong ▷ *n* prolongation of a note, by playing technique or electronics
SUSTAINED > SUSTAIN
SUSTAINER *n* rocket engine that maintains the velocity of a space vehicle after the booster has been jettisoned
SUSTAINS > SUSTAIN
SUSTINENT *adj* sustaining
SUSU *n* (in the Caribbean) savings fund shared by friends
SUSURRANT
> SUSURRATE
SUSURRATE *vb* make a soft rustling sound
SUSURROUS *adj* full of murmuring sounds
SUSURRUS > SUSURRATE
SUSUS > SUSU
SUTILE *adj* involving sewing
SUTLER *n* (formerly) a merchant who accompanied an army in order to sell provisions to the soldiers
SUTLERIES > SUTLER
SUTLERS > SUTLER
SUTLERY > SUTLER
SUTOR *n* cobbler
SUTORIAL > SUTOR
SUTORIAN > SUTOR
SUTORS > SUTOR
SUTRA *n* Sanskrit sayings or collections of sayings
SUTRAS > SUTRA
SUTTA *n* Buddhist scripture
SUTTAS > SUTTA
SUTTEE *n* former Hindu custom whereby a widow burnt herself to death on her husband's funeral pyre
SUTTEEISM > SUTTEE
SUTTEES > SUTTEE
SUTTLE *vb* work as sutler
SUTTLED > SUTTLE

SUTTLES > SUTTLE

SUTTLETIE same as > SUBTLETY

SUTTLING > SUTTLE

SUTTLY > SUBTLE

SUTURAL > SUTURE

SUTURALLY > SUTURE

SUTURE n stitch joining the edges of a wound ▷ vb join (the edges of a wound, etc) by means of sutures

SUTURED > SUTURE

SUTURES > SUTURE

SUTURING > SUTURE

SUZERAIN n state or sovereign with limited authority over another self-governing state

SUZERAINS > SUZERAIN

SVARAJ same as > SWARAJ

SVARAJES > SVARAJ

SVASTIKA same as > SWASTIKA

SVASTIKAS > SVASTIKA

SVEDBERG n unit used in physics

SVEDBERGS > SVEDBERG

SVELTE adj attractively or gracefully slim

SVELTELY > SVELTE

SVELTER > SVELTE

SVELTEST > SVELTE

SWAB n small piece of cotton wool used to apply medication, clean a wound, etc ▷ vb clean (a wound) with a swab

SWABBED > SWAB

SWABBER n person who uses a swab

SWABBERS > SWABBER

SWABBIE same as > SWABBY

SWABBIES > SWABBY

SWABBING > SWAB

SWABBY n seaman

SWABS > SWAB

SWACK adj flexible

SWACKED adj in a state of intoxication, stupor, or euphoria induced by drugs or alcohol

SWAD n loutish person

SWADDIE same as > SWADDY

SWADDIES > SWADDY

SWADDLE vb wrap (a baby) in swaddling clothes ▷ n swaddling clothes

SWADDLED > SWADDLE

SWADDLER > SWADDLE

SWADDLERS > SWADDLE

SWADDLES > SWADDLE

SWADDLING > SWADDLE

SWADDY n private soldier

SWADS > SWADDLE

SWAG n stolen property ▷ vb sway from side to side

SWAGE n shaped tool or die used in forming cold metal by hammering ▷ vb form (metal) with a swage

SWAGED > SWAGE

SWAGER > SWAGE

SWAGERS > SWAGE

SWAGES > SWAGE

SWAGGED > SWAG

SWAGGER vb walk or behave arrogantly ▷ n arrogant walk or manner ▷ adj elegantly fashionable

SWAGGERED > SWAGGER

SWAGGERER > SWAGGER

SWAGGERS > SWAGGER

SWAGGIE same as > SWAGGER

SWAGGIES > SWAGGIE

SWAGGING > SWAG

SWAGING > SWAGE

SWAGMAN n tramp who carries his belongings in a bundle on his back

SWAGMEN > SWAGMAN

SWAGS > SWAG

SWAGSHOP n shop selling cheap goods

SWAGSHOPS > SWAGSHOP

SWAGSMAN same as > SWAGMAN

SWAGSMEN > SWAGSMAN

SWAIL same as > SWALE

SWAILS > SWAIL

SWAIN n suitor

SWAINING n acting as suitor

SWAININGS > SWAINING

SWAINISH > SWAIN

SWAINS > SWAIN

SWALE n moist depression in a tract of land, usually with rank vegetation ▷ vb sway

SWALED > SWALE

SWALES > SWALE

SWALIER > SWALE

SWALIEST > SWALE

SWALING > SWALE

SWALINGS > SWALE

SWALLET n hole where water goes underground

SWALLETS > SWALLET

SWALLOW vb cause to pass down one's throat ▷ n swallowing

SWALLOWED > SWALLOW

SWALLOWER > SWALLOW

SWALLOWS > SWALLOW

SWALY > SWALE

SWAM > SWIM

SWAMI n Hindu religious teacher

SWAMIES > SWAMI

SWAMIS > SWAMI

SWAMP n watery area of land, bog ▷ vb cause (a boat) to fill with water and sink

SWAMPED > SWAMP

SWAMPER n person who lives or works in a swampy region, esp in the southern US

SWAMPERS > SWAMPER

SWAMPIER > SWAMP

SWAMPIEST > SWAMP

SWAMPING > SWAMP

SWAMPISH > SWAMP

SWAMPLAND n

permanently waterlogged area

SWAMPLESS > SWAMP

SWAMPS > SWAMP

SWAMPY > SWAMP

SWAMY same as > SWAMI

SWAN n large usu white water bird with a long graceful neck ▷ vb wander about idly

SWANG > SWING

SWANHERD n person who herds swans

SWANHERDS > SWANHERD

SWANK vb show off or boast ▷ n showing off or boasting

SWANKED > SWANK

SWANKER > SWANK

SWANKERS > SWANK

SWANKEST > SWANK

SWANKEY same as > SWANKY

SWANKEYS > SWANKY

SWANKIE same as > SWANKY

SWANKIER > SWANKY

SWANKIES > SWANKY

SWANKIEST > SWANKY

SWANKILY > SWANKY

SWANKING > SWANK

SWANKPOT same as > SWANK

SWANKPOTS > SWANKPOT

SWANKS > SWANK

SWANKY adj expensive and showy, stylish ▷ n lively person

SWANLIKE > SWAN

SWANNED > SWAN

SWANNERY n place where swans are kept and bred

SWANNIE n (in NZ) type of all-weather heavy woollen shirt

SWANNIER > SWANNY

SWANNIES > SWANNIE

SWANNIEST > SWANNY

SWANNING > SWAN

SWANNINGS > SWAN

SWANNY adj swanlike

SWANPAN n Chinese abacus

SWANPANS > SWANPAN

SWANS > SWAN

SWANSDOWN n fine soft feathers of a swan

SWANSKIN n skin of a swan with the feathers attached

SWANSKINS > SWANSKIN

SWANSONG n beautiful song fabled to be sung by a swan before it dies

SWANSONGS > SWANSONG

SWAP vb exchange (something) for something else ▷ n exchange

SWAPPED > SWAP

SWAPPER > SWAP

SWAPPERS > SWAP

SWAPPING > SWAP

SWAPPINGS > SWAP

SWAPS > SWAP

SWAPT > SWAP

SWAPTION another name for > SWAP

SWAPTIONS > SWAPTION

SWARAJ n (in British India) self-government

SWARAJES > SWARAJ

SWARAJISM > SWARAJ

SWARAJIST > SWARAJ

SWARD n stretch of short grass ▷ vb cover or become covered with grass

SWARDED > SWARD

SWARDIER > SWARDY

SWARDIEST > SWARDY

SWARDING > SWARD

SWARDS > SWARD

SWARDY adj covered with sward

SWARE > SWEAR

SWARF n material removed by cutting tools in the machining of metals, stone, etc ▷ vb faint

SWARFED > SWARF

SWARFING > SWARF

SWARFS > SWARF

SWARM n large group of bees or other insects ▷ vb move in a swarm

SWARMED > SWARM

SWARMER > SWARM

SWARMERS > SWARM

SWARMING > SWARM

SWARMINGS > SWARM

SWARMS > SWARM

SWART adj swarthy

SWARTH same as > SWART

SWARTHIER > SWARTHY

SWARTHILY > SWARTHY

SWARTHS > SWARTH

SWARTHY adj dark-complexioned

SWARTNESS > SWART

SWARTY > SWART

SWARVE same as > SWARF

SWARVED > SWARF

SWARVES > SWARF

SWARVING > SWARF

SWASH n rush of water up a beach following each break of the waves ▷ vb (esp of water or things in water) to wash or move with noisy splashing

SWASHED > SWASH

SWASHER n braggart

SWASHERS > SWASHER

SWASHES > SWASH

SWASHIER > SWASHY

SWASHIEST > SWASHY

SWASHING > SWASH

SWASHINGS > SWASH

SWASHWORK n type of work done on lathe

SWASHY adj slushy

SWASTICA same as > SWASTIKA

SWASTICAS > SWASTICA

SWASTIKA n symbol in the shape of a cross with the arms bent at right angles, used as the emblem of Nazi Germany

SWASTIKAS > SWASTIKA

SWAT vb strike or hit sharply ▷ n swatter

S

SWATCH n sample of cloth
SWATCHES > SWATCH
SWATH n width of one sweep of a scythe or of the blade of a mowing machine
SWATHABLE > SWATHE
SWATHE vb bandage or wrap completely ▷ n bandage or wrapping
SWATHED > SWATHE
SWATHER > SWATHE
SWATHERS > SWATHE
SWATHES > SWATHE
SWATHIER > SWATH
SWATHIEST > SWATH
SWATHING > SWATHE
SWATHS > SWATH
SWATHY > SWATH
SWATS > SWAT
SWATTED > SWAT
SWATTER n device for killing insects, esp a meshed flat attached to a handle ▷ vb splash
SWATTERED > SWATTER
SWATTERS > SWATTER
SWATTIER same as > SWOTTIER
SWATTIEST same as > SWOTTIEST
SWATTING > SWAT
SWATTINGS > SWAT
SWATTY same as > SWOTTY
SWAY vb swing to and fro or from side to side ▷ n power or influence
SWAYABLE > SWAY
SWAYBACK n abnormal sagging in the spine of older horses
SWAYBACKS > SWAYBACK
SWAYED > SWAY
SWAYER > SWAY
SWAYERS > SWAY
SWAYFUL > SWAY
SWAYING > SWAY
SWAYINGS > SWAY
SWAYL same as > SWEAL
SWAYLED > SWAYL
SWAYLING > SWAYL
SWAYLINGS > SWAYL
SWAYLS > SWAYL
SWAYS > SWAY
SWAZZLE n small metal instrument used to produce a shrill voice
SWAZZLES > SWAZZLE
SWEAL vb scorch
SWEALED > SWEAL
SWEALING > SWEAL
SWEALINGS > SWEAL
SWEALS > SWEAL
SWEAR vb use obscene or blasphemous language
SWEARD same as > SWORD
SWEARDS > SWEARD
SWEARER > SWEAR
SWEARERS > SWEAR
SWEARIER > SWEARY
SWEARIEST > SWEARY
SWEARING > SWEAR
SWEARINGS > SWEAR
SWEARS > SWEAR
SWEARWORD n word

considered obscene or blasphemous
SWEARY adj inclined to swear or characterized by swear-words
SWEAT n salty liquid given off through the pores of the skin ▷ vb have sweat coming through the pores
SWEATBAND n strip of cloth tied around the forehead or wrist to absorb sweat
SWEATBOX n device for causing tobacco leaves, fruit, or hides to sweat
SWEATED adj made by exploited labour
SWEATER n (woollen) garment for the upper part of the body
SWEATERS > SWEATER
SWEATIER > SWEATY
SWEATIEST > SWEATY
SWEATILY > SWEATY
SWEATING > SWEAT
SWEATINGS > SWEAT
SWEATLESS > SWEAT
SWEATS > SWEAT
SWEATSHOP n place where employees work long hours in poor conditions for low pay
SWEATSUIT n knitted suit worn by athletes for training
SWEATY adj covered with sweat
SWEDE n kind of turnip
SWEDES > SWEDE
SWEDGER n Scots dialect word for sweet
SWEDGERS > SWEDGER
SWEE vb sway
SWEED > SWEE
SWEEING > SWEE
SWEEL same as > SWEAL
SWEELED > SWEEL
SWEELING > SWEEL
SWEELS > SWEEL
SWEENEY n police flying squad
SWEENEYS > SWEENEY
SWEENIES > SWEENY
SWEENY n wasting of the shoulder muscles of a horse
SWEEP vb remove dirt from (a floor) with a broom ▷ n sweeping
SWEEPBACK n rearward inclination of a component or surface
SWEEPER n device used to sweep carpets, consisting of a long handle attached to a revolving brush
SWEEPERS > SWEEPER
SWEEPIER > SWEEP
SWEEPIEST > SWEEP
SWEEPING > SWEEP
SWEEPINGS npl debris, litter, or refuse
SWEEPS > SWEEP
SWEEPY > SWEEP
SWEER variant of > SWEIR

SWEERED > SWEER
SWEERING > SWEER
SWEERS > SWEER
SWEERT > SWEER
SWEES > SWEE
SWEET adj tasting of or like sugar ▷ n shaped piece of food consisting mainly of sugar ▷ vb sweeten
SWEETCORN n variety of maize, the kernels of which are eaten when young
SWEETED > SWEET
SWEETEN vb make (food or drink) sweet or sweeter
SWEETENED > SWEETEN
SWEETENER n sweetening agent that does not contain sugar
SWEETENS > SWEETEN
SWEETER > SWEET
SWEETEST > SWEET
SWEETFISH n small Japanese fish
SWEETIE n lovable person
SWEETIES > SWEETIE
SWEETING n variety of sweet apple
SWEETINGS > SWEETING
SWEETISH > SWEET
SWEETLIP n type of Australian fish with big lips
SWEETLIPS > SWEETLIP
SWEETLY n sweet
SWEETMAN n (in the Caribbean) a man kept by a woman
SWEETMEAL adj (of biscuits) sweet and wholemeal
SWEETMEAT n sweet delicacy such as a small cake
SWEETMEN > SWEETMAN
SWEETNESS > SWEET
SWEETS > SWEET
SWEETSHOP n shop selling confectionery
SWEETSOP n small West Indian tree
SWEETSOPS > SWEETSOP
SWEETVELD n grazing field with high-quality grass
SWEETWOOD n tropical tree
SWEETY same as > SWEETIE
SWEIR vb swear ▷ adj lazy
SWEIRED > SWEIR
SWEIRER > SWEIR
SWEIREST > SWEIR
SWEIRING > SWEIR
SWEIRNESS > SWEIR
SWEIRS > SWEIR
SWEIRT > SWEIR
SWELCHIE n whirlpool in Orkney
SWELCHIES > SWELCHIE
SWELL vb expand or increase ▷ n swelling or being swollen ▷ adj excellent or fine
SWELLDOM n fashionable society
SWELLDOMS > SWELLDOM

SWELLED > SWELL
SWELLER > SWELL
SWELLERS > SWELL
SWELLEST > SWELL
SWELLFISH popular name for > PUFFER
SWELLHEAD n conceited person
SWELLING > SWELL
SWELLINGS > SWELL
SWELLISH > SWELL
SWELLS > SWELL
SWELT vb die
SWELTED > SWELT
SWELTER vb feel uncomfortably hot ▷ n hot and uncomfortable condition
SWELTERED > SWELTER
SWELTERS > SWELTER
SWELTING > SWELT
SWELTRIER > SWELTRY
SWELTRY adj sultry
SWELTS > SWELT
SWEPT > SWEEP
SWEPTBACK adj (of an aircraft wing) having the leading edge inclined backwards towards the rear
SWEPTWING adj (of an aircraft) having wings swept backwards
SWERF same as > SWARF
SWERFED > SWERF
SWERFING > SWERF
SWERFS > SWERF
SWERVABLE > SWERVE
SWERVE vb turn aside from a course sharply or suddenly ▷ n swerving
SWERVED > SWERVE
SWERVER > SWERVE
SWERVERS > SWERVE
SWERVES > SWERVE
SWERVING > SWERVE
SWERVINGS > SWERVE
SWEVEN n vision or dream
SWEVENS > SWEVEN
SWEY same as > SWEE
SWEYED > SWEY
SWEYING > SWEY
SWEYS > SWEY
SWIDDEN n area of land where slash-and-burn techniques have been used to prepare it for cultivation
SWIDDENS > SWIDDEN
SWIES > SWY
SWIFT adj moving or able to move quickly ▷ n fast-flying bird with pointed wings ▷ adv swiftly or quickly ▷ vb make tight
SWIFTED > SWIFT
SWIFTER n line run around the ends of capstan bars to prevent their falling out of their sockets
SWIFTERS > SWIFTER
SWIFTEST > SWIFT
SWIFTIE n trick, ruse, or deception
SWIFTIES > SWIFTY

SWIFTING > SWIFT
SWIFTLET n type of small Asian swift
SWIFTLETS > SWIFTLET
SWIFTLY > SWIFT
SWIFTNESS > SWIFT
SWIFTS > SWIFT
SWIFTY same as > SWIFTIE
SWIG n large mouthful of drink ▷ vb drink in large mouthfuls
SWIGGED > SWIG
SWIGGER > SWIG
SWIGGERS > SWIG
SWIGGING > SWIG
SWIGS > SWIG
SWILER n (in Newfoundland) a seal hunter
SWILERS > SWILER
SWILL vb drink greedily ▷ n sloppy mixture containing waste food, fed to pigs
SWILLED > SWILL
SWILLER > SWILL
SWILLERS > SWILL
SWILLING > SWILL
SWILLINGS > SWILL
SWILLS > SWILL
SWIM vb move along in water by movements of the limbs ▷ n act or period of swimming
SWIMMABLE > SWIM
SWIMMER > SWIM
SWIMMERET n any of the small paired appendages on the abdomen of crustaceans
SWIMMERS npl swimming costume
SWIMMIER > SWIMMY
SWIMMIEST > SWIMMY
SWIMMILY > SWIMMY
SWIMMING > SWIM
SWIMMINGS > SWIM
SWIMMY adj dizzy
SWIMS > SWIM
SWIMSUIT n woman's swimming garment that leaves the arms and legs bare
SWIMSUITS > SWIMSUIT
SWIMWEAR n swimming costumes
SWIMWEARS > SWIMWEAR
SWINDGE same as > SWINGE
SWINDGED > SWINDGE
SWINDGES > SWINDGE
SWINDGING > SWINDGE
SWINDLE vb cheat (someone) out of money ▷ n instance of swindling
SWINDLED > SWINDLE
SWINDLER > SWINDLE
SWINDLERS > SWINDLE
SWINDLES > SWINDLE
SWINDLING > SWINDLE
SWINE n contemptible person
SWINEHERD n person who looks after pigs

SWINEHOOD > SWINE
SWINELIKE > SWINE
SWINEPOX n acute infectious viral disease of pigs
SWINERIES > SWINERY
SWINERY n pig farm
SWINES > SWINE
SWING vb move to and fro, sway ▷ n swinging
SWINGARM n main part of the rear suspension on a motorcycle
SWINGARMS > SWINGARM
SWINGBEAT n type of modern dance music that combines soul, rhythm and blues, and hip-hop
SWINGBIN n rubbish bin with a lid that swings shut after being opened
SWINGBINS > SWINGBIN
SWINGBOAT n piece of fairground equipment consisting of a boat-shaped carriage for swinging in
SWINGBY n act of spacecraft passing close to planet
SWINGBYS > SWINGBY
SWINGE vb beat, flog, or punish
SWINGED > SWINGE
SWINGEING > SWINGE
SWINGER n person regarded as being modern and lively
SWINGERS > SWINGER
SWINGES > SWINGE
SWINGIER > SWINGY
SWINGIEST > SWINGY
SWINGING > SWING
SWINGINGS > SWING
SWINGISM n former resistance to use of agricultural machines
SWINGISMS > SWINGISM
SWINGLE n flat-bladed wooden instrument used for beating and scraping flax ▷ vb use a swingle on
SWINGLED > SWINGLE
SWINGLES > SWINGLE
SWINGLING > SWINGLE
SWINGMAN n musician specializing in swing music
SWINGMEN > SWINGMAN
SWINGS > SWING
SWINGTAIL as in swingtail cargo aircraft kind of cargo aircraft
SWINGTREE n crossbar in a horse's harness
SWINGY adj lively and modern
SWINISH > SWINE
SWINISHLY > SWINE
SWINK vb toil or drudge ▷ n toil or drudgery
SWINKED > SWINK
SWINKER > SWINK
SWINKERS > SWINK
SWINKING > SWINK
SWINKS > SWINK

SWINNEY variant of > SWEENY
SWINNEYS > SWINNEY
SWIPE vb strike (at) with a sweeping blow ▷ n hard blow
SWIPED > SWIPE
SWIPER > SWIPE
SWIPERS > SWIPE
SWIPES npl beer, esp when poor or weak
SWIPEY adj drunk
SWIPIER > SWIPEY
SWIPIEST > SWIPEY
SWIPING > SWIPE
SWIPLE same as > SWIPPLE
SWIPLES > SWIPLE
SWIPPLE n part of a flail that strikes the grain
SWIPPLES > SWIPPLE
SWIRE n neck
SWIRES > SWIRE
SWIRL vb turn with a whirling motion ▷ n whirling motion
SWIRLED > SWIRL
SWIRLIER > SWIRL
SWIRLIEST > SWIRL
SWIRLING > SWIRL
SWIRLS > SWIRL
SWIRLY > SWIRL
SWISH vb move with a whistling or hissing sound ▷ n whistling or hissing sound ▷ adj fashionable, smart
SWISHED > SWISH
SWISHER > SWISH
SWISHERS > SWISH
SWISHES > SWISH
SWISHEST > SWISH
SWISHIER > SWISHY
SWISHIEST > SWISHY
SWISHING > SWISH
SWISHINGS > SWISH
SWISHY adj moving with a swishing sound
SWISS n type of muslin
SWISSES > SWISS
SWISSING n method of treating cloth
SWISSINGS > SWISSING
SWITCH n device for opening and closing an electric circuit ▷ vb change abruptly
SWITCHED > SWITCH
SWITCHEL n type of beer
SWITCHELS > SWITCHEL
SWITCHER > SWITCH
SWITCHERS > SWITCH
SWITCHES > SWITCH
SWITCHIER > SWITCH
SWITCHING > SWITCH
SWITCHMAN n person who operates railway points
SWITCHMEN > SWITCHMAN
SWITCHY > SWITCH
SWITH adv swiftly
SWITHE same as > SWITH
SWITHER vb hesitate or be indecisive ▷ n state of

hesitation or uncertainty
SWITHERED > SWITHER
SWITHERS > SWITHER
SWITHLY > SWITH
SWITS same as > SWITCH
SWITSES > SWITS
SWIVE vb have sexual intercourse with (a person)
SWIVED > SWIVE
SWIVEL vb turn on a central point ▷ n coupling device that allows an attached object to turn freely
SWIVELED > SWIVEL
SWIVELING > SWIVEL
SWIVELLED > SWIVEL
SWIVELS > SWIVEL
SWIVES > SWIVE
SWIVET n nervous state
SWIVETS > SWIVET
SWIVING > SWIVE
SWIZ n swindle or disappointment
SWIZZ same as > SWIZ
SWIZZED > SWIZZ
SWIZZES > SWIZZ
SWIZZING > SWIZZ
SWIZZLE n unshaken cocktail ▷ vb stir a swizzle stick in (a drink)
SWIZZLED > SWIZZLE
SWIZZLER > SWIZZLE
SWIZZLERS > SWIZZLE
SWIZZLES > SWIZZLE
SWIZZLING > SWIZZLE
SWOB less common word for > SWAB
SWOBBED > SWOB
SWOBBER > SWOB
SWOBBERS > SWOB
SWOBBING > SWOB
SWOBS > SWOB
SWOFFER > SWOFFING
SWOFFERS > SWOFFING
SWOFFING n sport of saltwater fly-fishing
SWOFFINGS > SWOFFING
SWOLLEN > SWELL
SWOLLENLY > SWELL
SWOLN > SWELL
SWOON n faint ▷ vb faint because of shock or strong emotion
SWOONED > SWOON
SWOONER > SWOON
SWOONERS > SWOON
SWOONIER > SWOONY
SWOONIEST > SWOONY
SWOONING > SWOON
SWOONINGS > SWOON
SWOONS > SWOON
SWOONY adj romantic or sexy
SWOOP vb sweep down or pounce on suddenly ▷ n swooping
SWOOPED > SWOOP
SWOOPER > SWOOP
SWOOPERS > SWOOP
SWOOPIER > SWOOP
SWOOPIEST > SWOOP
SWOOPING > SWOOP
SWOOPS > SWOOP

S

SWOOPY > SWOOP

SWOOSH *vb* make a swirling or rustling sound when moving or pouring out ▷ *n* swirling or rustling sound or movement

SWOOSHED > SWOOSH
SWOOSHES > SWOOSH
SWOOSHING > SWOOSH
SWOP *same as* > SWAP
SWOPPED > SWOP
SWOPPER > SWOP
SWOPPERS > SWOP
SWOPPING > SWOP
SWOPPINGS > SWOP
SWOPS > SWOP
SWOPT > SWOP
SWORD *n* weapon with a long sharp blade ▷ *vb* bear a sword
SWORDBILL *n* South American hummingbird
SWORDED > SWORD
SWORDER *n* fighter with sword
SWORDERS > SWORDER
SWORDFISH *n* large fish with a very long upper jaw
SWORDING > SWORD
SWORDLESS > SWORD
SWORDLIKE > SWORD
SWORDMAN *same as* > SWORDSMAN
SWORDMEN > SWORDMAN
SWORDPLAY *n* action or art of fighting with a sword
SWORDS > SWORD
SWORDSMAN *n* person skilled in the use of a sword
SWORDSMEN > SWORDSMAN
SWORDTAIL *n* type of small freshwater fish of Central America
SWORE > SWEAR
SWORN > SWEAR
SWOT *vb* study (a subject) intensively ▷ *n* person who studies hard
SWOTS > SWOT
SWOTTED > SWOT
SWOTTER *same as* > SWOT
SWOTTERS > SWOT
SWOTTIER > SWOTTY
SWOTTIEST > SWOTTY
SWOTTING > SWOT
SWOTTINGS > SWOT
SWOTTY *adj* given to studying hard, esp to the exclusion of other activities
SWOUN *same as* > SWOON
SWOUND *same as* > SWOUND
SWOUNDED > SWOUND
SWOUNDING > SWOUND
SWOUNDS *less common spelling of* > ZOUNDS
SWOUNE *same as* > SWOON
SWOUNED > SWOUNE
SWOUNES > SWOUNE
SWOUNING > SWOUNE
SWOUNS > SWOUN
SWOWND *same as* > SWOON
SWOWNDS > SWOWND
SWOWNE *same as* > SWOON

SWOWNES > SWOWNE
SWOZZLE *same as* > SWAZZLE
SWOZZLES > SWOZZLE
SWUM > SWIM
SWUNG > SWING
SWY *n* Australian gambling game involving two coins
SYBARITE *n* lover of luxury ▷ *adj* luxurious or sensuous
SYBARITES > SYBARITE
SYBARITIC > SYBARITE
SYBBE *same as* > SIB
SYBBES > SYBBE
SYBIL *same as* > SIBYL
SYBILS > SYBIL
SYBO *n* spring onion
SYBOE *same as* > SYBO
SYBOES > SYBOE
SYBOTIC *adj* of a swineherd
SYBOTISM > SYBOTIC
SYBOTISMS > SYBOTIC
SYBOW *same as* > SYBO
SYBOWS > SYBOW
SYCAMINE *n* mulberry tree mentioned in the Bible, thought to be the black mulberry
SYCAMINES > SYCAMINE
SYCAMORE *n* tree with five-pointed leaves and two-winged fruits
SYCAMORES > SYCAMORE
SYCE *n* (formerly, in India) a servant employed to look after horses, etc
SYCEE *n* silver ingots formerly used as a medium of exchange in China
SYCEES > SYCEE
SYCES > SYCE
SYCOMORE *same as* > SYCAMORE
SYCOMORES > SYCOMORE
SYCONIA > SYCONIUM
SYCONIUM *n* fleshy fruit of the fig
SYCOPHANT *n* person who uses flattery to win favour from people with power or influence
SYCOSES > SYCOSIS
SYCOSIS *n* chronic inflammation of the hair follicles
SYE *vb* strain
SYED > SYE
SYEING > SYE
SYEN *same as* > SCION
SYENITE *n* light-coloured coarse-grained plutonic igneous rock
SYENITES > SYENITE
SYENITIC > SYENITE
SYENS > SYEN
SYES > SYE
SYKE *same as* > SIKE
SYKER *adv* surely
SYKES > SYKE
SYLI *n* Finnish unit of volume
SYLIS > SYLI

SYLLABARY *n* table or list of syllables
SYLLABI > SYLLABUS
SYLLABIC *adj* of or relating to syllables ▷ *n* syllabic consonant
SYLLABICS > SYLLABIC
SYLLABIFY *vb* divide (a word) into syllables
SYLLABISE *same as* > SYLLABIZE
SYLLABISM *n* use of a writing system consisting of characters for syllables
SYLLABIZE *vb* divide into syllables
SYLLABLE *n* part of a word pronounced as a unit
SYLLABLED > SYLLABLE
SYLLABLES > SYLLABLE
SYLLABUB *n* dessert of beaten cream, sugar, and wine
SYLLABUBS > SYLLABUB
SYLLABUS *n* list of subjects for a course of study
SYLLEPSES > SYLLEPSIS
SYLLEPSIS *n* (in grammar or rhetoric) the use of a single sentence construction in which a verb, adjective, etc is made to cover two syntactical functions
SYLLEPTIC > SYLLEPSIS
SYLLOGE *n* collection or summary
SYLLOGES > SYLLOGE
SYLLOGISE *same as* > SYLLOGIZE
SYLLOGISM *n* form of logical reasoning consisting of two premises and a conclusion
SYLLOGIST > SYLLOGISM
SYLLOGIZE *vb* reason or infer by using syllogisms
SYLPH *n* slender graceful girl or woman
SYLPHIC > SYLPH
SYLPHID *n* little sylph
SYLPHIDE *same as* > SYLPHID
SYLPHIDES > SYLPHIDE
SYLPHIDS > SYLPHID
SYLPHIER > SYLPH
SYLPHIEST > SYLPH
SYLPHINE > SYLPH
SYLPHISH > SYLPH
SYLPHLIKE > SYLPH
SYLPHS > SYLPH
SYLPHY > SYLPH
SYLVA *n* trees growing in a particular region
SYLVAE > SYLVA
SYLVAN *adj* relating to woods and trees ▷ *n* inhabitant of the woods, esp a spirit
SYLVANER *n* German variety of grape

SYLVANERS > SYLVANER
SYLVANITE *n* silver-white mineral
SYLVANS > SYLVAN
SYLVAS > SYLVA
SYLVATIC *adj* growing, living, or occurring in a wood or beneath a tree
SYLVIA *n* songbird
SYLVIAS > SYLVIA
SYLVIINE > SYLVIA
SYLVIN *same as* > SYLVITE
SYLVINE *same as* > SYLVITE
SYLVINES > SYLVINE
SYLVINITE *n* rock containing sylvine
SYLVINS > SYLVIN
SYLVITE *n* soluble colourless, white, or coloured mineral
SYLVITES > SYLVITE
SYMAR *same as* > CYMAR
SYMARS > SYMAR
SYMBION *same as* > SYMBIONT
SYMBIONS > SYMBION
SYMBIONT *n* organism living in a state of symbiosis
SYMBIONTS > SYMBIONT
SYMBIOSES > SYMBIOSIS
SYMBIOSIS *n* close association of two species living together to their mutual benefit
SYMBIOTE *same as* > SYMBIONT
SYMBIOTES > SYMBIOTE
SYMBIOTIC > SYMBIOSIS
SYMBIOTS > SYMBIOT
SYMBOL *n* sign or thing that stands for something else ▷ *vb* be a symbol
SYMBOLE *same as* > CYMBAL
SYMBOLED > SYMBOL
SYMBOLES > SYMBOL
SYMBOLIC *adj* of or relating to a symbol or symbols
SYMBOLICS *n* study of beliefs
SYMBOLING > SYMBOL
SYMBOLISE *same as* > SYMBOLIZE
SYMBOLISM *n* representation of something by symbols
SYMBOLIST *n* person who uses or can interpret symbols ▷ *adj* of, relating to, or characterizing symbolism or symbolists
SYMBOLIZE *vb* be a symbol of
SYMBOLLED > SYMBOL
SYMBOLOGY *n* use, study, or interpretation of symbols
SYMBOLS > SYMBOL

SYMITAR same as > SCIMITAR

SYMITARE same as > SCIMITAR

SYMITARES > SYMITARE

SYMITARS > SYMITAR

SYMMETRAL > SYMMETRY

SYMMETRIC adj (of a disease) affecting both sides of the body

SYMMETRY n state of having two halves that are mirror images of each other

SYMPATHIN n substance released at certain sympathetic nerve endings

SYMPATHY n compassion for someone's pain or distress

SYMPATICO adj nice

SYMPATRIC adj (of biological speciation or species) existing in the same geographical areas

SYMPATRY n existing of organisms together without interbreeding

SYMPETALY n quality of having petals that are united

SYMPHILE n insect that lives in the nests of social insects and is fed and reared by the inmates

SYMPHILES > SYMPHILE

SYMPHILY n presence of different kinds of animal in ants' nests

SYMPHONIC > SYMPHONY

SYMPHONY n composition for orchestra, with several movements

SYMPHYSES > SYMPHYSIS

SYMPHYSIS n growing together of parts or structures

SYMPHYTIC > SYMPHYSIS

SYMPLAST n continuous system of protoplasts, linked by plasmodesmata and bounded by the cell wall

SYMPLASTS > SYMPLAST

SYMPLOCE n word repetition in successive clauses

SYMPLOCES > SYMPLOCE

SYMPODIA > SYMPODIUM

SYMPODIAL > SYMPODIUM

SYMPODIUM n main axis of growth in the grapevine and similar plants

SYMPOSIA > SYMPOSIUM

SYMPOSIAC adj of, suitable for, or occurring at a symposium

SYMPOSIAL > SYMPOSIUM

SYMPOSIUM n conference for discussion of a particular topic

SYMPTOM n sign indicating the presence of an illness

SYMPTOMS > SYMPTOM

SYMPTOSES > SYMPTOSIS

SYMPTOSIS n wasting condition

SYMPTOTIC > SYMPTOSIS

SYN Scots word for > SINCE

SYNAGOG same as > SYNAGOGUE

SYNAGOGAL > SYNAGOGUE

SYNAGOGS > SYNAGOG

SYNAGOGUE n Jewish place of worship and religious instruction

SYNALEPHA n elision of vowels in speech

SYNANDRIA npl peculiar bunchings of stamens

SYNANGIA > SYNANGIUM

SYNANGIUM n junction between arteries

SYNANON n type of therapy given to drug addicts

SYNANONS > SYNANON

SYNANTHIC > SYNANTHY

SYNANTHY n abnormal joining between flowers

SYNAPHEA n continuity in metre of verses of poem

SYNAPHEAS > SYNAPHEA

SYNAPHEIA same as > SYNAPHEA

SYNAPSE n gap where nerve impulses pass between two nerve cells ▷ vb create a synapse

SYNAPSED > SYNAPSE

SYNAPSES > SYNAPSIS

SYNAPSID n prehistoric mammal-like reptile

SYNAPSIDS > SYNAPSID

SYNAPSING > SYNAPSE

SYNAPSIS n association in pairs of homologous chromosomes at the start of meiosis

SYNAPTASE n type of enzyme

SYNAPTE n litany in Greek Orthodox Church

SYNAPTES > SYNAPTE

SYNAPTIC adj of or relating to a synapse

SYNARCHY n joint rule

SYNASTRY n coincidence of astrological influences

SYNAXARIA npl readings in the Greek Orthodox Church

SYNAXES > SYNAXIS

SYNAXIS n early Christian meeting

SYNC n synchronization ▷ vb synchronize

SYNCARP n fleshy multiple fruit

SYNCARPS > SYNCARP

SYNCARPY n quality of consisting of united carpels

SYNCED > SYNC

SYNCH same as > SYNC

SYNCHED > SYNCH

SYNCHING > SYNCH

SYNCHRO n type of electrical device

SYNCHRONY n state of being synchronous

SYNCHROS > SYNCHRO

SYNCHS > SYNCH

SYNCHYSES > SYNCHYSIS

SYNCHYSIS n muddled meaning

SYNCING > SYNC

SYNCLINAL > SYNCLINE

SYNCLINE n downward slope of stratified rock in which the layers dip towards each other from either side

SYNCLINES > SYNCLINE

SYNCOM n communications satellite in stationary orbit

SYNCOMS > SYNCOM

SYNCOPAL > SYNCOPE

SYNCOPATE vb stress the weak beats in (a rhythm) instead of the strong ones

SYNCOPE n omission of one or more sounds or letters from the middle of a word

SYNCOPES > SYNCOPE

SYNCOPIC > SYNCOPE

SYNCOPTIC > SYNCOPE

SYNCRETIC adj of the tendency of languages to reduce their use of inflection

SYNCS > SYNC

SYNCYTIA > SYNCYTIUM

SYNCYTIAL > SYNCYTIUM

SYNCYTIUM n mass of cytoplasm containing many nuclei and enclosed in a cell membrane

SYND same as > SYNE

SYNDACTYL adj (of certain animals) having two or more digits growing fused together ▷ n animal with this arrangement of digits

SYNDED > SYND

SYNDESES > SYNDESIS

SYNDESIS n use of syndetic constructions

SYNDET n synthetic detergent

SYNDETIC adj denoting a grammatical construction in which two clauses are connected by a conjunction

SYNDETON n syndetic construction

SYNDETONS > SYNDETON

SYNDETS > SYNDET

SYNDIC n business or legal agent of some universities or other institutions

SYNDICAL adj relating to the theory that syndicates of workers should seize the means of production

SYNDICATE n group of people or firms undertaking a joint business project ▷ vb publish (material) in several newspapers

SYNDICS > SYNDIC

SYNDING > SYND

SYNDINGS > SYND

SYNDROME n combination of symptoms indicating a particular disease

SYNDROMES > SYNDROME

SYNDROMIC > SYNDROME

SYNDS > SYND

SYNE vb rinse ▷ n rinse ▷ adv since

SYNECHIA n abnormality of the eye

SYNECHIAS > SYNECHIA

SYNECIOUS adj having male and female organs together on a branch

SYNECTIC > SYNECTICS

SYNECTICS n method of identifying and solving problems that depends on creative thinking

SYNED > SYNE

SYNEDRIA > SYNEDRION

SYNEDRIAL > SYNEDRION

SYNEDRION n assembly of judges

SYNEDRIUM same as > SYNEDRION

SYNERESES > SYNERESIS

SYNERESIS n process in which a gel contracts on standing and exudes liquid

SYNERGIA same as > SYNERGY

SYNERGIAS > SYNERGIA

SYNERGIC > SYNERGY

SYNERGID n type of cell in embryo

SYNERGIDS > SYNERGID

SYNERGIES > SYNERGY

SYNERGISE same as > SYNERGIZE

SYNERGISM same as > SYNERGY

SYNERGIST n drug, muscle, etc, that increases the action of another ▷ adj of or relating to synergism

SYNERGIZE vb act in synergy

SYNERGY n working together of two or more people, substances, or things to produce an effect greater than the sum of their individual effects

SYNES > SYNE

SYNESES > SYNESIS

SYNESIS n grammatical construction in which the inflection or form of a word is conditioned by the meaning rather than the syntax

SYNESISES > SYNESIS

SYNFUEL n synthetic fuel

SYNFUELS > SYNFUEL

SYNGAMIC > SYNGAMY

SYNGAMIES > SYNGAMY

S

SYNGAMOUS > SYNGAMY

SYNGAMY n sexual reproduction

SYNGAS n mixture of carbon monoxide and hydrogen

SYNGASES > SYNGAS

SYNGASSES > SYNGAS

SYNGENEIC adj with identical genes

SYNGENIC > SYNGENEIC

SYNGRAPH n document signed by several parties

SYNGRAPHS > SYNGRAPH

SYNING > SYNE

SYNIZESES > SYNIZESIS

SYNIZESIS n contraction of two vowels originally belonging to separate syllables into a single syllable

SYNKARYA > SYNKARYON

SYNKARYON n nucleus of a fertilized egg

SYNOD n church council

SYNODAL adj of or relating to a synod ▷ n money paid to a bishop by less senior members of the clergy at a synod

SYNODALS > SYNOD

SYNODIC adj relating to or involving a conjunction or two successive conjunctions of the same star, planet, or satellite

SYNODICAL > SYNOD

SYNODS > SYNOD

SYNODSMAN n layman at synod

SYNODSMEN > SYNODSMAN

SYNOECETE same as > SYNOEKETE

SYNOECISE same as > SYNOECIZE

SYNOECISM n union

SYNOECIZE vb unite

SYNOEKETE n insect that lives in the nests of social insects without receiving any attentions from the inmates

SYNOICOUS variant of > SYNECIOUS

SYNONYM n word with the same meaning as another

SYNONYME same as > SYNONYM

SYNONYMES > SYNONYME

SYNONYMIC > SYNONYM

SYNONYMS > SYNONYM

SYNONYMY n study of synonyms

SYNOPSES > SYNOPSIS

SYNOPSIS n summary or outline

SYNOPSISE same as > SYNOPSIZE

SYNOPSIZE vb make a synopsis of

SYNOPTIC adj of or relating to a synopsis ▷ n any of the three synoptic Gospels

SYNOPTICS > SYNOPTIC

SYNOPTIST > SYNOPTIC

SYNOVIA n clear thick fluid that lubricates the body joints

SYNOVIAL adj of or relating to the synovia

SYNOVIAS > SYNOVIA

SYNOVITIC > SYNOVITIS

SYNOVITIS n inflammation of the membrane surrounding a joint

SYNROC n titanium-ceramic substance that can incorporate nuclear waste in its crystals

SYNROCS > SYNROC

SYNTACTIC adj relating to or determined by syntax

SYNTAGM same as > SYNTAGMA

SYNTAGMA n syntactic unit or a word or phrase forming a syntactic unit

SYNTAGMAS > SYNTAGMA

SYNTAGMIC > SYNTAGMA

SYNTAGMS > SYNTAGM

SYNTAN n synthetic tanning substance

SYNTANS > SYNTAN

SYNTAX n way in which words are arranged to form phrases and sentences

SYNTAXES > SYNTAX

SYNTECTIC > SYNTEXIS

SYNTENIC > SYNTENY

SYNTENIES > SYNTENY

SYNTENY n presence of two or more genes on the same chromosome

SYNTEXIS n liquefaction

SYNTH n type of electrophonic musical instrument operated by a keyboard and pedals

SYNTHASE n enzyme that catalyses a synthesis process

SYNTHASES > SYNTHASE

SYNTHESES > SYNTHESIS

SYNTHESIS n combination of objects or ideas into a whole

SYNTHETIC adj (of a substance) made artificially ▷ n synthetic substance or material

SYNTHON n molecule used in synthesis

SYNTHONS > SYNTHON

SYNTHPOP n pop music using synthesizers

SYNTHPOPS > SYNTHPOP

SYNTHRONI npl combined thrones for bishops and their subordinates

SYNTHS > SYNTH

SYNTONIC adj emotionally in harmony with one's environment

SYNTONIES > SYNTONY

SYNTONIN n substance in muscle

SYNTONINS > SYNTONIN

SYNTONISE same as > SYNTONIZE

SYNTONIZE vb make frequencies match

SYNTONOUS same as > SYNTONIC

SYNTONY n matching of frequencies

SYNURA n variety of microbe

SYNURAE > SYNURA

SYPE same as > SIPE

SYPED > SYPE

SYPES > SYPE

SYPH shortening of > SYPHILIS

SYPHER vb lap (a chamfered edge of one plank over that of another) in order to form a flush surface

SYPHERED > SYPHER

SYPHERING > SYPHER

SYPHERS > SYPHER

SYPHILIS n serious sexually transmitted disease

SYPHILISE same as > SYPHILIZE

SYPHILIZE vb infect with syphilis

SYPHILOID > SYPHILIS

SYPHILOMA n tumour or gumma caused by infection with syphilis

SYPHON same as > SIPHON

SYPHONED > SYPHON

SYPHONING > SYPHON

SYPHONS > SYPHON

SYPHS > SYPH

SYPING > SYPE

SYRAH n type of French red wine

SYRAHS > SYRAH

SYREN same as > SIREN

SYRENS > SYREN

SYRETTE n small disposable syringe

SYRETTES > SYRETTE

SYRINGA n mock orange or lilac

SYRINGAS > SYRINGA

SYRINGE n device for withdrawing or injecting fluids, consisting of a hollow cylinder, a piston, and a hollow needle ▷ vb wash out or inject with a syringe

SYRINGEAL > SYRINX

SYRINGED > SYRINGE

SYRINGES > SYRINX

SYRINGING > SYRINGE

SYRINX n vocal organ of a bird, which is situated in the lower part of the trachea

SYRINXES > SYRINX

SYRPHIAN same as > SYRPHID

SYRPHIANS > SYRPHIAN

SYRPHID n type of fly

SYRPHIDS > SYRPHID

SYRTES > SYRTIS

SYRTIS n area of quicksand

SYRUP n solution of sugar in water ▷ vb bring to the consistency of syrup

SYRUPED > SYRUP

SYRUPIER > SYRUPY

SYRUPIEST > SYRUPY

SYRUPING > SYRUP

SYRUPLIKE > SYRUP

SYRUPS > SYRUP

SYRUPY adj thick and sweet

SYSADMIN n computer system administrator

SYSADMINS > SYSADMIN

SYSOP n person who runs a system or network

SYSOPS > SYSOP

SYSSITIA n ancient Spartan communal meal

SYSSITIAS > SYSSITIA

SYSTALTIC adj (esp of the action of the heart) characterized by alternate contractions and dilations

SYSTEM n method or set of methods

SYSTEMED adj having system

SYSTEMIC adj affecting the entire animal or body ▷ n systemic pesticide, fungicide, etc

SYSTEMICS > SYSTEMIC

SYSTEMISE same as > SYSTEMIZE

SYSTEMIZE vb give a system to

SYSTEMS > SYSTEM

SYSTOLE n regular contraction of the heart as it pumps blood

SYSTOLES > SYSTOLE

SYSTOLIC > SYSTOLE

SYSTYLE n building with different types of columns

SYSTYLES > SYSTYLE

SYTHE same as > SITH

SYTHES > SYTHE

SYVER n street drain or the grating over it

SYVERS > SYVER

SYZYGAL > SYZYGY

SYZYGETIC > SYZYGY

SYZYGIAL > SYZYGY

SYZYGIES > SYZYGY

SYZYGY n either of the two positions of a celestial body when sun, earth, and the body lie in a straight line

Tt

TA *interj* thank you ▷ *n* thank you

TAAL *n* language: usually, by implication, Afrikaans

TAALS > TAAL

TAATA *child's word for* > FATHER

TAATAS > TAATA

TAB *n* small flap or projecting label ▷ *vb* supply with a tab

TABANID *n* stout-bodied fly, the females of which have mouthparts specialized for sucking blood

TABANIDS > TABANID

TABARD *n* short sleeveless tunic decorated with a coat of arms, worn in medieval times

TABARDED *adj* wearing a tabard

TABARDS > TABARD

TABARET *n* hard-wearing fabric of silk or similar cloth with stripes of satin or moire, used esp for upholstery

TABARETS > TABARET

TABASHEER *n* dried bamboo sap, used medicinally

TABASHIR *same as* > TABASHEER

TABASHIRS > TABASHIR

TABBED > TAB

TABBIED > TABBY

TABBIES > TABBY

TABBINET *same as* > TABINET

TABBINETS > TABBINET

TABBING > TAB

TABBIS *n* silken cloth

TABBISES > TABBIS

TABBOULEH *n* kind of Middle Eastern salad made with cracked wheat, mint, parsley, and usually cucumber

TABBOULI *same as* > TABBOULEH

TABBOULIS > TABBOULI

TABBY *vb* make (eg a material) appear wavy ▷ *n* female domestic cat

TABBYHOOD *n* spinsterhood

TABBYING > TABBY

TABEFIED > TABEFY

TABEFIES > TABEFY

TABEFY *vb* emaciate or become emaciated

TABEFYING > TABEFY

TABELLION *n* scribe or notary authorized by the Roman Empire

TABER *old variant of* > TABOR

TABERD *same as* > TABARD

TABERDAR *n* holder of a scholarship at Queen's College, Oxford

TABERDARS > TABERDAR

TABERDS > TABERD

TABERED > TABER

TABERING > TABER

TABERS > TABER

TABES *n* wasting of a bodily organ or part

TABESCENT *adj* progressively emaciating

TABETIC > TABES

TABETICS > TABES

TABI *n* thick-soled Japanese sock, worn with sandals

TABID *adj* emaciated

TABINET *n* type of tabbied fabric

TABINETS > TABINET

TABLA *n* one of a pair of Indian drums played with the hands

TABLAS > TABLA

TABLATURE *n* any of a number of forms of musical notation, esp for playing the lute, consisting of letters and signs indicating rhythm and fingering

TABLE *n* piece of furniture with a flat top supported by legs ▷ *vb* submit (a motion) for discussion by a meeting

TABLEAU *n* silent motionless group arranged to represent some scene

TABLEAUS > TABLEAU

TABLEAUX > TABLEAU

TABLED > TABLE

TABLEFUL > TABLE

TABLEFULS > TABLE

TABLELAND *n* high plateau

TABLELESS > TABLE

TABLEMATE *n* someone with whom one shares a table

TABLES > TABLE

TABLESFUL > TABLE

TABLET *n* medicinal pill ▷ *vb* make (something) into a tablet

TABLETED > TABLET

TABLETING > TABLET

TABLETOP *n* upper surface of a table

TABLETOPS > TABLETOP

TABLETS > TABLET

TABLETTED > TABLET

TABLEWARE *n* articles such as dishes, plates, knives, forks, etc, used at meals

TABLEWISE *adv* in the form of a table

TABLIER *n* (formerly) part of a dress resembling an apron

TABLIERS > TABLIER

TABLING > TABLE

TABLINGS > TABLE

TABLOID *n* small-sized newspaper with many photographs and a concise, usu sensational style

TABLOIDS > TABLOID

TABLOIDY *adj* characteristic of a tabloid newspaper; trashy

TABOGGAN *same as* > TOBOGGAN

TABOGGANS > TABOGGAN

TABOO *n* prohibition resulting from religious or social conventions ▷ *adj* forbidden by a taboo ▷ *vb* place under a taboo

TABOOED > TABOO

TABOOING > TABOO

TABOOLEY *variant of* > TABBOULEH

TABOOLEYS > TABOOLEY

TABOOS > TABOO

TABOR *vb* play the tabor

TABORED > TABOR

TABORER > TABOR

TABORERS > TABOR

TABORET *n* low stool, originally in the shape of a drum

TABORETS > TABORET

TABORIN *same as* > TABORET

TABORINE *same as* > TABOURIN

TABORINES > TABORINE

TABORING > TABOR

TABORINS > TABORIN

TABORS > TABOR

TABOULEH *variant of* > TABBOULEH

TABOULEHS > TABOULEH

TABOULI *same as* > TABBOULEH

TABOULIS > TABOULI

TABOUR *same as* > TABOR

TABOURED > TABOUR

TABOURER > TABOUR

TABOURERS > TABOUR

TABOURET *same as* > TABORET

TABOURETS > TABOURET

TABOURIN *same as* > TABORET

TABOURING > TABOUR

TABOURINS > TABOURIN

TABOURS > TABOUR

TABRERE *same as* > TABOR

TABRERES > TABRERE

TABRET *n* smaller version of a tabor

TABRETS > TABRET

TABS > TAB

TABU *same as* > TABOO

TABUED > TABU

TABUING > TABU

TABULA *n* tablet for writing on

TABULABLE > TABULATE

TABULAE > TABULA

TABULAR *adj* arranged in a table

TABULARLY > TABULAR

TABULATE *vb* arrange (information) in a table ▷ *adj* having a flat surface

TABULATED > TABULATE

TABULATES > TABULATE

TABULATOR *n* key on a typewriter or word processor that sets stops so that data can be arranged and presented in columns

TABULI *variant of* > TABBOULEH

TABULIS > TABULI

TABUN *n* organic compound used in chemical warfare as a lethal nerve gas

TABUNS > TABUN

TABUS > TABU

TACAHOUT *n* abnormal outgrowth on the tamarisk plant

TACAHOUTS > TACAHOUT

TACAMAHAC *n* any of several strong-smelling resinous gums obtained from certain trees, used in making ointments, incense, etc

TACAN n electronic ultrahigh-frequency navigation system for aircraft which gives a continuous indication of bearing and distance from a transmitting station

TACANS > TACAN

TACE same as > TASSET

TACES > TACE

TACET n direction on a musical score indicating that a particular instrument or singer does not take part in a movement or part of a movement

TACH n device for measuring speed

TACHE n buckle, clasp, or hook

TACHES > TACHE

TACHINA as in tachina fly bristly fly

TACHINID n type of fly

TACHINIDS > TACHINID

TACHISM same as > TACHISME

TACHISME n type of action painting evolved in France in which haphazard dabs and blots of colour are treated as a means of instinctive or unconscious expression

TACHISMES > TACHISME

TACHISMS > TACHISM

TACHIST > TACHISM

TACHISTE > TACHISME

TACHISTES > TACHISME

TACHISTS > TACHIST

TACHO same as > TACHOGRAM

TACHOGRAM n graphical record of readings

TACHOS > TACHO

TACHS > TACH

TACHYLITE same as > TACHYLYTE

TACHYLYTE n black basaltic glass often found on the edges of intrusions of basalt

TACHYON n hypothetical elementary particle capable of travelling faster than the velocity of light

TACHYONIC > TACHYON

TACHYONS > TACHYON

TACHYPNEA n abnormally rapid breathing

TACIT adj implied but not spoken

TACITLY > TACIT

TACITNESS > TACIT

TACITURN adj habitually uncommunicative

TACK n short nail with a large head ▷ vb fasten with tacks

TACKBOARD n noticeboard

TACKED > TACK

TACKER > TACK

TACKERS > TACK

TACKET n nail, esp a hobnail

TACKETS > TACKET

TACKETY > TACKET

TACKEY same as > TACKY

TACKIER > TACKY

TACKIES npl tennis shoes or plimsolls

TACKIEST > TACKY

TACKIFIED > TACKIFY

TACKIFIER > TACKIFY

TACKIFIES > TACKIFY

TACKIFY vb give (eg rubber) a sticky feel

TACKILY > TACKY

TACKINESS > TACKY

TACKING > TACK

TACKINGS > TACK

TACKLE vb deal with (a task) ▷ n act of tackling an opposing player

TACKLED > TACKLE

TACKLER > TACKLE

TACKLERS > TACKLE

TACKLES > TACKLE

TACKLESS > TACK

TACKLING > TACKLE

TACKLINGS > TACKLE

TACKS > TACK

TACKSMAN n leaseholder, esp a tenant in the Highlands who sublets

TACKSMEN > TACKSMAN

TACKY adj slightly sticky

TACMAHACK same as > TACAMAHAC

TACNODE n in maths, point at which two branches of a curve have a common tangent, each branch extending in both directions of the tangent

TACNODES > TACNODE

TACO n tortilla fried until crisp, served with a filling

TACONITE n fine-grained sedimentary rock containing magnetite, haematite, and silica, which occurs in the Lake Superior region: a low-grade iron ore

TACONITES > TACONITE

TACOS > TACO

TACRINE n drug used to treat Alzheimer's disease

TACRINES > TACRINE

TACT n skill in avoiding giving offence

TACTFUL > TACT

TACTFULLY > TACT

TACTIC n method or plan to achieve an end

TACTICAL adj of or employing tactics

TACTICIAN > TACTICS

TACTICITY n quality of regularity in the arrangement of repeated units within a polymer chain

TACTICS n art of directing military forces in battle

TACTILE adj of or having the sense of touch

TACTILELY > TACTILE

TACTILIST n artist whose work strives to appeal to the sense of touch

TACTILITY > TACTILE

TACTION n act of touching

TACTIONS > TACTION

TACTISM another word for > TAXIS

TACTISMS > TACTISM

TACTLESS > TACT

TACTS > TACT

TACTUAL adj caused by touch

TACTUALLY > TACTUAL

TAD n small bit or piece

TADDIE short for > TADPOLE

TADDIES > TADDIE

TADPOLE n limbless tailed larva of a frog or toad

TADPOLES > TADPOLE

TADS > TAD

TAE Scots form of the verb > TOE

TAED > TAE

TAEDIUM archaic spelling of > TEDIUM

TAEDIUMS > TAEDIUM

TAEING > TAE

TAEKWONDO n Korean martial art

TAEL n unit of weight, used in the Far East, having various values between one to two and a half ounces

TAELS > TAEL

TAENIA n (in ancient Greece) a narrow fillet or headband for the hair

TAENIAE > TAENIA

TAENIAS > TAENIA

TAENIASES > TAENIASIS

TAENIASIS n infestation with tapeworms

TAENIATE adj ribbon-like

TAENIOID adj ribbon-like

TAES > TAE

TAFFAREL same as > TAFFRAIL

TAFFARELS > TAFFAREL

TAFFEREL same as > TAFFRAIL

TAFFERELS > TAFFEREL

TAFFETA n shiny silk or rayon fabric

TAFFETAS same as > TAFFETA

TAFFETY same as > TAFFETA

TAFFIA same as > TAFIA

TAFFIAS > TAFFIA

TAFFIES > TAFFY

TAFFRAIL n rail at the back of a ship or boat

TAFFRAILS > TAFFRAIL

TAFFY same as > TOFFEE

TAFIA n type of rum, esp from Guyana or the Caribbean

TAFIAS > TAFIA

TAG n label bearing information ▷ vb attach a tag to

TAGALONG n one who trails behind, esp uninvited; a hanger-on

TAGALONGS > TAGALONG

TAGAREEN n junk shop

TAGAREENS > TAGAREEN

TAGBOARD n sturdy form of cardboard

TAGBOARDS > TAGBOARD

TAGETES n any of a genus of plants with yellow or orange flowers, including the French and African marigolds

TAGGANT n microscopic material added to substance to identify it

TAGGANTS > TAGGANT

TAGGED > TAG

TAGGEE n one who has been made to wear a tag

TAGGEES > TAGGEE

TAGGER n one who marks with a tag

TAGGERS > TAGGER

TAGGIER > TAGGY

TAGGIEST > TAGGY

TAGGING > TAG

TAGGINGS > TAG

TAGGY adj (of wool, hair, etc) matted

TAGHAIRM n form of divination once practised in the Highlands of Scotland

TAGHAIRMS > TAGHAIRM

TAGINE n large, heavy N African cooking pot with a conical lid

TAGINES > TAGINE

TAGLESS adj having no tag

TAGLIKE adj resembling a tag

TAGLINE n funny line of joke

TAGLINES > TAGLINE

TAGLIONI n type of coat

TAGLIONIS > TAGLIONI

TAGMA n distinct region of the body of an arthropod, such as the head, thorax, or abdomen of an insect

TAGMATA > TAGMA

TAGMEME n class of speech elements all of which may fulfil the same grammatical role in a sentence

TAGMEMES > TAGMEME

TAGMEMIC > TAGMEME

TAGMEMICS > TAGMEME

TAGRAG same as > RAGTAG

TAGRAGS > TAGRAG

TAGS > TAG

TAGUAN n large nocturnal flying squirrel of high forests in the East Indies that uses its long tail as a rudder

TAGUANS > TAGUAN

TAHA n type of South African bird

TAHAS > TAHA

TAHINA same as > TAHINI

TAHINAS > TAHINA

TAHINI *n* paste made from ground sesame seeds, used esp in Middle Eastern cookery

TAHINIS > TAHINI

TAHR *n* goatlike bovid mammal of mountainous regions of S and SW Asia, having a shaggy coat and curved horns

TAHRS > TAHR

TAHSIL *n* administrative division of a zila in certain states in India

TAHSILDAR *n* officer in charge of the collection of revenues, etc, in a tahsil

TAHSILS > TAHSIL

TAI *n* a type of sea bream

TAIAHA *n* carved weapon in the form of a staff, now used in Māori ceremonial oratory

TAIAHAS > TAIAHA

TAIG *n* often derogatory term for Roman Catholic

TAIGA *n* belt of coniferous forest extending across much of subarctic North America, Europe, and Asia

TAIGAS > TAIGA

TAIGLACH *same as* > TEIGLACH

TAIGLE *vb* entangle or impede

TAIGLED > TAIGLE

TAIGLES > TAIGLE

TAIGLING > TAIGLE

TAIGS > TAIG

TAIHOA *interj* hold on! no hurry!

TAIKO *n* large Japanese drum

TAIKONAUT *n* astronaut from the People's Republic of China

TAIKOS > TAIKO

TAIL *n* rear part of an animal's body, usu forming a flexible appendage ▷ *adj* at the rear ▷ *vb* follow (someone) secretly

TAILARD *n* one having a tail

TAILARDS > TAILARD

TAILBACK *n* queue of traffic stretching back from an obstruction

TAILBACKS > TAILBACK

TAILBOARD *n* removable or hinged rear board on a truck etc

TAILBONE *nontechnical name for* > COCCYX

TAILBONES > TAILBONE

TAILCOAT *n* man's black coat having a horizontal cut over the hips and a tapering tail with a vertical slit up to the waist

TAILCOATS > TAILCOAT

TAILED > TAIL

TAILENDER *n* (in cricket) the batter last in the batting order

TAILER *n* one that tails

TAILERON *n* aileron located on the tailplane of an aircraft

TAILERONS > TAILERON

TAILERS > TAILER

TAILFAN *n* fanned structure at the hind end of a lobster or related crustacean, formed from the telson and uropods

TAILFANS > TAILFAN

TAILFIN *n* decorative projection at back of car

TAILFINS > TAILFIN

TAILFLIES > TAILFLY

TAILFLY *n* in angling, the lowest fly on a wet-fly cast

TAILGATE *n* door at the rear of a hatchback vehicle ▷ *vb* drive very close behind (a vehicle)

TAILGATED > TAILGATE

TAILGATER > TAILGATE

TAILGATES > TAILGATE

TAILING *n* part of a beam, rafter, projecting brick or stone, etc, embedded in a wall

TAILINGS *npl* waste left over after certain processes, such as from an ore-crushing plant or in milling grain

TAILLAMP *n* rear light

TAILLAMPS > TAILLAMP

TAILLE *n* (in France before 1789) a tax levied by a king or overlord on his subjects

TAILLES > TAILLE

TAILLESS > TAIL

TAILLEUR *n* woman's suit

TAILLEURS > TAILLEUR

TAILLIE *n* (in law) the limitation of an estate or interest to a person and the heirs of his body

TAILLIES > TAILLIE

TAILLIGHT *same as* > TAILLAMP

TAILLIKE *adj* resembling a tail

TAILOR *n* person who makes men's clothes ▷ *vb* cut or style (a garment) to specific requirements

TAILORED > TAILOR

TAILORESS *n* female tailor

TAILORING > TAILOR

TAILORS > TAILOR

TAILPIECE *n* piece added at the end of something, for example a report

TAILPIPE *vb* attach an object, esp a tin can, to the tail of an animal

TAILPIPED > TAILPIPE

TAILPIPES > TAILPIPE

TAILPLANE *n* small stabilizing wing at the rear of an aircraft

TAILRACE *n* channel that carries water away from a water wheel, turbine, etc

TAILRACES > TAILRACE

TAILS *adv* with the side of a coin that does not have a portrait of a head on it uppermost

TAILSKID *n* runner under the tail of an aircraft

TAILSKIDS > TAILSKID

TAILSLIDE *n* backwards descent of an aeroplane after stalling while in an upward trajectory

TAILSPIN *n* uncontrolled spinning dive of an aircraft

TAILSPINS > TAILSPIN

TAILSTOCK *n* casting that slides on the bed of a lathe in alignment with the headstock and is locked in position to support the free end of a workpiece

TAILWATER *n* water flowing in a tailrace

TAILWHEEL *n* wheel fitted to the rear of a vehicle, esp the landing wheel under the tail of an aircraft

TAILWIND *n* wind coming from the rear

TAILWINDS > TAILWIND

TAILYE *same as* > TAILLIE

TAILYES > TAILYE

TAILZIE *same as* > TAILLIE

TAILZIES > TAILZIE

TAIN *n* tinfoil used in backing mirrors

TAINS > TAIN

TAINT *vb* spoil with a small amount of decay, contamination, or other bad quality ▷ *n* something that taints

TAINTED > TAINT

TAINTING > TAINT

TAINTLESS > TAINT

TAINTS > TAINT

TAINTURE *n* contamination; staining

TAINTURES > TAINTURE

TAIPAN *n* large poisonous Australian snake

TAIPANS > TAIPAN

TAIRA *same as* > TAYRA

TAIRAS > TAIRA

TAIS > TAI

TAISCH *n* (in Scotland) apparition of a person whose death is imminent

TAISCHES > TAISCH

TAISH *same as* > TAISCH

TAISHES > TAISH

TAIT *same as* > TATE

TAITS > TAIT

TAIVER *same as* > TAVER

TAIVERED > TAIVER

TAIVERING > TAIVER

TAIVERS > TAIVER

TAIVERT *adj* Scots word meaning confused or bewildered

TAJ *n* tall conical cap worn as a mark of distinction by Muslims

TAJES > TAJ

TAJINE *same as* > TAGINE

TAJINES > TAJINE

TAK Scots variant spelling of > TAKE

TAKA *n* standard monetary unit of Bangladesh, divided into 100 paise

TAKABLE > TAKE

TAKAHE *n* very rare flightless New Zealand bird

TAKAHES > TAKAHE

TAKAMAKA *same as* > TACAMAHAC

TAKAMAKAS > TAKAMAKA

TAKAS > TAKA

TAKE *vb* remove from a place ▷ *n* one of a series of recordings from which the best will be used

TAKEABLE > TAKE

TAKEAWAY *adj* (of food) sold for consumption away from the premises ▷ *n* shop or restaurant selling meals for eating elsewhere

TAKEAWAYS > TAKEAWAY

TAKEDOWN *n* disassembly

TAKEDOWNS > TAKEDOWN

TAKEN > TAKE

TAKEOFF *n* act or process of making an aircraft airborne

TAKEOFFS > TAKEOFF

TAKEOUT *n* shop or restaurant that sells such food

TAKEOUTS > TAKEOUT

TAKEOVER *n* act of taking control of a company by buying a large number of its shares

TAKEOVERS > TAKEOVER

TAKER *n* person who agrees to take something that is offered

TAKERS > TAKER

TAKES > TAKE

TAKEUP *n* the claiming or acceptance of something, esp a state benefit, that is due or available

TAKEUPS > TAKEUP

TAKHI *n* type of wild Mongolian horse

TAKHIS > TAKHI

TAKI *same as* > TAKHI

TAKIER > TAKY

TAKIEST > TAKY

TAKIN *n* massive bovid mammal of mountainous regions of S Asia, having a shaggy coat, short legs, and horns that point backwards and upwards

TAKING > TAKE

TAKINGLY > TAKE

TAKINGS > TAKE

TAKINS > TAKIN

TAKIS > TAKI

TAKKIES *same as* > TACKIES

TAKS > TAK

TAKY *adj* appealing

TALA *n* standard monetary

unit of Samoa, divided into 100 sene

TALAK same as > TALAQ

TALAKS > TALAK

TALANT old variant of > TALON

TALANTS > TALANT

TALAPOIN n smallest of the guenon monkeys of swampy central W African forests, having olive-green fur and slightly webbed digits

TALAPOINS > TALAPOIN

TALAQ n Muslim form of divorce

TALAQS > TALAQ

TALAR n ankle-length robe

TALARIA npl winged sandals, such as those worn by Hermes

TALARS > TALAR

TALAS > TALA

TALAUNT old variant of > TALON

TALAUNTS > TALAUNT

TALAYOT n ancient Balearic stone tower

TALAYOTS > TALAYOT

TALBOT n (formerly) an ancient breed of large hound, usually white or light-coloured, having pendulous ears and strong powers of scent

TALBOTS > TALBOT

TALBOTYPE n early type of photographic process (invented by W H Fox Talbot) or a photograph produced using it

TALC n talcum powder ▷ vb apply talc to ▷ adj of, or relating to, talc

TALCED > TALC

TALCIER > TALCY

TALCIEST > TALCY

TALCING > TALC

TALCKED > TALCKY

TALCKIER > TALCKY

TALCKIEST > TALCKY

TALCKING > TALCKY

TALCKY same as > TALCY

TALCOSE > TALC

TALCOUS > TALC

TALCS > TALC

TALCUM n white, grey, brown, or pale green mineral, found in metamorphic rocks. It is used in the manufacture of talcum powder and electrical insulators

TALCUMS > TALCUM

TALCY adj like, containing, or covered in talc

TALE n story

TALEA n rhythmic pattern in certain mediaeval choral compositions

TALEAE > TALEA

TALEFUL adj having many tales

TALEGALLA n brush turkey, of New Guinea and

Australia

TALEGGIO n Italian cheese

TALEGGIOS > TALEGGIO

TALENT n natural ability

TALENTED > TALENT

TALENTS > TALENT

TALER same as > THALER

TALERS > TALER

TALES n group of persons summoned from among those present in court or from bystanders to fill vacancies on a jury panel

TALESMAN > TALES

TALESMEN > TALES

TALEYSIM > TALLITH

TALI > TALUS

TALIGRADE adj (of mammals) walking on the outer side of foot

TALION n system or legal principle of making the punishment correspond to the crime

TALIONIC adj of or relating to talion

TALIONS > TALION

TALIPAT same as > TALIPOT

TALIPATS > TALIPAT

TALIPED adj having a club foot ▷ n club-footed person

TALIPEDS > TALIPED

TALIPES n congenital deformity of the foot by which it is twisted in any of various positions

TALIPOT n palm tree of the East Indies, having large leaves that are used for fans, thatching houses, etc

TALIPOTS > TALIPOT

TALISMAN n object believed to have magic power

TALISMANS > TALISMAN

TALK vb express ideas or feelings by means of speech ▷ n speech or lecture

TALKABLE > TALK

TALKATHON n epic bout of discussion or speechifying

TALKATIVE adj fond of talking

TALKBACK n broadcast in which telephone comments or questions from the public are transmitted live

TALKBACKS > TALKBACK

TALKBOX n voice box

TALKBOXES > TALKBOX

TALKED > TALK

TALKER > TALK

TALKERS > TALK

TALKFEST n lengthy discussion

TALKFESTS > TALKFEST

TALKIE n early film with a soundtrack

TALKIER > TALKY

TALKIES > TALKIE

TALKIEST > TALKY

TALKINESS n quality or condition of being talky

TALKING n speech; the act of speaking

TALKINGS > TALKING

TALKS > TALK

TALKTIME n length of time a mobile phone can be used before its battery runs out

TALKTIMES > TALKTIME

TALKY adj containing too much dialogue or inconsequential talk

TALL adj higher than average

TALLAGE n tax levied by the Norman and early Angevin kings on their Crown lands and royal towns ▷ vb levy a tax (upon)

TALLAGED > TALLAGE

TALLAGES > TALLAGE

TALLAGING > TALLAGE

TALLAISIM > TALLITH

TALLAT same as > TALLET

TALLATS > TALLAT

TALLBOY n high chest of drawers

TALLBOYS > TALLBOY

TALLENT n plenty

TALLENTS > TALLENT

TALLER > TALL

TALLEST > TALL

TALLET n loft

TALLETS > TALLET

TALLGRASS n long grass in North American prairie

TALLIABLE adj taxable

TALLIATE vb levy a tax

TALLIATED > TALLIATE

TALLIATES > TALLIATE

TALLIED > TALLY

TALLIER > TALLY

TALLIERS > TALLY

TALLIES > TALLY

TALLIS variant of > TALLITH

TALLISES > TALLIS

TALLISH adj quite tall

TALLISIM > TALLITH

TALLIT variant of > TALLITH

TALLITES > TALLIT

TALLITH n white shawl with fringed corners worn over the head and shoulders by Jewish males during religious services

TALLITHES > TALLITH

TALLITHIM > TALLITH

TALLITHS > TALLITH

TALLITIM > TALLIT

TALLITOT > TALLIT

TALLITOTH > TALLITH

TALLITS > TALLIT

TALLNESS > TALL

TALLOL n oily liquid used for making soaps, lubricants, etc

TALLOLS > TALLOL

TALLOT same as > TALLET

TALLOTS > TALLOT

TALLOW n hard animal fat

used to make candles ▷ vb cover or smear with tallow

TALLOWED > TALLOW

TALLOWING > TALLOW

TALLOWISH > TALLOW

TALLOWS > TALLOW

TALLOWY > TALLOW

TALLS > TALL

TALLY vb (of two things) correspond ▷ n record of a debt or score

TALLYHO n cry of a participant at a hunt to encourage the hounds when the quarry is sighted ▷ vb to make the cry of tallyho

TALLYHOED > TALLYHO

TALLYHOS > TALLYHO

TALLYING > TALLY

TALLYMAN n scorekeeper or recorder

TALLYMEN > TALLYMAN

TALLYSHOP n shop that allows customers to pay in instalments

TALMA n short cloak

TALMAS > TALMA

TALMUD n primary source of Jewish religious law, consisting of the Mishnah and the Gemara

TALMUDIC > TALMUD

TALMUDISM > TALMUD

TALMUDS > TALMUD

TALON n bird's hooked claw

TALONED > TALON

TALONS > TALON

TALOOKA same as > TALUK

TALOOKAS > TALOOKA

TALPA n sebaceous cyst

TALPAE > TALPA

TALPAS > TALPA

TALUK n subdivision of a district

TALUKA same as > TALUK

TALUKAS > TALUKA

TALUKDAR n person in charge of a taluk

TALUKDARS > TALUKDAR

TALUKS > TALUK

TALUS n bone of the ankle that articulates with the leg bones to form the ankle joint

TALUSES > TALUS

TALWEG same as > THALWEG

TALWEGS > TALWEG

TAM n type of hat

TAMABLE > TAME

TAMAL same as > TAMALE

TAMALE n Mexican dish made of minced meat mixed with crushed maize and seasonings, wrapped in maize husks and steamed

TAMALES > TAMALE

TAMALS > TAMAL

TAMANDU same as > TAMANDUA

TAMANDUA n small arboreal edentate mammal

TAMANDUAS > TAMANDUA
TAMANDUS > TAMANDU
TAMANOIR *n* anteater
TAMANOIRS > TAMANOIR
TAMANU *n* poon tree
TAMANUS > TAMANU
TAMARA *n* powder consisting of cloves, cinnamon, fennel, coriander, etc, used in certain cuisines
TAMARACK *n* North American larch, with reddish-brown bark, bluish-green needle-like leaves, and shiny oval cones
TAMARACKS > TAMARACK
TAMARAO *same as* **>** TAMARAU
TAMARAOS > TAMARAO
TAMARAS > TAMARA
TAMARAU *n* small rare member of the cattle tribe of lowland areas of Mindoro in the Philippines
TAMARAUS > TAMARAU
TAMARI *n* Japanese variety of soy sauce
TAMARILLO *n* shrub with a red oval edible fruit
TAMARIN *n* small monkey of South and Central American forests
TAMARIND *n* tropical tree
TAMARINDS > TAMARIND
TAMARINS > TAMARIN
TAMARIS > TAMARI
TAMARISK *n* evergreen shrub with slender branches and feathery flower clusters
TAMARISKS > TAMARISK
TAMASHA *n* (in India) a show
TAMASHAS > TAMASHA
TAMBAC *same as* **>** TOMBAC
TAMBACS > TAMBAC
TAMBAK *same as* **>** TOMBAC
TAMBAKS > TAMBAK
TAMBALA *n* unit of Malawian currency
TAMBALAS > TAMBALA
TAMBER *same as* **>** TIMBRE
TAMBERS > TAMBER
TAMBOUR *n* embroidery frame, consisting of two hoops over which the fabric is stretched while being worked *⊳ vb* embroider (fabric or a design) on a tambour
TAMBOURA *n* instrument with a long neck, four strings, and no frets, used in Indian music to provide a drone
TAMBOURAS > TAMBOURA
TAMBOURED > TAMBOUR
TAMBOURER *n* one who embroiders on a tambour
TAMBOURIN *n* 18th-century Provençal folk dance
TAMBOURS > TAMBOUR
TAMBUR *n* old Turkish

stringed instrument
TAMBURA *n* Middle-Eastern stringed instrument with a long neck, related to the tambur
TAMBURAS > TAMBURA
TAMBURIN *same as* **>** TAMBURIN
TAMBURINS > TAMBURIN
TAMBURS > TAMBUR
TAME *adj* (of animals) brought under human control *⊳ vb* make tame
TAMEABLE > TAME
TAMED > TAME
TAMEIN *n* Burmese skirt
TAMEINS > TAMEIN
TAMELESS > TAME
TAMELY > TAME
TAMENESS > TAME
TAMER > TAME
TAMERS > TAME
TAMES > TAME
TAMEST > TAME
TAMIN *n* thin woollen fabric
TAMINE *same as* **>** TAMIN
TAMINES > TAMINE
TAMING *n* act of making (something) tame
TAMINGS > TAMING
TAMINS > TAMIN
TAMIS *same as* **>** TAMMY
TAMISE *n* type of thin cloth
TAMISES > TAMIS
TAMMAR *n* small scrub wallaby of Australia, with a thick dark-coloured coat
TAMMARS > TAMMAR
TAMMIE *n* short for tam-o'shanter, a traditional Scottish hat
TAMMIED > TAMMY
TAMMIES > TAMMY
TAMMY *n* glazed woollen or mixed fabric, used for linings, undergarments, etc *⊳ vb* (esp formerly) to strain (sauce, soup, etc) through a tammy
TAMMYING > TAMMY
TAMOXIFEN *n* drug that antagonizes the action of oestrogen and is used to treat breast cancer and some types of infertility in women
TAMP *vb* pack down by repeated taps
TAMPALA *n* Asian plant (Amaranthus tricolor), eaten as food
TAMPALAS > TAMPALA
TAMPAN *n* biting mite
TAMPANS > TAMPAN
TAMPED > TAMP
TAMPER *vb* interfere *⊳ n* person or thing that tamps, esp an instrument for packing down tobacco in a pipe
TAMPERED > TAMPER
TAMPERER > TAMPER
TAMPERERS > TAMPER
TAMPERING > TAMPER

TAMPERS > TAMPER
TAMPING *adj* very angry *⊳ n* act or instance of tamping
TAMPINGS > TAMPING
TAMPION *n* plug placed in a gun's muzzle when the gun is not in use to keep out moisture and dust
TAMPIONS > TAMPION
TAMPON *n* absorbent plug of cotton wool inserted into the vagina during menstruation *⊳ vb* use a tampon
TAMPONADE > TAMPON
TAMPONAGE > TAMPON
TAMPONED > TAMPON
TAMPONING > TAMPON
TAMPONS > TAMPON
TAMPS > TAMP
TAMS > TAM
TAMWORTH *n* any of a hardy rare breed of long-bodied reddish pigs
TAMWORTHS > TAMWORTH
TAN *n* brown coloration of the skin from exposure to sunlight *⊳ vb* (of skin) go brown from exposure to sunlight *⊳ adj* yellowish-brown
TANA *n* small Madagascan lemur
TANADAR *n* commanding officer of an Indian police station
TANADARS > TANADAR
TANAGER *n* American songbird with a short thick bill and a brilliantly coloured male plumage
TANAGERS > TANAGER
TANAGRA *n* type of tanager
TANAGRAS > TANAGRA
TANAGRINE *adj* of or relating to the tanager
TANALISED *adj* having been treated with the trademarked timber preservative Tanalith
TANALIZED *same as* **>** TANALISED
TANAS > TANA
TANBARK *n* bark of certain trees, esp the oak and hemlock, used as a source of tannin
TANBARKS > TANBARK
TANDEM *n* bicycle for two riders, one behind the other
TANDEMS > TANDEM
TANDOOR *n* type of Indian clay oven
TANDOORI *adj* (of food) cooked in an Indian clay oven *⊳ n* Indian method of cooking meat or vegetables on a spit in a clay oven
TANDOORIS > TANDOORI
TANDOORS > TANDOOR
TANE *old Scottish variant of* **>** TAKEN
TANG *n* strong taste or smell *⊳ vb* cause to ring

TANGA *n* triangular loincloth worn by indigenous peoples in tropical America
TANGAS > TANGA
TANGED > TANG
TANGELO *n* hybrid produced by crossing a tangerine tree with a grapefruit tree
TANGELOS > TANGELO
TANGENCE *n* touching
TANGENCES > TANGENCE
TANGENCY > TANGENT
TANGENT *n* line that touches a curve without intersecting it
TANGENTAL > TANGENT
TANGENTS > TANGENT
TANGERINE *n* small orange-like fruit of an Asian citrus tree *⊳ adj* reddish-orange
TANGHIN *n* strong poison formerly used in Madagascar to determine the guilt or otherwise of crime suspects
TANGHININ *n* active ingredient in tanghin
TANGHINS > TANGHIN
TANGI *n* Māori funeral ceremony
TANGIBLE *adj* able to be touched *⊳ n* tangible thing or asset
TANGIBLES > TANGIBLE
TANGIBLY > TANGIBLE
TANGIE *n* water spirit of Orkney, appearing as a figure draped in seaweed, or as a seahorse
TANGIER > TANGY
TANGIES > TANGIE
TANGIEST > TANGY
TANGINESS > TANGY
TANGING > TANG
TANGIS > TANGI
TANGLE *n* confused mass or situation *⊳ vb* twist together in a tangle
TANGLED > TANGLE
TANGLER > TANGLE
TANGLERS > TANGLE
TANGLES > TANGLE
TANGLIER > TANGLE
TANGLIEST > TANGLE
TANGLING *n* act or condition of tangling
TANGLINGS > TANGLING
TANGLY > TANGLE
TANGO *n* S American dance *⊳ vb* dance a tango
TANGOED > TANGO
TANGOING > TANGO
TANGOIST > TANGO
TANGOISTS > TANGO
TANGOLIKE > TANGO
TANGOS > TANGO
TANGRAM *n* Chinese puzzle in which a square, cut into a parallelogram, a square, and five triangles, is formed into figures
TANGRAMS > TANGRAM

t

TANGS > TANG

TANGUN n small and sturdy Tibetan pony

TANGUNS > TANGUN

TANGY adj having a pungent, fresh, or briny flavour or aroma

TANH n hyperbolic tangent

TANHS > TANH

TANIST n heir apparent of a Celtic chieftain chosen by election during the chief's lifetime: usually the worthiest of his kin

TANISTRY > TANIST

TANISTS > TANIST

TANIWHA n mythical Māori monster that lives in water

TANIWHAS > TANIWHA

TANK n container for liquids or gases ▷ vb put or keep in a tank

TANKA n Japanese verse form consisting of five lines, the first and third having five syllables, the others seven

TANKAGE n capacity or contents of a tank or tanks

TANKAGES > TANKAGE

TANKARD n large beer-mug, often with a hinged lid

TANKARDS > TANKARD

TANKAS > TANKA

TANKED > TANK

TANKER n ship or truck for carrying liquid in bulk

TANKERS > TANKER

TANKFUL n quantity contained in a tank

TANKFULS > TANKFUL

TANKIA n type of boat used in Canton

TANKIAS > TANKIA

TANKIES > TANKY

TANKING n heavy defeat

TANKINGS > TANKING

TANKINI n woman's two-piece swimming costume consisting of a vest or camisole top and bikini briefs

TANKINIS > TANKINI

TANKLESS > TANK

TANKLIKE > TANK

TANKS > TANK

TANKSHIP same as **>** TANKER

TANKSHIPS > TANKSHIP

TANKY n die-hard communist

TANLING n suntanned person

TANLINGS > TANLING

TANNA n Indian police station or army base

TANNABLE > TAN

TANNAGE n act or process of tanning

TANNAGES > TANNAGE

TANNAH same as **>** TANNA

TANNAHS > TANNAH

TANNAS > TANNA

TANNATE n any salt or ester of tannic acid

TANNATES > TANNATE

TANNED > TAN

TANNER > TAN

TANNERIES > TANNERY

TANNERS > TAN

TANNERY n place where hides are tanned

TANNEST > TAN

TANNIC adj of, containing, or produced from tannin or tannic acid

TANNIE n in S Africa, title of respect used to refer to an elderly woman

TANNIES > TANNIE

TANNIN n vegetable substance used in tanning

TANNING > TAN

TANNINGS > TAN

TANNINS > TANNIN

TANNISH > TAN

TANNOY n sound-amplifying apparatus used as a public-address system esp in a large building, such as a university ▷ vb announce (something) using a Tannoy system

TANNOYED > TANNOY

TANNOYING > TANNOY

TANNOYS > TANNOY

TANOREXIC n person obsessed with maintaining a tan

TANREC same as **>** TENREC

TANRECS > TANREC

TANS > TAN

TANSIES > TANSY

TANSY n yellow-flowered plant

TANTALATE n any of various salts of tantalic acid formed when the pentoxide of tantalum dissolves in an alkali

TANTALIC adj of or containing tantalum, esp in the pentavalent state

TANTALISE same as **>** TANTALIZE

TANTALISM **>** TANTALISE

TANTALITE n heavy brownish mineral consisting of a tantalum oxide of iron and manganese in orthorhombic crystalline form

TANTALIZE vb torment by showing but withholding something desired

TANTALOUS adj of or containing tantalum in the trivalent state

TANTALUM n hard greyish-white metallic element

TANTALUMS > TANTALUM

TANTALUS n case in which bottles of wine and spirits may be locked with their contents tantalizingly visible

TANTARA n blast, as on a trumpet or horn

TANTARARA same as **>** TANTARA

TANTARAS > TANTARA

TANTI adj old word for worthwhile

TANTIVIES > TANTIVY

TANTIVY adv at full speed ▷ interj hunting cry, esp at full gallop

TANTO adv too much

TANTONIES > TANTONY

TANTONY n runt

TANTRA n sacred books of Tantrism, written between the 7th and 17th centuries AD, mainly in the form of a dialogue between Siva and his wife

TANTRAS > TANTRA

TANTRIC > TANTRA

TANTRISM n teaching of tantra

TANTRISMS > TANTRISM

TANTRUM n childish outburst of temper

TANTRUMS > TANTRUM

TANUKI n animal similar to a raccoon, found in Japan

TANUKIS > TANUKI

TANYARD n part of a tannery

TANYARDS > TANYARD

TANZANITE n blue gemstone

TAO n (in Confucian philosophy) the correct course of action

TAONGA n treasure

TAONGAS > TAONGA

TAOS > TAO

TAP vb knock lightly and usu repeatedly ▷ n light knock

TAPA n inner bark of the paper mulberry

TAPACOLO n small bird of Chile and Argentina

TAPACOLOS > TAPACOLO

TAPACULO same as **>** TAPACOLO

TAPACULOS > TAPACULO

TAPADERA n leather covering for the stirrup on an American saddle

TAPADERAS > TAPADERA

TAPADERO same as **>** TAPADERA

TAPADEROS > TAPADERO

TAPALO n Latin American scarf, often patterned and brightly coloured

TAPALOS > TAPALO

TAPAS npl (in Spanish cookery) light snacks or appetizers, usually eaten with drinks

TAPE n narrow long strip of material ▷ vb record on magnetic tape

TAPEABLE > TAPE

TAPED > TAPE

TAPELESS > TAPE

TAPELIKE > TAPE

TAPELINE n tape or length of metal marked off in inches, centimetres, etc, used principally for measuring and fitting garments

TAPELINES > TAPELINE

TAPEN adj made of tape

TAPENADE n savoury paste made from capers, olives, and anchovies, with olive oil and lemon juice

TAPENADES > TAPENADE

TAPER > TAPE

TAPERED > TAPE

TAPERER > TAPE

TAPERERS > TAPE

TAPERING > TAPE

TAPERINGS > TAPE

TAPERNESS n state or quality of being tapered

TAPERS > TAPE

TAPERWISE adv in the manner of a taper

TAPES > TAPE

TAPESTRY n fabric decorated with coloured woven designs ▷ vb portray in tapestry

TAPET n example of tapestry

TAPETA > TAPETUM

TAPETAL > TAPETUM

TAPETI n forest rabbit of Brazil

TAPETIS > TAPETI

TAPETS > TAPET

TAPETUM n layer of nutritive cells in the sporangia of ferns and anthers of flowering plants that surrounds developing spore cells

TAPEWORM n long flat parasitic worm living in the intestines of vertebrates

TAPEWORMS > TAPEWORM

TAPHOLE n hole in a furnace for running off molten metal or slag

TAPHOLES > TAPHOLE

TAPHONOMY n study of the processes affecting an organism after death that result in its fossilization

TAPHOUSE n inn or bar

TAPHOUSES > TAPHOUSE

TAPING > TAPE

TAPIOCA n beadlike starch made from cassava root, used in puddings

TAPIOCAS > TAPIOCA

TAPIR n piglike mammal of tropical America and SE Asia, with a long snout

TAPIROID > TAPIR

TAPIRS > TAPIR

TAPIS n tapestry or carpeting, esp as formerly used to cover a table in a council chamber

TAPISES > TAPIS

TAPIST n person who records (read out) printed matter in an audio format for the benefit of visually impaired people

TAPISTS > TAPIST

TAPLASH n dregs of beer

TAPLASHES > TAPLASH

TAPPA same as > TAPA

TAPPABLE > TAP

TAPPAS > TAPPA

TAPPED > TAP

TAPPER n person who taps

TAPPERS > TAPPER

TAPPET n short steel rod in an engine, transferring motion from one part to another

TAPPETS > TAPPET

TAPPICE vb hide

TAPPICED > TAPPICE

TAPPICES > TAPPICE

TAPPICING > TAPPICE

TAPPING > TAP

TAPPINGS > TAP

TAPPIT adj crested; topped

TAPROOM n public bar in a hotel or pub

TAPROOMS > TAPROOM

TAPROOT n main root of a plant, growing straight down

TAPROOTED > TAPROOT

TAPROOTS > TAPROOT

TAPS > TAP

TAPSMAN n old word for a barman

TAPSMEN > TAPSMAN

TAPSTER n barman

TAPSTERS > TAPSTER

TAPSTRESS > TAPSTER

TAPSTRY adj relating to tapestry

TAPU adj sacred ▷ n Māori religious or superstitious restriction on something ▷ vb put a tapu on something

TAPUED > TAPU

TAPUING > TAPU

TAPUS > TAPU

TAQUERIA n restaurant specializing in tacos

TAQUERIAS > TAQUERIA

TAR n thick black liquid distilled from coal etc ▷ vb coat with tar

TARA same as > TARO

TARAIRE n type of New Zealand tree

TARAIRES > TARAIRE

TARAKIHI n common edible sea fish of New Zealand waters

TARAKIHIS > TARAKIHI

TARAMA n cod roe

TARAMAS > TARAMA

TARAMEA n variety of New Zealand speargrass

TARAMEAS > TARAMEA

TARAND n northern animal of legend, now supposed to have been the reindeer

TARANDS > TARAND

TARANTARA same as > TANTARA

TARANTAS same as > TARANTASS

TARANTASS n large horse-drawn four-wheeled Russian carriage without springs

TARANTISM n nervous disorder marked by uncontrollable bodily movement, widespread in S Italy during the 15th to 17th centuries: popularly thought to be caused by the bite of a tarantula

TARANTISM > TARANTISM

TARANTULA n large hairy spider with a poisonous bite

TARAS > TARA

TARAXACUM n perennial plant with dense heads of small yellow flowers and seeds with a feathery attachment

TARBOGGIN same as > TOBOGGAN

TARBOOSH n felt or cloth brimless cap, usually red and often with a silk tassel, formerly worn by Muslim men

TARBOUCHE same as > TARBOOSH

TARBOUSH same as > TARBOOSH

TARBOY n boy who applies tar to the skin of sheep cut during shearing

TARBOYS > TARBOY

TARBUSH same as > TARBOOSH

TARBUSHES > TARBUSH

TARCEL same as > TARCEL

TARCELS > TARCEL

TARDIED > TARDY

TARDIER > TARDY

TARDIES > TARDY

TARDIEST > TARDY

TARDILY > TARDY

TARDINESS > TARDY

TARDIVE adj tending to develop late

TARDO adj (of music) slow; to be played slowly

TARDY adj slow or late ▷ vb delay or impede (something or someone)

TARDYING > TARDY

TARDYON n particle travelling slower than the speed of light

TARDYONS > TARDYON

TARE n weight of the wrapping or container of goods ▷ vb weigh (a package, etc) in order to calculate the amount of tare

TARED > TARE

TARES > TARE

TARGA as in targa top denotes removable hard roof on a car

TARGE vb interrogate

TARGED > TARGE

TARGES > TARGE

TARGET n object or person a missile is aimed at ▷ vb aim or direct

TARGETED > TARGET

TARGETEER n soldier armed with a small round shield

TARGETING > TARGET

TARGETS > TARGET

TARGING > TARGE

TARIFF n tax levied on imports ▷ vb impose punishment for a criminal offence

TARIFFED > TARIFF

TARIFFING > TARIFF

TARIFFS > TARIFF

TARING > TARE

TARINGS > TARE

TARLATAN n open-weave cotton fabric, used for stiffening garments

TARLATANS > TARLATAN

TARLETAN same as > TARLATAN

TARLETANS > TARLETAN

TARMAC See also > MACADAM

TARMACKED > TARMAC

TARMACS > TARMAC

TARN n small mountain lake

TARNAL adj damned ▷ adv extremely

TARNALLY > TARNAL

TARNATION euphemism for > DAMNATION

TARNISH vb make or become stained or less bright ▷ n discoloration or blemish

TARNISHED > TARNISH

TARNISHER > TARNISH

TARNISHES > TARNISH

TARNS > TARN

TARO n plant with a large edible rootstock

TAROC old variant of > TAROT

TAROCS > TAROC

TAROK old variant of > TAROT

TAROKS > TAROK

TAROS > TARO

TAROT n special pack of cards used mainly in fortune-telling ▷ adj relating to tarot cards

TAROTS > TAROT

TARP informal word for > TARPAULIN

TARPAN n European wild horse common in prehistoric times but now extinct

TARPANS > TARPAN

TARPAPER n paper coated or impregnated with tar

TARPAPERS > TARPAPER

TARPAULIN n (sheet of) heavy waterproof fabric

TARPON n large silvery clupeoid game fish found in warm Atlantic waters

TARPONS > TARPON

TARPS > TARP

TARRAGON n aromatic herb

TARRAGONS > TARRAGON

TARRAS same as > TRASS

TARRASES > TARRAS

TARRE vb old word meaning to provoke or goad

TARRED > TAR

TARRES > TARRE

TARRIANCE archaic word for > DELAY

TARRIED > TARRY

TARRIER > TARRY

TARRIERS > TARRY

TARRIES > TARRY

TARRIEST > TARRY

TARRINESS > TAR

TARRING > TAR

TARRINGS > TAR

TARROCK n seabird

TARROCKS > TARROCK

TARROW vb exhibit reluctance

TARROWED > TARROW

TARROWING > TARROW

TARROWS > TARROW

TARRY vb linger or delay ▷ n stay ▷ adj covered in or resembling tar

TARRYING > TAR

TARS > TAR

TARSAL adj of the tarsus or tarsi ▷ n tarsal bone

TARSALGIA n pain in the tarsus

TARSALS > TARSAL

TARSEAL n bitumen surface of a road

TARSEALS > TARSEAL

TARSEL same as > TERCEL

TARSELS > TARSEL

TARSI > TARSUS

TARSIA another term for > INTARSIA

TARSIAS > TARSIA

TARSIER n small nocturnal primate of the E Indies, which has very large eyes

TARSIERS > TARSIER

TARSIOID adj resembling a tarsier

TARSIPED n generic term for a number of marsupials

TARSIPEDS > TARSIPED

TARSUS n bones of the heel and ankle collectively

TART n pie or flan with a sweet filling ▷ adj sharp or bitter ▷ adj (of a flavour, food, etc) sour, acid, or astringent ▷ vb (of food, drink, etc) become tart (sour)

TARTAN n design of straight lines crossing at right angles, esp one associated with a Scottish clan

TARTANA n small Mediterranean sailing boat

TARTANAS > TARTANA
TARTANE same as **>** TARTANA
TARTANED > TARTAN
TARTANES > TARTANE
TARTANRY n derogatory term for excessive use of tartan and other Scottish imagery to produce a distorted sentimental view of Scotland and its history
TARTANS > TARTAN
TARTAR n hard deposit on the teeth
TARTARE n mayonnaise sauce mixed with hard-boiled egg yolks, chopped herbs, capers, and gherkins
TARTARES > TARTARE
TARTARIC adj of or derived from tartar or tartaric acid
TARTARISE same as **>** TARTARIZE
TARTARIZE vb impregnate or treat with tartar or tartar emetic
TARTARLY adj resembling a tartar
TARTAROUS adj consisting of, containing, or resembling tartar
TARTARS > TARTAR
TARTED > TART
TARTER > TART
TARTEST > TART
TARTIER > TARTY
TARTIEST > TARTY
TARTILY > TARTY
TARTINE n slice of bread with butter or jam spread on it
TARTINES > TARTINE
TARTINESS > TARTY
TARTING > TART
TARTISH > TART
TARTISHLY > TART
TARTLET n individual pastry case with a filling of fruit or other sweet or savoury mixture
TARTLETS > TARTLET
TARTLY > TART
TARTNESS > TART
TARTRATE n any salt or ester of tartaric acid
TARTRATED adj being in the form of a tartrate
TARTRATES > TARTRATE
TARTS > TART
TARTUFE same as **>** TARTUFFE
TARTUFES > TARTUFFE
TARTUFFE n person who hypocritically pretends to be deeply pious
TARTUFFES > TARTUFFE
TARTUFO n Italian mousse-like chocolate dessert
TARTUFOS > TARTUFO
TARTY adj resembling a promiscuous woman; provocative in a cheap and bawdy way
TARWEED n resinous

Californian plant with a pungent scent
TARWEEDS > TARWEED
TARWHINE n bream of E Australia, silver in colour with gold streaks
TARWHINES > TARWHINE
TARZAN n man with great physical strength, agility, and virility
TARZANS > TARZAN
TAS > TA
TASAR same as **>** TUSSORE
TASARS > TASAR
TASBIH n form of Islamic prayer
TASBIHS > TASBIH
TASER vb use a Taser (trademark) stun gun on (someone)
TASERED > TASER
TASERING > TASER
TASERS > TASER
TASH vb stain or besmirch
TASHED > TASH
TASHES > TASH
TASHING > TASH
TASIMETER n device for measuring small temperature changes. It depends on the changes of pressure resulting from expanding or contracting solids
TASIMETRY > TASIMETER
TASK n piece of work to be done **▷** vb give someone a task to do
TASKBAR n area of computer screen showing what programs are running
TASKBARS > TASKBAR
TASKED > TASK
TASKER > TASK
TASKERS > TASK
TASKING > TASK
TASKINGS > TASK
TASKLESS > TASK
TASKS > TASK
TASKWORK n hard or unpleasant work
TASKWORKS > TASKWORK
TASLET same as **>** TASSET
TASLETS > TASLET
TASS n cup, goblet, or glass
TASSE same as **>** TASSET
TASSEL n decorative fringed knot of threads **▷** vb adorn with a tassel or tassels
TASSELED > TASSEL
TASSELING > TASSEL
TASSELL same as **>** TASSEL
TASSELLED > TASSEL
TASSELLS > TASSELL
TASSELLY > TASSEL
TASSELS > TASSEL
TASSES > TASSE
TASSET n piece of armour consisting of one or more plates fastened on to the bottom of a cuirass to

protect the thigh
TASSETS > TASSET
TASSIE same as **>** TASS
TASSIES > TASSIE
TASTABLE > TASTE
TASTE n sense by which the flavour of a substance is distinguished in the mouth **▷** vb distinguish the taste of (a substance)
TASTEABLE > TASTE
TASTED > TASTE
TASTEFUL adj having or showing good taste
TASTELESS adj bland or insipid
TASTER n person employed to test the quality of food or drink by tasting it
TASTERS > TASTER
TASTES > TASTE
TASTEVIN n small shallow cup for wine tasting
TASTEVINS > TASTEVIN
TASTIER > TASTY
TASTIEST > TASTY
TASTILY > TASTY
TASTINESS > TASTY
TASTING > TASTE
TASTINGS > TASTE
TASTY adj pleasantly flavoured
TAT n tatty or tasteless article(s) **▷** vb make (something) by tatting
TATAHASH n stew containing potatoes and cheap cuts of meat
TATAMI n thick rectangular mat of woven straw, used as a standard to measure a Japanese room
TATAMIS > TATAMI
TATAR n brutal person
TATARS > TATAR
TATE n small tuft of fibre
TATER n potato
TATERS > TATER
TATES > TATE
TATH vb (of cattle) to defecate
TATHED > TATH
TATHING > TATH
TATHS > TATH
TATIE same as **>** TATTIE
TATIES > TATIE
TATLER old variant of **>** TATTLER
TATLERS > TATLER
TATOU n armadillo
TATOUAY n large armadillo of South America
TATOUAYS > TATOUAY
TATOUS > TATOU
TATS > TAT
TATSOI n variety of Chinese cabbage
TATSOIS > TATSOI
TATT same as **>** TAT
TATTED > TAT
TATTER vb make or become torn
TATTERED > TATTER
TATTERING > TATTER

TATTERS > TATTER
TATTERY same as **>** TATTERED
TATTIE Scot or dialect word for **>** POTATO
TATTIER > TATTY
TATTIES > TATTIE
TATTIEST > TATTY
TATTILY > TATTY
TATTINESS > TATTY
TATTING > TAT
TATTINGS > TAT
TATTLE n gossip or chatter **▷** vb gossip or chatter
TATTLED > TATTLE
TATTLER n person who tattles
TATTLERS > TATTLER
TATTLES > TATTLE
TATTLING > TATTLE
TATTLINGS > TATTLE
TATTOO n pattern made on the body by pricking the skin and staining it with indelible inks **▷** vb make such a pattern on the skin
TATTOOED > TATTOO
TATTOOER > TATTOO
TATTOOERS > TATTOO
TATTOOING > TATTOO
TATTOOIST > TATTOO
TATTOOS > TATTOO
TATTOW old variant of **>** TATTOO
TATTOWED > TATTOW
TATTOWING > TATTOW
TATTOWS > TATTOW
TATTS > TATT
TATTY adj worn out, shabby, tawdry, or unkempt
TATU old variant of **>** TATTOO
TATUED > TATU
TATUING > TATU
TATUS > TATU
TAU n 19th letter in the Greek alphabet
TAUBE n type of German aeroplane
TAUBES > TAUBE
TAUGHT > TEACH
TAUHINU New Zealand name for **>** POPLAR
TAUHINUS > TAUHINU
TAUHOU same as **>** SILVEREYE
TAUHOUS > TAUHOU
TAUIWI n Māori term for the non-Māori people of New Zealand
TAUIWIS > TAUIWI
TAULD vb old Scots variant of told
TAUNT vb tease with jeers **▷** n jeering remark **▷** adj (of the mast or masts of a sailing vessel) unusually tall
TAUNTED > TAUNT
TAUNTER > TAUNT
TAUNTERS > TAUNT
TAUNTING > TAUNT
TAUNTINGS > TAUNT
TAUNTS > TAUNT

TAUON n negatively charged elementary particle

TAUONS > TAUON

TAUPATA n New Zealand shrub or tree, with shiny dark green leaves

TAUPATAS > TAUPATA

TAUPE adj brownish-grey ▷ n brownish-grey colour

TAUPES > TAUPE

TAUPIE same as > TAWPIE

TAUPIES > TAUPIE

TAUREAN adj born under or characteristic of Taurus

TAURIC same as > TAUREAN

TAURIFORM adj in the form of a bull

TAURINE adj of, relating to, or resembling a bull ▷ n derivative of the amino acid, cysteine, obtained from the bile of animals

TAURINES > TAURINE

TAUS > TAU

TAUT adj drawn tight ▷ vb Scots word meaning to tangle

TAUTAUG same as > TAUTOG

TAUTAUGS > TAUTAUG

TAUTED > TAUT

TAUTEN vb make or become taut

TAUTENED > TAUTEN

TAUTENING > TAUTEN

TAUTENS > TAUTEN

TAUTER > TAUT

TAUTEST > TAUT

TAUTING > TAUT

TAUTIT adj Scots word meaning tangled

TAUTLY > TAUT

TAUTNESS > TAUT

TAUTOG n large dark-coloured wrasse, used as a food fish

TAUTOGS > TAUTOG

TAUTOLOGY n use of words which merely repeat something already stated

TAUTOMER n either of the two forms of a chemical compound that exhibits tautomerism

TAUTOMERS > TAUTOMER

TAUTONYM n taxonomic name in which the generic and specific components are the same

TAUTONYMS > TAUTONYM

TAUTONYMY > TAUTONYM

TAUTS > TAUT

TAV n 23rd and last letter in the Hebrew alphabet

TAVA n thick Indian frying pan

TAVAH variant of > TAVA

TAVAHS > TAVAH

TAVAS > TAVA

TAVER vb wander about

TAVERED > TAVER

TAVERING > TAVER

TAVERN n pub

TAVERNA n (in Greece) a guesthouse that has its own bar

TAVERNAS > TAVERNA

TAVERNER n keeper of a tavern

TAVERNERS > TAVERNER

TAVERNS > TAVERN

TAVERS > TAVER

TAVERT adj bewildered or confused

TAVS > TAV

TAW vb convert skins into leather

TAWA n tall timber tree from New Zealand, with edible purple berries

TAWAI n New Zealand beech

TAWAIS > TAWAI

TAWAS > TAWA

TAWDRIER > TAWDRY

TAWDRIES > TAWDRY

TAWDRIEST > TAWDRY

TAWDRILY > TAWDRY

TAWDRY adj cheap, showy, and of poor quality ▷ n gaudy finery of poor quality

TAWED > TAW

TAWER > TAW

TAWERIES > TAWERY

TAWERS > TAW

TAWERY n place where tawing is carried out

TAWHAI same as > TAWAI

TAWHAIS > TAWHAI

TAWHIRI n small New Zealand tree with wavy green glossy leaves

TAWHIRIS > TAWHIRI

TAWIE adj easily persuaded or managed

TAWIER > TAWIE

TAWIEST > TAWIE

TAWING > TAW

TAWINGS > TAW

TAWNEY same as > TAWNY

TAWNEYS > TAWNEY

TAWNIER > TAWNY

TAWNIES > TAWNY

TAWNIEST > TAWNY

TAWNILY > TAWNY

TAWNINESS > TAWNY

TAWNY adj yellowish-brown ▷ n light brown to brownish-orange colour

TAWPIE n foolish or maladroit girl

TAWPIES > TAWPIE

TAWS same as > TAWSE

TAWSE n leather strap with one end cut into thongs, formerly used by schoolteachers to hit children who had misbehaved ▷ vb punish (someone) with or as if with a tawse

TAWSED > TAWSE

TAWSES > TAWSE

TAWSING > TAWSE

TAWT same as > TAUT

TAWTED > TAWT

TAWTIE > TAWT

TAWTIER > TAWT

TAWTIEST > TAWT

TAWTING > TAWT

TAWTS > TAWT

TAX n compulsory payment levied by a government on income, property, etc to raise revenue ▷ vb levy a tax on

TAXA > TAXON

TAXABLE adj capable of being taxed ▷ n person, income, property, etc, that is subject to tax

TAXABLES > TAXABLE

TAXABLY > TAXABLE

TAXACEOUS adj relating to a family of coniferous trees that includes the yews

TAXAMETER old variant of > TAXIMETER

TAXATION n levying of taxes

TAXATIONS > TAXATION

TAXATIVE > TAXATION

TAXED > TAX

TAXEME n any element of speech that may differentiate one utterance from another with a different meaning

TAXEMES > TAXEME

TAXEMIC > TAXEME

TAXER > TAX

TAXERS > TAX

TAXES > TAX

TAXI n car with a driver that may be hired to take people to any specified destination ▷ vb (of an aircraft) run along the ground before taking off or after landing

TAXIARCH n soldier in charge of a Greek taxis

TAXIARCHS > TAXIARCH

TAXICAB same as > TAXI

TAXICABS > TAXICAB

TAXIDERMY n art of stuffing and mounting animal skins to give them a lifelike appearance

TAXIED > TAXI

TAXIES > TAXIS

TAXIING > TAXI

TAXIMAN n taxi driver

TAXIMEN > TAXIMAN

TAXIMETER n meter fitted to a taxi to register the fare, based on the length of the journey

TAXING adj demanding, onerous

TAXINGLY > TAXING

TAXINGS > TAX

TAXIPLANE n aircraft that is available for hire

TAXIS n movement of a cell or organism in a particular direction in response to an external stimulus ancient Greek army unit

TAXITE n type of volcanic rock

TAXITES > TAXITE

TAXITIC > TAXITE

TAXIWAY n marked path along which aircraft taxi to or from a runway, parking area, etc

TAXIWAYS > TAXIWAY

TAXLESS > TAX

TAXMAN n collector of taxes

TAXMEN > TAXMAN

TAXOL n trademarked anti-cancer drug

TAXOLS > TAXOL

TAXON n any taxonomic group or rank

TAXONOMER > TAXONOMY

TAXONOMIC > TAXONOMY

TAXONOMY n classification of plants and animals into groups

TAXONS > TAXON

TAXOR > TAX

TAXORS > TAX

TAXPAID adj (of taxable products, esp wine) having had the applicable tax paid already

TAXPAYER n person or organization that pays taxes

TAXPAYERS > TAXPAYER

TAXPAYING > TAXPAYER

TAXUS n genus of conifers

TAXWISE adv regarding tax

TAXYING > TAXI

TAY Irish dialect word for > TEA

TAYASSUID n peccary

TAYBERRY n hybrid shrub produced by crossing a blackberry, raspberry, and loganberry

TAYRA n large arboreal musteline mammal, of Central and South America, with a dark brown body and paler head

TAYRAS > TAYRA

TAYS > TAY

TAZZA n wine cup with a shallow bowl and a circular foot

TAZZAS > TAZZA

TAZZE > TAZZA

TCHICK vb make a click by creating a vacuum in the mouth with the tongue pressed againt the palate then suddenly breaking the seal by withdrawing part of the tongue from the palate

TCHICKED > TCHICK

TCHICKING > TCHICK

TCHICKS > TCHICK

TCHOTCHKE n trinket

TE n (in tonic sol-fa) seventh degree of any major scale

TEA n drink made from infusing the dried leaves of an Asian bush in boiling water ▷ vb take tea

TEABAG n porous bag of tea leaves for infusion

TEABAGS > TEABAG

TEABERRY n berry of the wintergreen

TEABOARD n tea tray

TEABOARDS > TEABOARD

TEABOWL n small bowl used (instead of a teacup) for serving tea

TEABOWLS > TEABOWL

TEABOX n box for storing tea

TEABOXES > TEABOX

TEABREAD n loaf-shaped cake that contains dried fruit which has been steeped in cold tea before baking: served sliced and buttered

TEABREADS > TEABREAD

TEACAKE n flat bun, usually eaten toasted and buttered

TEACAKES > TEACAKE

TEACART n trolley from which tea is served

TEACARTS > TEACART

TEACH vb tell or show (someone) how to do something

TEACHABLE > TEACH

TEACHABLY > TEACH

TEACHER n person who teaches, esp in a school

TEACHERLY > TEACHER

TEACHERS > TEACHER

TEACHES > TEACH

TEACHIE old form of > TETCHY

TEACHING > TEACH

TEACHINGS > TEACH

TEACHLESS adj unable to be taught

TEACUP n cup out of which tea may be drunk

TEACUPFUL n amount a teacup will hold, about four fluid ounces

TEACUPS > TEACUP

TEAD old word for > TORCH

TEADE same as > TEAD

TEADES > TEADE

TEADS > TEAD

TEAED > TEA

TEAGLE vb raise or hoist using a tackle

TEAGLED > TEAGLE

TEAGLES > TEAGLE

TEAGLING > TEAGLE

TEAHOUSE n restaurant, esp in Japan or China, where tea and light refreshments are served

TEAHOUSES > TEAHOUSE

TEAING > TEA

TEAK n very hard wood of an E Indian tree

TEAKETTLE n kettle for boiling water to make tea

TEAKS > TEAK

TEAKWOOD another word for > TEAK

TEAKWOODS > TEAKWOOD

TEAL n kind of small duck

TEALIGHT n small candle

TEALIGHTS > TEALIGHT

TEALIKE adj resembling tea

TEALS > TEAL

TEAM n group of people forming one side in a game ▷ vb make or cause to make a team

TEAMAKER n person or thing that makes tea

TEAMAKERS > TEAMAKER

TEAMED > TEAM

TEAMER > TEAM

TEAMERS > TEAM

TEAMING > TEAM

TEAMINGS > TEAM

TEAMMATE n fellow member of a team

TEAMMATES > TEAMMATE

TEAMS > TEAM

TEAMSTER n commercial vehicle driver

TEAMSTERS > TEAMSTER

TEAMWISE adv in respect of a team; in the manner of a team

TEAMWORK n cooperative work by a team

TEAMWORKS > TEAMWORK

TEAPOT n container with a lid, spout, and handle for making and serving tea

TEAPOTS > TEAPOT

TEAPOY n small table or stand with a tripod base

TEAPOYS > TEAPOY

TEAR n drop of fluid appearing in and falling from the eye ▷ vb rip a hole in ▷ vb shed tears

TEARABLE > TEAR

TEARAWAY n wild or unruly person

TEARAWAYS > TEARAWAY

TEARDOWN n demolition; disassembly

TEARDOWNS > TEARDOWN

TEARDROP same as > TEAR

TEARDROPS > TEARDROP

TEARED > TEAR

TEARER > TEAR

TEARERS > TEAR

TEARFUL adj weeping or about to weep

TEARFULLY > TEARFUL

TEARGAS n gas or vaopr that makes the eyes smart and water ▷ vb deploy teargas against

TEARGASES > TEARGAS

TEARIER > TEARY

TEARIEST > TEARY

TEARILY > TEARY

TEARINESS > TEARY

TEARING > TEAR

TEARLESS > TEAR

TEAROOM same as > TEASHOP

TEAROOMS > TEAROOM

TEARS > TEAR

TEARSHEET n page in a newspaper or periodical that is cut or perforated so that it can be easily torn out

TEARSTAIN n stain or streak left by tears

TEARSTRIP n part of packaging torn to open it

TEARY adj characterized by, covered with, or secreting tears

TEAS > TEA

TEASABLE > TEASE

TEASE vb make fun of (someone) in a provoking or playful way ▷ n person who teases

TEASED > TEASE

TEASEL n plant with prickly leaves and flowers ▷ vb tease (a fabric)

TEASELED > TEASEL

TEASELER > TEASEL

TEASELERS > TEASEL

TEASELING > TEASEL

TEASELLED > TEASEL

TEASELLER > TEASEL

TEASELS > TEASEL

TEASER n annoying or difficult problem

TEASERS > TEASER

TEASES > TEASE

TEASHOP n restaurant where tea and light refreshments are served

TEASHOPS > TEASHOP

TEASING > TEASE

TEASINGLY > TEASE

TEASINGS > TEASE

TEASPOON n small spoon for stirring tea

TEASPOONS > TEASPOON

TEAT n nipple of a breast or udder

TEATASTER n person assessing teas by tasting them

TEATED > TEAT

TEATIME n late afternoon

TEATIMES > TEATIME

TEATS > TEAT

TEAWARE n implements and vessels for brewing and serving tea

TEAWARES > TEAWARE

TEAZE old variant of > TEASE

TEAZED > TEAZE

TEAZEL same as > TEASEL

TEAZELED > TEAZEL

TEAZELING > TEAZEL

TEAZELLED > TEAZEL

TEAZELS > TEAZEL

TEAZES > TEAZE

TEAZING > TEAZE

TEAZLE same as > TEASEL

TEAZLED > TEAZLE

TEAZLES > TEAZLE

TEAZLING > TEAZLE

TEBBAD n sandstorm

TEBBADS > TEBBAD

TEC short for > DETECTIVE

TECH n technical college

TECHED adj showing slight insanity

TECHIE n person who is skilled in the use of technology ▷ adj relating to or skilled in the use of technology

TECHIER > TECHY

TECHIES > TECHIE

TECHIEST > TECHY

TECHILY > TECHY

TECHINESS > TECHY

TECHNIC another word for > TECHNIQUE

TECHNICAL adj of or specializing in industrial, practical, or mechanical arts and applied sciences ▷ n small armed military truck

TECHNICS n study or theory of industry and industrial arts

TECHNIKON n technical college

TECHNIQUE n method or skill used for a particular task

TECHNO n type of electronic dance music with a very fast beat

TECHNOPOP n pop music sharing certain features with techno

TECHNOS > TECHNO

TECHS > TECH

TECHY same as > TECHIE

TECKEL n dachshund

TECKELS > TECKEL

TECS > TEC

TECTA > TECTUM

TECTAL > TECTUM

TECTIFORM adj in the form of a roof

TECTITE same as > TEKTITE

TECTITES > TECTITE

TECTONIC adj denoting or relating to construction or building

TECTONICS n study of the earth's crust and the forces affecting it

TECTONISM > TECTONIC

TECTORIAL as in tectorial membrane membrane in the inner ear that covers the organ of Corti

TECTRICES > TECTRIX

TECTRIX another name for > COVERT

TECTUM n any roof-like structure in the body, esp the dorsal area of the midbrain

TECTUMS > TECTUM

TED vb shake out (hay), so as to dry it

TEDDED > TED

TEDDER n machine equipped with a series of small rotating forks for tedding hay

TEDDERED > TEDDER

TEDDERING > TEDDER

TEDDERS > TEDDER

TEDDIE same as > TEDDY

TEDDIES > TEDDY

TEDDING > TED

TEDDY n teddy bear

TEDIER > TEDY
TEDIEST > TEDY
TEDIOSITY > TEDIOUS
TEDIOUS adj causing fatigue or boredom
TEDIOUSLY > TEDIOUS
TEDISOME old Scottish variant of > TEDIOUS
TEDIUM n monotony
TEDIUMS > TEDIUM
TEDS > TED
TEDY same as > TEDIOUS
TEE n small peg from which a golf ball can be played at the start of each hole ▷ vb position (the ball) ready for striking, on or as if on a tee
TEED > TEE
TEEING > TEE
TEEK adj in Indian English, well
TEEL same as > SESAME
TEELS > TEEL
TEEM vb be full of
TEEMED > TEEM
TEEMER > TEEM
TEEMERS > TEEM
TEEMFUL > TEEM
TEEMING > TEEM
TEEMINGLY > TEEM
TEEMLESS > TEEM
TEEMS > TEEM
TEEN n affliction or woe ▷ n teenager ▷ vb set alight
TEENAGE adj (of a person) aged between 13 and 19 ▷ n this period of time
TEENAGED adj (of a person) aged between 13 and 19
TEENAGER n person aged between 13 and 19
TEENAGERS > TEENAGER
TEENAGES > TEENAGE
TEEND same as > TIND
TEENDED > TEEND
TEENDING > TEEND
TEENDS > TEEND
TEENE same as > TEEN
TEENED > TEEN
TEENER > TEEN
TEENERS > TEEN
TEENES > TEENE
TEENFUL > TEEN
TEENIER > TEENY
TEENIEST > TEENY
TEENING > TEEN
TEENS > TEEN
TEENSIER > TEENSY
TEENSIEST > TEENSY
TEENSY same as > TEENY
TEENTIER > TEENTY
TEENTIEST > TEENTY
TEENTSIER > TEENTSY
TEENTSY same as > TEENY
TEENTY same as > TEENY
TEENY adj extremely small
TEENYBOP adj of, or relating to, a young teenager who avidly follows fashions in music and clothes
TEEPEE same as > TEPEE
TEEPEES > TEEPEE
TEER vb smear; daub

TEERED > TEER
TEERING > TEER
TEERS > TEER
TEES > TEE
TEETER vb wobble or move unsteadily
TEETERED > TEETER
TEETERING > TEETER
TEETERS > TEETER
TEETH > TOOTH
TEETHE vb (of a baby) grow his or her first teeth
TEETHED > TEETHE
TEETHER n object for an infant to bite on during teething
TEETHERS > TEETHER
TEETHES > TEETHE
TEETHING > TEETHE
TEETHINGS > TEETHING
TEETHLESS > TEETH
TEETOTAL adj drinking no alcohol ▷ vb advocate total abstinence from alcohol
TEETOTALS > TEETOTAL
TEETOTUM n spinning top bearing letters of the alphabet on its four sides
TEETOTUMS > TEETOTUM
TEF n annual grass, of NE Africa, grown for its grain
TEFF same as > TEF
TEFFS > TEFF
TEFILLAH n either of the pair of blackened square cases containing parchments inscribed with biblical passages, bound by leather thongs to the head and left arm, and worn by Jewish men during weekday morning prayers
TEFILLIN > TEFILLAH
TEFLON n a trademark for polytetrafluoroethylene when used in nonstick cooking vessels
TEFLONS > TEFLON
TEFS > TEF
TEG n two-year-old sheep
TEGG same as > TEG
TEGGS > TEGG
TEGMEN n either of the leathery forewings of the cockroach and related insects
TEGMENTA > TEGMENTUM
TEGMENTAL > TEGMENTUM
TEGMENTUM n one of the hard protective sometimes hairy or resinous specialized leaves surrounding the buds of certain plants
TEGMINA > TEGMEN
TEGMINAL > TEGMEN
TEGS > TEG
TEGU n large South American lizard
TEGUA n type of moccasin
TEGUAS > TEGUA
TEGUEXIN same as > TEGU
TEGUEXINS > TEGUEXIN
TEGULA n one of a pair of

coverings of the forewings of certain insects
TEGULAE > TEGULA
TEGULAR adj of, relating to, or resembling a tile or tiles
TEGULARLY > TEGULAR
TEGULATED adj overlapping in the manner of roof tiles
TEGUMEN same as > TEGMEN
TEGUMENT n protective layer around an ovule
TEGUMENTS > TEGUMENT
TEGUMINA > TEGUMEN
TEGUS > TEGU
TEHR same as > TAHR
TEHRS > TEHR
TEHSIL n administrative region in some S Asian countries
TEHSILDAR n person who administrates a tehsil
TEHSILS > TEHSIL
TEIGLACH npl morsels of dough boiled in honey, eaten as a dessert
TEIID n member of the Teiidae family of lizards
TEIIDS > TEIID
TEIL n lime tree
TEILS > TEIL
TEIN n monetary unit of Kazakhstan
TEIND Scot and northern English word for > TITHE
TEINDED > TEIND
TEINDING > TEIND
TEINDS > TEIND
TEINS > TEIN
TEKKIE variant of > TECHIE
TEKKIES > TEKKIE
TEKNONYMY n practice of naming a child after his or her parent
TEKTITE n small dark glassy object found in several areas around the world, thought to be a product of meteorite impact
TEKTITES > TEKTITE
TEKTITIC > TEKTITE
TEL same as > TELL
TELA n any delicate tissue or weblike structure
TELAE > TELA
TELAMON n column in the form of a male figure, used to support an entablature
TELAMONES > TELAMON
TELAMONS > TELAMON
TELARY adj capable of spinning a web
TELCO n telecommunications company
TELCOS > TELCO
TELD same as > TAULD
TELE same as > TELLY
TELECAST vb broadcast by television ▷ n television broadcast

TELECASTS > TELECAST
TELECHIR n robot arm controlled by a human operator
TELECHIRS > TELECHIR
TELECINE n apparatus for producing a television signal from cinematograph film
TELECINES > TELECINE
TELECOM n telecommunications
TELECOMS same as > TELECOM
TELEDU n badger of SE Asia and Indonesia, having dark brown hair with a white stripe along the back and producing a fetid secretion from the anal glands when attacked
TELEDUS > TELEDU
TELEFAX another word for > FAX
TELEFAXED > TELEFAX
TELEFAXES > TELEFAX
TELEFILM n TV movie
TELEFILMS > TELEFILM
TELEGA n rough four-wheeled cart used in Russia
TELEGAS > TELEGA
TELEGENIC adj having or showing a pleasant television image
TELEGONIC > TELEGONY
TELEGONY n supposed influence of a previous sire on offspring borne by a female to other sires
TELEGRAM n formerly, a message sent by telegraph ▷ vb send a telegram
TELEGRAMS > TELEGRAM
TELEGRAPH n formerly, a system for sending messages over a distance along a cable ▷ vb communicate by telegraph
TELEMAN n noncommissioned officer in the US navy, usually charged with communications duties
TELEMARK n turn in which one ski is placed far forward of the other and turned gradually inwards ▷ vb perform a telemark turn
TELEMARKS > TELEMARK
TELEMATIC adj of, or relating to, the branch of science concerned with the use of technological devices to transmit information over long distances
TELEMEN > TELEMAN
TELEMETER n any device for recording or measuring a distant event and transmitting the data to a receiver or observer ▷ vb obtain and transmit (data) from a distant source, esp from a spacecraft

TELEMETRY *n* use of electronic devices to record or measure a distant event and transmit the data to a receiver

TELEOLOGY *n* belief that all things have a predetermined purpose

TELEONOMY *n* condition of having a fundamental purpose

TELEOSAUR *n* type of crocodile from the Jurassic period

TELEOST *n* bony fish with rayed fins and a swim bladder ▷ *adj* of, relating to, or belonging to this type of fish

TELEOSTS > TELEOST

TELEPATH *n* person who is telepathic ▷ *vb* practise telepathy

TELEPATHS > TELEPATH

TELEPATHY *n* direct communication between minds

TELEPHEME *n* any message sent by telephone

TELEPHONE *n* device for transmitting sound over a distance along wires ▷ *vb* call or talk to (a person) by telephone ▷ *adj* of or using a telephone

TELEPHONY *n* system of telecommunications for the transmission of speech or other sounds

TELEPHOTO *n* short for telephoto lens: a compound camera lens that produces a magnified image of distant objects

TELEPIC *n* feature-length film made for television

TELEPICS > TELEPIC

TELEPLAY *n* play written for television

TELEPLAYS > TELEPLAY

TELEPOINT *n* system providing a place where a cordless telephone can be connected to a telephone network

TELEPORT *vb* (in science fiction) to transport (a person or object) across a distance instantaneously

TELEPORTS > TELEPORT

TELERAN *n* electronic navigational aid in which the image of a ground-based radar system is televised to aircraft in flight so that a pilot can see the position of his aircraft in relation to others

TELERANS > TELERAN

TELERGIC > TELERGY

TELERGIES > TELERGY

TELERGY *n* name for the form of energy supposedly transferred during telepathy

TELES > TELE

TELESALE > TELESALES

TELESALES *n* selling of a product or service by telephone

TELESCOPE *n* optical instrument for magnifying distant objects ▷ *vb* shorten

TELESCOPY *n* branch of astronomy concerned with the use and design of telescopes

TELESEME *n* old-fashioned electric signalling system

TELESEMES > TELESEME

TELESES > TELESIS

TELESHOP *vb* buy goods by telephone or Internet

TELESHOPS > TELESHOP

TELESIS *n* purposeful use of natural and social processes to obtain specific social goals

TELESM *n* talisman

TELESMS > TELESM

TELESTIC *adj* relating to a hierophant

TELESTICH *n* short poem in which the last letters of each successive line form a word

TELESTICS *n* ancient pseudoscientific art of animating statues, idols, etc, or causing them to be inhabited by a diety

TELETEX *n* international means of communicating text between a variety of terminals

TELETEXES > TELETEX

TELETEXT *n* system which shows information and news on television screens

TELETEXTS > TELETEXT

TELETHON *n* lengthy television programme to raise charity funds, etc

TELETHONS > TELETHON

TELETRON *n* system for showing enlarged televisual images in eg sports stadiums

TELETRONS > TELETRON

TELETYPE *vb* send typed message by telegraph

TELETYPED > TELETYPE

TELETYPES > TELETYPE

TELEVIEW *vb* watch television

TELEVIEWS > TELEVIEW

TELEVISE *vb* broadcast on television

TELEVISED > TELEVISE

TELEVISER > TELEVISE

TELEVISES > TELEVISE

TELEVISOR *n* apparatus through which one transmits or receives televisual images

TELEWORK *vb* work from home, communicating by computer, telephone etc

TELEWORKS > TELEWORK

TELEX *n* international communication service using teleprinters ▷ *vb* transmit by telex

TELEXED > TELEX

TELEXES > TELEX

TELEXING > TELEX

TELFER *n* an overhead transport system

TELFERAGE *n* overhead transport system in which an electrically driven truck runs along a single rail or cable, the load being suspended in a separate car beneath

TELFERED > TELFER

TELFERIC > TELFER

TELFERING > TELFER

TELFERS > TELFER

TELFORD *n* road built using a method favoured by Thomas Telford (1757-1834)

TELFORDS > TELFORD

TELIA > TELIUM

TELIAL > TELIUM

TELIC *adj* directed or moving towards some goal

TELICALLY > TELIC

TELIUM *n* spore-producing body of some rust fungi in which the teliospores are formed

TELL *vb* make known in words ▷ *n* large mound resulting from the accumulation of rubbish on a long-settled site, esp one with mudbrick buildings, particularly in the Middle East

TELLABLE > TELL

TELLAR *same as* > TILLER

TELLARED > TELLAR

TELLARING > TELLAR

TELLARS > TELLAR

TELLEN *same as* > TELLIN

TELLENS > TELLEN

TELLER *n* narrator ▷ *vb* (of a plant) to produce tillers

TELLERED > TELLER

TELLERING > TELLER

TELLERS > TELLER

TELLIES > TELLY

TELLIN *n* slim marine bivalve molluscs that live in intertidal sand

TELLING > TELL

TELLINGLY > TELL

TELLINGS > TELL

TELLINOID > TELLIN

TELLINS > TELLIN

TELLS > TELL

TELLTALE *n* person who reveals secrets ▷ *adj* revealing

TELLTALES > TELLTALE

TELLURAL *adj* tellurial; of or relating to the earth

TELLURATE *n* any salt or ester of telluric acid

TELLURIAN *same as* > TELLURION

TELLURIC *adj* of, relating to, or originating on or in the earth or soil

TELLURIDE *n* any compound of tellurium, esp one formed between tellurium and a more electropositive element or group

TELLURION *n* instrument that shows how day and night and the seasons result from the tilt of the earth, its rotation on its axis, and its revolution around the sun

TELLURISE *same as* > TELLURIZE

TELLURITE *n* any salt or ester of tellurous acid

TELLURIUM *n* brittle silvery-white nonmetallic element

TELLURIZE *vb* mix or combine with tellurium

TELLUROUS *adj* of or containing tellurium, esp in a low valence state

TELLUS *n* earth

TELLUSES > TELLUS

TELLY *n* television

TELLYS > TELLY

TELNET *n* computer system allowing one user to access remotely other computers on the same network ▷ *vb* use a telnet system

TELNETED > TELNET

TELNETING > TELNET

TELNETS > TELNET

TELNETTED > TELNET

TELOI > TELOS

TELOME *n* fundamental unit of a plant's structure

TELOMERE *n* either of the ends of a chromosome

TELOMERES > TELOMERE

TELOMES > TELOME

TELOMIC > TELOME

TELOPHASE *n* final stage of mitosis, during which a set of chromosomes is present at each end of the cell and a nuclear membrane forms around each, producing two new nuclei

TELOS *n* objective; ultimate purpose

TELOTAXES > TELOTAXIS

TELOTAXIS *n* movement of an organism in response to one particular stimulus, overriding any response to other stimuli present

TELPHER *same as* > TELFERAGE

TELPHERED > TELPHER

TELPHERIC > TELPHER

TELPHERS > TELPHER

TELS > TEL

TELSON *n* last segment or an appendage on the last segment of the body of crustaceans and arachnids

TELSONIC > TELSON

TELSONS > TELSON

TELT *same as* > TAULD

TEMAZEPAM *n* sedative in the form of a gel-like capsule, which is taken orally or melted and injected by drug users

TEMBLOR *n* earthquake or earth tremor

TEMBLORES > TEMBLOR

TEMBLORS > TEMBLOR

TEME *old variant of* > TEAM

TEMED > TEME

TEMENE > TEMENOS

TEMENOS *n* sacred area, esp one surrounding a temple

TEMERITY *n* boldness or audacity

TEMEROUS > TEMERITY

TEMES > TEME

TEMP *same as* > TEMPORARY

TEMPED > TEMP

TEMPEH *n* fermented soya beans

TEMPEHS > TEMPEH

TEMPER *n* outburst of anger ▷ *vb* make less extreme

TEMPERA *n* painting medium for powdered pigments

TEMPERAS > TEMPERA

TEMPERATE *adj* (of climate) not extreme ▷ *vb* temper

TEMPERED *adj* (of a scale) having the frequency differences between notes adjusted in accordance with the system of equal temperament

TEMPERER > TEMPER

TEMPERERS > TEMPER

TEMPERING > TEMPER

TEMPERS > TEMPER

TEMPEST *n* violent storm ▷ *vb* agitate or disturb violently

TEMPESTED > TEMPEST

TEMPESTS > TEMPEST

TEMPI > TEMPO

TEMPING > TEMP

TEMPLAR *n* lawyer, esp a barrister, who lives or has chambers in the Inner or Middle Temple in London

TEMPLARS > TEMPLAR

TEMPLATE *n* pattern used to cut out shapes accurately

TEMPLATES > TEMPLATE

TEMPLE *n* building for worship

TEMPLED > TEMPLE

TEMPLES > TEMPLE

TEMPLET *same as* > TEMPLATE

TEMPLETS > TEMPLET

TEMPO *n* rate or pace

TEMPORAL *adj* of time ▷ *n* any body part relating to or near the temple or temples

TEMPORALS > TEMPORAL

TEMPORARY *adj* lasting only for a short time ▷ *n* person, esp a secretary or other office worker, employed on a temporary basis

TEMPORE *adv* in the time of

TEMPORISE *same as* > TEMPORIZE

TEMPORIZE *vb* gain time by negotiation or evasiveness

TEMPOS > TEMPO

TEMPS > TEMP

TEMPT *vb* entice (a person) to do something wrong

TEMPTABLE > TEMPT

TEMPTED > TEMPT

TEMPTER > TEMPT

TEMPTERS > TEMPT

TEMPTING *adj* attractive or inviting

TEMPTINGS > TEMPTING

TEMPTRESS *n* woman who sets out to allure or seduce a man or men

TEMPTS > TEMPT

TEMPURA *n* Japanese dish of seafood or vegetables dipped in batter and deep-fried, often at the table

TEMPURAS > TEMPURA

TEMS *same as* > TEMSE

TEMSE *vb* sieve

TEMSED > TEMSE

TEMSES > TEMSE

TEMSING > TEMSE

TEMULENCE *n* drunkenness

TEMULENCY *same as* > TEMULENCE

TEMULENT > TEMULENCE

TEN *n* one more than nine ▷ *adj* amounting to ten

TENABLE *adj* able to be upheld or maintained

TENABLY > TENABLE

TENACE *n* holding of two nonconsecutive high cards of a suit, such as the ace and queen

TENACES > TENACE

TENACIOUS *adj* holding fast

TENACITY > TENACIOUS

TENACULA > TENACULUM

TENACULUM *n* surgical or dissecting instrument for grasping and holding parts, consisting of a slender hook mounted in a handle

TENAIL *same as* > TENAILLE

TENAILLE *n* low outwork in the main ditch between two bastions

TENAILLES > TENAILLE

TENAILLON *n* outwork shoring up a ravelin

TENAILS > TENAIL

TENANCIES > TENANCY

TENANCY *n* temporary possession or use of lands or property owned by somebody else, in return for payment

TENANT *n* person who rents land or a building ▷ *vb* hold (land or property) as a tenant

TENANTED > TENANT

TENANTING > TENANT

TENANTRY *n* tenants collectively

TENANTS > TENANT

TENCH *n* freshwater game fish of the carp family

TENCHES > TENCH

TEND *vb* be inclined

TENDANCE *n* care and attention

TENDANCES > TENDANCE

TENDED > TEND

TENDENCE *same as* > TENDENCY

TENDENCES > TENDENCE

TENDENCY *n* inclination to act in a certain way

TENDENZ *same as* > TENDENCY

TENDENZEN > TENDENZ

TENDER *adj* not tough ▷ *vb* offer ▷ *n* such an offer

TENDERED > TENDER

TENDERER > TENDER

TENDERERS > TENDER

TENDEREST > TENDER

TENDERING > TENDER

TENDERISE *same as* > TENDERIZE

TENDERIZE *vb* soften (meat) by pounding or treatment with a special substance

TENDERLY > TENDER

TENDERS > TENDER

TENDING > TEND

TENDINOUS *adj* of, relating to, possessing, or resembling tendons

TENDON *n* strong tissue attaching a muscle to a bone

TENDONS > TENDON

TENDRE *n* care

TENDRES > TENDRE

TENDRESSE *n* feeling of love; tenderness

TENDRIL *n* slender stem by which a climbing plant clings

TENDRILED > TENDRIL

TENDRILS > TENDRIL

TENDRON *n* shoot

TENDRONS > TENDRON

TENDS > TEND

TENDU *n* position in ballet

TENDUS > TENDU

TENE *same as* > TEEN

TENEBRAE *n* darkness

TENEBRIO *n* type of small mealworm

TENEBRIOS > TENEBRIO

TENEBRISM *n* school, style, or method of painting, adopted chiefly by 17th-century Spanish and Neapolitan painters, esp Caravaggio, characterized by large areas of dark colours, usually relieved with a shaft of light

TENEBRIST > TENEBRISM

TENEBRITY *n* darkness; gloominess

TENEBROSE *same as* > TENEBROUS

TENEBROUS *adj* gloomy, shadowy, or dark

TENEMENT *n* (esp in Scotland or the US) building divided into several flats

TENEMENTS > TENEMENT

TENENDUM *n* part of a deed that specifies the terms of tenure

TENENDUMS > TENENDUM

TENES > TENE

TENESMIC > TENESMUS

TENESMUS *n* bowel disorder

TENET *n* doctrine or belief

TENETS > TENET

TENFOLD *n* one tenth

TENFOLDS > TENFOLD

TENGE *n* standard monetary unit of Kazakhstan, divided into 100 tiyn

TENGES > TENGE

TENIA *same as* > TAENIA

TENIACIDE *n* substance, esp a drug, that kills tapeworms

TENIAE > TENIA

TENIAFUGE *same as* > TENIACIDE

TENIAS > TENIA

TENIASES > TENIASIS

TENIASIS *same as* > TAENIASIS

TENIOID > TENIA

TENNE *n* tawny colour

TENNER *n* ten-pound note

TENNERS > TENNER

TENNES > TENNE

TENNIES > TENNY

TENNIS *n* game in which players use rackets to hit a ball back and forth over a net

TENNISES > TENNIS

TENNIST *n* tennis player

TENNISTS > TENNIST

TENNO *n* formal title of the Japanese emperor, esp when regarded as a divine religious leader

TENNOS > TENNO

TENNY *same as* > TENNE

TENON *n* projecting end on a piece of wood fitting into a slot in another ▷ *vb* form a tenon on (a piece of wood)

TENONED > TENON

TENONER > TENON

TENONERS > TENON

TENONING > TENON

TENONS > TENON

t

TENOR n (singer with) the second highest male voice ▷ adj (of a voice or instrument) between alto and baritone

TENORIST n musician playing any tenor instrument

TENORISTS > TENORIST

TENORITE n black mineral found in copper deposits and consisting of copper oxide in the form of either metallic scales or earthy masses. Formula: CuO

TENORITES > TENORITE

TENORLESS > TENOR

TENOROON n tenor bassoon

TENOROONS > TENOROON

TENORS > TENOR

TENOTOMY n surgical division of a tendon

TENOUR old variant of > TENOR

TENOURS > TENOUR

TENPENCE n sum of money equivalent to ten pennies

TENPENCES > TENPENCE

TENPENNY adj (of a nail) three inches in length

TENPIN n one of the pins used in tenpin bowling

TENPINS > TENPIN

TENREC n small mammal resembling hedgehogs or shrews

TENRECS > TENREC

TENS > TEN

TENSE adj emotionally strained ▷ vb make or become tense ▷ n form of a verb showing the time of action

TENSED > TENSE

TENSELESS > TENSE

TENSELY > TENSE

TENSENESS > TENSE

TENSER > TENSE

TENSES > TENSE

TENSEST > TENSE

TENSIBLE adj capable of being stretched

TENSIBLY > TENSIBLE

TENSILE adj of tension

TENSILELY > TENSILE

TENSILITY > TENSILE

TENSING > TENSE

TENSION n hostility or suspense ▷ vb tighten

TENSIONAL > TENSION

TENSIONED > TENSION

TENSIONER > TENSION

TENSIONS > TENSION

TENSITIES > TENSITY

TENSITY rare word for > TENSION

TENSIVE adj of or causing tension or strain

TENSON n type of French lyric poem

TENSONS > TENSON

TENSOR n any muscle that can cause a part to become firm or tense

TENSORIAL > TENSOR

TENSORS > TENSOR

TENT n portable canvas shelter ▷ vb camp in a tent

TENTACLE n flexible organ of many invertebrates, used for grasping, feeding, etc

TENTACLED > TENTACLE

TENTACLES > TENTACLE

TENTACULA > TENTACLE

TENTAGE n tents collectively

TENTAGES > TENTAGE

TENTATION n method of achieving the correct adjustment of a mechanical device by a series of trials

TENTATIVE adj provisional or experimental ▷ n investigative attempt

TENTED > TENT

TENTER > TENT

TENTERED > TENT

TENTERING > TENT

TENTERS > TENT

TENTFUL n number of people or objects that can fit in a tent

TENTFULS > TENTFUL

TENTH n (of) number ten in a series ▷ adj coming after the ninth in numbering or counting order, position, time, etc ▷ adv after the ninth person, position, event, etc

TENTHLY same as > TENTH

TENTHS > TENTH

TENTIE adj wary

TENTIER > TENTIE

TENTIEST > TENTIE

TENTIGO n morbid preoccupation with sex

TENTIGOS > TENTIGO

TENTING > TENT

TENTINGS > TENT

TENTLESS > TENT

TENTLIKE > TENT

TENTMAKER n maker of tents

TENTORIA > TENTORIUM

TENTORIAL > TENTORIUM

TENTORIUM n tough membrane covering the upper part of the cerebellum

TENTS > TENT

TENTWISE adv in the manner of a tent

TENTY same as > TENTIE

TENUE n deportment

TENUES > TENUIS

TENUIOUS same as > TENUOUS

TENUIS n (in the grammar of classical Greek) any of the voiceless stops as represented by kappa, pi, or tau (k, p, t)

TENUITIES > TENUOUS

TENUITY > TENUOUS

TENUOUS adj slight or flimsy

TENUOUSLY > TENUOUS

TENURABLE > TENURE

TENURE n (period of) the holding of an office or position ▷ vb to assign a tenured position to

TENURED adj having tenure of office

TENURES > TENURE

TENURIAL > TENURE

TENURING > TENURE

TENUTI > TENUTO

TENUTO adv (of a note) to be held for or beyond its full time value ▷ vb note sustained thus

TENUTOS > TENUTO

TENZON same as > TENSON

TENZONS > TENZON

TEOCALLI n any of various truncated pyramids built by the Aztecs as bases for their temples

TEOCALLIS > TEOCALLI

TEOPAN n enclosure surrounding a teocalli

TEOPANS > TEOPAN

TEOSINTE n tall Central American annual grass, related to maize and grown for forage in the southern US

TEOSINTES > TEOSINTE

TEPA n type of tree native to South America

TEPAL n any of the subdivisions of a perianth that is not clearly differentiated into calyx and corolla

TEPALS > TEPAL

TEPAS > TEPA

TEPEE n cone-shaped tent, formerly used by Native Americans

TEPEES > TEPEE

TEPEFIED > TEPEFY

TEPEFIES > TEPEFY

TEPEFY vb make or become tepid

TEPEFYING > TEPEFY

TEPHIGRAM n chart depicting variations in atmospheric conditions relative to altitude

TEPHILLAH same as > TEFILLAH

TEPHILLIN > TEPHILLAH

TEPHRA n solid matter ejected during a volcanic eruption

TEPHRAS > TEPHRA

TEPHRITE n variety of basalt

TEPHRITES > TEPHRITE

TEPHRITIC > TEPHRITE

TEPHROITE n manganese silicate

TEPID adj slightly warm

TEPIDARIA npl in Ancient Rome, the warm rooms of the baths

TEPIDER > TEPID

TEPIDEST > TEPID

TEPIDITY > TEPID

TEPIDLY > TEPID

TEPIDNESS > TEPID

TEPOY same as > TEAPOY

TEPOYS > TEPOY

TEQUILA n Mexican alcoholic drink

TEQUILAS > TEQUILA

TEQUILLA same as > TEQUILA

TEQUILLAS > TEQUILLA

TERABYTE n large unit of computer memory

TERABYTES > TERABYTE

TERAFLOP n measure of processing speed, consisting of a thousand billion floating-point operations a second

TERAFLOPS > TERAFLOP

TERAGLIN n edible marine fish of Australia which has fine scales and is blue in colour

TERAGLINS > TERAGLIN

TERAHERTZ n large unit of electrical frequency

TERAI n felt hat with a wide brim worn in subtropical regions

TERAIS > TERAI

TERAKIHI same as > TARAKIHI

TERAKIHIS > TERAKIHI

TERAOHM n unit of resistance equal to 10^{12}ohms

TERAOHMS > TERAOHM

TERAPH n any of various small household gods or images venerated by ancient Semitic peoples

TERAPHIM > TERAPH

TERAPHIMS > TERAPH

TERAS n monstrosity; teratism

TERATA > TERAS

TERATISM n malformed animal or human, esp in the fetal stage

TERATISMS > TERATISM

TERATOGEN n any substance, organism, or process that causes malformations in a fetus

TERATOID adj resembling a monster

TERATOMA n tumour or group of tumours composed of tissue foreign to the site of growth

TERATOMAS > TERATOMA

TERAWATT n unit of power equal to one million megawatts

TERAWATTS > TERAWATT

TERBIA n amorphous white insoluble powder

TERBIAS > TERBIA

TERBIC > TERBIUM

TERBIUM n rare metallic element

TERBIUMS > TERBIUM

TERCE n third of the seven canonical hours of the divine office, originally fixed at the third hour of the day, about 9 am

TERCEL n male falcon or hawk, esp as used in falconry

TERCELET same as > TERCEL

TERCELETS > TERCELET

TERCELS > TERCEL

TERCES > TERCE

TERCET n group of three lines of verse that rhyme together or are connected by rhyme with adjacent groups of three lines

TERCETS > TERCET

TERCIO n regiment of Spanish or Italian infantry

TERCIOS > TERCIO

TEREBENE n mixture of hydrocarbons prepared from oil of turpentine and sulphuric acid, used to make paints and varnishes and medicinally as an expectorant and antiseptic

TEREBENES > TEREBENE

TEREBIC as in terebic acid white crystalline carboxylic acid produced by the action of nitric acid on turpentin

TEREBINTH n small anacardiaceous tree with winged leafstalks and clusters of small flowers, and yielding a turpentine

TEREBRA n ancient Roman device used for boring holes in defensive walls

TEREBRAE > TEREBRA

TEREBRANT n type of hymenopterous insect

TEREBRAS > TEREBRA

TEREBRATE adj (of animals, esp insects) having a boring or penetrating organ, such as a sting ⊳ vb bore

TEREDINES > TEREDO

TEREDO n marine mollusc that bores into and destroys submerged timber

TEREDOS > TEREDO

TEREFA same as > TREF

TEREFAH same as > TREF

TEREK n type of sandpiper

TEREKS > TEREK

TERES n shoulder muscle

TERETE adj (esp of plant parts) smooth and usually cylindrical and tapering

TERETES > TERETE

TERF old variant of > TURF

TERFE old variant of > TURF

TERFES > TERFE

TERFS > TERF

TERGA > TERGUM

TERGAL > TERGUM

TERGITE n constituent part of a tergum

TERGITES > TERGITE

TERGUM n cuticular plate

covering the dorsal surface of a body segment of an arthropod

TERIYAKI adj basted with soy sauce and rice wine and broiled over an open fire ⊳ n dish prepared in this way

TERIYAKIS > TERIYAKI

TERM n word or expression ⊳ vb name or designate

TERMAGANT n unpleasant and bad-tempered woman

TERMED > TERM

TERMER same as > TERMOR

TERMERS > TERMER

TERMINAL adj (of an illness) ending in death ⊳ n place where people or vehicles begin or end a journey

TERMINALS > TERMINAL

TERMINATE vb bring or come to an end

TERMINER n person or thing that limits or determines

TERMINERS > TERMINER

TERMING > TERM

TERMINI > TERMINUS

TERMINISM n philosophical theory

TERMINIST > TERMINISM

TERMINUS n railway or bus station at the end of a line

TERMITARY n termite nest

TERMITE n white antlike insect that destroys timber

TERMITES > TERMITE

TERMITIC > TERMITE

TERMLESS adj without limit or boundary

TERMLIES > TERMLY

TERMLY n publication issued once a term

TERMOR n person who holds an estate for a term of years or until he dies

TERMORS > TERMOR

TERMS > TERM

TERMTIME n time during a term, esp a school or university term

TERMTIMES > TERMTIME

TERN n gull-like sea bird with a forked tail and pointed wings

TERNAL > TERN

TERNARIES > TERNARY

TERNARY adj consisting of three parts ⊳ n group of three

TERNATE adj (esp of a leaf) consisting of three leaflets or other parts

TERNATELY > TERNATE

TERNE n alloy of lead containing tin (10·20 per cent) and antimony (1·5·2 per cent) ⊳ vb coat with this alloy

TERNED > TERNE

TERNES > TERNE

TERNING > TERNE

TERNION n group of three

TERNIONS > TERNION

TERNS > TERN

TERPENE n any one of a class of unsaturated hydrocarbons, such as the carotenes, that are found in the essential oils of many plants

TERPENES > TERPENE

TERPENIC > TERPENE

TERPENOID > TERPENE

TERPINEOL n terpene alcohol with an odour of lilac, present in several essential oils

TERPINOL same as > TERPINEOL

TERPINOLS > TERPINOL

TERRA n (in legal contexts) earth or land

TERRACE n row of houses built as one block ⊳ vb form into or provide with a terrace

TERRACED > TERRACE

TERRACES > TERRACE

TERRACING n series of terraces, esp one dividing a slope into a steplike system of flat narrow fields

TERRAE > TERRA

TERRAFORM vb engage in planetary engineering to enhance the capacity of an extraterrestrial planetary environment to sustain life

TERRAIN same as > TERRANE

TERRAINS > TERRAIN

TERRAMARA n neolithic Italian pile-dwelling

TERRAMARE > TERRAMARA

TERRANE n series of rock formations, esp one having a prevalent type of rock

TERRANES > TERRANE

TERRAPIN n small turtle-like reptile

TERRAPINS > TERRAPIN

TERRARIA > TERRARIUM

TERRARIUM n enclosed container for small plants or animals

TERRAS same as > TRASS

TERRASES > TERRAS

TERRAZZO n floor of marble chips set in mortar and polished

TERRAZZOS > TERRAZZO

TERREEN old variant of > TUREEN

TERREENS > TERREEN

TERRELLA n magnetic globe designed to simulate and demonstrate the earth's magnetic fields

TERRELLAS > TERRELLA

TERRENE adj of or relating to the earth ⊳ n land

TERRENELY > TERRENE

TERRENES > TERRENE

TERRET n either of the two metal rings on a harness

saddle through which the reins are passed

TERRETS > TERRET

TERRIBLE adj very serious ⊳ n something terrible

TERRIBLES > TERRIBLE

TERRIBLY adv in a terrible manner

TERRICOLE n plant or animal living on land

TERRIER n any of various breeds of small active dog

TERRIERS > TERRIER

TERRIES > TERRY

TERRIFIC adj great or intense

TERRIFIED > TERRIFY

TERRIFIER > TERRIFY

TERRIFIES > TERRIFY

TERRIFY vb fill with fear

TERRINE n earthenware dish with a lid

TERRINES > TERRINE

TERRIT same as > TERRET

TERRITORY n district

TERRITS > TERRIT

TERROIR n combination of factors, including soil, climate, and environment, that gives a wine its distinctive character

TERROIRS > TERROIR

TERROR n great fear

TERRORFUL > TERROR

TERRORISE same as > TERRORIZE

TERRORISM n use of violence and intimidation to achieve political ends

TERRORIST n person who employs terror or terrorism, esp as a political weapon

TERRORIZE vb force or oppress by fear or violence

TERRORS > TERROR

TERRY n fabric with small loops covering both sides, used esp for making towels

TERSE adj neat and concise

TERSELY > TERSE

TERSENESS > TERSE

TERSER > TERSE

TERSEST > TERSE

TERSION n action of rubbing off or wiping

TERSIONS > TERSION

TERTIA same as > TERCIO

TERTIAL same as > TERTIARY

TERTIALS > TERTIAL

TERTIAN adj (of a fever or the symptoms of a disease, esp malaria) occurring every other day ⊳ n tertian fever or symptoms

TERTIANS > TERTIAN

TERTIARY adj third in degree, order, etc ⊳ n any of the tertiary feathers

TERTIAS > TERTIA

TERTIUM as in tertium quid unknown or indefinite thing related in some way to two known or definite things, but distinct from both

TERTIUS n third (in a group)

TERTIUSES > TERTIUS

TERTS n card game using 32 cards

TERVALENT same as > TRIVALENT

TERYLENE n tradename for a synthetic polyester fibre or fabric based on terephthalic acid, characterized by lightness and crease resistance and used for clothing, sheets, ropes, sails, etc

TERYLENES > TERYLENE

TERZETTA n tercet

TERZETTAS > TERZETTA

TERZETTI > TERZETTO

TERZETTO n trio, esp a vocal one

TERZETTOS > TERZETTO

TES > TE

TESLA n derived SI unit of magnetic flux density equal to a flux of 1 weber in an area of 1 square metre.

TESLAS > TESLA

TESSELATE vb cover with small tiles

TESSELLA n little tessera

TESSELLAE > TESSELLA

TESSELLAR adj of or relating to tessellae

TESSERA n small square tile used in mosaics

TESSERACT n cube inside another cube

TESSERAE > TESSERA

TESSERAL > TESSERA

TESSITURA n general pitch level of a piece of vocal music

TESSITURE > TESSITURA

TEST vb try out to ascertain the worth, capability, or endurance of ▷ n critical examination

TESTA n hard outer layer of a seed

TESTABLE > TEST

TESTACEAN n microscopic animal with hard shell

TESTACIES > TESTATE

TESTACY > TESTATE

TESTAE > TESTA

TESTAMENT n proof or tribute

TESTAMUR n certificate proving an examination has been passed

TESTAMURS > TESTAMUR

TESTATE adj having left a valid will ▷ n person who dies and leaves a legally valid will

TESTATES > TESTATE

TESTATION > TESTATOR

TESTATOR n maker of a will

TESTATORS > TESTATOR

TESTATRIX same as > TESTATOR

TESTATUM n part of a purchase deed

TESTATUMS > TESTATUM

TESTCROSS vb subject to a testcross, a genetic test for ascertaining whether an individual is homozygous or heterozygous

TESTE n witness

TESTED > TEST

TESTEE n person subjected to a test

TESTEES > TESTEE

TESTER n person or thing that tests or is used for testing

TESTERN vb give (someone) a teston

TESTERNED > TESTERN

TESTERNS > TESTERN

TESTERS > TESTER

TESTES > TESTIS

TESTICLE n either of the two male reproductive glands

TESTICLES > TESTICLE

TESTIER > TESTY

TESTIEST > TESTY

TESTIFIED > TESTIFY

TESTIFIER > TESTIFY

TESTIFIES > TESTIFY

TESTIFY vb give evidence under oath

TESTILY > TESTY

TESTIMONY n declaration of truth or fact ▷ vb testify

TESTINESS > TESTY

TESTING > TEST

TESTINGS > TEST

TESTIS same as > TESTICLE

TESTON n French silver coin of the 16th century

TESTONS > TESTON

TESTOON same as > TESTON

TESTOONS > TESTOON

TESTRIL same as > TESTRILL

TESTRILL n sixpence

TESTRILLS > TESTRILL

TESTRILS > TESTRIL

TESTS > TEST

TESTUDO n form of shelter used by the ancient Roman Army for protection against attack from above, consisting either of a mobile arched structure or of overlapping shields held by the soldiers over their heads

TESTUDOS > TESTUDO

TESTY adj irritable or touchy

TET same as > TETH

TETANAL > TETANUS

TETANIC adj of, relating to, or producing tetanus or the spasms of tetanus ▷ n tetanic drug or agent

TETANICAL > TETANUS

TETANICS > TETANIC

TETANIES > TETANY

TETANISE same as > TETANIZE

TETANISED > TETANISE

TETANISES > TETANISE

TETANIZE vb induce tetanus in (a muscle)

TETANIZED > TETANIZE

TETANIZES > TETANIZE

TETANOID > TETANUS

TETANUS n acute infectious disease producing muscular spasms and convulsions

TETANUSES > TETANUS

TETANY n abnormal increase in the excitability of nerves and muscles resulting in spasms of the arms and legs, caused by a deficiency of parathyroid secretion

TETCHED same as > TECHED

TETCHIER > TETCHY

TETCHIEST > TETCHY

TETCHILY > TETCHY

TETCHY adj cross and irritable

TETE n elaborate hairstyle

TETES > TETE

TETH n ninth letter of the Hebrew alphabet transliterated as t and pronounced more or less like English t with pharyngeal articulation

TETHER n rope or chain for tying an animal to a spot ▷ vb tie up with rope

TETHERED > TETHER

TETHERING > TETHER

TETHERS > TETHER

TETHS > TETH

TETOTUM same as > TEETOTUM

TETOTUMS > TETOTUM

TETRA n brightly coloured tropical freshwater fish

TETRACID adj (of a base) capable of reacting with four molecules of a monobasic acid

TETRACIDS > TETRACID

TETRACT n sponge spicule with four rays

TETRACTS > TETRACT

TETRAD n group or series of four

TETRADIC > TETRAD

TETRADITE n person who believes that the number four has supernatural significance

TETRADS > TETRAD

TETRAGON n figure with four angles and four sides

TETRAGONS > TETRAGON

TETRAGRAM n any word of four letters

TETRALOGY n series of four related works

TETRAMER n four-molecule polymer

TETRAMERS > TETRAMER

TETRAPLA n book containing versions of the same text in four languages

TETRAPLAS > TETRAPLA

TETRAPOD n any vertebrate that has four limbs

TETRAPODS > TETRAPOD

TETRAPODY n metrical unit consisting of four feet

TETRARCH n ruler of one fourth of a country

TETRARCHS > TETRARCH

TETRARCHY > TETRARCH

TETRAS > TETRA

TETRAXON n four-pointed spicule

TETRAXONS > TETRAXON

TETRI n currency unit of Georgia

TETRIS > TETRI

TETRODE n electronic valve having four electrodes, namely a cathode, control grid, screen grid, and anode

TETRODES > TETRODE

TETRONAL n sedative drug

TETRONALS > TETRONAL

TETROXID same as > TETROXIDE

TETROXIDE n any oxide that contains four oxygen atoms per molecule

TETROXIDS > TETROXID

TETRYL n yellow crystalline explosive solid used in detonators

TETRYLS > TETRYL

TETS > TET

TETTER n blister or pimple ▷ vb cause a tetter to erupt (on)

TETTERED > TETTER

TETTERING > TETTER

TETTEROUS > TETTER

TETTERS > TETTER

TETTIX n cicada

TETTIXES > TETTIX

TEUCH Scots variant of > TOUGH

TEUCHAT Scots variant of > TEWIT

TEUCHATS > TEUCHAT

TEUCHER > TEUCH

TEUCHEST > TEUCH

TEUCHTER n in Scotland, derogatory word used by Lowlanders for a Highlander

TEUCHTERS > TEUCHTER

TEUGH same as > TEUCH

TEUGHER > TEUGH

TEUGHEST > TEUGH

TEUGHLY > TEUGH

TEUTONISE same as > TEUTONIZE

TEUTONIZE vb make or become German or Germanic

TEVATRON n machine used in nuclear research

TEVATRONS > TEVATRON

TEW vb work hard

TEWART same as > TUART
TEWARTS > TEWART
TEWED > TEW
TEWEL n horse's rectum
TEWELS > TEWEL
TEWHIT same as > TEWIT
TEWHITS > TEWHIT
TEWING > TEW
TEWIT n lapwing
TEWITS > TEWIT
TEWS > TEW
TEX n unit of weight used to measure yarn density
TEXAS n structure on the upper deck of a paddle-steamer containing the officers' quarters and the wheelhouse
TEXASES > TEXAS
TEXES > TEX
TEXT n main body of a book as distinct from illustrations etc ▷ vb send a text message to (someone)
TEXTBOOK n standard book on a particular subject ▷ adj perfect
TEXTBOOKS > TEXTBOOK
TEXTED > TEXT
TEXTER n person who communicates by text messaging
TEXTERS > TEXTER
TEXTILE n fabric or cloth, esp woven ▷ adj of (the making of) fabrics
TEXTILES > TEXTILE
TEXTING > TEXT
TEXTINGS > TEXTING
TEXTLESS > TEXT
TEXTORIAL adj of or relating to weaving or weavers
TEXTPHONE n phone designed to translate speech into text and vice versa
TEXTS > TEXT
TEXTUAL adj of, based on, or relating to, a text or texts
TEXTUALLY > TEXTUAL
TEXTUARY adj of, relating to, or contained in a text ▷ n textual critic
TEXTURAL > TEXTURE
TEXTURE n structure, feel, or consistency ▷ vb give a distinctive texture to (something)
TEXTURED > TEXTURE
TEXTURES > TEXTURE
TEXTURING > TEXTURE
TEXTURISE same as > TEXTURIZE
TEXTURIZE vb texture
THACK Scots word for > THATCH
THACKED > THACK
THACKING > THACK
THACKS > THACK
THAE Scots word for > THOSE
THAGI same as > THUGGEE
THAGIS > THAGI
THAIM Scots variant of

> THEM
THAIRM n catgut
THAIRMS > THAIRM
THALAMI > THALAMUS
THALAMIC > THALAMUS
THALAMUS n either of the two contiguous egg-shaped masses of grey matter at the base of the brain
THALASSIC adj of or relating to the sea
THALE as in thale cress a cruciferous wall plant
THALER n former German, Austrian, or Swiss silver coin
THALERS > THALER
THALI n meal consisting of several small meat or vegetable dishes accompanied by rice, bread, etc, and sometimes by a starter or a sweet
THALIAN adj of or relating to comedy
THALIS > THALI
THALLI > THALLUS
THALLIC adj of or containing thallium, esp in the trivalent state
THALLINE > THALLUS
THALLIOUS > THALLIUM
THALLIUM n highly toxic metallic element
THALLIUMS > THALLIUM
THALLOID > THALLUS
THALLOUS adj of or containing thallium, esp in the monovalent state
THALLUS n undifferentiated vegetative body of algae, fungi, and lichens
THALLUSES > THALLUS
THALWEG n longitudinal outline of a riverbed from source to mouth
THALWEGS > THALWEG
THAN prep used to introduce the second element of a comparison ▷ n old variant of "then" (that time)
THANA same as > TANA
THANADAR same as > TANADAR
THANADARS > THANADAR
THANAGE n state of being a thane
THANAGES > THANAGE
THANAH same as > TANA
THANAHS > THANAH
THANAS > THANA
THANATISM n belief that the soul ceases to exist when the body dies
THANATIST > THANATISM
THANATOID adj like death
THANATOS n Greek personification of death
THANE n Anglo-Saxon or medieval Scottish nobleman
THANEDOM > THANE

THANEDOMS > THANE
THANEHOOD > THANE
THANES > THANE
THANESHIP > THANE
THANG n thing
THANGKA n (in Tibetan Buddhism) a religious painting on a scroll
THANGKAS > THANGKA
THANGS > THANG
THANK vb express gratitude to
THANKED > THANK
THANKEE interj thank you
THANKER > THANK
THANKERS > THANK
THANKFUL adj grateful
THANKING > THANK
THANKINGS > THANK
THANKIT as in be thankit thank God
THANKLESS adj unrewarding or unappreciated
THANKS npl words of gratitude ▷ interj polite expression of gratitude
THANKYOU n conventional expression of gratitude
THANKYOUS > THANKYOU
THANNA same as > TANA
THANNAH same as > TANA
THANNAHS > THANNAH
THANNAS > THANNA
THANS > THAN
THAR same as > TAHR
THARM n stomach
THARMS > THARM
THARS > THAR
THAT pron used to refer to something already mentioned or familiar, or further away
THATAWAY adv that way
THATCH n roofing material of reeds or straw ▷ vb roof (a house) with reeds or straw
THATCHED > THATCH
THATCHER > THATCH
THATCHERS > THATCH
THATCHES > THATCH
THATCHIER > THATCH
THATCHING > THATCH
THATCHT old variant of > THATCHED
THATCHY > THATCH
THATNESS n state or quality of being 'that'
THAUMATIN n type of natural sweetener
THAW vb make or become unfrozen ▷ n thawing
THAWED > THAW
THAWER > THAW
THAWERS > THAW
THAWIER > THAWY
THAWIEST > THAWY
THAWING > THAW
THAWINGS > THAW
THAWLESS > THAW
THAWS > THAW
THAWY adj tending to thaw
THE det definite article,

used before a noun
THEACEOUS adj relating to a family of evergreen trees and shrubs of tropical and warm regions, which includes the tea plant
THEANDRIC adj both divine and human
THEARCHIC > THEARCHY
THEARCHY n rule or government by God or gods
THEATER same as > THEATRE
THEATERS > THEATER
THEATRAL adj of or relating to the theatre
THEATRE n place where plays etc are performed
THEATRES > THEATRE
THEATRIC adj of or relating to the theatre
THEATRICS n art of staging plays
THEAVE n young ewe
THEAVES > THEAVE
THEBAINE n poisonous white crystalline alkaloid, found in opium but without opioid actions
THEBAINES > THEBAINE
THEBE n inner satellite of Jupiter discovered in 1979
THEBES > THEBE
THECA n enclosing organ, cell, or spore case, esp the capsule of a moss
THECAE > THECA
THECAL > THECA
THECATE > THECA
THECODONT adj (of mammals and certain reptiles) having teeth that grow in sockets ▷ n extinct reptile
THEE pron refers to the person addressed: used mainly by members of the Society of Friends ▷ vb use the word "thee"
THEED > THEE
THEEING > THEE
THEEK Scots variant of > THATCH
THEEKED > THEEK
THEEKING > THEEK
THEEKS > THEEK
THEELIN trade name for > ESTRONE
THEELINS > THEELIN
THEELOL n estriol
THEELOLS > THEELOL
THEES > THEE
THEFT n act or an instance of stealing
THEFTLESS > THEFT
THEFTS > THEFT
THEFTUOUS adj tending to commit theft
THEGITHER Scots variant of > TOGETHER
THEGN same as > THANE
THEGNLY > THEGN
THEGNS > THEGN
THEIC n person who drinks excessive amounts of tea

THEICS > THEIC
THEIN old variant of > THANE
THEINE another name for > CAFFEINE
THEINES > THEINE
THEINS > THEIN
THEIR det of, belonging to, or associated in some way with them
THEIRS pron (thing or person) belonging to them
THEIRSELF pron dialect form of themselves: reflexive form of they or them
THEISM n belief in a God or gods
THEISMS > THEISM
THEIST > THEISM
THEISTIC > THEISM
THEISTS > THEISM
THELEMENT n old contraction of "the element"
THELF n old contraction of "the element"
THELITIS n inflammation of the nipple
THELVES > THELF
THELYTOKY n type of reproduction resulting in female offspring only
THEM pron refers to people or things other than the speaker or those addressed
THEMA n theme
THEMATA > THEMA
THEMATIC adj of, relating to, or consisting of a theme or themes ▷ n thematic vowel
THEMATICS > THEMATIC
THEME n main idea or subject being discussed ▷ vb design, decorate, arrange, etc, in accordance with a theme
THEMED > THEME
THEMELESS > THEME
THEMES > THEME
THEMING > THEME
THEMSELF pron reflexive form of one, whoever, anybody
THEN adv at that time ▷ pron that time ▷ adj existing or functioning at that time ▷ n that time
THENABOUT adv around then
THENAGE old variant of > THANAGE
THENAGES > THENAGE
THENAL adj of or relating to the thenar
THENAR n palm of the hand ▷ adj of or relating to the palm or the region at the base of the thumb
THENARS > THENAR
THENCE adv from that place or time
THENS > THEN
THEOCON n person who believes that religion should play a greater role in politics
THEOCONS > THEOCON
THEOCRACY n government by a god or priests
THEOCRASY n mingling into one of deities or divine attributes previously regarded as distinct
THEOCRAT > THEOCRACY
THEOCRATS > THEOCRACY
THEODICY n branch of theology concerned with defending the attributes of God against objections resulting from physical and moral evil
THEOGONIC > THEOGONY
THEOGONY n origin and descent of the gods
THEOLOG same as > THEOLOGUE
THEOLOGER n theologian
THEOLOGIC > THEOLOGY
THEOLOGS > THEOLOG
THEOLOGUE n theologian
THEOLOGY n study of religions and religious beliefs
THEOMACHY n battle among the gods or against them
THEOMANCY n divination or prophecy by an oracle or by people directly inspired by a god
THEOMANIA n religious madness, esp when it takes the form of believing oneself to be a god
THEONOMY n state of being governed by God
THEOPATHY n religious emotion engendered by the contemplation of or meditation upon God
THEOPHAGY n sacramental eating of a god
THEOPHANY n manifestation of a deity to man in a form that, though visible, is not necessarily material
THEORBIST > THEORBO
THEORBO n obsolete form of the lute, having two necks, one above the other, the second neck carrying a set of unstopped sympathetic bass strings
THEORBOS > THEORBO
THEOREM n proposition that can be proved by reasoning
THEOREMIC > THEOREM
THEOREMS > THEOREM
THEORETIC adj of, or based on, a theory
THEORIC n theory; conjecture
THEORICS > THEORIC
THEORIES > THEORY
THEORIQUE same as > THEORIC
THEORISE same as > THEORIZE
THEORISED > THEORISE
THEORISER > THEORISE
THEORISES > THEORISE
THEORIST n originator of a theory
THEORISTS > THEORIST
THEORIZE vb form theories, speculate
THEORIZED > THEORIZE
THEORIZER > THEORIZE
THEORIZES > THEORIZE
THEORY n set of ideas to explain something
THEOSOPH n proponent of theosophy
THEOSOPHS > THEOSOPH
THEOSOPHY n religious or philosophical system claiming to be based on intuitive insight into the divine nature
THEOTOKOI > THEOTOKOS
THEOTOKOS n mother of God
THEOW n slave in Anglo-Saxon Britain
THEOWS > THEOW
THERALITE n type of igneous rock
THERAPIES > THERAPY
THERAPIST n person skilled in a particular type of therapy
THERAPSID n extinct reptile: considered to be the ancestors of mammals
THERAPY n curing treatment
THERBLIG n basic unit of work in an industrial process
THERBLIGS > THERBLIG
THERE adv in or to that place ▷ n that place
THEREAT adv at that point or time
THEREAWAY adv in that direction
THEREBY adv by that means
THEREFOR adv for this, that, or it
THEREFORE adv consequently, that being so
THEREFROM adv from that or there
THEREIN adv in or into that place or thing
THEREINTO adv into that place, circumstance, etc
THEREMIN n electronic musical instrument, played by moving the hands through electromagnetic fields created by two metal rods
THEREMINS > THEREMIN
THERENESS n quality of having existence
THEREOF adv of or concerning that or it
THEREON archaic word for > THEREUPON
THEREOUT another word for > THEREFROM
THERES > THERE
THERETO adv that or it
THEREUNTO adv to that
THEREUPON adv immediately after that
THEREWITH adv with or in addition to that
THERIAC n ointment or potion of varying composition, used as an antidote to a poison
THERIACA same as > THERIAC
THERIACAL > THERIAC
THERIACAS > THERIACA
THERIACS > THERIAC
THERIAN n animal of the class Theria, a subclass of mammals
THERIANS > THERIAN
THERM n unit of measurement of heat public bath
THERMAE npl public baths or hot springs, esp in ancient Greece or Rome
THERMAL adj of heat ▷ n rising current of warm air
THERMALLY > THERMAL
THERMALS > THERMAL
THERME old variant of > THERM
THERMEL n type of thermometer measuring temperature by means of thermoelectic current
THERMELS > THERMEL
THERMES > THERME
THERMETTE n device, used outdoors, for boiling water rapidly
THERMIC same as > THERMAL
THERMICAL same as > THERMAL
THERMIDOR as in lobster thermidor dish of cooked lobster
THERMION n electron or ion emitted by a body at high temperature
THERMIONS > THERMION
THERMIT variant of > THERMITE
THERMITE as in thermite process process for reducing metallic oxides
THERMITES > THERMITE
THERMITS > THERMIT
THERMOS n trademark term for a type of stoppered vacuum flask used to preserve the temperature of its contents
THERMOSES > THERMOS
THERMOSET n material (esp a synthetic plastic or resin) that hardens permanently after one

application of heat and pressure

THERMOTIC *adj* of or because of heat

THERMS > THERM

THEROID *adj* of, relating to, or resembling a beast

THEROLOGY *n* study of mammals

THEROPOD *n* bipedal carnivorous saurischian dinosaur with strong hind legs and grasping hands

THEROPODS > THEROPOD

THESAURAL > THESAURUS

THESAURI > THESAURUS

THESAURUS *n* book containing lists of synonyms and related words

THESE *det* form of this used before a plural noun

THESES > THESIS

THESIS *n* written work submitted for a degree

THESP *short for* > THESPIAN

THESPIAN *adj* of or relating to drama and the theatre ▷ *n* actor or actress

THESPIANS > THESPIAN

THESPS > THESP

THETA *n* eighth letter of the Greek alphabet

THETAS > THETA

THETCH *old variant spelling of* > THATCH

THETCHED > THETCH

THETCHES > THETCH

THETCHING > THETCH

THETE *n* member of the lowest order of freeman in ancient Athens

THETES > THETE

THETHER *old variant of* > THITHER

THETIC *adj* (in classical prosody) of, bearing, or relating to a metrical stress

THETICAL *another word for* > THETIC

THEURGIC > THEURGY

THEURGIES > THEURGY

THEURGIST > THEURGY

THEURGY *n* intervention of a divine or supernatural agency in the affairs of man

THEW *n* muscle, esp if strong or well-developed

THEWED *adj* strong; muscular

THEWES > THEW

THEWIER > THEW

THEWIEST > THEW

THEWLESS > THEW

THEWS > THEW

THEWY > THEW

THEY *pron* people or things other than the speaker or people addressed

THIAMIN *same as* > THIAMINE

THIAMINE *n* vitamin found in the outer coat of

rice and other grains

THIAMINES > THIAMINE

THIAMINS > THIAMIN

THIASUS *n* congregation of people who have gathered to sing and dance in honour of a god

THIASUSES > THIASUS

THIAZIDE *n* diuretic drug

THIAZIDES > THIAZIDE

THIAZIN *same as* > THIAZINE

THIAZINE *n* any of a group of organic compounds containing a ring system composed of four carbon atoms, a sulphur atom, and a nitrogen atom

THIAZINES > THIAZINE

THIAZINS > THIAZIN

THIAZOL *same as* > THIAZOLE

THIAZOLE *n* colourless liquid with a pungent smell that contains a ring system composed of three carbon atoms, a sulphur atom, and a nitrogen atom

THIAZOLES > THIAZOLE

THIAZOLS > THIAZOL

THIBET *n* coloured woollen cloth

THIBETS > THIBET

THIBLE *n* stick for stirring porridge

THIBLES > THIBLE

THICK *adj* of great or specified extent from one side to the other ▷ *vb* thicken

THICKED > THICK

THICKEN *vb* make or become thick or thicker

THICKENED > THICKEN

THICKENER > THICKEN

THICKENS > THICKEN

THICKER > THICK

THICKEST > THICK

THICKET *n* dense growth of small trees

THICKETED *adj* covered in thicket

THICKETS > THICKET

THICKETY > THICKET

THICKHEAD *n* stupid or ignorant person

THICKIE *same as* > THICKO

THICKIES > THICKY

THICKING > THICK

THICKISH > THICK

THICKLEAF *n* succulent plant with sessile or short-stalked fleshy leaves

THICKLY > THICK

THICKNESS *n* state of being thick

THICKO *n* slow-witted unintelligent person

THICKOES > THICKO

THICKOS > THICKO

THICKS > THICK

THICKSET *adj* stocky in build

THICKSETS > THICKSET

THICKSKIN *n* insensitive person

THICKY *same as* > THICKO

THIEF *n* person who steals

THIEFLIKE *adj* like a thief

THIEVE *vb* steal

THIEVED > THIEVE

THIEVERY > THIEVE

THIEVES > THIEVE

THIEVING *adj* given to stealing other people's possessions

THIEVINGS > THIEVING

THIEVISH > THIEF

THIG *vb* beg

THIGGER > THIG

THIGGERS > THIG

THIGGING > THIG

THIGGINGS > THIG

THIGGIT *Scots inflection of* > THIG

THIGH *n* upper part of the human leg

THIGHBONE *same as* > FEMUR

THIGHED *adj* having thighs

THIGHS > THIGH

THIGS > THIG

THILK *pron* that same

THILL *another word for* > SHAFT

THILLER *n* horse that goes between the thills of a cart

THILLERS > THILLER

THILLS > THILL

THIMBLE *n* cap protecting the end of the finger (when sewing ▷ *vb* use a thimble

THIMBLED > THIMBLE

THIMBLES > THIMBLE

THIMBLING > THIMBLE

THIN *adj* not thick ▷ *vb* make or become thin ▷ *adv* in order to produce something thin

THINCLAD *n* track-and-field athlete

THINCLADS > THINCLAD

THINDOWN *n* reduction in the amount of particles, esp protons, of very high energy reaching and penetrating the earth's atmosphere from outer space

THINDOWNS > THINDOWN

THINE *adj* (something) of or associated with you (thou) ▷ *pron* something belonging to you (thou) ▷ *det* of, belonging to, or associated in some way with you (thou)

THING *n* material object

THINGAMY *n* person or thing the name of which is unknown

THINGHOOD *n* existence; state or condition of being a thing

THINGIER > THINGY

THINGIES > THINGY

THINGIEST > THINGY

THINGNESS *n* state of being a thing

THINGS > THING

THINGUMMY *n* person or thing the name of which is unknown, temporarily forgotten, or deliberately overlooked

THINGY *adj* existing in reality; actual

THINK *vb* consider, judge, or believe

THINKABLE *adj* able to be conceived or considered

THINKABLY > THINKABLE

THINKER > THINK

THINKERS > THINK

THINKING > THINK

THINKINGS > THINK

THINKS > THINK

THINLY > THIN

THINNED > THIN

THINNER > THIN

THINNERS > THIN

THINNESS > THIN

THINNEST > THIN

THINNING > THIN

THINNINGS > THIN

THINNISH > THIN

THINS > THIN

THIO *adj* of, or relating to, sulphur

THIOFURAN *another name for* > THIOPHEN

THIOL *n* any of a class of sulphur-containing organic compounds with the formula RSH, where R is an organic group

THIOLIC > THIOL

THIOLS > THIOL

THIONATE *n* any salt or ester of thionic acid

THIONATES > THIONATE

THIONIC *adj* of, relating to, or containing sulphur

THIONIN *same as* > THIONINE

THIONINE *n* crystalline derivative of thiazine used as a violet dye to stain microscope specimens

THIONINES > THIONINE

THIONINS > THIONIN

THIONYL *n* of, consisting of, or containing the divalent group SO

THIONYLS > THIONYL

THIOPHEN *n* colourless liquid heterocyclic compound found in the benzene fraction of coal tar and manufactured from butane and sulphur

THIOPHENE *same as* > THIOPHEN

THIOPHENS > THIOPHEN

THIOPHIL *adj* having an attraction to sulphur

THIOTEPA *n* drug used in chemotherapy

THIOTEPAS > THIOTEPA

THIOUREA *n* white water-soluble crystalline substance with a bitter taste

THIOUREAS > THIOUREA

THIR Scots word for > THESE

THIRAM n antifungal agent

THIRAMS > THIRAM

THIRD adj of number three in a series ▷ n one of three equal parts ▷ adv in the third place ▷ vb divide (something) by three

THIRDED > THIRD

THIRDHAND adv from the second of two intermediaries

THIRDING > THIRD

THIRDINGS > THIRD

THIRDLY > THIRD

THIRDS > THIRD

THIRDSMAN n intermediary

THIRDSMEN > THIRDSMAN

THIRL vb bore or drill

THIRLAGE n obligation imposed upon tenants of certain lands requiring them to have their grain ground at a specified mill

THIRLAGES > THIRLAGE

THIRLED > THIRL

THIRLING > THIRL

THIRLS > THIRL

THIRST n desire to drink ▷ vb feel thirst

THIRSTED > THIRST

THIRSTER > THIRST

THIRSTERS > THIRSTER

THIRSTFUL > THIRST

THIRSTIER > THIRSTY

THIRSTILY > THIRSTY

THIRSTING > THIRST

THIRSTS > THIRST

THIRSTY adj feeling a desire to drink

THIRTEEN n three plus ten ▷ adj amounting to thirteen ▷ det amounting to thirteen

THIRTEENS > THIRTEEN

THIRTIES > THIRTY

THIRTIETH adj being the ordinal number of thirty in counting order, position, time, etc: often written 30th ▷ n one of 30 approximately equal parts of something

THIRTY n three times ten ▷ adj amounting to thirty ▷ det amounting to thirty

THIRTYISH adj around thirty years of age

THIS pron used to refer to a thing or person nearby, just mentioned, or about to be mentioned ▷ adj used to refer to the present time

THISAWAY adv this way

THISNESS n state or quality of being this

THISTLE n prickly plant with dense flower heads

THISTLES > THISTLE

THISTLIER > THISTLE

THISTLY > THISTLE

THITHER adv or towards that place

THITHERTO adv until that time

THIVEL same as > THIBLE

THIVELS > THIVEL

THLIPSES > THLIPSIS

THLIPSIS n compression, esp of part of the body

THO short for > THOUGH

THOFT n bench (in a boat) upon which a rower sits

THOFTS > THOFT

THOLE n wooden pin set in the side of a rowing boat to serve as a fulcrum for rowing ▷ vb bear or put up with

THOLED > THOLE

THOLEIITE n type of volcanic rock

THOLEPIN same as > THOLE

THOLEPINS > THOLEPIN

THOLES > THOLE

THOLI > THOLUS

THOLING > THOLE

THOLOBATE n structure supporting a dome

THOLOI > THOLOS

THOLOS n dry-stone beehive-shaped tomb associated with the Mycenaean culture of Greece in the 16th to the 12th century BC

THOLUS n domed tomb

THON Scot word for > YON

THONDER Scot word for > YONDER

THONG n thin strip of leather etc

THONGED adj fastened with a thong

THONGS > THONG

THORACAL another word for > THORACIC

THORACES > THORAX

THORACIC adj of, near, or relating to the thorax

THORAX n part of the body between the neck and the abdomen

THORAXES > THORAX

THORIA > THORIUM

THORIAS > THORIUM

THORIC > THORIUM

THORITE n yellow, brownish, or black radioactive mineral consisting of tetragonal thorium silicate. It occurs in coarse granite and is a source of thorium

THORITES > THORITE

THORIUM n radioactive metallic element

THORIUMS > THORIUM

THORN n prickle on a plant ▷ vb jag or prick (something) as if with a thorn

THORNBACK n European ray with a row of spines along the back and tail

THORNBILL n South American hummingbird

THORNBIRD n small S American bird

THORNBUSH n tree, shrub, or bush with thorns

THORNED > THORN

THORNIER > THORNY

THORNIEST > THORNY

THORNILY > THORNY

THORNING > THORN

THORNLESS > THORN

THORNLIKE > THORN

THORNS > THORN

THORNSET adj set with thorns

THORNTREE n tree with thorns

THORNY adj covered with thorns

THORO (nonstandard) variant spelling of > THOROUGH

THORON n radioisotope of radon that is a decay product of thorium

THORONS > THORON

THOROUGH adj complete ▷ n passage

THOROUGHS > THOROUGH

THORP n small village

THORPE same as > THORP

THORPES > THORPE

THORPS > THORP

THOSE det form of that used before a plural noun

THOTHER pron old contraction of the other

THOU pron used when talking to one person ▷ n one thousandth of an inch ▷ vb use the word thou

THOUED > THOU

THOUGH adv nevertheless

THOUGHT > THINK

THOUGHTED adj with thoughts

THOUGHTEN adj convinced

THOUGHTS > THINK

THOUING > THOU

THOUS > THOU

THOUSAND n ten hundred ▷ adj amounting to a thousand ▷ det amounting to a thousand

THOUSANDS > THOUSAND

THOWEL old variant of > THOLE

THOWELS > THOWEL

THOWL old variant of > THOLE

THOWLESS adj lacking in vigour

THOWLS > THOWEL

THRAE same as > FRAE

THRAIPING n thrashing

THRALDOM same as > THRALL

THRALDOMS > THRALDOM

THRALL n state of being in the power of another person ▷ vb enslave or dominate

THRALLDOM same as > THRALL

THRALLED > THRALL

THRALLING > THRALL

THRALLS > THRALL

THRANG n throng ▷ vb throng ▷ adj crowded

THRANGED > THRANG

THRANGING > THRANG

THRANGS > THRANG

THRAPPLE n throat or windpipe ▷ vb throttle

THRAPPLED > THRAPPLE

THRAPPLES > THRAPPLE

THRASH vb beat, esp with a stick or whip ▷ n party

THRASHED > THRASH

THRASHER same as > THRESHER

THRASHERS > THRASHER

THRASHES > THRASH

THRASHING n severe beating

THRASONIC adj bragging or boastful

THRAVE n twenty-four sheaves of corn

THRAVES > THRAVE

THRAW vb twist (something); make something thrawn

THRAWARD adj contrary or stubborn

THRAWART same as > THRAWARD

THRAWED > THRAW

THRAWING > THRAW

THRAWN adj crooked or twisted

THRAWNLY > THRAWN

THRAWS > THRAW

THREAD n fine strand or yarn ▷ vb pass thread through

THREADED > THREAD

THREADEN adj made of thread

THREADER > THREAD

THREADERS > THREAD

THREADFIN n spiny-finned tropical marine fish

THREADIER > THREADY

THREADING > THREAD

THREADS slang word for > CLOTHES

THREADY adj of, relating to, or resembling a thread or threads

THREAP vb scold

THREAPED > THREAP

THREAPER > THREAP

THREAPERS > THREAP

THREAPING > THREAP

THREAPIT variant past participle of > THREAP

THREAPS > THREAP

THREAT n declaration of intent to harm

THREATED > THREAT

THREATEN vb make or be a threat to

THREATENS > THREATEN

THREATFUL > THREAT

THREATING > THREAT

THREATS > THREAT

THREAVE same as
> THRAVE
THREAVES > THREAVE
THREE n one more than
two ▷ adj amounting to
three ▷ det amounting to
three
THREEFOLD adv (having)
three times as many or as
much ▷ adj having three
times as many or as much
THREENESS n state or
quality of being three
THREEP same as > THREAP
THREEPEAT n third
consecutive win of a
particular sporting
championship ▷ vb win a
sporting championship for
the third consecutive time
THREEPED > THREEP
THREEPER > THREAP
THREEPERS > THREAP
THREEPING > THREEP
THREEPIT variant past
participle of > THREEP
THREEPS > THREEP
THREES > THREE
THREESOME n group of
three
THRENE n dirge; threnody
THRENES > THRENE
THRENETIC > THRENE
THRENODE same as
> THRENODY
THRENODES > THRENODE
THRENODIC > THRENODY
THRENODY n lament for
the dead
THRENOS n threnody;
lamentation
THRENOSES > THRENOS
THREONINE n essential
amino acid that occurs in
certain proteins
THRESH vb beat (wheat
etc) to separate the grain
from the husks and straw
▷ n act of threshing
THRESHED > THRESH
THRESHEL n flail
THRESHELS > THRESHEL
THRESHER n any of a
genus of large sharks
occurring in tropical and
temperate seas. They have
a very long whiplike tail
THRESHERS > THRESHER
THRESHES > THRESH
THRESHING > THRESH
THRESHOLD n bar forming
the bottom of a doorway
THRETTIES > THRETTY
THRETTY nonstandard
variant of > THIRTY
THREW > THROW
THRICE adv three times
THRID old variant of
> THREAD
THRIDACE n sedative
made from lettuce juice
THRIDACES > THRIDACE
THRIDDED > THRID
THRIDDING > THRID
THRIDS > THRID

THRIFT n wisdom and
caution with money
THRIFTIER > THRIFTY
THRIFTILY > THRIFTY
THRIFTS > THRIFT
THRIFTY adj not wasteful
with money
THRILL n sudden feeling of
excitement ▷ vb (cause to)
feel a thrill
THRILLANT another word
for > THRILLING
THRILLED > THRILL
THRILLER n book, film,
etc with an atmosphere of
mystery or suspense
THRILLERS > THRILLER
THRILLIER > THRILLY
THRILLING adj very
exciting or stimulating
THRILLS > THRILL
THRILLY adj causing
thrills
THRIMSA same as
> THRYMSA
THRIMSAS > THRIMSA
THRIP same as > THRIPS
THRIPS n small
slender-bodied insect with
piercing mouthparts that
feeds on plant sap
THRIPSES > THRIPS
THRISSEL Scots variant of
> THISTLE
THRISSELS > THRISSEL
THRIST old variant of
> THIRST
THRISTED > THRIST
THRISTING > THRIST
THRISTLE Scots variant of
> THISTLE
THRISTLES > THRISTLE
THRISTS > THRIST
THRISTY > THRIST
THRIVE vb flourish or
prosper
THRIVED > THRIVE
THRIVEN > THRIVE
THRIVER > THRIVE
THRIVERS > THRIVE
THRIVES > THRIVE
THRIVING > THRIVE
THRIVINGS > THRIVE
THRO same as > THROUGH
THROAT n passage from
the mouth and nose to the
stomach and lungs ▷ vb
vocalize in the throat
THROATED > THROAT
THROATIER > THROATY
THROATILY > THROATY
THROATING > THROAT
THROATS > THROAT
THROATY adj (of the voice)
hoarse
THROB vb pulsate
repeatedly ▷ n throbbing
THROBBED > THROB
THROBBER > THROB
THROBBERS > THROB
THROBBING > THROB
THROBLESS > THROB
THROBS > THROB
THROE n pang or pain ▷ n

endure throes
THROED > THROE
THROEING > THROE
THROES npl violent pangs
or pains
THROMBI > THROMBUS
THROMBIN n enzyme that
acts on fibrinogen in blood
causing it to clot
THROMBINS > THROMBIN
THROMBOSE vb become or
affect with a thrombus
THROMBUS n clot of
coagulated blood that
forms within a blood vessel
or inside the heart and
remains at the site of its
formation, often impeding
the flow of blood
THRONE n ceremonial seat
of a monarch or bishop ▷ vb
place or be placed on a
throne
THRONED > THRONE
THRONES > THRONE
THRONG vb crowd ▷ n great
number of people or things
crowded together ▷ adj
busy
THRONGED > THRONG
THRONGFUL > THRONG
THRONGING > THRONG
THRONGS > THRONG
THRONING > THRONE
THRONNER n person who is
good at doing odd jobs
THRONNERS > THRONNER
THROPPLE vb strangle or
choke
THROPPLED > THROPPLE
THROPPLES > THROPPLE
THROSTLE n song thrush
THROSTLES > THROSTLE
THROTTLE n device
controlling the amount of
fuel entering an engine ▷ vb
strangle
THROTTLED > THROTTLE
THROTTLER > THROTTLE
THROTTLES > THROTTLE
THROUGH prep from end to
end or side to side of ▷ adj
finished
THROUGHLY adv
thoroughly
THROVE > THRIVE
THROW vb hurl through the
air ▷ n throwing
THROWAWAY adj done or
said casually ▷ vb get rid of
or discard ▷ n handbill or
advertisement distributed
in a public place
THROWBACK n person or
thing that reverts to an
earlier type ▷ vb remind
someone of (something he
or she said or did
previously) in order to
upset him or her
THROWDOWN n challenge to
a physical or artistic
competition
THROWE old variant of
> THROE

THROWER > THROW
THROWERS > THROW
THROWES > THROWE
THROWING > THROW
THROWINGS > THROW
THROWN > THROW
THROWS > THROW
THROWSTER n person who
twists silk or other fibres
into yarn
THRU same as > THROUGH
THRUM vb strum
rhythmically but without
expression on (a musical
instrument) ▷ n in textiles,
unwoven ends of wap
thread
THRUMMED > THRUM
THRUMMER > THRUM
THRUMMERS > THRUM
THRUMMIER > THRUMMY
THRUMMING > THRUM
THRUMMY adj made of
thrums
THRUMS > THRUM
THRUPENNY as in thrupenny
bit twelve-sided British coin
of nickel-brass, valued at
three old pence, obsolete
since 1971
THRUPUT n quantity of
raw material or
information processed in a
given period
THRUPUTS > THRUPUT
THRUSH n brown songbird
THRUSHES > THRUSH
THRUST vb push forcefully
▷ n forceful stab
THRUSTED > THRUST
THRUSTER n person or
thing that thrusts
THRUSTERS > THRUSTER
THRUSTFUL > THRUST
THRUSTING > THRUST
THRUSTOR variant of
> THRUSTER
THRUSTORS > THRUSTOR
THRUSTS > THRUST
THRUTCH n narrow,
fast-moving stream ▷ vb
thrust
THRUTCHED > THRUTCH
THRUTCHES > THRUTCH
THRUWAY n thoroughfare
THRUWAYS > THRUWAY
THRYMSA n gold coin used
in Anglo-Saxon England
THRYMSAS > THRYMSA
THUD n dull heavy sound
▷ vb make such a sound
THUDDED > THUD
THUDDING > THUD
THUDS > THUD
THUG n violent man, esp a
criminal
THUGGEE n methods and
practices of the thugs of
India
THUGGEES > THUGGEE
THUGGERY > THUG
THUGGISH > THUG
THUGGISM > THUG
THUGGISMS > THUG

THUGGO n tough and violent person

THUGGOS > THUGGO

THUGS > THUG

THUJA n coniferous tree of North America and East Asia, with scalelike leaves, small cones, and an aromatic wood

THUJAS > THUJA

THULIA n oxide of thulium

THULIAS > THULIA

THULITE n rose-coloured zoisite sometimes incorporated into jewellery

THULITES > THULITE

THULIUM n malleable ductile silvery-grey element

THULIUMS > THULIUM

THUMB n short thick finger set apart from the others ▷ vb touch or handle with the thumb

THUMBED > THUMB

THUMBHOLE n hole for putting the thumb into

THUMBIER > THUMBY

THUMBIEST > THUMBY

THUMBING > THUMB

THUMBKIN same as > THUMBKIN

THUMBKINS n thumbscrew

THUMBLESS > THUMB

THUMBLIKE > THUMB

THUMBLING n extremely small person

THUMBNAIL n nail of the thumb ▷ adj concise and brief

THUMBNUT n nut with projections enabling it to be turned by the thumb and forefinger

THUMBNUTS > THUMBNUT

THUMBPOT n tiny flowerpot

THUMBPOTS > THUMBPOT

THUMBS > THUMB

THUMBTACK n short tack with a broad smooth head for fastening papers to a drawing board, etc

THUMBY adj clumsy; uncoordinated

THUMP n (sound of) a dull heavy blow ▷ vb strike heavily

THUMPED > THUMP

THUMPER > THUMP

THUMPERS > THUMP

THUMPING adj huge or excessive

THUMPS > THUMP

THUNDER n loud noise accompanying lightning ▷ vb rumble with thunder

THUNDERED > THUNDER

THUNDERER > THUNDER

THUNDERS > THUNDER

THUNDERY > THUNDER

THUNDROUS > THUNDER

THUNK another word for > THUD

THUNKED > THUNK

THUNKING > THUNK

THUNKS > THUNK

THURIBLE same as > CENSER

THURIBLES > THURIBLE

THURIFER n person appointed to carry the censer at religious ceremonies

THURIFERS > THURIFER

THURIFIED > THURIFY

THURIFIES > THURIFY

THURIFY vb burn incense near or before an altar, shrine, etc

THURL same as > THIRL

THURLS > THURL

THUS adv in this manner ▷ n aromatic gum resin

THUSES > THUS

THUSLY adv in such a way; thus

THUSNESS n state or quality of being thus

THUSWISE adj in this way; thus

THUYA same as > THUJA

THUYAS > THUYA

THWACK n whack ▷ vb beat with something flat ▷ interj exclamation imitative of this sound

THWACKED > THWACK

THWACKER > THWACK

THWACKERS > THWACK

THWACKING > THWACK

THWACKS > THWACK

THWAITE n piece of land cleared from forest or reclaimed from wasteland

THWAITES > THWAITE

THWART vb foil or frustrate ▷ n seat across a boat ▷ adj passing or being situated across ▷ adv across

THWARTED > THWART

THWARTER > THWART

THWARTERS > THWART

THWARTING > THWART

THWARTLY > THWART

THWARTS > THWART

THY adj of or associated with you (thou) ▷ det belonging to or associated in some way with you (thou)

THYINE adj of relating to the sandarac tree

THYLACINE n extinct doglike Tasmanian marsupial

THYLAKOID n small membranous sac within a chloroplast

THYLOSE old variant of > TYLOSIS

THYLOSES > THYLOSIS

THYLOSIS same as > TYLOSIS

THYME n aromatic herb

THYMES > THYME

THYMEY > THYME

THYMI > THYMUS

THYMIC adj of or relating to the thymus

THYMIDINE n crystalline nucleoside of thymine, found in DNA

THYMIER > THYME

THYMIEST > THYME

THYMINE n white crystalline pyrimidine base found in DNA

THYMINES > THYMINE

THYMOCYTE n lymphocyte found in the thymus

THYMOL n substance obtained from thyme, used as an antiseptic

THYMOLS > THYMOL

THYMOSIN n hormone secreted by the thymus

THYMOSINS > THYMOSIN

THYMUS n small gland at the base of the neck

THYMUSES > THYMUS

THYMY > THYME

THYRATRON n gas-filled tube that has three electrodes and can be switched between an 'off' state and an 'on' state. It has been superseded, except for application involving high-power switching, by the thyristor

THYREOID same as > THYROID

THYREOIDS > THYREOID

THYRISTOR n any of a group of semiconductor devices, such as the silicon-controlled rectifier, that can be switched between two states

THYROID n (of) a gland in the neck controlling body growth ▷ adj of or relating to the thyroid gland

THYROIDAL > THYROID

THYROIDS > THYROID

THYROXIN same as > THYROXINE

THYROXINE n principal hormone produced by the thyroid gland

THYROXINS > THYROXIN

THYRSE n type of inflorescence, occurring in the lilac and grape, in which the main branch is racemose and the lateral branches cymose

THYRSES > THYRSE

THYRSI > THYRSUS

THYRSOID > THYRSE

THYRSUS same as > THYRSE

THYSELF pron reflexive form of thou

TI same as > TE

TIAN n traditional French vegetable stew or earthenware dish it is cooked in

TIANS > TIAN

TIAR same as > TIARA

TIARA n semicircular jewelled headdress

TIARAED > TIARA

TIARAS > TIARA

TIARS > TIAR

TIBIA n inner bone of the lower leg

TIBIAE > TIBIA

TIBIAL > TIBIA

TIBIAS > TIBIA

TIC n spasmodic muscular twitch

TICAL n former standard monetary unit of Thailand, replaced by the baht in 1928

TICALS > TICAL

TICCA adj (of a thing or the services of a person) having been acquired for temporary use in exchange for payment

TICCED > TIC

TICCING > TIC

TICE vb tempt or allure; entice

TICED > TICE

TICES > TICE

TICH same as > TITCH

TICHES > TICH

TICHIER > TICHY

TICHIEST > TICHY

TICHY same as > TITCHY

TICING > TICE

TICK n mark (·) used to check off or indicate the correctness of something ▷ vb mark with a tick

TICKED > TICK

TICKEN same as > TICKING

TICKENS > TICKEN

TICKER n heart

TICKERS > TICKER

TICKET n card or paper entitling the holder to admission, travel, etc ▷ vb attach or issue a ticket to

TICKETED > TICKET

TICKETING > TICKET

TICKETS npl death or ruin

TICKEY n South African threepenny piece, which was replaced by the five-cent coin in 1961

TICKEYS > TICKEY

TICKIES > TICKY

TICKING n strong material for mattress covers

TICKINGS > TICKING

TICKLACE n (in Newfoundland) a kittiwake

TICKLACES > TICKLACE

TICKLE vb touch or stroke (a person) to produce laughter ▷ n tickling

TICKLED > TICKLE

TICKLER n difficult or delicate problem

TICKLERS > TICKLER

TICKLES > TICKLE

TICKLIER > TICKLE

TICKLIEST > TICKLE

TICKLING > TICKLE

TICKLINGS > TICKLE

TICKLISH adj sensitive to tickling

TICKLY > TICKLE

TICKS > TICK

TICKSEED another name for > COREOPSIS

TICKSEEDS > TICKSEED

TICKTACK n bookmakers' sign language ▷ vb make a ticking sound

TICKTACKS > TICKTACK

TICKTOCK n ticking sound made by a clock ▷ vb make a ticking sound

TICKTOCKS > TICKTOCK

TICKY same as > TICKEY

TICS > TIC

TICTAC same as > TICKTACK

TICTACKED > TICTAC

TICTACS > TICTAC

TICTOC same as > TICKTOCK

TICTOCKED > TICTOC

TICTOCS > TICTOC

TID n girl

TIDAL adj (of a river, lake, or sea) having tides

TIDALLY > TIDAL

TIDBIT same as > TITBIT

TIDBITS > TIDBIT

TIDDIER > TIDDY

TIDDIES > TIDDY

TIDDIEST > TIDDY

TIDDLE vb busy oneself with inconsequential tasks

TIDDLED > TIDDLE

TIDDLER n very small fish

TIDDLERS > TIDDLER

TIDDLES > TIDDLE

TIDDLEY same as > TIDDLY

TIDDLEYS > TIDDLEY

TIDDLIER > TIDDLY

TIDDLIES > TIDDLY

TIDDLIEST > TIDDLY

TIDDLING > TIDDLE

TIDDLY adj tiny ▷ n alcoholic beverage

TIDDY n four of trumps in the card game gleek

TIDE n rise and fall of the sea caused by the gravitational pull of the sun and moon ▷ vb carry or be carried with or as if with the tide

TIDED > TIDE

TIDELAND n land between high-water and low-water marks

TIDELANDS > TIDELAND

TIDELESS > TIDE

TIDELIKE > TIDE

TIDELINE n high-water mark left by the retreating tide

TIDELINES > TIDELINE

TIDEMARK n mark left by the highest or lowest point of a tide

TIDEMARKS > TIDEMARK

TIDEMILL n watermill powered by the force of the tide

TIDEMILLS > TIDEMILL

TIDERIP same as > RIPTIDE

TIDERIPS > TIDERIP

TIDES > TIDE

TIDESMAN n customs official at a port

TIDESMEN > TIDESMAN

TIDEWATER n water that advances and recedes with the tide

TIDEWAVE n undulation of the earth's water levels as the tide moves around it

TIDEWAVES > TIDEWAVE

TIDEWAY n strong tidal current or its channel, esp the tidal part of a river

TIDEWAYS > TIDEWAY

TIDIED > TIDY

TIDIER > TIDY

TIDIES > TIDY

TIDIEST > TIDY

TIDILY > TIDY

TIDINESS > TIDY

TIDING > TIDE

TIDINGS npl news

TIDIVATE same as > TITIVATE

TIDIVATED > TITIVATE

TIDIVATES > TITIVATE

TIDS > TID

TIDY adj neat and orderly ▷ vb put in order ▷ n small container for odds and ends

TIDYING > TIDY

TIDYTIPS n herb with flowers resembling those of the daisy

TIE vb fasten or be fastened with string, rope, etc ▷ n long narrow piece of material worn knotted round the neck

TIEBACK n length of cord, ribbon, or other fabric used for tying a curtain to one side

TIEBACKS > TIEBACK

TIEBREAK n deciding game in drawn match

TIEBREAKS > TIEBREAK

TIECLASP n clip, often ornamental, which holds a tie in place against a shirt

TIECLASPS > TIECLASP

TIED > TIE

TIEING same as > TIE

TIELESS > TIE

TIEPIN n ornamental pin used to pin the two ends of a tie to a shirt

TIEPINS > TIEPIN

TIER n one of a set of rows placed one above and behind the other ▷ vb be or arrange in tiers

TIERCE same as > TERCE

TIERCED adj (of a shield) divided into three sections of similar size but different colour

TIERCEL same as > TERCEL

TIERCELET another name for > TERCEL

TIERCELS > TIERCEL

TIERCERON n (in Gothic architecture) a type of rib on a vault

TIERCES > TIERCE

TIERCET same as > TERCET

TIERCETS > TIERCET

TIERED > TIER

TIERING > TIER

TIERS > TIER

TIES > TIE

TIETAC n fastener for holding a tie in place

TIETACK same as > TIETAC

TIETACKS > TIETACK

TIETACS > TIETAC

TIFF n petty quarrel ▷ vb have or be in a tiff

TIFFANIES > TIFFANY

TIFFANY n sheer fine gauzy fabric

TIFFED > TIFF

TIFFIN n (in India) a light meal, esp at midday ▷ vb take tiffin

TIFFINED > TIFFIN

TIFFING > TIFF

TIFFINGS > TIFF

TIFFINING > TIFFIN

TIFFINS > TIFFIN

TIFFS > TIFF

TIFOSI > TIFOSO

TIFOSO n fanatical fan (esp an Italian F1 fan)

TIFT (Scots) variant of > TIFF

TIFTED > TIFT

TIFTING > TIFT

TIFTS > TIFT

TIG n child's game

TIGE n trunk of an architectural column

TIGER n large yellow-and-black striped Asian cat

TIGEREYE n golden brown silicified variety of crocidolite, used as an ornamental stone

TIGEREYES > TIGEREYE

TIGERISH > TIGER

TIGERISM n arrogant and showy manner

TIGERISMS > TIGERISM

TIGERLIKE adj resembling a tiger

TIGERLY adj of or like a tiger

TIGERS > TIGER

TIGERWOOD n striped wood used in cabinetmaking

TIGERY > TIGER

TIGES > TIGE

TIGGED > TIG

TIGGING > TIG

TIGHT adj stretched or drawn taut ▷ adv in a close, firm, or secure way

TIGHTASS n inhibited or excessively self-controlled person

TIGHTEN vb make or become tight or tighter

TIGHTENED > TIGHTEN

TIGHTENER > TIGHTEN

TIGHTENS > TIGHTEN

TIGHTER > TIGHT

TIGHTEST > TIGHT

TIGHTISH > TIGHT

TIGHTKNIT adj closely integrated

TIGHTLY > TIGHT

TIGHTNESS > TIGHT

TIGHTROPE n rope stretched taut on which acrobats perform

TIGHTS npl one-piece clinging garment covering the body from the waist to the feet

TIGHTWAD n stingy person

TIGHTWADS > TIGHTWAD

TIGHTWIRE n wire tightrope

TIGLIC as in tiglic acid syrupy liquid or crystalline colourless unsaturated carboxylic acid

TIGLON same as > TIGON

TIGLONS > TIGLON

TIGON n hybrid offspring of a male tiger and a female lion

TIGONS > TIGON

TIGRESS n female tiger

TIGRESSES > TIGRESS

TIGRIDIA n type of tropical American plant

TIGRIDIAS > TIGRIDIA

TIGRINE adj of, characteristic of, or resembling a tiger

TIGRISH > TIGER

TIGRISHLY > TIGER

TIGROID adj resembling a tiger

TIGS > TIG

TIK n South African slang term for crystal meth

TIKA same as > TIKKA

TIKANGA n Māori ways or customs

TIKANGAS > TIKANGA

TIKAS > TIKA

TIKE same as > TYKE

TIKES > TIKE

TIKI n small carving of a grotesque person worn as a pendant ▷ vb take a scenic tour around an area

TIKIED > TIKI

TIKIING > TIKI

TIKIS > TIKI

TIKKA adj marinated in spices and dry-roasted ▷ n act of marking a tikka on the forehead

TIKKAS > TIKKA

TIKOLOSHE same as > TOKOLOSHE

TIKS > TIK

TIKTAALIK n extinct species thought to be a missing link between water and land animals

TIL another name for
> SESAME

TILAK n coloured spot or mark worn by Hindus, esp on the forehead, often indicating membership of a religious sect, caste, etc, or (in the case of a woman) marital status

TILAKS > TILAK

TILAPIA n type of fish

TILAPIAS > TILAPIA

TILBURIES > TILBURY

TILBURY n light two-wheeled horse-drawn open carriage, seating two people

TILDE n mark (~) used in Spanish to indicate that the letter 'n' is to be pronounced in a particular way

TILDES > TILDE

TILE n flat piece of ceramic, plastic, etc used to cover a roof, floor, or wall ▷ vb cover with tiles

TILED > TILE

TILEFISH n large brightly coloured deep-sea percoid food fish

TILELIKE adj like a tile

TILER > TILE

TILERIES > TILERY

TILERY n place where tiles are produced

TILES > TILE

TILING n tiles collectively

TILINGS > TILING

TILL prep until ▷ vb cultivate (land) ▷ n drawer for money, usu in a cash register ▷ n unstratified glacial deposit consisting of rock fragments of various sizes

TILLABLE > TILL

TILLAGE n act, process, or art of tilling

TILLAGES > TILLAGE

TILLED > TILL

TILLER n on boats, a handle fixed to the top of a rudderpost to serve as a lever in steering ▷ vb use a tiller

TILLERED > TILLER

TILLERING > TILLER

TILLERMAN n one working a tiller

TILLERMEN
> TILLERMAN

TILLERS > TILL

TILLICUM n (in the Pacific Northwest) a friend

TILLICUMS > TILLICUM

TILLIER > TILL

TILLIEST > TILL

TILLING > TILL

TILLINGS > TILL

TILLITE n rock formed from hardened till

TILLITES > TILLITE

TILLS > TILL

TILLY > TILL

TILS > TIL

TILT vb slant at an angle ▷ n slope

TILTABLE > TILT

TILTED > TILT

TILTER > TILT

TILTERS > TILT

TILTH n (condition of) land that has been tilled

TILTHS > TILTH

TILTING > TILT

TILTINGS > TILT

TILTMETER n instrument for measuring the tilt of the earth's surface

TILTROTOR n aircraft with rotors that can be tilted

TILTS > TILT

TILTYARD n (formerly) an enclosed area for tilting

TILTYARDS > TILTYARD

TIMARAU same as
> TAMARAU

TIMARAUS > TIMARAU

TIMARIOT n one holding a fief in feudal Turkey

TIMARIOTS > TIMARIOT

TIMBAL n type of kettledrum

TIMBALE n mixture of meat, fish, etc, in a rich sauce, cooked in a mould lined with potato or pastry

TIMBALES > TIMBALE

TIMBALS > TIMBAL

TIMBER n wood as a building material ▷ adj made out of timber ▷ vb provide with timbers ▷ interj lumberjack's shouted warning when a tree is about to fall

TIMBERED adj made of or containing timber or timbers

TIMBERING n timbers collectively

TIMBERMAN n any of various longicorn beetles that have destructive wood-eating larvae

TIMBERMEN
> TIMBERMAN

TIMBERS > TIMBER

TIMBERY > TIMBER

TIMBO n Amazonian vine from which a useful insecticide can be derived

TIMBOS > TIMBO

TIMBRAL adj relating to timbre

TIMBRE n distinctive quality of sound of a voice or instrument

TIMBREL n tambourine

TIMBRELS > TIMBREL

TIMBRES > TIMBRE

TIME n past, present, and future as a continuous whole ▷ vb note the time taken by

TIMEBOMB n bomb containing a timing mechanism that determines the time it will detonate

TIMEBOMBS > TIMEBOMB

TIMECARD n card used with a time clock

TIMECARDS > TIMECARD

TIMED > TIME

TIMEFRAME n period of time within which certain events are scheduled to occur

TIMELESS adj unaffected by time

TIMELIER > TIMELY

TIMELIEST > TIMELY

TIMELINE n graphic representation showing the passage of time as a line

TIMELINES > TIMELINE

TIMELY adj at the appropriate time ▷ adv at the right or an appropriate time

TIMENOGUY n taut rope on a ship

TIMEOUS adj in good time

TIMEOUSLY > TIMEOUS

TIMEOUT n in sport, interruption in play during which players rest, discuss tactics, or make substitutions

TIMEOUTS > TIMEOUT

TIMEPASS n way of passing the time ▷ vb pass the time

TIMEPIECE n watch or clock

TIMER n device for measuring time, esp a switch or regulator that causes a mechanism to operate at a specific time

TIMERS > TIMER

TIMES > TIME

TIMESAVER n something that saves time

TIMESCALE n period of time within which events occur or are due to occur

TIMESHARE n time-shared property

TIMESTAMP vb (of a computer) add a record of the date and time of an event to (data)

TIMETABLE n plan showing the times when something takes place, the departure and arrival times of trains or buses, etc ▷ vb set a time when a particular thing should be done

TIMEWORK n work paid for by the length of time taken, esp by the hour or the day

TIMEWORKS > TIMEWORK

TIMEWORN adj showing the adverse effects of overlong use or of old age

TIMID adj easily frightened

TIMIDER > TIMID

TIMIDEST > TIMID

TIMIDITY > TIMID

TIMIDLY > TIMID

TIMIDNESS > TIMID

TIMING n ability to judge when to do or say something so as to make the best effect

TIMINGS > TIMING

TIMIST n one concerned with time

TIMISTS > TIMIST

TIMOCRACY n political unit or system in which possession of property serves as the first requirement for participation in government

TIMOLOL n relaxant medicine used (for example) to reduce blood pressure

TIMOLOLS > TIMOLOL

TIMON n apparatus by which a vessel is steered

TIMONEER n helmsman; tillerman

TIMONEERS > TIMONEER

TIMONS > TIMON

TIMOROUS adj timid

TIMORSOME adj timorous; timid

TIMOTHIES > TIMOTHY

TIMOTHY as in timothy grass perennial grass of temperate regions, having erect stiff stems and cylindrical flower spikes: grown for hay and pasture

TIMOUS same as
> TIMEOUS

TIMOUSLY > TIMOUS

TIMPANA n traditional Maltese baked pasta and pastry dish

TIMPANI npl set of kettledrums

TIMPANIST > TIMPANI

TIMPANO n kettledrum

TIMPANUM same as
> TYMPANUM

TIMPANUMS > TIMPANUM

TIMPS same as > TIMPANI

TIN n soft metallic element ▷ vb put (food) into tins

TINA n (slang) crystal meth

TINAJA n large jar for cooling water

TINAJAS > TINAJA

TINAMOU n type of bird of Central and S America, with small wings, a heavy body, and an inconspicuous plumage

TINAMOUS > TINAMOU

TINAS > TINA

TINCAL another name for
> BORAX

TINCALS > TINCAL

TINCHEL n in Scotland, a circle of deer hunters who gradually close in on their quarry

TINCHELS > TINCHEL

TINCT vb tint ▷ adj tinted or coloured

TINCTED > TINCT

TINCTING > TINCT

TINCTS > TINCT

TINCTURE n medicinal extract in a solution of alcohol ▷ vb give a tint or colour to

TINCTURED > TINCTURE

TINCTURES > TINCTURE

TIND vb set alight

TINDAL n petty officer

TINDALS > TINDAL

TINDED > TIND

TINDER n dry easily-burning material used to start a fire

TINDERBOX n formerly, small box for tinder, esp one fitted with a flint and steel

TINDERS > TINDER

TINDERY > TINDER

TINDING > TIND

TINDS > TIND

TINE n prong of a fork or antler ▷ vb lose

TINEA n any fungal skin disease, esp ringworm

TINEAL > TINEA

TINEAS > TINEA

TINED > TINE

TINEID n type of moth of the family which includes the clothes moths

TINEIDS > TINEID

TINES > TINE

TINFOIL n paper-thin sheet of metal, used for wrapping foodstuffs

TINFOILS > TINFOIL

TINFUL n contents of a tin or the amount a tin will hold

TINFULS > TINFUL

TING same as > THING

TINGE n slight tint ▷ vb give a slight tint or trace to

TINGED > TINGE

TINGEING > TINGE

TINGES > TINGE

TINGING > TINGE

TINGLE n (feel) a prickling or stinging sensation ▷ vb feel a mild prickling or stinging sensation, as from cold or excitement

TINGLED > TINGLE

TINGLER > TINGLE

TINGLERS > TINGLE

TINGLES > TINGLE

TINGLIER > TINGLE

TINGLIEST > TINGLE

TINGLING > TINGLE

TINGLINGS > TINGLE

TINGLISH adj exciting

TINGLY > TINGLE

TINGS > TING

TINGUAITE n type of igneous rock

TINHORN n cheap pretentious person, esp a gambler with extravagant claims ▷ adj cheap and showy

TINHORNS > TINHORN

TINIER > TINY

TINIES npl small children

TINIEST > TINY

TINILY > TINY

TININESS > TINY

TINING > TINE

TINK shortened form of > TINKER

TINKED > TINK

TINKER n derogatory term for travelling mender of pots and pans ▷ vb fiddle with (an engine etc) in an attempt to repair it

TINKERED > TINKER

TINKERER > TINKER

TINKERERS > TINKER

TINKERING > TINKER

TINKERMAN n football coach who continually changes the team line-up or formation between games

TINKERMEN > TINKERMAN

TINKERS > TINKER

TINKERTOY n children's construction set

TINKING > TINK

TINKLE vb ring with a high tinny sound like a small bell ▷ n this sound or action

TINKLED > TINKLE

TINKLER same as > TINKER

TINKLERS > TINKLER

TINKLES > TINKLE

TINKLIER > TINKLE

TINKLIEST > TINKLE

TINKLING > TINKLE

TINKLINGS > TINKLE

TINKLY > TINKLE

TINKS > TINK

TINLIKE > TIN

TINMAN n one who works with tin or tin plate

TINMEN > TINMAN

TINNED > TIN

TINNER n tin miner

TINNERS > TINNER

TINNIE same as > TINNY

TINNIER > TINNY

TINNIES > TINNY

TINNIEST > TINNY

TINNILY > TINNY

TINNINESS > TINNY

TINNING > TIN

TINNINGS > TIN

TINNITUS n ringing, hissing, or booming sensation in one or both ears, caused by infection of the middle or inner ear, a side effect of certain drugs, etc

TINNY adj (of sound) thin and metallic ▷ n can of beer

TINPLATE n thin steel sheet coated with a layer of tin that protects the steel from corrosion ▷ vb coat (a metal or object) with a layer of tin, usually either by electroplating or by dipping in a bath of molten tin

TINPLATED > TINPLATE

TINPLATES > TINPLATE

TINPOT adj worthless or unimportant ▷ n pot made of tin

TINPOTS > TINPOT

TINS > TIN

TINSEL n decorative metallic strips or threads ▷ adj made of or decorated with tinsel ▷ vb decorate with or as if with tinsel

TINSELED > TINSEL

TINSELING > TINSEL

TINSELLED > TINSEL

TINSELLY > TINSEL

TINSELRY n tinsel-like material

TINSELS > TINSEL

TINSEY old variant of > TINSEL

TINSEYS > TINSEY

TINSMITH n person who works with tin or tin plate

TINSMITHS > TINSMITH

TINSNIPS n metal cutters

TINSTONE n black or brown stone

TINSTONES > TINSTONE

TINT n (pale) shade of a colour ▷ vb give a tint to

TINTACK n tin-plated tack

TINTACKS > TINTACK

TINTED > TINT

TINTER > TINT

TINTERS > TINT

TINTIER > TINTY

TINTIEST > TINTY

TINTINESS > TINTY

TINTING > TINT

TINTINGS > TINT

TINTLESS > TINT

TINTOOKIE n in informal Australian English, fawning or servile person

TINTS > TINT

TINTY adj having many tints

TINTYPE another name for > FERROTYPE

TINTYPES > TINTYPE

TINWARE n objects made of tin plate

TINWARES > TINWARE

TINWORK n objects made of tin

TINWORKS n place where tin is mined, smelted, or rolled

TINY adj very small

TIP n narrow or pointed end of anything ▷ vb put a tip on

TIPCART n cart that can be tipped to empty out its contents

TIPCARTS > TIPCART

TIPCAT n game in which a short sharp-ended piece of wood (the cat) is tipped in the air with a stick

TIPCATS > TIPCAT

TIPI variant spelling of > TEPEE

TIPIS > TIPI

TIPLESS > TIP

TIPOFF n warning or hint, esp given confidentially and based on inside information

TIPOFFS > TIPOFF

TIPPABLE > TIP

TIPPED > TIP

TIPPEE n person who receives a tip, esp regarding share prices

TIPPEES > TIPPEE

TIPPER n person who gives or leaves a tip

TIPPERS > TIPPER

TIPPET n scarflike piece of fur, often made from a whole animal skin, worn, esp formerly, round a woman's shoulders

TIPPETS > TIPPET

TIPPIER > TIPPY

TIPPIEST > TIPPY

TIPPING > TIP

TIPPINGS > TIP

TIPPLE vb drink alcohol habitually, esp in small quantities ▷ n alcoholic drink

TIPPLED > TIPPLE

TIPPLER > TIPPLE

TIPPLERS > TIPPLE

TIPPLES > TIPPLE

TIPPLING > TIPPLE

TIPPY adj extremely fashionable or stylish

TIPPYTOE same as > TIPTOE

TIPPYTOED > TIPPYTOE

TIPPYTOES > TIPPYTOE

TIPS > TIP

TIPSHEET n list of advice or instructions

TIPSHEETS > TIPSHEET

TIPSIER > TIPSY

TIPSIEST > TIPSY

TIPSIFIED > TIPSIFY

TIPSIFIES > TIPSIFY

TIPSIFY vb make tipsy

TIPSILY > TIPSY

TIPSINESS > TIPSY

TIPSTAFF n court official

TIPSTAFFS > TIPSTAFF

TIPSTAVES > TIPSTAFF

TIPSTER n person who sells tips about races

TIPSTERS > TIPSTER

TIPSTOCK n detachable section of a gunstock, usually gripped by the left hand of the user

TIPSTOCKS > TIPSTOCK

TIPSY adj slightly drunk

TIPT > TIP

TIPTOE vb walk quietly with the heels off the ground

TIPTOED > TIPTOE

TIPTOEING > TIPTOE

TIPTOES > TIPTOE

TIPTOP adj of the highest quality or condition ▷ adv of the highest quality or condition ▷ *n* best in quality ▷ *n* very top; pinnacle

TIPTOPS > TIPTOP

TIPTRONIC *n* type of gearbox that has both automatic and manual options

TIPULA *n* crane fly

TIPULAS > TIPULA

TIPUNA *n* ancestor

TIPUNAS > TIPUNA

TIRADE *n* long angry speech

TIRADES > TIRADE

TIRAGE *n* drawing of wine from a barrel prior to bottling

TIRAGES > TIRAGE

TIRAMISU *n* Italian dessert made with sponge soaked in coffee and Marsala, topped with soft cheese and powdered chocolate

TIRAMISUS > TIRAMISU

TIRASSE *n* mechanism in an organ connecting two pedals, so that both may be depressed at once

TIRASSES > TIRASSE

TIRE *vb* reduce the energy of, as by exertion

TIRED *adj* exhausted

TIREDER > TIRED

TIREDEST > TIRED

TIREDLY > TIRED

TIREDNESS > TIRED

TIRELESS *adj* energetic and determined

TIRELING *n* fatigued person or animal

TIRELINGS > TIRELING

TIRES > TIRE

TIRESOME *adj* boring and irritating

TIREWOMAN *n* an obsolete term for lady's maid

TIREWOMEN > TIREWOMAN

TIRING > TIRE

TIRINGS > TIRE

TIRITI *n* another name for the Treaty of Waitangi

TIRITIS > TIRITI

TIRL *vb* turn

TIRLED > TIRL

TIRLING > TIRL

TIRLS > TIRL

TIRO *same as* > TYRO

TIROES > TIRO

TIRONIC *variant of* > TYRONIC

TIROS > TIRO

TIRR *vb* strip or denude

TIRRED > TIRR

TIRRING > TIRR

TIRRIT *n* panic; scare

TIRRITS > TIRRIT

TIRRIVEE *n* outburst of bad temper; rumpus

TIRRIVEES > TIRRIVEE

TIRRIVIE *same as* > TIRRIVEE

TIRRIVIES > TIRRIVIE

TIRRS > TIRR

TIS > TI

TISANE *n* infusion of dried or fresh leaves or flowers, as camomile

TISANES > TISANE

TISICK *n* splutter; cough

TISICKS > TISICK

TISSUAL *adj* relating to tissue

TISSUE *n* substance of an animal body or plant ▷ *vb* weave into tissue

TISSUED > TISSUE

TISSUES > TISSUE

TISSUEY > TISSUE

TISSUING > TISSUE

TISSULAR *adj* relating to tissue

TISWAS *n* state of anxiety or excitement

TISWASES > TISWAS

TIT *n* any of various small songbirds; informal term for a female breast ▷ *vb* jerk or tug

TITAN *n* person who is huge, strong, or very important

TITANATE *n* any salt or ester of titanic acid

TITANATES > TITANATE

TITANESS *n* person who is huge, strong, or very important

TITANIA > TITANIUM

TITANIAS > TITANIA

TITANIC *adj* huge or very important

TITANIS *n* large predatory flightless prehistoric bird

TITANISES > TITANIS

TITANISM *n* titanic power

TITANISMS > TITANISM

TITANITE *another name for* > SPHENE

TITANITES > TITANITE

TITANIUM *n* strong light metallic element used to make alloys

TITANIUMS > TITANIUM

TITANOUS *adj* of or containing titanium, esp in the trivalent state

TITANS > TITAN

TITBIT *n* tasty piece of food

TITBITS > TITBIT

TITCH *n* small person

TITCHES > TITCH

TITCHIER > TITCHY

TITCHIEST > TITCHY

TITCHY *adj* very small

TITE *adj* immediately

TITELY *adv* immediately

TITER *same as* > TITRE

TITERS > TITER

TITFER *n* hat

TITFERS > TITFER

TITHABLE *adj* (until 1936) liable to pay tithes

TITHE *n* esp formerly, one tenth of one's income or produce paid to the church as a tax ▷ *vb* charge or pay a tithe

TITHED > TITHE

TITHER > TITHE

TITHERS > TITHE

TITHES > TITHE

TITHING > TITHE

TITHINGS > TITHING

TITHONIA *n* Central American herb with flowers resembling sunflowers

TITHONIAS > TITHONIA

TITI *n* small omnivorous New World monkey of South America, with long beautifully coloured fur and a long nonprehensile tail

TITIAN *n* reddish gold colour

TITIANS > TITIAN

TITILLATE *vb* excite or stimulate pleasurably

TITIS > TITI

TITIVATE *vb* smarten up

TITIVATED > TITIVATE

TITIVATES > TITIVATE

TITIVATOR > TITIVATE

TITLARK *another name for* > PIPIT

TITLARKS > TITLARK

TITLE *n* name of a book, film, etc ▷ *vb* give a title to

TITLED *adj* aristocratic

TITLELESS > TITLE

TITLER *n* one who writes titles

TITLERS > TITLE

TITLES > TITLE

TITLING > TITLE

TITLINGS > TITLE

TITLIST *n* titleholder

TITLISTS > TITLIST

TITMAN *n* (of pigs) the runt of a litter

TITMEN > TITMAN

TITMICE > TITMOUSE

TITMOSE *old spelling of* > TITMOUSE

TITMOUSE *n* any small active songbird

TITOKI *n* New Zealand evergreen tree with a spreading crown and glossy green leaves

TITOKIS > TITOKI

TITRABLE > TITRATE

TITRANT *n* solution in a titration that is added from a burette to a measured quantity of another solution

TITRANTS > TITRANT

TITRATE *vb* measure the volume or concentration of (a solution) by titration

TITRATED > TITRATE

TITRATES > TITRATE

TITRATING > TITRATE

TITRATION *n* operation in which a measured amount of one solution is added to a known quantity of another solution until the reaction between the two is complete

TITRATOR *n* device used to perform titration

TITRATORS > TITRATOR

TITRE *n* concentration of a solution as determined by titration

TITRES > TITRE

TITS > TIT

TITTED > TIT

TITTER *vb* laugh in a suppressed way ▷ *n* suppressed laugh

TITTERED > TITTER

TITTERER > TITTER

TITTERERS > TITTER

TITTERING > TITTER

TITTERS > TITTER

TITTIE *n* sister; young woman

TITTIES > TITTIE

TITTING > TIT

TITTISH *adj* testy

TITTIVATE *same as* > TITIVATE

TITTLE *n* very small amount ▷ *vb* chatter; tattle

TITTLEBAT *n* child's name for the stickleback fish

TITTLED > TITTLE

TITTLES > TITTLE

TITTLING > TITTLE

TITTUP *vb* prance or frolic ▷ *n* caper

TITTUPED > TITTUP

TITTUPING > TITTUP

TITTUPPED > TITTUP

TITTUPPY *same as* > TITTUPY

TITTUPS > TITTUP

TITTUPY *adj* spritely; lively

TITTY *same as* > TITTIE

TITUBANCY *n* staggering or stumbling

TITUBANT *adj* staggering

TITUBATE *vb* stagger

TITUBATED > TITUBATE

TITUBATES > TITUBATE

TITULAR *adj* in name only ▷ *n* bearer of a title

TITULARLY > TITULAR

TITULARS > TITULAR

TITULARY *same as* > TITULAR

TITULE *same as* > TITLE

TITULED > TITULE

TITULES > TITULE

TITULI > TITULUS

TITULING > TITULE

TITULUS *n* (in crucifixion) a sign attached to the top of the cross on which were written the condemned man's name and crime

TITUP *same as* > TITTUP

TITUPED > TITUP

TITUPING > TITUP

TITUPPED > TITUP

TITUPPING > TITUP

TITUPS > TITUP

TITUPY *same as* > TITTUPY

TIVY *same as* > TANTIVY

TIX *npl* tickets

TIYIN *n* monetary unit of Uzbekistan and Kyrgyzstan

TIYINS > TIYIN

TIZWAS *same as* > TISWAS

TIZWASES > TIZWAS

TIZZ *same as* > TIZZY

TIZZES > TIZZ

TIZZIES > TIZZY

TIZZY *n* confused or agitated state

TJANTING *n* pen-like tool used in batik for applying molten wax to fabric

TJANTINGS > TJANTING

TMESES > TMESIS

TMESIS *n* interpolation of a word or group of words between the parts of a compound word

TO *prep* indicating movement towards, equality or comparison, etc ▷ *adv* a closed position

TOAD *n* animal like a large frog

TOADEATER *rare word for* > TOADY

TOADFISH *n* spiny-finned bottom-dwelling marine fish of tropical and temperate seas, with a flattened tapering body and a wide mouth

TOADFLAX *n* plant with narrow leaves and yellow-orange flowers

TOADGRASS *another name for* > TOADRUSH

TOADIED > TOADY

TOADIES > TOADY

TOADISH > TOAD

TOADLESS *adj* having no toads

TOADLIKE > TOAD

TOADRUSH *n* annual rush growing in damp lowlands

TOADS > TOAD

TOADSTONE *n* amygdaloidal basalt occurring in the limestone regions of Derbyshire

TOADSTOOL *n* poisonous fungus like a mushroom

TOADY *n* ingratiating person ▷ *vb* be ingratiating

TOADYING > TOADY

TOADYISH > TOADY

TOADYISM > TOADY

TOADYISMS > TOADY

TOAST *n* sliced bread browned by heat ▷ *vb* brown (bread) by heat

TOASTED > TOAST

TOASTER > TOAST

TOASTERS > TOAST

TOASTIE *same as* > TOASTY

TOASTIER > TOASTY

TOASTIES > TOASTY

TOASTIEST > TOASTY

TOASTING > TOAST

TOASTINGS > TOAST

TOASTS > TOAST

TOASTY *n* toasted sandwich ▷ *adj* tasting or smelling like toast

TOAZE *variant spelling of* > TOZE

TOAZED > TOAZE

TOAZES > TOAZE

TOAZING > TOAZE

TOBACCO *n* plant with large leaves dried for smoking

TOBACCOES > TOBACCO

TOBACCOS > TOBACCO

TOBIES > TOBY

TOBOGGAN *n* narrow sledge for sliding over snow ▷ *vb* ride a toboggan

TOBOGGANS > TOBOGGAN

TOBOGGIN *variant spelling of* > TOBOGGAN

TOBOGGINS > TOBOGGIN

TOBY *n* water stopcock at the boundary of a street and house section

TOC *n* in communications code, signal for letter t

TOCCATA *n* rapid piece of music for a keyboard instrument

TOCCATAS > TOCCATA

TOCCATE > TOCCATA

TOCCATINA *n* short toccata

TOCHER *n* dowry ▷ *vb* give a dowry to

TOCHERED > TOCHER

TOCHERING > TOCHER

TOCHERS > TOCHER

TOCK *n* sound made by a clock ▷ *vb* (of a clock) make such a sound

TOCKED > TOCK

TOCKIER > TOCKY

TOCKIEST > TOCKY

TOCKING > TOCK

TOCKLEY *slang word for* > PENIS

TOCKLEYS > TOCKLEY

TOCKS > TOCK

TOCKY *adj* muddy

TOCO *n* punishment

TOCOLOGY *n* branch of medicine concerned with childbirth

TOCOS > TOCO

TOCS > TOC

TOCSIN *n* warning signal

TOCSINS > TOCSIN

TOD *n* unit of weight, used for wool, etc, usually equal to 28 pounds ▷ *vb* produce a tod

TODAY *n* this day ▷ *adv* on this day

TODAYS > TODAY

TODDE *same as* > TOD

TODDED > TOD

TODDES > TODDE

TODDIES > TODDY

TODDING > TOD

TODDLE *vb* walk with short unsteady steps ▷ *n* act or an instance of toddling

TODDLED > TODDLE

TODDLER *n* child beginning to walk

TODDLERS > TODDLER

TODDLES > TODDLE

TODDLING > TODDLE

TODDY *n* sweetened drink of spirits and hot water

TODGER *n* penis

TODGERS > TODGER

TODIES > TODY

TODS > TOD

TODY *n* small bird of the Caribbean, with a red-and-green plumage and long straight bill

TOE *n* digit of the foot ▷ *vb* touch or kick with the toe

TOEA *n* monetary unit of Papua New Guinea, worth one-hundredth of a kina

TOEAS > TOEA

TOEBIE *n* South African slang for sandwich

TOEBIES > TOEBIE

TOECAP *n* strengthened covering for the toe of a shoe

TOECAPS > TOECAP

TOECLIP *n* clip on a bicycle pedal into which the toes are inserted to prevent the foot from slipping

TOECLIPS > TOECLIP

TOED > TOE

TOEHOLD *n* small space on a mountain for supporting the toe of the foot in climbing

TOEHOLDS > TOEHOLD

TOEIER > TOEY

TOEIEST > TOEY

TOEING > TOE

TOELESS *adj* not having toes

TOELIKE > TOE

TOENAIL *n* thin hard clear plate covering part of the upper surface of the end of each toe ▷ *vb* join (beams) by driving nails obliquely

TOENAILED > TOENAIL

TOENAILS > TOENAIL

TOEPIECE *n* part of a shoe that covers the toes

TOEPIECES > TOEPIECE

TOEPLATE *n* metal reinforcement of the part of the sole of a shoe or boot underneath the toes

TOEPLATES > TOEPLATE

TOERAG *n* contemptible person

TOERAGGER *same as* > TOERAG

TOERAGS > TOERAG

TOES > TOE

TOESHOE *n* ballet pump with padded toes

TOESHOES > TOESHOE

TOETOE *same as* > TOITOI

TOETOES > TOETOE

TOEY *adj* (of a person) nervous or anxious

TOFF *n* well-dressed or upper-class person

TOFFEE *n* chewy sweet made of boiled sugar

TOFFEES > TOFFEE

TOFFIER > TOFFY

TOFFIES > TOFFY

TOFFIEST > TOFFY

TOFFISH *adj* belonging to or characteristic of the upper class

TOFFS *adj* like a toff

TOFFY *same as* > TOFFEE

TOFORE *prep* before

TOFT *n* homestead

TOFTS > TOFT

TOFU *n* soft food made from soya-bean curd

TOFUS > TOFU

TOFUTTI *n* tradename for any of a variety of nondairy, soya-based food products, esp frozen desserts

TOFUTTIS > TOFUTTI

TOG *n* unit for measuring the insulating power of duvets ▷ *vb* dress oneself, esp in smart clothes

TOGA *n* garment worn by citizens of ancient Rome ▷ *vb* wear a toga

TOGAE > TOGA

TOGAED > TOGA

TOGAS > TOGA

TOGATE *adj* clad in a toga

TOGATED *same as* > TOGATE

TOGAVIRUS *n* one of family of viruses

TOGE *old variant of* > TOGA

TOGED > TOGE

TOGES > TOGE

TOGETHER *adv* in company ▷ *adj* organized

TOGGED > TOG

TOGGER *vb* play football ▷ *n* football player

TOGGERED > TOGGER

TOGGERIES > TOGGERY

TOGGERING > TOGGER

TOGGERS > TOGGER

TOGGERY *n* clothes

TOGGING > TOG

TOGGLE *n* small bar-shaped button inserted through a loop for fastening ▷ *vb* supply or fasten with a toggle or toggles

TOGGLED > TOGGLE

TOGGLER > TOGGLE

TOGGLERS > TOGGLE

TOGGLES > TOGGLE

TOGGLING > TOGGLE

TOGS > TOG

TOGUE *n* large North American freshwater game fish

TOGUES > TOGUE

TOHEROA *n* large edible mollusc of New Zealand with a distinctive flavour

TOHEROAS > TOHEROA

TOHO *n* (to a hunting dog) an instruction to stop

TOHUNGA *n* Māori priest

TOHUNGAS > TOHUNGA

TOIL n hard work ▷ vb work hard
TOILE n transparent linen or cotton fabric
TOILED > TOIL
TOILER > TOIL
TOILERS > TOIL
TOILES > TOILE
TOILET n a bowl connected to a drain for receiving and disposing of urine and faeces ▷ vb go to the toilet
TOILETED > TOILET
TOILETING > TOILET
TOILETRY n object or cosmetic used to clean or groom oneself
TOILETS > TOILET
TOILETTE same as > TOILET
TOILETTES > TOILETTE
TOILFUL same as > TOILSOME
TOILFULLY > TOILFUL
TOILINET n type of fabric with a woollen weft and a cotton or silk warp
TOILINETS > TOILINET
TOILING > TOIL
TOILINGS > TOIL
TOILLESS > TOIL
TOILS > TOIL
TOILSOME adj requiring hard work
TOILWORN adj fatigued, wearied by work
TOING as in toing and froing state of going back and forth
TOINGS > TOING
TOISE n obsolete French unit of length roughly equal to 2m
TOISEACH n ancient Celtic nobleman
TOISEACHS > TOISEACH
TOISECH same as > TOISEACH
TOISECHS > TOISECH
TOISES > TOISE
TOISON n fleece
TOISONS > TOISON
TOIT vb walk or move in an unsteady manner, as from old age
TOITED > TOIT
TOITING > TOIT
TOITOI n tall grasses with feathery fronds
TOITOIS > TOITOI
TOITS > TOIT
TOKAMAK n reactor used in thermonuclear experiments
TOKAMAKS > TOKAMAK
TOKAY n small gecko of S and SE Asia, having a retractile claw at the tip of each digit
TOKAYS > TOKAY
TOKE n draw on a cannabis cigarette ▷ vb take a draw on a cannabis cigarette
TOKED > TOKE

TOKEN n sign or symbol ▷ adj nominal or slight
TOKENED > TOKEN
TOKENING > TOKEN
TOKENISM n policy of making only a token effort, esp to comply with a law
TOKENISMS > TOKENISM
TOKENS > TOKEN
TOKER > TOKE
TOKERS > TOKE
TOKES > TOKE
TOKING > TOKE
TOKO same as > TOCO
TOKOLOGY same as > TOCOLOGY
TOKOLOSHE n (in Bantu folklore) a malevolent mythical manlike animal of short stature
TOKOLOSHI variant of > TOKOLOSHE
TOKOMAK variant spelling of > TOKAMAK
TOKOMAKS > TOKOMAK
TOKONOMA n recess off a living room
TOKONOMAS > TOKONOMA
TOKOS > TOKO
TOKOTOKO n ceremonial carved Māori walking stick
TOKOTOKOS > TOKOTOKO
TOKTOKKIE n large South African beetle
TOLA n unit of weight, used in India, equal to 180 ser or 180 grains
TOLAN n white crystalline derivative of acetylene
TOLANE same as > TOLAN
TOLANES > TOLANE
TOLANS > TOLAN
TOLAR n standard monetary unit of Slovenia, divided into 100 stotin
TOLARJEV > TOLAR
TOLARJI > TOLAR
TOLARS > TOLAR
TOLAS > TOLA
TOLBOOTH same as > TOLLBOOTH
TOLBOOTHS > TOLBOOTH
TOLD > TELL
TOLE same as > TOLL
TOLED > TOLE
TOLEDO n type of sword originally made in Toledo
TOLEDOS > TOLEDO
TOLERABLE adj bearable
TOLERABLY > TOLERABLE
TOLERANCE n acceptance of other people's rights to their own opinions or actions
TOLERANT adj able to tolerate the beliefs, actions, opinions, etc, of others
TOLERATE vb allow to exist or happen
TOLERATED > TOLERATE
TOLERATES > TOLERATE
TOLERATOR > TOLERATE

TOLES > TOLE
TOLEWARE n enamelled or lacquered metal ware, usually gilded
TOLEWARES > TOLEWARE
TOLIDIN same as > TOLIDINE
TOLIDINE n compound used in dyeing and in chemical analysis, esp as an indicator of the presence of free chlorine in water
TOLIDINES > TOLIDINE
TOLIDINS > TOLIDIN
TOLING > TOLE
TOLINGS > TOLE
TOLL vb ring (a bell) slowly and regularly, esp to announce a death ▷ n tolling
TOLLABLE > TOLL
TOLLAGE same as > TOLL
TOLLAGES > TOLLAGE
TOLLBAR n bar blocking passage of a thoroughfare, raised on payment of a toll
TOLLBARS > TOLLBAR
TOLLBOOTH n booth or kiosk at which a toll is collected
TOLLDISH n dish used to measure out the portion of grain given to a miller as payment for his or her work
TOLLED > TOLL
TOLLER > TOLL
TOLLERS > TOLLER
TOLLEY n large shooting marble used in a game of marbles
TOLLEYS > TOLLEY
TOLLGATE n gate across a toll road or bridge at which travellers must pay
TOLLGATES > TOLLGATE
TOLLHOUSE n small house at a tollgate occupied by a toll collector
TOLLIE same as > TOLLY
TOLLIES > TOLLY
TOLLING > TOLL
TOLLINGS > TOLL
TOLLMAN n man who collects tolls
TOLLMEN > TOLLMAN
TOLLS > TOLL
TOLLWAY n road on which users must pay tolls to travel
TOLLWAYS > TOLLWAY
TOLLY n castrated calf
TOLSEL n tolbooth
TOLSELS > TOLSEL
TOLSEY n tolbooth
TOLSEYS > TOLBOOTH
TOLT n type of obsolete English writ
TOLTER vb struggle or move with difficulty, as in mud
TOLTERED > TOLTER
TOLTERING > TOLTER
TOLTERS > TOLTER
TOLTS > TOLT
TOLU n sweet-smelling

balsam obtained from a South American tree, used in medicine and perfume
TOLUATE n any salt or ester of any of the three isomeric forms of toluic acid
TOLUATES > TOLUATE
TOLUENE n colourless volatile flammable liquid obtained from petroleum and coal tar
TOLUENES > TOLUENE
TOLUIC as in toluic acid white crystalline derivative of toluene existing in three isomeric forms
TOLUID n white crystalline derivative of glycocoll
TOLUIDE variant of > TOLUID
TOLUIDES > TOLUIDE
TOLUIDIDE n chemical deriving from toluene
TOLUIDIN n type of dye
TOLUIDINE n compound used in dye production
TOLUIDINS > TOLUIDIN
TOLUIDS > TOLUID
TOLUOL another name for > TOLUENE
TOLUOLE another name for > TOLUENE
TOLUOLES > TOLUOLE
TOLUOLS > TOLUOL
TOLUS > TOLU
TOLUYL n of, consisting of, or containing any of three isomeric groups CH_3C_6 H_4CO-, derived from a toluic acid by removal of the hydroxyl group
TOLUYLS > TOLUYL
TOLYL n of, consisting of, or containing any of three isomeric groups, $CH_3C_6H_4-$, derived from toluene
TOLYLS > TOLYL
TOLZEY n tolbooth
TOLZEYS > TOLZEY
TOM n male cat ▷ adj (of an animal) male ▷ vb prostitute oneself
TOMAHAWK n fighting axe of the Native Americans
TOMAHAWKS > TOMAHAWK
TOMALLEY n fat from a lobster, called "liver", and eaten as a delicacy
TOMALLEYS > TOMALLEY
TOMAN n gold coin formerly issued in Persia
TOMANS > TOMAN
TOMATILLO n Mexican plant bearing edible berries of the same name
TOMATO n red fruit used in salads and as a vegetable
TOMATOES > TOMATO
TOMATOEY > TOMATO
TOMB n grave
TOMBAC n any of various brittle alloys containing copper and zinc and sometimes tin and arsenic:

used for making cheap jewellery, etc
TOMBACK *variant spelling of* > TOMBAC
TOMBACKS > TOMBAC
TOMBACS > TOMBAC
TOMBAK *same as* > TOMBAC
TOMBAKS > TOMBAK
TOMBAL *adj* like or relating to a tomb
TOMBED > TOMB
TOMBIC *adj* of or relating to tombs
TOMBING > TOMB
TOMBLESS > TOMB
TOMBLIKE > TOMB
TOMBOC *n* weapon
TOMBOCS > TOMBOC
TOMBOLA *n* lottery with tickets drawn from a revolving drum
TOMBOLAS > TOMBOLA
TOMBOLO *n* narrow sand or shingle bar linking a small island with another island or the mainland
TOMBOLOS > TOMBOLO
TOMBOY *n* girl who acts or dresses like a boy
TOMBOYISH > TOMBOY
TOMBOYS > TOMBOY
TOMBS > TOMB
TOMBSTONE *n* gravestone
TOMCAT *vb* (of a man) to be promiscuous
TOMCATS > TOMCAT
TOMCATTED > TOMCAT
TOMCOD *n* small fish resembling the cod
TOMCODS > TOMCOD
TOME *n* large heavy book
TOMENTA > TOMENTUM
TOMENTOSE > TOMENTUM
TOMENTOUS > TOMENTUM
TOMENTUM *n* feltlike covering of downy hairs on leaves and other plant parts
TOMES > TOME
TOMFOOL *n* fool ▷ *vb* act the fool
TOMFOOLED > TOMFOOL
TOMFOOLS > TOMFOOL
TOMIA > TOMIUM
TOMIAL > TOMIUM
TOMIUM *n* sharp edge of a bird's beak
TOMMED > TOM
TOMMIED > TOMMY
TOMMIES > TOMMY
TOMMING > TOM
TOMMY *n* private in the British Army ▷ *vb* (formerly) to exploit workers by paying them in goods rather than in money
TOMMYING > TOMMY
TOMMYROT *n* utter nonsense
TOMMYROTS > TOMMYROT
TOMO *n* shaft formed by the action of water on limestone or volcanic rock
TOMOGRAM *n* x-ray

photograph of a selected plane section of the human body or some other solid object
TOMOGRAMS > TOMOGRAM
TOMOGRAPH *n* device for making tomograms
TOMORROW *n* (on) the day after today ▷ *adv* on the day after today
TOMORROWS > TOMORROW
TOMOS > TOMO
TOMPION *same as* > TAMPION
TOMPIONS > TOMPION
TOMPON *same as* > TAMPON
TOMPONED > TOMPON
TOMPONING > TOMPON
TOMPONS > TOMPON
TOMS > TOM
TOMTIT *n* small European bird that eats insects and seeds
TOMTITS > TOMTIT
TON *n* unit of weight equal to 2240 pounds or 1016 kilograms (long ton) or, in the US, 2000 pounds or 907 kilograms (short ton); style; distinction
TONAL *adj* written in a key
TONALITE *n* igneous rock found in the Italian Alps
TONALITES > TONALITE
TONALITIC *adj* relating to or consisting of tonalite
TONALITY *n* presence of a musical key in a composition
TONALLY > TONAL
TONANT *adj* very loud
TONDI > TONDO
TONDINI > TONDINO
TONDINO *n* small tondo
TONDINOS > TONDINO
TONDO *n* circular easel painting or relief carving
TONDOS > TONDO
TONE *n* sound with reference to its pitch, volume, etc ▷ *vb* harmonize (with)
TONEARM *same as* > PICKUP
TONEARMS > TONEARM
TONED > TONE
TONELESS *adj* having no tone
TONEME *n* phoneme that is distinguished from another phoneme only by its tone
TONEMES > TONEME
TONEMIC > TONEME
TONEPAD *n* keypad used to transmit information by generating tones that can be recognised by a central system as corresponding to particular digits
TONEPADS > TONEPAD
TONER *n* cosmetic applied to the skin to reduce oiliness
TONERS > TONER
TONES > TONE

TONETIC *adj* (of a language) distinguishing words semantically by distinction of tone as well as by other sounds
TONETICS *npl* area of linguistics concentrating on the use of tone to distinguish words semantically
TONETTE *n* small musical instrument resembling a recorder
TONETTES > TONETTE
TONEY *variant spelling of* > TONY
TONG *n* (formerly) a secret society of Chinese Americans ▷ *vb* gather or seize with tongs ▷ *n* (formerly) a Chinese secret society
TONGA *n* light two-wheeled vehicle used in rural areas of India
TONGAS > TONGA
TONGED > TONG
TONGER *n* one who uses tongs to gather oysters
TONGERS > TONGER
TONGING > TONG
TONGMAN *another word for* > TONGER
TONGMEN > TONGMAN
TONGS *npl* large pincers for grasping and lifting
TONGSTER *n* tong member
TONGSTERS > TONGSTER
TONGUE *n* muscular organ in the mouth, used in speaking and tasting ▷ *vb* use the tongue
TONGUED > TONGUE
TONGUELET *n* small tongue
TONGUES > TONGUE
TONGUING > TONGUE
TONGUINGS > TONGUE
TONIC *n* medicine to improve body tone ▷ *adj* invigorating
TONICALLY > TONIC
TONICITY *n* state, condition, or quality of being tonic
TONICS > TONIC
TONIER > TONY
TONIES > TONY
TONIEST > TONY
TONIGHT *n* (in or during) the night or evening of this day ▷ *adv* in or during the night or evening of this day
TONIGHTS > TONIGHT
TONING > TONE
TONINGS > TONE
TONISH > TON
TONISHLY > TON
TONITE *n* explosive used in quarrying
TONITES > TONITE
TONK *vb* strike with a heavy blow ▷ *n* effete or effeminate man
TONKA as in *tonka bean* tall

leguminous tree of tropical America, having fragrant black almond-shaped seeds
TONKED > TONK
TONKER > TONK
TONKERS > TONK
TONKING > TONK
TONKS > TONK
TONLET *n* skirt of a suit of armour, consisting of overlapping metal bands
TONLETS > TONLET
TONNAG *n* type of (usually tartan) shawl
TONNAGE *n* weight capacity of a ship
TONNAGES > TONNAGE
TONNAGS > TONNAG
TONNE *same as* > TON
TONNEAU *n* detachable cover to protect the rear part of an open car when it is not carrying passengers
TONNEAUS > TONNEAU
TONNEAUX > TONNEAU
TONNELL *old spelling of* > TUNNEL
TONNELLS > TONNELL
TONNER *n* something, for example a vehicle, that weighs one ton
TONNERS > TONNE
TONNES > TONNE
TONNISH > TON
TONNISHLY > TON
TONOMETER *n* instrument for measuring the pitch of a sound, esp one consisting of a set of tuning forks
TONOMETRY > TONOMETER
TONOPLAST *n* membrane enclosing a vacuole in a plant cell
TONS > TON
TONSIL *n* small gland in the throat
TONSILAR > TONSIL
TONSILLAR > TONSIL
TONSILS > TONSIL
TONSOR *n* barber
TONSORIAL *adj* of a barber or his trade
TONSORS > TONSOR
TONSURE *n* shaving of all or the top of the head as a religious or monastic practice ▷ *vb* shave the head of
TONSURED > TONSURE
TONSURES > TONSURE
TONSURING > TONSURE
TONTINE *n* annuity scheme by which several subscribers accumulate and invest a common fund out of which they receive an annuity that increases as subscribers die until the last survivor takes the whole
TONTINER *n* subscriber to a tontine
TONTINERS > TONTINER
TONTINES > TONTINE

TONUS n normal tension of a muscle at rest

TONUSES > TONUS

TONY adj stylish or distinctive ▷ n stylish or distinctive person

TOO adv also, as well

TOOART variant spelling of > TUART

TOOARTS > TOOART

TOOK > TAKE

TOOL n implement used by hand ▷ vb work on with a tool

TOOLBAG n bag for storing or carrying tools

TOOLBAGS > TOOLBAG

TOOLBAR n horizontal row or vertical column of selectable buttons displayed on a computer screen, allowing the user to select a variety of functions

TOOLBARS > TOOLBAR

TOOLBOX n box for storing or carrying tools

TOOLBOXES > TOOLBOX

TOOLED > TOOL

TOOLER > TOOL

TOOLERS > TOOL

TOOLHEAD n adjustable attachment for a machine tool that holds the tool in position

TOOLHEADS > TOOLHEAD

TOOLHOUSE another word for > TOOLSHED

TOOLIE n adult who gatecrashes schools to make advances to the students

TOOLIES > TOOLIE

TOOLING n any decorative work done with a tool, esp a design stamped onto a book cover, piece of leatherwork, etc

TOOLINGS > TOOLING

TOOLKIT n set of tools designed to be used together or for a particular purpose

TOOLKITS > TOOLKIT

TOOLLESS adj having no tools

TOOLMAKER n person who makes tools

TOOLMAN n person who works with tools

TOOLMEN > TOOLMAN

TOOLROOM n room, as in a machine shop, where tools are made or stored

TOOLROOMS > TOOLROOM

TOOLS > TOOL

TOOLSET n set of predefined tools associated with a particular computer application

TOOLSETS > TOOLSET

TOOLSHED n small shed in the garden or yard of a house used for storing tools, esp those for gardening

TOOLSHEDS > TOOLSHED

TOOM vb empty (something) ▷ adj empty

TOOMED > TOOM

TOOMER > TOOM

TOOMEST > TOOM

TOOMING > TOOM

TOOMS > TOOM

TOON n large meliaceous tree of the East Indies and Australia, having clusters of flowers from which a dye is obtained

TOONIE n Canadian two-dollar coin

TOONIES > TOONIE

TOONS > TOON

TOORIE n tassel or bobble on a bonnet

TOORIES > TOORIE

TOOSHIE adj angry

TOOSHIER > TOOSHIE

TOOSHIEST > TOOSHIE

TOOT n short hooting sound ▷ vb (cause to) make such a sound

TOOTED > TOOT

TOOTER > TOOT

TOOTERS > TOOT

TOOTH n bonelike projection in the jaws of most vertebrates for biting and chewing

TOOTHACHE n pain in or near a tooth

TOOTHCOMB n comb with fine teeth set closely together

TOOTHED adj having a tooth or teeth

TOOTHFISH as in Patagonian toothfish Chilean sea bass

TOOTHFUL n little (esp alcoholic) drink

TOOTHFULS > TOOTHFUL

TOOTHIER > TOOTHY

TOOTHIEST > TOOTHY

TOOTHILY > TOOTHY

TOOTHING > TOOTH

TOOTHINGS > TOOTH

TOOTHLESS > TOOTH

TOOTHLIKE > TOOTH

TOOTHPICK n small stick for removing scraps of food from between the teeth

TOOTHS > TOOTH

TOOTHSOME adj delicious or appetizing in appearance, flavour, or smell

TOOTHWASH n tooth-cleaning liquid

TOOTHWORT n parasitic plant

TOOTHY adj having or showing numerous, large, or prominent teeth

TOOTING > TOOT

TOOTLE vb hoot softly or repeatedly ▷ n soft hoot or series of hoots

TOOTLED > TOOTLE

TOOTLER > TOOTLE

TOOTLERS > TOOTLE

TOOTLES > TOOTLE

TOOTLING > TOOTLE

TOOTS Scots version of > TUT

TOOTSED > TOOTS

TOOTSES > TOOTS

TOOTSIE same as > TOOTSY

TOOTSIES > TOOTSY

TOOTSING > TOOTS

TOOTSY same as > TOOTS

TOP n highest point or part ▷ adj at or of the top ▷ vb form a top on

TOPALGIA n pain restricted to a particular spot: a neurotic or hysterical symptom

TOPALGIAS > TOPALGIA

TOPARCH n ruler of a small state or realm

TOPARCHS > TOPARCH

TOPARCHY > TOPARCH

TOPAZ n semiprecious stone in various colours

TOPAZES > TOPAZ

TOPAZINE adj like topaz

TOPCOAT n overcoat

TOPCOATS > TOPCOAT

TOPCROSS n class of hybrid

TOPE vb drink alcohol regularly ▷ n small European shark

TOPECTOMY n (formerly) the surgical removal of part of the cerebral cortex to relieve certain psychiatric disorders

TOPED > TOPE

TOPEE n lightweight hat worn in tropical countries

TOPEES > TOPEE

TOPEK same as > TUPIK

TOPEKS > TOPEK

TOPER > TOPE

TOPERS > TOPE

TOPES > TOPE

TOPFLIGHT adj superior or excellent quality; outstanding

TOPFUL variant spelling of > TOPFULL

TOPFULL adj full to the top

TOPH n variety of sandstone

TOPHE variant spelling of > TOPH

TOPHES > TOPHE

TOPHI > TOPHUS

TOPHS > TOPH

TOPHUS n deposit of sodium urate in the helix of the ear or surrounding a joint

TOPI same as > TOPEE

TOPIARIAN > TOPIARY

TOPIARIES > TOPIARY

TOPIARIST > TOPIARY

TOPIARY n art of trimming trees and bushes into decorative shapes ▷ adj of or relating to topiary

TOPIC n subject of a conversation, book, etc

TOPICAL adj relating to current events

TOPICALLY > TOPICAL

TOPICS > TOPIC

TOPING > TOPE

TOPIS > TOPI

TOPKICK n (formerly) sergeant

TOPKICKS > TOPKICK

TOPKNOT n crest, tuft, decorative bow, etc, on the top of the head

TOPKNOTS > TOPKNOT

TOPLESS adj (of a costume or woman) with no covering for the breasts

TOPLINE vb headline; be the main focus of a newspaper story

TOPLINED > TOPLINE

TOPLINER > TOPLINE

TOPLINERS > TOPLINE

TOPLINES > TOPLINE

TOPLINING > TOPLINE

TOPLOFTY adj haughty or pretentious

TOPMAKER n wool dealer

TOPMAKERS > TOPMAKER

TOPMAKING > TOPMAKER

TOPMAN n sailor positioned in the rigging of the topsail

TOPMAST n mast next above a lower mast on a sailing vessel

TOPMASTS > TOPMAST

TOPMEN > TOPMAN

TOPMINNOW n small American freshwater cyprinodont fish

TOPMOST adj highest or best

TOPNOTCH adj excellent

TOPO n picture of a mountain with details of climbing routes superimposed on it

TOPOGRAPH n type of x-ray photograph

TOPOI > TOPO

TOPOLOGIC > TOPOLOGY

TOPOLOGY n geometry of the properties of a shape which are unaffected by continuous distortion

TOPONYM n name of a place

TOPONYMAL > TOPONYMY

TOPONYMIC > TOPONYMY

TOPONYMS > TOPONYMY

TOPONYMY n study of place names

TOPOS > TOPO

TOPOTYPE n specimen plant or animal taken from an area regarded as the typical habitat

TOPOTYPES > TOPOTYPE

TOPPED > TOP

TOPPER n top hat

TOPPERS > TOPPER

TOPPIER > TOPPY

TOPPIEST > TOPPY

TOPPING > TOP

TOPPINGLY > TOP

TOPPINGS > TOP

TOPPLE vb (cause to) fall over

TOPPLED > TOPPLE

TOPPLES > TOPPLE

TOPPLING > TOPPLE

TOPPY *adj* (of audio reproduction) having too many high-frequency sounds

TOPS > TOP

TOPSAIL *n* square sail carried on a yard set on a topmast

TOPSAILS > TOPSAIL

TOPSCORE *vb* score the highest in a sports match or competition

TOPSCORED > TOPSCORE

TOPSCORES > TOPSCORE

TOPSIDE *n* lean cut of beef from the thigh containing no bone

TOPSIDER *n* person in charge

TOPSIDERS > TOPSIDER

TOPSIDES > TOPSIDE

TOPSMAN *n* chief drover

TOPSMEN > TOPSMAN

TOPSOIL *n* surface layer of soil ▷ *vb* spread topsoil on (land)

TOPSOILED > TOPSOIL

TOPSOILS > TOPSOIL

TOPSPIN *n* spin imparted to make a ball bounce or travel exceptionally far, high, or quickly, as by hitting it with a sharp forward and upward stroke

TOPSPINS > TOPSPIN

TOPSTITCH *vb* stitch a line the outside of a garment, running close to a seam

TOPSTONE *n* stone forming the top of something

TOPSTONES > TOPSTONE

TOPWORK *vb* graft shoots or twigs onto the main branches of (for example, a fruit tree) to modify its yield

TOPWORKED > TOPWORK

TOPWORKS > TOPWORK

TOQUE *same as* > TUQUE

TOQUES > TOQUE

TOQUET *same as* > TOQUE

TOQUETS > TOQUET

TOQUILLA *another name for* > JIPIJAPA

TOQUILLAS > TOQUILLA

TOR *n* high rocky hill

TORA *variant spelling of* > TORAH

TORAH *n* whole body of traditional Jewish teaching, including the Oral Law

TORAHS > TORAH

TORAN *n* (in Indian architecture) an archway, usually wooden and often ornately carved

TORANA *same as* > TORAN

TORANAS > TORANA

TORANS > TORAN

TORAS > TORA

TORBANITE *n* type of oil shale

TORC *same as* > TORQUE

TORCH *n* small portable battery-powered lamp ▷ *vb* deliberately set (a building) on fire

TORCHABLE > TORCH

TORCHED > TORCH

TORCHER > TORCH

TORCHERE *n* tall narrow stand for holding a candelabrum

TORCHERES > TORCHERE

TORCHERS > TORCH

TORCHES > TORCH

TORCHIER *n* standing lamp with a bowl for casting light upwards and so giving all-round indirect illumination

TORCHIERE *same as* > TORCHIER

TORCHIERS > TORCHIER

TORCHIEST > TORCHY

TORCHING > TORCH

TORCHINGS > TORCH

TORCHLIKE > TORCH

TORCHON as in *torchon lace* coarse linen or cotton lace with a simple openwork pattern

TORCHONS > TORCHON

TORCHWOOD *n* rutaceous tree or shrub of Florida and the Caribbean, with hard resinous wood used for torches

TORCHY *adj* sentimental; maudlin; characteristic of a torch song

TORCS > TORC

TORCULAR *n* tourniquet

TORCULARS > TORCULAR

TORDION *n* old triple-time dance for two people

TORDIONS > TORDION

TORE *same as* > TORUS

TOREADOR *n* bullfighter

TOREADORS > TOREADOR

TORERO *n* bullfighter, esp one on foot

TOREROS > TORERO

TORES > TORE

TOREUTIC > TOREUTICS

TOREUTICS *n* art of making detailed ornamental reliefs, esp in metal, by embossing and chasing

TORGOCH *n* type of char

TORGOCHS > TORGOCH

TORI > TORUS

TORIC *adj* of, relating to, or having the form of a torus

TORICS > TORIC

TORIES > TORY

TORII *n* gateway, esp one at the entrance to a Japanese Shinto temple

TORMENT *vb* cause (someone) great suffering ▷ *n* great suffering

TORMENTA > TORMENTUM

TORMENTED > TORMENT

TORMENTER *same as* > TORMENTOR

TORMENTIL *n* creeping plant with yellow four-petalled flowers

TORMENTOR *n* person or thing that torments

TORMENTS > TORMENT

TORMENTUM *n* type of Roman catapult

TORMINA *n* complaints

TORMINAL > TORMINA

TORMINOUS > TORMINA

TORN > TEAR

TORNADE *same as* > TORNADO

TORNADES > TORNADE

TORNADIC > TORNADO

TORNADO *n* violent whirlwind

TORNADOES > TORNADO

TORNADOS > TORNADO

TORNILLO *n* shrub found in Mexico and some southwestern states of the US

TORNILLOS > TORNILLO

TORO *n* bull

TOROID *n* surface generated by rotating a closed plane curve about a coplanar line that does not intersect the curve

TOROIDAL > TOROID

TOROIDS > TOROID

TOROS > TORO

TOROSE *adj* (of a cylindrical part) having irregular swellings

TOROSITY > TOROSE

TOROT > TORAH

TOROTH > TORAH

TOROUS *same as* > TOROSE

TORPEDO *n* self-propelled underwater missile ▷ *vb* attack or destroy with or as if with torpedoes

TORPEDOED > TORPEDO

TORPEDOER > TORPEDO

TORPEDOES > TORPEDO

TORPEDOS > TORPEDO

TORPEFIED > TORPEFY

TORPEFIES > TORPEFY

TORPEFY *n* make torpid

TORPID *adj* sluggish and inactive

TORPIDITY > TORPID

TORPIDLY > TORPID

TORPIDS *n* series of boat races held at Oxford University during Lent

TORPITUDE *another word for* > TORPOR

TORPOR *n* torpid state

TORPORS > TORPOR

TORQUATE > TORQUES

TORQUATED > TORQUES

TORQUE *n* force causing rotation ▷ *vb* apply torque to (something)

TORQUED > TORQUE

TORQUER > TORQUE

TORQUERS > TORQUE

TORQUES *n* distinctive

band of hair, feathers, skin, or colour around the neck of an animal

TORQUESES > TORQUES

TORQUING > TORQUE

TORR *n* unit of pressure equal to one millimetre of mercury (133.3 newtons per square metre)

TORREFIED > TORREFY

TORREFIES > TORREFY

TORREFY *vb* dry (drugs, ores, etc) by subjection to intense heat

TORRENT *n* rushing stream ▷ *adj* like or relating to a torrent

TORRENTS > TORRENT

TORRET *same as* > TERRET

TORRETS > TORRET

TORRID *adj* very hot and dry

TORRIDER > TORRID

TORRIDEST > TORRID

TORRIDITY > TORRID

TORRIDLY > TORRID

TORRIFIED > TORRIFY

TORRIFIES > TORRIFY

TORRIFY *same as* > TORREFY

TORRS > TORR

TORS > TOR

TORSADE *n* ornamental twist or twisted cord, as on hats

TORSADES > TORSADE

TORSE *same as* > TORSO

TORSEL *n* wooden beam along the top of a wall for distributing the weight of something laid upon it

TORSELS > TORSEL

TORSES > TORSE

TORSI > TORSO

TORSION *n* twisting of a part by equal forces being applied at both ends but in opposite directions

TORSIONAL > TORSION

TORSIONS > TORSION

TORSIVE *adj* twisted

TORSK *n* fish with a single long dorsal fin

TORSKS > TORSK

TORSO *n* trunk of the human body

TORSOS > TORSO

TORT *n* civil wrong or injury for which damages may be claimed

TORTA *n* (in mining) a flat circular pile of silver ore

TORTAS > TORTA

TORTE *n* rich cake, originating in Austria, usually decorated or filled with cream, fruit, nuts, and jam

TORTELLI *npl* type of stuffed pasta

TORTEN > TORTE

TORTES > TORTE

TORTILE *adj* twisted or coiled

TORTILITY > TORTILE

t

TORTILLA n thin Mexican pancake
TORTILLAS > TORTILLA
TORTILLON another word for > STUMP
TORTIOUS adj having the nature of or involving a tort
TORTIVE adj twisted
TORTOISE n slow-moving land reptile with a dome-shaped shell
TORTOISES > TORTOISE
TORTONI n rich ice cream often flavoured with sherry
TORTONIS > TORTONI
TORTRICES > TORTRIX
TORTRICID n type of small moth of the family which includes the codling moth
TORTRIX n type of moth
TORTRIXES > TORTRIX
TORTS > TORT
TORTUOUS adj winding or twisting
TORTURE vb cause (someone) severe pain or mental anguish ▷ n severe physical or mental pain
TORTURED > TORTURE
TORTURER > TORTURE
TORTURERS > TORTURE
TORTURES > TORTURE
TORTURING > TORTURE
TORTUROUS > TORTURE
TORULA n species of fungal microorganisms
TORULAE > TORULA
TORULAS > TORULA
TORULI > TORULUS
TORULIN n vitamin found in yeast
TORULINS > TORULIN
TORULOSE adj (of something cylindrical) alternately swollen and pinched along its length
TORULOSES > TORULOSIS
TORULOSIS n infection by one of the torula
TORULUS n socket in an insect's head in which its antenna is attached
TORUS n large convex moulding approximately semicircular in cross section, esp one used on the base of a classical column
TORY n ultraconservative or reactionary person ▷ adj ultraconservative or reactionary
TOSA n large reddish dog, originally bred for fighting
TOSAS > TOSA
TOSE same as > TOZE
TOSED > TOSE
TOSES > TOSE
TOSH n nonsense ▷ vb tidy or trim
TOSHACH n military leader of a clan
TOSHACHS > TOSHACH

TOSHED > TOSH
TOSHER > TOSH
TOSHERS > TOSH
TOSHES > TOSH
TOSHIER > TOSHY
TOSHIEST > TOSHY
TOSHING > TOSH
TOSHY adj neat; trim
TOSING > TOSE
TOSS vb throw lightly ▷ n tossing
TOSSED > TOSS
TOSSEN old past participle of > TOSS
TOSSER n stupid or despicable person
TOSSERS > TOSSER
TOSSES > TOSS
TOSSIER > TOSSY
TOSSIEST > TOSSY
TOSSILY > TOSSY
TOSSING > TOSS
TOSSINGS > TOSS
TOSSPOT n habitual drinker
TOSSPOTS > TOSSPOT
TOSSUP n an instance of tossing up a coin
TOSSUPS > TOSSUP
TOSSY adj impudent
TOST old past participle of > TOSS
TOSTADA n crispy deep-fried tortilla topped with meat, cheese, and refried beans
TOSTADAS > TOSTADA
TOSTADO same as > TOSTADA
TOSTADOS > TOSTADO
TOT n small child ▷ vb total
TOTABLE > TOTE
TOTAL n whole, esp a sum of parts ▷ adj complete ▷ vb amount to
TOTALED > TOTAL
TOTALING > TOTAL
TOTALISE same as > TOTALIZE
TOTALISED > TOTALISE
TOTALISER > TOTALISE
TOTALISES > TOTALISE
TOTALISM n practice of a dictatorial one party state that regulates every form of life
TOTALISMS > TOTALISM
TOTALIST > TOTALISM
TOTALISTS > TOTALISM
TOTALITY n whole amount
TOTALIZE vb combine or make into a total
TOTALIZED > TOTALIZE
TOTALIZER > TOTALIZE
TOTALIZES > TOTALIZE
TOTALLED > TOTAL
TOTALLING > TOTAL
TOTALLY > TOTAL
TOTALS > TOTAL
TOTANUS another name for > REDSHANK
TOTANUSES > TOTANUS
TOTAQUINE n mixture of

quinine and other alkaloids derived from cinchona bark, used as a substitute for quinine in treating malaria
TOTARA n tall coniferous forest tree of New Zealand, with a hard durable wood
TOTARAS > TOTARA
TOTE vb carry (a gun etc) ▷ n act of or an instance of toting
TOTEABLE > TOTE
TOTED > TOTE
TOTEM n tribal badge or emblem
TOTEMIC > TOTEM
TOTEMISM n belief in kinship of groups or individuals having a common totem
TOTEMISMS > TOTEMISM
TOTEMIST > TOTEMISM
TOTEMISTS > TOTEMISM
TOTEMITE > TOTEMITE
TOTEMITES > TOTEMITE
TOTEMS > TOTEM
TOTER > TOTE
TOTERS > TOTE
TOTES > TOTE
TOTHER n other
TOTIENT n quantity of numbers less than, and sharing no common factors with, a given number
TOTIENTS > TOTIENT
TOTING > TOTE
TOTITIVE n number less than, and having no common factors with, a given number
TOTITIVES > TOTITIVE
TOTS > TOT
TOTTED > TOT
TOTTER vb move unsteadily ▷ n act or an instance of tottering
TOTTERED > TOTTER
TOTTERER > TOTTER
TOTTERERS > TOTTER
TOTTERING > TOTTER
TOTTERS > TOTTER
TOTTERY > TOTTER
TOTTIE adj very small
TOTTIER > TOTTY
TOTTIES > TOTTY
TOTTIEST > TOTTY
TOTTING > TOT
TOTTINGS > TOT
TOTTY n people, esp women, collectively considered as sexual objects ▷ adj very small
TOUCAN n tropical American bird with a large bill
TOUCANET n type of small toucan
TOUCANETS > TOUCANET
TOUCANS > TOUCAN
TOUCH vb come into contact with ▷ n sense by which an object's qualities are perceived when they come into contact with

part of the body ▷ adj of a non-contact version of particular sport
TOUCHABLE > TOUCH
TOUCHBACK n play in which the ball is put down by a player behind his own goal line when the ball has been put across the goal line by an opponent
TOUCHDOWN n moment at which a landing aircraft or spacecraft comes into contact with the landing surface ▷ vb (of an aircraft or spacecraft) to land
TOUCHE interj acknowledgment of the striking home of a remark or witty reply
TOUCHED adj emotionally moved
TOUCHER > TOUCH
TOUCHERS > TOUCH
TOUCHES > TOUCH
TOUCHHOLE n hole in the breech of early cannon and firearms through which the charge was ignited
TOUCHIER > TOUCHY
TOUCHIEST > TOUCHY
TOUCHILY > TOUCHY
TOUCHING adj emotionally moving ▷ prep relating to or concerning
TOUCHINGS > TOUCH
TOUCHLESS > TOUCH
TOUCHLINE n side line of the pitch in some games
TOUCHMARK n maker's mark stamped on pewter objects
TOUCHPAD n part of laptop computer functioning like mouse
TOUCHPADS > TOUCHPAD
TOUCHTONE adj of or relating to a telephone dialling system in which each of the buttons pressed generates a tone of a different pitch, which is transmitted to the exchange
TOUCHUP n renovation or retouching, as of a painting
TOUCHUPS > TOUCHUP
TOUCHWOOD n something, esp dry wood, used as tinder
TOUCHY adj easily offended
TOUGH adj strong or resilient ▷ n rough violent person
TOUGHED > TOUGH
TOUGHEN vb make or become tough or tougher
TOUGHENED > TOUGHEN
TOUGHENER > TOUGHEN
TOUGHENS > TOUGHEN
TOUGHER > TOUGH
TOUGHEST > TOUGH
TOUGHIE n person who is tough
TOUGHIES > TOUGHIE

TOUGHING > TOUGH
TOUGHISH > TOUGH
TOUGHLY > TOUGH
TOUGHNESS n quality or an instance of being tough
TOUGHS > TOUGH
TOUGHY same as > TOUGHIE
TOUK same as > TUCK
TOUKED > TOUK
TOUKING > TOUK
TOUKS > TOUK
TOUN n town
TOUNS > TOUN
TOUPEE n small wig
TOUPEED adj wearing a toupee
TOUPEES > TOUPEE
TOUPET same as > TOUPEE
TOUPETS > TOUPET
TOUR n journey visiting places of interest along the way ▷ vb make a tour (of)
TOURACO n brightly coloured crested arboreal African bird
TOURACOS > TOURACO
TOURED > TOUR
TOURER n large open car with a folding top, usually seating a driver and four passengers
TOURERS > TOURER
TOURIE same as > TOORIE
TOURIES > TOURIE
TOURING > TOUR
TOURINGS > TOUR
TOURISM n tourist travel as an industry
TOURISMS > TOURISM
TOURIST n person travelling for pleasure ▷ adj of or relating to tourists or tourism
TOURISTA variant of > TOURIST
TOURISTAS > TOURISTA
TOURISTED adj busy with tourists
TOURISTIC > TOURIST
TOURISTS > TOURIST
TOURISTY adj informal term for full of tourists or tourist attractions
TOURNEDOS n thick round steak of beef
TOURNEY n knightly tournament ▷ vb engage in a tourney
TOURNEYED > TOURNEY
TOURNEYER > TOURNEY
TOURNEYS > TOURNEY
TOURNURE n outline or contour
TOURNURES > TOURNURE
TOURS > TOUR
TOURTIERE n type of meat pie
TOUSE vb tangle, ruffle, or disarrange; treat roughly
TOUSED > TOUSE
TOUSER > TOUSE
TOUSERS > TOUSE
TOUSES > TOUSE

TOUSIER > TOUSY
TOUSIEST > TOUSY
TOUSING > TOUSE
TOUSINGS > TOUSE
TOUSLE vb make (hair or clothes) ruffled and untidy ▷ n disorderly, tangled, or rumpled state
TOUSLED > TOUSLE
TOUSLES > TOUSLE
TOUSLING > TOUSLE
TOUSTIE adj irritable; testy
TOUSTIER > TOUSTIE
TOUSTIEST > TOUSTIE
TOUSY adj tousled
TOUT vb seek business in a persistent manner ▷ n person who sells tickets for a popular event at inflated prices
TOUTED > TOUT
TOUTER > TOUT
TOUTERS > TOUT
TOUTIE adj childishly irritable or sullen
TOUTIER > TOUTIE
TOUTIEST > TOUTIE
TOUTING > TOUT
TOUTS > TOUT
TOUZE variant spelling of > TOUSE
TOUZED > TOUZE
TOUZES > TOUZE
TOUZIER > TOUZY
TOUZIEST > TOUZY
TOUZING > TOUZE
TOUZLE rare spelling of > TOUSLE
TOUZLED > TOUZLE
TOUZLES > TOUZLE
TOUZLING > TOUZLE
TOUZY variant spelling of > TOUSY
TOVARICH same as > TOVARISCH
TOVARISCH n comrade: a term of address
TOVARISH same as > TOVARISCH
TOW vb drag, esp by means of a rope ▷ n towing
TOWABLE > TOW
TOWAGE n charge made for towing
TOWAGES > TOWAGE
TOWARD same as > TOWARDS
TOWARDLY adj compliant
TOWARDS prep in the direction of
TOWAWAY n vehicle which has been towed away (because, for example, it was illegally parked)
TOWAWAYS > TOWAWAY
TOWBAR n metal bar on a car for towing vehicles
TOWBARS > TOWBAR
TOWBOAT n another word for tug (the boat)
TOWBOATS > TOWBOAT
TOWED > TOW
TOWEL n cloth for drying

things ▷ vb dry or wipe with a towel
TOWELED > TOWEL
TOWELETTE n paper towel
TOWELHEAD n offensive term for someone who wears a turban
TOWELING > TOWEL
TOWELINGS > TOWEL
TOWELLED > TOWEL
TOWELLING n material used for making towels
TOWELS > TOWEL
TOWER n tall structure, often forming part of a larger building
TOWERED adj having a tower or towers
TOWERIER > TOWERY
TOWERIEST > TOWERY
TOWERING adj very tall or impressive
TOWERLESS adj not having a tower
TOWERLIKE adj like a tower
TOWERS > TOWER
TOWERY adj with towers
TOWHEAD n often disparaging term for a person with blond or yellowish hair
TOWHEADED adj having blonde or yellowish hair
TOWHEADS > TOWHEAD
TOWHEE n N American brownish-coloured sparrow
TOWHEES > TOWHEE
TOWIE n truck used for towing
TOWIER > TOW
TOWIES > TOWIE
TOWIEST > TOW
TOWING > TOW
TOWINGS > TOW
TOWKAY n sir
TOWKAYS > TOWKAY
TOWLINE same as > TOWROPE
TOWLINES > TOWLINE
TOWMON same as > TOWMOND
TOWMOND n old word for year
TOWMONDS > TOWMOND
TOWMONS > TOWMON
TOWMONT same as > TOWMOND
TOWMONTS > TOWMONT
TOWN n group of buildings larger than a village
TOWNEE same as > TOWNIE
TOWNEES > TOWNEE
TOWNFOLK same as > TOWNSFOLK
TOWNHALL adj of a variety of the Asian plant moschatel
TOWNHOME another word for > TOWNHOUSE
TOWNHOMES > TOWNHOME
TOWNHOUSE n terraced house in an urban area, esp

a fashionable one, often having the main living room on the first floor with an integral garage on the ground floor
TOWNIE n often disparaging term for a resident in a town, esp as distinct from country dwellers
TOWNIER > TOWNY
TOWNIES > TOWNY
TOWNIEST > TOWNY
TOWNISH > TOWN
TOWNLAND n division of land of various sizes
TOWNLANDS > TOWNLAND
TOWNLESS > TOWN
TOWNLET n small town
TOWNLETS > TOWNLET
TOWNLIER > TOWNLY
TOWNLIEST > TOWNLY
TOWNLING n person who lives in a town
TOWNLINGS > TOWNLING
TOWNLY adj characteristic of a town
TOWNS > TOWN
TOWNSCAPE n view of an urban scene
TOWNSFOLK n people of a town
TOWNSHIP n small town
TOWNSHIPS > TOWNSHIP
TOWNSKIP n old term for a mischievous and roguish child who frequents city streets
TOWNSKIPS > TOWNSKIP
TOWNSMAN n inhabitant of a town
TOWNSMEN > TOWNSMAN
TOWNWEAR n clothes suitable for wearing while persuing activities usually associated with towns
TOWNY adj characteristic of a town
TOWPATH n path beside a canal or river, originally for horses towing boats
TOWPATHS > TOWPATH
TOWPLANE n aeroplane that tows gliders
TOWPLANES > TOWPLANE
TOWROPE n rope or cable used for towing a vehicle or vessel
TOWROPES > TOWROPE
TOWS > TOW
TOWSACK n sack made from tow
TOWSACKS > TOWSACK
TOWSE same as > TOUSE
TOWSED > TOWSE
TOWSER > TOWSE
TOWSERS > TOWSE
TOWSES > TOWSE
TOWSIER > TOWSY
TOWSIEST > TOWSY
TOWSING > TOWSE
TOWSY same as > TOUSY
TOWT vb sulk
TOWTED > TOWT

TOWTING > TOWT

TOWTS > TOWT

TOWY > TOW

TOWZE same as > TOUSE

TOWZED > TOWZE

TOWZES > TOWZE

TOWZIER > TOWZY

TOWZIEST > TOWZY

TOWZING > TOWZE

TOWZY same as > TOUSY

TOXAEMIA n blood poisoning

TOXAEMIAS > TOXAEMIA

TOXAEMIC > TOXAEMIA

TOXAPHENE n amber waxy solid with a pleasant pine odour, consisting of chlorinated terpenes, esp chlorinated camphene: used as an insecticide

TOXEMIA same as > TOXAEMIA

TOXEMIAS > TOXEMIA

TOXEMIC > TOXAEMIA

TOXIC adj poisonous ▷ n toxic substance

TOXICAL adj toxic

TOXICALLY > TOXIC

TOXICANT n toxic substance ▷ adj poisonous

TOXICANTS > TOXICANT

TOXICITY n degree of strength of a poison

TOXICOSES > TOXICOSIS

TOXICOSIS n any disease or condition caused by poisoning

TOXICS > TOXIC

TOXIGENIC adj producing poison

TOXIN n poison of bacterial origin

TOXINE nonstandard variant spelling of > TOXIN

TOXINES > TOXINE

TOXINS > TOXIN

TOXOCARA n parasitic worm infesting the intestines of cats and dogs

TOXOCARAL adj relating to toxocara

TOXOCARAS > TOXOCARA

TOXOID n toxin that has been treated to reduce its toxicity and is used in immunization to stimulate production of antitoxins

TOXOIDS > TOXOID

TOXOPHILY n archer

TOY n something designed to be played with ▷ adj designed to be played with ▷ vb play, fiddle, or flirt

TOYED > TOY

TOYER > TOY

TOYERS > TOY

TOYETIC adj (of a film or television franchise) able to generate revenue via spin-off toy products

TOYING > TOY

TOYINGS > TOY

TOYISH adj resembling a toy

TOYISHLY > TOYISH

TOYLESOME old spelling of > TOILSOME

TOYLESS > TOY

TOYLIKE > TOY

TOYLSOM old spelling of > TOILSOME

TOYMAN n man who sells toys

TOYMEN > TOYMAN

TOYO n Japanese straw-like material made out of rice paper and used to make hats

TOYON n shrub related to the rose

TOYONS > TOYON

TOYOS > TOYO

TOYS > TOY

TOYSHOP n shop selling toys

TOYSHOPS > TOYSHOP

TOYSOME adj playful

TOYTOWN adj having an unreal and picturesque appearance

TOYWOMAN n woman who sells toys

TOYWOMEN > TOYWOMAN

TOZE vb tease out; (of wool, etc) card

TOZED > TOZE

TOZES > TOZE

TOZIE n type of shawl

TOZIES > TOZIE

TOZING > TOZE

TRABEATE same as > TRABEATED

TRABEATED adj constructed with horizontal beams as opposed to arches

TRABECULA n any of various rod-shaped structures that divide organs into separate chambers

TRABS npl training shoes

TRACE vb locate or work out (the cause of something) ▷ n track left by something

TRACEABLE > TRACE

TRACEABLY > TRACE

TRACED > TRACE

TRACELESS > TRACE

TRACER n projectile which leaves a visible trail

TRACERIED > TRACERY

TRACERIES > TRACERY

TRACERS > TRACER

TRACERY n pattern of interlacing lines

TRACES > TRACE

TRACEUR n parkour participant

TRACEURS > TRACEUR

TRACHEA n windpipe

TRACHEAE > TRACHEA

TRACHEAL > TRACHEA

TRACHEARY adj using tracheae to breathe

TRACHEAS > TRACHEA

TRACHEATE > TRACHEA

TRACHEID n element of xylem tissue consisting of an elongated lignified cell with tapering ends and large pits

TRACHEIDE same as > TRACHEID

TRACHEIDS > TRACHEID

TRACHEOLE n small trachea found in some insects

TRACHINUS n weever fish

TRACHITIS n another spelling of tracheitis (inflammation of the trachea)

TRACHLE vb (of hair, clothing, etc) make untidy; dishevel; rumple

TRACHLED > TRACHLE

TRACHLES > TRACHLE

TRACHLING > TRACHLE

TRACHOMA n chronic contagious disease of the eye characterized by inflammation of the inner surface of the lids and the formation of scar tissue

TRACHOMAS > TRACHOMA

TRACHYTE n light-coloured fine-grained volcanic rock

TRACHYTES > TRACHYTE

TRACHYTIC adj (of the texture of certain igneous rocks) characterized by a parallel arrangement of crystals, which mark the flow of the lava when still molten

TRACING n traced copy

TRACINGS > TRACING

TRACK n rough road or path ▷ vb follow the trail or path of

TRACKABLE > TRACK

TRACKAGE n collective term for the railway tracks in general, or those in a given area or belonging to a particular company, etc

TRACKAGES > TRACKAGE

TRACKBALL n device consisting of a small ball, mounted in a cup, which can be rotated to move the cursor around the screen

TRACKBED n foundation on which railway tracks are laid

TRACKBEDS > TRACKBED

TRACKED > TRACK

TRACKER > TRACK

TRACKERS > TRACK

TRACKING n act or process of following something or someone

TRACKINGS > TRACKING

TRACKLESS adj having or leaving no trace or trail

TRACKMAN n workman who lays and maintains railway track

TRACKMEN > TRACKMAN

TRACKPAD same as

> TOUCHPAD

TRACKPADS > TRACKPAD

TRACKROAD another word for > TOWPATH

TRACKS > TRACK

TRACKSIDE n area alongside a track

TRACKSUIT n warm loose-fitting suit worn by athletes etc, esp during training

TRACKWAY n path or track

TRACKWAYS > TRACKWAY

TRACT n wide area ▷ vb track

TRACTABLE adj easy to manage or control

TRACTABLY > TRACTABLE

TRACTATE n short tract

TRACTATES > TRACTATE

TRACTATOR n person who writes tracts

TRACTED > TRACT

TRACTILE adj capable of being drawn out

TRACTING > TRACT

TRACTION n pulling, esp by engine power

TRACTIONS > TRACTION

TRACTIVE > TRACTION

TRACTOR n motor vehicle with large rear wheels for pulling farm machinery

TRACTORS > TRACTOR

TRACTRIX n (in geometry) type of curve

TRACTS > TRACT

TRACTUS n anthem sung in some RC masses

TRACTUSES > TRACTUS

TRAD n traditional jazz, as revived in the 1950s

TRADABLE > TRADE

TRADE n buying, selling, or exchange of goods ▷ vb buy and sell ▷ adj intended for or available only to people in industry or business

TRADEABLE > TRADE

TRADED > TRADE

TRADEFUL adj (of shops, for example) full of trade

TRADELESS > TRADE

TRADEMARK n (legally registered) name or symbol used by a firm to distinguish its goods ▷ vb label with a trademark

TRADENAME n name used by a trade to refer to a commodity, service, etc

TRADEOFF n exchange, esp as a compromise

TRADEOFFS > TRADEOFF

TRADER n person who engages in trade

TRADERS > TRADER

TRADES > TRADE

TRADESMAN n skilled worker

TRADESMEN

> TRADESMAN

TRADING > TRADE

TRADINGS > TRADE

TRADITION n handing down from generation to generation of customs and beliefs

TRADITIVE adj traditional

TRADITOR n Christian who betrayed his fellow Christians at the time of the Roman persecutions

TRADITORS > TRADITOR

TRADS > TRAD

TRADUCE vb slander

TRADUCED > TRADUCE

TRADUCER > TRADUCE

TRADUCERS > TRADUCE

TRADUCES > TRADUCE

TRADUCIAN > TRADUCE

TRADUCING > TRADUCE

TRAFFIC n vehicles coming and going on a road ▷ vb trade, usu illicitly

TRAFFICKY adj (of a street, area, town, etc) busy with motor vehicles

TRAFFICS > TRAFFIC

TRAGAL > TRAGUS

TRAGEDIAN n person who acts in or writes tragedies

TRAGEDIES > TRAGEDY

TRAGEDY n shocking or sad event

TRAGELAPH n mythical animal: a cross between a goat and a stag

TRAGI > TRAGUS

TRAGIC adj of or like a tragedy ▷ n tragedian

TRAGICAL same as > TRAGIC

TRAGICS > TRAGIC

TRAGOPAN n pheasant of S and SE Asia, with a brilliant plumage and brightly coloured fleshy processes on the head

TRAGOPANS > TRAGOPAN

TRAGULE n mouse deer

TRAGULES > TRAGULE

TRAGULINE adj like or characteristic of a tragule

TRAGUS n cartilaginous fleshy projection that partially covers the entrance to the external ear

TRAHISON n treason

TRAHISONS > TRAHISON

TRAIK vb trudge; trek with difficulty

TRAIKED > TRAIK

TRAIKING > TRAIK

TRAIKIT > TRAIK

TRAIKS > TRAIK

TRAIL n path, track, or road ▷ vb drag along the ground

TRAILABLE adj capable of being trailed

TRAILED > TRAIL

TRAILER n vehicle designed to be towed by another vehicle ▷ vb use a trailer to advertise (something)

TRAILERED > TRAILER

TRAILERS > TRAILER

TRAILHEAD n place where a trail begins

TRAILING adj (of a plant) having a long stem which spreads over the ground or hangs loosely

TRAILLESS adj without trail

TRAILS > TRAIL

TRAILSIDE adj beside a trail

TRAIN vb instruct in a skill ▷ n line of railway coaches or wagons drawn by an engine

TRAINABLE > TRAIN

TRAINBAND n company of English militia from the 16th to the 18th century

TRAINED > TRAIN

TRAINEE n person being trained ▷ adj (of a person) undergoing training

TRAINEES > TRAINEE

TRAINER n person who trains an athlete or sportsman

TRAINERS npl shoes in the style of those used for sports training

TRAINFUL n quantity of people or cargo that would be capable of filling a train

TRAINFULS > TRAINFUL

TRAINING n process of bringing a person to an agreed standard of proficiency by practice and instruction

TRAININGS > TRAINING

TRAINLESS > TRAIN

TRAINLOAD n quantity of people or cargo sufficient to fill a train

TRAINMAN n man who works on a train

TRAINMEN > TRAINMAN

TRAINS > TRAIN

TRAINWAY n railway track; channel in a built-up area through which a train passes

TRAINWAYS > TRAINWAY

TRAIPSE vb walk wearily ▷ n long or tiring walk

TRAIPSED > TRAIPSE

TRAIPSES > TRAIPSE

TRAIPSING > TRAIPSE

TRAIT n characteristic feature

TRAITOR n person guilty of treason or treachery

TRAITORLY adj of or characteristic of a traitor

TRAITORS > TRAITOR

TRAITRESS > TRAITOR

TRAITS > TRAIT

TRAJECT vb transport or transmit

TRAJECTED > TRAJECT

TRAJECTS > TRAJECT

TRAM same as > TRAMMEL

TRAMCAR same as > TRAM

TRAMCARS > TRAMCAR

TRAMEL variant spelling of > TRAMMEL

TRAMELED > TRAMEL

TRAMELING > TRAMEL

TRAMELL variant spelling of > TRAMMEL

TRAMELLED > TRAMELL

TRAMELLS > TRAMELL

TRAMELS > TRAMEL

TRAMLESS > TRAM

TRAMLINE n tracks on which a tram runs

TRAMLINED adj having tramlines

TRAMLINES > TRAMLINE

TRAMMED > TRAM

TRAMMEL n hindrance to free action or movement ▷ vb hinder or restrain

TRAMMELED > TRAMMEL

TRAMMELER > TRAMMEL

TRAMMELS > TRAMMEL

TRAMMIE n conductor or driver of a tram

TRAMMIES > TRAMMIE

TRAMMING > TRAM

TRAMP vb travel on foot, hike ▷ n homeless person who travels on foot

TRAMPED > TRAMP

TRAMPER n person who tramps

TRAMPERS > TRAMPER

TRAMPET variant spelling of > TRAMPETTE

TRAMPETS > TRAMPET

TRAMPETTE n small trampoline

TRAMPIER > TRAMPY

TRAMPIEST > TRAMPY

TRAMPING > TRAMP

TRAMPINGS > TRAMP

TRAMPISH > TRAMP

TRAMPLE vb tread on and crush ▷ n action or sound of trampling

TRAMPLED > TRAMPLE

TRAMPLER > TRAMPLE

TRAMPLERS > TRAMPLE

TRAMPLES > TRAMPLE

TRAMPLING > TRAMPLE

TRAMPOLIN n variant of trampoline: a tough canvass sheet suspended by springs from a frame, used by acrobats, gymnasts, etc

TRAMPS > TRAMP

TRAMPY adj (of woman) disreputable

TRAMROAD same as > TRAMWAY

TRAMROADS > TRAMROAD

TRAMS > TRAM

TRAMWAY same as > TRAMLINE

TRAMWAYS > TRAMWAY

TRANCE n unconscious or dazed state ▷ vb put into or as into a trance

TRANCED > TRANCE

TRANCEDLY > TRANCE

TRANCES > TRANCE

TRANCEY adj (of music) characteristic of the trance sub-genre

TRANCHE n portion of something large, esp a sum of money

TRANCHES > TRANCHE

TRANCHET n stoneage cutting tool

TRANCHETS > TRANCHET

TRANCIER > TRANCEY

TRANCIEST > TRANCEY

TRANCING > TRANCE

TRANECT n ferry

TRANECTS > TRANECT

TRANGAM n bauble or trinket

TRANGAMS > TRANGAM

TRANGLE n (in heraldry) a small fesse

TRANGLES > TRANGLE

TRANK n short form of tranquillizer: drug that calms a person

TRANKS > TRANK

TRANKUM same as > TRANGAM

TRANKUMS > TRANKUM

TRANNIE n transistor radio

TRANNIES > TRANNY

TRANNY same as > TRANNIE

TRANQ same as > TRANK

TRANQS > TRANQ

TRANQUIL adj calm and quiet

TRANS n short from of translation

TRANSACT vb conduct or negotiate (a business deal)

TRANSACTS > TRANSACT

TRANSAXLE n combined axle and gearbox

TRANSCEND vb rise above

TRANSCODE vb convert (digital computer data) from one format to another

TRANSDUCE vb change one form of energy to another

TRANSE n way through; passage

TRANSECT n sample strip of land used to monitor plant distribution and animal populations within a given area ▷ vb cut or divide crossways

TRANSECTS > TRANSECT

TRANSENNA n screen around a shrine

TRANSEPT n either of the two shorter wings of a cross-shaped church

TRANSEPTS > TRANSEPT

TRANSES > TRANSE

TRANSEUNT adj (of a mental act) causing effects outside the mind

TRANSFARD old past participle of > TRANSFER

TRANSFECT vb transfer genetic material isolated from a cell or virus into another cell

TRANSFER *vb* move or send from one person or place to another ▷ *n* transferring

TRANSFERS > TRANSFER

TRANSFIX *vb* astound or stun

TRANSFIXT > TRANSFIX

TRANSFORM *vb* change the shape or character of ▷ *n* result of a mathematical transformation

TRANSFUSE *vb* give a transfusion to

TRANSGENE *n* gene that is transferred from an organism of one species to an organism of another species by genetic engineering

TRANSHIP *same as* > TRANSSHIP

TRANSHIPS > TRANSHIP

TRANSHUME *vb* (of livestock) move to suitable grazing grounds according to the season

TRANSIENT *same as* > TRANSEUNT

TRANSIRE *n* document allowing goods to pass through customs

TRANSIRES > TRANSIRE

TRANSIT *n* passage or conveyance of goods or people ▷ *vb* make transit

TRANSITED > TRANSIT

TRANSITS > TRANSIT

TRANSLATE *vb* turn from one language into another

TRANSMEW *old variant of* > TRANSMUTE

TRANSMEWS > TRANSMEW

TRANSMIT *vb* pass (something) from one person or place to another

TRANSMITS > TRANSMIT

TRANSMOVE *vb* change the form, character, or substance of

TRANSMUTE *vb* change the form or nature of

TRANSOM *n* horizontal bar across a window

TRANSOMED > TRANSOM

TRANSOMS > TRANSOM

TRANSONIC *adj* of or relating to conditions when travelling at or near the speed of sound

TRANSPIRE *vb* become known

TRANSPORT *vb* convey from one place to another ▷ *n* business or system of transporting

TRANSPOSE *vb* interchange two things ▷ *n* matrix resulting from interchanging the rows and columns of a given matrix

TRANSSHIP *vb* transfer or be transferred from one ship or vehicle to another

TRANSUDE *vb* (of a fluid)

ooze or pass through interstices, pores, or small holes

TRANSUDED > TRANSUDE

TRANSUDES > TRANSUDE

TRANSUME *vb* make an official transcription of

TRANSUMED > TRANSUME

TRANSUMES > TRANSUME

TRANSUMPT *n* official transcription

TRANSVEST *vb* wear clothes traditionally associated with the opposite sex

TRANT *vb* travel from place to place selling goods

TRANTED > TRANT

TRANTER > TRANT

TRANTERS > TRANT

TRANTING > TRANT

TRANTS > TRANT

TRAP *n* device for catching animals ▷ *vb* catch

TRAPAN *same as* > TREPAN

TRAPANNED > TRAPAN

TRAPANNER > TRAPAN

TRAPANS > TRAPAN

TRAPBALL *n* old ball game in which a ball is placed in a see-saw device called a trap, flicked up by a batsman hitting one end of the trap, and then hit with a bat

TRAPBALLS > TRAPBALL

TRAPDOOR *n* door in floor or roof

TRAPDOORS > TRAPDOOR

TRAPE *same as* > TRAIPSE

TRAPED > TRAPE

TRAPES *same as* > TRAIPSE

TRAPESED > TRAPES

TRAPESES > TRAPES

TRAPESING > TRAPES

TRAPEZE *n* horizontal bar suspended from two ropes, used by circus acrobats ▷ *vb* swing on a trapeze

TRAPEZED > TRAPEZE

TRAPEZES > TRAPEZE

TRAPEZIA > TRAPEZIUM

TRAPEZIAL > TRAPEZIUM

TRAPEZII > TRAPEZIUS

TRAPEZING > TRAPEZE

TRAPEZIST *n* trapeze artist

TRAPEZIUM *same as* > TRAPEZOID

TRAPEZIUS *n* either of two flat triangular muscles, one covering each side of the back and shoulders, that rotate the shoulder blades

TRAPEZOID *same as* > TRAPEZIUM

TRAPFALL *n* trapdoor that opens under the feet

TRAPFALLS > TRAPFALL

TRAPING > TRAPE

TRAPLIKE > TRAP

TRAPLINE *n* line of traps

TRAPLINES > TRAPLINE

TRAPNEST *n* nest that holds a hen in place so that the number of eggs it alone produces can be counted

TRAPNESTS > TRAPNEST

TRAPPEAN *adj* of, relating to, or consisting of igneous rock, esp a basalt

TRAPPED > TRAP

TRAPPER *n* person who traps animals for their fur

TRAPPERS > TRAPPER

TRAPPIER > TRAPPY

TRAPPIEST > TRAPPY

TRAPPING > TRAP

TRAPPINGS *npl* accessories that symbolize an office or position

TRAPPOSE *adj* of or relating to traprock

TRAPPOUS *same as* > TRAPPOSE

TRAPPY *adj* having many traps

TRAPROCK *another name for* > TRAP

TRAPROCKS > TRAPROCK

TRAPS > TRAP

TRAPT *old past participle of* > TRAP

TRAPUNTO *n* type of quilting that is only partly padded in a design

TRAPUNTOS > TRAPUNTO

TRASH *n* anything worthless ▷ *vb* attack or destroy maliciously

TRASHCAN *n* dustbin

TRASHCANS > TRASHCAN

TRASHED *adj* drunk

TRASHER > TRASH

TRASHERS > TRASH

TRASHERY > TRASH

TRASHES > TRASH

TRASHIER > TRASHY

TRASHIEST > TRASHY

TRASHILY > TRASHY

TRASHING > TRASH

TRASHMAN *another name for* > BINMAN

TRASHMEN > TRASHMAN

TRASHTRIE *n* trash

TRASHY *adj* cheap, worthless, or badly made

TRASS *n* variety of the volcanic rock tuff, used to make a hydraulic cement

TRASSES > TRASS

TRAT *n* type of fishing line holding a series of baited hooks

TRATS > TRAT

TRATT *short for* > TRATTORIA

TRATTORIA *n* Italian restaurant

TRATTORIE > TRATTORIA

TRATTS > TRATT

TRAUCHLE *n* work or a task that is tiring, monotonous, and lengthy ▷ *vb* walk or work slowly and wearily

TRAUCHLED *adj* exhausted

by long hard work or concern

TRAUCHLES > TRAUCHLE

TRAUMA *n* emotional shock

TRAUMAS > TRAUMA

TRAUMATA > TRAUMA

TRAUMATIC > TRAUMA

TRAVAIL *n* labour or toil ▷ *vb* suffer or labour painfully, esp in childbirth

TRAVAILED > TRAVAIL

TRAVAILS > TRAVAIL

TRAVE *n* stout wooden cage in which difficult horses are shod

TRAVEL *vb* go from one place to another, through an area, or for a specified distance ▷ *n* travelling, esp as a tourist

TRAVELED *same as* > TRAVELLED

TRAVELER *same as* > TRAVELLER

TRAVELERS > TRAVELER

TRAVELING > TRAVEL

TRAVELLED *adj* having experienced or undergone much travelling

TRAVELLER *n* person who makes a journey or travels a lot

TRAVELOG *n* film, lecture, or brochure on travel

TRAVELOGS > TRAVELOG

TRAVELS > TRAVEL

TRAVERSAL > TRAVERSE

TRAVERSE *vb* pass or go over

TRAVERSED > TRAVERSE

TRAVERSER > TRAVERSE

TRAVERSES > TRAVERSE

TRAVERTIN *n* porous rock

TRAVES > TRAVE

TRAVESTY *n* grotesque imitation or mockery ▷ *vb* make or be a travesty of

TRAVIS *same as* > TREVISS

TRAVISES > TRAVIS

TRAVOIS *n* sled used for dragging logs

TRAVOISE *same as* > TRAVOIS

TRAVOISES > TRAVOISE

TRAWL *n* net dragged at deep levels behind a fishing boat ▷ *vb* fish with such a net

TRAWLED > TRAWL

TRAWLER *n* trawling boat

TRAWLERS > TRAWLER

TRAWLEY *same as* > TROLLEY

TRAWLEYS > TRAWLEY

TRAWLING > TRAWL

TRAWLINGS > TRAWL

TRAWLNET *n* large net, usually in the shape of a sock or bag, drawn at deep levels behind special boats (trawlers)

TRAWLNETS > TRAWLNET

TRAWLS > TRAWL

TRAY *n* flat board, usu with

a rim, for carrying things

TRAYBIT *n* threepenny bit

TRAYBITS > TRAYBIT

TRAYFUL *n* as many or as much as will fit on a tray

TRAYFULS > TRAYFUL

TRAYNE *old spelling of* > TRAIN

TRAYNED > TRAINE

TRAYNES > TRAYNE

TRAYNING > TRAYNE

TRAYS > TRAY

TRAZODONE *n* drug used to treat depression

TREACHER *n* traitor; treacherous person

TREACHERS > TREACHER

TREACHERY *n* wilful betrayal

TREACHOUR *same as* > TREACHER

TREACLE *n* thick dark syrup produced when sugar is refined ▷ *vb* add treacle to

TREACLED > TREACLE

TREACLES > TREACLE

TREACLIER > TREACLY

TREACLING > TREACLE

TREACLY > TREACLE

TREAD *vb* set one's foot on ▷ *n* way of walking or dancing

TREADED > TREAD

TREADER > TREAD

TREADERS > TREAD

TREADING > TREAD

TREADINGS > TREAD

TREADLE *n* lever worked by the foot to turn a wheel ▷ *vb* work (a machine) with a treadle

TREADLED > TREADLE

TREADLER > TREADLE

TREADLERS > TREADLE

TREADLES > TREADLE

TREADLESS *adj* (of a tyre, for example) having no tread

TREADLING > TREADLE

TREADMILL *n* cylinder turned by treading on steps projecting from it

TREADS > TREAD

TREAGUE *n* agreement to stop fighting

TREAGUES > TREAGUE

TREASON *n* betrayal of one's sovereign or country

TREASONS > TREASON

TREASURE *n* collection of wealth, esp gold or jewels ▷ *vb* prize or cherish

TREASURED > TREASURE

TREASURER *n* official in charge of funds

TREASURES > TREASURE

TREASURY *n* storage place for treasure

TREAT *vb* deal with or regard in a certain manner ▷ *n* pleasure, entertainment, etc given or paid for by someone else

TREATABLE > TREAT

TREATED > TREAT

TREATER > TREAT

TREATERS > TREAT

TREATIES > TREATY

TREATING > TREAT

TREATINGS > TREAT

TREATISE *n* formal piece of writing on a particular subject

TREATISES > TREATISE

TREATMENT *n* medical care

TREATS > TREAT

TREATY *n* signed contract between states

TREBBIANO *n* grape used to make wine

TREBLE *adj* triple ▷ *n* (singer with or part for) a soprano voice ▷ *vb* increase three times

TREBLED > TREBLE

TREBLES > TREBLE

TREBLING > TREBLE

TREBLY > TREBLE

TREBUCHET *n* large medieval siege engine for hurling missiles consisting of a sling on a pivoted wooden arm set in motion by the fall of a weight

TREBUCKET *same as* > TREBUCHET

TRECENTO *n* 14th century, esp with reference to Italian art and literature

TRECENTOS > TRECENTO

TRECK *same as* > TREK

TRECKED > TRECK

TRECKING > TRECK

TRECKS > TRECK

TREDDLE *variant spelling of* > TREADLE

TREDDLED > TREDDLE

TREDDLES > TREDDLE

TREDDLING > TREDDLE

TREDILLE *same as* > TREDRILLE

TREDILLES > TREDILLE

TREDRILLE *n* card game for three players

TREE *n* large perennial plant with a woody trunk

TREED > TREE

TREEHOUSE *n* house built in tree

TREEING > TREE

TREELAWN *n* narrow band of grass between a road and a pavement, usually planted with trees

TREELAWNS > TREELAWN

TREELESS > TREE

TREELIKE > TREE

TREEN *adj* made of wood ▷ *n* art of making treenware

TREENAIL *n* dowel used for pinning planks or timbers together

TREENAILS > TREENAIL

TREENS > TREEN

TREENWARE *n* dishes and other household utensils

made of wood, as by pioneers in North America

TREES > TREE

TREESHIP *n* state of being a tree

TREESHIPS > TREESHIP

TREETOP *n* top of a tree

TREETOPS > TREETOP

TREEWARE *n* books, magazines, or other reading materials that are printed on paper made from wood pulp as opposed to texts in the form of computer software, CD-ROM, audio books, etc

TREEWARES > TREEWARE

TREEWAX *n* yellowish wax secreted by an oriental scale insect

TREEWAXES > TREEWAX

TREF *adj* in Judaism, ritually unfit to be eaten

TREFA *same as* > TREF

TREFAH *same as* > TREF

TREFOIL *n* plant, such as clover, with a three-lobed leaf

TREFOILED > TREFOIL

TREFOILS > TREFOIL

TREGETOUR *n* juggler

TREHALA *n* edible sugary substance obtained from the pupal cocoon of an Asian weevil

TREHALAS > TREHALA

TREHALOSE *n* white crystalline disaccharide that occurs in yeast and certain fungi

TREIF *same as* > TREF

TREIFA *same as* > TREF

TREILLAGE *n* latticework

TREILLE *another word for* > TRELLIS

TREILLES > TREILLE

TREK *n* long difficult journey, esp on foot ▷ *vb* make such a journey

TREKKED > TREK

TREKKER > TREK

TREKKERS > TREK

TREKKING *n* as in *pony trekking* the act of riding ponies cross-country

TREKKINGS > TREKKING

TREKS > TREK

TRELLIS *n* framework of horizontal and vertical strips of wood ▷ *vb* interweave (strips of wood, etc) to make a trellis

TRELLISED > TRELLIS

TRELLISES > TRELLIS

TREMA *n* mark consisting of two dots placed over the second of two adjacent vowels to indicate it is to be pronounced separately rather than forming a diphthong with the first

TREMAS > TREMA

TREMATIC *adj* relating to the gills

TREMATODE *n* parasitic

flatworm

TREMATOID > TREMATODE

TREMBLANT *adj* (of jewels) set in such a way that they shake when the wearer moves

TREMBLE *vb* shake or quiver ▷ *n* trembling

TREMBLED > TREMBLE

TREMBLER *n* device that vibrates to make or break an electrical circuit

TREMBLERS > TREMBLER

TREMBLES *n* disease of cattle and sheep characterized by muscular incoordination and tremor, caused by ingestion of white snakeroot or rayless goldenrod

TREMBLIER > TREMBLE

TREMBLING > TREMBLE

TREMBLY > TREMBLE

TREMIE *n* large metal hopper and pipe used to distribute freshly mixed concrete over an underwater site.

TREMIES > TREMIE

TREMOLANT *another word for* > TREMOLO

TREMOLITE *n* white or pale green mineral of the amphibole group consisting of calcium magnesium silicate

TREMOLO *n* quivering effect in singing or playing

TREMOLOS > TREMOLO

TREMOR *n* involuntary shaking ▷ *vb* tremble

TREMORED > TREMOR

TREMORING > TREMOR

TREMOROUS > TREMOR

TREMORS > TREMOR

TREMULANT *n* device on an organ by which the wind stream is made to fluctuate in intensity producing a tremolo effect

TREMULATE *vb* produce a tremulous sound

TREMULOUS *adj* trembling, as from fear or excitement

TRENAIL *same as* > TREENAIL

TRENAILS > TRENAIL

TRENCH *n* long narrow ditch, esp one used as a shelter in war ▷ *adj* of or involving military trenches ▷ *vb* make a trench in (a place)

TRENCHAND *old variant of* > TRENCHANT

TRENCHANT *adj* incisive

TRENCHARD *same as* > TRENCHER

TRENCHED > TRENCH

TRENCHER *n* wooden plate for serving food

TRENCHERS > TRENCHER

TRENCHES > TRENCH

TRENCHING > TRENCH

TREND n general tendency or direction ▷ vb take a certain trend
TRENDED > TREND
TRENDIER > TRENDY
TRENDIES > TRENDY
TRENDIEST > TRENDY
TRENDIFY vb render fashionable
TRENDILY > TRENDY
TRENDING > TREND
TRENDOID n follower of trends
TRENDOIDS > TRENDOID
TRENDS > TREND
TRENDY n consciously fashionable (person) ▷ adj consciously fashionable
TRENDYISM > TRENDY
TRENISE n one of the figures in a quadrille
TRENISES > TRENISE
TRENTAL n mass said in remembrance of a person 30 days after his or her death
TRENTALS > TRENTAL
TREPAN same as > TREPHINE
TREPANG n any of various large sea cucumbers of tropical Oriental seas, the body walls of which are used as food by the Japanese and Chinese
TREPANGS > TREPANG
TREPANNED > TREPAN
TREPANNER > TREPAN
TREPANS > TREPAN
TREPHINE n surgical sawlike instrument for removing circular sections of bone, esp from the skull ▷ vb remove a circular section of bone from (esp the skull)
TREPHINED > TREPHINE
TREPHINER > TREPHINE
TREPHINES > TREPHINE
TREPID adj trembling
TREPIDANT adj trembling
TREPONEMA n anaerobic spirochaete bacterium that causes syphilis
TREPONEME same as > TREPONEMA
TRES adj very
TRESPASS vb go onto another's property without permission ▷ n trespassing
TRESS n lock of hair, esp a long lock of woman's hair ▷ vb arrange in tresses
TRESSED adj having a tress or tresses as specified
TRESSEL variant spelling of > TRESTLE
TRESSELS > TRESSEL
TRESSES > TRESS
TRESSIER > TRESS
TRESSIEST > TRESS
TRESSING > TRESS
TRESSOUR same as > TRESSURE
TRESSOURS > TRESSOUR

TRESSURE n narrow inner border on a shield, usually decorated with fleurs-de-lys
TRESSURED > TRESSURE
TRESSURES > TRESSURE
TRESSY > TRESS
TREST old variant of > TRESTLE
TRESTLE n board fixed on pairs of spreading legs, used as a support
TRESTLES > TRESTLE
TRESTS > TREST
TRET n (formerly) an allowance according to weight granted to purchasers for waste due to transportation
TRETINOIN n retinoid drug used to treat certain skin conditions
TRETS > TRET
TREVALLY n any of various food and game fishes
TREVALLYS > TREVALLY
TREVET same as > TRIVET
TREVETS > TREVET
TREVIS variant spelling of > TREVISS
TREVISES > TREVIS
TREVISS n partition in a stable for keeping animals apart
TREVISSES > TREVISS
TREW old variant spelling of > TRUE
TREWS npl close-fitting tartan trousers
TREWSMAN n Highlander
TREWSMEN > TREWSMAN
TREY n any card or dice throw with three spots
TREYBIT same as > TRAYBIT
TREYBITS > TREYBIT
TREYS > TREY
TREZ same as > TREY
TREZES > TREZ
TRIABLE adj liable to be tried judicially
TRIAC n device for regulating the amount of electric current allowed to reach a circuit
TRIACID adj (of a base) capable of reacting with three molecules of a monobasic acid
TRIACIDS > TRIACID
TRIACS > TRIAC
TRIACT adj having three rays
TRIACTINE same as > TRIACT
TRIAD n group of three
TRIADIC n something that has the characteristics of a triad
TRIADICS > TRIADIC
TRIADISM > TRIAD
TRIADISMS > TRIAD
TRIADIST > TRIAD
TRIADISTS > TRIAD
TRIADS > TRIAD

TRIAGE n (in a hospital) the principle or practice of sorting emergency patients into categories of priority for treatment ▷ vb sort (patients) into categories of priority for treatment
TRIAGED > TRIAGE
TRIAGES > TRIAGE
TRIAGING > TRIAGE
TRIAL n investigation of a case before a judge
TRIALISM n belief that man consists of body, soul, and spirit
TRIALISMS > TRIALISM
TRIALIST same as > TRIALLIST
TRIALISTS > TRIALIST
TRIALITY > TRIALISM
TRIALLED > TRIAL
TRIALLING > TRIAL
TRIALLIST n person who takes part in a competition
TRIALOGUE n dialogue between three people
TRIALS > TRIAL
TRIALWARE n computer software that can be used without charge for a limited evaluation period
TRIANGLE n geometric figure with three sides
TRIANGLED > TRIANGLE
TRIANGLES > TRIANGLE
TRIAPSAL adj (of a church) having three apses
TRIARCH n one of three rulers of a triarchy
TRIARCHS > TRIARCH
TRIARCHY n government by three people
TRIASSIC adj of, denoting, or formed in the first period of the Mesozoic era
TRIATHLON n athletic contest in which each athlete competes in three different events: swimming, cycling, and running
TRIATIC n rope between a ship's mastheads
TRIATICS > TRIATIC
TRIATOMIC adj a molecule having three atoms
TRIAXIAL adj having three axes ▷ n sponge spicule with three axes
TRIAXIALS > TRIAXIAL
TRIAXON another name for > TRIAXIAL
TRIAXONS > TRIAXON
TRIAZIN same as > TRIAZINE
TRIAZINE n any of three azines that contain three nitrogen atoms in their molecules
TRIAZINES > TRIAZINE
TRIAZINS > TRIAZIN
TRIAZOLE n heterocyclic compound

TRIAZOLES > TRIAZOLE
TRIAZOLIC > TRIAZOLE
TRIBADE n lesbian, esp one who practises tribadism
TRIBADES > TRIBADE
TRIBADIC > TRIBADE
TRIBADIES > TRIBADY
TRIBADISM n lesbian practice in which one partner lies on top of the other and simulates the male role in heterosexual intercourse
TRIBADY another word for > TRIBADISM
TRIBAL adj of or denoting a tribe or tribes ▷ n member of a tribal community
TRIBALISM n loyalty to a tribe
TRIBALIST > TRIBALISM
TRIBALLY > TRIBAL
TRIBALS > TRIBAL
TRIBASIC adj (of an acid) containing three replaceable hydrogen atoms in the molecule
TRIBBLE n frame for drying paper
TRIBBLES > TRIBBLE
TRIBE n group of clans or families believed to have a common ancestor
TRIBELESS > TRIBE
TRIBES > TRIBE
TRIBESMAN n member of a tribe
TRIBESMEN > TRIBESMAN
TRIBLET n spindle or mandrel used in making rings, tubes, etc
TRIBLETS > TRIBLET
TRIBOLOGY n study of friction, lubrication, and wear between moving surfaces
TRIBRACH n metrical foot of three short syllables
TRIBRACHS > TRIBRACH
TRIBULATE vb trouble
TRIBUNAL n board appointed to inquire into a specific matter
TRIBUNALS > TRIBUNAL
TRIBUNARY > TRIBUNE
TRIBUNATE n office or rank of a tribune
TRIBUNE n people's representative, esp in ancient Rome
TRIBUNES > TRIBUNE
TRIBUTARY n stream or river flowing into a larger one ▷ adj (of a stream or river) flowing into a larger one
TRIBUTE n sign of respect or admiration
TRIBUTER n miner
TRIBUTERS > TRIBUTER
TRIBUTES > TRIBUTE

TRICAR n car with three wheels

TRICARS > TRICAR

TRICE n moment ▷ vb haul up or secure

TRICED > TRICE

TRICEP same as > TRICEPS

TRICEPS n muscle at the back of the upper arm

TRICEPSES > TRICEPS

TRICERION n candlestick with three arms

TRICES > TRICE

TRICHINA n parasitic nematode worm, occurring in the intestines of pigs, rats, and man and producing larvae that form cysts in skeletal muscle

TRICHINAE > TRICHINA

TRICHINAL > TRICHINA

TRICHINAS > TRICHINA

TRICHITE n any of various needle-shaped crystals that occur in some glassy volcanic rocks

TRICHITES > TRICHITE

TRICHITIC > TRICHITE

TRICHOID adj resembling a hair

TRICHOME n any hairlike outgrowth from the surface of a plant

TRICHOMES > TRICHOME

TRICHOMIC > TRICHOME

TRICHORD n musical instrument with three strings

TRICHORDS > TRICHORD

TRICHOSES > TRICHOSIS

TRICHOSIS n any abnormal condition or disease of the hair

TRICHROIC n state of having three colours

TRICHROME adj three-coloured

TRICING > TRICE

TRICK n deceitful or cunning action or plan ▷ vb cheat or deceive

TRICKED > TRICK

TRICKER > TRICK

TRICKERS > TRICK

TRICKERY n practice or an instance of using tricks

TRICKIE Scots form of > TRICKY

TRICKIER > TRICKY

TRICKIEST > TRICKY

TRICKILY > TRICKY

TRICKING > TRICK

TRICKINGS > TRICK

TRICKISH same as > TRICKY

TRICKLE vb (cause to) flow in a thin stream or drops ▷ n gradual flow

TRICKLED > TRICKLE

TRICKLES > TRICKLE

TRICKLESS > TRICK

TRICKLET n tiny trickle

TRICKLETS > TRICKLET

TRICKLIER > TRICKLE

TRICKLING > TRICKLE

TRICKLY > TRICKLE

TRICKS > TRICK

TRICKSIER > TRICKSY

TRICKSILY > TRICKSY

TRICKSOME adj full of tricks

TRICKSTER n person who deceives or plays tricks

TRICKSY adj playing tricks habitually

TRICKY adj difficult, needing careful handling

TRICLAD n type of worm having a tripartite intestine

TRICLADS > TRICLAD

TRICLINIA n plural of triclinium: in Ancient Rome, reclining couch

TRICLINIC adj relating to or belonging to the crystal system characterized by three unequal axes, no pair of which are perpendicular

TRICLOSAN n drug used to treat skin infections

TRICOLOR same as > TRICOLOUR

TRICOLORS > TRICOLOR

TRICOLOUR n three-coloured striped flag ▷ adj having or involving three colours

TRICORN n cocked hat with opposing brims turned back and caught in three places ▷ adj having three horns or corners

TRICORNE same as > TRICORN

TRICORNES > TRICORNE

TRICORNS > TRICORN

TRICOT n thin rayon or nylon fabric knitted or resembling knitting, used for dresses, etc

TRICOTINE n twill-weave woollen fabric resembling gabardine

TRICOTS > TRICOT

TRICROTIC adj (of the pulse) having a tracing characterized by three elevations with each beat

TRICTRAC n game similar to backgammon

TRICTRACS > TRICTRAC

TRICUSPID adj having three points, cusps, or segments ▷ n tooth having three cusps

TRICYCLE n three-wheeled cycle ▷ vb ride a tricycle

TRICYCLED > TRICYCLE

TRICYCLER > TRICYCLE

TRICYCLES > TRICYCLE

TRICYCLIC adj (of a chemical compound) containing three rings in the molecular structure ▷ n antidepressant drug having a tricyclic molecular structure

TRIDACNA n giant clam

TRIDACNAS > TRIDACNA

TRIDACTYL adj having three digits on one hand or foot

TRIDARN n sideboard with three levels

TRIDARNS > TRIDARN

TRIDE old spelling of the past tense of > TRY

TRIDENT n three-pronged spear ▷ adj having three prongs

TRIDENTAL adj having three prongs, teeth, etc

TRIDENTED adj having three prongs

TRIDENTS > TRIDENT

TRIDUAN adj three days long

TRIDUUM n period of three days for prayer before a feast

TRIDUUMS > TRIDUUM

TRIDYMITE n form of silica

TRIE old spelling of > TRY

TRIECIOUS adj (of a plant) having male, female, and hermaphroditic flowers

TRIED > TRY

TRIELLA n three nominated horse races in which the punter bets on selecting the three winners

TRIELLAS > TRIELLA

TRIENE n chemical compound containing three double bonds

TRIENES > TRIENE

TRIENNIA > TRIENNIUM

TRIENNIAL adj happening every three years ▷ n relating to, lasting for, or occurring every three years

TRIENNIUM n period or cycle of three years

TRIENS n Byzantine gold goin worth one third of a solidus

TRIENTES > TRIENS

TRIER n person or thing that tries

TRIERARCH n citizen responsible for fitting out a state trireme, esp in Athens

TRIERS > TRIER

TRIES > TRY

TRIETERIC adj occurring once every two years

TRIETHYL adj consisting of three groups of ethyls

TRIFACIAL adj relating to the trigeminal nerve

TRIFECTA n form of betting in which the punter selects the first three place-winners in a horse race in the correct order

TRIFECTAS > TRIFECTA

TRIFF adj terrific; very good indeed

TRIFFER > TRIFF

TRIFFEST > TRIFF

TRIFFIC adj terrific; very good indeed

TRIFFID n any of a species of fictional plants that supposedly grew to a gigantic size, were capable of moving about, and could kill humans

TRIFFIDS > TRIFFID

TRIFFIDY adj resembling a triffid

TRIFID adj divided or split into three parts or lobes

TRIFLE n insignificant thing or amount ▷ vb deal (with) as if worthless

TRIFLED > TRIFLE

TRIFLER > TRIFLE

TRIFLERS > TRIFLE

TRIFLES > TRIFLE

TRIFLING adj insignificant

TRIFLINGS > TRIFLE

TRIFOCAL adj having three focuses ▷ n glasses that have trifocal lenses

TRIFOCALS > TRIFOCAL

TRIFOLD less common word for > TRIPLE

TRIFOLIES > TRIFOLY

TRIFOLIUM n leguminous plant with leaves divided into three leaflets and dense heads of small white, yellow, red, or purple flowers

TRIFOLY same as > TREFOIL

TRIFORIA > TRIFORIUM

TRIFORIAL > TRIFORIUM

TRIFORIUM n arcade above the arches of the nave, choir, or transept of a church

TRIFORM adj having three parts

TRIFORMED same as > TRIFORM

TRIG adj neat or spruce ▷ vb make or become spruce

TRIGAMIES > TRIGAMY

TRIGAMIST > TRIGAMY

TRIGAMOUS > TRIGAMY

TRIGAMY n condition of having three spouses

TRIGEMINI npl facial nerves

TRIGGED > TRIG

TRIGGER n small lever releasing a catch on a gun or machine ▷ vb set (an action or process) in motion

TRIGGERED > TRIGGER

TRIGGERS > TRIGGER

TRIGGEST > TRIG

TRIGGING > TRIG

TRIGLOT n person who can speak three languages

TRIGLOTS > TRIGLOT

TRIGLY > TRIG

TRIGLYPH n stone block in a Doric frieze, having three vertical channels

TRIGLYPHS > TRIGLYPH
TRIGNESS > TRIG
TRIGO n wheat field
TRIGON n (in classical Greece or Rome) a triangular harp or lyre
TRIGONAL adj triangular
TRIGONIC > TRIGON
TRIGONOUS adj (of stems, seeds, and similar parts) having a triangular cross section
TRIGONS > TRIGON
TRIGOS > TRIGO
TRIGRAM n three-letter inscription
TRIGRAMS > TRIGRAM
TRIGRAPH n combination of three letters used to represent a single speech sound or phoneme, such as eau in French beau
TRIGRAPHS > TRIGRAPH
TRIGS > TRIG
TRIGYNIAN adj relating to the Trigynia order of plants
TRIGYNOUS adj (of a plant) having three pistils
TRIHEDRA > TRIHEDRON
TRIHEDRAL adj having or formed by three plane faces meeting at a point ▷ n figure formed by the intersection of three lines in different planes
TRIHEDRON n figure determined by the intersection of three planes
TRIHYBRID n hybrid that differs from its parents in three genetic traits
TRIHYDRIC adj (of an alcohol or similar compound) containing three hydroxyl groups
TRIJET n jet with three engines
TRIJETS > TRIJET
TRIJUGATE adj in three pairs
TRIJUGOUS same as > TRIJUGATE
TRIKE n tricycle
TRIKES > TRIKE
TRILBIES > TRILBY
TRILBY n man's soft felt hat
TRILBYS > TRILBY
TRILD old past tense of > TRILL
TRILEMMA n quandary posed by three alternative courses of action
TRILEMMAS > TRILEMMA
TRILINEAR adj consisting of, bounded by, or relating to three lines
TRILITH same as > TRILITHON
TRILITHIC > TRILITHON
TRILITHON n structure consisting of two upright stones with a third placed across the top, such as

those of Stonehenge
TRILITHS > TRILITH
TRILL n rapid alternation between two notes ▷ vb play or sing a trill
TRILLED > TRILL
TRILLER > TRILL
TRILLERS > TRILL
TRILLING > TRILL
TRILLINGS > TRILL
TRILLION n one million million ▷ adj amounting to a trillion
TRILLIONS > TRILLION
TRILLIUM n plant of Asia and North America that has three leaves at the top of the stem with a single white, pink, or purple three-petalled flower
TRILLIUMS > TRILLIUM
TRILLO n (in music) a trill
TRILLOES > TRILL
TRILLS > TRILL
TRILOBAL > TRILOBE
TRILOBATE adj (esp of a leaf) consisting of or having three lobes or parts
TRILOBE n three-lobed thing
TRILOBED adj having three lobes
TRILOBES > TRILOBE
TRILOBITE n small prehistoric sea animal
TRILOGIES > TRILOGY
TRILOGY n series of three related books, plays, etc
TRIM adj neat and smart ▷ vb cut or prune into good shape ▷ n decoration
TRIMARAN n three-hulled boat
TRIMARANS > TRIMARAN
TRIMER n polymer or a molecule of a polymer consisting of three identical monomers
TRIMERIC > TRIMER
TRIMERISM > TRIMER
TRIMEROUS adj (of plants) having parts arranged in groups of three
TRIMERS > TRIMER
TRIMESTER n period of three months
TRIMETER n verse line consisting of three metrical feet ▷ adj designating such a line
TRIMETERS > TRIMETER
TRIMETHYL adj having three methyl groups
TRIMETRIC adj of, relating to, or consisting of a trimeter or trimeters
TRIMIX n gas mixture of nitrogen, helium and oxygen used by deep-sea divers
TRIMIXES > TRIMIX
TRIMLY > TRIM
TRIMMED > TRIM
TRIMMER > TRIM
TRIMMERS > TRIM

TRIMMEST > TRIM
TRIMMING > TRIM
TRIMMINGS > TRIM
TRIMNESS > TRIM
TRIMORPH n substance, esp a mineral, that exists in three distinct forms
TRIMORPHS > TRIMORPH
TRIMOTOR n vehicle with three motors
TRIMOTORS > TRIMOTOR
TRIMS > TRIM
TRIMTAB n small control surface attached to the trailing edge of a main control surface to enable the pilot to balance an aircraft
TRIMTABS > TRIMTAB
TRIN n triplet
TRINAL > TRINE
TRINARY adj made up of three parts
TRINDLE vb move heavily on (or as if on) wheels
TRINDLED > TRINDLE
TRINDLES > TRINDLE
TRINDLING > TRINDLE
TRINE n aspect of 120° between two planets, an orb of 8° being allowed ▷ adj of or relating to a trine ▷ vb put in a trine aspect
TRINED > TRINE
TRINES > TRINE
TRINGLE n slim rod
TRINGLES > TRINGLE
TRINING > TRINE
TRINITIES > TRINITY
TRINITRIN n pale yellow viscous explosive liquid substance made from glycerol and nitric and sulphuric acids
TRINITY n group of three
TRINKET n small or worthless ornament or piece of jewellery ▷ vb ornament with trinkets
TRINKETED > TRINKET
TRINKETS > TRINKET
TRINKETRY > TRINKET
TRINKETS > TRINKET
TRINKUM n trinket or bauble
TRINKUMS > TRINKUM
TRINODAL adj having three nodes
TRINOMIAL adj consisting of or relating to three terms ▷ n polynomial consisting of three terms
TRINS > TRIN
TRIO n group of three
TRIODE n electronic valve having three electrodes, a cathode, an anode, and a grid
TRIODES > TRIODE
TRIOL n any of a class of alcohols that have three hydroxyl groups per molecule
TRIOLEIN n naturally occurring glyceride of oleic

acid, found in fats and oils
TRIOLEINS > TRIOLEIN
TRIOLET n verse form of eight lines
TRIOLETS > TRIOLET
TRIOLS > TRIOL
TRIONES n seven stars of the constellation Ursa Major
TRIONYM another name for > TRINOMIAL
TRIONYMAL > TRIONYM
TRIONYMS > TRIONYM
TRIOR old form of > TRIER
TRIORS > TRIOR
TRIOS > TRIO
TRIOSE n simple monosaccharide produced by the oxidation of glycerol
TRIOSES > TRIOSE
TRIOXID same as > TRIOXIDE
TRIOXIDE n any oxide that contains three oxygen atoms per molecule
TRIOXIDES > TRIOXIDE
TRIOXIDS > TRIOXIDE
TRIOXYGEN technical name for > OXYGEN
TRIP n journey to a place and back, esp for pleasure ▷ vb (cause to) stumble
TRIPACK n pack of three
TRIPACKS > TRIPACK
TRIPART adj composed of three parts
TRIPE n stomach of a cow used as food
TRIPEDAL adj having three feet
TRIPERIES > TRIPERY
TRIPERY n place where tripe is prepared
TRIPES > TRIPE
TRIPEY > TRIPE
TRIPHASE adj having three phases
TRIPHONE n group of three phonemes
TRIPHONES > TRIPHONE
TRIPIER > TRIPE
TRIPIEST > TRIPE
TRIPITAKA n three collections of books making up the Buddhist canon of scriptures
TRIPLANE n aeroplane having three wings arranged one above the other
TRIPLANES > TRIPLANE
TRIPLE adj having three parts ▷ vb increase three times ▷ n something that is, or contains, three times as much as normal
TRIPLED > TRIPLE
TRIPLES > TRIPLE
TRIPLET n one of three babies born at one birth
TRIPLETS > TRIPLET
TRIPLEX n building divided into three separate dwellings
TRIPLEXES > TRIPLEX

TRIPLIED > TRIPLY
TRIPLIES > TRIPLY
TRIPLING > TRIPLE
TRIPLINGS > TRIPLE
TRIPLITE n brownish-red phosphate
TRIPLITES > TRIPLITE
TRIPLOID adj having or relating to three times the haploid number of chromosomes ▷ n triploid organism
TRIPLOIDS > TRIPLOID
TRIPLOIDY n triploid state
TRIPLY vb give a reply to a duply
TRIPLYING > TRIPLY
TRIPOD n three-legged stand, stool, etc
TRIPODAL > TRIPOD
TRIPODIC > TRIPOD
TRIPODIES > TRIPODY
TRIPODS > TRIPOD
TRIPODY n metrical unit consisting of three feet
TRIPOLI n lightweight porous siliceous rock derived by weathering and used in a powdered form as a polish, filter, etc
TRIPOLIS > TRIPOLI
TRIPOS n final examinations for an honours degree at Cambridge University
TRIPOSES > TRIPOS
TRIPPANT adj (in heraldry) in the process of tripping
TRIPPED > TRIP
TRIPPER n tourist
TRIPPERS > TRIPPER
TRIPPERY adj like a tripper
TRIPPET n any mechanism that strikes or is struck at regular intervals, as by a cam
TRIPPETS > TRIPPET
TRIPPIER > TRIPPY
TRIPPIEST > TRIPPY
TRIPPING > TRIP
TRIPPINGS > TRIP
TRIPPLE vb canter
TRIPPLED > TRIPPLE
TRIPPLER > TRIPPLE
TRIPPLERS > TRIPPLE
TRIPPLES > TRIPPLE
TRIPPLING > TRIPPLE
TRIPPY adj suggestive of or resembling the effect produced by a hallucinogenic drug
TRIPS > TRIP
TRIPSES > TRIPSIS
TRIPSIS n act of kneading the body to promote circulation, suppleness, etc
TRIPTAN n drug used to treat migraine
TRIPTANE n colourless highly flammable liquid
TRIPTANES > TRIPTANE
TRIPTANS > TRIPTAN
TRIPTOTE n word that has

only three cases
TRIPTOTES > TRIPTOTE
TRIPTYCA variant of > TRIPTYCH
TRIPTYCAS > TRIPTYCA
TRIPTYCH n painting or carving on three hinged panels, often forming an altarpiece
TRIPTYCHS > TRIPTYCH
TRIPTYQUE n customs permit for the temporary importation of a motor vehicle
TRIPUDIA > TRIPUDIUM
TRIPUDIUM n ancient religious dance
TRIPWIRE n wire that activates a trap, mine, etc, when tripped over
TRIPWIRES > TRIPWIRE
TRIPY > TRIPE
TRIQUETRA n ornament in the shape of three intersecting ellipses roughly forming a triangle
TRIRADIAL adj having or consisting of three rays or radiating branches
TRIREME n ancient Greek warship with three rows of oars on each side
TRIREMES > TRIREME
TRISAGION n old hymn
TRISCELE variant spelling of > TRISKELE
TRISCELES > TRISCELE
TRISECT vb divide into three parts, esp three equal parts
TRISECTED > TRISECT
TRISECTOR > TRISECT
TRISECTS > TRISECT
TRISEME n metrical foot of a length equal to three short syllables
TRISEMES > TRISEME
TRISEMIC > TRISEME
TRISERIAL adj arranged in three rows or series
TRISHAW another name for > RICKSHAW
TRISHAWS > TRISHAW
TRISKELE n three-limbed symbol
TRISKELES > TRISKELE
TRISKELIA n plural of singular triskelion: three-limbed symbol
TRISMIC > TRISMUS
TRISMUS n state of being unable to open the mouth because of sustained contractions of the jaw muscles, caused by tetanus
TRISMUSES > TRISMUS
TRISODIUM adj containing three sodium atoms
TRISOME n chromosome occurring three times (rather than twice) in a cell
TRISOMES > TRISOME
TRISOMIC > TRISOMY
TRISOMICS n study of

trisomy
TRISOMIES > TRISOMY
TRISOMY n condition of having one chromosome of the set represented three times in an otherwise diploid organism, cell, etc
TRIST variant spelling of > TRISTE
TRISTATE adj (of a digital computer chip) having high, low, and floating output states
TRISTE adj sad
TRISTESSE n sadness
TRISTEZA n disease affecting citrus trees
TRISTEZAS > TRISTEZA
TRISTFUL same as > TRISTE
TRISTICH n poem, stanza, or strophe that consists of three lines
TRISTICHS > TRISTICH
TRISUL n trident symbol of Siva
TRISULA same as > TRISUL
TRISULAS > TRISULA
TRISULS > TRISUL
TRITANOPE n person who cannot distinguish the colour blue
TRITE adj (of a remark or idea) commonplace and unoriginal ▷ n (on a lyre) the third string from the highest in pitch
TRITELY > TRITE
TRITENESS > TRITE
TRITER > TRITE
TRITES > TRITE
TRITEST > TRITE
TRITHEISM n belief in three gods, esp in the Trinity as consisting of three distinct gods
TRITHEIST > TRITHEISM
TRITHING n tripartition
TRITHINGS > TRITHING
TRITIATE vb replace normal hydrogen atoms in (a compound) by those of tritium
TRITIATED > TRITIATE
TRITIATES > TRITIATE
TRITICAL n trite; hackneyed
TRITICALE n fertile hybrid cereal
TRITICISM n something trite
TRITICUM n type of cereal grass of the genus which includes the wheats
TRITICUMS > TRITICUM
TRITIDE n tritium compound
TRITIDES > TRITIDE
TRITIUM n radioactive isotope of hydrogen
TRITIUMS > TRITIUM
TRITOMA another name for > KNIPHOFIA

TRITOMAS > TRITOMA
TRITON n any of various chiefly tropical marine gastropod molluscs, having large beautifully-coloured spiral shells
TRITONE n musical interval consisting of three whole tones
TRITONES > TRITONE
TRITONIA n type of plant with typically scarlet or orange flowers
TRITONIAS > TRITONIA
TRITONS > TRITON
TRITURATE vb grind or rub into a fine powder or pulp ▷ n powder or pulp resulting from this grinding
TRIUMPH n (happiness caused by) victory or success ▷ vb be victorious or successful
TRIUMPHAL adj celebrating a triumph
TRIUMPHED > TRIUMPH
TRIUMPHER > TRIUMPH
TRIUMPHS > TRIUMPH
TRIUMVIR n (esp in ancient Rome) a member of a triumvirate
TRIUMVIRI > TRIUMVIR
TRIUMVIRS > TRIUMVIR
TRIUMVIRY n triumvirate
TRIUNE adj constituting three in one, esp the three persons in one God of the Trinity ▷ n group of three
TRIUNES > TRIUNE
TRIUNITY > TRIUNE
TRIVALENT adj having a valency of three
TRIVALVE n animal having three valves
TRIVALVED adj having three valves
TRIVALVES > TRIVALVE
TRIVET n metal stand for a pot or kettle
TRIVETS > TRIVET
TRIVIA npl trivial things or details
TRIVIAL adj of little importance
TRIVIALLY > TRIVIAL
TRIVIUM n (in medieval learning) the lower division of the seven liberal arts, consisting of grammar, rhetoric, and logic
TRIVIUMS > TRIVIUM
TRIWEEKLY adv every three weeks ▷ n triweekly publication
TRIZONAL > TRIZONE
TRIZONE n area comprising three zones
TRIZONES > TRIZONE
TROAD same as > TROD
TROADE same as > TROD
TROADES > TROADE
TROADS > TROAD
TROAK old form of > TRUCK
TROAKED > TROAK
TROAKING > TROAK

TROAKS > TROAK
TROAT vb (of a rutting buck) to call or bellow
TROATED > TROAT
TROATING > TROAT
TROATS > TROAT
TROCAR n surgical instrument for removing fluid from bodily cavities, consisting of a puncturing device situated inside a tube
TROCARS > TROCAR
TROCHAIC adj of, relating to, or consisting of trochees ▷ n verse composed of trochees
TROCHAICS > TROCHAIC
TROCHAL adj shaped like a wheel
TROCHAR old variant spelling of > TROCAR
TROCHARS > TROCHAR
TROCHE another name for > LOZENGE
TROCHEE n metrical foot of one long and one short syllable
TROCHEES > TROCHEE
TROCHES > TROCHE
TROCHI > TROCHUS
TROCHIL same as > TROCHILUS
TROCHILI > TROCHILUS
TROCHILIC adj relating to the movement of a hummingbird's wings
TROCHILS > TROCHIL
TROCHILUS n any of several Old World warblers
TROCHISK another word for > TROCHE
TROCHISKS > TROCHISK
TROCHITE n joint of a crinoid
TROCHITES > TROCHITE
TROCHLEA n any bony or cartilaginous part with a grooved surface over which a bone, tendon, etc, may slide or articulate
TROCHLEAE > TROCHLEA
TROCHLEAR as in trochlear nerve either one of the fourth pair of cranial nerves, which supply the superior oblique muscle of the eye
TROCHLEAS > TROCHLEA
TROCHOID n curve described by a fixed point on the radius or extended radius of a circle as the circle rolls along a straight line ▷ adj rotating or capable of rotating about a central axis
TROCHOIDS > TROCHOID
TROCHUS n hoop (used in exercise)
TROCHUSES > TROCHUS
TROCK same as > TRUCK
TROCKED > TROCK
TROCKEN adj dry (used of wine, esp German wine)

TROCKING > TROCK
TROCKS > TROCK
TROD vb past participle of tread ▷ n path
TRODDEN > TREAD
TRODE same as > TROD
TRODES > TRODE
TRODS > TROD
TROELIE same as > TROOLIE
TROELIES > TROELIE
TROELY same as > TROOLIE
TROFFER n trough-like fixture for holding in place and reflecting light from a fluorescent tube
TROFFERS > TROFFER
TROG vb walk, esp aimlessly or heavily
TROGGED > TROG
TROGGING > TROG
TROGGS n loyalty; fidelity
TROGON n bird of tropical and subtropical regions of America, Africa, and Asia. They have a brilliant plumage, short hooked bill, and long tail
TROGONS > TROGON
TROGS > TROG
TROIKA n Russian vehicle drawn by three horses abreast
TROIKAS > TROIKA
TROILISM n sexual activity involving three people
TROILISMS > TROILISM
TROILIST > TROILISM
TROILISTS > TROILISM
TROILITE n iron sulphide present in most meteorites
TROILITES > TROILITE
TROILUS n type of large butterfly
TROILUSES > TROILUS
TROIS Scots form of > TROY
TROKE same as > TRUCK
TROKED > TROKE
TROKES > TROKE
TROKING > TROKE
TROLAND n unit of light intensity in the eye
TROLANDS > TROLAND
TROLL n giant or dwarf in Scandinavian folklore ▷ vb fish by dragging a lure through the water
TROLLED > TROLL
TROLLER > TROLL
TROLLERS > TROLL
TROLLEY n small wheeled table for food and drink ▷ vb transport on a trolley
TROLLEYED > TROLLEY
TROLLEYS npl men's underpants
TROLLIED > TROLLY
TROLLIES > TROLLY
TROLLING > TROLL
TROLLINGS > TROLL
TROLLIUS n plant with globe-shaped flowers

TROLLOP n promiscuous or slovenly woman ▷ vb behave like a trollop
TROLLOPED > TROLLOP
TROLLOPEE n loose dress or gown
TROLLOPS > TROLLOP
TROLLOPY > TROLLOP
TROLLS > TROLL
TROLLY same as > TROLLEY
TROLLYING > TROLLY
TROMBONE n brass musical instrument with a sliding tube
TROMBONES > TROMBONE
TROMINO n shape made from three squares, each joined to the next along one full side
TROMINOES > TROMINO
TROMINOS > TROMINO
TROMMEL n revolving cylindrical sieve used to screen crushed ore
TROMMELS > TROMMEL
TROMP vb trample
TROMPE n apparatus for supplying the blast of air in a forge, consisting of a thin column down which water falls, drawing in air through side openings
TROMPED > TROMP
TROMPES > TROMPE
TROMPING > TROMP
TROMPS > TROMP
TRON n public weighing machine
TRONA n greyish mineral that consists of hydrated sodium carbonate and occurs in salt deposits
TRONAS > TRONA
TRONC n pool into which waiters, waitresses, hotel workers, etc, pay their tips
TRONCS > TRONC
TRONE same as > TRON
TRONES > TRONE
TRONK n jail
TRONKS > TRONK
TRONS > TRON
TROOLIE n large palm leaf
TROOLIES > TROOLIE
TROOP n large group ▷ vb move in a crowd
TROOPED > TROOP
TROOPER n cavalry soldier
TROOPERS > TROOPER
TROOPIAL same as > TROUPIAL
TROOPIALS > TROOPIAL
TROOPING > TROOP
TROOPS > TROOP
TROOPSHIP n ship used to transport military personnel
TROOSTITE n reddish or greyish mineral that is a variety of willemite in which some of the zinc is replaced by manganese
TROOZ same as > TREWS
TROP adv too, too much

TROPAEOLA n plural of singular tropaeolum (a garden plant)
TROPARIA > TROPARION
TROPARION n short hymn
TROPE n figure of speech ▷ vb use tropes (in speech or writing)
TROPED > TROPE
TROPEOLIN n type of dye
TROPES > TROPE
TROPHESY n disorder of the nerves relating to nutrition
TROPHI n pl collective term for the mandibles and other parts of an insect's mouth
TROPHIC adj of or relating to nutrition
TROPHIED > TROPHY
TROPHIES > TROPHY
TROPHY n cup, shield, etc given as a prize ▷ adj regraded as a highly desirable symbol of wealth or success ▷ vb award a trophy to (someone)
TROPHYING > TROPHY
TROPIC n either of two lines of latitude at 23π°N (tropic of Cancer) or 23π°S (tropic of Capricorn)
TROPICAL adj of or in the tropics ▷ n tropical thing or place
TROPICALS > TROPICAL
TROPICS > TROPIC
TROPIN n andrenal androgen
TROPINE n white crystalline poisonous hygroscopic alkaloid obtained by heating atropine or hyoscyamine with barium hydroxide
TROPINES > TROPINE
TROPING > TROPE
TROPINS > TROPIN
TROPISM n tendency of a plant or animal to turn or curve in response to an external stimulus
TROPISMS > TROPISM
TROPIST > TROPISM
TROPISTIC > TROPISM
TROPISTS > TROPISM
TROPOLOGY n use of figurative language in speech or writing
TROPONIN n muscle-tissue protein involved in the contraction of muscle contraction
TROPONINS > TROPONIN
TROPPO adv too much ▷ adj mentally affected by a tropical climate
TROSSERS old form of > TROUSERS
TROT vb (of a horse) move at a medium pace, lifting the feet in diagonal pairs ▷ n trotting
TROTH n pledge of devotion, esp a betrothal

▷ vb promise to marry (someone)

TROTHED > TROTH
TROTHFUL > TROTH
TROTHING > TROTH
TROTHLESS > TROTH
TROTHS > TROTH
TROTLINE n long line suspended across a stream, river, etc, to which shorter hooked and baited lines are attached
TROTLINES > TROTLINE
TROTS > TROT
TROTTED > TROT
TROTTER n pig's foot
TROTTERS > TROTTER
TROTTING > TROT
TROTTINGS > TROT
TROTTOIR n pavement
TROTTOIRS > TROTTOIR
TROTYL n trinitrotoluene; a yellow solid: used chiefly as a high explosive and is also an intermediate in the manufacture of dyestuffs
TROTYLS > TROTYL
TROUBLE n (cause of) distress or anxiety ▷ vb (cause to) worry
TROUBLED > TROUBLE
TROUBLER > TROUBLE
TROUBLERS > TROUBLE
TROUBLES > TROUBLE
TROUBLING > TROUBLE
TROUBLOUS adj unsettled or agitated
TROUCH n rubbish
TROUCHES > TROUCH
TROUGH n long open container, esp for animals' food or water ▷ vb eat, consume, or take greedily
TROUGHED > TROUGH
TROUGHING > TROUGH
TROUGHS > TROUGH
TROULE old variant of > TROLL
TROULED > TROULE
TROULES > TROULE
TROULING > TROULE
TROUNCE vb defeat utterly
TROUNCED > TROUNCE
TROUNCER > TROUNCE
TROUNCERS > TROUNCE
TROUNCES > TROUNCE
TROUNCING > TROUNCE
TROUPE n company of performers ▷ vb (esp of actors) to move or travel in a group
TROUPED > TROUPE
TROUPER n member of a troupe
TROUPERS > TROUPER
TROUPES > TROUPE
TROUPIAL n any of various American orioles
TROUPIALS > TROUPIAL
TROUPING > TROUPE
TROUSE npl close-fitting breeches worn in Ireland
TROUSER adj of trousers ▷ vb take (something, esp money), often surreptitiously or unlawfully ▷ n of or relating to trousers
TROUSERED > TROUSERS
TROUSERS npl two-legged outer garment with legs reaching usu to the ankles
TROUSES > TROUSE
TROUSSEAU n bride's collection of clothing etc for her marriage
TROUT n game fish related to the salmon ▷ vb fish for trout
TROUTER > TROUT
TROUTERS > TROUT
TROUTFUL adj (of a body of water) full of trout
TROUTIER > TROUT
TROUTIEST > TROUT
TROUTING > TROUT
TROUTINGS > TROUT
TROUTLESS > TROUT
TROUTLET n small trout
TROUTLETS > TROUTLET
TROUTLING n small trout
TROUTS > TROUT
TROUTY > TROUT
TROUVERE n any of a group of poets of N France during the 12th and 13th centuries who composed chiefly narrative works
TROUVERES > TROUVERE
TROUVEUR same as > TROUVERE
TROUVEURS > TROUVEUR
TROVE as in treasure-trove valuable articles, such as coins, bullion, etc, found hidden in the earth or elsewhere and of unknown ownership
TROVER n (formerly) the act of wrongfully assuming proprietary rights over personal goods or property belonging to another
TROVERS > TROVER
TROVES > TROVE
TROW vb think, believe, or trust
TROWED > TROW
TROWEL n hand tool with a wide blade for spreading mortar, lifting plants, etc ▷ vb use a trowel on (plaster, soil, etc)
TROWELED > TROWEL
TROWELER > TROWEL
TROWELERS > TROWEL
TROWELING > TROWEL
TROWELLED > TROWEL
TROWELLER > TROWEL
TROWELS > TROWEL
TROWING > TROW
TROWS > TROW
TROWSERS old spelling of > TROUSERS
TROWTH variant spelling of > TROTH
TROWTHS > TROWTH
TROY as in troy weight system of weights used for

precious metals and gemstones, based on the grain, which is identical to the avoirdupois grain

TROYS > TROY
TRUANCIES > TRUANT
TRUANCY > TRUANT
TRUANT n pupil who stays away from school without permission ▷ adj being or relating to a truant ▷ vb play truant
TRUANTED > TRUANT
TRUANTING > TRUANT
TRUANTLY > TRUANT
TRUANTRY > TRUANT
TRUANTS > TRUANT
TRUCAGE n art forgery
TRUCAGES > TRUCAGE
TRUCE n temporary agreement to stop fighting ▷ vb make a truce
TRUCED > TRUCE
TRUCELESS > TRUCE
TRUCES > TRUCE
TRUCHMAN n interpreter; translator
TRUCHMANS > TRUCHMAN
TRUCHMEN > TRUCHMAN
TRUCIAL > TRUCE
TRUCING > TRUCE
TRUCK n railway goods wagon ▷ vb exchange (goods); barter
TRUCKABLE > TRUCK
TRUCKAGE n conveyance of cargo by truck
TRUCKAGES > TRUCKAGE
TRUCKED > TRUCK
TRUCKER n truck driver
TRUCKERS > TRUCKER
TRUCKFUL n amount of something that can be conveyed in a truck
TRUCKFULS > TRUCKFUL
TRUCKIE n truck driver
TRUCKIES > TRUCKIE
TRUCKING n transportation of goods by lorry
TRUCKINGS > TRUCKING
TRUCKLE vb yield weakly or give in ▷ n small wheel
TRUCKLED > TRUCKLE
TRUCKLER > TRUCKLE
TRUCKLERS > TRUCKLE
TRUCKLES > TRUCKLE
TRUCKLINE n organisation that conveys freight by truck
TRUCKLING > TRUCKLE
TRUCKLOAD n amount carried by a truck
TRUCKMAN n truck driver
TRUCKMEN > TRUCKMAN
TRUCKS > TRUCK
TRUCKSTOP n place providing fuel, oil, and often service facilities for truck drivers
TRUCULENT adj aggressively defiant
TRUDGE vb walk heavily or wearily ▷ n long tiring walk
TRUDGED > TRUDGE

TRUDGEN n type of swimming stroke that uses overarm action, as in the crawl, and a scissors kick
TRUDGENS > TRUDGEN
TRUDGEON nonstandard variant of > TRUDGEN
TRUDGEONS > TRUDGEON
TRUDGER > TRUDGE
TRUDGERS > TRUDGE
TRUDGES > TRUDGE
TRUDGING > TRUDGE
TRUDGINGS > TRUDGE
TRUE adj in accordance with facts
TRUEBLUE n staunch royalist or Conservative
TRUEBLUES > TRUEBLUE
TRUEBORN adj being such by birth
TRUEBRED adj thoroughbred
TRUED > TRUE
TRUEING > TRUE
TRUELOVE n person that one loves
TRUELOVES > TRUELOVE
TRUEMAN n honest person
TRUEMEN > TRUEMAN
TRUENESS > TRUE
TRUEPENNY n truthful person
TRUER > TRUE
TRUES > TRUE
TRUEST > TRUE
TRUFFE rare word for > TRUFFLE
TRUFFES > TRUFFE
TRUFFLE n edible underground fungus ▷ vb hunt for truffles
TRUFFLED > TRUFFLE
TRUFFLES > TRUFFLE
TRUFFLING > TRUFFLE
TRUG n long shallow basket used by gardeners
TRUGO n game similar to croquet, originally improvised in Victoria from the rubber discs used as buffers on railway carriages
TRUGOS > TRUGO
TRUGS > TRUG
TRUING > TRUE
TRUISM n self-evident truth
TRUISMS > TRUISM
TRUISTIC > TRUISM
TRULL n prostitute
TRULLS > TRULL
TRULY adv in a true manner
TRUMEAU n section of a wall or pillar between two openings
TRUMEAUX > TRUMEAU
TRUMP adj (card) of the suit outranking the others ▷ vb play a trump card on (another card) ▷ n suit outranking the others
TRUMPED > TRUMP
TRUMPERY n something useless or worthless ▷ adj useless or worthless

TRUMPET n valved brass instrument with a flared tube ▷ vb proclaim loudly
TRUMPETED > TRUMPET
TRUMPETER n person who plays the trumpet, esp one whose duty it is to play fanfares, signals, etc
TRUMPETS > TRUMPET
TRUMPING > TRUMP
TRUMPINGS > TRUMP
TRUMPLESS > TRUMP
TRUMPS > TRUMP
TRUNCAL adj of or relating to the trunk
TRUNCATE vb cut short ▷ adj cut short
TRUNCATED adj (of a cone, pyramid, prism, etc) having an apex or end removed by a plane intersection that is usually nonparallel to the base
TRUNCATES > TRUNCATE
TRUNCHEON n club formerly carried by a policeman ▷ vb beat with a truncheon
TRUNDLE vb move heavily on wheels ▷ n act or an instance of trundling
TRUNDLED > TRUNDLE
TRUNDLER n golf or shopping trolley
TRUNDLERS > TRUNDLER
TRUNDLES > TRUNDLE
TRUNDLING > TRUNDLE
TRUNK n main stem of a tree ▷ vb lop or truncate
TRUNKED > TRUNK
TRUNKFISH n tropical fish, having the body encased in bony plates with openings for the fins, eyes, mouth, etc
TRUNKFUL > TRUNK
TRUNKFULS > TRUNK
TRUNKING n cables that take a common route through an exchange building linking ranks of selectors
TRUNKINGS > TRUNKING
TRUNKLESS > TRUNK
TRUNKS npl shorts worn by a man for swimming
TRUNKWORK n visiting someone secretly in a trunk
TRUNNEL same as > TREENAIL
TRUNNELS > TRUNNEL
TRUNNION n one of a pair of coaxial projections attached to opposite sides of a container, cannon, etc, to provide a support about which it can turn in a vertical
TRUNNIONS > TRUNNION
TRUQUAGE variant of > TRUCAGE
TRUQUAGES > TRUQUAGE
TRUQUEUR n art forger
TRUQUEURS > TRUQUEUR
TRUSS vb tie or bind up ▷ n

device for holding a hernia, etc in place
TRUSSED > TRUSS
TRUSSER > TRUSS
TRUSSERS > TRUSS
TRUSSES > TRUSS
TRUSSING n system of trusses, esp for strengthening or reinforcing a structure
TRUSSINGS > TRUSSING
TRUST vb believe in and rely on ▷ n confidence in the truth, reliability, etc of a person or thing ▷ adj of or relating to a trust or trusts
TRUSTABLE > TRUST
TRUSTED > TRUST
TRUSTEE n person holding property on another's behalf ▷ vb act as a trustee
TRUSTEED > TRUSTEE
TRUSTEES > TRUSTEE
TRUSTER > TRUST
TRUSTERS > TRUST
TRUSTFUL adj inclined to trust others
TRUSTIER > TRUSTY
TRUSTIES > TRUSTY
TRUSTIEST > TRUSTY
TRUSTILY > TRUSTY
TRUSTING same as > TRUSTFUL
TRUSTLESS adj untrustworthy
TRUSTOR n person who sets up a trust
TRUSTORS > TRUSTOR
TRUSTS > TRUST
TRUSTY adj faithful or reliable ▷ n trustworthy convict to whom special privileges are granted
TRUTH n state of being true
TRUTHFUL adj honest
TRUTHIER > TRUTHY
TRUTHIEST > TRUTHY
TRUTHLESS > TRUTH
TRUTHLIKE n truthful
TRUTHS > TRUTH
TRUTHY adj truthful
TRY vb make an effort or attempt ▷ n attempt or effort
TRYE adj very good; select
TRYER variant of > TRIER
TRYERS > TRYER
TRYING > TRY
TRYINGLY > TRY
TRYINGS > TRY
TRYKE variant spelling of > TRIKE
TRYKES > TRYKE
TRYMA n drupe produced by the walnut and similar plants, in which the endocarp is a hard shell and the epicarp is dehiscent
TRYMATA > TRYMA
TRYOUT n a trial or test, as of an athlete or actor
TRYOUTS > TRYOUT
TRYP n parasitic protozoan

TRYPAN as in trypan blue dye obtained from tolidine that is absorbed by the macrophages of the reticuloendothelial system and is therefore used for staining cells in biological research
TRYPS > TRYP
TRYPSIN n enzyme occurring in pancreatic juice
TRYPSINS > TRYPSIN
TRYPTIC > TRYPSIN
TRYSAIL n small fore-and-aft sail set on a sailing vessel to help keep her head to the wind in a storm
TRYSAILS > TRYSAIL
TRYST n arrangement to meet ▷ vb meet at or arrange a tryst
TRYSTE variant spelling of > TRYST
TRYSTED > TRYST
TRYSTER > TRYST
TRYSTERS > TRYST
TRYSTES > TRYSTE
TRYSTING > TRYST
TRYSTS > TRYST
TRYWORKS n furnace for rendering blubber
TSADDIK variant of > ZADDIK
TSADDIKIM > TSADDIK
TSADDIKS > TSADDIK
TSADDIQ variant of > ZADDIK
TSADDIQIM > TSADDIQ
TSADDIQS > TSADDIQ
TSADE variant spelling of > SADHE
TSADES > TSADE
TSADI variant of > SADHE
TSADIS > TSADI
TSAMBA n Tibetan dish made from roasted barley and tea
TSAMBAS > TSAMBA
TSANTSA n (among the Shuar subgroup of the Jivaro people of Ecuador) shrunken head of an enemy kept as a trophy
TSANTSAS > TSANTSA
TSAR n Russian emperor
TSARDOM > TSAR
TSARDOMS > TSAR
TSAREVICH n tsar's son
TSAREVNA n daughter of a Russian tsar
TSAREVNAS > TSAREVNA
TSARINA n wife of a Russian tsar
TSARINAS > TSARINA
TSARISM n system of government by a tsar, esp in Russia until 1917
TSARISMS > TSARISM
TSARIST > TSARISM
TSARISTS > TSARISM
TSARITSA same as > TSARINA
TSARITSAS > TSARITSA

TSARITZA variant spelling of > TSARITSA
TSARITZAS > TSARITZA
TSARS > TSAR
TSATSKE variant of > TCHOTCHKE
TSATSKES > TSATSKE
TSESSEBE South African variant of > SASSABY
TSESSEBES > TSESSEBE
TSETSE n any of various bloodsucking African dipterous flies which transmit the pathogens of various diseases
TSETSES > TSETSE
TSIGANE variant of > TZIGANE
TSIGANES > TSIGANE
TSIMMES variant spelling of > TZIMMES
TSITSITH n tassels or fringes of thread attached to the four corners of the tallith
TSK vb utter the sound "tsk", usu in disapproval
TSKED > TSK
TSKING > TSK
TSKS > TSK
TSKTSK same as > TSK
TSKTSKED > TSKTSK
TSKTSKING > TSKTSK
TSKTSKS > TSKTSK
TSOORIS variant of > TSURIS
TSORES variant of > TSURIS
TSORIS variant of > TSURIS
TSORRISS variant of > TSURIS
TSOTSI n Black street thug or gang member
TSOTSIS > TSOTSI
TSOURIS variant of > TSURIS
TSOURISES > TSOURIS
TSUBA n sword guard of a Japanese sword
TSUBAS > TSUBA
TSUNAMI n tidal wave, usu caused by an earthquake under the sea
TSUNAMIC > TSUNAMI
TSUNAMIS > TSUNAMI
TSURIS n grief or strife
TSURISES > TSURIS
TSUTSUMU n Japanese art of wrapping gifts
TSUTSUMUS > TSUTSUMU
TUAN n lord
TUANS > TUAN
TUART n eucalyptus tree of Australia, yielding a very durable light-coloured timber
TUARTS > TUART
TUATARA n large lizard-like New Zealand reptile
TUATARAS > TUATARA
TUATERA variant spelling of > TUATARA
TUATERAS > TUATERA

t

TUATH n territory of an ancient Irish tribe

TUATHS > TUATH

TUATUA n edible marine bivalve of New Zealand waters

TUATUAS > TUATUA

TUB n open, usu round container ▷ vb wash (oneself or another) in a tub

TUBA n valved low-pitched brass instrument

TUBAE > TUBA

TUBAGE n insertion of a tube

TUBAGES > TUBAGE

TUBAIST > TUBA

TUBAISTS > TUBA

TUBAL adj of or relating to a tube

TUBAR another word for > TUBULAR

TUBAS > TUBA

TUBATE less common word for > TUBULAR

TUBBABLE > TUB

TUBBED > TUB

TUBBER > TUB

TUBBERS > TUB

TUBBIER > TUBBY

TUBBIEST > TUBBY

TUBBINESS > TUBBY

TUBBING > TUB

TUBBINGS > TUB

TUBBISH adj fat

TUBBY adj (of a person) short and fat

TUBE n hollow cylinder

TUBECTOMY n excision of the Fallopian tubes

TUBED > TUBE

TUBEFUL n quantity (of something) that a tube can hold

TUBEFULS > TUBEFUL

TUBELESS adj without a tube

TUBELIKE adj resembling a tube

TUBENOSE n seabird with tubular nostrils on its beak

TUBENOSES > TUBENOSE

TUBER n fleshy underground root of a plant such as a potato

TUBERCLE n small rounded swelling

TUBERCLED adj having tubercles

TUBERCLES > TUBERCLE

TUBERCULA n plural of tuberculum (another name for "turbercle")

TUBERCULE variant of > TUBERCLE

TUBEROID adj resembling a tuber

TUBEROSE same as > TUBEROUS

TUBEROSES > TUBEROSE

TUBEROUS adj (of plants) forming, bearing, or resembling a tuber or tubers

TUBERS > TUBER

TUBES > TUBE

TUBEWORK n collective term for tubes or tubing

TUBEWORKS > TUBEWORK

TUBEWORM n undersea worm

TUBEWORMS > TUBEWORM

TUBFAST n period of fasting and sweating in a tub, intended as a cure for disease

TUBFASTS > TUBFAST

TUBFISH another name for > GURNARD

TUBFISHES > TUBFISH

TUBFUL n amount a tub will hold

TUBFULS > TUBFUL

TUBICOLAR adj tube-dwelling

TUBICOLE n tube-dwelling creature

TUBICOLES > TUBICOLE

TUBIFEX n type of small reddish freshwater worm

TUBIFEXES > TUBIFEX

TUBIFICID n type of threadlike annelid worm

TUBIFORM same as > TUBULAR

TUBING n length of tube

TUBINGS > TUBING

TUBIST > TUBA

TUBISTS > TUBA

TUBLIKE > TUB

TUBS > TUB

TUBULAR adj of or shaped like a tube

TUBULARLY > TUBULAR

TUBULATE vb form or shape into a tube

TUBULATED > TUBULATE

TUBULATES > TUBULATE

TUBULATOR > TUBULATE

TUBULE n any small tubular structure, esp in an animal or plant

TUBULES > TUBULE

TUBULIN n protein forming the basis of microtubules

TUBULINS > TUBULIN

TUBULOSE adj tube-shaped; consisting of tubes

TUBULOUS adj tube-shaped

TUBULURE n tube leading into a retort or other receptacle

TUBULURES > TUBULURE

TUCHUN n (formerly) a Chinese military governor or warlord

TUCHUNS > TUCHUN

TUCK vb push or fold into a small space ▷ n stitched fold ▷ vb touch or strike

TUCKAHOE n type of edible root

TUCKAHOES > TUCKAHOE

TUCKED > TUCK

TUCKER n food ▷ vb weary or tire completely

TUCKERBAG n in Australia, bag or box used for carrying food

TUCKERBOX same as > TUCKERBAG

TUCKERED > TUCKER

TUCKERING > TUCKER

TUCKERS > TUCKER

TUCKET n flourish on a trumpet

TUCKETS > TUCKET

TUCKING > TUCK

TUCKS > TUCK

TUCKSHOP n shop, esp one in or near a school, where food such as cakes and sweets are sold

TUCKSHOPS > TUCKSHOP

TUCOTUCO n colonial burrowing South American rodent

TUCOTUCOS > TUCOTUCO

TUCUTUCO variant spelling of > TUCOTUCO

TUCUTUCOS > TUCUTUCO

TUCUTUCU same as > TUCOTUCO

TUCUTUCUS > TUCUTUCU

TUFA n porous rock formed as a deposit from springs

TUFACEOUS > TUFA

TUFAS > TUFA

TUFF n porous rock formed from volcanic dust or ash

TUFFE old form of > TUFT

TUFFES > TUFFE

TUFFET n small mound or seat

TUFFETS > TUFFET

TUFFS > TUFF

TUFOLI n type of tubular pasta

TUFT n bunch of feathers, grass, hair, etc held or growing together at the base ▷ vb provide or decorate with a tuft or tufts

TUFTED adj having a tuft or tufts

TUFTER > TUFT

TUFTERS > TUFT

TUFTIER > TUFT

TUFTIEST > TUFT

TUFTILY > TUFT

TUFTING > TUFT

TUFTINGS > TUFT

TUFTS > TUFT

TUFTY > TUFT

TUG vb pull hard ▷ n hard pull

TUGBOAT same as > TUG

TUGBOATS > TUGBOAT

TUGGED > TUG

TUGGER > TUG

TUGGERS > TUG

TUGGING > TUG

TUGGINGLY > TUG

TUGGINGS > TUG

TUGHRA n Turkish Sultan's official emblem

TUGHRAS > TUGHRA

TUGHRIK same as > TUGRIK

TUGHRIKS > TUGHRIK

TUGLESS > TUG

TUGRA variant of > TUGHRA

TUGRAS > TUGRA

TUGRIK n standard monetary unit of Mongolia, divided into 100 möngös

TUGRIKS > TUGRIK

TUGS > TUG

TUI n New Zealand honeyeater that mimics human speech and the songs of other birds

TUILLE n (in a suit of armour) hanging plate protecting the thighs

TUILLES > TUILLE

TUILLETTE n little tuille

TUILYIE vb fight

TUILYIED > TUILYIE

TUILYIES > TUILYIE

TUILZIE variant form of > TUILYIE

TUILZIED > TUILZIE

TUILZIES > TUILZIE

TUINA n form of massage originating in China

TUINAS > TUINA

TUIS > TUI

TUISM n practice of putting the interests of another before one's own

TUISMS > TUISM

TUITION n instruction, esp received individually or in a small group

TUITIONAL > TUITION

TUITIONS > TUITION

TUKTOO same as > TUKTU

TUKTOOS > TUKTOO

TUKTU (in Canada) another name for > CARIBOU

TUKTUS > TUKTU

TULADI n large trout found in Canada and northern areas of the US

TULADIS > TULADI

TULAREMIA n infectious disease of rodents

TULAREMIC > TULAREMIA

TULBAN old form of > TURBAN

TULBANS > TULBAN

TULCHAN n skin of a calf placed next to a cow to induce it to give milk

TULCHANS > TULCHAN

TULE n type of bulrush found in California

TULES > TULE

TULIP n plant with bright cup-shaped flowers

TULIPANT n turban

TULIPANTS > TULIPANT

TULIPLIKE > TULIP

TULIPS > TULIP

TULIPWOOD n light soft wood of the tulip tree, used in making furniture and veneer

TULLE n fine net fabric of silk etc

TULLES > TULLE

TULLIBEE n cisco of the Great Lakes of Canada

TULLIBEES > TULLIBEE
TULPA *n* being or object created through willpower and visualization techniques
TULPAS > TULPA
TULWAR *n* Indian sabre
TULWARS > TULWAR
TUM *informal or childish word for >* STOMACH
TUMBLE *vb* (cause to) fall, esp awkwardly or violently ▷ *n* fall
TUMBLEBUG *n* type of dung beetle
TUMBLED > TUMBLE
TUMBLER *n* stemless drinking glass
TUMBLERS > TUMBLER
TUMBLES > TUMBLE
TUMBLESET *n* somersault
TUMBLING > TUMBLE
TUMBLINGS > TUMBLING
TUMBREL *n* farm cart for carrying dung, esp one that tilts backwards to deposit its load
TUMBRELS > TUMBREL
TUMBRIL *same as* **>** TUMBREL
TUMBRILS > TUMBRIL
TUMEFIED > TUMEFY
TUMEFIES > TUMEFY
TUMEFY *vb* make or become tumid
TUMEFYING > TUMEFY
TUMESCE *vb* swell
TUMESCED > TUMESCE
TUMESCENT *adj* swollen or becoming swollen
TUMESCES > TUMESCE
TUMESCING > TUMESCE
TUMID *adj* (of an organ or part of the body) enlarged or swollen
TUMIDITY > TUMID
TUMIDLY > TUMID
TUMIDNESS > TUMID
TUMMIES > TUMMY
TUMMLER *n* comedian or other entertainer employed to encourage audience participation or to encourage guests at a resort to take part in communal activities
TUMMLERS > TUMMLER
TUMMY *n* stomach
TUMOR *same as* **>** TUMOUR
TUMORAL > TUMOUR
TUMORLIKE > TUMOUR
TUMOROUS > TUMOUR
TUMORS > TUMOR
TUMOUR *n* abnormal growth in or on the body
TUMOURS > TUMOUR
TUMP *n* small mound or clump ▷ *vb* make a tump around
TUMPED > TUMP
TUMPHIES > TUMPHY
TUMPHY *n* dolt; fool
TUMPIER > TUMP
TUMPIEST > TUMP

TUMPING > TUMP
TUMPLINE *n* (in the US and Canada, esp formerly) leather or cloth band strung across the forehead or chest and attached to a pack or load in order to support it
TUMPLINES > TUMPLINE
TUMPS > TUMP
TUMPY > TUMP
TUMS > TUM
TUMSHIE *n* turnip
TUMSHIES > TUMSHIE
TUMULAR *adj* of, relating to, or like a mound
TUMULARY *same as* **>** TUMULAR
TUMULI > TUMULUS
TUMULOSE *adj* abounding in small hills or mounds
TUMULOUS *same as* **>** TUMULOSE
TUMULT *n* uproar or commotion ▷ *vb* stir up a commotion
TUMULTED > TUMULT
TUMULTING > TUMULT
TUMULTS > TUMULT
TUMULUS *n* burial mound
TUMULUSES > TUMULUS
TUN *n* large beer cask ▷ *vb* put into or keep in tuns
TUNA *n* large marine food fish
TUNABLE *adj* able to be tuned
TUNABLY > TUNABLE
TUNAS > TUNA
TUNBELLY *n* large round belly
TUND *vb* beat; strike
TUNDED > TUND
TUNDING > TUND
TUNDISH *n* type of funnel
TUNDISHES > TUNDISH
TUNDRA *n* vast treeless Arctic region with permanently frozen subsoil
TUNDRAS > TUNDRA
TUNDS > TUND
TUNDUN *n* wooden instrument used by Native Australians in religious rites
TUNDUNS > TUNDUN
TUNE *n* (pleasing) sequence of musical notes ▷ *vb* adjust (a musical instrument) so that it is in tune
TUNEABLE *same as* **>** TUNABLE
TUNEABLY > TUNEABLE
TUNED > TUNE
TUNEFUL *adj* having a pleasant tune
TUNEFULLY > TUNEFUL
TUNELESS *adj* having no melody or tune
TUNER *n* part of a radio or television receiver for selecting channels
TUNERS > TUNER
TUNES > TUNE
TUNESMITH *n* composer

of light or popular music and songs
TUNEUP *n* adjustments made to an engine to improve its performance
TUNEUPS > TUNEUP
TUNG *as in tung oil* fast-drying oil obtained from the seeds of a central Asian euphorbiaceous tree, used in paints, varnishes, etc, as a drying agent and to give a water-resistant finish
TUNGS > TUNG
TUNGSTATE *n* salt of tungstic acid
TUNGSTEN *n* greyish-white metal
TUNGSTENS > TUNGSTEN
TUNGSTIC *adj* of or containing tungsten, esp in a high valence state
TUNGSTITE *n* yellow earthy rare secondary mineral that consists of tungsten oxide and occurs with tungsten ores
TUNGSTOUS *adj* of or containing tungsten in a low valence state
TUNIC *n* close-fitting jacket forming part of some uniforms
TUNICA *n* tissue forming a layer or covering of an organ or part, such as any of the tissue layers of a blood vessel wall
TUNICAE > TUNICA
TUNICATE *n* minute primitive marine chordate animal ▷ *adj* of, relating to this animal ▷ *vb* wear a tunic
TUNICATED > TUNICATE
TUNICATES > TUNICATE
TUNICIN *n* cellulose-like substance found in tunicates
TUNICINS > TUNICIN
TUNICKED *adj* wearing a tunic
TUNICLE *n* liturgical vestment worn by the subdeacon and bishops at High Mass and other religious ceremonies
TUNICLES > TUNICLE
TUNICS > TUNIC
TUNIER > TUNY
TUNIEST > TUNY
TUNING *n* set of pitches to which the open strings of a guitar, violin, etc, are tuned
TUNINGS > TUNING
TUNNAGE *same as* **>** TONNAGE
TUNNAGES > TUNNAGE
TUNNED > TUN
TUNNEL *n* underground passage ▷ *vb* make a tunnel (through)
TUNNELED > TUNNEL
TUNNELER > TUNNEL

TUNNELERS > TUNNEL
TUNNELING > TUNNEL
TUNNELLED > TUNNEL
TUNNELLER > TUNNEL
TUNNELS > TUNNEL
TUNNIES > TUNNY
TUNNING > TUN
TUNNINGS > TUN
TUNNY *same as* **>** TUNA
TUNS > TUN
TUNY *adj* having an easily discernable melody
TUP *n* male sheep ▷ *vb* cause (a ram) to mate with a ewe, or (of a ram) to mate with (a ewe)
TUPEK *same as* **>** TUPIK
TUPEKS > TUPEK
TUPELO *n* large tree of deep swamps and rivers of the southern US
TUPELOS > TUPELO
TUPIK *n* tent of seal or caribou skin used for shelter by the Inuit in summer
TUPIKS > TUPIK
TUPLE *n* row of values in a relational database
TUPLES > TUPLE
TUPPED > TUP
TUPPENCE *same as* **>** TWOPENCE
TUPPENCES > TUPPENCE
TUPPENNY *same as* **>** TWOPENNY
TUPPING > TUP
TUPS > TUP
TUPTOWING *n* study of Greek grammar
TUPUNA *same as* **>** TIPUNA
TUPUNAS > TUPUNA
TUQUE *n* knitted cap with a long tapering end
TUQUES > TUQUE
TURACIN *n* red pigment found in touraco feathers
TURACINS > TURACIN
TURACO *same as* **>** TOURACO
TURACOS > TURACO
TURACOU *variant of* **>** TOURACO
TURACOUS > TURACOU
TURBAN *n* Muslim, Hindu, or Sikh man's head covering, made by winding cloth round the head
TURBAND *old variant of* **>** TURBAN
TURBANDS > TURBAND
TURBANED > TURBAN
TURBANNED > TURBAN
TURBANS > TURBAN
TURBANT *old variant of* **>** TURBAN
TURBANTS > TURBANT
TURBARIES > TURBARY
TURBARY *n* land where peat or turf is cut or has been cut
TURBETH *variant of* **>** TURPETH
TURBETHS > TURBETH

TURBID adj muddy, not clear

TURBIDITE n sediment deposited by a turbidity current

TURBIDITY > TURBID

TURBIDLY > TURBID

TURBINAL same as > TURBINATE

TURBINALS > TURBINAL

TURBINATE adj of or relating to any of the thin scroll-shaped bones situated on the walls of the nasal passages ▷ n turbinate bone

TURBINE n machine or generator driven by gas, water, etc turning blades

TURBINED adj having a turbine

TURBINES > TURBINE

TURBIT n crested breed of domestic pigeon

TURBITH variant of > TURPETH

TURBITHS > TURBITH

TURBITS > TURBIT

TURBO n compressor in an engine

TURBOCAR n car driven by a gas turbine

TURBOCARS > TURBOCAR

TURBOFAN n engine in which a large fan driven by a turbine forces air rearwards to increase the thrust

TURBOFANS > TURBOFAN

TURBOJET n gas turbine in which the exhaust gases provide the propulsive thrust to drive an aircraft

TURBOJETS > TURBOJET

TURBOND old variant of > TURBAN

TURBONDS > TURBOND

TURBOPROP n gas turbine for driving an aircraft propeller

TURBOS > TURBO

TURBOT n large European edible flatfish

TURBOTS > TURBOT

TURBULENT adj involving a lot of sudden changes and conflicting elements

TURCOPOLE n lightly armed and highly mobile class of Crusader

TURD n piece of excrement

TURDINE adj of, relating to, or characteristic of thrushes

TURDION variant of > TORDION

TURDIONS > TURDION

TURDOID same as > TURDINE

TURDS > TURD

TURDUCKEN n boned turkey stuffed with a boned chicken

TUREEN n serving dish for soup

TUREENS > TUREEN

TURF n short thick even grass ▷ vb cover with turf

TURFED > TURF

TURFEN adj made of turf

TURFGRASS n grass grown for lawns

TURFIER > TURFY

TURFIEST > TURFY

TURFINESS > TURFY

TURFING > TURF

TURFINGS > TURF

TURFITE same as > TURFMAN

TURFITES > TURFITE

TURFLESS > TURF

TURFLIKE > TURF

TURFMAN n person devoted to horse racing

TURFMEN > TURFMAN

TURFS > TURF

TURFSKI n ski down a grassy hill on skis modified with integral wheels

TURFSKIS > TURFSKI

TURFY adj of, covered with, or resembling turf

TURGENCY > TURGENT

TURGENT obsolete word for > TURGID

TURGENTLY > TURGENT

TURGID adj (of language) pompous

TURGIDER > TURGID

TURGIDEST > TURGID

TURGIDITY > TURGID

TURGIDLY > TURGID

TURGITE n red or black mineral consisting of hydrated ferric oxide

TURGITES > TURGITE

TURGOR n normal rigid state of a cell, caused by pressure of the cell contents against the cell wall or membrane

TURGORS > TURGOR

TURION n perennating bud produced by many aquatic plants

TURIONS > TURION

TURISTA n traveller's diarrhoea

TURISTAS > TURISTA

TURK n obsolete derogatory term for a violent, brutal, or domineering person

TURKEY n large bird bred for food

TURKEYS > TURKEY

TURKIES old form of > TURQUOISE

TURKIESES > TURKIES

TURKIS old form of > TURQUOISE

TURKISES > TURKIS

TURKOIS old form of > TURQUOISE

TURKOISES > TURKOIS

TURKS > TURK

TURLOUGH n seasonal lake or pond

TURLOUGHS > TURLOUGH

TURM n troop of horsemen

TURME variant of > TURM

TURMERIC n yellow spice obtained from the root of an Asian plant

TURMERICS > TURMERIC

TURMES > TURME

TURMOIL n agitation or confusion ▷ vb make or become turbulent

TURMOILED > TURMOIL

TURMOILS > TURMOIL

TURMS > TURM

TURN vb change the position or direction (of) ▷ n turning

TURNABLE > TURN

TURNABOUT n act of turning so as to face a different direction

TURNAGAIN n revolution

TURNBACK n one who turns back (from a challenge, for example)

TURNBACKS > TURNBACK

TURNCOAT n person who deserts one party or cause to join another

TURNCOATS > TURNCOAT

TURNCOCK n (formerly) official employed to turn on the water for the mains supply

TURNCOCKS > TURNCOCK

TURNDOWN adj capable of being or designed to be folded or doubled down ▷ n instance of turning down

TURNDOWNS > TURNDOWN

TURNDUN another name for > TUNDUN

TURNDUNS > TURNDUN

TURNED > TURN

TURNER n person or thing that turns, esp a person who operates a lathe

TURNERIES > TURNERY

TURNERS > TURNER

TURNERY n objects made on a lathe

TURNHALL n building in which gymnastics is taught and practised

TURNHALLS > TURNHALL

TURNING n road or path leading off a main route

TURNINGS > TURNING

TURNIP n root vegetable with orange or white flesh ▷ vb sow (a field) with turnips

TURNIPED > TURNIP

TURNIPING > TURNIP

TURNIPS > TURNIP

TURNIPY adj like a turnip

TURNKEY n jailer ▷ adj denoting a project, as in civil engineering, in which a single contractor has responsibility for the complete job from the start to the time of installation or occupancy

TURNKEYS > TURNKEY

TURNOFF n road or other way branching off from the main

TURNOFFS > TURNOFF

TURNON n something sexually exciting

TURNONS > TURNON

TURNOUT n number of people appearing at a gathering

TURNOUTS > TURNOUT

TURNOVER n total sales made by a business over a certain period

TURNOVERS > TURNOVER

TURNPIKE n road where a toll is collected at barriers

TURNPIKES > TURNPIKE

TURNROUND n act or process in which a ship, aircraft, etc, unloads passengers and freight at end of a trip and reloads for next trip

TURNS > TURN

TURNSKIN n old name for a werewolf

TURNSKINS > TURNSKIN

TURNSOLE n any of various plants having flowers that are said to turn towards the sun

TURNSOLES > TURNSOLE

TURNSPIT n (formerly) a servant or small dog whose job was to turn the spit on which meat, poultry, etc, was roasting

TURNSPITS > TURNSPIT

TURNSTILE n revolving gate for admitting one person at a time

TURNSTONE n shore bird

TURNTABLE n revolving platform

TURNUP n the turned-up fold at the bottom of some trouser legs

TURNUPS > TURNUP

TUROPHILE n person who loves cheese

TURPETH n convolvulaceous plant of the East Indies, having roots with purgative properties

TURPETHS > TURPETH

TURPITUDE n wickedness

TURPS n colourless, flammable liquid

TURQUOIS variant of > TURQUOISE

TURQUOISE adj blue-green ▷ n blue-green precious stone

TURRET n small tower

TURRETED adj having or resembling a turret or turrets

TURRETS > TURRET

TURRIBANT old variant of > TURBAN

TURRICAL adj of, relating to, or resembling a turret

TURTLE n sea tortoise

TURTLED > TURTLE

TURTLER > TURTLE

t

TURTLERS > TURTLE

TURTLES > TURTLE

TURTLING > TURTLE

TURTLINGS > TURTLE

TURVES > TURF

TUSCHE n substance used in lithography for drawing the design and as a resist in silk-screen printing and lithography

TUSCHES > TUSCHE

TUSH interj exclamation of disapproval or contempt ▷ vb utter the interjection "tush"

TUSHED > TUSH

TUSHERIES > TUSHERY

TUSHERY n use of affectedly archaic language in novels, etc

TUSHES > TUSH

TUSHIE n pair of buttocks

TUSHIES > TUSHIE

TUSHING > TUSH

TUSHKAR variant of > TUSKAR

TUSHKARS > TUSHKAR

TUSHKER variant of > TUSKAR

TUSHKERS > TUSHKER

TUSHY variant of > TUSHIE

TUSK n long pointed tooth of an elephant, walrus, etc ▷ vb stab, tear, or gore with the tusks

TUSKAR n peat-cutting spade

TUSKARS > TUSKAR

TUSKED > TUSK

TUSKER n any animal with prominent tusks, esp a wild boar or elephant

TUSKERS > TUSKER

TUSKIER > TUSK

TUSKIEST > TUSK

TUSKING > TUSK

TUSKINGS > TUSK

TUSKLESS > TUSK

TUSKLIKE > TUSK

TUSKS > TUSK

TUSKY > TUSK

TUSSAC as in tussac grass kind of grass

TUSSAH same as > TUSSORE

TUSSAHS > TUSSAH

TUSSAL > TUSSIS

TUSSAR variant of > TUSSORE

TUSSARS > TUSSAR

TUSSEH variant of > TUSSORE

TUSSEHS > TUSSEH

TUSSER same as > TUSSORE

TUSSERS > TUSSER

TUSSIS technical name for a > COUGH

TUSSISES > TUSSIS

TUSSIVE > TUSSIS

TUSSLE vb fight or scuffle ▷ n energetic fight, struggle, or argument

TUSSLED > TUSSLE

TUSSLES > TUSSLE

TUSSLING > TUSSLE

TUSSOCK n tuft of grass

TUSSOCKED adj having tussocks

TUSSOCKS > TUSSOCK

TUSSOCKY > TUSSOCK

TUSSOR variant of > TUSSORE

TUSSORE n strong coarse brownish Indian silk obtained from the cocoons of an Oriental saturniid silkworm

TUSSORES > TUSSORE

TUSSORS > TUSSOR

TUSSUCK variant of > TUSSOCK

TUSSUCKS > TUSSUCK

TUSSUR variant of > TUSSORE

TUSSURS > TUSSUR

TUT interj an exclamation of mild reprimand, disapproval, or surprise ▷ vb express disapproval by the exclamation of "tut-tut." ▷ n payment system based on measurable work done rather that time spent doing it

TUTANIA n alloy of low melting point containing tin, antimony, copper and used mostly for decorative purposes

TUTANIAS > TUTANIA

TUTEE n one who is tutored, esp in a university

TUTEES > TUTEE

TUTELAGE n instruction or guidance, esp by a tutor

TUTELAGES > TUTELAGE

TUTELAR same as > TUTELARY

TUTELARS > TUTELAR

TUTELARY adj having the role of guardian or protector ▷ n tutelary person, deity, or saint

TUTENAG n zinc alloy

TUTENAGS > TUTENAG

TUTIORISM n (in Roman Catholic moral theology) the doctrine that in cases of moral doubt it is best to follow the safer course or that in agreement with the law

TUTIORIST > TUTIORISM

TUTMAN n one who does tutwork

TUTMEN > TUTMAN

TUTOR n person teaching individuals or small groups ▷ vb act as a tutor to

TUTORAGE > TUTOR

TUTORAGES > TUTOR

TUTORED > TUTOR

TUTORESS n female tutor

TUTORIAL n period of instruction with a tutor ▷ adj of or relating to a tutor

TUTORIALS > TUTORIAL

TUTORING > TUTOR

TUTORINGS > TUTOR

TUTORISE variant spelling of > TUTORIZE

TUTORISED > TUTORISE

TUTORISES > TUTORISE

TUTORISM > TUTOR

TUTORISMS > TUTOR

TUTORIZE vb tutor

TUTORIZED > TUTOR

TUTORIZES > TUTORIZE

TUTORS > TUTOR

TUTORSHIP > TUTOR

TUTOYED adj addressed in a familiar way

TUTOYER vb speak to someone on familiar terms

TUTOYERED > TUTOYER

TUTOYERS > TUTOYER

TUTRESS same as > TUTORESS

TUTRESSES > TUTRESS

TUTRICES > TUTRIX

TUTRIX n female tutor; tutoress

TUTRIXES > TUTRIX

TUTS Scots version of > TUT

TUTSAN n woodland shrub of Europe and W Asia

TUTSANS > TUTSAN

TUTSED > TUTS

TUTSES > TUTS

TUTSING > TUTS

TUTTED > TUT

TUTTI adv be performed by the whole orchestra or choir ▷ n piece of tutti music

TUTTIES > TUTTY

TUTTING > TUT

TUTTINGS > TUT

TUTTIS > TUTTI

TUTTY n finely powdered impure zinc oxide obtained from the flues of zinc-smelting furnaces and used as a polishing powder

TUTU n short stiff skirt worn by ballerinas

TUTUED adj wearing tutu

TUTUS > TUTU

TUTWORK n work paid using a tut system

TUTWORKER > TUTWORK

TUTWORKS > TUTWORK

TUX short for > TUXEDO

TUXEDO n dinner jacket

TUXEDOED adj wearing a tuxedo

TUXEDOES > TUXEDO

TUXEDOS > TUXEDO

TUXES > TUX

TUYER variant of > TUYERE

TUYERE n water-cooled nozzle through which air is blown into a cupola, blast furnace, or forge

TUYERES > TUYERE

TUYERS > TUYER

TUZZ n tuft or clump of hair

TUZZES > TUZZ

TWA Scots word for > TWO

TWADDLE n silly or pretentious talk or writing ▷ vb talk or write in a silly or pretentious way

TWADDLED > TWADDLE

TWADDLER > TWADDLE

TWADDLERS > TWADDLE

TWADDLES > TWADDLE

TWADDLIER > TWADDLE

TWADDLING > TWADDLE

TWADDLY > TWADDLE

TWAE same as > TWA

TWAES > TWAE

TWAFALD Scots variant of > TWOFOLD

TWAIN n two

TWAINS > TWAIN

TWAITE n herring-like food fish

TWAITES > TWAITE

TWAL n twelve

TWALPENNY n shilling

TWALS > TWAL

TWANG n sharp ringing sound ▷ vb (cause to) make a twang

TWANGED > TWANG

TWANGER > TWANG

TWANGERS > TWANG

TWANGIER > TWANG

TWANGIEST > TWANG

TWANGING > TWANG

TWANGINGS > TWANG

TWANGLE vb make a continuous loose twanging sound (on a musical instrument, for example)

TWANGLED > TWANGLE

TWANGLER > TWANGLE

TWANGLERS > TWANGLE

TWANGLES > TWANGLE

TWANGLING > TWANGLE

TWANGS > TWANG

TWANGY > TWANG

TWANK vb make an sharply curtailed twang

TWANKAY n variety of Chinese green tea

TWANKAYS > TWANKAY

TWANKIES > TWANKY

TWANKS > TWANK

TWANKY same as > TWANKAY

TWAS > TWA

TWASOME same as > TWOSOME

TWASOMES > TWASOME

TWAT n taboo term for female genitals

TWATS > TWAT

TWATTLE rare word for > TWADDLE

TWATTLED > TWATTLE

TWATTLER > TWATTLE

TWATTLERS > TWATTLE

TWATTLES > TWATTLE

TWATTLING > TWATTLE

TWAY old variant of > TWAIN

TWAYBLADE n type of orchid

TWAYS > TWAY

TWEAK vb pinch or twist sharply ▷ n tweaking

TWEAKED > TWEAK
TWEAKER n engineer's small screwdriver, used for fine adjustments
TWEAKERS > TWEAKER
TWEAKIER > TWEAK
TWEAKIEST > TWEAK
TWEAKING > TWEAK
TWEAKINGS > TWEAK
TWEAKS > TWEAK
TWEAKY > TWEAK
TWEE adj too sentimental, sweet, or pretty
TWEED n thick woollen cloth
TWEEDIER > TWEEDY
TWEEDIEST > TWEEDY
TWEEDILY adv in a manner characteristic of upper-class people who live in the country
TWEEDLE vb improvise aimlessly on a musical instrument
TWEEDLED > TWEEDLE
TWEEDLER > TWEEDLE
TWEEDLERS > TWEEDLE
TWEEDLES > TWEEDLE
TWEEDLING > TWEEDLE
TWEEDS > TWEED
TWEEDY adj of or made of tweed
TWEEL variant of > TWILL
TWEELED > TWEEL
TWEELING > TWEEL
TWEELS > TWEEL
TWEELY > TWEE
TWEEN same as > BETWEEN
TWEENAGE adj (of a child) between about eight and fourteen years old
TWEENAGER n child of approximately eight to fourteen years of age
TWEENER same as > TWEENAGER
TWEENERS > TWEENER
TWEENESS > TWEE
TWEENIE same as > TWEENY
TWEENIES > TWEENY
TWEENS > TWEEN
TWEENY n maid who assists both cook and housemaid
TWEER variant of > TWIRE
TWEERED > TWEER
TWEERING > TWEER
TWEERS > TWEER
TWEEST > TWEE
TWEET vb chirp ▷ interj imitation of the thin chirping sound made by small birds
TWEETED > TWEET
TWEETER n loudspeaker reproducing high-frequency sounds
TWEETERS > TWEETER
TWEETING > TWEET
TWEETS > TWEET
TWEEZE vb take hold of or pluck (hair, small objects, etc) with or as if with tweezers

TWEEZED > TWEEZE
TWEEZER same as > TWEEZERS
TWEEZERS npl small pincer-like tool
TWEEZES > TWEEZE
TWEEZING > TWEEZE
TWELFTH n (of) number twelve in a series ▷ adj of or being number twelve in a series
TWELFTHLY adv after the eleventh person, position, event, etc
TWELFTHS > TWELFTH
TWELVE n two more than ten ▷ adj amounting to twelve ▷ det amounting to twelve
TWELVEMO another word for > DUODECIMO
TWELVEMOS > TWELVEMO
TWELVES > TWELVE
TWENTIES > TWENTY
TWENTIETH adj coming after the nineteenth in numbering or counting order, position, time, etc ▷ n one of 20 approximately equal parts of something
TWENTY n two times ten ▷ adj amounting to twenty ▷ det amounting to twenty
TWENTYISH adj around 20
TWERP n silly person
TWERPIER > TWERP
TWERPIEST > TWERP
TWERPS > TWERP
TWERPY > TWERP
TWIBIL same as > TWIBILL
TWIBILL n mattock with a blade shaped like an adze at one end and like an axe at the other
TWIBILLS > TWIBILL
TWIBILS > TWIBIL
TWICE adv two times
TWICER n someone who does something twice
TWICERS > TWICER
TWICHILD n person in his or her dotage
TWIDDLE vb fiddle or twirl in an idle way ▷ n act or instance of twiddling
TWIDDLED > TWIDDLE
TWIDDLER > TWIDDLE
TWIDDLERS > TWIDDLE
TWIDDLES > TWIDDLE
TWIDDLIER > TWIDDLE
TWIDDLING > TWIDDLE
TWIDDLY > TWIDDLE
TWIER variant of > TUYERE
TWIERS > TWIER
TWIFOLD variant of > TWOFOLD
TWIFORKED adj having two forks; bifurcate
TWIFORMED adj having two forms
TWIG n small branch or shoot ▷ vb realize or understand
TWIGGED > TWIG

TWIGGEN adj made of twigs
TWIGGER > TWIG
TWIGGERS > TWIG
TWIGGIER > TWIGGY
TWIGGIEST > TWIGGY
TWIGGING > TWIG
TWIGGY adj of or relating to a twig or twigs
TWIGHT old variant of > TWIT
TWIGHTED > TWIGHT
TWIGHTING > TWIGHT
TWIGHTS > TWIGHT
TWIGLESS > TWIG
TWIGLET n small twig
TWIGLETS > TWIGLET
TWIGLIKE > TWIG
TWIGLOO n temporary shelter made from twigs, branches, leaves, etc
TWIGLOOS > TWIGLOO
TWIGS > TWIG
TWIGSOME adj covered with twigs; twiggy
TWILIGHT n soft dim light just after sunset ▷ adj of or relating to the period towards the end of the day
TWILIGHTS > TWILIGHT
TWILIT > TWILIGHT
TWILL n fabric woven to produce parallel ridges ▷ adj (in textiles) of or designating a weave in which the weft yarns are worked around two or more warp yarns to produce an effect of parallel diagonal lines or ribs ▷ vb weave in this fashion
TWILLED > TWILL
TWILLIES > TWILLY
TWILLING > TWILL
TWILLINGS > TWILL
TWILLS > TWILL
TWILLY n machine having a system of revolving spikes for opening and cleaning raw textile fibres
TWILT variant of > QUILT
TWILTED > TWILT
TWILTING > TWILT
TWILTS > TWILT
TWIN n one of a pair, esp of two children born at one birth ▷ vb pair or be paired
TWINBERRY n creeping wooden plant
TWINBORN adj born as a twin
TWINE n string or cord ▷ vb twist or coil round
TWINED > TWINE
TWINER > TWINE
TWINERS > TWINE
TWINES > TWINE
TWINGE n sudden sharp pain or emotional pang ▷ vb have or cause to have a twinge
TWINGED > TWINGE
TWINGEING > TWINGE
TWINGES > TWINGE
TWINGING > TWINGE

TWINIER > TWINE
TWINIEST > TWINE
TWINIGHT adj (of a baseball double-header) held in the late afternoon and evening
TWINING > TWINE
TWININGLY > TWINE
TWININGS > TWINE
TWINJET n jet aircraft with two engines
TWINJETS > TWINJET
TWINK n white correction fluid for deleting written text ▷ vb twinkle
TWINKED > TWINK
TWINKIE n stupid person
TWINKIES > TWINKIE
TWINKING > TWINK
TWINKLE vb shine brightly but intermittently ▷ n flickering brightness
TWINKLED > TWINKLE
TWINKLER > TWINKLE
TWINKLERS > TWINKLE
TWINKLES > TWINKLE
TWINKLING n very short time
TWINKLY > TWINKLE
TWINKS > TWINK
TWINLING old name for > TWIN
TWINLINGS > TWINLING
TWINNED > TWIN
TWINNING > TWIN
TWINNINGS > TWIN
TWINS > TWIN
TWINSET n matching jumper and cardigan
TWINSETS > TWINSET
TWINSHIP n condition of being a twin or twins
TWINSHIPS > TWIN
TWINTER n animal that is 2 years old
TWINTERS > TWINTER
TWINY > TWINE
TWIRE vb look intently at with (or as if with) difficulty
TWIRED > TWIRE
TWIRES > TWIRE
TWIRING > TWIRE
TWIRL vb turn or spin around quickly ▷ n whirl or twist
TWIRLED > TWIRL
TWIRLER > TWIRL
TWIRLERS > TWIRL
TWIRLIER > TWIRL
TWIRLIEST > TWIRL
TWIRLING > TWIRL
TWIRLS > TWIRL
TWIRLY > TWIRL
TWIRP same as > TWERP
TWIRPIER > TWIRP
TWIRPIEST > TWIRP
TWIRPS > TWIRP
TWIRPY > TWIRP
TWISCAR variant of > TUSKAR
TWISCARS > TWISCAR
TWIST vb turn out of the natural position ▷ n twisting

TWISTABLE > TWIST
TWISTED > TWIST
TWISTER n swindler
TWISTERS > TWISTER
TWISTIER > TWIST
TWISTIEST > TWIST
TWISTING > TWIST
TWISTINGS > TWIST
TWISTOR n variable corresponding to the coordinates of a point in space and time
TWISTORS > TWISTOR
TWISTS > TWIST
TWISTY > TWIST
TWIT vb poke fun at (someone) ▷ n foolish person
TWITCH vb move spasmodically ▷ n nervous muscular spasm
TWITCHED > TWITCH
TWITCHER n bird-watcher who tries to spot as many rare varieties as possible
TWITCHERS > TWITCHER
TWITCHES > TWITCH
TWITCHIER > TWITCHY
TWITCHILY > TWITCHY
TWITCHING > TWITCH
TWITCHY adj nervous, worried, and ill-at-ease
TWITE n N European finch with a brown streaked plumage
TWITES > TWITE
TWITS > TWIT
TWITTED > TWIT
TWITTEN n narrow alleyway
TWITTENS > TWITTEN
TWITTER vb (of birds) utter chirping sounds ▷ n act or sound of twittering
TWITTERED > TWITTER
TWITTERER > TWITTER
TWITTERS > TWITTER
TWITTERY > TWITTER
TWITTING > TWIT
TWITTINGS > TWIT
TWIXT same as > BETWIXT
TWIZZLE vb spin around
TWIZZLED > TWIZZLE
TWIZZLES > TWIZZLE
TWIZZLING > TWIZZLE
TWO n one more than one
TWOCCER > TWOCCING
TWOCCERS > TWOCCING
TWOCCING n act of breaking into a motor vehicle and driving it away
TWOCCINGS > TWOCCING
TWOCKER > TWOCCING
TWOCKERS > TWOCCING
TWOCKING same as > TWOCCING
TWOCKINGS > TWOCCING
TWOER n (in a game) something that scores two
TWOERS > TWOER
TWOFER n single ticket allowing the buyer entrance to two events, attractions, etc, for

substantially less than the cost were he or she to pay for each individually
TWOFERS > TWOFER
TWOFOLD adj having twice as many or as much ▷ adv by twice as many or as much ▷ n folding piece of theatrical scenery
TWOFOLDS > TWOFOLD
TWONESS n state or condition of being two
TWONESSES > TWONESS
TWONIE same as > TOONIE
TWONIES > TWONIE
TWOONIE variant of > TOONIE
TWOONIES > TWOONIE
TWOPENCE n sum of two pennies
TWOPENCES > TWOPENCE
TWOPENNY adj cheap or tawdry
TWOS > TWO
TWOSEATER n vehicle providing seats for two people
TWOSOME n group of two people
TWOSOMES > TWOSOME
TWOSTROKE adj relating to or designating an internal-combustion engine whose piston makes two strokes for every explosion
TWP adj stupid
TWYER same as > TUYERE
TWYERE variant of > TUYERE
TWYERES > TWYERE
TWYERS > TWYER
TWYFOLD adj twofold
TYCHISM n theory that chance is an objective reality at work in the universe, esp in evolutionary adaptations
TYCHISMS > TYCHISM
TYCOON n powerful wealthy businessman; shogun
TYCOONATE n office or rule of a tycoon
TYCOONERY > TYCOON
TYCOONS > TYCOON
TYDE old variant of the past participle of > TIE
TYE n trough used in mining to separate valuable material from dross ▷ vb (in mining) isolate valuable material from dross using a tye
TYED > TYE
TYEE n large northern Pacific salmon
TYEES > TYEE
TYEING > TYE
TYER > TYE
TYERS > TYE
TYES > TYE
TYG n mug with two handles
TYGS > TYG

TYIN variant of > TYIYN
TYING > TIE
TYIYN n money unit of Kyrgyzstan
TYIYNS > TYIYN
TYKE n often offensive term for small cheeky child
TYKES > TYKE
TYKISH > TYKE
TYLECTOMY n excision of a breast tumour
TYLER variant of > TILER
TYLERS > TYLER
TYLOPOD n mammal with padded feet, such as a camel or llama
TYLOPODS > TYLOPOD
TYLOSES > TYLOSIS
TYLOSIN n broad spectrum antibiotic
TYLOSINS > TYLOSIN
TYLOSIS n bladder-like outgrowth from certain cells in woody tissue that extends into and blocks adjacent conducting xylem cells
TYLOTE n knobbed sponge spicule
TYLOTES > TYLOTE
TYMBAL same as > TIMBAL
TYMBALS > TYMBAL
TYMP n blast furnace outlet through which molten metal flows
TYMPAN same as > TYMPANUM
TYMPANA > TYMPANUM
TYMPANAL adj relating to the tympanum
TYMPANI same as > TIMPANI
TYMPANIC adj of, relating to, or having a tympanum ▷ n part of the temporal bone in the mammalian skull that surrounds the auditory canal
TYMPANICS > TYMPANIC
TYMPANIES > TYMPANY
TYMPANIST > TIMPANI
TYMPANO > TYMPANI
TYMPANS > TYMPAN
TYMPANUM n cavity of the middle ear
TYMPANUMS > TYMPANUM
TYMPANY n distention of the abdomen
TYMPS > TYMP
TYND variant of > TIND
TYNDE variant of > TIND
TYNE variant of > TINE
TYNED variant of > TYNE
TYNES > TYNE
TYNING > TYNE
TYPABLE > TYPE
TYPAL rare word for > TYPICAL
TYPE n class or category ▷ vb print with a typewriter or word processor
TYPEABLE > TYPE
TYPEBAR n one of the bars in a typewriter that carry the type and are operated

by keys
TYPEBARS > TYPEBAR
TYPECASE n compartmental tray for storing printer's type
TYPECASES > TYPECASE
TYPECAST vb continually cast (an actor or actress) in similar roles
TYPECASTS > TYPECAST
TYPED > TYPE
TYPEFACE n style of the type
TYPEFACES > TYPEFACE
TYPES > TYPE
TYPESET vb set (text for printing) in type
TYPESETS > TYPESET
TYPESTYLE another word for > TYPEFACE
TYPEWRITE vb write by means of a typewriter
TYPEWROTE > TYPEWRITE
TYPEY variant of > TYPY
TYPHLITIC > TYPHLITIS
TYPHLITIS n inflammation of the caecum
TYPHOID adj of or relating to typhoid fever
TYPHOIDAL > TYPHOID
TYPHOIDIN n culture of dead typhoid bacillus for injection into the skin to test for typhoid fever
TYPHOIDS > TYPHOID
TYPHON n whirlwind
TYPHONIAN > TYPHON
TYPHONIC > TYPHOON
TYPHONS > TYPHON
TYPHOON n violent tropical storm
TYPHOONS > TYPHOON
TYPHOSE adj relating to typhoid
TYPHOUS > TYPHUS
TYPHUS n infectious feverish disease
TYPHUSES > TYPHUS
TYPIC same as > TYPICAL
TYPICAL adj true to type, characteristic
TYPICALLY > TYPICAL
TYPIER > TYPY
TYPIEST > TYPY
TYPIFIED > TYPIFY
TYPIFIER > TYPIFY
TYPIFIERS > TYPIFY
TYPIFIES > TYPIFY
TYPIFY vb be typical of
TYPIFYING > TYPIFY
TYPING n work or activity of using a typewriter or word processor
TYPINGS > TYPING
TYPIST n person who types with a typewriter or word processor
TYPISTS > TYPIST
TYPO n typographical error
TYPOGRAPH n person skilled in the art of

composing type and printing from it

TYPOLOGIC > TYPOLOGY

TYPOLOGY n doctrine or study of types or of the correspondence between them and the realities which they typify

TYPOMANIA n obsession with typology

TYPOS > TYPO

TYPP n unit of thickness of yarn

TYPPS > TYPP

TYPTO vb learn Greek conjugations

TYPTOED > TYPTO

TYPTOING > TYPTO

TYPTOS > TYPTO

TYPY adj (of an animal) typifying the breed

TYRAMINE n colourless crystalline amine derived from phenol

TYRAMINES > TYRAMINE

TYRAN vb act as a tyrant

TYRANED > TYRAN

TYRANING > TYRAN

TYRANNE variant of > TYRAN

TYRANNED > TYRANNE

TYRANNES > TYRANNE

TYRANNESS n female tyrant

TYRANNIC > TYRANNY

TYRANNIES > TYRANNY

TYRANNING > TYRANNE

TYRANNIS n tyrannical government

TYRANNISE same as > TYRANNIZE

TYRANNIZE vb exert power (over) oppressively or cruelly

TYRANNOUS > TYRANNY

TYRANNY n tyrannical rule

TYRANS > TYRAN

TYRANT n oppressive or cruel ruler ▷ vb act the tyrant

TYRANTED > TYRANT

TYRANTING > TYRANT

TYRANTS > TYRANT

TYRE n rubber ring, usu inflated, over the rim of a vehicle's wheel to grip the road ▷ vb fit a tyre or tyres to (a wheel, vehicle, etc)

TYRED > TYRE

TYRELESS > TYRE

TYRES > TYRE

TYRING > TYRE

TYRO n novice or beginner

TYROCIDIN n antibiotic

TYROES > TYRO

TYRONES > TYRO

TYRONIC > TYRO

TYROPITTA n Greek cheese pie

TYROS > TYRO

TYROSINE n aromatic nonessential amino acid

TYROSINES > TYROSINE

TYSTIE n black guillemot

TYSTIES > TYSTIE

TYTE variant spelling of > TITE

TYTHE variant of > TITHE

TYTHED > TYTHE

TYTHES > TYTHE

TYTHING > TYTHE

TZADDI same as > SADHE

TZADDIK variant of > ZADDIK

TZADDIKIM > TZADDIK

TZADDIKS > TZADDIK

TZADDIQ variant of > ZADDIK

TZADDIQIM > TZADDIQ

TZADDIQS > TZADDIQ

TZADDIS > TZADDI

TZAR same as > TSAR

TZARDOM > TZAR

TZARDOMS > TZAR

TZAREVNA variant of > TSAREVNA

TZAREVNAS > TZAREVNA

TZARINA variant of > TSARINA

TZARINAS > TZARINA

TZARISM variant of > TSARISM

TZARISMS > TZARISM

TZARIST > TZARISM

TZARISTS > TZARISM

TZARITZA variant of > TSARITSA

TZARITZAS > TZARITZA

TZARS > TZAR

TZATZIKI n Greek dip made from yogurt, chopped cucumber, and mint

TZATZIKIS > TZATZIKI

TZETSE variant of > TSETSE

TZETSES > TZETSE

TZETZE variant of > TSETSE

TZETZES > TZETZE

TZIGANE n type of Gypsy music

TZIGANES > TZIGANE

TZIGANIES > TZIGANY

TZIGANY variant of > TZIGANE

TZIMMES n traditional Jewish stew

TZITZIS variant of > TSITSITH

TZITZIT variant of > TZITZIT

TZITZITH variant of > TSITSITH

TZURIS variant of > TSURIS

t

Uu

UAKARI *n* type of monkey

UAKARIS > UAKARI

UBEROUS *adj* abundant

UBERTIES > UBERTY

UBERTY *n* abundance

UBIETIES > UBIETY

UBIETY *n* condition of being in a particular place

UBIQUE *adv* everywhere

UBIQUITIN *n* type of polypeptide

UBIQUITY *n* state of apparently being everywhere at once; omnipresence

UBUNTU *n* quality of compassion and humanity

UBUNTUS > UBUNTU

UCKERS *n* type of naval game

UDAL *n* form of freehold possession of land existing in northern Europe before the introduction of the feudal system and still used in Orkney and Shetland

UDALLER *n* person possessing a udal

UDALLERS > UDALLER

UDALS > UDAL

UDDER *n* large baglike milk-producing gland of cows, sheep, or goats

UDDERED > UDDER

UDDERFUL > UDDER

UDDERLESS > UDDER

UDDERS > UDDER

UDO *n* stout perennial plant of Japan and China with berry-like black fruits and young shoots that are edible when blanched

UDOMETER *n* archaic term for an instrument for measuring rainfall or snowfall

UDOMETERS > UDOMETER

UDOMETRIC > UDOMETER

UDOMETRY > UDOMETER

UDON *n* (in Japanese cookery) large noodles made of wheat flour

UDONS > UDON

UDOS > UDO

UDS *interj* God's or God save

UEY *n* u-turn

UEYS > UEY

UFO *n* flying saucer

UFOLOGIES > UFOLOGY

UFOLOGIST > UFOLOGY

UFOLOGY *n* study of UFOs

UFOS > UFO

UG *vb* hate

UGALI *n* type of stiff porridge made by mixing corn meal with boiling water: the basic starch constituent of a meal

UGALIS > UGALI

UGGED > UG

UGGING > UG

UGH *interj* exclamation of disgust ▷ *n* sound made to indicate disgust

UGHS > UGH

UGLIED > UGLY

UGLIER > UGLY

UGLIES > UGLY

UGLIEST > UGLY

UGLIFIED > UGLIFY

UGLIFIER > UGLIFY

UGLIFIERS > UGLIFY

UGLIFIES > UGLIFY

UGLIFY *vb* make or become ugly or more ugly

UGLIFYING > UGLIFY

UGLILY > UGLY

UGLINESS > UGLY

UGLY *adj* of unpleasant appearance ▷ *vb* make ugly

UGLYING > UGLY

UGS > UG

UGSOME *adj* loathsome

UH *interj* used to express hesitation

UHLAN *n* member of a body of lancers first employed in the Polish army and later in W European armies

UHLANS > UHLAN

UHURU *n* national independence

UHURUS > UHURU

UILLEAN as in *uillean pipes* bagpipes developed in Ireland and operated by squeezing bellows under the arm

UILLEANN *same as* > UILLEAN

UINTAHITE *same as* > UINTAITE

UINTAITE *n* variety of asphalt

UINTAITES > UINTAITE

UITLANDER *n* foreigner

UJAMAA as in *ujamaa village* communally organized village in Tanzania

UJAMAAS > UJAMAA

UKASE *n* (in imperial Russia) a decree from the tsar

UKASES > UKASE

UKE *short form of* > UKULELE

UKELELE *same as* > UKULELE

UKELELES > UKELELE

UKES > UKE

UKULELE *n* small guitar with four strings

UKULELES > UKULELE

ULAMA *n* body of Muslim scholars or religious leaders

ULAMAS > ULAMA

ULAN *same as* > UHLAN

ULANS > ULAN

ULCER *n* open sore on the surface of the skin or mucous membrane. ▷ *vb* make or become ulcerous

ULCERATE *vb* make or become ulcerous

ULCERATED > ULCERATE

ULCERATES > ULCERATE

ULCERED > ULCER

ULCERING > ULCER

ULCEROUS *adj* of, like, or characterized by ulcers

ULCERS > ULCER

ULE *n* rubber tree

ULEMA *same as* > ULAMA

ULEMAS > ULEMA

ULES > ULE

ULEX *n* variety of shrub

ULEXES > ULEX

ULEXITE *n* type of mineral

ULEXITES > ULEXITE

ULICES > ULEX

ULICON *same as* > EULACHON

ULICONS > ULICON

ULIGINOSE *same as* > ULIGINOUS

ULIGINOUS *adj* marshy

ULIKON *same as* > EULACHON

ULIKONS > ULIKON

ULITIS *n* gingivitis

ULITISES > ULITIS

ULLAGE *n* volume by which a liquid container falls short of being full ▷ *vb* create ullage in

ULLAGED > ULLAGE

ULLAGES > ULLAGE

ULLAGING > ULLAGE

ULLING *n* process of filling

ULLINGS > ULLING

ULMACEOUS *adj* relating to the family of deciduous trees and shrubs which includes the elms

ULMIN *n* substance found in decaying vegetation

ULMINS > ULMIN

ULNA *n* inner and longer of the two bones of the human forearm

ULNAD *adv* towards the ulna

ULNAE > ULNA

ULNAR > ULNA

ULNARE *n* bone in the wrist

ULNARIA > ULNARE

ULNAS > ULNA

ULOSES > ULOSIS

ULOSIS *n* formation of a scar

ULOTRICHY *n* state of having woolly or curly hair

ULPAN *n* Israeli study centre

ULPANIM > ULPAN

ULSTER *n* man's heavy double-breasted overcoat

ULSTERED *adj* wearing an ulster

ULSTERS > ULSTER

ULTERIOR *adj* (of an aim, reason, etc) concealed or hidden

ULTIMA *n* final syllable of a word

ULTIMACY > ULTIMATE

ULTIMAS > ULTIMA

ULTIMATA > ULTIMATUM

ULTIMATE *adj* final in a series or process ▷ *n* most significant, highest, furthest, or greatest thing ▷ *vb* end

ULTIMATED > ULTIMATE

ULTIMATES > ULTIMATE

ULTIMATUM *n* final warning stating that action will be taken unless certain conditions are met

ULTIMO *adv* in or during the previous month

ULTION *n* vengeance

ULTIONS > ULTION

ULTRA *n* person who has extreme or immoderate beliefs or opinions ▷ *adj* extreme or immoderate, esp in beliefs or opinions

ULTRACHIC *adj* extremely chic

ULTRACOLD *adj* extremely cold

ULTRACOOL *adj* extremely cool

ULTRADRY adj extremely dry

ULTRAFAST adj extremely fast

ULTRAFINE adj extremely fine

ULTRAHEAT vb sterilize through extreme heat treatment

ULTRAHIGH as in ultrahigh frequency radio-frequency band or radio frequency lying between 3000 and 300 megahertz

ULTRAHIP adj extremely trendy

ULTRAHOT adj extremely hot

ULTRAISM n extreme philosophy, belief, or action

ULTRAISMS > ULTRAISM

ULTRAIST > ULTRAISM

ULTRAISTS > ULTRAISM

ULTRALEFT adj of the extreme political Left or extremely radical

ULTRALOW adj extremely low

ULTRAPOSH adj extremely posh

ULTRAPURE adj extremely pure

ULTRARARE adj extremely rare

ULTRARED obsolete word for > INFRARED

ULTRAREDS > ULTRARED

ULTRARICH adj extremely rich

ULTRAS > ULTRA

ULTRASAFE adj extremely safe

ULTRASLOW adj extremely slow

ULTRASOFT adj extremely soft

ULTRATHIN adj extremely thin

ULTRATINY adj extremely small

ULTRAWIDE adj extremely wide

ULU n type of knife

ULULANT > ULULATE

ULULATE vb howl or wail

ULULATED > ULULATE

ULULATES > ULULATE

ULULATING > ULULATE

ULULATION > ULULATE

ULUS > ULU

ULVA n genus of seaweed

ULVAS > ULVA

ULYIE Scots variant of > OIL

ULYIES > ULYIE

ULZIE Scots variant of > OIL

ULZIES > ULZIE

UM interj representation of a common sound made when hesitating in speech ▷ vb hesitate while speaking

UMAMI n savoury flavour

UMAMIS > UMAMI

UMANGITE n type of mineral

UMANGITES > UMANGITE

UMBEL n umbrella-like flower cluster with the stalks springing from the central point

UMBELED same as > UMBELLED

UMBELLAR > UMBEL

UMBELLATE > UMBEL

UMBELLED adj having umbels

UMBELLET same as > UMBELLULE

UMBELLETS > UMBELLET

UMBELLULE n any of the small secondary umbels that make up a compound umbel

UMBELS > UMBEL

UMBER adj dark brown to reddish-brown ▷ n type of dark brown earth containing ferric oxide (rust) ▷ vb stain with umber

UMBERED > UMBER

UMBERING > UMBER

UMBERS > UMBER

UMBERY > UMBER

UMBILICAL adj of the navel

UMBILICI > UMBILICUS

UMBILICUS n navel

UMBLE as in umble pie (formerly) a pie made from the heart, entrails, etc, of a deer

UMBLES another term for > NUMBLES

UMBO n small hump projecting from the centre of the cap in certain mushrooms

UMBONAL > UMBO

UMBONATE > UMBO

UMBONES > UMBO

UMBONIC > UMBO

UMBOS > UMBO

UMBRA n shadow, esp the shadow cast by the moon onto the earth during a solar eclipse

UMBRACULA npl umbrella-like structures

UMBRAE > UMBRA

UMBRAGE n displeasure or resentment ▷ vb shade

UMBRAGED > UMBRAGE

UMBRAGES > UMBRAGE

UMBRAGING > UMBRAGE

UMBRAL > UMBRA

UMBRAS > UMBRA

UMBRATED adj shown in a faint manner

UMBRATIC > UMBRA

UMBRATILE adj shadowy

UMBRE same as > UMBRETTE

UMBREL n umbrella

UMBRELLA n portable device used for protection against rain, consisting of a folding frame covered in material attached to a central rod ▷ adj containing or covering many different organizations, ideas, etc

UMBRELLAS > UMBRELLA

UMBRELLO same as > UMBRELLA

UMBRELLOS > UMBRELLO

UMBRELS > UMBREL

UMBRERE n helmet visor

UMBRERES > UMBRERE

UMBRES > UMBRE

UMBRETTE n African wading bird

UMBRETTES > UMBRETTE

UMBRIERE same as > UMBRERE

UMBRIERES > UMBRIERE

UMBRIL same as > UMBRERE

UMBRILS > UMBRIL

UMBROSE same as > UMBROUS

UMBROUS adj shady

UMFAZI n African married woman

UMFAZIS > UMFAZI

UMIAC variant of > UMIAK

UMIACK variant of > UMIAK

UMIACKS > UMIACK

UMIACS > UMIAC

UMIAK n Inuit boat made of skins

UMIAKS > UMIAK

UMIAQ same as > UMIAK

UMIAQS > UMIAQ

UMLAUT n mark (¨) placed over a vowel, esp in German, to indicate a change in its sound ▷ vb modify by umlaut

UMLAUTED > UMLAUT

UMLAUTING > UMLAUT

UMLAUTS > UMLAUT

UMLUNGU n White man: used esp as a term of address

UMLUNGUS > UMLUNGU

UMM same as > UM

UMMA n Muslim community

UMMAH same as > UMMA

UMMAHS > UMMAH

UMMAS > UMMA

UMMED > UM

UMMING > UM

UMP short for > UMPIRE

UMPED > UMP

UMPH same as > HUMPH

UMPIE informal word for > UMPIRE

UMPIES > UMPY

UMPING > UMP

UMPIRAGE > UMPIRE

UMPIRAGES > UMPIRE

UMPIRE n official who rules on the playing of a game ▷ vb act as umpire in (a game)

UMPIRED > UMPIRE

UMPIRES > UMPIRE

UMPIRING > UMPIRE

UMPS > UMP

UMPTEEN adj very many ▷ det very many

UMPTEENTH n latest in a tediously long series

UMPTIETH same as > UMPTEENTH

UMPTY same as > UMPTEEN

UMPY same as > UMPIE

UMQUHILE adv formerly

UMRA n pilgrimage to Mecca that can be made at any time of the year

UMRAH same as > UMRA

UMRAHS > UMRAH

UMRAS > UMRA

UMS > UM

UMTEENTH same as > UMPTEENTH

UMU n type of oven

UMUS > UMU

UMWELT n environmental factors, collectively, that are capable of affecting the behaviour of an animal or individual

UMWELTS > UMWELT

UMWHILE same as > UMQUHILE

UN pron spelling of 'one' intended to reflect a dialectal or informal pronunciation

UNABASHED adj not ashamed or embarrassed

UNABATED adv without any reduction in force ▷ adj without losing any original force or violence

UNABATING adj not growing less in strength

UNABETTED adj without assistance

UNABIDING adj not lasting

UNABJURED adj not denied

UNABLE adj lacking the necessary power, ability, or authority (to do something)

UNABORTED adj not aborted

UNABRADED adj not eroded

UNABUSED adj not abused

UNABUSIVE adj not abusive

UNACCRUED adj not accrued

UNACCUSED adj not charged with wrongdoing

UNACERBIC adj not acerbic

UNACHING adj not aching

UNACIDIC adj not acidic

UNACTABLE adj unable to be acted

UNACTED adj not acted or performed

UNACTIVE adj inactive

UNADAPTED adj not adapted

UNADDED adj not added

UNADEPT adj not adept

UNADEPTLY > UNADEPT

UNADMIRED adj not admired

UNADOPTED adj (of a road) not maintained by a local authority

UNADORED adj not adored

UNADORNED adj not decorated

UNADULT adj not mature

UNADVISED adj rash or unwise

UNAFRAID adj not frightened or nervous

UNAGED adj not old

UNAGEING adj not ageing

UNAGILE adj not agile

UNAGING same as > UNAGEING

UNAGREED adj not agreed

UNAI same as > UNAU

UNAIDABLE adj unable to be helped

UNAIDED adv without any help or assistance ▷ adj without having received any help

UNAIDEDLY > UNAIDED

UNAIMED adj not aimed or specifically targeted

UNAIRED adj not aired

UNAIS > UNAI

UNAKIN adj not related

UNAKING Shakespearean form of > UNACHING

UNAKITE n type of mineral

UNAKITES > UNAKITE

UNALARMED adj not alarmed

UNALERTED adj not alerted

UNALIGNED adj not aligned

UNALIKE adj not similar

UNALIST n priest holding only one benefice

UNALISTS > UNALIST

UNALIVE adj unaware

UNALLAYED adj not allayed

UNALLEGED adj not alleged

UNALLIED adj not allied

UNALLOWED adj not allowed

UNALLOYED adj not spoiled by being mixed with anything else

UNALTERED adj not altered

UNAMASSED adj not amassed

UNAMAZED adj not greatly surprised

UNAMENDED adj not amended

UNAMERCED adj not amerced

UNAMIABLE adj not amiable

UNAMUSED adj not entertained, diverted, or laughing

UNAMUSING adj not entertaining

UNANCHOR vb remove anchor

UNANCHORS > UNANCHOR

UNANELED adj not having received extreme unction

UNANIMITY > UNANIMOUS

UNANIMOUS adj in complete agreement

UNANNEXED adj not annexed

UNANNOYED adj not annoyed

UNANXIOUS adj not anxious

UNAPPAREL vb undress

UNAPPLIED adj not applied

UNAPT adj not suitable or qualified

UNAPTLY > UNAPT

UNAPTNESS > UNAPT

UNARCHED adj not arched

UNARGUED adj not debated

UNARISEN adj not having risen

UNARM less common word for > DISARM

UNARMED adj without weapons

UNARMING > UNARM

UNARMORED adj without armour

UNARMS > UNARM

UNAROUSED adj not aroused

UNARRAYED adj not arrayed

UNARTFUL adj not artful

UNARY adj consisting of, or affecting, a single element or component

UNASHAMED adj not embarrassed, esp when doing something some people might find offensive

UNASKED adv without being asked to do something ▷ adj (of a question) not asked, although sometimes implied

UNASSAYED adj untried

UNASSUMED adj not assumed

UNASSURED adj insecure

UNATONED adj not atoned for

UNATTIRED adj unclothed

UNATTUNED adj unaccustomed

UNAU n two-toed sloth

UNAUDITED adj not having been audited

UNAUS > UNAU

UNAVENGED adj not avenged

UNAVERAGE adj not average

UNAVERTED adj not averted

UNAVOIDED adj not avoided

UNAVOWED adj not openly admitted

UNAWAKE adj not awake

UNAWAKED adj not aroused

UNAWARDED adj not awarded

UNAWARE adj not aware or conscious ▷ adv by surprise

UNAWARELY > UNAWARE

UNAWARES adv by surprise

UNAWED adj not awed

UNAWESOME adj not awesome

UNAXED adj not axed

UNBACKED adj (of a book, chair, etc) not having a back

UNBAFFLED adj not baffled

UNBAG vb take out of a bag

UNBAGGED > UNBAG

UNBAGGING > UNBAG

UNBAGS > UNBAG

UNBAITED adj not baited

UNBAKED adj not having been baked

UNBALANCE vb upset the equilibrium or balance of ▷ n imbalance or instability

UNBALE vb remove from bale

UNBALED > UNBALE

UNBALES > UNBALE

UNBALING > UNBALE

UNBAN vb stop banning or permit again

UNBANDAGE vb remove bandage from

UNBANDED adj not fastened with a band

UNBANKED adj not having been banked

UNBANNED > UNBAN

UNBANNING > UNBAN

UNBANS > UNBAN

UNBAPTISE same as > UNBAPTIZE

UNBAPTIZE vb remove the effect of baptism

UNBAR vb take away a bar or bars from

UNBARBED adj without barbs

UNBARE vb expose

UNBARED > UNBARE

UNBARES > UNBARE

UNBARING > UNBARE

UNBARK vb strip bark from

UNBARKED > UNBARK

UNBARKING > UNBARK

UNBARKS > UNBARK

UNBARRED > UNBAR

UNBARRING > UNBAR

UNBARS > UNBAR

UNBASED adj not having a base

UNBASHFUL adj not shy

UNBASTED adj not basted

UNBATED adj (of a sword, lance, etc) not covered with a protective button

UNBATHED adj unwashed

UNBE vb make non-existent

UNBEAR vb release (horse) from the bearing rein

UNBEARDED adj not having a beard

UNBEARED > UNBEAR

UNBEARING > UNBEAR

UNBEARS > UNBEAR

UNBEATEN adj having suffered no defeat

UNBED vb remove from bed

UNBEDDED > UNBED

UNBEDDING > UNBED

UNBEDS > UNBED

UNBEEN > UNBE

UNBEGET vb deprive of existence

UNBEGETS > UNBEGET

UNBEGGED adj not obtained by begging

UNBEGOT adj unbegotten

UNBEGUILE vb undeceive

UNBEGUN adj not commenced

UNBEING n non-existence

UNBEINGS > UNBEING

UNBEKNOWN adv without the knowledge (of a person) ▷ adj not known (to)

UNBELIEF n disbelief or rejection of belief

UNBELIEFS > UNBELIEF

UNBELIEVE vb disbelieve

UNBELOVED adj unhappy in love

UNBELT vb unbuckle the belt of (a garment)

UNBELTED > UNBELT

UNBELTING > UNBELT

UNBELTS > UNBELT

UNBEMUSED adj not bemused

UNBEND vb become less strict or more informal in one's attitudes or behaviour

UNBENDED > UNBEND

UNBENDING adj rigid or inflexible

UNBENDS > UNBEND

UNBENIGN adj not benign

UNBENT adj not bent or bowed

UNBEREFT adj not bereft

UNBERUFEN adj not called for

UNBESEEM vb be unbefitting to

UNBESEEMS > UNBESEEM

UNBESPEAK vb annul

UNBESPOKE adj not bespoken

UNBIAS vb free from prejudice

UNBIASED adj not having or showing prejudice or favouritism

UNBIASES > UNBIAS

UNBIASING > UNBIAS

UNBIASSED same as > UNBIASED

UNBIASSES > UNBIAS

UNBID same as > UNBIDDEN

UNBIDDEN adj not ordered or asked

UNBIGOTED adj not bigoted

UNBILLED adj not having been billed

UNBIND vb set free from bonds or chains

UNBINDING > UNBIND

UNBINDS > UNBIND

UNBISHOP vb remove from the position of bishop

UNBISHOPS > UNBISHOP
UNBITT vb remove (cable) from the bitts
UNBITTED > UNBITT
UNBITTEN adj not having been bitten
UNBITTER adj not bitter
UNBITTING > UNBITT
UNBITTS > UNBITT
UNBLAMED vb not blamed
UNBLENDED adj not blended
UNBLENT same as > UNBLENDED
UNBLESS vb deprive of a blessing
UNBLESSED adj deprived of blessing
UNBLESSES > UNBLESS
UNBLEST same as > UNBLESSED
UNBLIND vb rid of blindness
UNBLINDED > UNBLIND
UNBLINDS > UNBLIND
UNBLOCK vb remove a blockage from
UNBLOCKED > UNBLOCK
UNBLOCKS > UNBLOCK
UNBLOODED adj not bloodied
UNBLOODY adj not covered with blood
UNBLOTTED adj not blotted
UNBLOWED same as > UNBLOWN
UNBLOWN adj (of a flower) still in the bud
UNBLUNTED adj not blunted
UNBLURRED adj not blurred
UNBOARDED adj not boarded
UNBOBBED adj not bobbed
UNBODIED adj having no body
UNBODING adj having no presentiment
UNBOILED adj not boiled
UNBOLT vb unfasten a bolt of (a door)
UNBOLTED adj (of grain, meal, or flour) not sifted
UNBOLTING > UNBOLT
UNBOLTS > UNBOLT
UNBONDED adj not bonded
UNBONE vb remove bone from
UNBONED adj (of meat, fish, etc) not having had the bones removed
UNBONES > UNBONE
UNBONING > UNBONE
UNBONNET vb remove the bonnet from
UNBONNETS > UNBONNET
UNBOOKED adj not reserved
UNBOOKISH adj not studious
UNBOOT vb remove boots from

UNBOOTED > UNBOOT
UNBOOTING > UNBOOT
UNBOOTS > UNBOOT
UNBORE adj unborn
UNBORN adj not yet born
UNBORNE adj not borne
UNBOSOM vb relieve (oneself) of (secrets or feelings) by telling someone
UNBOSOMED > UNBOSOM
UNBOSOMER > UNBOSOM
UNBOSOMS > UNBOSOM
UNBOTTLE vb allow out of bottle
UNBOTTLED > UNBOTTLE
UNBOTTLES > UNBOTTLE
UNBOUGHT adj not purchased
UNBOUNCY adj not bouncy
UNBOUND adj (of a book) not bound within a cover
UNBOUNDED adj having no boundaries or limits
UNBOWED adj not giving in or submitting
UNBOWING adj not bowing
UNBOX vb empty a box
UNBOXED > UNBOX
UNBOXES > UNBOX
UNBOXING > UNBOX
UNBRACE vb remove tension or strain from
UNBRACED > UNBRACE
UNBRACES > UNBRACE
UNBRACING > UNBRACE
UNBRAID vb remove braids from
UNBRAIDED > UNBRAID
UNBRAIDS > UNBRAID
UNBRAKE vb stop reducing speed by releasing brake
UNBRAKED > UNBRAKE
UNBRAKES > UNBRAKE
UNBRAKING > UNBRAKE
UNBRANDED adj not having a brand name
UNBRASTE archaic past form of > UNBRACE
UNBRED adj not taught or instructed
UNBREECH vb remove breech from
UNBRIDGED adj not spanned by a bridge
UNBRIDLE vb remove the bridle from (a horse)
UNBRIDLED adj (of feelings or behaviour) not controlled in any way
UNBRIDLES > UNBRIDLE
UNBRIEFED adj not instructed
UNBRIGHT adj not bright
UNBRIZZED same as > UNBRUISED
UNBROILED adj not broiled
UNBROKE same as > UNBROKEN
UNBROKEN adj complete or whole
UNBROWNED adj not browned

UNBRUISED adj not bruised
UNBRUSED same as > UNBRUISED
UNBRUSHED adj not brushed
UNBUCKLE vb undo the buckle or buckles of
UNBUCKLED > UNBUCKLE
UNBUCKLES > UNBUCKLE
UNBUDDED adj not having buds
UNBUDGING adj not moving
UNBUILD vb destroy
UNBUILDS > UNBUILD
UNBUILT > UNBUILD
UNBULKY adj not bulky
UNBUNDLE vb separate (hardware from software) for sales purposes
UNBUNDLED > UNBUNDLE
UNBUNDLER > UNBUNDLE
UNBUNDLES > UNBUNDLE
UNBURDEN vb relieve (one's mind or oneself) of a worry by confiding in someone
UNBURDENS > UNBURDEN
UNBURIED > UNBURY
UNBURIES > UNBURY
UNBURNED same as > UNBURNT
UNBURNT adj not burnt
UNBURROW vb remove from a burrow
UNBURROWS > UNBURROW
UNBURTHEN same as > UNBURDEN
UNBURY vb unearth
UNBURYING > UNBURY
UNBUSTED adj unbroken
UNBUSY adj not busy
UNBUTTON vb undo by unfastening the buttons of (a garment)
UNBUTTONS > UNBUTTON
UNCAGE vb release from a cage
UNCAGED adj at liberty
UNCAGES > UNCAGE
UNCAGING > UNCAGE
UNCAKE vb remove compacted matter from
UNCAKED > UNCAKE
UNCAKES > UNCAKE
UNCAKING > UNCAKE
UNCALLED adj not called
UNCANDID adj not frank
UNCANDLED adj not illuminated by candle
UNCANDOUR n lack of candour
UNCANNED adj not canned
UNCANNIER > UNCANNY
UNCANNILY > UNCANNY
UNCANNY adj weird or mysterious
UNCANONIC adj unclerical
UNCAP vb remove a cap or top from (a container)
UNCAPABLE same as > INCAPABLE
UNCAPE vb remove the cape from

UNCAPED > UNCAPE
UNCAPES > UNCAPE
UNCAPING > UNCAPE
UNCAPPED > UNCAP
UNCAPPING > UNCAP
UNCAPS > UNCAP
UNCARDED adj not carded
UNCARED as in uncared for not cared (for)
UNCAREFUL adj careless
UNCARING adj thoughtless
UNCART vb remove from a cart
UNCARTED > UNCART
UNCARTING > UNCART
UNCARTS > UNCART
UNCARVED adj not carved
UNCASE vb display
UNCASED > UNCASE
UNCASES > UNCASE
UNCASHED adj not cashed
UNCASING as > UNCASE
UNCASKED adj removed from a cask
UNCAST adj not cast
UNCATCHY adj not catchy
UNCATE same as > UNCINATE
UNCATERED adj not catered
UNCAUGHT adj not caught
UNCAUSED adj not brought into existence by any cause
UNCE same as > OUNCE
UNCEASING adj continuing without a break
UNCEDED adj not ceded
UNCERTAIN adj not able to be accurately known or predicted
UNCES > UNCE
UNCESSANT same as > INCESSANT
UNCHAIN vb remove a chain or chains from
UNCHAINED > UNCHAIN
UNCHAINS > UNCHAIN
UNCHAIR vb unseat from chair
UNCHAIRED > UNCHAIR
UNCHAIRS > UNCHAIR
UNCHANCY adj unlucky, ill-omened, or dangerous
UNCHANGED adj remaining the same
UNCHARGE vb unload
UNCHARGED adj (of land or other property) not subject to a charge
UNCHARGES > UNCHARGE
UNCHARITY n lack of charity
UNCHARM vb disenchant
UNCHARMED > UNCHARM
UNCHARMS > UNCHARM
UNCHARNEL vb exhume
UNCHARRED adj not charred
UNCHARTED adj (of an area of sea or land) not having had a map made of it, esp because it is unexplored
UNCHARY adj not cautious
UNCHASTE adj not chaste

u

UNCHASTER > UNCHASTE

UNCHECK *vb* remove check mark from

UNCHECKED *adj* not prevented from continuing or growing ▷ *adv* without being stopped or hindered

UNCHECKS > UNCHECK

UNCHEERED *adj* miserable

UNCHEWED *adj* not chewed

UNCHIC *adj* not chic

UNCHICLY > UNCHIC

UNCHILD *vb* deprive of children

UNCHILDED > UNCHILD

UNCHILDS > UNCHILD

UNCHILLED *adj* not chilled

UNCHOKE *vb* unblock

UNCHOKED > UNCHOKE

UNCHOKES > UNCHOKE

UNCHOKING > UNCHOKE

UNCHOSEN *adj* not chosen

UNCHRISOM *adj* unchristened

UNCHURCH *vb* excommunicate

UNCI > UNCUS

UNCIA *n* twelfth part

UNCIAE > UNCIA

UNCIAL *adj* of or written in letters that resemble modern capitals, as used in Greek and Latin manuscripts of the third to ninth centuries ▷ *n* uncial letter or manuscript

UNCIALLY > UNCIAL

UNCIALS > UNCIAL

UNCIFORM *adj* having the shape of a hook ▷ *n* any hook-shaped structure or part, esp a small bone of the wrist

UNCIFORMS > UNCIFORM

UNCINAL *same as* > UNCINATE

UNCINARIA *same as* > HOOKWORM

UNCINATE *adj* shaped like a hook

UNCINATED > UNCINATE

UNCINI > UNCINUS

UNCINUS *n* small hooked structure, such as any of the hooked chaetae of certain polychaete worms

UNCIPHER *vb* decode

UNCIPHERS > UNCIPHER

UNCITED *adj* not quoted

UNCIVIL *adj* impolite, rude or bad-mannered

UNCIVILLY > UNCIVIL

UNCLAD *adj* having no clothes on

UNCLAIMED *adj* not having been claimed

UNCLAMP *vb* remove clamp from

UNCLAMPED > UNCLAMP

UNCLAMPS > UNCLAMP

UNCLARITY *adj* lack of clarity

UNCLASP *vb* unfasten the clasp of (something)

UNCLASPED > UNCLASP

UNCLASPS > UNCLASP

UNCLASSED *adj* not divided into classes

UNCLASSY *adj* not classy

UNCLAWED *adj* not clawed

UNCLE *n* brother of one's father or mother ▷ *vb* refer to as uncle

UNCLEAN *adj* lacking moral, spiritual, or physical cleanliness

UNCLEANED *adj* not cleaned

UNCLEANER > UNCLEAN

UNCLEANLY *adv* in an unclean manner ▷ *adj* characterized by an absence of cleanliness

UNCLEAR *adj* confusing or hard to understand

UNCLEARED *adj* not cleared

UNCLEARER > UNCLEAR

UNCLEARLY > UNCLEAR

UNCLED > UNCLE

UNCLEFT *adj* not cleft

UNCLENCH *vb* relax from a clenched position

UNCLES > UNCLE

UNCLESHIP *n* position of an uncle

UNCLEW *vb* undo

UNCLEWED > UNCLEW

UNCLEWING > UNCLEW

UNCLEWS > UNCLEW

UNCLICHED *adj* not cliched

UNCLIMBED *adj* not climbed

UNCLINCH *same as* > UNCLENCH

UNCLING > UNCLE

UNCLIP *vb* remove clip from

UNCLIPPED > UNCLIP

UNCLIPS > UNCLIP

UNCLIPT *archaic past form of* > UNCLIP

UNCLOAK *vb* remove cloak from

UNCLOAKED > UNCLOAK

UNCLOAKS > UNCLOAK

UNCLOG *vb* remove an obstruction from (a drain, etc)

UNCLOGGED > UNCLOG

UNCLOGS > UNCLOG

UNCLOSE *vb* open or cause to open

UNCLOSED > UNCLOSE

UNCLOSES > UNCLOSE

UNCLOSING > UNCLOSE

UNCLOTHE *vb* take off garments from

UNCLOTHED > UNCLOTHE

UNCLOTHES > UNCLOTHE

UNCLOUD *vb* clear clouds from

UNCLOUDED > UNCLOUD

UNCLOUDS > UNCLOUD

UNCLOUDY *adj* not cloudy

UNCLOVEN *adj* not cleaved

UNCLOYED *adj* not cloyed

UNCLOYING *adj* not cloying

UNCLUTCH *vb* open from tight grip

UNCLUTTER *vb* tidy and straighten up

UNCO *adj* awkward ▷ *n* awkward or clumsy person

UNCOATED *adj* not covered with a layer

UNCOATING *n* process whereby a virus exposes its genome in order to replicate

UNCOBBLED *adj* not cobbled

UNCOCK *vb* remove from a cocked position

UNCOCKED > UNCOCK

UNCOCKING > UNCOCK

UNCOCKS > UNCOCK

UNCODED *adj* not coded

UNCOER > UNCO

UNCOERCED *adj* unforced

UNCOES > UNCO

UNCOEST > UNCO

UNCOFFIN *vb* take out of a coffin

UNCOFFINS > UNCOFFIN

UNCOIL *vb* unwind or untwist

UNCOILED > UNCOIL

UNCOILING > UNCOIL

UNCOILS > UNCOIL

UNCOINED *adj* (of a metal) not made into coin

UNCOLORED *adj* not coloured

UNCOLT *vb* divest of a horse

UNCOLTED > UNCOLT

UNCOLTING > UNCOLT

UNCOLTS > UNCOLT

UNCOMBED *adj* not combed

UNCOMBINE *vb* break apart

UNCOMELY *adj* not attractive

UNCOMFIER > UNCOMFY

UNCOMFY *adj* not comfortable

UNCOMIC *adj* not comical

UNCOMMON *adj* not happening or encountered often

UNCONCERN *n* apathy or indifference

UNCONFINE *vb* remove restrictions from

UNCONFORM *adj* dissimilar

UNCONFUSE *vb* remove confusion from

UNCONGEAL *vb* become liquid again

UNCOOKED *adj* raw

UNCOOL *adj* unsophisticated

UNCOOLED *adj* not cooled

UNCOPE *vb* unmuzzle

UNCOPED > UNCOPE

UNCOPES > UNCOPE

UNCOPING > UNCOPE

UNCORD *vb* release from cords

UNCORDED > UNCORD

UNCORDIAL *adj* unfriendly

UNCORDING > UNCORD

UNCORDS > UNCORD

UNCORK *vb* remove the cork from (a bottle)

UNCORKED > UNCORK

UNCORKING > UNCORK

UNCORKS > UNCORK

UNCORRUPT *adj* not corrupt

UNCOS > UNCO

UNCOSTLY *adj* inexpensive

UNCOUNTED *adj* unable to be counted

UNCOUPLE *vb* disconnect or become disconnected

UNCOUPLED > UNCOUPLE

UNCOUPLER > UNCOUPLE

UNCOUPLES > UNCOUPLE

UNCOURTLY *adj* not courtly

UNCOUTH *adj* lacking in good manners, refinement, or grace

UNCOUTHER > UNCOUTH

UNCOUTHLY > UNCOUTH

UNCOVER *vb* reveal or disclose

UNCOVERED *adj* not covered

UNCOVERS > UNCOVER

UNCOWL *vb* remove hood from

UNCOWLED > UNCOWL

UNCOWLING > UNCOWL

UNCOWLS > UNCOWL

UNCOY *adj* not modest

UNCOYNED *same as* > UNCOINED

UNCRACKED *adj* not cracked

UNCRATE *vb* remove from a crate

UNCRATED > UNCRATE

UNCRATES > UNCRATE

UNCRATING > UNCRATE

UNCRAZY *adj* not crazy

UNCREATE *vb* unmake

UNCREATED > UNCREATE

UNCREATES > UNCREATE

UNCREWED *adj* not crewed

UNCROPPED *adj* not cropped

UNCROSS *vb* cease to cross

UNCROSSED > UNCROSS

UNCROSSES > UNCROSS

UNCROWDED *adj* (of a confined space, area, etc) not containing too many people or things

UNCROWN *vb* take the crown from

UNCROWNED *adj* having the powers, but not the title, of royalty

UNCROWNS > UNCROWN

UNCRUDDED *adj* uncurdled

UNCRUMPLE *vb* remove creases from

UNCRUSHED *adj* not crushed

UNCTION *n* act of anointing with oil in sacramental ceremonies

UNCTIONS > UNCTION

UNCTUOUS *adj* pretending to be kind and concerned

UNCUFF *vb* remove handcuffs from

UNCUFFED > UNCUFF

UNCUFFING > UNCUFF

UNCUFFS > UNCUFF

UNCULLED *adj* not culled

UNCURABLE *same as* > INCURABLE

UNCURABLY > UNCURABLE

UNCURB *vb* remove curbs from (a horse)

UNCURBED > UNCURB

UNCURBING > UNCURB

UNCURBS > UNCURB

UNCURDLED *adj* not curdled

UNCURED *adj* not cured

UNCURIOUS *adj* not curious

UNCURL *vb* move or cause to move out of a curled or rolled up position

UNCURLED > UNCURL

UNCURLING > UNCURL

UNCURLS > UNCURL

UNCURRENT *adj* not current

UNCURSE *vb* remove curse from

UNCURSED > UNCURSE

UNCURSES > UNCURSE

UNCURSING > UNCURSE

UNCURTAIN *vb* reveal

UNCURVED *adj* not curved

UNCUS *n* hooked part or process, as in the human cerebrum

UNCUT *adj* not shortened or censored

UNCUTE *adj* not cute

UNCYNICAL *adj* not cynical

UNDAM *vb* free from a dam

UNDAMAGED *adj* not spoilt or damaged

UNDAMMED > UNDAM

UNDAMMING > UNDAM

UNDAMNED *adj* not damned

UNDAMPED *adj* (of an oscillating system) having unrestricted motion

UNDAMS > UNDAM

UNDARING *adj* not daring

UNDASHED *adj* not dashed

UNDATABLE *adj* not able to be dated

UNDATE *vb* remove date from

UNDATED *adj* (of a manuscript, letter, etc) not having an identifying date

UNDAUNTED *adj* not put off, discouraged, or beaten

UNDAWNING *adj* not dawning

UNDAZZLE *vb* recover from a daze

UNDAZZLED > UNDAZZLE

UNDAZZLES > UNDAZZLE

UNDE *same as* > UNDEE

UNDEAD *adj* alive

UNDEAF *vb* restore hearing to

UNDEAFED > UNDEAF

UNDEAFING > UNDEAF

UNDEAFS > UNDEAF

UNDEALT *adj* not dealt (with)

UNDEAR *adj* not dear

UNDEBASED *adj* not debased

UNDEBATED *adj* not debated

UNDECAGON *n* polygon having eleven sides

UNDECAYED *adj* not rotten

UNDECEIVE *vb* reveal the truth to (someone previously misled or deceived)

UNDECENT *same as* > INDECENT

UNDECIDED *adj* not having made up one's mind

UNDECIMAL *adj* based on the number 11

UNDECK *vb* remove decorations from

UNDECKED > UNDECK

UNDECKING > UNDECK

UNDECKS > UNDECK

UNDEE *adj* wavy

UNDEEDED *adj* not transferred by deed

UNDEFACED *adj* not spoilt

UNDEFIDE *same as* > UNDEFIED

UNDEFIED *adj* not challenged

UNDEFILED *adj* not defiled

UNDEFINED *adj* not defined or made clear

UNDEIFIED > UNDEIFY

UNDEIFIES > UNDEIFY

UNDEIFY *vb* strip of the status of a deity

UNDELAYED *adj* not delayed

UNDELETE *vb* restore (a deleted computer file or text)

UNDELETED *adj* not deleted, or restored after being deleted

UNDELETES > UNDELETE

UNDELIGHT *n* absence of delight

UNDELUDED *adj* not deluded

UNDENIED *adj* not denied

UNDENTED *adj* not dented

UNDER *adv* indicating movement to or position beneath the underside or base ▷ *prep* less than

UNDERACT *vb* play (a role) without adequate emphasis

UNDERACTS > UNDERACT

UNDERAGE *adj* below the required or standard age ▷ *n* shortfall

UNDERAGED *adj* not old enough

UNDERAGES > UNDERAGE

UNDERARM *adj* denoting a style of throwing, bowling, or serving in which the hand is swung below shoulder level ▷ *adv* in an underarm style ▷ *n* armpit

UNDERARMS > UNDERARM

UNDERATE > UNDEREAT

UNDERBAKE *vb* bake insufficiently

UNDERBEAR *vb* endure

UNDERBID *vb* submit a bid lower than that of (others)

UNDERBIDS > UNDERBID

UNDERBIT > UNDERBITE

UNDERBITE *vb* use insufficient acid in etching

UNDERBODY *n* underpart of a body, as of an animal or motor vehicle

UNDERBORE > UNDERBEAR

UNDERBOSS *n* person who is second in command

UNDERBRED *adj* of impure stock

UNDERBRIM *n* part of a hat

UNDERBUD *vb* produce fewer buds than expected

UNDERBUDS > UNDERBUD

UNDERBUSH *n* undergrowth or underbrush

UNDERBUY *vb* buy (stock in trade) in amounts lower than required

UNDERBUYS > UNDERBUY

UNDERCARD *n* event supporting a main event

UNDERCART *n* aircraft undercarriage

UNDERCAST *vb* cast beneath

UNDERCLAD *adj* not wearing enough clothes

UNDERCLAY *n* grey or whitish clay rock containing fossilized plant roots and occurring beneath coal seams. When used as a refractory, it is known as fireclay

UNDERCLUB *vb* use a golf club that will not hit the ball as far as required

UNDERCOAT *n* coat of paint applied before the final coat ▷ *vb* apply an undercoat to a surface

UNDERCOOK *vb* cook for too short a time or at too low a temperature

UNDERCOOL *vb* cool insufficiently

UNDERCUT *vb* charge less than (a competitor) to obtain trade ▷ *n* act or an instance of cutting underneath

UNDERCUTS > UNDERCUT

UNDERDAKS *npl* underpants

UNDERDECK *n* lower deck of a vessel

UNDERDID > UNDERDO

UNDERDO *vb* do (something) inadequately

UNDERDOER > UNDERDO

UNDERDOES > UNDERDO

UNDERDOG *n* person or team in a weak or underprivileged position

UNDERDOGS > UNDERDOG

UNDERDONE *adj* not cooked enough

UNDERDOSE *vb* give insufficient dose

UNDERDRAW *vb* sketch the subject before painting it on the same surface

UNDERDREW > UNDERDRAW

UNDEREAT *vb* not eat enough

UNDEREATS > UNDEREAT

UNDERFED > UNDERFEED

UNDERFEED *vb* give too little food to ▷ *n* apparatus by which fuel, etc, is supplied from below

UNDERFELT *n* thick felt laid under a carpet to increase insulation

UNDERFIRE *vb* bake insufficiently

UNDERFISH *vb* catch fewer fish than the permitted maximum amount

UNDERFLOW *n* undercurrent

UNDERFONG *vb* receive

UNDERFOOT *adv* under the feet

UNDERFUND *vb* provide insufficient funding

UNDERFUR *n* layer of dense soft fur occurring beneath the outer coarser fur in certain mammals, such as the otter and seal

UNDERFURS > UNDERFUR

UNDERGIRD *vb* strengthen or reinforce by passing a rope, cable, or chain around the underside of (an object, load, etc)

UNDERGIRT > UNDERGIRD

UNDERGO *vb* experience, endure, or sustain

UNDERGOD *n* subordinate god

UNDERGODS > UNDERGOD

UNDERGOER > UNDERGO

UNDERGOES > UNDERGO

UNDERGONE > UNDERGO

UNDERGOWN *n* gown worn under another article of clothing

UNDERGRAD *n* person studying for a first degree; undergraduate

UNDERHAIR *n* lower layer of animal's hair

UNDERHAND *adj* sly, deceitful, and secretive ▷ *adv* in an underhand manner or style

UNDERHEAT *vb* heat insufficiently

u

UNDERHUNG adj (of the lower jaw) projecting beyond the upper jaw

UNDERIVED adj not derived

UNDERJAW n lower jaw

UNDERJAWS > UNDERJAW

UNDERKEEP vb suppress

UNDERKEPT > UNDERKEEP

UNDERKILL n less force than is needed to defeat enemy

UNDERKING n ruler subordinate to a king

UNDERLAID adj laid underneath

UNDERLAIN > UNDERLIE

UNDERLAP vb project under the edge of

UNDERLAPS > UNDERLAP

UNDERLAY n felt or rubber laid beneath a carpet to increase insulation and resilience ▷ vb place (something) under or beneath

UNDERLAYS > UNDERLAY

UNDERLEAF n (in liverworts) any of the leaves forming a row on the underside of the stem: usually smaller than the two rows of lateral leaves and sometimes absent

UNDERLET vb let for a price lower than expected or justified

UNDERLETS > UNDERLET

UNDERLIE vb lie or be placed under

UNDERLIER > UNDERLIE

UNDERLIES > UNDERLIE

UNDERLINE vb draw a line under ▷ n line underneath, esp under written matter

UNDERLING n subordinate

UNDERLIP n lower lip

UNDERLIPS > UNDERLIP

UNDERLIT adj lit from beneath

UNDERLOAD vb load incompletely

UNDERMAN vb supply with insufficient staff ▷ n subordinate man

UNDERMANS > UNDERMAN

UNDERMEN > UNDERMAN

UNDERMINE vb weaken gradually

UNDERMOST adj being the furthest under ▷ adv in the lowest place

UNDERN n time between sunrise and noon

UNDERNOTE n undertone

UNDERNS > UNDERN

UNDERPAID adj not paid as much as the job deserves

UNDERPART n lower part or underside of something such as an animal

UNDERPASS n section of a road that passes under

another road or a railway line

UNDERPAY vb pay someone insufficiently

UNDERPAYS > UNDERPAY

UNDERPEEP vb peep under

UNDERPIN vb give strength or support to

UNDERPINS > UNDERPIN

UNDERPLAY vb achieve (an effect) by deliberate lack of emphasis

UNDERPLOT n subsidiary plot in a literary or dramatic work

UNDERPROP vb prop up from beneath

UNDERRAN > UNDERRUN

UNDERRATE vb underestimate

UNDERRIPE adj not quite ripe

UNDERRUN vb run beneath

UNDERRUNS > UNDERRUN

UNDERSAID > UNDERSAY

UNDERSAY vb say by way of response

UNDERSAYS > UNDERSAY

UNDERSEA adv below the surface of the sea

UNDERSEAL n coating of tar etc applied to the underside of a motor vehicle to prevent corrosion ▷ vb apply such a coating to a motor vehicle

UNDERSEAS same as > UNDERSEA

UNDERSELF n subconscious or person within

UNDERSELL vb sell at a price lower than that of another seller

UNDERSET n ocean undercurrent ▷ vb support from underneath

UNDERSETS > UNDERSET

UNDERSHOT adj (of the lower jaw) projecting beyond the upper jaw

UNDERSIDE n bottom or lower surface

UNDERSIGN vb sign the bottom (of a document)

UNDERSIZE adj smaller than normal

UNDERSKY n lower sky

UNDERSOIL another word for > SUBSOIL

UNDERSOLD > UNDERSELL

UNDERSONG n accompanying secondary melody

UNDERSPIN n backspin

UNDERTAKE vb agree or commit oneself to (something) or to do (something)

UNDERTANE Shakespearean past participle of > UNDERTAKE

UNDERTAX vb tax insufficiently

UNDERTIME n time spent by an employee at work in non-work-related activities like socializing, surfing the internet, making personal telephone calls, etc

UNDERTINT n slight, subdued, or delicate tint

UNDERTONE n quiet tone of voice

UNDERTOOK past tense of > UNDERTAKE

UNDERTOW n strong undercurrent flowing in a different direction from the surface current

UNDERTOWS > UNDERTOW

UNDERUSE vb use less than normal

UNDERUSED > UNDERUSE

UNDERUSES > UNDERUSE

UNDERVEST another name for > VEST

UNDERVOTE n vote cast but invalid

UNDERWAY adj in progress ▷ adv in progress

UNDERWEAR n clothing worn under the outer garments and next to the skin

UNDERWENT past tense of > UNDERGO

UNDERWING n hind wing of an insect, esp when covered by the forewing

UNDERWIRE vb support with wire underneath

UNDERWIT n half-wit

UNDERWITS > UNDERWIT

UNDERWOOD n small trees, bushes, ferns, etc growing beneath taller trees in a wood or forest

UNDERWOOL n lower layer of an animal's coat

UNDERWORK vb do less work than expected

UNDESERT n lack of worth

UNDESERTS > UNDESERT

UNDESERVE vb fail to deserve

UNDESIRED adj not desired

UNDEVOUT adj not devout

UNDID > UNDO

UNDIES npl underwear, esp women's

UNDIGHT vb remove

UNDIGHTS > UNDIGHT

UNDIGNIFY vb divest of dignity

UNDILUTED adj (of a liquid) not having any water added to it

UNDIMMED adj (of eyes, light, etc) still bright or shining

UNDINE n female water spirit

UNDINES > UNDINE

UNDINISM n obsession with water

UNDINISMS > UNDINISM

UNDINTED adj not dinted

UNDIPPED adj not dipped

UNDIVIDED adj total and whole-hearted

UNDIVINE adj not divine

UNDO vb open, unwrap

UNDOABLE adj impossible

UNDOCILE adj not docile

UNDOCK vb take out of a dock

UNDOCKED > UNDOCK

UNDOCKING > UNDOCK

UNDOCKS > UNDOCK

UNDOER > UNDO

UNDOERS > UNDO

UNDOES > UNDO

UNDOING n cause of someone's downfall

UNDOINGS > UNDOING

UNDONE adj not done or completed

UNDOOMED adj not doomed

UNDOTTED adj not dotted

UNDOUBLE vb stretch out

UNDOUBLED > UNDOUBLE

UNDOUBLES > UNDOUBLE

UNDOUBTED adj certain or indisputable

UNDRAINED adj not drained

UNDRAPE vb remove drapery from

UNDRAPED > UNDRAPE

UNDRAPES > UNDRAPE

UNDRAPING > UNDRAPE

UNDRAW vb open (curtains)

UNDRAWING > UNDRAW

UNDRAWN > UNDRAW

UNDRAWS > UNDRAW

UNDREADED adj not feared

UNDREAMED adj not thought of or imagined

UNDREAMT same as > UNDREAMED

UNDRESS vb take off clothes from (oneself or another) ▷ n partial or complete nakedness ▷ adj characterized by or requiring informal or normal working dress or uniform

UNDRESSED adj partially or completely naked

UNDRESSES > UNDRESS

UNDREST same as > UNDRESSED

UNDREW > UNDRAW

UNDRIED adj not dried

UNDRILLED adj not drilled

UNDRIVEN adj not driven

UNDROSSY adj pure

UNDROWNED adj not drowned

UNDRUNK adj not drunk

UNDUBBED adj (of a film, etc) not dubbed

UNDUE adj greater than is reasonable; excessive

UNDUG adj not having been dug

UNDULANCE > UNDULANT

UNDULANCY > UNDULANT

UNDULANT adj resembling waves

UNDULAR > UNDULATE
UNDULATE *vb* move in waves ▷ *adj* having a wavy or rippled appearance, margin, or form
UNDULATED > UNDULATE
UNDULATES > UNDULATE
UNDULATOR > UNDULATE
UNDULLED *adj* not dulled
UNDULOSE *same as* > UNDULOUS
UNDULOUS *adj* undulate
UNDULY *adv* excessively
UNDUTEOUS *same as* > UNDUTIFUL
UNDUTIFUL *adj* not dutiful
UNDY *same as* > UNDEE
UNDYED *adj* not dyed
UNDYING *adj* never ending, eternal
UNDYINGLY > UNDYING
UNDYNAMIC *adj* not dynamic
UNEAGER *adj* nonchalant
UNEAGERLY > UNEAGER
UNEARED *adj* not ploughed
UNEARNED *adj* not deserved
UNEARTH *vb* reveal or discover by searching
UNEARTHED > UNEARTH
UNEARTHLY *adj* ghostly or eerie
UNEARTHS > UNEARTH
UNEASE > UNEASY
UNEASES > UNEASY
UNEASIER > UNEASY
UNEASIEST > UNEASY
UNEASILY > UNEASY
UNEASY *adj* (of a person) anxious or apprehensive
UNEATABLE *adj* (of food) so rotten or unattractive as to be unfit to eat
UNEATEN *adj* (of food) not having been consumed
UNEATH *adv* not easily
UNEATHES > UNEATH
UNEDGE *vb* take the edge off
UNEDGED > UNEDGE
UNEDGES > UNEDGE
UNEDGING > UNEDGE
UNEDIBLE *variant of* > INEDIBLE
UNEDITED *adj* not edited
UNEFFACED *adj* not destroyed
UNELATED *adj* not elated
UNELECTED *adj* not elected
UNEMPTIED *adj* not emptied
UNENDED *adj* without end
UNENDING *adj* not showing any signs of ever stopping
UNENDOWED *adj* not endowed
UNENGAGED *adj* not engaged
UNENJOYED *adj* not enjoyed
UNENSURED *adj* not

ensured
UNENTERED *adj* not having been entered previously
UNENVIED *adj* not envied
UNENVIOUS *adj* not envious
UNENVYING *adj* not envying
UNEQUABLE *adj* unstable
UNEQUAL *adj* not equal in quantity, size, rank, value, etc ▷ *n* person who is not equal
UNEQUALED *adj* (in US English) not equalled
UNEQUALLY > UNEQUAL
UNEQUALS > UNEQUAL
UNERASED *adj* not rubbed out
UNEROTIC *adj* not erotic
UNERRING *adj* never mistaken, consistently accurate
UNESPIED *adj* unnoticed
UNESSAYED *adj* untried
UNESSENCE *vb* deprive of being
UNETH *same as* > UNEATH
UNETHICAL *adj* morally wrong
UNEVADED *adj* not evaded
UNEVEN *adj* not level or flat
UNEVENER > UNEVEN
UNEVENEST > UNEVEN
UNEVENLY > UNEVEN
UNEVOLVED *adj* not evolved
UNEXALTED *adj* not exalted
UNEXCITED *adj* not aroused to pleasure, interest, agitation, etc
UNEXCUSED *adj* not excused
UNEXOTIC *adj* not exotic
UNEXPERT *same as* > INEXPERT
UNEXPIRED *adj* not having expired
UNEXPOSED *adj* not having been exhibited or brought to public notice
UNEXTINCT *adj* not extinct
UNEXTREME *adj* not extreme
UNEYED *adj* unseen
UNFABLED *adj* not fictitious
UNFACT *n* event or thing not provable
UNFACTS > UNFACT
UNFADABLE *adj* incapable of fading
UNFADED *adj* not faded
UNFADING *adj* not fading
UNFAILING *adj* continuous or reliable
UNFAIR *adj* not right, fair, or just ▷ *vb* disfigure
UNFAIRED > UNFAIR
UNFAIRER > UNFAIR
UNFAIREST > UNFAIR
UNFAIRING > UNFAIR

UNFAIRLY > UNFAIR
UNFAIRS > UNFAIR
UNFAITH *n* lack of faith
UNFAITHS > UNFAITH
UNFAKED *adj* not faked
UNFALLEN *adj* not fallen
UNFAMED *adj* not famous
UNFAMOUS *adj* not famous
UNFANCIED > UNFANCY
UNFANCY *vb* consider (a sportsperson or team) unlikely to win or succeed
UNFANNED *adj* not fanned
UNFASTEN *vb* undo, untie, or open or become undone, untied, or opened
UNFASTENS > UNFASTEN
UNFAULTY *adj* not faulty
UNFAVORED *adj* (in US English) not favoured
UNFAZED *adj* not disconcerted
UNFEARED *adj* unafraid
UNFEARFUL *adj* not scared
UNFEARING *adj* having no fear
UNFED *adj* not fed
UNFEED *adj* unpaid
UNFEELING *adj* without sympathy
UNFEIGNED *adj* not feigned
UNFELLED *adj* not cut down
UNFELT *adj* not felt
UNFELTED *adj* not felted
UNFENCE *vb* remove a fence from
UNFENCED *adj* not enclosed by a fence
UNFENCES > UNFENCE
UNFENCING > UNFENCE
UNFERTILE *same as* > INFERTILE
UNFETTER *vb* release from fetters, bonds, etc
UNFETTERS > UNFETTER
UNFEUDAL *adj* not feudal
UNFEUED *adj* not feued
UNFIGURED *adj* not numbered
UNFILDE *archaic form of* > UNFILED
UNFILED *adj* not filed
UNFILIAL *adj* not filial
UNFILLED *adj* (of a container, receptacle, etc) not having become or been made full
UNFILMED *adj* not filmed
UNFINE *adj* not fine
UNFIRED *adj* not fired
UNFIRM *adj* soft or unsteady
UNFISHED *adj* not used for fishing
UNFIT *adj* unqualified or unsuitable ▷ *vb* make unfit
UNFITLY *adv* in an unfit way
UNFITNESS > UNFIT
UNFITS > UNFIT
UNFITTED *adj* unsuitable
UNFITTER > UNFIT

UNFITTEST > UNFIT
UNFITTING *adj* not fitting
UNFIX *vb* unfasten, detach, or loosen
UNFIXED *adj* not fixed
UNFIXES > UNFIX
UNFIXING > UNFIX
UNFIXITY *n* instability
UNFIXT *variant of* > UNFIXED
UNFLAPPED *adj* not agitated or excited
UNFLASHY *adj* not flashy
UNFLAWED *adj* perfect
UNFLEDGED *adj* (of a young bird) not having developed adult feathers
UNFLESH *vb* remove flesh from
UNFLESHED > UNFLESH
UNFLESHES > UNFLESH
UNFLESHLY *adj* immaterial
UNFLEXED *adj* unbent
UNFLOORED *adj* without flooring
UNFLUSH *vb* lose the colour caused by flushing
UNFLUSHED > UNFLUSH
UNFLUSHES > UNFLUSH
UNFLUTED *adj* not fluted
UNFLYABLE *adj* unable to be flown
UNFOCUSED *adj* blurry
UNFOILED *adj* not thwarted
UNFOLD *vb* open or spread out from a folded state
UNFOLDED > UNFOLD
UNFOLDER > UNFOLD
UNFOLDERS > UNFOLD
UNFOLDING > UNFOLD
UNFOLDS > UNFOLD
UNFOND *adj* not fond
UNFOOL *vb* undeceive
UNFOOLED > UNFOOL
UNFOOLING > UNFOOL
UNFOOLS > UNFOOL
UNFOOTED *adj* untrodden
UNFORBID *adj* archaic word meaning unforbidden
UNFORCED *adj* not forced or having been forced
UNFORGED *adj* genuine
UNFORGOT *adj* archaic word meaning unforgotten
UNFORKED *adj* not forked
UNFORM *vb* make formless
UNFORMAL *same as* > INFORMAL
UNFORMED *adj* in an early stage of development
UNFORMING > UNFORM
UNFORMS > UNFORM
UNFORTUNE *n* misfortune
UNFOUGHT *adj* not fought
UNFOUND *adj* not found
UNFOUNDED *adj* not based on facts or evidence
UNFRAMED *adj* not framed
UNFRANKED *adj* not franked
UNFRAUGHT *adj* not fraught

u

UNFREE vb remove freedom from
UNFREED > UNFREE
UNFREEDOM n lack of freedom
UNFREEING > UNFREE
UNFREEMAN n person who is not a freeman
UNFREEMEN > UNFREEMAN
UNFREES > UNFREE
UNFREEZE vb thaw or cause to thaw
UNFREEZES > UNFREEZE
UNFRETTED adj not worried
UNFRIEND n enemy
UNFRIENDS > UNFRIEND
UNFROCK vb deprive (a priest in holy orders) of his or her priesthood
UNFROCKED > UNFROCK
UNFROCKS > UNFROCK
UNFROZE > UNFREEZE
UNFROZEN > UNFREEZE
UNFUELLED adj not fuelled
UNFUMED adj not fumigated
UNFUNDED adj not funded
UNFUNNIER > UNFUNNY
UNFUNNY adj not funny
UNFURL vb unroll or unfold
UNFURLED > UNFURL
UNFURLING > UNFURL
UNFURLS > UNFURL
UNFURNISH vb clear
UNFURRED adj not adorned with fur
UNFUSED adj not fused
UNFUSSIER > UNFUSSY
UNFUSSILY > UNFUSSY
UNFUSSY adj not characterized by overelaborate detail
UNGAG vb restore freedom of speech to
UNGAGGED > UNGAG
UNGAGGING > UNGAG
UNGAGS > UNGAG
UNGAIN adj inconvenient
UNGAINFUL > UNGAIN
UNGAINLY adj lacking grace when moving ▷ adv clumsily
UNGALLANT adj not gallant
UNGALLED adj not annoyed
UNGARBED adj undressed
UNGARBLED adj clear
UNGATED adj without gate
UNGAUGED adj not measured
UNGAZED as in ungazed at/ ungazed upon not gazed (at or upon)
UNGAZING adj not gazing
UNGEAR vb disengage
UNGEARED > UNGEAR
UNGEARING > UNGEAR
UNGEARS > UNGEAR
UNGELDED adj not gelded
UNGENIAL adj unfriendly
UNGENTEEL adj impolite

UNGENTLE adj not gentle
UNGENTLY > UNGENTLE
UNGENUINE adj false
UNGERMANE adj inappropriate
UNGET vb get rid of
UNGETS > UNGET
UNGETTING > UNGET
UNGHOSTLY adj not ghostly
UNGIFTED adj not talented
UNGILD vb remove gilding from
UNGILDED > UNGILD
UNGILDING > UNGILD
UNGILDS > UNGILD
UNGILT > UNGILD
UNGIRD vb remove belt from
UNGIRDED > UNGIRD
UNGIRDING > UNGIRD
UNGIRDS > UNGIRD
UNGIRT adj not belted
UNGIRTH vb release from a girth
UNGIRTHED > UNGIRTH
UNGIRTHS > UNGIRTH
UNGIVING adj inflexible
UNGLAD adj not glad
UNGLAZED adj not glazed
UNGLOSSED adj not glossed
UNGLOVE vb remove glove(s)
UNGLOVED > UNGLOVE
UNGLOVES > UNGLOVE
UNGLOVING > UNGLOVE
UNGLUE vb remove adhesive from
UNGLUED > UNGLUE
UNGLUES > UNGLUE
UNGLUING > UNGLUE
UNGOD vb remove status of being a god from
UNGODDED > UNGOD
UNGODDING > UNGOD
UNGODLIER > UNGODLY
UNGODLIKE adj not godlike
UNGODLILY > UNGODLY
UNGODLY adj unreasonable or outrageous
UNGODS > UNGOD
UNGORD same as > UNGORED
UNGORED adj not gored
UNGORGED same as > UNGORED
UNGOT same as > UNGOTTEN
UNGOTTEN adj not obtained or won
UNGOWN vb remove gown (from)
UNGOWNED > UNGOWN
UNGOWNING > UNGOWN
UNGOWNS > UNGOWN
UNGRACED adj not graced
UNGRADED adj not graded
UNGRASSED adj not covered with grass
UNGRAVELY adj in a light-hearted manner
UNGRAZED adj not grazed

UNGREASED adj not greased
UNGREEDY adj not greedy
UNGREEN adj not environmentally friendly
UNGROOMED adj not groomed
UNGROUND adj not crushed
UNGROUPED adj not placed in a group
UNGROWN adj not fully developed
UNGRUDGED adj not grudged
UNGUAL adj of, relating to, or affecting the fingernails or toenails
UNGUARD vb expose (to attack)
UNGUARDED adj not protected
UNGUARDS > UNGUARD
UNGUENT n ointment
UNGUENTA > UNGUENTUM
UNGUENTS > UNGUENT
UNGUENTUM same as > UNGUENT
UNGUES > UNGUIS
UNGUESSED adj unexpected
UNGUIDED adj (of a missile, bomb, etc) not having a flight path controlled either by radio signals or internal preset or self-actuating homing devices
UNGUIFORM adj shaped like a nail or claw
UNGUILTY adj innocent
UNGUINOUS adj fatty
UNGUIS n nail, claw, or hoof, or the part of the digit giving rise to it
UNGULA n truncated cone, cylinder, etc
UNGULAE > UNGULA
UNGULAR > UNGULA
UNGULATE n hoofed mammal
UNGULATES > UNGULATE
UNGULED adj hoofed
UNGUM vb remove adhesive from
UNGUMMED > UNGUM
UNGUMMING > UNGUM
UNGUMS > UNGUM
UNGYVE vb release from shackles
UNGYVED > UNGYVE
UNGYVES > UNGYVE
UNGYVING > UNGYVE
UNHABLE same as > UNABLE
UNHACKED adj not hacked
UNHAILED adj not hailed
UNHAIR vb remove the hair from (a hide)
UNHAIRED > UNHAIR
UNHAIRER > UNHAIR
UNHAIRERS > UNHAIR
UNHAIRING > UNHAIR
UNHAIRS > UNHAIR
UNHALLOW vb desecrate
UNHALLOWS > UNHALLOW

UNHALSED adj not hailed
UNHALVED adj not divided in half
UNHAND vb release from one's grasp
UNHANDED > UNHAND
UNHANDIER > UNHANDY
UNHANDILY > UNHANDY
UNHANDING > UNHAND
UNHANDLED adj not handled
UNHANDS > UNHAND
UNHANDY adj not skilful with one's hands
UNHANG vb take down from hanging position
UNHANGED adj not executed by hanging
UNHANGING > UNHANG
UNHANGS > UNHANG
UNHAPPIED > UNHAPPY
UNHAPPIER > UNHAPPY
UNHAPPIES > UNHAPPY
UNHAPPILY > UNHAPPY
UNHAPPY adj sad or depressed ▷ vb make unhappy
UNHARBOUR vb force out of shelter
UNHARDY adj fragile
UNHARMED adj not hurt or damaged in any way
UNHARMFUL adj not harmful
UNHARMING adj not capable of harming
UNHARNESS vb remove the harness from (a horse, etc)
UNHARRIED adj not harried
UNHASP vb unfasten
UNHASPED > UNHASP
UNHASPING > UNHASP
UNHASPS > UNHASP
UNHASTING adj not rushing
UNHASTY adj not speedy
UNHAT vb doff one's hat
UNHATCHED adj (of an egg) not having broken to release the fully developed young
UNHATS > UNHAT
UNHATTED > UNHAT
UNHATTING > UNHAT
UNHAUNTED adj not haunted
UNHEAD vb remove the head from
UNHEADED adj not having a heading
UNHEADING > UNHEAD
UNHEADS > UNHEAD
UNHEAL vb expose
UNHEALED adj not having healed physically, mentally, or emotionally
UNHEALING adj not healing
UNHEALS > UNHEAL
UNHEALTH n illness
UNHEALTHS > UNHEALTH
UNHEALTHY adj likely to cause poor health

UNHEARD adj not listened to

UNHEARSE vb remove from a hearse

UNHEARSED > UNHEARSE

UNHEARSES > UNHEARSE

UNHEART vb discourage

UNHEARTED > UNHEART

UNHEARTS > UNHEART

UNHEATED adj not having been warmed up

UNHEDGED adj unprotected

UNHEEDED adj noticed but ignored

UNHEEDFUL adj not heedful

UNHEEDILY adv carelessly

UNHEEDING adj not heeding

UNHEEDY adj not heedful

UNHELE same as > UNHEAL

UNHELED > UNHELE

UNHELES > UNHELE

UNHELING > UNHELE

UNHELM vb remove the helmet of (oneself or another)

UNHELMED > UNHELM

UNHELMING > UNHELM

UNHELMS > UNHELM

UNHELPED adj without help

UNHELPFUL adj doing nothing to improve a situation

UNHEPPEN adj awkward

UNHEROIC adj not heroic

UNHERST archaic past form of > UNHEARSE

UNHEWN adj not hewn

UNHIDDEN adj not hidden

UNHINGE vb derange or unbalance (a person or his or her mind)

UNHINGED > UNHINGE

UNHINGES > UNHINGE

UNHINGING > UNHINGE

UNHIP adj not at all fashionable or up to date

UNHIPPER > UNHIP

UNHIPPEST > UNHIP

UNHIRABLE adj not fit to be hired

UNHIRED adj not hired

UNHITCH vb unfasten or detach

UNHITCHED > UNHITCH

UNHITCHES > UNHITCH

UNHIVE vb remove from a hive

UNHIVED > UNHIVE

UNHIVES > UNHIVE

UNHIVING > UNHIVE

UNHOARD vb remove from a hoard

UNHOARDED > UNHOARD

UNHOARDS > UNHOARD

UNHOLIER > UNHOLY

UNHOLIEST > UNHOLY

UNHOLILY > UNHOLY

UNHOLPEN same as > UNHELPED

UNHOLY adj immoral or wicked

UNHOMELY adj not homely

UNHONEST same as > DISHONEST

UNHONORED adj not honoured

UNHOOD vb remove hood from

UNHOODED > UNHOOD

UNHOODING > UNHOOD

UNHOODS > UNHOOD

UNHOOK vb unfasten the hooks of (a garment)

UNHOOKED > UNHOOK

UNHOOKING > UNHOOK

UNHOOKS > UNHOOK

UNHOOP vb remove hoop(s) from

UNHOOPED > UNHOOP

UNHOOPING > UNHOOP

UNHOOPS > UNHOOP

UNHOPED adj unhoped-for

UNHOPEFUL adj not hopeful

UNHORSE vb knock or throw from a horse

UNHORSED > UNHORSE

UNHORSES > UNHORSE

UNHORSING > UNHORSE

UNHOSTILE adj not hostile

UNHOUSE vb remove from a house

UNHOUSED > UNHOUSE

UNHOUSES > UNHOUSE

UNHOUSING > UNHOUSE

UNHUMAN adj inhuman or not human

UNHUMANLY > UNHUMAN

UNHUMBLED adj not humbled

UNHUNG > UNHANG

UNHUNTED adj not hunted

UNHURRIED adj done at a leisurely pace, without any rush or anxiety

UNHURT adj not injured in an accident, attack, etc

UNHURTFUL adj not hurtful

UNHUSK vb remove the husk from

UNHUSKED > UNHUSK

UNHUSKING > UNHUSK

UNHUSKS > UNHUSK

UNI n (in informal English) university

UNIALGAL adj microbiological term

UNIAXIAL adj (esp of plants) having an unbranched main axis

UNIBODY adj of a vehicle in which frame and body are one unit

UNIBROW n informal word for eyebrows that meet above the nose

UNIBROWS > UNIBROW

UNICITIES > UNICITY

UNICITY n oneness

UNICOLOR same as > UNICOLOUR

UNICOLOUR adj of one colour

UNICORN n imaginary horselike creature with one horn growing from its forehead

UNICORNS > UNICORN

UNICYCLE n one-wheeled vehicle driven by pedals, used in a circus ▷ vb ride a unicycle

UNICYCLED > UNICYCLE

UNICYCLES > UNICYCLE

UNIDEAED adj not having ideas

UNIDEAL adj not ideal

UNIFACE n type of tool

UNIFACES > UNIFACE

UNIFIABLE > UNIFY

UNIFIC adj unifying

UNIFIED > UNIFY

UNIFIER > UNIFY

UNIFIERS > UNIFY

UNIFIES > UNIFY

UNIFILAR adj composed of, having, or using only one wire, thread, filament, etc

UNIFORM n special identifying set of clothes for the members of an organization, such as soldiers ▷ adj regular and even throughout, unvarying ▷ vb fit out (a body of soldiers, etc) with uniforms

UNIFORMED > UNIFORM

UNIFORMER > UNIFORM

UNIFORMLY > UNIFORM

UNIFORMS > UNIFORM

UNIFY vb make or become one

UNIFYING > UNIFY

UNIFYINGS > UNIFY

UNIJUGATE adj (of a compound leaf) having only one pair of leaflets

UNILINEAL same as > UNILINEAR

UNILINEAR adj developing in a progressive sequence

UNILLUMED adj not illuminated

UNILOBAR adj having one lobe

UNILOBED same as > UNILOBAR

UNIMBUED adj not imbued

UNIMPEDED adj not stopped or disrupted by anything

UNIMPOSED adj not imposed

UNINCITED adj unprovoked

UNINDEXED adj not indexed

UNINJURED adj not having sustained any injury

UNINSTALL vb remove from a computer system

UNINSURED adj not covered by insurance

UNINURED adj unaccustomed

UNINVITED adj not having been asked ▷ adv without having been asked

UNINVOKED adj not invoked

UNION n uniting or being united ▷ adj of a trade union

UNIONISE same as > UNIONIZE

UNIONISED > UNIONISE

UNIONISER > UNIONISE

UNIONISES > UNIONISE

UNIONISM n principles of trade unions

UNIONISMS > UNIONISM

UNIONIST n member or supporter of a trade union ▷ adj of or relating to union or unionism, esp trade unionism

UNIONISTS > UNIONIST

UNIONIZE vb organize (workers) into a trade union

UNIONIZED > UNIONIZE

UNIONIZER > UNIONIZE

UNIONIZES > UNIONIZE

UNIONS > UNION

UNIPAROUS adj (of certain animals) producing a single offspring at each birth

UNIPED n person or thing with one foot

UNIPEDS > UNIPED

UNIPLANAR adj situated in one plane

UNIPOD n one-legged support, as for a camera

UNIPODS > UNIPOD

UNIPOLAR adj of, concerned with, or having a single magnetic or electric pole

UNIPOTENT adj able to form only one type of cell

UNIQUE n person or thing that is unique

UNIQUELY > UNIQUE

UNIQUER > UNIQUE

UNIQUES > UNIQUE

UNIQUEST > UNIQUE

UNIRAMOSE same as > UNIRAMOUS

UNIRAMOUS adj (esp of the appendages of crustaceans) consisting of a single branch

UNIRONED adj not ironed

UNIRONIC adj not ironic

UNIS > UNI

UNISERIAL adj in or relating to a single series

UNISEX adj designed for use by both sexes ▷ n condition of seeming not to belong obviously either to one sex or the other from the way one behaves or dresses

UNISEXES > UNISEX

UNISEXUAL adj of one sex only

u

UNISIZE *adj* in one size only

UNISON *n* complete agreement

UNISONAL > UNISON

UNISONANT > UNISON

UNISONOUS > UNISON

UNISONS > UNISON

UNISSUED *adj* not issued

UNIT *n* single undivided entity or whole

UNITAGE > UNIT

UNITAGES > UNIT

UNITAL > UNIT

UNITARD *n* all-in-one skintight suit

UNITARDS > UNITARD

UNITARIAN *n* supporter of unity or centralization ▷ *adj* of or relating to unity or centralization

UNITARILY > UNITARY

UNITARY *adj* consisting of a single undivided whole

UNITE *vb* make or become an integrated whole ▷ *n* English gold coin minted in the Stuart period, originally worth 20 shillings

UNITED *adj* produced by two or more people or things in combination

UNITEDLY > UNITED

UNITER > UNITE

UNITERS > UNITE

UNITES > UNITE

UNITIES > UNITY

UNITING > UNITE

UNITINGS > UNITE

UNITION *n* joining

UNITIONS > UNITION

UNITISE *same as* > UNITIZE

UNITISED > UNITISE

UNITISER *same as* > UNITIZER

UNITISERS > UNITISER

UNITISES > UNITISE

UNITISING > UNITISE

UNITIVE *adj* tending to unite or capable of uniting

UNITIVELY > UNITIVE

UNITIZE *vb* convert (an investment trust) into a unit trust

UNITIZED > UNITIZE

UNITIZER *n* person or thing that arranges units into batches

UNITIZERS > UNITIZER

UNITIZES > UNITIZE

UNITIZING > UNITIZE

UNITRUST *n* type of income-producing trust fund

UNITRUSTS > UNITRUST

UNITS > UNIT

UNITY *n* state of being one

UNIVALENT *adj* (of a chromosome during meiosis) not paired with its homologue

UNIVALVE *adj* relating to, designating, or possessing a mollusc shell that consists of a single piece (valve) ▷ *n* gastropod mollusc or its shell

UNIVALVED > UNIVALVE

UNIVALVES > UNIVALVE

UNIVERSAL *adj* of or typical of the whole of mankind or of nature ▷ *n* something which exists or is true in all places and all situations

UNIVERSE *n* whole of all existing matter, energy, and space

UNIVERSES > UNIVERSE

UNIVOCAL *adj* unambiguous or unmistakable ▷ *n* word or term that has only one meaning

UNIVOCALS > UNIVOCAL

UNJADED *adj* not jaded

UNJAM *vb* remove blockage from

UNJAMMED > UNJAM

UNJAMMING > UNJAM

UNJAMS > UNJAM

UNJEALOUS *adj* not jealous

UNJOINED *adj* not joined

UNJOINT *vb* disjoint

UNJOINTED > UNJOINT

UNJOINTS > UNJOINT

UNJOYFUL *adj* not joyful

UNJOYOUS *adj* not joyous

UNJUDGED *adj* not judged

UNJUST *adj* not fair or just

UNJUSTER > UNJUST

UNJUSTEST > UNJUST

UNJUSTLY > UNJUST

UNKED *adj* alien

UNKEELED *adj* without a keel

UNKEMPT *adj* (of the hair) not combed

UNKEMPTLY > UNKEMPT

UNKEND *same as* > UNKENNED

UNKENNED *adj* unknown

UNKENNEL *vb* release from a kennel

UNKENNELS > UNKENNEL

UNKENT *same as* > UNKENNED

UNKEPT *adj* not kept

UNKET *same as* > UNKED

UNKID *same as* > UNKED

UNKIND *adj* unsympathetic or cruel

UNKINDER > UNKIND

UNKINDEST > UNKIND

UNKINDLED *adj* not kindled

UNKINDLY > UNKIND

UNKING *vb* strip of sovereignty

UNKINGED > UNKING

UNKINGING > UNKING

UNKINGLY *adj* not kingly

UNKINGS > UNKING

UNKINK *vb* straighten out

UNKINKED > UNKINK

UNKINKING > UNKINK

UNKINKS > UNKINK

UNKISS *vb* cancel (a previous action) with a kiss

UNKISSED *adj* not kissed

UNKISSES > UNKISS

UNKISSING > UNKISS

UNKNELLED *adj* not tolled

UNKNIGHT *vb* strip of knighthood

UNKNIGHTS > UNKNIGHT

UNKNIT *vb* make or become undone, untied, or unravelled

UNKNITS > UNKNIT

UNKNITTED > UNKNIT

UNKNOT *vb* disentangle or undo a knot or knots in

UNKNOTS > UNKNOT

UNKNOTTED > UNKNOT

UNKNOWING *adj* unaware or ignorant

UNKNOWN *adj* not known ▷ *n* unknown person, quantity, or thing

UNKNOWNS > UNKNOWN

UNKOSHER *adj* not conforming to Jewish religious law

UNLABELED *adj* not labelled

UNLABORED *adj* not laboured

UNLACE *vb* loosen or undo the lacing of (shoes, garments, etc)

UNLACED *adj* not laced

UNLACES > UNLACE

UNLACING > UNLACE

UNLADE *less common word for* > UNLOAD

UNLADED > UNLADE

UNLADEN *adj* not laden

UNLADES > UNLADE

UNLADING > UNLADE

UNLADINGS > UNLADE

UNLAID > UNLAY

UNLASH *vb* untie or unfasten

UNLASHED > UNLASH

UNLASHES > UNLASH

UNLASHING > UNLASH

UNLAST *archaic variant of* > UNLACED

UNLASTE *archaic variant of* > UNLACED

UNLATCH *vb* open or unfasten or come open or unfastened by the lifting or release of a latch

UNLATCHED > UNLATCH

UNLATCHES > UNLATCH

UNLAW *vb* penalize

UNLAWED > UNLAW

UNLAWFUL *adj* not permitted by law

UNLAWING > UNLAW

UNLAWS > UNLAW

UNLAY *vb* untwist (a rope or cable) to separate its strands

UNLAYING > UNLAY

UNLAYS > UNLAY

UNLEAD *vb* strip off lead

UNLEADED *adj* (of petrol) containing less tetraethyl lead, in order to reduce environmental pollution ▷ *n* petrol containing a reduced amount of tetraethyl lead

UNLEADEDS > UNLEADED

UNLEADING > UNLEAD

UNLEADS > UNLEAD

UNLEAL *adj* treacherous

UNLEARN *vb* try to forget something learnt or to discard accumulated knowledge

UNLEARNED *same as* > UNLEARNT

UNLEARNS > UNLEARN

UNLEARNT *adj* denoting knowledge or skills innately present rather than learnt

UNLEASED *adj* not leased

UNLEASH *vb* set loose or cause (something bad)

UNLEASHED > UNLEASH

UNLEASHES > UNLEASH

UNLED *adj* not led

UNLESS *conj* except under the circumstances that ▷ *prep* except

UNLET *adj* not rented

UNLETHAL *adj* not deadly

UNLETTED *adj* unimpeded

UNLEVEL *adj* not level ▷ *vb* make unbalanced

UNLEVELED > UNLEVEL

UNLEVELS > UNLEVEL

UNLEVIED *adj* not levied

UNLICH *Spenserian form of* > UNLIKE

UNLICKED *adj* not licked

UNLID *vb* remove lid from

UNLIDDED > UNLID

UNLIDDING > UNLID

UNLIDS > UNLID

UNLIGHTED *adj* not lit

UNLIKABLE *adj* not likable

UNLIKE *adj* dissimilar or different ▷ *prep* not like or typical of ▷ *n* person or thing that is unlike another

UNLIKED *adj* not liked

UNLIKELY *adj* improbable

UNLIKES > UNLIKE

UNLIMBER *vb* disengage (a gun) from its limber

UNLIMBERS > UNLIMBER

UNLIME *vb* detach

UNLIMED > UNLIME

UNLIMES > UNLIME

UNLIMING > UNLIME

UNLIMITED *adj* apparently endless

UNLINE *vb* remove the lining from

UNLINEAL *adj* not lineal

UNLINED *adj* not having any lining

UNLINES > UNLINE

UNLINING > UNLINE

UNLINK *vb* undo the link or links between

UNLINKED > UNLINK

UNLINKING > UNLINK

UNLINKS > UNLINK

UNLISTED adj not entered on a list

UNLIT adj (of a fire, cigarette, etc) not lit and therefore not burning

UNLIVABLE adj not fit for living in

UNLIVE vb live so as to nullify, undo, or live down (past events or times)

UNLIVED > UNLIVE

UNLIVELY adj lifeless

UNLIVES > UNLIVE

UNLIVING > UNLIVE

UNLOAD vb remove (cargo) from (a ship, truck, or plane)

UNLOADED > UNLOAD

UNLOADER > UNLOAD

UNLOADERS > UNLOAD

UNLOADING > UNLOAD

UNLOADS > UNLOAD

UNLOBED adj without lobes

UNLOCATED adj not located

UNLOCK vb unfasten (a lock or door)

UNLOCKED adj not locked

UNLOCKING > UNLOCK

UNLOCKS > UNLOCK

UNLOGICAL same as > ILLOGICAL

UNLOOKED adj not looked (at)

UNLOOSE vb set free or release

UNLOOSED > UNLOOSE

UNLOOSEN same as > UNLOOSE

UNLOOSENS > UNLOOSEN

UNLOOSES > UNLOOSE

UNLOOSING > UNLOOSE

UNLOPPED adj not chopped off

UNLORD vb remove from position of being lord

UNLORDED > UNLORD

UNLORDING > UNLORD

UNLORDLY adv not in a lordlike manner

UNLORDS > UNLORD

UNLOSABLE adj unable to be lost

UNLOST adj not lost

UNLOVABLE adj too unpleasant or unattractive to be loved

UNLOVE vb stop loving

UNLOVED adj not loved by anyone

UNLOVELY adj unpleasant in appearance or character

UNLOVES > UNLOVE

UNLOVING adj not feeling or showing love and affection

UNLUCKIER > UNLUCKY

UNLUCKILY > UNLUCKY

UNLUCKY adj having bad luck, unfortunate

UNLYRICAL adj not lyrical

UNMACHO adj not macho

UNMADE adj (of a bed) with the bedclothes not

smoothed and tidied

UNMAILED adj not sent by post

UNMAIMED adj not injured

UNMAKABLE adj unable to be made

UNMAKE vb undo or destroy

UNMAKER > UNMAKE

UNMAKERS > UNMAKE

UNMAKES > UNMAKE

UNMAKING > UNMAKE

UNMAKINGS > UNMAKE

UNMAN vb cause to lose courage or nerve

UNMANACLE vb release from manacles

UNMANAGED adj not managed

UNMANFUL adj unmanly

UNMANLIER > UNMANLY

UNMANLIKE adj not worthy of a man

UNMANLY adj not masculine or virile

UNMANNED adj having no personnel or crew

UNMANNING > UNMAN

UNMANNISH adj not mannish

UNMANS > UNMAN

UNMANTLE vb remove mantle from

UNMANTLED > UNMANTLE

UNMANTLES > UNMANTLE

UNMANURED adj not treated with manure

UNMAPPED adj not charted

UNMARD same as > UNMARRED

UNMARKED adj having no signs of damage or injury

UNMARRED adj not marred

UNMARRIED adj not married

UNMARRIES > UNMARRY

UNMARRY vb divorce

UNMASK vb remove the mask or disguise from

UNMASKED > UNMASK

UNMASKER > UNMASK

UNMASKERS > UNMASK

UNMASKING > UNMASK

UNMASKS > UNMASK

UNMATCHED adj not equalled or surpassed

UNMATED adj not mated

UNMATTED adj not matted

UNMATURED adj not matured

UNMEANING adj having no meaning

UNMEANT adj unintentional

UNMEEK adj not submissive

UNMEET adj not meet

UNMEETLY > UNMEET

UNMELLOW adj not mellow

UNMELTED adj not melted

UNMENDED adj not mended

UNMERITED adj not merited or deserved

UNMERRY adj not merry

UNMESH vb release from mesh

UNMESHED > UNMESH

UNMESHES > UNMESH

UNMESHING > UNMESH

UNMET adj unfulfilled

UNMETED adj unmeasured

UNMEW vb release from confinement

UNMEWED > UNMEW

UNMEWING > UNMEW

UNMEWS > UNMEW

UNMILKED adj not milked

UNMILLED adj not milled

UNMINDED adj disregarded

UNMINDFUL adj careless, heedless, or forgetful

UNMINED adj not mined

UNMINGLE vb separate

UNMINGLED > UNMINGLE

UNMINGLES > UNMINGLE

UNMIRY adj not swampy

UNMISSED adj unnoticed

UNMITER same as > UNMITRE

UNMITERED > UNMITER

UNMITERS > UNMITER

UNMITRE vb divest of a mitre

UNMITRED > UNMITRE

UNMITRES > UNMITRE

UNMITRING > UNMITRE

UNMIX vb separate

UNMIXABLE adj incapable of being mixed

UNMIXED > UNMIX

UNMIXEDLY > UNMIXED

UNMIXES > UNMIX

UNMIXING > UNMIX

UNMIXT same as > UNMIX

UNMOANED adj unmourned

UNMODISH adj passé

UNMOLD same as > UNMOULD

UNMOLDED > UNMOLD

UNMOLDING > UNMOLD

UNMOLDS > UNMOLD

UNMOLTEN adj not molten

UNMONEYED adj poor

UNMONIED same as > UNMONEYED

UNMOOR vb weigh the anchor or drop the mooring of (a vessel)

UNMOORED > UNMOOR

UNMOORING > UNMOOR

UNMOORS > UNMOOR

UNMORAL adj outside morality

UNMORALLY > UNMORAL

UNMORTISE vb release from mortise

UNMOTIVED adj without motive

UNMOULD vb change shape of

UNMOULDED > UNMOULD

UNMOULDS > UNMOULD

UNMOUNT vb dismount

UNMOUNTED > UNMOUNT

UNMOUNTS > UNMOUNT

UNMOURNED adj not mourned

UNMOVABLE adj not movable

UNMOVABLY > UNMOVABLE

UNMOVED adj not affected by emotion, indifferent

UNMOVEDLY > UNMOVED

UNMOVING adj still and motionless

UNMOWN adj not mown

UNMUFFLE vb remove a muffle or muffles from

UNMUFFLED > UNMUFFLE

UNMUFFLES > UNMUFFLE

UNMUSICAL adj (of a person) unable to appreciate or play music

UNMUZZLE vb take the muzzle off (a dog, etc)

UNMUZZLED > UNMUZZLE

UNMUZZLES > UNMUZZLE

UNNAIL vb unfasten by removing nails

UNNAILED > UNNAIL

UNNAILING > UNNAIL

UNNAILS > UNNAIL

UNNAMABLE adj that cannot or must not be named

UNNAMED adj not mentioned by name

UNNANELD same as > UNANELED

UNNATIVE adj not native

UNNATURAL adj strange and frightening because not usual

UNNEATH adj archaic word for underneath

UNNEEDED adj not needed

UNNEEDFUL adj not needful

UNNERVE vb cause to lose courage, confidence, or self-control

UNNERVED > UNNERVE

UNNERVES > UNNERVE

UNNERVING > UNNERVE

UNNEST vb remove from a nest

UNNESTED > UNNEST

UNNESTING > UNNEST

UNNESTS > UNNEST

UNNETHES same as > UNNEATH

UNNETTED adj not having or not enclosed in a net

UNNOBLE vb strip of nobility

UNNOBLED > UNNOBLE

UNNOBLES > UNNOBLE

UNNOBLING > UNNOBLE

UNNOISY adj quiet

UNNOTED adj not noted

UNNOTICED adj without being seen or noticed

UNNUANCED adj without nuances

UNOAKED adj (of wine) not matured in an oak barrel

UNOBEYED adj not obeyed

UNOBVIOUS adj unapparent

UNOFFERED adj not offered

UNOFTEN adv infrequently

UNOILED adj not lubricated with oil

u

UNOPEN adj not open

UNOPENED adj closed, barred, or sealed

UNOPPOSED adj not opposed

UNORDER vb cancel an order

UNORDERED adj not ordered

UNORDERLY adj not orderly or disorderly

UNORDERS > UNORDER

UNORNATE same as > INORNATE

UNOWED same as > UNOWNED

UNOWNED adj not owned

UNPACED adj without the aid of a pacemaker

UNPACK vb remove the contents of (a suitcase, trunk, etc)

UNPACKED > UNPACK

UNPACKER > UNPACK

UNPACKERS > UNPACK

UNPACKING > UNPACK

UNPACKS > UNPACK

UNPADDED adj not padded

UNPAGED adj (of a book) having no page numbers

UNPAID adj without a salary or wage

UNPAINED adj not suffering pain

UNPAINFUL adj painless

UNPAINT vb remove paint from

UNPAINTED > UNPAINT

UNPAINTS > UNPAINT

UNPAIRED adj not paired up

UNPALSIED adj not affected with palsy

UNPANEL vb unsaddle

UNPANELS > UNPANEL

UNPANGED adj without pain or sadness

UNPANNEL same as > UNPANEL

UNPANNELS > UNPANNEL

UNPAPER vb remove paper from

UNPAPERED > UNPAPER

UNPAPERS > UNPAPER

UNPARED adj not pared

UNPARTED adj not parted

UNPARTIAL same as > IMPARTIAL

UNPATCHED adj not patched

UNPATHED adj not having a path

UNPAVED adj not covered in paving

UNPAY vb undo

UNPAYABLE adj incapable of being paid

UNPAYING > UNPAY

UNPAYS > UNPAY

UNPEELED adj not peeled

UNPEERED adj unparalleled

UNPEG vb remove the peg

or pegs from, esp to unfasten

UNPEGGED > UNPEG

UNPEGGING > UNPEG

UNPEGS > UNPEG

UNPEN vb release from a pen

UNPENNED > UNPEN

UNPENNIED adj not having pennies

UNPENNING > UNPEN

UNPENS > UNPEN

UNPENT archaic past form of > UNPEN

UNPEOPLE vb empty of people

UNPEOPLED > UNPEOPLE

UNPEOPLES > UNPEOPLE

UNPERCH vb remove from a perch

UNPERCHED > UNPERCH

UNPERCHES > UNPERCH

UNPERFECT same as > IMPERFECT

UNPERPLEX vb remove confusion from

UNPERSON n person whose existence is officially denied or ignored

UNPERSONS > UNPERSON

UNPERVERT vb free (someone) from perversion

UNPICK vb undo (the stitches) of (a piece of sewing)

UNPICKED adj (of knitting, sewing, etc) having been unravelled or picked out

UNPICKING > UNPICK

UNPICKS > UNPICK

UNPIERCED adj not pierced

UNPILE vb remove from a pile

UNPILED > UNPILE

UNPILES > UNPILE

UNPILING > UNPILE

UNPILOTED adj unguided

UNPIN vb remove a pin or pins from

UNPINKED adj not decorated with a perforated pattern

UNPINKT same as > UNPINKED

UNPINNED > UNPIN

UNPINNING > UNPIN

UNPINS > UNPIN

UNPITIED adj not pitied

UNPITIFUL adj pitiless

UNPITTED adj not having had pits removed

UNPITYING adj not pitying

UNPLACE same as > DISPLACE

UNPLACED adj not given or put in a particular place

UNPLACES > UNPLACE

UNPLACING > UNPLACE

UNPLAGUED adj not plagued

UNPLAINED adj unmourned

UNPLAIT vb remove plaits from

UNPLAITED > UNPLAIT

UNPLAITS > UNPLAIT

UNPLANKED adj not planked

UNPLANNED adj not intentional or deliberate

UNPLANTED adj not planted

UNPLAYED adj not played

UNPLEASED adj not pleased or displeased

UNPLEATED adj not pleated

UNPLEDGED adj not pledged

UNPLIABLE adj not easily bent

UNPLIABLY > UNPLIABLE

UNPLIANT adj not pliant

UNPLOWED adj not ploughed

UNPLUCKED adj not plucked

UNPLUG vb disconnect (a piece of electrical equipment) by taking the plug out of the socket

UNPLUGGED adj using acoustic rather than electric instruments

UNPLUGS > UNPLUG

UNPLUMB vb remove lead from

UNPLUMBED adj not measured

UNPLUMBS > UNPLUMB

UNPLUME vb remove feathers from

UNPLUMED > UNPLUME

UNPLUMES > UNPLUME

UNPLUMING > UNPLUME

UNPOETIC adj not poetic

UNPOINTED adj not pointed

UNPOISED adj not poised

UNPOISON vb extract poison from

UNPOISONS > UNPOISON

UNPOLICED adj without police control

UNPOLISH vb remove polish from

UNPOLITE same as > IMPOLITE

UNPOLITIC another word for > IMPOLITIC

UNPOLLED adj not included in an opinion poll

UNPOPE vb strip of popedom

UNPOPED > UNPOPE

UNPOPES > UNPOPE

UNPOPING > UNPOPE

UNPOPULAR adj generally disliked or disapproved of

UNPOSED adj not posed

UNPOSTED adj not sent by post

UNPOTABLE adj undrinkable

UNPOTTED adj not planted in a pot

UNPRAISE vb withhold praise from

UNPRAISED > UNPRAISE

UNPRAISES > UNPRAISE

UNPRAY vb withdraw (a prayer)

UNPRAYED > UNPRAY

UNPRAYING > UNPRAY

UNPRAYS > UNPRAY

UNPREACH vb retract (a sermon)

UNPRECISE same as > IMPRECISE

UNPREDICT vb retract (a previous prediction)

UNPREPARE vb make unprepared

UNPRESSED adj not pressed

UNPRETTY adj unattractive

UNPRICED adj having no fixed or marked price

UNPRIEST vb strip of priesthood

UNPRIESTS > UNPRIEST

UNPRIMED adj not primed

UNPRINTED adj not printed

UNPRISON vb release from prison

UNPRISONS > UNPRISON

UNPRIZED adj not treasured

UNPROBED adj not examined

UNPROP vb remove support from

UNPROPER same as > IMPROPER

UNPROPPED > UNPROP

UNPROPS > UNPROP

UNPROVED adj not having been established as true, valid, or possible

UNPROVEN adj not established as true by evidence or demonstration

UNPROVIDE vb fail to supply requirements for

UNPROVOKE vb remove provocation from

UNPRUNED adj not pruned

UNPUCKER vb remove wrinkles from

UNPUCKERS > UNPUCKER

UNPULLED adj not pulled

UNPURE same as > IMPURE

UNPURELY > UNPURE

UNPURGED adj not purged

UNPURSE vb relax (lips) from pursed position

UNPURSED > UNPURSE

UNPURSES > UNPURSE

UNPURSING > UNPURSE

UNPURSUED adj not followed

UNPUZZLE vb figure out

UNPUZZLED > UNPUZZLE

UNPUZZLES > UNPUZZLE

UNQUAKING adj not quaking

UNQUALIFY vb disqualify

UNQUEEN vb depose from

the position of queen

UNQUEENED > UNQUEEN

UNQUEENLY adv not in a queenlike manner

UNQUEENS > UNQUEEN

UNQUELLED adj not quelled

UNQUIET adj anxious or uneasy ▷ n state of unrest ▷ vb disquiet

UNQUIETED > UNQUIET

UNQUIETER > UNQUIET

UNQUIETLY > UNQUIET

UNQUIETS > UNQUIET

UNQUOTE interj expression used to indicate the end of a quotation that was introduced with the word 'quote' ▷ vb close (a quotation), esp in printing

UNQUOTED > UNQUOTE

UNQUOTES > UNQUOTE

UNQUOTING > UNQUOTE

UNRACED adj not raced

UNRACKED adj not stretched

UNRAISED adj not raised

UNRAKE vb unearth through raking

UNRAKED adj not raked

UNRAKES > UNRAKE

UNRAKING > UNRAKE

UNRANKED adj not ranked

UNRATED adj not rated

UNRAVAGED adj not ravaged

UNRAVEL vb reduce (something knitted or woven) to separate strands

UNRAVELED > UNRAVEL

UNRAVELS > UNRAVEL

UNRAZED adj not razed

UNRAZORED adj unshaven

UNREACHED adj not reached

UNREAD adj (of a book or article) not yet read

UNREADIER > UNREADY

UNREADILY > UNREADY

UNREADY adj not ready or prepared

UNREAL adj (as if) existing only in the imagination

UNREALISE same as > UNREALIZE

UNREALISM n abstractionism

UNREALITY n quality or state of being unreal, fanciful, or impractical

UNREALIZE vb make unreal

UNREALLY > UNREAL

UNREAPED adj not reaped

UNREASON n irrationality or madness ▷ vb deprive of reason

UNREASONS > UNREASON

UNREAVE vb unwind

UNREAVED > UNREAVE

UNREAVES > UNREAVE

UNREAVING > UNREAVE

UNREBATED adj not refunded

UNREBUKED adj not rebuked

UNRECKED adj disregarded

UNRED same as > UNREAD

UNREDREST adj not redressed

UNREDUCED adj not reduced

UNREDY same as > UNREADY

UNREEL vb unwind from a reel

UNREELED > UNREEL

UNREELER n machine that unwinds something from a reel

UNREELERS > UNREELER

UNREELING > UNREEL

UNREELS > UNREEL

UNREEVE vb withdraw (a rope) from a block, thimble, etc

UNREEVED > UNREEVE

UNREEVES > UNREEVE

UNREEVING > UNREEVE

UNREFINED adj (of substances such as petroleum, ores, and sugar) not processed into a pure or usable form

UNREFUTED adj not refuted

UNREIN vb free from reins

UNREINED > UNREIN

UNREINING > UNREIN

UNREINS > UNREIN

UNRELATED adj not connected with each other

UNRELAXED adj not relaxed

UNREMOVED adj not removed

UNRENEWED adj not renewed

UNRENT adj not torn

UNRENTED adj not rented

UNREPAID adj not repaid

UNREPAIR less common word for > DISREPAIR

UNREPAIRS > UNREPAIR

UNRESERVE n candour

UNREST n rebellious state of discontent

UNRESTED adj not rested

UNRESTFUL adj restless

UNRESTING adj not resting

UNRESTS > UNREST

UNRETIRE vb resume work after retiring

UNRETIRED > UNRETIRE

UNRETIRES > UNRETIRE

UNREVISED adj not revised

UNREVOKED adj not revoked

UNRHYMED adj not rhymed

UNRIBBED adj not ribbed

UNRID adj unridden

UNRIDABLE adj not capable of being ridden

UNRIDDEN adj not or never ridden

UNRIDDLE vb solve or

puzzle out

UNRIDDLED > UNRIDDLE

UNRIDDLER > UNRIDDLE

UNRIDDLES > UNRIDDLE

UNRIFLED adj (of a firearm or its bore) not rifled

UNRIG vb strip (a vessel) of standing and running rigging

UNRIGGED > UNRIG

UNRIGGING > UNRIG

UNRIGHT n wrong

UNRIGHTS > UNRIGHT

UNRIGS > UNRIG

UNRIMED same as > UNRHYMED

UNRINGED adj not having or wearing a ring

UNRINSED adj not rinsed

UNRIP vb rip open

UNRIPE adj not fully matured

UNRIPELY > UNRIPE

UNRIPENED same as > UNRIPE

UNRIPER > UNRIPE

UNRIPEST > UNRIPE

UNRIPPED > UNRIP

UNRIPPING > UNRIP

UNRIPS > UNRIP

UNRISEN adj not risen

UNRIVALED adj (in US English) matchless or unrivalled

UNRIVEN adj not torn apart

UNRIVET vb remove rivets from

UNRIVETED > UNRIVET

UNRIVETS > UNRIVET

UNROASTED adj not roasted

UNROBE same as > DISROBE

UNROBED > UNROBE

UNROBES > UNROBE

UNROBING > UNROBE

UNROLL vb open out or unwind (something rolled or coiled) or (of something rolled or coiled) become opened out or unwound

UNROLLED > UNROLL

UNROLLING > UNROLL

UNROLLS > UNROLL

UNROOF vb remove the roof from

UNROOFED > UNROOF

UNROOFING > UNROOF

UNROOFS > UNROOF

UNROOST vb remove from a perch

UNROOSTED > UNROOST

UNROOSTS > UNROOST

UNROOT less common word for > UPROOT

UNROOTED > UNROOT

UNROOTING > UNROOT

UNROOTS > UNROOT

UNROPE vb release from a rope

UNROPED > UNROPE

UNROPES > UNROPE

UNROPING > UNROPE

UNROSINED adj not coated with rosin

UNROTTED adj not rotted

UNROTTEN adj not rotten

UNROUGED adj not coloured with rouge

UNROUGH adj not rough

UNROUND vb release (lips) from a rounded position

UNROUNDED adj articulated with the lips spread

UNROUNDS > UNROUND

UNROUSED adj not roused

UNROVE > UNREEVE

UNROVEN > UNREEVE

UNROYAL adj not royal

UNROYALLY > UNROYAL

UNRUBBED adj not rubbed

UNRUDE adj not rude

UNRUFFE same as > UNROUGH

UNRUFFLE vb calm

UNRUFFLED adj calm and unperturbed

UNRUFFLES > UNRUFFLE

UNRULE n lack of authority

UNRULED adj not ruled

UNRULES > UNRULE

UNRULIER > UNRULY

UNRULIEST > UNRULY

UNRULY adj difficult to control or organize

UNRUMPLED adj neat

UNRUSHED adj unhurried

UNRUSTED adj not rusted

UNS > UN

UNSADDLE vb remove the saddle from (a horse)

UNSADDLED > UNSADDLE

UNSADDLES > UNSADDLE

UNSAFE adj dangerous

UNSAFELY > UNSAFE

UNSAFER > UNSAFE

UNSAFEST > UNSAFE

UNSAFETY n lack of safety

UNSAID adj not said or expressed

UNSAILED adj not sailed

UNSAINED adj not blessed

UNSAINT vb remove status of being a saint from

UNSAINTED > UNSAINT

UNSAINTLY adj not saintly

UNSAINTS > UNSAINT

UNSALABLE adj not capable of being sold

UNSALABLY > UNSALABLE

UNSALTED adj not seasoned, preserved, or treated with salt

UNSALUTED adj not saluted

UNSAMPLED adj not sampled

UNSAPPED adj not undermined

UNSASHED adj not furnished with a sash

UNSATABLE adj not able to be sated; insatiable

UNSATED adj not sated

UNSATIATE adj insatiable

u

UNSATING adj not satisfying

UNSAVED adj not saved

UNSAVORY same as >UNSAVOURY

UNSAVOURY adj distasteful or objectionable

UNSAWED same as >UNSAWN

UNSAWN adj not cut with a saw

UNSAY vb retract or withdraw (something said or written)

UNSAYABLE adj that cannot be said

UNSAYING >UNSAY

UNSAYS >UNSAY

UNSCALE same as >DESCALE

UNSCALED >UNSCALE

UNSCALES >UNSCALE

UNSCALING >UNSCALE

UNSCANNED adj not scanned

UNSCARRED adj not scarred

UNSCARY adj not scary

UNSCATHED adj not harmed or injured

UNSCENTED adj not filled or impregnated with odour or fragrance

UNSCOURED adj not scoured

UNSCREW vb loosen (a screw or lid) by turning it

UNSCREWED >UNSCREW

UNSCREWS >UNSCREW

UNSCYTHED adj not cut with a scythe

UNSEAL vb remove or break the seal of

UNSEALED >UNSEAL

UNSEALING >UNSEAL

UNSEALS >UNSEAL

UNSEAM vb open or undo the seam of

UNSEAMED >UNSEAM

UNSEAMING >UNSEAM

UNSEAMS >UNSEAM

UNSEARED adj not seared

UNSEASON vb affect unfavourably

UNSEASONS >UNSEASON

UNSEAT vb throw or displace from a seat or saddle

UNSEATED >UNSEAT

UNSEATING >UNSEAT

UNSEATS >UNSEAT

UNSECRET adj not secret

UNSECULAR adj not secular

UNSECURED adj (of a loan, etc) secured only against general assets and not against a specific asset

UNSEDUCED adj not seduced

UNSEEABLE adj not able to be seen

UNSEEDED adj (of a player in a sport) not given a top player's position in the

opening rounds of a tournament

UNSEEING adj not noticing or looking at anything

UNSEEL vb undo seeling

UNSEELED >UNSEEL

UNSEELIE npl evil malevolent fairies ▷ adj of or belonging to the unseelie

UNSEELING >UNSEEL

UNSEELS >UNSEEL

UNSEEMING adj unseemly

UNSEEMLY adj not according to expected standards of behaviour ▷ adv in an unseemly manner

UNSEEN adj hidden or invisible ▷ adv without being seen ▷ n passage which is given to students for translation without them having seen it in advance

UNSEENS >UNSEEN

UNSEIZED adj not seized

UNSELDOM adv frequently

UNSELF vb remove self-centredness from ▷ n lack of self

UNSELFED >UNSELF

UNSELFING >UNSELF

UNSELFISH adj concerned about other people's wishes and needs rather than one's own

UNSELFS >UNSELF

UNSELL vb speak unfavourably and off-puttingly of (something or someone)

UNSELLING >UNSELL

UNSELLS >UNSELL

UNSELVES >UNSELF

UNSENSE vb remove sense from

UNSENSED >UNSENSE

UNSENSES >UNSENSE

UNSENSING >UNSENSE

UNSENT adj not sent

UNSERIOUS adj not serious

UNSERVED adj not served

UNSET adj not yet solidified or firm ▷ vb displace

UNSETS >UNSET

UNSETTING >UNSET

UNSETTLE vb change or become changed from a fixed or settled condition

UNSETTLED adj lacking order or stability

UNSETTLES >UNSETTLE

UNSEVERED adj not severed

UNSEW vb undo stitching of

UNSEWED >UNSEW

UNSEWING >UNSEW

UNSEWN >UNSEW

UNSEWS >UNSEW

UNSEX vb deprive (a person) of the attributes of his or her sex, esp to make a woman more callous

UNSEXED >UNSEX

UNSEXES >UNSEX

UNSEXING >UNSEX

UNSEXIST adj not sexist

UNSEXUAL adj not sexual

UNSEXY adj not sexually attractive

UNSHACKLE vb release from shackles

UNSHADED adj not shaded

UNSHADOW vb remove shadow from

UNSHADOWS >UNSHADOW

UNSHAKED same as >UNSHAKEN

UNSHAKEN adj (of faith or feelings) not having been weakened

UNSHALE vb expose

UNSHALED >UNSHALE

UNSHALES >UNSHALE

UNSHALING >UNSHALE

UNSHAMED same as >UNASHAMED

UNSHAPE vb make shapeless

UNSHAPED >UNSHAPE

UNSHAPELY adj not shapely

UNSHAPEN adj having no definite shape

UNSHAPES >UNSHAPE

UNSHAPING >UNSHAPE

UNSHARED adj not shared

UNSHARP adj not sharp

UNSHAVED adj not shaved

UNSHAVEN adj (of a man who does not have a beard) having stubble on his chin because he has not shaved recently

UNSHEATHE vb pull (a weapon) from a sheath

UNSHED adj not shed

UNSHELL vb remove from a shell

UNSHELLED >UNSHELL

UNSHELLS >UNSHELL

UNSHENT adj undamaged

UNSHEWN adj unshown

UNSHIFT vb release the shift key on a keyboard

UNSHIFTED >UNSHIFT

UNSHIFTS >UNSHIFT

UNSHIP vb be or cause to be unloaded, discharged, or disembarked from a ship

UNSHIPPED >UNSHIP

UNSHIPS >UNSHIP

UNSHIRTED adj not wearing a shirt

UNSHOCKED adj not shocked

UNSHOD adj not wearing shoes

UNSHOE vb remove shoes from

UNSHOED same as >UNSHOD

UNSHOEING >UNSHOE

UNSHOES >UNSHOE

UNSHOOT Shakespearean variant of >UNSHOUT

UNSHOOTED >UNSHOOT

UNSHOOTS >UNSHOOT

UNSHORN adj not cut

UNSHOT adj not shot

UNSHOUT vb revoke (an earlier statement) by shouting a contrary one

UNSHOUTED >UNSHOUT

UNSHOUTS >UNSHOUT

UNSHOWN adj not shown

UNSHOWY adj not showy

UNSHRIVED same as >UNSHRIVEN

UNSHRIVEN adj not shriven

UNSHROUD vb uncover

UNSHROUDS >UNSHROUD

UNSHRUBD adj not having shrubs

UNSHRUNK adj not shrunk

UNSHUNNED adj not shunned

UNSHUT vb open

UNSHUTS >UNSHUT

UNSHUTTER vb remove shutters from

UNSICKER adj unsettled

UNSICKLED adj not cut with a sickle

UNSIFTED adj not strained

UNSIGHING adj not lamented

UNSIGHT vb obstruct vision of

UNSIGHTED adj not sighted

UNSIGHTLY adj unpleasant to look at

UNSIGHTS >UNSIGHT

UNSIGNED adj (of a letter etc) anonymous

UNSILENT adj not silent

UNSIMILAR adj not similar

UNSINEW vb weaken

UNSINEWED >UNSINEW

UNSINEWS >UNSINEW

UNSINFUL adj without sin

UNSISTING adj Shakespearean term, possibly meaning insisting

UNSIZABLE adj of inadequate size

UNSIZED adj not made or sorted according to size

UNSKILFUL adj lacking dexterity or proficiency

UNSKILLED adj not having or requiring any special skill or training

UNSKIMMED adj not skimmed

UNSKINNED adj not skinned

UNSLAIN adj not killed

UNSLAKED adj not slaked

UNSLICED adj not sliced

UNSLICK adj not slick

UNSLING vb remove or release from a slung position

UNSLINGS >UNSLING

UNSLUICE vb let flow

UNSLUICED >UNSLUICE

UNSLUICES >UNSLUICE

UNSLUNG >UNSLING

UNSMART adj not smart

UNSMILING adj not wearing or assuming a smile

UNSMITTEN adj not smitten

UNSMOKED adj not smoked

UNSMOOTH vb roughen

UNSMOOTHS > UNSMOOTH

UNSMOTE same as **>** UNSMITTEN

UNSNAG vb remove snags from

UNSNAGGED > UNSNAG

UNSNAGS > UNSNAG

UNSNAP vb unfasten (the snap or catch) of (something)

UNSNAPPED > UNSNAP

UNSNAPS > UNSNAP

UNSNARL vb free from a snarl or tangle

UNSNARLED > UNSNARL

UNSNARLS > UNSNARL

UNSNECK vb unlatch

UNSNECKED > UNSNECK

UNSNECKS > UNSNECK

UNSNUFFED adj not snuffed

UNSOAKED adj not soaked

UNSOAPED adj not rubbed with soap

UNSOBER adj not sober

UNSOBERLY > UNSOBER

UNSOCIAL adj avoiding the company of other people

UNSOCKET vb remove from a socket

UNSOCKETS > UNSOCKET

UNSOD same as **>** UNSODDEN

UNSODDEN adj not soaked

UNSOFT adj hard

UNSOILED adj not soiled

UNSOLACED adj not comforted

UNSOLD adj not sold

UNSOLDER vb remove soldering from

UNSOLDERS > UNSOLDER

UNSOLEMN adj unceremonious

UNSOLID adj not solid

UNSOLIDLY > UNSOLID

UNSOLVED adj not having been solved or explained

UNSONCY same as **>** UNSONSY

UNSONSIE same as **>** UNSONSY

UNSONSY adj unfortunate

UNSOOTE adj not sweet

UNSOOTHED adj not soothed

UNSORTED adj not sorted

UNSOUGHT adj not sought after

UNSOUL vb cause to be soulless

UNSOULED > UNSOUL

UNSOULING > UNSOUL

UNSOULS > UNSOUL

UNSOUND adj unhealthy or unstable

UNSOUNDED adj not sounded

UNSOUNDER > UNSOUND

UNSOUNDLY > UNSOUND

UNSOURCED adj without a source

UNSOURED adj not soured

UNSOWED same as **>** UNSOWN

UNSOWN adj not sown

UNSPAR vb open

UNSPARED adj not spared

UNSPARING adj very generous

UNSPARRED > UNSPAR

UNSPARS > UNSPAR

UNSPEAK obsolete word for **>** UNSAY

UNSPEAKS > UNSPEAK

UNSPED adj not achieved

UNSPELL vb release from a spell

UNSPELLED > UNSPELL

UNSPELLS > UNSPELL

UNSPENT adj not spent

UNSPHERE vb remove from its, one's, etc, sphere or place

UNSPHERED > UNSPHERE

UNSPHERES > UNSPHERE

UNSPIDE same as **>** UNSPIED

UNSPIED adj unnoticed

UNSPILLED same as **>** UNSPILT

UNSPILT adj not spilt

UNSPLIT adj not split

UNSPOILED adj not damaged or harmed

UNSPOILT same as **>** UNSPOILED

UNSPOKE > UNSPEAK

UNSPOKEN adj not openly expressed

UNSPOOL vb unwind from spool

UNSPOOLED > UNSPOOL

UNSPOOLS > UNSPOOL

UNSPOTTED adj without spots or stains

UNSPRAYED adj not sprayed

UNSPRUNG adj without springs

UNSPUN adj not spun

UNSQUARED adj not made into a square shape

UNSTABLE adj lacking stability or firmness

UNSTABLER > UNSTABLE

UNSTABLY > UNSTABLE

UNSTACK vb remove from a stack

UNSTACKED > UNSTACK

UNSTACKS > UNSTACK

UNSTAID adj not staid

UNSTAINED adj not stained

UNSTALKED adj without a stalk

UNSTAMPED adj not stamped

UNSTARCH vb remove starch from

UNSTARRED adj not marked with a star

UNSTARRY adj not resembling or characteristic of a star from the entertainment world

UNSTATE vb deprive of state

UNSTATED adj not having been articulated or uttered

UNSTATES > UNSTATE

UNSTATING > UNSTATE

UNSTAYED adj unhindered

UNSTAYING adj nonstop

UNSTEADY adj not securely fixed **▷** vb make unsteady

UNSTEEL vb make (the heart, feelings, etc) more gentle or compassionate

UNSTEELED > UNSTEEL

UNSTEELS > UNSTEEL

UNSTEMMED adj without a stem

UNSTEP vb remove (a mast) from its step

UNSTEPPED > UNSTEP

UNSTEPS > UNSTEP

UNSTERILE adj not free from living, esp pathogenic, microorganisms

UNSTICK vb free or loosen (something stuck)

UNSTICKS > UNSTICK

UNSTIFLED adj not suppressed

UNSTILLED adj not reduced

UNSTINTED adj not stinted

UNSTIRRED adj not stirred

UNSTITCH vb remove stitching from

UNSTOCK vb remove stock from

UNSTOCKED adj without stock

UNSTOCKS > UNSTOCK

UNSTONED adj not stoned

UNSTOP vb remove the stop or stopper from

UNSTOPPED adj not obstructed or stopped up

UNSTOPPER vb unplug

UNSTOPS > UNSTOP

UNSTOW vb remove from storage

UNSTOWED > UNSTOW

UNSTOWING > UNSTOW

UNSTOWS > UNSTOW

UNSTRAP vb undo the straps fastening (something) in position

UNSTRAPS > UNSTRAP

UNSTRESS n weak syllable

UNSTRING vb remove the strings of

UNSTRINGS > UNSTRING

UNSTRIP vb strip

UNSTRIPED adj (esp of smooth muscle) not having stripes

UNSTRIPS > UNSTRIP

UNSTRUCK adj not struck

UNSTRUNG adj emotionally distressed

UNSTUCK adj freed from being stuck, glued, fastened, etc

UNSTUDIED adj natural or spontaneous

UNSTUFFED adj not stuffed

UNSTUFFY adj well-ventilated

UNSTUFT same as **>** UNSTUFFED

UNSTUNG adj not stung

UNSTYLISH adj unfashionable

UNSUBDUED adj not subdued

UNSUBJECT adj not subject

UNSUBTLE adj not subtle

UNSUBTLY > UNSUBTLE

UNSUCCESS n failure

UNSUCKED adj not sucked

UNSUIT vb make unsuitable

UNSUITED adj not appropriate for a particular task or situation

UNSUITING > UNSUIT

UNSUITS > UNSUIT

UNSULLIED adj (of a reputation, etc) not stained or tarnished

UNSUMMED adj not calculated

UNSUNG adj not acclaimed or honoured

UNSUNK adj not sunken

UNSUNNED adj not subjected to sunlight

UNSUNNY adj not sunny

UNSUPPLE adj rigid

UNSURE adj lacking assurance or self-confidence

UNSURED adj not assured

UNSURELY > UNSURE

UNSURER > UNSURE

UNSUREST > UNSURE

UNSUSPECT adj not open to suspicion

UNSWADDLE same as **>** UNSWATHE

UNSWATHE vb unwrap

UNSWATHED > UNSWATHE

UNSWATHES > UNSWATHE

UNSWAYED adj not swayed

UNSWEAR vb retract or revoke (a sworn oath)

UNSWEARS > UNSWEAR

UNSWEET adj not sweet

UNSWEPT adj not swept

UNSWOLLEN adj not swollen

UNSWORE > UNSWEAR

UNSWORN > UNSWEAR

UNTACK vb remove saddle and harness, etc, from

UNTACKED > UNTACK

UNTACKING > UNTACK

UNTACKLE vb remove tackle from

UNTACKLED > UNTACKLE

UNTACKLES > UNTACKLE

u

UNTACKS > UNTACK
UNTACTFUL *adj* not tactful
UNTAGGED *adj* without a label
UNTAILED *adj* tailless
UNTAINTED *adj* not tarnished, contaminated, or polluted
UNTAKEN *adj* not taken
UNTAMABLE *adj* (of an animal or person) not capable of being tamed, subdued, or made obedient
UNTAMABLY > UNTAMABLE
UNTAME *vb* undo the taming of
UNTAMED *adj* not brought under human control
UNTAMES > UNTAME
UNTAMING > UNTAME
UNTANGLE *vb* free from tangles or confusion
UNTANGLED > UNTANGLE
UNTANGLES > UNTANGLE
UNTANNED *adj* not tanned
UNTAPPED *adj* not yet used
UNTARRED *adj* not coated with tar
UNTASTED *adj* not tasted
UNTAUGHT *adj* without training or education
UNTAX *vb* stop taxing
UNTAXED *adj* not subject to taxation
UNTAXES > UNTAX
UNTAXING > UNTAX
UNTEACH *vb* cause to disbelieve (teaching)
UNTEACHES > UNTEACH
UNTEAM *vb* disband a team
UNTEAMED > UNTEAM
UNTEAMING > UNTEAM
UNTEAMS > UNTEAM
UNTEMPER *vb* soften
UNTEMPERS > UNTEMPER
UNTEMPTED *adj* not tempted
UNTENABLE *adj* (of a theory, idea, etc) incapable of being defended
UNTENABLY > UNTENABLE
UNTENANT *vb* remove (a tenant)
UNTENANTS > UNTENANT
UNTENDED *adj* not cared for or attended to
UNTENDER *adj* not tender
UNTENT *vb* remove from a tent
UNTENTED > UNTENT
UNTENTING > UNTENT
UNTENTS > UNTENT
UNTENTY *adj* inattentive
UNTENURED *adj* not having tenure
UNTESTED *adj* not having been tested or examined
UNTETHER *vb* untie
UNTETHERS > UNTETHER
UNTHANKED *adj* not thanked

UNTHATCH *vb* remove the thatch from
UNTHAW *same as* > THAW
UNTHAWED *adj* not thawed
UNTHAWING > UNTHAW
UNTHAWS > UNTHAW
UNTHINK *vb* reverse one's opinion about
UNTHINKS > UNTHINK
UNTHOUGHT > UNTHINK
UNTHREAD *vb* draw out the thread or threads from (a needle, etc)
UNTHREADS > UNTHREAD
UNTHRIFT *n* unthrifty person
UNTHRIFTS > UNTHRIFT
UNTHRIFTY *adj* careless with money
UNTHRONE *less common word for* > DETHRONE
UNTHRONED > UNTHRONE
UNTHRONES > UNTHRONE
UNTIDIED > UNTIDY
UNTIDIER > UNTIDY
UNTIDIES > UNTIDY
UNTIDIEST > UNTIDY
UNTIDILY > UNTIDY
UNTIDY *adj* messy and disordered ▷ *vb* make untidy
UNTIDYING > UNTIDY
UNTIE *vb* open or free (something that is tied)
UNTIED > UNTIE
UNTIEING > UNTIE
UNTIES > UNTIE
UNTIL *prep* in or throughout the period before
UNTILE *vb* strip tiles from
UNTILED > UNTILE
UNTILES > UNTILE
UNTILING > UNTILE
UNTILLED *adj* not tilled
UNTILTED *adj* not tilted
UNTIMED *adj* not timed
UNTIMELY *adj* occurring before the expected or normal time ▷ *adv* prematurely or inopportunely
UNTIMEOUS *same as* > UNTIMELY
UNTIN *vb* remove tin from
UNTINGED *adj* not tinged
UNTINNED *adj* not tinned
UNTINNING > UNTIN
UNTINS > UNTIN
UNTIPPED *adj* not tipped
UNTIRABLE *adj* not able to be fatigued
UNTIRED *adj* not tired
UNTIRING *adj* (of a person or their actions) continuing or persisting without declining in strength or vigour
UNTITLED *adj* without a title
UNTO *prep* to
UNTOILING *adj* not labouring

UNTOLD *adj* incapable of description
UNTOMB *vb* exhume
UNTOMBED > UNTOMB
UNTOMBING > UNTOMB
UNTOMBS > UNTOMB
UNTONED *adj* not toned
UNTORN *adj* not torn
UNTOUCHED *adj* not changed, moved, or affected
UNTOWARD *adj* causing misfortune or annoyance
UNTRACE *vb* remove traces from
UNTRACED *adj* not traced
UNTRACES > UNTRACE
UNTRACING > UNTRACE
UNTRACK *vb* remove from track
UNTRACKED *adj* not tracked
UNTRACKS > UNTRACK
UNTRADED *adj* not traded
UNTRAINED *adj* without formal or adequate training or education
UNTRAPPED *adj* not trapped
UNTREAD *vb* retrace (a course, path, etc)
UNTREADED > UNTREAD
UNTREADS > UNTREAD
UNTREATED *adj* (of an illness, etc) not having been dealt with
UNTRENDY *adj* not trendy
UNTRESSED *adj* not having a tress
UNTRIDE *same as* > UNTRIED
UNTRIED *adj* not yet used, done, or tested
UNTRIM *vb* deprive of elegance or adornment
UNTRIMMED > UNTRIM
UNTRIMS > UNTRIM
UNTROD > UNTREAD
UNTRODDEN > UNTREAD
UNTRUE *adj* incorrect or false
UNTRUER > UNTRUE
UNTRUEST > UNTRUE
UNTRUISM *n* something that is false
UNTRUISMS > UNTRUISM
UNTRULY > UNTRUE
UNTRUSS *vb* release from or as if from a truss
UNTRUSSED > UNTRUSS
UNTRUSSER *n* person who untrusses
UNTRUSSES > UNTRUSS
UNTRUST *n* mistrust
UNTRUSTS > UNTRUST
UNTRUSTY *adj* not trusty
UNTRUTH *n* statement that is not true, lie
UNTRUTHS > UNTRUTH
UNTUCK *vb* become or cause to become loose or not tucked in
UNTUCKED > UNTUCK
UNTUCKING > UNTUCK

UNTUCKS > UNTUCK
UNTUFTED *adj* not having tufts
UNTUMBLED *adj* not tumbled
UNTUNABLE *adj* not tuneful
UNTUNABLY > UNTUNABLE
UNTUNE *vb* make out of tune
UNTUNED > UNTUNE
UNTUNEFUL *adj* not tuneful
UNTUNES > UNTUNE
UNTUNING > UNTUNE
UNTURBID *adj* clear
UNTURF *vb* remove turf from
UNTURFED > UNTURF
UNTURFING > UNTURF
UNTURFS > UNTURF
UNTURN *vb* turn in a reverse direction
UNTURNED *adj* not turned
UNTURNING > UNTURN
UNTURNS > UNTURN
UNTUTORED *adj* without formal education
UNTWILLED *adj* not twilled
UNTWINE *vb* untwist, unravel, and separate
UNTWINED > UNTWINE
UNTWINES > UNTWINE
UNTWINING > UNTWINE
UNTWIST *vb* twist apart and loosen
UNTWISTED > UNTWIST
UNTWISTS > UNTWIST
UNTYING > UNTIE
UNTYINGS > UNTIE
UNTYPABLE *adj* incapable of being typed
UNTYPICAL *adj* not representative or characteristic of a particular type, person, etc
UNUNBIUM *n* chemical element
UNUNBIUMS > UNUNBIUM
UNUNITED *adj* separated
UNUNUNIUM *n* chemical element
UNURGED *adj* not urged
UNUSABLE *adj* not in good enough condition to be used
UNUSABLY > UNUSABLE
UNUSED *adj* not being or never having been used
UNUSEFUL *adj* useless
UNUSHERED *adj* not escorted
UNUSUAL *adj* uncommon or extraordinary
UNUSUALLY > UNUSUAL
UNUTTERED *adj* not uttered
UNVAIL *same as* > UNVEIL
UNVAILE *same as* > UNVEIL
UNVAILED > UNVAIL
UNVAILES > UNVAIL

u

UNVAILING > UNVAIL

UNVAILS > UNVAIL

UNVALUED adj not appreciated or valued

UNVARIED adj not varied

UNVARYING adj always staying the same

UNVEIL vb ceremonially remove the cover from (a new picture, plaque, etc)

UNVEILED > UNVEIL

UNVEILER n person who removes a veil

UNVEILERS > UNVEILER

UNVEILING n ceremony involving the removal of a veil covering a statue

UNVEILS > UNVEIL

UNVEINED adj without veins

UNVENTED adj not vented

UNVERSED adj not versed

UNVESTED adj not vested

UNVETTED adj not thoroughly examined

UNVEXED adj not annoyed

UNVEXT same as > UNVEXED

UNVIABLE adj not capable of succeeding, esp financially

UNVIEWED adj not viewed

UNVIRTUE n state of having no virtue

UNVIRTUES > UNVIRTUE

UNVISITED adj not visited

UNVISOR vb remove visor from

UNVISORED > UNVISOR

UNVISORS > UNVISOR

UNVITAL adj not vital

UNVIZARD same as > UNVISOR

UNVIZARDS > UNVIZARD

UNVOCAL adj not vocal

UNVOICE vb pronounce without vibration of the vocal cords

UNVOICED adj not expressed or spoken

UNVOICES > UNVOICE

UNVOICING > UNVOICE

UNVULGAR adj not vulgar

UNWAGED adj (of a person) not having a paid job

UNWAKED same as > UNWAKENED

UNWAKENED adj not roused from sleep

UNWALLED adj not surrounded by walls

UNWANING adj not waning

UNWANTED adj not wanted or welcome

UNWARDED adj not warded

UNWARE same as > UNAWARE

UNWARELY > UNWARE

UNWARES same as > UNAWARES

UNWARIE same as > UNWARY

UNWARIER > UNWARY

UNWARIEST > UNWARY

UNWARILY > UNWARY

UNWARLIKE adj not warlike

UNWARMED adj not warmed

UNWARNED adj not warned

UNWARPED adj not warped

UNWARY adj not careful or cautious and therefore likely to be harmed

UNWASHED adj not washed as in the great unwashed the masses

UNWASHEDS > UNWASHED

UNWASHEN same as > UNWASHED

UNWASTED adj not wasted

UNWASTING adj not wasting

UNWATCHED adj (of an automatic device, such as a beacon) not manned

UNWATER vb dry out

UNWATERED > UNWATER

UNWATERS > UNWATER

UNWATERY adj not watery

UNWAXED adj not treated with wax, esp of oranges or lemons, not sprayed with a protective coating of wax

UNWAYED adj having no routes

UNWEAL n ill or sorrow

UNWEALS > UNWEAL

UNWEANED adj not weaned

UNWEAPON vb disarm

UNWEAPONS > UNWEAPON

UNWEARIED adj not abating or tiring

UNWEARY adj not weary

UNWEAVE vb undo (weaving)

UNWEAVES > UNWEAVE

UNWEAVING > UNWEAVE

UNWEBBED adj not webbed

UNWED adj not wed

UNWEDDED adj not wedded

UNWEEDED adj not weeded

UNWEENED adj unknown

UNWEETING same as > UNWITTING

UNWEIGHED adj (of quantities purchased, etc) not measured for weight

UNWEIGHT vb remove weight from

UNWEIGHTS > UNWEIGHT

UNWELCOME adj unpleasant and unwanted

UNWELDED adj not welded

UNWELDY same as > UNWIELDY

UNWELL adj not healthy, ill

UNWEPT adj not wept for or lamented

UNWET adj not wet

UNWETTED same as > UNWET

UNWHIPPED adj not whipped

UNWHIPT same as > UNWHIPPED

UNWHITE adj not white

UNWIELDLY same as > UNWIELDY

UNWIELDY adj too heavy, large, or awkward to be easily handled

UNWIFELY adj not like a wife

UNWIGGED adj without a wig

UNWILFUL adj complaisant

UNWILL vb will the reversal of (something that has already occurred)

UNWILLED adj not intentional

UNWILLING adj reluctant

UNWILLS > UNWILL

UNWIND vb relax after a busy or tense time

UNWINDER > UNWIND

UNWINDERS > UNWIND

UNWINDING > UNWIND

UNWINDS > UNWIND

UNWINGED adj without wings

UNWINKING adj vigilant

UNWIPED adj not wiped

UNWIRE vb remove wiring from

UNWIRED > UNWIRE

UNWIRES > UNWIRE

UNWIRING > UNWIRE

UNWISDOM n imprudence

UNWISDOMS > UNWISDOM

UNWISE adj foolish

UNWISELY > UNWISE

UNWISER > UNWISE

UNWISEST > UNWISE

UNWISH vb retract or revoke (a wish)

UNWISHED adj not desired

UNWISHES > UNWISH

UNWISHFUL adj not wishful

UNWISHING > UNWISH

UNWIST adj unknown

UNWIT vb divest of wit

UNWITCH vb release from witchcraft

UNWITCHED > UNWITCH

UNWITCHES > UNWITCH

UNWITS > UNWIT

UNWITTED > UNWIT

UNWITTILY > UNWITTY

UNWITTING adj not intentional

UNWITTY adj not clever and amusing

UNWIVE vb remove a wife from

UNWIVED > UNWIVE

UNWIVES > UNWIVE

UNWIVING > UNWIVE

UNWOMAN vb remove womanly qualities from

UNWOMANED > UNWOMAN

UNWOMANLY adj not womanly

UNWOMANS > UNWOMAN

UNWON adj not won

UNWONT adj unaccustomed

UNWONTED adj out of the ordinary

UNWOODED adj not wooded

UNWOOED adj not wooed

UNWORDED adj not expressed in words

UNWORK vb destroy (work previously done)

UNWORKED adj not worked

UNWORKING > UNWORK

UNWORKS > UNWORK

UNWORLDLY adj not concerned with material values or pursuits

UNWORMED adj not rid of worms

UNWORN adj not having deteriorated through use or age

UNWORRIED adj not bothered or perturbed

UNWORTH n lack of value

UNWORTHS > UNWORTH

UNWORTHY adj not deserving or worthy

UNWOUND past tense and past participle of > UNWIND

UNWOUNDED adj not wounded

UNWOVE > UNWEAVE

UNWOVEN > UNWEAVE

UNWRAP vb remove the wrapping from (something)

UNWRAPPED > UNWRAP

UNWRAPS > UNWRAP

UNWREAKED adj unavenged

UNWREATHE vb untwist from a wreathed shape

UNWRINKLE vb remove wrinkles from

UNWRITE vb cancel (what has been written)

UNWRITES > UNWRITE

UNWRITING > UNWRITE

UNWRITTEN adj not printed or in writing

UNWROTE > UNWRITE

UNWROUGHT adj not worked

UNWRUNG adj not twisted

UNYEANED adj not having given birth

UNYOKE vb release (an animal, etc) from a yoke

UNYOKED > UNYOKE

UNYOKES > UNYOKE

UNYOKING > UNYOKE

UNYOUNG adj not young

UNZEALOUS adj unenthusiastic

UNZIP vb unfasten the zip of (a garment) or (of a zip or a garment with a zip) to become unfastened

UNZIPPED > UNZIP

UNZIPPING > UNZIP

UNZIPS > UNZIP

UNZONED adj not divided into zones

UP adv indicating movement to or position at a higher place ▷ adj of a high or higher position ▷ vb increase or raise

UPADAISY same as > UPSADAISY

u

UPAITHRIC *adj* without a roof

UPAS *n* large Javan tree with whitish bark and poisonous milky sap

UPASES >UPAS

UPBEAR *vb* sustain

UPBEARER >UPBEAR

UPBEARERS >UPBEAR

UPBEARING >UPBEAR

UPBEARS >UPBEAR

UPBEAT *adj* cheerful and optimistic ▷ *n* unaccented beat

UPBEATS >UPBEAT

UPBIND *vb* bind up

UPBINDING >UPBIND

UPBINDS >UPBIND

UPBLEW >UPBLOW

UPBLOW *vb* inflate

UPBLOWING >UPBLOW

UPBLOWN >UPBLOW

UPBLOWS >UPBLOW

UPBOIL *vb* boil up

UPBOILED >UPBOIL

UPBOILING >UPBOIL

UPBOILS >UPBOIL

UPBORE >UPBEAR

UPBORNE *adj* held up

UPBOUND *adj* travelling upwards

UPBOUNDEN *same as* >UPBOUND

UPBOW *n* stroke of the bow from its tip to its nut on a stringed instrument

UPBOWS >UPBOW

UPBRAID *vb* scold or reproach

UPBRAIDED >UPBRAID

UPBRAIDER >UPBRAID

UPBRAIDS >UPBRAID

UPBRAST *same as* >UPBURST

UPBRAY *vb* shame

UPBRAYED >UPBRAY

UPBRAYING >UPBRAY

UPBRAYS >UPBRAY

UPBREAK *vb* escape upwards

UPBREAKS >UPBREAK

UPBRING *vb* rear

UPBRINGS >UPBRING

UPBROKE >UPBREAK

UPBROKEN >UPBREAK

UPBROUGHT >UPBRING

UPBUILD *vb* build up

UPBUILDER >UPBUILD

UPBUILDS >UPBUILD

UPBUILT >UPBUILD

UPBURNING *adj* burning upwards

UPBURST *vb* burst upwards

UPBURSTS >UPBURST

UPBY *same as* >UPBYE

UPBYE *adv* yonder

UPCAST *n* material cast or thrown up ▷ *adj* directed or thrown upwards ▷ *vb* throw or cast up

UPCASTING >UPCAST

UPCASTS >UPCAST

UPCATCH *vb* catch up

UPCATCHES >UPCATCH

UPCAUGHT >UPCATCH

UPCHEER *vb* cheer up

UPCHEERED >UPCHEER

UPCHEERS >UPCHEER

UPCHUCK *vb* vomit

UPCHUCKED >UPCHUCK

UPCHUCKS >UPCHUCK

UPCLIMB *vb* ascend

UPCLIMBED >UPCLIMB

UPCLIMBS >UPCLIMB

UPCLOSE *vb* close up

UPCLOSED >UPCLOSE

UPCLOSES >UPCLOSE

UPCLOSING >UPCLOSE

UPCOAST *adv* up the coast

UPCOIL *vb* make into a coil

UPCOILED >UPCOIL

UPCOILING >UPCOIL

UPCOILS >UPCOIL

UPCOME *vb* come up

UPCOMES >UPCOME

UPCOMING *adj* coming soon

UPCOUNTRY *adj* of or from the interior of a country ▷ *adv* towards or in the interior of a country ▷ *n* interior part of a region or country

UPCOURT *adv* up basketball court

UPCURL *vb* curl up

UPCURLED >UPCURL

UPCURLING >UPCURL

UPCURLS >UPCURL

UPCURVE *vb* curve upwards

UPCURVED >UPCURVE

UPCURVES >UPCURVE

UPCURVING >UPCURVE

UPDART *vb* dart upwards

UPDARTED >UPDART

UPDARTING >UPDART

UPDARTS >UPDART

UPDATE *vb* bring up to date ▷ *n* act of updating or something that is updated

UPDATED >UPDATE

UPDATER >UPDATE

UPDATERS >UPDATE

UPDATES >UPDATE

UPDATING >UPDATE

UPDIVE *vb* leap upwards

UPDIVED >UPDIVE

UPDIVES >UPDIVE

UPDIVING >UPDIVE

UPDO *n* type of hairstyle

UPDOS >UPDO

UPDOVE >UPDIVE

UPDRAFT *n* upwards air current

UPDRAFTS >UPDRAFT

UPDRAG *vb* drag up

UPDRAGGED >UPDRAG

UPDRAGS >UPDRAG

UPDRAUGHT *n* upward movement of air or other gas

UPDRAW *vb* draw up

UPDRAWING >UPDRAW

UPDRAWN >UPDRAW

UPDRAWS >UPDRAW

UPDREW >UPDRAW

UPDRIED >UPDRY

UPDRIES >UPDRY

UPDRY *vb* dry up

UPDRYING >UPDRY

UPEND *vb* turn or set (something) on its end

UPENDED >UPEND

UPENDING >UPEND

UPENDS >UPEND

UPFIELD *adj* in sport, away from the defending team's goal

UPFILL *vb* fill up

UPFILLED >UPFILL

UPFILLING >UPFILL

UPFILLS >UPFILL

UPFLING *vb* throw upwards

UPFLINGS >UPFLING

UPFLOW *vb* flow upwards

UPFLOWED >UPFLOW

UPFLOWING >UPFLOW

UPFLOWS >UPFLOW

UPFLUNG >UPFLING

UPFOLD *vb* fold up

UPFOLDED >UPFOLD

UPFOLDING >UPFOLD

UPFOLDS >UPFOLD

UPFOLLOW *vb* follow

UPFOLLOWS >UPFOLLOW

UPFRONT *adj* open and frank ▷ *adv* (of money) paid out at the beginning of a business arrangement

UPFURL *vb* roll up

UPFURLED >UPFURL

UPFURLING >UPFURL

UPFURLS >UPFURL

UPGANG *n* climb

UPGANGS >UPGANG

UPGATHER *vb* draw together

UPGATHERS >UPGATHER

UPGAZE *vb* gaze upwards

UPGAZED >UPGAZE

UPGAZES >UPGAZE

UPGAZING >UPGAZE

UPGIRD *vb* belt up

UPGIRDED >UPGIRD

UPGIRDING >UPGIRD

UPGIRDS >UPGIRD

UPGIRT >UPGIRD

UPGO *vb* ascend

UPGOES >UPGO

UPGOING >UPGO

UPGOINGS >UPGO

UPGONE >UPGO

UPGRADE *vb* promote (a person or job) to a higher rank

UPGRADED >UPGRADE

UPGRADER >UPGRADE

UPGRADERS >UPGRADE

UPGRADES >UPGRADE

UPGRADING >UPGRADE

UPGREW >UPGROW

UPGROW *vb* grow up

UPGROWING >UPGROW

UPGROWN >UPGROW

UPGROWS >UPGROW

UPGROWTH *n* process of developing or growing upwards

UPGROWTHS >UPGROWTH

UPGUSH *vb* flow upwards

UPGUSHED >UPGUSH

UPGUSHES >UPGUSH

UPGUSHING >UPGUSH

UPHAND *adj* lifted by hand

UPHANG *vb* hang up

UPHANGING >UPHANG

UPHANGS >UPHANG

UPHAUD *Scots variant of* >UPHOLD

UPHAUDING >UPHAUD

UPHAUDS >UPHAUD

UPHEAP *vb* computing term

UPHEAPED >UPHEAP

UPHEAPING >UPHEAP

UPHEAPS >UPHEAP

UPHEAVAL *n* strong, sudden, or violent disturbance

UPHEAVALS >UPHEAVAL

UPHEAVE *vb* heave or rise upwards

UPHEAVED >UPHEAVE

UPHEAVER >UPHEAVE

UPHEAVERS >UPHEAVE

UPHEAVES >UPHEAVE

UPHEAVING >UPHEAVE

UPHELD >UPHOLD

UPHILD *archaic past form of* >UPHOLD

UPHILL *adj* sloping or leading upwards ▷ *adv* up a slope ▷ *n* difficulty

UPHILLS >UPHILL

UPHOARD *vb* hoard up

UPHOARDED >UPHOARD

UPHOARDS >UPHOARD

UPHOIST *vb* raise

UPHOISTED >UPHOIST

UPHOISTS >UPHOIST

UPHOLD *vb* maintain or defend against opposition

UPHOLDER >UPHOLD

UPHOLDERS >UPHOLD

UPHOLDING >UPHOLD

UPHOLDS >UPHOLD

UPHOLSTER *vb* fit (a chair or sofa) with padding, springs, and covering

UPHOORD *vb* heap up

UPHOORDED >UPHOORD

UPHOORDS >UPHOORD

UPHOVE >UPHEAVE

UPHROE *variant spelling of* >EUPHROE

UPHROES >UPHROE

UPHUDDEN >UPHAUD

UPHUNG >UPHANG

UPHURL *vb* throw upwards

UPHURLED >UPHURL

UPHURLING >UPHURL

UPHURLS >UPHURL

UPJET *vb* stream upwards

UPJETS >UPJET

UPJETTED >UPJET

UPJETTING >UPJET

UPKEEP *n* act, process, or cost of keeping something in good repair

UPKEEPS >UPKEEP

UPKNIT *vb* bind

UPKNITS >UPKNIT

UPKNITTED >UPKNIT

UPLAID > UPLAY
UPLAND adj of or in an area of high or relatively high ground ▷ n area of high or relatively high ground
UPLANDER n person hailing from the uplands
UPLANDERS > UPLANDER
UPLANDISH > UPLAND
UPLANDS > UPLAND
UPLAY vb stash
UPLAYING > UPLAY
UPLAYS > UPLAY
UPLEAD vb lead upwards
UPLEADING > UPLEAD
UPLEADS > UPLEAD
UPLEAN vb lean on something
UPLEANED > UPLEAN
UPLEANING > UPLEAN
UPLEANS > UPLEAN
UPLEANT > UPLEAN
UPLEAP vb jump upwards
UPLEAPED > UPLEAP
UPLEAPING > UPLEAP
UPLEAPS > UPLEAP
UPLEAPT > UPLEAP
UPLED > UPLEAD
UPLIFT vb raise or lift up ▷ n act or process of improving moral, social, or cultural conditions ▷ adj (of a bra) designed to lift and support the breasts
UPLIFTED > UPLIFT
UPLIFTER > UPLIFT
UPLIFTERS > UPLIFT
UPLIFTING adj acting to raise moral, spiritual, cultural, etc, levels
UPLIFTS > UPLIFT
UPLIGHT n lamp or wall light designed or positioned to cast its light upwards ▷ vb light in an upward direction
UPLIGHTED > UPLIGHT
UPLIGHTER n lamp or wall light designed or positioned to cast its light upwards
UPLIGHTS > UPLIGHT
UPLINK n transmitter on the ground that sends signals up to a communications satellite ▷ vb send (data) to a communications satellite
UPLINKED > UPLINK
UPLINKING > UPLINK
UPLINKS > UPLINK
UPLIT > UPLIGHT
UPLOAD vb transfer (data or a program) from one's own computer into the memory of another computer
UPLOADED > UPLOAD
UPLOADING > UPLOAD
UPLOADS > UPLOAD
UPLOCK vb lock up
UPLOCKED > UPLOCK
UPLOCKING > UPLOCK
UPLOCKS > UPLOCK
UPLOOK vb look up

UPLOOKED > UPLOOK
UPLOOKING > UPLOOK
UPLOOKS > UPLOOK
UPLYING adj raised
UPMAKE vb make up
UPMAKER > UPMAKE
UPMAKERS > UPMAKE
UPMAKES > UPMAKE
UPMAKING > UPMAKE
UPMAKINGS > UPMAKE
UPMANSHIP n one-upmanship
UPMARKET adj expensive and of superior quality ▷ vb make something upmarket
UPMARKETS > UPMARKET
UPMOST another word for > UPPERMOST
UPO prep upon
UPON prep on
UPPED > UP
UPPER adj higher or highest in physical position, wealth, rank, or status ▷ n part of a shoe above the sole
UPPERCASE adj capitalized ▷ vb capitalize or print in capitals
UPPERCUT n short swinging upward punch delivered to the chin ▷ vb hit (an opponent) with an uppercut
UPPERCUTS > UPPERCUT
UPPERMOST adj highest in position, power, or importance ▷ adv in or into the highest place or position
UPPERPART n highest part
UPPERS > UPPER
UPPILE vb pile up
UPPILED > UPPILE
UPPILES > UPPILE
UPPILING > UPPILE
UPPING > UP
UPPINGS > UP
UPPISH adj snobbish, arrogant, or presumptuous
UPPISHLY > UPPISH
UPPITY adj snobbish, arrogant, or presumptuous
UPPROP vb support
UPPROPPED > UPPROP
UPPROPS > UPPROP
UPRAISE vb lift up
UPRAISED > UPRAISE
UPRAISER > UPRAISE
UPRAISERS > UPRAISE
UPRAISES > UPRAISE
UPRAISING > UPRAISE
UPRAN > UPRUN
UPRATE vb raise the value, rate, or size of, upgrade
UPRATED > UPRATE
UPRATES > UPRATE
UPRATING > UPRATE
UPREACH vb reach up
UPREACHED > UPREACH
UPREACHES > UPREACH
UPREAR vb lift up
UPREARED > UPREAR
UPREARING > UPREAR

UPREARS > UPREAR
UPREST n uprising
UPRESTS > UPREST
UPRIGHT adj vertical or erect ▷ adv vertically or in an erect position ▷ n vertical support, such as a post ▷ vb make upright
UPRIGHTED > UPRIGHT
UPRIGHTLY > UPRIGHT
UPRIGHTS > UPRIGHT
UPRISAL > UPRISE
UPRISALS > UPRISE
UPRISE vb rise up
UPRISEN > UPRISE
UPRISER > UPRISE
UPRISERS > UPRISE
UPRISES > UPRISE
UPRISING n rebellion or revolt
UPRISINGS > UPRISING
UPRIST same as > UPREST
UPRISTS > UPRIST
UPRIVER adv towards or near the source of a river ▷ n area located upstream
UPRIVERS > UPRIVER
UPROAR n disturbance characterized by loud noise and confusion ▷ vb cause an uproar
UPROARED > UPROAR
UPROARING > UPROAR
UPROARS > UPROAR
UPROLL vb roll up
UPROLLED > UPROLL
UPROLLING > UPROLL
UPROLLS > UPROLL
UPROOT vb pull up by or as if by the roots
UPROOTAL > UPROOT
UPROOTALS > UPROOT
UPROOTED > UPROOT
UPROOTER > UPROOT
UPROOTERS > UPROOT
UPROOTING > UPROOT
UPROOTS > UPROOT
UPROSE > UPRISE
UPROUSE vb rouse or stir up
UPROUSED > UPROUSE
UPROUSES > UPROUSE
UPROUSING > UPROUSE
UPRUN vb run up
UPRUNNING > UPRUN
UPRUNS > UPRUN
UPRUSH n upward rush, as of consciousness ▷ vb rush upwards
UPRUSHED > UPRUSH
UPRUSHES > UPRUSH
UPRUSHING > UPRUSH
UPRYST same as > UPREST
UPS > UP
UPSADAISY interj expression of reassurance often uttered when someone stumbles or is lifted up
UPSCALE adj of or for the upper end of an economic or social scale ▷ vb upgrade
UPSCALED > UPSCALE
UPSCALES > UPSCALE

UPSCALING > UPSCALE
UPSEE n drunken revel
UPSEES > UPSEE
UPSELL vb persuade a customer to buy a more expensive or additional item
UPSELLING > UPSELL
UPSELLS > UPSELL
UPSEND vb send up
UPSENDING > UPSEND
UPSENDS > UPSEND
UPSENT > UPSEND
UPSET adj emotionally or physically disturbed or distressed ▷ vb tip over ▷ n unexpected defeat or reversal
UPSETS > UPSET
UPSETTER > UPSET
UPSETTERS > UPSET
UPSETTING > UPSET
UPSEY same as > UPSEE
UPSEYS > UPSEY
UPSHIFT vb move up (a gear)
UPSHIFTED > UPSHIFT
UPSHIFTS > UPSHIFT
UPSHOOT vb shoot upwards
UPSHOOTS > UPSHOOT
UPSHOT n final result or conclusion
UPSHOTS > UPSHOT
UPSIDE n upper surface or part
UPSIDES > UPSIDE
UPSIES > UPSY
UPSILON n 20th letter in the Greek alphabet
UPSILONS > UPSILON
UPSITTING n sitting up of a woman after childbirth
UPSIZE vb increase in size
UPSIZED > UPSIZE
UPSIZES > UPSIZE
UPSIZING > UPSIZE
UPSKILL vb improve the aptitude for work of (a person) by additional training
UPSKILLED > UPSKILL
UPSKILLS > UPSKILL
UPSLOPE adv up a or the slope
UPSOAR vb soar up
UPSOARED > UPSOAR
UPSOARING > UPSOAR
UPSOARS > UPSOAR
UPSOLD > UPSELL
UPSPAKE > UPSPEAK
UPSPEAK vb speak with rising intonation
UPSPEAKS > UPSPEAK
UPSPEAR vb grow upwards in a spear-like manner
UPSPEARED > UPSPEAR
UPSPEARS > UPSPEAR
UPSPOKE > UPSPEAK
UPSPOKEN > UPSPEAK
UPSPRANG > UPSPRING
UPSPRING vb spring up or come into existence ▷ n leap forwards or upwards

u

UPSPRINGS > UPSPRING
UPSPRUNG > UPSPRING
UPSTAGE *adj* at the back half of the stage ▷ *vb* draw attention to oneself from (someone else) ▷ *adv* on, at, or to the rear of the stage ▷ *n* back half of the stage
UPSTAGED > UPSTAGE
UPSTAGER > UPSTAGE
UPSTAGERS > UPSTAGE
UPSTAGES > UPSTAGE
UPSTAGING > UPSTAGE
UPSTAIR *same as*
> UPSTAIRS
UPSTAIRS *adv* to or on an upper floor of a building ▷ *n* upper floor ▷ *adj* situated on an upper floor
UPSTAND *vb* rise
UPSTANDS > UPSTAND
UPSTARE *vb* stare upwards
UPSTARED > UPSTARE
UPSTARES > UPSTARE
UPSTARING > UPSTARE
UPSTART *n* person who has risen suddenly to a position of power and behaves arrogantly ▷ *vb* start up, as in surprise, etc
UPSTARTED > UPSTART
UPSTARTS > UPSTART
UPSTATE *adv* towards, in, from, or relating to the outlying or northern sections of a state, esp New York State ▷ *n* outlying, esp northern, sections of a state
UPSTATER > UPSTATE
UPSTATERS > UPSTATE
UPSTATES > UPSTATE
UPSTAY *vb* support
UPSTAYED > UPSTAY
UPSTAYING > UPSTAY
UPSTAYS > UPSTAY
UPSTEP *n* type of vocal intonation
UPSTEPPED > UPSTEP
UPSTEPS > UPSTEP
UPSTIR *vb* stir up ▷ *n* commotion
UPSTIRRED > UPSTIR
UPSTIRS > UPSTIR
UPSTOOD > UPSTAND
UPSTREAM *adj* in or towards the higher part of a stream ▷ *vb* stream upwards
UPSTREAMS > UPSTREAM
UPSTROKE *n* upward stroke or movement, as of a pen or brush
UPSTROKES > UPSTROKE
UPSURGE *n* rapid rise or swell ▷ *vb* surge up
UPSURGED > UPSURGE
UPSURGES > UPSURGE
UPSURGING > UPSURGE
UPSWAY *vb* swing in the air
UPSWAYED > UPSWAY
UPSWAYING > UPSWAY
UPSWAYS > UPSWAY

UPSWEEP *n* curve or sweep upwards ▷ *vb* sweep, curve, or brush or be swept, curved, or brushed upwards
UPSWEEPS > UPSWEEP
UPSWELL *vb* swell up or cause to swell up
UPSWELLED > UPSWELL
UPSWELLS > UPSWELL
UPSWEPT > UPSWEEP
UPSWING *n* recovery period in the trade cycle ▷ *vb* swing or move up
UPSWINGS > UPSWING
UPSWOLLEN > UPSWELL
UPSWUNG > UPSWING
UPSY *same as* > UPSEE
UPTA *same as* > UPTER
UPTAK *same as* > UPTAKE
UPTAKE *n* numbers taking up something such as an offer or the act of taking it up ▷ *vb* take up
UPTAKEN > UPTAKE
UPTAKES > UPTAKE
UPTAKING > UPTAKE
UPTAKS > UPTAK
UPTALK *n* style of speech in which every sentence ends with a rising tone, as if the speaker is always asking a question ▷ *vb* talk in this manner
UPTALKED > UPTALK
UPTALKING > UPTALK
UPTALKS > UPTALK
UPTEAR *vb* tear up
UPTEARING > UPTEAR
UPTEARS > UPTEAR
UPTEMPO *adj* fast ▷ *n* uptempo piece
UPTEMPOS > UPTEMPO
UPTER *adj* of poor quality
UPTHREW > UPTHROW
UPTHROW *n* upward movement of rocks on one side of a fault plane relative to rocks on the other side ▷ *vb* throw upwards
UPTHROWN > UPTHROW
UPTHROWS > UPTHROW
UPTHRUST *n* upward push
UPTHRUSTS > UPTHRUST
UPTHUNDER *vb* make a noise like thunder
UPTICK *n* rise or increase
UPTICKS > UPTICK
UPTIE *vb* tie up
UPTIED > UPTIE
UPTIES > UPTIE
UPTIGHT *adj* nervously tense, irritable, or angry
UPTIGHTER > UPTIGHT
UPTILT *vb* tilt up
UPTILTED > UPTILT
UPTILTING > UPTILT
UPTILTS > UPTILT
UPTIME *n* time during which a machine, such as a computer, actually operates
UPTIMES > UPTIME

UPTITLING *n* practice of conferring grandiose job titles to employees performing relatively menial jobs
UPTOOK > UPTAKE
UPTORE > UPTEAR
UPTORN > UPTEAR
UPTOSS *vb* throw upwards
UPTOSSED > UPTOSS
UPTOSSES > UPTOSS
UPTOSSING > UPTOSS
UPTOWN *adv* towards, in, or relating to some part of a town that is away from the centre ▷ *n* such a part of town, esp a residential part
UPTOWNER > UPTOWN
UPTOWNERS > UPTOWN
UPTOWNS > UPTOWN
UPTRAIN *vb* train up
UPTRAINED > UPTRAIN
UPTRAINS > UPTRAIN
UPTREND *n* upward trend
UPTRENDS > UPTREND
UPTRILLED *adj* trilled high
UPTURN *n* upward trend or improvement ▷ *vb* turn or cause to turn over or upside down
UPTURNED > UPTURN
UPTURNING > UPTURN
UPTURNS > UPTURN
UPTYING > UPTIE
UPVALUE *vb* raise the value of
UPVALUED > UPVALUE
UPVALUES > UPVALUE
UPVALUING > UPVALUE
UPWAFT *vb* waft upwards
UPWAFTED > UPWAFT
UPWAFTING > UPWAFT
UPWAFTS > UPWAFT
UPWARD *same as*
> UPWARDS
UPWARDLY > UPWARD
UPWARDS *adv* from a lower to a higher place, level, condition, etc
UPWELL *vb* well up
UPWELLED > UPWELL
UPWELLING > UPWELL
UPWELLS > UPWELL
UPWENT > UPGO
UPWHIRL *vb* spin upwards
UPWHIRLED > UPWHIRL
UPWHIRLS > UPWHIRL
UPWIND *adv* into or against the wind ▷ *adj* going against the wind ▷ *vb* wind up
UPWINDING > UPWIND
UPWINDS > UPWIND
UPWOUND > UPWIND
UPWRAP *vb* wrap up
UPWRAPS > UPWRAP
UPWROUGHT *adj* wrought up
UR *interj* hesitant utterance used to fill gaps in talking
URACHI > URACHUS
URACHUS *n* cord of tissue connected to the bladder

URACHUSES > URACHUS
URACIL *n* pyrimidine present in all living cells, usually in a combined form, as in RNA
URACILS > URACIL
URAEI > URAEUS
URAEMIA *n* accumulation of waste products, normally excreted in the urine, in the blood: causes severe headaches, vomiting, etc
URAEMIAS > URAEMIA
URAEMIC > URAEMIA
URAEUS *n* sacred serpent represented on the headdresses of ancient Egyptian kings and gods
URAEUSES > URAEUS
URALI *n* type of plant
URALIS > URALI
URALITE *n* amphibole mineral, similar to hornblende, that replaces pyroxene in some igneous and metamorphic rocks
URALITES > URALITE
URALITIC > URALITE
URALITISE *same as*
> URALITIZE
URALITIZE *vb* turn into uralite
URANIA *n* uranium dioxide
URANIAN *adj* heavenly
URANIAS > URANIA
URANIC *adj* of or containing uranium, esp in a high valence state
URANIDE *n* any element having an atomic number greater than that of protactinium
URANIDES > URANIDE
URANIN *n* type of alkaline substance
URANINITE *n* blackish heavy radioactive mineral consisting of uranium oxide in cubic crystalline form together with radium, lead, helium, etc: occurs in coarse granite
URANINS > URANIN
URANISCI > URANISCUS
URANISCUS *n* palate
URANISM *n* homosexuality
URANISMS > URANISM
URANITE *n* any of various minerals containing uranium, esp torbernite or autunite
URANITES > URANITE
URANITIC > URANITE
URANIUM *n* radioactive silvery-white metallic element, used chiefly as a source of nuclear energy
URANIUMS > URANIUM
URANOLOGY *n* study of the universe and planets
URANOUS *adj* of or containing uranium, esp in a low valence state
URANYL *n* of, consisting of,

or containing the divalent ion UO, $^{2+}$ or the group -UO,

URANYLIC > URANYL
URANYLS > URANYL
URAO n type of mineral
URAOS > URAO
URARE same as > URALI
URARES > URARE
URARI same as > URALI
URARIS > URARI
URASE same as > UREASE
URASES > URASE
URATE n any salt or ester of uric acid
URATES > URATE
URATIC > URATE
URB n urban area
URBAN adj of or living in a city or town
URBANE adj characterized by courtesy, elegance, and sophistication
URBANELY > URBANE
URBANER > URBANE
URBANEST > URBANE
URBANISE same as > URBANIZE
URBANISED > URBANISE
URBANISES > URBANISE
URBANISM n character of city life
URBANISMS > URBANISM
URBANIST n person who studies towns and cities
URBANISTS > URBANIST
URBANITE n resident of an urban community
URBANITES > URBANITE
URBANITY n quality of being urbane
URBANIZE vb make (a rural area) more industrialized and urban
URBANIZED > URBANIZE
URBANIZES > URBANIZE
URBIA n urban area
URBIAS > URBIA
URBS > URB
URCEOLATE adj shaped like an urn or pitcher
URCEOLI > URCEOLUS
URCEOLUS n organ of a plant
URCHIN n mischievous child
URCHINS > URCHIN
URD n type of plant with edible seeds
URDE adj (in heraldry) having points
URDEE > URDE
URDS > URD
URDY n heraldic line pattern
URE same as > AUROCHS
UREA n white soluble crystalline compound found in urine
UREAL > UREA
UREAS > UREA
UREASE n enzyme occurring in many plants, esp fungi, that converts urea to ammonium carbonate

UREASES > UREASE
UREDIA > UREDIUM
UREDIAL > UREDIUM
UREDINE > UREDO
UREDINES > UREDO
UREDINIA > UREDINIUM
UREDINIAL > UREDINIUM
UREDINIUM same as > UREDIUM
UREDINOUS > UREDO
UREDIUM n spore-producing body of some rust fungi in which uredospores are formed
UREDO less common name for > URTICARIA
UREDOS > UREDO
UREDOSORI npl spore-producing bodies of some rust fungi in which uredospores are formed; uredia
UREIC > UREA
UREIDE n any of a class of organic compounds derived from urea by replacing one or more of its hydrogen atoms by organic groups
UREIDES > UREIDE
UREMIA same as > URAEMIA
UREMIAS > UREMIA
UREMIC > UREMIA
URENA n plant genus
URENAS > URENA
URENT adj burning
UREOTELIC adj excreting urea
URES > URE
URESES > URESIS
URESIS n urination
URETER n tube that conveys urine from the kidney to the bladder
URETERAL > URETER
URETERIC > URETER
URETERS > URETER
URETHAN same as > URETHANE
URETHANE n short for the synthetic material polyurethane
URETHANES > URETHANE
URETHANS > URETHAN
URETHRA n canal that carries urine from the bladder out of the body
URETHRAE > URETHRA
URETHRAL > URETHRA
URETHRAS > URETHRA
URETIC adj of or relating to the urine
URGE n strong impulse, inner drive, or yearning ▷ vb plead with or press (a person to do something)
URGED > URGE
URGENCE > URGENT
URGENCES > URGENT
URGENCIES > URGENT
URGENCY > URGENT
URGENT adj requiring speedy action or attention

URGENTLY > URGENT
URGER > URGE
URGERS > URGE
URGES > URGE
URGING > URGE
URGINGLY > URGE
URGINGS > URGE
URIAL n type of sheep
URIALS > URIAL
URIC adj of or derived from urine
URICASE n type of enzyme
URICASES > URICASE
URIDINE n nucleoside present in all living cells in a combined form, esp in RNA
URIDINES > URIDINE
URIDYLIC as in uridylic acid nucleotide consisting of uracil, ribose, and a phosphate group. It is a constituent of RNA
URINAL n sanitary fitting used by men for urination
URINALS > URINAL
URINANT adj having the head downwards
URINARIES > URINARY
URINARY adj of urine or the organs that secrete and pass urine ▷ n reservoir for urine
URINATE vb discharge urine
URINATED > URINATE
URINATES > URINATE
URINATING > URINATE
URINATION > URINATE
URINATIVE > URINATE
URINATOR > URINATE
URINATORS > URINATE
URINE n pale yellow fluid excreted by the kidneys to the bladder and passed as waste from the body ▷ vb urinate
URINED > URINE
URINEMIA same as > UREMIA
URINEMIAS > URINEMIA
URINEMIC > URINEMIA
URINES > URINE
URINING > URINE
URINOLOGY same as > UROLOGY
URINOSE same as > URINOUS
URINOUS adj of, resembling, or containing urine
URITE n part of the abdomen
URITES > URITE
URMAN n forest
URMANS > URMAN
URN n vase used as a container for the ashes of the dead ▷ vb put in an urn
URNAL > URN
URNED > URN
URNFIELD n cemetery full of individual cremation urns ▷ adj (of a number of Bronze Age cultures) characterized by cremation

in urns, which began in E Europe about the second millennium BC and by the seventh century BC had covered almost all of mainland Europe
URNFIELDS > URNFIELD
URNFUL n capacity of an urn
URNFULS > URNFUL
URNING n homosexual man
URNINGS > URNING
URNLIKE > URN
URNS > URN
UROBILIN n brownish pigment found in faeces and sometimes in urine
UROBILINS > UROBILIN
UROBOROS same as > OUROBOROS
UROCHORD n notochord of a larval tunicate, typically confined to the tail region
UROCHORDS > UROCHORD
UROCHROME n yellowish pigment that colours urine
URODELAN > URODELE
URODELANS > URODELAN
URODELE n amphibian of the order which includes the salamanders and newts
URODELES > URODELE
URODELOUS > URODELE
UROGENOUS adj producing or derived from urine
UROGRAPHY n branch of radiology concerned with X-ray examination of the kidney and associated structures
UROKINASE n biochemical catalyst
UROLAGNIA n sexual arousal involving urination
UROLITH n calculus in the urinary tract
UROLITHIC > UROLITH
UROLITHS > UROLITH
UROLOGIC > UROLOGY
UROLOGIES > UROLOGY
UROLOGIST > UROLOGY
UROLOGY n branch of medicine concerned with the urinary system and its diseases
UROMERE n part of the abdomen
UROMERES > UROMERE
UROPOD n paired appendage that arises from the last segment of the body in lobsters and related crustaceans and forms part of the tail fan
UROPODAL > UROPOD
UROPODOUS > UROPOD
UROPODS > UROPOD
UROPYGIA > UROPYGIUM
UROPYGIAL > UROPYGIUM
UROPYGIUM n hindmost part of a bird's body, from which the tail feathers grow

u

UROSCOPIC > UROSCOPY
UROSCOPY n examination of the urine
UROSES > UROSIS
UROSIS n urinary disease
UROSOME n abdomen of arthropods
UROSOMES > UROSOME
UROSTEGE n part of a serpent's tail
UROSTEGES > UROSTEGE
UROSTOMY n type of urinary surgery
UROSTYLE n bony rod forming the last segment of the vertebral column of frogs, toads, and related amphibians
UROSTYLES > UROSTYLE
URP dialect word for > VOMIT
URPED > URP
URPING > URP
URPS > URP
URSA n she-bear
URSAE > URSA
URSID n meteor
URSIDS > URSID
URSIFORM adj bear-shaped or bearlike in form
URSINE adj of or like a bear
URSON n type of porcupine
URSONS > URSON
URTEXT n earliest form of a text as established by linguistic scholars as a basis for variants in later texts still in existence
URTEXTS > URTEXT
URTICA n type of nettle
URTICANT n something that causes itchiness and irritation
URTICANTS > URTICANT
URTICARIA n skin condition characterized by the formation of itchy red or whitish raised patches, usually caused by an allergy
URTICAS > URTICA
URTICATE adj characterized by the presence of weals ▷ vb sting
URTICATED > URTICATE
URTICATES > URTICATE
URUBU n type of bird
URUBUS > URUBU
URUS another name for the > AUROCHS
URUSES > URUS
URUSHIOL n poisonous pale yellow liquid occurring in poison ivy and the lacquer tree
URUSHIOLS > URUSHIOL
URVA n Indian mongoose
URVAS > URVA
US pron refers to the speaker or writer and another person or other people
USABILITY > USABLE
USABLE adj able to be used
USABLY > USABLE

USAGE n regular or constant use
USAGER n person who has the use of something in trust
USAGERS > USAGER
USAGES > USAGE
USANCE n period of time permitted by commercial usage for the redemption of foreign bills of exchange
USANCES > USANCE
USAUNCE same as > USANCE
USAUNCES > USAUNCE
USE vb put into service or action ▷ n using or being used
USEABLE same as > USABLE
USEABLY > USABLE
USED adj second-hand
USEFUL adj able to be used advantageously or for several different purposes ▷ n odd-jobman or general factotum
USEFULLY > USEFUL
USEFULS > USEFUL
USELESS adj having no practical use
USELESSLY > USELESS
USER n continued exercise, use, or enjoyment of a right, esp in property
USERNAME n name given by computer user to gain access
USERNAMES > USERNAME
USERS > USER
USES > USE
USHER n official who shows people to their seats, as in a church ▷ vb conduct or escort
USHERED > USHER
USHERESS n female usher
USHERETTE n female assistant in a cinema who shows people to their seats
USHERING > USHER
USHERINGS > USHER
USHERS > USHER
USHERSHIP > USHER
USING > USE
USNEA n type of lichen
USNEAS > USNEA
USQUABAE n whisky
USQUABAES > USQUABAE
USQUE n whisky
USQUEBAE same as > USQUABAE
USQUEBAES > USQUEBAE
USQUES > USQUE
USTION n burning
USTIONS > USTION
USTULATE adj charred
USUAL adj of the most normal, frequent, or regular type ▷ n ordinary or commonplace events
USUALLY adv most often, in most cases
USUALNESS > USUAL
USUALS > USUAL

USUCAPION n method of acquiring property
USUCAPT > USUCAPION
USUCAPTED > USUCAPION
USUCAPTS > USUCAPION
USUFRUCT n right to use and derive profit from a piece of property belonging to another, provided the property itself remains undiminished and uninjured in any way
USUFRUCTS > USUFRUCT
USURE vb be involved in usury
USURED > USURE
USURER n person who lends funds at an exorbitant rate of interest
USURERS > USURER
USURES > USURE
USURESS n female usurer
USURESSES > USURESS
USURIES > USURY
USURING > USURE
USURIOUS > USURY
USUROUS > USURY
USURP vb seize (a position or power) without authority
USURPED > USURP
USURPEDLY > USURP
USURPER > USURP
USURPERS > USURP
USURPING > USURP
USURPINGS > USURP
USURPS > USURP
USURY n practice of lending money at an extremely high rate of interest
USWARD adv towards us
USWARDS same as > USWARD
UT n syllable used in the fixed system of solmization for the note C
UTA n side-blotched lizard
UTAS n eighth day of a festival
UTASES > UTAS
UTE same as > UTILITY
UTENSIL n tool or container for practical use
UTENSILS > UTENSIL
UTERI > UTERUS
UTERINE adj of or affecting the womb
UTERITIS n inflammation of the womb
UTEROTOMY n surgery on the uterus
UTERUS n womb
UTERUSES > UTERUS
UTES > UTE
UTILE obsolete word for > USEFUL
UTILIDOR n above-ground insulated casing for pipes carrying water, sewerage and electricity in permafrost regions
UTILIDORS > UTILIDOR
UTILISE same as > UTILIZE

UTILISED > UTILISE
UTILISER > UTILISE
UTILISERS > UTILISE
UTILISES > UTILISE
UTILISING > UTILISE
UTILITIES > UTILITY
UTILITY n usefulness ▷ adj designed for use rather than beauty
UTILIZE vb make practical use of
UTILIZED > UTILIZE
UTILIZER > UTILIZE
UTILIZERS > UTILIZE
UTILIZES > UTILIZE
UTILIZING > UTILIZE
UTIS n uproar
UTISES > UTIS
UTMOST n the greatest possible degree or amount ▷ adj of the greatest possible degree or amount
UTMOSTS > UTMOST
UTOPIA n real or imaginary society, place, state, etc, considered to be perfect or ideal
UTOPIAN adj of or relating to a perfect or ideal existence ▷ n idealistic social reformer
UTOPIANS > UTOPIAN
UTOPIAS > UTOPIA
UTOPIAST > UTOPIA
UTOPIASTS > UTOPIA
UTOPISM > UTOPIA
UTOPISMS > UTOPIA
UTOPIST > UTOPIA
UTOPISTIC > UTOPIA
UTOPISTS > UTOPIA
UTRICLE n larger of the two parts of the membranous labyrinth of the internal ear
UTRICLES > UTRICLE
UTRICULAR > UTRICLE
UTRICULI > UTRICULUS
UTRICULUS same as > UTRICLE
UTS > UT
UTTER vb express (something) in sounds or words ▷ adj total or absolute
UTTERABLE > UTTER
UTTERANCE n something uttered
UTTERED > UTTER
UTTERER > UTTER
UTTERERS > UTTER
UTTEREST > UTTER
UTTERING > UTTER
UTTERINGS > UTTER
UTTERLESS > UTTER
UTTERLY adv extremely
UTTERMOST same as > UTMOST
UTTERNESS > UTTER
UTTERS > UTTER
UTU n reward
UTUS > UTU
UVA n grape or fruit resembling this
UVAE > UVA

UVAROVITE *n* emerald-green garnet found in chromium deposits: consists of calcium chromium silicate

UVAS > UVA

UVEA *n* part of the eyeball consisting of the iris, ciliary body, and choroid

UVEAL > UVEA

UVEAS > UVEA

UVEITIC > UVEITIS

UVEITIS *n* inflammation of the uvea

UVEITISES > UVEITIS

UVEOUS > UVEA

UVULA *n* small fleshy part of the soft palate that hangs in the back of the throat

UVULAE > UVULA

UVULAR *adj* of or relating to the uvula ▷ *n* uvular consonant

UVULARLY > UVULAR

UVULARS > UVULAR

UVULAS > UVULA

UVULITIS *n* inflammation of the uvula

UXORIAL *adj* of or relating to a wife

UXORIALLY > UXORIAL

UXORICIDE *n* act of killing one's wife

UXORIOUS *adj* excessively fond of or dependent on one's wife

u

Vv

VAC vb clean with a vacuum cleaner
VACANCE n vacant period
VACANCES > VACANCE
VACANCIES > VACANCY
VACANCY n unfilled job
VACANT adj (of a toilet, room, etc) unoccupied
VACANTLY > VACANT
VACATABLE > VACATE
VACATE vb cause (something) to be empty by leaving
VACATED > VACATE
VACATES > VACATE
VACATING > VACATE
VACATION n time when universities and law courts are closed ▷ vb take a vacation
VACATIONS > VACATION
VACATUR n annulment
VACATURS > VACATUR
VACCINA same as > VACCINIA
VACCINAL adj of or relating to vaccine or vaccination
VACCINAS > VACCINA
VACCINATE vb inject with a vaccine
VACCINE n substance designed to cause a mild form of a disease to make a person immune to the disease itself
VACCINEE n person who has been vaccinated
VACCINEES > VACCINEE
VACCINES > VACCINE
VACCINIA technical name for > COWPOX
VACCINIAL > VACCINIA
VACCINIAS > VACCINIA
VACCINIUM n shrub genus
VACHERIN n soft cheese made from cows' milk
VACHERINS > VACHERIN
VACILLANT adj indecisive
VACILLATE vb keep changing one's mind or opinions
VACKED > VAC
VACKING > VAC
VACS > VAC
VACUA > VACUUM
VACUATE vb empty
VACUATED > VACUATE
VACUATES > VACUATE
VACUATING > VACUATE
VACUATION > VACUATE

VACUIST n person believing in the existence of vacuums in nature
VACUISTS > VACUIST
VACUITIES > VACUITY
VACUITY n absence of intelligent thought or ideas
VACUOLAR > VACUOLE
VACUOLATE > VACUOLE
VACUOLE n fluid-filled cavity in the cytoplasm of a cell
VACUOLES > VACUOLE
VACUOUS adj not expressing intelligent thought
VACUOUSLY > VACUOUS
VACUUM n empty space from which all or most air or gas has been removed ▷ vb clean with a vacuum cleaner
VACUUMED > VACUUM
VACUUMING > VACUUM
VACUUMS > VACUUM
VADE vb fade
VADED > VADE
VADES > VADE
VADING > VADE
VADOSE adj of or derived from water occurring above the water table
VAE same as > VOE
VAES > VAE
VAG n vagrant
VAGABOND n person with no fixed home, esp a beggar
VAGABONDS > VAGABOND
VAGAL adj of, relating to, or affecting the vagus nerve
VAGALLY > VAGAL
VAGARIES > VAGARY
VAGARIOUS adj characterized or caused by vagaries
VAGARISH > VAGARY
VAGARY n unpredictable change
VAGGED > VAG
VAGGING > VAG
VAGI > VAGUS
VAGILE adj able to move freely
VAGILITY > VAGILE
VAGINA n (in female mammals) passage from the womb to the external genitals
VAGINAE > VAGINA
VAGINAL > VAGINA
VAGINALLY > VAGINA

VAGINANT adj sheathing
VAGINAS > VAGINA
VAGINATE adj (esp of plant parts) having a sheath
VAGINATED > VAGINATE
VAGINITIS n inflammation of the vagina
VAGINOSES > VAGINOSIS
VAGINOSIS n bacterial vaginal infection
VAGINULA n little sheath
VAGINULAE > VAGINULA
VAGINULE same as > VAGINULA
VAGINULES > VAGINULE
VAGITUS n new-born baby's cry
VAGITUSES > VAGITUS
VAGOTOMY n surgical division of the vagus nerve
VAGOTONIA n pathological overactivity of the vagus nerve
VAGOTONIC > VAGOTONIA
VAGRANCY n state or condition of being a vagrant
VAGRANT n person with no settled home ▷ adj wandering
VAGRANTLY > VAGRANT
VAGRANTS > VAGRANT
VAGROM same as > VAGRANT
VAGS > VAG
VAGUE adj not clearly explained ▷ vb wander
VAGUED > VAGUE
VAGUELY > VAGUE
VAGUENESS > VAGUE
VAGUER > VAGUE
VAGUES > VAGUE
VAGUEST > VAGUE
VAGUING > VAGUE
VAGUS n tenth cranial nerve, which supplies the heart, lungs, and viscera
VAHANA n vehicle
VAHANAS > VAHANA
VAHINE n Polynesian woman
VAHINES > VAHINE
VAIL vb lower (something, such as a weapon), esp as a sign of deference or submission
VAILED > VAIL
VAILING > VAIL
VAILS > VAIL

VAIN adj excessively proud, esp of one's appearance
VAINER > VAIN
VAINESSE n vainness
VAINESSES > VAINESSE
VAINEST > VAIN
VAINGLORY n boastfulness or vanity
VAINLY > VAIN
VAINNESS > VAIN
VAIR n fur, probably Russian squirrel, used to trim robes in the Middle Ages
VAIRE adj of Russian squirrel fur
VAIRIER > VAIR
VAIRIEST > VAIR
VAIRS > VAIR
VAIRY > VAIR
VAIVODE n European ruler
VAIVODES > VAIVODE
VAKAS n Armenian priestly garment
VAKASES > VAKAS
VAKEEL n ambassador
VAKEELS > VAKEEL
VAKIL same as > VAKEEL
VAKILS > VAKIL
VALANCE n piece of drapery round the edge of a bed ▷ vb provide with a valance
VALANCED > VALANCE
VALANCES > VALANCE
VALANCING > VALANCE
VALE n valley ▷ sentence substitute farewell
VALENCE same as > VALENCY
VALENCES > VALENCE
VALENCIA n type of fabric
VALENCIAS > VALENCIA
VALENCIES > VALENCY
VALENCY n power of an atom to make molecular bonds
VALENTINE n (person to whom one sends) a romantic card on Saint Valentine's Day, 14th February
VALERATE n salt of valeric acid
VALERATES > VALERATE
VALERIAN n herb used as a sedative
VALERIANS > VALERIAN
VALERIC adj of, relating to, or derived from valerian
VALES > VALE

VALET n man's personal male servant ▷ vb act as a valet (for)

VALETA n old-time dance in triple time

VALETAS > VALETA

VALETE n farewell

VALETED > VALET

VALETES > VALET

VALETING > VALET

VALETINGS > VALET

VALETS > VALET

VALGOID > VALGUS

VALGOUS same as > VALGUS

VALGUS adj denoting a deformity of a limb ▷ n abnormal position of a limb

VALGUSES > VALGUS

VALI n Turkish civil governor

VALIANCE > VALIANT

VALIANCES > VALIANT

VALIANCY > VALIANT

VALIANT adj brave or courageous ▷ n brave person

VALIANTLY > VALIANT

VALIANTS > VALIANT

VALID adj soundly reasoned

VALIDATE vb make valid

VALIDATED > VALIDATE

VALIDATES > VALIDATE

VALIDER > VALID

VALIDEST > VALID

VALIDITY > VALID

VALIDLY > VALID

VALIDNESS > VALID

VALINE n essential amino acid

VALINES > VALINE

VALIS > VALI

VALISE n small suitcase

VALISES > VALISE

VALIUM as in valium picnic refers to a day on the New York Stock Exchange when business is slow

VALKYR variant of > VALKYRIE

VALKYRIE n (in Norse mythology) beatiful maiden who collects dead heroes on the battlefield to take to Valhalla

VALKYRIES > VALKYRIES

VALKYRS > VALKYR

VALLAR adj pertaining to a rampart

VALLARY > VALLAR

VALLATE adj surrounded with a wall

VALLATION n act or process of building fortifications

VALLECULA n any of various natural depressions or crevices

VALLEY n low area between hills, often with a river running through it

VALLEYED adj having a valley

VALLEYS > VALLEY

VALLHUND as in Swedish vallhund breed of dog

VALLHUNDS > VALLHUND

VALLONIA same as > VALONIA

VALLONIAS > VALLONIA

VALLUM n Roman rampart or earthwork

VALLUMS > VALLUM

VALONEA same as > VALONIA

VALONEAS > VALONEA

VALONIA n acorn cups and unripe acorns of a particular oak

VALONIAS > VALONIA

VALOR same as > VALOUR

VALORISE same as > VALORIZE

VALORISED > VALORISE

VALORISES > VALORISE

VALORIZE vb fix and maintain an artificial price for (a commodity) by governmental action

VALORIZED > VALORIZE

VALORIZES > VALORIZE

VALOROUS > VALOUR

VALORS > VALOR

VALOUR n bravery ▷ n courageous person

VALOURS > VALOUR

VALPROATE n medicament derived from valproic acid

VALPROIC as in valproic acid synthetic crystalline compound, used as an anticonvulsive

VALSE another word for > WALTZ

VALSED > VALSE

VALSES > VALSE

VALSING > VALSE

VALUABLE adj having great worth ▷ n valuable article of personal property, esp jewellery

VALUABLES > VALUABLE

VALUABLY > VALUABLE

VALUATE vb value or evaluate

VALUATED > VALUATE

VALUATES > VALUATE

VALUATING > VALUATE

VALUATION n assessment of worth

VALUATOR n person who estimates the value of objects, paintings, etc

VALUATORS > VALUATOR

VALUE n importance, usefulness ▷ vb assess the worth or desirability of

VALUED > VALUE

VALUELESS adj having or possessing no value

VALUER > VALUE

VALUERS > VALUE

VALUES > VALUE

VALUING > VALUE

VALUTA n value of one currency in terms of its exchange rate with

another

VALUTAS > VALUTA

VALVAL same as > VALVULAR

VALVAR same as > VALVULAR

VALVASSOR same as > VAVASOR

VALVATE adj furnished with a valve or valves

VALVE n device to control the movement of fluid through a pipe ▷ vb provide with a valve

VALVED > VALVE

VALVELESS > VALVE

VALVELET same as > VALVULE

VALVELETS > VALVELET

VALVELIKE > VALVE

VALVES > VALVE

VALVING > VALVE

VALVULA same as > VALVULE

VALVULAE > VALVULA

VALVULAR adj of or having valves

VALVULE n small valve or a part resembling one

VALVULES > VALVULE

VAMBRACE n piece of armour used to protect the arm

VAMBRACED > VAMBRACE

VAMBRACES > VAMBRACE

VAMOOSE vb leave a place hurriedly

VAMOOSED > VAMOSE

VAMOOSES > VAMOSE

VAMOOSING > VAMOSE

VAMOSE same as > VAMOOSE

VAMOSED > VAMOSE

VAMOSES > VAMOSE

VAMOSING > VAMOSE

VAMP n sexually attractive woman who seduces men ▷ vb (of a woman) to seduce (a man)

VAMPED > VAMP

VAMPER > VAMP

VAMPERS > VAMP

VAMPIER > VAMP

VAMPIEST > VAMP

VAMPING > VAMP

VAMPINGS > VAMP

VAMPIRE n (in folklore) corpse that rises at night to drink the blood of the living ▷ vb assail

VAMPIRED > VAMPIRE

VAMPIRES > VAMPIRE

VAMPIRIC > VAMPIRE

VAMPIRING > VAMPIRE

VAMPIRISE same as > VAMPIRIZE

VAMPIRISH > VAMPIRE

VAMPIRISM n belief in the existence of vampires

VAMPIRIZE vb suck blood from

VAMPISH > VAMP

VAMPISHLY > VAMP

VAMPLATE n piece of metal

mounted on a lance to protect the hand

VAMPLATES > VAMPLATE

VAMPS > VAMP

VAMPY > VAMP

VAN n motor vehicle for transporting goods ▷ vb send in a van

VANADATE n any salt or ester of a vanadic acid

VANADATES > VANADATE

VANADIATE same as > VANADATE

VANADIC adj of or containing vanadium, esp in a trivalent or pentavalent state

VANADIUM n metallic element, used in steel

VANADIUMS > VANADIUM

VANADOUS adj of or containing vanadium

VANASPATI n hydrogenated vegetable fat commonly used in India as a substitute for butter

VANDA n type of orchid

VANDAL n person who deliberately damages property

VANDALIC > VANDAL

VANDALISE same as > VANDALIZE

VANDALISH > VANDAL

VANDALISM n wanton or deliberate destruction caused by a vandal or an instance of such destruction

VANDALIZE vb cause damage to (personal or public property) deliberately

VANDALS > VANDAL

VANDAS > VANDA

VANDYKE n short pointed beard ▷ vb cut with deep zigzag indentations

VANDYKED > VANDYKE

VANDYKES > VANDYKE

VANDYKING > VANDYKE

VANE n flat blade on a rotary device such as a weathercock or propeller

VANED > VANE

VANELESS > VANE

VANES > VANE

VANESSA n type of butterfly

VANESSAS > VANESSA

VANESSID n type of butterfly ▷ adj relating to this butterfly

VANESSIDS > VANESSID

VANG n type of rope or tackle on a sailing ship

VANGS > VANG

VANGUARD n unit of soldiers leading an army

VANGUARDS > VANGUARD

VANILLA n seed pod of a tropical climbing orchid, used for flavouring ▷ adj flavoured with vanilla

VANILLAS > VANILLA

VANILLIC adj of, resembling, containing, or derived from vanilla or vanillin

VANILLIN n white crystalline aldehyde found in vanilla

VANILLINS > VANILLIN

VANISH vb disappear suddenly or mysteriously ▷ n second and weaker of the two vowels in a falling diphthong

VANISHED > VANISH

VANISHER > VANISH

VANISHERS > VANISH

VANISHES > VANISH

VANISHING > VANISH

VANITAS n type of Dutch painting

VANITASES > VANITAS

VANITIED adj with vanity units or mirrors

VANITIES > VANITY

VANITORY n vanity unit

VANITY n (display of) excessive pride

VANLOAD n amount van will carry

VANLOADS > VANLOAD

VANMAN n man in control of a van

VANMEN > VANMAN

VANNED > VAN

VANNER n horse used to pull delivery vehicles

VANNERS > VANNER

VANNING > VAN

VANNINGS > VAN

VANPOOL n van-sharing group

VANPOOLS > VANPOOL

VANQUISH vb defeat (someone) utterly

VANS > VAN

VANT archaic word for > VANGUARD

VANTAGE n state, position, or opportunity offering advantage ▷ vb benefit

VANTAGED > VANTAGE

VANTAGES > VANTAGE

VANTAGING > VANTAGE

VANTBRACE n armour for the arm

VANTBRASS > VAMBRACE

VANTS > VANT

VANWARD adv in or towards the front

VAPID adj lacking character, dull

VAPIDER > VAPID

VAPIDEST > VAPID

VAPIDITY > VAPID

VAPIDLY > VAPID

VAPIDNESS > VAPID

VAPOR same as > VAPOUR

VAPORABLE > VAPOR

VAPORED > VAPOR

VAPORER > VAPOR

VAPORERS > VAPOR

VAPORETTI > VAPORETTO

VAPORETTO n steam-powered passenger boat, as used on the canals in Venice

VAPORIFIC adj producing, causing, or tending to produce vapour

VAPORING > VAPOR

VAPORINGS > VAPOR

VAPORISE same as > VAPORIZE

VAPORISED > VAPORISE

VAPORISER same as > VAPORIZER

VAPORISES > VAPORISE

VAPORISH > VAPOR

VAPORIZE vb change into a vapour

VAPORIZED > VAPORIZE

VAPORIZER n substance that vaporizes or a device that causes vaporization

VAPORIZES > VAPORIZE

VAPORLESS > VAPOR

VAPORLIKE > VAPOR

VAPOROUS same as > VAPORIFIC

VAPORS > VAPOR

VAPORWARE n new software that has not yet been produced

VAPORY > VAPOR

VAPOUR n moisture suspended in air as steam or mist ▷ vb evaporate

VAPOURED > VAPOUR

VAPOURER > VAPOUR

VAPOURERS > VAPOUR

VAPOURING > VAPOUR

VAPOURISH > VAPOUR

VAPOURS > VAPOUR

VAPOURY > VAPOUR

VAPULATE vb strike

VAPULATED > VAPULATE

VAPULATES > VAPULATE

VAQUERO n cattlehand

VAQUEROS > VAQUERO

VAR n unit of reactive power of an alternating current

VARA n unit of length used in Spain, Portugal, and South America

VARACTOR n semiconductor diode that acts as a voltage-dependent capacitor

VARACTORS > VARACTOR

VARAN n type of lizard

VARANS > VARAN

VARAS > VARA

VARDIES > VARDY

VARDY n verdict

VARE n rod

VAREC n ash obtained from kelp

VARECH same as > VAREC

VARECHS > VARECH

VARECS > VAREC

VARES > VARE

VAREUSE n type of coat

VAREUSES > VAREUSE

VARGUENO n type of Spanish cabinet

VARGUENOS > VARGUENO

VARIA n collection or miscellany, esp of literary works

VARIABLE adj not always the same, changeable ▷ n something that is subject to variation

VARIABLES > VARIABLE

VARIABLY > VARIABLE

VARIANCE n act of varying

VARIANCES > VARIANCE

VARIANT adj differing from a standard or type ▷ n something that differs from a standard or type

VARIANTS > VARIANT

VARIAS > VARIA

VARIATE n random variable or a numerical value taken by it ▷ vb vary

VARIATED > VARIATE

VARIATES > VARIATE

VARIATING > VARIATE

VARIATION n something presented in a slightly different form

VARIATIVE > VARIATE

VARICEAL adj relating to a varix

VARICELLA n chickenpox

VARICES > VARIX

VARICOID same as > CIRSOID

VARICOSE adj of or resulting from varicose veins

VARICOSED same as > VARICOSE

VARICOSES > VARICOSIS

VARICOSIS n any condition characterized by distension of the veins

VARIED > VARY

VARIEDLY > VARY

VARIEGATE vb alter the appearance of, esp by adding different colours

VARIER n person who varies

VARIERS > VARIER

VARIES > VARY

VARIETAL adj of or forming a variety, esp a biological variety ▷ n wine labelled with the name of the grape from which it is pressed

VARIETALS > VARIETAL

VARIETIES > VARIETY

VARIETY n state of being diverse or various

VARIFOCAL adj gradated to permit any length of vision between near and distant ▷ n lens of this type

VARIFORM adj varying in form or shape

VARIOLA n smallpox

VARIOLAR > VARIOLA

VARIOLAS > VARIOLA

VARIOLATE vb inoculate with the smallpox virus ▷ adj marked or pitted with or as if with the scars of smallpox

VARIOLE n any of the rounded masses that make up the rock variolite

VARIOLES > VARIOLE

VARIOLITE n type of basic igneous rock

VARIOLOID adj resembling smallpox ▷ n mild form of smallpox occurring in persons with partial immunity

VARIOLOUS adj relating to or resembling smallpox

VARIORUM adj containing notes by various scholars or critics or various versions of the text ▷ n edition or text of this kind

VARIORUMS > VARIORUM

VARIOUS adj of several kinds

VARIOUSLY > VARIOUS

VARISCITE n green secondary mineral

VARISIZED adj of different sizes

VARISTOR n type of semiconductor device

VARISTORS > VARISTOR

VARITYPE vb produce (copy) on a Varityper ▷ n copy produced on a Varityper

VARITYPED > VARITYPE

VARITYPES > VARITYPE

VARIX n tortuous dilated vein

VARLET n menial servant

VARLETESS n female varlet

VARLETRY n the rabble

VARLETS > VARLET

VARLETTO same as > VARLET

VARLETTOS > VARLETTO

VARMENT same as > VARMINT

VARMENTS > VARMENT

VARMINT n irritating or obnoxious person or animal

VARMINTS > VARMINT

VARNA n any of the four Hindu castes

VARNAS > VARNA

VARNISH n solution of oil and resin, put on a surface to make it hard and glossy ▷ vb apply varnish to

VARNISHED > VARNISH

VARNISHER > VARNISH

VARNISHES > VARNISH

VARNISHY > VARNISH

VAROOM same as > VROOM

VAROOMED same as > VAROOM

VAROOMING same as > VAROOM

VAROOMS same as > VAROOM

VARROA n small parasite

VARROAS > VARROA

VARS > VAR

VARSAL adj universal

VARSITIES > VARSITY

VARSITY n university
VARTABED n position in the Armenian church
VARTABEDS >VARTABED
VARUS adj denoting a deformity of a limb ▷ n abnormal position of a limb
VARUSES >VARUS
VARVE n typically thin band of sediment deposited annually in glacial lakes
VARVED adj having layers of sedimentary deposit
VARVEL n piece of falconry equipment
VARVELLED adj having varvels
VARVELS >VARVEL
VARVES >VARVE
VARY vb change
VARYING >VARY
VARYINGLY >VARY
VARYINGS >VARY
VAS n vessel or tube that carries a fluid
VASA >VAS
VASAL >VAS
VASCULA >VASCULUM
VASCULAR adj relating to vessels
VASCULUM n metal box used by botanists in the field for carrying botanical specimens
VASCULUMS >VASCULUM
VASE n ornamental jar, esp for flowers
VASECTOMY n surgical removal of part of the vas deferens, as a contraceptive method
VASELIKE >VASE
VASELINE n translucent gelatinous substance obtained from petroleum
VASELINES >VASELINE
VASES >VASE
VASIFORM >VAS
VASOMOTOR adj (of a drug, agent, nerve, etc) affecting the diameter of blood vessels
VASOSPASM n sudden contraction of a blood vessel
VASOTOCIN n chemical found in birds, reptiles, and some amphibians
VASOTOMY n surgery on the vas deferens
VASOVAGAL adj relating to blood vessels and the vagus nerve
VASSAIL archaic variant of >VASSAL
VASSAILS >VASSAIL
VASSAL n man given land by a lord in return for military service ▷ vb or relating to a vassal ▷ vb vassalize
VASSALAGE n condition of being a vassal or the obligations to which a vassal was liable

VASSALESS >VASSAL
VASSALISE same as >VASSALIZE
VASSALIZE vb make a vassal of
VASSALLED >VASSAL
VASSALRY n vassalage
VASSALS >VASSAL
VAST adj extremely large ▷ n immense or boundless space
VASTER >VAST
VASTEST >VAST
VASTIDITY n vastness
VASTIER >VASTY
VASTIEST >VASTY
VASTITIES >VAST
VASTITUDE n condition or quality of being vast
VASTITY >VAST
VASTLY >VAST
VASTNESS >VAST
VASTS >VAST
VASTY archaic or poetic word for >VAST
VAT n large container for liquids ▷ vb place, store, or treat in a vat
VATABLE adj subject to VAT
VATFUL n amount enough to fill a vat
VATFULS >VATFUL
VATIC adj of, relating to, or characteristic of a prophet
VATICAL same as >VATIC
VATICIDE n murder of a prophet
VATICIDES >VATICIDE
VATICINAL adj foretelling or prophesying
VATMAN n Customs and Excise employee
VATMEN >VATMAN
VATS >VAT
VATTED >VAT
VATTER n person who works with vats; blender
VATTERS >VATTER
VATTING >VAT
VATU n standard monetary unit of Vanuatu
VATUS >VATU
VAU same as >VAV
VAUCH vb move fast
VAUCHED >VAUCH
VAUCHES >VAUCH
VAUCHING >VAUCH
VAUDOO same as >VOODOO
VAUDOOS >VAUDOO
VAUDOUX same as >VOODOO
VAULT n secure room for storing valuables ▷ vb jump over (something) by resting one's hand(s) on it.
VAULTAGE n group of vaults
VAULTAGES >VAULTAGE
VAULTED >VAULT
VAULTER >VAULT
VAULTERS >VAULT
VAULTIER >VAULTY
VAULTIEST >VAULTY

VAULTING n arrangement of ceiling vaults in a building ▷ adj excessively confident
VAULTINGS >VAULTING
VAULTLIKE >VAULT
VAULTS >VAULT
VAULTY adj arched
VAUNCE >ADVANCE
VAUNCED >VAUNCE
VAUNCES >VAUNCE
VAUNCING >VAUNCE
VAUNT vb describe or display (success or possessions) boastfully ▷ n boast
VAUNTAGE archaic variant of >VANTAGE
VAUNTAGES >VAUNTAGE
VAUNTED >VAUNT
VAUNTER >VAUNT
VAUNTERS >VAUNT
VAUNTERY n bravado
VAUNTFUL >VAUNT
VAUNTIE same as >VAUNTY
VAUNTIER >VAUNT
VAUNTIEST >VAUNT
VAUNTING >VAUNT
VAUNTINGS >VAUNT
VAUNTS >VAUNT
VAUNTY adj proud
VAURIEN n rascal
VAURIENS >VAURIEN
VAUS >VAU
VAUT same as >VAULT
VAUTE same as >VAULT
VAUTED >VAUTE
VAUTES >VAUTE
VAUTING >VAUT
VAUTS >VAUT
VAV n sixth letter of the Hebrew alphabet
VAVASOR n (in feudal society) vassal who also has vassals himself
VAVASORS >VAVASOR
VAVASORY n lands held by a vavasor
VAVASOUR same as >VAVASOUR
VAVASOURS >VAVASOUR
VAVASSOR same as >VAVASOR
VAVASSORS >VAVASSOR
VAVS >VAV
VAW n Hebrew letter
VAWARD n vanguard
VAWARDS >VAWARD
VAWNTIE >VAUNTY
VAWNTIER >VAWNTIE
VAWNTIEST >VAWNTIE
VAWS >VAW
VAWTE same as >VAULT
VAWTED >VAWTE
VAWTES >VAWTE
VAWTING >VAWTE
VEAL n calf meat ▷ vb cover with a veil
VEALE same as >VEIL
VEALED >VEAL
VEALER n young bovine animal of up to 14 months old grown for veal

VEALERS >VEALER
VEALES >VEALE
VEALIER >VEAL
VEALIEST >VEAL
VEALING >VEAL
VEALS >VEAL
VEALY >VEAL
VECTOR n quantity that has size and direction, such as force ▷ vb direct or guide (a pilot) by directions transmitted by radio
VECTORED >VECTOR
VECTORIAL >VECTOR
VECTORING >VECTOR
VECTORISE same as >VECTORIZE
VECTORIZE vb computing term
VECTORS >VECTOR
VEDALIA n Australian ladybird which is a pest of citrus fruits
VEDALIAS >VEDALIA
VEDETTE n small patrol vessel
VEDETTES >VEDETTE
VEDUTA n painting of a town or city
VEDUTE >VEDUTA
VEDUTISTA n artist who creates vedutas
VEDUTISTI >VEDUTISTA
VEE n letter 'v'
VEEJAY n video jockey
VEEJAYS >VEEJAY
VEENA same as >VINA
VEENAS >VEENA
VEEP n vice president
VEEPEE n vice president
VEEPEES >VEEPEE
VEEPS >VEEP
VEER vb change direction suddenly ▷ n change of course or direction
VEERED >VEER
VEERIES >VEERY
VEERING >VEER
VEERINGLY >VEER
VEERINGS >VEER
VEERS >VEER
VEERY n tawny brown North American thrush
VEES >VEE
VEG n vegetable or vegetables ▷ vb relax
VEGA n tobacco plantation
VEGAN n person who eats no meat, fish, eggs, or dairy products ▷ adj suitable for a vegan
VEGANIC adj farmed without the use of animal products or byproducts
VEGANISM >VEGAN
VEGANISMS >VEGAN
VEGANS >VEGAN
VEGAS >VEGA
VEGELATE n type of chocolate
VEGELATES >VEGELATE
VEGEMITE n informal word for a child

V

VEGEMITES > VEGEMITE
VEGES > VEG
VEGETABLE n edible plant ▷ adj of or like plants or vegetables
VEGETABLY > VEGETABLE
VEGETAL adj of or relating to plant life ▷ n vegetable
VEGETALLY > VEGETAL
VEGETALS > VEGETAL
VEGETANT adj causing growth or vegetation-like
VEGETATE vb live a dull boring life with no mental stimulation
VEGETATED > VEGETATE
VEGETATES > VEGETATE
VEGETE adj lively
VEGETIST n vegetable cultivator or enthusiast
VEGETISTS > VEGETIST
VEGETIVE adj dull or passive ▷ n vegetable
VEGETIVES > VEGETIVE
VEGGED > VEG
VEGGES > VEG
VEGGIE n vegetable ▷ adj vegetarian
VEGGIES > VEGGIE
VEGGING > VEG
VEGIE variant of > VEGGIE
VEGIES > VEGIE
VEGO adj vegetarian ▷ n vegetarian
VEGOS > VEGO
VEHEMENCE > VEHEMENT
VEHEMENCY > VEHEMENT
VEHEMENT adj expressing strong feelings
VEHICLE n machine for carrying people or objects
VEHICLES > VEHICLE
VEHICULAR > VEHICLE
VEHM n type of medieval German court
VEHME > VEHM
VEHMIC > VEHM
VEHMIQUE > VEHM
VEIL n piece of thin cloth covering the head or face ▷ vb cover with or as if with a veil
VEILED adj disguised
VEILEDLY > VEILED
VEILER > VEIL
VEILERS > VEIL
VEILIER > VEIL
VEILIEST > VEIL
VEILING n veil or the fabric used for veils
VEILINGS > VEILING
VEILLESS > VEIL
VEILLEUSE n small night-light
VEILLIKE > VEIL
VEILS > VEIL
VEILY > VEIL
VEIN n tube that takes blood to the heart ▷ vb diffuse over or cause to diffuse over in streaked patterns
VEINAL > VEIN

VEINED > VEIN
VEINER n wood-carving tool
VEINERS > VEINER
VEINIER > VEIN
VEINIEST > VEIN
VEINING n pattern or network of veins or streaks
VEININGS > VEINING
VEINLESS > VEIN
VEINLET n any small vein or venule
VEINLETS > VEINLET
VEINLIKE > VEIN
VEINOUS > VEIN
VEINS > VEIN
VEINSTONE another word for > GANGUE
VEINSTUFF another word for > GANGUE
VEINULE less common spelling of > VENULE
VEINULES > VEINULE
VEINULET same as > VEINLET
VEINULETS > VEINULET
VEINY > VEIN
VELA > VELUM
VELAMEN n thick layer of dead cells that covers the aerial roots of certain orchids
VELAMINA > VELAMEN
VELAR adj of, relating to, or attached to a velum ▷ n velar sound
VELARIA > VELARIUM
VELARIC > VELAR
VELARISE same as > VELARIZE
VELARISED > VELARISE
VELARISES > VELARISE
VELARIUM n awning used to protect the audience in ancient Roman theatres and amphitheatres
VELARIZE vb pronounce or supplement the pronunciation of (a speech sound) with articulation at the soft palate
VELARIZED > VELARIZE
VELARIZES > VELARIZE
VELARS > VELAR
VELATE adj having or covered with velum
VELATED same as > VELATE
VELATURA n overglaze
VELATURAS > VELATURA
VELCRO n tradename for a fastening consisting of two strips of nylon fabric that form a strong bond when pressed together
VELCROS > VELCRO
VELD n high grassland in southern Africa
VELDS > VELD
VELDSKOEN n leather ankle boot
VELDT same as > VELD
VELDTS > VELDT
VELE same as > VEIL

VELES > VELE
VELETA same as > VALETA
VELETAS > VELETA
VELIGER n free-swimming larva of many molluscs
VELIGERS > VELIGER
VELITES npl light-armed troops in ancient Rome, drawn from the poorer classes
VELL vb cut turf
VELLEITY n weakest level of desire or volition
VELLENAGE n (in Medieval Europe) status of being a villein
VELLET n velvet
VELLETS > VELLET
VELLICATE vb twitch, pluck, or pinch
VELLON n silver and copper alloy used in old Spanish coins
VELLONS > VELLON
VELLS > VELL
VELLUM n fine calfskin parchment ▷ adj made of or resembling vellum
VELLUMS > VELLUM
VELLUS as in vellus hair short fine unpigmented hair covering the human body
VELOCE adv be played rapidly
VELOCITY n speed of movement in a given direction
VELODROME n arena with a banked track for cycle racing
VELOUR n fabric similar to velvet
VELOURS same as > VELOUR
VELOUTE n rich white sauce or soup made from stock, egg yolks, and cream
VELOUTES > VELOUTE
VELOUTINE n type of velvety fabric
VELSKOEN n type of shoe
VELSKOENS > VELSKOEN
VELUM n any of various membranous structures
VELURE n velvet or a similar fabric ▷ vb cover with velure
VELURED > VELURE
VELURES > VELURE
VELURING > VELURE
VELVERET n type of velvet-like fabric
VELVERETS > VELVERET
VELVET n fabric with a thick soft pile ▷ vb cover with velvet
VELVETED > VELVET
VELVETEEN n cotton velvet
VELVETIER > VELVET
VELVETING > VELVET
VELVETS > VELVET
VELVETY > VELVET
VENA n vein in the body

VENAE > VENA
VENAL adj easily bribed
VENALITY > VENAL
VENALLY > VENAL
VENATIC adj of, relating to, or used in hunting
VENATICAL same as > VENATIC
VENATION n arrangement of the veins in a leaf or in the wing of an insect
VENATIONS > VENATION
VENATOR n hunter
VENATORS > VENATOR
VEND vb sell
VENDABLE > VEND
VENDABLES > VEND
VENDACE n either of two small whitefish occurring in lakes in Scotland and NW England
VENDACES > VENDACE
VENDAGE n vintage
VENDAGES > VENDAGE
VENDANGE same as > VENDAGE
VENDANGES > VENDANGE
VENDED > VEND
VENDEE n person to whom something, esp real property, is sold
VENDEES > VENDEE
VENDER same as > VENDOR
VENDERS > VENDER
VENDETTA n long-lasting quarrel between people in which they attempt to harm each other
VENDETTAS > VENDETTA
VENDEUSE n female salesperson
VENDEUSES > VENDEUSE
VENDIBLE adj saleable or marketable ▷ n saleable object
VENDIBLES > VENDIBLE
VENDIBLY > VENDIBLE
VENDING > VEND
VENDINGS > VEND
VENDIS same as > VENDACE
VENDISES > VENDIS
VENDISS same as > VENDACE
VENDISSES > VENDIS
VENDITION > VEND
VENDOR n person who sells goods such as newspapers or hamburgers from a stall or cart
VENDORS > VENDOR
VENDS > VEND
VENDUE n public sale
VENDUES > VENDUE
VENEER n thin layer of wood etc covering a cheaper material ▷ vb cover (a surface) with a veneer
VENEERED > VENEER
VENEERER > VENEER
VENEERERS > VENEER
VENEERING n material used as veneer or a

veneered surface
VENEERS > VENEER
VENEFIC adj having poisonous effects
VENEFICAL same as **>** VENEFIC
VENENATE vb poison
VENENATED > VENENATE
VENENATES > VENENATE
VENENE n medicine from snake venom
VENENES > VENENE
VENENOSE adj poisonous
VENERABLE adj worthy of deep respect
VENERABLY > VENERABLE
VENERATE vb hold (a person) in deep respect
VENERATED > VENERATE
VENERATES > VENERATE
VENERATOR > VENERATE
VENEREAL adj transmitted by sexual intercourse
VENEREAN n sex addict
VENEREANS > VENEREAN
VENEREOUS adj libidinous
VENERER n hunter
VENERERS > VENERER
VENERIES > VENERY
VENERY n pursuit of sexual gratification
VENETIAN n Venetian blind
VENETIANS > VENETIAN
VENEWE same as **>** VENUE
VENEWES > VENEWE
VENEY n thrust
VENEYS > VENEY
VENGE vb avenge
VENGEABLE > VENGE
VENGEABLY > VENGE
VENGEANCE n revenge
VENGED > VENGE
VENGEFUL adj wanting revenge
VENGEMENT > VENGE
VENGER > VENGE
VENGERS > VENGE
VENGES > VENGE
VENGING > VENGE
VENIAL adj (of a sin or fault) easily forgiven
VENIALITY > VENIAL
VENIALLY > VENIAL
VENIDIUM n genus of flowering plants
VENIDIUMS > VENIDIUM
VENIN n any of the poisonous constituents of animal venoms
VENINE same as **>** VENIN
VENINES > VENINE
VENINS > VENIN
VENIRE n list from which jurors are selected
VENIREMAN n person summoned for jury service
**VENIREMEN
 >** VENIREMAN
VENIRES > VENIRE
VENISON n deer meat
VENISONS > VENISON
VENITE n musical setting

for the 95th psalm
VENITES > VENITE
VENNEL n lane
VENNELS > VENNEL
VENOGRAM n X-ray of a vein
VENOGRAMS > VENOGRAM
VENOLOGY n study of veins
VENOM n malice or spite
 ▷ vb poison
VENOMED > VENOM
VENOMER > VENOM
VENOMERS > VENOM
VENOMING > VENOM
VENOMLESS > VENOM
VENOMOUS > VENOM
VENOMS > VENOM
VENOSE adj having veins
VENOSITY n excessive quantity of blood in the venous system or in an organ or part
VENOUS adj of veins
VENOUSLY > VENOUS
VENT n outlet releasing fumes or fluid ▷ vb express (an emotion) freely
VENTAGE n small opening
VENTAGES > VENTAGE
VENTAIL n (in medieval armour) a covering for the lower part of the face
VENTAILE same as **>** VENTAIL
VENTAILES > VENTAILE
VENTAILS > VENTAIL
VENTANA n window
VENTANAS > VENTANA
VENTAYLE same as **>** VENTAIL
VENTAYLES > VENTAYLE
VENTED > VENT
VENTER > VENT
VENTERS > VENT
VENTIDUCT n air pipe
VENTIFACT n pebble that has been shaped by wind-blown sand
VENTIGE same as **>** VENTAGE
VENTIGES > VENTIGE
VENTIL n valve on a musical instrument
VENTILATE vb let fresh air into
VENTILS > VENTIL
VENTING > VENT
VENTINGS > VENT
VENTLESS > VENT
VENTOSE adj full of wind
VENTOSITY n flatulence
VENTOUSE n apparatus sometimes used to assist the delivery of a baby
VENTOUSES > VENTOUSE
VENTRAL adj relating to the front of the body ▷ n ventral fin
VENTRALLY > VENTRAL
VENTRALS > VENTRAL
VENTRE same as **>** VENTURE
VENTRED > VENTRE
VENTRES > VENTRE
VENTRICLE n cavity in an

organ such as the heart
VENTRING > VENTRE
VENTRINGS > VENTRE
VENTROUS > VENTRE
VENTS > VENT
VENTURE n risky undertaking, esp in business ▷ vb do something risky
VENTURED > VENTURE
VENTURER > VENTURE
VENTURERS > VENTURE
VENTURES > VENTURE
VENTURI n tube used to control the flow of fluid
VENTURING > VENTURE
VENTURIS > VENTURI
VENTUROUS adj adventurous
VENUE n place where an organized gathering is held
VENUES > VENUE
VENULAR > VENULE
VENULE n any of the small branches of a vein
VENULES > VENULE
VENULOSE > VENULE
VENULOUS > VENULE
VENUS n type of marine bivalve mollusc
VENUSES > VENUS
VENVILLE n type of parish tenure
VENVILLES > VENVILLE
VERA as in aloe vera plant substance used in skin and hair preparations
VERACIOUS adj habitually truthful
VERACITY n truthfulness
VERANDA n porch or portico along the outside of a building
VERANDAED > VERANDA
VERANDAH same as **>** VERANDA
VERANDAHS > VERANDAH
VERANDAS > VERANDA
VERAPAMIL n calcium-channel blocker used in the treatment of some types of irregular heart rhythm
VERATRIA same as **>** VERATRINE
VERATRIAS > VERATRIA
VERATRIN same as **>** VERATRINE
VERATRINE n white poisonous mixture obtained from the seeds of sabadilla
VERATRINS > VERATRIN
VERATRUM n genus of herbs
VERATRUMS > VERATRUM
VERB n word that expresses the idea of action, happening, or being
VERBAL adj spoken ▷ n abuse or invective ▷ vb implicate (someone) in a crime by quoting alleged admission of guilt in court
VERBALISE same as

 > VERBALIZE
VERBALISM n exaggerated emphasis on the importance of words
VERBALIST n person who deals with words alone, rather than facts, ideas, feeling, etc
VERBALITY > VERBAL
VERBALIZE vb express (something) in words
VERBALLED > VERBAL
VERBALLY > VERBAL
VERBALS > VERBAL
VERBARIAN n inventor of words
VERBASCUM See **>** MULLEIN
VERBATIM adj word for word ▷ adv using exactly the same words
VERBENA n plant with sweet-smelling flowers
VERBENAS > VERBENA
VERBERATE vb lash
VERBIAGE n excessive use of words
VERBIAGES > VERBIAGE
VERBICIDE n person who destroys a word
VERBID n any nonfinite form of a verb or any nonverbal word derived from a verb
VERBIDS > VERBID
VERBIFIED > VERBIFY
VERBIFIES > VERBIFY
VERBIFY another word for **>** VERBALIZE
VERBILE n person who is best stimulated by words
VERBILES > VERBILE
VERBING n use of nouns as verbs
VERBINGS > VERBING
VERBLESS > VERB
VERBOSE adj speaking at tedious length
VERBOSELY > VERBOSE
VERBOSER > VERBOSE
VERBOSEST > VERBOSE
VERBOSITY > VERBOSE
VERBOTEN adj forbidden
VERBS > VERB
VERD as in verd antique dark green mottled impure variety of serpentine marble
VERDANCY > VERDANT
VERDANT adj covered in green vegetation
VERDANTLY > VERDANT
VERDELHO n type of grape
VERDELHOS > VERDELHO
VERDERER n judicial officer responsible for the maintenance of law and order in the royal forests
VERDERERS > VERDERER
VERDEROR same as **>** VERDERER
VERDERORS > VERDEROR
VERDET n type of verdigris
VERDETS > VERDET

V

VERDICT n decision of a jury

VERDICTS > VERDICT

VERDIGRIS n green film on copper, brass, or bronze

VERDIN n small W North American tit having grey plumage with a yellow head

VERDINS > VERDIN

VERDIT same as > VERDICT

VERDITE n type of rock used in jewellery

VERDITER n blue-green pigment made from copper

VERDITERS > VERDITER

VERDITES > VERDITE

VERDITS > VERDIT

VERDOY n floral or leafy shield decoration

VERDURE n flourishing green vegetation

VERDURED > VERDURE

VERDURES > VERDURE

VERDUROUS > VERDURE

VERECUND adj shy or modest

VERGE n grass border along a road ▷ vb move in a specified direction

VERGED > VERGE

VERGENCE n inward or outward turning movement of the eyes in convergence or divergence

VERGENCES > VERGENCE

VERGENCY adj inclination

VERGER n church caretaker

VERGERS > VERGER

VERGES > VERGE

VERGING > VERGE

VERGLAS n thin film of ice on rock

VERGLASES > VERGLAS

VERIDIC same as > VERIDICAL

VERIDICAL adj truthful

VERIER > VERY

VERIEST > VERY

VERIFIED > VERIFY

VERIFIER > VERIFY

VERIFIERS > VERIFY

VERIFIES > VERIFY

VERIFY vb check the truth or accuracy of

VERIFYING > VERIFY

VERILY adv in truth

VERISM n extreme naturalism in art or literature

VERISMO n school of composition that originated in Italian opera

VERISMOS > VERISMO

VERISMS > VERISM

VERIST > VERISM

VERISTIC > VERISM

VERISTS > VERISM

VERITABLE adj rightly called, without exaggeration

VERITABLY > VERITABLE

VERITAS n truth

VERITATES > VERITAS

VERITE adj involving a high degree of realism or naturalism ▷ n this kind of realism in film

VERITES > VERITE

VERITIES > VERITY

VERITY n true statement or principle

VERJUICE n acid juice of unripe grapes, apples, or crab apples ▷ vb make sour

VERJUICED > VERJUICE

VERJUICES > VERJUICE

VERKRAMP adj bigoted or illiberal

VERLAN n variety of French slang in which the syllables are inverted

VERLANS > VERLAN

VERLIG adj enlightened

VERLIGTE n (during apartheid) a White political liberal

VERLIGTES > VERLIGTE

VERMAL > VERMIS

VERMEIL n gilded silver, bronze, or other metal, used esp in the 19th century ▷ vb decorate with vermeil ▷ adj vermilion

VERMEILED > VERMEIL

VERMEILLE variant of > VERMEIL

VERMEILS > VERMEIL

VERMELL same as > VERMEIL

VERMELLS > VERMELL

VERMES > VERMIS

VERMIAN > VERMIS

VERMICIDE n any substance used to kill worms

VERMICULE n small worm

VERMIFORM adj shaped like a worm

VERMIFUGE n any drug or agent able to destroy or expel intestinal worms

VERMIL same as > VERMEIL

VERMILIES > VERMILY

VERMILION adj orange-red ▷ n mercuric sulphide, used as an orange-red pigment

VERMILLED > VERMIL

VERMILS > VERMIL

VERMILY > VERMEIL

VERMIN npl animals, esp insects and rodents, that spread disease or cause damage

VERMINATE vb breed vermin

VERMINED adj plagued with vermin

VERMINOUS adj relating to, infested with, or suggestive of vermin

VERMINS > VERMIN

VERMINY > VERMIN

VERMIS n middle lobe connecting the two halves of the cerebellum

VERMOULU adj worm-eaten

VERMOUTH n wine flavoured with herbs

VERMOUTHS > VERMOUTH

VERMUTH same as > VERMOUTH

VERMUTHS > VERMUTH

VERNACLE same as > VERNICLE

VERNACLES > VERNACLE

VERNAL adj occurring in spring

VERNALISE same as > VERNALIZE

VERNALITY > VERNAL

VERNALIZE vb subject (ungerminated or germinating seeds) to low temperatures

VERNALLY > VERNAL

VERNANT > VERNAL

VERNATION n way in which leaves are arranged in the bud

VERNICLE n veronica

VERNICLES > VERNICLE

VERNIER n movable scale on a graduated measuring instrument for taking readings in fractions

VERNIERS > VERNIER

VERNIX n white substance covering the skin of a foetus

VERNIXES > VERNIX

VERONAL n a long-acting barbiturate used medicinally

VERONALS > VERONAL

VERONICA n plant with small blue, pink, or white flowers

VERONICAS > VERONICA

VERONIQUE adj (of a dish) garnished with seedless white grapes

VERQUERE n type of backgammon game

VERQUERES > VERQUERE

VERQUIRE variant of > VERQUERE

VERQUIRES > VERQUIRE

VERRA Scot word for > VERY

VERREL n ferrule

VERRELS > VERREL

VERREY same as > VAIR

VERRUCA n wart, usu on the foot

VERRUCAE > VERRUCA

VERRUCAS > VERRUCA

VERRUCOSE adj covered with warts

VERRUCOUS same as > VERRUCOSE

VERRUGA same as > VERRUCA

VERRUGAS > VERRUGA

VERRY same as > VAIR

VERS n verse

VERSAL n embellished letter

VERSALS > VERSAL

VERSANT n side or slope of a mountain or mountain range

VERSANTS > VERSANT

VERSATILE adj having many skills or uses

VERSE n group of lines forming part of a song or poem ▷ vb write verse

VERSED adj thoroughly knowledgeable (about)

VERSELET n small verse

VERSELETS > VERSELET

VERSEMAN n man who writes verse

VERSEMEN > VERSEMAN

VERSER n versifier

VERSERS > VERSER

VERSES > VERSE

VERSET n short, often sacred, verse

VERSETS > VERSET

VERSICLE n short verse

VERSICLES > VERSICLE

VERSIFIED > VERSIFY

VERSIFIER > VERSIFY

VERSIFIES > VERSIFY

VERSIFORM adj changing in form

VERSIFY vb write in verse

VERSIN same as > VERSINE

VERSINE n mathematical term

VERSINES > VERSINE

VERSING > VERSE

VERSINGS > VERSE

VERSINS > VERSIN

VERSION n form of something, such as a piece of writing, with some differences from other forms

VERSIONAL > VERSION

VERSIONER n translator

VERSIONS > VERSION

VERSO n left-hand page of a book

VERSOS > VERSO

VERST n unit of length used in Russia

VERSTE same as > VERST

VERSTES > VERSTE

VERSTS > VERST

VERSUS prep in opposition to or in contrast with

VERSUTE adj cunning

VERT n right to cut green wood in a forest ▷ vb turn

VERTEBRA n one of the bones that form the spine

VERTEBRAE > VERTEBRA

VERTEBRAL > VERTEBRA

VERTEBRAS > VERTEBRA

VERTED > VERT

VERTEX n point on a geometric figure where the sides form an angle

VERTEXES > VERTEX

VERTICAL adj straight up and down ▷ n vertical direction

VERTICALS > VERTICAL

VERTICES > VERTEX

VERTICIL n circular

arrangement of parts about an axis, esp leaves around a stem
VERTICILS > VERTICIL
VERTICITY n ability to turn
VERTIGO n dizziness, usu when looking down from a high place
VERTIGOES > VERTIGO
VERTIGOS > VERTIGO
VERTING > VERT
VERTIPORT n type of airport
VERTS > VERT
VERTU same as > VIRTU
VERTUE same as > VIRTU
VERTUES > VERTUE
VERTUOUS > VERTU
VERTUS > VERTU
VERVAIN n plant with spikes of blue, purple, or white flowers
VERVAINS > VERVAIN
VERVE n enthusiasm or liveliness
VERVEL same as > VARVEL
VERVELLED > VERVEL
VERVELS > VERVEL
VERVEN same as > VERVAIN
VERVENS > VERVEN
VERVES > VERVE
VERVET n variety of a South African guenon monkey
VERVETS > VERVET
VERY adv more than usually, extremely ▷ adj absolute, exact
VESICA n bladder
VESICAE > VESICA
VESICAL adj of or relating to a vesica, esp the urinary bladder
VESICANT n any substance that causes blisters ▷ adj acting as a vesicant
VESICANTS > VESICANT
VESICATE vb blister
VESICATED > VESICATE
VESICATES > VESICATE
VESICLE n sac or small cavity, esp one containing fluid
VESICLES > VESICLE
VESICULA n vesicle
VESICULAE > VESICULA
VESICULAR > VESICLE
VESPA n type of wasp
VESPAS > VESPA
VESPER n evening prayer, service, or hymn
VESPERAL n liturgical book containing the prayers, psalms, and hymns used at vespers
VESPERALS > VESPERAL
VESPERS npl service of evening prayer
VESPIARY n nest or colony of social wasps or hornets
VESPID n insect of the

family that includes the common wasp and hornet ▷ adj of or belonging to this family
VESPIDS > VESPID
VESPINE adj of, relating to, or resembling a wasp or wasps
VESPOID adj like a wasp
VESSAIL archaic variant of > VESSEL
VESSAILS > VESSAIL
VESSEL n container or ship ▷ adj contained in a vessel
VESSELED > VESSEL
VESSELS > VESSEL
VEST n undergarment worn on the top half of the body ▷ vb give (authority) to (someone)
VESTA n short friction match, usually of wood
VESTAL adj pure, chaste ▷ n chaste woman
VESTALLY > VESTAL
VESTALS > VESTAL
VESTAS > VESTA
VESTED adj having an existing right to the immediate or future possession of property
VESTEE n person having a vested interest something
VESTEES > VESTEE
VESTIARY n room for storing clothes or dressing in, such as a vestry ▷ adj of or relating to clothes
VESTIBULA > VESTIBULE
VESTIBULE n small entrance hall
VESTIGE n small amount or trace
VESTIGES > VESTIGE
VESTIGIA > VESTIGIUM
VESTIGIAL adj remaining after a larger or more important thing has gone
VESTIGIUM n trace
VESTIMENT same as > VESTMENT
VESTING > VEST
VESTINGS > VEST
VESTITURE n investiture
VESTLESS > VEST
VESTLIKE > VEST
VESTMENT n garment or robe, esp one denoting office, authority, or rank
VESTMENTS > VESTMENT
VESTRAL > VESTRY
VESTRIES > VESTRY
VESTRY n room in a church used as an office by the priest or minister
VESTRYMAN n member of a church vestry
VESTRYMEN > VESTRYMAN
VESTS > VEST
VESTURAL > VESTURE
VESTURE n garment or something that seems like a garment ▷ vb clothe

VESTURED > VESTURE
VESTURER n person in charge of church vestments
VESTURERS > VESTURER
VESTURES > VESTURE
VESTURING > VESTURE
VESUVIAN n match for lighting cigars
VESUVIANS > VESUVIAN
VET vb check the suitability of ▷ n military veteran
VETCH n climbing plant with a beanlike fruit used as fodder
VETCHES > VETCH
VETCHIER > VETCHY
VETCHIEST > VETCHY
VETCHLING n type of climbing plant
VETCHY adj consisting of vetches
VETERAN n person with long experience in a particular activity, esp military service ▷ adj long-serving
VETERANS > VETERAN
VETIVER n tall hairless grass of tropical and subtropical Asia
VETIVERS > VETIVER
VETIVERT n oil from the vetiver
VETIVERTS > VETIVERT
VETKOEK n South African cake
VETKOEKS > VETKOEK
VETO n official power to cancel a proposal ▷ vb enforce a veto against
VETOED > VETO
VETOER > VETO
VETOERS > VETO
VETOES > VETO
VETOING > VETO
VETOLESS > VETO
VETS > VET
VETTED > VET
VETTER > VET
VETTERS > VET
VETTING n as in positive vetting checking a person's background to assess their suitability of an important post
VETTINGS > VETTING
VETTURA n Italian mode of transport
VETTURAS > VETTURA
VETTURINI > VETTURINO
VETTURINO n person who drives a vettura
VEX vb frustrate, annoy
VEXATION n something annoying
VEXATIONS > VEXATION
VEXATIOUS adj vexing
VEXATORY > VEX
VEXED adj annoyed and puzzled
VEXEDLY > VEXED
VEXEDNESS > VEXED
VEXER > VEX

VEXERS > VEX
VEXES > VEX
VEXIL same as > VEXILLUM
VEXILLA > VEXILLUM
VEXILLAR > VEXILLUM
VEXILLARY > VEXILLUM
VEXILLATE > VEXILLUM
VEXILLUM n vane of a feather
VEXILS > VEXIL
VEXING > VEX
VEXINGLY > VEX
VEXINGS > VEX
VEXT same as > VEXED
VEZIR same as > VIZIER
VEZIRS > VEZIR
VIA prep by way of ▷ n road
VIABILITY > VIABLE
VIABLE adj able to be put into practice
VIABLY > VIABLE
VIADUCT n bridge over a valley
VIADUCTS > VIADUCT
VIAE > VIA
VIAL n small bottle for liquids ▷ vb put into a vial
VIALED > VIAL
VIALFUL > VIAL
VIALFULS > VIAL
VIALING > VIAL
VIALLED > VIAL
VIALLING > VIAL
VIALS > VIAL
VIAMETER n device to measure distance travelled
VIAMETERS > VIAMETER
VIAND n type of food, esp a delicacy
VIANDS > VIAND
VIAS > VIA
VIATIC same as > VIATICAL
VIATICA > VIATICUM
VIATICAL adj of or denoting a road or a journey ▷ n purchase of a terminal patient's life assurance policy so that he or she may make use of the proceeds
VIATICALS > VIATICAL
VIATICUM n Holy Communion given to a person who is dying or in danger of death
VIATICUMS > VIATICUM
VIATOR n traveller
VIATORES > VIATOR
VIATORIAL adj pertaining to travelling
VIATORS > VIATOR
VIBE n feeling or flavour of the kind specified
VIBES npl vibrations
VIBEX n mark under the skin
VIBEY adj lively and vibrant
VIBICES > VIBEX
VIBIER > VIBEY
VIBIEST > VIBEY
VIBIST n person who plays a vibraphone in a jazz band or group

V

VIBISTS > VIBIST
VIBRACULA npl bristle-like polyps in certain bryozoans
VIBRAHARP n type of percussion instrument
VIBRANCE n vibrancy
VIBRANCES > VIBRANCE
VIBRANCY > VIBRANT
VIBRANT adj vigorous in appearance, energetic ▷ n trilled or rolled speech sound
VIBRANTLY > VIBRANT
VIBRANTS > VIBRANT
VIBRATE vb move back and forth rapidly
VIBRATED > VIBRATE
VIBRATES > VIBRATE
VIBRATILE > VIBRATE
VIBRATING > VIBRATE
VIBRATION n vibrating
VIBRATIVE > VIBRATE
VIBRATO n rapid fluctuation in the pitch of a note
VIBRATOR n device that produces vibratory motion
VIBRATORS > VIBRATOR
VIBRATORY > VIBRATE
VIBRATOS > VIBRATO
VIBRIO n curved or spiral rodlike bacterium
VIBRIOID > VIBRIO
VIBRION same as > VIBRIO
VIBRIONIC > VIBRIO
VIBRIONS > VIBRION
VIBRIOS > VIBRIO
VIBRIOSES > VIBRIOSIS
VIBRIOSIS n bacterial disease
VIBRISSA n any of the bristle-like sensitive hairs on the face of many mammals
VIBRISSAE > VIBRISSA
VIBRISSAL > VIBRISSA
VIBRONIC adj of, concerned with, or involving both electronic and vibrational energy levels of a molecule
VIBS npl type of climbing shoes
VIBURNUM n subtropical shrub with white flowers and berry-like fruits
VIBURNUMS > VIBURNUM
VICAR n member of the clergy in charge of a parish
VICARAGE n vicar's house
VICARAGES > VICARAGE
VICARATE same as > VICARIATE
VICARATES > VICARATE
VICARESS n rank of nun
VICARIAL adj of or relating to a vicar, vicars, or a vicariate
VICARIANT n any of several closely related species, etc, each of which exists in a separate geographical area

VICARIATE n office, rank, or authority of a vicar
VICARIES > VICARY
VICARIOUS adj felt indirectly by imagining what another person experiences
VICARLY > VICAR
VICARS > VICAR
VICARSHIP same as > VICARIATE
VICARY n office of a vicar
VICE n immoral or evil habit or action ▷ adj serving in place of ▷ vb grip (something) with or as if with a vice ▷ prep instead of
VICED > VICE
VICEGERAL adj of or relating to a person who deputizes for another
VICELESS > VICE
VICELIKE > VICE
VICENARY adj relating to or consisting of 20
VICENNIAL adj occurring every 20 years
VICEREGAL adj of a viceroy
VICEREINE n wife of a viceroy
VICEROY n governor of a colony who represents the monarch
VICEROYS > VICEROY
VICES > VICE
VICESIMAL same as > VIGESIMAL
VICHIES > VICHY
VICHY n French mineral water
VICIATE same as > VITIATE
VICIATED > VICIATE
VICIATES > VICIATE
VICIATING > VICIATE
VICINAGE n residents of a particular neighbourhood
VICINAGES > VICINAGE
VICINAL adj neighbouring
VICING > VICE
VICINITY n surrounding area
VICIOSITY same as > VITIOSITY
VICIOUS adj cruel and violent
VICIOUSLY > VICIOUS
VICOMTE n French nobleman
VICOMTES > VICOMTE
VICTIM n person or thing harmed or killed
VICTIMISE same as > VICTIMIZE
VICTIMIZE vb punish unfairly
VICTIMS > VICTIM
VICTOR n person who has defeated an opponent, esp in war or in sport
VICTORESS same as > VICTRESS
VICTORIA n large sweet

plum, red and yellow in colour
VICTORIAS > VICTORIA
VICTORIES > VICTORY
VICTORINE n woman's article of clothing
VICTORS > VICTOR
VICTORY n winning of a battle or contest
VICTRESS n female victor
VICTRIX same as > VICTRESS
VICTRIXES > VICTRIX
VICTUAL vb supply with or obtain victuals
VICTUALED > VICTUAL
VICTUALER > VICTUAL
VICTUALS npl food and drink
VICUGNA same as > VICUNA
VICUGNAS > VICUGNA
VICUNA n S American animal like the llama
VICUNAS > VICUNA
VID same as > VIDEO
VIDAME n French nobleman
VIDAMES > VIDAME
VIDE interj look
VIDELICET adv namely: used to specify items
VIDENDA > VIDENDUM
VIDENDUM n that which is to be seen
VIDEO vb record (a TV programme or event) on video ▷ adj relating to or used in producing television images ▷ n recording and showing of films and events using a television set, video tapes, and a video recorder
VIDEODISC variant of > VIDEODISK
VIDEODISK n disk on which information is stored in digital form
VIDEOED > VIDEO
VIDEOFIT n computer-generated picture of a person sought by the police
VIDEOFITS > VIDEOFIT
VIDEOGRAM n audiovisual recording
VIDEOING > VIDEO
VIDEOLAND n world of television and televised images
VIDEOS > VIDEO
VIDEOTAPE vb record (a TV programme) on video tape
VIDEOTEX n information system that displays data from a distant computer on a screen
VIDEOTEXT n means of representing on a TV screen information that is held in a computer
VIDETTE same as > VEDETTE
VIDETTES > VIDETTE

VIDICON n small television camera used in closed-circuit television
VIDICONS > VIDICON
VIDIMUS n inspection
VIDIMUSES > VIDIMUS
VIDS > VID
VIDUAGE n widows collectively
VIDUAGES > VIDUAGE
VIDUAL adj widowed
VIDUITIES > VIDUITY
VIDUITY n widowhood
VIDUOUS adj empty
VIE vb compete (with someone)
VIED > VIE
VIELLE n stringed musical instrument
VIELLES > VIELLE
VIENNA as in vienna loaf or vienna steak associated with Vienna
VIER > VIE
VIERS > VIE
VIES > VIE
VIEW n opinion or belief ▷ vb think of (something) in a particular way
VIEWABLE > VIEW
VIEWDATA n interactive form of videotext
VIEWDATAS > VIEWDATA
VIEWED > VIEW
VIEWER n person who watches television
VIEWERS > VIEWER
VIEWIER > VIEWY
VIEWIEST > VIEWY
VIEWINESS > VIEWY
VIEWING n act of watching television
VIEWINGS > VIEWING
VIEWLESS adj (of windows, etc) not affording a view
VIEWLY adj pleasant on the eye
VIEWPHONE n videophone
VIEWPOINT n person's attitude towards something
VIEWS > VIEW
VIEWY adj having fanciful opinions or ideas
VIFDA same as > VIVDA
VIFDAS > VIFDA
VIG n interest on a loan that is paid to a moneylender
VIGA n rafter
VIGAS > VIGA
VIGESIMAL adj relating to or based on the number 20
VIGIA n navigational hazard marked on a chart although its existence has not been confirmed
VIGIAS > VIGIA
VIGIL n night-time period of staying awake to look after a sick person, pray, etc
VIGILANCE n careful attention
VIGILANT adj watchful in

case of danger

VIGILANTE *n* person who takes it upon himself or herself to enforce the law

VIGILS > VIGIL

VIGNERON *n* person who grows grapes for winemaking

VIGNERONS > VIGNERON

VIGNETTE *n* small illustration placed at the beginning or end of a chapter or book ▷ *vb* portray in a vignette

VIGNETTED > VIGNETTE

VIGNETTER *n* device used in printing vignettes

VIGNETTES > VIGNETTE

VIGOR *same as* > VIGOUR

VIGORISH *n* type of commission

VIGORO *n* women's game similar to cricket

VIGOROS > VIGORO

VIGOROSO *adv* in music, emphatically

VIGOROUS *adj* having physical or mental energy

VIGORS > VIGOR

VIGOUR *n* physical or mental energy

VIGOURS > VIGOUR

VIGS > VIG

VIHARA *n* type of Buddhist temple

VIHARAS > VIHARA

VIHUELA *n* obsolete plucked stringed instrument of Spain, related to the guitar

VIHUELAS > VIHUELA

VIKING *n* Dane, Norwegian, or Swede who raided by sea most of N and W Europe between the 8th and 11th centuries

VIKINGISM > VIKING

VIKINGS > VIKING

VILAYET *n* major administrative division of Turkey

VILAYETS > VILAYET

VILD *same as* > VILE

VILDE *same as* > VILE

VILDLY > VILD

VILDNESS > VILD

VILE *adj* very wicked

VILELY > VILE

VILENESS > VILE

VILER > VILE

VILEST > VILE

VILIACO *n* scoundrel

VILIACOES > VILIACO

VILIACOS > VILIACO

VILIAGO *same as* > VILIACO

VILIAGOES > VILIAGO

VILIAGOS > VILIAGO

VILIFIED > VILIFY

VILIFIER > VILIFY

VILIFIERS > VILIFY

VILIFIES > VILIFY

VILIFY *vb* attack the character of

VILIFYING > VILIFY

VILIPEND *vb* treat or regard with contempt

VILIPENDS > VILIPEND

VILL *n* township

VILLA *n* large house with gardens

VILLADOM > VILLA

VILLADOMS > VILLA

VILLAE > VILLA

VILLAGE *n* small group of houses in a country area

VILLAGER *n* inhabitant of a village ▷ *adj* backward, unsophisticated, or illiterate

VILLAGERS > VILLAGER

VILLAGERY *n* villages

VILLAGES > VILLAGE

VILLAGIO *same as* > VILIACO

VILLAGIOS > VILLAGIO

VILLAGREE *variant of* > VILLAGERY

VILLAIN *n* wicked person

VILLAINS > VILLAIN

VILLAINY *n* evil or vicious behaviour

VILLAN *same as* > VILLEIN

VILLANAGE > VILLAN

VILLANIES > VILLANY

VILLANOUS > VILLAIN

VILLANS > VILLAN

VILLANY *same as* > VILLAINY

VILLAR > VILL

VILLAS > VILLA

VILLATIC *adj* of or relating to a villa, village, or farm

VILLEIN *n* peasant bound in service to his lord

VILLEINS > VILLEIN

VILLENAGE *n* villein's status

VILLI > VILLUS

VILLIACO *n* coward

VILLIACOS > VILLIACO

VILLIAGO *same as* > VILIACO

VILLIAGOS > VILLIAGO

VILLIFORM *adj* having the form of a villus or a series of villi

VILLOSE *same as* > VILLOUS

VILLOSITY *n* state of being villous

VILLOUS *adj* (of plant parts) covered with long hairs

VILLOUSLY > VILLOUS

VILLS > VILL

VILLUS *n* one of the finger-like projections in the small intestine of many vertebrates

VIM *n* force, energy

VIMANA *n* Indian mythological chariot of the gods

VIMANAS > VIMANA

VIMEN *n* long flexible shoot

that occurs in certain plants

VIMINA > VIMEN

VIMINAL > VIMEN

VIMINEOUS *adj* having, producing, or resembling long flexible shoots

VIMS > VIM

VIN *n* French wine

VINA *n* stringed musical instrument related to the sitar

VINACEOUS *adj* of, relating to, or containing wine

VINAL *n* type of manmade fibre

VINALS > VINAL

VINAS > VINA

VINASSE *n* residue left in a still after distilling spirits, esp brandy

VINASSES > VINASSE

VINCA *n* type of trailing plant with blue flowers

VINCAS > VINCA

VINCIBLE *adj* capable of being defeated or overcome

VINCIBLY > VINCIBLE

VINCULA > VINCULUM

VINCULUM *n* horizontal line drawn above a group of mathematical terms

VINCULUMS > VINCULUM

VINDALOO *n* type of very hot Indian curry

VINDALOOS > VINDALOO

VINDEMIAL *adj* relating to a grape harvest

VINDICATE *vb* clear (someone) of guilt

VINE *n* climbing plant, esp one producing grapes ▷ *vb* form like a vine

VINEAL *adj* relating to wines

VINED > VINE

VINEGAR *n* acid liquid made from wine, beer, or cider ▷ *vb* apply vinegar to

VINEGARED > VINEGAR

VINEGARS > VINEGAR

VINEGARY *adj* containing vinegar

VINELESS > VINE

VINELIKE > VINE

VINER *n* vinedresser

VINERIES > VINERY

VINERS > VINER

VINERY *n* hothouse for growing grapes

VINES > VINE

VINEW *vb* become mouldy

VINEWED > VINEW

VINEWING > VINEW

VINEWS > VINEW

VINEYARD *n* plantation of grape vines, esp for making wine

VINEYARDS > VINEYARD

VINIC *adj* of, relating to, or contained in wine

VINIER > VINE

VINIEST > VINE

VINIFERA *n* species of vine

VINIFERAS > VINIFERA

VINIFIED > VINIFY

VINIFIES > VINIFY

VINIFY *vb* convert into wine

VINIFYING > VINIFY

VINING > VINE

VINO *n* wine

VINOLENT *adj* drunken

VINOLOGY *n* scientific study of vines

VINOS > VINO

VINOSITY *n* distinctive and essential quality and flavour of wine

VINOUS *adj* of or characteristic of wine

VINOUSLY > VINOUS

VINS > VIN

VINT *vb* sell (wine)

VINTAGE *n* wine from a particular harvest of grapes ▷ *adj* best and most typical ▷ *vb* gather (grapes) or make (wine)

VINTAGED > VINTAGE

VINTAGER *n* grape harvester

VINTAGERS > VINTAGER

VINTAGES > VINTAGE

VINTAGING > VINTAGE

VINTED > VINT

VINTING > VINT

VINTNER *n* dealer in wine

VINTNERS > VINTNER

VINTRIES > VINTRY

VINTRY *n* place where wine is sold

VINTS > VINT

VINY > VINE

VINYL *n* type of plastic, used in mock leather and records ▷ *adj* of or containing a particular group of atoms

VINYLIC > VINYL

VINYLS > VINYL

VIOL *n* early stringed instrument preceding the violin

VIOLA *n* stringed instrument lower in pitch than a violin

VIOLABLE > VIOLATE

VIOLABLY > VIOLATE

VIOLAS > VIOLA

VIOLATE *vb* break (a law or agreement) ▷ *adj* violated or dishonoured

VIOLATED > VIOLATE

VIOLATER > VIOLATE

VIOLATERS > VIOLATE

VIOLATES > VIOLATE

VIOLATING > VIOLATE

VIOLATION > VIOLATE

VIOLATIVE > VIOLATE

VIOLATOR > VIOLATE

VIOLATORS > VIOLATE

VIOLD *archaic or poetic past form of* > VIAL

V

VIOLENCE n use of physical force, usu intended to cause injury or destruction

VIOLENCES > VIOLENCE

VIOLENT adj using or involving physical force with the intention of causing injury or destruction ▷ vb coerce

VIOLENTED > VIOLENT

VIOLENTLY > VIOLENT

VIOLENTS > VIOLENT

VIOLER n person who plays the viol

VIOLERS > VIOLER

VIOLET n plant with bluish-purple flowers ▷ adj bluish-purple

VIOLETS > VIOLET

VIOLIN n small four-stringed musical instrument played with a bow

VIOLINIST n person who plays the violin

VIOLINS > VIOLIN

VIOLIST n person who plays the viola

VIOLISTS > VIOLIST

VIOLONE n double-bass member of the viol family

VIOLONES > VIOLONE

VIOLS > VIOL

VIOMYCIN n type of antibiotic

VIOMYCINS > VIOMYCIN

VIOSTEROL n type of vitamin

VIPER n poisonous snake

VIPERFISH n predatory deep-sea fish

VIPERINE same as > VIPEROUS

VIPERISH same as > VIPEROUS

VIPEROUS adj of, relating to, or resembling a viper

VIPERS > VIPER

VIRAEMIA n condition in which virus particles circulate and reproduce in the bloodstream

VIRAEMIAS > VIRAEMIA

VIRAEMIC > VIRAEMIA

VIRAGO n aggressive woman

VIRAGOES > VIRAGO

VIRAGOISH > VIRAGO

VIRAGOS > VIRAGO

VIRAL adj of or caused by a virus

VIRALLY > VIRAL

VIRANDA same as > VERANDA

VIRANDAS > VIRANDA

VIRANDO same as > VERANDA

VIRANDOS > VIRANDO

VIRE vb turn

VIRED > VIRE

VIRELAI same as > VIRELAY

VIRELAIS > VIRELAI

VIRELAY n old French verse form

VIRELAYS > VIRELAY

VIREMENT n administrative transfer of funds from one part of a budget to another

VIREMENTS > VIREMENT

VIREMIA same as > VIRAEMIA

VIREMIAS > VIREMIA

VIREMIC > VIREMIA

VIRENT adj green

VIREO n American songbird

VIREONINE > VIREO

VIREOS > VIREO

VIRES > VIRE

VIRESCENT adj greenish or becoming green

VIRETOT as in on the viretot in a rush

VIRETOTS > VIRETOT

VIRGA n wisps of rain or snow that evaporate before reaching the earth

VIRGAS > VIRGA

VIRGATE adj long, straight, and thin ▷ n obsolete measure of land area, usually taken as equivalent to 30 acres

VIRGATES > VIRGATE

VIRGE n rod

VIRGER n rod-bearer

VIRGERS > VIRGER

VIRGES > VIRGE

VIRGIN n person, esp a woman, who has not had sexual intercourse ▷ adj not having had sexual intercourse ▷ vb behave like a virgin

VIRGINAL adj like a virgin ▷ n early keyboard instrument like a small harpsichord

VIRGINALS > VIRGINAL

VIRGINED > VIRGIN

VIRGINIA n type of flue-cured tobacco grown originally in Virginia

VIRGINIAS > VIRGINIA

VIRGINING > VIRGIN

VIRGINITY n condition or fact of being a virgin

VIRGINIUM former name for > FRANCIUM

VIRGINLY > VIRGIN

VIRGINS > VIRGIN

VIRGULATE adj rod-shaped or rodlike

VIRGULE another name for > SLASH

VIRGULES > VIRGULE

VIRICIDAL > VIRICIDE

VIRICIDE n substance that destroys viruses

VIRICIDES > VIRICIDE

VIRID adj verdant

VIRIDIAN n green pigment consisting of a hydrated form of chromic oxide

VIRIDIANS > VIRIDIAN

VIRIDITE n greenish mineral

VIRIDITES > VIRIDITE

VIRIDITY n quality or state of being green

VIRILE adj having the traditional male characteristics of physical strength and a high sex drive

VIRILELY > VIRILE

VIRILISE same as > VIRILIZE

VIRILISED > VIRILISE

VIRILISES > VIRILISE

VIRILISM n abnormal development in a woman of male secondary sex characteristics

VIRILISMS > VIRILISM

VIRILITY > VIRILE

VIRILIZE vb cause male characteristics to appear in female

VIRILIZED > VIRILIZE

VIRILIZES > VIRILIZE

VIRILOCAL adj living with husband's family

VIRING > VIRE

VIRINO n entity postulated to be the causative agent of BSE

VIRINOS > VIRINO

VIRION n virus in infective form, consisting of an RNA particle within a protein covering

VIRIONS > VIRION

VIRL same as > FERRULE

VIRLS > VIRL

VIROGENE n type of viral gene

VIROGENES > VIROGENE

VIROID n any of various infective RNA particles

VIROIDS > VIROID

VIROLOGIC > VIROLOGY

VIROLOGY n study of viruses

VIROSE adj poisonous

VIROSES > VIROSIS

VIROSIS n viral disease

VIROUS same as > VIROSE

VIRTU n taste or love for curios or works of fine art

VIRTUAL adj having the effect but not the form of

VIRTUALLY adv practically, almost

VIRTUE n moral goodness

VIRTUES > VIRTUE

VIRTUOSA n female virtuoso

VIRTUOSAS > VIRTUOSA

VIRTUOSE > VIRTUOSA

VIRTUOSI > VIRTUOSO

VIRTUOSIC > VIRTUOSO

VIRTUOSO n person with impressive esp musical skill ▷ adj showing exceptional skill or brilliance

VIRTUOSOS > VIRTUOSO

VIRTUOUS adj morally good

VIRTUS > VIRTU

VIRUCIDAL > VIRUCIDE

VIRUCIDE same as > VIRICIDE

VIRUCIDES > VIRUCIDE

VIRULENCE n quality of being virulent

VIRULENCY same as > VIRULENCE

VIRULENT adj extremely bitter or hostile

VIRUS n microorganism that causes disease in humans, animals, and plants

VIRUSES > VIRUS

VIRUSLIKE > VIRUS

VIRUSOID n small plant virus

VIRUSOIDS > VIRUSOID

VIS n power, force, or strength

VISA n permission to enter a country, shown by a stamp on the passport ▷ vb enter a visa into (a passport)

VISAED > VISA

VISAGE n face

VISAGED > VISAGE

VISAGES > VISAGE

VISAGIST same as > VISAGISTE

VISAGISTE n person who designs and applies face make-up

VISAGISTS > VISAGIST

VISAING > VISA

VISARD same as > VIZARD

VISARDS > VISARD

VISAS > VISA

VISCACHA n South American rodent

VISCACHAS > VISCACHA

VISCARIA n type of perennial plant

VISCARIAS > VISCARIA

VISCERA npl large abdominal organs

VISCERAL adj instinctive

VISCERATE vb disembowel

VISCID adj sticky

VISCIDITY > VISCID

VISCIDLY > VISCID

VISCIN n sticky substance found on plants

VISCINS > VISCIN

VISCOID adj (of a fluid) somewhat viscous

VISCOIDAL same as > VISCOID

VISCOSE same as > VISCOUS

VISCOSES > VISCOSE

VISCOSITY n state of being viscous

VISCOUNT n British nobleman ranking between an earl and a baron

VISCOUNTS > VISCOUNT

VISCOUNTY > VISCOUNT

VISCOUS adj thick and sticky

VISCOUSLY > VISCOUS

V

VISCUM n shrub genus
VISCUMS > VISCUM
VISCUS n internal organ
VISE vb advise or award a visa to ▷ n (in US English) vice
VISED > VISE
VISEED > VISE
VISEING > VISE
VISELIKE > VICE
VISES > VISE
VISHING n telephone scam used to gain access to credit card numbers or bank details
VISHINGS > VISHING
VISIBLE adj able to be seen ▷ n visible item of trade
VISIBLES > VISIBLE
VISIBLY > VISIBLE
VISIE same as > VIZY
VISIED > VISIE
VISIEING > VISIE
VISIER > VISIE
VISIERS > VISIE
VISIES > VISIE
VISILE n person best stimulated by vision
VISILES > VISILE
VISING > VISE
VISION n ability to see ▷ vb see or show in or as if in a vision
VISIONAL adj of, relating to, or seen in a vision, apparition, etc
VISIONARY adj showing foresight ▷ n visionary person
VISIONED > VISION
VISIONER n visionary
VISIONERS > VISIONER
VISIONING > VISION
VISIONIST n type of visionary
VISIONS > VISION
VISIT vb go or come to see ▷ n instance of visiting
VISITABLE > VISIT
VISITANT n ghost or apparition ▷ adj paying a visit
VISITANTS > VISITANT
VISITATOR n official visitor
VISITE n type of cape
VISITED > VISIT
VISITEE n person who is visited
VISITEES > VISITEE
VISITER variant of > VISITOR
VISITERS > VISITER
VISITES > VISITE
VISITING > VISIT
VISITINGS > VISIT
VISITOR n person who visits a person or place
VISITORS > VISITOR
VISITRESS n female visitor
VISITS > VISIT
VISIVE adj visual

VISNE n neighbourhood
VISNES > VISNE
VISNOMIE same as > VISNOMY
VISNOMIES > VISNOMY
VISNOMY n method of judging character from facial features
VISON n type of mink
VISONS > VISON
VISOR n transparent part of a helmet that pulls down over the face ▷ vb cover, provide, or protect with a visor
VISORED > VISOR
VISORING > VISOR
VISORLESS > VISOR
VISORS > VISOR
VISTA n (beautiful) extensive view ▷ vb make into vistas
VISTAED > VISTA
VISTAING > VISTA
VISTAL > VISTA
VISTALESS > VISTA
VISTAS > VISTA
VISTO same as > VISTA
VISTOS > VISTO
VISUAL adj done by or used in seeing ▷ n sketch to show the proposed layout of an advertisement, as in a newspaper
VISUALISE same as > VISUALIZE
VISUALIST n visualiser
VISUALITY > VISUAL
VISUALIZE vb form a mental image of
VISUALLY > VISUAL
VISUALS > VISUAL
VITA n curriculum vitae
VITACEOUS adj of a family of flowering plants that includes the grapevine
VITAE > VITA
VITAL adj essential or highly important ▷ n bodily organs that are necessary to maintain life
VITALISE same as > VITALIZE
VITALISED > VITALISE
VITALISER > VITALISE
VITALISES > VITALISE
VITALISM n philosophical doctrine that the phenomena of life cannot be explained in purely mechanical terms
VITALISMS > VITALISM
VITALIST > VITALISM
VITALISTS > VITALISM
VITALITY n physical or mental energy
VITALIZE vb fill with life or vitality
VITALIZED > VITALIZE
VITALIZER > VITALIZE
VITALIZES > VITALIZE
VITALLY > VITAL
VITALNESS > VITAL
VITALS > VITAL

VITAMER n type of chemical
VITAMERS > VITAMER
VITAMIN n one of a group of substances that are essential in the diet for specific body processes
VITAMINE same as > VITAMIN
VITAMINES > VITAMINE
VITAMINIC > VITAMIN
VITAMINS > VITAMIN
VITAS > VITA
VITASCOPE n early type of film projector
VITATIVE adj fond of life
VITE adv musical direction
VITELLARY > VITELLUS
VITELLI > VITELLUS
VITELLIN n phosphoprotein that is the major protein in egg yolk
VITELLINE adj of or relating to the yolk of an egg
VITELLINS > VITELLIN
VITELLUS n yolk of an egg
VITESSE n speed
VITESSES > VITESSE
VITEX n type of herb
VITEXES > VITEX
VITIABLE > VITIATE
VITIATE vb spoil the effectiveness of
VITIATED > VITIATE
VITIATES > VITIATE
VITIATING > VITIATE
VITIATION > VITIATE
VITIATOR > VITIATE
VITIATORS > VITIATE
VITICETA > VITICETUM
VITICETUM n place where vines are cultivated
VITICIDE n vine killer
VITICIDES > VITICIDE
VITILIGO n area of skin that is white from albinism or loss of melanin pigmentation
VITILIGOS > VITILIGO
VITIOSITY n viciousness
VITIOUS adj mistaken
VITRAGE n light fabric
VITRAGES > VITRAGE
VITRAIL n stained glass
VITRAIN n type of coal occurring as horizontal glassy bands of a nonsoiling friable material
VITRAINS > VITRAIN
VITRAUX > VITRAIL
VITREOUS adj like or made from glass
VITREUM n vitreous body
VITREUMS > VITREUM
VITRIC adj of, relating to, resembling, or having the nature of glass
VITRICS n glassware
VITRIFIED > VITRIFY
VITRIFIES > VITRIFY
VITRIFORM adj having the form or appearance of glass
VITRIFY vb change or be

changed into glass or a glassy substance
VITRINE n glass display case or cabinet for works of art, curios, etc
VITRINES > VITRINE
VITRIOL n language expressing bitterness and hatred ▷ vb attack or injure with or as if with vitriol
VITRIOLED > VITRIOL
VITRIOLIC adj (of language) severely bitter or harsh
VITRIOLS > VITRIOL
VITTA n tubelike cavity containing oil that occurs in the fruits of certain plants
VITTAE > VITTA
VITTATE > VITTA
VITTLE obsolete or dialect spelling of > VICTUAL
VITTLED > VITTLE
VITTLES obsolete or dialect spelling of > VICTUALS
VITTLING > VITTLE
VITULAR same as > VITULINE
VITULINE adj of or resembling a calf or veal
VIVA interj long live (a person or thing) ▷ n examination in the form of an interview ▷ vb examine (a candidate) in a spoken interview
VIVACE adv in a lively manner ▷ adj performed in a lively manner ▷ n piece of music to be performed in this way
VIVACES > VIVACE
VIVACIOUS adj full of energy and enthusiasm
VIVACITY n quality of being vivacious
VIVAED > VIVA
VIVAING > VIVA
VIVAMENTE adv in a lively manner
VIVANDIER n sutler
VIVARIA > VIVARIUM
VIVARIES > VIVARY
VIVARIUM n place where animals are kept in natural conditions
VIVARIUMS > VIVARIUM
VIVARY same as > VIVARIUM
VIVAS > VIVA
VIVAT interj long live ▷ n expression of acclamation
VIVATS > VIVAT
VIVDA n method of drying meat
VIVDAS > VIVDA
VIVE interj long live
VIVELY adv in a lively manner
VIVENCIES > VIVENCY
VIVENCY n physical or mental energy
VIVER n fish pond
VIVERRA n civet genus

V

VIVERRAS > VIVERRA
VIVERRID > VIVERRINE
VIVERRIDS > VIVERRINE
VIVERRINE n type of mammal of Eurasia and Africa ▷ adj of this family of mammals
VIVERS > VIVER
VIVES n disease found in horses
VIVIANITE n type of mineral
VIVID adj very bright
VIVIDER > VIVID
VIVIDEST > VIVID
VIVIDITY > VIVID
VIVIDLY > VIVID
VIVIDNESS > VIVID
VIVIFIC adj giving life
VIVIFIED > VIVIFY
VIVIFIER > VIVIFY
VIVIFIERS > VIVIFY
VIVIFIES > VIVIFY
VIVIFY vb animate, inspire
VIVIFYING > VIVIFY
VIVIPARA n animals that produce offspring that develop as embryos within the female parent
VIVIPARY n act of giving birth producing offspring that have developed as embryos
VIVISECT vb subject (an animal) to vivisection
VIVISECTS > VIVISECT
VIVO adv with life and vigour
VIVRES n provisions
VIXEN n female fox
VIXENISH > VIXEN
VIXENLY > VIXEN
VIXENS > VIXEN
VIZAMENT n consultation
VIZAMENTS > VIZAMENT
VIZARD n means of disguise ▷ vb conceal by means of a disguise
VIZARDED > VIZARD
VIZARDING > VIZARD
VIZARDS > VIZARD
VIZCACHA same as > VISCACHA
VIZCACHAS > VIZCACHA
VIZIED > VIZY
VIZIER n high official in certain Muslim countries
VIZIERATE n position, rank, or authority of a vizier
VIZIERIAL > VIZIER
VIZIERS > VIZIER
VIZIES > VIZY
VIZIR same as > VIZIER
VIZIRATE > VIZIR
VIZIRATES > VIZIR
VIZIRIAL > VIZIR
VIZIRS > VIZIR
VIZIRSHIP > VIZIR
VIZOR same as > VISOR
VIZORED > VIZOR
VIZORING > VIZOR
VIZORLESS > VIZOR

VIZORS > VIZOR
VIZSLA n breed of Hungarian hunting dog with a smooth rusty-gold coat
VIZSLAS > VIZSLA
VIZY vb look
VIZYING > VIZY
VIZZIE same as > VIZY
VIZZIED > VIZZIE
VIZZIEING > VIZZIE
VIZZIES > VIZZIE
VLEI n area of low marshy ground, esp one that feeds a stream
VLEIS > VLEI
VLIES > VLY
VLOG n video weblog
VLOGGER n person who keeps a video blog
VLOGGERS > VLOGGER
VLOGGING n action of keeping a video blog
VLOGGINGS > VLOGGING
VLOGS > VLOG
VLY same as > VLEI
VOAR n spring
VOARS > VOAR
VOCAB n vocabulary
VOCABLE n word regarded simply as a sequence of letters or spoken sounds ▷ adj capable of being uttered
VOCABLES > VOCABLE
VOCABLY > VOCABLE
VOCABS > VOCAB
VOCABULAR > VOCABLE
VOCAL adj relating to the voice ▷ n piece of jazz or pop music that is sung
VOCALESE n style of jazz singing
VOCALESES > VOCALESE
VOCALIC adj of, relating to, or containing a vowel or vowels
VOCALICS n non-verbal aspects of voice
VOCALION n type of musical instrument
VOCALIONS > VOCALION
VOCALISE same as > VOCALIZE
VOCALISED > VOCALISE
VOCALISER > VOCALISE
VOCALISES > VOCALISE
VOCALISM n exercise of the voice, as in singing or speaking
VOCALISMS > VOCALISM
VOCALIST n singer
VOCALISTS > VOCALIST
VOCALITY > VOCAL
VOCALIZE vb express with the voice
VOCALIZED > VOCALIZE
VOCALIZER > VOCALIZE
VOCALIZES > VOCALIZE
VOCALLY > VOCAL
VOCALNESS > VOCAL
VOCALS > VOCAL
VOCATION n profession or trade

VOCATIONS > VOCATION
VOCATIVE n (in some languages) case of nouns used when addressing a person ▷ adj relating to, used in, or characterized by calling
VOCATIVES > VOCATIVE
VOCES > VOX
VOCODER n type of synthesizer that uses the human voice as an oscillator
VOCODERS > VOCODER
VOCULAR > VOCULE
VOCULE n faint noise made when articulating certain sounds
VOCULES > VOCULE
VODCAST vb podcast with video
VODCASTED > VODCAST
VODCASTER > VODCAST
VODCASTS > VODCAST
VODDIES > VODDY
VODDY n vodka
VODKA n (Russian) spirit distilled from potatoes or grain
VODKAS > VODKA
VODOU variant of > VOODOO
VODOUN same as > VODUN
VODOUNS > VODOUN
VODOUS > VODOU
VODUN n voodoo
VODUNS > VODUN
VOE n (in Orkney and Shetland) a small bay or narrow creek
VOEMA n vigour or energy
VOEMAS > VOEMA
VOERTSAK variant of > VOETSEK
VOERTSEK variant of > VOETSEK
VOES > VOE
VOETSAK same as > VOETSEK
VOETSEK interj S African offensive expression of rejection
VOGIE adj conceited
VOGIER > VOGIE
VOGIEST > VOGIE
VOGUE n popular style ▷ adj popular or fashionable ▷ vb bring into vogue
VOGUED > VOGUE
VOGUEING n dance style of the late 1980s
VOGUEINGS > VOGUEING
VOGUER > VOGUE
VOGUERS > VOGUE
VOGUES > VOGUE
VOGUEY > VOGUE
VOGUIER > VOGUE
VOGUIEST > VOGUE
VOGUING same as > VOGUEING
VOGUINGS > VOGUING
VOGUISH > VOGUE
VOGUISHLY > VOGUE
VOICE n (quality of) sound made when speaking or

singing ▷ vb express verbally
VOICED adj articulated with accompanying vibration of the vocal cords
VOICEFUL > VOICE
VOICELESS adj without a voice
VOICEMAIL n facility of leaving recorded message by telephone
VOICEOVER n spoken commentary by unseen narrator on film
VOICER > VOICE
VOICERS > VOICE
VOICES > VOICE
VOICING > VOICE
VOICINGS > VOICE
VOID adj not legally binding ▷ n feeling of deprivation ▷ vb make invalid
VOIDABLE adj capable of being voided
VOIDANCE n annulment, as of a contract
VOIDANCES > VOIDANCE
VOIDED adj (of a design) with a hole in the centre of the same shape as the design
VOIDEE n light meal eaten before bed
VOIDEES > VOIDEE
VOIDER > VOID
VOIDERS > VOID
VOIDING > VOID
VOIDINGS > VOID
VOIDNESS > VOID
VOIDS > VOID
VOILA interj word used to express satisfaction
VOILE n light semitransparent fabric
VOILES > VOILE
VOIP n voice-over internet protocol
VOIPS > VOIP
VOISINAGE n district or neighbourhood
VOITURE n type of vehicle
VOITURES > VOITURE
VOITURIER n driver of a voiture
VOIVODE n type of military leader
VOIVODES > VOIVODE
VOL n heraldic wings
VOLA n palm of hand or sole of foot
VOLABLE adj quick-witted
VOLAE > VOLA
VOLAGE adj changeable
VOLANT adj in a flying position
VOLANTE n Spanish horse carriage
VOLANTES > VOLANTE
VOLAR adj of or relating to the palm of the hand or the sole of the foot
VOLARIES > VOLARY
VOLARY n large bird enclosure

VOLATIC adj flying
VOLATILE adj liable to sudden change, esp in behaviour ▷ n volatile substance
VOLATILES > VOLATILE
VOLCANIAN same as > VOLCANIC
VOLCANIC adj of or relating to volcanoes
VOLCANICS n types of rock
VOLCANISE same as > VOLCANIZE
VOLCANISM n processes that result in the formation of volcanoes
VOLCANIST n person who studies volcanoes
VOLCANIZE vb subject to the effects of or change by volcanic heat
VOLCANO n mountain with a vent through which lava is ejected
VOLCANOES > VOLCANO
VOLCANOS > VOLCANO
VOLE n small rodent ▷ vb to win by taking all the tricks in a deal
VOLED > VOLE
VOLENS as in nolens volens whether willing or unwilling
VOLERIES > VOLERY
VOLERY same as > VOLARY
VOLES > VOLE
VOLET n type of veil
VOLETS > VOLET
VOLING > VOLE
VOLITANT adj flying or moving about rapidly
VOLITATE vb flutter
VOLITATED > VOLITATE
VOLITATES > VOLITATE
VOLITIENT > VOLITION
VOLITION n ability to decide things for oneself
VOLITIONS > VOLITION
VOLITIVE adj of, relating to, or emanating from the will ▷ n (in some languages) a verb form or mood used to express a wish or desire
VOLITIVES > VOLITIVE
VOLK n people or nation, esp the nation of Afrikaners
VOLKS > VOLK
VOLKSLIED n German folk song
VOLKSRAAD n Boer assembly in South Africa in the 19th century
VOLLEY n simultaneous discharge of ammunition ▷ vb discharge (ammunition) in a volley
VOLLEYED > VOLLEY
VOLLEYER > VOLLEY
VOLLEYERS > VOLLEY
VOLLEYING > VOLLEY
VOLLEYS > VOLLEY
VOLOST n (in the former Soviet Union) a rural soviet

VOLOSTS > VOLOST
VOLPINO n Italian breed of dog
VOLPINOS > VOLPINO
VOLPLANE vb glide in an aeroplane
VOLPLANED > VOLPLANE
VOLPLANES > VOLPLANE
VOLS > VOL
VOLT n unit of electric potential ▷ vb (in fencing) make a quick movement to avoid a thrust
VOLTA n quick-moving Italian dance popular during the 16th and 17th centuries
VOLTAGE n electric potential difference expressed in volts
VOLTAGES > VOLTAGE
VOLTAIC adj producing an electric current
VOLTAISM another name for > GALVANISM
VOLTAISMS > VOLTAISM
VOLTE same as > VOLT
VOLTED > VOLT
VOLTES > VOLTE
VOLTI adv musical direction
VOLTIGEUR n French infantry member
VOLTING > VOLT
VOLTINISM n number of annual broods of an animal
VOLTMETER n instrument for measuring voltage
VOLTS > VOLT
VOLUBIL same as > VOLUBLE
VOLUBLE adj talking easily and at length
VOLUBLY > VOLUBLE
VOLUCRINE adj relating to birds
VOLUME n size of the space occupied by something ▷ vb billow or surge in volume
VOLUMED > VOLUME
VOLUMES > VOLUME
VOLUMETER n any instrument for measuring the volume of a solid, liquid, or gas
VOLUMETRY n act of measuring by volume
VOLUMINAL > VOLUME
VOLUMING > VOLUME
VOLUMISE same as > VOLUMIZE
VOLUMISED > VOLUMISE
VOLUMISER same as > VOLUMIZER
VOLUMISES > VOLUMISE
VOLUMIST n author
VOLUMISTS > VOLUMIST
VOLUMIZE vb create volume in something
VOLUMIZED > VOLUMIZE
VOLUMIZER n product used to give extra body to hair
VOLUMIZES > VOLUMIZE

VOLUNTARY adj done by choice ▷ n organ solo in a church service
VOLUNTEER n person who offers voluntarily to do something ▷ vb offer one's services
VOLUSPA n Icelandic mythological poem
VOLUSPAS > VOLUSPA
VOLUTE n spiral or twisting turn, form, or object ▷ adj having the form of a volute
VOLUTED > VOLUTE
VOLUTES > VOLUTE
VOLUTIN n granular substance found in cells
VOLUTINS > VOLUTIN
VOLUTION n rolling, revolving, or spiral form or motion
VOLUTIONS > VOLUTION
VOLUTOID > VOLUTE
VOLVA n cup-shaped structure that sheathes the base of the stalk of certain mushrooms
VOLVAE > VOLVA
VOLVAS > VOLVA
VOLVATE > VOLVA
VOLVE vb turn over
VOLVED > VOLVE
VOLVES > VOLVE
VOLVING > VOLVE
VOLVOX n freshwater protozoan
VOLVOXES > VOLVOX
VOLVULI > VOLVULUS
VOLVULUS n abnormal twisting of the intestines causing obstruction
VOMER n thin flat bone forming part of the separation between the nasal passages in mammals
VOMERINE > VOMER
VOMERS > VOMER
VOMICA n pus-containing cavity
VOMICAE > VOMICA
VOMICAS > VOMICA
VOMIT vb eject (the contents of the stomach) through the mouth ▷ n matter vomited
VOMITED > VOMIT
VOMITER > VOMIT
VOMITERS > VOMIT
VOMITING > VOMIT
VOMITINGS > VOMIT
VOMITIVE same as > VOMITORY
VOMITIVES > VOMITIVE
VOMITO n form of yellow fever
VOMITORIA n entrances in an amphitheatre
VOMITORY adj causing vomiting ▷ n vomitory agent
VOMITOS > VOMITO
VOMITOUS adj arousing feelings of disgust
VOMITS > VOMIT

VOMITUS n matter that has been vomited
VOMITUSES > VOMITUS
VONGOLE npl (in Italian cookery) clams
VOODOO n religion involving ancestor worship and witchcraft ▷ adj of or relating to voodoo ▷ vb affect by or as if by the power of voodoo
VOODOOED > VOODOO
VOODOOING > VOODOO
VOODOOISM same as > VOODOO
VOODOOIST > VOODOO
VOODOOS > VOODOO
VOORKAMER n front room of a house
VOORSKOT n advance payment made to a farmer for crops
VOORSKOTS > VOORSKOT
VOR vb (in dialect) warn
VORACIOUS adj craving great quantities of food
VORACITY > VORACIOUS
VORAGO n chasm
VORAGOES > VORAGO
VORANT adj devouring
VORLAGE n skiing position
VORLAGES > VORLAGE
VORPAL adj sharp
VORRED > VOR
VORRING > VOR
VORS > VOR
VORTEX n whirlpool
VORTEXES > VORTEX
VORTICAL > VORTEX
VORTICES > VORTEX
VORTICISM n art movement in 20th-century England
VORTICIST > VORTICISM
VORTICITY n rotational spin in a fluid
VORTICOSE adj rotating quickly
VOSTRO as in vostro account bank account held by a foreign bank with a British bank
VOTABLE > VOTE
VOTARESS n female votary
VOTARIES > VOTARY
VOTARIST variant of > VOTARY
VOTARISTS > VOTARIST
VOTARY n person dedicated to religion or to a cause ▷ adj ardently devoted to the services or worship of God
VOTE n choice made by a participant in a shared decision ▷ vb make a choice by a vote
VOTEABLE > VOTE
VOTED > VOTE
VOTEEN n devotee
VOTEENS > VOTEEN
VOTELESS > VOTE
VOTER n person who can or does vote

V

VOTERS > VOTER
VOTES > VOTE
VOTING > VOTE
VOTINGS > VOTE
VOTIVE adj done or given to fulfil a vow ▷ n votive offering
VOTIVELY > VOTIVE
VOTIVES > VOTIVE
VOTRESS > VOTARESS
VOTRESSES > VOTRESS
VOUCH vb give personal assurance ▷ n act of vouching
VOUCHED > VOUCH
VOUCHEE n person summoned to court to defend a title
VOUCHEES > VOUCHEE
VOUCHER n ticket used instead of money to buy specified goods ▷ vb summon someone to court as a vouchee
VOUCHERED > VOUCHER
VOUCHERS > VOUCHER
VOUCHES > VOUCH
VOUCHING > VOUCH
VOUCHSAFE vb give, entrust
VOUDON variant of > VOODOO
VOUDONS > VOUDON
VOUDOU same as > VOODOO
VOUDOUED > VOUDOU
VOUDOUING > VOUDOU
VOUDOUN variant of > VOODOO
VOUDOUNS > VOUDOUN
VOUDOUS > VOUDOU
VOUGE n form of pike used by foot soldiers in the 14th century and later
VOUGES > VOUGE
VOULGE n type of medieval weapon
VOULGES > VOULGE
VOULU adj deliberate
VOUSSOIR n wedge-shaped stone or brick that is used with others to construct an arch
VOUSSOIRS > VOUSSOIR
VOUTSAFE same as > VOUCHSAFE
VOUTSAFED > VOUTSAFE
VOUTSAFES > VOUTSAFE
VOUVRAY n dry white French wine
VOUVRAYS > VOUVRAY
VOW n solemn and binding promise ▷ vb promise solemnly
VOWED > VOW

VOWEL n speech sound made without obstructing the flow of breath ▷ vb say as a vowel
VOWELISE same as > VOWELIZE
VOWELISED > VOWELISE
VOWELISES > VOWELISE
VOWELIZE vb mark the vowel points in (a Hebrew word or text)
VOWELIZED > VOWELIZE
VOWELIZES > VOWELIZE
VOWELLED > VOWEL
VOWELLESS > VOWEL
VOWELLING > VOWEL
VOWELLY > VOWEL
VOWELS > VOWEL
VOWER > VOW
VOWERS > VOW
VOWESS n nun
VOWESSES > VOWESS
VOWING > VOW
VOWLESS > VOW
VOWS > VOW
VOX n voice or sound
VOXEL n term used in computing imaging
VOXELS > VOXEL
VOYAGE n long journey by sea or in space ▷ vb make a voyage
VOYAGED > VOYAGE
VOYAGER > VOYAGE
VOYAGERS > VOYAGE
VOYAGES > VOYAGE
VOYAGEUR n French canoeman who transported furs from trading posts in the North American interior
VOYAGEURS > VOYAGEUR
VOYAGING > VOYAGE
VOYEUR n person who obtains pleasure from watching people undressing or having sex
VOYEURISM > VOYEUR
VOYEURS > VOYEUR
VOZHD n Russian leader
VOZHDS > VOZHD
VRAIC n type of seaweed
VRAICKER n person who gathers vraic
VRAICKERS > VRAICKER
VRAICKING n act of gathering vraic
VRAICS > VRAIC
VRIL n life force
VRILS > VRIL
VROOM interj exclamation imitative of a car engine revving up ▷ vb move noisily and at high speed

VROOMED > VROOM
VROOMING > VROOM
VROOMS > VROOM
VROT adj South African slang for rotten
VROU n Afrikaner woman, esp a married woman
VROUS > VROU
VROUW n woman
VROUWS > VROUW
VROW same as > VROUW
VROWS > VROW
VUG n small cavity in a rock or vein, usually lined with crystals
VUGG same as > VUG
VUGGIER > VUG
VUGGIEST > VUG
VUGGS > VUGG
VUGGY > VUG
VUGH same as > VUG
VUGHIER > VUGH
VUGHIEST > VUGH
VUGHS > VUGH
VUGHY > VUG
VUGS > VUG
VULCAN n blacksmith
VULCANIAN adj of or relating to a volcanic eruption
VULCANIC same as > VOLCANIC
VULCANISE same as > VULCANIZE
VULCANISM same as > VOLCANISM
VULCANIST same as > VOLCANIST
VULCANITE n vulcanized rubber
VULCANIZE vb strengthen (rubber) by treating it with sulphur
VULCANS > VULCAN
VULGAR adj showing lack of good taste, decency, or refinement ▷ n common and ignorant person
VULGARER > VULGAR
VULGAREST > VULGAR
VULGARIAN n vulgar (rich) person
VULGARISE same as > VULGARIZE
VULGARISM n coarse word or phrase
VULGARITY n condition of being vulgar
VULGARIZE vb make vulgar or too common
VULGARLY > VULGAR
VULGARS > VULGAR
VULGATE n commonly recognized text or version

▷ adj generally accepted
VULGATES > VULGATE
VULGO adv generally
VULGUS n the common people
VULGUSES > VULGUS
VULN vb wound
VULNED > VULN
VULNERARY adj of, relating to, or used to heal a wound ▷ n vulnerary drug or agent
VULNERATE vb wound
VULNING > VULN
VULNS > VULN
VULPICIDE n person who kills foxes
VULPINE adj of or like a fox
VULPINISM > VULPINE
VULPINITE n type of granular anhydrite
VULSELLA n forceps
VULSELLAE > VULSELLA
VULSELLUM variant of > VULSELLA
VULTURE n large bird that feeds on the flesh of dead animals
VULTURES > VULTURE
VULTURINE adj of, relating to, or resembling a vulture
VULTURISH > VULTURE
VULTURISM n greed
VULTURN n type of turkey
VULTURNS > VULTURN
VULTUROUS same as > VULTURINE
VULVA n woman's external genitals
VULVAE > VULVA
VULVAL > VULVA
VULVAR > VULVA
VULVAS > VULVA
VULVATE > VULVA
VULVIFORM > VULVA
VULVITIS n inflammation of the vulva
VUM vb swear
VUMMED > VUM
VUMMING > VUM
VUMS > VUM
VUTTIER > VUTTY
VUTTIEST > VUTTY
VUTTY adj dirty
VUVUZELA n South African instrument blown by football fans
VUVUZELAS > VUVUZELA
VYING > VIE
VYINGLY > VIE
VYINGS > VIE

Ww

WAAC *n* (formerly) member of the Women's Auxiliary Army Corp

WAACS > WAAC

WAB *same as* > WEB

WABAIN *same as* > OUABAIN

WABAINS > WABAIN

WABBIT *adj* weary

WABBLE *same as* > WOBBLE

WABBLED > WABBLE

WABBLER > WABBLE

WABBLERS > WABBLE

WABBLES > WABBLE

WABBLIER > WABBLE

WABBLIEST > WABBLE

WABBLING > WABBLE

WABBLY > WABBLE

WABOOM *another word for* > WAGENBOOM

WABOOMS > WABOOM

WABS > WAB

WABSTER *Scots form of* > WEBSTER

WABSTERS > WABSTER

WACK *n* friend

WACKE *n* any of various soft earthy rocks that resemble or are derived from basaltic rocks

WACKER *same as* > WACK

WACKERS > WACKER

WACKES > WACKE

WACKEST > WACK

WACKIER > WACKY

WACKIEST > WACKY

WACKILY > WACKY

WACKINESS > WACKY

WACKO *adj* mad or eccentric ▷ *n* mad or eccentric person

WACKOS > WACKO

WACKS > WACK

WACKY *adj* eccentric or funny

WAD *n* black earthy ore of manganese ▷ *n* small mass of soft material ▷ *vb* form (something) into a wad

WADABLE > WADE

WADD *same as* > WAD

WADDED > WAD

WADDER > WAD

WADDERS > WAD

WADDIE *same as* > WADDY

WADDIED > WADDY

WADDIES > WADDY

WADDING > WAD

WADDINGS > WAD

WADDLE *vb* walk with short swaying steps ▷ *n* swaying walk

WADDLED > WADDLE

WADDLER > WADDLE

WADDLERS > WADDLE

WADDLES > WADDLE

WADDLIER > WADDLE

WADDLIEST > WADDLE

WADDLING > WADDLE

WADDLY > WADDLE

WADDS > WADD

WADDY *n* heavy wooden club used by Australian Aborigines ▷ *vb* hit with a waddy

WADDYING > WADDY

WADE *vb* walk with difficulty through water or mud ▷ *n* act or an instance of wading

WADEABLE > WADE

WADED > WADE

WADER *n* long-legged water bird

WADERS *npl* long waterproof boots which completely cover the legs, worn by anglers for standing in water

WADES > WADE

WADI *n* (in N Africa and Arabia) river which is dry except in the wet season

WADIES > WADY

WADING > WADE

WADINGS > WADE

WADIS > WADI

WADMAAL *same as* > WADMAL

WADMAALS > WADMAAL

WADMAL *n* coarse thick woollen fabric, formerly woven esp in Orkney and Shetland, for outer garments

WADMALS > WADMAL

WADMEL *same as* > WADMAL

WADMELS > WADMEL

WADMOL *same as* > WADMAL

WADMOLL *same as* > WADMAL

WADMOLLS > WADMOLL

WADMOLS > WADMOL

WADS > WAD

WADSET *vb* pledge or mortgage

WADSETS > WADSET

WADSETT *same as* > WADSET

WADSETTED > WADSET

WADSETTER > WADSET

WADSETTS > WADSETT

WADT *same as* > WAD

WADTS > WADT

WADY *same as* > WADI

WAE *old form of* > WOE

WAEFUL *old form of* > WOEFUL

WAENESS *n* sorrow

WAENESSES > WAENESS

WAES > WAE

WAESOME *adj* sorrowful

WAESUCK *interj* alas

WAESUCKS *interj* alas

WAFER *n* thin crisp biscuit ▷ *vb* seal, fasten, or attach with a wafer

WAFERED > WAFER

WAFERING > WAFER

WAFERS > WAFER

WAFERY > WAFER

WAFF *n* gust or puff of air ▷ *vb* flutter or cause to flutter

WAFFED > WAFF

WAFFIE *n* person regarded as having little worth to society

WAFFIES > WAFFIE

WAFFING > WAFF

WAFFLE *vb* speak or write in a vague wordy way ▷ *n* vague wordy talk or writing

WAFFLED > WAFFLE

WAFFLER > WAFFLE

WAFFLERS > WAFFLE

WAFFLES > WAFFLE

WAFFLIER > WAFFLE

WAFFLIEST > WAFFLE

WAFFLING > WAFFLE

WAFFLINGS > WAFFLE

WAFFLY > WAFFLE

WAFFS > WAFF

WAFT *vb* drift or carry gently through the air ▷ *n* something wafted

WAFTAGE > WAFT

WAFTAGES > WAFT

WAFTED > WAFT

WAFTER *n* device that causes a draught

WAFTERS > WAFTER

WAFTING > WAFT

WAFTINGS > WAFT

WAFTS > WAFT

WAFTURE *n* act of wafting or waving

WAFTURES > WAFTURE

WAG *vb* move rapidly from side to side ▷ *n* wagging movement

WAGE *n* payment for work done, esp when paid weekly ▷ *vb* engage in (an activity)

WAGED > WAGE

WAGELESS > WAGE

WAGENBOOM *n* S African tree

WAGER *vb* bet on the outcome of something ▷ *n* bet on the outcome of an event or activity

WAGERED > WAGER

WAGERER > WAGER

WAGERERS > WAGER

WAGERING > WAGER

WAGERS > WAGER

WAGES > WAGE

WAGGA *n* blanket or bed covering made out of sacks stitched together

WAGGAS > WAGGA

WAGGED > WAG

WAGGER > WAG

WAGGERIES > WAGGERY

WAGGERS > WAG

WAGGERY *n* quality of being humorous

WAGGING > WAG

WAGGISH *adj* jocular or humorous

WAGGISHLY > WAGGISH

WAGGLE *vb* move with a rapid shaking or wobbling motion ▷ *n* rapid shaking or wobbling motion

WAGGLED > WAGGLE

WAGGLER *n* float only the bottom of which is attached to the fishing line

WAGGLERS > WAGGLER

WAGGLES > WAGGLE

WAGGLIER > WAGGLE

WAGGLIEST > WAGGLE

WAGGLING > WAGGLE

WAGGLY > WAGGLE

WAGGON *same as* > WAGON

WAGGONED > WAGGON

WAGGONER *same as* > WAGONER

WAGGONERS > WAGGONER

WAGGONING > WAGGON

WAGGONS > WAGGON

WAGHALTER *n* person likely to be hanged

WAGING > WAGE

WAGMOIRE *obsolete word for* > QUAGMIRE

WAGMOIRES > WAGMOIRE

WAGON *n* four-wheeled vehicle for heavy loads ▷ *vb* transport by wagon

WAGONAGE n money paid for transport by wagon

WAGONAGES >WAGONAGE

WAGONED >WAGON

WAGONER n person who drives a wagon

WAGONERS >WAGONER

WAGONETTE n light four-wheeled horse-drawn vehicle with two lengthwise seats facing each other behind a crosswise driver's seat

WAGONFUL >WAGON

WAGONFULS >WAGON

WAGONING >WAGON

WAGONLESS >WAGON

WAGONLOAD n load that is or can be carried by a wagon

WAGONS >WAGON

WAGS >WAG

WAGSOME another word for >WAGGISH

WAGTAIL n small long-tailed bird

WAGTAILS >WAGTAIL

WAGYU n Japanese breed of beef cattle

WAGYUS >WAGYU

WAHCONDA n supreme being

WAHCONDAS >WAHCONDA

WAHINE n Māori woman, esp a wife

WAHINES >WAHINE

WAHOO n food and game fish of tropical seas

WAHOOS >WAHOO

WAI n in New Zealand, water

WAIATA n Māori song

WAIATAS >WAIATA

WAID >WEIGH

WAIDE >WEIGH

WAIF n young person who is, or seems, homeless or neglected ▷vb treat as a waif

WAIFED >WAIF

WAIFING >WAIF

WAIFISH >WAIF

WAIFLIKE >WAIF

WAIFS >WAIF

WAIFT n piece of lost property found by someone other than the owner

WAIFTS >WAIFT

WAIL vb cry out in pain or misery ▷n mournful cry

WAILED >WAIL

WAILER >WAIL

WAILERS >WAIL

WAILFUL >WAIL

WAILFULLY >WAIL

WAILING >WAIL

WAILINGLY >WAIL

WAILINGS >WAIL

WAILS >WAIL

WAILSOME >WAIL

WAIN vb transport ▷n farm wagon

WAINAGE n carriages, etc, for transportation of goods

WAINAGES >WAINAGE

WAINED >WAIN

WAINING >WAIN

WAINS >WAIN

WAINSCOT n wooden lining of the lower part of the walls of a room ▷vb line (a wall of a room) with a wainscot

WAINSCOTS >WAINSCOT

WAIR vb spend

WAIRED >WAIR

WAIRING >WAIR

WAIRS >WAIR

WAIRSH variant spelling of >WERSH

WAIRSHER >WAIRSH

WAIRSHEST >WAIRSH

WAIRUA n in New Zealand, spirit or soul

WAIRUAS >WAIRUA

WAIS >WAI

WAIST n part of the trunk between the ribs and the hips

WAISTBAND n band of material sewn on to the waist of a garment to strengthen it

WAISTBELT n belt

WAISTCOAT n sleeveless garment which buttons up the front, usu worn over a shirt and under a jacket

WAISTED adj having a waist or waistlike part

WAISTER n sailor performing menial duties

WAISTERS >WAISTER

WAISTING n act of wasting

WAISTINGS >WAISTING

WAISTLESS >WAIST

WAISTLINE n (size of) the waist of a person or garment

WAISTS >WAIST

WAIT vb remain inactive in expectation (of something) ▷n act or period of waiting

WAITE old form of >WAIT

WAITED >WAIT

WAITER n man who serves in a restaurant etc ▷vb serve at table

WAITERAGE n service

WAITERED >WAITER

WAITERING n act of serving at table

WAITERS >WAITER

WAITES >WAITE

WAITING >WAIT

WAITINGLY >WAIT

WAITINGS >WAIT

WAITLIST n waiting list

WAITLISTS >WAITLIST

WAITRESS n woman who serves people with food and drink in a restaurant ▷vb work as a waitress

WAITRON n waiter or waitress

WAITRONS >WAITRON

WAITS >WAIT

WAITSTAFF n waiters and waitresses collectively

WAIVE vb refrain from enforcing (a law, right, etc)

WAIVED >WAIVE

WAIVER n act or instance of voluntarily giving up a claim, right, etc

WAIVERS >WAIVER

WAIVES >WAIVE

WAIVING >WAIVE

WAIVODE same as >VOIVODE

WAIVODES >WAIVODE

WAIWODE same as >VOIVODE

WAIWODES >WAIWODE

WAKA n Māori canoe

WAKAME n edible seaweed

WAKAMES >WAKAME

WAKANDA n supernatural quality said by Native American people to be held by natural objects

WAKANDAS >WAKANDA

WAKAS >WAKA

WAKE vb rouse from sleep or inactivity ▷n vigil beside a corpse the night before the funeral

WAKEBOARD n short surfboard for a rider towed behind a motorboat ▷vb ride a wakeboard

WAKED >WAKE

WAKEFUL adj unable to sleep

WAKEFULLY >WAKEFUL

WAKELESS adj (of sleep) deep or unbroken

WAKEMAN n watchman

WAKEMEN >WAKEMAN

WAKEN vb wake

WAKENED >WAKEN

WAKENER >WAKEN

WAKENERS >WAKEN

WAKENING >WAKEN

WAKENINGS >WAKEN

WAKENS >WAKEN

WAKER >WAKE

WAKERIFE adj watchful

WAKERS >WAKE

WAKES >WAKE

WAKF same as >WAQF

WAKFS >WAKF

WAKIKI n Melanesian shell currency

WAKIKIS >WAKIKI

WAKING >WAKE

WAKINGS >WAKE

WALD Scots form of >WELD

WALDFLUTE n organ flute stop

WALDGRAVE n (in medieval Germany) an officer with jurisdiction over a royal forest

WALDHORN n organ reed stop

WALDHORNS >WALDHORN

WALDO n gadget for manipulating objects by remote control

WALDOES >WALDO

WALDOS >WALDO

WALDRAPP n type of ibis

WALDRAPPS >WALDRAPP

WALDS >WALD

WALE same as >WEAL

WALED >WALE

WALER >WALE

WALERS >WALE

WALES >WALE

WALI same as >VALI

WALIER >WALY

WALIES >WALY

WALIEST >WALY

WALING >WALE

WALIS >WALI

WALISE same as >VALISE

WALISES >WALISE

WALK vb move on foot with at least one foot always on the ground ▷n short journey on foot, usu for pleasure

WALKABLE >WALK

WALKABOUT n informal walk among the public by royalty etc

WALKATHON n long walk done, esp for charity

WALKAWAY n easily achieved victory

WALKAWAYS >WALKAWAY

WALKED >WALK

WALKER n person who walks

WALKERS >WALKER

WALKIES as in go walkies a walk

WALKING adj (of a person) considered to possess the qualities of something inanimate as specified ▷n act of walking

WALKINGS >WALKING

WALKMILL same as >WAULKMILL

WALKMILLS >WALKMILL

WALKOUT n strike

WALKOUTS >WALKOUT

WALKOVER n easy victory

WALKOVERS >WALKOVER

WALKS >WALK

WALKUP n building with stairs to upper floors

WALKUPS >WALKUP

WALKWAY n path designed for use by pedestrians

WALKWAYS >WALKWAY

WALKYRIE variant of >VALKYRIE

WALKYRIES >WALKYRIE

WALL n structure of brick, stone, etc used to enclose, divide, or support ▷vb enclose or seal with a wall or walls

WALLA same as >WALLAH

WALLABA n type of S American tree

WALLABAS >WALLABA

WALLABIES >WALLABY

WALLABY n marsupial like a small kangaroo

WALLAH n person involved with or in charge of a

specified thing

WALLAHS > WALLAH

WALLAROO n large stocky Australian kangaroo of rocky regions

WALLAROOS > WALLAROO

WALLAS > WALLA

WALLBOARD n thin board made of materials, such as compressed wood fibres or gypsum plaster, between stiff paper, and used to cover walls, partitions, etc

WALLCHART n chart on wall

WALLED > WALL

WALLER > WALL

WALLERS > WALL

WALLET n small folding case for paper money, documents, etc

WALLETS > WALLET

WALLEYE n fish with large staring eyes

WALLEYED > WALLEYE

WALLEYES > WALLEYE

WALLFISH n snail

WALLIE same as > WALLY

WALLIER > WALLY

WALLIES > WALLY

WALLIEST > WALLY

WALLING > WALL

WALLINGS > WALL

WALLOP vb hit hard ▷ n hard blow

WALLOPED > WALLOP

WALLOPER n person or thing that wallops

WALLOPERS > WALLOPER

WALLOPING n thrashing ▷ adj large or great

WALLOPS > WALLOP

WALLOW vb revel in an emotion ▷ n act or instance of wallowing

WALLOWED > WALLOW

WALLOWER > WALLOW

WALLOWERS > WALLOW

WALLOWING > WALLOW

WALLOWS > WALLOW

WALLPAPER n decorative paper to cover interior walls ▷ vb cover (walls) with wallpaper

WALLS > WALL

WALLSEND n type of coal

WALLSENDS > WALLSEND

WALLWORT n type of plant

WALLWORTS > WALLWORT

WALLY n stupid person ▷ adj fine, pleasing, or splendid

WALLYBALL n ball game played on court

WALLYDRAG n worthless person or animal

WALNUT n edible nut with a wrinkled shell ▷ adj made from the wood of a walnut tree

WALNUTS > WALNUT

WALRUS n large sea mammal with long tusks

WALRUSES > WALRUS

WALTIER > WALTY

WALTIEST > WALTY

WALTY adj (of a ship) likely to roll over

WALTZ n ballroom dance ▷ vb dance a waltz

WALTZED > WALTZ

WALTZER n person who waltzes

WALTZERS > WALTZER

WALTZES > WALTZ

WALTZING > WALTZ

WALTZINGS > WALTZ

WALTZLIKE > WALTZ

WALY same as > WALLY

WAMBENGER another name for > TUAN

WAMBLE vb move unsteadily ▷ n unsteady movement

WAMBLED > WAMBLE

WAMBLES > WAMBLE

WAMBLIER > WAMBLE

WAMBLIEST > WAMBLE

WAMBLING > WAMBLE

WAMBLINGS > WAMBLE

WAMBLY > WAMBLE

WAME n belly, abdomen, or womb

WAMED > WAME

WAMEFOU Scots variant of > WAMEFUL

WAMEFOUS > WAMEFOU

WAMEFUL n bellyful

WAMEFULS > WAMEFUL

WAMES > WAME

WAMMUL n dog

WAMMULS > WAMMUL

WAMMUS same as > WAMUS

WAMMUSES > WAMMUS

WAMPEE n type of Asian fruit tree

WAMPEES > WAMPEE

WAMPISH vb wave

WAMPISHED > WAMPISH

WAMPISHES > WAMPISH

WAMPUM n shells woven together, formerly used by Native Americans for money and ornament

WAMPUMS > WAMPUM

WAMPUS same as > WAMUS

WAMPUSES > WAMPUS

WAMUS n type of cardigan or jacket

WAMUSES > WAMUS

WAN adj pale and sickly looking ▷ vb make or become wan

WANCHANCY adj infelicitous

WAND n thin rod, esp one used in performing magic tricks

WANDER vb move about without a definite destination or aim ▷ n act or instance of wandering

WANDERED > WANDER

WANDERER > WANDER

WANDERERS > WANDER

WANDERING > WANDER

WANDEROO n macaque monkey of India and Sri Lanka, having black fur with a ruff of long greyish fur on each side of the face

WANDEROOS > WANDEROO

WANDERS > WANDER

WANDLE adj supple

WANDLIKE > WAND

WANDOO n eucalyptus tree of W Australia, having white bark and durable wood

WANDOOS > WANDOO

WANDS > WAND

WANE vb decrease gradually in size or strength

WANED > WANE

WANES > WANE

WANEY > WANE

WANG n cheekbone

WANGAN same as > WANIGAN

WANGANS > WANGAN

WANGLE vb get by devious methods ▷ n act or an instance of wangling

WANGLED > WANGLE

WANGLER > WANGLE

WANGLERS > WANGLE

WANGLES > WANGLE

WANGLING > WANGLE

WANGLINGS > WANGLE

WANGS > WANG

WANGUN same as > WANIGAN

WANGUNS > WANGUN

WANHOPE n delusion

WANHOPES > WANHOPE

WANIER > WANY

WANIEST > WANY

WANIGAN n provisions for camp

WANIGANS > WANIGAN

WANING > WANE

WANINGS > WANE

WANION n vehemence

WANIONS > WANION

WANK vb slang word for masturbate ▷ n instance of masturbating ▷ adj bad, useless, or worthless

WANKED > WANK

WANKER n slang word for worthless or stupid person

WANKERS > WANKER

WANKIER > WANKY

WANKIEST > WANKY

WANKING > WANK

WANKLE adj unstable

WANKS > WANK

WANKSTA n derogatory slang word for a person who acts or dresses like a gangster but who is not involved in crime

WANKSTAS > WANKSTA

WANKY adj slang word for pretentious

WANLE same as > WANDLE

WANLY > WAN

WANNA vb spelling of **want to** intended to reflect a dialectal or informal pronunciation

WANNABE adj wanting to be, or be like, a particular person or thing ▷ n person who wants to be, or be like, a particular person or thing

WANNABEE same as > WANNABE

WANNABEES > WANNABEE

WANNABES > WANNABE

WANNED > WAN

WANNEL same as > WANDLE

WANNER > WAN

WANNESS > WAN

WANNESSES > WAN

WANNEST > WAN

WANNIGAN same as > WANIGAN

WANNIGANS > WANNIGAN

WANNING > WAN

WANNION same as > WANION

WANNIONS > WANNION

WANNISH adj rather wan

WANS > WAN

WANT vb need or long for ▷ n act or instance of wanting

WANTAGE n shortage

WANTAGES > WANTAGE

WANTAWAY n footballer who wants to transfer to another club

WANTAWAYS > WANTAWAY

WANTED > WANT

WANTER > WANT

WANTERS > WANT

WANTHILL n molehill

WANTHILLS > WANTHILL

WANTIES > WANTY

WANTING adj lacking ▷ prep without

WANTON adj without motive, provocation, or justification ▷ n sexually unrestrained or immodest woman ▷ vb behave in a wanton manner

WANTONED > WANTON

WANTONER > WANTON

WANTONERS > WANTON

WANTONEST > WANTON

WANTONING > WANTON

WANTONISE same as > WANTONIZE

WANTONIZE vb behave wantonly

WANTONLY > WANTON

WANTONS > WANTON

WANTS > WANT

WANTY adj belt

WANWORDY adj without merit

WANWORTH n inexpensive purchase

WANWORTHS > WANWORTH

WANY > WANE

WANZE vb wane

WANZED > WANZE

WANZES > WANZE

WANZING > WANZE

WAP vb strike

WAPENSHAW n showing of weapons

WAPENTAKE n subdivision of certain shires or counties, esp in the

W

Midlands and North of England

WAPINSHAW same as > WAPENSHAW

WAPITI n large N American deer, now also common in New Zealand

WAPITIS > WAPITI

WAPPED > WAP

WAPPEND adj tired

WAPPER vb blink

WAPPERED > WAPPER

WAPPERING > WAPPER

WAPPERS > WAPPER

WAPPING > WAP

WAPS > WAP

WAQF n endowment in Muslim law

WAQFS > WAQF

WAR n fighting between nations ▷ adj of, like, or caused by war ▷ vb conduct a war

WARAGI n Ugandan alcoholic drink made from bananas

WARAGIS > WARAGI

WARATAH n Australian shrub with crimson flowers

WARATAHS > WARATAH

WARB n dirty or insignificant person

WARBIER > WARB

WARBIEST > WARB

WARBIRD n vintage military aeroplane

WARBIRDS > WARBIRD

WARBLE vb sing in a trilling voice ▷ n act or an instance of warbling

WARBLED > WARBLE

WARBLER n any of various small songbirds

WARBLERS > WARBLER

WARBLES > WARBLE

WARBLING > WARBLE

WARBLINGS > WARBLE

WARBONNET n headband with trailing feathers worn by certain North American Indian warriors

WARBS > WARB

WARBY > WARB

WARCRAFT n skill in warfare

WARCRAFTS > WARCRAFT

WARD n room in a hospital for patients needing a similar kind of care ▷ vb guard or protect

WARDCORN n payment of corn

WARDCORNS > WARDCORN

WARDED > WARD

WARDEN n person in charge of a building and its occupants ▷ vb act as a warden

WARDENED > WARDEN

WARDENING > WARDEN

WARDENRY > WARDEN

WARDENS > WARDEN

WARDER vb guard ▷ n prison officer

WARDERED > WARDER

WARDERING > WARDER

WARDERS > WARDER

WARDIAN as in wardian case type of glass container for housing delicate plants

WARDING > WARD

WARDINGS > WARD

WARDLESS > WARD

WARDMOTE n assembly of the citizens or liverymen of an area

WARDMOTES > WARDMOTE

WARDOG n veteran warrior

WARDOGS > WARDOG

WARDRESS n female officer in charge of prisoners in a jail

WARDROBE n cupboard for hanging clothes in

WARDROBED > WARDROBE

WARDROBER n person in charge of someone's wardrobe

WARDROBES > WARDROBE

WARDROOM n officers' quarters on a warship

WARDROOMS > WARDROOM

WARDROP obsolete form of > WARDROBE

WARDROPS > WARDROP

WARDS > WARD

WARDSHIP n state of being a ward

WARDSHIPS > WARDSHIP

WARE n articles of a specified type or material ▷ vb spend or squander

WARED > WARE

WAREHOU n any of several edible saltwater New Zealand fish

WAREHOUS > WAREHOU

WAREHOUSE n building for storing goods prior to sale or distribution ▷ vb store or place in a warehouse, esp a bonded warehouse

WARELESS adj careless

WAREROOM n store-room

WAREROOMS > WAREROOM

WARES npl goods for sale

WAREZ npl illegally copied computer software which has had its protection codes de-activated

WARFARE vb engage in war ▷ n fighting or hostilities

WARFARED > WARFARE

WARFARER > WARFARE

WARFARERS > WARFARE

WARFARES > WARFARE

WARFARIN n crystalline compound, used as a medical anticoagulant

WARFARING > WARFARE

WARFARINS > WARFARIN

WARHABLE adj able to fight in war

WARHEAD n explosive front part of a missile

WARHEADS > WARHEAD

WARHORSE n (formerly) a horse used in battle

WARHORSES > WARHORSE

WARIBASHI n disposable chopsticks

WARIER > WARY

WARIEST > WARY

WARILY > WARY

WARIMENT n caution

WARIMENTS > WARIMENT

WARINESS > WARY

WARING > WARE

WARISON n (esp formerly) a bugle note used as an order to a military force to attack

WARISONS > WARISON

WARK Scots form of > WORK

WARKED > WARK

WARKING > WARK

WARKS > WARK

WARLESS > WAR

WARLIKE adj of or relating to war

WARLING n one who is not liked

WARLINGS > WARLING

WARLOCK n man who practises black magic

WARLOCKRY n witchcraft

WARLOCKS > WARLOCK

WARLORD n military leader of a nation or part of a nation

WARLORDS > WARLORD

WARM adj moderately hot ▷ vb make or become warm ▷ n warm place or area

WARMAKER n one who wages war

WARMAKERS > WARMAKER

WARMAN n one experienced in warfare

WARMBLOOD n type of horse

WARMED > WARM

WARMEN > WARMAN

WARMER > WARM

WARMERS > WARM

WARMEST > WARM

WARMING > WARM

WARMINGS > WARM

WARMISH > WARM

WARMLY > WARM

WARMNESS > WARM

WARMONGER n person who encourages war

WARMOUTH n type of fish

WARMOUTHS > WARMOUTH

WARMS > WARM

WARMTH n mild heat

WARMTHS > WARMTH

WARMUP n preparatory exercise routine

WARMUPS > WARMUP

WARN vb make aware of possible danger or harm

WARNED > WARN

WARNER > WARN

WARNERS > WARN

WARNING n something that warns ▷ adj giving or serving as a warning

WARNINGLY > WARNING

WARNINGS > WARNING

WARNS > WARN

WARP vb twist out of shape ▷ n state of being warped

WARPAGE > WARP

WARPAGES > WARP

WARPATH n route taken by Native Americans on a warlike expedition

WARPATHS > WARPATH

WARPED > WARP

WARPER > WARP

WARPERS > WARP

WARPING > WARP

WARPINGS > WARP

WARPLANE n any aircraft designed for and used in warfare

WARPLANES > WARPLANE

WARPOWER n ability to wage war

WARPOWERS > WARPOWER

WARPS > WARP

WARPWISE adv (weaving) in the direction of the warp

WARRAGAL same as > WARRIGAL

WARRAGALS > WARRAGAL

WARRAGLE same as > WARRIGAL

WARRAGLES > WARRAGLE

WARRAGUL same as > WARRIGAL

WARRAGULS > WARRAGUL

WARRAN same as > WARRANT

WARRAND same as > WARRANT

WARRANDED > WARRAND

WARRANDS > WARRAND

WARRANED > WARRAN

WARRANING > WARRAN

WARRANS > WARRAN

WARRANT n (document giving) official authorization ▷ vb make necessary

WARRANTED > WARRANT

WARRANTEE n person to whom a warranty is given

WARRANTER > WARRANT

WARRANTOR n person or company that provides a warranty

WARRANTS > WARRANT

WARRANTY n (document giving) a guarantee

WARRAY vb wage war on

WARRAYED > WARRAY

WARRAYING > WARRAY

WARRAYS > WARRAY

WARRE same as > WAR

WARRED > WAR

WARREN n series of burrows in which rabbits live

WARRENER n gamekeeper or keeper of a warren

WARRENERS > WARRENER

WARRENS > WARREN

WARREY same as > WARRAY

WARREYED > WARREY

WARREYING > WARREY

WARREYS > WARREY

WARRIGAL n dingo ▷ adj wild

WARRIGALS > WARRIGAL

WARRING > WAR

WARRIOR n person who fights in a war
WARRIORS > WARRIOR
WARRISON same as > WARISON
WARRISONS > WARRISON
WARS > WAR
WARSAW n type of grouper fish
WARSAWS > WARSAW
WARSHIP n ship designed and equipped for naval combat
WARSHIPS > WARSHIP
WARSLE dialect word for > WRESTLE
WARSLED > WARSLE
WARSLER > WARSLE
WARSLERS > WARSLE
WARSLES > WARSLE
WARSLING > WARSLE
WARST obsolete form of > WORST
WARSTLE dialect form of > WRESTLE
WARSTLED > WARSTLE
WARSTLER > WARSTLE
WARSTLERS > WARSTLE
WARSTLES > WARSTLE
WARSTLING > WARSTLE
WART n small hard growth on the skin
WARTED > WART
WARTHOG n wild African pig with heavy tusks, wartlike lumps on the face, and a mane of coarse hair
WARTHOGS > WARTHOG
WARTIER > WART
WARTIEST > WART
WARTIME n time of war ▷ adj of or in a time of war
WARTIMES > WARTIME
WARTLESS > WART
WARTLIKE > WART
WARTS > WART
WARTWEED n type of plant
WARTWEEDS > WARTWEED
WARTWORT another word for > WARTWEED
WARTWORTS > WARTWORT
WARTY > WART
WARWOLF n Roman engine of war
WARWOLVES > WARWOLF
WARWORK n work contributing to war effort
WARWORKS > WARWORK
WARWORN adj worn down by war
WARY adj watchful or cautious
WARZONE n area where a war is taking place or there is some other violent conflict
WARZONES > WARZONE
WAS > BE
WASABI n Japanese cruciferous plant cultivated for its thick green pungent root
WASABIS > WASABI
WASE n pad to relieve

pressure of load carried on head
WASES > WASE
WASH vb clean (oneself, clothes, etc) with water and usu soap ▷ n act or process of washing
WASHABLE n thing that can be washed ▷ adj (esp of fabrics or clothes) capable of being washed without deteriorating
WASHABLES > WASHABLE
WASHAWAY another word for > WASHOUT
WASHAWAYS > WASHAWAY
WASHBALL n ball of soap
WASHBALLS > WASHBALL
WASHBASIN n basin for washing the face and hands
WASHBOARD n board having a surface, usually of corrugated metal, on which esp formerly, clothes were scrubbed
WASHBOWL same as > WASHBASIN
WASHBOWLS > WASHBOWL
WASHCLOTH n small piece of cloth used to wash the face and hands
WASHDAY n day on which clothes and linen are washed, often the same day each week
WASHDAYS > WASHDAY
WASHED > WASH
WASHEN > WASH
WASHER n ring put under a nut or bolt or in a tap as a seal ▷ vb fit with a washer
WASHERED > WASHER
WASHERIES > WASHERY
WASHERING > WASHER
WASHERMAN n man who washes clothes for a living
WASHERMEN > WASHERMAN
WASHERS > WASHER
WASHERY n plant at a mine where water or other liquid is used to remove dirt from a mineral, esp coal
WASHES > WASH
WASHHAND as in washhand basin, washhand stand for the washing of hands
WASHHOUSE n (formerly) building in which laundry was done
WASHIER > WASHY
WASHIEST > WASHY
WASHILY > WASHY
WASHIN n increase in the angle of attack of an aircraft wing towards the wing tip
WASHINESS > WASHY
WASHING n clothes to be washed
WASHINGS > WASHING
WASHINS > WASHIN
WASHLAND n frequently-flooded plain

WASHLANDS > WASHLAND
WASHOUT n complete failure
WASHOUTS > WASHOUT
WASHPOT n pot for washing things in
WASHPOTS > WASHPOT
WASHRAG same as > WASHCLOTH
WASHRAGS > WASHRAG
WASHROOM n toilet
WASHROOMS > WASHROOM
WASHSTAND n piece of furniture designed to hold a basin for washing the face and hands in
WASHTUB n tub or large container used for washing anything, esp clothes
WASHTUBS > WASHTUB
WASHUP n outcome of a process
WASHUPS > WASHUP
WASHWIPE n windscreen spray-cleaning mechanism
WASHWIPES > WASHWIPE
WASHWOMAN n woman who washes clothes for a living
WASHWOMEN > WASHWOMAN
WASHY adj overdiluted or weak
WASP n stinging insect with a slender black-and-yellow striped body
WASPIE n tight-waited corset
WASPIER > WASP
WASPIES > WASPIE
WASPIEST > WASP
WASPILY > WASP
WASPINESS > WASP
WASPISH adj bad-tempered
WASPISHLY > WASPISH
WASPLIKE > WASP
WASPNEST n nest of wasp
WASPNESTS > WASPNEST
WASPS > WASP
WASPY > WASP
WASSAIL n formerly, festivity when much drinking took place ▷ vb drink health of (a person) at a wassail
WASSAILED > WASSAIL
WASSAILER > WASSAIL
WASSAILRY > WASSAIL
WASSAILS > WASSAIL
WASSERMAN n man-shaped sea monster
WASSERMEN > WASSERMAN
WASSUP sentence substitute what is happening?
WAST singular form of the past tense of > BE
WASTABLE > WASTE
WASTAGE n loss by wear or waste
WASTAGES > WASTAGE
WASTE vb use pointlessly or thoughtlessly ▷ n act of wasting or state of being

wasted ▷ adj rejected as worthless or surplus to requirements
WASTED > WASTE
WASTEFUL adj extravagant
WASTEL n fine bread or cake
WASTELAND n barren or desolate area of land
WASTELOT n piece of waste ground in a city
WASTELOTS > WASTELOT
WASTELS > WASTEL
WASTENESS > WASTE
WASTER vb waste ▷ n layabout
WASTERED > WASTER
WASTERFUL Scots variant of > WASTEFUL
WASTERIE same as > WASTERY
WASTERIES > WASTERIE
WASTERING > WASTER
WASTERS > WASTER
WASTERY n extravagance
WASTES > WASTE
WASTEWAY n open ditch
WASTEWAYS > WASTEWAY
WASTEWEIR another name for > SPILLWAY
WASTFULL obsolete form of > WASTEFUL
WASTING adj reducing the vitality and strength of the body
WASTINGLY > WASTING
WASTINGS > WASTING
WASTNESS n obsolete form of wasteness
WASTREL n lazy or worthless person
WASTRELS > WASTREL
WASTRIE same as > WASTERY
WASTRIES > WASTRIE
WASTRIFE n wastefulness
WASTRIFES > WASTRIFE
WASTRY n wastefulness
WASTS > WAST
WAT adj wet; drunken
WATAP n stringy thread made by Native Americans from the roots of conifers
WATAPE same as > WATAP
WATAPES > WATAPE
WATAPS > WATAP
WATCH vb look at closely ▷ n portable timepiece for the wrist or pocket
WATCHABLE adj interesting, enjoyable, or entertaining
WATCHBAND n watch strap
WATCHBOX n sentry's box
WATCHCASE n protective case for a watch, generally of metal such as gold, silver, brass, or gunmetal
WATCHCRY n slogan used to rally support
WATCHDOG n dog kept to guard property
WATCHDOGS > WATCHDOG
WATCHED > WATCH

W

WATCHER n person who watches

WATCHERS > WATCHER

WATCHES > WATCH

WATCHET n shade of blue

WATCHETS > WATCHET

WATCHEYE n eye with a light-coloured iris

WATCHEYES > WATCHEYE

WATCHFUL adj vigilant or alert

WATCHING > WATCH

WATCHLIST n list of things to be monitored

WATCHMAN n man employed to guard a building or property

WATCHMEN > WATCHMAN

WATCHOUT n lookout

WATCHOUTS > WATCHOUT

WATCHWORD n word or phrase that sums up the attitude of a particular group

WATE > WIT

WATER n clear colourless tasteless liquid that falls as rain and forms rivers etc ▷ vb put water on or into

WATERAGE n transportation of cargo by means of ships, or the charges for such transportation

WATERAGES > WATERAGE

WATERBED n watertight mattress filled with water

WATERBEDS > WATERBED

WATERBIRD n any aquatic bird

WATERBUCK n any of various antelopes of the swampy areas of Africa, having long curved ridged horns

WATERBUS n boat offering regular transport service

WATERDOG n dog trained to hunt in water

WATERDOGS > WATERDOG

WATERED > WATER

WATERER > WATER

WATERERS > WATER

WATERFALL n place where the waters of a river drop vertically

WATERFOWL n bird that swims on water, such as a duck or swan

WATERHEAD n source of river

WATERHEN another name for > GALLINULE

WATERHENS > WATERHEN

WATERIER > WATERY

WATERIEST > WATERY

WATERILY > WATERY

WATERING > WATER

WATERINGS > WATER

WATERISH > WATER

WATERJET n jet of water

WATERJETS > WATERJET

WATERLEAF n carved column design

WATERLESS > WATER

WATERLILY n any of various aquatic plants having large leaves and showy flowers that float on the surface of the water

WATERLINE n level to which a ship's hull will be immersed when afloat

WATERLOG vb flood with water

WATERLOGS > WATERLOG

WATERLOO n total defeat

WATERLOOS > WATERLOO

WATERMAN n skilled boatman

WATERMARK n faint translucent design in a sheet of paper ▷ vb mark (paper) with a watermark

WATERMEN > WATERMAN

WATERPOX n chickenpox

WATERS > WATER

WATERSHED n important period or factor serving as a dividing line

WATERSIDE n area of land beside a river or lake

WATERSKI vb ski on water towed behind motorboat

WATERSKIS > WATERSKI

WATERWAY n river, canal, or other navigable channel used as a means of travel or transport

WATERWAYS > WATERWAY

WATERWEED n any of various weedy aquatic plants

WATERWORK n machinery, etc for storing, purifying, and distributing water

WATERWORN adj worn smooth by the action or passage of water

WATERY adj of, like, or containing water

WATERZOOI n type of Flemish stew

WATS > WAT

WATT n unit of power

WATTAGE n electrical power expressed in watts

WATTAGES > WATTAGE

WATTAPE same as > WATAP

WATTAPES > WATTAPE

WATTER > WAT

WATTEST > WAT

WATTHOUR n unit of energy equal to the power of one watt operating for an hour

WATTHOURS > WATTHOUR

WATTLE n branches woven over sticks to make a fence ▷ adj made of, formed by, or covered with wattle ▷ vb construct from wattle

WATTLED > WATTLE

WATTLES > WATTLE

WATTLESS > WATT

WATTLING > WATTLE

WATTLINGS > WATTLE

WATTMETER n meter for measuring electric power in watts

WATTS > WATT

WAUCHT same as > WAUGHT

WAUCHTED > WAUCHT

WAUCHTING > WAUCHT

WAUCHTS > WAUCHT

WAUFF same as > WAFF

WAUFFED > WAUFF

WAUFFING > WAUFF

WAUFFS > WAUFF

WAUGH vb bark

WAUGHED > WAUGH

WAUGHING > WAUGH

WAUGHS > WAUGH

WAUGHT vb drink in large amounts

WAUGHTED > WAUGHT

WAUGHTING > WAUGHT

WAUGHTS > WAUGHT

WAUK vb full (cloth)

WAUKED > WAUK

WAUKER > WAUK

WAUKERS > WAUK

WAUKING > WAUK

WAUKMILL same as > WAULKMILL

WAUKMILLS > WAULKMILL

WAUKRIFE variant of > WAKERIFE

WAUKS > WAUK

WAUL vb cry or wail plaintively like a cat

WAULED > WAUL

WAULING > WAUL

WAULINGS > WAUL

WAULK same as > WAUK

WAULKED > WAULK

WAULKER > WAULK

WAULKERS > WAULK

WAULKING > WAULK

WAULKMILL n cloth-fulling mill

WAULKS > WAULK

WAULS > WAUL

WAUR obsolete form of > WAR

WAURED > WAUR

WAURING > WAUR

WAURS > WAUR

WAURST > WAUR

WAVE vb move the hand to and fro as a greeting or signal ▷ n moving ridge on water

WAVEBAND n range of wavelengths or frequencies used for a particular type of radio transmission

WAVEBANDS > WAVEBAND

WAVED > WAVE

WAVEFORM n shape of the graph of a wave or oscillation obtained by plotting the value of some changing quantity against time

WAVEFORMS > WAVEFORM

WAVEFRONT n surface associated with a propagating wave and passing through all points in the wave that have the same phase

WAVEGUIDE n solid rod of dielectric or a hollow metal tube, usually of rectangular cross section, used as a path to guide microwaves

WAVELESS > WAVE

WAVELET n small wave

WAVELETS > WAVELET

WAVELIKE > WAVE

WAVELLITE n greyish-white, yellow, or brown mineral

WAVEMETER n instrument for measuring the frequency or wavelength of radio waves

WAVEOFF n signal or instruction to an aircraft not to land

WAVEOFFS > WAVEOFF

WAVER vb hesitate or be irresolute ▷ n act or an instance of wavering

WAVERED > WAVER

WAVERER > WAVER

WAVERERS > WAVER

WAVERIER > WAVERY

WAVERIEST > WAVERY

WAVERING > WAVER

WAVERINGS > WAVER

WAVEROUS same as > WAVERY

WAVERS > WAVER

WAVERY adj lacking firmness

WAVES > WAVE

WAVESHAPE another word for > WAVEFORM

WAVESON n goods floating on waves after shipwreck

WAVESONS > WAVESON

WAVEY n snow goose or other wild goose

WAVEYS > WAVEY

WAVICLE n origin of wave

WAVICLES > WAVICLE

WAVIER > WAVY

WAVIES > WAVY

WAVIEST > WAVY

WAVILY > WAVY

WAVINESS > WAVY

WAVING > WAVE

WAVINGS > WAVE

WAVY adj having curves ▷ n snow goose or other wild goose

WAW another name for > VAV

WAWA n speech ▷ vb speak

WAWAED > WAWA

WAWAING > WAWA

WAWAS > WAWA

WAWE same as > WAW

WAWES > WAWE

WAWL same as > WAUL

WAWLED > WAWL

WAWLING > WAWL

WAWLINGS > WAWL

WAWLS > WAWL

WAWS > WAW

WAX n solid shiny fatty or oily substance used for sealing, making candles, etc ▷ vb coat or polish with wax

WAXABLE > WAX

WAXBERRY n waxy fruit of the wax myrtle or the snowberry

WAXBILL n any of various chiefly African finchlike weaverbirds
WAXBILLS >WAXBILL
WAXCLOTH another name for >OILCLOTH
WAXCLOTHS >WAXCLOTH
WAXED >WAX
WAXEN adj made of or like wax
WAXER >WAX
WAXERS >WAX
WAXES >WAX
WAXEYE n small New Zealand bird with a white circle round its eye
WAXEYES >WAXEYE
WAXFLOWER n any of various plants with waxy flowers
WAXIER >WAXY
WAXIEST >WAXY
WAXILY >WAXY
WAXINESS >WAXY
WAXING >WAX
WAXINGS >WAX
WAXLIKE >WAX
WAXPLANT n climbing shrub of E Asia and Australia
WAXPLANTS >WAXPLANT
WAXWEED n type of wild flower
WAXWEEDS >WAXWEED
WAXWING n type of songbird
WAXWINGS >WAXWING
WAXWORK n lifelike wax model of a (famous) person
WAXWORKER >WAXWORK
WAXWORKS >WAXWORK
WAXWORM n waxmoth larva
WAXWORMS >WAXWORM
WAXY adj resembling wax in colour, appearance, or texture
WAY n manner or method ▷ vb travel
WAYBILL n document stating the nature, origin, and destination of goods being transported
WAYBILLS >WAYBILL
WAYBOARD n thin geological seam separating larger strata
WAYBOARDS >WAYBOARD
WAYBREAD n plantain
WAYBREADS >WAYBREAD
WAYED >WAY
WAYFARE vb travel
WAYFARED >WAYFARE
WAYFARER n traveller
WAYFARERS >WAYFARER
WAYFARES >WAYFARE
WAYFARING >WAYFARE
WAYGOING n leaving
WAYGOINGS >WAYGOING
WAYGONE adj travel-weary
WAYGOOSE same as >WAYZGOOSE
WAYGOOSES >WAYGOOSE
WAYING >WAY
WAYLAID >WAYLAY

WAYLAY vb lie in wait for and accost or attack
WAYLAYER >WAYLAY
WAYLAYERS >WAYLAY
WAYLAYING >WAYLAY
WAYLAYS >WAYLAY
WAYLEAVE n access to property granted by a landowner for payment
WAYLEAVES >WAYLEAVE
WAYLEGGO interj away here! let go!
WAYLESS >WAY
WAYMARK n symbol or signpost marking the route of a footpath ▷ vb mark out with waymarks
WAYMARKED >WAYMARK
WAYMARKS >WAYMARK
WAYMENT vb express grief
WAYMENTED >WAYMENT
WAYMENTS >WAYMENT
WAYPOINT n stopping point on route
WAYPOINTS >WAYPOINT
WAYPOST n signpost
WAYPOSTS >WAYPOST
WAYS >WAY
WAYSIDE n side of a road
WAYSIDES >WAYSIDE
WAYWARD adj erratic, selfish, or stubborn
WAYWARDLY >WAYWARD
WAYWISER n device for measuring distance
WAYWISERS >WAYWISER
WAYWODE n Slavonic governor
WAYWODES >WAYWODE
WAYWORN adj worn or tired by travel
WAYZGOOSE n works outing made annually by a printing house
WAZIR another word for >VIZIER
WAZIRS >WAZIR
WAZOO n slang word for person's bottom
WAZOOS >WAZOO
WAZZOCK n foolish or annoying person
WAZZOCKS >WAZZOCK
WE pron speaker or writer and one or more others
WEAK adj lacking strength
WEAKEN vb make or become weak
WEAKENED >WEAKEN
WEAKENER >WEAKEN
WEAKENERS >WEAKEN
WEAKENING >WEAKEN
WEAKENS >WEAKEN
WEAKER >WEAK
WEAKEST >WEAK
WEAKFISH n any of several sea trouts
WEAKISH >WEAK
WEAKISHLY >WEAK
WEAKLIER >WEAKLY
WEAKLIEST >WEAKLY
WEAKLING n feeble person or animal
WEAKLINGS >WEAKLING

WEAKLY adv feebly ▷ adj weak or sickly
WEAKNESS n being weak
WEAKON n subatomic particle
WEAKONS >WEAKON
WEAKSIDE n (in basketball) side of court away from ball
WEAKSIDES >WEAKSIDE
WEAL n raised mark left on the skin by a blow
WEALD n open or forested country
WEALDS >WEALD
WEALS >WEAL
WEALSMAN n statesman
WEALSMEN >WEALSMAN
WEALTH n state of being rich
WEALTHIER >WEALTHY
WEALTHILY >WEALTHY
WEALTHS >WEALTH
WEALTHY adj possessing wealth
WEAMB same as >WAME
WEAMBS >WEAMB
WEAN vb accustom (a baby or young mammal) to food other than mother's milk
WEANED >WEAN
WEANEL n recently-weaned child or animal
WEANELS >WEANEL
WEANER n person or thing that weans
WEANERS >WEANER
WEANING >WEAN
WEANINGS >WEAN
WEANLING n child or young animal recently weaned
WEANLINGS >WEANLING
WEANS >WEAN
WEAPON vb arm ▷ n object used in fighting
WEAPONED >WEAPON
WEAPONEER n person associated with the use or maintenance of weapons, esp nuclear weapons
WEAPONING >WEAPON
WEAPONISE same as >WEAPONIZE
WEAPONIZE vb adapt (a chemical, bacillus, etc) in such a way that it can be used as a weapon
WEAPONRY n weapons collectively
WEAPONS >WEAPON
WEAR vb have on the body as clothing or ornament ▷ n clothes suitable for a particular time or purpose
WEARABLE adj suitable for wear or able to be worn ▷ n any garment that can be worn
WEARABLES >WEARABLE
WEARED >WEAR
WEARER >WEAR
WEARERS >WEAR
WEARIED >WEARY
WEARIER >WEARY

WEARIES >WEARY
WEARIEST >WEARY
WEARIFUL same as >WEARISOME
WEARILESS adj not wearied or able to be wearied
WEARILY >WEARY
WEARINESS >WEARY
WEARING adj tiring ▷ n act of wearing
WEARINGLY >WEARING
WEARINGS >WEAR
WEARISH adj withered
WEARISOME adj tedious
WEARPROOF adj resistant to damage from normal wear or usage
WEARS >WEAR
WEARY adj tired or exhausted ▷ vb make or become weary
WEARYING >WEARY
WEASAND former name for the >TRACHEA
WEASANDS >WEASAND
WEASEL n small carnivorous mammal with a long body and short legs ▷ vb use ambiguous language to avoid speaking directly or honestly
WEASELED >WEASEL
WEASELER >WEASEL
WEASELERS >WEASEL
WEASELING >WEASEL
WEASELLED >WEASEL
WEASELLER >WEASEL
WEASELLY >WEASEL
WEASELS >WEASEL
WEASELY >WEASEL
WEASON Scots form of >WEASAND
WEASONS >WEASON
WEATHER n day-to-day atmospheric conditions of a place ▷ vb (cause to) be affected by the weather
WEATHERED adj affected by exposure to the action of the weather
WEATHERER >WEATHER
WEATHERLY adj (of a sailing vessel) making very little leeway when close-hauled, even in a stiff breeze
WEATHERS >WEATHER
WEAVE vb make (fabric) by interlacing (yarn) on a loom
WEAVED >WEAVE
WEAVER n person who weaves, esp as a means of livelihood
WEAVERS >WEAVER
WEAVES >WEAVE
WEAVING >WEAVE
WEAVINGS >WEAVE
WEAZAND same as >WEASAND
WEAZANDS >WEAZAND
WEAZEN same as >WIZEN
WEAZENED >WEAZEN
WEAZENING >WEAZEN

W

WEAZENS > WEAZEN
WEB n net spun by a spider ▷ vb cover with or as if with a web
WEBBED > WEB
WEBBIE n person who is well versed in the use of the World Wide Web
WEBBIER > WEBBY
WEBBIES > WEBBIE
WEBBIEST > WEBBY
WEBBING n anything that forms a web
WEBBINGS > WEBBING
WEBBY adj of, relating to, resembling, or consisting of a web
WEBCAM n camera that transmits images over the internet
WEBCAMS > WEBCAM
WEBCAST n broadcast of an event over the internet ▷ vb make such a broadcast
WEBCASTED > WEBCAST
WEBCASTER > WEBCAST
WEBCASTS > WEBCAST
WEBER n SI unit of magnetic flux
WEBERS > WEBER
WEBFED adj (of printing press) printing from rolls of paper
WEBFEET > WEBFOOT
WEBFOOT n foot having the toes connected by folds of skin
WEBFOOTED > WEBFOOT
WEBHEAD n person who uses the Internet a lot
WEBHEADS > WEBHEAD
WEBIFIED > WEBIFY
WEBIFIES > WEBIFY
WEBIFY vb convert (information) to a format capable of being displayed on the Internet
WEBIFYING > WEBIFY
WEBINAR n interactive seminar conducted over the World Wide Web
WEBINARS > WEBINAR
WEBISODE n episode (of a television series) intended for on-line viewing
WEBISODES > WEBISODE
WEBLESS > WEB
WEBLIKE > WEB
WEBLISH n shorthand form of English that is used in text messaging, chat rooms, etc
WEBLISHES > WEBLISH
WEBLOG n person's online journal
WEBLOGGER > WEBLOG
WEBLOGS > WEBLOG
WEBMAIL n system of electronic mail that allows account holders to access their mail via an internet site rather than downloading it
WEBMAILS > WEBMAIL

WEBMASTER n person responsible for the administration of a website on the World Wide Web
WEBPAGE n page on website
WEBPAGES > WEBPAGE
WEBRING n group of websites organized in a circular structure
WEBRINGS > WEBRING
WEBS > WEB
WEBSITE n group of connected pages on the World Wide Web
WEBSITES > WEBSITE
WEBSTER archaic word for > WEAVER
WEBSTERS > WEBSTER
WEBWHEEL n wheel containing a plate or web instead of spokes
WEBWHEELS > WEBWHEEL
WEBWORK n work done using the World Wide Web
WEBWORKS > WEBWORK
WEBWORM n type of caterpillar
WEBWORMS > WEBWORM
WEBZINE n magazine published on the Internet
WEBZINES > WEBZINE
WECHT n agricultural tool
WECHTS > WECHT
WED vb marry
WEDDED > WED
WEDDER dialect form of > WEATHER
WEDDERED > WEDDER
WEDDERING > WEDDER
WEDDERS > WEDDER
WEDDING > WED
WEDDINGS > WEDDING
WEDEL variant of > WEDELN
WEDELED > WEDEL
WEDELING > WEDEL
WEDELN n succession of high-speed turns performed in skiing ▷ vb perform a wedeln
WEDELNED > WEDELN
WEDELNING > WEDELN
WEDELNS > WEDELN
WEDELS > WEDEL
WEDGE n piece of material thick at one end and thin at the other ▷ vb fasten or split with a wedge
WEDGED > WEDGE
WEDGELIKE > WEDGE
WEDGES > WEDGE
WEDGEWISE adv in manner of a wedge
WEDGIE n wedge-heeled shoe
WEDGIER > WEDGE
WEDGIES > WEDGIE
WEDGIEST > WEDGE
WEDGING > WEDGE
WEDGINGS > WEDGE
WEDGY > WEDGE
WEDLOCK n marriage
WEDLOCKS > WEDLOCK
WEDS > WED

WEE adj small or short ▷ n instance of urinating ▷ vb urinate
WEED n plant growing where undesired ▷ vb clear of weeds
WEEDED > WEED
WEEDER > WEED
WEEDERIES > WEEDERY
WEEDERS > WEED
WEEDERY n weed-ridden area
WEEDICIDE n weed-killer
WEEDIER > WEEDY
WEEDIEST > WEEDY
WEEDILY > WEEDY
WEEDINESS > WEEDY
WEEDING > WEED
WEEDINGS > WEED
WEEDLESS > WEED
WEEDLIKE > WEED
WEEDS npl widow's mourning clothes
WEEDY adj (of a person) thin and weak
WEEING > WEE
WEEK n period of seven days, esp one beginning on a Sunday ▷ adv seven days before or after a specified day
WEEKDAY n any day of the week except Saturday or Sunday
WEEKDAYS > WEEKDAY
WEEKE same as > WICK
WEEKEND n Saturday and Sunday ▷ vb spend or pass a weekend
WEEKENDED > WEEKEND
WEEKENDER n person spending a weekend holiday in a place, esp habitually
WEEKENDS adv at the weekend, esp regularly or during every weekend
WEEKES > WEEKE
WEEKLIES > WEEKLY
WEEKLONG adj lasting a week
WEEKLY adv happening, done, etc once a week ▷ n newspaper or magazine published once a week ▷ adj happening once a week or every week
WEEKNIGHT n evening or night of a weekday
WEEKS > WEEK
WEEL Scot word for > WELL
WEELS > WEEL
WEEM n underground home
WEEMS > WEEM
WEEN vb think or imagine (something)
WEENED > WEEN
WEENIE adj very small ▷ n wiener
WEENIER > WEENY
WEENIES > WEENIE
WEENIEST > WEENY
WEENING > WEEN
WEENS > WEEN
WEENSIER > WEENSY

WEENSIEST > WEENSY
WEENSY same as > WEENY
WEENY adj very small
WEEP vb shed tears ▷ n spell of weeping
WEEPER n person who weeps, esp a hired mourner
WEEPERS > WEEPER
WEEPHOLE n small drain hole in wall
WEEPHOLES > WEEPHOLE
WEEPIE > WEEPY
WEEPIER > WEEPY
WEEPIES > WEEPY
WEEPIEST > WEEPY
WEEPILY > WEEPY
WEEPINESS > WEEPY
WEEPING adj (of plants) having slender hanging branches
WEEPINGLY > WEEPING
WEEPINGS > WEEPING
WEEPS > WEEP
WEEPY adj liable to cry ▷ n sentimental film or book
WEER > WEE
WEES > WEE
WEEST > WEE
WEET dialect form of > WET
WEETE same as > WIT
WEETED > WEETE
WEETEN same as > WIT
WEETER > WEET
WEETEST > WEET
WEETING > WEET
WEETINGLY > WEET
WEETLESS obsolete variant of > WITLESS
WEETS > WEET
WEEVER n type of small fish
WEEVERS > WEEVER
WEEVIL n small beetle that eats grain etc
WEEVILED same as > WEEVILLED
WEEVILLED adj weevil-ridden
WEEVILLY another word for > WEEVILLED
WEEVILS > WEEVIL
WEEVILY another word for > WEEVILLED
WEEWEE vb urinate
WEEWEED > WEEWEE
WEEWEEING > WEEWEE
WEEWEES > WEEWEE
WEFT n cross threads in weaving ▷ vb form weft
WEFTAGE n texture
WEFTAGES > WEFTAGE
WEFTE n forsaken child
WEFTED > WEFT
WEFTES > WEFTE
WEFTING > WEFT
WEFTS > WEFT
WEFTWISE adv in the direction of the weft
WEID n sudden illness
WEIDS > WEID
WEIGELA n type of shrub
WEIGELAS > WEIGELA
WEIGELIA same as > WEIGELA
WEIGELIAS > WEIGELA

WEIGH vb have a specified weight
WEIGHABLE > WEIGH
WEIGHAGE n duty paid for weighing goods
WEIGHAGES > WEIGHAGE
WEIGHED > WEIGH
WEIGHER > WEIGH
WEIGHERS > WEIGH
WEIGHING > WEIGH
WEIGHINGS > WEIGH
WEIGHMAN n person responsible for weighing goods
WEIGHMEN > WEIGHMAN
WEIGHS > WEIGH
WEIGHT n heaviness of an object ▷ vb add weight to
WEIGHTAGE same as > WEIGHTING
WEIGHTED > WEIGHT
WEIGHTER > WEIGHT
WEIGHTERS > WEIGHT
WEIGHTIER > WEIGHTY
WEIGHTILY > WEIGHTY
WEIGHTING n extra allowance paid in special circumstances
WEIGHTS > WEIGHT
WEIGHTY adj important or serious
WEIL n whirlpool
WEILS > WEIL
WEINER same as > WIENER
WEINERS > WEINER
WEIR vb ward off ▷ n river dam
WEIRD adj strange or bizarre ▷ vb warn beforehand
WEIRDED > WEIRD
WEIRDER > WEIRD
WEIRDEST > WEIRD
WEIRDIE same as > WEIRDO
WEIRDIES > WEIRDIE
WEIRDING > WEIRD
WEIRDLY > WEIRD
WEIRDNESS > WEIRD
WEIRDO n peculiar person
WEIRDOES > WEIRDO
WEIRDOS > WEIRDO
WEIRDS > WEIRD
WEIRDY n weird person
WEIRED > WEIR
WEIRING > WEIR
WEIRS > WEIR
WEISE same as > WISE
WEISED > WEISE
WEISES > WEISE
WEISING > WEISE
WEIZE same as > WISE
WEIZED > WEIZE
WEIZES > WEIZE
WEIZING > WEIZE
WEKA n flightless New Zealand rail
WEKAS > WEKA
WELAWAY same as > WELLAWAY
WELCH same as > WELSH
WELCHED > WELCH
WELCHER > WELCH
WELCHERS > WELCH

WELCHES > WELCH
WELCHING > WELCH
WELCOME vb greet with pleasure ▷ n kindly greeting ▷ adj received gladly
WELCOMED > WELCOME
WELCOMELY > WELCOME
WELCOMER > WELCOME
WELCOMERS > WELCOME
WELCOMES > WELCOME
WELCOMING > WELCOME
WELD vb join (pieces of metal or plastic) by softening with heat ▷ n welded joint
WELDABLE > WELD
WELDED > WELD
WELDER > WELD
WELDERS > WELD
WELDING > WELD
WELDINGS > WELD
WELDLESS > WELD
WELDMENT n unit composed of welded pieces
WELDMENTS > WELDMENT
WELDOR > WELD
WELDORS > WELDOR
WELDS > WELD
WELFARE n wellbeing
WELFARES > WELFARE
WELFARISM n policies or attitudes associated with a welfare state
WELFARIST > WELFARISM
WELK vb wither; dry up
WELKE obsolete form of > WELK
WELKED > WELK
WELKES > WELKE
WELKIN n sky, heavens, or upper air
WELKING > WELK
WELKINS > WELKIN
WELKS > WELK
WELKT adj twisted
WELL adv satisfactorily ▷ adj in good health ▷ interj exclamation of surprise, interrogation, etc ▷ n hole sunk into the earth to reach water, oil, or gas ▷ vb flow upwards or outwards
WELLADAY interj alas
WELLADAYS interj alas
WELLANEAR interj alas
WELLAWAY interj alas!
WELLAWAYS interj alas
WELLBEING n state of being well, happy, or prosperous
WELLBORN adj having been born into a wealthy family
WELLCURB n stone surround at top of well
WELLCURBS > WELLCURB
WELLDOER n moral person
WELLDOERS > WELLDOER
WELLED > WELL
WELLHEAD n source of a well or stream
WELLHEADS > WELLHEAD

WELLHOLE n well shaft
WELLHOLES > WELLHOLE
WELLHOUSE n housing for well
WELLIE n wellington boot
WELLIES > WELLY
WELLING > WELL
WELLINGS > WELL
WELLNESS n state of being in good physical and mental health
WELLS > WELL
WELLSITE n site of well
WELLSITES > WELLSITE
WELLY n energy or commitment
WELS n type of catfish
WELSH vb fail to pay a debt or fulfil an obligation
WELSHED > WELSH
WELSHER > WELSH
WELSHERS > WELSH
WELSHES > WELSH
WELSHING > WELSH
WELT same as > WEAL
WELTED > WELT
WELTER n jumbled mass ▷ vb roll about, writhe, or wallow
WELTERED > WELTER
WELTERING > WELTER
WELTERS > WELTER
WELTING > WELT
WELTINGS > WELT
WELTS > WELT
WEM same as > WAME
WEMB same as > WAME
WEMBS > WEMB
WEMS > WEM
WEN n cyst on the scalp
WENA pron South African word for you
WENCH n young woman ▷ vb frequent the company of prostitutes
WENCHED > WENCH
WENCHER > WENCH
WENCHERS > WENCH
WENCHES > WENCH
WENCHING > WENCH
WEND vb go or travel
WENDED > WEND
WENDIGO n evil spirit or cannibal
WENDIGOS > WENDIGO
WENDING > WEND
WENDS > WEND
WENGE n type of tree found in central and West Africa
WENGES > WENGE
WENNIER > WEN
WENNIEST > WEN
WENNISH > WEN
WENNY > WEN
WENS > WEN
WENT n path
WENTS > WENT
WEPT > WEEP
WERE vb form of the past tense of **be** used after we, you, they, or a plural noun
WEREGILD same as > WERGILD
WEREGILDS > WEREGILD

WEREWOLF n (in folklore) person who can turn into a wolf
WERGELD same as > WERGILD
WERGELDS > WERGELD
WERGELT same as > WERGILD
WERGELTS > WERGELT
WERGILD n price set on a man's life in successive Anglo-Saxon and Germanic law codes, to be paid as compensation by his slayer
WERGILDS > WERGILD
WERNERITE another name for > SCAPOLITE
WERO n challenge made by an armed Māori warrior to a visitor to a marae
WEROS > WERO
WERRIS slang word for > URINATION
WERRISES > WERRIS
WERSH adj tasteless
WERSHER > WERSH
WERSHEST > WERSH
WERT singular form of the past tense of > BE
WERWOLF same as > WEREWOLF
WERWOLVES > WERWOLF
WESAND same as > WEASAND
WESANDS > WESAND
WESKIT informal word for > WAISTCOAT
WESKITS > WESKIT
WESSAND same as > WEASAND
WESSANDS > WESSAND
WEST n part of the horizon where the sun sets ▷ adj in the west ▷ adv in, to, or towards the west ▷ vb move in westerly direction
WESTABOUT adv in, to, or towards the west
WESTBOUND adj going towards the west
WESTED > WEST
WESTER vb move or appear to move towards the west ▷ n strong wind or storm from the west
WESTERED > WESTER
WESTERING > WESTER
WESTERLY adj of or in the west ▷ adv towards the west ▷ n wind blowing from the west
WESTERN adj of or in the west ▷ n film or story about cowboys in the western US
WESTERNER n person from the west of a country or area
WESTERNS > WESTERN
WESTERS > WESTER
WESTIE n informal word for a young working-class person from the western suburbs of Sydney
WESTIES > WESTIE

w

WESTING n movement, deviation, or distance covered in a westerly direction

WESTINGS > WESTING

WESTLIN Scots word for > WESTERN

WESTLINS adv to or in west

WESTMOST adj most western

WESTS > WEST

WESTWARD adv towards the west ▷ n westward part or direction ▷ adj moving, facing, or situated in the west

WESTWARDS same as > WESTWARD

WET adj covered or soaked with water or another liquid ▷ n moisture or rain ▷ vb make wet

WETA n type of wingless insect

WETAS > WETA

WETBACK n Mexican labourer who enters the US illegally

WETBACKS > WETBACK

WETHER n male sheep, esp a castrated one

WETHERS > WETHER

WETLAND n area of marshy land

WETLANDS > WETLAND

WETLY > WET

WETNESS > WET

WETNESSES > WET

WETPROOF adj waterproof

WETS > WET

WETSUIT n body suit for diving

WETSUITS > WETSUIT

WETTABLE > WET

WETTED > WET

WETTER > WET

WETTERS > WET

WETTEST > WET

WETTIE n wetsuit

WETTIES > WETTIE

WETTING > WET

WETTINGS > WET

WETTISH > WET

WETWARE n humorous term for the brain

WETWARES > WETWARE

WEX obsolete form of > WAX

WEXE obsolete form of > WAX

WEXED > WEX

WEXES > WEX

WEXING > WEX

WEY n measurement of weight

WEYARD obsolete form of > WEIRD

WEYS > WEY

WEYWARD obsolete form of > WEIRD

WEZAND obsolete form of > WEASAND

WEZANDS > WEZAND

WHA Scot word for > WHO

WHACK vb strike with a resounding blow ▷ n such a blow

WHACKED > WHACK

WHACKER > WHACK

WHACKERS > WHACK

WHACKIER > WHACKY

WHACKIEST > WHACKY

WHACKING adj huge ▷ n severe beating ▷ adv extremely

WHACKINGS > WHACKING

WHACKO n mad person

WHACKOES > WHACKO

WHACKOS > WHACKO

WHACKS > WHACK

WHACKY variant spelling of > WACKY

WHAE same as > WHA

WHAISLE Scots form of > WHEEZE

WHAISLED > WHAISLE

WHAISLES > WHAISLE

WHAISLING > WHAISLE

WHAIZLE same as > WHAISLE

WHAIZLED > WHAIZLE

WHAIZLES > WHAIZLE

WHAIZLING > WHAIZLE

WHAKAIRO n art of carving

WHAKAIROS > WHAKAIRO

WHAKAPAPA n genealogy

WHALE n large fish-shaped sea mammal ▷ vb hunt for whales

WHALEBACK n something shaped like the back of a whale

WHALEBOAT n narrow boat from 20 to 30 feet long having a sharp prow and stern, formerly used in whaling

WHALEBONE n horny substance hanging from the upper jaw of toothless whales

WHALED > WHALE

WHALELIKE > WHALE

WHALEMAN n person employed in whaling

WHALEMEN > WHALEMAN

WHALER n ship or person involved in whaling

WHALERIES > WHALERY

WHALERS > WHALER

WHALERY n whaling

WHALES > WHALE

WHALING n hunting of whales for food and oil ▷ adv extremely

WHALINGS > WHALING

WHALLY adj (of eyes) with light-coloured irises

WHAM interj expression indicating suddenness or forcefulness ▷ n forceful blow or impact or the sound produced by such a blow or impact ▷ vb strike or cause to strike with great force

WHAMMED > WHAM

WHAMMIES > WHAMMY

WHAMMING > WHAM

WHAMMO n sound of a sudden collision

WHAMMOS > WHAMMO

WHAMMY n devastating setback

WHAMO same as > WHAMMO

WHAMPLE n strike

WHAMPLES > WHAMPLE

WHAMS > WHAM

WHANAU n (in Māori societies) a family, esp an extended family

WHANAUS > WHANAU

WHANG vb strike or be struck so as to cause a resounding noise ▷ n resounding noise produced by a heavy blow

WHANGAM n imaginary creature

WHANGAMS > WHANGAM

WHANGED > WHANG

WHANGEE n tall woody grass grown for its stems, which are used for bamboo canes

WHANGEES > WHANGEE

WHANGING > WHANG

WHANGS > WHANG

WHAP same as > WHOP

WHAPPED > WHAP

WHAPPER same as > WHOPPER

WHAPPERS > WHAPPER

WHAPPING > WHAP

WHAPS > WHAP

WHARE n Māori hut or dwelling place

WHARENUI n (in New Zealand) meeting house

WHARENUIS > WHARENUI

WHAREPUNI n (in a Māori community) a tall carved building used as a guesthouse

WHARES > WHARE

WHARF n platform at a harbour for loading and unloading ships ▷ vb put (goods, etc) on a wharf

WHARFAGE n accommodation for ships at wharves

WHARFAGES > WHARFAGE

WHARFED > WHARF

WHARFIE n person employed to load and unload ships

WHARFIES > WHARFIE

WHARFING > WHARF

WHARFINGS > WHARF

WHARFS > WHARF

WHARVE n wooden disc or wheel on a shaft serving as a flywheel or pulley

WHARVES > WHARVE

WHAT pron which thing ▷ interj exclamation of anger, surprise, etc ▷ adv in which way, how much ▷ n part; portion

WHATA n building on stilts or a raised platform for storing provisions

WHATAS > WHATA

WHATEN adj what; what

kind of

WHATEVER pron everything or anything that ▷ adj intensive form of what ▷ det intensive form of what ▷ interj expression used to show indifference or dismissal

WHATNA another word for > WHATEN

WHATNESS n what something is

WHATNOT n similar unspecified thing

WHATNOTS > WHATNOT

WHATS > WHAT

WHATSIS US form of > WHATSIT

WHATSISES > WHATSIS

WHATSIT n person or thing the name of which is unknown, temporarily forgotten, or deliberately overlooked

WHATSITS > WHATSIT

WHATSO n of whatever kind

WHATTEN same as > WHATEN

WHAUP n curlew

WHAUPS > WHAUP

WHAUR Scot word for > WHERE

WHAURS > WHAUR

WHEAL same as > WEAL

WHEALS > WHEAL

WHEAR obsolete variant of > WHERE

WHEARE obsolete variant of > WHERE

WHEAT n grain used in making flour, bread, and pasta

WHEATEAR n small songbird

WHEATEARS > WHEATEAR

WHEATEN n type of dog ▷ adj made of the grain or flour of wheat

WHEATENS > WHEATEN

WHEATIER > WHEATY

WHEATIEST > WHEATY

WHEATLAND n region where wheat is grown

WHEATLESS > WHEAT

WHEATMEAL n brown, but not wholemeal, flour

WHEATS > WHEAT

WHEATWORM n parasitic nematode worm that forms galls in the seeds of wheat

WHEATY adj having a wheat-like taste

WHEE interj exclamation of joy, thrill, etc

WHEECH vb move quickly

WHEECHED > WHEECH

WHEECHING > WHEECH

WHEECHS > WHEECH

WHEEDLE vb coax or cajole

WHEEDLED > WHEEDLE

WHEEDLER > WHEEDLE

WHEEDLERS > WHEEDLE

WHEEDLES > WHEEDLE

WHEEDLING > WHEEDLE

WHEEL n disc that revolves on an axle ⊳ vb push or pull (something with wheels)
WHEELBASE n distance between a vehicle's front and back axles
WHEELED adj having or equipped with a wheel or wheels
WHEELER n horse or other draught animal nearest the wheel
WHEELERS > WHEELER
WHEELIE n manoeuvre on a bike in which the front wheel is raised off the ground
WHEELIER > WHEELY
WHEELIES > WHEELIE
WHEELIEST > WHEELY
WHEELING > WHEEL
WHEELINGS > WHEEL
WHEELLESS adj having no wheels
WHEELMAN n helmsman
WHEELMEN > WHEELMAN
WHEELS > WHEEL
WHEELSMAN same as > WHEELMAN
WHEELSMEN > WHEELSMAN
WHEELWORK n arrangement of wheels in a machine, esp a train of gears
WHEELY adj resembling a wheel
WHEEN n few
WHEENGE Scots form of > WHINGE
WHEENGED > WHEENGE
WHEENGES > WHEENGE
WHEENGING > WHEENGE
WHEENS > WHEEN
WHEEP vb fly quickly and lightly
WHEEPED > WHEEP
WHEEPING > WHEEP
WHEEPLE vb whistle weakly
WHEEPLED > WHEEPLE
WHEEPLES > WHEEPLE
WHEEPLING > WHEEPLE
WHEEPS > WHEEP
WHEESH vb silence (a person, noise, etc) or be silenced
WHEESHED > WHEESH
WHEESHES > WHEESH
WHEESHING > WHEESH
WHEESHT same as > WHEESH
WHEESHTED > WHEESHT
WHEESHTS > WHEESHT
WHEEZE vb breathe with a hoarse whistling noise ⊳ n wheezing sound
WHEEZED > WHEEZE
WHEEZER > WHEEZE
WHEEZERS > WHEEZE
WHEEZES > WHEEZE
WHEEZIER > WHEEZE
WHEEZIEST > WHEEZE
WHEEZILY > WHEEZE

WHEEZING > WHEEZE
WHEEZINGS > WHEEZE
WHEEZLE vb make hoarse breathing sound
WHEEZLED > WHEEZLE
WHEEZLES > WHEEZLE
WHEEZLING > WHEEZLE
WHEEZY > WHEEZE
WHEFT same as > WAFT
WHEFTS > WHEFT
WHELK n edible snail-like shellfish
WHELKED adj having or covered with whelks
WHELKIER > WHELK
WHELKIEST > WHELK
WHELKS > WHELK
WHELKY > WHELK
WHELM vb engulf entirely with or as if with water
WHELMED > WHELM
WHELMING > WHELM
WHELMS > WHELM
WHELP n pup or cub ⊳ vb (of an animal) give birth
WHELPED > WHELP
WHELPING > WHELP
WHELPLESS > WHELP
WHELPS > WHELP
WHEMMLE vb overturn
WHEMMLED > WHEMMLE
WHEMMLES > WHEMMLE
WHEMMLING > WHEMMLE
WHEN adv at what time? ⊳ pron at which time ⊳ n question of when
WHENAS conj while; inasmuch as
WHENCE n point of origin ⊳ adv from what place or source ⊳ pron from what place, cause, or origin
WHENCES > WHENCE
WHENCEVER adv out of whatsoever place, cause or origin
WHENEVER adv at whatever time
WHENS > WHEN
WHENUA n land
WHENUAS > WHENUA
WHENWE n White immigrant from Zimbabwe, caricatured as being tiresomely over-reminiscent of happier times
WHENWES > WHENWE
WHERE adv in, at, or to what place? ⊳ pron in, at, or to which place ⊳ n question as to the position, direction, or destination of something
WHEREAS n testimonial introduced by whereas
WHEREASES > WHEREAS
WHEREAT adv at or to which place
WHEREBY pron by which ⊳ adv how? by what means?
WHEREFOR adv for which
WHEREFORE adv why ⊳ n explanation or reason

WHEREFROM adv from what or where? whence? ⊳ pron from which place
WHEREIN adv in what place or respect? ⊳ pron in which place or thing
WHEREINTO adv into what place? ⊳ pron into which place
WHERENESS n state of having a place
WHEREOF adv of what or which person or thing? ⊳ pron of which person or thing
WHEREON adv on what thing or place? ⊳ pron on which thing, place, etc
WHEREOUT adv out of which
WHERES > WHERE
WHERESO adv in or to unspecified place
WHERETO adv towards what (place, end, etc)? ⊳ pron which
WHEREUNTO same as > WHERETO
WHEREUPON adv upon what?
WHEREVER adv at whatever place ⊳ pron at, in, or to every place or point which
WHEREWITH pron with or by which ⊳ adv with what?
WHERRET vb strike (someone) a blow ⊳ n blow, esp a slap on the face
WHERRETED > WHERRET
WHERRETS > WHERRET
WHERRIED > WHERRY
WHERRIES > WHERRY
WHERRIT vb worry or cause to worry
WHERRITED > WHERRIT
WHERRITS > WHERRIT
WHERRY n any of certain kinds of half-decked commercial boats, such as barges, used in Britain ⊳ vb travel in a wherry
WHERRYING > WHERRY
WHERRYMAN > WHERRY
WHERRYMEN > WHERRY
WHERVE same as > WHARVE
WHERVES > WHERVE
WHET vb sharpen (a tool) ⊳ n act of whetting
WHETHER conj used to introduce any indirect question
WHETS > WHET
WHETSTONE n stone for sharpening tools
WHETTED > WHET
WHETTER > WHET
WHETTERS > WHET
WHETTING > WHET
WHEUGH same as > WHEW
WHEUGHED > WHEUGH
WHEUGHING > WHEUGH
WHEUGHS > WHEUGH
WHEW interj exclamation expressing relief, delight,

etc ⊳ vb express relief
WHEWED > WHEW
WHEWING > WHEW
WHEWS > WHEW
WHEY n watery liquid that separates from the curd when milk is clotted
WHEYEY > WHEY
WHEYFACE n pale bloodless face
WHEYFACED > WHEYFACE
WHEYFACES > WHEYFACE
WHEYIER > WHEY
WHEYIEST > WHEY
WHEYISH > WHEY
WHEYLIKE > WHEY
WHEYS > WHEY
WHICH pron used to request or refer to a choice from different possibilities ⊳ adj used with a noun in requesting that the particular thing being referred to is further identified or distinguished
WHICHEVER pron any out of several ⊳ adj any out of several ⊳ det any (one, two, etc, out of several)
WHICKER vb (of a horse) to whinny or neigh
WHICKERED > WHICKER
WHICKERS > WHICKER
WHID vb move quickly
WHIDAH same as > WHYDAH
WHIDAHS > WHIDAH
WHIDDED > WHID
WHIDDER vb move with force
WHIDDERED > WHIDDER
WHIDDERS > WHIDDER
WHIDDING > WHID
WHIDS > WHID
WHIFF n puff of air or odour ⊳ vb come, convey, or go in whiffs
WHIFFED > WHIFF
WHIFFER > WHIFF
WHIFFERS > WHIFF
WHIFFET n insignificant person
WHIFFETS > WHIFFET
WHIFFIER > WHIFFY
WHIFFIEST > WHIFFY
WHIFFING > WHIFF
WHIFFINGS > WHIFF
WHIFFLE vb think or behave in an erratic or unpredictable way
WHIFFLED > WHIFFLE
WHIFFLER n person who whiffles
WHIFFLERS > WHIFFLER
WHIFFLERY n frivolity
WHIFFLES > WHIFFLE
WHIFFLING > WHIFFLE
WHIFFS > WHIFF
WHIFFY adj smelly
WHIFT n brief emission of air
WHIFTS > WHIFT
WHIG vb go quickly
WHIGGED > WHIG
WHIGGING > WHIG

WHIGS > WHIG
WHILE n period of time
WHILED > WHILE
WHILERE adv a while ago
WHILES adv at times
WHILING > WHILE
WHILK archaic and dialect word for > WHICH
WHILLIED > WHILLY
WHILLIES > WHILLY
WHILLY vb influence by flattery
WHILLYING > WHILLY
WHILLYWHA variant of > WHILLY
WHILOM adv formerly ▷ adj one-time
WHILST same as > WHILE
WHIM n sudden fancy ▷ vb have a whim
WHIMBERRY n whortleberry
WHIMBREL n small European curlew with a striped head
WHIMBRELS > WHIMBREL
WHIMMED > WHIM
WHIMMIER > WHIMMY
WHIMMIEST > WHIMMY
WHIMMING > WHIM
WHIMMY adj having whims
WHIMPER vb cry in a soft whining way ▷ n soft plaintive whine
WHIMPERED > WHIMPER
WHIMPERER > WHIMPER
WHIMPERS > WHIMPER
WHIMPLE same as > WIMPLE
WHIMPLED > WHIMPLE
WHIMPLES > WHIMPLE
WHIMPLING > WHIMPLE
WHIMS > WHIM
WHIMSEY same as > WHIMSY
WHIMSEYS > WHIMSEY
WHIMSICAL adj unusual, playful, and fanciful
WHIMSIED > WHIMSY
WHIMSIER > WHIMSY
WHIMSIES > WHIMSY
WHIMSIEST > WHIMSY
WHIMSILY > WHIMSY
WHIMSY n capricious idea ▷ adj quaint, comical, or unusual, often in a tasteless way
WHIN n gorse
WHINBERRY same as > WHIMBERRY
WHINCHAT n type of songbird
WHINCHATS > WHINCHAT
WHINE n high-pitched plaintive cry ▷ vb make such a sound
WHINED > WHINE
WHINER > WHINE
WHINERS > WHINE
WHINES > WHINE
WHINEY same as > WHINY
WHINGDING same as > WINGDING

WHINGE vb complain ▷ n complaint
WHINGED > WHINGE
WHINGEING > WHINGE
WHINGER > WHINGE
WHINGERS > WHINGE
WHINGES > WHINGE
WHINGIER > WHINGY
WHINGIEST > WHINGY
WHINGING > WHINGE
WHINGY adj complaining peevishly, whining
WHINIARD same as > WHINYARD
WHINIARDS > WHINIARD
WHINIER > WHINY
WHINIEST > WHINY
WHININESS > WHINY
WHINING > WHINE
WHININGLY > WHINE
WHININGS > WHINE
WHINNIED > WHINNY
WHINNIER > WHINNY
WHINNIES > WHINNY
WHINNIEST > WHINNY
WHINNY vb neigh softly ▷ n soft neigh ▷ adj covered in whin
WHINNYING > WHINNY
WHINS > WHIN
WHINSTONE n any dark hard fine-grained rock, such as basalt
WHINY adj high-pitched and plaintive
WHINYARD n sword
WHINYARDS > WHINYARD
WHIO n New Zealand mountain duck with blue plumage
WHIOS > WHIO
WHIP n cord attached to a handle, used for beating animals or people ▷ vb strike with a whip, strap, or cane
WHIPBIRD n any of several birds having a whistle ending in a whipcrack note
WHIPBIRDS > WHIPBIRD
WHIPCAT n tailor
WHIPCATS > WHIPCAT
WHIPCORD n strong worsted or cotton fabric with a diagonally ribbed surface
WHIPCORDS > WHIPCORD
WHIPCORDY adj whipcord-like
WHIPJACK n beggar imitating a sailor
WHIPJACKS > WHIPJACK
WHIPLASH n quick lash of a whip
WHIPLESS adj without a whip
WHIPLIKE > WHIP
WHIPPED > WHIP
WHIPPER > WHIP
WHIPPERS > WHIP
WHIPPET n racing dog like a small greyhound
WHIPPETS > WHIPPET
WHIPPIER > WHIPPY

WHIPPIEST > WHIPPY
WHIPPING > WHIP
WHIPPINGS > WHIP
WHIPPY adj springy
WHIPRAY n stingray
WHIPRAYS > WHIPRAY
WHIPS > WHIP
WHIPSAW n any saw with a flexible blade, such as a bandsaw ▷ vb saw with a whipsaw
WHIPSAWED > WHIPSAW
WHIPSAWN > WHIPSAW
WHIPSAWS > WHIPSAW
WHIPSNAKE n thin snake like leather whip
WHIPSTAFF n ship's steering bar
WHIPSTALL n stall in which an aircraft goes into a nearly vertical climb, pauses, slips backwards momentarily, and drops suddenly with its nose down
WHIPSTER n insignificant but pretentious or cheeky person, esp a young one
WHIPSTERS > WHIPSTER
WHIPSTOCK n handle of a whip
WHIPT old past tense of > WHIP
WHIPTAIL n type of lizard
WHIPTAILS > WHIPTAIL
WHIPWORM n parasitic worm living in the intestines of mammals
WHIPWORMS > WHIPWORM
WHIR n prolonged soft swish or buzz, as of a motor working or wings flapping ▷ vb make or cause to make a whir
WHIRL vb spin or revolve ▷ n whirling movement
WHIRLBAT n thing moved with a whirl
WHIRLBATS > WHIRLBAT
WHIRLED > WHIRL
WHIRLER > WHIRL
WHIRLERS > WHIRL
WHIRLIER > WHIRLY
WHIRLIES n illness induced by excessive use of alcohol or drugs
WHIRLIEST > WHIRLY
WHIRLIGIG same as > WINDMILL
WHIRLING > WHIRL
WHIRLINGS > WHIRL
WHIRLPOOL n strong circular current of water
WHIRLS > WHIRL
WHIRLWIND n column of air whirling violently upwards in a spiral ▷ adj much quicker than normal
WHIRLY adj characterized by whirling
WHIRR same as > WHIR
WHIRRED > WHIR
WHIRRET vb strike with sharp blow
WHIRRETED > WHIRRET

WHIRRETS > WHIRRET
WHIRRIED > WHIRRY
WHIRRIES > WHIRRY
WHIRRING > WHIR
WHIRRINGS > WHIR
WHIRRS > WHIRR
WHIRRY vb move quickly
WHIRRYING > WHIRRY
WHIRS > WHIR
WHIRTLE same as > WORTLE
WHIRTLES > WHIRTLE
WHISH less common word for > SWISH
WHISHED > WHISH
WHISHES > WHISH
WHISHING > WHISH
WHISHT interj hush! be quiet! ▷ adj silent or still ▷ vb make or become silent
WHISHTED > WHISHT
WHISHTING > WHISHT
WHISHTS > WHISHT
WHISK vb move or remove quickly ▷ n quick movement
WHISKED > WHISK
WHISKER n any of the long stiff hairs on the face of a cat or other mammal
WHISKERED adj having whiskers
WHISKERS > WHISKER
WHISKERY adj having whiskers
WHISKET same as > WISKET
WHISKETS > WHISKET
WHISKEY n Irish or American whisky
WHISKEYS > WHISKEY
WHISKIES > WHISKY
WHISKING > WHISK
WHISKS > WHISK
WHISKY n spirit distilled from fermented cereals
WHISPER vb speak softly, without vibration of the vocal cords ▷ n soft voice
WHISPERED > WHISPER
WHISPERER n person or thing that whispers
WHISPERS > WHISPER
WHISPERY > WHISPER
WHISS vb hiss
WHISSED > WHISS
WHISSES > WHISS
WHISSING > WHISS
WHIST same as > WHISHT
WHISTED > WHIST
WHISTING > WHIST
WHISTLE vb produce a shrill sound, esp by forcing the breath through pursed lips ▷ n whistling sound
WHISTLED > WHISTLE
WHISTLER n person or thing that whistles
WHISTLERS > WHISTLER
WHISTLES > WHISTLE
WHISTLING > WHISTLE
WHISTS > WHIST
WHIT n smallest particle

WHITE *adj* of the colour of snow ▷ *n* colour of snow
WHITEBAIT *n* small edible fish
WHITEBASS *n* type of fish
WHITEBEAM *n* type of tree
WHITECAP *n* wave with a white broken crest
WHITECAPS > WHITECAP
WHITECOAT *n* person who wears a white coat
WHITECOMB *n* fungal disease infecting the combs of certain fowls
WHITED as in *whited sepulchre* hypocrite
WHITEDAMP *n* mixture of poisonous gases, mainly carbon monoxide, occurring in coal mines
WHITEFACE *n* white stage make-up
WHITEFISH *n* type of fish
WHITEFLY *n* tiny whitish insect that is harmful to greenhouse plants
WHITEHEAD *n* type of pimple with a white head
WHITELIST *n* list of e-mail contacts from whom messages are regarded as acceptable by the user ▷ *vb* put (an email contact) on a whitelist
WHITELY > WHITE
WHITEN *vb* make or become white or whiter
WHITENED > WHITEN
WHITENER *n* substance that makes something white or whiter
WHITENERS > WHITENER
WHITENESS > WHITE
WHITENING > WHITEN
WHITENS > WHITEN
WHITEOUT *n* atmospheric condition in which blizzards or low clouds make it very difficult to see
WHITEOUTS > WHITEOUT
WHITEPOT *n* custard or milk pudding
WHITEPOTS > WHITEPOT
WHITER > WHITE
WHITES *npl* white clothes, as worn for playing cricket
WHITEST > WHITE
WHITETAIL *n* type of deer
WHITEWALL *n* pneumatic tyre having white sidewalls
WHITEWARE *n* white ceramics
WHITEWASH *n* substance for whitening walls ▷ *vb* cover with whitewash
WHITEWING *n* type of bird
WHITEWOOD *n* light-coloured wood often prepared for staining
WHITEY same as > WHITY
WHITEYS > WHITEY
WHITHER same as > WUTHER
WHITHERED > WHITHER
WHITHERS > WHITHER

WHITIER > WHITY
WHITIES > WHITY
WHITIEST > WHITY
WHITING *n* edible sea fish
WHITINGS > WHITING
WHITISH > WHITE
WHITLING *n* type of trout
WHITLINGS > WHITLING
WHITLOW *n* inflamed sore on a finger or toe, esp round a nail
WHITLOWS > WHITLOW
WHITRACK *n* weasel or stoat
WHITRACKS > WHITRACK
WHITRET *n* variant of whittret
WHITRETS > WHITRET
WHITRICK *n* dialect word for a male weasel
WHITRICKS > WHITRICK
WHITS > WHIT
WHITSTER *n* person who whitens clothes
WHITSTERS > WHITSTER
WHITTAW same as > WHITTAWER
WHITTAWER *n* person who treats leather
WHITTAWS > WHITTAW
WHITTER variant spelling of > WITTER
WHITTERED > WHITTER
WHITTERS > WHITTER
WHITTLE *vb* cut or carve (wood) with a knife ▷ *n* knife, esp a large one
WHITTLED > WHITTLE
WHITTLER > WHITTLE
WHITTLERS > WHITTLE
WHITTLES > WHITTLE
WHITTLING > WHITTLE
WHITTRET *n* male weasel
WHITTRETS > WHITTRET
WHITY *adj* of a white colour ▷ *n* derogatory term for a White person
WHIZ same as > WHIZZ
WHIZBANG *n* small-calibre shell
WHIZBANGS > WHIZBANG
WHIZZ *vb* make a loud buzzing sound ▷ *n* loud buzzing sound
WHIZZBANG same as > WHIZBANG
WHIZZED > WHIZZ
WHIZZER > WHIZZ
WHIZZERS > WHIZZ
WHIZZES > WHIZZ
WHIZZIER > WHIZZY
WHIZZIEST > WHIZZY
WHIZZING > WHIZZ
WHIZZINGS > WHIZZ
WHIZZO same as > WHIZZY
WHIZZY *adj* using sophisticated technology to produce vivid effects
WHO *pron* which person
WHOA *interj* command used, esp to horses, to stop or slow down
WHODUNIT same as > WHODUNNIT

WHODUNITS > WHODUNIT
WHODUNNIT *n* detective story, play, or film
WHOEVER *pron* any person who
WHOLE *adj* containing all the elements or parts ▷ *n* complete thing or system
WHOLEFOOD *n* food that has been processed as little as possible ▷ *adj* of or relating to wholefood
WHOLEMEAL *adj* (of flour) made from the whole wheat grain
WHOLENESS > WHOLE
WHOLES > WHOLE
WHOLESALE *adv* dealing by selling goods in large quantities to retailers ▷ *n* business of selling goods in large quantities and at lower prices to retailers for resale
WHOLESOME *adj* physically or morally beneficial
WHOLISM same as > HOLISM
WHOLISMS > WHOLISM
WHOLIST same as > HOLIST
WHOLISTIC same as > HOLISTIC
WHOLISTS > WHOLIST
WHOLLY *adv* completely or totally
WHOLPHIN *n* whale-dolphin hybrid
WHOLPHINS > WHOLPHIN
WHOM *pron* objective form of *who*
WHOMBLE same as > WHEMMLE
WHOMBLED > WHOMBLE
WHOMBLES > WHOMBLE
WHOMBLING > WHOMBLE
WHOMEVER *pron* objective form of *whoever*
WHOMMLE same as > WHEMMLE
WHOMMLED > WHOMMLE
WHOMMLES > WHOMMLE
WHOMMLING > WHOMMLE
WHOMP *vb* strike; thump
WHOMPED > WHOMP
WHOMPING > WHOMP
WHOMPS > WHOMP
WHOMSO *pron* whom; whomever
WHOOBUB same as > HUBBUB
WHOOBUBS > WHOOBUB
WHOOF same as > WOOF
WHOOFED > WHOOF
WHOOFING > WHOOF
WHOOFS > WHOOF
WHOOP *n* shout or cry to express excitement ▷ *vb* emit a whoop
WHOOPED > WHOOP
WHOOPEE *n* cry of joy
WHOOPEES > WHOOPEE
WHOOPER *n* type of swan
WHOOPERS > WHOOPER
WHOOPIE same as

> WHOOPEE
WHOOPIES > WHOOPIE
WHOOPING > WHOOP
WHOOPINGS > WHOOPING
WHOOPLA *n* commotion; fuss
WHOOPLAS > WHOOPLA
WHOOPS *interj* exclamation of surprise or of apology
WHOOPSIE *n* animal excrement
WHOOPSIES > WHOOPSIE
WHOOSH *n* hissing or rushing sound ▷ *vb* make or move with a hissing or rushing sound
WHOOSHED > WHOOSH
WHOOSHES > WHOOSH
WHOOSHING > WHOOSH
WHOOSIS *n* thingamajig
WHOOSISES > WHOOSIS
WHOOT obsolete variant of > HOOT
WHOOTED > WHOOT
WHOOTING > WHOOT
WHOOTS > WHOOT
WHOP *vb* strike, beat, or thrash ▷ *n* heavy blow or the sound made by such a blow
WHOPPED > WHOP
WHOPPER *n* anything unusually large
WHOPPERS > WHOPPER
WHOPPING *n* beating as punishment ▷ *adj* unusually large ▷ *adv* extremely
WHOPPINGS > WHOPPING
WHOPS > WHOP
WHORE *n* prostitute ▷ *vb* be or act as a prostitute
WHORED > WHORE
WHOREDOM *n* activity of whoring or state of being a whore
WHOREDOMS > WHOREDOM
WHORES > WHORE
WHORESON *n* bastard ▷ *adj* vile or hateful
WHORESONS > WHORESON
WHORING > WHORE
WHORISH > WHORE
WHORISHLY > WHORE
WHORL *n* ring of leaves or petals
WHORLBAT same as > WHIRLBAT
WHORLBATS > WHORLBAT
WHORLED > WHORL
WHORLS > WHORL
WHORT *n* small shrub bearing blackish edible sweet berries
WHORTLE *n* whortleberry
WHORTLES > WHORTLE
WHORTS > WHORT
WHOSE *pron* of whom or of which ▷ *det* of whom? belonging to whom?
WHOSEVER *pron* belonging to whoever
WHOSIS *n* thingamajig
WHOSISES > WHOSIS

W

WHOSO *archaic word for*
> WHOEVER

WHOSOEVER *same as*
> WHOEVER

WHOT *obsolete variant of*
> HOT

WHOW *interj* wow

WHUMMLE *vb variant of* whemmle

WHUMMLED > WHUMMLE

WHUMMLES > WHUMMLE

WHUMMLING > WHUMMLE

WHUMP *vb* make a dull thud ▷ *n* dull thud

WHUMPED > WHUMP

WHUMPING > WHUMP

WHUMPS > WHUMP

WHUNSTANE *Scots variant of*
> WHINSTONE

WHUP *vb* defeat totally

WHUPPED > WHUP

WHUPPING > WHUP

WHUPPINGS > WHUPPING

WHUPS > WHUP

WHY *adv* for what reason ▷ *pron* because of which ▷ *n* reason, purpose, or cause of something

WHYDAH *n* type of black African bird

WHYDAHS > WHYDAH

WHYDUNIT *same as*
> WHYDUNNIT

WHYDUNITS > WHYDUNIT

WHYDUNNIT *n* novel, film, etc, concerned with the motives of the criminal rather than his or her identity

WHYEVER *adv* for whatever reason

WHYS > WHY

WIBBLE *vb* wobble

WIBBLED > WIBBLE

WIBBLES > WIBBLE

WIBBLING > WIBBLE

WICCA *n* cult or practice of witchcraft

WICCAN *n* member of wicca

WICCANS > WICCAN

WICCAS > WICCA

WICE *Scots form of* > WISE

WICH *n* variant of wych

WICHES > WICH

WICK *n* cord through a lamp or candle which carries fuel to the flame ▷ *adj* lively or active ▷ *vb* (of a material) draw in (water, fuel, etc)

WICKAPE *same as*
> WICKAPE

WICKAPES > WICKAPE

WICKED *adj* morally bad ▷ *n* wicked person

WICKEDER > WICKED

WICKEDEST > WICKED

WICKEDLY > WICKED

WICKENS > WICKEN

WICKEN *same as*
> QUICKEN

WICKENS > WICKEN

WICKER *adj* made of woven cane ▷ *n* slender flexible twig or shoot, esp of willow

WICKERED > WICKER

WICKERS > WICKER

WICKET *n* set of three cricket stumps and two bails

WICKETS > WICKET

WICKIES > WICKY

WICKING > WICK

WICKINGS > WICK

WICKIUP *n* crude shelter made of brushwood, mats, or grass and having an oval frame

WICKIUPS > WICKIUP

WICKLESS > WICK

WICKS > WICK

WICKTHING *n* creeping animal, such as a woodlouse

WICKY *same as* > QUICKEN

WICKYUP *same as*
> WICKIUP

WICKYUPS > WICKYUP

WICOPIES > WICOPY

WICOPY *n* any of various North American trees, shrubs, or herbaceous plants

WIDDER *same as* > WIDOW

WIDDERS > WIDDER

WIDDIE *same as* > WIDDY

WIDDIES > WIDDY

WIDDLE *vb* urinate ▷ *n* urine

WIDDLED > WIDDLE

WIDDLES > WIDDLE

WIDDLING > WIDDLE

WIDDY *vb* rope made of twigs

WIDE *adj* large from side to side ▷ *adv* the full extent ▷ *n* (in cricket) a bowled ball ruled to be outside a batsman's reach

WIDEAWAKE *n* hat with a low crown and a very wide brim

WIDEBAND *n* wide bandwidth transmission medium

WIDEBODY *n* aircraft with a wide fuselage

WIDELY > WIDE

WIDEN *vb* make or become wider

WIDENED > WIDEN

WIDENER > WIDEN

WIDENERS > WIDEN

WIDENESS > WIDE

WIDENING > WIDEN

WIDENS > WIDEN

WIDEOUT *n* footballer who catches passes from the quarterback

WIDEOUTS > WIDEOUT

WIDER > WIDE

WIDES > WIDE

WIDEST > WIDE

WIDGEON *same as*
> WIGEON

WIDGEONS > WIDGEON

WIDGET *n* any small device, the name of which is unknown or forgotten

WIDGETS > WIDGET

WIDGIE *n* female larrikin or bodgie

WIDGIES > WIDGIE

WIDISH > WIDE

WIDOW *n* woman whose husband is dead and who has not remarried ▷ *vb* cause to become a widow

WIDOWBIRD *n* whydah

WIDOWED > WIDOW

WIDOWER *n* man whose wife is dead and who has not remarried

WIDOWERED > WIDOWER

WIDOWERS > WIDOWER

WIDOWHOOD > WIDOW

WIDOWING > WIDOW

WIDOWMAN *n* widower

WIDOWMEN > WIDOWMAN

WIDOWS > WIDOW

WIDTH *n* distance from side to side

WIDTHS > WIDTH

WIDTHWAY *adj* across the width

WIDTHWAYS *same as*
> WIDTHWISE

WIDTHWISE *adv* in the direction of the width

WIEL *same as* > WEEL

WIELD *vb* hold and use (a weapon)

WIELDABLE > WIELD

WIELDED > WIELD

WIELDER > WIELD

WIELDERS > WIELD

WIELDIER > WIELDY

WIELDIEST > WIELDY

WIELDING > WIELD

WIELDLESS *adj* unwieldy

WIELDS > WIELD

WIELDY *adj* easily handled, used, or managed

WIELS > WIEL

WIENER *n* kind of smoked beef or pork sausage, similar to a frankfurter

WIENERS > WIENER

WIENIE *same as* > WIENER

WIENIES > WIENIE

WIFE *n* woman to whom a man is married ▷ *vb* marry

WIFED > WIFE

WIFEDOM *n* state of being a wife

WIFEDOMS > WIFEDOM

WIFEHOOD > WIFE

WIFEHOODS > WIFE

WIFELESS > WIFE

WIFELIER > WIFE

WIFELIEST > WIFE

WIFELIKE > WIFE

WIFELY > WIFE

WIFES > WIFE

WIFEY *n* wife

WIFEYS > WIFEY

WIFIE *n* woman

WIFIES > WIFIE

WIFING > WIFE

WIFTIER > WIFTY

WIFTIEST > WIFTY

WIFTY *adj* scatterbrained

WIG *n* artificial head of hair ▷ *vb* furnish with a wig

WIGAN *n* stiff fabric

WIGANS > WIGAN

WIGEON *n* duck found in marshland

WIGEONS > WIGEON

WIGGA *same as* > WIGGER

WIGGAS > WIGGA

WIGGED > WIG

WIGGER *n* white youth who adopts Black youth culture

WIGGERIES > WIGGERY

WIGGERS > WIGGER

WIGGERY *n* wigs

WIGGIER > WIGGY

WIGGIEST > WIGGY

WIGGING > WIG

WIGGINGS > WIG

WIGGLE *vb* move jerkily from side to side ▷ *n* wiggling movement

WIGGLED > WIGGLE

WIGGLER > WIGGLE

WIGGLERS > WIGGLE

WIGGLES > WIGGLE

WIGGLIER > WIGGLE

WIGGLIEST > WIGGLE

WIGGLING > WIGGLE

WIGGLY > WIGGLE

WIGGY *adj* eccentric

WIGHT *vb* blame ▷ *n* human being ▷ *adj* strong and brave

WIGHTED > WIGHT

WIGHTING > WIGHT

WIGHTLY *adv* swiftly

WIGHTS > WIGHT

WIGLESS > WIG

WIGLET *n* small wig

WIGLETS > WIGLET

WIGLIKE > WIG

WIGMAKER *n* person who makes wigs

WIGMAKERS > WIGMAKER

WIGS > WIG

WIGWAG *vb* move (something) back and forth ▷ *n* system of communication by flag semaphore

WIGWAGGED > WIGWAG

WIGWAGGER > WIGWAG

WIGWAGS > WIGWAG

WIGWAM *n* Native American's tent

WIGWAMS > WIGWAM

WIKI *n* website consisting mainly of user-generated content

WIKIS > WIKI

WIKIUP *same as*
> WICKIUP

WIKIUPS > WIKIUP

WILCO *interj* expression in telecommunications etc, indicating that the message just received will be complied with

WILD *same as* > WIELD

WILDCARD *n* person given entry to competition without qualifying

WILDCARDS > WILDCARD

WILDCAT *n* European wild

animal like a large domestic cat ▷ *adj* risky and financially unsound ▷ *vb* drill for petroleum or natural gas in an area having no known reserves

WILDCATS > WILDCAT

WILDED > WILD

WILDER *vb* lead or be led astray

WILDERED > WILDER

WILDERING > WILDER

WILDERS > WILDER

WILDEST > WILD

WILDFIRE *n* highly flammable material, such as Greek fire, formerly used in warfare

WILDFIRES > WILDFIRE

WILDFOWL *n* wild bird that is hunted for sport or food

WILDFOWLS > WILDFOWL

WILDGRAVE *same as* > WALDGRAVE

WILDING *n* uncultivated plant, esp the crab apple, or a cultivated plant that has become wild

WILDINGS > WILDING

WILDISH > WILD

WILDLAND *n* land which has not been cultivated

WILDLANDS > WILDLAND

WILDLIFE *n* wild animals and plants collectively

WILDLIFES > WILDLIFE

WILDLING *same as* > WILDING

WILDLINGS > WILDLING

WILDLY > WILD

WILDNESS > WILD

WILDS > WILD

WILDWOOD *n* wood or forest growing in a natural uncultivated state

WILDWOODS > WILDWOOD

WILE *n* trickery, cunning, or craftiness ▷ *vb* lure, beguile, or entice

WILED > WILE

WILEFUL *adj* deceitful

WILES > WILE

WILFUL *adj* headstrong or obstinate

WILFULLY > WILFUL

WILGA *n* small drought-resistant tree of Australia

WILGAS > WILGA

WILI *n* spirit

WILIER > WILY

WILIEST > WILY

WILILY > WILY

WILINESS > WILY

WILING > WILE

WILIS > WILI

WILJA > WILTJA

WILJAS > WILTJA

WILL *vb* used as an auxiliary to form the future tense or to indicate intention, ability, or expectation ▷ *n* strong determination

WILLABLE *adj* able to be wished or determined by the will

WILLED *adj* having a will as specified

WILLEMITE *n* secondary mineral consisting of zinc silicate

WILLER > WILL

WILLERS > WILL

WILLEST > WILL

WILLET *n* large American shore bird

WILLETS > WILLET

WILLEY *same as* > WILLY

WILLEYED > WILLEY

WILLEYING > WILLEY

WILLEYS > WILLEY

WILLFUL *same as* > WILFUL

WILLFULLY > WILLFUL

WILLIAM *as in sweet william* flowering plant

WILLIAMS > WILLIAM

WILLIE *n* informal word for a penis

WILLIED > WILLY

WILLIES > WILLY

WILLING *adj* ready or inclined (to do something)

WILLINGER > WILLING

WILLINGLY > WILLING

WILLIWAU *same as* > WILLIWAW

WILLIWAUS > WILLIWAU

WILLIWAW *n* sudden strong gust of cold wind blowing offshore from a mountainous coast

WILLIWAWS > WILLIWAW

WILLOW *n* tree with thin flexible branches ▷ *vb* (of raw textile fibres) to open and clean in a machine having a system of rotating spikes

WILLOWED > WILLOW

WILLOWER *n* willow

WILLOWERS > WILLOWER

WILLOWIER > WILLOWY

WILLOWING > WILLOW

WILLOWISH > WILLOW

WILLOWS > WILLOW

WILLOWY *adj* slender and graceful

WILLPOWER *n* ability to control oneself and one's actions

WILLS > WILL

WILLY *vb* clean in willowing-machine

WILLYARD *adj* timid

WILLYART *same as* > WILLYARD

WILLYING > WILLY

WILLYWAW *same as* > WILLIWAW

WILLYWAWS > WILLYWAW

WILT *vb* (cause to) become limp or lose strength ▷ *n* act of wilting or state of becoming wilted

WILTED > WILT

WILTING > WILT

WILTJA *n* Aboriginal shelter

WILTJAS > WILTJA

WILTS > WILT

WILY *adj* crafty or sly

WIMBLE *n* any of a number of hand tools, such as a brace and bit or a gimlet, used for boring holes ▷ *vb* bore (a hole) with or as if with a wimble

WIMBLED > WIMBLE

WIMBLES > WIMBLE

WIMBLING > WIMBLE

WIMBREL *same as* > WHIMBREL

WIMBRELS > WIMBREL

WIMMIN *n* common intentional literary misspelling spelling of 'women'

WIMP *n* feeble ineffectual person ▷ *vb* as in *wimp out* fail to complete something through fear

WIMPED > WIMP

WIMPIER > WIMP

WIMPIEST > WIMP

WIMPINESS > WIMP

WIMPING > WIMP

WIMPISH > WIMP

WIMPISHLY > WIMP

WIMPLE *n* garment framing the face, worn by medieval women and now by nuns ▷ *vb* ripple or cause to ripple or undulate

WIMPLED > WIMPLE

WIMPLES > WIMPLE

WIMPLING > WIMPLE

WIMPS > WIMP

WIMPY > WIMP

WIN *vb* come first in (a competition, fight, etc) ▷ *n* victory, esp in a game

WINCE *vb* draw back, as if in pain ▷ *n* wincing

WINCED > WINCE

WINCER > WINCE

WINCERS > WINCE

WINCES > WINCE

WINCEY *n* plain- or twill-weave cloth, usually having a cotton or linen warp and a wool filling

WINCEYS > WINCEY

WINCH *n* machine for lifting or hauling using a cable or chain wound round a drum ▷ *vb* lift or haul using a winch

WINCHED > WINCH

WINCHER > WINCH

WINCHERS > WINCH

WINCHES > WINCH

WINCHING > WINCH

WINCHMAN *n* man who operates winch

WINCHMEN > WINCHMAN

WINCING > WINCE

WINCINGS > WINCE

WINCOPIPE *n* type of plant

WIND *n* current of air ▷ *vb* render short of breath

WINDABLE *n* able to be wound

WINDAC *same as* > WINDAS

WINDACS > WINDAC

WINDAGE *n* deflection of a projectile as a result of the effect of the wind

WINDAGES > WINDAGE

WINDAS *n* windlass

WINDASES > WINDAS

WINDBAG *n* person who talks much but uninterestingly

WINDBAGS > WINDBAG

WINDBELL *n* light bell made to be sounded by wind

WINDBELLS > WINDBELL

WINDBILL *n* bill of exchange cosigned by a guarantor

WINDBILLS > WINDBILL

WINDBLAST *n* strong gust of wind

WINDBLOW *n* trees uprooted by wind

WINDBLOWN *adj* blown about by the wind

WINDBLOWS > WINDBLOW

WINDBORNE *adj* (of plant seeds, etc) borne on the wind

WINDBOUND *adj* (of a sailing vessel) prevented from sailing by an unfavourable wind

WINDBREAK *n* fence or line of trees providing shelter from the wind

WINDBURN *n* irritation and redness of the skin caused by prolonged exposure to winds of high velocity

WINDBURNS > WINDBURN

WINDBURNT > WINDBURN

WINDCHILL *n* chilling effect of wind and low temperature

WINDED > WIND

WINDER *n* person or device that winds, as an engine for hoisting the cages in a mine shaft

WINDERS > WINDER

WINDFALL *n* unexpected good luck

WINDFALLS > WINDFALL

WINDFLAW *n* squall

WINDFLAWS > WINDFLAW

WINDGALL *n* soft swelling in the area of the fetlock joint of a horse

WINDGALLS > WINDGALL

WINDGUN *n* air gun

WINDGUNS > WINDGUN

WINDHOVER *dialect name for* > KESTREL

WINDIER > WINDY

WINDIEST > WINDY

WINDIGO *same as* > WENDIGO

WINDIGOS > WINDIGO

WINDILY > WINDY

WINDINESS > WINDY

WINDING > WIND

WINDINGLY > WINDING

WINDINGS > WIND

W

WINDLASS n winch worked by a crank ▷ vb raise or haul (a weight, etc) by means of a windlass

WINDLE vb wind something round continuously

WINDLED >WINDLE

WINDLES >WINDLE

WINDLESS >WIND

WINDLING >WINDLE

WINDLINGS >WINDLE

WINDMILL n machine for grinding or pumping driven by sails turned by the wind ▷ vb move or cause to move like the arms of a windmill

WINDMILLS >WINDMILL

WINDOCK same as >WINNOCK

WINDOCKS >WINDOCK

WINDORE n window

WINDORES >WINDORE

WINDOW n opening in a wall to let in light or air ▷ vb furnish with windows

WINDOWED >WINDOW

WINDOWING >WINDOW

WINDOWS >WINDOW

WINDOWY >WINDOW

WINDPIPE n tube linking the throat and the lungs

WINDPIPES >WINDPIPE

WINDPROOF n wind-resistant

WINDRING adj winding

WINDROW n long low ridge or line of hay or a similar crop, designed to achieve the best conditions for drying or curing ▷ vb put (hay or a similar crop) into windrows

WINDROWED >WINDROW

WINDROWER >WINDROW

WINDROWS >WINDROW

WINDS >WIND

WINDSAIL n sail rigged as an air scoop over a hatch or companionway to catch breezes and divert them below

WINDSAILS >WINDSAIL

WINDSES npl ventilation shafts within mines

WINDSHAKE n crack between the annual rings in wood

WINDSHIP n ship propelled by wind

WINDSHIPS >WINDSHIP

WINDSOCK n cloth cone on a mast at an airfield to indicate wind direction

WINDSOCKS >WINDSOCK

WINDSTORM n storm consisting of violent winds

WINDSURF vb sail standing on a board equipped with a mast, sail, and boom

WINDSURFS >WINDSURF

WINDSWEPT adj exposed to the wind

WINDTHROW n uprooting of trees by wind

WINDTIGHT adj impenetrable by wind

WINDUP n prank or hoax

WINDUPS >WINDUP

WINDWARD n direction from which the wind is blowing ▷ adj of or in the direction from which the wind blows ▷ adv towards the wind

WINDWARDS adv in the direction of the wind

WINDWAY n part of wind instrument

WINDWAYS >WINDWAY

WINDY adj denoting a time or conditions in which there is a strong wind

WINE n alcoholic drink made from fermented grapes ▷ adj of a dark purplish-red colour ▷ vb give wine to

WINEBERRY another name for >MAKO

WINED >WINE

WINEGLASS n glass for wine, usually with a small bowl on a stem with a flared base

WINELESS >WINE

WINEMAKER n maker of wine

WINEPRESS n any equipment used for squeezing the juice from grapes in order to make wine

WINERIES >WINERY

WINERY n place where wine is made

WINES >WINE

WINESAP n variety of apple

WINESAPS >WINESAP

WINESHOP n shop where wine is sold

WINESHOPS >WINESHOP

WINESKIN n skin of a sheep or goat sewn up and used as a holder for wine

WINESKINS >WINESKIN

WINESOP n old word for an alcoholic

WINESOPS >WINESOP

WINEY adj having the taste or qualities of wine

WING n one of the limbs or organs of a bird, insect, or bat that are used for flying ▷ vb fly

WINGBACK n football position

WINGBACKS >WINGBACK

WINGBEAT n complete cycle of moving the wing by a bird in flight

WINGBEATS >WINGBEAT

WINGBOW n distinctive band of colour marking the wing of a bird

WINGBOWS >WINGBOW

WINGCHAIR n chair with forward projections from back

WINGDING n noisy lively party or festivity

WINGDINGS >WINGDING

WINGE same as >WHINGE

WINGED adj furnished with wings

WINGEDLY >WINGED

WINGEING >WINGE

WINGER n player positioned on a wing

WINGERS >WINGER

WINGES >WINGE

WINGIER >WINGY

WINGIEST >WINGY

WINGING >WING

WINGLESS adj having no wings or vestigial wings

WINGLET n small wing

WINGLETS >WINGLET

WINGLIKE >WING

WINGMAN n player in the wing position in Australian Rules

WINGMEN >WINGMAN

WINGOVER n manoeuvre in which the direction of flight of an aircraft is reversed by putting it into a climbing turn until nearly stalled, the nose then being allowed to fall while continuing the turn

WINGOVERS >WINGOVER

WINGS >WING

WINGSPAN n distance between the wing tips of an aircraft, bird, or insect

WINGSPANS >WINGSPAN

WINGSUIT n type of skydiving suit

WINGSUITS >WINGSUIT

WINGTIP n outermost edge of a wing

WINGTIPS >WINGTIP

WINGY adj having wings

WINIER >WINY

WINIEST >WINY

WINING >WINE

WINISH >WINE

WINK vb close and open (an eye) quickly as a signal ▷ n winking

WINKED >WINK

WINKER n person or thing that winks

WINKERS >WINKER

WINKING >WINK

WINKINGLY >WINK

WINKINGS >WINK

WINKLE n shellfish with a spiral shell ▷ vb extract or prise out

WINKLED >WINKLE

WINKLER n one who forces person or thing out

WINKLERS >WINKLER

WINKLES >WINKLE

WINKLING >WINKLE

WINKS >WINK

WINLESS adj not having won anything

WINN n penny

WINNA vb will not

WINNABLE >WIN

WINNARD n heron

WINNARDS >WINNARD

WINNED >WIN

WINNER n person or thing that wins

WINNERS >WINNER

WINNING adj (of a person) charming, attractive, etc

WINNINGLY >WINNING

WINNINGS >WIN

WINNLE same as >WINNLE

WINNLES >WINNLE

WINNOCK n window

WINNOCKS >WINNOCK

WINNOW vb separate (chaff) from (grain) ▷ n device for winnowing

WINNOWED >WINNOW

WINNOWER >WINNOW

WINNOWERS >WINNOW

WINNOWING >WINNOW

WINNOWS >WINNOW

WINNS >WINN

WINO n destitute person who habitually drinks cheap wine

WINOES >WINO

WINOS >WINO

WINS >WIN

WINSEY same as >WINCEY

WINSEYS >WINSEY

WINSOME adj charming or winning

WINSOMELY >WINSOME

WINSOMER >WINSOME

WINSOMEST >WINSOME

WINTER n coldest season ▷ vb spend the winter

WINTERED >WINTER

WINTERER >WINTER

WINTERERS >WINTER

WINTERFED vb past tense of 'winterfeed' (to feed (livestock) in winter when the grazing is not rich enough)

WINTERIER >WINTERY

WINTERING >WINTER

WINTERISE same as >WINTERIZE

WINTERISH >WINTER

WINTERIZE vb prepare (a house, car, etc) to withstand winter conditions

WINTERLY same as >WINTRY

WINTERS >WINTER

WINTERY same as >WINTRY

WINTLE vb reel; stagger

WINTLED >WINTLE

WINTLES >WINTLE

WINTLING >WINTLE

WINTRIER >WINTRY

WINTRIEST >WINTRY

WINTRILY >WINTRY

WINTRY adj of or like winter

WINY same as >WINEY

WINZE n steeply inclined shaft, as for ventilation between levels

WINZES >WINZE

WIPE vb clean or dry by rubbing ▷ n wiping

WIPEABLE *adj* able to be wiped

WIPED > WIPE

WIPEOUT *n* instance of wiping out

WIPEOUTS > WIPEOUT

WIPER *n* any piece of cloth, such as a handkerchief, towel, etc, used for wiping

WIPERS > WIPER

WIPES > WIPE

WIPING > WIPE

WIPINGS > WIPE

WIPPEN *n* part of hammer action in piano

WIPPENS > WIPPEN

WIRABLE *adj* that can be wired

WIRE *n* thin flexible strand of metal ▷ *vb* fasten with wire

WIRED *adj* excited or nervous

WIREDRAW *vb* convert (metal) into wire by drawing through successively smaller dies

WIREDRAWN > WIREDRAW

WIREDRAWS > WIREDRAW

WIREDREW > WIREDRAW

WIREFRAME *n* visual representation of the structure of a web page

WIREGRASS *n* fine variety of grass

WIREHAIR *n* type of terrier

WIREHAIRS > WIREHAIR

WIRELESS *adj* (of a computer network) connected by radio rather than by cables or fibre optics ▷ *n* old-fashioned name for radio ▷ *vb* send by wireless

WIRELIKE > WIRE

WIREMAN *n* person who installs and maintains electric wiring, cables, etc

WIREMEN > WIREMAN

WIREPHOTO *n* facsimile of a photograph transmitted electronically via a telephone system

WIRER *n* person who sets or uses wires to snare rabbits and similar animals

WIRERS > WIRER

WIRES > WIRE

WIRETAP *vb* make a connection to a telegraph or telephone wire in order to obtain information secretly

WIRETAPS > WIRETAP

WIREWAY *n* tube for electric wires

WIREWAYS > WIREWAY

WIREWORK *n* functional or decorative work made of wire

WIREWORKS *n* factory where wire or articles of wire are made

WIREWORM *n* destructive wormlike beetle larva

WIREWORMS > WIREWORM

WIREWOVE *adj* woven out of wire

WIRIER > WIRY

WIRIEST > WIRY

WIRILDA *n* SE Australian acacia tree with edible seeds

WIRILDAS > WIRILDA

WIRILY > WIRY

WIRINESS > WIRY

WIRING *n* system of wires ▷ *adj* used in wiring

WIRINGS > WIRING

WIRRA *interj* exclamation of sorrow or deep concern

WIRRAH *n* Australian saltwater fish with bright blue spots

WIRRAHS > WIRRAH

WIRRICOW *same as* > WORRICOW

WIRRICOWS > WIRRICOW

WIRY *adj* lean and tough

WIS *vb* know or suppose (something)

WISARD *obsolete spelling of* > WIZARD

WISARDS > WISARD

WISDOM *n* good sense and judgment

WISDOMS > WISDOM

WISE *vb* guide ▷ *adj* having wisdom ▷ *n* manner

WISEACRE *n* person who wishes to seem wise

WISEACRES > WISEACRE

WISEASS *n* person who thinks he or she is being witty or clever

WISEASSES > WISEASS

WISECRACK *n* clever, sometimes unkind, remark ▷ *vb* make a wisecrack

WISED > WISE

WISEGUY *n* person who wants to seem clever

WISEGUYS > WISEGUY

WISELIER > WISE

WISELIEST > WISE

WISELING *n* one who claims to be wise

WISELINGS > WISELING

WISELY > WISE

WISENESS > WISE

WISENT *n* European bison

WISENTS > WISENT

WISER > WISE

WISES > WISE

WISEST > WISE

WISEWOMAN *n* witch

WISEWOMEN > WISEWOMAN

WISH *vb* want or desire ▷ *n* expression of a desire

WISHA *interj* expression of surprise

WISHBONE *n* V-shaped bone above the breastbone of a fowl

WISHBONES > WISHBONE

WISHED > WISH

WISHER > WISH

WISHERS > WISH

WISHES > WISH

WISHFUL *adj* too optimistic

WISHFULLY > WISHFUL

WISHING > WISH

WISHINGS > WISH

WISHLESS > WISH

WISHT *variant of* > WHISHT

WISING > WISE

WISKET *n* basket

WISKETS > WISKET

WISP *n* light delicate streak ▷ *vb* move or act like a wisp

WISPED > WISP

WISPIER > WISPY

WISPIEST > WISPY

WISPILY > WISPY

WISPINESS > WISPY

WISPING > WISP

WISPISH > WISP

WISPLIKE > WISP

WISPS > WISP

WISPY *adj* thin, fine, or delicate

WISS *vb* urinate

WISSED > WIS

WISSES > WIS

WISSING > WIS

WIST *vb* know

WISTARIA *same as* > WISTERIA

WISTARIAS > WISTARIA

WISTED > WIST

WISTERIA *n* climbing shrub with blue or purple flowers

WISTERIAS > WISTERIA

WISTFUL *adj* sadly longing

WISTFULLY > WISTFUL

WISTING > WIST

WISTITI *n* marmoset

WISTITIS > WISTITI

WISTLY *adv* intently

WISTS > WIST

WIT *vb* detect ▷ *n* ability to use words or ideas in a clever and amusing way

WITAN *n* assembly of higher ecclesiastics and important laymen, including king's thegns, that met to counsel the king on matters such as judicial problems

WITANS > WITAN

WITBLITS *n* illegally distilled strong alcoholic drink

WITCH *n* person, usu female, who practises (black) magic ▷ *vb* cause or change by or as if by witchcraft

WITCHED > WITCH

WITCHEN *n* rowan tree

WITCHENS > WITCHEN

WITCHERY *n* practice of witchcraft

WITCHES > WITCH

WITCHETTY *n* edible larva of certain Australian moths and beetles

WITCHHOOD > WITCH

WITCHIER > WITCHY

WITCHIEST > WITCHY

WITCHING *adj* relating to or appropriate for witchcraft ▷ *n* witchcraft

WITCHINGS > WITCHING

WITCHKNOT *n* knot in hair

WITCHLIKE > WITCH

WITCHWEED *n* type of plant that is a serious pest of grain crops in parts of Africa and Asia

WITCHY *adj* like a witch

WITE *vb* blame

WITED > WITE

WITELESS *adj* witless

WITES > WITE

WITGAT *n* type of S African tree

WITGATS > WITGAT

WITH *prep* indicating presence alongside, possession, means of performance, characteristic manner, etc ▷ *n* division between flues in chimney

WITHAL *adv* as well

WITHDRAW *vb* take or move out or away

WITHDRAWN *adj* unsociable

WITHDRAWS > WITHDRAW

WITHDREW *past tense of* > WITHDRAW

WITHE *n* strong flexible twig, esp of willow, suitable for binding things together ▷ *vb* bind with withes

WITHED > WITHE

WITHER *vb* wilt or dry up

WITHERED > WITHER

WITHERER > WITHER

WITHERERS > WITHER

WITHERING > WITHER

WITHERITE *n* white, grey, or yellowish mineral

WITHEROD *n* American shrub

WITHERODS > WITHEROD

WITHERS *npl* ridge between a horse's shoulder blades

WITHES > WITHE

WITHHAULT > WITHHOLD

WITHHELD > WITHHOLD

WITHHOLD *vb* refrain from giving

WITHHOLDS > WITHHOLD

WITHIER > WITHY

WITHIES > WITHY

WITHIEST > WITHY

WITHIN *adv* in or inside ▷ *prep* in or inside ▷ *n* something that is within

WITHING > WITHE

WITHINS > WITHIN

WITHOUT *prep* not accompanied by, using, or having ▷ *adv* outside ▷ *n* person who is without

WITHOUTEN *obsolete form of* > WITHOUT

WITHOUTS > WITHOUT

WITHS > WITH

WITHSTAND *vb* oppose or resist successfully

WITHSTOOD
>WITHSTAND
WITHWIND n bindweed
WITHWINDS
>WITHWIND
WITHY n willow tree, esp an osier ▷ adj (of people) tough and agile
WITHYWIND same as
>WITHWIND
WITING >WITE
WITLESS adj foolish
WITLESSLY >WITLESS
WITLING n person who thinks himself witty
WITLINGS >WITLING
WITLOOF n chicory
WITLOOFS >WITLOOF
WITNESS n person who has seen something happen ▷ vb see at first hand
WITNESSED >WITNESS
WITNESSER >WITNESS
WITNESSES >WITNESS
WITNEY n type of blanket; heavy cloth
WITNEYS >WITNEY
WITS >WIT
WITTED adj having wit
WITTER vb chatter pointlessly or at unnecessary length ▷ n pointless chat
WITTERED >WITTER
WITTERING >WITTER
WITTERS >WITTER
WITTICISM n witty remark
WITTIER >WITTY
WITTIEST >WITTY
WITTILY >WITTY
WITTINESS >WITTY
WITTING adj deliberate
WITTINGLY >WITTING
WITTINGS >WIT
WITTOL n man who tolerates his wife's unfaithfulness
WITTOLLY >WITTOL
WITTOLS >WITTOL
WITTY adj clever and amusing
WITWALL n golden oriole
WITWALLS >WITWALL
WITWANTON vb be disrespectfully witty
WIVE vb marry (a woman)
WIVED >WIVE
WIVEHOOD obsolete variant of >WIFEHOOD
WIVEHOODS >WIVEHOOD
WIVER another word for >WIVERN
WIVERN same as >WYVERN
WIVERNS >WIVERN
WIVERS >WIVER
WIVES >WIFE
WIVING >WIVE
WIZ shortened form of >WIZARD
WIZARD n magician ▷ adj superb
WIZARDLY >WIZARD

WIZARDRY n magic or sorcery
WIZARDS >WIZARD
WIZEN vb make or become shrivelled ▷ n archaic word for 'weasand' (the gullet)
WIZENED adj shrivelled or wrinkled
WIZENING >WIZEN
WIZENS >WIZEN
WIZES >WIZ
WIZIER same as >VIZIER
WIZIERS >WIZIER
WIZZEN same as >WIZEN
WIZZENS >WIZEN
WIZZES >WIZ
WO archaic spelling of >WOE
WOAD n blue dye obtained from a plant, used by the ancient Britons as a body dye
WOADED adj coloured blue with woad
WOADS >WOAD
WOADWAX n small Eurasian leguminous shrub
WOADWAXEN n small leguminous shrub with yellow flowers producing a yellow dye
WOADWAXES >WOADWAX
WOALD same as >WELD
WOALDS >WOALD
WOBBEGONG n Australian shark with brown-and-white skin
WOBBLE vb move unsteadily ▷ n wobbling movement or sound
WOBBLED >WOBBLE
WOBBLER >WOBBLE
WOBBLERS >WOBBLE
WOBBLES >WOBBLE
WOBBLIER >WOBBLY
WOBBLIES >WOBBLY
WOBBLIEST >WOBBLY
WOBBLING >WOBBLE
WOBBLINGS >WOBBLE
WOBBLY adj unsteady ▷ n temper tantrum
WOBEGONE same as >WOEBEGONE
WOCK same as >WOK
WOCKS >WOCK
WODGE n thick lump or chunk
WODGES >WODGE
WOE n grief
WOEBEGONE adj looking miserable
WOEFUL adj extremely sad
WOEFULLER >WOEFUL
WOEFULLY >WOEFUL
WOENESS >WOE
WOENESSES >WOE
WOES >WOE
WOESOME adj woeful
WOF n fool
WOFS >WOF
WOFUL same as >WOEFUL
WOFULLER >WOFUL
WOFULLEST >WOFUL
WOFULLY >WOFUL
WOFULNESS >WOFUL

WOG n derogatory word for a foreigner, esp one who is not White
WOGGISH >WOG
WOGGLE n ring of leather through which a Scout neckerchief is threaded
WOGGLES >WOGGLE
WOGS >WOG
WOIWODE same as >VOIVODE
WOIWODES >WOIWODE
WOK n bowl-shaped Chinese cooking pan, used for stir-frying
WOKE >WAKE
WOKEN >WAKE
WOKKA as in wokka board wobble board: a piece of fibreboard used as a musical instrument
WOKS >WOK
WOLD same as >WELD
WOLDS >WOLD
WOLF n wild predatory canine mammal ▷ vb eat ravenously
WOLFBERRY n type of shrub
WOLFED >WOLF
WOLFER same as >WOLVER
WOLFERS >WOLFER
WOLFFISH n type of large northern deep-sea fish with large sharp teeth
WOLFHOUND n very large breed of dog
WOLFING >WOLF
WOLFINGS >WOLF
WOLFISH >WOLF
WOLFISHLY >WOLF
WOLFKIN n young wolf
WOLFKINS >WOLFKIN
WOLFLIKE >WOLF
WOLFLING n young wolf
WOLFLINGS >WOLFLING
WOLFRAM another name for >TUNGSTEN
WOLFRAMS >WOLFRAM
WOLFS >WOLF
WOLFSBANE n type of poisonous N temperate plant with yellow hoodlike flowers
WOLFSKIN n skin of wolf used for clothing, etc
WOLFSKINS >WOLFSKIN
WOLLIES >WOLLY
WOLLY n pickled cucumber or olive
WOLVE vb hunt for wolves
WOLVED >WOLVE
WOLVER n person who hunts wolves
WOLVERENE same as >WOLVERINE
WOLVERINE n carnivorous mammal of Arctic regions
WOLVERS >WOLVER
WOLVES >WOLF
WOLVING >WOLVE
WOLVINGS >WOLVE
WOLVISH same as >WOLFISH

WOLVISHLY >WOLVISH
WOMAN n adult human female ▷ adj female ▷ vb provide with a woman or women
WOMANED >WOMAN
WOMANHOOD n state of being a woman
WOMANING >WOMAN
WOMANISE same as >WOMANIZE
WOMANISED >WOMANISE
WOMANISER >WOMANISE
WOMANISES >WOMANISE
WOMANISH adj effeminate
WOMANISM n feminism among black women
WOMANISMS >WOMANISM
WOMANIST >WOMANISM
WOMANISTS >WOMANISM
WOMANIZE vb (of a man) to indulge in many casual affairs with women
WOMANIZED >WOMANIZE
WOMANIZER >WOMANIZE
WOMANIZES >WOMANIZE
WOMANKIND n all women considered as a group
WOMANLESS >WOMAN
WOMANLIER >WOMANLY
WOMANLIKE adj like a woman
WOMANLY adj having qualities traditionally associated with a woman
WOMANNESS >WOMAN
WOMANS >WOMAN
WOMB vb enclose ▷ n hollow organ in female mammals where babies are conceived and develop
WOMBAT n small heavily-built burrowing Australian marsupial
WOMBATS >WOMBAT
WOMBED >WOMB
WOMBIER >WOMBY
WOMBIEST >WOMBY
WOMBING >WOMB
WOMBLIKE >WOMB
WOMBS >WOMB
WOMBY adj hollow; spacious
WOMEN >WOMAN
WOMENFOLK npl women collectively
WOMENKIND same as >WOMANKIND
WOMERA same as >WOOMERA
WOMERAS >WOMERA
WOMMERA same as >WOOMERA
WOMMERAS >WOMMERA
WOMMIT n foolish person
WOMMITS >WOMMIT
WOMYN same as >WOMAN
WON n standard monetary unit of North Korea, divided into 100 chon ▷ vb live or dwell
WONDER vb be curious about ▷ n wonderful thing ▷ adj spectacularly successful

W

WONDERED > WONDER
WONDERER > WONDER
WONDERERS > WONDER
WONDERFUL *adj* very fine
WONDERING > WONDER
WONDERKID *n* informal word for an exceptionally successful young person
WONDEROUS *obsolete variant of >* WONDROUS
WONDERS > WONDER
WONDRED *adj* splendid
WONDROUS *adj* wonderful ▷ *adv* (intensifier)
WONGA *n* money
WONGAS > WONGA
WONGI *vb* talk informally
WONGIED > WONGI
WONGIING > WONGI
WONGIS > WONGI
WONING > WON
WONINGS > WON
WONK *n* person who is obsessively interested in a specified subject
WONKIER > WONKY
WONKIEST > WONKY
WONKS > WONK
WONKY *adj* shaky or unsteady
WONNED > WON
WONNER > WON
WONNERS > WON
WONNING > WON
WONNINGS > WON
WONS > WON
WONT *adj* accustomed ▷ *n* custom ▷ *vb* become or cause to become accustomed
WONTED *adj* accustomed or habituated (to doing something)
WONTEDLY > WONTED
WONTING > WONT
WONTLESS > WONT
WONTON *n* dumpling filled with spiced minced pork
WONTONS > WONTON
WONTS > WONT
WOO *vb* seek the love or affection of (a woman)
WOOBUT *same as >* WOUBIT
WOOBUTS > WOOBUT
WOOD *n* substance trees are made of, used in carpentry and as fuel ▷ *adj* made of or using wood ▷ *vb* (of land) plant with trees
WOODBIN *n* box for firewood
WOODBIND *same as >* WOODBINE
WOODBINDS > WOODBIND
WOODBINE *n* honeysuckle
WOODBINES > WOODBINE
WOODBINS > WOODBIN
WOODBLOCK *n* hollow block of wood used as a percussion instrument
WOODBORER *n* type of beetle whose larvae bore into and damage wood

WOODBOX *n* box for firewood
WOODBOXES > WOODBOX
WOODCHAT *n* European and N African songbird with a black-and-white plumage, a reddish-brown crown and a hooked bill
WOODCHATS > WOODCHAT
WOODCHIP *n* textured wallpaper
WOODCHIPS > WOODCHIP
WOODCHOP *n* wood-chopping competition, esp at a show
WOODCHOPS > WOODCHOP
WOODCHUCK *n* N American marmot with coarse reddish-brown fur
WOODCOCK *n* game bird
WOODCOCKS > WOODCOCK
WOODCRAFT *n* ability and experience in matters concerned with living in a wood or forest
WOODCUT *n* (print made from) an engraved block of wood
WOODCUTS > WOODCUT
WOODED *adj* covered with trees
WOODEN *adj* made of wood ▷ *vb* fell or kill (a person or animal)
WOODENED > WOODEN
WOODENER > WOODEN
WOODENEST > WOODEN
WOODENING > WOODEN
WOODENLY > WOODEN
WOODENS > WOODEN
WOODENTOP *n* dull, foolish, or unintelligent person
WOODFREE *adj* (of high-quality paper) made from pulp that has been treated chemically, removing impurities
WOODGRAIN *n* grain in wood
WOODHEN *another name for >* WEKA
WOODHENS > WOODHEN
WOODHOLE *n* store area for wood
WOODHOLES > WOODHOLE
WOODHORSE *n* frame for holding wood being sawn
WOODHOUSE *n* shed for firewood
WOODIE *n* gallows rope
WOODIER > WOODY
WOODIES > WOODIE
WOODIEST > WOODY
WOODINESS > WOODY
WOODING > WOOD
WOODLAND *n* forest ▷ *adj* living in woods
WOODLANDS > WOODLAND
WOODLARK *n* type of Old World lark
WOODLARKS > WOODLARK
WOODLESS > WOOD
WOODLICE > WOODLOUSE
WOODLORE *n* woodcraft skills

WOODLORES > WOODLORE
WOODLOT *n* area restricted to the growing of trees
WOODLOTS > WOODLOT
WOODLOUSE *n* small insect-like creature with many legs
WOODMAN *same as >* WOODSMAN
WOODMEAL *n* sawdust powder
WOODMEALS > WOODMEAL
WOODMEN > WOODMAN
WOODMICE > WOODMOUSE
WOODMOUSE *n* field mouse
WOODNESS > WOOD
WOODNOTE *n* natural musical note or song, like that of a wild bird
WOODNOTES > WOODNOTE
WOODPILE *n* heap of firewood
WOODPILES > WOODPILE
WOODPRINT *another name for >* WOODCUT
WOODRAT *n* pack-rat
WOODRATS > WOODRAT
WOODREEVE *n* steward responsible for wood
WOODROOF *same as >* WOODRUFF
WOODROOFS > WOODROOF
WOODRUFF *n* plant with small sweet-smelling white flowers and sweet-smelling leaves
WOODRUFFS > WOODRUFF
WOODRUSH *n* type of plant, chiefly of the N hemisphere, with grasslike leaves and small brown flowers
WOODS *npl* closely packed trees forming a forest or wood
WOODSCREW *n* metal screw that tapers to a point so that it can be driven into wood by a screwdriver
WOODSHED *n* small outbuilding where firewood, garden tools, etc, are stored
WOODSHEDS > WOODSHED
WOODSHOCK *n* type of bird
WOODSIA *n* type of small fern with tufted rhizomes and wiry fronds
WOODSIAS > WOODSIA
WOODSIER > WOODSY
WOODSIEST > WOODSY
WOODSKIN *n* canoe made of bark
WOODSKINS > WOODSKIN
WOODSMAN *n* person who lives in a wood or who is skilled at woodwork or carving
WOODSMEN > WOODSMAN
WOODSPITE *n* green woodpecker
WOODSTONE *n* type of stone resembling wood
WOODSTOVE *n* wood-burning stove
WOODSY *adj* of, reminiscent

of, or connected with woods
WOODTONE *n* colour matching that of wood
WOODTONES > WOODTONE
WOODWALE *n* green woodpecker
WOODWALES > WOODWALE
WOODWARD *n* person in charge of a forest or wood
WOODWARDS > WOODWARD
WOODWAX *same as >* WOODWAXEN
WOODWAXEN *same as >* WOADWAXEN
WOODWAXES > WOODWAX
WOODWIND *n* (of) a type of wind instrument made of wood ▷ *adj* of or denoting a type of wind instrument, such as the oboe
WOODWINDS > WOODWIND
WOODWORK *n* parts of a room or building made of wood
WOODWORKS > WOODWORK
WOODWORM *n* insect larva that bores into wood
WOODWORMS > WOODWORM
WOODWOSE *n* hairy wildman of the woods
WOODWOSES > WOODWOSE
WOODY *adj* (of a plant) having a very hard stem
WOODYARD *n* place where timber is cut and stored
WOODYARDS > WOODYARD
WOOED > WOO
WOOER > WOO
WOOERS > WOO
WOOF *vb* (of dogs) bark or growl
WOOFED > WOOF
WOOFER *n* loudspeaker reproducing low-frequency sounds
WOOFERS > WOOFER
WOOFIER > WOOFY
WOOFIEST > WOOFY
WOOFING > WOOF
WOOFS > WOOF
WOOFTER *n* derogatory term for a male homosexual
WOOFTERS > WOOFTER
WOOFY *adj* with close, dense texture
WOOHOO *interj* expression of joy, approval, etc
WOOING > WOO
WOOINGLY > WOO
WOOINGS > WOO
WOOL *n* soft hair of sheep, goats, etc
WOOLD *vb* wind (rope)
WOOLDED > WOOLD
WOOLDER *n* stick for winding rope
WOOLDERS > WOOLDER
WOOLDING > WOOLD
WOOLDINGS > WOOLD
WOOLDS > WOOLD
WOOLED *same as >* WOOLLED

WOOLEN same as
>WOOLLEN
WOOLENS >WOOLEN
WOOLER same as
>WOOLDER
WOOLERS >WOOLER
WOOLFAT same as
>LANOLIN
WOOLFATS >WOOLFAT
WOOLFELL n skin of a
sheep or similar animal
with the fleece still
attached
WOOLFELLS >WOOLFELL
WOOLHAT n poor white
person in S States
WOOLHATS >WOOLHAT
WOOLIE n wool garment
WOOLIER >WOOLY
WOOLIES >WOOLY
WOOLIEST >WOOLY
WOOLINESS >WOOLY
WOOLLED adj (of animals)
having wool
WOOLLEN adj relating to or
consisting partly or wholly
of wool ▷ n garment or
piece of cloth made wholly
or partly of wool, esp a
knitted one
WOOLLENS >WOOLLEN
WOOLLIER >WOOLLY
WOOLLIES >WOOLLY
WOOLLIEST >WOOLLY
WOOLLIKE >WOOL
WOOLLILY >WOOLLY
WOOLLY adj of or like wool
▷ n knitted woollen
garment
WOOLMAN n wool trader
WOOLMEN >WOOLMAN
WOOLPACK n cloth or
canvas wrapping used to
pack a bale of wool
WOOLPACKS >WOOLPACK
WOOLS >WOOL
WOOLSACK n sack
containing or intended to
contain wool
WOOLSACKS >WOOLSACK
WOOLSEY n cotton and
wool blend
WOOLSEYS >WOOLSEY
WOOLSHED n large building
in which sheep shearing
takes place
WOOLSHEDS >WOOLSHED
WOOLSKIN n sheepskin
with wool still on
WOOLSKINS >WOOLSKIN
WOOLWARD adv with
woollen side touching the
skin
WOOLWORK n embroidery
with wool
WOOLWORKS >WOOLWORK
WOOLY same as >WOOLLY
WOOMERA n notched stick
used by Australian
Aborigines to aid the
propulsion of a spear
WOOMERANG same as
>WOOMERA
WOOMERAS >WOOMERA
WOON same as >WON

WOONED >WOON
WOONING >WOON
WOONS >WOON
WOOPIE n well-off older
person
WOOPIES >WOOPIE
WOOPS vb (esp of small
child) vomit
WOOPSED >WOOPS
WOOPSES >WOOPS
WOOPSING >WOOPS
WOORALI less common name
for >CURARE
WOORALIS >WOORALI
WOORARA same as
>WOURALI
WOORARAS >WOORARA
WOORARI same as
>WOURALI
WOORARIS >WOORARI
WOOS >WOO
WOOSE same as >WUSS
WOOSEL same as >OUZEL
WOOSELL same as >OUZEL
WOOSELLS >WOOSELL
WOOSELS >WOOSEL
WOOSES >WOOSE
WOOSH same as >WHOOSH
WOOSHED >WOOSH
WOOSHES >WOOSH
WOOSHING >WOOSH
WOOT vb wilt thou?
WOOTZ n Middle-Eastern
steel
WOOTZES >WOOTZ
WOOZIER >WOOZY
WOOZIEST >WOOZY
WOOZILY >WOOZY
WOOZINESS >WOOZY
WOOZY adj weak, dizzy, and
confused
WOP same as >WHOP
WOPPED >WOP
WOPPING >WOP
WOPS >WOP
WORCESTER n type of
woollen fabric
WORD n smallest single
meaningful unit of speech
or writing ▷ vb express in
words
WORDAGE n words
considered collectively, esp
a quantity of words
WORDAGES >WORDAGE
WORDBOOK n book
containing words, usually
with their meanings
WORDBOOKS >WORDBOOK
WORDBOUND adj unable to
find words to express sth
WORDBREAK n point at
which a word is divided
when it runs over from one
line of print to the next
WORDED >WORD
WORDGAME n any game
involving the formation,
discovery, or alteration of a
word or words
WORDGAMES >WORDGAME
WORDIER >WORDY
WORDIEST >WORDY
WORDILY >WORDY

WORDINESS >WORDY
WORDING n choice and
arrangement of words
WORDINGS >WORDING
WORDISH adj talkative
WORDLESS adj inarticulate
or silent
WORDLORE n knowledge
about words
WORDLORES >WORDLORE
WORDPLAY n verbal wit
based on the meanings and
ambiguities of words
WORDPLAYS >WORDPLAY
WORDS >WORD
WORDSMITH n person
skilled in using words
WORDY adj using too many
words
WORE >WEAR
WORK n physical or mental
effort directed to making or
doing something ▷ adj of
or for work ▷ vb (cause to)
do work
WORKABLE adj able to
operate efficiently
WORKABLY >WORKABLE
WORKADAY n working day
▷ adj ordinary
WORKADAYS
>WORKADAY
WORKBAG n container for
implements, tools, or
materials, esp sewing
equipment
WORKBAGS >WORKBAG
WORKBENCH n heavy table
at which a craftsman or
mechanic works
WORKBOAT n boat used for
tasks
WORKBOATS >WORKBOAT
WORKBOOK n exercise book
or textbook used for study,
esp a textbook with spaces
for answers
WORKBOOKS >WORKBOOK
WORKBOX same as
>WORKBAG
WORKBOXES >WORKBOX
WORKDAY another word for
>WORKADAY
WORKDAYS >WORKDAY
WORKED adj made or
decorated with evidence of
workmanship
WORKER n person who
works in a specified way
WORKERIST n supporter
of working-class politics
WORKERS >WORKER
WORKFARE n scheme
under which the
government of a country
requires unemployed
people to do community
work or undergo job
training in return for
social-security payments
WORKFARES >WORKFARE
WORKFLOW n rate of
progress of work
WORKFLOWS >WORKFLOW
WORKFOLK npl working

people, esp labourers on a
farm
WORKFOLKS same as
>WORKFOLK
WORKFORCE n total
number of workers
WORKFUL adj hardworking
WORKGIRL n young female
manual worker
WORKGIRLS >WORKGIRL
WORKGROUP n collection of
networked computers
WORKHORSE n person or
thing that does a lot of dull
or routine work
WORKHOUR n time set aside
for work
WORKHOURS >WORKHOUR
WORKHOUSE n (in England,
formerly) institution where
the poor were given food
and lodgings in return for
work
WORKING n operation or
mode of operation of
something ▷ adj relating to
or concerned with a person
or thing that works
WORKINGS >WORKING
WORKLESS >WORK
WORKLOAD n amount of
work to be done, esp in a
specified period
WORKLOADS >WORKLOAD
WORKMAN n manual worker
WORKMANLY adj
appropriate to or befitting
a good workman
WORKMATE n person who
works with another person
WORKMATES >WORKMATE
WORKMEN >WORKMAN
WORKOUT n session of
physical exercise for
training or fitness
WORKOUTS >WORKOUT
WORKPIECE n piece of
metal or other material
that is in the process of
being worked on or made
or has actually been cut or
shaped by a hand tool or
machine
WORKPLACE n place, such
as a factory or office, where
people work
WORKPRINT n unfinished
print of cinema film
WORKROOM n room in
which work, usually
manual labour, is done
WORKROOMS >WORKROOM
WORKS >WORK
WORKSAFE adj (of an
internet link) suitable for
viewing in the workplace
WORKSHEET n sheet of
paper containing exercises
to be completed by a
student
WORKSHOP n room or
building for a
manufacturing process
▷ vb perform (a play) with
no costumes, set, or

musical accompaniment

WORKSHOPS > WORKSHOP

WORKSHY adj not inclined to work

WORKSOME adj hardworking

WORKSPACE n area set aside for work

WORKTABLE n table at which writing, sewing, or other work may be done

WORKTOP n surface in a kitchen, used for food preparation

WORKTOPS > WORKTOP

WORKUP n medical examination

WORKUPS > WORKUP

WORKWEAR n clothes, such as overalls, as worn for work in a factory, shop, etc

WORKWEARS > WORKWEAR

WORKWEEK n number of hours or days in a week actually or officially allocated to work

WORKWEEKS > WORKWEEK

WORKWOMAN n female manual worker

WORKWOMEN > WORKWOMAN

WORLD n planet earth ▷ adj of the whole world

WORLDBEAT n popular music from outside western mainstream

WORLDED adj incorporating worlds

WORLDLIER > WORLDLY

WORLDLING n person who is primarily concerned with worldly matters or material things

WORLDLY adj not spiritual ▷ adv in a worldly manner

WORLDS > WORLD

WORLDVIEW n comprehensive view of human life and the universe

WORLDWIDE adj applying or extending throughout the world

WORM n small limbless invertebrate animal ▷ vb rid of worms

WORMCAST n coil of earth excreted by a burrowing worm

WORMCASTS > WORMCAST

WORMED > WORM

WORMER > WORM

WORMERIES > WORMERY

WORMERS > WORM

WORMERY n piece of apparatus, having a glass side or sides, in which worms are kept for study

WORMFLIES > WORMFLY

WORMFLY n type of lure dressed on a double hook, the barbs of which sit one above the other and back-to-back

WORMGEAR n gear with screw thread

WORMGEARS > WORMGEAR

WORMHOLE n hole made by a worm in timber, plants, or fruit

WORMHOLED > WORMHOLE

WORMHOLES > WORMHOLE

WORMIER > WORMY

WORMIEST > WORMY

WORMIL n burrowing larva of type of fly

WORMILS > WORMIL

WORMINESS > WORMY

WORMING > WORM

WORMISH > WORM

WORMLIKE > WORM

WORMROOT n plant used to cure worms

WORMROOTS > WORMROOT

WORMS n disease caused by parasitic worms living in the intestines

WORMSEED n any of various plants having seeds or other parts used in medicine to treat worm infestation

WORMSEEDS > WORMSEED

WORMWOOD n bitter plant

WORMWOODS > WORMWOOD

WORMY adj infested with or eaten by worms

WORN > WEAR

WORNNESS n quality or condition of being worn

WORRAL n type of lizard

WORRALS > WORRAL

WORREL same as > WORRAL

WORRELS > WORREL

WORRICOW n frightening creature

WORRICOWS > WORRICOW

WORRIED > WORRY

WORRIEDLY > WORRY

WORRIER > WORRY

WORRIERS > WORRY

WORRIES > WORRY

WORRIMENT n anxiety or the trouble that causes it

WORRISOME adj causing worry

WORRIT vb tease or worry

WORRITED > WORRIT

WORRITING > WORRIT

WORRITS > WORRIT

WORRY vb (cause to) be anxious or uneasy ▷ n (cause of) anxiety or concern

WORRYCOW same as > WORRICOW

WORRYCOWS > WORRYCOW

WORRYGUTS n person who tends to worry, esp about insignificant matters

WORRYING > WORRY

WORRYINGS > WORRY

WORRYWART same as > WORRYGUTS

WORSE vb defeat

WORSED > WORSE

WORSEN vb make or grow worse

WORSENED > WORSEN

WORSENESS n state or condition of being worse

WORSENING > WORSEN

WORSENS > WORSEN

WORSER archaic or nonstandard word for > WORSE

WORSES > WORSE

WORSET n worsted fabric

WORSETS > WORSET

WORSHIP vb show religious devotion to ▷ n act or instance of worshipping

WORSHIPED > WORSHIP

WORSHIPER n worshipper

WORSHIPS > WORSHIP

WORSING > WORSE

WORST n worst thing ▷ vb defeat

WORSTED n type of woollen yarn or fabric

WORSTEDS > WORSTED

WORSTING > WORST

WORSTS > WORST

WORT n any of various unrelated plants, esp ones formerly used to cure diseases

WORTHED > WORTH

WORTHFUL adj worthy

WORTHIED > WORTHY

WORTHIER > WORTHY

WORTHIES > WORTHY

WORTHIEST > WORTHY

WORTHILY > WORTHY

WORTHING > WORTH

WORTHLESS adj without value or usefulness

WORTHS > WORTH

WORTHY adj deserving admiration or respect ▷ n notable person ▷ vb make worthy

WORTHYING > WORTHY

WORTLE n plate with holes for drawing wire through

WORTLES > WORTLE

WORTS > WORT

WOS > WO

WOSBIRD n illegitimate child

WOSBIRDS > WOSBIRD

WOST wit, to know

WOT wit, to know

WOTCHA same as > WOTCHER

WOTCHER sentence substitute slang term of greeting

WOTS > WOT

WOTTED > WOT

WOTTEST > WOT

WOTTETH > WOT

WOTTING > WOT

WOUBIT n type of caterpillar

WOUBITS > WOUBIT

WOULD > WILL

WOULDEST same as > WOULDST

WOULDS same as > WOULDST

WOULDST singular form of the past tense of > WILL

WOUND vb injure ▷ n injury

WOUNDABLE > WOUND

WOUNDED adj suffering from wounds

WOUNDEDLY > WOUNDED

WOUNDER > WOUND

WOUNDERS > WOUND

WOUNDILY > WOUNDY

WOUNDING > WOUND

WOUNDINGS > WOUND

WOUNDLESS > WOUND

WOUNDS > WOUND

WOUNDWORT n type of plant formerly used for dressing wounds

WOUNDY adj extreme

WOURALI n plant from which curare is obtained

WOURALIS > WOURALI

WOVE > WEAVE

WOVEN n article made from woven cloth

WOVENS > WOVEN

WOW interj exclamation of astonishment ▷ n astonishing person or thing ▷ vb be a great success with

WOWED > WOW

WOWEE stronger form of > WOW

WOWF adj mad

WOWFER > WOWF

WOWFEST > WOWF

WOWING > WOW

WOWS > WOW

WOWSER n puritanical person

WOWSERS > WOWSER

WOX > WAX

WOXEN > WAX

WRACK n seaweed ▷ vb strain or shake (something) violently

WRACKED > WRACK

WRACKFUL n ruinous

WRACKING > WRACK

WRACKS > WRACK

WRAITH n ghost

WRAITHS > WRAITH

WRANG Scot word for > WRONG

WRANGED > WRANG

WRANGING > WRANG

WRANGLE vb argue noisily ▷ n noisy argument

WRANGLED > WRANGLE

WRANGLER n one who wrangles

WRANGLERS > WRANGLER

WRANGLES > WRANGLE

WRANGLING > WRANGLE

WRANGS > WRANG

WRAP vb fold (something) round (a person or thing) so as to cover ▷ n garment wrapped round the shoulders

WRAPOVER adj (of a garment, esp a skirt) not sewn at one side, but worn wrapped round the body and fastened so that

W

the open edges overlap ▷ n such a garment

WRAPOVERS > WRAPOVER

WRAPPAGE n material for wrapping

WRAPPAGES > WRAPPAGE

WRAPPED > WRAP

WRAPPER vb cover with wrapping ▷ n cover for a product

WRAPPERED > WRAPPER

WRAPPERS > WRAPPER

WRAPPING > WRAP

WRAPPINGS > WRAP

WRAPROUND same as > WRAPOVER

WRAPS > WRAP

WRAPT same as > RAPT

WRASSE n colourful sea fish

WRASSES > WRASSE

WRASSLE same as > WRESTLE

WRASSLED > WRASSLE

WRASSLES > WRASSLE

WRASSLING > WRASSLE

WRAST same as > WREST

WRASTED > WRAST

WRASTING > WRAST

WRASTLE same as > WRESTLE

WRASTLED > WRASTLE

WRASTLES > WRASTLE

WRASTLING > WRASTLE

WRASTS > WRAST

WRATE > WRITE

WRATH n intense anger ▷ adj incensed ▷ vb make angry

WRATHED > WRATH

WRATHFUL adj full of wrath

WRATHIER > WRATHY

WRATHIEST > WRATHY

WRATHILY > WRATHY

WRATHING > WRATH

WRATHLESS > WRATH

WRATHS > WRATH

WRATHY same as > WRATHFUL

WRAWL vb howl

WRAWLED > WRAWL

WRAWLING > WRAWL

WRAWLS > WRAWL

WRAXLE vb wrestle

WRAXLED > WRAXLE

WRAXLES > WRAXLE

WRAXLING > WRAXLE

WRAXLINGS > WRAXLE

WREAK vb inflict (vengeance, etc) or to cause (chaos, etc)

WREAKED > WREAK

WREAKER > WREAK

WREAKERS > WREAK

WREAKFUL adj seeking revenge

WREAKING > WREAK

WREAKLESS adj unrevengeful

WREAKS > WREAK

WREATH n twisted ring or band of flowers or leaves used as a memorial or tribute

WREATHE vb form into or take the form of a wreath by intertwining or twisting together

WREATHED > WREATHE

WREATHEN adj twisted into wreath

WREATHER > WREATHE

WREATHERS > WREATHE

WREATHES > WREATHE

WREATHIER > WREATHY

WREATHING > WREATHE

WREATHS > WREATH

WREATHY adj twisted into wreath

WRECK vb destroy ▷ n remains of something that has been destroyed or badly damaged, esp a ship

WRECKAGE n wrecked remains

WRECKAGES > WRECKAGE

WRECKED adj in a state of intoxication, stupor, or euphoria, induced by drugs or alcohol

WRECKER n formerly, person who lured ships onto the rocks in order to plunder them

WRECKERS > WRECKER

WRECKFISH n large sea perch

WRECKFUL adj causing wreckage

WRECKING > WRECK

WRECKINGS > WRECK

WRECKS > WRECK

WREN n small brown songbird

WRENCH vb twist or pull violently ▷ n violent twist or pull

WRENCHED > WRENCH

WRENCHER > WRENCH

WRENCHERS > WRENCH

WRENCHES > WRENCH

WRENCHING > WRENCH

WRENS > WREN

WREST vb twist violently ▷ n act or an instance of wresting

WRESTED > WREST

WRESTER > WREST

WRESTERS > WREST

WRESTING > WREST

WRESTLE vb fight, esp as a sport, by grappling with and trying to throw down an opponent ▷ n act of wrestling

WRESTLED > WRESTLE

WRESTLER > WRESTLE

WRESTLERS > WRESTLE

WRESTLES > WRESTLE

WRESTLING n sport in which each contestant tries to overcome the other either by throwing or pinning him or her to the ground or by forcing a submission

WRESTS > WREST

WRETCH n despicable person

WRETCHED adj miserable or unhappy

WRETCHES > WRETCH

WRETHE same as > WREATHE

WRETHED > WRETHE

WRETHES > WRETHE

WRETHING > WRETHE

WRICK variant spelling (chiefly Brit) of > RICK

WRICKED > WRICK

WRICKING > WRICK

WRICKS > WRICK

WRIED > WRY

WRIER > WRY

WRIES > WRY

WRIEST > WRY

WRIGGLE vb move with a twisting action ▷ n wriggling movement

WRIGGLED > WRIGGLE

WRIGGLER > WRIGGLE

WRIGGLERS > WRIGGLE

WRIGGLES > WRIGGLE

WRIGGLIER > WRIGGLE

WRIGGLING > WRIGGLE

WRIGGLY > WRIGGLE

WRIGHT n maker

WRIGHTS > WRIGHT

WRING vb twist, esp to squeeze liquid out of

WRINGED > WRING

WRINGER same as > MANGLE

WRINGERS > WRINGER

WRINGING > WRING

WRINGS > WRING

WRINKLE n slight crease, esp one in the skin due to age ▷ vb make or become slightly creased

WRINKLED > WRINKLE

WRINKLES > WRINKLE

WRINKLIER > WRINKLE

WRINKLIES npl derogatory word for old people

WRINKLING > WRINKLE

WRINKLY > WRINKLE

WRIST n joint between the hand and the arm

WRISTBAND n band around the wrist, esp one attached to a watch or forming part of a long sleeve

WRISTIER > WRISTY

WRISTIEST > WRISTY

WRISTLET n band or bracelet worn around the wrist

WRISTLETS > WRISTLET

WRISTLOCK n wrestling hold in which a wrestler seizes his opponent's wrist and exerts pressure against the joints of his hand, arm, or shoulder

WRISTS > WRIST

WRISTY adj (of a player's style of hitting the ball in cricket, tennis, etc) characterized by considerable movement of the wrist

WRIT n written legal command

WRITABLE > WRITE

WRITATIVE adj inclined to write a lot

WRITE vb mark paper etc with symbols or words

WRITEABLE > WRITE

WRITER n author

WRITERESS n female writer

WRITERLY adj of or characteristic of a writer

WRITERS > WRITER

WRITES > WRITE

WRITHE vb twist or squirm in or as if in pain ▷ n act or an instance of writhing

WRITHED > WRITHE

WRITHEN adj twisted

WRITHER > WRITHE

WRITHERS > WRITHE

WRITHES > WRITHE

WRITHING > WRITHE

WRITHINGS > WRITHE

WRITHLED adj wrinkled

WRITING > WRITE

WRITINGS > WRITE

WRITS > WRIT

WRITTEN > WRITE

WRIZLED adj wrinkled

WROATH n unforeseen trouble

WROATHS > WROATH

WROKE > WREAK

WROKEN > WREAK

WRONG adj incorrect or mistaken ▷ adv in a wrong manner ▷ n something immoral or unjust ▷ vb treat unjustly

WRONGDOER n person who acts immorally or illegally

WRONGED > WRONG

WRONGER > WRONG

WRONGERS > WRONG

WRONGEST > WRONG

WRONGFUL adj unjust or illegal

WRONGING > WRONG

WRONGLY > WRONG

WRONGNESS > WRONG

WRONGOUS adj unfair

WRONGS > WRONG

WROOT obsolete form of > ROOT

WROOTED > WROOT

WROOTING > WROOT

WROOTS > WROOT

WROTE > WRITE

WROTH adj angry

WROTHFUL same as > WRATHFUL

WROUGHT adj (of metals) shaped by hammering or beating

WRUNG > WRING

WRY adj drily humorous ▷ vb twist or contort

WRYBILL n New Zealand plover whose bill is bent to one side enabling it to search for food beneath stones

WRYBILLS >WRYBILL
WRYER >WRY
WRYEST >WRY
WRYING >WRY
WRYLY >WRY
WRYNECK n woodpecker that has a habit of twisting its neck round
WRYNECKS >WRYNECK
WRYNESS >WRY
WRYNESSES >WRY
WRYTHEN adj twisted
WUD Scots form of >WOOD
WUDDED >WUD
WUDDING >WUD
WUDJULA n Australian word for a non-Aboriginal person
WUDJULAS >WUDJULA
WUDS >WUD
WUDU n practice of ritual washing before daily prayer
WUDUS >WUDU
WUKKAS npl Australian taboo slang expression for no problems
WULFENITE n yellow,

orange, red, or grey lustrous secondary mineral
WULL obsolete form of >WILL
WULLED >WILL
WULLING >WILL
WULLS >WILL
WUNNER same as >ONER
WUNNERS >WUNNER
WURLEY n Aboriginal hut
WURLEYS >WURLEY
WURLIE same as >WURLEY
WURLIES >WURLIE
WURST n large sausage, esp of a type made in Germany, Austria, etc
WURSTS >WURST
WURTZITE n zinc sulphide
WURTZITES >WURTZITE
WURZEL n root
WURZELS >WURZEL
WUS n casual term of address
WUSES >WUS
WUSHU n Chinese martial arts
WUSHUS >WUSHU
WUSS n feeble or effeminate

person
WUSSES >WUSS
WUSSIER >WUSSY
WUSSIES >WUSSY
WUSSIEST >WUSSY
WUSSY adj feeble or effeminate ▷ n feeble person
WUTHER vb (of wind) blow and roar
WUTHERED >WUTHER
WUTHERING adj (of a wind) blowing strongly with a roaring sound
WUTHERS >WUTHER
WUXIA n genre of Chinese fiction and film, concerning the adventures of sword-wielding chivalrous heroes
WUXIAS >WUXIA
WUZZLE vb mix up
WUZZLED >WUZZLE
WUZZLES >WUZZLE
WUZZLING >WUZZLE
WYANDOTTE n heavy American breed of

domestic fowl
WYCH n type of tree having flexible branches
WYCHES >WYCH
WYE n y-shaped pipe
WYES >WYE
WYLE vb entice
WYLED >WYLE
WYLES >WYLE
WYLIECOAT n petticoat
WYLING >WYLE
WYN n rune equivalent to English 'w'
WYND n narrow lane or alley
WYNDS >WYND
WYNN same as >WYN
WYNNS >WYNN
WYNS >WYN
WYTE vb blame
WYTED >WYTE
WYTES >WYTE
WYTING >WYTE
WYVERN n heraldic beast having a serpent's tail and a dragon's head and a body with wings and two legs
WYVERNS >WYVERN

Xx

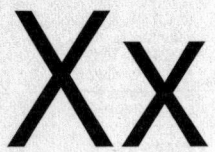

XANTHAM *n* acacia gum
XANTHAMS > XANTHAM
XANTHAN *same as* > XANTHAM
XANTHANS > XANTHAM
XANTHATE *n* any salt or ester of xanthic acid
XANTHATES > XANTHATE
XANTHEIN *n* soluble part of the yellow pigment that is found in the cell sap of some flowers
XANTHEINS > XANTHEIN
XANTHENE *n* yellowish crystalline heterocyclic compound used as a fungicide
XANTHENES > XANTHENE
XANTHIC *adj* of, containing, or derived from xanthic acid
XANTHIN *n* any of a group of yellow or orange carotene derivatives that occur in the fruit and flowers of certain plants
XANTHINE *n* crystalline compound related in structure to uric acid and found in urine, blood, certain plants, and certain animal tissues
XANTHINES > XANTHINE
XANTHINS > XANTHIN
XANTHISM *n* condition of skin, fur, or feathers in which yellow coloration predominates
XANTHISMS > XANTHISM
XANTHOMA *n* presence in the skin of fatty yellow or brownish plaques or nodules, esp on the eyelids, caused by a disorder of lipid metabolism
XANTHOMAS > XANTHOMA
XANTHONE *n* crystalline compound
XANTHONES > XANTHONE
XANTHOUS *adj* of, relating to, or designating races with yellowish hair and a light complexion
XANTHOXYL *n* South American plant
XEBEC *n* small three-masted Mediterranean vessel with both square and lateen sails, formerly used by Algerian pirates and later used for commerce

XEBECS > XEBEC
XENIA *n* influence of pollen upon the form of the fruit developing after pollination
XENIAL > XENIA
XENIAS > XENIA
XENIC *adj* denoting the presence of bacteria
XENIUM *n* diplomatic gift
XENOBLAST *n* type of mineral deposit
XENOCRYST *n* crystal included within an igneous rock as the magma cooled but not formed from it
XENOGAMY *n* fertilization by the fusion of male and female gametes from different individuals of the same species
XENOGENIC *adj* relating to the supposed production of offspring completely unlike either parent
XENOGENY *n* offspring unlike either parent
XENOGRAFT *n* tissue graft obtained from a donor of a different species from the recipient
XENOLITH *n* fragment of rock differing in origin, composition, structure, etc, from the igneous rock enclosing it
XENOLITHS > XENOLITH
XENOMANIA *n* passion for foreign things
XENOMENIA *n* menstruation from unusual orifices
XENON *n* colourless odourless gas found in very small quantities in the air
XENONS > XENON
XENOPHILE *n* person who likes foreigners or things foreign
XENOPHOBE *n* person who hates or fears foreigners or strangers
XENOPHOBY *n* hatred or fear of foreigners or strangers
XENOPHYA *n* parts of shell or skeleton formed by foreign bodies
XENOPUS *n* African frog
XENOPUSES > XENOPUS
XENOTIME *n* yellow-brown mineral

XENOTIMES > XENOTIME
XENURINE *adj* relating to a type of armadillo
XERAFIN *n* Indian coin
XERAFINS > XERAFIN
XERANSES > XERANSIS
XERANSIS *n* gradual loss of tissue moisture
XERANTIC > XERANSIS
XERAPHIN *same as* > XERAFIN
XERAPHINS > XERAPHIN
XERARCH *adj* (of a sere) having its origin in a dry habitat
XERASIA *n* dryness of the hair
XERASIAS > XERASIA
XERIC *adj* of, relating to, or growing in dry conditions
XERICALLY > XERIC
XERISCAPE *n* landscape designed to conserve water
XEROCHASY *n* release of seeds or pollen on drying
XERODERMA *n* any abnormal dryness of the skin as the result of diminished secretions from the sweat or sebaceous glands
XEROMA *n* excessive dryness of the cornea
XEROMAS > XEROMA
XEROMATA > XEROMA
XEROMORPH *n* xerophilous plant
XEROPHAGY *n* fasting by eating only dry food
XEROPHILE *n* plant or animal who likes living in dry surroundings
XEROPHILY > XEROPHILE
XEROPHYTE *n* xerophilous plant, such as a cactus
XEROSERE *n* sere that originates in dry surroundings
XEROSERES > XEROSERE
XEROSES > XEROSIS
XEROSIS *n* abnormal dryness of bodily tissues, esp the skin, eyes, or mucous membranes
XEROSTOMA *n* abnormal lack of saliva; dryness of the mouth
XEROTES *same as* > XEROSIS
XEROTIC > XEROSIS

XEROX *n* tradename for a machine employing a xerographic copying process ▷ *vb* produce a copy (of a document, etc) using such a machine
XEROXED > XEROX
XEROXES > XEROX
XEROXING > XEROX
XERUS *n* ground squirrel
XERUSES > XERUS
XI *n* 14th letter in the Greek alphabet
XIPHOID *adj* shaped like a sword ▷ *n* part of the sternum
XIPHOIDAL > XIPHOID
XIPHOIDS > XIPHOID
XIPHOPAGI *n* Siamese twins joined at the lower sternum
XIS > XI
XOANA > XOANON
XOANON *n* primitive image of a god, carved, esp originally, in wood, and supposed to have fallen from heaven
XRAY *n* code word for the letter X
XRAYS > XRAY
XU *n* Vietnamese currency unit
XYLAN *n* yellow polysaccharide consisting of xylose units: occurs in straw husks and other woody tissue
XYLANS > XYLAN
XYLEM *n* plant tissue that conducts water and minerals from the roots to all other parts
XYLEMS > XYLEM
XYLENE *n* type of hydrocarbon
XYLENES > XYLENE
XYLENOL *n* synthetic resin made from xylene
XYLENOLS > XYLENOL
XYLIC > XYLEM
XYLIDIN *same as* > XYLIDINE
XYLIDINE *n* mixture of six isomeric amines derived from xylene and used in dyes
XYLIDINES > XYLIDINE
XYLIDINS > XYLIDIN
XYLITOL *n* crystalline alcohol used as sweetener

XYLITOLS >XYLITOL
XYLOCARP n fruit, such as a coconut, having a hard woody pericarp
XYLOCARPS >XYLOCARP
XYLOGEN same as >XYLEM
XYLOGENS >XYLOGEN
XYLOGRAPH n engraving in wood ▷ vb print (a design, illustration, etc) from a wood engraving
XYLOID adj of, relating to, or resembling wood
XYLOIDIN n type of explosive
XYLOIDINE same as >XYLOIDIN

XYLOIDINS >XYLOIDIN
XYLOL another name (not in technical usage) for >XYLENE
XYLOLOGY n study of the composition of wood
XYLOLS >XYLOL
XYLOMA n hard growth in fungi
XYLOMAS >XYLOMA
XYLOMATA >XYLOMA
XYLOMETER n device for measuring the specific gravity of wood
XYLONIC adj denoting an acid formed from xylose
XYLONITE n type of plastic

XYLONITES >XYLONITE
XYLOPHAGE n creature that eats wood
XYLOPHONE n musical instrument made of a row of wooden bars played with hammers
XYLORIMBA n large xylophone with an extended range of five octaves
XYLOSE n white crystalline dextrorotatory sugar found in the form of xylan in wood and straw
XYLOSES >XYLOSE
XYLOTOMY n preparation

of sections of wood for examination by microscope
XYLYL n group of atoms
XYLYLS >XYLYL
XYST n long portico, esp one used in ancient Greece for athletics
XYSTER n surgical instrument for scraping bone
XYSTERS >XYSTER
XYSTI >XYSTUS
XYSTOI >XYSTOS
XYSTOS same as >XYST
XYSTS >XYST
XYSTUS same as >XYST

X

Yy

YA *pron* you

YAAR *n* in informal Indian English, a friend

YAARS > YAAR

YABA *n* informal word for 'yet another bloody acronym'

YABAS > YABA

YABBA *n* form of methamphetamine

YABBAS > YABBA

YABBER *vb* talk or jabber ▷ *n* talk or jabber

YABBERED > YABBER

YABBERING > YABBER

YABBERS > YABBER

YABBIE *same as* > YABBY

YABBIED > YABBY

YABBIES > YABBY

YABBY *n* small freshwater crayfish ▷ *vb* go out to catch yabbies

YABBYING > YABBY

YACCA *n* Australian plant with a woody stem, stiff grasslike leaves, and a spike of small white flowers

YACCAS > YACCA

YACHT *n* large boat with sails or an engine, used for racing or pleasure cruising ▷ *vb* sail in a yacht

YACHTED > YACHT

YACHTER > YACHT

YACHTERS > YACHT

YACHTIE *n* yachtsman

YACHTIES > YACHTIE

YACHTING *n* sport or practice of navigating a yacht

YACHTINGS > YACHTING

YACHTMAN *same as* > YACHTSMAN

YACHTMEN > YACHTMAN

YACHTS > YACHT

YACHTSMAN *n* person who sails a yacht

YACHTSMEN > YACHTSMAN

YACK *same as* > YAK

YACKA *same as* > YACCA

YACKAS > YACKA

YACKED > YACK

YACKER *same as* > YAKKA

YACKERS > YACKER

YACKING > YACK

YACKS > YACK

YAD *n* hand-held pointer used for reading the sefer torah

YADS > YAD

YAE *same as* > AE

YAFF *vb* bark

YAFFED > YAFF

YAFFING > YAFF

YAFFLE *n* woodpecker with a green back and wings, and a red crown

YAFFLES > YAFFLE

YAFFS > YAFF

YAG *n* artificial crystal

YAGER *same as* > JAEGER

YAGERS > YAGER

YAGGER *n* pedlar

YAGGERS > YAGGER

YAGI *n* type of highly directional aerial

YAGIS > YAGI

YAGS > YAG

YAH *interj* exclamation of derision or disgust ▷ *n* affected upper-class person

YAHOO *n* crude coarse person

YAHOOISM > YAHOO

YAHOOISMS > YAHOO

YAHOOS > YAHOO

YAHRZEIT *n* (in Judaism) the anniversary of the death of a close relative, on which it is customary to kindle a light and recite the Kaddish

YAHRZEITS > YAHRZEIT

YAHS > YAH

YAIRD *Scots form of* > YARD

YAIRDS > YAIRD

YAK *n* Tibetan ox with long shaggy hair ▷ *vb* talk continuously about unimportant matters

YAKHDAN *n* box for carrying ice on a pack animal

YAKHDANS > YAKHDAN

YAKIMONO *n* grilled food

YAKIMONOS > YAKIMONO

YAKITORI *n* Japanese dish consisting of small pieces of chicken skewered and grilled

YAKITORIS > YAKITORI

YAKKA *n* work

YAKKAS > YAKKA

YAKKED > YAK

YAKKER *same as* > YAKKA

YAKKERS > YAKKER

YAKKING > YAK

YAKOW *n* animal bred from a male yak and a domestic cow

YAKOWS > YAKOW

YAKS > YAK

YAKUZA *n* Japanese criminal organization involved in illegal gambling, extortion, gun-running, etc

YALD *adj* vigorous

YALE *n* mythical beast with the body of an antelope (or similar animal) and swivelling horns

YALES > YALE

YAM *n* tropical root vegetable

YAMALKA *same as* > YARMULKE

YAMALKAS > YAMALKA

YAMEN *n* (in imperial China) the office or residence of a public official

YAMENS > YAMEN

YAMMER *vb* whine in a complaining manner ▷ *n* yammering sound

YAMMERED > YAMMER

YAMMERER > YAMMER

YAMMERERS > YAMMER

YAMMERING > YAMMER

YAMMERS > YAMMER

YAMPIES > YAMPY

YAMPY *n* foolish person

YAMS > YAM

YAMULKA *same as* > YARMULKE

YAMULKAS > YAMULKA

YAMUN *same as* > YAMEN

YAMUNS > YAMUN

YANG *n* (in Chinese philosophy) one of two complementary principles maintaining harmony in the universe

YANGS > YANG

YANK *vb* pull or jerk suddenly ▷ *n* sudden pull or jerk

YANKED > YANK

YANKEE *n* code word for the letter Y

YANKEES > YANKEE

YANKER > YANK

YANKERS > YANK

YANKIE *n* shrewish woman

YANKIES > YANKIE

YANKING > YANK

YANKS > YANK

YANQUI *n* slang word for American

YANQUIS > YANQUI

YANTRA *n* diagram used in meditation

YANTRAS > YANTRA

YAOURT *n* yoghurt

YAOURTS > YAOURT

YAP *vb* bark with a high-pitched sound ▷ *n* high-pitched bark ▷ *interj* imitation or representation of the sound of a dog yapping or people jabbering

YAPOCK *same as* > YAPOK

YAPOCKS > YAPOCK

YAPOK *n* type of opossum

YAPOKS > YAPOK

YAPON *same as* > YAUPON

YAPONS > YAPON

YAPP *n* type of book binding

YAPPED > YAP

YAPPER > YAP

YAPPERS > YAP

YAPPIE *n* young aspiring professional

YAPPIER > YAP

YAPPIES > YAPPIE

YAPPIEST > YAP

YAPPING > YAP

YAPPINGLY > YAP

YAPPS > YAPP

YAPPY > YAP

YAPS > YAP

YAPSTER > YAP

YAPSTERS > YAP

YAQONA *n* Polynesian shrub

YAQONAS > YAQONA

YAR *adj* nimble

YARCO *n* derogatory dialect word for a young working-class person who wears casual sports clothes

YARCOS > YARCO

YARD *n* unit of length equal to 36 inches or about 91.4 centimetres ▷ *vb* draft (animals), esp to a saleyard

YARDAGE *n* length measured in yards

YARDAGES > YARDAGE

YARDANG *n* ridge formed by wind erosion

YARDANGS > YARDANG

YARDARM *n* outer end of a ship's yard

YARDARMS > YARDARM

YARDBIRD *n* inexperienced, untrained, or clumsy soldier, esp one employed on menial duties

YARDBIRDS > YARDBIRD

YARDED > YARD

YARDER > YARD

YARDERS > YARD

YARDING n group of animals displayed for sale

YARDINGS > YARDING

YARDLAND n archaic unit of land

YARDLANDS > YARDLAND

YARDMAN n farm overseer

YARDMEN > YARDMAN

YARDS > YARD

YARDSTICK n standard against which to judge other people or things

YARDWAND same as > YARDSTICK

YARDWANDS > YARDWAND

YARDWORK n garden work

YARDWORKS > YARDWORK

YARE adj ready, brisk, or eager ▷ adv readily or eagerly

YARELY > YARE

YARER > YARE

YAREST > YARE

YARFA n peat

YARFAS > YARFA

YARK vb make ready

YARKED > YARK

YARKING > YARK

YARKS > YARK

YARMELKE same as > YARMULKE

YARMELKES > YARMELKE

YARMULKA same as > YARMULKE

YARMULKAS > YARMULKA

YARMULKE n skullcap worn by Jewish men

YARMULKES > YARMULKE

YARN n thread used for knitting or making cloth ▷ vb thread with yarn

YARNED > YARN

YARNER > YARN

YARNERS > YARN

YARNING > YARN

YARNS > YARN

YARPHA n peat

YARPHAS > YARPHA

YARR n wild white flower

YARRAMAN n horse

YARRAMANS > YARRAMAN

YARRAMEN > YARRAMAN

YARRAN n type of small hardy tree of inland Australia

YARRANS > YARRAN

YARROW n wild plant with flat clusters of white flowers

YARROWS > YARROW

YARRS > YARR

YARTA Shetland word for > HEART

YARTAS > YARTA

YARTO same as > YARTA

YARTOS > YARTO

YASHMAC same as > YASHMAK

YASHMACS > YASHMAC

YASHMAK n veil worn by a Muslim woman to cover her face in public

YASHMAKS > YASHMAK

YASMAK same as > YASHMAK

YASMAKS > YASHMAK

YATAGAN same as > YATAGHAN

YATAGANS > YATAGAN

YATAGHAN n Turkish sword with a curved single-edged blade

YATAGHANS > YATAGHAN

YATE n type of small eucalyptus tree yielding a very hard timber

YATES > YATE

YATTER vb talk at length ▷ n continuous chatter

YATTERED > YATTER

YATTERING > YATTER

YATTERS > YATTER

YAUD Scots word for > MARE

YAUDS > YAUD

YAULD adj alert, spritely, or nimble

YAUP variant spelling of > YAWP

YAUPED > YAUP

YAUPER > YAUP

YAUPERS > YAUP

YAUPING > YAUP

YAUPON n southern US evergreen holly shrub with spreading branches, scarlet fruits, and oval leaves

YAUPONS > YAUPON

YAUPS > YAUP

YAUTIA n Caribbean plant cultivated for its edible leaves and underground stems

YAUTIAS > YAUTIA

YAW vb (of an aircraft or ship) turn to one side or from side to side while moving ▷ n act or movement of yawing

YAWED > YAW

YAWEY > YAWS

YAWING > YAW

YAWL n two-masted sailing boat ▷ vb howl, weep, or scream harshly

YAWLED > YAWL

YAWLING > YAWL

YAWLS > YAWL

YAWMETER n instrument for measuring an aircraft's yaw

YAWMETERS > YAWMETER

YAWN vb open the mouth wide and take in air deeply, often when sleepy or bored ▷ n act of yawning

YAWNED > YAWN

YAWNER > YAWN

YAWNERS > YAWN

YAWNIER > YAWN

YAWNIEST > YAWN

YAWNING > YAWN

YAWNINGLY > YAWN

YAWNINGS > YAWN

YAWNS > YAWN

YAWNSOME adj boring

YAWNY > YAWN

YAWP vb gape or yawn, esp audibly ▷ n shout, bark, yelp, or cry

YAWPED > YAWP

YAWPER > YAWP

YAWPERS > YAWP

YAWPING > YAWP

YAWPINGS > YAWP

YAWPS > YAWP

YAWS n infectious tropical skin disease

YAWY > YAWS

YAY interj exclamation indicating approval, congratulation, or triumph ▷ n cry of approval

YAYS > YAY

YBET archaic past participle of > BEAT

YBLENT archaic past participle of > BLEND

YBORE archaic past participle of > BEAR

YBOUND archaic past participle of > BIND

YBOUNDEN archaic past participle of > BIND

YBRENT archaic past participle of > BURN

YCLAD archaic past participle of > CLOTHE

YCLED archaic past participle of > CLOTHE

YCLEEPE archaic form of > CLEPE

YCLEEPED > YCLEEPE

YCLEEPES > YCLEEPE

YCLEEPING > YCLEEPE

YCLEPED same as > YCLEPT

YCLEPT adj having the name of

YCOND archaic past participle of > CON

YDRAD archaic past participle of > DREAD

YDRED archaic past participle of > DREAD

YE pron you ▷ adj the

YEA interj yes ▷ adv indeed or truly ▷ sentence substitute aye ▷ n cry of agreement

YEAD vb proceed

YEADING > YEAD

YEADS > YEAD

YEAH n positive affirmation

YEAHS > YEAH

YEALDON n fuel

YEALDONS > YEALDON

YEALING n person of the same age as oneself

YEALINGS > YEALING

YEALM vb prepare for thatching

YEALMED > YEALM

YEALMING > YEALM

YEALMS > YEALM

YEAN vb (of a sheep or goat) to give birth to (offspring)

YEANED > YEAN

YEANING > YEAN

YEANLING n young of a goat or sheep

YEANLINGS > YEANLING

YEANS > YEAN

YEAR n time taken for the earth to make one revolution around the sun, about 365 days

YEARBOOK n reference book published annually containing details of the previous year's events

YEARBOOKS > YEARBOOK

YEARD vb bury

YEARDED > YEARD

YEARDING > YEARD

YEARDS > YEARD

YEAREND n end of the year

YEARENDS > YEAREND

YEARLIES > YEARLY

YEARLING n animal between one and two years old ▷ adj being a year old

YEARLINGS > YEARLING

YEARLONG adj throughout a whole year

YEARLY adv (happening) every year or once a year ▷ adj occurring, done, or appearing once a year or every year ▷ n publication, event, etc, that occurs once a year

YEARN vb want (something) very much

YEARNED > YEARN

YEARNER > YEARN

YEARNERS > YEARN

YEARNING n intense or overpowering longing, desire, or need

YEARNINGS > YEARNING

YEARNS > YEARN

YEARS > YEAR

YEAS > YEA

YEASAYER n person who usually agrees with proposals

YEASAYERS > YEASAYER

YEAST n fungus used to make bread rise and to ferment alcoholic drinks ▷ vb froth or foam

YEASTED > YEAST

YEASTIER > YEASTY

YEASTIEST > YEASTY

YEASTILY > YEASTY

YEASTING > YEAST

YEASTLESS > YEAST

YEASTLIKE > YEAST

YEASTS > YEAST

YEASTY adj of, resembling, or containing yeast

YEBO interj yes ▷ sentence substitute expression of affirmation

YECCH same as > YECH

YECCHS > YECCH

YECH n expression of disgust

YECHIER > YECHY

YECHIEST > YECHY

YECHS > YECH

YECHY > YECH

YEDE same as > YEAD

YEDES > YEDE

YEDING > YEDE

YEED same as > YEAD

YEEDING > YEED

YEEDS > YEED
YEELIN n person of the same age as oneself
YEELINS > YEELIN
YEGG n burglar or safe-breaker
YEGGMAN same as **>** YEGG
YEGGMEN > YEGGMAN
YEGGS > YEGG
YEH same as **>** YEAH
YELD adj (of an animal) barren or too young to bear young
YELDRING n yellowhammer (bird)
YELDRINGS > YELDRING
YELDROCK same as **>** YELDRING
YELDROCKS > YELDROCK
YELK n yolk of an egg
YELKS > YELK
YELL vb shout or scream in a loud or piercing way **>** n loud cry of pain, anger, or fear
YELLED > YELL
YELLER > YELL
YELLERS > YELL
YELLING > YELL
YELLINGS > YELL
YELLOCH vb yell
YELLOCHED > YELLOCH
YELLOCHS > YELLOCH
YELLOW n colour of gold, a lemon, etc **>** adj of this colour **>** vb make or become yellow
YELLOWED > YELLOW
YELLOWER > YELLOW
YELLOWEST > YELLOW
YELLOWFIN n type of tuna
YELLOWIER > YELLOW
YELLOWING > YELLOW
YELLOWISH > YELLOW
YELLOWLY > YELLOW
YELLOWS n any of various fungal or viral diseases of plants, characterized by yellowish discoloration and stunting
YELLOWY > YELLOW
YELLS > YELL
YELM same as **>** YEALM
YELMED > YELM
YELMING > YELM
YELMS > YELM
YELP n a short sudden cry **>** vb utter a sharp or high-pitched cry of pain
YELPED > YELP
YELPER > YELP
YELPERS > YELP
YELPING > YELP
YELPINGS > YELP
YELPS > YELP
YELT n young sow
YELTS > YELT
YEMMER southwest English form of **>** EMBER
YEMMERS > YEMMER
YEN n monetary unit of Japan **>** vb have a longing
YENNED > YEN
YENNING > YEN

YENS > YEN
YENTA n meddlesome woman
YENTAS > YENTA
YENTE same as **>** YENTA
YENTES > YENTE
YEOMAN n farmer owning and farming his own land
YEOMANLY adj of, relating to, or like a yeoman **>** adv in a yeomanly manner, as in being brave, staunch, or loyal
YEOMANRY n yeomen
YEOMEN > YEOMAN
YEP n affirmative statement
YEPS > YEP
YERBA n stimulating South American drink made from dried leaves
YERBAS > YERBA
YERD vb bury
YERDED > YERD
YERDING > YERD
YERDS > YERD
YERK vb tighten stitches
YERKED > YERK
YERKING > YERK
YERKS > YERK
YERSINIA n plague bacterium
YERSINIAE > YERSINIA
YERSINIAS > YERSINIA
YES interj expresses consent, agreement, or approval **>** n answer or vote of yes **>** sentence substitute used to express acknowledgment, affirmation, consent, agreement, or approval or to answer when one is addressed **>** vb reply in the affirmative
YESES > YES
YESHIVA n traditional Jewish school devoted chiefly to the study of rabbinic literature and the Talmud
YESHIVAH same as **>** YESHIVA
YESHIVAHS > YESHIVAH
YESHIVAS > YESHIVA
YESHIVOT > YESHIVA
YESHIVOTH > YESHIVA
YESK vb hiccup
YESKED > YESK
YESKING > YESK
YESKS > YESK
YESSED > YES
YESSES > YES
YESSING > YES
YEST archaic form of **>** YEAST
YESTER adj of or relating to yesterday
YESTERDAY n the day before today **>** adv on or during the day before today
YESTEREVE n yesterday evening
YESTERN same as **>** YESTER

YESTREEN n yesterday evening
YESTREENS > YESTREEN
YESTS > YEST
YESTY archaic form of **>** YEASTY
YET adv up until then or now
YETI n large legendary manlike creature alleged to inhabit the Himalayan Mountains
YETIS > YETI
YETT n gate or door
YETTIE n young, entrepreneurial, and technology-based (person)
YETTIES > YETTIE
YETTS > YETT
YEUK vb itch
YEUKED > YEUK
YEUKIER > YEUKY
YEUKIEST > YEUKY
YEUKING > YEUK
YEUKS > YEUK
YEUKY > YEUK
YEVE vb give
YEVEN > YEVE
YEVES > YEVE
YEVING > YEVE
YEW n evergreen tree with needle-like leaves and red berries
YEWEN adj made of yew
YEWS > YEW
YEX vb hiccup
YEXED > YEX
YEXES > YEX
YEXING > YEX
YFERE adv together
YGLAUNST archaic past participle of **>** GLANCE
YGO archaic past participle of **>** GO
YGOE archaic past participle of **>** GO
YIBBLES adv perhaps
YICKER vb squeal or squeak
YICKERED > YICKER
YICKERING > YICKER
YICKERS > YICKER
YID n offensive word for a Jew
YIDAKI n long wooden wind instrument played by the Aboriginal peoples of Arnhem Land
YIDAKIS > YIDAKI
YIDS > YID
YIELD vb produce or bear **>** n amount produced
YIELDABLE > YIELD
YIELDED > YIELD
YIELDER > YIELD
YIELDERS > YIELD
YIELDING adj submissive
YIELDINGS > YIELD
YIELDS > YIELD
YIKE n argument, squabble, or fight **>** vb argue, squabble, or fight
YIKED > YIKE
YIKES interj expression of

surprise, fear, or alarm
YIKING > YIKE
YIKKER vb squeal or squeak
YIKKERED > YIKKER
YIKKERING > YIKKER
YIKKERS > YIKKER
YILL n ale
YILLS > YILL
YIN Scots word for **>** ONE
YINCE Scots form of **>** ONCE
YINDIE n person who combines a lucrative career with non-mainstream tastes
YINDIES > YINDIE
YINS > YIN
YIP n emit a high-pitched bark
YIPE same as **>** YIPES
YIPES interj expression of surprise, fear, or alarm
YIPPED > YIP
YIPPEE interj exclamation of joy or pleasure
YIPPER n golfer who suffers from a failure of nerve
YIPPERS > YIPPER
YIPPIE n young person sharing hippy ideals
YIPPIES > YIPPIE
YIPPING > YIP
YIPPY same as **>** YIPPIE
YIPS > YIP
YIRD vb bury
YIRDED > YIRD
YIRDING > YIRD
YIRDS > YIRD
YIRK same as **>** YERK
YIRKED > YIRK
YIRKING > YIRK
YIRKS > YIRK
YIRR vb snarl, growl, or yell
YIRRED > YIRR
YIRRING > YIRR
YIRRS > YIRR
YIRTH n earth
YIRTHS > YIRTH
YITE n European bunting with a yellowish head and body and brown streaked wings and tail
YITES > YITE
YITIE same as **>** YITE
YITIES > YITIE
YITTEN adj frightened
YLEM n original matter from which the basic elements are said to have been formed following the explosion postulated in the big bang theory of cosmology
YLEMS > YLEM
YLIKE Spenserian form of **>** ALIKE
YLKE archaic spelling of **>** ILK
YLKES > YLKE
YMOLT Spenserian past participle of **>** MELT
YMOLTEN Spenserian past participle of **>** MELT

YMPE *Spenserian form of*
> IMP
YMPES > YMPE
YMPING > YMPE
YMPT > YMPE
YNAMBU *n* South American
bird
YNAMBUS > YNAMBU
YO *interj* expression used as
a greeting or to attract
someone's attention
▷ *sentence substitute*
expression used as a
greeting, to attract
someone's attention, etc
▷ *n* cry of greeting
YOB *n* bad-mannered
aggressive youth
YOBBERIES > YOBBERY
YOBBERY *n* behaviour
typical of aggressive surly
youths
YOBBISH *adj* typical of
aggressive surly youths
YOBBISHLY > YOBBISH
YOBBISM > YOB
YOBBISMS > YOB
YOBBO *same as* > YOB
YOBBOES > YOBBO
YOBBOS > YOBBO
YOBS > YOB
YOCK *vb* chuckle
YOCKED > YOCK
YOCKING > YOCK
YOCKS > YOCK
YOD *n* tenth letter in the
Hebrew alphabet
YODE > YEAD
YODEL *vb* sing with abrupt
changes between a normal
and a falsetto voice ▷ *n* act
or sound of yodelling
YODELED > YODEL
YODELER > YODEL
YODELERS > YODEL
YODELING > YODEL
YODELLED > YODEL
YODELLER > YODEL
YODELLERS > YODEL
YODELLING > YODEL
YODELS > YODEL
YODH *same as* > YOD
YODHS > YODH
YODLE *variant spelling of*
> YODEL
YODLED > YODLE
YODLER > YODLE
YODLERS > YODLE
YODLES > YODLE
YODLING > YODLE
YODS > YOD
YOGA *n* Hindu method of
exercise and discipline
aiming at spiritual, mental,
and physical wellbeing
YOGAS > YOGA
YOGEE *same as* > YOGI
YOGEES > YOGEE
YOGH *n* character used in
Old and Middle English to
represent a palatal fricative
YOGHOURT *variant form of*
> YOGURT
YOGHOURTS > YOGHOURT

YOGHS > YOGH
YOGHURT *same as*
> YOGURT
YOGHURTS > YOGHURT
YOGI *n* person who
practises yoga
YOGIC > YOGA
YOGIN *same as* > YOGI
YOGINI > YOGI
YOGINIS > YOGI
YOGINS > YOGIN
YOGIS > YOGI
YOGISM > YOGI
YOGISMS > YOGI
YOGURT *n* slightly sour
custard-like food made
from milk that has had
bacteria added to it, often
sweetened and flavoured
with fruit
YOGURTS > YOGURT
YOHIMBE *n* bark used in
herbal medicine
YOHIMBES > YOHIMBE
YOHIMBINE *n* alkaloid
found in the bark of a
tropical African tree
YOICK *vb* urge on
foxhounds
YOICKED > YOICK
YOICKING > YOICK
YOICKS *interj* cry used by
huntsmen to urge on the
hounds to the fox ▷ *vb* urge
on foxhounds
YOICKSED > YOICKS
YOICKSES > YOICKS
YOICKSING > YOICKS
YOJAN *n* Indian unit of
distance
YOJANA *same as* > YOJAN
YOJANAS > YOJANA
YOJANS > YOJAN
YOK *vb* chuckle
YOKE *n* wooden bar put
across the necks of two
animals to hold them
together ▷ *vb* put a yoke on
YOKED > YOKE
YOKEL *n* derogatory term
for a person who lives in the
country and is usu simple
and old-fashioned
YOKELESS > YOKE
YOKELISH > YOKEL
YOKELS > YOKEL
YOKEMATE *n* colleague
YOKEMATES > YOKEMATE
YOKER *vb* spit
YOKERED > YOKER
YOKERING > YOKER
YOKERS > YOKE
YOKES > YOKE
YOKING > YOKE
YOKINGS > YOKE
YOKKED > YOK
YOKKING > YOK.
YOKOZUNA *n* grand
champion sumo wrestler
YOKOZUNAS > YOKOZUNA
YOKS > YOK
YOKUL *Shetland word for*
> YES
YOLD *archaic past participle*

of > YIELD
YOLDRING *n*
yellowhammer (bird)
YOLDRINGS > YOLDRING
YOLK *n* yellow part of an
egg that provides food for
the developing embryo
YOLKED > YOLK
YOLKIER > YOLK
YOLKIEST > YOLK
YOLKLESS > YOLK
YOLKS > YOLK
YOLKY > YOLK
YOM *n* day
YOMIM > YOM
YOMP *vb* walk or trek
laboriously, esp heavily
laden and over difficult
terrain
YOMPED > YOMP
YOMPING > YOMP
YOMPS > YOMP
YON *adj* that or those over
there ▷ *adv* yonder ▷ *pron*
that person or thing
YOND *same as* > YON
YONDER *adv* over there
▷ *adj* situated over there
▷ *det* being at a distance,
either within view or as if
within view ▷ *n* person
YONDERLY > YONDER
YONDERS > YONDER
YONI *n* female genitalia,
regarded as a divine symbol
of sexual pleasure
YONIC *adj* resembling a
vulva
YONIS > YONI
YONKER *same as*
> YOUNKER
YONKERS > YONKER
YONKS *npl* very long time
YONNIE *n* stone
YONNIES > YONNIE
YONT *same as* > YON
YOOF *n* non-standard
spelling of youth, used
humorously or facetiously
YOOFS > YOOF
YOOP *n* sob
YOOPS > YOOP
YORE *n* time long past ▷ *adv*
in the past
YORES > YORE
YORK *vb* bowl or try to bowl
(a batsman) by pitching the
ball under or just beyond
the bat
YORKED > YORK
YORKER *n* ball that pitches
just under the bat
YORKERS > YORKER
YORKIE *n* Yorkshire terrier
YORKIES > YORKIE
YORKING > YORK
YORKS > YORK
YORLING *as in yellow yorling*
yellowhammer
YORLINGS > YORLING
YORP *vb* shout
YORPED > YORP
YORPING > YORP
YORPS > YORP

YOTTABYTE *n* very large
unit of computer memory
YOU *pron* person or people
addressed ▷ *n* personality
of the person being
addressed
YOUK *vb* itch
YOUKED > YOUK
YOUKING > YOUK
YOUKS > YOUK
YOUNG *adj* in an early stage
of life or growth ▷ *n* young
people in general; offspring
YOUNGER > YOUNG
YOUNGERS *n* young people
YOUNGEST > YOUNG
YOUNGISH > YOUNG
YOUNGLING *n* young
person, animal, or plant
YOUNGLY *adv* youthfully
YOUNGNESS > YOUNG
YOUNGS > YOUNG
YOUNGSTER *n* young
person
YOUNGTH *n* youth
YOUNGTHLY *adj* youthful
YOUNGTHS > YOUNGTH
YOUNKER *n* young man
YOUNKERS > YOUNKER
YOUPON *same as* > YAUPON
YOUPONS > YOUPON
YOUR *adj* of, belonging to,
or associated with you
YOURN *dialect form of*
> YOURS
YOURS *pron* something
belonging to you
YOURSELF *pron* reflexive
form of *you*
YOURT *same as* > YURT
YOURTS > YOURT
YOUS *pron* refers to more
than one person including
the person or persons
addressed but not
including the speaker
YOUSE *same as* > YOUS
YOUTH *n* time of being
young
YOUTHEN *vb* render more
youthful-seeming
YOUTHENED > YOUTHEN
YOUTHENS > YOUTHEN
YOUTHFUL *adj* vigorous or
active
YOUTHHEAD *same as*
> YOUTHHOOD
YOUTHHOOD *n* youth
YOUTHIER > YOUTHY
YOUTHIEST > YOUTHY
YOUTHLESS > YOUTH
YOUTHLY *adv* young
YOUTHS > YOUTH
YOUTHSOME *archaic variant*
of > YOUTHFUL
YOUTHY *Scots word for*
> YOUNG
YOW *vb* howl
YOWE *Scot word for* > EWE
YOWED > YOW
YOWES > YOWE
YOWIE *n* legendary
Australian apelike creature
YOWIES > YOWIE

YOWING > YOW
YOWL n loud mournful cry ▷ vb produce a loud mournful wail or cry
YOWLED > YOWL
YOWLER > YOWL
YOWLERS > YOWL
YOWLEY n yellowhammer (bird)
YOWLEYS > YOWLEY
YOWLING > YOWL
YOWLINGS > YOWL
YOWLS > YOWL
YOWS > YOW
YPERITE n mustard gas
YPERITES > YPERITE
YPIGHT archaic past participle of > PITCH
YPLAST archaic past participle of > PLACE
YPLIGHT archaic past participle of > PLIGHT
YPSILOID > YPSILON
YPSILON same as > UPSILON
YPSILONS > YPSILON
YRAPT Spenserian form of > RAPT
YRAVISHED archaic past participle of > RAVISH
YRENT archaic past participle of > REND
YRIVD archaic past participle of > RIVE
YRNEH n unit of reciprocal inductance
YRNEHS > YRNEH
YSAME Spenserian word for > TOGETHER
YSHEND Spenserian form of > SHEND
YSHENDING > YSHEND
YSHENDS > YSHEND
YSHENT > YSHEND
YSLAKED archaic past participle of > SLAKE
YTOST archaic past participle of > TOSS
YTTERBIA n colourless hygroscopic substance used in certain alloys and ceramics

YTTERBIAS > YTTERBIA
YTTERBIC > YTTERBIUM
YTTERBITE n rare mineral
YTTERBIUM n soft silvery element
YTTERBOUS > YTTERBIUM
YTTRIA n insoluble solid used mainly in incandescent mantles
YTTRIAS > YTTRIA
YTTRIC > YTTRIUM
YTTRIOUS > YTTRIUM
YTTRIUM n silvery metallic element used in various alloys
YTTRIUMS > YTTRIUM
YU n jade
YUAN n standard monetary unit of the People's Republic of China
YUANS > YUAN
YUCA same as > YUCCA
YUCAS > YUCA
YUCCA n tropical plant with spikes of white leaves
YUCCAS > YUCCA
YUCCH interj expression of disgust
YUCH interj expression of disgust
YUCK interj exclamation indicating contempt, dislike, or disgust ▷ vb chuckle
YUCKED > YUCK
YUCKER > YUCK
YUCKERS > YUCK
YUCKIER > YUCKY
YUCKIEST > YUCKY
YUCKINESS > YUCKY
YUCKING > YUCK
YUCKO adj disgusting ▷ interj exclamation of disgust
YUCKS > YUCK
YUCKY adj disgusting, nasty
YUFT n Russia leather
YUFTS > YUFT
YUG same as > YUGA
YUGA n (in Hindu

cosmology) one of the four ages of mankind
YUGARIE variant spelling of > EUGARIE
YUGARIES > YUGARIE
YUGAS > YUGA
YUGS > YUG
YUK same as > YUCK
YUKATA n light kimono
YUKATAS > YUKATA
YUKE vb itch
YUKED > YUKE
YUKES > YUKE
YUKIER > YUKY
YUKIEST > YUKY
YUKING > YUKE
YUKKED > YUK
YUKKIER > YUKKY
YUKKIEST > YUKKY
YUKKING > YUK
YUKKY same as > YUCKY
YUKO n score of five points in judo
YUKOS > YUKO
YUKS > YUK
YUKY adj itchy
YULAN n Chinese magnolia often cultivated for its showy white flowers
YULANS > YULAN
YULE n Christmas, the Christmas season, or Christmas festivities
YULES > YULE
YULETIDE n Christmas season
YULETIDES > YULETIDE
YUM interj expression of delight
YUMMIER > YUMMY
YUMMIES > YUMMY
YUMMIEST > YUMMY
YUMMINESS > YUMMY
YUMMO adj tasty ▷ interj exclamation of delight or approval
YUMMY adj delicious ▷ interj exclamation indicating pleasure or delight, as in anticipation of delicious food ▷ n delicious food item

YUMP vb leave the ground when driving over a ridge
YUMPED > YUMP
YUMPIE n young upwardly mobile person
YUMPIES > YUMPIE
YUMPING > YUMP
YUMPS > YUMP
YUNX n wryneck
YUNXES > YUNX
YUP n informal affirmative statement
YUPON same as > YAUPON
YUPONS > YUPON
YUPPIE n young highly-paid professional person, esp one who has a materialistic way of life ▷ adj typical of or reflecting the values of yuppies
YUPPIEDOM > YUPPIE
YUPPIEISH > YUPPIE
YUPPIES > YUPPY
YUPPIFIED > YUPPIFY
YUPPIFIES > YUPPIFY
YUPPIFY vb make yuppie in nature
YUPPY same as > YUPPIE
YUPS > YUP
YUPSTER > YINDIE
YUPSTERS > YUPSTER
YURT n circular tent consisting of a framework of poles covered with felt or skins, used by Mongolian and Turkic nomads of E and central Asia
YURTA same as > YURT
YURTAS > YURT
YURTS > YURT
YUS > YU
YUTZ n Yiddish word meaning fool
YUTZES > YUTZ
YUZU n type of citrus fruit
YUZUS > YUZU
YWIS adv certainly
YWROKE archaic past participle of > WREAK

Zz

ZA n pizza
ZABAIONE n light foamy dessert
ZABAIONES > ZABAIONE
ZABAJONE same as > ZABAIONE
ZABAJONES > ZABAJONE
ZABETA n tariff
ZABETAS > ZABETA
ZABRA n small sailing vessel
ZABRAS > ZABRA
ZABTIEH n Turkish police officer
ZABTIEHS > ZABTIEH
ZACATON n coarse grass
ZACATONS > ZACATON
ZACK n Australian five-cent piece
ZACKS > ZACK
ZADDICK adj righteous
ZADDIK n Hasidic Jewish leader
ZADDIKIM > ZADDIK
ZADDIKS > ZADDIK
ZAFFAR same as > ZAFFER
ZAFFARS > ZAFFAR
ZAFFER n impure cobalt oxide, used to impart a blue colour to enamels
ZAFFERS > ZAFFER
ZAFFIR same as > ZAFFER
ZAFFIRS > ZAFFIR
ZAFFRE same as > ZAFFER
ZAFFRES > ZAFFRE
ZAFTIG adj ripe or curvaceous
ZAG vb change direction sharply
ZAGGED > ZAG
ZAGGING > ZAG
ZAGS > ZAG
ZAIBATSU n group or combine comprising a few wealthy families that controls industry, business, and finance in Japan
ZAIKAI n Japanese business community
ZAIKAIS > ZAIKAI
ZAIRE n currency used in the former Zaïre
ZAIRES > ZAIRE
ZAITECH n investment in financial markets by a company to supplement its main income
ZAITECHS > ZAITECH
ZAKAT n annual tax on Muslims to aid the poor in the Muslim community
ZAKATS > ZAKAT

ZAKOUSKA > ZAKOUSKI
ZAKOUSKI same as > ZAKUSKI
ZAKUSKA > ZAKUSKI
ZAKUSKI npl hors d'oeuvres, consisting of tiny open sandwiches spread with caviar, smoked sausage, etc
ZAMAN n tropical tree
ZAMANG same as > ZAMAN
ZAMANGS > ZAMANG
ZAMANS > ZAMAN
ZAMARRA n sheepskin coat
ZAMARRAS > ZAMARRA
ZAMARRO same as > ZAMARRA
ZAMARROS > ZAMARRO
ZAMBO n offensive word for a Black person
ZAMBOMBA n drum-like musical instrument
ZAMBOMBAS > ZAMBOMBA
ZAMBOORAK n small swivel-mounted cannon
ZAMBOS > ZAMBO
ZAMBUCK n St John ambulance attendant, esp at a sports meeting
ZAMBUCKS > ZAMBUCK
ZAMBUK same as > ZAMBUCK
ZAMBUKS > ZAMBUK
ZAMIA n type of plant of tropical and subtropical America, with a short thick trunk, palmlike leaves, and short stout cones
ZAMIAS > ZAMIA
ZAMINDAR n (in India) the owner of an agricultural estate
ZAMINDARI n (in India) a large agricultural estate
ZAMINDARS > ZAMINDAR
ZAMINDARY same as > ZAMINDARI
ZAMOUSE n West African buffalo
ZAMOUSES > ZAMOUSE
ZAMPOGNA n Italian bagpipes
ZAMPOGNAS > ZAMPOGNA
ZAMPONE n sausage made from pig's trotters
ZAMPONI > ZAMPONE
ZAMZAWED adj (of tea) having been left in the pot to stew
ZANAMIVIR n drug used to treat influenza

ZANANA same as > ZENANA
ZANANAS > ZANANA
ZANDER n European freshwater pikeperch, valued as a food fish
ZANDERS > ZANDER
ZANELLA n twill fabric
ZANELLAS > ZANELLA
ZANIED > ZANY
ZANIER > ZANY
ZANIES > ZANY
ZANIEST > ZANY
ZANILY > ZANY
ZANINESS > ZANY
ZANJA n irrigation canal
ZANJAS > ZANJA
ZANJERO n irrigation supervisor
ZANJEROS > ZANJERO
ZANTE n type of wood
ZANTES > ZANTE
ZANTHOXYL variant spelling of > XANTHOXYL
ZANY adj comical in an endearing way ▷ n clown or buffoon, esp one in old comedies who imitated other performers with ludicrous effect ▷ vb clown
ZANYING > ZANY
ZANYISH > ZANY
ZANYISM > ZANY
ZANYISMS > ZANY
ZANZA same as > ZANZE
ZANZAS > ZANZA
ZANZE n African musical instrument
ZANZES > ZANZE
ZAP vb kill (by shooting) ▷ n energy, vigour, or pep ▷ interj exclamation used to express sudden or swift action
ZAPATA adj (of a moustache) drooping
ZAPATEADO n Spanish dance with stamping and very fast footwork
ZAPATEO n Cuban folk dance
ZAPATEOS > ZAPATEO
ZAPOTILLA n shoe
ZAPPED > ZAP
ZAPPER n remote control for a television etc
ZAPPERS > ZAPPER
ZAPPIER > ZAPPY
ZAPPIEST > ZAPPY
ZAPPING > ZAP
ZAPPY adj energetic
ZAPS > ZAP

ZAPTIAH same as > ZAPTIEH
ZAPTIAHS > ZAPTIAH
ZAPTIEH n Turkish police officer
ZAPTIEHS > ZAPTIEH
ZARAPE n blanket-like shawl
ZARAPES > ZARAPE
ZARATITE n green amorphous mineral
ZARATITES > ZARATITE
ZAREBA n stockade or enclosure of thorn bushes around a village or campsite
ZAREBAS > ZAREBA
ZAREEBA same as > ZAREBA
ZAREEBAS > ZAREEBA
ZARF n (esp in the Middle East) a holder, usually ornamental, for a hot coffee cup
ZARFS > ZARF
ZARI n thread made from fine gold or silver wire
ZARIBA same as > ZAREBA
ZARIBAS > ZARIBA
ZARIS > ZARI
ZARNEC n sulphide of arsenic
ZARNECS > ZARNEC
ZARNICH same as > ZARNEC
ZARNICHS > ZARNICH
ZARZUELA n type of Spanish vaudeville or operetta, usually satirical in nature
ZARZUELAS > ZARZUELA
ZAS > ZA
ZASTRUGA variant spelling of > SASTRUGA
ZASTRUGI > ZASTRUGA
ZATI n type of macaque
ZATIS > ZATI
ZAX variant of > SAX
ZAXES > ZAX
ZAYIN n seventh letter of the Hebrew alphabet
ZAYINS > ZAYIN
ZAZEN n (in Zen Buddhism) deep meditation undertaken whilst sitting upright with legs crossed
ZAZENS > ZAZEN
ZEA n corn silk
ZEAL n great enthusiasm or eagerness

ZEALANT *archaic variant of* > ZEALOT
ZEALANTS > ZEALANT
ZEALFUL > ZEAL
ZEALLESS > ZEAL
ZEALOT *n* fanatic or extreme enthusiast
ZEALOTISM > ZEALOT
ZEALOTRY *n* extreme or excessive zeal or devotion
ZEALOTS > ZEALOT
ZEALOUS *adj* extremely eager or enthusiastic
ZEALOUSLY > ZEALOUS
ZEALS > ZEAL
ZEAS > ZEAL
ZEATIN *n* cytokinin derived from corn
ZEATINS > ZEATIN
ZEBEC *variant spelling of* > XEBEC
ZEBECK *same as* > ZEBEC
ZEBECKS > ZEBECK
ZEBECS > ZEBEC
ZEBRA *n* black-and-white striped African animal of the horse family
ZEBRAFISH *n* striped tropical fish
ZEBRAIC *adj* like a zebra
ZEBRANO *n* type of striped wood
ZEBRANOS > ZEBRANO
ZEBRAS > ZEBRA
ZEBRASS *n* offspring of a male zebra and a female ass
ZEBRASSES > ZEBRASS
ZEBRAWOOD *n* tree yielding striped hardwood used in cabinetwork
ZEBRINA *n* trailing herbaceous plant
ZEBRINAS > ZEBRINA
ZEBRINE > ZEBRA
ZEBRINES > ZEBRA
ZEBRINNY *n* offspring of a male horse and a female zebra
ZEBROID > ZEBRA
ZEBRULA *n* offspring of a male zebra and a female horse
ZEBRULAS > ZEBRULA
ZEBRULE *same as* > ZEBRULA
ZEBRULES > ZEBRULE
ZEBU *n* Asian ox with a humped back and long horns
ZEBUB *n* large African fly
ZEBUBS > ZEBUB
ZEBUS > ZEBU
ZECCHIN *same as* > ZECCHINO
ZECCHINE *same as* > ZECCHINO
ZECCHINES > ZECCHINE
ZECCHINI > ZECCHINO
ZECCHINO *n* former gold coin
ZECCHINOS > ZECCHINO
ZECCHINS > ZECCHIN
ZECHIN *same as* > ZECCHINO

ZECHINS > ZECHIN
ZED *n* British and New Zealand spoken form of the letter *z*
ZEDOARIES > ZEDOARY
ZEDOARY *n* dried rhizome of a tropical Asian plant, used as a stimulant and a condiment
ZEDS > ZED
ZEE *the US word for* > ZED
ZEES > ZEE
ZEIN *n* protein occurring in maize and used in the manufacture of plastics
ZEINS > ZEIN
ZEITGEBER *n* agent or event that sets or resets the biological clock
ZEITGEIST *n* spirit or attitude of a specific time or period
ZEK *n* Soviet prisoner
ZEKS > ZEK
ZEL *n* Turkish cymbal
ZELANT *alternative form of* > ZEALANT
ZELANTS > ZELANT
ZELATOR *same as* > ZELATRIX
ZELATORS > ZELATOR
ZELATRICE *same as* > ZELATRIX
ZELATRIX *n* nun who monitors the behaviour of younger nuns
ZELKOVA *n* type of elm tree
ZELKOVAS > ZELKOVA
ZELOSO *adv* with zeal
ZELOTYPIA *n* morbid zeal
ZELS > ZEL
ZEMINDAR *same as* > ZAMINDAR
ZEMINDARI > ZEMINDAR
ZEMINDARS > ZEMINDAR
ZEMINDARY *n* jurisdiction of a zemindar
ZEMSTVA > ZEMSTVO
ZEMSTVO *n* (in tsarist Russia) an elective provincial or district council established in most provinces of Russia by Alexander II in 1864 as part of his reform policy
ZEMSTVOS > ZEMSTVO
ZENAIDA *n* dove
ZENAIDAS > ZENAIDA
ZENANA *n* (in the East, esp in Muslim and Hindu homes) part of a house reserved for the women and girls of a household
ZENANAS > ZENANA
ZENDIK *n* unbeliever or heretic
ZENDIKS > ZENDIK
ZENITH *n* highest point of success or power
ZENITHAL > ZENITH
ZENITHS > ZENITH
ZEOLITE *n* any of a large group of glassy secondary minerals
ZEOLITES > ZEOLITE

ZEOLITIC > ZEOLITE
ZEP *n* type of long sandwich
ZEPHYR *n* soft gentle breeze
ZEPHYRS > ZEPHYR
ZEPPELIN *n* large cylindrical airship
ZEPPELINS > ZEPPELIN
ZEPPOLE *n* Italian fritter
ZEPPOLES > ZEPPOLE
ZEPPOLI > ZEPPOLE
ZEPS > ZEP
ZERDA *n* fennec
ZERDAS > ZERDA
ZEREBA *same as* > ZAREBA
ZEREBAS > ZEREBA
ZERIBA *same as* > ZAREBA
ZERIBAS > ZERIBA
ZERK *n* grease fitting
ZERKS > ZERK
ZERO *n* (symbol representing) the number o ▷ *adj* having no measurable quantity or size ▷ *vb* adjust (an instrument or scale) so as to read zero ▷ *det* no (thing) at all
ZEROED > ZERO
ZEROES > ZERO
ZEROING > ZERO
ZEROS > ZERO
ZEROTH *adj* denoting a term in a series that precedes the term otherwise regarded as the first term
ZERUMBET *n* plant stem used as stimulant and condiment
ZERUMBETS > ZERUMBET
ZEST *n* enjoyment or excitement ▷ *vb* give flavour, interest, or piquancy to
ZESTED > ZEST
ZESTER *n* kitchen utensil used to scrape fine shreds of peel from citrus fruits
ZESTERS > ZESTER
ZESTFUL > ZEST
ZESTFULLY > ZEST
ZESTIER > ZEST
ZESTIEST > ZEST
ZESTILY > ZEST
ZESTING > ZEST
ZESTLESS > ZEST
ZESTS > ZEST
ZESTY > ZEST
ZETA *n* sixth letter in the Greek alphabet, a consonant, transliterated as *z*
ZETAS > ZETA
ZETETIC *adj* proceeding by inquiry ▷ *n* investigation
ZETETICS > ZETETIC
ZETTABYTE *n* 10^{21} or 2^{70} bytes
ZEUGMA *n* figure of speech in which a word is used to modify or govern two or more words although appropriate to only one of them or making a different sense with each

ZEUGMAS > ZEUGMA
ZEUGMATIC > ZEUGMA
ZEUXITE *n* ferriferous mineral
ZEUXITES > ZEUXITE
ZEX *n* tool for cutting roofing slate
ZEXES > ZEX
ZEZE *n* stringed musical instrument
ZEZES > ZEZE
ZHO *same as* > ZO
ZHOMO *n* female zho
ZHOMOS > ZHOMO
ZHOS > ZHO
ZIBELINE *n* sable or the fur of this animal ▷ *adj* of, relating to, or resembling a sable
ZIBELINES > ZIBELINE
ZIBELLINE *same as* > ZIBELINE
ZIBET *n* large civet of S and SE Asia, having tawny fur marked with black spots and stripes
ZIBETH *same as* > ZIBET
ZIBETHS > ZIBETH
ZIBETS > ZIBET
ZIFF *n* beard
ZIFFIUS *n* sea monster
ZIFFIUSES > ZIFFIUS
ZIFFS > ZIFF
ZIG *same as* > ZAG
ZIGAN *n* gypsy
ZIGANKA *n* Russian dance
ZIGANKAS > ZIGANKA
ZIGANS > ZIGAN
ZIGGED > ZIG
ZIGGING > ZIG
ZIGGURAT *n* (in ancient Mesopotamia) a temple in the shape of a pyramid
ZIGGURATS > ZIGGURAT
ZIGS > ZIG
ZIGZAG *n* line or course having sharp turns in alternating directions ▷ *vb* move in a zigzag ▷ *adj* formed in or proceeding in a zigzag ▷ *adv* in a zigzag manner
ZIGZAGGED > ZIGZAG
ZIGZAGGER > ZIGZAG
ZIGZAGGY > ZIGZAG
ZIGZAGS > ZIGZAG
ZIKKURAT *same as* > ZIGGURAT
ZIKKURATS > ZIKKURAT
ZIKURAT *same as* > ZIGGURAT
ZIKURATS > ZIKURAT
ZILA *n* administrative district in India
ZILAS > ZILA
ZILCH *n* nothing
ZILCHES > ZILCH
ZILL *n* finger cymbal
ZILLA *same as* > ZILA
ZILLAH *same as* > ZILA
ZILLAHS > ZILLAH
ZILLAS > ZILLA
ZILLION *n* extremely large but unspecified number**

Z

ZILLIONS > ZILLION
ZILLIONTH > ZILLION
ZILLS > ZILL
ZIMB *same as* **>** ZEBUB
ZIMBI *n* cowrie shell used as money
ZIMBIS > ZIMBI
ZIMBS > ZIMB
ZIMOCCA *n* bath sponge
ZIMOCCAS > ZIMOCCA
ZIN *short form of* **>** ZINFANDEL
ZINC *n* bluish-white metallic element used in alloys and to coat metal ▷ *vb* coat with zinc
ZINCATE *n* any of a class of salts derived from the amphoteric hydroxide of zinc
ZINCATES > ZINCATE
ZINCED > ZINC
ZINCIC > ZINC
ZINCIER > ZINC
ZINCIEST > ZINC
ZINCIFIED > ZINCIFY
ZINCIFIES > ZINCIFY
ZINCIFY *vb* coat with zinc
ZINCING > ZINC
ZINCITE *n* red or yellow mineral consisting of zinc oxide in hexagonal crystalline form
ZINCITES > ZINCITE
ZINCKED > ZINC
ZINCKIER > ZINC
ZINCKIEST > ZINC
ZINCKIFY *same as* **>** ZINCIFY
ZINCKING > ZINC
ZINCKY > ZINC
ZINCO *n* printing plate made from zincography
ZINCODE *n* positive electrode
ZINCODES > ZINCODE
ZINCOID > ZINC
ZINCOS > ZINCO
ZINCOUS > ZINC
ZINCS > ZINC
ZINCY > ZINC
ZINDABAD *interj* long live: used as part of a slogan in India, Pakistan, etc
ZINE *n* magazine or fanzine
ZINEB *n* organic insecticide
ZINEBS > ZINEB
ZINES > ZINE
ZINFANDEL *n* type of Californian wine
ZING *n* quality in something that makes it lively or interesting ▷ *vb* make or move with or as if with a high-pitched buzzing sound
ZINGANI > ZINGANO
ZINGANO *n* gypsy
ZINGARA *same as* **>** ZINGARO
ZINGARE > ZINGARA
ZINGARI > ZINGARO
ZINGARO *n* Italian Gypsy
ZINGED > ZING

ZINGEL *n* small freshwater perch
ZINGELS > ZINGEL
ZINGER > ZING
ZINGERS > ZING
ZINGIBER *n* ginger plant
ZINGIBERS > ZINGIBER
ZINGIER > ZINGY
ZINGIEST > ZINGY
ZINGING > ZING
ZINGS > ZING
ZINGY *adj* vibrant
ZINKE *n* cornett
ZINKED > ZINC
ZINKENITE *n* steel-grey metallic mineral consisting of a sulphide of lead and antimony
ZINKES > ZINKE
ZINKIER > ZINC
ZINKIEST > ZINC
ZINKIFIED > ZINCIFY
ZINKIFIES > ZINKIFY
ZINKIFY *vb* coat with zinc
ZINKING > ZINC
ZINKY > ZINC
ZINNIA *n* plant of tropical and subtropical America, with solitary heads of brightly coloured flowers
ZINNIAS > ZINNIA
ZINS > ZIN
ZIP *same as* **>** ZIPPER
ZIPLESS > ZIP
ZIPLOCK *adj* fastened with interlocking plastic strips ▷ *vb* seal (a ziplock storage bag)
ZIPLOCKED > ZIPLOCK
ZIPLOCKS > ZIPLOCK
ZIPPED > ZIP
ZIPPER *n* fastening device operating by means of two parallel rows of metal or plastic teeth on either side of a closure that are interlocked by a sliding tab ▷ *vb* fasten with a zipper
ZIPPERED *adj* provided or fastened with a zip
ZIPPERING > ZIPPER
ZIPPERS > ZIPPER
ZIPPIER > ZIPPY
ZIPPIEST > ZIPPY
ZIPPING > ZIP
ZIPPO *n* nothing
ZIPPOS > ZIPPO
ZIPPY *adj* full of energy
ZIPS > ZIP
ZIPTOP *adj* (of a bag) closed with a zip
ZIRAM *n* industrial fungicide
ZIRAMS > ZIRAM
ZIRCALLOY *n* alloy of zirconium containing small amounts of tin, chromium, and nickel. It is used in pressurized-water reactors
ZIRCALOY *same as* **>** ZIRCALLOY
ZIRCALOYS > ZIRCALOY
ZIRCON *n* mineral used as a gemstone and in industry

ZIRCONIA *n* white oxide of zirconium, used as a pigment for paints, a catalyst, and an abrasive
ZIRCONIAS > ZIRCONIA
ZIRCONIC > ZIRCONIUM
ZIRCONIUM *n* greyish-white metallic element that is resistant to corrosion
ZIRCONS > ZIRCON
ZIT *n* spot or pimple
ZITE *same as* **>** ZITI
ZITHER *n* musical instrument consisting of strings stretched over a flat box and plucked to produce musical notes
ZITHERIST > ZITHER
ZITHERN *same as* **>** ZITHER
ZITHERNS > ZITHERN
ZITHERS > ZITHER
ZITI *n* type of pasta
ZITIS > ZITI
ZITS > ZIT
ZIZ *same as* **>** ZIZZ
ZIZANIA *n* aquatic grass
ZIZANIAS > ZIZANIA
ZIZEL *n* chipmunk
ZIZELS > ZIZEL
ZIZIT *same as* **>** ZIZITH
ZIZITH *variant spelling of* **>** TSITSITH
ZIZYPHUS *n* jubejube tree
ZIZZ *n* short sleep ▷ *vb* take a short sleep, snooze
ZIZZED > ZIZZ
ZIZZES > ZIZZ
ZIZZING > ZIZZ
ZIZZLE *vb* sizzle
ZIZZLED > ZIZZLE
ZIZZLES > ZIZZLE
ZIZZLING > ZIZZLE
ZLOTE > ZLOTY
ZLOTIES > ZLOTY
ZLOTY *n* monetary unit of Poland
ZLOTYCH *same as* **>** ZLOTY
ZLOTYS > ZLOTY
ZO *n* Tibetan breed of cattle, developed by crossing the yak with common cattle
ZOA > ZOON
ZOAEA *same as* **>** ZOEA
ZOAEAE > ZOAEA
ZOAEAS > ZOAEA
ZOARIA > ZOARIUM
ZOARIAL > ZOARIUM
ZOARIUM *n* colony of zooids
ZOBO *same as* **>** ZO
ZOBOS > ZOBO
ZOBU *same as* **>** ZO
ZOBUS > ZOBU
ZOCALO *n* plaza in Mexico
ZOCALOS > ZOCALO
ZOCCO *n* plinth
ZOCCOLO *same as* **>** ZOCCO
ZOCCOLOS > ZOCCOLO
ZOCCOS > ZOCCO
ZODIAC *n* imaginary belt in the sky within which the sun, moon, and planets

appear to move, divided into twelve equal areas, called signs of the zodiac, each named after a constellation
ZODIACAL > ZODIAC
ZODIACS > ZODIAC
ZOEA *n* free-swimming larva of a crab or related crustacean, which has well-developed abdominal appendages and may bear one or more spines
ZOEAE > ZOEA
ZOEAL > ZOEA
ZOEAS > ZOAEA
ZOECHROME *same as* **>** ZOETROPE
ZOECIA > ZOECIUM
ZOECIUM *same as* **>** ZOOECIUM
ZOEFORM > ZOEA
ZOETIC *adj* pertaining to life
ZOETROPE *n* cylinder-shaped toy with a sequence of pictures on its inner surface which, when viewed through the vertical slits spaced regularly around it while the toy is rotated, produce an illusion of animation
ZOETROPES > ZOETROPE
ZOETROPIC > ZOETROPE
ZOFTIG *adj* ripe or curvaceous
ZOIATRIA *n* veterinary surgery
ZOIATRIAS > ZOIATRIA
ZOIATRICS *n* veterinary surgery
ZOIC *adj* relating to or having animal life
ZOISITE *n* grey, brown, or pink mineral
ZOISITES > ZOISITE
ZOISM *n* belief in magical animal powers
ZOISMS > ZOISM
ZOIST > ZOISM
ZOISTS > ZOISM
ZOL *n* South African slang for a cannabis cigarette
ZOLPIDEM *n* drug used to treat insomnia
ZOLPIDEMS > ZOLPIDEM
ZOLS > ZOL
ZOMBI *same as* **>** ZOMBIE
ZOMBIE *n* person who appears to be lifeless, apathetic, or totally lacking in independent judgment
ZOMBIES > ZOMBIE
ZOMBIFIED > ZOMBIFY
ZOMBIFIES > ZOMBIFY
ZOMBIFY *vb* turn into a zombie
ZOMBIISM > ZOMBIE
ZOMBIISMS > ZOMBIE
ZOMBIS > ZOMBI
ZOMBORUK *n* small swivel-mounted cannon
ZOMBORUKS > ZOMBORUK
ZONA *n* zone or belt

Z

ZONAE > ZONA

ZONAL *adj* of, relating to, or of the nature of a zone

ZONALLY > ZONAL

ZONARY *same as* > ZONAL

ZONATE *adj* marked with, divided into, or arranged in zones

ZONATED *same as* > ZONATE

ZONATION *n* arrangement in zones

ZONATIONS > ZONATION

ZONDA *n* South American wind

ZONDAS > ZONDA

ZONE *n* area with particular features or properties ▷ *vb* divide into zones

ZONED > ZONE

ZONELESS > ZONE

ZONER *n* something which divides other things into zones

ZONERS > ZONER

ZONES > ZONE

ZONETIME *n* standard time of the time zone in which a ship is located at sea, each zone extending 7½° to each side of a meridian

ZONETIMES > ZONETIME

ZONING > ZONE

ZONINGS > ZONE

ZONK *vb* strike resoundingly

ZONKED *adj* highly intoxicated with drugs or alcohol

ZONKING > ZONK

ZONKS > ZONK

ZONOID *adj* resembling a zone

ZONULA *n* small zone or belt

ZONULAE > ZONULA

ZONULAR > ZONULE

ZONULAS > ZONULA

ZONULE *n* small zone, band, or area

ZONULES > ZONULE

ZONULET *n* small belt

ZONULETS > ZONULET

ZONURE *n* lizard with ringed tail

ZONURES > ZONURE

ZOO *n* place where live animals are kept for show

ZOOBIOTIC *adj* parasitic on or living in association with an animal

ZOOBLAST *n* animal cell

ZOOBLASTS > ZOOBLAST

ZOOCHORE *n* plant with the spores or seeds dispersed by animals

ZOOCHORES > ZOOCHORE

ZOOCHORY > ZOOCHORE

ZOOCYTIA > ZOOCYTIUM

ZOOCYTIUM *n* outer sheath of some social infusorians

ZOOEA *same as* > ZOEA

ZOOEAE > ZOOEA

ZOOEAL > ZOOEA

ZOOEAS > ZOOEA

ZOOECIA > ZOOECIUM

ZOOECIUM *n* part of a polyzoan colony that houses the feeding zooids

ZOOEY > ZOO

ZOOGAMETE *n* gamete that can move independently

ZOOGAMIES > ZOOGAMY

ZOOGAMOUS > ZOOGAMY

ZOOGAMY *n* sexual reproduction in animals

ZOOGENIC *adj* produced from animals

ZOOGENIES > ZOOGENY

ZOOGENOUS *same as* > ZOOGENIC

ZOOGENY *n* doctrine of formation of animals

ZOOGLEA *same as* > ZOOGLOEA

ZOOGLEAE > ZOOGLEA

ZOOGLEAL > ZOOGLEA

ZOOGLEAS > ZOOGLEA

ZOOGLOEA *n* mass of bacteria adhering together by a jelly-like substance derived from their cell walls

ZOOGLOEAE > ZOOGLOEA

ZOOGLOEAL > ZOOGLOEA

ZOOGLOEAS > ZOOGLOEA

ZOOGLOEIC > ZOOGLOEA

ZOOGONIES > ZOOGONY

ZOOGONOUS > ZOOGONY

ZOOGONY *same as* > ZOOGENY

ZOOGRAFT *n* animal tissue grafted onto a human body

ZOOGRAFTS > ZOOGRAFT

ZOOGRAPHY *n* branch of zoology concerned with the description of animals

ZOOID *n* any independent animal body, such as an individual of a coral colony

ZOOIDAL > ZOOID

ZOOIDS > ZOOID

ZOOIER > ZOO

ZOOIEST > ZOO

ZOOKEEPER *n* person who cares for animals in a zoo

ZOOKS *short form of* > GADZOOKS

ZOOLATER > ZOOLATRY

ZOOLATERS > ZOOLATRY

ZOOLATRIA *same as* > ZOOLATRY

ZOOLATRY *n* (esp in ancient or primitive religions) the worship of animals as the incarnations of certain deities, symbols of particular qualities or natural forces, etc

ZOOLITE *n* fossilized animal

ZOOLITES > ZOOLITE

ZOOLITH *n* fossilized animal

ZOOLITHIC > ZOOLITH

ZOOLITHS > ZOOLITH

ZOOLITIC > ZOOLITE

ZOOLOGIC > ZOOLOGY

ZOOLOGIES > ZOOLOGY

ZOOLOGIST > ZOOLOGY

ZOOLOGY *n* study of animals

ZOOM *vb* move or rise very rapidly ▷ *n* sound or act of zooming

ZOOMANCY *n* divination through observing the actions of animals

ZOOMANIA *n* extreme or excessive devotion to animals

ZOOMANIAS > ZOOMANIA

ZOOMANTIC > ZOOMANCY

ZOOMED > ZOOM

ZOOMETRIC > ZOOMETRY

ZOOMETRY *n* branch of zoology concerned with the relative length or size of the different parts of an animal or animals

ZOOMING > ZOOM

ZOOMORPH *n* representation of an animal form

ZOOMORPHS > ZOOMORPH

ZOOMORPHY > ZOOMORPH

ZOOMS > ZOOM

ZOON *same as* > ZOOM

ZOONAL > ZOON

ZOONED > ZOON

ZOONIC *adj* concerning animals

ZOONING > ZOON

ZOONITE *n* segment of an articulated animal

ZOONITES > ZOONITE

ZOONITIC > ZOONITE

ZOONOMIA *same as* > ZOONOMY

ZOONOMIAS > ZOONOMIA

ZOONOMIC > ZOONOMY

ZOONOMIES > ZOONOMY

ZOONOMIST > ZOONOMY

ZOONOMY *n* science of animal life

ZOONOSES > ZOONOSIS

ZOONOSIS *n* any infection or disease that is transmitted to man from lower vertebrates

ZOONOTIC > ZOONOSIS

ZOONS > ZOON

ZOOPATHY *n* science of animal diseases

ZOOPERAL > ZOOPERY

ZOOPERIES > ZOOPERY

ZOOPERIST > ZOOPERY

ZOOPERY *n* experimentation on animals

ZOOPHAGAN *n* carnivore

ZOOPHAGY *n* eating other animals

ZOOPHILE *n* person who is devoted to animals and their protection from practices such as vivisection

ZOOPHILES > ZOOPHILE

ZOOPHILIA *n* morbid condition in which a person has a sexual attraction to animals

ZOOPHILIC > ZOOPHILE

ZOOPHILY *same as* > ZOOPHILIA

ZOOPHOBE > ZOOPHOBIA

ZOOPHOBES > ZOOPHOBIA

ZOOPHOBIA *n* unusual or morbid dread of animals

ZOOPHORI > ZOOPHORUS

ZOOPHORIC > ZOOPHORUS

ZOOPHORUS *n* frieze with animal figures

ZOOPHYTE *n* any animal resembling a plant, such as a sea anemone

ZOOPHYTES > ZOOPHYTE

ZOOPHYTIC > ZOOPHYTE

ZOOPLASTY *n* surgical transplantation to man of animal tissues

ZOOS > ZOO

ZOOSCOPIC > ZOOSCOPY

ZOOSCOPY *n* condition causing hallucinations of animals

ZOOSPERM *n* any of the male reproductive cells released in the semen during ejaculation

ZOOSPERMS > ZOOSPERM

ZOOSPORE *n* asexual spore of some algae and fungi that moves by means of flagella

ZOOSPORES > ZOOSPORE

ZOOSPORIC > ZOOSPORE

ZOOSTEROL *n* any of a group of animal sterols, such as cholesterol

ZOOT *as in* *zoot suit* man's suit consisting of baggy trousers with tapered bottoms and a long jacket with wide padded shoulders

ZOOTAXIES > ZOOTAXY

ZOOTAXY *n* science of the classification of animals

ZOOTECHNY *n* science of breeding animals

ZOOTHECIA *n* outer layers of certain protozoans

ZOOTHEISM *n* treatment of an animal as a god

ZOOTHOME *n* group of zooids

ZOOTHOMES > ZOOTHOME

ZOOTIER > ZOOTY

ZOOTIEST > ZOOTY

ZOOTOMIC > ZOOTOMY

ZOOTOMIES > ZOOTOMY

ZOOTOMIST > ZOOTOMY

ZOOTOMY *n* branch of zoology concerned with the dissection and anatomy of animals

ZOOTOXIC > ZOOTOXIN

ZOOTOXIN *n* toxin, such as snake venom, that is produced by an animal

ZOOTOXINS > ZOOTOXIN

ZOOTROPE *same as* > ZOETROPE

ZOOTROPES > ZOOTROPE

ZOOTROPHY n nourishment of animals

ZOOTY adj showy

ZOOTYPE n animal figure used as a symbol

ZOOTYPES > ZOOTYPE

ZOOTYPIC > ZOOTYPE

ZOOZOO n wood pigeon

ZOOZOOS > ZOOZOO

ZOPILOTE n small American vulture

ZOPILOTES > ZOPILOTE

ZOPPA adj syncopated

ZOPPO same as > ZOPPA

ZORBING n activity of travelling downhill inside a large air-cushioned hollow ball

ZORBINGS > ZORBING

ZORBONAUT n person who engages in the activity of zorbing

ZORGITE n copper-lead selenide

ZORGITES > ZORGITE

ZORI n Japanese sandal

ZORIL same as > ZORILLA

ZORILLA n skunk-like African musteline mammal having a long black-and-white coat

ZORILLAS > ZORILLA

ZORILLE same as > ZORILLA

ZORILLES > ZORILLE

ZORILLO same as > ZORILLE

ZORILLOS > ZORILLO

ZORILS > ZORIL

ZORINO n skunk fur

ZORINOS > ZORINO

ZORIS > ZORI

ZORRO n hoary fox

ZORROS > ZORRO

ZOS > ZO

ZOSTER n shingles; herpes zoster

ZOSTERS > ZOSTER

ZOUAVE n (formerly) member of a body of French infantry composed of Algerian recruits

ZOUAVES > ZOUAVE

ZOUK n style of dance music that combines African and Latin American rhythms and uses electronic instruments and modern studio technology

ZOUKS > ZOUK

ZOUNDS interj mild oath indicating surprise or indignation

ZOWIE interj expression of pleasurable surprise

ZOYSIA n type of grass with short stiffly pointed leaves, often used for lawns

ZOYSIAS > ZOYSIA

ZUCCHETTI > ZUCCHETTO

ZUCCHETTO n small round skullcap worn by clergymen and varying in colour according to the rank of the wearer

ZUCCHINI n courgette

ZUCCHINIS > ZUCCHINI

ZUCHETTA same as > ZUCCHETTO

ZUCHETTAS > ZUCHETTA

ZUCHETTO same as > ZUCCHETTO

ZUCHETTOS > ZUCHETTO

ZUFFOLI > ZUFFOLO

ZUFFOLO same as > ZUFOLO

ZUFOLI > ZUFOLO

ZUFOLO n small flute

ZUGZWANG n (in chess) position in which one player can move only with loss or severe disadvantage ▷ vb manoeuvre (one's opponent) into a zugzwang

ZUGZWANGS > ZUGZWANG

ZULU n (in the NATO phonetic alphabet) used to represent z

ZULUS > ZULU

ZUMBOORUK n small swivel-mounted cannon

ZUPA n confederation of Serbian villages

ZUPAN n head of a zupa

ZUPANS > ZUPAN

ZUPAS > ZUPA

ZURF same as > ZARF

ZURFS > ZURF

ZUZ n ancient Hebrew silver coin

ZUZIM > ZUZ

ZUZZIM > ZUZ

ZWANZIGER n silver coin formerly used in Southern Germany and Austria until the end of the 19th century

ZWIEBACK n small type of rusk, which has been baked first as a loaf, then sliced and toasted, usually bought ready-made

ZWIEBACKS > ZWIEBACK

ZYDECO n type of Black Cajun music

ZYDECOS > ZYDECO

ZYGA > ZYGON

ZYGAENID adj of the burnet moth genus

ZYGAENOID same as > ZYGAENID

ZYGAL > ZYGON

ZYGANTRA > ZYGANTRUM

ZYGANTRUM n vertebral articulation in snakes and some lizards

ZYGOCACTI n branching cactuses

ZYGODONT adj possessing paired molar cusps

ZYGOID same as > DIPLOID

ZYGOMA n slender arch of bone that forms a bridge between the cheekbone and the temporal bone on each side of the skull of mammals

ZYGOMAS > ZYGOMA

ZYGOMATA > ZYGOMA

ZYGOMATIC adj of or relating to the zygoma

ZYGON n brain fissure

ZYGOPHYTE n plant that reproduces by means of zygospores

ZYGOSE > ZYGOSIS

ZYGOSES > ZYGOSIS

ZYGOSIS n (in bacteria) the direct transfer of DNA between two cells that are temporarily joined

ZYGOSITY > ZYGOSIS

ZYGOSPERM same as > ZYGOSPORE

ZYGOSPORE n thick-walled sexual spore formed from the zygote of some fungi and algae

ZYGOTE n fertilized egg cell

ZYGOTENE n second stage of the prophase of meiosis, during which homologous chromosomes become associated in pairs (bivalents)

ZYGOTENES > ZYGOTENE

ZYGOTES > ZYGOTE

ZYGOTIC > ZYGOTE

ZYLONITE variant spelling of > XYLONITE

ZYLONITES > ZYLONITE

ZYMASE n mixture of enzymes that is obtained as an extract from yeast and ferments sugars

ZYMASES > ZYMASE

ZYME n ferment

ZYMES > ZYME

ZYMIC > ZYME

ZYMITE n priest who uses leavened bread during communion

ZYMITES > ZYMITE

ZYMOGEN n any of a group of compounds that are inactive precursors of enzymes and are activated by a kinase

ZYMOGENE same as > ZYMOGEN

ZYMOGENES > ZYMOGENE

ZYMOGENIC adj of, or relating to a zymogen

ZYMOGENS > ZYMOGEN

ZYMOGRAM n band of electrophoretic medium showing a pattern of enzymes following electrophoresis

ZYMOGRAMS > ZYMOGRAM

ZYMOID adj relating to a ferment

ZYMOLOGIC > ZYMOLOGY

ZYMOLOGY n chemistry of fermentation

ZYMOLYSES > ZYMOLYSIS

ZYMOLYSIS n process of fermentation

ZYMOLYTIC > ZYMOLYSIS

ZYMOME n glutinous substance that is insoluble in alcohol

ZYMOMES > ZYMOME

ZYMOMETER n instrument for estimation the degree of fermentation

ZYMOSAN n insoluble carbohydrate found in yeast

ZYMOSANS > ZYMOSAN

ZYMOSES > ZYMOSIS

ZYMOSIS same as > ZYMOLYSIS

ZYMOTIC adj of, relating to, or causing fermentation ▷ n disease

ZYMOTICS > ZYMOTIC

ZYMURGIES > ZYMURGY

ZYMURGY n branch of chemistry concerned with fermentation processes in brewing, etc

ZYTHUM n Ancient Egyptian beer

ZYTHUMS > ZYTHUM

ZYZZYVA n American weevil

ZYZZYVAS > ZYZZYVA

ZZZ n informal word for sleep

ZZZS > ZZZ

z